Standard Catalog of® 9th Edition

WORLD PAPER MONEY

Volume One Specialized Issues

Based on the original writings of Albert Pick

Edited by

Neil Shafer & George S. Cuhaj

Randy Thern
Numismatic Cataloging Supervisor

Special Consultants

Colin R. Bruce II, Kishore Jhunjhunwalla, John Kleeberg, Arthur C. Matz, Alistair Robb, Joel Shafer, Alim Sumana

Published by

700 E. State Street • Iola, WI 54990-0001
Telephone: 715/445-2214

Please call or write for our free catalog of publications. Our toll-free number to place an order or obtain a free catalog is 800-258-0929 or please use our regular business telephone, 715-445-2214.

Library of Congress Catalog Number: 83-83100
ISBN: 0-87349-466-0

Printed in the United States of America

TABLE OF CONTENTS

INCHES 1 2 3 4 5 6 7

ACKNOWLEDGMENTS

The contributions to this catalog have been many and varied. Accordingly, we wish to acknowledge the invaluable input provided by collectors, scholars and dealers in the world paper money field. We wish to single out the following individuals and organizations for their contributions to this work through the submission of notes for illustration, descriptive information and valuations.

Esko Ahlrory
Walter D. Allan
David Amey
Michael Anderson
Jorge E. Arbelaez
Efrain Archilla-Diez
Keith Austin
Douglas B. Ball
Cem Barlok
Adriaan C. F. Beck
Wolfgang Bertsch
Milt Blackburn
Ed Bohannon
Joseph E. Boling
Jean Bricaud
Robert Brooks
Colin R. Bruce II
Edvardo Colantonio
Scott Cordry
Guido Crapanzano
Ricard De Leon
C. M. Desai
Duane D. Douglas
Wilhelm Eglseer
Jos. F.M. Eijsermans
Esko Ekman
George A. Fisher Jr.
Wolfgang A. Frick
Gary Ganguillet
Arcelio Gomez-Prado
Bernardo Gonzales-White
Urs Graf
R. H. Griffen
Lee Gordon
Rune Gustafsson
Agus Halim
Flemming Lyngbeck Hansen
Dr. James A. Haxby
William G. Henderson
Dick Herman
Lowell C. Horwedel
Kishore Jhunjunwalla
William M. Judd
Peter Karstrom
Alex Keglyan
Olaf Keiner
Josef Klaus
John Kleeberg
Chester L. Krause
Lee Shin Song
Claire Lobel
Alan Luedeking
Ma Tak Wo
John T. Martin
Martin MacDaeid
Arthur C. Matz
Leo May
A. L. T. McCammon
Bill McNatt
Howard Mitchell
Michael Morris
Richard Murdoch
Claud Murphy Jr.
Tanju Mutlu
Eric P. Newman
C. M. Nielsen
Don Olmstead
Juan J. Paris
Antonio Pedraza
Aac. de Albergaria Pinheiro
Rudolph Richter
John Rishel
Alistair F. Robb
Alan Sadd
Carlton "Fred" Schwan
Timothy R. G. Sear
Joel Shafer
Mort Shafer
Brian A. Silsbee
Arlie Slabaugh
George Slusarczuk
Gary F. Snover
Mauricio Soto
William F. Spengler
Jimmie C. Steelman
Tim Steiner
Mel Steinberg
Alim A. Sumana
Steven Tan
Fred Tang
Anthony Tumonis
Michael Vort-Ronald
A. Wang
St. Westdal
Michael J. Whelihan
Yu Chien Hua
Christof Zellweger
Earl Ziegler

INSTITUTIONS

American Numismatic Association
American Numismatic Society
International Bank Note Society
Smithsonian Institution

PUBLICATIONS

The Stateman's Year-Book, 2001.
137th Edition

Barry Turner, editor. The Stateman's Year-Book Office, The Macmillan Press Ltd., 4-6 Crinan Street. London N1 9SQ, England. (Statistical and Historical Annual of the States of the World).

INTRODUCTION

Although paper money collecting is undoubtedly nearly as old as paper money itself, this segment of the numismatic hobby has begun to reach a popularity approaching that of coin collecting only since the latter half of the 1970s. While coins and paper money are alike in that both have served as legal obligations to facilitate commerce, long-time paper money enthusiasts know the similarity ends there.

Coins were historically guaranteed by the intrinsic value of their metallic content - at least until recent years when virtually all circulating coins have become little more than legal tender tokens, containing no precious metals except for the many commemoratives never meant to be circulated - while paper money possesses a value only when it is accepted for debts or converted into hard money. With many notes issued, this conversion privilege was limited and ultimately negated by the imposition of redemption cutoff dates.

Such conditions made collecting of bank notes a risky business, particularly with notes possesing face value of more than a nominal sum. This is why in most instances, except where issues were withdrawn shortly after release or became virtually worthless because of hyper-inflation, early high denomination notes are extremely difficult to locate, especially in uncirculated or high grades of preservation.

The development of widespread collector interest in paper money of most nations was long inhibited by a near total absence of adequate documentary literature. No more than three decades ago collectors could refer only to a few catalogs and dealer price lists of limited scope, most of which were incomplete and difficult to acquire, or they could build their own knowledge through personal collecting pursuits and contact with fellow collectors.

This situation was corrected somewhat over the past 25 years with a number of new special catalogs covering the more popularly collected countries. Still, many areas remained uncataloged, and no single volume existed that provided comprehensive, detailed, illustrated listings of issues from all countries of the world.

The earlier catalogs authored by Albert Pick chronicling issues of Europe and the Americas were assembled as stepping stones to the ultimate objective which became reality with publication of the first Standard Catalog of World Paper Money in 1975. That work provided collectors with complete listings and up-to-date valuations of all Pick's recorded government note issues of the 20th century, incorporating his previously unpublished manuscripts on Africa, Asia and Oceania, plus many earlier issues.

This totally revised and updated ninth edition is part of the most comprehensive world paper money reference ever assembled, presenting details about various early provincial and state government notes as well as many kinds of issues sponsored by commercial banks, regional authorities and in some cases military administrations.

Falling within the scope of Volume I are selected issues of major banks (many of which circulated equally with government notes in their respective countries), issues of quasi-government institutions with fairly wide circulation (national pawn shops, some railroads and others), notes issued by state or regional authority with somewhat more restricted circulation, and siege notes from the 1500s (Leyden) to modern times as issued by military occupations and with a very restricted area of circulation.

Coverage in this Specialized Issues volume is widespread and includes regional and bank issues from countries like Albania, Austria, Bolivia, various British Caribbean islands, Costa Rica, Cuba, Dominican Republic, El Salvador, Fiji, Greece, Guatemala, Guernsey, Honduras, Indian States, Italian States, Jamaica, Japan, Jersey, Lagos, Macao, Netherlands, Nicaragua, Paraguay, Rhodesia, South Africa, Spain, Trinidad and others. Extensive presentations are included for Argentina, Brazil, Chile, China, Colombia, Denmark, Ecuador, France, German States, India banks, Indonesia regionals, Mexico, Netherlands East Indies, New Zealand, Papal States, Peru, Philippines (guerrilla issues), Portugal, Russia, banks of Spain, Sweden, Switzerland, Uruguay and Venezuela.

GENERALISUES

Coverage InVoume 2 and 3

Legal tender notes issued by recognized national governments, and which enjoyed wide circulation in their respective countries, are covered in Volumes 2 and 3. General issues, Volume 2 covers the era from the late 1300's to 1960, and Volume 3 covers all notes issued since 1961.

Users of this current Volume 1 interested in acquiring the General Issues, Volume 2 and 3 are invited to contact the publisher. Inquiries should be directed to Standard Catalog of World Paper Money, Krause Publications, Book Division, 700 E. State St., Iola, WI 54990.

The recent sales of specimen notes and proofs from the archives of the American Bank Note Company (1990- 91) have given rise to many new listings as well as descriptions of pieces not previously available for cataloging. In such cases where substantive information for a previously unlisted type, variety or date range was found, the catalog listing will include the designation referring to specimens, proofs, or archive copies. It is assumed that such pieces may exist for most of the other notes already listed in the catalog; however, as with all previous editions, they will not be mentioned.

This extensively revised and updated ninth edition also includes hundreds of new and/or improved illustrations, increased specimen listings, expanded varities in Indonesia and much more valuable information throughout.

Index

NUMERICS

A

B

C

D

E

F

G

H

M

N

O

P

Q

R

S

T

U

V

W

Y

Z

STANDARD INTERNATIONAL NUMERAL SYSTEMS

PREPARED ESPECIALLY FOR THE **STANDARD CATALOG OF WORLD PAPER MONEY**

WESTERN	0	½	1	2	3	4	5	6	7	8	9	10	50	100	500	1000
ROMAN			I	II	III	IV	V	VI	VII	VIII	IX	X	L	C	D	M
ARABIC-TURKISH	٠	١/٢	١	٢	٣	٤	٥	٦	٧	٨	٩	١٠	٥٠	١٠٠	٥٠٠	١٠٠٠
MALAY—PERSIAN	٠	١/٢	١	٢	٣	۴	۵	٦ or ۶	٧	٨	٩	١٠	۵٠	١٠٠	۵٠٠	١٠٠٠
EASTERN ARABIC	۰	۱/۲	۱	۲	۳	۴	۵	۶	۷	۸	۹	۱۰	۵۰	۱۰۰	۵۰۰	۱۰۰۰
HYDERABAD ARABIC	٠	١/٢	١	٢	٣	۴	۵	۶	٧	٨	٩	١٠	۵٠	١٠٠	۵٠٠	١٠٠٠
INDIAN (Sanskrit)	०	१/२	१	२	३	४	५	६	७	८	९	१०	५०	१००	५००	१०००
ASSAMESE	০	১/২	১	২	৩	৪	৫	৬	৭	৮	৯	১০	৫০	১০০	৫০০	১০০০
BENGALI	০	১/২	১	২	৩	৪	৫	৬	৭	৮	৯	১০	৫০	১০০	৫০০	১০০০
GUJARATI	૦	૧/૨	૧	૨	૩	૪	૫	૬	૭	૮	૯	૧૦	૫૦	૧૦૦	૫૦૦	૧૦૦૦
KUTCH	०	१/२	१	२	३	४	५	६	७	८	९	१०	५०	१००	५००	१०००
DEVAVNAGRI	०	१/२	१	२	३	४	५	६ or ६	७	८	९ or ९	१०	५०	१००	५००	१०००
NEPALESE	०	१/२	१ or १	२	३	४	५ or ५	६	७	८ or ८	९ or ९ or ९	१०	५०	१००	५००	१०००
TIBETAN	༠	༡/༢	༡	༢	༣	༤	༥	༦	༧	༨	༩	༡༠	༥༠	༡༠༠	༥༠༠	༡༠༠༠
MONGOLIAN	᠐	᠑/᠒	᠑	᠒	᠓	᠔	᠕	᠖	᠗	᠘	᠙	᠑᠐	᠕᠐	᠑᠐᠐	᠕᠐᠐	᠑᠐᠐᠐
BURMESE	၀	၁/၂	၁	၂	၃	၄	၅	၆	၇	၈	၉	၁၀	၅၀	၁၀၀	၅၀၀	၁၀၀၀
THAI-LAO	๐	๑/๒	๑	๒	๓	๔	๕	๖	๗	๘	๙	๑๐	๕๐	๑๐๐	๕๐๐	๑๐๐๐
JAVANESE	꧐		꧑	꧒	꧓	꧔	꧕	꧖	꧗	꧘	꧙	꧑꧐	꧕꧐	꧑꧐꧐	꧕꧐꧐	꧑꧐꧐꧐
ORDINARY CHINESE JAPANESE-KOREAN	零	半	一	二	三	四	五	六	七	八	九	十	十五	百	百五	千
OFFICIAL CHINESE			壹	貳	叁	肆	伍	陸	柒	捌	玖	拾	拾伍	佰	佰伍	仟
COMMERCIAL CHINESE			〡	〢	〣	〤	〥	〦	〧	〨	〩	十	〥十	〡百	〥百	〡千
KOREAN		반	일	이	삼	사	오	육	찰	팔	구	십	오십	백	오백	천
GEORGIAN			ა	ბ	გ	დ	ე	ვ	ზ	ჱ	თ	ი	ნ	რ	ფ	ჩ
			11 ია	20 კ	30 ლ	40 მ	50 ნ	60 ჲ	70 ო	80 პ	90 ჟ	100 რ	200 ს 300 ტ	400 უ	600 ქ 700 ღ	800 ყ
ETHIOPIAN	◆		፩	፪	፫	፬	፭	፮	፯	፰	፱	፲	፶	፻	፭፻	፲፻
				20 ፳	30 ፴	40 ፵		60 ፷	70 ፸	80 ፹	90 ፺					
HEBREW			א	ב	ג	ד	ה	ו	ז	ח	ט	י	נ	ק	תק	
				20 כ	30 ל	40 מ		60 ס	70 ע	80 פ	90 צ		200 ר 300 ש	400 ת	600 תר 700 תש	800 תת
GREEK			Α	Β	Γ	Δ	Ε	ΣΤ	Ζ	Η	Θ	Ι	Ν	Ρ	Ο	͵Α
				20 Κ	30 Λ	40 Μ	60 Ξ	70 Ο	80 Π		200 Σ	300 Τ	400 Υ	600 Χ	700 Ψ	800 Ω

DATING

Determining a note's date of issue is a basic consideration of attribution. As the reading of dates is subject not only to the vagaries of numeric styling, but to variations in dating roots caused by the observation of differing religious eras or regal periods from country to country, and in some instances even within a given country, making this determination can sometimes be quite difficult. Most countries outside the North Africa and Oriental sphere rely on Western date numerals and Christian era (AD) reckoning, although in a few instances note dating has been tied to the year of a reign or government.

Countries of the Arabic sphere generally date their issues to the Mohammedan era (AH) which commenced on July 16, 622 AD, when the prophet Mohammed fled from Mecca to Medina. As their calendar is reckoned by the lunar year of 354 days, which is about three percent (precisely 3.03 percent) shorter than the Christian year, a formula is required to convert the dating to its Western equivalent. To convert an AH date to the approximate AD date, subtract three percent of the AH date (round to the closest whole number) from the AH date, then add 621.

The Mohammedan calendar is not always based on the lunar year (AH), however, causing some confusion, particularly in Afghanistan and Iran (Persia) where a calendar based on the solar year (SH) was introduced around 1920. These dates can be converted to AD by simply adding 621. In 1976 the government of Iran implemented a new solar calendar based on the founding of the Iranian monarchy in 559 BC. The first year observed on the new calendar was 2535 (MS), which commenced on March 20, 1976.

China - Republic 9th year, 1st month, 15th day (15.1.1920), read r. to l.

Russia - 1 October 1920

Thailand (Siam) - 1 December 2456

Korea - 4288 (1955)

Poland - 28 February 1919

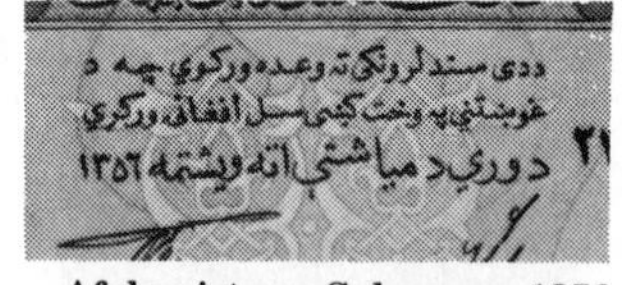

Afghanistan - Solar year 1356

Israel - 1973, 5733

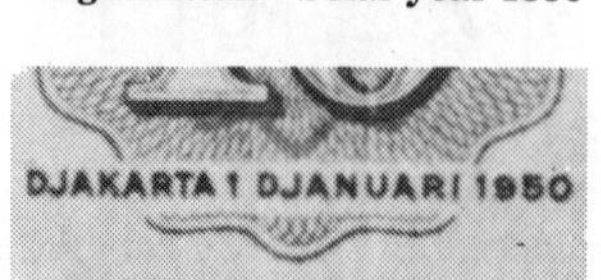

Indonesia - January 1950

Egypt - 1967 December 2

Greece - 5 March 1943

Several different eras of reckoning, including Christian and Mohammedan (AH), have been used to date paper money of the Indian subcontinent. The two basic systems are the Vikrama Samvat era (VS), which dates from October 18, 58 BC, and the Sa-ka era (SE), the origin of which is reckoned from March 3, 78 AD. Dating according to both eras appears on the notes of the various native states and countries of the area.

Thailand (Siam) has observed three different eras of dating. The most predominant is the Buddhist era (BE) which originated in 543 BC. Next is the Bangkok or Ratanakosindsok era (RS) dating from 1781 AD (dates consists of only three numerals), followed by the Chula- Sakarat era (CS) which dates from 638 AD, with the latter also observed in Burma.

Other calendars include that of the Ethiopian era (EE) which commenced 7 years, 8 months after AD dating, and that of the Jewish people which commenced on October 7, 3761 BC. Korea claims a legendary dating from 2333 BC which is acknowledged on some issues of paper money.

The following table indicates the year dating for the various eras which correspond to 1998 by Christian calendar reckoning, but it must be remembered that there are overlaps between the eras in some instances.

Christian era (AD)	—1998
Mohammedan era (AH)	—AH1419
Solar year (SH)	—SH1377
Monarchic Solar era (MS)	—MS2557
Vikrama Samvat (VS)	—VS2055
Saka era (SE)	—SE1920
Buddhist era (BE)	—BE2541
Bangkok era (RS)	—RS217
Chula-Sakarat era (CS)	—CS1360
Ethiopian era (EE)	—EE1990
Jewish era	—5758
Korean era	—4331
Javanese Aji Saka era (AS)	—AS1931
Fasli era (FE)	—FE1408

Paper money of Oriental origin - principally Japan, Korea, China, Turkestan and Tibet - is generally dated to the year of the government, dynastic, regional or cyclical eras, with the dates indicated in Oriental characters which usually read from right to left. In recent years, however, some dating has been according to the Christian calendar, and in Western numerals.

More detailed guides to the application of the less prevalent dating systems than those described, and others of strictly local nature, along with the numeral designations employed, are presented in conjunction with the appropriate listings.

Some notes carry dating according to both the locally observed and Christian eras. This is particularly true in the Arabic sphere, where the Mohammedan date may be indicated in Arabic numerals and the Christian date in Western numerals, or both dates may be represented in either Arabic or Western numerals.

In general the date actually carried on a given paper money issue is indicated. Notes issued by special Law or Decree will have L or D preceding the date. Dating listed which does not actually appear on a given note is generally bracketed by parentheses. Undated issues are indicated by the presence of the letters ND along with the year of issue in parentheses, if it is known.

Timing differentials between the 354-day Mohammedan and 365-day Christian year cause situations whereby paper money bearing dates for both eras exist with two year dates from one calendar in combination with a single date from the other.

HOW TO USE THIS CATALOG

Catalog listings consist of all regular and provisional notes attaining wide circulation in their respective countries for the period covered. Notes have been listed under the historical country name. Thus Dahomey is not under Benin, and so on, as had been the case in past catalogs. Where catalog numbers have changed, and you may find some renumbering in this edition, the old catalog numbers appear in parentheses directly below the new number. The listings continue to be grouped by issue range rather than by denomination, and a slight change in the listing format should make the bank name, issue dates as well as catalog numbers and denominations easier to locate. These changes have been made to make the catalog as easy to use as possible for you.

The editors and publisher make no claim to absolute completeness, just as they acknowledge that some errors and pricing inequities will appear. Correspondence is invited with interested persons who have notes previously unlisted or who have information to enhance the presentation of existing listings in succeeding editions of this catalog.

Catalog Format

Listings proceed generally according to the following sequence: country, geographic or political, chronology, bank name and sometimes alphabetically or by date of first note issue. Release within the bank, most often in date order, but sometimes by printer first.

Catalog number — The basic reference number at the beginning of each listing for each note. For this Modern Issues volume the regular listings require no prefix letters except when 'A' or 'B' appear within the catalog number. (Military and Regional prefixes are explained later in this section.)

Denomination — the value as shown on the note, in western numerals. When denominations are only spelled out, consult the numerics chart.

Date — the actual issue date as printed on the note in day-month-year order. Where more than one date appears on a note, only the latest is used. Where the note has no date, the designation ND is used, followed by a year date in parentheses when it is known. If a note is dated by the law or decree of authorization, the date appears with an L or D and is italicized.

Descriptions of the note are broken up into one or more items as follows:

Color — the main color(s) of the face, and the underprint are given first. If the colors of the back are different, then they follow the face design description.

Design — The identification and location of the main design elements if known. Back design elements identified if known.

If design elements and or signatures are the same for an issue group then they are printed only once at the heading of the issue, and apply for the group that follows.

Printer — often a local printer has the name shown in full. Abbreviations are used for the most prolific printers. Refer to the list of printer abbreviations elsewhere in this introduction. In these listings the use of the term "imprint" refers to the logo or the printer's name as usually appearing in the bottom frame or below in the margin of the note.

Valuations — are generally given under the grade headings of Good, Fine and Extremely Fine for early notes; and Very Good, Very Fine and Uncirculated for the later issues. Listings that do not follow these two patterns are clearly indicated. UNC followed by a value is used usually for specimens and proofs when lower grade headings are used for a particular series of issued notes.

Catalog prefix or suffix letters

A catalog number preceded by a capital 'A' indicated the incorporation of an earlier listing as required by type or date; a capital letter following the catalog number usually shows the addition of a later issue. Both may indicate newly discovered lower or higher denominations to a series. Listings of notes for regional circulation are distinguished from regular national issues with the prefix letter 'R'; military issues use a 'M' prefix; foreign exchange certificates are assigned a 'FX' prefix. Varieties, specific date or signature listings are shown with small letters 'a' following a number within their respective entries. Some standard variety letters include: 'p' for proof notes, 'r' for remainder notes, 's' for specimen notes and 'x' for errors.

Denominations

The denomination as indicated on many notes issued by a string of countries stretching from eastern Asia, through western Asia and on across northern Africa, often appears only in unfamiliar non-Western numeral styles. With the listings that follow, denominations are always indicated in Western numerals.

A comprehensive chart keying Western numerals to their non-Western counterparts is included elsewhere in this introduction as an aid to the identification of note types. This compilation features not only the basic numeral systems such as Arabic, Japanese and Indian, but also the more restricted systems such as Burmese, Ethiopian, Siamese, Tibetan, Hebrew, Mongolian and Korean. Additionally, the list includes other localized variations that have been applied to some paper money issues.

In consulting the numeral systems chart to determine the denomination of a note, one should remember that the actual numerals styles employed in any given area, or at a particular time, may vary significantly from these basic representations. Such variations can be deceptive to the untrained eye, just as variations from Western numeral styles can prove deceptive to individuals not acquainted with the particular style employed.

Dates and Date Listing Policy

In previous editions of this work it was the goal to provide a sampling of the many date varieties that were believed to exist. In recent times, as particular dates (and usually signature combinations) were known to be scarcer, that particular series was expanded to include listings of individual dates. At times this idea has been fully incorporated, but with some series it is not practicable, especially when just about every day in a given month could have been an issue date for the notes.

Accordingly, where it seems justifiable that date spans can be realistically filled with individual dates, this has been done.

In order to accommodate the many new dates, the idea of providing small letters to break them up into narrower spans of years has been used. Within these small letter date spans, the aim has been to include no more than five or six dates. If it appears that there are too many dates for a series, with no major differences in value, then a general inclusive date span is used (beginning and ending) and individual dates within this span are not shown.

For those notes showing only a general date span, the only important dates become those that expand the range of years, months or days earlier or later. But even they would have no impact on the values shown.

Because a specific date is not listed does not necessarily mean it is rare. It may be just that it has not been reported. Those date varieties known to be scarcer are cataloged separately. Newly reported dates in a wide variety of listings are constantly being reported. This indicates that research into the whole area is very active, and a steady flow of new dates is fully expected upon publication of this edition.

Abbreviations

Certain abbreviations have been adopted for words occurring frequently in note descriptions. Following is a list of these:

#	-	number (catalog or serial)
bldg.	-	building
ctr.	-	center
dk.	-	dark
FV	-	face value
Gen.	-	General
govt.	-	government
Kg.	-	king
l.	-	left
lg.	-	large
lt.	-	light
m/c	-	multicolored
ND	-	no date
ovpt.	-	overprint
portr.	-	portrait
Qn.	-	queen
r.	-	right
sign.	-	signature or signatures
sm.	-	small
unpt.	-	underprint (background printing)
wmk.	-	watermark
w/	-	with
w/o	-	without

Valuations

Valuations are given for most notes in three grades. Earlier issues are usually valued in the grade headings of Good, Fine and Extremely Fine; later issues take the grade headings of Very Good, Very Fine and Uncirculated. While it is true that some early notes cannot be valued in Extremely Fine and some later notes have no premium value in Very Good, it is felt that this coverage provides the best uniformity of value data to the collecting community. There are exceptional cases where headings are adjusted for either single notes or a series that really needs special treatment. We have endeavored to print the grade headings often for ease of reference.

Valuations are determined generally from a consensus of individuals submitting prices for evaluation. Some notes have

NO values; this does not necessarily mean they are expensive or even rare; but it shows that no pricing information was forthcoming. A number of notes have a 'Rare' designation, and no values. Such notes are generally not available on the market, and when they do appear the price is a matter between buyer and seller. No book can provide guidance in these instances except to indicate rarity.

Valuations used in this book are based on the IBNS grading standards and are stated in U.S. dollars. They serve only as aids in evaluating paper money since actual market conditions throughout the worldwide collector community are constantly changing. In addition, particularly choice examples of many issues listed often bring higher premiums than values listed.

Unless otherwise presented, values are given for types only, without regard for date or signature. In a number of instances there could be dates or signature varieties worth a substantial premium over the listed value.

FV (for Face Value) is used as a value designation on older but still redeemable legal tender notes in lower conditions. FV may appear in one or both condition columns before Uncirculated, depending on the relative age and availability of the note in question.

Collection care

The proper preservation of a collection should be of paramount importance to all in the hobby - dealers, collectors and scholars. Only a person who has housed notes in a manner giving pleasure to him or herself and others will keep alive the pleasure of collecting for future generations. The same applies to the way of housing as to the choice of the collecting specialty: it is chiefly a question of what most pleases the individual collector.

Arrangement and sorting of a collection is most certainly a basic requirement. Storing the notes in safe paper envelopes and filing boxes should, perhaps, be considered only when building a new section of a collection, for accommodating varieties or for reasons of saving space when the collection has grown quickly.

Many paper money collections are probably housed in some form of plastic-pocketed album, which are today manufactured in many different sizes and styles to accommodate many types of world paper money. Because the number of bank note collectors has grown continually over the past twenty-five years, some specialty manufacturers of albums have developed a paper money selection. The notes, housed in clear plastic pockets, individually or in groups, can be viewed and exchanged without difficulty. These albums are not cheap, but the notes displayed in this manner do make a lasting impression on the viewer. A large collection will hardly be accommodated in its entirety in this manner, thus many collectors limit themselves to partial areas or especially valuable notes, which are displayed thus.

A word of concern: certain types of plastic and all vinyl used for housing notes may cause notes to become brittle over time, or cause an irreversible and harmful transfer of oils from the vinyl onto the bank notes.

The high demand for quality that stamp collectors make on their products cannot be transferred to the paper money collecting fraternity. A postage stamp is intended for a single use, then is relegated to a collection. With paper money, it is nearly impossible to acquire uncirculated specimens from a number of countries because of export laws or internal bank procedures. Bends from excessive counting, or even staple holes, are commonplace. Once acquiring a circulated note, the collector must endeavor to maintain its state of preservation.

The fact that there is a classification and value difference between notes with greater use or even damage is a matter of course. It is part of the opinion and personal taste of the individual collector to decide what is considered worthy of collecting and what to pay for such items.

For the purposed of strengthening and mending torn paper money, under no circumstances should one use plain cellophane tape or a similar material. These tapes warp easily, with sealing marks forming at the edges, and the tape frequently discolors. Only with the greatest of difficulty (and often not at all) can these tapes be removed, and damage to the note or the printing is almost unavoidable. The best material for mending tears is an archival tape recommended for the treatment and repair of documents.

There are collectors who, with great skill, remove unsightly spots, repair badly damaged notes, replace missing pieces and otherwise restore or clean a note. Before venturing to tackle such work, one should first experiment with cheap duplicates and not endanger a collection piece. Really difficult work of this nature should be left to the experienced restorer. There is also the question of morality of tampering with a note to improve its condition, either by repairing, starching, ironing, pressing or other methods to possibly deceive a potential future buyer. Such a question must, in the final analysis, be left to the individual collector.

IBNS GRADING STANDARDS FOR WORLD PAPER MONEY

The following introduction and Grading Guide is the result of work prepared under the guidance of the Grading Committee of the International Bank Note Society (IBNS.) It has been adopted as the official grading standards of that society.

Introduction

Grading is the most controversial component of paper money collecting today. Small differences in grade can mean significant differences in value. The process of grading is so subjective and dependent on external influences such as lighting, that even a very experienced individual may well grade the same note differently on separate occasions.

To facilitate communication between sellers and buyers, it is essential that grading terms and their meanings be as standardized and as widely used as possible. This standardization should reflect common usage as much as practicable. One difficulty with grading is that even the actual grades themselves are not used everywhere by everyone. For example, in Europe the grade 'About Uncirculated' (AU) is not in general use, yet in North America it is widespread. The European term 'Good VF' may roughly correspond to what individuals in North America call 'Extremely Fine' (EF).

The grades and definitions as set forth below cannot reconcile all the various systems and grading terminology variants. Rather, the attempt is made here to try and diminish the controversy with some common-sense grades and definitions that aim to give more precise meaning to the grading language of paper money.

How to look at a banknote

In order to ascertain the grade of a note, it is essential to examine it out of a holder and under a good light. Move the note around so that light bounces off at different angles. Try holding the note obliquely, so the note is even with your eye as you look up at the light. Hard-to-see folds or slight creases will show up under such examination. Some individuals also lightly feel along the surface of the note to detect creasing.

Cleaning, Washing, Pressing of Banknotes

a) Cleaning, washing or pressing paper money is generally harmful and reduces both the grade and the value of a note. At the very least, a washed or pressed note may lose its original sheen and its surface may become lifeless and dull. The defects a note had, such as folds and creases, may not necessarily be completely eliminated and their telltale marks can be detected under a good light. Carelessly washed notes may also have white streaks where the folds or creases were (or still are).

b) Processing of a note which started out as Extremely Fine will automatically reduce it at least one full grade.

Unnatural Defects

Glue, tape or pencil marks may sometimes be successfully removed. While such removal will leave a cleaned surface, it will improve the overall appearance of the note without concealing any of its defects. Under such circumstnces, the grade of that note may also be improved.

The words “pinholes”. “staple holes”, “trimmed”, “writing on face”, “tape marks”, etc. should always be added to the description of a note. It is realized that certain countries routinely staple their notes together in groups before issue. In such cases, the desription can include a comment such as "usual stple holes" or something similar. After all, not everyone knows that certain notes cannot be found otherwise.

The major point of this section is that one cannot lower the overall grade of a note with defects simply because of the defects. The price will reflect the lowered worth of a defective note, but the description must always include the specific defects.

The Term *Uncirculated*

The word *Uncirculated* is use in the grading guide only as a qualitive measurement of the appearance of a note. It has nothing at all to do with whether or not an issuer has actually released the note to circulation1. Thus, the term About Uncirculated is justified and acceptable because so many notes that have never seen hand to hand use have been mishandled so that they are available at best in AU condition. Either a note is uncirculated in condition or it is not; there can be no degrees of uncirculated. Highlights or defects in color, centering and the like may be included in a description but the fact that a note is or is not in uncirculated condition should not be a disputable point.

Grading Guide — Definitions of Terms

UNCIRCULATED: A perfectly preserved note, never mishandled by the issuing authority, a bank teller, the public or a collector.

Paper is clean and firm, without discoloration. Corners are sharp and square without any evidence of rounding. (Rounded corners are often a tell-tale sign of a cleaned or "doctored" note.)

NOTE: Some note issuers are most often available with slight evidence of very light counting folds which do not "break" the paper. Also, French-painted notes usually have a slight ripple in the paper. Many collectors and dealers refer to such notes as AU-UNC.

ABOUT UNCIRCULATED: A virtually perfect note, with some minor handling. May show very slight evidence of bank counting folds at a corner or one light fold through the center, but not both. An AU note cannot be creased, a crease being a hard fold which has usually "broken" the surface of the note.

Paper is clean and bright with original sheen. Corners are not rounded.

NOTE: Europeans will refer to an About Uncirculated or AU note as "EF-Unc" or as just "EF". The Extremely Fine note described below will often be referred to as "GVF" or "Good Very Fine".

EXTREMELY FINE: A very attractive note, with light handling. May have a maximum of three light folds or one strong crease.

Paper is clean and firm, without discoloration. Corners are sharp and square without any evidence of rounding. (Rounded corners are often a tell-tale sign of a cleaned or "doctored" note.)

VERY FINE: An attractive note, but with more evidence of handling and wear. May have several folds both vertically and horizontally.

Paper may have minimal dirt, or possible color smudging. Paper itself is still relatively crisp and not floppy.

There are no tears into the border area, although the edges do show slight wear. Corners also show wear but not full rounding.

FINE: A note that shows considerable circulation, with many folds, creases and wrinkling.

Paper is not excessively dirty but may have some softness. Edges may show much handling, with minor tears in the border area. Tears may not extend into the design. There will be no center hole because of excessive folding.

Colors are clear but not very bright. A staple hole or two would not be considered unusual wear in a Fine note. Overall appearance is still on the desirable side.

VERY GOOD: A well used note, abused but still intact.

Corners may have much wear and rounding, tiny nicks, tears may extend into the design, some discoloration may be present, staining may have occurred, and asmall hole may sometimes be seen at center from excessive folding.

Staple and pinholes are usually present, and the note itself is quite limp but NO pieces of the note can be missing. A note in VG condition may still have an overall not unattractive appearance.

GOOD: A well worn and heavily used note. Normally damage from prolonged circulation will include strong multiple folds and creases, stains, pinholes and/or staple holes, dirt, discoloration, edge tears, center hole, rounded corners and an overall unattractive appearance. No large pieces of the note may be missing. Graffiti is commonly seen on notes in G condition.

FAIR: A totally limp, dirty and very well used note. Larger pieces may be half torn off or missing besides the defects mentioned under the Good category. Tears will be larger, obscured portions of the note will be bigger.

POOR: A "rag" with severe damage because of wear, staining, pieces missing, grafiti, larger holes. May have tape holding pieces of the note together. Trimming may have taken place to remove rough edges. A poor note is desirable only as a "filler" or when such a note is the only one known of that particular issue.

The above Introduction and Grading Guide is the result of work prepared under the guidance of the Grading Committee of the International Bank Note Society. It was adopted officially in 1986

BANKNOTE PRINTERS

Printers' names, abbreviations or monograms will usually appear as part of the frame design or below it on face and/or back. In some instances the engraver's name may also appear in a similar location on a note. The following abbreviations identify printers for many of the notes listed in this volume:

ABNC . . . . American Bank Note Company (USA)
BABN(C) . . . . British American Bank Note Co., Ltd. (Canada)
B&S . . . . Bouligny & Schmidt (Mexico)
BCdE . . . . Banco Central de Ecuador
BEPP . . . . Bureau of Engraving & Printing, Peking (China)
BF . . . . Banque de France (France)
BFL . . . . Barclay & Fry Ltd. (England)
BWC . . . . Bradbury, Wilkinson & Co. (England)
CABB . . . . Compania Americana de Billetes de Banco (ABNC)
CABNC . . . . Canada Bank Note Company (Canada)
CBC . . . . Columbian Banknote Co. (USA)
CBNC . . . . Canadian Bank Note Company (Canada)
CCBB . . . . Compania Columbiana de Billetes de Banco (CBC)
CdM- . . . . Casa da Moeda (Brazil)
CdM- . . . . Casa de Moneda (Argentina, Chile, etc.)
CHB . . . . Chung Hua Book Co. (China)
CMN . . . . Casa de Moneda de la Nacion (Argentina)
CMPA . . . . Commercial Press (China)
CNBB . . . . Compania Nacional de Billetes de Banco (NBNC)
CONB . . . . Continental Bank Note Company (USA)
CPF . . . . Central Printing Factory (China)
CSABB . . . . Compania Sud/Americana de Billetes de Banco . . . . (Argentina)
CS&E . . . . Charles Skipper & East (England)
DLR . . . . De La Rue (England)
DTB . . . . Dah Tung Book Co., and Ta Tung Printing (China)
E&C . . . . Evans & Cogswell (CSA)
EAW . . . . E. A. Wright (USA)
FCO . . . . Francois- Charles Oberthur
FLBN . . . . Franklin-Lee Bank Note Company (USA)
FNMT . . . . Fabrica Nacional de Moneda y Timbre (Spain)
G&D . . . . Giesecke & Devrient (Germany)
HBNC . . . . Hamilton Bank Note Company (USA)
HKB . . . . Hong Kong Banknote (Hong Kong)
HKP . . . . Hong Kong Printing Press (Hong Kong)
H&L . . . . Hoyer & Ludwig, Richmond, Virginia (CSA)
HLBNC . . . . Homer Lee Bank Note Co. (USA)
H&S . . . . Harrison & Sons Ltd. (England)
IBB . . . . Imprenta de Billetes-Bogota (Colombia)
IBSFB . . . . Imprenta de Billetes-Santa Fe de Bogota (Colombia)
IBNC . . . . International Bank Note Company (USA)
IPS . . . . Roma(Italy)
JBNC . . . . Jeffries Bank Note Company (USA)
JEZ . . . . Joh. Enschede en Zonen (Netherlands)
K&B . . . . Keatinge & Ball (CSA)
KBNC . . . . Kendall Bank Note Company, New York (USA)
LN . . . . Litografia Nacional (Columbia)
NAL . . . . Nissen & Arnold (England)
NBNC . . . . National Bank Note Company (USA)
OCV . . . . Officina Carte-Valori (Italy)
ODBI . . . . Officina Della Banca D'Italia (Italy)
OFZ . . . . Orell Fussli, Zurich (Switzerland)
P&B . . . . Perkins & Bacon (England)
PBC . . . . Perkins, Bacon & Co. (England)
PB&P . . . . Perkins, Bacon & Petch (England)
SBNC . . . . Security Banknote Company (USA)
TDLR . . . . Thomas De La Rue (England)
UPC . . . . Union Printing Co. (China)
UPP . . . . Union Publishers & Printers Fed. Inc. (China)
USBNC . . . . United States Banknote Corp. (USA)
WDBN . . . . Western District Banknote Fed. Inc.
W&S . . . . Waterlow & Sons Ltd. (England)
WPCo . . . . Watson Printing Co. (China)
WWS . . . . W. W. Sprague & Co. Ltd. (England)

International Bank Note Society

The International Bank Note Society (IBNS) was formed in 1961 to promote the collecting of world paper money. A membership in excess of 2,000 in over 100 nations around the globe draw on the services of the Society in advancing their knowledge and collections.

The benefits of Society membership include the quarterly IBNS Journal, a magazine featuring learned writings on the notes of the world, their history, artistry and technical background. Additionally each member receives a directory which lists the membership by name as well as geographic location. Collector specialties are also given. A newsletter is published to announce events in a timely fashion, as well a semi-annual auctions of bank notes. Finally, an attribution service is offered by the society for persons with paper money they are unable to identify.

One of the greatest benefits of IBNS membership is the facility for correspondence with other members around the world, for purposes of exchanging notes, information and assistance with research projects.

Application for Membership in the INTERNATIONAL BANK NOTE SOCIETY

Name ______________________________

Last First Initial

Street ______________________________

____

City Province or State

____

Country Postal Code

Type of Membership:

Individual: ❑ $20.00 per year
Junior (Ages 11-17): ❑ $10.00 per year
Family (includes children under 18): ❑ $25.00 per year

Payment in US Dollars payable to IBNS.

Check ❑ Other ❑ Money Order ❑

Do you wish your name and address to appear in our Membership Directory? Yes ❑ No ❑

Collecting Interest ______________________________

____

____

Mail to: Milan Alusic
P.O. Box 1642
Racine, Wisconsin
U.S.A. 53401

The Republic of Albania, a Balkan republic bounded by the rump Yugoslav state of Montenegro and Serbia, Macedonia, Greece and the Adriatic Sea, has an area of 11,100 sq. mi. (28,748 sq. km.) and a population of 3.5 million. Capital: Tirana. The country is mostly agricultural, although recent progress has been made in the manufacturing and mining sectors. Petroleum, chrome, iron, copper, cotton textiles, tobacco and wood products are exported.

Since it had been part of the Greek and Roman Empires, little is known of the early history of Albania. After the disintegration of the Roman Empire, Albania was overrun by Goths, Byzantines, Venetians and Turks. Skanderbeg, the national hero, resisted the Turks and established an independent Albania in 1443, but in 1468 the country again fell to the Turks and remained part of the Ottoman Empire for more than 400 years.

Independence was re-established by revolt in 1912, and the present borders established in 1913 by a conference of European powers which, in 1914, placed Prince William of Wied on the throne; popular discontent forced his abdication within months. In 1920, following World War I occupancy by several nations, a republic was set up. Ahmet Zogu seized the presidency in 1925, and in 1928 proclaimed himself king with the title of Zog I. King Zog fled when Italy occupied Albania in 1939 and enthroned King Victor Emanuel of Italy. Upon the surrender of Italy to the Allies in 1943, German troops occupied the country. They withdrew in 1944, and communist partisans seized power, naming Gen. Enver Hoxha provisional president. In 1946, following a victory by the communist front in the 1945 elections, a new constitution modeled on that of the USSR was adopted. In accordance with the constitution of Dec. 28, 1976, the official name of Albania was changed from the People's Republic of Albania to the People's Socialist Republic of Albania. A general strike by trade unions in 1991 forced the communist government to resign. A new government was elected in March 1992. In 1997 Albania had a major financial crisis which caused civil disturbances and the fall of the administration.

MONETARY SYSTEM:

1 Frank = 100 Qindtar

REGIONAL - BERAT

BASHKIA E BERATIT

1925 ISSUE

		VG	VF	UNC
S101	**50 QINDTAR** 19.12.1925.	—	Rare	—

DHOMA TREGETARE E BERATIT

1924 ISSUE

#S102 and S103 Mercury w/cadeuces at ctr. Dancing crowned Liberty oval hand stamp on back.

		VG	VF	UNC
S102	**0.50 LIRË ITALIANE** April 1924. Red on yellow unpt.			
	a. Issued note.	—	—	—
	r. Remainder w/o sign. or oval hand stamp.	30.00	60.00	125.00

		VG	VF	UNC
S103	**1 LIRË ITALIANE** 1924. Black on red unpt.			
	a. April 1924.	—	—	—
	b. May 1924.	—	—	—
	r1. As a. Remainder w/o sign., serial # or oval hand stamp.	30.00	60.00	125.00
	r2. As b. Remainder w/o sign. or oval hand stamp.	30.00	60.00	125.00

REGIONAL - ELBASAN

BASHKIA E ELBASANIT

1924 ISSUE

		VG	VF	UNC
S104	**0.10 FRANGA ARGJENT** 1.6.1924. Black on red unpt. Double-headed eagle. Black circular double-headed eagle hand stamp on back w/imprint: Bashkija e Elbasanit.	—	Rare	—

1925 ISSUE

		VG	VF	UNC
S104A	**0.10 FRANGA ARGJENT** 1.4.1925. Black on red unpt. Double-headed eagle. Similar to #S104.	—	Rare	—
S104B	**0.20 FRANGA ARGJENT** 1.4.1925. Red on gray unpt. Double-headed eagle. Circular double-headed eagle hand stamp on back.	—	Rare	—
S104C	**0.40 FRANGA ARGJENT** 1.4.1925. Red on black unpt. Double-headed eagle. Circular double-headed eagle hand stamp on front.	—	—	—

REGIONAL - GJIROKASTËR

BASHKI E GJIROKASTRES

CA 1920 ISSUE

		VG	VF	UNC
S105	**1 FRANGA** ND. Black. Circular double-headed eagle hand stamp on back.	—	Rare	—

REGIONAL - KORÇË

Established by the French in 1917.

MONETARY SYSTEM

1 Franc = 100 Centimes
1 Skender = 100 Qint

SHQIPËRIË VETQEVERITARE - KORÇË

1917 FIRST ISSUE, SERIES A

#S106 and S107 w/title: *SHQIPËRIË VETQEVERITARE, KORÇË.* Double-headed eagle at ctr. Printer: A. A. Vangheli - Korytza.

		VG	VF	UNC
S106	**1/2 FRANC** 1.3.1917. Brown on aqua unpt. Back aqua; circular purple hand stamp at r.	7.50	20.00	50.00

		VG	VF	UNC
S107	**1 FRANC** 1.3.1917.	7.50	20.00	50.00

1917 SECOND ISSUE, SERIES B

#S108 and S109 w/title: *SHQIPËRIË VETQEVERITARE, KORÇË.* Double-headed eagle at ctr.

		VG	VF	UNC
S108	**1/2 FRANC** 25.3.1917. Brown on aqua unpt. Back aqua; circular purple hand stamp at r.	10.00	25.00	60.00

S109 1 FRANC | VG 10.00 | VF 25.00 | UNC 60.00
25.3.1917. Black on brown-orange unpt. Back brown; circular purple hand stamp at r.

1917 THIRD ISSUE, SERIES C

#S110 and S111 w/title: *REPUBLIKA SHQIPETARË, KORÇË*. Double-headed eagle at ctr.

S110 1/2 FRANC | VG 12.50 | VF 35.00 | UNC 80.00
10.10.1917.

S111 1 FRANC | VG 12.50 | VF 35.00 | UNC 80.00
10.10.1917.

1918 FIRST ISSUE, SERIES D

		VG	VF	UNC
S112	1/2 FRANC Feb. 1918.	30.00	75.00	160.00
S113	1 FRANC Feb. 1918.	30.00	75.00	160.00

1918 SECOND ISSUE, SERIES A

#S114 and S115 w/circular hand stamp at upper r. Town view on back.

S114 0.50 FRANC | VG 12.50 | VF 30.00 | UNC 60.00
1.11.1918. Dk. green and dk. blue. Back dk. green.

S115 1 FRANC | VG 12.50 | VF 30.00 | UNC 60.00
1.11.1918. Red-brown and dk. blue. Back red-brown.

1918 THIRD ISSUE, SERIES B

#S116 and S117 w/circular handstamp at upper r. Town view on back.

		VG	VF	UNC
S116	0.50 FRANC 1.12.1918. Dk. green and dk. blue. Like #S114.	15.00	45.00	110.00
S117	1 FRANC 1.12.1918. Red-brown and dk. blue. Like #S115.	15.00	45.00	110.00

1918 FOURTH ISSUE, SERIES C

#S118 and S119 w/circular hand stamp at upper r. Town view on back.

		VG	VF	UNC
S118	0.50 FRANC 10.12.1918. Dk. green and dk. blue. Like #S114 and S116.	30.00	70.00	160.00
S119	1 FRANC 10.12.1918. Red-brown and dk. blue. Like #S115 and S117.	30.00	70.00	160.00

TERRITOIRE DE KORITZA - KORÇË

1920 FIRST ISSUE

#S120 and S121 w/title: *TERRITOIRE DE KORITZA* monochrome, circular hand stamp: *Commandement Militaire de Korytza-Armee d'Orient*. Circular hand stamp: *Direksiae Finances - Korçë* on back.

S120 0.50 CENTIMES | VG 10.00 | VF 30.00 | UNC 70.00
Mar. 1920. Black. Brown paper.

S121 1 FRANC | VG 10.00 | VF 30.00 | UNC 70.00
Mar. 1920. Black. Red paper.

1920 SECOND ISSUE

		GOOD	FINE	XF
S122	1 FRANC 1.4.1920. M/c.	30.00	70.00	180.00
S123	5 FRANCS 1.4.1920. M/c.	50.00	120.00	300.00

1920 THIRD ISSUE

		GOOD	FINE	XF
S124	1 FRANC 1.8.1920.	30.00	70.00	180.00

1921 FIRST ISSUE

#S130 and S131 w/title: *KATUNDAR'I E KORÇËS*.

		VG	VF	UNC
S130	1/2 SKENDER 1.8.1921. Dk. brown and red on yellow unpt. Skanderbeg at l.			
	a. Issued note.	60.00	150.00	350.00
	r. Remainder w/o serial #.	—	—	200.00

		VG	VF	UNC
S131	1 SKENDER 1.8.1921. Red and black on green unpt. Skanderbeg at l.	60.00	125.00	300.00
S131A	2 SKENDER 1.8.1921. Similar to #131.	100.00	200.00	450.00

1921 SECOND ISSUE

#S132-S135 farmer plowing, w/title: *KATUNDARI E KORÇËS.* Skanderbeg on horseback on back.

		GOOD	FINE	XF
S132	25 QINT 9.11.1921.	50.00	100.00	225.00
S133	50 QINT 9.11.1921.	50.00	100.00	225.00

		GOOD	FINE	XF
S134	1 SKENDER 9.11.1921.	50.00	100.00	225.00
S135	20 SKENDER 9.11.1921. Yellow.	75.00	125.00	300.00

1923 ISSUE

		GOOD	FINE	XF
S137	25 FR. ARG. 1.1.1923. Red and green. W/title: *BASHKIJAE KORÇËS.* Double-headed eagle on back.	40.00	100.00	225.00

REGIONAL - SHKODËR

SIGURIM ARKE - SHKODRES PERMBE

1920 ISSUE

#S141-S144 black on red unpt. W/title: *SIGURIM ARKE I PERLIMT ARES SE SHKODRËS PERMBI.* Brown paper.

		VG	VF	UNC
S141	5 QINDTAR 30.1.1920.	20.00	50.00	100.00

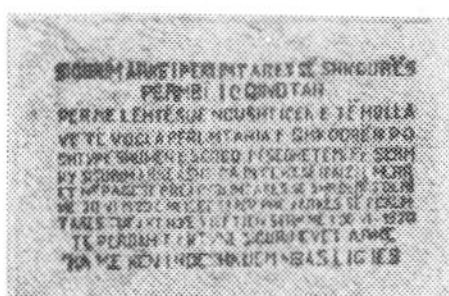

		VG	VF	UNC
S142	10 QINDTAR 30.1.1920.	20.00	50.00	100.00

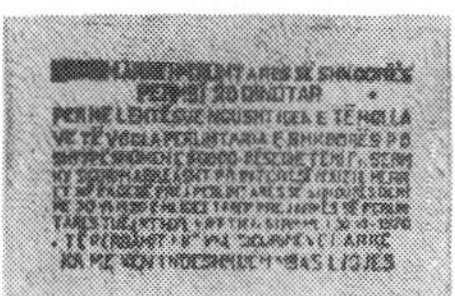

		VG	VF	UNC
S143	20 QINDTAR 30.1.1920.	20.00	50.00	100.00
S144	50 QINDTAR 30.1.1920.	30.00	85.00	175.00

REGIONAL - VLORË

BASHKIA E VLORËS

1924 FIRST ISSUE

#S151-S153 w/title: *BASHKIA E VLORËS.* Double-headed eagle at ctr. in unpt.

		GOOD	FINE	XF
S151	10 QINDTAR 1.5.1924.	30.00	90.00	180.00

		GOOD	FINE	XF
S152	25 QINDTAR 1.5.1924.	30.00	90.00	180.00

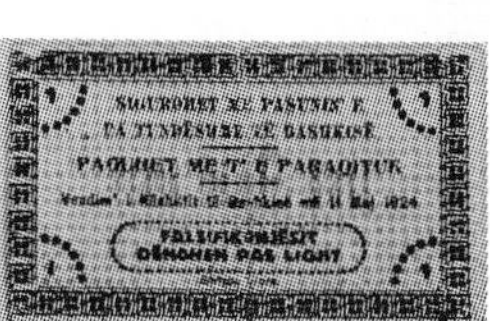

		GOOD	FINE	XF
S153	1 FRANK 11.5.1924. Black on orange unpt.	30.00	90.00	180.00

1924 SECOND ISSUE

#S163 and S164 w/title: *BASHKIA E VLORËS.* Portr. man at l.

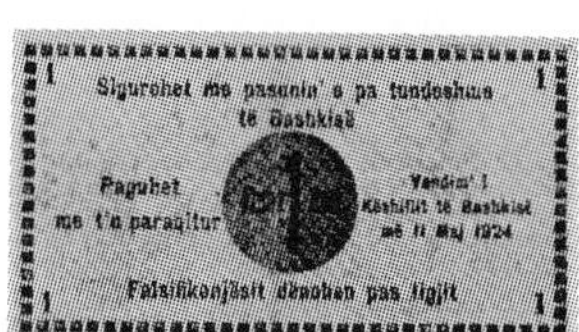

		GOOD	FINE	XF
S163	1 FRANK 11.5.1924. Brown and red on gray unpt.	50.00	150.00	250.00

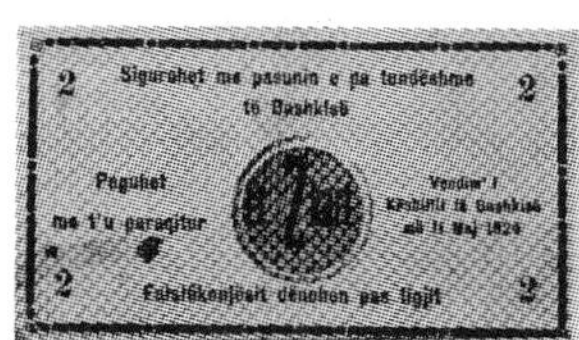

		GOOD	FINE	XF
S164	2 FRANK 11.5.1924. Blue and brown on green unpt.	60.00	150.00	250.00

SIEGE

SHQIPËRIA SHEMENDEFER(I)
ALBANIA RAILWAY

Railway issue by Turkish Gen. Esat Pasha besieged by Montenegrin forces in 1913.

MONETARY SYSTEM:

1 Grush = 40 Para

1913 ND ISSUE

#S181-S184 steam passenger train w/mountains in background (sideways). Uniface. These notes also come in uncut sheets.

		VG	VF	UNC
S181	5 PARA ND (1913).	75.00	175.00	400.00
S182	10 PARA ND (1913). Black.	8.00	30.00	75.00

S183 **1/2 GRUSH**

	VG	VF	UNC
ND (1913) Dk. blue.	10.00	32.50	80.00

S184 **1 GRUSH**

	GOOD	FINE	XF
ND (1913). Purple.	8.00	30.00	75.00

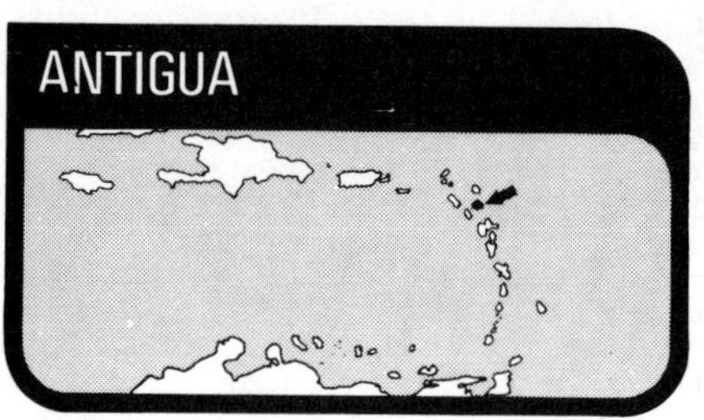

The Associated State of Antigua, located on the eastern edge of the Leeward Islands in the Caribbean Sea, has an area of 171 sq.mi. (442 sq. km). Capital: St. John's. Antigua and its dependencies, Barbuda and Redonda, comprised a presidency of the Leeward Islands.

Antigua was discovered by Columbus in 1493, settled by the British in 1632, occupied by the French in 1666, and ceded to Britain in 1667.

RULERS:

British

MONETARY SYSTEM:

1 British West Indies Dollar = 4 Shillings - 2 Pence
5 British West Indies Dollars = 1 Pound - 10 Pence

NOTE: For later issues see British East Caribbean Territories in Vol. 2 and East Caribbean States in Vol. 3.

BRITISH ADMINISTRATION

BARCLAYS BANK (DOMINION, COLONIAL AND OVERSEAS)

Formerly The Colonial Bank.

1926 PROVISIONAL ISSUE

S105 **5 DOLLARS**

	GOOD	FINE	XF
1926. Black on pink and green unpt. Arms at ctr.	—	Rare	—

1937 PROVISIONAL ISSUE

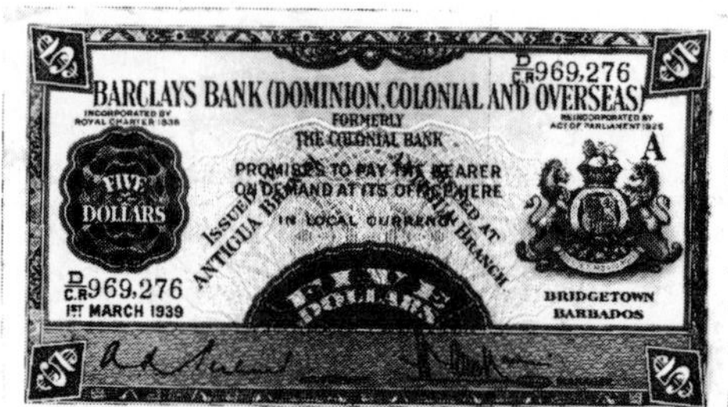

S108 **5 DOLLARS**

1937-40. Purple on m/c unpt. Arms at r. Office of issue: Bridgetown, Barbados. Ovpt: *ISSUED AT ANTIGUA BRANCH.* Printer: BWC.

	GOOD	FINE	XF
a. 1.5.1937.	250.00	600.00	1500.
b. 1.3.1939.	225.00	525.00	1350.
c. 1.3.1940.	200.00	500.00	1250.

COLONIAL BANK

Later became Barclays Bank.

1900 ISSUE

S112 **5 DOLLARS**

	GOOD	FINE	XF
To 1926. Arms at upper ctr. Printer: P&B.	Reported Not Confirmed		

ROYAL BANK OF CANADA

1913 PROVISIONAL ISSUE

S115 **5 DOLLARS**

2.1.1913. Black on green unpt. Portr. C. E. Neill at l., arms at ctr., portr. H. S. Holt at r. Back green; royal crest at ctr. Blue ovpt: *ANTIGUA* at l. and r., ovpt: *PAYABLE AT ST. JOHN'S ANTIGUA* at l. ctr. Printer: ABNC.

	GOOD	FINE	XF
a. Issued note	—	—	—
p. Proof.	—	Unc	450.00
s. Specimen.	—	Unc	2000.

1920 REGULAR ISSUE

S116 **5 DOLLARS = 1 POUND - 10 PENCE**

2.1.1920. Black on green unpt. Steamship at ctr. Back green; royal crest at ctr. Printer: ABNC.

	GOOD	FINE	XF
a. Issued note.	350.00	1000.	—
p. Proof.	—	Unc	450.00

1938 ISSUE

		GOOD	FINE	XF
S117	**5 DOLLARS = 1 POUND/10 PENCE** 3.1.1938. Black on green unpt. Similar to #S116 but reduced size. Printer: CBNC.			
	a. Issued note.	250.00	600.00	—
	p. Proof.	—	Unc	450.00

The Argentine Republic, located in South America, has an area of 1,068,301 sq. mi. (2,766,889 sq. km.) and a population of 37.03 million. Capital: Buenos Aires. Its varied topography ranges from the subtropical lowlands of the north to the towering Andean Mountains in the west and the windswept Patagonian steppe in the south. The rolling, fertile pampas of central Argentina are ideal for agriculture and grazing, and support most of the republic's population. Meat packing, flour milling, textiles, sugar refining and dairy products are the principal industries. Oil is found in Patagonia, but most of the mineral requirements must be imported.

Argentina was discovered in 1516 by the Spanish navigator Juan de Solis. A permanent Spanish colony was established at Buenos Aires in 1580, but the colony developed slowly. When Napoleon conquered Spain, the Argentines set up their own government in the name of the Spanish king on May 25, 1810. Independence was formally declared on July 9, 1816.

MONETARY SYSTEM:

1 Peso = 8 Reales = 100 Centavos

ARRANGEMENT

Listings for Argentina are divided into six major sections. The first contains early government, government-controlled institutions and banks for the period 1820-1864. The second contains such notes issued between 1865 and 1903. Presented at the beginning of each of these sections are government or Treasury issues, followed by bank issues according to the headings found on the notes. The third section consists of notes falling under a National Bank system called *Bancos Nacionales Garantidos,* first issued in 1888. The fourth lists earlier provincial issues, and the fifth lists all regional and private bank issues in alphabetical sequence. The sixth lists all later provincial issues, from 1890 to 2002.

The following chart indicates the contents of each of these six major sections:

Section I, 1820-64

GOVERNMENT

Government of the Province of Buenos Aires
Customs Notes of 1820-1821 . . . . . #S101-S120
Provincia de Buenos Aires, 1823 . . . . . #121-S123
Argentine Confederation
Treasury Notes, 1853-1854 . . . . . #S151-S166
Customs Bonds-Gobierno Nacional, 1855-1859 . . . . . #S170-S172, S181-S211
República Argentina
Treasury Notes, 1860-61 . . . . . #S216-S231

EARLY BANCOS

Banco de Buenos Ayres, 1822-1829 . . . . . #S301-S336
Banco Nacional, 1826 . . . . . #S337-S359
Banco Nacional de las Provincias Unidas del Rio de la Plata, 1829-1840 . . . . . #S360-S376
Casa de Moneda - notes titled *La Provincia de Buenos Aires,* 1841-1851 . . . . . #S377-S401
Banco y Casa de Moneda - notes titled *La Provincia de Buenos Aires,* 1853-1854 . . . . . #S402-S414
- as above, notes titled *El Estado de Buenos Aires,* 1856-1858 . . . . . #S415-S435
- as above, in its own name 1864 . . . . . #S441-S450

Section II, 1865-1903

TREASURY

Treasury Bills, 1876 . . . . . #S461-S464
Bonos de Tesoro, Provincia de Buenos Aires, 1880 . . . . . #S464A-S464C
Treasury Notes, 1890 . . . . . #S465-S466

BANKS

Banco de la Provincia de Buenos Aires, 1865, 1869-1891 . . . . . #S467-S470, S500-S579
- as above, notes titled *La Provincia de Buenos Aires,* 1867, 1869 . . . . . #S471-S499
Banco Británico de la América del Sud, 1894 . . . . . #S601
Banco Hipotecario de la Provincia de Buenos Aires, 1891 . . . . . #S611-S632
Banco Nacional, 1873-1883 . . . . . #S641-S720
Banco Provincial de Córdoba, 1873-1891 . . . . . #S721-S757
Banco Provincial de Entre-Rios, 1885 . . . . . #S760-S772
Banco Provincial de Salta, 1884-1903 . . . . . #S786-S797
Banco Provincial de Santa Fé, 1874-1882 . . . . . #S798-S835
Banco Provincial de Tucumán, 1888 . . . . . #S841-S846

Section III, 1888

BANCOS NACIONALES GARANTIDOS

Banco Alemán Transatlántico . . . . . #S1008
Banco Británico de la América del Sud . . . . . #S1020
Banco Buenos Aires . . . . . #S1024-S1027
Banco Carabassa . . . . . #S1040
Banco Constructor de la Plata . . . . . #S1041-S1043
Banco Frances del Rio de la Plata . . . . . #S1057
Banco Inglés de Rio de Janeiro . . . . . #S1063-S1065
Banco de Italia y Rio de la Plata . . . . . #S1078
Banco Londres y Rio de la Plata . . . . . #S1090
Banco Nacional . . . . . #S1091-S1100
Banco de la Provincia de Buenos Aires . . . . . #S1101-S1109
Banco Provincial de Catamarca . . . . . #S1111-S1116
Banco Provincial de Córdoba . . . . . #S1121-S1129
Banco Provincial de Corrientes . . . . . #S1131-S1137
Banco Provincial de Entre Rios . . . . . #S1141-S1146
Banco Provincial de La Rioja . . . . . #S1151-S1157
Banco de la Provincia de Mendoza . . . . . #S1161-S1165

Banco Provincial de Salta .... #S1171-S1175
Banco Provincial de San Juan .... #S1181-S1186
Banco Provincial de Santa Fé .... #S1191-S1200
Banco de la Provincia de Santiago del Estero .... #S1201-S1207
Banco Provincial de Tucumán .... #S1211-S1216
Banco de San Luis .... #S1221-S1226
Nuevo Banco Italiano .... #S1236-S1237

Section IV, 1823-76

PROVINCIAL

Province of Catamarca, 1849 .... #S1251
Province of Córdoba, 1829 .... #S1263
Province of Corrientes, 1826-1861 .... #S1281-S1348
Province of Entre-Rios, 1826 .... #S1361-S1366
Province of Mendoza, 1839 .... #S1381
Province of San Luis, 1871 .... #S1394-S1396
Province of Santa Fé, 1823 .... #S1401-S1403
Province of Santiago del Estero, 1870-1876 .... #S1411-S1421

Section V, 1866-84

REGIONAL AND PRIVATE BANKS

Banco Argentino, 1866-1873 .... #S1451-S1545
Banco J. Benites e Hijo, 1867-1868 .... #S1551-S1565
Banco del Chaco, 1884 .... #S1566
Banco Comercial de Corrientes, 1867-1868 .... #S1571-S1584
Banco Comercial de Santa Fé, 1867-1869 .... #S1590-S1598
Banco del Comercio, 1869 .... #S1601-S1608
Banco de Consignaciones de Frutos del Pais .... #S1610
Banco de Corrientes, 1873 .... #S1611-S1620
Banco de Cuyo, 1892 .... #S1631-S1644
Banco Entre-Riano, 1864-1872 .... #S1651-S1668
Banco Hipotecario de la Provincia de Córdoba, ND .... #S1671-S1672
Banco Hipotecario de las Provincias Ligadas del Norte, 1841 .... #S1679-S1683
Banco Industrial de la Provincia de La Rioja .... #S1691-S1695
Banco del Litoral, 1871-1880 .... #S1701-S1718
Banco de Londres y Rio de la Plata, 1866-1869 .... #S1721-S1745
Banco Mauá & Ca., 1865-1868 .... #S1745A-S1747C
Banco Mendez Hermanos y Cia .... #S1747E-S1747M
Banco de Mendoza, 1871-1882 .... #S1748-S1758
Banco Muñoz & Rodriguez & Ca., 1883 .... #S1760-S1763
(Banco) Oxandaburu y Garvino, 1867-1869 .... #S1771-S1778
Banco Oxandaburu y Garbino, 1869 .... #S1781-S1794
Banco Domingo Garbino, 1869 .... #S1801-S1806
Banco Paraná, 1868 .... #S1811-S1819
Banco Rio Cuarto, 1874 .... #S1821-S1826
Banco del Rio de la Plata, 1868-1869 .... #S1831-S1848
Banco (del) Rosario de Santa Fé, 1865-1869 .... #S1851-S1856
Banco de San Juan, 1873-1878 .... #S1860-S1900
Banco de San Luis, 1894 .... #S1901-S1904
Banco Solanas & Cia., 1874 .... #S1912-S1918
Banco de Victoria, 1873 .... #S1923
Caja de Ahorros de Rosario, 1870 .... #S1931
Credito Popular, 1906 .... #S1944
Credito Territorial, 1877 .... #S1951
Credito Territorial de Santa Fé, 1869 .... #S1963
Daniel Gonzalez y Compa., 1866-1868 .... #S1971-S1976
Miguel Lanieri, 1871 .... #S1982-S1983
Banco Lanieri, 1871 .... #S1983A
Otero y Cia. (and Banco Otero y Cia.), 1868-1880 .... #S1984-S2004

Section VI, 1890-1932, 1985-96

PROVINCIAL 1890-1932

Province of Corrientes, 1891 .... #S2015
Province of Jujuy, 1903-1932 .... #S2021-S2035
Province of Mendoza, 1893-1923 .... #S2042-S2096H
Province of Salta, 1907-1933 .... #S2097-S2142
Province of San Juan, 1896-1923 .... #S2151-S2194
Province of Santa Fé, 1890 .... #S2214-S2217
Province of Santiago del Estero .... #S2221
Province of Tucumán, 1900-1920 .... #S2235-S2248

PROVINCIAL BONOS 1985-2002

Province of Catamarca .... #S2351-S2353
Province of Jujuy .... #S2401-S2413
Province of La Rioja .... #S2501-S2507
Province of Mendoza .... #S2371-S2381
Province of Salta .... #S2601-S2630
Province of San Juan .... #S2651-S2654
Province of Tucumán .... #S2701-S2719

SECTION I

Early Forerunners of Paper Money, 1813-18

Several kinds of paper issues took place shortly after Argentinian independence, but these did not constitute true paper money. They represented loans to the government, and could serve in only a very limited capacity as payment for customs or certain debts.

GOVERNMENT

GOVERNMENT OF THE PROVINCE OF BUENOS AIRES

Probably the earliest issues that could have circulated were the Customs Notes of the Ministerio de Hacienda, 1820-1821. There were two distinct types, similar in general appearance but with differing legends in the circular design at top ctr.

1820 CUSTOMS NOTES FIRST ISSUE

#S101-S106 legend in circular design: *PROVINCIA DE BUENOS-AYRES*. Text on notes: *PAPEL VILLETE O AMORTIZAVLE* above *VALE POR*...line. Issued under Decrees of 27 May and 29 November 1820. Black on white paper. Several wmk. varieties. Circle w/oval hand stamp of arms and text at upper ctr. Printed sign.

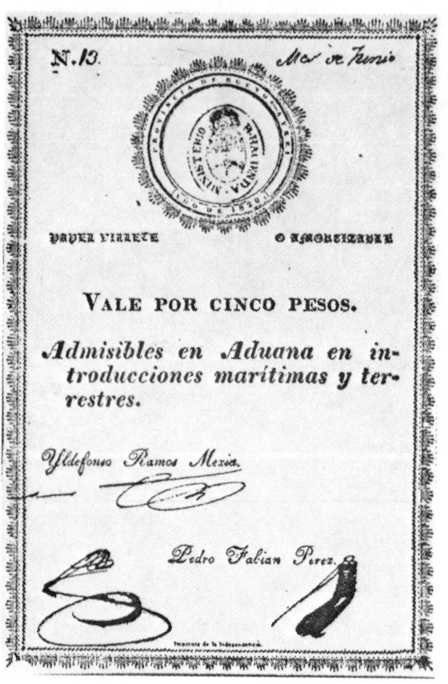

		Good	Fine	XF
S101	**5 PESOS** 1820.	250.00	450.00	750.00
S102	**10 PESOS** 1820.	250.00	450.00	750.00
S103	**20 PESOS** 1820.	250.00	450.00	750.00
S104	**40 PESOS** 1820.	275.00	500.00	800.00
S105	**50 PESOS** 1820.	250.00	450.00	750.00
S106	**100 PESOS** 1820.	250.00	450.00	750.00

1820 CUSTOMS NOTES SECOND ISSUE

#S107-S113 like previous issue, but handwritten sign.

		Good	Fine	XF
S107	**5 PESOS** 1820.	200.00	400.00	700.00
S108	**10 PESOS** 1820.	200.00	400.00	700.00
S109	**20 PESOS** 1820.	200.00	400.00	700.00
S110	**40 PESOS** 1820.	250.00	450.00	750.00
S111	**50 PESOS** 1820.	200.00	400.00	700.00
S112	**100 PESOS** 1820.	200.00	400.00	700.00
S113	**100 PESOS** 1821.	200.00	400.00	700.00

1820; 1821 CUSTOMS NOTES THIRD ISSUE

#S114-S120 legend in circular design: *PAPEL MONEDA DE LA PROVINCIA DE BUENOS-AYRES*. W/o text: *PAPEL VILLETE* etc. above *VALE ...* line. Similar to previous issue. All except #S116 w/handwritten sign.

		Good	Fine	XF
S114	**10 PESOS** 1820.	250.00	450.00	750.00
S115	**20 PESOS** 1820.	250.00	450.00	750.00
S116	**100 PESOS** 1820. Printed sign.	250.00	450.00	750.00
S117	**100 PESOS** 1820.	250.00	450.00	750.00
S118	**10 PESOS** 1821.	250.00	450.00	750.00
S119	**20 PESOS** 1821.	250.00	450.00	750.00
S120	**100 PESOS** 1821.	250.00	450.00	750.00

PROVINCIA DE BUENOS AIRES

1823 ISSUE

#S121-S123 issued by the government of the Province in 1823. Payable in metallic money. Black printing.

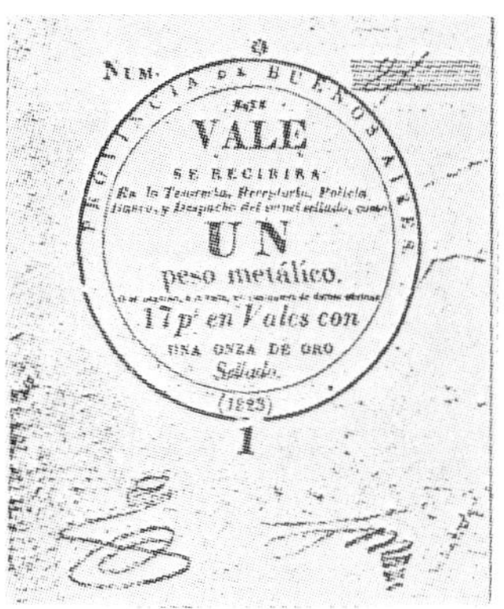

		GOOD	FINE	XF
S121	**1 PESO** 1823. Circle w/text and value at ctr.	200.00	400.00	700.00

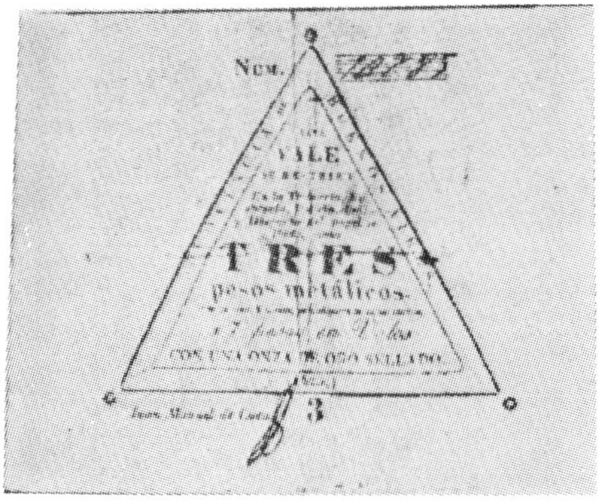

		GOOD	FINE	XF
S122	**3 PESOS** 1823. Triangle w/text and value at ctr.	—	Rare	—
S123	**5 PESOS** 1823. Pentagon w/text and value at ctr.	—	Rare	—

ARGENTINE CONFEDERATION

Formed in 1852, upon its separation from the Province of Buenos Aires in 1854 it became a separate entity with its capital at Paraná. Plans for paper money issues began in 1853. Several different kinds were made from 1853 through 1861.

1853-54 ND TREASURY NOTES ISSUE

#S151-S154 authorized by decree of January 30, 1854 while the government was waiting for copper coins to arrive from Europe.

		GOOD	FINE	XF
S151	**1/2 REAL**	Reported Not Confirmed		

		GOOD	FINE	XF
S152	**1 REAL** ND. Black. Ram at bottom ctr. Uniface.	—	Rare	—
S153	**2 REALES** ND.	Reported Not Confirmed		
S154	**4 REALES** ND.	Reported Not Confirmed		

ADMINISTRACIÓN DE HACIENDA Y CREDITO

1853 ND TREASURY NOTES

#S155-S159 Black. Handwritten date 9 December 1853. Uniface. Issue controlled by the *Administración de Hacienda y Credito*.

		GOOD	FINE	XF
S155	**1 PESO** 1853. Horse at bottom ctr. Squarish format.	100.00	225.00	450.00
S156	**5 PESOS** 1853. Horses and cow at top ctr., clasped hands at bottom ctr.	150.00	325.00	700.00

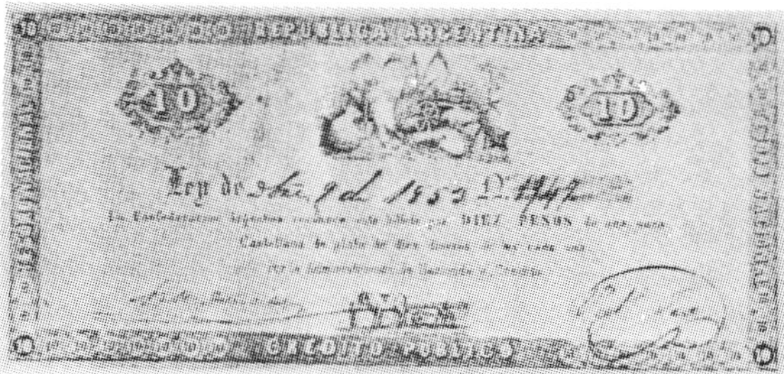

		GOOD	FINE	XF
S157	**10 PESOS** 1853. Cows, plants and bales at top ctr., cow at bottom ctr.	250.00	450.00	850.00
S158	**20 PESOS** 1853.	Reported Not Confirmed		
S159	**50 PESOS** 1853.	Reported Not Confirmed		
S160	**100 PESOS** 1853.	Reported Not Confirmed		

185X ND TREASURY NOTES

#S161-S166 Black. Specimens only. Printer: PBC.

		GOOD	FINE	XF
S161	**1 PESO** 185x. Farm tools at upper ctr. Specimen.	—	Rare	—

		GOOD	FINE	XF
S162	**5 PESOS** 185x. Allegorical figures at upper ctr. Specimen.	—	Rare	—

		GOOD	FINE	XF
S163	**10 PESOS** 185x. Bull at upper ctr. Specimen.	—	Rare	—
S164	**20 PESOS**	Reported Not Confirmed		

		GOOD	FINE	XF
S165	**50 PESOS** 185x. Allegory of Commerce at upper ctr. Specimen.	—	Rare	—
S166	**100 PESOS** 185x.	Reported Not Confirmed		

CUSTOM BONDS - GOBIERNO NACIONAL

Seven different issues of bonds good for partial payment of customs duties and payable to bearer at fixed percentages were made from 1857 to 1859.

DECRETO DE 15 DE NOVIEMBRE DE 1855

		Good	Fine	XF
S170	**10 PESOS** *D.1855.*	—	Rare	—
S171	**100 PESOS** *D.1855.*	—	Rare	—
S172	**200 PESOS** *D.1855.*	—	Rare	—

DECRETO DE 7 DE MAYO DE 1857

#S181-S184 black. Uniface. Various handwritten dates in 1857. Interest payable at 1% per month.

		Good	Fine	XF
S181	**10 PESOS** 1857.	10.00	30.00	70.00
S182	**20 PESOS** 1857.	10.00	30.00	70.00
S183	**50 PESOS** 1857.	10.00	30.00	70.00

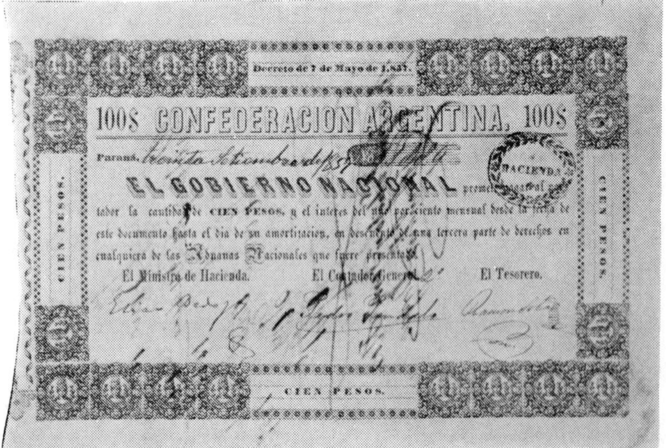

		Good	Fine	XF
S184	**100 PESOS** 1857. 20 tiny portr. medalets make up part of border design.	10.00	30.00	70.00

DECRETOS DE 7 DE MAYO Y 5 DE JUNIO 1857

#S185-S188 like previous issue. Various handwritten dates into 1859. Interest payable at 2% per month.

		Good	Fine	XF
S185	**10 PESOS** 1857-59.			
	a. Issued note.	10.00	30.00	70.00
	x. Error w/*descento* in text.	20.00	60.00	125.00
S186	**20 PESOS** 1857-59.	10.00	30.00	70.00

		Good	Fine	XF
S187	**50 PESOS** 1857-59.	10.00	30.00	70.00
S188	**100 PESOS** 1857-59. Similar to #S184, but only 18 portr. medalets in border design.	10.00	30.00	70.00

1857 FIRST ISSUE

#S189-S191 payable from October 1, 1857.

		Good	Fine	XF
S189	**25 PESOS** 1857.	Reported Not Confirmed		
S190	**50 PESOS** 1857.	Reported Not Confirmed		

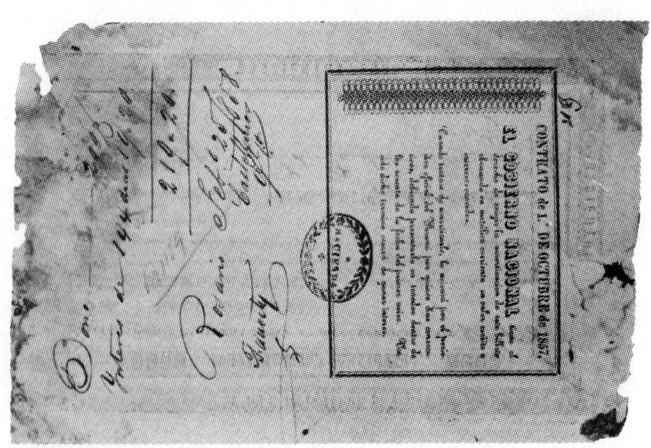

		Good	Fine	XF
S191	**200 PESOS** 1857.	10.00	30.00	70.00

1857 SECOND ISSUE

#S192-S195 payable from January 1, 1858.

		Good	Fine	XF
S192	**20 PESOS** 1857.	10.00	30.00	70.00

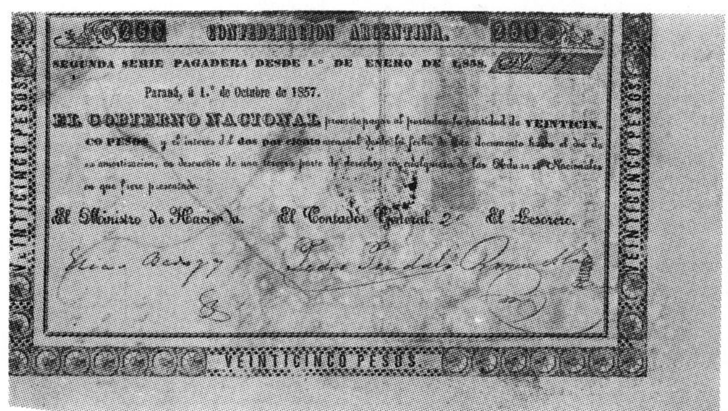

		Good	Fine	XF
S193	25 Pesos 1857.	10.00	30.00	70.00
S194	50 Pesos 1857.	10.00	30.00	70.00
S195	200 Pesos 1857.	10.00	30.00	70.00

1857 Third Issue

#S196-S198 payable from January 1, 1859.

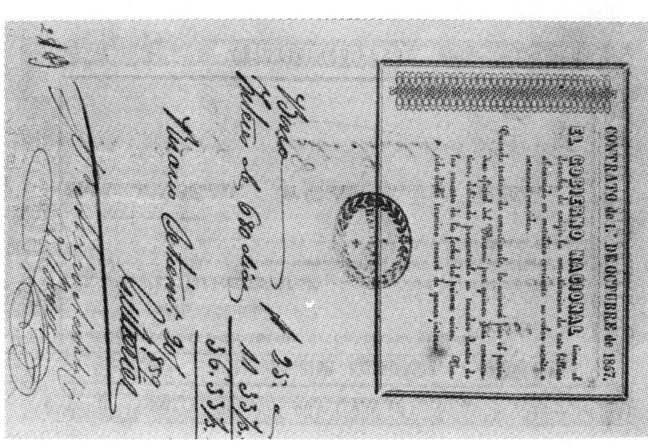

		Good	Fine	XF
S196	25 Pesos 1857.	10.00	30.00	70.00
S197	50 Pesos 1857.	10.00	30.00	70.00
S198	200 Pesos 1857.	10.00	30.00	70.00

1859 Issue

#S201-S203 black. Uniface. Issued in 1859 to help finance the war between the Confederation and the State of Buenos Aires. No law or contract is shown. Various handwritten dates in 1859.

		Good	Fine	XF
S201	20 Pesos 1859.	10.00	30.00	70.00

		Good	Fine	XF
S202	50 Pesos 1859.	10.00	30.00	70.00
S203	100 Pesos 1859.	10.00	30.00	70.00

Contrato de 10 de Mayo de 1859

#S204-S206 black. Uniface. Interest was set at 1-1/2% per month.

		Good	Fine	XF
S204	100 Pesos 1859.	10.00	30.00	70.00
S205	200 Pesos 1859.	10.00	30.00	70.00

		Good	Fine	XF
S206	500 Pesos 1859. Border design like #S188 and #S211.	20.00	50.00	110.00

Ley Septiembre 29 de 1859

#S207 single form was issued, with space for various handwritten denominations. Interest rate was 6% annually.

		Good	Fine	XF
S207	Various Amounts 1859. Black. Uniface.	—	Rare	—

Ley de 30 de Septiembre de 1859

#S208-S211 black. Uniface. Notes have various handwritten dates in 1859. Interest rate was 2% per month.

		Good	Fine	XF
S208	10 Pesos 1859.	10.00	30.00	70.00

		Good	Fine	XF
S209	**20 Pesos** 1859.	10.00	30.00	70.00
S210	**50 Pesos** 1859.	10.00	30.00	70.00

		Good	Fine	XF
S211	**100 Pesos** 1859. Similar to #S188.	10.00	25.00	50.00

República Argentina

In October of 1860, the Argentine Confederation adopted the name REPUBLICA ARGENTINA. For a time that year, the war between the Confederation and Buenos Aires ceased and the two were joined. But by June 1861 relations between them had ruptured once again, and fighting began in earnest. The final defeat of Buenos Aires by the Confederation in September, 1861, brought about unification and the end of the Confederation.

Treasury

Ley de 1 de Octubre de 1860

#S216-S223 various handwritten dates in 1860 and 1861. Most have blue ovpt: *PAGADO No.* in oval on face or back.

		Good	Fine	XF
S216	**1/2 Peso** 1860-61. Like #S224 but w/o ovpt: *1861.*	Reported Not Confirmed		
S217	**1 Peso** 1860-61. Like #S225 but w/o ovpt: *1861.*	Reported Not Confirmed		
S218	**2 Pesos** 1860-61. Like #S226 but w/o ovpt: *1861.*	Reported Not Confirmed		
S219	**5 Pesos** 1860-61. Like #S227 but w/o ovpt: *1861.*	—	Rare	—
S220	**10 Pesos** 1860-61. Black. Green paper. Denomination in oval at upper ctr.	15.00	40.00	85.00

		Good	Fine	XF
S221	**20 Pesos** 1860-61. Black. Greenish yellow paper. Arms at upper ctr.			
	a. Issued note.	15.00	40.00	85.00
	b. Oval hand stamp: *PAGADO.*	12.00	30.00	65.00

		Good	Fine	XF
S222	**50 Pesos** 1860-61. Black. Lt. tan paper. Seated woman in oval at l.			
	a. Issued note.	15.00	40.00	85.00
	b. Oval hand stamp: *PAGADO.*	12.00	30.00	65.00

		Good	Fine	XF
S223	**100 Pesos** 1860-61. Black and pink. Seated allegorical man w/bales at ctr.	15.00	40.00	85.00

Ley de 1 de Octubre de 1860; 1861 Issue

#S224-S231 like previous issue but blue oval ovpt: *EMISION DE 15 DE OCTUBRE 1861* at r. Handwritten date 15 Octubre 1861. Oval hand stamped seal.

		Good	Fine	XF
S224	**1/2 Peso** 1861. Black.	30.00	70.00	125.00

		Good	Fine	XF
S225	**1 Peso** 1861. Brown-violet.			
	a. Issued note.	35.00	85.00	150.00
	b. Oval hand stamp: *PAGADO.*	30.00	70.00	125.00
S226	**2 Pesos** 1861. Blue.	30.00	70.00	125.00

		Good	Fine	XF
S227	**5 Pesos** 1861. Orange.	30.00	65.00	110.00
S228	**10 Pesos** 1861. Like #S220.	15.00	40.00	85.00
S229	**20 Pesos** 1861.	30.00	65.00	110.00
S230	**50 Pesos** 1861.	50.00	125.00	—
S231	**100 Pesos** 1861. Black on pink unpt. Wmk: Denomination and bank crest. Uniface.	75.00	—	—

Banco de Buenos-Ayres

1822 First Issue

Consisted of a form on which the various specified denominations were written. Practically the entire issue was redeemed and no original examples are known. Reprints of the blank form were made by the Compania Sud-Americana de Billetes de Banco around 1900.

#S301-S306 black. Uniface.

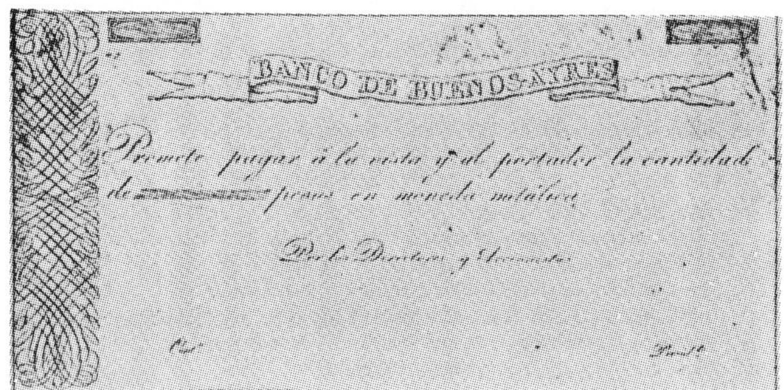

		Good	Fine	XF
S301	**20 Pesos** ND (1822).	—	—	—
S302	**50 Pesos** ND (1822).	—	—	—
S303	**100 Pesos** ND (1822).	—	—	—
S304	**200 Pesos** ND (1822).	—	—	—
S305	**500 Pesos** ND (1822).	—	—	—
S306	**1000 Pesos** ND (1822).	—	—	—

June 1823 Second Issue

Consisted of 2 emissions separately designed and dated.

		Good	Fine	XF
S307	**1 Peso** 9.6.1823. Black. Uniface. 1 bank seal (rayed sun in circle) at l.	—	Rare	—

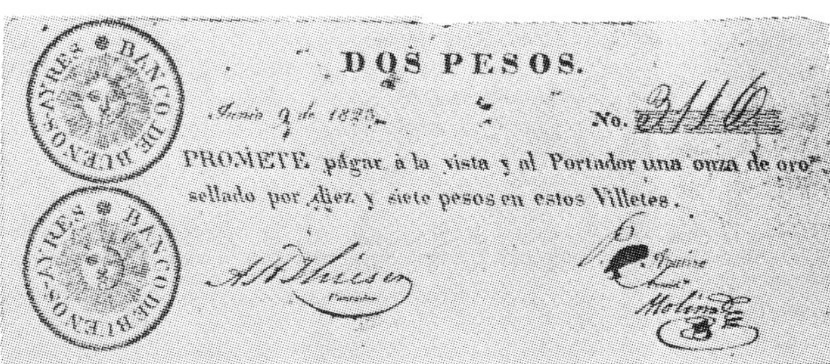

		Good	Fine	XF
S308	**2 Pesos** 9.6.1823. Similar to #S307 except 2 bank seals at l.	—	Rare	—

Nov. 1823 "Second" Issue

		Good	Fine	XF
S309	**1 Peso** 20.11.1823. Black. Uniface. 1 bank seal at ctr., heavy border.	—	Rare	—

		Good	Fine	XF
S310	**2 Pesos** 20.11.1823. Similar to #S309 except 2 bank seals, one partly over the other, at ctr.	—	Rare	—

1823-24 Third Issue

#S311-S319 black. Uniface. Notes printed in London.

		Good	Fine	XF
S311	**1 Peso** ND. Rose paper. National arms at top ctr. Hand sign. V. Alvarez.	—	Rare	—

NOTE: For 1 Peso notes like #S311 but w/different sign., see #S320.

#S312-S316 hand dated either 1.8.1823 or 1.3.1824. Arms at l. White paper.

		Good	Fine	XF
S312	**5 Pesos** 1823-24.	—	Rare	—

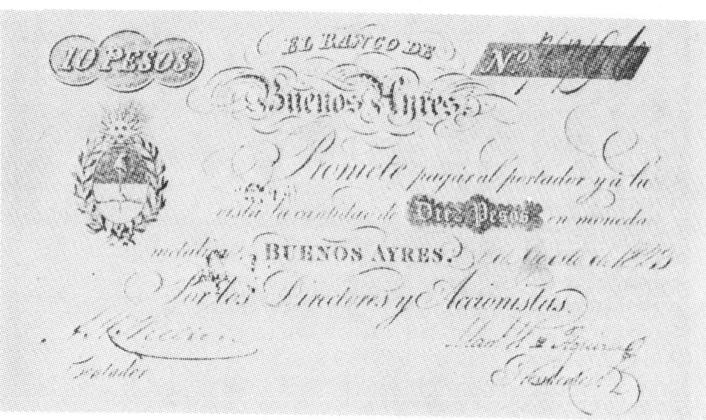

		Good	Fine	XF
S313	**10 Pesos** 1823-24.	—	Rare	—
S314	**20 Pesos** 1823-24.	—	Rare	—
S315	**50 Pesos** 1823-24.	—	Rare	—
S316	**100 Pesos** 1823-24.	—	Rare	—

NOTE: For notes like #S312-S313 and S315-316 but dated in 1826, see #S321-S324.

#S317-S319 *Deleted.*

1826 Third Issue (Continuation)

The Banco de las Provincias Unidas del Rio de la Plata was formed on January 28, 1826. It was to take over the issuance of bank notes from the Banco de Buenos-Ayres. The first issue of this newly created bank consisted of notes printed from plates for the Third Issue of the Banco de Buenos-Ayres.

		Good	Fine	XF
S320	**1 Peso** ND. Black. Like #S311 but different sign.			
	a. Rose paper.	150.00	350.00	850.00
	b. White paper.	150.00	350.00	850.00

#S321-S324 like S312-S313 and S315-S316 except for having handwritten dates in 1826.

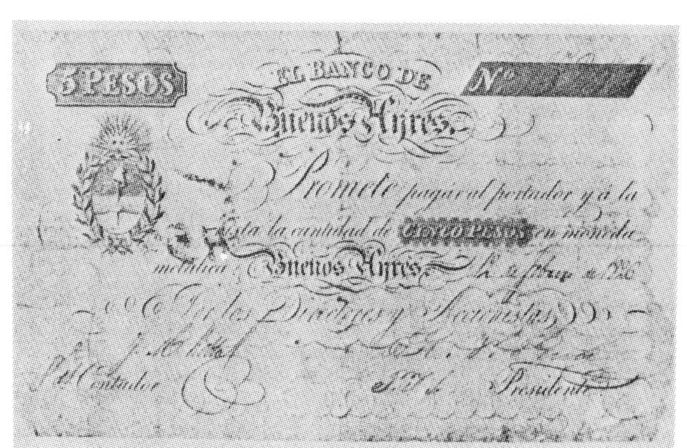

		Good	Fine	XF
S321	**5 Pesos** 1826.	—	Rare	—

		Good	Fine	XF
S322	**10 Pesos** 1826.	—	Rare	—
S323	**50 Pesos** 1826.	—	Rare	—
S324	**100 Pesos** 1826.	—	Rare	—

#S325-S327 *Deleted.*

1827 Fourth Issue

#S328-S336 carry the name of Banco de Buenos-Ayres but were issued by the Banco Nacional. Notes had been ordered by the former in 1825 but because of a Brazilian blockade they were not delivered until March 1827. Black on thin white paper. Uniface. Printer: Fairman, Draper, Underwood and Co., Philadelphia. Some notes later reprinted from the same plates in Buenos Aires on thicker paper. Notes hand dated from 1827-28 or 1829. Reprints of all values except the 1 Peso were made by the Compania Sud-Americana de Billetes de Banco around 1900.

		Good	Fine	XF
S328	**1 Peso** 1827-29. Portr. S. Bolívar at l., allegorical figures at ctr., portr. G. Washington at r.			
	a. Issued note.	125.00	300.00	650.00
	r. Unsigned remainder.	—	50.00	200.00

		Good	Fine	XF
S329	**5 Pesos** 1827-28. Portr. B. Franklin at l., allegorical woman at upper ctr., 2 horseback riders at bottom ctr., portr. W. Penn at r.	—	—	—

		Good	Fine	XF
S330	**10 Pesos** 1827-28. Eagle w/shield at ctr., portr. S. Bolívar at upper r., portr. G. Washington at lower r.	—	Rare	—

		Good	Fine	XF
S331	**20 Pesos** 1827-28. Portr. S. Bolívar at l., beehive at ctr., portr. G. Washington at upper r.	—	Rare	—
S332	**50 Pesos** 1827-28. Portr. S. Bolívar at upper l., G. Washington at lower l., allegorical figures and denomination at ctr.	—	Rare	—

		Good	Fine	XF
S333	**100 Pesos** 1827-28. Standing woman at l., allegorical woman at ctr., man at r.	—	Rare	—

		Good	Fine	XF
S334	**150 Pesos** 1827-29. Standing woman near portr. G. Washington at l., allegorical women at ctr. and r.	—	Rare	—

		Good	Fine	XF
S335	**500 Pesos** 1827-29. Allegorical woman w/bales at ctr.	—	Rare	—
S336	**1000 Pesos** 1827-29. Allegorical woman w/2 children at l., eagle at ctr., woman standing w/scale at r.	—	Rare	—

NOTE: No original notes of #S336 are known, only the reprints.

Banco Nacional

1826 1 Peso Issues

Notes with the "short form" bank name were first issued in 1826, though the notes bore no date. Two distinct types were made, and both were marked for issue in Buenos Aires or Provincia Oriental (later to become Uruguay).

#S337-S341 black. Uniface. Arms at ctr.

		Good	Fine	XF
S337	**1 Peso** ND (1826). Square format. Text: *CAJA DE* at lower l. (w/o any indication of circulating area).	—	—	—
S338	**1 Peso** ND (1826). Like #S337 except text: *CAJA DE* printed and *B.A.* (for Buenos Aires) filled in by hand at lower l.	—	—	—
S339	**1 Peso** ND (1826). Like #S337 except printed text: *CAJA DE P.O.* (for Provincia Oriental) at lower l.	—	—	—
S340	**1 Peso** ND (1826). Rectangular format. Printed *CAJA DE B.A.* at lower l.	—	—	—

		Good	Fine	XF
S341	**1 Peso** ND (1826). Like #S340 except printed text: *CAJA DE P.O.* at lower l.	—	—	—

1826 Fractional Issue

Issued in 1826 and 1827 without numerals, sign. or date. Printed in sheets of 32 subjects. Various colors are are known. Denominations are in parts of a Real. Corners are decorated with flowers, leaves or other design elements.

		Good	Fine	XF
S342	**10 Decimos** ND. Black, green or red-orange.	—	Rare	—

		Good	Fine	XF
S343	**20 Decimos** ND. Leaves in corners. Orange or brown.	—	Rare	—
S344	**20 Decimos** ND. Pointed arches in corners. Blue, ochre or green.	—	Rare	—

1826 "Whole Denomination" Issues

Two distinct issues were made during 1826. The first had the heading *BANCO NACIONAL*, and the second *EL BANCO NACIONAL*. Notes were hand dated 12.2.1826, 15.7.1826, or 1.12.1826. All are very rare or no longer known as original notes. Reprints (in both colors, red and black) were made by the Compania Sud-Americana de Billetes de Banco around 1900.

#S345-S354 heading: *BANCO NACIONAL*.

#S345-S349 black. Uniface.

#S345-S347 National Arms at l.

		Good	Fine	XF
S345	**5 Pesos** 1826.	—	Rare	—
S346	**10 Pesos** 1826.	Reported Not Confirmed		
S347	**20 Pesos** 1826.	—	Rare	—

NOTE: #S347 is known only as reprints; no originals have survived.

#S348-S349 National Arms at ctr.

Notice

Readers with unlisted dates, color or signature varieties are invited to submit photocopies of their notes to: Standard Catalog of World Paper Money, Krause Publications, 700 East State St. Iola WI 54990-0001 U.S.A. or by email: thernr@krause.com. Email submissions of material for possible inclusion need to be 100% jpeg attachments at 300 dpi.

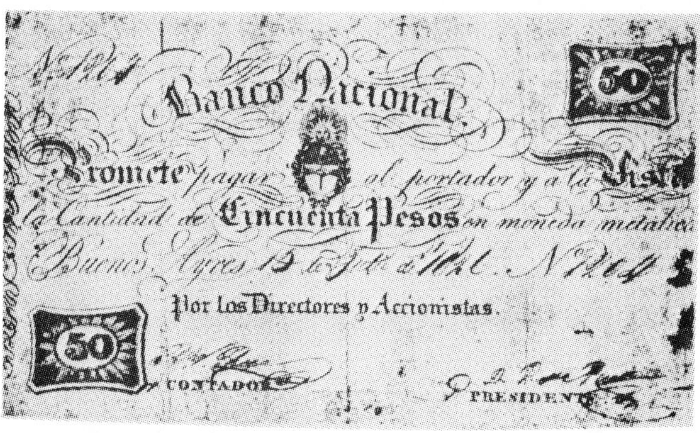

		Good	Fine	XF
S348	**50 Pesos** 1826.	—	Rare	—
S349	**100 Pesos** 1826.	—	Rare	—

#S350-S354 red. Uniface. Like previous issue.

		Good	Fine	XF
S350	**5 Pesos** 1826.	—	Rare	—
S351	**10 Pesos** 1826.	Reported Not Confirmed		
S352	**20 Pesos** 1826.	—	Rare	—
S353	**50 Pesos** 1826.	—	Rare	—

NOTE: #S350, S352, S353 known only as reprints.

		Good	Fine	XF
S354	**100 Pesos** 1826.	—	Rare	—

#S355-S359 heading: *EL BANCO NACIONAL*. Arms at ctr. Uniface.

		Good	Fine	XF
S355	**10 Pesos** 1826. Red.	Reported Not Confirmed		
S356	**20 Pesos** 1826. Red.	Reported Not Confirmed		
S357	**50 Pesos** 1826. Black.	—	Rare	—
S358	**100 Pesos** 1826. Black.	—	Rare	—

		Good	Fine	XF
S359	**150 Pesos** 1826. Black.	—	Rare	—

NOTE: #S357-359 known only as reprints.

Banco Nacional de las Provincias Unidas del Rio de la Plata

Notes with the "long form" bank name were first issued in 1829. Several issues followed using similar designs but with revalidations.

1829 Issue

#S360-S367 black on various colors of paper. Uniface. Printer: Perkins and Heath, London (w/o imprint). Some were also printed from the same plates in Buenos Aires.

		Good	Fine	XF
S360	**1 Peso** 1.3.1829; 1.9.1829; 12.2.1830. Arms at ctr., standing woman at r.			
	a. Red paper.	65.00	150.00	325.00
	b. 1.9.1829. White paper.	65.00	150.00	325.00

NOTE: The 1830 date is very rare.

#S361-363, S365-366 arms at l., 3 allegorical women seated at upper ctr.

#S361-S363 text at bottom reads: *POR EL PRESIDENTE Y DIRECTORES.*

		Good	Fine	XF
S361	**5 Pesos** 1.3.1829; 1.9.1829. Lt. blue paper.	—	—	—
S362	**10 Pesos** 1.3.1829; 1.9.1829. Green paper.	—	Rare	—
S363	**20 Pesos** 1.3.1829; 1.9.1829. Yellow paper.	—	Rare	—

#S364-S367 text at bottom reads: *POR LOS DIRECTORES Y ACCIONISTAS.*

		Good	Fine	XF
S364	**50 Pesos** 1.3.1829; 1.9.1829. 3 allegorical women at l., arms at ctr. White paper.	—	Rare	—
S365	**100 Pesos** 1.3.1829; 1.9.1829. White paper.	—	Rare	—
S366	**200 Pesos** 1.3.1829; 1.9.1829. White paper.	—	Rare	—
S367	**500 Pesos** 1.3.1829. Arms at ctr. White paper.	—	Rare	—

1834 Renovacion Transitional Issue

Starting in 1834 the Banco Nacional reissued some of the lower denominations of the previous issue. Higher values as well as certain lower value notes were not issues of the Banco Nacional but were instead under the control of the newly formed Casa de Moneda. Such notes are so indicated in the listings. The Casa de Moneda was created by decree on May 30, 1836.

		Good	Fine	XF
S368	**1 Peso** 1834-38. Like #S360 but *RENOVACION 1834* twice on face in small circles at l. and r.			
	a. 29.8.1834. Serial #1 to 418,000. Banco Nacional.	60.00	175.00	400.00
	b. 29.8.1834. Serial #418,001 to 1,000,000. Casa de Moneda.	20.00	75.00	200.00
	c. 8.12.1838. 1,443,000 notes issued by Casa de Moneda.	15.00	60.00	175.00

#S369-S376 like #S361-367. All except #S376 have *RENOVACION 1834* printed twice on face at bottom l. and r. beneath curved lines. All on white paper except #S370.

		Good	Fine	XF
S369	**5 Pesos** 29.8.1834. Like #S361. Black.			
	a. Serial #1 to 115,000. Banco Nacional.	200.00	500.00	—
	b. Serial #115,001 to 278,000. Casa de Moneda.	100.00	300.00	—
S370	**5 Pesos** 8.12.1838. Like #S369 but red 416,000 notes issued by Casa de Moneda.	—	Rare	—
S371	**10 Pesos** 1834-38. Like #S362.			
	a. 29.8.1834. Serial #1 to 49,000. Banco Nacional.	—	Rare	—
	b. 29.8.1834. Serial #49,001 to 246,000. Casa de Moneda.	150.00	400.00	—
	c. 8.12.1838. 349 notes issued by Casa de Moneda.	—	Rare	—
S372	**20 Pesos** 1834-38. Like #S363.			
	a. 29.8.1834. Serial #1 to 39,000. Banco Nacional.	—	Rare	—
	b. 29.8.1834. Serial #39,001 to 125,000. Casa de Moneda.	200.00	500.00	—
	c. 8.12.1838. 38,000 notes issued by Casa de Moneda.	175.00	400.00	—
S373	**50 Pesos** 1829-38. Like #S364. All issued by Casa de Moneda.			
	a. 1.9.1829. Serial #1 to 20,000.	200.00	500.00	—
	b. 29.8.1834. Serial #20,001 to 30,000.	200.00	500.00	—
	c. 8.12.1838. 103,000 notes issued.	200.00	500.00	—
S374	**100 Pesos** 1.9.1829; 29.8.1834. Like #S365. All issued by Casa de Moneda.	—	Rare	—

NOTE: 57,000 notes dated 1.9.1829; 39,000 dated 29.8.1834.

		Good	Fine	XF
S375	**200 Pesos** 29.8.1834; 8.12.1838. Like #S366. All issued by Casa de Moneda.	—	Rare	—

NOTE: 19,165 notes dated 29.8.1834; 37,000 dated 8.12.1838.

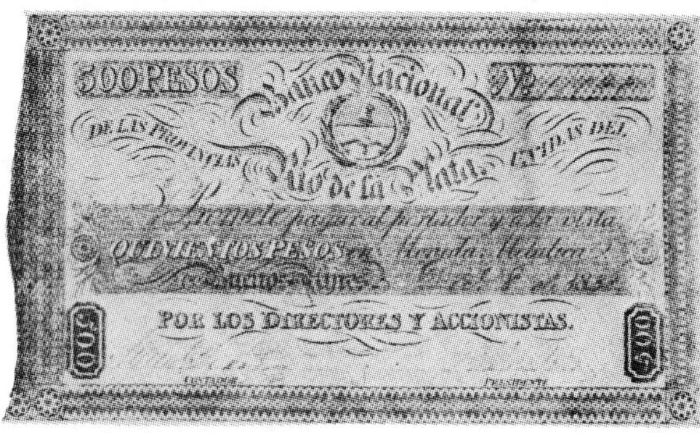

		Good	Fine	XF
S376	**500 Pesos** 8.12.1838; 28.3.1840. Like #S367. 44,000 notes issued by Casa de Moneda.	—	Rare	—

Casa de Moneda

Notes w/title: *LA PROVINCIA DE BUENOS AYRES*

The Casa de Moneda functioned as the issuing arm of the government from its creation in 1836 until a reorganization changing it to the Banco y Casa de Moneda in 1853. Notes issued by the Casa de Moneda from 1841 to 1851 had political slogans as part of the text w/title: *LA PROVINCIA DE BUENOS AYRES.* The Casa de Moneda is indicated as the issuer near the bottom.

1841 Issue

Each denomination has a different date in 1841. The year date is sometimes printed in full, or the last 1 or 2 numerals may be handwritten.

#S377-S378 black. Uniface. Handwritten sign. Printer: PBP.

		Good	Fine	XF
S377	**1 Peso** 1.1.1841. Allegorical women w/shields at ctr.			
	a. *1841* fully printed. Orange paper.	20.00	75.00	175.00
	b. *1841* fully printed. Pinkish purple paper. W/o imprint.	20.00	75.00	175.00
	c. *184* printed. Orange paper. W/imprint.	20.00	75.00	175.00
	d. *184* printed. Pinkish purple paper.	20.00	75.00	175.00
	s. Specimen.	—	—	—

		GOOD	FINE	XF
S378	**5 PESOS**			
	1.2.1841. Ostriches at ctr. Fully printed date. Orange paper.			
	a. Issued note.	40.00	100.00	250.00
	s. Specimen.	—	—	—

#S379-S383 printer: Wilson & Sons, London.

Some of these notes were also printed later in Buenos Aires. All w/heading at top: *Viva La Federacion!*

		GOOD	FINE	XF
S379	**10 PESOS**			
	1.3.1841. Cow and sheep at ctr. Orange paper.			
	a. *1841* fully printed.	70.00	250.00	—
	b. *184* printed.	70.00	250.00	—

		GOOD	FINE	XF
S380	**20 PESOS**			
	1.4.1841. Horse at lower ctr. Orange paper.			
	a. *1841* fully printed.	—	—	—
	b. *184* printed.	—	—	—
	s. Specimen.	—	—	—

		GOOD	FINE	XF
S381	**50 PESOS**			
	1.5.1841. Cows at ctr. *18* printed. Orange paper.	—	—	—

		GOOD	FINE	XF
S382	**100 PESOS**			
	1.6.1841. Municipal Council bldg. at ctr. *18* printed. Orange paper.	—	—	—

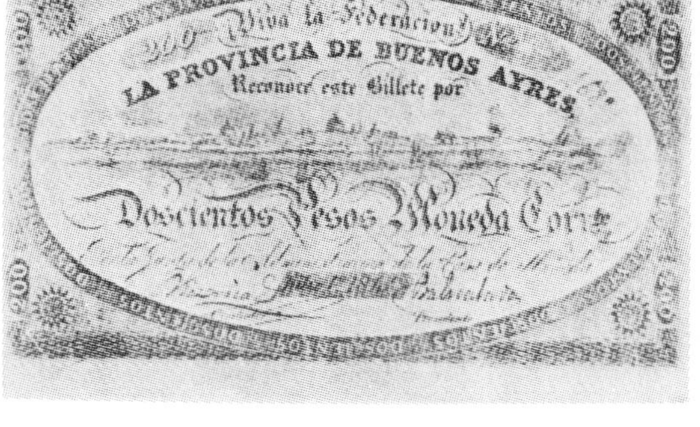

		GOOD	FINE	XF
S383	**200 PESOS**			
	1.7.1841. View of Buenos Aires at ctr. *1841* fully printed. Pinkish purple paper.	—	Rare	—

1844 ISSUES

#S384-S387 orange. Uniface. 2-line political heading at top: *VIVA LA CONFEDERACION ARGENTINA! MUERAN LOS SALVAGES UNITARIOS!* Printer: plates by PB&P; notes printed in Buenos Aires.

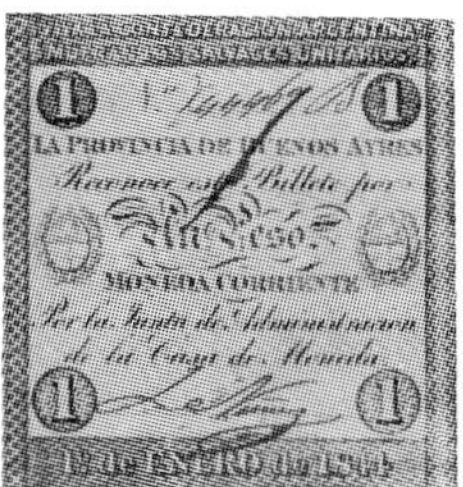

		GOOD	FINE	XF
S384	**1 PESO**			
	1.1.1844. Arms at l. and r. Square format.			
	a. Yellow paper.	12.50	35.00	85.00
	b. Textured or plain white paper.	20.00	60.00	150.00
	c. Lt. blue paper.	50.00	100.00	250.00

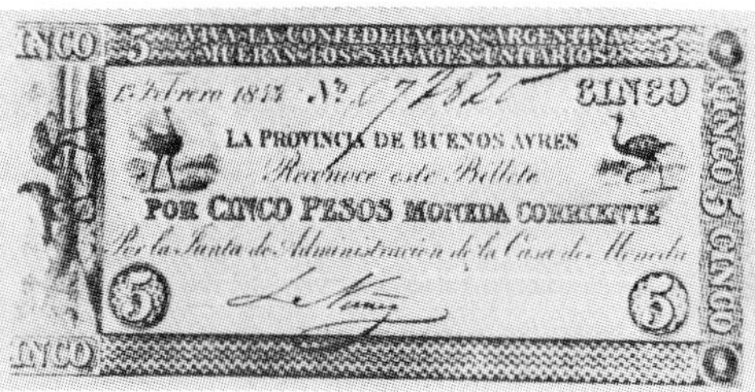

		GOOD	FINE	XF
S385	**5 PESOS**			
	1.2.1844. Ostriches at l. border and at l. and r. One hand sign.			
	a. Yellow paper.	40.00	80.00	160.00
	b. Textured or plain white paper.	50.00	95.00	225.00
	c. Two hand sign. (first 29,000 issued).	50.00	95.00	225.00

		GOOD	FINE	XF
S386	**10 PESOS**			
	1.3.1844. Sheep at l. border, arms at lower l., sheep and horse at ctr.			
	a. Yellow paper.	200.00	450.00	—
	b. Textured or plain white paper.	250.00	550.00	—
S387	**20 PESOS**			
	1.4.1844. 2 horses at bottom l. and r.			
	a. Yellow paper.	250.00	550.00	—
	b. Textured white paper.	275.00	600.00	—

#S388-S391 black. Like #S384-S387. White paper except for some of #S388 printed on yellow paper.

		GOOD	FINE	XF
S388	**1 PESO**			
	1.1.1844. Like #S384.			
	a. Yellow paper.	40.00	80.00	175.00
	b. White paper.	15.00	40.00	100.00
S389	**5 PESOS**			
	1.2.1844. Like #S385.	65.00	125.00	300.00

		GOOD	FINE	XF
S390	**10 PESOS** 1.3.1844. Like #S386.	—	—	—

		GOOD	FINE	XF
S391	**20 PESOS** 1.4.1844. Like #S387.	—	—	—

NOTE: For notes similar to #S388-S391 but w/o political headings at top, see #S402-S406.

1845-47 ISSUES

Higher values were issued to supplement those of lower value issued earlier.

#S392-S394 and S396 printer: plates by PB&P. #S395 printer: plates by Wilson & Sons. All printed in Buenos Aires. Uniface.

#S393-S395 black.

		GOOD	FINE	XF
S392	**50 PESOS** 1.5.1845. Orange on yellow paper. Cow at upper l., bull and cow at ctr., cow at upper r.	—	Rare	—
S393	**50 PESOS** 1.5.1845. Like #S392. White paper.	—	Rare	—

		GOOD	FINE	XF
S394	**100 PESOS** 1.6.1845. Yellow paper. Municipal Council bldg. at ctr.			
	a. Background lines *CIEN PESOS* repeated many times.	—	Rare	—
	b. Background of parallel lines w/o words.	—	Rare	—

NOTE: For issue similar to #S394 but w/o political headings at top, see #S408.

		GOOD	FINE	XF
S395	**500 PESOS** 1.9.1845. Yellow paper. Ships at ctr., allegorical women standing at l. and r.			
	a. *184* of date printed (first 498 notes).	Reported Not Confirmed		
	b. Entire date printed.	—	Rare	—
S396	**1000 PESOS** Sept.1847. Orange on white paper. Standing allegorical woman w/anchor at ctr. Printer: plate by PB&P. Printed in Buenos Aires.			
	a. Numerals of serial # printed.	—	Rare	—
	b. Numerals entered by hand.	Reported Not Confirmed		

NOTE: For issue similar to #S396b but w/o political headings at top, see #S412.

1848-51 ISSUES

#S397-S399 black. White paper. Uniface. Printer: plates, PB&P. Printed in Buenos Aires.

		GOOD	FINE	XF
S397	**50 PESOS** 1.10.1848. Bull at ctr.	—	Rare	—
S398	**100 PESOS** 1.11.1848. Allegorical woman seated in oval at ctr., ship in background.	—	Rare	—
S399	**200 PESOS** 1.7.1848. View of Buenos Aires city at ctr.	—	Rare	—

NOTE: For notes similar to #S397-S399 but w/o political headings at top, see #S407, S409 and S410.

		GOOD	FINE	XF
S400	**500 PESOS** 1.8.1849. View of Buenos Aires, Mercury flying above. Printer: plate by PB&P.			
	a. Red.	Reported Not Confirmed		
	b. Black.	Reported Not Confirmed		

NOTE: #S400 is known only in reprint form (ca.1900).

		GOOD	FINE	XF
S401	**500 PESOS** 1.12.1851. Red. White paper. Seated allegorical woman, 2 children and shields at ctr. Printer: plate by PB&P. Printed in Buenos Aires.	—	Rare	—

NOTE: For note similar to #S401 but w/o political headings at top, see #S411.

BANCO Y CASA DE MONEDA

After the fall of dictator General Manuel Rosas in 1852, there was a banking reorganization, and by the end of 1853 the Banco y Casa de Moneda was formed to be the issuing entity for the State of Buenos Aires. On April 8, 1854, Buenos Aires separated from the Confederacion Argentina. Its first issue consisted of notes dated from 1844-1851 using old plates from the Casa de Moneda. But before these notes were printed, the plates were altered to cross out or erase completely the political headings at the top.

1854 ND ISSUES

#S402-S412 w/old dates 1844-51, political headings obliterated or erased.

		VG	VF	UNC
S402	**1 PESO** ND (1854 - old date 1.1.1844). Like #S388 but only the second political heading erased (error?).	60.00	150.00	—

		GOOD	FINE	XF
S403	**1 PESO** ND (1854 - old date 1.1.1844). Like #S388 but both political headings obliterated.			
	a. Both headings erased completely.	10.00	30.00	80.00
	b. Both headings crossed out by ovpt.	10.00	30.00	80.00
S404	**5 PESOS** ND (1854 - old date 1.2.1844). Like #S389 but both political headings crossed out by ovpt.	35.00	120.00	—

		Good	Fine	XF
S405	**10 Pesos** ND (1854 - old date 1.3.1844). Like #S390 but both political headings crossed out by ovpt.	50.00	175.00	—
S406	**20 Pesos** ND (1854 - old date 1.4.1844). Like #S391 but both political headings crossed out by ovpt.	100.00	300.00	—
S407	**50 Pesos** ND (1854 - old date 1.10.1848). Like #S397 but both political headings erased completely.	—	Rare	—
S408	**100 Pesos** ND (1854 - old date 1.6.1845). Like #S394 but both political headings crossed out by ovpt.	Reported Not Confirmed		
S409	**100 Pesos** ND (1854 - old date 1.11.1848). Like #S398 but both political headings erased completely.	—	Rare	—
S410	**200 Pesos** ND (1854 - old date 1.7.1848). Like #S399 but both political headings crossed out by ovpt.	—	Rare	—
S411	**500 Pesos** ND (1854 - old date 1.12.1851). Like #S401 but both political headings erased completely.	—	Rare	—
S412	**1000 Pesos** ND (1854 - old date 9.1847). Like #S396b but both political headings erased completely.	Reported Not Confirmed		

NOTE: Reprints of #S411 and S412 are known in red.

La Provincia De Buenos Aires

1853 Issue

A plate was prepared by PB&P for a proposed 1853 issue of what would have been the first Argentine 5000 Pesos note. It was lost en route to Buenos Aires. Specimens may exist.

		Good	Fine	XF
S413	**5000 Pesos** 1.3.1853.	Reported Not Confirmed		

1854 Issue

		Good	Fine	XF
S414	**200 Pesos** 1.1.1854. Black. View of Buenos Aires at ctr. Uniface. Printer: BWC. Specimen.	—	Rare	—

El Estado De Buenos Ayres

All notes with this heading were issued by the Banco y Casa de Moneda.

1856 Issue

#S415-S425 dated except for #S423. Black. Uniface except for #S425. Printer: plates by Pickett London (w/o imprint except for #S424 and S425). Notes printed in Buenos Aires.

		Good	Fine	XF
S415	**1 Peso** 1.5.1856. Arms at ctr.	20.00	50.00	120.00

		Good	Fine	XF
S416	**5 Pesos** 1.5.1856. Shepherd and sheep at l., arms at ctr. One or two sign.	30.00	100.00	250.00

		Good	Fine	XF
S417	**10 Pesos** 1.5.1856. Allegorical woman standing at l., arms at upper l., farm tools at ctr.			
	a. 1 sign.	40.00	125.00	275.00
	b. 2 sign.	70.00	200.00	375.00

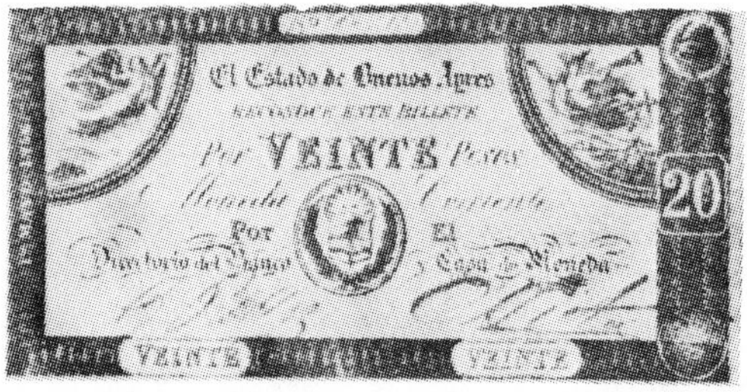

		Good	Fine	XF
S418	**20 Pesos** 1.5.1856. Allegory of Victory at upper l., arms at ctr., flying Mercury at upper r. Liberty cap in upper r. corner.	—	—	—

		Good	Fine	XF
S419	**50 Pesos** 1.5.1856. Arms at upper l., caduceus w/sword at ctr., Liberty cap at lower r.	—	Rare	—

		Good	Fine	XF
S420	**100 Pesos** 1.5.1856. Train and boats at l., arms at upper r.	—	Rare	—
S421	**200 Pesos** 1.5.1856. Mercury flying over bundles and ship at ctr., arms at r.	—	Rare	—

A word on pricing

When a note is marked RARE in the price columns, this note seldom appears on the market, or few are known in private hands. When dashes are in the price column, means that the note has not traded on the open market recently and a definitive value could not accurately be determined. Rare does not always mean expensive. A dashed price does not mean expensive or rare.

		Good	Fine	XF
S422	**500 Pesos** 1.5.1856. Arms at upper l., Greek soldier carrying sheep at ctr., Liberty cap at upper r.	—	Rare	—
S423	**1000 Pesos** ND (1.5.1856). Arms and kangaroo at l., llama at r.	—	Rare	—

NOTE: #S423 is known only as reprints made in 1900 by the CSABB in Buenos Aires.

		Good	Fine	XF
S424	**5000 Pesos** 1.5.1856. Allegorical woman w/staff at l., Neptune riding chariot at r. Uniface.	—	Rare	—
S425	**5000 Pesos** 1.5.1856. Face like #S424. Back design blue background, w/wording: *BANCO Y CASA DE MONEDA DE BUENOS AIRES.*	—	Rare	—

NOTE: #S425 is the first Argentine note to have printing on the back.

1857 Issue

Several higher values were reissued beginning in 1857. All backs are printed in different colors but with the same design as the face.

#S426-S428 printer: plates by PBC. Notes printed in Buenos Aires.

		Good	Fine	XF
S426	**500 Pesos** 1.8.1857. Black. Farm tools at l., Neptune w/seahorses at ctr., beehive at r. Back red.	—	Rare	—

NOTE: Beware of good quality counterfeits.

		Good	Fine	XF
S427	**1000 Pesos** 1.8.1857. Black. Allegorical woman w/plants and farm tools at ctr., arms at lower ctr. Back green.			
	a. Handwritten serial # (1857-65).	—	Rare	—
	b. Printed serial # (1866-67). Blue *1000* added on back.	—	Rare	—

		Good	Fine	XF
S428	**5000 Pesos** 1.8.1857. Black. Neptune in chariot at upper ctr., arms below. Back blue.			
	a. Handwritten serial # (1857-64).	—	Rare	—
	b. Printed serial # (1865-67).	—	Rare	—

1858 Issue

#S429-S435 arms at ctr., higher values #S433-S435 w/cannon and flags. Black. White paper. Uniface. Printer: plates by PBC. Notes printed in Buenos Aires.

		Good	Fine	XF
S429	**1 Peso** 25.5.1858.			
	a. Issued note.	15.00	45.00	100.00
	s. Specimen.	—	—	—

		Good	Fine	XF
S430	**5 Pesos** 25.5.1858. Cow at l.			
	a. Issued note.	15.00	50.00	140.00
	s. Specimen.	—	—	—
S431	**10 Pesos** 25.5.1858. Cows at l. and r.	25.00	75.00	175.00
S432	**20 Pesos** 25.5.1858. Sheep at l. and r.	75.00	200.00	425.00

		Good	Fine	XF
S433	**50 Pesos** 25.5.1858. Allegory w/3 women at l. and r.	—	—	—
S434	**100 Pesos** 25.5.1858. Farm tools, sheep and ship at l.	—	—	—

		GOOD	FINE	XF
S435	**200 PESOS** 25.5.1858. Sailing ship at l. and r.	—	Rare	—

1864 TRANSITIONAL ISSUE

The 1864 issue was the only one to carry the name *EL BANCO Y CASA DE MONEDA DE BUENOS AYRES* as the main heading. However, by that time the issuing institution was the Banco de la Provincia de Buenos Aires. This bank name was applied to the backs of all notes from 20 to 200 Pesos. Plans called for values of 500, 1000 and 5000 Pesos to be part of this issue but they were never released. Prints using original artwork were made in 1969.

#S441-S447 arms at upper l., bank name on back.

#S441-S443 uniface.

		GOOD	FINE	XF
S441	**1 PESO** 1.1.1864.			
	a. Green paper.	12.00	40.00	90.00
	b. Tan paper.	7.00	30.00	65.00
S442	**5 PESOS** 1.1.1864. Green paper.	15.00	50.00	125.00
S443	**10 PESOS** 1.1.1864. Blue paper.	17.00	60.00	150.00

#S444-S447 bank name on back.

		GOOD	FINE	XF
S444	**20 PESOS** 1.1.1864. Pinkish violet paper. Back green.	20.00	75.00	175.00

#S445-S447 w/cannon and flags.

		GOOD	FINE	XF
S445	**50 PESOS** 1.1.1864. Horse and cow at l. and ctr. r. Salmon paper. Back blue.	—	—	—

		GOOD	FINE	XF
S446	**100 PESOS** 1.1.1864. Similar to #S445 but sheep added in circle at bottom ctr. Back black.			
	a. Rose paper.	—	—	—
	b. White paper.	—	—	—
S447	**200 PESOS** 1.1.1864. Like #S446. Back maroon.			
	a. Blue-violet paper.	—	—	—
	b. White paper.	—	—	—
S448	**500 PESOS** 1.1.(1864). Similar to #S446. Bull at lower ctr. Olive or white paper. (Prints only).	—	—	—
S449	**1000 PESOS** 1.1.1864. Similar to #S448. 3 horse heads at lower ctr. Orange paper. (Prints only).	—	—	—
S450	**5000 PESOS** 1.1.1864. Similar to #S449. Yellow paper. (Prints only).	—	—	—

NOTE: No originals of #S448, S449 and S450 were printed or issued.

SECTION II

TREASURY

LEY DE 10 DE OCTOBRE DE 1876 TREASURY BILL ISSUE

The inconvertibility of notes into specie which began in 1876 started a monetary crisis in Argentina. The government then issued Customs Notes very similar in characteristics to the Customs Notes used in 1820-21.

#S461 and S462 arms w/cannon and flags at ctr. Printer: Alberto Larsen Bs.As.

		GOOD	FINE	XF
S461	**50 PESOS FUERTES** ND (1876). Black and lt. green. Back lt. green; 2 allegorical figures. Series A.	—	Rare	—

		GOOD	FINE	XF
S462	**100 PESOS FUERTES** ND (1876). Black, maroon and green. Allegorical women at l. and r. Back maroon; arms twice. Series B.	—	Rare	—

#S463 and S464 arms surrounded by 14 provincial arms at ctr. Arms at l. ctr. on back. Printer: Guillermo Kraft Bs.As.

		GOOD	FINE	XF
S463	**50 PESOS** ND (1876). Blue.	—	Rare	—
S464	**100 PESOS** ND (1876). Like #S463. Ochre. Back maroon.	—	Rare	—

BONOS DEL TESORO, PROVINCIA DE BUENOS AYRES

8% interest bearing notes.

LEY DE 10 DE MAYO DE 1880/DECRETO DE 11 DE MAYO DE 1880

All notes have sailor at l., Agriculture at ctr., and soldier at r. Backs are brown; founders of Banco de la Provincia de Buenos Aires at ctr. Each note has 38 interest coupons attached. Printer: ABNC.

		GOOD	FINE	XF
S464A	**500 PESOS** *L.1880.* Black on brown unpt. Specimen.	—	—	—
S464B	**1000 PESOS** *L.1880.* Black on green unpt. Specimen.	—	—	—
S464C	**5000 PESOS** *L.1880.* Black on blue unpt. Specimen.	—	—	—

1890 TREASURY NOTES ISSUE

These notes were issued by the Treasury through the Caja de Conversion. They were equal in value to notes issued by the Bancos Nacionales Garantidos (see later section).

#S465-S466 issued w/red seal like Bancos Nacionales Garantidos. Printer: BWC (w/o imprint).

		GOOD	FINE	XF
S465	**50 PESOS** 15.9.1890. Black on green unpt. Dr. J. Celman at l, allegorical man w/trident at r., arms at ctr.	Reported Not Confirmed		

		GOOD	FINE	XF
S466	**500 PESOS** 15.9.1890. Black on lt. blue and brown unpt. Allegorical woman w/portr. Gen. M. Belgrano at l., arms at ctr. Back blue; allegorical women w/arms at ctr.	—	—	—

BANK ISSUES

BANCO DE LA PROVINCIA DE BUENOS AIRES

1865 ISSUE

#S467-S470 issued in Pesos Fuertes, redeemable in gold and worth more than the regular circulating currency. Reprints of the face sides in original colors were made by the bank in 1975.

		GOOD	FINE	XF
S467	**20 PESOS FUERTES** 1.7.1865. Black and green. Liberty and Mercury at l., arms at ctr.	—	Rare	—

		GOOD	FINE	XF
S468	**50 PESOS FUERTES** 1.7.1865. Black, maroon and green. Sailing ship at l., train at r. Back black and green.	—	Rare	—

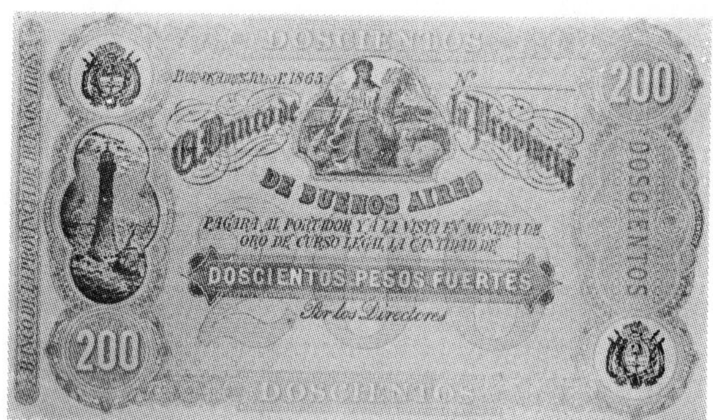

		GOOD	FINE	XF
S469	**200 PESOS FUERTES** 1.7.1865. Black, green and salmon. Lighthouse at l., arms at upper l. and lower r., allegorical woman w/agricultural plants at ctr.	—	Rare	—

NOTE: #S469 known only as partially finished proof and reprint forms.

		GOOD	FINE	XF
S470	**500 PESOS FUERTES** 1.7.1865. Black, maroon and orange. Liberty at l., arms at ctr., Justice at r.	—	Rare	—

NOTE: #S470 known only in reprint form.

LA PROVINCIA DE BUENOS AYRES

1867 ISSUE

An issue in regular currency (not Pesos Fuertes) was prepared in 1867.

#S471-S480 printer: BWC. Imprint only on #S475, S477 and S479.

#S471-S475 uniface.

		GOOD	FINE	XF
S471	**1 PESO** 1.4.1867. Black. Ram at ctr.	10.00	30.00	75.00

		GOOD	FINE	XF
S472	**5 PESOS** 1.4.1867. Black. Dog at l. and r.	15.00	50.00	100.00

		GOOD	FINE	XF
S473	**10 PESOS** 1.4.1867. Black on blue unpt. Cow at l., arms at r.	30.00	75.00	175.00

		GOOD	FINE	XF
S474	**20 PESOS** 1.4.1867. Black on green unpt. Horse at l. and r., arms at upper ctr.	50.00	150.00	—

		GOOD	FINE	XF
S475	**50 PESOS** 1.4.1867. Black on green unpt. Rider on horseback w/lasso at l.	200.00	425.00	—

		GOOD	FINE	XF
S476	**100 PESOS** 1.4.1867. Black on rose unpt. Portr. woman at ctr. Back rose.	200.00	425.00	—

		GOOD	FINE	XF
S477	**200 PESOS** 1.4.1867. Black on blue unpt. Portr. seated woman at l., arms at r. Back blue.	—	Rare	—
S478	**500 PESOS** 1.4.1867. Black on green unpt. Arms at l. and r., standing woman and sheep at ctr. Back gray.	—	Rare	—
S479	**1000 PESOS** 1.4.1867. Black on green and salmon unpt. Woman w/shovel at l., flags above, arms at r. Back green and salmon.	—	Rare	—

		GOOD	FINE	XF
S480	**5000 PESOS** 1.4.1867. Black on maroon, blue and salmon unpt. Standing woman w/sheaf and sickle at l. Back blue and salmon.	—	Rare	—

1869 ISSUE

#S481-S499 printer: ABNC. Imprint in Spanish: *Compania Americana de Billetes de Banco, Nueva York* except on #S490, S495 and S496.

		GOOD	FINE	XF
S481	**1 PESO** 1.1.1869. Black. Woman at lower l. and r., ram and ewes at upper ctr. Uniface.			
	a. Handwritten sign. (1870-75). Red or blue serial #.	3.50	15.00	40.00
	b. Printed sign. (1877-83).	3.50	15.00	40.00

		GOOD	FINE	XF
S482	**5 PESOS**			
	1.1.1869 (1869-76). Black. Seated man at lower l. and r., bull at top ctr. Handwritten sign. Uniface.	7.00	30.00	65.00
S483	**5 PESOS**			
	1.1.1869 (1876-83). Black on lt. blue and salmon unpt. Like #S482.			
	a. Handwritten sign. (1876-77).	5.00	25.00	70.00
	b. Printed sign. (1877-83).	5.00	20.00	50.00
S484	**10 PESOS**			
	1.1.1869 (1870-76). Black on lt. blue unpt., w/*DIEZ*. F. Varela at lower l., horse at upper ctr., portr. woman at lower r. Uniface. Handwritten sign.	8.00	35.00	150.00

		GOOD	FINE	XF
S485	**10 PESOS**			
	1.1.1869 (1876-83). Black on blue and ochre unpt. w/*X*. Like #S484.			
	a. Handwritten sign. (1876-77).	6.00	35.00	125.00
	b. Printed sign., red or blue serial # (1877-83).	6.00	20.00	100.00
S486	**20 PESOS**			
	1.1.1869 (1869-74). Black on green unpt. and back numerals. Seated allegorical woman at lower l. and r., Gen. J. Lavalle at ctr. Handwritten sign.	17.50	75.00	250.00

		GOOD	FINE	XF
S487	**20 PESOS**			
	1.1.1869 (1874-83). Black on green and salmon unpt. Like #S486 but uniface.			
	a. Handwritten sign. (1874-77).	9.00	75.00	250.00
	b. Printed sign. (1877-83).	9.00	75.00	250.00
	p. Proof.	—	—	—
	s. Specimen.	—	—	—

		GOOD	FINE	XF
S488	**50 PESOS**			
	1.1.1869 (1869-74). Black on rose unpt. and back numerals. *L 50 L* protector in unpt. Gaucho w/guitar at lower l., 2 allegorical women at upper ctr., Gen G. de las Heras at lower r. Handwritten sign.			
	a. Issued note.	90.00	400.00	—
	p. Proof.	—	—	—

		GOOD	FINE	XF
S489	**50 PESOS**			
	1.1.1869 (1874-77). Black on green and maroon unpt. Like #S488 but *CINCUENTA* protector in unpt. Uniface.	125.00	450.00	—

		GOOD	FINE	XF
S490	**50 PESOS**			
	1.1.1869 (1877-83). Black on green and brown unpt. Gaucho w/guitar at lower l., cherub at ctr., Gen. de las Heras at lower r. Uniface. Printed sign. Imprint in English.			
	a. Issued note.	100.00	400.00	—
	s. Specimen.	—	—	—

		GOOD	FINE	XF
S491	**100 PESOS**			
	1.1.1869 (1869-76). Black on ochre unpt. Woman seated at lower l., 2 allegorical women at upper ctr., Gen. J. M. Paz at lower r. Uniface. Handwritten sign.			
	a. Issued note.	150.00	500.00	—
	p. Proof.	—	—	—
	s. Specimen.	—	—	—
S492	**100 PESOS**			
	1.1.1869 (1876-83). Black on green and salmon unpt. Like #S491.			
	a. Handwritten sign. (1876-77)	150.00	500.00	—
	b. Printed sign. (1877-83).	150.00	500.00	—
S493	**200 PESOS**			
	1.1.1869 (1869-76). Black on ochre unpt. Gen. C. M. de Alvear at l., corral at ctr., Pallas Athena at r. Orange back. Handwritten sign.			
	a. Issued note.	—	—	—
	p. Proof.	—	—	—

S494 200 PESOS — GOOD / FINE / XF

1.1.1869 (1876-77). Black on brownish red and lt. blue unpt. Like #S493. — — —

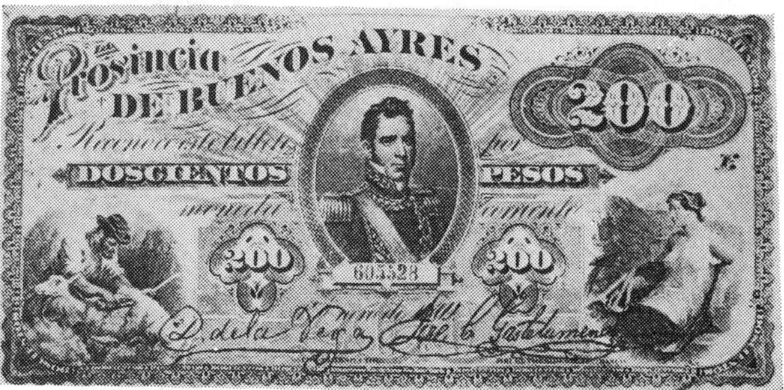

S495 200 PESOS — GOOD / FINE / XF

1.1.1869 (1877-83). Black on green unpt. Dog at lower l., Portr. Gen. C. M. Alvear at ctr. Navigation at r. Back red and blue. Printed sign. Imprint in English. — — —

S496 200 PESOS — GOOD / FINE / XF

1.1.1869 (1879-83). Black on green unpt. Man shearing sheep at l., portr. Gen. C. M. Alvear at ctr., Navigation at r. Back gray-brown. Printed sign. Imprint in English. — — —

S497 500 PESOS — GOOD / FINE / XF

1.1.1869 (1869-83). Black on red unpt. Slaughterhouse at upper l., Gen. J. M. de Pueyrredon at lower r. Back red. Handwritten sign. — — —

S498 1000 PESOS

1.1.1869 (1869-83). Black on lt. blue unpt. Navigator at l., ship at ctr., Adm. G. Brown at r. Back lt. blue. Handwritten sign.

	GOOD	FINE	XF
a. Issued note.	—	Rare	—
p. Proof.	—	—	—

S499 5000 PESOS — GOOD / FINE / XF

1.1.1869 (1869-83). Black on green unpt. Horses at upper l., Dr. D. Sarsfield at lower l., child head at ctr. r., seated allegorical woman by lg. globe at lower r. Back green. Handwritten sign. — Rare —

EL BANCO DE LA PROVINCIA DE BUENOS AIRES

1869 ISSUE

This issue consists of notes in Centesimos Fuertes and Pesos Fuertes. Lower values (#S500-S504) use the spelling AYRES; #S505-S511 use the form AIRES in the title. Printer: ABNC. Imprint appears in English on #S500-S504, in English and Spanish on #S510, and in Spanish on #S505-S509, and S511. In 1876 some notes of all denominations were revalidated; these are cataloged as a separate group.

S500 8 CENTESIMOS FUERTES

1.1.1869. Black on ochre unpt. Pallas Athena at l. Back orange; small bust of Athena at ctr. Handwritten sign.

	GOOD	FINE	XF
a. 2 sign.	10.00	30.00	100.00
b. 1 sign.	8.00	25.00	75.00

S501 10 CENTESIMOS FUERTES

1.1.1869. Black on green unpt. Mercury at r. Back green; portr. Indian woman at ctr. Handwritten sign.

	GOOD	FINE	XF
a. Issued note, 2 sign.	25.00	90.00	250.00
b. Issued note, 1 sign.	12.00	50.00	150.00
r. Unsigned remainder.	—	35.00	60.00

S502 16 CENTESIMOS FUERTES
1.1.1869. Black on red-orange unpt. Col. L. Argerich at ctr. Back red-orange; steam locomotive at ctr. Handwritten sign.

	GOOD	FINE	XF
a. 2 sign.	35.00	90.00	250.00
b. 1 sign.	30.00	85.00	225.00

S503 20 CENTESIMOS FUERTES
1.1.1869. Black on gray-brown unpt. Girl at l. Back brown; dog on safe at ctr. Handwritten sign.

	GOOD	FINE	XF
	30.00	85.00	225.00

S504 40 CENTESIMOS FUERTES
1.1.1869. Black on lt. blue unpt. Young woman at ctr. Back blue; steamship at lower ctr. Handwritten sign.

	GOOD	FINE	XF
a. 2 sign.	35.00	90.00	250.00
b. 1 sign.	30.00	85.00	225.00

S505 10 PESOS FUERTES
1.1.1869. Black on ochre unpt. Gen J. de Arenales at l., gaucho on horseback w/cows at r. Back orange. Handwritten sign.

	GOOD	FINE	XF
a. Issued note.	—	Rare	—
p. Proof.	—	—	—
s. Specimen.	—	—	—

S506 20 PESOS FUERTES
1.1.1869. Black on ochre unpt. Allegorical woman and child at lower l., wagon train at ctr., Dr. M. Moreno at lower r. Back brown. Handwritten sign.

	GOOD	FINE	XF
a. Issued note.	—	Rare	—
s. Specimen ovpt: *MUESTRA*.	—	—	—

S507 50 PESOS FUERTES
1.1.1869. Black on red-orange unpt. Steam locomotive at l., wagons and campfire at ctr., Col. C. Saavedra at r. Back red. Handwritten sign.

	GOOD	FINE	XF
a. Issued note.	—	Rare	—
p. Proof.	—	—	—

S508 100 PESOS FUERTES
1.1.1869. Black on green unpt. Dr. B. Rivadavia at lower l., gaucho w/horse at ctr., allegorical woman at lower r. Back green. Handwritten sign.

	GOOD	FINE	XF
	—	Rare	—

S509 200 PESOS FUERTES
1.1.1869. Black on purple-rose unpt. Gen. M. Belgrano at lower l., steam passenger train at upper ctr., allegory of Industry at r. Handwritten sign.

	GOOD	FINE	XF
a. Issued note.	—	Rare	—
p. Proof.	—	—	—
s. Specimen w/ or w/o ovpt: *MUESTRA*.	—	—	—

S510 200 PESOS FUERTES
1.1.1869. Black on green unpt. Gen M. Belgrano at l., sailing ship at ctr., allegorical woman and child at r. Handwritten sign. Back brown; cattle and sheep. Specimen ovpt: *MUESTRA*.

	GOOD	FINE	XF
	—	Rare	—

S511 500 PESOS FUERTES
1.1.1869. Black on lt. blue unpt. Allegorical woman at l., man, dog and woman pounding corn at ctr., Gen. J. de San Martin at r. Back blue. Handwritten sign. Specimen ovpt: *MUESTRA*.

	GOOD	FINE	XF
	—	—	—

LEY DE 25 SEPTIEMBRE DE 1876 PROVISIONAL ISSUE

#S512-S523 ovpt: *LEY DE 25 SETBRE. (25.9) 1876* in circular seal on face.

		GOOD	FINE	XF
S512	**8 CENTESIMOS FUERTES** ND (- old date 1.1.1869). Black on ochre unpt. Ovpt. on #S500.			
	a. 1 handwritten sign.	8.00	25.00	90.00
	b. 1 printed sign.	6.00	20.00	70.00

		GOOD	FINE	XF
S513	**10 CENTESIMOS FUERTES** ND (- old date 1.1.1869). Black on green unpt. Ovpt. on #S501.			
	a. 1 handwritten sign.	12.00	50.00	150.00
	b. 1 printed sign.	10.00	40.00	125.00
S514	**16 CENTESIMOS FUERTES** ND (- old date 1.1.1869). Black on gray-brown unpt. Ovpt. on #S502.			
	a. 1 handwritten sign.	17.50	60.00	175.00
	b. 1 printed sign.	17.50	60.00	175.00

		GOOD	FINE	XF
S515	**20 CENTESIMOS FUERTES** ND (- old date 1.1.1869). Black on ochre unpt. Ovpt. on #S503.			
	a. 1 handwritten sign.	30.00	100.00	250.00
	b. 1 printed sign.	17.50	75.00	175.00
S516	**40 CENTESIMOS FUERTES** ND (- old date 1.1.1869). Black on lt. blue unpt. Ovpt. on #S504.			
	a. 1 handwritten sign.	30.00	100.00	250.00
	b. 1 printed sign.	30.00	100.00	250.00

		GOOD	FINE	XF
S517	**10 PESOS FUERTES** ND (- old date 1.1.1869). Black on ochre unpt. Ovpt. on #S505.			
	a. 2 handwritten sign.	—	Rare	—
	b. 2 printed sign.	—	Rare	—

#S518-S523 2 handwritten sign.

		GOOD	FINE	XF
S518	**20 PESOS FUERTES** ND (- old date 1.1.1869). Black on ochre unpt. Ovpt. on #S506.	—	Rare	—
S519	**50 PESOS FUERTES** ND (- old date 1.1.1869). Black on red-orange unpt. Ovpt. on #S507.	—	Rare	—
S520	**100 PESOS FUERTES** ND (- old date 1.1.1869). Black on green unpt. Ovpt. on #S508.	—	Rare	—
S521	**200 PESOS FUERTES** ND (- old date 1.1.1869). Black on purple-rose unpt. Ovpt. on #S509.	—	Rare	—
S522	**200 PESOS FUERTES** ND (- old date 1.1.1869). Black on green unpt. Ovpt. on #S510.	—	Rare	—
S523	**500 PESOS FUERTES** ND (- old date 1.1.1869). Black on pale blue unpt. Ovpt. on #S511.	Reported Not Confirmed		

1871 ISSUE

The 1871 emission was prepared in order to fill in several denominations not included in the previous issue. The notes were issued from 1876 to 1883. Printer ABNC.

NOTE: Some 1 and 4 Pesos were ovpt. in 1876.

		GOOD	FINE	XF
S524	**1 PESO FUERTE** 1.1.1871. Black on ochre unpt. Sailor at lower l., Gen. M. Pinto at ctr., peasant woman at r. Back brown.			
	a. Handwritten sign.	35.00	125.00	300.00
	b. Printed sign.	50.00	150.00	350.00

		GOOD	FINE	XF
S525	**2 PESOS FUERTES** 1.1.1871. Black on green unpt. Brigadier Gen. M. Rodriguez at l., dog head at ctr. Back dk. brown. Handwritten sign.	150.00	500.00	—
S526	**4 PESOS FUERTES** 1.1.1871. Black on lt. blue unpt. Horses at l., Dr. M. Garcia at r. Back blue.			
	a. Handwritten sign.	120.00	350.00	—
	b. Printed sign.	120.00	350.00	—

#S527-S528 ovpt: *LEY DE 25 SETBRE 1876* in seal on face, like #S512-S523.

		GOOD	FINE	XF
S527	**1 PESO FUERTE** ND (- old date 1.1.1871). Ovpt. on #S524.			
	a. Handwritten sign.	35.00	150.00	400.00
	b. Printed sign.	50.00	175.00	450.00

		Good	Fine	XF
S528	**4 Pesos Fuertes** ND (- old date 1.1.1871). Ovpt. on #S526.			
	a. Handwritten sign.	125.00	350.00	—
	b. Printed sign.	125.00	350.00	—
	s. Specimen.	—	—	—

1881 Issue

		Good	Fine	XF
S529	**5 Pesos Fuertes** 14.1.1881. Black on m/c unpt. Gaucho riding horseback at l., portr. Dr. A. Alsina at ctr., woman seated at r. Back dk. brown; steam passenger train at station. Specimen (not issued).	—	—	—

Ley 8 Noviembre de 1881; 1883 Issue

This issue was originally backed by gold, but in 1885 a law was passed stopping any convertibility of paper money. Some denominations were ovpt. showing this law.

#S530-S544 printer: ABNC.

#S530-S534 black. Uniface. Not issued.

#S530

#S531

		Good	Fine	XF
S530	**8 Centesimos Oro** 1.1.1883. Pallas Athena at l., Dr. N. Avellaneda at r. Specimen.	—	—	—
S531	**10 Centesimos Oro** 1.1.1883. Dr. D. Sarmiento at l., Mercury at r. Specimen.	—	—	—

		Good	Fine	XF
S532	**16 Centesimos Oro** 1.1.1883. Gen. B. Mitre at l., Col. L. Argerich at r. Specimen.	—	—	—

		Good	Fine	XF
S533	**20 Centesimos Oro** 1.1.1883. Girl at l., Dr. S. Derqui at r. Specimen.	—	—	—

		Good	Fine	XF
S534	**40 Centesimos Oro** 1.1.1883. Young woman at l., Justice J. Urquiza at r.	—	—	—
	p. Proof.	—	—	—
	s. Specimen.	—	—	—

#S535-S543 printed sign.

		Good	Fine	XF
S535	**1 Peso Oro** 1.1.1883. Black on maroon unpt. Gen. M. Rodriguez at l., farm tools at ctr., Gen. M. Pinto at r. Uniface.			
	a. 1 sign.	35.00	175.00	400.00
	b. 2 sign.	50.00	200.00	500.00
	p. Proof.	—	—	—
	s. Specimen.	—	—	—

		Good	Fine	XF
S536	**2 Pesos Oro** 1.1.1883. Black on rose unpt. A. Alsina at l., horse at ctr., F. Varela at r. Uniface.			
	a. 1 sign.	100.00	400.00	—
	b. 2 sign.	100.00	400.00	—
	p. Proof.	—	—	—
	s. Specimen.	—	—	—

#S537-S543 2 printed sign.

		Good	Fine	XF
S537	**4 Pesos Oro** 1.1.1883. Black on cream unpt. Dr. M. Alberti at l., cow at ctr., J. Castelli at r. Uniface.			
	a. Issued note.	125.00	425.00	—
	p. Proof.	—	—	—
	s. Specimen.	—	—	—

		Good	Fine	XF
S538	**5 Pesos Oro** 1.1.1883. Black on green unpt. Gen. J. Lavalle at l., ram at ctr., Gen. J. M. Paz at r. Uniface.			
	a. Issued note.	125.00	425.00	—
	p. Proof.	—	—	—
	s. Specimen.	—	—	—

S539 10 PESOS ORO
1.1.1883. Black on lt. blue unpt. Gen. J. A. de Arenales at l., wagon train at ctr., Gen G. Las Heras at r. Back maroon.

	GOOD	FINE	XF
a. Issued note.	150.00	500.00	—
p. Proof.	—	—	—
s. Specimen.	—	—	—

S540 20 PESOS ORO
1.1.1883. Black on rose unpt. Col. C. Saavedra at l., man and woman at ctr., Gen J. M. de Pueyrredon at r. Back maroon-bronze.

	GOOD	FINE	XF
a. Issued note.	—	—	—
p. Proof.	—	—	—
s. Face on lt. brown unpt. Back brown. Specimen.	—	—	—

S541 50 PESOS ORO
1.1.1883. Black on cream unpt. Gen. C. de Alvear at l., navigator at ctr., Adm. G. Brown at r. Back orange.

	GOOD	FINE	XF
a. Issued note.	—	—	—
p. Proof.	—	—	—
s. Specimen.	—	—	—

S542 100 PESOS ORO
1.1.1883. Black on rose unpt. D. Sarsfield at l., reclining allegorical woman at ctr., M. Moreno at r. Back rose; train.

	GOOD	FINE	XF
a. Issued note.	—	—	—
p. Proof.	—	—	—
s. Specimen.	—	—	—

A word on date ranges

Often date ranges or specific dates are listed. These have been observed or reported by our contributors. If a note is outside the published range, it only means that it is a newly reported date, and not necessarily worthy of a premium value.

S543 200 PESOS ORO
1.1.1883. Black on lt. blue unpt. B. Rivadavia at lower l., sailing ship at ctr., M. Garcia at lower r. Back blue; bank founders at ctr.

	GOOD	FINE	XF
a. Issued note.	—	—	—
p. Proof.	—	—	—

S544 500 PESOS ORO
1.1.1883. Black on green unpt. Gen M. Belgrano at lower l., gaucho on horseback at ctr., J. de San Martin at lower r. Back green; allegory of the Republic at ctr.

	GOOD	FINE	XF
p. Proof. ND.	—	—	—
s. Specimen. 1.1.1883.	—	—	—

1885 PROVISIONAL ISSUE

#S545-S553 ovpt: *LEY 14 OCTUBRE 1885 GOBIERNO NACIONAL/INTERVENCION* in circle on face.

S545 1 PESO ORO
ND (- old date 1.1.1883). Black on maroon unpt. Ovpt. on #S535.

	GOOD	FINE	XF
a. 1 sign.	35.00	150.00	350.00
b. 2 sign.	Reported Not Confirmed		

S546 2 PESOS ORO
ND (- old date 1.1.1883). Black on rose unpt. Ovpt. on #S536.

	GOOD	FINE	XF
a. 1 sign.	125.00	400.00	—
b. 2 sign.	125.00	400.00	—

		GOOD	FINE	XF
S547	**4 PESOS ORO** ND (- old date 1.1.1883). Black on cream unpt. Ovpt. on #S537.	125.00	400.00	—
S548	**5 PESOS ORO** ND (- old date 1.1.1883). Black on green unpt. Ovpt. on #S538.	125.00	400.00	—
S549	**10 PESOS ORO** ND (- old date 1.1.1883). Ovpt. on #S539.	150.00	—	—
S550	**20 PESOS ORO** ND (- old date 1.1.1883). Black on rose unpt. Ovpt. on #S540.	175.00	—	—
S551	**50 PESOS ORO** ND (- old date 1.1.1883). Black on cream unpt. Ovpt. on #S541.	225.00	—	—
S552	**100 PESOS ORO** ND (- old date 1.1.1883). Black on rose unpt. Ovpt. on #S542.	250.00	—	—
S553	**200 PESOS ORO** ND (- old date 1.1.1883). Black on lt. blue unpt. Ovpt. on #S543.	300.00	—	—

LEY DE 5 DE NOVIEMBRE DE 1881; 1885 REGULAR ISSUE

The purpose of the 1885 issue was to replace earlier notes with denominations in *PESOS DE ORO* to notes in Pesos but in *Moneda Nacional Oro.* All issued notes of this issue carry the 1885 circular ovpt. in circle on face. All backs have bank name. Printer: ABNC.

		GOOD	FINE	XF
S561	**1 PESO** 1.1.1885. Black on salmon and green unpt. Gen. M. Rodriguez at l., llamas at ctr., Gen. M. Pinto at r. Back blue.			
	a. Issued note.	40.00	125.00	350.00
	s. Specimen.	—	—	—

		GOOD	FINE	XF
S562	**2 PESOS** 1.1.1885. Black on ochre and green unpt. Similar to #S536. Back green.			
	a. Issued note.	110.00	400.00	—
	s. Specimen.	—	—	—

		GOOD	FINE	XF
S563	**5 PESOS** 1.1.1885. Black on rose and green unpt. Similar to #S538 except cows at ctr. Back maroon.			
	a. Issued note.	125.00	425.00	—
	s. Specimen.	—	—	—

		GOOD	FINE	XF
S564	**10 PESOS** 1.1.1885. Black on maroon and lt. blue unpt. Similar to #S539. Back green.			
	a. Issued note.	200.00	700.00	—
	s. Specimen.	—	—	—

		GOOD	FINE	XF
S565	**20 PESOS** 1.1.1885. Black on maroon and lt. blue unpt. Similar to #S540. Back maroon.			
	a. Issued note.	225.00	800.00	—
	s. Specimen.	—	—	—

		GOOD	FINE	XF
S566	**50 PESOS** 1.1.1885. Black on orange, ochre and rose unpt. Similar to #S541. Back maroon.			
	a. Issued note.	275.00	950.00	—
	s. Specimen.	—	—	—

		GOOD	FINE	XF
S567	**100 PESOS** 1.1.1885. Black on cream, blue and lt. blue unpt. Similar to #S542. Back blue and black; farmers herding cattle and sheep at ctr.			
	a. Issued note.	400.00	1200.	—
	s. Specimen.	—	—	—

		GOOD	FINE	XF
S568	**200 PESOS** 1.1.1885. Black on maroon, green and bronze unpt. Similar to #S543. Back maroon and black.			
	a. Issued note.	450.00	1500.	—
	s. Specimen.	—	—	—

		GOOD	FINE	XF
S569	**500 PESOS** 1.1.1885. Black on red, green and maroon unpt. similar to #S544. Back red and black; men and horses at l.			
	a. Issued note.	—	Rare	—
	p. Proof.	—	—	—
	s. Specimen.	—	—	—

NOTE: #S569a is known from a single example w/sign. and circular ovpt. in the Banco de la Provincia museum in Buenos Aires.

1891 CERTIFICADOS DE DEPOSITO ISSUE

This issue consisted of money substitutes needed because of a political and monetary crisis occurring in 1890. First printings of the 1 and 5 Pesos did not carry the title: *CERTIFICADO DE DEPOSITO* and were not issued. Printer: Talleres del Museo de La Plata. All notes except the 1 Peso (#S571 and S573) carry this imprint on the back.

All noted under Law of 7 August 1891.

		GOOD	FINE	XF
S571	**1 PESO** *L.1891.* Blue on ochre and violet unpt. Arms at l., Mercury and woman in chariot w/lions at r. Back gray; allegorical group at ctr.	—	Rare	—

		GOOD	FINE	XF
S572	**5 PESOS** *L.1891.* Black. Arms at upper l., cows at lower l., seated woman at r. Face proof only.	—	—	—

#S573-S579 w/text: *CERTIFICADO DE DEPOSITO* as part of face.

		GOOD	FINE	XF
S573	**1 PESO** *L.1891.* Similar to #S571.			
	a. Issued note.	8.00	15.00	40.00
	b. Punched hole cancelled.	—	Unc	8.00

		GOOD	FINE	XF
S574	**2 PESOS** *L.1891.* Black on lt. blue and ochre unpt. Indian pouring water from jug at l., arms at r. Back green; animals, grain, peasants and carts.	—	Rare	—

		GOOD	FINE	XF
S575	**5 PESOS** *L.1891.* Black on ochre and lt. blue unpt. Arms at upper l., cow at lower l., peasant carrying grain at r. Back blue and green; manager, woman and cows.			
	a. Issued note.	25.00	60.00	125.00
	b. Punched hole cancelled.	—	Unc	22.00
	r. Remainder w/o sign.	—	Unc	100.00

		GOOD	FINE	XF
S576	**10 PESOS** *L.1891.* Black on salmon and green unpt. Portr. Liberty at l., arms at r. Back gray and maroon; horse head at l. and r.	—	Rare	—

		GOOD	FINE	XF
S577	**50 PESOS** *L.1891.* Black on green and maroon unpt. Sailing ship at l., arms at ctr., allegorical man at r. Back green; 3 cows.	—	Rare	—

		Good	Fine	XF
S578	**100 Pesos** *L.1891.* Black on maroon and cream unpt. Ox-cart at l., arms at r. Back lt. blue, gray and black; horses.	—	Rare	—

		Good	Fine	XF
S579	**500 Pesos** *L.1891.* Black on blue-gray and ivory unpt. Arms at lower l., field workers at upper r. Back blue-gray and black.	—	Rare	—

Banco Británico de la América del Sud

1888 Conformes por Oro Issue

This issue took place from 1888 to 1897; notes were hand dated. Only one denomination is presently known, and in a single example.

		Good	Fine	XF
S601	**1000 Pesos** 16.3.1894. Black on rose unpt. Back rose. Hand sign.	—	Rare	—

Banco Hipotecario de la Provincia de Buenos Aires

This issue was yet another attempt to meet the financial crisis of the 1890 period. Two series were prepared but only the first was issued. The notes saw limited circulation but at a big discount.

Ley de 14 de Julio de 1891

#S611-S623 w/text: *MONEDA NACIONAL DE CURSO LEGAL.*

#S611-S632 arms on face, legal text on back. Printer: Talleres del Museo de La Plata. Imprint on back.

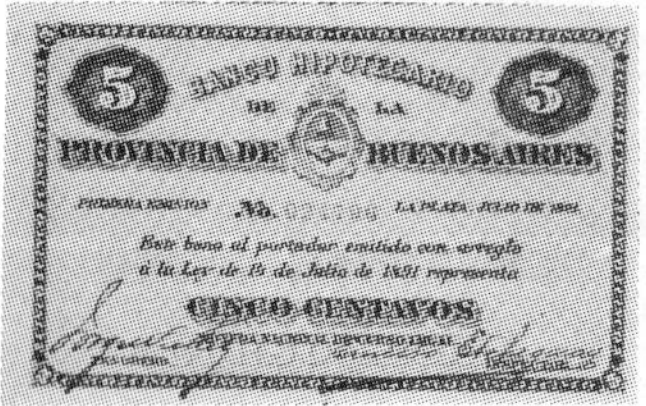

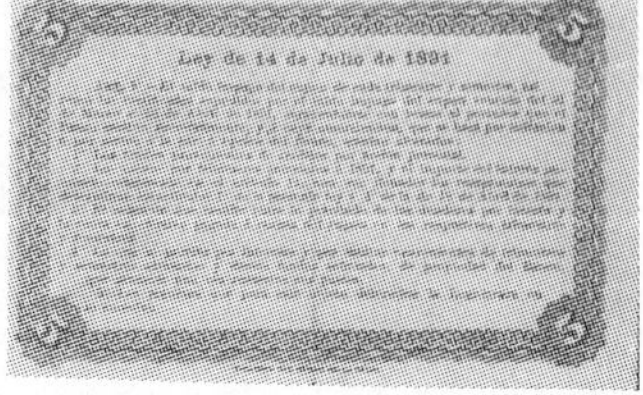

		Good	Fine	XF
S611	**5 Centavos** 7.1891. Black on sepia unpt. Arms at upper ctr. Back maroon.	5.00	12.00	30.00
S612	**10 Centavos** 7.1891.	Reported Not Confirmed		
S613	**20 Centavos** 7.1891. Black on rose unpt. Arms at l. Back orange.	5.00	15.00	35.00
S614	**50 Centavos** 7.1891. Black on lt. blue unpt. Arms at upper ctr. Back green.	7.50	20.00	45.00

		Good	Fine	XF
S615	**1 Peso** 7.1891. Black on dull maroon unpt. Arms at lower l. Back dull maroon.	8.50	25.00	75.00
S616	**2 Pesos** 7.1891. Black on ochre unpt. Arms at ctr. Back maroon.	20.00	60.00	175.00

		Good	Fine	XF
S617	**5 Pesos** 7.1891. Black on lt. blue unpt. Arms at ctr. Back orange.	10.00	30.00	100.00
S618	**10 Pesos** 7.1891. Black on ochre unpt. Arms at ctr. Back maroon.	20.00	75.00	200.00
S619	**20 Pesos** 7.1891. Black on blue-green unpt. Arms at l. Back green.	12.00	35.00	125.00
S620	**50 Pesos** 7.1891. Black on beige and lt. blue unpt. Arms at r. Back blue.	25.00	90.00	225.00

		Good	Fine	XF
S621	**100 Pesos** 7.1891. Black on maroon and lt. blue unpt. Arms at r. Back blue.	50.00	110.00	300.00

		GOOD	FINE	XF
S622	**200 PESOS**			
	7.1891. Black on green unpt. Arms at ctr. Back sepia.	—	Rare	—
S623	**500 PESOS**			
	7.1891. Black on green and ochre unpt. Arms at ctr. Back blue.	60.00	150.00	350.00

#S624-S632 w/text: *MONEDA NACIONAL ORO SELLADO*. Unpt. wording different from previous issue, otherwise notes are similar. Specimens only.

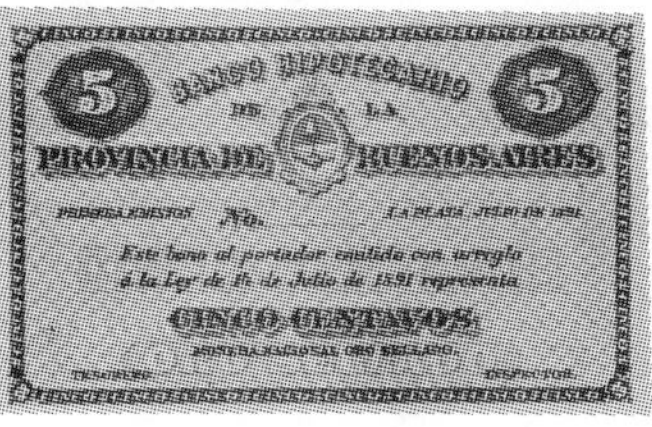

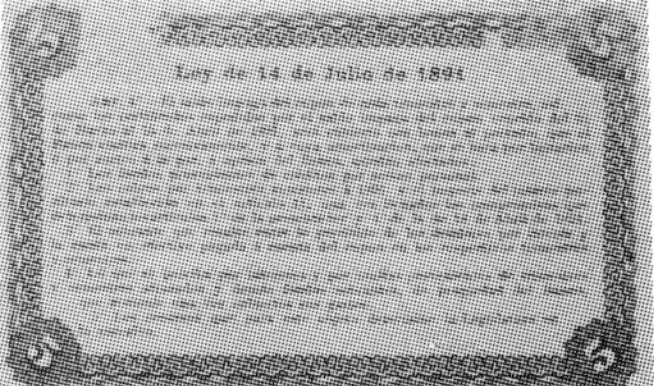

		GOOD	FINE	XF
S624	**5 CENTAVOS**			
	7.1891. Black on sepia unpt. Similar to #S611.	10.00	30.00	65.00
S625	**10 CENTAVOS**			
	7.1891.	Reported Not Confirmed		
S626	**20 CENTAVOS**			
	7.1891. Black on rose unpt. Similar to #S613.	10.00	30.00	65.00
S627	**50 CENTAVOS**			
	7.1891. Black on lt. blue unpt. Similar to #S614.	15.00	40.00	90.00

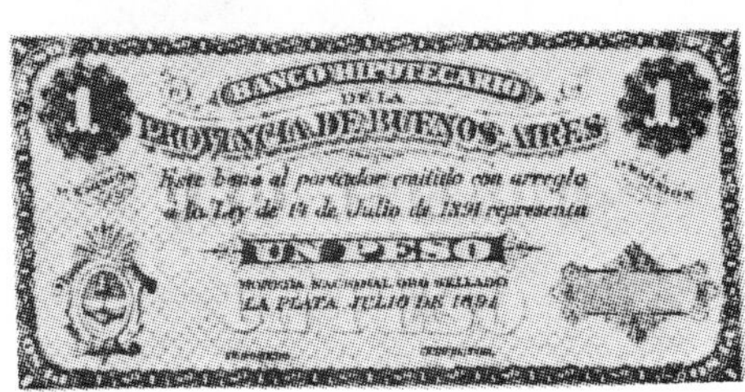

		GOOD	FINE	XF
S628	**1 PESO**			
	7.1891. Black on blue unpt. Similar to #S615.	15.00	40.00	100.00
S629	**5 PESOS**			
	7.1891. Black on green unpt. Similar to #S617.	20.00	50.00	110.00
S630	**10 PESOS**			
	7.1891. Black on green unpt. Similar to #S618.	40.00	150.00	350.00
S631	**20 PESOS**			
	7.1891. Black on maroon unpt. Similar to #S619.	25.00	60.00	125.00
S632	**50 PESOS**			
	7.1891. Similar to #S620.	Reported Not Confirmed		

BANCO NACIONAL

1873 ISSUE

The 1873 dated issue was large and with many variations. It consisted of 19 different denominations of notes which come with or without overprints and stampings from different branches of issue. The varieties break down into 4 major face and 3 back variants. Various combinations of faces and backs are shown for each note. Faces are indicated by numbers and backs with capital letters according to the following descriptions:

Faces:

1. As printed, w/o revalidation or ovpt.
2. Vertical ovpt: *Ley de 24 Octubre 1876.*
3. Ovpt: *Ley... 1876* plus sign. *Delgado Gerente* underneath.
4. Ovpt: *Moneda Nacional Oro Ley de 5 Noviembre 1881* in oval, plus lg. capital letter (A-V) which may indicate branch office. (Specific designations of letter to branch office are not known.)

Backs:

A. As printed, w/o revalidation or ovpt.
B. Branch office stamp and hand sign. of manager.
C. Branch office stamp and 1879 date printed.

17 branch offices used these notes in varying amounts. Values shown are for the most common. Branch names are as follows:

Catamarca . . . . GualeguaychúSalta
Concepción del Uruguay . . . . JujuySan Juan
Concordia . . . . La RiojaSan Luís
Córdoba . . . . MendozaSantiago del Estero
Corrientes . . . . ParanáTucumán
Gualeguay . . . . Rosario

#S641-S659 series A-D. Printer: ABNC.

		GOOD	FINE	XF
S641	**4 CENTAVOS FUERTES**			
	1.8.1873. Black on green unpt. Dog and safe at upper ctr., arms below. Uniface.			
	a. Face 1, back A.	10.00	25.00	55.00
	b. Face 1, back C.	15.00	30.00	75.00
	c. Face 2, back A.	15.00	30.00	75.00
	d. Face 2, back B.	15.00	30.00	75.00
	e. Face 2, back C.	15.00	30.00	75.00
	f. Face 3, back A.	15.00	30.00	75.00
	g. Face 3, back B.	12.00	27.00	60.00
	h. Face 3, back C.	12.00	27.00	60.00
	s. Specimen.	—	—	—

		GOOD	FINE	XF
S642	**5 CENTAVOS FUERTES**			
	1.8.1873. Black on blue unpt. Arms at ctr. Uniface.			
	a. Face 1, back A.	10.00	25.00	55.00
	b. Face 1, back C.	10.00	25.00	55.00
	c. Face 2, back A.	12.00	30.00	70.00
	d. Face 2, back B.	12.00	30.00	70.00
	e. Face 2, back C.	12.00	30.00	70.00
	f. Face 3, back A.	12.00	30.00	70.00
	g. Face 3, back B.	12.00	30.00	70.00
	h. Face 3, back C.	10.00	25.00	55.00
	s. Specimen.	—	—	—

		GOOD	FINE	XF
S643	**10 CENTAVOS FUERTES**			
	1.8.1873. Black on ochre unpt. Arms at ctr. Uniface.			
	a. Face 1, back A.	15.00	30.00	75.00
	b. Face 1, back C.	20.00	40.00	90.00
	c. Face 2, back A.	25.00	50.00	110.00
	d. Face 2, back B.	25.00	50.00	110.00
	e. Face 2, back C.	25.00	50.00	110.00
	f. Face 3, back A.	25.00	50.00	110.00
	g. Face 3, back B.	25.00	50.00	110.00
	h. Face 3, back C.	20.00	40.00	90.00
	s. Specimen.	—	—	—

S644 20 CENTAVOS FUERTES
1.8.1873. Black. Gaucho on horseback herding cows at ctr., arms below. Back blue; arms of the 14 provinces of the Republic.

	GOOD	FINE	XF
a. Face 1, back A.	15.00	30.00	100.00
b. Face 1, back C.	15.00	30.00	100.00
c. Face 2, back A.	25.00	50.00	150.00
d. Face 2, back B.	25.00	50.00	150.00
e. Face 2, back C.	25.00	50.00	150.00
f. Face 3, back A.	25.00	50.00	150.00
g. Face 3, back B.	25.00	50.00	150.00
h. Face 3, back C.	15.00	30.00	100.00

S645 25 CENTAVOS FUERTES
1.8.1873. Black. Sheep at lower l., arms at upper ctr., cow at lower r. Back red; similar to #S644.

	GOOD	FINE	XF
a. Remainder w/o sign.	150.00	450.00	—
p. Proof.	—	—	—
s. Specimen.	—	—	—

NOTE: It appears likely that #S645 was never signed or issued because of the disappearance of a box containing them and some 50 Centavos notes at the customs office. No issued example is presently known.

S646 40 CENTAVOS FUERTES
1.8.1873. Black on ochre unpt. Allegorical woman at l. and r. Back green; similar to #S644.

	GOOD	FINE	XF
a. Face 1, back A.	25.00	50.00	150.00
b. Face 1, back C.	25.00	50.00	150.00
c. Face 2, back A.	30.00	60.00	200.00
d. Face 2, back B.	30.00	60.00	200.00
e. Face 2, back C.	30.00	60.00	200.00
f. Face 3, back A.	30.00	60.00	200.00
g. Face 3, back B.	30.00	60.00	200.00
h. Face 3, back C.	25.00	50.00	150.00
p. Proof.	—	—	—

S647 50 CENTAVOS FUERTES
1.8.1873. Black. Horses at l., arms at ctr., farmer scene at r. Back green; similar to #S644.

	GOOD	FINE	XF
a. Face 1, back A.	150.00	600.00	—
p. Proof.	—	—	—
s. Specimen.	—	—	—

NOTE: Very few of #S647 was signed and released (see NOTE following #S645).

S648 75 CENTAVOS FUERTES
1.8.1873. Black on ochre unpt. Ostriches running at lower l., arms at ctr., portr. J. M. de. Pueyrredon at lower r. Back brown; similar to #S644.

	GOOD	FINE	XF
a. Face 1, back A.	Reported Not Confirmed		
b. Face 1, back C.	40.00	150.00	400.00
c. Face 2, back A.	40.00	150.00	400.00
d. Face 2, back B.	50.00	160.00	450.00
e. Face 2, back C.	40.00	150.00	400.00
f. Face 3, back A.	50.00	160.00	450.00
g. Face 3, back B.	40.00	150.00	400.00
h. Face 3, back C.	40.00	150.00	400.00
p. Proof.	—	—	—
s. Specimen.	—	—	—

NOTE: An issue of 75 Centavos notes is reported to have been printed by Guillermo Kraft, Bs. As. but no examples are known.

S649 1 PESO FUERTE
1.8.1873. Black on salmon unpt. Gen. M. Necochea at l., arms at ctr., ox-cart at r. Back brown; similar to #S644.

	GOOD	FINE	XF
a. Face 1, back A.	65.00	175.00	450.00
b. Face 1, back C.	65.00	175.00	450.00
c. Face 2, back A.	65.00	175.00	500.00
d. Face 2, back B.	65.00	175.00	450.00
e. Face 2, back C.	65.00	175.00	500.00
f. Face 3, back A.	65.00	175.00	500.00
g. Face 3, back B.	65.00	175.00	450.00
h. Face 3, back C.	65.00	175.00	450.00
i. Face 4, back A. Blue or red ovpt.	65.00	175.00	450.00
p. Proof.	—	—	—
s. Specimen.	—	—	—

S650 2 PESOS FUERTES

1.8.1873. Black on rose and green unpt. Train at upper l. ctr., arms at ctr., train at upper ctr. r., Dr. A. Saenz at lower r. Back blue; similar to #S644.

	Good	Fine	XF
a. Face 1, back A.	85.00	200.00	500.00
b. Face 1, back C.	85.00	200.00	500.00
c. Face 2, back A.	85.00	200.00	500.00
d. Face 2, back B.	85.00	200.00	500.00
e. Face 2, back C.	85.00	200.00	500.00
f. Face 3, back A.	85.00	200.00	500.00
g. Face 3, back B.	85.00	200.00	500.00
h. Face 3, back C.	85.00	200.00	500.00
i. Face 4, back A. Blue or red ovpt.	85.00	200.00	500.00
p. Proof.	—	—	—
s. Specimen.	—	—	—

S651 3 PESOS FUERTES

1.8.1873. Black on sepia and lt. green unpt. Arms at l., allegorical woman at ctr., portr. B. Rivadavia at r. Back yellow-brown; similar to #S644.

	Good	Fine	XF
a. Face 1, back C.	200.00	600.00	—
p. Proof.	—	—	—
s. Specimen.	—	—	—

S652 5 PESOS FUERTES

1.8.1873. Black on lt. blue and ochre unpt. Ship at upper l., arms at ctr., ship at upper r., Dean Funes at lower r. Back violet; similar to #S644.

	Good	Fine	XF
a. Face 1, back A.	—	Rare	—
b. Face 1, back C.	—	Rare	—
c. Face 2, back A.	—	Rare	—
d. Face 2, back B.	—	Rare	—
e. Face 2, back C.	—	Rare	—
f. Face 3, back A.	—	Rare	—
g. Face 3, back B.	—	Rare	—
h. Face 3, back C.	—	Rare	—
p. Proof.	—	—	—
s. Specimen.	—	—	—

S653 10 PESOS FUERTES

1.8.1873. Black on blue-green unpt. Arms at lower l., woman w/sheep at ctr., Gen. A. Balcerce at lower r. Back brown; similar to #S644.

	Good	Fine	XF
a. Face 1, back A.	—	Rare	—
b. Face 1, back C.	—	Rare	—
c. Face 2, back A.	—	Rare	—
d. Face 2, back B.	—	Rare	—
e. Face 2, back C.	—	Rare	—
f. Face 3, back A.	—	Rare	—
g. Face 3, back B.	—	Rare	—
h. Face 3, back C.	—	Rare	—

S654 15 PESOS FUERTES

1.8.1873. Black on green unpt. portr. woman at lower l., arms at ctr., portr. Gen. M. Rodriguez at lower r. Back green; similar to #S644.

	Good	Fine	XF
a. Face 1, back C.	Reported Not Confirmed		
p. Proof.	—	—	—
s. Specimen w/ or w/o ovpt: *SPECIMEN.*	—	—	—

S655 20 PESOS FUERTES

1.8.1873. Black on brown unpt. N. Pena at l., sailor at ctr., arms at r. Back blue; similar to #S644.

	Good	Fine	XF
a. Face 1, back A.	—	Rare	—
b. Face 1, back C.	—	Rare	—
c. Face 2, back A.	—	Rare	—
d. Face 2, back B.	—	Rare	—
e. Face 2, back C.	—	Rare	—
f. Face 3, back A.	—	Rare	—
g. Face 3, back B.	—	Rare	—
h. Face 3, back C.	—	Rare	—
p. Proof.	—	—	—
s. Specimen.	—	—	—

S656 50 PESOS FUERTES

1.8.1873. Black on green unpt. Allegory of Work at l., arms at ctr., Fray J. de ro at r. Back brown; similar to #S644.

	Good	Fine	XF
a. Face 1, back A.	—	Rare	—
b. Face 1, back C.	—	Rare	—
c. Face 2, back A.	—	Rare	—
d. Face 2, back B.	—	Rare	—
e. Face 2, back C.	—	Rare	—
f. Face 3, back A.	—	Rare	—
g. Face 3, back B.	—	Rare	—
h. Face 3, back C.	—	Rare	—
p. Proof.	—	—	—
s. Specimen.	—	—	—

		GOOD	FINE	XF
S657	**100 PESOS FUERTES**			
	1.8.1873. Black on ochre unpt. Allegory of Sciences at l., arms at ctr., Gen. M. Rodriguez at r. Back black and green; 14 provincial flags and national arms.			
	a. Issued note.	Reported Not Confirmed		
	p. Proof.	—	—	—
	s. Specimen.	—	—	—

NOTE: No issued example of any kind is known for #S657.

		GOOD	FINE	XF
S658	**200 PESOS FUERTES**			
	1.8.1873. Black on ochre unpt. Allegorical woman and child at l., J. Paso at ctr., arms at r. Back black and ochre; similar to #S657.			
	a. Issued note.	Reported Not Confirmed		
	p. Proof.	—	—	—
	s. Specimen.	—	—	—

NOTE: No issued example of any kind is known for #S658.

		GOOD	FINE	XF
S659	**500 PESOS FUERTES**			
	1.8.1873. Black on violet unpt. 2 women w/flag at l., arms flanked by cherubs at ctr., Dr. B. Rivadavia at lower r. Back black and dk. brown; similar to #S657.			
	a. Issued note.	Reported Not Confirmed		
	p. Proof.	—	—	—
	s. Specimen.	—	—	—

NOTE: No issued example of any kind is known for #S659. Since this and #S658 were not sent to any branch offices, it is likely that if they were issued, it was only with face 1 and back A.

1879 ISSUE

#S661-S664 vertical ovpt: *Ley de 24 Octubre 1876* and sign. *Delgado gerente* underneath at l. These special denominations were made to facilitate the exchange of notes denominated in Reales Bolivianos. 4-1/2 Centavos = 1/2 Real, 9 Centavos = 1 Real, 18 Centavos = 2 Reales, and 36 Centavos = 4 Reales Bolivianos. Printer: Guillermo Kraft, Bueno Aires.

Backs come either w/o branch office stamping or w/such stamping and date *1879*. Additionally, some notes w/branch office indicated on back will have sign. of branch manager added. Branches which stamped some of these notes are as follows:

Catamarca	Gualeguaychú	Salta
Concepción del Uruguay	Jujuy	San Juan
Concordia	La Rioja	San Luís
Córdoba	Mendoza	Santiago del Estero
Corrientes	Paraná	Tucumán
Gualeguay	Rosario	

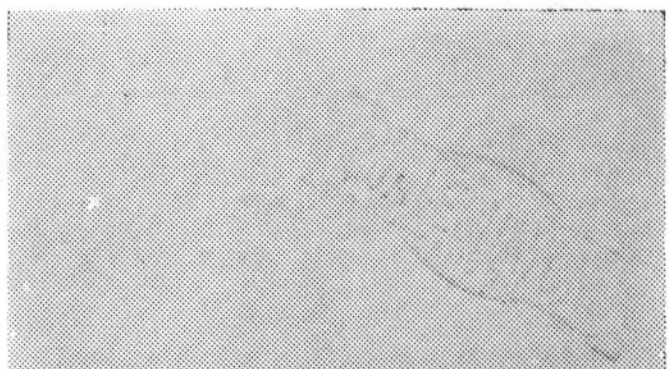

		GOOD	FINE	XF
S661	**4-1/2 CENTAVOS FUERTES**			
	2.1.1879. Black on lt. blue unpt. Arms at ctr. Uniface. Vertical red ovpt.			
	a. W/o branch office stamping on back.	15.00	35.00	85.00
	b. Branch office and date *1879* stamped on back.	20.00	40.00	95.00

		GOOD	FINE	XF
S662	**9 CENTAVOS FUERTES**			
	2.1.1879. Black on lt. green unpt. Girl and dog at ctr. Vertical red ovpt. Back brown.			
	a. W/o branch office stamping on back.	20.00	40.00	90.00
	b. Branch office and date *1879* stamped on back.	25.00	50.00	125.00

		GOOD	FINE	XF
S663	**18 CENTAVOS FUERTES**			
	2.1.1879. Black on ochre unpt. Girl at l., ship, arms and train at ctr., boy at r. Vertical dk. blue ovpt. Back ochre; 14 provincial arms.			
	a. W/o branch office stamping on back.	85.00	175.00	350.00
	b. Branch office and date *1879* stamped on back.	85.00	175.00	350.00

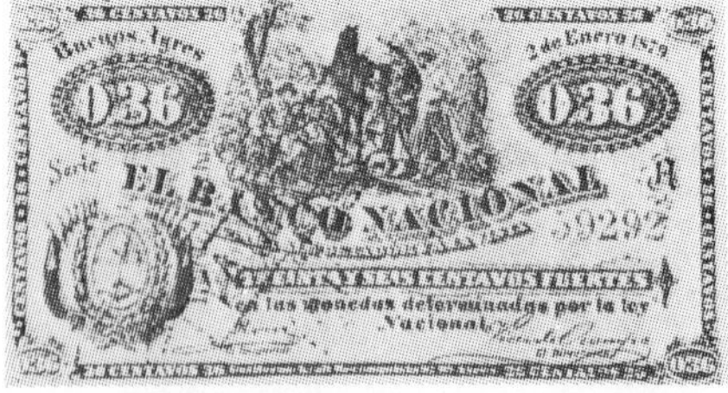

		GOOD	FINE	XF
S664	**36 CENTAVOS FUERTES**			
	2.1.1879. Black on salmon unpt. Arms at lower l., gauchos and horse at ctr. Vertical red ovpt. Back blue; similar at #S663.			
	a. W/o branch office stamping on back.	75.00	150.00	300.00
	b. Branch office and date *1879* stamped on back.	75.00	150.00	300.00

1880 FIRST ISSUE

These were made to circulate in the northern provinces. Once again, their purpose was to facilitate the exchange of notes denominated in Pesos Bolivianos and fractions thereof. Each note had text stating its equivalent in *Chirolas* of specified value. The value of a *Chirola* fluctuated with the price of silver on the international market. It was also affected by the silver content in the Bolivian coinage.

Two issues of Centavos/Chirolas notes were made, and both are dated 1.3.1880. The difference is the stated value of the Chirola, the first being @ 14 centavos and the second @ 16 centavos. Printer: Guillermo Kraft, Buenos Aires.

All notes except #S668 have the same vertical ovpt: *1876.* and sign. as the previous issue. All back designs contain the 14 provincial arms. Some are stamped with branch office names and date *1879* from the following offices:

Catamarca	Mendoza	San Luís
Jujuy	Salta	Santiago del Estero
La Rioja	San Juan	Tucumán

#S665-S668 Chirola = 14 Centavos Fuertes.

		GOOD	FINE	XF
S665	14 CENTAVOS FUERTES = 1 CHIROLA 1.3.1880. Black on violet unpt. Girl at l., arms at upper r. Vertical red ovpt. Back lt. gray.			
	a. W/o branch office stamping on back.	150.00	400.00	—
	b. W/branch office and date *1879* stamped on back.	150.00	400.00	—
S666	28 CENTAVOS FUERTES = 2 CHIROLAS 1.3.1880. Black on brown-orange unpt. Gaucho on horseback at l., arms at lower ctr., seated Liberty at r. Vertical red ovpt. Back green.			
	a. W/o branch office stamping on back.	150.00	400.00	—
	b. W/branch office and date *1879* stamped on back.	150.00	400.00	—

		GOOD	FINE	XF
S667	56 CENTAVOS FUERTES = 4 CHIROLAS 1.3.1880. Black on brown-orange unpt. Gaucho on horseback at l., arms at lower ctr., seated Liberty at r. Vertical red ovpt. Back green.			
	a. W/o branch office stamping on back.	150.00	400.00	—
	b. W/branch office and date *1879* stamped on back.	150.00	400.00	—
S668	5 PESOS-60 CENTAVOS FUERTES =40 CHIROLAS 1.3.1880. Black on ochre unpt. Arms, gaucho and cows at l. W/o vertical ovpt. Back green; arms.			
	a. W/o branch office stamping on back.	—	Rare	—
	b. W/branch office and date *1879* stamped on back.	—	Rare	—

1880 SECOND ISSUE

#S669-S671 Chirola = 16 Centavos Fuertes.

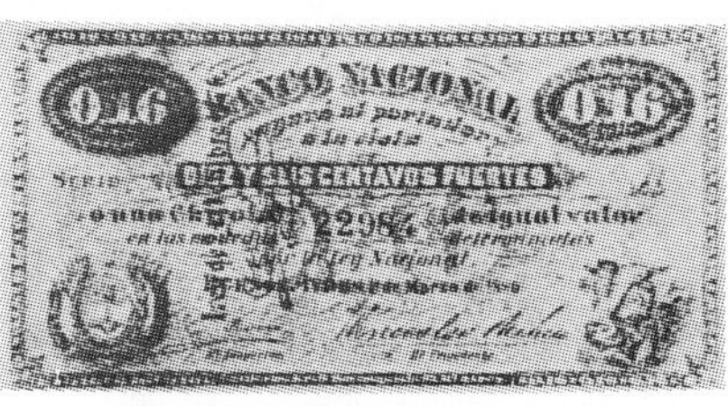

		GOOD	FINE	XF
S669	16 CENTAVOS FUERTES = 1 CHIROLA 1.3.1880. Black on maroon unpt. Arms at lower l., cow's head at lower r. Vertical dk. blue ovpt. Back maroon.			
	a. W/o branch office stamping on back.	150.00	400.00	—
	b. W/branch office and date *1879* stamped on back.	150.00	400.00	—

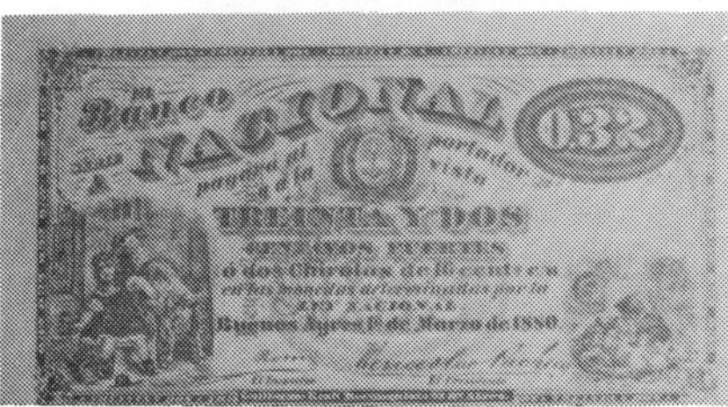

		GOOD	FINE	XF
S670	32 CENTAVOS FUERTES = 2 CHIROLAS 1.3.1880. Black on green unpt. Baby and goat at l., arms at ctr., domestic animals at r. Vertical red ovpt. Back lt. brown.			
	a. W/o branch office stamping on back.	150.00	400.00	—
	b. W/branch office and date *1879* stamped on back.	150.00	400.00	—

		GOOD	FINE	XF
S671	64 CENTAVOS FUERTES = 4 CHIROLAS 1.3.1880. Black on rose unpt. Arms at l., sailing ship in storm at ctr. Vertical blue or black ovpt. Back maroon.			
	a. W/o branch office stamping on back.	175.00	500.00	—
	b. W/branch office and date *1879* stamped on back.	175.00	500.00	—

1883 FIRST ISSUE

#S676-S684 may have lg. capital letter from A to V possibly indicating branch office. The exact designation of letter to office is not known. Also a reissue of these notes (#S685-S693) took place w/circular revalidation ovpt: *GOBIERNO NACIONAL-INTERVENCION* around *Ley 14 de Octubre de 1885* (similar to #S545-S553). Printer: ABNC.

		GOOD	FINE	XF
S676	1 PESO 1.1.1883. Black on orange unpt. Portr. woman at l., reclining allegorical woman and globe at ctr., Gen. M. Rodriguez at r. Back orange.			
	a. Issued note.	40.00	150.00	350.00
	s. Specimen.	—	—	—

		GOOD	FINE	XF
S677	2 PESOS 1.1.1883. Black on ochre unpt. Woman at l., portr. B. Rivadavia upper ctr., Liberty at lower r. Back brownish maroon.			
	a. Issued note.	80.00	250.00	600.00
	p. Proof. Back brown.	—	—	—
	s. Specimen.	—	—	—

		GOOD	FINE	XF
S678	5 PESOS 1.1.1883. Black on blue-green unpt. Gen. R. Pena at upper l., 2 cherubs at ctr., standing allegorical woman at r. Back blue-green.			
	a. Issued note.	100.00	350.00	850.00
	p. Proof. Back green.	—	—	—
	s. Specimen.	—	—	—

		GOOD	FINE	XF
S679	10 PESOS 1.1.1883. Black on deep rose unpt. Portr. woman's head at l. and r., J. A. Roca at ctr. Back deep rose; arms w/flags and cannon.			
	a. Issued note.	175.00	—	—
	p. Proof.	—	—	—
	s. Specimen.	—	—	—

S680 20 PESOS
1.1.1883. Black on lt. green unpt. Allegorical woman w/staff, bird and plants at ctr., Dean Funes at lower r. Back grayish green.

	GOOD	FINE	XF
a. Issued note.	200.00	—	—
p. Proof.	—	—	—
s. Specimen.	—	—	—

S681 50 PESOS
1.1.1883. Black on rose unpt. Cherub at l., farm implements at ctr., M. Gonzalez B. facing l. at r. Back rose.

	GOOD	FINE	XF
p. Proof.	—	—	—
s. Specimen.	—	—	—

S682 100 PESOS
1.1.1883. Black on pink unpt. 2 allegorical women overlooking ships at l., J. J. Paso at r. Back black and violet; flowers.

	GOOD	FINE	XF
p. Proof.	—	—	—
s. Specimen.	—	—	—

S683 200 PESOS
1.1.1883. Black on ochre unpt. Woman and horse at l., A. P. Saenz at r. Back black and maroon; 2 allegorical women at ctr.

	GOOD	FINE	XF
p. Proof. Back brown.	—	—	—
s. Specimen.	—	—	—

S684 500 PESOS
1.1.1883. Black on green and rose unpt. Arms at lower l., woman reclining at upper ctr., Gen. J. de San Martín at lower r. Back black and orange; woman in oval at ctr. Specimen.

GOOD	FINE	XF
—	—	—

1885 FIRST PROVISIONAL ISSUE

#S685-S693 w/circular revalidation ovpt: *1885* on face.

		GOOD	FINE	XF
S685	**1 PESO** ND (- old date 1.1.1883). Black on orange unpt. Ovpt. on #S676.	40.00	150.00	400.00
S686	**2 PESOS** ND (- old date 1.1.1883). Black on ochre unpt. Ovpt. on #S677.	80.00	250.00	700.00
S687	**5 PESOS** ND (- old date 1.1.1883). Black on blue-green unpt. Ovpt. on #S678.	100.00	300.00	1000.
S688	**10 PESOS** ND (- old date 1.1.1883). Black on deep rose unpt. Ovpt. on #S679.	150.00	—	—
S689	**20 PESOS** ND (- old date 1.1.1883). Black on green unpt. Ovpt. on #S680.	200.00	—	—
S690	**50 PESOS** ND (- old date 1.1.1883). Black on rose unpt. Ovpt. on #S681.	—	—	—
S691	**100 PESOS** ND (- old date 1.1.1883). Black on pink unpt. Ovpt. on #S682.	—	—	—
S692	**200 PESOS** ND (- old date 1.1.1883). Black on ochre unpt. Ovpt. on #S683.	Reported Not Confirmed		
S693	**500 PESOS** ND (- old date 1.1.1883). Black on green and rose unpt. Ovpt. on #S684.	Reported Not Confirmed		

1883 SECOND ISSUE

#S694-S713 w/arms at ctr. Printer: BWC.

#S694-S703 were also reissued w/circular revalidation ovpt: *1885* (#S704-S713) similar to the 1883 First Issue w/arms at ctr. Printer: BWC.

S694 1 PESO
1.1.1883. Black on green unpt. Sailor at l., Gen. M. Rodriguez at r. Back rose and green; head of Liberty.

GOOD	FINE	XF
40.00	100.00	300.00

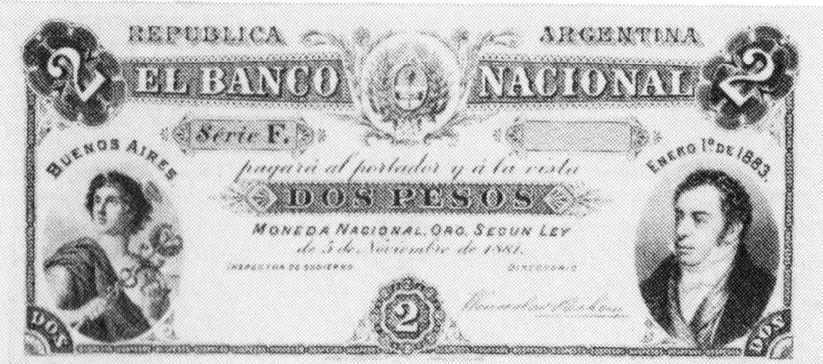

S695 2 PESOS
1.1.1883. Black on green unpt. Mercury w/caduceus at l., Dr. B. Rivadavia at r. Back rose, green and violet; similar to #S694 but head w/Phrygian cap.

	GOOD	FINE	XF
a. Issued note.	80.00	300.00	750.00
p. Proof.	—	—	—

		Good	Fine	XF
S696	**5 Pesos** 1.1.1883. Black on rose unpt. Gen. R. Pena at l., cows at r. Back rose; similar to #S695.			
	a. Issued note.	100.00	250.00	600.00
	p. Proof.	—	—	—

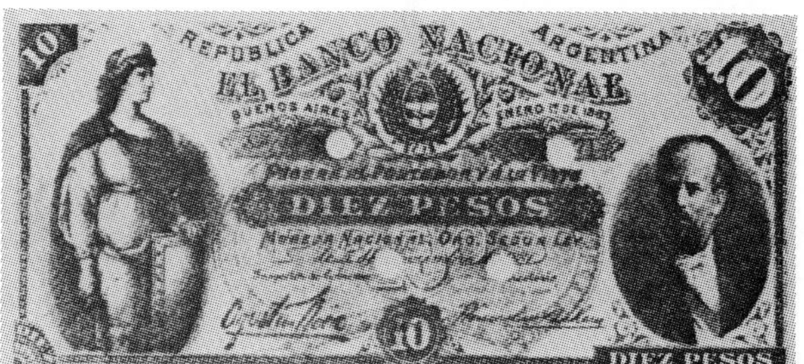

		Good	Fine	XF
S697	**10 Pesos** 1.1.1883. Black on green and lt. blue unpt. Liberty standing at l., President J. A. Roca at r. Back green; 14 provincial arms.	—	Rare	—
S698	**10 Pesos** 1.1.1883. Black on yellow and lt. blue unpt. Generally similar to #S697 but many plate differences. Back lt. green.	—	Rare	—
S699	**20 Pesos** 1.1.1883. Black on green and lt. blue unpt. Standing Liberty at l., Dean Funes at r. Back brown; woman's head.	—	Rare	—
S700	**50 Pesos** 1.1.1883. Black on ochre and rose unpt. Group of 4 persons at l., Gen. A. Balcarce at r. Back lt. blue.	—	Rare	—

		Good	Fine	XF
S701	**100 Pesos** 1.1.1883. Black on ochre unpt. Liberty at l., J. J. Paso at r. Back rose.	—	Rare	—

		Good	Fine	XF
S702	**200 Pesos** 1.1.1883. Black on green unpt. Allegory of Art at l., A. P. Saenz at r. Back black, brown and blue; hay wagon at ctr. Specimen.	—	Rare	—
S703	**500 Pesos** 1.1.1883. Black on green and ochre unpt. Gen J. de San Martín at r., allegory of Painting at l. Back green. Specimen.	—	Rare	—

1885 Second Provisional Issue

#S704-S713 w/circular revalidation ovpt: *1885* on face.

		Good	Fine	XF
S704	**1 Peso** ND (- old date 1.1.1883). Black on green unpt. Ovpt. on #S694.	40.00	100.00	300.00
S705	**2 Pesos** ND (- old date 1.1.1883). Black on green unpt. Ovpt. on #S695.	80.00	250.00	600.00
S706	**5 Pesos** ND (- old date 1.1.1883). Black on rose unpt. Ovpt. on #S696.	100.00	300.00	700.00
S707	**10 Pesos** ND (- old date 1.1.1883). Black on green unpt. Ovpt. on #S697.	—	Rare	—

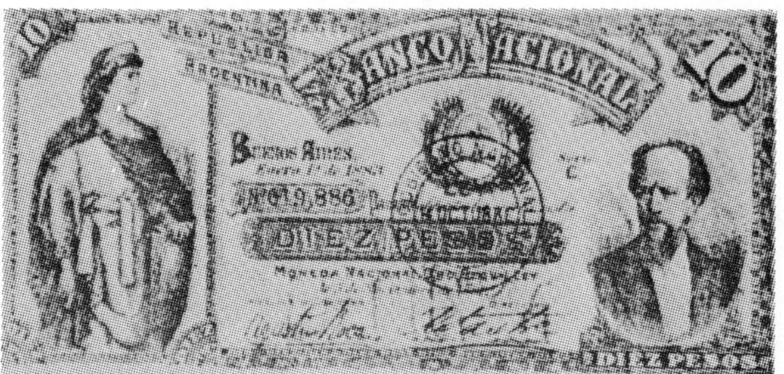

		Good	Fine	XF
S708	**10 Pesos** ND (- old date 1.1.1883). Black on yellow and lt. blue unpt. Ovpt. on #S698.	—	Rare	—
S709	**20 Pesos** ND (- old date 1.1.1883). Black on green and lt. blue unpt. Ovpt. on #S699.	—	Rare	—
S710	**50 Pesos** ND (- old date 1.1.1883). Black on ochre and rose unpt. Ovpt. on #S700.	—	Rare	—
S711	**100 Pesos** ND (- old date 1.1.1883). Black on ochre unpt. Ovpt. on #S701.	—	Rare	—
S712	**200 Pesos** ND (- old date 1.1.1883). Black on green unpt. Ovpt. on #S702.	Reported Not Confirmed		
S713	**500 Pesos** ND (- old date 1.1.1883). Black on green and ochre unpt. Ovpt. on #S703.	Reported Not Confirmed		

1883 Third Issue

A third issue was prepared for this bank, but apparently not placed into circulation. All known examples are either specimens or proofs. All faces have the shorter version of the bank name. All backs carry the long version. Printer: ABNC.

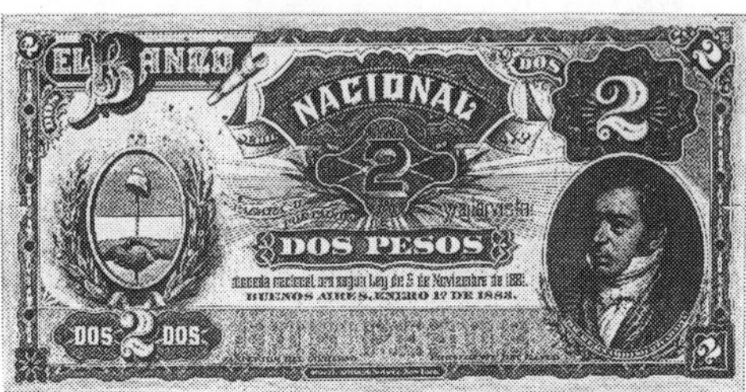

		Good	Fine	XF
S715	**2 Pesos** 1.1.1883. Black on blue and lt. orange unpt. Arms at l., Dr. B. Rivadavia at r. Back deep blue; lg. numeral at ctr. Specimen w/o serial #.	—	—	—

		Good	Fine	XF
S716	**5 Pesos** 1.1.1883. Black on green, brown and lt. red unpt. Col. Borrego at l., Raphael's "Angel" at ctr., arms at r. Back brown. Specimen w/o serial #.	—	—	—

		GOOD	FINE	XF
S717	**10 PESOS** 1.1.1883. Black on green and brown unpt. Justice seated at l., arms at ctr., J. A. Roca in uniform at r. Back deep green. Specimen w/o serial #.	—	—	—

		GOOD	FINE	XF
S718	**20 PESOS** 1.1.1883. Black on m/c unpt. Arms at l., allegorical woman at ctr., man at r. Specimen.	—	—	—

		GOOD	FINE	XF
S720	**500 PESOS** 1.1.1883. Mules going down mountain trail at r. on back. Proof.	—	—	—

BANCO PROVINCIAL DE CÓRDOBA

1873 FIRST ISSUE

#S721-S724 printer: BWC.

		GOOD	FINE	XF
S721	**1/2 REAL BOLIVIANO** 27.3.1873. Green. Portr. woman at l., bird at r. Head at l. and r. on back.	100.00	300.00	—

		GOOD	FINE	XF
S722	**1 REAL BOLIVIANO** 27.3.1873. Green. Woman and chipmunk at l. Back like #S721.	100.00	300.00	—
S723	**2 REALES BOLIVIANOS** 27.3.1873. Black on brown unpt. Dog.	125.00	—	—
S724	**4 REALES BOLIVIANOS** 27.3.1873. Black. Arms at lower l., galloping horse at ctr.	125.00	—	—

NOTE: #S721-S724 come w/ or w/o ovpt: *INSPECCION DE BANCOS* on back.

#S725-S727 printer: Lit. S. Martín, Buenos Aires.

		GOOD	FINE	XF
S725	**1 PESO BOLIVIANO** 27.3.1873. Black. Reclining allegorical woman at upper ctr., woman's head at upper r. Uniface.	75.00	250.00	—
S726	**5 PESOS BOLIVIANOS** 27.3.1873. Black on rose unpt. Gaucho.	—	—	—
S727	**10 PESOS BOLIVIANOS** 27.3.1873. Black.	—	—	—

NOTE: #S725-S727 come w/ or w/o ovpt: *INSPECCION DE BANCOS* on back.

1873 SECOND ISSUE

#S728 and S729 printer: Lit. S. Martín.

		GOOD	FINE	XF
S728	**50 CENTAVOS** 27.3.1873. Sheep.	—	—	—
S729	**1 PESO** 27.3.1873. Black on green unpt. Allegorical group.	—	—	—

NOTE: #S728 and S729 come w/ or w/o ovpt: *INSPECCION DE BANCOS* or *BOLNOS*.

1873 THIRD ISSUE

		GOOD	FINE	XF
S730	**1 PESO FUERTE** 27.3.1873. Allegorical group.	—	—	—

1881 FIRST ISSUE

Two different issues were made in 1881 for this bank. The first was locally printed, and the second was produced in England.

S731-S735 printer: Mackern & McLean, Buenos Aires.

		GOOD	FINE	XF
S731	**1 PESO** 1.1.1881.	Reported Not Confirmed		
S732	**5 PESOS** 1.1.1881.	Reported Not Confirmed		
S733	**10 PESOS** 1.1.1881. Black w/rose *10*. Dean G. Funes at l., provincial cathedral at r.			
	a. W/o ovpt.	100.00	300.00	—
	b. Ovpt: *Ley 14 Octubre 1885.*	100.00	300.00	—
S734	**20 PESOS** 1.1.1881.	Reported Not Confirmed		

		GOOD	FINE	XF
S735	**50 PESOS**			
	1.1.1881. Black w/rose *50.* Portr. Gen. J. Paz at l., train, arms and wagons at ctr. r. Back green; Liberty.			
	a. W/o ovpt.	200.00	500.00	—
	b. Ovpt: *Ley 14 Octubre 1885.*	200.00	500.00	—

1881 SECOND ISSUE

#S736-S740 printer: W&S.

		GOOD	FINE	XF
S736	**1 PESO**			
	1.1.1881. Black on gray unpt. 6 people at lower l., man watching girl pounding corn at ctr. Back orange.			
	a. W/o ovpt.	75.00	200.00	—
	b. Ovpt: *Ley 14 Octubre 1885.*	75.00	200.00	—

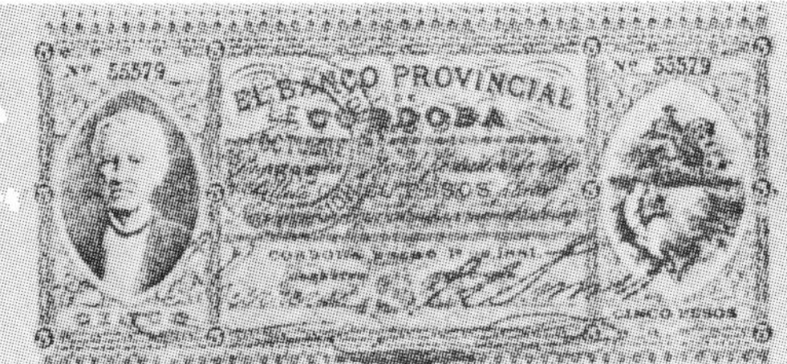

		GOOD	FINE	XF
S737	**5 PESOS**			
	1.1.1881. Black on gray and brown unpt. Portr. M. Fragueiro at l., gaucho on horseback at r. Back blue.			
	a. W/o ovpt.	150.00	400.00	—
	b. Ovpt: *Ley 14 Octubre 1885.*	150.00	400.00	—

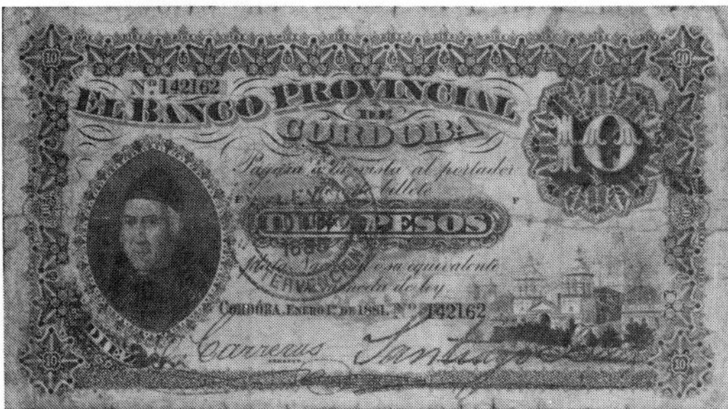

		GOOD	FINE	XF
S738	**10 PESOS**			
	1.1.1881. Black on lt. blue unpt. Like #S733. Back brown; arms at upper ctr.			
	a. W/o ovpt.	—	—	—
	b. Ovpt: *Ley 14 Octubre 1885.*	175.00	500.00	—
S739	**20 PESOS**			
	1.1.1881.	Reported Not Confirmed		
S740	**50 PESOS**			
	1.1.1881.	Reported Not Confirmed		

1889 ISSUE

Bonos

Circulating bonds issued by the *Sección Hipotecaria Agricola e Industrial* of the bank.

#S741-S744 printer: ABNC.

		GOOD	FINE	XF
S741	**1 PESO**			
	1.1.1889. Black on green unpt. Portr. J. Ceilman at lower l., cherubs at ctr., farmer and horse at r. Back green; building at ctr.			
	a. Issued note.	35.00	75.00	150.00
	s. Specimen.	—	—	—

		GOOD	FINE	XF
S742	**5 PESOS**			
	1.1.1889. Black on yellow and brown unpt. Portr. D. Sarsfield at l., seated allegorical woman w/gear and tools at r. Back brown; structure w/2 tall pillars at ctr.	40.00	100.00	250.00

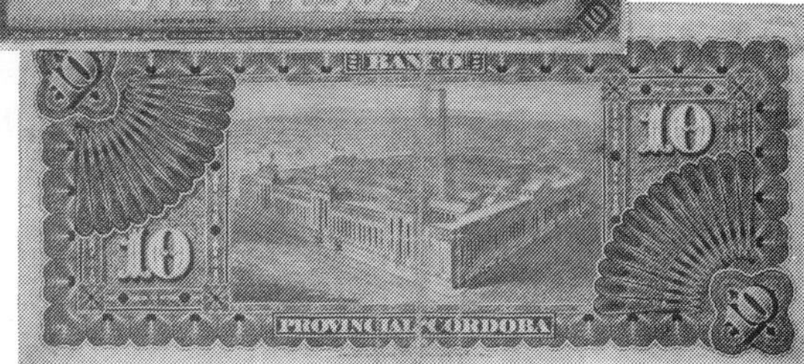

		GOOD	FINE	XF
S743	**10 PESOS**			
	1.1.1889. Black on blue and yellow unpt. Statue of Freedom at l., Gen. J. M. Paz at r. Back blue; govt. bldg. at ctr.	60.00	150.00	—

		GOOD	FINE	XF
S744	**20 PESOS**			
	1.1.1889. Black on orange and yellow unpt. M. Fraguiero at lower l., seated allegorical woman w/pitcher at r. Scene w/bridge and mountains at ctr. on back.			
	p1. Proof. Back orange.	—	—	—
	p2. Proof. Back green.	—	—	—

1891 ISSUE

		Good	Fine	XF
S755	**50 PESOS** 20.4.1891 (handwritten date). Arms at l. Uniface. Printer: La Minerva, Córdoba.	—	Rare	—
S756	**100 PESOS** 20.4.1891. Like #S755.	—	Rare	—
S757	**200 PESOS** 20.4.1891. Like #S755.	—	Rare	—

BANCO PROVINCIAL DE ENTRE-RÍOS

Two different issues were made for this bank in 1885. The first was locally printed, and the second was made in New York. The first issue does not bear the ovpt: *Ley 14 Octubre 1885* but all notes of the second issue do have this ovpt. on the face.

FIRST ISSUE - SERIES A

#S761-S766 text w/incorrect date: *8 de Noviembre de 1881*. Printer: La Union de Stiller y Laass, Buenos Aires.

		Good	Fine	XF
S760	**1 PESO** 1.4.1885. Black on red-orange unpt. 2 allegorical figures at lower l., portr. Gen. E. Racedo at upper ctr., steam train at lower r. Back maroon; provincial arms.			
	a. Issued note.	40.00	150.00	—
	s. Specimen ovpt: *MUESTRA*.	—	—	—

		Good	Fine	XF
S761	**1 PESO** 1.4.1885. Gen. E. Racedo at lower l., provincial arms at upper ctr., steam train at lower r.			
	a. Issued note.	—	—	—
	s. Specimen.	—	—	—

		Good	Fine	XF
S762	**2 PESOS** 1.4.1885. Black on lt. blue unpt. Portr. A. Crespo at l., farm implements and plants at ctr. r. Back blue-green; arms.			
	a. Issued note.	80.00	300.00	—
	s. Specimen ovpt: *MUESTRA*.	—	—	—

		Good	Fine	XF
S763	**5 PESOS** 1.4.1885. Black on blue-green unpt. Gen. J. de Urquiza at lower l., arms at ctr., view of Paraná at lower r. Back blue; Liberty.			
	a. Issued note.	150.00	450.00	—
	s. Specimen ovpt: *MUESTRA*.	—	—	—

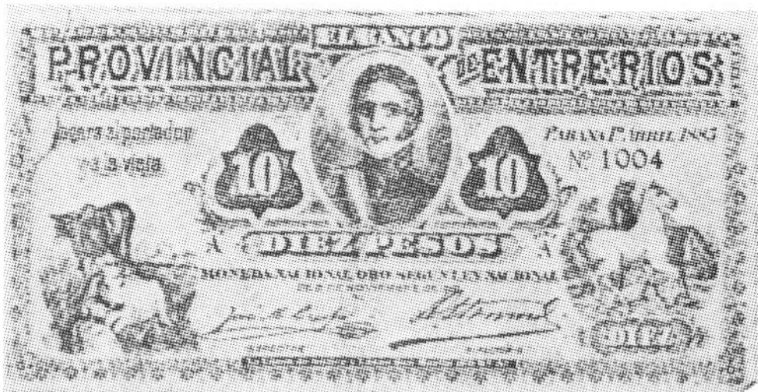

		Good	Fine	XF
S764	**10 PESOS** 1.4.1885. Black. Cows at lower l., portr. Gen. L. Sola at upper ctr., horses at r.			
	a. Issued note.	—	Rare	—
	s. Specimen ovpt: *MUESTRA*.	—	—	—
S765	**20 PESOS** 1.4.1885. Black on ochre unpt. Gen. E. Racedo as an old man.			
	a. Issued note.	—	Rare	—
	s. Specimen ovpt: *MUESTRA*.	—	—	—
S766	**50 PESOS** 1.4.1885.	Reported Not Confirmed		

SECOND ISSUE - SERIES B

#S767-S772 text w/corrected date: *5 de noviembre de 1881*. W/circular 1885 revalidation ovpt. on face. Printer: ABNC.

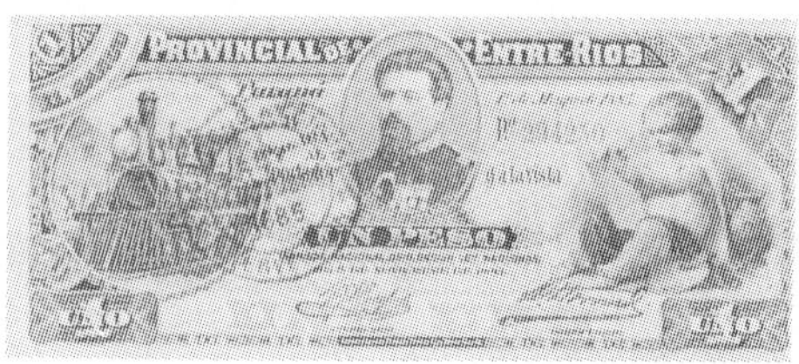

		Good	Fine	XF
S767	**1 PESO** 1.5.1885. Black on rose and green unpt. Steam train at l., portr. Gen. E. Racedo at top ctr., young allegorical figure at r. Back green; similar to #S760.			
	a. Issued note.	20.00	85.00	350.00
	s. Specimen.	—	—	—

		Good	Fine	XF
S768	**2 PESOS** 1.5.1885. Black on ochre and green unpt. A. Crespo at ctr., allegory of Farming at r. Back red; arms at ctr.			
	a. Issued note.	80.00	350.00	—
	s. Specimen.	—	—	—

		Good	Fine	XF
S769	**5 Pesos** 1.5.1885. Black on green and rose unpt. Provincial arms and allegory of Navigation at l., J. de Urquiza at r. Back maroon; similar to #S763.			
	a. Issued note.	150.00	450.00	—
	s. Specimen.	—	—	—

		Good	Fine	XF
S770	**10 Pesos** 1.5.1885. Black on blue and orange unpt. Gaucho herding cows at l., cherub at upper ctr. r., portr. Gen. L. Sola at r. Back blue; arms at ctr.			
	a. Issued note.	200.00	—	—
	p. Proof.	—	—	—
	s. Specimen.	—	—	—

		Good	Fine	XF
S771	**20 Pesos** 1.5.1885. Black on pink and green unpt. Gen. L. Mansilla at l., Raphael's Angel at ctr., open law book at r. Back brown; arms at ctr. Proof.	—	—	—
S772	**50 Pesos** 1.5.1885.	Reported Not Confirmed		

Banco Provincial de Salta

1884 Issue

#S786-S789 w/ovpt: *Ley 14 Octubre 1885* on face. Printer: G&D.

		Good	Fine	XF
S786	**1 Peso** 1.1.1884. Black on green unpt. Cow and ram at ctr. Back green.			
	a. Issued note.	75.00	250.00	—
	b. Cancelled, perforated: *PAGADO.*	60.00	200.00	—

		Good	Fine	XF
S787	**5 Pesos** 1.1.1884. Black on rose and lt. blue unpt. Cows at ctr. Back red.	200.00	750.00	—
S788	**10 Pesos** 1.1.1884. Man w/horse at r. Proof.	—	—	—
S789	**20 Pesos** 1.1.1884.	Reported Not Confirmed		

#S791-S794 Deleted.

Ley de Octubre 30 de 1891; 1899 Issue

		Good	Fine	XF
S796	**1 Peso** 25.7.1899. Black on brown unpt. Gen. A. de Arenales at l., provincial arms at upper ctr. Back orange; cow's head at l. and r., plantation and field at ctr.	20.00	50.00	150.00

1903, 1907 Renovacion Provisional Issue

		Good	Fine	XF
S797	**1 Peso** 1903 (- old date 25.7.1899). Black ovpt: *RENOVACION AÑO 1903* on back of #S796.	50.00	100.00	250.00
S797A	**1 Peso** 1907 (-old date 25.7.1899). Black ovpt.: *RENOVACION AÑO 1907 on* back of #S796.	50.00	100.00	250.00

Banco Provincial de Santa Fé

1874 First Issue

#S798-S802 issued in Pesos Fuertes. Printer: Litografia E. Fleuti, Rosario.

		Good	Fine	XF
S798	**5 Centavos Fuertes** 1.9.1874. Black. Sheep at lower l., arms at upper ctr.	—	—	—
S799	**10 Centavos Fuertes** 1.9.1874. Blue. Arms at top ctr., deer at r.	—	—	—
S800	**20 Centavos Fuertes** 1.9.1874. Blue. Horse at l., arms at top ctr.	—	—	—
S801	**37-1/2 Centavos Fuertes** 1.9.1874. Arms at top ctr., cow at r.	—	—	—
S802	**1 Peso Fuerte** 1.9.1874. Black on green unpt. Plowman at r.	—	—	—

1874 Second Issue

		Good	Fine	XF
S804	**1 Real Plata Boliviana** 1.11.1874. Black. Horses at lower l., provincial arms at ctr. Uniface. Rosario issue. Imprint: *Lito E. Fleuti Rosario.*	30.00	75.00	150.00
S805	**1 Real Boliviano** 1.11.1874. Like #S804 but rose paper. Santa Fe issue.	—	—	—
S806	**4 Reales Bolivianos** 1.11.1874. Black. Arms at ctr., puma at r. Rosario issue.	—	—	—
S807	**4 Reales Bolivianos** 1.11.1874. Black on rose paper. Like #S806. Santa Fe issue.	—	—	—
S808	**1 Peso Boliviano** 1.11.1874. Black on yellow-ochre paper. Farmer plowing w/oxen at l., arms at top ctr. Back brown. Rosario issue.	—	—	—
S809	**1 Peso Boliviano** 1.11.1874. Black on green unpt. Like #S808. Back blue. Santa Fe issue.	—	—	—

		GOOD	FINE	XF
S810	**10 PESOS BOLIVIANOS** 1.11.1874. Black. Steam train at upper l., arms at top ctr., ship at r. Rosario issue.	—	—	—
S811	**10 PESOS BOLIVIANOS** 1.11.1874. Black on yellow unpt. Like #S810. Back violet. Santa Fe issue.	—	—	—

1875 FIRST ISSUE

#S811A-S818 printer: ABNC.

		GOOD	FINE	XF
S811A	**50 CENTAVOS PLATA BOLIVIANA** 1.1.1875. Black on salmon unpt. Like #S812. Rosario issue. Series A; B.	—	—	—

		GOOD	FINE	XF
S812	**50 CENTAVOS PLATA BOLIVIANA** 1.1.1875. Black on yellow unpt. Provincial arms at lower l., horse at upper ctr., child at lower r. Santa Fe issue. Series A; B.			
	a. Issued note.	150.00	450.00	—
	p. Proof.	—	—	—
	s. Specimen.	—	—	—

		GOOD	FINE	XF
S813	**1 PESO PLATA BOLIVIANA** 1.1.1875. Black on green unpt. Portr. child at l., farmer w/horse plowing at ctr., provincial arms at r. Back green. Rosario issue. Series A; B.	—	—	—
S814	**1 PESO PLATA BOLIVIANA** 1.1.1875. Black on orange unpt. Like #S815. Back orange. Santa Fe issue. Series A; B.	—	—	—
S814A	**5 PESOS PLATA BOLIVIANA** 1.1.1875. Black on orange unpt. Like #S815. Back orange; dog at ctr. Rosario issue. Proof.	—	—	—

		GOOD	FINE	XF
S815	**5 PESOS PLATA BOLIVIANA** 1.1.1875. Black on green unpt. Farmer w/pig at l., steam tractor at ctr., provincial arms at r. Santa Fe issue. Series A; B.	—	—	—
S816	**10 PESOS PLATA BOLIVIANA** 1.1.1875. Black on green unpt. Provincial arms at l., gaucho and ostrich at ctr., J. B. Alberdi at r. Back green. Rosario issue. Series A; B.	—	—	—

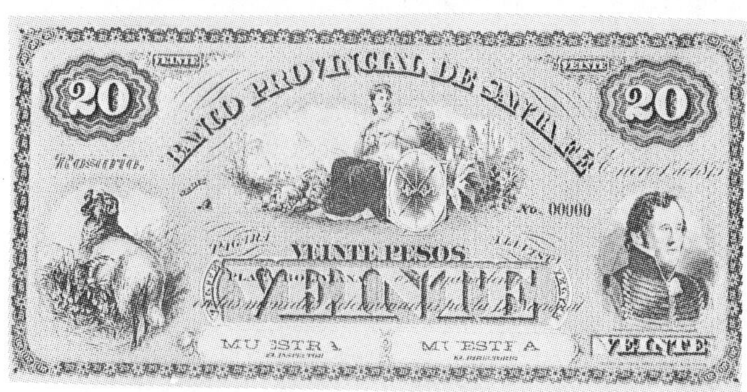

		GOOD	FINE	XF
S817	**20 PESOS PLATA BOLIVIANA** 1.1.1875. Sheep at lower l., seated allegorical woman at ctr., General E. Lopez at lower r. Back brown; steam locomotive at ctr. Rosario issue. Series A.	—	—	—
S818	**50 PESOS PLATA BOLIVIANA** 1.1.1875. Black on maroon unpt. Dog at l., gauchos roping steer at upper ctr., G. Urquiza at r. Back maroon; cow's head at ctr. Rosario issue. Series A.	—	—	—

1875 SECOND ISSUE

#S819-S821 printers: E. Fleuti or D. Boldt.

		GOOD	FINE	XF
S819	**1/2 REAL PLATA BOLIVIANA** 1.1.1875. Provincial arms at l., Liberty at r.			
	a. Handwritten sign. Black serial #.	—	—	—
	b. Stamped sign., black or red serial #.	—	—	—

		GOOD	FINE	XF
S820	**1 REAL PLATA BOLIVIANA** 1875 (1.11.1874). Black. Like #S804 but slightly narrower shield of arms, ornament added to l. of *SERIE UNA* at top, and imprint changed to *Lito A Vapor Fleuti Rosario.*	40.00	100.00	350.00

		GOOD	FINE	XF
S821	**10 PESOS PLATA BOLIVIANA** 1.1.1875. Black on green unpt. Provincial arms at upper l., vaqueros driving cattle at upper ctr., dog w/pheasant at lower r. Back green. Printer: Fleuti, Rosario.			
	a. Issued note.	75.00	200.00	600.00
	r. Remainder.	—	—	50.00

1875 THIRD ISSUE

#S822-S824 are dated 1875 but were actually contracted for and issued in 1881. Printer: A. Pech, Buenos Aires.

		Good	Fine	XF
S822	**1 Peso Plata Boliviana** 1.1.1875. Black on blue unpt. Similar to #S813. Back blue. Rosario issue. Series C.	75.00	400.00	—
S823	**1 1/2 Pesos = 12 Reales Plata Boliviana** 1.1.1875. Child at l., cattle at ctr., provincial arms at r. Rosario issue. Series A. Specimen.	—	—	—
S824	**2 Pesos Plata Boliviana** 1.1.1875. Black on brown unpt. Provincial arms at l., seated woman at ctr., dog at r. Back brown. Rosario issue. Series A.			
	a. Issued note.	—	—	—
	b. Stamped: *SUCURSAL* 4 times on back (for Santa Fé).	—	—	—

NOTE: #S822-S824 were stamped w/designation for Santa Fé as needed, on the back.

1881 Issue

		Good	Fine	XF
S825	**1 Real Plata Boliviana** 1.1.1881. Black. Standing woman w/basket and cornucopia at l., provincial arms at lower r. Uniface. Printer: Fleuti (Rosario).	75.00	175.00	—

1882 Issue

All notes of this issue are dated at Rosario but some notes destined for Santa Fe have that city name in red ovpt. on face. Issues for Rosario and Santa Fé come w/o or w/ovpt: *Ley 14 Octubre 1885*.

#S826-S830D issued at Rosario. Printer: ABNC.

		Good	Fine	XF
S826	**1 Peso** 1.1.1882. Black on lt. brown unpt. Provincial arms at l., vaqueros driving cattle at ctr., portr. girl at r. Back brown.			
	a. W/o ovpt.	60.00	275.00	—
	b. Ovpt: *Ley 14 Octubre 1885.*	60.00	275.00	—

		Good	Fine	XF
S827	**1 1/2 Pesos** 1.1.1882. Black on green unpt. Provincial arms at l., horse and dogs at ctr., gaucho at r. Back green.			
	a. W/o ovpt.	100.00	400.00	—
	b. Ovpt: *Ley 14 Octubre 1885.*	100.00	400.00	—
S828	**5 Pesos** 1.1.1882. Black on blue unpt. Gaucho at lower l., factory at ctr., provincial arms at r. Back blue.			
	a. W/o ovpt.	200.00	500.00	—
	b. Ovpt: *Ley 14 Octubre 1885.*	200.00	500.00	—
	s. Specimen.	—	—	—
S829	**10 Pesos** 1.1.1882. Black on rose unpt. J. B. Alberdi at l., gaucho on horseback, Indian on food, and animals at ctr., provincial arms at r. Back red.			
	a. W/o ovpt.	200.00	750.00	—
	b. Ovpt: *Ley 14 Octubre 1885.*	200.00	750.00	—
	p. Proof back, green.	—	—	—

		Good	Fine	XF
S830	**20 Pesos** 1.1.1882. Black on ochre unpt. Portr. Gen. E. Lopez at l., provincial arms at l. ctr., steam freight train at ctr. r. Back ochre.			
	a. W/o ovpt.	—	Rare	—
	b. Ovpt: *Ley 14 Octubre 1885.*	—	Rare	—
	s. Specimen.	—	—	—

		Good	Fine	XF
S830A	**50 Pesos** 1.1.1882. Black on orange unpt. Provincial arms and allegorical woman w/scales at l., portr. Urquiza at r. Back orange. Series A. Proof.	—	—	—
S830C	**200 Pesos** 1.1.1882. Black on dk. brown unpt. Seated allegorical woman at l., Raphael's Angel at upper ctr., provincial arms at r. Back dk. brown; seated allegorical woman w/sheep at ctr. Series A. Proof.	—	—	—

		Good	Fine	XF
S830D	**500 Pesos** 1.1.1882. Black on brown unpt. Seated allegorical woman at l., and upper ctr., griffin at l. and r. of provincial arms at bottom ctr., men in harbor scene at r. Back brown; horse at ctr. Series A. Proof.	—	—	—

#S831-S835 w/red ovpt: *Santa Fé* on face.

		Good	Fine	XF
S831	**1 Peso** 1.1.1882. Like #S826.			
	a. W/o ovpt.	60.00	150.00	—
	b. Ovpt: *Ley 14 Octubre 1885.*	60.00	150.00	—
S832	**1 1/2 Pesos** 1.1.1882. Like #S827.	—	—	—
S833	**5 Pesos** 1.1.1882. Like #S828.			
	a. W/o ovpt.	200.00	500.00	—
	b. Ovpt: *Ley 14 Octubre 1885.*	200.00	500.00	—
S834	**10 Pesos** 1.1.1882. Like #S829.			
	a. W/o ovpt.	200.00	750.00	—
	b. Ovpt: *Ley 14 Octubre 1885.*	200.00	750.00	—
S835	**20 Pesos** 1.1.1882. Like #S830.			
	a. W/o ovpt.	—	Rare	—
	b. Ovpt: *Ley 14 Octubre 1885.*	—	Rare	—

BANCO PROVINCIAL DE TUCUMÁN

1888 ISSUE

#S841-S846 all come w/ovpt: *Ley 14 Octubre 1885* on face. Printer: CSABB, Buenos Aires.

		GOOD	FINE	XF
S841	1 PESO 1.3.1888. Black on ochre unpt. House of Tucumán at l., Gov. L. Quinteros at lower r. Back maroon.	50.00	200.00	500.00

		GOOD	FINE	XF
S842	2 PESOS 1.3.1888. Black on rose unpt. Gov. Col. M. Paz at upper ctr. Back red.	80.00	400.00	—
S843	5 PESOS 1.3.1888. J. B. Alberdi at l., steam train at ctr.	—	—	—

		GOOD	FINE	XF
S844	10 PESOS 1.3.1888. Black on ochre and lt. blue unpt. N. Avellaneda at l., steam train leaving tunnel at ctr.	—	—	—

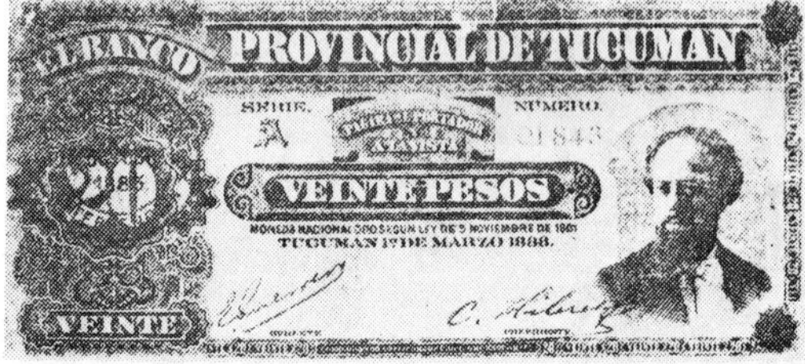

		GOOD	FINE	XF
S845	20 PESOS 1.3.1888. Man at lower r.	—	—	—
S846	50 PESOS 1.3.1888.	Reported Not Confirmed		

SECTION III

BANCOS NACIONALES GARANTIDOS

(Guaranteed National Banks)

In a further effort at unifying the currency, Argentina passed a law on November 3, 1887, stating that any corporation or society with capital of 250,000 pesos in national money could function as a bank and issue notes guaranteed by national public funds. Such notes would be legal in all parts of the country.

Not all denominations were printed by all banks participating. In a few instances notes were prepared for issue but withheld from circulation and later destroyed. All notes of any given denomination were uniform except for bank name and series designation. Printer: BWC.

Descriptions of each denomination are given below:

1 PESO 1.1.1888. Black on pink unpt. Portr. Adm. G. Brown at l., arms at ctr., 3 cherubs at r. Back rose; allegory of Arts and Sciences.

2 PESOS. 1.1.1888. Black on grayish brown unpt. 2 cherubs and anchor at l., arms at upper ctr., portr. Gen. C. de Alvear at r. Back maroon; allegory of Commerce.

5 PESOS.... 1.1.1888. Black on green and rose unpt. Portr. Dr. D. Sarsfield and allegorical woman at l., arms at ctr. Back green; allegory of Science.

10 PESOS 1.1.1888. Black on blue unpt. Portr. Dr. J. Roca at l., arms at ctr., cherub and cow at r. Back blue; fruit gathering.

20 PESOS...1.1.1888. Black on brown and yellow unpt. Portr. Dr. W. Pacheco at l., arms at upper ctr., winged Victory and cherubs at r. Back maroon; vaqueros roping cattle.

50 PESOS.. 1.1.1888. Black on blue and yellow unpt. Arms at ctr., portr. Dr. M. Celman and mythological figure w/trident at r. Back green; ranch working.

100 PESOS1.1.1888. Black on sepia unpt. Portr. Dr. M. Moreno at l., arms at upper ctr., allegorical woman at r. Back maroon; teaching Indians.

200 PESOS1.1.1888. Black on sepia unpt. Allegorical winged woman at l., arms at upper ctr., Portr. Dr. B. Rivadavia at r. Back maroon; horses.

500 PESOS1.1.1888. Black on m/c unpt. Allegorical woman and portr. Gen. M. Belgrano at l., arms at ctr. Back blue; exportation.

1000 PESOS. 1.1.1888. Black on m/c unpt. Portr. Gen. J. de San Martín and allegory of Victory w/2 angels at l., arms at ctr. Back green; allegory of Agriculture and 3 children.

Because of various financial conditions, occurrences and crises, various issues were overprinted with revalidations at certain times. All known ovpt. are listed under their respective banks. The ovpts. appear as follows:

LEY 6 SETIEMBRE 1890

LEY 16 OCTUBRE 1891

LEY 29 OCTUBRE DE 1891

(used only on #S1098)

LEY 8 ENERO DE 1894

LEY 20 DE SETIEMBRE DE 1897

NOTE: Only those notes w/o any of these ovpt. are issues of the Bancos. All ovpt. notes are in reality issues of the Caja de Conversion.

BANCO ALEMÁN TRANSATLÁNTICO

SERIES 010

		GOOD	FINE	XF
S1008	200 PESOS 1.1.1888.	—	Rare	—

BANCO BRITÁNICO DE LA AMÉRICA DEL SUD

SERIES 024

		GOOD	FINE	XF
S1020	1000 PESOS 1.1.1888.	—	Rare	—

NOTE: A single example is known of #S1020 and it has only 1 sign. A total of 250 notes of this issue were made.

BANCO BUENOS AIRES

SERIES 013

		GOOD	FINE	XF
S1024	**10 PESOS** 1.1.1888.	—	Rare	—

		GOOD	FINE	XF
S1026	**50 PESOS** 1.1.1888.	—	Rare	—
S1027	**1000 PESOS** 1.1.1888.	—	Rare	—

BANCO CARABASSA

SERIES ?

		GOOD	FINE	XF
S1040	**1000 PESOS** 1.1.1888.	—	—	—

NOTE: #S1040 was prepared for issue but not released. All were later destroyed.

BANCO CONSTRUCTOR DE LA PLATA

SERIES ?

		GOOD	FINE	XF
S1041	**1 PESO** 1.1.1888.	—	—	—
S1043	**5 PESOS** 1.1.1888.	—	—	—

NOTE: #S1041 and S1043 were prepared for issue but not released. All were later destroyed.

BANCO FRANCES DEL RIO DE LA PLATA

SERIES 020

		GOOD	FINE	XF
S1057	**100 PESOS** 1.1.1888.	—	—	—

NOTE: #S1057 was prepared for issue but not released. All were later destroyed.

BANCO INGLÉS DE RIO DE JANEIRO

SERIES 017

		GOOD	FINE	XF
S1063	**5 PESOS** 1.1.1888.	—	—	—
S1064	**10 PESOS** 1.1.1888.	—	—	—
S1065	**20 PESOS** 1.1.1888.	—	—	—

NOTE: #S1063-S1065 were prepared for issue but not released. All were later destroyed.

BANCO DE ITALIA Y RIO DE LA PLATA

SERIES 017

		GOOD	FINE	XF
S1078	**200 PESOS** 1.1.1888.	—	—	—

NOTE: #S1078 was prepared for issue but not released. All were later destroyed.

BANCO LONDRES Y RIO DE LA PLATA

SERIES ?

		GOOD	FINE	XF
S1090	**1000 PESOS** 1.1.1888.	—	—	—

NOTE: #S1090 was prepared for issue but not released. All were later destroyed.

BANCO NACIONAL

SERIES 001

		GOOD	FINE	XF
S1091	**1 PESO** 1.1.1888.			
	a. W/o ovpt.	10.00	30.00	100.00
	b. Ovpt: *Ley 8.1.1894.*	10.00	30.00	100.00
	c. Ovpt: *Ley 20.9.1897.*	10.00	30.00	100.00
S1092	**2 PESOS** 1.1.1888.			
	a. W/o ovpt.	15.00	40.00	150.00
	b. Ovpt: *Ley 16.10.1891.*	25.00	60.00	200.00
	c. Ovpt: *Ley 8.1.1894.*	15.00	40.00	150.00

		GOOD	FINE	XF
S1093	**5 PESOS** 1.1.1888.			
	a. W/o ovpt.	20.00	50.00	200.00
	b. Ovpt: *Ley 6.9.1890.*	40.00	100.00	300.00
	c. Ovpt: *Ley 16.10.1891.*	35.00	85.00	250.00
	d. Ovpt: *Ley 8.1.1894.*	20.00	50.00	200.00

		GOOD	FINE	XF
S1094	**10 PESOS** 1.1.1888.			
	a. W/o ovpt.	35.00	150.00	325.00
	b. Ovpt: *Ley 6.9.1890.*	45.00	150.00	350.00
	c. Ovpt: *Ley 16.10.1891.*	50.00	150.00	400.00
	d. Ovpt: *Ley 8.1.1894.*	35.00	150.00	325.00
S1095	**20 PESOS** 1.1.1888.			
	a. W/o ovpt.	75.00	300.00	—
	b. Ovpt: *Ley 6.9.1890.*	85.00	350.00	—

S1096 50 Pesos
1.1.1888.

	Good	Fine	XF
a. W/o ovpt.	150.00	500.00	—
b. Ovpt: *Ley 6.9.1890.*	200.00	700.00	—

S1097 100 Pesos
1.1.1888.

	Good	Fine	XF
a. W/o ovpt.	200.00	—	—
b. Ovpt: *Ley 6.9.1890.*	225.00	—	—
c. Ovpt: *Ley 16.10.1891.*	250.00	—	—
d. Ovpt: *Ley 8.1.1894.*	275.00	—	—

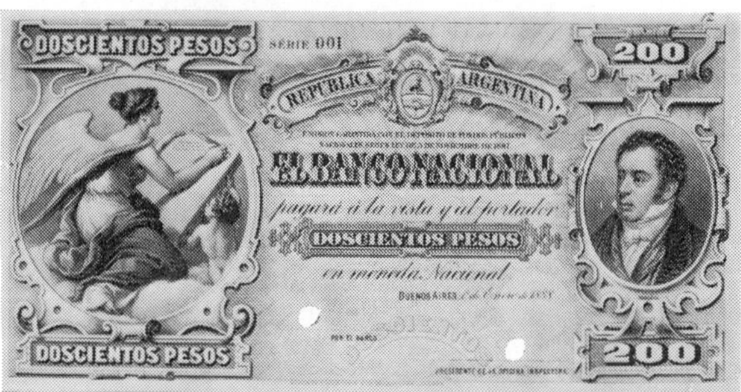

S1098 200 Pesos
1.1.1888.

	Good	Fine	XF
a. W/o ovpt.	—	—	—
b. Ovpt: *Ley 6.9.1890.*	—	—	—
c. Ovpt: *Ley 16.10.1891.*	—	—	—
d. Ovpt: *Ley 29.10.1891.*	—	—	—

S1099 500 Pesos
1.1.1888.

	Good	Fine	XF
a. W/o ovpt.	—	—	—
b. Ovpt: *Ley 6.9.1890.*	—	—	—
c. Ovpt: *Ley 16.10.1891.*	—	—	—

S1100 1000 Pesos
1.1.1888.

	Good	Fine	XF
a. W/o ovpt.	—	—	—
b. Ovpt: *Ley 6.9.1890.*	—	—	—
c. Ovpt: *Ley 16.10.1891.*	—	—	—

Banco de la Provincia de Buenos Aires

Series 002

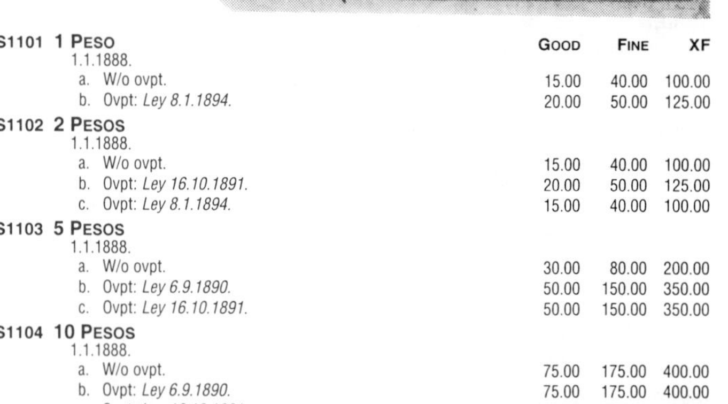

S1101 1 Peso
1.1.1888.

	Good	Fine	XF
a. W/o ovpt.	15.00	40.00	100.00
b. Ovpt: *Ley 8.1.1894.*	20.00	50.00	125.00

S1102 2 Pesos
1.1.1888.

	Good	Fine	XF
a. W/o ovpt.	15.00	40.00	100.00
b. Ovpt: *Ley 16.10.1891.*	20.00	50.00	125.00
c. Ovpt: *Ley 8.1.1894.*	15.00	40.00	100.00

S1103 5 Pesos
1.1.1888.

	Good	Fine	XF
a. W/o ovpt.	30.00	80.00	200.00
b. Ovpt: *Ley 6.9.1890.*	50.00	150.00	350.00
c. Ovpt: *Ley 16.10.1891.*	50.00	150.00	350.00

S1104 10 Pesos
1.1.1888.

	Good	Fine	XF
a. W/o ovpt.	75.00	175.00	400.00
b. Ovpt: *Ley 6.9.1890.*	75.00	175.00	400.00
c. Ovpt: *Ley 16.10.1891*	100.00	225.00	550.00

S1105 20 Pesos
1.1.1888.

	Good	Fine	XF
a. W/o ovpt.	85.00	300.00	1000.
b. Ovpt: *Ley 6.9.1890.*	85.00	300.00	1000.

S1106 50 PESOS

1.1.1888.	GOOD	FINE	XF
a. W/o ovpt.	200.00	700.00	—
b. Ovpt: *Ley 6.9.1890.*	250.00	800.00	—

S1107 100 PESOS

1.1.1888.	GOOD	FINE	XF
a. W/o ovpt.	225.00	750.00	—
b. Ovpt: *Ley 6.9.1890.*	250.00	1000.	—

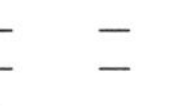

S1108 200 PESOS

1.1.1888.	GOOD	FINE	XF
a. W/o ovpt.	—	—	—
b. Ovpt: *Ley 6.9.1890.*	—	—	—

S1109 500 PESOS

1.1.1888.	GOOD	FINE	XF
	—	—	—

BANCO PROVINCIAL DE CATAMARCA

SERIES 014

	GOOD	FINE	XF
S1111 1 PESO			
1.1.1888.			
a. W/o ovpt.	15.00	40.00	100.00
b. Ovpt: *Ley 20.9.1897.*	20.00	50.00	125.00
S1112 2 PESOS			
1.1.1888.			
a. W/o ovpt.	35.00	85.00	200.00
b. Ovpt: *Ley 8.1.1894.*	30.00	75.00	175.00
S1113 5 PESOS			
1.1.1888.			
a. W/o ovpt.	55.00	150.00	350.00
b. Ovpt: *Ley 16.10.1891.*	70.00	175.00	400.00
S1114 10 PESOS			
1.1.1888.	140.00	300.00	700.00

	GOOD	FINE	XF
S1115 20 PESOS			
1.1.1888.	150.00	450.00	—
S1116 50 PESOS			
1.1.1888.	—	—	—

BANCO PROVINCIAL DE CÓRDOBA

SERIES 004

S1121 1 PESO

1.1.1888.	GOOD	FINE	XF
a. W/o ovpt.	15.00	40.00	100.00
b. Ovpt: *Ley 8.1.1894.*	15.00	40.00	100.00

S1122 2 PESOS

1.1.1888.	GOOD	FINE	XF
a. W/o ovpt.	15.00	40.00	100.00
b. Ovpt: *Ley 16.10.1891.*	30.00	75.00	175.00
c. Ovpt: *Ley 8.1.1894.*	15.00	40.00	100.00

	GOOD	FINE	XF
S1123 5 PESOS			
1.1.1888.			
a. W/o ovpt.	30.00	85.00	225.00
b. Ovpt: *Ley 6.9.1890.*	40.00	100.00	250.00
c. Ovpt: *Ley 16.10.1891.*	50.00	120.00	275.00
S1124 10 PESOS			
1.1.1888.			
a. W/o ovpt.	80.00	200.00	500.00
b. Ovpt: *Ley 16.10.1891.*	100.00	250.00	600.00

	GOOD	FINE	XF
S1125 20 PESOS			
1.1.1888.	125.00	350.00	—
S1126 50 PESOS			
1.1.1888.	—	—	—

		Good	Fine	XF
S1127	100 Pesos 1.1.1888.	—	—	—
S1128	200 Pesos 1.1.1888.	—	—	—
S1129	500 Pesos 1.1.1888.	—	—	—

Banco Provincial de Corrientes

Series 015

		Good	Fine	XF
S1131	1 Peso 1.1.1888.			
	a. W/o ovpt.	15.00	40.00	100.00
	b. Ovpt: *Ley 8.1.1894.*	Reported Not Confirmed		
	c. Ovpt: *Ley 20.9.1897.*	10.00	30.00	95.00
S1132	2 Pesos 1.1.1888.			
	a. W/o ovpt.	30.00	75.00	175.00
	b. Ovpt: *Ley 16.10.1891.*	40.00	100.00	250.00
	c. Ovpt: *Ley 8.1.1894.*	20.00	50.00	125.00
S1133	5 Pesos 1.1.1888.	50.00	125.00	300.00
S1134	10 Pesos 1.1.1888.	125.00	300.00	650.00
S1135	20 Pesos 1.1.1888.	150.00	400.00	—
S1136	50 Pesos 1.1.1888.	—	—	—
S1137	100 Pesos 1.1.1888.	—	—	—

Banco Provincial de Entre Rios

Two different issues were made for this bank in 1885. The first was locally printed, and the second was made in New York. The first issue does not bear the ovpt: *Ley 14 Octubre 1885* but all notes of the second issue do have this ovpt. on the face.

Series 005

		Good	Fine	XF
S1141	1 Peso 1.1.1888.			
	a. W/o ovpt.	8.00	25.00	100.00
	b. Ovpt: Ley 8.1.1894.	8.00	25.00	100.00
	c. Ovpt: Ley 20.9.1897.	15.00	40.00	110.00

		Good	Fine	XF
S1142	2 Pesos 1.1.1888.			
	a. W/o ovpt.	17.50	45.00	150.00
	b. Ovpt: *Ley 16.10.1891.*	40.00	100.00	250.00
	c. Ovpt: *Ley 8.1.1894.*	15.00	40.00	125.00
S1143	5 Pesos 1.1.1888.	50.00	150.00	350.00
S1144	10 Pesos 1.1.1888.	80.00	200.00	450.00
S1145	20 Pesos 1.1.1888.	150.00	350.00	—
S1146	50 Pesos 1.1.1888.	—	—	—

Banco Provincial de La Rioja

Series 012

		Good	Fine	XF
S1151	1 Peso 1.1.1888.			
	a. W/o ovpt.	15.00	40.00	100.00
	b. Ovpt: *Ley 8.1.1894.*	15.00	40.00	100.00
S1152	2 Pesos 1.1.1888.			
	a. W/o ovpt.	25.00	60.00	150.00
	b. Ovpt: *Ley 16.10.1891.*	30.00	80.00	200.00
	c. Ovpt: *Ley 8.1.1894.*	20.00	50.00	125.00
S1153	5 Pesos 1.1.1888.	55.00	160.00	350.00
S1154	10 Pesos 1.1.1888.			
	a. W/o ovpt.	140.00	300.00	650.00
	b. Ovpt: *Ley 6.9.1890.*	150.00	320.00	700.00
S1155	20 Pesos 1.1.1888.	200.00	450.00	—
S1156	50 Pesos 1.1.1888.	—	—	—
S1157	100 Pesos 1.1.1888.	—	—	—

Banco de la Provincia de Mendoza

The correct name of this bank is Banco de la Provincia de Mendoza. Through printer's error some notes with title: *Banco Provincial de Mendoza* were made and sent to Argentina.

Series 008

		Good	Fine	XF
S1161	1 Peso 1.1.1888.			
	a. W/o ovpt.	15.00	40.00	100.00
	b. Ovpt: *Ley 20.9.1897.*	15.00	40.00	100.00
S1162	2 Pesos 1.1.1888.			
	a. W/o ovpt.	20.00	50.00	125.00
	b. Ovpt: *Ley 6.9.1890.*	60.00	165.00	400.00
	c. Ovpt: *Ley 8.1.1894.*	60.00	165.00	400.00
S1163	5 Pesos 1.1.1888.			
	a. W/o ovpt.	60.00	165.00	400.00
	b. Ovpt: *Ley 6.9.1890.*	75.00	250.00	600.00
S1164	10 Pesos 1.1.1888.			
	a. W/o ovpt.	100.00	225.00	550.00
	b. Ovpt: *Ley 6.9.1890.*	150.00	350.00	—
	c. Ovpt: *Ley 16.10.1891.*	150.00	350.00	—
S1165	20 Pesos 1.1.1888.			
	a. W/o ovpt.	175.00	425.00	—
	b. Ovpt: *Ley 6.9.1890.*	200.00	450.00	—

Banco Provincial de Salta

Series 006

		Good	Fine	XF
S1171	1 Peso 1.1.1888.			
	a. W/o ovpt.	10.00	25.00	90.00

	Good	Fine	XF
b. Ovpt: *Ley 8.1.1894.*	10.00	25.00	90.00
c. Ovpt: *Ley 20.9.1897.*	10.00	25.00	90.00
S1172 2 Pesos 1.1.1888.			
a. W/o ovpt.	20.00	50.00	125.00
b. Ovpt: *Ley 16.10.1891.*	35.00	100.00	275.00
c. Ovpt: *Ley 8.1.1894.*	20.00	50.00	125.00
S1173 5 Pesos 1.1.1888.	45.00	125.00	300.00
S1174 10 Pesos 1.1.1888.	65.00	175.00	400.00
S1175 20 Pesos 1.1.1888.	150.00	350.00	—

Banco Provincial de San Juan

Series 011

	Good	Fine	XF
S1181 1 Peso 1.1.1888.			
a. W/o ovpt.	15.00	40.00	100.00
b. Ovpt: *Ley 8.1.1894.*	15.00	40.00	100.00
c. Ovpt: *Ley 20.9.1897.*	20.00	50.00	125.00
S1182 2 Pesos 1.1.1888.			
a. W/o ovpt.	25.00	60.00	150.00
b. Ovpt: *Ley 16.10.1891.*	35.00	100.00	275.00
c. Ovpt: *Ley 8.1.1894.*	25.00	60.00	150.00
S1183 5 Pesos 1.1.1888.			
a. W/o ovpt.	60.00	165.00	400.00
b. Ovpt: *Ley 6.9.1890.*	70.00	175.00	425.00
S1184 10 Pesos 1.1.1888.			
a. W/o ovpt.	140.00	300.00	650.00
b. Ovpt: *Ley 6.9.1890.*	150.00	320.00	700.00
c. Ovpt: *Ley 16.10.1891.*	200.00	500.00	—
S1185 20 Pesos 1.1.1888.	200.00	500.00	—
S1186 50 Pesos 1.1.1888.			
a. W/o ovpt.	—	—	—
b. Ovpt: *Ley 6.9.1890.*	—	—	—

Banco Provincial de Santa Fé

Series 003

	Good	Fine	XF
S1191 1 Peso 1.1.1888.			
a. W/o ovpt.	15.00	40.00	100.00
b. Ovpt: *Ley 20.9.1897.*	10.00	25.00	90.00

	Good	Fine	XF
S1192 2 Pesos 1.1.1888.			
a. W/o ovpt.	20.00	50.00	125.00
b. Ovpt: *Ley 8.1.1894.*	25.00	60.00	150.00
S1193 5 Pesos 1.1.1888.	35.00	100.00	300.00

	Good	Fine	XF
S1194 10 Pesos 1.1.1888.			
a. W/o ovpt.	65.00	175.00	400.00
b. Ovpt: *Ley 16.10.1891.*	80.00	200.00	475.00
S1195 20 Pesos 1.1.1888.	150.00	350.00	—
S1196 50 Pesos 1.1.1888.			
a. W/o ovpt.	—	—	—
b. Ovpt: *Ley 6.9.1890.*	—	—	—
S1197 100 Pesos 1.1.1888.	—	—	—
S1198 200 Pesos 1.1.1888.	—	—	—
S1199 500 Pesos 1.1.1888.	—	—	—
S1200 1000 Pesos 1.1.1888.	—	—	—

Banco de la Provincia de Santiago del Estero

Series 009

	Good	Fine	XF
S1201 1 Peso 1.1.1888.			
a. W/o ovpt.	20.00	50.00	125.00
b. Ovpt: *Ley 8.1.1894.*	20.00	50.00	125.00

	Good	Fine	XF
S1202 2 Pesos 1.1.1888.			
a. W/o ovpt.	25.00	60.00	150.00
b. Ovpt: *Ley 16.10.1891.*	35.00	100.00	275.00
c. Ovpt: *Ley 8.1.1894.*	25.00	60.00	150.00
S1203 5 Pesos 1.1.1888.			
a. W/o ovpt.	80.00	200.00	450.00
b. Ovpt: *Ley 6.9.1890.*	100.00	225.00	550.00
S1204 10 Pesos 1.1.1888.	175.00	425.00	—
S1205 20 Pesos 1.1.1888.	275.00	575.00	—
S1206 50 Pesos 1.1.1888.	—	—	—
S1207 100 Pesos 1.1.1888.	—	—	—

Banco Provincial de Tucumán

Series 007

	Good	Fine	XF
S1211 1 Peso 1.1.1888.			
a. W/o ovpt.	20.00	50.00	125.00
b. Ovpt: *Ley 20.9.1897.*	25.00	60.00	150.00

	Good	Fine	XF
S1212 2 Pesos 1.1.1888.			
a. W/o ovpt.	25.00	60.00	150.00
b. Ovpt: *Ley 8.1.1894.*	30.00	85.00	200.00
S1213 5 Pesos 1.1.1888.	60.00	165.00	375.00
S1214 10 Pesos 1.1.1888.			

	Good	Fine	XF
a. W/o ovpt.	90.00	240.00	550.00
b. Ovpt: *Ley 6.9.1890.*	120.00	250.00	575.00
S1215 20 Pesos 1.1.1888.	175.00	375.00	—
S1216 50 Pesos 1.1.1888.	—	—	—

Banco de San Luis

Series 016

	Good	Fine	XF
S1221 1 Peso 1.1.1888.			
a. W/o ovpt.	25.00	60.00	150.00
b. Ovpt: *Ley 8.1.1894.*	25.00	60.00	150.00
S1222 2 Pesos 1.1.1888.			
a. W/o ovpt.	45.00	125.00	300.00
b. Ovpt: *Ley 16.10.1891.*	70.00	175.00	400.00
c. Ovpt: *Ley 8.1.1894.*	45.00	125.00	300.00
S1223 5 Pesos 1.1.1888.	75.00	250.00	600.00
S1224 10 Pesos 1.1.1888.	150.00	320.00	700.00
S1225 20 Pesos 1.1.1888.	250.00	650.00	—
S1226 50 Pesos 1.1.1888.	—	—	—

Nuevo Banco Italiano

Series ?

	Good	Fine	XF
S1236 50 Pesos 1.1.1888.	—	—	—
S1237 100 Pesos 1.1.1888.	—	—	—

NOTE: #S1236 and S1237 were prepared for issue but not released. All were later destroyed.

Section IV

PROVINCIAL

Province of Catamarca

1849 Issue

	Good	Fine	XF
S1251 1 Real June 1849. Black. Arms at r. W/text: *Mueran los salvajes Unitarios* at l.	—	—	—

Province of Córdoba

1829 Issue

	Good	Fine	XF
S1263 10 Pesos 1829. Black. Handwritten sign.	—	—	—

NOTE: Issues are reported for 1853 and 1858.

Province of Corrientes

1826 Issue

	Good	Fine	XF
S1281 1 Peso 30.5.1826.	—	—	—

1827 Issue

	Good	Fine	XF
S1291 1 Peso 29.5.1827.	—	—	—
S1292 2 Pesos 29.5.1827.	—	—	—

1841 Treasury Notes Issue

	Good	Fine	XF
S1301 1 Peso 23.7.1841.	—	—	—
S1302 5 Pesos 23.7.1841.	—	—	—
S1304 20 Pesos 23.7.1841.	—	—	—

1843 Issue

	Good	Fine	XF
S1311 1 Peso 1843. Black. W/o date stamping on back.	—	—	—
S1312 1 Peso 1843. Similar to #S1311 but date stamping: *1843* on back.	—	—	—
S1313 1 Peso 1843. Stamped arms at ctr. Longer text than on #S1311. Date stamping: *1843* on back.	—	—	—

1852 Issue

#S1321, S1324, and S1325 w/text: *VIVA LA CONFEDERACIÓN!*

	Good	Fine	XF
S1321 1 Real 1852. Black. Goat at upper l. and r., stamped arms at ctr.	—	—	—

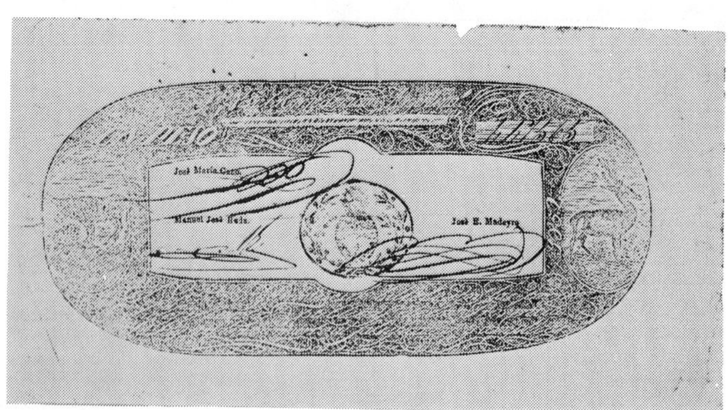

	Good	Fine	XF
S1324 1 Peso 1852. Black. Calf at l., deer at r.	—	—	—
S1325 5 Pesos 1852. Black. Horse and ship.	—	—	—

1857 Issue

	Good	Fine	XF
S1335 5 Pesos 1857. Black. Eagle and Ceres head.	—	—	—
S1336 10 Pesos 1857. Black.	—	—	—

1861 Issue

	Good	Fine	XF
S1344 4 Reales 1861. Black.	—	—	—

NOTE: #S1344 issued for the Casa de Moneda and Banco de la Provincia de Corrientes.

	Good	Fine	XF
S1345 1 Peso 1861. Arms at top ctr.	—	—	—
S1348 20 Pesos 1861.	—	—	—

NOTE: #S1345 and S1348 issued for the Junta de Administración de la Casa de Moneda.

NOTE: An 1865 dated issue is reported.

PROVINCE OF ENTRE-RIOS

1826 ISSUE

		GOOD	FINE	XF
S1361	**1 REAL** 11.10.1826.	—	Rare	—

1868 ISSUE

		GOOD	FINE	XF
S1366	**2 PESOS** 1868.	—	—	—

1876 ISSUE

#S1374-S1375 issued at Concepción del Uruguay. Printer: Lit. San Martín.

		GOOD	FINE	XF
S1372	**10 CENTAVOS** 1.3.1876. Black. Girl at l.	—	—	—
S1373	**20 CENTAVOS** 1.3.1876. Black. Shield at upper l., Male portr. at lower l.	—	—	—

		GOOD	FINE	XF
S1374	**50 CENTAVOS** 1.3.1876. Brown and black. Portr. woman's head at l. and r. Uniface.	—	—	—

		GOOD	FINE	XF
S1375	**1 PESO FUERTE** 1.3.1876. Black. Cat's head at upper l., arms at lower ctr., star w/value at upper r. Back blue.	—	—	—

PROVINCE OF MENDOZA

LAW OF 21.6.1839

		GOOD	FINE	XF
S1381	**1/4 REAL** ND.	—	—	—

PROVINCE OF SAN LUIS

1871 ISSUE

		GOOD	FINE	XF
S1394	**4 REALES** 27.9.1871. Red-orange.	—	—	—
S1395	**1 PESO** 27.9.1871.	—	—	—
S1396	**5 PESOS** 27.9.1871.	—	—	—

PROVINCE OF SANTA FÉ

LAW OF 23.8.1823

		GOOD	FINE	XF
S1401	**1 PESO = 8 REALES**	—	—	—
S1402	**2 PESOS 1 REAL = 17 REALES**	—	—	—
S1403	**4 PESOS 2 REALES = 34 REALES**	—	—	—

PROVINCE OF SANTIAGO DEL ESTERO

1870 ISSUE

		GOOD	FINE	XF
S1411	**50 PESOS** 5.8.1870.	—	—	—

1876 ISSUE

#S1416-S1420 uniface. Printer: G. Kraft.

		GOOD	FINE	XF
S1416	**5 CENTAVOS FUERTES** 30.9.1876. Blue-green paper.	50.00	130.00	—
S1418	**20 CENTAVOS FUERTES** 30.9.1876. Black. Jaguars at upper ctr.	60.00	200.00	—

		GOOD	FINE	XF
S1420	**1 PESO FUERTE** 30.9.1876. Blue on buff paper. Dog at top ctr.	60.00	200.00	—

		GOOD	FINE	XF
S1421	**5 PESOS FUERTES** 1876. Red-orange. Group of people at ctr.	—	—	—

SECTION V

Regional and Private Banks

BANCO ARGENTINO

Head office at Rosario; branches at Concordia, Córdoba, Paraná and Santa Fé. Notes issued periodically from 1866-1873. Two kinds of issues were made, the bulk being in Pesos Bolivianos and a small part in Pesos Fuertes. Colors vary according to branch and issue. Most notes were made by the American Bank Note Company, the imprint of which appears in Spanish or English. There are also paper differences.

ABNC BANK NOTE DESIGNS

Designs of notes made by ABNC are uniform for all issues; thus they are described here w/o reference to any particular issue.

Notes in Pesos Plata Boliviana:

1/2 REAL	Arms at top ctr.
1 REAL	Sailing ship at top ctr.
4 REALES	Woman in costume at lower l., dog and safe at upper ctr., woman w/sheaf at lower r.
1 PESO	Ostrich at l., woman and man watering horses at ctr.
5 PESOS	People w/spyglass at l., bull at ctr., woman w/spyglass at r.
10 PESOS	Woman at l., horses at upper ctr.
20 PESOS	Seated woman at l., steam train at station at ctr. r.
50 PESOS	Woman's head at l. and r., sheep at ctr.

Notes in Pesos Fuertes:

50 CENTAVOS	Rooster at ctr.
2 PESOS	Seated woman at l., leopard at upper ctr.
20 PESOS	Seated woman at l., steam train at station at ctr. r.

Other issues are described when listed.

1871-73 CONCORDIA ISSUES

		GOOD	FINE	XF
S1451	**1/2 REAL PLATA BOLIVIANA** 187x. Black on green paper. Dog's head at ctr. Uniface.	25.00	100.00	—

#S1456-S1463 back green. Printer: ABNC.

		GOOD	FINE	XF
S1456	**1/2 REAL PLATA BOLIVIANA** 187x, 1871, 1873. Black on green unpt.	15.00	60.00	—
S1457	**1 REAL PLATA BOLIVIANA** 1871, 1873. Black on green unpt.	15.00	60.00	—
S1458	**4 REALES PLATA BOLIVIANA** 1.7.1873. Black on blue unpt.	20.00	75.00	—
S1459	**1 PESO PLATA BOLIVIANA** 1.7.1873. Black on green unpt.	20.00	80.00	—
S1460	**5 PESOS PLATA BOLIVIANA** 1.7.1873. Black on blue unpt.	20.00	80.00	—
S1461	**10 PESOS PLATA BOLIVIANA** 1.7.1873. Black on green unpt.	15.00	80.00	175.00
S1463	**50 PESOS PLATA BOLIVIANA** 1.7.1873. Black on green unpt.	25.00	120.00	—

CONCORDIA ND PROVISIONAL ISSUE

#S1466 and S1467 Rosario issues ovpt: *CONCORDIA*.

No.	Denomination	Good	Fine	XF
S1466	**50 CENTAVOS FUERTES** ND (- old date 1.5.1866). Black on salmon paper. W/vertical ovpt. *CONCORDIA* at l. ctr. on #S1530.	25.00	90.00	—
S1467	**1 PESO FUERTE** ND (- old date 1.12.1866). Black on blue paper. W/vertical ovpt: *CONCORDIA* at l. and ctr. r. on #S1531.	30.00	110.00	—

1871-73 CÓRDOBA ISSUES

No.	Denomination	Good	Fine	XF
S1471	**1/2 REAL PLATA BOLIVIANA** 187x. Dog. (Not issued).	20.00	75.00	—

No.	Denomination	Good	Fine	XF
S1472	**1 REAL PLATA BOLIVIANA** 187x. Black. Horse's head at upper l. (Not issued).	20.00	75.00	150.00
S1473	**1/2 REAL PLATA BOLIVIANA** 1871. Woman's head.	20.00	75.00	—

#S1476-S1486 printer: ABNC.

No.	Denomination	Good	Fine	XF
S1476	**1/2 REAL PLATA BOLIVIANA** 187x; 1872; 1873. Black on brown unpt. Back orange.	10.00	60.00	—

No.	Denomination	Good	Fine	XF
S1477	**1 REAL PLATA BOLIVIANA** 187x; 1872; 1873. Black on brown unpt. Back orange.	15.00	60.00	—
S1478	**1 REAL PLATA BOLIVIANA** 1.7.1873.	—	—	—
S1479	**1 PESO PLATA BOLIVIANA** 1.7.1873. Black on brown unpt. Back gold.	20.00	80.00	150.00
S1481	**10 PESOS PLATA BOLIVIANA** 1.7.1873. Black on gold unpt. Back gold.	15.00	60.00	120.00
S1482	**20 PESOS PLATA BOLIVIANA** 1.7.1873. Black on brown unpt. Back orange.	25.00	115.00	—
S1483	**50 PESOS PLATA BOLIVIANA** 1.7.1873. Black on brown unpt. Back gold.	30.00	135.00	—

1873 CÓRDOBA PESO FUERTE ISSUE

No.	Denomination	Good	Fine	XF
S1486	**50 CENTAVOS FUERTES** 1.7.1873. Rooster at ctr.	25.00	95.00	—

GUALEGUAY ND PROVISIONAL ISSUE

No.	Denomination	Good	Fine	XF
S1488	**1 PESO** ND (- old date 1.9.1866). Black. 3 winged figures at upper ctr. W/ovpt: *GUALEGUAY* at upper ctr. Uniface. Printer: A. Larsch.	—	—	—

1873 PARANÁ PLATA BOLIVIANA ISSUES

No.	Denomination	Good	Fine	XF
S1491	**1/2 REAL PLATA BOLIVIANA** 187x. Gray and black. Dog's head at ctr. Uniface.	20.00	75.00	150.00

#S1496-S1503 w/red backs. Printer: ABNC.

No.	Denomination	Good	Fine	XF
S1496	**1/2 REAL PLATA BOLIVIANA** 1.7.1873. Black on orange unpt.	25.00	70.00	—
S1497	**1 REAL PLATA BOLIVIANA** 1.7.1873. Black on rose unpt.	—	—	—

No.	Denomination	Good	Fine	XF
S1498	**4 REALES PLATA BOLIVIANA** 1.7.1873. Black on red unpt.	20.00	80.00	—
S1499	**1 PESO PLATA BOLIVIANA** 1866, 1.7.1873. Black on red unpt.	30.00	115.00	—
S1501	**10 PESOS PLATA BOLIVIANA** 1.7.1873. Black on red unpt.			

No.	Denomination	Good	Fine	XF
S1502	**20 PESOS PLATA BOLIVIANA** 1.7.1873. Allegorical woman seated at upper l., steam train at passenger station at upper ctr. r.	—	—	—

No.	Denomination	Good	Fine	XF
S1503	**50 PESOS PLATA BOLIVIANA** 1.7.1873. Black on rose unpt. Woman at lower l., sheep at upper ctr., woman at lower r.	—	—	—

1873 PARANÁ PESO FUERTE ISSUE

No.	Denomination	Good	Fine	XF
S1506	**50 CENTAVOS FUERTES** 1.7.1873.	—	—	—

PARANÁ ND PROVISIONAL ISSUES

#S1511-S1514 are Rosario notes w/ovpt: *PARANÁ*.

No.	Denomination	Good	Fine	XF
S1511	**5 PESOS** ND (- old date 1866).	—	—	—
S1512	**10 PESOS** ND (- old date 1872).	—	—	—

No.	Denomination	Good	Fine	XF
S1513	**10 PESOS** ND (- old date 13.7.1872). Black on red unpt. Portr. seated woman at l., train vertically at r. w/ovpt: *PARANÁ* twice, at l. and ctr. r. Uniface. Printer: Lit. Alb. Larsch, Buenos Aires.	—	—	—
S1514	**20 PESOS** ND (- old date 1866).	—	—	—

ROSARIO ISSUES

1866-72 ISSUES

#S1516-S1518 black. Uniface. Printer: Lito. C. Held, Rosario.

		GOOD	FINE	XF
S1516	**1/2 REAL PLATA BOLIVIANA** 1.1.1867. Black. Ram at upper ctr.	—	—	—
S1517	**1/2 REAL PLATA BOLIVIANA** 1.7.1869. Unsigned remainder.	—	—	—
S1518	**1 PESO PLATA BOLIVIANA** 1.7.1869. Black. Uniface.	15.00	50.00	100.00
S1519	**1 REAL PLATA BOLIVIANA** 187x. Black on purple paper. Horse head at upper l. Uniface.	—	—	—

1869-1873 ISSUE

#S1521-S1529 printer: ABNC.

		GOOD	FINE	XF
S1521	**1/2 REAL PLATA BOLIVIANA** 1869; 1871; 1873. Black on blue unpt.	25.00	85.00	—

		GOOD	FINE	XF
S1522	**1 REAL PLATA BOLIVIANA** 187x; 1871; 1873. Black on blue unpt.	20.00	80.00	—
S1523	**4 REALES PLATA BOLIVIANA** 1.7.1867; 1.12.1868. Black. Uniface.	20.00	80.00	—

#S1524 *Deleted.* See #S1531.

		GOOD	FINE	XF
S1525	**1 PESO PLATA BOLIVIANA** 1.7.1873. Black. Like #S1524.	15.00	40.00	100.00

		GOOD	FINE	XF
S1526	**5 PESOS PLATA BOLIVIANA** 1.9.1866; 1.11.1866.			
	a. Black on lt. orange paper. Back green.	20.00	100.00	200.00
	b. 1.11.1866. Black on brown unpt. White paper.	40.00	125.00	225.00

		GOOD	FINE	XF
S1527	**10 PESOS PLATA BOLIVIANA** 1866; 1872; 1873. Black.	20.00	100.00	200.00
S1529	**50 PESOS PLATA BOLIVIANA** 1866; 1873. Black on green paper.	75.00	200.00	—

1866; 1867 ROSARIO PESO FUERTE ISSUE

		GOOD	FINE	XF
S1530	**50 CENTAVOS FUERTES** 1.5.1866; 1.6.1866; 2.7.1866; 18.1866. Black on peach paper.	20.00	75.00	—
S1531	**1 PESO FUERTE** 1.11.1867-1.7.1868. Black on blue paper. Back brown.	25.00	100.00	—

		GOOD	FINE	XF
S1532	**2 PESOS FUERTES** 1866; 1.1.1867. Black on yellow paper. Back red.	50.00	175.00	—

		GOOD	FINE	XF
S1534	**20 PESOS FUERTES** 1866; 1873. Black.	60.00	175.00	—

187X SANTA FÉ ISSUE

		GOOD	FINE	XF
S1536	**1/2 REAL PLATA BOLIVIANA** 187x. Blue. Dog's head at ctr. Uniface.	20.00	60.00	125.00

NOTE: Higher values are reported, not confirmed.

SANTA FÉ ND PROVISIONAL ISSUE

#S1543-S1545 Rosario issue w/ovpt: *SANTA FÉ*.

		GOOD	FINE	XF
S1543	**2 PESOS FUERTES** ND (- old date 1.9.1866). W/vertical ovpt: *SANTA FE* twice at l. and ctr. r. on #S1532.	100.00	300.00	—
S1545	**10 PESOS FUERTES** ND (- old date 1.10.1866). #S1527 w/blue ovpt: *SANTA FE* vertically. Back blue.	—	—	—

NOTE: Other values are reported w/ovpt: *SANTA FE* but not confirmed.

BANCO J. BENITES E HIJO

Issued at Gualeguaychú.

1867 ISSUE

#S1551-S1553 uniface. Printer: Lit. San Martin.

		GOOD	FINE	XF
S1551	1/2 REAL BOLIVIANO 1.1.1867. Black on yellow paper. Standing woman and 2 cherubs at l.	50.00	150.00	—
S1552	1 REAL BOLIVIANO 1.1.1867. Black on dk. green paper. 3 cherubs and numeral at l.	60.00	200.00	—

		GOOD	FINE	XF
S1553	2 REALES BOLIVIANOS 1.1.1867. Black and gray. Justice seated at l., dog and lock box at upper ctr.	75.00	250.00	—

#S1556-S1565 printer: ABNC.

		GOOD	FINE	XF
S1556	1 PESO MONEDA BOLIVIANA 15.10.1867. Black on brown unpt. Portr. girl and birds at lower l., vaqueros roping cattle at ctr., portr. girl w/rabbits at lower r. Back green.	40.00	200.00	—

		GOOD	FINE	XF
S1557	5 PESOS MONEDA BOLIVIANA 15.10.1867. Black on red unpt. Man at lower l., gauchos at top ctr., seated women at lower r. Back gold.			
	a. Issued note.	40.00	200.00	—
	b. Ovpt: *GUALEGUAY.*	—	—	—

		GOOD	FINE	XF
S1559	20 PESOS MONEDA BOLIVIANA 15.10.1867. Black on green unpt. Allegorical woman reclining on bales at lower l., woman w/pigeon at ctr., allegorical woman reclining w/shield at lower r. Back red-orange.			
	a. Issued note.	65.00	250.00	—
	p. Proof.	—	—	—

		GOOD	FINE	XF
S1560	50 PESOS MONEDA BOLIVIANA 15.10.1868. Black on green unpt. Allegorical woman standing at l., man at upper ctr., woodsman at r. Back blue.	—	—	—

1868 ISSUE

		GOOD	FINE	XF
S1562	1 PESO FUERTE 15.10.1868. Black on orange unpt. Allegorical woman seated at l., ship and steam passenger train flanking portr. woman at upper ctr., woman at lower r. Back green. Proof.	—	—	—

		GOOD	FINE	XF
S1563	5 PESOS FUERTES 15.10.1868. Black on blue unpt. Man at l., 3 allegorical women at ctr., woman with bird at r. Back green. Proof.	—	—	—
S1564	20 PESOS FUERTES 15.10.1868. Black on brown unpt. Man at l., modes of transportation at ctr., young girl at r. Back green. Archive copy.	—	—	—

		GOOD	FINE	XF
S1565	100 PESOS FUERTES 15.10.1867. Black on orange unpt. Portr. woman at lower l., allegorical woman w/sheep at upper ctr., cattle at lower r. Back brown. Proof.	—	—	—

A word on date ranges

Often date ranges or specific dates are listed. These have been observed or reported by our contributors. If a note is outside the published range, it only means that it is a newly reported date, and not necessarily worthy of a premium value.

BANCO DEL CHACO

Issued at Villa Ocampo, Province of Santa Fé.

1884 ISSUE

		GOOD	FINE	XF
S1566	1 PESO 1.10.1884. Black on red and green unpt. Portr. woman at ctr. between dog's head at l., cow's head at r. Back green and red. Printer: BWC.	20.00	75.00	175.00

BANCO COMERCIAL DE CORRIENTES

1867 ISSUE

#S1571-S1577 w/stamped and hand sign. Uniface.

		GOOD	FINE	XF
S1571	6 1/4 CENTESIMOS 1.2.1867. Black on blue paper. Rooster at upper ctr. Printer: Lit. San Martín.			
	a. Issued note.	15.00	50.00	—
	r. Unsigned remainder w/counterfoil.	—	—	20.00

#S1572-S1576 printer: Lit. Alb. Larsch, Buenos Aires.

		GOOD	FINE	XF
S1572	12 1/2 CENTESIMOS 1.2.1867. Black. Yellow paper. Dog at upper ctr. facing r.			
	a. Issued note.	20.00	75.00	175.00
	r. Unsigned remainder w/counterfoil.	—	—	—

		GOOD	FINE	XF
S1573	25 CENTESIMOS 1.2.1867. Black on gray unpt. Jaguar at upper ctr. facing r.	30.00	90.00	—
S1574	50 CENTESIMOS 1.2.1867. Black on yellowish brown paper. Swan at upper ctr.	45.00	—	—

		GOOD	FINE	XF
S1575	1 PESO FUERTE 1.2.1867. Black on brown unpt. Horse galloping at upper ctr. facing l.			
	a. Issued note.	45.00	110.00	—
	r1. Unsigned remainder w/counterfoil.	—	35.00	70.00
	r2. Unsigned remainder w/o counterfoil.	—	20.00	45.00

		GOOD	FINE	XF
S1576	5 PESOS FUERTES 1.2.1867. Black on brown unpt. Viking at l., bull at upper ctr.			
	a. Issued note.	50.00	100.00	—
	r1. Unsigned remainder w/counterfoil.	—	—	—
	r2. Unsigned remainder w/o counterfoil.	—	—	—

		GOOD	FINE	XF
S1577	10 PESOS FUERTES 1.2.1867. Black on orange unpt. Liberty head at lower l., cows at top ctr., dog on safe at lower r. Uniface. Printer: Lit. San Martín.			
	a. Issued note.	175.00	—	—
	r1. Unsigned remainder w/counterfoil.	—	—	—
	r2. Unsigned remainder w/o counterfoil.	—	—	—

1868 ISSUE

#S1581-S1584 w/stamped sign.

		GOOD	FINE	XF
S1581	12 1/2 CENTESIMOS ND. Black on gray unpt. Dog at upper ctr. facing l.	30.00	125.00	—

		GOOD	FINE	XF
S1582	25 CENTESIMOS 1.3.1868. Black on gray unpt. Jaguar at upper ctr. facing l.	30.00	125.00	—

		GOOD	FINE	XF
S1583	50 CENTESIMOS 1.3.1868. Black. Cow at upper ctr.	40.00	110.00	—

		GOOD	FINE	XF
S1584	1 PESO FUERTE 1.3.1868. Black on brown unpt. Seated allegorical woman w/child at lower l., cow's head at upper ctr. r.	40.00	150.00	—

BANCO COMERCIAL DE SANTA FÉ

Issued at Rosario.

1867 ISSUE

		GOOD	FINE	XF
S1590	1 PESO PLATA BOLIVIANA 1.5.1867. Black on rose unpt. Cherub w/chickens at lower l., villagers at upper ctr. Printer: Lit. San Martín, Bs As.	—	—	—

1869 ISSUE

#S1593-S1598 printer: ABNC.

		GOOD	FINE	XF
S1593	**4 REALES PLATA BOLIVIANA** 2.1.1869. Black on green unpt. Girl's head at upper ctr.			
	a. Issued note.	30.00	150.00	—
	s. Specimen.	—	—	—

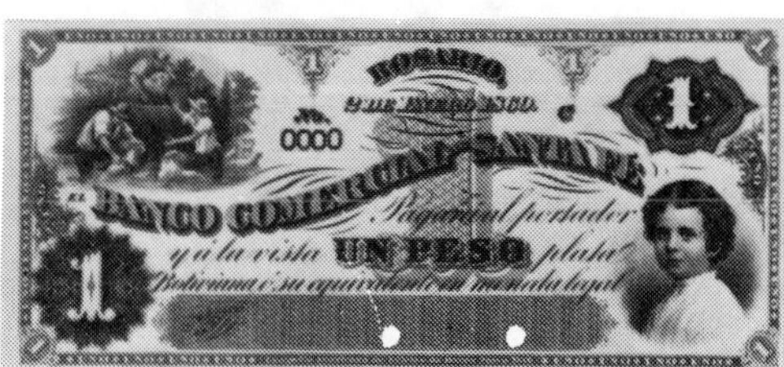

		GOOD	FINE	XF
S1594	**1 PESO PLATA BOLIVIANA** 2.1.1869. Black on orange unpt. Men shearing sheep at upper l., young boy at lower r.			
	a. Issued note.	40.00	150.00	—
	r. Unsigned remainder.	—	25.00	60.00
	s. Specimen.	—	—	—
S1595	**5 PESOS PLATA BOLIVIANA** 2.1.1869. Black on green unpt. Anchor and boxes at l., galloping horse at ctr., young boy at r. Back brown.	60.00	200.00	—

		GOOD	FINE	XF
S1596	**10 PESOS PLATA BOLIVIANA** 2.1.1869. Black on brown unpt. Young sailor at lower l., gauchos roping cattle at upper ctr., young woman at lower r. Back brown. Specimen.	—	—	—

		GOOD	FINE	XF
S1597	**20 PESOS PLATA BOLIVIANA** 2.1.1869. Black on orange unpt. Gaucho at lower l., cow's head at ctr., man at r. Back brown. Specimen.	—	—	—

		GOOD	FINE	XF
S1598	**50 PESOS PLATA BOLIVIANA** 2.1.1869. Black on blue or green unpt. Horse w/children at lower l., woman w/marine implements at ctr., cow at lower r. Specimen.	—	—	—

BANCO DEL COMERCIO

Issued at Gualeguay.

1869 ISSUE

		GOOD	FINE	XF
S1601	**1/2 REAL** 1.7.1869. Red or brown serial #.	—	—	
S1604	**4 REALES** 1.7.1869. Black. Man standing w/numeral at l. Local print.	—	—	—

#S1606-S1608 printer: ABNC.

		GOOD	FINE	XF
S1606	**5 PESOS BOLIVIANOS** 1.7.1869. Black on blue unpt. Man and boy at lower l., seated allegorical woman at upper ctr., 2 sailors, one w/spyglass at lower r. Back red.			
	a. Issued note.	—	—	—
	r. Unsigned remainder.	40.00	150.00	—
	s. Specimen.	—	—	—

		GOOD	FINE	XF
S1607	**10 PESOS BOLIVIANOS** 1.7.1869. Black on brown unpt. Farmer and sheep at lower l., seated woman at upper ctr., child at lower r. Back green; portr. woman's head at each corner.			
	a. Issued note.	—	—	—
	r. Unsigned remainder.	40.00	150.00	—

		GOOD	FINE	XF
S1608	**20 PESOS BOLIVIANOS** 1.7.1869. Black on red-brown unpt. Sailor at lower l., monument at top ctr., anchor at lower r. Back brown.			
	a. Issued note.	—	—	—
	r. Unsigned remainder.	60.00	175.00	—
	s. Specimen.	—	—	—

BANCO DE CONSIGNACIONES DE FRUTOS DEL PAÍS

Issued at La Plata.

1890S ISSUE

		GOOD	FINE	XF
S1610	**100 PESOS** 189x. Man at l.	—	—	—

BANCO DE CORRIENTES

1873 ISSUE

#S1611-S1620 printer: Guillermo Kraft, Buenos Aires.

		Good	Fine	XF
S1611	**6 1/4 Centavos Fuertes** 15.3.1873. Black on rose paper. Heron.	—	—	—
S1612	**12 1/2 Centavos Fuertes** 15.3.1873. Black on ochre unpt. Deer.	—	—	—
S1613	**25 Centavos Fuertes** 15.3.1873. Black on lilac unpt. Puma group.	—	—	—

		Good	Fine	XF
S1614	**50 Centavos Fuertes** 15.3.1873. Green. Ostrich at l.	50.00	150.00	—
S1615	**1 Peso Fuerte** 15.3.1873. Black on pink unpt. Dog at upper ctr.	—	—	—

		Good	Fine	XF
S1616	**5 Pesos Fuertes** 15.3.1873. Black on orange unpt. Bull at lower l. Back green.	75.00	200.00	—

		Good	Fine	XF
S1617	**10 Pesos Fuertes** 15.3.1873. Black on blue unpt. Horse at upper l. Back red.	—	—	—
S1620	**100 Pesos Fuertes** 15.3.1873. Black on green and yellow unpt. Gauchos.	—	Rare	—

NOTE: An 1876 issue is also reported.

BANCO DE CUYO

1868 MENDOZA ISSUE

		Good	Fine	XF
S1628	**20 Pesos Plata Boliviana** 1.7.1868. Black. Mountains and sailing ship at l. and r. ctr., allegorical woman at l. and r.	—	—	—

1892 SAN JUAN ISSUE

		Good	Fine	XF
S1631	**10 Centavos** 15.7.1892.	—	—	—
S1633	**50 Centavos** 15.7.1892. Brown-yellow. Man at l.	—	—	—

18XX ISSUE

#S1636-S1644 printer: BWC. Series C.

s Fuertes. #S1636-S1640 uniface.

		Good	Fine	XF
S1636	**5 Centavos Fuertes** 18xx. Black. Plant at top ctr., armadillo at r. Proof.	—	—	—

		Good	Fine	XF
S1637	**10 Centavos Fuertes** 18xx. Black. Bird at l., grapes at r. Proof.	—	—	—

		Good	Fine	XF
S1638	**20 Centavos Fuertes** 18xx. Black on green unpt. Woman's head at l. Proof.	—	—	—
S1639	**50 Centavos Fuertes** 18xx. Black on blue unpt. Woman's head at upper l. Proof.	—	—	—

		Good	Fine	XF
S1640	**1 Peso Fuerte** 18xx. Black on lilac unpt. Woman's head at upper l., young goat at lower l. Proof.	—	—	—

		Good	Fine	XF
S1641	**5 Pesos Fuertes** 18xx. Black on red, orange and green unpt. Woman's head at l., gaucho herding cattle at upper ctr. Back brown and blue; head at l. and r. Proof.	—	—	—

		Good	Fine	XF
S1642	**10 Pesos Fuertes** 18xx. Black on orange, lilac and green unpt. Woman's head at l., pathway and mountains at upper ctr. Back green, blue and brown; similar to #S1641. Proof.	—	—	—

S1642A 20 PESOS FUERTES	GOOD	FINE	XF
18xx. Black. Proof.	—	—	—

S1643 50 PESOS FUERTES	GOOD	FINE	XF
18xx. Black on red and green unpt. Woman's head at l., longhorn steers at ctr. Back violet and green; similar to #S1641. Proof.	—	—	—

S1644 100 PESOS FUERTES	GOOD	FINE	XF
18xx. Black on pink and green unpt. Woman's head at l., pack mules at r. Back orange and green; 7 heads. Proof.	—	—	—

BANCO ENTRE-RIANO

Issued at Concepción del Uruguay.

1864 ISSUE

S1651 5 CENTAVOS	GOOD	FINE	XF
15.3.1864. Black. Animal at ctr.			
a. Issued note.	40.00	200.00	—
b. Ovpt: *GUALEGUAY*.	—	—	—

S1652 10 CENTAVOS	GOOD	FINE	XF
15.3.1864. Black on blue paper. Ostrich at top ctr.			
a. Issued note.	40.00	200.00	—
b. Ovpt: *GUALEGUAY*.	—	—	—
S1653 20 CENTAVOS			
15.3.1864. Cow's head at l. Printer: Lit. Megey, Williams, Montevideo.	—	—	—

S1655 1 PESO FUERTE	GOOD	FINE	XF
15.3.1864. Black on green unpt. Dog walking r. vertically at l. Uniface. Printer: Lit. Mege y Williams, Montevideo.			
a. Issued note.	—	—	—
b. Ovpt: *GUALEGUAY*.	—	—	—

1866 ISSUE

S1657 1 REAL BOLIVIANO	GOOD	FINE	XF
15.5.1866. Black. Pampas cat at ctr.			
a. Issued note.	40.00	200.00	—
b. Ovpt.: *CONCORDIA* on back.	—	—	—

1870 ISSUE

#S1661-S1665 printer: CNBB.

S1661 1 PESO MONEDA BOLIVIANA	GOOD	FINE	XF
1.6.1870. Black. Seated woman at l., farmers herding animals at ctr., boat at r. Back brown; cow head at upper l. and r.			
a. Issued note.	80.00	300.00	—
b. W/ovpt: *CONCORDIA*.	—	—	—

S1662 5 PESOS MONEDA BOLIVIANA	GOOD	FINE	XF
1.6.1870. Black. Man at lower l., men and horses at ctr., woman w/barrels and sheaves at lower r. Back green; horse at ctr. Proof.	—	—	—

		Good	Fine	XF
S1663	**10 Pesos Moneda Boliviana** 1.6.1870. Black. Standing Liberty at l., 2 seated allegorical women w/scales and flags at ctr., woman at r. Back red; basket of fruit at l., basket of corn at r.			
	a. Issued note.	65.00	300.00	—
	b. W/ovpt: *CONCORDIA.*	—	—	—
	c. W/ovpt: *VICTORIA.*	—	—	—

		Good	Fine	XF
S1664	**20 Pesos Moneda Boliviana** 1.6.1870. Black. Mercury at lower l., Prosperity, Justice and Liberty seated at ctr., standing woman at r. Back blue; woman and child at lower ctr.	—	—	—
S1665	**100 Pesos Moneda Boliviana** 1.6.1870. Black. Urquiza at upper ctr., standing allegorical woman at lower l., standing Liberty w/staff at lower r. Back black and gold; cannon, anchor and other implements at ctr. Proof.	—	—	—

1872 Issue

#S1666 and S1668 printer: Lit. San Martín.

		Good	Fine	XF
S1666	**1/2 Real Boliviano** 8.1.1872. Black on blue paper. Rooster at upper l.			
	a. Issued note.	60.00	200.00	—
	b. W/ovpt: *VICTORIA* on back.	—	—	—

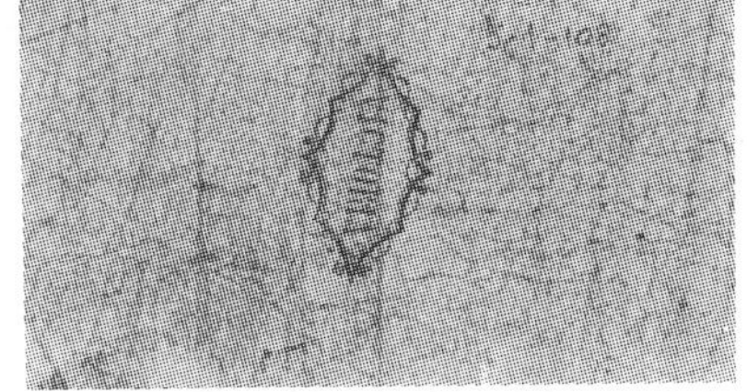

		Good	Fine	XF
S1668	**2 Reales Boliviano** 8.1.1872. Black on yellow paper. Puma at upper ctr.			
	a. Issued note.	60.00	200.00	—
	b. W/ovpt: *VICTORIA* on back.	—	—	—

Banco Hipotecario de la Provincia de Córdoba

ND Issue

		Good	Fine	XF
S1671	**1 Decimo** ND. Rose and blue unpt. Arms.	—	—	—
S1672	**10 Centavos Pesos Bolivianos** ND. Black on brown unpt. Arms; V. Sobremonte.	—	—	—

Banco Hipotecario de las Provincias Ligadas del Norte

1841 Issue

In 1841 several provinces formed what was called the Coalition of the North, and a bank was established to issue notes for circulation in the member provinces. They were Catamarca, Jujuy, La Rioja, Salta and Tucumán.

		Good	Fine	XF
S1679	**1 Real** 9.3.1841. Black. Stamping *RECURSO* in brown at l.	—	—	—
S1680	**2 Reales** 9.3.1841. Black. Similar to #S1679. Stamping in green.	—	—	—
S1681	**4 Reales** 9.3.1841. Similar to #S1679. Text states that 10% interest was to be paid after termination of the war. Stamping in red-orange.	—	—	—

		Good	Fine	XF
S1682	**1 Peso** 9.3.1841. Similar text to #S1681. Stamping in brown.	—	—	—
S1683	**1 Peso** 1841. Black. Woman at ctr. W/o stamping.	—	—	—

Banco Industrial de la Provincia de La Rioja

1884 Issue

		Good	Fine	XF
S1691	**1 Peso** 1884.	—	—	—
S1692	**2 Pesos** 1884.	—	—	—
S1693	**5 Pesos** 1884.	—	—	—
S1694	**10 Pesos** 1884.	—	—	—
S1695	**20 Pesos** 1884.	—	—	—

Banco del Litoral

Issued at Paraná.

1871-75 Issues

		Good	Fine	XF
S1701	**1/2 Real Plata Boliviana** 1.2.1875. Black. Animals at lower l. Printer: Lit. Fleuti, Rosario.	—	—	—

		Good	Fine	XF
S1702	**1 Real Plata Boliviana** 21.7.1871. Black. Uniface.	50.00	200.00	—

		Good	Fine	XF
S1703	**1 Real Plata Boliviana** 1.1.1874. Swans at ctr.	50.00	200.00	—
S1704	**1 Real Plata Boliviana** 1.10.1875. Black on orange paper. Swans at r. Uniface.	—	—	—
S1705	**4 Reales Plata Boliviana** 21.7.1871. Black. Man at l., dog and safe at ctr., girl at r.	—	—	—
S1706	**1 Peso Plata Boliviana** 1.7.1874. Black on green paper. Allegory of Navigation seated on bale leaning on anchor at l., allegory of Industry w/wheel seated at r. Back purple; horse head at l. and r. Ovpt.: *VICTORIA* at r. Series C. Printer: Fleuti.	—	—	—

Provisional ND Issue

#S1711-S1715 values in Pesos Fuertes ovpt. on Plata Boliviana notes.

		Good	Fine	XF
S1711	**4 1/2 Centavos on 1/2 Real** ND (- old date 1.2.1875). W/purple ovpt. stamped across face on #S1701.	50.00	200.00	—

		Good	Fine	XF
S1712	**9 Centavos on 1 Real** ND (- old date 1.10.1875). W/purple ovpt. stamped across face on #S1703.	50.00	200.00	—

		Good	Fine	XF
S1714	**37 1/2 Centavos on 4 Reales** ND (- old date 21.7.1871). W/red ovpt. on #S1705.			
	a. Issued note.	65.00	250.00	—
	b. Ovpt: *VICTORIA*.	—	—	—

		Good	Fine	XF
S1715	**75 Centavos on 1 Peso** ND (- old date 1.7.1874). Ovpt. on #S1706.	—	—	—

Ley de 24 de Octubre de 1876; 1880 Issue

		Good	Fine	XF
S1718	**4-1/2 Centavos** 31.12.1880. Portr. dog's head facing r. at ctr. Series A. Printer: E. Fleuti.	—	—	—

Banco de Londres y Rio de la Plata

Córdoba Issues

#S1721-S1729 printer: BWC.

		Good	Fine	XF
S1721	**1/2 Real Moneda Boliviana** 15.11.1869. Black. Steam locomotive at ctr. Uniface.	15.00	60.00	—
S1722	**1 Real Moneda Boliviana** 15.11.1869. Black on yellow paper. Dog's head at l.	20.00	75.00	—
S1723	**1 Real Moneda Boliviana** 1869. Black on brown unpt. Horse.	30.00	90.00	—

		Good	Fine	XF
S1724	**2 Reales Moneda Boliviana** 15.11.1869. Black. Rooster at upper l.	40.00	125.00	—
S1725	**4 Reales Moneda Boliviana** 1869. Black. Sheep.	50.00	150.00	—

		Good	Fine	XF
S1726	**1 Peso Moneda Boliviana** 15.11.1869. Black on brown unpt. Horse's head at l.	50.00	145.00	—
S1727	**10 Pesos Moneda Boliviana** 15.11.1869.	—	—	—
S1728	**20 Pesos Moneda Boliviana** 15.11.1869.	—	—	—
S1729	**50 Pesos Moneda Boliviana** 15.11.1869.	—	—	—

NOTE: W/ or w/o ovpt: *INSPECCION DE BANCOS* on back.

Rosario Issues

1866-69 Issues

#S1731-S1739 uniface.

		Good	Fine	XF
S1731	**1 Real Plata Boliviana** 15.9.1866. Black.	30.00	90.00	—

		Good	Fine	XF
S1732	**1 1/2 Reales Plata Boliviana** 15.9.1866. Black.	40.00	120.00	—

		Good	Fine	XF
S1734	**4 Reales Plata Boliviana** 1.1.1867. Black on gray unpt. Goat's head at ctr.	50.00	200.00	—
S1735	**1 Peso Moneda Boliviana** 15.11.1869. Man at ctr.	—	—	—
S1737	**10 Pesos Plata Boliviana** 15.9.1866. Man at top ctr.	—	—	—
S1738	**10 Pesos Plata Boliviana** 15.11.1869.	—	—	—
S1738A	**20 Pesos Plata Boliviana** 15.11.1869.	—	—	—
S1739	**50 Pesos Plata Boliviana** 15.11.1869. Cherub at l., man at top ctr.	—	—	—

1866 ISSUE

		GOOD	FINE	XF
S1739A	**25 CENTAVOS** 1.7.1866. Black. Condor at l.	40.00	175.00	—

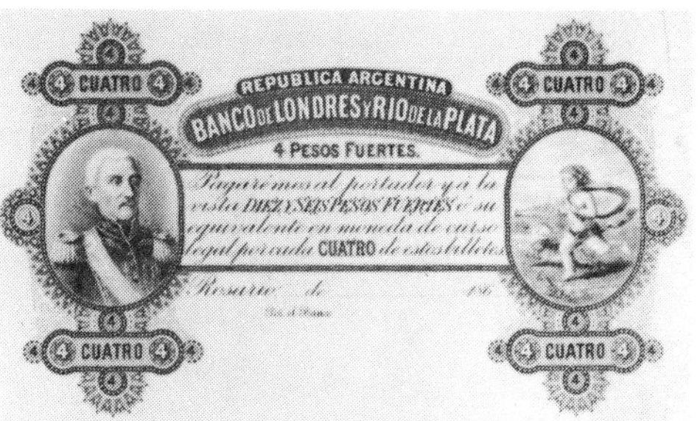

		GOOD	FINE	XF
S1739E	**4 PESOS FUERTES** 186x. Portr. Belgrano at l., cherub at r.	—	—	—

		GOOD	FINE	XF
S1740	**50 PESOS FUERTES** 15.9.1866. Similar to #S1739E.	—	—	—

1871 ISSUE

		GOOD	FINE	XF
S1741	**10 PESOS** 10.11.1871.	—	—	—
S1742	**20 PESOS** 10.11.1871.	—	—	—
S1743	**50 PESOS** 10.11.1871.	—	—	—

1872-74 ISSUE

		GOOD	FINE	XF
S1744	**1/2 REAL** 25.9.1872. Arms at r.	—	—	—
S1745	**10 PESOS FUERTES** 1.6.1874. Belgrano at l.	—	—	—

BANCO MAUÁ & CIA.

1865 ISSUE

		GOOD	FINE	XF
S1745A	**5 CENTAVOS** 1.7.1865. Black. Printer: Lito L. Therier, Rosario.	—	—	—

1867 PESO BOLIVIANO ISSUE

#S1746 and S1747 printer: ABNC.

		GOOD	FINE	XF
S1746	**1 PESO PLATA BOLIVIANA** 2.1.1867. Black on green unpt.			
	a. Issued note.	60.00	150.00	—
	p. Proof.	—	—	—

		GOOD	FINE	XF
S1747	**2 PESOS PLATA BOLIVIANA** 2.1.1867. Black on green unpt.			
	a. Issued note.	75.00	200.00	—
	p. Proof.	—	—	—
	s. Specimen ovpt: *MUESTRA*.	—	—	—

1860'S PESO FUERTE ISSUE

		GOOD	FINE	XF
S1747C	**20 CENTESIMOS FUERTES** 186x. Portr. man at l., gaucho on horseback at top ctr. r. Series B.	—	—	—

BANCO MENDEZ HERMANOS Y CIA.

PROVISIONAL ISSUE

#S1747E-S1747G w/ovpt new bank name on notes of the Banco Muñoz & Rodriguez & Ca.

		GOOD	FINE	XF
S1747E	**1 PESO** Ovpt. on #S1761.	—	—	—
S1747F	**5 PESOS** Ovpt. on #S1762.	—	—	—
S1747G	**10 PESOS** Ovpt. on #S1763.	—	—	—

REGULAR ISSUE

#S1747K-S1747M issued 1886-88. Possibly also issued w/1885 circular stamping.

		GOOD	FINE	XF
S1747K	**1 PESO** 188x.	—	—	—
S1747L	**5 PESOS** 188x.	—	—	—
S1747M	**10 PESOS** 188x.	—	—	—

BANCO DE MENDOZA

1876; 1877 ISSUE

#S1748-S1755 printer: H. Simon.

		GOOD	FINE	XF
S1748	**1/2 REAL MONEDA BOLIVIANA** 1.1.1877. Blue. Helmeted Athena at l. Series A.			
	a. Issued note.	—	—	—
	r. Unsigned remainder.	—	—	—

		GOOD	FINE	XF
S1749	**1 REAL MONEDA BOLIVIANA** 1.1.1876; 1.1.1877. Black. Gaucho on horseback roping cattle at ctr. Series B.			
	a. Issued note.	—	—	—
	r. Unsigned remainder.	—	—	—

	GOOD	FINE	XF
S1750 2 REALES MONEDA BOLIVIANA			
1.1.1876; 1.1.1877. Brown. Seated allegorical woman and child at l. Uniface. Series C.			
a. Issued note.	—	—	—
r. Unsigned remainder.	—	—	—
s. Specimen.	—	—	—

	GOOD	FINE	XF
S1751 4 REALES MONEDA BOLIVIANA			
1.1.1876; 1.1.1877. Black on green unpt. Gaucho standing w/horse and dog at ctr. Series D.			
a. Issued note.	—	—	—
r. Unsigned remainder.	—	—	—
S1752 1 PESO BOLIVIANO			
1.1.1877. Black on blue unpt. Back blue.			
a. Issued note.	—	—	—
r. Unsigned remainder.	—	—	—

	GOOD	FINE	XF
S1753 5 PESOS BOLIVIANOS			
1.1.1877. Black on green unpt. Bldg., people at upper ctr.			
a. Issued note.	—	—	—
r. Unsigned remainder.	—	—	—
S1755 20 PESOS BOLIVIANOS			
1.1.1877.	—	Rare	—

1877 ISSUE

#S1756-S1758 hand dated. Printer: CNBB.

	GOOD	FINE	XF
S1756 1 PESO MONEDA BOLIVIANA			
ca. 1877.	—	—	—

	GOOD	FINE	XF
S1757 5 PESOS MONEDA BOLIVIANA			
ca. 1877. Brown on rose unpt. Military encampment at ctr., steam passenger train crossing stone arch bridge w/cattle below in stream at lower l., woman at lower r.			
r. Unsigned remainder.	—	—	—
s. Specimen, punched hole cancelled.	—	—	—
S1758 10 PESOS MONEDA BOLIVIANA			
ca. 1877.	—	—	—

BANCO MUÑOZ & RODRIGUEZ & CA.

Issued at Tucumán.

1883 FIRST ISSUE

	GOOD	FINE	XF
S1760 7 PESOS			
1.6.1883. Allegory of the Republic at l., arms at r.	—	—	—

1883 SECOND ISSUE

#S1761-S1763 printer: ABNC.

	GOOD	FINE	XF
S1761 1 PESO			
30.6.1883. Black on brown unpt. Portr. girl and dog at l., allegorical woman at ctr., Gen. J. de San Martín at r. Back brown. Series A.			
a. Issued note.	—	—	—
s. Specimen.	—	—	—

	GOOD	FINE	XF
S1762 5 PESOS			
30.6.1883. Black on rose unpt. Portr. girl w/rabbits at l., 2 farmers w/horse plowing at ctr., B. Rivadavia at r. Back rose. Series A.			
p. Proof w/o unpt.	—	—	—
s. Specimen.	—	—	—

	VG	VF	UNC
S1763 10 PESOS			
30.6.1883. Black on blue unpt. Portr. C. Columbus at l., steam passenger train at ctr., Gen. Belgrano at r. Back blue. Series A.			
p. Proof.	—	—	—
s. Specimen.	—	—	—

NOTE: It is reported that #S1761-S1763 may also have ovpt. w/1855 circular stamping. Also, these notes are reported ovpt. w/earlier bank name *Banco Mendez Hermanos y Cia.* on face and back. The Banco Muñoz & Rodriguez & Ca. became absorbed by the Banco Provincial de Tucumán listed earlier (see #S841-S846).

(BANCO) OXANDABURU Y GARVINO

Issued at Gualeguaychú.

1867 ISSUE

#S1771-S1778 printer: Lit. San Martín. Bank name w/*GARVINO*.

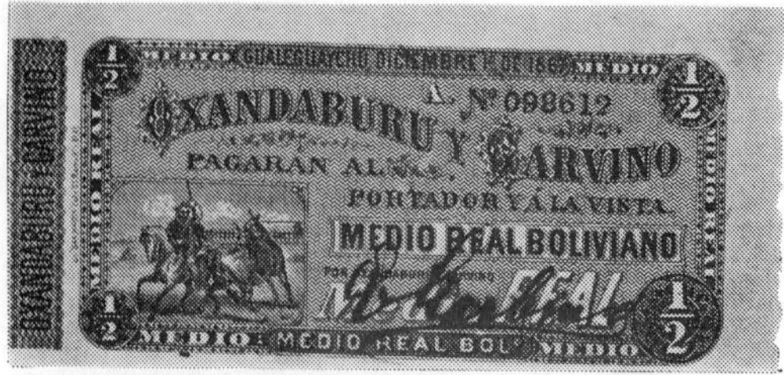

	VG	VF	UNC
S1771 1/2 REAL BOLIVIANO			
1.12.1867. Black. Gaucho on horseback w/bull at l. Uniface.			
a. Issued note.	4.00	10.00	25.00
r. Unsigned remainder.	—	—	10.00

	GOOD	FINE	XF
S1772 1 REAL BOLIVIANO			
1.12.1867. Black. Blue paper.			
a. Issued note.	—	—	—
r. Unsigned remainder.	—	—	—

		GOOD	FINE	XF
S1774	**4 REALES BOLIVIANOS** 1.12.1867. Lt. red. Bull's head at ctr.			
	a. Issued note.	—	—	—
	r. Unsigned remainder.	—	—	10.00

		GOOD	FINE	XF
S1775	**1 PESO BOLIVIANO** 1.12.1867. Black on red unpt. Fox stealing a duck at lower l., portr. woman w/2 children at ctr., bull at lower r.			
	a. Issued note.	—	Rare	—
	r. Unsigned remainder w/counterfoil.	—	—	—

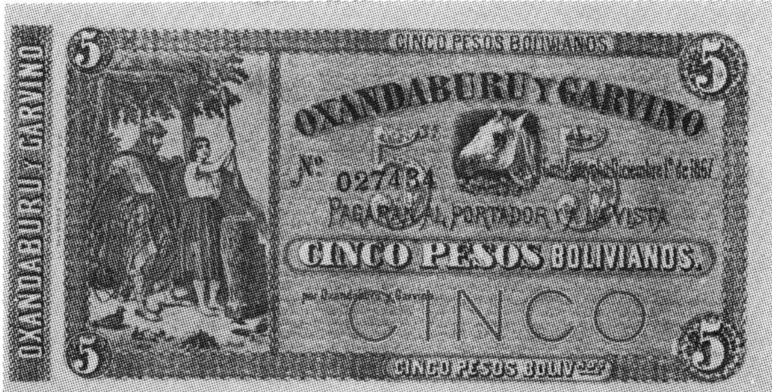

		VG	VF	UNC
S1776	**5 PESOS BOLIVIANOS** 1.12.1867. Brown on red-violet and rose unpt. Gaucho and woman at l., horse's head at ctr.			
	a. Issued note.	—	400.00	—
	b. Unsigned remainder.	—	5.00	12.00

		VG	VF	UNC
S1778	**20 PESOS BOLIVIANOS** 1.12.1867. Red on green unpt. 2 gauchos and woman at ctr. Back brown. Unsigned remainder.	—	—	20.00

Notice

Readers with unlisted dates, color or signature varieties are invited to submit photocopies of their notes to: Standard Catalog of World Paper Money, Krause Publications, 700 East State St. Iola WI 54990-0001 U.S.A. or by email: thernr@krause.com. Email submissions of material for possible inclusion need to be 100% jpeg attachments at 300 dpi.

BANCO OXANDABURU Y GARBINO

1869 PESO BOLIVIANA ISSUE

#S1781-S1785 issued in Pesos Bolivianos. Printer: ABNC. Bank name w/*GARBINO*.

		VG	VF	UNC
S1781	**4 REALES BOLIVIANOS** 2.1.1869. Black on brown unpt. Dog's head at ctr. Uniface.			
	a. Issued note.	65.00	300.00	—
	r. Unsigned remainder.	—	—	6.00

		VG	VF	UNC
S1782	**1 PESO BOLIVIANA** 2.1.1869. Black on green unpt. Girl at lower l., cow and calf at ctr., seated woman and child at lower r. Uniface.			
	a. Issued note.	—	—	—
	r. Unsigned remainder.	—	—	10.00

		VG	VF	UNC
S1783	**5 PESOS BOLIVIANOS** 2.1.1869. Black on green unpt. Seated allegorical woman w/sickle and sheaf at lower l., workers, men on horseback at ctr., sailor at lower r. Back brown.			
	a. Issued note.	—	—	—
	r. Unsigned remainder.	—	—	12.00

		VG	VF	UNC
S1784	**10 PESOS BOLIVIANOS** 2.1.1869. Black on red unpt. Gaucho seated at lower l., man watching woman mashing corn at ctr., 3 horse heads at lower r. Back brown.			
	a. Issued note.	—	—	—
	r. Unsigned remainder.	—	—	25.00
S1785	**20 PESOS BOLIVIANOS** 2.1.1869. Black on red unpt. Gaucho at l., wagons in camp at ctr., woman at r. Back brown.	—	Rare	—

#S1791-S1794 printer: ABNC. Bank name w/*GARBINO*.

1869 PESO FUERTE ISSUE

		VG	VF	UNC
S1791	**1 PESO FUERTE** 2.1.1869. Black on blue unpt. Girl at lower l., horse's head at ctr., anchor at lower r. Uniface. Unsigned remainder.	—	—	10.00

S1792 5 Pesos Fuertes
2.1.1869. Black on green unpt. Girl at lower l. and r., dog on safe at upper l. ctr. Back green. Unsigned remainder.

VG	VF	Unc
—	—	12.00

S1794 200 Pesos Fuertes
2.1.1869. Black on red-brown unpt. Gauchos and carriage at ctr. Back red-brown. Unsigned remainder.

VG	VF	Unc
—	—	20.00

Banco Domingo Garbino

Provisional ND Issue

#S1801-S1806 w/red vertical ovpt: *BANCO DOMINGO GARBINO* on face of Banco Oxandaburu y Garbino issues. All notes have handwritten sign.

S1801 4 Reales
ND (- old date 2.1.1869). Ovpt. new bank name on #S1781.

VG	VF	Unc
—	Rare	—

S1802 1 Peso
ND (- old date 2.1.1869). Ovpt. new bank name on #S1791.

VG	VF	Unc
5.00	10.00	25.00

S1803 5 Pesos
ND (- old date 2.1.1869). Ovpt. new bank name on #S1792.

VG	VF	Unc
10.00	20.00	60.00

S1804 10 Pesos
ND (- old date 2.1.1869). Ovpt. new bank name on #S1784.

VG	VF	Unc
75.00	250.00	—

S1805 20 Pesos
ND (- old date 2.1.1869). Ovpt. new bank name on #S1785.

VG	VF	Unc
50.00	200.00	—

S1806 20 Pesos
ND (- old date 2.1.1869). Ovpt. new bank name on #S1794.

VG	VF	Unc
75.00	250.00	—

Banco Paraná

1868 ND; 1868-69 Issues

#S1811-S1819 printer: Lit. San Martín. Names of branches are part of the oval stamping on back.

S1811 1/2 Real Boliviano
1.4.1868. Blue. Rooster at upper ctr.

	Good	Fine	XF
a. Issued note.	2.00	7.50	—
b. Hand stamped: *LA PAZ.*	—	—	—
c. Hand stamped: *VICTORIA.*	—	—	—
d. Hand stamped: *1869* in oval.	—	—	—

S1812 1 Real Boliviano
1.4.1868. Red. Dog's head at l., dog facing r. at ctr.

	Good	Fine	XF
a. Issued note.	2.50	12.50	—
b. Hand stamped: *LA PAZ.*	—	—	—
c. Hand stamped: *VICTORIA.*	—	—	—
d. Hand stamped: *1869* in oval.	—	—	—

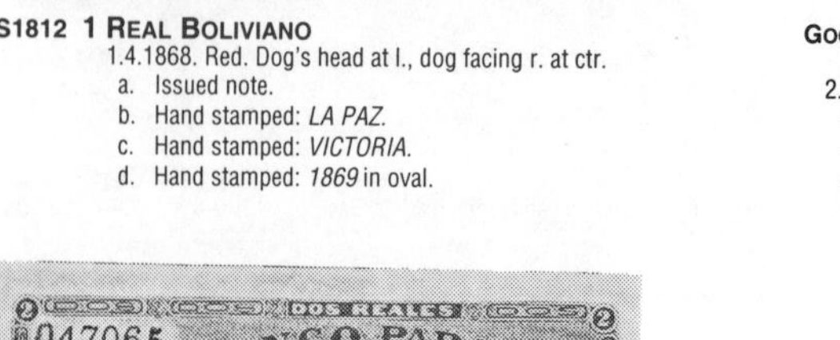

S1813 2 REALES BOLIVIANOS
1.4.1869. Purple. Standing allegorical woman at l., puma at lower r.

	GOOD	FINE	XF
a. Issued note.	3.00	17.50	—
b. Hand stamped: *LA PAZ.*	—	—	—
c. Hand stamped: *VICTORIA.*	—	—	—
d. Hand stamped: *1869* in oval.	—	—	—

S1814 4 REALES BOLIVIANOS
1.4.1868. Brown. Ram at lower l., portr. boy w/sheep at upper ctr.

	GOOD	FINE	XF
a. Issued note.	4.00	17.50	—
b. Hand stamped: *LA PAZ.*	—	—	—
c. Hand stamped: *VICTORIA.*	—	—	—
d. Hand stamped: *1869* in oval.	—	—	—

S1815 1 PESO BOLIVIANO
ND (1868). Black and green. Seated woman w/anchor at loading dock at lower l., 2 horses at ctr., man w/horse and child at lower r. Series A.

	GOOD	FINE	XF
a. Issued note.	4.00	15.00	—
b. Hand stamped: *LA PAZ.*	—	—	—
c. Hand stamped: *VICTORIA.*	—	—	—
d. Hand stamped: *1869* in oval.	—	—	—

S1816 1 PESO BOLIVIANO
ND (1868). Black and red. Like #S1815. *Se. A.*

	GOOD	FINE	XF
a. Issued note.	5.00	15.00	—
b. Hand stamped: *LA PAZ.*	—	—	—
c. Hand stamped: *VICTORIA.*	—	—	—
d. Hand stamped: *1869* in oval.	—	—	—

S1817 5 PESOS MONEDA BOLIVIANA
1.4.1868. Purple on green unpt. Bull at lower l.

	GOOD	FINE	XF
a. Issued note.	5.00	25.00	—
b. Hand stamped: *LA PAZ.*	—	—	—
c. Hand stamped: *VICTORIA.*	—	—	—
d. Hand stamped: *1869* in oval.	—	—	—

S1818 10 PESOS PLATA BOLIVIANA
1.4.1868. Black on tan unpt. Seated allegorical woman w/shield and sailing ships at upper ctr., arms below. Animals and old train at ctr. on back.

	GOOD	FINE	XF
a. Issued note.	40.00	100.00	—
b. Hand stamped: *LA PAZ.*	—	—	—
c. Hand stamped: *VICTORIA.*	—	—	—
d. Hand stamped: *1869* in oval.	—	—	—

S1819 20 PESOS MONEDA BOLIVIANA
1.4.1868. Black on blue-gray unpt. Cherubs at lower l. and r., paddlewheel steamer at upper ctr. Back brown; sailing ship at ctr., sm. head of Mercury at r.

	GOOD	FINE	XF
a. Issued note.	8.00	35.00	—
b. Hand stamped: *LA PAZ.*	—	—	—
c. Hand stamped: *VICTORIA.*	—	—	—
d. Hand stamped: *1869* in oval.	—	—	—

BANCO RIO CUARTO

1874 ISSUE

	GOOD	FINE	XF
S1821 1/2 REAL BOLIVIANA 1.4.1874. Black. Woman at l.	—	—	—
S1822 1 REAL BOLIVIANA 1.4.1874. Woman.	—	—	—
S1823 2 REALES BOLIVIANA 1.4.1874. Woman.	—	—	—

	GOOD	FINE	XF
S1825 1 PESO BOLIVIANA 1.4.1874. Black on blue and green unpt. Portr. woman at upper l., allegorical woman reclining w/scroll at ctr., man and sheep at lower r. Back green. Printer: ABNC.	—	Rare	—

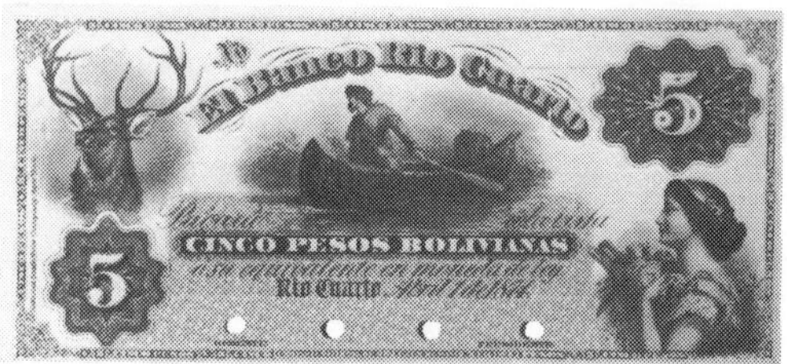

		Good	Fine	XF
S1826	**5 Pesos Bolivianas** 1.4.1874. Black on brown unpt. Stag head at upper l., man in canoe at ctr., woman at lower r. Back brown. Printer: CNBB. Proof.	—	—	—

Banco del Rio de la Plata

Issued at Gualeguay.

1868 First Issue

		Good	Fine	XF
S1831	**1/2 Real Plata Boliviana** 3.10.1868. Brown. Horse's head at upper ctr.			
	a. Issued note.	40.00	250.00	—
	b. Ovpt: *CONCEPCION DEL URUGUAY.*	—	—	—

		Good	Fine	XF
S1832	**1 Peso Plata Boliviana** 3.10.1868. Black. Cow's head at upper ctr.			
	a. Issued note.	40.00	250.00	—
	b. Ovpt: *CONCEPCION DEL URUGUAY.*	—	—	—

		Good	Fine	XF
S1833	**2 Reales Plata Boliviana** 3.10.1868. Black. Goat's head at upper ctr. Printer: Lito. Hongsfeld, Buenos Aires.			
	a. Issued note.	40.00	250.00	—
	b. Ovpt: *CONCEPCION DEL URUGUAY.*	—	—	—

		Good	Fine	XF
S1834	**4 Reales Plata Boliviana** 3.10.1868. Black. Portr. Liberty at l.	40.00	250.00	—

		Good	Fine	XF
S1835	**1 Peso Plata Boliviana** 3.10.1868. Black on violet paper. Woman standing at ctr. w/sheep. Printer: Lit. San Martín.			
	a. Issued note.	40.00	250.00	—
	b. Ovpt: *CONCEPCION DEL URUGUAY.*	—	—	—

		Good	Fine	XF
S1836	**2 Pesos Plata Boliviana** 3.10.1868. Black on violet paper. Dog on safe at upper ctr. Printer: Lit. San Martín.			
	a. Issued note.	40.00	250.00	—
	b. Ovpt: *CONCEPCION DEL URUGUAY.*	—	—	—

		Good	Fine	XF
S1837	**5 Pesos Plata Boliviana** 3.10.1868. Black and dull red on yellow paper. Portr. seated allegorical woman w/scales at l.			
	a. Issued note.	50.00	250.00	—
	b. Ovpt: *CONCEPCION DEL URUGUAY.*	—	—	—
S1838	**10 Pesos Plata Boliviana** 3.10.1868. Black, green and rose on orange paper. Woman standing at l.			
	a. Issued note.	—	—	—
	b. Ovpt: *CONCEPCION DEL URUGUAY.*	—	—	—

1868 Second Issue

		Good	Fine	XF
S1843	**1 Peso Plata Boliviano** 28.9.1868. Black on orange unpt. Uniface. Printer: Lit. Mege y Willems, Montevideo.	40.00	250.00	—

1869 ISSUE

		GOOD	FINE	XF
S1848	**5 PESOS MONEDA BOLIVIANA** 9.1.1869. Black on brown unpt. Dk. blue paper. Uniface. Printer: Lit. San Martín.	85.00	300.00	—

BANCO (DEL) ROSARIO DE SANTA FÉ

Established 1865.

1865-69 ISSUES

#S1851, S1853-S1856 printer: Lit. C. Held, Rosario.

		GOOD	FINE	XF
S1851	**1 REAL PLATA BOLIVIANA** 1.10.1869. Black on lt. yellow unpt. Heading w/*DEL*. Uniface.			
	a. Stamped sign.	40.00	200.00	—
	b. Handwritten sign.	—	—	—
S1853	**1 PESO PLATA BOLIVIANA** 1865-67. Angels at top ctr.	—	—	—

		GOOD	FINE	XF
S1854	**1 PESO PLATA BOLIVIANA** 1.10.1869. Black. Gauchos at top ctr.			
	a. Stamped sign.	40.00	200.00	—
	b. Handwritten sign.	75.00	300.00	—

		GOOD	FINE	XF
S1856	**10 PESOS PLATA BOLIVIANA** 1.10.1869. Black on red unpt. Girl's head at lower l. and lower r., gaucho roping cattle at top ctr.			
	a. Stamped sign. Red or brown serial #.	—	—	—
	b. Handwritten sign. Green or blue serial #.	—	—	—

BANCO DE SAN JUAN

1860S SAN JUAN, CATAMARCA AND TUCUMÁN ISSUE

		GOOD	FINE	XF
S1860	**2 REALES** 186x. Printer: G. Kraft, Bs. As.	—	—	—

1870S CATAMARCA ISSUE

		GOOD	FINE	XF
S1862	**1 PESO BOLIVIANO** 187x. Black and red on green unpt. Horses at ctr. Back blue. Printer: Guillermo Kraft. Proof stamped *MUESTRA*.	—	—	400.00

1873 SAN JUAN PESO PLATA BOLIVIANA ISSUE

		GOOD	FINE	XF
S1864	**4 REALES PLATA BOLIVIANA** 1.7.1873.	—	—	—

		GOOD	FINE	XF
S1873	**1 PESO PLATA BOLIVIANA** 18xx. Black on green unpt. Woman holding spool of yarn at l. Uniface. Series C. Proof.	—	—	—

1876 SAN JUAN PESO FUERTE ISSUE

#S1876-S1883 printer: BWC. Series D.

		GOOD	FINE	XF
S1876	**5 CENTAVOS FUERTES** 3.1.1876. Black. Portr. woman at l. Uniface. Proof.			
S1877	**10 CENTAVOS FUERTES** 3.1.1876. 3.1.1876. Proof.	—	—	—
S1878	**20 CENTAVOS FUERTES** 3.1.1876. Proof.	—	—	—

		GOOD	FINE	XF
S1880	**1 PESO FUERTE** 3.1.1876. Black on green unpt. Bird at l. Back red, green and tan; 2 heads.	—	—	—
S1881	**5 PESOS FUERTES** 18xx.	—	—	—
S1882	**10 PESOS FUERTES** 18xx.	—	—	—

		GOOD	FINE	XF
S1883	**20 PESOS FUERTES** 18xx. Black on orange unpt. Cow's head, allegorical woman's head and shield at upper r. Back red and green. 6 heads of Liberty.	—	—	—
S1884	**50 PESOS FUERTES** 187x. Black on yellow unpt. Gathering of people at lower l. Printer: G. Kraft, Bs. As. Series A.	—	—	—

1874-76 TUCUMÁN PESO BOLIVIANA ISSUE

		GOOD	FINE	XF
S1886	5 CENTAVOS MONEDA BOLIVIANA (ca.1874). Specimen.	—	—	—
S1887	1 REAL MONEDA BOLIVIANA 1876.	—	—	—
S1888	1 1/2 REALES MONEDA BOLIVIANA 1876.	—	—	—
S1891	1 PESO MONEDA BOLIVIANA 1.7.1874. Seal of branch at San Juan.	—	—	—

1876 TUCUMÁN PESO FUERTE ISSUE

		GOOD	FINE	XF
S1892	10 CENTAVOS FUERTES 3.1.1876. Black on green paper.	—	—	—
S1896	60 CENTAVOS FUERTES 1.10.1878. Payable in national money or 4 chirolas of 15 Centavos each in Bolivian money.	—	—	—
S1897	1 PESO FUERTE (ca. 1876).	—	—	—
S1900	20 PESOS FUERTES (ca. 1876).	—	—	—

BANCO DE SAN LUIS

1894 ISSUE

		GOOD	FINE	XF
S1901	1 PESO 17.3.1894. Green.	—	—	—

		GOOD	FINE	XF
S1902	2 PESOS 17.3.1894. Black on gold unpt. Back green. Series B.	—	—	100.00

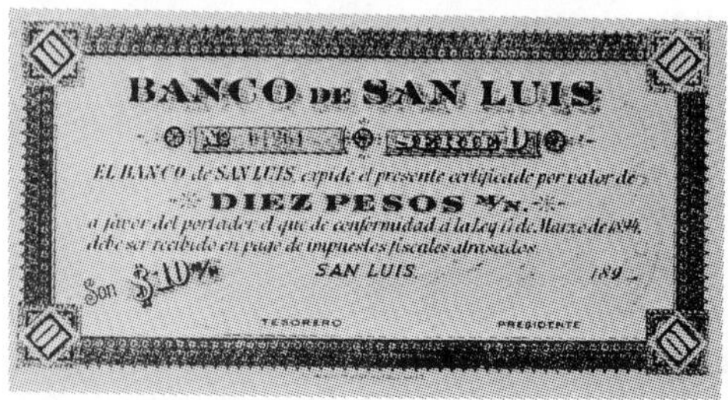

		GOOD	FINE	XF
S1904	10 PESOS 17.3.1894. Black on gold unpt. Back blue. Series D.	—	—	120.00

BANCO SOLANAS & CIA.

1874 ISSUE

#S1912-S1915 uniface. Printer: A. Godel. Unsigned remainders.

		GOOD	FINE	XF
S1912	1 REAL PLATA BOLIVIANA 1.8.1874. Green and black. Ram at ctr.	—	90.00	300.00

		GOOD	FINE	XF
S1913	2 REALES PLATA BOLIVIANA 1.8.1874. Blue and black. Bull at ctr.	—	90.00	300.00

		GOOD	FINE	XF
S1915	1 PESO BOLIVIANO 1.8.1874. Brown and black. Allegorical woman at l., gaucho on horseback chasing ostriches at ctr. r. Back gray.	—	90.00	300.00

#S1916-S1918 printer: ABNC.

		GOOD	FINE	XF
S1916	5 PESOS MONEDA BOLIVIANA 1.8.1874. Black on brown unpt. 3 allegorical women at l., sheep under trees at upper ctr., allegorical woman at r. Back brown. Proof.	—	—	—
S1918	20 PESOS MONEDA BOLIVIANA 1.8.1874. Black on brown unpt. Woman, ducks and horse at l., dog on safe at ctr., 2 allegorical women w/sailing ships behind at r. Back brown. Proof.	—	—	—

BANCO DE VICTORIA

1873 ISSUE

		GOOD	FINE	XF
S1923	1 PESO 1.4.1873. Black. Man at l.	—	Rare	—

CAJA DE AHORROS DE ROSARIO

1870 ISSUE

		GOOD	FINE	XF
S1931	1 REAL BOLIVIANA 1870.	—	—	—

CREDITO POPULAR

1906 BONO DE CREDITO ISSUE

		GOOD	FINE	XF
S1944	5 PESOS 8.6.1906. Black on brown unpt. Standing allegorical woman and cherub at l. Back blue-black.	30.00	200.00	—

CREDITO TERRITORIAL

Issued at Concepción del Uruguay, Province of Entre-Rios.

1877 ISSUE

		GOOD	FINE	XF
S1951	1 PESO FUERTE June 1877. Black on salmon unpt. Arms at upper ctr., steam train at lower ctr. Ovpt: *Law 5.6.1879* on back. Printer: Lit. San Martín, Buenos Aires.	—	Rare	—

CREDITO TERRITORIAL DE SANTA FÉ

LAW OF 28.9.1869

		GOOD	FINE	XF
S1958	**1 REAL PLATA BOLIVIANA** 1.1.1870. Black. Lg. ornate "1" in unpt. at ctr. Printer: C. (?), Rosario.	—	—	—

		GOOD	FINE	XF
S1963	**1 PESO PLATA BOLIVIANA** ND (ca. 1869). Black and orange. Woman's head at l., galloping horse at upper ctr. facing l. Uniface. Printer: Lit. San Martín.	—	Rare	—

DANIEL GONZALEZ Y COMPA.

1860S ISSUE

Issued in the Province of Mendoza. The firm operated from 1866 to 1879.

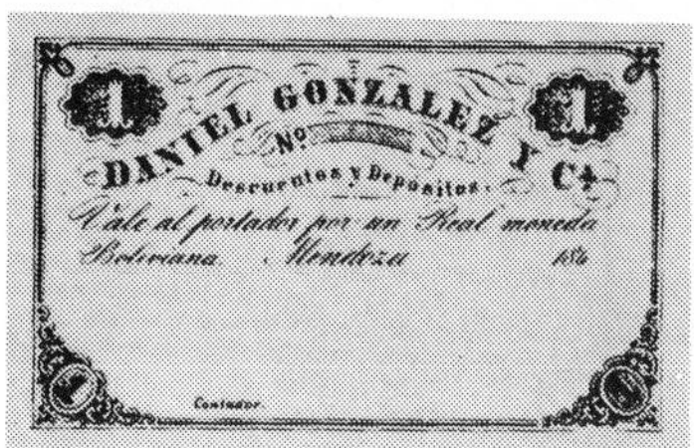

		GOOD	FINE	XF
S1971	**1 REAL MONEDA BOLIVIANA** 186x. Uniface.			
	a. Lt. green w/o wmk.	—	—	—
	b. Lt. green w/wmk.	—	—	—
	c. Dk. green. W/o wmk.	—	—	—
	d. Dk. green w/wmk.	—	—	—
S1972	**2 REALES MONEDA BOLIVIANA** 186x. Red-orange. Uniface.			
	a. W/o wmk.	—	—	—
	b. W/wmk.	—	—	—

#S1974-S1976 printer: ABNC.

		GOOD	FINE	XF
S1974	**1 PESO PLATA BOLIVIANA** 1.3.1866; 1.9.1868. Black on green unpt. Condor at ctr. w/wings spread across face. Back red-brown.			
	a. Black on green unpt. and border. Issued note.	—	—	—
	p. Black on orange unpt. and border. Proof.	—	—	—

		GOOD	FINE	XF
S1975	**5 PESOS PLATA BOLIVIANA** 186x. Black on blue unpt. Young girl's head at lower l. and lower r., Agriculture at upper ctr. Back blue. Proof.	—	—	—

		GOOD	FINE	XF
S1976	**10 PESOS PLATA BOLIVIANA** 186x. Black. Girl at lower l., gauchos herding cattle at ctr., young woman at lower r. Back brown.			
	p1. Brown unpt. Face proof.	—	—	—
	p2. Red-orange unpt. Face proof.	—	—	—

MIGUEL LANIERI

Notes issued at Victoria, Province of Entre-Rios.

1871 ISSUES

#S1982 and S1983 back stamped w/issuer's name and design in back oval.

		GOOD	FINE	XF
S1982	**4 REALES BOLIVIANOS** 1.11.1871. Black. Cow's head at ctr., boat at upper r. Uniface.	40.00	200.00	—

		GOOD	FINE	XF
S1983	**4 REALES BOLIVIANOS** 1.11.1871. Black. Dog's head at l., ship at ctr. Back blue.	40.00	200.00	—

		GOOD	FINE	XF
S1983A	**1 PESO BOLIVIANO** 1.11.1871. Black. Indian seated at lower l., steamship at top ctr.	—	—	—

OTERO Y CIA.

Issued at Córdoba.

1867 ISSUE

		GOOD	FINE	XF
S1984	**1/2 REAL PLATA BOLIVIANA** 31.11.1867.	—	—	—
S1985	**1 REAL PLATA BOLIVIANA** 1.6.1867; 31.11.1867.	—	—	—
S1986	**2 REALES PLATA BOLIVIANA** 1.6.1867; 31.11.1867.	—	—	—
S1987	**4 REALES PLATA BOLIVIANA** 1.6.1867; 31.11.1867.	—	—	—
S1988	**1 PESO PLATA BOLIVIANA** 31.11.1867.	—	—	—

	GOOD	FINE	XF
S1989 5 PESOS PLATA BOLIVIANA 31.11.1867.	—	—	—
S1990 10 PESOS PLATA BOLIVIANA 31.11.1867.	—	—	—

1868 ISSUE

#S1991-S1999 printer: ABNC.

	GOOD	FINE	XF
S1991 1 PESO PLATA BOLIVIANA 1.1.1868. Black on orange unpt. Arms of Córdoba at upper l., horses at upper ctr., winged allegorical woman w/numeral *1* at lower r. Proof.	—	—	—

	GOOD	FINE	XF
S1992 5 PESOS PLATA BOLIVIANA 1.1.1868. Black on red-orange unpt. Girl's head at upper l., 5 cherubs w/numeral *5* at ctr., arms of Córdoba at lower r.			
p. Proof.	—	—	—
s. Specimen.	—	—	—

	GOOD	FINE	XF
S1993 10 PESOS BOLIVIANOS 1.1.1868. Black on green unpt. Girl tending cows at upper l., 2 horse's heads at upper ctr. r., man smoking at lower r. Proof.	—	—	—

1869 ISSUE

	GOOD	FINE	XF
S1996 1/2 REAL PLATA BOLIVIANA 1.4.1869. Black. Text across face. Proof.	—	—	—

	GOOD	FINE	XF
S1997 1 REAL PLATA BOLIVIANA 1.4.1869. Black. Arms of Córdoba at ctr. Uniface.	40.00	125.00	—

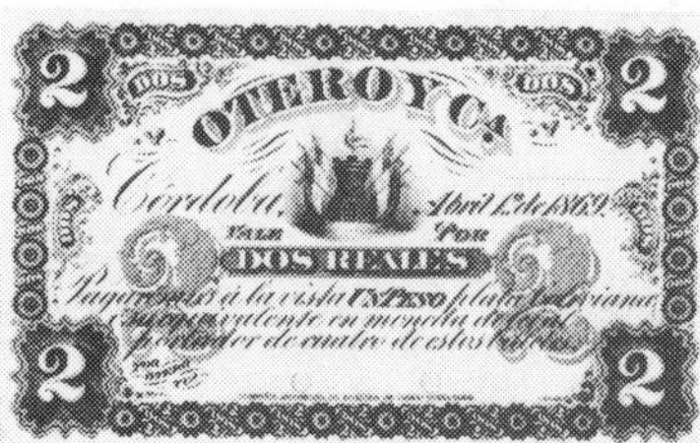

	GOOD	FINE	XF
S1998 2 REALES PLATA BOLIVIANA 1.4.1869. Black. Arms of Córdoba at upper ctr. Proof.	—	—	—
S1998A4 REALES PLATA BOLIVIANA 1.4.1869.	—	—	—

1872 ISSUE

	GOOD	FINE	XF
S1999 4 REALES PLATA BOLIVIANA 1.1.1872. Portr. girl at lower l. and lower r., arms of Córdoba at ctr. Proof.	—	—	—

BANCO OTERO Y CIA.

1880 ISSUE

#S2001-S2004 portr. Gen. M. Paz at l. Printer: BWC.

	GOOD	FINE	XF
S2001 1 PESO PLATA 2.1.1880. Black on green unpt.	—	—	—
S2002 5 PESOS PLATA 2.1.1880. Black on carmine unpt. Gauchos.	—	—	—
S2003 10 PESOS PLATA 2.1.1880. Black.	—	—	—

	GOOD	FINE	XF
S2004 20 PESOS PLATA 2.1.1880. Black. Man watching woman mashing corn at r. Male portr. at l. Proof.	—	Unc	350.00

SECTION VI

PROVINCIAL

PROVINCE OF CORRIENTES

BILLETES DE TESORERIA ND ISSUE

TREASURY BILLS

LEY PROMULGADA EL 16 DE NOVIEMBRE DE 1891

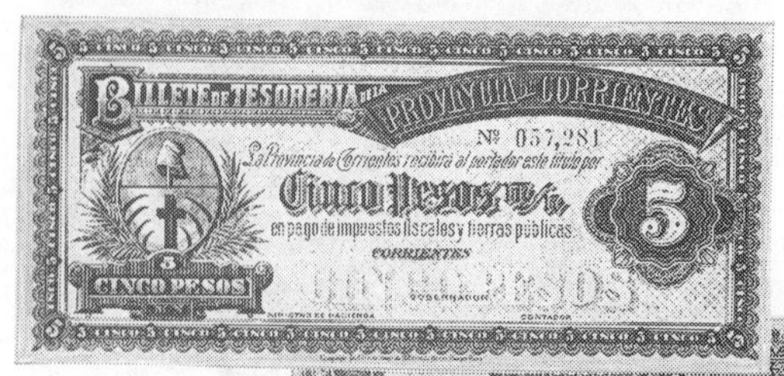

		GOOD	FINE	XF
S2015	**5 PESOS** *L.1891.* Black on brown unpt. Provincial arms at l. Back blue, farmer and dog at l. Printer: CSABB.	15.00	35.00	100.00

PROVINCE OF JUJUY

1903; 1905 OBLIGACIONES DE TESORERIA ISSUE

TREASURY OBLIGATIONS

#S2021-S2024 printer: CSABB.

		GOOD	FINE	XF
S2021	**5 CENTAVOS** 1.1.1903. Black on brown unpt. Provincial arms at l. Back brown.	8.00	20.00	60.00

		GOOD	FINE	XF
S2022	**10 CENTAVOS** 1.1.1903. Black on lt. green unpt. Provincial arms at upper l.	10.00	25.00	75.00

		GOOD	FINE	XF
S2023	**50 CENTAVOS** 1.1.1903. Black on lt. brown unpt. Provincial arms at upper ctr.	10.00	25.00	75.00

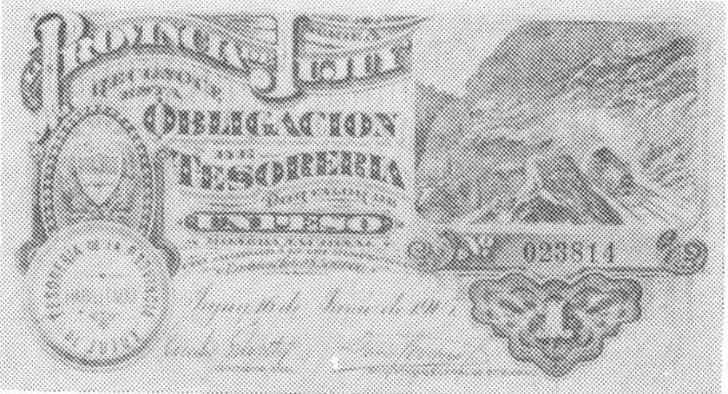

		GOOD	FINE	XF
S2024	**1 PESO** 16.6.1905. Red. Provincial arms at l., steam train emerging from tunnel at r. Back red and green; plantation at l.	12.00	30.00	85.00

LEYES 529 & 530 DE 20.4.1928; 1928 ISSUE

		GOOD	FINE	XF
S2025	**20 CENTAVOS** *L.1928.* Black on blue-gray unpt.	—	—	—

1932 TITULOS DE CRÉDITO INTERNO ISSUE

INTERNAL CREDIT CLAIMS

		GOOD	FINE	XF
S2035	**1 PESO** 8.11.1932. Black on red-brown unpt. Provincial arms at upper l. Back red. Series A.	20.00	40.00	75.00

PROVINCE OF MENDOZA

LEY DEL 28 DE NOVIEMBRE DE 1892; 1893 ISSUE

#S2042-S2046 printer: J. Peuser, Buenos Aires.

		GOOD	FINE	XF
S2042	**10 CENTAVOS** 1.1.1893. Black on green unpt. Arms at lower l. Back blue. Series D.	8.00	15.00	50.00
S2044	**50 CENTAVOS** 1.1.1893. Series C.			
	a. Issued note.	—	—	—
	s. Specimen ovpt: *MUESTRA.*	—	—	—

		GOOD	FINE	XF
S2045	**1 PESO** 1.1.1893. Arms at top ctr. Series A.			
	a. Issued note.	8.00	20.00	60.00
	s. Specimen ovpt: *MUESTRA.*	—	—	—
S2046	**5 PESOS** 1.1.1893. Series B.			
	a. Issued note.	—	—	—
	s. Specimen ovpt: *MUESTRA.*	—	—	—

LEY 28.11.1892 Y 25.4.1895; 1893 ISSUE

#S2051 and S2052 printer: CSABB.

		GOOD	FINE	XF
S2051	**1 PESO** 1.1.1893. Series A.			
	a. Issued note.	—	—	—
	s. Specimen ovpt: *MUESTRA.*	—	—	—
S2052	**5 PESOS** 1.1.1893. Series B.			
	a. Issued note.	—	—	—
	s. Specimen ovpt: *MUESTRA.*	—	—	—

LEY DE 25 DE ABRIL DE 1895; 1897 ISSUE

#S2056 and S2057 printer: J. Peuser, Buenos Aires.

		GOOD	FINE	XF
S2056	**1 PESO** Nov. 1897. Series E.			
	a. Issued note.	—	—	—
	s. Specimen ovpt: *MUESTRA.*	—	—	—

		GOOD	FINE	XF
S2057	**5 PESOS** Nov. 1897. Black on gold unpt. Arms at l. Aqueduct on back. Series F.			
	a. Issued note.	15.00	30.00	80.00
	s. Specimen ovpt: *MUESTRA.*	—	—	—

LEY NO. 74; 1898 ISSUE

#S2059 and S2060 printer: J. Peuser.

		GOOD	FINE	XF
S2059	**1 PESO** May 1898. Black on green unpt. Series 1.			
	a. Issued note.	—	—	—
	s. Specimen ovpt: *MUESTRA.*	—	—	—
S2060	**5 PESOS** May 1898. Series 2.			
	a. Issued note.	—	—	—
	s. Specimen ovpt: *MUESTRA.*	—	—	—

LEY DEL 25 DE ABRIL DE 1895; 1899 ISSUE

#S2065 and S2066 printer: CSABB.

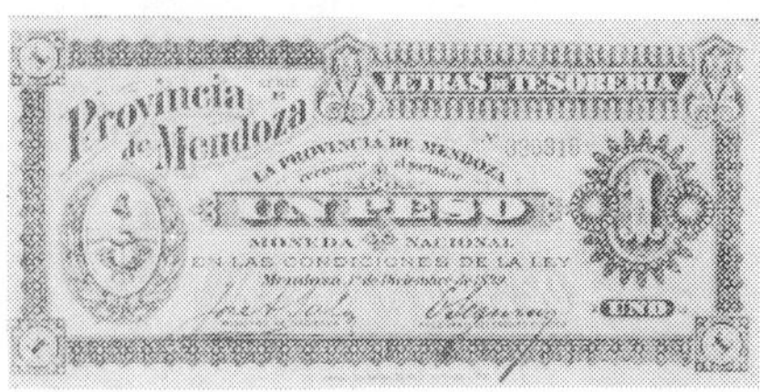

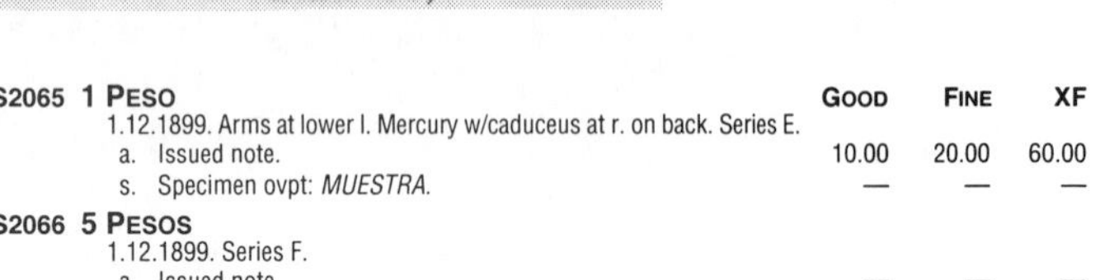

		Good	Fine	XF
S2065	**1 Peso** 1.12.1899. Arms at lower l. Mercury w/caduceus at r. on back. Series E.			
	a. Issued note.	10.00	20.00	60.00
	s. Specimen ovpt: *MUESTRA.*	—	—	—
S2066	**5 Pesos** 1.12.1899. Series F.			
	a. Issued note.	—	—	—
	s. Specimen ovpt: *MUESTRA.*	—	—	—

Ley No. 210 del 22 de Junio de 1901; First Issue

#S2075 and S2075A printer: CSABB.

		Good	Fine	XF
S2075	**1 Peso** June 1901. Black on green and orange unpt. Arms at top ctr. Back blue; Athena at r. Series B; C.	7.00	12.00	45.00
S2075A	**5 Pesos** June 1901. Woman seated near barrels at l., arms at r. Mountains on back. Series A.			
	a. Issued note.	—	—	—
	s. Specimen ovpt: *MUESTRA.*	—	—	—

1901 Second Issue

#S2076 and S2077 printer: G. Kraft, Buenos Aires.

		Good	Fine	XF
S2076	**1 Peso** June 1901. Black on blue and orange unpt. Like #S2075 but different printer. Series C.			
	a. Issued note.	7.00	12.00	45.00
	s. Specimen ovpt: *MUESTRA.*	—	—	—
S2077	**5 Pesos** June 1901. Series B.	—	—	—

Ley No. 645; 1914 Issues

#S2081-S2094 printer: Guillermo Kraft, Buenos Aires.

		Good	Fine	XF
S2081	**50 Centavos** December 1914. Black and brown on tan unpt. Liberty head at upper l., arms at lower r. w/circular ovpt: *POR CANJE* on face. Back orange-brown. Series A.			
	a. Issued note.	8.00	20.00	50.00
	s. Specimen ovpt: *MUESTRA.*	—	—	—

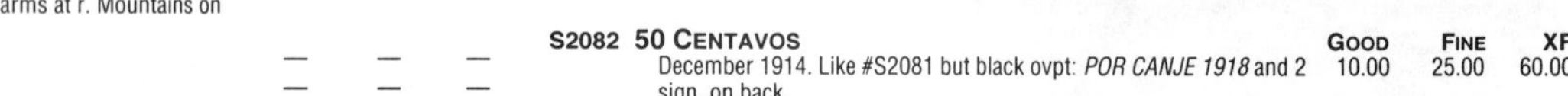

		Good	Fine	XF
S2082	**50 Centavos** December 1914. Like #S2081 but black ovpt: *POR CANJE 1918* and 2 sign. on back.	10.00	25.00	60.00

		Good	Fine	XF
S2083	**50 Centavos** December 1914. Brown, green and black. Arms at top ctr. Back green; girl at ctr. Black ovpt: *CANJE* twice. Series B; C.	8.00	20.00	50.00

		Good	Fine	XF
S2084	**50 Centavos** December 1914. Blue and dk. green. Arms at l., portr. woman at lower r. Series A-P.			
	a. Issued note.	10.00	25.00	60.00
	s. Specimen.	—	—	—

S2085 1 PESO

December 1914. Black on blue and orange unpt. Similar to #S2076 but different law and sign. Text changed on back. Series A.

	GOOD	FINE	XF
	8.00	20.00	50.00

S2086 1 PESO

December 1914. Like #S2085 but black ovpt: *POR CANJE 1918* and 2 sign. on back.

	GOOD	FINE	XF
a. Issued note.	8.00	15.00	40.00
s. Specimen.	—	—	—

S2087 1 PESO

December 1914. Black and violet on peach unpt. Arms at ctr. Back red; black ovpt: *CANJE* twice. Series B; C.

	GOOD	FINE	XF
	7.50	15.00	40.00

S2088 1 PESO

December 1914. Black and red on olive unpt. Standing Justice at l., winged allegorical man at r. Back brown; monument at ctr. Series A-P.

	GOOD	FINE	XF
a. Issued note.	8.00	15.00	40.00
s. Specimen.	—	—	—

S2088A 5 PESOS

December 1914. Series A.

	GOOD	FINE	XF
	—	—	—

S2089 5 PESOS

December 1914. Allegorical woman reclining by barrels at l., arms at r. Mountains on back. Ovpt: *CANJE* twice. Series B.

	GOOD	FINE	XF
	12.00	40.00	125.00

S2090 5 PESOS

December 1914. Black and green. Seated allegorical woman flanking child at ctr. Woman on back. Series A-P.

	GOOD	FINE	XF
a. Issued note.	12.00	40.00	125.00
s. Specimen.	—	—	—

S2091 10 PESOS

December 1914. Grayish green on lt. gray unpt. Seated woman and globe at ctr. Back blue; building and hills on back. Series A-P.

	GOOD	FINE	XF
a. Issued note.	20.00	75.00	—
s. Specimen.	—	—	—

S2092 20 PESOS

December 1914. Allegorical woman reclining by barrels at l., arms at r. Mountains at ctr. on back. Series A-P.

	GOOD	FINE	XF
a. Issued note.	—	—	—
s. Specimen.	—	—	—

S2092A 20 PESOS

December 1914. Ovpt: *POR CANJE (1923-24).* on back. Series A-P.

	GOOD	FINE	XF
	—	—	—

S2093 50 PESOS

December 1914. Black on yellow-green unpt. Liberty at ctr., arms above. Back brown-violet; ovpt: *POR CANJE (1923-24).* Series A-P.

	GOOD	FINE	XF
a. Issued note.	—	—	—
s. Specimen.	—	—	—

S2094 100 PESOS

December 1914. Allegorical woman reclining by barrels at l., arms at r. Allegorical woman seated, child standing at ctr. on back. Series A; B.

	GOOD	FINE	XF
a. Issued note.	—	—	—
s. Specimen.	—	—	—

S2094A 100 PESOS

December 1914. Green on yellow unpt. Arms at lower ctr. Ovpt: *POR CANJE (1923-24)* on back. Series A-P.

	GOOD	FINE	XF
a. Issued note.	—	—	—
s. Specimen, punched hole cancelled.	—	—	—

S2095 500 PESOS

December 1914. Black and green on gray unpt. Back red. Series A-R.

	GOOD	FINE	XF
a. Issued note.	—	—	—
s. Specimen.	—	—	—

		GOOD	FINE	XF
S2095A	**500 PESOS** December 1914. Justice w/sword and balance scales at ctr. Two children w/produce at ctr. on back. Ovpt.: *POR CANJE* (1923-24). Series A-P.	—	—	—
S2095B	**1000 PESOS** December 1914. Series A.	—	—	—

LEY NO. 650; 1914 ISSUE

#S2095C-S2095G printer: Guillermo Kraft, Bs. As.

		GOOD	FINE	XF
S2095C	**1 PESO** December 1914. Brown-orange. Series A.	—	—	—
S2095D	**5 PESOS** December 1914. Black on green unpt. Series A.	—	—	—
S2095E	**10 PESOS** December 1914. Black on red unpt. Series A; B.	—	—	—
S2095F	**20 PESOS** December 1914. Black and violet on yellow unpt. Series A; B.	—	—	—
S2095G	**50 PESOS** December 1914. Black and brown on brown unpt. Reclining figure w/implements at l., arms at r. Series A.	—	—	—

DECRETO DE 26 DE OCTOBRE DE 1923

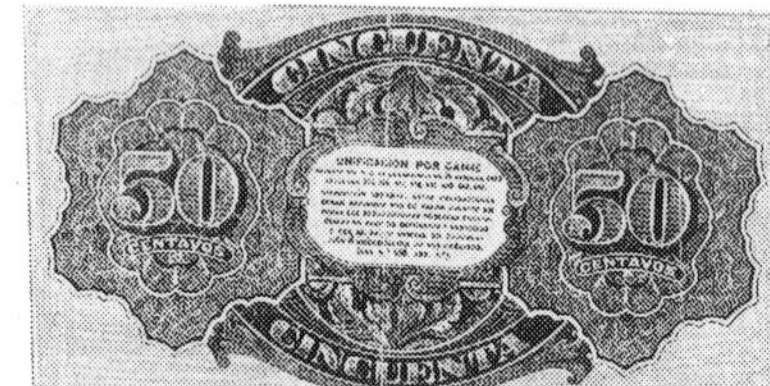

		GOOD	FINE	XF
S2096	**50 CENTAVOS** *D.1923.* Like #S2084, including 1914 date on face. Decree date on back.	—	—	—
S2096A	**1 PESO** *D.1923.* Like #S2088, including 1914 date on face. Decree date on back.	—	—	—

1908 CRÉDITO Y HABILITACIÓN INDUSTRIAL ISSUE

#S2096F-S2096H w/square back ovpt: *HABILITADA - Leyes 389 y 437.*

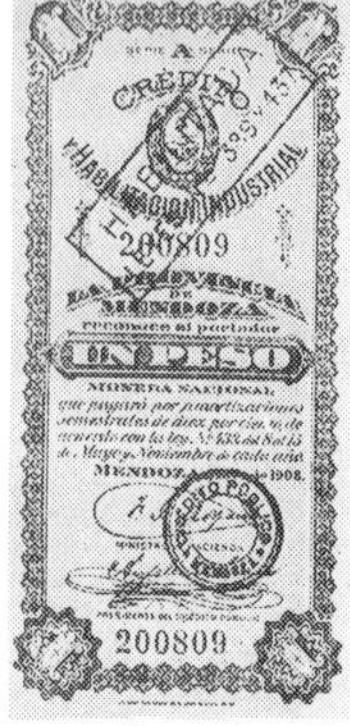

		GOOD	FINE	XF
S2096F	**1 PESO** May 1908. Black on green unpt. Arms at upper ctr. w/circular ovpt: *CREDITO PUBLICO MENDOZA.* Allegory of Industry seated at upper ctr. on back. Series A. Printer: CSABB.	—	—	—
S2096G	**5 PESOS** May 1908.	Reported Not Confirmed		
S2096H	**20 PESOS** May 1908.	Reported Not Confirmed		

Notice

Readers with unlisted dates, color or signature varieties are invited to submit photocopies of their notes to: Standard Catalog of World Paper Money, Krause Publications, 700 East State St. Iola WI 54990-0001 U.S.A. or by email: thernr@krause.com. Email submissions of material for possible inclusion need to be 100% jpeg attachments at 300 dpi.

PROVINCE OF SALTA

1891 PROVINCIAL ISSUE

#S2097-S2100 specimen hand stamped: *MUESTRA.*

		GOOD	FINE	XF
S2097	**1 PESO** 30.10.1891. M/c. Portr. Gen. R. Alvarado at lower l., allegorical woman w/sheep at lower r. Back blue. Series A. Specimen.	—	—	—

		GOOD	FINE	XF
S2098	**2 PESOS** 30.10.1891. M/c. Portr. Dr. Pedro J. Frías at l., woman w/cornucopia at r. Back brown. Series B. Specimen.	—	—	—

		GOOD	FINE	XF
S2099	**5 PESOS** 30.10.1891. M/c. Portr. Gen. E. Frías at l., soldiers on horseback at r. Back green. Series C. Specimen.	—	—	—

		GOOD	FINE	XF
S2100	**10 PESOS** 30.10.1891. M/c. Portr. Gen. M. Guemes at l., monument of allegorical woman w/flag at r. Back red-brown. Series D. Specimen.	—	—	—

OBLIGACIONES DE LA PROVINCIA; 1907 ISSUE

OBLIGATIONS OF THE PROVINCE; 1907 ISSUE

		GOOD	FINE	XF
S2101	**1 PESO** 30.4.1907. Black on orange unpt. Gen. A. de Apenales at l.	12.00	30.00	80.00

1916 ISSUE

	GOOD	FINE	XF
S2111 1 PESO 31.8.1916. Black on brown unpt. Sm. head in star at ctr. Back brown; cow's head at ctr. Printer: CSABB.	12.00	30.00	80.00
S2112 2 PESOS 31.8.1916. Black on green unpt.	15.00	40.00	90.00

1921 ISSUE

	GOOD	FINE	XF
S2121 1 PESO 30.9.1921. Green. Red circular ovpt: *EMISION 30 SETIEMBRE 1921 SERIE D* at lower r. Provincial arms at ctr. on back.	12.00	30.00	80.00

LAWS OF 20.7.1921, 5.6.1922 AND 30.9.1922; 1927 ISSUE

	GOOD	FINE	XF
S2131 1 PESO 6.1927. Portr. Gen. Guemes at l. Round hand stamp: *EMISION DE JUNIO AÑO 1927* at lower ctr. Chilean railroad at ctr., provincial arms at r. on back. Printer: Peuser.	15.00	40.00	80.00

LAWS OF 30.9.1922 AND 24.1.1928; 1928 ISSUE

#S2136 and S2137 circular red hand stamp at top ctr: *EMISION DE MARZO AÑO 1928*. Printer: Peuser.

	GOOD	FINE	XF
S2136 1 PESO 3.1928. Black on blue unpt. Like #S2131. Back blue.	10.00	25.00	60.00

	GOOD	FINE	XF
S2137 2 PESOS 3.1928. Black on red unpt. Like #S2136. Back red.	15.00	30.00	70.00

1931 RENOVACION PROVISIONAL ISSUE

	GOOD	FINE	XF
S2139 1 PESO 10.1931. Black on blue unpt. Like #S2136 but red circular emission date stamping at upper ctr. on face. Ovpt.: *RENOVACION 1931* in rectangular box at upper ctr. on back.	—	—	—

LAWS OF 5.6.1922, 30.9.1922, 24.1.1928 AND 20.10.1932

	GOOD	FINE	XF
S2141 1 PESO *L.1932.* Black on green unpt. Like #S2136. Back green.	10.00	25.00	60.00

1933 ISSUE

	GOOD	FINE	XF
S2142 1 PESO 1.1933. Black on blue unpt. Like #S2136 but red circular emission date stamping at ctr. on face.	—	—	—
S2143 2 PESOS 1.1933. Similar to #S2142.	—	—	—

PROVINCE OF SAN JUAN

LEY DE 15 DE JULIO DE 1893 LETRAS DE TESORERIA ISSUE

TREASURY LETTERS OF CREDIT

	GOOD	FINE	XF
S2151 1 PESO 31.12.1896. Black on brown unpt. Arms at l. Black square ovpt: *CREDITO PUBLICO / RENOVACION / SAN JUAN* at ctr. Back brown; grinder at upper ctr. Series G. Printer: CSABB.	12.00	30.00	80.00

LEY DE 25 DE JULIO DE 1894

	GOOD	FINE	XF
S2155 50 PESOS *L. 1894.* Black on green unpt. Portr. Laprida at l., arms at r. Series E. Printer: CSABB.	—	—	—

LEY DE 17 DE ENERO DE DE 1898; 1899 ISSUE

#S2161-S2163 printer: CSABB.

S2161 5 Centavos
15.5.1899. Black on green unpt. Arms at l. Back blue. Series D.

Good	Fine	XF
10.00	22.50	60.00

S2162 10 Centavos
15.5.1899. Black on brown unpt. Arms at l. Back brown. Series C.

Good	Fine	XF
10.00	20.00	70.00

S2163 20 Centavos
15.5.1899. Black on lt. green unpt. Arms at r. Back olive-gray. Series B.

Good	Fine	XF
12.00	35.00	90.00

Ley de 17 de Enero de de 1898; 1909 Issue

#S2174 and S2175 printer: CSABB.

S2174 50 Centavos
1.7.1909. Black on brown unpt.

Good	Fine	XF
10.00	25.00	75.00

	Good	Fine	XF
S2175 1 Peso 1.7.1909. Black on green unpt. Arms at l. Back green; girl and grapes at ctr. Series D.			
a. Issued note.	12.00	30.00	75.00
b. Red stamping in rectangle on face: *Credito Público/Renovación.*	—	—	—
S2177 5 Pesos 1.7.1909. Black on lt. brown unpt. Red ovpt: *CREDITO PUBLICO / RENOVACION* across face. Back brown; two standing women at r. Printer: G. Kraft, BsAires.	—	—	—
S2178 10 Pesos 1.7.1909. Black on brown unpt. O. Rawson at l., arms at ctr. Red diagonal ovpt: *CREDITO PUBLICO / RENOVACION.*	—	—	—
S2179 20 Pesos 1.7.1909. Portr. Sarmiento. Series A.	—	—	—

Ley de 30 de Junio de 1923

#S2184 and S2188 printer: Peuser, Buenos Aires.

S2184 50 Centavos
1.9.1923. Black on brown unpt. Like #S2185. Back green. Series A.

Good	Fine	XF
10.00	20.00	75.00

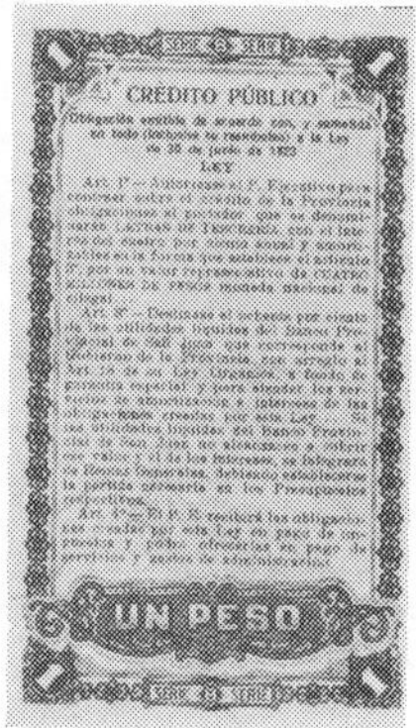

	Good	Fine	XF
S2185 1 Peso 1.9.1923. Black on green unpt. Arms at ctr. Back blue. Series B.	10.00	20.00	75.00
S2187 5 Pesos 1.9.1923. Black on lt. brown unpt. Like #S2185. Back lt. violet. Series D.	20.00	50.00	—
S2188 10 Pesos 1.9.1923. Black on ochre unpt. Like #S2185. Back black and violet. Series E.	20.00	50.00	—

Ley de 20 de Diciembre 1893; Obligaciones del Monte de Piedad 1894-95 Issue

Obligations of the National Pawn Shop

#S2191-S2194 printer: CSABB.

S2191 5 Centavos
30.1.1894. Black on lt. brown unpt. Arms at l. Sign. at ctr. r. Back brown. Series 4.

Good	Fine	XF
10.00	25.00	70.00

	Good	Fine	XF
S2192 5 Centavos 30.9.1895. Similar to #S191 but sign. at l. ctr., and different text on back. Series 4.	10.00	20.00	65.00
S2193 10 Centavos 30.9.1895. Black on green unpt. Arms at l. Back green. Series 3.	12.00	30.00	75.00

S2194 20 Centavos
30.9.1895. Black on brown unpt. Arms at lower r. Back brown. Series 2.

Good	Fine	XF
12.00	30.00	75.00

Province of Santa Fé

1890 Billetes de Tesoreria Issue

Treasury Bills

#S2214-S2217 printer: CSABB.

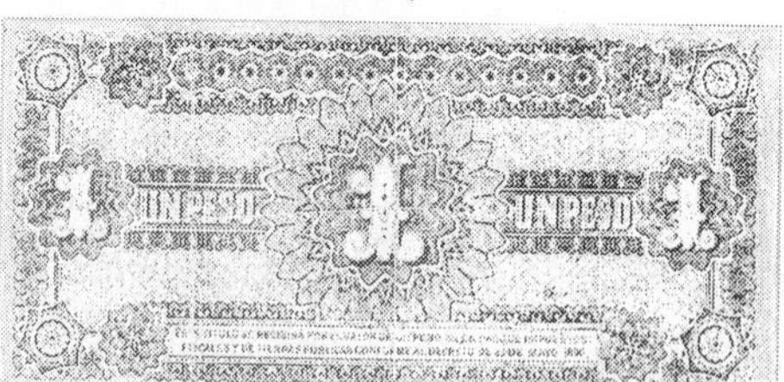

S2214 1 Peso
23.5.1890. Black on orange unpt. Provincial arms at lower l. Series E.

Good	Fine	XF
—	—	—

		GOOD	FINE	XF
S2215	2 PESOS 23.5.1890. Provincial arms at upper r. Farmer w/dog at ctr. on back. Series F.	—	—	—

		GOOD	FINE	XF
S2216	5 PESOS 23.5.1890. Black on green unpt. Provincial arms at upper l. Back green; deer at ctr. Series A.	30.00	100.00	—
S2217	10 PESOS 23.5.1890. Black on blue unpt. Provincial arms at l. Back blue; eagle at ctr. Series B.	30.00	100.00	—

PROVINCE OF SANTIAGO DEL ESTERO

LEY 17.4.1891 TITULO DE CREDITO ISSUE

		GOOD	FINE	XF
S2221	1 PESO *L.1891.* Black on brown unpt. Arms at lower l. Back blue. Printer: CSABB.	75.00	225.00	—

PROVINCE OF TUCUMÁN

LEY 30.3.1900 LETRAS DE TESORERIA ISSUE

TREASURY LETTERS OF CREDIT

#S2235 and S2236 printer: CSABB.

		GOOD	FINE	XF
S2235	1 PESO ND. Black on brown unpt. Portr. B. de Monteagudo at l., arms above. Back brown; field scene at ctr. Series A.	12.00	35.00	90.00

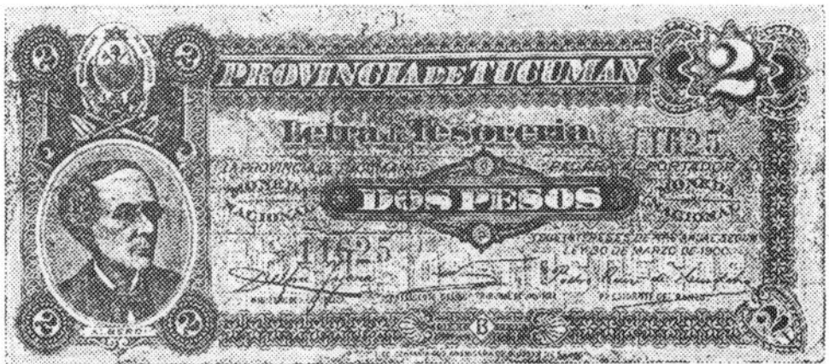

		GOOD	FINE	XF
S2236	2 PESOS *L.1900.* Black on brown unpt. Portr. Alberdi at l. Back brown; tunnels under river at ctr.	—	—	—

LEY DE 12 DE JULIO DE 1915 TITULOS DE DEUDA PÚBLICA, BONOS DE FOMENTO ISSUE

CERTIFICATES OF PUBLIC DEBT, DEVELOPMENT BONDS

#S2245 and S2246 vertical format. Printer: CSABB.

		GOOD	FINE	XF
S2245	1 PESO 1.11.1915. Black on green unpt. Arms at upper ctr. Back brown; building at top. Series A; D; F; H.	12.00	30.00	80.00
S2246	2 PESOS 1.11.1915.	—	—	—

LEY DEL 1920

#S2247 and S2248 rectangular ovpt: *Emision de Canje Año 1920* on back. Printer: CSABB.

		GOOD	FINE	XF
S2247	1 PESO 8.4.1920. Series F.	—	—	—

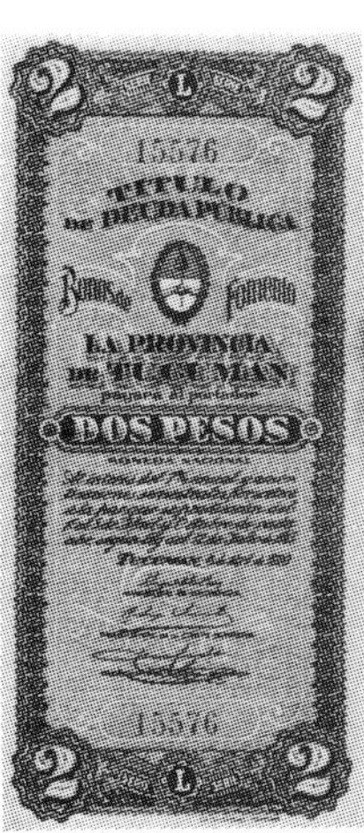

		GOOD	FINE	XF
S2248	2 PESOS 8.4.1920. Similar to #S2246.	12.00	30.00	80.00
S2249	2 PESOS 1923 (- old date 1920). Like #S2248 but w/1923 date on face and ovpt. on back.	25.00	50.00	150.00

PROVINCIAL BONOS, 1985-2002

PROVINCE OF BUENOS AIRES

LEY NO. 12.727; ND ISSUE

#S2310-S2314 Riogo Rocha at r. Text, building on back. Printer: Ciccone.

		VG	VF	UNC
S2310	1 PESO ND.	1.00	2.00	5.00
S2311	2 PESOS ND.	1.00	4.00	10.00
S2312	5 PESOS ND.	2.00	6.00	15.00

		VG	VF	UNC
S2313	10 PESOS ND.	3.00	8.00	20.00
S2314	20 PESOS ND.	5.00	10.00	30.00

PROVINCE OF CATAMARCA

LEY 4748 (EXP. DATE 30.11.1998) - TITULO PUBLICO AL PORTADOR; 1993 ND ISSUE

#S2351-S2353 arms at upper r. Printer: Ciccone.

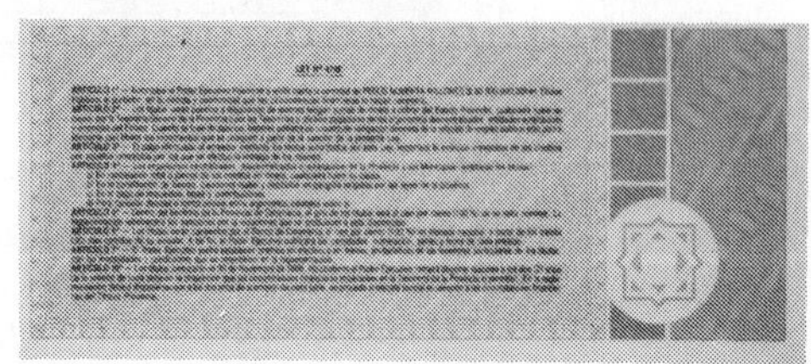

		VG	VF	UNC
S2351	1 PESO ND (1993). Dk. blue-gray on lt. blue and m/c unpt. Mountain highway at ctr. r. Dk. blue-gray text on back. Serie A.	.30	.60	3.00

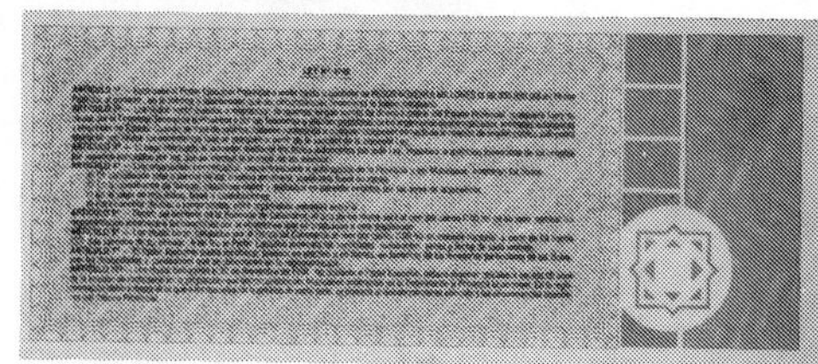

		VG	VF	UNC
S2352	5 PESOS ND (1993). Green on lt. blue and m/c unpt. Barn at ctr. r. Green text on back. Serie A.	1.00	2.00	10.00

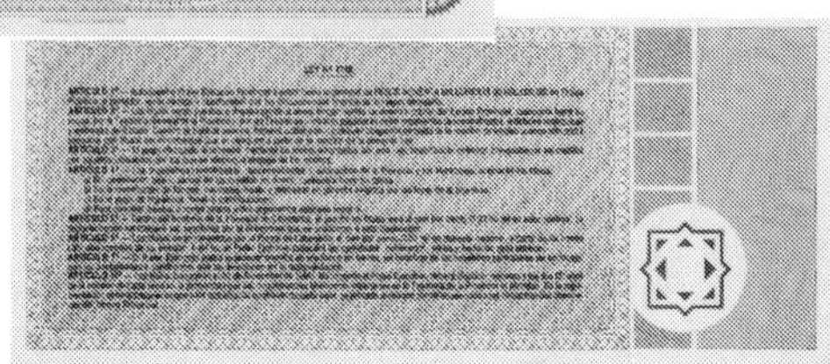

		VG	VF	UNC
S2353	10 PESOS ND (1993). Dk. brown on pink and m/c unpt. Cathedral at ctr. r. Dk. brown text on back. Serie A.	2.00	4.00	20.00

2002 ND ISSUE

#S2354-S2356 printer: Casa de Moneda.

		VG	VF	UNC
S2354	1 PESO ND (2001). Blue and violet. Violet and ochre on back. Mountain highway at l. ctr. Serie B.	1.00	2.00	5.00
S2355	5 PESOS ND (2001). Series C.	2.00	6.00	15.00
S2356	10 PESOS ND (2001). Serie C.	4.00	10.00	25.00

PROVINCE OF CORDOBA

LEY 8472 (EXP. DATE 1.8.97); ND ISSUE

#S2375-S2378 Provincial arms at upper left, interest coupons at right. Text on back.

		VG	VF	UNC
S2375	5 PESOS 1.8.1995. Black on lt. green unpt. Serie A.	1.00	5.00	12.00
S2376	10 PESOS 1.8.1995. Serie A.	4.00	10.00	25.00
S2377	20 PESOS 1.8.1995.	4.00	20.00	45.00
S2378	50 PESOS 1.8.1995.	8.00	40.00	100.00

LEY 8472 (EXP. DATE 1.1.98); ND ISSUE

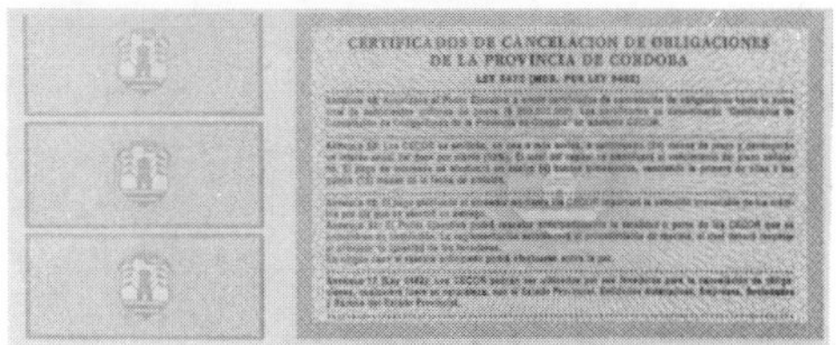

		VG	VF	UNC
S2379	5 PESOS 1.1.1996. Serie B.	1.00	3.00	10.00
S2380	10 PESOS 1.1.1998. Serie B.	2.00	10.00	25.00
S2381	20 PESOS 1.1.1996. Serie B.	4.00	20.00	45.00

LEY 8472 (EXP. DATE 1.8.97); ND ISSUE

#S2375-S2378 Provincial arms at upper left, interest coupons at right. Text on back.

		VG	VF	UNC
S2382	5 PESOS ND (2002). Cabildo Hictorico de Cordoba at r. Text on back.	1.00	5.00	15.00

PROVINCE OF CORRIENTES

LEY NO. 1/99 (EXP. DATE 17.11.2000); ND ISSUE

#S2390-S2392 national coat of arms at r., provincial map at ctr. Text on back. Printer: Casa de Moneda.

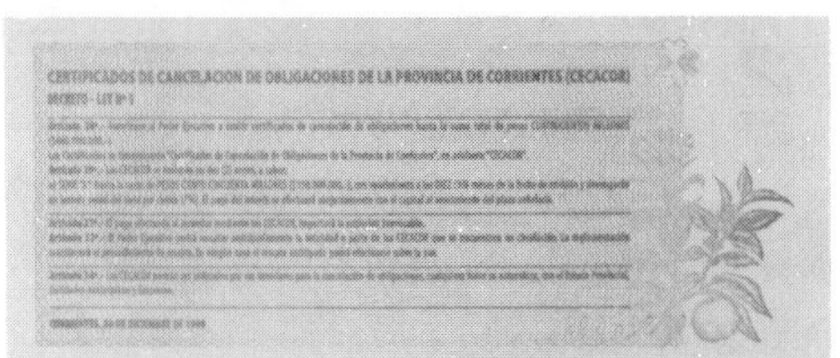

		VG	VF	UNC
S2390	2 PESOS 17.1.2000. Blue and red on m/c unpt. Serie A.	1.00	2.00	5.00
S2391	5 PESOS 17.1.2000. Serie A.	2.00	4.00	12.00
S2392	10 PESOS 17.1.2000. Purple and green on m/c unpt. Serie A.	2.00	4.00	12.00

LEY NO. 1/99 (EXP. DATE 31.1.2002); ND ISSUE

#S2393-S2395 Provincial coat of arms at r., map at ctr. Text on back. Printer: Casa de Moneda.

		VG	VF	UNC
S2393	2 PESOS 1.8.2000.	1.00	2.00	5.00
S2394	5 PESOS 1.8.2000. Gray and brown on m/c unpt. Serie B.	2.00	4.00	10.00
S2395	10 PESOS 31.1.2002.	3.00	6.00	15.00

A word on pricing

When a note is marked RARE in the price columns, this note seldom appears on the market, or few are known in private hands. When dashes are in the price column, means that the note has not traded on the open market recently and a definitive value could not accurately be determined. Rare does not always mean expensive. A dashed price does not mean expensive or rare.

PROVINCE OF FORMOSA

LEY 9/95; ND ISSUE.

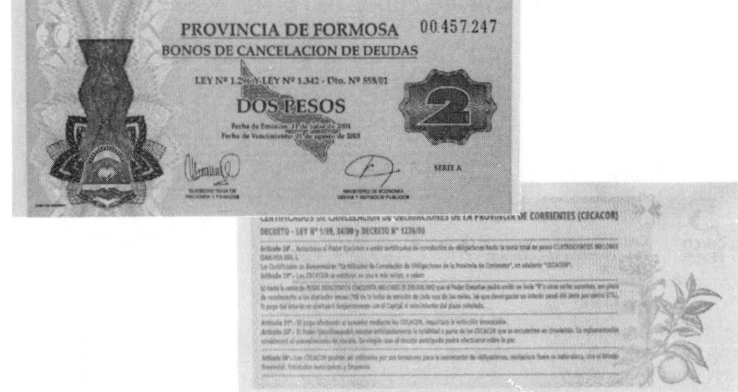

		VG	VF	UNC
S2399	2 PESOS ND.	1.00	2.00	5.00
S2399A	5 PESOS ND.	1.00	4.00	10.00

PROVINCE OF JUJUY
TITULO PUBLICO AL PORTADOR ISSUES

LEY NO. 4248 (EXP. DATE 31.12.1988)

#S2401-S2405 military formation at ctr. Printer: Ciccone.

		VG	VF	UNC
S2401	10 CENTAVOS ND (1986). Brown on orange-brown and m/c unpt. Lt. red text on back.	.05	.10	.50
S2402	50 CENTAVOS ND (1986). Brown on blue and m/c unpt. Violet text on back.	.10	.20	.75
S2403	1 AUSTRAL ND (1986). Blue on aqua and m/c unpt. Lilac text on back.	.10	.25	1.00
S2404	5 AUSTRALES ND (1986). Brown on pink and m/c unpt. Tan text on back.	.15	.35	1.50
S2405	10 AUSTRALES ND (1986). Deep blue on lt. blue and m/c unpt. Aqua text on back.	.20	.50	2.25
S2406	50 AUSTRALES ND. Green. Military formation at l., arms in unpt. at ctr. r. Printer: CdM.	.30	.80	4.00

LEY NO. 4434/89 (EXP. DATE 31.12.1989); ND ISSUE

		VG	VF	UNC
S2407	100 AUSTRALES ND. Pink on lt. blue and m/c unpt. Like #S2401-5. Printer: Ciccone.	.40	1.00	5.00

LEY NO. 1422 (EXP. DATE 1.10.1990); ND ISSUE

#S2408-S2412 like #S2406.

		VG	VF	UNC
S2408	50 AUSTRALES ND. Green. Like #S2406 except for law date.	.25	.75	3.50

LEY NO. 4439 (EXP. DATE 31.12.1991); ND ISSUE

		VG	VF	UNC
S2409	500 AUSTRALES ND. Black text on pink, tan and m/c unpt.	.10	.25	1.25
S2410	1000 AUSTRALES ND. Lilac.	.20	.50	2.50

LEY NO. 4488 (EXP. DATE 31.12.1991); ND ISSUE

		VG	VF	UNC
S2411	1000 AUSTRALES ND. Lilac. Like #S2410.	.20	.50	2.00

LEY NO. 4499 (EXP. DATE 31.12.1990); ND ISSUE

		VG	VF	UNC
S2412	5000 AUSTRALES ND. Lt. blue.	.50	1.25	6.50

LEY NO. 4516/90 (EXP. DATE 31.12.1991); ND ISSUE

		VG	VF	UNC
S2413	10,000 AUSTRALES ND.	1.00	2.50	10.00

LEY NO. 4824 (EXP. DATE 1.4.2007); ND ISSUE

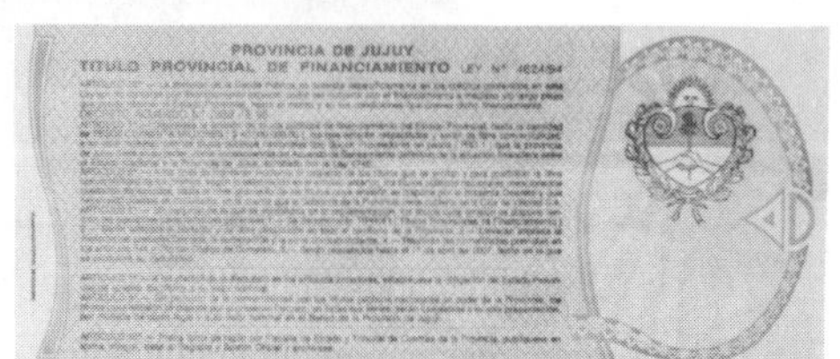

		VG	VF	UNC
S2414	1 PESO ND. Municipal bldg. at r. Text on back. Printer: Ciccone.	1.00	2.00	4.00

PROVINCE OF LA RIOJA

LEY NO. 4534 - BONO CANCELACION DE DEUDA; 1986 ND ISSUE

#S2501-S2507 portr. of J. Facundo Quiroga at r. Provincial arms at ctr. Printer: CdM-A.

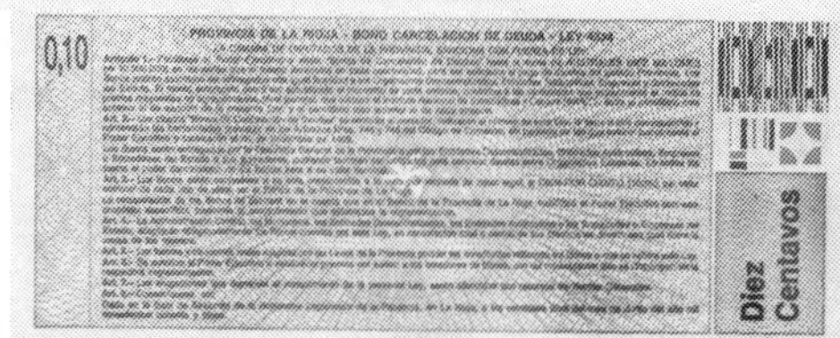

		VG	VF	UNC
S2501	10 CENTAVOS ND (1986). Orange w/dk. brown text on m/c unpt.	.05	.10	.50
S2502	50 CENTAVOS ND (1986). Purple.	.10	.20	.75
S2503	1 AUSTRAL (1986). ND. Green.			
	a. *Un Austral* written out above denomination at lower ctr.	.10	.30	1.25
	b. W/o *Un Austral.*	.10	.25	1.00
S2504	5 AUSTRALES ND (1986). Brown.	.15	.35	1.50
S2505	10 AUSTRALES ND (1986). Black text on blue and m/c unpt. Dk. blue text on back.	.20	.50	2.25
S2506	50 AUSTRALES ND. Purple.	.25	.75	3.50
S2507	100 AUSTRALES ND. Red and black on m/c unpt.	.25	1.00	5.00

PROVINCE OF MENDOZA

CERTIFICADOS DE CANCELACION DE OBLIGACIONES LEY 8472 (MODIFIED BY LAW 8482)

1995 ISSUE

		GOOD	FINE	XF
S2521	5 PESOS 1.8.1995. Arms at upper l.	—	—	—

1996 ISSUE

		GOOD	FINE	XF
S2531	5 PESOS 1.1.1996. Arms at ctr.	—	—	—

PROVINCE OF RIO NEGRO

DECRETO LEY 9.95

#S2550-S2552 Arms at l. Text on back. Printer: CdM-A.

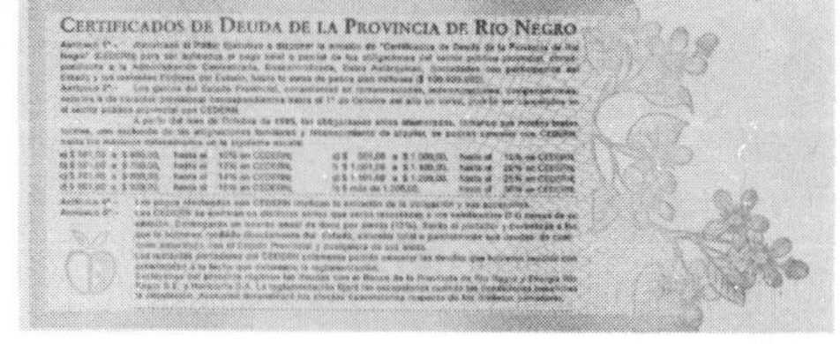

		VG	VF	UNC
S2550	1 PESO ND.	1.00	2.00	5.00
S2551	2 PESOS ND.	1.00	3.00	8.00
S2552	5 PESOS ND.	2.00	4.00	12.00

PROVINCE OF SALTA

LEY NO. 6228 - BONO DE CANCELACION DE DEUDA; 1985 ND ISSUE

#S2601-S2605 provincial arms at upper l. Redeemable 31.12.1987. Printer: CdM-A.

		VG	VF	UNC
S2601	50 PESOS ARGENTINOS ND (1985). (Not issued).	.15	.50	2.00

#S2602-S2605 black text.

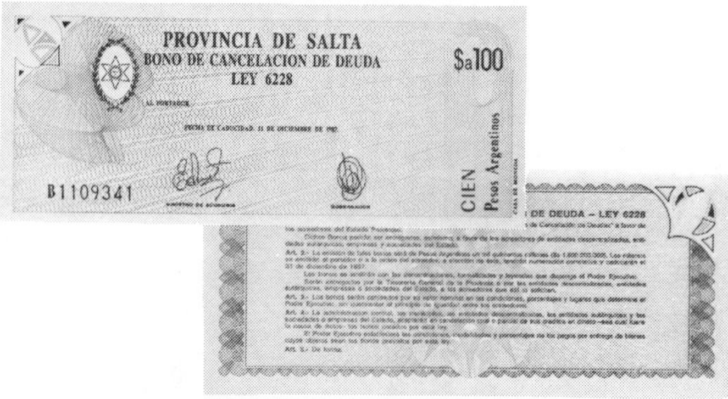

		VG	VF	UNC
S2602	100 PESOS ARGENTINOS ND (1985). Green, blue and m/c.	.20	.50	2.50
S2603	500 PESOS ARGENTINOS ND (1985). Ochre, orange and m/c.	.25	.75	3.50
S2604	1000 PESOS ARGENTINOS ND (1985). Pink, lt. blue and m/c.			
	a. Bottom line of text on back ends w/o *DECRETO...*	.25	1.00	5.00
	b. Bottom line ends: *Decreto 1059 del 30 de Mayo de 1985.*	.50	1.25	6.00
S2605	5000 PESOS ARGENTINOS ND (1985). Blue, lt. blue and m/c.			
	a. As #S2604a.	.50	1.50	7.00
	b. As #S2604b.	.50	1.75	8.50

1986 ND PROVISIONAL ISSUE

Currency Reform

1 Austral = 1,000 Pesos Argentinos

#S2606-S2608 brownish black ovpt. new denomination at r. on similar notes like #S2603-S2605 but bottom line of text on back ends w/*Decreto 1605 del 15 de Agosto de 1985.*

		VG	VF	UNC
S2606	50 CENTAVOS ON 500 PESOS ARGENTINOS ND (1986). Ochre, orange and m/c. Ovpt. on #S2603.	.10	.20	.75

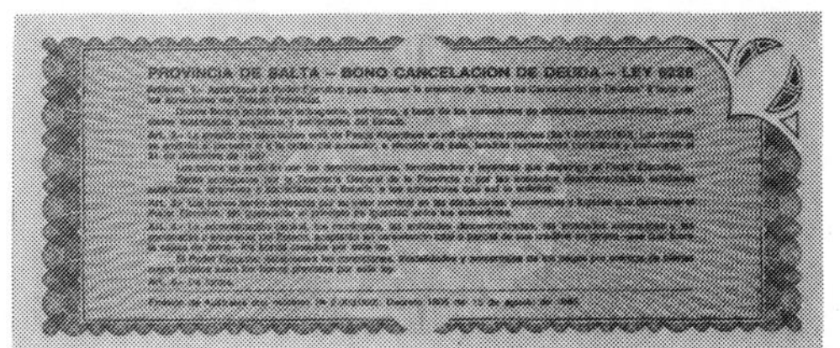

		VG	VF	UNC
S2607	**1 AUSTRAL ON 1000 PESOS ARGENTINOS** ND (1986). Pink, lt. blue and m/c. Ovpt. on #S2604.	.10	.25	1.00
S2608	**5 AUSTRALES ON 5000 PESOS ARGENTINOS** ND (1986). Blue, lt. blue and m/c. Ovpt. on #S2605.	.15	.25	1.50

LEY 6628; 1986 ND ISSUE

#S2611-S2613 provincial arms at upper l. Printer: CdM-A.

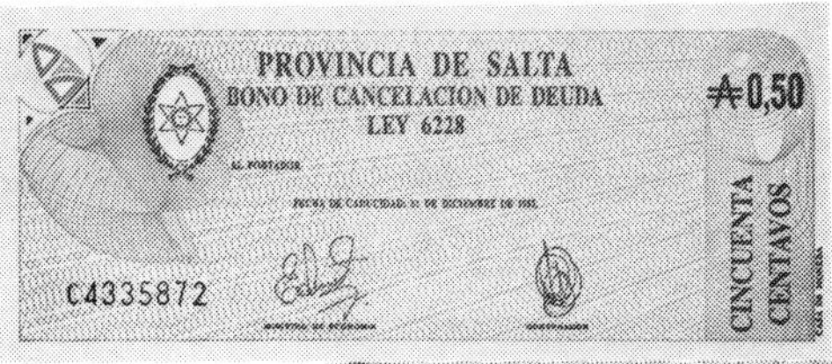

		VG	VF	UNC
S2611	**50 CENTAVOS** ND (1986). Dk. brown on m/c unpt. Bottom line of text on back ends: *Decreto 2248 del 18 de Noviembre de 1985.*	.05	.10	.25

		VG	VF	UNC
S2612	**1 AUSTRAL** ND (1986). Like #S2611.			
	a. Bottom line of text on back ends: *Decreto 2248 del 16 de Noviembre de 1985.*	.05	.10	.35
	b. Bottom line ends: *Decreto 1984/86.*	.05	.10	.25
	c. Bottom line ends: *Decreto 245/87.*	.05	.10	.25
	d. Bottom line ends: *Decreto 949/87.*	.05	.10	.25
	e. Bottom line ends: *Decreto 1520/87.*	.05	.10	.25
S2613	**5 AUSTRALES** ND (1986). Like #S2611.			
	a. Bottom line of text on back ends: *Decreto 2248 del 16 de Noviembre de 1985.*	.10	.20	.50
	b. Bottom line on back ends: *Decreto 1984/86.*	.05	.15	.40
	c. Bottom line ends: *Decreto 2291/86.*	.05	.15	.40
	d. Bottom line ends: *Decreto 245/87.*	.05	.15	.40
	e. Bottom line ends: *Decreto 949/87.*	.05	.15	.40
	f. Bottom line ends: *Decreto 1520/87.*	.05	.15	.40
	g. Bottom line ends: *Decreto 2292/87.*	.05	.15	.40

LEYES NO. 6228-6495 (REDEEMABLE 31.10.1991)

#S2621-S2627 provincial arms at upper l. Printer: CdM-A.

NOTE: Each denomination has a different geometric design at r.

		VG	VF	UNC
S2621	**10 AUSTRALES** ND. Black on violet, pale olive-green and m/c unpt.			
	a. Bottom line of text on back ends: *Decreto 359.88.*	.05	.10	.35
	b. Bottom line ends: *Decreto 1556/88 del 01/09/88.*	.05	.10	.35
S2622	**50 AUSTRALES** ND. Red and black on lilac and m/c unpt. Bottom line of text on back ends: *Decreto 1274/88.*	.05	.15	.50
S2623	**100 AUSTRALES** ND. Dk. olive-green on pale green and m/c unpt.			
	a. Bottom line of text on back ends: *Decreto 1895/88 del 05/10/88.*	.10	.20	.75
	b. Bottom line ends: *Decreto 28/89.*	.10	.20	.75
	c. Bottom line ends: *Decreto 887/89 del 31/05/89.*	.10	.20	.75
	d. Bottom line ends: *Decreto 1161/89.*	.10	.20	.75
S2624	**500 AUSTRALES** ND. Brown, olive-gray and black on lilac and m/c unpt.			
	a. Bottom line of text on back ends: *Decreto 1161/89.*	.10	.25	1.00
	b. Bottom line ends: *Decreto 1420 del 31 de Julio de 1989.*	.10	.25	1.00
S2625	**1000 AUSTRALES** ND. Blue-gray and black on lt. blue and m/c unpt.			
	a. Bottom line of text on back ends: *Decreto 1420 del 31 de Julio de 1989.*	.20	.50	2.00
	b. Bottom line ends: *Decreto 1624 del 26 de Septiembre de 1989.*	.20	.50	2.00
	c. Bottom line ends: *Decreto 2075 del 12 de Diciembre de 1989.*	.20	.50	2.00
S2626	**5000 AUSTRALES** ND. Brownish black and violet on m/c unpt.			
	a. Bottom line of text on back ends: *Decreto 35 del 8 de Enero de 1990.*	.50	1.25	6.50
	b. Bottom line ends: *Decreto 277 del 23 de Febrero de 1990.*	.50	1.25	6.50

#S2627 and S2628 replacement notes: Serial # prefix *L99* and *M99*.

		VG	VF	UNC
S2627	**10,000 AUSTRALES** ND. Brownish-black on m/c unpt.			
	a. Bottom line of text on back ends: *Decreto 277 del 23 de Febrero de 1990.*	1.00	2.50	12.50
	b. Bottom line ends: *Decreto 472 del 23 de Marzo de 1990.*	1.00	2.50	12.50
	c. Bottom line ends: *Decreto 858 del 18 Mayo de 1990.*	1.00	2.50	12.50
	d. Bottom line ends: *Decreto 2620/90.*	1.00	2.50	12.50
S2628	**50,000 AUSTRALES** ND (1990-91). Brownish black on m/c unpt.			
	a. Bottom line of text on back ends: *Decreto 1710/90.*	3.50	12.50	50.00
	b. Bottom line ends: *Decreto 2620/90.*	3.50	12.50	50.00
	c. Bottom line ends: *Decreto 628/91.*	3.50	12.50	50.00

LEYES NO. 6228-6623; 1991 ND ISSUE

#S2629 and S2630 replacement notes serial # prefix *L99* and *M99*.

NOTE: #S2629-S2630a redeemable 31.10.1991.

NOTE: #S2630b redeemable 31.03.1992.

		GOOD	FINE	XF
S2629	**10,000 AUSTRALES** ND (1991). Brownish black on m/c unpt. Bottom line of text on back ends: *Decreto 702/91.*	1.00	2.50	12.50

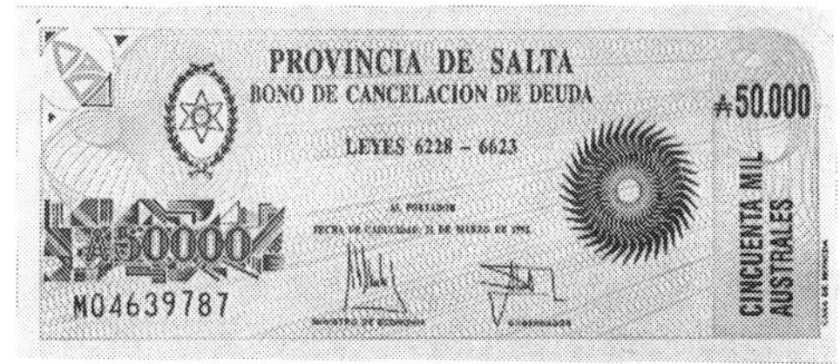

		VG	VF	UNC
S2630	**50,000 AUSTRALES** ND (1991). Brownish black on m/c unpt.			
	a. Bottom line of text on back ends: *Decreto 702/91.*	3.50	12.50	50.00
	b. Bottom line ends: *Decreto 1039/91 y 1133/91.*	3.50	12.50	50.00

PROVINCE OF SAN JUAN

DECRETO ACUERDO NO 0059/95 (EXP. DATE 31.7.1995)

#S2651-S2654 arms at l. Wmk. paper. Printer: Ciccone Calcografica.

		VG	VF	UNC
S2651	**1 PESO** ND (1995). Deep blue-violet and red on m/c unpt.	.25	1.25	3.50

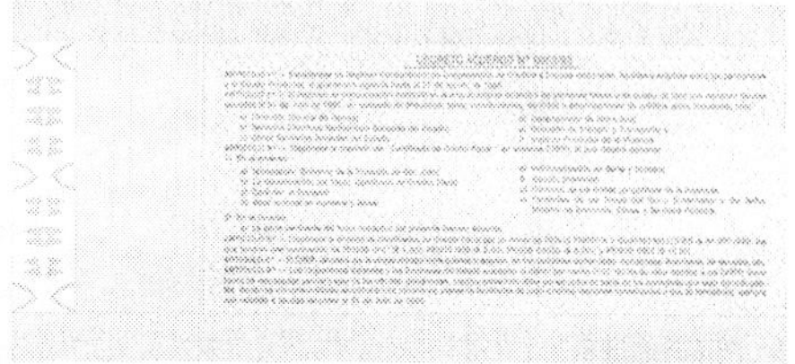

		VG	VF	UNC
S2652	**2 PESOS** ND (1995). Blue and red on m/c unpt.	.50	3.00	6.00

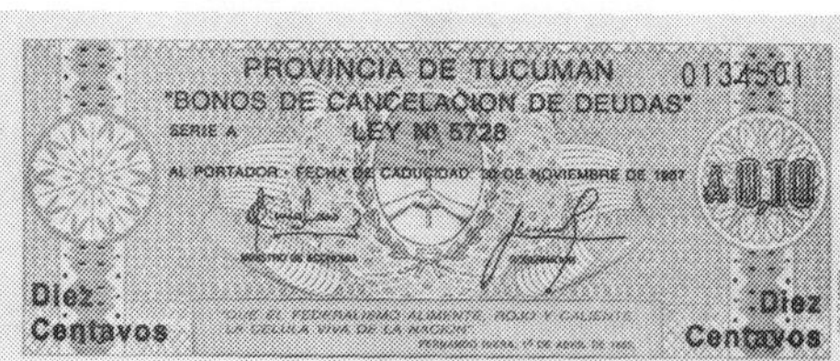

		VG	VF	UNC
S2653	**5 PESOS** ND (1995). Dk. green and deep red on m/c unpt.	1.00	6.00	12.50

		VG	VF	UNC
S2654	**10 PESOS** ND (1995). Brown-violet and deep blue-green on m/c unpt.	2.00	12.00	25.00

PROVINCE OF TUCUMÁN

BONO DE CANCELACION DE DEUDAS
LEY NO. 5728 (EXP. DATE30.11.1987; 1985 ISSUE

#S2701-S2706 arms at ctr. in unpt. 3-line legend at bottom ctr. Printer: CdM.

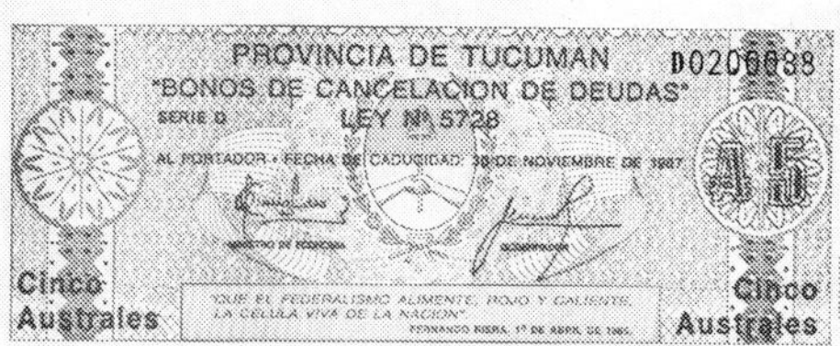

		VG	VF	UNC
S2701	**10 CENTAVOS** 1.4.1985. Dk. brown text on pink, green and m/c unpt. Red-brown text on back.			
	a. Bottom line of text on back w/o *Decreto.*	.05	.15	.50
	b. Bottom line of text on back w/*Decreto* and number.	.05	.15	.50
S2702	**50 CENTAVOS** 1.4.1985. Dk. brown on lilac and m/c unpt. Like #S2701. Violet text on back.	.10	.20	.75
S2703	**1 AUSTRAL** 1.4.1985. Dk. brown text on lilac and m/c unpt. Like #S2701.	.10	.25	1.00

		VG	VF	UNC
S2704	**5 AUSTRALES** 1.4.1985. Like #S2703.			
	a. Bottom line of text on back w/o *Decreto.*	.10	.25	1.50
	b. Bottom line of text on back w/*Decreto* and number.	.10	.25	1.25
S2705	**10 AUSTRALES** 1.4.1985. Lt. blue, pink and m/c unpt. Like #S2701.			
	a. Bottom line of text on back w/o *Decreto.*	.15	.50	2.25
	b. Bottom line of text on back w/*Decreto* and number.	.15	.50	1.75

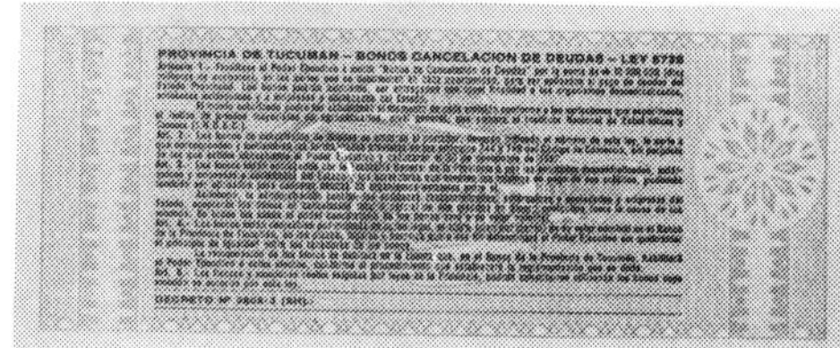

		VG	VF	UNC
S2706	**50 AUSTRALES** 1.4.1985. Like #S2704.	.15	.50	2.50

LEY NO. 5728 (EXP. DATE 30.11.1991); ND ISSUE

#S2711-S2714 similar to #S2701-S2706. Printer: CdM.

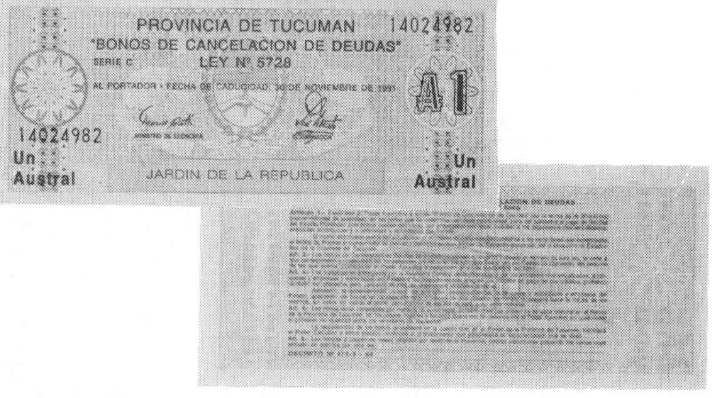

		VG	VF	UNC
S2711	**1 AUSTRAL** ND. Green.			
	a. No text at bcttom ctr.	.05	.10	.35
	b. *JARDIN DE LA REPÚBLICA* at bottom ctr.	.05	.10	.25
S2712	**5 AUSTRALES** ND. Pink.			
	a. No text at bottom ctr.	.05	.15	.50
	b. *JARDIN DE LA REPÚBLICA* at bottom ctr.	.05	.15	.50
S2713	**10 AUSTRALES** ND. Lt. blue.			
	a. No text at bottom ctr.	.10	.20	.50
	b. *JARDIN DE LA REPÚBLICA* at bottom ctr.	.10	.20	.50
S2714	**50 AUSTRALES** ND. Black text on lilac and tan unpt. *JARDIN DE LA REPÚBLICA* at bottom ctr.	.10	.20	.75

#S2715-S2719 house of Tucumán at ctr., arms at r.

		VG	VF	UNC
S2715	**100 AUSTRALES** ND. Red-violet, black and m/c.	.10	.25	1.00

	VG	VF	UNC
S2716 500 AUSTRALES ND. Lt. blue. Series H.	.20	.50	2.00

	VG	VF	UNC
S2717 5000 AUSTRALES ND. Black on lt. green and m/c unpt. Series I.	.50	1.50	6.50

	VG	VF	UNC
S2718 10,000 AUSTRALES ND. Black on lt. reddish brown and m/c unpt. Series J.	1.00	2.50	12.50

	VG	VF	UNC
S2719 50,000 AUSTRALES ND (1990). Black text on light red-violet and m/c unpt. Back dk. blue-green text on lt. blue and m/c unpt. Printer: CdM. Wmk: Multiple oval arms.	1.00	2.50	12.50

LEY NO. 5728 (EXP. DATE 30.11.1995); ND ISSUE

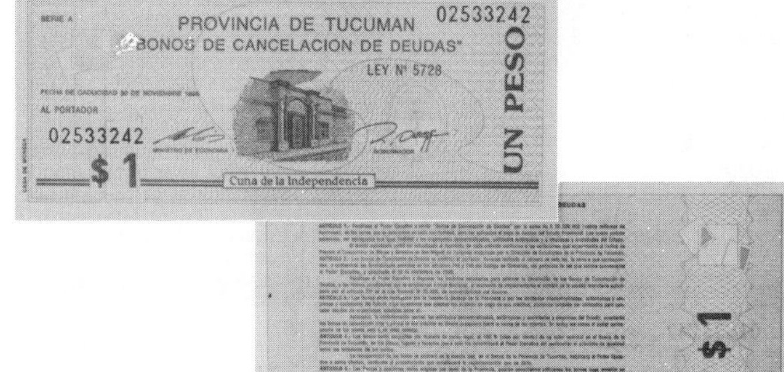

	VG	VF	UNC
S2720 1 PESO ND. House of Tucuman at ctr. Text on back. Printer: Casa de Moneda.	1.00	4.00	10.00

LEY NO. 5728 (EXP. DATE 31.12.2003); ND ISSUE

#S2721-S2773 House of Tucuman at r. Text on back. Printer: Ciccone.

	VG	VF	UNC
S2721 2 PESOS ND.	1.00	2.00	5.00
S2722 5 PESOS ND.	1.00	4.00	10.00
S2753 10 PESOS	4.00	10.00	20.00

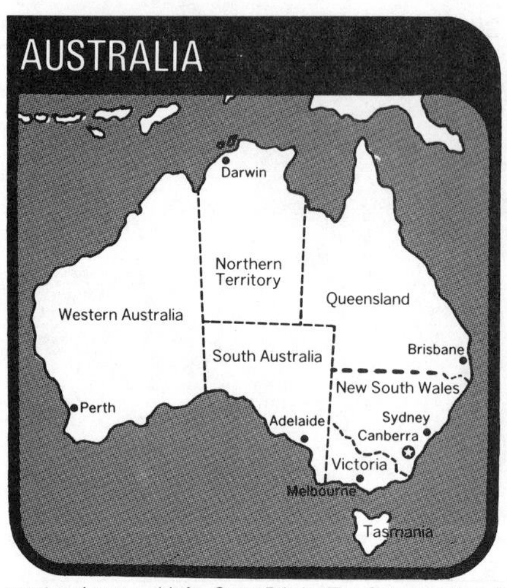

The Commonwealth of Australia, the smallest continent and largest island in the world, is located south of Indonesia between the Indian and Pacific oceans. It has an area of 2,967,909 sq. mi. (7,686,849 sq. km.) and a population of 18.84 million. Capital: Canberra. Due to its early and sustained isolation, Australia is the habitat of such curious and unique fauna as the kangaroo, koala, platypus, wombat and barking lizard. The continent possesses extensive mineral deposits, the most important of which are gold, coal, silver, nickel, uranium, lead and zinc. Livestock raising, mining and manufacturing are the principal industries. Chief exports are wool, meat, wheat, iron ore, coal and nonferrous metals.

The first caucasians to see Australia probably were Portuguese and Spanish navigators of the late 16th century. In 1770, Captain James Cook explored the east coast and annexed it for Great Britain. The Colony of New South Wales was founded by Captain Arthur Phillip on Jan. 26, 1788, a date now celebrated as Australia Day. Dates of creation of six colonies that now comprise the states of the Australian Commonwealth are: New South Wales, 1823; Tasmania, 1825; Western Australia, 1838; South Australia, 1842; Victoria, 1851; Queensland, 1859. A constitution providing for federation of the colonies was approved by the British Parliament in 1900; the Commonwealth of Australia came into being in 1901. Australia passed the Statute of Westminster Adoption Act on Oct. 9, 1942, which officially established Australia's complete autonomy in external and internal affairs, thereby formalizing a situation that had existed for years.

During WWII Australia was the primary supply and staging area for Allied forces in the South Pacific Theatre.

Australia is a member of the Commonwealth of Nations. Elizabeth II is Head of State as Queen of Australia.

RULERS:

British

MONETARY SYSTEM:

1 Shilling = 12 Pence
1 Pound = 20 Shillings = 2 Dollars
1 Pound = 20 Shillings; to 1966
1 Dollar = 100 Cents, 1966-

PRIVATE BANKS

Although prolific in number of issues, few notes of the early banks have survived or have been accurately recorded except for the very late issues ca. 1910 bearing the superscribed ovpt: *AUSTRALIAN NOTE.* The pioneer work in this field is *Australian Bank Notes 1817-1963* by G.W. Tomlinson published in 1963. The latest reference work is *Banks of Issue in Australia* by Michael P. Vort-Ronald published in 1982. The following listing of banks of issue is taken from the latter reference.

BANKS OF ISSUE	HEAD OFFICE	DATES
Australian and European Bank Limited	Melbourne	1874-1879
Australian Banking Company Limited	Sydney	1886-1891
Australian Bank of Commerce Limited	Sydney	1910-1931
Australian Joint Stock Bank Limited	Sydney	1853-1910
Bank of Adelaide	Adelaide ***	1865-1980
Bank of Australasia ***	London	1835-1951
Bank of Australia	Sydney	1826-1843
Bank of Newcastle	Newcastle	1828-1829
Bank of New South Wales ***	Sydney	1817-1982
Bank of New Zealand	Wellington	1861-
Bank of North Queensland Limited	Brisbane	1888-1917
Bank of Parramatta **	Parramatta	1830's
Bank of Queensland Limited	London	1863-1866
Bank of South Australia Limited	London	1836-1892
Bank of Tasmania	Launceston	1853-1885
Bank of Van Diemen's Land Limited	Hobart	1823-1891
Bank of Victoria Limited ***	Melbourne	1853-1927
Bank of Western Australia	Perth	1837-1841
Bathurst Bank	Bathurst	1835-1840
City Bank of Sydney ***	Sydney	1863-1918
City of Melbourne Bank Limited	Melbourne	1873-1895
Colonial Bank	Hobart	1840-1843
Colonial Bank of Australasia Limited	Melbourne	1856-1918
Commercial Bank of Australia Limited ***	Melbourne	1866-1982
Commercial Bank of South Australia	Adelaide	1878-1886
Commercial Bank of Tasmania Limited ***	Hobart	1829-1921
Commercial Banking Company of Sydney Limited ***	Sydney	1834-1982
Cornwall Bank	Launceston	1828-1835
Derwent Bank	Hobart	1827-1849
English, Scottish & Australian (Chartered) Bank Limited	London	1852-1970
Excelsior Bank *	Sydney	1880-1893
Federal Bank of Australia Limited	Melbourne	1881-1893
London Bank of Australia Limited ***	London	1852-1921
Mercantile Bank of Australia	Melbourne	1885-1892
Mercantile Bank of Sydney	Sydney	1869-1892
Metropolitan Bank Limited	Melbourne	1888-1891
National Bank of Australasia Limited ***	Melbourne	1858-1982
National Bank of Tasmania Limited	Launceston	1885-1918
New South Wales Government	Sydney	1893
Oriental Bank Corporation	London	1851-1884
Port Phillip Bank	Melbourne	1839-1843
Producers' Bank, Sydney **	Sydney	1851-1861?
Provincial and Suburban Bank Limited	Melbourne	1872-1879
Queensland Government	Brisbane	1866-1869
Queensland Government ***	Brisbane	1893-1910
Queensland National Bank Limited	Brisbane	1872-1948
Royal Bank of Australia (Boyd's)	London	1840-1850
Royal Bank of Australia Limited ***	Melbourne	1888-1927
Royal Bank of Queensland Limited	Brisbane	1885-1917
Sydney & County Bank Limited	Sydney	1881-1882
Sydney Bank **	Sydney	1826
Sydney Banking Company	Sydney	1839-1843
Sydney Deposit Bank	Sydney	1885-1892
Tamar Bank	Launceston	1834-1838
Tasmanian Bank	Hobart	1826-1829
Town and Country Bank	Adelaide	1881-1886
Union Bank of Australia Limited ***	London	1837-1951
Waterloo Company	Sydney	1822-1834
Western Australian Bank ***	Perth	1841-1927

Many of the above banks issued notes at branch offices and some were located in other states.

* A bank which had not become a bank of issue, but whose note forms have been observed.

** Not regarded as a legitimate or genuine bank, or bank of issue.

*** Various notes issued by fifteen banks and the Queensland Government (marked "****" in the listing of private banks) were used by the Australian Government from 1910-1914. These superscribed notes were vertically ovpt: *AUSTRALIAN NOTE* and w/a promise to pay in gold, with the date 1st December 1910. For further details and illu8strations see Vol. 2.

The Bank of Australasia

1 Pound, 1.7.1896, Melbourne issue

Commercial Banking Co. of Sydney

10 Pounds, 1878, Sydney issue

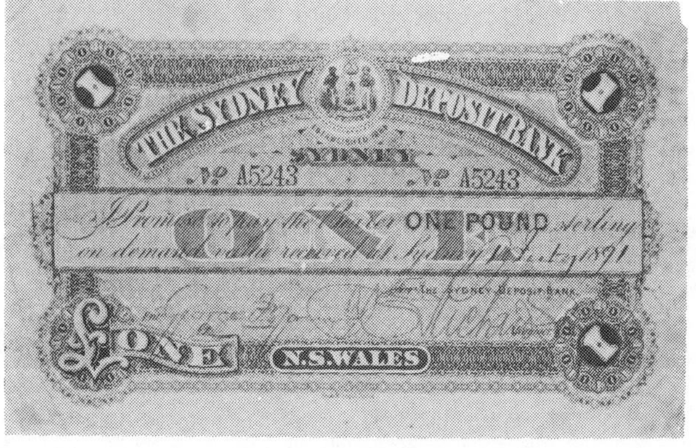

The Sydney Deposit Bank

1 Pound, 1.1.1891, Sydney issue

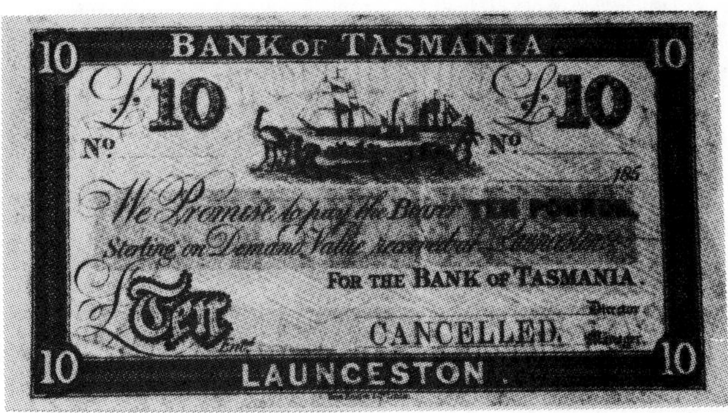

Bank of Tasmania

10 Pounds, 185x, Launceston issue

BRITISH ADMINISTRATION

GOVERNMENT OF NEW SOUTH WALES

1893 ND TREASURY ISSUE

#S1001-S1005 arms at top ctr.

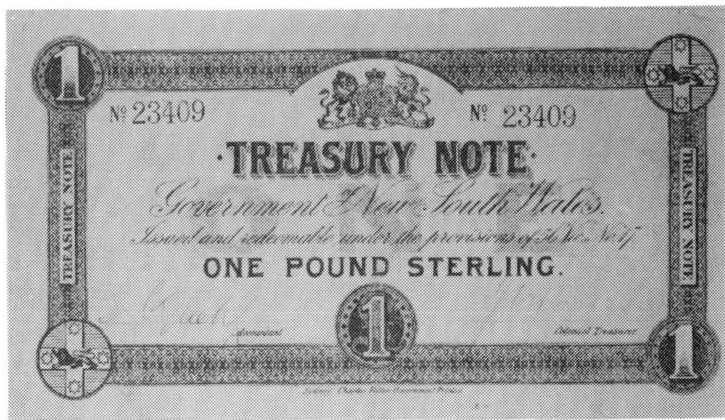

		GOOD	FINE	XF
S1001	**1 POUND** ND (1893). Black.	—	15,000.	—

NOTE: Aug. 1990 Spink auction, $10,500 in VF.

		GOOD	FINE	XF
S1002	**5 POUNDS** ND (1893). Brown.	—	Unc	16,500.
S1003	**10 POUNDS** ND (1893). Yellow.	—	Unc	17,000.
S1004	**20 POUNDS** ND (1893). Green.	—	Unc	18,000.
S1005	**50 POUNDS** ND (1893). Lt. blue.	—	Unc	20,000.

QUEENSLAND

1866 TREASURY ISSUE

#S1006-S1007 medallic portr. of Qn. Victoria at upper ctr.

		GOOD	FINE	XF
S1006	**1 POUND** 1.11.1866. Lt. blue. Back violet.	—	45,000.	—
S1007	**5 POUNDS** 1866. Pink. Back brown.	—	50,000.	—

1893 SUPERSCRIBED ISSUE

Ovpt: *GOVERNMENT OF QUEENSLAND/TREASURY NOTE* payable on demand on face or back on issues of eight different private banks.

#S1008-S1011 Ovpt. on Australia Joint Stock Bank. All are rare.

		GOOD	FINE	XF
S1008	**1 POUND** 2.6.1893.	—	90,000.	—
S1009	**5 POUNDS** 2.6.1893.	—	100,000.	—
S1010	**10 POUNDS** 2.6.1893.	—	110,000.	—
S1011	**20 POUNDS** 2.6.1893.	—	125,000.	—

#S1012-S1015 Ovpt. on Bank of Australasia.

		GOOD	FINE	XF
S1012	**1 POUND** 2.6.1893.	—	90,000.	—
S1013	**5 POUNDS** 2.6.1893.	—	100,000.	—
S1014	**10 POUNDS** 2.6.1893.	—	110,000.	—
S1015	**50 POUNDS** 1893.	—	125,000.	—

#S1016-S1019 Ovpt. on Bank of New South Wales.

		GOOD	FINE	XF
S1016	**1 POUND** 2.6.1893.	—	90,000.	—
S1017	**5 POUNDS** 2.6.1893.	—	100,000.	—
S1018	**10 POUNDS** 2.6.1893.	—	110,000.	—
S1019	**20 POUNDS** 2.6.1893.	—	125,000.	—

#S1020-S1023 Ovpt. on Bank of North Queensland.

		GOOD	FINE	XF
S1020	**1 POUND** 2.6.1893.	—	90,000.	—
S1021	**5 POUNDS** 2.6.1893.	—	100,000.	—
S1022	**10 POUNDS** 2.6.1893.	—	110,000.	—
S1023	**20 POUNDS** 2.6.1893.	—	125,000.	—

#S1024-S1027 Ovpt. on Commercial Banking Co. of Sydney.

		GOOD	FINE	XF
S1024	**1 POUND** 2.6.1893.	—	90,000.	—
S1025	**5 POUNDS** 2.6.1893.	—	100,000.	—
S1026	**10 POUNDS** 2.6.1893.	—	110,000.	—
S1027	**20 POUNDS** 2.6.1893.	—	125,000.	—

#S1028-S1031 Ovpt. on Queensland National Bank.

		GOOD	FINE	XF
S1028	**1 POUND** 2.6.1893.	—	90,000.	—
S1029	**5 POUNDS** 2.6.1893.	—	100,000.	—
S1030	**10 POUNDS** 2.6.1893.	—	110,000.	—

		Good	Fine	XF
S1031	**20 Pounds** 2.6.1893.	—	125,000.	—

#S1032-S1035 Ovpt. on Royal Bank of Queensland.

		Good	Fine	XF
S1032	**1 Pound** 2.6.1893.	—	90,000.	—
S1033	**5 Pounds** 2.6.1893.	—	100,000.	—
S1034	**10 Pounds** 2.6.1893.	—	110,000.	—
S1035	**20 Pounds** 2.6.1893.	—	125,000.	—

#S1036-S1039 Ovpt. on Union Bank of Australia.

		Good	Fine	XF
S1036	**1 Pound** 2.6.1893.	—	90,000.	—
S1037	**5 Pounds** 2.6.1893.	—	100,000.	—
S1038	**10 Pounds** 2.6.1893.		110,000.	
S1039	**20 Pounds** 2.6.1893.	—	125,000.	—

1893; 1899 Brisbane Regular Issue

#S1040-S1047 arms at upper l.

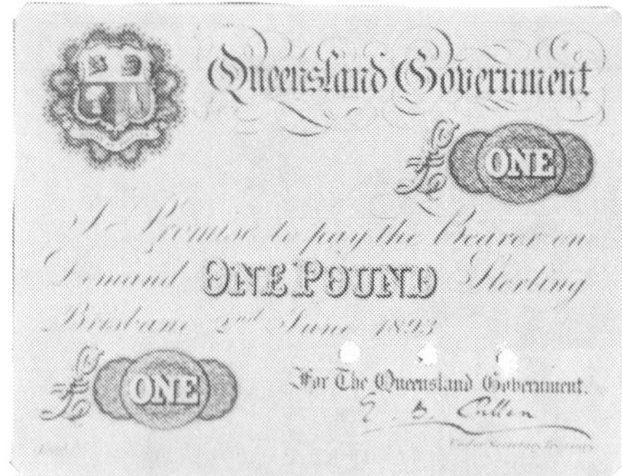

		Good	Fine	XF
S1040	**1 Pound** 2.6.1893. Black and green.	—	10,000.	—

		Good	Fine	XF
S1041	**5 Pounds** 2.1.1899; 2.1.1902; 1.7.1903. Black and green.	—	12,500.	—
S1042	**10 Pounds** 1893-99.	—	20,000.	—
S1043	**20 Pounds** 1893-99.	—	25,000.	—

1905 Issue

		Good	Fine	XF
S1044	**1 Pound** 1905-10. Black on green unpt. Back blue.	—	9000.	—
S1045	**5 Pounds** 1905-10. Black on pink unpt. Back brown.	—	17,000.	—
S1046	**10 Pounds** 1905-10.	—	20,000.	—
S1047	**20 Pounds** 1905-10.	—	23,000.	—

The Republic of Austria, a parliamentary democracy located in mountainous central Europe, has an area of 32,374 sq. mi. (83,849 sq. km.). Capital: Vienna.

The territories later to be known as Austria were overrun in pre-Roman times by various tribes, including the Celts. Upon the fall of the Roman Empire, the country became a margravate of Charlemagne's Empire. Ottokar, King of Bohemia, gained possession in 1252, only to lose the territory to Rudolf of Habsburg in 1276. Thereafter, until World War I, the story of Austria was that of the ruling Habsburgs, German emperors from 1438-1806. From 1815-1867 it was a member of the "Deutsche Bund" (German Union).

During World War I, the Austro-Hungarian Empire was one of the Central Powers with Germany, Bulgaria and Turkey. At the end of the war, the Empire was dismembered and Austria established as an independent republic.

RULERS:

Franz Joseph, 1848-1916
Karl I, 1916-1918

MONETARY SYSTEM:

1 Krone = 100 Heller 1892-1924

Banks

Wiener Commissions Bank

1888 Cassa-Scheine - Interest Bearing Notes Issue

		Good	Fine	XF
S56	**1000 Gulden** 12.1.(?) 1888/7x. Seated allegorical figures at l. and r.	—	—	—

Regional - Federal States, 1918-23; 1945

Banks:

Kärten (Carinthia)

Kärnten (Carinthia)

1918 Issue

#S101-S105 arms at ctr. on back.

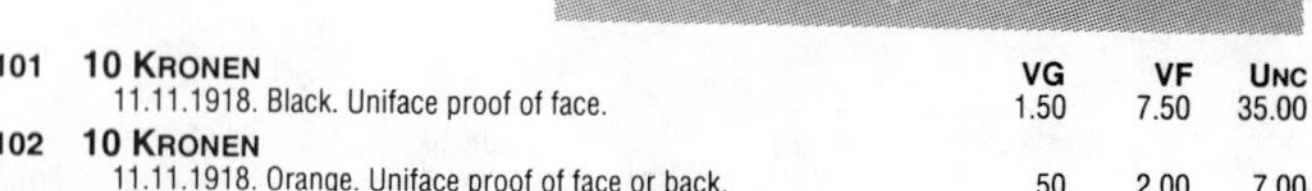

		VG	VF	Unc
S101	**10 Kronen** 11.11.1918. Black. Uniface proof of face.	1.50	7.50	35.00
S102	**10 Kronen** 11.11.1918. Orange. Uniface proof of face or back.	.50	2.00	7.00

		VG	VF	Unc
S103	**20 Kronen** 11.11.1918. Blue. Printed on both sides, w/serial #. (Not issued).	1.00	5.00	15.00

		VG	VF	UNC
S104	**100 KRONEN** 11.11.1918. Black. Uniface proof of face.	5.00	20.00	50.00
S105	**100 KRONEN** 11.11.1918. Orange.			
	a. Uniface proof of face or back.	2.00	5.00	12.00
	b. Proof of both sides.	4.00	10.00	25.00

1920 ISSUE

		VG	VF	UNC
S106	**10 HELLER** 1.3.1920. Black and red on lt. brown unpt.	.10	.20	.30
S107	**20 HELLER** 1.3.1920. Black and blue on lt. brown unpt.	.10	.20	.30
S108	**50 HELLER** 1.3.1920. Black and green on lt. brown unpt.	.10	.20	.30

1945 REICHSGAU KÄRNTEN ISSUE

		VG	VF	UNC
S108A	**50 REICHSMARK** 15.4.1945. Purple on off-white paper. Uniface.	50.00	150.00	325.00

NOTE: #S108A was issued during the last weeks of WWII.

NIEDERÖSTERREICH (LOWER AUSTRIA)

MAY 1920 ISSUE

		VG	VF	UNC
S109	**10 HELLER** May 1920. Dk. green. Mountain scene w/Semmering railway bridge.			
	a. Issued note.	.10	.20	.30
	p. Uniface proof of back, picture dk. green.	1.00	5.00	10.00

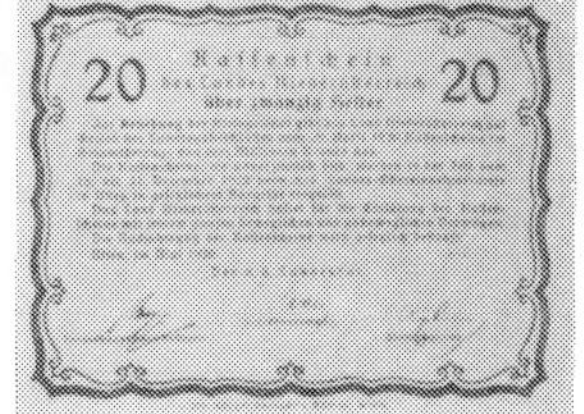

		VG	VF	UNC
S110	**20 HELLER** May 1920. Blue-gray. Steamer on the Danube below Abbey of Melk.			
	a. Issued note.	.10	.20	.30
	p. Uniface proof of back, picture dk. green.	1.00	5.00	10.00

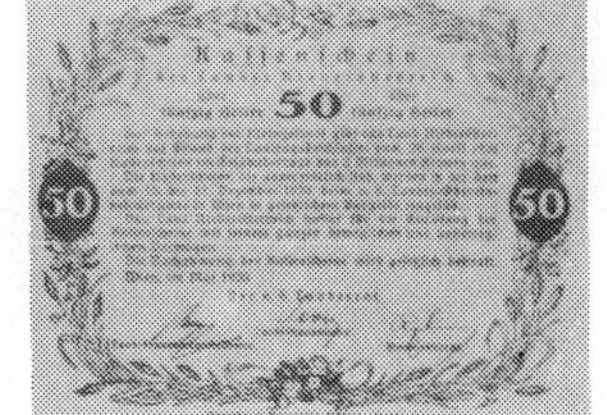

		VG	VF	UNC
S111	**50 HELLER** May 1920. Brown. Farmer plowing w/horses.			
	a. Issued note.	.10	.20	.30
	p. Uniface proof of back, picture dk. green.	1.00	5.00	10.00

JULY 1920 ISSUE

		VG	VF	UNC
S112	**10 HELLER** July 1920. Green to dk. green. Farmer's wife w/cows.			
	a. *II. AUFLAGE* (2nd issue).	.10	.20	.30
	b. Uniface proof on orange, green, red-brown, blue or lilac tinted paper.	3.00	10.00	17.50
	x. Error, picture on both sides (one inverted).	3.00	10.00	17.50

		VG	VF	UNC
S113	**20 HELLER** July 1920. Blue to dk. blue. Landscape w/horse-drawn cart.			
	a. *II. AUFLAGE* (2nd issue).	.10	.20	.30
	p. Uniface proof on white, brown, red-brown or lilac tinted paper.	4.00	12.00	20.00
	x1. Error, picture on both sides.	4.00	12.00	20.00
	x2. Error, mountains missing.	.50	1.50	3.00

		VG	VF	UNC
S114	**50 HELLER** July 1920. Brown. Castle at ctr.			
	a. *II, AUFLAGE* (2nd issue).	.10	.20	.30
	p. Uniface proof on green, blue, red-brown or lilac tinted paper.	2.00	9.00	15.00
	x1. Error, picture on both sides, brown (back inverted).	4.00	10.00	17.50
	x2. Error, picture on both sides, lt. blue (proof print).	3.00	9.00	15.00

OBERÖSTERREICH (UPPER AUSTRIA)

1920-21 ISSUES

		VG	VF	UNC
S115	**20 HELLER** 1.3.1920. Arms at ctr. on back.			
	a. Blue-green on white paper.	.10	.20	.30
	b. Green-blue on bluish paper.	.10	.20	.30
	c. Blue on gray paper.	1.00	2.25	3.00
	d. Violet.	.25	1.00	1.50
	p1. Green. Proof.	4.00	10.00	15.00
	p2. Brown. Proof.	5.00	12.00	17.50
	p3. Black. Uniface proof of face or back.	—	—	20.00
S116	**50 HELLER** 1.3.1920.			
	a. Dk. brown.	.10	.20	.30
	b. Red.	.10	.20	.40
S117	**10 HELLER** 1.6.1920. Uniface.			
	a. Pink.	.10	.20	.30
	b. Gray-violet.	.10	.20	.30
S118	**80 HELLER** 21.6.1920. Red and gray.	.10	.20	.40
S119	**10 HELLER** 1921.			
	a. Red.	.05	.10	.20
	b. Green.	.05	.10	.20
	c. Orange.	.10	.25	1.00
	d. Brown.	.05	.10	.20
	e. Blue.	.05	.10	.20

		VG	VF	UNC
S120	**20 HELLER**			
	1921. Village at upper l. Rural views on back.			
	a. Brown.	.05	.10	.20
	b. Violet.	.05	.10	.20
	c. Black.	.05	.10	.20
	d. Green.	.05	.10	.20
	x. Error, different picture of Steyr w/fountain on back. Printed in nine different colors. Value for each.	10.00	30.00	50.00

		VG	VF	UNC
S121	**50 HELLER**			
	1.2.1921. Orange.	.10	.20	.30

ÖSTERREICH OB DER ENNS (AUSTRIA ABOVE THE ENNS)

1918 ISSUE

		VG	VF	UNC
S122	**5 KRONEN**			
	30.11.1918. Brown on green.	1.00	5.00	10.00
S123	**10 KRONEN**			
	30.11.1918. Green on blue-gray.	2.00	7.00	18.00
S124	**20 HELLER**			
	30.11.1918. Blue on gray-brown.	3.00	9.00	25.00

		VG	VF	UNC
S125	**50 KRONEN**			
	30.11.1918. Brown on lt. brown.	4.00	20.00	50.00

SALZBURG

1919 ISSUES

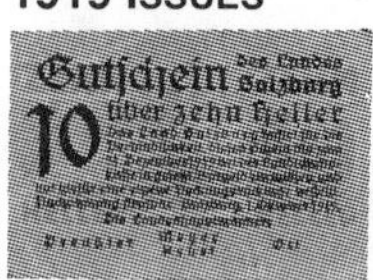
#S126

#S128

		VG	VF	UNC
S126	**10 HELLER**			
	1.10.1919. Blue on green. Uniface.			
	a. Issued note.	.10	.20	.30
	b. Error, w/o unpt.	.50	3.00	4.50
S127	**20 HELLER**			
	1.10.1919. Black on yellow. Uniface.	.10	.20	.30
S128	**50 HELLER**			
	1.10.1919. Blue on pink. Uniface.			
	a. Issued note.	.10	.20	.30
	p. Black. 90 x 60mm. Proof.	—	—	35.00
	x. Error, w/o unpt.	1.00	3.00	4.50

1920 ISSUE

		VG	VF	UNC
S129	**10 HELLER**			
	May 1920. Black and red. Salzburg ca. 1500.			
	a. Issued note.	.10	.20	.30
	x1. Error, face w/o red printing.	.50	3.00	4.50
	x2. Error, back w/o red printing.	.50	3.00	4.50

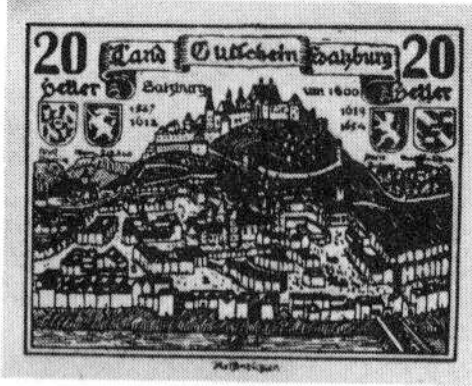

		VG	VF	UNC
S130	**20 HELLER**			
	May 1920. Black and red. Salzburg ca. 1600.			
	a. Issued note.	.10	.20	.40
	x1. Error, face w/o red printing.	.50	3.00	4.50
	x2. Error, back w/o red printing.	.50	3.00	4.50

		VG	VF	UNC
S131	**50 HELLER**			
	May 1920. Black and red. Salzburg ca. 1700.			
	a. Issued note.	.10	.20	.40
	x1. Error, face w/o red printing.	.50	3.00	4.50
	x2. Error, back w/o red printing.	.50	3.00	4.50

1921 ISSUES

		VG	VF	UNC
S132	**5 KRONEN**			
	1921. Mirabell Palace. (Not issued).			
	a. Printing on face brown, unpt. red-brown, picture on back brown. Printer's name at ctr. w/ and w/o serial #.	.50	3.50	7.50
	b. Like "a" but printer's and designer's name at l. and r.	.50	4.50	9.00
	c. Like "a" but w/o printer's name, and picture on back in lilac.	1.00	6.00	11.00
	d. Printing on face brown on green unpt.	4.00	15.00	22.50
S133	**20 KRONEN**			
	1921. Summer Riding School in Salzburg on back. (Not issued).			
	a. Like #S132a.	1.00	3.50	7.50
	b. Like #S132b.	1.00	3.50	7.50
	c. Like #S132c.	2.00	5.00	9.00
	d. Like #S132d.	10.00	15.00	22.50

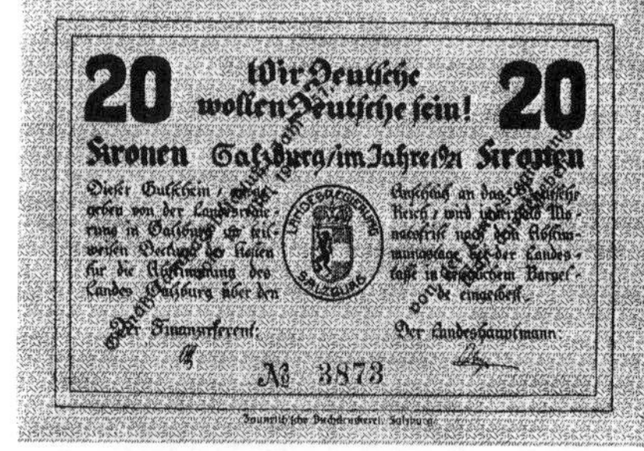

		VG	VF	UNC
S134	**20 KRONEN**			
	1921. Crowned arms at ctr. Residence in Salzburg on back.			
	a. Like #S132a.	1.00	3.50	7.50
	b. Like #S132b.	1.00	4.50	9.00
	c. Like #S132c.	2.00	6.00	12.00
	d. Like #S132d.	10.00	15.00	22.50

NOTE: Other varieties of #S132-S134 were printed, mostly unfinished pieces.

STEIERMARK (STYRIA)

1919 ISSUE

		VG	VF	UNC
S135	**10 HELLER**			
	17.10.1919. Blue on tan unpt.	.10	.20	.30
S136	**20 HELLER**			
	17.10.1919. Green on yellow-green unpt.	.10	.20	.30

		VG	VF	UNC
S137	**50 HELLER** 17.10.1919. Red-brown on gray-green unpt.	.10	.20	.30

		VG	VF	UNC
S138	**50 HELLER** 17.10.1919. Red-brown. *II AUFLAGE* (2nd issue).			
	a. Blue unpt.	.10	.20	.50
	b. Green unpt.	.10	.20	.50
	c. Yellow-brown unpt.	.10	.20	.50
	d. Pink unpt.	.10	.20	.50

TIROL (TYROL)

1919 ISSUE

#S139-S141 imperial eagle at ctr. on back.

		VG	VF	UNC
S139	**10 HELLER** 1.9.1919. Orange.	.10	.20	.40
S140	**20 HELLER** 1.9.1919. Gray.	.10	.20	.40

		VG	VF	UNC
S141	**50 HELLER** 1.9.1919. Green.	.10	.20	.40

1920 ISSUE

#S142-S144 imperial eagle at ctr. on back.

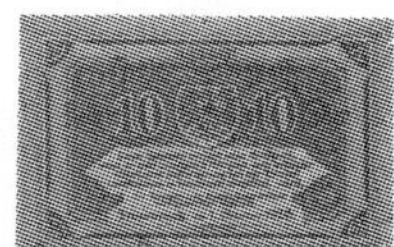

		VG	VF	UNC
S142	**10 HELLER** 1.10.1920. Green.	.10	.20	.40

		VG	VF	UNC
S143	**20 HELLER** 1.10.1920. Brown.	.10	.20	.40
S144	**50 HELLER** 1.10.1920. Blue.	.10	.20	.40

VORARLBERG

1919 ISSUE

		VG	VF	UNC
S145	**10 HELLER** 1.10.1919. Green. Shield at ctr. on back.	.10	.20	.40

		VG	VF	UNC
S146	**20 HELLER** 1.10.1919. Lt. brown. Shield at ctr. on back.	.10	.20	.40
S147	**50 HELLER** 1.10.1919. Blue.	.10	.20	.40

1921 ISSUE

		VG	VF	UNC
S148	**50 HELLER** 1.5.1921. Shield at upper ctr. Feldkirch Katzeturm (cat's tower) at l. ctr. on back.			
	a. Brown.	.10	.30	.60
	b. Violet.	.10	.30	.60
	c. Brown. Card stock.	—	—	15.00
	d. Violet. Card stock.	—	—	15.00
	x1. Brown. Error, back inverted.	2.00	5.00	10.00
	x2. Violet. Error, back inverted.	2.00	5.00	10.00

DONAUSTAAT (DANUBE STATE)

After WWI a buffer state to be known as Donaustaat (Danube State) was planned in central Europe. Monetary plans were well underway and notes were partially printed with denominational numerals but w/o unit name. The Donaustaat idea did not come to fruition and later on (1923-37), the unfinished notes were ovpt. and issued as Austrian lottery tickets. A small number of each denomination were not so used, and are very much scarcer than the lottery ovpt. pieces.

1923-37 LOTTERY TICKETS

		VG	VF	UNC
S151	**10** ND. Green and red-brown. Girl's head at r.			
	a. Unfinished note.	—	—	60.00
	b. W/lottery ovpt.	2.00	5.00	9.00

S152 20

	VG	VF	UNC
ND. Green and violet. Girl's head at r.			
a. Unfinished note.	—	—	60.00
b. W/lottery ovpt.	1.00	3.00	5.00

S153 50

	VG	VF	UNC
ND. Blue and violet. Woman's head at r. Back blue and brown.			
a. Unfinished note.	—	—	60.00
b. W/lottery ovpt.	2.00	5.00	9.00

S154 100

	VG	VF	UNC
ND. Blue and brown. Woman's head at r. Back blue and gray-green.			
a. Unfinished note.	—	—	75.00

	VG	VF	UNC
b. W/lottery ovpt.	2.00	5.00	9.00

S155 1000

	VG	VF	UNC
ND. Green and blue. Girl's head at r. Back blue and red-brown.			
a. Unfinished note.	—	—	100.00
b. W/lottery ovpt.	2.00	5.00	10.00

S156 10,000

	VG	VF	UNC
ND. Red, brown and olive. Back blue, lilac, violet and olive. Heads of 11 children.			
a. Unfinished note.	—	—	55.00
b. W/lottery ovpt.	2.00	7.00	15.00

NOTE: Many lottery text varieties and stampings exist. Illustrated pieces are only examples.

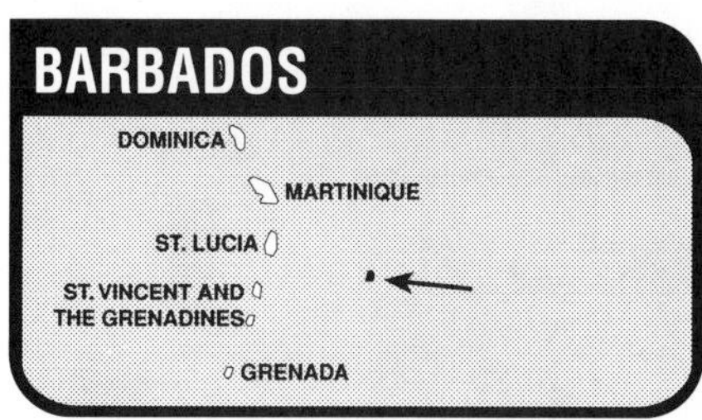

Barbados, an independent state within the British Commonwealth, is located in the Windward Islands of the West Indies east of St. Vincent. The coral island has an area of 166 sq. mi. (431 sq. km) and a population of 269,000. Capital: Bridgetown. The economy is based on sugar and tourism. Sugar, petroleum products, molasses and rum are exported.

Barbados was named by the Portuguese who achieved the first landing on the island in 1563. British sailors landed at the site of present-day Holetown in 1624. Barbados was under uninterrupted British control from the time of the first British settlement in 1627 until it obtained independence on Nov. 30, 1966. It is a member of the Commonwealth of Nations. Elizabeth II is Head of State, as Queen of Barbados.

Barbados was included in the issues of the British Caribbean Territories - Eastern Group and later the East Caribbean Currency Authority until 1973.

RULERS:

British to 1966

MONETARY SYSTEM:

1 British West Indies Dollar = 4 Shillings - 2 Pence
5 British West Indies Dollars = 1 Pound - 10 Pence

BRITISH ADMINISTRATION

BARCLAYS BANK (DOMINION, COLONIAL AND OVERSEAS)

Formerly the Colonial Bank.

1922 ISSUE

#S101-S103 arms at ctr. Lg. ovpt. *B* at upper r. Printer: BWC.

		Good	Fine	XF
S101	**5 DOLLARS** 1922; 1.9.1926; 1.2.1934. Black on pink and blue-green unpt. Back green.	400.00	800.00	—
S102	**20 DOLLARS** 1922; 1926.	—	Rare	—

		Good	Fine	XF
S103	**100 DOLLARS** 1922; 1926; 1935.			
	a. Issued note. 1922; 1926.	—	Rare	—
	r. Remainder perforated: *CANCELLED*. 1.1.1935.	—	Unc	2000.

1937 ISSUE

#S111-S113 arms at r. Lg. ovpt. *B* at upper r. Printer: BWC.

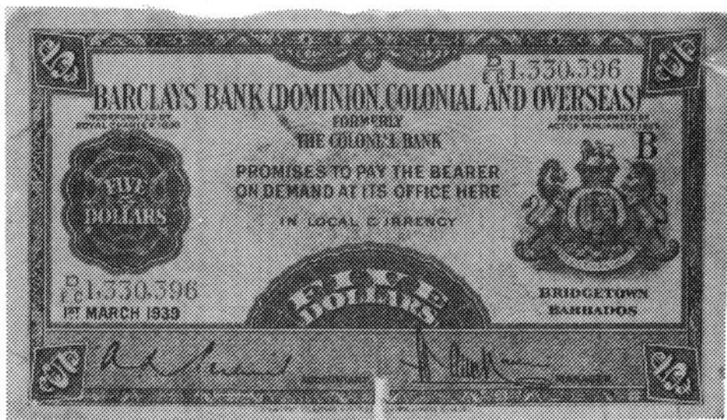

		Good	Fine	XF
S111	**5 DOLLARS** 1937-49. Purple on m/c unpt.			
	a. Sign. titles: *ACCOUNTANT* and *MANAGER*. 1.3.1937-1.3.1940.	200.00	400.00	850.00
	b. Sign. titles: *ASSISTANT MANAGER* and *MANAGER*. 1.10.1949.	250.00	500.00	1250.
	s. Specimen. 1.5.1937.	—	Unc	750.00
S112	**20 DOLLARS** 1.1.1937; 1.3.1940. Brown.	450.00	1350.	—
S113	**100 DOLLARS** 1.1.1937; 1.3.1940. Green.	—	Rare	—

NOTE: Also issued w/various branch office ovpt.

CANADIAN BANK OF COMMERCE

Special designs in large size for British West Indies territories; not intended for circulation in Canada.

1922 ISSUE

#S120-S123 vertical black ovpt: *BARBADOS* at l. and r. Printers: ABNC and CBNC.

		Good	Fine	XF
S120	**5 DOLLARS** 2.1.1922. Black on green and red-orange unpt. Seated woman w/lyre and jug at ctr. Back orange; Mercury and allegorical woman flanking bank arms at ctr. Printer: ABNC.	250.00	600.00	—
S121	**5 DOLLARS** 2.1.1922. Black on green and red-orange unpt. Like #S120. Printer: CBNC.	250.00	600.00	—
S122	**20 DOLLARS** 2.1.1922; 1.7.1940. Black on red-brown and green unpt. Seated woman and globe at ctr. Back blue; like #S121.	750.00	1500.	—
S123	**100 DOLLARS** 2.1.1922. Black on blue and olive unpt. Seated woman w/book and lamp at l. ctr. Back brown; like #S121.	—	Rare	—

NOTE: A similar issue of #S123 was made for Trinidad.

1940 ISSUE

		Good	Fine	XF
S131	**5 DOLLARS** 1.7.1940. Black on green and red-orange unpt. Allegorical group at ctr. Back orange. Printer: CBNC.	150.00	500.00	1000.

NOTE: Design of #S131 is similar to a regular Canadian issue made by this bank, though color and wording on the face distinguish it from the actual Canadian counterpart.

COLONIAL BANK

Later became Barclays Bank.

1882 ISSUE

		Good	Fine	XF
S141	**5 DOLLARS** 1.7.1882; 1.6.1912. Brown. Arms at upper ctr., *B* in circle at upper l. and r. Back green. Printer: P&B.	—	Rare	—

1918 ISSUE

#S151-153 arms at upper ctr. Lg. ovpt: *B* at upper r. Printer: PBC.

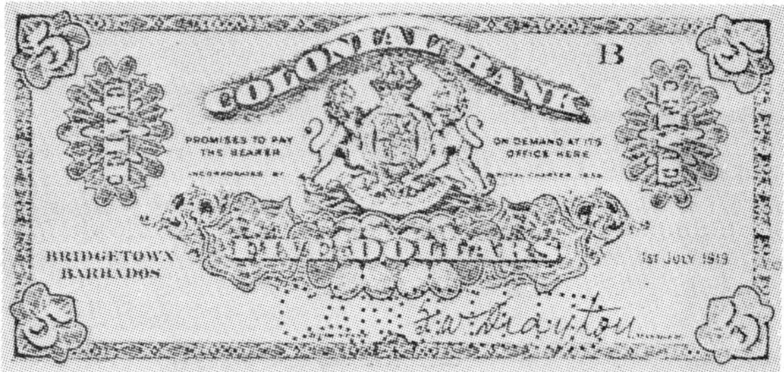

		Good	Fine	XF
S151	**5 Dollars** 1918; 1919. Black on orange unpt. Back green.			
	a. Issued note. 1.1.1918.	1250.	—	—
	s. Specimen perforated: *CANCELLED*. 1.7.1919.	—	Unc	3000.
S152	**20 Dollars** 191x.	—	Rare	—
S153	**100 Dollars** 191x.	—	Rare	—

NOTE: #S152 and S153 are reported to have dates to 1920, but no specifics are known.

Royal Bank of Canada

1909 Provisional Issue

#S161-S163 vertical ovpt: *BARBADOS* at l. and r., smaller vertical ovpt: *PAYABLE AT BRIDGETOWN, BARBADOS* at ctr. on regular Canadian issues #S1371, S1375b and S1377 of this bank. Printer: ABNC.

		Good	Fine	XF
S161	**5 Dollars** 2.1.1909. Black on green and yellow unpt. Ovpt. on Canada #S1371.	600.00	1800.	—
S162	**20 Dollars** 2.1.1909. Black on blue and yellow unpt. Ovpt. on Canada #S1375b.	—	Rare	—

		Good	Fine	XF
S163	**100 Dollars** 2.1.1909. Black on red-orange unpt. Ovpt. on Canada #S1377.			
	a. Issued note.	—	Rare	—
	s. Specimen.	—	—	—

1920 Issue

Designed specifically for circulation in the West Indies.

#S171-S173 crowned supported arms at ctr. on back. Lg. size notes. Printer: ABNC.

		Good	Fine	XF
S171	**5 Dollars = 1 Pound - 10 Pence** 2.1.1920. Black on green unpt. Passenger steamship at ctr. Back green.	325.00	850.00	—
S172	**20 Dollars = 4 Pounds - 3 Shillings - 4 Pence** 2.1.1920. Black on blue unpt. Sugar cane harvesting at ctr. Back blue.	—	Rare	—
S173	**100 Dollars = 20 Pounds - 16 Shillings - 8 Pence** 2.1.1920. Black on orange unpt. Seated woman w/island behind. Back orange.	—	Rare	—

1938 Issue

#S181 and S182 similar to previous issue but reduced size. Printer: CBNC.

		Good	Fine	XF
S181	**5 Dollars = 1 Pound - 10 Pence** 3.1.1938. Similar to #S171.	175.00	400.00	900.00
S182	**20 Dollars = 4 Pounds - 3 Shillings - 4 Pence** 3.1.1938. Black on orange unpt. Ox cart at ctr. Back rose.	700.00	1750.	—

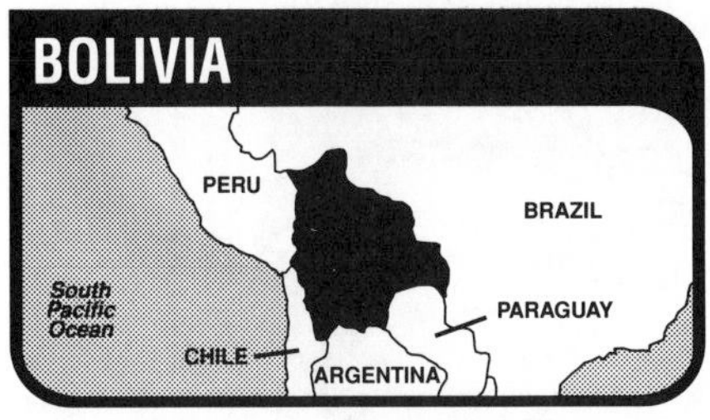

The Republic of Bolivia, a landlocked country in west central South America, has an area of 424,165 sq. mi. (1,098,581 sq. km.) and a population of 8.33 million. Capitals: La Paz (administrative); Sucre (constitutional). Mining is the principal industry and tin the most important metal. Minerals, petroleum, natural gas, cotton and coffee are exported.

The Incas, who ruled one of the world's greatest dynasties, incorporated the area that is now western Bolivia into their empire about 1200AD. Their control was maintained until the Spaniards arrived in 1535 and reduced the predominantly Indian population to slavery. When Napoleon occupied Madrid in 1808 and placed his brother Joseph on the Spanish throne, a fervor of revolutionary activity quickened in Bolivia, culminating with the 1809 proclamation of independence. Sixteen years of struggle ensued before the republic, named for the famed liberator General Simón Bolívar, was established on August 6, 1825. Since then, Bolivia has had more than 60 revolutions, 70 presidents and 11 constitutions.

RULERS:

Spanish to 1825

MONETARY SYSTEM:

1 Boliviano = 100 (Centavos) to 1965

SPECIMEN NOTES:

All specimen, *muestra, muestra sin valor* and *especimen* notes always have serial #'s of zero.

BANKS

Banco Agricola .... #S101-S106
Banco Boliviano.. #S111-S116
Banco de Bolivia y Londres... #S121-S126
Banco del Comercio .... #S131-S136
Banco Francisco Argandoña... #S141-S150
Banco Industrial de La Paz .... #S151-S156
Banco Industrial.. #S161-S166
Banco Mercantil.. #S171-S177
Banco Nacional de Bolivia.. #S181-S217
Banco Potosí... #S221-S236

REPUBLIC

BANCO AGRICOLA

Issued at La Paz.

1903 ISSUE

#S101-S106 printer: BWC.

S101 1 BOLIVIANO — GOOD / FINE / XF

22.11.1903. Black on lt. brown and rose unpt. Bldg. at l., allegorical woman w/sickle and sheaf at r. Back brown; farmers loading wagon at ctr.

	GOOD	FINE	XF
a. Series E-K.	40.00	100.00	350.00
s. Specimen. Uniface.	—	—	—

S102 5 BOLIVIANOS — GOOD / FINE / XF

22.11.1903. Black on lt. brown and rose unpt. Sheep grazing on hillside at ctr., bank at lower r. Back blue; oxen driven wagon at ctr.

	GOOD	FINE	XF
a. Series B.	100.00	225.00	—
s. Specimen. Uniface.	—	—	—

S103 10 BOLIVIANOS — GOOD / FINE / XF

22.11.1903. Black on m/c unpt. Winged man w/rake at l., sheep behind portr. S. Bolívar at lower r.

	GOOD	FINE	XF
a. Issued note.	—	—	—
s. Specimen. Uniface.	—	Unc	300.00

S104 20 BOLIVIANOS — GOOD / FINE / XF

22.11.1903. Black on m/c unpt. Bank at l., farm woman w/bucket on shoulder and cattle at r. Sheep at ctr. on back.

	GOOD	FINE	XF
a. Issued note.	—	—	—
s. Specimen. Uniface.	—	Unc	450.00

S105 50 BOLIVIANOS — GOOD / FINE / XF

22.11.1903. Black on red and m/c unpt. Woman w/basket on head and holding sickle at l., bank at ctr. Back green; bull, cow and calf at ctr.

	GOOD	FINE	XF
a. Issued note.	—	Rare	—
s. Specimen. Uniface.	—	—	—

S106 100 BOLIVIANOS

22.11.1903. Similar to #S105. — Reported Not Confirmed

BANCO BOLIVIANO

Authorized by dictator Gen. Mariano Melgarejo on 24.1.1867; established 1868. Later became part of the Banco Nacional de Bolivia.

1868 ISSUE

		GOOD	FINE	XF
S111	**1 PESO FUERTE** 6.11.1868. Black on dk. green unpt. Seated allegorical women at l. and r. of shield w/arms, condor above. Back green. Printer: CNBB. Series C.	—	—	—

NOTE: For provisional issue ovpt. new bank name see #S181.

S112	**5 PESOS FUERTES** 18xx (ca.1868). Black on brown unpt. 3 allegorical women w/bust of Gen. A. J. de Sucre at ctr. Back brown. Proof.	—	—	—

		GOOD	FINE	XF
S113	**10 PESOS FUERTES** 18xx (ca.1868). Black on orange unpt. 2 allegorical young girls at bottom l., mountain scene at ctr., young girl at bottom r. Back orange. Proof.	—	—	—

		GOOD	FINE	XF
S114	**20 PESOS FUERTES** 18xx (ca.1868). Black on blue unpt. Spaniard at l., men and horses at ctr., allegorical woman w/flowers at lower r. Back blue. Proof.	—	—	—

		GOOD	FINE	XF
S115	**50 PESOS FUERTES** 19.10.1868. Black on red-orange unpt. Cotton boll at l. Justice seated w/scales at upper ctr., portr. woman at r. Back red-orange.			
	a. Issued note.	—	Rare	—
	p. Proof.	—	—	—

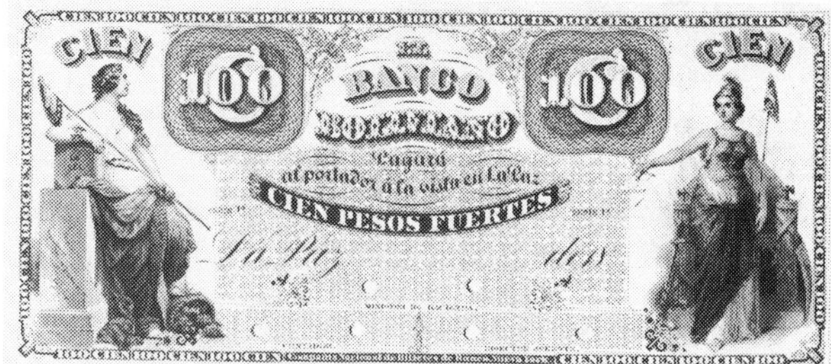

		GOOD	FINE	XF
S116	**100 PESOS FUERTES** 18xx (ca.1868). Black on green unpt. Liberty at l., helmeted Minerva at r. Back green. Proof.	—	—	—

BANCO DE BOLIVIA Y LONDRES

Issued at La Paz.

1909 ISSUE

#S121-S126 sign. varieties. Printer: W&S.

		GOOD	FINE	XF
S121	**1 BOLIVIANO** 1.2.1909. Black on yellow-red unpt. Portr. Sra. Argandoña (La Princesa de la Glorieta) at ctr. Back green; 2 Indians and burro at ctr. Series A.	75.00	200.00	450.00
S122	**5 BOLIVIANOS** 1.2.1909.	—	—	—

		GOOD	FINE	XF
S123	**10 BOLIVIANOS** 1.2.1909. Black on yellow and violet unpt. Portr. Sra. Argandoña (La Princesa de la Glorieta) at l., llamas in pasture at r. Back dk. green, like #S121. Series A.	—	Rare	—
S124	**20 BOLIVIANOS** 1.2.1909.	—	Rare	—
S125	**50 BOLIVIANOS** 1.2.1909.	—	Rare	—
S126	**100 BOLIVIANOS** 1.2.1909.	—	—	—

NOTE: For notes of this bank ovpt: *Banco de la Nación Boliviana*, see #96-101 in Vol. 2.

BANCO DEL COMERCIO

Issued at Oruro.

1900 ISSUE

#S131-S136 sign. varieties. Arms at ctr. on back. Series A. Printer: BWC.

		GOOD	FINE	XF
S131	**1 BOLIVIANO** 1.1.1900. Black on green and pink unpt. 2 miners standing at l., portr. S. Bolívar at r. Back blue.	7.00	15.00	75.00

		GOOD	FINE	XF
S132	**5 BOLIVIANOS** 1.1.1900. Black on green and blue unpt. Allegorical woman and child at l., portr. Gen. A. Nariño at lower r. Back green.	20.00	75.00	250.00
S133	**10 BOLIVIANOS** 1.1.1900. Black on pink and green unpt. Woman seated at l., portr. C. Columbus at lower r. Back red.	40.00	200.00	750.00
S134	**20 BOLIVIANOS** 1.1.1900. Black on blue and pink unpt. Portr. helmeted Minerva at lower l., allegory of Art seated at r. Back purple.	150.00	500.00	—
S135	**50 BOLIVIANOS** 1.1.1900. Black on orange and green unpt. Llamas in Potosí street at l., Mercury seated at r. Back brown.	200.00	700.00	—
S136	**100 BOLIVIANOS** 1.1.1900.		Reported Not Confirmed	

BANCO FRANCISCO ARGANDOÑA

1893 ISSUE

#S141-S146 portr. Francisco Argandoña as a young man at l.; arms at top ctr. or top ctr. r. Printer: BWC.

		GOOD	FINE	XF
S141	**1 BOLIVIANO** 1.7.1893. Black on pale blue and yellow-orange unpt. Child w/pick at r. Back green; 2 seated allegorical women flanking arms at ctr. Series L.	200.00	600.00	—

		GOOD	FINE	XF
S142	**5 BOLIVIANOS** 1.7.1893. Black on blue and red unpt. Portr. w/cherub at l., arms at upper ctr. r. Back dk. brown; Castillo de la Glorieta at Sucre at ctr.	100.00	250.00	—

		GOOD	FINE	XF
S143	**10 BOLIVIANOS** 1.7.1893. Black on grayish violet and orange unpt. 2 cherubs holding portr. at l., arms at upper ctr., bull's head at lower r. Back red; like #S142. Series A; B.	—	Rare	—

		GOOD	FINE	XF
S144	**20 BOLIVIANOS** 1.7.1893. Black on pale green and orange unpt. Arms at upper ctr., 2 allegorical women w/easel and lyre at r. Back blue and dk. blue. Like #S142.			
	p. Proof.	—	Unc	400.00
	s1. Specimen perforated: *SPECIMEN/BW&Co/LONDON.*	—	Unc	450.00
	s2. Specimen perforated: *SPECIMEN.*	—	Unc	450.00

#S144A *Deleted.* See #S144.

		Good	Fine	XF
S145	**50 Bolivianos** 1.7.1893. Black on brown and orange unpt. Stylized plant at l., arms at upper ctr., portr. w/cherub at r. Back orange; cattle drinking at pond.			
	p. Unfinished proof.	—	—	—
	s. Specimen perforated: *SPECIMEN.*	—	Unc	600.00

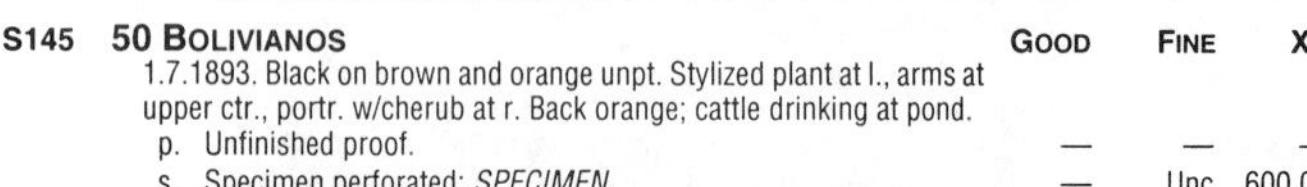

		Good	Fine	XF
S146	**100 Bolivianos** 1.7.1893. Black on green and red unpt. Arms at upper ctr., Clotilde Urioste Velasco (Mrs. F. Argandoña) seated at lower r. Back dk. brown; arms at l., reclining allegorical woman on clouds at ctr., legend at r.			
	p. Proof.	—	Unc	400.00
	s. Specimen perforated: *SPECIMEN.*	—	Unc	600.00

NOTE: 500 Bolivianos denomination for this bank is reported, not confirmed.

1898 Issue

#S147 and S148 similar to #S141 and S142 but w/older portr. Argandoña w/coat at l. Printer: BWC.

		Good	Fine	XF
S147	**1 Boliviano** 1898; 1909. Black on red and lilac unpt. 2 seated allegorical women flanking arms at ctr.			
	a. Series B-Z. 1.1.1898.	40.00	90.00	—
	b. Series CC-FF. 1.1.1909.	20.00	50.00	175.00

		Good	Fine	XF
S148	**5 Bolivianos** 1.1.1898. Dk. gray on pale green unpt. Back dk. brown; bldg. at ctr.	40.00	150.00	—

1905 Issue

		Good	Fine	XF
S149	**5 Bolivianos** 1.1.1905. Black on pink, lilac and lt. blue unpt. Mercury w/Argandoña portr. at l., arms at upper ctr., Mrs. Argandoña w/allegory Fame at r. Back blue; like #S142. Series A-G. Larger size. Printer: BWC.	30.00	100.00	325.00

Note: Beware of good and dangerous contemporary counterfeits.

1907 Issue

		Good	Fine	XF
S150	**5 Bolivianos** 1.1.1907. Black on lt. green, brown, red, lt. blue and yellow unpt. Like #S149. Back blue. Series A-G. Printer: BWC.	30.00	100.00	325.00

Banco Industrial de La Paz

Became Banco Industrial in 1906.

1900 Issue

#S151-S156 helmeted arms of La Paz at ctr. on back. Sign. varieties. Printer: ABNC.

		Good	Fine	XF
S151	**1 Boliviano** 1900; 1905. Black on yellow unpt. 2 Indian women and children at l. Back olive.			
	a. Series A-G. 1.6.1900.	70.00	175.00	400.00
	b. 1.1.1905.	80.00	200.00	450.00
	s. Specimen. 1.6.1900.	—	Unc	200.00

		Good	Fine	XF
S152	**5 Bolivianos** 1900; 1905. Black on yellow and red-orange unpt. Man on horseback leading pack animals, Indian w/rifle at r. Back red-orange.			
	a. Series A. 1.6.1900.	100.00	300.00	—
	b. Series B. 1.1.1905.	125.00	350.00	—
	s. Specimen. 1.6.1900.	—	Unc	200.00

		Good	Fine	XF
S152A	**5 Bolivianos** 1.1.1905. Like #S152 but *DE LA PAZ* crossed out on face and back.	—	—	—

		Good	Fine	XF
S153	**10 Bolivianos** 1.6.1900; 1.1.1905. Black on yellow and brown unpt. Woman holding parasol at l., 2 Indians at r. Back brown.			
	a. 1.6.1900.	—	Rare	—
	b. Series B. 1.1.1905.	—	Rare	—
	s. Specimen. 1.6.1900.	—	Unc	200.00

		Good	Fine	XF
S154	**20 Bolivianos** 1.6.1900. Black on green and yellow unpt. 2 allegorical women w/barrels and other commodities at l. Back green. Proof or specimen.	—	Unc	225.00

		Good	Fine	XF
S155	**50 Bolivianos** 1.6.1900. Black on olive-green and yellow unpt. 3 Indians at ctr. Back blue. Proof or specimen.	—	Unc	250.00

		Good	Fine	XF
S156	**100 Bolivianos** 1.6.1900. Black on orange and yellow unpt. Allegorical woman w/globe and cherub at ctr. Back red. Proof or specimen.	—	Unc	300.00

Banco Industrial

New name for Banco Industrial de La Paz in 1906. Later became part of the Banco Nacional de Bolivia.

1906; 1907 Issue

#S161-S166 sign. varieties.

#S161, S163-S166 printer: ABNC.

		Good	Fine	XF
S161	**1 Boliviano** 1906; 1907. Black on yellow unpt. Similar to #S151. Back dk. brown.			
	a. Series H-P. 1.1.1906.	30.00	75.00	225.00
	b. 1.1.1907.	35.00	85.00	250.00

		Good	Fine	XF
S162	**5 Bolivianos** 1.1.1907. Black on yellow and red-orange unpt. Horseback rider roping horse at l., standing figure at r. Back red-orange. Printer: W&S.	50.00	200.00	500.00
S163	**10 Bolivianos** 1.1.1907. Group of people.	—	Rare	—
S164	**20 Bolivianos** 1.1.1906.	Reported Not Confirmed		
S165	**50 Bolivianos** 1.1.1906.	Reported Not Confirmed		
S166	**100 Bolivianos** 1.1.1906.	Reported Not Confirmed		

Banco Mercantil

Issued at Oruro.

1906 Issue

#S171-S177 sign. varieties. Printer: ABNC.

		Good	Fine	XF
S171	**1 Boliviano** 1906; 1911. Black on green unpt. Girl at l., arms at r. Back olive or lighter green; bldg. and farm animals at ctr.			
	a. Series C-O. 1.7.1906.	35.00	80.00	175.00
	b. Series R-Y. 1.7.1911.	50.00	110.00	250.00

#S172 *Deleted.* See #S173.

		Good	Fine	XF
S173	**5 Bolivianos** 1906; 1911. Black on yellow, brown and yellow-green unpt. Miners at ctr. Back brown; arms w/church and monument in circle w/Potosí mountain at ctr.			
	a. Series A-D. 1.7.1906.	60.00	140.00	300.00
	b. Series D-G. 1.7.1911.	50.00	100.00	250.00

		Good	Fine	XF
S174	**10 Bolivianos** 1906; 1911. Black on red-orange and yellow unpt. People including mother and child, and hut at ctr. Back red-orange; clock tower and bldg. at ctr.			
	a. Series A; B. 1.7.1906.	80.00	300.00	—
	b. Series B. 1.7.1911.	90.00	300.00	—

		Good	Fine	XF
S175	**20 Bolivianos** 1.7.1906. Black on green and yellow unpt. 3 allegorical figures at ctr. Back blue; Plaza of Cochabamba at ctr.	400.00	900.00	—

		Good	Fine	XF
S176	**50 Bolivianos** 1.7.1906. Black on brown unpt. 2 young girls at ctr. Back brown; viaduct w/mountain in background.			
	r. Remainder. Numbered, w/o sign.	—	—	—
	p. Proof.	—	—	—
	s. Specimen.	—	—	—

		Good	Fine	XF
S177	**100 Bolivianos** 19xx. Black on orange and yellow unpt. Young woman at l. Back red; manufacturing scene at ctr.			
	a. Issued note.	—	—	—
	p. Proof.	—	—	—
	s. Specimen.	—	—	—

Banco Nacional de Bolivia

Authorized in 1871; took over assets of the Banco Boliviano in 1872.

1872 Provisional Issue

#S181 w/ovpt. new bank name on notes of the Banco Boliviano.

		Good	Fine	XF
S181	**1 Peso** 1.8.1872. Ovpt: *BANCO NACIONAL DE BOLIVIA* across ctr. on face and back on #S111. Series D.	200.00	550.00	—

NOTE: Higher values are reported, not confirmed.

1873 Cobija Issue

#S184-S189 were payable in Cobija or Valparaiso (now within Chile as a result of the War of the Pacific, 1879). Printer: ABNC.

		Good	Fine	XF
S184	**1 Boliviano** 17.2.1873. Black on dk. brown unpt. Like #S191, but w/different text at ctr. Back brown.			
	a. Issued note.	—	Rare	—
	p1. Proof. Orange unpt., back orange.	—	Unc	350.00
	p2. Proof. Red ovpt: *EMISION DEL LITORAL* across lower ctr.	—	—	—

		Good	Fine	XF
S185	**5 Bolivianos** 187x (ca.1873). Black. Like #S192, but w/different text at ctr.			
	p1. Proof. Blue unpt. Back blue.	—	Unc	400.00
	p2. Uniface proof. Green unpt.	—	—	—

		GOOD	FINE	XF
S186	**10 BOLIVIANOS**			
	187x (ca.1873). Black. Like #S193, but w/different text at ctr.			
	p1. Proof. Green unpt. Back blue.	—	Unc	400.00
	p2. Uniface proof. Green unpt. Red ovpt: *EMISION DEL LITORAL* across lower ctr.	—	—	—
	p3. Uniface proof. Brown unpt.	—	—	—

		GOOD	FINE	XF
S187	**20 BOLIVIANOS**			
	187x (ca.1873). Black on tan unpt. Sucre at lower l., Potosí city scene w/mountain across upper ctr., seated woman w/globe at lower r. Back tan. Proof.	—	Unc	450.00

		GOOD	FINE	XF
S188	**50 BOLIVIANOS**			
	187x (ca.1873). Black on orange unpt. Like #S195, but different text at ctr. Back orange. Proof.	—	Unc	450.00

		GOOD	FINE	XF
S189	**100 BOLIVIANOS**			
	187x (ca.1873). Black. River and mountains at lower l., Potosí mountain scene in oval w/eagle and flags flanked by 2 allegorical women at upper ctr., sailing ships at lower r.			
	p1. Proof. Deep orange unpt. Back deep orange.	—	Unc	450.00
	p2. Uniface proof. Brown unpt. Series C.	—	—	—

A word on pricing

When a note is marked RARE in the price columns, this note seldom appears on the market, or few are known in private hands. When dashes are in the price column, means that the note has not traded on the open market recently and a definitive value could not accurately be determined. Rare does not always mean expensive. A dashed price does not mean expensive or rare.

1873 La Paz Provisional Issue

		GOOD	FINE	XF
S190	**1 BOLIVIANO**			
	17.2.1873. Red handwritten ovpt: *La Paz*/Cobija on #S184.	—	Rare	—

1874 Antofagasta Issue

#S191-S195 payable at Antofagasta. Printer: ABNC.

		GOOD	FINE	XF
S191	**1 BOLIVIANO**			
	187x (ca.1874). Black on green unpt. Man and llamas at l., mountain and town at ctr., man at r. Back green.			
	a. Red ovpt: *EMISION DEL LITORAL* across lower ctr. on face and in circular form at ctr. on back.	—	Rare	—
	p. Proof.	—	Unc	350.00
	s. Specimen.	—	Unc	400.00

		GOOD	FINE	XF
S192	**5 BOLIVIANOS**			
	187x (ca.1874). Black on red-orange unpt. Miners at lower l., Potosí mountain scene in oval flanked by 2 seated allegorical women at upper ctr., Indian woman at lower r. Back red-orange.			
	a. Blue ovpt: *EMISION DEL LITORAL* across lower ctr. on face and in circular form at ctr. on back.	—	—	—
	p. Proof.	—	—	—
	s. Specimen.	—	Unc	400.00

		GOOD	FINE	XF
S193	**10 BOLIVIANOS**			
	187x (ca.1874). Black on orange unpt. Allegorical woman and plants at lower l., condor at upper ctr., Agriculture seated at lower r. Back orange.			
	a. Blue ovpt: *EMISION DEL LITORAL* across lower ctr. on face and in circular form at ctr. on back.	—	Rare	—
	p. Proof.	—	—	—
	s. Specimen.	—	Unc	400.00

		Good	Fine	XF
S195	**50 Bolivianos** 187x (ca.1874). Black on blue unpt. Bolívar at lower l., Potosí mountain scene in oval flanked by 2 seated allegorical women at upper ctr., seated allegorical woman w/pole and cap at lower r. Back blue. Proof.	—	—	—

1875 La Paz Issue

#S197-S198 printer: ABNC.

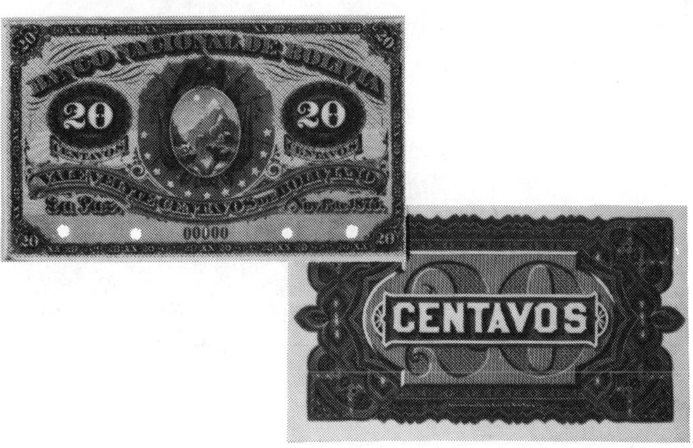

		Good	Fine	XF
S197	**20 Centavos** 1.11.1875. Black on green unpt. Potosí mountain scene in oval at ctr. Back green; value at ctr.			
	a. Issued note.	—	Rare	—
	p. Uniface proof.	—	Unc	200.00
	s. Specimen ovpt: *MUESTRA* or *SPECIMEN*, punched hole cancelled. Series A.	—	Unc	300.00

		Good	Fine	XF
S198	**40 Centavos** 1.11.1875. Black on orange unpt. Raphael's Angel at ctr. Back orange; value at ctr.			
	a. Issued note.	—	Rare	—
	p. Uniface proof.	—	Unc	250.00
	s. Specimen ovpt: *MUESTRA*, punched hole cancelled.	—	Unc	350.00

1877 Sucre Issue

#S199-S204 printer: ABNC.

		Good	Fine	XF
S199	**1 Boliviano** 1.1.1877. Black on red and green unpt. Mountain and city of Potosí at ctr. Back brown; Indian w/llamas at l., Indian at r.			
	a. Issued note.	75.00	200.00	600.00
	p. Proof.	—	—	—
	s. Specimen.	—	—	—

		Good	Fine	XF
S200	**5 Bolivianos** 1.1.1877. Black on lt. blue and tan unpt. Similar to #S185 and #S192, but w/major plate changes. Back blue. Series A.			
	a. Issued note.	—	—	—
	p. Proof.	—	—	—
	s. Specimen.	—	—	—

		Good	Fine	XF
S201	**10 Bolivianos** 1.1.1877. Black on red and green unpt. Allegorical woman at l. and r. of bank at ctr. Back green. Series A.			
	p. Proof.	—	—	—
	s. Specimen.	—	—	—

		Good	Fine	XF
S202	**20 Bolivianos** 1.1.1877. Black on orange unpt. Similar to #S187, but w/major plate changes. Back black and orange; Indian w/llamas at ctr.			
	p. Proof.	—	—	—
	s. Specimen. Series A.	—	—	—

		Good	Fine	XF
S203	**50 Bolivianos** 1.1.1877. Black on red-orange unpt. Similar to #S188 and #S195, but w/major plate changes. Back black and red-orange; mule team in mountains at ctr. Series A. Proof.	—	—	—

		GOOD	FINE	XF
S204	**100 BOLIVIANOS** 1.1.1877. Black on magenta unpt. Indian woman and Potosí mountain scene in oval at l., clock tower and monument at ctr., sailing ships at r. Back black and magenta; men and horses at ctr. Series A. Proof.	—	—	—

1882-83 SUCRE ISSUE

#S205-S210 printer: ABNC.

		GOOD	FINE	XF
S205	**1 BOLIVIANO** 1.1.1883. Black on green and red unpt. Condor at upper ctr., portr. S. Bolívar at lower r. Back brown; reclining allegorical woman at ctr.			
	a. Issued note. Series A1-R1.	10.00	25.00	125.00
	p. Proof. Series AA.	—	—	—
	s. Specimen. Series S1; T1; DD.	—	—	—

		GOOD	FINE	XF
S206	**5 BOLIVIANOS** 1.1.1883. Black on orange and blue unpt. Justice at l., 2 allegorical women paying homage to bust of A. J. de Sucre at ctr., 2 men at r. Back blue; seated Justice allegory w/condor at ctr.			
	a. Series B.	75.00	350.00	—
	p. Proof. Series B.	—	—	—
	s. Specimen. Series B1.	—	—	—

NOTE: Many counterfeits (including illus.) of #S206 were made.

		GOOD	FINE	XF
S207	**10 BOLIVIANOS** 1.1.1883. Black on green and red unpt. Allegorical woman at l., men and llamas at ctr., allegorical woman at r. Back green; allegorical woman feeding condor at ctr. Series B. Proof.	—	—	—

		GOOD	FINE	XF
S208	**20 BOLIVIANOS** 1.1.1883. Black on brown and red unpt. Reclining woman at l. ctr., 2 young girls at r. Back black and brown; allegorical woman w/child and globe at ctr.			
	a. Issued note.	—	—	—
	p. Proof.	—	Unc	300.00
	s. Specimen.	—	—	—

		GOOD	FINE	XF
S209	**50 BOLIVIANOS** 1.1.1883. Black on red-orange unpt. Indian woman at l., seated allegorical woman w/globe at ctr., portr. Sucre at r. Back black and red-orange; reclining allegorical woman w/ancient oil lamp at ctr.			
	p. Proof.	—	—	—
	s. Specimen, punched hole cancelled.	—	—	—

		GOOD	FINE	XF
S210	**100 BOLIVIANOS** 1.1.1882; 1.1.1883. Black on orange unpt. "Reception of Columbus" at l., allegorical woman w/pitcher at ctr. r. Back orange and black; standing Liberty w/shield and faces at ctr.			
	p. Proof.	—	—	—
	s. Specimen.	—	—	—

NOTE: The 1882 date of #S210 was prepared in error according to ABNC records.

1892-94 ISSUE

#S211-S213 printer: ABNC.

		Good	Fine	XF
S211	1 Boliviano 1892; 1894. Black on yellow and orange unpt. Miners at lower l., helmeted Athena at ctr. Back brown-orange; young woman and sheep at ctr.			
	a. Serial # at lower l. and upper r. 1.1.1892. Series L-Z; AA-HH.	15.00	30.00	100.00
	b. Serial # at upper l. and r. 1.1.1892. Series II-ZZ; A1-L1.	15.00	30.00	100.00
	c. 1.1.1894.	Reported Not Confirmed		
	s. Specimen. As a. Series A.	—	—	

		Good	Fine	XF
S212	5 Bolivianos 1.1.1892. Black on green and yellow unpt. Horse at l., seated woman w/2 children at r. Back dk. brown; seated woman w/sheaf and 2 sheep at ctr.			
	a. Issued note.	40.00	120.00	300.00
	p. Proof.	—	—	—

		Good	Fine	XF
S213	10 Bolivianos 1.1.1894. Black on blue and yellow unpt. Man w/oxen plowing at ctr., seated woman at r. Back green; woman, child and cows at ctr.			
	a. Issued note.	80.00	200.00	400.00
	p. Proof.	—	—	—

NOTE: Higher values are reported, not confirmed.

1904 Issue

#S214 and S215 printer: BWC.

		Good	Fine	XF
S214	5 Bolivianos 1.1.1904. Black on peach and lt. green unpt. Portr. S. Bolívar at top ctr. Back brown; girl at ctr. Series A; B.			
	a. Issued note.	200.00	600.00	—
	s. Specimen perforated: *CANCELLED.*	—	—	—
S215	10 Bolivianos 1.1.1904.	—	—	—

NOTE: Higher values are reported, not confirmed.

1910 Issue

		Good	Fine	XF
S217	20 Bolivianos 1910. Black on brown and m/c unpt. Allegorical woman seated at l. Portr. allegorical woman at ctr. on back.			
	a. Issued note.	—	Rare	—
	p. Uniface back proof.	—	Unc	100.00

Banco Potosí

Issued at Sucre.

1887 Issue

#S221-S226 printer: ABNC.

		Good	Fine	XF
S221	1 Boliviano 1.1.1887. Black on green and pink unpt. Seated allegorical woman leaning on trunk at l., A. Ballivian at r. Back brown; people in village square at ctr.			
	a. Issued note. Red serial #. Series A-O.	15.00	35.00	85.00
	b. Issued note. Black serial #. Series P-W.	15.00	35.00	85.00
	r. Remainder.	—	Unc	45.00
	s. Specimen. Series A; I; P.	—	Unc	100.00

		Good	Fine	XF
S222	5 Bolivianos 1.1.1887. Black on blue and orange unpt. Arms at l., steam freight train at ctr., child writing at lower r. Back blue; Justice seated at ctr.			
	a. Issued note.	50.00	125.00	400.00
	s. Specimen.	—	Unc	100.00

S223 10 BOLIVIANOS
1.1.1887. Black on rose and green unpt. Ox-drawn cart at ctr., seated Justice at r. Back green; allegorical woman at ctr.

	GOOD	FINE	XF
a. Issued note.	80.00	250.00	—
s. Specimen.	—	Unc	150.00

S224 20 BOLIVIANOS
1.1.1887. Black on red and ochre unpt. Woman in hammock at l., allegorical woman at r. Back brown and black; group of angels and fish at ctr.

	GOOD	FINE	XF
a. Issued note.	200.00	500.00	—
s. Specimen.	—	Unc	200.00

S225 50 BOLIVIANOS
1.1.1887. Black on m/c unpt. Woman emptying pitcher at l., men w/llamas at ctr., portr. Gen. A. Nariño at r. Back orange and black; condor at ctr.

	GOOD	FINE	XF
a. Issued note.	—	Rare	—
s. Specimen.	—	—	—

S226 100 BOLIVIANOS
1.1.1887. Black on orange and gray unpt. Scene of Potosí at ctr., portr. S. Bolívar at upper r. Back orange and black; miners at ctr.

	GOOD	FINE	XF
p. Proof.	—	—	—
s. Specimen.	—	—	—

1894 ISSUE

#S231-S236 printer: BWC.

S231 1 BOLIVIANO
1.1.1894. Black on pink, orange, and green unpt. Kneeling child at l., portr. Gen A. Nariño at r. Back dk. brown on yellow unpt.; indians and llamas at ctr. Unsigned remainders.

GOOD	FINE	XF
—	Unc	20.00

NOTE: A hoard of uncirculated remainders of #S231 numbering in the thousands was located during 1984.

S232 5 BOLIVIANOS
1.1.1894. Black on lt. blue and yellow unpt. Arms at l., steam locomotive at upper ctr., cupid painting at r. Back blue on yellow unpt; allegorical woman at ctr.

GOOD	FINE	XF
75.00	175.00	350.00

S233 10 BOLIVIANOS
1.1.1894. Black on pale green and red-orange unpt. Ox-drawn cart at upper ctr., allegorical woman w/musical instruments at r. Back deep green; allegory of Culture.

	GOOD	FINE	XF
p. Proof.	—	—	—
s. Specimen.	—	—	—

		GOOD	FINE	XF
S234	**20 BOLIVIANOS** 1.1.1894. Black on tan and red-orange unpt. Woman w/sheep at l., portr. helmeted Roman warrior at r. Back brown and black; cherubs on dock at ctr.			
	p. Proof.	—	—	—
	s. Specimen.	—	—	—

		GOOD	FINE	XF
S235	**50 BOLIVIANOS** 1.1.1894. Black on red unpt. Man harvesting at l., animals in town at ctr., portr. C. Columbus at r. Back black and orange on yellow unpt.; American eagle at ctr.			
	a. Issued note.	—	Rare	—
	r. Unsigned or partially signed remainder w/serial #.	—	Unc	1000.
	s. Uniface specimen w/ or w/o perforated: *SPECIMEN* w/o serial #.	—	—	—

		GOOD	FINE	XF
S236	**100 BOLIVIANOS** 1.1.1894. Black on orange unpt. Potosí at ctr., portr. S. Bolívar at upper r. Back orange and black; mine opening w/donkey drawn ore car and miners at ctr. Printer: BWC.			
	a. Black on orange unpt.	—	Rare	—
	r. Unsigned remainder w/o serial #.	—	—	1000.
	s. Uniface specimen w/ or w/o perforated: *SPECIMEN* w/o serial #. Purple on yellow-green unpt.	—	—	—

The Republic of Bosnia-Herzegovina borders Croatia to the north and west, Serbia to the east and Montenegro in the southeast with only 12.4 miles of coastline. The total land area is 19,735 sq. mi. (51,129 sq. km.). It has a population of 4.34 million. Capital: Sarajevo. Electricity, mining and agriculture are leading industries.

Bosnia's first ruler of importance was the Ban Kulin, 1180-1204. Stephen Kotromanió was invested with Bosnia, held loyalty to Hungary and extended his rule to the principality of Hum or Zahumlje, the future Herzegovina. His daughter Elisabeth married Louis the Great and he died in the same year. His nephew Tvrtko succeeded and during the weakening of Serbian power he assumed the title *Stephen Tvrtko, in Christ God King of the Serbs and Bosnia and the Coastland.* Later he assumed the title of *King of Dalmatia and Croatia,* but died before he could consolidate power. Successors also asserted their right to the Serbian throne.

In 1459 the Turks invaded Serbia. Bosnia was invaded in 1463 and Herzegovina in 1483. During Turkish rule Islam was accepted rather than Catholicism. During the 16th and 17th centuries Bosnia was an important Turkish outpost in continuing warfare with the Habsburgs and Venice. When Hungary was freed of the Turkish yoke, the imperialists penetrated Bosnia, and in 1697 Prince Eugene captured Sarajevo. Later, by the Treaty of Karlowitz in 1699, the northern boundary of Bosnia became the northernmost limit of the Turkish empire while the eastern area was ceded to Austria, but later restored to Turkey in 1739 lasting until 1878 following revolts of 1821, 1828, 1831 and 1862. On June 30, 1871 Serbia and Montenegro declared war on Turkey and were quickly defeated. The Turkish war with Russia led to the occupation by Austria-Hungary. Insurgents attempted armed resistance and Austria-Hungary invaded, quelling the uprising in 1878. The Austrian occupation provided a period of prosperity while at the same time prevented relations with Serbia and Croatia. Strengthening political and religious movements from within forced the annexation by Austria on Oct. 7, 1908. Hungary's establishment of a dictatorship in Croatia following the victories of Serbian forces in the Balkan War roused the whole Yugoslav population of Austria-Hungary to feverish excitement. The Bosnian group, mainly students, devoted its efforts to revolutionary ideas. After Austria's Balkan front collapsed in Oct. 1918 the union with Yugoslavia developed and on Dec. 1, 1918 the former Kingdom of the Serbs, Croats and Slovenes was proclaimed (later to become the Kingdom of Yugoslavia on Oct. 3, 1929).

After the defeat of Germany in WWII during which Bosnia was under the control of Pavelic of Croatia, a new Socialist Republic was formed under Marshal Tito having six constituent republics all subservient, quite similar to the constitution of the U.S.S.R. Military and civil loyalty was with Tito. In Jan. 1990 the Yugoslav government announced a rewriting of the constitution, abolishing the Communist Party's monopoly of power. Opposition parties were legalized in July 1990. On Oct. 15, 1991 the National Assembly adopted a Memorandum on Sovereignty that envisaged Bosnian autonomy within a Yugoslav Federation. In March 1992 an agreement was reached under EC auspices by Moslems, Serbs and Croats to set up 3 autonomous ethnic communities under a central Bosnian authority. Independence was declared on April 5, 1992. The 2 Serbian members of government resigned and fighting broke out between all 3 ethnic communities. The Dayton (Ohio, USA) Peace Accord was signed in 1995 which recognized the Federation of Bosnia-Herzegovina and the Srpska (Serbian) Republic. Both governments maintain separate military forces, schools, etc., providing humanitarian aid while a treaty allowed NATO "Peace Keeping" forces be deployed in Dec. 1995 replacing the United Nations troops previously acting in a similar role.

RULERS:

Ottoman, until 1878
Austrian, 1878-1918
Yugoslavian, 1918-1941

MONETARY SYSTEM:

1 Dinar = 100 Para 1992-1998
1 Convertible Marka = 1 Deutschemark
1 Convertible Marka = 100 Convertible Pfeniga, 1998-

PARTISAN - WWII

ZEMALJSKO ANTIFASISTICKO VIJECE BOSNE I HERCEGOVINE

BOSNIA AND HERZEGOVINA ANTI-FASCIST AUTHORITY

DECREE 15.1.1943; NARODNOG OSLOBODENJA ISSUE

NATIONAL BONDS

#S134-S138 brown, red and lt. blue. Star in sprays w/long ribbons w/text: *SMRT FASIZMO - SLOBODA NARODU* at upper ctr. Series BH and I/V.

		GOOD	FINE	XF
S134	**100 DINARA = 100 KUNA**	100.00	250.00	—
S135	**500 DINARA = 500 KUNA**	100.00	250.00	—
S136	**1000 DINARA = 1000 KUNA** *D.1943.* 12 stylized soldiers in attack ranks in unpt.	100.00	250.00	—
S137	**5000 DINARA = 5000 KUNA**	100.00	250.00	—
S138	**10,000 DINARA = 10,000 KUNA**	100.00	250.00	—

The Federative Republic of Brazil, which comprises half the continent of South America, is the only Latin American country deriving its culture and language from Portugal. It has an area of 3,286,470 sq. mi. (8,511,965 sq. km.) and a population of 169.2 million. Capital: Brasília. The economy of Brazil is as varied and complex as any in the developing world. Agriculture is a mainstay of the economy, although but 4 percent of the area is under cultivation. Known mineral resources are almost unlimited in variety and size of reserves. A large, relatively sophisticated industry ranges from basic steel and chemical production to finished consumer goods. Coffee, cotton, iron ore and cocoa are the chief exports.

Brazil was discovered and claimed for Portugal by Admiral Pedro Alvares Cabral in 1500. Portugal established a settlement in 1532 and proclaimed the area a royal colony in 1549. During the Napoleonic Wars, Dom João VI established the seat of Portuguese government in Rio de Janeiro. When he returned to Portugal, his son Dom Pedro I declared Brazil's independence on Sept. 7, 1822, and became emperor of Brazil. The Empire of Brazil was maintained until 1889 when a republic was established. The Federative Republic was established in 1946 by terms of a constitution drawn up by a constituent assembly. Following a coup in 1964, the armed forces retained overall control under dictatorship until a civilian government was restored on March 15, 1985. The current constitution was adopted in 1988.

MONETARY SYSTEM:

1 Milreis = 1000 Reis, 1833-1942
1 Cruzeiro = 100 Centavos, 1942-1967

ARRANGEMENT

Listings for Brazil in this volume are divided into six major sections. The first contains provincial notes for the period 1808 to 1857. The second contains notes titled *Banco do Brazil* (actually from three separate banks with this name), issued from 1808 to 1890. The third lists issues from banks under the Empire, from 1850 to 1885. The fourth is a listing of regional issues from 1892 to 1897. Fifth is another section on bank issues, this time under the Republic, from 1889 to 1893. The sixth section is comprised of later regional issues from 1924 to 1966.

The following chart indicates specific contents of each of these sections:

Section I, 1808-1857

PROVINCIAL ISSUES

Bahia, 1828 .... #S101-S104
Ceará, 1857 .... #S111
Minas Geraes, 1808-1818 .... #S121-S145
República Rio Grandense, 1838 .... #S151

Section II, 1808-1890

BANCO DO BRAZIL

First Banco do Brazil, 1808-1829 .... #S171-S224
Second Banco do Brazil, 1851-1853 .... #S227-S229
Third Banco do Brazil, 1853-1890 .... #S231-S358

Section III, 1850-1885

BANK ISSUES EMPIRE

Banco da Bahia, 1858-1860 .... #S381-S390
Banco Commercial e Agricola, 1858-1859 .... #S401-S419
Banco Commercial da Bahia, 1850 .... #S421
Banco Commercial do Maranhão, 1854 .... #S424
Banco do Maranhão, 1857-1885 .... #S425-S430
Banco do Rio Grande do Sul, 1859 .... #S436
Banco Rural e Hypothecario, 1859 .... #S441-S443
Novo Banco de Pernambuco, 1858 .... #S447-S450

Section IV, 1892-1897

REGIONAL ISSUES

Alagoas, 1895 .... #S471-S473
Amazonas, 1892 .... #S477-S478
Maranhão, 1894 .... #S481
Pernambuco, 1895-1898 .... #S486-S498
Rio Grande do Norte, 1897 .... #S501-S506
Sergipe, 1897 .... #S511-S515

Section V, 1889-1893

BANK ISSUES REPUBLIC

Banco da Bahia, 1890 .... #S521-S522
Banco do Brazil, 1890 .... #S526-S535
Banco do Café, 1890 .... #S541-S542
Banco de Crédito Popular do Brazil, 1891-1892 .... #S546-S555
Banco Emissor da Bahia, 1890 .... #S561-S566
Banco Emissor do Norte, 1890 .... #S571-S580
Banco Emissor de Pernambuco, 1890 .... #S581-S586
Banco Emissor do Sul, 1890 .... #S591-S593
Banco dos Estados Unidos do Brazil, 1890 .... #S596-S607B
Banco Industrial dos Estados do Sul, 1891 .... #S608-S609
Banco Mercantil de Santos, 1890 .... #S611-S616
Banco Nacional do Brazil no Rio de Janeiro, 1890 .... #S621-S630
Banco da República dos Estados Unidos do Brazil, 1889-1891 .... #S631-S650
Banco da República do Brazil, 1893 .... #S656-S680
Banco de São Paulo, 1889 .... #S681-S683
Banco Sul Americano de Pernambuco, 1890 .... #S686-S689
Banco Uniao Ibero Americano, 1891 .... #S691
Banco Uniao de São Paulo, 1890 .... #S693-S711

Section VI, 1924-1966

REGIONAL ISSUES

Minas Geraes, 1930 .... #S751-S764
Rio Grande do Sul, 1930-1934, 1959-1966 .... #S771-S854
São Paulo, 1932 .... #S861-S876
Revolution Issue, 1924 .... #S881

SECTION I, 1808-57

EMPIRE - PROVINCIAL ISSUES

BAHIA

PROVINCIA DA BAHIA

Issued to redeem the copper coins in circulation throughout the Province.

LAW OF 27.11.1827/DECREE OF 24.12.1827; 1828 ISSUE

#S101-S104 black. Imperial arms at upper ctr. Uniface.

		GOOD	FINE	XF
S101	**10 MIL REIS** 1828.	—	Rare	—
S102	**25 MIL REIS** 1828.	—	Rare	—
S103	**50 MIL REIS** 1828.	—	Rare	—

		GOOD	FINE	XF
S104	**100 MIL REIS** 1828.	—	Rare	—

NOTE: A second issue consisting of the same denominations is reported, not confirmed.

CEARÁ

PROVINCIA DO CEARÁ

1857 TREASURY NOTES ISSUE

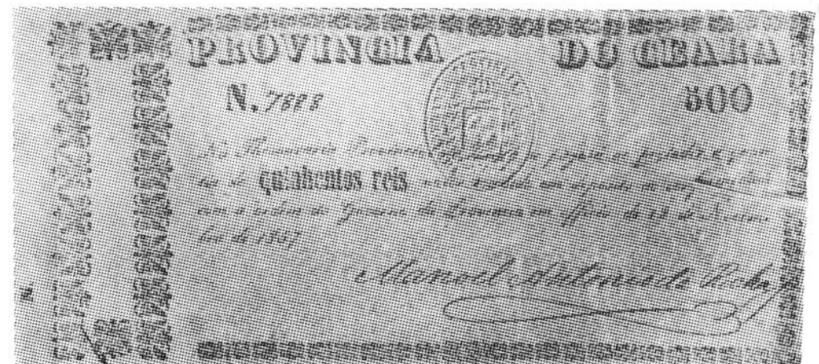

		GOOD	FINE	XF
S111	**500 REIS** 12.11.1857. Black. Embossed oval provincial arms at upper ctr.	—	Rare	—

MINAS GERAES

CAPITANIA DE MINAS GERAES

Issued under Royal Letter of 13.5.1808.

1808 ND GOLD EXCHANGE NOTES ISSUE

#S121-S126 black. Denomination at top between two ornaments. White paper, uniface.

		GOOD	FINE	XF
S121	**37 1/2 REIS = 1 VINTEM DE OURO** ND (1808).	—	Rare	—
S122	**75 REIS = 2 VINTENS DE OURO** ND (1808).	—	Rare	—

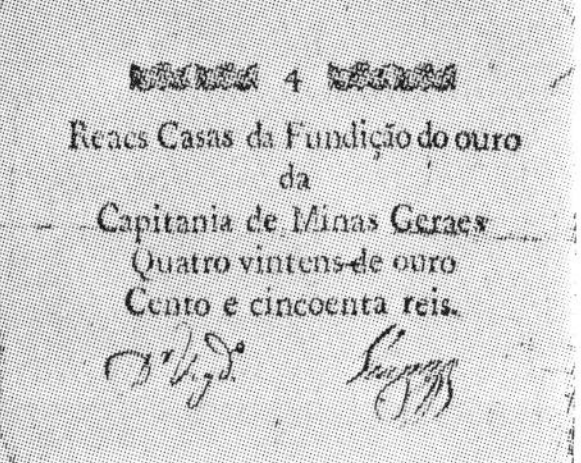

		Good	Fine	XF
S123	**150 Reis = 4 Vintens de Ouro** ND (1808).	—	Rare	—
S124	**300 Reis = 8 Vintens de Ouro** ND (1808).	—	Rare	—
S125	**450 Reis = 12 Vintens de Ouro** ND (1808).	—	Rare	—
S126	**600 Reis = 16 Vintens de Ouro** ND (1808).	—	Rare	—

1809 ND Issue

#S131-S136 black. Crowned arms of Portugal in half wreath at upper ctr. White paper, uniface.

		Good	Fine	XF
S131	**37 1/2 Reis = 1 Vintem de Ouro** ND (1809).	—	Rare	—
S132	**75 Reis = 2 Vintens de Ouro** ND (1809).	—	Rare	—
S133	**150 Reis = 4 Vintens de Ouro** ND (1809).	—	Rare	—
S134	**300 Reis = 8 Vintens de Ouro** ND (1809).	—	Rare	—
S135	**450 Reis = 12 Vintens de Ouro** ND (1809).	—	Rare	—

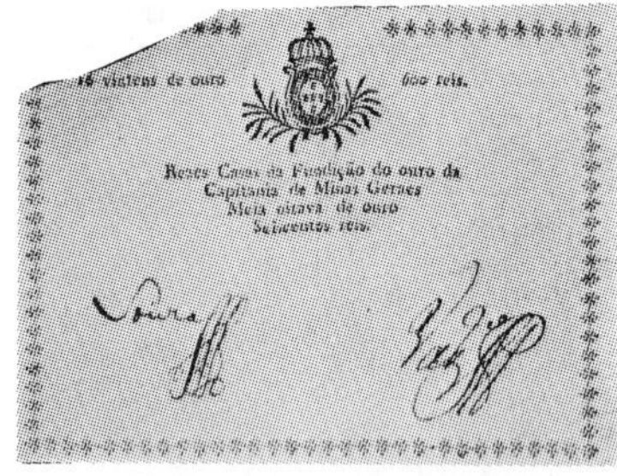

		Good	Fine	XF
S136	**600 Reis = 16 Vintens de Ouro** ND (1809).	—	Rare	—

1818 ND Issue

Printed in 1818 at Rio de Janeiro but apparently not issued as no examples in issued condition are known.

		Good	Fine	XF
S141	**37 1/2 Reis = 1 Vintem de Ouro** (ca. 1818).	—	—	—
S142	**75 Reis = 2 Vintens de Ouro** (ca. 1818).	—	—	—
S143	**150 Reis = 4 Vintens de Ouro** (ca. 1818).	—	—	—
S144	**300 Reis = 8 Vintens de Ouro** (ca. 1818).	—	—	—
S145	**450 Reis = 12 Vintens de Ouro** (ca. 1818).	—	—	—

NOTE: The 600 Reis denomination was not printed as part of this issue.

República Rio-Grandense, 1835-1845

Because of a local war situation in the province of São Pedro do Rio Grande do Sul, the copper coin in circulation could not be satisfactorily recalled. A revolutionary republic was proclaimed on September 20, 1835, lasting until February 28, 1845. During that time an issue of paper notes was made to facilitate the recall of copper coins.

1838 Conhecimientos Issue

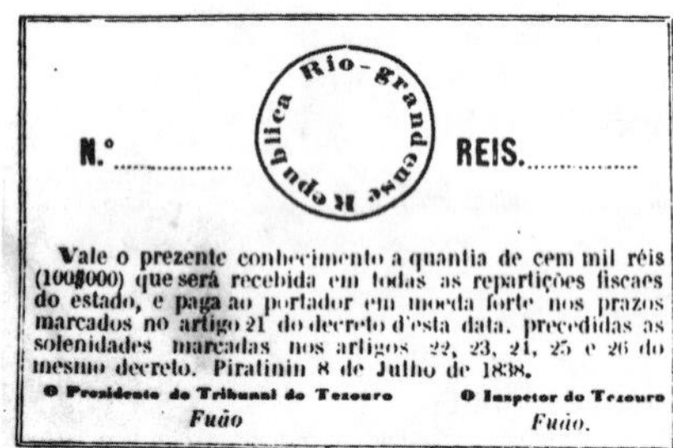

N.° .... Republica Rio-grandense REIS.............

Vale o prezente conhecimento a quantia de cem mil réis (100$000) que será recebida em todas as repartições fiscaes do estado, e paga ao portador em moeda forte nos prazos marcados no artigo 21 do decreto d'esta data, precedidas as solenidades marcadas nos artigos 22, 23, 24, 25 e 26 do mesmo decreto. Piratinin 8 de Julho de 1838.

O Presidente do Tribunal do Tezouro — Fulão
O Inspetor do Tezouro — Fulão.

		Good	Fine	XF
S151	**100 Reis** 6.7.1838. Black.	—	Rare	—

Section II, 1808-90

Banco do Brazil - During the 19th century there were three separate institutions established with the same bank name. The first came in 1808 by royal letter. It issued banknotes up to the time of its closing in 1829. A second bank (Banco do Brazil no Rio de Janeiro) was formed in 1851 by the Viscount of Mauá. Several notes from this bank are reported, not confirmed (see listing).

The Banco do Brazil no Rio de Janeiro merged with the Banco Commercial no Rio de Janeiro in 1853 to form the third Banco do Brazil which became operational that year as a private bank. It issued a variety of notes, employing printers in Brazil, England and the United States. A number of branches were established and these, too, issued specially designed as well as overprinted regular notes in their names. Some notes of this bank remained in circulation until the end of the century.

A fourth Banco do Brazil was formed in 1905; this bank exists today. Its note issues of 1923 and 1930 are found in Vol. 2.

Banco do Brazil (First)

1810-13 Issue

#S171-S188 black. Neptune reclining, water jug at upper l. Uniface.

		Good	Fine	XF
S171	**4 Mil Reis** ND (1813-29).	—	Rare	—
S172	**6 Mil Reis** ND (1813-29).	—	Rare	—

		Good	Fine	XF
S173	**8 Mil Reis** ND (1813-29).	—	Rare	—
S174	**10 Mil Reis** ND (1813-29).	—	Rare	—
S175	**12 Mil Reis** ND (1813-29).	—	Rare	—
S176	**20 Mil Reis** ND (1813-29).	—	Rare	—
S177	**30 Mil Reis** ND (1810-29).	—	Rare	—

		Good	Fine	XF
S178	**40 Mil Reis** ND (1810-29).	—	Rare	—
S179	**50 Mil Reis** ND (1810-29).	—	Rare	—
S180	**60 Mil Reis** ND (1810-29).	—	Rare	—
S181	**70 Mil Reis** ND (1810-29).	—	Rare	—
S182	**80 Mil Reis** ND (1810-29).	—	Rare	—
S183	**90 Mil Reis** ND (1810-29).	—	Rare	—
S184	**100 Mil Reis** ND (1810-29). Value in shaded area at ctr. r.	—	Rare	—
S185	**100 Mil Reis** ND (1810-29). Value in open area at ctr. r.	—	Rare	—
S186	**200 Mil Reis** ND (1810-29).	—	Rare	—
S187	**300 Mil Reis** ND (1810-29).	—	Rare	—
S188	**400 Mil Reis** ND (1810-29).	—	Rare	—

NOTE: Higher values are reported, not confirmed.

Decree of 4.7.1828

#S201-S202 black. Allegorical figures and ship at upper ctr. Dates filled in by hand. Uniface.

		Good	Fine	XF
S201	**1 Mil Reis** 1828-29.	—	Rare	—

		GOOD	FINE	XF
S202	2 MIL REIS 1828-29.	—	Rare	—

DECREE OF 23.9.1829

#S206-S224 allegorical figures at l., ctr. and r. Back w/4 portr. in circles. Printers: Perkins & Heath or Perkins & Bacon. Some notes have one name, others have both names. Notes hand dated. Uniface.

#S206-S216 black.

		GOOD	FINE	XF
S206	1 MIL REIS 1829-33.	—	Rare	—
S207	2 MIL REIS 1829-30.	—	Rare	—
S208	4 MIL REIS 1829-30.	—	Rare	—
S209	6 MIL REIS 1829-30.	—	Rare	—
S210	8 MIL REIS 1829-30.	—	Rare	—
S211	10 MIL REIS 1829-30.	—	Rare	—
S212	12 MIL REIS 1829-30.	—	Rare	—
S213	20 MIL REIS 1829-30.	—	Rare	—

		GOOD	FINE	XF
S214	30 MIL REIS 1829-30.	—	Rare	—
S215	40 MIL REIS 1829-30.	—	Rare	—
S216	50 MIL REIS 1829-30.	—	Rare	—
S217	60 MIL REIS 1829-30. Blue.	—	Rare	—
S218	70 MIL REIS 1829-30. Gray.	—	Rare	—
S219	80 MIL REIS 1829-30. Yellow.	—	Rare	—
S220	90 MIL REIS 1829-30. Blue.	—	Rare	—
S221	100 MIL REIS 1829-30. Sepia.	—	Rare	—
S222	200 MIL REIS 1829-30. Green.	—	Rare	—
S223	300 MIL REIS 1829-30. Green.	—	Rare	—
S224	400 MIL REIS 1829-30. Green.	—	Rare	—

BANCO DO BRAZIL NO RIO DE JANEIRO (SECOND)

1851 ND ISSUE

		GOOD	FINE	XF
S227	200 MIL REIS ND. Issued at Rio de Janeiro.	Reported Not Confirmed		
S228	100 MIL REIS ND. Issued at São Paulo branch.	Reported Not Confirmed		
S229	100 MIL REIS ND. Issued at São Pedro de Rio Grande do Sul branch.	Reported Not Confirmed		

BANCO DO BRAZIL (THIRD)

DECREE OF 31.8.1853 (1853-54)

#S231-S236 black. Uniface. Printer: CMRJ.

		GOOD	FINE	XF
S231	20 MIL REIS ND (1854-55). View of naval arsenal at ctr.	—	Rare	—
S232	30 MIL REIS ND (1853-55). Gaucho at ctr.	—	Rare	—
S233	50 MIL REIS ND (1854-55). Indian woman in hammock at ctr.	—	Rare	—

		GOOD	FINE	XF
S234	100 MIL REIS ND (1854-55). Manned rowboat, 2 swans at ctr.	—	Rare	—

		GOOD	FINE	XF
S235	200 MIL REIS ND (1854-55). Reclining sailor at ctr.	—	Rare	—

		GOOD	FINE	XF
S236	500 MIL REIS ND (1854-55). Standing woman at l. and r., allegory of Abundance at upper ctr.	—	Rare	—

1856-57 ND FIRST ISSUE

#S241-S245 black. Uniface.

		GOOD	FINE	XF
S241	**20 MIL REIS** ND (1856). View of Rio de Janeiro at upper ctr.	—	Rare	—
S242	**30 MIL REIS** ND (1856). Different view of Rio de Janeiro at upper ctr. Rose paper.	—	Rare	—
S243	**50 MIL REIS** ND (1857). Allegory of Abundance at upper ctr.	—	Rare	—
S244	**100 MIL REIS** ND (1856). City of Santos at upper ctr. Yellow paper.	—	Rare	—

		GOOD	FINE	XF
S245	**200 MIL REIS** ND (1856). Shore of Icarai at upper ctr. Green paper.			
	a. Issued note.	—	Rare	—
	b. Cancelled, perforated: *SEM VALOR.*	—	—	—

1856 ND SECOND ISSUE

#S246-S247 black. Uniface.

		GOOD	FINE	XF
S246	**20 MIL REIS** ND (1856). Different view of Rio de Janeiro at upper ctr.	12.00	30.00	60.00
S247	**50 MIL REIS** ND (1856). Scene of Rio de Janeiro at ctr. Green paper.	—	Rare	—

1857 ND ISSUE

		GOOD	FINE	XF
S248	**20 MIL REIS** ND (1857-60). Black and green on brown unpt. Liberty standing w/flag at l., coffee worker at r. Back green. Printer: BWC.	—	Rare	—

1860'S ND ISSUE

#S251-S256 printer: ABNC.

		GOOD	FINE	XF
S251	**25 MIL REIS** ND. Black and red. 2 sailors dockside w/sailing ship at anchor at lower l., St. Sebastian and allegory of Transport at top ctr., portr. C. Columbus at lower r. Back red.			
	a. Issued note.	—	Rare	—
	p. Proof.	—	—	—
	s. Specimen.	—	—	—

		GOOD	FINE	XF
S252	**30 MIL REIS** ND. Black and brown. St. Sebastian at lower l., horse at top ctr., seated allegorical woman at lower r. Back brown.			
	a. Issued note.	—	Rare	—
	p. Proof.	—	—	—
	s. Specimen.	—	—	—

S253 50 MIL REIS | GOOD | FINE | XF

ND. Black and green. St. Sebastian at lower l., explorer landing at upper ctr., portr. girl w/pups at lower r. Back green.

	GOOD	FINE	XF
a. Issued note.	—	Rare	—
p. Proof.	—	—	—
s. Specimen.	—	—	—

S254 100 MIL REIS

ND. Black and blue. St. Sebastian at lower l., steam passenger train at upper ctr., allegory of Justice at lower r. Back blue.

	GOOD	FINE	XF
a. Issued note.	—	Rare	—
p. Proof.	—	—	—
s. Specimen.	—	—	—

S255 200 MIL REIS

ND. Black and yellow unpt. Seated woman at lower l., allegory of Abundance at top ctr., St. Sebastian at lower r. Back red; steam passenger train at station at upper ctr.

	GOOD	FINE	XF
a. Issued note.	—	Rare	—
p. Proof.	—	—	—
s. Specimen.	—	—	—

S256 500 MIL REIS

ND. Black and orange. Portr. Liberty at lower l., St. Sebastian and field workers at upper ctr., portr. woman at lower r. Back orange; sailor in oval at ctr.

	GOOD	FINE	XF
a. Issued note.	—	Rare	—
p. Proof.	—	—	—
s. Specimen.	—	—	—

NOTE: #S254, S255 and S256 were reissued in 1890 with sign. of A. A. Vieira da Costa. For a listing of those notes and a new issue of 1890 by the Banco do Brazil see #S526-S528, and S531-S535.

A word on pricing

When a note is marked RARE in the price columns, this note seldom appears on the market, or few are known in private hands. When dashes are in the price column, means that the note has not traded on the open market recently and a definitive value could not accurately be determined. Rare does not always mean expensive. A dashed price does not mean expensive or rare.

BAHIA

1856 ND ISSUE

#S261-S266 black. View of Bahia at upper ctr. Uniface. Printer: Bradbury and Evans.

		GOOD	FINE	XF
S261	**10 MIL REIS** ND (1856). White paper.	—	Rare	—
S262	**20 MIL REIS** ND (1856). Red paper.	—	Rare	—
S263	**50 MIL REIS** ND (1856). Yellow paper.	—	Rare	—
S264	**100 MIL REIS** ND (1856). Green paper.	—	Rare	—
S265	**200 MIL REIS** ND (1856). Lt. brown paper.	—	Rare	—
S266	**500 MIL REIS** ND (1856). Rose paper.	—	Rare	—

NOTE: A second issue consisting of 10, 20, 50, 100 and 200 Mil Reis notes is reported, not confirmed.

MARANHÃO

1856 ND ISSUE

#S276-S280 black. Allegory of Commerce with Brazilian flag at upper ctr. Uniface. Printer: Knowles and Foster (w/o imprint).

		GOOD	FINE	XF
S276	**10 MIL REIS** ND (1856). Red paper.	—	Rare	—
S277	**20 MIL REIS** ND (1856). Green paper.	—	Rare	—

		GOOD	FINE	XF
S278	**50 MIL REIS** ND (1856). Green paper.	—	Rare	—
S279	**100 MIL REIS** ND (1856). Brown paper.	—	Rare	—
S280	**200 MIL REIS** ND (1856). White paper.	—	Rare	—

NOTE: A second issue consisting of 10, 20, 50, 100 and 200 Mil Reis notes is reported but not confirmed.

OURO PRETO

1856 ND ISSUE

#S291 is a special design for branch issues.

		Good	Fine	XF
S291	**10 Mil Reis** ND (1856). Black. Beehive at upper ctr. Uniface.	—	Rare	—

#S292-S296 ovpt: *CAIXA FILIAL DO OURO PRETO* on face of Banco do Brazil issues.

S292	**20 Mil Reis** ND (1856). Black. Ovpt. on #S231.	—	Rare	—
S293	**30 Mil Reis** ND (1856). Black. Ovpt. on #S232.	—	Rare	—
S294	**50 Mil Reis** ND (1856). Black. Ovpt. on #S233.	—	Rare	—
S295	**100 Mil Reis** ND (1856). Black. Ovpt. on #S234.	—	Rare	—
S296	**200 Mil Reis** ND (1856). Black. Ovpt. on #S235.	—	Rare	—

1857 ND Issue

#S301 is a special design for this issue.

		Good	Fine	XF
S301	**20 Mil Reis** ND (1857). Black. Shoreline of Botafogo at ctr. Uniface. Printer: Knowles & Foster (w/o imprint).	—	Rare	—

#S302-S304 ovpt: *CAIXA FILIAL DO OURO PRETO* on face of Banco do Brazil issues.

		Good	Fine	XF
S302	**50 Mil Reis** ND (1857). Black. Ovpt. on #S243.	—	Rare	—

		Good	Fine	XF
S303	**100 Mil Reis** ND (1857). Black. Ovpt. on #S244.	—	Rare	—

		Good	Fine	XF
S304	**200 Mil Reis** ND (1857). Black. Ovpt. on #S245.	—	Rare	—

NOTE: Two other issues (10, 20 and 30 Mil Reis, and 20 and 50 Mil Reis) for this branch are reported, not confirmed.

Pará

1856 ND First Issue

#S311-S315 black. Woman with globe and plants at upper ctr. Uniface. Printer: Knowles & Foster (w/o imprint).

		Good	Fine	XF
S311	**10 Mil Reis** ND (1856). Yellow paper.	—	Rare	—
S312	**20 Mil Reis** ND (1856). Green paper.	—	Rare	—
S313	**50 Mil Reis** ND (1856). Yellow paper.	—	Rare	—
S314	**100 Mil Reis** ND (1856). Gray paper.	—	Rare	—

		Good	Fine	XF
S315	**200 Mil Reis** ND (1856). Red paper.	—	Rare	—

1856 ND Second Issue

#S316-S318 black. Uniface. Printer: Knowles & Foster (w/o imprint).

		Good	Fine	XF
S316	**10 Mil Reis** ND (1856). Woman w/globe at upper ctr. Green paper.	—	Rare	—

		Good	Fine	XF
S317	**20 Mil Reis** ND (1856). Allegory of Arts at upper ctr. Rose paper.	—	Rare	—

		Good	Fine	XF
S318	**50 Mil Reis** ND (1856). Horses galloping at upper ctr. Red paper.	—	Rare	—
S319	**100 Mil Reis** ND.		Reported Not Confirmed	
S320	**200 Mil Reis** ND.		Reported Not Confirmed	

PERNAMBUCO

1856 ND FIRST ISSUE

#S321-S326 black. View of Recife at upper ctr. Uniface. Printer: Bradbury & Evans (w/o imprint).

		GOOD	FINE	XF
S321	**10 MIL REIS** ND (1856). White paper.	—	Rare	—
S322	**20 MIL REIS** ND (1856). Gray paper.	—	Rare	—

		GOOD	FINE	XF
S323	**50 MIL REIS** ND (1856). Rose paper.	—	Rare	—
S324	**100 MIL REIS** ND (1856). Yellow paper.	—	Rare	—
S325	**200 MIL REIS** ND (1856). Green paper.	—	Rare	—
S326	**500 MIL REIS** ND (1856). Brown paper.	—	Rare	—

1856 ND SECOND ISSUE

#S327 and S328 black. Uniface. Printer: Knowles & Foster (w/o imprint).

		GOOD	FINE	XF
S327	**10 MIL REIS** ND (1856). Sailboat at l. and r., city view of Recife at upper ctr.	—	Rare	—

		GOOD	FINE	XF
S328	**50 MIL REIS** ND (1856). View of Recife w/bridge at upper ctr. Yellow paper.	—	Rare	—

NOTE: 20, 100 and 200 Mil Reis notes for the Second Issue are reported, not confirmed.

RIO GRANDE DO SUL

1856 ND FIRST ISSUE

#S331-S335 black. Like #S311-S315 (Pará issue). Uniface. Printer: Knowles & Foster (w/o imprint).

		GOOD	FINE	XF
S331	**10 MIL REIS** ND (1856). Green paper.	—	Rare	—

		GOOD	FINE	XF
S332	**20 MIL REIS** ND (1856). Brown paper.	—	Rare	—
S333	**50 MIL REIS** ND (1856). Gray paper.	—	Rare	—
S334	**100 MIL REIS** ND (1856). Rose paper.	—	Rare	—
S335	**200 MIL REIS** ND (1856). Yellow paper.	—	Rare	—

1856 ND SECOND ISSUE

		GOOD	FINE	XF
S338	**50 MIL REIS** ND (1856). Black. Ox-cart and palm at l. and r., horses galloping at upper ctr. Green paper. Uniface. Printer: Knowles & Foster (w/o imprint).	—	Rare	—

NOTE: 10 and 20 Mil Reis notes for the Second Issue are reported, not confirmed.

1860 ND ISSUE

		GOOD	FINE	XF
S340	**100 MIL REIS** ND (ca.1860). Black. Small bldgs at l. and r., gaucho roping longhorn steers at upper ctr. Printer: Bradbury & Evans. Proof.	—	—	—

SÃO PAULO

NOTE: There were 5 separate issues from the São Paulo branch. The first two were made in Rio de Janeiro, and the rest were printed in England. This accounts for the split in the various issues as listed.

1856 ND FIRST ISSUE

#S341 is a special design for branch issues.

		GOOD	FINE	XF
S341	**10 MIL REIS** ND (1856). Black. Like #S291.	—	Rare	—

#S342-S346 ovpt: *CAIXA FILIAL DE S. PAULO* on face at top on regular Banco do Brazil issues.

		GOOD	FINE	XF
S342	**20 MIL REIS** ND (1856). Black. Ovpt. on $S231.	—	Rare	—
S343	**30 MIL REIS** ND (1856). Black. Ovpt. on #S232.	—	Rare	—

S344 50 Mil Reis — Good — Fine Rare — XF —
ND (1856). Black. Ovpt. on #S233.

S345 100 Mil Reis — Good — Fine Rare — XF —
ND (1856). Black. Ovpt. on #S234.

S346 500 Mil Reis — Good — Fine Rare — XF —
ND (1856). Black. Ovpt. on #S236.

1856 ND Second Issue

S347 50 Mil Reis — Good — Fine Rare — XF —
ND (1856). Ovpt: *CAIXA FILIAL DE S. PAULO* on #S243.

1856 ND Third Issue

S348 10 Mil Reis — Good — Fine Rare — XF —
ND (1856). Black. Like #S311-S315. Yellow paper. Uniface. Printer: Knowles & Foster (w/o imprint).

1856 ND Fourth Issue

#S351 is a special design for this issue.

S351 10 Mil Reis — Good — Fine Rare — XF —
ND (1856). Black. View of Santos at ctr. Uniface. Printer: Knowles & Foster (w/o imprint).

#S352-S356 ovpt: *CAIXA FILIAL DE S. PAULO* on regular Banco do Brazil issues.

S352 20 Mil Reis — Good — Fine Rare — XF —
ND (1856). Black. Ovpt. on #S241.

S353 30 Mil Reis — Good — Fine Rare — XF —
ND (1856). Black. Ovpt. on #S242.

S354 50 Mil Reis — Good — Fine Rare — XF —
ND (1856). Black. Ovpt. on #S243.

S355 100 Mil Reis — Good — Fine Rare — XF —
ND (1856). Black. Ovpt. on #S244.

S356 200 Mil Reis — Good — Fine Rare — XF —
ND (1856). Black. Ovpt. on #S245.

1856 ND Fifth Issue

S357 20 Mil Reis — Good / Fine / XF: Reported Not Confirmed
ND (1856).

S358 50 Mil Reis — Good — Fine Rare — XF —
ND (1856). Black. Ovpt: *CAIXA FILIAL DE S. PAULO* on #S247.

Section III, 1850-85 Empire Bank Issues

Banco da Bahia

1858 ND Issue

#S381-S386 black. White paper. Uniface. Printer: Knowles & Foster (w/o imprint). Rare as issued notes.

S381 10 Mil Reis — Good — Fine Rare — XF —
ND (1858). Sailing ship at l., group of allegorical women and children at top ctr. Series 1.

		Good	Fine	XF
S382	**20 Mil Reis** ND (1858). Dock workers at upper ctr. Series 1.	—	Rare	—

		Good	Fine	XF
S383	**25 Mil Reis** ND (1858). Mule train at upper ctr. Series 2.	—	Rare	—
S384	**50 Mil Reis** ND (1858). Man riding mule at upper ctr. Series 1.	—	Rare	—
S385	**100 Mil Reis** ND (1858). Ox-cart in rural scene at upper ctr.	—	Rare	—
S386	**200 Mil Reis** ND (1858).		Reported Not Confirmed	

1860's ND Issue

#S387-S390 like previous issue but are printed in different colors, on tinted paper, and have printing on the backs.

		Good	Fine	XF
S387	**25 Mil Reis** ND (ca. 1860). Black, green and rose. Like #S383. Gray paper. Back green and rose. Series 3 or 4.	75.00	125.00	200.00

		Good	Fine	XF
S388	**50 Mil Reis** ND (ca. 1860). Black, green and rose. Like #S384. Pink paper. Back green and rose. Series 2, 3 or 4.	75.00	125.00	200.00

		Good	Fine	XF
S389	**100 Mil Reis** ND (ca. 1860). Black and green. Like #S385. Yellow paper. Back green. Series 3 or 4.	—	Rare	—
S390	**200 Mil Reis** ND (ca. 1860).		Reported Not Confirmed	

Banco Commercial e Agricola

1858 ND First Issue

#S401-S403 black. Sailing ships at l. Uniface. Printer: CMRJ.

		Good	Fine	XF
S401	**20 Mil Reis** ND (1858). Village scene at upper ctr. Blue paper.	—	Rare	—

		Good	Fine	XF
S402	**30 Mil Reis** ND (1858). Cow at upper ctr. Lilac paper.	—	Rare	—

		Good	Fine	XF
S403	**50 Mil Reis** ND (1858). Mercury seated at upper ctr. White paper.	—	Rare	—

NOTE: Higher values of 100, 200, 500 Mil Reis are reported, not confirmed.

1858 ND Second Issue

#S411-S416 black. Uniface. Printer: PBC.

		Good	Fine	XF
S411	**20 Mil Reis** ND (1858). Seated allegorical woman at upper ctr. Blue paper.	—	Rare	—

#S412-S416 white paper.

		Good	Fine	XF
S412	**30 Mil Reis** ND (1858). Allegory of Abundance at upper ctr.	—	Rare	—

		Good	Fine	XF
S413	**50 Mil Reis** ND (1858). Discovery of Brazil at upper ctr.	—	Rare	—
S414	**100 Mil Reis** ND (1858). 3 allegorical women (Arts) at upper ctr.	—	Rare	—
S415	**200 Mil Reis** ND (1858). Seated woman at upper ctr.	—	Rare	—

		Good	Fine	XF
S416	**500 Mil Reis** ND (1858). Standing woman at upper ctr.	—	Rare	—

Campos

1859 ND Issue

		Good	Fine	XF
S418	**10 Mil Reis** ND (1859). Black. 2 seated women at upper ctr. Rose paper. Uniface. Printer: PBC.	—	Rare	—

Vassouras

1858 ND Issue

		Good	Fine	XF
S419	**10 Mil Reis** ND (1858). Black. Like #S418. Blue paper.	—	Rare	—

NOTE: Higher values of 20, 30, 50, and 100 Mil Reis for this issue are reported, not confirmed.

BANCO COMMERCIAL DA BAHIA

1850 ISSUE

		GOOD	FINE	XF
S421	100 MIL REIS 26.10.1850 (date filled in by hand). Black. Standing allegorical woman w/sickle at l., seated man w/bales at upper l. ctr., portr. woman at r., allegorical woman below, portr. man at bottom. Uniface. Printer: TCC.	—	Rare	—

BANCO COMMERCIAL DO MARANHÃO

DECREE OF 24 MARCH 1849; 1854 ISSUE

		GOOD	FINE	XF
S424	100 MIL REIS 1.4.1854 (date filled in by hand). Black. Uniface.	—	Rare	—

NOTE: 5, 10, 20, and 50 Mil Reis notes are reported, not confirmed.

BANCO DO MARANHÃO

DECREE OF 25.11.1857

		GOOD	FINE	XF
S425	20 MIL REIS *D.1857.* Deep aqua on gray unpt. Uniface.	—	—	—

NOTE: Other notes of the First or Second Series of 10, 25, 50, 100, 200 and 500 Mil Reis are reported, not confirmed.

DECREE OF 25.11.1857/DECISION OF 9.7.1885

#S427-S430 Mercury seated at l. White paper. Uniface. Printer: BWC.

		GOOD	FINE	XF
S427	25 MIL REIS ND (1885). Black.	Reported Not Confirmed		

		GOOD	FINE	XF
S428	50 MIL REIS ND (1885). Black and green on yellow unpt.	—	Rare	—
S429	100 MIL REIS ND (1885). Black and red.	—	Rare	—
S430	200 MIL REIS ND (1885). Black and blue.	—	Rare	—

BANCO DO RIO GRANDE DO SUL

1859 ND ISSUE

		GOOD	FINE	XF
S436	10 MIL REIS ND (1859). Black. Mercury in allegory of Commerce at ctr. Uniface. Printer: Knowles & Foster (w/o imprint).			
	a. White paper.	—	—	—
	b. Yellow paper.	—	—	—
	c. Green paper.	—	—	—
	d. Blue paper.	—	—	—

BANCO RURAL E HYPOTHECARIO

1859 ND ISSUE

#S441-S443 black. Uniface. Printer: PBC.

		GOOD	FINE	XF
S441	20 MIL REIS ND (1859). Seated allegorical woman at upper ctr. Blue paper.	—	Rare	—

		GOOD	FINE	XF
S442	**30 MIL REIS** ND (1859). Neptune and 2 seahorses at upper ctr. White paper.	—	Rare	—

		GOOD	FINE	XF
S443	**50 MIL REIS** ND (1859). Standing allegorical woman at upper ctr. White paper.	—	Rare	—

NOTE: 100, 200 and 500 Mil Reis notes are reported, not confirmed.

NOVO BANCO DE PERNAMBUCO

1858 ND ISSUE

#S447-S448 black. White paper. Uniface. Printer: Knowles & Foster (w/o imprint).

		GOOD	FINE	XF
S447	**10 MIL REIS** ND (1858). Winged arms w/horse at upper ctr.	—	Rare	—

		GOOD	FINE	XF
S448	**20 MIL REIS** ND (1858). Winged arms w/3 bunches of grapes at upper ctr.	—	Rare	—
S450	**100 MIL REIS** ND (1858). Black. Specimen.	—	Unc	150.00

NOTE: 50 and 200 Mil Reis notes are reported, not confirmed.

SECTION IV, 1892-97 REPUBLIC REGIONAL ISSUES

ALAGOAS

APÓLICES DO ESTADO/SECURITIES OF THE STATE

LAW OF 5.8.1895

		GOOD	FINE	XF
S471	**100 REIS** *L.1895.* Blue on green unpt. State arms at l. Back blue; woman at ctr.	8.00	25.00	65.00
S472	**200 REIS** *L.1895.* Black on rose. unpt. Like #S471. Back black.	10.00	30.00	75.00
S473	**500 REIS** *L.1895.* Coral on green unpt. Like #S471. Back coral.	12.00	40.00	100.00

AMAZONAS

TITULOS DE DIVIDA/TITLES OF DEBT

LAW OF 15.12.1891; 1892 ND ISSUE

		GOOD	FINE	XF
S477	**2 MIL REIS** ND (1892).	Reported Not Confirmed		
S478	**5 MIL REIS** ND (1892).	Reported Not Confirmed		

MARANHÃO

TITULOS DE DIVIDA AO PORTADOR/TITLES OF DEBT TO BEARER

LAW OF 25.6.1894

		GOOD	FINE	XF
S481	**10 MIL REIS** *L.1894.* Black.	60.00	150.00	—

PERNAMBUCO

APÓLICES DA DIVIDA PÚBLICA/SECURITIES OF THE PUBLIC DEBT

LAW OF 22.6.1895

#S486-S488 state arms at l. Printer: J. E. Purcell, Recife.

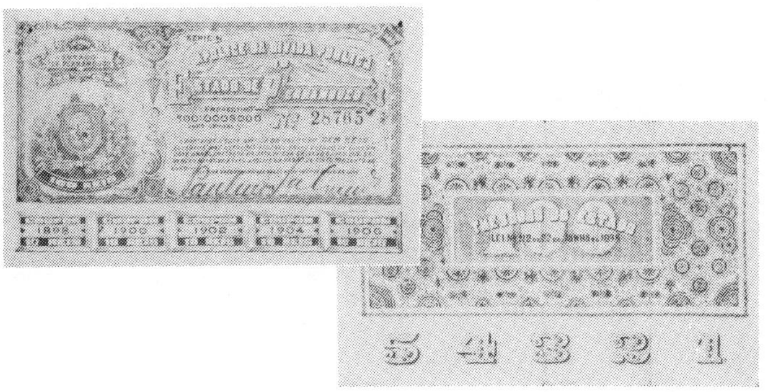

		GOOD	FINE	XF
S486	**100 REIS** *L.1895.* Blue-black on orange unpt. Back blue-black.	3.00	10.00	30.00
S487	**200 REIS** *L.1895.* Red on red-brown unpt. Back red-brown.	4.00	15.00	40.00
S488	**500 REIS** *L.1895.* Dull green on brown unpt. Back dk. green.	5.00	20.00	50.00

LAW OF 19.11.1896; 1897 ISSUE

#S491-S492 arms at upper l. Printer: J. E. Purcell, Recife.

		GOOD	FINE	XF
S491	**50 MIL REIS** 4.1.1897. Black and blue. Back lt. blue.	—	—	—
S492	**100 MIL REIS** 1897.	Reported Not Confirmed		

LAW OF 30.6.1898

#S496-S498 like #S486-S488. Printer: Barbosa Primo & Ca., Recife.

		GOOD	FINE	XF
S496	**100 REIS** *L.1898.* Green unpt. Like #S486.	8.00	25.00	60.00
S497	**200 REIS** *L.1898.* Like #S487.	10.00	30.00	65.00
S498	**500 REIS** *L.1898.* Like #S488.	12.00	35.00	75.00

RIO GRANDE DO NORTE

APÓLICES DA DIVIDA PÚBLICA/SECURITIES OF THE PUBLIC DEBT

LAW OF 15.12.1896; 1897 ND ISSUE

#S501-S506 printer: J. E. Purcell, Recife.

		GOOD	FINE	XF
S501	**100 REIS** ND (1897). Blue-green. Dog at lower l.	—	—	—
S502	**200 REIS** ND (1897). Red-brown. Lion at l.	—	—	—
S503	**500 REIS** ND (1897). Black on green unpt. Woman w/sheaf and sickle at l., conch shell at r. Back dk. brown.			
	a. Issued note.	—	—	—
	b. Unsigned remainder.	—	—	—

		GOOD	FINE	XF
S505	**5 MIL REIS** ND (1897). Black and orange. Indian wearing feathered headdress at l. Back violet.	—	—	—

		GOOD	FINE	XF
S506	**10 MIL REIS** ND (1897). Black. Young girl at l. Back coral.	—	—	—

SERGIPE

APÓLICES DO ESTADO/SECURITIES OF THE STATE

LAW OF 27.2.1897

#S511-S515 state arms at l. (man w/hot air balloon and basket). Printer: J. E. Purcell, Recife.

		GOOD	FINE	XF
S511	**100 REIS** *L.1897.* Dk. brown and green. Back brown.	—	—	—

		GOOD	FINE	XF
S512	**200 REIS** *L.1897.* Lt. and dk. coral. Back blue.	—	—	—
S513	**500 REIS** *L.1897.* Orange and blue. Back blue.	—	—	—
S514	**1 MIL REIS** *L.1897.* Brown and red. Back brown.	—	—	—
S515	**5 MIL REIS** *L.1897.* Violet and green.	—	—	—

SECTION V, 1889-93
REPUBLIC - BANK ISSUES

BANCO DA BAHIA

1890 ND PROVISIONAL ISSUE

#S521 and S522 ovpt. new bank name on Imperial Treasury Notes.

		GOOD	FINE	XF
S521	**50 MIL REIS** ND (1890). Black on orange yellow unpt. Ovpt. on Estampa 6, #A253 in Vol. 2.	—	Rare	—
S522	**100 MIL REIS** ND (1890). Black on red and green unpt. Ovpt. on Estampa 5, #A247 in Vol. 2.	—	Rare	—

BANCO DO BRAZIL

In 1893 this bank became part of the Banco da República do Brazil. A reissue of part of the last issue of notes of the Banco do Brazil (ca. 1857) was authorized by decree of 8.3.1890. Printer: ABNC.

REISSUE

		GOOD	FINE	XF
S525	**50 MIL REIS** ND (1890). Like #S253. Proof.	—	—	—

#S526-S528 like earlier issue but w/sign. of Anto. Arnaldo Vieira da Costa.

		GOOD	FINE	XF
S526	**100 MIL REIS** ND (1890). Like #S254 except for sign.	175.00	—	—

		GOOD	FINE	XF
S527	**200 MIL REIS** ND (1890). Like #S255 except for sign.	225.00	—	—
S528	**500 MIL REIS** ND (1890). Like #S256 except for sign.	300.00	—	—

LAW OF 24.11.1888/DECREE OF 8.3.1890

#S531-S532 printer: ABNC.

		GOOD	FINE	XF
S531	**10 MIL REIS** ND (1890). Black on orange and yellow unpt. 2 seated allegorical women at l. and r., 2 cherubs at ctr. Back black and orange; reclining woman w/lamp at ctr. Specimen.	—	Rare	—

		GOOD	FINE	XF
S532	**20 MIL REIS** ND (1890). Black on blue and m/c unpt. Portr. man and woman at upper l., seated allegory of Industry at upper r w/condor between above bank title. Back sepia; family pride of lions at ctr. Specimen.	—	Rare	—

#S533-S535 printer: W&S.

		GOOD	FINE	XF
S533	**50 MIL REIS** ND (1890). Black on m/c unpt. Portr. woman between 2 seated women at l., bull's head at lower r. Back blue; woman at ctr. Specimen.	—	Rare	—
S534	**200 MIL REIS** ND (1890). Black on m/c unpt. Standing woman at l., woman at ctr., allegory of Commerce at r. Back sepia; rural scene at ctr. Specimen.	—	Rare	—
S535	**500 MIL REIS** ND (1890). Black on m/c unpt. Woman at l., ship at ctr., standing woman at r. Back sepia; woman at ctr. Specimen.	—	Rare	—

BANCO DO CAFÉ

This organization issued mortgage letters to stimulate the sales of coffee very similar in design to actual banknotes.

DECREES OF 19.1.1890 AND 3.5.1890

#S541-S542 shield between 2 reclining allegorical women at ctr. Printer: ABNC.

		GOOD	FINE	XF
S541	**100 MIL REIS** *D. 1890.* Green on lilac unpt. Back lilac; squares showing months and value. Unsigned remainder w/serial #.	—	Unc	3.00

		GOOD	FINE	XF
S542	**500 MIL REIS** ND (1890). Purple on olive-brown unpt. Proof.	—	—	—

BANCO DE CRÉDITO POPULAR DO BRAZIL

DECREE OF 14.11.1890; 1891 ND PROVISIONAL ISSUE

#S546-S550 ovpt. new bank name on notes of the Banco dos Estados Unidos do Brazil.

#S546-S549 printers: G&D, and Laemmert & Co.

		GOOD	FINE	XF
S546	**5 MIL REIS** ND (1891). Black on m/c unpt. Ovpt. on #S601.	—	Rare	—
S547	**20 MIL REIS** ND (1891). Black on orange, brown and m/c unpt. Ovpt. on #S603.	—	Rare	—
S548	**100 MIL REIS** ND (1891). Ovpt. on #S605.	Reported Not Confirmed		
S549	**200 MIL REIS** ND (1891). Black on brown and m/c unpt. Ovpt. on #S606.	—	Rare	—
S550	**500 MIL REIS** ND (1891). Black on brown and yellow unpt. Ovpt. on #S607.	—	Rare	—

DECREES OF 8.3.1890 AND 14.11.1890; 1891-92 ND ISSUE

#S550A-S555 printer: ABNC.

		GOOD	FINE	XF
S550A	**1 MIL REIS** ND (ca.1891). Black on brown unpt. Steam passenger train at ctr. Back dk. brown; allegorical woman w/coins, scale and safe at ctr.			
	p. Proof	—	—	—
	s. Specimen.	—	—	—
S550B	**2 MIL REIS** ND (ca.1891). Black on green unpt. Steam train at l. and r., 2 children reading at ctr. Back green; woman at l. Proof.	—	—	—

		GOOD	FINE	XF
S551	**5 MIL REIS** ND (1892). Black on rose unpt. Seated allegorical woman w/flowers at l., woman and child at r. Back sepia; woman at ctr. Proof.	—	—	—
S551A	**10 MIL REIS** ND (ca.1891). Black on olive-green and yellow unpt. Justice at l., street scene w/tree and mountain behind at r. Back olive-green. Proof.	—	—	—

S551B 20 Mil Reis | Good | Fine | XF
ND (ca. 1891). Black on orange and yellow unpt. Portr. girl at l., Indian woman seated in small boat at r. Back orange.

	Good	Fine	XF
p. Proof.	—	—	—
s. Specimen.	—	—	—

S552 50 Mil Reis | Good | Fine | XF
ND (1892). Black on yellow and brown unpt. Basket and tree at l., woman seated at r. Back red-brown.

	Good	Fine	XF
p. Proof.	—	—	—
s. Specimen.	—	—	—

S553 100 Mil Reis | Good | Fine | XF
ND (1892). Black on yellow and purple unpt. Lion's head at l., reclining woman at r. Back red-brown; rural scene w/sheep at ctr. Proof. | — | — | —

S554 200 Mil Reis | Good | Fine | XF
ND (ca.1891). Black on orange and yellow unpt. Allegory of Electricity at l., equestrians, oxen teams and train at r. Back orange; miners at ctr. Proof. | — | — | —

S555 500 Mil Reis | Good | Fine | XF
ND (ca.1891). Black on blue and yellow unpt. Allegorical woman w/book and globe at upper l., young girl at upper r. Back blue and black; allegorical woman at r.

	Good	Fine	XF
p. Proof.	—	—	—
s. Specimen.	—	—	—

Banco Emissor da Bahia

1890 ND Provisional Issue

#S561-S564 ovpt. new bank name on Imperial Treasury Notes.

		Good	Fine	XF
S561	**10 Mil Reis** ND (1890). Black on green and orange unpt. Ovpt. on Estampa 8, #A262 in Vol. 2.	—	Rare	—

		Good	Fine	XF
S562	**20 Mil Reis** ND (1890). Black on orange and green unpt. Ovpt. on Estampa 8, #A263 in Vol. 2.	—	Rare	—

		Good	Fine	XF
S563	**50 Mil Reis** ND (1890). Black on orange and yellow unpt. Ovpt. on Estampa 6, #A253 in Vol. 2.	—	Rare	—
S564	**100 Mil Reis** ND (1890). Black on red and yellow unpt. Ovpt. on Estampa 5, #A247 in Vol. 2.	—	Rare	—

1892 ND Issue

#S565-S565B printer: ABNC.

S565 10 Mil Reis | Good | Fine | XF
ND (ca.1892). Black on blue and yellow unpt. 2 standing allegorical women at r. Back blue.

	Good	Fine	XF
p. Proof.	—	—	—
s. Specimen.	—	—	—

S565A 20 Mil Reis | Good | Fine | XF
ND (ca.1892). Black on brown and yellow unpt. Standing Liberty at ctr. Back brown. Proof. | — | — | —

		GOOD	FINE	XF
S565B	**50 MIL REIS** ND (ca.1892). Black on orange and yellow unpt. Reclining allegorical woman w/flag, lion and sailing ship in background at l. Back orange. Proof.	—	—	—

DECREES OF 17.1.1890 AND 12.5.1890

		GOOD	FINE	XF
S566	**100 MIL REIS** ND (1890). Black on lt. blue and rose unpt. Seated woman at l., cupid and constellation at r. Back dk. brown; bank at ctr. Printer: CMRJ. (Not issued).	—	Rare	—

BANCO EMISSOR DO NORTE

1890 ND PROVISIONAL ISSUE

#S571-S573 ovpt. new bank name on Imperial Treasury Notes.

		GOOD	FINE	XF
S571	**10 MIL REIS** ND (1890). Black on green and orange unpt. Ovpt. on Estampa 8, #A262 in Vol. 2.	—	Rare	—
S572	**50 MIL REIS** ND (1890). Black on orange and yellow unpt. Ovpt. on Estampa 6, #A253 in Vol. 2.	—	Rare	—
S573	**100 MIL REIS** ND (1890). Black on red and green unpt. Ovpt. on Estampa 5, #A247 in Vol. 2.	—	Rare	—

DECREES OF 8.3.1890 AND 19.6.1890

#S576-S580 printer: ABNC. (Not issued).

		GOOD	FINE	XF
S576	**10 MIL REIS** ND. Black on m/c unpt. 2 allegorical women seated at l., national arms at r. Back red; ornate bldg. at ctr. Specimen.	—	—	—

		GOOD	FINE	XF
S577	**20 MIL REIS** ND. Black on blue and yellow unpt. Minerva at l., 2 seated allegorical women flanking national arms at ctr., palm at r. Back blue; palm-lined street w/bank at l. Proof.	—	—	—

		GOOD	FINE	XF
S578	**50 MIL REIS** ND. Black on green and yellow unpt. Justice at l., national arms at l. ctr., railroad workers and steam passenger train at r. Back green; bank at ctr. Specimen.	—	—	—

		GOOD	FINE	XF
S579	**100 MIL REIS** ND. Black on yellow and orange unpt. National arms at ctr., allegory of Navigation at r. Back brick red; bank at ctr. r.			
	p. Proof.	—	—	—
	s. Specimen.	—	—	—

DECREE 19.6.1890

		GOOD	FINE	XF
S580	**10 MIL REIS** *D.1890.* Black on blue and yellow unpt. 2 standing allegorical women at r. Back green. Proof.	—	—	—

BANCO EMISSOR DE PERNAMBUCO

1890 ND PROVISIONAL ISSUE

#S581-S582 ovpt. new bank name on Imperial Treasury Notes.

		GOOD	FINE	XF
S581	**100 MIL REIS** ND (1890). Black on red and green unpt. Ovpt. on Estampa 5, #A247 in Vol. 2.	—	Rare	—
S582	**200 MIL REIS** ND (1890). Black on blue and yellow unpt. Ovpt. on Estampa 6, #A254 in Vol. 2.	—	Rare	—

DECREES OF 8.3.1890 AND 18.10.1890

S586 100 MIL REIS | GOOD | FINE | XF
ND. Black on ochre unpt. Dog's head at l., reclining allegorical woman at r. Back sepia; entrance to port of Recife at ctr. Printer: Companhia de Artes Graphicas do Brazil. Estampa 1, Series 1. (Not issued). | — | Rare | —

BANCO EMISSOR DO SUL

1890 ND PROVISIONAL ISSUE

#S591-S593 ovpt. new bank name on Imperial Treasury Notes.

		GOOD	FINE	XF
S591	**10 MIL REIS** ND (1890). Black on green and orange unpt. Ovpt. on Estampa 8, #A262 in Vol. 2.	—	Rare	—
S592	**50 MIL REIS** ND (1890). Black on orange and green unpt. Ovpt. on Estampa 6, #A253 in Vol. 2.	—	Rare	—
S593	**100 MIL REIS** ND (1890). Black on red and green unpt. Ovpt. on Estampa 5, #A247 in Vol. 2.	—	Rare	—

BANCO DOS ESTADOS UNIDOS DO BRAZIL

In December 1890, this bank became part of the Banco da República dos Estados Unidos do Brazil.

1890 ND PROVISIONAL ISSUE

#S596-S599 ovpt. new bank name on Imperial Treasury Notes.

		GOOD	FINE	XF
S596	**10 MIL REIS** ND (1890). Black on green and orange unpt. Red ovpt. on Estampa 8, #A262 in Vol. 2.	—	Rare	—
S597	**20 MIL REIS** ND (1890). Black on orange and green unpt. Wine ovpt. on Estampa 8, #A263 in Vol. 2.	—	Rare	—
S598	**50 MIL REIS** ND (1890). Black on orange and yellow unpt. Lt. blue ovpt. on Estampa 6, #A253 in Vol. 2.	—	Rare	—

		GOOD	FINE	XF
S599	**200 MIL REIS** ND (1890). Black on blue and yellow unpt. Red ovpt. on Estampa 6, #A254 in Vol. 2.	—	Rare	—

DECREES OF 17.1.1890 AND 8.3.1890

#S601-S606 printers: G&D, and Laemmert & Co.

		GOOD	FINE	XF
S601	**5 MIL REIS** ND (1890). Black on m/c unpt. Standing woman and national arms at ctr. Back green; national arms at ctr. (Not issued).	—	Rare	—

		GOOD	FINE	XF
S602	**10 MIL REIS** ND (1890). Black on rose Standing allegory of Agriculture at l., palm tree at r. Back m/c; arms at ctr. a. Ovpt: *CIRCULA EM TODOS OS ESTADOS DA REPUBLICA* on back. b. Ovpt: *PAGAVEL EM OURO NOS TERMOS DO DECRETO no. 253, DE 8 DE MARCO DE 1890* on face.	— 	Rare 	—

		GOOD	FINE	XF
S603	**20 MIL REIS** ND (1890). Black on orange, brown and m/c unpt. Sailing ship in port at lower l., standing allegory of Navigation at r. Back blue and orange; arms at ctr. (Not issued).	—	Rare	—
S604	**50 MIL REIS** ND (1890). Black on m/c unpt. Woman at l., ship and steam train at r. Back m/c; arms at ctr. (Not issued).	—	Rare	—
S605	**100 MIL REIS** ND.	Reported Not Confirmed		

		GOOD	FINE	XF
S606	**200 MIL REIS** ND (1890). Black on brown and m/c unpt. Liberty within coffee plant sprays at ctr. Back m/c; arms. (Not issued).	—	Rare	—

#S607-S607B like later Banco da República dos Estados Unidos issue for #S607A and S607B. Printer: ABNC. (Not issued).

		Good	Fine	XF
S607	**30 Mil Reis** ND (ca.1890). Black on brown and yellow unpt. Woman at l., steam powered ship in rough seas at l. ctr., girl smelling flowers at r. Back dk. brown. Proof.	—	—	—

		Good	Fine	XF
S607A	**50 Mil Reis** ND (ca.1890). Black on green unpt. Like #S647, but w/old bank name.			
	p. Proof.	—	—	—
	s. Specimen.	—	—	—

		Good	Fine	XF
S607B	**500 Mil Reis** ND (1890). Black on green and yellow unpt. Like #S650, but w/old bank name. Proof.	—	—	—

Banco Industrial dos Estados do Sul

Obrigacoes ao Portador (Obligations to Bearer)

1891 Issue

		Good	Fine	XF
S608	**10 Mil Reis** 1.10.1891. Black and gray. Steam passenger train at upper ctr. Back red-brown; list of encashment values and dates. Printer: Companhia Editora Fluminense Rio de Janeiro.	—	Rare	—
S609	**10 Mil Reis** 1.10.1891. Black and gray. Like #S608 but w/o imprint at bottom.	—	Rare	—

Banco Mercantil de Santos

Law of 24.11.1888/Decree of 8.3.1890

#S611-S616 (not issued).

#S611-S612 printer: ABNC.

		Good	Fine	XF
S611	**10 Mil Reis** ND. Black on yellow and ochre unpt. Like #S531.			
	p. Proof.	—	—	—
	s. Specimen.	—	—	—

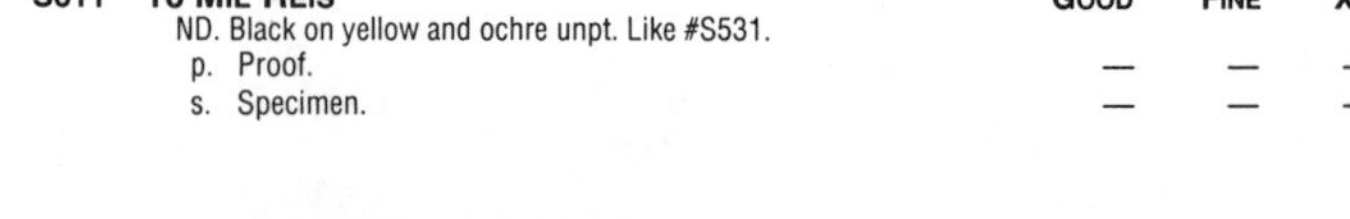

		Good	Fine	XF
S612	**20 Mil Reis** ND. Black on yellow and ochre unpt. Like #S532.			
	p. Proof.	—	—	—
	s. Specimen.	—	—	—

#S613-S616 printer: W&S.

		Good	Fine	XF
S613	**50 Mil Reis** ND. Black on m/c unpt. Like #S533. (Not issued).	—	Rare	—
S614	**100 Mil Reis** ND. Black on yellow and blue unpt. Woman at l., 3 allegorical women at ctr., coffee workers at r. Back blue; steer's head at ctr. (Not issued).	—	Rare	—
S615	**200 Mil Reis** ND. Black on m/c unpt. Like #S534. (Not issued).	—	Rare	—
S616	**500 Mil Reis** ND. Black on m/c unpt. Like #S535. (Not issued).	—	Rare	—

Banco Nacional do Brazil no Rio de Janeiro

In December 1890, this bank became part of the Banco da República dos Estados Unidos do Brazil.

1890 ND Provisional Issue

#S621-S624 ovpt. new bank name and other inscription on Imperial Treasury Notes. Ovpt. work printed by Laemmert & Co.

		Good	Fine	XF
S621	**10 Mil Reis** ND (1890). Black on orange and green unpt. Ovpt. on Estampa 7, #A258 in Vol. 2.	—	Rare	—

		Good	Fine	XF
S622	**100 Mil Reis** ND (1890). Black on red and green unpt. Ovpt. on Estampa 5, #A247 in Vol. 2.	—	Rare	—

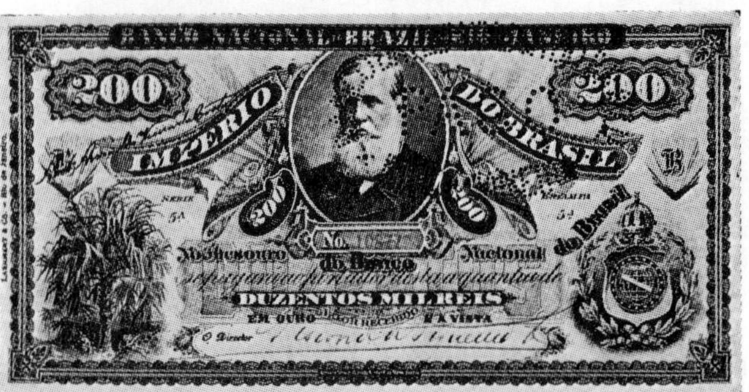

		Good	Fine	XF
S623	**200 Mil Reis** ND (1890). Black on red and blue unpt. Ovpt. on Estampa 5, #A248 in Vol. 2.	—	Rare	—

		GOOD	FINE	XF
S624	**500 MIL REIS** ND (1890). Black on orange and blue unpt. Ovpt. on Estampa 5, #A249 in Vol. 2.	—	Rare	—

LAW OF 24.11.1888/DECREE OF 8.3.1890

#S625-S626 printer: ABNC.

		GOOD	FINE	XF
S625	**10 MIL REIS** ND (1890). Black on orange and yellow unpt. Like #S531.			
	p. Proof.	—	—	—
	s. Specimen.	—	—	—

		GOOD	FINE	XF
S626	**20 MIL REIS** ND (1890). Black on blue and m/c unpt. Like #S532.			
	p. Proof.	—	—	—
	s. Specimen.	—	—	—

#S627-S630 printer: W&S.

		GOOD	FINE	XF
S627	**30 MIL REIS** ND (1890). Black on orange unpt. Woman at l., steam passenger train and mountains at r. Back dk. brown. (Not issued).	—	Rare	—

		GOOD	FINE	XF
S628	**100 MIL REIS** ND (1890). Black on yellow and blue unpt. Like #S614.	—	Rare	—

		GOOD	FINE	XF
S629	**200 MIL REIS** ND (1890). Black on m/c unpt. Like #S534.	—	Rare	—

		GOOD	FINE	XF
S630	**500 MIL REIS** ND (1890). Black on m/c unpt. Like #S535.	—	Rare	—

BANCO DA REPÚBLICA DOS ESTADOS UNIDOS DO BRAZIL

This bank resulted from the amalgamation of the Banco dos Estados Unidos do Brazil and the Banco Nacional late in 1890. Later it bacame the Banco da República do Brazil.

1891 ND PROVISIONAL ISSUES

#S631-S634 black ovpt. new bank name on notes of the Banco Nacional do Brazil.

		Good	Fine	XF
S631	**20 Mil Reis** ND (1891). Black on blue and m/c unpt. Ovpt. new bank name in circle around vignette at l., on #S626.	—	Rare	—
S632	**100 Mil Reis** ND (1891). Black on yellow and blue unpt. Ovpt. on #S628.	—	Rare	—

		Good	Fine	XF
S633	**200 Mil Reis** ND (1891). Black on m/c unpt. Ovpt. on #S629.	—	Rare	—
S634	**500 Mil Reis** ND (1891). Black on m/c unpt. Ovpt. on #S630.	—	Rare	—

#S635 ovpt. new bank name on note of the Banco dos Estados Unidos do Brazil.

		Good	Fine	XF
S635	**500 Mil Reis** ND (1891). Ovpt. on #S607B.	—	Rare	—

Decrees of 14.1.1889 and 7.12.1889

		Good	Fine	XF
S637	**500 Mil Reis** ND. Black on green and yellow unpt. Woman's head over standing sailor at l., mint bldg. at l. ctr., Minerva at lower r. Back deep red and black; girl at l. Printer: Cia. de Billetes de Banco, F. Rieusset. Specimen.	—	—	—

NOTE: #S637 is most likely a Specimen of a proposed issue that never gained approval. The authorization decrees are also missing from all references.

Decrees of 17.1.1890 and 7.12.1890

#S641-S644 printer: ABNC.

		Good	Fine	XF
S641	**10 Mil Reis** ND (1891). Black on yellow and blue unpt. 2 standing allegorical women at r. Back blue. Serial #1 to 85,712.			
	a. Issued note.	100.00	225.00	—
	r. Remainder, punched hole cancelled.	—	—	—

		Good	Fine	XF
S642	**20 Mil Reis** ND (1891). Black on yellow unpt. Woman leaning on shield on pedestal between flags at ctr. Back sepia. Series 1. Serial #1 to 100,000.	—	Rare	—

NOTE: #S642 but Series 2 is an issue of the Banco da República do Brazil. See #S657.

		Good	Fine	XF
S643	**50 Mil Reis** ND (1891). Black on orange and yellow unpt. Seated allegorical woman w/flag, lion and sailing ship in background at l. Back orange. Like #S565B. Serial #1 to 79,000.			
	a. Issued note.	—	Rare	—
	p. Proof.	—	—	—

		Good	Fine	XF
S644	**200 Mil Reis** ND (1891). Black on green unpt. Similar to #S637 except for printer. Serial #1 to 70,500.	—	Rare	—

NOTE: Higher serial # of #S641, S643 and S644 were issued by the Banco da República do Brazil before its own notes were ready. See #S656, S658 and S659.

Decree of 8.3.1890

#S645 and S646 printer: G&D.

S645 10 MIL REIS — GOOD / FINE / XF

ND (1891). Black on m/c unpt. Face like #S602. Back similar to #S602. Serial #1 to 78,680.

	GOOD	FINE	XF
a. Issued note.	—	Rare	—
b. Punched hole cancelled, hand stamped: *AMOSTRA.*	—	—	—

DECREE OF 7.12.1890

S646 30 MIL REIS — GOOD / FINE / XF

ND (1891). Black on m/c unpt. 2 seated allegorical figures at ctr. Back m/c. Serial #1 to 58,668.

	GOOD	FINE	XF
a. Issued note.	—	Rare	—
b. Punched hole cancelled, hand stamped: *AMOSTRA.*	—	—	—

#S647-S650 printer: ABNC.

S647 50 MIL REIS — GOOD / FINE / XF

ND (1891). Black on green unpt. Allegorical woman leaning on anchor at l., reclining woman at r. Back blue. Serial #1 to 100,000 in First Series, 1 to 13,000 in Second Series.

	GOOD	FINE	XF
a. Issued note.	—	Rare	—
p. Proof.	—	—	—
s. Specimen.	—	—	—

S648 100 MIL REIS — GOOD / FINE / XF

ND (1891). Black on yellow and ochre unpt. Reclining allegorical woman w/Liberty pole and globe at l., standing allegorical woman w/pedestal and shield w/arms at r. Back sepia; national arms at ctr. Serial #1 to 43,000.

	GOOD	FINE	XF
a. Issued note.	—	Rare	—
p. Proof.	—	—	—
s. Specimen.	—	—	—

S649 200 MIL REIS — GOOD / FINE / XF

ND (1891). Black on orange and yellow unpt. Steam passenger train at l., 2 standing allegorical women at r. Back black and orange; palace in Rio de Janeiro at ctr. Serial #1 to 17,000.

	GOOD	FINE	XF
a. Issued note.	—	Rare	—
b. Cancelled, hand stamped: *AMOSTRA.*	—	—	—
s. Specimen.	—	—	—

S650 500 MIL REIS — GOOD / FINE / XF

ND (1891). Black on green and yellow unpt. Sailing ship at l., woman seated at ctr., standing woman at r. Back black and green; docks and arsenal at Rio de Janeiro at ctr. Serial #1 to 69,000.

	GOOD	FINE	XF
a. Issued note.	—	Rare	—
s. Specimen.	—	—	—

NOTE: For a reissue of notes #S645-S650 with higher serial #, see Banco da República do Brazil, #S661-S666.

NOTE: A 50 and 100 Mil Reis under a decree of 1892, are reported, not confirmed.

BANCO DA REPÚBLICA DO BRAZIL

Formed in 1892; formerly the Banco da República dos Estados Unidos do Brazil.

1893 ND FIRST EMERGENCY ISSUE

#S656-S659 is an emergency reissue of notes of the Banco da República dos Estados Unidos do Brazil. #S641-S644. #S656, S658 and S659 have higher serial #, #S657 is a different series. Printer: ABNC.

		GOOD	FINE	XF
S656	**10 MIL REIS** ND (1893). Like #S641 but serial #85,713 to 99,423.	—	Rare	—
S657	**20 MIL REIS** ND (1893). Like #S642 but Series 2 and serial #1 to 8000.	—	Rare	—
S658	**50 MIL REIS** ND (1893). Like #S643 but serial #79,001 to 87,000.	—	Rare	—
S659	**200 MIL REIS** ND (1893). Like #S644 but serial #70,501 to 74,000.	—	Rare	—

1893 ND SECOND EMERGENCY ISSUE

#S661-S666 is an emergency reissue of notes of the Banco da República dos Estados Unidos do Brazil, S645-S650.

		GOOD	FINE	XF
S661	**10 MIL REIS** ND (1893). Like #S645 but serial #78,681 to 100,000 in First Series, and 1 to 15,247 in Second Series.	—	Rare	—
S662	**30 MIL REIS** ND (1893). Like #S646 but serial #58,669 to 65,000.	—	Rare	—
S663	**50 MIL REIS** ND (1893). Like #S647 but serial #13,001 to 24,000. Second Series.	—	Rare	—
S664	**100 MIL REIS** ND (1893). Like #S648 but serial # 43,001 to 92,500.	—	Rare	—
S665	**200 MIL REIS** ND (1893). Like #S649 but serial #17,001 to 21,000.	—	Rare	—

S666 500 MIL REIS — GOOD / FINE / XF

ND (1893). Like #S650 but serial #69,001 to 71,004.

	GOOD	FINE	XF
a. Issued note.	—	Rare	—
r. Remainder cancelled, hand stamped: *AMOSTRA.*	—	—	—

Decree of 17.12.1892; 1893 ND Issue

#S671-S672 printers: G&D, and Laemmert & Co.

		Good	Fine	XF
S671	**10 Mil Reis** ND (1893). Black on brown, blue and m/c unpt. Star around Liberty at l., seated woman at r. Back brown and lt. blue; arms at r.			
	a. Issued note.	—	Rare	—
	s. Specimen ovpt. and perforated: *AMOSTRA.*	—	Rare	—
S672	**50 Mil Reis** ND (1893). Black on green and m/c unpt. Woman in profile at l., sailing ship near lighthouse at r. Back m/c; arms at l. ctr.	—	Rare	—

Law of 23.9.1893

#S674-S680 printers: G&D, and Laemmert & Co.

		Good	Fine	XF
S674	**10 Mil Reis** ND (1893). Like #S671 except for authorization date.	—	Rare	—

		Good	Fine	XF
S675	**20 Mil Reis** ND (1893). Black on lt. blue and m/c unpt. Seated Justice w/shield of arms at r. Back blue and orange; arms at r.	—	Rare	—

		Good	Fine	XF
S676	**30 Mil Reis** ND (1893). Black on red, lt. blue and m/c unpt. Palm and sailing ship at lower l., seated allegory of Industry and Commerce at r. Back red, blue and m/c; arms at l.	—	Rare	—

		Good	Fine	XF
S677	**50 Mil Reis** ND (1893). Like #S672 except for authorization date.	—	Rare	—

		Good	Fine	XF
S678	**100 Mil Reis** ND (1893). Black on m/c unpt. Reclining allegorical woman at lower l. and r., portr. woman's head in profile at upper ctr. Back black and rose; view of the port at Rio de Janeiro at ctr.	—	Rare	—

		Good	Fine	XF
S679	**200 Mil Reis** ND (1893). Black on m/c unpt. Arms at l. ctr., 2 allegorical women and shield w/arms at r. Back black and green; view of loading area on docks at Rio de Janeiro.	—	Rare	—

		Good	Fine	XF
S680	**500 Mil Reis** ND (1893). Black on m/c unpt. Eagle between reclining Minerva and Neptune at ctr. Lighthouse, globe and anchor at lower r. Back black and rose; sailing ships at anchor in port of Rio de Janeiro.	—	Rare	—

Banco de São Paulo

1889 ND Provisional Issue

#S681-S683 ovpt. new bank name and other details on Imperial Treasury Notes. Ovpt. work printed by Laemmert & Co.

		Good	Fine	XF
S681	**10 Mil Reis** ND (1889). Black on orange and green unpt. Ovpt. on Estampa 7, #A258 in Vol. 2.	—	Rare	—

		Good	Fine	XF
S682	**100 Mil Reis** ND (1889). Black on red and green unpt. Ovpt. on Estampa 5, #A247 in Vol. 2.	—	Rare	—

		GOOD	FINE	XF
S683	500 MIL REIS ND (1889). Black on orange and blue unpt. Ovpt. on Estampa 5, #A249 in Vol. 2.	—	Rare	—

BANCO SUL AMERICANO DE PERNAMBUCO

DECREES OF 17.1.1890 AND 7.3.1890

#S686-S689 printer: ABNC. No notes of this bank were released to circulation.

		GOOD	FINE	XF
S686	10 MIL REIS ND. Black on m/c unpt. Sailing ships at port of Recife at l., 2 sailors at r. Back purple. (Not issued).	—	Rare	—

		GOOD	FINE	XF
S687	20 MIL REIS ND. Black on m/c unpt. Back blue. (Not issued).	—	Rare	—

NOTE: The face design for #S687 is not known.

		GOOD	FINE	XF
S688	50 MIL REIS ND. Black on m/c unpt. Portr. woman between 2 reclining allegorical women at l. ctr., Mercury seated at r. Back green. (Not issued).	—	Rare	—

		GOOD	FINE	XF
S689	200 MIL REIS ND. Black on m/c unpt. Seated woman at l. ctr., sailor at ctr. r., 2 standing allegorical women at r. Back yellow. (Not issued).	—	Rare	—

BANCO UNIÃO IBERO AMERICANO

1891 OBRIGACOES (OBLIGATIONS) ISSUE

		GOOD	FINE	XF
S691	20 MIL REIS 8.7.1891. Blue and red. 3 allegorical women and 2 shields w/arms at upper l. Back red-brown; table of redemption dates and values.	—	Rare	—

BANCO UNIÃO DE SÃO PAULO

DECREE OF 17.1.1890; FIRST ISSUE

#S693-S694 printers: Laemmert & Co., and G&D.

		GOOD	FINE	XF
S693	100 MIL REIS ND (1890). Black on green unpt. Reclining Indian w/lion at l., sailing ships at port of Santos at upper ctr. Back green; national arms at ctr.	—	Rare	—
S694	200 MIL REIS ND (1890). Black on rose unpt. Like #S693. Back sepia.	—	Rare	—

DECREE OF 8.3.1890; FIRST ISSUE

		Good	Fine	XF
S694A	**500 Mil Reis** ND (1890). Black on green unpt. Seated woman w/shield of arms at l. Back like #S693.	—	Rare	—

Decree of 8.3.1890; Second Issue

#S695-S700 national arms at ctr. on back. Printers: Laemmert & Co., and G&D.

		Good	Fine	XF
S695	**10 Mil Reis** ND (1890). Black on sepia and m/c unpt. Allegorical figure of Electricity at l., steam passenger train at lower r. Back sepia, orange and m/c.			
	a. Issued note.	—	Rare	—
	r. Remainder punched hole cancelled, hand stamped: *AMOSTRA.*	—	—	—
S696	**20 Mil Reis** ND (1890). Similar to #S695.	—	Rare	—
S697	**50 Mil Reis** ND (1890). Similar to #S695.	—	Rare	—

		Good	Fine	XF
S698	**100 Mil Reis** ND (1890). Black on lilac and m/c unpt. Standing allegorical woman and cupid at l., Mercury in circle at lower r. Back brown and m/c.			
	a. Issued note.	—	Rare	—
	r. Remainder punched hole cancelled, hand stamped: *AMOSTRA.*	—	—	—
S699	**200 Mil Reis** ND (1890). Similar to #S698.	—	Rare	—
S700	**500 Mil Reis** ND (1890). Similar to #S698.	—	Rare	—

Decree of 8.3.1890; Third Issue

#S705-S711 not issued. Printer: ABNC.

		Good	Fine	XF
S705	**10 Mil Reis** ND (ca.1892). Black on green and yellow unpt. Seated allegorical woman w/marine implements at l., cherub at r. Back green.			
	p. Proof.	—	—	—
	s. Specimen.	—	—	—

		Good	Fine	XF
S706	**20 Mil Reis** ND (ca.1892). Black on orange and yellow unpt. Cherub at lower l., seated allegorical woman w/eagle at l. ctr. Back orange or green.			
	p. Proof.	—	—	—
	s. Specimen.	—	—	—

		Good	Fine	XF
S707	**30 Mil Reis** ND (ca.1892). Black on brown and yellow unpt. Women at l. and r. Back brown or green; bust of allegorical woman at l. and ctr. r.			
	p. Proof.	—	—	—
	s. Specimen.	—	—	—

		Good	Fine	XF
S708	**50 Mil Reis** ND (ca.1892). Black on blue and yellow unpt. Cherub representing Electricity at l., cherub at ctr., woman w/quill pen at r. Back blue or green; cherub's head at top ctr.			
	p. Proof.	—	—	—
	s. Specimen.	—	—	—

		Good	Fine	XF
S709	**100 Mil Reis** ND (ca.1892). Black on orange and yellow unpt. Miner at l. and r., 2 men conversing at ctr. Back red or green.			
	p. Proof.	—	—	—
	s. Specimen.	—	—	—

		GOOD	FINE	XF
S710	**200 MIL REIS** ND (ca.1892). Black on orange and yellow unpt. Plant at lower l., dog at upper l., allegorical woman and child at ctr., allegorical woman at r. Back orange or green; young girl at ctr.			
	p. Proof.	—	—	—
	s. Specimen.	—	—	—

		GOOD	FINE	XF
S711	**500 MIL REIS** ND (ca.1892). Black on olive-green and yellow unpt. Standing allegorical woman w/scales at l., oxen team pulling wagon at ctr. r. Back olive or green; steam train and cowboys on horseback at r.			
	p. Proof.	—	—	—
	s. Specimen.	—	—	—

SECTION VI, 1924-66
PROVINCIAL ISSUES

ESTADO DE MINAS GERAES

OBRIGACOES DO THESOURO DO ESTADO

OBLIGATIONS OF THE TREASURY OF THE STATE

LAW OF 16.10.1930

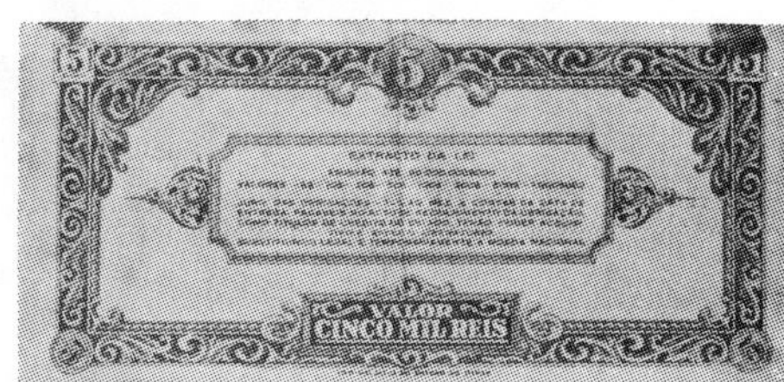

		GOOD	FINE	XF
S751	**5 MIL REIS** *L. 1930.* Black-green on tan unpt. Back green. Printer: Imp. Official do Estado de Minas.	25.00	75.00	150.00

NOTE: Values of 10, 20, 50, 100, 200, 500 Mil Reis and 1 Conto de Reis are reported, not confirmed.

PREVIDENCIA DOS SERVIDORES DO ESTADO DE MINAS GERAES

1930 ISSUE

		GOOD	FINE	XF
S761	**2 MIL REIS** 21.10.1930. Brown and pink on pink unpt. Back gray.	20.00	50.00	110.00

		GOOD	FINE	XF
S762	**5 MIL REIS** 20.10.1930. Brown and orange on orange unpt. Back gray.	20.00	50.00	110.00
S763	**10 MIL REIS** 31.10.1930. Brown and gray on gray unpt. Back gray.	25.00	70.00	150.00
S764	**20 MIL REIS** 31.10.1930. Brown and lt. pink on lt. pink unpt. Back gray.	25.00	70.00	150.00

ESTADO DO RIO GRANDE DO SUL

THESOURO DO ESTADO/TREASURY OF THE STATE

1930 ISSUE - SERIES A

#S771-S777 arms at r. Imprint: Lith. da Livraria do Globo, Porto Alegre.

		GOOD	FINE	XF
S771	**5 MIL REIS** 31.10.1930. Black and red on m/c unpt. Back dull red.	25.00	60.00	130.00
S772	**10 MIL REIS** 31.10.1930. Like #S771. Back blue.	25.00	60.00	130.00
S773	**20 MIL REIS** 31.10.1930. Like #S771. Back violet.	25.00	70.00	150.00
S774	**50 MIL REIS** 31.10.1930. Like #S771. Back yellow.	27.50	75.00	200.00

		GOOD	FINE	XF
S775	**100 MIL REIS** 31.10.1930. Like #S771. Back green.	40.00	80.00	200.00
S776	**200 MIL REIS** 31.10.1930. Like #S771.	60.00	125.00	250.00
S777	**500 MIL REIS** 31.10.1930. Like #S771.	75.00	150.00	300.00

1931 Issue - Series B

#S781-S787 State Treasury on back. Imprint as previous issue.

		Good	Fine	XF
S781	**5 Mil Reis** 1.5.1931. Dk. blue-gray on olive unpt. Portr. O. Aranha at l. Back dk. blue.	25.00	50.00	110.00
S782	**10 Mil Reis** 1.5.1931. Black on blue unpt. Portr. G. Vargas at l. Back green.	30.00	60.00	130.00
S783	**20 Mil Reis** 1.5.1931. Black on rose unpt. Portr. A. Brasil at l. Back red.	40.00	80.00	175.00
S784	**50 Mil Reis** 1.5.1931. Black on green and m/c unpt. Portr. B. de Medeiros at l. Back dk. violet.	50.00	90.00	200.00
S785	**100 Mil Reis** 1.5.1931. Black on m/c unpt. Portr. S. Martins at l.	60.00	110.00	225.00
S786	**200 Mil Reis** 1.5.1931. Black on m/c unpt. Portr. J. de Castilhos at l.	75.00	125.00	240.00
S787	**500 Mil Reis** 1.5.1931. Black on m/c unpt. Portr. P. Machado at l.	100.00	175.00	350.00

NOTE: 1931 Issue - Series C: A complete set has been reported with designs similar to Series B, D and E.

1932 Issue - Series D

#S791-S797 designs and imprint like previous issue.

		Good	Fine	XF
S791	**5 Mil Reis** 1.5.1932. Black on rose and m/c unpt. Like #S781. Back red-brown.	15.00	30.00	70.00

		Good	Fine	XF
S792	**10 Mil Reis** 1.5.1932. Black on brown, green and m/c unpt. Like #S782. Back olive.	25.00	50.00	125.00

		Good	Fine	XF
S793	**20 Mil Reis** 1.5.1932. Black on blue, yellow and m/c unpt. Like #S783. Back red.	40.00	80.00	200.00
S794	**50 Mil Reis** 1.5.1932. Black on m/c unpt. Like #S784. Back dk. blue.	50.00	90.00	225.00
S795	**100 Mil Reis** 1.5.1932. Black on m/c unpt. Like #S785. Back wine.	60.00	110.00	250.00

		Good	Fine	XF
S796	**200 Mil Reis** 1.5.1932. Black on m/c unpt. Like #S786. Back blue.	75.00	150.00	300.00
S797	**500 Mil Reis** 1.5.1932. Black on m/c unpt. Like #S787. Back dk. violet.	100.00	175.00	400.00

1933 Issue - Series E

#S801-S807 designs and imprint like previous 2 issues.

		Good	Fine	XF
S801	**5 Mil Reis** 1.5.1933. Blue on m/c unpt. Like #S781 and S791. Back dk. blue.	20.00	40.00	105.00
S802	**10 Mil Reis** 1.5.1933. Blue on m/c unpt. Like #S782 and S792. Back violet.	25.00	50.00	125.00
S803	**20 Mil Reis** 1.5.1933. Violet on m/c unpt. Like #S783 and S793. Back lt. brown.	40.00	80.00	200.00
S804	**50 Mil Reis** 1.5.1933. Black on m/c unpt. Like #S784 and S794. Back wine.	50.00	90.00	225.00
S805	**100 Mil Reis** 1.5.1933. Black on m/c unpt. Like #S785 and S795. Back dk. red.	60.00	110.00	250.00
S806	**200 Mil Reis** 1.5.1933. Black on m/c unpt. Like #S786 and S796. Back red-brown.	75.00	125.00	275.00
S807	**500 Mil Reis** 1.5.1933. Black on m/c unpt. Like #S787 and S797. Back green.	100.00	175.00	375.00

1934 Issue - Series F

#S811-S817 same portr. as previous issues but they are at ctr. instead of at l. Back is the Palace of Piratini. Imprint as previous issues.

		Good	Fine	XF
S811	**5 Mil Reis** 1.5.1934. Black on green and m/c unpt. Back violet.	25.00	50.00	125.00
S812	**10 Mil Reis** 1.5.1934. Black on m/c unpt. Back olive.	30.00	60.00	150.00
S813	**20 Mil Reis** 1.5.1934. Black on m/c unpt. Back lt. brown.	40.00	80.00	200.00
S814	**50 Mil Reis** 1.5.1934. Black on orange and m/c unpt. Back brown.	50.00	90.00	225.00
S815	**100 Mil Reis** 1.5.1934. Black on m/c unpt. Back dk. red.	60.00	110.00	250.00
S816	**200 Mil Reis** 1.5.1934. Black on m/c unpt. Back blue.	75.00	125.00	275.00
S817	**500 Mil Reis** 1.5.1934. Black on m/c unpt.	100.00	175.00	375.00

Letras do Tesouro

Treasury Letters

These notes were issued while Leonel Brizola was governor of the state; acceptance was only grudgingly given, and the notes became derisively known as "brizoletas."

Law of 30.7.1959; 1960-63 Issue

#S821-S830 arms of the old República Rio Grandense of 1835 at top ctr. Imprint: Lit. Globo S. A.-P. Alegre.

		Good	Fine	XF
S821	**50 Cruzeiros** 1962-66. Green.			
	a. Sm. date: 15.1.1960; 1.7.1962.	20.00	45.00	100.00
	b. Lg. date: 25.4.1966.	20.00	45.00	100.00

		GOOD	FINE	XF
S822	**100 CRUZEIROS** 14.1.1963; 29.1.1963; 3.2.1963. Blue on gray unpt.	20.00	45.00	100.00
S823	**200 CRUZEIROS** 10.2.1960; 25.4.1966. Green and pink.	—	—	—
S824	**500 CRUZEIROS** (ca.1962). Brown.	—	—	—
S825	**1000 CRUZEIROS** (ca.1962). Green and cream. Value expressed as *1 MIL CRUZEIROS*.	—	—	—
S826	**1000 CRUZEIROS** (ca.1962). Dk. green and lt. yellow. Value expressed as *1000 CRUZEIROS*.	—	—	—
S827	**5000 CRUZEIROS** (ca.1962). Brown and green.	—	—	—

		GOOD	FINE	XF
S828	**10,000 CRUZEIROS** (ca.1962). Dk. and lt. green.	—	—	—
S829	**50,000 CRUZEIROS** (ca.1962). Sepia and yellow.	—	—	—
S830	**100,000 CRUZEIROS** (ca.1962). Dk. brown and yellow.	—	—	—

LAW OF 30.7.1959/DECREE OF 31.8.1961

#S844-S849 similar to previous issue but red ovpt: *LEGALIDADE* and black ovpt. of decree date on face. Printer: TDLR, S.A.

		GOOD	FINE	XF
S844	**500 CRUZEIROS** *D. 1961*. Brown on gray unpt.	25.00	50.00	110.00
S845	**1000 CRUZEIROS** *D. 1961*. Blue on gray unpt.	25.00	50.00	110.00
S846	**5000 CRUZEIROS** *D. 1961*.	—	—	—
S847	**10,000 CRUZEIROS** *D. 1961*.	—	—	—
S848	**50,000 CRUZEIROS** *D. 1961*.	—	—	—
S849	**100,000 CRUZEIROS** *D. 1961*.	—	—	—

LAW OF 6.12.1965/DECREE OF 21.12.1965; 1966 ISSUE

#S851-S854 similar to previous issues. Imprint: Lit. Globo S.A.- P. Alegre.

		GOOD	FINE	XF
S851	**5000 CRUZEIROS** (ca.1966).	—	—	—
S852	**10,000 CRUZEIROS** 23.9.1966.	—	—	—
S853	**50,000 CRUZEIROS** (ca.1966).	—	—	—
S854	**100,000 CRUZEIROS** (ca.1966).	—	—	—

ESTADO DE SÃO PAULO

BONUS DO THESOURO (BONDS OF THE TREASURY)

DECREE OF 14.7.1932; FIRST ISSUE

#S861-S866 imprint: *Comp. Melmoramentos de São Paulo* (Weiszflog Irmaos Incorporada) S. Paulo-Rio-Cayeiras.

		GOOD	FINE	XF
S861	**5 MIL REIS** *D.1932*. Dk. blue on orange unpt. Portr. D. J. Velho at ctr. Back brown.			
	a. W/o imprint.	20.00	40.00	100.00
	b. W/imprint.	18.00	35.00	90.00

		GOOD	FINE	XF
S862	**10 MIL REIS** *D.1932*. Olive. Like #S81. Back green.	35.00	70.00	150.00
S863	**20 MIL REIS** *D.1932*. Blue and lt. brown. Like #S861. Back orange.	40.00	80.00	200.00
S864	**50 MIL REIS** *D.1932*. Blue and violet. Like #S861. Back green.	50.00	100.00	250.00

		GOOD	FINE	XF
S865	**100 MIL REIS** *D.1932*. Black on m/c unpt. Portr. F. D. Paes Leme at ctr. Back blue-green.	65.00	150.00	325.00

DECREE OF 14.7.1932; SECOND ISSUE

It is reported that the Second Issue was in circulation only 3 days, then withdrawn. #S871-S876 printer like previous issue.

		GOOD	FINE	XF
S871	**5 MIL REIS** *D.1932*. Blue on orange unpt. Portr. A. Barroso at r. Back brown.	—	—	—

		GOOD	FINE	XF
S872	**10 MIL REIS** *D.1932*. Blue. Portr. Marques de Tamandare at r. Back yellow.	—	—	—
S873	**20 MIL REIS** *D.1932*. Blue-green on orange unpt. Gen. Osorio at r. Back green on rose unpt.; coffee gathering at ctr.	—	—	—

		GOOD	FINE	XF
S874	**50 MIL REIS** *D.1932*. Blue on orange unpt. Portr. Marshal F. Peixoto at upper ctr. Back blue on orange unpt. Like #S873.	—	—	—

		Good	Fine	XF
S875	**100 Mil Reis** *D.1932.* Blue on brown unpt. Duke of Caxias at l. Back blue on yellow unpt.	—	—	—

		Good	Fine	XF
S876	**200 Mil Reis** *D.1932.* Blue on orange unpt. Portr. R. Barbosa at upper ctr. Back green on orange unpt.	—	—	—

Revolution 1924

O Governo Revolucionario do Brazil Revolutionary Government

1924 Issue

		Good	Fine	XF
S881	**5 Mil Reis** 5.7.1924. Dk. blue. Pale pink tinted paper. Justice at ctr.			
	a. Finished note.	85.00	225.00	—
	b. Unfinished note.	—	—	75.00

NOTE: Most of #S881 was not finished or issued.

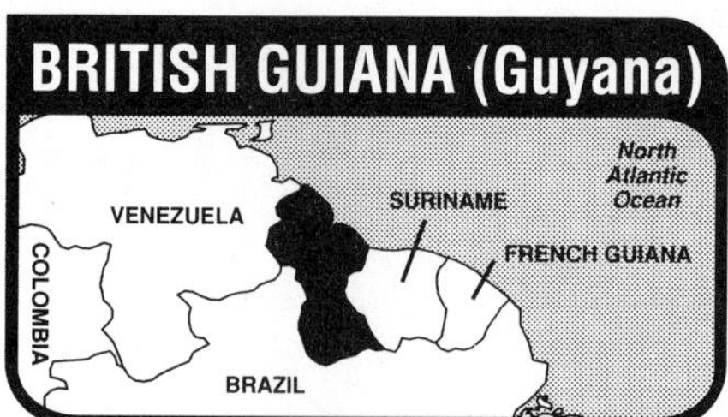

British Guiana was a British Crown Colony in Northern South America with an area of 89,480 sq. mi. Capital: Georgetown. The economy was mainly agricultural. Chief exports were sugar, molasses, rum and forest products.

The original area of Guyana, which included present-day Surinam, French Guiana, and parts of Brazil and Venezuela, was sighted by Columbus in 1498. The first European settlement was made late in the 16th century by the Dutch. For the next 150 years, possession alternated between the Dutch and the British, with a short interval of French control. The British exercised de facto control after 1796, although the area, which included the Dutch colonies of Essequebo, Demerary and Berbice, was not ceded to them by the Dutch until 1814. From 1803 to 1831, Essequebo and Demerary were administered separately from Berbice. The three colonies were united in the British Crown Colony of British Guiana in 1831. British Guiana won internal self-government in 1952.

For later issues see Guyana listings in Volume 3, Modern issues.

RULERS:

British to 1966

MONETARY SYSTEM:

1 Joe = 22 Guilders to 1836
1 Dollar = 4 Shillings-2 Pence, 1837-1965

British Administration

Barclays Bank (Dominion, Colonial and Overseas)

Formerly the Colonial Bank. Issued at Demerara.

1926 Issue

#S101-S103 arms at upper ctr. Lg. ovpt: *B.G.* at upper r. Arms at ctr. on back. Printer: BWC.

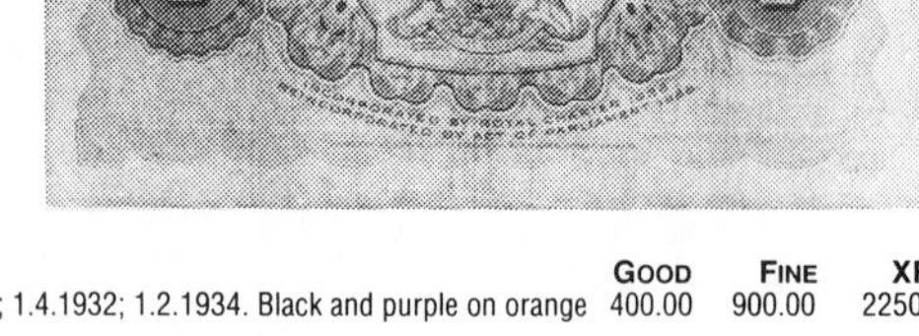

		Good	Fine	XF
S101	**5 Dollars** 1.9.1926; 1.11.1928; 1.4.1932; 1.2.1934. Black and purple on orange unpt. Back green.	400.00	900.00	2250.
S102	**10 Dollars** 1.9.1926; 1.4.1932.	—	Rare	—
S102A	**20 Dollars** 1.9.1926. Specimen.	—	Rare	—

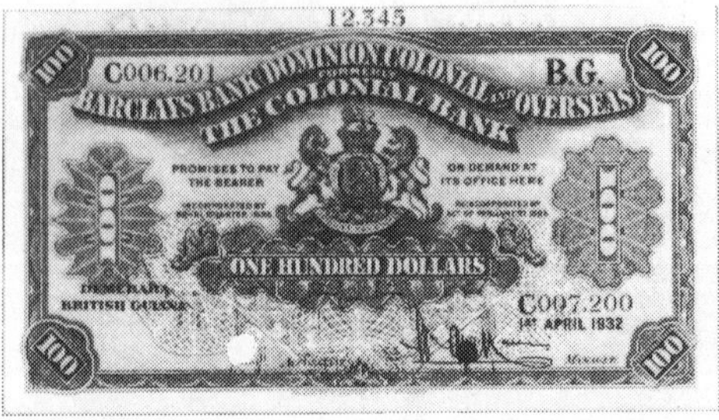

		Good	Fine	XF
S103	**100 Dollars** 1.9.1926; 1.4.1932. Specimen.	—	Rare	—

1937 Issue

#S104-S106 arms at r. Lg. ovpt: *B.G.* at upper r. Arms at ctr. on back. Printer: BWC.

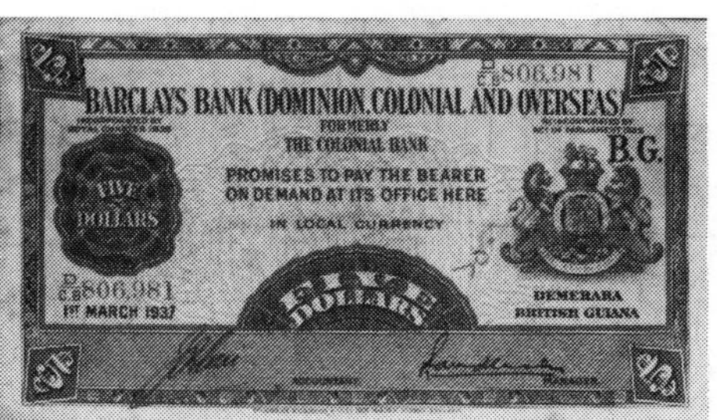

		GOOD	FINE	XF
S104	**5 DOLLARS**			
	1.3.1937-1.3.1940. Purple.			
	a. Issued note.	250.00	450.00	800.00
	s. Proof.	—	Unc	750.00

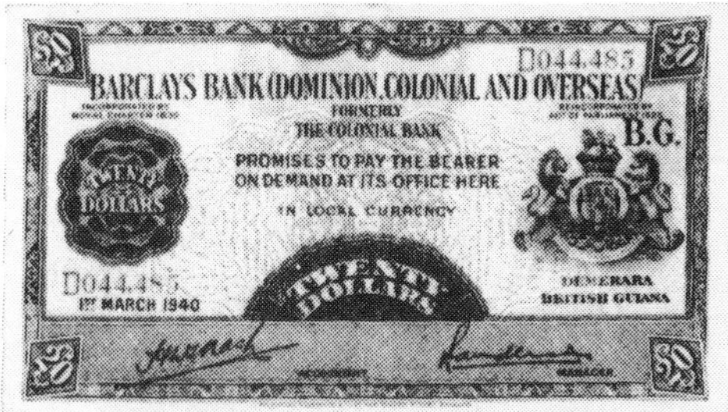

		GOOD	FINE	XF
S105	**20 DOLLARS**			
	1.3.1937; 1.5.1937; 1.3.1940. Brown.	500.00	1350.	—
S106	**100 DOLLARS**			
	1.3.1937; 1.5.1937; 1.3.1940. Specimen.	—	Rare	—

BRITISH GUIANA BANK

1902 ISSUE

#S111-S113 figure resembling seated Britannia at upper l. Printer: PBC.

		GOOD	FINE	XF
S111	**5 DOLLARS**			
	1.3.1902; 2.9.1907. Black. Back red-brown.	—	Rare	—

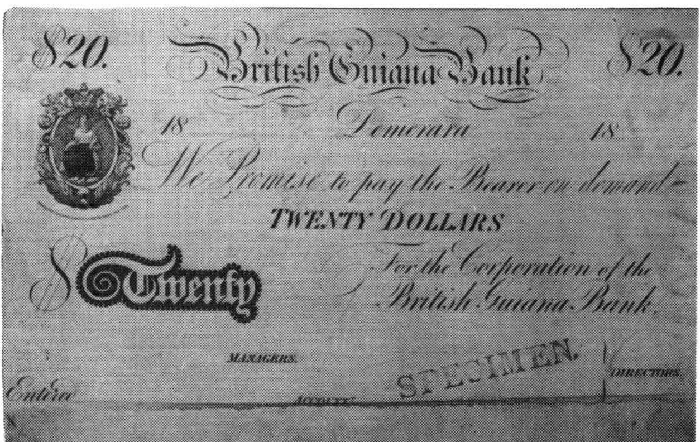

		GOOD	FINE	XF
S112	**20 DOLLARS**			
	18xx. Specimen.	—	Rare	—
S113	**100 DOLLARS**			
		—	Rare	—

COLONIAL BANK

Later (in 1925) became Barclays Bank. Issued at Georgetown, Demerary.

1900; 1917 ISSUE

#S116-S118 arms at upper ctr., *G* at upper l. and r. Printer: PBC.

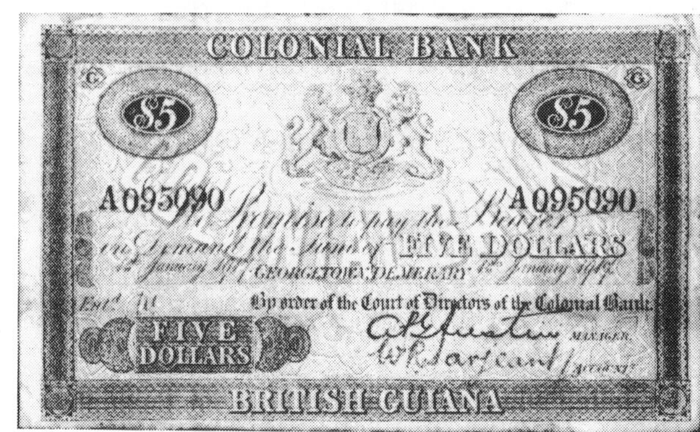

		GOOD	FINE	XF
S116	**5 DOLLARS**			
	1.1.1917. Black and red. Back green.			
	a. Issued note.	750.00	2200.	—
	s. Specimen.	—	Unc	1100.

		GOOD	FINE	XF
S117	**20 DOLLARS**			
	ND (ca.1900). Black on yellow unpt. Back blue. Specimen.	—	Unc	2250.

		GOOD	FINE	XF
S118	**100 DOLLARS**			
	19xx (ca.1900). Black on green unpt. Back red. Specimen.	—	Unc	2800.

1917 ISSUE

#S126-S128 arms at upper ctr. Lg. ovpt: *B.G.* at upper r. Printer: PBC.

		GOOD	FINE	XF
S126	**5 DOLLARS**			
	(ca.1917).	—	Rare	—

		GOOD	FINE	XF
S127	**20 DOLLARS** 1.2.1917.	—	Rare	—
S128	**100 DOLLARS** (ca.1917).	—	Rare	—

ROYAL BANK OF CANADA

Notes designed specifically for circulation in the West Indies issued at Georgetown.

1909 PROVISIONAL ISSUE

#S130-S133 vertical ovpt: *BRITISH GUIANA* at l. and r., smaller text vertical ovpt: *Payable at Georgetown, British Guiana* at ctr. on regular Canadian issues of this bank.

		GOOD	FINE	XF
S130	**100 DOLLARS** 2.1.1909. Black on red-orange unpt. Ovpt. on #S1377. Printer: ABNC	—	Rare	—

1913 PROVISIONAL ISSUE

#S131-S133 Printer: ABNC.

		GOOD	FINE	XF
S131	**5 DOLLARS** 2.1.1913. Black on green unpt. Ovpt. on #S1378.	500.00	1750.	—
S132	**20 DOLLARS** 2.1.1913. Black on blue unpt. Ovpt. on #S1380.	750.00	—	—
S133	**100 DOLLARS** 2.1.1913. Black on orange and lt. Ovpt. on #S1382.	—	Rare	—

1920 REGULAR ISSUE

#S136-S138 Georgetown issue. Larger size notes. Printer: ABNC.

		GOOD	FINE	XF
S136	**5 DOLLARS = 1 POUND-10 PENCE** 2.1.1920. Black on green unpt. Steamship at ctr. Back green.	300.00	750.00	—
S137	**20 DOLLARS = 4 POUNDS-3 SHILLINGS-4 PENCE** 2.1.1920. Black on blue unpt. Harvesting sugar cane at ctr. Back blue.	—	Rare	—

		GOOD	FINE	XF
S138	**100 DOLLARS = 20 POUNDS-16 SHILLINGS-8 PENCE** 2.1.1920. Black on orange unpt. Reclining woman w/island scene in background at ctr. Back orange.	—	Rare	—

1938 ISSUE

#S141 and S142 similar to #S136 and S137 but reduced size. Printer: CBNC.

		GOOD	FINE	XF
S141	**5 DOLLARS = 1 POUND-10 PENCE** 3.1.1938. Similar to #S136.	200.00	500.00	900.00

		GOOD	FINE	XF
S142	**20 DOLLARS = 4 POUNDS-3 SHILLINGS-4 PENCE** 3.1.1938. Black on orange-red unpt. Back rose. Similar to #S137.	600.00	1700.	—

BRITISH VIRGIN ISLANDS

The Colony of the Virgin Islands, a British colony situated in the Caribbean Sea northeast of Puerto Rico and west of the Leeward Islands, has an area of 59 sq. mi. (153 sq. km.). Capital: Road Town. The principal islands of the 36-island group are Tortola, Virgin Gorda, Anegada, and Jost Van Dyke.

Tortola, which has an area of about 24 sq. mi. (62 sq. km.), is the largest of thirty-six islands, in the British Virgin Islands, a presidency of the British Leeward Islands.

The Virgin Islands were discovered by Columbus in 1493, and named by him Las Virgenes, in honor of St. Ursula and her companions. It was settled by the Dutch in 1648, and was occupied by the British in 1666. They have held it ever since. The British Virgin Islands were formerly part of the administration of the Leeward Islands, but received a separate administration as a Crown Colony in 1950. A new constitution promulgated in 1967 provided for a ministerial form of government headed by the governor.

U.S.A. coins and currency continue to be the primary medium of exchange.

RULERS:
British

MONETARY SYSTEM
1 Shilling = 12 Pence
1 Pound = 20 Shillings

BRITISH ADMINISTRATION

GOVERNMENT OF THE BRITISH VIRGIN ISLANDS

1921 ISSUE

		GOOD	FINE	XF
S101	**2 SHILLINGS-6 PENCE** (ca. 1931).	Reported Not Confirmed		
S102	**5 SHILLINGS** (ca. 1931).	—	Rare	—
S103	**10 SHILLINGS** (ca. 1931).	—	Rare	—

NOTE: The above issue was reported by Dr. Arnold Keller, ca.1965.

BULGARIA-THRACE

Thrace, a name applied at various periods to areas of different extent, is a territory divided at present between Greece, Turkey and Bulgaria. Bulgaria's claim came as a result of the end of the first Balkan War of 1912, at which time it took control of most of Thrace.

The second Balkan War altered this status but the whole area remained in turmoil until after the end of World War I. At that point, Greece had taken most of Thrace, but the Allies believed Bulgaria needed an economic outlet to the Aegean Sea. Article 48 of the Treaty of Neuilly declared that Bulgaria had the right of transit over its former Thracian territory to the various ports assigned to Greece. Nothing worked out as planned, and the area was again reapportioned in 1923.

TITLES:

MONETARY SYSTEM:
1 Lev ЛЕВ = 100 Stotinki СТОТИНКИ

ALLIES & BULGARIAN ADMINISTRATION

THRACE-INTERALLIEE

1919 PROVISIONAL ISSUE

#S101-S114 Bulgarian National Bank notes w/Thrace Internationale adhesive stamp and embossed oval seal w/*THRACE-INTERALLIEE.*

ADHESIVE REVENUE STAMP VARIETIES:
Type A - Black on blue paper.
Type B - Black on white paper.

		GOOD	FINE	XF
S101	**1 LEV SREBRO** ND (1919-20). Adhesive stamp Type A and embossed seal on back of #14 (Vol. 2).	—	—	—
S102	**2 LEVA SREBRO** ND (1919-20). Adhesive stamp Type A and embossed seal on back of #15 (Vol. 2).	—	—	—
S105	**5 LEVA SREBRO** ND (1919-20). Adhesive stamp Type B and embossed seal on back of #16 (Vol. 2).	—	—	—
S106	**5 LEVA SREBRNI** ND (1919-20). Adhesive stamp Type B and embossed seal on back of #21 (Vol. 2).	—	—	—

		GOOD	FINE	XF
S107	**10 LEVA SREBRO** ND (1919-20). Adhesive stamp Type B and embossed seal on face of #17 (Vol. 2).	—	—	—
S108	**10 LEVA ZLATNI** ND (1919-20). Adhesive stamp Type B and embossed seal on back of #22a (Vol. 2).	—	—	—

		Good	Fine	XF
S109	**20 Leva Zlato** ND (1919-20). Adhesive stamp Type A and embossed seal on back of #18 (Vol. 2).	—	—	—
S110	**20 Leva Zlatni** ND (1919-20). Adhesive stamp Type A and embossed seal on back of #23 (Vol. 2).	—	—	—
S111	**50 Leva Zlato** ND (1919-20). Adhesive stamp Type A and embossed seal on back of #19 (Vol. 2).	—	—	—

		Good	Fine	XF
S112	**50 Leva Zlatni** ND (1919-20). Adhesive stamp Type A and embossed seal on back of #24 (Vol. 2).	—	—	—

#113 and 114 w/wide hologram foil strip at l. Reduced size.

		Good	Fine	XF
S113	**100 Leva Zlato** ND (1919-20). Adhesive stamp Type B and embossed seal on back of #20 (Vol. 2).	—	—	—
S114	**100 Leva Zlatni** ND (1919-20). Adhesive stamp Type B and embossed seal on back of #25 (Vol. 2).	—	—	—

NOTE: Higher denominations may exist.

NOTE: Apparently for a period of about six months, beginning in late 1919 until May 1920 (the end of Thrace Interallie) special revalidated notes of 1903, 1916, and 1917 were placed in circulation. No official documentation has been uncovered to this date for this particular series. Some authorities believe the entire issue to be spurious.

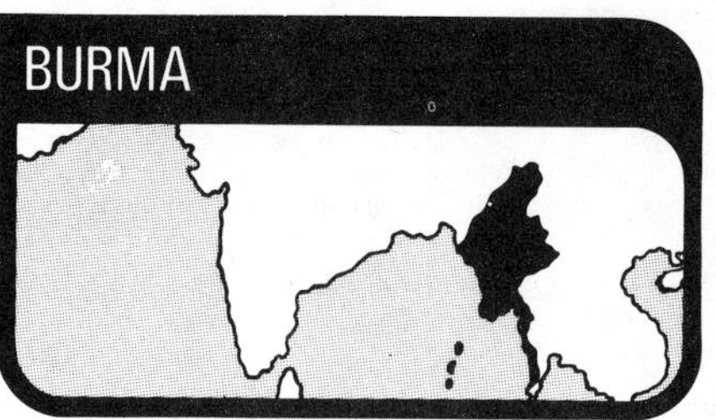

The Socialist Republic of the Union of Burma (now Myanmar), a country of Southeast Asia fronting on the Bay of Bengal and the Andaman Sea, has an area of 261,789 sq. mi. (676,552 sq. km.). Capital: Rangoon.

The first European to reach Burma, about 1435, was Nicolo Di Conti, a merchant of Venice. During the beginning of the reign of Bodawpaya (1782-1819AD) the kingdom comprised most of the same area as it does today including Arakan which was taken over in 1784-85. The British East India Company, while unsuccessful in its 1612 effort to establish posts along the Bay of Bengal, was enabled by the Anglo-Burmese Wars of 1824-86 to expand to the whole of Burma and to secure its annexation to British India. In 1937, Burma was separated from India, becoming a separate British colony with limited self-government. The Japanese occupied Burma in 1942, and in late 1943 Burma became an "independent and sovereign state" under Dr. Ba Maw who was appointed the Adipadi (head of state). Burma became an independent nation outside the British Commonwealth on Jan. 4, 1948, the constitution of 1948 providing for parliamentary democracy and the nationalization of certain industries. However, political and economic problems persisted, and on March 2, 1962, Gen. Ne Win took over the government, suspended the constitution, installed himself as chief of state, and pursued a socialistic program with nationalization of nearly all industry and trade. The country name was officially changed to Myanmar in 1989.

Shan States are located in eastern Burma along the Chinese, Thai and Lao borders in what is called the Golden Triangle. The Shan are ethnically related to the Thai and Lao, and are often referred to as Tai. A Shan National Army was organized in 1961 to fight the Burmese and to create an independent country for the Shan people. This army collapsed in the mid-1960s, but other groups are always being formed.

Government of Tailand

Shan National Army

1964-65 ND Issue

#S101-S103 militant arms at l., globe within tigers (brand of heroin label) at r. on face. Text is in local T'ai language. (Not issued).

		VG	VF	Unc
S101	**1 Tep** ND (1964-65). Blue. Worker at l., factory at ctr., tools at r. on back.	8.00	40.00	100.00

S102 **5 TEP**

ND (1964-65). Violet. Farm tractor at l., logging at ctr., rural scene at r. on back.

VG	VF	UNC
4.00	20.00	50.00

S103 **10 TEP**

ND (1964-65). Brown. Ambulance at l., hospital at ctr., medical workers at r. on back.

VG	VF	UNC
8.00	40.00	100.00

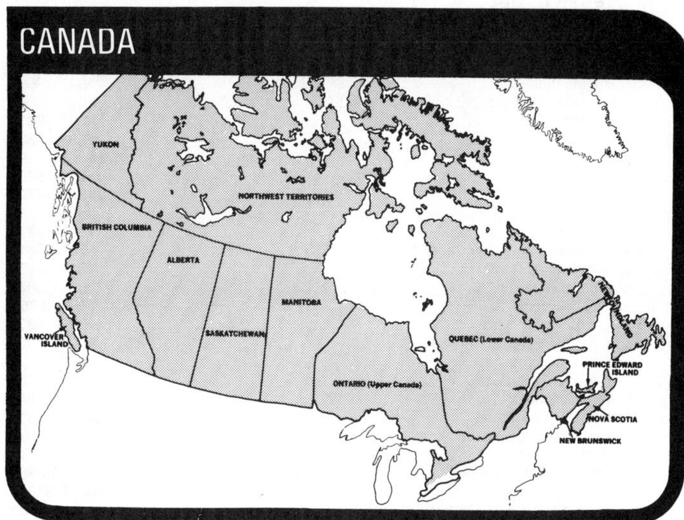

Canada is located to the north of the United States, and spans the full breadth of the northern portion of North America from Atlantic to Pacific oceans, except for the State of Alaska. It has a total area of 3,850,000 sq. mi. (9,970,610 sq. km.) and a population of 30.68 million. Capital: Ottawa.

Jacques Cartier, a French explorer, took possession of Canada for France in 1534, and for more than a century the history of Canada was that of a French colony. Samuel de Champlain helped to establish the first permanent colony in North America, in 1604 at Port Royal, Acadia - now Annapolis Royal, Nova Scotia. Four years later he founded the settlement of Quebec.

The British settled along the coast to the south while the French, motivated by a grand design, pushed into the interior. France's plan for a great American empire was to occupy the Mississippi heartland of the country, and from there to press in upon the narrow strip of English coastal settlements from the rear. Inevitably, armed conflict erupted between the French and the British; consequently, Britain acquired Hudson Bay, Newfoundland and Nova Scotia from the French in 1713. British control of the rest of New France was secured in 1763, largely because of James Wolfe's great victory over Montcalm near Quebec in 1759.

During the American Revolution, Canada became a refuge for great numbers of American Royalists, most of whom settled in Ontario, thereby creating an English majority west of the Ottawa River. The ethnic imbalance contravened the effectiveness of the prevailing French type of government, and in 1791 the Constitutional act was passed by the British parliament, dividing Canada at the Ottawa River into two parts, each with its own government: Upper Canada, chiefly English and consisting of the southern section of what is now Ontario; and Lower Canada, chiefly French and consisting principally of the southern section of Quebec. Subsequent revolt by dissidents in both sections caused the British government to pass the Union act, July 23, 1840, which united Lower and Upper Canada (as Canada East and Canada West) to form the Province of Canada, with one council and one assembly in which the two sections had equal numbers.

The union of the two provinces did not encourage political stability; the equal strength of the French and British made the task of government all but impossible. A further change was made with the passage of the British North American act, which took effect on July 1, 1867, and established Canada as the first federal union in the British Empire. Four provinces entered the union at first: Upper Canada as Ontario, Lower Canada as Quebec, Nova Scotia and New Brunswick. The Hudson's Bay Company's territories were acquired in 1869 out of which were formed the provinces of Manitoba, Saskatchewan and Alberta. British Columbia joined in 1871 and Prince Edward Island in 1873. Canada took over the Arctic Archipelago in 1895. In 1949 Newfoundland came into the confederation. Canada is a member of the Commonwealth. Elizabeth II is Head of State as Queen of Canada.

RULERS:

British 1763-

MONETARY SYSTEM:

French:
12 Deniers = 1 Sou (sols)
20 Sous or Sols = 1 Livre Coloniale
1 Liard = 3 Deniers
1 Ecu = 6 Livres
1 Louis D'or = 4 Ecus
English:
4 Farthings = 1 Penny
12 Pence = 1 Shilling
20 Shillings = 1 Pound
Canadian Decimal Currency
100 Cents = 1 Dollar

ARRANGEMENT

Canada listings in this volume include sections covering French colonial issues, Provincial (British) issues, Chartered Bank issues (including Hudsons Bay Company), and Spurious and Expired banks. The following outline indicates exact location of the various issuers by catalog number.

FRENCH COLONIAL

BRITISH COLONIAL

British Army

PROVINCIAL ISSUES

CHARTERED BANKS

Bank of British Columbia . . . #S201-S219
Bank of British North America . . . #S221-S435
Bank of Hamilton . . . #S441-S468
Bank of Montreal . . . #S471-S564
Bank of New Brunswick . . . #S571-S599
Bank of Nova Scotia . . . #S601-S633
Bank of Ottawa . . . #S636-S664
Bank of Toronto . . . #S666-S693
Bank of Vancouver . . . #S696-S700
Bank of Yarmouth . . . #S701-S704
Banque Canadienne Nationale . . . #S706-S717
Banque d'Hochelaga . . . #S721-S815
Banque Internationale du Canada . . . #S816-S818
Banque Jacques Cartier . . . #S821-S837
Banque Nationale . . . #S841-S875
Bank of the People . . . #S875A-S875E
Banque du Peuple . . . #S876-S909
Banque Provinciale du Canada . . . #S911-S922
Banque de St. Hyacinthe . . . #S924-S929
Banque de St. Jean . . . #S931-S935
Banque Ville Marie . . . #S936-S946
Barclays Bank (Canada) . . . #S947-S951
Canadian Bank of Commerce . . . #S952-S972
City Bank . . . #S972A-S972C
Commercial Bank of Canada . . . #S973-S996
Commercial Bank of Manitoba . . . #S997-S1000
Commercial Bank of the Midland District . . . #S1000A-S1000W
Commercial Bank of Windsor . . . #S1001-S1004
Crown Bank of Canada . . . #S1006-S1009
Dominion Bank . . . #S1011-S1036
Eastern Townships Bank . . . #S1041-S1057
Exchange Bank of Yarmouth . . . #S1058-S1060
Farmers Bank of Canada . . . #S1061-S1065
Gore Bank . . . #S1066-S1069
Halifax Banking Company . . . #S1070-S1086
Home Bank of Canada . . . #S1087-S1091
Hudsons Bay Company . . . #S1095-S1121
Imperial Bank of Canada . . . #S1122-S1145H
Merchants Bank of Canada . . . #S1146-S1173
Merchants' Bank of Halifax . . . #S1174-S1189
Merchants Bank of Prince Edward Island . . . #S1191-S1196
Metropolitan Bank . . . #S1197-S1201
Molsons Bank . . . #S1202-S1243
Montreal Bank . . . #S1243A-S1243K
Niagara District Bank . . . #S1243L-S1243V
Northern Bank . . . #S1244-S1247
Northern Crown Bank . . . #S1248-S1251
Ontario Bank . . . #S1252-S1286
Peoples Bank of Halifax . . . #S1287-S1290
Peoples Bank of New Brunswick . . . #S1291-S1302
Quebec Bank . . . #S1306-S1368
Royal Bank of Canada . . . #S1369-S1394
St. Lawrence Bank . . . #S1395-S1399
St. Stephens Bank . . . #S1400-S1430
Sovereign Bank of Canada . . . #S1431-S1434
Standard Bank of Canada . . . #S1435-S1447
Sterling Bank of Canada . . . #S1448-S1453
Summerside Bank of Prince Edward Island . . . #S1454-S1465
Traders Bank of Canada . . . #S1466-S1482
Union Bank of Canada . . . #S1483-S1507
Union Bank of Halifax . . . #S1511-S1521
Union Bank of Lower Canada . . . #S1521A-S1521J
Union Bank of Prince Edward Island . . . #S1522-S1533
United Empire Bank of Canada . . . #S1534-S1535
Western Bank of Canada . . . #S1536-S1538
Weyburn Security Bank . . . #S1539-S1541

SPURIOUS OR EXPIRED BANKS

The following notes are irredeemable.

Bank of Acadia . . . #S1542-S1545
Accommodation Bank . . . #S1546-S1547
Agricultural Bank, Montreal . . . #S1548-S1550
Agricultural Bank, Toronto . . . #S1551-S1564
Arman's Bank . . . #S1565-S1567
Banque De Boucherville . . . #S1568
Bank of Brantford . . . #S1569-S1576
British Canadian Bank . . . #S1577-S1578
Canada Bank, Montreal . . . #S1579-S1580
Canada Bank, Toronto . . . #S1581-S1583
Bank of Canada, Montreal . . . #S1584-S1595
Banque Canadienne . . . #S1596-S1599
Central Bank of Canada . . . #S1600-S1602
Central Bank of New Brunswick . . . #S1603-S1617
Charlotte County Bank . . . #S1618-S1622
Bank of Charlottetown . . . #S1623-S1625
City Bank, Banque de la Cité . . . #S1626-S1656
City Bank of Montreal . . . #S1656A
Bank of Clifton . . . #S1657-S1665
Colonial Bank of Canada . . . #S1666-S1680
Colonial Bank of Chatham . . . #S1681-S1683
Commercial Bank, Brockville . . . #S1684-S1685
Commercial Bank, Kingston, U.C. . . . #S1686-S1689
Commercial Bank, Montreal, L.C. . . . #S1689A-S1689C
Commercial Bank of Fort Erie, U.C. . . . #S1690-S1696
Commercial Bank of Montreal, L.C. . . . #S1697-S1702
Commercial Bank of New Brunswick . . . #S1703-S1720
Commercial Branch Bank of Canada, Collingwood, C.W. . . . #S1721-S1722
Consolidated Bank of Canada, Montreal . . . #S1723-S1728
Bank of the County of Elgin, St. Thomas, C.W. . . . #S1729-S1732
Eastern Bank of Canada, St. John, N.B. . . . #S1733-S1734
Exchange Bank, Quebec, L.C. . . . #S1735
Exchange Bank of Canada, Montreal, L.C. . . . #S1736-S1742
Exchange Bank of Canada, Windsor . . . #S1743
Exchange Bank of Toronto, U.C. . . . #S1744-S1747
Exchange Bank Company of Chippewa, U.C. . . . #S1748-S1749
Farmer's Bank, Toronto, U.C. . . . #S1750
Farmers' Bank of Malden, U.C. . . . #S1751-S1753
Farmer's Joint Stock Banking Co., Toronto, U.C. . . . #S1754-S1769
Farmers J.S. Banking Co., Toronto, U.C. . . . #S1770
Farmers Bank of Rustico. P.E.I. . . . #S1771-S1776
Farmers Bank of St. Johns, L.C. . . . #S1777-S1781
Federal Bank of Canada, Toronto . . . #S1782-S1788
Bank of Fredericton, N.B. . . . #S1789-S1793
Free Holders Bank of the Midland District, Bath, U.C. . . . #S1794-S1795
Goderich Bank, U.C. . . . #S1796-S1797
Gore Bank of Hamilton, U.C. . . . #S1798-S1800
Hart's Bank, Three Rivers, L.C. . . . #S1801-S1807
Henry's Bank, L.C. . . . #S1808-S1813
International Bank of Canada, Toronto, C.W. . . . #S1814-S1828
Kingston Bank, L.C. . . . #S1829
Bank of Liverpool, N.S. . . . #S1830-S1833
Bank of London in Canada . . . #S1834-S1838
Lower Canada Bank, Montreal, L.C. . . . #S1839-S1841
Bank of Lower Canada, Quebec, L.C. . . . #S1842-S1846
MacDonald & Co., Victoria, B.C. . . . #S1847-S1852
Maritime Bank of the Dominion of Canada, St. Johns, N.B. . . . #S1853-S1859
Mechanics Bank, Montreal, L.C. . . . #S1860-S1862
Mechanics Bank, Montreal, C.E. . . . #S1863-S1865
Mechanics Bank of Saint John's, L.C. . . . #S1866-S1874
Mercantile Banking Corporation, Halifax, N.S. . . . #S1875
Merchants Bank, Montreal, C.E. . . . #S1875A-S1875I
Merchants Bank, Toronto, U.C. . . . #S1876-S1879
Merchants Exchange Bank, Goderich, C.W. . . . #S1880
Metropolitan Bank, Montreal . . . #S1881-S1885
Montreal Bank, C.W. . . . #S1886
Newcastle Banking Company, Amherst, U.C. . . . #S1887-S1888
New Castle District Loan Company, Peterborough, U.C. . . . #S1889-S1892
Niagara Suspension Bridge Bank, Queenston, U.C. . . . #S1893-S1908
Bank of Ottawa (Banque de Ottawa), Montreal, L.C. . . . #S1909-S1914
Phenix Bank, Phillipsburg, L.C. . . . #S1915-S1918
Pictou Bank, N.S. . . . #S1919-S1921
Bank of Prince Edward Island, Charlottetown . . . #S1922-S1933
Provincial Bank, London . . . #S1934-S1935
Provincial Bank of Canada, Stanstead, C.E. . . . #S1936-S1938
Bank of Quebec, Lower Canada . . . #S1939
Royal Canadian Bank, Toronto, C.W. . . . #S1940-S1952
Saint Francis Bank, Stanstead, C.E. . . . #S1953-S1954
Banque St. Jean Baptiste, Montreal . . . #S1955-S1957
St. Lawrence Bank & Lumber Co., Malbaie, L.C. . . . #S1958-S1959
St. Stephens Joint Stock Banking Comp'y . . . #S1959A
Bank of Saskatchewan, Moose Jaw . . . #S1960-S1962
Stadacona Bank, Quebec City . . . #S1963-S1966
Tattersall Bank, Montreal, L.C. . . . #S1967
Union Bank, Montreal, L.C. . . . #S1968-S1988
Union Bank of Montreal, L.C. . . . #S1989-1990
Bank of Upper Canada, Kingston, U.C. . . . #S1991-S1996
Bank of Upper Canada, York, U.C. . . . #S1997-S2037
Bank of Western Canada, Clifton, C.W. . . . #S2038-S2041
Westmorland Bank of New Brunswick, Bend of the Petticodiac . . . #S2042-S2050
Zimmerman Bank, Elgin, C.W. . . . #S2051-S2076

FRENCH ADMINISTRATION

NEW FRANCE

Playing Card Money, 1685-1728

Introduced because of a shortage of regular currency, playing card money was used about 75 years in French Canada. Whole and partial cards were used; few examples are presently known, probably because of severe penalties for retention after their redemption period.

CARD MONEY, 1729-57

Pieces of plain cardboard w/sign. of Governor and Intendant, also their seals.

		Good	Fine	XF
S101	**7 Sols-6 Deniers** 1749.	—	Rare	—

#102

#104

#106

		Good	Fine	XF
S102	**15 Sols** 1749; 1757.	—	Rare	—
S103	**20 Sols** 1734.	—	Rare	—
S104	**30 Sols** 1733; 1738; 1752; 1757.	—	Rare	—
S105	**3 Livres** 1742; 1747; 1749.	—	Rare	—
S106	**6 Livres** 1729; 1735; 1749.	—	Rare	—

		GOOD	FINE	XF
S107	12 LIVRES 1729-49.	—	Rare	—

		GOOD	FINE	XF
S108	24 LIVRES 1729-49.	—	Rare	—

ORDONNANCES OR TREASURY NOTES, 1753-60

Treasury notes were issued to supplement card money.

		GOOD	FINE	XF
S111	20 SOLS 1754; 1757-59.	—	Rare	—

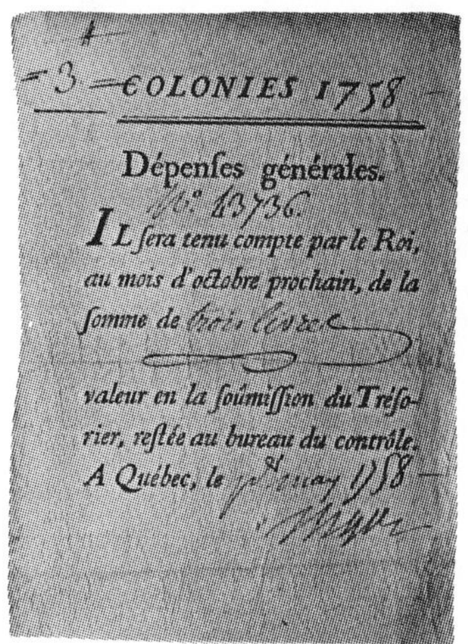

3 COLONIES 1758

Dépenſes générales.

IL ſera tenu compte par le Roi, au mois d'octobre prochain, de la ſomme de

valeur en la ſoumiſſion du Treſorier, reſtée au bureau du contrôle. A Québec, le

		GOOD	FINE	XF
S112	3 LIVRES 1756; 1758; 1760.	—	Rare	—

		GOOD	FINE	XF
S113	6 LIVRES 1758; 1759.	—	Rare	—
S114	12 LIVRES 1757-59.	—	Rare	—
S115	24 LIVRES 1756.	—	Rare	—

		GOOD	FINE	XF
S116	48 LIVRES 1753; 1758.	—	Rare	—
S117	96 LIVRES 1757; 1759.	—	Rare	—

BRITISH ADMINISTRATION

BRITISH ARMY

The British government expended large sums to finance the War of 1812, especially for pay and troop supplies. Because of difficulties in sending to Canada the required monetary instruments which would ordinarily have provided funds, it was decided to issue Army Bills, orders redeemable in government bills of exchange on London. Several issues were made.

Small denomination notes bore no interest; only those of 25 Dollars and higher had interest due. The Bills circulated to a fair extent, and after the war they were rapidly redeemed with the provinces paying the interest and the British treasury the principal.

The notes themselves mention several currencies: dollars, piastres, and often shillings. Notes are found hand signed, numbered and issued, or as unsigned remainders w/o serial # or sign.

1813 FIRST ARMY BILL ISSUE

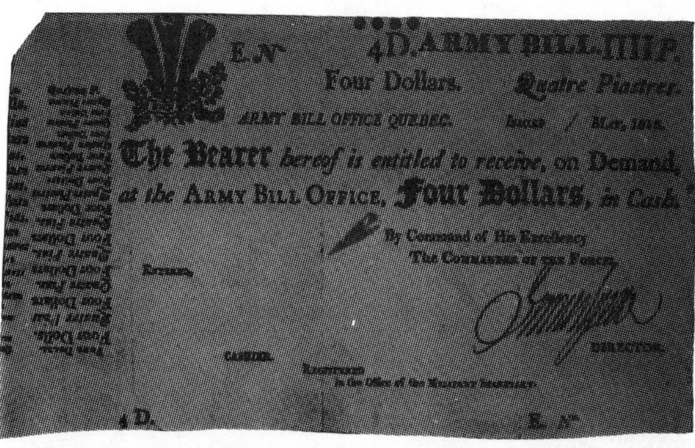

		GOOD	FINE	XF
S118A	4 DOLLARS May and June 1813. Plumes at upper l.	—	Rare	—

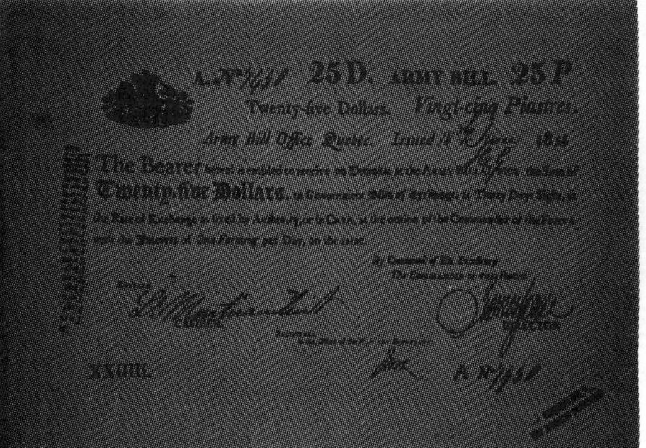

		GOOD	FINE	XF
S118B	25 DOLLARS 15.6.1813; 17.4.1813.	—	Rare	—

	Good	Fine	XF
S118C 50 Dollars ca.1813.	—	Rare	—
S118D 100 Dollars ca.1813.	—	Rare	—
S118E 400 Dollars ca.1813.	—	Rare	—

1813 Second Army Bill Issue

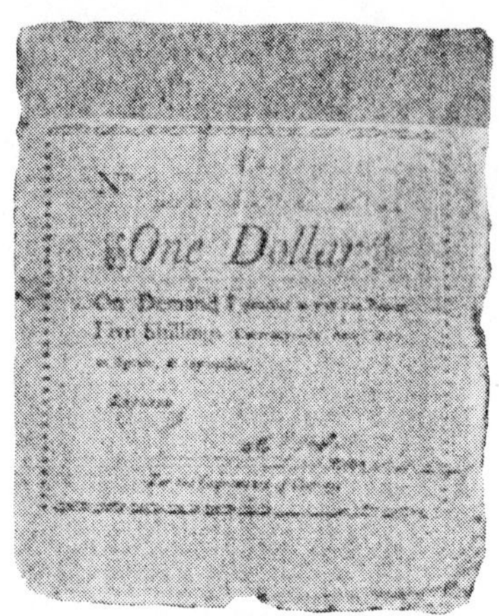

	Good	Fine	XF
S119A 1 Dollar ca.1813-14.	—	Rare	—
S119B 2 Dollars ca.1813-14.	Reported Not Confirmed		
S119C 8 Dollars ca.1813-14.	Reported Not Confirmed		
S119D 10 Dollars ca.1813-14.	Reported Not Confirmed		
S119E 12 Dollars ca.1813-14.	Reported Not Confirmed		
S119F 16 Dollars ca.1813-14.	Reported Not Confirmed		
S119G 20 Dollars ca.1813-14.	Reported Not Confirmed		

1814 Army Bill Issue

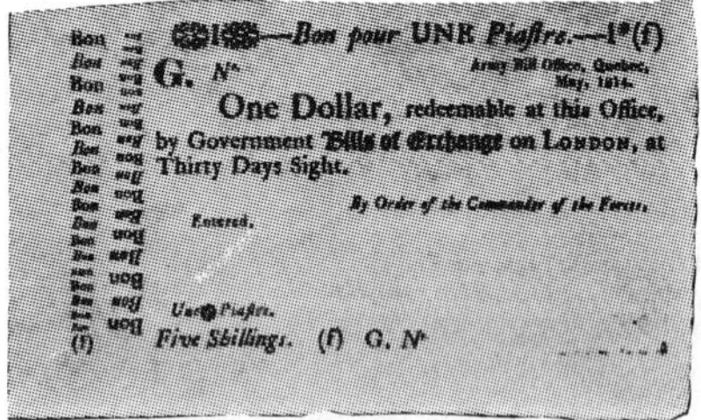

S120A 1 Dollar = 1 Piastre = 5 Shillings March or May 1814.	Good	Fine	XF
a. Issued note.	—	Rare	—
r. Remainder.	—		

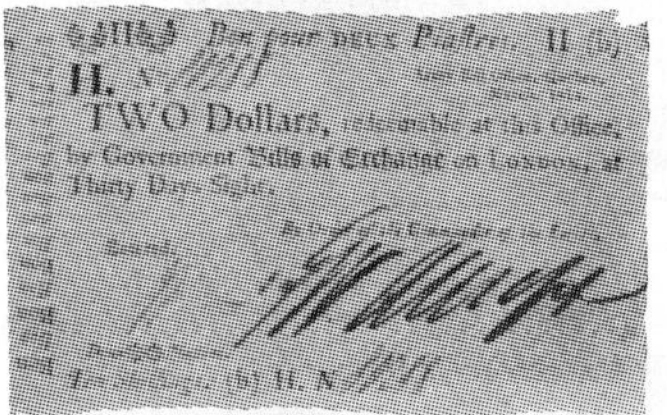

S120B 2 Dollars = 2 Piastres = 10 Shillings March 1814.	Good	Fine	XF
a. Issued note.	—	Rare	—
r. Remainder.	—		

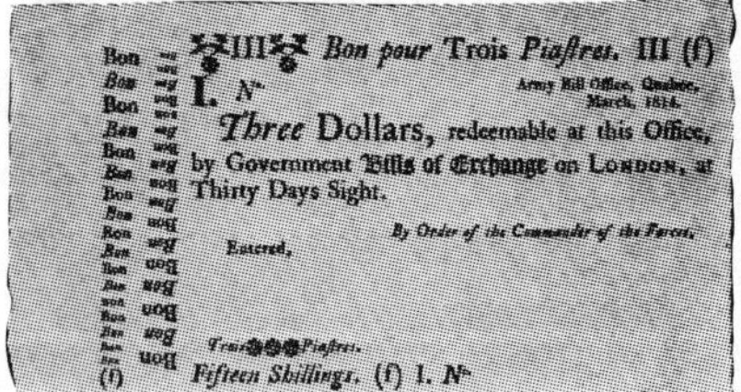

S120C 3 Dollars = 3 Piastres-15 Shillings March 1814.	Good	Fine	XF
a. Issued note.	—	Rare	—
r. Remainder.	—	—	800.00

S120D 5 Dollars = 5 Piastres = 25 Shillings May 1814.	Good	Fine	XF
a. Issued note.	—	Rare	—
r. Remainder.	—	—	800.00

	Good	Fine	XF
S120E 10 Dollars = 10 Piastres = 50 Shillings March or August 1814.	—	Rare	—

1815 Army Bill Issue

	Good	Fine	XF
S120J 10 Dollars January 1815. Cornucopias at upper l.	—	Rare	—

#S120M *Deleted.* See United States - Michigan Territory, #S1346.

Provincial

British Columbia

Treasury

1862 Issue

Pound Sterling System

	Good	Fine	XF
S126 5 Dollars 1862.	Reported Not Confirmed		
S127 10 Dollars 1862.	Reported Not Confirmed		
S128 25 Dollars 1862.	Reported Not Confirmed		

NOTE: Only one of each of #S126-S128 is believed to exist.

Nova Scotia

Treasury

1812 Issue

Issued at Halifax.

Pound Sterling System

	Good	Fine	XF
S132 1 Pound 10.9.1812.	700.00	—	—

#S133 *Deleted.* See #S134C.

A word on date ranges

Often date ranges or specific dates are listed. These have been observed or reported by our contributors. If a note is outside the published range, it only means that it is a newly reported date, and not necessarily worthy of a premium value.

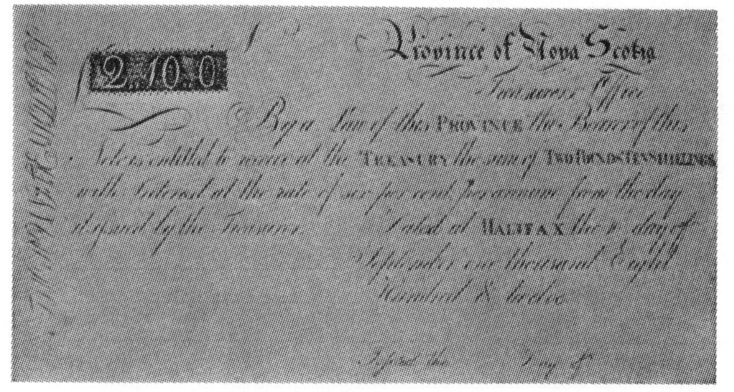

	Good	Fine	XF
S134 2 Pounds-10 Shillings 10.9.1812.	1000.	—	—
S134A 5 Pounds 10.9.1812.	1500.	—	—
S134B 50 Pounds 10.9.1812.	2000.	—	—

1813 Issue

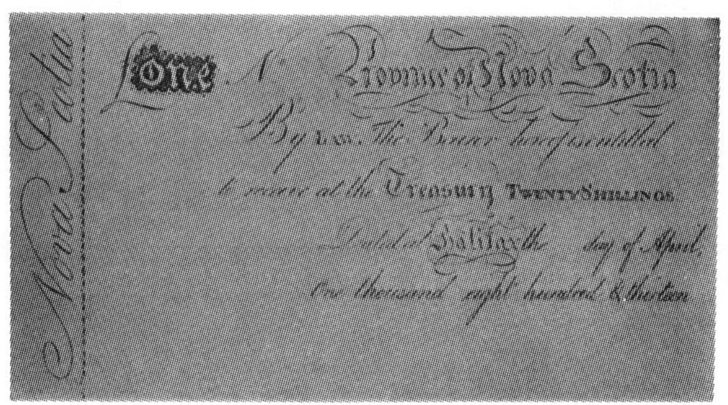

	Good	Fine	XF
S134C 1 Pound 30.4.1813.	700.00	—	—
S134D 2 Pounds 30.4.1813.	1000.	—	—
S134E 5 Pounds 1813-17.	1250.	—	—

1817; 1823 Issue

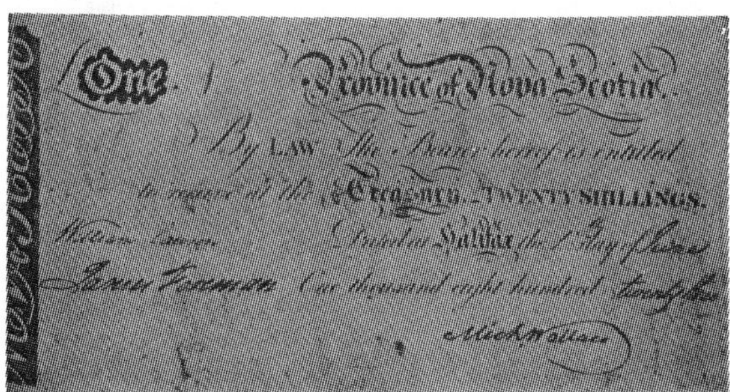

	Good	Fine	XF
S134F 1 Pound 1.6.1823.	600.00	—	—
S134G 2 Pounds 1817-23.	800.00	—	—
S134H 5 Pounds 1817-23.	1000.	—	—

1820 Issue

Dollar System

	Good	Fine	XF
S134I 1 Dollar 5.9.1820.			
a. Issued note.	700.00	—	—
x. Counterfeit.	—	—	—

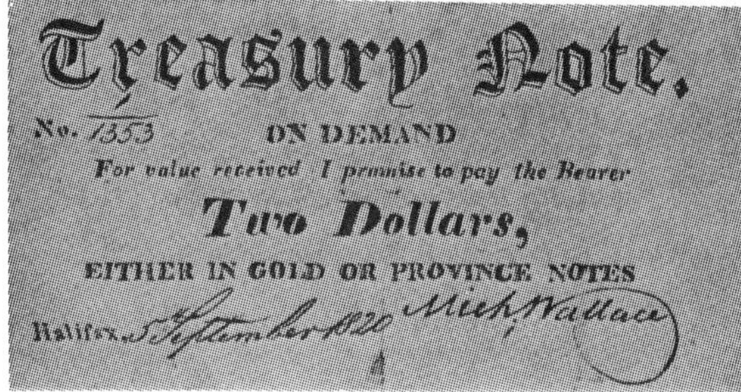

	Good	Fine	XF
S135 2 Dollars 5.9.1820.			
a. Issued note.	—	Rare	—
x. Counterfeit.	—	—	—

1824; 1830 Issue

Dollar/Pound Sterling System

	Good	Fine	XF
S135A 5 Shillings = 1 Dollar 1830.	—	Rare	—

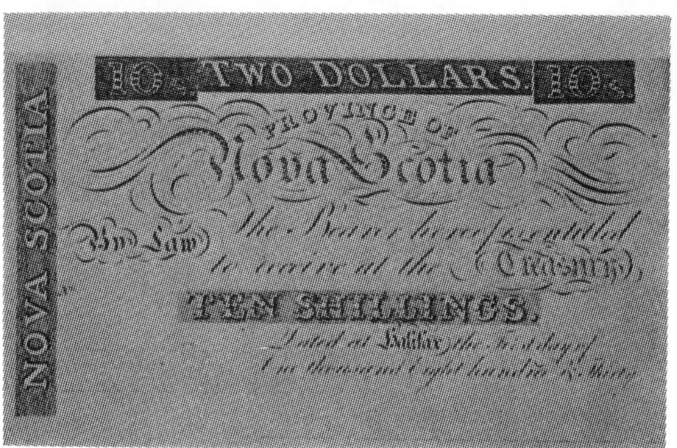

	Good	Fine	XF
S136 10 Shillings = 2 Dollars 1830.	—	Rare	—
S137 1 Pound 1824-.	—	Rare	—
S137A 2 Pounds 1824-.	—	Rare	—
S137B 5 Pounds 1824-.	—	Rare	—

1825; 1828 Issue

Pound Sterling System

#S138 and S138D lithographic issue. Printer: Peter Maverick of New York.

	Good	Fine	XF
S138 1 Pound 1.8.1825.	—	Rare	—

	Good	Fine	XF
S138D 20 Shillings = 1 Pound 1828; 1.6.1829; 1.3.1832.	—	Rare	—

1838 Issue

	Good	Fine	XF
S138E 1 Pound 1838. Printer: RW & H.	—	Rare	—

1848 Issue

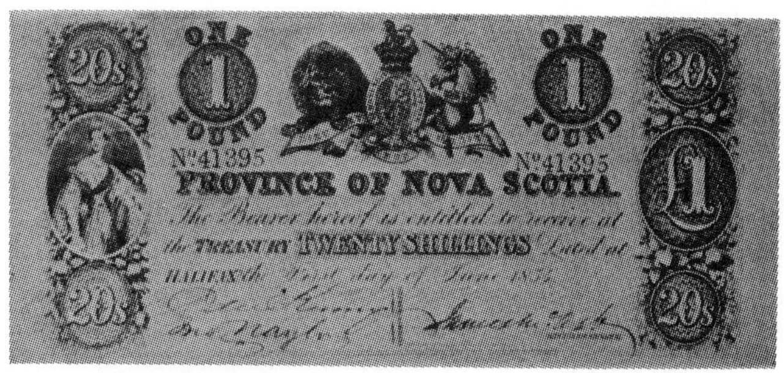

	Good	Fine	XF
S139 1 Pound = 20 Shillings 1.5.1848; 1.6.1853; 1.6.1854. Black. Portr. Qn. Victoria at l., supported royal arms at upper ctr. Handwritten or printed serial #. Printer: P, B&P.	150.00	525.00	1750.

1861 Issue

		Good	Fine	XF
S140	**5 Dollars** 1.6.1861; 1.5.1865; 1.5.1866; 1.8.1866. Black on green unpt. Portr. Qn. Victoria at lower l., kneeling Indian at r. of shield at upper ctr., portr. Prince Albert at lower r. Back orange; St. George slaying dragon at ctr. Printer: ABNC.	175.00	625.00	2250.

Ontario

Provisional Government of Upper Canada

Issued by William Lyon Mackenzie after he fled to New York State following the collapse of the 1837 Rebellion in Upper Canada. Navy Island is located in the Niagara River about 3 miles up river from Niagara Falls.

1837 Issues

#S141-S143A blue tint paper.

		Good	Fine	XF
S141	**1 Dollar** 27.12.1837. Black.	—	Rare	—
S142	**2 Dollars** 27.12.1837. Black.	850.00	—	—
S143	**10 Dollars** 27.12.1837. Black. Lg. letters.	1000.	—	—
S143A	**10 Dollars** 27.12.1837. Black. Sm. letters.	1000.	—	—

Island of Saint John

Treasury

1790 Issue

#S144-S150 black. Uniface.

		Good	Fine	XF
S144	**1 Shilling** 20.11.1790.	300.00	1000.	2500.
S145	**1 Shilling-6 Pence** 20.11.1790.	300.00	1000.	2500.
S146	**2 Shillings-6 Pence** 20.11.1790.	300.00	1000.	2500.
S147	**5 Shillings** 20.11.1790.	300.00	1000.	2500.
S148	**10 Shillings** 20.11.1790.	300.00	1000.	2500.
S149	**20 Shillings** 20.11.1790.	300.00	1000.	2500.
S150	**40 Shillings** 20.11.1790.	300.00	1000.	2500.

Prince Edward Island

Treasury

Issued at Charlotte Town.

1848-58 Issue

Pound Sterling System

#S151-S157 supported royal arms at top ctr. Uniface.

		Good	Fine	XF
S151	**5 Shillings** 1855; 1866. Black. Sailing ship at top ctr., seal on ice at upper r.	240.00	1000.	3000.
S152	**10 Shillings** 1855; 1866. Black. Farmer plowing w/horses at upper ctr., ship building at upper r.	240.00	1000.	3000.

		Good	Fine	XF
S153	**1 Pound** 1848; 9.3.1870. Black. Farmer raking straw at lower l., sheaf of wheat at r.	300.00	1000.	3600.
S154	**2 Pounds** 23.7.1858. Black. Provincial Provincial Legislature bldg. at top ctr.	300.00	1000.	3600.
S155	**5 Pounds** 1858. Black. Provincial Seal at upper ctr.	300.00	1000.	3600.

1872 Issue

Dollar System

#S156 and S157 supported royal arms at ctr. Back green. Printer: BABNC.

		Good	Fine	XF
S156	**10 Dollars** 1872. Black on green unpt. Prince Arthur at lower l., seated Britannia at lower r.	425.00	1250.	4400.
S157	**20 Dollars** 1872. Plow at lower l., sailors w/sailing ship in background at lower r.	425.00	1250.	4400.

NOTE: For other bank issues refer to Canada - "Chartered" or "Spurious & Expired" bank listings.

Province of Canada

Provincial Debentures

185x Issue

#S161-S164 uniface. Printer: RW & H.

		Good	Fine	XF
S161	**1 Dollar = 5 Shillings** 185x. Black w/red *ONE* protector. Seated female w/farm tools at top ctr. Proof.	—	Unc	750.00
S162	**2 Dollars = 10 Shillings** 185x. Black w/red *TWO* protector. 2 seated females at top ctr. Proof.	—	Unc	750.00
S162A	**5 Dollars = 1 Pound-5 Shillings** 185x. Black w/red *FIVE* protector. 3 cherubs and 2 seated allegorical women w/ornate *5* at top ctr.	—	Unc	750.00
S163	**10 Dollars = 2 Pounds-10 Shillings** 185x. Britannia and arms at top ctr. Proof.	—	Unc	750.00
S164	**20 Dollars = 5 Pounds** 185x. Supported royal arms at top ctr. Proof.	—	Unc	750.00

NOTE: Do not confuse the rare Provincial Debentures with the more commonly available County Debentures 1850-54 of similar design issued by the Municipal Council at Brockville.

1849-62 Provisional Issue

#S171-S176 Bank of Montreal notes issued at various offices between 1849-62 w/green or blue ovpt: *PROVINCIAL NOTE/LEGAL TENDER* and vertical ovpt: *PAYABLE IN. . .* Several different issues were ovpt., but only in the listed denominations. All are very rare.

		Good	Fine	XF
S171	**4 Dollars** 1852-59.			
	a. Ovpt: *PAYABLE IN MONTREAL.*	—	Rare	—
	b. Ovpt: *PAYABLE IN TORONTO.*	—	Rare	—
S172	**5 Dollars** 1844-59.			
	a. Ovpt: *PAYABLE IN MONTREAL.*	—	Rare	—
	b. Ovpt: *PAYABLE IN TORONTO.*	—	Rare	—
S173	**10 Dollars** 1842-59.			
	a. Ovpt: *PAYABLE IN MONTREAL.*	—	Rare	—
	b. Ovpt: *PAYABLE IN TORONTO.*	—	Rare	—
S174	**20 Dollars** 18xx.			
	a. Ovpt: *PAYABLE IN MONTREAL.*	—	Rare	—
	b. Ovpt: *PAYABLE IN TORONTO.*	—	Rare	—
S175	**50 Dollars** 18xx.			
	a. Ovpt: *PAYABLE IN MONTREAL.*	—	Rare	—
	b. Ovpt: *PAYABLE IN TORONTO.*	—	Rare	—
S176	**100 Dollars** 1861.			
	a. Ovpt: *PAYABLE IN MONTREAL.*	—	Rare	—
	b. Ovpt: *PAYABLE IN TORONTO.*	—	Rare	—

NOTE: For Province of Canada regular issue see Vol. 2, #A26-A33.

Private and Chartered Banks

Bank of British Columbia 1862-94

Operated from 1862-94.

1862-63 Issue

#S201-S204 Coin portr. Qn. Victoria at upper l., standing Britannia w/seated woman at upper ctr. Black on blue unpt. Printer: Rixon & Arnold.

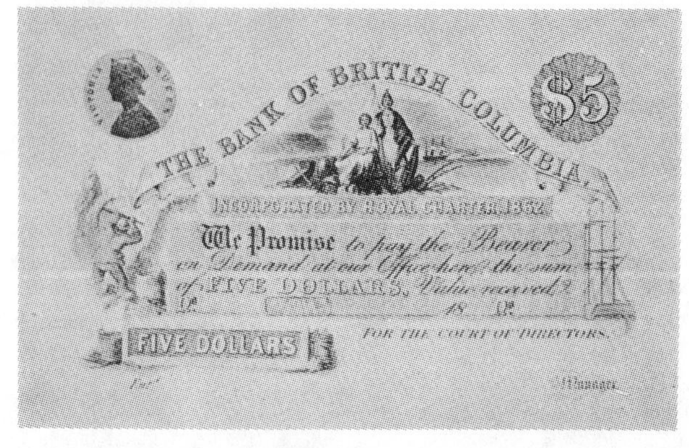

		VG	VF	UNC
S201	**5 DOLLARS** 28.11.1862-6.1.1863. Miner w/pickaxe at l.			
	a. W/*VICTORIA* after l.h. serial #.	—	3650.	—
	b. W/o *VICTORIA* after l.h. serial #.	—	3650.	—
S202	**20 DOLLARS** 28.11.1862. Miner pouring ore at l.	—	3650.	—

		VG	VF	UNC
S203	**50 DOLLARS** 28.11.1862. Miner at crank at l.	—	3650.	—
		GOOD	FINE	XF
S204	**100 DOLLARS** 6.1.1863. Miner w/sledge hammer at l.	—	—	—

NOTE: All issued notes of #S204 were redeemed.

1863-75 ISSUE

#S206-S210 black on blue unpt. Various portr. frame w/Qn. Victoria at upper l., standing Britannia w/seated woman at upper ctr. Printer: Wm. Brown & Co.

		VG	VF	UNC
S206	**1 DOLLAR** 24.6.1863; 30.6.1863.	2800.	4200.	—

		VG	VF	UNC
S207	**5 DOLLARS** 31.3.1864.	—	—	—
S208	**10 DOLLARS** 15.5.1873.	—	—	—
S209	**20 DOLLARS** 23.5.1875.	—	—	—
S210	**50 DOLLARS** 23.5.1875.	—	—	—

1879 ISSUE

#S211-S215 Black. Sailing ship at lower l., coin portr. Qn. Victoria at upper ctr., mine head at lower r. Back green. Printer: Wm. Brown & Co.

		VG	VF	UNC
S211	**5 DOLLARS** 1.6.1879.	—	Rare	—

		VG	VF	UNC
S212	**10 DOLLARS** 1.6.1879.	—	Rare	—
S213	**20 DOLLARS** 1.6.1879.	—	Rare	—
S214	**50 DOLLARS** 1.6.1879.	—	Rare	—
S215	**100 DOLLARS** 1.6.1879.	—	Rare	—

1894 ISSUE

#S216-S219 serial # printed on back in very lg. red numerals. Printer: ABNC.

		VG	VF	UNC
S216	**5 DOLLARS** 1.1.1894. Black on yellow and green unpt. Standing Britannia w/seated woman at upper ctr. Back green.			
	a. Issued note.	—	Rare	—
	p. Face and back proofs.	—	—	1250.
	s. Specimen.	—	—	1500.

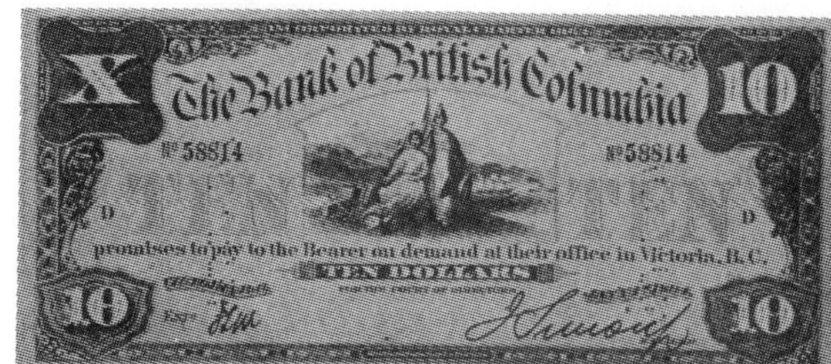

		VG	VF	UNC
S217	**10 DOLLARS** 1.1.1894. Black on yellow and blue unpt. Similar to #S216. Back blue.			
	a. Issued note.	—	Rare	—
	p. Face and back proofs.	—	—	1250.
	s. Specimen.	—	—	1500.

		VG	VF	UNC
S218	**20 DOLLARS** 1.1.1894. Black on yellow and brown unpt. Miners at upper ctr. Back dk. brown.			
	a. Issued note.	—	Rare	—
	p. Face and back proofs.	—	—	1250.
	s. Specimen.	—	—	1500.

		VG	VF	UNC
S219	**50 DOLLARS** 1.1.1894. Black on yellow and deep red unpt. Supported royal arms at top ctr. Back brownish red.			
	a. Issued note.	—	Rare	—
	p. Face and back proofs.	—	—	1250.
	s. Specimen.	—	—	1500.

BANK OF BRITISH NORTH AMERICA

BRANTFORD

1852-53 ISSUE

#S221 and S222 black. Uniface. Printer: PB&P.

		VG	VF	UNC
S221	**4 DOLLARS = 1 POUND** 1.7.1853. Standing Britannia w/shield at l., reclining allegory at upper ctr., seated allegory Commerce at r. Proof.	—	Unc	300.00

		GOOD	FINE	XF
S222	**5 DOLLARS = 1 POUND-5 SHILLINGS** 5.7.1852. Green unpt. Sheep and plough at l.	150.00	550.00	—

1871 ISSUE

#S226-S228 black, supported royal arms at ctr. Uniface. Printer: PBC.

		VG	VF	UNC
S226	**5 DOLLARS** 29.11.1871. Britannia at lower l. Qn. Victoria at lower r.	315.00	525.00	—
S227	**10 DOLLARS** 31.1.1871. Proof.	—	—	245.00
S228	**20 DOLLARS** 31.1.1871. Proof.	—	—	350.00

CANADA - EAST

1852 ISSUE

#S231 and S232 black w/red numeral protector on face. Uniface. Printer: PBC.

		VG	VF	UNC
S231	**1 DOLLAR = 5 SHILLINGS** 1.12.1852.			
	a. Montreal.	425.00	850.00	—
	b. Quebec.	Reported Not Confirmed		
S232	**2 DOLLARS = 10 SHILLINGS** 1.12.1852.			
	a. Montreal. Black ovpt: *BYTOWN* at ctr.	425.00	850.00	—
	b. Quebec.	425.00	850.00	—

1856 ISSUE

#S236 and S237 black w/blue word protector on coins at face. Uniface. Printer: PBC.

		VG	VF	UNC
S236	**1 DOLLAR = 5 SHILLINGS** 1.1.1856.			
	a. Montreal. Blue ovpt: *OTTAWA* at ctr. and ends.	425.00	850.00	—
	b. Quebec. Red ovpt: *PAYABLE IN OTTAWA.*	425.00	850.00	—
S237	**2 DOLLARS = 10 SHILLINGS** 1.1.1856.			
	a. Montreal. Blue ovpt: *OTTAWA* at ctr. and ends.	425.00	850.00	—
	b. Quebec.	425.00	850.00	—

CANADA - WEST

1852 ISSUE

#S241 black. Uniface. Printer: PBC.

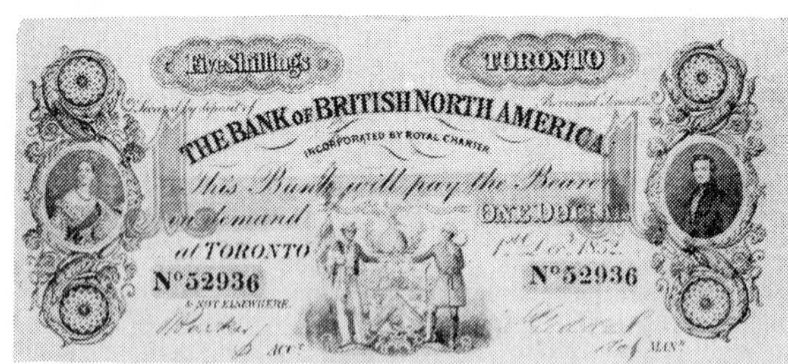

		GOOD	FINE	XF
S241	**1 DOLLAR = 5 SHILLINGS** 1.12.1852.			
	a. Brantford.	275.00	850.00	—
	b. Hamilton. Blue numeral on face.	185.00	550.00	—
	c. Blue word on face.	185.00	550.00	—
	d. Toronto. Red numeral on face.	275.00	850.00	—

1856 ISSUE

#S246 and S247 black w/blue word protector on face. Uniface. Printer: PBC.

		GOOD	FINE	XF
S246	**1 DOLLAR = 5 SHILLINGS** 1.1.1856.			
	a. Brantford.	275.00	850.00	—
	b. Hamilton.	185.00	550.00	—
	c. Kingston.	185.00	550.00	—
	d. London.	185.00	550.00	—
	e. Toronto.	185.00	550.00	—
S247	**2 DOLLARS = 10 SHILLINGS** 1.1.1856. *2* at upper l. and r.			
	a. Brantford.	275.00	850.00	—
	b. Hamilton.	185.00	550.00	—
	c. Kingston.	185.00	550.00	—
	d. Toronto.	185.00	550.00	—

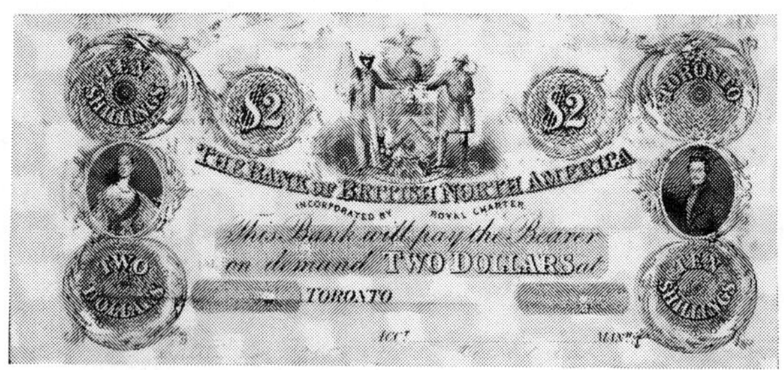

		GOOD	FINE	XF
S248	**2 DOLLARS = 10 SHILLINGS** ND. Text: *TEN SHILLINGS* at upper l.			
	a. Kingston. Proof.	—	Unc	350.00
	b. Toronto. Proof.	—	Unc	350.00

FREDERICTON

1847 ISSUE

		GOOD	FINE	XF
S251	**4 DOLLARS = 1 POUND** 1.9.1847. Black. Britannia at l., beehive at upper ctr., reclining allegory Commerce at r., supported royal arms at bottom ctr. Uniface. Printer: PB&P. Proof.	—	Unc	2000.

HALIFAX

1838 ISSUE

#S256 and S257 black. Bank crest at upper ctr. Uniface. Printer: PB&P.

		GOOD	FINE	XF
S256	**5 POUNDS** ND (1838). Proof.	—	Unc	500.00
S257	**7 POUNDS-10 SHILLINGS** ND (1838). Proof.	—	Unc	500.00

1841-72 ISSUE

		GOOD	FINE	XF
S259	**5 POUNDS** 18xx. Black. Printer: PBC. Proof.	—	Unc	800.00

1865-74 ISSUE

#S261-S264 black w/green word protector on face. Uniface. Printer: PBC.

		GOOD	FINE	XF
S261	**4 DOLLARS** 1872; 1.12.1874. Proof.	—	Unc	350.00

		VG	VF	UNC
S262	**5 DOLLARS** 1870-74.			
	a. Red ovpt: *HALIFAX* at l. and r. and text ovpt: *PAYABLE IN DOMINION CURRENCY* across top. 1.7.1871.	550.00	1050.	—
	p. Proof. 1.7.1870; 2.1.1871; 1.11.1871; 1.12.1874.	—	—	350.00
S263	**10 DOLLARS** 1.7.1870; 1.7.1871; 1.12.1874. Proof.	—	—	350.00

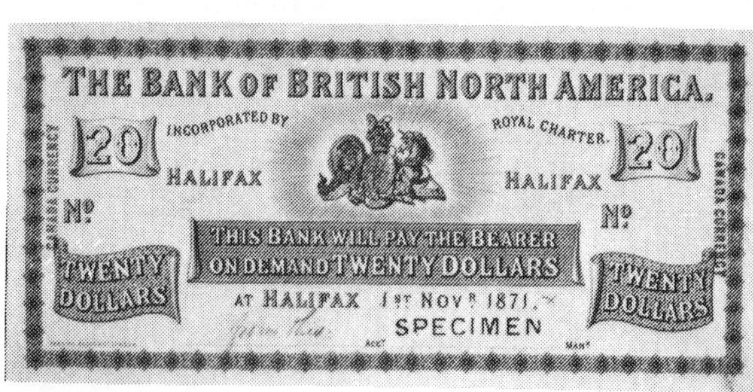

		VG	VF	UNC
S264	**20 DOLLARS** 24.5.1865; 1.11.1871. Supported royal arms at upper ctr. Proof.	—	—	350.00

#S266-S267 *Deleted*. See #S283-S284.

HAMILTON

1845-56 ISSUE

#S271-S274 black. Uniface. Printer: PBC.

		GOOD	FINE	XF
S271	**4 DOLLARS = 1 POUND** 1845-55.			
	a. 1.11.1845.	200.00	600.00	—
	b. Green word on face and back. 1.11.1852.	200.00	600.00	—
	c. Blue word on face w/blue ovpt: *PARIS.* 1.5.1855.	200.00	600.00	—
S272	**5 DOLLARS = 1 POUND-5 SHILLINGS** 1.11.1845; 1.5.1855. Blue word on face.	200.00	600.00	—
S273	**10 DOLLARS = 2 POUNDS-10 SHILLINGS** 1.5.1853. Blue word on face.	225.00	650.00	—
S274	**50 DOLLARS = 12 POUNDS-10 SHILLINGS** 1.3.1856. Blue word on face. Proof.	—	Unc	350.00

1874-75 ISSUE

#S275 and S275A. Black. Supported royal arms. Uniface. Printer: PBC.

		GOOD	FINE	XF
S275	**5 DOLLARS** 1.6.1874; 1.5.1875. Proof.	—	Unc	210.00

		VG	VF	UNC
S275A	**10 DOLLARS** 1.6.1874. Proof.	425.00	850.00	—

HAMILTON/BRANTFORD AGENCY

1852 ISSUE

		GOOD	FINE	XF
S276	**5 DOLLARS = 25 SHILLINGS** 1.3.1852. Black. Bank crest at l., beehive at upper ctr., sheep and plow at r., small supported royal arms at bottom ctr. Uniface. Printer: PBC.	200.00	600.00	—

HAMILTON/DUNDAS AGENCY

1852-53 ISSUE

#S280-S282 black. Small supported royal arms at bottom ctr. Uniface. Printer: PBC.

		VG	VF	UNC
S280	**4 DOLLARS = 1 POUND** 18xx. Proof.	—	—	400.00
S281	**5 DOLLARS = 1 POUND-5 SHILLINGS** 1.3.1852; 1.3.1856. Britannia at l., allegory Commerce in crowned ornate frame at r. Proof.	—	—	350.00
S282	**10 DOLLARS = 2 POUNDS-10 SHILLINGS** 2.2.1853. Sheep and plow at l., cherubs at upper ctr., Indian camp at r. Proof.	—	—	400.00

HAMILTON/SIMCOE AGENCY

1845 ISSUE

#S283 and S284 black. Small supported royal arms at bottom ctr. Uniface. Printer: PBC.

		GOOD	FINE	XF
S283	**4 DOLLARS = 1 POUND** 1845-48. Seated allegory Agriculture at l., reclining allegorical woman at upper ctr., seated allegorical woman at r.			
	a. 1.1.1845.	200.00	600.00	—
	p. 1.1.1848. Proof.	—	Unc	300.00
S284	**5 DOLLARS = 1 POUND-5 SHILLINGS** 1.1.1848. Proof.	—	Unc	300.00

#S286 and S287 *Deleted*. See #S275-S275A.

KINGSTON

1840S-1853 ISSUE

#S291-S295 black. Uniface. Printer: PBC.

		GOOD	FINE	XF
S291	**4 DOLLARS** 184x-1853. Seated Indian at Commerce at upper ctr., seated woman at r.			
	a. 1.2.1852.	200.00	650.00	—
	c. Green unpt. 1.7.1853.	200.00	650.00	—
	p. Proof. 184x.	—	Unc	300.00
	r. Remainder. 1.7.1853.	—	Unc	300.00
S292	**5 DOLLARS** 184x-1852. Qn. Victoria, allegorical women, Indian.			
	a. 4.8.1852.	200.00	650.00	—
	p. Proof. 184x.	—	Unc	300.00
S293	**10 DOLLARS** 184x. Harbor scene, allegorical women, bank crest. Proof.	—	Unc	325.00

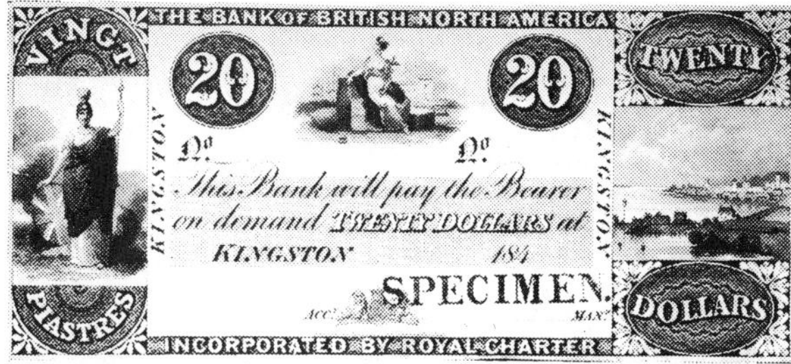

		GOOD	FINE	XF
S294	**20 DOLLARS** 184x. Britannia at l., Commerce seated at upper ctr., harbor scene at r. Proof.	—	Unc	400.00
S295	**50 DOLLARS** 184x. Commerce, Britannia, Agriculture. Proof.	—	Unc	475.00

1872; 1875 ISSUE

#S296-S298 black. Uniface. Printer: PBC.

		VG	VF	UNC
S296	**4 DOLLARS** 4.5.1872. Justice at l., supported royal arms at ctr., woman w/sheaf and sickle at r.	425.00	850.00	—

		VG	VF	UNC
S297	**5 DOLLARS** 1.5.1875. Britannia seated at l., supported royal arms at upper ctr., Victoria seated at r.			
	p. Proof.	—	—	210.00
	x. Counterfeit w/engraved sign.	—	—	—
S298	**10 DOLLARS** 6.5.1872. Supported royal arms at upper ctr. Proof.	—	—	245.00

LONDON

1854-56 ISSUE

#S301-S303 black w/blue word protector. Supported royal arms at bottom ctr. Uniface. Printer: PBC.

		GOOD	FINE	XF
S301	**4 DOLLARS = 1 POUND** 1854-56. Seated Britannia w/lion at l., bank crest at ctr., seated allegory Justice at r.			
	a. Red ovpt: *NAPANEE*. 1.1.1856.	200.00	650.00	—
	p. Proof. 1.3.1854.	—	Unc	150.00
S302	**5 DOLLARS = 25 SHILLINGS** 1.3.1854. Sheep and plow at l., 3 seated allegories at upper ctr., seated Britannia at r.	200.00	650.00	—
S303	**10 DOLLARS = 50 SHILLINGS** 1.3.1854. Agriculture, seated Agriculture, seated woman w/harp. Proof.	—	Unc	175.00

1866-75 ISSUE

#S305-S308 black. Uniface. Printer: PBC.

		VG	VF	UNC
S305	**4 DOLLARS** 3.8.1875. Like #S296. Proof.	—	—	275.00

		VG	VF	UNC
S306	**5 DOLLARS** 1866-75. Like #S297.			
	a. 3.8.1875.	350.00	625.00	—
	p1. Proof. 23.4.1866.	—	—	210.00
	p2. Proof. 1.8.1872.	—	—	210.00

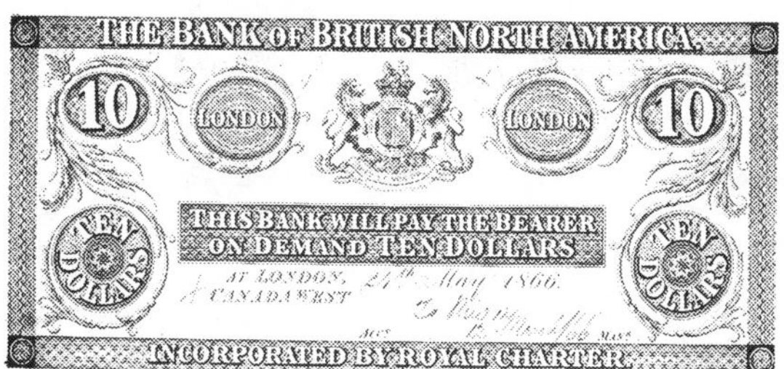

		VG	VF	UNC
S307	**10 DOLLARS** 24.5.1866. Like #S298. Proof.	—	—	245.00
S308	**20 DOLLARS** 3.8.1875. Supported royal arms at upper ctr. Proof.	—	—	315.00

MONTREAL

Issued for general circulation, redeemable at any branch office.

1838 ISSUE

#S311-S313 black. Bank crest at ctr. Uniface. Printer: PBC.

		GOOD	FINE	XF
S311	**1 DOLLAR** 1.9.1838.	125.00	400.00	1100.
S312	**10 DOLLARS** 18xx. Proof.	—	Unc	400.00
S313	**50 DOLLARS** ND (1838). Proof.	—	Unc	400.00

1841-54 ISSUE

#S316-S320 black. Small supported royal arms at bottom ctr. Uniface. Printer: PBC.

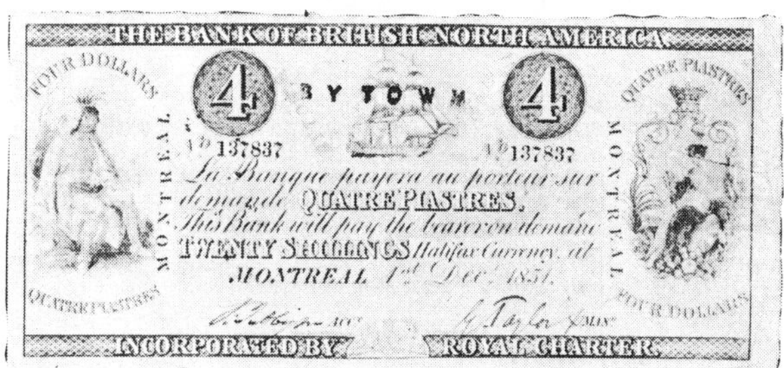

		GOOD	FINE	XF
S316	**4 DOLLARS = 20 SHILLINGS** 1841-52. Seated Indian at l., sailing ship at upper ctr., seated allegory Commerce in crowned ornate frame at r.			
	a. Black and red ovpt: *BYTOWN* and *PARIS*. 1.1.1841-1.1.1847.	200.00	650.00	—
	b. Black and red ovpt: *BYTOWN* and *PARIS*. 1.12.1851.	200.00	650.00	—
	c. Green word on face and black. Black and red ovpt: *BYTOWN* and *PARIS*. 1.12.1852.	200.00		650.00

		Good	Fine	XF
S317	**5 Dollars = 1 Pound-5 Shillings** 1841-54. Brock's monument at l., sailing ship upper ctr., seated Qn. Victoria at r.			
	a. 1.1.1841.	200.00	650.00	—
	b. Green word on face and back. 21.1.1854.	200.00	650.00	—
S318	**10 Dollars = 2 Pounds-10 Shillings** 184x. Indian camp at l., allegory Commerce at upper ctr., harbor scene at r.	—	Unc	235.00
S319	**20 Dollars = 5 Pounds** 184x. View of Montreal at l., 3 allegorical women at upper ctr., monument and houses at r. Proof.	—	Unc	275.00
S320	**50 Dollars = 12 Pounds-10 Shillings** 184x. Bank crest at l., steamship at upper ctr., monument and houses in Montreal at r. Proof.	—	Unc	300.00

1865-73 Issue

#S321-S325 black. Uniface. Printer: PBC.

		VG	VF	Unc
S321	**4 Dollars** 1.12.1873.	425.00	850.00	—
S322	**5 Dollars** 1.8.1870; 8.4.1872. Seated Britannia at lower l., supported royal arms at upper ctr., Queen Victoria on throne at lower r. Proof.	—	—	200.00
S323	**10 Dollars** 1865-70. Supported royal arms at upper ctr.			
	a. 1.8.1870.	425.00	850.00	—
	p. Proof. 30.11.1865.	—	—	245.00
S324	**20 Dollars** 1.12.1865. Sheep, beehive and tools at upper ctr. Proof.	—	—	300.00
S325	**50 Dollars** 1.1.1866. Standing woman w/lute at l., supported royal arms at upper ctr., seated allegorical woman at r. Proof.	—	—	315.00

Ottawa

1863-73 Issue

#S326-S329 black. Uniface. Printer: PBC.

		VG	VF	Unc
S326	**4 Dollars** 1871-73. Portr. seated Justice at lower l., supported arms at upper ctr., portr. woman lower r.			
	a. Blue ovpt: *ARNPRIOR* at l. and r. 1.12.1873.	425.00	850.00	—
	p. Proof. 1.12.1871.	—	—	275.00
S327	**5 Dollars** 10.8.1865; 31.1.1871; 1.5.1872. Proof.	—	—	210.00
S328	**10 Dollars** 1.9.1865; 31.1.1871. Proof.	—	—	245.00
S329	**20 Dollars** 31.1.1871. Supported royal arms. Proof.	—	—	315.00

Quebec

1838 Issue

#S331 and S332 black. Bank crest at upper ctr. Uniface. Printer: PB&P.

		Good	Fine	XF
S331	**1 Dollar** 1.9.1838.	125.00	450.00	750.00
S332	**10 Dollars** 18xx. Proof.	—	Unc	600.00

1841-53 Issue

#S336-S338 black. Small supported royal arms at bottom ctr. Uniface. Printer: PB&P.

		Good	Fine	XF
S336	**4 Dollars = 20 Shillings** 1.1.1853. Seated allegory Commerce in crowned ornate frame at l., seated Indian at r.			
	a. Issued note.	200.00	600.00	—
	p. Proof. 18xx.	—	Unc	150.00
S337	**5 Dollars = 1 Pound-5 Shillings** 1.1.1841. Seated Qn. Victoria at l., seated allegorical woman w/sickle at r.	200.00	600.00	—
S338	**10 Dollars = 2 Pounds-10 Shillings** 1.1.1841. Sheep and plow at l., sailing ship at r.	200.00	600.00	—

1871 Issue

		Good	Fine	XF
S341	**4 Dollars** 22.11.1871. Black. Small supported royal arms at bottom ctr. Uniface. Printer: PBC.	200.00	550.00	—

St. John, New Brunswick

1837 Issue

#S346 and S347 black. Bank crest at upper ctr. Uniface. Printer: PB&P.

		Good	Fine	XF
S346	**1 Dollar = 5 Shillings** 1.7.1837.	200.00	650.00	—
S347	**2 Dollars = 10 Shillings** ND (1837). Proof.	—	Unc	350.00

1853-71 Issue

#S351-S356 black w/green word protector on face. Small supported royal arms at bottom ctr. Uniface. Printer: PBC.

		VG	VF	Unc
S351	**1 Dollar = 5 Shillings** 1854-62. Seated Justice at l., bank crest at upper ctr., seated Commerce w/lute at r.			
	a. Issued note. 1.12.1859; 1.12.1862.	425.00	900.00	—
	p. Proof. 2.1.1854.	—	—	350.00

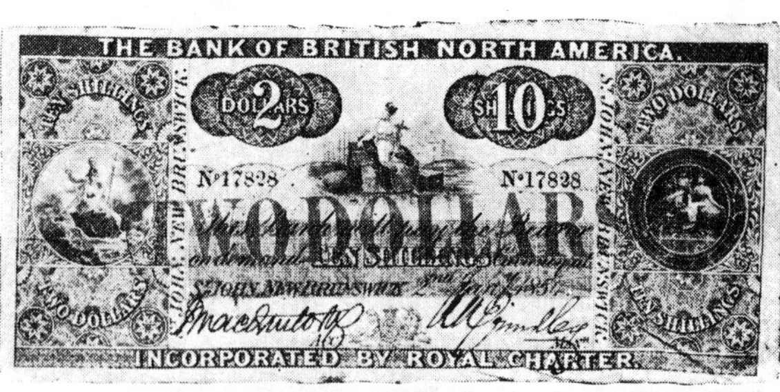

		VG	VF	Unc
S352	**2 Dollars = 10 Shillings** 1.2.1854. Seated Britannia at l., small seated allegory Commerce at upper ctr., Commerce, Britannia and Agriculture in circles at r.	425.00	900.00	—
S353	**4 Dollars = 1 Pound** 1.1.1853; 1.2.1871. Bank crest at l., sailing ship at upper ctr., standing allegorical woman w/anchor by beehive at r. Proof.	—	—	350.00

NOTE: Counterfeit dated 1846 exists.

		VG	VF	Unc
S354	**5 Dollars = 1 Pound-5 Shillings** 1862; 1869. Similar to #S353. Red ovpt: *V V.*			
	a. Issued note. 1.12.1862.	425.00	900.00	—
	p. Proof. 1.9.1869.	—	—	350.00
S355	**20 Dollars = 5 Pounds** 18xx. Portr. Qn. Victoria at l., 2 allegorical women at upper ctr., reclining allegorical woman w/sailing ship in background at r. Proof.	—	—	350.00
S356	**40 Dollars = 10 Pounds** 18xx. Portr. Qn. Victoria at l., bank crest at upper ctr. Proof.	—	—	350.00

1866; 1868 Issue

#S361 and S362 black w/green word protector on face and back. W/o frame. Red ovpt: *S.* Printer: PBC.

		VG	VF	Unc
S361	**1 Dollar** 31.8.1866; 1.12.1868.	500.00	1000.	—
S362	**2 Dollars** 1.12.1868.	500.00	1000.	—

1866-72 Issue

#S366-S370 black. Uniface. Printer: PBC.

		VG	VF	Unc
S366	**4 Dollars** 1871-72.			
	a. Blue ovpt: *FREDERICTON* at l. and r. and blue ovpt: *MONCTON* across ctr. 31.5.1872.	600.00	1400.	—
	p. Proof. 31.5.1871.	—	—	350.00
S367	**5 Dollars** 1.5.1871; 1.5.1872. Proof.	—	—	265.00
S368	**10 Dollars** 1.1.1870; 18.6.1872. Proof.	—	—	300.00
S369	**20 Dollars** 29.4.1871; 29.4.1872. Supported royal arms. Proof.	—	—	315.00
S370	**50 Dollars** 1.9.1866; 1.1.1870. Proof.	—	—	350.00

St. John, Newfoundland

1837-47 Issue

#S371 and S372 black. Bank crest at upper ctr. Uniface. Printer: PB&P.

		Good	Fine	XF
S371	**1 Pound** 20.3.1837.	450.00	1400.	—
S372	**5 Pounds** 1.7.1847. Proof.	—	Unc	425.00

St. Stephen

1872 Issue

		Good	Fine	XF
S376	**4 Dollars = 1 Pound** 12.8.1872. Black. Bank crest at l., sailing ship at upper ctr., standing allegorical woman w/anchor by beehive at r., small supported royal arms at bottom ctr. Uniface. Printer: PBC. Proof.	—	Unc	350.00

Toronto

1840s Dollar Issue

#S381-S385 black. Uniface. Printer: PBC.

		Good	Fine	XF
S381	**4 Dollars** 184x. Proof.	—	Unc	275.00
S382	**5 Dollars** 184x. Proof.	—	Unc	275.00
S383	**10 Dollars** 184x. Proof.	—	Unc	275.00
S384	**20 Dollars** 184x. Proof.	—	Unc	275.00
S385	**50 Dollars** 184x. Proof.	—	Unc	275.00

1846-65 DOLLAR/POUND ISSUE

#S386-S388 printer: PBC.

		VG	VF	UNC
S386	**4 DOLLARS = 1 POUND** 1846-52. Seated Commerce at l., bank crest at r.			
	a. 1.11.1852.	425.00	850.00	—
	p. Proof. 1.1.1846.	—	—	250.00

		VG	VF	UNC
S387	**5 DOLLARS = 1 POUND-5 SHILLINGS = 25 SHILLINGS** 1.1.1846. Mountains, village at l., seated Commerce in crowned ornate frame at r.	—	—	250.00
S387A	**5 DOLLARS = 25 SHILLINGS** 4.1.1865. Like #S387. Proof.	—	—	280.00
S388	**10 DOLLARS = 50 SHILLINGS** 1864.	425.00	850.00	—

1864-71 ISSUE

#S390-S393 black. Uniface. Printer: PBC.

		VG	VF	UNC
S390	**3 DOLLARS** 8.12.1871. Seated Justice at lower l., supported royal arms at upper ctr., allegorical woman w/sheaf and sickle at lower r.			
	a. Issued note.	—	—	—
	p. Proof.	—	—	275.00
S391	**5 DOLLARS** 1865-71. Seated Britannia w/lion at lower l., supported royal arms at upper ctr., seated Qn. Victoria at lower r.			
	a. Blue vertical ovpt: *DUNNVILLE* at l. and r. 4.1.1865.	315.00	700.00	—
	p. Proof. 31.1.1871.	—	—	210.00
S392	**10 DOLLARS** 1864-71. Supported royal arms at upper ctr.			
	a. 23.4.1864.	425.00	850.00	—
	p. Proof. 1.1.1871.	—	—	245.00
S393	**20 DOLLARS** 31.1.1871. Supported royal arms at upper ctr. Proof.	—	—	250.00

VICTORIA

1859-67 ISSUE

#S396 and S397 black w/green word protector on face and back. W/o frame. Uniface. Printer: PBC.

		GOOD	FINE	XF
S396	**1 DOLLAR** 1859-67. Portr. Qn. Victoria at lower l., seated Britannia at upper ctr.			
	a. 1.12.1859.	100.00	250.00	—
	p1. Proof. 18xx.	—	Unc	350.00
	p2. Proof. 2.12.1867.	—	Unc	350.00
	s. Specimen. 1.12.1859.	—	Unc	200.00
S397	**2 DOLLARS** 2.1.1860. Seated Indian at l., seated Commerce at upper ctr., standing Britannia w/shield at r. Proof.			
	a. Issued note.	—	—	2450.
	p. Proof.	—	Unc	200.00

1859-68 ISSUE

#S401-S404 black. Uniface. Printer: PBC.

		GOOD	FINE	XF
S401	**5 DOLLARS** 1859-67. Seated Britannia w/lion at lower l., supported royal arms at upper ctr., seated Qn. Victoria at lower r.			
	a. Issued note. 1859.	—	—	2450.
	p. Proof. 23.4.1867.	—	Unc	250.00
	s. Specimen. 27.9.1859.	—	Unc	650.00
S402	**10 DOLLARS** 1860-67. Supported royal arms at upper ctr.			
	a. Issued note. 3.2.1860.	—	—	2450.
	p. Proof. 23.4.1867; 16.10.1873.	—	Unc	250.00
	s. Specimen. 3.2.1860.	—	Unc	250.00
S403	**20 DOLLARS** 5.3.1860. Sheep, beehive and tools at upper ctr. Specimen.			
	a. Issued note. 5.3.1860.	—	—	2450.
	s. Specimen. 1.1.1868.	—	Unc	650.00
S404	**20 DOLLARS** 1.1.1868. Supported royal at upper ctr. Proof.	—	Unc	250.00

1861-72 ISSUE

#S406-S408 black. Branch name to be filled in. Uniface. Printer: PBC.

		GOOD	FINE	XF
S406	**100 DOLLARS** 1861-72. Cherubs at lower l. and lower r., supported royal arms at ctr.			
	a. 1.8.1861; 15.8.1865.	—	Unc	475.00
	b. 5.9.1861; 22.1.1871.	—	Unc	475.00
	p1. Proof. 22.11.1866.	—	Unc	275.00
	p2. Proof. 15.4.1872.	—	Unc	275.00
	s. Specimen. 15.8.1861.	—	Unc	475.00
S407	**500 DOLLARS** 1.8.1861; 15.8.1861; 5.9.1961. Seated allegory w/caduceus at l. and r., supported royal arms at ctr. Proof.	—	Unc	850.00

		GOOD	FINE	XF
S408	**1000 DOLLARS** 1.8.1861; 15.8.1861; 5.9.1861. Seated and kneeling allegorical woman at l. and r., supported royal arms at upper ctr. Proof.	—	Unc	1050.

MONTREAL

Issued for general circulation, redeemable at any branch office.

1876-77 ISSUE

#S411-S416 except #S413b black on green unpt. Seated Britannia w/lion at lower l., supported royal arms at ctr., seated Qn. Victoria at lower r. Back green. Sign. varieties. Printer: BABNC.

		VG	VF	UNC
S411	**4 DOLLARS** 3.7.1877.	700.00	1550.	—
S412	**5 DOLLARS** 3.7.1877.	350.00	675.00	—

NOTE: Counterfeits abundant.

		VG	VF	UNC
S413	**10 DOLLARS** 1876-77.			
	a. Black on green unpt. 3.7.1877.	500.00	975.00	—
	b. Blue on reddish brown unpt. 3.7.1877.	550.00	1200.	—
	p. Proof. 1.7.1876.	—	—	350.00
S414	**20 DOLLARS** 3.7.1877.	500.00	975.00	—
S415	**50 DOLLARS** 3.7.1877.	1050.	2100.	—
S416	**100 DOLLARS** 3.7.1877.	1050.	2100.	—

1884 ISSUE

		VG	VF	UNC
S421	**5 DOLLARS** 1.5.1884. Blue on orange unpt. Portr. elderly Qn. Victoria at ctr. Back black. Printer: PBC.	1050.	2100.	—

1886; 1889 ISSUE

#S426 and S427 black on green unpt. Back green; bank crest at ctr. Sign. varieties. Printer: BABNC.

		GOOD	FINE	XF
S426	**5 DOLLARS** 28.5.1886. Portr. Prince of Wales at lower l., bank crest at ctr., portr. elderly Qn. Victoria at lower r.			
	a. Handsigned at r.	25.00	100.00	250.00
	b. Printed sign. at r.	25.00	100.00	250.00

		GOOD	FINE	XF
S427	**10 DOLLARS** 3.7.1889. Portr. elderly Qn. Victoria at ctr.			
	a. Handsigned at r.	35.00	150.00	300.00
	b. Printed sign. at r.	35.00	150.00	300.00

1911 ISSUE

#S431-S435 lg. bank arms at ctr. on back. Sign. varieties. Printer: W&S.

		GOOD	FINE	XF
S431	**5 DOLLARS** 3.7.1911. Black on green unpt. Royal crest at l., portr. Kg. George V at lower ctr., Canadian crest at r. Back green.			
	a. Sign. Stikeman at r.	55.00	200.00	500.00
	b. Sign. Mackenzie at r.	55.00	200.00	500.00

		GOOD	FINE	XF
S432	**10 DOLLARS** 3.7.1911. Black on blue-green unpt. Supported royal arms at l., portr. Qn. Mary at ctr., bank crest at r. Back blue.			
	a. Sign. Stikeman at r.	55.00	225.00	550.00
	b. Sign. Mackenzie at r.	55.00	225.00	550.00

		GOOD	FINE	XF
S433	**20 DOLLARS** 3.7.1911. Black on red-orange unpt. Royal crest at l., portr. Kg. Edward VII at ctr., Canadian crest at r. Back carmine.			
	a. Sign. Mackenzie at r.	425.00	850.00	—
	s. Sign. Stikeman at r. Specimen.	—	Unc	500.00

		GOOD	FINE	XF
S434	**50 DOLLARS** 3.7.1911. Black on lilac unpt. Portr. Qn. Alexandra at bottom ctr. Back purple.			
	a. Sign. Mackenzie at r.	425.00	850.00	—
	s1. Sign. Stikeman at r. Specimen.	—	Unc	500.00
	s2. Sign. Mackenzie at r. Specimen.	—	Unc	500.00

		GOOD	FINE	XF
S435	**100 DOLLARS** 3.7.1911. Orange. Royal crest at l., portr. Qn. Victoria at ctr., bank crest at r. Back brown.			
	a. Sign. Mackenzie at r.	630.00	1400.	—
	s. Sign. Mackenzie at r. Specimen.	—	Unc	750.00

NOTE: Specimen notes from salesman's sample books exist in other colors than noted above.

BANK OF HAMILTON

1872-73 ISSUE

#S441-S446 black on green unpt. Back green; Hamilton City crest at ctr. Printer: BABNC.

		VG	VF	UNC
S441	**4 DOLLARS** 1.9.1872; 2.9.1872. D. McInnes at lower l., steam passenger train at top l. ctr., machinist at lathe at lower r.	975.00	2100.	—
S442	**5 DOLLARS** 1.9.1872; 2.9.1872. D. McInnes at lower l., blacksmith and woman w/lg. ornate 5 at r.	975.00	2100.	—
S443	**10 DOLLARS** 1.9.1872; 2.9.1872. 2 allegorical women seated w/lg. ornate *X* at l., D. McInnes at upper ctr. r.	975.00	2100.	—
S444	**20 DOLLARS** 2.1.1873. D. McInnes at l., seated allegorical woman at r. Proof.	—	—	500.00
S445	**50 DOLLARS** 2.1.1873. D. McInnes at upper l., milkmaid w/cows at lower r. Proof.	—	—	500.00
S446	**100 DOLLARS** 2.1.1873. D. McInnes at upper ctr. Proof.	—	—	500.00

1887 ISSUE

		VG	VF	UNC
S447	**5 DOLLARS** 1.3.1887. Black on green unpt. J. Stuart at l., workers, factories at r. Back green; Hamilton City crest at ctr. Printer: BABNC. Proof.	—	—	500.00

		VG	VF	UNC
S448	**5 DOLLARS** 1.12.1887. Black. Portr. J. Stuart at l., view overlooking Hamilton at ctr. Back green; Hamilton City crest at ctr. Printer: CBNC.			
	a. Issued note w/ochre unpt.	975.00	2100.	—
	p1. Face proof w/blue unpt.	—	—	500.00
	p2. Face proof w/green unpt.	—	—	500.00
	p3. Back proof blue.	—	—	—

1892 ISSUE

#S451-S455 printer: Western Bank Note Co., Chicago.

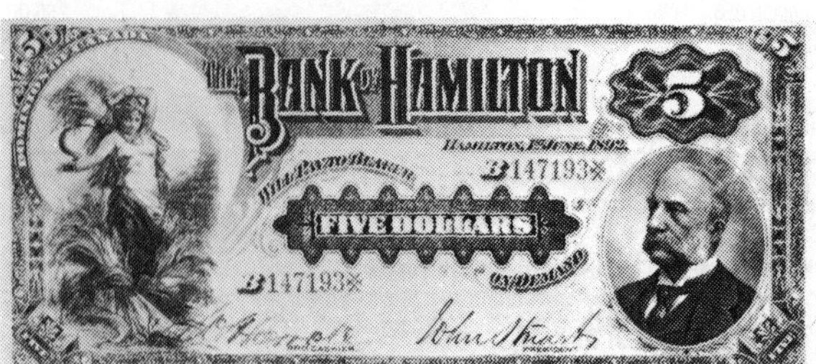

		GOOD	FINE	XF
S451	**5 DOLLARS** 1.6.1892. Black on green unpt. Agriculture at l., portr. J. Stuart at lower r. Back green; head office bldg. at ctr.	300.00	600.00	900.00
S452	**10 DOLLARS** 1.6.1892. Black on green unpt. Horseshoe and Niagara Falls at upper ctr., Commerce at r. Back red-brown; head office bldg. at ctr.	115.00	500.00	—

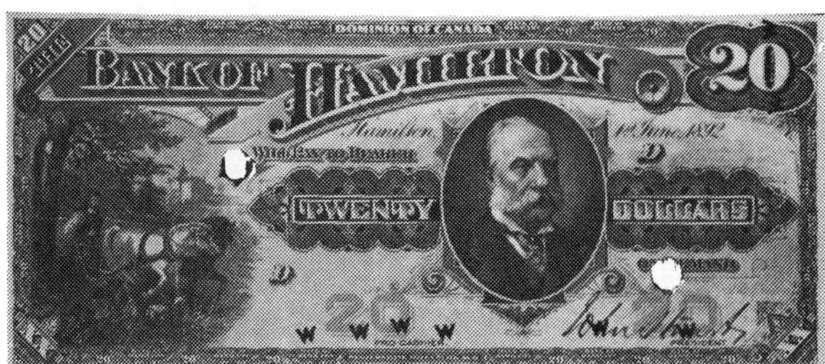

		Good	Fine	XF
S453	**20 Dollars** 1.6.1892. Black on ochre unpt. Farmer plowing w/horses at lower l., portr. J. Stuart at ctr. r. Back brown; stag's head at ctr. Proof, punched hole cancelled.	—	Unc	625.00
S454	**50 Dollars** 1.6.1892. Black on olive-green unpt. Portr. J. Stuart at upper l., tugboat at ctr. Back olive-green; Indians hunting buffalo at ctr. Specimen.	—	Unc	850.00
S455	**100 Dollars** 1.6.1892. Black on red-brown unpt. Steam passenger train at l. ctr., J. Stuart at lower r. Back dull red. Specimen.	—	Unc	850.00

1904 Issue

#S456-S460 printer: Western Bank Note Company, Chicago.

		VG	VF	Unc
S456	**5 Dollars** 2.1.1904. Black on green unpt. Seated Qn. Alexandra w/cherubs at l. Back green.	425.00	—	—
S457	**10 Dollars** 2.1.1904. Black on orange unpt. Seated Qn. Alexandra w/cherubs at l. ctr. Back orange.	850.00	—	—
S458	**20 Dollars** 2.1.1904. Black on olive unpt. Kg. Edward VII at lower ctr. Back brown.	1100.	—	—
S459	**50 Dollars** 2.1.1904. Black on blue unpt. Seated Qn. Alexandra w/cherubs at lower r. Back blue.	1650.	—	—
S460	**100 Dollars** 2.1.1904. Brown. Kg. Edward VII at lower l.	2800.	—	—

1909-14 Issue

#S461-S465 red ovpt: *E E* or *S S* on 1909 issue; *C C* or *E E* on 1914 issue. Printer: ABNC.

		Good	Fine	XF
S461	**5 Dollars** 1909; 1914. Black on green unpt. Reclining Britannia, Agriculture and Industry at ctr. Back green.			
	a. 1.6.1909.	30.00	125.00	350.00
	b. 1.6.1914.	25.00	87.50	250.00

		Good	Fine	XF
S462	**10 Dollars** 1.6.1909; 1.6.1914. Black on brown and yellow unpt. Seated allegorical woman between agriculture and industrial backgrounds at l. ctr. Back brown.	45.00	175.00	500.00
S463	**20 Dollars** 1909; 1914. Black on blue unpt. Reclining Britannia as #S461 at ctr. r. Back slate gray.			
	a. 1.6.1914.	75.00	300.00	—
	s. Specimen. 1.6.1909.	—	Unc	525.00

		Good	Fine	XF
S464	**50 Dollars** 1909-14. Black on red unpt. Seated allegorical woman as at #S462 at ctr. Back red-orange; bust of woman at ctr.			
	a. 1.6.1914.	125.00	525.00	—
	p. Proof. 1.6.1909.	—	Unc	350.00
S465	**100 Dollars** 1.6.1909; 1.6.1914. Black on olive-green unpt. Reclining Britannia as #S461 at l. ctr.	425.00	1750.	—

1922 Jubilee Issue

#S466-S468, 50th Anniversary of the Bank

#S466-S468 printer: ABNC.

		Good	Fine	XF
S466	**5 Dollars** 1.3.1922. Black on green unpt. Reclining Britannia as #S461 at ctr. Back green.	135.00	525.00	1200.
S467	**10 Dollars** 1.3.1922. Black on orange unpt. Seated allegorical woman as #S462 at ctr. Back orange.	120.00	400.00	1000.

		Good	Fine	XF
S468	**25 Dollars** 1.3.1922. Black on m/c unpt. 2 allegorical women at l. Back purple.			
	a. Issued note.	725.00	2000.	3000.
	p. Face and back proofs.	—	Unc	1000.

NOTE: While #S466-S468 constitute the 1922 Jubilee issue, only #S468 shows commemorative text *JUBILEE ISSUE* on face.

Bank of Montreal

1820s Issue

#S471-S473 black. Uniface. Printer: Graphic.

		Good	Fine	XF
S471	**1 Dollar** 1.8.1823-1.5.1825. Seated Britannia, sailing ship at upper ctr.	315.00	1050.	—
S472	**2 Dollars** 1.12.1826. Seated Britannia and Indian at upper ctr.	315.00	1050.	—
S473	**5 Dollars** 18xx. Seated woman and sailing ship at upper ctr. Proof.	—	Unc	350.00

1830-35 Issue

#S474 and S475 black. Uniface. Sign. varieties. Printer: Fairman, Draper and Underwood.

		Good	Fine	XF
S474	**1 Dollar** 1.7.1831. Indian w/ornate *ONE* at top ctr. above child's head. Sir W. Raleigh at r.			
	a. *MONTREAL* at lower r.	315.00	1050.	—
	b. Text: *PAYABLE AT QUEBEC* at top.	315.00	1050.	—
S474A	**2 Dollars = 10 Shillings** 1.6.183x. Woman in ornate *Z* at upper ctr., 2 coins below, standing Justice at upper r. Text: *PAYABLE AT QUEBEC.* Proof.	—	Unc	425.00
S474B	**5 Dollars = 1 Pound-5 Shillings** 1.6.183x. Portr. C. Columbus at l., 2 allegorical women, child and eagle in ornate *5* at upper ctr., bird below. Text: *PAYABLE AT QUEBEC.* Proof.	—	Unc	425.00
S475	**10 Dollars = 2 Pounds-10 Shillings** 1.6.1835. Seated allegorical woman at upper ctr., man's head in circular frame below, ornate 10's in all 4 corners.			
	a. *MONTREAL* at lower l.	315.00	1050.	—
	b. Text: *PAYABLE AT QUEBEC* at top.	315.00	1050.	—

1835-37 Issue

#S476-S482 black. Uniface. Sign. varieties. Printer: RWH & C.

		Good	Fine	XF
S476	**1 Dollar = 5 Shillings** 1.1.1835-1.1.1837. 2 men w/livestock at l., portr. Kg. William IV at upper ctr., St. George slaying dragon at upper r.			
	a. *MONTREAL* engraved. Black stamp: *PAYABLE AT QUEBEC.*	275.00	900.00	—
	b. Stamp: *PAYABLE AT QUEBEC.* 18xx.	275.00	900.00	—
	c. Text: *PAYABLE AT QUEBEC* engraved. 18xx.	275.00	900.00	—
S477	**2 Dollars = 10 Shillings** 3.6.1837. Indian woman at upper l., sailing ships at upper ctr., Indian brave aiming bow and arrow at upper r.			
	a. *MONTREAL* engraved. Black stamp: *PAYABLE AT AT QUEBEC.*	275.00	900.00	—
	b. Stamp: *PAYABLE AT QUEBEC.* 18xx.	275.00	900.00	—
	c. Text: *PAYABLE AT QUEBEC* engraved. 18xx.	275.00	900.00	—

		Good	Fine	XF
S478	**5 Dollars = 1 Pound-5 Shillings** 18xx. Reclining Greek god by fountain at ctr. above lion on crown. *MONTREAL* engraved. Proof.	—	Unc	350.00
S479	**10 Dollars = 2 Pounds-10 Shillings** 18xx. Sailing ships at upper and lower l., griffin, allegorical man and woman at ctr. *MONTREAL* engraved. Proof.	—	Unc	350.00
S480	**20 Dollars = 5 Pounds** 18xx. Seated Indian at l., seated woman w/crowned shield at upper ctr., Justice at r. *MONTREAL* engraved. Proof.	—	Unc	350.00
S481	**50 Dollars = 12 Pounds-10 Shillings** 18xx. *MONTREAL* engraved. Proof.	—	Unc	350.00
S482	**100 Dollars = 25 Pounds** 18xx. Female in chariot drawn by lions at top ctr., Commerce at lower l. and r. *MONTREAL* engraved. Proof.	—	Unc	350.00

1842-49 Issues

#S483-S486 black. Small "dog and safe" vignette at bottom ctr. Uniface. Sign. varieties.

		Good	Fine	XF
S483	**1 Dollar = 5 Shillings** 1842-49. Bison at top ctr., plants at r.			
	a. 1847.	240.00	850.00	—
	b. Red handstamp: *BELLEVILLE*. Printer: RWH & Co. 2.8.1842.	225.00	800.00	—
	c. Red handstamp: *BELLEVILLE*. Printers: Danforth, Underwood, New York and Underwood, Bald, Spencer, Hufty, New York. 2.8.1843-2.8.1847.	275.00	1000.	—
	d. Fully engraved date. Red ovpt: *BROCKMAN, BYTOWN, HAMILTON, LONDON,* and *ST. THOMAS*. Red word on face and back. Printer: RWH & E. 1.5.1849.	—	—	—
	p. Partially engraved date. Printer: RW & H. Proof. 2.4.184x.	—	Unc	525.00
S484	**2 Dollars = 10 Shillings** 1847-49. Seated Mercury w/lion at top ctr.			
	a. 1847.	240.00	850.00	—
	b. Red handstamped: *BELLEVILLE*. Printers: Danforth, Underwood, New York and Underwood, Bald, Spencer, Hufty, New York. 2.8.1843-2.8.1847.	275.00	1000.	—
	c. Fully engraved date. Red ovpt: *BROCKVILLE, BYTOWN, HAMILTON, LONDON,* and *ST. THOMAS*. Red word on face and back. Printer: RWH & E. 1.5.1849.	275.00	1000.	—
	p1. Partially engraved date. Printer: RWH & E. Proof. 2.4.184x.	—	Unc	525.00
	p2. Red handstamped: *BELLEVILLE*. Printer: RWH & C. Proof. 2.8.184x.	—	Unc	525.00
S485	**5 Dollars = 1 Pound-5 Shillings** 1842-49. Plants at l., royal crest at ctr., plants at r.			
	a. 1843-47.	250.00	850.00	—
	b. Red handstamped: *BELLEVILLE*. Printers: Danforth, Underwood, New York and Underwood, Bald, Spencer, Hufty, New York. 2.8.1843-2.8.1847.	275.00	1000.	—
	c. Fully engraved date. Red ovpt: *BROCKVILLE, BYTOWN, HAMILTON, LONDON,* and *ST. THOMAS*. Red word on face and back. Printer: RWH & E. 1.5.1849.	250.00	850.00	—
	p1. Partially engraved date. Printer: RW & H. Proof. 2.4.184x.	—	Unc	525.00
	p2. Red handstamped: *BELLEVILLE*. Printer: RWH & E. Proof. 2.8.184x.	—	Unc	525.00
S486	**10 Dollars = 2 Pounds-10 Shillings** 1842-49. Woman at upper l., seated Indian at top ctr., plants at r.			
	a. Red handstamped: *BELLEVILLE*. Printers: Danforth, Underwood, New York and Underwood, Bald, Spencer, Hufty, New York. 2.8.1843-2.8.1847.	—	—	—
	b. Red handstamped: *BELLEVILLE*. Printer: RWH & Co. 2.8.1842.	225.00	775.00	—
	c. Fully engraved date. Red ovpt: *BROCKVILLE, BYTOWN, HAMILTON, LONDON,* and *ST. THOMAS*. Red word protector on face and back. Printer: RWH & E. 1.5.1849.	275.00	1000.	—
	p. Partially engraved date. Printer: RW & H. Proof. 2.4.184x.	—	Unc	525.00

1844-61 Issue

#S487-S495 black. Montreal arms at bottom ctr. Uniface. Sign. varieties.

		Good	Fine	XF
S487	**1 Dollar = 5 Shillings** 1846-49. Standing woman in ornate outlined 1 at l. and r., sailing ships in harbor at upper ctr.			
	a. Quebec. Red numeral protector on face and back. 1.5.1846.	175.00	700.00	—
	b. Montreal. Red word protector on face and back. Fully engraved date. 1.1.1849.	145.00	700.00	—
	c. Quebec. Red word protector on face and back. Fully engraved date. 1.1.1849.	100.00	500.00	—
	d. Hamilton. Green word protector on face and back. Red ovpt: *BRANTFORD*. Fully engraved date. Printers: RWH & E and ABNC. 1.1.1849.	225.00	450.00	—
	e. Montreal. Green word protector on face and back. Green ovpt: *LONDON* and blue handstamped: *S* handstamp. Fully engraved date. Printers: RWH & E and ABNC. 1.1.1849.	275.00	525.00	—
	f. Quebec. Green word protector on face and back. Fully engraved date. Printers: RWH & E and ABNC. 1.1.1849.	110.00	525.00	—
	g. Toronto. Green word protector on face and back. Fully engraved date. Red ovpt: *BRANTFORD* and *COBOURG*. Printer: RWH & E and ABNC. 1.1.1849.	175.00	525.00	—
	h. Montreal. Partially engraved date. Printer: RWH & C. 18xx.	100.00	475.00	—
	p. As h. Proof.	—	Unc	525.00
S488	**2 Dollars = 10 Shillings** 1846-49. Standing woman in ornate outlined *2* at l. and r. Ornate *2* between seated Britannia and standing Justice at upper ctr.			
	a. Quebec. Red numeral protector on face and back. 1.5.1846.	210.00	700.00	—
	b. Montreal. Red word protector on face and back. 1.1.1849.	145.00	700.00	—
	c. Cobourg. Green word protector on face and back. Red ovpt: *LINDSAY*. Fully engraved date. Printers: RWH & E and ABNC. 1.1.1849.	130.00	550.00	—
	d. Montreal. Green word protector on face and back. Fully engraved date. Printers: RWH & E and ABNC. 1.1.1849.	110.00	525.00	—
	e. Quebec. Green word protector on face and back. Fully engraved date. Printers: RWH & E and ABNC. 1.1.1849.	110.00	525.00	—
	f. Toronto. Red ovpt: *SIMCOE*. Green word protector on face and back. Fully engraved date. Printers: RWH & E and ABNC. 1.1.1849.	110.00	525.00	—
	p. Montreal. Partially engraved date. Printer: RWH & Co. Proof. 18xx.	—	Unc	425.00
S489	**3 Dollars = 15 Shillings** 1844. Standing woman in ornate outlined *3* at l. and r., floating allegorical woman w/crest at upper ctr.			
	a. Montreal. Partially engraved date. Printer: RWH & C. 1.1.1844.	675.00	2300.	—
	b. Quebec. 1.5.1844.	675.00	2300.	—
S490	**4 Dollars = 1 Pound** 18xx. Standing Britannia in ornate outlined *4* at l., supported royal arms at top ctr., standing Justice in ornate outlined *4* at r. Partially engraved date. Montreal. Printer: RWH & C. Proof.	—	Unc	425.00
S491	**5 Dollars = 1 Pound-5 Shillings** 1.1.1844. Young woman at lower l. and r., woman seated in ornate *V* at ctr. Partially engraved date. Red numeral protector on face and back. Montreal. Printer: RWH & C. Proof.	200.00	875.00	—
S492	**10 Dollars = 2 Pounds-10 Shillings** 1846.52. Seated woman at lower l. and r., 2 women seated in ornate *X* at ctr.			
	a. Montreal. Partially engraved date. Blue ovpt: *T T* and green *M M*. Green word protector on face and back. Printer: RWH & C. 1.1.1849.	215.00	875.00	—
	b. Quebec. 1.5.1846-1.5.1852.	215.00	875.00	—
S493	**20 Dollars = 5 Pounds** 18xx. Standing Indian w/drawn bow at l., deer at upper ctr., Indian princess at r. Partially engraved date. Montreal. Printer: RWH & Co. Proof.	—	Unc	425.00
S494	**50 Dollars = 1 Pound-10 Shillings** 18xx. Victoria at l., sailing ship at ctr., Prince Consort at r. Partially engraved date. Montreal. Printer: RWH & C. Proof.	—	Unc	425.00
S495	**100 Dollars = 25 Pounds** 1.8.1861. Standing Justice at l., seated Victoria at upper ctr., seated Commerce at r. Partially engraved date. Green word protector on face and back. Montreal. Printer: RWH & C.	250.00	1050.	—

1851-53 Issue

Type I: W/denomination panel at lower l.

Type II: W/additional *ONE, 2, 5* or *10* numeral protectors behind denomination panel at lower l.

#S496-S500 black. Bank crest, 2 Indians w/shield at upper l. Uniface. Sign. and ovpt. varieties. Printer: PBC.

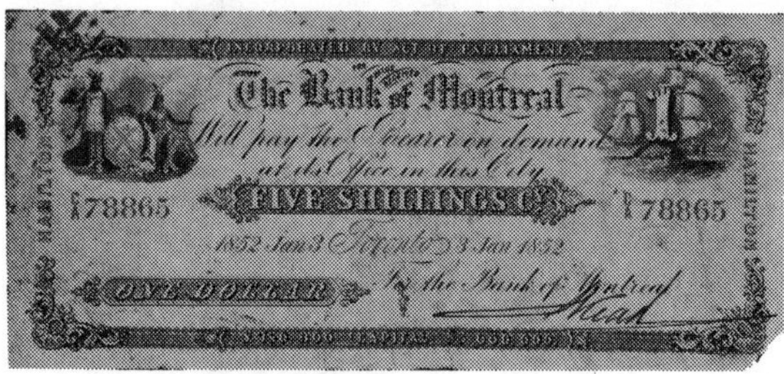

		Good	Fine	XF
S496	**1 Dollar = 5 Shillings** 1852. Sailing ships at upper r.			
	a. Type I: Montreal-Montreal. 1.1.1852.	200.00	700.00	—
	b. Type I: Toronto-Kingston. 6.6.1852.	200.00	700.00	—
	c. Type II: Montreal-Montreal. 1.1.1852.	200.00	700.00	—
S497	**2 Dollars = 10 Shillings** 1851-1852. Commerce at upper r.			
	a. Type I: LONDON/Montreal-Montreal. 1.3.1852.	200.00	700.00	—
	b. Type I: Toronto-Bytown. 5.3.1852.	200.00	700.00	—
	c. Type I: Toronto-Hamilton. 3.1.1852.	275.00	775.00	—
	d. Type I: Toronto-Toronto. 1.1.1851.	—	Unc	700.00
	e. Type II: 1852.	200.00	700.00	—
	f. Type III: Lg. green *TWO* in unpt. LONDON/Montreal-Montreal. 1.3.1852.	300.00	850.00	—
S498	**4 Dollars = 20 Shillings** 1851-52. Abundance at upper r.			
	a. Type I: Toronto-Toronto. 1.7.1851.	—	Unc	425.00
	b. Type I: THREE RIVERS/Montreal-Montreal. 1.4.1852.	350.00	975.00	—
	c. Type II: 1852.	350.00	975.00	—
S499	**5 Dollars = 25 Shillings** 3.4.1852-1.3.1853. Indians horseback at upper r.			
	a. Type I: Quebec-Quebec. 3.4.1852; 1.3.1853.	200.00	700.00	—
	b. Type II: 1852-53.	200.00	700.00	—
S500	**10 Dollars = 50 Shillings** 1852. Paddle wheel steamboat at upper r.			
	a. Type I: Toronto-Bytown. 5.5.1852.	350.00	975.00	—
	b. Type II: Toronto-London. 5.5.1852.	350.00	975.00	—

1853-57 Issues

#S501-S502 black. Bank crest at upper l. Back blue. Sign. varieties. Printer: Toppan, Carpenter, Casilear & Co.

		Good	Fine	XF
S501	**1 Dollar** 1853-57. Portr. Qn. Victoria at lower r.			
	a. *GODERICH* engraved. Red ovpt: *LONDON* in date. Green *BRANTFORD* ovpt. 1.8.1856.	275.00	560.00	—
	b. *PICTON* engraved. Red ovpt: *KINGSTON* in date. 1.8.1856.	200.00	550.00	—
	c. *WHITBY* engraved. Red ovpt: *BOWMANVILLE* in date. 1.8.1856.	200.00	600.00	—
	d. *WOODSTOCK* engraved. Red ovpt: *LONDON* in date. 1.8.1856.	200.00	600.00	—
	e. *BROCKVILLE* engraved. Red ovpt: *BROCKVILLE* in date. 2.1.1857; 2.2.1857.	200.00	550.00	—
	f. *LONDON* engraved. Red ovpt: *LONDON* in date. *T T* at top. 2.1.1857; 2.2.1857.	200.00	550.00	—
	g. *OTTAWA* engraved. Red ovpt: *OTTAWA* in date. 2.1.1857; 2.2.1857.	200.00	550.00	—
	h. *PORT HOPE* engraved. Red ovpt: *COBOURG* in date w/additional red ovpt: *LINDSAY*. 2.1.1857; 2.2.1857.	200.00	550.00	—
	p. *MONTREAL* engraved. Face proof.	—	Unc	350.00
	r. *TORONTO* engraved. Red ovpt: *TORONTO* in date. Remainder. 1.2.1853.	—	—	600.00

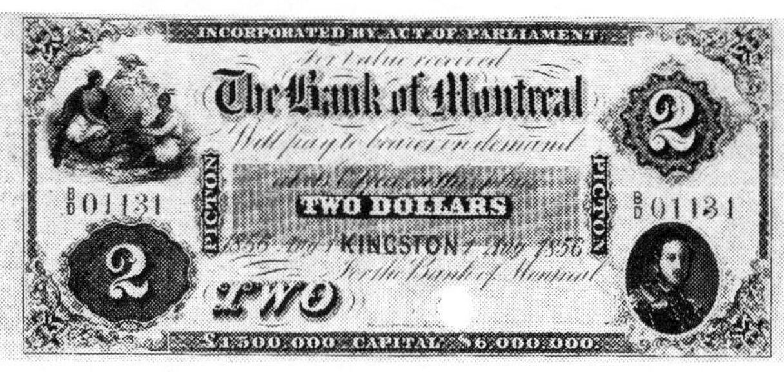

		Good	Fine	XF
S502	**2 Dollars** 1856-57. Portr. Prince Consort at lower r.			
	a. *LONDON* engraved. Red ovpt: *LONDON* in date. *T T* at top. 1.8.1856.	200.00	550.00	—
	b. *PERTH* engraved. Red ovpt: *OTTAWA* in date. 1.8.1856.	200.00	550.00	—
	c. *PICTON* engraved. Red ovpt: *KINGSTON* in date. 1.8.1856.	200.00	550.00	—
	d. *SIMCOE* engraved. Red ovpt: *BRANTFORD* in date. 1.8.1856.	200.00	550.00	—
	e. *OTTAWA* engraved. Red ovpt: *OTTAWA* in date. 2.1.1857; 2.2.1857.	200.00	550.00	—
	p. *QUEBEC* engraved. Face proof.	—	Unc	275.00

NOTE: All notes dated 1858 or 1864 are counterfeits.

1859 Issue

#S503-S507 black on green unpt., plain or fully tinted lg. numerals, ovpt. branch name across ctr. in red or blue. Sign. varieties. Printed backs green; St. George and dragon at ctr. Printers: RWH & E and ABNC.

		VG	VF	Unc
S503	**1 Dollar** 3.1.1859. Bank crest at upper ctr. portr. Qn. Victoria at lower l., reclining allegory Ceres w/produce at lower r.			
	a. Printed back.	625.00	1350.	—
	b. Uniface.	600.00	1125.	—

		VG	VF	Unc
S504	**2 Dollars** 3.1.1859. Portr. Qn. Victoria and Prince Albert at upper ctr., St. George slaying dragon at lower l., bank crest at lower r.			
	a. Printed back.	625.00	1350.	—
	b. Uniface.	600.00	1125.	—
S505	**4 Dollars** 3.1.1859. Portr. Wellington at upper ctr., bank crest at lower l., reclining Britannia at lower r.			
	a. Printed back.	625.00	1450.	—
	b. Uniface.	600.00	1125.	—
S506	**5 Dollars** 3.1.1859. Head office facade at upper ctr., bank crest at lower l., seated blacksmith at lower r.			
	a. Printed back.	625.00	1350.	—
	b. Uniface.	600.00	1125.	—
S507	**10 Dollars** 3.1.1859. Portr. R. Peel at upper ctr., reclining allegorical woman at lower l., bank crest at lower r.	625.00	1350.	—

1862 Issue

#S508-S510 black on green unpt. w/branch name in red or blue. Uniface. Sign. varieties. Printer: ABNC.

		Good	Fine	XF
S508	**1 Dollar** 1.8.1862. Similar to #S503.	200.00	550.00	1125.
S508A	**2 Dollars** 1.8.1862. Similar to #S504.	325.00	900.00	2250.
S509	**5 Dollars** 1.8.1862. Similar to #S506 but w/angular view of head office facade at upper ctr.	325.00	900.00	2250.
S510	**10 Dollars** 1.8.1862. Similar to #S507.	325.00	900.00	2250.

NOTE: All notes dated 1858 or 1864 are counterfeits.

1871 Issue

#S511-S516 black on green unpt. Back green; St. George slaying dragon at ctr. Sign. varieties. Printer: BABNC.

		Good	Fine	XF
S511	**4 Dollars** 6.2.1871. Woman and cherubs w/ornate *4* at ctr., R. B. Angus at lower l., E. H. King at lower r.	375.00	1050.	—

		Good	Fine	XF
S512	**5 Dollars** 2.1.1871. Seated Britannia w/lion, ornate *V* w/*5* at ctr., portr. T. Ryan at l., portr. E. H. King at r.	375.00	1075.	—
S513	**10 Dollars** 1.3.1871. Cherubs w/ornate *X* at ctr., portr. T. Ryan at lower l., portr. E. H. King at lower r.	400.00	1125.	—
S514	**20 Dollars** 3.3.1871. E. H. King at ctr.	500.00	1400.	—
S515	**50 Dollars** 5.5.1871. Allegorical woman seated on lg. ornate *L* at ctr., R. B. Angus at lower l., E. H. King at lower r.	500.00	1400.	—
S516	**100 Dollars** 6.6.1871. Justice seated within lg. ornate *C* at ctr., R. B. Angus at l., E. H. King at r.	500.00	1400.	—

1882 Issue

#S517-S519 black on green unpt. Back green; St. George slaying dragon at ctr. Sign. varieties. Printer: BABNC.

		Good	Fine	XF
S517	**5 Dollars** 2.1.1882. Britannia w/lion, lg. ornate *V* w/*5* at ctr., portr. W. J. Buchanan at lower l., portr. C. F. Smithers at lower r.	525.00	1500.	—

		Good	Fine	XF
S518	**10 Dollars** 2.1.1882. Cherubs w/lg. ornate *X* at ctr., portr. Dr. G. W. Campbell at lower l., portr. C. F. Smithers at lower r.	475.00	1350.	—
S519	**20 Dollars** 2.1.1882. Portr. C. F. Smithers at ctr.	625.00	1750.	—

1888 Issue

#S520 andd S521 black on green unpt. Back green. Sign. varieties. Printer: BABNC.

		Good	Fine	XF
S520	**5 Dollars** 2.1.1888. Britannia w/lion, lg. ornate *V* w/*5* at ctr., W. J. Buchanan at lower l., D. Smith at lower r.	425.00	1200.	—
S521	**10 Dollars** 2.1.1888. Cherubs w/lg. ornate *X* at ctr., portr. G. Drummond at lower l., D. Smith at lower r.	425.00	1200.	—

1891 Issue

#S522-S525 black on green unpt. Back green. Sign. varieties. Printer: ABNC.

#S522-S524 bank crest at ctr.

		VG	VF	UNC
S522	**5 Dollars** 2.1.1891. E. Clouston at lower l., Toronto Branch office bldg. at ctr. on back.	850.00	1900.	—
S523	**10 Dollars** 2.1.1891. G. Drummond at lower l., D. Smith at lower r. Montreal Head Office bldg. at ctr. on back.	1050.	1900.	—
S524	**20 Dollars** 2.1.1891. E. Clouston at l., D. Smith at r. Back similar to #S523.	1050.	1900.	—
S525	**50 Dollars** 2.1.1891. Lg. script "£" at ctr., G. Drummond at lower l., D. Smith at lower r. Back similar to #S523.	1050.	1900.	—

1892 Issue

#S526 and S527 black on green unpt. Back green. Sign. varieties. Printer: CBNC.

		VG	VF	UNC
S526	**50 Dollars** 2.1.1892. Portr. E. S. Clouston at l., portr. D. Smith at ctr., bank crest at lower r. Montreal Head Office bldg. at ctr. on back.	1550.	2800.	—
S527	**100 Dollars** 2.1.1892. E. S. Clouston at upper l., bank crest at ctr., D. Smith at lower r. Montreal Head Office bldg. at l. on back.	1550.	2800.	—

1895 Issue

#S528-S530 black on green unpt. Back green. Sign. varieties. Printer: BABNC.

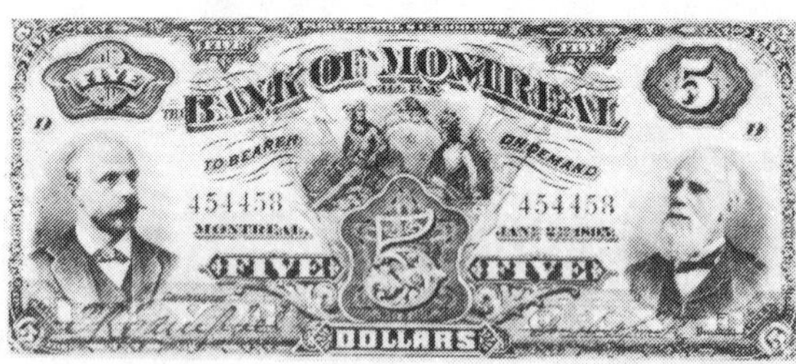

		VG	VF	UNC
S528	**5 Dollars** 2.1.1895. E. S. Clouston at lower l., bank crest at upper ctr., D. Smith at lower r. Tornonto Branch Office bldg. at ctr. on back.	185.00	550.00	—
S529	**10 Dollars** 2.1.1895. Bank crest at upper l. over D. Smith, G. Drummond at lower r. Montreal Head Office bldg. at ctr. on back.	775.00	1675.	—
S530	**20 Dollars** 2.1.1895. D. Smith at lower l., bank crest at ctr., E. S. Clouston at lower r. Back similar to #S529.	775.00	1675.	—

1903 Issue

#S531 and S532 back black and green. "Double Size." Sign. varieties. Printer: W&S.

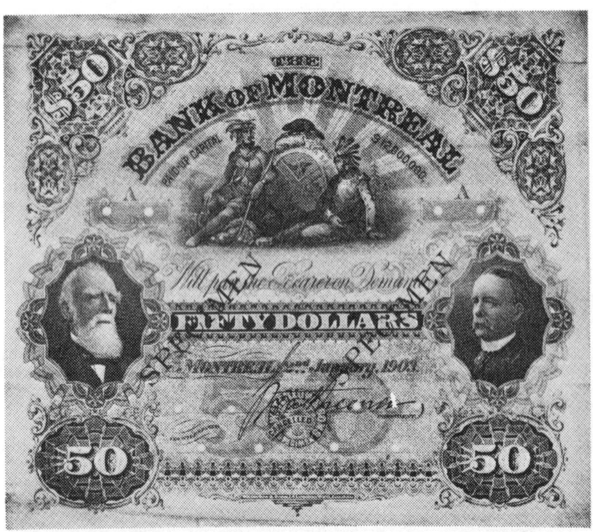

		VG	VF	UNC
S531	**50 Dollars** 2.1.1903. Black, orange and green. Portr. D. Smith at l., bank crest at upper ctr., portr. G. Drummund at r. Montreal Head Office bldg. at l., Toronto branch at r. on back.			
	a. Issued note.	3500.	7700.	—
	s. Specimen perforated: *SPECIMEN.*	—	—	—
S532	**100 Dollars** 2.1.1903. Black, gold and rose. Portr. D. Smith at l., bank crest at top ctr., portr. G. Drummund at r. Montreal Head Office bldg. at ctr. on back.			
	a. Issued note.	3850.	8400.	—
	s. Specimen perforated: *SPECIMEN.*	—	—	—

1904 Issue

#S533-S535 black on olive-green unpt. Back green. Sign. varieties. Printer: ABNC.

		VG	VF	UNC
S533	**5 Dollars** 2.1.1904. E. S. Clouston lower l., bank crest at upper ctr., G. Drummond at lower r. Montreal Head Office bldg. at ctr. on back.	85.00	225.00	550.00

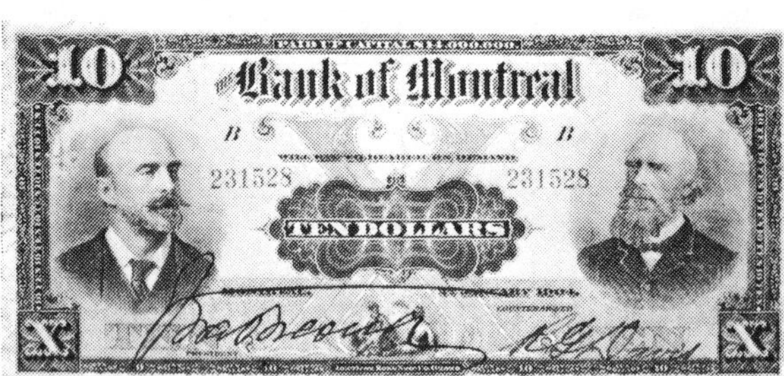

		VG	VF	UNC
S534	**10 Dollars** 2.1.1904. E. S. Clouston at l., bank crest at bottom ctr., D. Smith at r. Toronto Bank Branch Office bldg. at ctr. on back.	100.00	275.00	700.00
S535	**20 Dollars** 2.1.1904. Portr. E. S. Clouston at lower l., bank crest at ctr., portr. G. Drummond at lower r. Montreal Head Office bldg. at ctr. on back.	100.00	275.00	700.00

1911 Issue

#S536 and S537 black on olive-green unpt. Back olive-green. Sign. varieties. Printer: ABNC.

		VG	VF	UNC
S536	**5 Dollars** 3.1.1911. E.S. Clouston at lower l., bank crest at upper ctr., R.B. Angus at lower r. Montreal Head Office bldg. at ctr. on back.	125.00	250.00	800.00
S537	**20 Dollars** 3.1.1911. Similar to #S536.	150.00	325.00	975.00

1912 Issue

#S538-S542 black on olive-green unpt. Back green. Sign. varieties. Printer: ABNC.

		VG	VF	UNC
S538	**5 Dollars** 3.9.1912. V. Meredith at lower l., bank crest at upper ctr., R. B. Angus at lower r. Montreal Head Office bldg. at ctr. on back.	125.00	275.00	850.00
S539	**10 Dollars** 3.9.1912. V. Meredith at l., bank crest at bottom ctr., D. Smith at r. Toronto Branch Office bldg. at ctr. on back.	165.00	350.00	1200.
S540	**20 Dollars** 3.9.1912. V. Meredith at lower l., bank crest at upper ctr., R. B. Angus at lower r. Montreal Head Office bldg. at ctr. on back.	155.00	385.00	1400.
S541	**50 Dollars** 3.9.1912. Similar to #S539.	250.00	500.00	—
S542	**100 Dollars** 3.9.1912. V. Meredith at lower l., bank crest at upper ctr., R. B. Angus at lower r. Back similar to #S540.	250.00	500.00	—

1914 Issue

#S543-S547 black on olive-green unpt. Sir F. Williams-Taylor at lower l., bank crest at ctr., V. Meredeith at lower r. Back green. Sign. varieties. Printer: ABNC.

		VG	VF	UNC
S543	**5 Dollars** 3.11.1914. Montreal Head Office bldg. at ctr. on back.	15.00	45.00	135.00
S544	**10 Dollars** 3.11.1914. Toronto Branch Office bldg. at ctr. on back.	17.50	50.00	150.00
S545	**20 Dollars** 3.11.1914. Montreal Head Office bldg. at ctr. on back.	42.00	85.00	280.00
S546	**50 Dollars** 3.11.1914. Toronto Branch Office bldg. at ctr. on back.	150.00	300.00	1050.
S547	**100 Dollars** 3.11.1914. Montreal Head Office bldg. at ctr. on back.	175.00	350.00	1200.

1923 ISSUE

#S548-S552 black on olive-green unpt. Sir F. Williams-Taylor at lower l., bank crest at lower ctr., V. Meredeith at lower r. Back green. Printer: CBNC.

		VG	VF	UNC
S548	**5 DOLLARS** 2.1.1923. Montreal Head Office bldg. on back.	15.00	30.00	100.00

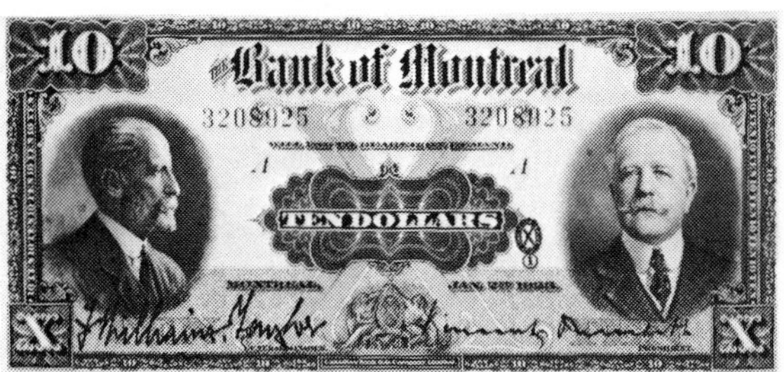

		VG	VF	UNC
S549	**10 DOLLARS** 2.1.1923. Toronto Branch Office bldg. at ctr. on back.	20.00	37.50	125.00
S550	**20 DOLLARS** 2.1.1923. Montreal Head Office bldg. at ctr. on back.	25.00	50.00	200.00
S551	**50 DOLLARS** 2.1.1923. Toronto Branch Office bldg. at ctr. on back.	150.00	325.00	1125.

		VG	VF	UNC
S552	**100 DOLLARS** 2.1.1923. Montreal Head Office bldg. at ctr. on back.	150.00	325.00	1125.

1931 ISSUE

#S553-S557 black on olive-green unpt. Back green. Sign. varieties. Printer: CBNC.

		VG	VF	UNC
S553	**5 DOLLARS** 2.1.1931. W. A. Bog at lower l., bank crest at upper ctr., C. B. Gordon at lower r. Montreal Head Office bldg. at ctr. on back.	15.00	30.00	90.00

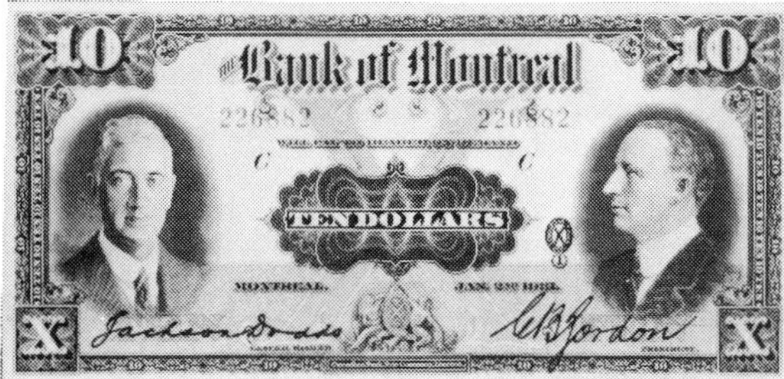

		VG	VF	UNC
S554	**10 DOLLARS** 2.1.1931. J. Dodds at l., bank crest at bottom ctr., C. B. Gordon at r. Toronto Branch Office bldg. at ctr. on back.	17.50	45.00	135.00
S555	**20 DOLLARS** 2.1.1931. J. Dodds at l., bank crest at upper ctr., C. B. Gordon at r. Montreal Head Office bldg. at ctr. on back.	275.00	700.00	1500.
S556	**50 DOLLARS** 2.1.1931. Similar to #S554.	80.00	150.00	550.00
S557	**100 DOLLARS** 2.1.1931. Similar to #S553.	100.00	225.00	700.00

1935 ISSUE

#S558-S560 black olive-green unpt. Back green. Sign. varieties. Like #S553-S555 but reduced size.

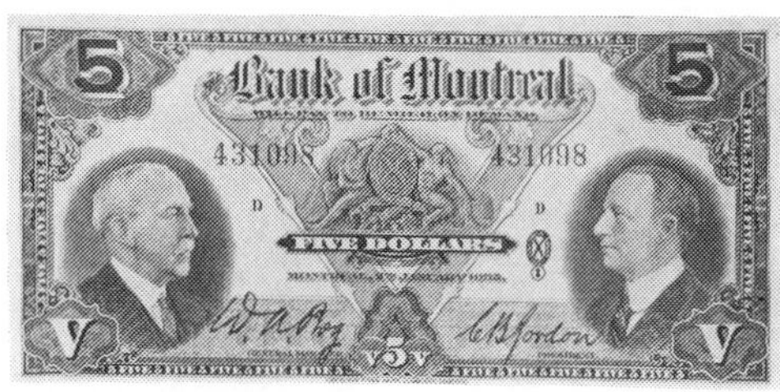

		VG	VF	UNC
S558	**5 DOLLARS** 2.1.1935. Like #S553.			
	a. Sign. W. A. Bog and C. B. Gordon.	15.00	35.00	125.00
	b. Sign. J. Dodds and C. B. Gordon.	15.00	35.00	125.00

		VG	VF	UNC
S559	**10 DOLLARS** 2.1.1935. Like #S554.			
	a. Sign. W. A. Bog and C. B. Gordon.	13.50	32.50	100.00
	b. Sign. J. Dodds and C. B. Gordon.	15.00	35.00	125.00
S560	**20 DOLLARS** 2.1.1935. Like #S555.			
	a. Sign. W. A. Bog and C. B. Gordon.	18.50	35.00	125.00
	b. Sign. J. Dodds and C. B. Gordon.	18.50	35.00	125.00

1938 ISSUE

#S561-S563 black on olive-green unpt. Back green. Sign. varieties. Printer: CBNC.

		VG	VF	UNC
S561	**5 DOLLARS** 3.1.1938. J. Dodds at lower l., bank crest at upper ctr., C. B. Gordon at lower r. Montreal Head Office bldg. on back.			
	a. Sign. J. Dodds and C. B. Gordon.	15.00	35.00	125.00
	b. Sign. G. W. Spinney and C. B. Gordon.	15.00	35.00	125.00

		VG	VF	UNC
S562	**10 DOLLARS** 3.1.1938. G. W. Spinney at l., bank crest at bottom ctr., C. B. Gordon at r. Toronto Branch Office on back.			
	a. Sign. J. Dodds and C. B. Gordon.	13.50	32.50	100.00
	b. Sign. G. W. Spinney and C. B. Gordon.	13.50	32.50	100.00
S563	**20 DOLLARS** 3.1.1938. Similar to #S562. Montreal Head Office bldg. on back.			
	a. Sign. J. Dodds and C. B. Gordon.	20.00	50.00	150.00
	b. Sign. G. W. Spinney and C. B. Gordon.	20.00	50.00	150.00

1942 Issue

		VG	VF	Unc
S564	**5 Dollars** 7.12.1942. Black on olive-green unpt. B. C. Gardner at lower l., bank crest at upper ctr., G. W. Spinney at lower r. Back green; Montreal Head Office bldg. on back. Printer: CBNC.	20.00	50.00	150.00

Bank of New Brunswick 1820-1906

1820-32 Issue

Pound Sterling System.

#S571-S574 standing Britannia at l., cherubs and women around seated Britannia at top ctr., 2 cherubs, cask and bale at lower ctr. Large size, 185 x 100mm. Back blue; 2 women's heads at upper and lower l. and r., 2 cherubs, cask and bale at upper and lower ctr. Printer: Perkins, Fairman & Heath.

		Good	Fine	XF
S571	**5 Shillings** 26.12.1820. Black on green unpt.	375.00	1250.	—
S572	**1 Pound** 1.1.1831. Black.	375.00	1250.	—
S573	**2 Pounds** 1.12.1832. Black.	375.00	1250.	—
S574	**10 Pounds** 18xx. Black. Proof.	—	Unc	500.00

1838-59 Issues

#S575-S580 standing Britannia at l., cherubs and women around Britannia at ctr., 2 cherubs, cask and bale at lower ctr. Back like #S571-S574. Reduced size, 170 x 72mm. Printer: New England Bank Note Co.

		Good	Fine	XF
S575	**5 Shillings** 1.6.1849-1.10.1856.	375.00	1250.	—
S575A	**5 Shillings** 1.12.1858; 1.10.1859. Red ovpt: *ONE DOLLAR*.	375.00	1250.	—
S576	**1 Pound** 1.10.1845-1.7.1852.	375.00	1250.	—
S577	**2 Pounds** 18xx. Proof.	—	Unc	500.00
S578	**5 Pounds** 14.9.1838.	45.00	150.00	—

NOTE: All known examples of apparently issued notes of #S578 are counterfeits. Genuine examples are found in sheets of proof notes.

		Good	Fine	XF
S579	**10 Pounds** 18xx. Proof.	—	Unc	275.00
S580	**25 Pounds** 1.11.1860.	575.00	1950.	—

1860-84 Issue

Dollar System

#S581-S587 similar to #S575-S580. Printer: ABNC.

		Good	Fine	XF
S581	**1 Dollar** 1.11.1860; 1.7.1863; 1.9.1868.	425.00	1400.	—
S582	**2 Dollars** 1.9.1868. Proof.	—	Unc	500.00
S583	**5 Dollars** 1860-84.			
	a. 1.11.1860; 1.7.1863; 1.9.1868.	425.00	1400.	—
	p. Proof. 1.1.1884.	—	Unc	500.00
S584	**10 Dollars** 1860-80.			
	a. 1.11.1860.	425.00	1400.	—
	p. Proof. 1.7.1880.	—	Unc	500.00

		Good	Fine	XF
S585	**20 Dollars** 1.11.1860; 1.9.1868. 2 sign. varieties.	475.00	1550.	—
S586	**50 Dollars** 1.11.1860.	475.00	1550.	—
S587	**100 Dollars** 1.11.1860.	475.00	1540.	—

1892 Issues

#S591-S594 black on green and yellow unpt. Women and cherubs around seated Britannia at ctr.

		VG	VF	Unc
S591	**5 Dollars** 25.3.1892. J. S. Lewin at lower l., bank crest at lower r. Back blue.	1050.	2100.	—
S592	**5 Dollars** 25.3.1892. Like #S591 but w/red Roman numeral *V V* on face.	1125.	2175.	—
S593	**10 Dollars** 25.3.1892. Sailor and provincial crest at lower l., J. S. Lewin at lower r. Back green.	1125.	2175.	—
S594	**10 Dollars** 25.3.1892. Like #S593 but w/red Roman Numerals *X X* on face.	1200.	2250.	—

1903-06 Issue

#S596-S599 bank facade at ctr. on back. Printer: ABNC.

		Good	Fine	XF
S596	**5 Dollars** 2.1.1904. Black on yellow-green and pink unpt. J. Manchester at lower l., suspension bridge, view of St. John at ctr., bank crest at lower r.			
	a. Sign. title: *MANAGER* at l.	425.00	1400.	—
	b. Sign. title: *FOR GENERAL MANAGER* at l.	425.00	1400.	—
S597	**10 Dollars** 1.9.1903. Black on yellow-green and green unpt. Sailor and provincial crest at l. Britannia, women and cherubs at ctr., portr. J. Manchester at lower r.			
	a. Sign. title: *MANAGER* at l.	425.00	1400.	—
	b. Sign. title: *FOR GENERAL MANAGER* at l.	425.00	1400.	—
S598	**20 Dollars** 2.1.1906. Black and blue. J. Manchester at l., reclining allegorical woman w/bale and casks at ctr., bank crest at r.			
	a. Sign. title: *MANAGER* at l.	525.00	1750.	—
	b. Sign. title: *FOR GENERAL MANAGER* at l.	525.00	1750.	—

		Good	Fine	XF
S599	**50 Dollars** 2.1.1906. Black and green. Seated allegory Commerce at l., bank crest at ctr., J. Manchester at r.			
	a. Sign. title: *MANAGER* at l.	525.00	1750.	—
	b. Sign. title: *FOR GENERAL MANAGER* at l.	525.00	1750.	—

Bank of Nova Scotia

1832-52 Issues

Pound Sterling System.

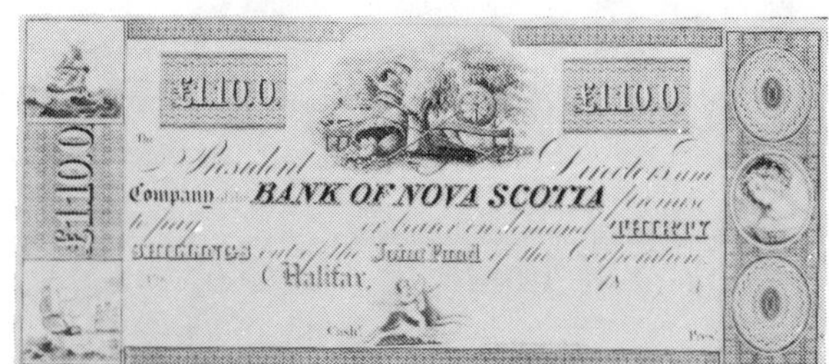

		Good	Fine	XF
S601	**1 Pound-10 Shillings** 18xx. Black. Sailing ships at top and bottom l., farm implements, produce at top ctr., child riding deer at bottom ctr., portr. Ceres at r. Proof.	—	Unc	500.00
S602	**2 Pounds** 18xx. Black. Proof.	—	Unc	500.00

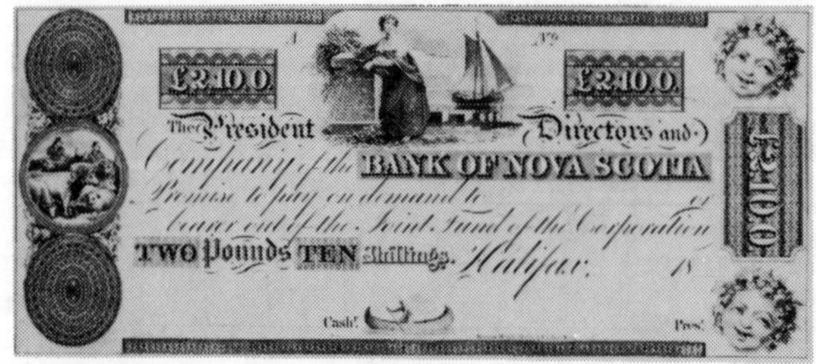

S603 2 POUNDS-10 SHILLINGS — GOOD — | FINE Unc | XF 500.00
18xx. Black. Standing allegorical woman w/sailing ship in background at upper ctr., man in canoe at bottom ctr., 2 men w/livestock at l., cherub's face at top and bottom r. Proof.

S604 5 POUNDS
3.4.1837. Black. 3 cherubs at top ctr., blacksmith at l., alchemist at r. Portr. Ceres at lower ctr. — 450.00 | 1475. | —

S605 5 POUNDS
2.6.1834; 1.1.1852. Black. Like #S604 but w/horse's head at lower ctr. — 450.00 | 1475. | —

#S606 *Deleted.* See #S612.

S607 5 POUNDS-5 SHILLINGS
2.5.1840. Black. St. George slaying dragon at top ctr., man and boy at l., sailing ship at r. — 550.00 | 1750. | —

S608 6 POUNDS
1.7.1840. Black. Allegorical male on chariot at top ctr., men harvesting wheat at l., steamboat at bottom ctr., man on horseback and farmer at r. — 550.00 | 1750. | —

S609 7 POUNDS
1.8.1840. Black. Halifax harbor at top ctr., sailor w/flag at l., deer at bottom ctr., milkmaid at r. — 550.00 | 1750. | —

S610 7 POUNDS-10 SHILLINGS
1.8.1840. Black. Crest at top ctr., standing Justice at l., dog w/key at bottom ctr., woman w/lyre at r. — 550.00 | 1750. | —

S611 10 POUNDS — GOOD | FINE | XF
1.1.1839; 1.1.1852. Black. Portr. Kg. William IV at l., royal arms at upper ctr., allegory Navigation at r. — 450.00 | 1475. | —

1864 ISSUE

Dollar System.

S612 20 DOLLARS — VG | VF | UNC
1.1.1864. Black and green. Royal arms at top ctr. Printer: Blades, East & Blades, London. — 1250. | 2375. | —

1870; 1871 ISSUE

#S616 and S617 printer: BABNC.

S616 4 DOLLARS — GOOD | FINE | XF
1.7.1870; 1.7.1871. Black on green unpt. Beehive and flowers at upper ctr.
- a. Issued note. — 625.00 | 1750. | —
- b. Red ovpt: *CANADA CURRENCY* twice. 1.7.1870. — 625.00 | 1750. | —

S617 5 DOLLARS
1.7.1870; 1.7.1871; 2.7.1877. Black and green. St. George slaying dragon at upper ctr.
- a. Issued note. — 625.00 | 1750. | —
- b. Red ovpt: *CANADA CURRENCY* twice. 1.7.1870. — 625.00 | 1750. | —

S617A 20 DOLLARS
1.7.1871; 1.1.1877. Black on green unpt. Printer: ABNC. — Reported Not Confirmed

S617B 4 DOLLARS
2.7.1877. Black on green unpt. Like #S616 but w/*PROVINCE OF - NOVA SCOTIA* at top ctr. — 625.00 | 1750. | —

1877 ISSUE

S618 5 DOLLARS — GOOD — | FINE Unc | XF 700.00
2.7.1881. Black on blue unpt. Pallas at upper l., Portr. J. Howe at ctr., bank crest at lower r. *FIVE* at lower l. and r. of portr. Back green. Proof.

1881-1929 ISSUES

#S618-S620 printer: ABNC.

S618A 5 DOLLARS — GOOD | FINE | XF
2.7.1881. Like #S618 but w/o *FIVE* at lower l. and r. of portr. Back brown.
- a. Issued note. — 525.00 | 1750. | —
- b. Red ovpt: *WINNIPEG* twice. — 725.00 | 2400. | —

S618B 5 DOLLARS
2.7.1881. Black on blue, green and ochre unpt. Large curved *FIVE* under portr. — 525.00 | 1750. | —

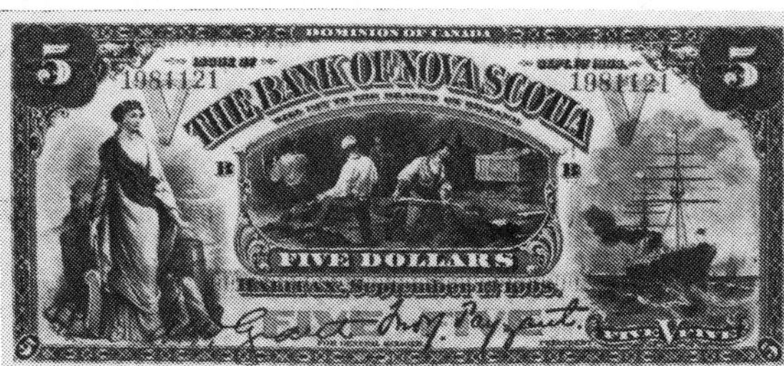

S619 5 DOLLARS — VG | VF | UNC
1898-1908. Black on green and orange unpt. Mining scene at ctr., standing allegorical woman at l., steamship at r.
- a. W/or w/o red ovpt: *SS.* 1.6.1898. — 125.00 | 225.00 | —
- b. W/o orange Roman numerals *V*s. 1.9.1908. — 42.50 | 105.00 | 350.00
- c. W/orange Roman numeral *V*'s at upper l. and r. 1.9.1908. — 60.00 | 150.00 | 315.00

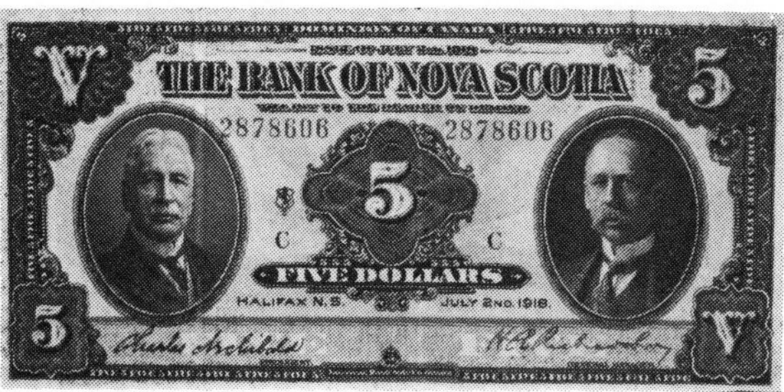

S620 5 DOLLARS — VG | VF | UNC
2.7.1918. Black on green unpt. Portr. J. Y. Payzant at l., portr. H. A. Richardson at r. — 35.00 | 87.50 | 275.00

#S621-S622 printer: CBNC.

S621 5 DOLLARS — VG | VF | UNC
2.1.1924. Black on red and green unpt. Portr. G. S. Campbell at l., portr. J .A. McLeod at r. — 20.00 | 50.00 | 175.00

S622 5 DOLLARS — VG | VF | UNC
2.1.1929. Black on red and green unpt. — 20.00 | 50.00 | 175.00

S623 10 DOLLARS — VG | VF | UNC
1877-1929. Black on ochre and blue unpt. Printer: ABNC or CBNC.
- a. Back green. 2.7.1877. — 550.00 | 975.00 | —
- b. Back green. 2.1.1903. — 100.00 | 200.00 | 775.00
- c. As b. 2.1.1917. — 27.50 | 82.50 | 275.00
- d. As b. 2.1.1919. — 27.50 | 82.50 | 275.00
- e. Back blue. 2.1.1924. — 21.00 | 50.00 | 140.00
- f. Back gray. 2.1.1929. — 17.50 | 37.50 | 125.00

#S624 *Deleted.* See #S671A.

#S625-S627 printer: ABNC.

S625 20 DOLLARS
1.1.1882. Proof. — — | — | 625.00

S626 20 DOLLARS
2.7.1896. Black on pink and blue unpt. Allegorical woman, globe and cherub at ctr. — 1400. | 3000. | —

S627 20 DOLLARS
1.11.1897. Black on yellow-green and rose unpt. Allegorical women at l. and r., portr. of woman at upper ctr. — 1400. | 3000. | —

#S628-S631 printer: ABNC or CBNC.

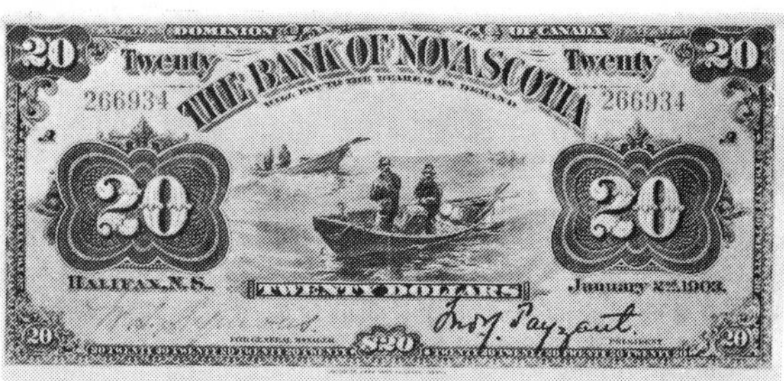

		VG	VF	UNC
S628	**20 DOLLARS**			
	1903; 1918. Black on yellow-green and rose unpt. Fishermen in boats at ctr. w/*HALIFAX, N.S.* at lower l. and date at lower r. Back olive.			
	a. 2.1.1903.	140.00	325.00	900.00
	b. 1.2.1918.	30.00	70.00	385.00

		VG	VF	UNC
S629	**20 DOLLARS**			
	1925; 1929. W/*HALIFAX, N.S.* at upper l. and date at upper r.			
	a. Back green. 2.1.1925.	30.00	85.00	300.00
	b. Back orange. 2.1.1929.	25.00	75.00	275.00

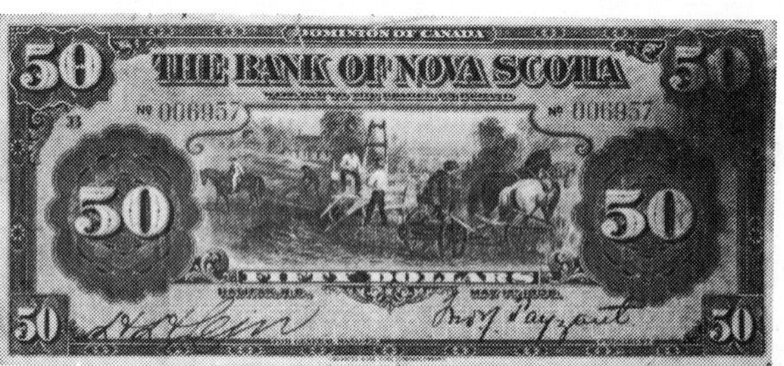

		VG	VF	UNC
S630	**50 DOLLARS**			
	1.5.1906; 2.7.1920; 2.1.1925. Black on olive and red unpt. Threshing scene at ctr. Back slate.			
	a. 1.5.1906.	625.00	975.00	—
	b. 2.7.1920.	425.00	900.00	2800.
	c. 2.1.1925.	500.00	950.00	3150.
S631	**100 DOLLARS**			
	1899-1929. Black on yellow-green and rose unpt. Liberty seated w/lion at l. ctr., seated Art and Industry at ctr. r. Back brown.			
	a. 1.8.1899.	750.00	1750.	—
	b. 3.1.1911.	700.00	1500.	—
	c. 2.1.1919; 2.1.1925; 2.1.1929.	425.00	975.00	—

1935 ISSUE

#S632 and S633 like previous issue but reduced size. Printer: CBNC.

		VG	VF	UNC
S632	**5 DOLLARS**			
	2.1.1935. Black on red and green unpt. Portr. J. A. McLeod at l., portr. H. F. Patterson at r. Back green; seal at ctr.	10.00	25.00	125.00

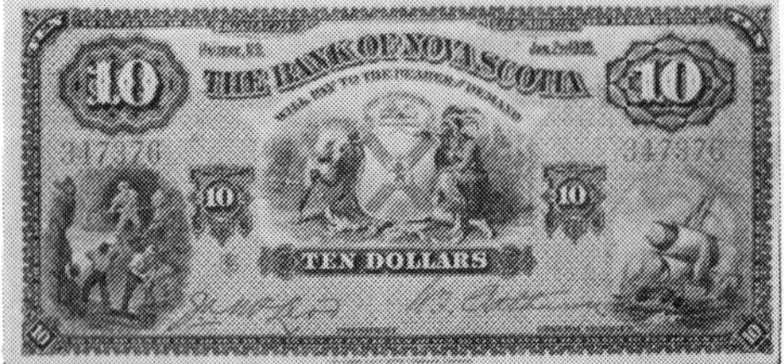

		VG	VF	UNC
S633	**10 DOLLARS**			
	2.1.1935. Black on ochre and blue unpt. Like #S623. Back slate gray; bank seal at ctr.	15.00	30.00	150.00

BANK OF OTTAWA

Issued at Ottawa, Ontario.

1874 ISSUE

#S636-S638 black on green unpt. Crest of Ottawa at upper ctr. Back green. Printer: BABNC.

		GOOD	FINE	XF
S636	**4 DOLLARS**			
	2.11.1874. G. Bryson at lower l., J. Maclaren at lower r.	500.00	1475.	—
S637	**5 DOLLARS**			
	2.11.1874. G. Bryson at upper l., J. Maclaren at upper r.	465.00	1400.	—
S638	**10 DOLLARS**			
	2.11.1874. Similar to #S636 and S637. Face proof.	—	Unc	350.00

1880 ISSUE

#S641 and S642 black on olive unpt. Back brown. Printer: ABNC.

		VG	VF	UNC
S641	**5 DOLLARS**			
	2.11.1880. Girl w/lamb at l., loggers at ctr., woman w/pen at r. Rafting at l. on back.			
	a. Issued note.	975.00	1950.	—
	s. Specimen.	—	—	500.00

		VG	VF	UNC
S642	**10 DOLLARS**			
	2.11.1880. Portr. blacksmith at l., Justice w/2 oval shields at ctr., portr. sailor at r. Indian maiden at ctr. on back.			
	a. Issued note.	1025.	2025.	—
	s. Specimen.	—	—	500.00

1888-91 ISSUE

#S646-S649 black on green unpt. Back green. Printer: BABNC.

		VG	VF	UNC
S646	**5 DOLLARS**			
	2.1.1888. Lumberjack felling tree at l., cattle at ctr., J. Maclaren at r.			
	a. Issued note.	900.00	2000.	—
	p. Proof.	—	—	500.00
S647	**10 DOLLARS**			
	2.1.1888. J. Maclaren at ctr. Crest at ctr. on back. Proof.	—	—	500.00
S648	**20 DOLLARS**			
	2.1.1891. Loggers, J. Maclaren and Canal Locks No. 2 at ctr. Proof.	—	—	500.00
S649	**50 DOLLARS**			
	2.1.1891. Proof.	—	—	600.00

1895-1900 ISSUE

#S651 and S652 reclining allegorical woman at ctr., C. Magee at l., Parliament bldg. at r. Back green; Ottawa Crest at ctr. Printer: BABNC.

		VG	VF	UNC
S651	**5 DOLLARS**			
	1895; 1900.			
	a. Black on green unpt. 2.1.1895.	900.00	1900.	—
	b. Black on ochre unpt. 1.6.1900.	900.00	1900.	—
S652	**10 DOLLARS**			
	1895-1900.			
	a. Black on green unpt. 2.1.1895.	1150.	2300.	—
	b. Black on ochre unpt. 1.6.1900.	1150.	2300.	—

1903 ISSUE

#S653-S656 back green; Ottawa Crest at ctr. Printer: BABNC.

		VG	VF	UNC
S653	**5 DOLLARS** 2.1.1903. Black on ochre unpt. Steam locomotive at l., Parliament bldg. at ctr. r.			
	a. Issued note.	850.00	1675.	—
	p. Proof.	—	—	600.00
S654	**10 DOLLARS** 2.1.1903. Black on olive unpt. Head office bldg. at l., cattle scene at ctr. Parliament bldg. at r.			
	a. Large tint.	900.00	1750.	—
	b. Modified smaller tint.	900.00	1750.	—
S655	**20 DOLLARS** 2.1.1903. Black and green. Loggers, portr. G. Bryson and Canal Locks No. 2 at ctr.	1050.	2025.	—
S656	**50 DOLLARS** 2.1.1903. Black and green. Farmer w/horse and dog at l., Parliament bldg. above portr. G. Bryson at ctr., 3 horses' heads at r.	1050.	2025.	—

1906 ISSUE

#S657-S658 printer: ABNC.

		VG	VF	UNC
S657	**5 DOLLARS** 1906; 1917. Logging camp scene at ctr.			
	a. Black on green unpt. Sign. Hay at r. 1.6.1906.	525.00	1050.	—
	b. Black on green unpt. Sign. Maclaren at r.	525.00	1050.	—
	c. Black on yellow and green unpt. Sign. Maclaren at r. 1.6.1906.	525.00	1050.	—
	d. Black on yellow and green unpt. Sign. Bryson at r. 1.6.1917.	500.00	1200.	—
S658	**10 DOLLARS** 1.6.1906. Dairy farm scene at ctr.			
	a. Black on green unpt. Sign. Hay at r.	525.00	1050.	—
	b. Black on green unpt. Sign. Maclaren at r.	525.00	1050.	—
	c. Black on yellow and green unpt. Sign. Maclaren at r.	525.00	1050.	—

1912-13 ISSUES

#S661-S664 Ottawa Crest at ctr. on back.

#S661 and S662 printer: W&S.

		GOOD	FINE	XF
S661	**5 DOLLARS** 1.6.1912. Black on blue unpt. Logging camp scene at ctr. Back olive-green.	200.00	725.00	1600.

		GOOD	FINE	XF
S662	**5 DOLLARS** 1.9.1913. Black on blue-green and ochre unpt. Like #S661. Back brown.	115.00	420.00	1050.
S663	**10 DOLLARS** 1.8.1913. Dairy farm scene at ctr. Back green. Printer: ABNC.			
	a. Black on green unpt.	210.00	700.00	—
	b. Black on ochre and green unpt.	210.00	700.00	—
S664	**10 DOLLARS** 1.9.1913. Black on green unpt. Cattle under trees at ctr. Back green. Printer: BABNC.	210.00	700.00	1675.

BANK OF TORONTO

NOTE: A number of spurious notes falsely altered from other bank issues to the Bank of Toronto exist, including a $1 and $4 from the Colonial Bank of Canada 1859-1862 and $2 from the International Bank of Canada 1858.

1856-65 PROVINCE OF CANADA ISSUES

#S666-S674 small Toronto Crest at bottom ctr. Qn. Victoria and Prince Albert medallion at ctr. on back.

		GOOD	FINE	XF
S666	**1 DOLLAR** 3.7.1856. Justice at l., seated farmer at upper ctr., seated Indian at lower r. Back orange.			
	a. Black w/blue *ONE* protector.	335.00	1050.	—
	b. Black w/green *ONE* protector.	335.00	1050.	—
S667	**1 DOLLAR** 2.7.1859. Black w/green *ONE* protector on face and back. Like #S666.			
	a. Issued note.	110.00	525.00	—
	b. Blue ovpt: *MONTREAL* twice.	110.00	525.00	—
	c. Red ovpt: *PETERBORO* twice.	110.00	525.00	—
	d. Blue ovpt: *PORT HOPE* twice.	110.00	525.00	—
S668	**2 DOLLARS** 3.7.1856. 2 children w/sheaves at lower l., steam train and wagons at wharf at top ctr., allegorical woman at r. Back orange.			
	a. Black w/blue *TWO* protector.	325.00	1050.	—
	b. Black w/green *TWO* protector.	325.00	1050.	—
S669	**2 DOLLARS** 2.7.1859. Black w/green *TWO* protector on face and back. Like #S668.	175.00	700.00	—
S670	**4 DOLLARS** 3.7.1856. Farmer w/scythe at lower l., 3 allegorical women at top ctr., Indian Chief Red Jacket at lower r. Back orange.			
	a. Black w/blue *FOUR* protector.	335.00	1250.	—
	b. Blue ovpt: *BARRIE* twice.	335.00	1250.	—
	c. Black w/green *FOUR* protector.	335.00	1250.	—
S671	**4 DOLLARS** 2.7.1859. Black w/green *FOUR* protector on face and back. Like #S670. Uniface.			
	a. Issued note.	300.00	975.00	—
	b. Blue ovpt: *BARRIER* twice.	300.00	975.00	—
	c. Blue ovpt: *COBOURG* twice.	300.00	975.00	—
	d. Blue ovpt: *MONTREAL* twice.	300.00	975.00	—
S672	**5 DOLLARS** 3.7.1856. Woman at lower l., royal arms at upper ctr., Commerce w/lg. 5 sideways at lower r. Back orange.			
	a. Black w/blue *V - V* protector.	325.00	1050.	—
	b. Black w/green *V - V* protector.	325.00	1050.	—
S673	**5 DOLLARS** 3.1.1857. Like #S672. Blue ovpt: *COBOURG* twice.	—	Rare	—
S674	**5 DOLLARS** 1859-65. Like #S672. Uniface.			
	a. Black w/green *V - V* protector on face and back. 2.7.1859.	250.00	975.00	—
	b. Black w/blue *V - V* protector on face and back. 3.7.1865.	250.00	975.00	—
S675	**10 DOLLARS** 185x. Beaver at lower l., Toronto Crest at upper ctr., steam passenger train at lower r. Back orange. Proof.	—	Unc	350.00
S676	**10 DOLLARS** 2.7.1859. Black w/green *TEN* protector on face and back. Like #S675. Uniface.			
	a. Issued note.	300.00	975.00	—
	b. Blue ovpt: *COLLINGWOOD* twice.	305.00	975.00	—
	c. Blue ovpt: *ST. CATHARINES* twice.	305.00	975.00	—

1876-80 DOMINION OF CANADA ISSUE

#S681-S684 *DOMINION OF CANADA* replaces *PROVINCE OF CANADA* below bank title. Printer: ABNC.

		GOOD	FINE	XF
S681	**4 DOLLARS** 1.1.1876. Black on green and pink unpt. Man's portr. at lower l., allegorical woman w/2 children at ctr., portr. W. Gooderham at lower r. Uniface.			
	a. Issued note.	375.00	1250.	—
	b. Blue ovpt: *COLLINGWOOD* twice.	375.00	1250.	—
	c. Blue ovpt: *ST. CATHARINES* twice.	375.00	1250.	—

#S682-S684 back blue; Qn. Victoria and Prince Albert medallion at ctr.

		GOOD	FINE	XF
S682	**5 DOLLARS** 1.7.1880. Black w/green *FIVE* protector. Like #S672.			
	a. Issued note.	305.00	975.00	—
	b. Blue ovpt: *ST. CATHARINES* twice.	305.00	975.00	—
S683	**10 DOLLARS** 1.7.1880. Black. Like #S675. Proof.	—	Unc	315.00
S684	**20 DOLLARS** 1.7.1880. Black. Portr. Qn. Victoria at lower l., steam passenger train at ctr., milkmaid by cow and calf at lower r.	—	Unc	315.00

NOTE: Counterfeit notes of this issue exist w/ovpt: *PETERBORO* or *PORT HOPE* but no genuine notes w/these particular ovpt. are currently known.

1887-1929 ISSUE

#S686-S689 printer: ABNC or CBNC.

		GOOD	FINE	XF
S686	**5 DOLLARS** 1890-1929. Black on yellow unpt. Like #S682.			
	a. Issued note. 1.7.1890; Ovpt: *BRANTFORD*. 1.2.1906. 1.7.1890.	135.00	450.00	—
	b1.	125.00	425.00	—
	b2. Ovpt: *CARDINAL*. 1.7.1890.	1350.	—	—
	c. Blue ovpt: *COLDWATER* (Ontario). 1.7.1890.	—	Rare	—
	d. Ovpt: *CREEMORE*. 1.7.1890.	—	Rare	—

		Good	Fine	XF
e.	Ovpt: *ELMVALE.* 1.7.1890.	—	Rare	—
f.	Blue ovpt: *GANANOQUE* (Ontario). 1.7.1890.	—	Rare	—
g.	Ovpt: *KEENE.* 1.7.1890.	—	Rare	—
h.	Blue ovpt: *LONDON.* 1.7.1890.	200.00	—	—
i.	Ovpt: *MILLBROOK.* 1.7.1890.	200.00	—	—
j.	Ovpt: *MONTREAL.* 1.7.1890.	200.00	—	—
k.	Ovpt: *NIAGARA FALLS CENTRE.* 1.7.1890.	200.00	—	—
l.	Ovpt: *OIL SPRINGS.* 1.7.1890.	200.00	—	—
m.	Ovpt: *OMOMEE.* 1.7.1890.	200.00	—	—
n.	Ovpt: *PETERBORO.* 1.7.1890.	—	Rare	—
o.	Blue ovpt: *POINT ST. CHARLES* (Quebec). 1.7.1890.	—	Rare	—
p.	Ovpt: *PORT HOPE.* 1.7.1890.	—	Rare	—
q.	Ovpt: *ST. CATHARINES.* 1.7.1890.	—	Rare	—
r.	Ovpt: *SUDBURY.* 1.7.1890.	—	Rare	—
s.	Blue ovpt: *VICTORIA HARBOUR* (Ontario). 1.7.1890.	—	Rare	—
t.	Blue ovpt: *WINNIPEG.* 1.7.1890.	—	Rare	—
u.	Ovpt: *GASPE.* 1.2.1906.	—	Rare	—
v.	Ovpt: *POINT ST. CHARLES.* 1.2.1906.	—	Rare	—
w.	Ovpt: *ST. CATHARINES.* 1.2.1906.	—	Rare	—
x.	Ovpt: *WATERLOO.* 1.2.1906.	—	Rare	—
y.	1.2.1911.	175.00	700.00	—
z.	1.2.1912.	60.00	175.00	450.00
aa.	1.2.1914.	60.00	175.00	450.00
ab.	1.2.1917.	27.50	85.00	265.00
ac.	1.2.1923.	17.50	55.00	175.00
ad.	1.10.1929.	17.50	55.00	175.00

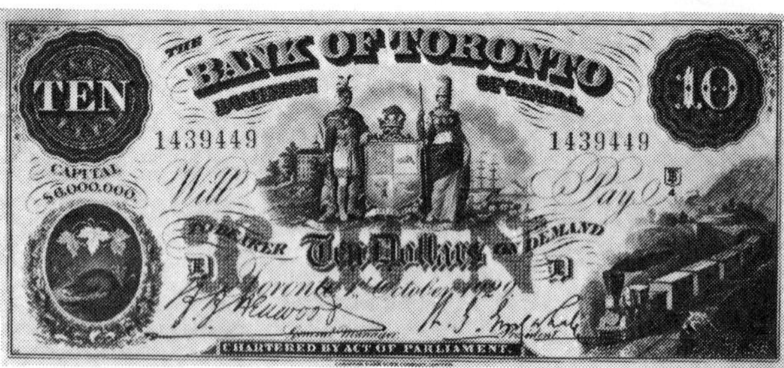

S687 10 Dollars

1887-1929. Black on yellow unpt. Like #S683.

		Good	Fine	XF
a.	1.7.1887.	250.00	700.00	—
b.	1.6.1892.	150.00	425.00	—
c.	Blue ovpt: *KING STREET WEST BR.* (Toronto). 1.7.1887.	—	Rare	—
d.	Blue ovpt: *LONDON.* 1.7.1887.	—	Rare	—
e.	Ovpt: *LONDON FF.* 1.7.1887.	—	Rare	—
f.	Ovpt: *CARTWRIGHT.* 1.6.1892.	—	Rare	—
g.	Ovpt: *COPPER CLIFF.* 1.6.1892.	—	Rare	—
h.	Ovpt: *KING STREET WEST BR.* 1.6.1892.	—	Rare	—

		Good	Fine	XF
i.	Ovpt: *LONDON.* 1.6.1892.	—	Rare	—
j.	1.6.1902.	150.00	425.00	—
k.	1.2.1906.	150.00	425.00	—
l.	1.2.1911.	165.00	450.00	—
m.	1.2.1912; 1.2.1914.	70.00	225.00	—
n.	1.2.1917; 1.2.1923; 1.10.1929.	35.00	100.00	275.00

S688 20 Dollars

1887-1923. Black on yellow unpt. Like #S684.

		Good	Fine	XF
a.	1.7.1887.	275.00	775.00	—
b.	Blue ovpt: *PARRY SOUND.* 1.7.1887.	—	Rare	—

		Good	Fine	XF
c.	Blue ovpt: *WINNIPEG.* 1.7.1887.	—	Rare	—
d.	1.2.1906; 2.2.1913.	200.00	550.00	—
e.	1.2.1917; 1.2.1923; 1.10.1929.	45.00	125.00	375.00

S689 50 Dollars

1890-1929. Black on yellow unpt. Bull's head at lower l., City Hall at ctr., cattle at lower r.

		Good	Fine	XF
a.	1.2.1906; 1.2.1914.	375.00	1100.	—
b.	2.2.1920; 1.10.1929.	175.00	725.00	1250.
p.	Proof. 1.7.1890; 2.2.1913.	—	Unc	350.00
s.	Specimen. 1.2.1906.	—	Unc	400.00

1935-37 Issue

#S691-S693 like S686-S688 but reduced size. Printer: CBNC.

S691 5 Dollars

1935; 1937. Black on yellow unpt. Like #S686.

		VG	VF	Unc
a.	Sign. H. B. Henwood and W. G. Gooderham. 2.1.1935.	21.00	45.00	185.00
b.	Sign. H. B. Henwood and J. R. Lamb. 2.1.1937.	21.00	45.00	185.00
c.	Sign. F. H. Marsh and J. R. Lamb. 2.1.1937.	21.00	45.00	185.00

S692 10 Dollars

1935; 1937. Black on yellow unpt. Like #S687.

		VG	VF	Unc
a.	Sign. H. B. Henwood and W. G. Gooderham. 2.1.1935.	25.00	50.00	200.00
b.	Sign. H. B. Henwood and J. R. Lamb. 2.1.1937.	25.00	50.00	200.00
c.	Sign. F. H. Marsh and J. R. Lamb. 2.1.1937.	25.00	50.00	200.00

S693 20 Dollars

	VG	VF	Unc
2.1.1935. Black on yellow unpt. Like #S688.	32.50	75.00	300.00

BANK OF VANCOUVER

1910 ISSUE

#S696-S700 Parliament bldg., Victoria on back. Printer: BABNC.

		GOOD	FINE	XF
S696	**5 DOLLARS** 2.5.1910. Black on green and yellow-green unpt. Ships in harbor at ctr. Back green.			
	a. Issued note.	2000.	6300.	—
	p. Proof.	—	Unc	700.00
S697	**10 DOLLARS** 2.5.1910. Black on green and red-brown unpt. Lumberjacks cutting down fir tree at l. Back brown.			
	a. Issued note.	2350.	8400.	—
	p. Proof.	—	Unc	700.00
S698	**20 DOLLARS** 2.5.1910. Black on yellow-orange and red unpt. Fishermen in boats at ctr. Back red.			
	a. Issued note.	2350.	8400.	—
	p. Proof.	—	Unc	700.00
S699	**50 DOLLARS** 2.5.1910. Black on blue unpt. Miners at ctr. r. Back blue	—	Unc	700.00

		GOOD	FINE	XF
S700	**100 DOLLARS** 2.5.1910. Black on olive-green unpt. Harvesting grain at ctr. Proof.	—	Unc	700.00

BANK OF YARMOUTH

1860 ISSUE

		GOOD	FINE	XF
S701	**20 DOLLARS** 1.12.1860. Black on green unpt. Farmer planting at lower l., portr. Princess of Wales between lion and unicorn at top ctr., ship in dry dock at r. Back orange. Printer: ABNC.			
	a. Issued note.	875.00	2800.	—
	b. Red ovpt: *CANADIAN CURRENCY.*	875.00	2800.	—

1870-91 ISSUE

#S702-S704 black on green unpt. Back green. Sign. varieties. Printer: BABNC.

		GOOD	FINE	XF
S702	**4 DOLLARS** 1.7.1870. Allegorical woman at sea borne by 2 porpoises at l. Indian maiden at r.			
	a. Issued note.	900.00	2800.	—
	b. Red ovpt: *CANADIAN CURRENCY.*	900.00	2800.	—
	p. Face proof.	—	Unc	750.00
S703	**5 DOLLARS** 1870; 1891. Anchor at upper l., sailing ships at upper ctr., allegorical woman w/flag, sailing ships in background at lower r.			
	a. 1.7.1870.	900.00	2800.	—
	b. Red ovpt: *CANADIAN CURRENCY.*	900.00	2800.	—
	c. 1.7.1891.	900.00	2800.	—
S704	**10 DOLLARS** 1870; 1891. Oval portr. of Qn. Victoria in "Widow's Weeds" between lion and unicorn at lower ctr.			
	a. 1.7.1870.	900.00	2800.	—
	b. Red ovpt: *CANADIAN CURRENCY.*	900.00	2800.	—
	c. 1.7.1891.	900.00	2800.	—

BANQUE CANADIENNE NATIONALE

Merged with La Banque Provinciale du Canada in 1979 to form the National Bank of Canada.

1925 ISSUE

#S706-S710 portr. J. A. Vaillancourt at l., portr. B. Leman at r. Provincial crests on back. Printer: CBNC.

		VG	VF	UNC
S706	**5 DOLLARS** 1.2.1925. Black on green unpt. Monument at ctr. Back green.	35.00	70.00	—
S707	**10 DOLLARS** 1.2.1925. Black on brown unpt. Similar to #S706 but w/different monument at ctr. Back brown.	35.00	85.00	—
S708	**20 DOLLARS** 1.2.1925. Black on blue unpt. Similar to #S706 but w/different monument at ctr. Back blue.	87.50	175.00	—

		VG	VF	UNC
S709	**50 DOLLARS** 1.2.1925. Black on olive unpt. Similar to #S706 but w/Maisonneuve monument at ctr. Back olive.	210.00	420.00	—

		VG	VF	UNC
S710	**100 DOLLARS** 1.2.1925. Black on purple unpt. Back purple. Specimen.	315.00	630.00	—

1929 ISSUE

#S711-S715 portr. F. L. Beique at l., portr. B. Leman. at r. Provincial crests at ctr. on back. Printer: CBNC.

		VG	VF	UNC
S711	**5 DOLLARS** 1.2.1929. Black on green unpt. Similar to #S706. Back green.	35.00	70.00	—
S712	**10 DOLLARS** 1.2.1929. Black on brown unpt. Similar to #S707. Back brown.	35.00	75.00	—

		VG	VF	UNC
S713	**20 DOLLARS** 1.2.1929. Black on blue unpt. Similar to #S708. Back blue.	105.00	210.00	—

		VG	VF	UNC
S714	**50 DOLLARS** 1.2.1929. Black on olive unpt. Similar to #S709. Back olive.	315.00	550.00	—
S715	**100 DOLLARS** 1.2.1929. Black on purple unpt. Similar to #S710. Back purple. Specimen.	—	—	700.00

1935 Issue

#S716 and S717 similar to #S711 and S712 but reduced size. Printer: CBNC.

		VG	VF	Unc
S716	5 Dollars 2.1.1935. Similar to #S711.	21.00	45.00	175.00

		VG	VF	Unc
S717	10 Dollars 2.1.1935. Similar to #S712.	25.00	55.00	210.00

Banque d'Hochelaga

1874-77 Issues

#S721-S727 black on green unpt. L. Tourville at lower r. Back green. Sign. varieties. Printer: BABNC.

		VG	VF	Unc
S721	4 Dollars 2.1.1874. 3 horses' heads at lower l., milkmaid w/cows at top ctr.	975.00	1950.	—
S722	4 Dollars 2.7.1877. Like #S721. Blue ovpt: *TROIS-RIVIERES.*	850.00	1825.	—
S723	5 Dollars 2.1.1874. Steam passenger train, ships at dockside. Face proof.	—	—	350.00
S724	10 Dollars 2.1.1874. Shepherd boy at l., J. Cartier landing at ctr. Face proof.	—	—	350.00
S725	20 Dollars 1.11.1875. Dog on strong box at lower l., woman operating telegraph at upper ctr. Face proof.	—	—	350.00
S726	50 Dollars 1.11.1875. Woman w/sheaf at l., fisherman, sailing ships at ctr. Face proof.	—	—	350.00
S727	100 Dollars 1.11.1875. Dog by safe at lower l., sailing ships dockside, factories at upper ctr. Face proof.	—	—	350.00

1880 Issue

#S781-S785 black on green unpt. Similar to #S723-S727 but w/Qn. Victoria in "Widow's Weeds" at lower r. Back green. Sign. varieties. Printers: BABNC.

		VG	VF	Unc
S781	5 Dollars 1.9.1880. Face proof.	—	—	350.00
S782	10 Dollars 1.9.1880. Face proof.	—	—	350.00
S783	20 Dollars 1.9.1880. Face proof.	—	—	350.00
S784	50 Dollars 1.9.1880. Face proof.	—	—	350.00
S785	100 Dollars 1.9.1880. Face proof.	—	—	350.00

1889 Issue

#S786-S790 Proofs (uniface) and Specimens (printed on both sides) only. Provincial crest at ctr. on back. Printer: CABNC.

		VG	VF	Unc
S786	5 Dollars 1.6.1889. Black on m/c unpt. Steam, sailing ships at l.			
	a. Issued note.	1000.	2000.	—
	p1. Black. Proof.	—	—	210.00
	p2. Black on m/c unpt. Proof.	—	—	525.00
	s. Back blue. Specimen.	—	—	700.00

		VG	VF	Unc
S787	10 Dollars 1.6.1889. Farmers plowing w/horses at l., portr. S. de Chaplain at r.			
	p1. Black. Proof.	—	—	280.00
	p2. Black on m/c unpt. Proof.	—	—	525.00
	s. Back orange. Specimen.	—	—	700.00

		VG	VF	Unc
S788	20 Dollars 1.6.1889. Horses w/Roebling suspension bridge in background at l., Prince of Wales at r.			
	p. Black on m/c unpt. Proof.	—	—	525.00
	s. Back green. Specimen.	—	—	700.00

		VG	VF	Unc
S789	50 Dollars 1.6.1889. Prince of Wales at l., family on house raft at r.			
	p. Black on m/c unpt. Proof.	—	—	525.00
	s. Back green. Specimen.	—	—	700.00

		VG	VF	Unc
S790	100 Dollars 1.6.1889. Portr. S. de Champlain at upper l., Indians on bluff overlooking steam passenger train at r.			
	p. Black on m/c unpt. Proof.	—	—	525.00
	s. Back green. Specimen.	—	—	700.00

1894 Issue

#S791 and S792 black on green unpt. Portr. M. J. Pendergast at l., L. H. St. Charles at r. Sign. varieties. Printer: BABNC.

		VG	VF	Unc
S791	5 Dollars 1.6.1894. Sailing ships in Montreal Harbor at top ctr. Face proof.	—	—	350.00
S792	10 Dollars 1.6.1894. Cartier landing at ctr. Face proof.	—	—	350.00

A word on date ranges

Often date ranges or specific dates are listed. These have been observed or reported by our contributors. If a note is outside the published range, it only means that it is a newly reported date, and not necessarily worthy of a premium value.

1898; 1907 ISSUE

#S796-S800 sign. varieties. Printer: ABNC.

		GOOD	FINE	XF
S796	**5 DOLLARS** 2.5.1898; 1.3.1907. Black on olive unpt. M. J. Pendergast at l., steamship at upper ctr., L. H. St. Charles at r. Back green; provincial arms at ctr.	510.00	1675.	—
S797	**10 DOLLARS** 1898; 1907. Black on olive unpt. Maissoneuve monument at l., portr. L. H. St. Charles at ctr. r. Back carmine; provincial arms at ctr.			
	a. Issued note. 2.5.1898.	510.00	1675.	—
	p1. Black. Face proof. 1.3.1907.	—	Unc	175.00
	p2. Black on olive unpt. Face proof. 2.5.1898; 1.3.1907.	—	Unc	280.00

		GOOD	FINE	XF
S798	**20 DOLLARS** 1898; 1907. Black on olive unpt. Farmer's loading hay at l. ctr., portr. L. H. St. Charles at r. Back blue; provincial arms at l., Maissoneuve monument at ctr. r.			
	p1. Black. Proof. 2.5.1898; 1.3.1907.	—	Unc	175.00
	p2. Black on olive unpt. Proof. 2.5.1898.	—	Unc	350.00

		GOOD	FINE	XF
S799	**50 DOLLARS** 1898; 1907. M. J. Pendergast at lower l., L. H. St. Charles at lower r. Back olive; Maissoneuve monument at ctr.			
	p1. Black on green and olive-green unpt. Face proof. 2.5.1898; 1.3.1907.	—	Unc	350.00
	p2. Black. Face proof. 1.3.1907.	—	Unc	175.00
S800	**100 DOLLARS** 1898; 1907. Dock scene w/ship by elevator bldg., L. H. St. Charles at upper r. Back green; Maissoneuve monument at ctr.			
	p1. Black on olive unpt. Face proof. 2.5.1898; 1.3.1907.	—	Unc	350.00
	p2. Black. Face proof. 1.3.1907.	—	Unc	210.00

1911 ISSUE

#S801-S805 similar to #S796-S800. Sign. varieties. Printer: ABNC.

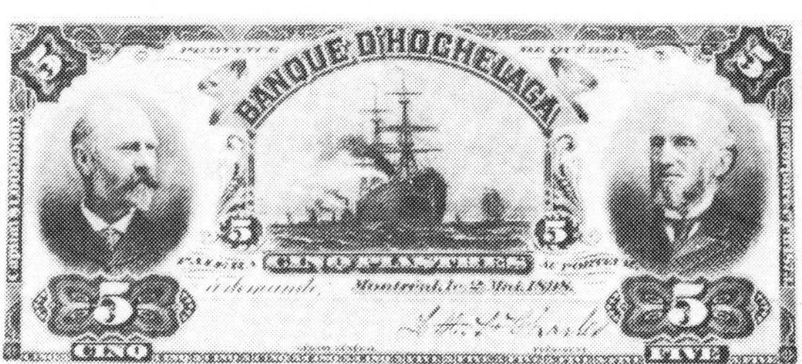

		GOOD	FINE	XF
S801	**5 DOLLARS** 25.2.1911. Back green; provincial arms at ctr.			
	p. Face and back proofs.	—	Unc	175.00
	s. Specimen.	—	Unc	300.00

		GOOD	FINE	XF
S802	**10 DOLLARS** 25.2.1911. Back red; provincial arms at ctr.			
	a. Issued note.	425.00	1400.	—
	p. Face and back proofs.	—	Unc	250.00
S803	**20 DOLLARS** 25.2.1911. Back blue; provincial arms at ctr. Face and back proofs.	—	Unc	250.00
S804	**50 DOLLARS** 25.2.1911. Back olive; arms at l., Maissoneuve monument at ctr. Face and back proofs.	—	Unc	250.00

		GOOD	FINE	XF
S805	**100 DOLLARS** 25.2.1911. Back green; Maissoneuve monument. Face proof.	—	Unc	250.00

1914 ISSUE

#S806-S810 J. A. Vaillancourt at l. Provincial arms at ctr. on back. Sign. varieties. Printer: W&S.

		GOOD	FINE	XF
S806	**5 DOLLARS** 1.1.1914. Black on lt. blue unpt. Place d'Arms at ctr., Maissoneuve monument at lower r. Back blue-green.	25.00	75.00	225.00

		GOOD	FINE	XF
S807	**10 DOLLARS** 1.1.1914. Black on yellow-orange unpt. Quebec City at ctr., Champlain monument at lower r. Back yellow-brown.	35.00	125.00	275.00

		GOOD	FINE	XF
S808	**20 DOLLARS** 1.1.1914. Black on blue-green unpt. Parliament bldgs. at ctr., J. Cartier at r. Back green.	300.00	975.00	—

		Good	VF	XF
S809	**50 Dollars** 1.1.1914. Black on salmon unpt. Horse-drawn reaper in in wheat field at ctr., farmer broadcasting seeds at r. Back brown.	300.00	975.00	—

		Good	Fine	XF
S810	**100 Dollars** 1.1.1914. Black on lilac unpt. Lake Moraine scene at ctr., De La Verendrye monument at lower r. Back slate.	300.00	975.00	—

1917-20 Issue

#S811-S815 portr. J. A. Vaillancourt at l., portr. B. Leman at r. Provincial arms at ctr. on back. Sign. varieties. Printer: ABNC.

		Good	Fine	XF
S811	**5 Dollars** 2.1.1917. Black on olive unpt. 4 figure statue at ctr. Back olive.	35.00	115.00	275.00

		Good	Fine	XF
S812	**10 Dollars** 2.1.1917. Black on brown unpt. Similar to #S811. Back brown.	40.00	135.00	350.00
S813	**20 Dollars** 2.1.1917. Black on blue unpt. Seated allegorical woman w/flag and Canadian shield of arms at ctr. Back blue.	125.00	425.00	1050.
S814	**50 Dollars** 2.1.1920. Black on red unpt. Maissoneuve monument at ctr. Back red.	235.00	770.00	—

		Good	Fine	XF
S815	**100 Dollars** 2.1.1920. Black on purple unpt. Back purple.	235.00	770.00	—

Banque Internationale du Canada

Issued in Montreal, Quebec.

Absorbed by the Home Bank of Canada in 1913.

1911 Issue

#S816-S818 w/red ovpt: *M M* and blue ovpt: *QUEBEC*. Bank seal w/globe at ctr. on back. Printer: ABNC.

		Good	Fine	XF
S816	**5 Dollars** 2.10.1911. Black on green and yellow unpt. Portr. R. Forget at ctr. Back green.	950.00	3250.	—

		Good	Fine	XF
S817	**10 Dollars** 17.10.1911. Black, orange and yellow. Portr. R. Forget at l., portr. R. Bickerdike at r. Back brown.	950.00	3250.	—
S818	**20 Dollars** 17.10.1911. Black, olive and yellow. Similar to #S817. Back brown.	950.00	3250.	—

Banque Jacques Cartier

1862 Issue

#S821-S824 black on green unpt. J. Cartier at ctr. Back green. Printer: ABNC.

		Good	Fine	XF
S821	**1 Dollar** 2.1.1862. Portr. Qn. Victoria at lower l., portr. R. Trudeau at lower r.	845.00	2800.	—
S822	**2 Dollars** 2.1.1862. Portr. Princess Eugenie at lower l., portr. Prince of Wales at lower r.	845.00	2800.	—
S823	**5 Dollars** 2.1.1862.	Reported Not Confirmed		
S824	**10 Dollars** 2.1.1862.	Reported Not Confirmed		

1870 Issue

#S826 and S827 portr. Qn. Victoria at l., portr. Prince Albert ctr.

		VG	VF	Unc
S826	**4 Dollars** 2.5.1870. Seated allegorical woman, sailing ships at lower l., beaver at lower r.			
	a. Ornate black *4*'s at upper l and r.	2800.	—	—
	b. Green *FOUR* over ornate black *4*'s at upper l. and r.	2800.	—	—
S827	**5 Dollars** 1870-80. R. Trudeau at lower l., A. Desjardins at lower r.			
	a. 2.5.1870.	2800.	—	—
	b. Blue ovpt: *VICTORIAVILLE.* 1.6.1880.	2800.	—	—
S828	**20 Dollars** 2.5.1870; 2.5.1871. Dog's head at lower l., blacksmith w/horses at lower r. Face proof.	—	—	350.00
S829	**50 Dollars** 2.5.1870. Woman w/parchment at l., woman reaping grain at r. Face proof.	—	—	350.00
S830	**10 Dollars** 2.5.1870. Qn. Victoria in "Widow's Weeds" at l., anchor, barrel and bales at r. Face proof.	—	—	350.00

1886-89 Issues

#S831-S834 J. Cartier at l., bank bldg. facade at r. Printer: CABNC.

		VG	VF	Unc
S831	**5 Dollars** 1.6.1886. Black on green unpt. Farm family w/animals at ctr. Face proof.	—	—	500.00
S832	**5 Dollars** 1.6.1889. Black on blue-green and ochre unpt. Like #S831. Face proof.	—	—	500.00
S833	**10 Dollars** 1.6.1886. Indians on bluff, steam passenger train below.			
	a. Black on orange and blue unpt.	2800.	—	—
	p. Face proof. Black on green unpt.	—	—	500.00

		VG	VF	UNC
S834	**10 DOLLARS** 1.6.1889. Black on blue-green and ochre unpt. Like #S833.			
	a. Issued note.	—	Rare	—
	p. Face proof.	—	—	500.00

1895 ISSUE

#S836-S837 black on green unpt. A. L. Demontigny at lower l., A. Desjardins at lower r. Back green; Indian on bluff. Printer: BABNC.

		VG	VF	UNC
S836	**5 DOLLARS** 2.1.1895. J. Cartier, Montreal views at ctr. Face proof.	—	—	350.00
S837	**10 DOLLARS** 2.1.1895. J. Cartier w/shipmates at ctr. Face proof.	—	—	350.00

BANQUE NATIONALE

1860 ISSUE

#S841-S844 black on green unpt. Uniface. Sign. varieties. Printer: ABNC.

		GOOD	FINE	XF
S841	**1 DOLLAR** 1860. Standing male citizen at lower l., Quebec City arms at upper ctr., J. Cartier at lower r.			
	a. Partially engraved date, handsigned sheet #. 28.4.1860.	210.00	700.00	1550.
	b. Engraved date, printed sheet #. 28.4.1860.	125.00	425.00	910.00
	c. As b. 25.5.1860.	175.00	550.00	1050.
S842	**2 DOLLARS** 1860. 2 allegorical women at lower l., Quebec City arms at upper ctr., oval portr. J. Cartier at r.			
	a. Partially engraved date, handsigned sheet #. 28.4.1860.	210.00	700.00	1550.
	b. Engraved date, printed sheet #. 28.4.1860.	195.00	550.00	1125.
	c. As b. 25.5.1860.	225.00	775.00	1550.
S843	**5 DOLLARS** 1860. Farm tools at lower l., farmers plowing w/horses at top ctr., woman w/cornucopia at lower r.			
	a. Partially engraved date, handsigned sheet #. 28.4.1860.	250.00	850.00	1675.
	b. Engraved date, printed sheet #. 28.4.1860.	225.00	775.00	1550.
S844	**10 DOLLARS** 1860. St. John the Baptist w/lamb at lower l., steam passenger train at top ctr., seated Britannia w/Upper Canada shield of arms at lower r.			
	a. Partially engraved date, handsigned sheet #. 28.4.1860.	250.00	850.00	1675.
	b. Engraved date, printed sheet #. 28.4.1860.	225.00	775.00	1550.

1870-71 ISSUE

#S846-S850 black on green unpt. Back green. Sign. varieties. Printer: BABNC.

		GOOD	FINE	XF
S846	**4 DOLLARS** 1870-71. Beehive at upper l., paddle wheel steamboat "Quebec" at bottom ctr., sailor at lower r.			
	a. Issued note. 28.5.1870.	200.00	700.00	1475.
	b. Red ovpt: *OTTAWA.*	200.00	700.00	1475.
	c. Red ovpt: *SHERBROOKE.*	200.00	700.00	1475.
	s. Specimen. 28.5.1871; 2.10.1871.	—	Unc	700.00
S847	**6 DOLLARS** 28.5.1870. Elderly woman teaching girl knitting at lower l., girl w/cattle at top ctr., oval portr. S. de Champlain at lower r.			
	a. Issued note.	1175.	4200.	—
	b. Red ovpt: *OTTAWA.*	1175.	4200.	—
	c. Red ovpt: *SHERBROOKE.*	1175.	4200.	—
S848	**20 DOLLARS** 2.10.1871. Farmer feeding horses at lower l., Quebec City arms at top ctr., young sailor climbing rope ladder at lower r. Black ovpt: *XX.*	350.00	1050.	2800.

		GOOD	FINE	XF
S849	**50 DOLLARS** 2.10.1871. Farmer carrying cornstalks at l., reclining woman w/waterjug at top ctr., Agriculture at r. Black ovpt: *XX.*	350.00	1050.	2800.
S850	**100 DOLLARS** 2.10.1871. Sailors looking to sea at top ctr. Black ovpt: *XX.*	450.00	1250.	2725.

1873 ISSUE

#S851 and S852 black on green unpt. Back green. Printer: BABNC.

		GOOD	FINE	XF
S851	**5 DOLLARS** 2.1.1873. Plow and agricultural produce at lower l., shipbuilders at upper ctr., seated Britannia w/shield of *5*at lower r.	250.00	800.00	1950.
S852	**10 DOLLARS** 2.1.1873. St. John the Baptist w/lamb at lower l., agricultural produce and tools at upper ctr., anchor at lower r.	250.00	800.00	1950.

1883 ISSUE

#S856-S857 black on green unpt. J. R. Thibaudeau at lower r. Back green. Red ovpt: *A D* and blue ovpt: *P.* Sign. varieties. Printer: BABNC.

		VG	VF	UNC
S856	**5 DOLLARS** 1.3.1883. S. de Champlain at lower l., paddle wheel steamboat "Quebec" at upper ctr.	700.00	1325.	—
S857	**10 DOLLARS** 1.3.1883. J. Cartier at l., farmer plowing w/horses at upper ctr.	700.00	1325.	—

1891 ISSUE

#S861 and S862 black on green unpt. A. Gaboury at lower r. Red ovpt: *A D* and *R* or blue ovpt: *P.* Sign. varieties. Back green; Quebec City arms at ctr. Printer: BABNC.

		VG	VF	UNC
S861	**5 DOLLARS** 2.1.1891. S. de Champlain at lower l., steam train at upper ctr.	700.00	1325.	—
S862	**10 DOLLARS** 2.1.1891. J. Cartier at lower l., farmer plowing w/horses at upper ctr.	700.00	1325.	—

1897 ISSUE

#S866 and S867 black on orange unpt. Sign. varieties. Back green; Quebec City arms at ctr. Printer: BABNC.

		GOOD	FINE	XF
S866	**5 DOLLARS** 2.1.1897. S. de Champlain at lower l., steam passenger train at upper ctr., Britannia leaning on globe, flag at lower r.			
	a. R.h. sign. title: *PRESIDENT.*	70.00	225.00	625.00
	b. R.h. sign. title: *PRÉSIDENT.*	65.00	200.00	500.00

		GOOD	FINE	XF
S867	**10 DOLLARS** 2.1.1897. J. Cartier at lower l., farmer plowing w/horses at upper ctr., Qn. Victoria in "Widow's Weeds" at lower r.			
	a. R.h. sign. title: *PRESIDENT.*	90.00	300.00	770.00
	b. R.h. sign. title: *PRÉSIDENT.*	70.00	225.00	625.00

1922 ISSUE

#S871-S875 Back green; Quebec City arms at ctr. Printer: BABNC.

#S871-S873, and S875 portr. G. E. Amyot at r.

		VG	VF	UNC
S871	**5 DOLLARS** 2.11.1922. Black on olive unpt. Monument at l.			
	a. Issued note.	770.00	1550.	—
	s. Specimen.	—	—	225.00

		VG	VF	UNC
S872	**10 DOLLARS** 2.11.1922. Black and orange. Portr. J. Cartier sighting land at l. Specimen.	—	—	250.00
S873	**20 DOLLARS** 2.11.1922. Black and orange. Quebec Citadel at l.			
	a. Issued note.	1125.	2300.	—
	s. Specimen.	—	—	250.00
S874	**50 DOLLARS** 2.11.1922. Black and brown. Portr. G. E. Amyot at ctr. Specimen.	—	—	275.00
S875	**100 DOLLARS** 2.11.1922. Black and brown. Specimen.	—	—	300.00

BANK OF THE PEOPLE

Issued at Toronto, Upper Canada.

1836-40 ISSUE

#S875A-S875E black. Printer: Durand, Burton & Edmonds, N. York.

		GOOD	FINE	XF
S875A	**1 DOLLAR = 5 SHILLINGS** 12.10.1836. Seated allegorical woman at l., sailboats in Toronto harbor at upper ctr., small steamboat at bottom ctr., seated allegorical male w/chest and anchor at r.			
	a. Issued note.	650.00	1750.	—
	p. Partially engraved date. Proof.	—	Unc	625.00
S875B	**2 DOLLARS = 10 SHILLINGS** 18xx. Paddle wheel steamboat at l., seated allegorical woman at top ctr., small passenger train at bottom ctr. Sail boats in Toronto harbor at r. Proof.	—	Unc	625.00
S875C	**3 DOLLARS** 9.10.1840. 3 seated allegorical women at top ctr.	700.00	2000.	—
S875D	**4 DOLLARS = 20 SHILLINGS** 9.10.1840. Portr. J. Fox at l., reclining Indian maiden at top ctr.	675.00	1950.	—
S875E	**8 DOLLARS = 2 POUNDS** 8.6.1840. Supported royal arms at top ctr., small horse's head at bottom ctr.	1375.	3925.	—
S875F	**10 DOLLARS** 18xx. Portr. J. Fox at l., reclining allegorical woman w/lion shield and farm tools, ships in background at upper ctr., small crown at bottom ctr., standing young farm girl at r. Proof.	—	Unc	625.00

BANQUE DU PEUPLE

Issued at Montreal, Lower Canada.

1835-36 ISSUE

#S876-S879 black. Back blue; standing male citizen at ctr. Sign. varieties. Printer: RWH & Co.

		GOOD	FINE	XF
S876	**1 DOLLAR** 11.7.1835; 2.8.1836. Seated shepherd boy at l.; men w/cattle and sheep at upper ctr., small child riding deer at bottom ctr., cherub at r.	185.00	625.00	—
S877	**2 DOLLARS** 11.7.1835. Portr. of man at l, two allegorical women at upper ctr., small man in canoe at bottom ctr., seated allegorical male at r.	180.00	625.00	—
S878	**5 DOLLARS** 1835. Portr. L.-J. Papineau at l., woman in lion drawn chariot at upper ctr., small sailing ship at bottom ctr.			
	a. Title: *Cassier* at lower l. 11.7.1835.	250.00	850.00	—
	r. Company name at lower l. Remainder. 18xx.	—	Unc	500.00
S879	**10 DOLLARS** 1836. Sailing ship and Commerce at upper ctr., portr. L.-J. Papineau at r.			
	a. Title: *Cassier* at lower l. 2.3.1836.	250.00	850.00	—
	r. Company name at lower l. Remainder. 18xx.	—	Unc	500.00

1838 ISSUE

		GOOD	FINE	XF
S881	**5 DOLLARS** 1.7.1838. Black. Seated woman w/lamb at l., farm family at top ctr., 5 Spanish 8 reales coins vertically at r. Back blue; standing citizen at l., farmer picking corn at r. Printer: RWH & Co.			
	a. Printed date: 18xx.	100.00	350.00	—
	b. Printed date: 1838.	275.00	850.00	—

1839 ISSUE

#S882 and S883 black. Company name at lower l. Dollars only. Printer: Durand & Co.

		GOOD	FINE	XF
S882	**1 DOLLAR** 1.10.1839. Portr. Christ child at l. and r., angel w/shield of Britannia, cherub at upper ctr. Back blue; Spanish 8 Reales coin at l., Agriculture at ctr., standing male citizen at r.	145.00	700.00	—
S883	**2 DOLLARS** 1.10.1839. Seated woman w/shield at l., angel w/shield of Britannia at upper ctr. Back blue; 2 Spanish 8 reales coins at l.	165.00	775.00	—

1845 ISSUE

#S884 and S885 black. Dollars and shillings. Printer: Durand & Co.

		GOOD	FINE	XF
S884	**1 DOLLAR = 5 SHILLINGS** 1.3.1845. Like #S882 but w/bilingual denominations and w/*Cash* at lower l.	235.00	700.00	—

		GOOD	FINE	XF
S885	**2 DOLLARS = 10 SHILLINGS** 1.3.1845. Like #S883 but w/bilingual denominations and w/*Cash* at lower l.	300.00	770.00	—

1845-50 ISSUE

#S886-S893 black. Blue ovpt: *TORONTO*. Sign. variety. Printer: TCC.

		GOOD	FINE	XF
S886	**1 DOLLAR = 5 SHILLINGS** 1.9.1846-1.3.1850. Cooper making barrel at l., farm boy w/wheat sheaf and cradle at top ctr., 4 cherubs w/lg. "1" at lower r. Back blue; standing citizen at l. and r.	215.00	735.00	—

		GOOD	FINE	XF
S887	**2 DOLLARS = 10 SHILLINGS** 1.9.1846; 1.3.1850. Farmer sharpening scythe at lower l., blacksmith and logger at upper ctr., dog at lower r. Back blue; standing male citizen at ctr.	220.00	770.00	—
S888	**4 DOLLARS = 20 SHILLINGS** 1.5.1847. Seated carpenter at l., milkmaids by cows at top ctr. r., blacksmith at r. Back blue; portr. of young woman at ctr.	280.00	910.00	—
S889	**5 DOLLARS = 1 POUND-5 SHILLINGS** 184x. Seated Commerce at l., woman w/sheaves in lg. ornate *V* at ctr., allegorical seated woman on globe w/trumpet at r. Face proof.	—	Unc	350.00
S890	**10 DOLLARS = 2 POUNDS-10 SHILLINGS** 184x. 2 allegorical women w/ornate *X* at l. and r., Qn. Victoria and Prince Albert w/cherubs along top. Face proof.	—	Unc	350.00
S891	**20 DOLLARS = 5 POUNDS** 1.3.1845. Sailor w/telescope at l., small steamboat at bottom ctr., man plowing w/horses at upper r.	355.00	1200.	—
S892	**50 DOLLARS = 12 POUNDS-10 SHILLINGS** 1.3.1845. Canal boat at l., reclining sailor w/flag, sailing ship in background at upper ctr., young girl's bust at bottom ctr., paddle wheel steamboat at r.	355.00	1200.	—
S893	**100 DOLLARS = 25 POUNDS** 184x. Portr. of woman at l., Montreal harbor at ctr., small shield at bottom ctr., portr. of woman at r. Face proof.	—	Unc	350.00

1854-70 ISSUES

#S896-S902 dollars and pound/shillings. Sign. varieties. Printer: TCC.

		GOOD	FINE	XF
S896	**1 DOLLAR = 5 SHILLINGS** 2.5.1870. Black. Like #S886 but w/green *ONE* protector on face only. Back blue.			
	a. Inscription above signature.	200.00	625.00	—
	b. Inscription deleted.	200.00	625.00	—
S897	**2 DOLLARS = 10 SHILLINGS** 2.5.1870. Black. Like #S887 but w/green *TWO* protector on face only. Back blue.	210.00	735.00	—
S898	**4 DOLLARS = 20 SHILLINGS** 2.1.1854. Black. Like #S888 but w/green *FOUR* protector on face only. Back blue.	250.00	850.00	—
S899	**4 DOLLARS = 20 SHILLINGS** 2.5.1870. Black on green unpt. Like #S898 but back green. Printers: TCC and BABNC.	270.00	875.00	—
S900	**5 DOLLARS = 1 POUND-5 SHILLINGS** 2.5.1870. Black on green unpt. Like #S889 but back green.	Reported Not Confirmed		
S901	**10 DOLLARS = 2 POUNDS-10 SHILLINGS** 2.5.1870. Black on green unpt. Like #S890 but back green.	Reported Not Confirmed		
S902	**20 DOLLARS = 5 POUNDS** 2.5.1870. Black on green unpt. Like #S891 but back green. Red ovpt: *S* twice.	335.00	1125.	—

1882 ISSUE

#S903 and S904 black on green unpt. Back blue. Dollars and pounds/shillings. Sign. varieties. Printers: TCC and BABNC.

		GOOD	FINE	XF
S903	5 DOLLARS = 1 POUND-5 SHILLINGS 2.5.1882. Blue ovpt: *QUEBEC* twice.	270.00	875.00	—
S904	10 DOLLARS = 2 POUNDS-10 SHILLINGS 2.5.1882. Red ovpt: *D M* twice.	315.00	975.00	—

1885-92 ISSUE

#S906-S909 black on green unpt. Back blue. Dollars only. Sign. varieties.

		GOOD	FINE	XF
S906	5 DOLLARS 1885-1892. Face like #S900.			
	a. Blue numbers. Blue ovpt: *QUEBEC* twice. Printers: TCC and BABNC. 6.11.1885.	300.00	850.00	—
	b. As a. 2.7.1892.	350.00	1000.	—
	c. Red numbers. Red ovpt: *S S*. Printers: TCC and CBNC. 6.11.1885.	285.00	875.00	—

		GOOD	FINE	XF
S907	10 DOLLARS 2.5.1888. Face like #S901. Blue numbers. Printers: TCC and BABNC. Face proof.	—	Unc	350.00
S908	50 DOLLARS 6.11.1885. Face like #S892.			
	a. Red numbers. Printers: TCC and CABNC.	335.00	1125.	—
	p. Face proof. Blue numbers. Printers: TCC and BABNC.	—	Unc	350.00
S909	100 DOLLARS 6.11.1885. Face like #S893.			
	a. Blue numbers. Printers: TCC and BABNC.	—	Unc	350.00
	p. Face proof. Red numbers. Printers: TCC and CABNC.	—	Unc	350.00

BANQUE PROVINCIALE DU CANADA

Issued at Montreal, Quebec.

1900 ISSUE

#S911 and S912 black on green unpt. Supported bank crest at ctr. Sign. varieties. Printer: BABNC.

		GOOD	FINE	XF
S911	5 DOLLARS 2.7.1900. Farm woman w/cow and calf at lower l., lumberjack chopping tree at lower r. Indians on bluff at ctr. on back.	375.00	1250.	2800.
S912	10 DOLLARS 2.7.1900. 2 allegorical women at lower l., steamship at lower r.	—	Unc	350.00

1907 ISSUE

#S913 and S914 T. Bienvenu at lower l., H. Laporte at lower r. Back green; head office bldg. facade at ctr. Sign. varieties. Printer: BABNC.

		VG	VF	UNC
S913	5 DOLLARS 1.6.1907. Steam passenger train at station at ctr.			
	a. Black on green unpt.	455.00	910.00	—
	b. Black on brown unpt. Face proof.	—	—	350.00

		GOOD	FINE	XF
S914	10 DOLLARS 1.6.1907. Black on green unpt. Steamboat "Montreal" at ctr.	840.00	1750.	—

1913; 1928 ISSUE

#S916-S918 portr. H. Laporte at l. or l. ctr., portr. T. Bienvenu at r. or ctr. r. Head office bldg. facade at ctr. on back. All notes w/2 portr. Sign. varieties. Printer: ABNC or CBNC.

		VG	VF	UNC
S916	5 DOLLARS 1913-28. Back green.			
	a. Black on orange and green unpt. 2.1.1913.	210.00	420.00	1400.
	b. 31.1.1919.	105.00	210.00	700.00
	c. Black on green and yellow unpt. 31.1.1919.	35.00	87.50	350.00
	d. 1.8.1928.	25.00	70.00	225.00

		VG	VF	UNC
S917	10 DOLLARS 1913-28.			
	a. Black on orange and yellow-green unpt. Back orange. 2.1.1913.	65.00	140.00	545.00
	b. 31.1.1919.	75.00	175.00	700.00
	c. Black on brown and yellow unpt. Back brown. 31.1.1919.	25.00	65.00	280.00
	d. 1.8.1928.	25.00	65.00	280.00

		VG	VF	UNC
S918	20 DOLLARS 1.8.1928. Black on blue unpt. Back blue.	75.00	155.00	600.00

1935 ISSUE

#S919 and S920 portr. S. J. B. Roland at ctr. Bank bldg. at ctr. on back. Reduced size notes. Printer: BABNC.

		VG	VF	UNC
S919	5 DOLLARS 2.1.1935. Brown. Back green.	16.50	50.00	200.00

		VG	VF	UNC
S920	10 DOLLARS 2.1.1935. Black. Back olive-green.	18.50	35.00	110.00

1936 ISSUE

#S921 and S922 portr. C. A. Roy at ctr. Bank bldg. at ctr. on back. Printer: CBNC.

		VG	VF	UNC
S921	5 DOLLARS 1.9.1936. Black on yellow and blue unpt.			
	a. Back blue.	16.50	50.00	200.00
	b. Back green.	37.50	87.50	280.00
	p. Proof.	—	—	—

		VG	VF	UNC
S922	10 DOLLARS 1.9.1936. Black on yellow and orange unpt.			
	a. Back orange.	25.00	75.00	225.00
	b. Back green.	21.00	27.50	135.00
	p. Face proof w/green tint.	—	—	—

BANQUE DE ST. HYACINTHE

Issued at St. Hyacinthe, Quebec.

1874 ISSUE

#S924-S926 black on green unpt. Back green. Printer: BABNC.

		VG	VF	UNC
S924	4 DOLLARS 2.1.1874. Farmer w/cornstalks at l., shepherd boy at ctr., P. Bachand at r. Face proof.	—	—	350.00
S925	5 DOLLARS 2.1.1874. Allegorical woman at lower l., farmer watering livestock at top ctr., G. C. Dessaulles at lower r. Face proof.	—	—	350.00
S926	10 DOLLARS 2.1.1874. St. John the Baptist w/lamb at lower l., farmer plowing w/horses at lower ctr. G. C. Dessaulles at lower r. Face proof.	—	—	350.00

1880-92 Issue

#S927 and S928 sign. varieties. Printer: BABNC.

		VG	VF	Unc
S927	**5 Dollars** 1.7.1880. Black on green unpt. Similar to #S925. Back green.	2100.	4400.	—
S928	**10 Dollars** 1.7.1880. Black on green unpt. Similar to #S926. Back green.	2250.	4700.	—
S929	**20 Dollars** 2.1.1892. Black on yellow-green and green unpt. Shepherdess w/sheep at l., crowned Canadian arms at l. ctr., allegorical woman at lower r. Back brown. Printer: CBNC and BABNC.	2250.	4700.	—

Banque de St. Jean

Issued at St. Jean, Quebec.

1873-1900 Issue

#S931-S933 black on green unpt. St. John the Baptist w/lamb at r. Back green. Sign. varieties. Printer: BABNC.

		VG	VF	Unc
S931	**4 Dollars** 1.9.1873. Supported ornate *4* w/shield at l., L. Molleur at upper ctr. r.	2100.	4400.	—
S932	**5 Dollars** 1873; 1900. L. Molleur at l., workers, factories w/lg. ornate, *5* at top ctr.			
	a. 1.9.1873.	2450.	5150.	—
	b. 1.4.1900.	2100.	4400.	—
S933	**10 Dollars** 1873; 1881. L. Molleur at upper l., 2 seated allegorical women w/lg. ornate *X* at bottom ctr.			
	a. 1.9.1873.	2450.	5150.	—
	b. 1.4.1881.	2100.	4400.	—

1906 Issue

#S934 and S935 black on green unpt. Similar to #S932 and S933 but w/J. Cartier replacing L. Molleur at l. Printer: BABNC.

		VG	VF	Unc
S934	**5 Dollars** 1.4.1906. Similar to #S932.	2100.	4400.	—
S935	**10 Dollars** 1.4.1906. Similar to #S933.	2100.	4400.	—

Banque Ville-Marie

Issued at Montreal, Quebec.

1873-90 Issue

#S936-S939 black on green unpt. Montreal harbor at upper ctr. Back green. Red ovpt: *TROIS-RIVIERES* and *SOREL*, red ovpt: *F* and blue ovpt: *N N*. Sign. varieties. Printer: BABNC.

		Good	Fine	XF
S936	**4 Dollars** 1873-79. St. John the Baptist w/lamb at lower r.			
	a. Red ovpt: *TROIS-RIVIERES*. 2.1.1873.	550.00	1675.	—
	p. Face proof. 1.8.1879.	—	Unc	425.00
S937	**5 Dollars** 1873-85. S. de Champlain at lower l.			
	a. 2.1.1873.	550.00	1825.	—
	b. 1.10.1885.	550.00	1825.	—
	p. Face proof. 1.8.1879.	—	Unc	425.00
S938	**10 Dollars** 1873-85. J. Cartier shipboard sighting land at lower l.			
	a. 2.1.1873.	550.00	1825.	—
	p. Face proof. 1.10.1885.	—	Unc	425.00
S939	**50 Dollars** 1885-90. Young "Lucy" at lower l., St. John the Baptist w/lamb at lower r.			
	a. 1.10.1885.	575.00	2800.	—
	p. Face proof. 1.9.1890.	—	Unc	425.00

1889 Issues

#S941-S943 black on green unpt. Red serial #. Blue ovpt: *W W*. Sign. varieties. Printer: CABNC.

		VG	VF	Unc
S941	**5 Dollars** 2.1.1889. Montreal harbor at l. ctr., portr. D. Maisonneuve at lower r.	1200.	2250.	—

		VG	VF	Unc
S942	**10 Dollars** 2.1.1889. Steam powered sailing ship at lower l., portr. D. Maisonneuve at lower r.	1325.	2600.	—
S943	**20 Dollars** 2.1.1889. D. Maisonneuve at upper l., *20* between griffins at ctr. r.	1325.	2600.	—

#S944-S946 like S941-943. Blue serial #. Printer: BABNC.

		VG	VF	Unc
S944	**5 Dollars** 2.1.1889.	1325.	2600.	—
S945	**10 Dollars** 2.1.1889.	1200.	2250.	—
S946	**20 Dollars** 2.1.1889.	1200.	2250.	—

Barclays Bank (Canada)

1929 Issue

#S947-S949 seated allegorical female w/globe at ctr. Bank bldg. facade at ctr. on back. Sign. varieties. Printer: CBNC.

		VG	VF	Unc
S947	**5 Dollars** 3.9.1929. Black on green unpt. Back green.			
	a. Sign. J. R. Bruce and R. L. Bordon.	275.00	575.00	2000.
	b. Sign. F. H. Dickenson and R. L. Bordon.	275.00	575.00	2000.
	c. Sign. H. A. Stevenson and R. L. Bordon.	275.00	575.00	2000.
S948	**10 Dollars** 3.9.1929. Black on orange unpt.			
	a. Sign. J. R. Bruce and R. L. Bordon.	275.00	575.00	2000.
	b. Sign. F. H. Dickenson and R. L. Bordon.	275.00	575.00	2000.
	c. Sign. H. A. Stevenson and R. L. Bordon.	275.00	575.00	2000.
S949	**20 Dollars** 3.9.1929. Black on blue unpt. Back blue.			
	a. Sign. J. R. Bruce and R. L. Bordon.	315.00	660.00	2250.
	b. Sign. H. A. Stevenson and R. L. Bordon.	315.00	660.00	2250.

1935 Issue

#S950 and S951 similar to #S947 and S948 but reduced size.

		VG	VF	Unc
S950	**5 Dollars** 2.1.1935. Black on green unpt. Back green.			
	a. Sign. H. A. Stevenson and R. L. Bordon.	32.50	125.00	500.00
	s. Sign. H. A. Stevenson and A. A. Magee. Specimen.	—	—	700.00
S951	**10 Dollars** 2.1.1935. Black on orange unpt. Back orange.			
	a. Sign. H. A. Stevenson and R. L. Bordon.	32.50	125.00	500.00
	b. Sign. H. A. Stevenson and A. A. Magee.	32.50	125.00	500.00

CANADIAN BANK OF COMMERCE

Issued at Toronto, Ontario.

1867-71 ISSUE

#S952-S957 black on green unpt. Back green. Some notes of 1867 have blue ovpt: *GUELPH, HAMILTON, LONDON* or *ST. CATHARINES*, and red ovpt: *G* with blue ovpt: *ST. CATHARINES*. Sign. varieties. Printer: BABNC.

		VG	VF	UNC
S952	**1 DOLLAR** 1.5.1867. Woman on shell drawn by dolphins at upper l., sm. woman's bust at bottom ctr., Indian maiden at lower r.	425.00	1050.	—

		VG	VF	UNC
S953	**2 DOLLARS** 1.5.1867. Anchor, crate and barrel at lower l., sm. beaver at bottom ctr., seated allegorical woman at wharf at lower r.	700.00	1750.	—

		VG	VF	UNC
S954	**4 DOLLARS** 1.7.1870. Elderly woman teaching young girl to knit at lower l., cattle at ctr., beehive at lower r.	600.00	2000.	—

		VG	VF	UNC
S955	**5 DOLLARS** 1867-71. Portr. Qn. Victoria in "Widow's Weeds" at ctr.			
	a. 1.5.1867.	700.00	2100.	—
	b. Text: *CAPITAL $4,000,000* at bottom. 1.5.1871.	700.00	2100.	—
	c. Text: *CAPITAL $6,000,000* at bottom. 1.5.1871.	700.00	2100.	—

NOTE: #S955b counterfeits w/E. J. Smith as Cashier are abundant.

		VG	VF	UNC
S956	**10 DOLLARS** 1867-71. Supported royal arms at upper ctr.			
	a. 1.5.1867.	—	Rare	—
	b. Text: *CAPITAL $4,000,000* at bottom. 1.5.1871.	—	Rare	—
	c. Text: *CAPITAL $6,000,000* at bottom. 1.5.1871.	—	Rare	—

NOTE: #S956c counterfeits are abundant.

		VG	VF	UNC
S957	**50 DOLLARS** 1.7.1870. Reclining allegory Intelligence at lower l., seated allegory Science w/child holding torch upwards at r.			
	a. Text: *CAPITAL $4,000,000* at bottom.	—	Rare	—
	b. Text: *CAPITAL $6,000,000* at bottom.	—	Rare	—

NOTE: Only 12 examples of #S957 were outstanding in 1922.

1879; 1887 ISSUES

#S958-S959 black on green unpt. Back green. Sign. varieties. Printer: BABNC.

#S958 and S958A Canadian arms at ctr.

		VG	VF	UNC
S958	**5 DOLLARS** 1.1.1879. Rectangular frame around portr. W. McMaster at ctr. Canadian arms on back.	2100.	—	—

		VG	VF	UNC
S958A	**5 DOLLARS** 1.1.1879. Similar to #S958 but w/oval frame around portr.	2100.	—	—

		VG	VF	UNC
S959	**10 DOLLARS** 3.1.1887. Portr. W. McMaster at l., steam ship at ctr., portr. H. W. Darling at r. Lathework, counters and bank name on back.	—	—	—

NOTE: #S959 was withdrawn shortly afer issue because the green tint pattern blurred easily.

1888; 1893 ISSUES

Sign. varieties. Printer: ABNC.

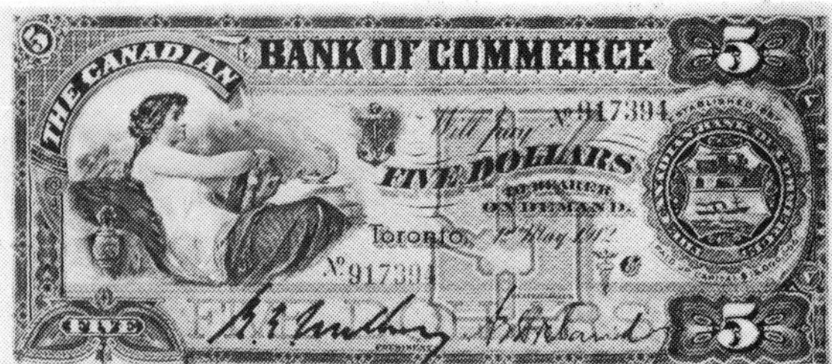

S960 5 DOLLARS

1888-1912. Black on orange and yellow-brown unpt. Reclining allegorical woman w/lamp at l., bank seal at r. Back red-brown.

	VG	VF	UNC
a. 2.1.1888.	425.00	850.00	—
b. 2.1.1892.	140.00	280.00	—
c. Red ovpt: *D D.* 2.1.1892.	—	500.00	—
d. Blue, green or purple ovpt: *YUKON* twice. 2.1.1892.	2100.	3500.	—
e. 2.1.1901.	140.00	280.00	—
f. Red ovpt: *DAWSON* twice. 2.1.1901.	—	2950.	—
g. W/or w/o red ovpt: *E E* or *H H.* 2.1.1906.	140.00	280.00	—
h. 8.1.1907.	80.00	205.00	—
i. 1.5.1912.	80.00	205.00	—

S961 10 DOLLARS

1888-1912. Black on yellow and red unpt. Bank seal at l., cherubs around portr. of Minerva at ctr., seated child painting at r. Back blue.

	VG	VF	UNC
a. 2.1.1888.	420.00	980.00	—
b. 2.1.1892.	140.00	280.00	—
c. Blue, green or purple ovpt: *YUKON* twice. 2.1.1892.	2100.	—	—
d. 2.1.1901.	87.50	175.00	—
e. Red ovpt: *DAWSON* twice. 2.1.1901.	—	2950.	—
f. 2.1.1906.	140.00	280.00	—
g. 8.1.1907; 1.5.1912.	80.00	155.00	—

S962 20 DOLLARS

1888-1912. Black on orange and green unpt. Reclining child w/dolphin, sailing ships in background at l., bank seal at ctr. r., seated allegorical woman w/globe and urn at lower r. Back orange.

	VG	VF	UNC
a. 2.1.1888.	840.00	—	—
b. 2.1.1892.	840.00	—	—
c. Red, green or orange ovpt: *YUKON* twice. 2.1.1892.	2100.	—	—
d. 2.1.1901.	350.00	—	—
e. Brown ovpt: *YUKON* twice. 2.1.1901.	2100.	—	—
f. Red or green ovpt: *DAWSON* twice. 2.1.1901.	—	3425.	—
g. 2.1.1906.	350.00	—	—
h. 8.1.1907.	350.00	—	—
i. 1.5.1912.	80.00	157.50	—
p. Proof. 2.1.1901; 1.5.1912.			

S963 50 DOLLARS

1893-1912. Black on yellow and brown unpt. Reclining allegorical woman w/spilled urn and lyre at ctr. Back brown.

	VG	VF	UNC
a. 3.7.1893.	1050.	—	—
b. Red, green or orange ovpt: *YUKON* twice. 3.7.1893.	—	Rare	—
c. 2.1.1901.	1050.	—	—
d. Red or green ovpt: *DAWSON* twice. 2.1.1901.	—	Rare	—
e. 2.1.1906.	1050.	—	—
f. 8.1.1907; 1.5.1912.	840.00	—	—
p. Proof. 2.1.1907; 1.5.1912.	—	—	—
s. Specimen. 2.1.1901; 2.1.1906; 1.5.1912.	—	—	—

S964 100 DOLLARS

1888-1912. Black on orange and blue unpt. Seated allegorical woman w/books and globe at ctr. Back dk. green.

	VG	VF	UNC
a. 1.5.1912.	500.00	—	—
p. Face proof. 2.1.1888; 2.1.1901; 2.1.1906; 8.1.1907.	—	—	350.00
s. Specimen. 2.1.1901.	—	—	—

1917 ISSUES

#S965-S969 various allegorical figures. Bank seal between standing Mercury and Ceres at ctr. on back. Printers: ABNC, Ottawa and CBNC.

S965 5 DOLLARS

2.1.1917. Black. Allegorical group of standing Agriculture, Mercury and Invention at ctr. Back olive-green.

	VG	VF	UNC
a. Red and green seal.	45.00	105.00	425.00
b. M/c seal.	87.50	175.00	625.00

S965A 5 DOLLARS

2.1.1917. Black on green and m/c unpt. Like #S965. Back olive-green.

	VG	VF	UNC
a. Sign. B. E. Walker and J. Aird.	35.00	75.00	300.00
b. Sign. J. Aird and F. M. Gibson.	35.00	75.00	300.00
c. Sign. J. Aird and S. H. Logan w/title: *General Manager.*	37.50	100.00	315.00
d. As c, but w/title: *GENERAL MANAGER.*	20.00	40.00	175.00

S966 10 DOLLARS

	VG	VF	UNC
2.1.1917. Black. Allegories standing Juno w/bull at upper l., reclining woman at lower l. ctr., seated women w/goats at lower r., cherubs w/shield w/"X" at lower l. and r. M/c seal. Back blue.	45.00	100.00	425.00

S966A 10 DOLLARS

2.1.1917. Black on orange and m/c unpt. Back blue.

	VG	VF	UNC
a. W/o imprint. Sign. of B. E. Walker and J. Aird.	35.00	75.00	300.00
b. W/imprint. Sign. as a.	35.00	75.00	300.00
c. Sign. J. Aird and C. W. Rowley w/title: *General Manager.*	35.00	75.00	300.00
d. As c, but w/title: *GENERAL MANAGER.*	35.00	75.00	300.00
e. Sign. J. Aird and S. H. Logan w/title: *General Manager.*	35.00	75.00	300.00
f. As e, but w/title: *GENERAL MANAGER.*	25.00	55.00	175.00

		VG	VF	UNC
S967	**20 DOLLARS**			
	2.1.1917. Black. Neptune reclining w/trident at l., seated sea maidens at lower ctr. r., seated Mercury and maiden at r. Back orange.	85.00	195.00	625.00
S967A	**20 DOLLARS**			
	2.1.1917. Black on yellow and m/c unpt. Back orange.			
	a. Sign. B. E. Walker and J. Aird.	87.50	175.00	625.00
	b. Sign. J. Aird and A. St. L. Trigge.	140.00	315.00	1200.
	c. Sign. J. Aird and S. H. Logan w/title: *General Manager.*	37.50	75.00	275.00
	d. As c, but w/title: *GENERAL MANAGER.*	37.50	75.00	275.00

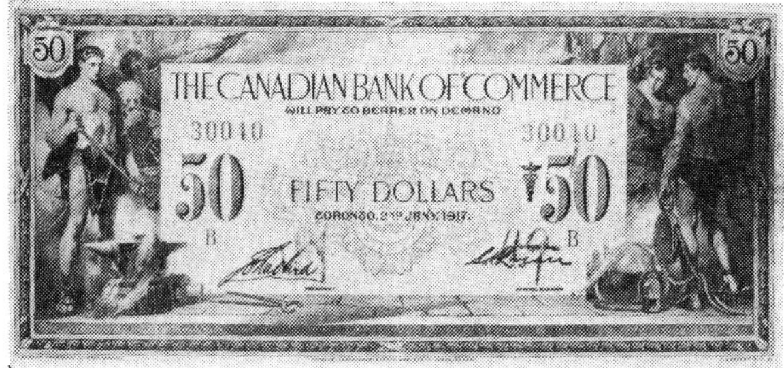

		VG	VF	UNC
S968	**50 DOLLARS**			
	2.1.1917. Black. Standing Vulcan, herculean youth at l., standing herculean youths at r. Back brown.	175.00	300.00	1125.
S968A	**50 DOLLARS**			
	2.1.1917. Black on olive-green and m/c unpt. Back brown.			
	a. Sign. B. E. Walker and J. Aird.	125.00	210.00	840.00
	b. Sign. J. Aird and S. H. Logan.	125.00	210.00	840.00

		VG	VF	UNC
S969	**100 DOLLARS**			
	2.1.1917. Black. Seated Mercury, standing Manufacturing at l., 3 seated goddesses at lower l. ctr., standing pioneer, explorer at r. Back purple.	105.00	210.00	625.00

1935 ISSUE

#S970-S972 similar to S965A-S967A but reduced size. Printer: CBNC.

		VG	VF	UNC
S970	**5 DOLLARS**			
	2.1.1935. Back olive-green. Similar to #S965A.			
	a. Sign. J. Aird and S. H. Logan.	10.00	25.00	150.00
	b. Sign. S. H. Logan and A. E. Arscott.	14.00	32.50	250.00

		VG	VF	UNC
S971	**10 DOLLARS**			
	2.1.1935. Back blue. Similar to #S966A.			
	a. Sign. J. Aird and S. H. Logan.	30.00	65.00	150.00
	b. Sign. S. H. Logan and A. E. Arscott.	25.00	45.00	185.00

		VG	VF	UNC
S972	**20 DOLLARS**			
	2.1.1935. Back orange. Similar to #S967A.	28.00	63.00	235.00

CITY BANK

Issued at St. John. New Brunswick.

1836-38 ISSUE

#S972A-S972F black. Uniface. Printer: New England Bank Note Co.

		GOOD	FINE	XF
S972A	**2 SHILLINGS-6 PENCE**			
	1.1.1838. Steam passenger train at top ctr. over small steamboat.	515.00	1400.	—

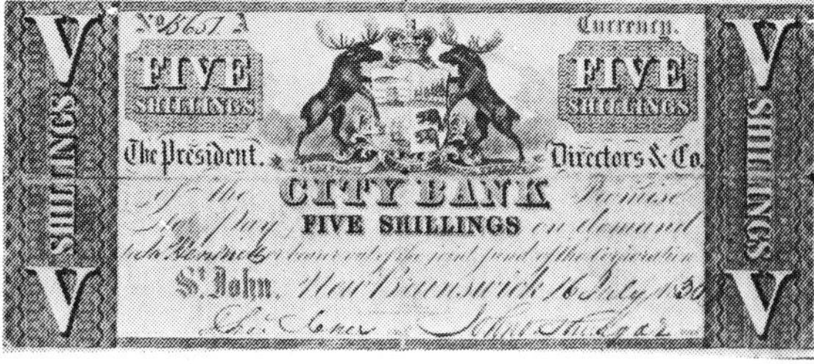

		GOOD	FINE	XF
S972B	**5 SHILLINGS**			
	16.7.1836. Crest w/moose supporters at top ctr.	515.00	1400.	—

		GOOD	FINE	XF
S972C	**1 POUND**			
	16.7.1836. Waterfront scene at top ctr.	515.00	1400.	—
S972D	**5 POUNDS**			
	18xx. Town, fence and cattle at top ctr. Face proof.	—	Unc	625.00
S972E	**10 DOLLARS**			
	18xx. Supported royal arms at top ctr. Face proof.	—	Unc	625.00
S972F	**20 DOLLARS**			
	18xx. Military encampment at top ctr. Face proof.	—	Unc	625.00

COMMERCIAL BANK OF CANADA

Issued at Kingston, Province of Canada.

1857 REGULAR ISSUES

#S973-S977 black on yellow unpt. Printer: TCC.

		GOOD	FINE	XF
S973	**1 DOLLAR** 2.1.1857. Seated Indian w/rifle at lower l, steam passenger train in countryside at upper ctr., portr. Indian maiden in oval frame at r. Uniface.			
	a. *BROCKVILLE* at bottom.	190.00	665.00	—
	b. *HAMILTON* at bottom.	190.00	665.00	—
	c. *LONDON* at bottom. Handstamp: *C* on back.	190.00	665.00	—
	d. *TORONTO* at bottom. Black handstamp: *W.*	190.00	665.00	—
S974	**2 DOLLARS** 2.1.1857. Chickens at lower l., cow and calf in stream at upper ctr., farm woman feeding chickens at lower r. Uniface.			
	a. *HAMILTON* at ends.	190.00	665.00	—
	b. *LONDON* at ends.	190.00	665.00	—
S975	**5 DOLLARS** 2.1.1857. Surveyors at l., steam passenger train in countryside at upper ctr., seated man w/pick and shovel at lower r. *KINGSTON* at ends. Red ovpt: *LONDON.* Uniface.			
	a. Brown back w/lathework and bank name.	190.00	665.00	—
S976	**5 DOLLARS** 2.1.1857. Like #975 but w/*LONDON* at ends. Uniface.			
	a. Brown back w/lathework and bank name.	170.00	665.00	—
S977	**10 DOLLARS** 2.1.1857. Portr. Qn. Victoria at lower l., 2 standing men w/sailor seated on anchor at upper ctr., portr. Princess Eugenie at lower r. *GALT* at ends. Back brown.	235.00	770.00	—

1857 MONTREAL BRANCH ISSUE

#S978-S983 black on yellow unpt. Printer: TCC.

		GOOD	FINE	XF
S978	**1 DOLLAR** 2.1.1857. Standing Indian at l., seated farmer w/scythe at ctr., farm woman w/sheaf at lower r. *MONTREAL* at bottom. Uniface.	275.00	840.00	—
S979	**2 DOLLARS** 2.1.1857. Seated Indian maiden w/shield, cattle and sheep at water's edge. *MONTREAL* at ends. Uniface. Face proof.	—	Unc	350.00
S980	**5 DOLLARS** 2.1.1857. Portr. of C. Columbus at l., sailing ships in harbor at ctr., sailor w/sextant at r. *MONTREAL* at ends. Back brown. Face proof.	—	Unc	350.00
S981	**10 DOLLARS** 2.1.1857. Woman, Montreal arms at l., harbor scene at ctr., bust of Wellington at r. *MONTREAL* at bottom. Back brown.	275.00	840.00	—
S982	**100 DOLLARS** 2.1.1857. Bank bldg. at upper ctr., portr. Princess Eugenie at lower r. *MONTREAL* at bottom. Back brown. Face proof.	—	Unc	420.00
S983	**1000 DOLLARS = 250 POUNDS** 2.1.1857. Portr. Princess Eugenie at ctr. *MONTREAL* at ctr. r. Back brown. Face proof.	—	Unc	625.00

1857-61 REGULAR ISSUE

		GOOD	FINE	XF
S986	**1 DOLLAR** 1860-61. Like #S973. Uniface.			
	a. *BELLEVILLE* at ends. 2.1.1860.	160.00	500.00	—
	b. *BROCKVILLE* at ends. Black handstamp: *K.* 2.1.1860.	160.00	500.00	—
	c. *INGERSOLL* at ends. 2.1.1860.	160.00	500.00	—
	d. *KINGSTON* at ends. 2.1.1860.	160.00	500.00	—
	e. *LONDON* at ends. 2.1.1860.	160.00	500.00	—
	f. *PERTH* at ends. 2.1.1860.	160.00	500.00	—
	g. *TORONTO* at ends. 2.1.1860.	160.00	500.00	—
	h. *WINDSOR* at ends. 2.1.1860.	160.00	500.00	—
	p. *KINGSTON* at ends. Proof. 2.1.1861.	—	Unc	275.00

		GOOD	FINE	XF
S987	**2 DOLLARS** 2.1.1860. Like #S974.			
	a. *BELLEVILLE* at ends.	160.00	500.00	—
	b. *HAMILTON* at ends.	135.00	420.00	—
	c. *KINGSTON* at ends.	160.00	500.00	—
	d. *LONDON* at ends.	160.00	500.00	—
	e. *WINDSOR* at ends.	160.00	500.00	—
	p1. *PORT HOPE* at ends. Proof.	—	Unc	275.00
	p2. *PRESCOTT* at ends. Proof.	—	Unc	275.00

		GOOD	FINE	XF
S988	**5 DOLLARS** 2.1.1860. Like #S975.			
	p1. *CHATHAM* at ends. Proof.	—	Unc	275.00
	p2. *KINGSTON* at ends. Proof.	—	Unc	275.00

1860-62 MONTREAL BRANCH ISSUE

#S991-S996 black on green unpt. Uniface.

#S991-S993 printer: TCC.

		GOOD	FINE	XF
S991	**1 DOLLAR** 2.1.1860. Like #S978. *MONTREAL* at bottom. Proof.	—	Unc	350.00
S992	**2 DOLLARS** 2.1.1860. Like #S979. *MONTREAL* at bottom. Proof.	—	Unc	350.00
S993	**5 DOLLARS** 2.1.1860. Like #S980. *MONTREAL* at bottom. Proof.	—	Unc	350.00
S994	**10 DOLLARS** 2.1.1860. Like #S981. *MONTREAL* at bottom. Printer: TCC and ABNC. Proof.	—	Unc	425.00
S995	**100 DOLLARS** 2.1.1862. Like #S982. *MONTREAL* at bottom. Printer: ABNC. Proof.	—	Unc	525.00
S996	**1000 DOLLARS** 2.1.1860. Similar to #S983. *MONTREAL* at ctr. r. W/o imprint. Proof.	—	Unc	875.00

COMMERCIAL BANK OF MANITOBA

Issued at Winnipeg, Manitoba.

1885 ISSUE

#S997 and S998 printer: CABNC.

		VG	VF	UNC
S997	**5 DOLLARS** 1.5.1885. Black on green unpt. Standing allegorical woman w/shield at upper l., Indian camp at ctr., portr. Qn. Victoria at r. Back brown.	3150.	—	—
S998	**10 DOLLARS** 1.5.1885. Black and yellow. Standing allegorical woman w/shield at upper l., farmers reaping grain at ctr. r. Back green.	3150.	—	—

1891 ISSUE

#S999 and S1000 black on green unpt. Head office bldg. at lower l., D. McArthur at lower r. Back green. Sign. varieties. Printer: BABNC.

		VG	VF	UNC
S999	**5 DOLLARS** 2.1.1891. Horse drawn reaper at ctr. Steam passenger train at station at ctr. on back.	3150.	—	—
S1000	**10 DOLLARS** 2.1.1891. Plowing w/horses at ctr. Crest at ctr. on back.	3150.	—	—

COMMERCIAL BANK OF THE MIDLAND DISTRICT

Issued at Kingston, Upper Canada.

1832-35 ISSUE

Dollar/Shilling System.

#S1000A and S1000B black. Uniface. Printer: Rawdon, Clark & Co.

		GOOD	FINE	XF
S1000A	**1 DOLLAR = 5 SHILLINGS** 1832-33. Paddle wheel steamboat at upper ctr., cherub face at upper and lower r. Proof.			
	a. 1.11.1833.	375.00	1050.	—
	p. Proof. 2.8.1832.	—	Unc	350.00
S1000B	**2 DOLLARS = 10 SHILLINGS** 1.3.1833; 1.1.1835. Woman seated at l., 2 allegorical women w/shield w/lg. *2* at upper ctr., town, harbor view sideways at r.	375.00	1050.	—

1836 ISSUE

#S1000C-S1000D black. Uniface. Printer: RWH & E.

		GOOD	FINE	XF
S1000C	**1 DOLLAR = 5 SHILLINGS** 1.3.1836. Indian seated at l., milk maid churning butter at ctr., farm woman w/grain at r.	375.00	1050.	—
S1000D	**2 DOLLARS = 10 SHILLINGS** 1.3.1836. Harbor scene at l., allegorical man by urn at ctr., allegorical man at upper r., allegorical woman at lower r.	375.00	1050.	—

1843 ISSUE

#S1000E-S1000H black. Uniface. Printer: RWH & C or RWH & E.

#S1000E-S1000G oval portr. Prince Consort at l., Qn. Victoria at r.

		GOOD	FINE	XF
S1000E	**1 DOLLAR = 5 SHILLINGS** 1.7.1843. Indian maiden stepping out of canoe at top ctr.	375.00	1050.	—
S1000F	**2 DOLLARS = 10 SHILLINGS** 1.7.1843. Seated Britannia and Agriculture at top ctr.	375.00	1050.	—
S1000G	**5 DOLLARS = 25 SHILLINGS** 1.7.1843. 2 seated allegorical women w/cherubs w/lg. ornate *5* at top ctr.	360.00	1050.	—
S1000H	**10 DOLLARS = 50 SHILLINGS** 1.7.1843. Portr. Qn. Victoria at l. Proof.	—	Unc	350.00

1847-54 ISSUES

Dollar/Pound Sterling System.

#S1000J-S1000Q black. Red ovpt: *TORONTO* or *BROCKVILLE*. Uniface. Printer: RWH & Co. or RWH & E.

		GOOD	FINE	XF
S1000J	**1 DOLLAR = 5 SHILLINGS** 1.7.1846; 1.7.1847; 1.7.1848; 1.7.1853; 1.7.1854. Farmer w/sickle and sheave at lower l., reclining allegorical woman w/lg. ornate *1* at upper ctr., standing sailor w/telescope at lower r.	375.00	1050.	—
S1000K	**2 DOLLARS = 10 SHILLINGS** 18xx. Justice and Liberty at l., 2 seated allegorical women w/cornucopia at top ctr., Agriculture and Commerce at r.			
	a. Issued note.	375.00	1050.	—
	p. Proof.	—	Unc	350.00

#S1000L-S1000N oval portr. Qn. Victoria at l., Prince Consort at r.

S1000L	**5 DOLLARS = 1 POUND-5 SHILLINGS** 18xx. Reclining allegorical woman on lg. ornate *5* supported by 4 cherubs at top ctr. Proof.	—	Unc	350.00
S1000M	**10 DOLLARS = 2 POUNDS-10 SHILLINGS** 18xx. Seated allegorical woman w/lg. ornate *10* at top ctr. Proof.	—	Unc	350.00
S1000N	**20 DOLLARS = 5 POUNDS** 18xx. Woman seated w/lg. ornate *20* at top ctr. Proof.	—	Unc	420.00
S1000P	**50 DOLLARS = 12 POUNDS-10 SHILLINGS** 18xx. Portr. Qn. Victoria on royal crest at l. Proof.	—	Unc	420.00
S1000Q	**100 DOLLARS = 25 POUNDS** 18xx. Allegorical woman at top ctr., royal crest at r. Proof.	—	Unc	420.00

1854 ISSUE

#S1000R and S1000S black. Uniface. Printer: RWH & Co.

		VG	VF	UNC
S1000R	**5 DOLLARS** 18xx. Mercury seated w/lion at top ctr., portr. of woman at r. Proof.	—	—	350.00

		VG	VF	UNC
S1000S	**10 DOLLARS** 2.1.1854. Allegorical male in flight holding cornucopia spilling coins at top ctr. r., sailing ships at lower r.	85.00	150.00	—

1854 BROCKVILLE ISSUE

		VG	VF	UNC
S1000T	**4 DOLLARS** 2.5.1854. Black. Green panel w/branch name at upper l. and r. Portr. of young woman lower l. and at lower r., steam passenger train in countryside at top ctr.	420.00	840.00	—

1854 HAMILTON ISSUE

		VG	VF	UNC
S1000U	**4 DOLLARS** 2.5.1854. Like #S1000T.	420.00	840.00	—

1854 LONDON ISSUE

		VG	VF	UNC
S1000V	**4 DOLLARS** 2.5.1854. Like #S1000T.	420.00	840.00	—

1854 ST. CATHERINES ISSUE

		VG	VF	UNC
S1000W	**4 DOLLARS** 2.5.1854. Like #S1000T.	420.00	840.00	—

1854 TORONTO ISSUE

		VG	VF	UNC
S1000X	**4 DOLLARS** 2.5.1854. Like #S1000T. Proof.	—	—	350.00

COMMERCIAL BANK OF WINDSOR

Issued at Windsor, Nova Scotia.

1860 ISSUE

		VG	VF	UNC
S1001	**20 DOLLARS** 186x. Black on green unpt. 2 children holding sheaves at lower l., steam passenger train at station at upper ctr., standing sailor w/lion at lower r. Back green. Printer: ABNC. Proof.	—	—	700.00

1870-98 ISSUE

#S1002-S1003A black on green unpt. Back green. Printer: BABNC.

		VG	VF	UNC
S1002	**4 DOLLARS** 1870-71. Reclining woman spilling water jar at bottom ctr., Niagara Falls in background.			
	a. 1.7.1871.	2100.	—	—
	p. Proof. 1.9.1870.	—	—	625.00
S1003	**5 DOLLARS** 1.9.1870; 1.7.1871; 1.7.1898. Proof.	—	—	625.00
S1003A	**10 DOLLARS** 1870-98.			
	a. 1.7.1871.	2100.	—	—
	p. Proof. 1.9.1870; 1.7.1898.	—	—	625.00

#S1004 *Deleted*. See #S1001.

CROWN BANK OF CANADA

Issued at Toronto, Ontario.

1904 ISSUE

#S1006-S1009 printer: BABNC.

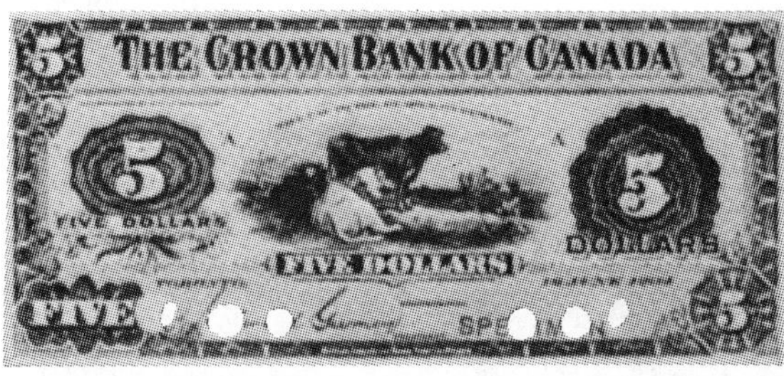

		VG	VF	UNC
S1006	**5 DOLLARS** 1.6.1904. Black on green and yellow unpt. Cattle at ctr. Back brown; crown.	2450.	—	—
S1007	**10 DOLLARS** 1.6.1904. Black on brown and yellow unpt. Lion on mountain at l. Back blue; crown. Face proof.	—	—	700.00
S1008	**20 DOLLARS** 1.6.1904. Black on red and blue unpt. Seated allegorical man, child and 2 reclining women at l. ctr. Back red; crown. Face proof.	—	—	700.00
S1009	**50 DOLLARS** 1.6.1904. Black on red and yellow unpt. Parliament bldg. at l. ctr. Back red-brown; crown. Face proof.	—	—	700.00

DOMINION BANK

Issued at Toronto, Ontario.

1871-73 ISSUE

#S1011-S1016 black on green unpt. Back green. Sign. varieties. Printer: BABNC.

		VG	VF	UNC
S1011	**4 DOLLARS** 1.2.1871. Portr. Prince Arthur at lower l., farmer watering livestock at top ctr., seated Britannia w/shield w/lg. ornate *4* at lower r.	1050.	1900.	—

		VG	VF	UNC
S1012	**5 DOLLARS** 1.2.1871. Supported oval portr. of Qn. Victoria in "Widow's Weeds" at ctr.	1050.	1900.	—
S1013	**10 DOLLARS** 1.5.1871. Girl at l., paddle wheel steamboat at top ctr., lumberjack at lower r.	1125.	2100.	—
S1014	**20 DOLLARS** 1.5.1871. Blacksmith shoeing horses at lower l., farm machinery at upper ctr., lumberjack at lower r.	1125.	2100.	—
S1015	**50 DOLLARS** 1.5.1871. Face proof.	—	—	560.00
S1016	**100 DOLLARS** 1.10.1873. Reclining woman spilling water jar at ctr., Niagara Falls in background.	1125.	2100.	—

1876-88 ISSUE

#S1017-S1020 sign. varieties.

#S1017-S1019 printer: ABNC.

		VG	VF	UNC
S1017	**4 DOLLARS** 1.1.1876. Black on green and red unpt. Laureate woman's bust at l., seated allegorical woman w/children at ctr., girl's bust at r. Back brown.	850.00	1900.	—
S1018	**5 DOLLARS** 1.1.1881. Black on blue unpt. Seated woman w/sheaf at l., 2 seated allegorical women at r. Back blue.	850.00	1900.	—
S1019	**10 DOLLARS** 2.1.1888. Black on brown and green unpt. Allegorical woman w/fasces at l., seated allegorical women by beehive at upper ctr. r. Back brown; reclining Indian at ctr.	1125.	2100.	—
S1020	**50 DOLLARS** 1.7.1881. Black on green unpt. J. Cartier sighting land at lower l., ships dockside at top ctr., Qn. Victoria in "Widow's Weeds" at lower r. Back green. Printer: BABNC.	1125.	2100.	—

1891; 1898 ISSUE

#S1021-S1022 black on green unpt. Back green. Printer: BABNC.

		VG	VF	UNC
S1021	**5 DOLLARS** 1.7.1891. Lighthouse, boats at l., farmer reaping grain w/horses at ctr., power lines and cattle at r.	975.00	1825.	—
S1022	**10 DOLLARS** 1.7.1898. Portr. F. Smith at lower l., cattle at ctr. r.	1050.	2100.	—

1896-1901 ISSUE

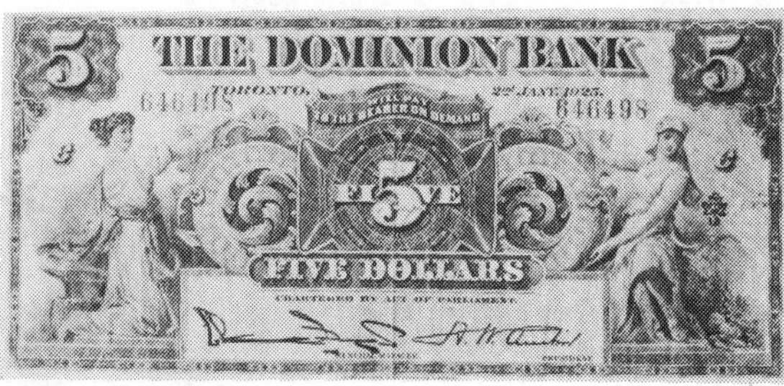

		VG	VF	UNC
S1023	**5 DOLLARS** 1896-1925. Black on green unpt. Woman kneeling at l., woman seated at r. Back green; Greek god at ctr.			
	a. 1.1.1896; 1.1.1898.	770.00	1675.	—
	b. 2.1.1900.	700.00	1550.	—
	c. 2 sign. varieties. 3.7.1905.	100.00	210.00	—
	d. 2 sign. varieties. 2.1.1925.	70.00	157.50	630.00
S1024	**10 DOLLARS** 1900-10. Black on yellow-green and green unpt. Reclining Britannia w/lion at ctr. Back red, yellow-green and green; beaver at ctr.			
	a. 2.1.1900.	210.00	420.00	—
	b. 2 sign. varieties. 3.1.1910.	65.00	135.00	455.00

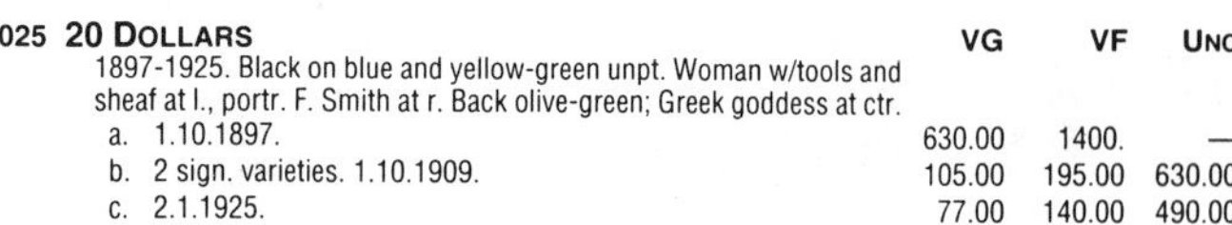

		VG	VF	UNC
S1025	**20 DOLLARS** 1897-1925. Black on blue and yellow-green unpt. Woman w/tools and sheaf at l., portr. F. Smith at r. Back olive-green; Greek goddess at ctr.			
	a. 1.10.1897.	630.00	1400.	—
	b. 2 sign. varieties. 1.10.1909.	105.00	195.00	630.00
	c. 2.1.1925.	77.00	140.00	490.00

		VG	VF	UNC
S1026	**50 DOLLARS** 1901; 1925. Black on brown, purple and green unpt. Beehive at l., livestock at r. Back m/c; beaver at ctr.			
	a. 2.7.1901.	280.00	560.00	—
	b. 2.1.1925.	195.00	350.00	—

1925 ISSUE

		VG	VF	UNC
S1027	**10 DOLLARS** 2.1.1925. Black on yellow and green unpt. Like #S1024. Back yellow and green. 2 sign. varieties.	42.00	90.00	300.00
S1027A	**50 DOLLARS** 2.1.1925. Black on blue, olive-green and m/c unpt. Like #S1026.	42.00	90.00	300.00

1931 ISSUE

#S1028-S1032 portr. A. W. Austin at l., portr. C. A. Bogert at r. Map of Canada on back. Printer: CBNC.

		VG	VF	UNC
S1028	**5 DOLLARS** 1.2.1931. Black on blue and orange unpt. Back green. 2 sign. varieties.	40.00	75.00	300.00

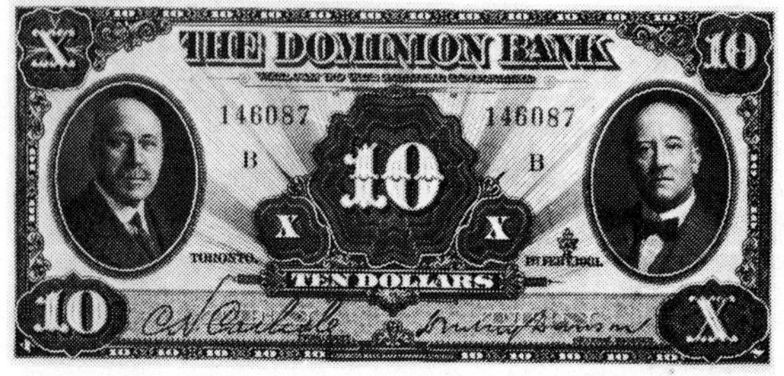

		VG	VF	UNC
S1029	**10 DOLLARS** 1.2.1931. Black on blue and orange unpt. Back blue. 2 sign. varieties.	55.00	110.00	420.00

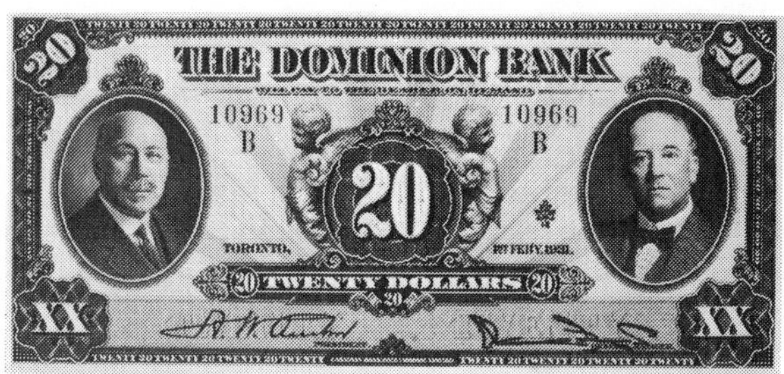

		VG	VF	UNC
S1030	**20 DOLLARS** 1.2.1931. Black on purple and orange unpt. Back purple.	55.00	185.00	600.00
S1031	**50 DOLLARS** 1.2.1931. Black on yellow, pink and orange unpt. Back orange. Specimen.	—	—	525.00
S1032	**100 DOLLARS** 1.2.1931. Black on olive and orange unpt. Back red-brown.	280.00	630.00	—

1935 ISSUE

#S1033 and S1034 similar to #S1028 and S1029 but reduced size w/portr. D. Danson at l., portr. C. H. Carlisle at r. Printer: CBNC.

		VG	VF	UNC
S1033	**5 DOLLARS** 2.1.1935 Black on green and orange unpt. Back green.	17.50	37.50	150.00
S1034	**10 DOLLARS** 2.1.1935. Black on yellow, pink and orange unpt. Back orange.	20.00	52.50	185.00

1938 ISSUE

#S1035 and S1036 similar to #S1033 and S1034 but w/portr. C. H. Carlisle at l., portr. R. Rae at r. Printer: CBNC.

		VG	VF	UNC
S1035	**5 DOLLARS** 3.1.1938. Black on orange and brown unpt. Back brown.	21.00	42.00	185.00

		VG	VF	UNC
S1036	**10 DOLLARS** 3.1.1938. Black on blue and yellow unpt. Back olive.	30.00	65.00	250.00

EASTERN TOWNSHIPS BANK

Began operations in Sherbrooke, Quebec Province in 1859. Taken over by the Canadian Bank of Commerce in 1912.

1859 ISSUE

#S1041-S1046 black on green unpt. Sign. varieties. Printer: ABNC.

		GOOD	FINE	XF
S1041	**1 DOLLAR** 1.8.1859. Portr. Qn. Victoria at lower l., Magog River Falls at upper ctr., standing Indian at upper r.			
	a. Partially engraved date. Red word protector on back.	450.00	1825.	—
	b. Engraved date, hand signed sign. of B. Pomroy at r. Red ovpt: *STANBRIDGE.*	450.00	1825.	—
	c. As b. Red ovpt: *STANSTEAD.*	450.00	1825.	—
	d. As b. Red ovpt: *WATERLOO.*	450.00	1825.	—
	e. Engraved date and printed sign. of B. Pomroy at r.	450.00	1825.	—

		GOOD	FINE	XF
S1042	**2 DOLLARS** 1.8.1859. Portr. Qn. Victoria at lower l., cattlemen on horseback w/herd at top ctr., portr. Prince Consort at lower r.			
	a. Partially engraved date. Red word protector on back.	450.00	1825.	—
	b. Engraved date; hand signed sign. of B. Pomroy at r. Red ovpt: *STANBRIDGE.*	450.00	1825.	—
	c. As b. Red ovpt: *STANSTEAD.*	450.00	1825.	—
	d. As b. Red ovpt: *WATERLOO.*	450.00	1825.	—
	e. Engraved date and printed sign. of B. Pomroy at r.	450.00	1825.	—

		GOOD	FINE	XF
S1043	**4 DOLLARS** 1859-61. Portr. Prince of Wales at lower l., Magog River Falls at upper ctr., portr. B. Pomroy at lower r. Red word protector on back.			
	a. Partially engraved date. Red ovpt: *WATERLOO.* 1.8.1859.	455.00	1825.	—
	b. Engraved date; hand signed sign. of B. Pomroy at r. 1.2.1861.	455.00	1825.	—
	c. Engraved date; printed sign. of B. Pomroy at r. 1.2.1861.	455.00	1825.	—

		GOOD	FINE	XF
S1044	**5 DOLLARS** 1.8.1859. Seated allegorical woman at lower l., horse, colt and farmer at top ctr., farmer w/scythe at lower r.			
	a. Partially engraved date. Red word protector on back.	550.00	1900.	—
	b. Engraved date; hand signed sign. of B. Pomroy at r. Red ovpt: *STANBRIDGE.*	550.00	1900.	—
	c. As b. Red ovpt: *STANSTEAD.*	550.00	1900.	—
	d. As b. Red ovpt: *WATERLOO.*	550.00	1900.	—
	e. Engraved date and printed sign. of B. Pomroy at r.	550.00	1900.	—

		GOOD	FINE	XF
S1045	**10 DOLLARS** 1.8.1859. Hunter w/dog by campfire at lower l., reclining shepherd boy at top ctr., steam train at lower r.			
	a. Partially engraved date. Red word protector on back.	650.00	2100.	—
	b. Engraved date; hand signed sign. of B. Pomroy at r. Red ovpt: *STANBRIDGE.*	650.00	2100.	—
	c. As b. Red ovpt: *STANSTEAD.*	650.00	2100.	—
	d. As b. Red ovpt: *WATERLOO.*	650.00	2100.	—
	e. Engraved date and printed sign. of B. Pomroy at r.	650.00	2100.	—

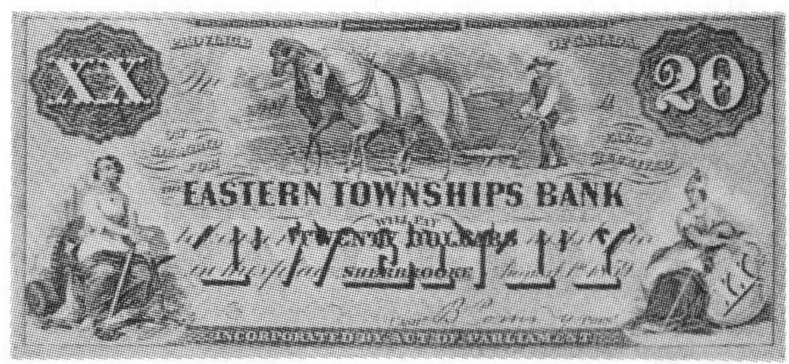

		Good	Fine	XF
S1046	**20 Dollars** 1.8.1859.			
	a. Partially engraved date. Red word protector on back.	650.00	2100.	—
	b. Engraved date; hand signed sign. of B. Pomroy at r. Red ovpt: *STANBRIDGE.*	650.00	2100.	—
	c. As b. Red ovpt: *STANSTEAD.*	650.00	2100.	—
	d. As b. Red ovpt: *WATERLOO.*	650.00	2100.	—
	e. Engraved date and printed sign. of B. Pomroy at r.	650.00	2100.	—

1873 Issue

#S1047-S1051 black on green unpt. Back green; blacksmith shoeing horse at ctr. Sign. varieties. Printer: BABNC.

		Good	Fine	XF
S1047	**4 Dollars** 1.7.1873. Farm animals at lower l., Magog River Falls at upper ctr., portr. B. Pomroy at lower r.	650.00	2100.	—

		Good	Fine	XF
S1048	**5 Dollars** 1.7.1873. Portr. Wm. Farwell at lower l., paddle wheel steamboat at upper ctr., lumberjack at lower r.	650.00	2100.	—

		Good	Fine	XF
S1049	**10 Dollars** 1.7.1873. Portr. Wm. Farwell at lower l., farmer watering livestock at top ctr., portr. B. Pomroy at lower r.	650.00	2100.	—

		Good	Fine	XF
S1050	**50 Dollars** 1.7.1873; 1.7.1874. Steam passenger train at upper l.. portr. Wm. Farwell at upper ctr. r., portr. B. Pomroy at lower r.	700.00	2250.	—

		Good	Fine	XF
S1051	**100 Dollars** 1.7.1873; 1.7.1874. Portr. Wm. Farwell at l., Magog River Falls at top ctr., portr. B. Pomroy at r.	700.00	2250.	—

1879; 1893 Issue

#S1052-S1055 black on green unpt. Back green. Sign. varieties. Printer: BABNC.

		Good	Fine	XF
S1052	**4 Dollars** 1.7.1879. Similar to #S1047 but w/portr. R. W. Heneker at lower r.	550.00	1900.	—
S1053	**5 Dollars** 1879; 1902. Like #S1048.			
	a. 1.7.1879.	550.00	1900.	—
	b. 2.7.1902.	375.00	1200.	—

		Good	Fine	XF
S1054	**10 Dollars** 1.7.1879; 2.1.1893. Similar to #S1049 but w/portr. R. W. Heneker at lower r.	575.00	2100.	—

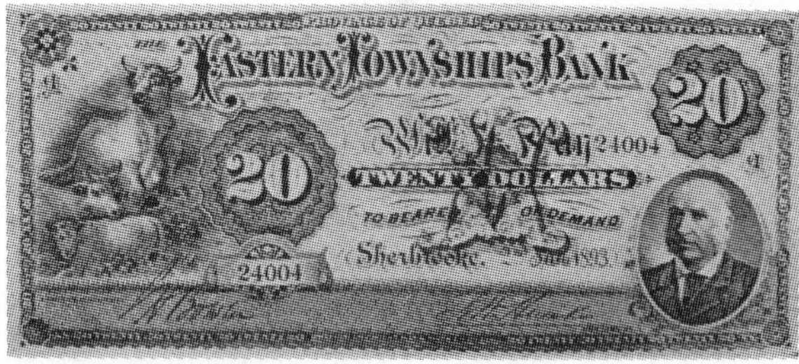

		Good	Fine	XF
S1055	**20 Dollars** 2.1.1893. Cattle at l., portr. R. W. Heneker at lower r. Bull's head at ctr. on back.	650.00	2100.	—

1906 Issue

#S1056 and S1057 back green on m/c unpt; bank crest. Sign. varieties. Printer: ABNC.

		Good	Fine	XF
S1056	**5 Dollars** 2.1.1906. Black on red and yellow unpt. Portr. J. Mackinnon at l., steam train in countryside at ctr. r.	240.00	900.00	1775.

		GOOD	FINE	XF
S1057	**10 DOLLARS** 2.1.1906. Black on orange and green unpt. Portr. Wm. Farwell at l., miners drilling at ctr.	240.00	900.00	1775.

EXCHANGE BANK OF YARMOUTH

Established in Yarmouth, Nova Scotia in 1867. Absorbed by Bank of Montreal in 1903.

1869; 1870 ISSUE

#S1058-S1060 1871 w/red ovpt: *S* and *CANADIAN CURRENCY; 1890-1902* w/red ovpt: *S*. Printer: ABNC.

		VG	VF	UNC
S1058	**5 DOLLARS** 1870-1900. Black. Sailing ships at l., sailor, man and boy on shore, fishermen in background at top ctr., young sailor at r. Back blue.			
	a. Issued note. Green unpt. 1.7.1871; 1.7.1890.	3150.	—	—
	b. Red-orange unpt. 1.7.1900.	3150.	—	—
	p. Proof. 1.8.1870.	—	—	700.00

		VG	VF	UNC
S1059	**10 DOLLARS** 1870-1900. Black. Seated allegorical woman at lower l., ships, wharf scene at top ctr., ship's carpenter at lower r. Back green.			
	a. Issued note. Green unpt. 1.7.1871; 1.7.1890.	3150.	—	—
	b. Ochre unpt. 1.7.1900.	3150.	—	—
	p. Proof. 1.8.1870.	—	—	700.00
S1060	**20 DOLLARS** 1869-1902. Black. 2 sailors dockside at lower l., wharf scene, steam passenger train, wagons at top ctr., man mounted on horse drinking at lower r. Back green.			
	a. Green unpt. 1.7.1871.	3150.	—	—
	b. Orange unpt. 1.7.1901.	3150.	—	—
	p. Blue unpt. Proof. 1.8.1869.	—	—	700.00

NOTE: All the notes of the Exchange Bank of Yarmouth are extremely rare and usually are found punched hole cancelled.

FARMERS BANK OF CANADA

Established in Toronto, Ontario in 1906. Failed in 1910.

1907 ISSUE

#S1061-S1065 sign. varieties. Printer: BABNC.

		VG	VF	UNC
S1061	**5 DOLLARS** 2.1.1907; 1.9.1908. Black on green unpt. Farmer watering livestock at upper l. Back green.	1750.	—	—
S1062	**10 DOLLARS** 2.1.1907. Black on orange unpt. Sheep grazing at upper ctr. Back green; bull's head at ctr.	3150.	—	—
S1063	**25 DOLLARS** 1907-08. Black on gold unpt. Portr. Sir W. Laurier at l., J. P. Whitney at r. Back gold.			
	a. 1.9.1908.	4200.	—	—
	p. Face proof. 2.1.1907.	—	—	1050.
S1064	**50 DOLLARS** 2.1.1907. Black on olive-green unpt. Farmers plowing w/horses at ctr. Back green; woman w/sickle in field at ctr. Face proof.	—	—	630.00
S1065	**100 DOLLARS** 2.1.1907. Black on red unpt. Farmer storing hay into barn at l. ctr. Back green; farmer w/boy sharpening tools on grindstone at l. Face proof.	—	—	700.00

GORE BANK

Established in Hamilton, Upper Canada in 1835. Absorbed by the Canadian Bank of Commerce in 1870.

1836 ISSUE

#S1066-S1069 black. Uniface. Sign. varieties. Printer: New England Bank Note Co.

		VG	VF	UNC
S1066	**1 DOLLAR** 1836-56. Wentworth County Court House at top ctr.			
	a. Partially engraved date. 6.2.1840; 1.11.1849; 1.3.1850.	630.00	—	—
	b. Fully engraved date. 2.9.1850; 2.6.1856.	350.00	900.00	—

		VG	VF	UNC
S1067	**2 DOLLARS** 1836-56. Seated Britannia w/lion, reclining allegorical woman, unicorn at top ctr.			
	a. Partially engraved date. 9.12.1845.	700.00	—	—
	b. Fully engraved date. 2.9.1850; 2.9.1852; 2.6.1856.	350.00	900.00	—
S1068	**4 DOLLARS** 1836-56. Supported royal arms at top ctr.			
	a. Partially engraved date. 7.11.1836; 7.1839; 1.3.1850.	700.00	—	—
	b. Fully engraved date. 2.9.1852.	420.00	1050.	—
S1069	**10 DOLLARS** 1836-56. Sailing ship at l., St. George slaying dragon at top ctr.			
	a. Partially engraved date. 16.11.1836; 3.1.1839.	770.00	—	—
	b. Fully engraved date. 2.9.1852.	420.00	1050.	—

HALIFAX BANKING COMPANY

Established in Halifax, Nova Scotia, 1825. Merged w/the Canadian Bank of Commerce in 1903.

1825 ISSUE

Pound Sterling System.

		GOOD	FINE	XF
S1070	**1 POUND-10 SHILLINGS** 1.9.1825; 1.9.1826. Black. Uniface. Printer: Maverick.	900.00	3150.	—

1833 ISSUE

#S1071-S1074 black on blue unpt. Uniface. Printer: New England Bank Note Company, Boston.

		GOOD	FINE	XF
S1071	**5 POUNDS** 18xx. Cattle at l., sailing ship, cask and bales at bottom ctr., farm implements, sailing ship at upper l. and upper r.	—	Unc	1125.

		Good	Fine	XF
S1072	**6 Pounds** 18xx. Sailing ships at upper l. and lower r., standing Britannia at top l. ctr., farm implements at bottom ctr., farmers harvesting at r. Remainder.	—	Unc	1125.

		Good	Fine	XF
S1073	**6 Pounds-10 Shillings** 18xx. Fishing vessel at l., beehive at upper l. ctr., farm tools at bottom ctr., whaling scene over cattle w/whaling scene below at r. Remainder.	—	Unc	1125.

		Good	Fine	XF
S1074	**7 Pounds-10 Shillings** 18xx. Allegorical woman at l., sailing ships at upper l. ctr., casks and sailing ship at bottom ctr., cattle at r. Remainder.	—	Unc	1125.

1863 Issue

Dollar System.

		VG	VF	Unc
S1075	**20 Dollars** 9.12.1863. Black on green unpt. Sailing ships in Halifax harbor at upper ctr. Printer: ABNC.			
	a. Handwritten or printed serial #.	2800.	—	—
	b. Red ovpt: *July 1, 1871* and *CANADA CURRENCY.*	2800.	—	—

1871 Issue

		VG	VF	Unc
S1076	**20 Dollars** 14.9.1871. Like #S1075 but *CANADA CURRENCY* and date engraved. Printer: ABNC.	2800.	—	—

1872; 1880 Issue

#S1077-S1079A black on green unpt. Sailing ships in Halifax harbor at ctr. Back green. Printer: ABNC.

		VG	VF	Unc
S1077	**4 Dollars** 1.10.1872; 1.10.1880.	3150.	—	—

		VG	VF	Unc
S1078	**5 Dollars** 1872; 1880.			
	a. 1.10.1872; 1.10.1880.	3150.	—	—
	b. Slightly modified panels, and imprint: *BABNC* added. 1.10.1880.	3150.	—	—

		VG	VF	Unc
S1079	**10 Dollars** 1872; 1880.			
	a. 1.10.1872; 1.10.1880.	3150.	—	—
	b. Imprint: *CBNC* added. 1.10.1880.	3150.	—	—
S1079A	**20 Dollars** 1.10.1880. Black on green unpt. Sailing ships in Halifax harbor. Back green. Imprint *CNBC.* Proof.	—	—	350.00

1887-94 Issue

#S1080-S1083 Fishermen, fishing vessel at l., sailing ships in Halifax harbor at ctr. Halifax crest at r. Halifax crest on back. Printer: CABNC.

		VG	VF	Unc
S1080	**5 Dollars** 1.1.1887. Black.			
	a. Green unpt. Back green.	3150.	—	—
	b. Red unpt. Back brown.	3150.	—	—
	p. Black unpt. Back brown. Proof.	—	—	350.00
S1081	**5 Dollars** 1.1.1894. Black on blue unpt. Like #S1080 but w/imprint: *BABNC.*	3150.	—	—

		VG	VF	UNC
S1082	**10 DOLLARS** 2.7.1890. Black on green unpt. Back green.	3150.	—	—

		VG	VF	UNC
S1083	**20 DOLLARS** 2.7.1890. Black on green unpt. Back green.	3150.	—	—

1896-98 ISSUE

#S1083A-S1086 black on green unpt. R. Uniake at r. Back green. Printer: BABNC.

		VG	VF	UNC
S1083A	**5 DOLLARS** 2.7.1896. H. N. Wallace at l., sailing ships in Halifax harbor at ctr. Halifax crest at l. on back. Proof.	—	—	350.00

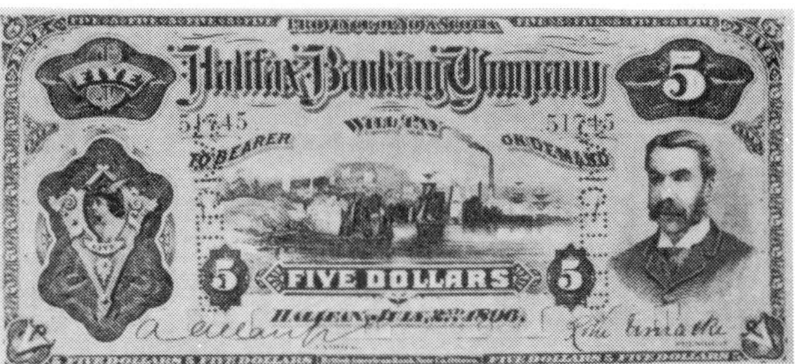

		VG	VF	UNC
S1084	**5 DOLLARS** 2.7.1896. Head of Mercury in ornate *V* at l., sailing ships in Halifax harbor at ctr. Halifax crest at l. on back.	3150.	—	—

		VG	VF	UNC
S1085	**10 DOLLARS** 1.7.1898. Ocean freighter, boats at lower l.	3150.	—	—

		VG	VF	UNC
S1086	**20 DOLLARS** 1.7.1898. Halifax crest at l.	3150.	—	—

HOME BANK OF CANADA

Established under charter in Toronto, Ontario in 1905, failed in 1923.

1904-20 ISSUE

#S1087-S1091 backs black on red, green and brown unpt. Children reading at ctr. Sign. varieties. Printer: ABNC.

		GOOD	FINE	XF
S1087	**5 DOLLARS** 1904-20. Black on red unpt. Portr. Major Gen. I. Brock at l., seated woman w/sailing ships in background at ctr. r.			
	a. Blue ovpt: *S S.* 1.3.1904.	425.00	1400.	—
	b. 2.3.1914.	425.00	1400.	—
	c. 1.3.1917.	425.00	1400.	—
	d. 1.3.1920.	425.00	1400.	—

		GOOD	FINE	XF
S1088	**10 DOLLARS** 1904-20. Black on green unpt. Fenian Raid monument at l., woman w/farm animals at ctr. r.			
	a. Red ovpt: *S S.* 1.3.1904.	425.00	1400.	—
	b. 2.3.1914.	425.00	1400.	—
	c. 1.3.1917.	425.00	1400.	—
	d. 1.3.1920.	425.00	1400.	—

		GOOD	FINE	XF
S1089	**20 DOLLARS** 1904-20. Black on brown unpt. Riel Rebellion monument at l., agricultural scene at ctr. r.			
	a. 1.3.1920.	525.00	1750.	—
	s. Specimen. 1.3.1904; 2.3.1914.	—	Unc	700.00
S1090	**50 DOLLARS** 1.3.1904; 2.3.1914. Black on blue unpt. Boer War monument at l., farmer w/horse and children scene at ctr. r. Specimen.	—	Unc	840.00
S1091	**100 DOLLARS** 1904-17. Black and olive. S. de Champlain monument at l., portr. of Minerva at upper ctr. r.			
	a. 1.3.1917.	525.00	1750.	—
	p. Face proof. 2.3.1914.	—	Unc	420.00
	s. Specimen. 1.3.1904.	—	Unc	840.00

HUDSONS BAY COMPANY

1820-70 YORK FACTORY ISSUES

Notes were first dated and signed in London before being shipped to York Factory. Upon issue the notes were dated and countersigned. In the case of #S1095c, they also bear a blue machine date stamp of the Red River Settlement. London dates appear first; actual issue dates follow.

		GOOD	FINE	XF
S1095	**1 SHILLING** 1821-70. Blue.			
	a. 1.5.1821-1.9.1833.	750.00	—	—
	b. 3.5.1837-4.3.1846.	—	—	—
	c. 1.5.1846-1.5.1870.	450.00	—	—
	r. Remainder w/counterfoil. 1.5.1846-1.5.18(70).	—	—	550.00

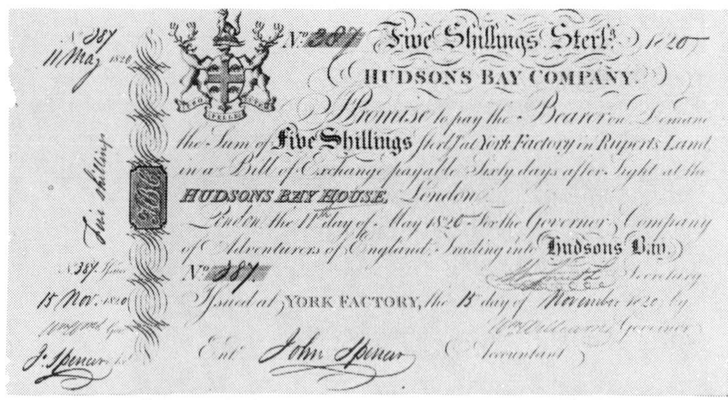

		GOOD	FINE	XF
S1096	**5 SHILLINGS**			
	1820-28. Black.			
	a. 4.5.1820-1.9.1828.	650.00	—	—
	r. Remainder w/counterfoil. 11.5.1820-1.6.1821.	—	—	400.00
S1097	**5 SHILLINGS**			
	1832-66. Red-brown.	650.00	—	—
	b. 27.5.1832-25.8.1840.	—	—	—
	c. 1.5.1845-1.3.1866.	550.00	—	—

NOTE: Later dated notes are usually found hand cancelled.

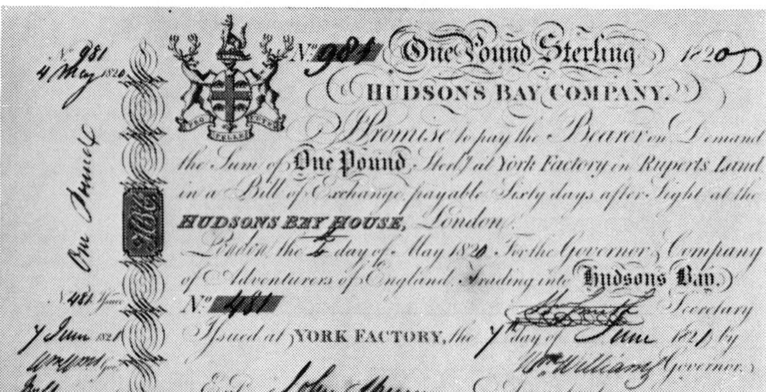

		GOOD	FINE	XF
S1098	**1 POUND**			
	1820-70. Black.			
	a. 1.5.1820-1.9.1824.	650.00	1250.	—
	b. 1.5.1832-25.8.1832.	650.00	1250.	—
	c. 9.5.1832-6.7.1846.	—	—	—
	d. 1.5.1850-20.10.1857.	450.00	1000.	—
	e. 26.7.1858-1.6.1869.	—	—	—
	r1. Remainder. 4.5.1820-7.6.1821.	—	—	500.00
	r2. Remainder w/counterfoil 1.6.1870-18xx.	—	400.00	—
S1099	**5 POUNDS**			
	7.10.1870.	—	—	—

1870 FT. GARRY, N.W.T. PROMISSORY NOTE ISSUE

All are on thin, brownish paper w/hand sign. of accountant rubber stamp of Governor of Assinboia. Smaller size than York Factory issues.

		GOOD	FINE	XF
S1100	**5 SHILLINGS** 2.5.1870.	—	Rare	—
S1101	**1 POUND** 2.5.1870.	—	Rare	—
S1102	**5 POUNDS** 10.5.1870.	—	Rare	—
S1103	**10 POUNDS** 16.5.1870.	—	Rare	—

1870 RED RIVER PROMISSORY NOTE ISSUE

		GOOD	FINE	XF
S1104	**1 SHILLING** 1870.	—	Rare	—

DEASE POST, BR. COLUMBIA CARD MONEY ISSUE

		GOOD	FINE	XF
S1106	**25 CENTS** ND. White.	—	Rare	—
S1107	**50 CENTS** ND. Green.	—	Rare	—
S1108	**1 DOLLAR** ND. Red.	—	Rare	—
S1109	**5 DOLLARS** ND. Blue.	—	Rare	—

FORT GRAHAME POST CARD MONEY ISSUE

		GOOD	FINE	XF
S1110	**25 CENTS** ND. White.	—	Rare	—
S1112	**1 DOLLAR** ND. Red.	—	Rare	—
S1113	**5 DOLLARS** ND. Blue.	—	Rare	—

LAIRD POST CARD MONEY ISSUE

		GOOD	FINE	XF
S1114	**1 DOLLAR** ND. Red.	—	Rare	—
S1115	**5 DOLLARS** ND. Blue.	—	Rare	—

MCDAMES CREEK POST CARD MONEY ISSUE

		GOOD	FINE	XF
S1116	**5 DOLLARS** ND. Blue. Text reads *H.B.C. B.C. District.*	—	Rare	—
S1117	**5 DOLLARS** ND. Blue. Text reads *H.B.C. CASSIAR.*	—	Rare	—

MISCELLANEOUS (NO POST NAME) CARD MONEY ISSUE

		GOOD	FINE	XF
S1118	**1 DOLLAR** ND. Red-orange.	—	Rare	—
S1119	**5 DOLLARS** ND. Blue. Back olive.	—	Rare	—
S1120	**5 DOLLARS** ND. Blue. Back dk. brown.	—	—	—
S1121	**10 DOLLARS** ND. Deep red. Back dk. brown.	—	—	—

NOTE: #S1120 and S1121 are thought to be modern fantasy reproductions.

IMPERIAL BANK OF CANADA

Established in Toronto, Ontario in 1873. Merged w/the Canadian Bank of Commerce in 1961 forming the Canadian Imperial Bank of Commerce.

1875-1886 ISSUES

#S1122-S1129 sign. varieties. Printer: BABNC.

#S1122-S1126 W. H. Merritt at l., H. S. Howland at r.

		VG	VF	UNC
S1122	**4 DOLLARS** 1.3.1875. Black on green unpt. Supported ornate *4* on royal crest at ctr. Blue ovpt: *Z Z.*	850.00	1675.	—
S1123	**5 DOLLARS** 1.3.1875. Black w/green *V-FIVE-V* protector in unpt. Farmer plowing w/horses at ctr. Blue ovpt: *Z Z.*	550.00	1050.	—
S1124	**5 DOLLARS** 1.11.1876. Black on green unpt. Similar to #S1123 but guilloche replaces *V-FIVE-V.*	550.00	1050.	—
S1125	**5 DOLLARS** 1886-96. Black on green unpt. Supported lg. ornate 5 and tilted royal crest at ctr.			
	a. 2.8.1886.	550.00	1050.	—
	b. 2.8.1890.	550.00	1050.	—
	c. Black on ochre unpt. Back orange. 1.10.1895.	625.00	1400.	—
	d. Black and ochre. Back orange 1.10.1896.	550.00	1050.	—
S1126	**10 DOLLARS** 1.3.1875. Black on green unpt. Bank crest between lion and reclining Indian at top ctr. Blue ovpt: *Z Z.*	550.00	1125.	—
S1127	**20 DOLLARS** 1876-1906. Black on green unpt. Farmer mowing w/horses at l., H. S. Howland at lower r.			
	a. 1.11.1876.	625.00	1400.	—
	b. 1.5.1906.	625.00	1400.	—
S1128	**50 DOLLARS** 1.11.1876. Black on green unpt. W. H. Merritt at upper ctr. Face proof.	—	—	350.00
S1129	**100 DOLLARS** 1.11.1876. Black on green unpt. Supported Canadian crest at upper ctr. Face proof.	—	—	350.00

1902 ISSUE

#S1130-S1135 sign. varieties. Printer: W & S.

		VG	VF	UNC
S1130	**5 DOLLARS** 1902-10. Black on ochre unpt. Woman by chest at l., portr. Prince Edward at top ctr., Canadian crest at r. Back green; seated woman w/tablet at ctr.			
	a. 1.10.1902; 1.5.1906.	315.00	630.00	—
	b. 1.1.1910.	250.00	500.00	—

		VG	VF	UNC
S1131	**10 DOLLARS** 1902-10. Black on blue unpt. Cherubs at l. and r. of portr. Qn. Alexandria at l., supported royal arms at upper ctr. r. Back yellow-brown; seated woman w/cherub at ctr.			
	a. 1.1.1910.	210.00	560.00	—
	s. Specimen. 1.10.1902.	—	—	625.00

1902; 1907 DOUBLE SIZE NOTE ISSUES

#S1132-S1135 are extra lg. size.

		GOOD	FINE	XF
S1132	**20 DOLLARS** 1.10.1902. Blue on orange and violet unpt. Seated woman w/child, beehive at lower l., George Vas Duke of York at upper ctr. Back red-orange; woman w/fruit basket at ctr.			
	a. Issued note.	2800.	7000.	—
	s. Specimen.	—	—	—

		GOOD	FINE	XF
S1133	**50 DOLLARS** 1902-10. Black on gold and green unpt. Qn. Alexandria at ctr., seated allegorical woman at lower r. Back deep red; standing Commerce, sailing ship in background at ctr. on back.			
	a. 2.1.1907.	2800.	7000.	—
	s. Specimen. 1.10.1902.	—	Unc	2450.
S1134	**100 DOLLARS** 1.10.1902. Blue on lilac, brown and yellow unpt. Kg. Edward VIII over steam train at l., supported ornate *100* at ctr., T. R. Merritt over steam ship at r. Back ochre; bank bldg. at ctr. Specimen.	—	Unc	2450.
S1135	**100 DOLLARS** 2.1.1907. Black on red and gold unpt. Like #S1134. Back blue. Specimen.	—	Unc	2450.

1915-17 ISSUES

#S1136-S1141 printer: BABNC.

		GOOD	FINE	XF
S1136	**5 DOLLARS** 1.10.1915. Black on yellow, green and orange unpt. Like #S1125.	110.00	385.00	1050.

#S1137-S1141 black on green unpt.

		GOOD	FINE	XF
S1137	**5 DOLLARS** 1916; 1920. Like #S1136.			
	a. 3.1.1916.	35.00	125.00	300.00
	b. 2.1.1920.	35.00	125.00	300.00

		GOOD	FINE	XF
S1138	**10 DOLLARS** 1915; 1920. Like #S1126.			
	a. 1.10.1915.	35.00	125.00	300.00
	b. 2 sign. varieties. 2.1.1920.	25.00	87.50	225.00

		GOOD	FINE	XF
S1139	**20 DOLLARS** 1915; 1920. Like #S1127.			
	a. 1.10.1915.	70.00	225.00	600.00
	b. 2.1.1920.	70.00	225.00	600.00
S1140	**50 DOLLARS** 2.1.1917. Like #S1128.	350.00	1200.	—

		GOOD	FINE	XF
S1141	**100 DOLLARS** 1917; 1920. Like #S1129.			
	a. 2.1.1917.	350.00	1200.	—
	b. 2.1.1920.	350.00	1200.	—
	x. Counterfeit. 2.1.1917.	—	65.00	125.00

1923 ISSUE

#S1142-S1145A lion over crown on back. 2 sign. varieties. Printer: CBNC.

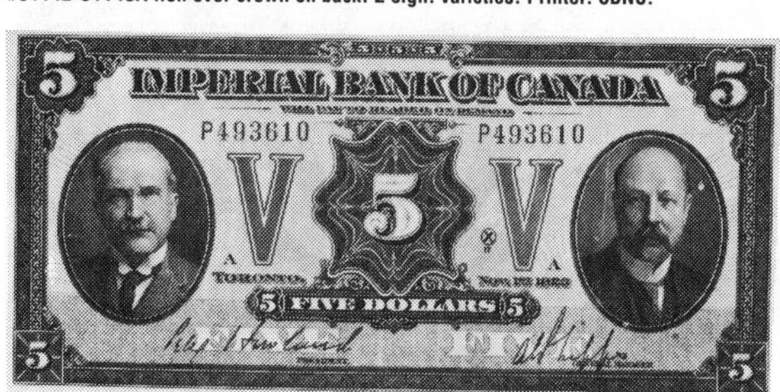

		VG	VF	UNC
S1142	**5 DOLLARS** 1.11.1923. Black on green unpt. Portr. P. Howland at l., portr. A. H. Phipps at r. Back green.	50.00	100.00	375.00

		VG	VF	UNC
S1143	**10 DOLLARS** 1.11.1923. Black on blue unpt. Similar to #S1142. Back blue.	50.00	100.00	375.00

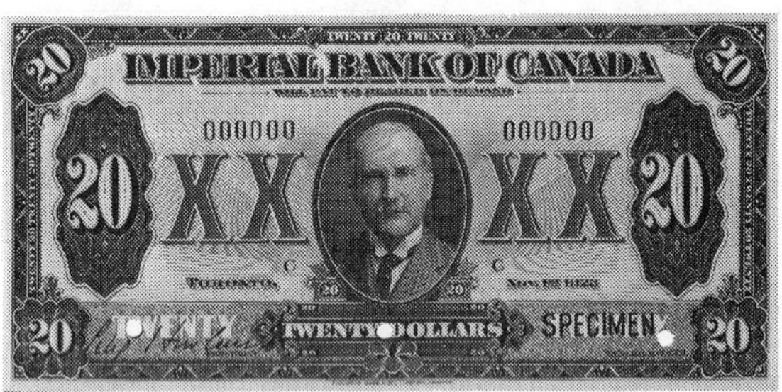

		VG	VF	UNC
S1144	**20 DOLLARS** 1.11.1923. Black on brown unpt. Portr. P. Howland at ctr. Back brown.	55.00	125.00	450.00

		VG	VF	UNC
S1145	**50 DOLLARS** 1.11.1923. Black on orange unpt. Portr. P. Howland at r. Back orange.	150.00	600.00	—

		VG	VF	UNC
S1145A	**100 DOLLARS** 1.11.1923. Black on olive-green unpt. Portr. P. Howland at l. Back olive-green. Specimen.	—	—	775.00

1933 ISSUE

#S1145B-S1145D lion over crown on back. Printer: CBNC.

		VG	VF	UNC
S1145B	**5 DOLLARS** 1.11.1933. Black on green unpt. Portr. A. H. Phipps at l., portr. F. A. Ralph at r. Back green.	40.00	85.00	325.00
S1145C	**10 DOLLARS** 1.11.1933. Black and blue. Similar to #S1145B. Back blue.	75.00	140.00	625.00
S1145D	**20 DOLLARS** 1.11.1933. Black and brown. Portr. A. H. Phipps at ctr. Back brown. Specimen.	—	—	350.00

1934 ISSUE

#S1145E and S1145F similar to #S1145B and S1145C. Printer: CBNC.

		VG	VF	UNC
S1145E	**5 DOLLARS** 1.11.1934. Black on green unpt.			
	a. Sign. A. H. Phipps and F. A. Ralph.	15.00	32.50	165.00
	b. Sign. H. J. Jaffray and F. A. Ralph.	15.00	32.50	165.00

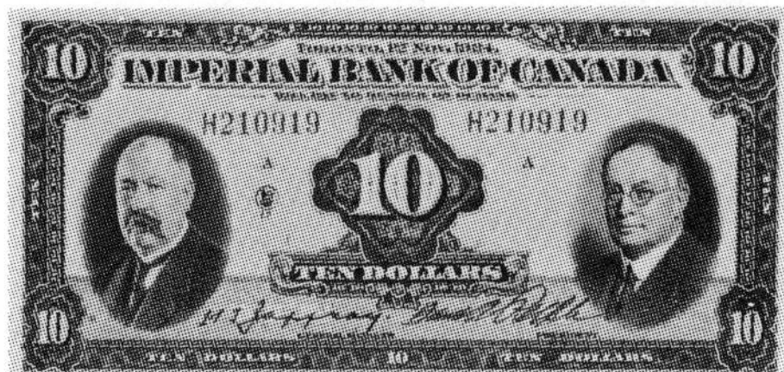

		VG	VF	UNC
S1145F	**10 DOLLARS** 1.11.1934. Black on blue unpt.			
	a. Sign. A. H. Phipps and F. A. Ralph.	21.00	37.50	175.00
	b. Sign. H. J. Jaffray and F. A. Ralph.	25.00	50.00	200.00

1939 ISSUE

#S1145G-S1145H reduced size notes. H. J. Jaffray at l., A. H. Phipps at r. Lion over crown on back.

		VG	VF	UNC
S1145G	**5 DOLLARS** 3.1.1939. Black on green unpt. Back green.	21.00	37.50	175.00
S1145H	**10 DOLLARS** 3.1.1939. Black on blue unpt. Back blue.	25.00	45.00	200.00

MERCHANTS BANK OF CANADA

Established in Montreal, Quebec in 1864. Suffered lg. losses resulting in being sold to the Bank of Montreal in 1922.

1868-73 ISSUE

#S1146-S1151 black on green unpt. Sign. varieties. Back green. Printers: ABNC and BABNC.

		GOOD	FINE	XF
S1146	**1 DOLLAR** 2.3.1868. 2 sailors on wharf at lower l., steam passenger train dockside at upper ctr., H. Allan at lower r.			
	a. Issued note.	200.00	625.00	—
	b. Blue ovpt: *PERTH.*	200.00	625.00	—
	c. Blue ovpt: *TORONTO.*	200.00	625.00	—
S1147	**2 DOLLARS** 2.3.1868. Portr. Prince of Wales at l., sailing ship and steamboat at upper ctr., H. Allan at lower r.			
	a. Issued note.	210.00	700.00	—
	b. Blue ovpt: *PERTH.*	210.00	700.00	—
	c. Blue ovpt: *TORONTO.*	210.00	700.00	—

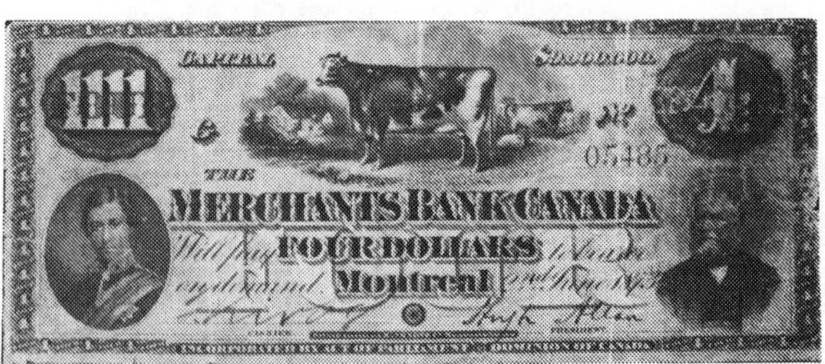

		GOOD	FINE	XF
S1148	**4 DOLLARS** 1870; 1873. Portr. Prince of Wales at lower l., cow at upper ctr., H. Allan at lower r.			
	a. 2.5.1870.	165.00	550.00	—
	b. 2.6.1873.	165.00	550.00	—
S1149	**5 DOLLARS** 1868; 1873. H. Allan at lower l., reclining sailor w/anchor at top ctr., Prince of Wales at lower r.			
	a. Issued note. 2.3.1868.	180.00	600.00	—
	b. Blue ovpt: *PERTH.*	180.00	600.00	—
	c. Blue ovpt: *TORONTO.*	180.00	600.00	—
	p. Face proof. 1.8.1873.	—	Unc	420.00
S1150	**10 DOLLARS** 1.8.1871. River boat pilot at lower l., head office bldg. at ctr., H. Allan at lower r.	310.00	1050.	—
S1151	**20 DOLLARS** 1.8.1873. Earl of Dufferin at lower l., steam passenger train crossing stone arch bridge at ctr. H. Allan at lower r. Face proof.	—	Unc	420.00

1886 ISSUE

#S1152-S1155 black on green unpt. Sign. varieties. H. Allan at lower r. Back green. Printer: BABNC.

		Good	Fine	XF
S1152	**5 Dollars** 2.7.1886. 2 sailors on wharf at lower l., steam sailing ship at top ctr.	100.00	335.00	770.00
S1153	**10 Dollars** 2.7.1886. Similar to #S1150 but w/H. Allan at lower r.	105.00	350.00	975.00
S1154	**50 Dollars** 2.7.1886. Portr. Earl of Dufferin at l., paddle wheel steamboat "Quebec" at ctr. Face proof.	—	Unc	420.00
S1155	**100 Dollars** 2.7.1886. Portr. Qn. Victoria in "Widow's Weeds" at l., ship at ctr. Face proof.	—	Unc	420.00

1900; 1903 Issue

#S1156-S1159 sign. varieties. Printer: ABNC.

		VG	VF	Unc
S1156	**5 Dollars** 1.1.1900. Black on m/c unpt. Reclining allegorical woman holding sextant at l., clipper ships at ctr. Back black and m/c; portr. gypsy woman at ctr. 2 sign. varieties.	300.00	775.00	—
S1157	**10 Dollars** 1.1.1900. Black on m/c unpt. 2 seated allegorical women, steam train, factories in background at ctr. Back black on m/c unpt.; seated Justice w/reclining male and female. 2 sign. varieties. Specimen.	—	—	350.00
S1158	**20 Dollars** 2.1.1903. Black on green and orange unpt. Steer's head at l. Back black on m/c unpt.; bank crest at ctr. Specimen.	—	—	420.00
S1159	**50 Dollars** 2.1.1903. Black on red and olive unpt. Stag at l., young woman at r. Back black on m/c unpt.; bank crest at ctr. Specimen.	—	—	420.00

1906; 1907 Issue

#S1160-S1164 black on green unpt. Back green. Sign. varieties. Printer: BABNC.

		Good	Fine	XF
S1160	**5 Dollars** 1.2.1906. River boat pilot at lower l., steam passenger ship at top ctr., portr. H. Montagu Allan at lower r. 2 beavers at ctr. on back.	60.00	200.00	500.00
S1161	**10 Dollars** 1.2.1906. Indian on horseback at lower l., farmer reaping w/horses at ctr., portr. H. Montagu Allan at lower r. Sailor w/telescope at ctr. on back.	60.00	200.00	500.00

		Good	Fine	XF
S1162	**20 Dollars** 1.6.1907. Steer's head at l. Sheep at pond at ctr. on back.	150.00	500.00	—
S1163	**50 Dollars** 1.6.1907. Stag at l., bank crest at lower r.	425.00	1400.	—
S1164	**100 Dollars** 1.6.1907. Steam passenger ship at l., H. Montagu Allan at r. Ancient scene w/Greek woman watching youth painting jug at ctr. on back.	425.00	1400.	—

1916 Issue

#S1165 and S1166 black on green unpt. Portr. D. C. Macrow at lower l., H. Montagu Allan at lower r. Sign. varieties. Back green. Printer: BABNC.

		Good	Fine	XF
S1165	**5 Dollars** 1.2.1916. Steam passenger ship at upper ctr. 2 beavers at ctr. on back.	35.00	125.00	275.00

		Good	Fine	XF
S1166	**10 Dollars** 1.2.1916. Farmer reaping w/horses at ctr. Sailor on watch at ctr. on back.	35.00	125.00	275.00

1917 Issue

#S1167-S1171 black on green unpt. Back green; bank crest at ctr. 2 sign. varieties. Printer: ABNC.

		Good	Fine	XF
S1167	**5 Dollars** 3.1.1917. Portr. H. Montagu Allan at l., voyagers loading canoes at ctr., portr. D. C. Macrow at r.	150.00	525.00	900.00

		Good	Fine	XF
S1168	**10 Dollars** 3.1.1917. Similar to #S1167 but w/ocean freighter and steam passenger train dockside at ctr.	325.00	1100.	1800.
S1169	**20 Dollars** 3.1.1917. Steer's head at l.	325.00	975.00	1400.
S1170	**50 Dollars** 3.1.1917. Stag at l., young woman at r.	375.00	1250.	1950.
S1171	**100 Dollars** 3.1.1917. Similar to #S1167 and S1168 but w/seated woman w/winged wheel at ctr.	375.00	1250.	1950.

1919 Issue

#S1172 and S1173 bank crest at ctr. on back. Printer: ABNC.

		VG	VF	Unc
S1172	**5 Dollars** 1.11.1919. Black on green unpt. Portr. Prince of Wales at lower ctr.	200.00	500.00	—
S1173	**10 Dollars** 1.11.1919. Black on blue unpt. Portr. Sir H. Allan at ctr.	385.00	700.00	—

MERCHANTS' BANK OF HALIFAX

Established in Halifax, Nova Scotia in 1869. Changed name to the Royal Bank of Canada in 1901.

1864 ISSUES

#S1174 and S1175 back black. Printer: Blades, East & Blades.

		GOOD	FINE	XF
S1174	**20 DOLLARS** 31.3.1864. Black w/orange *TWENTY DOLLARS* protector. W/o border frames.	735.00	2450.	—

		GOOD	FINE	XF
S1175	**20 DOLLARS** 1.10.1864. Like #S1174 but w/border frames.	735.00	2450.	—

1869; 1870 ISSUE

		GOOD	FINE	XF
S1175A	**4 DOLLARS** 1.7.1870. Black on green unpt. Steam sailing ships at l., ctr. and at r. Green ovpt: *CANADIAN CURRENCY, 1 JULY, 1871.*	650.00	2100.	—
S1176	**5 DOLLARS** 1.7.1870. Black on orange unpt. Steam sailing ship at ctr.			
	a. Issued note.	650.00	2100.	—
	b. Green ovpt: *CANADIAN CURRENCY, 1 JULY, 1871.*	650.00	2100.	—
S1177	**20 DOLLARS** 1.10.1869. Black on orange unpt. Steam sailing ship at top ctr.			
	a. Issued note.	650.00	2100.	—
	b. Green ovpt: *CANADIAN CURRENCY, 1 JULY, 1871.*	650.00	2100.	—

1871-74 ISSUE

#S1178, S1179, and S1181 like #S1175A-S1177 but w/*CANADA CURRENCY* engraved. Sign. varieties. Also known w/ovpt: *SUMMERSIDE*. Printer: Blades, East & Blades.

		GOOD	FINE	XF
S1178	**4 DOLLARS** 1.7.1871; 1.1.1872; 1.10.1873. Black on green and orange unpt. Back orange.	550.00	1750.	—

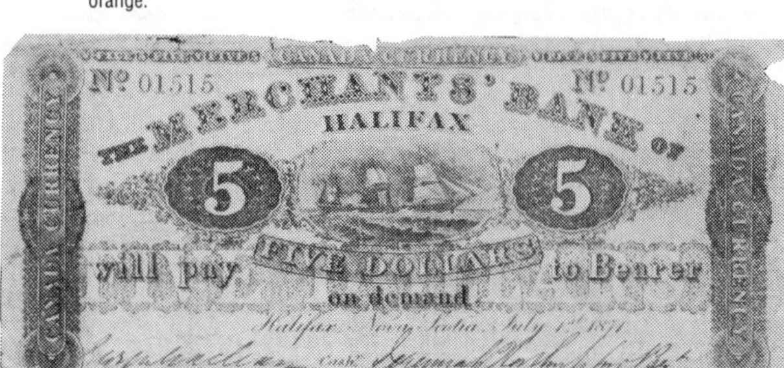

		GOOD	FINE	XF
S1179	**5 DOLLARS** 1.7.1871; 1.1.1872; 1.10.1873. Black on orange unpt. Back green.	550.00	1750.	—
S1180	**10 DOLLARS** 1.1.1874. Black on green and orange unpt. Steam sailing ship at upper ctr. Back orange.	725.00	1950.	—
S1181	**20 DOLLARS** 1.10.1873. Black on orange unpt. Back black.	725.00	1950.	—

1878; 1879 ISSUE

#S1182 and 1183 w/*DOMINION OF CANADA* engraved at top ctr. Back orange. Printer: Blades, East & Blades.

		GOOD	FINE	XF
S1182	**4 DOLLARS** 1.1.1879. Black on yellow-green and red unpt. Sloop at lower l., steam powered sailing ships at top ctr., bank bldg. at lower r.	550.00	1750.	—
S1183	**10 DOLLARS** 1.1.1878. Black on green and orange unpt. Similar to #S1180.	550.00	1750.	—

1880; 1883 ISSUE

#S1184-S1186 printer: ABNC.

		VG	VF	UNC
S1184	**5 DOLLARS** 1880-96. Black on orange and green unpt. Portr. allegorical woman at l., steam powered sailing ship at ctr., bank bldg. at r. Back brown.			
	a. 1.7.1880; 1.5.1890.	850.00	1675.	—
	b. 2.1.1892.	900.00	1825.	—
	p. Proof. 2.1.1896.	—	—	420.00

		VG	VF	UNC
S1185	**10 DOLLARS** 1880-96. Black on yellow-orange and blue unpt. Sailing ship at l., bank bldg. at lower r. Back green.			
	a. 2.1.1896.	400.00	1400.	—
	p. Proof. 1.7.1880.	—	—	425.00
	s. Specimen. 2.1.1893.	—	—	850.00
S1186	**20 DOLLARS** 1883-98. Black on blue and orange unpt. Back brown.			
	a. 21.1.1883.	400.00	1400.	—
	s. Specimen. 1.1.1898.	—	—	700.00

1894; 1899 ISSUE

#S1187-S1189 T. E. Kenny at r. Bank bldg. at ctr. on back. Printer: ABNC.

		VG	VF	UNC
S1187	**5 DOLLARS** 1894-99. Black on green unpt. D. H. Duncan at lower l. Back green.			
	a. 1.6.1894; 2.1.1899.	400.00	1400.	—
	p. Proof. 2.1.1896.	—	—	500.00
	s. Specimen. 2.1.1896.	—	—	—
S1188	**50 DOLLARS** 18.7.1899. Black on yellow and blue unpt. Miners at upper ctr. Back blue. Proof.	—	—	700.00
S1189	**100 DOLLARS** 3.7.1899. Black on yellow and orange unpt. Seated allegorical woman w/tablet and child at l. Back orange. Proof.	—	—	700.00

MERCHANTS BANK OF PRINCE EDWARD ISLAND

Chartered in Charlottetown, P.E.I. in 1871. Absorbed by the Canadian Bank of Commerce in 1906.

1871-91 ISSUE

#S1191-S1195 black on green unpt. Back green. Red ovpt: *CANADA CURRENCY*. Printer: BABNC.

		GOOD	FINE	XF
S1191	**1 DOLLAR** 1871-89. Farmer plowing w/horses at upper l., sailor on watch at lower r.			
	a. Partially engraved date. 1.11.1871.	850.00	2800.	—
	b. Fully engraved date. 1.9.1877.	850.00	2800.	—
	c. Fully engraved date. 1.8.1889.	850.00	2800.	—

		GOOD	FINE	XF
S1192	**2 DOLLARS** 1871; 1877. Anchor at lower l., paddle wheel steamboat at top ctr., 3 horse's heads at lower r.			
	a. Partially engraved date. 1.9.1871.	850.00	2800.	—
	b. Fully engraved date. 1.9.1877.	850.00	2800.	—

A word on date ranges

Often date ranges or specific dates are listed. These have been observed or reported by our contributors. If a note is outside the published range, it only means that it is a newly reported date, and not necessarily worthy of a premium value.

		GOOD	FINE	XF
S1193	**5 DOLLARS** 1877; 1892. Young sailor climbing rope ladder at lower l., farm woman w/livestock at upper ctr., standing allegorical woman at lower r.			
	a. Fully engraved date. 1.9.1877.	850.00	2800.	—
	p. Partially engraved date. Face proof. 18xx.	—	Unc	490.00
	s. Specimen. Fully engraved date. 1.3.1892.	—	Unc	850.00

		GOOD	FINE	XF
S1194	**10 DOLLARS** 1891; 1892. Young woman at lower l., steam train emerging from tunnel at ctr., portr. Prince of Wales at lower r.			
	a. Fully engraved date. 1.3.1892.	850.00	2800.	—
	p. Partially engraved date. Face proof. 18xx.	—	Unc	490.00
	s. Specimen. Fully engraved date. 6.11.1891.	—	Unc	850.00

		GOOD	FINE	XF
S1195	**20 DOLLARS** 1891; 1892. Portr. Qn. Victoria in "Widow's Weeds" at lower ctr.			
	p. Partially engraved date. Face proof. 18xx.	—	Unc	490.00
	s. Fully engraved date. Specimen. 6.11.1891; 1.3.1892.	—	Unc	850.00

1900 ISSUE

		GOOD	FINE	XF
S1196	**5 DOLLARS** 2.1.1900. Black on pink and green unpt. 2 allegorical women at lower l., steamship at upper ctr., standing Indian maiden w/spear at lower r. Face proof. Printer: BABNC.	—	Unc	700.00

METROPOLITAN BANK

Established in Toronto, Ontario in 1902. Merged with the Bank of Nova Scotia in 1914.

1902 ISSUE

#S1197-S1201 royal crest on back. Sign. varieties. Printer: ABNC.

		VG	VF	UNC
S1197	**5 DOLLARS** 5.11.1902. Black on yellow and red unpt. Child standing between 2 reclining allegorical women at ctr. Back green. 3 sign. varieties.			
	a. Issued note.	1250.	—	—
	b. W/red ovpt: *S S*.	1250.	—	—
	c. W/red ovpt: *Q Q*.	1250.	—	—
S1198	**10 DOLLARS** 1902; 1909. Black on yellow-green and green unpt. Steam sailing ship at ctr. 3 sign. varieties.			
	a. 5.11.1902.	1550.	—	—
	b. As a. W/*S S*.	1550.	—	—
	c. As a. W/red ovpt: *Q Q*.	1550.	—	—
	d. 5.11.1909.	1550.	—	—

		VG	VF	UNC
S1199	**20 DOLLARS** 1902; 1909. Black on yellow-green and green unpt. Trolley at ctr. Back olive-green.			
	a. 5.11.1909.	1750.	—	—
	s. Specimen. 5.11.1902.	—	—	850.00
S1200	**50 DOLLARS** 1902; 1909. Black and brown. Steam train at station at ctr. Back orange.			
	p. Face proof. 5.11.1909.	—	—	350.00
	s. Specimen. 5.11.1902.	—	—	850.00
S1201	**100 DOLLARS** 1902; 1912. Black, yellow-green and red. Mining scene at ctr. Back gray.			
	s1. Specimen. 5.11.1902.	—	—	850.00
	s2. Specimen. 5.11.1912.	—	—	850.00

MOLSONS BANK

Established in Montreal, Canada East in 1837. The Molsons were also involved as brewers and distillers. Suspended banking operations until 1853, later chartered in 1855. Acquired by the Bank of Montreal in 1925.

1837 ISSUE

Dollar System.

#S1202-S1204 black. Back brown. Unsigned remainders. Printer: RWH & Co.

		GOOD	FINE	XF
S1202	**1 DOLLAR** 15.9.1837. Farmers w/livestock at l., standing allegorical woman at ctr., cherub w/basket at r.	225.00	770.00	1675.
S1203	**2 DOLLARS** 15.9.1837.	250.00	850.00	1950.
S1204	**5 DOLLARS** 15.9.1837. Paddle wheel steamboat at l., royal crest at upper ctr., seated Archimedes w/globe at r.	225.00	770.00	1675.

1853 ISSUE

Dollar/Pound Sterling System.

#S1205-S1209 black. Red ovpt: *PAYABLE AT MONTREAL*, blue ovpt: *ST. C.* Printer: Toppan, Carpenter & Casilear.

		GOOD	FINE	XF
S1205	**1 DOLLAR = 5 SHILLINGS** 1.10.1853. Seated Agriculture at upper l., 3 ships at ctr., seated Commerce at upper r. Back brown.	215.00	735.00	—

		GOOD	FINE	XF
S1206	**2 DOLLARS = 10 SHILLINGS** 1.10.1853. Portr. Prince Consort at lower l., seated allegorical woman w/farming scene in background at upper ctr., portr. Qn. Victoria at lower r. Back olive.	215.00	735.00	—
S1207	**5 DOLLARS = 25 SHILLINGS** 1.10.1853. 3 allegorical women w/anchor at l., seated allegorical woman w/cattle at upper ctr. Back brown.	250.00	850.00	—
S1208	**20 DOLLARS = 5 POUNDS** 1.10.1853. Standing Indian in ornate frame at l., sailing ships at top ctr., standing male citizen at lower r. Back brown. Remainder.	—	375.00	—
S1209	**50 DOLLARS = 12 POUNDS-10 SHILLINGS** 1.10.1853. Back brown. Harvest scene at l., portr. Qn. Victoria at ctr., steam passenger train at r. Face proof.	—	Unc	350.00

1855 ISSUES

#S1210-S1218 w/engraved *Chartered by Act of Parliament* sign. varieties. Printers: Toppan, Carpenter, Casilear, Toppan, Carpenter & Co. and ABNC.

		GOOD	FINE	XF
S1210	**1 DOLLAR = 5 SHILLINGS** 1.1.1855. Black. Like #S1205. Back orange. Montreal issue.			
	a. Issued note w/o protector.	210.00	700.00	—
	b. Green *ONE* protector on face and back.	210.00	700.00	—
S1211	**1 DOLLAR = 5 SHILLINGS** 1.10.1855. Black. Like #S1210. Back blue. Toronto issue.			
	a. Issued note w/o protector.	210.00	700.00	—
	b. Blue ovpt: *LONDON*. Green *ONE* protector on face and back.	230.00	770.00	—
	c. Blue ovpt: *PAYABLE AT LONDON*. Green *ONE* protector.	230.00	770.00	—
	d. Red ovpt: *PAYABLE AT MONTREAL*. Green *ONE* protector.	230.00	770.00	—
S1212	**2 DOLLARS = 10 SHILLINGS** 1.10.1855. Black. Like #S1206. Montreal issue. Face proof.	—	Unc	280.00

		GOOD	FINE	XF
S1213	**4 DOLLARS = 1 POUND** 1.10.1855. Black. Portr. of young woman at l., 4 cherubs w/o ornate 4 at ctr., 3 standing allegorical women at r. Back green. Montreal issue.			
	a. W/o protector.	325.00	1050.	—
	b. Green *FOUR* protector on face and back.	225.00	770.00	—
S1214	**4 DOLLARS = 1 POUND** 1.10.1855. Black. Like #S1213. Back blue. Toronto issue.			
	a. W/o protector.	280.00	910.00	—
	b. Blue ovpt: *PAYABLE AT LONDON* and green *FOUR* protector on face and back.	225.00	770.00	—
S1215	**5 DOLLARS = 25 SHILLINGS** 1.10.1855. Black. Like #S1207. Back green. Montreal issue.			
	a. W/o protector.	325.00	1050.	—
	b. Green *FIVE* protector on face and back.	280.00	910.00	—
S1216	**5 DOLLARS = 25 SHILLINGS** 1.10.1855. Like #S1215. Green *FIVE* protector on face and back. Toronto issue.	280.00	910.00	—
S1217	**20 DOLLARS = 5 POUNDS** 1.10.1855. Black. Like #S1208. Back orange. Montreal issue.			
	p1. W/o unpt. Face proof.	—	Unc	280.00
	p2. Green unpt. Face proof	—	Unc	350.00
S1218	**50 DOLLARS = 1 POUND-10 SHILLINGS** 1.10.1855. Black. Like #1209. Back orange. Montreal issue.			
	p1. W/o unpt. Face proof.	—	Unc	280.00
	p2. Green unpt. Face proof.	—	Unc	350.00

1857 ISSUE

Dollar System.

#S1219 and S1220 black on green unpt. Back green. Printer: RWH & E.

		GOOD	FINE	XF
S1219	**1 DOLLAR** 1.10.1857. Portr. young woman at l., reclining woman holding lg. ornate *1* at upper ctr., sailor w/sextant at lower r.	200.00	700.00	—
S1220	**2 DOLLARS** 1.10.1857. Portr. young woman at lower l., lg. ornate *2* between seated Britannia and Justice at upper l. ctr., woman w/sheaf and sickle in lg. *2* at r.	200.00	700.00	—

1871 ISSUE

#S1221 and S1222 black on green unpt. Back green. Sign. varieties. Blue ovpt: *TORONTO*. Printer: BABNC.

		VG	VF	UNC
S1221	**6 DOLLARS** 1.11.1871. Portr. J. H. R. Molson at upper l., 2 beavers at lower ctr., portr. W. Molson at upper r.	5250.	—	—

		VG	VF	UNC
S1222	**7 DOLLARS** 1.11.1871. Portr. J. H. R. Molson at lower l., ship builders at ctr., portr. W. Molson at lower r.	5250.	—	—

1872 ISSUE

#S1223-S1225 black on green unpt. Portr. J. H. R. Molson at l., portr. W. Molson at r. Back green. Sign. varieties. Printer: BABNC.

		GOOD	FINE	XF
S1223	**4 DOLLARS** 1872; 1875. Cherubs w/lg. ornate *4* at upper ctr. r.			
	a. 1.6.1872.	350.00	1125.	—
	b. 1.6.1875.	350.00	1125.	—
S1224	**5 DOLLARS** 1872-1901.			
	a. 1.6.1880.	240.00	840.00	—
	b. 2.7.1890; 3.1.1893.	280.00	900.00	—
	c. 2.7.1898.	210.00	700.00	—
	d. 3.7.1899; 2.1.1900; 2.7.1901.	150.00	500.00	—
	p. Face proof. 1.6.1872.	—	Unc	315.00

		GOOD	FINE	XF
S1225	**10 DOLLARS** 1872-1901. Cherubs w/lg. ornate *X* at bottom ctr.			
	a. 1.6.1880.	280.00	910.00	—
	b. 2.7.1890.	220.00	770.00	—
	c. 2.7.1898; 3.7.1899.	210.00	700.00	—
	d. 2.1.1900; 2.7.1901.	150.00	500.00	—
	p. Face proof. 1.6.1872.	—	Unc	315.00

1891; 1899 ISSUE

#S1226 and S1227 black on green unpt. Printer: BABNC.

		GOOD	FINE	XF
S1226	**20 DOLLARS** 1899; 1901. Like #S1217.			
	a. Issued note. 3.7.1899.	450.00	1475.	—
	p. Uniface proof. 1.10.1901.	—	—	—
S1226A	**50 DOLLARS = 12 POUNDS-10 SHILLINGS** 2.1.1887. Like #S1218.	—	Unc	350.00
S1227	**50 DOLLARS** 2.1.1891. Like #S1218.	450.00	1475.	—

1903; 1904 ISSUE

#S1228-S1230 back green. Sign. varieties. Printer: BABNC.

#S1228 and S1229 portr. W. M. Macpherson at l., portr. W. Molson at r.

		VG	VF	UNC
S1228	**5 DOLLARS** 1903; 1904. Black on brown and green unpt. Woman w/cherub in lg. ornate *5* at ctr.			
	a. 2.1.1903.	100.00	335.00	—
	b. 2.1.1904.	100.00	335.00	—
S1229	**10 DOLLARS** 1903; 1904. Black on brown and green unpt. Lg. ornate *X* between reclining Indian and woman at ctr.			
	a. 2.1.1903.	150.00	525.00	—
	b. 2.1.1904.	150.00	525.00	—
S1230	**20 DOLLARS** 2.1.1904. Black on green and orange unpt. Blacksmith at lower l., steamship "C. P. Lake" at top ctr., woman w/flower basket at lower r.	335.00	700.00	2450.

1905 ISSUE

#S1231-S1232 black on yellow and green unpt. Back green. Printer: BABNC.

		VG	VF	UNC
S1231	**5 DOLLARS** 2.10.1905. Like #S1228 but w/lg. ornate *V - V* in unpt.			
	a. L.h. portr. shoulders turned r.	125.00	265.00	—
	b. L.h. portr. shoulders turned front.	100.00	225.00	—
S1232	**10 DOLLARS** 2.10.1905. Like #S1229 but w/lg. ornate *X - X* in unpt.			
	a. L.h. portr. shoulders turned r.	125.00	265.00	—
	b. L.h. portr. shoulders turned front.	100.00	225.00	—

1908 ISSUE

#S1233 and S1234 black on olive-green unpt. Portr. Sir W. Molson Macpherson at l., portr. W. Molson at r. Back green; bank crest at ctr. Sign. varieties. Printer: ABNC.

		VG	VF	UNC
S1233	5 DOLLARS 2.1.1908.	105.00	210.00	—

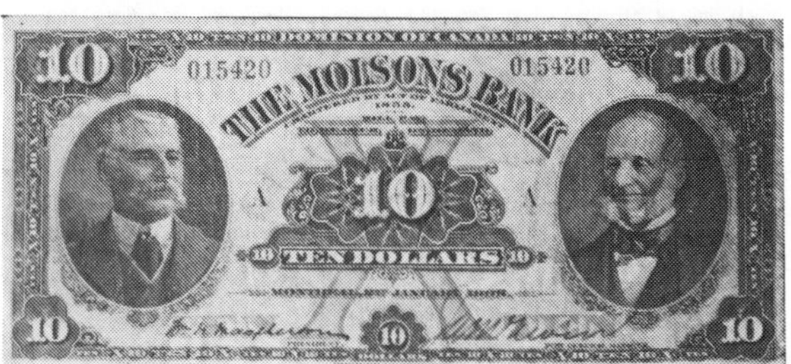

		VG	VF	UNC
S1234	10 DOLLARS 2.1.1908.	110.00	225.00	—

1912 ISSUE

#S1235 and S1236 bank crest at ctr. on back. Sign. varieties. Printer: W&S.

		VG	VF	UNC
S1235	5 DOLLARS 2.1.1912. Black on green unpt. 2 beehives at l., portr. W. Molson at ctr., 2 steers at r. Back green.	50.00	125.00	400.00
S1236	10 DOLLARS 2.1.1912. Black on lilac unpt. Steam passenger ship at l., portr. Sir W. Molson Macpherson at ctr., steam passenger train at r. Back blue.	115.00	250.00	750.00

1914 ISSUE

#S1237 and S1238 black on green unpt. Back green; bank crest. Sign. varieties. Printer: BABNC.

		GOOD	FINE	XF
S1237	50 DOLLARS 2.1.1914. Steam locomotive at l., portr. W. Molson at ctr., waterfalls at r.	400.00	1250.	—
S1238	100 DOLLARS 2.1.1914. Portr. bearded man at ctr.	400.00	1250.	—

1916 ISSUE

		GOOD	FINE	XF
S1239	10 DOLLARS 3.1.1916. Black on green unpt. Riverfront factories at ctr., portr. Sir W. Molson Macpherson at r. Back blue. Sign. varieties. Printer: W & S.	40.00	125.00	275.00

1918 ISSUE

#S1240 and S1241 portr. W. M. Macpherson at l., portr. W. Molson at r. Sign. varieties. Printer: ABNC.

		GOOD	FINE	XF
S1240	5 DOLLARS 2.7.1918. Black on green unpt. Back green.	40.00	125.00	325.00
S1241	10 DOLLARS 2.7.1918. Black on orange unpt. Back orange.	35.00	100.00	265.00

1922 ISSUE

#S1242 and S1243 black on green unpt. Back green; bank crest at ctr. Printer: BABNC.

		VG	VF	UNC
S1242	5 DOLLARS 3.7.1922. Portr. F. W. Molson at r.	25.00	75.00	300.00

		VG	VF	UNC
S1243	10 DOLLARS 3.7.1922. Portr. M. Molson at ctr.	27.50	85.00	350.00

MONTREAL BANK

Established in Montreal, Lower Canada in 1817.

1817-19 ISSUE

#S1243A-S1243D black. Uniface. Printer: A. Reed E.W. Con.

		VG	VF	UNC
S1243A	5 DOLLARS 18xx. 5 coins at l., Montreal at top ctr. Proof.	—	Unc	280.00
		GOOD	FINE	XF
S1243B	10 DOLLARS 1.1.1818. 5 coins and Nelson's monument at l.	385.00	1325.	—
S1243C	20 DOLLARS 10.10.1817; 1.1.1818. Montreal harbor, sailing ships at top ctr.	385.00	1325.	—
S1243D	50 DOLLARS 18xx. Royal crest at top ctr. Proof.	—	Unc	280.00

1818-20 ISSUE

#S1243E-S1243I black. Uniface. Printer: Leney & Rollison.

		Good	Fine	XF
S1243E	**1 Dollar** 1.3.1819; 1.4.1819. Montreal prison at top ctr.	315.00	1050.	—
S1243F	**2 Dollars** 1.12.1818; 1.3.1819; 1.4.1819; 5.1.1820. Paddle wheel steamboat at top ctr.	295.00	950.00	—

		Good	Fine	XF
S1243G	**5 Dollars** 1.2.1819; 5.3.1819; 11.3.1819. Tree and farm tools at top ctr.	295.00	950.00	—

		Good	Fine	XF
S1243H	**10 Dollars** 1.1.1818. Indian hunting in forest at top ctr.	385.00	1325.	—
S1243I	**100 Dollars** 18xx. Beehive at top ctr. Proof.	—	Unc	280.00

1821-22 Issue

#S1243J-S1243K black. Uniface. Printer: Reed & Stiles.

		Good	Fine	XF
S1243J	**1 Dollar** 18xx. Britannia, harbor scene in background at top ctr. Proof.	—	Unc	525.00

		Good	Fine	XF
S1243K	**5 Dollars** 2.10.1821. Woman on shell drawn by sea horses at top ctr.	300.00	1000.	—

1822-29 Issue

#S1243L-S1243O black. Uniface. Printer: Graphic Company.

		Good	Fine	XF
S1243L	**10 Dollars** 1.7.1829. Sailing ships at top ctr.	300.00	1000.	—
S1243M	**20 Dollars** 1.6.1822. Seated woman w/20 at top ctr.	300.00	1000.	—
S1243N	**50 Dollars** 18xx. Seated Commerce at top ctr. Unsigned remainder.	—	450.00	—

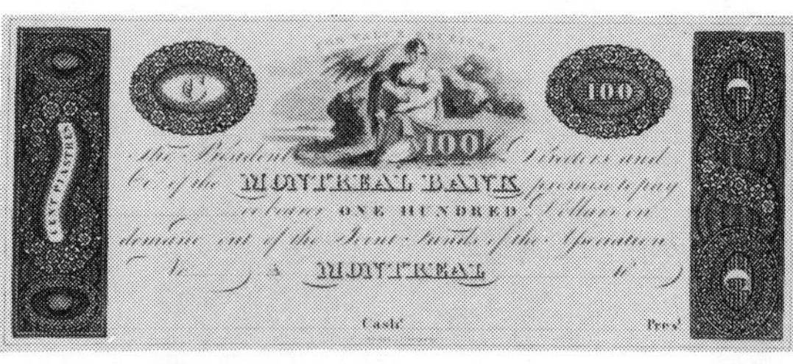

		Good	Fine	XF
S1243O	**100 Dollars** 1.6.1822. Woman seated on block w/100 at top ctr.	300.00	1000.	—

Niagara District Bank

Began operations in St. Catharines, Upper Canada in 1853. Merged with the Imperial Bank of Canada in 1873.

1854-55 Issue

#S1243P-S1243R black. Uniface. All notes w/text: *Secured by Deposit of Provincial Securities* at bottom. Printer: Danforth, Wright & Co.

		Good	Fine	XF
S1243P	**1 Dollar** 1854-55. Milkmaid at lower l., supported royal arms at top ctr.			
	a. 1854-55.	575.00	1950.	—
	b. Raised to $5.	315.00	1050.	—
	c. Raised to $10.	315.00	1050.	—
S1243Q	**2 Dollars** 18xx. Prince Consort at l. Proof.	—	Unc	500.00
S1243R	**5 Dollars** 18xx. Shipbuilding scene at l., Qn. Victoria at ctr. Proof.	—	Unc	500.00

1855-62 Issue

#S1243S-S1243W uniface. Sign. varieties. Printers: Danforth, Wright & Co. and ABNC.

		Good	Fine	XF
S1243S	**1 Dollar = 5 Shillings** 1855; 1862. Black. Horseshoe Falls at Niagara at upper l. Red word protector on face and back.			
	a. W/o unpt. Partially engraved. 2.7.1855.	505.00	1400.	—
	b. Green unpt. Fully engraved date. 2.1.1862.	415.00	1200.	—

		Good	Fine	XF
S1243T	**2 Dollars = 10 Shillings** 185x; 1862. Black. Portr. of Qn. Victoria at upper l., woman kneeling viewing plaque w/shipbuilding scene at bottom ctr., steam locomotive at lower r. Red word protector on face and back.			
	a. Green unpt. Fully engraved date. 2.1.1862.	415.00	1200.	—
	p. W/o unpt. Partially engraved date. Proof. 2.7.185x.	—	Unc	500.00
S1243U	**4 Dollars = 20 Shillings** 1855; 1862. Black. Man's portr. at lower l., paddle wheel, steamship and sailing ship at bottom ctr., ship in canal at lower r. Red word protector on face and back.			
	a. W/o unpt. Partially engraved date. 2.7.1855.	575.00	1550.	—
	b. Green unpt. Fully engraved date. 2.1.1862.	510.00	1400.	—
S1243V	**5 Dollars = 1 Pound-5 Shillings** 185x; 1862. Black. Man's portr. at lower l., 3 men dock-side at bottom ctr. Red word protector on face and back.			
	a. Green unpt. Fully engraved date. 2.1.1862.	415.00	1200.	—
	p. W/o unpt. Partially engraved date. Proof. 2.7.185x.	—	Unc	500.00
S1243W	**10 Dollars** 18xx. Black on green unpt. Sailor, woman and child at lower l., seated Justice at ctr., reclining woman at lower r. Partially engraved date. Face proof.	—	Unc	700.00

1872 Issue

#S1243X-S1243Z black on green unpt. Portr. W. H. Merritt at l., portr. J. R. Benson at r. Back green. Printer: BABNC.

		Good	Fine	XF
S1243X	**4 Dollars** 1.7.1872. Farm girl watering cattle at top ctr.	420.00	1400.	—
S1243Y	**5 Dollars** 1.7.1872. Paddle wheel steamboat at top ctr.	345.00	1125.	—
S1243Z	**10 Dollars** 1.7.1872. Niagara Falls at bottom ctr.	420.00	1400.	—

Northern Bank

Established in Winnipeg, Manitoba in 1905. Amalgamated with the Crown Bank of Canada in 1905 to become the Northern Crown Bank.

1905 Issue

#S1244-S1247 back green. Printer: BABNC.

		GOOD	FINE	XF
S1244	5 DOLLARS 1.11.1905. Black on green unpt. Farmer w/horses at ctr.	1375.	4550.	—
S1245	10 DOLLARS 1.11..1905. Black on red-brown unpt. Farmer w/horse drawn reaper at l. ctr.	1150.	3850.	—
S1246	20 DOLLARS 1.11.1905. Black on brown unpt. 2 bison on flatland at ctr.	1150.	3850.	—
S1247	50 DOLLARS 1.11.1905. Black on ochre unpt. Farm tools at lower l., farmer watering horses at ctr. Proof.	—	Unc	750.00

THE NORTHERN CROWN BANK

Formerly the Northern Bank and the Crown Bank of Canada.

1908-14 ISSUE

#S1248-S1251 royal crown over flower and leaves at bottom ctr. on back. Printer: BABNC.

		VG	VF	UNC
S1248	5 DOLLARS 1908; 1914. Black on olive and red unpt. Farmer w/horses at l. ctr. Back reddish-brown.			
	a. 2.7.1908.	1050.	2240.	—
	b. 2.7.1914.	1120.	2450.	—
S1249	10 DOLLARS 1908; 1914. Black on yellow and green unpt. Farmer w/horse drawn reaper at l. ctr. Back blue.			
	a. 2.7.1908.	1120.	2450.	—
	b. 2.7.1914.	1190.	2310.	—

		VG	VF	UNC
S1250	20 DOLLARS 2.7.1908. Black on peach and blue unpt. Bison on prairie at ctr. Back orange.	1400.	—	—
S1251	50 DOLLARS 2.7.1908. Black on yellow and red unpt. Lion in mountains. Back purple. Proof.	—	—	420.00

ONTARIO BANK

Established in Bowmanville, Canada West in 1857. Facing failure in 1906 it was absorbed by the Bank of Montreal.

1857 BOWMANVILLE ISSUE

#S1252-S1255 black on green unpt. Red ovpt: *MONTREAL* (twice) and blue ovpt: *PRESCOTT, TORONTO,* (twice) or *ALEXANDRIA.* Blue sheet number and *BOWMANVILLE* at bottom. Back green. Sign. varieties. Printers: RWH & E and ABNC.

		GOOD	FINE	XF
S1252	1 DOLLAR 15.8.1857. Agricultural produce at l., cattle at top ctr., shearing sheep at lower r.	230.00	770.00	—
S1253	2 DOLLARS 15.8.1857. Standing blacksmith w/sledge hammer by anvil at l., seated woman w/dog by cattle at ctr.	240.00	840.00	—
S1254	5 DOLLARS 15.8.1857. Portr. J. Cartier at l.; farmer sharpening scythe at ctr., bull's head at lower r. Face proof.	—	Unc	350.00
S1255	10 DOLLARS 15.8.1857. Barges at l., seated Indian and crest at ctr., cattle driving scene at r. Face proof.	—	Unc	350.00

1857 MONTREAL ISSUE

#S1256-S1259 like #S1252-S1255. Black on green unpt. Red ovpt: *OSHAWA* and blue ovpt: *TORONTO.* Blue sheet number and *MONTREAL* at bottom. Back green. Sign. varieties. Printers RWH & E and ABNC.

		GOOD	FINE	XF
S1256	1 DOLLAR 15.8.1857.	230.00	770.00	—
S1257	2 DOLLARS 15.8.1857.	250.00	875.00	—
S1258	5 DOLLARS 15.8.1857. Face proof.	—	Unc	350.00
S1259	10 DOLLARS 15.8.1857. Face proof.	—	Unc	350.00

1861 FIRST BOWMANVILLE ISSUE

Guelph-Dundas ovpts.

#S1260-S1263 like #S1252-S1255. Black on green unpt. Red ovpt: *GUELPH* and *DUNDAS* and blue ovpt: *TORONTO.* One red sheet number and *BOWMANVILLE* at bottom. Back green. Sign. varieties. Printers: RWH & E and ABNC.

		GOOD	FINE	XF
S1260	1 DOLLAR 15.8.1861.	265.00	875.00	—
S1261	2 DOLLARS 15.8.1861.	265.00	875.00	—
S1262	5 DOLLARS 15.8.1861.	265.00	875.00	—
S1263	10 DOLLARS 15.8.1861.	265.00	875.00	—

1861 SECOND BOWMANVILLE ISSUE

Hamilton-Lindsay ovpts.

#S1264-S1267 like #S1252-S1255. Black on green unpt. Blue ovpt: *HAMILTON* and *LINDSAY.* Two red sheet numbers and *BOWMANVILLE* at bottom. Back green. Sign. varieties. Printers: RWH & E and ABNC.

		GOOD	FINE	XF
S1264	1 DOLLAR 15.8.1861.	200.00	630.00	—
S1265	2 DOLLARS 15.8.1861.	200.00	630.00	—
S1266	5 DOLLARS 15.8.1861. Face proof.	—	Unc	350.00
S1267	10 DOLLARS 15.8.1861. Face proof.	—	Unc	350.00

1861 THIRD BOWMANVILLE ISSUE

Guelph-Whitby ovpts.

#S1268-S1271 like #S1252-S1255. Black on green unpt. Red ovpt: *GUELPH* and *MONTREAL* and blue ovpt: *WHITBY.* Two blue sheet numbers and *BOWMANVILLE* at bottom. Back green. Sign. varieties. Printers: RWH & E and ABNC.

		GOOD	FINE	XF
S1268	1 DOLLAR 15.8.1861.	200.00	630.00	—
S1269	2 DOLLARS 15.8.1861.	200.00	630.00	—
S1270	5 DOLLARS 15.8.1861. Face proof.	—	Unc	350.00
S1271	10 DOLLARS 15.8.1861. Face proof.	—	Unc	350.00

1860 ISSUE

#S1272-S1274 black on green unpt. Back green. Printer: ABNC.

		GOOD	FINE	XF
S1272	20 DOLLARS 3.8.1860. Young woman resting on hay at upper l., farm boy resting w/sheep at upper r. over portr. Prince Albert. Face proof.	—	Unc	420.00
S1273	50 DOLLARS 3.8.1860. Standing allegorical woman by beehive at l., portr. Prince of Wales at ctr., allegorical woman holding grapes and cornucopia at lower r. Face proof.	—	Unc	420.00
S1274	100 DOLLARS 3.8.1860. Portr. Prince of Wales at lower l., 2 reclining allegorical women at top ctr. Face proof.	—	Unc	420.00

1870 ISSUE

#S1275-S1277 black on green unpt. Blue ovpt: *LINDSAY, PETERBORO, MONTREAL* or *OSHAWA.* Back green. Sign. varieties. Printer: BABNC.

		VG	VF	UNC
S1275	4 DOLLARS 1.8.1870. Farmer plowing w/horses at lower l., portr. Prince Arthur at lower r.	420.00	840.00	—
S1276	5 DOLLARS 1.11.1870. Portr. Prince Arthur at lower l., farm woman w/sickle at ctr., portr. young woman at lower r.	420.00	770.00	—
S1277	10 DOLLARS 1.11.1870. Woodsman at lower l., seated girl holding scroll at lower r.	420.00	770.00	—

NOTE: Counterfeits exist of #S1277.

1882 ISSUE

#S1278-S1280 black on green unpt. Back green; crest at ctr. Sign. varieties. Printer: BABNC.

		VG	VF	UNC
S1278	5 DOLLARS 3.7.1882. Young woman at lower l., Indian girl w/shield at ctr., steam train at r.	1120.	—	—

		VG	VF	Unc
S1279	**10 Dollars** 3.7.1882. Portr. Prince Arthur at l., dockside scene at ctr., girl at r. Face proof.	—	Unc	350.00
S1280	**10 Dollars** 3.7.1882. Cattle grazing at l., girl at r. Face proof.	—	Unc	350.00
S1281	**100 Dollars** 3.7.1882. Portr. Prince of Wales at l., allegorical women at ctr. Face proof.	—	Unc	350.00

1888 Issue

#S1282-S1285 sign. varieties. Printer: ABNC.

		VG	VF	Unc
S1282	**5 Dollars** 1.6.1888. Black on yellow and orange unpt. Farmer haying, horses at lower l., portr. Indian brave at ctr., standing allegorical woman w/wheel at r. Back orange.			
	a. Issued note.	770.00	1475.	—
	b. Red ovpt: *1903* (twice).	975.00	1825.	—
S1283	**10 Dollars** 1.6.1888. Black on yellow-green and orange unpt. "Calmady children" at upper l., seated allegorical woman at ctr., sailor boy at upper r. Back olive.			
	a. Issued note.	910.00	1750.	—
	b. Red ovpt: *1903* (twice).	910.00	1750.	—
S1284	**20 Dollars** 1.6.1888. Black on yellow and blue unpt. Portr. 2 laureate allegorical women at l., seated woman amongst sheep at ctr. r. Back green. Face proof.	—	—	420.00
S1285	**50 Dollars** 1.6.1888. Black on yellow-green and red unpt. Reclining woman w/spilt jug at l., crouching sailor by anchor at r. Back brown. Face proof.	—	—	420.00

1898 Issue

		Good	Fine	XF
S1286	**5 Dollars** 1.1.1898. Black on green unpt. Portr. young woman at upper l., woman and cherubs at ctr., bull's head at r. Sign. varieties. Printer: BABNC.	550.00	1325.	—

People's Bank of Halifax

Established in Halifax, Nova Scotia in 1864. Absorbed by the Bank of Montreal in 1905.

1864-1903 Issue

#S1287-S1289 back green. Printer: BABNC.

		VG	VF	Unc
S1287	**4 Dollars** 1.7.1870. Black on green unpt. Seated Commerce at l., supported royal arms at lower r. Red ovpt: *1871* and *CANADA CURRENCY* seal.			
	a. Issued note.	1250.	2525.	—
	p. Face proof.	—	—	500.00
S1288	**5 Dollars** 1870-1901. Black on green unpt. Seated woman holding trident w/ship in background at lower l., horses' heads at r.			
	a. Red ovpt: *1871* and *CANADA CURRENCY* seal.	1550.	3150.	—
	b. 1.7.1882-1.10.1900.	1550.	3150.	—
	c. Overall green unpt. 1.10.1901.	1550.	3150.	—
	p. Face proof. 18xx.	—	—	500.00
S1289	**10 Dollars** 1880-1903. Black. Woman and telegraph.			
	a. 1.11.1894.	1825.	3775.	—
	b. Orange unpt. 1.10.1900.	1825.	3775.	—
	c. 1.10.1901.	1825.	3775.	—
	p1. Green unpt. Face proof. 1.9.1880.	—	—	500.00
	p2. Green unpt. Face proof. 2.7.1903.	—	—	500.00
S1290	**20 Dollars** 1864-1903. Black on green unpt. Portr. Princess of Wales at l., portr. Qn. Victoria between reclining Indian woman and lion at ctr., 2 sailors on watch at lower r. Back blue. Printer: ABNC.			
	a. Issued note. 1.11.1898.	1750.	2950.	—
	p. Face proof. 25.5.1864; 2.7.1903.	—	—	425.00
	s. Specimen. 27.5.1870.	—	—	—

Peoples Bank of New Brunswick

Established in Fredericton, New Brunswick in 1864. Absorbed by the Bank of Montreal in 1907.

1864-73 Issue

#S1291-S1293 black on green unpt. Portr. of man at lower l. Partially engraved date. Uniface. Printer: ABNC.

		Good	Fine	XF
S1291	**1 Dollar** 1.9.1864; 1.5.1867. Lion w/shield at ctr., portr. Qn. Victoria at lower r.	355.00	1200.	—
S1292	**2 Dollars** 1873. Britannia and Justice at ctr., portr. Qn. Victoria at lower r.	355.00	1200.	—
S1293	**5 Dollars** 18xx. Arms at ctr., sailboat at lower r. Proof.	—	Unc	500.00

1874; 1881 Issue

#S1294-S1296 black on green unpt. Fully engraved date. Back green. Sign. varieties. Printers: ABNC and BABNC.

		VG	VF	Unc
S1294	**1 Dollar** 2.1.1874; 1.12.1881. Similar to #S1291.			
	a. 2.1.1874.	700.00	1475.	—
	b. 1.12.1881.	850.00	1675.	—
S1295	**2 Dollars** 2.1.1874; 1.12.1881. Similar to #S1292.			
	a. 2.1.1874.	850.00	1675.	—
	b. 1.12.1881.	625.00	1475.	—
S1295A	**5 Dollars** 2.1.1874. Similar to #S1293.	700.00	1750.	—
S1296	**10 Dollars** 1.12.1881. Prince of Wales at lower l., seated Liberty w/torch at l. ctr., sailing ship at upper ctr. r., portr. man at lower r.	975.00	2100.	—

1885 Issue

#S1297 and S1298 black on green unpt. Portr. Qn. Victoria in "Widow's Weeds" at r. Back green. Printer: BABNC.

		VG	VF	Unc
S1297	**1 Dollar** 2.1.1885. Anchor at lower l., steam train at ctr.	850.00	1675.	—
S1298	**5 Dollars** 2.11.1885. Portr. Prince Arthur at l., sailing ship at ctr.	975.00	2100.	—

1897; 1904 Issue

#S1299 and S1300 legislative bldg. at l., A. F. Randolph at r. Back green. Sign. varieties. Printer: BABNC.

		VG	VF	Unc
S1299	**5 Dollars** 1897; 1904.			
	a. Black on red-brown unpt. 22.6.1897.	975.00	1675.	—
	b. Black on ochre unpt. 1.7.1904.	1250.	2450.	—
S1300	**10 Dollars** 1897; 1904.			
	a. Black on red-brown unpt. 22.6.1897.	1250.	2450.	—
	b. Black on ochre unpt. 1.7.1904.	1250.	2450.	—

1897 Issue

#S1301 and S1302 printers: ABNC and BABNC.

		VG	VF	Unc
S1301	**20 Dollars** 22.6.1897. Black on blue unpt. Standing Justice at l., St. George slaying dragon at ctr., portr. Duke of Wellington at lower r. Back blue.	1250.	2450.	—
S1302	**50 Dollars** 1897; 1905. Portr. Qn. Victoria at l., reclining Commerce at top ctr. r., cattle at lower r.			
	a. Black on green unpt. Partially engraved date, completed by red handstamp: *Nov. 2, 1905.* Back green. 6.10.1905.	1250.	2800.	—
	p. Black on blue unpt. Fully engraved date. Face proof. 22.6.1897.	—	—	500.00

#S1303-S1305 *Deleted.* See #S1936-S1938.

Québec Bank

Began operations in 1818 as a private partnership in Quebec, Lower Canada. Chartered in 1822. Merged with the Royal Bank of Canada in 1917.

1818 Issue

Dollar System.

#S1306-S1310 black. Uniface. Printer: Maverick.

NOTE: Counterfeits exist w/engraved sign. and date 1 May 1819.

		Good	Fine	XF
S1306	**1 Dollar** 1818; 1819.	—	—	—
S1307	**3 Dollars** 20.10.1818. Farm at upper l.	525.00	1675.	—
S1308	**5 Dollars** 1818; 1819.	—	—	—
S1309	**10 Dollars** 1818; 1819. Crossed cornucopias at upper l.	—	—	—
S1310	**100 Dollars** 1818; 1819.	—	—	—

1819 Issue

#S1311-S1317 black. Uniface proofs. No issued notes known today. Printer: Graphic Co.

		Good	Fine	XF
S1311	**1 Dollar** 1819-31.	—	Unc	500.00

		GOOD	FINE	XF
S1312	**2 DOLLARS** 1819-37.	—	Unc	500.00
S1313	**5 DOLLARS** 1819-34.	—	Unc	500.00

		GOOD	FINE	XF
S1314	**10 DOLLARS** 1819-34.	—	Unc	500.00
S1315	**20 DOLLARS** 1819-33.	Reported Not Confirmed		
S1316	**50 DOLLARS** 1819-33.	—	Unc	500.00
S1317	**100 DOLLARS** 1819-33.	—	Unc	500.00

1835 ISSUE

#S1318-S1319 black. Sign. varieties. Printer: Rawdon, Wright & Co.

		VG	VF	UNC
S1318	**1 DOLLAR** 1835; 1836. Man w/3 children, seated woman w/early steam passenger train in background at top ctr., small steamship at bottom.	775.00	1675.	—
S1319	**5 DOLLARS** 1.6.18xx. Proof.	—	Unc	500.00

1837 SCRIP ISSUE

		GOOD	FINE	XF
S1320	**6 PENCE = 12 SOUS** 1.6.1837. Black. Printer: Jones.	235.00	800.00	—

#S1320A and S1320B black. Uniface. Sign. varieties. Printer: RW & H.

		VG	VF	UNC
S1320A	**1/4 DOLLAR** 1.10.1837. Cherubs at l. and r. of portr. woman at ctr., reverse of Spanish 2 reales coin at r.	775.00	1475.	—
S1320B	**1/2 DOLLAR** 1.10.1837. Reverse of Spanish 4 reales coin at l., portr. woman at l. and r. of sailing ship over dog's head at ctr.	775.00	1475.	—

1837-60 ISSUES

#S1321-S1328 black. Uniface. Printer for all except #S1323: RWH & Co.

		VG	VF	UNC
S1321	**1 DOLLAR** 18xx. Proof.	—	Unc	280.00
S1322	**2 DOLLARS** 18xx. Proof.	—	Unc	280.00

		GOOD	FINE	XF
S1323	**2 DOLLARS** 1858-59. Beehive at l., supported royal arms at top ctr., Indian paddling canoe at lower ctr., standing Britannia at r. Green ovpt: *QUEBEC* and *C. E.* Green word protector on face. Printer: Harris & Sealey, New York. Spurious issue.	60.00	200.00	—
S1324	**5 DOLLARS** 18xx. Proof.	—	Unc	280.00
S1325	**10 DOLLARS** 18xx. Proof.	—	Unc	280.00
S1326	**20 DOLLARS** 18xx. 3 allegories above ship and factory at ctr., sailing ship at r.			
	p. Proof.	—	Unc	280.00
	r. Blue ovpt: *OTTAWA* Green word protector on face. Dated w/blue printed #. Unsigned remainder. 1.11.18xx.	—	—	560.00

#S1327 and S1328 sailing ships whaling at l.

		GOOD	FINE	XF
S1327	**50 DOLLARS** 18xx. Sailing ships, wharf scene at l., 2 allegories above dog by strongbox at ctr.			
	p. Proof.	—	Unc	280.00
	r. Blue ovpt: *OTTAWA*. Green word protector on face. Dated w/blue printed #. Unsigned remainder. 1.11.18xx.	—	—	560.00
S1328	**100 DOLLARS** 18xx. Seahorses pulling Neptune and woman at top ctr., schooner at r.			
	p. Proof.	—	Unc	280.00
	r. Blue ovpt: *OTTAWA*. Green word protector on face. Dated w/blue printed #. Unsigned remainder. 1.11.18xx.	—	—	560.00

1843-65 ISSUES

Dollar/Pound Sterling System.

#S1329-S1335B black. Sign. varieties.

#S1329-S1332 and #S1334-S1335 printer: RWH & Co.

		GOOD	FINE	XF
S1329	**1 DOLLAR = 5 SHILLINGS** 1.11.18xx. 2 allegorical women flanking shield at upper ctr., dog's head at lower ctr. Uniface. Proof.	—	Unc	280.00
S1330	**1 DOLLAR = 5 SHILLINGS** 1.11.1855-1861. Like #S1329. Red word protector on face and back. Blue hand stamp: *OTTAWA*.	190.00	630.00	1470.

		GOOD	FINE	XF
S1331	**2 DOLLARS = 10 SHILLINGS** 1.11.1852-1860. Standing Britannia at lower l., seated allegorical man and woman at top ctr., milkmaid w/bucket at lower r. Uniface.	220.00	775.00	—
S1332	**2 DOLLARS = 10 SHILLINGS** 1.11.1850. Like #S1331. Red word protector on face and back. Blue hand stamp: *OTTAWA*.	240.00	840.00	—
S1333	**2 DOLLARS = 10 SHILLINGS** 1.11.1865. Like #S1331. Black text: *PAYABLE IN TORONTO* at top, *TORONTO* at ends, and *FOR THE QUEBEC BANK* at lower l. Back green. Printer RWH & E.			
	a. Red word and green numeral protectors on face and back.	165.00	840.00	—
	b. Green word and green numeral protectors on face only.	165.00	840.00	—
S1334	**5 DOLLARS = 1 POUND-5 SHILLINGS** 1.11.18xx. Seated woman w/shield w/lg. ornate *5* at l., 2 men w/beehive and shield above 2 small ships at ctr., 3 cherubs in oval at r. Uniface. Proof.	—	Unc	280.00
S1335	**5 DOLLARS = 1 POUND-5 SHILLINGS** 1.11.1847; 1860-61. Like #S1334. Red word protector on face and back. Blue hand stamp: *OTTAWA*.	205.00	700.00	—
S1335A	**10 DOLLARS = 2 POUNDS-10 SHILLINGS** 1.11.18xx. Bust of helmeted Greek soldier at l., sailing ships at ctr., portr. Qn. Victoria at r. Proof.	—	Unc	280.00
S1335B	**10 DOLLARS = 2 POUNDS-10 SHILLINGS** 1.11.1849. Like #S1335A. Red word protector on face and back. Blue hand stamp: *OTTAWA*.	165.00	840.00	—

1843-62 ISSUES

Dollar System.

#S1336-S1341 black. Uniface. Sign. varieties.

		GOOD	FINE	XF
S1336	**1 DOLLAR** 1.11.18xx. Bust of Greek god at l., Indians hunting on horseback at top ctr., woman and anchor in lg. ornate *1* at r. Blue hand stamp: *BYTOWN*. Printer: RW & H. Proof.	—	Unc	280.00
S1337	**2 DOLLARS** 1.11.18xx. Royal crest at top ctr., bust of helmeted Roman Soldier at r. Blue handstamp: *BYTOWN*. Printer: RW & H. Proof.	—	Unc	280.00
S1338	**4 DOLLARS** 1.11.18xx. Bust of helmeted Roman soldier at l. and r., sailing ships in harbor over mermaid at ctr. Blue handstamp: *BYTOWN*. Printer: RW & H. Proof.	—	Unc	280.00
S1339	**4 DOLLARS** 1849-62. Like #S1338.			
	a. Red word protector on face and back Printer: RWH & Co. 1.11.1849-1852.	235.00	800.00	—
	b. Printer: RWH & E. 1.2.1862.	225.00	775.00	—

		Good	Fine	XF
S1340	**5 Dollars** 1852-54. Man w/shield at l., facing griffins at top ctr., portr. Qn. Victoria at r.			
	a. Blue hand stamp: *BYTOWN.* Printer like #S1336. 1.11.1852-1853.	235.00	800.00	—
	b. Printer: RWH & E. 1.2.1854.	225.00	775.00	—
S1341	**10 Dollars** 1849-62. Bust of helmeted Greek soldier at l., sailing ships at upper l. ctr., Qn. Victoria at r.			
	a. Blue handstamp: *BYTOWN.* Printer: RW & H. 1.11.1853.	235.00	800.00	—
	b. Red word protector on face and back. Printer: RW & H. 1.11.1849-1852.	225.00	775.00	—
	c. Printer: RWH & E. 1.2.1862.	225.00	775.00	—

1858 Spurious Issue

		VG	VF	Unc
S1341A	**2 Dollars** 1858; 1859. Black. Beehive, farm tools at l., supported royal arms at top ctr., standing Britannia at r. Green word protector on face. Green ovpt: *QUEBEC* and *C.E.* Uniface. Printer: Harris & Sealey Engravers.	150.00	315.00	—

1856 Issue

Dollar/Pound Sterling System.

#S1342-S1344 uniface. Sign. varieties. Printer: TCC.

		Good	Fine	XF
S1342	**1 Dollar = 5 Shillings** 185x, 1859. Anchor, barrel at l., woodsman over St. George slaying dragon at ctr., beehive, flowers at r.			
	a. Green word protector on face. (No notes known). 2.1.185x.	—	—	—
	b. Black on green unpt. 2.1.1859.	275.00	975.00	—
	p. Black. Proof. 2.1.185x.	—	Unc	275.00

		Good	Fine	XF
S1343	**4 Dollars = 1 Pound** 1856-59. Men w/cattle and wagons at lower l., men w/cattle at lower ctr. steam train at lower r.			
	a. Black. 2.1.1856.	225.00	775.00	—
	b. Green word protector on face only. (No notes known). 2.1.185x.	—	—	—
	c. Black on green unpt. 2.1.1859.	280.00	975.00	—
S1344	**10 Dollars = 2 Pounds-10 Shillings** 185x, 1859.			
	a. Green word protector on face only. (No notes known). 2.1.185x.	—	—	—
	b. Black on green unpt. (No notes known). 2.1.1859.	—	—	—
	p. Black. Proof. 2.1.185x.	—	Unc	280.00

1863 Issue

#S1345-S1349 black on green unpt. Except for #S1347a, blue ovpt: *GASPE, OTTAWA, PAYABLE IN TORONTO, ST. CATHARINES PAYABLE IN TORONTO, PAYABLE IN MONTREAL, OTTAWA PAYABLE IN MONTREAL* or *THREE RIVERS.* Sign. varieties. Printer: ABNC.

#S1345-S1348 bank crest at upper or top ctr.

		VG	VF	Unc
S1345	**1 Dollar** 2.1.1863. Portr. of sailor at l., 3 lumberjacks at lower r.	350.00	775.00	—
S1346	**2 Dollars** 2.1.1863. Shipbuilding scene at lower l., sailing ships at lower r.	595.00	1125.	—
S1347	**4 Dollars** 2.1.1863. Sailor, woman and child at lower l., seated Britannia w/shield w/lg. *4* at lower r.	595.00	1125.	—
S1347A	**4 Dollars** Similar to #S1347 but w/lg. ornate "4's" at l. and r. of bank crest. Blue ovpt: *TORONTO.*	630.00	1200.	—
S1348	**5 Dollars** 2.1.1863. 2 beavers at lower l. Seated woman w/telescope at lower r.	840.00	1600.	—
S1349	**10 Dollars** 2.1.1863. Reclining woman at lower l., bank crest at lower r.	840.00	1600.	—

1870 Issue

		VG	VF	Unc
S1350	**4 Dollars** 1.10.1870. Black on green unpt. Sir N. F. Belleau at lower l., bank crest at upper ctr., young sailor at lower r. Blue ovpt: *OTTAWA, TORONTO,* or *THREE RIVERS.* Sign. varieties. Printer: BABNC.	490.00	1050.	—

1873; 1888 Issue

#S1351-S1353 sign. varieties. Printers: ABNC and BABNC.

		VG	VF	Unc
S1351	**4 Dollars** 2.1.1873. Black on green unpt. Similar to #S1347A. Red ovpt: *A A* or blue ovpt: *B B.*	630.00	1200.	—
S1352	**5 Dollars** 1873-88. Black on green unpt. Similar to #S1348.			
	a. Red ovpt: *A A* or blue ovpt: *B B.* 2.1.1873.	770.00	1475.	—
	b. Purple hand stamp: *D* or *B.* 3.1.1888.	770.00	1475.	—
	c. Black on brown unpt. 3.1.1888.	805.00	1600.	—
S1353	**10 Dollars** 3.1.1888. Black on green unpt. Similar to #S1349. Red ovpt: *A A* or blue ovpt: *B B.* Purple hand stamp: *D* or *B.*	910.00	1750.	—

1898 Issue

#S1354-S1359 sign. varieties. Printer: ABNC.

		VG	VF	Unc
S1354	**5 Dollars** 3.1.1898. Black on green unpt. Paddle wheel steamboat and modern ship at ctr. Back green; bank crest at ctr.	630.00	1350.	—
S1355	**10 Dollars** 3.1.1898. Black on olive-green unpt. Docks at Quebec City at ctr. Back blue; bank crest at ctr.	630.00	1325.	—

#S1356-S1359 black on yellow and olive-green unpt.

		VG	VF	Unc
S1356	**10 Dollars** 3.1.1898. Like #S1355. Back green; bank crest at ctr.	630.00	1325.	—
S1357	**20 Dollars** 3.1.1898. Cherub on winged wheel at l., falls at r. Back olive; Quebec City - Prescott Gate at ctr.	910.00	1750.	—
S1358	**50 Dollars** 3.1.1898. Seated woman w/globe at ctr. Back olive; Quebec Cty - Kent Gate at ctr.	910.00	1750.	—
S1359	**100 Dollars** 3.1.1898. Reclining woman w/spear and bank crest at l. ctr. Back olive; Quebec City - Hope Gate at ctr.	910.00	1750.	—

1901 Issue

		VG	VF	Unc
S1360	**5 Dollars** 2.7.1901. Black on yellow and olive unpt. Seated woman w/lion and shield at ctr. Back green; bank crest at ctr. Sign. varieties. Printer: ABNC.	630.00	1325.	—

1908; 1911 Issues

#S1361-S1368 black on yellow and olive unpt. Back green. Sign. varieties. Printer: ABNC.

		VG	VF	Unc
S1361	**5 Dollars** 1.6.1908. Similar to #S1360. Red ovpt: *M M.* Bank crest on back.			
	a. W/o text: *FOUNDED 1818* at top.	425.00	1000.	3150.
	b. W/text: *FOUNDED 1818* at top.	425.00	975.00	3150.
S1362	**5 Dollars** 1.6.1908. Like #S1361a. Quebec City - Prescott Gate on back.	525.00	1025.	—

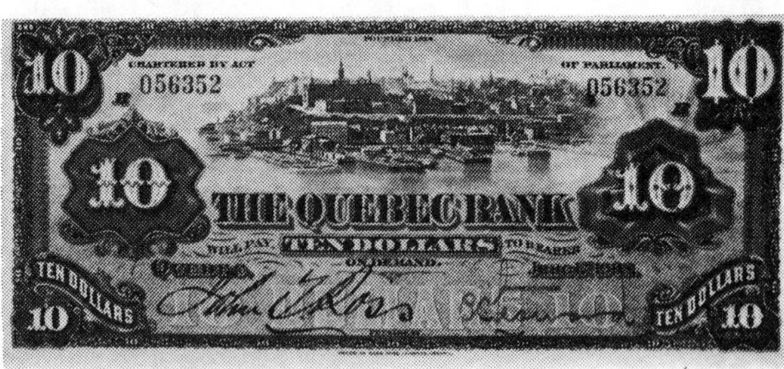

		VG	VF	Unc
S1363	**10 Dollars** 1.6.1908. Similar to #S1355. Bank crest on back.			
	a. W/o text: *FOUNDED 1818* at top.	490.00	1025.	3150.
	b. W/text: *FOUNDED 1818* at top.	490.00	980.00	3150.
S1364	**10 Dollars** 1.6.1908. Like #S1363a. Quebec City - Hope Gate on back.	525.00	1025.	—
S1365	**20 Dollars** 3.1.1911. Similar to #S1357. Quebec City - Prescott Gate on back. W/text: *Founded 1818* at top.	840.00	1765.	—
S1366	**20 Dollars** 3.1.1911. Like #S1365. Bank crest on back.	1015.	2100.	—
S1367	**50 Dollars** 3.1.1911. Similar to #S1358. Quebec City - Kent Gate on back. W/text: *Founded 1818* at top.	840.00	1775.	—
S1368	**100 Dollars** 3.1.1911. Similar to #S1359. Quebec City - Hope Gate on back. W/text: *Founded 1818* at top.	840.00	1775.	—

Royal Bank of Canada

Formerly the Merchants Bank of Halifax. Became Royal Bank of Canada in 1901. Established branch offices in the Caribbean. See also Antigua, Barbados, British Guiana, Dominica, Grenada, Jamaica, St. Kitts, St. Lucia and Trinidad listings.

1901; 1909 Issue

#S1369-S1377 sign. varieties. Royal crest at ctr. on back. Printer: ABNC.

		Good	Fine	XF
S1369	**5 Dollars** 2.1.1901. Black on m/c unpt. Seated woman w/2 children at l. Back green and m/c.	100.00	335.00	1100.

S1370 5 DOLLARS
2.1.1901. Black on green and yellow-green unpt. Like #S1369. Back green. 55.00 165.00 500.00

		GOOD	FINE	XF
S1371	**5 DOLLARS** 2.1.1909. Black on green and yellow unpt. Like #S1370.			
	a. Black 5's on face.	65.00	175.00	500.00
	b. Green 5's on face.	25.00	85.00	200.00
S1372	**10 DOLLARS** 2.1.1901. Black on m/c unpt. Seated allegorical woman at r. Back blue and m/c.	115.00	385.00	910.00

		GOOD	FINE	XF
S1373	**10 DOLLARS** 2.1.1909. Black on m/c unpt. Like #S1372. Back green and m/c.	145.00	500.00	1125.
S1373A	**10 DOLLARS** 2.1.1909. Black on green and yellow unpt. Like #S1373. Back olive and yellow.	65.00	210.00	525.00
S1374	**20 DOLLARS** 2.1.1901. Black on m/c unpt. Seated woman w/lion and shield at ctr. Back yellow-brown and m/c.			
	a. Issued note.	155.00	525.00	1250.
	p. Proof.	—	Unc	350.00
S1375	**20 DOLLARS** 2.1.1909. Black on m/c unpt. Like #S1374. Back green and m/c. Specimen.	—	Unc	875.00
S1375A	**20 DOLLARS** 2.1.1909. Black on blue and yellow unpt. like #S1375.	200.00	665.00	1325.
S1376	**50 DOLLARS** 2.1.1901; 2.1.1909. Black on m/c unpt. Steam sailing ship at r. Back yellow-brown and m/c.			
	p. Proof.	—	Unc	350.00
	s. Specimen.	—	Unc	875.00
S1377	**100 DOLLARS** 2.1.1909. Black on red-orange unpt. Seated Commerce in oval frame at r. Back red-orange. Face proof.	—	Unc	350.00

1913 ISSUE

#S1378-S1382 supported royal arms at ctr. on back. Sign. varieties. Printer: ABNC or CBNC.

		VG	VF	UNC
S1378	**5 DOLLARS** 2.1.1913. Black on green unpt. of E. L. Pease at l., Canadian arms at ctr., H. S. Holt at r. Back green.	35.00	90.00	300.00

		VG	VF	UNC
S1379	**10 DOLLARS** 2.1.1913. Black on yellow-green and blue unpt. "H. M. C. S. Bellerophon" at ctr. Back yellow-orange.	35.00	125.00	500.00

		VG	VF	UNC
S1380	**20 DOLLARS** 2.1.1913. Black on blue unpt. Steam passenger train in prairies at ctr. Back blue.	70.00	175.00	600.00

		VG	VF	UNC
S1381	**50 DOLLARS** 2.1.1913. Black on green and yellow unpt. E. L. Pease at l. Back olive.	200.00	500.00	—

		VG	VF	UNC
S1382	**100 DOLLARS** 2.1.1913. Black on orange and yellow-green unpt. H. S. Holt at r. Back red.	500.00	1000.	—

1927 ISSUE

#S1383-S1387 Canadian arms at ctr. Sign. varieties. Printer: CBNC.

#S1383-S1385 C. E. Neill at l., H. S. Holt at r.

		VG	VF	UNC
S1383	**5 DOLLARS** 3.1.1927. Black on green unpt. Back green.	20.00	50.00	250.00
S1384	**10 DOLLARS** 3.1.1927. Black on orange unpt. Back orange.	20.00	50.00	250.00

		VG	VF	UNC
S1385	**20 DOLLARS** 3.1.1927. Black on blue unpt. Back blue.	25.00	75.00	300.00

		VG	VF	UNC
S1386	**50 DOLLARS** 3.1.1927. Black on purple unpt. E. L. Pease at l. Back purple.	125.00	265.00	1000.
S1387	**100 DOLLARS** 3.1.1927. Black on olive unpt. H. S. Holt at r.	160.00	335.00	1250.

1933 ISSUE

#S1388-S1390 M. W. Wilson at l., H. Holt at r. Royal crest at ctr. on back. Printer: CBNC.

		VG	VF	UNC
S1388	**5 DOLLARS** 3.7.1933. Black on green unpt. Back green.	25.00	75.00	300.00
S1389	**10 DOLLARS** 3.7.1933. Black on orange unpt. Back orange.	25.00	75.00	300.00
S1390	**20 DOLLARS** 3.7.1933. Black on blue unpt. Back blue. Specimen.	—	—	525.00

1935 ISSUE

#S1391-S1393 like #S1388-S1390, but reduced size. Printer: BABNC.

		VG	VF	UNC
S1391	**5 DOLLARS** 2.1.1935. Black on green unpt. Back green.	10.00	21.00	100.00

		VG	VF	UNC
S1392	**10 DOLLARS** 2.1.1935. Black on orange unpt. Back orange.	14.00	25.00	110.00

		VG	VF	UNC
S1393	**20 DOLLARS** 2.1.1935. Black on blue unpt. Back blue.	17.50	35.00	200.00

1943 ISSUE

		VG	VF	UNC
S1394	**5 DOLLARS** 2.1.1943. Black on green unpt. S. G. Dobson at l., M. Wilson at r. Back green; royal crest at ctr. Printer: BABNC.	24.50	60.00	195.00

ST. LAWRENCE BANK

Established in Toronto, Ontario in 1872. Changed its name to the Standard Bank of Canada in 1876.

1872 ISSUES

#S1395-S1399 black on green unpt. Printer: BABNC.

		VG	VF	UNC
S1395	**4 DOLLARS** 2.12.1872. Deer at lower l., portr. of J. C. Fitch at upper l. ctr., steam passenger train, ships dockside at top ctr. r. Face proof.	—	—	500.00
S1396	**4 DOLLARS** 2.12.1872. Similar to #S1395 but w/o portr. Fitch. Face proof.	—	—	500.00
S1396A	**5 DOLLARS** 2.12.1872. J. Cartier sighting land at l., portr. J. C. Fitch at lower r. Face proof.	—	—	500.00

		VG	VF	UNC
S1397	**5 DOLLARS** 2.12.1872. Cartier sighting land at l., portr. Prince Arthur at lower r. Face proof.	—	—	500.00
S1398	**10 DOLLARS** 2.12.1872. Portr. K. F. Lockhart at upper l. cherubs w/lg. ornate *X* at lower ctr., portr. J. C. Fitch at upper r. Face proof.	—	—	500.00
S1399	**10 DOLLARS** 2.12.1872. Allegorical woman at upper l., denomination quilloche replacing portr. J. C. Fitch at upper r. Face proof.	—	—	500.00

ST. STEPHENS BANK

Established in St. Stephen, New Brunswick in 1836. Sold to the Bank of British North America in 1910.

1830S FIRST ISSUE

Pound Sterling System.

#S1400-S1402 black. Supported royal arms at upper ctr. Uniface. Printer: New England Bank Note Company.

		VG	VF	UNC
S1400	**1 POUND** 18xx. Shipbuilding at l. Proof.	—	—	350.00
S1401	**5 POUNDS** 18xx. Standing Britannia w/shield at l. Proof.	—	—	350.00
S1402	**10 POUNDS** 18xx. Beehive at l. Proof.	—	—	350.00

1830S SECOND ISSUE

Dollar System.

#S1403 and S1404 black. Uniface. Printer: New England Bank Note Company.

		VG	VF	UNC
S1403	**1 DOLLAR** 18xx. Ships at ctr., seated woman at r. Proof.	—	Unc	350.00

		GOOD	FINE	XF
S1404	**2 DOLLARS** 1.9.1836. Allegorical women at l., seated woman w/produce at top ctr. r., portr. woman at r.	355.00	1200.	—

1846-60 ISSUE

#S1405-S1407 black. W/o word protectors. Uniface. Printer: New England Bank Note Company.

		GOOD	FINE	XF
S1405	**1 DOLLAR** 1.1.1846; 1.9.1853. Sailing ships, at upper l., seated Indian woman at r.	355.00	1190.	—
S1406	**2 DOLLARS** 18xx. Sailing ships at upper l., woman at well at r. Proof.	—	Unc	350.00
S1407	**3 DOLLARS** 18xx. Harvesting at l., steamboat at r. Proof.	—	Unc	350.00

1840S ISSUE

#S1408-S1410 w/red word protector on face and back. Designs like previous 3 notes.

		GOOD	FINE	XF
S1408	**1 DOLLAR** 18xx. Like #S1405. (No notes known).	—	—	—
S1409	**2 DOLLARS** 18xx. Like #S1406. Remainder.	—	Unc	875.00
S1410	**3 DOLLARS** 18xx. Like #S1407. (No notes known).	—	—	—

1852 ISSUE

#S1411-S1412 black. Printer: Boston Bank Note Company.

		VG	VF	UNC
S1411	**5 DOLLARS** 1.6.1852. Tug and sailing ships at l., 2 Indians near falls at ctr., farmer w/sheaf at r. Remainder.			
	p. Face proof. 18xx.	—	—	350.00
	r. Unsigned remainder. 1.6.1852.	—	—	875.00
S1412	**10 DOLLARS** 1.6.1852; 18xx. Indian in canoe at upper l. ctr., shipbuilding at r. Face proof.	—	—	350.00

1860 ISSUES

#S1413 and S1418 black on green unpt. Printer: ABNC.

		VG	VF	UNC
S1413	**1 DOLLAR** 1.7.1860. Black on green unpt. Portr. Wm. Todd at lower l., bear attacking hunters in boat at upper ctr. sailor boy at lower r. Uniface.	875.00	1750.	—
S1414	**1 DOLLAR** 1.7.1860. Like #S1413 but back green.	875.00	1750.	—

#S1415 and S1416 uniface.

		VG	VF	UNC
S1415	**2 DOLLARS** 1.7.1860. Black on green unpt. St. George slaying dragon at lower l., portr. Wm. Todd at lower r. Proof.	—	—	350.00
S1416	**3 DOLLARS** 1.7.1860. Black on green unpt. Seated allegorical woman w/tablet at lower l., portr. Qn. Victoria at upper ctr., seated Britannia w/shield w/lg. 3. at lower r.	875.00	1750.	—

		VG	VF	UNC
S1417	**5 DOLLARS** 1.7.1860. Black on green unpt. 2 sailors on dock at lower l., lion w/shield at upper ctr., portr. Qn. Victoria at lower r. Uniface. Proof.	—	—	350.00
S1417A	**5 DOLLARS** 1.7.1860. Like #S1417 but back green.	—	—	350.00
S1418	**10 DOLLARS** 1.7.1860. Black on green unpt. Beehieve at lower l., sailor at upper ctr., supported royal arms at lower r. Uniface. Proof.	—	—	350.00
S1418A	**10 DOLLARS** 1.7.1860. Like #S1418 but back green.	—	—	350.00

1873-86 ISSUE

#S1419-S1423 like previous issue but w/slightly modified unpt. Back green. Printers: ABNC and BABNC.

		GOOD	FINE	XF
S1419	**1 DOLLAR** 1.10.1873; 1.3.1880; 1.2.1886. Like #S1413.	260.00	910.00	—
S1420	**2 DOLLARS** 1873-86. Like #S1415.			
	a. 1.10.1873; 1.3.1880.	270.00	945.00	—
	b. 1.2.1886.	205.00	700.00	1680.

		GOOD	FINE	XF
S1421	**3 DOLLARS** 1.10.1873; 1.3.1880; 1.2.1886. Like #S1416.	205.00	700.00	—
S1422	**5 DOLLARS** 1.2.1886. Like #S1417.	465.00	1330.	—
S1423	**10 DOLLARS** 1.2.1886. Like #S1418.	465.00	1330.	—

1863 ISSUE

#S1424-S1427 black on green unpt. Payable by Z. Chipman or at Bank of New York, payable in U.S. funds. Back green.

		GOOD	FINE	XF
S1424	**1 DOLLAR** 1.5.1863. Portr. W. Todd at lower l., steam passenger train at lower r.			
	a. W/text: *TO Z. CHIPMAN.*	475.00	975.00	—
	b. W/text: *TO THE BANK OF NEW YORK.*	475.00	975.00	—

#S1425-S1427 portr. W. Todd at lower r.

		GOOD	FINE	XF
S1425	**2 DOLLARS** 1.5.1863. Portr. girl w/puppies at lower l., cattle at upper ctr.			
	a. W/text: *TO Z. CHIPMAN.*	475.00	975.00	—
	b. W/text: *TO THE BANK OF NEW YORK.*	475.00	975.00	—

		GOOD	FINE	XF
S1426	**3 DOLLARS** 1.5.1863. Lumberjacks at upper l.			
	a. W/text: *TO Z. CHIPMAN.*	475.00	975.00	—
	b. W/text: *TO THE BANK OF NEW YORK.*	475.00	975.00	—

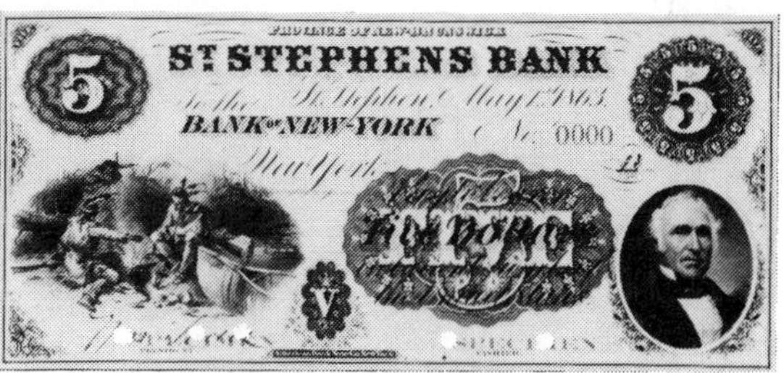

		GOOD	FINE	XF
S1427	**5 DOLLARS** 1.5.1863. Indians by campfire, canoe at lower l.			
	a. W/text: *TO Z. CHIPMAN.*	475.00	975.00	—
	b. W/text: *TO THE BANK OF NEW YORK.*	475.00	975.00	—

1892 ISSUE

#S1428-S1430 black on green unpt. Back green. Printers: BABNC and ABNC.

		VG	VF	UNC
S1428	**5 DOLLARS** 2.1.1892; 2.1.1903. Lighthouse and ships at lower l., reclining woman at ctr., steam train at lower r.	950.00	1675.	—
S1429	**10 DOLLARS** 2.1.1892; 2.1.1903. Sailing ships at lower l., men unloading railroad boxcar at top ctr., seated Britannia w/Indian girl at lower r.	950.00	1675.	—
S1430	**20 DOLLARS** 2.1.1892; 2.1.1903. Allegorical woman at l., farmer watering livestock at ctr., sailor at r. Face proof.	—	—	350.00

Notice

Readers with unlisted dates, color or signature varieties are invited to submit photocopies of their notes to: Standard Catalog of World Paper Money, Krause Publications, 700 East State St. Iola WI 54990-0001 U.S.A. or by email: thernr@krause.com. Email submissions of material for possible inclusion need to be 100% jpeg attachments at 300 dpi.

SOVEREIGN BANK OF CANADA

Established in Montreal, Quebec in 1901. Liquidated in 1908. Notes issued on Toronto Branch Office.

1902-07 ISSUE

#S1431-S1434 sign. varieties. Printer: ABNC.

		GOOD	FINE	XF
S1431	**5 DOLLARS** 1902-05. Black on green and yellow-green unpt., Bank seal at l., portr. Kg. Edward VII at lower ctr. Back black and m/c; bank crest at ctr.			
	a. Red ovpt: *M M.* 1.5.1902.	315.00	1050.	2485.
	b. 1.5.1905.	340.00	1155.	2730.
S1432	**10 DOLLARS** 1902-07. Black on red-orange and yellow-green unpt. Seated Britannia w/lion and shield at ctr. Back black and m/c; bank crest at ctr.			
	a. 1.5.1905.	535.00	1750.	—
	s1. Red ovpt: *M.* Specimen. 1.5.1902.	—	Unc	1000.
	s2. Specimen. 1.5.1907.	—	Unc	1000.
S1433	**20 DOLLARS** 1.5.1907. Black on green unpt. Bank seal at l., portr. Kg. Edward VII at r. Back orange. Specimen.	—	Unc	850.00
S1434	**50 DOLLARS** 1.5.1906; 1.5.1907. Black on blue and yellow-green unpt. Portr. Kg. Edward VII at l. Back green; bank bldg. at ctr. Specimen.	—	Unc	850.00

STANDARD BANK OF CANADA

Formerly the St. Lawrence Bank. Absorbed the Western Bank of Canada in 1909. Amalgamated with the Sterling Bank of Canada in 1924 and unified with the Canadian Bank of Commerce.

1876-81 ISSUE

#S1435-S1438 black on green unpt. Back green. Sign. varieties. Printer: BABNC.

		GOOD	FINE	XF
S1435	**4 DOLLARS** 1.11.1876. Portr. T. Gibbs at lower l., steam train, ships dockside at top ctr. r.	475.00	1540.	—
S1436	**5 DOLLARS** 1.11.1876. J. Cartier sighting land at l., T. Gibbs at lower r.	555.00	1770.	—
S1437	**10 DOLLARS** 1.11.1876. Farmer haying cows at upper l., T. Gibbs at lower r.	555.00	1770.	—
S1438	**50 DOLLARS** 1.12.1881. T. Gibbs at lower l., woman w/telegraph at ctr. Face proof.	—	Unc	750.00

1890 ISSUE

#S1439 and S1440 like #S1437 and S1438. Black on green unpt. Back green. Sign. varieties. Printer: BABNC.

		GOOD	FINE	XF
S1439	**10 DOLLARS** 1.12.1890. Like #S1437.	405.00	1330.	—
S1440	**50 DOLLARS** 1.12.1890. Like #S1438.	405.00	1330.	—

1891 ISSUE

		GOOD	FINE	XF
S1441	**5 DOLLARS** 1.5.1891. 2 allegorical women at l., oval portr. woman at upper ctr., seated woman w/flower basket at lower r. Bank seal at l., standing Justice w/royal shield at ctr. on back. Sign. varieties. Printer: ABNC.			
	a. Black on yellow and blue unpt. Back brown.	350.00	1200.	—
	b. Black on yellow and green unpt. Back green.	350.00	1200.	—
	c. Black on yellow and red unpt. Back green.	350.00	1200.	—
	d. Black on yellow and red unpt. Back red.	135.00	455.00	1190.

1900 ISSUE

		GOOD	FINE	XF
S1442	**10 DOLLARS** 1.5.1900. Black on gold unpt. Similar to #S1437, but w/W. Cowan at lower r. Back green. Sign varieties. Printer: BABNC.	205.00	700.00	1750.

1914 ISSUE

#S1443-S1446 bank crest at ctr. on back. Sign. varieties. Printer: ABNC.

		GOOD	FINE	XF
S1443	**5 DOLLARS** 1914-19. Black on orange unpt. Portr. laureate allegorical woman at ctr. Back green.			
	a. 2.1.1914; 2.1.1918.	60.00	200.00	—
	b. 2.1.1919.	30.00	100.00	250.00
S1444	**10 DOLLARS** 1914-19. Black on olive unpt. Portr. W. F. Cowan at ctr. Back brown.			
	a. 2.1.1914; 2.1.1918.	80.00	265.00	700.00
	b. 2.1.1919.	70.00	225.00	600.00

		GOOD	FINE	XF
S1445	**20 DOLLARS** 1914-19. Black on green unpt. Portr. 2 allegorical women at ctr. Back olive.			
	a. 2.1.1914; 2.1.1918.	150.00	500.00	1250.
	b. 2.1.1919.	175.00	600.00	1500.

		GOOD	FINE	XF
S1446	**100 DOLLARS** 1914-18. Black on yellow-brown unpt. Similar to #S1444. Back brown-violet.			
	a. 2.1.1914.	410.00	1400.	—
	b. 2.1.1918. Proof	—	Unc	400.00

1924 ISSUE

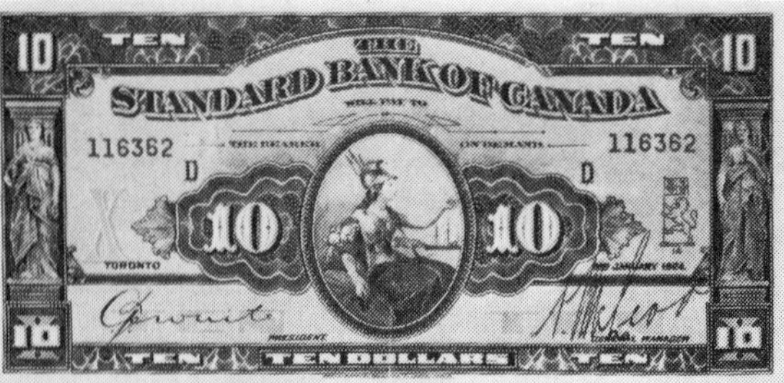

		GOOD	FINE	XF
S1447	**10 DOLLARS** 2.1.1924. Seated Britannia at lower ctr., statues of Industry at l., Agriculture at r. Back green. Printer: BABNC.			
	a. Black on yellow-brown unpt.	42.00	140.00	298.00
	b. Black on yellow-orange unpt.	25.00	85.00	210.00

STERLING BANK OF CANADA

Chartered in 1905 in Toronto, Ontario. Merged with the Standard Bank of Canada in 1924.

1906 ISSUE

#S1448-S1451 back green. Sign. varieties. Printer: BABNC.

		Good	Fine	XF
S1448	**5 Dollars** 25.4.1906. Black on green unpt. Steam ships, sailboats at upper ctr. Royal crest at ctr. on back.	230.00	770.00	1610.
S1449	**10 Dollars** 25.4.1906. Black on yellow and yellow-orange unpt. Seated woman w/flag at l. Seated Britannia at ctr. on back.	150.00	500.00	900.00
S1450	**20 Dollars** 25.4.1906. Black on green unpt. Lion and lioness at r.	675.00	2250.	—
S1451	**50 Dollars** 25.4.1906. Black on blue unpt. Allegorical woman w/shield, Parliament bldg. in background at ctr. Face proof.	—	Unc	600.00

1914 Issue

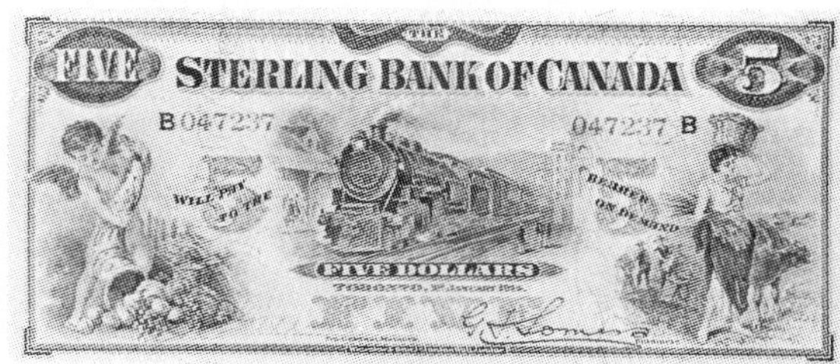

		VG	VF	Unc
S1452	**5 Dollars** 1.1.1914. Black on yellow unpt. Cherub emptying cornucopia at lower l., steam passenger train at ctr., farmers harvesting, woman w/basket on head at lower r. Back orange-red; portr. Princess Patricia of Connaught at ctr. Sign. varieties. Printer: W & S.	350.00	735.00	2310.

1921 Issue

		VG	VF	Unc
S1453	**10 Dollars** 3.1.1921. Black on gold unpt. Standing allegorical woman w/anchor at l., standing allegorical woman w/cornucopia at r. Back blue; lg. *10* between Indian and woodsman at ctr. Sign. varieties. Printer: BABNC.	525.00	1050.	—

Summerside Bank of Prince Edward Island

Established in 1866 in Summerside, P.E.I. Absorbed by the Bank of New Brunswick in 1901.

1866 Issue

Dollar/Pound Sterling System.

#S1454-S1456 black. Partially engraved date. Back brown. Printer: ABNC.

		Good	Fine	XF
S1454	**1 Dollar = 4 Shillings-2 Pence** 2.4.1866. 3 children w/colt at lower l., farmer by milkmaid milking cow at ctr., boy w/sheep at lower r.	840.00	2800.	—
S1455	**2 Dollars = 8 Shillings-4 Pence** 18xx. Shipbuilding at lower l., royal crest at ctr., dog by safe at lower r. Face proof.	—	Unc	750.00
S1456	**8 Dollars = 33 Shillings-4 Pence** 22.1.1866. Cooper making barrels at lower l., sailing ships at upper ctr., sailing ships at lower r.	—	5250.	—

1872 Issue

Dollar System.

#S1457-S1461 black. Fully engraved date. #S1457-S1459 like #S1454-S1455. Back brown. Printer: ABNC.

		Good	Fine	XF
S1457	**1 Dollar** 1.2.1872. Green word protector on face and back.			
	a. Issued note w/o red ovpt.	1470.	4900.	—
	b. Red ovpt: *CANADA CURRENCY* at both ends.	1470.	4900.	—
S1459	**2 Dollars** 1.2.1872. Green word protector on face and back.	1470.	4900.	—
S1460	**5 Dollars** 1.2.1872. Sailor w/lion, bales and flag at lower l., paddle wheel steamer at upper ctr. seated Britannia w/shield w/lg. *5* at lower r. Green word protector on face and back.	1845.	5250.	—
S1461	**10 Dollars** 1.2.1872. Similar to #S1456. Green word protector on face and back.	1845.	5250.	—

1884-1900 Issues

#S1462-S1465 black on green unpt. Printer: BABNC.

		Good	Fine	XF
S1462	**1 Dollar** 1.12.1884. Farm girl w/cow and calf at lower l., boy watering horse at ctr., sailors on lookout at lower r. Back green.	1470.	4900.	—
S1463	**1 Dollar** 1.12.1884. Face like #S1462. Uniface.	1470.	4900.	—
S1464	**5 Dollars** 1.7.1891. Farm tools at lower l., fishermen and boats at upper ctr., seated Britannia w/shield w/lg. *5* at lower r. Back green; 3 horses' heads at l. Face proof.	—	Unc	750.00
S1465	**10 Dollars** 1.9.1900. Seated woman w/cornucopia at lower l., sheep grazing at upper ctr., steamships at r. Back green. Face proof.	—	Unc	750.00

Traders Bank of Canada

Opened in Toronto, Ontario in 1885. Merged with the Royal Bank of Canada in 1912.

1885; 1886 Issue

#S1466-S1469 black on green unpt. Portr. of H. S. Strathy at l., portr. A. Manning at r. Back green. Sign. varieties. Printer: BABNC.

		Good	Fine	XF
S1466	**5 Dollars** 2.7.1885. Farmer w/cattle at ctr. Face proof.	—	Unc	500.00
S1467	**10 Dollars** 2.7.1885. Allegorical figures w/lg. ornate *X* at lower ctr. Face proof.	—	Unc	500.00
S1468	**50 Dollars** 1.3.1886. Allegorical women w/globe at ctr. Face proof.	—	Unc	500.00
S1469	**100 Dollars** 1.3.1886. Ships dockside at ctr. Face proof.	—	Unc	500.00

1890; 1903 Issue

#S1470 and S1471 black on green unpt. Back green. Sign. varieties. Printer: BABNC.

		Good	Fine	XF
S1470	**5 Dollars** 2.1.1893. Similar to #S1466 but w/portr. W. Bell at r.	205.00	700.00	1750.
S1471	**20 Dollars** 2.1.1890. Portr. H. S. Strathy at l., seated allegorical woman w/machinery at ctr., W. Bell at r. Proof w/face and back on one card.	—	Unc	500.00

1897; 1907 Issue

#S1472-S1476 black on green unpt. Portr. of H. S. Strathy at lower l., portr. C. D. Warren at lower r. Sign. varieties. Printer: BABNC.

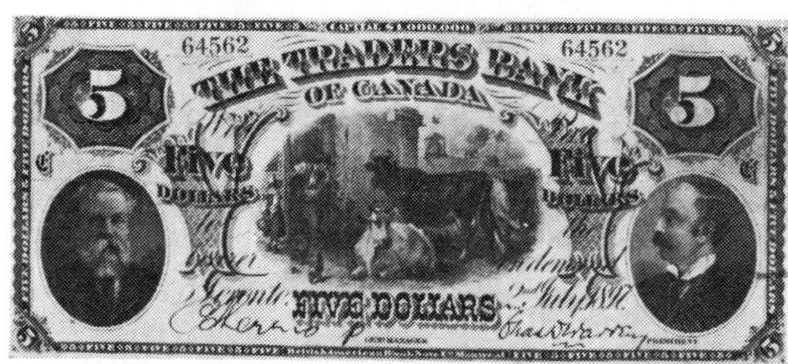

		VG	VF	Unc
S1472	**5 Dollars** 2.1.1897; 2.7.1897; 1.11.1907. Similar to #S1470.	325.00	675.00	2175.
S1473	**10 Dollars** 2.1.1897; 2.7.1897; 1.11.1907. Similar to #S1467.	450.00	1050.	—
S1474	**20 Dollars** 1.11.1907. Similar to #S1471. Face proof.	—	—	350.00
S1475	**50 Dollars** 2.1.1897; 2.7.1897. Similar to #S1468. Face proof.	—	—	350.00
S1476	**100 Dollars** 2.1.1897. Similar to #S1469. Face proof.	—	—	350.00

1909 Issue

#S1477-S1481 bank bldg. at ctr. on back. Sign. varieties. Printers: ABNC or BABNC.

		VG	VF	Unc
S1477	**5 Dollars** 2.1.1909. Black on yellow and green unpt. Sailing ships dockside at ctr. Back green. Face proof.	—	—	350.00

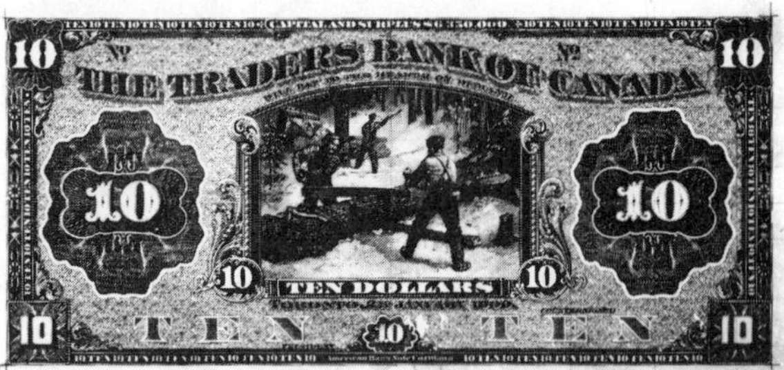

		GOOD	FINE	XF
S1478	**10 DOLLARS** 2.1.1909. Black on m/c unpt. Woodsmen cutting logs at ctr. Back green, red and brown.	365.00	1175.	3000.
S1479	**20 DOLLARS** 2.1.1909. Black on m/c unpt. Steam passenger train at station at ctr. Back brown, green and red. Face proof.	—	Unc	350.00
S1480	**50 DOLLARS** 2.1.1909. Black on m/c unpt. Sailing ship in stormy sea at ctr. Back blue, brown and purple. Face proof.	—	Unc	350.00
S1481	**100 DOLLARS** 2.1.1909. Black on m/c unpt. Cowboy rounding up cattle at ctr. Back orange and m/c. Face proof.	—	Unc	350.00

1910 ISSUE

		GOOD	FINE	XF
S1482	**5 DOLLARS** 1.11.1910. Black on red, green and purple unpt. Farmer reaping grain w/horses at ctr. Back olive on blue and brown unpt; bank bldg. at ctr. Sign. varieties. Printer: ABNC.	350.00	1200.	2800.

UNION BANK OF CANADA

Formerly the Union Bank of Lower Canada. Purchased by the Royal Bank of Canada in 1925.

1886 ISSUE

#S1483-S1487 sign. varieties. Printer: Canada Bank Note Co.

		GOOD	FINE	XF
S1483	**5 DOLLARS** 2.8.1886. Black on ochre unpt. Hillside village scene at l., livestock at ctr., portr. Qn. Victoria at lower r. Back green; facing griffins at l. and r. Face proof.	425.00	1400.	—
S1484	**10 DOLLARS** 2.8.1886. Black on ochre unpt. Quebec Citadel at l., farmer reaping grain w/horses at ctr., portr. Qn. Victoria at lower r. Back blue; like #S1483.	425.00	1400.	—
S1485	**20 DOLLARS** 2.8.1886. Black on red-orange unpt. Farmers plowing w/horses at ctr. Back brown. Face proof.	—	Unc	420.00
S1486	**50 DOLLARS** 2.8.1886. Black on red-orange unpt. Raphael's "angel" (w/o wings) at lower l., Quebec Citadel at r. Back brown. Face proof.	—	Unc	420.00
S1487	**100 DOLLARS** 2.8.1886. Black on red-orange unpt. Standing allegorical woman at l. and at r. Back brown. Face proof.	—	Unc	420.00

1893 ISSUE

#S1488-S1492 black on green unpt. Bank crest at ctr., portr. A. Thomson at lower r. Sign. varieties. Printer: BABNC.

		GOOD	FINE	XF
S1488	**5 DOLLARS** 1.6.1893. Sailing ship at lower l.	150.00	500.00	1260.
S1489	**10 DOLLARS** 1.6.1893. Farm tools at lower l.	125.00	425.00	1000.
S1490	**20 DOLLARS** 1.6.1893. 3 horse heads at l. Face proof.	—	Unc	500.00
S1491	**50 DOLLARS** 1.6.1893. Face proof.	—	Unc	500.00
S1492	**100 DOLLARS** 1.6.1893. Similar to #S1491. Face proof.	—	Unc	500.00

1903; 1907 QUEBEC BRANCH ISSUE

#S1493 and S1494 bank crest at ctr. on back. Sign. varieties. Printer: ABNC.

		GOOD	FINE	XF
S1493	**5 DOLLARS** 1903-07. Black on m/c unpt. Farmers harvesting w/horse drawn reapers at ctr.			
	a. 1.6.1903. Red serial #.	165.00	560.00	1190.
	b. 1.6.1903. Blue serial #.	165.00	560.00	1190.
S1493A	**5 DOLLARS** 1.6.1907. Black on various shades of green unpt. Like #S1493.	80.00	265.00	665.00
S1494	**10 DOLLARS** 1.6.1903; 1.6.1907. Black on m/c unpt. Cowboy roping steer at ctr.	230.00	770.00	1610.

1912 WINNIPEG ISSUE

#S1495 and S1496 sign. varieties. Printer: ABNC or CBNC.

		VG	VF	UNC
S1495	**5 DOLLARS** 1.7.1912. Like #S1493.			
	a. Black on m/c unpt.	65.00	140.00	455.00
	b. Black on dk. green and m/c unpt. L.h. sign. J. Galt. Blue ovpt: *NORTHWEST TERRITORIES.*	1000.	2000.	—
	c. Black on dk. green and m/c unpt. L. h. sign. W. R. Allan. W/o ovpt.	55.00	125.00	385.00

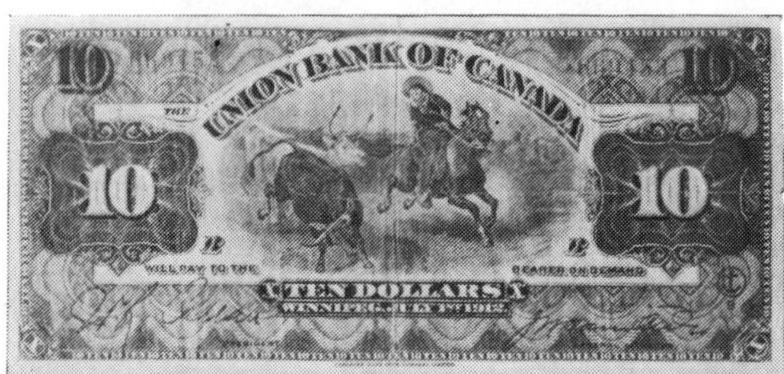

		VG	VF	UNC
S1496	**10 DOLLARS** 1.7.1912. Black on m/c unpt. Like #S1494.	55.00	125.00	350.00

1907 QUEBEC ISSUE

Higher values of 1886 design resumed.

#S1497-S1499 black on green unpt. Back brown. Printer: BABNC.

		VG	VF	UNC
S1497	**20 DOLLARS** 1.6.1907. Like #S1485. Face proof.	—	Unc	350.00
S1498	**50 DOLLARS** 1.6.1907. Similar to #S1486 but w/young girl w/feather at lower l. Face proof.	—	Unc	350.00
S1499	**100 DOLLARS** 1.6.1907. Like #S1487. Face proof.	—	Unc	350.00

1912 WINNIPEG ISSUE

#S1500-S1502 black on green unpt. Back green.

		VG	VF	UNC
S1500	**20 DOLLARS** 1.7.1912. Like #S1485.	490.00	1025.	—
S1501	**50 DOLLARS** 1.7.1912. Like #S1498.	700.00	1400.	—
S1502	**5 DOLLARS** 1.7.1912. Like #S1487.	910.00	1820.	—

QUEBEC

1921 ISSUE

#S1503-S1507 black on m/c unpt. Portr. J. W. Hamilton at l., portr. W. R. Allan at r. Printer: ABNC.

		GOOD	FINE	XF
S1503	**5 DOLLARS** 1.7.1921. Back green.			
	a. Issued note.	85.00	275.00	700.00
	p. Face proof.	—	Unc	350.00

		Good	Fine	XF
S1504	**10 Dollars**			
	1.7.1921. Back red.			
	a. Issued note.	45.00	140.00	385.00
	p. Face proof.	—	Unc	350.00
S1505	**20 Dollars**			
	1.7.1921. Back blue.			
	p. Face proof.	—	Unc	350.00
	s. Specimen.	—	Unc	700.00
S1506	**50 Dollars**			
	1.7.1921. Back brown.			
	p. Face proof.	—	Unc	350.00
	s. Specimen.	—	Unc	700.00
S1507	**100 Dollars**			
	1.7.1921. Back olive.			
	p. Face proof.	—	Unc	350.00
	s. Specimen.	—	Unc	700.00

Union Bank of Halifax

Established in Halifax, Nova Scotia in 1856. Took over the Commerical Bank of Windsor in 1902. Absorbed by the Royal Bank of Canada in 1910.

1861 Issue

#S1511 printer: RWH & E.

		Good	Fine	XF
S1511	**5 Dollars**			
	1.9.1861; 18.9.1861. Black. Cargo at upper and lower l., 2 seated allegorical woman at top ctr. w/small portr. Qn. Victoria below. Red word protector on face. Back red-brown; medallic portr. Qn. Victoria and Prince Albert at ctr.	945.00	3150.	—

1870 Issue

#S1514 and S1515 black on green unpt. Back green. Printer: BABNC.

		Good	Fine	XF
S1514	**4 Dollars**			
	1.6.1870. Farmer plowing w/horses at top ctr., small flower below. Face proof.	—	Unc	420.00
S1515	**5 Dollars**			
	1.6.1870. Bank bldg. at top ctr., small flower below. Face proof.	—	Unc	350.00

1871; 1904 Issues

#S1516-S1521 printer: BABNC.

#S1516-S1517 black on green unpt. Back green.

		Good	Fine	XF
S1516	**4 Dollars**			
	1.7.1871. Steam sailing ship at upper l., dog's head at lower r. Face proof.	—	Unc	350.00

		Good	Fine	XF
S1517	**5 Dollars**			
	1871-1909. Bank bldg. at ctr. Fishermen at ctr. on back.			
	a. 1.7.1886; 1.5.1909.	840.00	2800.	—
	p. Face proof. 1.7.1871; 1.7.1882; 1.4.1900.	—	Unc	350.00
S1518	**10 Dollars**			
	1871-1900. Supported royal arms at upper ctr. Fishermen at ctr. on back.			
	a. Black on ochre unpt. 1.4.1900.	840.00	2800.	—
	p1. Black on green unpt. Face proof. 1.7.1871.	—	Unc	350.00
	p2. As a. Face proof.	—	Unc	350.00
S1519	**20 Dollars**			
	1871-1900. Seated woman on deck at lower l., fishermen shipboard at ctr., anchor at lower r. Boy w/fish and dog at ctr. on back.			
	p1. Black on green unpt. Face proof. 1.7.1871.	—	Unc	350.00
	p2. Black on ochre unpt. Face proof. 1.4.1900.	—	Unc	425.00
S1520	**50 Dollars**			
	1.9.1904. Black on blue unpt. Lighthouse view in Trinidad at l., Indian and sailor w/shield at ctr. r. Face proof.	—	Unc	350.00
S1521	**100 Dollars**			
	1.9.1904. Black on brown unpt. Fisherman and wife looking at ocean, portr. of sailor at ctr. r. Face proof.	—	Unc	420.00

Union Bank of Lower Canada

Opened in Quebec, Canada East in 1865. Purchased Quebec Provident and Savings Bank in 1872. Became Union Bank of Canada in 1886.

1866 Issue

varieties. Printer: ABNC. #S1521A-S1521D Canadian arms between man w/flag and Indian at ctr. Back green. Sign. varieties. Printer: ABNC.

		Good	Fine	XF
S1521A	**1 Dollar**			
	1.3.1866. Man at l., shipbuilder w/broadaxe at lower r.			
	a. Black on green unpt. W/green word protectors and numeral. Lg. red ovpt: *S S*, blue ovpt: *OTTAWA* or *MONTREAL* twice.	300.00	980.00	—
	b. Black w/green word protector on face. Lg. red ovpt: *S S*, also w/blue ovpt: *THREE RIVERS* twice.	365.00	1200.	—

		Good	Fine	XF
S1521B	**2 Dollars**			
	1.3.1866. Anchor at lower l., man at r.			
	a. Black on green unpt. W/green word and numeral protectors. Lg. red ovpt: *S S*, blue ovpt: *OTTAWA* or *MONTREAL*. twice.	610.00	1950.	—
	b. Black w/green word protector on face. Lg. red ovpt: *S S*, also w/blue ovpt: *THREE RIVERS* twice.	435.00	1200.	—
S1521C	**4 Dollars**			
	1.3.1866. Black on green unpt. W/green word and numeral protectors. Sailors dock side at lower l., man at lower r. Lg. red ovpt: *S S*, blue ovpt: *OTTAWA* or *MONTREAL* twice.	610.00	1950.	—
S1521D	**5 Dollars**			
	1.3.1866. Black on green unpt. W/green word and numeral protectors. Man at l., sailors on lookout at lower r. Lg. red ovpt: *S S*, blue ovpt: *OTTAWA* or *MONTREAL* twice.	610.00	1950.	—

1870-71 Issue

#S1521E-S1521J black on green unpt. Canadian arms between man w/flag and Indian at ctr. Back green. Sign. varieties. Red ovpt: *MONTREAL* twice. Printer: BABNC.

		Good	Fine	XF
S1521E	**4 Dollars**			
	1.9.1870. Portr. Qn. Victoria at lower l., sailors dockside at lower r.	405.00	1330.	—

		Good	Fine	XF
S1521F	**5 Dollars**			
	1.8.1871. Sailors on lookout at lower l., woman supported by 2 porpoises at lower r.	400.00	1300.	—
S1521G	**10 Dollars**			
	1.12.1872. Seated allegorical woman w/flag dockside at lower l., sailor boy climbing rope ladder at lower r. Face proof.	—	Unc	420.00
S1521H	**20 Dollars**			
	1.9.1870.	405.00	1330.	—
S1521I	**50 Dollars**			
	1.12.1871. Face proof.	—	Unc	420.00
S1521J	**100 Dollars**			
	1.12.1871. Face proof.	—	Unc	420.00

UNION BANK OF PRINCE EDWARD ISLAND

Established in Charlottetown, P.E.I. in 1860. Absorbed by the Bank of Nova Scotia in 1883.

1864-65 ISSUE

Dollar/Pound Sterling System.

#S1522-S1525 black w/green word protector on face and back. Partially engraved date. Printer: ABNC.

		GOOD	FINE	XF
S1522	**1 DOLLAR = 4 SHILLINGS-2 PENCE** 18xx. Sailors dockside at lower l., lion w/shield at ctr., seated woman w/sheep at lower r. Face proof.	—	Unc	2000.

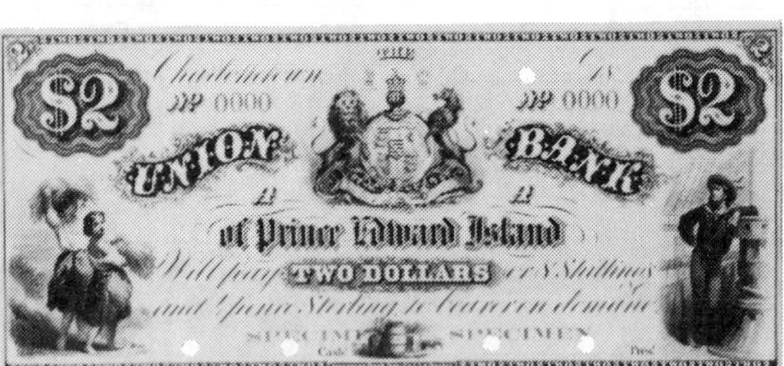

		GOOD	FINE	XF
S1523	**2 DOLLARS = 8 SHILLINGS-4 PENCE** 1.6.1864. 2 children w/sheaves at lower l., supported royal arms at ctr., sailor at lower r. Green *TWO DOLLARS* protector on face and back.	735.00	2450.	—

		GOOD	FINE	XF
S1524	**5 DOLLARS = 20 SHILLINGS-10 PENCE** 2.1.1865. St. George slaying dragon at lower l., seated milkmaid w/cows at upper ctr., steam sailing ship at lower r. Green *5 FIVE 5* protector on face and back.	735.00	2450.	—
S1525	**20 DOLLARS = 4 POUNDS-3 SHILLINGS-4 PENCE** 18xx. Portr. Princess of Wales at lower l., P.E.I. arms at top ctr., Prince of Wales at lower r. Green *TWENTY* protector on face and back.			
	a. Issued note.	1050.	3500.	—
	p. Face proof.	—	Unc	700.00

1872 ISSUE

#S1526-S1530 black. Fully engraved date. Green word protector on face and back. Similar to previous issue. Printer: ABNC.

		GOOD	FINE	XF
S1526	**1 DOLLAR** 1.1.1872. Similar to #S1522.			
	a. Issued note w/o ovpt.	565.00	1825.	—
	b. Red ovpt: *CANADA CURRENCY* twice.	565.00	1825.	—
#S1527	***Deleted.* See #S1526b.**			
S1528	**2 DOLLARS** 1.1.1872. Similar to #S1523.	565.00	1825.	—
S1529	**5 DOLLARS** 1.1.1872. Similar to #S1524. Face proof.	—	Unc	500.00
S1530	**20 DOLLARS** 1.1.1872. Similar to #S1525.			
	a. Issued note.	700.00	2300.	—
	p. Face proof.	—	Unc	700.00

1875 ISSUE

#S1531-S1533 black on green unpt. Ovpt: *U* upper l., *B* upper r. Printer: BABNC.

		GOOD	FINE	XF
S1531	**1 DOLLAR** 1.3.1875. Codfish at lower l., steam locomotive at ctr., seals at lower r.	430.00	1400.	—
S1532	**2 DOLLARS** 1875-77. River pilot at lower l., dog on strong box at upper ctr., woman w/sheaf at lower r.			
	a. 1.3.1875.	750.00	2100.	—
	p. Face proof. 1877.	—	Unc	420.00
S1533	**5 DOLLARS** 1875-77. St. George slaying dragon at lower l., farm tools and produce at upper ctr., seated allegorical woman w/telescope at lower r.			
	a. 1.3.1875.	750.00	2100.	—
	p. Face proof. 1877.	—	Unc	420.00

UNITED EMPIRE BANK OF CANADA

Formerly the Pacific Bank of Canada. Merged with the Union Bank of Canada.

1906 ISSUE

#S1534 and S1535 sign. varieties. Printer: ABNC.

		GOOD	FINE	XF
S1534	**5 DOLLARS** 1.8.1906. Black on green unpt. Seated Britannia between 2 world globes at ctr. Back green.	1625.	4550.	—

		GOOD	FINE	XF
S1535	**10 DOLLARS** 1.8.1906. Black on yellow-green unpt. Seated Justice at upper l. Back blue; 2 beavers at ctr.	1625.	4550.	—

WESTERN BANK OF CANADA

Chartered in Oshawa, Ontario in 1882. Merged with the Standard Bank of Canada in 1909.

1882; 1890 ISSUE

#S1536-S1538 black on green unpt. R. S. Hamlin at l., J. Cowan at r. Sign. varieties. Printer: BABNC.

		GOOD	FINE	XF
S1536	**5 DOLLARS** 2.10.1882. Farm tools and produce at bottom ctr.	550.00	1750.	—
S1537	**10 DOLLARS** 2.10.1882. Shepherdess w/sheep at ctr.	675.00	2100.	—
S1538	**20 DOLLARS** 2.7.1890. Seated Ceres w/cornucopia at ctr.	850.00	2450.	—

WEYBURN SECURITY BANK

Established in Weyburn, Saskatchewan in 1910. Merged with the Imperial Bank of Canada in 1931.

1911 ISSUE

#S1539-S1541 sign. varieties. Printer: ABNC or CBNC.

		GOOD	FINE	XF
S1539	**5 DOLLARS** 3.1.1911. Black on green unpt. Steam passenger train at depot at ctr. Back green.	250.00	840.00	1470.
S1540	**10 DOLLARS** 3.1.1911. Black on yellow-green unpt. Seated allegorical figures at l. ctr. and ctr. r. Back green.	320.00	1050.	1750.

		Good	Fine	XF
S1541	**20 Dollars** 3.1.1911. Black on orange unpt. Oval portr. woman at ctr. supported by 2 cherubs. Back orange.	—	2100.	—

Spurious and Expired Banks

The Bank of Acadia

Established in Liverpool, Nova Scotia in 1872 and expired within 4 months.

1872 Issue

#S1542-S1545 black on green unpt. Uniface. Printer: BABNC.

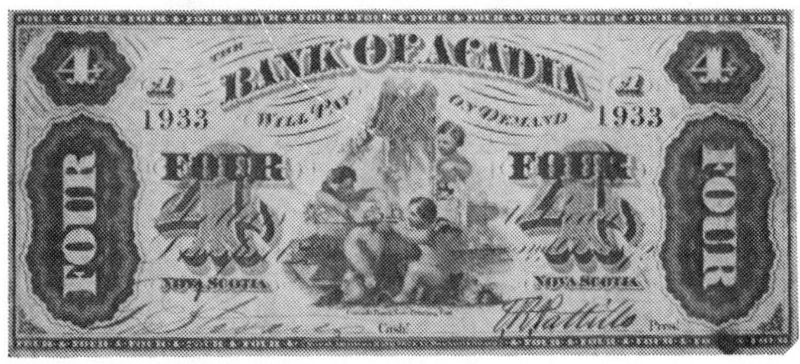

		Good	Fine	XF
S1542	**4 Dollars** 2.12.1872. Cherubs w/lg. ornate *4* at ctr.	135.00	350.00	1000.
S1543	**5 Dollars** 2.12.1872. Sailing ships at upper l. ctr.	165.00	400.00	1200.
S1544	**10 Dollars** 2.12.1872. Cherubs w/lg. ornate *X* at ctr.	165.00	400.00	1200.
S1545	**20 Dollars** 2.12.1872. Sailing ship at upper l., paddle wheel steamboat at lower ctr.	700.00	2100.	—

The Accommodation Bank

1837 Spurious Issue

Dollar/Pound Sterling System.

#S1546-S1547 black. Seated Justice w/lion at ctr. Uniface. Printer: RWH & Co.

		Good	Fine	XF
S1546	**4 Dollars = 20 Shillings** 18(37). W/o redeemable clause above Justice. Unsigned remainder w/o serial # or date.	52.50	140.00	335.00

		Good	Fine	XF
S1547	**4 Dollars = 20 Shillings** 18(37). W/redeemable clause above Justice.			
	a. Completed note.	210.00	630.00	1400.
	r. Remainder w/o serial # or date.	52.50	140.00	335.00

The Agricultural Bank (Montreal, L.C.)

1841 Issue

#S1548-S1550 black. Uniface. Various handwritten dates 1841-46. Printer: Burton and Gurley.

		VG	VF	Unc
S1548	**1 Dollar** 1841-46 Standing Indian at l., farmer plowing w/oxen at top ctr., standing allegorical female at r.	225.00	425.00	

		VG	VF	Unc
S1549	**2 Dollars** 1841-46. Farmer w/grain by tree at l., seated Agriculture at top ctr., standing allegorical helmeted woman at r.	225.00	425.00	—

		VG	VF	Unc
S1550	**3 Dollars** 1841-46. Farm woman w/rake at l., seated Agriculture w/shield at top ctr., farmer plowing w/oxen at r.	350.00	700.00	—

The Agricultural Bank

Established in Toronto, Upper Canada in 1834.

1834 Issue

#S1551-S1556 black. Uniface. Printer: RWH & Co.

		VG	VF	Unc
S1551	**1 Dollar = 5 Shillings** 1.4.1834; 1.7.1835. Horse at upper ctr., woman holding sheaf of grain at r.	25.00	75.00	210.00

		VG	VF	Unc
S1552	**2 Dollars = 10 Shillings** 8.8.1834-21.9.1937. Farmers w/livestock at l. and r., beehive, cornucopia, sheaf of grain and spinning wheel at upper ctr.			
	a. W/o clause: *One year after date.*	25.00	75.00	210.00

	VG	VF	UNC
b. W/additional clause: *One year after date* under lg. *2*'s (21.9.1837).	32.50	87.50	225.00

S1553 4 DOLLARS = 20 SHILLINGS
1.4.1833-1.3.1837. Plow at l., seated allegorical woman and Indian holding shield at upper ctr., sheaf of grain at r.

	VG	VF	UNC
a. W/o clause: *One year after date.*	60.00	175.00	400.00
b. W/additional clause: *One year after date* (1.3.1837).	70.00	210.00	550.00

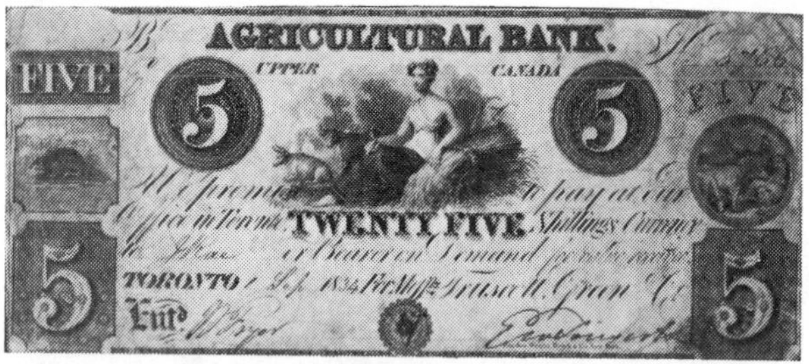

	VG	VF	UNC
S1554 5 DOLLARS = 25 SHILLINGS 8.8.1834-1.12.1834. Beaver at l., seated Agriculture at ctr., farmer w/livestock at r.	50.00	140.00	335.00

	VG	VF	UNC
S1555 10 DOLLARS = 50 SHILLINGS 1.1.1834-1.1.1835. Farmers harvesting grain at upper ctr., portr. Kg. William IV at r.	400.00	1000.	—

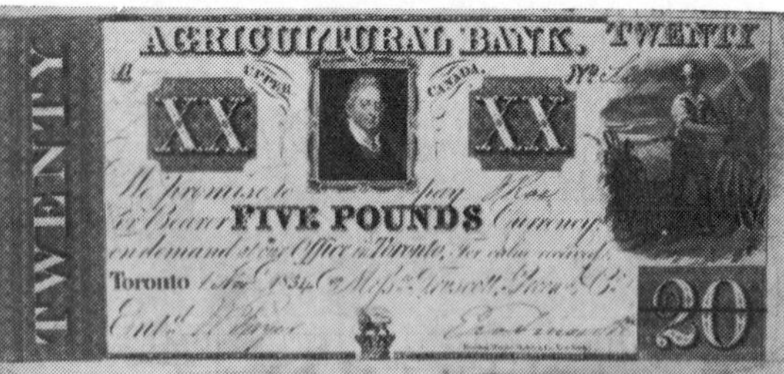

	GOOD	FINE	XF
S1556 20 DOLLARS = 5 POUNDS 1.9.1834; 1.11.1834. Portr. Kg. William IV at upper ctr., farmer picking corn at upper r.	525.00	1400.	—

1835 ISSUE

#S1557-S1560 black. Uniface. W/text: *FOR GEO. TRUSCOTT* engraved at bottom. Hand stamped black: *B*, red *C* or black *H*. Printer: New England Bank Note Comp., Boston.

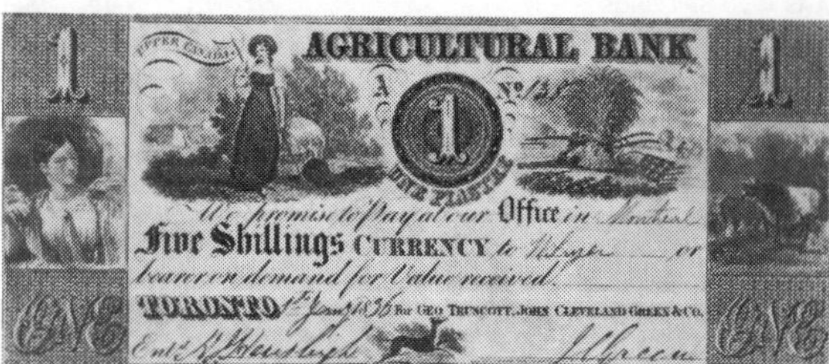

	VG	VF	UNC
S1557 1 DOLLAR = 5 SHILLINGS 1.10.1835; 1.11.1835; 1.12.1835; 1.1.1836. Portr. girl at l., farm woman raking hay at upper l. ctr., sheaf of grain and plow at upper ctr. r., cattle at r., small deer at bottom ctr.	14.00	28.00	105.00

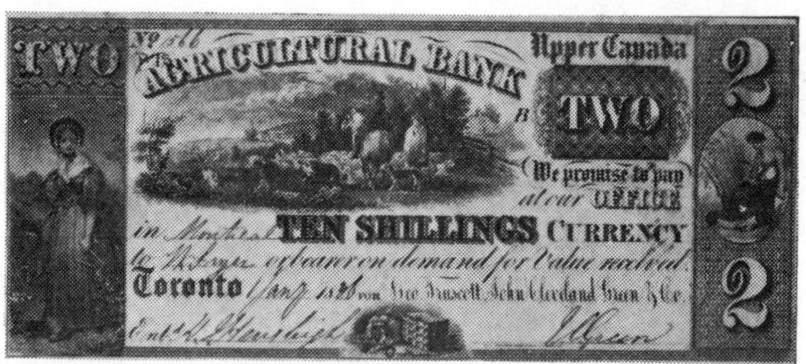

	VG	VF	UNC
S1558 2 DOLLARS = 10 SHILLINGS 1.10.1835-1.1.1836. Milkmaid at l., men w/cattle, horse and dog at upper l. ctr., farm woman w/sickle at r., small strong box at bottom ctr.	14.00	28.00	105.00

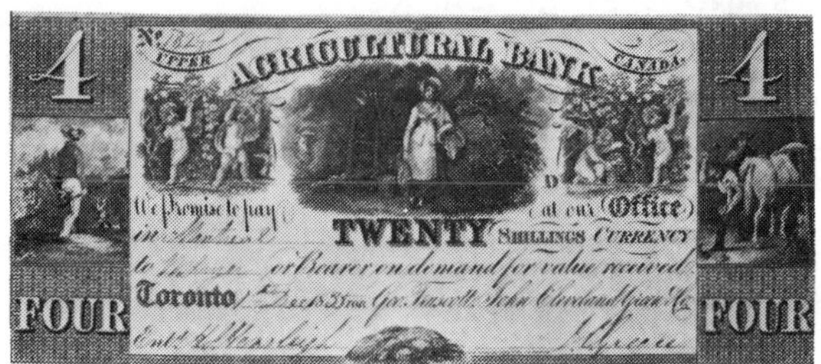

	VG	VF	UNC
S1559 4 DOLLARS = 20 SHILLINGS 1.10.1835-1.11.1836. Boy raking at l., milkmaid between cherubs at ctr., blacksmith shoeing horse at r., farm produce at bottom ctr.	28.00	52.50	122.50

	VG	VF	UNC
S1560 5 DOLLARS = 25 SHILLINGS 1.10.1835-1.1.1836. Female group w/seated helmeted Britannia at l., farmers harvesting at upper ctr., seated Britannia at r., produce at bottom ctr.	14.00	35.00	105.00

1837 ISSUE

#S1561-S1565 w/*THE* added to bank name and w/o *FOR GEO. TRUSCOTT*.

	VG	VF	UNC
S1561 1 DOLLAR = 5 SHILLINGS 1.10.1837. Like #S1557.	8.00	20.00	60.00

	VG	VF	UNC
S1562 2 DOLLARS = 10 SHILLINGS 1.10.1837. Like #S1558.	8.00	20.00	60.00

	VG	VF	UNC
S1563 4 DOLLARS = 20 SHILLINGS 1.10.1837. Like #S1559.	21.50	42.50	85.00

		VG	VF	UNC
S1564	**5 DOLLARS = 25 SHILLINGS** 1.10.1837. Like #S1560.	8.00	20.00	60.00

ARMAN'S BANK

Established in Montreal, Lower Canada.

1837 ISSUE

Pence/Sou System.

#S1565-S1567 black. Cornucopia at bottom ctr. Uniface.

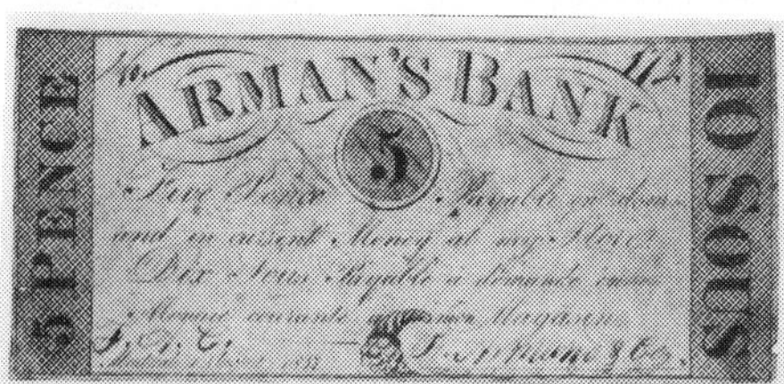

		GOOD	FINE	XF
S1565	**5 PENCE = 10 SOUS** 1.8.1837.	125.00	400.00	—

		GOOD	FINE	XF
S1566	**10 PENCE = 20 SOUS** 1.8.1837.	125.00	400.00	—

		GOOD	FINE	XF
S1567	**15 PENCE = 30 SOUS** 1.8.1837.	125.00	400.00	—

BANQUE DE BOUCHERVILLE

Established in Boucherville, Lower Canada.

1830S ISSUE

		VG	VF	UNC
S1568	**1 PIASTRE** 18xx. Black. Uniface. Unsigned remainder. Printer: Bourne Sc.	21.00	60.00	155.00

Notice

Readers with unlisted dates, color or signature varieties are invited to submit photocopies of their notes to: Standard Catalog of World Paper Money, Krause Publications, 700 East State St. Iola WI 54990-0001 U.S.A. or by email: thernr@krause.com. Email submissions of material for possible inclusion need to be 100% jpeg attachments at 300 dpi.

BANK OF BRANTFORD

Established in Brantford, Canada West in 1857. Most of the issue was circulated in the U.S.A.

1859 ISSUE

#S1569-S1572 black on green unpt. Uniface. Printer: ABNC.

		VG	VF	UNC
S1569	**1 DOLLAR** 1.11.1859. St. George slaying dragon at lower l., farm girl w/calves at upper ctr., cattle at lower r.			
	a. Partially engraved date.	28.00	52.50	175.00
	b. Engraved date.	28.00	52.50	175.00
	c. Blue ovpt: *Issued.../Honiton 1st May, 1862* and *CARROLE* on #S1569a.	42.00	77.00	245.00
	d. Ovpt. as c. but w/*KINGSMILL.*	42.00	77.00	245.00

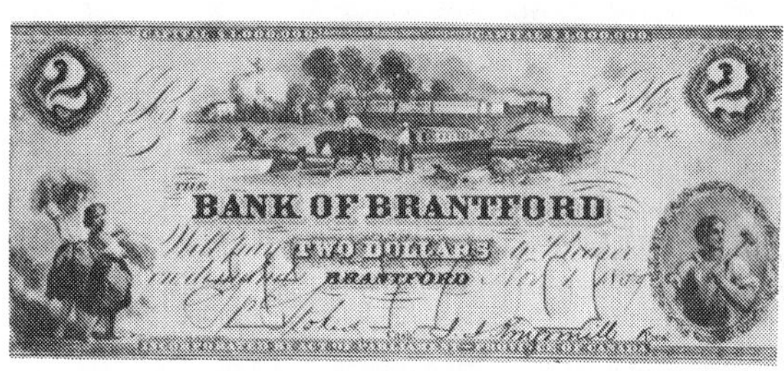

		VG	VF	UNC
S1570	**2 DOLLARS** 1.11.1859. 2 young girls w/sheaves of grain at lower l., boat in locks, steam passenger train in background at upper ctr., blacksmith w/hammer at lower r.			
	a. Partially engraved date.	28.00	52.50	175.00
	b. Engraved date.	28.00	52.50	175.00
	c. Blue ovpt: *Issued.../Honiton, 1st May, 1862* on #S1570b.	32.50	75.00	140.00
	d. Purple ovpt. as c, but w/*Westbrook.*	42.50	135.00	—

		VG	VF	UNC
S1571	**4 DOLLARS** 1.11.1859. Portr. Lord Elgin at lower l., mill along canal at top ctr., portr. young girl at lower r.			
	a. Partially engraved date.	42.00	105.00	210.00
	b. Engraved date.	42.00	105.00	210.00
	c. Blue ovpt: *Issued.../Honiton, 1st May, 1862* on #S1571b.	42.00	105.00	210.00
	d. Purple ovpt. as c, but w/*Westbrook.*	70.00	210.00	—

		VG	VF	UNC
S1572	**5 DOLLARS** 1.11.1859. Portr. Qn. Victoria at lower l., steam passenger train, boats and horses at top ctr., portr. child w/rabbits at lower r.			
	a. Partially engraved date.	12.50	35.00	100.00
	b. Engraved date.	12.50	35.00	100.00
	c. Blue ovpt: *Issued.../Honiton, 1st May, 1862* on #S1572b.	20.00	55.00	175.00
	d. Purple ovpt. as c, but w/*Westbrook.*	42.50	125.00	—

1859 Sault Ste. Marie Branch Issue

#S1573-S1576 black on red unpt. Uniface. Unsigned remainders. Printer: ABNC.

		VG	VF	Unc
S1573	**1 Dollar** 1.11.1859. Like #S1569b.	—	—	70.00
S1574	**2 Dollars** 1.11.1859. Like #S1570b.	—	—	125.00
S1575	**4 Dollars** 1.11.1859. Like #S1571b.	—	—	140.00
S1576	**5 Dollars** 1.11.1859. Like #S1572b.	—	—	70.00

British Canadian Bank

Established in Winnipeg, Manitoba in 1882. Notes issued on Toronto, Ontario branch.

1884 Issue

#S1577 and S1578 black on green unpt. Back green. Printer: BABNC.

		VG	VF	Unc
S1577	**5 Dollars** 15.9.1884. Steam train, ships dockside at l. Face proof.	—	—	800.00

		VG	VF	Unc
S1578	**10 Dollars** 15.9.1884. Portr. Qn. Victoria at upper l., seated Britannia w/lion and child at lower r. Face proof.	—	—	800.00

Canada Bank

Possibly established in Montreal, Lower Canada.

1790s Issue

#S1577 and S1578 black. Beaver by tree stump w/sailing ship in background at upper l. Uniface. Various handwritten dates. Printer: Albby Sc., London.

No.	Denomination	Good	Fine	XF
S1579	**5 Shillings** 10.8.1792.			
	a. Issued note.	200.00	700.00	1750.
	r. Unsigned remainder. 179x.	150.00	500.00	1250.
S1580	**Pounds(s)** 179x. Unsigned remainder.	325.00	1100.	2750.

Canada Bank, The

Established in Toronto, Canada West. Later became the Canadian Bank of Commerce.

1855 Issue

#S1580A-S1583 black. Uniface. Printer: Danforth, Wright & Co.

		VG	VF	Unc
S1580A	**1 Dollar** 1.11.1855. Portr. Qn. Victoria at lower l., Falls at Niagara at upper ctr. r., portr. Prince Albert at lower r. Face proof.	—	—	750.00
S1581	**1 Dollar = 5 Shillings** 1.11.1855. Portr. Qn. Victoria at lower l., Roebling Bridge at upper ctr. r., portr. Prince Albert at lower r. Face proof.	—	—	750.00
S1582	**2 Dollars = 10 Shillings** 1.11.1855. Woman w/sickle at l., royal crest at ctr. Face proof.	—	—	750.00
S1583	**5 Dollars = 1 Pound-5 Shillings** 1.11.1855. Cattle watering in pond at ctr. Face proof.	—	—	750.00

Bank of Canada

Began operations in Montreal, Lower Canada in 1818.

1818-22 Issue

#S1584-S1591 black. Partially engraved date. Uniface. Printer: Reed.

No.	Denomination	Good	Fine	XF
S1584	**1 Dollar** 1.8.1818; 6.11.1819. Seated Goddess of Plenty w/cornucopia and lg. *1* at top ctr., agricultural tools at bottom ctr.	65.00	315.00	840.00

No.	Denomination	Good	Fine	XF
S1585	**2 Dollars** 1.2.1822. Seated allegorical woman w/cornucopia and lg. *2* at top ctr., agricultural tools at bottom ctr.	12.00	60.00	157.50
S1586	**10 Dollars** 18xx. Hillside citadel and town at top ctr. Prince of Wales crest at bottom ctr. Proof.	—	Unc	350.00
S1587	**50 Dollars** 25.8.1818. Supported royal arms at upper ctr., small beaver at bottom ctr.	84.00	420.00	910.00

No.	Denomination	Good	Fine	XF
S1588	**100 Dollars** 18xx. Supported royal arms at upper ctr., small sailing ship at bottom ctr. Proof.	—	Unc	350.00

1820s Issue

#S1589-S1591 w/curved *AT THE MECHANICS BANK IN THE CITY OF N. YORK* above vignette.

No.	Denomination	Good	Fine	XF
S1589	**2 Dollars** 18xx. Seated female holding sword and lg. *2* at top ctr., small sailing ship at bottom ctr. Proof.	—	Unc	350.00
S1590	**5 Dollars** 18xx. Female afloat holding lg. *5* at upper ctr. Small paddle wheel steamboat at bottom ctr. Proof.	—	Unc	350.00
S1591	**20 Dollars** 18xx. Supported royal arms at upper ctr., small shield at bottom ctr. Proof.	—	Unc	350.00

1818 Issue

#S1591A-S1593 black. Engraved date. Uniface. Printer: Graphic.

No.	Denomination	Good	Fine	XF
S1591A	**1 Dollar** 1.10.1818. Couple in horse-drawn sleigh at upper ctr.	75.00	250.00	600.00
S1592	**2 Dollars** 1.10.1818. Seated woman w/sickle at top ctr., 2 coins at bottom ctr.	75.00	250.00	600.00
S1593	**5 Dollars** 1.10.1818; 6.1.1820; 4.6.1823. Seated Indian w/lion at top ctr., 5 coins at bottom ctr., *V* in guilloche at upper l., *5* at upper r.	75.00	250.00	600.00

1818 New York City Branch Issue

#S1593A, S1593C and S1593E black w/*MECHANICS BANK*, engraved date.

No.	Denomination	Good	Fine	XF
S1593A	**1 Dollar** 1.10.1818. Like #S1591A.	75.00	250.00	600.00
S1593C	**3 Dollars** 1.10.1818. Boat, seated native and man at top ctr	75.00	250.00	600.00
S1593E	**5 Dollars** 1820-23. Like #S1593 but w/*5* in guilloche at upper l., *V* at upper r. Partially engraved date w/o engraved payee's name.	75.00	245.00	595.00
S1593G	**10 Dollars** 1.10.1818. Sailing ship, 3 seated allegorical persons at top ctr.	75.00	250.00	600.00

1822 Issue

#S1594 and S1595 black. Engraved date. Uniface. Printer: Graphic.

No.	Denomination	Good	Fine	XF
S1594	**1 Dollar** 1.1.1822. Coin of Kg. George IV at top ctr.	75.00	250.00	600.00

		Good	Fine	XF
S1595	**2 Dollars** 1.1.1822. 2 coins of Kg. George IV at top ctr.	75.00	250.00	600.00

Banque Canadienne

Established in St. Hyacinthe, Lower Canada in 1836. Failed in 1838.

1836 Issue

#S1596 and S1599 black. Hand written dates. Printer: RWH & Co.

		VG	VF	Unc
S1596	**1 Dollar = 1 Piastre** 23.8.1836. Men w/livestock at l., cornucopia, sheaf of grain and spinning wheel at top ctr., farmer plowing w/horse at r. Back blue-green.	150.00	325.00	—
S1597	**2 Dollars = 2 Piastres** 23.8.1836. Standing Britannia w/anchor at upper l., seated female, cattle and sheaves at upper ctr. Back blue-green.	150.00	325.00	—
S1598	**5 Dollars = 5 Piastres** 23.8.1836. Indian shooting bow and arrow at upper l., sailing ship at upper ctr., sailing ship, steam passenger train (sideways) at r. Back green.	250.00	575.00	—

		VG	VF	Unc
S1599	**10 Dollars = 10 Piastres = 2 Pounds-10 Shillings** 23.8.1836. Portr. Kg. William IV at l., steam passenger train, produce, tools and waterfall at top ctr., beehive at r., small man in canoe at bottom ctr. Back green.	250.00	575.00	—

Central Bank of Canada

Incorporated in Toronto, Ontario in 1883. Failed in 1887.

1884; 1887 Issue

#S1600-S1602 black on green unpt. D. Blain at l. Printer: BABNC.

		VG	VF	Unc
S1600	**5 Dollars** 1.1.1884. Allegorical female w/cherubs at r. Back green; horses at trough.	350.00	850.00	—
S1601	**10 Dollars** 1.1.1884. Man plowing w/horses at r. Back green.	500.00	1050.	—
S1602	**50 Dollars** 3.1.1887. A. A. Allen at lower r. Face proof.	—	—	350.00

Central Bank of New Brunswick

Established in Fredericton, New Brunswick in 1834. Failed in 1866.

1847; 1851 Issue

Pound Sterling System.

		Good	Fine	XF
S1603	**5 Shillings** 1.11.1847. Blue. Blacksmith at anvil at l., seated Justice at top ctr., cargo and ships below. Back gray.	475.00	1550.	—
S1604	**1 Pound** 1.5.1847. Black. Indian seated w/rifle at l., supported royal arms at top ctr., small paddle wheel steamboat below.	350.00	1150.	—
S1604A	**1 Pound** 1.10.1847. Blue. Like #S1604. Back gray.	350.00	1150.	—
S1605	**5 Pounds** 1.5.1847. Black. Portr. Kg. William IV at l., St. George slaying dragon at top ctr. Back blue.	350.00	1150.	—
S1605A	**5 Pounds** 2.1.1851; 1.11.1857. Blue. Like #S1605. Back gray.	350.00	1150.	—

1847 Issue

Dollar/Pound Sterling System.

		Good	Fine	XF
S1605B	**1 Dollar = 5 Shillings** 10.11.1847. Blue. Like #S1603. Back green.	425.00	1400.	—

1852-53 Issue

#S1606-S1608 blue. Back orange.

		Good	Fine	XF
S1606	**1 Dollar = 5 Shillings** 1.10.1852; 1.5.1853. Like #S1605B.	325.00	1050.	—
S1607	**1 Pound** 18xx. Like #S1604.	425.00	1400.	—
S1608	**5 Pounds** 1.5.1853. Like #S1605.	375.00	1300.	—

1856-57 Issue

#S1609-S1611 black. Uniface.

		Good	Fine	XF
S1609	**1 Dollar = 5 Shillings** 1.6.1856. Like #S1603.	420.00	1400.	—
S1610	**1 Pound** 1.8.1857; 1.10.1857. Like #S1604.	315.00	1050.	—
S1611	**5 Pounds** 18xx. Like #S1605. Proof.	—	Unc	750.00

1860 Issue

Dollar System.

#S1612-S1617 black on green unpt. Uniface.

		Good	Fine	XF
S1612	**1 Dollar** 1.11.1860. Portr. man at lower l., lion w/shield at upper ctr., portr. Qn. Victoria at lower r.	420.00	1400.	—
S1613	**2 Dollars** 1.11.1860. Portr. man at lower l., 2 allegorical females w/lg. *2* at ctr., portr. Qn. Victoria at lower r.	420.00	1400.	—
S1614	**3 Dollars** 1.11.1860. Portr. Prince of Wales at lower l., allegorical female at l., sailing ship at upper ctr. r., portr. man at r.	1260.	2800.	—
S1615	**5 Dollars** 1.11.1860. Portr. man at lower l., supported royal arms at top ctr., sailboat at lower r. Face proof.	—	Unc	750.00
S1616	**20 Dollars** 18xx. Standing Justice at l., St. George slaying dragon at ctr., portr. Duke of Wellington at lower r. Green *TWENTY* protector.			
	p. Green. Curved outline *TWENTY*. Face proof.	—	Unc	750.00
	r. Unsigned remainder.	600.00	—	—
S1617	**50 Pounds** 18xx. Portr. Qn. Victoria at l., reclining Goddess of Plenty w/sailing ship in background at top ctr., steam passenger train on viaduct at lower r. Face proof.	—	Unc	750.00

Charlotte County Bank

Established in St. Andrews, New Brunswick in 1825. Ceased operation in 1860's.

1852-59 Issue

#S1618-1622 black. Standing Britannia at l., Navigation reclining at shoreline at top and bottom ctr. Partially engraved dates. Back red-brown. Printer: Perkins and Heath.

		VG	VF	Unc
S1618	**5 Shillings** 12.9.1853-26.8.1856.	840.00	—	—
S1619	**1 Pound** 1.9.1852; 8.11.1859.	840.00	—	—
S1620	**3 Pounds** 1.9.1852.	1260.	—	—
S1621	**5 Pounds** 18xx. Face proof.	—	—	600.00
S1622	**10 Pounds** 18xx. Face proof.	—	—	600.00

BANK OF CHARLOTTETOWN

"Established" in Charlottetown, P.E.I. in 1852.

1850S ISSUE

Pound Sterling/Dollar System.

#S1623 printers: RWH & E and New England Banknote Co.

		VG	VF	UNC
S1623	5 POUNDS = 16 DOLLARS 66 CENTS 18xx. Black. Uniface. Roses, shamrocks and thistles at l., supported royal arms at upper ctr., sailing ship at upper and lower r.			
	p1. W/*Payable at S. Draper's New York;* w/3 denomination: P.E.I. *5 Pounds;* Canada - *4 Pounds.* U.S. - *SIXTEEN DOLLARS.* Proof.	—	—	750.00
	p2. W/*Redeemed at S. Draper's New York and at Wm. Elliott & Cos. British Consulate Boston;* w/3 denominations: P.E.I. - *5 Pounds;* Canada - *4.3.4. Pounds;* U.S. - *SIXTEEN DOLLARS, 66 CENTS.* Proof.	—	—	750.00

1852 ISSUE

Dollar System.

#S1623A-S1625 black. Roses, shamrocks and thistle at l., sailing ship at upper and lower r. Uniface. Printers: RWH & E and New England Bank Note Co.

		VG	VF	UNC
S1623A	1 DOLLAR 1.5.1852. Seated Britannia w/shield at top ctr. Proof.	—	—	750.00
S1624	2 DOLLARS 1.5.1852. Reclining sailor w/sailing ship in background at top ctr.	1750.	—	—

		VG	VF	UNC
S1625	3 DOLLARS 1.5.1852. Seated Agriculture at top ctr.	2500.	—	—

THE CITY BANK/LA BANQUE DE LA CITÉ

Began operations in Montreal, Lower Canada in 1833.

MONTREAL

1833-40 ISSUE

#S1626-S1631 black. Lg. red ovpt: *EASTERN TOWNSHIPS.* Printer: RWH & Co.

		GOOD	FINE	XF
S1626	1 DOLLAR = 1 PIASTRE 10.10.1833. Portr. Kg. William IV at l., Indian shooting bow and arrow at ctr. Back red: *CITY BANK/MONTREAL* between identical standing woman at l. and at r.	325.00	1050.	—

		GOOD	FINE	XF
S1627	2 DOLLARS = 2 PIASTRES 18xx. Indian in canoe at upper ctr., portr. Kg. William IV at lower r. Proof.	—	Unc	350.00

		GOOD	FINE	XF
S1628	5 DOLLARS 18xx. Portr. Kg. William IV at l., seated Archimedes moving the earth at top ctr., supported royal arms (sideways) at r. Face proof.	—	Unc	350.00
S1629	10 DOLLARS 18xx. Portr. Kg. William IV at l., supported royal arms at upper ctr., woman w/sheaf of wheat at r., small steamboat at bottom ctr.			
	p. Face proof.	—	Unc	350.00
	x. Counterfeit.	32.50	100.00	—

NOTE: Counterfeits exist w/text: *OF PARLIAMENT* below portr. of Kg. William IV in military dress at l.

		GOOD	FINE	XF
S1630	20 DOLLARS 18xx. Portr. Kg. William IV between lion and unicorn at upper ctr. Face proof.	—	Unc	500.00

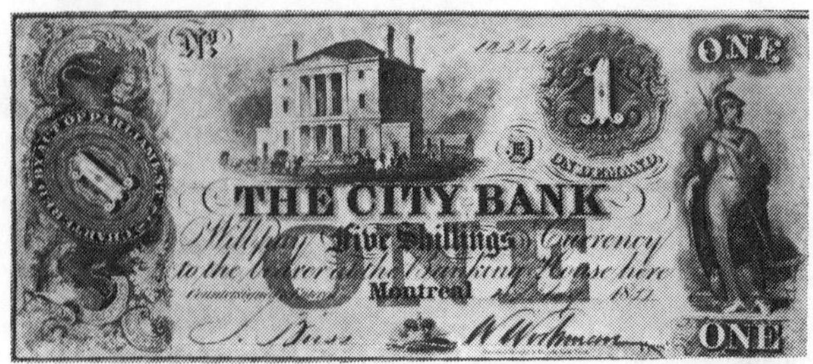

		GOOD	FINE	XF
S1631	100 DOLLARS 18xx. Portr. Kg. William IV at top ctr. St. George slaying dragon at l. and r. Face proof.	—	Unc	500.00

1851-53 ISSUE

Dollar/Pound Sterling System.

#S1632-S1637 black. Uniface.

		GOOD	FINE	XF
S1632	1 DOLLAR = 5 SHILLINGS 1.5.1851; 2.5.1851. Counter w/lion and unicorn (sideways) at l., bank bldg. at upper l. ctr., standing Britannia at r. Red word protector on face and back.	350.00	1150.	—
S1632A	2 DOLLARS = 10 SHILLINGS 18xx. Bank bldg. Red word protector on face and back. Proof.	—	Unc	350.00

S1633 4 DOLLARS = 1 POUND — GOOD 275.00 — FINE 1050. — XF —
1.2.1853. Portr. Qn. Victoria at l., bank bldg. at top ctr.

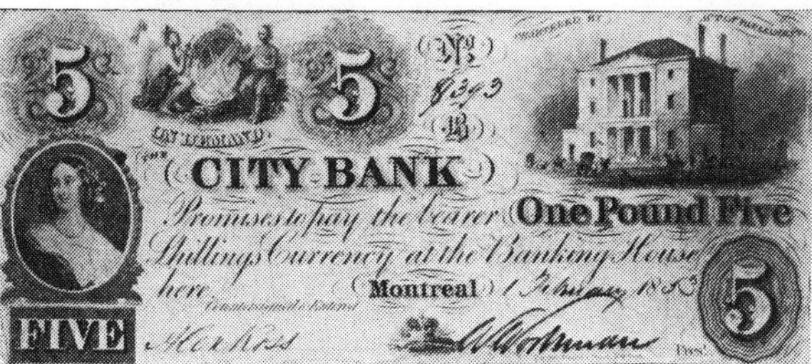

S1634 5 DOLLARS = 1 POUND-5 SHILLINGS — GOOD 275.00 — FINE 1050. — XF —
1.2.1853. Female portr. at l., 2 Indians holding shield at upper l., bank bldg. at upper r.

		GOOD	FINE	XF
S1635	**10 DOLLARS = 2 POUNDS-10 SHILLINGS** 18xx. Bank bldg. at top ctr. Red word protector on face and back. Proof.	—	Unc	350.00
S1635A	**20 DOLLARS = 5 POUNDS** 18xx. Woman at l., bank bldg. at ctr. Red word protector on face and back. Proof.	—	Unc	425.00
S1636	**50 DOLLARS = 12 POUNDS-10 SHILLINGS** 18xx. Bank bldg. at ctr. Red word protector on face and back. Proof.	—	Unc	425.00
S1637	**100 DOLLARS = 25 POUNDS** 18xx. Portr. Prince Albert at l., bank bldg. at ctr., portr. Qn. Victoria at r. Red word protector on face and back. Proof.	—	Unc	425.00

TORONTO

1850-54 ISSUE

#S1638-S1642 black. Uniface. 1861 and 1865 w/green word protector on face and back. Printers: RWH & Co. and RWH & E.

S1638 1 DOLLAR — GOOD 200.00 — FINE 650.00 — XF —
1.10.1850-2.10.1865. Seated Liberty w/shield at top ctr., portr. Qn. Victoria at r.

S1639 2 DOLLARS — GOOD 325.00 — FINE 1050. — XF —
31.12.1852; 1.9.1854; 1.8.1856. Seated Navigation w/shield at top ctr., portr. Qn. Victoria at r.

S1640 5 DOLLARS — GOOD 325.00 — FINE 1050. — XF —
31.12.1852. Supported royal arms (sideways) at l., Archimedes moving the earth at top ctr., portr. Kg. William IV at r.

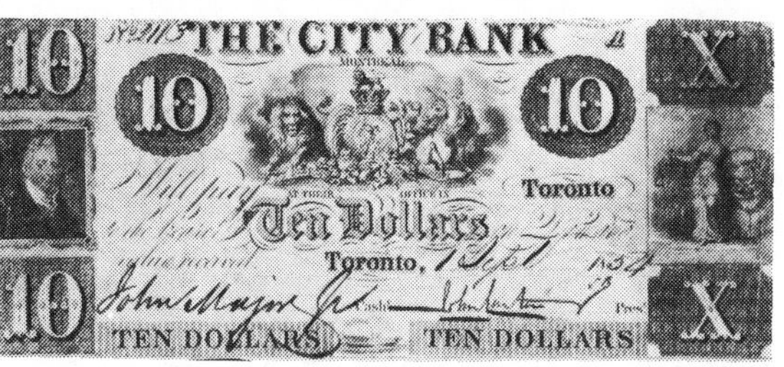

S1641 10 DOLLARS — GOOD 325.00 — FINE 1050. — XF —
1.9.1854. Portr. Kg. William IV at l., supported royal arms at upper ctr., standing Justice at r.

S1642 20 DOLLARS — GOOD — — FINE Unc — XF 500.00
18xx. Allegorical female l., portr. Kg. William IV at ctr. Face proof.

QUEBEC

1850S ISSUE

#S1643 and S1644 black. Uniface. Printer: RWH & Co.

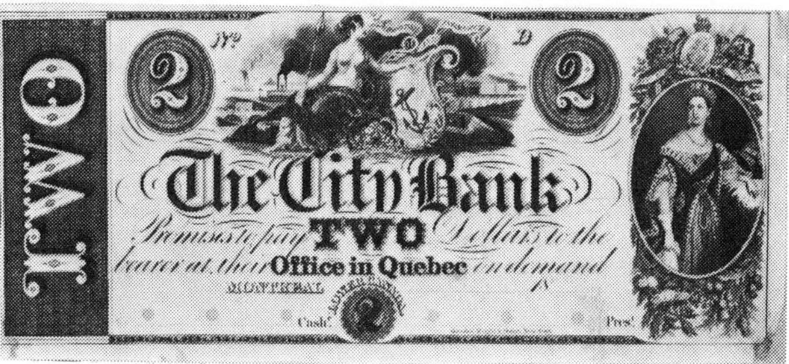

		GOOD	FINE	XF
S1643	**2 DOLLARS** 18xx. Like #S1639. Proof.	—	Unc	450.00
S1644	**4 DOLLARS = 1 POUND** 18xx. Portr. Qn. Victoria at l., bank bldg. at top ctr. Red word protector on face. Proof.	—	Unc	425.00

1857 FIRST ISSUE

#S1645-S1649 black. Portr. man at l. and another at r. Back orange; w/*CITY BANK MONTREAL*. Green word protector on face and back. Blue ovpt: *TORONTO*. Blue hand stamp: *MINES*. Printer: TCC, Montreal.

S1645 1 DOLLAR — GOOD 85.00 — FINE 300.00 — XF —
1.1.1857. Settlers and Indians holding frame portr. Qn. Victoria at ctr.

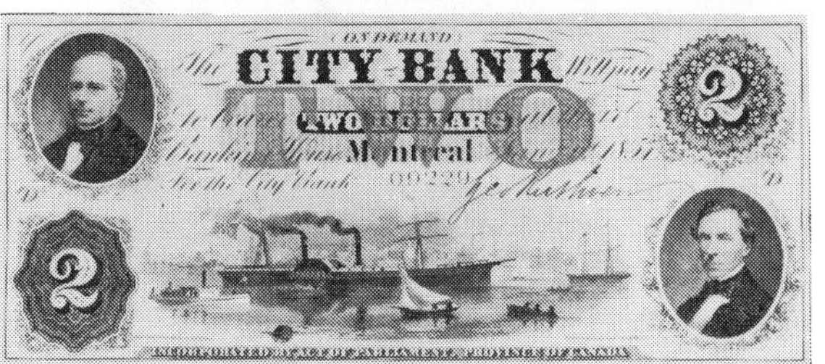

S1646 2 DOLLARS | GOOD | FINE | XF
1.1.1857. Ships and boats in harbor at bottom ctr. | 95.00 | 325.00 | —

S1647 4 DOLLARS | GOOD | FINE | XF
1.1.1857. Reclining Commerce and farmer seated holding shield at top ctr.
a. Issued note w/o ovpt. | 250.00 | 650.00 | —
b. Blue ovpt: *MINES.* | — | — | —

c. Blue ovpt: *TORONTO.* | — | — | —

S1648 5 DOLLARS | GOOD | FINE | XF
1.1.1857. Farmers waving at steam passenger train at top ctr. | 150.00 | 500.00 | —

S1649 10 DOLLARS | GOOD | FINE | XF
1.1.1857. St. George slaying a dragon at top ctr. | 250.00 | 850.00 | —

S1649A 20 DOLLARS
1.1.1857. Livestock by stream at ctr. | 250.00 | 850.00 | —

1857 SECOND ISSUE

#S1650-S1654 black. Uniface. Green word protector on face. Blue ovpt: *QUEBEC* or *TORONTO*. Printer: TCC, Montreal.

S1650 1 DOLLAR | GOOD | FINE | XF
1.1.1857.
a. Issued note w/o ovpt. | 75.00 | 250.00 | —
b. Blue ovpt: *QUEBEC.* | — | — | —

S1651 2 DOLLARS | GOOD | FINE | XF
1.1.1857. Face like #S1646. | 100.00 | 300.00 | —

S1652 4 DOLLARS
1.1.1857. Face like #S1647. | 125.00 | 400.00 | —

S1653 5 DOLLARS
1.1.1857. Face like #S1648. | 125.00 | 400.00 | —

S1654 10 DOLLARS
1.1.1857. Face like #S1649. | 150.00 | 500.00 | —

S1655 5 DOLLARS | GOOD | FINE | XF
1.1.1857. Black on green unpt. Green *W* and panel added to *FIVE.* Red ovpt: *ST. CATHARINES.* Back green; *CITY BANK MONTREAL.* Printers: TCC and BABNC. | 150.00 | 700.00 | —

1857 SPURIOUS ISSUE

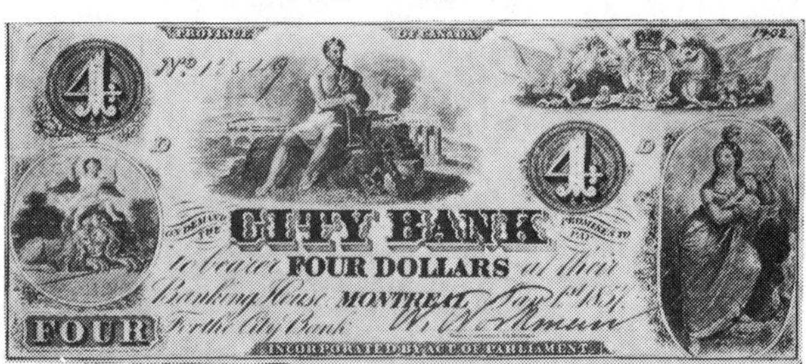

S1656 4 DOLLARS | VG | VF | UNC
1.1.1857. Black. Portr. cherub w/lion at l., seated blacksmith at top ctr., supported royal arms at upper r. above portr. Indian princess at lower r. Uniface. Printer: TCC. | 100.00 | 225.00 | —

CITY BANK OF MONTREAL

1861 SPURIOUS ISSUE

#S1656A printers: Jocelyn, Draper, Welsh & Co. and ABNC.

S1656A 5 DOLLARS | GOOD | FINE | XF
9.2.1861. Orange-brown. Farm family at l., Cornelia Jocelyn at lower r. Uniface. | 85.00 | 250.00 | —

NOTE: Altered from a Colonial Bank of Canada issue.

BANK OF CLIFTON

Formerly the Zimmerman Bank.

1859 FIRST ISSUE

#S1657-S1659 black. Roebling bridge at Niagara Falls top ctr. Partially engraved date. Red word protector on face and back. Uniface. Printer: ABNC.

S1657 1 DOLLAR | VG | VF | UNC
1.10.1859; 1.11.1859. Clifton House hotel at lower l., seated Industry at lower r. | 20.00 | 45.00 | 125.00

S1658 3 DOLLARS | VG | VF | UNC
1.10.1859; 1.11.1859. Clifton House hotel at lower l., portr. Qn. Victoria at lower r. | 40.00 | 100.00 | 225.00

		VG	VF	UNC
S1659	**5 DOLLARS** 1.10.1859; 1.11.1859. Seated farm woman w/sickle at upper l, steam passenger train at lower r.	20.00	45.00	125.00

1859 SECOND ISSUE

#S1660-S1662 black. Fully engraved date. Curved black ovpt: *OTTAWA, ILL.* and stars. Red word protector on face and back.

		VG	VF	UNC
S1660	**1 DOLLAR** 1.10.1859. Like #S1657.	17.50	31.50	98.00

		VG	VF	UNC
S1661	**3 DOLLARS** 1.10.1859. Clifton House hotel at lower l., portr. Qn. Victoria at lower r.	40.00	85.00	200.00
S1662	**5 DOLLARS** 1.10.1859. Like #S1659.	17.50	32.50	100.00

1860 ISSUE

Overprint Varieties.

Blue oval ovpt: *Sassenberg & Co., Buenos Ayres.*

Black ovpts: *Redeemed by Frederick Lau & Co. Bankers, 162 Fulton St. N.Y. at 3/4 per cent; Redeemable in Chicago at the office of Chadwick & Co.; Redeemable in bankable funds at the office of Chadwick & Co. 5 Clark Street under the - house Chicago, Ill.* Blue hand stamp: *3.*

#S1663-S1665 black on red unpt. St. George slaying dragon at ctr. Uniface. Printer: NYBNC.

		VG	VF	UNC
S1663	**1 DOLLAR** 1860-61.			
	a. 1.9.1860.	15.00	28.00	90.00
	b. 1.9.1861.	10.00	25.00	75.00

		VG	VF	UNC
S1664	**2 DOLLARS** 1860-61.			
	a. 1.9.1860.	15.00	28.00	90.00
	b. 1.9.1861.	10.00	25.00	75.00
S1665	**5 DOLLARS** 1860-61.			
	a. 1.9.1860.	15.00	28.00	90.00
	b. 1.9.1861.	10.00	25.00	75.00

NOTE: 1861 variety w/handwritten *1* engraved *0* in date for all denominations.

COLONIAL BANK OF CANADA

Chartered in Toronto, Canada West in 1856. Began operations in 1858 and failed within 6 months.

1859 FIRST ISSUE

#S1666-S1674 black on orange-brown unpt. W/2 sign. Uniface. Various hand stamped letters and numbers are encountered. Printers: Jocelyn, Draper, Welch & Co. and ABNC.

		VG	VF	UNC
S1666	**1 DOLLAR** 4.4.1859-8.7.1859. Portr. woman at lower l., lumberjack at top ctr.	17.50	42.50	105.00

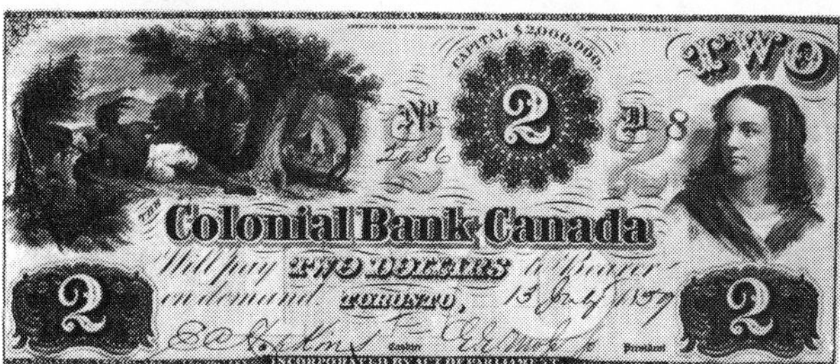

		VG	VF	UNC
S1667	**2 DOLLARS** 4.4.1859-14.7.1859. Indians on bluff at upper l., young woman at r.	17.50	42.50	105.00

		VG	VF	UNC
S1668	**3 DOLLARS** 4.4.1859-6.7.1859. St. George slaying dragon at lower l., 3 allegorical women at top ctr., C. Jocelyn at lower r.	52.50	122.50	297.50

		VG	VF	UNC
S1669	**4 DOLLARS** 4.4.1859-24.6.1859. Standing Justice at l., portr. Qn. Victoria at ctr.	45.50	112.50	227.50
S1670	**5 DOLLARS** 4.4.1859-4.7.1859. Farm family under tree at lower l., C. Jocelyn at lower r.	17.50	42.50	105.00
S1671	**10 DOLLARS** 4.4.1859; 1.5.1859. Steam passenger train at station at upper l., Indian maiden at lower r.	50.00	100.00	300.00

		VG	VF	UNC
S1672	**20 DOLLARS** 2.5.1859; 4.8.1859. St. George slaying dragon at upper l., farmers hay at ctr., C. Jocelyn at lower r.			
	a. Issued note.	840.00	1750.	—
	r. Unsigned remainder.	350.00	700.00	—

S1673 50 Dollars | VG | VF | Unc
2.5.1859; 4.8.1859. St. George slaying dragon at lower l., sailing ships at top ctr., C. Jocelyn at lower r.

	VG	VF	UNC
a. Issued note.	420.00	840.00	—
r. Unsigned remainder.	105.00	225.00	—

S1674 100 Dollars
2.5.1859; 4.8.1859. Paddle wheel steamship at l., portr. Qn. Victoria at lower r.

	VG	VF	UNC
a. Issued note.	420.00	840.00	—
r. Unsigned remainder.	105.00	225.00	—

1859 Second Issue

#S1675-S1680 black on pink unpt. W/text: *For the Colonial Bank* w/1 sign. Various hand stamped letters and numbers are encountered. Uniface. Printer: Jocelyn, Draper, Welch & Co. and ABNC monogram.

		VG	VF	UNC
S1675	**1 Dollar** 4.5.1859. Like #S1666.	17.50	42.00	105.00
S1676	**2 Dollars** 4.5.1859. Like #S1667.	87.50	175.00	560.00
S1677	**3 Dollars** 4.5.1859. Like #S1668.	42.00	105.00	210.00
S1678	**4 Dollars** 4.5.1859. Like #S1669.	42.00	105.00	210.00

		VG	VF	UNC
S1679	**5 Dollars** 4.5.1859. Like #S1670.	17.50	42.50	105.00

		VG	VF	UNC
S1680	**10 Dollars** 20.10.1859. Like #S1671.	50.00	105.00	350.00

Colonial Bank of Chatham

Established in Chatham, Upper Canada in 1837. Notes were circulated in Western New York.

1837 Issue

#S1681-S1683 black. Small crouching lion at bottom ctr. Uniface. Printer: RWH & Co.

		Good	Fine	XF
S1680A	**2 Dollars = 10 Shillings** 3.2.1837. Cherubs at l. and r., standing Justice, seated Agriculture by arms at upper ctr., lion head at bottom ctr.	950.00	2000.	—

		Good	Fine	XF
S1681	**3 Dollars = 15 Shillings** 3.2.1837. Seated Justice at top ctr., portr. Indian chief at upper r.	950.00	2000.	—

		Good	Fine	XF
S1682	**5 Dollars = 25 Shillings** 3.2.1837. Supported royal arms at top ctr., portr. Kg. William IV at r.	950.00	2000.	—

		Good	Fine	XF
S1683	**10 Dollars = 50 Shillings** 3.2.1837. Britannia in chariot drawn by lions at ctr., standing farm woman at r.	950.00	2000.	—

Commercial Bank (Brockville, U.C.)

Notes were circulated in Upper Canada, Michigan and Ohio.

1834-36 Issue

#S1684 and S1685 black. W/text: *For Messrs. Sims, Colburn and Co.* Uniface. Printer: Burton and Edmonds.

S1684 5 DOLLARS = 25 SHILLINGS
3.11.1836. Seated allegorical man w/spilt urn at upper ctr., sailing ship at lower r., cargo and sailing ship at bottom ctr., sailing ship at lower r.

VG	VF	UNC
850.00	—	—

S1685 10 DOLLARS = 50 SHILLINGS
2.9.1834. Standing Liberty at upper l., portr. Kg. William IV at upper l. ctr., seated Agriculture at upper r.

VG	VF	UNC
850.00	—	—

COMMERCIAL BANK (KINGSTON, U.C.)

1837 FIRST SPURIOUS ISSUE

#S1686-S1689 black. W/text: *for the Foreign and Domestic Exchange Company.* Uniface. Printer: Jas. Harris, N.Y.
#S1686-S1688 handwritten: *Commercial* and *Kingston.*

S1686 1 DOLLAR
18.7.1837. Portr. G. Washington at l., seated Mercury w/sailing ship in background at top ctr., portr. B. Franklin at r., Indian in canoe at bottom ctr.

GOOD	FINE	XF
250.00	850.00	—

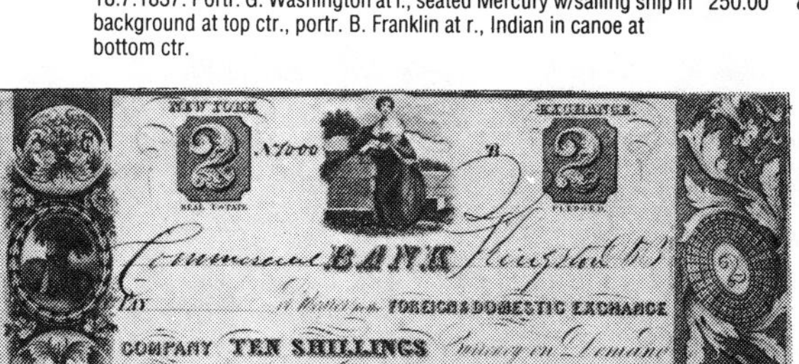

S1687 2 DOLLARS = 10 SHILLINGS
30.7.1837. Grain sheaves at l., standing Agriculture w/grain at top ctr., floral design w/counter at r.

GOOD	FINE	XF
250.00	850.00	—

S1688 3 DOLLARS = 15 SHILLINGS
21.6.1837; 26.6.1837. Horse's head at l., seated woman w/mill in background at top ctr., cargo and sailing ship at bottom ctr., floral design w/counter at r.

GOOD	FINE	XF
250.00	850.00	—

1837 SECOND SPURIOUS ISSUE

S1689 1 DOLLAR
25.7.1837. Like #S1686 but w/*COMMERICAL* and *KINGSTON* engraved.

GOOD	FINE	XF
275.00	950.00	—

COMMERCIAL BANK (MONTREAL, L.C.)

1837 ISSUE

#S1689A-S1689C black. Uniface. Printer: RW & H.

		GOOD	FINE	XF
S1689A	**3 DOLLARS** 1837. Dock scene at l., blacksmith and 2 women at top ctr., woman w/wheat at r.	Reported Not Confirmed		
S1689B	**5 DOLLARS** 1837. Youth at l., seated woman at ctr., blacksmith at r.	Reported Not Confirmed		
S1689C	**10 DOLLARS** 1.6.1837. Seated woman w/shield at l., blacksmith and 2 women at top ctr., cherub w/stone slab at r., small crouching lion at bottom ctr.	30.00	110.00	225.00

COMMERCIAL BANK OF FORT ERIE, U.C.

1837 SPURIOUS ISSUE

#S1690-S1696 black. Encountered w/various spurious sign. and dates in 1850s. Uniface. Printer: RWH & Co.

S1690 1 DOLLAR
10.1.1837. St. George slaying dragon at upper l., steamship at upper ctr. r., portr. Kg. William IV at r., small deer at bottom ctr.

VG	VF	UNC
100.00	200.00	—

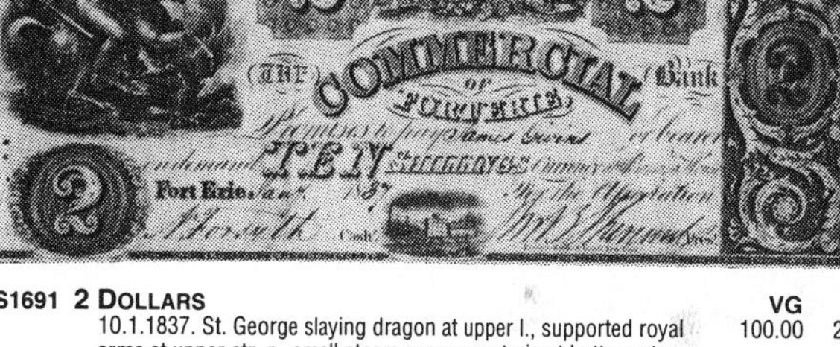

S1691 2 DOLLARS
10.1.1837. St. George slaying dragon at upper l., supported royal arms at upper ctr. r., small steam passenger train at bottom ctr.

VG	VF	UNC
100.00	200.00	—

S1692 3 DOLLARS
10.1.1837. Standing Britannia at upper l., farmers sowing seed and cultivating w/horses at upper l. ctr., St. George slaying dragon at upper r., small steamboat at bottom ctr. Unsigned remainder.

VG	VF	UNC
175.00	335.00	—

S1693 4 DOLLARS
20.7.1836; 20.1.1837. Supported royal arms at top ctr., farmers havesting wheat at r., small steamboat at bottom ctr.

VG	VF	UNC
150.00	300.00	—

S1694 5 Dollars — VG | VF | Unc
20.7.1836; 20.1.1837; 20.8.1837. Portr. Kg. William IV at upper l. ctr., St. George slaying dragon at upper r., small beaver at bottom ctr. — 100.00 | 200.00 | —

S1695 10 Dollars — VG | VF | Unc
18xx. Supported royal arms at top ctr., cherub at r., small dog's head at bottom ctr. Unsigned remainder. — 300.00 | 600.00 | —

S1696 20 Dollars — VG | VF | Unc
18xx. 2 allegorical women seated w/sailing ships in background at upper ctr., supported royal arms turned sideways at r., small dog's head at bottom ctr. Unsigned remainder. — 300.00 | 600.00 | —

Commercial Bank of Montreal, L.C.

Established in Montreal, Lower Canada operating for a short period until 1837.

1835 Issue

Dollar/Pound Sterling System.

#S1697-S1700 black. Uniface. Printer: RWH & E.

S1697 5 Dollars = 1 Pound-5 Shillings — Good | Fine | XF
21.8.1835; 1.9.1835. St. George slaying a dragon at l., steam passenger train at r. — 275.00 | 900.00 | —

S1698 10 Dollars = 2 Pounds-10 Shillings
21.8.1835; 1.9.1835. Indian maiden at upper l., early steam passenger train at r. Proof. — 275.00 | 900.00 | —

S1699 20 Dollars = 5 Pounds — Good | Fine | XF
10.10.1835. Standing allegorical vulcan standing by seated allegorical woman at upper l., allegorical man presenting offering to seated woman at r. — 300.00 | 975.00 | —

S1700 50 Dollars = 12 Pounds-10 Shillings — Good | Fine | XF
10.10.1835. Allegorical nude woman and cherub w/serpents below at upper l. — 300.00 | 975.00 | —

1836 Issue

Dollar/Piastre System.

#S1701 and S1702 black. Uniface. Printer: Underwood, Bald, Spencer & Hufty. Unissued remainders.

S1701 1 Dollar = 1 Piastre — Good | Fine | XF
1.6.1836. Farm woman w/sickle at l., young man w/dog at upper ctr., farm woman w/sheaves of grain at r. — 200.00 | 700.00 | —

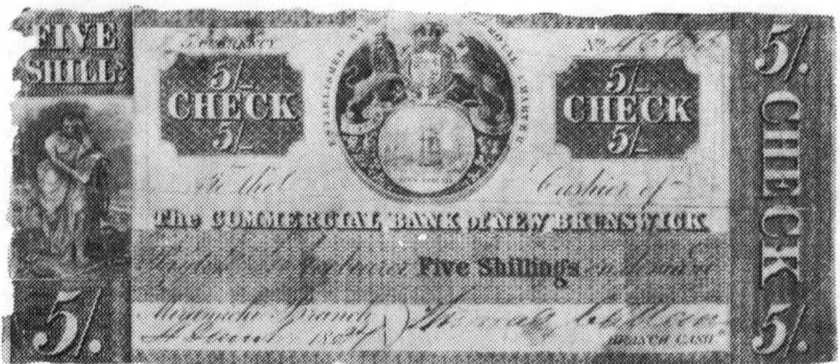

S1702 2 Dollars = 2 Piastres — Good | Fine | XF
1.6.1836. Woman w/cornucopia at l., steam passenger train passing by houses at upper l. ctr., standing Justice at r. — 250.00 | 900.00 | —

Commercial Bank of New Brunswick

Established in St. John, New Brunswick in 1834. Failed in 1868.

#S1703-S1705 black. Supported royal arms above sailing ship medal at top ctr. Back green. Printer: New England Bank Note Company.

Fredericton

1800s Issue

S1703 1 Pound — Good | Fine | XF
18xx. Sailing ships at l. Face proof. — — | Unc | 500.00

#S1704 and S1705 small lion on crown at bottom ctr.

S1704 2 Pounds
18xx. Sailing ships at l. Face proof. — — | Unc | 500.00

S1705 5 Pounds
18xx. Standing Britannia w/shield at l. Face proof. — — | Unc | 500.00

Miramichi

#S1706 and S1707 black. Supported royal arms above sailing ship medal at top ctr. Back green. Printer: New England Bank Note Company.

1837 Issue

S1706 5 Shillings — Good | Fine | XF
4.12.1837. Allegorical woman at l. — 300.00 | 1050. | —

		GOOD	FINE	XF
S1707	**7 SHILLINGS-6 PENCE** 4.12.1837. Allegorical woman w/lyre and cornucopia at l.	300.00	1050.	—

ST. JOHN

1850s ISSUE

#S1708-S1713 black. Supported royal arms above sailing ship medal at top ctr. Back green: small lion on crown at bottom ctr. Printer: New England Bank Note Company.

		GOOD	FINE	XF
S1708	**5 SHILLINGS** 18xx. Sailing ships by lighthouse at l., 2 farmers harvesting grain at r. Sailing ships at l. and r. on back. Face proof.	—	Unc	350.00

		GOOD	FINE	XF
S1709	**1 POUND** 1.6.1850; 1.7.1852; 1.6.1853; 1.11.1853. Ship, cargo and fasces at l.			
	a. Issued note.	365.00	1050.	—
	p. Face proof.	—	Unc	700.00
S1710	**2 POUNDS** 18xx. Sailing ships at l. Face proof.	—	Unc	500.00
S1711	**5 POUNDS** 1.6.1853. Seated Britannia at l.			
	a. Issued note.	275.00	1050.	—
	p. Face proof.	—	Unc	700.00
S1712	**10 POUNDS** 18xx. Sailing ship at l. Face proof.	—	Unc	500.00
S1713	**25 POUNDS** 18xx. Sailing ships at l. Face proof.	—	Unc	600.00

1860 ISSUE

Dollar/Pound Sterling System.

#S1714-S1720 black on green unpt. Back green. Printer: ABNC.

		GOOD	FINE	XF
S1714	**1 DOLLAR = 5 SHILLINGS** 1.11.1860. Sailing ship at l.			
	a. Issued note.	100.00	500.00	1050.
	p. Face proof.	—	Unc	700.00
S1715	**2 DOLLARS = 10 SHILLINGS** 1.11.1860. Shipbuilding at r.			
	a. Issued note.	200.00	650.00	1050.
	p. Face proof.	—	Unc	700.00
S1716	**4 DOLLARS = 1 POUND** 1.11.1860. Ship, cargo and faces at l.			
	a. Issued note.	200.00	650.00	1125.
	p. Face proof.	—	Unc	700.00
S1717	**8 DOLLARS = 2 POUNDS** 1.11.1860. Young girl w/basket of flowers at lower r. Face proof.	—	Unc	850.00
S1718	**20 DOLLARS = 5 POUNDS** 1.11.1860. Ship at lower l., pilot at ship's wheel at lower r. Face proof.	—	Unc	350.00
S1719	**50 DOLLARS = 12 POUNDS-10 SHILLINGS** 1.11.1860. Seated allegorical woman at lower r. Face proof.	—	Unc	350.00
S1720	**100 DOLLARS = 25 POUNDS** 1.11.1860. Fisherman on schooner at lower r.	—	Unc	350.00

COMMERCIAL BRANCH BANK OF CANADA, COLLINGWOOD, P.C.

1861 SPURIOUS ISSUE

#S1721 and S1722 black on green unpt. Printer: Union Bank Note Company.

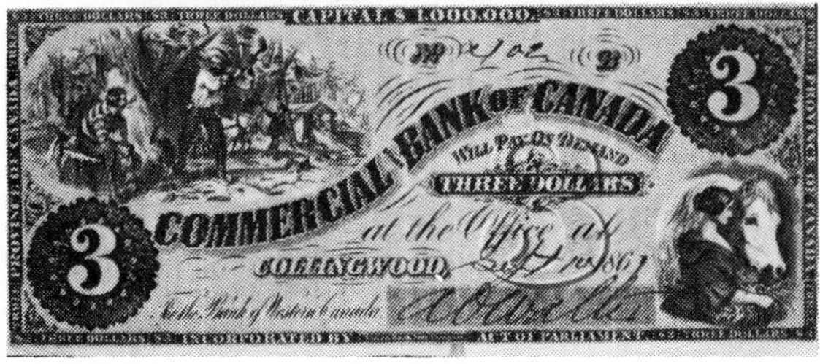

		VG	VF	UNC
S1721	**3 DOLLARS** 10.9.1861. Lumberjacks at upper l., woman feeding horse at lower r.	250.00	400.00	—

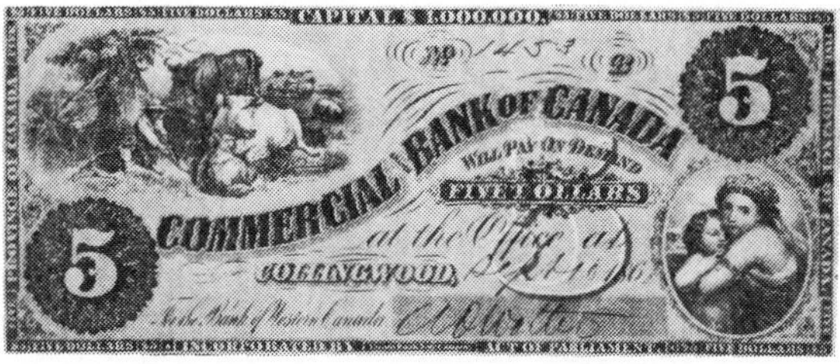

		VG	VF	UNC
S1722	**5 DOLLARS** 10.9.1861; 10.7.1862. Farmer and child seated under tree w/cattle at upper l., woman hugging child at lower r.	200.00	350.00	—

THE CONSOLIDATED BANK OF CANADA

Created out of a merger of the City Bank and Royal Canadian Bank in Montreal, Quebec in 1876. Failed in 1879.

1876 ISSUE

#S1723-S1728 black on green unpt. Supported bank crest at upper ctr. Back green; shield at l. and another at r. Printer: BABNC. Additional blue ovpts: *SEAFORTH* and *SHERBROOKE* reported.

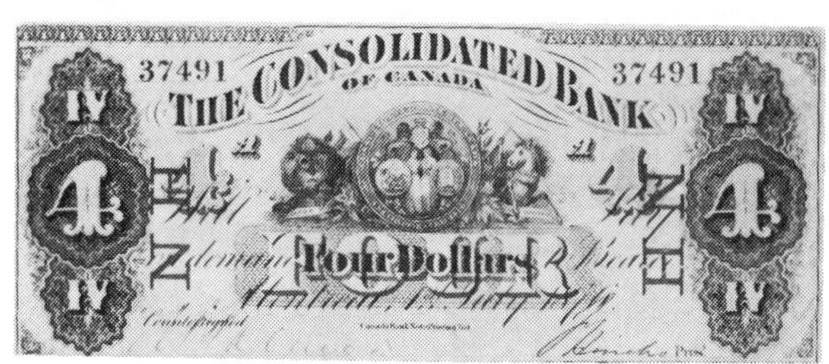

		VG	VF	UNC
S1723	**4 DOLLARS** 1.7.1876.			
	a. Issued note w/o ovpt.	275.00	700.00	—
	b. W/blue ovpt: *B-B.*	275.00	700.00	—
	c. W/blue ovpt: *C-C.*	275.00	700.00	—
	d. W/blue ovpt: *D-D.*	275.00	700.00	—
	e. W/blue ovpt: *N-N.*	275.00	700.00	—

		VG	VF	UNC
	f. W/vertical blue ovpt: *NH-NH.*	275.00	700.00	—
	g. W/vertical blue ovpt: *BELLEVILLE*	275.00	700.00	—
	h. W/vertical blue ovpt: *GALT* twice.	275.00	700.00	—
	i. W/vertical blue ovpt: *HAMILTON* twice.	275.00	700.00	—
	j. W/vertical blue ovpt: *ST. CATHARINES* twice.	275.00	700.00	—

		VG	VF	UNC
S1724	**5 DOLLARS** 1.7.1876.			
	a. Issued note w/o ovpt.	150.00	325.00	—
	b. W/blue ovpt: *N N.*	150.00	325.00	—

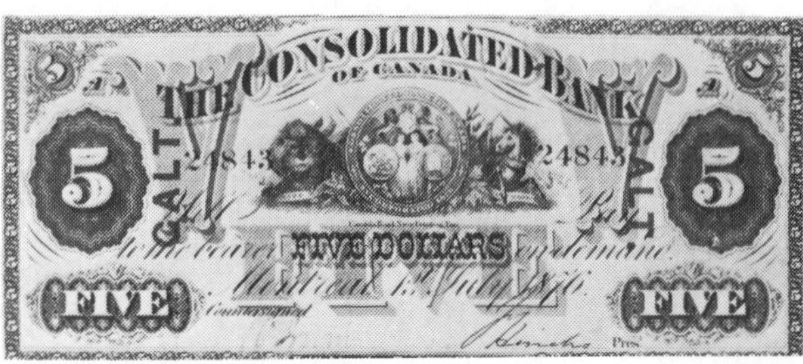

c. W/vertical blue ovpt: *GALT* twice.	150.00	325.00	—

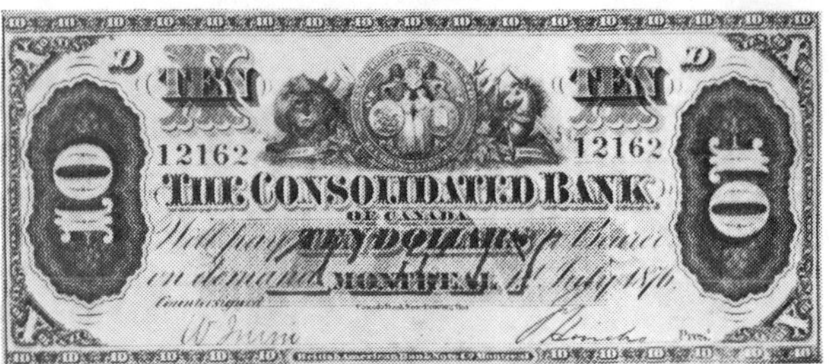

	VG	VF	UNC
S1725 10 DOLLARS			
1.7.1876.	150.00	325.00	—

	VG	VF	UNC
S1726 20 DOLLARS			
1.7.1876.			
a. Issued note.	700.00	1500.	—
p. Face proof.	—	—	450.00

	VG	VF	UNC
S1727 50 DOLLARS			
1.7.1876. Face proof.	—	—	450.00

	VG	VF	UNC
S1728 100 DOLLARS			
1.7.1876.	700.00	1470.	—

Notice

Readers with unlisted dates, color or signature varieties are invited to submit photocopies of their notes to: Standard Catalog of World Paper Money, Krause Publications, 700 East State St. Iola WI 54990-0001 U.S.A. or by email: thernr@krause.com. Email submissions of material for possible inclusion need to be 100% jpeg attachments at 300 dpi.

THE BANK OF THE COUNTY OF ELGIN

Established in St. Thomas, Canada West in 1855. Closed in 1862.

1856-57 ISSUE

#S1729-S1732 black. Uniface. Also encountered cut cancelled w/lower r. hand sign. removed. Red word protector on face and back. Printer: TCC.

	GOOD	FINE	XF
S1729 1 DOLLAR			
1.7.1856; 1.8.1856; 1.9.1856. Bank bldg. at lower l., farmer driving livestock at top ctr., rooster w/hens and chicks at lower r.			
a. Issued note.	400.00	1200.	—
b. Cut cancelled.	250.00	850.00	—

#S1730-S1732 bank bldg. at lower r.

	GOOD	FINE	XF
S1730 2 DOLLARS			
1.8.1856; 31.1.18357. Portr. E. Ermatinger at lower l., steam passenger train at top l. ctr.			
a. Issued note.	425.00	1400.	—
b. Cut cancelled.	325.00	1050.	—

	GOOD	FINE	XF
S1731 5 DOLLARS			
25.6.1856; 1.8.1856. Portr. Duke of Wellington at lower l., farmer w/livestock at top ctr.			
a. Issued note.	625.00	1750.	—
b. Cut cancelled.	425.00	1275.	—

	GOOD	FINE	XF
S1732 10 DOLLARS			
1.8.1856. Portr. E. Ermatinger at lower l., farm family watching steam passenger train at top ctr.			
a. Issued note.	525.00	1825.	—
b. Cut cancelled.	375.00	1200.	—

EASTERN BANK OF CANADA

Incorporated in St. John, New Brunswick in 1928. Ceased operations in 1932.

1929 ISSUE

#S1733 and S1734 bank seal at ctr. on back. Printer: CNBC.

		GOOD	FINE	XF
S1733	**5 DOLLARS** 15.5.1929. Black on green unpt. Ship and steam train at dockside at ctr. Back orange. Proof.	—	Unc	600.00
S1734	**10 DOLLARS** 15.5.1929. Black on brown unpt. Allegorical woman reclining at ctr. Back brown. Proof.	—	Unc	600.00

THE EXCHANGE BANK, QUEBEC, L.C.

1839; 1844 ISSUE

		VG	VF	UNC
S1735	**1 DOLLAR** 1839; 1844. Black. Reclining allegorical woman at top ctr. Uniface.			
	a. 29.9.1839.	1125.	—	—
	b. 21.5.1844.	1125.	—	—

THE EXCHANGE BANK OF CANADA

Established in Montreal, Quebec in 1871. Failed in 1883.

1872-73 ISSUE

#S1736-S1742 black on green unpt. T. Caverhill at l., M. H. Gault at r. Back green; beehive and flowers at ctr. Additional ovpts: Blue *EXTER, X* over *BRUSSELS:* purple C.

		GOOD	FINE	XF
S1736	**4 DOLLARS** 1.10.1872; 1.11.1872. Seated Justice at ctr.			
	a. Issued note w/o ovpt.	225.00	775.00	—
	b. Vertical blue ovpt: *AYLMER* twice.	225.00	775.00	—
	c. Vertical blue ovpt: *BRUSSELS* twice.	225.00	775.00	—
	d. Vertical blue ovpt: *HAMILTON* twice.	225.00	775.00	—

		GOOD	FINE	XF
S1737	**5 DOLLARS** 1.10.1872; 1.11.1872. Seated Industry at ctr. r.			
	a. Issued note w/o ovpt.	225.00	775.00	—
	b. Vertical blue ovpt: *AYLMER* twice.	225.00	775.00	—
	c. Vertical blue ovpt: *BRUSSELS* twice.	225.00	775.00	—
	d. Vertical blue ovpt: *HAMILTON* twice.	225.00	775.00	—
	e. Vertical blue ovpt: *PARKHILL* twice.	225.00	775.00	—

	f. Lg. ovpt: *L-L*.	225.00	775.00	—

		VG	VF	UNC
S1738	**6 DOLLARS** 1.10.1872; 1.11.1872. Paddle wheel steamboat at upper ctr.			
	a. Issued note w/o ovpt.	2800.	—	—
	b. Vertical blue ovpt: *VALLEYFIELD* twice.	2800.	—	—

		GOOD	FINE	XF
S1739	**10 DOLLARS** 1.10.1872; 1.11.1872. lg. *X* in unpt. at ctr.			
	a. Issued note w/o ovpt.	425.00	1400.	—
	b. Vertical blue ovpt: *ALYMER* twice.	425.00	1400.	—
	c. Vertical blue ovpt: *BEDFORD* twice.	425.00	1400.	—
	d. Vertical blue ovpt: *HAMILTON* twice.	425.00	1400.	—
S1740	**25 DOLLARS** 1.10.1872; 1.11.1872. Trade and Transportation at ctr. Face proof.	—	Unc	1500.

		GOOD	FINE	XF
S1741	**50 DOLLARS** 2.1.1873. Face proof.	—	Unc	500.00
S1742	**100 DOLLARS** 2.1.1873. Reclining allegorical woman w/split water jug at top ctr. Face proof.	—	Unc	500.00

THE EXCHANGE BANK OF CANADA, WINDSOR, ONTARIO

1864 ISSUE

		GOOD	FINE	XF
S1743	**1 DOLLAR** 8.6.1864. Black. Standing Britannia at lower l., early steam passenger train at ctr., supported royal arms at r. Uniface.	225.00	525.00	—

THE EXCHANGE BANK OF TORONTO, U.C.

1855 ISSUE

#S1744-S1747 black. Crest at l. Uniface. Printer: RWH & E. Unsigned remainders.

S1744 1 DOLLAR | VG 22.50 | VF 42.50 | UNC 150.00
1.5.1855. Stag at l. of seated Indian w/lg. *1* at upper ctr., farmer w/sheaf and sickle at lower r.

S1745 2 DOLLARS | VG 22.50 | VF 42.50 | UNC 150.00
1.5.1855. Farmer's harvesting grain w/cradles at upper ctr., sailing ship at lower r.

S1746 5 DOLLARS | VG 22.50 | VF 42.50 | UNC 150.00
1.5.1855. Sailing ship at top ctr., standing Navigation at lower r.

S1747 10 DOLLARS | VG 22.50 | VF 42.50 | UNC 150.00
1.5.1855. Various ships at upper ctr., deer at upper r., bison at lower r.

THE EXCHANGE BANK COMPANY OF CHIPPEWA, U.C.

Notes circulated in Buffalo, New York.

1837 SPURIOUS ISSUE

#S1748 and S1749 black. Uniface. Printer: RWH & Co.

	GOOD	FINE	XF
S1748 5 DOLLARS 2.1.1837. Produce and farm implements at top ctr., Indian at r., beaver at bottom ctr.			
a. Issued note.	325.00	1050.	—
r. Remainder w/o serial #. 18xx.	325.00	1050.	—

	GOOD	FINE	XF
S1749 10 DOLLARS 18xx. Livestock at top ctr., Seated Commerce at r., small steamboat at bottom ctr.			
r. Remainder w/o serial #.	325.00	1050.	—

THE FARMER'S BANK, TORONTO, U.C.

1843 SPURIOUS ISSUE

S1750 5 DOLLARS = 1 POUND-5 SHILLINGS | VG 700.00 | VF — | UNC —
3.8.1843. Black. Plow at l., kneeling cherub writing on stone slab at top ctr., woman w/bow at r. *New York - Exchange* at top border. Uniface. Printer: SC .N.Y.

FARMERS' BANK OF MALDEN

Issued at Malden, Upper Canada.

1800S ISSUE

#S1751-S1753 black. Uniface. Printer: Draper, Toppan, Longacre & Co.

S1751 1 DOLLAR = 5 SHILLINGS | VG — | VF Unc | UNC 850.00
18xx. Steamboat at l., rural scene at upper ctr., Indian maiden at r. Proof.

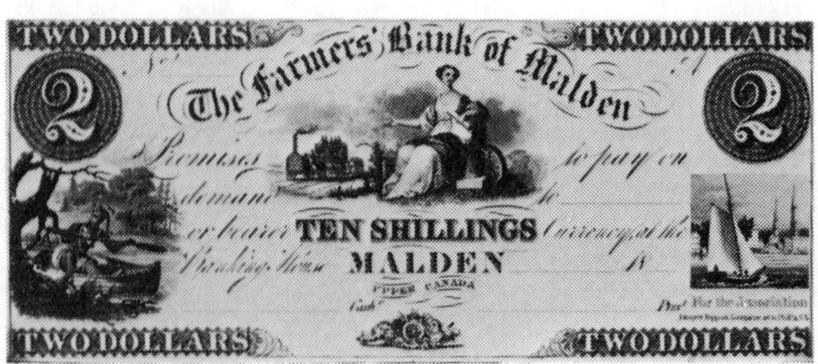

	VG	VF	UNC
S1752 2 DOLLARS = 10 SHILLINGS 18xx. Indian in canoe at lower l., seated allegorical woman w/early steam passenger train in background at upper ctr., sailboat at lower r. Proof.	—	Unc	850.00
S1753 3 DOLLARS = 15 SHILLINGS 18xx. Man seated w/flag at lower l., livestock at upper ctr., farm woman w/sheaf and sickle at upper r. Proof.	—	Unc	850.00

FARMER'S JOINT STOCK BANKING CO.

Established in Toronto, Upper Canada in 1835. Failed in early 1850s.

1835-37 ISSUES

Dollar/Pound Sterling System.

#S1754-S1759 black. Uniface. Printer: New England Bank Note Company, Boston.

		GOOD	FINE	XF
S1754	**1 DOLLAR = 5 SHILLINGS** 1.9.1835. Seated allegorical woman at l., farmers harvesting grain between cattle and man on horseback by man w/dog at upper ctr., woman at lower r.	100.00	350.00	—
S1755	**2 DOLLARS = 10 SHILLINGS** 11.9.1837. Ship, cargo and fasces at l., seated woman w/haying in background at upper l. ctr., standing Britannia w/shield at lower r.	100.00	350.00	—
S1756	**4 DOLLARS = 1 POUND** 18xx. Indian at l., woman w/sheaf and dog at top ctr., seated Britannia at lower r.			
	a. Issued note.	75.00	250.00	—
	p. Face proof.	—	Unc	350.00

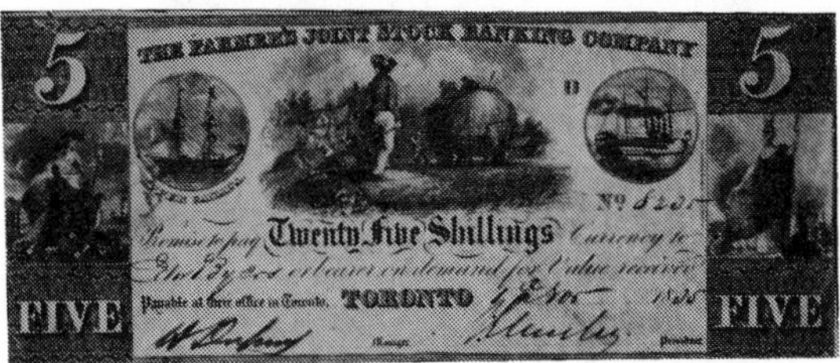

		GOOD	FINE	XF
S1757	**5 DOLLARS = 25 SHILLINGS** 1.11.1835. Abundance at l., farmers loading hay wagon between ships at upper ctr., standing Britannia w/shield at r.	100.00	350.00	—

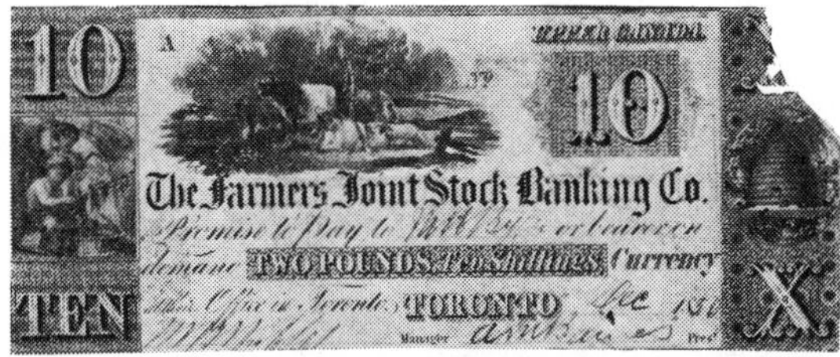

		GOOD	FINE	XF
S1758	**10 DOLLARS = 2 POUNDS-10 SHILLINGS** December 1835. 2 cherubs picking grapes at l., livestock at top l. ctr., beehive at r.	100.00	350.00	—
S1759	**50 DOLLARS = 12 POUNDS-10 SHILLINGS** 18xx. Woman w/flowers, farmers planting at l., maids by cows at ctr., sheaf at r. Proof.	—	Unc	300.00

GREEN BAY, WISCONSIN

1849 ISSUE

Dollar System.

#S1760-S1769 lion and unicorn supporters at top ctr. Printer: RWH & E.

#S1760, S1762-S1765 black. Uniface.

#S1760-S1762 *THE BRANCH OF* and *Office in Green Bay, Wisconsin* engraved.

		VG	VF	UNC
S1760	**1 DOLLAR** 1.2.1849. Standing Britannia at lower l., supported royal arms at top ctr., young woman at lower r., small griffin w/key at bottom ctr.	1400.	—	—

		VG	VF	UNC
S1761	**2 DOLLARS** 1.2.1849. Blacksmith by anvil at lower l., supported portr. Prince Consort at top ctr., standing Navigation at lower r., small supported royal arms at bottom ctr.	1400.	—	—

		VG	VF	UNC
S1762	**5 DOLLARS** 1.2.1849. Standing Britannia and Justice at lower l., supported portr. of Qn. Victoria at top ctr., Minerva standing by seated Prosperity at lower r., small crown on swords at bottom ctr.	1400.	—	—

TORONTO

1849 FIRST ISSUE

Dollar/Pound Sterling System.

#S1763-1765 also w/red ovpt: *KINGSTON*, various letters and numerical handstamps.

		VG	VF	UNC
S1763	**1 DOLLAR = 5 SHILLINGS** 1.2.1849. Like #S1760.	22.50	42.50	125.00
S1764	**2 DOLLARS = 10 SHILLINGS** 1.2.1849. Like #S1761.	22.50	42.50	125.00

		VG	VF	UNC
S1765	**5 DOLLARS = 25 SHILLINGS** 1.2.1849. Like #S1762.	22.50	42.50	125.00

1849 SECOND ISSUE

#S1766-S1769 black. Red word protector on face and back. . . .*at their Office in* engraved. Uniface.

		VG	VF	UNC
S1766	**1 DOLLAR** 1.2.1849. Like #S1760.	15.00	32.50	90.00

S1767 2 DOLLARS VG 15.00 VF 32.50 UNC 90.00
1.2.1849. Like #S1761.

S1768 3 DOLLARS VG 35.00 VF 80.00 UNC 160.00
1.2.1849. Standing Britannia and Justice at lower l., Neptune and Liberty in chariot at top ctr., blacksmith, seaman and farmer w/lg. ornate *3* at lower r.

S1769 5 DOLLARS VG 15.00 VF 32.50 UNC 90.00
1.2.1849. Like #S1762.

FARMERS J.S. BANKING CO., TORONTO, U.C.

1800S SPURIOUS ISSUE

S1770 10 DOLLARS = 10 PIASTRES
18xx. Black. Portr. J. Fox at l., seated woman holding lion shield at upper ctr., woman in grain field at r. Uniface. Printer: Casilear, Durand, Burton & Edmonds. Unsigned remainder.

	VG	VF	UNC
a. Printed date: 18xx.	—	—	125.00
b. Printed date: 1849.	—	—	150.00

FARMERS BANK OF RUSTICO, P.E.I.

1864 ISSUE

Pound Sterling/Piastre System.

#S1771-S1773 black on green unpt. Uniface. Printer: ABNC.

S1771 4 SHILLINGS = 1 PIASTRE VG 1750. VF — UNC —
2.11.1864. 2 scythes on sheaf of wheat at l., farmer plowing w/2 horses at upper ctr., 3 men shearing sheep at lower r.

S1772 8 SHILLINGS = 2 PIASTRES VG — VF Unc UNC 750.00
2.11.1864. Farm boy carrying cornstalks at lower l., farm family w/cattle and hen w/chicks at upper ctr., driving cattle below railroad bridge at lower r. Proof.

S1773 1 POUND = 5 PIASTRAS VG — VF Unc UNC 750.00
2.11.1864. Chickens at upper l., farmer watering livestock at top ctr., milkmaid by livestock at lower r. Proof.

1872 ISSUE

Dollar/Piastre System.

#S1774-S1776 like #S1771-S1773. Printers: ABNC, BABNC.

S1774 1 DOLLAR = 1 PIASTRE VG 1250. VF — UNC —
2.1.1872. Like #S1771.

S1775 2 DOLLARS = 2 PIASTRES VG 1400. VF — UNC —
2.1.1872. Like #S1772.

S1776 5 DOLLARS = 5 PIASTRES VG 1750. VF — UNC —
2.1.1872. Like #S1773.

FARMERS BANK OF ST. JOHNS, L.C.

1837 ISSUE

#S1777-S1779 black. Uniface.

S1777 1 DOLLAR VG 500.00 VF — UNC —
4.12.1837; 5.12.1837. Standing Britannia at l., early steam passenger train at top ctr., sheaf of grain at r., small farm implements at bottom ctr.

		VG	VF	UNC
S1778	**1 DOLLAR 25 CENTS** 5.12.1837. Seated Agriculture w/steamboat in background at upper l. ctr., standing Indian brave w/rifle at r.	975.00	—	—
S1778A	**1 DOLLAR 50 CENTS** 5.12.1837. Seated allegorical women at lower l., seated woman w/Indian brave w/rifle at ctr., farmer plowing w/horses at r.	975.00	—	—

		VG	VF	UNC
S1779	**2 DOLLARS** 4.12.1837. Seated Mercury by shoreline w/sailing ship in background at l., cherubs sculpting busts at top ctr., Phoenix at lower r., small dog lying by strongbox at bottom ctr.	500.00	—	—

1838 ISSUE

#S1779A-S1781 black. Uniface. Printer: Lowe.

		VG	VF	UNC
S1779A	**3 DOLLARS** 18xx. Standing Indian woman w/bow & arrow at l., man standing w/papers, bldg. in background at ctr., seated Indian w/plaque at r. Unsigned remainder.	—	300.00	—

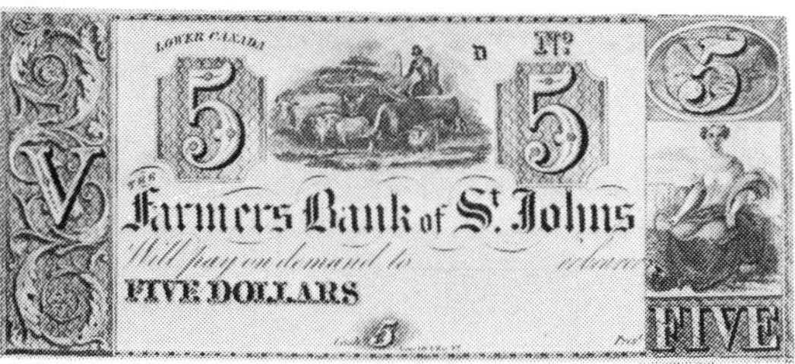

		VG	VF	UNC
S1780	**5 DOLLARS** 21.5.1838. Farmer w/livestock at top ctr., seated Agriculture w/sheaf and sickle at r.			
	a. Issued note.	500.00	—	—
	r. Unsigned remainder.	—	300.00	—
S1781	**10 DOLLARS** 18xx. Farmer plowing w/horses at top ctr., seated allegorical man at r. Unsigned remainder.	—	300.00	—

FEDERAL BANK OF CANADA, TORONTO

Chartered in Toronto, Ontario in 1874. Closed in late 1880's.

1874-82 ISSUE

#S1782-S1787 black on green unpt. H. S. Strathey at lower l., N. Alexandra at lower r. Back green. Printer: BABNC.

		GOOD	FINE	XF
S1782	**4 DOLLARS** 1.7.1874. Cherubs w/ornate 4 at ctr.	150.00	500.00	—

		GOOD	FINE	XF
S1783	**5 DOLLARS** 1.7.1874. Blacksmiths by anvil, ornate *5* w/factories in background at ctr.	110.00	325.00	—

		GOOD	FINE	XF
S1784	**10 DOLLARS** 1.7.1874; 1.1.1877. 2 allegorical women seated by ornate *X* w/factories in background.	150.00	500.00	—

		GOOD	XF	UNC
S1785	**50 DOLLARS** 1.1.1877. Steam passenger train at station at ctr. Face proof.	—	—	425.00

		VG	VF	UNC
S1786	**100 DOLLARS** 1.9.1882. Canadian arms at ctr. Face proof.	—	—	425.00

1884 ISSUE

#S1787 and S1788 black on green unpt. Portr. S. Nordheimer at lower l., H. S. Strathey at lower r. Back green. Printer: BABNC.

		VG	VF	UNC
S1787	**5 DOLLARS** 1.1.1884. Similar to #S1783. Face proof.	—	—	500.00
S1788	**10 DOLLARS** 1.1.1884. Similar to #S1784. Face proof.	—	—	500.00

BANK OF FREDERICTON, N.B.

Founded in Fredericton, New Brunswick in 1836. Merged with the Commercial Bank of New Brunswick in 1839.

1837-38 ISSUE

#S1789-S1793 black. Printer: New England Bank Note Co.

		VG	VF	UNC
S1789	**5 SHILLINGS** 8.5.1837. Seated girl w/sheaf at l., paddle wheel steamboat and sailboats at top ctr., seated Indian brave at r. Back blue.	1400.	—	—

		VG	VF	UNC
S1790	**5 SHILLINGS** 6.3.1838. Similar to #S1789 but w/hunter at r. Back blue.	1400.	—	—
S1791	**10 SHILLINGS** 18xx. Blacksmith at l., sailing ships at top l. ctr., lion and shield at r. Proof.	—	—	650.00
S1792	**1 POUND** 18xx. 2 farmers harvesting grain at l., farmer sowing seed w/horses in background at top ctr. Proof.	—	—	650.00
S1793	**5 POUNDS** 18xx. Seated Justice at l., farmer by horseman and livestock at top ctr. Proof.	—	—	650.00

FREE HOLDERS BANK OF THE MIDLAND DISTRICT

Established in Bath, Upper Canada in late 1830s. Operated for less than one month.

1800S ISSUE

#S1794 and S1795 black. Uniface. Printer: RWH & Co. Unsigned remainders.

S1794 1 DOLLAR = 5 SHILLINGS | VG 575.00 | VF — | UNC —
18xx. Supported royal arms at top ctr., woman w/sheaf at upper r., farmers w/livestock at lower r., small reclining Agriculture w/sheaf and sickle at bottom ctr.

S1795 5 DOLLARS = 25 SHILLINGS | VG 575.00 | VF — | UNC —
18xx. Beehive, cornucopia, produce, sheaf and spinning wheel at top ctr., small child riding deer at bottom ctr.

GODERICH BANK, U.C.

1834 ISSUE

#S1796 and S1797 black. Uniface. Printer: C. P. Harrison.

S1796 1 DOLLAR = 5 SHILLINGS | GOOD 300.00 | FINE — | XF —
12.9.1834.

S1797 2 DOLLARS = 10 SHILLINGS | GOOD 300.00 | FINE — | XF —
12.9.1834. Lion (sideways) at l., seated Mercury by cargo w/sailing ships in background at upper l.

GORE BANK OF HAMILTON, U.C.

1800S SPURIOUS ISSUE

#S1798-S1800 black. Uniface. Printer: Casilear, Durand, Burton & Edmonds. Unsigned remainders.

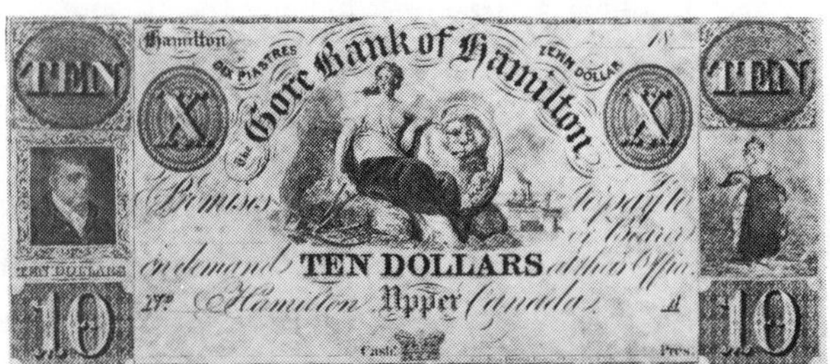

S1798 10 DOLLARS | GOOD — | FINE 42.50 | XF 125.00
18xx. Portr. J. Fox at l., seated woman w/lion shield at upper ctr., young woman w/sheaf at r.

S1799 20 DOLLARS | GOOD — | FINE 42.50 | XF 125.00
18xx. Allegorical woman w/shield and spear at l., portr. Kg. William IV at upper l. ctr., steers at upper r.

S1800 50 DOLLARS | GOOD — | FINE 42.50 | XF 125.00
18xx. Identical allegorical woman at l. and at r., supported portr. of Kg. William IV at top ctr.

HART'S BANK

Established in Three Rivers, Lower Canada in 1835. Closed in 1847.

1837 ISSUE

#S1801-S1804 black. Uniface. Printer: Bourne. Unsigned remainders.

		VG	VF	UNC
S1801	5 PENCE = 10 SOUS 1.10.1837.	15.00	55.00	150.00
S1802	10 PENCE = 20 SOUS 1.10.1837.	15.00	55.00	150.00
S1803	20 PENCE = 40 SOUS 1.10.1837.	15.00	55.00	150.00
S1804	2 SHILLINGS-6 PENCE = 60 SOUS 1.10.1837. Man smoking pipe at r.	15.00	55.00	150.00

1838 ISSUE

#S1805-S1807 black. 2 people in horse drawn sleigh at upper l. ctr. Back orange; 2 men portr. (sideways). Printer: Bourne.

S1805 1 DOLLAR | VG | VF | UNC
28.7.1838. Paddle wheel steamboat (sideways) at l., seated Indian maiden at r., small steamboat at bottom ctr.
a. Issued note. | 425.00 | — | —
rp. Uniface reprint. | — | 42.50 | 125.00

S1806 3 DOLLARS | VG | VF | UNC
20.8.1838. Seated Indian maiden at l., couple in horse drawn sleigh at top ctr., small ship, casks at bottom ctr.
a. Issued note. | 450.00 | — | —
rp. Uniface reprint. | — | 75.00 | 225.00

S1807 5 DOLLARS | VG — | VF 42.50 | UNC 125.00
18xx. Like #S1806. Uniface reprint.

HENRY'S BANK, L.C.

LA PRAIRIE

1837 ISSUE

Dollar/Pound/Ecu System.

#S1808-S1809 black. Uniface.

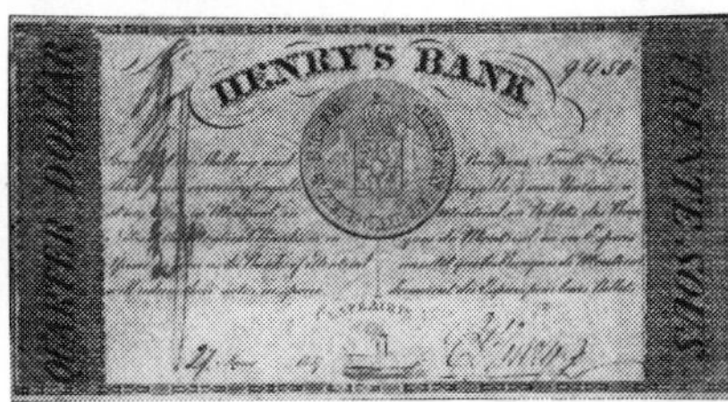

	S1808 1/4 DOLLAR = 1 SHILLING-3 PENCE = 30 SOUS	VG	VF	UNC
	27.6.1837. Reverse of Mexican 2 reales coin at upper ctr.			
a.	Issued note.	17.50	38.50	100.00
rp.	Reprint.	—	7.50	20.00

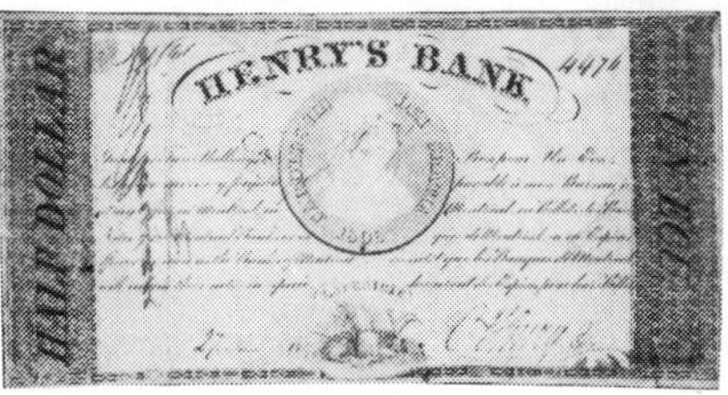

	S1809 1/2 DOLLAR = 2 SHILLINGS-6 PENCE = 1 ECU	VG	VF	UNC
	27.6.1837. Obverse of Spanish Colonial coin of Charles IV at upper ctr.			
a.	Issued note.	17.50	38.50	100.00
rp.	Reprint.	—	7.50	20.00

1837 ISSUE

Dollar/Piastre System.

#S1810 and S1813 black. Uniface. Printer: Burton, Gurley & Edmunds, N.Y.

S1810 1 DOLLAR	VG	VF	UNC
19.6.1837; 27.6.1837. Identical standing allegorical woman at l. and at r., seated w/anchor at upper ctr., small steamboat at bottom ctr.	25.00	60.00	200.00

S1811 2 DOLLARS	VG	VF	UNC
19.6.1837; 27.6.1837. Woman w/sheaf at l., seated woman w/sheaf by cattle at upper ctr., cow and sheep at r., small shield w/*2* at bottom ctr.	25.00	60.00	200.00

MONTREAL

1837 ISSUE

#S1812 and S1813 printer: Burton, Gurley & Edmunds, N.Y.

S1812 5 DOLLARS	GOOD	FINE	XF
27.6.1837. Village coastal view tipped sideways at l., seated allegorical male by shoreline w/sailing ship in background at upper ctr., farmer w/sheaf at r., small ship, casks at bottom ctr.	55.00	150.00	350.00

S1813 10 DOLLARS	GOOD	FINE	XF
27.6.1837. Allegorical woman w/eagle at upper ctr., small shield w/*X* at bottom ctr.	67.50	175.00	425.00

INTERNATIONAL BANK OF CANADA

Established in Toronto, Canada West in 1858. Failed in 1859.

1858 FIRST ISSUE

#S1814-S1825 uniface. Printer: Danforth, Wright & Co., New York and Philadelphia.

#S1814-S1817 black. 2 sign. Uniface.

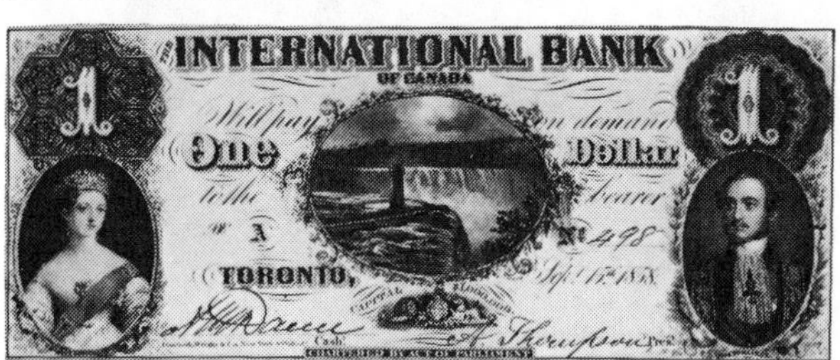

	S1814 1 DOLLAR	VG	VF	UNC
	15.9.1858. Portr. Qn. Victoria at lower l., Niagara and Horseshoe Falls at ctr., portr. Prince Consort at lower r.			
a.	Issued note.	60.00	125.00	400.00
r.	Remainder.	—	—	225.00

	S1815 1 DOLLAR	VG	VF	UNC
	15.9.1858. Portr. Qn. Victoria at lower l., Roebling Suspension Bridge at Niagara Falls ctr., portr. Prince Consort at lower r.			
a.	Issued note.	60.00	125.00	400.00
r.	Remainder.	—	—	225.00

	S1816 2 DOLLARS	VG	VF	UNC
	15.9.1858. Allegorical woman at upper l., supported royal arms at top ctr. r.			
a.	Issued note.	85.00	175.00	600.00
r.	Remainder.	—	—	275.00

	VG	VF	UNC
S1817 5 DOLLARS			
15.9.1858. Small supported royal arms at l., cattle watering along river at ctr.			
a. Issued note.	85.00	175.00	600.00
r. Remainder.	—	—	275.00

#S1818-S1821 black w/red protector. 2 sign. Uniface.

	VG	VF	UNC
S1818 1 DOLLAR			
15.9.1858. Like #S1814 but w/red *1 1* protector.			
a. Issued note.	70.00	150.00	500.00
r. Remainder.	—	—	275.00
S1819 1 DOLLAR			
15.9.1858. Like #S1815 but w/red *ONE* protector.			
a. Issued note.	70.00	150.00	500.00
r. Remainder.	—	—	275.00
S1820 2 DOLLARS			
15.9.1858. Like #S1816 but w/red *TWO* protector.			
a. Issued note.	70.00	150.00	500.00
r. Remainder.	—	—	275.00
S1821 5 DOLLARS			
15.9.1858. Like #S1817 but w/red *FIVE* protector.			
a. Issued note.	70.00	150.00	500.00
r. Remainder.	—	—	275.00

1858 SECOND ISSUE

#S1822-S1825 black. 1 sign. Uniface.

S1822 1 DOLLAR	VG	VF	UNC
15.9.1858. Like #S1814.			
a. Green protector. Blue serial #. Sign. J. H. Markell.	22.50	42.50	150.00
b. Red serial #. Sign. J. C. Fitch.	10.00	30.00	75.00
c. Brown protector. Blue serial #. Sign. J. H. Markell.	22.50	42.50	150.00
d. Red serial #. Sign. J. H. Markell.	22.50	42.50	150.00
e. Sign. J. C. Fitch.	10.00	22.50	75.00
f. Red protector. Sm. blue serial #. Sign. J. H. Markell.	17.50	35.00	125.00
g. Sm. blue serial #. Sign. J. C. Fitch.	22.50	42.50	150.00
h. Lg. blue serial #. Sign. J. C. Fitch.	10.00	22.50	75.00
i. Ochre protector. Red serial #. Sign. J. H. Markell.	25.00	65.00	225.00
j. Sign. J. C. Fitch.	25.00	50.00	175.00
k. Sm. blue serial #. Sign. J. C. Fitch.	22.50	42.50	150.00
l. Lg. blue serial #. Sign. J. C. Fitch.	25.00	50.00	175.00
m. Blue protector. Red serial #. Sign. J. H. Markell.	25.00	50.00	175.00
n. Sign. J. C. Fitch.	15.00	35.00	110.00

S1823 1 DOLLAR	VG	VF	UNC
15.9.1858. Like #S1815.			
a. Green protector. Blue serial 1. Sign. J. H. Markell.	28.00	52.50	165.00
b. Red serial #. Sign. J. C. Fitch.	15.00	30.00	100.00
c. Brown protector. Blue serial #. Sign. J. H. Markell.	22.50	42.50	150.00
d. Red serial #. Sign. J. H. Markell.	25.00	50.00	165.00
e. Sign. J. C. Fitch.	10.00	22.50	70.00
f. Red protector. Sm. blue serial #. Sign. J. H. Markell.	22.50	42.50	150.00
g. Sm. blue serial #. Sign. J. C. Fitch.	25.00	52.50	165.00
h. Lg. blue serial #. Sign. J. C. Fitch.	10.00	22.50	75.00
i. Ochre protector. Red serial #. Sign. J. H. Markell.	25.00	65.00	225.00
j. Sign. J. C. Fitch.	25.00	50.00	165.00
k. Sm. blue serial #. Sign. J. C. Fitch.	17.50	37.50	110.00
l. Lg. blue serial #. Sign. J. C. Fitch.	25.00	50.00	165.00
m. Blue protector. Red serial #. Sign. J. H. Markell.	25.00	50.00	165.00
n. Sign. J. C. Fitch.	15.00	35.00	110.00

S1824 2 DOLLARS	VG	VF	UNC
15.9.1858. Like #S1816.			
a. Green protector. Blue serial #. Sign. J. H. Markell.	27.50	52.50	175.00
b. Red serial #. Sign. J. C. Fitch.	15.00	32.50	100.00
c. Brown protector. Blue serial #. Sign. J. H. Markell.	22.50	42.50	150.00
d. Red serial #. Sign. J. H. Markell.	25.00	50.00	175.00
e. Sign. J. C. Fitch.	10.00	22.50	75.00
f. Red protector. Sm. blue serial #. Sign. J. H. Markell.	25.00	52.50	175.00
g. Sm. blue serial #. Sign. J. C. Fitch.	22.50	42.50	150.00
h. Lg. blue serial #. Sign. J. C. Fitch.	10.00	22.50	75.00
i. Ochre protector. Red serial #. Sign. J. H. Markell.	25.00	75.00	225.00
j. Sign. J. C. Fitch.	25.00	50.00	175.00
k. Sm. blue serial #. Sign. J. C. Fitch.	17.50	37.50	125.00
l. Lg. blue serial #. Sign. J. C. Fitch.	25.00	50.00	175.00
m. Blue protector. Red serial #. Sign. J. H. Markell.	25.00	50.00	175.00
n. Sign. J. C. Fitch.	17.50	35.00	125.00

S1825 5 DOLLARS	VG	VF	UNC
15.9.1858. Like #S1817.			
a. Green protector. Blue serial #. Sign. J. H. Markell.	27.50	52.50	175.00
b. Red serial #. Sign. J. C. Fitch.	10.00	27.50	75.00
c. Brown protector. Blue serial #. Sign. J. H. Markell	17.50	35.00	125.00
d. Red serial #. Sign. J. H. Markell.	25.00	50.00	175.00
e. Sign. J. C. Fitch.	10.00	22.50	75.00
f. Red protector. Sm. blue serial #. Sign. J. H. Markell.	17.50	35.00	125.00
g. Sm. blue serial #. Sign. J. C. Fitch.	10.00	22.50	75.00
h. Lg. blue serial #. Sign. J. C. Fitch.	10.00	35.00	75.00
i. Ochre protector. Red serial #. Sign. J. H. Markell.	22.50	60.00	200.00
j. Sign. J. C. Fitch.	25.00	50.00	175.00
k. Sm. blue serial #. Sign. J. C. Fitch.	15.00	32.50	90.00
l. Lg. blue serial #. Sign. J. C. Fitch.	25.00	50.00	175.00
m. Blue protector. Red serial #. Sign. J. H. Markell.	25.00	50.00	175.00
n. Sign. J. C. Fitch.	15.00	35.00	110.00

1859 ISSUE

#S1826-S1828 black w/green word or number protector on back. Back green. Printer: ABNC.

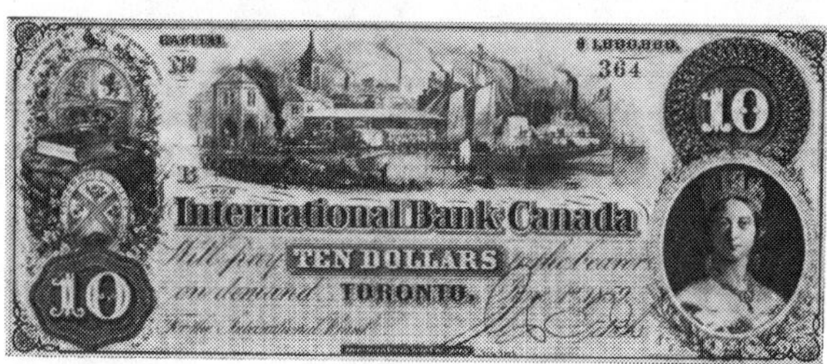

S1826 10 DOLLARS	VG	VF	UNC
1.6.1859. Crests, crown on book at l., town along river, boat at top ctr., portr. Qn. Victoria at lower r.	60.00	150.00	650.00

S1827 20 DOLLARS	VG	VF	UNC
1.6.1859. Beavers at lower l., paddle wheel steamboat at top ctr., youthful Prince of Wales at lower r.	400.00	800.00	—

S1828 50 DOLLARS	VG	VF	UNC
1.6.1859. Navigation at lower l., buffalo hunting at top ctr., seated Britannia w/arms of Canada at lower r.	60.00	150.00	500.00

KINGSTON BANK

Supposedly issued from Kingston, Lower Canada.

1837 SPURIOUS ISSUE

		VG	VF	UNC
S1829	**5 DOLLARS** 1837; 12.10.1841; 3.8.1843. Black. Seated allegorical woman at l., cattle, plow and early steam passenger train at top ctr. r., cornucopia, caduceus and chest w/ships in background at bottom ctr. Uniface.			
	a. Fully signed. 1837.	100.00	235.00	—
	r. Remainder. 1837; 1841; 1843.	90.00	200.00	—

NOTE: #S1829 exists w/additional ovpt: *New York Safety Fund* to infer being an issue of the Kingston Bank in New York.

BANK OF LIVERPOOL

Established in Liverpool, Nova Scotia in 1871. Purchased by the Bank of Nova Scotia in 1879.

1871 ISSUE

#S1830-S1833 black on green unpt. 3 sign. varieties. Back green. Printer: BABNC.

		GOOD	FINE	XF
S1830	**4 DOLLARS** 1.11.1871. Young sailor climbing ship's rigging at lower l., shipbuilders at upper ctr., pilot at ship's wheel at lower r.	350.00	1125.	—

		GOOD	FINE	XF
S1831	**5 DOLLARS** 1.11.1871. Lumberjack felling tree at l., splitting logs at r.	300.00	1050.	—

		GOOD	FINE	XF
S1832	**10 DOLLARS** 1.11.1871. Agriculture at l., fishing ships at top ctr., sailor at lower r.	430.00	1475.	—

		GOOD	FINE	XF
S1833	**20 DOLLARS** 1.11.1871. Bull's head at lower l., shipwrecked sailors at top ctr., 3 horses' heads at lower r.	600.00	1750.	—

BANK OF LONDON IN CANADA

Established in London, Ontario in 1884. Taken over by the Bank of Toronto in 1887-88.

1883 ISSUE

#S1834-S1838 black on green unpt. Back green. Printer: BABNC.

		GOOD	FINE	XF
S1834	**5 DOLLARS** 1.12.1883. Farm tools and produce at l., H. Taylor at ctr., dog on strongbox at r.			
	a. Issued note.	725.00	2800.	—
	r. Remainder unsigned at r. w/2 cut *PAID* cancellations.	—	—	2450.

		GOOD	FINE	XF
S1835	**10 DOLLARS** 1.12.1883. H. Taylor at lower l., allegorical woman w/flowers at lower r.			
	a. Issued note.	1100.	3500.	—
	r. Remainder unsigned at r. w/2 cut *PAID* cancellations.	—	—	2450.

		GOOD	FINE	XF
S1836	**20 DOLLARS** 1.12.1883. Allegorical woman w/cornstalks at l., H. Taylor at ctr. Remainder unsigned at r. w/2 cut *PAID* cancellations.	—	—	2100.

		GOOD	FINE	XF
S1837	**50 DOLLARS** 1.12.1883. Horses and pigeons at l., H. Taylor at ctr. r., seated allegorical woman at lower r. Remainder unsigned at r. w/2 cut *PAID* cancellations.	—	—	2100.

S1838 100 Dollars | Good | Fine | XF
1.12.1883. Cows at l., H. Taylor at ctr., woman operating telegraph at r. Remainder unsigned at r. w/2 cut *PAID* cancellations. | — | — | 2100.

Lower Canada Bank

Supposedly issued at Montreal, Lower Canada.

1837 Spurious Issue

#S1839-S1841 black. Sea creatures at upper and lower l., small clasped hands at bottom ctr. Uniface. Printer: RWH & Co.

S1839 1 Dollar	Good	Fine	XF
18xx. Hercules wrestling lion at top ctr., woman w/sheaves at upper r.			
a. Issued note.	175.00	350.00	—
p. Proof.	—	Unc	275.00

S1840 2 Dollars	Good	Fine	XF
4.11.1837. Allegorical man slaying dragon at top ctr., allegorical man and woman w/coins at r.	150.00	500.00	—

S1841 3 Dollars	Good	Fine	XF
18xx. Seated Homer at top ctr., cherub w/basket of fruit at r. Proof.	—	Unc	280.00

Bank of Lower Canada

Issued at Quebec, Lower Canada.

1839-51 Issue

#S1842-S1846 black. Uniface. Standing Britannia at r. Various dates 1839-51 and sign. of questionable authenticity. Printer: Harris & Sealey, N. York.

#S1842-S1844 small Indian in canoe at bottom ctr.

S1842 1 Dollar	VG	VF	Unc
1839-51. Beehive and farm tools at l., supported royal arms at top ctr. *D. Birdsey* omitted.			
b. W/o *D. Birdsey*.	140.00	275.00	425.00
p. *W/A. Messrs. D. Birdsey & Cie* engraved at lower l. Proof.	—	—	280.00

S1843 2 Dollars	VG	VF	Unc
1839-51. Supported royal arms at upper ctr.	140.00	300.00	—

S1844 3 Dollars	VG	VF	Unc
1839-51. Small supported arms at l., seated allegorical man giving key to kneeling man, Minerva at top ctr.	175.00	—	—

#S1845 and S1846 supported royal arms at bottom ctr.

S1845 5 Dollars	VG	VF	Unc
1839-51. Indian brave at upper l., 2 trains at dockside at upper ctr. r.	175.00	300.00	560.00

S1846 10 Dollars	VG	VF	Unc
1839-51. Seated Mercury w/sailing ship in background at top ctr.	210.00	365.00	665.00

Macdonald & Co.

Established in Victoria, British Columbia in 1859. Failed in 1864.

1863 Issue

#S1847-S1849 black. Indian maiden facing l. at lower l., supported royal arms at top ctr., Indian brave facing w/arm raised at lower r. Uniface. Printer: Britton & Co., S.F.

S1847 1 Dollar	VG	VF	Unc
6.9.1863.	85.00	200.00	—

S1848 5 DOLLARS VG 140.00 VF 250.00 UNC —
6.9.1863.

S1849 10 DOLLARS VG 165.00 VF 280.00 UNC —
6.9.1863.

#S1850-S1852 similar to #S1847-S1849 but Indian maiden facing r. at lower l. and Indian brave facing l. w/arm down at lower r.

S1850 1 DOLLAR 265.00 500.00 —
6.9.1863. Remainder.

S1851 5 DOLLARS VG 265.00 VF 500.00 UNC —
6.9.1863.

S1852 10 DOLLARS Reported Not Confirmed
6.9.1863.

MARITIME BANK OF THE DOMINION OF CANADA

Established in St. John, New Brunswick in 1872. Failed in 1887.

1873; 1875 ISSUE

#S1853-S1856 black on green unpt. Back green; anchor, barrels and bale. 2 sign. varieties. Printer: BABNC.

S1853 4 DOLLARS VG 2800. VF — UNC —
2.1.1873. J. Domville at lower l., sailing ship at ctr., J. H. R. Rowley at lower r.

S1854 5 DOLLARS VG — VF — UNC 560.00
2.1.1873. J. Domville at lower l., steam sailing ship at ctr., J. H. R. Rowley at lower r. Face proof.

S1855 10 DOLLARS VG — VF — UNC 560.00
2.1.1873. Sailing ship at lower l., J. Robertson at ctr., young sailor climbing ship's rigging at lower r. Face proof.

S1856 50 DOLLARS — — 560.00
1.6.1875. Major Gen. J. W. Domville at l., supported Great Seal of Canada at ctr., J. Domville at r. Face proof.

1881; 1882 ISSUE

#S1857-S1859 black on green unpt. Back green; anchor, barrels and bale.

S1857 5 DOLLARS VG VF UNC
3.10.1881. Sailor at lower l., sailing ship at dockside at ctr., seated woman w/telescope by lg. ornate *5* at lower r.

	VG	VF	UNC
a. W/o ovpt.	1400.	—	—
b. Ovpt: Lg. red *V*.	1750.	—	—

S1858 10 DOLLARS VG 2100. VF — UNC —
3.10.1881. Sailing ship at lower l., portr. Qn. Victoria at ctr., young sailor climbing ship's rigging at lower r.

S1859 20 DOLLARS — — 560.00
1.1.1882. Dock scene at l., steamship at ctr., allegorical woman w/flag and bale at r. Face proof.

MECHANICS BANK, MONTREAL

Established in Montreal, Canada East in 1865. Failed in 1879.

1837 SPURIOUS ISSUE

#S1860-S1862 black. Uniface. Printer: RWH & Co.

S1860 3 DOLLARS GOOD 33.00 FINE 112.00 XF 280.00
1.6.1837. Dock scene, steamboat at l., blacksmith at anvil w/2 women at top ctr., woman w/wheat at r.

S1861 5 DOLLARS GOOD 25.00 FINE 85.00 XF 210.00
1.5.1837; 1.6.1837. Seated youth w/tools at l., seated woman leaning on lg. gear at top ctr., blacksmith at anvil at r.

S1862 10 DOLLARS
1.5.1837; 1.6.1837. Seated woman w/rake at l., blacksmith at anvil w/2 women at top ctr., cherub kneeling inscribing stone at r.

	GOOD	FINE	XF
S1862	25.00	85.00	210.00

MECHANICS BANK, MONTREAL, C.E.

Established in Montreal, Canada East in 1865. Failed in 1879.

1872 ISSUE

#S1863-S1865 black on green unpt. Back blue-green. Sign. varieties. Printer: BABNC.

S1863 4 DOLLARS
1.6.1872. Blacksmith w/man and 2 horses at l., carpenters at bottom ctr., machinist at lower r.

	VG	VF	UNC
a. Purple hand stamp: circled *A*.	100.00	200.00	—
b. Blue ovpt: *A-A*.	100.00	200.00	—

	VG	VF	UNC
c. Blue ovpt: *B-B*.	100.00	200.00	—
d. Blue ovpt: *L- L*.	100.00	200.00	—
e. Vertical blue ovpt: *ALEXANDRIA* twice.	100.00	200.00	—
f. Vertical blue ovpt: *BEAUHARNOIS* twice.	100.00	200.00	—

S1864 5 DOLLARS
1.6.1872. Farmer watering livestock at upper l., stonecutters at lower r.

	VG	VF	UNC
a. Purple hand stamp: circled *A-A*.	63.00	140.00	—
b. Blue ovpt: *A-A*.	63.00	140.00	—
c. Vertical blue ovpt: *ALEXANDRIA* twice.	63.00	140.00	—
d. Vertical blue ovpt: *BEAUHARNOIS* twice.	63.00	140.00	—

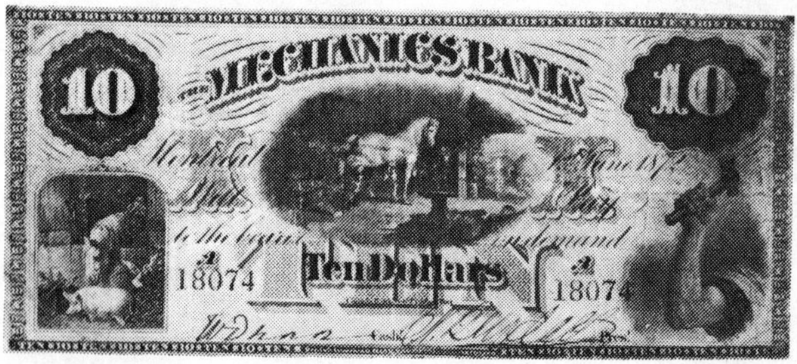

S1865 10 DOLLARS
1.6.1872. Livestock at lower l., blacksmith shoeing horse at ctr., arm w/hammer at lower r.

	VG	VF	UNC
S1865	300.00	750.00	—

MECHANICS BANK OF ST. JOHN'S, L.C.

1837 FIRST SPURIOUS ISSUE

#S1866-S1868 black. Uniface. Printer: RWH & Co.

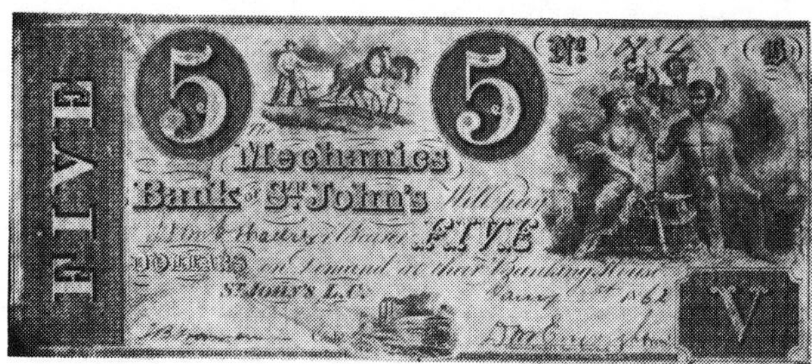

S1866 5 DOLLARS
20.5.1837. Man plowing w/horses at upper l. ctr., standing Mercury behind seated allegorical man and woman at upper r.

	GOOD	FINE	XF
S1866	68.00	227.50	560.00

S1867 10 DOLLARS
20.5.1837; 21.5.1837. Seated woman leaning on gear at l., steam passenger trains along river at top l. ctr., sailing ships at upper r.

S1868 20 DOLLARS
20.5.1837. Blacksmith at l., paddle wheel steamship at top ctr., allegorical woman at r.

	GOOD	FINE	XF
S1867	110.00	280.00	700.00
S1868	110.00	280.00	700.00

1837 SECOND SPURIOUS ISSUE

#S1869-S1871 black. *A. Messrs. H. N. Warren & Cie a St. John's* engraved at lower l. Hand sign. H. N. Warren & Cie vertically. Uniface. Printer: RWH & Co.

S1869 1 DOLLAR
18xx. Seated woman leaning against gear at l., steam passenger trains along river at top ctr., seated young man w/tools at r.

	GOOD	FINE	XF
a. Issued note.	—	—	—
r. Unsigned remainder.	35.00	122.50	—

S1870 2 DOLLARS
1.7.1837; 29.11.1837. Woman w/wheat sheaf at l., blacksmith at anvil w/2 women at top ctr., farmer harvesting wheat w/scythe at r.

	GOOD	FINE	XF
S1870	35.00	122.50	—

		Good	Fine	XF
S1871	**3 Dollars** 18xx. Paddle wheel steamship at top ctr., blacksmith at anvil at r. Unsigned remainder.	50.00	175.00	—

NOTE: #S1869-1871 are encountered w/various spurious dates and sign.

1837 Third Spurious Issue

#S1872-S1874 like #S1869-1871. Black. *A Messrs. T. H. Perry & Cie a St. John's* engraved at lower l. hand sign. T. H. Perry & Cia vertically. Uniface. Printer: RWH & Co.

		Good	Fine	XF
S1872	**1 Dollar** 29.11.1837. Like #S1869.	35.00	122.50	—
S1873	**2 Dollars** 18xx. Similar to #S1870. Unsigned remainder.	35.00	122.50	—

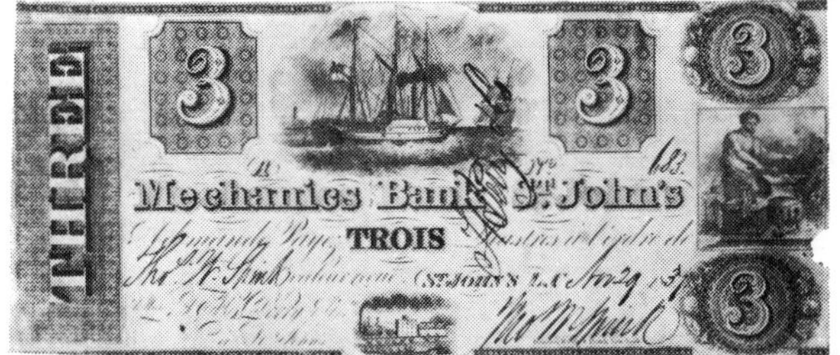

		Good	Fine	XF
S1874	**3 Dollars** 29.11.1837. Like #S1870.	50.00	175.00	—

Mercantile Banking Corporation

Payable at Halifax, Nova Scotia.

1878 Issue

		Good	Fine	XF
S1875	**10 Dollars** 1.1.1878. Black. Sailing ship at ctr. Uniface. Printer: Chas. Skipper & East. Face proof.	—	Unc	840.00

Merchants Bank, C.E.

1840s ND Issue

#S1875A-S1875C black. Uniface. Printer: RW & H.

		Good	Fine	XF
S1875A	**5 Dollars** 18xx. Commerce, anchor, ship at upper ctr., child w/deer at r.	100.00	350.00	—

Merchants Bank, Montreal, L.C.

1840s ND Issue

		Good	Fine	XF
S1875B	**10 Dollars** 18xx. Commerce, ship at upper ctr., woman in waves at r.	Reported Not Confirmed		
S1875C	**20 Dollars** 18xx. Commerce, ship at upper ctr., dock scene at r.	Reported Not Confirmed		

Merchants Bank, C.E.

1864 Issue

#S1875D-S1875I black on green unpt. Printer: ABNC.

		Good	Fine	XF
S1875D	**1 Dollar** 1.6.1864. Sailors dockside at lower l., train and wagons at wharf at ctr., portr. H. Allan at r.			
	a. Issued note.	400.00	800.00	—
	p. Proof.	—	—	—
S1875E	**2 Dollars** 1.6.1864. Portr. Prince of Wales at l., steamships and sailing ships at ctr., portr. H. Allan at r.			
	a. Issues note.	400.00	800.00	—
	p. Proof.	—	—	—

#S1875F-S1875I portr. H. Allan at lower l.

		Good	Fine	XF
S1875F	**5 Dollars** 1.6.1864. Sailor w/anchor at upper ctr., Prince of Wales as a small boy at lower r.			
	a. Issued note.	500.00	900.00	—
	p. Proof.	—	—	—
S1875G	**10 Dollars** 1.6.1864. Train, men and cattle at ctr., sailor w/telescope at lower r.			
	a. Issued note.	700.00	1200.	—
	p. Proof.	—	—	—
S1875H	**50 Dollars** 1.6.1864. Paddle wheel steamer at ctr. r. Proof.	—	Unc	750.00
S1875I	**100 Dollars** 1.6.1864. Paddle wheel steamer at ctr., dog at lower r. Proof.	—	Unc	750.00

Merchants Bank, Toronto, U.C.

1836; 1837 Spurious Issue

#S1876-S1879 black. Uniface. Printer: Terry, Pelton & Co.

		Good	Fine	XF
S1876	**1 Dollar** 1836-37. Allegorical woman at upper l., portr. of cherub at upper l. ctr., 3 allegorical women at upper r. ctr., portr. of young woman at lower r., small sailing ships at bottom ctr.			
	a. Issued note. 5.12.1836; 1.6.1837; 14.6.1837.	60.00	200.00	—
	r. Unsigned remainder. 18xx.	—	Unc	500.00

		Good	Fine	XF
S1877	**2 Dollars** 1.6.1837; 4.7.1837. Sailing ship and tugboat at l., 2 allegorical women at top ctr., portr. of young woman at lower r., small eagle at bottom ctr.			
	a. Issued note.	60.00	200.00	—
	r. Unsigned remainder. 18xx.	—	Unc	500.00

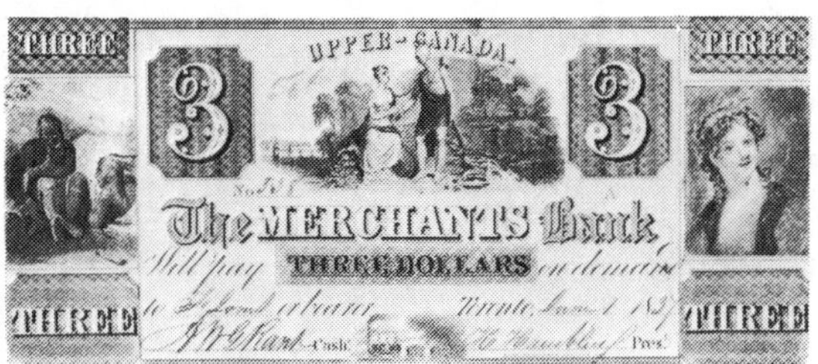

		Good	Fine	XF
S1878	**3 Dollars** 1.6.1837. 2 Indians reclining at l., seated woman by Indian brave at upper ctr., portr. of young woman at r., small early steam passenger train at bottom ctr.			
	a. Issued note.	75.00	250.00	—
	r. Unsigned remainder. 18xx.	—	Unc	500.00

		Good	Fine	XF
S1879	**5 Dollars** 1.6.1837; 4.7.1837. Seated woman by Indian brave at l., dock scene at top ctr., small crest between men at bottom ctr.	240.00	800.00	—

Merchants Exchange Bank, Goderich, C.W.

1853 Spurious Issue

#S1880 printer: Wellstood, Hanks, Hay and Whiting.

		Good	Fine	XF
S1880	**1 Dollar** 1.1.1853. Black. Eagle and shield at l., Agriculture and Justice w/eagle and shield at upper ctr., sailing ship at lower r. Uniface.	350.00	1200.	—

Metropolitan Bank

Established in Montreal, Quebec in 1871. Liquidated in 1876.

1872 Issue

#S1881-S1885 black on green unpt. Portr. M. Cuvellier at lower l., portr. H. Starnes at lower r. Back green. Printer: BABNC.

		VG	VF	Unc
S1881	**4 Dollars** 1.2.1872. Supported shield at upper ctr.	1750.	—	—

		VG	VF	Unc
S1882	**5 Dollars** 1.2.1872. 2 blacksmiths w/lg. ornate *5* at ctr. Red ovpt: *OB.*	1750.	—	—

		VG	VF	Unc
S1883	**10 Dollars** 1.5.1872. 2 allegorical women seated w/lg. ornate *X* at top ctr. r.	1750.	—	—
S1884	**50 Dollars** 1.5.1872. Face proof.	—	—	490.00
S1885	**100 Dollars** 1.5.1872. Face proof.	—	—	490.00

Montreal Bank, C.W.

1848 Spurious Issue

		VG	VF	Unc
S1886	**5 Dollars** 10.10.1848; 1.4.1853. Black. Farmer w/livestock at l. paddle wheel steamboat at upper r. Uniface.	250.00	525.00	—

Newcastle Banking Company

Established in Amherst, Upper Canada in 1836.

1836 Issue

#S1886A-S1888 black. Uniface.

		Good	Fine	XF
S1886A	**1 Dollar = 5 Shillings** 20.1.1836. Sheaves of wheat, plow and cattle at upper ctr.	100.00	335.00	805.00

		Good	Fine	XF
S1887	**2 Dollars = 10 Shillings** 20.1.1836; 15.2.1836. Sheaves of wheat and farm tools at upper ctr.	100.00	335.00	805.00

		Good	Fine	XF
S1888	**4 Dollars = 20 Shillings** 20.1.1836; 15.2.1836. Seated Agriculture w/farm tools and produce at upper ctr.	125.00	400.00	975.00

New Castle District Loan Company, Peterborough, U.C.

1836 Issue

#S1889-S1892 black. Uniface. Printer: RWH & Co.

		Good	Fine	XF
S1889	**1 Dollar = 5 Shillings** 18xx. Naval commander at upper l., seated Abundance w/sheaf and cattle in background at ctr., standing Navigation at r., small beaver at bottom ctr. Unsigned remainder.	68.00	227.50	—

	S1890 2 DOLLARS = 10 SHILLINGS	GOOD	FINE	XF
	27.8.1836; 8.10.1836. Portr. Kg. William IV at upper l., man w/cradle in grain below, reclining woman at top ctr., small arm w/hammer at bottom ctr.			
a.	Issued note.	68.00	227.50	—
r.	Unsigned remainder. 18xx.	85.00	275.00	600.00

S1891 4 DOLLARS = 20 SHILLINGS = 1 POUND	GOOD	FINE	XF
15.2.1836-27.8.1836. 2 men w/livestock at l., supported portr. Kg. William IV at upper ctr., blacksmith at r., small ship, cask at bottom ctr.	35.00	125.00	300.00

S1892 10 DOLLARS = 50 SHILLINGS	GOOD	FINE	XF
6.8.1836; 27.8.1836. 2 men w/livestock at l., St. George slaying dragon at upper ctr., Indian brave w/drawn bow at lower r., small paddle wheel steamboat at bottom ctr.	35.00	120.00	300.00

NIAGARA SUSPENSION BRIDGE BANK, QUEENSTON, U.C.

Established in Queenston, Upper Canada in 1836. Failed in 1841.

1836 ISSUE

#S1893-S1908 mythical Niagara suspension bridge at top l. ctr. or ctr. r. Uniface. Printer: RWH & Co.

S1893 1 DOLLAR = 5 SHILLINGS	GOOD	FINE	XF
18xx. St. George slaying dragon at upper l., portr. Kg. William. IV at r.	30.00	105.00	—

#S1894-S1895A black. Uniface. W/handwritten text: *PAYABLE AT THE BANK* along bridge vignette.

	GOOD	FINE	XF
S1894 3 DOLLARS = 15 SHILLINGS 20.12.1836; 1839. Standing Navigation at l., Indian brave paddling canoe at upper r., dog's head at bottom ctr.	45.00	175.00	—
S1895 5 DOLLARS = 25 SHILLINGS 18xx. Standing Indian brave w/drawn bow at upper r., paddle wheel steamboat at bottom ctr.	30.00	105.00	—

1837-39 ISSUE

#S1896-S1898 black. Like #S1893-S1895 but w/engraved text: *PAYABLE AT THE BANK* along upper border.

	GOOD	FINE	XF
S1896 1 DOLLAR = 5 SHILLINGS 3.4.1837. Like #S1893.	20.00	70.00	—
S1897 3 DOLLARS = 15 SHILLINGS 18xx. Like #S1894.	20.00	85.00	—
S1898 5 DOLLARS = 25 SHILLINGS 20.7.1839. Like #S1895.	20.00	70.00	—

1840 ISSUE

#S1899-S1902 black. Similar to #S1896-S1898. Back orange.

S1899 1 DOLLAR = 5 SHILLINGS	VG	VF	UNC
13.10.1840. Like #S1896.	35.00	122.50	—

S1900 3 DOLLARS = 15 SHILLINGS	VG	VF	UNC
13.10.1840. Like #S1897.	42.00	140.00	—

S1901 5 DOLLARS = 25 SHILLINGS	VG	VF	UNC
13.10.1840. W/small *Queenston* to l. of paddle wheel steamboat at bottom ctr., *U.C.* at r.	35.00	122.50	—

1841 ISSUES

#S1902-S1908 black. Uniface.

S1902 1 DOLLAR = 5 SHILLINGS	VG	VF	UNC
1.7.1841. Like #S1896.	35.00	122.50	—

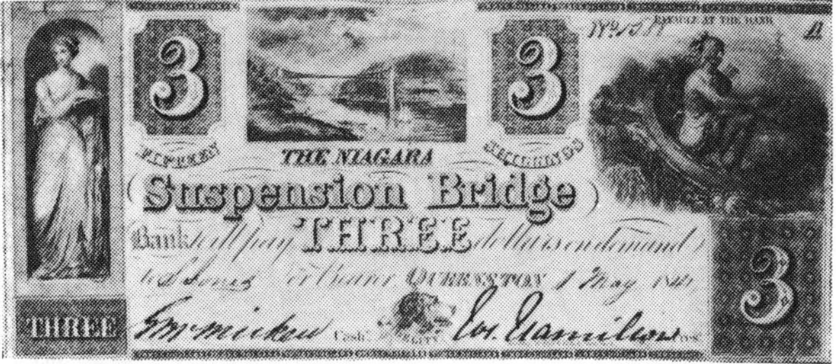

S1903 3 DOLLARS = 15 SHILLINGS	VG	VF	UNC
1.3.1841; 1.5.1841; 1.7.1841. Like #S1894.	45.50	157.50	—

		VG	VF	UNC
S1904	**5 DOLLARS = 25 SHILLINGS**			
	1841. Like #S1895.			
	a. *QUEENSTON* above ship at bottom; *U.* at l., *C* at r.	87.50	227.50	—
	b. 1.3.1841; 1.5.1841; 1.7.1841. *Queenston* at l. of ship at bottom; *U.C.* at r.	35.00	122.50	—
	c. *QUEENSTON* above ship at bottom; *UPPER CANADA.*	192.50	385.00	—
	r. As a. Remainder. 18xx.	56.00	140.00	—

#S1905-S1908 w/o text: *PAYABLE AT THE BANK.*

		VG	VF	UNC
S1905	**10 DOLLARS = 50 SHILLINGS**			
	4.1.1841. Mythical Niagara Suspension Bridge at top l. ctr., St. George slaying dragon at upper r., *U.C.* at bottom ctr.			
	a. Issued note.	122.50	332.50	—
	r. Remainder.	63.00	157.50	—
S1906	**10 DOLLARS = 50 SHILLINGS**			
	4.1.1841. Like #S1905 but w/*UPPER CANADA* at bottom ctr.			
	a. Issued note.	122.50	332.50	—
	r. Remainder.	63.00	157.50	—

		VG	VF	UNC
S1907	**20 DOLLARS = 5 POUNDS**			
	4.1.1841. Mythical Niagara Suspension Bridge at lower l., goddess rising from water at top l. ctr., Greek god reclining by fountain w/bathers at upper r., *U.C.* at bottom ctr.			
	a. Issued note.	140.00	420.00	—
	r. Remainder.	122.50	280.00	—
S1908	**20 DOLLARS = 5 POUNDS**			
	4.1.1841. Like #S1906 but w/*UPPER CANADA* at bottom ctr.			
	a. Issued note.	140.00	420.00	—
	r. Remainder.	122.50	280.00	—

BANK OF OTTAWA, (BANQUE DE OTTAWA), MONTREAL,L.C.

1837 FIRST SPURIOUS ISSUE

#S1909-S1914 Printer: Burton, Gurley, Edmonds, New York.

		GOOD	FINE	XF
S1909	**5 DOLLARS** 15.4.1837; 15.5.1837. Black. Royal crest w/lion and unicorn at top ctr., portr. Kg. William IV at r., small horse's head at bottom ctr. Back blue.	157.50	525.00	—

1837 SECOND SPURIOUS ISSUE

#S1910-S1911 black. Engraved text: *Accepted for MESSRS. JOSEPH C. FRINK & CO.* at bottom l. ctr. Back blue.

		GOOD	FINE	XF
S1910	**1 DOLLAR** 10.8.1837; 11.10.1837. Standing woman pouring wine at upper l., 3 allegorical women seated at top, helmeted allegorical woman w/eagle at upper r., small crown at bottom ctr.	150.00	500.00	—

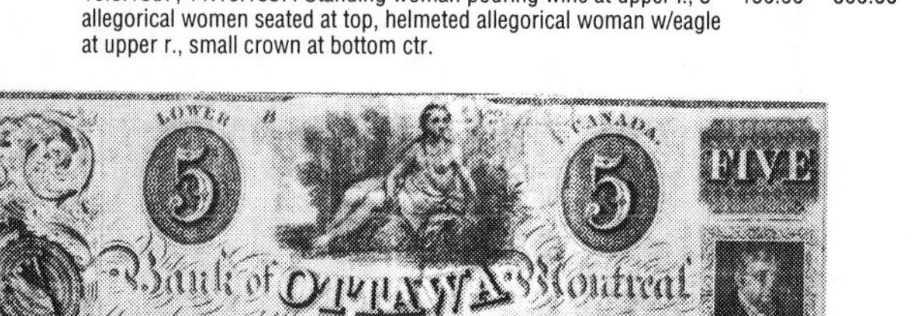

		GOOD	FINE	XF
S1911	**5 DOLLARS = 1 POUND-5 SHILLINGS** 18xx. Indian maiden reclining at top ctr., portr. Kg. William IV at r. Remainder.	130.00	400.00	—

1837 THIRD SPURIOUS ISSUE

		GOOD	FINE	XF
S1911A	**1 DOLLAR** 18.5.1837 like #S1910 but *Accepted for D. F. Merril & Co.* at lower r.	—	—	—

1837 FOURTH SPURIOUS ISSUE

#S1912-S1914 black. W/engraved *Accepted for* ___ at bottom l. or r. *SECURED BY REAL ESTATE* hand stamp. Uniface.

		GOOD	FINE	XF
S1912	**1 DOLLAR** 1.11.1837. Like #S1910 and S1911A.	135.00	420.00	—

		GOOD	FINE	XF
S1913	**3 DOLLARS** 4.1.1838. Standing allegorical woman w/foot on globe at l., mill at top ctr., bust of young woman at r., small horse head at bottom ctr.	190.00	630.00	—

		Good	Fine	XF
S1914	**10 Dollars** 1.4.1837. 3 cherubs w/woman kneeling at stone marker w/*TEN* at upper l., young woman w/spear at r.	87.50	700.00	—

Phenix Bank, Phillipsburg, L.C.

1837 Spurious Issue

Dollar System.

#S1915-S1918 small black. Paddle wheel steamboat (sideways) at l., Phoenix at upper r., small dog lying by strongbox at bottom ctr. w/adjoining text: *THE STATE OF VERMONT* at ctr. Uniface. Printer: Jas Harris.

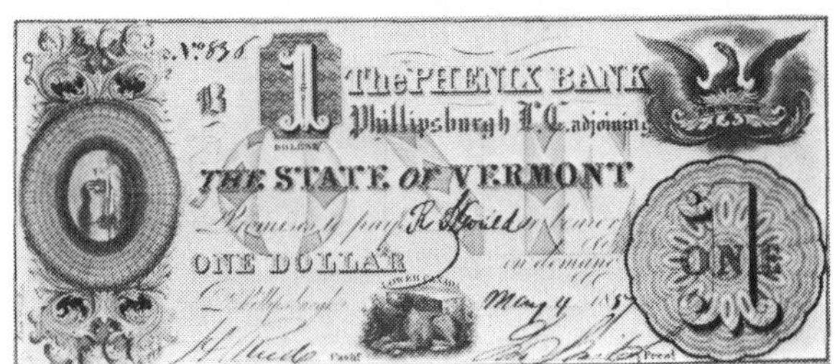

		VG	VF	Unc
S1915	**1 Dollar** 4.5.1837.	420.00	840.00	—

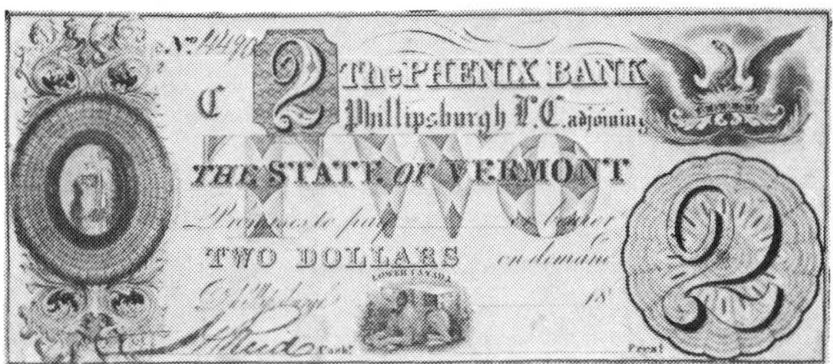

		VG	VF	Unc
S1916	**2 Dollars** Remainder. 18xx.	500.00	1000.	—
S1917	**3 Dollars** 4.5.1837.	675.00	1400.	—

1841 Spurious Issue

Dollar/Pound Sterling System.

		VG	VF	Unc
S1918	**1 Dollar = 5 Shillings** 8.10.1841. Like #S1915.	500.00	1000.	—

Pictou Bank

Established in Pictou, Nova Scotia in 1873. Failed in 1887.

1874 Issue

#S1919-S1921 black on green unpt. Back green. Printer: BABNC.

		VG	VF	Unc
S1919	**4 Dollars** 2.1.1874. Anchor by cargo at lower l., steam passenger train at dock side at top ctr., sailor raising flag at lower r.			
	a. Issued note.	1120.	2240.	—
	r. Remainder.	—	—	910.00

		VG	VF	Unc
S1920	**5 Dollars** 1874; 1882. Farmer w/dog feeding horse grain at lower l., sailing ships at upper ctr., standing sailor at lower r.			
	a. Issued note. 2.1.1874.	1000.	2100.	—
	r. Remainder. 2.1.1874; 2.1.1882.	—	200.00	600.00

		VG	VF	Unc
S1921	**10 Dollars** 1874; 1882. Miners at top l. ctr., sailing ships at lower r.			
	a. Issued note. 2.1.1882.	975.00	2075.	—
	p. Face proof. 2.1.1874.	—	—	350.00
	r1. Remainder. 2.1.1874.	—	—	900.00
	r2. Remainder. 2.1.1882.	—	—	775.00

Bank of Prince Edward Island

Established in Charlotte Town, P.E.I. in 1856. Liquidated in 1881.

1856 Issue

Pound Sterling System.

#S1922-S1925 black. Uniface. Printers: New England Bank Note Co. and RWH & E.

		Good	Fine	XF
S1922	**5 Shillings** 18.8.1856; 7.4.1857. Sailing ship at l., seated woman w/dog and cattle at top ctr.	230.00	770.00	—

		Good	Fine	XF
S1923	**10 Shillings** 13.8.1856; 7.4.1857. Farmer plowing w/horses at top ctr.	280.00	910.00	—

S1924 1 POUND GOOD 355.00 FINE 1190. XF —
18.8.1856; 1.1.1857. Seated Agriculture, sheaf w/sailing ship in background at top ctr.

S1925 5 POUNDS GOOD 505.00 FINE 1680. XF —
13.8.1856. Portr. Qn. Victoria at upper l., suppored royal arms at top ctr., portr. Prince Consort at upper r.

1859 ISSUE

#S1926-S1928 black. Uniface. ABNC monogram added.

		GOOD	FINE	XF
S1926 2 POUNDS	1.1.1859; 1.12.1863. Like #S1922.	280.00	910.00	—
S1927 10 SHILLINGS	1.1.1859; 2.1.1860; 1.1.1862. Like #S1923.	280.00	910.00	—

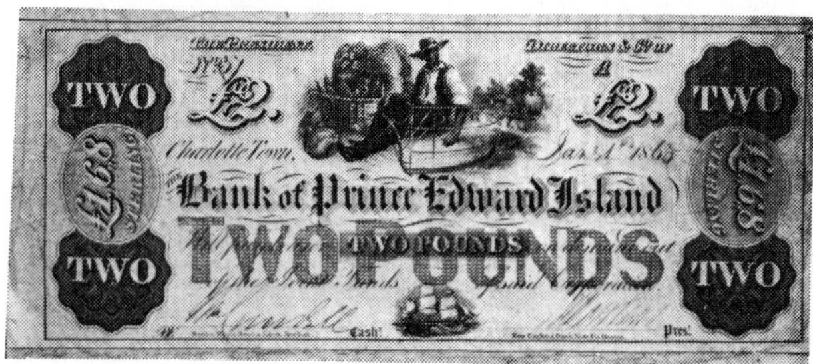

S1928 2 POUNDS GOOD 280.00 FINE 910.00 XF —
1.1.1859; 1.1.1863. Farmer seated w/produce at top ctr.

1872 ISSUE

Dollar System.

#S1929-S1933 black on green unpt. Back green. Printer: BABNC.

S1929 1 DOLLAR
1.1.1872; 1.1.1877. Farm woman harvesting grain w/sickle at ctr.

	VG	VF	UNC
a. 1.1.1872.	65.00	200.00	700.00
b. Vertical red ovpt: *CANADA CURRENCY* twice on #S1929a.	82.50	250.00	800.00
c. 1.1.1877.	45.00	135.00	450.00
d. Vertical red ovpt: *CANADA CURRENCY* twice on #S1929c.	57.50	175.00	600.00

S1930 2 DOLLARS
1.1.1872; 1.1.1877. Anchor by cargo at lower l., horse watering in stream at upper ctr., cattle at lower r.

	VG	VF	UNC
a. 1.1.1872.	65.00	200.00	700.00
b. Vertical red ovpt: *CANADA CURRENCY* twice on #S1930a.	82.50	250.00	800.00
c. 1.1.1877.	45.00	135.00	450.00
d. Vertical red ovpt: *CANADA CURRENCY* twice on #S1930c.	57.50	175.00	600.00

S1931 5 DOLLARS
1.1.1872; 1.1.1877. Farmer watering livestock at top ctr., young woman's head at bottom ctr.

	VG	VF	UNC
a. 1.1.1872.	300.00	525.00	2250.
b. Vertical red ovpt: *CANADA CURRENCY* twice on #S1931a.	300.00	525.00	2250.
c. 1.1.1877.	227.50	525.00	1600.
d. Vertical red ovpt: *CANADA CURRENCY* twice on #S1931c.	200.00	420.00	1600.

S1932 10 DOLLARS
1.1.1872. Sailor at bottom l., fishing boats at top ctr., beehive at lower r.

	VG	VF	UNC
a. Issued note.	105.00	210.00	700.00
r. Remainder w/1 sign.	63.00	122.50	385.00

S1933 20 DOLLARS
1.1.1872. Portr. Qn. Victoria at upper l., seated woman w/trident ship in dry dock in background at top ctr., portr. Prince of Wales at upper r.

	VG	VF	UNC
a. Issued note.	110.00	227.50	840.00
r. Remainder w/1 sign.	87.50	200.00	625.00

PROVINCIAL BANK

Incorporated in London, Ontario in 1884. Never opened for business.

1884 ISSUE

#S1934 and S1935 black on green unpt. Back green. Printer: BABNC.

		VG	VF	UNC
S1934 5 DOLLARS	1.8.1884. Lord Dufferin at l., farmer watering livestock at ctr., barge in locks at r. Face proof.	—	—	500.00
S1935 10 DOLLARS	1.8.1884. Lord Dufferin at l., farm scene at ctr., beavers at r. Face proof.	—	—	500.00

PROVINCIAL BANK OF CANADA

Established in Stanstead, Canada East in 1856. Closed in 1863.

1856 ISSUE

#S1936-S1938 black. Uniface. Printer: Danforth Wright & Co.

#S1936 and S1937 small supported royal arms at l.

S1936 1 DOLLAR VG 425.00 VF 900.00 UNC —
1.4.1856. Supported royal arms at ctr. Red numeral protector on face and back.

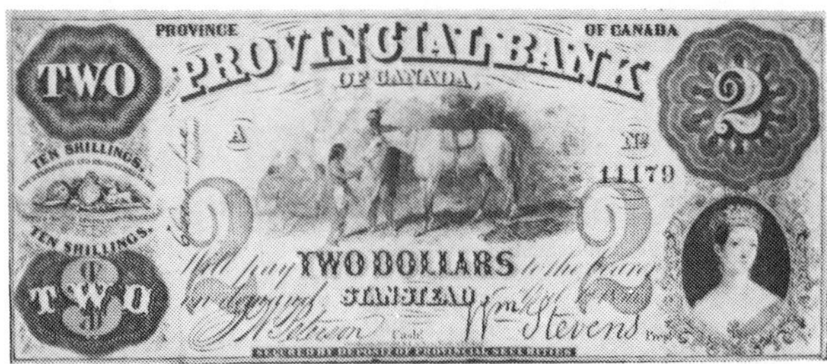

S1937 2 DOLLARS

	VG	VF	UNC
1.4.1856. Indians w/horse at ctr., portr. Qn. Victoria at lower r. Red numeral protector on face and back.	350.00	800.00	—

S1938 5 DOLLARS

	VG	VF	UNC
1.4.1856. Indian family overlooking factories at lower l., portr. Prince Consort at bottom ctr. r. Red Roman numeral protector on face and back.	425.00	900.00	—

BANK OF QUÉBEC, LOWER CANADA

1841 SPURIOUS ISSUE

S1939 2 PIASTRES

	VG	VF	UNC
2.1.1841. Black. Beehive and farm implements at l., supported royal arms at upper ctr., standing Britannia at r. Uniface. Printer: Harris & Sealey. Remainder.	235.00	500.00	—

ROYAL CANADIAN BANK

Established in Toronto in 1864. Merged with the City Bank in 1876 to become The Consolidated Bank of Canada.

1865 FIRST ISSUE

#S1940-S1943 black on green unpt. Supported bank seal at upper ctr. Partially engraved date. Back brown. Red ovpt: *C*. Black K hand stamp: *K*. Printer: ABNC.

S1940 1 DOLLAR

	VG	VF	UNC
4.7.1865. Portr. Duke of Wellington at lower l., standing sailor at lower r.	625.00	1200.	—

S1941 2 DOLLARS

	VG	VF	UNC
4.7.1865. Portr. Prince of Wales at lower l., reclining farm woman w/basket of produce at lower r.	625.00	1200.	—

S1942 5 DOLLARS

	VG	VF	UNC
4.7.1865. Princess of Wales at lower l., woman seated w/telescope at lower r. Face proof.	—	—	315.00

S1943 10 DOLLARS

	VG	VF	UNC
4.7.1865. Portr. Qn. Victoria at lower l., woman w/scale and sword on dock at lower r. Face proof.	—	—	315.00

1865 SECOND ISSUE

S1943A 1 DOLLAR

	VG	VF	UNC
26.7.1865. Like #S1940.			
a. Blue serial #.	700.00	1325.	—
b. Red serial #.	700.00	1325.	—

	VG	VF	UNC
c. Vertical red ovpt: *COBOURG* twice.	700.00	1325.	—
d. Blue ovpt: *T T.*	700.00	1325.	—

S1944 2 DOLLARS

	VG	VF	UNC
26.7.1865. Like #S1941.			
a. Blue serial #.	700.00	1330.	—
b. Red serial #.	700.00	1330.	—
c. Vertical red ovpt: *PARIS* twice.	550.00	1150.	—

S1944A 5 DOLLARS

	VG	VF	UNC
26.7.1865. Like #S1942.			
a. Blue serial #.	850.00	1675.	—
b. Blue ovpt: *OTTAWA.*	700.00	1500.	—
c. Blue ovpt: *T T.*	700.00	1500.	—

1865 THIRD ISSUE

#S1944B-S1946 black on green unpt. Supported bank seal at upper ctr. Back green. Printer: CONB.

S1944B 2 DOLLARS

	VG	VF	UNC
26.7.1865. Prince Albert at lower l., farmer at lower r.			
a. W/text: *AT ITS BANKING HOUSE IN TORONTO* above bank seal.	875.00	1750.	—
b. W/text: *AT ITS AGENCY IN MONTREAL* above bank seal.	Reported Not Confirmed		

1865 SECOND ISSUE

S1945 5 DOLLARS

	VG	VF	UNC
26.7.1865. Young woman at lower l., Indian on horseback at lower r.			
a. W/text: *AT ITS BANKING HOUSE IN TORONTO* above bank seal.	875.00	1750.	—
b. W/text: *AT ITS AGENCY IN MONTREAL* above bank seal.	700.00	1325.	—
c. Blue ovpt: *T-T.*	700.00	1750.	—

		VG	VF	UNC
S1946	**10 DOLLARS** 26.7.1865. Portr. Qn. Victoria at lower l., Indian brave at lower r.			
	a. W/text: *AT ITS BANKING HOUSE IN TORONTO* above bank seal.	Reported Not Confirmed		
	s. W/text: *AT ITS AGENCY IN MONTREAL* above bank seal. Specimen.	—	—	700.00

1870 ISSUE

#S1947-S1952 black on green unpt. Back green. Printer: BABNC.

		VG	VF	UNC
S1947	**4 DOLLARS** 1.7.1870. 2 sailors at dock side at lower l., supported bank crest at upper ctr., beaver on shoreline at lower r. 1 serial #.			
	a. Issued note.	700.00	1330.	—
	b. Vertical blue ovpt: *Montreal* twice.	700.00	1330.	—
	c. Black hand stamp: *A*.	550.00	1150.	—
S1947A	**4 DOLLARS** 1.7.1870. Like #S1947 but w/lg. *4* at upper l. and at upper r. 2 serial #.	700.00	1330.	—

		VG	VF	UNC
S1948	**5 DOLLARS** 1.7.1872. Portr. T. McCracken at lower l., supported bank crest at top l. ctr.	875.00	1750.	—

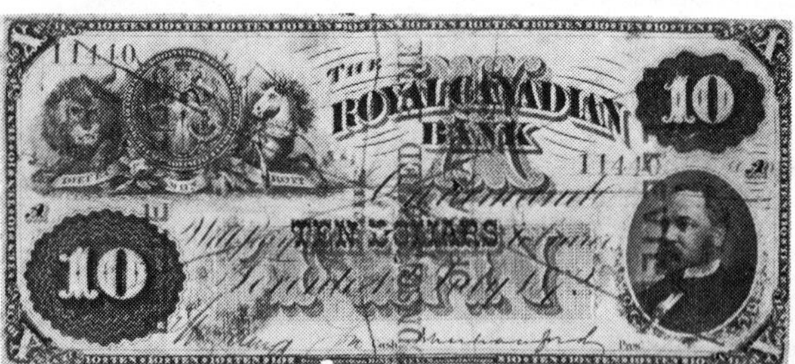

		VG	VF	UNC
S1949	**10 DOLLARS** 1.1.1872. Supported bank crest at upper l., portr. J. Crawford at lower r.			
	a. Issued note w/o ovpt.	980.00	2030.	—
	b. Vertical red ovpt: *BELLEVILLE* twice and *CONSOLIDATED BANK/OF CANADA*.	980.00	2030.	—
S1950	**20 DOLLARS** 2.10.1871. Allegorical woman at l., supported bank crest at ctr., sailor at r. Face proof.	—	—	350.00
S1951	**50 DOLLARS** 2.10.1871. Supported bank crest at ctr. Face proof.	—	—	350.00
S1952	**100 DOLLARS** 2.10.1871. Supported bank crest at ctr. Face proof.	—	—	350.00

SAINT FRANCIS BANK

Formed in Stanstead, Canada East in 1855. Never opened for business.

1850 ISSUE

#S1953 and S1954 black on red unpt. Back blue. Printer: RWH & Co.

		VG	VF	UNC
S1953	**5 DOLLARS** 185x. Portr. Indian brave seated at l., supported portr. Qn. Victoria at top ctr., portr. Prince Consort at lower r. Face proof.	—	—	600.00
S1954	**10 DOLLARS** 185x. Anchor by cargo at l., St. George slaying dragon at top ctr., portr. Qn. Victoria at lower r. Face proof.	—	—	600.00

BANQUE ST. JEAN BAPTISTE

Formed in Montreal, Quebec in 1875. Never opened for business.

1875 ISSUE

#S1955-S1957 black on green unpt. Back green. Printer: BABNC.

		VG	VF	UNC
S1955	**4 DOLLARS** 24.6.1875. Man at l., St. John the Baptist w/lamb at ctr., R. A. R. Hubert at r. Face proof.	—	—	420.00

		VG	VF	UNC
S1956	**5 DOLLARS** 24.6.1875. Allegorical woman reclining at lower l., St. John the Baptist seated by lamb at ctr., R. A. R. Hubert at lower r. Face proof.	—	—	600.00
S1957	**10 DOLLARS** 24.6.1875. St. John the Baptist seated by lamb at ctr., R. A. R. Hubert at r. Face proof.	—	—	600.00

ST. LAWRENCE BANK & LUMBER CO.

Supposedly issued at Malbay, Lower Canada.

1837 SPURIOUS ISSUE

#S1958 and S1959 black. Uniface. Printer: Underwood, Bald, Spencer & Hufty.

		VG	VF	UNC
S1958	**1 DOLLAR** 25.5.1837. Identical Roman bust in all corners, sawmill at top ctr., Indian at bottom ctr.	17.50	35.00	105.00

		VG	VF	UNC
S1959	**2 DOLLARS** 25.5.1837. Identical Roman busts (sideways) at l. and r., ferry St. Lawrence and 2 sailing ships between identical Roman busts at ctr., 2 Spanish 8 Reales coins at bottom ctr.	17.50	35.00	105.00

ST. STEPHENS JOINT STOCK BANKING CO.

Supposed to have been established in St. Stephen, New Brunswick in 1855.

1840S ISSUE

		VG	VF	UNC
S1959A	**3 DOLLARS** 18xx. Black. Man at lower l., sailing ships at upper l. ctr., steamboat and sailboat at lower r. Uniface. Printer: New England Bank Note Co. Remainder.	2450.	—	—

BANK OF SASKATCHEWAN

Formed at Moose Jaw, Saskatchewan in 1913. Never opened for business.

1913 ISSUE

#S1960-S1962 printer: ABNC.

		VG	VF	UNC
S1960	**5 DOLLARS** 1.5.1913. Black on yellow and dk. green unpt. Steam passenger train approaching farmer cultivating w/tractor at ctr. Back green; allegorical woman w/sheaf and sickle at ctr. Face proof.	—	—	700.00

		VG	VF	UNC
S1961	**10 DOLLARS** 1.5.1913. Black on brown and yellow unpt. Steam passenger train approaching railroad construction at ctr. Back green. Face proof.	—	—	700.00

		VG	VF	UNC
S1962	**20 DOLLARS** 1.5.1913. Black on red and yellow unpt. Steam freight trains at grain storage facility at ctr. Back green; steam threshing at ctr. Face proof.	—	—	700.00

STADACONA BANK

Established in Quebec City, Quebec in 1872. Liquidated in 1879.

1874 ISSUE

#S1963-S1966 black on green unpt. Back green. Printer: BABNC.

		GOOD	FINE	XF
S1963	**4 DOLLARS** 2.4.1874. Sailing ship at lower l., supported royal arms at top ctr., portr. A. Joseph at lower r.			
	a. Issued note w/o ovpt.	475.00	1575.	—
	b. Red ovpt: *L-L.*	475.00	1575.	—

		GOOD	FINE	XF
	c. Red ovpt: *P-P.*	475.00	1575.	—
	d. Vertical red ovpt: *ST. SAVEUR* twice.	475.00	1575.	—
S1964	**5 DOLLARS** 2.4.1874. S. de Champlain at lower l., steamboat at Québec at ctr., A. Joseph at lower r. Red ovpt: *E-E.*	625.00	1750.	—
S1965	**6 DOLLARS** 2.4.1874. Steam passenger train at upper l., A. Joseph at lower r. F ace proof.	—	Unc	800.00

		GOOD	FINE	XF
S1966	**10 DOLLARS** 2.4.1874. J. Cartier at lower l., A. Joseph at lower r. Red vertical ovpt: *FRASERVILLE* twice.	625.00	1750.	—

TATTERSALL BANK, MONTREAL, L.C.

Formed in Montreal, Lower Canada.

1830 ISSUE

		GOOD	FINE	XF
S1967	***DELETED.*** Advertising note.			

UNION BANK

Established in Montreal, Lower Canada in 1838. Later became the Union Bank of Montreal.

1838 FIRST ISSUE

Dollar/Piastre System.

#S1968-S1976 printer: Burton & Gurley.

#S1968-S1970 black. Uniface.

		GOOD	FINE	XF
S1968	**1 DOLLAR** 14.7.1838; 1.8.1838. Woman posing in art studio at top ctr., small anchor, ship and caduceus at bottom ctr.	50.00	210.00	—

		GOOD	FINE	XF
S1969	**2 DOLLARS** 14.7.1838. Seated Mercury w/sailing ship in background at top ctr., small road and sign post at bottom ctr.	50.00	210.00	—
S1970	**5 DOLLARS** 14.7.1838. Seated woman by Indian brave at top ctr., small crown at bottom ctr.	65.00	280.00	—

1838 SECOND ISSUE

#S1971-S1973 like #S1968-S1970 but w/back green.

		GOOD	FINE	XF
S1971	**1 DOLLAR** 1.8.1838.	60.00	265.00	—

		Good	Fine	XF
S1972	2 Dollars 1.8.1838.	60.00	265.00	—

		Good	Fine	XF
S1973	5 Dollars 1.8.1838.	75.00	300.00	—

1838 Third Issue

#S1974-S1976 like #S1971-S1973 but back blue.

		Good	Fine	XF
S1974	1 Dollar 1.8.1838.	60.00	265.00	—
S1975	2 Dollars 1.8.1838.	60.00	265.00	—
S1976	5 Dollars 1.8.1838.	75.00	300.00	—

1838 Fourth Issue

Dollar System.

#S1977-S1988 printer: RWH & Co.

#S1977-S1979 black. Back red-brown.

		Good	Fine	XF
S1977	1 Dollar 1.8.1838. Indian hunting buffalo at top ctr., Indian w/drawn bow at r., small portr. blacksmith at bottom ctr.	25.00	85.00	—

		Good	Fine	XF
S1978	2 Dollars 1.8.1838. Indian paddling canoe at top ctr., woman w/sheaf of wheat at r., clasped hands in spray at bottom.	25.00	85.00	—

		Good	Fine	XF
S1979	3 Dollars 1.8.1838. Seated allegorical woman surrounded by cherubs in clouds at top ctr., standing Indian maiden at upper r., small early steam passenger train at bottom ctr.	50.00	140.00	—

1838 Fifth Issue

#S1980-S1985 black. Back orange.

		Good	Fine	XF
S1980	1 Dollar 1.8.1838. Like #S1977.	40.00	125.00	—
S1981	2 Dollars 1.8.1838. Like #S1978.	30.00	100.00	—
S1982	3 Dollars 1.8.1838. Like #S1979.			
	a. Issued note.	60.00	175.00	—
	r. Unsigned remainder. 18xx.	—	Unc	625.00

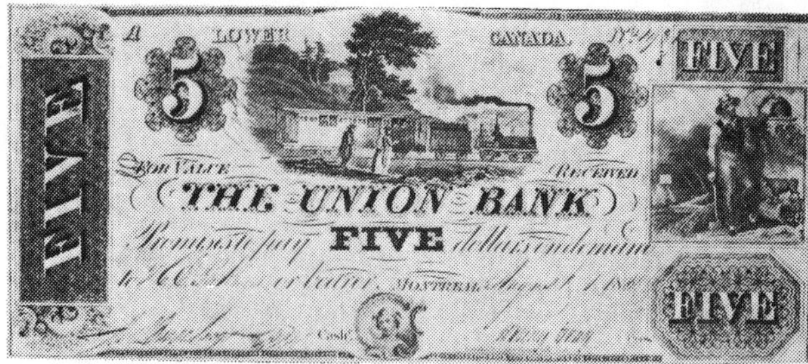

		Good	Fine	XF
S1983	5 Dollars 1.8.1838. Train at ctr., farmer w/implements, beehive and cornucopia at r.			
	a. Issued note.	50.00	140.00	—
	r. Unsigned remainder.	—	Unc	425.00

		Good	Fine	XF
S1984	10 Dollars 18xx. Steam passenger train and cargo at l., seated Indian brave overlooking ruins of Jamestown at top ctr. r., small griffin w/key at bottom ctr. Unsigned remainder.	105.00	350.00	770.00

		Good	Fine	XF
S1985	20 Dollars 18xx. Woman kneeling at l., steam passenger train at dockside at top ctr., allegorical woman at r. Unsigned remainder.	95.00	315.00	630.00

1838 Sixth Issue

#S1986-S1988A like #S1977-S1979 but back blue.

		Good	Fine	XF
S1986	1 Dollar 1.8.1838.	30.00	100.00	—
S1987	2 Dollars 1.8.1838.	30.00	100.00	—
S1988	3 Dollars 1.8.1838.	40.00	140.00	—
S1988A	5 Dollars 1.8.1838.	75.00	245.00	—

Union Bank of Montreal

Originally established as the Union Bank in Montreal, Lower Canada ca.1840.

1840 Issue

Dollar System.

#S1989-S1990 black. Back blue. Red ovpt: *G* at l. Printers: Danforth, Underwood & Co. and Underwood, Bald, Spencer & Hufty.

		Good	Fine	XF
S1989	50 Dollars 1.1.1840. Woman kneeling w/sickle at l., ships near harbor flanked by oval medallion portrs. facing inwards at top ctr., farm boy reclining at r.			
	a. 1.1.1840.	125.00	420.00	1050.
	r. Remainder. 18xx.	—	Unc	600.00

1840 DOLLAR/POUND ISSUE

		GOOD	FINE	XF
S1990	**100 DOLLARS = 25 POUNDS** 1.1.1840. Seated woman w/book at l., Indians along shoreline w/steamship in background flanked by oval medallion portrs. facing outwards at top ctr., portr. young man w/flag at r.	125.00	420.00	1050.

BANK OF UPPER CANADA, KINGSTON, U.C.

Established in Kingston, Upper Canada in 1819. Failed in 1822.

1819; 1820 ISSUE

Dollar System.

#S1991-S1995 black. Black ovpt: *Payable at the Bank of Canada in Montreal.* Uniface. Printer: Graphic.

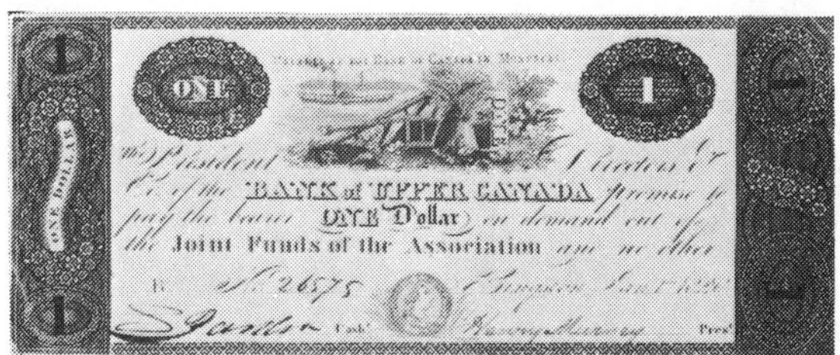

		GOOD	FINE	XF
S1991	**1 DOLLAR** 1.5.1819; 1.1.1820. Plow and sheaf w/paddle wheel steamboat in background at top ctr., coin at bottom ctr.			
	a. Partially engraved date. 29.3.1819; 1.5.1819.	75.00	157.50	—
	b. Engraved date. 1.1.1820.	35.00	75.00	245.00

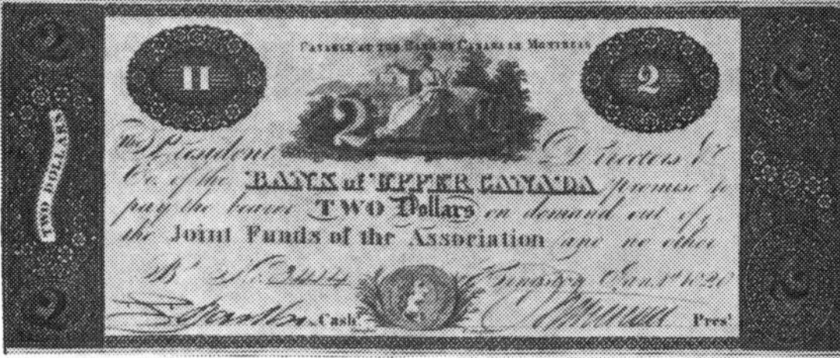

		VG	VF	UNC
S1992	**2 DOLLARS** 1.5.1819; 1.1.1820. Seated Justice w/trident at top ctr., 2 coins at bottom ctr.			
	a. Partially engraved date. 1.5.1819.	75.00	157.50	—
	b. Engraved date. 1.1.1820.	35.00	75.00	245.00

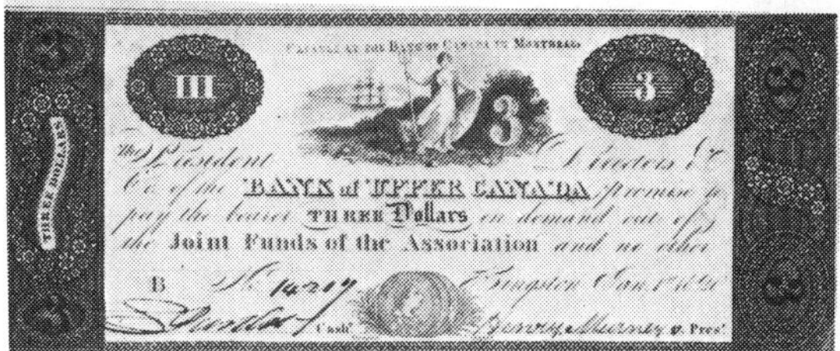

		VG	VF	UNC
S1993	**3 DOLLARS** 1.1.1820. Standing Britannia w/sailing ship in background at top ctr., 3 coins at bottom ctr.	52.50	87.50	265.00

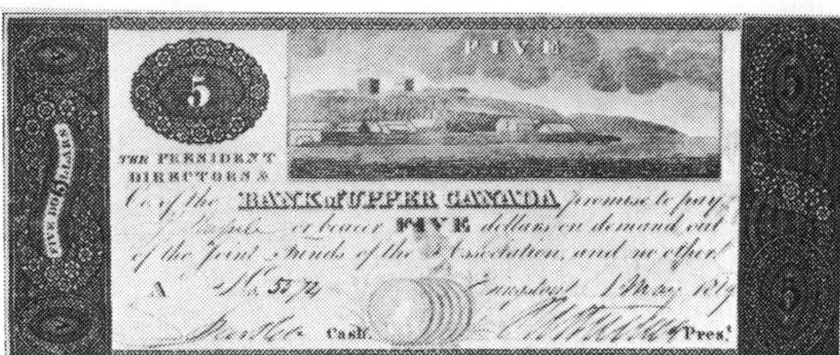

		GOOD	FINE	XF
S1994	**5 DOLLARS** 1819-22. Fort, shipbuilding along shoreline at upper r., 5 coins at bottom ctr.			
	a. Partially engraved date. 4.4.1822; 1.5.1822; 3.6.1822.	25.00	87.50	210.00
	b. As a. 18xx.	—	—	105.00

		GOOD	FINE	XF
S1995	**10 DOLLARS** 1819-22. Fort above Kingston Harbor at upper l. ctr.			
	a. Partially engraved date. 4.4.1819; 1.5.1819; 3.6.1822.	25.00	87.50	210.00
	b. As d. 18xx.	—	—	105.00

1820 ISSUE

Pound Sterling System.

		GOOD	FINE	XF
S1996	**6 PENCE** 23.8.1820. Black. Seated Britannia at upper l. Uniface.	335.00	1125.	—

BANK OF UPPER CANADA, YORK, U. C.

Established in York, Upper Canada in 1821. Failed in 1866.

1826-30 ISSUES

Dollar/Pound Sterling System.

#S1997-S2001 black. Uniface. Printer: Graphic.

		VG	VF	UNC
S1997	**1 DOLLAR = 5 SHILLINGS** 7.3.1829; 19.3.1831. Seated Britannia w/steamboat and beehive in background at top ctr., value at bottom ctr.	275.00	550.00	—
S1998	**2 DOLLARS = 10 SHILLINGS** 3.8.1827. Harbor view, lighthouse at top ctr., 2 coins at bottom ctr.	315.00	675.00	—

		VG	VF	UNC
S1999	**4 DOLLARS = 20 SHILLINGS** 3.11.1830; 2.11.1832. St. George slaying dragon at top ctr., 4 coins at bottom ctr.	385.00	800.00	—

		VG	VF	UNC
S2000	**5 DOLLARS = 25 SHILLINGS** 1826-32. View of York, lighthouse at top ctr. W/text: *FIVE DOLLARS - CINQUE PIASTRES* above counters at upper l. and r.			
	a. 2.8.1826; 3.1.1827; 9.1.1830.	280.00	560.00	—
	b. 19.9.1832.	385.00	800.00	—
S2000A	**5 DOLLARS = 25 SHILLINGS** 19.9.1832. Like #S2000 but w/text: *FIVE DOLLARS - CINQUE PIASTRES* below counters at upper l. and r.	315.00	665.00	—
S2001	**10 DOLLARS = 50 SHILLINGS** 1.11.1830. Harbor scene at top ctr.	385.00	805.00	—

1836-38 ISSUES

Dollar System.

#S2002-S2009 black. Uniface. W/text: *Payable at Toronto.* Printer: RWH & Co. or RWH & E.

		VG	VF	UNC
S2002	**1 DOLLAR** 18xx. Seated Justice at l., Neptune in horse drawn chariot and winged woman at top ctr., oval portr. Indian at bottom ctr. Proof.	—	—	280.00

		VG	VF	UNC
S2003	**2 DOLLARS** 6.11.1836. Standing Navigation at l., Indian brave w/drawn bow at upper ctr., allegorical woman at r., small bison at bottom ctr. .	450.00	840.00	—

S2004 4 DOLLARS | VG 450.00 | VF 840.00 | UNC —
3.5.1837. Standing Indian "Red Jacket" at upper l., supported royal arms at upper ctr., portr. Sir W. Raleigh at r.

S2005 5 DOLLARS | VG — | VF — | UNC 280.00
18xx. 3 seated allegorical women at l., Neptune w/woman in horse drawn shell at top ctr., standing Britannia holding anchor at upper r., small sailing ship at bottom ctr. Proof.

S2006 10 DOLLARS | VG 450.00 | VF 840.00 | UNC —
1.1.1838. 2 seated allegorical women w/sailing ship in background, Neptune w/woman in horse drawn shell at top ctr., portr. cherub at r., small sailing ship at bottom ctr.

#S2007-S2009 obelisk at r.

S2007 20 DOLLARS | VG — | VF — | UNC 350.00
18xx. Griffin and 3 allegorical women at top ctr., small griffin w/key at bottom ctr. Proof.

S2008 50 DOLLARS | VG — | VF — | UNC 350.00
18xx. Portr. cherub at l., steam train at dock side at top ctr. Proof.

S2009 100 DOLLARS | VG — | VF — | UNC 350.00
18xx. Supported royal arms at top ctr. Proof.

1849-51 ISSUES

Dollar/Pound Sterling System.

#S2010-S2017 black. Small St. George slaying dragon at bottom ctr. Toronto. Red word protector on face back. Uniface. Printer: RWH & Co.

S2010 1 DOLLAR = 5 SHILLINGS | VG 475.00 | VF 925.00 | UNC —
1.9.1849. Lion at l., seated Commerce w/ornate *1* at top ctr., woman w/dog and *1* at r.

S2011 2 DOLLARS = 10 SHILLINGS | VG — | VF — | UNC 280.00
18xx. Seated Agriculture at l., 2 griffins facing w/*2* between at ctr., portr. woman at r. Proof.

S2012 4 DOLLARS = 1 POUND | VG 425.00 | VF 775.00 | UNC —
1.11.1851; 5.8.1852; 7.11.1856. Portr. Qn. Victoria at l., seated Britannia by lion at top ctr., seated Agriculture at r.

S2013 5 DOLLARS = 1 POUND-5 SHILLINGS | VG 475.00 | VF 925.00 | UNC —
9.10.1849. Portr. Qn. Victoria at l., lion and shield at top ctr., portr. Prince Consort at r.

S2014 10 DOLLARS = 2 POUNDS-10 SHILLINGS | VG 475.00 | VF 925.00 | UNC —
18xx. Young woman w/wheat stalks at l., seated woman w/harp and sheaf at top ctr., standing Britannia at r.

S2015 20 DOLLARS = 5 POUNDS | VG — | VF — | UNC 280.00
18xx. Griffin at lower l., seated Mercury and woman w/caduceus at top ctr., Britannia at lower r. Proof.

S2016 50 DOLLARS = 12 POUNDS-10 SHILLINGS | VG — | VF — | UNC 280.00
18xx. Seated Agriculture at lower l., seated Abundance between lion and unicorn at top ctr., seated Britannia at lower r. Proof.

S2017 100 DOLLARS = 25 POUNDS | VG — | VF — | UNC 280.00
18xx. Portr. seated Qn. Victoria at lower l., supported portr. Qn. Victoria at top ctr., medallion portr. archaic male soldier at lower r. Proof.

1851-57 ISSUES

Dollar/Pound Sterling System.

#S2018 and S2020 black. Uniface. Printer: TCC.

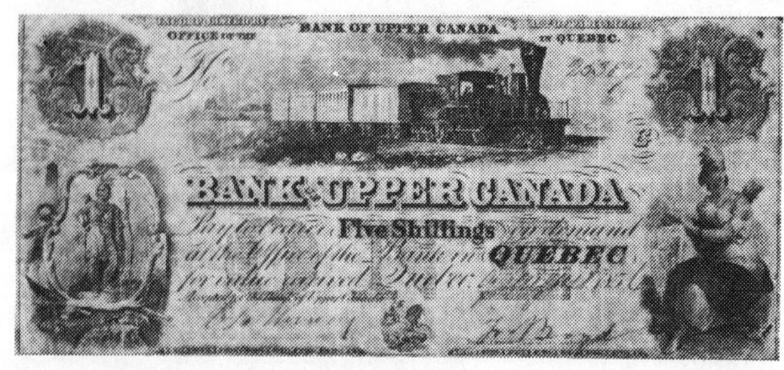

S2018 1 DOLLAR = 5 SHILLINGS
2.1.1851-18.5.1857. Ornate frame w/Indian brave at lower l., steam passenger train at top ctr., seated Indian maiden w/shield at lower r. Blue word on face.

	VG	VF	UNC
a. Kingston. 6.1.1851.	425.00	925.00	—
b. Montreal. 2.1.1851.	425.00	925.00	—
c. Quebec. 2.5.1854-18.5.1857.	385.00	770.00	—

S2019 2 DOLLARS = 10 SHILLINGS
2.1.1851-7.11.1856. Early steam passenger train at l., 2 herdsmen on horseback driving livestock at top ctr., 2 milkmaids milking cows at r.

	VG	VF	UNC
a. Brockville. 9.1.1851.	350.00	630.00	—
b. Quebec. 5.5.1852-7.11.1856.	385.00	770.00	—
p. Montreal. Proof. 185x.	—	—	280.00

S2020 5 DOLLARS = 1 POUND-5 SHILLINGS
9.5.1857. Horse galloping at l., supported portr. Qn. Victoria at upper ctr., dog lying by strongbox at r.

	VG	VF	UNC
a. Quebec. 9.5.1857.	420.00	875.00	—
p. Montreal. Proof. 185x.	—	—	280.00

#S2021 and S2022 black. Supported royal arms (sideways) at r. Uniface. Printer: RWH & Co.

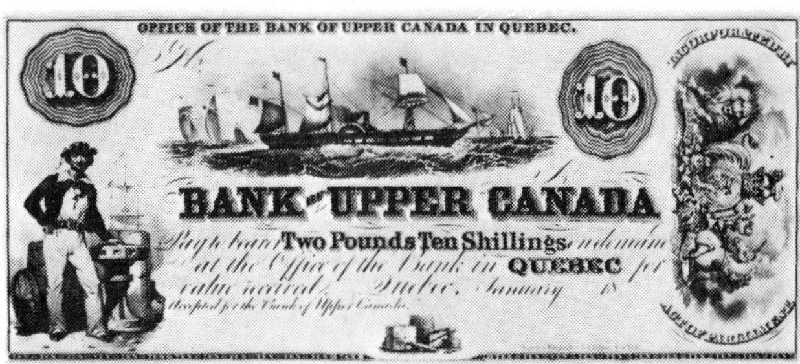

S2021 10 DOLLARS = 2 POUNDS-10 SHILLINGS
Jan. 18xx. Standing sailor at lower l., paddle wheel steam sailing ship at top ctr.

	VG	VF	UNC
p1. Montreal. Proof.	—	—	325.00
p2. Quebec. Proof.	—	—	325.00

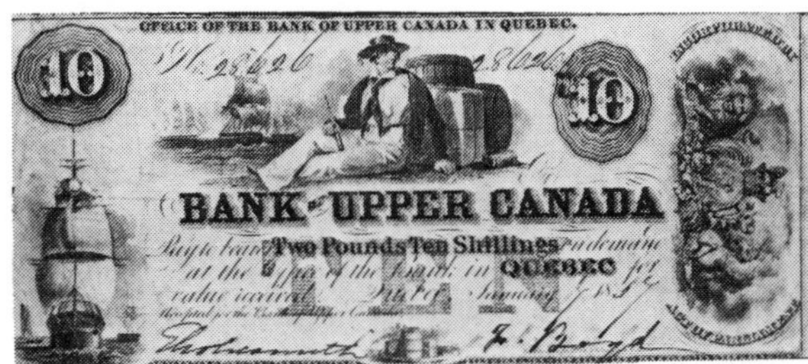

S2022 10 DOLLARS = 2 POUNDS-10 SHILLINGS
7.1.1857. 3 ships under full sail at lower l., seated sailor by cargo w/sailing ship in background at top ctr.

	VG	VF	UNC
a. Quebec. 7.1.1857.	475.00	925.00	—
p. Montreal. Proof. Jan. 185x.	—	—	315.00

#S2023 and S2024 young girl at lower l., seated Commerce and Britannia at upper ctr., herdsmen driving cattle under bridge at lower r. Toronto. Printer: RWH & E.

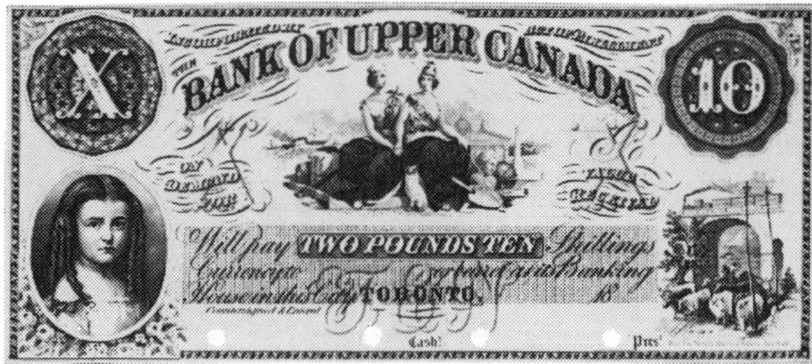

	VG	VF	UNC
S2023 10 DOLLARS = 2 POUNDS-10 SHILLINGS 18xx. Black on brown-orange unpt. Proof.	—	—	450.00
S2024 10 DOLLARS = 2 POUNDS-10 SHILLINGS 18xx. Black on green unpt. Proof.	—	—	450.00

1859 ISSUE

Dollar System.

#S2025-S2032 black on green unpt. 2 sign. Back green. Various numerical and branch ovpts. exist. Printers: RWH & E and ABNC.

S2025 1 DOLLAR
1.7.1859-2.7.1859. Seated Justice at lower l., St. George slaying dragon at upper ctr., seated Britannia w/crest of Upper Canada at lower r.

	VG	VF	UNC
a. Montreal. 1.7.1859.	420.00	875.00	—
b. Quebec. 1.7.1859.	385.00	770.00	—
c. Toronto. 1.7.1859. 18xx.	420.00	875.00	—
d. Toronto. 2.7.1859.	420.00	875.00	—

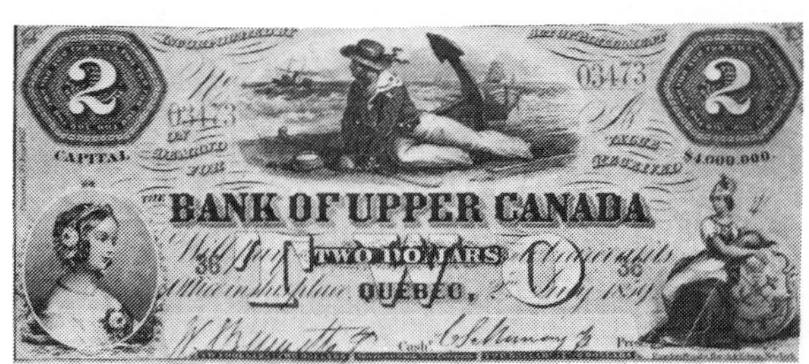

S2026 2 DOLLARS
2.7.1859. Portr. youthful Qn. Victoria at lower l., sailor reclining by anchor w/ships and boat in background at top ctr., seated Britannia w/crest of Upper Canada at lower r.

	VG	VF	UNC
a. Montreal. 2.7.1859.	420.00	875.00	—
b. Quebec. 2.7.1859.	385.00	770.00	—
c. Toronto. 2.7.1859.	385.00	770.00	—
p. Toronto. Proof. 18xx.	—	—	280.00

S2027 4 DOLLARS
4.7.1859. Young woman w/cornucopia at lower l., 2 allegorical women seated w/3 shields at upper ctr., blacksmith seated at lower r.

	VG	VF	UNC
a. Toronto. 4.7.1859.	385.00	770.00	—
p. Toronto. Proof. 18xx.	—	—	325.00

S2028 5 Dollars
5.7.1859. Standing sailor at lower l., 2 allegorical women seated w/3 shields at top ctr., portr. Prince of Wales at lower r.

	VG	VF	Unc
a. Montreal. 5.7.1859.	420.00	875.00	—
b. Quebec. 5.7.1859.	420.00	875.00	—
c. Toronto. 5.7.1859/18xx.	420.00	875.00	—
d. Toronto. 5.7.1859.	420.00	875.00	—

S2029 10 Dollars
6.7.1859. Youthful portr. Qn. Victoria at lower l., 2 allegorical women seated w/3 shields at top ctr., seated Britannia w/crest of Upper Canada at lower r.

	VG	VF	Unc
a. Montreal. 6.7.1859.	420.00	875.00	—
b. Quebec. 6.7.1859.	385.00	770.00	—
c. Toronto. 6.7.1859.	420.00	875.00	—
p. Toronto. Proof. 18xx.	—	—	325.00

S2030 20 Dollars

	VG	VF	Unc
18xx; 8.7.1859. Seated Justice and Britannia w/crest of Upper Canada at top ctr. r., stone mason at lower r. Toronto. Proof.	—	—	325.00

S2031 50 Dollars

	VG	VF	Unc
18xx; 8.7.1859. Farm implements at lower l., seated Justice and Britannia w/crest of Upper Canada at upper ctr., woman w/sheaf and sickle at lower r. Toronto. Proof.	—	—	325.00

S2032 100 Dollars

	VG	VF	Unc
18xx; 9.7.1859. Seated Justice and Britannia w/crest of Upper Canada at top ctr., seated woman by bale at lower r. Tornonto. Proof.	—	—	325.00

1861 Issue

#S2033-S2037 black on green unpt. 1 sign. Back green. Various branch name ovpt. w/ or w/o numbers in red or black exist. Toronto. Printers: RW & H and ABNC.

S2033 1 Dollar

	VG	VF	Unc
1.1.1861. Like #S2025.	280.00	630.00	—

S2034 2 Dollars

	VG	VF	Unc
1.1.1861. Like #S2026.	420.00	875.00	—

S2035 4 Dollars

	VG	VF	Unc
1.1.1861. Like #S2027.	385.00	800.00	—

S2036 5 Dollars

	VG	VF	Unc
1.1.1861. Like #S2028.	280.00	630.00	—

S2037 10 Dollars

	VG	VF	Unc
1.1.1861. Like #S2029.	385.00	800.00	—

BANK OF WESTERN CANADA

Established in Clifton, Canada West in 1859. Failed in 1863.

1859 ISSUE

#S2038-2041 black on red unpt. Red word protector on face and back. Black hand stamps: *X*, *SW* and *O*. Uniface. Printer: ABNC.

		VG	VF	UNC
S2038	1 DOLLAR 20.9.1859. Portr. Qn. Victoria at lower l., supported royal arms at top ctr., portr. Prince Consort at lower r.			
	a. R.h. sign. G. McMicken.	227.50	485.00	—
	b. R.h. sign. E. J. Richardson.	21.50	65.00	225.00

		VG	VF	UNC
S2039	2 DOLLARS 20.9.1859. Portr. Qn. Victoria at lower l., seated Britannia by lion at top ctr.			
	a. R.h. sign. G. McMicken.	227.50	485.00	—
	b. R.h. sign. E. J. Richardson.	21.50	65.00	225.00

		VG	VF	UNC
S2040	4 DOLLARS 20.9.1859. Portr. Prince Consort at lower l., lion w/shield at top ctr., portr. Qn. Victoria at lower r.			
	a. R.h. sign. G. McMicken.	262.50	490.00	—
	b. R.h. sign. E. J. Richardson.	22.50	70.00	250.00

		VG	VF	UNC
S2041	5 DOLLARS 20.9.1859. Portr. Prince Consort at l., St. George slaying dragon at top ctr., seated Britannia w/crest of Upper Canada at lower r.			
	a. R.h. sign. G. McMicken.	227.50	490.00	—
	b. R.h. sign. E. J. Richardson.	22.50	70.00	250.00

A word on pricing

When a note is marked RARE in the price columns, this note seldom appears on the market, or few are known in private hands. When dashes are in the price column, means that the note has not traded on the open market recently and a definitive value could not accurately be determined. Rare does not always mean expensive. A dashed price does not mean expensive or rare.

WESTMORLAND BANK OF NEW BRUNSWICK

Established in Bend of the Petticodiac, New Brunswick in 1854. Failed in 1867.

BEND OF PETTICODIAC

1854-59 ISSUE

#S2042-S2046 black. Bend of the Petticodiac. Uniface. Printer: RWH & E.

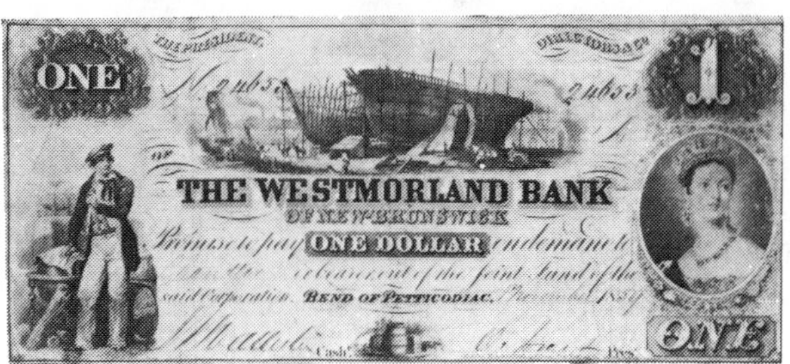

		VG	VF	UNC
S2042	1 DOLLAR 1.5.1854-1.11.1859. Standing sailor at lower l., shipbuilding at top ctr., portr. Qn. Victoria at r., small cask at bottom ctr.			
	a. L.h. sign. J. Johnson. 1.5.1854.	210.00	450.00	—
	b. L.h. sign. J. McAllister.	250.00	525.00	—

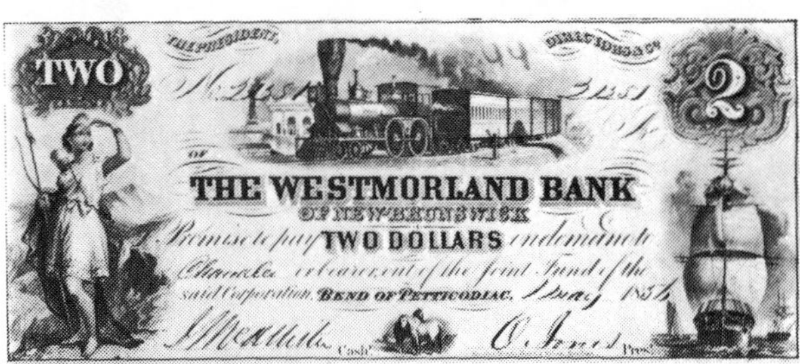

		VG	VF	UNC
S2043	2 DOLLARS 1.5.1854-1.11.1859. Indian maiden w/spear at lower l., steam passenger train at top ctr., 3 ships under full sail at lower r., 2 small horses at bottom ctr.			
	a. L.h. sign. J. Johnson. 1.5.1854.	280.00	560.00	—
	b. L.h. sign. J. McAllister.	315.00	595.00	—

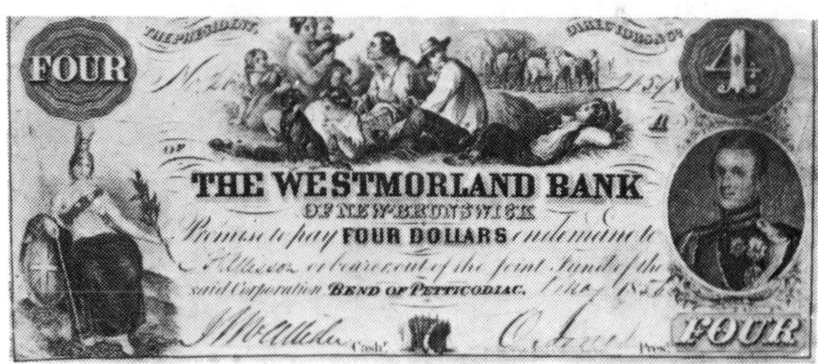

		VG	VF	UNC
S2044	4 DOLLARS 1.5.1854-1.11.1859. Seated Britannia w/shield at lower l., farm family w/horsedrawn hay wagon in background at top ctr., portr. Prince Consort at r., small shipbuilding at bottom ctr.			
	a. L.h. sign. J. Johnson. 1.5.1854.	250.00	525.00	—
	b. L.h. sign. J. McAllister.	250.00	525.00	—

		VG	VF	UNC
S2045	20 DOLLARS 1.5.1854-1.11.1859. Seated Britannia w/shield at lower l., woman w/rake and ornate *20* at upper ctr., seated Justice at lower r., small swords, crown on cushion at bottom ctr. 2 sign. varieties.	3150.	—	—
S2046	40 DOLLARS 18xx. Young woman at lower l., seated Justice and Britannia w/royal crest at upper ctr., 2 women at lower r., small shipbuilding at bottom ctr. Proof.	—	—	1500.

MONCTON

1861 ISSUE

#S2047-S2050 black on green unpt. Back blue. Printers: RWH & E and ABNC.

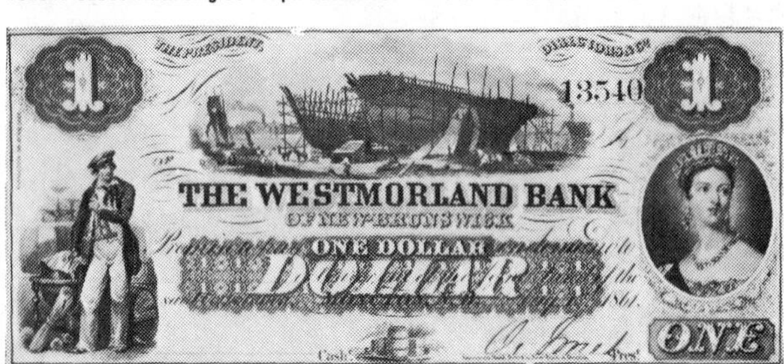

		VG	VF	UNC
S2047	1 DOLLAR 1.8.1861. Face like #S2042.			
	a. L.h. sign. J. McAllister.	25.00	55.00	300.00
	b. L.h. sign. W. C. Jones.	30.00	65.00	350.00
	c. L.h. sign. J. S. Trites.	32.50	70.00	375.00
	r. Unsigned remainder.	—	—	275.00

		VG	VF	UNC
S2048	2 DOLLARS 1.8.1861. Face like #S2043.			
	a. L.h. sign. J. McAllister.	25.00	55.00	175.00
	b. L.h. sign. W. C. Jones.	30.00	65.00	210.00
	c. L.h. sign. J. S. Trites.	32.50	70.00	230.00
	r. Unsigned remainder.	—	—	175.00

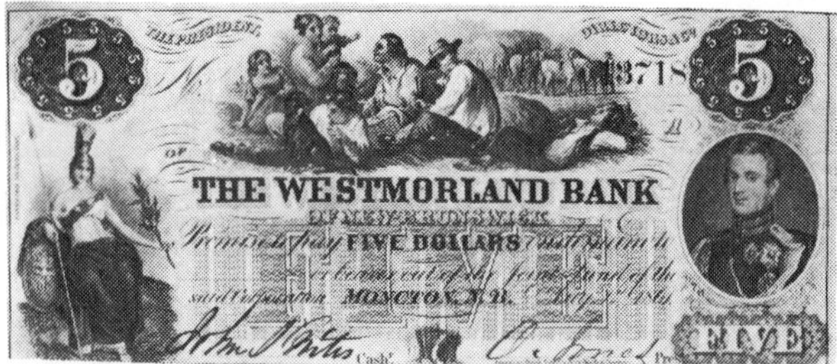

		VG	VF	UNC
S2049	5 DOLLARS 1.8.1861. Face like #S2044.			
	a. L.h. sign. J. McAllister.	25.00	55.00	175.00
	b. L.h. sign. W. C. Jones.	30.00	65.00	210.00
	c. L.h. sign. J. S. Trites.	32.50	70.00	230.00
	r. Unsigned remainder.	—	—	230.00
S2050	20 DOLLARS 1.8.1861. Face like #S2045.	2100.	—	—

ZIMMERMAN BANK

Established in Elgin, Canada West in 1854. Changed name to Bank of Clifton in 1859.

ELGIN

1854-55 ISSUE

#S2051-S2055 black. *ELGIN* at lower l. Uniface. Printers: Toppan, Carpenter, Casilear & Co. and Toppan Carpenter & Co.

		VG	VF	UNC
S2051	1 DOLLAR 2.11.1854. Clifton House at lower l., Roebling Suspension Bridge at Niagara at top ctr., seated Industry at lower r.	300.00	560.00	—
S2052	3 DOLLARS 185x. Like #S2057. Proof.	—	—	280.00

		VG	VF	UNC
S2053	5 DOLLARS 1.10.1855. Seated allegorical woman at upper l., Roebling Suspension Bridge at Niagara at top ctr. r., steam passenger train at lower r.	300.00	560.00	—
S2054	10 DOLLARS 185x. Similar to #S2065. Proof.	—	—	280.00
S2055	20 DOLLARS 185x. Similar to #S2066. Proof.	—	—	280.00

1856 ISSUE

#S2056-S2058 black. *ELGIN* at lower ctr. Red word protector on face and back. Uniface. Printer: Toppan, Carpenter, Casilear & Co. and Toppan Carpenter & Co.

		VG	VF	UNC
S2056	1 DOLLAR 7.6.1856; 1.12.1856. Roebling Suspension Bridge at Niagara at upper ctr., Clifton House at lower l., seated Industry at lower r.			
	a. Engraved date 185x. Retrograde protector on back.	87.50	175.00	560.00
	b. Normal protector on back.	87.50	175.00	560.00
	c. Engraved date 1856. Retrograde protector on back.	175.00	350.00	—
	d. Normal protector on back.	175.00	350.00	—

		VG	VF	UNC
S2057	3 DOLLARS 185x. Roebling Suspension Bridge at Niagara at upper ctr., Clifton House at lower l., portr. Qn. Victoria at lower r. Remainder.			
	a. Engraved date 185x. Retrograde protector on back.	122.50	227.50	700.00
	b. As #S2057a but w/normal protector on back.	122.50	227.50	700.00
	c. Engraved date 1856. Retrograde protector on back.	210.00	490.00	—
	d. As #S2057c but w/normal protector on back.	227.50	490.00	—

		VG	VF	UNC
S2058	5 DOLLARS 7.7.1856. Seated allegorical woman at upper r., Roebling Suspension Bridge at Niagara at upper ctr., steam passenger train at lower r.			
	a. Engraved date 185x. Retrograde protector on back.	87.50	175.00	560.00
	b. As #S2058a but w/normal protector on back.	87.50	175.00	560.00
	c. Engraved date 1856. Retrograde protector on back.	157.50	350.00	—
	d. As #S2058c but w/normal protector on back.	175.00	420.00	—
S2058A	10 DOLLARS 7.6.1856; 1.12.1856. Roebling Suspension Bridge at Niagara at l., portr. Prince Consort at ctr., woman w/sheaf at r.			
	a. Engraved date 185x. Retrograde protector on back.	Reported Not Confirmed		
	b. As #S2058a but w/normal protector on back.	Reported Not Confirmed		
	c. Engraved date 1856. Retrograde protector on back.	350.00	595.00	—
	d. As #S2058c but w/normal protector on back.	Reported Not Confirmed		

1850s First Issue

#S2059-S2061 black. Blue word protector. Uniface. Printer: Toppan, Carpenter, Casilear & Co. and Toppan Carpenter & Co.

		Good	Fine	XF
S2059	**1 Dollar** 185x. Like #S2056. Remainder.	30.00	100.00	250.00
S2060	**3 Dollars** 185x. Like #S2057. Remainder.	30.00	100.00	250.00
S2061	**5 Dollars** 185x. Like #S2058. Remainder.	30.00	100.00	87.50

1850s Second Issue

#S2062-S2066 black. Red numerical protector unpt. Uniface.

		Good	Fine	XF
S2062	**1 Dollar** 185x. Roebling Suspension Bridge at Niagara at upper ctr., Clifton House at lower l., seated Industry at lower r.	40.00	125.00	300.00

		Good	Fine	XF
S2063	**3 Dollars** 185x. Roebling Suspension Bridge at Niagara at upper ctr., Clifton House at lower l., portr. Qn. Victoria at lower r. Remainder.	50.00	160.00	350.00

		Good	Fine	XF
S2064	**5 Dollars** 1856. Roebling Suspension Bridge at Niagara at upper ctr., seated allegorical woman at upper l., steam passenger train at lower r.			
	a. Engraved date 185x.	40.00	125.00	300.00
	b. Engraved date 1856.	70.00	230.00	—

		Good	Fine	XF
S2065	**10 Dollars** 185x. Roebling Suspension Bridge at Niagara at top l., portr. Prince Consort at top ctr. r., woman w/sheaf at lower r. Remainder.	60.00	195.00	—

		Good	Fine	XF
S2066	**20 Dollars** 185x. Clifton House at lower l., Roebling Suspension Bridge at Niagara at upper ctr., woman w/telescope at lower r. Remainder.	60.00	195.00	455.00

1850s Third Issue

#S2067-S2071 black. Blue numerical protector. Uniface.

		Good	Fine	XF
S2067	**1 Dollar** 185x. Like #S2062. Remainder.			
	a. Engraved date 185x.	15.00	45.00	110.00
	b. Engraved date 1856.	70.00	230.00	—
S2068	**3 Dollars** 185x. Like #S2063. Remainder.	40.00	125.00	230.00
S2069	**5 Dollars** 185x. Like #S2064. Remainder.	15.00	45.00	110.00
S2070	**10 Dollars** 185x. Like #S2065. Remainder.	16.50	55.00	160.00
S2071	**20 Dollars** 185x. Like #S2066. Remainder.	16.50	55.00	160.00

Clifton

1850s Issue

#S2072-S2076 black. Red word protector. *CLIFTON* at lower ctr.

		VG	VF	Unc
S2072	**1 Dollar** 185x. Like #S2062. Remainder.	27.50	55.00	210.00

		VG	VF	Unc
S2073	**3 Dollars** 185x. Like #S2063. Remainder.	52.50	140.00	280.00

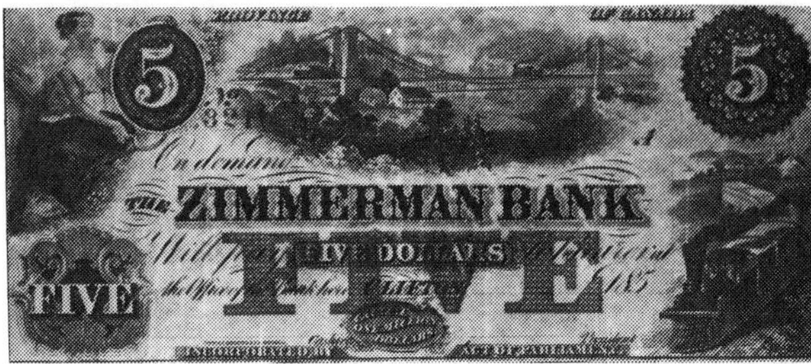

		VG	VF	Unc
S2074	**5 Dollars** 185x. Like #S2064. Remainder	27.50	55.00	210.00
S2075	**10 Dollars** 185x. Like #S2065. Remainder.	105.00	210.00	—

		VG	VF	Unc
S2076	**20 Dollars** 185x. Like #S2066. Remainder.	105.00	210.00	—

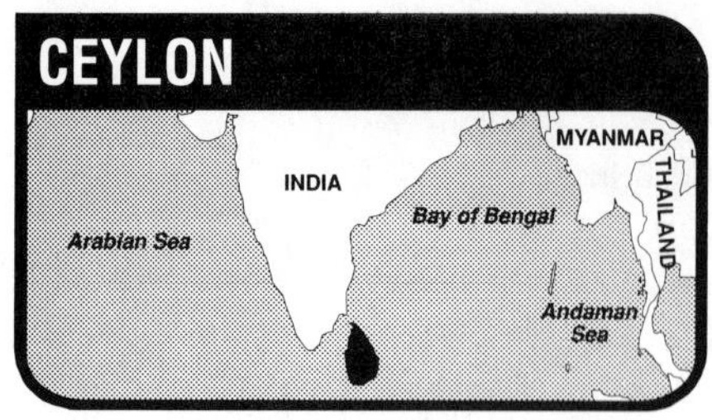

Ceylon, situated in the Indian Ocean 18 miles (29 km.) southeast of India, has an area of 25,332 sq. mi. (65,610 sq. km.). Capital: Colombo.

The earliest known inhabitants of Ceylon, the Veddahs, were subjugated by the Sinhalese from northern India in the 6th century B.C. Sinhalese rule was maintained until 1408, after which the island was controlled by China for 30 years. The Portuguese came to Ceylon in 1505 and maintained control of the coastal area for 150 years. The Dutch initially appeared off the coast of Ceylon in 1602. They soon entered into a treaty of commerce with the King of Kandy with the object of ousting the Portuguese and they obtained protection and free trade for cinnamon and pepper. In 1638 the native Prince Rajasinga II called upon the Dutch to help him against the Portuguese and they now took one place after another, including Galle in 1640 and Colombo in 1656. By the time Jaffna had fallen into their hands in 1658, they had taken possession of all the ports of Ceylon. The British seized the Dutch colonies in 1796, and made them a Crown Colony in 1802. In 1815, the British conquered the independent Kingdom of Kandy in the central part of the island. Constitutional changes in 1931 and 1946 granted the Ceylonese a measure of autonomy and a parliamentary form of government. Ceylon became a self-governing dominion of the British Commonwealth on Feb. 4, 1948. On May 22, 1972, the Ceylonese adopted a new constitution which declared Ceylon to be the Republic of Shri (Sri) Lanka - "Resplendent Island." Shri Lanka is a member of the Commonwealth of Nations. The president is Chief of State.

RULERS:

Portuguese, until 1658
Dutch, until 1796
British, 1796-1972

MONETARY SYSTEM:

1 Rixdollar = 48 Stuivers
1 Pound = 20 Shillings
1 Shilling = 12 Pence
1 Rupee = 100 Cents, ca. 1830-

Dutch Administration

Verenigde Oostindische Compagnie

United East India Company

KREDIT BRIEVEN: payable to the bearer on demand in Ceylonese copper coinage. There were three languages printed on the notes - Dutch, Sinhalese and Tamil. Each note was hand signed by three officials.

1785 First Issue

This issue totalled 25,000 Rixdollars face value.

		Good	Fine	XF
S11	**50 Rixdollars** 10.5.1785.	—	—	—
S12	**100 Rixdollars** 10.5.1785.	—	—	—
S13	**500 Rixdollars** 10.5.1785.	—	—	—
S14	**1000 Rixdollars** 10.5.1785.	—	—	—

1785 Second Issue

		Good	Fine	XF
S21	**5 Rixdollars** Oct. 1785.	—	—	—
S22	**10 Rixdollars** Oct. 1785.	—	—	—
S23	**20 Rixdollars** Oct. 1785.	—	—	—
S24	**50 Rixdollars** Oct. 1785.	—	—	—
S25	**100 Rixdollars** Oct. 1785.	—	—	—
S26	**200 Rixdollars** Oct. 1785.	—	—	—
S27	**500 Rixdollars** Oct. 1785.	—	—	—

NOTE: Third Issue Dec. 1785 and Fourth Issue May 1786: presumably in the same denominations as the Second Issue. In all there were 13 issues between 1787 and 1795, besides two special emissions for use at Batticaloa (1789 and 1790) and one for Trincomalee (1788).

1796 Issue

Interest Bearing Cash Notes

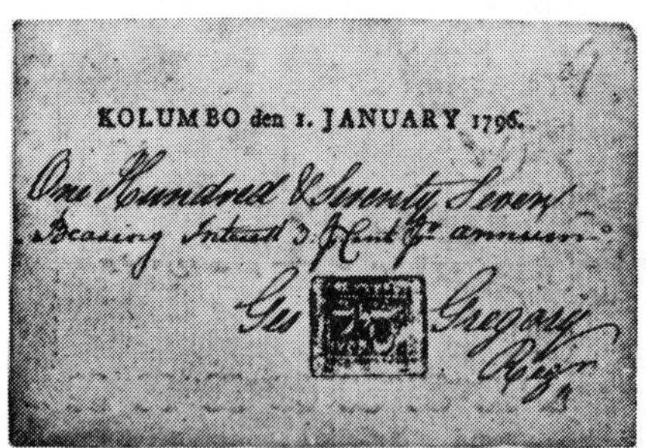

		Good	Fine	XF
S41	**1 Rixdollar** 1.1.1796. C/VOC monogram in circle at upper l. and lower r., tree in circle at lower l. and upper r.	—	—	—
S42	**2 Rixdollars** 1.1.1796.	—	—	—
S43	**3 Rixdollars** 1.1.1796.	—	—	—
S44	**4 Rixdollars** 1.1.1796.	—	—	—
S45	**5 Rixdollars** 1.1.1796.	—	—	—
S46	**10 Rixdollars** 1.1.1796.	—	—	—

British Administration

The British took over the debts of the Kredit Brieven in 1796. Notes in circulation at that time equalled 50,000 pounds sterling. The British issued interest-bearing certificates payable each half year.

Asiatic Banking Corporation

Founded around 1860; failed in 1866. Offices of Issue: Colombo and Kandy. Notes were also prepared for the Shanghai office. Refer to China listings.

1865 Colombo Issue

#S101-S104 bank arms at upper ctr. Printer: SE&C.

		Good	Fine	XF
S101	**10 Shillings/5 Rupees** 1.11.1865; 1.5.1866. Black on green unpt. Back green.	250.00	750.00	—

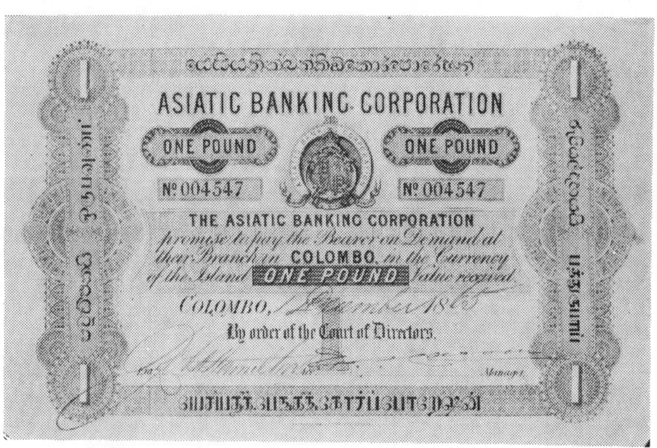

		Good	Fine	XF
S102	**1 Pound** 1.12.1865; 1.5.1866. Brown and black. Uniface.	300.00	1000.	—
S103	**5 Pounds** 1.9.1865. Orange and black.	400.00	1300.	—

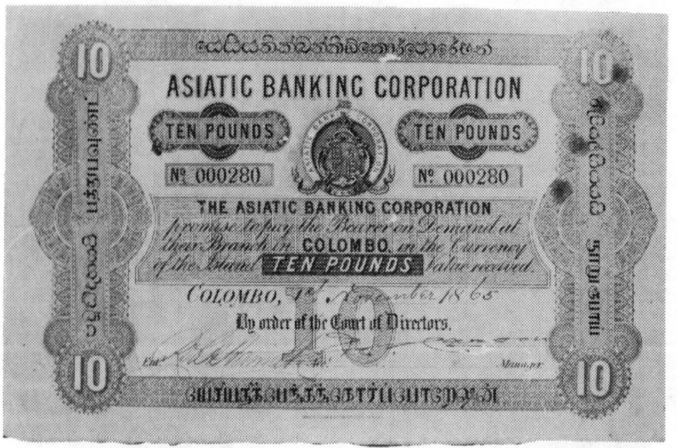

		Good	Fine	XF
S104	**10 Pounds** 1.11.1865. Lilac and black.	450.00	1500.	—

1865 Kandy Issue

#S106-S109 like Colombo issue. Printer: SE&C.

NOTE: #S106c dated in 1822 are fictitious.

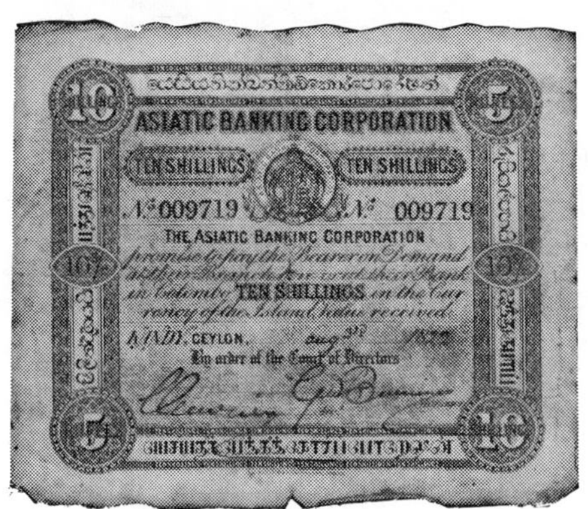

		Good	Fine	XF
S106	**10 Shillings/5 Rupees** 1865. Like #S101.			
	a. Dated 1865.	150.00	650.00	—
	b. Not dated.	75.00	450.00	—
	c. Dated 1822 (fictitious).	75.00	325.00	—

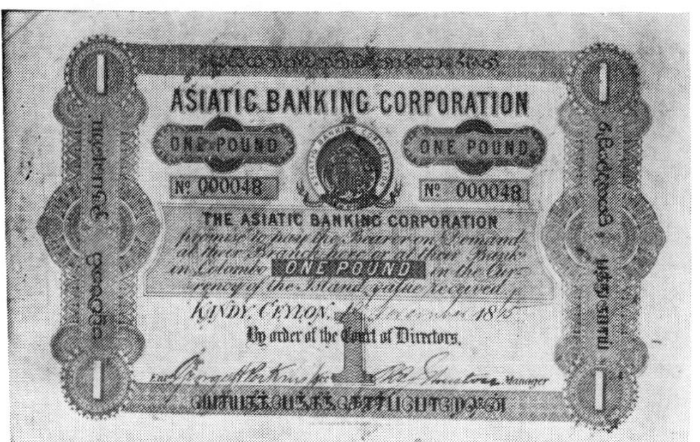

		Good	Fine	XF
S107	**1 Pound** 1.11.1865; 31.1.1866. Like #S102.	300.00	1000.	—
S108	**5 Pounds** 29.11.1865. Orange and black. Like #S103.	350.00	1300.	—
S109	**10 Pounds** ca. 1865. Lilac and black. Like #S104.	Reported Not Confirmed		

Bank of Ceylon

Established in 1841. Merged with the Oriental Bank in 1849.

1840's Issue

#S111-S115 black. Seated Britannia w/elephant in circle at l., supported bank arms at upper ctr. Uniface. Proofs only.

		Good	Fine	XF
S111	**1 Pound** 18xx. Proof.	—	Rare	—
S112	**5 Pounds** 18xx. Proof.	—	Rare	—
S113	**10 Pounds** 18xx. Proof.	—	Rare	—
S114	**20 Pounds** 18xx. Proof.	—	Rare	—

		Good	Fine	XF
S115	**50 Pounds** 18xx. Proof.	—	Rare	—

Chartered Mercantile Bank of India, London & China

Offices of issue: Colombo, Galle and Kandy.

1867 Colombo Issue

Pound Sterling System.

		Good	Fine	XF
S117	**10 Shillings** 1.1.1867. Green. Arms at top ctr.	—	Rare	—

1870's Colombo Issue

Rupee System.

#S121-S126 ca.1870-80. Arms at top ctr.

		Good	Fine	XF
S121	**5 Rupees** 1.11.1873; 1.1.1877; 7.1.1880. Red-brown on blue unpt.			
	a. Issued note.	—	Rare	—
	p. ND. Face proof.	—	—	250.00
	r. Back proof.	—	—	90.00
S122	**10 Rupees** ND.			
	p. Face proof.	—	—	350.00
	r. Back proof.	—	—	100.00
S123	**50 Rupees** ND			
	p. Face proof.	—	—	650.00
	r. Back proof.	—	—	100.00
S124	**100 Rupees** ND.			
	p. Face proof.	—	—	750.00
	r. Back proof.	—	—	110.00
S125	**500 Rupees** ND.			
	p. Face proof.	—	—	1000.
	r. Back proof.	—	—	125.00
S126	**1000 Rupees** ND.			
	p. Face proof.	—	—	1250.
	r. Back proof.	—	—	150.00

A word on pricing

When a note is marked RARE in the price columns, this note seldom appears on the market, or few are known in private hands. When dashes are in the price column, means that the note has not traded on the open market recently and a definitive value could not accurately be determined. Rare does not always mean expensive. A dashed price does not mean expensive or rare.

1880 Galle Issue

		Good	Fine	XF
S128	**10 Rupees** 1.7.1880. Blue on red-brown unpt. Arms at top ctr.	—	Rare	—

1873 Kandy Issue

		Good	Fine	XF
S129	**5 Rupees** 1.11.1873. Arms at top ctr.	—	Rare	—

Mercantile Bank of India, London & China

Offices of issue: Colombo and Kandy.

1870s Kandy/Colombo Issue

		Good	Fine	XF
S131	**5 Shillings** 1.7.18xx. Black on lt. blue unpt. Seated Britannia and symbols of commerce at upper ctr. Vertical ovpt: *ISSUED AT KANDY* at ctr.	—	Rare	—

Oriental Bank Corporation

Founded around 1850; failed in 1884. Offices of issue: Badulla, Colombo, Galle, Jaffna, Kandy and Newera Ellia.

1869 Badulla Issue

#S136-S139 printer: PBC.

		Good	Fine	XF
S136	**5 Rupees** 1869.	—	Rare	—
S137	**10 Rupees** 1869.	—	Rare	—
S138	**50 Rupees** 1869.	Reported Not Confirmed		
S139	**100 Rupees** 1869.	Reported Not Confirmed		

1866-81 Colombo Issues

		Good	Fine	XF
S141	**5 Rupees** 15.3.1866. Lt. blue. Supported arms at top ctr.	—	Rare	—

		Good	Fine	XF
S142	**5 Rupees** 1.1.1881. Black on red-violet unpt. Enthroned qn. at l., supported arms at upper ctr., portr. Mercury at r. Back lt. blue and red-violet. Printer: BWC.	—	Rare	—

		Good	Fine	XF
S143	**10 Rupees** 15.12.1877. Black. Arms at top ctr. Printer: PB&P.	—	Rare	—
S144	**50 Rupees** 1.1.1880.	—	Rare	—
S146	**100 Rupees** 1.1.1876. Blue-green. Arms at ctr. Printer: PB&P.	—	Rare	—

1866-67 Galle Issue

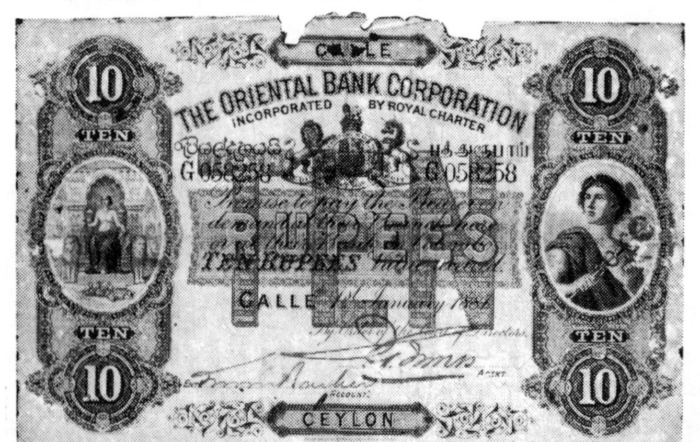

		Good	Fine	XF
S148	**10 Rupees** 1866; 1867. Black. Arms at top ctr.			
	a. Issued note. 15.2.1867.	—	Rare	—
	p. Proof. 15.6.1866.	—	Rare	—

1884 Galle Issue

#S151-S154 printer: BWC.

		Good	Fine	XF
S151	**5 Rupees** 1.1.1884.	—	Rare	—

		Good	Fine	XF
S152	**10 Rupees** 1.1.1881; 1.1.1884. Similar to #S142.	—	Rare	—
S153	**50 Rupees** 1.1.1884.	—	Rare	—
S154	**100 Rupees** 1.1.1884.	—	Rare	—

1881 Jaffna Issue

#S155-S155A printer: BWC.

		Good	Fine	XF
S155	**5 Rupees** 1.1.1881. Similar to #S142. Specimen.	—	—	—

S155A 10 RUPEES	GOOD	FINE	XF
1.1.1881. Like #S152. Specimen perforated: *CANCELLED*, BW & Co.	—	—	—

1873 KANDY ISSUE

#S156-S157 printer: BWC.

S156 5 RUPEES	GOOD	FINE	XF
1.7.1873. Black. Like #S141.	—	Rare	—

1881 KANDY ISSUE

S157 5 RUPEES	GOOD	FINE	XF
1.1.1881. Like #S142.	—	Rare	—

1881 NEWERA ELLIA ISSUE

S161 5 RUPEES	GOOD	FINE	XF
1.1.1881. Like #S142.	300.00	900.00	—

The Republic of Chile, a ribbon-like country on the Pacific coast of southern South America, has an area of 292,258 sq. mi. (756,945 sq. km.) and a population of 15.21 million. Capital: Santiago. Historically, the economic base of Chile has been the rich mineral deposits of its northern provinces. Copper, of which Chile has about 25 percent of the world's reserves, has accounted for more than 75 per cent of Chile's export earnings in recent years. Other important exports are iron ore, iodine, fruit and nitrate of soda.

Diego de Almargo was the first Spaniard to attempt to wrest Chile from the Incas and Araucanian tribes, 1536. He failed, and was followed by Pedro de Valdivia, a favorite of Pizarro, who founded Santiago in 1541. When the Napoleonic Wars involved Spain, leaving the constituent parts of the Spanish Empire to their own devices, Chilean patriots formed a national government and proclaimed the country's independence, Sept. 18, 1810. Independence, however, was not secured until Feb. 12, 1818, after a bitter struggle led by Generals Bernardo O'Higgins and José de San Martín.

In 1925, the constitution was ratified to strengthen the Executive branch at the expense of the Legislature.

MONETARY SYSTEM:

1 Peso = 100 Centavos
1 Condor = 100 Centavos

PROVINCIAL

Province of Valdivia .... #S101-S102

COMMERCIAL BANKS

Banco Agricola .... #S106-S112
Banco de Ahorros y Préstamos .... #S115-S116
Banco de la Alianza .... #S118-S128
Banco de Arauco .... #S130
Banco de José Bunster .... #S131-S134
Banco de Caupolican .... #S136-S139
Banco de Chile .... #S145-S147
Banco Comercial de Chile .... #S151-S163
Banco de Concepción .... #S166-S182
Banco Consolidado de Chile .... #S186-S191
Banco Constructor Hipotecario .... #S198
Banco Crédito Unido .... #S208-S211
Banco de Curicó .... #S218-S220
Banco de A. Edwards y Ca. .... #S231-S248
Banco de Escobar, Ossa y Ca. .... #S253-S257
Banco de Llanquihue .... #S263
Banco de D. Matte y Ca. .... #S278-S281
Banco de Matte, Mac-Clure i Ca. .... #S283
Banco de Melipilla .... #S296-S299
Banco Mobiliario .... #S306-S312
Banco de Montenegro I Ca. .... #S313-S314
Banco Nacional de Chile .... #S316-S338
Banco del Ñuble .... #S344-S346
Banco de Ossa y Ca. .... #S351-S358
Banco del Pobre .... #S361-S364
Banco Popular Hipotecario .... #S379
Banco de Rere .... #S388-S389
Banco San Fernando .... #S397-S400
Banco de Santiago .... #S411-S417
Banco de la Serena .... #S418
Banco Sud-Americano .... #S421
Banco del Sur .... #426-S432
Banco de Talca .... #S439-S443
Banco Banco de Tarapacá y Londres .... #S447-S455
Banco de la Union .... #S460-S467
Banco de Valparaiso .... #S477-S512

PROVINCE OF VALDIVIA

TESORERIA Y ADUANA UNIDAS VALDIVIA

UNITED TREASURY AND CUSTOMS

1840-44 ISSUE

#S101-S102 value printed at ctr. and handwritten at lower r., 2 sign., 2 oval monogram seals and 2 official seals inscribed for the issuing authority. Treasury seal at top ctr., also at the same location on back. Black.

		Good	Fine	XF
S101	4 Reales 1840-44.	250.00	550.00	—
S102	8 Reales 1840-44.	250.00	550.00	—

Commercial Banks

Banco Agricola

Founded in 1868; merged with other banks in 1894 to form the Banco de Chile.

1869-93 Issue

#S106-S112 printer: CABB (ABNC).

		Good	Fine	XF
S106	1 Peso 7.3.1887. Black on orange and red unpt. Girl at l., allegory of Agriculture at ctr., woman w/produce at r. Back brown.	—	Rare	—

#S108-S110 are known only as proofs.

S108	5 Pesos (ca.1870). Brown or gray back proof.	—	—	—

		Good	Fine	XF
S109	10 Pesos 18xx. Black on blue unpt. Farmer carrying hay for horse at l., cattle at ctr. Green or orange back. Proof.	—	—	—

		Good	Fine	XF
S110	20 Pesos 1869. Black on brown unpt. 2 allegorical children at bottom l., allegorical woman w/harvest at ctr., child w/rabbits at lower r. Back red-orange. Proof.	—	—	—

		Good	Fine	XF
S111	50 Pesos 20.4.1893. Black on blue unpt. Cherubs at l. and r., farmers loading ox-cart at upper ctr. Back green.	—	Rare	—

		Good	Fine	XF
S112	100 Pesos 18xx. Black on red unpt. Farmer at l., allegorical woman w/3 children at ctr. Back orange.			
	p. Proof.	—	Unc	450.00
	s. Specimen ovpt: *MUESTRA*.	—	Unc	450.00

NOTE: 2 Pesos denomination is reported, not confirmed.

Banco de Ahorros y Préstamos

Founded in 1890.

1893 Issue

		Good	Fine	XF
S115	10 Pesos 1893. Black on yellow unpt. Seated woman w/sword at l., seated Mercury at r. Back green; helmeted head at ctr. Printer: W&S.	100.00	300.00	—

		Good	Fine	XF
S116	20 Pesos 18xx. Black on orange and blue unpt. Woman seated w/scale, coins and safe at ctr. Back orange; young girl's head at ctr. Printer: ABNC.	—	—	—

NOTE: Other denominations are reported, not confirmed.

Banco de la Alianza

Founded in 1872.

1870's Provisional Issue

#S118 ovpt. new bank name on notes of the Banco Nacional de Chile.

		Good	Fine	XF
S118	20 Pesos ND (- old date 1872). Ovpt. on #S320.	—	Rare	—

1874-77 Regular Issue

#S121-S123 printer: ABNC.

#S121-S123 like Banco Nacional notes #S325, S318 and S319.

		Good	Fine	XF
S121	1 Peso 1877. Black on tan unpt. arms at lower l., palace at ctr., Liberty at lower r. Back green.	100.00	400.00	—

		GOOD	FINE	XF
S122	5 PESOS 1876-77. Black on orange unpt. Condor at l., arms at ctr., girl at r. Back green.	—	—	—

		GOOD	FINE	XF
S123	10 PESOS 1874 (hand dated). Black on green unpt. Girl at lower l., condor at upper ctr., arms at lower r. Back green.	—	—	—

1878; 1879 ISSUE

#S126-S128 printer: ABNC.

		GOOD	FINE	XF
S126	1 PESO 3.1.1879. Black on green and peach unpt. Bull's head at l., Liberty at ctr., arms at r. Back brown; woman at ctr.	100.00	350.00	—

		GOOD	FINE	XF
S127	5 PESOS 18xx (ca.1878). Black on green and orange unpt. Child at lower l., arms at ctr., horse at lower r. Back brown; girl at ctr.			
	p. Proof.	—	—	—
	s. Specimen.	—	—	—

#S128 like Banco Nacional note #S334.

		GOOD	FINE	XF
S128	10 PESOS 2.1.1878. Black on green and red-brown unpt. Valdivia at lower l., condor at ctr., arms at lower r. Back brown; Valdivia ovpt. showing guarantee and inconvertibility according at law, and sign. of Mint Superintendent at l.	250.00	—	—

BANCO DE ARAUCO

1870'S ISSUE

		GOOD	FINE	XF
S130	20 PESOS 18xx. Black on green and yellow unpt. Portr. woman w/book at l. ctr., portr. man at r. Back dk. brown. Printer: ABNC.			
	p. Proof.	—	—	—
	s. Specimen.	—	—	—

BANCO DE JOSÉ BUNSTER

Founded in 1882. Issued at Collipulli.

1882 ISSUE

#S131-S134 printer: ABNC.

		GOOD	FINE	XF
S131	1 PESO 18xx (ca. 1882-98). Black on yellow unpt. Woman leaning on wheel at l., Raphael's angel at upper ctr., portr. man at r. Back brown.	—	—	—

NOTE: #S131 is known as an issued note only w/ovpt: *EMISION FISCAL* and is listed in Vol. 2, #27A.

		GOOD	FINE	XF
S132	5 PESOS 18xx. Black on green unpt. Portr. man at l., galloping horse at ctr., seated allegorical woman at r. Back green. Proof.	—	—	—
S133	10 PESOS 18xx. Black on salmon unpt. Child w/sheep at r., man at ctr., 2 allegorical women at r. Back orange. Proof.	—	—	—

		GOOD	FINE	XF
S134	20 PESOS 18xx (ca.1882-98). Black on orange and yellow unpt. Bridges at l. ctr., portr. woman at r. Back brown: 3 children looking at book at ctr. Proof.	—	—	—

BANCO DE CAUPOLICAN

Founded in 1882. Issued at Rengo.

1884 ISSUE

#S136-S139 printer: ABNC.

		GOOD	FINE	XF
S136	1 PESO 2.7.1884. Black on green unpt. Woman at l., reclining woman w/globe at r. Back brown.			
	a. Issued note.	200.00	475.00	—
	p. Proof. 18xx.	—	—	—

		GOOD	FINE	XF
S137	5 PESOS ND. Black on orange unpt. Farm animals at l., N. American Indian head at ctr. Back blue. Specimen.	—	—	—

		GOOD	FINE	XF
S139	**20 PESOS** 18xx. Black on orange unpt. Reclining allegorical woman at ctr. Back green: plants at r.			
	r. Unsigned remainder.	15.00	25.00	50.00
	s. Specimen.	—	—	—

BANCO DE CHILE

Founded in 1894 and exists today.

1894-96 ISSUE

#S145-S147 printer: ABNC. Issued at Valparaiso.

		GOOD	FINE	XF
S145	**20 PESOS** ND (ca.1894). Black on green and yellow unpt. Bridges at l. and r., arms at ctr. Back brown; Valdivia at ctr.			
	a. Issued note.	—	Rare	—
	s. Specimen.	—	—	—

		GOOD	FINE	XF
S146	**50 PESOS** ND (ca.1896). Black on green and yellow unpt. Allegorical woman at l. and r. of arms at ctr.			
	p. Proof.	—	—	—
	s. Specimen.	—	—	—
S147	**100 PESOS** ND (ca.1896). Black on pink, yellow and orange unpt. Similar to #S146. Proof.	—	—	—

BANCO COMERCIAL DE CHILE

1890'S ISSUE

#S151-S156 printer: W&S.

		GOOD	FINE	XF
S151	**1 PESO** (ca.1890). Black on yellow and pink unpt. Woman w/basket on head at l., arms at r. Back green; condor at ctr.	—		—
S152	**2 PESOS** (ca.1890). Black on green and pink unpt. Arms at l., seated woman w/bales at ctr. Back red-brown; woman at ctr.	—	—	—

NOTE: #S151 and S152 are known issued only w/ovpt: *EMISION FISCAL* and are listed in Vol. 2, #30 and 31.

		GOOD	FINE	XF
S153	**5 PESOS** 18xx. Young girl at l., arms at ctr. r. Salesman's sample book. Specimen.	—	Unc	200.00

		GOOD	FINE	XF
S154	**10 PESOS** 1890. Black on green and orange unpt. Arms at upper l., woman reclining w/shield and caduceus at ctr. r. Back red-brown.	—	—	—

		GOOD	FINE	XF
S156	**50 PESOS** 18xx. 3 allegorical women at ctr. Proof.	—	—	—

1893 ISSUE

#S160-S163 Liberty and arms on face. Various vignettes of railroad bridges. Printer: BWC.

		GOOD	FINE	XF
S160	**10 PESOS** 8.6.1893. Black on green and rose unpt. Liberty at l., bridge at ctr., arms at r. Ox-cart on back. Series B.	—	—	—

NOTE: #S160 w/ovpt: *EMISION FISCAL* is listed in Vol. 2, #32.

		GOOD	FINE	XF
S161	**20 PESOS** 8.6.1893. Specimen.	—	—	—
S162	**50 PESOS** 8.6.1893. Specimen.	—	—	—

		GOOD	FINE	XF
S163	**100 PESOS** 8.6.1893. Series E. Specimen perforated *CANCELLED B.W. & Co.*	—	—	—

BANCO DE CONCEPCIÓN

Founded in 1871.

1870'S ISSUE

#S166-S170 like Banco del Sur, but w/different colors. Printer: CABB (ABNC).

		GOOD	FINE	XF
S166	**1 PESO** 18xx (ca.1872). Black on green unpt. Woman w/water jug at l., Gen. Freire at ctr., farmers harvesting grapes at r.			
	a. Back green.	—	—	—
	b. Back orange.	—	—	—

		GOOD	FINE	XF
S168	**5 PESOS** 18xx (ca.1872). Black on orange unpt. Ox team pulling hay wagon w/farmers at l., young girl at upper ctr., Gen. Freire at r. Back brown. Proof.	—	—	—

		Good	Fine	XF
S169	**10 Pesos** 18xx (ca.1872). Black on brown unpt. Portr. Gen. Freire at upper l., ox team and wagon at ctr., woman's head at lower r. Proof.	—	—	—

		Good	Fine	XF
S170	**20 Pesos** 18xx (ca.1872). Black on brown or blue unpt. 2 girls at lower l., Gen. Freire at upper ctr., anchor at lower r. Back brown. Face proof.	—	—	—
S172	**100 Pesos** 18xx (ca.1872). Black on violet unpt. Gen. Freire at l., waterfalls and volcano scene at ctr., beehive at lower r. Back lt. orange. Archive copy.	—	—	—

1880's Issue

#S176-S182 printer: ABNC.

		Good	Fine	XF
S176	**1 Peso** 2.1.1885. Black on green and m/c unpt. Reclining allegorical woman w/globe at l., portr. Pinto at r. Back red-brown; standing Indian at ctr.			
	a. Issued note.	125.00	250.00	—
	r. Unsigned remainder.	—	Unc	45.00
	s. Specimen.	—	Unc	200.00

NOTE: #S176 w/ovpt: *EMISION FISCAL* is listed in Vol. 2, #34.

		Good	Fine	XF
S178	**5 Pesos** Jan. 18xx. Black on blue and orange unpt. Cherubs at l. and r. of monument at ctr. Back green; horses at ctr. Specimen.	—	—	—
S179	**10 Pesos** Jan. 18xx. Black on blue and orange unpt. Train station at ctr. Back blue; allegorical woman (Concepción) at ctr. Specimen.	—	—	—

		Good	Fine	XF
S180	**20 Pesos** 2.7.1xxx (ca.1883). Black on orange and yellow unpt. Monument at l., women at l. and r. of value at ctr. Back red-orange; woman at ctr.			
	r. Unsigned remainder.	—	Unc	75.00
	s. Specimen.	—	Unc	200.00

		Good	Fine	XF
S182	**100 Pesos** 18xx (ca.1884). Black on orange and m/c unpt. Rail yard and town in background at r. Back deep red; 2 allegorical women.			
	p. Proof.	—	—	—
	s. Specimen.	—	—	—

Banco Consolidado de Chile

Founded in 1876. Issued at Valparaiso.

1877 Issue

#S186-S191 printer: ABNC.

		Good	Fine	XF
S186	**1 Peso** 3.1.1877. Black on blue and orange unpt. Liberty at l., Raphael's angel at ctr., 2 children holding scroll at r. Back blue; Commerce at ctr.	—	—	—

		Good	Fine	XF
S187	**2 Pesos** 3.1.1877. Black on green and brown unpt. Minerva at l., Mercury at r., 2 cherubs w/scroll at bottom ctr. Back blue; workers at ctr.			
	a. Issued note.	—	—	—
	s. Specimen.	—	Unc	250.00
S188	**5 Pesos** 3.1.1877. Black on blue and yellow unpt. Allegorical woman w/cherub at l., winged cherubs w/flowers and horn at ctr., cherubs w/scroll at r. Back blue; farmers and horses at ctr.			
	a. Issued note.	—	—	—
	s. Specimen.	—	Unc	250.00

		Good	Fine	XF
S189	**10 Pesos** 3.1.1877. Black on orange and green unpt. Condor at lower l., seated allegorical woman w/2 cherubs at ctr., 2 cherubs w/scroll at lower r. Back blue; train at ctr.			
	p. Proof.	—	—	—
	s. Specimen.	—	Unc	300.00
S190	**50 Pesos** ND (1877). Black on green and orange unpt. Allegorical woman at l., woman w/bales at ctr. cherubs w/scroll at r. Back blue; farmers plowing w/oxen at ctr.			
	p. Proof.	—	—	—
	s. Specimen.	—	Unc	350.00

		Good	Fine	XF
S191	**100 Pesos** ND (1877). Black on blue and orange unpt. Woman seated at l., cherub at ctr., cherubs w/scroll at r. Back blue; sheep and steer at ctr.			
	p. Proof.	—	—	—
	s. Specimen.	—	Unc	400.00

BANCO CONSTRUCTOR HIPOTECARIO

Founded in 1889. Issued at Santiago.

1894 ISSUE

		GOOD	FINE	XF
S198	10 PESOS 14.11.1894. Black on yellow and pink unpt. Liberty head at lower l., bldg. at ctr., arms at lower r. Back green; standing woman at ctr. Printer W&S. Salesman's sample book specimen.	—	Unc	85.00

NOTE: For #S198 w/circular ovpt: *BANCO POPULAR HIPOTECARIO* on back, see #S379.

BANCO CRÉDITO UNIDO

Issued at Santiago.

1889-94 ISSUE

		GOOD	FINE	XF
S208	10 PESOS 28.4.1889; 17.6.1889; 12.6.1894. Black on green and yellow unpt. Portr. uniformed man at l., galloping horse at ctr., monument at r. Back green. Printer: ABNC.			
	a. Issued note.	120.00	250.00	—
	p. Proof.	—	250.00	—

		GOOD	FINE	XF
S211	100 PESOS ND. Black on orange and yellow unpt. Man at l., portr. girl at ctr., equestrian statue at r. Back orange. Proof.	—	—	—

NOTE: Other denominations are reported, not confirmed.

BANCO DE CURICÓ

Founded in 1881. Issued at Curicó.

1882 ISSUE

#S218-S220 printer: ABNC.

		GOOD	FINE	XF
S218	5 PESOS 18xx (ca.1882). Black on green and peach unpt. Portr. Comandante E. Ramirez in uniform at ctr. Back brown; C. Columbus sighting land at ctr. Specimen.	—	Unc	250.00

NOTE: #S218 is known issued only w/ovpt: *EMISION FISCAL* and is listed in Vol. 2, #35.

		GOOD	FINE	XF
S219	10 PESOS 18xx (ca.1882). Black on pink unpt. Portr. Capt. A. Prat at l., 2 ships in battle at r. Back brown. Proof.	—	—	—

		GOOD	FINE	XF
S220	20 PESOS 18xx (ca.1882). Black on blue and yellow unpt. Woman w/sheaf at l., portr. Capt. A. Prat at l. ctr., bank above arms at lower r. Back brown; 2 ships engaged in warfare.			
	r. Unsigned remainder.	—	Unc	25.00
	s. Specimen.	—	—	175.00

BANCO DE A. EDWARDS Y CA.

Founded in 1867. Three different series of notes were made. Issued at Valparaiso.

1871; 1872 ISSUES

Peso System

#S231-S232 printer: William Brown & Co., London.

		GOOD	FINE	XF
S231	1 PESO 1.7.1871. Black. Railroad through mountains at ctr. Bank names and *UN PESO* 4 times on back in blue.	—	Rare	—
S232	1 PESO 1.7.1872. Like #S231. Back reads *1-UN PESO-1*.	—	Rare	—

1876-79 ISSUES

#S236-S243 printer: BWC.

		GOOD	FINE	XF
S236	1 PESO 3.1.1878. Black on blue unpt. Portr. girl at upper l., arms at lower r. Back blue; 2 portr. at ctr.	40.00	90.00	350.00
S237	1 PESO 1.7.1879. Black on green unpt. Like #S236.	30.00	80.00	250.00

		GOOD	FINE	XF
S238	**2 PESOS** 1.1.1878. Black on pink unpt. Portr. woman at l. Back pink.	90.00	300.00	—

		GOOD	FINE	XF
S239	**5 PESOS** 1876; 1877. Black on orange and blue unpt. Portr. woman at l., cherub w/sextant in sailboat at r. Back green, red and brown.			
	a. Issued note. 3.1.1876; 3.1.1877.	100.00	350.00	—
	r. Unsigned remainder. 3.1.1877.	—	Unc	75.00

		GOOD	FINE	XF
S240	**10 PESOS** 3.1.1876; 3.1.1877. Black on green and orange unpt. Portr. woman at l., cherub w/plow at r. Back green.	100.00	350.00	—
S243	**100 PESOS** 3.1.1876. Woman at l., cherubs at r. Specimen.	—	—	—

1890's ISSUE

Pound Sterling System

#S246-S248. Not issued. Printer: BWC.

		GOOD	FINE	XF
S246	**1 POUND STERLING** 189x. Portr. man at l., arms at lower r.	—	—	200.00
S247	**5 POUNDS STERLING** 189x.	Reported Not Confirmed		

		GOOD	FINE	XF
S248	**10 POUNDS STERLING** 189x. Like #S246 (Not issued).	—	—	200.00

BANCO DE ESCOBAR, OSSA Y CA.

Founded in 1866. Located in Santiago.

1887 ISSUE

#S253-S257 printer: ABNC. Unsigned remainders are encountered w/false sign.

		GOOD	FINE	XF
S253	**5 PESOS** 1.1.1887. Black on blue unpt. Seated woman w/sword at l., miners at ctr., woman and shoreline at r. Back blue. Unsigned remainder.	—	—	—

		GOOD	FINE	XF
S254	**10 PESOS** 18xx. Black on brown unpt. Girls at l. and r., miners at ctr. Back brown.			
	p. Proof.	—	Unc	300.00
	r. Unsigned remainder.	—	—	—
S255	**20 PESOS** 18xx. Black on rose-pink unpt. Standing woman at l., miners at upper ctr., girl at r. Back rose.	—	—	—

NOTE: #S254 and S255 were illegally ovpt: *EMISION FISCAL* and are listed in Vol. 2, #38 and 39. Both are known issued w/these spuriously applied ovpt.

		GOOD	FINE	XF
S256	**50 PESOS** 18xx (ca.1872). Black on green unpt. Girls at lower l. and r., miners digging at top ctr. Back green.	—	—	—

		GOOD	FINE	XF
S257	**100 PESOS** 18xx (ca.1872). Black on red-brown unpt. Miners at lower l. and r. Back red-brown.			
	r. Unsigned remainder.	—	—	—
	s. Specimen.	—	—	—

Banco de Llanquihue

Located at Puerto Montt.

1870's Issue

		Good	Fine	XF
S263	**10 Pesos** 18xx. Standing allegorical woman w/sickle at ctr. Printer: W&S. Salesman's sample book specimen.	—	Rare	—

NOTE: Other denominations are reported, not confirmed.

Banco de D. Matte y Ca.

Founded in 1875. Issued at Santiago.

Provisional Issue

		Good	Fine	XF
S271	**1 Peso**		Reported Not Confirmed	

1888; 1889 Regular Issue

#S278-S281 printer: ABNC.

		Good	Fine	XF
S278	**10 Pesos** 18xx (ca.1888). Black on yellow and green unpt. Farmer harvesting corn at l., girl and dog at r. Back pinkish red.			
	a. Issued note.	—	Rare	—
	p. Proof.	—	—	—

NOTE: #S278 w/ovpt: *EMISION FISCAL* is listed in Vol. 2, #32.

		Good	Fine	XF
S279	**20 Pesos** 18xx (ca.1888). Black on yellow and orange unpt. Liberty at l., allegorical woman and produce at top ctr., woman and grapes at r. Back red-brown.			
	r. Remainder.	—	7.00	20.00
	s. Specimen.	—	—	—
S280	**50 Pesos** 18xx (ca.1888). Black on blue and yellow unpt. Boy and wheat at l., Liberty and Justice at l. and r. of man w/boy and pack horse at ctr., girl w/flowers at r. Back green.			
	a. Issued note.	—	Rare	—
	p. Proof.	—	—	—

		Good	Fine	XF
S281	**100 Pesos** 1.3.1889. Black on green and yellow unpt. Train at l., Liberty and Justice at l. and r. of portr. Montt at top ctr., farm tools and grain at r. Back olive.			
	a. Issued note.	—	Rare	—
	p. Proof.	—	—	—

Banco de Matte, Mac-Clure i Ca.

Founded in 1871.

1875 Issue

		Good	Fine	XF
S283	**1 Peso** (ca.1875). Blue on violet paper. Gathering hay at l., man at ctr., ships at r. Printer: William Brown & Co.	—	—	—

NOTE: #S283 is known issued only w/ovpt: *EMISION FISCAL* and is listed in Vol. 2, #41.

Banco de Melipilla

Founded in 1879. Issued at Melipilla.

1879-87 Issue

#S296-S299 printer: ABNC.

		Good	Fine	XF
S296	**1 Peso** 18xx (ca.1879). Black on tan unpt. Girl w/sheep at l., roundup of horses at ctr., girl w/quill pen at r. Back blue-green; woman and child at ctr.			
	p. Proof.	—	—	—
	r. Remainder.	—	Unc	85.00

		Good	Fine	XF
S297	**5 Pesos** (ca.1887). Black on tan unpt. Seated woman at l., gathering hay at ctr., ducks at r. Back blue-green; seated woman. Proof.	—	—	—

NOTE: #S297 w/ovpt: *EMISION FISCAL* is listed in Vol. 2, #42.

		Good	Fine	XF
S298	**10 Pesos** 20.12.1887. Black on tan unpt. Beehives at l., reclining woman w/jug at ctr., farm animals at r. Back blue; farm implements at ctr.	—	Rare	—

		Good	Fine	XF
S299	**20 Pesos** 18xx (ca.1887). Black on red unpt. Griffins at lower l. and r., Justice w/money chest and cornucopia at ctr. Back red-orange; allegorical woman w/sheep at ctr. Series C.			
	a. Issued note.	—	Rare	—
	r. Unsigned remainder.	—	—	—

BANCO MOBILIARIO

Founded in 1869. Issued at Santiago.

1870-95 ISSUE

#S306-S312 printer: ABNC.

NOTE: #S306 and S308 w/ovpt: *EMISION FISCAL* are listed in Vol. 2, #34 and 34A.

		GOOD	FINE	XF
S306	**1 PESO** 2.1.187x. Black on green and gold unpt. 2 women at lower l., boy at ctr., woman at lower r. Back brown.			
	a. Issued note.	100.00	350.00	—
	s. Specimen.	—	—	—
S307	**5 PESOS** 2.1.18xx. Black. Woman reclining on sheaf at B., young girl at r. Back green. Archive copy.	—	—	—

		GOOD	FINE	XF
S308	**10 PESOS** 2.1.1890. Black. Boy at l., men w/llamas at lower r. Back blue.			
	a. Issued note.	—	Rare	—
	s. Specimen.	—	—	—

NOTE: #S306 and S308 w/ovpt: *EMISION FISCAL* are listed in Vol. 2, #34 and 34A.

		GOOD	FINE	XF
S309	**20 PESOS** 2.1.18xx (ca.1895). Black on yellow and purple unpt. Athena at lower l., condor at upper ctr., men w/llamas at lower r. Back purple.	—	—	—
S310	**50 PESOS** ND (ca.1870). Black on brown unpt. Condor at l., allegorical woman at r. Back brown. Archive copy.	—	—	—
S310A	**50 PESOS** 18xx (ca.1895). Black on brown and yellow unpt. Similar to #S310, but differnet design above bank name at upper ctr. Archive copy.	—	—	—

		GOOD	FINE	XF
S311	**100 PESOS** 18xx. Girl at lower l., condor at upper ctr., boy at lower r. Specimen.	—	—	—
S312	**500 PESOS** ND (18xx).	—	—	—

BANCO DE MONTENEGRO I CA.

Located at Chillán.

1869 ISSUE

#S313 and S314 printer: ABNC.

		GOOD	FINE	XF
S313	**1 PESO** Jan. 18xx (Feb. 1869). Black on brown unpt. Sailors w/bales at lower l., reclining allegorical woman at ctr., B. O'Higgins at r. Back blue-gray. Proof.	—	—	—
S314	**5 PESOS** 18xx. Black. Proof.	—	—	—

BANCO NACIONAL DE CHILE

Founded in 1865. Two different series of notes were issued at Valparaiso.

1872-77 ISSUE

#S316-S320 printer: CABB (ABNC).

NOTE: #S318 and S319 like Banco de la Alianza notes #S122 and S123.

		GOOD	FINE	XF
S316	**1 PESO** 3.6.1872. Black on brown unpt. Arms at lower l., man at ctr., Liberty head at lower r. Back green.	125.00	275.00	—

		GOOD	FINE	XF
S318	**5 PESOS** 2.1.1877. Black. on yellow unpt. Condor at l., arms at ctr., girl at r. Back green.	150.00	325.00	—

		GOOD	FINE	XF
S319	**10 PESOS** 2.2.1876. Black. Girl at lower l., condor at upper ctr., arms at lower r. Back green.			
	a. Issued note.	—	Rare	—
	p. Proof. 18xx.	—	—	—

NOTE: #S318 and S319 like Banco de la Alianza notes #S122 and S123.

		GOOD	FINE	XF
S320	**20 PESOS** 13.12.1872. Black on orange unpt. Man plowing w/oxen at l. (sideways), arms at ctr. Back green.			
	a. Issued note.	—	Rare	—
	p. Proof. 18xx.	—	—	—
S322	**100 PESOS** 18xx (ca.1865). Black on green unpt. Oxen team at l., arms at ctr. Proof.	—	—	—

1870'S ISSUE

		GOOD	FINE	XF
S325	**1 PESO** 2.1.187x (ca.1873). Black on brown unpt. Arms at lower l., palace at ctr., Liberty at lower r. Back green. Proof.	—	—	—

NOTE: #S325 is like Banco de la Alianza note #S121.

A word on pricing

When a note is marked RARE in the price columns, this note seldom appears on the market, or few are known in private hands. When dashes are in the price column, means that the note has not traded on the open market recently and a definitive value could not accurately be determined. Rare does not always mean expensive. A dashed price does not mean expensive or rare.

1878 Issue

#S331-S338 printer: ABNC.
#S331-S334, S336-S337 Valdivia at ctr. on back.
#S331 and S333 like Banco de la Alianza notes #S126 and S127, except w/Valdivia on face and back.

		Good	Fine	XF
S331	**1 Peso** 3.1.1878; 3.1.1887; 3.1.1888. Black on green and peach unpt. Bull's head at l., Valdivia at ctr., arms at r. Back brown.	65.00	150.00	—

		Good	Fine	XF
S332	**2 Pesos** 3.1.1878; 3.1.1888. Black on red-brown and green unpt. Valdivia at l., arms at ctr., girl w/flowers at r. Back brown.	85.00	200.00	—
S333	**5 Pesos** (ca.1879). Black on green and orange unpt. Valdivia at lower l., arms at ctr., head at r. Back brown.	—	—	—

NOTE: #S331-S333 w/ovpt: *EMISION FISCAL* are listed in Vol. 2, #45-47.

		Good	Fine	XF
S334	**10 Pesos** (ca.1879). Black on green and brown unpt. Valdivia at lower l., condor at upper ctr., arms at r. Back brown.	—	—	—

NOTE: #S334 like Banco de la Alianza note #S128.

		Good	Fine	XF
S335	**20 Pesos** 18xx. Black on green and orange unpt. Man plowing w/oxen at l. (sideways), arms at ctr., portr. Valdivia at lower r. Back brown; condor at ctr.			
	p. Proof.	—	—	—
	s. Specimen.	—	—	—
S336	**50 Pesos** 3.1.18xx. Black on blue and orange unpt. Valdivia at l., farmers plowing w/oxen at ctr., arms at r. Back brown. Specimen.	—	—	—

		Good	Fine	XF
S337	**100 Pesos** 3.1.18xx. Black on blue and orange unpt. Valdivia at lower l. ctr., wagon drawn by oxen at ctr., arms at lower r. Back brown. Specimen.	—	—	—

		Good	Fine	XF
S338	**500 Pesos** 3.1.18xx (ca.1879). Black on green and yellow unpt. Portr. Valdivia at l., cherub at upper ctr., allegorical woman w/hammer and anvil at upper r., arms at lower r. Back brown; Valdivia at l., cattle watering in pond.			
	p. Proof.	—	—	—
	s. Specimen.	—	—	—

Banco del Ñuble

Issued at Chillán.

1885-90 Issue

#S344 and S345 printer: CABB (ABNC).

		Good	Fine	XF
S344	**10 Pesos** 1.5.1885; 1.5.1890. Black on yellow and green unpt. Woman w/child, calf and cows at l. ctr. Back brown; woman w/sheaf at ctr.	75.00	150.00	325.00
S345	**20 Pesos** 18xx (ca.1888). Black on orange, pink and yellow unpt. Farmer w/team of oxen plowing field at ctr., Back w/cow at l.			
	p. Proof. Back orange.	—	—	—
	s. Specimen. Back blue.	—	—	—

		Good	Fine	XF
S346	**20 Pesos** ND. Silver ovpt.: *20-XX-VEINTE* on #S344.	—	—	—

Banco de Ossa y Ca.

Formerly Ossa i Ca. Later became part of Banco de Escobar Ossa y Ca.

1860's Issue

#S351-S356 printer: ABNC.

		Good	Fine	XF
S351	**5 Pesos** Jan. 186x. Allegory of Navigation at lower l., man at upper ctr., allegorical woman w/trident at lower r. Proof.	—	—	—
S352	**10 Pesos** Jan. 186x. Mercury at l., allegory of Navigation reclining at upper ctr., man at lower r. Specimen.	—	—	—

		Good	Fine	XF
S353	**20 Pesos** 1.186x. Black on orange unpt. Portr. woman w/rabbit at l., Paddle wheel steamship at ctr., portr. man at r. Back dk. brown.			
	p. Proof.	—	—	—
	s. Specimen.	—	—	—

		Good	Fine	XF
S354	**50 Pesos** Jan. 186x. Liberty and Minerva at lower l., dog on strongbox at upper ctr., man at lower r. Specimen.	—	—	—

		Good	Fine	XF
S355	**100 Pesos** Jan. 186x. Woman at lower l., cherubs at upper ctr., man at lower r. Proof.	—	—	—

Banco del Pobre

Founded in 1869. Issued at Santiago.

1876-78 Issue

#S361-S363 printer: CNBB (NBNC).

		Good	Fine	XF
S361	**1 Peso** 7.8.1877. Black and brown. Liberty and pedestal at l., 3 children reading at ctr., star in wreath at r. Back green.			
	a. Issued note.	—	—	—
	r. 187x. Remainder w/counterfoil. Series A; B.	—	Unc	20.00

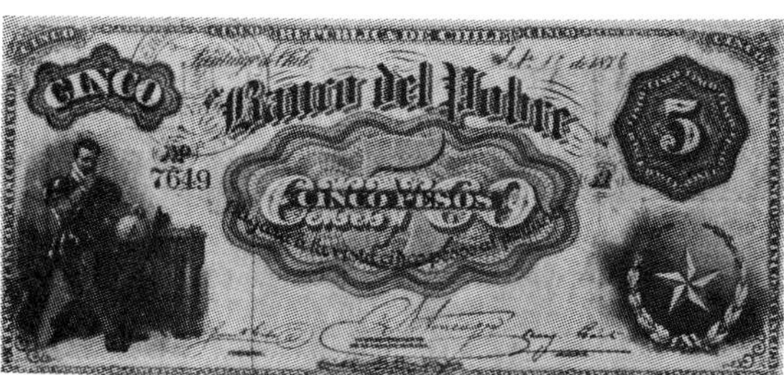

		Good	Fine	XF
S362	**5 Pesos** 16.9.1876. Black, brown and yellow. Spanish conquistador seated w/globe at l., star in wreath at lower r. Back green.			
	a. Issued note.	—	—	—
	r. Remainder.	—	Unc	20.00

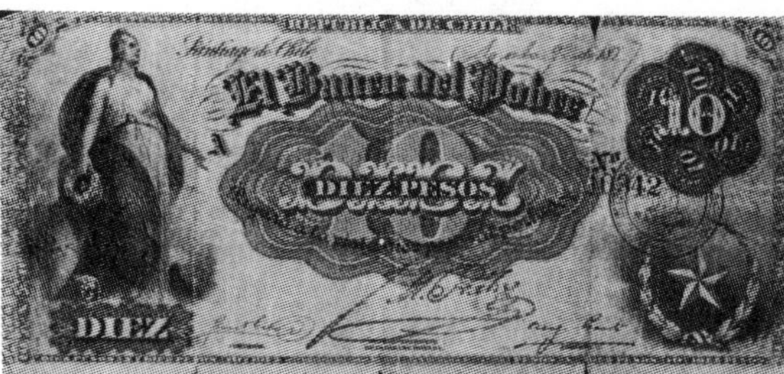

		Good	Fine	XF
S363	**10 Pesos** 9.8.1877. Black, brown and yellow. Liberty standing at l., star in wreath at r. Back green.			
	a. Issued note.	—	—	—
	r. Remainder.	—	Unc	20.00
S364	**20 Pesos** (ca.1878). Black. Steam passenger train at upper l., Liberty at ctr. r.	—	Rare	—

Banco Popular Hipotecario

1894 Provisional Issue

		Good	Fine	XF
S379	**10 Pesos** 14.11.1894. Ovpt. on Banco Constructor Hipotecario, #S198 w/old name barred out on face, and circular ovpt. w/new bank name at ctr. on back.	—	Rare	—

Banco de Rere

1890 Issue

#S388 and S389 printer: W&S.

		Good	Fine	XF
S388	**10 Pesos** 189x. Black on yellow unpt. Minerva standing at l., man plowing w/oxen at ctr. Back blue. Series A. Unsigned remainder.	—	—	—

		Good	Fine	XF
S389	**20 Pesos** 189x. Black on lt. brown unpt. Steam passenger train at upper l., helmeted woman at ctr. r. Unsigned remainder.	—	Unc	350.00

Banco San Fernando

Issued at San Fernando.

1891-99 Issue

#S397-S400 printer: ABNC.

		Good	Fine	XF
S397	**5 Pesos** 18xx (16.5.1899). Black on green unpt. Indian woman seated at l., horse's head at r. Back green.	—	—	—

S398 10 PESOS

1891. Ducks at l., seated Agriculture at ctr. r.

	GOOD	FINE	XF
a. Issued note.	—	—	—
s. Specimen. Back green.	—	—	—

S399 20 PESOS

18xx. Black on tan unpt. Agricultural tools at top ctr., seated allegorical woman by globe at lower r. Back brown.

GOOD	FINE	XF
—	—	—

S400 50 PESOS

18xx (4.4.1891). Black on gold unpt. Liberty and Justice seated w/shield at ctr. Back brown.

GOOD	FINE	XF
—	—	—

NOTE: Some authorities believe that all notes from this bank which appear to be in issued condition are in reality fraudulently dated and signed. The same is true for any notes w/ovpt: *EMISION FISCAL* as listed in Vol. 2, #50.

BANCO DE SANTIAGO

Issued at Santiago. Founded in 1884.

1883-86 ISSUE

#S411-S417 w/vertical face and horizontal back. Printer: CABB (ABNC).

S411 1 PESO

25.2.1886. Black on brown unpt. Woman w/fasces and portr. Tocornal at upper l., cherub at upper r. Back brown; sailing ship "Esmeralda" at ctr.

	GOOD	FINE	XF
a. Issued note.	—	—	—
s. Specimen w/counterfoil.	—	Unc	500.00

NOTE: #S411 w/ovpt: *EMISION FISCAL* is listed in Vol. 2, #51.

S414 10 PESOS

20.10.1883. Black on salmon unpt. Standing woman at l. holding man's portr.; woman and children at lower r. Back green.

	GOOD	FINE	XF
a. Issued note.	—	—	—
s. Specimen w/counterfoil.	—	Unc	850.00

S415 20 PESOS

25.2.1886. Black on blue unpt. Child at ctr. Back blue.

	GOOD	FINE	XF
a. Issued note w/red ovpt: *27.7.1986* date over old date.	100.00	250.00	—
s. Specimen w/counterfoil.	—	Unc	800.00

S417 100 PESOS

ND (ca.1884). Black on green unpt. Like #S414. Back orange.

	GOOD	FINE	XF
p. Proof.	—	—	—
s. Specimen w/counterfoil.	—	Unc	950.00

BANCO DE LA SERENA

1891 ISSUE

S418 10 PESOS

189x (ca.1891). Black on green and yellow unpt. Condor w/wings spread at upper l., miners at r. Back green; allegorical woman w/farm implements at ctr. Printer: ABNC.

	GOOD	FINE	XF
p. Proof.	—	—	—
s. Specimen.	—	—	—

Notice

Readers with unlisted dates, color or signature varieties are invited to submit photocopies of their notes to: Standard Catalog of World Paper Money, Krause Publications, 700 East State St. Iola WI 54990-0001 U.S.A. or by email: thernr@krause.com. Email submissions of material for possible inclusion need to be 100% jpeg attachments at 300 dpi.

BANCO SUD-AMERICANO

Founded in 1872. Issued at Santiago.

1873 ISSUE

		Good	Fine	XF
S421	**1 PESO** 16.4.1873. Black and brown. Seated woman and shield at top ctr. Back brown; Mercury standing on globe at ctr. Printer: CNBB (NBNC).	100.00	250.00	—

NOTE: Higher denominations are reported, not confirmed.

BANCO DEL SUR

Issued at Chillán.

1870 ISSUE

#S426-S430 similar to Banco de Concepción first issue but w/different colors. Printer: ABNC.

		Good	Fine	XF
S426	**1 PESO** 18xx (ca.1870). Black on green unpt. Similar to #S166. Back orange.	—	—	—

		Good	Fine	XF
S428	**5 PESOS** 18xx (ca.1870). Black on red-orange unpt. Similar to #S168. Back green. Proof.	—	—	—
S429	**10 PESOS** 18xx (ca.1870). Black on brown unpt. Similar to #S169. Back blue.	—	—	—
S430	**20 PESOS** 18xx (ca.1870). Black on orange unpt. Similar to #S170. Proof.	—	—	—
S432	**100 PESOS** 18xx (ca.1870). Similar to #S172. Archive copy.	—	—	—

#S434 *Deleted.*

BANCO DE TALCA

Founded in 1884. Issued at Talca.

1885-88 ISSUE

#S439-S443 mountain at upper ctr. r. on face. Printer: ABNC.

		Good	Fine	XF
S439	**5 PESOS** 18xx (ca.1885). Black on blue and orange unpt. Portr. man at l., allegorical woman w/staff at r. Back blue.			
	p. Proof.	—	—	—
	s. Specimen.	—	—	—

		Good	Fine	XF
S440	**10 PESOS** 18xx (ca. 1885). Black on green and orange unpt. Man at l., village market scene at r. Back green.			
	p. Proof.	—	—	—
	s. Specimen.	—	—	—

		Good	Fine	XF
S441	**20 PESOS** 18xx (ca.1888). Black on orange and yellow-green unpt. Portr. 2 women at upper l., portr. man at lower r. Back red-brown.			
	a. Issued note.	—	—	—
	p. Proof.	—	—	—
	s. Specimen.	—	—	—

		Good	Fine	XF
S443	**100 PESOS** 18xx (ca.1885). Black on brown, blue and orange unpt. Portr. man at l., allegorical woman at r. holding scales. Back orange.			
	p. Proof.	—	—	—
	s. Specimen.	—	—	—

BANCO DE TARAPACA Y LONDRES

IQUIQUE

1891 ISSUE

		Good	Fine	XF
S447	**10 PESOS** 21.3.1891. Red-orange. Bank arms at ctr. Value vertically in blue letters on back. Printer: R. Bini, Iquique.	—	—	—

NOTE: #S447 was ovpt. for acceptance w/o endorsement at the named bank or the Banco de Valparaiso.

PISAGUA

1891 ISSUE

#S453-S455 red-orange bank arms at ctr. Off-white paper. Printer: R. Bini, Iquique.

		Good	Fine	XF
S453	**5 PESOS** 20.5.1891. Unsigned remainder.	—	—	—

		GOOD	FINE	XF
S454	**10 PESOS** 20.5.1891. Unsigned remainder.	—	—	—

		GOOD	FINE	XF
S455	**20 PESOS** 20.5.1891. Unsigned remainder.	—	—	—

BANCO DE LA UNION

Founded in 1874. Issued at Santiago.

1870'S PROVISIONAL ISSUE

		GOOD	FINE	XF
S460	**1 PESO** ND (- old date Jan. 18xx). Black and silver ovpt. new bank name on #S313. Solid black circular ovpt. at ctr. on back. Remainder.	—	—	2500.

1881 ISSUE

#S462-S467 printer: CABB (ABNC).

		GOOD	FINE	XF
S462	**2 PESOS** 18xx. Black on brown and green unpt. Boy seated w/dog at l., chickens at r. Back brown.	—	—	—

		GOOD	FINE	XF
S463	**5 PESOS** 31.7.1878. Black on blue and orange unpt. B. O'Higgins at lower l., dog's head at ctr., allegorical woman at lower r. Back brown, Specimen.			
	a. Issued note.	—	—	—
	s. Specimen.	—	—	—

		GOOD	FINE	XF
S464	**10 PESOS** 1.1.1881. Black on blue and orange unpt. B. O'Higgins at upper l., angelic trumpeter w/globe at upper ctr., anchor at lower r. Back orange.	—	—	—
S465	**20 PESOS** 18xx. Black on green and orange unpt. Girl and dog at l., 2 horses at ctr., B. O'Higgins at r. Back orange-brown. Specimen.	—	—	—

		GOOD	FINE	XF
S466	**50 PESOS** 18xx. Black on green and gold unpt. Woman w/scroll at l., B. O'Higgins at ctr., seated woman w/bale at r. Back lt. orange. Specimen.	—	—	—

		GOOD	FINE	XF
S467	**100 PESOS** 18xx. Black on green and red unpt. Seated allegorical woman in tropical garden at ctr. Back blue. Specimen.	—	—	—

BANCO DE VALPARAISO

Founded in 1855. In 1894 it became part of the Banco de Chile. Several regular issues and one locally printed issue were made by this bank.

1870 ISSUE

		GOOD	FINE	XF
S477	**1 PESO** 18xx. Black. Like #S478. Proof.	—	Unc	400.00

		GOOD	FINE	XF
S478	**5 PESOS** 1.4.1870. Blue. National arms at top ctr.	—	Rare	—

1876-77 ISSUE

#S486-S488 Mercury standing on globe on back. Printer: CNBB (NBNC).

		GOOD	FINE	XF
S486	**1 PESO** 3.1.1876. Black and orange. Bank at upper ctr. Back green.	85.00	300.00	—

		GOOD	FINE	XF
S487	**2 PESOS** 3.1.1876. Black and blue. Bldg. at upper ctr. Back blue.	90.00	350.00	—

		GOOD	FINE	XF
S488	**5 PESOS** 3.1.1876. Black and green. Girl seated w/sheep, coastline at l., steam passenger train at r. in background at top ctr. Back green.	—	—	—

#S489-S491 printer: ABNC.

		GOOD	FINE	XF
S489	**10 PESOS** 2.7.1877. Black on green unpt. Dog's head at upper l., allegorical woman at l. and r. of shield at ctr. r. Back black on green unpt; 2 allegorical figures at ctr.			
	p. Proof.	—	—	—
	s. Specimen.	—	—	—
S490	**20 PESOS** 2.7.1877. Black on salmon and green unpt. Design like #S489. Back black on orange unpt. Archive copy.	—	—	—

		GOOD	FINE	XF
S491	**50 PESOS** 2.7.1877. Black on blue and orange unpt. Allegorical woman w/shield and eagle at ctr. Back black on blue-green unpt; allegorical woman w/bird at ctr. Proof.	—	—	—

		GOOD	FINE	XF
S492	**100 PESOS** 2.7.1877. Black on green and orange unpt. Seated allegorical woman, cherubs and Chilean arms at ctr., portr. woman w/tiara at r. Back black and green; Liberty standing at ctr. Specimen.	—	—	—

1881 ISSUE

		GOOD	FINE	XF
S498	**5 PESOS** 8.1.1881. Black on blue and orange unpt. Woman holding faces w/child at l.,2 young cherubs at top ctr., 2 cherubs w/shield at lower r. Back blue; farmers working at ctr.	—	—	—

1891 ISSUES

Local printings.

Issued at Pisagua.

#S511 and S512 printer: R. Bini, Iquique.

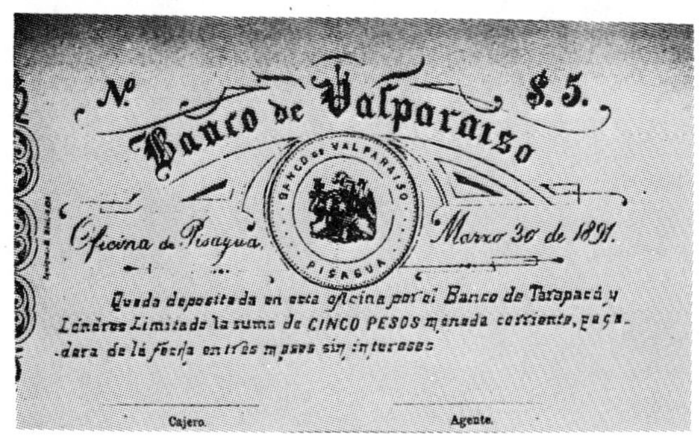

		GOOD	FINE	XF
S511	**5 PESOS** 30.3.1891; 15.5.1891. Blue. Circular bank arms at ctr. Uniface.	—	—	—

		GOOD	FINE	XF
S512	**5 PESOS** 1.7.1891. Black. Different oval arms at ctr. Uniface.	—	—	—

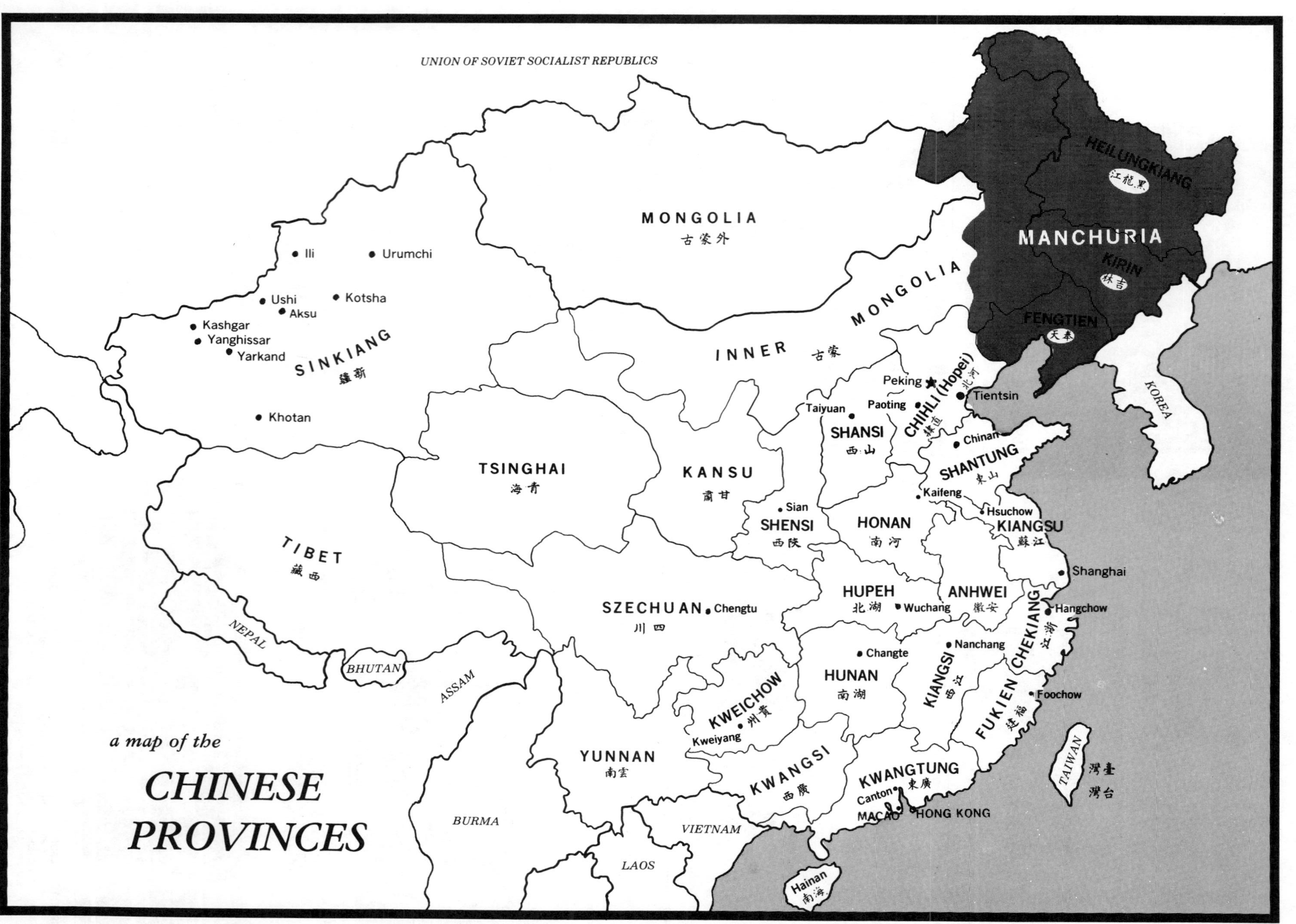
UNION OF SOVIET SOCIALIST REPUBLICS
MONGOLIA
古蒙外
MANCHURIA
HEILUNGKIANG
KIRIN
FENGTIEN
KOREA
INNER MONGOLIA
古蒙
SINKIANG
Ili
Urumchi
Ushi
Kotsha
Aksu
Kashgar
Yanghissar
Yarkand
Khotan
TSINGHAI
海青
KANSU
TIBET
藏西
CHIHLI (Hopei)
Peking
Tientsin
Paoting
Taiyuan
SHANSI
西山
Chinan
SHANTUNG
東山
Kaifeng
Sian
SHENSI
Hsuchow
KIANGSU
HONAN
南河
Shanghai
HUPEH
北湖
Wuchang
ANHWEI
Hangchow
CHEKIANG
SZECHUAN
Chengtu
川四
NEPAL
BHUTAN
ASSAM
Changte
Nanchang
HUNAN
南湖
KIANGSI
KWEICHOW
Kweiyang
FUKIEN
Foochow
TAIWAN
YUNNAN
KWANGSI
KWANGTUNG
Canton
MACAO
HONG KONG
BURMA
VIETNAM
LAOS
Hainan
a map of the
CHINESE
PROVINCES

CHINA (Chung Kuo) 中國

China's ancient civilization began in the Huang Ho basin about 1500 BC. The warring feudal states comprising early China were first united under Emperor Ch'in Shih Huang Ti (246-210 BC) who gave China its name and first central government. Subsequent dynasties alternated brilliant cultural achievements with internal disorder until the Empire was brought down by the revolution of 1911, and the Republic of China installed in its place. Chinese culture attained a pre-eminence in art, literature and philosophy, but a traditional backwardness in industry and administration ill prepared China for the demands of 19th century Western expansionism which exposed it to military and political humiliations, and mandated a drastic revision of political practice in order to secure an accommodation with the modern world.

The Republic of 1911 barely survived the stress of World War I, and was subsequently all but shattered by the rise of nationalism and the emergence of the Chinese Communist movement. Moscow, which practiced a policy of cooperation between Communists and other parties in movements for national liberation, sought to establish an entente between the Chinese Communist Party and the Kuomintang (National People's Party) of Sun Yat-sen. The ensuing cooperation was based on little more than the hope each had of using the other.

An increasingly uneasy association between the Kuomintang and the Chinese Communist Party developed and continued until April 12, 1927, when Chiang Kai-shek, Sun Yat-sen's political heir, instituted a bloody purge to stamp out the Communists within the Kuomintang and the government and virtually paralyzed their ranks throughout China. Some time after the mid-1927 purges, the Chinese Communist Party turned to armed force to resist Chiang Kai-shek and during the period of 1930-34 acquired control over large parts of Kiangsi, Fukien, Hunan and Hupeh. The Nationalist Nanking government responded with a series of campaigns against the Soviet power bases and, by October 1934, succeeded in driving the remnants of the Communist army to a refuge in Shensi Province.

Subsequently, the Communists under the leadership of Mao Tse-tung defeated the Nationalists and on September 21, 1949 formally established the Peoples Republic.

EMPERORS:

TE TSUNG 德宗

Reign title: Kuang Hsu 光緒 1875-1908, Years 1-34

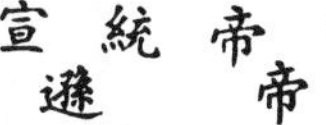

HSUAN T'UNG TI

(Hsun Ti)

Reign title: Hsuan T'ung 宣統 1908-1911

YUAN SHIH-KAI

Proposed reign title: Hung Hsien 憲洪 Dec. 15, 1915-March 21, 1916.

MONETARY SYSTEM:

Cash Coin System
1 Tael = 800-1600 Cash*

***NOTE: In theory, 1000 cash were equal to a tael of silver, but in actuality the rate varied from time to time and from place to place.**

Dollar System

1 Cent (fen, hsien) = 10 Cash (wen)
1 Chiao (hao) = 10 Cents
1 Dollar (yuan) = 100 Cents

Tael System

1 Fen (candareen) = 10 Li
1 Ch'ien (mace) = 10 Fen
1 Liang (tael) = 10 Ch'ien (mace)

MONETARY UNITS:

The dating and following charts have been adapted from *Chinese Banknotes* by Ward Smith and Brian Matravers. Calligraphy in special instances by Marian C. Smith.

Dollar Amounts		
Dollar *(Yuan)*	元 or 員	圓 or 圜
Half Dollar *(Pan Yuan)*	圓 半	
50¢ *(Chiao/Hao)*	角伍	毫伍
10¢ *(Chiao/Hao)*	角壹	毫壹
1¢ *(Fen/Hsien)*	分壹	仙壹

Copper and Cash Coin Amounts			
Copper *(Mei)*	枚	String *(Tiao)*	吊
Cash *(Wen)*	文	String *(Tiao)*	弔
String *(Kuan)*	貫	String *(Ch'uan)*	串

Tael Amounts	
Tael *(Liang)*	兩
Half Tael *(Pan Liang)*	兩半
5 Mace *(Wu Ch'ien)*	錢伍
1 Mace *(1 Ch'ien)*	錢壹
Ku Ping *(Tael)**	平庫

Common Prefixes			
Copper *(T'ung)*	銅	"Small money"	洋 小
Silver *(Yin)*	銀	"Big money"	洋 大
Gold *(Chin)*	金	"Big money"	洋 英

ARRANGEMENT

FOREIGN BANK ISSUES .... #S97-S757

The foreign bank issues are listed in a normal alphabetic listing of note issuing authority. The notes usually bear the Chinese text on one side and the respective English, Russian, or other foreign text on the opposite side.

This includes a full listing of the foreign note issuers complete with romanizations of and including the Chinese text as found on the notes. If a particular bank changed its name through the years, the successive note issues will be found listed under the new bank name.

The branch office overprints are mentioned under each each bank's entry and are illustrated throughout the listings as the bank office changes.

PROVINCIAL BANK ISSUES .... #S802-S3041

The Provincial Bank issues are listed alphabetically, using romanizations of the principal issuer's name in Chinese and, in addition, the various English names known to have been used for note issues.

COMMUNIST BANK ISSUES .... #S3050-S3781

The Communist Bank issues are listed alphabetically, using romanizations of the principal issuer's name in Chinese and, in addition, the various English names known to have been used for note issues.

MILITARY ISSUES...................................... #S3791-S3960

The Military issues are listed alphabetically, using romanizations of the principal issuer's name in Chinese and, in addition, the various English names known to have been used for note issues.

NUMERICAL CHARACTERS

NUMERALS

NUMBER	CONVENTIONAL		FORMAL		COMMERCIAL
1	一 正	元	壹	弌	〡
2	二		弍	貳	〢
3	三		叁	弎	〣
4	四		肆		〤
5	五		伍		〥
6	六		陸		〦
7	七		柒		〧
8	八		捌		〨
9	九		玖		〩
10	十		拾	什	十
20	十 二 or 廿		拾貳	念	〢十
25	五 十 二 or 五廿		伍拾貳		〢十〥
30	十 三 or 卅		拾叁		〣十
100	百 一		佰壹		〡百
1,000	千 一		仟壹		〡千
10,000	萬 一		萬壹		〡万
100,000	萬 十	億 一 (old)	萬拾	億壹	十万
1,000,000	萬百一	億 一 (new)	萬佰壹		〡百万

DATING:

Prior to the Republican era, Chinese notes were usually dated in reference to the year of reign of the current emperor. To arrive at the corresponding AD date, subtract one year from the year *(nien)* and add this number to the emperor's accession year.

YEARS OF THE REPUBLIC

Years of the Republic

Year		AD	Year		AD	Year		AD	Year		AD
1	一	- 1912	11	一十	- 1922	21	一十二	- 1932	31	一十三	- 1942
2	二	- 1913	12	二十	- 1923	21	二十二	- 1933	32	二十三	- 1943
3	三	- 1914	13	三十	- 1924	23	三十二	- 1934	33	三十三	- 1944
4	四	- 1915	14	四十	- 1925	24	四十二	- 1935	34	四十三	- 1945
5	五	- 1916	15	五十	- 1926	25	五十二	- 1936	35	五十三	- 1946
6	六	- 1917	16	六十	- 1927	26	六十二	- 1927	36	六十三	- 1947
7	七	- 1918	17	七十	- 1928	27	七十二	- 1938	37	七十三	- 1948
8	八	- 1919	18	八十	- 1929	28	八十二	- 1939	38	八十三	- 1949
9	九	- 1920	19	九十	- 1930	29	九十二	- 1940	39	九十三	- 1950
10	十	- 1921	20	十二	- 1931	30	十三	- 1941	40	十四	- 1951

NOTE: Chinese dates are normally read from right to left, except for the modern issues of the People's Republic of China from 1953 where the Western date is read from left to right.

CYCLICAL DATING:

Another method of dating is a 60-year, repeating cycle, outlined in the table below. The date is shown by the combination of two characters, the first of the top row and the second from the column at left. In this catalog, when a cyclical date is used, the abbreviation CD appears before the AD date.

This chart has been adapted from *Chinese Banknotes* by Ward Smith and Brian Matravers. Calligraphy by Marian C. Smith.

	庚	辛	壬	癸	甲	乙	丙	丁	戊	己
戌	1850 1910		1862 1922		1874 1934		1886 1946		1838 1898	
亥		1851 1911		1863 1923		1875 1935		1887 1947		1839 1899
子	1840 1900		1852 1912		1864 1924		1876 1936		1888 1948	
丑		1841 1901		1853 1913		1865 1925		1877 1937		1889 1949
寅	1830 1890		1842 1902		1854 1914		1866 1926		1878 1938	
卯		1831 1891		1843 1903		1855 1915		1867 1927		1879 1939
辰	1880 1940		1832 1892		1844 1904		1856 1916		1868 1928	
巳		1881 1941		1833 1893		1845 1905		1857 1917		1869 1929
午	1870 1930		1882 1942		1834 1894		1846 1906		1858 1918	
未		1871 1931		1883 1943		1835 1895		1847 1907		1859 1919
申	1860 1920		1872 1932		1884 1944		1836 1896		1848 1908	
酉		1861 1921		1873 1933		1885 1945		1837 1897		1849 1909

PORTRAIT ABBREVIATIONS:

SYS = Sun Yat-sen, 1867-1925
President of Canton Government
1917-25

CKS = Chiang Kai-shek, 1886-1975
President in Nanking, 1927-31
Head of Formosa Government, 1949-75

NOTE: Because of the frequency of the above appearing in listings of Chinese notes their initials are used only in reference to their portraits.

PRINTERS ABBREVIATIONS

ABNC - American Bank Note Co. .... 鈔美
BEPK - Bureau of Engraving & Printing, Yung Heng, Kirin .... 部政財
BEPP - Bureau of Engraving & Printing .... 書印衡永
BWC - Bradbury, Wilkinson & Co. .... Not used
CCLA - Ch'ing Lien, Changsha .... 蓮青
CEPA - China Engraving & Printing .... 版凹華中
CHBA - Chung Hua Book Co. .... 局書華中
CHCC - Ch'ien Chen Chi, Sian .... 集振乾
CHCP - Chao Hsiang Color .... 刷色祥兆
CMPA - Commercial Press .... 務商
CNPC - Ch'u Nan Printing Co. .... 南楚
CPFA - Central Printing Factory .... 廠製印央中
CPFT - Central Printing Factory, Taipei .... 北台
CPOF - Changsha Printing Office .... 刷印沙長
DOFS - Dept. of Finance, Sinkiang .... 廳政財
FRBC - First Republican Book .... 一第國民
HHEC - Hsin Hua, Hong Kong .... 華新
HKCL - Hsingkuo Co., Ltd. .... 國興
HKPA - Hong Kong Printing Press .... 字印港香
HODP - Hunan Official Document .... 紙官南湖
HSPS - Hsieh Shun, Shanghai .... 順協
HWPO - Han Wen, Shanghai .... 文漢
ILBC - I Lin Book, Sian .... 林藝
IPCL - International Printing Co., Ltd. .... 文蘇
IYPC - I Yang, Changsha .... 陽宜
JIPB - Japan Govt. Printing .... 局刷印(府政)
MLTA - Mo Lin T'ang, Pinkiang .... 堂林墨
NWE&PF - Northwest Engraving & Printing Factory .... 北西
PHCF - Pai Hua Chou Feng, Nanking .... 豐州花百
PYOG - Peiyang Official Gazette .... 報官洋北
PYPO - Peiyang Printing Office .... 刷印洋北
SASO - Shensi Army Service Office .... 軍陸西陜
SHPC - Shanghai Printing Co. .... 刷印海上
SOPO - Shantung Official .... 刷印官東山
STPO - Shantung Printing Office .... 刷印東山
TCPL - Tung Chi, Liaoning .... 記東
TTBC - Ta Tung (Dah Tung) Printing (Several branch plants) .... 局書東大
TWCC - Ts'ai Wen, Tsitsihar .... 文杉
TYPC - Ta Yeh (Dah Yip) Co. (Several branches) .... 司公業大
WHPP - Wu Han Book Co. .... 書印漢武
W&S - Waterlow & Sons, Ltd. .... 路德華國英
WTBC - Wen T'ung Book, Kiukiang .... 通文
YHBA - Yung Heng Book Co. .... 書印衡永
YMSO - Yunnan Military Supply .... 雷軍南雲
YOPO - Yunnan Official Printing .... 印官南雲
YSCL - Yue Sheng & Co., Ltd. .... 興裕

PLACE NAMES

The following list is designed for users unfamiliar with written Chinese who wish to check place names appearing on notes, usually as overprints. For this reason, the arrangement is based on the number of strokes in the first character, normally found at the right or top. This is a selected list. Some obscure locations have been omitted.

English names are a mixture of popular names or variants thereon, which appear on notes, and Wade-Giles romanizations for places which lack well established English names.

Chinese place names tend to be simple descriptive terms relating to a geographical feature, e.g., "north of the lake" (Hupei), "southern capital" (Nanking) or "on the sea" (Shanghai). Most provincial names show this characteristic. In the latter case, many are paired, which has the disadvantage to the western eye and ear of making them look and sound much the same. Hunan-Hupei, Honan-Hopei, Kwangtung-Kwangsi, Kiangsu-Kiangsi (plus Kiangnan on older notes) and Shantung-Shansi are not difficult to confuse. The most serious problem, however, is Shansi-Shensi. Here, the last characters are the same rather than the first but the first characters, if pronounced correctly, differ only in tone. Even the meanings are close, Shansi, literally, is "mountains west," while Shensi is "mountain passes west," although the first character in this instance is not often used in this meaning. The difference in English spelling is generally accepted convention. Chinese find no difficulty in keeping the two separated because the tonal difference is sufficient in the spoken language and written forms for the first characters are totally dissimilar.

Westerners who might be tempted to consider these or other problems in terminology as resulting from mysterious oriental mental processes should first appraise their own place names, which are rarely as logical or as simple. Inconsistent spellings of place names in romanization too, are primarily western rather than Chinese errors. If confusion does arise, the reasons are complex, and, in any event, no satisfactory solution has yet been found.

Kiukiang, Kiangsi	江九
Pa Pu, Kwangsi	步八
Szechuan (alt)	川
Ch'uan Sha, Kiangsi	沙川
Ch'uan K'ang, Szechuan	康川
Shansi	西山
Shantung	東山
Shanhaikuan Chihli/Hopei	關海山
Shanghai, Kiangsu	海上
Shang Jao, Kiangsi	饒上
Ta T'ung Shansi	同大
Ta Cheng Chihli/Hopei	城大
Ta Ch'en Fukien	陳大
Dairen, Liaoning	連大
Honan (alt)	州中
China (alt)	華中
China	國中
Newchwang Liaoning	莊牛
Niu T'ou Chihli/Hopei	頭牛
T'ai Ku Shansi	谷太
T'ai Yuan, Shansi	原太
Tientsin, Chihli/Hopei	津天
Wen An, Chihli/Hope	安文
Wu Ch'ang, Kirin	常五
Cheng yang, Honan	陽正
Tibet	藏西
Hsien Yu, Fukien	遊仙
Kansu	肅甘
Paotow, Suiyuan	頭包
Peiping, Chihli/Hopei	平北
Peking, Chihli/Hopei	京北
Pakhoi, Kwangtung	海北
Shih I, Chihli/Hopei	邑石
Shihkiachwang, Chihli/Hopei	莊家石
Szechuan	川四
T'ai T'ou Chihli/Hopei	頭台
Taiwan (alt)	灣台
Yung Ch'ing, Chihli/Hopei	清永
Yung Ning, Chihli/Hopei	寧永
Anhwei	徽安
Chengtu, Szechuan	都成
Kirin	林吉
Chi Hsien, Chihli/Hopei	縣吉
Kiangsi	西江
Kiangnan	南江
Kiangsu	蘇江
Sian, Shensi	安西
Sikang	康西
Ili, Sinkiang	犂伊
Swatow, Kwangtung	頭汕
Tulunnoerh, Chahar	倫多
Ch'ih Feng, Jehol	峯赤
Hsin Tien, Chihli/Hopei	店辛
Li Chia K'ou, Kwangsi	口家李
Sha P'ing, Shansi	坪沙
Kiangsu (al (literary)	吳
Changsha, Hunan	沙長
Changchun, Kirin	春長
Ch'ang Cheng (Great Wall)	城長
Ch'ang Li, Chihli/Hopei	黎昌
Chihli	隸直
Quemoy (Kinmen) Fukien	門金
Peking/Peiping, Chihli/Hopei	京北
Tsingtao, Shantung	島青
Chinghai (or Tsinghai)	海青
Fengtien	天奉
Feng Hsin, Kiangsi	新奉
Fou Cheng, Chihli/Hopei	城阜
Hangchow, Chekiang	州杭
Hopei	北河
Honan	南河
Ho Chien, Chihli/Hopei	間河
Hulun, Heilungkiang	倫呼
Kunming, Yunnan	明昆
Manchuria	省三東
Manchuria (alt.)	九北東
Wu Ning, Szechuan	寧武
Wu Han, Hupei	漢武
Yenan Shensi	安延
Chekiang	江浙
Chien Ch'ang, Kiangsi	昌建
Chien Yang, Kiangsu	陽建
Chungking, Szechuan	慶重
Harbin, Heilungkiang	賓爾哈
Hsin An, Chihli/Hopei	安信
Kuling, Kiangsi	嶺牯
Liuchow, Kwangsi	州柳
Nan Chiang, Szechuan	江南
Nanchang, Kiangsi	昌南
Nanking, Kiangsu	京南
Nan Kuan Chen, Chihli/Hopei	鎮關南
Nan Hsiung, Kwangtung	雄南
Nanning, Kwangsi	(甯)寧南
Paoting, Chihli/Hopei	定保
T'ai An, Shantung	安泰
Tihua, Sinkiang	化廸
Weihaiwei, Shantung	衛海威
Shansi (literary)	(晉)晋
Chin Tz'u Shansi	祠晋
Shensi (Literary)	秦
Chinwangtao, Shantung	島皇秦
Haikow Kwangtung	口海
Hailar, Heilungkiang	爾拉海
Hainan, Kwangtung	南海
Hong Kong	港香
Hsuchow, Kiangsu	州徐
Kwangsi (literary)	桂
Kweilin, Kwangsi	林桂
Urga, Mongolia	倫庫
Matsu, Fukien	祖馬
Ma T'ou Chen Shantung	鎮頭馬
Hupei (literary)	鄂
P'u T'ien Fukien	田莆
Shensi	西陝
Tongshan, Chihli/Hopei	山唐
T'ao Yuan Hunan	源桃
Chefoo, Shantung	台烟
Kalgan, Chihli/Hopei	口家張
Ch'ang Te, Hunan	德常
Tsingkiangpu, Kiangsu	浦江清
Ch'ung Ming, Kiangsu	明崇
Huai Hai, Kiangsu	海淮
Kuo Hsien, Shansi	縣崞
Liao Cheng, Shantung	城聊
Pi'ng Hsien, Kiangsi	縣萍
Pukow, Kiangsu	口浦
Mukden, Liaoning	京盛
Su Hsien, Anhwei	縣宿
Ts'ao Ts'un, Shantung	村曹
T'ung Cheng, Hopei	城通
Wuchow, Kwangsi	州梧
Yeh Hsien, Shantung	縣掖
Chi Ning, Chahar	寧集
Chingtechen, Kiangsi	鎮德景
Hei Ho, Heilungkiang	河黑
Heilungkiang	江龍黑
Hunan (literary)	湘
Hupei	北湖
Hunan	南湖
Anhwei (literary)	皖
Kaifeng, Honan	封開
Kweichow	州貴
Kweiyang, Kwangsi	陽貴
Lung Ch'ang Szechuan	昌隆
Ningpo, Chekiang	波甯
Sheng Fang Chihli/Hopei	芳勝
Wusih, Kiangsu	錫無
Yu Tz'u, Shansi	次榆
Kwangtung/ Kwangsi (lit)	粵
Yunnan	南雲
Fu An, Fukien	安福
Foochow, Fukien	州福
Fu I, Fukien	邑福
Fukien	建福
Fu Ch'ing, Fukien	清福
Amoy, Fukien	門厦
Sinkiang	疆新
Jui Ch'ang Kiangsi	昌瑞
Fukien (literary)	閩
P'eng Lai, Shantung	萊蓬
Po Hai, Chihli/Hopei	海渤
Suiyuan	遠綏
Tan Hsien, Shantung	縣單
Yangchow, Kiangsu	州揚
Chefoo (alt) Shantung	台煙
Chahar	爾哈察
Chao Hsien, Chihli/Hopei	縣趙
Chia Ting, Kiangsu	定嘉
Hankow, Hupei	口漢
Ningpo (alt) Chekiang	波寧
Ninghsia	夏寧
Pinkiang, Heilungkiang	江賓
Shou Kuang, Shantung	光壽
Tainan, Taiwan	南臺
Taiwan (alt)	灣臺
Yunnan	滇
Chengchow, Honan	州鄭
Jehol	河熱
Kuang An Chen Chihli/Hopei	鎮安廣
Kwangsi	西廣
Canton, Kwangtung	州廣
Kwangtung	東廣
Manchukuo	國洲滿
Manchouli, Heilungkiang	里洲滿
Shantung (literary)	魯
Hopei (literary)	冀
Kweichow (literary)	黔
Chui Tzu Shan, Jehol	山字錐
Liaoning (al	東遼
Liaoning	寧遼
Lungkow, Shantung	口龍
Lungchow, Kwangsi	州龍
Mongolia	古蒙
Meng Chiang (Mongolia)	疆蒙
Honan (literary)	豫
Macao	門澳
Chinan (Tsinan) Shantung	南濟
Yingkow, Liaoning	口營
Chenkiang, Kiangsu	江鎮
Fengchen, Suiyuan	鎮豐
Li Chiang Chihli/Hopei	港鯉
Kuantung, Liaoning	東關
Lanchow, Kansu	州蘭
Kansu (literary)	隴
Kiangsu (literary)	蘇
Soochow, Kiangsu	州蘇
Su Ch'ao Chen Honan	鎮橋蘇
Hsien Hsien Chihli/Hopei	縣獻
Lu Hsien Szechuan	縣瀘
Pa Hsien Chihli / Hopei	縣霸
Li Hsien Chihli / Hopei	縣蠡
Kiangsi (literary)	贛
Watlam, Kwangsi	林鬱
Yungtsun	遵永

The above chart listings are taken from "CHINESE BANKNOTES" by Ward D. Smith and Brian Matravers (published 1970).

FOREIGN BANKS

With the passage of the Age of Discovery it became apparent that the products of the East were very desirable in Europe. The British in India, the Dutch and Portuguese in the East Indies were the leaders in developing the trade of the area.

With the Portuguese settlement at Macao in 1557 the potential for developing the China trade came closer to reality. Because of the isolationist policy of the reigning dynasty in China it was to be many years before the European powers could gain a viable foothold for trade in China. The product that was to provide the opportunity for further exploitation was to be opium. The British developed a very lucrative trade in opium from India into China sponsored by the East India Co. Opium was illegal inside China but was brough in through smuggling and official connivance.

The Treaty of Nanking, signed August 29, 1842, was to open the China trade by having as one of its terms the opening of the ports of Amoy, Canton, Foochow, Ningpo and Shanghai to foreign trade and residence. The Treaty Ports, as these were called, were the stepping stones upon which general trade was developed. By 1911 there were 50 ports opened for trade in China.

With the development of Western trade in China it was thought necessary by the traders to establish Western banking. The first Western bank in China was a branch of the Commercial Bank of India in Canton in 1851 and later in Shanghai in 1855.

The ceding of Hong Kong to Great Britain in 1842 also provided a base for European banking practices. The Bank of Western India established a branch there in 1842.

Various banks of British background dominated the banking scene in China for most of the 50 years following the treaty of Nanking. Then came a German bank in 1889, a Russian bank in 1895, a Japanese bank in 1898, a U.S. bank in 1902, a French bank in 1902, a Belgian bank in 1903 and a Dutch bank in 1904. All of these banks were note issuers at one or more branches. The notes were issued to encourage doing business with that bank in the area represented. The banknotes circulated in direct competition with the regular Chinese issues of the period.

The foreign banks also provided loans for the Chinese government (both for the empire and later for the new republic). Many of these loans were very substantial amounts and required more than one of the foreign banks to accommodate the amount.

The notes of the foreign banks circulated until World War II and a number of these banks still maintain offices in Hong Kong.

American Oriental Banking Corporation
(American Oriental Bank of Shanghai)
#S97-S103

行銀豐美海上
Shang Hai Mei Feng Yin Hang

(American Oriental Bank of Tientsin)
#S105

行銀豐美津天
T'ien Ching Mei Feng Yin Hang

American Oriental Bank of Fukien
#S106-S109

行銀豐美建福
Fu Chien Mei Feng Yin Hang

American Oriental Bank of Szechuen
#S110-S110B

行銀豐美川四
Szu Ch'uan Mei Feng Yin Hang

Asia Banking Corporation
#S113-S117

行銀華友國美
Mei Kuo Yu Hua Yin Hang

Asiatic Banking Corporation
#S117A-S117B

行銀彰利海上
Shang Hai Li Chang Yin Hang

Asiatic Commercial Bank, Ltd.
#S118-S120

行銀華美
Mei Hua Yin Hang

Banque Belge Pour L'Etranger
#S123-S149

行銀比華
Hua Pi Yin Hang

British and Belgian Industrial Bank of China
#S150-S151

英行比實業銀
Ying Pi Shih Yeh Yin Hang

Bank of Canton, Ltd. (Eng)
#S152-S153N

司公限有行銀東廣
Kuang Tung Yin Hang Yu Hsien Kung Szu

Chartered Bank of India, Australia & China
#S154-S222

行銀理滙國中山金新度印
Yin Tu Hsin Chin Shan Chung Kuo Hui Li Yin Hang

行銀利加麥國中山金新度印
Yin Tu Hsin Chin Shan Chung Kuo Mai Chia Li Yin Hang

Chartered Mercantile Bank of India, London & China
#S223-S225C

行銀利有海上
Shang Hai Yu Li Yin Hang

China Specie Bank, Ltd.
#S228-S228D

行銀寶國華中
Chung Hua Kuo Pao Yin Hang

Chinese-American Bank of Commerce
#S230-S245

行銀業懋華中
Chung Hua Mou Yeh Yin Hang

Chinese Engineering & Mining Company Limited
#S246-S247A

司公限有務礦平開
K'ai P'ing K'uang Wu Yu Hsien Kung Szu

Chinese Italian Banking Corporation
#S248-S257

行銀義震
Chen I Yin Hang

Comptoir D' Escompte de Paris
#S257B

Not Available
Shang Hai Fa Lan Hsi Yin Hang

Credit Commercial Sino-Francaise
#S258-S260

行銀業振法中
Chung Fa Chen Yeh Yin Hang

Deutsch-Asiatische Bank
#S261-S303

行銀華德
Te Hua Yin Hang

Bank of East Asia Ltd.
#S303A-S303E

行銀亞東
Tung Ya Yin Hang

Exchange Bank of China
#S303J-S310

行銀業匯華中
Chung Hua Hui Yeh Yin Hang

Hong Kong & Shanghai Banking Corporation
Hong Kong & Shanghai Banking Company, Limited
#S311-S383

豐滙海上港香商英
Hsiang K'ang Shang Hai Hui Li Yin Hang

Industrial and Commercial Bank Ltd.
#S383A-S383I

行銀商工
Kung Shang Yin Hang

Banque Industrielle de Chine
#S384-S400

行銀業實法中
Chung Fa Shih Yeh Yin Hang

International Banking Corporation
#S401-S434

行銀旗花商美
Mei Shang Hua Ch'i Yin Hang

Banque de L'Indochine
#S436-S438

行銀理滙方東
Tung Fang Hui Li Yin Hang

Mercantile Bank of India Limited
#S441-S446

行銀利有
Yu Li Yin Hang

National Bank of China Limited
#S446B

行銀 理 滙華中港香
Hsiang K'ang Chung Hua Hui Li Yin Hang

National Commercial and Savings Bank, Ltd.
#S447-S456

行銀蓄儲業商民國港香
Hsiang K'ang Kuo Min Shang Yeh Ch'u Hsu Yin Hang

Netherlands Trading Society
#S457-S461

行銀囒和海上
Shang Hai Ho Lan Yin Hang

Oriental Bank Corporation
#S463-S463D

行銀理滙藩東
Tung Fan Hui Lu Yin Hang

Russo-Asiatic Bank, 1910-26
(РУССКО-АЗIАТСКI(БАНКЪ)
#S465-S502

行銀勝道商俄
O Shang Tao Sheng Yin Hang

Russo-Chinese Bank, 1895-10
(Banque Russo-Chinoise, РУССКО- КИТАЙСКIЙ БАНКЪ)
#S503-S554

行銀勝道俄華
Hua O Tao Sheng Yin Hang

Sino-Belgian Bank, 1902-20
(Banque Sino-Belge)
#S555-S574

行銀比華
Hua Pi Yin Hang

Sino-Scandinavian Bank
#S581-S600

行銀威華
Hua Wei Yin Hang

Bank of Taiwan
Bank of Taiwan, Limited
#S601-S634

行銀灣臺
T'ai Wan Yin Hang

Yokohama Specie Bank, Limited
#S635-S757

行銀金正濱橫
Heng Pin Cheng Chin Yin Hang

FOREIGN BANKS

AMERICAN ORIENTAL BANKING CORPORATION
AMERICAN ORIENTAL BANK OF SHANGHAI

行銀豐美海上 *Shang Hai Mei Feng Yin Hang*

Opened 1921. Most notes redeemed.

SHANGHAI BRANCH

1919 ISSUE

#S97-S100 ship, pagoda in background in circle at ctr. Printer: ABNC.

S97	**5 DOLLARS** 16.9.1919. DK. green on blue and m/c unpt. Specimen. *(S/M #S53-0.3).*	—	Unc	650.00
S98	**10 DOLLARS** 16.9.1919. Dk. blue on brown and m/c unpt. Specimen. *(S/M #S53-0.3).*	—	Unc	850.00

S100	**100 DOLLARS** 16.9.1919. Dk. brown on green and m/c unpt. Freighter, tug w/barge, sailboats and ferry in harbor on back. Specimen. *(S/M #S53-0.5).*	—	Unc	1850.

1924 ISSUE

#S101-S103 ship, pagoda in background in circle at ctr. Printer: ABNC.

		GOOD	FINE	XF
S101	**1 DOLLAR** 1924. *(S/M #S53-1).*	50.00	175.00	500.00
S102	**5 DOLLARS** 1924. *(S/M #S53-2).*			
	a. Issued note.	200.00	—	—
	p. Proof.	—	Unc	350.00
	s. Specimen.	—	Unc	500.00
S103	**10 DOLLARS** 1924. *(S/M #S53-4).*	Reported Not Confirmed		

AMERICAN ORIENTAL BANK OF TIENTSIN

行銀豐美津天 *T'ien Ching Mei Feng Yin Hang*

TIENTSIN BRANCH

1924 ISSUE

		GOOD	FINE	XF
S105	**5 DOLLARS** 16.9.1924. Black on m/c unpt. Back orange. Printer: ABNC. *(S/M #T127-).*			
	a. Issued note.	—	—	—
	p. Proof.	—	Unc	450.00
	s. Specimen.	—	Unc	600.00

AMERICAN ORIENTAL BANK OF FUKIEN

行銀豐美建福 *Fu Chien Mei Feng Yin Hang*

Opened 1922. Most notes redeemed.

FOOCHOW BRANCH 州福

1922 DAI FOOK ISSUE

		GOOD	FINE	XF
S106	**1 DOLLAR** 16.9.1922. Blue. *(S/M #F26-12).*	—	—	—
S106A	**5 DOLLARS** 16.9.1922. Blue. *(S/M #F26-12).*	—	—	—
S106B	**10 DOLLARS** 16.9.1922. Olive-green. Hand stamped: *SAMPLE. (S/M #F26-13).*	—	—	—

1922 ISSUE

#S107-S109 ship, pagoda in background in circle at ctr. Printer: ABNC.

		GOOD	FINE	XF
S107	**1 DOLLAR** 16.9.1922. Green on m/c unpt. *(S/M #F26-1).*			
	a. Issued note.	10.00	50.00	125.00
	p. Proof.	—	Unc	200.00
	s. Specimen.	—	Unc	300.00
S108	**5 DOLLARS** 16.9.1922. Brown on m/c unpt. *(S/M #F26-2).*	150.00	325.00	475.00

		GOOD	FINE	XF
S109	**10 DOLLARS** 6.9.1922. Brown on m/c unpt. *(S/M #F26-3).*			
	a. Issued note.	175.00	350.00	650.00
	p. Proof.	—	Unc	300.00
	s. Specimen.	—	Unc	550.00

AMERICAN ORIENTAL BANK OF SZECHUEN

行銀豐美川四
Szu Ch'uan Mei Feng Yin Hang

Opened in 1922. Later in 1932 it became the Mei Feng Bank.

CHUNGKING BRANCH 慶重

1922 ISSUE

#S110-S110B ship, pagoda in background in circle at ctr. Printer: ABNC.

		GOOD	FINE	XF
S110	**1 DOLLAR**			
	16.9.1922. Blue and gray on m/c unpt. Back brown. *(S/M #S101-1).*			
	a. Issued note.	150.00	375.00	—
	p. Proof.	—	Unc	250.00
	s. Specimen.	—	Unc	450.00
S110A	**5 DOLLARS**			
	16.9.1922. *(S/M #S101-2).*	200.00	400.00	—
S110B	**10 DOLLARS**			
	16.9.1922. Blue on m/c unpt. Back orange. *(S/M #S101-3).*			
	a. Issued note.	—	—	—
	p. Proof.	—	Unc	350.00
	s. Specimen.	—	Unc	450.00

ASIA BANKING CORPORATION

行銀華友國美

Mei Kuo Yu Hua Yin Hang

A subsidiary of the Guarantee Trust Co. of New York, which was organized in 1918. Absorbed by International Banking Corp., 1924.

NOTE-ISSUING BRANCHES:

Changsha, Hankow, Peking, Shanghai, Tientsin

1918 ISSUE

#S111-S116 camel caravan along Great Wall at ctr. Bank seal at ctr. on back. Printer ABNC.

		GOOD	FINE	XF
S111	**1 DOLLAR**			
	1918. Dk. green on m/c unpt.			
	a. *CHANGSHA. (S/M #Y35-1a).*	175.00	450.00	—
	b. *SHANGHAI. (S/M #Y35-1d).*	150.00	375.00	—
	c. *TIENTSIN. (S/M #Y35-1e).*	175.00	450.00	—
	s1. *CHANGSHA.* Specimen. *(S/M #Y35-1a).*	—	Unc	225.00
	s2. *PEKING.* Specimen. *(S/M #Y35-1c).*	—	Unc	225.00
	s3. *SHANGHAI.* Specimen. *(S/M #Y35-1d).*	—	Unc	225.00
	s4. *TIENTSIN.* Specimen. *(S/M #Y35-1e).*	—	Unc	225.00

		GOOD	FINE	XF
S112	**5 DOLLARS**			
	1918. Dk. blue on m/c unpt.			
	a. *PEKING. (S/M #Y35-2c).*	—	Rare	—
	b. *SHANGHAI. (S/M #Y35-2d).*	Reported Not Confirmed		
	s1. *HANKOW.* Specimen. *(S/M #Y35-2b).*	—	Unc	275.00
	s2. *PEKING.* Specimen. *(S/M #Y35-2c).*	—	Unc	275.00
	s3. *TIENTSIN.* Specimen. *(S/M #Y35-2e).*	—	Unc	275.00

		GOOD	FINE	XF
S113	**10 DOLLARS**			
	1918. Olive-brown on m/c unpt.			
	a. *PEKING. (S/M #Y35-3c).*	—	Rare	—
	b. *SHANGHAI. (S/M #Y35-3d).*	Reported Not Confirmed		
	c. *TIENTSIN. (S/M #Y35-3e).*	—	Rare	—
	s1. *PEKING.* Specimen. *(S/M #Y35-3c).*	—	Unc	325.00
	s2. *TIENTSIN.* Specimen. *(S/M #Y35-3e).*	—	Unc	325.00

		GOOD	FINE	XF
S114	**20 DOLLARS**			
	1918. Dk. brown on m/c unpt.			
	p. W/o branch name. Proof. *(S/M #Y35-).*	—	Unc	300.00
	s1. *PEKING.* Specimen. *(S/M #Y35-).*	—	—	—
	s2. *SHANGHAI.* Specimen. *(S/M #Y35-).*	—	Unc	300.00

		GOOD	FINE	XF
S115	**50 DOLLARS**			
	1918. Black on m/c unpt.			
	p. W/o branch name. Proof. *(S/M #Y35-).*	—	Unc	350.00
	s1. *PEKING.* Specimen. *(S/M #Y35-4c).*	—	Unc	450.00
	s2. *SHANGHAI.* Specimen. *(S/M #Y35-4d).*	—	Unc	350.00
	s3. *TIENTSIN.* Specimen. *(S/M #Y35-4e).*	—	Unc	450.00

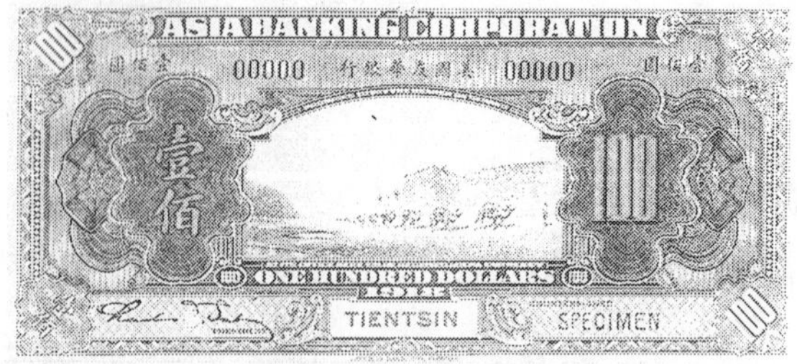

		GOOD	FINE	XF
S116	**100 DOLLARS**			
	1918. Orange on m/c unpt.			
	a. *SHANGHAI. (S/M #Y35-5d).*	Reported Not Confirmed		
	p. W/o branch name. Proof. *(S/M #Y35-).*	—	Unc	450.00
	s1. *PEKING.* Specimen. *(S/M #Y35-5c).*	—	Unc	550.00
	s2. *TIENTSIN.* Specimen. *(S/M #Y35-5e).*	—	Unc	550.00

#S117 *Deleted.* See #S116.

ASIATIC BANKING CORPORATION

行銀彰利海上

Shang Hai Li Chang Yin Hang

Founded ca.1860; failed in 1866. Other offices of issue were Colombo and Kandy. Refer to Ceylon listings.

SHANGHAI BRANCH 海上

1800's ISSUE

#S117A and S117B bank seal at upper ctr. Printer: Smith Elder & Co., Engravers, London.

		GOOD	FINE	XF
S117A	**10 TAELS**			
	18xx. Uniface. Proof. *(S/M #-).*	—	Unc	1250.

		GOOD	FINE	XF
S117B	**25 TAELS**			
	18xx. Uniface. Proof. *(S/M #-).*	—	Unc	1500.

ASIATIC COMMERCIAL BANK, LTD.

行銀華美

Mei Hua Yin Hang

An obscure institution. Its Chinese name, *Mei Hua Yin Hang,* means literally *American Bank.*

SHANGHAI BRANCH 海上

1926 ISSUE

#S118 and S120 printer: CHB.

		GOOD	FINE	XF
S118	**1 DOLLAR**			
	1926. Green and m/c. Back orange. *(S/M #M7-1).*	175.00	475.00	—

		GOOD	FINE	XF
S120	**10 DOLLARS**			
	1926. Green and m/c. Vessel at ctr. Back orange. *(S/M #M7-3).*	450.00	850.00	—

BANQUE BELGE POUR L'ETRANGER, SOCIÉTE ANONYME, 1913-35 (BANQUE SINO-BELGE)

行銀比華

Hua Pi Yin Hang

Formerly the Sino-Belgian Bank.

NOTE-ISSUING BRANCHES:

Hankow Peking Shanghai Tientsin

HANKOW BRANCH 口漢

1921 ISSUE

#S123-S127 ship dockside at ctr. Arms at ctr. on back. Printer: ABNC.

		GOOD	FINE	XF
S123	**1 DOLLAR = 1 PIASTRE**			
	1.7.1921. *(S/M #H185-1c).*	100.00	250.00	—

		GOOD	FINE	XF
S124	**5 DOLLARS = 5 PIASTRES**			
	1.7.1921. Olive-green on m/c unpt. *(S/M #H185-2c).*	125.00	275.00	750.00
S125	**10 DOLLARS = 10 PIASTRES**			
	1.7.1921. Deep gray on m/c unpt. *(S/M #H185-3c).*	175.00	350.00	900.00

		GOOD	FINE	XF
S126	**50 DOLLARS = 50 PIASTRES**			
	1.7.1921. Orange on m/c unpt. *(S/M #H185-4c).*	—	Rare	—
S127	**100 DOLLARS = 100 PIASTRES**			
	1.7.1921. *(S/M #H185-5c).*	Reported Not Confirmed		

PEKING BRANCH 京北

1921 ISSUE

#S128-S129A ship dockside at ctr. Arms at ctr. on back. Printer: ABNC. Punched hole cancelled w/hand stamp: *SPECIMEN.*

		GOOD	FINE	XF
S128	**5 DOLLARS = 5 PIASTRES**			
	1.7.1921. Green on m/c unpt. *(S/M #H185-2d).*	—	—	—

		GOOD	FINE	XF
S129	**10 DOLLARS = 10 PIASTRES** 1.7.1921. Yellow-orange on m/c unpt. *(S/M #H185-3d).*	—	—	—
S129A	**50 DOLLARS = 50 PIASTRES** 1.7.1921. Lt. blue on m/c unpt. *(S/M #H185-4d).*	—	—	—

SHANGHAI BRANCH 海上

1913 MEXICAN DOLLAR PROVISIONAL ISSUE

		GOOD	FINE	XF
S130	**5 MEXICAN DOLLARS** 1913 (-old date 15.7.1912). New Bank name ovpt. at top margin on #S567. Printer: G&D, Leipzig. *(S/M #H185-).*	—	Rare	—

1921 REGULAR ISSUE

#S135-S139 ship dockside at ctr. Printer: ABNC.

		GOOD	FINE	XF
S135	**1 DOLLAR = 1 PIASTRE** 1.7.1921. *(S/M #H185-1a).*	160.00	300.00	725.00
S136	**5 DOLLARS = 5 PIASTRES** 1.7.1921. Red and m/c. *(S/M #H185 -2a).*	225.00	525.00	—

		GOOD	FINE	XF
S137	**10 DOLLARS = 10 PIASTRES** 1.7.1921. *(S/M #H185-3a).*	125.00	350.00	—
S138	**50 DOLLARS = 50 PIASTRES** 1.7.1921. *(S/M #H185-4a).*	—	Rare	—
S139	**100 DOLLARS = 100 PIASTRES** 1.7.1921. *(S/M #H185-5a).*	—	Rare	—

TIENTSIN BRANCH 津天

1912 LOCAL DOLLAR ISSUE

		GOOD	FINE	XF
S142	**5 DOLLARS** 30.4.1913. Brown and blue. Port scene along bottom. Printer: G&D, Leipzig. Uniface. Specimen. *(S/M #H185 -).*	—	—	2000.

1921 LOCAL DOLLAR/PIASTRE ISSUE

#S145-S149 ship at ctr. Printer: ABNC.

		GOOD	FINE	XF
S145	**1 DOLLAR = 1 PIASTRE** 1.7.1921. *(S/M #H185-1b).*	125.00	350.00	—
S146	**5 DOLLARS = 5 PIASTRES** 1.7.1921. Blue and m/c. *(S/M #H185-2b).*	150.00	335.00	—
S147	**10 DOLLARS = 10 PIASTRES** 1.7.1921. *(S/M #H185-3b).*	175.00	525.00	—
S148	**50 DOLLARS = 50 PIASTRES** 1.7.1921. Orange and m/c. *(S/M #H185-4b).*	300.00	850.00	—
S149	**100 DOLLARS = 100 PIASTRES** 1.7.1921. *(S/M #H185-5b).*	350.00	1000.	—

BRITISH AND BELGIAN INDUSTRIAL BANK OF CHINA

英比實業銀行
Ying Pi Shih Yeh Yin Hang

CHANGSHA BRANCH 沙長

1913 ISSUE

		GOOD	FINE	XF
S150	**5 TAELS** 22.8.1913. Brown on yellow unpt. Back blue and orange. Remainder. *(S/M #Y12-1).*	—	—	1000.

NOTE: Crude forgeries exist of #S150.

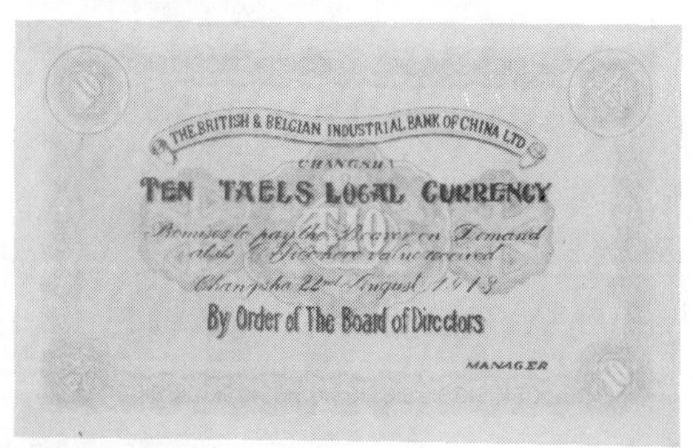

		GOOD	FINE	XF
S151	**10 TAELS** 22.8.1913. Remainder. *(S/M #Y12-2).*	—	Rare	—

BANK OF CANTON LIMITED

司公限有行銀東廣
Kuang Tung Yin Hang Yu Hsien Kung Szu

HANKOW BRANCH 口漢

1922 ISSUE

#S152-S152D Shanghai shoreline at ctr. View of Hong Kong at ctr. on back. Printer: ABNC.

		GOOD	FINE	XF
S152	**1 DOLLAR** 1.7.1922. Green on m/c unpt. Back blue. *(S/M #K63-21).*	—	—	—
S152A	**5 DOLLARS** 1.7.1922. Proof. *(S/M #K63-22).*	—	—	—
S152B	**10 DOLLARS** 1.7.1922. Proof. *(S/M #K63-23).*	—	—	—
S152C	**50 DOLLARS** 1.7.1922. Proof. *(S/M #K63-24).*	—	—	—
S152D	**100 DOLLARS** 1.7.122. Proof. *(S/M #K63-25).*	—	—	—

SHANGHAI BRANCH 海上

1917 ISSUE

#S153-S153E like #S152-S152D.

		GOOD	FINE	XF
S153	**1 DOLLAR** 1.7.1917. Proof. *(S/M #K63-1).*	—	—	—

		GOOD	FINE	XF
S153A	**5 DOLLARS** 1.7.1917. Black on m/c unpt. Back green. *(S/M #K63-2).*	—	—	—
S153B	**10 DOLLARS** 1.7.1917. Black on m/c unpt. Back blue. *(S/M #K63-3).*	—	—	—

		GOOD	FINE	XF
S153C	**50 DOLLARS** 1.7.1917. Black on m/c unpt. Back brown. *(S/M #K63-4).*	—	—	—
S153D	**100 DOLLARS** 1.7.1917. Proof. *(S/M #K63-5).*	—	—	—
S153E	**500 DOLLARS** 1.7.1917. Proof. *(S/M #K63-6).*	—	—	—

1920 ISSUE

		GOOD	FINE	XF
S153F	**1 DOLLAR** 1.1.1920. Dk. gray on red and green unpt. *(S/M #63-11).*	275.00	525.00	—

SWATOW BRANCH

1922 ISSUE

		GOOD	FINE	XF
S153J	**1 DOLLAR** 1.7.1922. *(S/M #K63-31).*	—	—	—
S153K	**5 DOLLARS** 1.7.1922. *(S/M #K63-32).*	—	—	—
S153L (S152L)	**10 DOLLARS** 1.7.1922. *(S/M #K63-33).*	—	—	—
S153M	**50 DOLLARS** 1.7.1922. *(S/M #K63-34).*	—	—	—
S153N	**100 DOLLARS** 1.7.1922. *(S/M #K63-35).*	—	—	—

CHARTERED BANK OF INDIA, AUSTRALIA & CHINA

行銀理滙國中山金新度印

Yin Tu Hsin Chin Shan Chung Kuo Hui Li Yin Hang

行銀利加麥國中山金新度印

Yin Tu Hsin Chin Shan Chung Kuo Mai Chia Li Yin Hang

NOTE-ISSUING BRANCHES:

Hankow Shanghai Peking Tientsin

NOTE: For the Hong Kong Branch issues see Vol. 2.

HANKOW BRANCH 口漢

1900 ISSUE

#S154-S156 supported royal arms at top ctr. Printer: WWS.

		GOOD	FINE	XF
S154	**1 DOLLAR** 1900-15. Red unpt. *(S/M #Y11-20a).*	—	Rare	—
S155	**5 DOLLARS** 1900-15. *(S/M #Y11-21a).*	—	Rare	—
S156	**10 DOLLARS** 1900-15. *(S/M #Y11-22a).*	—	Rare	—

1915; 1924 ISSUE

#S159-S162 supported royal arms at ctr. printer: W&S.

		GOOD	FINE	XF
S159	**5 DOLLARS** 1.3.1924. Green w/lg. red *FIVE* protector. *(S/M #Y11-30a).*	85.00	225.00	—

		GOOD	FINE	XF
S160	**10 DOLLARS** 31.3.1924. Dk. red w/lg. blue *TEN* protector. Back dk. red and black; bank at ctr. *(S/M #Y11-31a).*	125.00	250.00	—

		GOOD	FINE	XF
S161	**50 DOLLARS** 1.5.1924. Dk. blue. *(S/M #Y11-32a).*	200.00	750.00	—
S162	**100 DOLLARS** 1915-30. *(S/M #Y11-33a).*	250.00	900.00	—

#S165-S174 *Deleted.*

SHANGHAI BRANCH 海上

1863; 1874 ISSUE

Dollar System.

#S175-S178 printer: WWS.

		GOOD	FINE	XF
S175	**1 DOLLAR** 1863-74. *(S/M #Y11-1).*	—	Rare	—
S176	**5 DOLLARS** 1863-74. Gray. *(S/M #Y11-2).*	—	Rare	—
S177	**10 DOLLARS** 1863-74. *(S/M #Y11-3).*	—	Rare	—
S178	**25 DOLLARS** 1863-74. *(S/M #Y11-4).*	—	Rare	—

1881; 1885 ISSUE

#S181-S183 printer: WWS.

		GOOD	FINE	XF
S181	**1 DOLLAR** 1.3.1881; 17.11.1892. *(S/M #Y11-10).*	250.00	900.00	—
S182	**5 DOLLARS** 1885-99. *(S/M #Y11-11).*	—	Rare	—
S183	**10 DOLLARS** 1885-99. *(S/M #Y11-12).*	—	Rare	—

1911-22 ISSUE

#S184-S187 supported royal arms at top ctr. Printer: WWS.

		GOOD	FINE	XF
S184	**5 DOLLARS** 20.1.1914-1.10.1927. Blue on green and red unpt. *(S/M #Y11-30c).*	80.00	225.00	650.00
S185	**10 DOLLARS** 29.5.1913; 30.5.1918. Red and violet w/lg. purple *TEN* protector. Back green. *(S/M #Y11-31c).*	90.00	250.00	750.00
S185A	**10 DOLLARS** 2.5.1921; 1.9.1922; 2.5.1927; 1.10.1929. Like #S185 but back red-orange *(S/M #Y11-31c).*	80.00	250.00	700.00
S186	**50 DOLLARS** 1.6.1921; 2.5.1927. Orange and green. *(S/M #Y11-32c).*	300.00	950.00	—

		GOOD	FINE	XF
S187	**100 DOLLARS** 30.12.1911; 21.4.1914; 1.9.1922. Blue and red on pink and purple unpt. Back green. *(S/M #Y11-33c).*	400.00	1250.	—

1930'S ISSUE

		GOOD	FINE	XF
S188	**1 DOLLAR** 19xx. Brown on m/c unpt. Supported royal arms at top ctr. Bank bldg. at ctr. on back. Proof. *(S/M #Y11-).*	—	Rare	—

1898-1911 MEXICAN DOLLAR ISSUE

#S191-S193 supported royal arms at upper ctr. Sign. varieties. Printer: WWS.

		GOOD	FINE	XF
S191	**1 MEXICAN DOLLAR** 1898-1913. Black on pink unpt. Back green. *(S/M #Y11-).*			
	a. 15.8.1898; 11.5.1899.	150.00	425.00	950.00
	b. 13.4.1907; 22.5.1911; 22.7.1911; 14.5.1913; 19.6.1914.	125.00	375.00	850.00

		GOOD	FINE	XF
S192	**5 MEXICAN DOLLARS** 23.11.1900-2.4.1912. Green and red. Back green. *(S/M #Y11-).*	200.00	850.00	1750.

		GOOD	FINE	XF
S193	**10 MEXICAN DOLLARS** 1.6.1897; 1.11.1901; 1.6.1904; 8.4.1907. Red and purple. Back green. *(S/M #Y11-).*	300.00	950.00	1850.
S194	**50 MEXICAN DOLLARS** 30.12.1911. Orange on red unpt. w/ochre word protector. *(S/M #Y11-).*	—	Rare	—

		GOOD	FINE	XF
S194A	**100 MEXICAN DOLLARS** 1.11.1901; 30.12.1911. Purple on pink unpt. *(S/M #Y11-).*	—	—	—

1800'S TAEL ISSUE

#S195-S195C supported royal arms at upper ctr. Printer: Batho & Co., London.

		GOOD	FINE	XF
S195	**5 TAELS** 18xx. Brown. *(S/M #Y11-).*			
	a. Issued note.	—	Rare	—
	p. Proof.	—	—	—
S195A	**10 TAELS** 18xx. Blue. *(S/M #Y11-).*			
	a. Issued note.	—	Rare	—
	p. Proof.	—	—	—
	r. Remainder.	—	—	—
S195B	**25 TAELS** 18xx. Black. Proof. *(S/M #Y11-).*	—	Rare	—
S195C	**50 TAELS** 18xx. Gray-green. Proof. *(S/M #Y11-).*	—	Rare	—

1885-1911 ISSUE

#S196-S200 supported royal arms at upper ctr. Printer: WWS.

		GOOD	FINE	XF
S196	**5 TAELS** 14.12.1910; 26.1.1916. *(S/M #Y11-).*	350.00	1250.	—
S197	**10 TAELS** 1.1.1885; 31.10.1911. Dp. blue on lt. blue w/red *TEN.* protector. Back green. *(S/M #Y11-).*	500.00	1500.	—

		GOOD	FINE	XF
S198	**50 TAELS** 28.10.1911/18xx. Green w/purple *FIFTY* protector. Back green. *(S/M #Y11-).*	—	Rare	—
S199	**100 TAELS** 19xx. *(S/M #Y11-).*	—	—	—
S200	**500 TAELS** 19xx. *(S/M #Y11-).*	—	—	—

TIENTSIN BRANCH 津天

1917-29 ISSUES

#S200A-S206 supported royal arms at top ctr. Bank name repeated in unpt. Printer: WWS.

		GOOD	FINE	XF
S200A	**1 DOLLAR** 19xx. Back brown. Proof. *(S/M Y11-).*	—	—	—
S201	**5 DOLLARS** 1.10.1925; 1.7.1926. Green and blue. Back green. *(S/M #Y11-30d).*	100.00	600.00	—
S202	**5 DOLLARS** 2.5.1927; 1.10.1927. Green and blue. Back blue. *(S/M #Y11-30d).*	125.00	600.00	—

		GOOD	FINE	XF
S202A	**10 DOLLARS** 19xx. Brown w/curved purple word protector. Unsigned remainder. *(S/M #Y11-).*	—	—	—

		Good	Fine	XF
S203	**10 Dollars** 1917; 1926; 1928. Purple and red. *(S/M #Y11-31d).*			
	a. Issued note. 1.7.1926; 2.1.1928.	150.00	600.00	—
	r. Remainder perforated: *CANCELLED.* 1.7.1917; 1.7.1926.	—	Unc	1000.

		Good	Fine	XF
S204	**25 Dollars** 1.8.1917. Olive-green and red-orange on pink unpt. Remainder perforated: *CANCELLED. (S/M #Y11-).*	—	Unc	1200.
S205	**50 Dollars** 1.10.1929. *(S/M#Y11-).*	—	—	—
S206	**100 Dollars** 1.10.1925. Red and black w/lg. violet numeral protector. Perforated: *CANCELLED. (S/M #Y11-33d).*	—	—	—
S207	**100 Dollars** 1.10.1929. Red-orange and orange w/lg. violet numeral protector. *(S/M #Y11-33d).*	300.00	1200.	—

1920's Issue

#S208-S213 supported royal arms at upper ctr. above bank monogram in chain link sunburst unpt. Printer: WWS. Proof.

		Good	Fine	XF
S208	**5 Dollars** 19xx. Green and blue. *(S/M #Y11-).*	—	Unc	1000.
S209	**10 Dollars** 19xx. Brown and blue. *(S/M #Y11-).*	—	Unc	1000.
S210	**50 Dollars** 19xx. Black and green. *(S/M#Y11-).*	—	Unc	1100.

		Good	Fine	XF
S211	**100 Dollars** 19xx. Blue, green and violet. *(S/M #Y11-).*	—	Unc	1200.

		Good	Fine	XF
S213	**100 Dollars** 19xx. Sunburst unpt. Perforated: *CANCELLED. (S/M #Y11-).*	—	Unc	1200.

1930 Issue

#S215-S220 supported royal arms at upper ctr. Printer: W&S.

		Good	Fine	XF
S215	**5 Dollars** 12.6.1930. Purple and lt. brown. Helmeted Minerva at l., arms at ctr. Junk at ctr. on back. *(S/M #Y11-).*	75.00	300.00	850.00

		GOOD	FINE	XF
S216	**10 DOLLARS** 1.12.1930. Blue and black on yellow unpt. Portr. young helmeted Roman soldier at lower l., supported royal arms at ctr. Junk at ctr. r. on back. *(S/M #Y11-).*	150.00	350.00	900.00

		GOOD	FINE	XF
S220	**500 DOLLARS** 1.1.1930. Brown and black w/blue *500* at lower ctr., and old helmeted Roman soldier at lower l. Back brown; river boat at bottom ctr. Specimen. *(S/M #Y11-).*	—	Rare	—

1900'S "HONGPING" TAEL ISSUE

#S221-S222 supported royal arms at top ctr. Bank name repeated in unpt. Printer: WWS.

		GOOD	FINE	XF
S221	**5 HONGPING TAELS** 19xx. Rose and green. Proof. *(S/M #Y11-).*	—	Unc	1000.
S222	**10 HONGPING TAELS** 19xx. *(S/M #Y11-).*	Reported Not Confirmed		

CHARTERED MERCANTILE BANK OF INDIA, LONDON & CHINA

上海有利銀行

Shang Hai Yu Li Yin Hang

Later became Mercantile Bank of India Limited.

NOTE-ISSUING BRANCHES:

Hankow Shanghai

NOTE: For Hong Kong Branch issues see Vol. 2.

HANKOW BRANCH

1800S TAEL ISSUE

		GOOD	FINE	XF
S223	**5 TAELS** 18xx. *(S/M #S54-).*	—	—	—
S223A	**10 TAELS** 18xx. *(S/M #S54-).*	—	—	—
S223B	**50 TAELS** 18xx. *(S/M #S54-).*	—	—	—
S223C	**100 TAELS** 18xx. *(S/M #S54-).*	—	—	—

SHANGHAI BRANCH

1800S TAEL ISSUE

		GOOD	FINE	XF
S224	**5 TAELS** 18xx. Supported royal arms at upper ctr. *(S/M #S54-).*	—	—	—
S224A	**10 TAELS** 18xx. *(S/M #S54-).*	—	—	—
S224B	**25 TAELS** 18xx. *(S/M #S54-).*	—	—	—
S224C	**50 TAELS** 18xx. *(S/M #S54-).*	—	—	—
S224D	**100 TAELS** 18xx. *(S/M #S54-).*	—	—	—

		GOOD	FINE	XF
S224F	**1000 TAELS** 18xx. Seated Britannia, lion, shield, anchor at upper ctr. *(S/M #S54-).*	—	—	—

1881 MEXICAN DOLLAR ISSUE

		GOOD	FINE	XF
S225	**1 MEXICAN DOLLAR** 1.3.1881. Red-orange w/lg. ornate blue word protector. Supported royal arms at upper ctr. Printer: PB&C. *(S/M #S54-).*	—	Rare	—
S225A	**5 MEXICAN DOLLARS** 18xx. *(S/M #S54-).*	—	—	—
S225B	**10 MEXICAN DOLLARS** 18xx. *(S/M #S54-).*	—	—	—
S225C	**50 MEXICAN DOLLARS** 18xx. *(S/M #S54-).*	—	—	—

CHINA SPECIE BANK, LTD.

中華國寶銀行

Chung Hua Kuo Pao Yin Hang

1922 ISSUE

#S228-S228D steam passenger train, livestock, and windmills at ctr. on back. Shanghai. Printer: ABNC.

		GOOD	FINE	XF
S228	**1 DOLLAR** Oct. 1922. Dk. olive-green on m/c unpt. Cash coin at ctr. Back black. Proof. *(S/M #C261.5-1).*	—	—	—

		GOOD	FINE	XF
S228A	**5 DOLLARS** Oct. 1922. Blue on m/c unpt. 5-cash coins on face. Back red-orange. Proof. *(S/M #C261.5-2).*	—	—	—

#S228B-S228D 10-cash coins on face.

		GOOD	FINE	XF
S228B	**10 DOLLARS** Oct. 1922. Brown on m/c unpt. Back Blue. Proof. *(S/M #C261.5-3).*	—	—	—
S228C	**50 DOLLARS** Oct. 1922. Orange on m/c unpt. Back green. Proof. *(S/M #C261.5-4).*	—	—	—
S228D	**100 DOLLARS** Oct. 1922. Purple on m/c unpt. Back black. Proof. *(S/M #C261.5-5).*	—	—	—

CHINESE AMERICAN BANK OF COMMERCE

中華懋業銀行
Chung Hua Mou Yeh Yin Hang

Established 1919, liquidated 1927. Most notes redeemed.

NOTE-ISSUING BRANCHES:

Hankow	Harbin	Peking
Shanghai	Shangtung	Tientsin

1920 FIRST ISSUE

#S230-S234 black on m/c unpt. Shield in floral spray at l., Statue of Liberty in circular frame at r. Back green. Printer: ABNC.

		GOOD	FINE	XF
S230	**1 DOLLAR** 15.7.1920.			
	a. *HANKOW. (S/M #C271-1a).*	75.00	300.00	750.00
	s1. *PEKING.* Specimen, punched hole cancelled. *(S/M #C271-1c).*	—	—	—
	s2. *TIENTSIN.* Specimen, punched hole cancelled. *(S/M #C271-1b).*	—	—	—
	s3. W/o branch name. Specimen. *(S/M #C271-1).*	—	Unc	475.00

		GOOD	FINE	XF
S231	**5 DOLLARS** 15.7.1920.			
	a. *HARBIN. (S/M #C271-3.5b).*	—	—	—
	s1. *HARBIN.* Specimen. *(S/M #C271-3.5b).*	—	—	—
	s2. *PEKING.* Specimen, punched hole cancelled. *(S/M #C271-3.5c).*	—	—	—
	s3. *TIENTSIN.* Specimen, punched hole cancelled. *(S/M #C271-3f).*	—	—	—
	s4. W/o branch name. Specimen. *(S/M #C271-3.5).*	—	Unc	535.00
S232	**10 DOLLARS** 15.7.1920. Black on m/c unpt. Back green.			
	a. *PEKING. (S/M #C271.5c).*	225.00	675.00	1800.
	b. *SHANGHAI. (S/M #C271-4d).*	225.00	675.00	1800.
	s1. *PEKING.* Specimen. *(S/M #C271-5c).*	—	—	—
	s2. *SHANGHAI.* Specimen. *(S/M #C271-4d)*	—	Unc	550.00
	s3. *TIENTSIN.* Specimen, punched hole cancelled. *(S/M #C271-5f).*	—	—	—
	s4. W/o branch name. *(S/M #C271-5).*	—	Unc	600.00

		GOOD	FINE	XF
S233	**50 DOLLARS** 15.7.1920. W/o branch name. Specimen. *(S/M #C271-7).*	—	Unc	850.00
S234	**100 DOLLARS** 15.7.1920. W/o branch name. Specimen. *(S/M #C271-8).*	—	Unc	950.00

1920 SECOND ISSUE

		GOOD	FINE	XF
S235	**1 DOLLAR** 15.7.1920. Blue on m/c unpt. Statue of Liberty in oval frame in floral spray at r.			
	a. *HANKOW. (S/M #C271-2a).*	225.00	600.00	—
	b. *PEKING. (S/M #C271-2c).*	150.00	450.00	1350.
	c. *SHANGHAI. (S/M #C271-2d).*	150.00	450.00	1350.
	d. Like #S235a but back red. *SHANTUNG. (S/M #C271-2e).*	150.00	450.00	1350.
	s1. *TIENTSIN.* Specimen, punched hole cancelled. *(S/M #C271-2f).*	—	—	—
	s2. W/o branch name. Specimen. *(S/M #C271-2).*	—	Unc	425.00

		GOOD	FINE	XF
S236	**5 DOLLARS** 15.7.1920. Brown on m/c unpt. Statue of Liberty in oval frame at ctr. Back orange; shield in floral spray at ctr.			
	a. *HANKOW. (S/M #C271-3a).*	—	—	—
	s1. *PEKING.* Specimen. *(S/M #C271-3d).*	—	—	—
	s2. *SHANGHAI.* Specimen. *(S/M #C271-3d).*	—	Unc	350.00
	s3. *TIENTSIN.* Specimen, punched hole cancelled. *(S/M #C271-3f).*	—	—	—
	s4. W/o branch name. Specimen. *(S/M #C271-3).*	—	—	—

#S238 *Deleted.* See #S232.

#S239 *Deleted.* See #S235.

#S240 *Deleted.* See #S236.

#S241 *Deleted.* See #S232.

#S242 *Deleted.* See #S235.

CHINESE ENGINEERING AND MINING CO.

開平礦務有限公司

K'ai P'ing K'uang Wu Yu Hsien Kung Szu

This firm, after 1912 was called the Kailan Mining Administration, was the largest and best-known British owned mining enterprise in China.

1902 ISSUE

#S246-S247A Navigation seated w/anchor at ctr. w/pagoda and junks in background - Tongshan.

		GOOD	FINE	XF
S246	**1 DOLLAR** 1.3.1902. Black on green and yellow unpt. *(S/M #K1-1).*	70.00	200.00	—

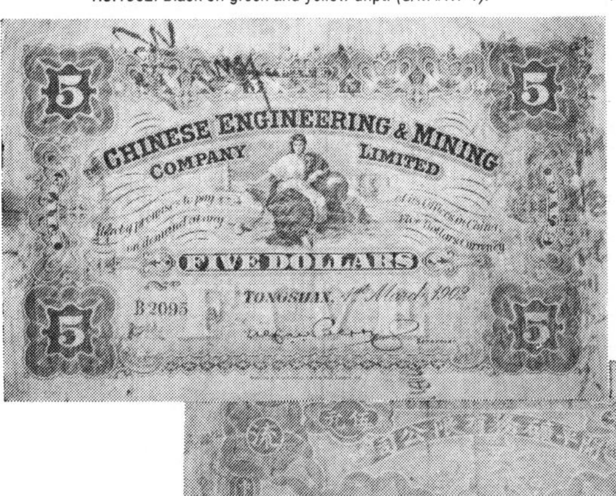

		GOOD	FINE	XF
S247	**5 DOLLARS** 1.3.1902. Black on green and yellow unpt. *(S/M #K1-2).*	—	—	—
S247A	**10 DOLLARS** 1.3.1902. Black on green and yellow unpt. *(S/M #K1-3).*			
	a. Issued note.	—	—	—
	r. Remainder.	—	—	200.00

CHINESE ITALIAN BANKING CORPORATION

震義銀行

Chen I Yin Hang

Opened 1920. Reorganized 1923 as Italian Bank of China.

1921 ISSUE

#S248-S250 inland marina at ctr. W/o sign. or serial #.

		GOOD	FINE	XF
S248	**1 YÜAN** 1.4.1921. *(S/M #C36-).*			
	r1. Unsigned remainder w/serial #.	—	—	700.00
	r2. Unsigned remainder w/o serial #.	—	—	400.00
S249	**5 YÜAN** 1.4.1921. *(S/M #C36-).*	—	Rare	—
S250	**10 YÜAN** 1.4.1921. *(S/M #C36-).*	—	Rare	—

#S253-S257 bridge at ctr. Remainders w/o sign. or branch office designation. Printer: ABNC.

		VG	VF	UNC
S253	**1 YÜAN** 15.9.1921. Green on m/c unpt. Back orange. *(S/M #C36-1).*	5.00	15.00	40.00

		VG	VF	UNC
S254	**5 YÜAN** 15.9.1921. Brown on m/c unpt. Back dk. green. *(S/M #C36-2).*	6.00	20.00	45.00

		VG	VF	UNC
S255	**10 YÜAN** 15.9.1921. Blue on m/c unpt. Back red-brown. *(S/M #C36-3).*	6.00	20.00	45.00
S256	**50 YÜAN** 15.9.1921. Black on m/c unpt. Back purple. *(S/M #C36-4).*	32.50	100.00	250.00
S257	**100 YÜAN** 15.9.1921. Violet on m/c unpt. *(S/M #C36-5).*	110.00	250.00	1100.

COMPTOIR D'ESCOMPTE DE PARIS

Shang Hai Fa Lan Hsi Yin Hang

1866 ISSUE

		VG	VF	UNC
S257B	**5 TAELS** 10.2.1866. Liberty seated between French and Colonial shields at upper ctr.	—	—	—

CREDIT COMMERCIAL SINO-FRANCAIS

中法振業銀行

Chung Fa Chen Yeh Yin Hang

PEKING BRANCH 京北

1923 ISSUE

#S258-S260 printer: BEPP.

		Good	Fine	XF
S258	**1 YÜAN** 1.8.1923. Violet on m/c unpt. Tower at ctr. *(S/M #C253-1).*	75.00	225.00	675.00

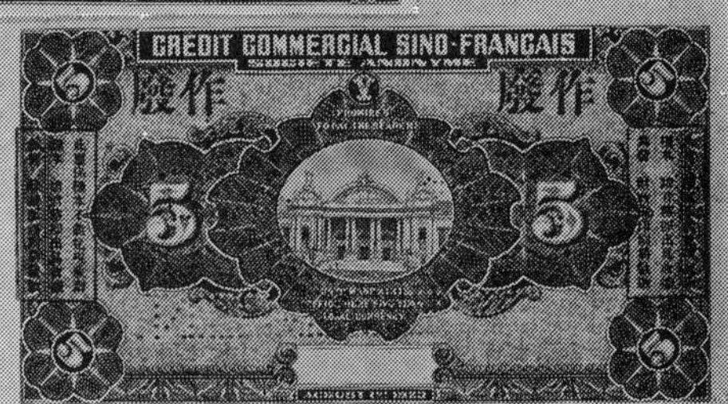

		Good	Fine	XF
S259	**5 YÜAN** 1.8.1923. Blue on m/c unpt. Gateway at ctr. *(S/M #C253-2).*			
	a. Issued note.	150.00	425.00	850.00
	s. Back w/o *PEKING.* Specimen.	—	Unc	275.00

		Good	Fine	XF
S260	**10 YÜAN** 1.8.1923. Brown on m/c unpt. City gate at ctr. Arch of Triumph at ctr. on back. *(S/M #C253-3).*			
	a. Issued note.	175.00	475.00	900.00
	s1. Back w/*PEKING.* Specimen.	—	Unc	350.00
	s2. Back w/o *PEKING.* Specimen.	—	Unc	275.00

DEUTSCH-ASIATISCHE BANK

行銀華德

Te Hua Yin Hang

NOTE-ISSUING BRANCHES:

Hankow, Shanghai, Tsingtao, Peking, Tientsin

NOTE: For Kiachou Branch issues see Vol. 2.

HANKOW BRANCH 口漢

1907 DOLLAR ISSUE

#S261-S303 eagle arms at upper l., facing Chinese dragons at lower l., Germania w/shield and spear at r. Wmk: G&D. Printer: G&D.

		Good	Fine	XF
S261	**1 DOLLAR** 1.3.1907. Blue on rose unpt. *(S/M #T101 -1a).*			
	a. Issued note.	435.00	925.00	—
	s. Specimen.	—	Unc	2500.
S262	**5 DOLLARS** 1.3.1907. Dk. green on pale purple unpt. *(S/M #T101-2a).*			
	a. Issued note.	500.00	1125.	—
	s. Specimen.	—	Unc	2500.
S263	**10 DOLLARS** 1.3.1907. Brown on blue unpt. *(S/M #T101-3a).*			
	a. Issued note.	465.00	1200.	—
	s. Specimen.	—	Unc	2500.
S264	**25 DOLLARS** 1.3.1907. Green on rose unpt. Specimen. *(S/M #T101-4a).*	—	Unc	2500.
S265	**50 DOLLARS** 1.3.1907. Purple on gray unpt. Specimen. *(S/M #T101-5a).*	—	Unc	2500.

1907 TAEL ISSUE

		Good	Fine	XF
S268	**1 TAEL** 1.3.1907. Gray on yellow unpt. Specimen. *(S/M #T101-10a).*	—	Unc	2500.
S269	**5 TAELS** 1.3.1907. Brown on green unpt. Specimen. *(S/M #T101-11a).*	—	Unc	2500.
S270	**10 TAELS** 1.3.1907. Blue on lt. brown unpt. Specimen. *(S/M #T101-12a).*	—	Unc	2500.
S271	**20 TAELS** 1.3.1907. Purple on blue-violet unpt. Specimen. *(S/M #T101-13a).*	—	Unc	2500.

PEKING BRANCH 京北

1907; 1914 DOLLAR ISSUE

		Good	Fine	XF
S272	**1 DOLLAR** 1.3.1907. Blue on rose unpt. Specimen. *(S/M #T101 -1b).*	—	Unc	2000.
S273	**5 DOLLARS** 1.3.1907. Dk. green on pale purple unpt. Specimen. *(S/M #T101-2b).*	—	Unc	2500.
S274	**10 DOLLARS** 1.3.1907. Brown on blue unpt. Specimen. *(S/M #T101-3b).*	—	Unc	2500.
S275	**25 DOLLARS** 1.3.1907. Green on rose unpt. Specimen. *(S/M #T101-4b).*	—	Unc	2500.
S276	**50 DOLLARS** 1.3.1907. Purple on gray unpt. Specimen. *(S/M #T101-5b).*	—	Unc	2500.
S277	**100 DOLLARS** 1.7.1914. Red on violet unpt. Back red and blue. Remainder. *(S/M #T101-24).*	—	Unc	1600.

1907 TAEL ISSUE

		Good	Fine	XF
S279	**1 TAEL** 1.3.1907. Gray on yellow unpt. Specimen. *(S/M #T101-10b).*	—	Unc	2500.

		Good	Fine	XF
S280	**5 TAELS** 1.3.1907. Brown on green unpt. Remainder. *(S/M #T101-11b).*	—	Unc	1400.
S281	**10 TAELS** 1.3.1907. Blue on lt. brown unpt. *(S/M #T101-12b).*	—	Unc	2500.
S282	**20 TAELS** 1.3.1907. Purple on violet-blue unpt. *(S/M #T101-13b).*	—	Unc	2250.

SHANGHAI BRANCH 海上

1907; 1914 DOLLAR ISSUE

		Good	Fine	XF
S283	**1 DOLLAR** 1.3.1907. Blue on rose unpt. *(S/M #T101 -1c).*			
	a. Issued note.	525.00	1200.	—
	s. Specimen.	—	Unc	3000.

		GOOD	FINE	XF
S284	**5 DOLLARS** 1.3.1907. Dk. green on pale purple unpt. *(S/M #T101-2c).*			
	a. Issued note.	600.00	1350.	—
	s. Specimen.	—	Unc	3000.
S285	**10 DOLLARS** 1.3.1907. Brown on blue unpt. *(S/M #T101-3c).*			
	a. Issued note.	675.00	1500.	—
	s. Specimen.	—	Unc	3000.
S286	**25 DOLLARS** 1.3.1907. Green on rose unpt. Specimen. *(S/M #T101-4c).*	—	Unc	3000.
S287	**50 DOLLARS** 1.3.1907. Purple on gray unpt. Specimen. *(S/M #T101-5c).*	—	Unc	3000.

		GOOD	FINE	XF
S288	**200 DOLLARS** 1.7.1914. Black on red unpt. Remainder. *(S/M #T101-26b).*	—	Unc	2250.

1907 TAEL ISSUE

		GOOD	FINE	XF
S289	**1 TAEL** 1.3.1907. Gray on yellow Specimen. *(S/M #T101-10c).*	—	Unc	3000.
S290	**5 TAELS** 1.3.1907. Brown on green Specimen. *(S/M #T101-11c).*	—	Unc	3000.
S291	**10 TAELS** 1.3.1907. Blue on lt. blue Specimen. *(S/M #T101-12c).*	—	Unc	3250.
S292	**20 TAELS** 1.3.1907. Purple on blue-violet unpt. Specimen. *(S/M #T101-13c).*	—	Unc	3250.

TIENTSIN BRANCH 津天

1907 DOLLAR ISSUE

		GOOD	FINE	XF
S293	**1 DOLLAR** 1.3.1907. Blue on rose unpt. *(S/M #T101 -1d).*			
	a. Issued note.	525.00	1275.	—
	s. Specimen.	—	Unc	2000.
S294	**5 DOLLARS** 1.3.1907. Dk. green on pale purple unpt. *(S/M #T101-2d).*			
	a. Issued note.	600.00	1350.	—
	s. Specimen.	—	Unc	2000.
S295	**10 DOLLARS** 1.3.1907. Brown on blue unpt. *(S/M #T101-3d).*			
	a. Issued note.	675.00	1500.	—
	s. Specimen.	—	Unc	2000.
S296	**25 DOLLARS** 1.3.1907. Green on rose unpt. *(S/M #T101-4d).*			
	a. Isssued note.	1000.	2500.	—
	s. Specimen.	—	Unc	2000.
S297	**50 DOLLARS** 1.3.1907. Purple on gray unpt. Specimen. *(S/M #T101-5d).*	—	Unc	2000.

1907 TAEL ISSUE

		GOOD	FINE	XF
S300	**1 TAEL** 1.3.1907. Gray on yellow unpt. Specimen. *(S/M #T101-10d).*	—	Unc	2000.
S301	**5 TAELS** 1.3.1907. Brown on green unpt. Specimen. *(S/M #T101-11d).*	—	Unc	2000.
S302	**10 TAELS** 1.3.1907. Blue on lt. brown unpt. Specimen. *(S/M #T101-12d).*	—	Unc	2250.
S303	**20 TAELS** 1.3.1907. Purple on blue-violet unpt. Specimen. *(S/M #T101-13d).*	—	Unc	2250.

TSINGTAO BRANCH 島青

Refer to Kiachou listings in Vol. 2.

BANK OF EAST ASIA LTD.

行銀亞東

Tung Ya Yin Hang

SHANGHAI BRANCH 海上

1924 ISSUE

#S303A-S303E Shanghai street scene at ctr. East Asia Bank bldg. in Hong Kong at ctr. on back, Printer: W&S.

		VG	VF	UNC
S303A	**1 DOLLAR** 1.1.1924. Brown on orange-brown unpt. Back brown. Specimen. *(S/M #T220.5-11).*	—	—	900.00
S303B	**5 DOLLARS** 1.1.1924. Orange on lt. green unpt. Back orange. Specimen. *(S/M #T220.5-12).*	—	—	1000.
S303C	**10 DOLLARS** 1.1.1924. Dk. green w/black text on lt. orange unpt. Back dk. green. Specimen. *(S/M #T220.5-13).*	—	—	1250.

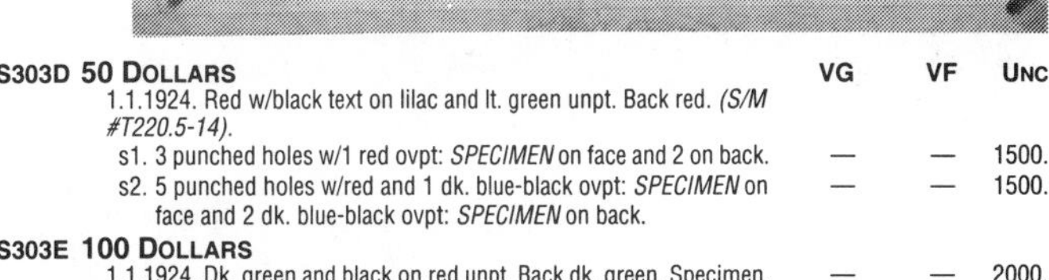

		VG	VF	UNC
S303D	**50 DOLLARS** 1.1.1924. Red w/black text on lilac and lt. green unpt. Back red. *(S/M #T220.5-14).*			
	s1. 3 punched holes w/1 red ovpt: *SPECIMEN* on face and 2 on back.	—	—	1500.
	s2. 5 punched holes w/red and 1 dk. blue-black ovpt: *SPECIMEN* on face and 2 dk. blue-black ovpt: *SPECIMEN* on back.	—	—	1500.
S303E	**100 DOLLARS** 1.1.1924. Dk. green and black on red unpt. Back dk. green. Specimen. *(S/M #T220.5-15).*	—	—	2000.

EXCHANGE BANK OF CHINA

行銀業匯華中

Chung Hua Hui Yeh Yin Hang

Established 1917.

PEKING BRANCH 京北

1920 ISSUE

S303J-S303N fortress gate at ctr. Printer: BEPP.

		VG	VF	UNC
S303J	**1 DOLLAR** 1.1.1920. Specimen. *(S/M #C256-1a).*	—	—	300.00
S303L	**10 DOLLARS** 1.1.1920. Brown. Specimen. *(S/M #C256-3a).*	—	—	365.00

		VG	VF	Unc
S303M	**50 Dollars**			
	1.1.1920. Specimen. *(S/M #C256-4a).*	—	—	400.00
S303N	**100 Dollars**			
	1.1.1920. Specimen. *(S/M #C256-5a).*	—	—	525.00

Tientsin Branch 津天

1920 Issue

#S304-S310 gate fortress at ctr. Printer: BEPP. Ovpt: *M* - Mukden, *P* - Peking or *T* - Tientsin.

		VG	VF	Unc
S304	**1 Dollar**			
	1.1.1920. Brown. *(S/M #C256-1b).*			
	a. Issued note.	25.00	80.00	200.00
	b. Ovpt: *M; P; P* w/*Yu* and *37; T* or *T* w/*Ta* and *35.*	20.00	70.00	150.00
	r. Unsigned remainder.	—	—	70.00
S305	**5 Dollars**			
	1.1.1920. Red. *(S/M #C256-2b).*			
	a. Issued note.	30.00	100.00	250.00
	b. Ovpt: *M; P; T; T* w/*Hsiang* or *34.*	20.00	80.00	160.00
	r. Unsigned remainder.	—	—	85.00
	s. Uniface specimens.	—	—	125.00

		VG	VF	Unc
S306	**10 Dollars**			
	1.1.1920. Blue. *(S/M #C256-3b).*			
	a. Issued note.	50.00	150.00	325.00
	b. Ovpt: *M; P; T; T* w/*Hsiang, T* w/*Piao; T'ung; 33; 38; TBJ* monogram.	30.00	90.00	180.00
	r. Unsigned remainder.	—	—	95.00
	s. Uniface specimens.	—	—	140.00

		VG	VF	Unc
S307	**50 Dollars**			
	1.1.1920. Violet. Specimen. *(S/M #C256-4b).*	—	—	300.00

		VG	VF	Unc
S308	**100 Dollars**			
	1.1.1920. Brown. Specimen. *(S/M #C256-5b).*	—	—	350.00

1928 Issue

#S309 and S310 steamship at ctr. Printer: BEPP.

		VG	VF	Unc
S309	**10 Cents**			
	1.5.1928. Green. *(S/M #C256-10).*			
	a. Ovpt: *M.*	10.00	35.00	100.00
	b. Ovpt: *P.*	10.00	35.00	100.00
	c. Ovpt: *T.*	10.00	35.00	100.00
S310	**20 Cents**			
	1.5.1928. Brown. *(S/M #C256-11).*			
	a. Ovpt: *M.*	15.00	45.00	135.00
	b. Ovpt: *P.*	15.00	45.00	135.00
	c. Ovpt: *T.*	15.00	45.00	135.00
	r. Remainder.	—	35.00	110.00

Hong Kong & Shanghai Banking Company, Limited
Hong Kong & Shanghai Banking Corp.

行銀理滙海上港香

Hsiang K'ang Shang Hai Hui Li Yin Hang

Color and design varieties exist for all issues of this bank. Various date and sign. varieties.

NOTE-ISSUING BRANCHES:

Amoy	Hankow	Shanghai
Chefoo	Peking	Tientsin

NOTE: For Hong Kong Branch issues see Vol. 2.

AMOY BRANCH 門厦

Established 1873.

1886 ISSUE

#S311-S313 printer: BFLT.

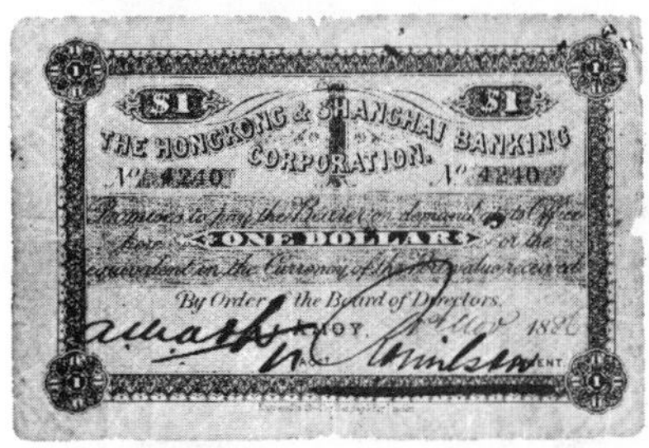

		GOOD	FINE	XF
S311	**1 DOLLAR** 1.1.1886. Brown and blue-green. *(S/M #Y13-20).*	225.00	1000.	—
S312	**5 DOLLARS** 1886-1904. *(S/M #Y13-21).*	—	Rare	—
S313	**10 DOLLARS** 1886-1904. *(S/M #Y13-22).*	—	Rare	—

CHEFOO BRANCH 台烟

Established 1910.

1922 ISSUE

#S315-S317 printer: TDLR.

		GOOD	FINE	XF
S315	**1 DOLLAR** 1.9.1922. Arms at l., bank bldg. at ctr. *(S/M #Y13-).*			
	a. Issued note.	250.00	950.00	—
	s. Specimen.	—	Unc	500.00

		GOOD	FINE	XF
S316	**5 DOLLARS** 1.9.1922. Arms at l., woman making lace at r. *(S/M #Y13-).*			
	a. Issued note.	300.00	900.00	—
	s. Specimen.	—	Unc	650.00

		GOOD	FINE	XF
S317	**10 DOLLARS** 1.9.1922. Blue, green and yellow. Woman making lace at upper l., arms at upper ctr. r. *(S/M #Y13-).*			
	a. Issued note.	200.00	700.00	1500.
	s. Specimen.	—	Unc	750.00

FOOCHOW BRANCH 州福

Established 1877.

1884 PROVISIONAL ISSUE

#S320-S325 ovpt. 6 Chinese characters in red on each side of supported bank arms and *BRANCH OFFICE OF THE BANK IN FOOCHOW* on Hong Kong notes. (See Vol. 2). Printer: Ashby & Co.

		GOOD	FINE	XF
S320	**1 DOLLAR** (ca.1884). *(S/M #Y13-).*	Reported Not Confirmed		
S321	**5 DOLLARS** (ca.1884). *(S/M #Y13-).*	Reported Not Confirmed		
S322	**10 DOLLARS** (ca.1884). *(S/M #Y13-).*	Reported Not Confirmed		

		GOOD	FINE	XF
S323	**25 DOLLARS** 1.12.1884. Green and red. Ovpt. on Hong Kong #121. *(S/M #Y13-).*	—	Rare	—
S324	**50 DOLLARS** 1.1.1884. Ovpt. on Hong Kong #127. *(S/M #Y13-).*	—	—	—
S325	**100 DOLLARS** (ca.1884). *(S/M #Y13-).*	Reported Not Confirmed		

1886-90'S REGULAR ISSUE

#S331 and S333 printer: BFLT.

		GOOD	FINE	XF
S326	**1 DOLLAR** 1.6.1886. Purple on red unpt. Qn. Victoria on back. Printer: BWC. *(S/M #Y13-).*	1000.	2250.	—

		GOOD	FINE	XF
S331	**5 DOLLARS** 188x. Green and red. Unissued remainder. *(S/M #Y13-).*	—	Rare	—
S333	**25 DOLLARS** 189x. Red-orange and green. Back red-orange; arms at ctr. Remainder, perforated: *CANCELLED. (S/M #Y13-).*	—	Rare	—

HANKOW BRANCH 口漢

Established 1868.

1921 ISSUE

#S336-S339 pagoda at l., rocks in ocean at r. Bank bldg. at ctr. on back. Printer: BWC.

		GOOD	FINE	XF
S336	**5 DOLLARS** 1.5.1921. Blue on m/c unpt. *(S/M #Y13-)*.	750.00	1750.	—
S337	**10 DOLLARS** 1.5.1921. Green on m/c unpt. Back blue. *(S/M #Y13-)*.			
	a. Issued note.	—	Rare	—
	s. Specimen.	—	Unc	300.00
S338	**50 DOLLARS** 1.5.1921. Specimen. *(S/M #Y13-)*.	—	Unc	400.00
S339	**100 DOLLARS** 1.5.1921. Brown and black on m/c unpt. Specimen. *(S/M #Y13-)*.	—	Unc	500.00

1870'S TAEL ISSUE

#S339A-S339C printer: BFL.

		GOOD	FINE	XF
S339A	**1 TAEL** 18xx. Black. Proof. *(S/M #Y13-)*.	—	—	—

		GOOD	FINE	XF
S339B	**5 TAELS** 18xx. Dk.green and green on pink unpt. Specimen. *(S/M #Y13-)*.	—	—	—
S339C	**10 TAELS** 18xx. Dk. blue and blue on yellow-orange unpt. Specimen. *(S/M #Y13-)*.	—	—	—

PEKING BRANCH 京北

Established 1885.

1907 ISSUE

		GOOD	FINE	XF
S339D	**5 DOLLARS** 1.6.1907. Blue and black on orange unpt. Similar to #S340. Printer: W&S.	—	Rare	—

1922 ISSUE

#S340-S343 printer: W&S.

		GOOD	FINE	XF
S340	**5 DOLLARS** 1.1.1922. Blue and yellow. Seated cherub w/cornucopia at lower l., bridge, landscape at upper ctr., bank arms at lower r. *(S/M #Y13-)*.			
	a. Issued note	600.00	1600.	—
	s. Specimen.	—	Unc	750.00

		GOOD	FINE	XF
S341	**10 DOLLARS** 1.1.1922. Olive and black. Man carrying water at lower l., bank arms at upper ctr., villagers at lower r. *(S/M #Y13-)*.			
	a. Issued note.	1000.	2250.	—
	s. Specimen.	—	Unc	950.00

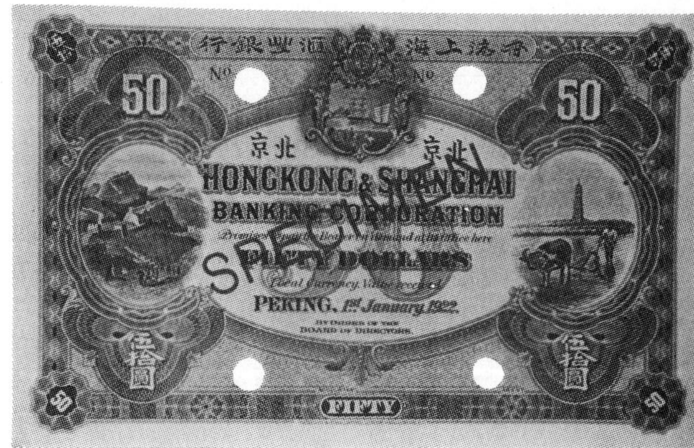

		GOOD	FINE	XF
S342	**50 DOLLARS** 1.1.1922. Brown and yellow. Landscape at l., bank arms at top ctr., man plowing w/ox at r. Specimen. *(S/M #Y13-)*.	—	Unc	1100.

		GOOD	FINE	XF
S343	**100 DOLLARS** 1.1.1922. Bank arms at upper l., bldg. at bottom ctr. Specimen. *(S/M #Y13-)*.	—	Unc	1250.

SHANGHAI BRANCH 海上

Established 1865.

1900-23 DOLLAR LOCAL CURRENCY ISSUES

#S350-S353 printer: BWC.

		GOOD	FINE	XF
S350	**1 DOLLAR** 1.1.1900. Blue on red unpt. *(S/M #Y13-)*.	175.00	450.00	—

#S351-S353 bank arms at upper or top ctr.

		Good	Fine	XF
S351	**5 Dollars** 1.1.1900; 1.1.1902. Blue and red. *FIVE* in unpt. at ctr. *(S/M #Y13-)*.	150.00	450.00	1400.

		Good	Fine	XF
S352	**5 Dollars** 1.7.1904-1.1.1912. Blue on yellow unpt. Back dk. red. *(S/M #Y13-31)*.	120.00	360.00	—
S352A	**5 Dollars** 1.3.1914-24.7.1920. Like #S352 but back maroon. *(S/M #Y13-31)*.	120.00	360.00	—

		Good	Fine	XF
S353	**5 Dollars** 1.3.1923. Blue on m/c unpt. *FIVE* in unpt. at lower ctr. *(S/M #Y13-40)*.	90.00	275.00	—

#S355-S358 printer: BWC.

		Good	Fine	XF
S355	**10 Dollars** 1.1.1900; 1.1.1902. Green and red. Children on back. *(S/M #Y13-)*.	200.00	600.00	—

#S356 Deleted.

		Good	Fine	XF
S357	**10 Dollars** 1.7.1904-15.6.1913. Green on m/c unpt. W/o *TEN* in unpt. Back red. *(S/M #Y13-32)*.	125.00	350.00	900.00

A word on date ranges

Often date ranges or specific dates are listed. These have been observed or reported by our contributors. If a note is outside the published range, it only means that it is a newly reported date, and not necessarily worthy of a premium value.

		Good	Fine	XF
S357A	**10 Dollars** 1.3.1914-24.7.1920. Like #S357 but back maroon. *(S/M #Y13-32)*.	125.00	350.00	900.00

		Good	Fine	XF
S358	**10 Dollars** 1.9.1923. Lt. green on m/c unpt. *TEN* in unpt. at lower ctr. *(S/M #Y13-41)*.	150.00	350.00	600.00

#S360-S364 printer: BWC.

S360	**10 Dollars** (ca.1904). Red on m/c unpt. Back red. *(S/M #Y13-33)*.	Reported Not Confirmed

		Good	Fine	XF
S361	**50 Dollars** 28.4.1914-24.7.1920. Red on m/c unpt. Back maroon; Minerva seated w/globe and shield at ctr. *(S/M #Y13-33)*.	200.00	650.00	—

		Good	Fine	XF
S362	**50 Dollars** 1.9.1923. *FIFTY* in unpt. at lower ctr. Specimen. *(S/M #Y13-42)*.	—	Unc	600.00

		GOOD	FINE	XF
S363	**100 DOLLARS** 4.12.1911-3.9.1919. Dk. brown on m/c unpt. Back red. *(S/M #Y13-34).*	185.00	465.00	—
S363A	**100 DOLLARS** 24.7.1920. Like #S363 but back maroon. *(S/M #Y13-34).*	185.00	465.00	—

		GOOD	FINE	XF
S363B	**100 DOLLARS** 19xx. Brown on lt. green unpt. *ONE HUNDRED* in unpt. at lower ctr. Back red-orange; allegorical woman seated. Specimen. *(S/M #Y13-).*	—	Unc	750.00

		GOOD	FINE	XF
S364	**100 DOLLARS** 1.9.1923. Smaller outlined *ONE HUNDRED* in unpt. at lower ctr. Specimen. *(S/M #Y13-43).*	—	Unc	500.00

1924 DOLLAR ISSUE

		GOOD	FINE	XF
S365	**5 DOLLARS** 1.1.1924. Black and brown on pale orange and lt. green unpt. Similar to #S359. Bank bldg. at ctr. on back. Printer: W&S. *(S/M #Y13-).*			
	a. Issued note.	200.00	600.00	—
	s. Specimen.	—	Unc	450.00
S365A	**10 DOLLARS** 1.1.1924. Green on m/c unpt. *TEN* in unpt. at lower ctr. Bank bldg. at ctr. on back. *(S/M #Y13-).*	75.00	225.00	500.00

1884-97 MEXICAN DOLLAR FIRST ISSUE

#S366-S368B bank arms at upper ctr. Arms at ctr. on back. Printer: BFLT.

		GOOD	FINE	XF
S366	**1 MEXICAN DOLLAR** 1.9.1884; 1.1.1885; 25.4.1892. Blue on red unpt. Back red. *(S/M #Y13-10).*	600.00	1800.	—

#S366A *Deleted.* See #S369.

		VG	VF	UNC
S367	**5 MEXICAN DOLLARS** 1.11.1890-1.3.1897. Brown on lt. blue unpt. *(S/M #Y13-11).*	700.00	2100.	—

		VG	VF	UNC
S368	**10 MEXICAN DOLLARS** 29.1.1897; 30.1.1897; 5.2.1897; 1.3.1897. Dk. olive-green on red unpt. Back red-orange. Handwritten or printed dates. *(S/M #Y13-12).*	800.00	2400.	—

		VG	VF	UNC
S368A	**50 MEXICAN DOLLARS** 18xx. Brown-orange on lt. green unpt. Back brown-orange; arms at ctr. Specimen perforated: *CANCELLED. (S/M #Y13-).*	—	Unc	650.00

		GOOD	FINE	XF
S368B	**100 MEXICAN DOLLARS** 18xx. W/o imprint. Proof. *(S/M #Y13-).*	—	—	—

1892 MEXICAN DOLLAR SECOND ISSUE

		VG	VF	UNC
S369	**1 MEXICAN DOLLAR** 1.9.1893; 4.1.1897; 1.3.1897; 1.1.1900. Blue one red-orange unpt.; engraved dates. Back red-orange w/arms at ctr. Printer: BFLT. *(S/M #Y13-10).*	200.00	800.00	—

1874; 1875 TAEL ISSUE

#S372-S376 printer: Ashby & Co.

		GOOD	FINE	XF
S372	**1 TAEL** 24.9.1874; 1.6.1888. Gray and blue. Arms at upper ctr. Back purple. *(S/M #Y13-1).*	400.00	2000.	—
S373	**5 TAELS** (ca.1875-99). *(S/M #Y13-2).*	1000.	3500.	—
S374	**10 TAELS** (ca.1875-99). *(S/M #Y13-3).*	—	Rare	—
S375	**50 TAELS** (ca.1875-99). *(S/M #Y13-4).*	Reported Not Confirmed		
S376	**100 TAELS** (ca.1875-99). *(S/M #Y13-5).*	Reported Not Confirmed		

TIENTSIN BRANCH 津天

Established 1881.

1901 DOLLAR ISSUE

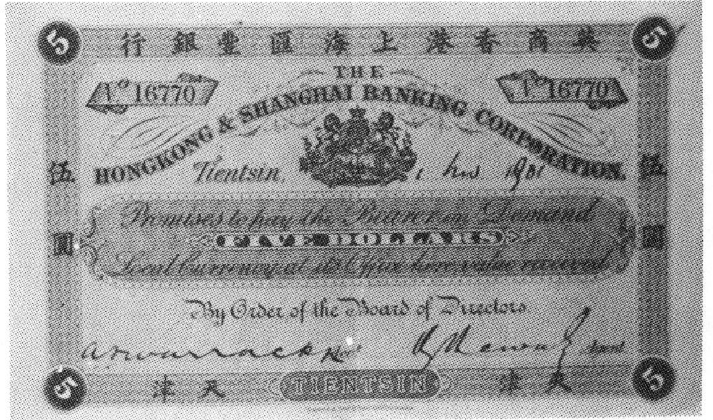

		GOOD	FINE	XF
S378	**5 DOLLARS** 1.11.1901. Brown and blue-green. Arms at upper ctr. Bank arms at ctr. on back. Printer: BFLT. *(S/M #Y13 -).*	500.00	1800.	—

1880'S MEXICAN DOLLAR ISSUE

#S379-S380A arms at upper ctr. Bank arms at ctr. on back. Unsigned remainders perforated: *CANCELLED.* Printer: BFLT.

		GOOD	FINE	XF
S379	**1 MEXICAN DOLLAR** 18xx. Brown on lt. blue unpt. Back red-orange.	—	Unc	900.00

		GOOD	FINE	XF
S380	**25 MEXICAN DOLLARS** 18xx. Dk. blue-black on red unpt. Back red-orange. *(S/M #Y13-).*	—	Unc	2000.
S380A	**50 MEXICAN DOLLARS** 18xx. Red-orange on olive-green unpt. Back red-orange. *(S/M #Y13-).*	—	Unc	2750.

1907 DOLLAR ISSUE

#S381-S383 printer: W&S.

		GOOD	FINE	XF
S381	**5 DOLLARS** 1.6.1907. Red and yellow. Arms at l., city gate at upper ctr., cherub at r. Back black and red. *(S/M #Y13-).*	500.00	1200.	—

1920 ISSUE

		VG	VF	UNC
S382	**5 DOLLARS** 1.1.1920. Like #S381 but back brown and green. *(S/M #Y13-).*	400.00	800.00	—
S383	**10 DOLLARS** 1.1.1920. Boy seated w/tablet at l., city gate at ctr., arms at r. *(S/M #Y13-).*	550.00	1350.	—

Industrial and Commercial Bank Ltd.

行銀商工
Kung Shang Yin Hang

Hankow Branch 口漢

1921 Issue

#S383A-S383C allegorical male "Industry" at ctr. Printer: ABNC.

		VG	VF	Unc
S383A	**1 Dollar** 1.1.1921. Dk. blue and m/c. *(S/M #K92-1a).*	—	—	—
S383B	**5 Dollars** 1.1.1921. Proof. *(S/M #K92-2a).*	—	—	—
S383C	**10 Dollars** 1.1.1921. Proof. *(S/M #K92-3a).*	—	—	—

Shanghai Branch 海上

1921 Issue

#S383F-S383I allegorical male "Industry" at ctr. Printer: ABNC.

		VG	VF	Unc
S383F	**1 Dollar** 1.1.1921. Proof. *(S/M #K92-1b).*	—	—	—
S383G	**5 Dollars** 1.1.1921. Proof. *(S/M #K92-2b).*	—	—	—
S383H	**10 Dollars** 1.1.1921. Proof. *(S/M #K92-3b).*	—	—	—
S383I	**50 Dollars** 1.1.1921. Proof. *(S/M #K92-4b).*	—	—	—

Banque Industrielle de Chine

行銀業實法中
Chung Fa Shih Yeh Yin Hang

Opened 1913. Failed 1921. Most notes redeemed.

NOTE-ISSUING BRANCHES:

Canton	Hankow	Mukden
Peking	Shanghai	Swatow
Tientsin		

Canton Branch 州廣

1914 Issue

#S384-S384D printer: BWC.

		VG	VF	Unc
S384	**1 Dollar** 1914. Specimen perforated: *CANCELLED. (S/M #C254-1-).*	—	—	1500.
S384A	**5 Dollars** 1914. Specimen perforated: *CANCELLED. (S/M #C254-2-).*	—	—	1750.
S384C	**50 Dollars** 1914. Specimen perforated: *CANCELLED. (S/M #C254-4-).*	—	—	2000.
S384D	**100 Dollars** 1914. Specimen perforated: *CANCELLED. (S/M #C254-5-).*	—	—	2250.

Hankow Branch 口漢

1920 Issue

#S385-S386C printer: BWC.

		VG	VF	Unc
S385	**1 Dollar** 14.7.1920. Dk. blue on m/c unpt. *(S/M #C254-1-).*			
	a. Issued note.	—	—	—
	s. Specimen perforated: *CANCELLED.*	—	—	750.00
S385A	**5 Dollars** 14.7.1920. Dk. blue on m/c unpt. Temple of Heaven at l. on back. *(S/M #C254-).*	—	—	—

		VG	VF	Unc
S386	**10 Dollars** 14.7.1920. City gate at r. on back. *(S/M #C254-).*	450.00	1350.	—
S386A	**50 Dollars** 14.7.1920. Specimen perforated: *CANCELLED. (S/M #C254-4-).*	—	—	975.00
S386C	**500 Dollars** 14.7.1920. Specimen perforated: *CANCELLED. (S/M #C254-6-).*	—	—	1200.

Mukden Branch 京盛

1920 Issue

#S388-S388B printer: BWC.

		VG	VF	Unc
S388	**50 Dollars** 1920. Specimen perforated: *CANCELLED. (S/M #C254-4-).*	—	—	825.00

		VG	VF	Unc
S388B	**100 Dollars** 1920. Specimen perforated: *CANCELLED. (S/M #C254-5-).*	—	—	975.00

Peking Branch 京北

1914-15 Issue

#S389-S394 printer: BWC.

S389 1 DOLLAR

	VG	VF	UNC
5.8.1915. Dk. blue on m/c unpt. Chinze at lower l. and lower r. City gate at top ctr. on back. *(S/M #C254-1a).*	350.00	1100.	—

S390 5 DOLLARS

	VG	VF	UNC
5.8.1915. Dk. blue on m/c unpt. Temple of Heaven at l. on back. *(S/M #C254-2a).*	325.00	900.00	—

S391 10 DOLLARS

1914-15. Black on m/c unpt. City gate at r. on back. *(S/M #C254-3a).*

	VG	VF	UNC
a. Issued note.	—	—	—
s. Specimen.	—	Unc	450.00

S392 50 DOLLARS

1914. Pagoda at l. on back. *(S/M #C254-4a).*

	VG	VF	UNC
a. Issued note.	—	—	—
r. Remainder perforated: *CANCELLED.*	—	Unc	650.00
s. Specimen.	—	Unc	650.00

S393 100 DOLLARS

5.8.1915. Great Wall at ctr. on back. *S/M #C254-5a).*

	VG	VF	UNC
a. Issued note.	—	Unc	850.00
s. Specimen.	—	—	—

S394 500 DOLLARS

	VG	VF	UNC
1914. Specimen. *(S/M #C254-6b).*	—	Unc	900.00

SHANGHAI BRANCH 海上

1914-16 ISSUE

#S395-S397 printer: BWC.

S395 1 DOLLAR

	VG	VF	UNC
1.10.1915. Dk. blue on m/c unpt. Chinze at lower l. and r. *(S/M #C254-1c).*	200.00	650.00	—

S396 5 DOLLARS

1.10.1915. Dk. blue on m/c unpt. *(S/M #C254-2c).*

	VG	VF	UNC
a. Issued note.	375.00	800.00	—
s. Specimen perforated: *CANCELLED.*	—	—	900.00

		VG	VF	UNC
S397	**10 DOLLARS** 2.10.1915. Black on m/c unpt. *(S/M #C254-3b).*	425.00	900.00	—
S397A	**50 DOLLARS** 1914. Specimen. *(S/M #C254-4c).*	—	—	1150.
S397B	**100 DOLLARS** 1914. Specimen. *(S/M #C254-5c).*	—	—	1350.
S397C	**500 DOLLARS** 1914. Specimen. *(S/M #C254-6c).*	—	—	1750.

SWATOW BRANCH 頭汕

1914-20 PROVISIONAL ISSUE

#S397D-S397G ovpt: *SWATOW MEXICAN DOLLARS, SWATOW/SHANGHAI*. Ovpt: *Lung Yin* and *Swatow/Shanghai* on back.

		VG	VF	UNC
S397D	**1 DOLLAR** 1914. Specimen perforated: *CANCELLED. (S/M #C254-1d).*	—	—	1050.
S397F	**10 DOLLARS** 1920. Ovpt. on #S397. *(S/M #C254-3d).*			
	a. Issued note.	—	—	—
	s. Specimen perforated: *CANCELLED.*	—	—	1200.
S397G	**50 DOLLARS** 1920. Specimen perforated: *CANCELLED. (S/M #C254-4d).*	—	—	1800.

TIENTSIN BRANCH 津天

1914-15 ISSUE

		VG	VF	UNC
S398	**1 DOLLAR** 1914-15. Blue and m/c. *(S/M #C254-1b).*	200.00	650.00	—

		VG	VF	UNC
S399	**5 DOLLARS** 1914. Specimen perforated: *CANCELLED. (S/M #C254-2b).*	—	—	750.00
S400	**10 DOLLARS** 1914-15. Red. Specimen. *(S/M #C254-3b).*	—	—	950.00
S400A	**50 DOLLARS** 1914. Specimen. *(S/M #C254-4b).*	—	—	1250.
S400B	**100 DOLLARS** 1914. Specimen. *(S/M #C254-5b).*	—	—	1500.

		VG	VF	UNC
S400C	**500 DOLLARS** 1914. Chinze at lower l. and lower r. Specimen. *(S/M #C254-6b).*	—	—	2000.

INTERNATIONAL BANKING CORPORATION

行銀旗花商美

Mei Shang Hua Ch'i Yin Hang

Notes issued 1905-1927. Most notes redeemed. Subsidiary of National City Bank of New York.

NOTE-ISSUING BRANCHES:

Canton	Peking	Tientsin
Hankow	Shanghai	

CANTON BRANCH 東廣

1909 ISSUE

#S401-S405 eagle on pedestal between 2 globes at ctr. on face and back. *Kuangtung*. Printer: ABNC.

		VG	VF	UNC
S401	**1 DOLLAR** 1.1.1909. Brown on m/c unpt. *(S/M #M10-10).*	200.00	700.00	—
S402	**5 DOLLARS** 1.1.1909. Green on m/c unpt. Specimen. *(S/M #M10-11).*	—	—	1000.
S403	**10 DOLLARS** 1.1.1909. Blue on m/c unpt. Specimen. *(S/M #M10-12).*	—	—	825.00
S404	**50 DOLLARS** 1.1.1909. Gray on m/c unpt. Specimen. *(S/M #M10-13).*	—	—	1200.

		VG	VF	UNC
S405	**100 DOLLARS** 1.1.1909. Violet on m/c unpt. Specimen. *(S/M #M10-14).*	—	—	1750.

HANKOW BRANCH 口漢

1918 ISSUE

#S406-S410 eagle on pedestal between 2 globes on face and back. Printer: ABNC.

		VG	VF	UNC
S406	**1 DOLLAR** 1.7.1918. *(S/M #M10-40a).*	60.00	175.00	—

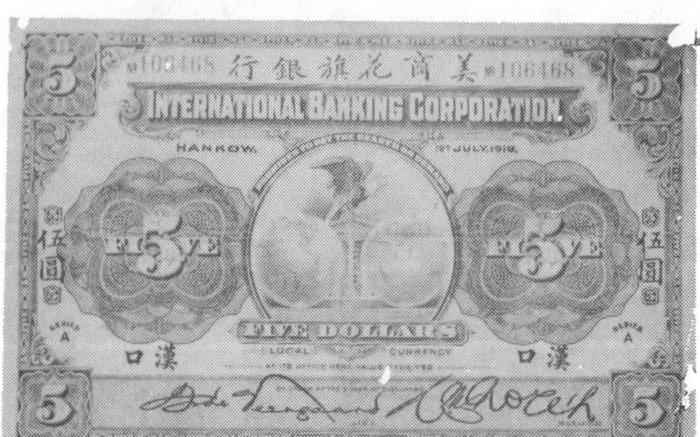

		VG	VF	UNC
S407	**5 DOLLARS** 1.7.1918. Olive and m/c. *(S/M #M10-41a).*	125.00	375.00	—

		VG	VF	UNC
S408	**10 DOLLARS** 1.7.1918. Gray and m/c. *(S/M #M10-42a).*	80.00	300.00	—
S409	**50 DOLLARS** 1.7.1918. Black and m/c. *(S/M #M10-43a).*	200.00	750.00	—
S410	**100 DOLLARS** 1.7.1918. *(S/M #M10-44a).*	250.00	550.00	—

1919 ISSUE

		VG	VF	UNC
S411	**1 DOLLAR** 1.7.1919. Eagle on pedestal between 2 globes at ctr. on face and back. Printer: ABNC. *(S/M #M10-50d).*	50.00	160.00	—

HARBIN BRANCH 賓爾哈

A 1 Dollar note has been reported, date unknown.

PEKING BRANCH 京北

1910 ISSUE

#S412-S416 eagle on pedestal between 2 globes on face and back. Printer: ABNC.

		VG	VF	UNC
S412	**1 DOLLAR** 1.1.1910. *(S/M #M10-20).*	50.00	120.00	—
S413	**5 DOLLARS** 1.1.1910. Black on m/c unpt. *(S/M #M10-21).*	90.00	350.00	—

		VG	VF	UNC
S414	**10 DOLLARS** 1.1.1910. Black on m/c unpt. *(S/M #M10-22).*	80.00	325.00	—
S415	**50 DOLLARS** 1.1.1910. Specimen. *(S/M #M10-23).*	—	Unc	300.00
S416	**100 DOLLARS** 1.1.1910. Specimen. *(S/M #M10-24).*	—	Unc	300.00

1917 ISSUE

		VG	VF	UNC
S416D	**50 DOLLARS** 1.1.1917. Black on m/c unpt. Eagle on pedestal between 2 globes at ctr. on face and back. Printer: ABNC. *(S/M #M10-).*	—	—	—

1919 ISSUE

		VG	VF	UNC
S417	**1 DOLLAR** 1.7.1919. Black on m/c unpt. Like #S411. *(S/M #M10-50c).*	25.00	60.00	140.00

SHANGHAI BRANCH 海上

1905 DOLLAR ISSUE

		VG	VF	UNC
S418	**1 DOLLAR** 1.1.1905. *(S/M #M10-1).*	40.00	150.00	300.00
S419	**5 DOLLARS** 1.1.1905. Green on m/c unpt. *(S/M #M10-2).*			
	a. Issued note.	60.00	250.00	650.00
	p. Proof.	—	—	475.00
	s. Specimen.	—	—	300.00
S420	**10 DOLLARS** 1.1.1905. Brown on m/c unpt. *(S/M #M10-3).*			
	a. Issued note.	70.00	300.00	750.00
	p. Proof.	—	—	600.00
	s. Specimen.	—	—	350.00
S421	**50 DOLLARS** 1.1.1905. *(S/M #M10-4).*	—	—	—

		VG	VF	UNC
S422	**100 DOLLARS** 1.1.1905. Blue on m/c unpt. Eagle on pedestal between 2 globes at l. Printer: ABNC. *(S/M #M10 -5).*			
	a. Issued note.	—	—	—
	p. Proof.	—	—	1800.
	s. Specimen.	—	—	1500.

1919 ISSUE

		VG	VF	UNC
S423	**1 DOLLAR** 1.7.1919. Orange on m/c unpt. Like #S411. 2 sign varieties. *(S/M #M10-50a).*			
	a. Issued note.	20.00	60.00	125.00
	p. Proof.	—	—	180.00
	s. Specimen.	—	—	120.00

1918 TAEL ISSUE

#S424-S428 eagle on pedestal between 2 globes on face and back. Printer: ABNC.

		VG	VF	UNC
S424	**1 TAEL** 1.1.1918. Orange on m/c unpt. *(S/M #M10-30).*	—	—	—

		VG	VF	UNC
S425	**5 TAELS** 1.1.1918. Black and gray on m/c unpt. *(S/M #M10-31).*			
	a. Issued note.	—	—	—
	p. Proof.	—	—	1500.
	s. Specimen.	—	—	1000.
S426	**10 TAELS** 1.1.1918. *(S/M #M10-32).*			
	p. Proof.	—	—	1500.
	s. Specimen.	—	—	1000.
S427	**50 TAELS** 1.1.1918. *(S/M #M10-33).*	—	—	—
S428	**100 TAELS** 1.1.1918. Black and gray on m/c unpt. Back brown. *(S/M #M10-34).*			
	p. Proof.	—	—	2500.
	s. Specimen.	—	—	2000.

TIENTSIN BRANCH 津天

1918 ISSUE

#S429-S433 eagle on pedestal between 2 globes on face and back. Printer: ABNC.

		VG	VF	UNC
S429	**1 DOLLAR** 1.7.1918. *(S/M #M10-40b).*	30.00	80.00	180.00
S430	**5 DOLLARS** 1.7.1918. Olive on m/c unpt. Back orange. *(S/M #M10-41b).*	100.00	375.00	—

		VG	VF	UNC
S431	**10 DOLLARS** 1.7.1918. Black and m/c. *(S/M #M10-42b).*	125.00	450.00	—
S432	**50 DOLLARS** 1.7.1918. Black and m/c. *(S/M #M10-43b).*	—	—	—
S433	**100 DOLLARS** 1.7.1918. *(S/M #M10-44b).*	—	—	—

1919 ISSUE

		VG	VF	UNC
S434	**1 DOLLAR** 1.7.1919. Black and m/c. Like #S411. *(S/M #M10-50b).*	25.00	65.00	125.00

BANQUE DE L'INDOCHINE

行銀理滙方東
Tung Fang Hui Li Yin Hang

NOTE-ISSUING BRANCHES:
Canton Shameen Shanghai

NOTE: For branch issues in other countries see Vol. 2.

CANTON SHAMEEN BRANCH 面沙東廣

DECRETS DES 21.1.1875, 20.2.1888 ET 16.5.1900

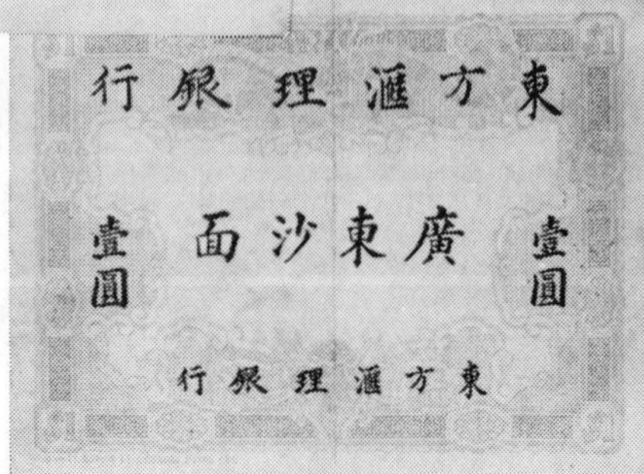

		VG	VF	UNC
S436	**1 DOLLAR = 1 PIASTRE** 15.1.1902. Red and green. Dragon border. Back black text on yellow. *(S/M #T204-1).*	—	Rare	—
S437	**5 DOLLARS = 5 PIASTRES** 1902. Red and green. Neptune reclining holding trident at at lower l. Back yellow w/black text. *(S/M #T204-2).*	—	Rare	—
S438	**10 DOLLARS = 10 PIASTRES** 1902. Red and green. Elephant columns at l. and r. 2 reclining women w/ox at l., tiger at r. at lower border. Back yellow w/black text. *(S/M #T204-3).*	—	Rare	—
S439	**100 DOLLARS = 100 PIASTRES** 1901. Red and green. Vasco da Gama at l., sailing ships at lower ctr., man w/paddle at r. Back yellow w/black text. Specimen. *(S/M #T204-4).*	—	Rare	—

SHANGHAI BRANCH 海上

DECRETS DES 21.1.1875, 20.2.1988 ET 16.5.1900

#S440-S440C red w/black text.

		VG	VF	UNC
S440	**1 DOLLAR = 1 PIASTRE** 15.1.1902. Similar to #S436. *(S/M #T204-).*	—	Rare	—
S440A	**5 DOLLARS = 5 PIASTRES** 1902. Similar to #S437. Back orange w/black text. *(S/M #T204-).*	—	Rare	—
S440B	**10 DOLLARS = 10 PIASTRES** 1902. Similar to #S438. *(S/M #T204-).*	—	Rare	—
S440C	**100 DOLLARS = 100 PIASTRES** 1901. Similar to #S439. Specimen. *(S/M #T204).*	—	Rare	—

MERCANTILE BANK OF INDIA LIMITED

行銀利有
Yu Li Yin Hang

Formerly the Chartered Mercantile Bank of India, London & China.

NOTE-ISSUING BRANCH:
Shanghai

NOTE: For Hong Kong Branch issues see Vol. 2.

SHANGHAI BRANCH 海上

1916 ISSUE

#S441-S446 portr. Mercury at ctr. on back. Printer: W&S.

		VG	VF	UNC
S441	**1 DOLLAR** c.1916. Yellow. Back green. *(S/M #S54-1).*	200.00	800.00	1800.

		VG	VF	UNC
S442	**5 DOLLARS** 1.7.1916. Green and m/c. Sampans along coastline at upper ctr. Back blue. *(S/M #S54-3).*	300.00	1200.00	—

		VG	VF	UNC
S443	**10 DOLLARS** 1.7.1916. Brown and black on m/c unpt. Landscape of multiple arch bridge and mountains at ctr. Back brown. *(S/M #S54-4).*	400.00	1500.	—

S444 50 DOLLARS

	VG	VF	UNC
1.7.1916. Sampans along coastline at ctr. *Cancelled. (S/M #S54-5).*	—	—	1400.

S445 100 DOLLARS

	VG	VF	UNC
1.7.1916. Shoreline, mountains in background at ctr. *Cancelled. (S/M #S54-6).*	—	—	2100.

1924 ISSUE

S446 1 DOLLAR

	VG	VF	UNC
1.7.1924. Black and m/c. Sampan near coastline at ctr. Back orange. Printer: BWC. *(S/M #S54-2).*	180.00	550.00	1000.

NATIONAL BANK OF CHINA

香港中華滙理銀行

Hsiang K'ang Chung Hua Hui Li Yin Hang

Established 1891, closed in 1911.

NOTE-ISSUING BRANCH:

Amoy

NOTE: For Hong Kong Branch issues see Vol. 2.

AMOY BRANCH 厦門

1890S ISSUE

S446B 5 DOLLARS

	VG	VF	UNC
189x. Red-brown w/black text on yellow unpt. Arms at ctr. Printer: W&S. Remainder. *(S/M #H97-2b).*	—	Rare	—

NATIONAL COMMERCIAL AND SAVINGS BANK, LTD.

香港國民商業儲蓄銀行

Hsiang K'ang Kuo Min Shang Yeh Ch'u Hsu Yin Hang

NOTE: Due to the shortage of its issues in circulation, this bank authorized notes torn in half to circulate at half the face value. Each half had to be signed by a bank officer to be acceptable. Many whole notes in collections today are two halves joined together.

NOTE-ISSUING BRANCHES:

Hankow Shanghai

HANKOW BRANCH 漢口

1924 ISSUE

#S447-S451 Great Wall at ctr. 2 globes at ctr. on back. Printer: ABNC.

		VG	VF	UNC
S447	**1 DOLLAR**			
	1.12.1924. Blue and m/c. *(S/M #H100-1b).*			
	a. Issued note.	150.00	450.00	1000.
	b. Repaired, joined w/mismatched serial #.	60.00	180.00	—
	s. Specimen.	—	—	—
S448	**5 DOLLARS**			
	1.12.1924. Blue and m/c. *(S/M #H100-2b).*			
	a. Issued note.	150.00	450.00	1000.
	b. Repaired, joined w/mismatched serial #.	75.00	225.00	—

		VG	VF	UNC
S449	**10 DOLLARS**			
	1.12.1924. Brown and m/c. *(S/M #H100-3b).*			
	a. Issued note.	300.00	900.00	1900.
	b. Repaired, joined w/mismatched serial #.	150.00	450.00	—
S450	**50 DOLLARS**			
	1.12.1924. Green and m/c. *(S/M #H100-4b).*			
	a. Issued note.	600.00	450.00	3600.
	b. Repaired, joined w/mismatched serial #.	300.00	900.00	—
S451	**100 DOLLARS**			
	1.12.1924. Red and m/c. *(S/M #H100-5b).*			
	a. Issued note.	750.00	2250.	5000.
	b. Repaired, joined w/mismatched serial #.	400.00	1200.	—

SHANGHAI BRANCH 上海

1924 ISSUE

#S452-S456 like #S447-S451.

		VG	VF	UNC
S452	**1 DOLLAR**			
	1.12.1924. Blue and m/c. *(S/M #H100-1a).*			
	a. Issued note.	70.00	200.00	450.00
	b. Repaired, joined w/mismatched serial #.	30.00	90.00	—

		VG	VF	UNC
S453	**5 DOLLARS** 1.12.1924. Blue and m/c. *(S/M #H100-2a).*			
	a. Issued note.	100.00	300.00	700.00
	b. Repaired, joined w/mismatched serial #.	50.00	150.00	—
S454	**10 SILVER YÜAN** 1.12.1924. Brown and m/c. *(S/M #H100-3a).*			
	a. Issued note.	110.00	335.00	750.00
	b. Repaired, joined w/mismatched serial #.	75.00	225.00	—
S455	**50 DOLLARS** 1.12.1924. Green and m/c. *(S/M #H100-4a).*			
	a. Issued note.	250.00	750.00	1600.
	b. Repaired, joined w/mismatched serial #.	150.00	450.00	—
S456	**100 DOLLARS** 1.12.1924. Red and m/c. *(S/M #H100-5a).*			
	a. Issued note.	300.00	900.00	2000.
	b. Repaired, joined w/mismatched serial #.	150.00	450.00	—

NETHERLANDS TRADING SOCIETY

行銀嘣和海上

Shang Hai Ho Lan Yin Hang

SHANGHAI BRANCH 海上

1909 ISSUE

#S457-S459 printer: BWC.

		VG	VF	UNC
S457	**1 DOLLAR** 1.1.1909. *(S/M #S51-1).*	—	—	—

		VG	VF	UNC
S458	**5 DOLLARS** 1.1.1909. Blue on violet and green unpt. Medieval oriental warrior at ctr. above arch bridge on back. *(S/M #S51-2).*	500.00	1500.	2250.
S459	**10 DOLLARS** 1.1.1909. Red. Like #S458. *(S/M #S51-3).*	600.00	1800.	2500.

1922 ISSUE

#S460 and S461 printer: BWC.

		VG	VF	UNC
S460	**50 DOLLARS** 1.1.1922. M/c. Medieval oriental warrior at l. on back. *(S/M #S51-).*			
	a. Issued note.	—	Rare	—
	s. Specimen.	—	—	1800.

		VG	VF	UNC
S461	**100 DOLLARS** 1.1.1922. Violet, blue and yellow. Medieval warrior at top ctr., bridge below. Back deep brown, tan and blue; arms at top ctr., w/lion at l. and r. *(S/M #S51-).*			
	a. Issued note.	—	Rare	—
	s. Specimen.	—	—	2250.

ORIENTAL BANK CORPORATION

行銀理滙藩東

Tung Fan Hui Li Yin Hang

NOTE-ISSUING BRANCH:
Shanghai

NOTE: For Hong Kong Branch issues see Vol. 2.

SHANGHAI BRANCH 海上

1865 ISSUE

#S463-S463D supported arms at upper ctr. Payable in sycee (silver ingots).

		GOOD	FINE	XF
S463	**5 TAELS** 1865. Specimen. *(S/M #T203-).*	—	—	—
S463A	**10 TAELS** 1865. Specimen. *(S/M #T203-).*	—	—	—
S463B	**50 TAELS** 1865. Specimen. *(S/M #T203-).*	—	—	—
S463C	**100 TAELS** 1865. Specimen. *(S/M #T203-).*	—	—	—

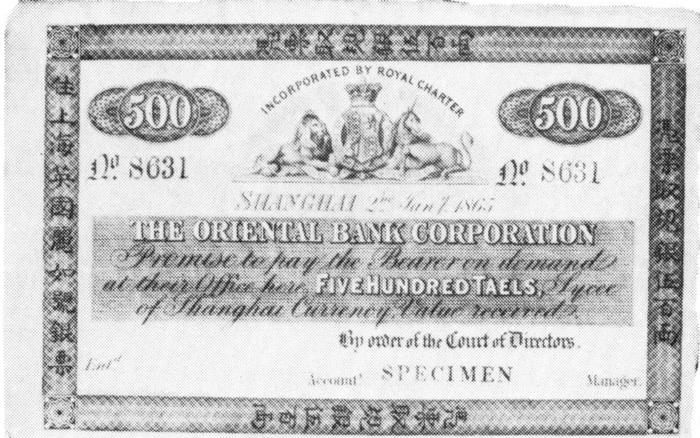

		GOOD	FINE	XF
S463D	**500 TAELS** 2.1.1865. Specimen. *(S/M #T203-).*	—	—	—

RUSSO-ASIATIC BANK, 1900-26

РУССКО-АЗІАТСКІИ БАНКЪ

行銀勝道商俄

O Hua (and Hua O) Tao Sheng Yin Hang

Formerly the Russo-Chinese Bank. Liquidated in 1928.

NOTE-ISSUING BRANCHES:

Harbin	Newchwang	Tientsin
Kuld'sha, Chuguchak & Kashgar	Shanghai	

HARBIN BRANCH 賓爾哈

1910 PROVISIONAL ISSUE

Dollar System.

#S465-S467 ovpt. denomination, new bank name and new office of issue on Tientsin Hong Ping Hua Pao Tael issue. Printer: BWC.

		GOOD	FINE	XF
S465	**50 DOLLARS** ND (1910). Ovpt. on #S549. *(S/M #05-).*	—	Rare	—

		VG	VF	UNC
S466	**100 DOLLARS** ND (1910). Ovpt. on #S550. *(S/M #05-).*	400.00	1200.	2500.
S467	**500 DOLLARS** ND (1910). Ovpt. on #S551. *(S/M #05-).*	—	Rare	—

1917 ISSUE

Ruble System.

1 Ruble = 100 Kopeks

#S473-S478 issued about 1917 in Harbin for use by the Chinese Eastern Railway. Printer: ABNC.

#S467 and S468 *Deleted.*

		VG	VF	UNC
S473	**50 KOPEKS** ND (1917). Green and orange. Steam passenger train at l. *(S/M #05-100).*			
	a. Issued note.	3.00	12.00	35.00
	p. Proof.	—	—	120.00
	s. Specimen.	—	—	80.00

#S474-S478 steam passenger train at ctr. on back.

		VG	VF	UNC
S474	**1 RUBLE** ND (1917). Orange-brown and m/c. Back brown. *(S/M #05-101).*			
	a. Issued note.	4.00	15.00	45.00
	p. Proof.	—	—	185.00
	s. Specimen.	—	—	125.00
S475	**3 RUBLES** ND (1917). Green and m/c. Back green. *(S/M #05-102).*			
	a. Issued note.	4.00	15.00	45.00
	p. Proof.	—	—	200.00
	s. Specimen.	—	—	135.00
S476	**10 RUBLES** ND (1917). Brown-orange and m/c. Back red. *(S/M #05-103).*			
	a. Issue note.	6.00	20.00	65.00
	p. Proof.	—	—	225.00
	s. Specimen.	—	—	150.00

#S477 *Deleted.*

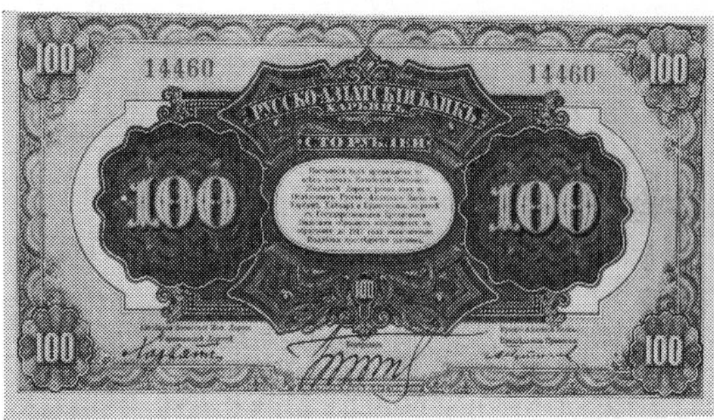

		VG	VF	UNC
S478	**100 RUBLES** ND (1917). Tan, green, and m/c. Back brown. *(S/M #05-105).*			
	a. Issued note.	35.00	100.00	275.00
	p. Proof.	—	—	550.00
	s. Specimen.	—	—	350.00

KULD'SHA, CHUGUCHAK & KASHGAR BRANCH

1913-17 ISSUE

#S479-S483 dragon at l., at ctr. and at r. Dragon at bottom ctr. on back. Printer: BWC.

		GOOD	FINE	XF
S479	**1 GOLD FEN** 1913-17. Blue on brown and green unpt. Back black on green and brown unpt. *(S/M #05-50).*	325.00	850.00	—

		GOOD	FINE	XF
S480	**2 GOLD FEN** 1913-17. Blue on m/c unpt. Back black on lt. green and pale lilac unpt. *(S/M #05-51).*	350.00	1000.	—
S481	**10 GOLD FEN = 1 MACE** 1913-24.7.1918. Blue on m/c unpt. Back black on blue and gold unpt. *(S/M #05-52).*			
	a. Issued note.	600.00	1500.	—
	s. Specimen.	—	—	—

		Good	Fine	XF
S482	**50 Gold Fen = 5 Mace** 1913-17. Specimen. *(S/M #O5-53).*	—	Rare	—
S483	**100 Gold Fen = 10 Mace** 1913-17. Specimen. *(S/M #O5-54).*	—	Rare	—

NOTE: One gold-based cent (fen) equalled 25 silver-based cents.

Newchwang Branch 莊牛

1910 Provisional Issue

#S484 and S484A ovpt. new branch office name in English.

		Good	Fine	XF
S484	**1 Dollar** ND (ca. 1910 -old date 1/14.3.1907). Ovpt. on #S517. *(S/M #O5-).*	—	—	—

NOTE: No known surviving examples.

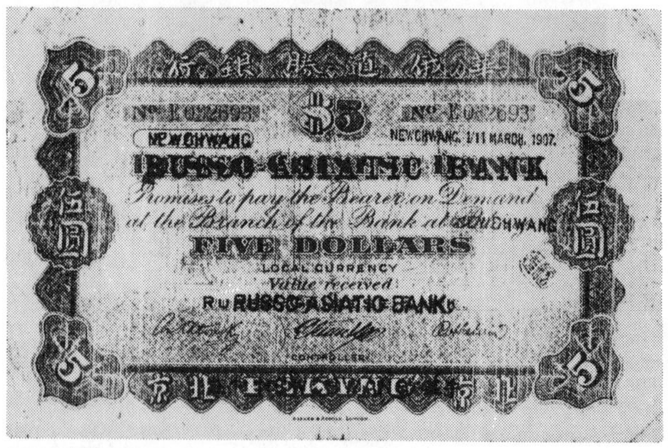

		Good	Fine	XF
S484A	**5 Dollars** ND (ca.1910 -old date 1/14.3.1907). Ovpt. on #S518. *(S/M #O5-).*	—	Rare	—

NOTE: See also #S517 and S518.

Shanghai Branch 海上

1914 Local Dollar Currency Issue

#S485-S489 facing dragons at l. and r. Bank bldg. at lower ctr. on back. W/o printed date w/*SHANGHAI 1/14 JANUARY* or *1/14 JULY 1914* hand stamped in lower margin. Printer: BWC.

		Good	Fine	XF
S485	**1 Dollar** 1/14.1.1914. Black and red. *(S/M #O5-80).*	160.00	475.00	1250.
S486	**5 Dollars** 1/14.1.1914. Black on m/c unpt. *(S/M #O5-81).*	300.00	950.00	—
S487	**10 Dollars** 1914. Black on m/c unpt. *(S/M #O5-82).*	—	—	—
S488	**50 Dollars** 1914. Black on m/c unpt. *(S/M #O5-83).*	—	—	—
S489	**100 Dollars** 1914. Black on m/c unpt. *(S/M #O5-84a).*	—	—	—

1914 Mexican Dollar Issue

#S490-S494 printer: ABNC.

		Good	Fine	XF
S490	**1 Mexican Dollar** 1914. Specimen. *(S/M #O5-60).*	—	—	—
S491	**5 Mexican Dollars** 1914. Specimen. *(S/M #O5-61).*	—	—	—
S492	**10 Mexican Dollars** 1914. Specimen. *(S/M #O5-62).*	—	—	—

		Good	Fine	XF
S493	**50 Mexican Dollars** 1914. Specimen. *(S/M #O5-63).*	—	—	—
S494	**100 Mexican Dollars** 1914. Specimen. *(S/M #O5-64.*	—	—	—

#S495-S499 *Deleted.*

Tientsin Branch 津天

1917 Issue

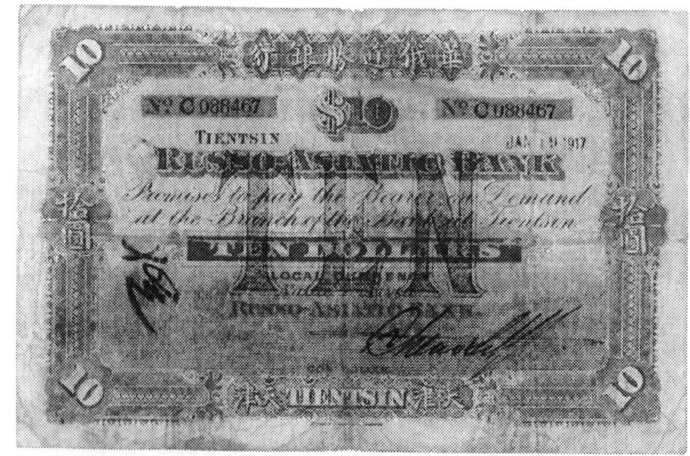

		Good	Fine	XF
S502	**10 Dollars** 19.1.1917. Red-orange. Printer: Nissen & Arnold, London. *(S/M #O5-).*	—	Rare	—

Russo-Chinese Bank, 1895-1910

РУССКО-КИТАЙСКІЙ БАНКЪ

行銀勝道俄華

Huo O Tao Sheng Yin Hang

NOTE-ISSUING BRANCHES:

Hankow	Peking
Shanghai	Tientsin

1898 Issue

		Good	Fine	XF
S503	**100 Cash** CD1898. Brown. Medieval characters in frame. Blue hand stamped seals. Uniface. *(S/M #O5-3).*	—	—	—
S504	**300 Cash** CD1898. Blue. Medieval characters in frame. Red hand stamped seals. Uniface. *(S/M #O5-5).*	800.00	2000.	—

1898 Kuping Tael Issue

		Good	Fine	XF
S506	**1 Kuping Tael** CD1898. *(S/M #O5-10).*	—	—	—

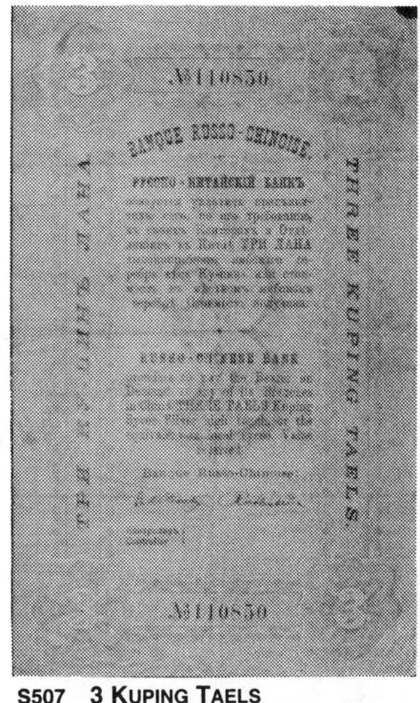

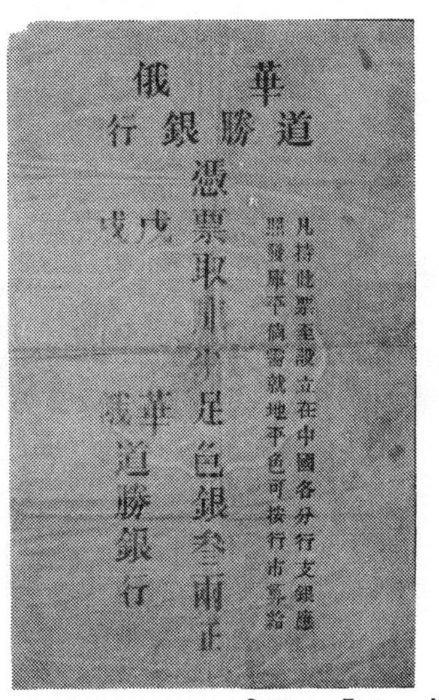

		GOOD	FINE	XF
S507	**3 KUPING TAELS** CD1898. *(S/M #O5-11)*	600.00	1800.	—
S508	**5 KUPING TAELS** CD1898. *(S/M #O5-12).*	600.00	1800.	—

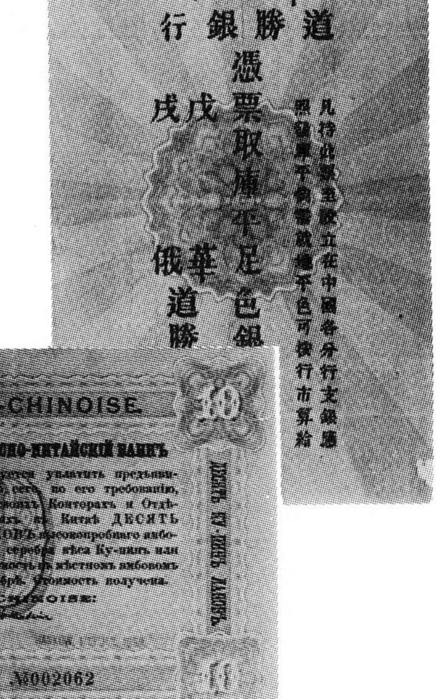

		GOOD	FINE	XF
S509	**10 KUPING TAELS** CD1898. *(S/M #O5-13).*	—	Rare	—
S510	**50 KUPING TAELS** CD1898. *(S/M #O5-14).*	—	Rare	—
S511	**100 KUPING TAELS** CD1898. *(S/M #O5-15).*	—	Rare	—

HANKOW BRANCH 口漢

1914 ISSUE

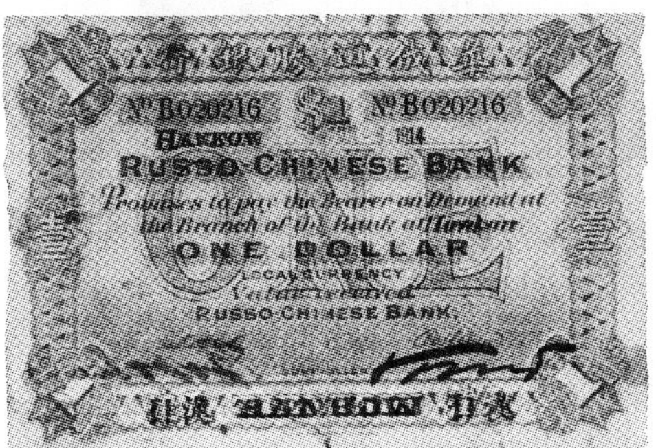

		GOOD	FINE	XF
S512	**1 DOLLAR** 6.6.1914. Ovpt. on #S546. *(S/M #O5-).*	—	Rare	—

NEWCHWANG BRANCH 莊牛

1907 PROVISIONAL ISSUE

#S517 and S518 ovpt. new branch office name in English.

		GOOD	FINE	XF
S517	**1 DOLLAR** 1/14.3.1907. Ovpt. on #S522. *(S/M #O5-).*	—	Rare	—
S518	**5 DOLLARS** 1/14.3.1907. Ovpt. on #S523. *(S/M #O5-).*	—	Rare	—

NOTE: See also #S484 and S484A.

PEKING BRANCH 京北

1903-14 ISSUE

#S522-S523 printers: Nissen & Arnold, London.

		GOOD	FINE	XF
S522	**1 DOLLAR** (ca. 1903-14). *(S/M #O5-).*	450.00	—	—

		GOOD	FINE	XF
S523	**5 DOLLARS** 1/14.9.1903. Orange on yellow unpt. *(S/M #05-).*	—	Rare	—

1907 CHINGPING TSUYIN TAEL ISSUE

#S531-S535 printer: BWC.

		GOOD	FINE	XF
S531	**1 TAEL** Yr. 33 (1907). Blue, brown and m/c. *(S/M #05-20).*			
	a. Issued note.	800.00	2000.	—
	s. Specimen.	—	—	—
S532	**5 TAELS** Yr. 33 (1907). Specimen. *(S/M #05-21).*	—	Rare	—
S533	**10 TAELS** Yr. 33 (1907). Specimen. *(S/M #05-22).*	—	Rare	—

		GOOD	FINE	XF
S534	**50 TAELS** Yr. 33 (1907). Specimen. *(S/M #05-23).*	—	Rare	—
S535	**100 TAELS** Yr. 33 (1907). Specimen. *(S/M #05-24).*	—	Rare	—

A word on pricing

When a note is marked RARE in the price columns, this note seldom appears on the market, or few are known in private hands. When dashes are in the price column, means that the note has not traded on the open market recently and a definitive value could not accurately be determined. Rare does not always mean expensive. A dashed price does not mean expensive or rare.

SHANGHAI BRANCH 上海

1901; 1902 MEXICAN DOLLAR ISSUE

#S536-S540 specimen ovpt. or perforated: ОБРАЗЕЦЪЧ

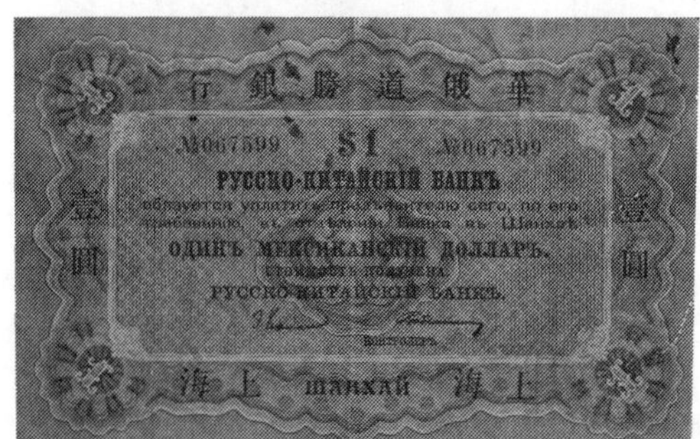

		GOOD	FINE	XF
S536	**1 MEXICAN DOLLAR** 1/14.3.1902; 1/14.8.1901. Brown and m/c. *(S/M #05-1).*			
	a. Issued note.	450.00	1250.	—
	s. Specimen.	—	—	—
S537	**5 MEXICAN DOLLARS** (ca. 1901). Grayish green on m/c unpt. *(S/M #05-)*			
	a. Issued note.	600.00	1800.	—
	s. Specimen.	—	—	—

		GOOD	FINE	XF
S538	**10 MEXICAN DOLLARS** (ca. 1901). Specimen. *(S/M #05-).*	—	—	—

		GOOD	FINE	XF
S539	**50 MEXICAN DOLLARS** (ca. 1901). Specimen. *(S/M #05-).*	—	—	—

S540 100 MEXICAN DOLLARS — GOOD — FINE — XF
(ca. 1901). Specimen. *(S/M #05-).* — — —

1909 ISSUE

#S541-S545 facing dragons at l. and r. Facing dragons at l. and r., bank bldg. at bottom ctr. on back. Printer: BWC.

		GOOD	FINE	XF
S541	**1 MEXICAN DOLLAR** 14.8.1909. Black, pink and blue. *(S/M #05-40).*	400.00	1200.	—

#S542-S545 specimen perforated: *SPECIMEN*.

		GOOD	FINE	XF
S542	**5 MEXICAN DOLLARS** 1909. Brown and m/c. Specimen. *(S/M #05-41).*	—	Unc	850.00
S543	**10 MEXICAN DOLLARS** 1909. Violet and m/c. Specimen. *(S/M #05-42).*	—	Unc	1000.

		GOOD	FINE	XF
S544	**50 MEXICAN DOLLARS** 1909. Brown and m/c. Specimen. *(S/M #05-43).*	—	Unc	1250.
S545	**100 MEXICAN DOLLARS** 1909. Green and m/c. Specimen. *(S/M #05-44).*	—	Unc	1500.

TIENTSIN BRANCH 津天

1907 DOLLAR ISSUE

		GOOD	FINE	XF
S546	**1 DOLLAR** (ca. 1907-14). Printer: Nissen & Arnold, London. *(S/M #05-).*	—	—	—

1907 HONG PING HUA PAO TAEL ISSUE

#S549-S553 dragon at ctr., facing dragons at l. and r., Bank bldg. at ctr. on back. Printer: BWC.

		VG	VF	UNC
S549	**1 TAEL** Yr. 33 (1907). Red and m/c. *(S/M #05-30).*			
	a. Issued note.	450.00	1200.	—
	s. Specimen.	—	Unc	750.00
S550	**5 TAELS** Yr. 33 (1907). Green. Specimen. *(S/M #05-31).*	—	Unc	900.00
S551	**10 TAELS** Yr. 33 (1907). Specimen. *(S/M #05-32).*	—	Unc	1050.
S552	**50 TAELS** Yr. 33 (1907). Specimen. *(S/M #05-33).*	—	Unc	1350.

		VG	VF	UNC
S553	**100 TAELS** Yr. 33 (1907). Specimen. *(S/M #05-34).*	—	Unc	1800.
S554	**500 TAELS** Yr. 33 (1907). Specimen.	—	Rare	—

BANQUE SINO-BELGE, 1902-20

行銀比華
Hua Pi Yin Hang

Formerly the Sino-Belgian Bank.

NOTE-ISSUING BRANCHES:

Hankow Shanghai Tientsin

HANKOW BRANCH 口漢

1902-08 ISSUE

		VG	VF	UNC
S555	**1 DOLLAR** 1902-08. *(S/M #H190-1c).*	Reported Not Confirmed		
S556	**5 DOLLARS** 1902-08. Orange and green. *(S/M #H190-2c).*	—	Rare	—
S557	**10 DOLLARS** 1902-08. Blue and rose. *(S/M #H190-3c).*	—	Rare	—
S558	**50 DOLLARS** 1902-08. *(S/M #H190-4c).*	Reported Not Confirmed		

SHANGHAI BRANCH 海上

1902-08 ISSUE

		VG	VF	UNC
S561	**1 DOLLAR** 1902-08. *(S/M #H190-1a).*	—	Rare	—
S562	**5 DOLLARS** 1902-08. Orange and green. *(S/M #H190-2a).*	—	Rare	—
S563	**10 DOLLARS** 1902-08. Blue and rose. *(S/M #H190-3a).*	—	Rare	—
S564	**50 DOLLARS** 1902-08. *(S/M #H190-4a).*	—	Rare	—

1908-12 MEXICAN DOLLAR ISSUE

#S567-S568 printer: GD.

		VG	VF	UNC
S567	**5 MEXICAN DOLLARS** 1.7.1908; 15.7.1912. Red and green. *(S/M #H190-).*	—	Rare	—

NOTE: The ovpt: *BANK BELGE POUR L'ETRANGER* in upper r. margin was applied later to #S567. Refer to #S130.

		VG	VF	UNC
S568	**10 MEXICAN DOLLARS** 1.7.1908; 15.7.1912. *(S/M #H190-).*	—	Rare	—

TIENTSIN BRANCH 津天

1902-08 ISSUE

		VG	VF	UNC
S571	**1 DOLLAR** 1902-08. *(S/M #H190-1b).*	—	Rare	—
S572	**5 DOLLARS** 1902-04. *(S/M #H190-2b).*	—	Rare	—
S573	**10 DOLLARS** 1902-04. *(S/M #H190-3b).*	—	Rare	—
S574	**50 DOLLARS** 1902-04. *(S/M #H190-4b).*	—	Rare	—

SINO-SCANDINAVIAN BANK

行銀威華
Hua Wei Yin Hang

NOTE-ISSUING BRANCHES:

Ch'ang Li (Yungchi currency)
Chinwangtao
Peking
Suiyan
Tientsin
Yungchi
Yungtsun

CH'ANG LI BRANCH 梁昌

1922 PROVISIONAL ISSUES

		VG	VF	UNC
S580	**1 YÜAN** 1.2.1922. Green. Ovpt. on #S585. *(S/M #H192-2c).*	15.00	30.00	60.00
S581	**5 YÜAN** 1.2.1922. Brown. Ovpt. on #S587. *(S/M #H192-4b).*	9.00	20.00	45.00

		VG	VF	UNC
S582	**10 YÜAN** 1.2.1922. Blue-black and rule. *(S/M #H192-5c).*			
	a. Ovpt. on #S588. *(S/M #H192-).*	8.00	15.00	40.00
	b. Ovpt. on #S590C. *(S/M #H192-).*	9.00	20.00	45.00
S583	**10 YÜAN** 1.2.1922. Blue and m/c. Ovpt. on #S589A. *(S/M #H192-6c).*	10.00	25.00	50.00

CHINWANGTAO BRANCH 島皇秦

1926 ISSUE

#S583A-S584B Great Wall at ctr. on back. Printer: BEPP.

		VG	VF	UNC
S583A	**16 COPPER COINS** 1926. Purple on orange unpt. Woocha tea house, bridge at l. *(S/M #H192-20b).*	—	—	—

#S584-S584B Woocha tea house, bridge at ctr.

		VG	VF	UNC
S584	**30 COPPER COINS** 1926. Purple and green. *(S/M #H192-21).*	30.00	80.00	150.00

		VG	VF	UNC
S584A	**48 COPPER COINS** 1926. Red on pale green unpt. *(S/M #H192-23b).*	—	—	—
S584B	**50 COPPER COINS** 1926. Violet on brown unpt. Back violet on pink unpt. *(S/M #H192-23.5).*	—	—	—

PEKING BRANCH 京北

1922 ISSUES

#S585 and S588 Viking ship at ctr. on back. Printer: BEPP.

		VG	VF	UNC
S585	**1 YÜAN** 1.2.1922. Green. Stone arch bridge at ctr. *(S/M #H192-2a).*	15.00	30.00	70.00
S586	**1 YÜAN** 1.2.1922. Green and m/c. Like #S585. *(S/M #H192-1a).*			
	a. Issued note.	18.00	35.00	80.00
	b. W/additional numerical ovpt: *10.*	20.00	40.00	90.00
S587	**5 YÜAN** 1.2.1922. Brown. Hillside pagoda, shoreline at ctr. *(S/M #H192-4a).*	18.00	35.00	80.00

		GOOD	FINE	XF
S588	**10 YÜAN** 1.2.1922. Blue-black and m/c. Hillside pagoda, shoreline at ctr. *(S/M #H192-6a).*	7.50	25.00	75.00

1922 PROVISIONAL ISSUE

		VG	VF	UNC
S589 (S587A)	**1 YÜAN** 1.2.1922. Green and m/c. Ovpt. on #S591. *(S/M #H192-1c).*	20.00	45.00	100.00
S589A	**10 YÜAN** 1.2.1922. Blue-black and m/c. Ovpt. on #S594. *(S/M #H192-5b).*	8.00	30.00	80.00

SUIYUAN BRANCH 遠綏

1922 PROVISIONAL ISSUE

#S590-S590C Suiyuan ovpt. w/rosettes, *YUNGCHI CURRENCY* across lower center and place name below serial #.

		GOOD	FINE	XF
S590	**1 YÜAN** 1.2.1922. Green. Ovpt. on #S585. *(S/M #H192-2b).*	12.50	37.50	110.00
S590A	**5 YÜAN** 1.2.1922. Brown. Ovpt. on #S587. *(S/M #H192-4c).*	12.50	37.50	110.00
S590B	**10 YÜAN** 1.2.1922. Blue-black and m/c. Ovpt. on #S588. *(S/M #H192-6-).*	12.50	37.50	—

1922 ISSUE

		GOOD	FINE	XF
S590C	**10 YÜAN** 1.2.1922. Blue-black and m/c. *(S/M #H192-6).*	—	—	—

TIENTSIN BRANCH 津天

1922 ISSUE

		GOOD	FINE	XF
S591	**1 YÜAN** 1.2.1922. Green and m/c. *(S/M #H192-1b).*	10.00	35.00	80.00

		GOOD	FINE	XF
S592	**5 YÜAN** 1.2.1922. Brown and m/c. *(S/M #H192-5a).*			
	a. Issued note.	5.00	10.00	30.00
	b. W/various Chinese control character ovpt. at upper l. and r. on face.	8.00	15.00	40.00
S593	**10 YÜAN** 1.2.1922. Blue-black and m/c. Coastline at ctr. *(S/M #H192-6b).*			
	a. Issued note.	5.00	15.00	42.50
	b. W/various Chinese control character ovpt. at upper l. and r. on face.	5.00	17.50	47.50
S594	**10 YÜAN** 1.2.1922. Blue-black and m/c. Ovpt. on #S588. *(S/M #H192-6b).*	5.00	17.50	47.50

1925 ISSUE

		GOOD	FINE	XF
S595	**10 CENTS** 1.10.1925. Green. Bridge at l. Back orange. Printer: BEPP. *(S/M #H192-10).*	4.00	8.00	20.00
S595A	**10 CENTS** 1.10.1925. Like #S595 but back dk. red w/different sign. variety at r. *(S/M #H192-).*	5.00	12.00	30.00

		GOOD	FINE	XF
S596	**20 CENTS** 1.10.1925. Orange. Bridge at l. Printer: BEPP. *(S/M #H192-11).*	8.00	20.00	50.00

YUNGCHI BRANCH

1925 PROVISIONAL ISSUE

		GOOD	FINE	XF
S596A	**5 YÜAN** 1.10.1925. Ovpt. on #S590A. *(S/M #H192-).*	—	—	—

YUNGTSUN BRANCH 遵永

1926 ISSUE

#S597-S600 Great Wall at ctr. on back. Printer: BEPP.

		GOOD	FINE	XF
S597	**16 COPPER COINS** 1926. Blue and orange. *(S/M #H192-20).*	20.00	60.00	180.00
S597A	**30 COPPER COINS** 1926. Bldg's, bridge at ctr. *(S/M #H192-).*	20.00	60.00	180.00

		GOOD	FINE	XF
S598	**32 COPPER COINS** 1926. Green and brown. Bridge at r. Remainder. *(S/M #H192-22).*	—	—	120.00

		GOOD	FINE	XF
S599	**48 COPPER COINS** 1926. Red on pale green unpt. Like #S584A. Remainder w/o serial #. *(S/M #H192-23a).*	—	—	150.00
S600	**80 COPPER COINS** 1926. *(S/M #H192-24).*	25.00	80.00	250.00

BANK OF TAIWAN (LIMITED)

行銀灣台

T'ai Wan Yin Hang

NOTE-ISSUING BRANCH

ES:

Amoy	Canton	Foochow
Hankow	Kiukiang	Shanghai

AMOY BRANCH 門厦

1905-09 PROVISIONAL ISSUE

#S601-S604 withdrawn silver certificates hand stamped for Amoy Branch. See Vol. 2.

		GOOD	FINE	XF
S601	**1 YEN** 10.1.1905. Hand stamped on #907. *(S/M #T71-1).*	—	Rare	—
S602	**5 YEN** 10.1.1905. Hand stamped on #908. *(S/M #T71-2).*	—	Rare	—
S603	**10 YEN** Nov. 1906. Hand stamped on #909. *(S/M #T71-12).*	—	Rare	—
S604	**50 YEN** Jan. 1909. Hand stamped on #910. *(S/M #T71-23).*	—	Rare	—

CANTON BRANCH

1911 "LOCAL CURRENCY" ISSUE

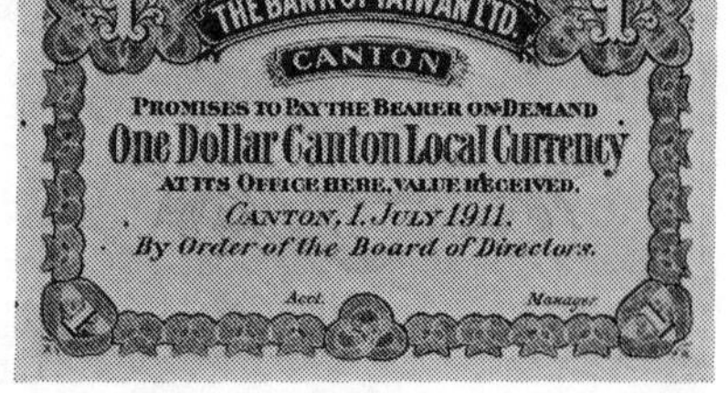

		GOOD	FINE	XF
S604A	**1 YEN** 1.7.1911. Facing dragons at upper l. and r. on back. *Kuangtung. (S/M #T71-).*	—	—	—

FOOCHOW BRANCH 州福

1906 ISSUE

#5605-S612 specimen, punched hole cancelled.

		GOOD	FINE	XF
S605	**1 DOLLAR** 7.3.1906. *(S/M #T71-10).*	—	Rare	—
S606	**5 DOLLARS** 7.3.1906. *(S/M #T71-11).*	—	Rare	—

		Good	Fine	XF
S607	**1 Dollar** Oct. 1906. *(S/M #T71-).*	—	Unc	2500.
S608	**5 Dollars** Oct. 1906. *(S/M #T71-).*	—	Rare	—

1914 Issue

		Good	Fine	XF
S609	**10 Dollars** April 1914. *(S/M #T71-53).*	—	Rare	—
S610	**10 Dollars** 1.8.1914. *(S/M #T71-54).*	—	Rare	—
S611	**50 Dollars** 1.8.1914. *(S/M #T71-55).*	—	Rare	—

1916 Issue

		Good	Fine	XF
S612	**50 Dollars** Jan. 1916. *(S/M #T71-67).*	—	Rare	—

Hankow Branch 口漢

1915-18 Issue

#S613-S615 specimen.

		Good	Fine	XF
S613	**1 Dollar** 1.5.1915. *(S/M #T71-60).*	—	Rare	—

		Good	Fine	XF
S614	**5 Dollars** 1.9.1917. *(S/M #T71-61).*	—	Rare	—
S615	**10 Dollars** 1.4.1918. *(S/M #T71-62).*	—	Rare	—

Kiukiang Branch 江九

1913 Issue

#S616-S618 specimen.

		Good	Fine	XF
S616	**1 Dollar** 4.6.1913. *(S/M #T71-44).*	—	Rare	—
S617	**5 Dollars** July 1913. *(S/M #T71-45).*	—	Rare	—
S618	**10 Dollars** July 1913. *(S/M #T71-46).*	—	Rare	—

1914 Issue

#S619-S621 specimen.

		Good	Fine	XF
S619	**1 Dollar** Feb. 1914. *(S/M #T71-50).*	—	Rare	—
S620	**5 Dollars** Feb. 1914. *(S/M #T71-51).*	—	Rare	—
S621	**10 Dollars** Feb. 1914. *(S/M #T71-52).*	—	Rare	—

Shanghai Branch 海上

1915 Issue

#S622-S624 specimen.

		Good	Fine	XF
S622	**1 Dollar** 1.12.1915. *(S/M #T71-).*	—	Rare	—
S623	**5 Dollars** 1.12.1915. *(S/M #T71-).*	—	Rare	—
S624	**10 Dollars** 1.12.1915. *(S/M #T71-).*	—	Rare	—

1916-17 "Local Currency" Issue

#S625-S626 specimen.

		Good	Fine	XF
S625	**5 Dollars** 1.6.1916. *(S/M #T71-65).*	—	Rare	—
S626	**10 Dollars** 1.11.1917. *(S/M #T71-66).*	—	Rare	—

Swatow Branch 頭汕

1908 Issue

#S627-S629 specimen.

		Good	Fine	XF
S627	**1 Dollar** 4.1.1908. *(S/M #T71-20).*	—	Rare	—
S628	**5 Dollars** 4.1.1908. *(S/M #T71-21).*	—	Rare	—
S629	**10 Dollars** 4.1.1908. *(S/M #T71-22).*	—	Rare	—

1911 Issue

#S630-S633 specimen.

		Good	Fine	XF
S630	**5 Dollars** 1.10.1911. *(S/M #T71-41).*	—	Rare	—
S631	**10 Dollars** 1.11.1911. *(S/M #T71-42).*	—	Rare	—
S632	**50 Dollars** Dec. 1911. *(S/M #T71-43).*	—	Rare	—
S633	**50 Dollars** 1.12.1911. *(S/M #T71-33)*	—	Rare	—

A word on pricing

When a note is marked RARE in the price columns, this note seldom appears on the market, or few are known in private hands. When dashes are in the price column, means that the note has not traded on the open market recently and a definitive value could not accurately be determined. Rare does not always mean expensive. A dashed price does not mean expensive or rare.

1912 ISSUE

		Good	Fine	XF
S634	**1 DOLLAR** 1.3.1912. Specimen. *(S/M #T71-40).*	—	Rare	—

YOKOHAMA SPECIE BANK, LIMITED

行銀金正濱橫

Heng Pin Cheng Chin Yin Hang

NOTE-ISSUING BRANCHES:

Tsinan	Harbin	Shanghai
Dairen	Newchwang	Tientsin
Hankow	Peking	Tsingtao

TSINAN (CHINAN) BRANCH 南濟

1920 ISSUE

		Good	Fine	XF
S635	**1 DOLLAR** 15.1.1920. Green and black. *(S/M #H31-125a).*	—	Rare	—
S636	**5 DOLLARS** 15.1.1920. Violet and black. *(S/M #H31-126a).*	—	Rare	—

		Good	Fine	XF
S637	**10 DOLLARS** 15.1.1920. Green and black. 107 x 173mm. *(S/M #H31-127a).*	—	Rare	—

DAIREN BRANCH 連大

1913 ISSUE

		Good	Fine	XF
S644	**100 DOLLARS** 1.2.1913. Violet and black. *(S/M #H31-76).*	—	Rare	—

1913 GOLD YEN ISSUE

		Good	Fine	XF
S645	**1 GOLD YEN** ND (1913). Brown and black. *(S/M #H31-71).*	—	Rare	—

		Good	Fine	XF
S646	**5 GOLD YEN** ND (1913). Brown and green. *(S/M #H31-73).*	—	Rare	—
S647	**10 GOLD YEN** ND (1913). Violet and black. *(S/M #H31-75).*	—	Rare	—

		Good	Fine	XF
S648	**100 GOLD YEN** ND (1915). Blue, gold and black. *(S/M #H31-103).*	—	Rare	—
S649	**1 GOLD YEN** ND (1916). Orange and black. *(S/M #H31-).*	—	Rare	—
S650	**5 GOLD YEN** ND (1916). Gray and black. *(S/M #H31-).*	—	Rare	—
S651	**10 GOLD YEN** ND (1917). Gray and black. *(S/M #H31-).*	—	Rare	—

1918 ND ISSUE

		Good	Fine	XF
S652	**10 SEN** ND (1918). Blue on brown unpt. Bank bldg. at r. Back green w/black text. *(S/M #H31-130a).*	150.00	350.00	600.00
S653	**50 SEN** ND (1918). Brown, green and black. Bank bldg. at r. *(S/M #H31-131a).*	—	Rare	—

1918 DOLLAR LOCAL CURRENCY ISSUES

		Good	Fine	XF
S654	**100 DOLLARS** 25.12.1918. Violet and black. Serial # at upper l. and upper r. *(S/M #H31-).*	—	Rare	—
S655	**100 DOLLARS** 25.12.1918 (1925). Violet and black. Serial # at upper l. and lower r. *(S/M #H31-).*	—	Rare	—

1927 ND PROVISIONAL ISSUES

		Good	Fine	XF
S656	**100 DOLLARS** ND (1927 -old date 1.6.1927). Ovpt. on Peking #S704. *(S/M #H31-).*	—	Rare	—

		Good	Fine	XF
S657	**100 DOLLARS** ND (1926 -old date 1.5.1925). Ovpt. on Tientsin #S731. *(S/M #H31-).*	—	Rare	—
S658	**100 DOLLARS** ND (1926 -old date 1.8.1917). Ovpt. on Tsingtao #S745. *(S/M #H31-).*	—	Rare	—

1930 REGULAR ISSUE

		GOOD	FINE	XF
S659	**1 DOLLAR** 1.4.1930. Brown and black. *(S/M #H31-).*	300.00	600.00	1200.
S660	**5 DOLLARS** 1.4.1930. Slate and black. *(S/M #H31 -).*	—	Rare	—
S661	**10 DOLLARS** 1.4.1930. Gold and black. *(S/M #H31 -).*	—	Rare	—

HANKOW BRANCH 口漢

1917 DOLLAR LOCAL CURRENCY ISSUE

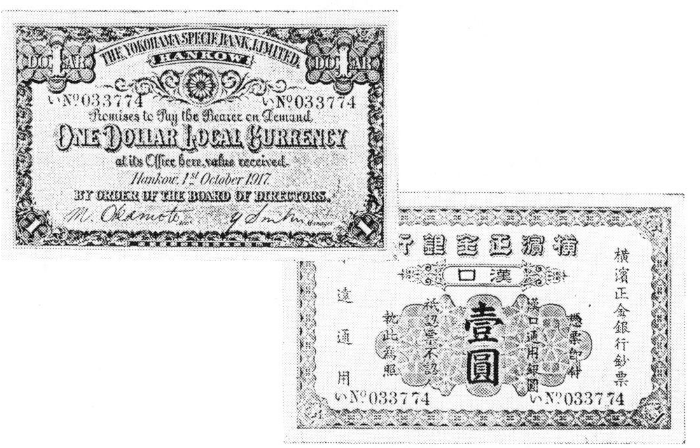

		GOOD	FINE	XF
S662	**1 DOLLAR** 1.10.1917. Blue and black. Back blue and yellow. *(S/M #H31-125b).*	225.00	400.00	750.00
S663	**5 DOLLARS** 1.10.1917. Olive-green and black. Back brown. *(S/M #H31-126b).*	—	Rare	—

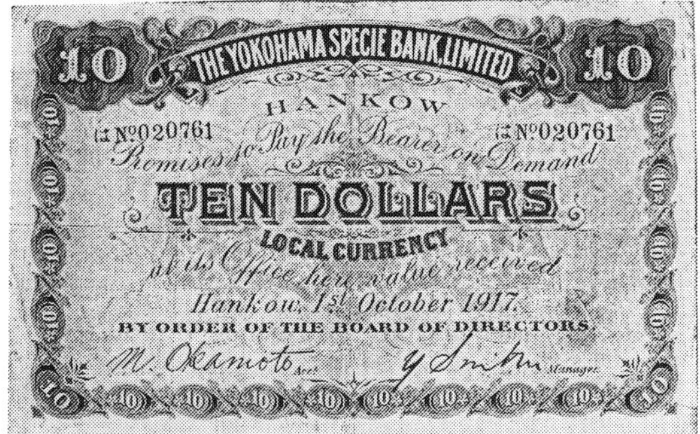

		GOOD	FINE	XF
S664	**10 DOLLARS** 1.10.1917. Green. Bank bldg. at lower ctr. Back brown and orange-yellow. *(S/M #H31-127b).*	—	Rare	—
S665	**100 DOLLARS** 1.10.1917. Brown and yellow. Bank bldg. at r. Back green and black. *(S/M #H31-128b).*	—	Rare	—

HARBIN BRANCH 賓爾哈

1921 DOLLAR LOCAL CURRENCY PROVISIONAL ISSUE

		GOOD	FINE	XF
S666	**1 DOLLAR** 1.5.1921. Ovpt. on Tsinan #S635. *(S/M #H31-).*	—	Rare	—

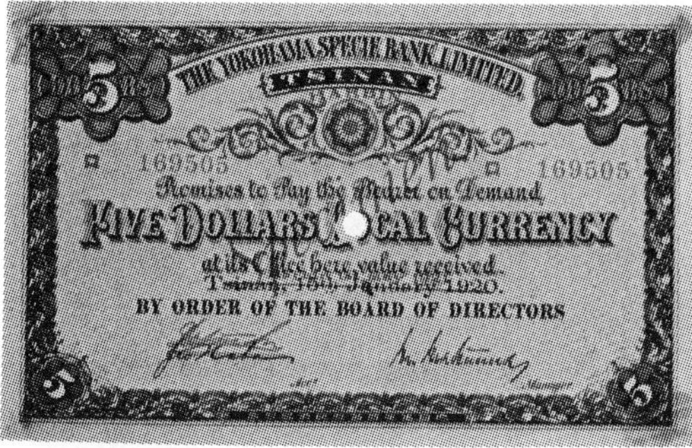

		GOOD	FINE	XF
S667	**5 DOLLARS** 1.5.1921. Ovpt. on Tsinan #S636. *(S/M #H31-).*	—	Rare	—
S668	**10 DOLLARS** 1.5.1921. Ovpt. on Tsinan #S637. *(S/M #H31-).*	—	Rare	—
S669	**50 DOLLARS** 1.5.1921. Ovpt. on Shanghai #S715. *(S/M #H31-).*	—	Rare	—
S670	**100 DOLLARS** 1.5.1921. Ovpt. on Shanghai #S716. *(S/M #H31-).*	—	Rare	—

1921 REGULAR ISSUE

		GOOD	FINE	XF
S671	**1 DOLLAR** 15.12.1921. Gray and black. *(S/M #H31-).*	—	Rare	—
S672	**5 DOLLARS** 15.12.1921. Gray and black. *(S/M #H31-).*	—	Rare	—

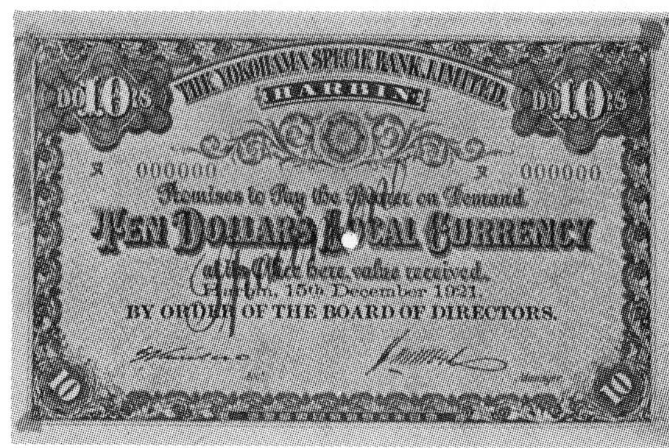

		GOOD	FINE	XF
S673	**10 DOLLARS** 15.12.1921. Gray and black. *(S/M #H31-).*	—	Rare	—
S674	**100 DOLLARS** 15.12.1921. Green and black. *(S/M #H31-).*	—	Rare	—

NEWCHWANG BRANCH 莊牛

1902 NEWCHANG TAEL ISSUE

		GOOD	FINE	XF
S675	**1 TAEL** 1.7.1902. Gold and black. *(S/M #H31-10a).*	—	Rare	—
S676	**5 TAELS** 1.7.1902. Green and black. *(S/M #H31-11a).*	—	Rare	—

		GOOD	FINE	XF
S677	**10 TAELS** 1.7.1902. Blue and black. *(S/M #H31-12a).*	—	Rare	—
S678	**50 TAELS** 1.7.1902. Brown and black. *(S/M #H31-13a).*	—	Rare	—
S679	**100 TAELS** 1.7.1902. Violet and black. *(S/M #H31-14a).*	—	Rare	—

1902 SMALL SILVER COIN ISSUE

#S680-S682 3 lg. characters in oval on each side of face.

		GOOD	FINE	XF
S680	**1 DOLLAR** 1.7.1902. Lt. green and black. *(S/M #H31-30).*	—	Rare	—
S681	**5 DOLLARS** 1.7.1902. Lt. green and black. *(S/M #H31-33).*	—	Rare	—
S682	**10 DOLLARS** 1.7.1902. Lt. green and black. *(S/M #H31-36).*	—	Rare	—

1902 DOLLAR LOCAL CURRENCY ISSUE

#S683-S685 western serial # on both face and back.

		GOOD	FINE	XF
S683	**1 DOLLAR** 1.7.1902. Black and brown. *(S/M #H31-).*	—	Rare	—
S684	**5 DOLLARS** 1.7.1902. Black and blue. *(S/M #H31-).*	—	Rare	—
S685	**10 DOLLARS** 1.7.1902. Black and yellow. *(S/M #H31-).*	—	Rare	—

#S686-S687 Chinese serial # on face, western serial # on back.

		GOOD	FINE	XF
S686	**1 DOLLAR** 1.7.1902. Red and black. *(S/M #H31-).*			
	a. Issued note.	225.00	600.00	1350.
	b. W/ovpt: OR *IN TIENTSIN.* Specimen.	—	Rare	—
S687	**5 DOLLARS** 1.7.1902. Purple and black. *(S/M #H31-).*			
	a. Issued note.	500.00	1000.	—
	b. W/ovpt: OR *IN TIENTSIN.* Specimen.	—	Rare	—

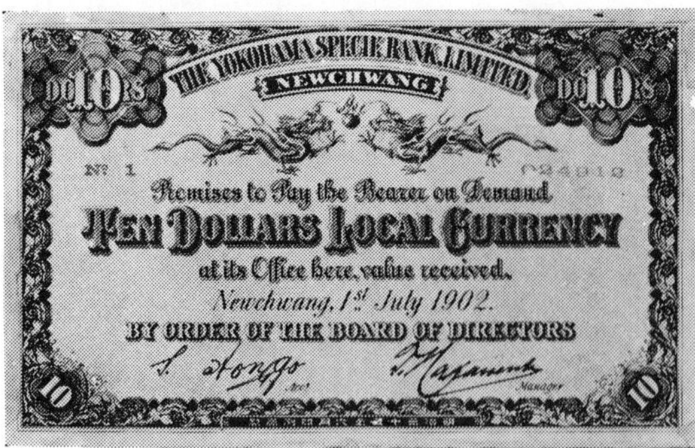

		Good	Fine	XF
S688	**10 Dollars** 1.7.1902. Black and gold. *(S/M #H31-).*	600.00	1250.	—

#S690-S692 ***Deleted.*** **See #S686a and S687a.**

Peking Branch 京北

1910 Dollar Local Currency Issue

		Good	Fine	XF
S695	**1 Dollar** 15.8.1910. Green and black. *(S/M #H31-60).*	—	Rare	—
S696	**5 Dollars** 15.8.1910. Red-brown and black. *(S/M #H31-61).*	—	Rare	—
S697	**10 Dollars** 15.8.1910. Red-brown and black. *(S/M #H31-62).*	—	Rare	—

		Good	Fine	XF
S698	**50 Dollars** 15.8.1910. Olive-green and black. *(S/M #H31-63).*	—	Rare	—

1920-27 Issue

		Good	Fine	XF
S700	**1 Dollar** 15.7.1920. Green and black. *(S/M #H31-).*	400.00	900.00	—
S702	**10 Dollars** 15.7.1920. Brown and black. *(S/M #H31-).*	750.00	1500.	—
S703	**50 Dollars** 15.12.1921. Green and black. *(S/M #H31-).*	—	Rare	—
S704	**100 Dollars** 1.6.1927. Orange and black. *(S/M #H31-).*	—	Rare	—

Shanghai Branch 海上

1902; 1907 Dollar Local Currency Issue

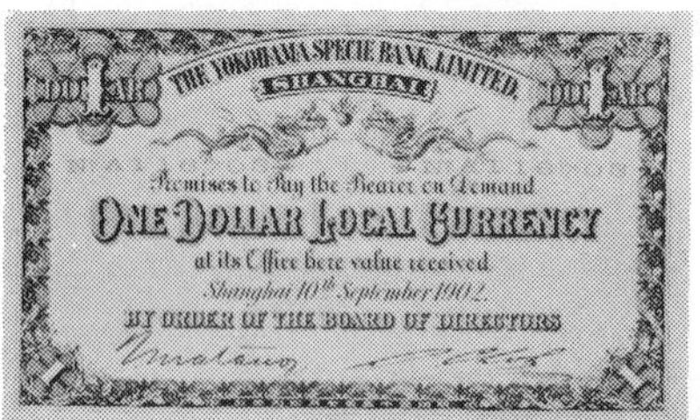

		Good	Fine	XF
S705	**1 Dollar** 10.9.1902. Brown and black. *(S/M #H31-32c).*	250.00	600.00	—
S706	**5 Dollars** 10.9.1902. Violet and black. *(S/M #H31-35c).*	450.00	900.00	—
S707	**10 Dollars** 10.9.1902. Gold and black. *(S/M #H31-38c).*	—	Rare	—
S708	**50 Dollars** 1.5.1907 (1909). Olive-green and black. black. *(S/M #H31-50).*	—	Rare	—
S709	**100 Dollars** 1.5.1907 (1909). Blue and black. *(S/M #H31-51).*	—	Rare	—

1914 Issue

		Good	Fine	XF
S711	**10 Dollars** 1.7.1914. Purple, orange and black. *(S/M #H31-80).*	—	Rare	—

1918 Issue

		Good	Fine	XF
S713	**5 Dollars** 15.6.1918. Violet and black. *(S/M #H31-140).*	—	Rare	—
S714	**10 Dollars** 15.6.1918. Purple and orange. *(S/M #H31-141).*	—	Rare	—
S715	**50 Dollars** 15.6.1918. Olive-green and black. *(S/M #H31-142).*	—	Rare	—
S716	**100 Dollars** 15.6.1918. Blue and black. *(S/M #H31-143).*	—	Rare	—

TIENTSIN BRANCH 津天

1902 DOLLAR LOCAL CURRENCY ISSUE

		GOOD	FINE	XF
S718	**1 DOLLAR** 1.7.1902. Red-brown and black. *(S/M #H31-32d).*	250.00	500.00	900.00
S719	**5 DOLLARS** 1.7.1902. Violet and black. *(S/M #H31-35d).*	—	Rare	—
S720	**10 DOLLARS** 1.7.1902. Gold and black. *(S/M #H31-38d).*	—	Rare	—

1918 ISSUE

		GOOD	FINE	XF
S721	**1 DOLLAR** 15.6.1918. Brown and black. *(S/M #H31-).*	150.00	450.00	—

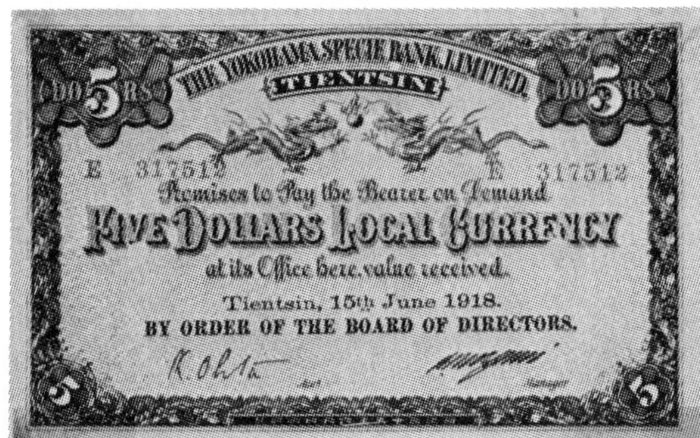

		GOOD	FINE	XF
S722	**5 DOLLARS** 15.6.1918. Blue and black. *(S/M #H31-).*	—	Rare	—
S723	**10 DOLLARS** 15.6.1918. Tan and black. *(S/M #H31-).*	—	Rare	—
S725	**100 DOLLARS** 1.3.1918. Green and black. *(S/M #H31-).*	—	Rare	—

1925 ISSUE

		GOOD	FINE	XF
S731	**100 DOLLARS** 1.5.1925. Green and black. Sign. varieties. *(S/M #H31-).*	—	Rare	—

1902 TAEL ISSUE

		GOOD	FINE	XF
S732	**5 TAELS** 1.7.1902. Green and black. *(S/M #H31-11b).*	—	Rare	—
S733	**10 TAELS** 1.7.1902. Blue and black. *(S/M #H31-12b).*	—	Rare	—
S734	**50 TAELS** 1.7.1902. Brown and black. *(S/M #H31-13b).*	—	Rare	—

		GOOD	FINE	XF
S735	**100 TAELS** 1.7.1902. Red-brown and black. *(S/M #H31-14b).*	—	Rare	—

1937 PROVISIONAL ISSUE

		GOOD	FINE	XF
S736	**1 DOLLAR** 1.4.1937. Ovpt. on Tsingtao #S757. *(S/M #H31-).*	—	Rare	—

Notice

Readers with unlisted dates, color or signature varieties are invited to submit photocopies of their notes to: Standard Catalog of World Paper Money, Krause Publications, 700 East State St. Iola WI 54990-0001 U.S.A. or by email: thernr@krause.com. Email submissions of material for possible inclusion need to be 100% jpeg attachments at 300 dpi.

		GOOD	FINE	XF
S737	**5 DOLLARS** 1.4.1937. Ovpt. on Tsingtao #S742. *(S/M #H31-).*	—	Rare	—

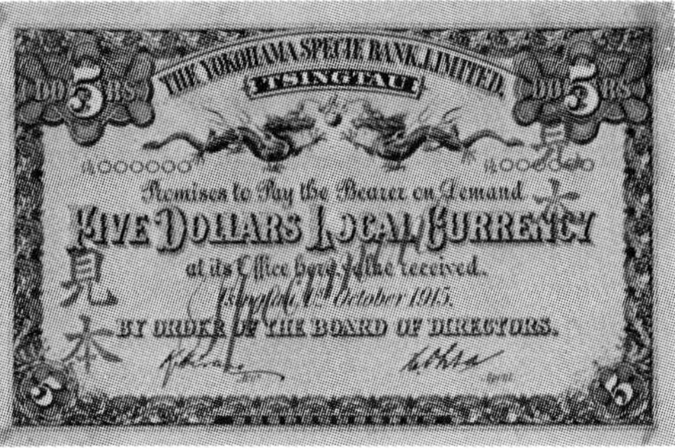

		GOOD	FINE	XF
S740	**100 DOLLARS** 1.4.1937. Ovpt. on Tsingtao #S745. *(S/M #H31-).*	—	Rare	—

TSINGTAO BRANCH 島青

1915; 1917 DOLLAR LOCAL CURRENCY ISSUE

		GOOD	FINE	XF
S741	**1 DOLLAR** 1.10.1915. Gray and black. *(S/M #H31-100).*	—	Rare	—

		GOOD	FINE	XF
S742	**5 DOLLARS** 1.10.1915. Orange and black. *(S/M #H31-101).*	—	Rare	—

		GOOD	FINE	XF
S743	**10 DOLLARS** 1.10.1915. Slate gray and black. *(S/M #H31-102).*	—	Rare	—
S745	**100 DOLLARS** 1.8.1917. Red-brown and black. *(S/M #H31-144).*	—	Rare	—

1918 ISSUE

		GOOD	FINE	XF
S746	**1 DOLLAR** 15.6.1918. Gray and black. *(S/M #H31-).*	—	Rare	—

1918 ND ISSUE

		GOOD	FINE	XF
S750	**10 SEN** ND (1918). Blue and brown. *(S/M #H31-130b).*			
	a. Agency period. (Block #1-1000).	100.00	275.00	500.00
	b. Branch period. (Block #1001-).	200.00	500.00	900.00

S751 50 SEN
ND (1918). Green and brown. *(S/M #H31-131b).* 250.00 500.00 1000.

1921 ISSUE

		GOOD	FINE	XF
S752	**1 DOLLAR** 15.12.1921. Black and violet. *(S/M #H31-).*	—	—	—

1922 ISSUE

		GOOD	FINE	XF
S753	**1 DOLLAR** 1.6.1922. Black and violet. *(S/M #H31-).*	—	Rare	—

1924 ISSUE

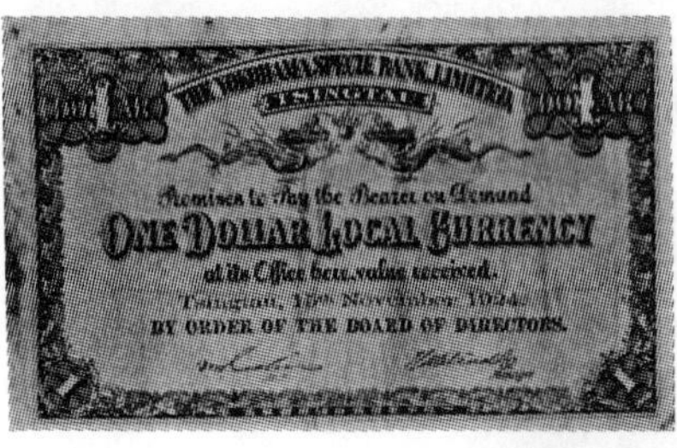

		GOOD	FINE	XF
S757	**1 DOLLAR** 15.11.1924. Black and violet. Serial # varieties. *(S/M #H31-150).*	—	Rare	—

#S758 and S759 *Deleted.*

PROVINCIAL BANKS

Some of the provincial bank note issuing authorities were originally established during the reigns of the last two Chinese emperors prior to the establishment of the new republic. As such they continued doing business as normal with notes circulating alongside those of the foreign banks, the various early military issues which were mainly overprinted notes of provincial authorities, and the rush of the endless local issuers during the next two decades of most major cities.

In some cases the old imperial notes were reissued with current years of the republic overprinted over the past emperor's name and year of reign.

The following listings, based on Ward Smith's writings, are inclusive of provincial issuers and the occasional municipal or local government issuer whose notes circulated beyond its local boundaries.

Bank of Anhwei Provincial Government #S802	號銀省徽安 *An Hui Sheng Yin Hao*
Anhwei Regional Bank #S805-S815	行銀方地徽安 *An Hui Ti Fang Yin Hang*
Anhwei Yu Huan Bank #S819-S823	局錢官皖裕徽安 *An Hui Yü Huan Kuan Ch'ien Chü*
Tsihar Hsing Yeh Bank #S825-S855	行銀業興爾哈察 *Ch'a Ha Erh Hsing Yeh Yin Hang*
Charhar Commercial Bank #S855E-S857B	局錢業商爾哈察 *Ch'a Ha Erh Shang Yeh Ch'ien Chu*
Changsha Bank #S858-S860	行 銀 沙 長 *Ch'ang Sha Yin Hang*
Chekiang Provincial Bank #S863-S869	行 銀 省 江 浙 *Che Chiang Sheng Yin Hang*
Chekiang Provincial Bank #S871-S893	行 銀 方 地 江 浙 *Che Chiang Ti Fang Yin Hang*
Kirin Government Bank #S895	局錢官林吉 *Chi Lin Kuan Ch'ien Chü*
Kirin Yung Heng Provincial Bank Yung Heng Provincial Bank of Kirin #S901-S1081F	局錢銀官衡永林吉 *Chi Lin Yung Heng Kuan Yin Ch'ien Chü*
Reconstruction Bank of Kiangsi #S1082A-S1082H	行銀設建西江 *Chiang Hsi Chien She Yin Hang*
Kiangse Government Bank #S1082L-S1085H	號總錢銀官西江 *Chiang Hsi Kuan Yin Ch'ien Tsung Hao*
Public Bank of Kiangsi #S1086-S1089	行銀立公西江 *Chiang Hsi Kung Li Yin Hang*
Kiangsi Provincial Bank #S1089C-S1089E	行銀省西江 *Chiang Hsi Sheng Yin Hang*
Kiangsi Regional Bank #S1090-S1093	行銀方地西江 *Chiang Hsi Ti Fang Yin Hang*
Kiangsi Finance Bureau #S1093D-S1096	廳政財西江 *Chiang Hsi Ts'ai Cheng T'ing*
Bank of Kiangsi #S1097-S1119	行 銀 西 江 *Chiang Hsi Yin Hang*
Yu Ming Bank of Kiangsi #S1125-S1160	行銀民裕西江 *Chiang Hsi Yü Min Yin Hang*
Kiangnan Yu-Ning Government Bank Yu Ning Imperial Bank #S1161-S1180	票鈔元局錢銀官寧裕 *Yü Ning Kuan Yin Ch'ien Chü Yüan Ch'ao P'iao*
Kiangnan Yü Su Silver Currency Bureau #S1183-S1185	局錢銀官寧裕南江 *Chiang Nan Yü Su Kuan Yin Ch'ien Chü*
Kiang Shun Government Bank #S1188	號銀官省江 *Chiang Sheng Kuan Yin Hao*
Kiangsu Farmers Bank Kingsu Farmers Bank #S1191-S1205	行銀民農省蘇江 *Chiang Su Sheng Nung Min Yin Hang*

Kiangsu Province
#S1208-S1213
券換兌省蘇江
Chiang Su Sheng Tui Huan Ch'üan

Nanking Exchange Office of the Financial Department, Kiangsu
#S1215-S1217
處換兌京政司南財蘇江
Chiang Su Ts'ai Cheng Szu Nan Ching Tui Huan Ch'üan

Kiangsu Finance Department
#S1220-S1224
廳政財蘇江
Chiang Su Ts'ai Cheng T'ing

Kiangsu Bank
#S1226-S1227
行 銀 蘇 江
Chiang Su Yin Hang

Yue Soo Imperial Bank
#S1228-S1234
局錢銀官蘇裕蘇江
Chiang Su Yü Su Kuan Yin Ch'ien Chü

Chihli Provincial Treasury
#S1238-S1243
券換兌庫金省隸直
Chih Li Sheng Chin K'u Tui Huan Ch'üan

Chihli Province
#S1247-S1252
券通流期定庫省隸直
Chih Li Sheng K'u Ting Ch'i Liu T'ung Ch'üan

Provincial Bank of Chihli
#S1254-S1290
局錢官省隸直
Chih Li Sheng Kuan Ch'ien Chü
行銀省隸直
Chih Li Sheng Yin Hang

Bank of Local Railways of Shansi and Suiyüan
#S1291-S1301
號銀路鐵方地綏晉
Chin Sui Ti Fang T'ieh Lu Yin Hao

Tsingtao City Agricultural and Industrial Bank
#S1302-S1302C
行銀工農市島青
Ch'ing Tao Shih Nung Kung Yin Hang

Tsingtao (Regional) City Bank
#S1302D-S1302L
行銀方地島青
Ch'ing Tao Ti Fang Yin Hang

Fengtien Industrial Bank
Hsin Yieh Bank
Shing Yeh Bank
Mukden Bank of Industrial Development
Fentien Hsing Yeh Bank
#S1303-S1325
行銀業興天奉
Feng T'ien Hsing Yeh Yin Hang

Hua Feng Official Currency Bureau
#S1327-S1329
號銀官豐華天奉
Feng T'ien Hua Feng Kuan Yin Hao

Fengtien Official Currency Bureau
#S1330-S1354
號銀官天奉
Feng T'ien Kuan Yin Hao

Fengtien Public Exchange Bank
Kung Tsi Bank of Fengtien
#S1355-S1380
號錢市平濟公天奉
Feng T'ien Kung Chi P'ing Shih Ch'ien Hao

Fengtien Agricultural and Industrial Bank
#S1383-S1393
行銀總業農天奉
Feng T'ien Nung Yeh Tsung Yin Hang

Fukien Provincial Bank
#S1395-S1431
行銀省建福
Fu Chien Sheng Yin Hang

Fukien Bank
#S1435-S1440
行銀建福
Fu Chien Yin Hang

Fu Lung Bank
#S1443-S1447
行銀隴富
Fu Luang Yin Hang

Hainan Bank
#S1451-S1459
行 銀 南 海
Hai Nan Yin Hang

Hio Lung Kiang Government Bank
#S1461-S1515
號銀官江龍黑
Hei Lung Chiang Kuan Yin Hao

Kwang Sing Company/Heilungchiang
Kuang Hsin Syndicate of Heilungkiang
#S1521-S1619G
司公信廣
Kuang Hsin Kung Szu
江龍黑
Hei Lung Chiang

Provincial Bank of Heilungkiang
#S1621-S1627
號銀官省江龍黑
Hei Lung Chiang Sheng Kuan Yin Hao

Amoor Government Bank
#S1631-S1653
號銀省江龍黑
Hei Lung Chiang Kuan Yin Hao
券元銀小
Hsiao Yin Yüan Ch'üan

Provincial Bank of Honan
#S1661-S1693
行銀省南河
Ho Nan Sheng Yin Hang
行銀南河
Ho Nan Yin Hang

Bank of Honan Province
Yü Ch'üan Bank of Honan
#S1691-S1700
局錢銀官泉豫南河
Ho Nan Yü Ch'üan Kuan Yin Ch'ien Chü

Hopei Province
#S1708
券通流時臨縣冀/省北河
Ho Pei Sheng/Chi Hsien Lin Shih Liu T'ung Chüan

Ho Pei Metropolitan Bank
#S1709-S1710B
局錢銀北河
Ho Pei Yin Ch'ien Chü

Bank of Hopei
#S1711-S1735
行銀北河
Ho Pei Yin Hang
行銀省北河
Ho Pei Sheng Yin Hang

Khotan District Administration
#S1737
印長政行區闐和
Ho Tien Ch'ü Hang Cheng Chang Yin

Khotan Administration Government Head Public Office
#S1738
Not Available
Ho T'ien Hsing Cheng Ch'ang Kung Shu Yin Liu(?) T'ung

Sikang Provincial Bank
#S1739-S1740
行銀省康西
Hsi K'ang Sheng Yin Hang

Subtreasury of Sinkiang - Official Note
#S1742
票官庫藩疆新
Hsin Chiang Fan k'u Kuan P'iao

Main Official Currency Bureau of Sinkiang
#S1742A-S1742B
局總錢官疆新
Hsin Chiang Kuan Ch'ien Tsung Chü

Sinkiang Commercial and Industrial Bank
#S1743-S1778
行銀業商疆新
Hsin Chiang Shang Yeh Yin Hang

Industrial and Commercial Bank of Sinkiang, Ili Branch
#S1778A-S1778H
票財行分梨伊行銀業商疆新
Hsin Chiańg Shang Yeh Yin Hang I Li Fen Hang Ts'ai P'iao

Sinkiang Sub-prefecture Administration Finance Department Treasury - Official Note
#S1779-S1780F
票官庫廳政財府政省疆新
Hsin Chiang Sheng Cheng Fu Ts'ai Cheng T'ing Ku Kuan P'iao

Sinkiang Province
#S1781-S1783
券庫金省疆新
Hsin Chiang Sheng Chin K'u Ch'üan

Sinkiang Provincial Bank
#S1786-S1807
行銀省疆新
Hsin Chiang Sheng Yin Hang

Treasury Department of Sinkiang - Official Note
#S1808
票官庫司疆新
Hsin Chiang Szu K'u Kuan P'iao

Provincial Treasury of Sinkiang - Official Note
#S1809-S1810
票官庫廳疆新
Hsin Chiang T'ing K'u Kuan P'iao

Sinkiang Finance Department Treasury
#S1811-S1882
票官庫廳政財府政省疆新
Hsin Chiang/Ts'ai Cheng Ting K'u Kuan P'iao

Monetary Bureau of Government Suchow
#S1891A-S1891C
局錢官市平州徐
Hsü Chou P'ing Shih Kuan Ch'ien Chü

Hulunpeierh Official Currency Bureau
#S1892A-S1892M
局錢商官爾貝倫呼
Hu Lun Pei Erh Kuan Shang Ch'ien Chü

Official Mint Hunan
Hunan Government Bank
#S1893-S1930
局錢官南湖
Hu Nan Kuan Ch'ien Chü

Hunan Provincial Treasury
#S1936-S1948
廳政財省南湖
Hu Nan Sheng Ts'ai Cheng T'ing

Hunan Provincial Bank
Provincial Bank of Hunan
#S1951-S1994
行銀省南湖
Hu Nan Sheng Yin Hang

Hunan Industrial Bank
#S1996-S2011
行銀業實南湖
Hu Nan Shih Yeh Yin Hang

Hunan Treasury
#S2016-S2020
券証庫金利有期定南湖
Hu Nan Ting Ch'i Yu Li Chin K'u Cheng Ch'üan

Hunan Bank
Hunan Provincial Bank
#S2022-S2078
行銀南湖
Hu Nan Yin Hang

Hupeh Government Cash Bank
Hupeh Provincial Bank
#S2081-S2098
局錢官北湖
Hu Pei Kuan Ch'ien Chü

Hupeh Provincial Bank
#S2101-S2124
行銀省北湖
Hu Pei Sheng Yin Hang

Hupeh Government Mint
#S2126-S2144
局元銀北湖
Hu Pei Yin Yüan Chü

Ili Official Currency Bureau
#S2145-S2153
局錢官犁伊
I Li Kuan Ch'ien Chü
局總錢官犁伊
I Li Kuan Ch'ien Tsung Chü

Hsing Yeh Bank of Jehol
Industrial Development Bank of Jehol
#S2155-S2222
行銀業興河熱
Je Ho Hsing Yeh Yin Hang
行銀業興
Hsing Yeh Yin Hang

Kan Sen Bank of Kiangsi
Provincial Bank of Kiangsi
#S2223-S2236
行銀省贛
Kan Sheng Yin Hang

Monetary Bureau of Government Kansu
#S2237-S2245
局錢官市平(省)肅甘
Kan Su (Sheng) P'ing Shih Kuan Ch'ien Chü

Kansu Provincial Bank
#S2246
局錢官市平(省)肅甘
Kan Su (Sheng) P'ing Shih Kuan Ch'ien Chü

Canton Municipal Bank
#S2251-S2285
行銀立市市州廣
Kuang Chou Shih Shih Li Yin Hang

Kwangsi Official Currency Bureau
#S2287-S2292
號錢銀官西廣
Kuang Hsi Kuan Yin Ch'ien Hao

Kwangsi Farmers Bank
#S2295-S2296
行銀民農西廣
Kuang Hsi Nung Min Yin Hang

Kwangsi Provincial Treasury Notes
#S2301-S2309
(券)庫金省西廣
Kuang Hsi Sheng Chin K'u (Ch'üan)

Kwangsi Provincial Government
#S2311-S2315
券通流幣輔省西廣
Kuang Hsi Sheng Fu Pi Liu T'ung Ch'üan

Provincial Bank of Kwangsi (or Kwangse)
#S2318-S2342
行銀省西廣
Kuang Hsi Sheng Yin Hang

Kwangsi Bank
#S2343-S2382
行銀西廣
Kuang Hsi Yin Hang

Kwangtung Currency Bureau
#S2385-S2394
局錢東廣
Kuang Tung Ch'ien Chü

Provincial Bank of Kwangtung Province
#S2395-S2408
行銀省東廣
Kuang Tung Sheng Yin Hang Tui Huan Ch'üan

Kwangtung Provincial Bank
#S2411-S2459
行銀省東廣
Kuang Tung Sheng Yin Hang

Kweichow Provincial Government General Treasury
#S2460-S2460C
庫金總府政省州貴
Kuei Chou Sheng Cheng Fu Tsung Chin K'u

Provincial Bank of Kweichow
#S2461-S2463
行銀省州貴
Kuei Chou Sheng Yin Hang

Kweichow Bank
Kueichow Bank
Bank of Kweichow
#S2465-S2484
行銀州貴
Kuei Chou Yin Hang

Ninghsia Provincial Bank
#S2488-S2489
行銀省夏寧
Ning Hsia Sheng Yin Hang

Hunan Pao Hsing Mineral Bank
Hunan Pow Shing Mining Bank
#S2490-S2490G
行銀業鑛興寶
Pao Hsing Kuang Yeh Yin Hang

Altai District
#S2490J-S2490L
券銀用通泰爾阿
O Erh T'ai T'ung Yung Yin Ch'uan

Peiping Municipal Bank
#S2491-S2501
行銀市平北
Pei P'ing Shih Yin Hang

Pei Yang Kin Fu Bank
#S2505
號銀武經洋北
Pei Yang Ching Wu Yin Hao

Commercial Guarantee Bank of Chihli
#S2509-S2518
行銀商保洋北
Pei Yang Pao Shang Yin Hang

Peiyang Tientsin Bank
#S2521-S2530
行銀津天洋北
Pei Yang T'ien Ching Yin Hang

Peiyang Currency Bureau
#S2531
局元銀洋北
Pei Yang Yin Yüan Chü

Frontier Bank
#S2535-S2585
行銀業邊
Pien Yeh Yin Hang

Market Stabilization Currency Bureau
#S2589-S2590
局錢官市平
P'ing Shih Kuan Ch'ien Chü

Shan Hsi Zing Fun Bank
#S2593-S2598
行銀豐秦西陝
Shan Hsi Ch'in Feng Yin Hang

Fu Ching Chien Chü/Shensi
Fu Ching Bank of Shensi
Fu Ching Bank
#S2601-S2618
局錢泰富西陝
Shan Hsi Fu Ch'in Ch'ien Chüan
行銀泰富西陝
Shan Hsi Fu Ch'in Yin Hang

Shansi Provincial Railway
#S2624
處事辦合聯行兩鐵省省西山
Shan Hsi Sheng Sheng T'ien Liang Hang Lian Ho Pan Shih Ch'u

Shanse Provincial Bank
Shansi Provincial Bank
#S2625-S2680
行銀省西山
Shan Hsi Sheng Yin Hang

Provincial Bank of Shensi
#S2681-S2693
行銀省西陝
Shan Hsi Sheng Yin Hang

Bank of Shansi
#S2694
券通流行銀西陝
Shan Hsi Yin Hang Liu T'ung Ch'üan

Shantung Commercial Bank
#S2695-S2700
行銀業商東山
Shan Tung Shang Yeh Yin Hang

Shan Tung Exchange Bureau
#S2703-S2713
局換錢官市平東山
Shan Tung P'ing Shih Kuan Ch'ien Tsung Chü

Shantung Provincial Treasury
#S2715-S2720
券庫金省東山
Shan Tung Sheng Chin K'u Ch'üan

Shantung Provincial Treasury
#S2723-S2725
券庫省東山
Shan Tung Sheng K'u Ch'uan

Shantung Min Sheng Bank
#S2731-S2742
行銀生民省東山
Shan Tung Sheng Min Sheng Yin Hang

Provincial Bank of Shantung
#S2745-S2763
行銀省東山
Shan Tung Sheng Yin Hang

Shan Tung Bank
Bank of Shantung
#S2765-S2772
行銀東山
Shan Tung Yin Hang

Suiyuan Provincial Bank
#S2774-S2802
局錢官市平遠綏
Sui Yüan P'ing Shih Kuan Ch'ien Chü

Szechuan Provincial Bank
#S2804-S2808
局錢官川四
Szu Ch'uan Kuan Ch'ien Chü

Szechuan Official Bank
#S2811-S2815
局銀官川四
Szu Ch'uan Kuan Yin Hao
號銀官川四
Szu Ch'uan Kuan Hao

Szechuan Provincial Government
#S2816-S2817
券庫設建府政省川四
Szu Ch'uan Sheng Cheng Fu Chien She K'u Ch'üan

Szechuan Provincial Bank
#S2819-S2824
行銀省川四
Szu Ch'uan Sheng Yin Hang

Szechuan Province
#S2827-S2829
券換兌川四
Szu Ch'uan Tui Huan Ch'üan

Szechuan Copper Currency Bureau
#S2830-S2832
局元銅/川四
Szu Ch'uan/T'ung Yüan Chü

Tihua Official Currency Bureau
#S2835-S2841
局錢官化廸
Ti Hua Kuan Ch'ien Chü

Tientsin Bank
#S2843
行銀津天
T'ien Ching Yin Hao

Bureau of Finance Ching Hai
Maintenance Note
#S2845-S2850
券持維廳政財
Ts'ai Cheng T'ing Wei Ch'ih Ch'üan

Fukien South - Eastern Bank
#S2851-S2853
建福/行銀南東
Tung Nan Yin Hang/Fu Chien

Provincial Bank of the Three Eastern Provinces
Bank of Manchuria
Provincial Bank of Manchuria
Eastern Provincial Bank
Toong San Sang Government Bank
#S2854-S2965
行銀省三東
Tung San Sheng Yin Hang
行銀官省三東
Tung San Sheng Kuan Yin Hang
號銀官省三東
Tung San Sheng Kuan Yin Hao
券兌 號銀官省三東
Tung San Sheng Kuan Yin Hui Tui Ch'üan

Provincial Bank of Honan
#S2971-S2985
局錢銀官泉豫
Yü Ch'üan Kuan Yin Ch'ien Chü

Yu Sien Bank
Yü Hsiang Bank
#S2988-S2994
行銀湘裕
Yün Hsiang Yin Hang

New Fu-Tien Bank
#S2996-S3004
行銀新滇富南雲
Yün Nan Fu T'ien Hsin Yin Hang

Fu-Tien Bank
Yunnan "Fu-Tien" Bank
Yunnan "Futten" Bank
#S3009-S3023
行銀滇富南雲
Yün Nan Fu T'ien Yin Hang
行銀滇富
Fu T'ien Yin Hang

Yunnan Official Currency Bureau
#S3023E
局錢官南雲
Yün Nan Kuan Ch'ien Chü

Yunnan Provincial Bank
#S3024-S3031D
票本額定圓銀行銀省南雲
Yün Nan Sheng Yin Hang Yin Yüan Ting O Pen Piao

Bank of Territorial Development of Yunnan
#S3033-S3037
行銀邊殖辦合商官南雲
Yün Nan Kuan Shang Ho Ban Chih Pien Yin Hang

Islamic Republic of Turkestan
United Islamic Republic of East Turkestan
Revolutionary or Supreme Government
#S3039-S3041

Islamic Republic of East Turkestan
#S3045-S3046

OVERPRINTS:

The various city or regional overprints are easily noted, being normally two or three Chinese characters usually in two or more places on a note and sometimes found in English on the other side of the note.

Various single Chinese control characters were applied, and appear in two or more places on a note. Sometimes western numerals were utilized and appear in circles, or outlined squares, etc.

監理官印

The most frequently encountered overprint in the Three Eastern Provinces and Manchurian series is a four Chinese character overprint in a 21mm square outline. This *Official Controller's Seal* overprint supervised the amount of issue of certain banks and guaranteed the notes.

In certain cases we find available an original printers' specimen, an issued note, an issued note with the official overprint along with a "local" specimen of a circulated note bearing normal serial numbers. The purpose of this overprint at present eludes the authors at this writing.

NOTE: Catalog # in ( ) are in reference to *CHINESE BANKNOTES* by Ward Smith and Brian Matravers, 1970, Shirjieh Publishers, Menlo Park, California.

BANK OF ANHWEI PROVINCIAL GOVERNMENT

號銀省徽安
An Hui Sheng Yin Hao

1925 ISSUE

		VG	VF	UNC
S802	**5 DOLLARS** 1925. Red and yellow. Industrial waterfront at l., train at r. Back red; bridge at ctr. *(S/M #A4-1).*	40.00	120.00	—

ANHWEI REGIONAL BANK

行銀方地徽安
An Hui Ti Fang Yin Hang

1937 ISSUE

#S804-S810 printer: TTBC.

		VG	VF	UNC
S804	**1 FEN** ND (ca. 1937). Red. 2 sign. var. *(S/M #A5-0.5).*	2.00	8.00	24.00

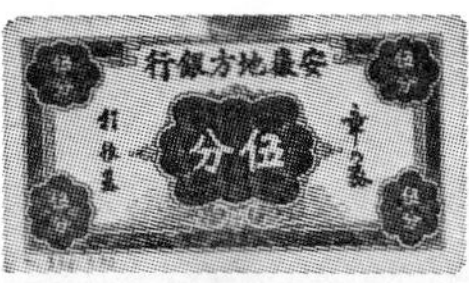

		VG	VF	UNC
S805	**5 FEN** ND (ca. 1937). Brown. Back red. *(S/M #A5-1).*	2.00	8.00	24.00

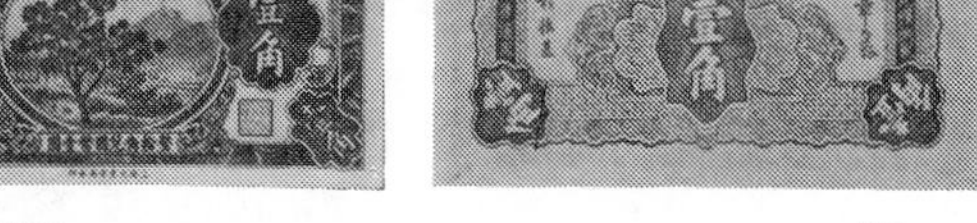

		VG	VF	UNC
S806	**1 CHIAO** ND (ca. 1937). Red. Tree at ctr. Back m/c. *(S/M #A5-2).*	1.50	5.00	15.00

		VG	VF	UNC
S807	**2 CHIAO** ND (ca. 1937). Blue. Tree at ctr. Back m/c. *(S/M #A5-3).*	5.00	15.00	45.00

		VG	VF	UNC
S808	**50 CHIAO** ND (ca. 1937). Violet. Landscape at ctr. Back green and m/c. *(S/M #A5-4).*	10.00	30.00	—
S810	**1 YÜAN** 1939. Red. Tree at l. Back red. *(S/M #A5-10).*	10.00	30.00	—

#S813-S815 printer: CHBA.

		VG	VF	UNC
S813	**1 CHIAO** ND. Red. Pagoda at ctr. Back m/c. *(S/M #A5-20).*	5.00	15.00	45.00

		VG	VF	UNC
S814	**2 CHIAO** ND. Blue. Pagoda at ctr. Back green. *(S/M #A5-21).*	5.00	15.00	45.00

		VG	VF	UNC
S815	**5 CHIAO** ND. Violet. Tree at ctr. Back m/c. *(S/M #A5-22).*	10.00	30.00	—

ANHWEI YU HUAN BANK

安徽裕皖官錢局

An Hui Yü Huan Kuan Ch'ien Chü

1907 DOLLAR ISSUE

#S819-S820 printer: CMPA.

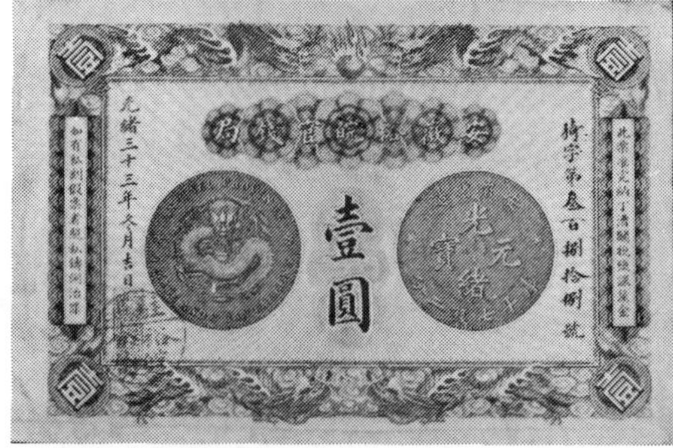

		GOOD	FINE	UNC
S819	**1 DOLLAR** 1907. Blue and yellow. Facing dragons in top and bottom border, dragon dollar at l. and r. of ctr. Back brown; black text. *(S/M #A6-1).*	37.50	110.00	—

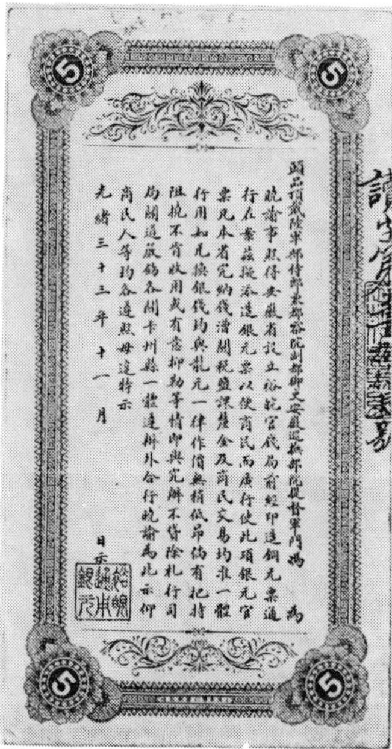

		GOOD	FINE	UNC
S820	**5 DOLLARS** 1907. Black and brown on blue unpt. Dragon dollar above facing dragons at l. and r. Back brown; black text. *(S/M #A6-2).*	62.50	185.00	—

1909 CASH ISSUE

		GOOD	FINE	UNC
S823	**1000 CASH** ND (ca. 1909). Blue and yellow. Facing dragons in upper border, waves at bottom. Back green. *(S/M #A6-10).*	50.00	150.00	—

TSIHAR HSING YEH BANK

察哈爾興業銀行

Ch'a Ha Erh Hsing Yeh Yin Hang

1920 DOLLAR ISSUE

		VG	VF	UNC
S825	**1 DOLLAR** 3.5.1920. Green. Mountain village at ctr. *Kalgan* vertically in Manchu at l., Chinese at r. Back green. *KALGAN.* Printer: BEPP. *(S/M #C1-1).*	20.00	75.00	—

		VG	VF	UNC
S826	**1 DOLLAR** 3.5.1920. Like #S825. *(S/M #C1-1).*			
	a. W/*Kalgan* in Chinese horizontally below vertical Chinese at l. and r.	20.00	75.00	—
	b. W/*Kalgan* in Chinese below serial # at upper l. and r.	20.00	75.00	—

#S829 *Deleted.* See #S833.

		VG	VF	UNC
S831	**10 COPPERS** 1921. Green. Farm scene at r. Back brown. *Kalgan. (S/M #C1-).*	20.00	75.00	—

		VG	VF	UNC
S832	**20 COPPERS** 1.6.1921; 1.6.1924. Yellow. Like #S831. Back blue. *KALGAN. (S/M #C1-11).*	20.00	75.00	—

1921 COPPER COIN ISSUE

		VG	VF	UNC
S833	**100 COPPERS** 1.6.1921. Yellow. Village at l. Back orange. *KALGAN. (S/M #C1-).*	30.00	90.00	—

1924 DOLLAR ISSUE

#S835-S837 printer: BEPP.

		VG	VF	UNC
S835	**10 CENTS** 1924. Brown and blue. Hilltop pagoda, shoreline at ctr. Back violet.			
	a. *KALGAN. (S/M #C1-20a).*	10.00	40.00	—
	b. *PEKING. (S/M #C1-20b).*	10.00	40.00	—
	c. *TULONNOERH. (S/M #C1-20c).*	10.00	40.00	—
	d. *KALGAN* w/additional square seal. *(S/M #C1-20d).*	10.00	40.00	—

		VG	VF	UNC
S836	**20 CENTS** 1924. Purple, brown and orange. Village at ctr. Back gray.			
	a. *KALGAN. (S/M #C1-21a).*	10.00	40.00	—
	b. *PEKING. (S/M #C1-21b).*	10.00	40.00	—
	c. *TULONNOERH. (S/M #C1-21c).*	10.00	40.00	—
	d. *KALGAN* w/additional square red seal. *(S/M #C1-21d).*	10.00	40.00	—

		VG	VF	UNC
S837	**50 CENTS** 1924. Blue and brown. Bridge at ctr. Back brown.			
	a. *KALGAN. (S/M #C1-22a).*	17.50	60.00	—
	b. *PEKING. (S/M #C1-22b).*	17.50	60.00	—
	c. *TULONNOERH. (S/M #C1-22c).*	17.50	60.00	—

NOTE: For #S835-S837 w/additional ovpt. see Military-Bank of the Northwest #S3861-S3863.

1925 COPPER COIN ISSUE

#S841-S844 printer: BEPP.

		VG	VF	UNC
S841	**10 COPPERS** 1925. Green. Back blue. *(S/M #C1-30).*	15.00	50.00	—
S842	**20 COPPERS** 1925. Brown. Back blue. *S/M #C1-31).*	15.00	50.00	—
S843	**40 COPPERS** 1925. Brown. Back violet. *(S/M #C1-32).*	15.00	50.00	—
S844	**100 COPPERS** 1925. Brown. Back red. *(S/M #C1-33).*	15.00	50.00	—

1926 COPPER COIN ISSUE

#S847-S850 mountain village at ctr. Printer: BEPP.

		VG	VF	UNC
S847	**10 COPPERS** 1926. Black. Back orange and blue. *PEKING. (S/M #C1-40).*	15.00	50.00	—

		VG	VF	UNC
S848	**20 COPPERS** 1926. Brown on lt. blue unpt. Back brown. *Peking/KALGAN.*			
	a. Sign. Pao Lien. *(S/M #C1-41a).*	15.00	50.00	—
	b. Sign. Li En Ching. *(S/M #C1-41b).*	15.00	50.00	—
	r. Remainder. *(S/M #C1-41c).*	—	20.00	60.00
S849	**50 COPPERS** 1926. Green and yellow. Back green. *(S/M #C1-42).*	18.00	55.00	—

		VG	VF	UNC
S850	**100 COPPERS** 1926. Red and green. Back red. *PEKING/KALGAN. (S/M #C1-).*	20.00	60.00	—

1927 ISSUE

#S853-S855 tower at ctr. Printer: BEPP.

		VG	VF	UNC
S853	**1 DOLLAR** 1.11.1927. Green and m/c. Back green.			
	a. *KALGAN. (S/M #C1-50b).*	12.50	40.00	120.00
	b. *PEKING. (S/M #C1-50).*	12.50	40.00	120.00
	r. Remainder. *(S/M #C1-).*	—	22.50	70.00

		VG	VF	UNC
S854	**5 DOLLARS** 1.11.1927. Orange and m/c. Back orange.			
	a. *PEKING. (S/M #C1-51).*	15.00	45.00	135.00
	r. Remainder. *(S/M #C1-).*	—	25.00	75.00
S855	**10 DOLLARS** 1.11.1927. *(S/M #C1-).*	Reported Not Confirmed		

CHARHAR COMMERCIAL BANK

局钱業商爾哈察

Ch'a Ha Erh Shang Yeh Ch'ien Chu

1933 ISSUE

#S855E and S855F hillside bldg. at ctr.

		VG	VF	UNC
S855E (S856)	**20 COPPERS** Yr.22 (1933). *Kalgan. (S/M #C3-0.2).*	6.00	18.00	55.00
S855F (S856A)	**100 COPPERS** Yr.22 (1933). Blue. *Kalgan. (S/M #C3-0.5).*	7.50	22.50	67.50

#S856B-S856D printer: BEPP.

		VG	VF	UNC
S856	**1 CHIAO** Yr. 22 (1933). Blue-gray. *Kalgan. (S/M #C3-0.7).*	—	—	—
S856A	**2 CHIAO** Yr. 22 (1933). Red. *Kalgan. (S/M #C3-0.8).*	—	—	—

		VG	VF	UNC
S856B	**1 YÜAN** 1.12.1933. Brown. Junks in harbor at ctr. r. Back brown; hilltop temple at ctr.			
	a. *Kalgan. (S/M #C3-1a).*	4.00	12.00	37.50
	b. *Peiping/Tientsin and various control numbers. (S/M #C3-1b).*	5.00	15.00	37.50
S856C	**5 YÜAN** 1.12.1933. Red.			
	a. *Kalgan. (S/M #C3-2a).*	4.00	12.00	36.00
	b. *Peiping/Tientsin and various control numbers. (S/M #C3-2b).*	5.00	15.00	45.00
S856D	**10 YÜAN** 1.12.1933. Purple on yellow unpt. Back green.			
	a. *Kalgan. (S/M #C3-3a).*	6.50	20.00	65.00
	b. *Peiping/Tientsin. (S/M #C3-3b).*	—	—	—

1935 ISSUE

		VG	VF	UNC
S856G	**30 COPPERS** Yr. 24 (1935). Green. Similar to #S855E. *Kalgan. (S/M #C3-6).*	—	—	—

		VG	VF	UNC
S856H	**40 COPPERS** Yr. 24 (1935). Dk. brown. Similar to #S855E. *Kalgan. (S/M #C3-7).*	—	—	—

#S857A-S857B hillside view at ctr. r. Steam ore train at ctr. on back. *Kalgan.* Printer: BEPP.

		VG	VF	UNC
S857A	**10 CENTS** 1935. Brown. *(S/M #C3-10).*	2.50	7.50	20.00
S857B	**20 CENTS** 1935. Green. *(S/M #C3-11).*	5.00	8.00	25.00

CHANGSHA BANK

行銀沙長

Ch'ang Sha Yin Hang

1928 ISSUE

#S858-S860 various control # ovpt. Printer: ABNC.

		VG	VF	UNC
S858	**1 DOLLAR** 1.1.1928. Purple on m/c unpt. Back purple. *HUNAN. (S/M #C14-1).*	45.00	135.00	—
S859	**5 DOLLARS** 1.1.1928. Green on m/c unpt. Pavilion at ctr. Back green. *HUNAN. (S/M #C14-2).*	37.50	110.00	—
S860	**10 DOLLARS** 1.1.1928. Brown on m/c unpt. Modern bldg. at ctr. Back brown. *HUNAN. (S/M #C14-3).*	60.00	180.00	—

NOTE: For #S858-S860 w/additional ovpt. see Hunan Provincial Bank #S1951-S1953.

CHEKIANG PROVINCIAL BANK

行銀省江浙

Che Chiang Sheng Yin Hang

1949 SILVER DOLLAR ISSUE

#S863-S867 printer: CPFT.

		VG	VF	UNC
S863	**10 CENTS** Yr. 38 (1949). Blue. Pagoda at l. Back blue. *(S/M #C24-1).*	7.50	22.50	67.50
S864	**20 CENTS** Yr. 38 (1949). Orange. *(S/M #C24-2).*	7.50	22.50	67.50
S865	**50 CENTS** Yr. 38 (1949). *(S/M #C24-3).*	10.00	30.00	—

		VG	VF	UNC
S866	**1 DOLLAR** Yr. 38 (1949). Red. Pagoda at l., SYS dollar at r. Back red; junk dollar at ctr. *(S/M #C24-10).*	5.00	15.00	45.00
S867	**5 DOLLARS** Yr. 38 (1949). Green. *(S/M #C24-11).*	30.00	90.00	—

1950 SILVER DOLLAR ISSUE

		VG	VF	UNC
S869	**5 DOLLARS** Yr. 39 (1950). Green. SYS at lower r. Pagoda at lower r. on back. *(S/M #C24-15).*	—	90.00	160.00

CHEKIANG PROVINCIAL BANK

行銀方地江浙

Che Chiang Ti Fang Yin Hang

1932 ISSUE

#S871-S876 printer: CEPA.

		VG	VF	UNC
S871	**10 CENTS** 1932. Green. Pavilion and pagoda at l., gateway at r. Back brown. *HANGCHOW. (S/M #C26-1).*	9.00	27.50	85.00

		VG	VF	UNC
S872	**20 CENTS** 1932. Blue. Like #S871. Back green. *HANGCHOW. (S/M #C26-2).*	12.00	35.00	110.00

		VG	VF	UNC
S874	**1 DOLLAR** 1932. Dk. green on m/c unpt. Bldg. on hillside at ctr. Back blue. *HANGCHOW. (S/M #C26-10).*	12.50	40.00	—

		VG	VF	UNC
S875	**5 DOLLARS** 1932. Blue on m/c unpt. Pagoda at ctr. Back green. *HANGCHOW. (S/M #C26-11).*	30.00	90.00	—

		VG	VF	UNC
S876	**10 DOLLARS** 1932. Violet on m/c unpt. Lakeside pavilion at ctr. Back orange. *HANGCHOW. (S/M #C26-12).*	40.00	120.00	—

1936 ISSUE

#S877-S879 printer: TTBC.

		VG	VF	UNC
S877	**10 CENTS** 1936. Green. Pagoda at l. Back m/c. *(S/M #C26-20).*	1.50	5.00	15.00

		VG	VF	UNC
S878	**20 CENTS** 1936. Blue. Pagoda at l. Back m/c. *(S/M #C26-21).*	2.50	7.50	22.50

		VG	VF	UNC
S879	**50 CENTS** 1936. Red. Pavilion at l. Back m/c. *(S/M #C26-22).*	2.50	7.50	25.00

1938 ND FIRST ISSUE

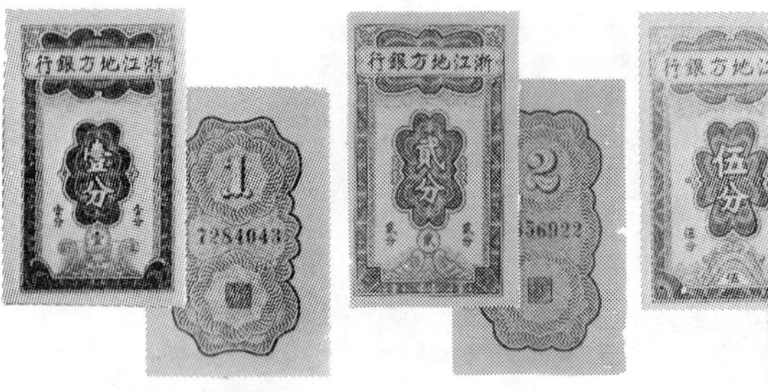

#S880 **#S881** **#S882**

		VG	VF	UNC
S880	**1 CENT** ND (ca. 1938). Blue. Back green. *(S/M #C26-30).*	1.00	3.25	10.00
S881	**2 CENTS** ND (ca. 1938). Green. Back blue. *(S/M #C26-31).*	1.00	4.00	12.00
S882	**5 CENTS** ND (ca. 1938). Red. Back blue. *(S/M #C26-33).*	1.00	3.25	10.00

1938 ND SECOND ISSUE

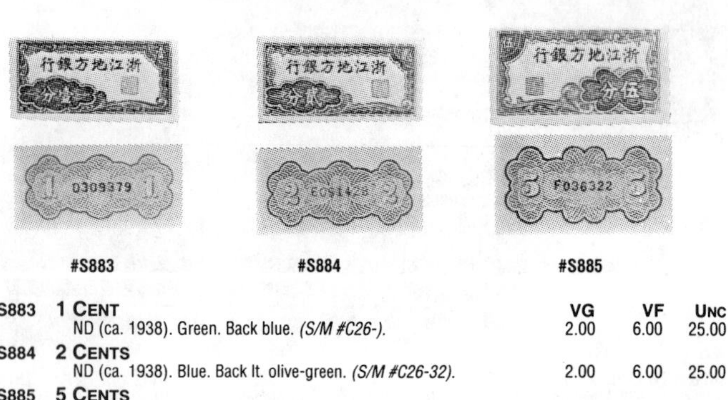

#S883 **#S884** **#S885**

		VG	VF	UNC
S883	**1 CENT** ND (ca. 1938). Green. Back blue. *(S/M #C26-).*	2.00	6.00	25.00
S884	**2 CENTS** ND (ca. 1938). Blue. Back lt. olive-green. *(S/M #C26-32).*	2.00	6.00	25.00
S885	**5 CENTS** ND (ca. 1938). Red. *(S/M #C26-34).*	2.00	6.00	20.00

1939 ISSUE

		VG	VF	UNC
S888	**1 YÜAN** 1939. Blue and yellow. Pavilion at l. Back blue. Printer: TTBC. *(S/M #C26-40).*	6.00	18.00	55.00

1941 ISSUE

		VG	VF	UNC
S893	**1 YÜAN** 1941. Blue. Pavilion at l. Back green and m/c. Printer: TTBC. *(S/M #C26-50).*	5.00	15.00	45.00

KIRIN GOVERNMENT BANK

吉林官錢局

Chi Lin Kuan Ch'ien Chü

1907-09 ISSUE

		VG	VF	UNC
S895	**1 DOLLAR** ND (ca. 1907-09). Black. Dragons at at upper l. and r. Vertical format. Uniface. *(S/M #C71-1).*	100.00	300.00	—

KIRIN YUNG HENG PROVINCIAL BANK
YUNG HENG PROVINCIAL BANK OF KIRIN

吉林永衡官銀錢號

Chi Lin Yung Heng Kuan Yin Ch'ien Chü

#S901-S951 issued in the year of the Emperor Kuang Hsu.

1898 ISSUE

		VG	VF	UNC
S901	1 TIAO Yr. 24 (1898). *(S/M #C76-0.1).*	Reported Not Confirmed		

1902 ISSUE

		VG	VF	UNC
S911	1 TIAO Yr. 28 (1902). *(S/M #C76-0.2).*	Reported Not Confirmed		

1904 ISSUE

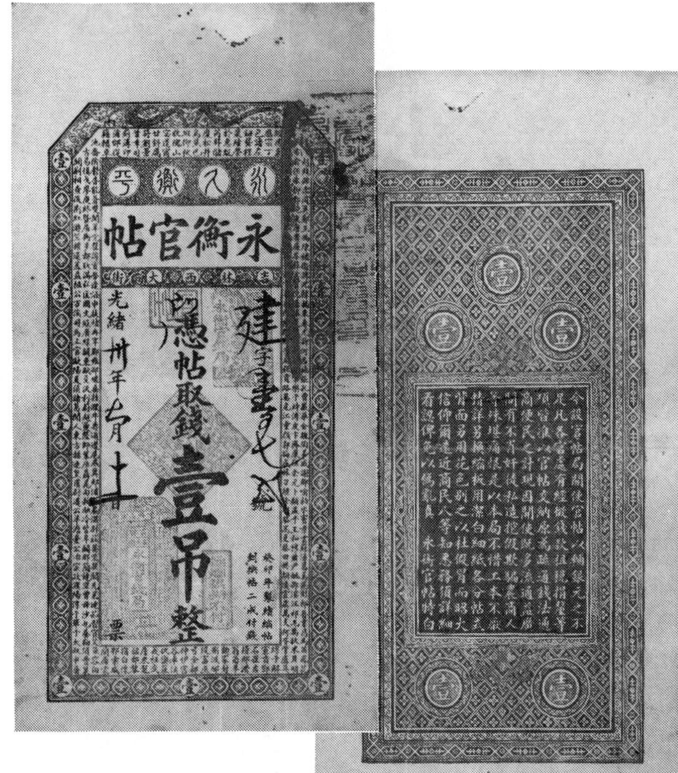

		VG	VF	UNC
S921	1 TIAO Yr. 30 (1904). Black. Back gray. Vertical format. *(S/M #C76-0.3).*	90.00	270.00	—

#S922 *Deleted.* See #S921.

1905 ISSUE

		VG	VF	UNC
S934	10 TIAO Yr. 31 (1905). *(S/M #C76-0.5).*	120.00	360.00	—
S935	50 TIAO Yr. 31 (1905). *(S/M #C76-0.6).*	Reported Not Confirmed		

1906 ISSUE

		VG	VF	UNC
S941	1 TIAO Yr. 32 (1906). *(S/M #C76-0.7).*	75.00	225.00	—
S942	2 TIAO Yr. 32 (1906). *(S/M #C76-0.8).*	75.00	225.00	—

1907 ISSUE

		VG	VF	UNC
S951	1 TIAO Yr. 33 (1907). *(S/M #C76-).*	Reported Not Confirmed		

1908 ISSUE

		VG	VF	UNC
S961	1 TIAO Yr. 34 (1908). Black. *(S/M #C76-1).*	125.00	375.00	—
S962	2 TIAO Yr. 34 (1908). *(S/M #C76-2).*	135.00	400.00	—
S963	3 TIAO Yr. 34 (1908). *(S/M #C76-3).*	150.00	450.00	—
S964	5 TIAO Yr. 34 (1908). *(S/M #C76-4).*	150.00	450.00	—
S965	10 TIAO Yr. 34 (1908). *(S/M #C76-5).*	165.00	500.00	—
S966	50 TIAO Yr. 34 (1908). *(S/M #C76-6).*	200.00	600.00	—
S967	100 TIAO Yr. 34 (1908). *(S/M #C76-7).*	Reported Not Confirmed		

1911 ISSUE

#S968-S974 issued in the year of the Emperor Hsuan T'ung.

		VG	VF	UNC
S968	1 TIAO Yr. 3 (1911). Black w/red seals. Back red. *(S/M #C76-10).*	60.00	180.00	—
S969	2 TIAO Yr. 3 (1911). *(S/M #C76-11).*	67.50	200.00	—
S970	3 TIAO Yr. 3 (1911). *(S/M #C76-12).*	75.00	225.00	—
S971	5 TIAO Yr. 3 (1911). *(S/M #C76-13).*	80.00	240.00	—
S972	10 TIAO Yr. 3 (1911). *(S/M #C76-14).*	90.00	270.00	—
S973	50 TIAO Yr. 3 (1911). *(S/M #C76-15).*	Reported Not Confirmed		
S974	100 TIAO Yr. 3 (1911). *(S/M #C76-).*	Reported Not Confirmed		

1913 ISSUE

		VG	VF	UNC
S976	2 TIAO 1913. *(S/M #C76-21).*	55.00	165.00	—
S977	3 TIAO 1913. *(S/M #C76-22).*	62.50	185.00	—
S978	5 TIAO (ca. 1913). *(S/M #C76-23).*	62.50	185.00	—
S979	10 TIAO (ca. 1913). *(S/M #C76-24).*	75.00	225.00	—
S980	50 TIAO (ca. 1913). *(S/M #C76-25).*	—	—	—
S981	100 TIAO (ca. 1913). *(S/M #C76-26).*	—	—	—

1916-17 PROVISIONAL ISSUE

#S981A issued in the year of the Republic. Ovpt: *Chung Hua Min Kuo* over *Hsuan T'ung* on #S968.

		VG	VF	UNC
S981A	1 TIAO 1916-17. Vertical format. *(S/M #C76-20).*	15.00	50.00	—

1917-18 ISSUE

#S982-S988 issued in the year of the Republic. Ovpt: Red seals. Printer: BEPK.

		VG	VF	UNC
S982	1 TIAO 1917-18. *(S/M #C76-30).*	10.00	30.00	90.00
S983	2 TIAO 1916-17. *(S/M #C76-31).*	25.00	75.00	—
S984	3 TIAO 1916-17. *(S/M #C76-32).*	30.00	90.00	—
S985	5 TIAO 1917-18. Dk. green w/black text. Back yellow-orange. *(S/M #C76-33).*	10.00	25.00	—

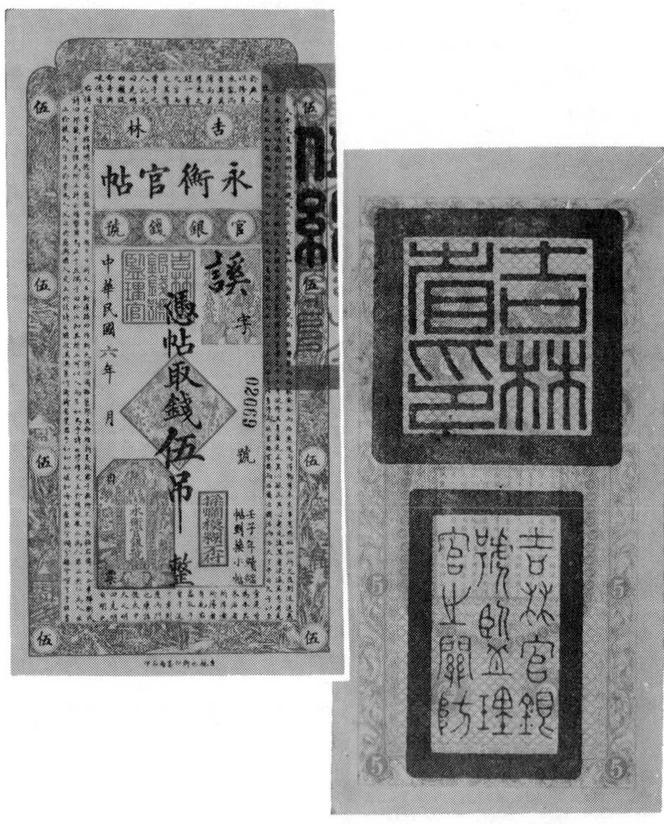

		VG	VF	UNC
S986	**10 TIAO** 1916-17. Yellow orange w/black text. Back blue and green. Vertical format. *(S/M #C76-34).*	8.00	20.00	—
S987	**50 TIAO** 1916-17. *(S/M #C76-35).*	20.00	60.00	—
S988	**100 TIAO** 1916-18. *(S/M #C76-36).*	—	—	—

1917 "BIG MONEY" ISSUE

#S989-S992 printer: BEPK.

		VG	VF	UNC
S989	**1 DOLLAR** 1917. *(S/M #C76-40).*	—	—	—
S990	**3 DOLLARS** 1917. *(S/M #C76-41).*	—	—	—

NOTE: For #S990 w/additional ovpt. see Frontier Bank #S2549.

		VG	VF	UNC
S991	**5 DOLLARS** 1917. *(S/M #C76-).*	—	—	—
S992	**10 DOLLARS** 1917. *(S/M #C76-).*	—	—	—

1917 "SMALL MONEY" ISSUE

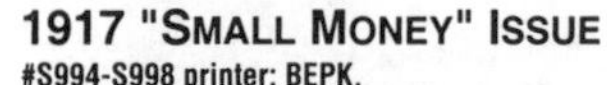

#S994-S998 printer: BEPK.

		VG	VF	UNC
S994	**1 YÜAN** 1917. *(S/M #C76-42).*	—	—	—

		VG	VF	UNC
S995	**3 YÜAN** 1917. *(S/M #C76-43).*	—	—	—
S996	**5 YÜAN** 1917. *(S/M #C76-44).*	—	—	—
S997	**10 YÜAN** 1917. *(S/M #C76-45).*	—	—	—
S998	**50 YÜAN** 1917. *(S/M #C76-46).*	—	—	—

1918 TIAO ISSUE

		VG	VF	UNC
S1003	**100 TIAO** 1918. Red. Back green. Printer: BEPK. *(S/M #C76-50).*	40.00	120.00	—

1918 FIRST "SMALL MONEY" ISSUE

		VG	VF	UNC
S1005	**5 CENTS** 1918. Blue-green. Back black. *(S/M #C76-).*	22.50	67.50	—

#S1006-S1008 printer: BEPK.

		VG	VF	UNC
S1006	**10 CENTS** 1918. Blue-green. Back black. *(S/M #C76-60).*			
	a. Issued note.	4.00	15.00	35.00
	s. Specimen.	—	—	45.00

		VG	VF	UNC
S1007	**20 CENTS** 1918. Violet and green. Bldg. at ctr. Back green. *(S/M #C76-62).*	8.00	25.00	50.00

NOTE: For #S1006 and S1007 w/additional ovpt. see Frontier Bank #S2545 and S2546.

		VG	VF	UNC
S1008	**50 CENTS** 1918. Blue and orange. Gateway at l. Back orange. *(S/M #C76-64).*	8.00	25.00	50.00

1918 SECOND "SMALL MONEY" ISSUE

#S1009-S1015 w/o imprint.

		VG	VF	UNC
S1009	**1 CHIAO** 1918. Black and green. Back olive; bldgs. at ctr. *(S/M #C76-61).*	17.50	50.00	—

NOTE: For #S1009 w/additional ovpt. see Frontier Bank #S2544.

		VG	VF	UNC
S1010	2 CHIAO 1918. Violet. *(S/M #C76-63).*	30.00	90.00	—
S1011	5 CHIAO 1918. Blue. Back red. *(S/M #C76-65).*	30.00	90.00	—
S1012	1 YÜAN 1918. *(S/M #C76-72).*	40.00	120.00	—
S1013	5 YÜAN 1918. *(S/M #C76-75).*	40.00	120.00	—
S1014	10 YÜAN 1918. *(S/M #C76-82).*	50.00	150.00	—
S1015	50 YÜAN 1918. *(S/M #C76-83).*	60.00	180.00	—

1918 DOLLAR ISSUE

#S1017-S1019 payment: *IN SUBSIDIARY COINS*. Printer: BEPA.

		VG	VF	UNC
S1017	1 DOLLAR 1918. Blue and green. Junks at ctr. Back orange. *(S/M #C76-71).*	20.00	60.00	—
S1018	5 DOLLARS 1918. Brown and blue. Back green. *(S/M #C76-74).*	20.00	60.00	—
S1019	10 DOLLARS 1918. *(S/M #C76-81).*	25.00	75.00	—

1918 "BIG MONEY" ISSUE

#S1020-S1022 printer: BEPA.

		VG	VF	UNC
S1020	1 DOLLAR 1918. Green. Deer by woods at river's edge at ctr. Back blue. *(S/M #C76-70).*			
	a. Issued note.	30.00	90.00	—
	s. Specimen.	—	—	125.00
S1021	5 DOLLARS 1918. *(S/M #C76-73).*	30.00	90.00	—
S1022	10 DOLLARS 1918. *(S/M #C76-80).*	50.00	150.00	—

1920 TIAO ISSUE

#S1023-S1029 printer: YHBA.

		VG	VF	UNC
S1023	1 TIAO 1920. *(S/M #C76-90).*	22.50	67.50	—
S1024	2 TIAO 1920. *(S/M #C76-91).*	30.00	90.00	—
S1025	3 TIAO 1920. *(S/M #C76-92).*	37.50	110.00	—

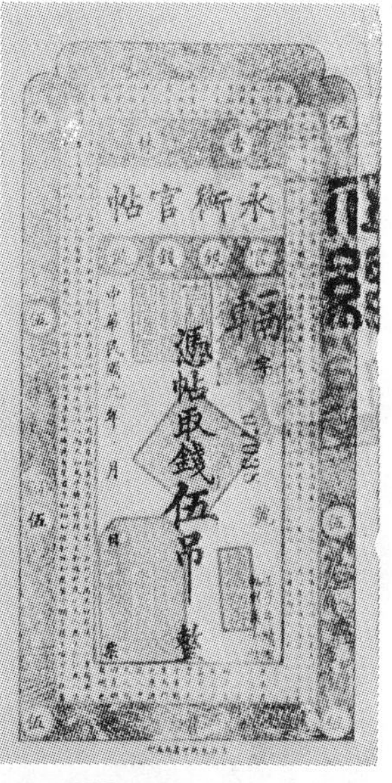

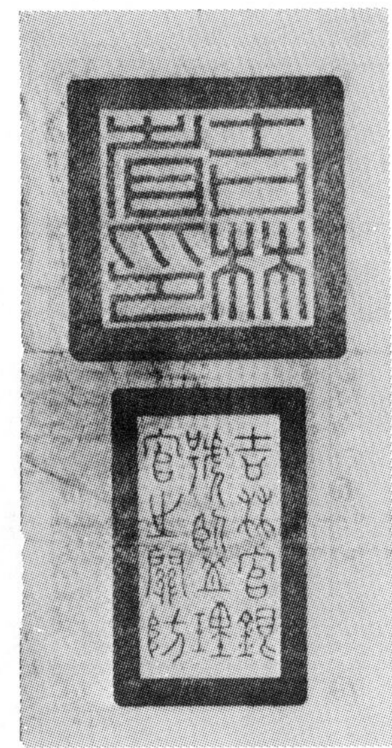

		VG	VF	UNC
S1026	5 TIAO 1920. Vertical format. *(S/M #C76-93).*	25.00	75.00	—
S1027	10 TIAO 1920. *(S/M #C76-94).*	25.00	75.00	—
S1028	50 TIAO 1920. *(S/M #C76-95).*	—	—	—
S1029	100 TIAO 1920. Red. Back green. *(S/M #C76-96).*	25.00	75.00	—
S1030	100 TIAO 1920. Orange. Back green. Printer: KOPB. *(S/M #C76-97).*	25.00	75.00	—

1921 DOLLAR ISSUE

#S1031-S1041 *Harbin*. Printer: BEPK.

		VG	VF	UNC
S1031	5 COPPERS 1921. *(S/M #C76-).*	10.00	30.00	—
S1032	10 COPPERS 1921. *(S/M #C76-).*	—	—	—
S1033	20 COPPERS 1921. *(S/M #C76-).*	—	—	—
S1034	50 COPPERS 1921. *(S/M #C76-).*	—	—	—
S1035	100 COPPERS 1921. Dk. brown on lt. green unpt. Great Wall at l. Back black. *(S/M #C76-).*	—	—	—
S1036	5 CENTS 1921. *(S/M #C76-).*	—	—	—
S1037	10 CENTS 1921. *(S/M #C76-).*	—	—	—
S1038	20 CENTS 1921. *(S/M #C76-).*	—	—	—
S1039	1 DOLLAR 1921. *(S/M #C76-).*	—	—	—
S1040	5 DOLLARS 1921. *(S/M #C76-).*	—	—	—
S1041	10 DOLLARS 1921. *(S/M #C76-).*	—	—	—

1923 "BIG MONEY" ISSUES

#S1044-S1050 *HARBIN*. Printer: BEPP.

		VG	VF	UNC
S1044	5 CENTS 1923. Blue-black on lt. green unpt. Village wall at l. Back dk. blue-green. *(S/M #C76-9.9).*	30.00	90.00	—
S1045	10 CENTS 1923. Dk blue on lt. blue unpt. Steam passenger train at l. Back dk. blue. *(S/M #C76-100).*	30.00	90.00	—

	VG	VF	UNC
S1046 20 CENTS 1923. Dk. blue on lt. orange unpt. Steamship, boats at l. Back purple. *(S/M #C76-101).*			
a. Issued note.	30.00	90.00	—
s. Specimen.	—	—	125.00

NOTE: For #S1045 and S1046 w/additional ovpt. see Frontier Bank #S2556 and S2557.

	VG	VF	UNC
S1048 1 DOLLAR 1923. *(S/M #C76-110).*	40.00	120.00	—
S1049 5 DOLLARS 1923. *(S/M #C76-112).*	40.00	120.00	—
S1050 10 DOLLARS 1923. *(S/M #C76-114).*	50.00	150.00	—

#S1051-S1053 *Harbin* w/additional red 4 Chinese character gov't. ovpt. Printer: ABNC.

	VG	VF	UNC
S1051 1 DOLLAR 1.12.1923. Orange and m/c. Back brown. *(S/M #C76-111).*	10.00	30.00	90.00

	VG	VF	UNC
S1052 5 DOLLARS 1.12.1923. Green and m/c. Pavilion at ctr. Back orange. *(S/M #C76-113).*	15.00	45.00	—
S1053 10 DOLLARS 1.12.1923. Violet and m/c. Back green. *(S/M #C76-115).*			
a. Issued note.	20.00	60.00	—
b. Cancelled.	—	—	60.00

NOTE: For #S1051-S1053 w/additional ovpt. see Frontier Bank #S2559-S2561.

1925 ISSUE

#S1055 and S1056 printer: Ministry of Finance.

	VG	VF	UNC
S1055 5 DOLLARS 1.9.1925. Green on pink unpt. Monument at r. Back green. Specimen. *(S/M #C76-119).*	—	—	125.00
S1056 10 DOLLARS 1925. Olive-green on yellow unpt. Temple of Divine Light at r. Back blue. Specimen. *(S/M #C76120).*	—	—	150.00

1926 "SMALL MONEY" ISSUE

#S1058-S1061 printer: YHBA.

	VG	VF	UNC
S1058 10 CENTS 1926. *(S/M #C76-122).*	20.00	60.00	—
S1059 20 CENTS 1926. *(S/M #C76-124).*	20.00	60.00	—
S1060 50 CENTS 1926. *(S/M #C76-126).*	30.00	90.00	—
S1061 1 DOLLAR 1926. *(S/M #C76-130).*	30.00	90.00	—

1926 "BIG MONEY" ISSUE

#S1062-S1065 printer: BEPK.

	VG	VF	UNC
S1062 5 CENTS 1926. Green and red. Farmer seated by cattle at ctr. Back green. *(S/M #C76-120).*	20.00	60.00	—

	VG	VF	UNC
S1063 10 CENTS 1926. Red and yellow. Battleship and dirigible at r. Back red. *(S/M #C76-121).*	20.00	60.00	—

	VG	VF	UNC
S1064 20 CENTS 1926. Red and yellow. Tower gate at l. Back red. *(S/M #C76-123).*	20.00	60.00	—

	VG	VF	UNC
S1065 50 CENTS 1926. Brown and red. Pavilion at ctr. Back brown. *(S/M #C76-125).*	20.00	60.00	180.00

#S1066-S1068 printer: ABNC.

		VG	VF	UNC
S1066	**1 DOLLAR** 1926. Black and m/c. House at l. Back black. *(S/M #C76-131).*	30.00	90.00	—
S1067	**5 DOLLARS** 1926. Blue and m/c. House at r. Back blue. *(S/M #C76-132).*	30.00	90.00	—
S1068	**10 DOLLARS** 1926. Green and m/c. Back green. *(S/M #C76-133).*	40.00	120.00	—

1928 PROVISIONAL TIAO ISSUE

		VG	VF	UNC
S1071	**1 TIAO** 1928. Black. Ovpt. on #S968. *(S/M #C76-140).*	10.00	40.00	—

1928 REGULAR TIAO ISSUE

#S1075-S1082 black text w/red printed seals on face and back. Printer: YHBA.

		VG	VF	UNC
S1075	**1 TIAO** 1928. Black. Back red. Vertical format. *(S/M #C76-141).*	5.00	15.00	35.00

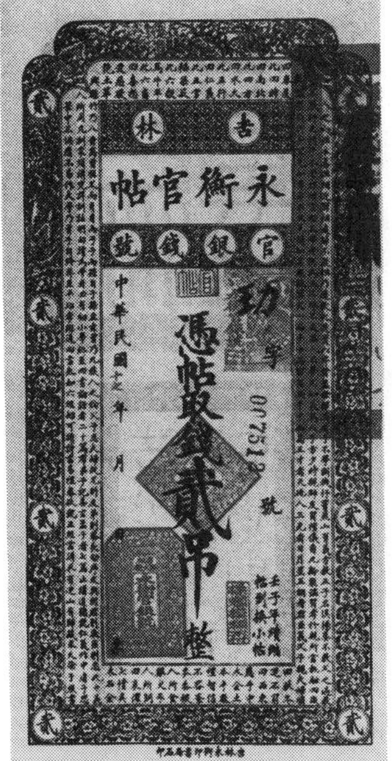

		VG	VF	UNC
S1076	**2 TIAO** 1928. Black. Back red. *(S/M #C76-142).*	8.00	25.00	75.00
S1077	**3 TIAO** 1928. Black. Back red. *(S/M #C76-143).*	5.00	20.00	40.00
S1078	**4 TIAO** 1928. *(S/M #C76-144).*	Reported Not Confirmed		
S1079	**5 TIAO** 1928. Dk. green. Back orange. *(S/M #C76-145).*			
	a. Red seals.	5.00	15.00	35.00
	b. Orange seals on face.	—	—	—

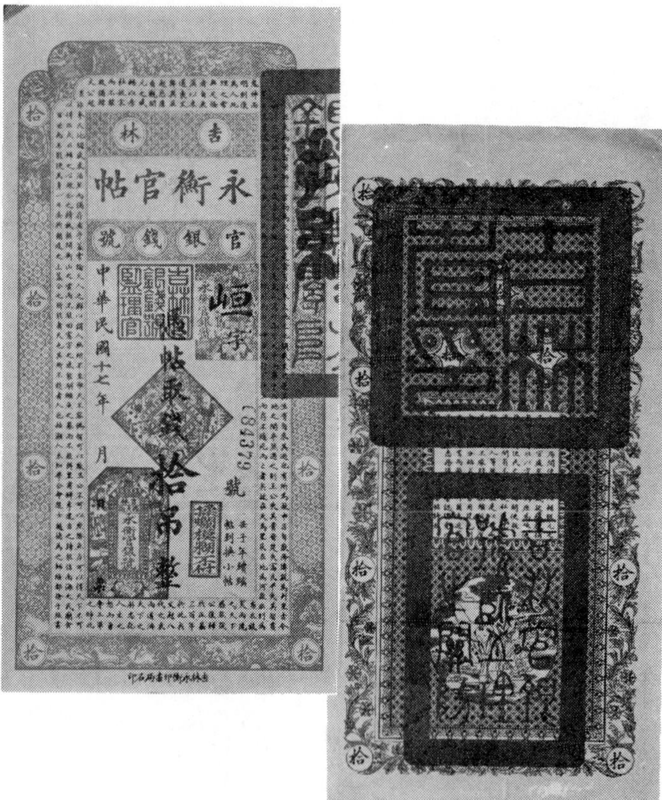

		VG	VF	UNC
S1080	**10 TIAO** 1928. Orange. Back green; 2 men carrying a canoe at bottom ctr. Vertical format. *(S/M #C76-146).*	4.00	12.50	30.00
S1081	**50 TIAO** 1928. Red. Back blue. *(S/M #C76-147).*	5.00	15.00	35.00

		VG	VF	UNC
S1081A	**100 TIAO** 1928. Orange. Back green; ornamental fence w/bldg. in background. Vertical format. *(S/M #C76-148).*	6.00	18.00	45.00

1932 "BIG MONEY" ISSUE

		VG	VF	UNC
S1081F	**5 DOLLARS** Yr. 21 (1932). Red-brown. *(S/M #C76-160).*	—	—	—

RECONSTRUCTION BANK OF KIANGSI

江西建設銀行

Chiang Hsi Chien She Yin Hang

1932 ISSUE

#S1082 *Deleted*. See #S1081A.

		VG	VF	UNC
S1082A	**10 COPPERS** 1932. Red on green unpt. Fortress at ctr. Back blue; steam passenger train at ctr. *(S/M #C90-0.1).*			
	a. Issued note.	12.50	35.00	—
	b. *Chiuchiang. (S/M #C90-0.1a).*	15.00	45.00	—
	c. *Chian. (S/M #C90-0.1b).*	15.00	45.00	—
	d. *Linch'uan. (S/M #C90-0.1c).*	15.00	45.00	—

1939 ISSUE

		VG	VF	UNC
S1082B	**1 CENT** ND (1939). Red. Back black. *(S/M #C90-0.5).*	6.50	20.00	—
S1082C	**2 CENTS** ND (1939). *(S/M #C90-0.6).*	8.00	25.00	—
S1082D	**5 CENTS** ND (1939). Red. Back blue. *(S/M #C90-1).*	6.50	20.00	—
S1082E	**10 CENTS** 1939. Blue. *(S/M #C90-10).*	7.50	25.00	—

		VG	VF	UNC
S1082F	**20 CENTS** 1939. Blue. Great Wall at r. Back blue and brown. *(S/M #C90-11).*	7.50	25.00	—

		VG	VF	UNC
S1082G	**50 CENTS** 1939. Red. Bldg. at ctr. Automobile at ctr. on back. *(S/M #C90-12).*	7.50	25.00	—
S1082H	**50 CENTS** 1939. Red. Radio towers at r. *(S/M #C90-13).*	10.00	30.00	—

KIANGSE GOVERNMENT BANK

江西官銀錢總號

Chiang Hsi Kuan Yin Ch'ien Tsung Hao

1907 CASH ISSUE

		VG	VF	UNC
S1082L	**1000 CASH** ND (ca. 1907). Dk. blue and red. Dragon at top, facing dragons at l. and r. Back red w/black text. *(S/M #C94-0.4).*	—	—	—

1907 DOLLAR ISSUE

#S1083-S1085 printer: CMPA.

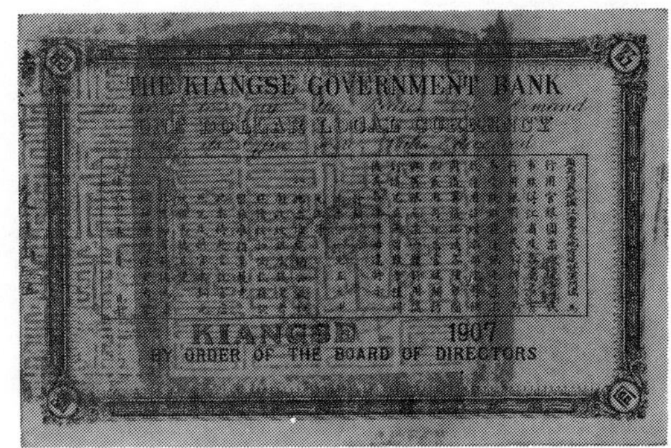

		VG	VF	UNC
S1083	**1 DOLLAR** Yr. 33 (1907). Black and blue. Back black w/red seal. *(S/M #C94-1).*	100.00	300.00	—
S1084	**5 DOLLARS** Yr. 33 (1907). Like #S1083. *(S/M #C94-2).*	Reported Not Confirmed		
S1085	**10 DOLLARS** Yr. 33 (1907). Like #S1083. *(S/M #C94-3).*	150.00	500.00	—

1907 TAEL ISSUE

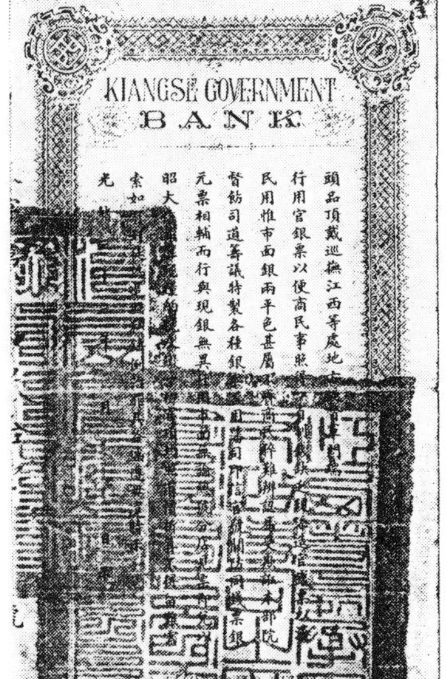

		VG	VF	UNC
S1085H	**100 TAELS** Yr. 33 (1907). Gray-black. Facing dragons at upper l. and r. Vertical format. *(S/M #C94-15).*	80.00	250.00	—

NOTE: "Chinese Banknotes" had titles switched in error for S/M #C94 and C95.

PUBLIC BANK OF KIANGSI

江西公立銀行

Chiang Hsi Kung Li Yin Hang

1905-07 ISSUE

		VG	VF	UNC
S1086	**1000 CASH** Yr. 31 (1905). *(S/M #C95-1).*	80.00	250.00	—
S1088	**1 TAEL** Yr. 33 (1907). *(S/M #C95-11).*	Reported Not Confirmed		
S1089	**100 TAELS** Yr. 33 (1907). *(S/M #C95-17).*	Reported Not Confirmed		

KIANGSI PROVINCIAL BANK

江西省銀行

Chiang Hsi Sheng Yin Hang

1949 ISSUE

		VG	VF	UNC
S1089C	**10 CENTS** July 1949. Dk. Blue. *(S/M #C98-3).*			
	a. Issued note.	2.50	8.50	25.00
	s. Specimen.	—	—	—
S1089D	**20 CENTS** July 1949. Brown-violet. *(S/M #C98-4).*	3.00	10.00	30.00

		VG	VF	UNC
S1089E	**50 CENTS** July 1949. Red. Specimen. *(S/M #C98-5).*	—	—	125.00

KIANGSI REGIONAL BANK

江西地方銀行

Chiang Hsi Ti Fang Yin Hang

ND PROVISIONAL ISSUE

#S1090-S1093 ovpt. new bank name on issues of Kan Sen Bank of Kiangsi.

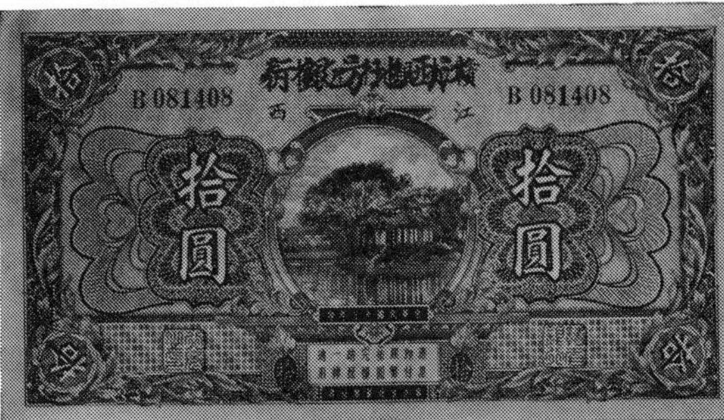

		VG	VF	UNC
S1090	**10 COPPERS** ND (- old date 1925). Ovpt. on #S2227A. *(S/M #C100-1).*	60.00	180.00	—
S1091	**1 DOLLAR** ND (- old date 1924). Ovpt. on #S2225. *(S/M #C100-10).*	Reported Not Confirmed		
S1092	**5 DOLLARS** ND (- old date 1924). Ovpt. on #S2226. *(S/M #C100-11).*	30.00	90.00	—

		VG	VF	UNC
S1093	**10 DOLLARS** ND (- old date 1924). Ovpt. on #S2227. *(S/M #C100-12).*	40.00	120.00	—

KIANGSI FINANCE BUREAU

江西財政廳

Chiang Hsi Ts'ai Cheng T'ing

1924 ISSUE

		VG	VF	UNC
S1093C	**1/2 DOLLAR** ND (1924). Brown on lt. blue unpt. Like #S1093D. Back red.	150.00	250.00	—

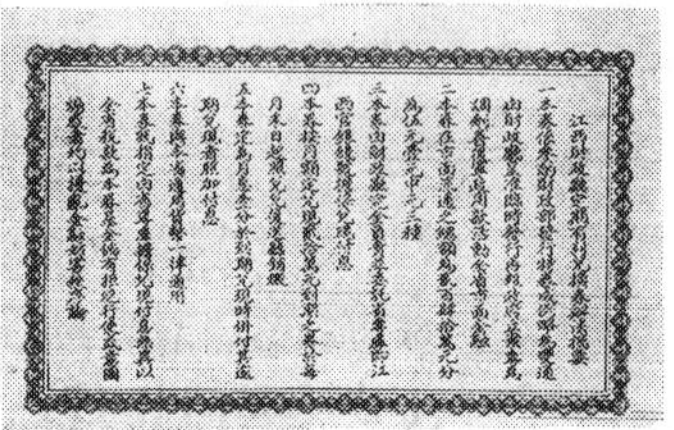

		VG	VF	UNC
S1093D	**1 YÜAN** 1.9. Yr. 13 (1924). Blue on purple unpt. Shoreline house at ctr. Back purple; text. *(S/M #C101-0.5).*	—	—	—

1926/27 ISSUE

		VG	VF	UNC
S1094	**1 YÜAN** Yr.15/16 (1926/27). Green and red. Pavilion at ctr. *(S/M #C101-1).*	50.00	150.00	—
S1095	**5 YÜAN** Yr. 15/16 (1926/27). *(S/M #C101-2).*	Reported Not Confirmed		
S1096	**10 YÜAN** Yr. 15/16 (1926/27). *(S/M #C101-3).*	Reported Not Confirmed		

BANK OF KIANGSI

江西銀行

Chiang Hsi Yin Hang

ND ISSUE

#S1097-S1099 printer: CCCA.

		VG	VF	UNC
S1097	**1 DOLLAR** ND. Orange and m/c. Back brown. *(S/M #C102-1).*	40.00	120.00	—

NOTE: For #S1097 w/additional ovpt. which was issued by the quasi-national Central Bank of China, see #181A, Vol. 2.

		VG	VF	UNC
S1098	**5 DOLLARS** ND. Green on m/c unpt. *(S/M #C102-2).*	—	—	—
S1099	**10 DOLLARS** ND. Blue and m/c. Back green. *(S/M #C102-3).*	50.00	150.00	—

1916 DOLLAR ISSUE

#S1100-S1101 printer: PHCF.

		VG	VF	UNC
S1100	**1 DOLLAR** 1916. Red and violet. Back black. *(S/M #C102-10).*	20.00	60.00	—

		VG	VF	UNC
S1101	**5 DOLLARS** 1916. Green and orange. Pavilion at l., tower at r. Back red and blue; village along shoreline at ctr. *(S/M #C102-11).*	15.00	40.00	90.00

		VG	VF	UNC
S1102	**10 DOLLARS** 1916. Orange and m/c. Tower at l. and r. Back blue and yellow; like #S1101. Printer: CMPA. *(S/M #C102-12).*	30.00	90.00	225.00

1919 COPPER COIN ISSUE

		VG	VF	UNC
S1105	**10 COPPERS** 1919. Blue and yellow. Back green. *KIUKIANG. (S/M #C102-20).*	30.00	90.00	250.00
S1108	**100 COPPERS** 1919. Blue and yellow. Pavilion, trees at r. Back maroon. *(S/M #C102-23).*	—	—	—

1926 COPPER COIN ISSUE

		VG	VF	UNC
S1115	**10 COPPERS** 1926. *(S/M #C102-31).*	30.00	90.00	250.00
S1119	**100 COPPERS** Blue. Bldg. at ctr. Back brown. *(S/M #C102-35).*	—	—	—

YU MING BANK OF KIANGSI

江西裕民銀行

Chiang Hsi Yü Min Yin Hang

1929 COPPER COIN ISSUE

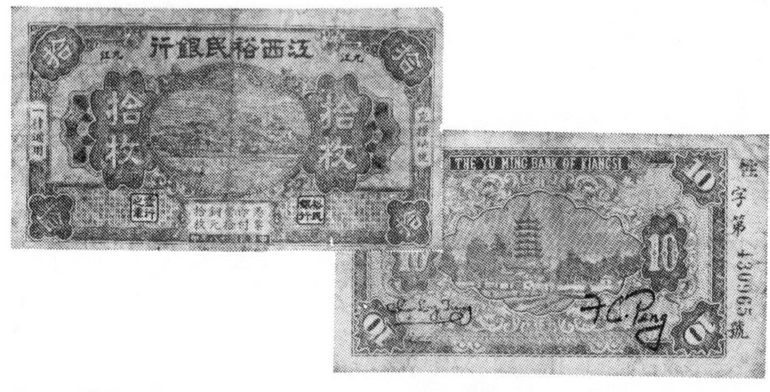

		VG	VF	UNC
S1121	**10 COPPERS** 1929. Dk. blue on green unpt. Hillside village at ctr. Back olive-green; pagoda at ctr.			
	a. *Chiuchiang. (S/M #C103-0.5a.).*	20.00	70.00	—
	b. *Chian. (S/M #C103-0.5b).*	20.00	70.00	—
S1124	**100 COPPERS** 1929. Brown. Back red. *(S/M #C103-0.9).*	20.00	70.00	—

ND DOLLAR ISSUE

#S1125 and S1126 printer: TTBC.

		VG	VF	UNC
S1125	**1 CENT** ND. Red. Back m/c. *(S/M #C103-1).*	3.00	9.00	25.00
S1126	**5 CENTS** ND. Blue. Back red. *(S/M #C103-2).*	6.00	17.50	50.00

1932 COPPER COIN ISSUE

		VG	VF	UNC
S1129	**10 COPPERS** 1932. Blue and green. House on rock formation surrounded by water at l. Back orange; house by bridge at ctr. *(S/M #C103-10).*	4.00	12.00	36.00

		VG	VF	UNC
S1130	**10 COPPERS** 1932. Red. Like #S1129. Back blue. *Kian. (S/M #C103-11).*	5.00	15.00	45.00
S1131	**10 COPPERS** 1932. Blue and yellow. Like #S1129 and S1130. Back red. *(S/M #C103-12).*	5.00	15.00	45.00
S1132	**100 COPPERS** 1932. Blue and yellow. *Kewu. (S/M #C103-15).*	6.50	20.00	60.00

1933 DOLLAR ISSUE

#S1122-S1137 printer: TTBC.

		VG	VF	UNC
S1133	**20 CENTS** 1933. Red. Pagoda, shoreline at r. Back brown; w/additional Chinese control characters. *(S/M #C103-20).*	6.50	20.00	50.00
S1134	**50 CENTS** 1933. Deep blue. Pavilion at ctr. Back red. 2 sign. varieties.			
	a. Issued note. *(S/M #C103-21a).*	4.00	12.00	30.00
	b. As a. Additional ovpt.: *Chian* w/control character *Wo. (S/M #C103-21b).*	6.50	20.00	60.00
	c. *Chian. (S/M #C103-21c).*	6.50	20.00	60.00
	d. *Chinchiang. (S/M #C103-21d).*	6.50	20.00	60.00
	e. *Chiatsu. (S/M #C103-21e).*	6.50	20.00	60.00
	f. *Shanghai* (blocked out w/black ovpt.). *(S/M #C103-21f).*	—	—	—

		VG	VF	UNC
S1135	**1 DOLLAR** 1933. Red. Hillside pagoda at l. ctr. Back brown. *(S/M #C103-30).*	7.00	21.00	—
S1136	**5 DOLLARS** 1933. Green. Like #S1135. Back orange. *(S/M #C103-31).*	35.00	110.00	—
S1137	**10 DOLLARS** 1933. Green. Back violet. *(S/M #C103-32).*	45.00	135.00	—

1934; 1935 ISSUE

#S1139 and S1140 printer: TTBC.

		VG	VF	UNC
S1138	**10 CENTS** 1934. Brown. Bldg., trees at upper ctr. Ovpt: *Yang Chuan. (S/M #C103-39).*	—	—	—

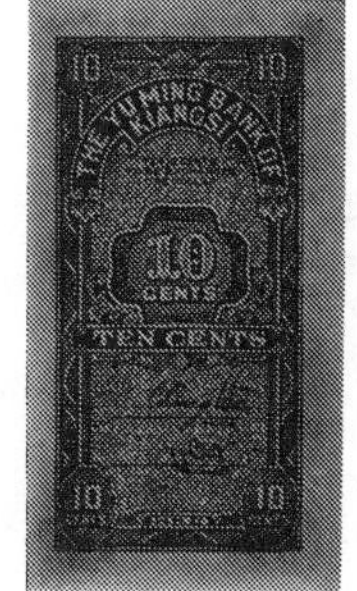

		VG	VF	UNC
S1139	**10 CENTS** 1934. Orange. Island at upper ctr. Back blue. 2 sign. varieties. Vertical format.	5.00	15.00	45.00
	a. Issued note. *(S/M #C103-40a).*	5.00	15.00	45.00
	b. W/additional Chinese control characters. *(S/M #103-40b).*	5.00	15.00	45.00
S1140	**20 CENTS** 1934. Orange. Back lt. brown. *(S/M #C103-41).*	6.00	18.00	55.00
S1141	**20 CENTS** 1934. Dk. green. Bldg., trees at upper ctr. Ovpt: *Yang Chuan. (S/M #C103-42).*	—	—	—

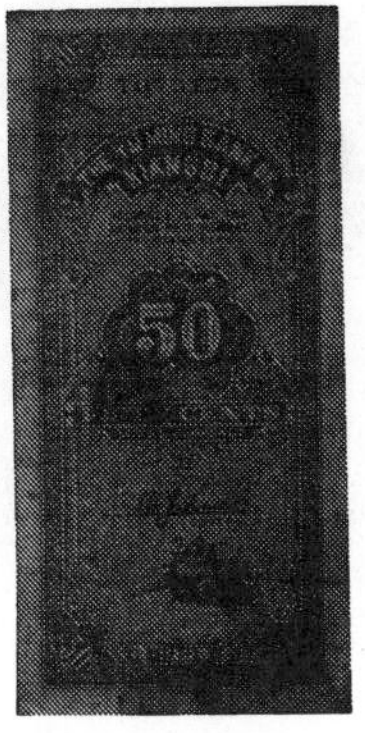

		VG	VF	UNC
S1143	**50 CENTS** 1935. Red. Tower at upper ctr. Back green. *Kanchou.* Vertical format. *(S/M #C103-45).*	7.00	21.00	65.00

1935 PROVISIONAL ISSUE

		VG	VF	UNC
S1146	**50 CENTS** 1935. Red. 7 character ovpt: "changed to 5 Chiao note" on #S1143. Back green. *(S/M #C103-46).*	7.00	21.00	65.00

1938 ISSUE

		VG	VF	UNC
S1151	**5 CENTS** 1938. Red. Sailboats at l., towers at r. Printer: TTBC. *(S/M #C103-50).*	7.00	21.00	65.00

NOTE: Denominations of 10, 20, 50 Cents, 1 and 5 Dollars have been reported, not confirmed.

1945 ISSUE

		VG	VF	UNC
S1158	**100 DOLLARS** 1945. Violet. Gazebo at l. Back red. *(S/M #C103-70).*	60.00	185.00	—
S1159	**200 DOLLARS** 1945. Violet. Pagoda at ctr. Back red. *(S/M #C103-71).*	75.00	225.00	—
S1160	**400 DOLLARS** 1945. Violet. Back violet.			
	a. Issued note. *(S/M #C103-72a).*	100.00	300.00	—
	b. *Nanchang. (S/M #C103-72b).*	100.00	300.00	—

KIANGNAN YU-NING GOVERNMENT BANK
YU NING IMPERIAL BANK

江南裕寧官銀錢局

Chiang Nan/Yü Ning Kuan Yin Ch'ien Chü (Yüan Ch'ao P'iao)

1903 CASH ISSUE

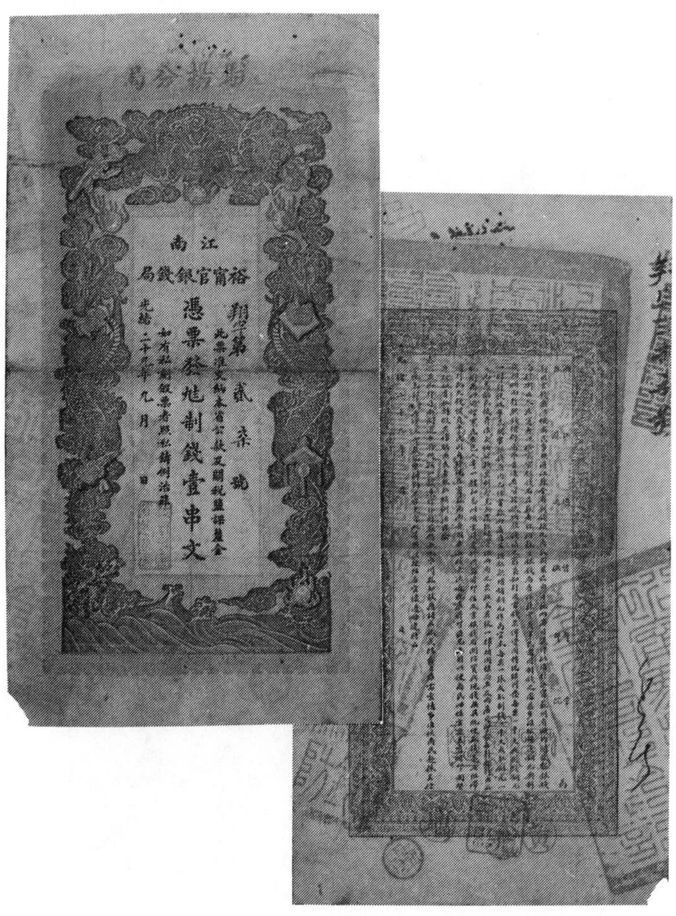

		VG	VF	UNC
S1161	**1 CH'UAN** Yr. 29 (1903). Green, blue and red. Dragons in frame. back black; red seals. Vertical format. *(S/M #C107-1).*	60.00	180.00	—

		VG	VF	UNC
S1162	1 CH'UAN Yr. 29 (1903). Green and m/c. Back red; red seals. *(S/M #C107-2).*	60.00	180.00	—
S1163	100 CASH Yr. 29 (1903). Green and m/c. Back red. *(S/M #C107-3).*	80.00	240.00	—
S1166	1000 CASH (ca. 1903). *(S/M #C107-).*	—	—	—

1905 SILVER DOLLAR ISSUE

#S1168 and S1169 printer: HWPO.

		VG	VF	UNC
S1168	1 DOLLAR Yr. 31 (1905). Black and m/c. Back red and black. *(S/M #C107-10).*	200.00	600.00	—

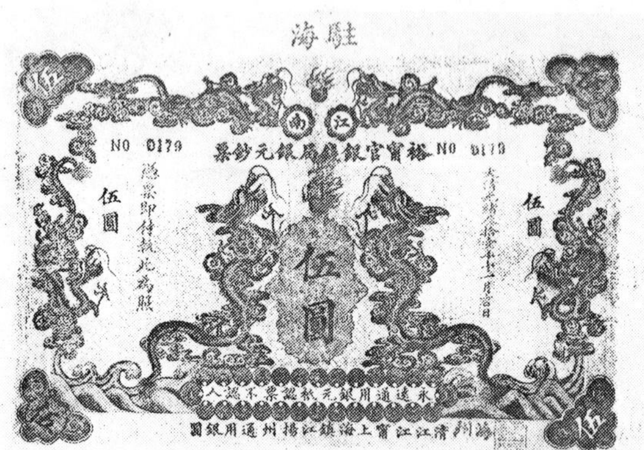

		VG	VF	UNC
S1169	5 DOLLARS Yr. 31 (1905). Black and red. Facing dragons at ctr. Back red and yellow; dragon dollar at l. and r. *(S/M #C107-11).*	250.00	750.00	—
S1170	10 DOLLARS Yr. 31 (1905). Black and red on m/c unpt. Facing dragons at ctr. between dragon dollar (obverse and reverse) on back. *(S/M #C107-12).*	500.00	1500.	—

1907 COPPER COIN ISSUES

#S1172-S1173 small facing dragons at top. Lg. facing dragons w/waves below on back. Printer: CMPA.

		VG	VF	UNC
S1172	10 COPPERS March Yr. 33 (1907). Brown and blue. Back red. *(S/M #C107-20).*	100.00	300.00	—
S1172A	20 COPPERS March Yr. 33 (1907). Dk. blue on ochre unpt. Back green and black. *(S/M #C107-20A).*	—	—	—

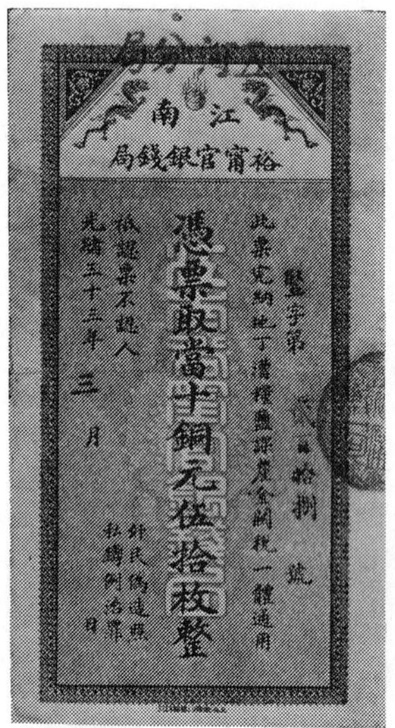

		VG	VF	UNC
S1173	50 COPPERS March Yr. 33 (1907). blue-green on tan unpt. Back blue. Vertical format. *(S/M #C107-21).*	100.00	300.00	—

		VG	VF	UNC
S1174	100 COPPERS 1.3. Yr. 33 (1907). Green and m/c. Facing dragons in frame. Back black; red seals. Vertical format. *(S/M #C107-23).*	60.00	180.00	—

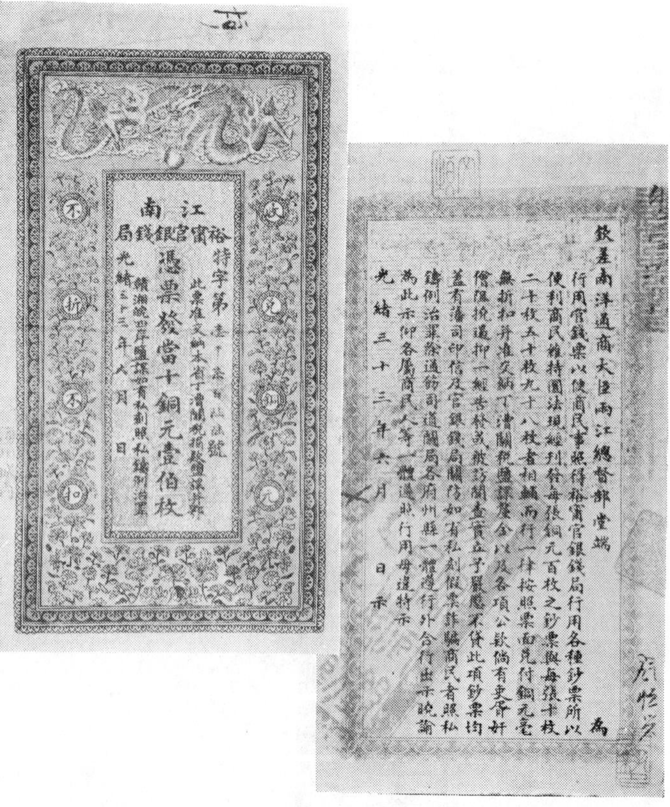

		VG	VF	UNC
S1175	100 COPPERS June Yr. 33 (1907). Red and m/c. Dragon at top. Back red. Vertical format.			
	a. Issued note. *(S/M #C107-22a).*	60.00	200.00	—
	b. *Ch'eng Yang. (S/M #C107-22b).*	120.00	360.00	—

1907 FIRST SILVER DOLLAR ISSUE

#S1177-S1179 facing dragons at ctr. Portr. viceroy at ctr. between dragon dollar obverse and reverse on back. Printer: HWPO.

		VG	VF	UNC
S1177	**1 DOLLAR** 1.7.1907. Purple and blue. Back brown and blue.			
	a. *Shanghai (S/M #C107-30a).*	200.00	600.00	—
	b. *Nanking. (S/M #C107-30b).*	200.00	600.00	—
	c. *Chiuchiang. (S/M #C107-30c).*	200.00	600.00	—
	d. *Nanking/Chiuchiang. (S/M #C107-30d).*	200.00	600.00	—
S1178	**5 DOLLARS** 1.7.1907. Blue and yellow. Back blue and yellow.			
	a. *Shanghai. (S/M #C107-31a).*	300.00	900.00	—
	b. *Nanking. (S/M #C107-31b).*	300.00	900.00	—
	c. *Ch'ing Chiang. (S/M #C107-31c).*	300.00	900.00	—
	d. *Ch'ing Chiang/Nanking. (S/M #C107-).*	300.00	900.00	—

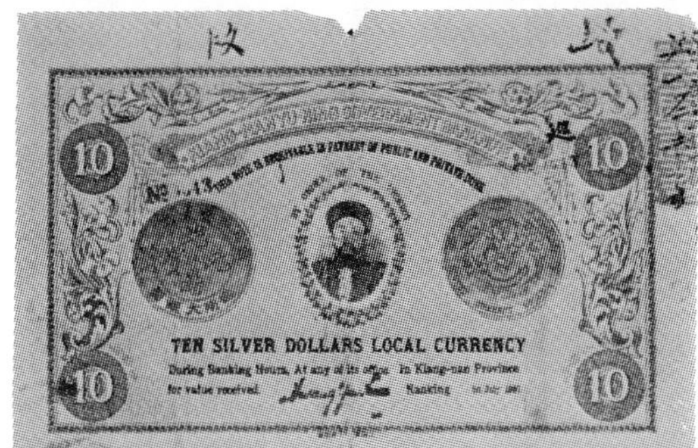

		VG	VF	UNC
S1179	**10 DOLLARS** 1.7.1907. *T'ungchow. (S/M #C107-32).*	375.00	1100.	—

1907 SECOND SILVER DOLLAR ISSUE

		VG	VF	UNC
S1180	**1 DOLLAR** 1.7.1907. Similar #S1177 but silver dragon dollar obverse and reverse on back replaced w/4 Chinese characters at l. and crossed flags at r.			
	a. *Shanghai. (S/M #C107-30a).*	300.00	900.00	—
	b. *Nanking. (S/M #C107-30b).*	300.00	900.00	—
	c. *Kiukiang. (S/M #C107-30c).*	300.00	900.00	—
	d. *Nanking/Shanghai. (S/M #C107-30d).*	300.00	900.00	—
	e. *Ch'ing Chiang/Nanking. (S/M #C107-30e).*	300.00	900.00	—
	f. *Kiukiang/Nanking. (S/M #C107-30f).*	300.00	900.00	—
	g. *Kiukiang/Nanking/Shanghai. (S/M #C107-30g).*	300.00	900.00	—

KIANGNAN YÜ SU SILVER CURRENCY BUREAU

Chiang Nan

江南裕蘇官銀錢局

Yü Su Kuan Yin Ch'ien Chü

1903 CASH ISSUE

		VG	VF	UNC
S1183	**100 CASH** Yr. 29 (1903). Red. Back black. *Kiangnan/Kiangsu. (S/M #C110-1).*	125.00	375.00	—
S1184	**500 CASH** Yr. 29 (1903). Green. Back green. *Kiangnan/Kiangsu. (S/M #C110-2).*	125.00	375.00	—

		VG	VF	UNC
S1185	**1000 CASH** Yr. 29 (1903); Yr. 30 (1904). Red w/black text. Facing dragons in frame. Back black. *Kiangnan/Kiangsu.* Vertical format. *(S/M #C110-3).*	175.00	525.00	—

KIANG SHUN GOVERNMENT BANK

江省官銀號

Chiang Sheng Kuan Yin Hao

1909 ISSUE

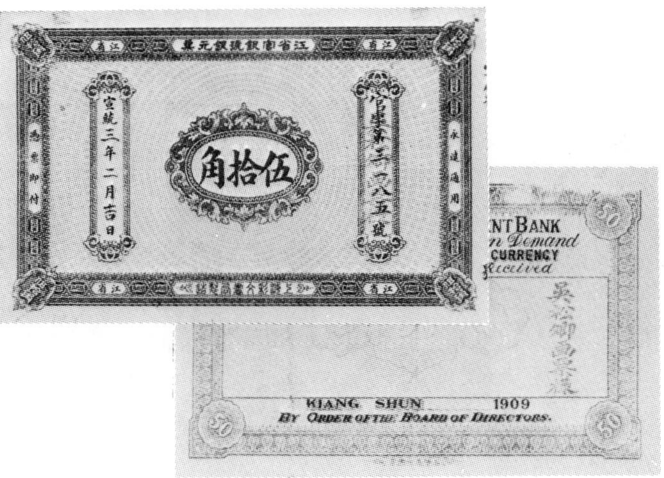

		VG	VF	UNC
S1188	**500 CENTS** 1909. Unissued remainder. *(S/M #C111-20).*	—	—	—

KIANGSU FARMERS BANK
KINGSU FARMERS BANK

江蘇省農民銀行

Chiang Su Sheng Nung Min Yin Hang

Formerly Government of Suchow - Monetary Bureau.

1933 PROVISIONAL ISSUE

#S1191-S1193 ovpt. on Government of Suchow - Monetary Bureau issue.

#S1192-S1198 vertical format.

S1191 10 CENTS

	VG	VF	UNC
1933. Ovpt. on #S1891A. *(S/M #C115-1).*	Reported Not Confirmed		

S1192 20 CENTS

	VG	VF	UNC
1933. Dk. blue. Ovpt. on #S1891B. *(S/M #C115-2).*			
a. Issued note.	15.00	45.00	—
b. W/additional ovpt. Chinese control character.	15.00	50.00	—

S1193 50 CENTS

	VG	VF	UNC
1933. Ovpt. on #S1891C. *(S/M #C115-3).*	10.00	30.00	—

1936 ISSUES

#S1194-S1198 pavilion w/pagoda in background.

#S1194a

#S1194b

S1194 10 CENTS

	VG	VF	UNC
1936. Red. Back green. Printer: TYPC.			
a. Issued note. *(S/M #C115-10a).*	5.00	15.00	45.00
b. Ovpt: *Su. (S/M #C115-10b).*	10.00	30.00	—

S1195 20 CENTS

	VG	VF	UNC
1936. Blue. Back brown. Printer: TYPC.			
a. Issued note. *(S/M #C115-11a).*	12.00	35.00	—
b. Ovpt: *SG SU. (S/M #C115-11b).*	15.00	45.00	—

S1196 50 CENTS

	VG	VF	UNC
1936. Printer: YSCL. *(S/M #C115-).*	15.00	45.00	—

S1198 50 CENTS

	VG	VF	UNC
1936. Brown. Back violet. Printer: TTBC. *(S/M #C115-12).*	15.00	45.00	—

1939 ISSUE

S1200 1 YÜAN

	VG	VF	UNC
1939. Red. Pavilion w/pagoda in background at r., Chinese character sign. at r. Printer: TTBC. *(S/M #C115-20).*			
a. Chinese sign. at r.	20.00	60.00	—
b. Chinese sign. seal at r..	20.00	60.00	—

1940 ISSUE

		VG	VF	UNC
S1202	1 YÜAN 1940. Green. Farmer plowing w/oxen at upper ctr. Back brown; pavilion w/pagoda in background at r. Printer: YSCL. *(S/M #C115-30).*	20.00	60.00	—

1941 ISSUES

		VG	VF	UNC
S1203	50 CENTS 1941. Brown-violet. Temple at upper ctr. Back green. Printer: Sin Kee Printing Co. *(S/M #C115-38).*	15.00	45.00	—

		VG	VF	UNC
S1203A	1 YÜAN 1941. Gray-green. Hillside village at ctr. Back olive-green; trees w/house in background at l. ctr. *(S/M #C115-39).*	20.00	60.00	—
S1203B (1203B)	1 YÜAN			

		VG	VF	UNC
S1204	1 YÜAN 1941. Green. Pagoda at ctr. Printer: TTBC. *(SM #C115-40).*	15.00	45.00	—
S1205	5 YÜAN 1941. Red. Back green. Printer: SHPC. *(S/M #C115-41).*	40.00	120.00	—

KIANGSU PROVINCE

江蘇省兌換券

Chiang Su Sheng Tui Huan Ch'üan

ND EXCHANGE NOTES ISSUE

		VG	VF	UNC
S1208	1 YÜAN ND. *(S/M #C116-1).*	Reported Not Confirmed		

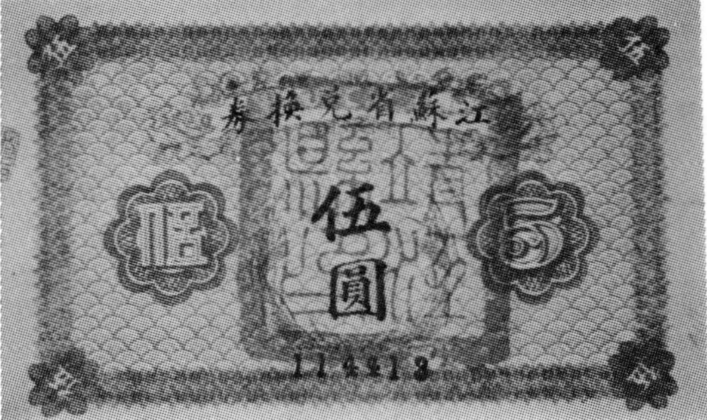

		GOOD	FINE	XF
S1209	5 YÜAN ND. *(S/M #C116-2).*	80.00	240.00	—
S1210	10 YÜAN ND. *(S/M #C116-3).*	80.00	240.00	—

1925 EXCHANGE NOTES ISSUE

		GOOD	FINE	XF
S1211	1 YÜAN 1925. Brown and green. Back yellow. *(S/M #C116-10).*	80.00	240.00	—
S1212	5 YÜAN 1925. Green and red. Back green. *(S/M #C116-11).*	80.00	240.00	—
S1213	10 YÜAN 1925. Blue and green. Back green. *(S/M #C116-12).*	80.00	240.00	—

NANKING EXCHANGE OFFICE OF THE FINANCIAL DEPARTMENT, KIANGSU

江蘇財政司南京兌換處

Chiang Su Ts'ai Cheng Szu Nan Ching Tui Huan Ch'üan

1912 ISSUE

#S1215-S1217 surviving are usually encountered cut diagonally and the halves have been taped back together. Whole uncut notes command a considerable premium.

		GOOD	FINE	XF
S1215	1 YÜAN 1912. Green on orange unpt. Back lilac. *(S/M #C118-1).*	150.00	450.00	—
S1216	5 YÜAN 1912. *(S/M #C118-2).*	Reported Not Confirmed		
S1217	10 YÜAN 1912. *(S/M #C118-3).*	225.00	675.00	—

KIANGSU FINANCE DEPARTMENT

江蘇財政廳

Chiang Su Ts'ai Cheng T'ing

1939 COPPER COIN ISSUE

		GOOD	FINE	XF
S1220	1 COPPER 1939. Red. Pagoda at l. *(S/M #C120-1).*	5.00	15.00	50.00

		GOOD	FINE	XF
S1221	**5 COPPERS** 1939. Brown. *(S/M #C120-2).*	5.00	15.00	50.00

		GOOD	FINE	XF
S1222	**10 COPPERS** 1939. Olive-green. Pagodas at r. *(S/M #C120-3).*	5.00	15.00	50.00

		GOOD	FINE	XF
S1223	**15 COPPERS** 1939. Brown. House at l. *(S/M #C120-4).*	8.00	25.00	75.00

		GOOD	FINE	XF
S1224	**30 COPPERS** 1939. Blue. House w/pagoda in background at r. *(S/M C120-5).*	10.00	30.00	90.00

KIANGSU BANK

江蘇銀行

Chiang Su Yin Hang

1913 ISSUE

#S1226-S1226B lions supporting globe. People near pagoda and bridge on back. Printer: BWC.

		GOOD	FINE	XF
S1226	**1 DOLLAR** 1.6.1913. Specimen. *(S/M #C121-1).*	—	Unc	300.00
S1226A	**5 DOLLARS** 1.6.1913. Specimen. *(S/M #C121-2).*	—	Unc	400.00

		GOOD	FINE	XF
S1226B	**10 DOLLARS** 1.6.1913. Specimen. *(S/M #C121-3).*	—	Unc	500.00

1927 ISSUE

		GOOD	FINE	XF
S1227	**1 DOLLAR** 1927. *(S/M #C121-10).*	Reported Not Confirmed		
S1227A	**5 DOLLARS** 1927. *(S/M #C121-11).*	Reported Not Confirmed		
S1227B	**10 DOLLARS** 1927. *(S/M #C121-12).*	Reported Not Confirmed		

YUE SOO IMPERIAL BANK

江蘇裕蘇官銀錢局

Chiang Su Yü Su Kuan Yin Ch'ien Chü

1906 SILVER DOLLAR ISSUE

#S1228-S1230 *Soochow*. Printer: HWPO.

		GOOD	FINE	XF
S1228	**1 DOLLAR** 1.9.1906. Green and red. Man at ctr. r. Back green and yellow; 2 dragons facing at upper ctr. *(S/M #C122-1).*	150.00	450.00	—
S1229	**5 DOLLARS** 1.9.1906. *(S/M #C122-2).*	—	—	—
S1230	**10 DOLLARS** 1.9.1906. Green and red. Back green and yellow. *(S/M #C122-3).*	175.00	525.00	—

1908 SILVER DOLLAR ISSUE

#S1232-S1235 facing dragons at ctr. on back. *Soochow*. Most notes encountered have been repaired after 2 corners were severed when cancelled. Printer: IPCL.

		GOOD	FINE	XF
S1232	**1 DOLLAR** 1.9.1908. Brown and green. Back black and violet. *(S/M #C122-10).*			
	a. Issued note.	150.00	450.00	—
	b. Clipped or repaired cancelled note.	60.00	180.00	—

		GOOD	FINE	XF
S1233	**5 DOLLARS** 1.9.1908. Brown and green. Back black and violet. *(S/M #C122-11).*			
	a. Issued note.	185.00	550.00	—
	b. Clipped or repaired cancelled note.	90.00	270.00	—
S1234	**10 DOLLARS** 1.9.1908. *(S/M #C122-12).*			
	a. Issued note.	—	—	—
	b. Clipped or repaired cancelled note.	100.00	300.00	—

CHIHLI PROVINCE

直隸省金庫兌換券

Chih Li Sheng Chin K'u Tui Huan Ch'ü

1924 TREASURY EXCHANGE NOTES ISSUE

		GOOD	FINE	XF
S1238	**1 DOLLAR** 1924. *(S/M #C160-1).*	Reported Not Confirmed		
S1239	**5 DOLLARS** 1924. *(S/M #C160-2).*	Reported Not Confirmed		
S1240	**10 DOLLARS** 1924. *(S/M #C160-3).*	Reported Not Confirmed		

1928 TREASURY EXCHANGE NOTES ISSUE

#S1241-S1243 printer: BEPP.

		GOOD	FINE	XF
S1241	**1 YÜAN** 1928. Orange. Bridge at ctr. *(S/M #C160-10).*			
	a. Issued note.	30.00	90.00	270.00
	r. Remainder.	—	Unc	150.00
S1242	**5 YÜAN** 1928. Green. *(S/M #C160-11).*			
	a. Issued note.	45.00	125.00	—
	r. Remainder.	—	Unc	180.00
S1243	**10 YÜAN** 1928. Blue. *(S/M #C160-12).*			
	a. Issued note.	60.00	180.00	—
	r. Remainder.	—	Unc	210.00

CHIHLI PROVINCE

券通流期定庫省隸直

Chih Li Sheng K'u Ting Ch'i Liu T'ung Ch'ü

1926 TERM CIRCULATING NOTES ISSUE

		GOOD	FINE	XF
S1247	**10 CENTS** 1926. Green. *(S/M #C162-1).*	35.00	110.00	—
S1248	**20 CENTS** 1926. Brown. *(S/M #C162-2).*	40.00	125.00	—

#S1251 and S1252 printer: SOPO.

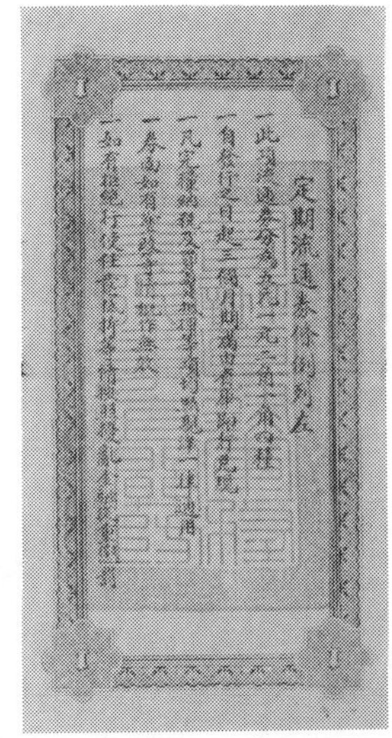

		VG	VF	UNC
S1251	**1 YÜAN** March 1926. Brown-violet on green unpt. Back brown-violet. Vertical format. *(S/M #C162-10).*			
	a. Issued note.	75.00	225.00	—
	r. Remainder.	—	25.00	75.00
S1252	**5 YÜAN** March 1926. Blue and violet. Like #S1251. Back blue and red. *(S/M #C162-11).*	60.00	180.00	—

PROVINCIAL BANK OF CHIHLI

局錢官省隸直

Chi Li Sheng Kuan Ch'ien Chü

行銀省隸直

Chih Li Sheng Yin Hang

1916 CASH ISSUE

		VG	VF	UNC
S1254	**200 CASH** 1916. Blue and m/c. Back brown and yellow. *Tientsin. (S/M #C163-1).*	60.00	180.00	—

1916 PROVISIONAL DOLLAR ISSUE

#S1257-S1260 ovpt. new bank name on Peiyang Tientsin Bank issue.

		VG	VF	UNC
S1257	**1 DOLLAR** 1916. Brown on m/c unpt. Ovpt. on #S2526. *(S/M #C163-5).*	—	—	—

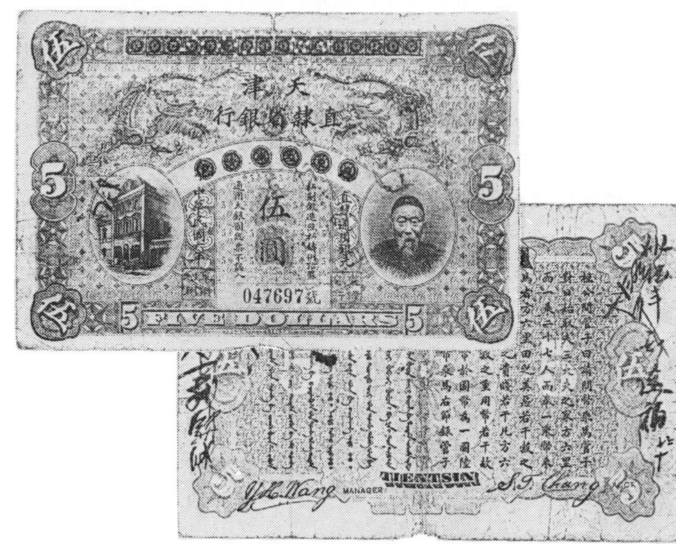

		VG	VF	UNC
S1258	**5 DOLLARS** 1916. Ovpt. on #S2528. Chinese character cancellation perforations. *(S/M #C163-6).*	—	—	—
S1259	**50 DOLLARS** 1916. Ovpt. on #S2529A. Remainder. *(S/M #C163-9).*	—	—	—

		VG	VF	UNC
S1260	**100 DOLLARS** 1916. Ovpt. on #S2530. Remainder. *(S/M #C163-10).*	—	—	—

1920 DOLLAR ISSUE

#S1263-S1265 house at ctr. *Tientsin.* Printer: ABNC.

		VG	VF	UNC
S1263	**1 DOLLAR** 1.12.1920. Black on dk. green and m/c unpt. Back dk. green.			

	VG	VF	UNC
a. Sign. Chen-Wang w/English titles. *(S/M #C163-20b).*	8.00	25.00	—
b. Sign. Ma-Chang w/o English titles. *(S/M #C163-20a).*	3.00	10.00	30.00
c. Sign. Wang-Wang. *(S/M #C163-20c).*	8.00	25.00	—
d. W/additional Chinese character control ovpt.	8.00	25.00	—

S1264 5 DOLLARS
1.12.1920. Black on dk. blue unpt. Back dk. blue.

	VG	VF	UNC
a. Sign. Chen-Wang w/English titles. *(S/M #C163-21b).*	10.00	30.00	—
b. Sign. Ma-Chang w/o English titles. *(S/M #C163-21a).*	8.00	25.00	—
c. Sign. Wang-Wang. *(S/M #C163-21c).*	15.00	45.00	—

S1265 10 DOLLARS
1.12.1920. Black on m/c unpt. Back brown.

	VG	VF	UNC
a. Sign. Chen-Wang w/English titles. *(S/M #C163-22b).*	15.00	45.00	—
b. Sign. Ma-Chang w/o English titles. *(S/M #C163-22a).*	10.00	30.00	—
c. Sign. Wang-Wang. *(S/M #C163-22c).*	15.00	45.00	—

1921 COPPER COIN ISSUE

#S1268 and S1269 face w/black text. Modern bldg. at ctr. on back. *Tientsin.*

	VG	VF	UNC
S1268 5 COPPERS 1921. Brown and blue. Back green. *(S/M #C163-30).*	35.00	110.00	—
S1269 10 COPPERS 1921. Brown and green. Back green. *(S/M #C163-31).*	35.00	110.00	—

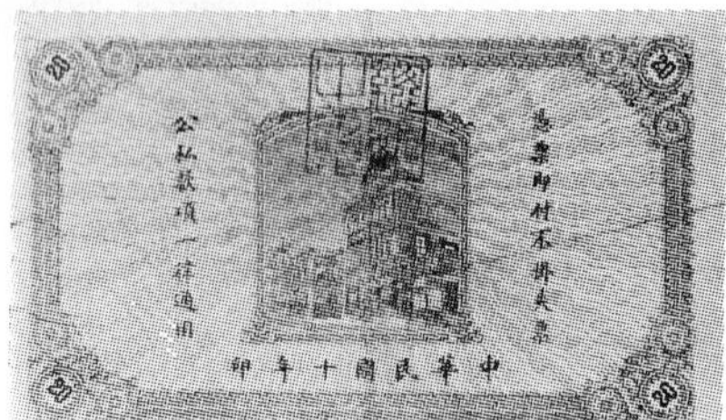

S1270 20 COPPERS
1921. Violet and yellow. Back green; lg. hand stamped sign. seal ovpt. *(S/M #C163-32).*

	VG	VF	UNC
a. Issued note.	42.50	125.00	—
b. W/2 sign. seals on back.	37.50	110.00	—
S1271 50 COPPERS 1921. Violet and orange. Back green. *(S/M #C163-33).*	50.00	150.00	—

1923 ISSUE

	VG	VF	UNC
S1271A 20 COPPERS 1923. Brown-violet on blue unpt. Back dk. green. *Tientsin. (S/M #C163-38).*	75.00	225.00	—
S1271C 100 COPPERS 1923. Purple on lt. green unpt. Temple at ctr. Back green; temple at ctr. *YUNG TSUN.*	—	—	—

1924 COPPER COIN ISSUE

#S1272-S1274A bridge w/house in background at ctr. Printer: BEPP.

S1272 10 COPPERS
1924. Blue on orange unpt. Back orange and brown.

	VG	VF	UNC
a. *Tientsin* w/vertical Chinese 10 characters ovpt. at l. and r. *(S/M #C163-40c).*	15.00	45.00	—
b. *Tientsin* w/vertical Chinese 5 characters ovpt. at l. and r. *(S/M #C163-40b).*	15.00	45.00	—
c. *Tientsin/Peking* w/vertical Chinese 5 characters ovpt. at l. and r. *(S/M #C163-40a).*	17.50	50.00	—
d. *Paoting. (S/M #C163-d).*	25.00	75.00	—
e. *Paoting/Tientsin. (S/M #C163-e).*	25.00	75.00	—

S1273 20 COPPERS
1924. Violet and green. W/ovpt. 10 vertical Chinese characters at l. and r. Back green and black.

	VG	VF	UNC
a. *Peking. (S/M #C163-41a).*	15.00	45.00	—
b. *Tientsin/Peking. (S/M #C163-41b).*	20.00	75.00	—
S1274 40 COPPERS 1924. Brown and green. Back violet. *Tientsin. (S/M #C163-42).*	25.00	75.00	—
S1274A 50 COPPERS 1924. *Peking. (S/M #C163-43).*	25.00	75.00	—

1925 COPPER COIN ISSUE

#S1275-S1278 bridge w/house in background at l. or at ctr. Printer: BEPP.

	VG	VF	UNC
S1275 10 COPPERS 1925. *(S/M #C163-50).*	Reported Not Confirmed		

S1276 20 COPPERS
1925. Violet and blue. Back black and green.

	VG	VF	UNC
a. *Tientsin. (S/M #C163-51b).*	15.00	45.00	—
b. *Tientsin/Peking. (S/M #C163-51a).*	17.00	50.00	—

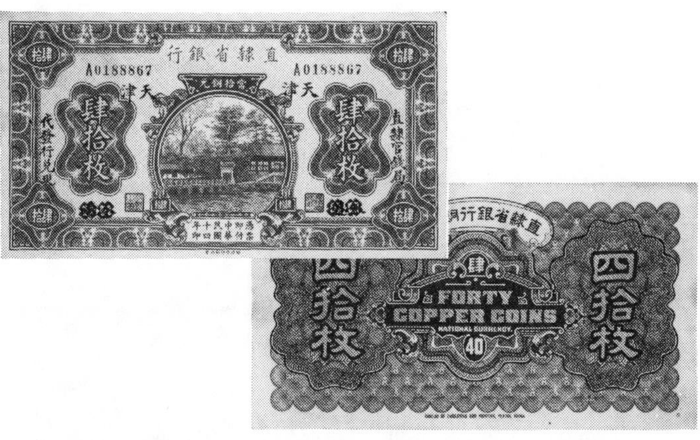

		VG	VF	UNC
S1276A	**40 COPPERS** 1925. Brown on lt. green unpt. Back black on violet unpt. *Tientsin/Yungstun. (S/M #C163-51.5).*	25.00	75.00	—
S1277	**50 COPPERS** 1925. Brown. Back green and black.			
	a. *Tientsin. (S/M #C163-52a).*	20.00	50.00	—
	b. *Yungtsun. (S/M #C163-52b).*	25.00	60.00	—

		VG	VF	UNC
S1278	**100 COPPERS** 1925. Green on red. unpt.			
	a. *Yungtsun. (S/M #C163-53a).*	30.00	90.00	—
	b. *Tientsin/Yungtsun. (S/M #C163-53b).*	35.00	110.00	—

1926 ISSUES

#S1279-S1280 printer: BEPP.

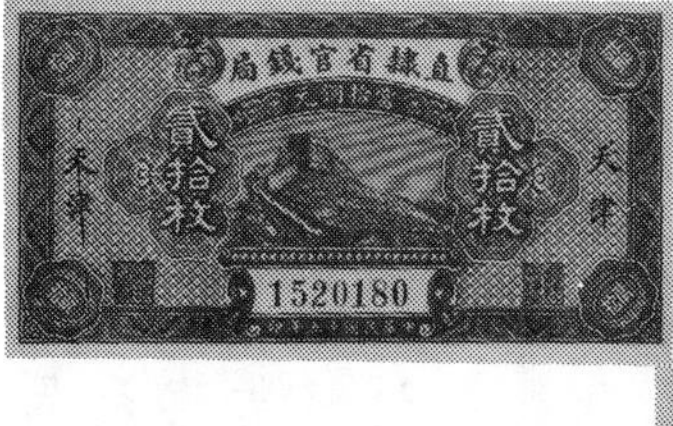

		VG	VF	UNC
S1279	**10 COPPERS** 1926. Bridge w/house in background at ctr. *Tientsin. (S/M #C163-60).*	20.00	60.00	—
S1280	**20 COPPERS** 1926. Violet and green. Back black and green. *Tientsin. (S/M #C163-62).*	10.00	30.00	—

		VG	VF	UNC
S1282	**20 COPPERS** 1926. Brown on violet and gray-green unpt. Great Wall at ctr. Back gray-green on brown unpt. *Tientsin. (S/M #C163-61).*	2.00	8.00	25.00

#S1285 and S1286 Great Wall at r. *Tientsin.*

		VG	VF	UNC
S1285	1926. Violet on brown and gray-green unpt. Back brown on gray-green unpt. *(S/M #C163-70).*	1.75	5.00	15.00
S1286	1926. Blue-green on brown and violet unpt. Back violet on blue-green unpt. *(S/M #C163-71).*	1.75	5.00	15.00

NOTE: For #S1285 and S1286 w/additional rectangular ovpt. see Military - Chihli Provincial #S3803 and S3804.

#S1288-S1290 city gate at ctr. Printer: BEPA.

		VG	VF	UNC
S1288	**1 YÜAN** 1.10.1926. Violet and m/c. Back violet.			
	a. *TIENTSIN. (S/M #C163-80a).*	3.00	10.00	30.00
	b. *HSUCHOW/TIENTSIN. (S/M #C163-80b).*	7.50	22.50	67.50

		VG	VF	UNC
S1289	**5 YÜAN** 1.10.1926. Blue-gray and m/c. Back blue-gray.			
	a. *TIENTSIN. (S/M #C163-81a).*	8.00	25.00	75.00
	b. *HSUCHOW. (S/M #C163-81b).*	12.50	40.00	120.00
S1290	**10 YÜAN** 1.10.1926. Red and m/c. Back red.			
	a. *TIENTSIN. (S/M #C163-82a).*	10.00	30.00	90.00
	b. *HSUCHOW. (S/M #C163-82b).*	12.50	40.00	120.00
	c. *HSUCHOW/TIENTSIN. (S/M #C163-82c).*	12.50	40.00	120.00

NOTE: For #S1288-S1290 w/additional red rectangular ovpt. see Military - Chihli Provincial #S3805-S3807.

BANK OF LOCAL RAILWAYS OF SHANSI AND SUIYÜAN

號銀路鐵方地綏晋

Chin Sui Ti Fang T'ieh Lu Yin Hao

1934 ISSUE

#S1291-S1296 steam passenger train at r. Printer: BEPP.

		VG	VF	UNC
S1291	**1 CHIAO = 10 CENTS** 1934. Deep olive-green. Back brown.			
	a. *Kiaocheng. (S/M #C180-1a).*	10.00	30.00	—
	b. *TAIYUAN. (S/M #C180-1b).*	10.00	30.00	—
S1292	**2 CHIAO = 20 CENTS** 1934. Dk. blue. *Taiyuan. (S/M #C180-2).*	12.00	35.00	—
S1293	**5 CHIAO = 50 CENTS** 1934. Violet. Back violet. *(S/M #C180-3).* (Not issued).	—	—	—

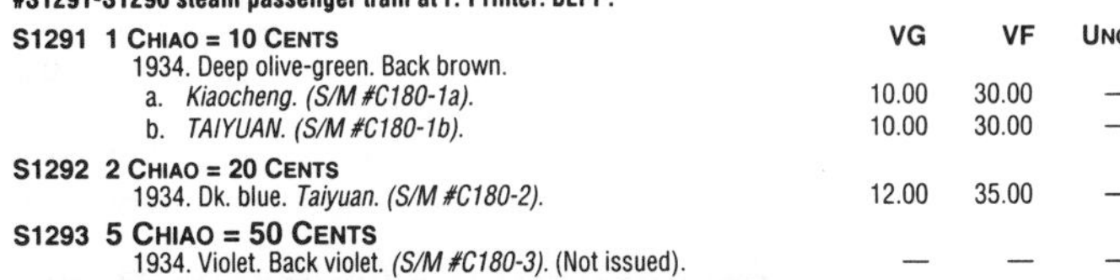

S1294 1 YÜAN

	VG	VF	UNC
1.7.1934. Purple on yellow unpt. Back purple.			
a. *HUNGCHUNG. (S/M #C180-10a).*	30.00	90.00	—
b. *SINHSIEN. (S/M #C180-10b).*	30.00	90.00	—
c. *TAIYUAN. (S/M #C180-10c).*	5.00	15.00	45.00
d. *YUTZE. (S/M #C180-10d).*	30.00	90.00	—
e. *KIAOCHENG. (S/M #C180-10e).*	30.00	90.00	—
f. *PINGYAO. (S/M #C180-10f).*	30.00	90.00	—
g. *YUCI. (S/M #C180-10g).*	15.00	45.00	—
r. Remainder w/o sign., serial # or place name.	--	—	75.00

S1295 5 YÜAN

	VG	VF	UNC
1934. Olive-green.			
a. *Taiyuan. (S/M #C180-11a).*	10.00	30.00	—
b. *Yuci. (S/M #C180-11b).*	15.00	45.00	—

S1296 10 YÜAN

	VG	VF	UNC
1934. Brown. *Taiyuan. (S/M #C180-12).*	25.00	75.00	—

1936 ISSUE

#S1297-S1301 printer: NWPF.

		VG	VF	UNC
S1297	**10 CENTS** 1936. Green. *(S/M #C180-20).* (Not issued).	15.00	45.00	—
S1298	**20 CENTS** 1936. Brown. Steam passenger train at ctr. *(S/M #C180-21).*	15.00	45.00	—

#S1299-S1301 steam passenger train at r.

		VG	VF	UNC
S1299	**50 CENTS** 1936. Blue. Back red. *(S/M #C180-22).*	3.00	10.00	30.00

S1300 1 YÜAN

	VG	VF	UNC
1936. Brown on ochre unpt.			
a. Issued note. *(S/M #C180-23a).*	5.00	15.00	45.00
b. W/2 additional black vertical Chinese 4 character ovpts. at l. and r. *(S/M #C180-23b).*	—	—	—

S1301 5 YÜAN

	VG	VF	UNC
1936. Dk. brown-violet on lt. blue and orange unpt. Back dk. brown on pale green unpt. *Shansi.*			
a. Issued note. *(S/M #C180-24a).*	5.00	15.00	45.00
b. W/2 additional black vertical Chinese 4 character ovpts. at l. and r. *(S/M #C180-24b).*	12.50	40.00	120.00

TSINGTAO CITY AGRICULTURAL AND INDUSTRIAL BANK

行銀工農市島青

Ch'ing Tao Shih Nung Kung Yin Hang

1933 ND PROVISIONAL COPPER COIN ISSUE

#S1302-S1302C ovpt. new bank name on Tsingtao City Bank - Tsingtao Regional Bank.

		VG	VF	UNC
S1302	**10 COPPERS** ND (1933 - old date 1924). ovpt. on #S1302D. *(S/M #C195-1).*	30.00	90.00	—
S1302A	**30 COPPERS** ND (1933 - old date 1924). Ovpt. on #S1302E. *(S/M #C195-).*	30.00	90.00	—

		VG	VF	UNC
S1302B	**50 COPPERS** ND (1933 - old date 1924). Ovpt. on #S1302F. *(S/M #C195-).*	30.00	90.00	—
S1302C	**100 COPPERS** ND (1933 - old date 1924). Ovpt. on #S1302G. *(S/M #C195-2).*	30.00	90.00	—

TSINGTAO CITY BANK
TSINGTAO REGIONAL BANK

行銀方地島青

Ch'ing Tao Ti Fang Yin Hang

1924 ISSUE

#S1302D-S1302F lg. bldg. at ctr. Printer: BEPP.

		VG	VF	UNC
S1302D	**10 COPPERS** 1924. *(S/M #C196-1).*	30.00	90.00	—
S1302E	**30 COPPERS** 1924. *(S/M #C196-1.3).*	30.00	90.00	—
S1302F	**50 COPPERS** 1924. Green on yellow unpt. Back green on ochre unpt. *(S/M #C196-1.5).*	30.00	90.00	—
S1302G	**100 COPPERS** 1924. *(S/M #C196-2).*	30.00	90.00	—

#S1302J-S1302L monument at ctr. Printer: BEPP. Specimen.

		VG	VF	UNC
S1302J	**1 YÜAN** 15.4.1924.*(S/M #C196-10).*	—	—	110.00
S1302K	**5 YÜAN** 15.4.1924. *(S/M #C196-11).*	—	—	125.00
S1302L	**10 YÜAN** 15.4.1924. *(S/M #C196-12).*	—	—	150.00

NOTE: For #S1302J-S1302L w/ovpt: *SHANTUNG* see Provincial Bank of Shantung #S2745-S2747.

FENGTIEN INDUSTRIAL BANK
HSIN YIEH BANK
SHING YEH BANK
MUKDEN BANK OF INDUSTRIALDEVELOPMENT
FENTIEN HSING YNG YEH BANK

行銀業興天奉

Feng T'ien Hsing Yeh Yin Hang

1913 FIRST ISSUE

#S1303-S1305 printer: PYOG.

		VG	VF	UNC
S1303	**1 DOLLAR** 1913. *(S/M #F7-1).*	100.00	300.00	—

		VG	VF	UNC
S1304	**5 DOLLARS** 1913. *(S/M #F7-2).*	125.00	375.00	—

		VG	VF	UNC
S1305	**10 DOLLARS** 1913. Bldg. at l. and r. on back. *(S/M #F7-3).*	100.00	300.00	—

1913 SECOND ISSUE

#S1307-S1309 printer: ABNC.

		VG	VF	UNC
S1307	**1 DOLLAR** 1913. *(S/M #F7-10).*	—	—	—
S1308	**5 DOLLARS** 1913. *(S/M #F7-11).*	—	—	—
S1309	**10 DOLLARS** 1913. *(S/M #F7-12).*	—	—	—

1914 ISSUE

#S1311-S1313 printer: PYPO.

		VG	VF	UNC
S1311	**1 DOLLAR** 1914. *(S/M #F7-20).*	75.00	225.00	—
S1312	**5 DOLLARS** 1914. *(S/M #F7-21).*	60.00	180.00	—
S1313	**10 DOLLARS** 1914. *(S/M #F7-22).*	75.00	225.00	—

1915 ISSUE

		VG	VF	UNC
S1315	**1 DOLLAR** 1915. Waterfront at l. and r. Street scene at ctr. on back. *(S/M #F7-).*	100.00	300.00	—

1917 ISSUE

		VG	VF	UNC
S1320	**1 DOLLAR** 1917. House amidst trees at ctr. *(S/M #F7-30).*	60.00	180.00	—
S1321	**5 DOLLARS** 1917. *(S/M #F7-31).*	60.00	180.00	—
S1322	**10 DOLLARS** 1917. *(S/M #F7-32).*	75.00	225.00	—

1918; 1919 BOND ISSUE

#S1323-S1325 printer: ABNC.

		VG	VF	UNC
S1323	**1 DOLLAR** 1919; 1920. Black. Pavilion at r. Back green on m/c unpt. Printer: ABNC. *(S/M #F7-40).*	45.00	135.00	—

		VG	VF	UNC
S1324	**5 DOLLARS** 1918. Orange. Tower at l. Back brown. *(S/M #F7-41).*	45.00	135.00	—
S1325	**10 DOLLARS** 1918. Green. Back brown. *(SM #F7-42).*	75.00	225.00	—

#S1326 *Deleted.* See #S1323.

HUA FENG OFFICIAL CURRENCY BUREAU

奉天華豐官銀號

Feng T'ien Hua Feng Kuan Yin Hao

1905 ISSUE

#S1327-S1329 printer: PYOG.

		GOOD	FINE	XF
S1327	**1 DOLLAR** Yr. 31 (1905). *(S/M #F8-1).*	75.00	225.00	—
S1328	**5 DOLLARS** Yr. 31 (1905). *(S/M #F8-2).*	100.00	300.00	—
S1329	**2 DOLLARS** Yr. 31 (1905). *(S/M #F8-3).*	125.00	375.00	—

FENGTIEN OFFICIAL CURRENCY BUREAU

奉天官銀號

Feng T'ien Kuan Yin Hao

1905 DOLLAR ISSUE

#S1330-S1337 printer: PYOG.

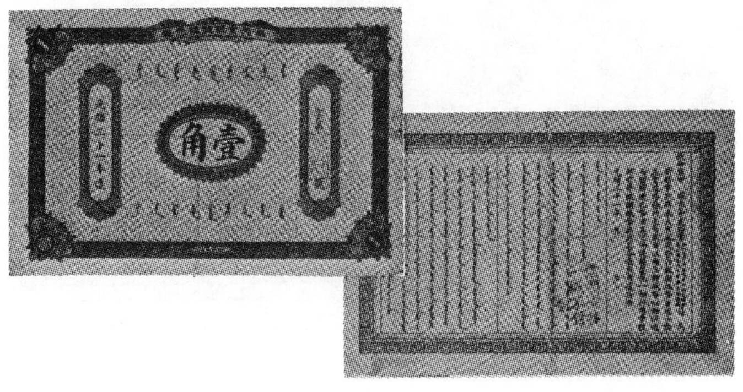

		GOOD	FINE	XF
S1330	**10 CENTS** Yr. 31 (1905). Green. Back orange. *(S/M #F10-1).*	50.00	150.00	—
S1331	**20 CENTS** Yr. 31 (1905). *(S/M #F10-2).*	50.00	150.00	—

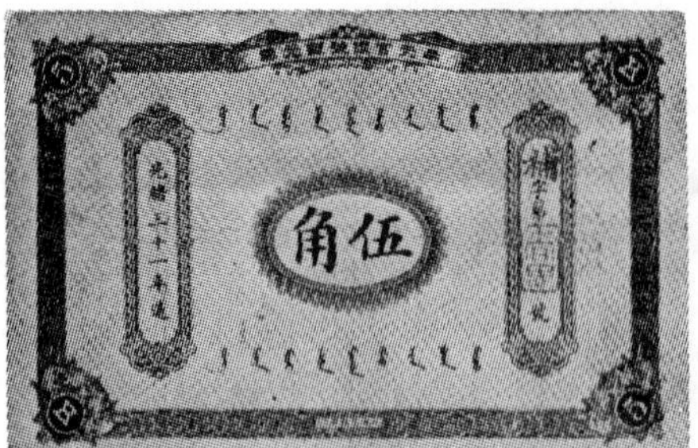

		GOOD	FINE	XF
S1332	**50 CENTS** Yr. 31 (1905). Green. Back orange. *(S/M #F10-3).*	57.50	170.00	—
S1333	**100 CENTS** Yr. 31 (1905). *(S/M #F10-4).*	90.00	270.00	—
S1335	**1 DOLLAR** Yr. 31 (1905). *(S/M #F10-10)*	90.00	270.00	—
S1336	**5 DOLLARS** Yr. 31 (1905). Green. Back orange. *(S/M #F10-11).*	90.00	270.00	—
S1337	**10 DOLLARS** Yr. 31 (1905). *(S/M #F10-12)*	100.00	300.00	—

#S1337A and S1338 *Deleted.* See #S1353 and S1354.

1905 TIAO ISSUE

#S1339-S1345 printer: PYOG.

		GOOD	FINE	XF
S1338	**1 TIAO** Yr. 31 (1905). (S/M #F10-).	—	Rare	—
S1339	**2 TIAO** Yr. 31 (1905). (S/M #F10-).	—	Rare	—
S1340	**3 TIAO** Yr. 31 (1905). (S/M #F10-).	—	Rare	—
S1341	**4 TIAO** Yr. 31 (1905). (S/M #F10-).	—	Rare	—
S1342	**5 TIAO** Yr. 31 (1905). (S/M #F10-).	—	Rare	—
S1343	**6 TIAO** Yr. 31 (1905). (S/M #F10-).	—	Rare	—
S1344	**7 TIAO** Yr. 31 (1905). (S/M #F10-).	—	Rare	—
S1345	**8 TIAO** Yr. 31 (1905). (S/M #F10-).	—	Rare	—
S1346	**10 TIAO** Yr. 31 (1905). Vertical format. (S/M #F10-).	—	Rare	—
S1347	**15 TIAO** Yr. 31 (1905). (S/M #F10-).	—	Rare	—
S1348	**20 TIAO** Yr. 31 (1905). (S/M #F10-).	—	Rare	—
S1349	**25 TIAO** Yr. 31 (1905). (S/M #F10-).	—	—	—
S1350	**30 TIAO** Yr. 31 (1905). (S/M #F10-).	—	—	—
S1351	**40 TIAO** Yr. 31 (1905). (S/M #F10-).	—	—	—
S1352	**50 TIAO** Yr. 31 (1905). (S/M #F10-).	—	—	—
S1352A	**60 TIAO** Yr. 31 (1905). (S/M #F10-).	—	—	—
S1352B	**70 TIAO** Yr. 31 (1905). (S/M #F10-).	—	—	—
S1352C	**100 TIAO** Yr. 31 (1905). (S/M #F10-).	—	—	—

1906 DOLLAR ISSUE

		GOOD	FINE	XF
S1353	**100 CENTS** Yr. 32 (1906). *(S/M #F10-).*	90.00	270.00	—
S1354	**10 DOLLARS** Yr. 32 (1906). *(S/M #F10-).*	100.00	300.00	—

NOTE: For previously listed 1908 Issue, #S1339-S1345, see #S2854-S2854F.

FENGTIEN PUBLIC EXCHANGE BANK
KUNG TSI BANK OF FENGTIEN

奉天公濟平市錢號

Feng T'ien Kung Chi P'ing Shih Ch'ien Hao

1918 COPPER COIN ISSUES

		VG	VF	UNC
S1355	**5 COPPERS** 1918. Green and yellow. Back green. *(S/M #F12-1).*	22.50	67.50	—

		VG	VF	UNC
S1356	**10 COPPERS** 1918. Dk. blue on yellow unpt. *(S/M #F12-2).*	22.50	67.50	—
S1357	**20 COPPERS** 1918. *(S/M #F12-3).*	25.00	75.00	—

		VG	VF	UNC
S1358	**50 COPPERS** 1918. Blue and tan. Back gray. *(S/M #F12-4).*	25.00	75.00	—

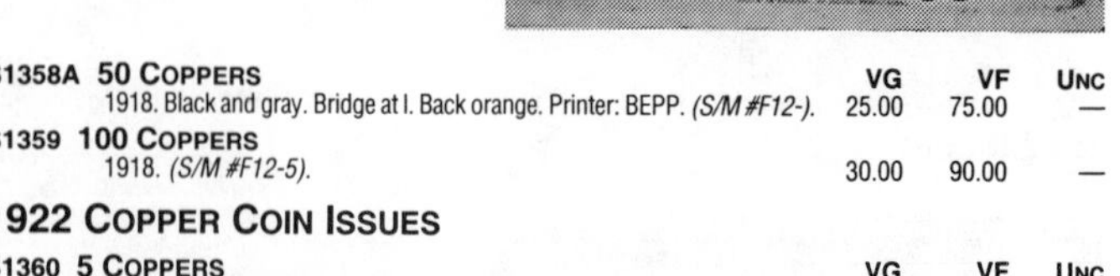

		VG	VF	UNC
S1358A	**50 COPPERS** 1918. Black and gray. Bridge at l. Back orange. Printer: BEPP. *(S/M #F12-).*	25.00	75.00	—
S1359	**100 COPPERS** 1918. *(S/M #F12-5).*	30.00	90.00	—

1922 COPPER COIN ISSUES

		VG	VF	UNC
S1360	**5 COPPERS** 1922. *(S/M #F12-10).*	10.00	30.00	—

		VG	VF	UNC
S1361	**10 COPPERS** 1922. Brown. Tower at l. Back blue. *(S/M #F12-11).*	8.00	25.00	—

		GOOD	FINE	XF
S1362	**20 COPPERS** 1922. Green. City tower gate at l. Back red. *(S/M #F12-12).*	6.00	20.00	—

		GOOD	FINE	XF
S1363	**50 COPPERS** 1922. Brown. Back orange. *(S/M #F12-13).*			
	a. Issued note.	8.00	25.00	75.00
	s. Specimen.	—	—	50.00
S1364	**100 COPPERS** 1922. Blue. Back green. *(S/M #F12-14).*	12.50	36.00	—

		GOOD	FINE	XF
S1365	**100 COPPERS** 1922. Black. City fortress gate at l. Back green. Engraved. *(S/M #F12-15).*	12.00	35.00	—

		VG	VF	UNC
S1370	**100 COPPERS** 1922. Dk. gray-green. Like #S1365 but lithograph. *(S/M #F12-).*	2.00	6.00	15.00

1923 COPPER COIN ISSUE

		GOOD	FINE	XF
S1371	**5 COPPERS** 1923. *(S/M #F12-20).*	5.00	15.00	—
S1372	**10 COPPERS** 1923. *(S/M #F12-21).*	6.00	18.00	—
S1373	**20 COPPERS** 1923. *(S/M #F12-22).*	7.50	22.50	—
S1374	**50 COPPERS** 1923. *(S/M #F12-23).*	7.50	22.50	—
S1375	**100 COPPERS** 1923. *(S/M #F12-24).*	7.50	22.50	—

1924 COPPER COIN ISSUE

		GOOD	FINE	XF
S1376	**5 COPPERS** 1924. *(S/M #F12-30).*	6.00	18.00	—

		GOOD	FINE	XF
S1377	**10 COPPERS** 1924. Brown-violet. Back blue. *(S/M #F12-31).*	3.00	10.00	30.00

		GOOD	FINE	XF
S1378	**20 COPPERS** 1924. *(S/M #F12-32).*	7.50	22.50	—
S1379	**50 COPPERS** 1924. *(S/M #F12-33).*	7.50	22.50	—
S1380	**100 COPPERS** 1924. *(S/M #F12-34).*	7.50	22.50	—

FENGTIEN AGRICULTURAL AND INDUSTRIAL BANK

行銀總業農天奉

Feng T'ien Nung Yeh Tsung Yin Hang

1911 ISSUE

		GOOD	FINE	XF
S1383	**50 CENTS** 1911. Printer: PYOG. *(S/M #F15-1).*	30.00	90.00	—

1912 ISSUE

#S1388-S1390 printer: PYOG.

		GOOD	FINE	XF
S1388	**1 DOLLAR** 1912. Red and green. *(S/M #F15-10).*	30.00	90.00	—
S1389	**5 DOLLARS** 1912. *(S/M #F15-11).*	40.00	120.00	—
S1390	**10 DOLLARS** 1912. *(S/M #F15-12).*	50.00	150.00	—
S1391	**1 DOLLAR** ND. *(S/M #F15-20).*	Reported Not Confirmed		
S1392	**5 DOLLARS** ND. *(S/M #F15-21).*	Reported Not Confirmed		
S1393	**10 DOLLARS** ND. *(S/M #F15-22).*	Reported Not Confirmed		

FUKIEN PROVINCIAL BANK

行銀省建福

Fu Chien Sheng Yin Hang

1925 ISSUE

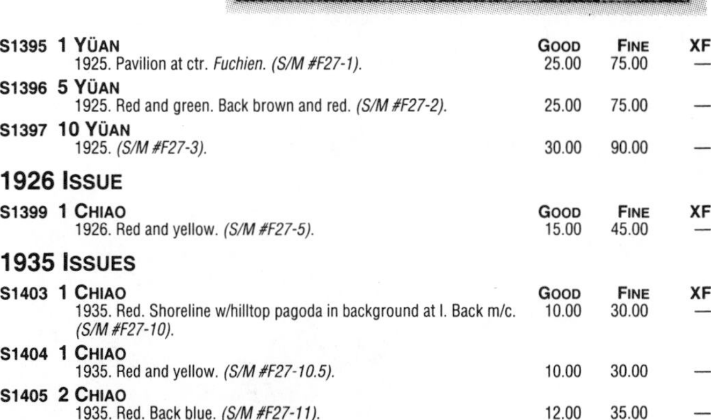

		GOOD	FINE	XF
S1395	**1 YÜAN** 1925. Pavilion at ctr. *Fuchien.* *(S/M #F27-1).*	25.00	75.00	—
S1396	**5 YÜAN** 1925. Red and green. Back brown and red. *(S/M #F27-2).*	25.00	75.00	—
S1397	**10 YÜAN** 1925. *(S/M #F27-3).*	30.00	90.00	—

1926 ISSUE

		GOOD	FINE	XF
S1399	**1 CHIAO** 1926. Red and yellow. *(S/M #F27-5).*	15.00	45.00	—

1935 ISSUES

		GOOD	FINE	XF
S1403	**1 CHIAO** 1935. Red. Shoreline w/hilltop pagoda in background at l. Back m/c. *(S/M #F27-10).*	10.00	30.00	—
S1404	**1 CHIAO** 1935. Red and yellow. *(S/M #F27-10.5).*	10.00	30.00	—
S1405	**2 CHIAO** 1935. Red. Back blue. *(S/M #F27-11).*	12.00	35.00	—

		GOOD	FINE	XF
S1406	2 CHIAO 1935. Blue and green. Village w/hilltop pagoda in background at r. *(S/M #F27-11.5).*	8.00	25.00	—
S1407	5 CHIAO 1935. Violet. Houses at l. Back blue and m/c. *(S/M #F27-12).*	7.50	22.50	—

		GOOD	FINE	XF
S1407A	5 CHIAO 1935. Green. Shoreline village w/hilltop pagoda in background, rural bldg. at r. Lg. *50* at upper l. and r. on back. *(S/M #F27-13).*	12.00	35.00	—
S1408	5 CHIAO 1935. Blue. Village at l. w/pagoda in background, pavilion at r. Back blue. *(S/M #F27-14).*	10.00	30.00	—

1936 ISSUE

		GOOD	FINE	XF
S1409	2 CHIAO 1936. Green. Back red. *(S/M #F27-20).*	8.00	25.00	—
S1410	5 CHIAO 1936. Orange. Back m/c. *(S/M #F27-21).*	12.00	35.00	—

1937 ISSUE

		GOOD	FINE	XF
S1412	1 CHIAO 1937. Red. Boat near island w/house and tower at l. ctr. Back orange and red. *(S/M #F27-30).*	3.00	10.00	27.00

1938-39 ISSUE

#S1415 and S1416 boat near island w/house and tower at l. ctr.

		GOOD	FINE	XF
S1415	1 FEN 1938. Red and blue. Like #S1412. Back red. *(S/M #F27-40).*	1.00	3.00	9.00
S1416	5 FEN 1938. Green. Back purple. *(S/M #F27-41).*	2.50	7.50	22.50

		GOOD	FINE	XF
S1420	1 YÜAN 1939. Red. Bridge at r. Back brown. *(S/M #F27-50).*	3.00	10.00	27.00

1940-41 ISSUE

		GOOD	FINE	XF
S1423	1 FEN 1940. Like #S1415. *(S/M #F27-60).*	1.50	5.00	15.00

		GOOD	FINE	XF
S1424	5 FEN 1940. Green. Like #S1416. Back purple. *(S/M #F27-61).*	1.25	4.00	12.00

		GOOD	FINE	XF
S1427	2 CHIAO 1941. Brown. Bridge at r. Back brown. *(S/M #F27-70).*	3.00	10.00	27.00

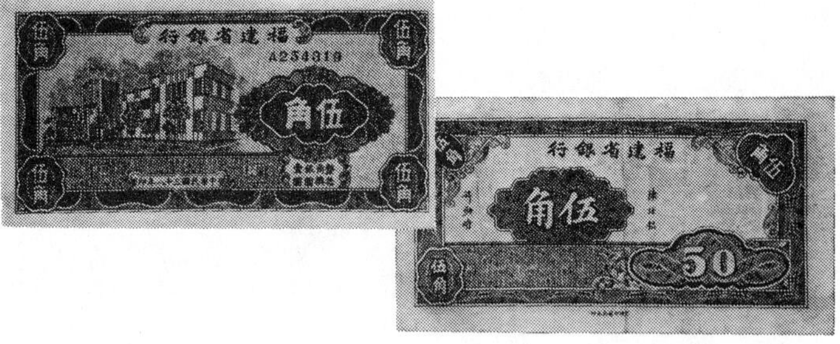

		GOOD	FINE	XF
S1428	5 CHIAO 1941. Red. Like #S1427. *(S/M #F27-71).*	3.00	10.00	27.00

1949 ISSUE

		GOOD	FINE	XF
S1430	5 FEN 1949. *(S/M #F27-79).*	3.00	10.00	30.00
S1431	1 CHIAO 1949. *(S/M #F27-80).*	2.50	7.50	22.50

		GOOD	FINE	XF
S1433	5 CHIAO 1949. Red on lt. orange unpt. Modern bldg. at l. Back green. *(S/M #F27-85).*	6.00	18.00	55.00

FUKIEN BANK

行銀建福

Fu Chien Yin Hang

ND FIRST DOLLAR ISSUE

#S1435-S1437 SYS memorial on back. Printer: ABNC.

		GOOD	FINE	XF
S1435	**1 DOLLAR** ND. Blue and m/c. Village w/mountains in background at ctr. Back blue. *AMOY. (S/M #F31-1).*	37.50	110.00	—
S1436	**5 DOLLARS** ND. Green and m/c. Back green. *AMOY. (S/M #F31-2).*	45.00	135.00	—
S1437	**10 DOLLARS** ND. *AMOY. (S/M #F31-3).*	60.00	180.00	—

ND SECOND DOLLAR ISSUE

		GOOD	FINE	XF
S1439	**5 DOLLARS** ND. Gateways, lg. tree at lower ctr.			
	a. *AMOY. (S/M #F31-12a).*	37.50	110.00	—
	b. *PAILOU. (S/M #F31-12b).*	45.00	135.00	—

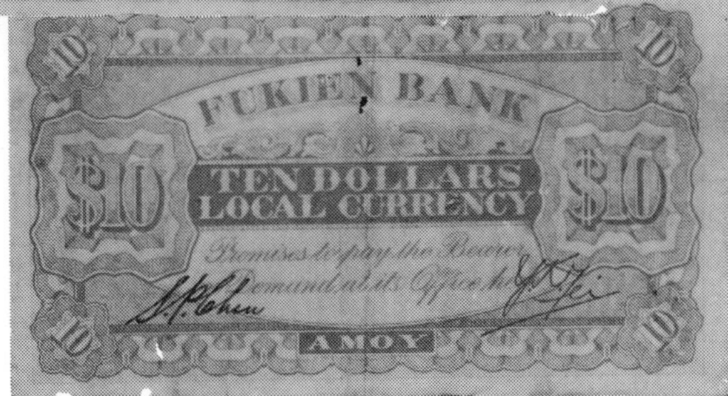

		GOOD	FINE	XF
S1440	**10 DOLLARS** ND. Gateway at ctr.			
	a. *AMOY. (S/M #F31-13a).*	50.00	150.00	—
	b. *PAILOU. (S/M #F31-13b).*	60.00	180.00	—

FU LUNG BANK

行銀隴富
Fu Lung Yin Hang

ND PROVISIONAL ISSUE

#S1443-S1447 ovpt. new bank name on Bank of the Northwest (Military issue).

		GOOD	FINE	XF
S1443	**10 CENTS** ND (- old date 1928). Blue on m/c unpt. Ovpt. on #S3885b. *(Kansu). (S/M #F441).*	17.50	55.00	—
S1444	**20 CENTS** ND (- old date 1928). Red on m/c unpt. Ovpt. on #S3886e. *(Kansu). (S/M #F442).*	17.50	55.00	—
S1445	**1 DOLLAR** ND (- old date 1928). Brown. Ovpt. on #S3887c. *(Kansu). (S/M #F4410).*	25.00	75.00	—
S1446	**5 DOLLARS** ND (- old date 1928). Deep green. Ovpt. on #S3888. *(S/M #F44-11).*	25.00	75.00	—
S1447	**10 DOLLARS** ND (- old date 1928). Red-brown. Ovpt. on #S3889. *(S/M #F44-12).*	37.50	110.00	—

HAINAN BANK

行 銀 南 海
Hai Nan Yin Hang

This was the last outpost and banking facility of retreating nationalist forces led by CKS.

1949 ISSUE

#S1451-S1459 SYS. Printer: HKPA.

		GOOD	FINE	XF
S1451	**1 CENT** 1949. Uniface. *(S/M #H3-1).*	Reported Not Confirmed		

		VG	VF	UNC
S1452	**2 CENTS** 1949. Brown. Uniface. *(S/M #H3-2).*	.05	.15	.50

		VG	VF	UNC
S1453	**5 CENTS** 1949. Red on tan unpt. Uniface. *(S/M #H3-3).*	.05	.15	.50
S1454	**10 CENTS** 1949. *(S/M #H3-4).*	Reported Not Confirmed		

		VG	VF	UNC
S1455	**20 CENTS** 1949. Green. Palm trees, islands at ctr. on back. *(S/M #H3-5).*	.05	.25	.75

		VG	VF	UNC
S1456	**50 CENTS** 1949. Maroon on lt. blue unpt. Back dk. blue; junk at ctr. *(S/M #H3-6).*	.10	.25	1.00

		VG	VF	UNC
S1457	**1 YÜAN** 1949. Brown-violet on lt. green unpt. Back brown-violet; palm trees, junks and islands at l. and r. *(S/M #H3-10).*	7.50	20.00	60.00
S1458	**5 YÜAN** 1949. Green on orange unpt. *(S/M #H3-11).*	Reported Not Confirmed		

		VG	VF	UNC
S1459	**10 YÜAN** 1949. Black on lilac unpt. Back red-violet; junk at ctr. *(S/M #H3-12).*	25.00	75.00	225.00

HIO LUNG KIANG GOVERNMENT BANK

黑龍江官銀號

Hei Lung Chiang Kuan Yin Hao

1909 "SMALL MONEY" ISSUE

#S1461-S1465 issued in the first year of the Emperor Hsuan T'ung w/western date 1909 on backs. Printer: PYOG.

No.	Description	VG	VF	UNC
S1461	**10 CENTS** 1909. *(S/M #H6-1).*	45.00	135.00	—
S1462	**20 CENTS** 1909. *(S/M #H6-2).*	45.00	135.00	—
S1463	**50 CENTS** 1909. *(S/M #H6-3).*	60.00	180.00	—

No.	Description	VG	VF	UNC
S1464	**100 CENTS** 1909. *(S/M #H6-4).*	75.00	225.00	—

1908 COPPER COIN ISSUE

No.	Description	VG	VF	UNC
S1465	**5 COPPERS** 1908. *(S/M #H6-10).*	—	—	—
S1466	**10 COPPERS** 1908. *(S/M #H6-11).*	—	—	—
S1467	**20 COPPERS** 1908. *(S/M #H6-12).*	—	—	—
S1468	**30 COPPERS** 1908. *(S/M #H6-13).*	—	—	—
S1469	**50 COPPERS** 1908. *(S/M #H6-14).*	—	—	—
S1470	**100 COPPERS** 1908. *(S/M #H6-15).*	—	—	—
S1471	**200 COPPERS** 1908. *(S/M #H6-16).*	—	—	—
S1472	**500 COPPERS** 1908. *(S/M #H6-17).*	—	—	—
S1473	**1000 COPPERS** 1908. *(S/M #H6-18).*	—	—	—

1913 COPPER COIN ISSUE

No.	Description	VG	VF	UNC
S1474	**5 COPPERS** Jan. 1913. Black. Back red. *(S/M #H6-20).*	25.00	75.00	—

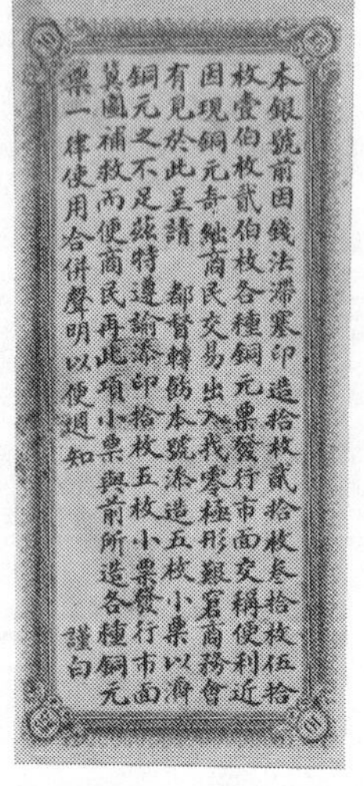

No.	Description	VG	VF	UNC
S1475	**10 COPPERS** Jan. 1913. Orange. Back olive-green. Vertical format. *(S/M #H6-21).*	17.50	50.00	—
S1476	**20 COPPERS** 1913. *(S/M #H6-22).*	—	—	—
S1477	**30 COPPERS** 1913. *(S/M #H6-23).*	—	—	—
S1478	**50 COPPERS** 1913. *(S/M #H6-24).*	—	—	—
S1479	**100 COPPERS** 1913. *(S/M #H6-25).*	—	—	—
S1480	**200 COPPERS** 1913. *(S/M #H6-26).*	—	—	—
S1481	**500 COPPERS** 1913. Violet and green. *(S/M #H6-27).*	—	—	—
S1482	**1000 COPPERS** 1913. *(S/M #H6-28).*	—	—	—

S1483-S1488 *Deleted*. See #S1629-S1634.

1914 "SMALL MONEY" ISSUE

No.	Description	VG	VF	UNC
S1489	**10 CENTS** 1914. *(S/M #H6-40).*	—	—	—
S1490	**20 CENTS** 1914. *(S/M #H6-41).*	—	—	—
S1491	**50 CENTS** 1914. *(S/M #H6-42).*	—	—	—
S1492	**100 CENTS** 1914. *(S/M #H6-43).*	—	—	—

NOTE: #S1489-S1492 probably another Amoor Government issue.

#S1495-S1500 *Deleted*. See #S1636-S1639B.

#S1501-S1503 *Deleted*. See #S1639C-S1639E.

#S1505-S1508 *Deleted*. See #S1641-S1645.

1918 TIAO ISSUE

No.	Description	VG	VF	UNC
S1511	**15 TIAO** 1918. *(S/M #H6-).*	—	—	—

No.	Description	VG	VF	UNC
S1512	**16 TIAO = 500 COPPERS** 1918. Black text on purple and green unpt. People around border. Back red-orange; fortress gateway at ctr. Vertical format. *(S/M #H6-80).*	—	—	—
S1513	**32 TIAO = 1000 COPPERS** July 1918. Black text. Dk. blue-green on yellow-orange unpt. Back green. *(S/M #H6-80.5).*	—	—	—
S1515	**50 TIAO** 1918. *(S/M #H6-81).*	Reported Not Confirmed		

KWANG SING COMPANY/HEILUNGCHIANG KUANG HSIN SYNDICATE OF HEILUNGKIANG

廣信公司

Kuang Hsin Kung Szu

黑龍江廣信公司

Hei Lung Chiang Kuang Hsin Kung Szu

1904 TIAO ISSUE

No.	Description	VG	VF	UNC
S1521	**1 TIAO** Yr. 30 (1904). *(S/M #H7-1).*	80.00	240.00	—
S1522	**2 TIAO** Yr. 30 (1904). *(S/M #H7-2).*	90.00	270.00	—
S1523	**3 TIAO** Yr. 30 (1904). *(S/M #H7-3).*	100.00	300.00	—
S1524	**5 TIAO** Yr. 30 (1904). *(S/M #H7-4).*	110.00	330.00	—
S1525	**10 TIAO** Yr. 30 (1904). *(S/M #H7-5).*	120.00	360.00	—
S1527	**100 TIAO** Yr. 30 (1904). *(S/M #H7-6).*	130.00	390.00	—

1904 TAEL ISSUE

No.	Description	VG	VF	UNC
S1529	**1 TAEL** Yr. 30 (1904). *(S/M #H7-10).*	150.00	450.00	—
S1530	**2 TAELS** Yr. 30 (1904). *(S/M #H7-11).*	180.00	540.00	—
S1531	**3 TAELS** Yr. 30 (1904). *(S/M #H7-12).*	200.00	600.00	—

		VG	VF	UNC
S1532	**5 TAELS** Yr. 30 (1904). *(S/M #H7-13).*	300.00	—	—
S1533	**10 TAELS** Yr. 30 (1904). *(S/M #H7-14).*	—	—	—
S1534	**30 TAELS** Yr. 30 (1904). *(S/M #H7-15).*	—	—	—
S1536	**50 TAELS** Yr. 30 (1904). *(S/M #H7-16).*	—	—	—

1906 TIAO ISSUE

		VG	VF	UNC
S1536F	**10 TIAO** Yr. 32 (1906). Orange and black. *(S/M #H7-16.9).*	—	—	—

1907 TIAO ISSUE

		VG	VF	UNC
S1537	**1 TIAO** Yr. 33 (1907). Red and green. Trees and people in frame border. Back red. *(S/M #H7-17).*	125.00	500.00	—
S1538	**5 TIAO** Yr. 33 (1907). Purple and black. 2 dragons. *(S/M #H7-17.1).*	—	—	—
S1539	**10 TIAO** Yr. 33 (1907). Red and black. 2 dragons. *(S/M #H7-17.2).*	—	—	—
S1539A	**50 TIAO** Yr. 33 (1907). Green and orange. *(S/M #H7-17.3).*	—	—	—

1908 TIAO ISSUE

		VG	VF	UNC
S1540	**1 TIAO** Yr. 34 (1908). Green and red. *(S/M #H7-17.6).*	—	—	—

1909 TIAO ISSUE

		VG	VF	UNC
S1540F	**5 TIAO** Yr. 35 (1909). Purple and black. 2 dragons. *(S/M #H7-17.8).*	—	—	—

1915 TIAO ISSUE

		VG	VF	UNC
S1541	**5 TIAO** 1915. Violet and black. *(S/M #H7-18).*	60.00	250.00	—

1916 TIAO ISSUE

		VG	VF	UNC
S1544	**1 TIAO** 1916. Red and green. *(S/M #H7-19).*	30.00	90.00	—
S1545	**2 TIAO** 1916. Red and blue. *(S/M #H7-19.5).*	—	—	—

1918 TIAO ISSUE

		VG	VF	UNC
S1550	**1 TIAO** 1918. *(S/M #H7-).*	45.00	135.00	—

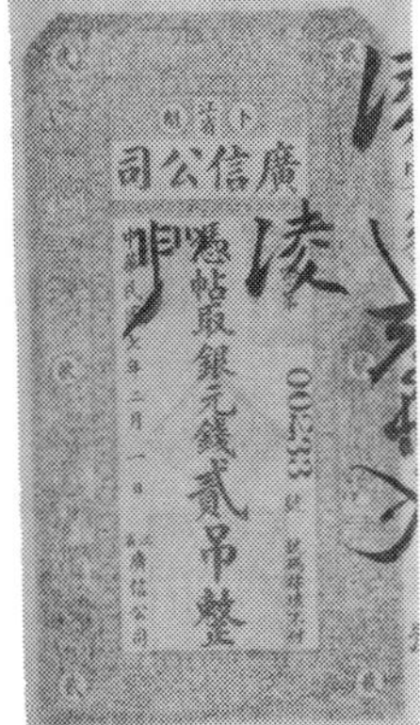

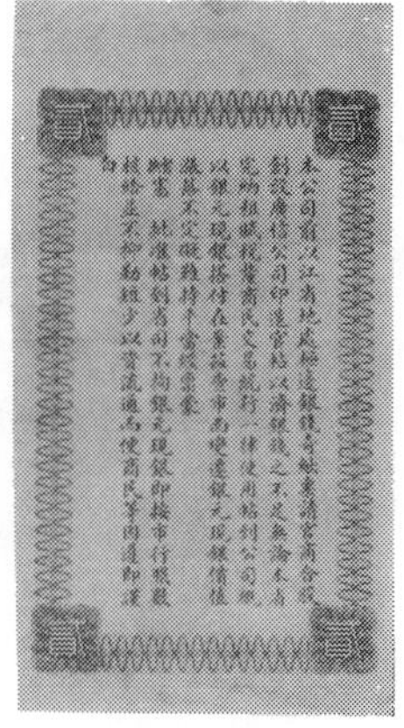

		VG	VF	UNC
S1551	**2 TIAO** 1.2.1918. Red. Back blue. Vertical format. *(S/M #H7-20).*	37.50	110.00	—
S1552	**3 TIAO** 1918. Blue. *(S/M #H7-22).*	45.00	135.00	—
S1553	**5 TIAO** 1918. *(S/M #H7-23).*	45.00	135.00	—
S1554	**10 TIAO** 1918. Red. *(S/M #H7-24).*	45.00	135.00	—
S1555	**100 TIAO** 1918. Red, blue and black. Back red. *(S/M #H7-28).*	60.00	180.00	—

1919 TIAO ISSUE

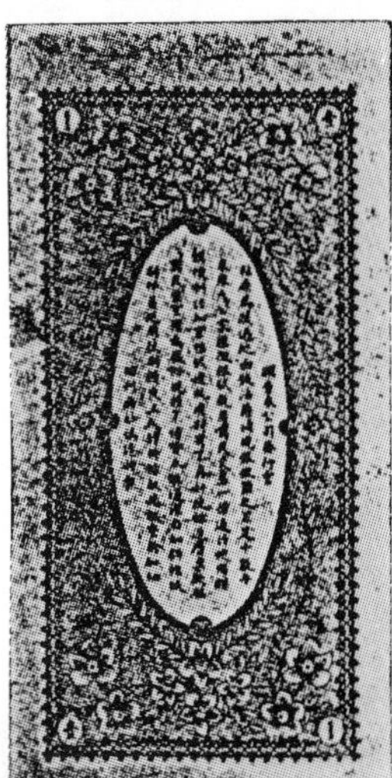

		VG	VF	UNC
S1559	**1 TIAO** 1.3.1919. Green. Back red. Vertical format. *(S/M #H7-30).*	25.00	75.00	—
S1560	**2 TIAO** 1919. Red. Back blue. *(S/M #H7-31).*	25.00	75.00	—
S1561	**3 TIAO** 1919. Blue. Back green. *(S/M #H7-32).*	25.00	75.00	—

		VG	VF	UNC
S1562	**5 TIAO** 1919. Violet. Man at l., woman at r. Back green. Vertical format. *(S/M #H7-33).*	25.00	75.00	—
S1563	**10 TIAO** 1919. Orange. Back violet. *(S/M #H7-34).*	25.00	75.00	—

1919 ND "SMALL MONEY" ISSUE

		VG	VF	UNC
S1565	**10 CENTS** ND (1919). Violet and blue. *(S/M #H7-35).*	17.50	55.00	—
S1566	**20 CENTS** ND (1919). Green and violet. *(S/M #H7-36).*	17.50	55.00	—

1919 "BIG MONEY" ISSUE

#S1568-S1570 printer: BEPP.

		VG	VF	UNC
S1568	**1 DOLLAR** 1919. Blue and violet. *(S/M #H7-37).*	30.00	90.00	—
S1569	**5 DOLLARS** 1919. Green. *37.5).*	45.00	135.00	—
S1570	**10 DOLLARS** 1919. Brown. *(S/M #H7-38).*	37.50	110.00	—
S1570A	**10 DOLLARS** 1919. Green. *(S/M #H7-).*	40.00	80.00	—

1919 HARBIN BRANCH ISSUE

		VG	VF	UNC
S1571	**1 DOLLAR** 1919. Brown. *(S/M #H7-).* Specimen.	—	—	200.00
S1571A	**5 DOLLARS** 1919. Orange. *(S/M #H7-).* Specimen.	—	—	200.00
S1571B	**10 DOLLARS** 1919. Brown. *(S/M #H7-).* Specimen.	—	—	200.00

1920 "SMALL MONEY" ISSUES

		VG	VF	UNC
S1572	**10 CENTS**			
	1920. Violet and blue. *(S/M #H7-39).*	12.00	35.00	—

#S1575-S1577 printer: BEPP.

		VG	VF	UNC
S1575	**10 CENTS**			
	1920. Green. Back orange and green.			
	a. *Heiho. (S/M #H7-40a).*	20.00	60.00	—
	b. *Hulun. (S/M #H7-40b).*	25.00	75.00	—
S1576	**20 CENTS**			
	1920. Green. Village at ctr. Back orange and green.			
	a. *Heiho. (S/M #H7-41a).*	30.00	90.00	—
	b. *Hulun. (S/M #H7-41b).*	30.00	90.00	—

		VG	VF	UNC
S1577	**50 CENTS**			
	1920. Green. Fortress towers at ctr. Back dk. brown on yellow-green and orange unpt.			
	a. *Heiho. (S/M #H7-42a).*	30.00	90.00	—
	b. *Hulun. (S/M #H7-42b).*	30.00	90.00	—

1920 TIAO ISSUE

		VG	VF	UNC
S1579	**1 TIAO**			
	1920. Red and green. *(S/M #H7-43).*	32.50	100.00	—

1921 TIAO ISSUE

		VG	VF	UNC
S1582	**50 TIAO**			
	1921. Green and red. *(S/M #H7-44).*	30.00	90.00	—
S1583	**100 TIAO**			
	1921. Blue and violet. *(S/M #H7-46).*	32.50	100.00	—
S1584	**100 TIAO**			
	1921. Red and black. *(S/M #H7-47).*	32.50	100.00	—

		VG	VF	UNC
S1585	**100 TIAO**			
	1921. Blue and red. Vertical format. *(S/M #H7-48).*	32.50	100.00	—

1922 TIAO ISSUE

		VG	VF	UNC
S1590	**50 TIAO**			
	1.1.1922. Green and red. Uniface. Vertical format. *(S/M #H7-50).*			
	a. Issued note.	30.00	90.00	—
	b. Cancelled.	7.50	25.00	75.00

1924 TIAO ISSUE

		VG	VF	UNC
S1596	**100 TIAO**			
	1922. Maroon, red, blue, and black. Like #S1555. Back red. *(S/M #H7-60).*	20.00	60.00	—

1924 "BIG MONEY" ISSUE

#S1601-S1603 statues of lions w/city tower gate in background at ctr. Printer: ABNC.

		VG	VF	UNC
S1601	**1 DOLLAR**			
	1.11.1924. Black and m/c. Back orange. *(S/M #H7-71a).*			
	a. *Harbin. (S/M #H7-71b).*	22.50	67.50	—
	b. *Harbin* w/official Chinese 4 character ovpt. *(S/M #H7-71c).*	22.50	67.50	—
S1602	**5 DOLLARS**			
	1.11.1924. Brown and m/c. Back green. *(S/M #H7-73a).*			
	a. *Harbin. (S/M #H7-73b).*	22.50	67.50	—
	b. *Harbin* w/official Chinese 4 character ovpt. *(S/M #H7-73c).*	22.50	67.50	—

		VG	VF	UNC
S1603	**10 DOLLARS**			
	1.11.1924. Red and m/c. Back blue. *(S/M #H7-75a).*			
	a. *Harbin. (S/M #H7-75b).*	30.00	90.00	—
	b. *Harbin* w/official Chinese 4 character ovpt. *(S/M #H7-75c).*	30.00	90.00	—
	c. W/o place name. *(S/M #H7-75-75d).*	25.00	75.00	—

1924 DOLLAR BOND ISSUE

#S1604-S1606 hillside shrine at ctr. Printer: ABNC.

	VG	VF	UNC
S1604 1 DOLLAR 1.12.1924. Green and m/c. Back green. *(S/M #H7-70).*	17.50	55.00	—
S1605 5 DOLLARS 1.12.1924. Black and m/c. Back orange. *(S/M #H7-72).*	25.00	75.00	—

	VG	VF	UNC
S1606 10 DOLLARS 1.12.1924. Olive-green and m/c. Back olive. *(S/M #H7-74).*	25.00	75.00	—

1925 TIAO ISSUE

	VG	VF	UNC
S1610 20 TIAO 1925. Brown. Back green. *(S/M #H7-80).*	22.50	67.50	—

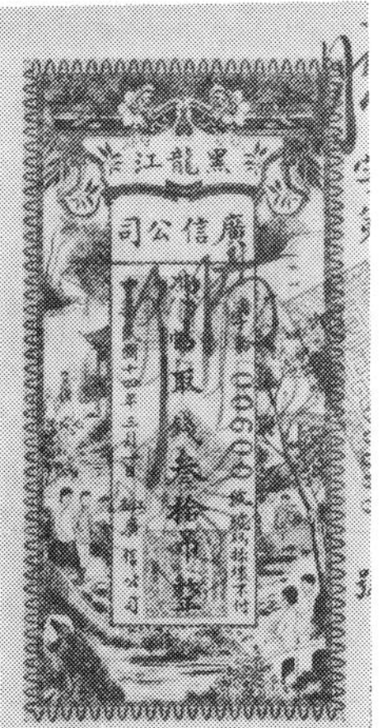

	VG	VF	UNC
S1611 30 TIAO 1.3.1925. Black. Back violet. Vertical format. *(S/M #H7-81).*	22.50	67.50	—

#S1613 Deleted. See #S1619G.

1925 DOLLAR ISSUE

#S1614 and S1614B w/10 Chinese characters "1 Yüan equals 12 Chiao" blackened. Printer: ABNC.

	VG	VF	UNC
S1614 1 DOLLAR 1925. Brown on m/c unpt. *(S/M #H7-93).*	—	—	—
S1614B 10 DOLLARS 1925. Green on m/c unpt. *(S/M #H7-95).*	—	—	—

1926 "BIG MONEY" ISSUE

	VG	VF	UNC
S1615 10 DOLLARS 1926. Dk. brown on m/c unpt. Hillside shrine at ctr. Specimen. *(S/M #H7-96).*	—	—	—

1929 "SMALL MONEY" ISSUE

	VG	VF	UNC
S1616 10 CENTS 1929. Orange. Bldgs. at l. Back blue. (S/M #H7-100).			
a. *Harbin.*	17.50	55.00	—
b. As a. W/official Chinese 4 character ovpt.	17.50	55.00	—
s. Specimen.	—	—	60.00

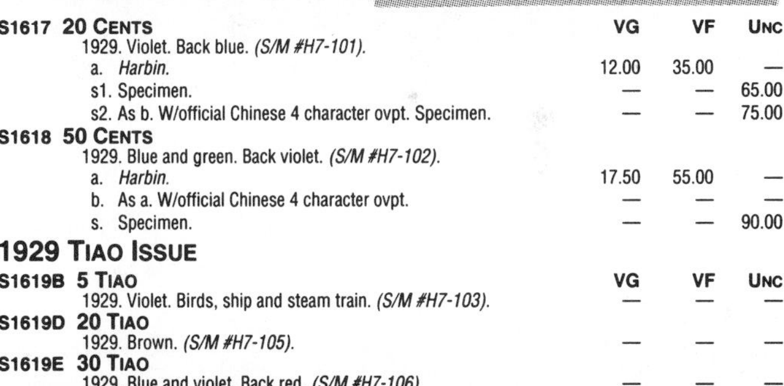

	VG	VF	UNC
S1617 20 CENTS 1929. Violet. Back blue. *(S/M #H7-101).*			
a. *Harbin.*	12.00	35.00	—
s1. Specimen.	—	—	65.00
s2. As b. W/official Chinese 4 character ovpt. Specimen.	—	—	75.00
S1618 50 CENTS 1929. Blue and green. Back violet. *(S/M #H7-102).*			
a. *Harbin.*	17.50	55.00	—
b. As a. W/official Chinese 4 character ovpt.	—	—	—
s. Specimen.	—	—	90.00

1929 TIAO ISSUE

	VG	VF	UNC
S1619B 5 TIAO 1929. Violet. Birds, ship and steam train. *(S/M #H7-103).*	—	—	—
S1619D 20 TIAO 1929. Brown. *(S/M #H7-105).*	—	—	—
S1619E 30 TIAO 1929. Blue and violet. Back red. *(S/M #H7-106).*	—	—	—

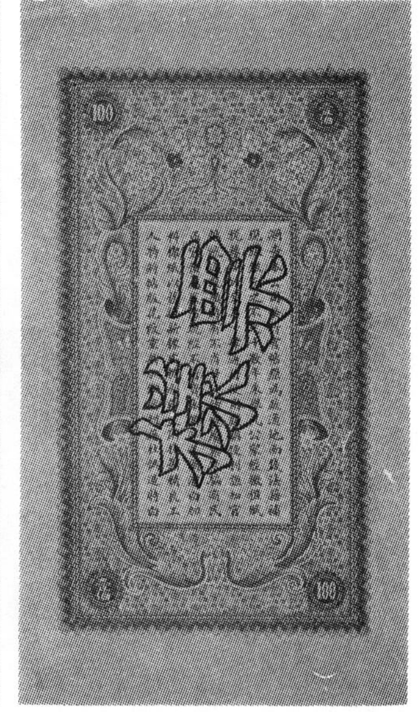

		VG	VF	UNC
S1619G	**100 TIAO** 1.1.1929. Blue and violet. Bird, rural view in left frame panels and deer, rural view in right frame panels. Back red. Vertical format. *(S/M #H7-90).*			
	a. Issued note.	35.00	65.00	110.00
	s. Specimen.	—	—	85.00

PROVINCIAL BANK OF HEILUNGKIANG

黑龍江省官銀號

Hei Lung Chiang Sheng Kuan Yin Hao

1929 ISSUE

#S1621-S1623 printer: TWCC.

		VG	VF	UNC
S1621	**10 CENTS** 1929. *(S/M #H11-1).*	Reported Not Confirmed		
S1622	**20 CENTS** 1929. *(S/M #H11-2).*	Reported Not Confirmed		
S1623	**50 CENTS** 1929. *(S/M #H11-3).*	Reported Not Confirmed		

1931 ISSUE

#S1624-S1628 forest at l., steam train at r. Printer: BEPP.

		VG	VF	UNC
S1624	**1 YÜAN** 1.6.1931. Brown. Specimen. *(S/M #H11-10).*	—	—	120.00
S1625	**5 YÜAN** 1.6.1931. Specimen. *(S/M #H11-11).*	—	—	150.00
S1626	**10 YÜAN** 1.6.1931. Specimen. *(S/M #H11-12).*	—	—	185.00

		VG	VF	UNC
S1627	**100 YÜAN** 1.6.1931. Specimen. *(S/M #H11-14).*	—	—	165.00

AMOOR GOVERNMENT BANK

黑龍江官銀號 小銀元券

Hei Lung Chiang Kuan Yin Hao Hsiao Yin Yüan Ch'üan

1913 ISSUE

		VG	VF	UNC
S1629	**1 CHIAO = 10 CENTS** 1913. *(S/M #H6-30).*	—	—	—
S1630	**2 CHIAO = 20 CENTS** 1913. *(S/M #H6-31).*	—	—	—

#S1631 *Deleted*. See #S1633.

		VG	VF	UNC
S1632	**10 CHIAO = 100 CENTS** 1913. *(S/M #H6-33).*	—	—	—

		VG	VF	UNC
S1633	**50 CHIAO = 500 CENTS** 1913. Lions facing globe at upper ctr. on face and back. *(S/M #H6-34).*	75.00	—	—
S1634	**100 CHIAO = 1000 CENTS** 1913. *(S/M #H6-35).*	—	—	—

NOTE: #S1629-S1634 were listed in *Chinese Banknotes* under Hio Lung Kiang Government Bank. Printer: FRBC.

1915 MANCHURIAN ISSUE

		VG	VF	UNC
S1636	**10 CENTS** 1.12.1915. Black and green on lt. orange unpt. Bldg. at ctr. Back blue. *(S/M #H6-50).*	50.00	150.00	—
S1637	**20 CENTS** 1.12.1915. Blue and m/c. *(S/M #H6-51).*	—	—	—
S1638	**50 CENTS** 1.12.1915. Green, yellow, and blue. Park scene at ctr. Back purple; w/text: *USABLE IN MANCHURIA* at bottom ctr. *(S/M #H6-52).*	37.50	110.00	—
S1639	**100 CENTS** 1.12.1915. *(S/M #H6-53 and H12-1).*	50.00	150.00	—
S1639A	**500 CENTS** 1.12.1915. *(S/M #H6-54).*	—	—	—
S1639B	**1000 CENTS** 1.12.1915. *(S/M #H6-55).*	—	—	—
S1639C	**1 DOLLAR** 1915. *(S/M #H6-60).*	Reported Not Confirmed		
S1639D	**5 DOLLARS** 1915. *(S/M #H6-61).*	Reported Not Confirmed		
S1639E	**10 DOLLARS** 1915. *(S/M #H6-62).*	Reported Not Confirmed		

NOTE: #S1636-S1639E were listed in *Chinese Banknotes* under Hio Lung Kiang Government Bank.

1916 ISSUE

#S1641 and S1642 flowers on back.

		VG	VF	UNC
S1641	**10 CENTS** 1916. Green and yellow. Back violet. *(S/M #H6-70 and H12-10).*	30.00	90.00	—
S1642	**20 CENTS** 1916. *(S/M #H6-71 and H12-11).*	37.50	110.00	—
S1643	**50 CENTS** 1916. Violet and green. *(S/M #H6-72).*	—	—	—

		VG	VF	UNC
S1645	**1 DOLLAR** 1916. Blue on yellow unpt. Lions supporting globe at upper ctr. Back black on tan unpt. Tower gate at ctr. on back. *(S/M #H6-73).*	40.00	120.00	—

	VG	VF	UNC
S1646 5 DOLLARS 1916. Blue on yellow unpt. Lions supporting globe at upper ctr. Back black on tan unpt.; tower gate at ctr. *(S/M #H6-74).*	—	—	—

#S1641-S1645 were listed in *Chinese Banknotes* under Hio Lung Kiang Government Bank.

1917 ISSUE

	VG	VF	UNC
S1648 1 DOLLAR 1917. *(S/M #H12-20).*	40.00	120.00	—
S1649 5 DOLLARS 1917. *(S/M #H12-21).*	50.00	150.00	—

1918 ISSUE

	VG	VF	UNC
S1649A 60 COPPERS 1918. Blue-gray.	50.00	150.00	
S1650 1000 COPPERS 1918. *(S/M #H12-30).*	100.00	300.00	—
S1651 50 CHIAO = 500 CENTS 1918. *(S/M #H12-35).*	Reported Not Confirmed		

1919 ISSUE

	VG	VF	UNC
S1653 50 CHIAO = 500 CENTS 1919. Lions facing globe at upper ctr. face and back. *(S/M #H12-42).*	90.00	270.00	—

AMOY INDUSTRIAL BANK

1940S ISSUE

	VG	VF	UNC
S1655 1 CENT ca.1940. Green. Pagoda at l.	—	—	35.00
S1656 5 CENTS ca.1940. Red. Pagoda at l.	—	—	35.00
S1657 10 CENTS ca.1940. Green. Pagoda at l.	—	—	75.00
S1658 50 CENTS ca.1940. Blue. Pagoda at r.	—	—	75.00

PROVINCIAL BANK OF HONAN

行銀省南河
Ho Nan Sheng Yin Hang
行銀南河
Ho Nan Yin Hang

1921 ISSUE

	GOOD	FINE	XF
S1661 10 COPPERS 1921. Blue and brown. *(S/M #H62-0.2).*	30.00	90.00	—
S1662 20 COPPERS 1921. *(S/M #H62-0.3).*	30.00	90.00	—
S1665 1 YÜAN 1921. *(S/M #H62-).*	40.00	120.00	—

NOTE: For earlier issues see Provincial Bank of Honan #S2971-S2985 and for similar issues see #S1695, S1700 and S1706.

1922 ISSUE

#S1669-S1671 printer: BEPP.

	GOOD	FINE	XF
S1669 10 COPPERS 1.8.1922. Blue on tan unpt. Back blue and black. *(S/M #H62-0.6).*	30.00	90.00	—
S1670 20 COPPERS 1.8.1922. Green on tan unpt. Back green and black. *(S/M #H62-0.7).*	30.00	90.00	—
S1671 50 COPPERS 1.8.1922. Violet on pink unpt. Back violet and lt. blue. *(S/M #H62-0.8).*	37.50	110.00	—

NOTE: For #S1669-S1671 w/10 Chinese characters ovpt. see #S1704-S1706.

#S1673-S1675 old Chinese man at ctr. Also exists w/additional Chinese character ovpt. Printer: BEPP.

	GOOD	FINE	XF
S1673 1 YÜAN 15.7.1922. Blue. Back blue and m/c. *(S/M #H62-1).*	10.00	30.00	80.00
S1674 5 YÜAN 15.7.1922. Orange. Back dk. red. *(S/M #H62-2).*	20.00	60.00	180.00

	GOOD	FINE	XF
S1675 10 YÜAN 15.7.1922. Green. Back green and m/c. *(S/M #H62-3).*	25.00	80.00	240.00

1923 ISSUES

#S1676-1685 pagoda at l., bldg. at r.

	GOOD	FINE	XF
S1676 10 COPPERS 1923. Blue. Back dk. brown. *(S/M #H62-8).*	10.00	30.00	60.00
S1677 10 COPPERS 1923. Blue. Back orange. *(S/M #H62-9).*	10.00	30.00	60.00
S1679 20 COPPERS 1923. Green. Back olive. *(S/M #H62-10).*			
a. Issued note.	10.00	30.00	60.00
b. Ovpt: *I.*	10.00	30.00	60.00
S1680 20 COPPERS 1923. Gray and blue. *(S/M #H62-10.5).*	10.00	30.00	60.00
S1681 20 COPPERS 1923. Green and gray. *(S/M #H62-10.7).*	10.00	30.00	60.00

	GOOD	FINE	XF
S1682 50 COPPERS 1923. Brown on pink unpt. Back red. *(S/M #H62-11).*			
a. Issued note.	3.00	10.00	30.00
b. Control letters ovpt: *GG; HH; OO; QQ; RR; SS; UU.*	3.00	10.00	30.00
S1683 50 COPPERS 1923. Brown on pink unpt. Back red. *(S/M #H62-15).*	4.50	12.50	40.00

S1685 100 COPPERS

1923. Orange and m/c. Back orange; shrine at ctr.

		GOOD	FINE	XF
a.	Issued note. *(S/M #H62-20c).*	4.00	12.50	40.00
b.	*Honan. (S/M #H62-20a).*	4.00	12.50	40.00
c.	*Tientsin. (S/M #H62-20b).*	4.00	12.50	40.00
r.	Remainder w/o serial #. *(S/M #H62-20-d).*	—	Unc	30.00

#S1688-S1690 printer: BEPP.

S1688 1 DOLLAR

15.7.1923. Red on m/c unpt. Shrine at ctr. Back brown-orange.

		GOOD	FINE	XF
a.	Issued note. *(S/M #H62-20c).*	3.50	10.00	30.00
b.	*HONAN. (S/M #H62-20a).*	4.00	12.50	40.00
c.	*TIENTSIN. (S/M #H62-20b).*	5.00	15.00	45.00
d.	*Hupei. (S/M #H62-20d).*	12.00	35.00	—
e.	*Paotow/HONAN. (S/M #H62-20e).*	12.00	35.00	—
f.	*PEKING. (SM #H62-20f).*	5.00	15.00	45.00
r.	Remainder w/o place name. *(S/M #H62-20g).*	—	Unc	30.00

S1689 5 DOLLARS

15.7.1923. Green on m/c unpt. Shrine at r. Back brown.

		GOOD	FINE	XF
a.	Issued note. *(S/M #H62-21c).*	6.00	17.50	55.00
b.	*HONAN. (S/M #H62-21a).*	6.00	17.50	55.00
c.	*TIENTSIN. (S/M #H62-21b).*	7.50	22.50	67.50
d.	*CHENGCHOW. (S/M #H62-21f).*	12.00	35.00	—
e.	*PEKING. (S/M #H62-21e).*	7.50	22.50	67.50
r.	Remainder w/o place name. *(S/M #H62-21g).*	—	Unc	42.50

S1690 10 DOLLARS

15.7.1923. Violet and m/c. Shrine at l. Back green.

		GOOD	FINE	XF
a.	Issued note. *(S/M #H62-22c).*	7.50	22.50	67.50
b.	*HONAN. (S/M #H62-22a).*	7.50	22.50	67.50
c.	*TIENTSIN. (S/M #H62-22b).*	8.50	25.00	—
d.	*CHENGCHOW. (S/M #H62-22f).*	12.00	35.00	—
e.	*PEKING. (S/M #H62-22e).*	10.00	30.00	—
r.	Remainder w/o place name. *(S/M #H62-22-g).*	—	Unc	60.00

NOTE: For #S1688-S1690 w/lg. red seal ovpt. on back see Military - Honan Province #S3858-S3860.

BANK OF HONAN PROVINCE
YÜ CH'ÜAN BANK OF HONAN

局錢銀官泉豫南河

Ho Nan Yü Ch'üan Kuan Yin Ch'ien Chü

1916 COPPER COIN ISSUE

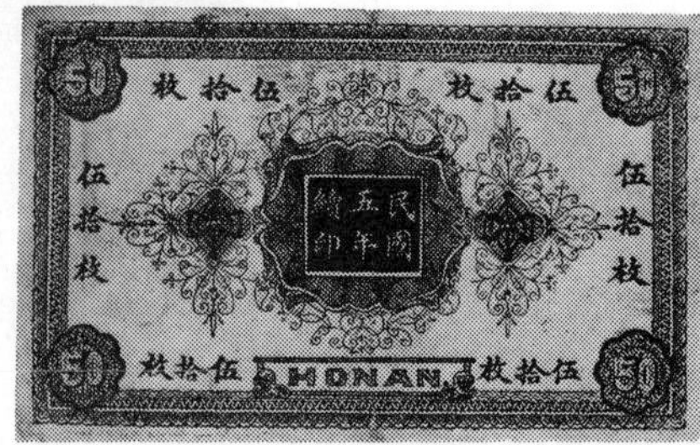

S1691 50 COPPERS

	GOOD	FINE	XF
1916. Brown on yellow unpt. Tower at ctr. Back brown. *HONAN. (SM #H62.5-3).*	90.00	270.00	—

1916 DOLLAR ISSUE

		Good	Fine	XF
S1695	**10 Dollars** 1.6.1916. Green on brown unpt. Tower at l., pagoda at r. Shrine at ctr. on back. *HONAN. (S/M #H62.5-8).*	90.00	270.00	—

NOTE: For earlier listings see Provincial Bank of Honan #S2971-S2985 and #S1661-S1690.

1922 Issues

#S1700 and S1701 old Chinese man at ctr.

		Good	Fine	XF
S1700	**100 Cents** 1.3.1922. Blue on yellow-green unpt. Back red and black. Printer: BEPP. *(S/M #H62.5-15).*	40.00	120.00	—
S1701	**100 Cents** 1.3.1922. Blue on yellow-green. Back orange and black. *(S/M #H62.5-16).*	40.00	120.00	—

ND Provisional Issue

#S1704-S1706 old Chinese man at ctr. w/additional Chinese 10 character bank name ovpt.

		Good	Fine	XF
S1704	**10 Coppers** ND (- old date 1.8.1922). Blue on tan unpt. Ovpt. on #S1669. *(S/M #H62.5-20).*	40.00	120.00	—
S1705	**20 Coppers** ND (- old date 1.8.1922). Green on tan unpt. Ovpt. on #S1670. *(S/M #H62.5-21).*	40.00	120.00	—
S1706	**50 Coppers** ND (- old date 1.8.1922). Violet on pink unpt. Ovpt. on #S1671. *(S/M #62.5-33).*	40.00	120.00	—

Hopei Province

券通流時臨縣冀／省北河

Ho Pei Sheng/Chi Hsien Lin Shih Liu T'ung Chüan

1938 Temporary Circulating Note Issue

		VG	VF	Unc
S1708	**10 Cents** 1938. Green. Mythical animals and gazebo at l. Back red. *(SM #H62.7-11).*	—	—	—
S1708A	**2 Chiao = 20 Cents** 1938.	—	—	—

Ho Pei Metropolitan Bank

局錢銀北河

Ho Pei Yin Ch'ien Chü

1929 Issue

#S1709 and S1709A *Pei P'ing.* Printer: BEPP.

		VG	VF	Unc
S1709	**20 Coppers** 1929. Dk. blue on pink unpt. Back dk. blue. *(S/M #H63-1).*	4.00	12.50	40.00
S1709A	**40 Coppers** 1929. *(S/M #H63-2).*	4.00	12.50	40.00

1931 Issue

		VG	VF	Unc
S1709D	**20 Coppers** 1931. Red-brown on pale blue unpt. Pagoda at ctr. Back red-brown. *(S/M #H63-5).*	4.00	12.00	37.50

1933 Issue

#S1709I-S1709K *Pei P'ing.* Printer: BEPP.

		VG	VF	Unc
S1709I	**20 Coppers** 1933. Black on pink unpt. Tea house behind bridge at ctr. Back black. *(S/M #H63-9).*	7.50	22.50	67.50
S1709J	**40 Coppers** 1933. Purple on green unpt. Back purple. *(S/M #H63-10).*	5.00	12.50	55.00
S1709K	**60 Coppers** 1933. *(S/M #H63-11).*	7.50	22.50	67.50

1934 Issue

		VG	VF	Unc
S1709N	**60 Coppers** 1934. *(S/M #H63-14).*	7.50	22.50	67.50

1935 Issue

		VG	VF	Unc
S1710C	**20 Coppers** 1935. Black on pink unpt. *Pei P'ing.* Printer: BEPP. *(S/M #H63-16).*	4.00	12.00	36.00

1936 Issue

#S1710D-S1710F *Pei P'ing.* Printer: BEPP.

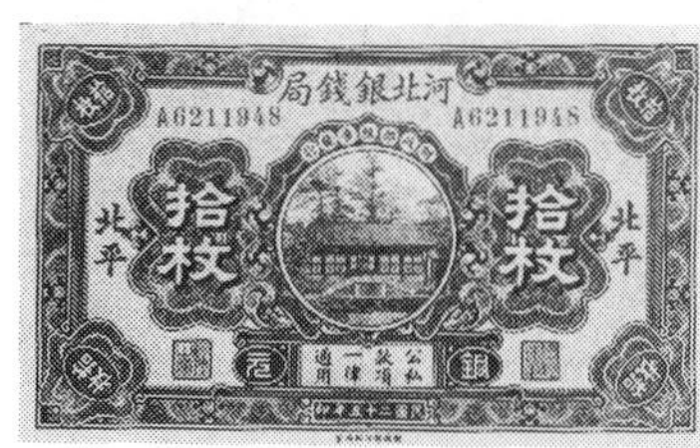

		VG	VF	Unc
S1710D	**10 Coppers** 1936. Purple on yellow unpt. Tea house behind bridge at ctr. Back purple. *(S/M #H63-20).*	3.00	10.00	30.00

		VG	VF	UNC
S1710E	20 COPPERS 1936. Black on red unpt. Back black. *(S/M #H63-21).*	3.00	10.00	30.00
S1710F	40 COPPERS 1936. *(S/M #H63-22).*	5.00	15.00	45.00

1938 ISSUE

#S1710J (S1710) and S1710K tea house behind bridge at ctr. Vertical format. Printer: PYPO.

		VG	VF	UNC
S1710J	4 COPPERS 1938. Dk. green. *(S/M #H63-30).*	2.50	8.00	25.00

#S1710

#S1710A

S1710K	6 COPPERS 1938. Brown. *(S/M #H63-31).*	2.50	8.00	25.00
S1710L	8 COPPERS 1938. *(S/M #H63-32).*	Reported Not Confirmed		
S1710M	20 COPPERS 1938. Dk. blue on pink unpt. Back dk. blue. *(S/M #H63-35).*	—	—	—
S1710N	40 COPPERS 1938. Brown. *(S/M #H63-36).*	—	—	—

BANK OF HOPEI
PROVINCIAL BANK OF HOPEI

河北省銀行
Ho Pei Yin Hang

河北銀行
Ho Pei Sheng Yin Hang

1929 ISSUE

#S1711 and S1712 printer: BEPP.

		GOOD	FINE	XF
S1711	10 CENTS 1.6.1929. Brown. Trees, house along shoreline at ctr. Back dk. brown. *(S/M #H64-1).*			
	a. *Peiping.* W/English title under sign. *(S/M #H64-1a).*	4.00	12.00	—
	b. *Peiping.* W/o English sign. titles. *(S/M #H64-1b).*	4.00	12.00	—
	c. *Tientsin.* W/English title under sign. *(S/M #H64-1c).*	4.00	12.00	—
	d. *Tientsin.* W/o English sign. titles. *(S/M #64-1d).*	4.00	12.00	—

		GOOD	FINE	XF
S1712	20 CENTS 1.6.1929. Blue. Hut at l. Back black.			
	a. *Peiping. (S/M #H64-2a).*	4.00	12.00	—
	b. *Tientsin. (S/M #H64-2b).*	4.00	12.00	—
	r. Unsigned remainders. *(S/M #H64-2c).*	—	Unc	30.00

1930 ISSUE

		GOOD	FINE	XF
S1715	1 YÜAN 1.5.1930. Brown. Great Wall at ctr. *Pei P'ing.* Printer: BEPP. *(S/M #H64-5).*	22.50	67.50	—

1932 COPPER COIN ISSUE

#S1716-S1720 hillside pagoda at l. *TIENTSIN.* Printer: BEPP.

		GOOD	FINE	XF
S1716	10 COPPERS 1.10.1932. Olive-green. *(S/M #H64-8).*	20.00	60.00	—

		GOOD	FINE	XF
S1717	20 COPPERS 1.10.1932. Orange-brown. *(S/M #H64-9).*	20.00	60.00	—
S1718	40 COPPERS 1.10.1932. Black and blue. Back black. *(S/M #H64-10).*	30.00	90.00	—

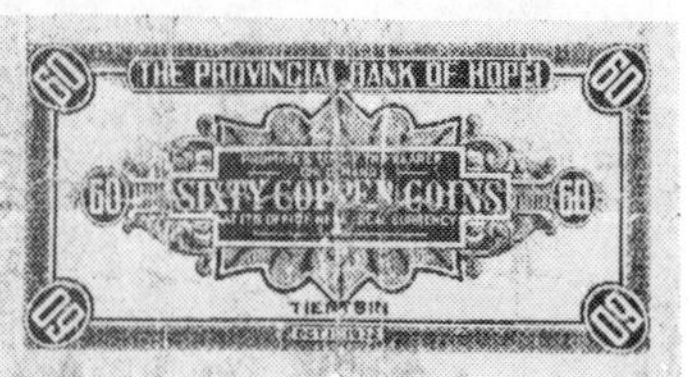

		GOOD	FINE	XF
S1719	60 COPPERS 1.10.1932. *(S/M #H64-11).*	30.00	100.00	—

		GOOD	FINE	XF
S1720	**100 COPPERS** 1.10.1932. Red. *(S/M #H64-12).*	30.00	90.00	—

1933 ISSUE

#S1723-S1724 pagoda at l. *TIENTSIN*. Printer: W&S.

		GOOD	FINE	XF
S1723	**1 YÜAN** 1.7.1933. Black on m/c unpt. Back green. *(S/M #H64-20).*	15.00	45.00	—
S1724	**5 YÜAN** 1.7.1933. Brown on m/c unpt. Back violet. *(S/M #H64-21).*			
	a. Issued note. *(S/M #H64-21a).*	10.00	30.00	—
	b. W/black numerical ovpt: *14. (S/M #H64-21b).*	10.00	30.00	—
	c. W/black numerical and red letter ovpt: *43g. (S/M #H64-21c).*	10.00	30.00	—
	d. W/green numerical ovpt: *34. (S/M #H64-21d).*	10.00	30.00	—
S1725	**10 YÜAN** 1.7.1933. Rose on m/c unpt. Back rose.			
	a. Issued note. *(S/M #H64-22a).*	20.00	60.00	—
	b. W/black numeral ovpt. *(S/M #H64-22b).*	20.00	60.00	—
	c. W/green numerical ovpt. *(S/M #C64-22c).*	20.00	60.00	—
	d. W/green numerical and black letter ovpt: *26g. (S/M #H64-22d).*	20.00	60.00	—

1934 ISSUE

#S1726-S1732 *Tientsin*. Printer: BEPP.

		GOOD	FINE	XF
S1726	**10 CENTS** 1934. Blue. *(S/M #H64-30).*	15.00	45.00	—
S1727	**20 CENTS** 1934. Brown. *(S/M #H64-31).*	15.00	45.00	—
S1728	**50 CENTS** 1934. Green. *(S/M #H64-32).*	12.00	35.00	—

#S1729-S1731 summer palace above shoreline at l. or r. *TIENTSIN*.

		GOOD	FINE	XF
S1729	**1 YÜAN** 1934. Orange and black. Back orange. *(S/M #H64-40).*	2.50	7.50	22.50
S1730	**2 YÜAN** 1934. Green.			
	a. Issued note. *(S/M #H64-41a).*	10.00	30.00	90.00
	b. W/additional numerical ovpt: *142. (S/M #H64-41b).*	12.00	35.00	105.00

		GOOD	FINE	XF
S1731	**5 YÜAN** 1934. Red. Like #S1730.			
	a. Issued note. *(S/M #H64-42a).*	10.00	30.00	—
	b. W/additional control # ovpt: *91; 148; 150* or letters: *TT. (S/M #H64-42b).*	10.00	30.00	—

		GOOD	FINE	XF
S1732	**10 YÜAN** 1934. Brown on lt. blue unpt. Summer palace at ctr. *TIENSTIN.*			
	a. Issued note. *(S/M #H64-43a).*	20.00	60.00	—
	b. W/additional numerical ovpt: *91. (S/M #H64-43b).*	20.00	60.00	—
	c. W/additional Chinese character ovpt: *Chin. (S/M #H64-43c).*	—	—	—
	d. W/additional Chinese character ovpt: *Mei. (S/M #H64-43d).*	—	—	—

1940 ISSUE

		GOOD	FINE	XF
S1735	**50 CENTS** 1940. Red. Back blue. *(S/M #H64-50).*	15.00	50.00	—

KHOTAN DISTRICT ADMINISTRATION

印長政行區闐和

Ho Tien Ch'ü Hang Cheng Chang Yin

1935-36 ISSUE

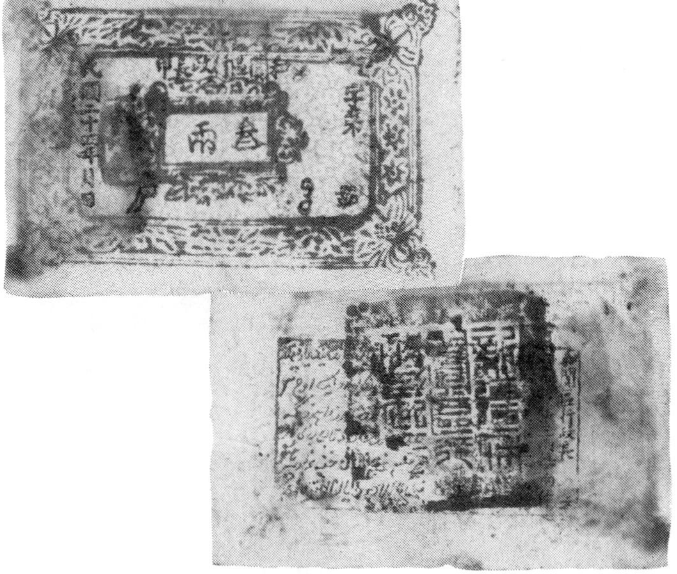

		GOOD	FINE	XF
S1737	**3 TAELS** 1935-36. Black text on red. Back w/lg. red hand stamped seal. *(S/M #H65.5-13).*	8.00	25.00	—

KHOTAN ADMINISTRATION GOVERNMENT HEAD PUBLIC OFFICE

Ho T'ien Hsing Cheng Ch'ang Kung Shu Yin Liu Chao Piao T'ung

1935 ISSUE

		GOOD	FINE	XF
S1738	**1 TAEL** 1934; 1935. Black text on pink unpt. W/violet rectangular hand stamp. Back purple; black text and lg. red hand stamped seal. *(S/M #H65.7-11)*.	15.00	45.00	—

SIKANG PROVINCIAL BANK

行銀省康西

Hsi K'ang Sheng Yin Hang

1939 ISSUE

#S1739-S1740 printer: BEPP.

		GOOD	FINE	XF
S1739	**1/2 YÜAN** 1939. Red on orange and blue unpt. Mountain scene at l. Tibetan headings on back. *(S/M #H75-1)*.	20.00	65.00	—

		GOOD	FINE	XF
S1740	**1 YÜAN** 1939. Green on lt. green unpt. Mountain fortress at ctr. Back blue on orange unpt. *(S/M #H75-10)*.	15.00	50.00	150.00
S1741	**5 YÜAN** 1939. *(S/M #H75-12)*.	—	—	—

SUBTREASURY OF SINKIANG - OFFICIAL NOTE

票官庫藩疆新

Hsin Chiang Fan k'u Kuan P'iao

1912 ISSUE

		GOOD	FINE	XF
S1742	**400 CASH** 1912. M/c. 2 dragons. Chinese and Turki text on back. Vertical format. *(S/M #-)*.	—	—	—

MAIN OFFICIAL CURRENCY BUREAU OF SINKIANG

局總錢官疆新

Hsin Chiang Kuan Ch'ien Tsung Chu

1908 ISSUE

		GOOD	FINE	XF
S1742A	**400 CASH** CD 1908. M/c. Dragons. Chinese and Turki text on back. Vertical format, 130 x 260mm. *(S/M #-)*.	—	—	—

1909 ISSUE

		GOOD	FINE	XF
S1742B	**400 CASH** 1909. Similar to S1742A. *(S/M #-)*.	—	—	—

SINKIANG COMMERCIAL AND INDUSTRIAL BANK

行銀業商疆新

Hsin Chiang Shang Yeh Yin Hang

1939 ISSUE

		GOOD	FINE	XF
S1743	**1 FEN** 1939. Olive-green. Back green. *(S/M #H123-1)*.	5.00	17.50	50.00
S1744	**3 FEN** 1939. Blue. Like #S1743. *(S/M #H123-2)*.	7.00	20.00	60.00
S1745	**5 FEN** 1939. Red-orange. *(S/M #H123-3)*.			
	a. W/*NO* before serial #.	8.00	25.00	75.00
	b. W/2 letter serial # prefix.	8.00	25.00	75.00

		GOOD	FINE	XF
S1746	**1 CHIAO** 1939. Green. Rural scene at r. *(S/M #H123-4)*.			
	a. Black sign. 2 varieties.	3.00	10.00	30.00
	b. Green sign.	3.00	10.00	30.00

		GOOD	FINE	XF
S1747	**2 CHIAO** 1939. Violet. City shops at r.			
	a. Back violet, black sign. *(S/M #H123-5)*.	5.50	16.50	50.00
	b. Back purple, black sign.	5.50	16.50	50.00

		GOOD	FINE	XF
S1748	**5 CHIAO** 1939. Red. Tower at l. Back red-brown; black sign. 2 varieties. *(S/M #H123-6).*	**5.50**	**16.50**	**50.00**
S1749	**1 YÜAN** 1939. Red. *(S/M #H123-10).*	12.50	37.50	110.00

		GOOD	FINE	XF
S1750	**3 YÜAN** 1939. Green. Radio transmitting bldg. at ctr. *(S/M #H123-11).*	26.50	80.00	—
S1751	**5 YÜAN** 1939. Orange face and back. Square Chinese sign. in red. *(S/M #H123-12).*	12.50	37.50	—
S1752	**10 YÜAN** 1939. *(S/M #H123-13).*	Reported Not Confirmed		

		GOOD	FINE	XF
S1753	**50 YÜAN** 1939. Brown and green. Men fishing at l., rural shoreline at r. Back brown; shepherd and sheep at ctr. *(S/M #H123-14).*	20.00	60.00	—

		GOOD	FINE	XF
S1754	**100 YÜAN** 1939. Red. Woman weaving at l., men farming at r. Back violet; offshore house at ctr. *(S/M #H123-15).*	20.00	60.00	—

1940 ISSUE

		GOOD	FINE	XF
S1758	**10 YÜAN** 1940. Red. Canyon at ctr. Black sign. on back. *(S/M #H123-20).*			
	a. W/*NO* before serial #. 2 sign. varieties.	15.00	45.00	—
	b. W/2 letter serial # prefix.	15.00	45.00	—

1943-45 ISSUE

		GOOD	FINE	XF
S1761	**1 YÜAN** 1943. Red. *(S/M #H123-30).*	17.50	55.00	—
S1762	**5 YÜAN** 1943. Green. Back red. *(S/M #H123-31).*	17.50	55.00	—
S1763	**10 YÜAN** 1943. Blue. Car and truck in city street at ctr. Rural house at ctr. on back. *(S/M #H123-32).*	17.50	55.00	—

1945 ISSUE

		GOOD	FINE	XF
S1765	**200 YÜAN** 1945. Violet. Portr. SYS at l. Back red; bridge over wooded stream at ctr. *(S/M #H123-40).*	7.00	20.00	60.00

1946 ISSUE

		GOOD	FINE	XF
S1768	**100 YÜAN** 1946. Red. Weaving at l., farming r. Back blue. *(S/M #H123-50).*	15.00	45.00	—

		GOOD	FINE	XF
S1769	**500 YÜAN** 1946. Brown. Portr. SYS at l. Back green; bank bldg. at ctr. *(S/M #H123-51).*	8.00	25.00	75.00

1947 ISSUE

#S1771-S1772 SYS at l.

		GOOD	FINE	XF
S1771	**2000 YÜAN** 1947. Red and blue. Back red; harvesting grain w/tractor at r. *(S/M #H123-60).*	10.00	30.00	—

		GOOD	FINE	XF
S1772	**5000 YÜAN** 1947. Blue on red unpt. Back blue; factories at r. *(S/M #H12361).*	10.00	30.00	—

#S1773 and S1774 SYS at upper ctr. Bank bldg. at upper ctr. on back. Vertical format.

		GOOD	FINE	XF
S1773	**10,000 YÜAN** 1947. Brown. *(S/M #H123-62).*	20.00	60.00	—
S1774	**20,000 YÜAN** 1947. Blue-green and yellow. Back blue. *(S/M #H123-63).*	10.00	30.00	90.00

1948 ISSUE

#S1776 and S1777 SYS at l.

		GOOD	FINE	XF
S1776	**100,000 YÜAN** 1948. Red and yellow. Back red; airplane above steam train passing through hills at r. *(S/M #H123-70).*	20.00	60.00	—

		GOOD	FINE	XF
S1777	**200,000 YÜAN** 1948. Violet and red. Like #S1771. Back violet. *(S/M #H123-71).*	12.50	40.00	—

		GOOD	FINE	XF
S1778	**500,000 YÜAN** 1948. Green. Similar to #S1774. *(S/M #H123-72).*	13.50	40.00	—

INDUSTRIAL AND COMMERCIAL BANK OF SINKIANG, ILI BRANCH

新疆商業銀行伊犁分行財票

Hsin Chiang Shang Yeh Yin Hang I Li Fen Hang Ts'ai P'iao

1947 ISSUE

#S1778A-S1778C w/Chinese bank name.

		VG	VF	UNC
S1778A	**2000 DOLLARS** 1947. Purple. Grain mill and electric power station of Ining. Back blue.	150.00	200.00	—
S1778B	**2500 DOLLARS** 1947. Red. Emin Pagoda of Turpan, farmer w/grapes. Back black.			
	a. W/o AH date.	100.00	150.00	—
	b. AH1366.	—	—	—
S1778C	**3000 DOLLARS** 1947. Dk. brown. Ili Branch of the Commercial and Industrial Bank at ctr. Back black.	—	—	—

1948 ISSUES

#S1778D-S1778H w/o Chinese text.

		VG	VF	UNC
S1778D	**100 DOLLARS** 1948. Violet. Turki text: *yüz = 100* at ctr. Back black.	90.00	150.00	—
S1778E	**300 DOLLARS** 1948. Purple. Value: *300* at ctr. Back red.	150.00	200.00	—
S1778F	**300 DOLLARS** 1948. Deep violet. Similar to #S1778E. Back black.	150.00	200.00	—
S1778G	**500 DOLLARS** 1948. Purple. Back green. Vertical format.	170.00	230.00	—
S1778H	**1000 DOLLARS** 1948. Red. Bldg. at ctr. Back black.	170.00	230.00	—

SINKIANG SUB-PREFECTURE ADMINISTRATION FINANCE DEPARTMENT TREASURY - OFFICIAL NOTE

新疆省政府財政廳庫官票

Hsin Chiang Sheng Cheng Fu Ts'ai Cheng Ting K'u Kuan Piao

1932 ISSUE

		GOOD	FINE	XF
S1779	**3 TAELS** 1932. Burgundy. Back blue-green; bldgs. at ctr. *Kashgar* and *Khotan*. *(S/M #H123.5-9)*.	20.00	50.00	100.00

		GOOD	FINE	XF
S1780	**5 TAELS** 1932. Blue on yellow unpt. w/red text. Back brown and dk. blue on lt. green unpt; snow capped mountains at ctr. *Kashgar* and *Khotan* . 177 x 103mm. *(S/M #H123.5-10)*.	8.50	25.00	75.00

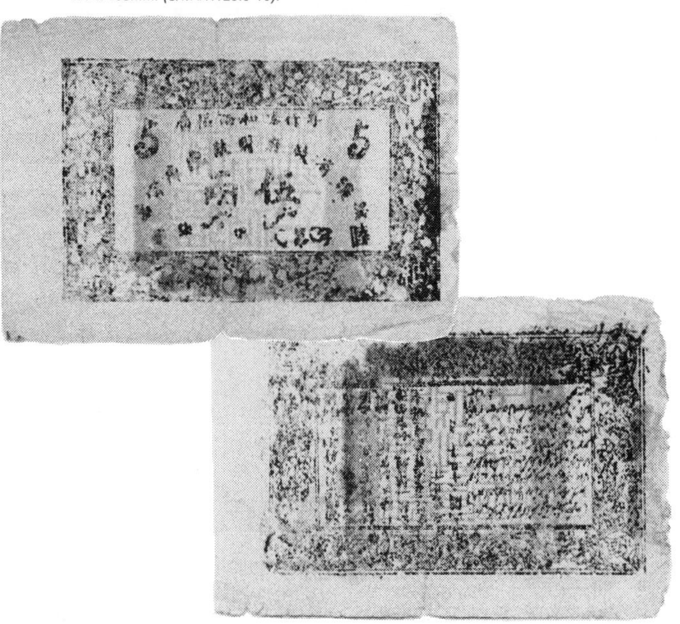

		GOOD	FINE	XF
S1780A	**50 TAELS** 1932. Red. *(S/M #H123.5-18)*.	—	—	—

***#S1780B Deleted.* See #S1780F.**

1934; 1935 ISSUES

		GOOD	FINE	XF
S1780C	**3 TAELS** 1934. Similar to #S1779. *Kashgar* and *Khotan*. *(S/M #H123.5-22)*.	—	—	—
S1780D	**5 TAELS** 1934; 1936. Floral branches in borders. *Kashgar* and *Khotan*. *(S/M #H123.5-23)*.	—	—	—

		GOOD	FINE	XF
S1780F	**50 TAELS** 1934-36. Pale olive-green w/black text. Back blue-gray. *Kashgar* and *Khotan*. *(S/M #H123.5-25)*.	32.50	100.00	—

SINKIANG PROVINCE

券庫金省疆新

Hsin Chiang Sheng Chin K'u Ch'üan

1931 TREASURY NOTE ISSUE

#S1781-S1783 printer: BEPP.

		GOOD	FINE	XF
S1781	**2 CH'IEN** 1931. Brown and green. Back green. *(S/M #H124-1)*.	37.50	110.00	—
S1782	**5 CH'IEN** 1931. Orange and green. Back blue. *(S/M #H124-2)*.	45.00	135.00	—
S1783	**1 TAEL** 1931. Orange and green. Back green. *(S/M #H124-3)*.	60.00	180.00	—

SINKIANG PROVINCIAL BANK

行銀省疆新

Hsin Chiang Sheng Yin Hang

1948 YÜAN ISSUE

		GOOD	FINE	XF
S1786	**1,000,000 YÜAN** 1948. Red. Portr. SYS at upper ctr. Back violet; bank bldg. at upper ctr. Vertical format. *(S/M #H125-1)*.	15.00	45.00	—
S1787	**3,000,000 YÜAN** 1948. Blue. Back violet. *(S/M #H125-2)*.	15.00	50.00	—
S1788	**6,000,000 YÜAN** 1948. Black, yellow and red. SYS at l. Back olive; bank bldg. at r. *(S/M #H125-3)*.	15.00	45.00	—
S1789	**10,000,000 YÜAN** 1948.	Reported Not Confirmed		

1949 GOLD YÜAN ISSUE

1 Gold Yüan = 600,000 *Fa Pi* Yüan

		GOOD	FINE	XF
S1790	**30,000,000 YÜAN = 50 GOLD YÜAN** 1949. Brown and red. Portr. SYS at ctr. r. Back brown; bank bldg. at ctr. *(S/M #H125-10).*	15.00	50.00	—

		GOOD	FINE	XF
S1791	**6,000,000 YÜAN = 10 GOLD YÜAN** 1949. Violet and red. Portr. SYS at r. Back red; bank bldg. at l. *(S/M #H125-11).*	12.50	40.00	—
S1793	**300,000,000 YÜAN = 500 GOLD YÜAN** 1949. *(S/M #H125-12).*	Reported Not Confirmed		

		GOOD	FINE	XF
S1794	**600,000,000 YÜAN = 1,000 GOLD YÜAN** 1949. Red and blue. Like #S1788. Back blue. *(S/M #H125-13).*	25.00	80.00	—
S1796	**3,000,000,000 YÜAN = 5,000 GOLD YÜAN** 1949. Dk. brown and red. Portr. SYS at lower ctr. Bank bldg. at r. on back. *(S/M #H125-14).*	65.00	150.00	—

		GOOD	FINE	XF
S1797	**6,000,000,000 YÜAN = 10,000 GOLD YÜAN** 1949. Purple and green. Portr. SYS at lower l. Back violet; bank bldg. at r. *(S/M #H125-15).*	40.00	120.00	—

1949; 1950 SILVER YÜAN ISSUE

		GOOD	FINE	XF
S1798	**1 FEN** 1949. Blue. Trees, hills at ctr. (S/M #H125-19).	12.50	50.00	150.00

		GOOD	FINE	XF
S1799	**5 FEN** 1949. Violet. *(S/M #H125-20).*	10.00	30.00	90.00

		GOOD	FINE	XF
S1800	**1 CHIAO = 10 CENTS** 1949. Red. Landscape, mountain at ctr. *(S/M #H125-21).*	20.00	80.00	—
S1801	**2 CHIAO = 20 CENTS** 1949. Violet. Landscape, mountains. *(S/M #H125-22).*	25.00	90.00	—

		GOOD	FINE	XF
S1803	**1 SILVER YÜAN** 1949. Blue. Farming w/horses at l. and r. Pine trees, mountains at lower l. ctr. on back. *(S/M #H125-30).*	25.00	90.00	—

		GOOD	FINE	XF
S1806	**10 SILVER YÜAN** 1950. Farming at l. and r. *(S/M #H125-35).*	20.00	80.00	—
S1807	**10 SILVER YÜAN** 1950. Steam passenger train at l., ship at r. *(S/M #H125-36).*	20.00	80.00	—

TREASURY DEPT. OF SINKIANG - OFFICIAL NOTE

票官庫司疆新

Hsin Chiang Szu K'u Kuan P'iao

1913 ISSUE

		GOOD	FINE	XF
S1808	**400 CASH** 1913. M/c. 2 dragons. Chinese and Turki text on back. Vertical format. *(S/M #-).*	—	—	—

PROVINCIAL TREASURY OF SINKIANG - OFFICIAL NOTE

票官庫廳疆新

Hsin Chiang T'ing K'u Kuan P'iao

1914; 1915 ISSUE

		GOOD	FINE	XF
S1809	**100 CASH** Yr. 3 (1914). Red and black. Chinze at l. and r. holding 2 crossed striped flags. Chinese and Turki text on back. Printed in Tihua. *(S/M #-).*	—	—	—
S1809A	**100 CASH** Yr. 4 (1915). Similar to S1809. *(S/M #-).*	—	—	—
S1810	**400 CASH** Yr. 4 (1915). Blue, black and yellow. 2 dragons. Chinese and Turki text on back. Vertical format. *(S/M #-).*	—	—	—

SINKIANG PROVISIONAL GOVERNMENT FINANCE DEPARTMENT TREASURY

票官庫廳政財疆新

Hsin Chiang/Ts'ai Cheng T'ingK'u Kuan P'iao

NOTE: Many plate and color varieties exist for many of these crude block printed issues.

1917 ISSUE

		GOOD	FINE	XF
S1811	**400 CASH** Yr. 6 (1917). Blue and yellow. Back green and orange. Printer: BEPP. *(S/M #H126-1).*	20.00	80.00	—

1919 ISSUE

#S1815 and S1817 printer: BEPP.

		GOOD	FINE	XF
S1815	**100 CASH** Yr. 8 (1919). Yellow. Back black. *(S/M #H126-10).*	12.50	40.00	—
S1817	**400 CASH** Yr. 8 (1919). Blue. Back black. *(S/M #H126-11).*	22.00	65.00	—

1920 ISSUE

		GOOD	FINE	XF
S1820	**100 CASH** Yr. 9 (1920). Green and black on red unpt. Back black and blue on yellow unpt. *(S/M #H126-20).*	15.00	50.00	—

		GOOD	FINE	XF
S1822	**400 CASH** Yr. 9 (1920). Green on pink unpt. w/black text. Back blue on deep yellow unpt. Vertical format. Printer: BEPP. *(S/M #H126-22).*			
	a. Olive-green.	12.50	40.00	—
	b. Bright green (poor quality).	—	—	—

1921 ISSUE

		GOOD	FINE	XF
S1825	**400 CASH** Yr. 10 (1921). Blue. Back yellow. Vertical format. Printer: BEPP. *(S/M #H126-30).*	12.50	40.00	—

1925 ISSUE

		GOOD	FINE	XF
S1830	**400 CASH** Yr. 14 (1925). Red. Back black. Printer: DOFS. *(S/M #H126-40).*	22.00	65.00	—

1927 ISSUE

		GOOD	FINE	XF
S1835	**400 CASH** Yr. 16 (1927). Red w/black text. Back blue. Printer: DOFS. *(S/M #H126-50).*	22.00	65.00	—

1928 ISSUE

		GOOD	FINE	XF
S1840	**400 CASH** Yr. 17 (1928). Red w/black text. Back blue; black text. Printer: DOFS *(S/M #H126-60).*	12.50	40.00	—

1930 ISSUE

		GOOD	FINE	XF
S1844	**400 CASH** Yr. 19 (1930). Red floral border w/black text. Back blue; cockerals in border w/black text. *(S/M #H126-62).*	20.00	60.00	—

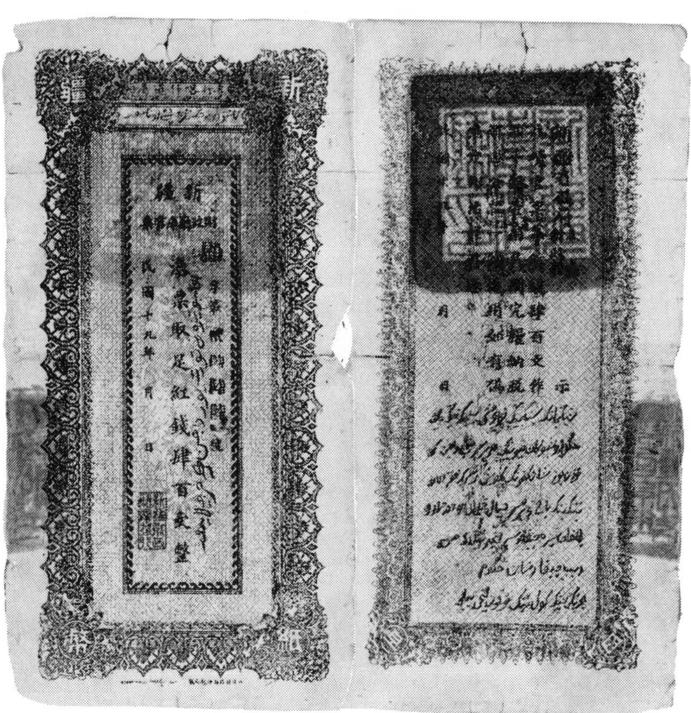

		Good	Fine	XF
S1845	**400 Cash** Yr. 19 (1930). Deep blue-green on pink unpt. w/black text. Vertical format. *(S/M #H126-65).*	12.50	40.00	—

1931 Issue

		Good	Fine	XF
S1850	**400 Cash** Yr. 20 (1931). Red w/black text. Similar to #S1844. Back blue w/black text. Vertical format. Printer: DOFS. *(S/M #H126-70).*	10.00	30.00	—

		Good	Fine	XF
S1851	**400 Cash** Yr. 20 (1931). Green on red unpt. w/black text. Back blue on yellow-orange unpt. Vertical format. *(S/M #H126-).*	10.00	30.00	90.00

1932 Issue

#S1856 and S1858 printer: DOFS.

		Good	Fine	XF
S1856	**100 Cash** Yr. 21 (1932). Blue. Back violet. Vertical format. *(S/M #H126-80).*	25.00	75.00	—
S1857	**100 Cash** Yr. 21 (1932). Brown. Back green. *(S/M #H126-80.5).*	5.00	15.00	50.00
S1858	**400 Cash** Yr. 21 (1932). Red. Back black. *(S/M #H126-81).*	22.00	65.00	—

#S1859-S1870 printer: BEPP.

		Good	Fine	XF
S1859	**400 Cash** Yr. 21 (1932). Gray and yellow. Back violet and green. *(S/M #H126-82).*	22.00	65.00	—
S1863	**2000 Cash** Yr. 21 (1932). Violet and green. Back violet and green. *(S/M #H126-83).*	25.00	75.00	—
S1864	**4000 Cash** Yr. 21 (1932). Violet and blue. Back brown and yellow. *(S/M #H126-84).*	25.00	75.00	—
S1868	**3 Taels** Yr. 21 (1932). Brown-violet on pale green unpt. Circles in border. Back deep blue-green w/black text. *(S/M #H126-90).*	15.00	50.00	—

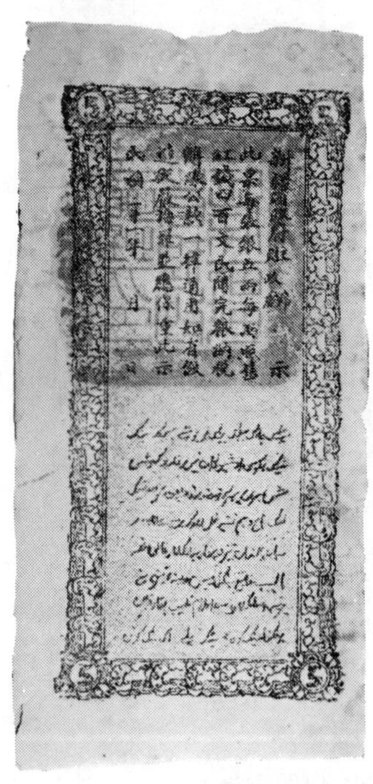

		Good	Fine	XF
S1869	**5 Taels** Yr. 21 (1932). Blue. Back black. Vertical format. *(S/M #H126-91).*	8.00	25.00	—
S1870	**10 Taels** Yr. 21 (1932). Dk. blue and green. Back lt. green. *(S/M #H126-92).*	30.00	90.00	—

1933 ISSUE

		GOOD	FINE	XF
S1875	**10 TAELS** Yr. 22 (1933). Dk. blue-black on lt. green unpt. Back green on yellow-orange unpt. Vertical format. *(S/M #H126-95).*	10.00	30.00	—
S1876	**50 TAELS** Yr. 22 (1933). *(S/M #H126-99).*	40.00	120.00	—

#S1879 *Deleted.* See #S1779.

1934 ISSUE

		GOOD	FINE	XF
S1880	**5 TAELS** Yr. 23 (1934). *(S/M #H126.5-12).*	45.00	135.00	—

		GOOD	FINE	XF
S1881	**10 TAELS** Yr. 23 (1934). Red w/black text. Back blue-gray. Vertical format. *(S/M #H126.5-13).*	—	Rare	—
S1882	**50 TAELS** Yr. 23 (1934). *(S/M #H126.5-15).*	50.00	150.00	—

#S1886 *Deleted.* See #S1780B.

SUNNING RAILWAY CO., LTD.

HSIN NING T'IEN LU KUNG SZU

#S1888-S1890 *Deleted.* (Local issue).

MONETARY BUREAU OF GOVERNMENT SUCHOW

局錢官市平州徐

Hsü Chou P'ing Shih Kuan Ch'ien Chü

1933 ISSUE

#S1891A-S1891C bldg. w/pagoda in background at top center. Various numerical and Chinese character ovpts. Printer: TTBC.

		GOOD	FINE	XF
S1891A	**10 CENTS** 1933. Red. Back green. *(S/M #H155-1).*			
	a. Issued note.	15.00	45.00	—
	b. W/additional control ovpt: *32; 60; Ho; Su.*	20.00	60.00	—
S1891B	**20 CENTS** 1933. Blue. Back brown. *(S/M #H155-2).*			
	a. Issued note.	20.00	60.00	—
	b. W/additional control ovpt: *25; 46; 61.*	22.00	65.00	—
S1891C	**50 CENTS** 1933. Brown. Back violet. *(S/M #H155-3).*	25.00	75.00	—

NOTE: For #S1891A-S1891C w/solid bar ovpt. see #S1191-S1193.

HULUNPEIERH OFFICIAL CURRENCY BUREAU

局錢商官爾貝倫呼

Hu Lun Pei Erh Kuan Shang Ch'ien Chü

1918 ISSUE

#S1892A-S1892C *Heilungkiang.* Printer: MLTA.

		GOOD	FINE	XF
S1892A	**5 CHIAO** 1918. Green. Back orange. *(S/M #H157-1).*	25.00	75.00	—
S1892B	**1 YÜAN** 1918. Violet and yellow. Back brown. *(S/M #H157-10).*	25.00	75.00	—
S1892C	**3 YÜAN** 1918. Green and yellow. Back brown. *(S/M #H157-11).*	30.00	90.00	—

#S1892D-S1892F *Heilungkiang.* Printer: MLCA.

		GOOD	FINE	XF
S1892D	**5 YÜAN** 1918. Blue and green. *(S/M #H157-12).*	30.00	90.00	—
S1892E	**10 YÜAN** 1918. Orange and red. Back orange. *(S/M #H157-13).*	37.50	110.00	—
S1892F	**25 YÜAN** 1918. Blue and yellow. Back violet and green. *(S/M #H157-14).*	50.00	150.00	—

1919 ISSUE

#S1892G-S1892M *Heilungkiang.* Printer: MLCA.

		GOOD	FINE	XF
S1892G	**5 CHIAO** 1919. Black and orange. *(S/M #H157-20).*	20.00	60.00	—

		GOOD	FINE	XF
S1892H	**1 YÜAN** 1919. Brown on yellow-green unpt. Bridge over river at ctr. Back brown. *(S/M #H157-30).*	30.00	90.00	—

		GOOD	FINE	XF
S1892I	3 YÜAN 1919. Black and yellow. *(S/M #H157-31).*			
	a. Red serial #.	75.00	225.00	—
	b. Black serial #.	75.00	225.00	—

		GOOD	FINE	XF
S1892J	5 YÜAN July 1919. Dk. blue on lt. blue unpt. Hillside pagoda at ctr. Back dk. blue on lt. olive-green unpt. *(S/M #H157-32).*	20.00	60.00	—

		GOOD	FINE	XF
S1892K	10 YÜAN 1919. Orange. Back orange and green. *(S/M #H157-33).*	30.00	100.00	—
S1892L	25 YÜAN 1919. Blue and red. Back violet and blue; shrines at ctr. *(S/M #H157-34).*	50.00	150.00	—

		GOOD	FINE	XF
S1892M	100 YÜAN 1919. Olive-gray on orange unpt. Back red on lt. green unpt. *(S/M #H157-35).*	165.00	500.00	—

OFFICIAL MINT HUNAN
HUNAN GOVERNMENT BANK

局錢官南湖

Hu Nan Kuan Ch'ien Chü

1903 ISSUE

		GOOD	FINE	XF
S1893	1 CH'UAN Yr. 29 (1903). Brown and green. *(S/M #H161-0.1).*	60.00	180.00	—

#S1895-S1904 facing dragons at upper l. and r., waves at bottom.

1904 ISSUE

		GOOD	FINE	XF
S1895	1 CH'UAN CD 1904. Purple and yellow. W/o rectangular frames. *(S/M #H61-0.2).*	100.00	300.00	—
S1896	1 CH'UAN CD 1904. Brown and blue. W/rectangular frames. Japanese imprint. *(S/M #H161-0.3).*	80.00	240.00	—
S1898	1 DOLLAR Yr. 30 (1904). Blue and red. *(S/M #H161-0.4).*	165.00	500.00	—
S1899	1 DOLLAR Yr. 30 (1904). Blue and green. *(S/M #H161-0.5).*	80.00	240.00	—
S1903	100 DOLLARS Yr. 30 (1904). *(S/M #H161-1).*	Reported Not Confirmed		
S1904	1 TAEL Yr. 30 (1904). Black and green. *(S/M #H161-4).*	60.00	180.00	—

1906 ISSUE

#S1907-S1913 facing dragons at upper l. and r., waves at bottom.

		GOOD	FINE	XF
S1907	100 COPPERS Yr. 32 (1906). Brown and green. *(S/M #H161-6).*	100.00	300.00	—
S1910	1 CH'UAN Yr. 32 (1906). Brown and black. Back orange. *(S/M #H161-10).*	120.00	360.00	—

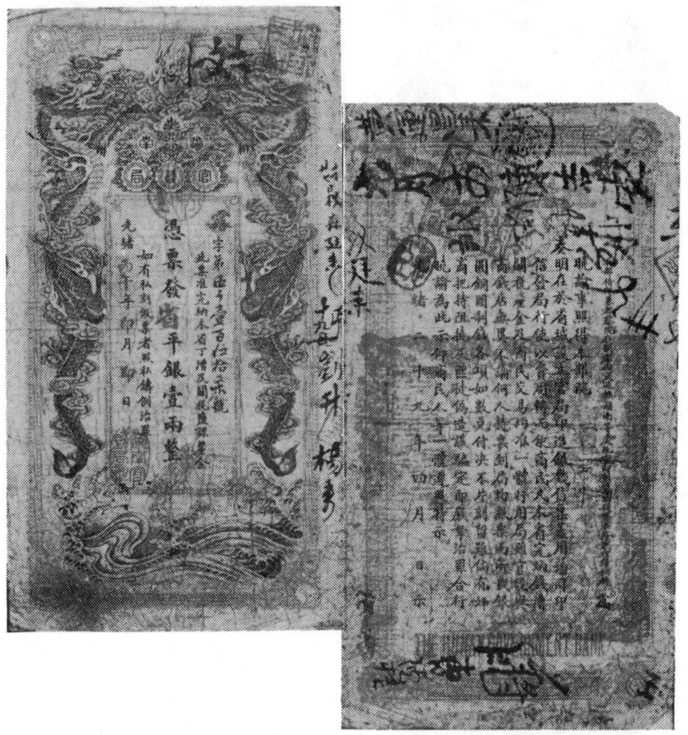

		GOOD	FINE	XF
S1913	1 TAEL CD 1906. Vertical format. *(S/M #H161-20).*	60.00	180.00	—

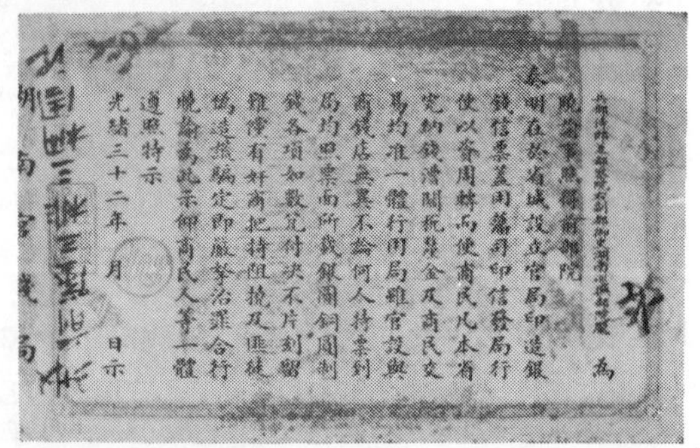

	GOOD	FINE	XF
S1914 5 TAELS Yr. 32 (1906). Blue and black. Printer: PYOP.			
a. Issued note. *(S/M #H161-22).*	35.00	110.00	—
x. *TEALS* error. *(S/M #H161-21).*	40.00	125.00	—

1908 ISSUE

	VG	VF	UNC
S1917 50 COPPERS Yr. 34 (1908). Printer: CMPA. *(S/M #H161-39).*	—	—	—

	VG	VF	UNC
S1918 100 COPPERS Yr. 34 (1908). Blue and gray on yellow unpt. Facing dragons at upper l. and r., house at l., road to factory at r.			
a. Issued note.	—	—	—
r. Remainder w/perforation and hand stamped cancellation. *(S/M #H161-40).*	—	—	100.00
S1919 500 COPPERS Yr. 34 (1908). Printer: CMPA. *(S/M #H161-).*	—	—	—
S1920 1000 COPPERS Yr. 34 (1908). Printer: CMPA. *(S/M #H161-).*	—	—	—
S1923 1 DOLLAR Yr. 34 (1908). Blue. Back orange. *(S/M #H161-50).*	50.00	150.00	—

#S1926 and S1927 dragons facing at top over house at l., road to factory at r. Printer: CMPA.

	GOOD	FINE	XF
S1926 1 TAEL Yr. 34 (1908). Black and blue. Back brown and red. *(S/M #H161-60).*	40.00	120.00	—

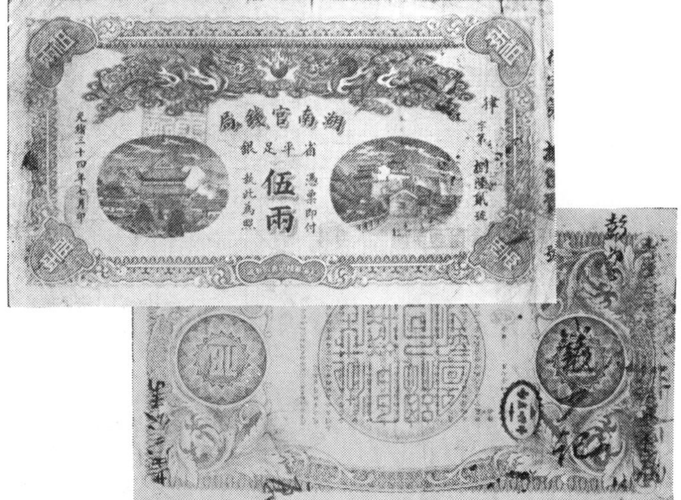

	GOOD	FINE	XF
S1927 5 TAELS Yr. 34 (1908). Violet and yellow. Similar to #S1918. Back blue and red. *(S/M #H161-61).*	150.00	400.00	—

1909 ISSUE

	GOOD	FINE	XF
S1929 1 TAEL 1909. *(S/M #H161-70).*	Reported Not Confirmed		
S1930 5 TAELS 1909. *(S/M #H161-71).*	Reported Not Confirmed		

HUNAN PROVINCIAL TREASURY

廳政財省南湖

Hu Nan Sheng Ts'ai Cheng T'ing

NOTE: For earlier issues see Yu Sien, Yu Hsiang, Hunan, and Hunan Provincial Bank listings.

1920 ISSUES

#S1936-S1940 bearer bond types. Printer: HODP.

	GOOD	FINE	XF
S1936 1 DOLLAR 1920. Brown. Back brown and red. *(S/M #H163-1).*	30.00	90.00	—
S1937 1 DOLLAR 1920. Blue and green. Back green and red. *(S/M #H163-2).*	30.00	90.00	—
S1938 5 DOLLARS 1920. Brown. Back orange and red. *(S/M #H163-3).*	30.00	90.00	—
S1939 5 DOLLARS 1920. Brown and green. Back blue and red. *(S/M #H163-4).*	30.00	90.00	—
S1940 10 DOLLARS 1920. Green. Back brown and red. *(S/M #H163-5).*	30.00	90.00	—

1926 ISSUE

	GOOD	FINE	XF
S1943 1 DOLLAR 1926. *(S/M #H163-10).*	Reported Not Confirmed		

1936 ISSUE

	GOOD	FINE	XF
S1948 10 SILVER YÜAN 1936. *(S/M #H163-).*	Reported Not Confirmed		

HUNAN PROVINCIAL BANK
PROVINCIAL BANK OF HUNAN

行銀省南湖

Hu Nan Sheng Yin Hang

ND PROVISIONAL ISSUE

#S1951-S1953 w/5 additional Chinese character ovpt. on Changsha Bank.

	GOOD	FINE	XF
S1951 1 YÜAN ND (- old date 1.1.1928). Ovpt. on #S858. *(S/M #H164-1).*			
a. W/Chinese 5 character ovpt. and Chinese sign.	20.00	70.00	—
b. W/Chinese 13 character ovpt. and English sign.	30.00	90.00	—

	GOOD	FINE	XF
S1952 5 YÜAN ND (- old date 1.1.1928). Ovpt. on #S859. *(S/M #H164-2).*			
a. Chinese sign.	50.00	150.00	—
b. W/13 character ovpt. and English sign. and additional Chinese character control ovpt.	50.00	150.00	—

	GOOD	FINE	XF
S1953 10 YÜAN ND (-old date 1.1.1928). Ovpt. on #S860. Chinese sign. *(S/M #H164-3).*	60.00	180.00	—

1930 ISSUE

		GOOD	FINE	XF
S1956	10 CENTS 1930. Green. Bldg. at ctr. *(S/M #H164-6).*	22.50	67.50	—
S1957	20 CENTS 1930. Purple. Bank bldg. at upper ctr. Gazebo at upper ctr. on back. Vertical format. *(S/M #H164-7).* format.	25.00	75.00	—
S1958	50 CENTS 1930. Red. Bank bldg. at ctr. *(S/M #H164-8).*	30.00	90.00	—

1932 ISSUE

		GOOD	FINE	XF
S1960	200 CASH 1932. Green. Back red and blue. Printer: TTBC. *(S/M #H164-10).*	30.00	90.00	—

1935 ISSUE

		GOOD	FINE	XF
S1965	200 CASH 1935. Green. Printer: TTGL. *(S/M #H164-15).*	30.00	90.00	—
S1970	50 CENTS 1935. Green and yellow. Back orange. Printer: CPOF. *(S/M #H164-20).*	22.50	67.50	—

1936 ISSUE

		GOOD	FINE	XF
S1975	200 CASH Green. Bldg. at ctr. Back m/c. *(S/M #H164-29).*	22.50	67.50	—
S1976	300 CASH 1936. Dk. brown. Bldg. w/tower at upper ctr. Back red. Vertical format. *(S/M #H164-30).*	30.00	90.00	—

		GOOD	FINE	XF
S1978	1000 CASH 1936. Red on pink unpt. Palace at upper ctr. *(S/M #H164-32).*	35.00	110.00	—
S1980	10 CENTS 1936. Green. *(S/M #H164-35).*	22.50	67.50	—
S1981	20 CENTS 1936. Green. Like #S1957. *(S/M #H164-36).*	22.50	67.50	—
S1982	50 CENTS 1936. Purple. Bldg. at l. Back orange. *(S/M #H164-37).*	25.00	75.00	—

1937 ISSUE

		VG	VF	UNC
S1984	5 CENTS 1937. Violet. Bldg. at l. Back orange. Printer: CMPA. *(S/M #H164-40).*	4.00	12.00	36.00

1938 ISSUE

#S1987-S1991 printer: CMPA.

		VG	VF	UNC
S1987	2 CENTS 1938. Orange. Rural house at ctr. Back dk. green. *(S/M #H164-50).*	6.00	17.50	55.00
S1988	3 CENTS 1938. Red. Back blue. *(S/M #H164-51).*	6.00	17.50	55.00

		VG	VF	UNC
S1989	10 CENTS 1938. Blue. Shelter at lower r. Back orange and brown. *(S/M #H164-52).*	2.50	7.50	22.50
S1990	20 CENTS 1938. Green. Back brown. *(S/M #H164-53).*	10.00	30.00	—
S1991	50 CENTS 1938. Brown. Railway girder bridge at ctr. Back green and blue. *(S/M #H164-54).*	10.00	30.00	—

1940 ISSUE

#S1992-S1994 printer: CMPA.

		VG	VF	UNC
S1992	10 CENTS 1940. Blue. Pavilion at l. Back brown and blue. *(S/M #H164-60).*	6.00	17.50	55.00

		VG	VF	UNC
S1993	20 CENTS 1940. Violet. Palace garden at l. Back green and m/c. *(S/M #H164-61).*	3.00	9.00	27.00
S1994	50 CENTS 1940. Red. Fortress gate at l. Back orange, dk. olive-green and dk. blue. *(S/M #H164-62).*			
	a. Issued note.	10.00	30.00	—
	s1. Specimen. Red Chinese character ovpt. on back. W/o serial # or sign. seals.	—	Unc	65.00
	s2. Specimen. Dk. blue Chinese character ovpt. on face. W/serial #.	—	Unc	75.00

1949 ISSUE

#S1994C and S1995 printer: CHB.

		VG	VF	UNC
S1994C	10 CENTS 1949. Gray. SYS at l. Back brown. *(S/M #H164-68).*	—	25.00	75.00
S1994D	20 CENTS 1949. Bldg. at l. *(S/M #H164-69).*	—	30.00	90.00
S1995	50 CENTS 1949. Red-violet. SYS at ctr. *(S/M #H164-70).*	—	20.00	60.00

HUNAN INDUSTRIAL BANK

行銀業實南湖

Hu Nan Shih Yeh Yin Hang

1912 TAEL ISSUE

#S1996 and S1997 printer: CNPC.

		GOOD	FINE	XF
S1996	1 TAEL 1912. Green and orange. Back black. *(S/M #H165-1).*	90.00	270.00	—

		GOOD	FINE	XF
S1997	5 TAELS 1912. Modern office bldg. at l., rural view w/mountains at r. *(S/M #H165-2).*	—	—	—

1912 COPPER COIN ISSUE

		GOOD	FINE	XF
S1998	100 COPPERS 1912. Blue. Back green. *(S/M #H165-).*	15.00	45.00	—

1912 YÜAN ISSUE

		GOOD	FINE	XF
S1998E	**1 YÜAN** 1912. *(S/M #H165-).*	—	—	—

1913 ISSUE

		GOOD	FINE	XF
S1999	**20 COPPERS** 1913. Brown and yellow. Back olive; sailing ship at ctr. *(S/M #H165-10).*	22.50	67.50	—
S2000	**30 COPPERS** 1913. Green and yellow. *HUNAN. (S/M #H165-).*	35.00	110.00	—

1916 COPPER COIN ISSUES

		GOOD	FINE	XF
S2005	**100 COPPERS** 1916. Black and orange. Bearded man at l., pagoda at r. Back orange; cattle at ctr. *Changsha. (S/M #H165-20).*	25.00	75.00	—
S2006	**100 COPPERS** 1916. Blue and green. Similar to #S2005. *(S/M #H165-21).*	20.00	60.00	—

1916 YÜAN ISSUE

		GOOD	FINE	XF
S2008	**1 DOLLAR** 1916. Green. Back brown. *Changsha. (S/M #H165-30).*	35.00	110.00	—

1917 COPPER COIN ISSUE

		GOOD	FINE	XF
S2011	**200 COPPERS** 1917. Countryside at l., house at r. House by shoreline at ctr. on back. *(S/M #H165-).*	45.00	135.00	—

HUNAN TREASURY

湖南定期有利金庫証券

Hu Nan Ting Ch'i Yu Li Chin K'u Cheng Chüan

1920 INTEREST-BEARING TERM CERTIFICATES ISSUES

#S2016-S2020 printer: HODP.

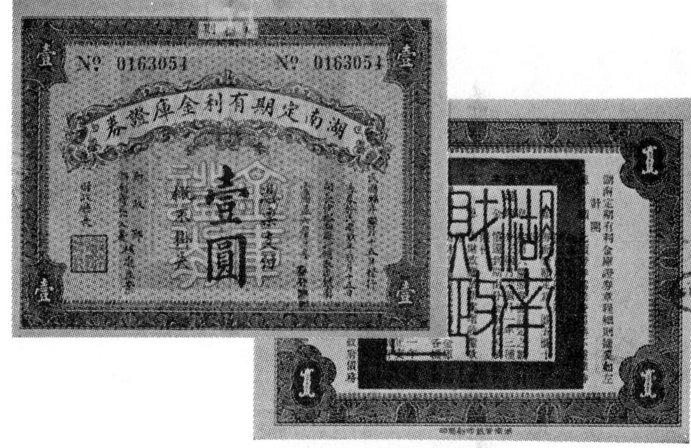

		VG	VF	UNC
S2016	**1 YÜAN** 15.2.1920. Blue and green. Back green and red. *(S/M #H166-1).*	30.00	90.00	—
S2017	**1 YÜAN** 1920. Brown. Back brown and red. *(S/M #H166-2).*	30.00	90.00	—

		VG	VF	UNC
S2018	**5 YÜAN** 15.2.1920. Brown and green. Back blue and red. *(S/M #H166-3).*	30.00	100.00	—
S2019	**5 YÜAN** 1920. Violet and yellow. Back orange and red. *(S/M #H166-4).*	17.00	50.00	—

		VG	VF	Unc
S2020	**10 Yüan** 1920. Green. Back brown and red. *(S/M #H166-5).*	20.00	60.00	—

Hunan Bank
Hunan Provincial Bank

湖南銀行
Hu Nan Yin Hang

1912 Copper Coin Issue

		Good	Fine	XF
S2022	**20 Coppers** Jan. 1912. *(S/M #H167-0.7).*	20.00	60.00	—
S2022A	**30 Coppers** 1912. Violet on ochre unpt. Back blue. *(S/M #H167-0.8).*	20.00	60.00	—

		Good	Fine	XF
S2023	**50 Coppers** Jan. 1912. Green and yellow. Back violet. Printer: SHBC. *(S/M #H167-1).*	20.00	60.00	—

		Good	Fine	XF
S2027	**100 Coppers** 1.1.1912. Green, black and brown. Facing peacocks at upper l. and r. Back gray-green. *(S/M #H167-2).*	15.00	45.00	—

1912 Yüan Issue

		Good	Fine	XF
S2029	**1 Yüan** 1912. Brown and m/c. Back brown. *(S/M #H167-10).*	15.00	45.00	—
S2030	**5 Yüan** 1912. Brown and m/c. Back brown. *(S/M #H167-11).*	20.00	60.00	—
S2031	**10 Yüan** 1912. Brown and m/c. Back brown. *(S/M #H167-12).*	25.00	75.00	—

1912 Tael Issue

#S2032-S2034 facing peacocks at upper l. and upper r.

		Good	Fine	XF
S2032	**1 Tael** 1.1.1912. Violet, black and brown. Back violet. *(S/M #H167-20).*	15.00	45.00	—

		Good	Fine	XF
S2033	**5 Taels** 1.1.1912. Violet and black. Back violet. *(S/M #H167-21).*	30.00	90.00	—
S2034	**10 Taels** 1.1.1912. Violet and black. Back violet. *(S/M #H167-22).*	50.00	150.00	—

1913 Copper Coin Issues

#S2036-S2041 black text. Lg. red circular seal on back.

		Good	Fine	XF
S2036	**20 Coppers** 1913. Green and yellow. Back blue. Printer: CMPA. *(S/M #H167-30).*	10.00	30.00	—
S2037	**30 Coppers** 1913. Brown on yellow unpt. Back blue. Printer: TYPC. *(S/M #H167-31).*	12.00	36.00	—
S2039	**100 Coppers** 1913. Blue on yellow unpt. Back green. Printer: CMPA. *(S/M #H167-32).*	12.00	35.00	—

		Good	Fine	XF
S2040	**100 Coppers** 1913. Blue on yellow-orange unpt. Back olive-green. *(S/M #H167-33).*	8.50	30.00	—
S2041	**100 Coppers** 1913. Like #S2040 but dk. blue on pink unpt. Back brown-violet. *(S/M #H167-34).*	8.50	30.00	—

1914 Copper Coin Issue

		Good	Fine	XF
S2042	**30 Coppers** 1914. Brown and green. *(S/M #H167-37).*	15.00	45.00	—

1915 Copper Coin Issue

#S2045-S2048 printer: CCLA.

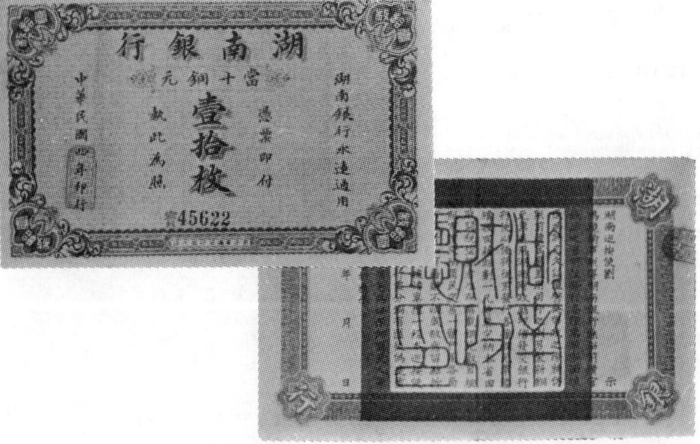

		Good	Fine	XF
S2045	**10 Coppers** 1915. Blue and red. Back green. *(S/M #H167-40).*	10.00	35.00	—
S2046	**20 Coppers** 1915. Green and orange. Back violet. *(S/M #H167-41).*	12.50	40.00	—

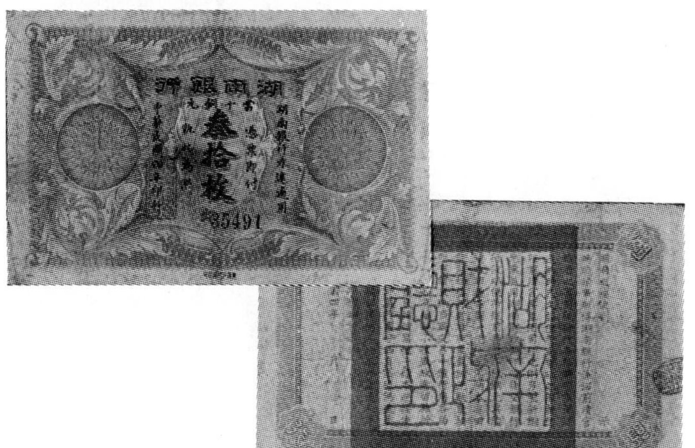

		Good	Fine	XF
S2047	**30 Coppers** 1915. Red and blue. Back brown. *(S/M #H167-42).*	15.00	45.00	—
S2048	**50 Coppers** 1915. Red and green. Back blue. *(S/M #H167-43).*	15.00	45.00	—

		Good	Fine	XF
S2050	**100 Coppers** 1.4.1915. Green. House at l., road to walled city at r. Back brown and m/c. Printer: ABNC. *(S/M #H167-44).*	12.00	35.00	—
S2053	**10 Cents** 1915. Brown and green. *(S/M #H167-47).*	—	—	—

1917 Copper Coin Issues

#S2056-S2060 temple at l., road to walled city at r. Bank bldg. at ctr. on back. *Changsha.* Printer: CMPA.

		Good	Fine	XF
S2056	**10 Coppers** 1.1.1917. Blue and red. Back olive. *(S/M #H167-50).*	7.00	20.00	60.00
S2057	**20 Coppers** 1.1.1917. Blue and brown. Back brown. *(S/M #H167-51).*	9.00	27.00	—

		Good	Fine	XF
S2058	**30 Coppers** 1.1.1917. Green and red. Back brown and blue. *(S/M #H167-52).*	10.00	30.00	—
S2059	**50 Coppers** 1.1.1917. Black and yellow. Back brown and green. *(S/M #H167-53).*	10.00	30.00	—
S2060	**100 Coppers** 1.1.1917. Brown and blue. Back green and yellow. *(S/M #H167-54).*	12.50	40.00	—
S2061	**100 Coppers** 1917. Green and orange. Uniface. *Hankow. (S/M #H167-55).*	12.50	40.00	—

1918 Copper Coin Issue

		Good	Fine	XF
S2065	**10 Coppers** 1918. Brown and green. Back blue and yellow. *(S/M #H167-60).*	12.50	40.00	—

1918 Dollar Issue

		Good	Fine	XF
S2067	**50 Cents** 1918. Green on orange unpt. Bldg. at ctr. Back blue. *(S/M #H167-69).*	25.00	75.00	—
S2068	**1 Dollar** 1918. Green and yellow. Back green. *(S/M #H167-70).*	15.00	45.00	—
S2069	**5 Dollars** 1918. Gray and green. *(S/M #H167-71).*	22.50	67.50	—

ND Dollar Issue

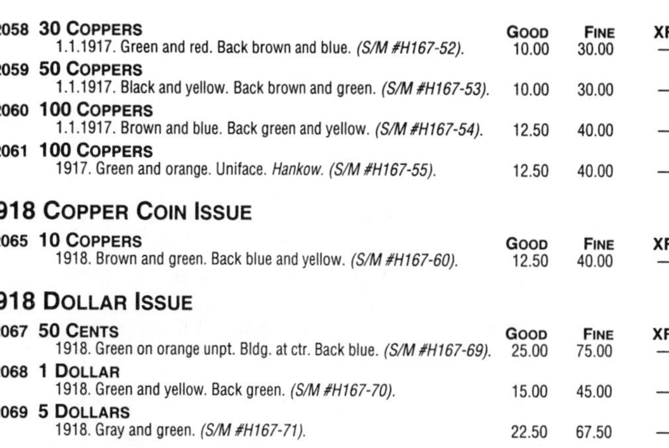

		Good	Fine	XF
S2073	**1 Dollar** ND. Green on violet unpt. Shrine at ctr. Back brown. Printer: BEPP. *HANKOW. (S/M #H167-76).*	40.00	120.00	—

		Good	Fine	XF
S2078	**5 Dollars** ND. Blue. Road to walled city at ctr. Printer: BEPP. W/o place name. Specimen. *(S/M #H167-77).*	—	Unc	75.00

HUPEH GOVERNMENT CASH BANK
HUPEH PROVINCIAL BANK

湖北官錢局
Hu Pei Kuan Ch'ien Chü

1896 ISSUE

		GOOD	FINE	XF
S2081	**1000 CASH** Yr. 22 (1896). Lt. blue w/black text and red seals. Facing dragons at l. and r. Vertical format. *(S/M #H171-0.5).*	60.00	180.00	—

1899 ISSUE

		GOOD	FINE	XF
S2085	**1 CH'UAN** Yr. 25 (1899); Yr. 26 (1900). Blue and yellow. Back brown. *(S/M #H171-1).*			
	a. Handwritten date. Yr. 25 (1899).	135.00	400.00	—
	b. Printed date. Yr. 26 (1900).	120.00	360.00	—

1904 ISSUE

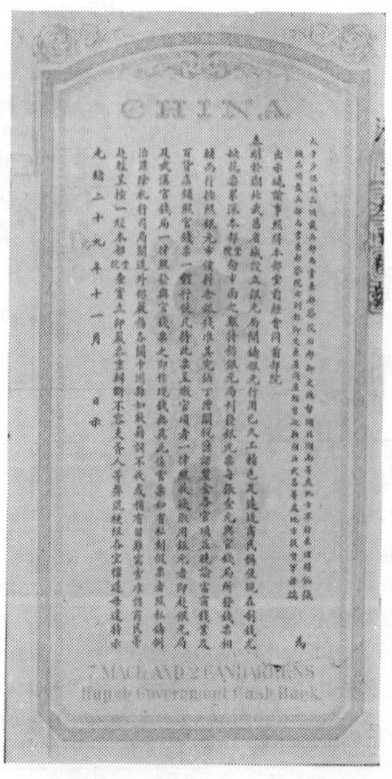

		GOOD	FINE	XF
S2090	**1 YÜAN** Yr. 30 (1904). Black and green. Dragons facing at upper l. and r. Back orange. Vertical format. *S/M #H171-10).*	75.00	225.00	—
S2091	**5 YÜAN** Yr. 30 (1904). *(S/M #H171-11).*	Reported Not Confirmed		

1904 TAEL ISSUE

		GOOD	FINE	XF
S2092	**10 TAELS** Yr. 30 (1904). Black on m/c unpt. 2 portr. w/2 dragons. *(S/M #H171-15).*	—	—	—

1906 ISSUE

		GOOD	FINE	XF
S2093	**1 CH'UAN** Yr. 32 (1906)/Yr. 25. Green and yellow. 2 facing dragons. Back orange. *(S/M #H171-17).*	—	—	—

1908 ISSUE

		GOOD	FINE	XF
S2094	**1 CH'UAN** Yr. 34 (1908)/Yr. 25. Green and yellow. Back orange. *(S/M #H171-20).*	75.00	225.00	—

1914 ISSUE

		GOOD	FINE	XF
S2098	**100 COPPERS** 1914. Green and black. House at l., tower at r. Back green; red seal. *(S/M #H171-30).*	4.00	12.00	36.00

HUPEH PROVINCIAL BANK

湖北省銀行
Hu Pei Sheng Yin Hang

1928 ISSUE

		GOOD	FINE	XF
S2101	**1 CHIAO = 10 CENTS** 1928. Dk. blue. Pagoda at upper ctr. Back orange. 3 sign. varieties. Vertical format. Printer: WHPP. *(S/M #H173-10).*	7.00	20.00	—

		GOOD	FINE	XF
S2102	**2 CHIAO = 20 CENTS** 1928. Red. Tower at ctr. Back brown. Printer: CCCA. 2 sign. varieties. *(S/M #H173-11).*	7.00	20.00	—

	Good	Fine	XF
S2103 5 Chiao = 50 Cents 1928. Green. Pagoda at l. Printer: WHPP. *(S/M #H173-12).*	15.00	50.00	—

1929 Issue

#S2104-S2106 *Hankow*. Printer: ABNC.

	Good	Fine	XF
S2104 1 Yüan 1929. Violet and m/c. Pagoda at r. Back blue. *(S/M #H173-20).*			
a. Issued note.	15.00	45.00	135.00
p. Proof.	—	Unc	185.00
S2105 5 Yüan 1929. Green and m/c. Pagoda at ctr. Back orange. *(S/M #H173-21a).*			
a. Issued note.	17.50	55.00	—
p. Proof.	—	Unc	225.00
S2106 10 Yüan 1929. Red and m/c. Pagoda at l. Back violet. *(S/M #H173-22a).*			
a. Issued note.	22.50	67.50	—
p. Proof.	—	Unc	265.00

NOTE: For #S2104-S2106 w/additional ovpt. see Agricultural Bank of the Four Provinces, #A88-A90 and Farmers Bank of China #466-468, Vol. 2.

1932 Issue

	Good	Fine	XF
S2108 5 Chiao = 50 Cents 1932. Green. Pagoda at l. Shoreline at ctr. on back. Printer: CCCA. *HANKOW. (S/M #H17-30).*	10.00	30.00	90.00

1936 Issue

#S2110 and S2112 printer: TYPC.

	Good	Fine	XF
S2110 1 Chiao = 10 Cents 1936. Blue. Tower at ctr. Back green and orange. *(S/M #H173-40).*	5.00	15.00	45.00

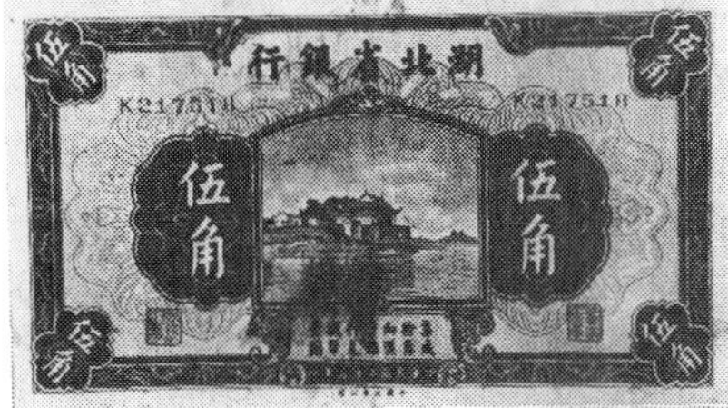

	Good	Fine	XF
S2112 50 Cents 1936. Blue. Waterfront bldg. at ctr. Back green; gateway at ctr. *(S/M #H173-41).*	5.00	15.00	45.00

1940 Issue

	Good	Fine	XF
S2115 5 Cents 1940. Orange. *(S/M #H173-50).*	7.50	22.50	67.50
S2119 1 Yüan 1940. *(S/M #H173-).*	Reported Not Confirmed		

1941 Issue

#S2122-S2125 printer: TTBC.

	Good	Fine	XF
S2122 1 Yüan 1941. Olive. *(S/M #H173-60).*	6.00	17.50	55.00

	Good	Fine	XF
S2123 5 Yüan 1941. Blue and yellow. Tower at ctr. Back blue. *(S/M #H173-61).*	8.00	25.00	75.00
S2124 10 Yüan 1941. Green. *(S/M #H173-62).*	12.50	37.50	110.00

Hupeh Government Mint

湖北銀元局

Hu Pei Yin Yüan Chü

1894 Issue

	Good	Fine	XF
S2126 1 Tiao Yr. 20 (1894). *(S/M #H175-1).*	90.00	270.00	—

		GOOD	FINE	XF
S2127	**5 TIAO** Yr. 20 (1894). *(S/M #H175-2).*	90.00	270.00	—
S2128	**10 TIAO** Yr. 20 (1894). *(S/M #H175-3).*	120.00	360.00	—
S2130	**1 TAEL** Yr. 20 (1894). *(S/M #H175-10.*	120.00	360.00	—
S2131	**3 TAELS** Yr. 20 (1894). *(S/M #H175-11.*	150.00	450.00	—
S2132	**5 TAELS** Yr. 20 (1894). *(S/M #H175-12.*	180.00	540.00	—
S2133	**10 TAELS** Yr. 20 (1894). *(S/M #H175-13.*	200.00	600.00	—

1899 ISSUE

		VG	VF	UNC
S2135	**1 DOLLAR = 7 MACE 2 CANDAREENS** Yr. 25 (1899). Green and m/c. Facing dragons holding obverse and reverse of silver dragon dollar at upper l. and r. Back orange; black text. Vertical format. *(S/M #H175-20).*	180.00	650.00	—
S2136	**5 DOLLARS** Yr. 25 (1899). *(S/M #H175-21).*	180.00	550.00	—
S2137	**10 DOLLARS** Yr. 25 (1899). *(S/M #H175-22).*	200.00	600.00	—

1900 ISSUE

		VG	VF	UNC
S2139	**1 DOLLAR** Yr. 26 (1900). *(S/M #H175-30).*	150.00	450.00	—
S2140	**5 DOLLARS** Yr. 26 (1900). *(S/M #H175-31).*	150.00	450.00	—
S2141	**10 DOLLARS** Yr. 26 (1900). *(S/M #H175-32).*	180.00	550.00	—

1909 ISSUE

		VG	VF	UNC
S2142	**1 DOLLAR** 1909. *(S/M #H175-40).*	120.00	360.00	—
S2143	**5 DOLLARS** 1909. *(S/M #H175-41).*	135.00	400.00	—
S2144	**10 DOLLARS** 1909. *(S/M #H175-42).*	175.00	525.00	—

ILI OFFICIAL CURRENCY BUREAU

局總錢官犂伊

I Li Kuan Ch'ien Tsung Chü

局錢官犂伊

I Li Kuan Ch'ien Chü

1899 ISSUE

		VG	VF	UNC
S2145	**200 CASH** Yr. 25 (1899). Cloth. *(S/M #I21.5-3).*	—	—	—
S2145A	**300 CASH** Yr. 25 (1899). Cloth. *(S/M #I21.5-4).*	—	—	—
S2145B	**500 CASH** Yr. 25 (1899). Cloth. *(S/M #I21.5-5).*			
S2145C	**1000 CASH** Yr. 25 (1899). Cloth. Vertical format. Uniface. *(S/M #I21.5-6).*			

1909 ISSUE

#S2149 and S2150 printer: PYOG.

		GOOD	FINE	XF
S2149	**1000 CASH** Yr. 1 (1909). Blue and black. Dragons facing at upper l. and r. Back brown. Vertical format. *(S/M #I22-1).*	60.00	180.00	—
S2150	**2000 CASH** Yr. 1 (1909). *(S/M #I22-2).*	80.00	240.00	—

1914 ISSUE

		GOOD	FINE	XF
S2152	**200 CASH** 1/1/1914. Black and green. Facing Chinze at top and bottom. Uniface. Vertical format. *(S/M #I22-12).*	—	—	—

1917 ISSUE

		VG	VF	UNC
S2153	**5 CH'IEN** 1917. Cloth. Vertical format. *(S/M #I21.5-15).*	180.00	540.00	—

HSING YEH BANK OF JEHOL
INDUSTRIAL DEVELOPMENT BANK OF JEHOL

行銀業興河熱
Je Ho Hsing Yeh Yin Hang
行銀業興
Hsing Yeh Yin Hang

ND ISSUE

#S2155-S2158 Temple at ctr. Landscape w/pagoda at ctr. on back.

		GOOD	FINE	XF
S2155	**10 COPPERS** ND. Olive. *(S/M #J1-0.5).*	30.00	90.00	—

		GOOD	FINE	XF
S2156	**20 COPPERS** ND. Dk. green. *(S/M #J1-1).*	30.00	90.00	—
S2158	**100 COPPERS** ND. Gray. Back gray. *(S/M #J1-2).*	30.00	100.00	—

1918; 1919 ISSUE

		GOOD	FINE	XF
S2160	**10 CENTS** 1918. *(S/M #J1-10).*	Reported Not Confirmed		
S2161	**20 CENTS** 1918. *(S/M #J1-11).*	Reported Not Confirmed		

		GOOD	FINE	XF
S2162	**30 CENTS** 1918. Purple and black on brown unpt. Temple at ctr. Back brown and blue; city gate at ctr.	40.00	120.00	—
S2163	**40 CENTS** 1918. *(S/M #J1-13).*	Reported Not Confirmed		
S2164	**50 CENTS** 1918. *(S/M #J1-14).*	Reported Not Confirmed		
S2165	**1 DOLLAR** 1919. *(S/M #J1-20).*	Reported Not Confirmed		
S2166	**5 DOLLARS** 1919. *(S/M #J1-21).*	Reported Not Confirmed		
S2167	**10 DOLLARS** 1919. *(S/M #J1-22).*	Reported Not Confirmed		

1920 ISSUES

#S2168-S2172 printer: BEPP.

		GOOD	FINE	XF
S2168	**1 DOLLAR** 1920. Green. House at ctr. Back orange; bldgs. at ctr. w/text: *EXCHANGE NOTE* at r.			
	a. *Chao Yang. (S/M #J1-30a).*	30.00	90.00	—
	b. *Chao Yang/Tientsin. (S/M #J1-30b).*	30.00	90.00	—
	c. *Chih Feng (Hsien). (S/M #J1-30c).*	30.00	90.00	—
	d. *Chih Feng/Tientsin. (S/M #J1-30n).*	30.00	90.00	—
	e. *Ching P'eng. (S/M #J1-30d).*	30.00	90.00	—
	f. *Chui Tzu Shan. (S/M #J1-30e).*	30.00	90.00	—
	g. *JEHOL. (S/M #J1-30f).*	12.50	37.50	—
	h. *JEHOL - Payable in Fengtien. (S/M #J1-30g).*	20.00	60.00	—
	i. *K'ai Lu. (S/M #J1-30h).*	30.00	90.00	—
	j. *Ling Yuan. (S/M #J1-30i).*	30.00	90.00	—
	k. *Ling Yuan/Tientsin. (S/M #J1-30j).*	30.00	90.00	—
	l. *Lung Hua. (S/M #J1-30k).*	30.00	90.00	—
	m. *P'ing Ch'uan. (S/M #J1-30l).*	30.00	90.00	—
	n. *P'ing Ch'uan/Tientsin. (S/M #J1-30m).*	30.00	90.00	—
	o. *Tientsin. (S/M #J1-30o).*	30.00	90.00	—

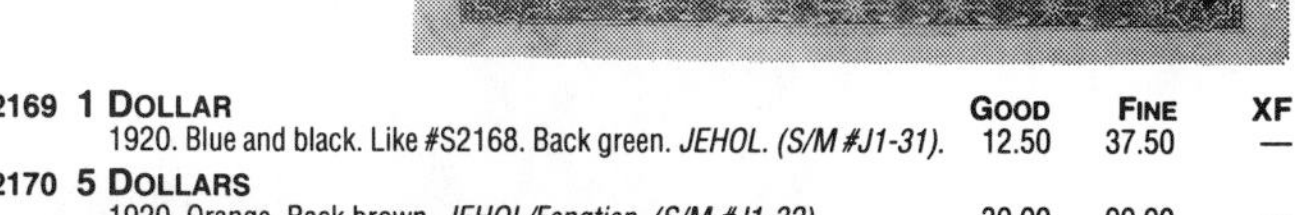

		GOOD	FINE	XF
S2169	**1 DOLLAR** 1920. Blue and black. Like #S2168. Back green. *JEHOL. (S/M #J1-31).*	12.50	37.50	—
S2170	**5 DOLLARS** 1920. Orange. Back brown. *JEHOL/Fengtien. (S/M #J1-32).*	30.00	90.00	—

		GOOD	FINE	XF
S2171	**5 DOLLARS** 1920. Brown. Like #S2169. Back orange.			
	a. *Chih Feng (Hsien). (S/M J1-33c).*	30.00	90.00	—
	b. *JEHOL. (S/M #J1-33f).*	12.00	35.00	—
	c. *K'ai Lu. (S/M #J1-33h).*	30.00	90.00	—

	GOOD	FINE	XF
S2172 10 DOLLARS			
1920. Brown. Like #S2168. Back violet.			
a. *JEHOL. (S/M #J1-34f).*	12.00	35.00	—
b. *Chih Feng/Tientsin. (S/M #J1-34n).*	30.00	90.00	—
c. *P'ing Ch'uan/Tientsin. (S/M #J1-34m).*	30.00	90.00	—
d. *P'ing Ch'uan/JEHOL. (S/M #J1-33p).*	30.00	90.00	—

1921 COPPER COIN ISSUE

#S2174-S2178 hillside fortress at ctr. Pagoda in trees at ctr. on back. Printer: BEPA.

	GOOD	FINE	XF
S2174 10 COPPERS ND (1921). Pale olive-green w/back text. *(S/M #J1-40).*	20.00	60.00	250.00
S2174A 10 COPPERS ND (1921). Orange w/black text. *(S/M #J1-40.5).*	20.00	60.00	250.00
S2175 20 COPPERS ND (1921). Orange w/black text. *(S/M #J1-41).*	20.00	60.00	—

	GOOD	FINE	XF
S2175A 20 COPPERS ND (1921). Dk. green w/black text. Similar to #S2175 w/Chinese characters "Copper Coin Exchange Money" in bottom ctr. panel. Violet ovpt: *Chao Yang. (S/M #J1-41.5).*	25.00	75.00	—

	GOOD	FINE	XF
S2176 50 COPPERS ND (1921). Brown w/black text. *(S/M #J1-42).*	25.00	75.00	—

	GOOD	FINE	XF
S2177 100 COPPERS ND (1921). Dull olive-green w/black text. *(S/M #J1-43).*	15.00	50.00	—
S2177A 100 COPPERS ND (1921). Dull purple w/black text.			
a. Issued note. *(S/M #J1-43.5a).*	15.00	50.00	—
b. W/additional Chinese character ovpt: *Chao Yang. (S/M #J1-43.5b).*	20.00	60.00	—

	GOOD	FINE	XF
S2177B 200 COPPERS ND (1921). Dk. blue w/black text. *(S/M #J1-43.7).*	30.00	90.00	—
S2178 500 COPPERS ND (1921). *(S/M #J1-44).*	40.00	120.00	—

1922 ISSUE

#S2179-S2181 printer: BEPP.

	GOOD	FINE	XF
S2179 1 YÜAN 1922. Specimen. *(S/M #J1-50).*	—	Unc	65.00
S2180 5 YÜAN 1922. Specimen. *S/M #J1-51).*	—	Unc	75.00
S2181 10 YÜAN 1922. Specimen. *(S/M #J1-52).*	—	Unc	85.00

1923 ISSUE

#S2183-S2185 printer: BEPP.

	GOOD	FINE	XF
S2183 1 YÜAN			
1.6.1923.			
a. *CHENG TE FU. (S/M #J1-60a).*	22.50	67.50	—
b. *KIEN P'ING HSIEN. (S/M #J1-60b).*	22.50	67.50	—
c. *CH'IH FENG HSIEN. (S/M #J1-60c).*	22.50	67.50	—
d. *FENG NING. (S/M #J1-60d).*	22.50	67.50	—
e. *LINGYUAN. (S/M #J1-60e).*	22.50	67.50	—
f. *LUNG HUA. (S/M #J1-60f).*	22.50	67.50	—
g. *P'ING CH'UAN. (S/M #J1-60g).*	22.50	67.50	—
h. *SUI TUNG HSIEN. (S/M #J1-60h).*	22.50	67.50	—
i. *WEI CH'ANG. (S/M #J1-60i).*	22.50	67.50	—
S2184 5 YÜAN			
1.6.1923. Green. Great wall at ctr.			
a. *KIEN P'ING HSIEN. (S/M #J1-61a).*	22.50	67.50	—
b. *FENG NING. (S/M #J1-61b).*	22.50	67.50	—
c. *CHAO YANG FU. (S/M #J1-61c).*	22.50	67.50	—
d. *CHING P'ENG. (S/M #J1-61 d).*	22.50	67.50	—
e. *FU HSING HSIEN. (S/M #J1-61e).*	22.50	67.50	—
f. *LUAN PING. (S/M #J1-61f).*	22.50	67.50	—
g. *LING SE. (S/M #J1-61g).*	22.50	67.50	—
h. *KAI LU. (S/M #J1-61h).*	22.50	67.50	—
i. *CH'IH FENG HSIEN. (S/M #J1-61i).*	22.50	67.50	—

		GOOD	FINE	XF
S2185	**10 YÜAN**			
	1.6.1923. Dk. blue. Great Wall at ctr.			
	a. *CHENGTEHFU. (S/M #J1-62a).*	30.00	90.00	—
	b. *CH'IH FENG HSIEN. (S/M #J1-62b).*	30.00	90.00	—
	c. *LINGYUAN. (S/M #J1-62c).*	30.00	90.00	—
	d. *PING CH'UAN. (S/M #J1-62d).*	30.00	90.00	—
	e. *WEI CH'ANG. (S/M #J1-62e).*	30.00	90.00	—
	f. *CHAO YANG FU. (S/M #J1-62f).*	30.00	90.00	—
	g. *FU HSING HSIEN. (S/M #H1-62g).*	30.00	90.00	—
	h. *LING SE. (S/M #J1-62h).*	30.00	90.00	—
	i. *KIEN P'ING HSIEN. (S/M #J1-62i).*	30.00	90.00	—

1925 ISSUE

#S2186-S2188 Great Wall at ctr. Printer: BEPP.

		GOOD	FINE	XF
S2186	**1 YÜAN**			
	1925. Violet.			
	a. Sign. P. C. Kao. *S/M #J1-70a).*	12.50	37.50	110.00
	b. Sign. Y. F. Wang. *(S/M #J1-70b).*	12.50	37.50	110.00
S2187	**5 YÜAN**			
	1925. Yellow. Great Wall at ctr.			
	a. Sign. P. C. Kao. *(S/M #J1-71a).*	12.50	37.50	110.00
	b. Sing. Y. F. Wang. *(S/M #J1-71b).*	12.50	37.50	110.00

		GOOD	FINE	XF
S2188	**10 YÜAN**			
	1925. Green. Like #S2187.			
	a. Sign. P. C. Kao. *(S/M #J1-72a).*	12.50	37.50	110.00
	b. Sign. Y. F. Wang. *(S/M #J1-72b).*	12.50	37.50	110.00

1926 ISSUE

#S2189 and S2190 printer: BEPP.

		GOOD	FINE	XF
S2189	**1 YÜAN**			
	1.9.1926. Green on m/c unpt. Bldg. at l. *(S/M #J1-73).*	30.00	100.00	—
S2190	**5 YÜAN**			
	1.9.1926. Blue on m/c unpt. *(S/M #J1-74).*	37.50	110.00	—

1927 ISSUE

		GOOD	FINE	XF
S2191	**10 CENTS**			
	1.4.1927. Black and yellow. Cottage at ctr. *(S/M #J1-76).*	24.00	72.00	—

		GOOD	FINE	XF
S2191C	**5 DOLLARS**			
	1.11.1927.	—	—	—

1928 ISSUE

		GOOD	FINE	XF
S2193	**10 CENTS**			
	1928. Orange and gray. Printer: BEPP. *(S/M #J1-78).*	24.00	72.00	—

#S2197-S2199 printer: BEPP.

S2197	**1 YÜAN** 1928. *(S/M #J1-80).*	Reported Not Confirmed
S2198	**5 YÜAN** 1928. *(S/M #J1-81).*	Reported Not Confirmed
S2199	**10 YÜAN** 1928. *(S/M #J1-82).*	Reported Not Confirmed

1929 FIRST ISSUE

#S2201-S2206 w/o imprint.

		GOOD	FINE	XF
S2201	**10 CENTS**			
	1929. Green and red. House at ctr. Back green. *(S/M #J1-90).*	25.00	80.00	—
S2202	**20 CENTS** 1929. *(S/M #J1-92).*	Reported Not Confirmed		
S2203	**50 CENTS** 1929. *(S/M #J1-94).*	Reported Not Confirmed		
S2204	**1 YÜAN** 1929. *(S/M #J1-100).*	Reported Not Confirmed		
S2205	**5 YÜAN** 1929. *(S/M #J1-101).*	Reported Not Confirmed		
S2206	**10 YÜAN** 1929. *(S/M #J1-102).*	Reported Not Confirmed		

1929 SECOND ISSUE

#S2207-S2209 printer: BEPP.

		GOOD	FINE	XF
S2207	**10 CENTS** 1929. *(S/M #J1-91).*	Reported Not Confirmed		
S2208	**20 CENTS** 1929. *(S/M #J1-93).*	Reported Not Confirmed		
S2209	**50 CENTS** 1929. *(S/M #J1-95).*	Reported Not Confirmed		
S2211	**5 YÜAN** 1929. *(S/M #J1-97).*	Reported Not Confirmed		

1930 ISSUE

#S2212 and S2212A waterfront bldgs. at l. and r.

#S2214-S2216 printer: BEPP.

		GOOD	FINE	XF
S2212	**10 CENTS** 1930. Red. *(S/M #J1-108).*	20.00	60.00	—
S2212A	**20 CENTS** 1930. Purple. *(S/M #J1-109).*	20.00	60.00	—
S2213	**50 CENTS** 1930. *(S/M #J1-110).*	30.00	90.00	—
S2214	**1 YÜAN** 1930. *(S/M #J1-120).*	Reported Not Confirmed		
S2215	**5 YÜAN** 1930. *(S/M #J1-121).*	Reported Not Confirmed		
S2216	**10 YÜAN** 1930. *(S/M #J1-122).*	Reported Not Confirmed		

1931 ISSUE

#S2220-S2222 printer: BEPP.

		GOOD	FINE	XF
S2217	**10 CENTS** 1931. Green and red. Like #S2201. Back green. *(S/M #J1-130).*	30.00	90.00	—
S2218	**20 CENTS** 1931. *(S/M #J1-131).*	Reported Not Confirmed		
S2219	**50 CENTS** 1931. *(S/M #J1-132).*	Reported Not Confirmed		
S2220	**1 YÜAN** 1931. *(S/M #J1-140).*	Reported Not Confirmed		
S2221	**5 YÜAN** 1931. *(S/M #J1-141).*	Reported Not Confirmed		
S2222	**10 YÜAN** 1931. *(S/M #J1-142).*	Reported Not Confirmed		

KAN SEN BANK OF KIANGSI
PROVINCIAL BANK OF KIANGSI

贛省銀行
Kan Sheng Yin Hang

1912 ISSUE

		GOOD	FINE	XF
S2223	**100 CENTS** 1912. Black and yellow. Facing dragons at top. Shoreline at ctr. on back. *Kiangsi.* Vertical format. *(S/M #K2-0.3).*	—	—	—

1923; 1924 ISSUE

		GOOD	FINE	XF
S2224	**10 CENTS** 1923. Orange. Similar to #S2223. *Kiangsi. (S/M #K2-0.6).*	—	—	—

#S2225-S2227 gazebo, house along shoreline. Village within wall at ctr. on back.

		GOOD	FINE	XF
S2225	**1 DOLLAR** 1924. Black on tan and m/c unpt. *(S/M #K2-1).*	60.00	180.00	—
S2226	**5 DOLLARS** 1924. Violet on m/c unpt. Back red. *(S/M #K2-2).*	45.00	135.00	—

		GOOD	FINE	XF
S2227	**10 DOLLARS** 1924. Green on m/c unpt. Back orange. *(S/M #K2-3).*	22.50	67.50	—

NOTE: #S2225-S2227 w/additional ovpt. see Kiangsi Regional Bank #S1090-S1093.

1925 ISSUE

		GOOD	FINE	XF
S2227A	**10 COPPERS** 1925. *(S/M #K2-5).*	20.00	60.00	—

		GOOD	FINE	XF
S2228	**10 CENTS** ND. Red and green. Pavilion in park at ctr. Back brown and yellow. *Nanchang. (S/M #K2-101).*	30.00	90.00	—

		GOOD	FINE	XF
S2231	**1 DOLLAR** ND. Green and m/c. Back brown. *Nanchang. (S/M #K2-20).*	40.00	120.00	—
S2232	**5 DOLLARS** ND. *Nanchang. (S/M #K2-21).*	40.00	120.00	—

		GOOD	FINE	XF
S2233	**10 DOLLARS** ND. Violet and m/c. Houses at ctr. Back green; houses along shoreline at ctr. *Nanchang. (S/M #K2-22).*	65.00	200.00	—

1926 ISSUE

		GOOD	FINE	XF
S2234	**1 DOLLAR** 1926. *(S/M #K2-30).*	Reported Not Confirmed		
S2235	**5 DOLLARS** 1926. *(S/M #K2-31).*	Reported Not Confirmed		
S2236	**10 DOLLARS** 1926. *(S/M #K2-32).*	Reported Not Confirmed		

MONETARY BUREAU OF GOVERNMENT KANSU

局錢官市平(省)肅甘

Kan Su (Sheng) P'ing Shih Kuan Ch'ien Chü

1928 ND ISSUE

		GOOD	FINE	XF
S2237	**10 COPPERS** ND (1928). *(S/M #K11-0.1).*	—	—	—

1932 ND ISSUE

		GOOD	FINE	XF
S2237D	**10 COPPERS** ND (1932). Green. Bldgs., mountains at ctr. *(S/M #K11-0.2).*	—	—	—
S2237E	**20 COPPERS** ND (1932). *(S/M #K11-0.3).*	—	—	—
S2237F	**50 COPPERS** ND (1932). *(S/M #K11-0.4).*	—	—	—

1932 ISSUE

		GOOD	FINE	XF
S2238	**50 COPPERS** 1932. Temple at ctr. *KANSU. (S/M #K11-0.5).*	15.00	45.00	—

1935 ISSUE

		GOOD	FINE	XF
S2240	**20 COPPERS** 1935. Blue and yellow. Back blue. Printer: TTBC. *Kansu Province. (S/M #K11-1).*	12.50	37.50	110.00
S2245	**50 CENTS** 1935. Red. Arch bridge at l., bridge to city at r. Back dk. green. *KANSU. (S/M #K11-10).*	12.50	37.50	—

KANSU PROVINCIAL BANK

局錢官市平(省)肅甘

Kan Su (Sheng) P'ing Shih Kuan Ch'ien Chü

1935 ISSUE

		GOOD	FINE	XF
S2246	**50 CENTS** 1935. Brown. Water wheels at ctr. Back blue. Printer: TTBC. *(S/M #K11-11).*	10.00	30.00	—

CANTON MUNICIPAL BANK

行銀立市市州廣

Kuang Chou Shih Shih Li Yin Hang

Founded in 1927. Notes were redeemed by the Central Bank of China in 1937.

1928 ISSUE

#S2251 *Deleted.*

#S2253-2255 arms at ctr. SYS at upper ctr. on back.

		GOOD	FINE	XF
S2253	**10 CENTS** 1.12.1928. Blue and red. Back red.			
	a. Chinese sign. in black.	15.00	45.00	—
	b. Red sign. over black sign.	15.00	45.00	—

#S2254 *Deleted.*

		GOOD	FINE	XF
S2255	**50 CENTS** 1.12.1928. Green and red.	—	—	—

1929-1932 DOLLAR ISSUE

#S2256-2259 face vertical. Back horizontal; SYS at ctr.

		GOOD	FINE	XF
S2256	**1 DOLLAR** 1931-32. Red-orange and green. Back orange. Printer: W&S.			
	a. 1.10.1931.	15.00	45.00	—
	b. 15.3.1932; 10.4.1932.	12.50	35.00	—

#S2257-2259 printer: ABNC.

		GOOD	FINE	XF
S2257	**5 DOLLARS** 1929; 1931. Red and m/c. Back green.			
	a. 1.9.1929.	25.00	75.00	—
	b. 1.7.1931.	20.00	50.00	—
S2258	**10 DOLLARS** 1929; 1931. Blue and m/c. Back brown.			
	a. 1.9.1929.	30.00	90.00	—
	b. 1.7.1931.	25.00	75.00	—
S2259	**50 DOLLARS** 1929; 1931. Violet and m/c. Back orange.			
	a. 1.9.1929.	—	—	—
	b. 1.7.1931.	80.00	180.00	—

1931 CENT ISSUE

		GOOD	FINE	XF
S2260	**10 CENTS** 1.10.1931. Green and red. 5-story bldg. at l. Back green.			
	a. Red seal centered below denomination.	—	—	—
	b. Red seal to l., new Chinese sign. at r. w/old Chinese sign. obliterated.	—	—	—

#S2265 *Deleted.* See #S2256a; #S2268 *Deleted.* See #S2257b; #S2269 *Deleted.* See #S2258b; #S2270 *Deleted.* See #S2259b.

1933 ISSUE

#S2276-2280 face vertical, back horizontal.

#S2276-2277 SYS at ctr. on face. Printer: ABNC.

		GOOD	FINE	XF
S2276	**10 CENTS** 1.5.1933. Red and yellow. Back blue; mausoleum of "72 Martyrs of the Yellow Flower Hill" at r.			
	a. Sign. Hsu and Ch'en.	—	—	—
	b. Sign. Huang and Ch'en.	—	—	—

		VG	VF	UNC
S2277	**20 CENTS** 1.5.1933. Orange on lt. blue unpt. Portr. SYS at ctr. Back black; modern bridge at l. ctr. *(S/M #K24-41).*	—	—	—

#S2278-S2280 SYS at ctr. on back.

		VG	VF	UNC
S2278	**1 DOLLAR** 1.5.1933. Lt. brown on pale green unpt. Monument at ctr. Back purple.			
	a. Chinese and English sign. w/red serial #. *(S/M #K24-50a).*	3.00	10.00	30.00
	b. Chinese sign. w/red serial #. *(S/M #K24-50c).*	3.00	10.00	30.00
	c. Chinese sign. w/dk. blue serial #. *(S/M #K24-50b).*	3.00	9.00	27.00
S2279	**5 DOLLARS** 1.5.1933. Green on pale lilac unpt. Lg. bldg. at upper ctr. Back red-violet.			
	a. Chinese and English sign. w/red serial #. *(S/M #K24-51a).*	4.00	12.00	35.00
	b. Chinese sign. w/red serial #. *(S/M #K24-51c).*	4.00	12.00	35.00
	c. Chinese sign. w/dk. blue serial #.*(S/M #K24-51b).*	3.00	9.00	27.00
S2280	**10 DOLLARS** 1.5.1933. Red on green and yellow unpt. Gov't. bldg. at ctr. Back olive.			
	a. Chinese and English sign. w/red serial #. *(S/M #K24-52a).*	26.50	80.00	240.00
	b. Chinese sign. w/red serial #. *(S/M #K24-52c).*	26.50	80.00	240.00
	c. Chinese sign. w/dk. blue serial #.*(S/M #K24-52b).*	20.00	60.00	180.00
S2281	**50 DOLLARS** 1933. Blue and black on m/c unpt. Public bldg. at ctr. Back orange. *(S/M #K24-53).*	25.00	75.00	—

1935 ISSUE

		VG	VF	UNC
S2285	**50 DOLLARS** 1935. Violet and m/c. *(S/M #K24-).*	Reported Not Confirmed		

KWANGSI OFFICIAL CURRENCY BUREAU

號錢銀官西廣

Kuang Hsi Kuan Yin Ch'ien Hao

1909 ISSUE

		VG	VF	UNC
S2287	**1 TAEL** Yr. 1 (1909). *Kweilin. (S/M #K31-1).*	120.00	360.00	—
S2289	**10 TAELS** Yr. 1 (1909). *Kweilin. (S/M #K31-2).*	135.00	400.00	—
S2290	**1 TAEL** Yr. 1 (1909). *Lungchow. (S/M #K31-10).*	120.00	360.00	—
S2292	**10 TAELS** Yr. 1 (1909). *Lungchow. (S/M #K31-11).*	135.00	400.00	—

KWANGSI FARMERS BANK

行銀民農西廣

Kuang Hsi Nung Min Yin Hang

1938 ISSUE

		VG	VF	UNC
S2295	**1 YÜAN** 1938. Blue. Mythical man at l., farming at r. Back red. *(S/M #K32-1).*	17.50	55.00	—

		VG	VF	UNC
S2296	**5 YÜAN** 1938. Green. Like #S2295. Back brown. *(S/M #K32-2).*	20.00	75.00	—

KWANGSI PROVINCIAL TREASURY NOTES

(券)庫金省西廣

Kuang Hsi Sheng Chin K'u (Ch'üan)

1923 ISSUE

		VG	VF	UNC
S2301	**1 YÜAN** 1923. *(S/M #K33-1).*	Reported Not Confirmed		
S2302	**5 YÜAN** 1923. *(S/M #K33-2).*	Reported Not Confirmed		
		GOOD	**FINE**	**XF**
S2303	**10 YÜAN** 1923. Green and brown. Back green. *(S/M #K33-3).*	50.00	150.00	300.00

NOTE: #S2301-S2303 are believed to be a military issue.

1931 ISSUE

		GOOD	FINE	XF
S2303A	**1 YÜAN** 1931. National star in all 4 corners. Vertical format.			
	a. *Kweilin. (S/M #K33-6a).*	—	—	—
	b. *Liuchow. (S/M #K33-6b).*	—	—	—
	c. *Nanning. (S/M #K33-6c).*	—	—	—
	d. *Wuchow. (S/M #K33-6d).*	—	—	—

NOTE: #S2303A is considered a military issue.

1934 ISSUE

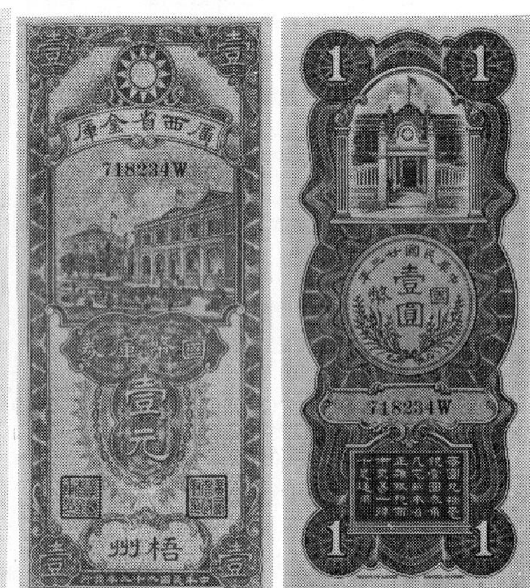

Nanning **Wuchow**

		GOOD	FINE	XF
S2304	**1 DOLLAR** 1934. Orange and m/c. Gov't. bldgs. at upper ctr. Back olive-green; bldg. above silver dollar at ctr. Vertical format. Printer: W&S.			
	a. Serial # suffix *N. Nanning. (S/M #K33-10a).*	10.00	30.00	100.00
	b. Serial # suffix *W. Wuchow. (S/M #K33-10b).*	10.00	30.00	100.00

1936 ISSUE

		GOOD	FINE	XF
S2309	**10 SILVER YÜAN** 1936. Blue and green. Back brown. Ovpt: *Kwangsi Bank. (S/M #K33-11).*	40.00	120.00	—

KWANGSI PROVINCIAL GOVERNMENT

券通流幣輔省西廣

Kuang Hsi Sheng Fu Pi Liu T'ung Ch'üan

1949 ISSUE

#S2311-S2315 printer: HKPA.

		VG	VF	UNC
S2311	**10 CENTS** ND (1949). Green and m/c. Bldg. at ctr. Back brown. *(S/M #K34-1).*	3.00	10.00	30.00

		VG	VF	UNC
S2312	**20 CENTS** ND (1949). Brown and m/c. Bldg. at r. Back red. *(S/M #K342).*	3.00	10.00	35.00

		VG	VF	UNC
S2313	**50 CENTS** ND (1949). Brown and m/c. Bldg. at ctr. Back brown. *(S/M #K34-3).*	3.00	10.00	30.00

		VG	VF	UNC
S2314	**100 CENTS** ND (1949). Green and m/c. Bldg. at r. Back brown. *(S/M #K34-4).*	6.00	17.50	55.00

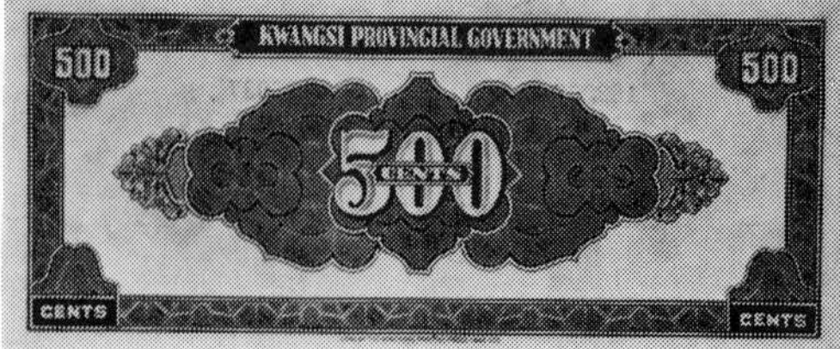

		VG	VF	UNC
S2315	**500 CENTS** ND (1949). Red and m/c. Bldg. at ctr. Back red. *(S/M #K34-5).*	12.50	37.50	110.00

PROVINCIAL BANK OF KWANGSI (KWANGSE)

行銀省西廣

Kuang Hsi Sheng Yin Hang

1922 ISSUE

		GOOD	FINE	XF
S2318	**10 CENTS** 1922. Green on red and lt. green unpt. Lake scene at ctr. Back brown on lt. blue unpt. *(S/M #K35-).*	—	—	—
S2323	**5 DOLLARS** 1922. Green. *(S/M #K35-).*	—	—	—

1926 ISSUES

#S2325-S2327 w/lg. rectangular ovpt. refer to Military - Chinese Republic Army, Navy and Air Force Sub. headquarters #S3828-S3830.

		GOOD	FINE	XF
S2325	**1 DOLLAR** Jan. 1926. Green and yellow. Pagoda at l., park at r. Back green and red; coliseum at ctr.			
	a. Deleted. See r.			
	b. *Kweilin. (S/M #K35-1b).*	12.00	35.00	—
	c. *Liuchow. (S/M #K35-1c).*	12.00	35.00	—
	d. *Lungchow. (S/M #K35-1d).*	12.00	35.00	—
	e. *NANNING. (S/M #K35-1e).*	12.00	35.00	—
	f. *Watlam. (S/M #K35-1f).*	12.00	35.00	—
	g. *WUCHOW. (S/M #K35-1g).*	12.00	35.00	—
	r. Remainder w/o place name. *(S/M #K35-1r).*	—	Unc	25.00

		GOOD	FINE	XF
S2326	**5 DOLLARS** Jan. 1926. Dk. blue and black on red unpt. Park at l., shoreline, boats at r. Back gray on green unpt; Great Wall at ctr.			
	a. Deleted. See r.			
	b. *Kweilin. (S/M #K35-2b).*	15.00	45.00	—
	c. *Liuchow. (S/M #K35-2c).*	15.00	45.00	—
	d. *Lungchow. (S/M #K35-2d).*	15.00	45.00	—
	e. Green *NANNING* on back. *(S/M #K35-2e).*	15.00	45.00	—
	f. *Watlam. (S/M #K35-2f).*	15.00	45.00	—
	h. *Pai Sze/WUCHOW. (S/M #K35-2g).*	15.00	45.00	—
	i. Black *NANNING* on back. *(S/M #K35-2e).*	15.00	45.00	—
	j. *WUCHOW. (S/M #K35-2g).*	15.00	45.00	—
	r. Remainder w/o place name. *(S/M #K35-2r).*	—	Unc	35.00

#S2366A *Deleted.* See #S2326j.

		GOOD	FINE	XF
S2327	**10 DOLLARS** Jan. 1926. Brown and black on olive-gray unpt. Like #S2326. Back blue-gray on lt. blue unpt.			
	a. Deleted. See r.			
	b. *Kweilin. (S/M #K35-3b).*	17.50	55.00	—
	c. *Liuchow. (S/M #K35-3c).*	17.50	55.00	—
	d. *Lungchow. (S/M #K35-3d).*	17.50	55.00	—
	e. *NANNING. (S/M #K35-3e).*	17.50	55.00	—
	f. *Watlam. (S/M #K35-3f).*	17.50	55.00	—
	g. *WUCHOW. (S/M #K35g).*	17.50	55.00	—
	r. Remainder w/o place name. *(S/M #K35-3r).*	—	Unc	35.00

#S2328 *Deleted.* See #2327g.

1928 ISSUE

		GOOD	FINE	XF
S2331	**1 CHIAO = 10 CENTS** 1928. *(S/M #K35-10).*	Reported Not Confirmed		

		GOOD	FINE	XF
S2332	**2 CHIAO = 20 CENTS** 1928. Blue on brown unpt. House by bridge at top ctr. Back blue-gray. *(S/M #K35-11).*	12.50	37.50	—

		GOOD	FINE	XF
S2333	**5 CHIAO = 50 CENTS** 1928. Green and m/c. Houses at top ctr. Back blue. *(S/M #K35-12).*	7.00	20.00	—

1928 LOCAL CURRENCY ISSUE

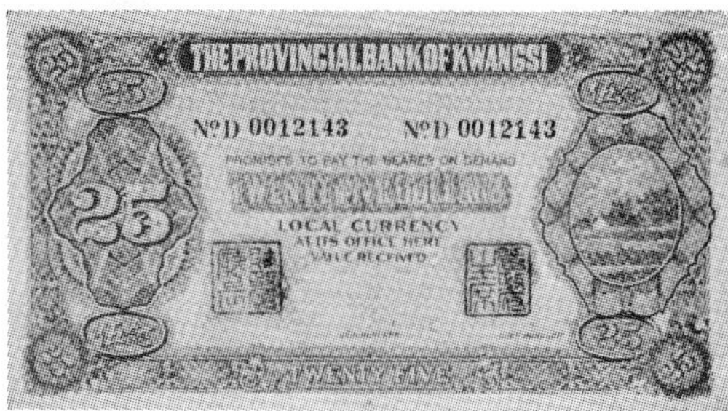

		GOOD	FINE	XF
S2337	**25 DOLLARS** 1928. Violet and m/c. Rural scene at r. *(S/M #K35-20).*			
	a. Issued note.	30.00	90.00	—
	r. Remainder w/o sign. seals.	—	—	60.00

1929 ISSUE

#S2339-S2342 river scene at ctr. Printer: ABNC.

		GOOD	FINE	XF
S2339	**1 DOLLAR** 1929. Black and m/c. Back red.			
	a. Deleted. See r.			
	b. *Kweilin. (S/M #K35-30b).*	2.50	8.00	25.00
	c. *Liuchow. (S/M #K35-30c).*	2.50	8.00	25.00
	d. *Lungchow. (S/M #K35-30d).*	2.50	8.00	25.00
	e. *Nanning. (S/M #K35-30e).*	2.50	8.00	25.00
	f. *Watlam. (S/M #K35-30f).*	2.50	8.00	25.00
	g. *Wuchow. (S/M #K35-30g).*	2.50	8.00	25.00
	h. *Wuchow* w/additional ovpt: *Pa Pu. (S/M #K35-30h).*	2.50	8.00	25.00
	i. *Chengchow. (S/M #K35-30).*	2.50	8.00	25.00
	r. Remainder w/o place name. *(S/M #K35-30r).*	—	Unc	20.00

S2340 5 Dollars
1929. Green and m/c. Back purple.

		Good	Fine	XF
a.	Deleted. See r.			
b.	*Kweilin. (S/M #K35-31b).*	2.00	7.00	20.00
c.	*Liuchow. (S/M #K35-31c).*	2.00	7.00	20.00
d.	*Lungchow. (S/M #K35-31d).*	2.00	7.00	20.00
e.	*Nanning. (S/M #K35-31e).*	2.00	7.00	20.00
f.	*Watlam. (S/M #K35-31f).*	2.00	7.00	20.00
g.	*Wuchow. (S/M #K35-31g).*	2.00	7.00	20.00
h.	*Wuchow* w/additional ovpt: *Pa Pu. (S/M #K35-31h).*	2.00	7.00	20.00
i.	*Chengchow. (S/M #K35-31).*	2.00	7.00	20.00
j.	*Pimlok. (S/M #K35-31).*	2.00	7.00	20.00
r.	Remainder w/o place name. *(S/M #K35-31r).*	—	Unc	20.00

S2341 10 Dollars
1929. Blue and m/c. Back brown.

		Good	Fine	XF
a.	Deleted. See r.			
b.	*Kweilin. (S/M #K35-32b).*	2.00	8.00	25.00
c.	*Liuchow. (S/M #K35-32c).*	2.00	8.00	25.00
d.	*Lungchow. (S/M #K35-32d).*	2.00	8.00	25.00
e.	*Nanning. (S/M #K35-32e).*	2.00	8.00	25.00
f.	*Watlam. (S/M #K35-32f).*	2.00	8.00	25.00
g.	*Wuchow. (S/M #K35-32g).*	2.00	8.00	25.00
h.	*Wuchow* w/additional ovpt: *Pa Pu. (S/M #K35-32h).*	2.00	8.00	25.00
i.	*Chengchow. (S/M #K35-32i).*	2.00	8.00	25.00
r.	Remainder w/o place name. *(S/M #K35-32r).*	—	Unc	22.50

1932 Issue

		Good	Fine	XF
S2342	**10 Cents** 1932. Brown and green. Back orange. *(S/M #K35-40).*	15.00	45.00	—

Kwangsi Bank

廣西銀行

Kuang Hsi Yin Hang

1904 Imperial Tael Issue

		Good	Fine	XF
S2343	**1 Tael** Yr. 30 (1904). *(S/M #K36-).*	—	—	—
S2344	**10 Taels** Yr. 30 (1904). *(S/M #K36-).*	—	—	—

1909 Imperial Issue

#S2345 and S2346 facing dragons at l. and r.

		Good	Fine	XF
S2345	**1 Yüan** Yr. 2 (1909). Black. Silver dollar at ctr. *(S/M #K36-).*	—	—	—
S2346	**5 Yüan** Yr. 2 (1909). Black. 5 silver dollars at ctr. Back green and black. *(S/M #K36-).*	60.00	180.00	—

1912 Military Hao Issue

		Good	Fine	XF
S2347	**1 Hao** June 1912. *(S/M #K36-).*	45.00	135.00	210.00
S2347A	**2 Hao** June 1912. *(S/M #K36-).*	50.00	150.00	225.00
S2347B	**5 Hao** June 1912. *(S/M #K36-).*	60.00	175.00	300.00

1912 Military Ch'iao Issue

		Good	Fine	XF
S2348 (S2347)	**10 Cents** Sept. 1912. *(S/M #K36-1).*	40.00	120.00	200.00
S2349	**20 Cents** Sept. 1912. *(S/M #K36-1.5).*	50.00	150.00	225.00

		Good	Fine	Unc
S2350	**50 Cents** Sept. 1912. *(S/M #K36-2).*	60.00	175.00	300.00

#S2351-S2353 mountain pass at l., modern bldg. along shoreline at r. Serial # varieties: w/ or w/o *No.*; single letter prefix. Various hand stamps in different colored inks.

S2351 1 Dollar
1912. Gray-green and purple-violet on yellow unpt. Back dk. brown on pale blue unpt.

		Good	Fine	XF
a.	*KWEILIN. (S/M #K36-10a).*	10.00	30.00	90.00
b.	*LIUCHOW. (S/M #K36-10b).*	8.50	25.00	75.00
c.	*LUNGCHOW. (S/M #K36-10c).*	4.00	12.00	35.00
d.	*NANNING.* (2 varieties for *Ning*). *(S/M #K36-10d).*	4.00	12.00	35.00
e.	*WUCHOW.* (or *Wu*). (S/M #K36-10e).	8.00	25.00	70.00
f.	*WATLAM. (S/M #K36-10f).*	8.00	25.00	70.00

S2352 5 Dollars
1912. Dk. brown and orange on lt. blue unpt. Back orange on pale green unpt.

		Good	Fine	XF
a.	*KWEILIN. (S/M #K36-11a).*	15.00	45.00	130.00
b.	*LIUCHOW. (S/M #K36-11b).*	15.00	45.00	130.00
c.	*LUNGCHOW. (S/M #K36-11c).*	10.00	30.00	90.00
d.	*NANNING. (S/M #K36-11d).*	10.00	30.00	90.00
e.	*WUCHOW. (S/M #K36-11e).*	15.00	45.00	130.00

S2353 10 Dollars
1912. Green on yellow unpt. Back green.

		Good	Fine	XF
a.	*KWEILIN. (S/M #K36-12a).*	22.50	75.00	—
b.	*LIUCHOW. (S/M #K36-12b).*	22.50	75.00	—
c.	*LUNGCHOW. (S/M #K36-12c).*	22.50	75.00	—
d.	*NANNING. (S/M #K36-12d).*	22.50	75.00	—
e.	*WUCHOW. (S/M #K36-12e).*	22.50	75.00	—

1915 Military Issue

#S2354 and S2354A like #S2351.

		Good	Fine	XF
S2354	**10 Cents** 1915. Blue and red. Back orange and blue. *KWEILIN. (S/M #K36-20).*	15.00	45.00	—
S2354A	**50 Cents** 1915. Green on yellow unpt. *(S/M #K36-22).*	15.00	45.00	—

1917 Military Issue

		Good	Fine	XF
S2355	**10 Cents** 1917. Like #S2351. *(S/M #K36-24).*	10.00	30.00	—

1918 Military Issue

		Good	Fine	XF
S2356	**50 Cents** 1918. *(S/M #K36-28).*	Reported Not Confirmed		

1920 Military Issue

#S2357-S2362 like #S2351.

		Good	Fine	XF
S2357	**10 Cents** Oct. 1920. Blue and orange. Back orange and blue. *WUCHOW. (S/M #K36-30).*	6.50	20.00	70.00

#S2358 *Deleted.* See #S2357.

		Good	Fine	XF
S2359	**20 Cents** 1920. Blue. Back blue. *(S/M #K36-31).*	15.00	45.00	—
S2361	**50 Cents** 1920. Green on yellow unpt. Back violet. *(S/M #K36-32).*	15.00	45.00	—

#S2362 *Deleted.* See #S2361.

1921 Military Issues

		Good	Fine	XF
S2363	**10 Cents** 1921. Blue and red. Back orange and blue. *KWEILIN. (S/M #K36-40).*	10.00	30.00	75.00

#S2365 and S2366 red octagonal seal: *ISSUED BY KWANGSI BANK - Tenth Year of the Republic of China* along w/oval hand stamp w/similar message in Chinese on back.

		Good	Fine	XF
S2365	**50 Cents** Feb. Yr. 10 (1921). Deep blue-green on orange unpt. Back violet on pale green unpt. *WUCHOW. (S/M #K36-41).*	7.00	20.00	—

		GOOD	FINE	XF
S2366	**1 DOLLAR** Yr. 10 (1921 - old date Yr. 1). Ovpt. on #S2351e. *WUCHOW*. *(S/M #K36-42)*.	—	—	—

		GOOD	FINE	XF
S2367	**2 DOLLARS** 1921. *KWEILIN*. *(S/M #K36-44)*.	80.00	250.00	—
S2368	**5 DOLLARS** 1921. Brown and orange. Back orange and green. *LUNGCHOW*. *(S/M #K36-50)*.	90.00	270.00	—

		GOOD	FINE	XF
S2369	**5 DOLLARS** 1921. Title: *KWEILIN BANK* on back. *KWEILIN*. *(S/M #K36-51)*.	90.00	300.00	—

1922 MILITARY DOLLAR ISSUES

		GOOD	FINE	XF
S2370	**10 CENTS** 1922. Gray. *Kweilin*. *(S/M #K36-55)*.	10.00	30.00	—
S2372	**50 CENTS** 1922. Green and orange. *(S/M #K36-56)*.	10.00	30.00	—
S2373	**1 DOLLAR** 1922. Blue and yellow. *(S/M #K36-57)*.	12.50	37.50	110.00
S2374	**1 DOLLAR** 1922. Gray. *Kweilin*. *(S/M #K36-58)*.	12.50	37.50	110.00
S2375	**2 DOLLARS** 1922. *Kweilin*. *(S/M #K36-59)*.	Reported Not Confirmed		

1923 MILITARY HAO ISSUE

		GOOD	FINE	XF
S2376	**1 HAO** 1923. Blue on pink unpt. Back red. *(S/M #K36-)*.	22.50	65.00	150.00

1936 PROVINCIAL ISSUE

		VG	VF	UNC
S2380	**1 CHIAO** 1936. Dk. blue. Bldg. at l. and r. Back red. Printer: HHEC. *(S/M #K36-60)*.	6.50	20.00	50.00

1938 ISSUES

		VG	VF	UNC
S2381	**5 CHIAO** 1936. Green. Bridge at l. Back orange and m/c. Printer: CMPA. *(S/M #K36-70)*.	4.00	12.00	36.00

		VG	VF	UNC
S2382	**5 CHIAO** ND. Violet. Shoreline at r. Back green and m/c. Printer: CMPA. *(S/M #K36-80)*.	17.50	55.00	—

KWANGTUNG CURRENCY BUREAU

廣東錢局

Kuang Tung Ch'ien Chü

1904 ISSUE

		GOOD	FINE	XF
S2385	**1 DOLLAR** Yr. 30 (1904). Black on ochre unpt. Back pale brown-orange; black text. Printer: PYOG. *(S/M #K51-1)*.	120.00	360.00	—

1905 ISSUE

		GOOD	FINE	XF
S2388	**1 DOLLAR** Yr. 31 (1905). Black on pale green. Back grayish purple. *(S/M #K51-20).*	120.00	360.00	—

1907 ISSUE

TYPE I

#S2389-S2391 dragon dollar coins not touching frame at l. or r. w/solid frame below house at bottom ctr. Rectangular frame, black text and 3 vertical rectangular hand stamps on back. Printer: PYOG.

		GOOD	FINE	XF
S2389	**1 DOLLAR** Yr. 33 (1907). Black. Back yellow-orange. *(S/M #K51-).*	120.00	360.00	—
S2390	**5 DOLLARS** Yr. 33 (1907). Black. Back lt. green. *(S/M #K51-).*	135.00	400.00	—

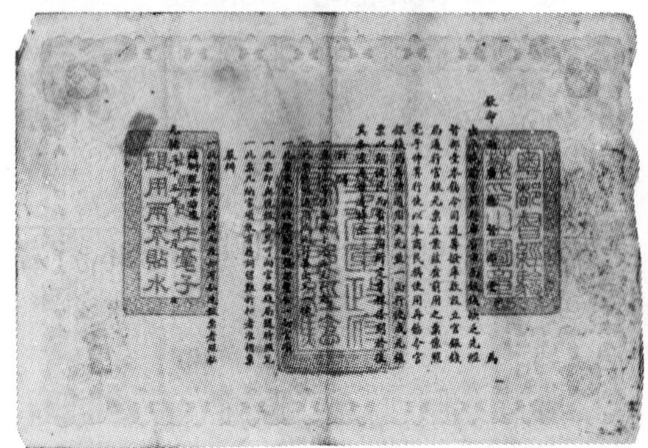

		GOOD	FINE	XF
S2391	**10 DOLLARS** Yr. 33 (1907). Black. Back red. *(S/M #K51-).*	225.00	675.00	—

TYPE II

#S2392-S2395 dragon dollar coins touch frame at l. and r. w/broken frame below house at bottom ctr. Backs w/text between scrollwork and ornate denominations; red seal w/black sign. at lower r. Printer: JIPB.

		GOOD	FINE	XF
S2392	**1 DOLLAR** Yr. 33 (1907). Black. *(S/M #K51-20a).*	120.00	360.00	—
S2393	**5 DOLLARS** Yr. 33 (1907). Black. *(S/M #K51-).*	135.00	400.00	—

		GOOD	FINE	XF
S2394	**10 DOLLARS** Yr. 33 (1907). Black. *(S/M #K51-).*	225.00	675.00	—

NOTE: #S2392 & S2394 w/additional lg. seal ovpt. are reported as a military reissue ca. 1911.

PROVINCIAL BANK OF KWANGTUNG PROVINCE

券換兌 行銀省東廣

Kuang Tung Sheng Yin Hang Tui Huan Ch'üan

1913 EXCHANGE NOTES ISSUE

#S2395-S2398 printer: ABNC.

		GOOD	FINE	XF
S2395	**50 CENTS** 1913. *Canton. (S/M #K55-1).*	60.00	180.00	—
S2396	**1 DOLLAR** 1913. Green and m/c. Back red. *Canton. (S/M #K55-10).*	100.00	300.00	—
S2397	**2 DOLLARS** 1913. *Canton. (S/M #K55-11).*	110.00	330.00	—

		GOOD	FINE	XF
S2398	**5 DOLLARS** 1.1.1913. Dk. green on m/c unpt. Lg. bldg. at ctr. *Canton. (S/M #K55-12).*			
	a. Issued note.	125.00	375.00	—
	b. Punched hole cancelled.	75.00	225.00	—
	p. Proof.	—	Unc	800.00
	s. Specimen.	—	Unc	500.00

		GOOD	FINE	XF
S2399	**10 DOLLARS** 1.1.1913. *Canton. (S/M #K55-13).*			
	p. Proof.	—	Unc	1250.
	s. Specimen.	—	Unc	750.00

NOTE: For #S2398 and S2399 w/additional ovpt., see Bank of China #29 and 29A, Vol. 2.

1918 EXCHANGE NOTES ISSUE

#S2401-S2405 *CANTON*. Printer: ABNC.

		GOOD	FINE	XF
S2401	**1 DOLLAR** 1.1.1918. Dk. blue on m/c unpt. Pagoda at ctr. Back dk. green.			
	a. 2 red sign. seals at l., lg. black sign. at r. w/o sign. title. *(S/M #K55-20).*	5.00	15.00	45.00
	b. 2 red sign. seals at l., sign. title: *GEN. MANAGER* at r. *(S/M #K55-20d).*	5.00	15.00	45.00
	c. English sign. 25mm square blue ovpt. at ctr. *(S/M #K55-20).*	2.00	6.00	18.00
	d. Sign. titles: *CASHIER* and *MANAGING DIRECTOR* below English sign. *(S/M #K55-20a).*	5.00	15.00	—
	e. *Sheng Li* at top ctr. English sign. w/o titles. *(S/M #K55-20b.).*	.50	2.50	7.50

	GOOD	FINE	XF
f. Lg. red hexagonal seal at l., black ovpt. w/pagoda at ctr. and w/additional 5 digit serial #. *(S/M #K55-20).*	8.00	25.00	—
g. Like e., but w/o 5 digit serial #. *(S/M #K55-20c).*	7.00	21.00	—
p. Proof.	—	Unc	75.00
s. Specimen.	—	Unc	50.00

NOTE: For #S2401 ovpt. 6 character new bank name see #469, Vol. 2.

		GOOD	FINE	XF
S2402	**5 DOLLARS** 1.1.1918. Orange on m/c unpt. Lg. bldg. at ctr., *Sheng Li* at top ctr. Back purple.			
	a. Sign. titles: *CASHIER* and *MANAGING DIRECTOR* below English sign. *(S/M #K55-21a).*	3.00	9.00	—
	b. English sign. w/o titles. *(S/M #K55-21b).*	1.00	3.00	9.00

	GOOD	FINE	XF
c. Lg. red seal at l., lg. black ovpt. w/pagoda at ctr. w/additional 5 digit serial #. *(S/M #K55-21).*	8.00	25.00	75.00
d. Like c, but w/o 5 digit serial #. *(S/M #K55-21c).*	5.00	15.00	45.00
p. Proof.	—	Unc	90.00
s. Specimen.	—	Unc	60.00

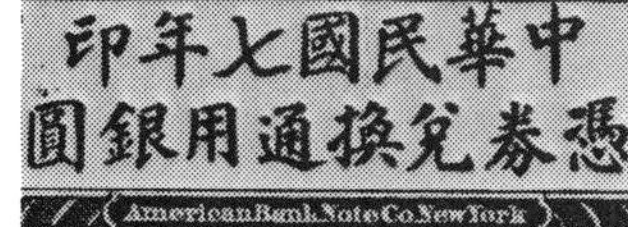

Large 7

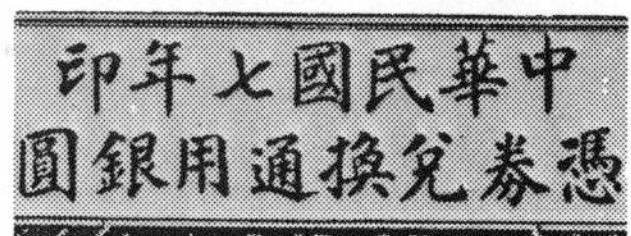

Small 7

		GOOD	FINE	XF
S2403	**10 DOLLARS** 1.1.1918. Dk. green on m/c unpt. Theatre at ctr. *Sheng Li* at l. and r. of bank name. Back orange.			
	a. Sign. titles: *CASHIER and MANAGING DIRECTOR* below English sign., lg. *7* in date. *(S/M #K55-22a).*	3.00	9.00	27.00
	b. Like a., but w/sm. *7* in date. *(S/M #K55-22a).*	3.00	9.00	27.00
	c. English sign. w/o titles,. lg. *7* in date. *(S/M #K55-22b).*	1.25	5.00	15.00
	d. English sign. w/o titles., sm. *7* in date. *(S/M #K55-22b).*	1.25	5.00	15.00
	e. *Swatow/CANTON. (S/M #K55-22).*	10.00	30.00	—

	GOOD	FINE	XF
f. Lg. red seal at l., lg. black ovpt. w/pagoda at ctr., sm. *7* in date, w/additional 5 digit serial #. *(S/M #K55-22).*	12.00	35.00	70.00
g. Like f., but sm. *7* in date. *(S/M #K55-22).*	12.00	35.00	70.00
h. Like f., but w/o 5 digit serial #. *(S/M #K55-22c).*	10.00	30.00	60.00
i. Like g., but w/o 5 digit serial #. *(S/M #K55-22c).*	10.00	30.00	60.00
p. Proof.	—	Unc	90.00
s. Specimen.	—	Unc	60.00

S2404 50 DOLLARS	GOOD	FINE	XF
1.1.1918. Dk. brown on m/c unpt. Pavilion, pool at ctr. *Sheng Li* at top ctr. Back olive-green.			
a. Sign. titles: *CASHIER* and *MANAGING DIRECTOR* below printed black English sign. *(S/M #K55-23a).*	5.00	15.00	45.00
b. Like a., but sign. at l. handwritten in various colors. *(S/M #K55-23a).*	8.00	20.00	55.00
c. English sign. w/o titles. *(S/M #K55-23b).*	2.50	7.50	22.50
d. Like c., but sign. at l. handwritten in various colors. *(S/M #K55-).*	10.00	25.00	70.00
e. Lg. red seal at l., lg. black ovpt. w/pagoda at ctr., w/additional 5 digit serial #. *(S/M #K55-23).*	17.00	50.00	—
f. Like e., but w/o 5 digit serial #. *(S/M #K55-23).*	15.00	45.00	—
s. Specimen.	—	Unc	75.00

S2405 100 DOLLARS	GOOD	FINE	XF
1.1.1918. Olive-green on m/c unpt. University at ctr. Back blue-black.			
a. Sign. titles: *CASHIER* and *MANAGING DIRECTOR* below printed black English sign. *(S/M #K55-24a).*	8.00	25.00	75.00
b. Like a., but sign. at r. handwritten in various colors. *(S/M #K55-24a).*	10.00	30.00	90.00
c. Printed English sign. w/o titles. *(S/M #K55-24b).*	4.00	10.00	25.00
d. English sign. w/o titles, but sign. at r. handwritten. *(S/M #K55-24b).*	5.00	20.00	65.00
e. Lg. red seal at l., lg. black ovpt. w/pagoda at ctr., w/additional 5 digit serial #. *(S/M #K55-24).*	20.00	50.00	100.00
f. Like e., but w/o 5 digit serial #. *(S/M #K55-24).*	16.00	40.00	80.00
p. Proof.	—	Unc	225.00
s. Specimen.	—	Unc	150.00

NOTE: Modern forged sign. titles of #S2401-S2405 exist.

1922 EXCHANGE NOTES ISSUE

#S2407-S2408 printer: ABNC.

S2407 20 CENTS	GOOD	FINE	XF
1.1.1922. Black. Tunnel at l. Back blue and m/c. *(S/M #K55-30).*			
a. Issued note.	1.00	3.00	9.00
s. Specimen.	—	Unc	35.00

S2408 50 CENTS	GOOD	FINE	XF
1.1.1922. Orange. Lg. bldg. at ctr. Back green. *(S/M #K55-31).*			
a. Issued note.	1.50	4.00	12.00
s. Specimen.	—	Unc	40.00

KWANGTUNG PROVINCIAL BANK

行銀省東廣

Kuang Tung Sheng Yin Hang

SIGNATURE VARIETIES:

A	B	C	D	E	F	G

1931 NATIONAL CURRENCY ISSUE

#S2411, S2414 and S2417 SYS at ctr. Bank bldg. at ctr. on back. Printer: ABNC.

S2411 1 DOLLAR	GOOD	FINE	XF
1931. Blue-gray on m/c unpt. Back blue.			
a. Sign. A-B. *(S/M #K56-2a).*	8.00	25.00	—
b. *HAIKOW. (S/M #K56-2b).*	15.00	45.00	—
c. *SWATOW. (S/M #K56-2c).*	15.00	45.00	—

S2414 5 DOLLARS	GOOD	FINE	XF
1931. Green on m/c unpt. Back green.			
a. Sign. A-B. *(S/M #K56-11a).*	10.00	30.00	—
b. *SWATOW. (S/M #K56-11b).*	20.00	60.00	—
c. Sign. D-E-F. *(S/M #K56-11c).*	15.00	45.00	—
d. *HAIKOW. (S/M #K56-11d).*	20.00	60.00	—

S2417 10 SILVER YÜAN	GOOD	FINE	XF
1931. Red-brown on m/c unpt. Back red-brown. Sign. A-B *(S/M #K56-).*	25.00	75.00	—

1931 LOCAL CURRENCY ISSUE

#S2421-S2424 SYS at r. Bank bldg. at ctr. on back. Printer: ABNC.

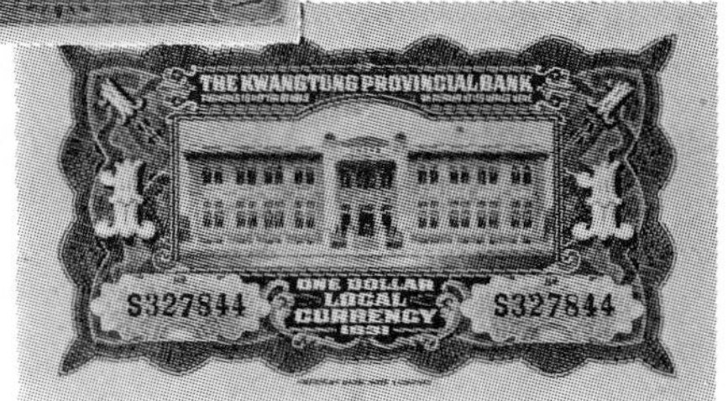

		VG	VF	UNC
S2421	**1 DOLLAR**			
	1931. Orange on m/c unpt. Back olive.			
	a. Sign. A-B. *(S/M #K56-1a).*	.30	1.00	3.00
	b. Sign. C-B. *(S/M #K56-1b).*	.30	1.00	3.00
	c. Sign. D-E. *(S/M #K56-1c).*	.50	1.50	4.50
	d. Sign. D-E-F. *(S/M #K56-1d).*	.30	1.00	3.00
	e. *SWATOW.* Sign. G-B. *(S/M #K56-1e).*	3.00	12.00	—

		VG	VF	UNC
	f. *PAK HOI.* Sign. G-B. *(S/M #K56-1f).*	3.00	12.00	—

		VG	VF	UNC
S2422	**5 DOLLARS**			
	1931. Green on m/c unpt. Back orange.			
	a. Sign. A-B. *(S/M #K56-10a).*	.50	1.50	4.50
	b. Sign. C-B. *(S/M #K56-10b).*	.30	1.00	3.00
	c. Sign. D-E. *(S/M #K56-10c).*	Reported Not Confirmed		
	d. Sign. D-E-F. *(S/M #K56-10d).*	.30	1.00	3.00
	e. *SWATOW. (S/M #K56-10e).*	3.00	12.00	—
	f. *PAK HOI. (S/M #K56-10f).*	3.00	12.00	—

		VG	VF	UNC
S2423	**10 DOLLARS**			
	1931. Red on m/c unpt. Back brown.			
	a. Sign. A-B. *(S/M #K56-14a).*	1.00	3.00	10.00
	b. Sign. C-B. *(S/M #K56-14b).*	1.00	3.00	10.00
	c. Sign. D-E. *(S/M #K56-14c).*	Reported Not Confirmed		
	d. Sign. D-E.F. *(S/M #K56-14d).*	1.00	3.00	10.00
	e. *Nan Hsiung. (S/M #K56-14e).*	4.00	15.00	—
	f. *SWATOW. (S/M #K56-14).*	3.00	12.00	—
	g. *PAK HOI (S/M #K56-14-).*	3.00	12.00	—

		VG	VF	UNC
S2424	**100 DOLLARS**			
	1931. Olive-brown on m/c unpt. Back blue. Sign. A-B. *(S/M #K56-17).*	6.00	20.00	60.00

1931 PROVISIONAL ISSUES

#S2425-S2429 ovpt: *LOCAL CURRENCY* on National currency issue.

S2425 1 Dollar	VG	VF	Unc
1931. Brown and m/c. Back brown.			
a. Sign. D-E-F. *(S/M #K56-3b).*	.50	1.50	4.50
b. Black ovpt. sign. D-E-F. *(S/M #K56-4b).*	.30	1.00	3.00
c. Sign. A-B. *(S/M #K56-4).*	.50	1.50	4.50
d. As c. *Nan Hsiung blocked out at lower l. and r. (S/M #K56-6).*	4.50	15.00	45.00

S2426 5 Dollars	VG	VF	Unc
1931. Red and m/c. Back red. Sign. D-E-F. *(S/M #K56-12b).*	1.00	3.50	11.00

S2427 5 Dollars	VG	VF	Unc
1931. Dk. blue and m/c. Back blue. Like #S2426. Sign. A-B. *(S/M #K56-13b).*			
a. Issued note.	1.00	3.50	11.00
b. *Nan Hsiung* blocked out at lower l. and r. *(S/M #K56-13).*	4.50	15.00	45.00

S2428 10 Dollars	VG	VF	Unc
1931. Violet and m/c. Back violet. Sign. A-B. *(S/M #K56-15b).*	1.50	4.50	12.50

S2429 10 Dollars	VG	VF	Unc
1931. Green and m/c. Back green. Like #S2428.			
a. Sign. D-E-F. *(S/M #K56-16b).*	1.00	3.50	10.00
b. Black ovpt. Sign. D-E-F. *(S/M #K56-16b).*	1.00	3.50	10.00

1932 Issue

#S2429A and S2430 SYS at l. Pagoda at ctr. on back. *Haikow* at l. and r. in frame.

S2429A 10 Cents	VG	VF	Unc
1932. Brown. *(S/M #K56-18).*	3.00	10.00	25.00

S2430 20 Cents	VG	VF	Unc
1932. Brown. *(S/M #K56-19).*	4.00	12.00	37.50

1934 Issue

#S2431-S2432 printer: HHEC.

S2431 10 Cents	VG	VF	Unc
1934. Red. Shoreline, sampan at l.			
a. W/o place name. *(S/M #K56-20a).*	.50	1.50	4.50
b. *PAK HOI. (S/M #K56-20b).*	1.00	3.50	10.00
c. *Swatow. (S/M #K56-20).*	1.00	3.50	10.00
S2432 50 Cents			
1934. Blue. Back red-violet. *(S/M #K56-21).*	1.00	3.00	9.00

1935 NATIONAL/FOREIGN CURRENCY ISSUE

#S2433-S2434 SYS at l. w/*Ta Yang* (foreign or Mexican coins) at l. and r. in frame. Pagoda at ctr. on back. Printer: HKPA.

		GOOD	FINE	XF
S2433	**10 CENTS** 1935. Brown. *(S/M #K56-29).*	2.00	6.00	18.00
S2434	**20 CENTS** 1935. Brown and violet. Back brown and green. *(S/M #K56-31).*	3.00	9.00	27.00

1935 LOCAL CURRENCY ISSUE

#S2436-S2438 SYS at r. Junk and sampan in harbor at ctr. on back. Printer: ABNC.

		VG	VF	UNC
S2436	**10 CENTS** 1935. Red on m/c unpt.			
	a. W/o place name. *(S/M #K56-30a).*	.25	1.00	3.00
	b. *PAK HOI. (S/M #K56-30b).*	1.00	3.00	9.00
	c. *SWATOW. (S/M #K56-30c).*	1.00	3.00	9.00
	p. As a. Proof.	—	—	50.00
	s1. As a. Specimen.	—	—	35.00
	s2. As b. Specimen.	—	—	45.00
	s3. As c. Specimen.	—	—	45.00

		VG	VF	UNC
S2437	**20 CENTS** 1935. Green on m/c unpt. Back green.			
	a. W/o place name, black sign. *(S/M #K56-32a).*	1.00	3.00	9.00
	b. Green sign. *(S/M #K56-32a).*	.25	1.00	3.00
	c. *PAK HOI. (S/M #K56-32b).*	1.00	3.00	9.00
	d. *SWATOW. (S/M #K56-32).*	1.00	3.00	9.00
	p1. As a. Proof.	—	—	70.00
	p2. As b. Proof.	—	—	50.00
	s1. As a. Specimen.	—	—	45.00
	s2. As b. Specimen.	—	—	35.00
	s3. As c. Specimen.	—	—	45.00
	s4. As d. Specimen.	—	—	45.00
	s5. Brown Chinese character ovpt. Specimen.	—	—	200.00
	s6. W/o sign. Specimen.	—	—	35.00

		VG	VF	UNC
S2438	**50 CENTS** 1935. Blue on m/c unpt. Back blue. *(S/M #K56-33).*			
	a. Issued note.	1.00	3.00	9.00
	p. W/o sign. Proof.	—	—	75.00
	s. W/o sign. Specimen.	—	—	50.00

1936 NATIONAL CURRENCY ISSUE

		VG	VF	UNC
S2440	**20 CENTS** 1936. Blue and m/c. Memorial bldg. at ctr. Back blue and brown. Printer: CHB.			
	a. Sign. A-B. *(S/M #K56-40).*	3.00	9.00	27.00
	b. Sign. D-E-F. *(S/M #K56-40).*	3.00	9.00	27.00

1936 LOCAL CURRENCY ISSUE

#S2442-S2443 printer: CHB.

		VG	VF	UNC
S2442	**1 DOLLAR** ND (1936). Red and green. Shoreline at r. Back green. *(S/M #K56-50).*	1.50	4.50	12.50

		VG	VF	UNC
S2443	**5 DOLLARS** ND (1936). Green and tan. Shoreline at ctr. Back green. *(S/M #K56-51).*	1.50	4.50	12.50

1939 HAINAN ISLAND DISTRICT ISSUE

#S2446 and S2447 issued during the Japanese occupation of Hainan Island.

SIGNATURE VARIETIES

1. Wu Shou Nan

2. Ch'iu Yüeh Sung

		VG	VF	UNC
S2446	**20 CENTS** 1939. Blue and m/c. Back red. *(S/M #K56-60).*	20.00	60.00	150.00
S2447	**1 DOLLAR** 1939. Red. SYS at r., SYS Memorial bldg. in Canton at ctr. Back blue and green. *(S/M #K56-70).*			
	a. Issued note.	25.00	75.00	200.00
	s. Specimen w/sign.	—	—	100.00

1940 ISSUE

#S2449 and S2450 issued during the Japanese occupation.

		VG	VF	UNC
S2449	**1 DOLLAR** 1940. Red. Similar to #S2447. Back blue and green. *(S/M #K56-80).*			
	a. Sign. 1.	20.00	60.00	150.00
	b. Sign. 2.	20.00	60.00	150.00
	s. Specimen w/o sign.	—	—	100.00

		VG	VF	UNC
S2450	**5 DOLLARS** 1940. Orange. SYS at r., Memorial to Canton martyrs at l. Back green. *(S/M #K56-81).*			
	a. Sign. 1.	40.00	120.00	300.00
	b. Sign. 2.	40.00	120.00	300.00

1949 ISSUE

#S2452-2459 SYS at l. Uniface. Printer: CHB.

		VG	VF	UNC
S2452	**1 CENT** 1949. Red. *(S/M #K57-1).*	.25	.75	2.50

		VG	VF	UNC
S2453	**5 CENTS** 1949. Violet and green. *(S/M #K57-2).*	.25	.75	2.50

#S2454-S2455 SYS at ctr. Gov't. bldg. at ctr. on back.

		VG	VF	UNC
S2454	**10 CENTS** 1949. Violet and brown. Back brown. *(S/M #K57-3).*	.25	.75	2.50

		VG	VF	UNC
S2455	**50 CENTS** 1949. Brown and blue. Back blue. *(S/M #K57-4).*	.25	.75	2.50

#S2456-S2459 SYS at l. Gov't. bldg. at ctr. on back.

		VG	VF	UNC
S2456	**1 YÜAN** 1949. Blue and green. Back blue. *(S/M #K57-10).*	.30	1.00	3.00
S2457	**5 YÜAN** 1949. Green. *(S/M #K57-11).*	.50	1.50	4.50
S2458	**10 YÜAN** 1949. Violet. *(S/M #K57-12).*	.50	1.50	4.50

		VG	VF	UNC
S2459	**100 YÜAN** 1949. Red. *(S/M #K57-13).*	1.50	5.00	15.00

KWEICHOW PROVINCIAL GOVERNMENT GENERAL TREASURY

貴州省政府總金庫

Kuei Chou Sheng Cheng Fu Tsung Chin K'u

1930 ISSUE

		GOOD	FINE	XF
S2460	**50 YÜAN** 1930. *(S/M #K70.5-11).*	—	—	—
S2460A	**100 DOLLARS** 1930. *(S/M #K70.5-12).*	—	—	—

1932 ISSUE

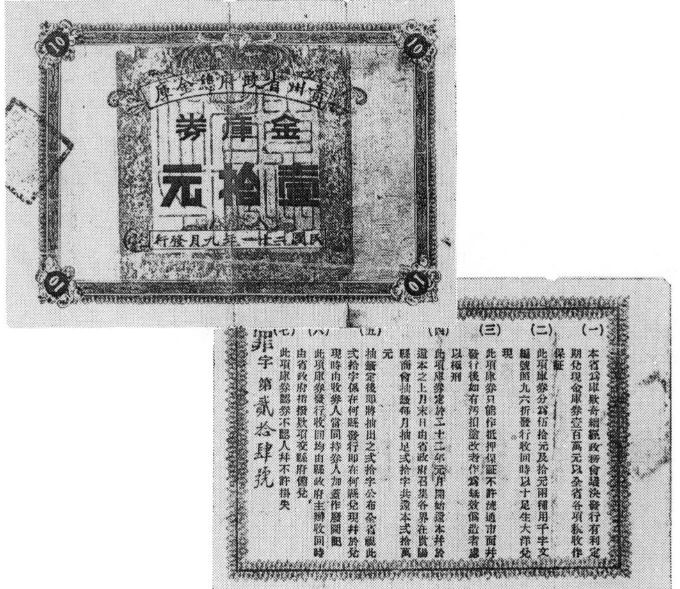

		GOOD	FINE	XF
S2460B	**10 YÜAN** 1932. *(S/M #K70.5-15).*	—	—	—
S2460C	**50 YÜAN** 1932. *(S/M #K70.5-16).*	—	—	—

PROVINCIAL BANK OF KWEICHOW

貴州省銀行
Kuei Chou Sheng Yin Hang

1949 ISSUE

#S2461-S2463 modern bldg. at ctr. on back. Printer: CPFA.

		GOOD	FINE	XF
S2461	**1 CENT** 1949. Orange. *(S/M #K71-1).*	2.25	8.00	15.00
S2462	**5 CENTS** 1949. Green and m/c. Back green. *(S/M #K71-2).*	5.00	15.00	40.00

		GOOD	FINE	XF
S2463	**10 CENTS** 1949. Red and blue. Back red *(S/M #K71-3).*	6.50	20.00	60.00

KWEICHOW BANK
KUEICHOW BANK
BANK OF KWEICHOW

貴州銀行
Kuei Chou Yin Hang

1912 ISSUE

#S2468-S2470 Birds of Paradise facing at upper l. and r. Printer: WTBC.

		GOOD	FINE	XF
S2465	**10 CENTS** 1912. Green. Back yellow. *(S/M #K72-1).*	22.50	75.00	—
S2466	**20 CENTS** 1912. Green. Back yellow. *(S/M #K72-2).*	22.50	75.00	—
S2467	**50 CENTS** 1912. Green. Back brown. *(S/M #K72-3).*	30.00	90.00	—

		GOOD	FINE	XF
S2468	**1 YÜAN** 1912. Blue, black and yellow.			
	a. Serial #. *(S/M #K72-10a).*	12.00	40.00	—
	b. W/o serial #. *(S/M #K72-10b).*	—	Unc	100.00

		GOOD	FINE	XF
S2469	**5 YÜAN** 1912. Blue and m/c. Like #S2468. Back orange. *(S/M #K72-11).*	30.00	100.00	—
S2470	**10 YÜAN** 1912. Green and m/c. Back green. *(S/M #K72-12).*	35.00	125.00	—

1918 ISSUE

		GOOD	FINE	XF
S2471	**10 CENTS** 1918. Green. *(S/M #K72-20).*	22.50	75.00	—
S2472	**20 CENTS** 1918. Blue. *(S/M #K72-21).*	30.00	90.00	—
S2473	**50 CENTS** 1918. Brown. Back yellow. *(S/M #K72-22).*	30.00	90.00	—

1922 ISSUE

		GOOD	FINE	XF
S2474	**1 YÜAN** 1.11.1922. Blue and green. Peacocks facing at ctr. Back green. *(S/M #K72-30).*	40.00	120.00	—
S2475	**10 YÜAN** 1.11.1922. Brown and green. Peacock facing at ctr. Back blue.	60.00	180.00	—

1925 ND ISSUE

		GOOD	FINE	XF
S2477	**10 CENTS** ND (1925). Green. Temple at r. Modern bldg. complex, shoreline on back. *(S/M #K72-40).*	15.00	45.00	—
S2478	**20 CENTS** ND (1925). Blue. *(S/M #K72-41).*	15.00	50.00	—

		GOOD	FINE	XF
S2479	**50 CENTS** ND (1925). Brown. Like #S2477. *(S/M #K72-).*	22.50	75.00	—

		GOOD	FINE	XF
S2480	**1 YÜAN** ND (1925). Blue and m/c. Bldgs. at l. and r. Back blue and red. *(S/M #K72-42).*	30.00	90.00	—
S2482 (S2485)	**10 YÜAN** ND (1925). Green. Pavilion, bridge at ctr. Back yellow-green; rural scenes at l. and r. *(S/M #K72-44).*	30.00	90.00	—

1930 ISSUE

		GOOD	FINE	XF
S2483	**50 CENTS** 1930. Bldg., trees at l. Bldg., bridge at ctr. on back. *(S/M #K72-50).*	20.00	60.00	—
S2484	**1 DOLLAR** 1930. Green. Back blue. *(S/M #K72-60).*	22.50	75.00	—

#S2485 *Deleted.* See #S2482.

#S2486 and S2487 *Deleted.* (local issue).

NINGHSIA PROVINCIAL BANK

行銀省夏寧

Ning Hsia Sheng Yin Hang

1942 ISSUE

#S2488-S2489 printer: BEPP.

		GOOD	FINE	XF
S2488	**10 CENTS** 1942. Red. Back violet. *(S/M #N16-1).*	30.00	90.00	—

		GOOD	FINE	XF
S2489	**20 CENTS** 1942. Green. *(S/M #N16-2).*	30.00	90.00	—

HUNAN PAO HSING MINERAL BANK
HUNAN POW SHING MINING BANK

司公礦煤興寶

(Hunan) Pao Hsing Kuang Yeh Yin Hang

1912 ISSUE

		GOOD	FINE	XF
S2490	**100 COPPERS** 1912. *(S/M #P10-0.3)*	—	—	—
S2490A	**1 DOLLAR** 1912. *(S/M #P10-0.7).* (Not issued).	—	—	—

1912 TAEL ISSUES

#S2490B bldgs. at l., rural scene at r. *Changsha.*

		GOOD	FINE	XF
S2490B	**1 TAEL** 1912. Black on tan unpt. Back blue on yellow unpt. *(S/M #P10-1).*	75.00	225.00	—

#S2490C-S2490E bldgs. at l., rural scene at r. *Changsha.*

		GOOD	FINE	XF
S2490C	**3 TAELS** 1912. *(S/M #P10-2).*	—	—	—
S2490D	**5 TAELS** 1912. *(S/M #P10-3).*	100.00	400.00	—

		GOOD	FINE	XF
S2490E	**10 TAELS** 1912. Black on ochre unpt. Back blue on red unpt. *(S/M #P10-4).*	125.00	—	—

		GOOD	FINE	XF
S2490G	**10 TAELS** 1912. Two flags above hemisphere at ctr. Bldgs. at mine at ctr. on back. *(S/M #P10-15).*	—	—	—

ALTAI DISTRICT

券銀用通泰爾阿

O Erh T'ai T'ung Yung Yin Ch'uan

1918 CURRENT SILVER NOTE ISSUE

#S2490J-S2490L horse drawn wagon w/people at ctr.

		GOOD	FINE	XF
S2490J	**1 YÜAN** 1918. Gray-violet. Back green. *(S/M #03-1).*	22.50	67.50	—
S2490K	**5 YÜAN** 1918. Olive-green. Back orange. *(S/M #03-2).*	22.50	67.50	—
S2490L	**10 YÜAN** 1918. Orange. Back blue. *(S/M #03-3).*	30.00	90.00	—

PEIPING MUNICIPAL BANK

行銀市平北

Pei P'ing Shih Yin Hang

1936 ISSUE

#S2491-S2498 printer: BEPP. Specimen.

		VG	VF	UNC
S2491	**20 COPPERS** 1936. Brown. *(S/M #P27-1).*	—	—	70.00

		VG	VF	UNC
S2492	**25 COPPERS** 1936. Blue. Pagoda at ctr. on back. *(S/M #P27-2).*	—	—	70.00

		GOOD	FINE	XF
S2495	**20 CENTS** 1936. Brown. Back brown and red. *(S/M #P27-10).*	—	—	75.00

		GOOD	FINE	XF
S2497	**1 YÜAN** 1936. Green and yellow. Shoreline, tower at ctr. Back green. *(S/M #P27-20).*	—	—	90.00

		GOOD	FINE	XF
S2498	**5 YÜAN** 1936. Orange. *(S/M #P27-21).*	—	—	110.00

1937 ISSUE

		GOOD	FINE	XF
S2501	**2 CENTS** 1937. Gateway at ctr. Printer: BEPP. *(S/M #P27-).*			
	a. Issued note.	12.00	35.00	—
	s. Specimen.	—	Unc	75.00

PEI-YANG KIN-FU BANK

北洋經武銀行

Pei Yang Ching Wu Yin Hao

1906 ISSUE

		GOOD	FINE	XF
S2505	**3 TAELS** CD 1906. Like #S2522. Printer: BWC. Vertical format. Specimen. *(S/M #-)*.	—	Unc	500.00

NOTE: Also see #S2521.

COMMERCIAL GUARANTEE BANK OF CHIHLI

北洋保商銀行

Pei Yang Pao Shang Yin Hang

ND ISSUE

#S2509-S2510 ship at lower l., lighthouse at bottom ctr., steam train at lower r.

		GOOD	FINE	XF
S2509	**5 DOLLARS** ND. Black and red. Back red and green. Remainder. *(S/M #P33-1)*.	32.50	100.00	300.00

		GOOD	FINE	XF
S2510	**10 DOLLARS** ND. Black and blue. Back blue and red. Remainder. *(S/M #P33-2)*.	50.00	160.00	500.00

1908-11 ISSUE

		GOOD	FINE	XF
S2510A	**1 DOLLAR** (ca.1908-11). Green. Back orange. Remainder. *(S/M #P33-)*.	32.50	100.00	300.00

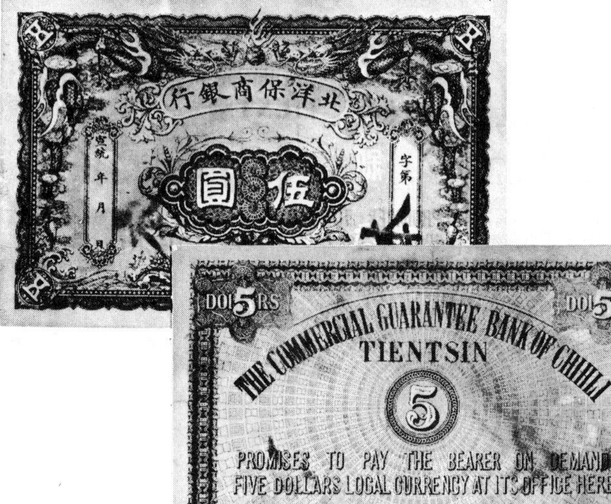

		GOOD	FINE	XF
S2511	**5 DOLLARS** (ca.1908-11). Brown and m/c. Back orange and green. Remainder. *(S/M #P33-3)*.	32.50	100.00	300.00
S2512	**10 SILVER YÜAN** (ca.1908-11). Brown. Back orange. Remainder. *(S/M #P33-4)*.	40.00	120.00	360.00
S2512A	**50 DOLLARS** (ca.1908-11). Violet. Back green and red. Remainder. *(S/M#P33-)*.	50.00	160.00	480.00

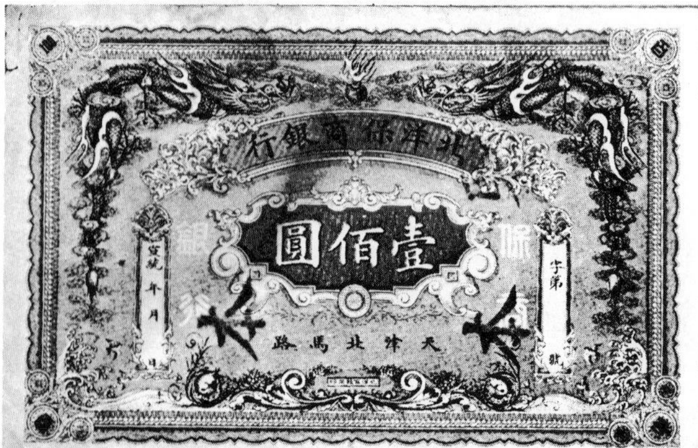

		GOOD	FINE	XF
S2513	**100 DOLLARS** (ca.1908-11). Green and m/c. Back green and red. Specimen. *(S/M #P33-5)*.	—	—	—

1912 ISSUE

		GOOD	FINE	XF
S2514	**1 TAEL** 1912. *(S/M #P33-)*.	—	—	—

		Good	Fine	XF
S2514A	**3 Taels**			
	1912. *(S/M #P33-).*	—	—	—
S2514B	**5 Taels**			
	1912. *(S/M #P33-).*	—	—	—
S2514C	**10 Taels**			
	1912. *(S/M #P33-).*	—	—	—
S2514D	**50 Taels**			
	1912. Blue and black. Back green and red. *(S/M #P33-).*	—	—	—

		Good	Fine	XF
S2514E	**100 Taels**			
	1912. Vertical format. *(S/M #P33-).*	—	—	—
S2514F	**500 Taels**			
	1912. Yellow and m/c. Back brown and green. Specimen. *(S/M #P33-).*	—	—	—

1919 Issue

#S2515-S2517A printer: ABNC.

		Good	Fine	XF
S2515	**1 Dollar**			
	1.1.1919. Purple on m/c unpt. Bank bldg. at l. w/o place name.			
	a. *Peiping. (S/M #P33-9a).*	30.00	100.00	—
	b. *Tientsin (S/M #P33-9b).*	30.00	100.00	—
	p. Proof.	—	Unc	150.00

		Good	Fine	XF
S2515A	**5 Dollars**			
	1.1.1919. Violet on m/c. unpt. Bank bldg. at r. Back violet.			
	a. *PEIPING. (S/M #P33-10a).*	40.00	120.00	—
	b. W/additional numerical ovpt: *3-5; 13. (S/M #P33-10b).*	40.00	120.00	—
	c. *TIENTSIN.* W/additional numerical ovpt: *21. (S/M #P33-10c).*	50.00	150.00	—

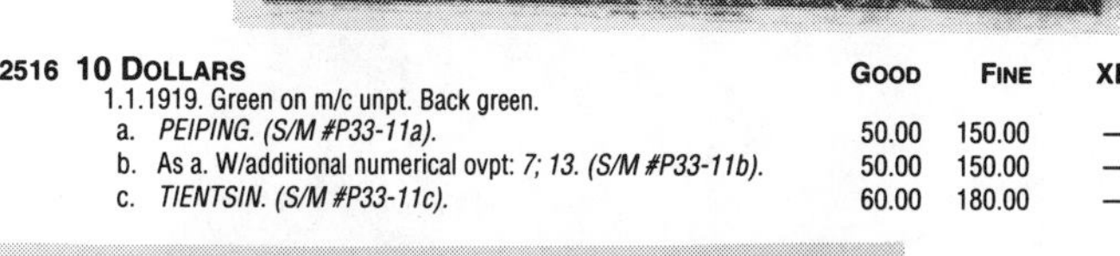

		Good	Fine	XF
S2516	**10 Dollars**			
	1.1.1919. Green on m/c unpt. Back green.			
	a. *PEIPING. (S/M #P33-11a).*	50.00	150.00	—
	b. As a. W/additional numerical ovpt: *7; 13. (S/M #P33-11b).*	50.00	150.00	—
	c. *TIENTSIN. (S/M #P33-11c).*	60.00	180.00	—

		Good	Fine	XF
S2516A	**5 Dollars**			
	1.1.1919. Similar to #S2516 but w/different guilloche. W/o place name. Proof. *(S/M #P33-11.5).*	—	Unc	175.00
S2517A	**10 Dollars**			
	1.1.1919. Similar to #S2516 but w/different guilloche. W/o place name. Proof. *(S/M #P33-12).*	—	Unc	200.00

1933 Issue

		Good	Fine	XF
S2518	**1 Dollar**			
	1.7.1933. Lilac and m/c. Great Wall at l. and r. Back brown. Printer: W&S.			
	a. *PEIPING.* Lg. sign. *(S/M #P33-20a).*	12.50	42.00	—
	b. *PEIPING.* Lg. sign. w/additional numerical ovpt: *55-88,* etc. *(S/M #P33-20c).*	12.50	42.00	—
	c. *PEIPING.* Sm. sign. *S/M #P33-20b).*	12.50	42.00	—
	d. *PEIPING.* Sm. sign. w/additional numerical ovpt: *55-88,* etc. *(S/M #P33-20d).*	12.50	42.00	—
	e. *TIENTSIN.* Lg. sign. *(S/M #P33-20e).*	12.50	42.00	—
	f. *TIENTSIN.* Lg. sign. w/additional numerical ovpt: *55-88,* etc. *(S/M #P33-20f).*	12.50	42.00	—
	g. *TIENTSIN.* Sm. sign. *(S/M #P33-20g).*	12.50	42.00	—
	h. *TIENTSIN.* Sm. sign. w/additional numerical ovpt: *55-88,* etc. *(S/M #P33-20h).*	12.50	42.00	—

PEIYANG TIENTSIN BANK

Pei Yang T'ien Ching Yin Hao

1910 TAEL ISSUE

#S2521-S2525 dragons facing above portr. Li Hung Chan w/harbor view at bottom.

		VG	VF	UNC
S2521	**1 TAEL** (ca. 1910). M/c. Back blue and orange. Remainder. *(S/M #P35-1).*	45.00	150.00	450.00

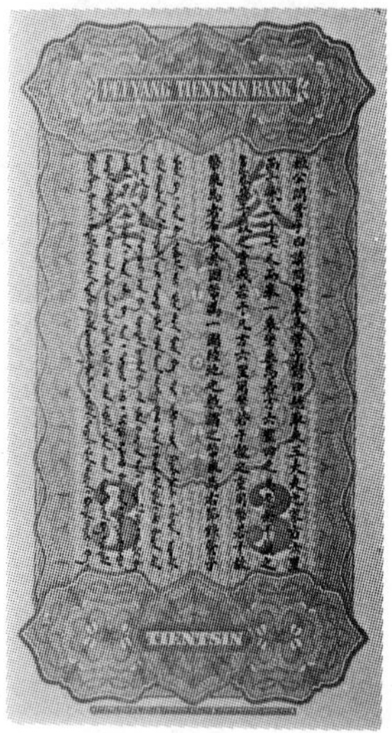

		VG	VF	UNC
S2522	**3 TAELS** (ca. 1910). Back red and green. Vertical format. Remainder. *(S/M #P35-2).*	—	200.00	600.00

NOTE: Also see #S2505.

S2523	**5 TAELS** (ca. 1910). Back red and green. Remainder. *(S/M #P35-3).*	—	180.00	550.00
S2524	**10 TAELS** (ca. 1910). Back orange and blue. Remainder. *(S/M #P35-4).*	—	225.00	675.00
S2525	**100 TAELS** (ca. 1910). Remainder. *(S/M #P35-5).*	—	300.00	900.00

1910 DOLLAR ISSUE

#S2526-S2530 dragons facing above bldg. at l., portr. Li Hung Chan at r. Printer: BWC.

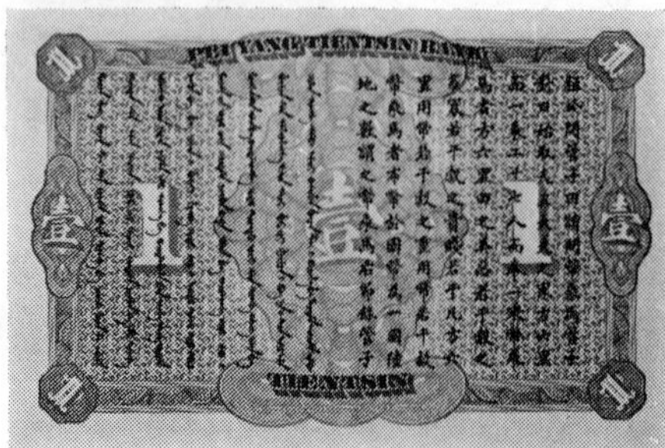

		VG	VF	UNC
S2526	**1 DOLLAR** (ca. 1910). Brown and m/c. Back brown and blue. Remainder. *(S/M #P35-10).*	—	125.00	375.00
S2527	**3 DOLLARS** (ca. 1910). Green and m/c. Back blue and yellow. Remainder. *(S/M #P35-11).*	—	125.00	375.00
S2528	**5 DOLLARS** (ca. 1910). Remainder. *(S/M #P35-12).*	—	150.00	450.00
S2529	**10 DOLLARS** (ca. 1910). Remainder. *(S/M #P35-13).*	—	180.00	540.00
S2529A	**50 DOLLARS** (ca. 1910). Similar to #S2530. Remainder. *(S/M #P35-13.5).*	—	225.00	675.00

		VG	VF	UNC
S2530	**100 DOLLARS** (ca. 1910). Red and m/c. Back green and red. Remainder. *(S/M #P35-14).*	—	300.00	900.00

NOTE: For #S2526 and S2530 w/additional ovpt. see Provincial Bank of Chihli #S1257-S1260.

PEIYANG CURRENCY BUREAU

北洋銀元局

Pei Yang Yin Yüan Chü

1905 ISSUE

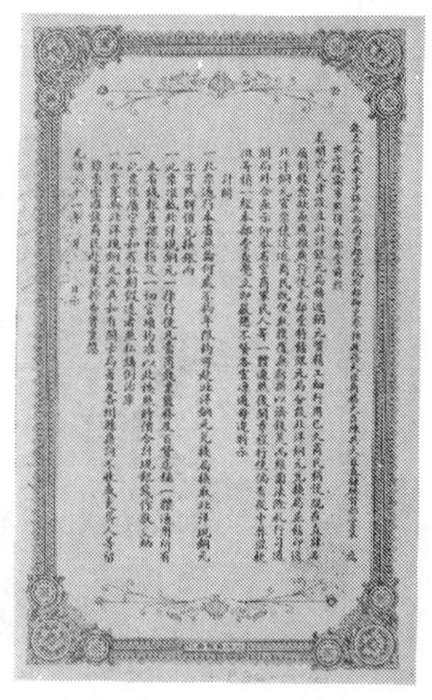

		GOOD	FINE	XF
S2531	**500 CASH** Yr. 31 (1905). Blue on yellow unpt. Dragons facing at upper l. and r. Orange text on back. Vertical format. *(S/M #P36-1).*	110.00	330.00	—

FRONTIER BANK

邊業銀行

Pien Yeh Yin Hang

1919 ISSUE

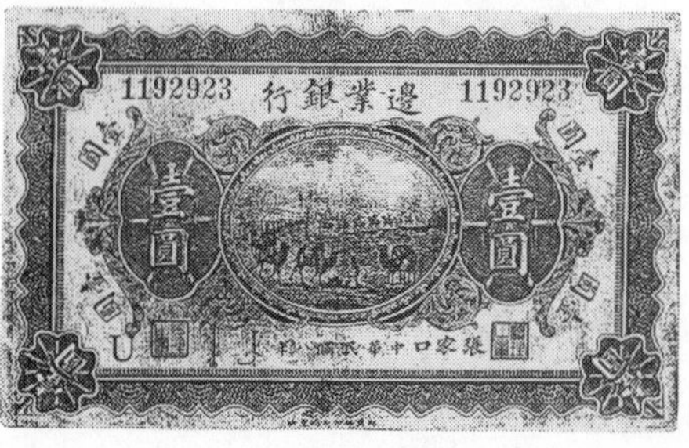

		GOOD	FINE	XF
S2535	**1 DOLLAR** 1919. Greenish black. Camel caravan at ctr. Back black on greenish black and red unpt. Printer: BEPP. Калганъ *(Kalgan).* Red letter ovpt: *U. (S/M #P42-).*	60.00	180.00	—

1920 ISSUE

		GOOD	FINE	XF
S2538	**10 CENTS** 1920. Brown and green. Back green and m/c. Printer: BEPP. *Kalgan. (S/M #P42-1).*	8.00	25.00	—
S2539	**20 CENTS** 1920. Gray and red. Back blue and m/c. *Kalgan. (S/M #P42-).*	10.00	30.00	—

1920 PROVISIONAL ISSUES

#S2544-S2546 ovpt. on Kirin Yung Heng Provincial Bank.

		GOOD	FINE	XF
S2544	**10 CENTS** ND (1920 -old date 1918). Ovpt. on #S1009. *(S/M #P42-2).*	17.50	55.00	—
S2545	**10 CENTS** ND (1920 -old date 1918). Ovpt. on #S1006. *(S/M #P42-3).*	17.50	55.00	—
S2546	**10 CENTS** ND (1920 -old date 1918). Ovpt. on #S1007. *(S/M #P42-4).*	18.50	55.00	—
S2549	**3 DOLLARS** ND (1920 -old date 1917). Ovpt. on #S990. *(S/M #P42-10).*	40.00	120.00	—

1921 REGULAR ISSUE

#S2551-S2553 printer: BEPP.

		GOOD	FINE	XF
S2551	**1 YÜAN** 1.4.1921. Brown. Camels at ctr. Back orange. *Harbin.* Uniface specimens. *(S/M #P42-20).*	—	Unc	85.00

		GOOD	FINE	XF
S2552	**5 YÜAN** 1.4.1921. Green. Camel caravan, tents at ctr. Back brown.			
	a. *Tientsin. (S/M #P42-21a).*	20.00	60.00	—
	s. *Harbin.* Uniface specimen. *(S/M #P42-21b).*	—	Unc	90.00

		GOOD	FINE	XF
S2553	**10 YÜAN** 1.4.1921. Violet. Camel caravan at ctr. Back orange. *Harbin. (S/M #P42-22).*			
	a. Issued note.	25.00	75.00	—
	s. Uniface specimen.	—	Unc	100.00

1924 ND PROVISIONAL ISSUE

#S2556-S2561 ovpt. on Kirin Yung Heng Provisional Bank.

		GOOD	FINE	XF
S2556	**10 CENTS** ND (1924 -old date 1923). Ovpt. on #S1045. *(S/M #P42-30).*	Reported Not Confirmed		
S2557	**20 CENTS** ND (1924 -old date 1923). Ovpt. on #S1046. *(S/M #P42-31).*	Reported Not Confirmed		
S2559	**1 YÜAN** ND (1924 -old date 1923). Ovpt. on #S1051. *(S/M #P42-40).*	30.00	100.00	—
S2560	**5 YÜAN** ND (1924 -old date 1923). Ovpt. on #S1052. *(S/M #P42-41).*	40.00	120.00	—
S2561	**10 YÜAN** ND (1924 -old date 1923). Ovpt. on #S1053. *(S/M #P42-42).*	45.00	135.00	—

1925 ISSUES

#S2563-S2566 printer: BEPP.

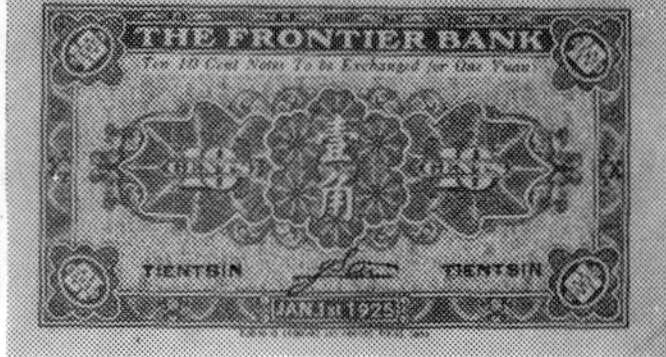

		GOOD	FINE	XF
S2563	**10 CENTS** 1.1.1925. Green.			
	a. *TIENTSIN. (S/M #P42-50).*	10.00	30.00	—
	b. *MUKDEN. (S/M #P42-50).*	10.00	30.00	—

		GOOD	FINE	XF
S2564	**10 CENTS** 1.1.1925. Orange. Harvesting at ctr.			
	a. *PEKING AND TIENTSIN CURRENCY. (S/M #P42-).*	6.00	18.00	—
	b. *MUKDEN. (S/M #P42-).*	6.00	18.00	—

		GOOD	FINE	XF
S2565	**20 CENTS** 1.1.1925. Orange. Harvesting at ctr.			
	a. *TIENTSIN. (S/M #P42-51).*	8.00	25.00	—
	b. *PEKING AND TIENTSIN CURRENCY. (S/M #P42-).*	8.00	25.00	—
	c. *MUKDEN. (S/M #P42-).*	8.00	25.00	—
S2566	**50 CENTS** 1.1.1925. Violet. Back violet and red. *MUKDEN. (S/M #P42-52).*	10.00	30.00	—

#S2568-S2575 printer: ABNC.

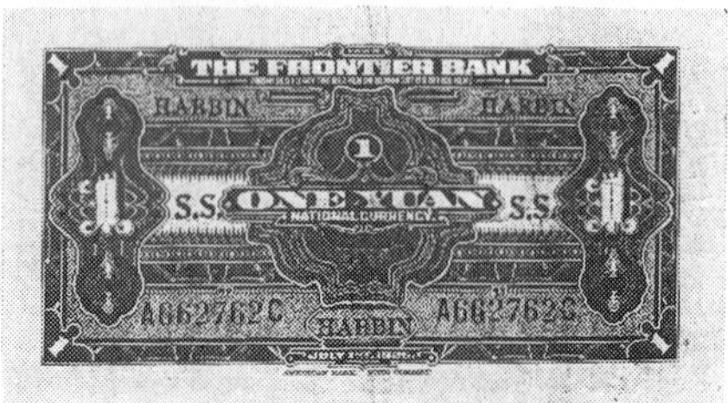

		VG	VF	UNC
S2568	**1 YÜAN**			
	1.7.1925. Green on m/c unpt. Hut at ctr. Back green.			
	a. *HARBIN.* W/additional Chinese 4 character ovpt. *(S/M #P42-60b).*	20.00	60.00	—
	s1. *HARBIN.* Specimen. *(S/M #P42-60a).*	—	—	75.00
	s2. As a. Specimen. *(S/M #P42-60b).*	—	—	75.00
	s3. *MUKDEN.* Specimen. *(S/M #P42-60c).*	—	—	75.00
S2569	**1 YÜAN**			
	1.7.1925. Brown on m/c unpt. Like #S2568. Back red-violet.			
	s1. *HARBIN.* Specimen. *(S/M #P42-61a).*	—	—	75.00
	s2. *HARBIN.* W/additional Chinese 4 character official ovpt. Specimen. *(S/M #P42-61b).*	—	—	75.00

		VG	VF	UNC
	s3. *MUKDEN.* Specimen. *(S/M #P42-61c).*	—	—	75.00

		VG	VF	UNC
S2570	**5 YÜAN**			
	1.7.1925. Brown on m/c unpt. House at ctr. Back brown.			
	a. *HARBIN. (S/M #P42-62a).*	25.00	75.00	—
	b. *THREE EASTERN PROVINCES. (S/M #P42-62b).*	32.50	100.00	—
	s1. *HARBIN.* W/additional Chinese 4 character official ovpt. Specimen. *(S/M #P42-62c).*	—	—	85.00
	s2. As. b. Specimen. *(S/M #P42-62b).*	—	—	100.00
	s3. *MUKDEN.* Specimen. *(S/M #P42-62d).*	—	—	85.00
S2571	**5 YÜAN**			
	1.7.1925. Orange on m/c unpt. Like #S2570. Back orange. *MUKDEN. (S/M #P42-63).*	25.00	75.00	—

		VG	VF	UNC
S2572	**10 YÜAN**			
	1.7.1925. Blue on m/c unpt.			
	a. *HARBIN. (S/M #P42-64a).*	25.00	75.00	—
	b. Like b., w/additional ovpt: *Harbin* above sign. and control character *Hei* at l. and r. *HARBIN* over control letters *S.S.* at l. and r. on back. *(S/M #P42-64d).*	30.00	90.00	—
	c. *HARBIN.* W/additional Chinese 4 character official ovpt. and *Harbin. (S/M #P42-64c).*	30.00	90.00	—
	s1. As c. Specimen. *(S/M #P42-64c).*	—	—	100.00
	s2. *THREE EASTERN PROVINCES.* Specimen. *(S/M #P42-64b).*	—	—	125.00

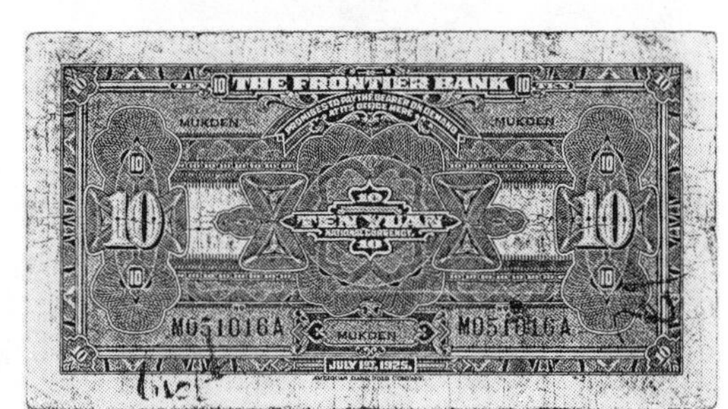

		VG	VF	UNC
S2573	**10 YÜAN**			
	1.7.1925. Dk. green and m/c. like #2572. Back green. *MUKDEN. (S/M #P42-65).*	8.00	25.00	—
S2574	**50 YÜAN**			
	1.7.1925. Olive. Back green. *(S/M #P42-66).*	—	—	—
S2575	**100 YÜAN**			
	1.7.1925. Blue. Back violet. *(S/M #P42-67).*	—	—	—

1929 ISSUES

		VG	VF	UNC
S2576	**10 CENTS**			
	1.12.1929. Brown and red. Back brown. *HARBIN.* W/additional Chinese 4 character official ovpt. Specimen. *(S/M #P42-70a).*	—	—	75.00

		VG	VF	UNC
S2577	**10 CENTS**			
	1.12.1929. Orange. Like #S2576. *MUKDEN. (S/M #P42-70b).*	15.00	45.00	—

		VG	VF	UNC
S2578	**20 CENTS** 1.12.1929. Red. Like #S2579. *HARBIN.* W/additional Chinese 4 character official ovpt. Specimen. *(S/M #P42-71a).*	—	—	75.00

		VG	VF	UNC
S2579	**20 CENTS** 1.12.1929. Green.*MUKDEN.* Specimen. *(S/M #P42-71b.)*	—	—	75.00

		VG	VF	UNC
S2580	**50 CENTS** 1.12.1929. Orange. *HARBIN.* W/additional Chinese 4 character official ovpt. *(S/M #P42-72a).*			
	a. Issued note.	20.00	60.00	—
	s. Specimen.	—	—	75.00
S2581	**50 CENTS** 1.12.1929. Brown. *MUKDEN.* Specimen. *(S/M #P42-72b.)*	—	—	75.00

1932 ISSUE

		VG	VF	UNC
S2585	**1 YÜAN** 1932. *(S/M #P42-).*	Reported Not Confirmed		

MARKET STABILIZATION CURRENCY BUREAU

局錢官市平

P'ing Shih Kuan Ch'ien Chüan

1924 COPPER COIN ISSUE

#S2589-S2590 gateway at ctr.

		VG	VF	UNC
S2589	**10 COPPERS** 13.7.1924. Brown and tan. Back blue. *Kiangsu. (S/M #P50-1).*	22.50	67.50	—

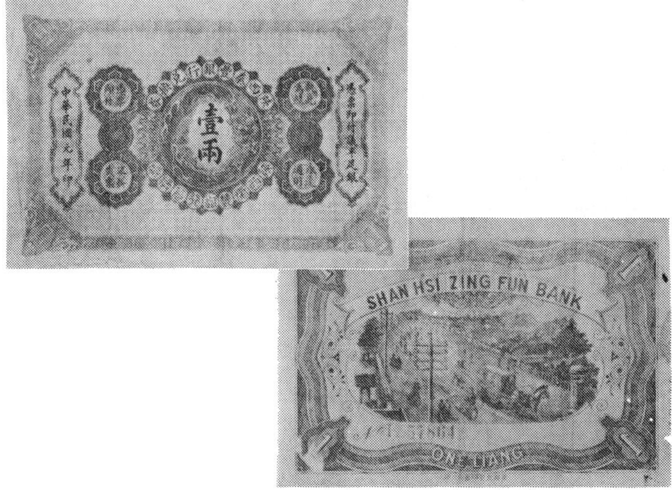

		VG	VF	UNC
S2590	**100 COPPERS** 13.7.1924. Red and tan. Back orange. *Kiangsu. (S/M #P50-2).*	30.00	90.00	—

SHAN HSI ZING FUN BANK

行銀豐泰西陝

Shan Hsi Ch'in Feng Yin Hang

1912 LIANG (TAEL) ISSUE

#S2593 and S2594 printer: CMPA.

		VG	VF	UNC
S2593	**1 LIANG (TAEL)** 1.5.1912. Violet and m/c. Back blue. Remainder. *(S/M #S16-1).*	—	80.00	240.00
S2594	**5 LIANG (TAELS)** 1.5.1912. Violet. Specimen. *(S/M #S16 -).*	—	—	300.00

1913 LIANG (TAEL) ISSUE

#S2597 and S2598 printer: CMPA.

S2597 5 LIANG (TAELS)

1913. Green and orange. 2 spheres at ctr. Uniface. *(S/M #S16-2).*

	VG	VF	UNC
r1. Remainder.	—	80.00	240.00
r2. Remainder w/perforations and cancellation ovpt.	—	60.00	200.00

S2598 10 LIANG (TAELS)

	VG	VF	UNC
1913. Black and violet. Back blue and green; ship at l., train at r. *(S/M #S16-3).*	30.00	90.00	275.00

FU CHING CHIEN CHÜ/SHENSI
FU CHING BANK OF SHENSI
FU CHING BANK

局钱泰富西陕

Shan Hsi Fu Ch'in Ch'ien Chü

行銀泰富西陕

Shan Hsi Fu Ch'in Yin Hang

局钱泰富

Fu Ch'in Ch'ien Chü

1919 TAEL ISSUE

S2598A 1TAELS

	GOOD	FINE	XF
1919. Green. Pagoda, bldgs at ctr. Back orange.	—	—	—

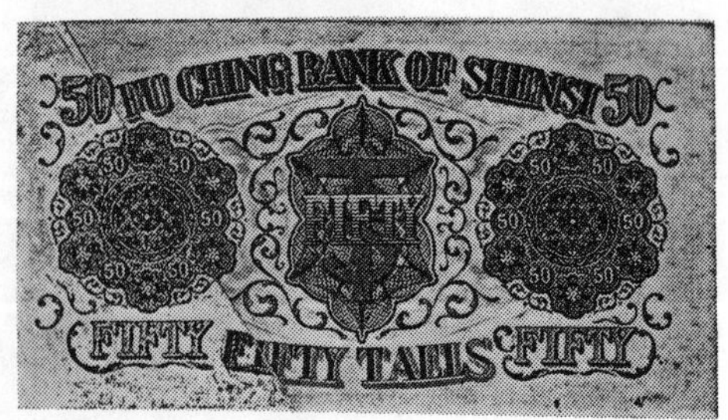

S2599 50 TAELS

	GOOD	FINE	XF
1919. Purple. Pagoda, bldgs. at ctr. Back brown on green upnt. Diagonally cut cancelled at ctr. r. *(S/M #S17-0-8).*	—	—	—

1922 YÜAN ISSUE

#S2600-S2600B fortress at ctr. Printer: BEPP.

S2600 1 YÜAN

	GOOD	FINE	XF
1922. Green. Back violet and m/c. *(S/M #S20-1).*	10.00	30.00	—

		GOOD	FINE	XF
S2600A	**5 YÜAN** 1922. Blue. Back violet and m/c. *(S/M #S20-2).*	15.00	45.00	—
S2600B	**10 YÜAN** 1922. Orange. Back violet and m/c. *(S/M #S20-3).*	17.50	50.00	—

NOTE: For #S2600-S2600B w/additional ovpt. see Military - National Army Combined Headquarters #S3918-S3920.

1923 CASH ISSUE

#S2601-S2603 mountain view at top. Printer: BEPP.

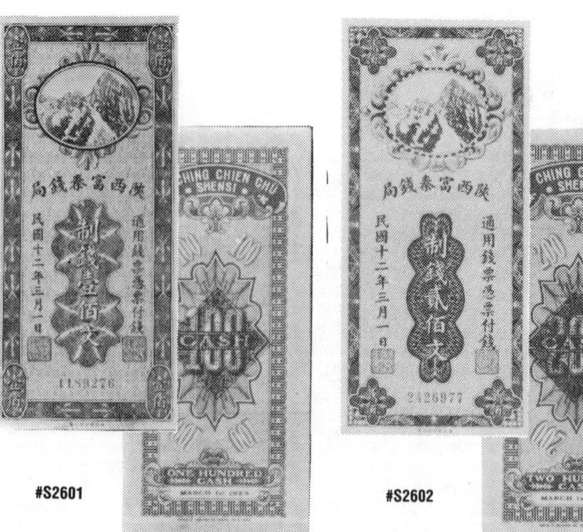

#S2601

#S2602

		GOOD	FINE	XF
S2601	**100 CASH** 1.3.1923. Violet. Back green and red. Vertical format. *(S/M #S17-1).*	20.00	60.00	180.00
S2602	**200 CASH** 1.3.1923. *(S/M #S17-1.3).*	25.00	80.00	240.00

		Good	Fine	XF
S2603	**500 Cash** 1.3.1923. Red-orange. Back olive on red-orange unpt. Vertical format. *(S/M #S17-1.6).*	30.00	90.00	270.00
S2604	**1000 Cash** 1923. *(S/M #S17-2).*	40.00	120.00	360.00

1926 Ch'uan Issue

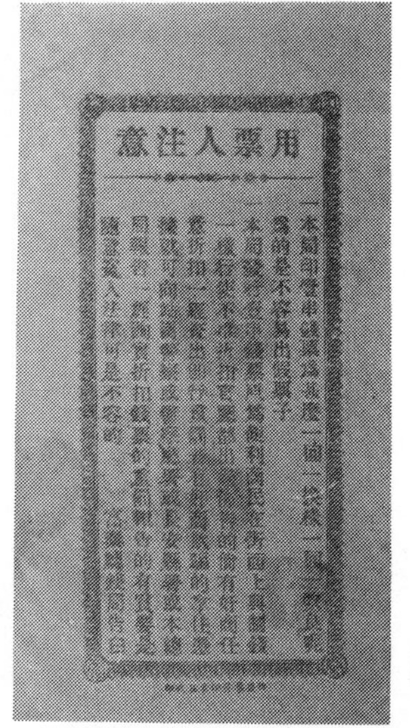

		Good	Fine	XF
S2606	**1 Ch'uan** 1926. Blue and yellow. Bldg. at top. Back brown. Printer: ILBC. Vertical format. *(S/M #S17-10).*	40.00	120.00	360.00

1927 Ch'uan Issue

		Good	Fine	XF
S2607	**1 Ch'uan** 1.2.1927. *(S/M #S17-15).*	—	—	—

		Good	Fine	XF
S2607A	**2 Ch'uan** 1.2.1927. Red. Temple at ctr. *(S/M #S17-16).*	—	—	—
S2607B	**2 Ch'uan** 1.2.1927. Dull red. Pagoda, trees at ctr. *(S/M #S17-17).*	—	—	—
S2608	**10 Cents** 1927. *(S/M #S17-20).*	20.00	60.00	—
S2609	**30 Cents** 1927. Green and red. Back blue. *(S/M #S17-21).*	30.00	90.00	—
S2610	**50 Cents** 1927. *(S/M #S17-22).*	30.00	90.00	—

NOTE: For #S2608-S2610 w/additional ovpt. see Military - National Army #S3907-S3909.

1928 Cash Issue

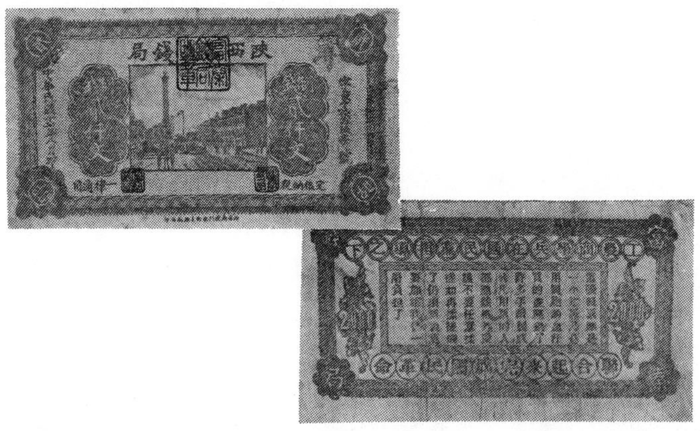

		Good	Fine	XF
S2614	**2000 Cash** Aug. 1928. Purple on lt. yellow-green unpt. Monument in city at ctr. *(S/M #S17-29).*	40.00	120.00	—
S2615	**2000 Cash** 1928. Red and yellow. Back red .*(S/M #S17-30).*	30.00	90.00	—

1931 Copper Coin Issue

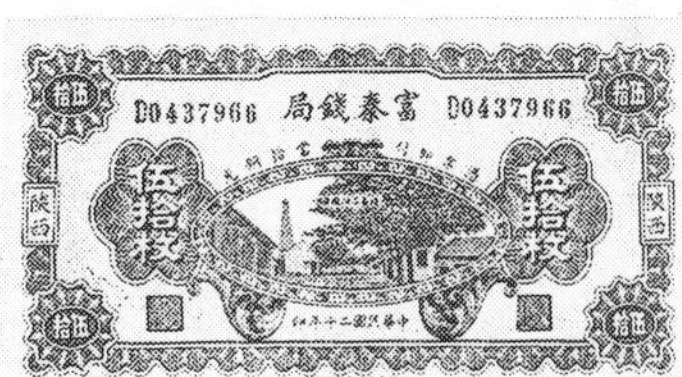

		Good	Fine	XF
S2616	**50 Coppers** 1931. Brown on pale green unpt. Farm bldgs. at ctr. Biplane at ctr. on back. *(S/M #S17-42).*	—	—	—

1935 Copper Coin Issue

		Good	Fine	XF
S2618	**20 Coppers** 1935. Specimen. *(S/M #S17-51).*	—	Unc	75.00

#S2621-S2623 *Deleted.* See #S2599-S2600B.

Shansi Provincial Railway

山西省省鐵兩行聯合辦事處

Shan Hsi Sheng T'ien Liang Hang Lian Ho Pan Shih Ch'u

1940 Issue

		Good	Fine	XF
S2624	**25 Cents** June 1940. Purple on pink unpt. Bldg. at l. Back red. *(S/M #S22.5-6).*	10.00	30.00	—

SHANSE PROVINCIAL BANK
SHANSI PROVINCIAL BANK

行銀省西山
Shan Hsi Sheng Yin Hang

1919 ISSUE

		GOOD	FINE	XF
S2625	**10 CENTS** 1919. *(S/M #S23-1).*	Reported Not Confirmed		
S2626	**20 CENTS** 1919. *(S/M #S23-2).*	Reported Not Confirmed		
S2627	**50 CENTS** 1919. *(S/M #S23-3).*	Reported Not Confirmed		

		GOOD	FINE	XF
S2628	**1 DOLLAR** 1919. Blue on green and ochre unpt. Rural house at ctr. Back blue; shoreline at ctr.			
	a. *TAIYUAN.* (3mm). Sign. Y. C. Yen and P. C. Hao w/o sign. titles. *(S/M #S23-10a).*	5.00	17.50	50.00
	b. *TAIYUAN.* (3mm). Sign. C. Y. Chia and J. C. Hsü w/titles *Co-Director* and *Director.*	5.00	17.50	50.00
	c. As b. *TAIYUAN.* (4mm). Sign. (?). P. Chi and J. C. Hsü w/titles.	5.00	17.50	50.00
	d. *TIENTSIN. (S/M #S23-10c).*	15.00	45.00	—
	s. *PEIPING.* Specimen. *S/M #S23-10b).*	—	Unc	80.00
S2628A	**1 DOLLAR** 1919. Blue on brown and purple unpt. Like #S2628. *SHANSI. (S/M #S23-10d).*	15.00	45.00	—

#S2629-S2632 printer: BEPP.

		GOOD	FINE	XF
S2629	**5 DOLLARS** 1919. Blue and brown. Back blue. *TAIYUAN. (S/M #S23-11).*	30.00	90.00	—

		GOOD	FINE	XF
S2630	**10 DOLLARS** 1919. Black on blue and brown unpt. Shoreline houses at ctr. Back blue.			
	a. *TAIYUAN. (S/M #S23-12a).*	35.00	110.00	—
	s. *PEIPING.* Specimen. *(S/M #S23-12b).*	—	Unc	125.00
S2631	**50 DOLLARS** 1919. *TAIYUAN. (S/M #S23-13).*	Reported Not Confirmed		
S2632	**100 DOLLARS** 1919. *TAIYUAN. (S/M #S23-14).*	Reported Not Confirmed		

1922 ISSUE

		GOOD	FINE	XF
S2632A	**10 CENTS** 1.3.1922. Brown on red unpt. Pavilion at l. Back green and dk. brown. Printer: BEPP. *(S/M #S23-15).*	17.50	55.00	—

1924 ISSUE

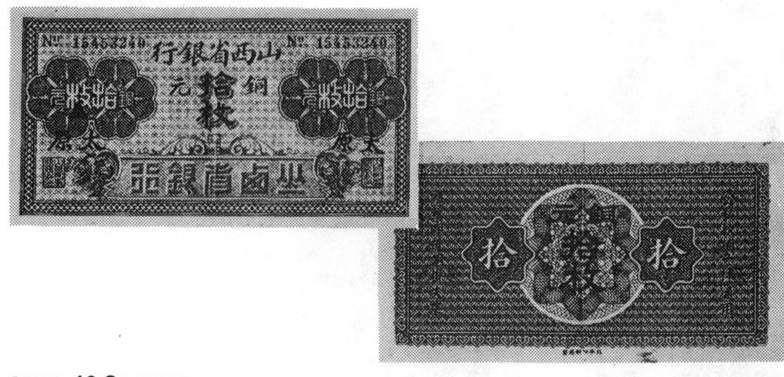

		GOOD	FINE	XF
S2633	**10 COPPERS** ND (1924). Brown on green unpt. Back dk. blue on red unpt.			
	a. *Fen Yang. (S/M #S23-20a).*	10.00	30.00	90.00
	b. Black. *P'ing Yao. (S/M #S23-20b).*	10.00	30.00	90.00
	c. Black. *Tai Yuan. (S/M #S23-20c).*	10.00	30.00	90.00
	d. Red. *Tai Yuan. (S/M #S23-20d).*	10.00	30.00	90.00
	e. *Yu Tz'u. (S/M #S23-20e).*	10.00	30.00	90.00
	f. Black. *Tai Hsien. (S/M #S23-20f).*	10.00	30.00	90.00

		GOOD	FINE	XF
S2634	**20 COPPERS** ND (1924). Blue-black on red-orange unpt. *(S/M #S23-21).*			
	a. *Tái Yuan. (S/M #S23-21a).*	10.00	30.00	90.00
	b. *Tái Hsien. (S/M #S23-21b).*	10.00	30.00	90.00
S2635	**50 COPPERS** ND (1924). *(S/M #S23-22).*	18.00	55.00	160.00
S2636	**100 COPPERS** ND (1924). Red on gray unpt. *Sin Hsien. (S/M #S23-23).*	18.00	55.00	160.00

1926 ISSUE

#S2637-S2641 printer: BEPP.

		GOOD	FINE	XF
S2637	**10 CENTS** 1926. Violet. Waterfront scene at r.			
	a. *PEIPING. (S/M #S23-30b).*	9.00	27.00	—
	b. *TIENTSIN. (S/M #S23-30a).*	9.00	27.00	—
	c. *TAIYUAN.* Sign. C. Y. Chia and J. C. Hsü w/titles: *Co-Director* and *Director. (S/M #S23-30c).*	8.00	25.00	—
	d. Sign. Y. C. Yen as *Co-Director* at l. and r. *(S/M #S23-30d).*	8.00	25.00	—
S2638	**10 CENTS** 1926. Dk. green. Like #S2637. Back green. *TAIYUAN. (S/M #S23-).*	8.00	25.00	—
S2639	**20 CENTS** 1926. Red. Rural house at r.			
	a. *TIENTSIN. (S/M #S23-30a).*	9.00	27.00	—
	b. *TAIYUAN.* As #S2637c. *(S/M #S23-30b).*	9.00	27.00	—
	c. *TAIYUAN.* As #S2637d. *(S/M #S23-30c).*	9.00	27.00	—
S2641	**1 DOLLAR** 1926. *(S/M #S23-40).*	Reported Not Confirmed		

1928 ISSUES

#S2644-S2648 printer: BEPP.

		GOOD	FINE	XF
S2644	**10 COPPERS** 1928. Blue-black on ochre and pale blue unpt. Temple at l. Back brown.			
	a. *Fen Hsiu. (S/M #S23-45a).*	10.00	30.00	—
	b. *Tai Yuan. (S/M #S23-45b).*	10.00	30.00	—
	c. *Sin Hsien. (S/M #S23-45c).*	10.00	30.00	—

		GOOD	FINE	XF
S2645	**20 COPPERS** 1928. Brown on m/c. Fortress at l.			
	a. *Fen Hsiu. (S/M #S23-46a).*	15.00	45.00	—
	b. *Tai Yuan. (S/M #S23-46b).*	15.00	45.00	—
S2647	**10 CENTS** 1928. Blue. Back green. *(S/M #S23-50).*	Reported Not Confirmed		

		GOOD	FINE	XF
S2648	**20 CENTS** 1928. Violet. Pagoda at l. *TAIYUAN. (S/M #S23-51).*	10.00	30.00	90.00
S2649	**20 CENTS** 1928. Violet. Back green. *TAIYUAN. (S/M #S23-52).*	10.00	30.00	—

		GOOD	FINE	XF
S2651	**1 DOLLAR** 1928. Brown. Hillside bldgs. at ctr. Back green. *TAIYUAN. (S/M #S23-53).*	15.00	40.00	80.00

		GOOD	FINE	XF
S2651A	**1 DOLLAR** 1928. Blue-violet on m/c unpt. River, city, tower along wall at r. *TAIYUAN. (S/M #S23-54).*	15.00	45.00	—
S2652	**5 DOLLARS** 1928. Dk. blue-gray. Bldg. w/clock tower at ctr. *TAIYUAN. (S/M #S23-55).*	15.00	50.00	—

		GOOD	FINE	XF
S2652A	**5 DOLLARS** 1928. Brown on ochre unpt. Hillside village at r. *TAIYUAN. (S/M #S23-56).*	20.00	60.00	—

		GOOD	FINE	XF
S2653	**10 DOLLARS** 1928. Dk. green. Bank bldg. at ctr. *TAIYUAN. (S/M #S23-57).*	30.00	90.00	—

		GOOD	FINE	XF
S2653A	**10 DOLLARS** 1928. Brown-violet on ochre and pale blue unpt. Bldgs. at r. Back brown on yellow unpt.; hillside village at l. *TAIYUAN. (S/M #S23-58).*	20.00	60.00	—

1930 ISSUES

#S2654-S2659 printer: BEPP.

		GOOD	FINE	XF
S2654	**10 CENTS** 1930. Brown. Hillside bldgs. at l. Bldg. w/clock tower on on back.			
	a. *TAIYUAN. (S/M #S23-60a).*	9.00	27.50	55.00
	b. *KIUSIU. (S/M #S23-60b).*	9.00	27.50	55.00
	c. *PINGYAO. (S/M #S23-60c).*	9.00	27.50	55.00
	d. *SUIYUAN. (S/M #S23-60d).*	9.00	27.50	55.00
	e. *TAIHSIEN. (S/M #S23-60e).*	9.00	27.50	55.00

		GOOD	FINE	XF
S2655	**20 CENTS** 1930. Brown. Shoreline, lg. bldg. in distance at l. Peking fortress gate at ctr. on back. *TAIYUAN. (S/M #S23-60.5).*	8.00	25.00	50.00
S2655A	**20 CENTS** 1930. Like #S2655 but deep olive-green.			
	a. *SUIYUAN. (S/M #S23-61a).*	8.00	25.00	75.00
	b. *FANTSAN. (S/M #S23-61b).*	8.00	25.00	75.00
	c. *TAIKU. (S/M #S23-61c).*	8.00	25.00	75.00
	d. *TAIYUAN. (S/M #S23-61d).*	8.00	25.00	75.00
S2656	**50 CENTS** 1930. Red. Back violet. *(S/M #S23-62).*	10.00	30.00	60.00

		GOOD	FINE	XF
S2657	**1 YÜAN** 1.8.1930. Brown on m/c unpt. Shoreline at ctr. Back brown.			
	a. *CHANGCHIH.* 2 sign. varieties. *(S/M #S23-70a).*	15.00	45.00	135.00
	b. *CH'UWO. (S/M #S23-70b).*	15.00	45.00	135.00
	c. *FENYANG. (S/M #S23-70c).*	15.00	45.00	135.00
	d. *HUNGTIEN. (S/M #S23-70d).*	15.00	45.00	135.00
	e. *KIAOCHENG. (S/M #S23-70e).*	15.00	45.00	135.00
	f. *KIEHSIU. (S/M #S23-70f).*	15.00	45.00	135.00
	g. *LINFEN. (S/M #S23-70g).*	15.00	45.00	135.00
	h. *PINGYAO. (S/M #S23-70h).*	15.00	45.00	135.00
	i. *SHOHSIEN. (S/M #S23-70i).*	15.00	45.00	135.00
	j. *SIAOYI. (S/M #S23-70j).*	15.00	45.00	135.00
	k. *SINHSIEN. (S/M #S23-70k).*	15.00	45.00	135.00
	l. *SUIYUAN. (S/M #S23-70l).*	15.00	45.00	135.00
	m. *TAIYUAN.* 2 sign. varieties. *(S/M #S23-70m).*	3.00	10.00	30.00
	n. *TATUNG. (S/M #S23-70n).*	15.00	45.00	135.00
	o. *TSING CHENG. (S/M #S23-70o).*	15.00	45.00	135.00
	p. *YUTZE. (S/M #S23-70p).*	15.00	45.00	135.00
	q. *CHIHSIEN. (S/M #S23-70q).*	15.00	45.00	135.00
	r. *WENSHUI. (S/M #S23-70r).*	15.00	45.00	135.00
	s. *YUNCHENG.* 2 sign. varieties. *(S/M #S23-70s).*	15.00	45.00	135.00
	t. *HUNGTUNG. (S/M #S23-70t).*	20.00	60.00	—
	u. *TAIKU.* 2 sign. varieties. *(S/M #S23-70u).*	20.00	60.00	—
	v. *CHIHSIEN. (S/M #S23-70x).*	20.00	60.00	—
	w. *YANGCHÜAN. (S/M #S23-70w).*	20.00	60.00	—
	x. *FANTSUN. (S/M #S23-70x).*	20.00	60.00	—
	y. *SINKIANG. (S/M #S23-70y).*	20.00	60.00	—
	z. *YINGHSIEN. (S/M #S23-70z).*	20.00	60.00	—
S2657A	**1 YÜAN** Violet w/bright m/c guilloches. Like #S2657 w/similar branch office ovpts. *(S/M #S23-70).*	25.00	60.00	120.00
S2657B	**1 YÜAN** Violet w/dull m/c guilloches. Like #S2657A w/similar branch office ovpts. *(S/M #23-70).*	25.00	60.00	120.00

NOTE: Confirmation of various branch ovpts. for #S2657A and S2657B is requested.

		GOOD	FINE	XF
S2658	**5 YÜAN** 1930. Yellow. *TAIYUAN. (S/M #S23-71).*	30.00	70.00	140.00
S2659	**10 YÜAN** 1930. Green. *TAIYUAN. (S/M #S23-72).*	32.00	80.00	160.00

#S2660 *Deleted.* See #S2654.

#S2663 *Deleted.* See #S2657A and #S2657B.

1932 ISSUE

#S2666-S2673 printer: BEPP.

		GOOD	FINE	XF
S2666	**10 COPPERS** 1932. Dk. brown. Pagodas at l., rural house at r. Back red. *TAIYUAN.*			
	a. Issued note. *(S/M #S23-75a).*	7.00	20.00	—
	b. W/additional 8 Chinese character ovpt. at l. and r. on back. *(S/M #S23-75b).*	7.00	20.00	—
S2667	**20 COPPERS** 1932. Black. Like #S2666. Back brown. *TAIYUAN.*			
	a. Issued note. *(S/M #S23-76a).*	8.00	25.00	—
	b. W/additional 6 Chinese character ovpt. at l. and r. on back. *(S/M #S23-76b).*	8.00	25.00	—
S2671	**1 YÜAN** 1932. Red and brown. Back brown. *(S/M #S23-80).*	10.00	30.00	—
S2672	**5 YÜAN** 1932. Yellow. *(S/M #S23-81).*	12.50	40.00	—

		GOOD	FINE	XF
S2673	**10 YÜAN** 1932. Green on m/c unpt. Railroad, ore cars, factory and workers at ctr. Back green.			
	a. *TAIYUAN. (S/M #S23-82a).*	20.00	60.00	—
	b. *T'AIKU. (S/M #S23-82b).*	20.00	60.00	—

1933 ISSUE

		GOOD	FINE	XF
S2675	**5 YÜAN** 1.9.1933. Red on lt. blue unpt. Watchtower at Peking at ctr. Back red; factories at ctr. Printer: BEPP.			
	a. *TAIYUAN.* Sign. Y. Fu - S. Wang. *(S/M #S23-90a).*	17.50	55.00	—
	b. *TAIYUAN.* Sign. Y. Fu - C. L. Lu. *(S/M #S23-90b).*	17.50	55.00	—
	c. *TAIKU.* Sign. Y. Fu - S. Wang. *(S/M #S23-90c).*	17.50	55.00	—
	d. *HUNGTUNG.* Sign. Y. Fu - S. Wang. *(S/M #S23-90d).*	17.50	55.00	—
	e. *PINGYAO.* Sign. Y. Fu - S. Wang. *(S/M #S23-90e).*	17.50	55.00	—

1936 ISSUE

#S2677 and S2678 pagoda at ctr. *SHANSI.* Printer: NWPF.

		GOOD	FINE	XF
S2677	**1 YÜAN** July 1936. Olive-green on lt. blue unpt. Back dk. blue. *(S/M #S23-99).*	5.00	15.00	—

1937 ND PROVISIONAL ISSUE

		GOOD	FINE	XF
S2678	**1 YÜAN** ND (1937 -old date July 1936). Olive-green on lt. blue unpt. Ovpt: 2 vertical sets of 4 Chinese characters at l. and r on #S2677. Different serial # on back. *(S/M #S23-100).*	15.00	45.00	—

1937 REGULAR ISSUE

#S2679-S2681 watchtower at Peking at l. or r. *SHANSI*. Printer: NWPF.

		GOOD	FINE	XF
S2679	**5 YÜAN** 1937. Brown on m/c unpt. Back orange; pavilion at ctr. *(S/M #S23-110).*	15.00	45.00	—

		GOOD	FINE	XF
S2680	**10 YÜAN** 1937. Black and m/c. Back green; mountain village. *(S/M #S23-111).*	15.00	45.00	—

PROVINCIAL BANK OF SHENSI

行銀省西陝

Shan Hsi Sheng Yin Hang

1930 ND PROVISIONAL ISSUE

#S2681-S2683 ovpt. new issuer's name.

		VG	VF	UNC
S2681	**1 DOLLAR** ND (1930 -old date 1.8.1928). Brown. Ovpt. on #S3887d. *SHENSI/SHANTUNG. (S/M #S24-1).*			
	a. Issued note.	35.00	110.00	—
	s. Specimen w/3 Chinese character ovpt., punched hole cancelled.	—	—	120.00
S2682	**5 DOLLARS** ND (1930 -old date 1.8.1928). Deep green. Ovpt. on #S3888c. *SHENSI/SHANTUNG. (S/M #S24-2).*			
	a. Issued note.	45.00	135.00	—
	s. Specimen as #S2681s.	—	—	150.00
S2683	**10 DOLLARS** ND (1930 -old date 1.8.1928). Red-brown. Ovpt. on #S3889d. *SHENSI/SHANTUNG. (S/M #S24-3).*			
	a. Issued note.	60.00	180.00	—
	s. Specimen as #S2681s.	—	—	175.00

1931 ISSUE

#S2684-S2686 printer: BEPP.

		VG	VF	UNC
S2684	**1 DOLLAR** 1931. Brown. Back brown. *SHENSI. (S/M #S24-10).*	22.50	67.50	—
S2685	**5 DOLLARS** 1931. Green. Back green. *SHENSI. (S/M #S24-11).*	30.00	90.00	—
S2686	**10 DOLLARS** 1931. Blue. Back blue; biplane at ctr. *SHENSI. (S/M #S24-12).*	35.00	110.00	—

1932 ISSUE

#S2687-S2688 barns w/tower at l. Printer: BEPP.

		VG	VF	UNC
S2687	**10 CENTS** 1.4.1932. Red. Back red; biplane at ctr. *SHENSI. (S/M #S24-20).*			
	a. Issued note.	15.00	45.00	—
	s. Specimen.	—	—	85.00

		VG	VF	UNC
S2688	**20 CENTS** 1.4.1932. Green. Back green; monoplane at ctr.*SHENSI. (S/M #S24-21).*			
	a. Issued note.	17.50	55.00	—
	s. Specimen.	—	—	100.00

1939 ND PROVISIONAL ISSUE

#S2691-S2692A ovpt. new bank name on unissued notes of Shensi Fu Ching Bank.

		VG	VF	UNC
S2691	**1 CHIAO = 10 CENTS ON 50 COPPERS** ND (1939 -old date Yr. 17). Blue. Rural bldg. at ctr. Back blue; biplane at ctr. *(S/M #S24-30).*	15.00	45.00	—
S2692	**2 CHIAO = 20 CENTS** ND (1939 -old date Yr. 17). Red. Back red. *(S/M #S24-31).*	17.50	50.00	—
S2692A	**5 CHIAO = 50 CENTS** ND (1939 -old date Yr. 17). Dull blue-green. Like #S2691. Back gray. *(S/M #S24-32).*	25.00	80.00	—

1949 ISSUE

		VG	VF	UNC
S2693	**20 CENTS** 1949. Pagoda at r. *(S/M #S24-42).*	—	—	—

BANK OF SHANSI

券通流 行銀西陝

Shan Hsi Yin Hang Liu T'ung Ch'üan

ND ISSUE

		VG	VF	UNC
S2694	**1 YÜAN** ND (ca.1912). Blue on yellow unpt. Back black. Remainder. *(S/M #S26.5-10).*	60.00	200.00	—

SHANTUNG COMMERCIAL BANK

山東商業銀行

Shan Tung Shang Yeh Yin Hang

1920 ND PROVISIONAL ISSUE

#S2695 and S2696 ovpt. new bank name on Shan Tung Bank.

		GOOD	FINE	XF
S2695	**5 DOLLARS** ND (1920). Ovpt. on #S2768. *(S/M #S42-0.5).*	22.50	67.50	—
S2696	**10 DOLLARS** ND (1920). Ovpt. on #S2769. *(S/M #S42-1).*	30.00	90.00	—

1926 REGULAR ISSUE

		GOOD	FINE	XF
S2700	**10 DOLLARS** 1926. Green and m/c. Back green. Printer: BEPP. *(S/M #S42-).*	—	—	—

SHANTUNG EXCHANGE BUREAU

山東平市官錢局

Shan Tung P'ing Shih Kuan Ch'ien Tsung Chü

1932 ISSUE

		GOOD	FINE	XF
S2703	**10 CENTS** 1932. Red. Printer: HTCN. *Chinan.* *(S/M #S41.5-11).*	12.00	35.00	—

1933 ISSUE

		GOOD	FINE	XF
S2708	**10 CENTS** 1933. Red. Printer: SSPC. *(S/M #S41.5-12).*	12.00	35.00	—

		GOOD	FINE	XF
S2708A	**20 CENTS** 1933. Dk. blue on blue unpt. Gateway at ctr. Vertical format. *(S/M #S41.5-13).*	12.00	35.00	—

1936 COPPER COIN ISSUE

		GOOD	FINE	XF
S2709	**10 COPPERS** Yr. 25 (1936). Dk. blue-gray on blue-gray unpt. 3 tower gate at ctr. Control letters A-A on back. *(S/M #S41.5-19).*	8.00	25.00	—

		GOOD	FINE	XF
S2710	**20 COPPERS** Yr. 25 (1936). Dk. green on green unpt. Waterfront village at l. *(S/M #S41.5-20).*	8.00	25.00	—

		GOOD	FINE	XF
S2711	**50 COPPERS** Yr. 25 (1936). Steam passenger train at ctr. *(S/M #S41.5-21).*			
	a. Control letters *A-A* on back.	10.00	30.00	—
	b. Control letters *B-B* on back.	10.00	30.00	—

		GOOD	FINE	XF
S2712	**100 COPPERS** Yr. 25 (1936). Red on yellow-orange unpt. Bldg. w/clock tower at ctr. *(S/M #S41.5-22).*	15.00	45.00	—

		GOOD	FINE	XF
S2713	**100 COPPERS** 1936. Brown on blue-green unpt. Bank bldg. at ctr. *(S/M #S41.5-23).*	22.50	70.00	—

SHANTUNG PROVINCIAL TREASURY

山東省金庫券

Shan Tung Sheng Chin K'u Ch'üan

1926 ISSUE

#S2718-S2720 house at l., gardening at r. Printer: SOPO.

		GOOD	FINE	XF
S2715	**10 CENTS** 1926. *(S/M #S43-1).*	Reported Not Confirmed		
S2716	**20 CENTS** 1926. *(S/M #S43-2).*	Reported Not Confirmed		

		GOOD	FINE	XF
S2718	**1 YÜAN** 1926. Orange and yellow. Back violet. *(S/M #S43-10).*	30.00	90.00	270.00
S2719	**5 YÜAN** 1926. Blue and green. Back green. *(S/M #S43-11).*	33.50	100.00	300.00

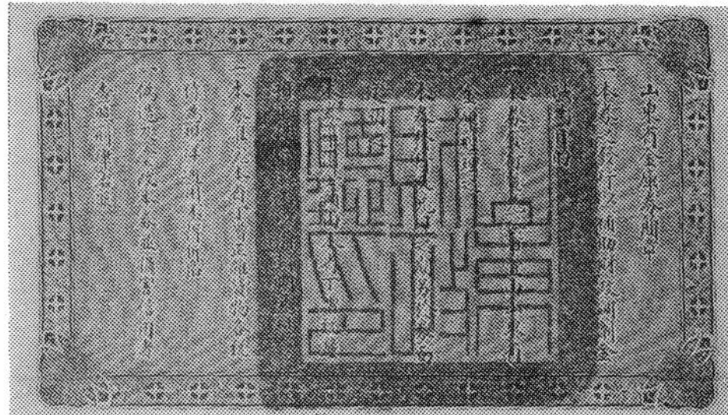

		GOOD	FINE	XF
S2720	**10 YÜAN** 1926. Gray and brown. Back brown. *(S/M #S43-12).*	45.00	135.00	400.00

SHANTUNG PROVINCIAL TREASURY

山東省庫券

Shan Tung Sheng K'u Ch'uan

1932 ISSUE

		GOOD	FINE	XF
S2723	**1 DOLLAR** 1932. Blue.			
	a. *Chefoo. (S/M #S43.5-10a).*	45.00	125.00	—
	b. *Shantung. (S/M #S43.5-10b).*	45.00	125.00	—
S2724	**5 DOLLARS** 1932. *Shantung. (S/M #S45.5-11).*	—	—	—
S2725	**10 DOLLARS** 1932. *Shantung. (S/M #S43.5-12).*	—	—	—

SHANTUNG MIN SHENG BANK

山東省民生銀行

Shan Tung Sheng Min Sheng Yin Hang

1936 ISSUE

#S2731-S2733 printer: SSPC.

		GOOD	FINE	XF
S2731	**10 CENTS** 1936. Brown. Sampan at ctr. Back brown. *(S/M #S45-1).*	5.00	15.00	—

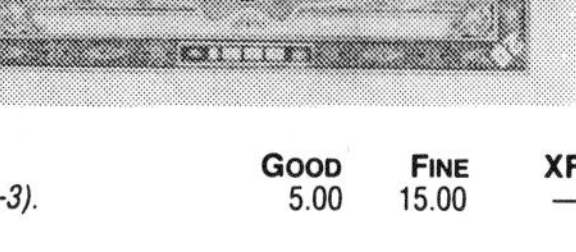

		GOOD	FINE	XF
S2732	**20 CENTS** 1936. Dk. gray-green. Shoreline at ctr. *(S/M #S45-3).*	5.00	15.00	—
S2733	**50 CENTS** 1936. Orange. *(S/M #S45-5).*	6.50	20.00	—
S2734	**1 DOLLAR** 1936. *(S/M #S45-10).*	Reported Not Confirmed		
S2735	**5 DOLLARS** 1936. *(S/M #S45-11).*	Reported Not Confirmed		
S2736	**10 DOLLARS** 1936. *(S/M #S45-12).*	Reported Not Confirmed		

1937 ISSUE

		GOOD	FINE	XF
S2737	**5 CENTS** 1937. *(S/M #S45-20).*	Reported Not Confirmed		
S2738	**10 CENTS** 1937. *(S/M #S45-21).*	Reported Not Confirmed		
S2739	**20 CENTS** 1937. *(S/M #S45-22).*	Reported Not Confirmed		

1940 ISSUE

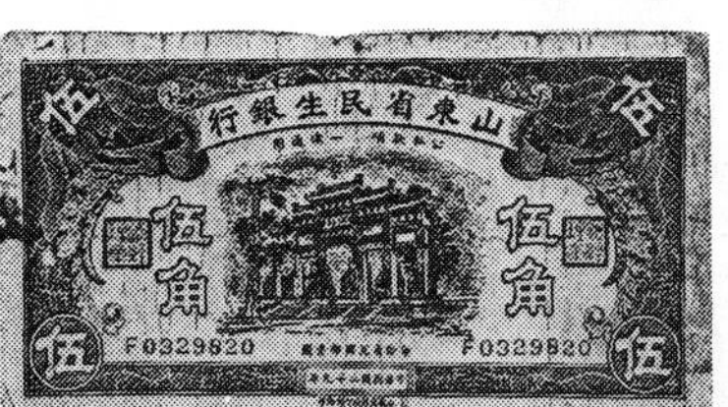

		GOOD	FINE	XF
S2740	**50 CENTS** 1940. Black. Gateway at ctr. *(S/M #S45-28).*	2.50	7.50	22.50

S2742 5 YÜAN — GOOD — FINE — XF

1940. Green on yellow unpt. Peasants cultivating at ctr. Back gray. Printer: SSPC. *(S/M #S45-32).*

	GOOD	FINE	XF
a. Issued note.	3.00	7.50	—
b. W/additional red serial # on back.	5.00	20.00	—

1943 ISSUE

S2744 10 YÜAN — GOOD 8.00 — FINE 25.00 — XF —

1943. Red on yellow unpt. Back brown. *(S/M #S45-40).*

NOTE: For #S2744 w/ovpt: *Yu Min Yin Hang* on back see #S3785 (Communist).

PROVINCIAL BANK OF SHANTUNG

山東省銀行

Shan Tung Sheng Yin Hang

1925 ND PROVISIONAL ISSUE

#S2745-S2747 Ovpt. new bank name on Tsingtao (Regional) City Bank. *SHANTUNG.*

		GOOD	FINE	XF
S2745 1 YÜAN	ND (1925 -old date 15.4.1924). Ovpt. on #S1302U. *(S/M #S46-1).*	15.00	45.00	—
S2746 5 YÜAN	ND (1925 -old date 15.4.1924). Ovpt. on #S1302K. *(S/M #S46-2).*	15.00	45.00	—

		GOOD	FINE	XF
S2747 10 YÜAN	ND (1925 -old date 15.4.1924). Ovpt. on #S1302L. *(S/M #S46-3).*	22.50	72.00	—

1925 TIAO ISSUE

#S2748 and S2749 railway city gate at ctr. on back.

		GOOD	FINE	XF
S2748 1 TIAO = 49 COPPER CENTS	Sept. 1925. Brown on blue unpt. Unsigned remainder. *(S/M #S46-7).*	—	Unc	200.00

		GOOD	FINE	XF
S2749 5 TIAO = 245 COPPER CENTS	Sept. 1925. Green. Back red. Unsigned remainder. *(S/M #S46-8).*	—	Unc	200.00

1925 FIRST REGULAR ISSUE

#S2751-S2753 monument at ctr. Printer: BEPP.

S2751 1 YÜAN — GOOD — FINE — XF

15.8.1925. Green and m/c. Back green.

	GOOD	FINE	XF
a. *SHANTUNG. (S/M #S46-20b).*	12.00	35.00	—
b. *SHANTUNG/TSINGTAO. (S/M #S46-20c).*	15.00	45.00	—
c. *CHINGTAO/Shantung. (S/M #S46-20d).*	15.00	45.00	—
d. W/o place name. *(S/M #S46-20a).*	—	Unc	50.00

		GOOD	FINE	XF
S2752	**5 YÜAN**			
	15.8.1925. Blue and m/c. Back blue.			
	a. *SHANTUNG. (S/M #S46-22a).*	15.00	45.00	135.00
	b. *CHINGTAO/SHANTUNG* w/additional serial #. *(S/M #S46-22b).*	17.50	50.00	—

NOTE: For #S2751 and S2752 w/additional ovpt. see Military - Chihli - Shantung #S3812a nd S3813.

S2753	**10 YÜAN**			
	15.8.1925. *(S/M #S46-24).*	Reported Not Confirmed		

1925 SECOND REGULAR ISSUE

#S2754-S2761 printer: ABNC.

		GOOD	FINE	XF
S2754	**10 CENTS**			
	1.10.1925. Yellow. Back blue. *(S/M #S46-10).*	10.00	30.00	—

		GOOD	FINE	XF
S2755	**20 CENTS**			
	1.10.1925. Black. Shoreline at ctr. Back blue and red. *TSINAN. (S/M #S46-11).*	12.00	35.00	—
S2756	**50 CENTS**			
	1.10.1925. Brown. Back brown and m/c. *TSINGTAO. (S/M #S46-).*	12.00	36.00	—

#S2757-S2759 house on top of hill at ctr.

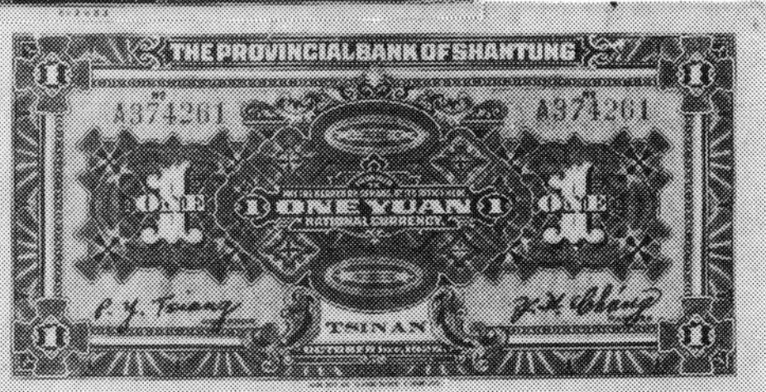

		GOOD	FINE	XF
S2757	**1 YÜAN**			
	1.10.1925. Blue and m/c. Back blue. *TSINAN. (S/M #S46-21).*	10.00	30.00	—
S2758	**5 YÜAN**			
	1.10.1925. Violet and m/c. Back violet.			
	a. *TSINAN. (S/M #S46-23a).*	8.00	25.00	—
	b. *TIENTSIN. (S/M #S46-23b).*	12.00	35.00	—
	c. *SHANGHAI. (S/M #S46-23c).*	15.00	45.00	—

		GOOD	FINE	XF
S2759	**10 YÜAN**			
	1.10.1925. Red and m/c. Back red. *TSINAN. (S/M #S46-25).*	10.00	30.00	90.00
S2760	**50 YÜAN**			
	1.10.1925. *(S/M #S46-26).*	Reported Not Confirmed		
S2761	**100 YÜAN**			
	1.10.1925. *(S/M #S46-27).*	Reported Not Confirmed		

1926 ISSUE

#S2762-S2763 printer: BEPP.

		GOOD	FINE	XF
S2762	**10 CENTS**			
	1.8.1926. Green. Rural house at ctr. Back brown and green.			
	a. *TSINAN. (S/M #S46-30a).*	12.00	35.00	—
	b. *TSINGTAU. (S/M #S46-30b).*	12.00	35.00	—
	c. *TIENTSIN. (S/M #S46-30c).*	12.00	35.00	—
S2763	**20 CENTS**			
	1.8.1926. Blue. *TSINAN. (S/M #S46-31).*	12.00	35.00	—

1926 TIAO ISSUE

		GOOD	FINE	XF
S2763B	**2 TIAO = 100 COPPER COINS**			
	Oct. 1926. Green. Similar to #S2749. *(S/M #S46-53).*	20.00	60.00	180.00
S2764	**10 TIAO = 500 COPPER COINS**			
	Oct. 1926. Red and blue. Similar to #S2749. Back red. *(S/M #S46-55).*	20.00	60.00	180.00

SHANTUNG BANK
BANK OF SHANTUNG

山東銀行
Shan Tung Yin Hang

1912 ISSUE

		VG	VF	UNC
S2765	**1 YÜAN**			
	1912. Black and m/c. Back black. Printer: CHCP. *Chinan. (S/M #S50-1).*	30.00	90.00	—

Note: Previously listed 1 and 3 Ch'uan notes #S2766 and #S2767 dated 1914 are modern fabrications.

ND DOLLAR ISSUE

#S2768 and S2769 house at l., pavilion at r.

		VG	VF	UNC
S2768	**5 DOLLARS**			
	ND. Blue and violet. Back green. *(S/M #S50-9).*	—	—	—

	VG	VF	UNC
S2769 10 SILVER YÜAN ND. *(S/M #S50-10).*	—	—	—

NOTE: For #S2768 and S2769 w/additional ovpt. see Shantung Commercial Bank #S2695-S2696.

1916 DOLLAR ISSUE

	VG	VF	UNC
S2770 1 DOLLAR 1916. *(S/M #S50-20).*	Reported Not Confirmed		
S2771 5 DOLLARS 1916. Like #S2768. *(S/M #S50-21).*	Reported Not Confirmed		

	VG	VF	UNC
S2772 10 SILVER YÜAN 1916. Violet and m/c. Like #S2769. Back green on pale gold unpt. *SHANTUNG. Specimen. Perforated 4 Chinese characters. (S/M #S50-22).*	—	—	125.00

SUIYUAN PROVINCIAL BANK

局錢官市平遠綏

Sui Yüan P'ing Shih Kuan Ch'ien Chü

1923 ISSUE

#S2774-S2775 printer: BEPP.

	VG	VF	UNC
S2774 20 COPPERS 1923. Violet and green. Back brown. *(S/M #S91-).*	—	—	65.00

	VG	VF	UNC
S2775 30 COPPERS 1923. Red and blue. Shoreline at l. Specimen. *(S/M #S91-1).*	—	—	75.00
S2778 10 CENTS 1923. Green. *(S/M #S91-).*	—	—	—
	GOOD	**FINE**	**XF**
S2779 20 CENTS 1923. Red. *(S/M #S91-).*	—	—	—

1925 ISSUE

#S2780 and S2781 two pavilions at l. Steam passenger train at ctr. on back.

	GOOD	FINE	XF
S2780 10 COPPERS 1925. Brown on green unpt. Back blue. *Paotow. (S/M #S91-).*	—	—	—
S2781 20 COPPERS 1925. Dk. olive-green on lt. oange unpt. Back lt. red-orange. *Kuei Sui. (S/M #S91-).*	12.00	35.00	—
S2782 60 COPPERS 1925. *(S/M #S91-).*	—	—	—

#S2785-S2786 printer: BEPP.

	GOOD	FINE	XF
S2785 1 YÜAN 1.2.1925. Gateway at ctr. *Suiyuan.* Specimen. *(S/M #S91-).*	—	Unc	100.00

	GOOD	FINE	XF
S2786 5 YÜAN 1.2.1925. House at ctr. *Suiyuan.* Specimen. *(S/M #S91-).*	—	Unc	110.00

1927 ISSUE

	GOOD	FINE	XF
S2789 50 COPPERS 1927. Shoreline at l. Steam passenger train at ctr. on back. *(S/M #S91-).*	—	Unc	100.00
s1. Chinese ovpt. Specimen.	—	Unc	100.00
s2. English ovpt: *SPECIMEN* on back.	—	Unc	100.00

1930 ISSUE

#S2791-S2793 printer: BEPP.

		GOOD	FINE	XF
S2791	**1 YÜAN** 1.7.1930. Green. Bridge to house at ctr. *Suiyuan. (S/M #S91-10).*			
	a. Issued note.	20.00	60.00	—
	s. Specimen.	—	Unc	100.00
S2792	**5 YÜAN** 1.7.1930. Blue. Pavilion on dock at ctr. *Suiyuan. (S/M #S91-11).*	22.50	—	—

		GOOD	FINE	XF
S2793	**10 YÜAN** 1.7.1930. Mountain fortress at ctr. *Suiyuan. (S/M #S91-12).*	25.00	75.00	—
	a. Issued note.	25.00	75.00	—
	s. Specimen.	—	Unc	150.00

1932 ISSUE

#S2795-S2801 printer: BEPP.

		GOOD	FINE	XF
S2795	**10 COPPERS** 1932. Blue. Back blue and yellow. *(S/M #S91-21).*	—	—	—
S2796	**20 COPPERS** 1932. Green. Back green. *(S/M #S91-22).*	—	—	—
S2798	**60 COPPERS** 1932. Violet and blue. Back violet. *(S/M #S91-24).*	—	—	—
S2800	**1 CHIAO = 10 CENTS** 1932. Green. Back green. *(S/M #S91-26).*	—	—	—
S2801	**2 CHIAO = 20 CENTS** 1932. Red. Back red. *(S/M #S91-28).*	—	—	—

1935 ISSUE

		GOOD	FINE	XF
S2802	**1 CHIAO = 10 CENTS** 1935. Blue on yellow unpt. Bldg. at ctr. Back blue. *(S/M #S91-31).*	—	—	—

SZECHUAN PROVINCIAL BANK

局錢官川四

Szu Ch'uan Kuan Ch'ien Chü

1923 ISSUE

		GOOD	FINE	XF
S2804	**1 DOLLAR** 1923. *(S/M #S96-1).*	Reported Not Confirmed		
S2805	**3 DOLLARS** 1923. *(S/M #S96-2).*	Reported Not Confirmed		

1924 CASH ISSUE

		GOOD	FINE	XF
S2808	**1000 CASH = 100 COPPERS** March 1924. Green. Pagoda at l., house at r. Back green; red seal ovpt. Remainder. *(S/M #S96-10).*	25.00	100.00	—

SZECHUAN OFFICIAL BANK

號銀官川四

Szu Ch'uan Kuan Yin

號銀官川四

Szu Ch'uan Kuan Yin Hao

ND DOLLAR ISSUE

		GOOD	FINE	XF
S2809	**1 DOLLAR** ND. Green and yellow. Back blue; painting of emperor and subjects. *(S/M #S100-1).*	15.00	45.00	—

1923 CASH ISSUE

		GOOD	FINE	XF
S2810	**1000 CASH** 1923. Blue and yellow. Back violet. *(S/M #S100-5).*	15.00	45.00	—

1923 DOLLAR ISSUE

		GOOD	FINE	XF
S2811	**1 DOLLAR** 1923. Blue. Painting of child up tree, 2 women below on back. Vertical format. *(S/M #S100-10).*	22.50	67.50	—

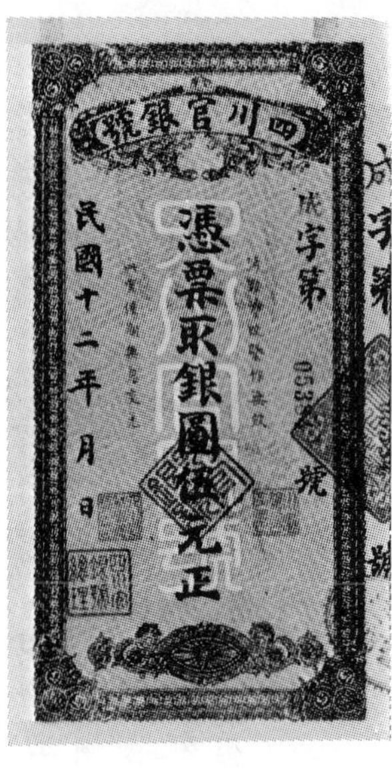

		GOOD	FINE	XF
S2812	**5 DOLLARS** 1923. Purple. Painting of trees on back. Vertical format. *(S/M #S100-11).*	30.00	90.00	—

1924 CASH ISSUE

		GOOD	FINE	XF
S2813	**200 CASH** 1924. *(S/M #S100-20).*	Reported Not Confirmed		
S2814	**500 CASH** 1924. *(S/M #S100-21).*	Reported Not Confirmed		
S2815	**1000 CASH** 1924. *(S/M #S100-22).*	22.50	67.50	—

SZECHUAN PROVINCIAL GOVERNMENT

四川省政府建設庫券

Szu Ch'uan Sheng Cheng Fu Chien She K'u Ch'üan

1936 RECONSTRUCTION NOTES

		GOOD	FINE	XF
S2816	**50 DOLLARS** 1936. Blue and green. Bldgs. at ctr. Back blue. *(S/M #S102-1).*	35.00	110.00	—
S2817	**100 DOLLARS** 1936. Orange and yellow. Bldgs. at l. and r. *(S/M #S102-2).*	45.00	135.00	—

NOTE: For #S2816 and S2817 w/additional ovpt. see Farmers Bank of China #472 and 473, Vol. 2.

SZECHUEN PROVINCIAL BANK

四川省銀行

Szu Ch'uan Sheng Yin Hang

1935 ND PROVISIONAL ISSUE

		GOOD	FINE	XF
S2819	**50 CENTS** ND (1935 -old date 1934). Green. Ovpt. new bank name on Bank of Chungking. *(S/M #S103-0.5).*	22.50	72.00	—

1936; 1937 REGULAR ISSUE

		GOOD	FINE	XF
S2821	**50 CENTS** 1.7.1936. Red. Bldgs. at upper ctr. Back brown and green. Vertical format. *(S/M #S103-1).*	15.00	50.00	—
S2823	**5 DOLLARS** 1.7.1937. Green and m/c. Mountains, tower at upper ctr. Back green. *(S/M #S103-10).*	17.50	55.00	—
S2824	**10 SILVER YÜAN** 1.7.1937. Violet and m/c. Back violet. *(S/M #S103-11).*	17.50	55.00	—

NOTE: For #S2823 and S2824 w/additional ovpt. see Farmers Bank of China #470 and 471, Vol. 2.

1949 ISSUE

#S2825-S2826 hillside village at top. Szechuan Republican coin on back.

		GOOD	FINE	XF
S2825	**5 CENTS** 1949. Green. *(S/M #S103.1-12).*	10.00	30.00	100.00
S2825A	**10 CENTS** 1949. Blue. *(S/M #S103.1-13).*	10.00	30.00	100.00

		GOOD	FINE	XF
S2826	**50 CENTS** 9149. Red. Vertical format. *(S/M #S103.1-16).*	10.00	30.00	100.00

SZECHUEN PROVINCE

四川兌換券

Szu Ch'uan Tui Huan Ch'üan

1921 ISSUE

#S2827-S2829 house at l., pagoda at r.

		GOOD	FINE	XF
S2827	**1 DOLLAR** 1921. Blue and green. Back green and red; shelter in trees at ctr.			
	a. *CHUNGKING. (S/M #S104.5-11a).*	15.00	50.00	—
	b. W/o place name. *(S/M #S104.5-11b).*	—	30.00	90.00

		Good	Fine	XF
S2828	**5 Dollars** 1921. Brown and green. Back red and blue.			
	a. *CHUNGKING. (S/M #S104.5-12a).*	45.00	135.00	—
	r. Remainder w/o place name. *(S/M #S104.5-12b).*	—	45.00	135.00
S2829	**10 Dollars** 1921. Green and yellow. Back brown and green.			
	a. *CHUNGKING. (S/M #S104.5-13a).*	50.00	150.00	—
	r. Remainder w/o place name. *(S/M #S104.5-13b).*	—	50.00	150.00

SZECHUAN COPPER CURRENCY BUREAU

局元銅/川四

Szu Ch'uan/T'ung Yüan Chü

1904 ISSUE

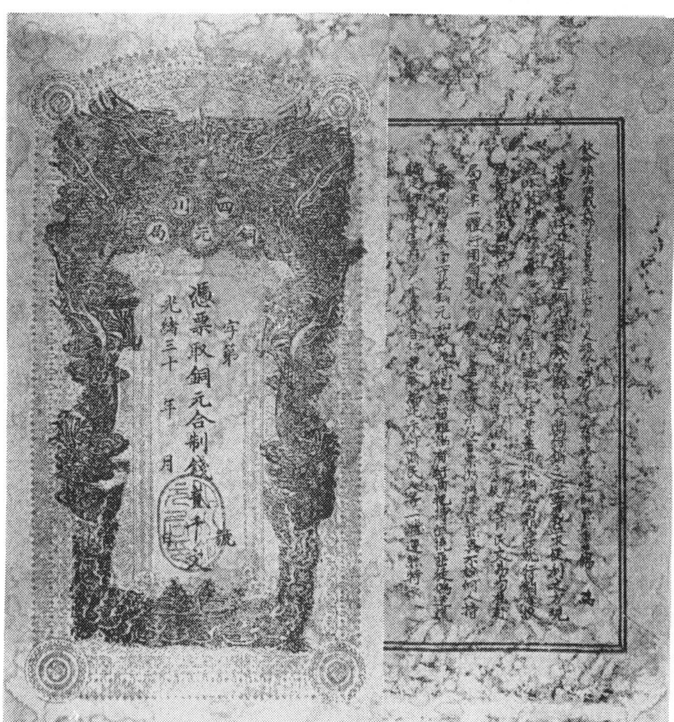

		Good	Fine	XF
S2830	**2000 Cash** Yr. 30 (1904). Dk. blue and red. Facing dragons at upper l. and r. Back black. *(S/M #S105-0.4).*	—	—	—

1908 ISSUE

		Good	Fine	XF
S2831	**1000 Cash** ND (ca.1908). Brown and black. *(S/M #S105-0.9).*	35.00	110.00	—
S2832	**2000 Cash** ND (ca.1908). Brown and black. Back blue. *(S/M #S105-1).*	45.00	135.00	—

TIHUA OFFICIAL CURRENCY BUREAU

局錢官化廸

Ti Hua Kuan Ch'ien Chü

1923 ISSUE

#S2833A-S2841 printed on cloth.

		Good	Fine	XF
S2833A	**40 Cash** 1923. Black. Crossed flags w/horizontal stripes at top, floral design at l. and r. *Ili. (S/M #T116-0.2).*	45.00	135.00	—

1924 ISSUE

		Good	Fine	XF
S2833B	**40 Cash** 1924. Black. Similar to #S2833A. *(S/M #T116-0.3).*	45.00	135.00	—

1925 ISSUE

		Good	Fine	XF
S2833C	**40 Cash** 1925. Black. *(S/M #T116-0.4).*	30.00	90.00	—

1926 ISSUE

		Good	Fine	XF
S2834	**40 Cash** 1926. Black and yellow. Uniface. *(S/M #T116-0.5).*	45.00	135.00	—

1927 ISSUE

		Good	Fine	XF
S2834A	**40 Cash** 1927. Black. *(S/M #T116-0.7).*	30.00	90.00	—

1928 ISSUE

		Good	Fine	XF
S2835	**40 Cash** 1928. *Sinkiang. (S/M #T116-1).*	30.00	90.00	—

1929 ISSUE

		Good	Fine	XF
S2836	**40 Cash** 1929. *Sinkiang. (S/M #T116-10).*	30.00	90.00	—

1930 ISSUE

		Good	Fine	XF
S2837	**40 Cash** 1930. Black and yellow. *Sinkiang. (S/M #T116-20).*	45.00	135.00	—

1931 ISSUE

		Good	Fine	XF
S2838	**40 Cash** 1931. Black and yellow. *Sinkinag. (S/M #T116-30).*	45.00	135.00	—

1932 ISSUE

		Good	Fine	XF
S2839	**40 Cash** 1932. Crossed flags w/sunburst in canton at top, floral design at l. and r., waves at bottom. Cloth. *Sinkiang. (S/M #T116-40).*	40.00	120.00	—
S2841	**100 Cash** 1932. Sun at top and bottom, leaves at l. and r. *Sinkiang. (S/M #T116-41).*	—	—	—

Notice

Readers with unlisted dates, color or signature varieties are invited to submit photocopies of their notes to: Standard Catalog of World Paper Money, Krause Publications, 700 East State St. Iola WI 54990-0001 U.S.A. or by email: thernr@krause.com. Email submissions of material for possible inclusion need to be 100% jpeg attachments at 300 dpi.

TIENTSIN BANK

行銀津天

T'ien Ching Yin Hao

1905 ISSUE

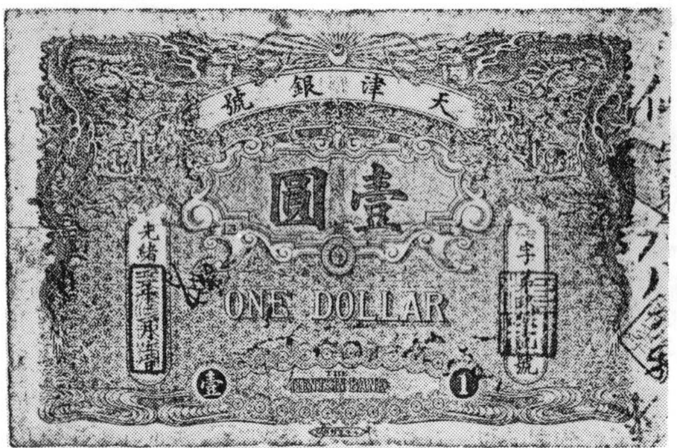

		GOOD	FINE	XF
S2843	**1 DOLLAR** Yr. 31 (1905). Green and red. Facing dragons at upper l. and r. Back blue. *(S/M #T170.5-11).*	90.00	300.00	—

BUREAU OF FINANCE CHING HAI (TSING HAI)

券持維廳政財

(Ch'ing Hai) Ts'ai Cheng T'ing Wei Ch'ih Ch'üan

1930 MAINTENANCE NOTES ISSUE

		GOOD	FINE	XF
S2845	**10 CENTS** 1930. *(S/M #T191-).*	—	—	—
S2846	**1 DOLLAR** 1930. Blue. *(S/M #T191-).*	—	—	—
S2847	**5 DOLLARS** 1930. Red. *(S/M #T191-).*	—	—	—

1935 MAINTENANCE NOTES ISSUE

#S2848-S2850 Chinghai Province. Printer: BEPP.

		GOOD	FINE	XF
S2848	**1 YÜAN** 1935. *(S/M #T191-1).*	Reported Not Confirmed		

		GOOD	FINE	XF
S2849	**5 YÜAN** 1935. Red. Bldgs. on hillside at ctr. Junks at ctr. on back. Remainder. *(S/M #T191-2).*	—	Unc	75.00
S2850	**10 YÜAN** 1935. *(S/M #T191-3).*	Reported Not Confirmed		

FUKIEN SOUTH - EASTERN BANK

建福/行銀南東

Tung Nan Yin Hang/Fu Chien

1928 ISSUE

#S2851 and S2853 *FUKIEN.*

		GOOD	FINE	XF
S2851	**1 DOLLAR** 1928. Shelter in park at ctr. Specimen. *(S/M #F30-11).*	—	Unc	150.00

		GOOD	FINE	XF
S2853	**10 DOLLARS** 1928. Bldg. at ctr. Specimen. *(S/M #F30-11).*	—	Unc	200.00

PROVINCIAL BANK OF THE THREE EASTERN PROVINCES
BANK OF MANCHURIA
БАНК МАНЬЧЖУРІИ
PROVINCIAL BANK OF MANCHURIA
EASTERN PROVINCIAL BANK
TOONG SAN SANG GOVERNMENT BANK

行銀省三東

Tung San Sheng Yin Hang

行銀官省三東

Tung San Sheng Kuan Yin Hang

號銀官省三東

Tung San Sheng Kuan Yin Hao

券兌滙號銀官省三東

Tung San Sheng Kuan Yin Hui Tui Ch'üan

1908 ISSUE

#S2854-S2854F printer: PYOG.

		GOOD	FINE	XF
S2854	**10 CENTS** Yr. 1 (1908). *(S/M #F10-20).*	40.00	120.00	—
S2854A	**20 CENTS** Yr. 1 (1908). *(S/M #F10-21).*	40.00	120.00	—
S2854B	**50 CENTS** Yr. 1 (1908). *(S/M #F10-22).*	40.00	120.00	—
S2854C	**100 CENTS** Yr. 1 (1908). *(S/M #F10-23).*	50.00	150.00	—
S2854D	**1 DOLLAR** Yr. 1 (1908). *(S/M #F10-24).*	50.00	150.00	—
S2854E	**5 DOLLARS** Yr. 1 (1908). *(S/M #F10-25).*	60.00	180.00	—
S2854F	**10 DOLLARS** Yr. 1 (1908). *(S/M #F10-26).*	70.00	210.00	—

1909 CHIAO ISSUE

		GOOD	FINE	XF
S2855	**1 CHIAO = 10 CENTS** 1.4.1909. M/c. *(S/M #T214-).*	40.00	125.00	—
S2856	**2 CHIAO = 20 CENTS** 1.4.1909. *(S/M #T214-).*	Reported Not Confirmed		
S2857	**5 CHIAO = 50 CENTS** 1.4.1909. *(S/M #T214-).*	Reported Not Confirmed		

		GOOD	FINE	XF
S2858	**10 CHIAO = 100 CENTS** 1.4.1909. Gray and orange. Back gray and green. *(S/M #T214-).*	50.00	150.00	—
S2859	**50 CHIAO = 500 CENTS** 1.4.1909. *(S/M #T214-).*	Reported Not Confirmed		
S2860	**100 CHIAO = 1000 CENTS** 1.4.1909. *(S/M #T214-).*	Reported Not Confirmed		

1910 CHIAO ISSUE

#S2861-S2866 printer: PYOG.

		GOOD	FINE	XF
S2861	**1 CHIAO = 10 CENTS** 1910. *(S/M #T214-1).*	Reported Not Confirmed		
S2862	**2 CHIAO = 20 CENTS** 1910. *(S/M #T214-2).*	Reported Not Confirmed		
S2863	**5 CHIAO = 50 CENTS** 1910. *(S/M #T214-3).*	Reported Not Confirmed		
S2864	**10 CHIAO = 100 CENTS** 1910. *(S/M #T214-4).*	Reported Not Confirmed		
S2865	**50 CHIAO = 500 CENTS** 1910. *(S/M #T214-5).*	Reported Not Confirmed		
S2866	**100 CHIAO = 1000 CENTS** 1910. *(S/M #T214-6).*	Reported Not Confirmed		

1912 CHIAO ISSUE

#S2867-S2868 printer: PYPO.

		GOOD	FINE	XF
S2867	**1 CHIAO = 10 CENTS** 1912. Gray and green. Back blue. *(S/M #T214-).*	33.00	100.00	—
S2868	**2 CHIAO = 20 CENTS** 1912. Tan. Back bistre. *(S/M #T214-).*	33.00	100.00	—

1913 CHIAO ISSUE

No.	Description	Good	Fine	XF
S2873	**1 CHIAO = 10 CENTS** 1913. *(S/M #T214-10).*	Reported Not Confirmed		
S2874	**2 CHIAO = 20 CENTS** 1913. *(S/M #T214-11).*	Reported Not Confirmed		
S2875	**5 CHIAO = 50 CENTS** 1913. *(S/M #T214-12).*	Reported Not Confirmed		
S2876	**10 CHIAO = 100 CENTS** 1913. *(S/M #T214-13).*	Reported Not Confirmed		
S2877	**50 CHIAO = 500 CENTS** 1913. *(S/M #T214-14).*	Reported Not Confirmed		
S2878	**100 CHIAO = 1000 CENTS** 1913. *(S/M #T214-15).*	Reported Not Confirmed		

1915 CHIAO ISSUE

No.	Description	Good	Fine	XF
S2880	**1/2 CHIAO = 5 CENTS** 1915. Blue and green. Steam passenger train at r. Back violet; wooded hills at ctr. *(S/M #T21420).*	10.00	30.00	90.00

No.	Description	Good	Fine	XF
S2881	**1 CHIAO = 10 CENTS** 1915. Blue and green. Wooded hills at r. Back brown; fortress gateway at ctr. *(S/M #T214-21).*	15.00	45.00	135.00

No.	Description	Good	Fine	XF
S2882	**2 CHIAO = 20 CENTS** 1915. Blue on yellow unpt. Wooded hills at r. Back brown; temple at ctr. *(S/M #T214-22a).*	15.00	45.00	135.00
S2882A	**2 CHIAO = 20 CENTS** 1915. Blue on pink unpt. Like #S2882. Back gray. *(S/M #T214-22b).*	15.00	45.00	135.00
S2883	**5 CHIAO = 50 CENTS** 1915. *(S/M #T214-23).*	Reported Not Confirmed		
S2884	**10 CHIAO = 100 CENTS** 1915. *(S/M #T214-24).*	Reported Not Confirmed		
S2885	**50 CHIAO = 500 CENTS** 1915. *(S/M #T214-25).*	Reported Not Confirmed		
S2886	**100 CHIAO = 1000 CENTS** 1915. *(S/M #T214-26).*	Reported Not Confirmed		

1916 ISSUE

#S2892-S2895 *MUKDEN*. Printer: BEPP.

No.	Description	Good	Fine	XF
S2887	**5 COPPERS** 1916. *(S/M #T214-30).*	Reported Not Confirmed		
S2888	**10 COPPERS** 1916. *(S/M #T214-31).*	Reported Not Confirmed		
S2889	**20 COPPERS** 1916. *(S/M #T214-32).*	Reported Not Confirmed		
S2890	**50 COPPERS** 1916. *(S/M #T214-33).*	Reported Not Confirmed		
S2891	**100 COPPERS** 1916. *(S/M #T214-34).*	Reported Not Confirmed		

No.	Description	Good	Fine	XF
S2892	**1 DOLLAR** 1.5.1916. Yellow. Wooded hillside. Back black. *(S/M #T214-40).*	15.00	45.00	—
S2893	**5 DOLLARS** 1.5.1916. *(S/M #T214-41).*	20.00	60.00	—
S2894	**10 DOLLARS** 1.5.1916. *(S/M #T214-42).*	25.00	75.00	—
S2895	**50 DOLLARS** 1.5.1916. *(S/M #T214-43).*	30.00	90.00	—

1917 ISSUE

#S2897-S2899 Temple of Heaven at ctr. on back. *Fengtien*. Printer: BEPP.

No.	Description	Good	Fine	XF
S2897	**1 DOLLAR** 1917. Orange. Back green and black. *(S/M #T214-50).*	30.00	90.00	—
S2898	**5 DOLLARS** 1917. Blue. Back green and Black. *(S/M #T214-51).*	30.00	90.00	—

No.	Description	Good	Fine	XF
S2899	**10 DOLLARS** 1917. Green. Back blue and black. *(S/M #T214-52).*	40.00	120.00	—

1918 ISSUE

#S2901-S2903 *Fengtien*. Printer: TCPL.

No.	Description	Good	Fine	XF
S2901	**10 CENTS** 1918. *(S/M #T214-60).*	Reported Not Confirmed		
S2902	**20 CENTS** 1918. *(S/M #T214-61).*	Reported Not Confirmed		
S2903	**50 CENTS** 1918. *(S/M #T214-62).*	Reported Not Confirmed		

1919 ISSUE

#S2908-S2912 printer: ABNC.

No.	Description	Good	Fine	XF
S2906	**50 CENTS** 1919. Printer: PYOG. *(S/M #T214-70).*	Reported Not Confirmed		
S2908	**1 TAEL** 1919. *(S/M #T214-80).*	Reported Not Confirmed		
S2909	**5 TAELS** 1919. *(S/M #T214-81).*	Reported Not Confirmed		
S2910	**10 TAELS** 1919. *(S/M #T214-82).*	Reported Not Confirmed		
S2911	**50 TAELS** 1919. *(S/M #T214-83).*	Reported Not Confirmed		
S2912	**100 TAELS** 1919. *(S/M #T214-84).*	Reported Not Confirmed		

1920 ISSUE

#S2916-S2918 bldgs. at ctr. *Harbin*. Printer: BEPP.

No.	Description	Good	Fine	XF
S2913	**10 CENTS** 1920. Printer: PYOG. *(S/M #T214-90).*	Reported Not Confirmed		

No.	Description	Good	Fine	XF
S2916	**1 DOLLAR** 1920. Green. Back blue w/black text. *(S/M #T214-100).*	15.00	45.00	—

S2917 5 DOLLARS

	GOOD	FINE	XF
1920. Ovpt: *HARBIN/BANK OF MANCHURIA* on back. Specimen. *(S/M #T214-101).*	—	Unc	175.00

S2918 10 DOLLARS

	GOOD	FINE	XF
1920. Specimen. *(S/M #T214-102).*	—	Unc	200.00

1921 ISSUES

#S2920-S2920C *FENGTIEN*. Printer: TCPL.

	GOOD	FINE	XF
S2920 5 CENTS 1921. *(S/M #T214-110).*	Reported Not Confirmed		
S2920A 10 CENTS 1921. *(S/M #T214-111).*	Reported Not Confirmed		
S2920B 20 CENTS 1921. *(S/M #T214-113).*	Reported Not Confirmed		
S2920C 50 CENTS 1921. *(S/M #T214-116).*	Reported Not Confirmed		

#S2921-S2924 bldgs. at l. *HARBIN*. Printer: BEPP.

S2921 5 CENTS

	GOOD	FINE	XF
1.1.1921. Violet and blue. Back blue and m/c. *(S/M #T214-).*			
a. Issued note.	10.00	30.00	—
b. W/official Chinese 4 character ovpt.	10.00	30.00	—

S2922 10 CENTS

	GOOD	FINE	XF
1.1.1921. Blue and yellow. Back orange and blue.			
a. Issued note. *(S/M #T214-112a).*	12.00	35.00	—
b. W/official Chinese 4 character ovpt. *(S/M #T214-112b).*	12.00	35.00	—

S2923 20 CENTS

	GOOD	FINE	XF
1.1.1921. Blue and yellow. Back violet and m/c. *(S/M #T214-114).*	15.00	45.00	—

S2925 20 CENTS

	GOOD	FINE	XF
1.1.1921. Brown on lt. blue unpt. Back dk. green and m/c. W/o imprint.			
a. Issued note. *(S/M #T214-115a).*	12.00	35.00	—
b. W/official Chinese 4 character ovpt. *(S/M #T214-115b).*	12.00	35.00	—

S2926 50 CENTS

	GOOD	FINE	XF
1.1.1921. *(S/M #T214-117).*	Reported Not Confirmed		

#S2927-S2929 *HARBIN*. Printer: ABNC.

S2927 1 DOLLAR

	GOOD	FINE	XF
July 1921. Yellow-orange and m/c. Bldg. at ctr. Back yellow-orange.			
a. Issued note. *(S/M #T214-120a).*	15.00	45.00	—
b. W/official Chinese 4 character ovpt. *(S/M #T214-120b).*	15.00	45.00	—
s. Specimen ovpt. on #S2927b. *(S/M #T214-120c).*	—	Unc	90.00

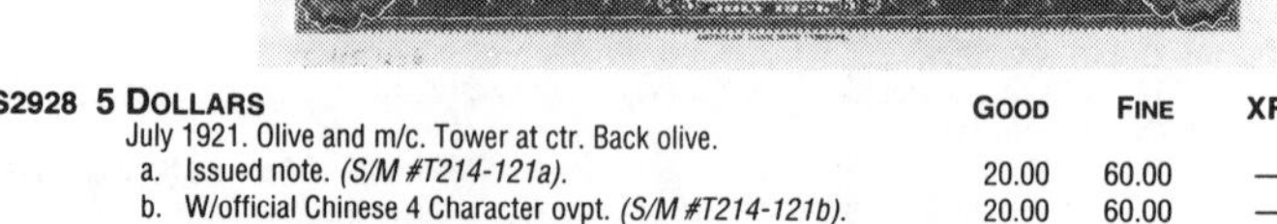

S2928 5 DOLLARS

	GOOD	FINE	XF
July 1921. Olive and m/c. Tower at ctr. Back olive.			
a. Issued note. *(S/M #T214-121a).*	20.00	60.00	—
b. W/official Chinese 4 Character ovpt. *(S/M #T214-121b).*	20.00	60.00	—
s. Specimen ovpt. on #S2928b. *(S/M #T214-121c).*	—	Unc	120.00

S2929 10 DOLLARS

	GOOD	FINE	XF
July 1921. Purple and m/c. Tower gates at ctr. Back violet.			
a. Issued note. *(S/M #T214-122a).*	25.00	75.00	—
b. W/official Chinese 4 character ovpt. at ctr. on face. *(S/M #T214-122b).*	17.00	50.00	—
s. Specimen ovpt. on #S2929b. *(S/M #T214-122c).*	—	Unc	100.00

1922 ISSUE

#S2931-S2935 *Fengtien*. Printer: TCPL.

		GOOD	FINE	XF
S2931	**5 COPPERS** 1922. *(S/M #T214-130).*	Reported Not Confirmed		
S2932	**10 COPPERS** 1922. *(S/M #T214-131).*	Reported Not Confirmed		
S2933	**20 COPPERS** 1922. *(S/M #T214-132).*	Reported Not Confirmed		
S2934	**50 COPPERS** 1922. *(S/M #T214-133).*	Reported Not Confirmed		
S2935	**100 COPPERS** 1922. *(S/M #T214-134).*	Reported Not Confirmed		

#S2936-S2938 Temple of Heaven at ctr. on back. *Fengtien*.

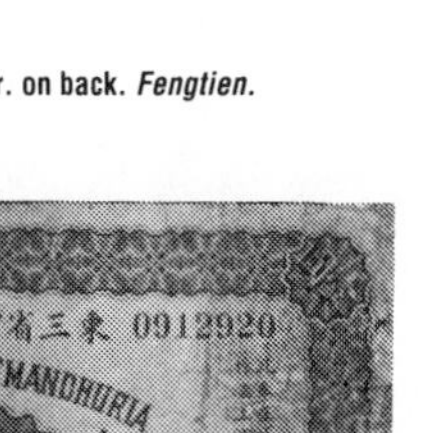

		GOOD	FINE	XF
S2936	**1 DOLLAR** 1922. Orange. Back green. *(S/M #T214-140).*	15.00	35.00	70.00
S2937	**5 DOLLARS** 1922. Dk. blue. Similar to #S2936. Back green. *(S/M #T214-141).*	25.00	75.00	—

		GOOD	FINE	XF
S2938	**10 DOLLARS** 1922. Green. Back blue. *(S/M #T214-142).*	25.00	75.00	—

#S2940-S2943 bldgs. at l. *Harbin*. W/o imprint.

		GOOD	FINE	XF
S2940	**5 CENTS** 1.4.1923. Blue and yellow. Back violet and m/c.			
	a. Issued note. *(S/M #T214-150a).*	12.00	36.00	105.00
	b. W/official Chinese 4 character ovpt. *(S/M #T214-150b).*	12.00	36.00	105.00

		GOOD	FINE	XF
	s. Specimen ovpt. on #S2940b. *(S/M #T214-150c).*	—	—	65.00

		GOOD	FINE	XF
S2941	**10 CENTS** 1.4.1923. Brown and yellow-green. Back brown, orange and green.			
	a. Issued note. *(S/M #T214-151a).*	5.00	15.00	45.00
	b. W/official Chinese 4 character ovpt. *(S/M #T214-151b).*	10.00	30.00	90.00
	s. Specimen ovpt. on #S2941b. *(S/M #T214-151c).*	—	—	75.00
S2942	**20 CENTS** 1.4.1923. *(S/M #T214-152).*	Reported Not Confirmed		
S2943	**50 CENTS** 1.4.1923. *(S/M #T214-153).*	Reported Not Confirmed		

#S2944-S2946 printer: BEPP.

S2944	**1 DOLLAR** 1923.	
	a. *Fengtien. (S/M #T214-160a).*	Reported Not Confirmed
	b. *Harbin. (S/M #T214-160b).*	Reported Not Confirmed
	c. *Tientsin. (S/M #T214-160c).*	Reported Not Confirmed
S2945	**5 DOLLARS** 1923.	
	a. *Fengtien. (S/M #T214-161a).*	Reported Not Confirmed
	b. *Harbin. (S/M #T214-161b).*	Reported Not Confirmed
	c. *Tientsin. (S/M #T214-161c).*	Reported Not Confirmed
S2946	**10 DOLLARS** 1923.	
	a. *Fengtien. (S/M #T214-162a).*	Reported Not Confirmed
	b. *Harbin. (S/M #T214-162b).*	Reported Not Confirmed
	c. *Tientsin. (S/M #T214-162c).*	Reported Not Confirmed

1924 ISSUE

#S2947-S2949 *Fengtien*. Printer: TCPL.

		GOOD	FINE	XF
S2947	**1 DOLLAR** 1924. *(S/M #T214-170).*	Reported Not Confirmed		
S2948	**5 DOLLARS** 1924. *(S/M #T214-172).*	Reported Not Confirmed		
S2949	**10 DOLLARS** 1924. *(S/M #T214-174).*	Reported Not Confirmed		

#S2951-S2955 tower at ctr. Printer: ABNC.

		VG	VF	UNC
S2951	**1 DOLLAR** 1.1.1924. Blue and m/c. Back green.			
	a. Issued note. *(S/M #T214-171a).*	12.00	36.00	—
	s. Specimen. *(S/M #T214-171b).*	—	—	25.00

S2952 5 DOLLARS
1.1.1924. Green and m/c. Back orange.

	VG	VF	UNC
a. Issued note. *(S/M #T214-173a).*	15.00	45.00	135.00
s. Specimen. *(S/M #T214-173b).*	—	—	110.00

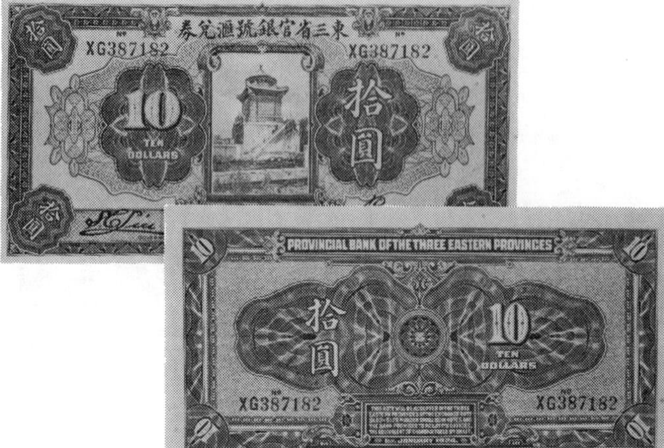

S2953 10 DOLLARS
1.1.1924. Dk. brown on pink, green, and m/c unpt. Back red. *(S/M #T214-175).*

	VG	VF	UNC
a. 171 x 86mm.	20.00	60.00	—
b. 165 x 84mm.	20.00	60.00	—

S2954 50 DOLLARS
1.1.1924. Green and m/c. Back brown. *(S/M #T214-176).*

	VG	VF	UNC
	40.00	120.00	—

S2955 100 DOLLARS
1.1.1924. Violet and m/c. Back black.

	VG	VF	UNC
	50.00	150.00	—

1929 FIRST ISSUE

#S2956-S2958 *Fengtien.* Printer: TCPL.

	VG	VF	UNC
S2956 10 CENTS 1929. *(S/M #T214-180).*	Reported Not Confirmed		
S2957 20 CENTS 1929. *(S/M #T214-182).*	Reported Not Confirmed		
S2958 50 CENTS 1929. *(S/M #T214-184).*	Reported Not Confirmed		

1929 SECOND ISSUE

#S2959-S2961 *MUKDEN.*

S2959 10 CENTS
1.12.1929. Green. Lg. bldg. at ctr.

	GOOD	FINE	XF
a. Issued note. *(S/M #T214-181a).*	8.00	25.00	—
b. W/additional control # ovpt: *2. (S/M #T214-181b).*	9.00	27.00	—

S2960 20 CENTS
1.12.1929. Brown. Bridge at ctr. *(S/M #T214-183).*

	GOOD	FINE	XF
	8.00	25.00	—

S2961 50 CENTS
1.12.1929. Blue. *(S/M #T214-185).*

	GOOD	FINE	XF
	10.00	30.00	—

#S2962-S2965 pavilion by pool at ctr. Printer: ABNC.

S2962 1 DOLLAR
Nov. 1929. Black and m/c. Back black.

	GOOD	FINE	XF
a. *THREE EASTERN PROVINCES. (S/M #T214-190c).*	15.00	45.00	—
b. *TIENTSIN/THREE EASTERN PROVINCES. (S/M #T214-190b).*	17.00	50.00	—
p1. As a. Proof.	—	Unc	200.00
p2. *TIENTSIN.* Proof.	—	Unc	375.00
r. Remainder w/o place name. *(S/M #T214-190a).*	—	Unc	75.00
s1. As a. Specimen.	—	Unc	125.00
s2. *TIENTSIN.* Specimen.	—	Unc	225.00

S2963 5 DOLLARS
Nov. 1929. Brown and m/c. Back brown.

	GOOD	FINE	XF
a. *THREE EASTERN PROVINCES. (S/M #T214-191c).*	25.00	75.00	—
b. *TIENTSIN/THREE EASTERN PROVINCES. (S/M #T214-191b).*	25.00	75.00	—
p1. As a. Proof.	—	Unc	225.00
p2. *TIENTSIN.* Proof.	—	Unc	450.00
r. Remainder w/o place name. *(S/M #T214-191a).*	—	Unc	85.00
s1. As a. Specimen.	—	Unc	150.00
s2. *TIENTSIN.* Specimen.	—	Unc	300.00

1929 FIRST ISSUE

#S2956-S2958 *Fengtien.* Printer: TCPL.

S2964 10 DOLLARS
Nov. 1929. Green and m/c. Back green.

	GOOD	FINE	XF
a. *THREE EASTERN PROVINCES. (S/M #T214-192c).*	20.00	60.00	—
b. *TIENTSIN/THREE EASTERN PROVINCES. (S/M #T214-192b).*	30.00	90.00	—
p1. As a. Proof.	—	Unc	275.00
p2. *TIENTSIN.* Proof.	—	Unc	600.00
r. Remainder w/o place name. *(S/M #T214-192a).*	—	Unc	100.00
s1. As a. Specimen.	—	Unc	175.00
s2. *TIENTSIN.* Specimen.	—	Unc	350.00

1929 Second Issue

#S2959-S2961 *MUKDEN*.

		Good	Fine	XF
S2965	**100 Dollars** Nov. 1929. Red and m/c.			
	a. *THREE EASTERN PROVINCES. (S/M #T214-193c).*	60.00	180.00	—
	b. *TIENTSIN/THREE EASTERN PROVINCES. (S/M #T214-193b).*	70.00	210.00	—
	p. As a. Proof.	—	Unc	675.00
	r. Remainder w/o place name. *(S/M #T214-193a).*	—	Unc	200.00
	s. As a. Specimen.	—	Unc	400.00

NOTE: For #S2962-S2965 w/additional ovpt. see Chanan Bank #J118-J119 and Central Bank of Manchukuo #J120-J122, Vol. 2.

Provincial Bank of Honan

豫泉官銀錢局

Yü Ch'üan Kuan Yin Ch'ien Chü

1904 Issue

		Good	Fine	XF
S2971	**500 Cash** Yr. 30 (1904). *(S/M #Y20-).*	Reported Not Confirmed		
S2972	**1000 Cash** Yr. 30 (1904). Red and green. Back black. *(S/M #Y20-1).*	75.00	225.00	—
S2973	**1000 Cash** Yr. 30 (1904). Orange and blue. *(S/M #Y20-).*	Reported Not Confirmed		
S2974	**2000 Cash** Yr. 30 (1904). *(S/M #Y20-).*	Reported Not Confirmed		

1918 Issue

#S2977 and S2978 portr. old man at lower l.

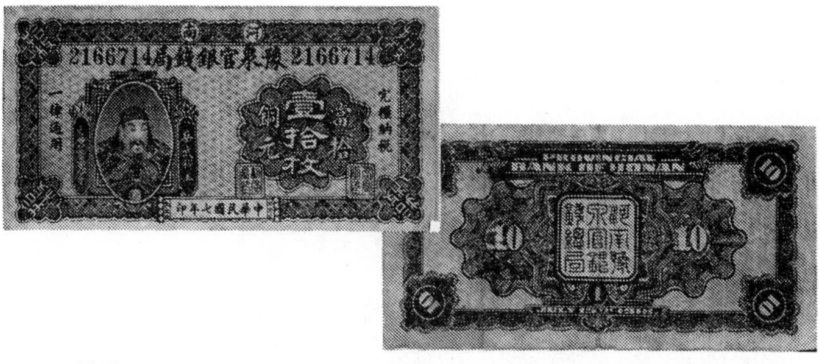

		Good	Fine	XF
S2977	**10 Coppers** 15.7.1918. Dk. olive-green on pink unpt. Like #S2978. Back red on yellow unpt. *(S/M #Y20-10).*	12.00	35.00	—

		Good	Fine	XF
S2978	**20 Coppers** 15.7.1918. Violet on tan unpt. Back dk. blue on olive-green unpt. *(S/M #Y20-11).*	12.50	37.50	75.00
S2979	**50 Coppers** 15.7.1918. *(S/M #20-12).*	Reported Not Confirmed		
S2980	**100 Coppers** 15.7.1918. *(S/M #Y20-13).*	Reported Not Confirmed		

#S2981-S2983 portr. old man at ctr. Printer: ABNC.

		Good	Fine	XF
S2981	**1 Dollar** 15.7.1918. Blue. Back blue on green and tan unpt. *(S/M #Y20-20).*	17.50	55.00	—
S2982	**5 Dollars** 15.7.1918. Orange. Back red on blue and brown unpt. *(S/M #Y20-21).*	22.50	67.50	—
S2983	**10 Dollars** 15.7.1918. Dk. red on blue and brown unpt. Back green on blue and tan unpt. *(S/M #Y20-22).*	25.00	75.00	—

1921 Issue

		Good	Fine	XF
S2985	**1 Dollar** 1921. Green. Back red and blue. *(S/M #Y20-30).*	18.50	55.00	—

NOTE: For #S2985 w/lg. square red seal ovpt. see Military - Hunan Province Treasury #S3855.

Yu Sien Bank
Yü Hsiang Bank

裕湘銀行

Yü Hsiang Yin Hang

The successor to Hunan Bank and predecessor of the Hunan Provincial Bank.

1918 Issue

#S2988-S2992 house at l., roadway to walled city at r. Bank bldg. at ctr. on back. Printer: CMPA. *CHANGSHA*.

		Good	Fine	XF
S2988	**10 Coppers** June 1918. Brown and blue. Back orange and blue. *(S/M #Y24-1).*	12.50	42.00	—
S2989	**10 Coppers** 1918. Brown and green. Back red and blue. *(S/M #Y24-2).*	12.50	42.00	—
S2990	**20 Coppers** 1918. Green and brown. Back blue and yellow. *(S/M #Y24-3).*	12.50	42.00	—

		Good	Fine	XF
S2992	**100 Coppers** June 1918. Green and orange. Back brown and blue. *(S/M #Y4-4).*	15.00	45.00	—

#S2994-S2995A house at l., roadway to walled city at r. *HUNAN // CHANGSHA*. Printer: ABNC.

		Good	Fine	XF
S2994	**1 Silver Dollar** 15.7.1918. Red. Back red and m/c. *(S/M #Y24-10).*			
	a. Issued note.	15.00	45.00	—
	p. W/o place name. Proof.	—	—	—

S2995 5 Silver Dollars

		Good	Fine	XF
S2995	5 Silver Dollars 15.7.1918. Dk. blue. Back dk. blue and m/c. *(S/M #Y24-11).*			
	a. Issued note.	30.00	90.00	—
	p. W/o place name. Proof.	—	—	—
S2995A	10 Silver Dollars 15.7.1918. W/o place name. Proof. *(S/M #Y24-12).*	—	—	—

New Fu-T'ien Bank
Yunnan Fu-T'ien Bank

雲南富滇新銀行

Yün Nan Fu T'ien Hsin Yin Hang

1929 Issue

#S2996-S3000 phoenix and horse facing above globes. Printer: ABNC.

		Good	Fine	XF
S2996	1 Dollar 1929. Blue and m/c. Back blue. *(S/M #Y67-1).*			
	a. Issued note.	5.00	17.50	—
	s. Specimen.	—	Unc	60.00
S2997	5 Dollars 1929. Brown and m/c. Back brown. *(S/M #Y67-2).*			
	a. Issued note.	10.00	30.00	—
	s. Specimen.	—	Unc	75.00

		Good	Fine	XF
S2998	10 Dollars 1929. Violet and m/c. Back violet. *(S/M #Y67-3).*			
	a. Issued note.	12.00	35.00	—
	s. Specimen.	—	Unc	85.00
S2999	50 Dollars 1929. Green and m/c. Back green. *(S/M #Y67-4).*			
	a. Issued note.	17.50	55.00	—
	s. Specimen.	—	Unc	110.00

		Good	Fine	XF
S3000	100 Dollars 1929. Red and m/c. Back red. *(S/M #Y67-5).*			
	a. Issued note.	17.50	55.00	—
	s. Specimen.	—	Unc	135.00

1933 Issue

		Good	Fine	XF
S3001	5 Cents 1933. Blue and red. Temple at ctr. Back blue. *(S/M #Y67-12).*	10.00	30.00	60.00
S3002	10 Cents 1933. Violet. Pagoda on hillside at ctr. *(S/M #Y67-).*	17.50	55.00	—
S3003	20 Cents 1933. Green on red unpt. *(S/M #Y67-).*	22.50	67.50	—
S3004	50 Cents 1933. Red and blue. *(S/M #Y67-).*	6.00	15.00	40.00

Fu-Tien Bank
Yunnan "Fu-Tien" Bank
Yunnan "Futten" Bank

雲南富滇銀行

Yün Nan Fu T'ien Yin Hang

富滇銀行

Fu Tien Yin Hang

1913 Issue

#S3009-S3010 crossed flags at top ctr. Printer: YOPO.

		Good	Fine	XF
S3009	5 Dollars 1913. Brown, green and red. Back dk. green and red. *(S/M #Y70-0.5).*	100.00	300.00	—

		GOOD	FINE	XF
S3009A	**10 DOLLARS** 1913. Blue and m/c. Back brown and yellow. *(S/M #Y70-1).*	100.00	300.00	—

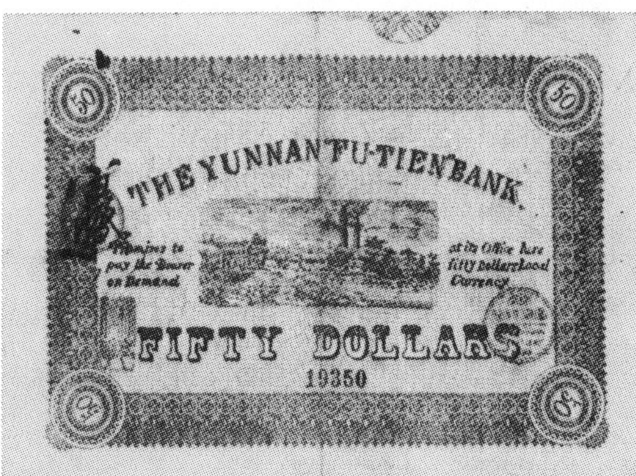

		GOOD	FINE	XF
S3009B	**50 DOLLARS** 1913 (?). City view at ctr. *(S/M #Y70-).*	—	—	—

		GOOD	FINE	XF
S3009C	**100 DOLLARS** 1913 (?). Antique steam passenger train at ctr. *(S/M #Y70-).*	—	—	—

NOTE: Confirmation of date of issue for #S3009B and S3009C is requested.

1916 COMMEMORATIVE ISSUE

#S3009E-S3009G, In Memory of the Chinese Republican Revolution in Yunnan Province

#S3009E-S3009G portr. general at r.

		GOOD	FINE	XF
S3009E	**1 YÜAN** Yr. 5 (1916). Black and olive-brown. Rural scene at l. Rural village on back. Specimen w/perforations. *(S/M #Y70-).*	—	Rare	—

		GOOD	FINE	XF
S3009F	**5 YÜAN** Yr. 5 (1916). Black and brown on pale blue unpt. Rural scene at l. Specimen w/perforations. *(S/M #Y70-).*	—	Rare	—

		GOOD	FINE	XF
S3009G	**10 YÜAN** Yr. 5 (1916). Black and blue-black. Gazebo at l. Back blue-gray; village. Specimen w/perforations. *(S/M #Y70-).*	—	Rare	—

1919 ISSUE

		GOOD	FINE	XF
S3010	**1 DOLLAR** 1919. Purple on lt. blue unpt. Back red on green unpt. *(S/M #Y70-).*	80.00	240.00	—

1921 ND ISSUE

#S3011-S3020 phoenix and horse facing above globes. Printer: ABNC.

		GOOD	FINE	XF
S3011	**10 CENTS** ND (1921). Black. Back blue and m/c. *(S/M #Y70-11).*	10.00	30.00	—

		GOOD	FINE	XF
S3012	**20 CENTS** ND (1921). Dk. blue. Back dk. blue on m/c unpt. *(S/M #Y70-12.)*			
	a. Issued note.	12.00	35.00	—
	b. Punched hole cancelled, hand stamps.	10.00	30.00	—

		GOOD	FINE	XF
S3013	**50 CENTS** ND (1921). Dk. green. Back green and m/c. 2 sign. varieties. *(S/M #Y70-13).*	12.00	35.00	—
S3014	**1 DOLLAR** ND (1921). Olive and m/c. Back green; gateway at ctr. *(S/M #Y70-20).*	45.00	135.00	—
S3015	**5 DOLLARS** ND (1921). Violet on m/c unpt. Back red-violet; gateway at ctr. *(S/M #Y70-21).*	Reported Not Confirmed		
S3016	**10 DOLLARS** ND (1921). *(S/M #Y70-22).*	Reported Not Confirmed		
S3017	**50 DOLLARS** *(S/M #Y70-23).* ND (1921).	Reported Not Confirmed		
S3018	**100 DOLLARS** ND (1921). *(S/M #Y70-24).*	Reported Not Confirmed		
S3019	**500 DOLLARS** ND (1921). *(S/M #Y70-25).*	Reported Not Confirmed		
S3020	**1000 DOLLARS** ND (1921). *(S/M #Y70-26).*	Reported Not Confirmed		

1927 ISSUE

#S3021-S3023 printer: YOPO.

		GOOD	FINE	XF
S3021	**1 DOLLAR** 1927. *(S/M #Y70-30).*	Reported Not Confirmed		
S3022	**5 DOLLARS** 1927. *(S/M #Y70-31).*	Reported Not Confirmed		

		GOOD	FINE	XF
S3023	**10 DOLLARS** 1927. Blue and green. Crossed flags at upper ctr. Back red and brown. *(S/M #Y70-32).*	40.00	120.00	—

1929 ISSUE

		GOOD	FINE	XF
S3023B	**5 DOLLARS** 1929. Dk. blue on pale orange unpt. Back red on pink unpt. w/black text. *(S/M #Y70-35).*	6.50	20.00	60.00

YUNNAN OFFICIAL CURRENCY BUREAU

局錢官南雲

Yün Nan Kuan Ch'ien Chü

1907 TAEL ISSUE

		GOOD	FINE	XF
S3023E3	**TAELS 6 MACE** Yr. 33 (1907). Black on orange unpt. Facing dragons at top, waves at bottom. Black text, lg. red square seal on back. *(S/M #Y70.5-13).*	—	—	—

YUNNAN PROVINCIAL BANK

票本額定圓

Yün Nan Sheng Yin Hang

銀行銀省南雲

Yin Yüan Ting O Pen P'iao

1949 SILVER YÜAN CASHIER'S CHECKS ISSUE

		VG	VF	UNC
S3024	**1 SILVER YÜAN** 1949. Red on lt. blue unpt. Back red; city gates at ctr. Printer: HKPA.			
	a. Issued note. *(S/M #Y71-0.4a).*	2.50	8.00	20.00

		VG	VF	UNC
	b. W/additional lg. red hand stamped sign. seal and violet Chinese 4 character ovpt.: *Ting O Pen P'iao. (S/M #Y71-0.4b).*	2.50	8.00	20.00

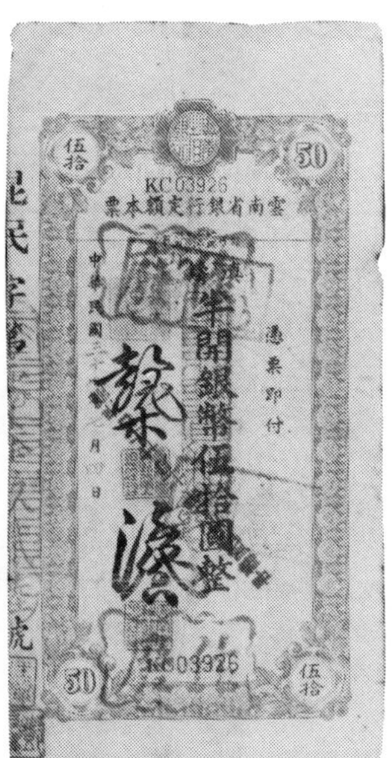

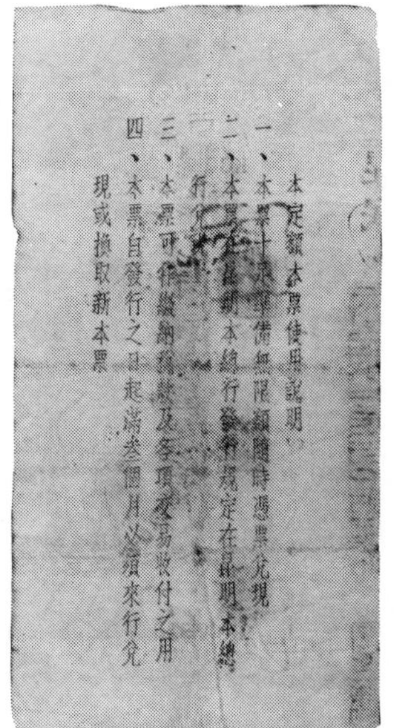

		VG	VF	UNC
S3025	**5 SILVER YÜAN** 1949. Red and blue. Uniface. Vertical format. *(S/M #Y71-)*.			
	a. Issued note.	15.00	45.00	—
	r1. Remainder w/o counterfoil.	—	10.00	30.00
	r2. Remainder w/counterfoil.	—	15.00	45.00
S3026	**10 SILVER YÜAN** 1949. Blue and yellow. Uniface .*(S/M #Y71-1)*.			
	a. Issued note.	20.00	60.00	—
	r1. Remainder w/o counterfoil.	—	12.00	35.00
	r2. Remainder w/counterfoil.	—	15.00	40.00

		VG	VF	UNC
S3027	**50 SILVER YÜAN** 4.7.1949; 1.12.1949. *Kumming. (S/M #Y71-3)*.			
	a. Issued note.	—	—	—
	b. Cancelled.	—	—	—
S3028	**100 SILVER YÜAN** 1.12.1949. *(S/M #Y71-4)*.			
	a. Issued note.	—	—	—
	b. Cancelled.	—	—	—

1949 CASHIER'S CHECKS (O PEN P'IAO) ISSUE

#S3029-S3029C Series A.

		VG	VF	UNC
S3029	**10 SILVER YÜAN** (ca.1949). Red w/black text. Embossed bank seal at top ctr. w/text. *Payable in Yunnan Provincial silver 1/2 dollars* on back. *(S/M #71-11)*.			
	a. Issued note.	—	—	—
	b. Cancelled.	—	—	—
S3029A	**20 SILVER DOLLARS** (ca. 1949). Green w/black text. *(S/M #71-12)*.	—	—	200.00
S3029B	**50 SILVER DOLLARS** (ca. 1949). *(S/M #71-13)*.	Reported Not Confirmed		
S3029C	**100 SILVER DOLLARS** 4.7.1949. *(S/M 71-14)*.	—	—	—

1949 KUNMING BRANCH CASHIER'S CHECKS ISSUE

#S3031 printer: HKPA.

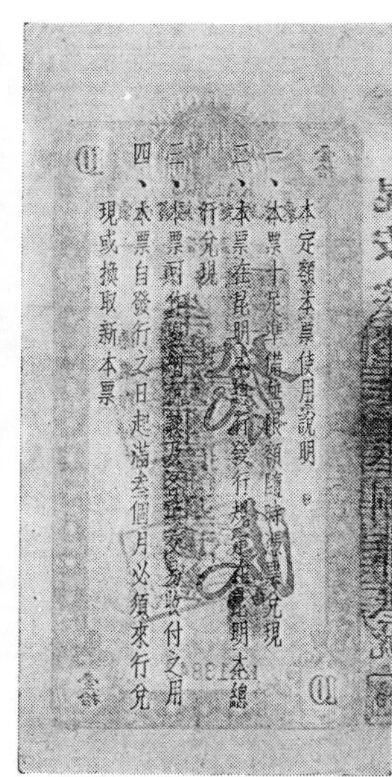

		VG	VF	UNC
S3031	**5 DOLLARS** 1.12.1949. Green w/black text. Uniface. *(S/M #Y71-21)*.	—	—	—
S3031A	**10 DOLLARS** (ca. 1949). *(S/M #Y71-22)*.	—	—	—
S3031B	**20 DOLLARS** (ca. 1949). *(S/M #Y71-23)*.	—	—	—
S3031C	**50 DOLLARS** 1.12.1949. Purple. *(S/M #Y71-24)*.	—	—	—
S3031D	**100 DOLLARS** (ca. 1949). *(S/M #Y71-25)*.	—	—	—

BANK OF TERRITORIAL DEVELOPMENT OF YUNNAN

雲南官商合辦殖邊銀行

Yün Nan Kuan Shang Ho Ban Chih Pien Yin Hang

雲南官商合辦殖邊銀行兌換券

Yün Nan Kuan Shang Ho Ban Chih Pien Yin Hang Tui Huan Ch'üan

1927 ISSUE

#S3033-S3037 monument by fortress at ctr. Hillside village at ctr. on back. *YUNNAN.* Printer: ABNC.

		VG	VF	UNC
S3033	**1 DOLLAR** 1.5.1927. Proof. *(S/M #Y70.7-1).*	—	—	—
S3034	**5 DOLLARS** 1.5.1927. Proof. *(S/M #Y70.7-2).*	—	—	—
S3035	**10 SILVER YÜAN** 1.5.1927. Proof. *(S/M #Y70.7-3).*	—	—	—
S3036	**50 DOLLARS** 1.5.1927. Proof. *(S/M #Y70.7-4).*	—	—	—

		VG	VF	UNC
S3037	**100 DOLLARS** 1.5.1927. *(S/M #Y70.7-5).*			
	p. Proof.	—	—	—
	s. Specimen.	—	—	—

ISLAMIC REPUBLIC OF TURKESTAN

UNITED ISLAMIC REPUBLIC OF EAST TURKESTAN

REVOLUTIONARY OR SUPREME GOVERNMENT, KHOTAN

1933 SILVER DACHIN ISSUE

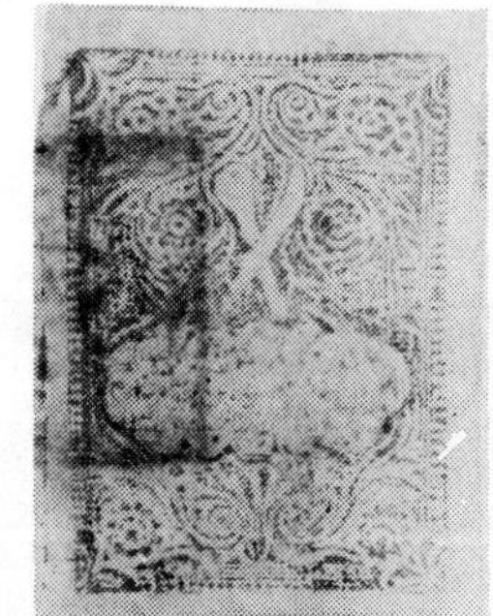

		VG	VF	UNC
S3039	**100 SILVER DACHIN** AH1352 (1933). Black w/red text. Back blue-green, blue text on red unpt. Cloth. *(S/M #-).*	20.00	60.00	—

1933 COPPER CASH ISSUE

		GOOD	FINE	XF
S3041	**400 COPPER CASH** AH1352 (1933). Blue, black text on red violet. Uniface. 2 reddish brown hand stamped seals on back *(S/M #-)*	27.50	85.00	—

ISLAMIC REPUBLIC OF EAST TURKESTAN

1933 ISSUE

		GOOD	FINE	XF
S3045	**5 MISCAL = 1/2 TAEL** ND (1933). *(S/M #-).*	—	—	—
S3046	**1 SAR = 1 TAEL** AH1352 (1933). Star and crescent at ctr. *(S/M #-).*			
	a. Cloth.	—	—	—
	b. Paper.	—	—	—

COMMUNIST BANKS

REPUBLIC PERIOD

An increasingly uneasy association between the Kuomintang and the Chinese Communist Party developed and continued until April 12, 1927, when Chiang Kai-shek, Sun Yat-sen's political heir, instituted a bloody purge to stamp out the Communists within the *Kuomintang* and the government and virtually paralyzed their ranks throughout China. Some time after the mid-1927 purges, the Chinese Communist Party turned to armed force to resist Chiang Kai-shek and during the period of 1930-34 acquired control over large parts of Kiangsi (Jiangxi), Fukien (Fujian), Hunan and Hupeh (Hbei). The Nationalist Nanking government responded with a series of campaigns against the soviet power bases and, by October 1934, succeeded in driving the remnants of the Communist army to a refuge in Shensi (Shaanxi) Province. There the Communists reorganized under the leadership of Mao Tse-tung, defeated the Nationalist forces, and on Sept. 21, 1949 established the Peoples Republic of China. Thereafter relations between Russia and Communist China steadily deteriorated until 1958 when China emerged as an independent center of Communist power.

SOVIET PERIOD

Prior to 1949, the Peoples Republic of China did not exist as such, but the Communists did control areas known as "Soviets." Most of the "Soviets" were established on the borders of two or more provinces and were named according to the provinces involved. Thus there were such "Soviets" as the Kiangsi-Hunan Soviet, the Hunan-Hupeh-Kiangsi Soviet, the Hupeh-Honan-Anhwei Soviet and others. In 1931 some of the "Soviets" in the southern Kiangsi area were consolidated into the Chinese Soviet Republic, which lasted until the Long March of 1934.

NOTE: The following listings are incomplete as other issuers exist which will be added when developed for future editions of this volume.

MONETARY SYSTEM:

10 Wen (Cash) = 1 Fen (Cent)
10 Fen (Cents) = 1 Chiao (Hao)
10 Chiao = 1 Yüan (Dollar)

Bank of Chang Chung
#S3050-S3057

行 銀 城 長
Ch'ang Chung Yin Hang

Bank of Eastern Chekiang
#S3058-S3059B

行 銀 東 浙
Che Tung Yin Hang

Bank of Kirin
#S3060-S3063A

行銀省林吉
Chi Lin Sheng Yin Hang

Bank of Chinan
#S3063F-S3105

行 銀 南 冀
Chi Nan Yin Hang

Kiangsi Workers and Farmers Bank
#S3108-S3111

行銀農工西江
Chiang Hsi Kung Nung Yin Hang

Kiang Hwai Bank of China
#S3116-S3134

行 銀 淮 江
Chiang Huai Yin Hang

Bank of Kiangnan (nau)
#S3135A-S3135B

行 銀 南 江
Chiang Nan Yin Hang

7th Administrative District Shansi-Chahar-Hopei Border Area Cooperative Society
#S3135P-S3135T

區政行七第區邊冀察晋
Chin Ch'a Chi Pien Chü Ti Ch'i Hsing Cheng Ch'ü

Bank of Shansi, Chahar and Hopei
#S3136-S3211

行銀區邊冀察晋
Chin Ch'a Chi Pien Chü Yin Hang

Szechuan-Shensi Provincial Soviet Workers and Farmers Bank
#S3215-S3224

行銀農工/府政埃維蘇省陝川
Ch'uan Shan Sheng Su Wei Ai Cheng Fu / Kung Nung Yin Hang

Bank of Soviet Szechuan-Shensi Provincial Workers and Farmers
#S3228-S3229

府政埃維蘇陝川
Ch'uan Shan Sheng Su Wei Ai Cheng Fu

Kung Nung Yin Hang

Chung Chou Farmers Bank
Farmers Bank of Chung Chou
#S3232-S3241

行銀民農州中
Chung Chou Nung Min Yin Hang

Chinese Soviet Republic /
Szechuan - Shensi Provincial Workers and Farmers Bank
#S3243

國和共埃維蘇華中
Chung Hua Su Wei Ai Kung Ho Kuo

Ch'uan Shan Sheng Kung Nung Yin Hang Ch'ien Hang

Chinese Soviet Republic National Bank
Chinese Soviet Republic Economic Reconstruction Bonds
#S3244-S3247

行銀家國國和共埃維蘇華中
Chung Hua Su Wei Ai Kung Ho Kuo Kuo Chi Yin Hang

Kuo Chi Yin Hang
Worker and Peasants Bank
#S3249

(行銀)省陝川國和共埃維蘇華中
Chung Hua Su Wei Ai Kung Ho Kuo Ch'uan Shan Sheng (Yin Hang)

Chinese Soviet Republic National Bank
#S3250-S3270

行銀家國國和共埃維蘇華中
Chung Hua Su Wei Ai Kung Ho Kuo Kuo Chia Yin Hang

行 銀 家 國
Kuo Chia Yin Hang

Chinese Soviet Republic National Bank/
Hunan-West Hupei Special Branch
#S3273-S3274

行分省贛湘行銀家國國和共埃維蘇華中
Chung Hua Su Wei Ai Kung Ho Kuo Kuo Chia Yin Hang

Hsiang O Hsi T'a Chü Feng Hang

行分區特西鄂湘行銀家國
(Short form) *Kuo Chia Yin Hang Hsiang O Hsi T'e Chü Fen Hang*

Chinese Soviet National Bank, Hunan-Kwangsi Province
Chung Hua Su Wei Ai Kung
#S3274A-S3275

行分區特西鄂湘行銀家國國和共埃維蘇華中
Ho Kuo Kuo Chia Yin Hang Hsiang Kan Sheng Fen Hang

Chinese Soviet Republic Government Bank
#S3276-S3288

行銀家國國和共埃維蘇華中
Chung Hua Su Wei Ai Kung Ho Kuo Kuo Chia Yin Hang

行 銀 家 國
Kuo Chia Yin Hang

Farmers Bank of Northwest China (Shansi)
Sibei(o) Nung Min Inxang
#S3289-S3325

行銀民農北西晋
Shan Hsi Pei Nung Min Yin Hang

Hunan-Hupei-Kiangsi Workers and Farmers Bank
#S3327-S3345

行銀農工省贛鄂湘
Hsiang O Kan Sheng Kung Nung Yin Hang

Hunan-Hupei Soviet Bank
#S3349

行銀埃維蘇省兩鄂湘
Hsiang O Liang Sheng Su Wei Ai Yin Hang

Provincial Treasury of Hupeh, East Hupeh, Branch
#S3351 and S3353

庫分東鄂庫省北湖
Hu Pei Sheng K'u O T'ung Fen K'u

Bank of Central China
#S3355-S3418

行銀中華
Hua Chung Yin Hang

Huainan Bank
#S3418B-S3419L

行銀南淮
Huai Nan Yin Hang

Northwest Anhwei Special District Soviet Bank
#S3421-S3423D

行銀埃維蘇區特地北西皖
Huan Hsi Pei Ti T'e Chü Su Wei Ai Yin Hang

Bank of Rehher Sheeng
#S3424-S3428

行銀省河熱
Je Ho Sheng Yin Hang

Northeast Kiangsi Soviet Bank
#S3433-S3438

行銀埃維蘇(省)北東贛
Kan Tung Pei (Sheng) Su Wei Ai Yin Hang

Northeast Kiangsi Soviet Bank / North Fukien Branch
#S3440-S3440C

行銀北閩行銀埃維蘇(省)北東贛
Kan Tung Pei Sheng Su Wei Ai Yin Hang / Min Pei Yin Hang

Kiangsi, Hunan, Anhwei Soviet Workers and Farmers Bank
#S3441

行銀農工埃蘇皖豫贛
Kan Yü Huan Su Wei Ai Kung Nung Yin Hang

Bank of Kuantung
#S3445-S3449

行銀東關
Kuan Tung Yin Hang

Bank of West Shantung
#S3450-S3462

行銀西魯
Lu Hsi Yin Hang

Fukien-Chekiang-Kiangsi Soviet Bank
#S3465-S3480

行銀埃維蘇省贛浙閩

Min Che Kan Sheng Su Wei Ai Yin Hang

Fukien-Chekiang-Kiangsi Soviet Bank/North Fukien Branch
#S3481-S3481B

行銀北閩/行銀埃維蘇省贛浙閩

Min Che Kan Sheng Su Wei Ai Yin Hang/Min Pei Yin Hang

Fukien-Kwangtung-Kiangsi Border Area Bank
#S3482

行銀區邊贛粵閩

Min Yüeh Kan Pien Chü Yin Hang

Southern Peoples Bank
#S3483-S3489

行銀民人方南

Nan Fang Jen Min Yin Hang

Inner Mongolia Peoples Bank
#S3494-S3506

行銀民人古蒙内

Nei Mung Ku Jen Min Yin Hang

Bank of Inner Mongolia
#S3507-S3507A

行銀蒙内

Nei Mung Yin Hang

Bank of Inner Chiang
#S3507J-S3507R

行銀省江嫩

Nen Chiang Sheng Yin Hang

West Hupeh Peasants Bank
#S3508A-S3508J

行銀民農西鄂

O Hsi Nung Min Yin Hang

North Hupeh Peasants Bank
#S3508P-S3508Q

行銀民農北鄂

O Pei Nung Min Yin Hang

East Hupei Workers and Peasants Bank
#S3509-S3512

行銀農工東鄂

O Tung Kung Nung Yin Hang

Southeast Hupei Workers, Peasants and Soldiers Bank
#S3515-S3525

行銀兵農工南東鄂

O Tung Nan Kung Nung Ping Yin Hang

Southeast Hupei Workers and Farmers Bank
#S3526-S3529

行銀農工南東鄂

O Tung Nan Kung Nung Yin Hang

Hupei-Honan-Anhwei Soviet Bank
#S3538

行銀埃維蘇省皖豫鄂

O Yü Huan Sheng Su Wei Ai Yin Hang

Hupei-Honan-Anhwei Province
Soviet Workers and Peasants Bank
#S3539-S3540C

行銀農工埃維蘇省皖豫鄂

O Yü Huan Sheng Su Wei Ai Kung Neng Yin Hang

Bank of Bai Hai, Bo Xai Inxang, B. X. Inxiang
Pei Hai Bank of China, Pei Hai Bank, Bank of Pei Hai
#S3541-S3623N

行銀海北

Pei Hai Yin Hang

P'ing Chiang Workers and Farmers Bank
#S3624-S3625

行銀農工縣江平

P'ing Chiang Hsien Kung Nung Yin Hang

Maojgungs Liutungkyan
#S3630-S3648

司公易貿/區邊寧甘陝

Shan Kan Ning Pien Ch'ü /Mao I Kung Szu

Shaan Gan Ning Bianky Inxan (g)

Shensi-Kansu-Ninghsia Border Area Bank
#S3651-S3670

行銀區邊寧甘陝

Shan Kan Ning Pien Ch'ü Yin Hang

Bank of Shantong
#S3671-S3675

行銀黨上

Shang Tang Yin Hang

Soviet Bank (Hopei-Honan-Anhwei Soviet Economic Commune)
#S3676-S3677

行銀埃維蘇

Su Wei Ai Yin Hang

Ta Chiang Bank/Dagiang Inxan(g)
#S3680-S3710

行銀江大

Ta Chiang Yin Hang

Eastern Mongolian Bank
#S3715-S3717

行銀蒙東

Tung Mung Yin Hang

Kwangsi-Kweichow-Yunnan Border District
Dian-Kian-Gui Bianky
#S3719-S3720

局易貿區邊桂黔滇

T'ien Ch'ien Kuei Pien Ch'ü Mao I Chü

Bank of Dung Bai
Bank of Dung Pai
Tung Pei Bank of China
#S3725-S3770

行銀北東

Tung Pei Yin Hang

Guangxua Shangdian
#S3775-S3781

店商華光安延

Yen An Kuang Hua Shang Tien

店商華光

Kuang Hua Shang Tien

NOTE: Colors may vary greatly even with significant changes in many issues due to the shortage of quality materials and access to modern printing facilities.

BANK OF CHANG CHUNG

行 銀 城 長

Ch'ang Chung Yin Hang

1948 ISSUE

		GOOD	FINE	XF
S3050	**100 YÜAN** 1948. Brown and yellow. Great Wall at l. Back green. *(S/M #C6-1).*	6.50	20.00	60.00

		GOOD	FINE	XF
S3052	**200 YÜAN** 1948. Black on orange unpt. Great Wall at l. Back red. *(S/M #C6-2).*	4.00	12.00	35.00
S3053	**500 YÜAN** 1948. Black on violet unpt. Mao Tse-tung at l. Back red. *(S/M #C6-3).*	5.00	15.00	45.00
S3053A	**500 YÜAN** 1948. Blue on lt. blue unpt. Like #S3053. Back red-brown. *(S/M #C6-).*	7.50	22.50	67.50
S3054	**500 YÜAN** 1948. Blue on orange unpt. Mao Tse-tung at l. Back brown. *(S/M #C6-4).*	5.00	15.00	45.00
S3055	**1000 YÜAN** 1948. Brown and yellow. Plowing w/horses. Red serial #. Back violet. *(S/M #C6-5).*	5.00	15.00	45.00
S3056	**1000 YÜAN** 1948. Brown and red. Like #S3055 but w/blue serial #. Back violet. *(S/M #C6-6).*	5.00	15.00	45.00

		Good	Fine	XF
S3057	**5000 Yüan** 1948. Black on blue unpt. Shanhaikuan city gate. Back blue. *(S/M #C6-7).*			
	a. Serial # at upper l., red control letters at upper r., red vertical Chinese characters. at l. and r. *(S/M #C6-7a).*	7.50	22.50	67.50
	b. Serial # at upper r., red control letters at upper l., black vertical Chinese characters at l. and r. *(S/M #C6-7b).*	7.50	22.50	67.50

Bank of Eastern Chekiang

浙東銀行

Che Tung Yin Hang

1945 Issue

		Good	Fine	XF
S3058	**2 Chiao** 1945. Vertical format. Uniface w/square seal stamping on back. *(S/M #C27-).*	10.00	30.00	90.00
S3058A	**5 Chiao = 50 Cents** 1945. 2 peasants operating foot-powered water conveyor at r. Uniface w/square seal stamping on back. *(S/M #C27-).*	10.00	30.00	90.00

		Good	Fine	XF
S3058B	**5 Chiao** 1945. Farming scene at ctr. r. *(S/M #C27-).*	7.50	22.50	60.00

		Good	Fine	XF
S3058C	**1 Yüan** 1945. Rural street scene at ctr. *(S/M #C27-).*	7.50	22.50	67.50

		Good	Fine	XF
S3058D	**1 Yüan** 1945. Rural scene at ctr. r. *(S/M #C27-).*	8.00	25.00	75.00

		Good	Fine	XF
S3058E	**1 Yüan** 1945. Uniface w/square seal stamping on back. *(S/M #C27-).*	15.00	45.00	135.00

		Good	Fine	XF
S3058F	**1 Yüan** 1945. Peasants operating foot-powered water conveyor at l. ctr. *(S/M #C27-).*	10.00	30.00	90.00

		Good	Fine	XF
S3058G	**5 Yüan** 1945. Rural scene at ctr. r. *(S/M #C27-).*	15.00	45.00	135.00

		Good	Fine	XF
S3058H	**10 Yüan** 1945. Black on brown unpt. Rural scene at ctr. r. Back brown. *(S/M #C27-).*	17.50	55.00	165.00

1945 Circulating Bearer Checks Emergency Issue

#S3059-S3059B vertical format.

S3059

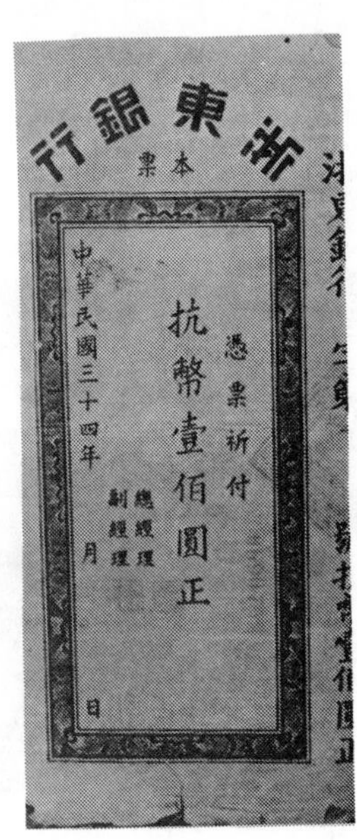

S3059A

		Good	Fine	XF
S3059	**50 Yüan** 1945. *(S/M #C27-).*	15.00	45.00	135.00

		GOOD	FINE	XF
S3059A	**50 YÜAN** 1945. *(S/M #C27-).*	—	—	—

		GOOD	FINE	XF
S3059B	**100 YÜAN** 1945. *(S/M #C27-).*	—	—	—

BANK OF KIRIN

吉林省銀行
Chi Lin Sheng Yin Hang

1946 ISSUE

		GOOD	FINE	XF
S3060	**5 YÜAN** 1946. Red. Back violet. *(S/M #C73-1).*	15.00	45.00	135.00

		GOOD	FINE	XF
S3061	**10 YÜAN** 1946. Olive. Biplane over city, river, bridges at ctr. Back maroon. *(S/M #C73-1.5).*	12.50	40.00	120.00
S3062	**50 YÜAN** 1946. Green. Back red. *(S/M #C73-2).*	17.50	55.00	165.00

		GOOD	FINE	XF
S3063	**100 YÜAN** 1946. Dk. blue or blue on red unpt. Back red. *(S/M #C73-).*	6.00	17.50	52.00
S3063A	**100 YÜAN** 1946. Purple on red unpt. Like #S3063. Back red. *(S/M #C73-).*	4.50	15.00	42.00

BANK OF CHINAN

濟南銀行
Chi Nan Yin Hang

1932 CIRCULATING CASHIERS CHECK ISSUE

		GOOD	FINE	XF
S3063F	**200 YÜAN** 1932. *(S/M #C81-).*	9.00	27.50	82.50
S3063G	**500 YÜAN** 1932. *(S/M #C81-).*	9.00	27.50	82.50

1939 REGULAR ISSUES

		GOOD	FINE	XF
S3064	**1 CHIAO = 10 CENTS** 1939. Greenish black. Steam passenger train crossing bridge w/mountains in background at lower l. Back brown. *(S/M #C81-0.1.*	3.50	10.00	30.00

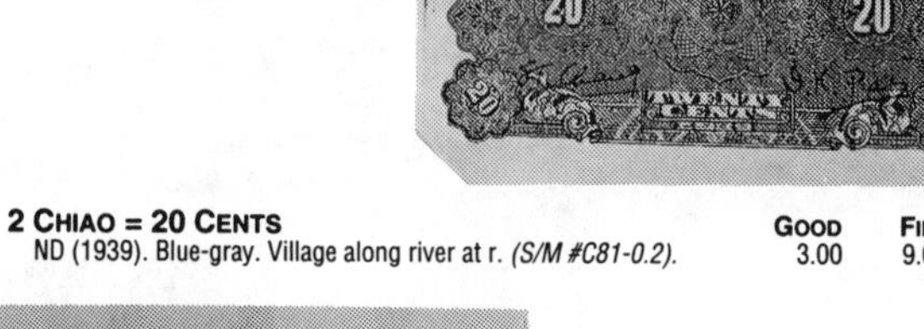

		GOOD	FINE	XF
S3065	**2 CHIAO = 20 CENTS** ND (1939). Blue-gray. Village along river at r. *(S/M #C81-0.2).*	3.00	9.00	27.00

		GOOD	FINE	XF
S3065A	**2 CHIAO 5 FEN = 25 CENTS** 1939. Purple. Towered bridge, mountain behind at l. Steam passenger train at ctr. on back. *(S/M #C81-0.3).*	7.50	22.50	67.50

		GOOD	FINE	XF
S3066	**5 CHIAO = 50 CENTS** 1939. Gray-green. City fortress gate at Peking at l. *(S/M #C81-0.4).*	3.00	9.00	27.00
S3066A	**5 CHIAO = 50 CENTS** 1939. Steam passenger train at l. *(S/M #C81-0.5).*	10.00	30.00	90.00

		Good	Fine	XF
S3067	**1 Yüan** 1939. Brown. Bldg., mountains at l. Ship at ctr. on back. *(S/M #C81-0.7).*	3.00	9.00	27.00

		Good	Fine	XF
S3068	**2 Yüan** 1939. Olive-green on pink unpt. Temple at r. Back violet-brown w/bank bldg. at ctr. *(S/M #C81-1).*	3.50	11.00	32.50
S3068A	**3 Yüan** 1939. Green. Gazebo on hill behind houses at l. Back red-orange. *(S/M #C81-1.1).*	9.00	27.00	80.00
S3069	**5 Yüan** 1939. Olive-green on pink unpt. Gazebo on hill behing houses at l., gateway by shoreline at r. Back brown; warships and planes at ctr. *T'ai Yüeh. (S/M #C81-1.3).*	1.50	4.00	12.00

		Good	Fine	XF
S3069A	**5 Yüan** 1939. Olive-green on pink unpt. Like #S3609. *(S/M #C81-1.4).*			
	a. Black ovpt: *T'ai Hang* at lower l. and r.	2.00	6.00	18.00
	b. W/*T'ai Yüeh* in oval frame.	9.00	27.00	80.00
	c. Red ovpt: *T'ai Yüeh* w/o frame.	6.00	18.00	55.00

#S3069B Deleted. See #S3069A.

		Good	Fine	XF
S3069C	**5 Yüan** 1939. Red and black on lt. green unpt. Like #S3069. Back green. *(S/M #C81-1.6).*			
	a. W/o place name.	1.50	4.00	12.00
	b. Black ovpt: *T'ai Hang* at l. and r.	6.00	18.00	55.00
S3069D	**5 Yüan** 1939. Steam passenger trains at l. Bldgs. at ctr. on back. *(S/M #C81-1.7).*	9.00	27.00	80.00
S3069E	**10 Yüan** 1939. Brown-violet on pale blue unpt. Like #S3070. Back black. *(S/M #C81-2).*	3.00	9.00	27.00

		Good	Fine	XF
S3070	**10 Yüan** 1939. Dk. green on pink unpt. Steam passenger train at ctr. Back red; tea house at ctr. *(S/M #C81-2.5).*			
	a. W/o place name. *(S/M #C81-2.5a).*	2.00	6.00	18.00
	b. Black *T'ai Yüeh. (S/M #C81-2.5b).*	7.50	22.50	67.50
	c. Red *T'ai Hang* at l. and r.	7.50	22.50	67.50
S3070A	**10 Yüan** 1939. Red on yellow unpt. Fortress at l., steam passenger train at r. *Ping Yüan. (S/M #C81-3).*	15.00	40.00	120.00
S3070B	**20 Yüan** 1939. Bldgs. at l. Bridge over river at ctr. on back. *T'ai Yüeh. (S/M #C81-4).*	10.00	30.00	90.00
S3070C	**20 Yüan** 1939. Bldg. at ctr. *(S/M #C81-5).*	10.00	30.00	90.00

		Good	Fine	XF
S3070D	**50 Yüan** 1939. Red-orange. Temple of Heaven at r. Like #S3084. Back green; temple at ctr. *(S/M #C81-6).*			
	a. W/o place name.	7.50	22.50	67.50
	b. *T'ai Hang.*	7.50	22.50	67.50
	c. *T'ai Yüeh.*	7.50	22.50	67.50
S3070E	**50 Yüan** 1939. Pagoda at r. *(S/M #C81-6.5).*			
	a. W/o place name.	10.00	30.00	90.00
	b. *P'ing Yüan.*	10.00	30.00	90.00

		Good	Fine	XF
S3070F	**100 Yüan** 1939. Deep blue on red unpt. Bldgs. at ctr. Back red; steam passenger train at ctr. *(S/M #C81-7).*			
	a. W/o place name.	9.00	28.00	85.00
	b. *T'ai Hang.*	10.00	30.00	90.00

1940 ISSUE

		GOOD	FINE	XF
S3071	**20 CENTS** 1940. Steam passenger train at lower r. *(S/M #C81-8).*	10.00	30.00	90.00

1941 ISSUE

#S3073-S3073B Seventeen-Arch bridge at Summer Palace at ctr.

		GOOD	FINE	XF
S3073	**10 COPPERS** 1941. Red-orange. *(S/M #C81-9.3).*			
	a. Back green.	7.50	22.50	67.50
	b. Back greenish black.	7.50	22.50	67.50

		GOOD	FINE	XF
S3073A	**20 COPPERS** 1941. Gray-green. Back brown. *(S/M #C81-9.5).*	6.00	18.00	55.00
S3073B	**20 COPPERS** 1941. Gray. Like #S3073A. Back dk. blue. *(S/M #C81-).*	7.50	22.50	67.50
S3073C	**20 COPPERS** 1941. Purple. Like #S3073B. *(S/M #C81-).*	7.50	22.50	67.50
S3073F	**50 COPPERS** 1941. *(S/M #C81-9.7).*			
	a. Purple.	—	—	—
	b. Gray-violet.	—	—	—

1942 ISSUES

#S3074-S3076 vertical format.

S3074

S3075

		GOOD	FINE	XF
S3074	**25 YÜAN** 1942. Green. Gazebo at upper ctr. *(S/M #C81-9.7).*	2.00	6.00	18.00
S3075	**50 YÜAN** 1942. Brown-violet. Steam passenger train at upper ctr. Back blue-gray. *(S/M #C81-10).*	3.00	9.00	27.00

		GOOD	FINE	XF
S3076	**100 YÜAN** 1942. Brown. Temple at upper ctr. Back blue. *(S/M #C81-11).*	3.50	10.00	33.00

		GOOD	FINE	XF
S3077	**100 YÜAN** 1942. Blue. Planting rice at l. Cultivating w/horses at l. and r. on back. *(S/M #C81-12).*			
	a. Back green.	9.00	28.00	85.00
	b. Back brown.	3.00	10.00	30.00
S3077A	**100 YÜAN** 1942. Deep brown. Like #S3077. *(S/M #C81-12.5).*			
	a. Back black.	9.00	28.00	85.00
	b. Back blue.	5.00	15.00	45.00

		GOOD	FINE	XF
S3078	**200 YÜAN** 1942. Blue. Peasant at l. Back brown; bldg. at ctr. *(S/M #C81-13).*	3.00	10.00	30.00
S3078A	**200 YÜAN** 1942. Violet-brown. Like #S3078. Back blue-gray. *(S/M #C81-13.5).*	5.00	15.00	45.00
S3079	**500 YÜAN** 1942. Blue-black. Fortress at l. Back brown. *(S/M #C81-14).*	6.00	18.00	55.00

		GOOD	FINE	XF
S3080	**1000 YÜAN** 1942. Green on pink unpt. Steam passenger train at ctr. Back red-brown; gateway along river at ctr. *(S/M #C81-15).*			
	a. 2 serial #.	6.00	18.00	55.00
	b. Block letters at l., serial # at r.	3.00	10.00	30.00

1943 EMERGENCY CIRCULATING CASHIERS CHECK ISSUE

		GOOD	FINE	XF
S3080F	**200 YÜAN** 1943. Red. Uniface. *(S/M #C81-).*	—	—	—

S3080G 500 YÜAN	GOOD	FINE	XF
1943. Blue-violet. Uniface. *(S/M #C81-).*	—	—	—

1943 REGULAR ISSUE

S3081 200 YÜAN	GOOD	FINE	XF
1943. Red on yellow unpt. Pagoda at l. *(S/M #C81-15.2).*	20.00	62.50	200.00
S3082 1000 YÜAN			
1943. Black on lilac unpt. Like #S3081. *(S/M #C87-15.4).*	26.50	80.00	240.00

1944 ISSUE

S3083 20 YÜAN	GOOD	FINE	XF
1944. Brown-violet. Factory bldgs. at l. Like #S3070B. *(S/M #C81-15.6).*	10.00	30.00	90.00

S3084 50 YÜAN	GOOD	FINE	XF
1944. Red-orange on yellow unpt. Temple of Heaven at r. Like #S3070D. Back deep green; temple at ctr.			
a. W/o place name. *(S/M #C81-15.8a).*	9.00	27.50	85.00
b. *T'ai Hang. (S/M #C81-15.8b).*	9.00	27.50	80.00
c. *T'ai Yüeh. (S/M #C81-15.8c).*	10.00	30.00	90.00

S3084A 100 YÜAN	GOOD	FINE	XF
1944. City square, gateway at ctr. Steam passenger train at ctr. on back. *(S/M #C81-15.9).*			
a. W/o place name.	8.50	25.00	80.00
b. *T'ai Hang.*	8.50	25.00	80.00

1945 ISSUES

S3085 5 YÜAN	GOOD	FINE	XF
1945. Bldg. on hillside at r. *(S/M #C81-16).*	10.00	30.00	90.00
S3086 10 YÜAN			
1945. Steam passenger train at r. *(S/M #C81-17).*	7.50	22.50	67.50
S3086A 25 YÜAN			
1945. Purple. Boat at ctr., pagoda at r. *(S/M #C81-18).*	20.00	62.50	200.00

S3086B 50 YÜAN	GOOD	FINE	XF
1945. Blue-black. Steam passenger train at r. Back brown; temple at l. ctr.			
a. W/o place name.	4.00	12.00	35.00
b. *T'ai Hang. (S/M #C81-19b).*	7.50	22.50	67.50
c. *P'ing Yüan. (S/M #C81-19c).*	4.00	12.00	35.00
p. Proof. Face and back.	—	Unc	100.00

S3087 100 YÜAN	GOOD	FINE	XF
1945. Blue. Tower at ctr. Back red; city gateway at ctr. *P'ing Yüan. (S/M #C81-20).*	6.00	18.00	55.00

S3088 100 YÜAN	GOOD	FINE	XF
1945. Red. City fortress gate at Peking at ctr. Back green. *(S/M #C81-21).*	8.00	25.00	75.00
S3089 100 YÜAN			
1945. Brown on yellow unpt. Like #S3088. Back blue-gray. *(S/M #C81-21.5).*			
a. White paper.	6.00	18.00	55.00
b. Buff paper.	6.00	18.00	55.00

S3090 500 YÜAN	GOOD	FINE	XF
1945. Brown and green. Plowing at ctr. Back blue; warship at ctr. *(S/M #C81-22).*	3.00	9.00	27.00
S3090A 500 YÜAN			
1945. Blue-green on pink unpt. Like #S3090. Back brown. *(S/M #C81-22.5).*	4.50	12.50	40.00
S3091 500 YÜAN			
1945. Green and yellow. Plowing. Back brown. *(S/M #C81-23).*			
a. Bold serial #.	4.50	12.50	40.00
b. Regular serial #.	5.00	15.00	50.00

1946 ISSUE

		GOOD	FINE	XF
S3093	**100 YÜAN** 1946. Blue-green on yellow unpt. Village gateway at ctr. Back brown; Temple of Heaven at ctr. *(S/M #C81-28).*	5.00	15.00	50.00

		GOOD	FINE	XF
S3095	**500 YÜAN** 1946. Gray-green. Bldg., steam passenger train at ctr. Back black.			
	a. Buff paper. *(S/M #C81-30a).*	3.00	10.00	30.00
	b. White paper. *(S/M #C81-30b).*	3.00	10.00	30.00
	p. Proof. Face and back.	—	Unc	80.00

1948 ISSUES

		GOOD	FINE	XF
S3099	**500 YÜAN** 1948. Red. Harvesting grain at r. Back blue. *(S/M #C81-40).*	2.00	6.00	18.00

		GOOD	FINE	XF
S3100	**500 YÜAN** 1948. Red on green and orange unpt. Steam passenger train at ctr. Pagoda at l. on back. *(S/M #C81-41).*	3.00	9.00	27.00

#S3101 *Deleted.* See #S3100.

		GOOD	FINE	XF
S3102	**500 YÜAN** 1948. Brown and green. Horse drawn cart at r. Back brown. *(S/M #C81-43).*	3.00	10.00	30.00

#S3103 *Deleted.* See #S3102.

		GOOD	FINE	XF
S3105	**2000 YÜAN** 1948. Green and yellow. Steam passenger train at r. Back brown. *(S/M #C81-44).*	4.00	12.50	37.50

KIANGSI WORKERS AND FARMERS BANK

江西工農銀行

Chiang Hsi Kung Nung Yin Hang

ND ISSUE

		GOOD	FINE	XF
S3108	**1 DOLLAR** ND. V. Lenin. K. Marx on back. *(S/M #C96-1).*	—	—	—

		GOOD	FINE	XF
S3109	**100 COPPERS** ND. Green. River front village at ctr. Back red; mountains and river at ctr. *(S/M #C96-8).*	30.00	100.00	—

NOTE: #S3109 w/denomination: 10 x 10 coppers coin.

		GOOD	FINE	XF
S3110	**500 COPPERS** ND. Green. Rural house at l., bldg. and tower at r. Back red; rural bldg. l. and view at r. *(S/M #C96-10).*	40.00	125.00	—

NOTE: #S3110 w/denomination: 50 x 10 coppers coin.

		GOOD	FINE	XF
S3111	**1000 COPPERS** ND. Bldgs. at l. and r. *(S/M #C96-20).*	50.00	150.00	—

KIANG HWAI BANK OF CHINA

行銀淮江

Chiang Huai Yin Hang

1941 ISSUES

#S3115 *Deleted.*

		GOOD	FINE	XF
S3116	**5 CHIAO = 50 CENTS** 1941. Blue-violet and red. Plowing w/ox. Back green. *(S/M #C104-2).*	10.00	30.00	90.00
S3117	**1 YÜAN** 1941. Dk. blue. Sawing wood, rice paddy at ctr. Back orange. *Su Chung. (S/M #C104-10a).*	10.00	35.00	105.00
S3117A	**1 YÜAN** 1941. Dk. blue. Like #S3117. Back orange. *Yan Fu (S/M #C104-10b).*	17.50	55.00	165.00

1941 PROVISIONAL ISSUE

#S3118 and S3118A ovpt: *Tso 5 Yüan* at l. and r.

		GOOD	FINE	XF
S3118	**5 YÜAN ON 1 YÜAN** 1941. Dk. blue. Ovpt on #3117. Back orange. *Su Chung. (S/M #C104-11).*	17.50	55.00	165.00

		GOOD	FINE	XF
S3118A	**5 YÜAN ON 1 YÜAN** 1941. Dk. blue. Ovpt. on #3117. Back orange. *Yan Fu. (S/M #C104-11b).*	22.50	67.50	200.00
S3119	**5 YÜAN** 1941. Red. Like #S3117. Back blue. *(S/M #C104-12).*	17.50	55.00	165.00

1943 ISSUES

		GOOD	FINE	XF
S3123	**2 CHIAO = 20 CENTS** 1943. Sampans at ctr. *(S/M #C104-19).*	10.00	30.00	90.00
S3124	**5 CHIAO = 50 CENTS** 1943. Blue. Plowing w/ox. Back brown. *(S/M #C104-20).*	10.00	30.00	90.00
S3125	**50 CENTS** 1943. Green. Sampans at l. ctr. Back red. *(S/M #C104-21).*	12.00	35.00	110.00
S3126	**1 YÜAN** 1943. Red. Rural scene. Back blue. *(S/M #C104-30).*	12.00	35.00	110.00

1944 ISSUES

		GOOD	FINE	XF
S3129	**1 YÜAN** 1944. Blue. Farmer and water wheel. Back violet. *(S/M #C104-40).*	12.00	35.00	110.00
S3130	**1 YÜAN** 1944. Brown. Planting rice. Back green. *(S/M #C104-41).*	12.00	35.00	110.00

		GOOD	FINE	XF
S3131	**5 YÜAN** 1944. Blue. Portr. Mao Tse-tung at r. Back violet; Great Wall at r.			
	a. W/o place name. *(S/M #C104-42a).*	18.50	55.00	165.00
	b. *Su Chung. (S/M #C104-42b).*	20.00	60.00	180.00
S3132	**10 YÜAN** 1944. Blue. Automobile. Back brown. *(S/M #C104-43).*	18.50	55.00	165.00

		GOOD	FINE	XF
S3133	**20 YÜAN** 1944. Green. Portr. Mao Tse-tung at r. Back violet on lt. green unpt. *(S/M #C104-44).*	20.00	60.00	180.00
S3134	**50 YÜAN** 1944. Red. Like #S3133. Back brown. Printer: KHPF. *(S/M #C104-45).*	30.00	90.00	270.00

NOTE: For #S3134 w/additional Chinese 4 characters ovpt. see Bank of Central China #S3356.

BANK OF KIANGNAN (NAU)

行銀南江

Chiang Nan Yin Hang

1945 ISSUE

		GOOD	FINE	XF
S3135A	**1 YÜAN = 1 DOLLAR** 1945. Blue-black. Peasants working in rice field at l. ctr. Back dk. red. *(S/M #C106-14).*	10.00	30.00	90.00

		GOOD	FINE	XF
S3135B	**5 YÜAN** 1945. Red on pink unpt. Arched bridge to house at l. Back dk. brown. *(S/M #C106-15).*	10.00	30.00	90.00

7TH ADMINISTRATIVE DISTRICT SHANSI-CHAHAR-HOPEI BORDER AREA COOPERATIVE SOCIETY ("ZINCHAGI DICIXINGZHENGKY")

區政行七第區邊冀察晋

Chin Ch'a Chi Pien Chü Ti Chi'i Hsing Cheng Ch'ü

1941 ISSUES

#S3135P and S3135Q bldgs. along river at upper ctr. Vertical format.

		GOOD	FINE	XF
S3135P	1 CHIAO = 10 CENTS 1941. Dk. blue. *(S/M #C167.5-11).*			
	a. Back pale olive-green.	3.00	10.00	30.00
	b. Back brown.	5.00	15.00	45.00
S3135Q	1 CHIAO = 10 CENTS 1941. Violet. Like #S3135P. Back red-orange. *(S/M #C167.5-12).*	3.00	10.00	30.00

		GOOD	FINE	XF
S3135R	2 CHIAO = 20 CENTS 1941. Dk. blue on orange unpt. Bldg. at lower r. Back red. *(S/M #C167.5-13).*	10.00	30.00	90.00

		GOOD	FINE	XF
S3135S	5 CHIAO = 50 CENTS 1941. Deep purple on yellow-green unpt. 2 people in boat near Seventeen-Arch bridge at Summer Palace. Back red-violet. Vertical format. *(S/M #C167.5-14).*	3.00	10.00	30.00

1942 ISSUE

		GOOD	FINE	XF
S3135T	5 CHIAO 1942. Brown-violet on pink unpt. Bldgs. w/steeples at upper ctr. Back violet. Vertical format. *(S/M #C167.5-16).*			
	a. Blue serial #.	8.00	25.00	75.00
	b. Red serial #.	8.00	25.00	75.00

A word on date ranges

Often date ranges or specific dates are listed. These have been observed or reported by our contributors. If a note is outside the published range, it only means that it is a newly reported date, and not necessarily worthy of a premium value.

BANK OF SHANSI, CHAHAR AND HOPEI

晉察冀邊區銀行

Chin Ch'a Chi Pien Ch'ü Yin Hang

1938 ISSUE

		GOOD	FINE	XF
S3136	1 CHIAO = 10 CENTS 1938. Brown. Gazebo at upper ctr. Back olive. Vertical format. *(S/M #C168-1).*	2.00	6.00	18.00
S3137	2 CHIAO = 20 CENTS 1938. Violet. Pagoda. Back green. Vertical format. *(S/M #C168-2).*	47.50	140.00	320.00

		GOOD	FINE	XF
S3138	5 CHIAO = 50 CENTS 1938. Purple. Pagoda at upper ctr. Back brown. Vertical format. *(S/M #C168-3).*	2.00	6.00	18.00
S3139	1 YÜAN 1938. Orange and black. Farmer plowing w/horse at l. Back lt. brown. *(S/M #C168-).*	15.00	45.00	135.00

		GOOD	FINE	XF
S3140	5 YÜAN 1938. Brown. Tower bridge at ctr. *(S/M #C168-).*	7.50	22.50	67.50

1939 ISSUES

S3143 10 COPPERS — GOOD 10.00 FINE 30.00 XF 90.00
1939. Green and blue. Summer palace. Back brown. *(S/M #C168-10).*

S3144 20 COPPERS — GOOD 5.50 FINE 15.00 XF 48.00
1939. Green. Statue of bull w/gazebo in background at upper ctr. Back brown. Vertical format. *(S/M #C168-11).*

S3147 1 YÜAN — GOOD 3.00 FINE 9.00 XF 27.00
1939. Olive-green on yellow-orange unpt. Peking Memorial at r. Back violet. *(S/M #C168-20).*

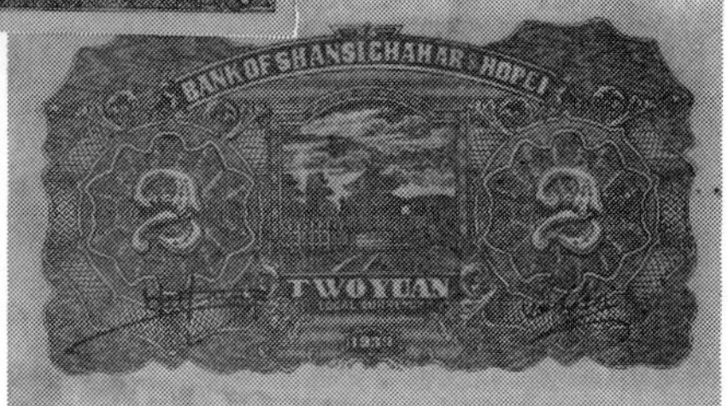

S3148 2 YÜAN — GOOD 3.50 FINE 10.00 XF 33.00
1939. Red-brown on yellow-orange unpt. Mountains at l., trees at r. Back olive. *(S/M #C168-21).*

S3149 5 YÜAN — GOOD 7.50 FINE 20.00 XF 62.50
1939. Red-orange on green unpt. Great Wall at l. and r., sky in background. Back brown and green; pavilion at ctr. Series A; B; C; D. *(S/M #C168-22).*

S3149A 5 YÜAN — GOOD 5.00 FINE 15.00 XF 50.00
1939. Red-orange on green unpt. Similar to #S3149 but w/o sky and clouds in background. Series E; F; G; H. *(S/M #C168-23).*

S3150 5 YÜAN — GOOD 18.50 FINE 55.00 XF 165.00
1939. City gate at ctr. *(S/M #C168-).*

1940 ISSUE

S3151 2 CHIAO = 20 CENTS — GOOD 1.50 FINE 4.00 XF 12.00
1940. Violet. Hills in Peking. Back orange. Vertical format. *(S/M #C168-30).*

S3152 5 CHIAO = 50 CENTS — GOOD 10.00 FINE 30.00 XF 90.00
1940. Red. Woman spinning at l., sheep at r. Back dk. blue. (I(S/M #C168-).

S3156 10 YÜAN — GOOD 5.00 FINE 15.00 XF 50.00
1940. Brown, black and m/c. Temple of Heaven at ctr. Back olive on lt. yellow-green. *(S/M #C168-40).*

1941 ISSUE

S3158 50 YÜAN — GOOD 15.00 FINE 45.00 XF 135.00
1941. Farmer by well at l., bridge over stream at r. Great Wall at ctr. on back. *(S/M #C168-).*

1943 ISSUE

S3160 10 YÜAN — GOOD 4.00 FINE 12.50 XF 37.50
1943. Red. Shepherd w/sheep. Back red. 2 sign. varieties. *(S/M #C168-50).*

S3161 50 Yüan — 1943. Brown and violet-gray. Rural scene at l., plowing w/ox at r. Back green. *(S/M #C168-51).* Good 7.50 · Fine 22.50 · XF 67.50

1944 Issue

		Good	Fine	XF
S3165	**50 Yüan** 1944. Brown on lt. blue unpt. Planting rice at ctr. *(S/M #C168-60).*	7.50	22.50	67.50
S3166	**100 Yüan** 1944. Violet. Planting rice. Back green. *(S/M #C168-61).*	7.50	22.50	67.50
S3167	**500 Yüan** 1944. Brown and red-brown. Plowing w/ox. Back brown. *(S/M #C168-62).*	7.50	22.50	67.50
S3168	**1000 Yüan** 1944. Red and brown. Planting rice. Back brown. *(S/M #C168-63).*	12.00	35.00	110.00
S3169	**5000 Yüan** 1944. Rural scene at r. Plow horse at ctr. on back. Specimen. *(S/M #C168-).*	—	Unc	200.00

1945 Issues

S3170 5 Yüan — 1945. Sampans at ctr. *Hopei, Liaoning* and *Jehol. (S/M #C168-).* Good 12.00 · Fine 35.00 · XF 110.00

S3171 5 Yüan — 1945. Olive on yellow unpt. Pagoda at ctr. Back brown. *(S/M #C168-70).* Good 5.00 · Fine 15.00 · XF 50.00

S3172 10 Yüan — 1945. Brown. Cultivating w/horse and an ox. Back orange. *Hopei, Liaoning* and *Jehol. (S/M #C168-71).* Good 8.00 · Fine 25.00 · XF 75.00

		Good	Fine	XF
S3172A	**10 Yüan** 1945. Brown. Like #S3172 but w/clouds in background. *(S/M #C168-71a).*	8.00	25.00	75.00
S3173	**10 Yüan** 1945. Red-brown on lt. blue unpt. Great Wall at ctr. Back purple. *(S/M #C168-72).*	3.00	9.00	27.00
S3174	**10 Yüan** 1945. Red. Sheep at l. Back violet. Hopei, Liaoning and Jehol. *(S/M #C168-73).*	10.00	30.00	90.00
S3174A	**10 Yüan** 1945. Brown-violet on ochre unpt. Like #S3174. Back brown. *(S/M #C168-73a).*	10.00	30.00	90.00
S3174B	**10 Yüan** 1945. Brown. Sheep at l. *(S/M #C168-).*			
	a. 2 serial *#.*	7.50	22.50	67.50
	b. 2 block *#.*	7.50	22.50	67.50

		Good	Fine	XF
S3174C	**10 Yüan** 1945. Brown-violet. Peasants cultivating at upper ctr. Back red-orange. Series 3; 5. W/o serial #. Vertical format. *(S/M #C168-73.5).*	2.00	6.00	18.00
S3175	**50 Yüan** 1945. Olive-green. Small river boat, shoreline houses. *(S/M #C168-74).*	8.00	25.00	75.00
S3176	**50 Yüan** 1945. Brown. Temple at ctr. Back brown. *(S/M #C168-75).*	6.50	20.00	60.00

S3177 50 Yüan — 1945. Brown-orange and deep brown. Back olive-green; plowing. *(S/M #C168-76).* Good 8.00 · Fine 25.00 · XF 75.00

#S3178 *Deleted.* See #S3176.

		Good	Fine	XF
S3179	**50 Yüan** 1945. Violet. Flock of sheep. Back olive-green. *Hopei, Liaoning* and *Jehol.* 2 serial # varieties. *(S/M #C168-).*	6.50	20.00	60.00
S3179A	**50 Yüan** 1945. Brown. Like #S3179. Back olive-green. *(S/M #C168-80).*	6.50	20.00	60.00

S3180 100 Yüan — 1945. Green. Plowing w/ox at lower r. Back brown. *(S/M #C168-81).* Good 6.00 · Fine 18.00 · XF 55.00

S3181 100 YÜAN

	GOOD	FINE	XF
1945. Brown-orange on yellow unpt. Planting rice at lower ctr. r. Back brown. *Chi Chung. (S/M #C168-).*	10.00	30.00	90.00

S3182 100 YÜAN

	GOOD	FINE	XF
1945. Brown on yellow unpt. Plowing w/horse at l., horse drawn cart at r. Back green. *(S/M #C168-82).*	4.00	12.00	35.00

S3183 100 YÜAN

	GOOD	FINE	XF
1945. Brown. Great Wall. Back green; hillside pagoda at ctr. *(S/M #C168-83).*	4.00	12.00	35.00

S3184 100 YÜAN

	GOOD	FINE	XF
1945. Orange-brown on yellow unpt. Harvesting rice at lower r. Back brown or orange-brown. *Hopei. (S/M #C168-84).*	8.00	25.00	75.00

S3185 200 YÜAN

	GOOD	FINE	XF
1945. Brown. Plowing w/horse at r.. Back blue; farmer and sheep at ctr. *(S/M #C168-85).*	6.50	20.00	60.00

S3186 500 YÜAN

	GOOD	FINE	XF
1945. Red and brown on yellow-green unpt. Bridge. Back brown; junk at ctr. *(S/M #C168-86).*	4.50	12.50	40.00

1946 ISSUES

S3190 10 YÜAN

	GOOD	FINE	XF
1946. Violet and red. Steam passenger train at ctr. r. Back violet. *Hopei, Liaoning* and *Jehol. (S/M #C168-90).*	10.00	30.00	90.00

S3191 50 YÜAN

	GOOD	FINE	XF
1946. Violet. Back red. *(S/M #C168-91).*	10.00	30.00	—

S3192 100 YÜAN

	GOOD	FINE	XF
1946. Red. Tea house at l. Back brown. *(S/M #C168-92).*	5.00	15.00	45.00

S3193 100 YÜAN

	GOOD	FINE	XF
1946. Green. Farmers at r. Back brown. *(S/M #C168-93).*	5.00	15.00	45.00

		Good	Fine	XF
S3194	**200 YÜAN** 1946. Red-brown and grayish green on lt. yellow-green unpt. Farmer w/irrigation bucket at r. Back lilac; men at ctr. *(S/M #C168-94).*	4.00	12.00	36.50
S3194A	**200 YÜAN** 1946. Steam passenger train at l. *Hopei, Liaoning* and *Jehol.* *(S/M #C168-).*	8.00	25.00	75.00

		Good	Fine	XF
S3195	**500 YÜAN** 1946. Red-brown and black on yellow unpt. Cattle w/rancher. Back brown. *(S/M #C168-95).*	8.00	25.00	75.00

		Good	Fine	XF
S3196	**500 YÜAN** 1946. Red and yellow. Harvesting at r. Back violet. *(S/M #C168-96).*	8.00	25.00	75.00
S3197	**500 YÜAN** 1946. Brown and black. Rural scenes at l. and r. Back brown. *Hopei, Liaoning* and *Jehol. (S/M #C168-97).*	8.00	25.00	75.00

		Good	Fine	XF
S3198	**500 YÜAN** 1946. Brown and black. Pack horse at l., plowing w/horse at r. Back blue and green. *(S/M #C168-100).*	5.00	15.00	48.00

		Good	Fine	XF
S3199	**500 YÜAN** 1946. Brown on lt. green and ochre unpt. Back pale brown-orange. *(S/M #C168-101).*			
	a. Issued note.	4.00	12.50	37.50
	b. W/2 additional square red hand stamped seals: *Wang Chun Chuan* at l. and *Li Run Tian* at r.	7.50	22.50	67.50

		Good	Fine	XF
S3200	**1000 YÜAN** 1946. Brown on yellow-orange and lt. green unpt. Automobile crossing girder bridge at ctr. Back tan on yellow unpt. *(S/M #C168-102).*	4.00	12.00	37.50

		Good	Fine	XF
S3201	**1000 YÜAN** 1946. Black on lt. blue unpt. Horses grazing. Back brown on ochre unpt. *(S/M #C168-103).*	5.00	15.00	48.00

1947 ISSUES

		Good	Fine	XF
S3205	**1000 YÜAN** 1947. Brown on lt. blue and ochre unpt. Gazebo at ctr. *(S/M #C168-110).*	5.00	15.00	48.00

S3206 1000 YÜAN

	GOOD	FINE	XF
1947. Violet. Horse pump at r. Back violet. *Hopei, Liaoning* and *Jehol. (S/M #C168-111).*	5.00	15.00	48.00

S3207 2000 YÜAN

	GOOD	FINE	XF
1947. Green. Steam passenger train at l. Back brown. *Hopei, Liaoning* and *Jehol. (S/M #C168-112).*	5.00	15.00	48.00

S3208 5000 YÜAN

	GOOD	FINE	XF
1947. Violet on green and yellow unpt. Junks at r. Back brown. *(S/M #C168-113).*	5.00	15.00	48.00

S3209 5000 YÜAN

	GOOD	FINE	XF
1947. Red and green. Plowing. Back brown. *(S/M #C168-114).*	4.00	12.50	37.50

S3210 5000 YÜAN

	GOOD	FINE	XF
1947. Brown and black. Junks at r. Like #S3208. Back brown. *(S/M #C168-115).*	3.00	10.00	30.00

S3211 5000 YÜAN

	GOOD	FINE	XF
1947. Brown-violet on yellow unpt. Bridge at l. Back red-brown. *Hopei, Liaoning* and *Jehol. (S/M #C168-116).*	2.50	8.50	25.00

SZECHUAN-SHENSI PROVINCIAL SOVIET WORKERS AND FARMERS BANK

川陝省蘇維埃政府/工農銀行

Ch'uan Shan Sheng Su Wei Ai Cheng Fu / Kung Nung Yin Hang

1932 ISSUE

#S3215-S3217 printed on cloth of various colors.

S3215 2 CH'UAN

	GOOD	FINE	XF
1932. Black.			
a. White cloth. *(S/M #C242-1a).*	90.00	275.00	825.00
b. Blue cloth. *(S/M #C242-1b).*	90.00	275.00	825.00

1933 ISSUE

#S3217-S3224 vertical format.

S3217 1 CH'UAN

	GOOD	FINE	XF
1933. Black. Gray cloth. Red oval validation hand stamp. *(S/M #C242-5).*	40.00	120.00	360.00

S3218 2 CH'UAN

	GOOD	FINE	XF
1933. Black. Back black; solid *2* in circle at ctr.			
a. White cloth. *(S/M #C242-10a).*	35.00	110.00	335.00
b. Blue cloth. *(S/M #C242-10b).*	42.50	130.00	390.00
c. Red oval validation hand stamp. *(S/M #C242-10-).*	33.50	100.00	300.00

S3219 3 CH'UAN

	GOOD	FINE	XF
1933. Black. Back black.			
a. White cloth. *(S/M #C242-11a).*	42.50	130.00	390.00

	GOOD	FINE	XF
b. Red oval validation ovpt. *(S/M #C242-11b).*	42.50	130.00	390.00
c. Blue cloth. *(S/M #C242-11c).*	42.50	130.00	390.00
d. Green cloth. *(S/M #C242-11d).*	52.50	160.00	480.00

NOTE: High quality counterfeits of #S3218 and S3219 printed on gray cloth are often encountered.

1933-35 ISSUE

	GOOD	FINE	XF
S3220 1 CH'UAN 1934. Blue. *(S/M #C242-20).*	75.00	225.00	—
S3221 3 CH'UAN 1934. Red. *(S/M #C242-21).*	50.00	150.00	—

	GOOD	FINE	XF
S3222 5 CH'UAN ND. Cloth. *(S/M #C242-).*	600.00	1750.	—

	GOOD	FINE	XF
S3223 10 CH'UAN ND. (1933?). Black on brown unpt. Cloth. *(S/M #C242-).*	700.00	2000.	—
S3224 300 CASH 1935. *(S/M #C242-30).*	Reported Not Confirmed		

BANK OF SOVIET SZECHUAN-SHENSI PROVINCIAL WORKERS AND FARMERS

川陝省蘇維埃政府/工農銀行

Ch'uan Shan Sheng Su Wei Ai Cheng Fu / Kung Nung Yin Hang

1933 ISSUE

	GOOD	FINE	XF
S3228 1 DOLLAR ND (1933). Blue w/red star at l. and r. of portr. Lenin at ctr. Back green; clenched fist smashing imperialists. *(S/M #C243-1).*	125.00	375.00	900.00

	GOOD	FINE	XF
S3229 1 DOLLAR ND (1933). Portr. Lenin at l., Marx at r. Tractors, factory at ctr. on back. *(S/M #C243-).*	250.00	750.00	1800.

CHUNG CHOU FARMERS BANK FARMERS BANK OF CHUNG CHOU

中州農民銀行

Chung Chou Nung Min Yin Hang

1946 ISSUE

	GOOD	FINE	XF
S3232 20 YÜAN 1946. Red. Rural river view at lower l. Back black; bldgs. at ctr. *(S/M #C252-12).*	5.50	16.00	48.00

S3233 50 YÜAN

	Good	Fine	XF
1946. Temple at l. *(S/M #C252-13).*	8.00	25.00	75.00

S3234 100 YÜAN

	Good	Fine	XF
1946. Dk. blue on pink unpt. Steam passenger train at ctr. Back deep blue-green; hillside shelter at ctr. *(S/M #C252-14).*	8.00	25.00	75.00

1948 ISSUES

S3235 2 YÜAN

	Good	Fine	XF
1948. Blue. *(S/M #C252-21).*			
a. Back red-brown.	6.50	20.00	60.00
b. Back black.	6.50	20.00	60.00

S3235A 2 YÜAN

	Good	Fine	XF
1948. Blue. Gazebos on bridge at r. Back brown-violet. *(S/M #C252-22).*	10.00	30.00	90.00

S3235B 3 YÜAN

	Good	Fine	XF
1948. Orange. Farmers planting rice at l. Back blue-green. *(S/M #C252-23).*	18.00	55.00	165.00

S3236 5 YÜAN

	Good	Fine	XF
1948. Black on pink unpt. Back red-brown; rural bldgs. at ctr. *(S/M #C252-24).*			
a. Issued note.	10.00	30.00	90.00
s. Specimen.	—	Unc	150.00

S3237 10 YÜAN

	Good	Fine	XF
1948. Green. Gazebo at l. *(S/M #C252-25).*	18.00	55.00	165.00

S3237A 10 YÜAN

	Good	Fine	XF
1948. Grayish black. Gazebo at ctr. Back brown.			
a. Back retrograde. *(S/M #C252-26a).*	2.00	6.00	18.00
b. Back normal. *(S/M #C252-26b).*	2.00	6.00	18.00

S3237B 10 YÜAN

	Good	Fine	XF
1948. Green. Peasants working in field at ctr. Back red-brown. *(S/M #C252-27).*	10.00	30.00	90.00

S3238 20 YÜAN

	Good	Fine	XF
1948. Gray-green. Boats at l. Back dk. gray-green. *(S/M #C252-28).*	10.00	30.00	90.00

S3240 100 YÜAN

	Good	Fine	XF
1948. Brown-violet on lt. yellow-green unpt. Gazebo on bridge at r. Back blue-green.			
a. Back blue-green. *(S/M #C252-30a).*	8.00	25.00	75.00
b. Back blue-gray. *(S/M #C252-30b).*	10.00	30.00	90.00
p. Proof. Face and back.	—	Unc	300.00
s. Specimen.	—	Unc	80.00

S3241 200 YÜAN

	Good	Fine	XF
1948. *(S/M #C252-31).*	20.00	60.00	180.00

CHINESE SOVIET REPUBLIC SZECHUAN-SHENSI PROVINCIAL WORKERS AND FARMERS BANK

行乾行銀農工省陝川/國和共埃維蘇華中

Chung Hua Su Wei Ai Kung Ho Kuo / Ch'uan Shan Sheng Kung Nung Yin Hang Ch'ien Hang

1933 ISSUE

S3243 1 YÜAN
1933. Green on yellow unpt. Portr. Stalin at ctr. Back green on lt. green unpt, red star between 2 soldiers at ctr.

	GOOD	FINE	XF
a. Paper. *(S/M #-).*	250.00	750.00	1800.
b. Cloth. *(S/M #-).*	300.00	900.00	2400.

CHINESE SOVIET REPUBLIC NATIONAL BANK

行銀 家國國和共埃維蘇華中行 銀 家 國

Chung Hua Su Wei Ai Kung Ho Kuo Kuo Chia Yin Hang Kuo Chia Yin Hang

1936 CHINESE SOVIET REPUBLIC ECONOMIC RECONSTRUCTION BONDS ISSUE

	GOOD	FINE	XF
S3244 50 CENTS 1936. Green. Flag and hemisphere Back red. *(S/M #C272-1).*	18.00	55.00	165.00
S3246 2 DOLLARS 1936. Green. Like #S3244. Back red. *(S/M #C272-10).*	20.00	60.00	180.00
S3247 5 DOLLARS 1936. Green. Back red. *(S/M #C272-).*	33.50	110.00	330.00

WORKER AND PEASANTS BANK

(行銀)省陝川國和共埃維蘇華中

Chung Hua Su Wei Ai Kung Ho Kuo Ch'uan Shan Sheng (Yin Hang)

1934 ISSUE

	GOOD	FINE	XF
S3249 3 CH'UAN 1934. Black, blue and orange. Star above 3 horses at ctr. Hammer and sickle above N. Lenin on back. Vertical format. *(S/M #C273-1).*	125.00	375.00	900.00

CHINESE SOVIET REPUBLIC NATIONAL BANK

行銀 家國國和共埃維蘇華中行 銀 家 國

Chung Hua Su Wei Ai Kung Ho Kuo Kuo Chia Yin Hang Kuo Chia Yin Hang

1932 ISSUE

	GOOD	FINE	XF
S3250 5 FEN 1932. Green. Soldiers at ctr. Back violet; arms at ctr. *(S/M #C274-1).*	4.00	12.50	37.50

	GOOD	FINE	XF
S3251 1 CHIAO 1932. Red. Back red. *(S/M #C274-2).*	8.00	25.00	75.00

S3251A 2 CHIAO
1932. Blue. Similar to #S3262. Back pale violet. *(S/M #C274-2.5).*

	GOOD	FINE	XF
a. W/*No.* printed on back.	12.50	40.00	120.00
b. W/*No. D* printed on back.	12.50	40.00	120.00
c. As a but printed on face.	12.50	40.00	120.00

#S3252 Deleted.

	GOOD	FINE	XF
S3253 1 YÜAN 1932-33. Lt. olive-brown on pale blue unpt. Portr. N. Lenin at ctr. Back green. *(S/M #C274-10).*	10.00	30.00	100.00

1933 ISSUES

S3255 1 CHIAO
1933. *(S/M #C274-20).* GOOD FINE XF

Reported Not Confirmed

	GOOD	FINE	XF
S3257 5 CHIAO 1933. Violet and green. Back red-brown. *(S/M #C274-21).*	5.00	15.00	45.00
S3258 5 CHIAO 1933. Like #S3257 but violet on ochre unpt. Back red-brown. *(S/M #C274-22).*	10.00	30.00	90.00
S3259 1 YÜAN 1933. Reddish brown and blue. Portr. N. Lenin at ctr. Like #S3253. Back deep green. *(S/M #C274-29).*	18.00	55.00	165.00

NOTE: #S3259 believed to be spurious issue by some authorities.

1934 ISSUES

		GOOD	FINE	XF
S3260	**10 COPPERS** 1934. Soldiers w/flag above sphere at ctr. *(S/M #C274-31).*	18.00	55.00	165.00

		GOOD	FINE	XF
S3262	**2 CHIAO** 1934. Blue and black on yellow unpt. Portr. N. Lenin at ctr. Back black; arms at ctr. *(S/M #C274-41).*	8.00	25.00	75.00
S3263	**5 CHIAO** 1934. *(S/M #C274-42).*	Reported Not Confirmed		
S3264	**1 YÜAN** 1934. N. Lenin. *(S/M #C274-50).*	20.00	60.00	180.00
S3265	**1 YÜAN** 1934. K. Marx. *(S/M #C274-51).*	30.00	90.00	270.00

#S3268 Deleted.

1936 ISSUE

		GOOD	FINE	XF
S3270	**1 YÜAN** 1936. Lenin. *(S/M #C274-70).*	20.00	60.00	180.00

CHINESE SOVIET REPUBLIC NATIONAL BANK

行分區特西鄂湘行銀家國國和共埃維蘇華中

Chung Hua Su Wei Ai Kung Ho Kuo Kuo Chia Yin Hang Hsiang O Hsi T'a Chü Fen Hang

行分區特西鄂湘行銀家國

(Short form) Kuo Chia Yin Hang Hsiang O Hsi T'e Chü Fen Hang

HUNAN - WEST HUPEI SPECIAL BRANCH

1931 ISSUE

		GOOD	FINE	XF
S3273	**1 CHIAO** 1931. Black. Bldg. at ctr. Back blue; rural hillside bldgs. at ctr. *(S/M #C275-1).*	—	—	—
S3273A	**2 CHIAO** 1931. Black. Temple at lower ctr. Back green; hammer and sickle on a star at ctr. *(S/M #C275-2).*	—	—	—
S3273B	**2 CHIAO** 1931. Black. Bldg. at lower ctr. Back red; village at ctr. *(S/M #C275-3).*	—	—	—
S3273C	**5 CHIAO** 1931. Temple of Heaven at ctr. *Changsha. (S/M #C275-4).*	—	—	—
S3274	**1 YÜAN** 1931. Hillside bldgs. at ctr. on back. *Changsha. (S/M #C275-2).*	—	—	—

CHINESE SOVIET REPUBLIC BANK OF HUNAN-KWANGSI PROVINCE

行分省贛湘行銀家國國和共埃維蘇華中

Chung Hua Su Wei Ai Kung Ho Kuo Kuo Chia Yin Hang Hsiang Kan Sheng Fen Hang

行銀家國

Kuo Chia Yin Hang

1933 ISSUE

		GOOD	FINE	XF
S3274A	**5 FEN** 1934. Red. Back dk. blue. *(S/M #C274-).*	6.50	20.00	60.00

1934 CHIAO ISSUES

		GOOD	FINE	XF
S3274B	**1 CHIAO** 1933. Red. Hammer and sickle on globe at ctr. Bldg. at ctr. on back.			
	a. Back brown. *(S/M #C274-40a).*	4.00	12.50	40.00
	b. Back black. *(S/M #C274-40b).*	10.00	30.00	90.00
	c. Back deep olive-green. *(S/M #C274-40c).*	15.00	45.00	135.00

		GOOD	FINE	XF
S3274C	**1 CHIAO** 1934. Brown. Like #S3274A. Back green. *(S/M #C274-40).*	15.00	45.00	135.00

1934 COPPER COIN ISSUE

		GOOD	FINE	XF
S3275	**10 COPPERS** 1934. Black. Soldiers w/flag above globe at ctr. *(S/M #C274-51).*	6.50	20.00	60.00

CANTON

1933 ISSUE

		GOOD	FINE	XF
S3275A	**2 CHIAO** 1933. Dk. brown. Youngsters w/flag on globe at ctr. Back red; temple at ctr. *(S/M #C274-42).*	30.00	90.00	270.00
S3275B	**1 YÜAN** 1933. N. Lenin at ctr. Back blue. *(S/M #C274-48).*	57.50	175.00	525.00

CHINESE SOVIET REPUBLIC GOVERNMENT BANK

行銀家國國和共埃維蘇華中

Chung Hua Su Wei Ai Kung Ho Kuo Kuo Chia Yin Hang

行銀家國

Kuo Chia Yin Hang

NORTHWEST

1935 ISSUE

		GOOD	FINE	XF
S3276	**5 FEN** 1935. Black. Uniface. *(S/M #C276-1).*	15.00	50.00	150.00
S3278	**2 CHIAO** 1935. Black. Worker holding up hammer and peasant holding up sickle, flag in background. Uniface. *(S/M #C276-2).*	20.00	60.00	180.00

S3279 2 Chiao | Good | Fine | XF
1935. Face like #3278. Back w/radiant star on shield behind horseman at ctr. Vertical format. Cloth. *(S/M #C276-3).* | 35.00 | 110.00 | 330.00

S3281 1 Yüan | Good | Fine | XF
1935. N. Lenin in star at ctr. Farmer, worker and soldier w/flag at ctr. on back. Cloth. *(S/M #C276-10).* | 100.00 | 275.00 | 600.00

1936 Issue

S3282 1 Fen | Good | Fine | XF
1936. Man in circular frame at l., denomination in oval frame at ctr. r. *(S/M #C276-3).* | 20.00 | 60.00 | 180.00

S3284 1 Chiao | Good | Fine | XF
1936. Black. J. Stalin at upper ctr. Vertical format. Uniface.
- a. Paper. *(S/M #C276-20a).* | 40.00 | 120.00 | 360.00
- b. Cloth. *(S/M #C276-20b).* | 45.00 | 135.00 | 400.00

S3285 2 Chiao | Good | Fine | XF
1936. Foot soldiers in trench about to advance behind leader. Uniface. *(S/M #C276-21).* | 30.00 | 90.00 | 270.00

S3286 5 Chiao | Good | Fine | XF
ND (1936). Crowd rallying at ctr. Uniface. *(S/M #C276-22).* | 37.50 | 110.00 | 330.00

S3287 1 Yüan
1936. *(S/M #C276-23).* | Reported Not Confirmed

S3288 2 Yüan
ND. *(S/M #C276-).* | Reported Not Confirmed

Farmers Bank of Northwest China (Shansi)
Sibei(o) Nung Min Inxang

晋西北農民銀行

Shan Hsi Pei Nung Min Yin Hang

1940 Issues

S3289 5 Fen | Good | Fine | XF
1940. Purplish black. Summer house at top ctr. Vertical format. Specimen. *(S/M #H76-0.3).* | — | Unc | 120.00

S3290 1 Chiao = 10 Cents
1940. Black. Bldg. at r. *(S/M #H76-0.5).* | 8.00 | 25.00 | 75.00

S3290A 5 Chiao = 50 Cents
1940. Pagoda at lower l. *(S/M #H76-0.7).* | 10.00 | 30.00 | 90.00

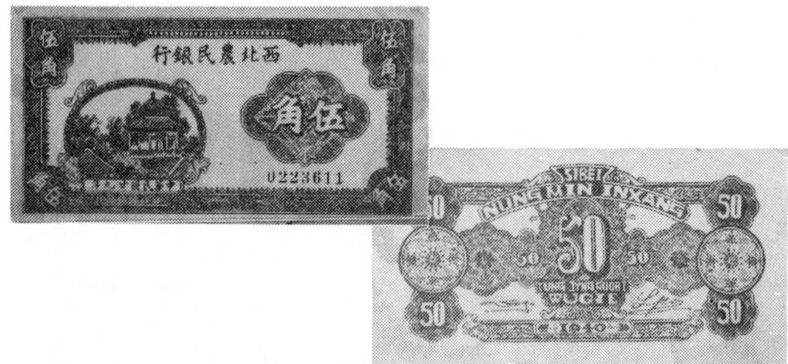

S3291 5 Chiao = 50 Cents | Good | Fine | XF
1940. Tan. Gazebo at l. Back blue-gray. *(S/M #H76-1).* | 15.00 | 45.00 | 135.00

S3292 5 Chiao = 50 Cents | Good | Fine | XF
1940. Dk. brown-violet. 4 people in boat at lower l. Back dk. brown-violet; like #S3291. *(S/M #H76-1.5).*
- a. Issued note. | 8.00 | 25.00 | 75.00
- b. Violet serial #. | 20.00 | 60.00 | 180.00

S3293 1 Yüan
1940. Black and pale olive-green. Farmers at l., bridge at r. Back brown-violet; 2 steam ships at ctr. *(S/M #H76-2).*
- a. Issued note w/ovpt. on 1st character of bank name. | 10.00 | 35.00 | 100.00
- b. W/o ovpt. on 1st character of bank name. | 35.00 | 110.00 | 330.00

		Good	Fine	XF
S3294	**1 Yüan** 1940. Dk. green and dk. brown. Farmer plowing w/horse at l., farmer at r. Back purple and red-orange; bldg. at ctr. *(S/M #H76-3).*			
	a. Issued note.	15.00	45.00	135.00
	s. Specimen.	—	Unc	150.00

		Good	Fine	XF
S3295	**2 Yüan** 1940. Dk. brown on pink unpt. Temple at ctr. Back dk. brown; gazebo at l., fortress gate at r. *(S/M #H76-4).*	4.00	12.50	37.50

		Good	Fine	XF
S3295A	**2 Yüan** 1940. Deep olive-green on yellow unpt. House at ctr. *(S/M #H76-4.5).*			
	a. Back brown-orange.	10.00	30.00	90.00
	b. Back yellow.	12.00	35.00	110.00

1941 Issue

		Good	Fine	XF
S3296	**5 Yüan** 1941. Black on ochre unpt. Rural scene at l. and r. Bridge by gazebo at ctr. on back. *(S/M #H76-5).*			
	a. Issued note.	18.00	55.00	165.00
	s. Specimen.	—	Unc	175.00

1942 Issue

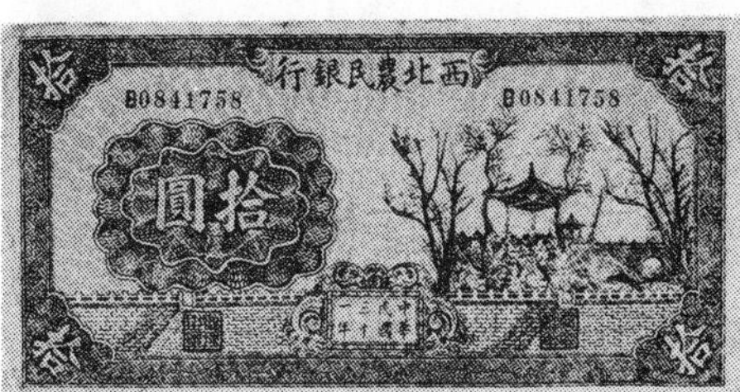

		Good	Fine	XF
S3297	**10 Yüan** 1942. Blue-black. Small shrines in woods near bridge at r. *(S/M #H76-).*	20.00	60.00	180.00

1943 Issues

		Good	Fine	XF
S3298	**50 Yüan** 1943. Blue-black. 3 peasants working at l., sheep grazing at r. *(S/M #H76-7).*			
	a. Issued note.	—	—	200.00
	s. Specimen.	—	Unc	175.00
S3298A	**50 Yüan** 1943. Red-brown on ochre unpt. Temple in trees at r. *(S/M #H76-9).*	20.00	60.00	180.00

		Good	Fine	XF
S3298B	**50 Yüan** 1943. Dk. blue. Like #S3298A. *(S/M #H76-).*			
	a. Back violet-brown.	15.00	45.00	135.00
	b. Blue italic serial # Back red.	8.00	25.00	75.00

		Good	Fine	XF
S3298C	**100 Yüan** 1943. Blue-gray. Great Wall at ctr. *(S/M #H76-9.7).*	33.50	100.00	300.00

		Good	Fine	XF
S3298D	**100 Yüan** 1943. Green. Sheep at r. *(S/M #H76-10).*			
	a. Back green.	20.00	60.00	180.00
	b. Back blue-black.	30.00	90.00	270.00

No.	Denomination / Description	Good	Fine	XF
S3298E	**100 Yüan** 1943. Brown. Like #S3298D. Back blue. *(S/M #H76-11).*	20.00	60.00	180.00

1945 Issues

No.	Denomination / Description	Good	Fine	XF
S3299A	**10 Yüan** 1945. Black. Boat passing under village bridge at upper ctr. Vertical format. *(S/M #H76-13).*	30.00	100.00	300.00

1943 Issues

No.	Denomination / Description	Good	Fine	XF
S3299B	**10 Yüan** 1945. Blue. Like #S3299A. Back green. *(S/M #H76-14).*	30.00	100.00	300.00

1945 Issues

No.	Denomination / Description	Good	Fine	XF
S3299C	**100 Yüan** 1945. Great Wall at ctr. Unissued remainder w/o serial # or seals. *(S/M #H76-16).*	—	Unc	100.00

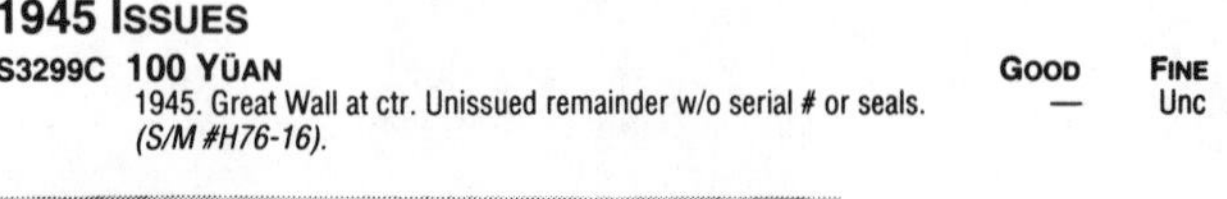

No.	Denomination / Description	Good	Fine	XF
S3300	**500 Yüan** 1945. Red and black. Yanan headquarters at ctr. Back blue; bldg at ctr. *(S/M #H76-20).*	15.00	45.00	135.00

No.	Denomination / Description	Good	Fine	XF
S3301	**500 Yüan** 1945. Blue-gray. Seated person at l., sheep at r. Back blue. *(S/M #H76-23).*	25.00	75.00	225.00

#S3301A *Deleted.* See #S3300.

1946 Issues

No.	Denomination / Description	Good	Fine	XF
S3304	**100 Yüan** 1946. Violet-brown on yellow-orange unpt. Cow, sheep and horse at r. Back brown; 3 people at ctr. *(S/M #H76-30).*	20.00	60.00	180.00
S3305	**500 Yüan** 1946. Pagoda at ctr. Temple on back. *(S/M #H76-30.5).*	20.00	60.00	180.00

No.	Denomination / Description	Good	Fine	XF
S3306	**500 Yüan** 1946. Brown on blue unpt. Pagoda at l. Back green; gazebo at ctr. *(S/M #H76-31).*	30.00	90.00	270.00
S3307	**1000 Yüan** 1946. Blue-gray on ochre unpt. Boat passing under village bridge at l. Specimen. *(S/M #H76-33).*	—	Unc	150.00

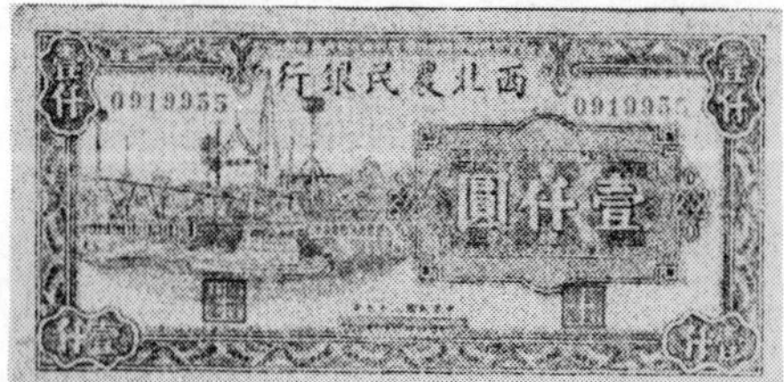

No.	Denomination / Description	Good	Fine	XF
S3308	**1000 Yüan** 1946. Blue-gray. Boat, bridge at l. Back red. *(S/M #H76-36).*	18.00	55.00	165.00

1947 Issues

#S3310 *Deleted.*

#S3311 *Deleted.*

No.	Denomination / Description	Good	Fine	XF
S3313	**1000 Yüan** 1947. Violet. Plowing w/ox. Back green. *(S/M #H76-42).*	25.00	75.00	225.00

#S3313A *Deleted.* See #S3314.

No.	Denomination / Description	Good	Fine	XF
S3314	**2000 Yüan** 1947. Brown-violet on ochre unpt. Farmer plowing w/ox at ctr. r. Back green. *(S/M #H76-43).*			
	a. Issued note.	35.00	110.00	330.00
	b. Brown rays in background.	15.00	50.00	150.00
S3315	**2000 Yüan** 1947. Blue. Sheep. Back red. *(S/M #H76-44).*	30.00	90.00	270.00

No.	Denomination / Description	Good	Fine	XF
S3316	**5000 Yüan** 1947. Lt. blue-black on pink unpt. Flock of sheep grazing at r. Back red. *(S/M #H76-45).*	18.00	55.00	165.00
S3317	**5000 Yüan** 1947. Violet. Farmer, cows. Back green. *(S/M #H76-46).*	25.00	75.00	225.00

No.	Denomination / Description	Good	Fine	XF
S3318	**10,000 Yüan** 1947. Black. Great Wall at l. and r. Back black; steer at l., sheep at r. *(S/M #H76-50).*	35.00	110.00	330.00

#S3320 *Deleted.*

1948 Issues

No.	Denomination / Description	Good	Fine	XF
S3321	**1000 Yüan** 1948. Black. Farm at l., hillside pagoda at r. Back red; temple at ctr.			
	a. Lg. serial #. *(S/M #H76-61a).*	20.00	60.00	180.00
	b. Sm. serial #. *(S/M #H76-61b).*	20.00	60.00	180.00

S3322 5000 YÜAN	GOOD	FINE	XF
1948. Black. Rural scene at l., pagoda at r. Back red. *(S/M #H76-62).*	20.00	60.00	180.00

S3323 10,000 YÜAN	GOOD	FINE	XF
1948. Blue-black. Irrigation system. Back red. *(S/M #H76-63).*			
a. Regular serial #.	6.50	20.00	60.00
b. Italic serial #.	30.00	90.00	270.00

S3324 10,000 YÜAN	GOOD	FINE	XF
1948. Black. Like #S3322. Back red. *(S/M #H76-64).*	1.65	5.00	15.00

S3325 50,000 YÜAN	GOOD	FINE	XF
1948. Purplish black. Camels at l., fortress at r. Specimen. *(S/M #H76-68).*	—	Unc	200.00

HUNAN-HUPEI-KIANGSI WORKERS AND FARMERS BANK

行銀農工省贛鄂湘

Hsiang O Kan Sheng Kung Nung Yin Hang

ND ISSUE

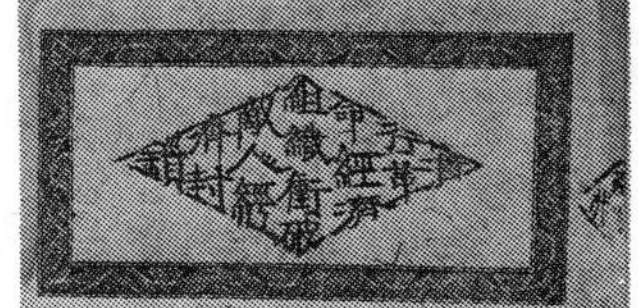

S3327 200 CASH	GOOD	FINE	XF
ND. Black. Pagoda at l., bldg. at r. Back red. *(S/M #H101-11).*			
a. Issued note.	12.50	40.00	120.00
r. Uniface remainder.	—	Unc	300.00

S3328 200 CASH	GOOD	FINE	XF
ND. Blue-green. Like #S3327. Back red. *(S/M #H101-2).*	35.00	110.00	330.00

1931 ISSUE

S3329 1 CH'UAN	GOOD	FINE	XF
1931. Blue. Printer: PCYC. *(S/M #H101-10).*	Reported Not Confirmed		

S3333 1 CHIAO	GOOD	FINE	XF
1931. Black. Rural family scenes at l. and r. *(S/M #H101-20).*			
a. Issued note.	50.00	150.00	450.00
b. Hand stamped Chinese characters in rectangular frame "Full Cash Paid."	30.00	90.00	270.00

S3333A 1 CHIAO	GOOD	FINE	XF
1931. Blue. Like #S3333. *(S/M #H101).*	100.00	300.00	900.00
S3333B 1 CHIAO			
1931. Green. Like #S3333A. *(S/M #H101-).*	100.00	300.00	900.00

S3335 5 CHIAO	GOOD	FINE	XF
1931. Black. Similar to #S3333. *(S/M #H101-21).*	—	Rare	—
S3336 1 DOLLAR			
1931. Black. *(S/M #H101-30).*	—	Rare	—

1932 ISSUE

		GOOD	FINE	XF
S3340	**2 CHIAO** 1932. Red on olive unpt. Back black. *(S/M #H101-40).*			
	a. Issued note.	30.00	90.00	270.00
	b. 3 character ovpt. in rectangle (Paid).	20.00	60.00	180.00
S3340A	**2 CHIAO** 1932. Red and black. Like #S3340. Back w/18 columns of text. *(S/M #H101-).*	30.00	90.00	270.00
S3340B	**2 CHIAO** 1932. Red and black. Like #S3340A but back w/25 columns of text. *(S/M #H101-).*	150.00	450.00	1350.
S3341	**3 CHIAO** 1932. Black w/red text. Portr. bearded man at l., pagoda at r. Back brown-violet; village at ctr. *(S/M #H101-41).*			
	a. Issued note.	60.00	200.00	600.00
	b. Hand stamped 3 Chinese characters in rectangular frame "Full Cash Paid."	45.00	135.00	400.00

NOTE: The old man depicted on #S3341 is not Karl Marx but copied from a locally issued earlier note.

1933 ISSUE

		GOOD	FINE	XF
S3344	**2 CHIAO** 1933. Dk. blue. Pagoda at l., temple at r. Back red; shoreline village, bridge and boats at ctr.			
	a. Issued note.	—	Rare	—
	b. Violet hand stamp 4 Chinese characters in rectangular frame.	75.00	225.00	675.00
S3345	**3 CHIAO** 1933. Red. *(S/M #H101-51).*	—	Rare	—

HUNAN-HUPEI SOVIET BANK

行銀埃維蘇省兩鄂湘

Hsiang O Liang Sheng Su Wei Ai Yin Hang

1931 ISSUE

		GOOD	FINE	XF
S3349	**1 YÜAN** 1931. *(S/M #H102-1).*	90.00	275.00	825.00

PROVINCIAL TREASURY OF HUPEH

庫分東鄂庫省北湖

Hu Pei Sheng K'u O T'ung Fen K'u

EAST HUPEH

1940-42 ISSUE

		GOOD	FINE	XF
S3351	**5 CHIAO** 1940. Blue-black on lt. blue unpt. Back violet. Specimen. *(S/M #H172.5-13).*	—	Unc	100.00
S3353	**1 YÜAN** 1942. Blue on m/c unpt. Back purple. Specimen. *(S/M #H172.5-24).*	—	Unc	100.00

BANK OF CENTRAL CHINA

行銀中華

Hua Chung Yin Hang

1944 ISSUE

		GOOD	FINE	XF
S3355	**10 YÜAN** 1944. Red. Logging at r. Back black and yellow. *(S/M #H180-1).*			
	a. 3mm serial #.	10.00	30.00	90.00
	b. 5mm serial #.	10.00	30.00	90.00

1944 PROVISIONAL ISSUE

		GOOD	FINE	XF
S3356	**50 YÜAN** 1944. Red. Ovpt. on #S3134. Back brown. *(S/M #H180-2).*	57.50	175.00	525.00

1945 REGULAR ISSUES

		GOOD	FINE	XF
S3358	**5 CHIAO = 50 CENTS** 1945. Villagers working at l. and r. *(S/M #H180-).*	5.00	15.00	48.00

		GOOD	FINE	XF
S3359	**5 CHIAO = 50 CENTS** 1945. Dk. blue. Temple w/pagoda in background at l. ctr. Back red. *(S/M #H180-9).*	5.00	15.00	48.00

		GOOD	FINE	XF
S3360	**1 YÜAN** 1945. Blue. Steam passenger train at r. Back red. *(S/M #H180-20).*	8.00	25.00	75.00

		GOOD	FINE	XF
S3361	**1 YÜAN** 1945. Blue. Junks at l., ships at r. Back brown. *(S/M #H180-21).*	5.00	15.00	45.00
S3361A	**1 YÜAN** 1945. Red. Like #S3361.	5.00	15.00	45.00
S3362	**2 YÜAN** 1945. Violet. Planting rice. Back green. *(S/M #H180-23).*	8.00	25.00	75.00
S3363	**2 YÜAN** 1945. Blue. Like #S3362. Back brown. *(S/M #H180-24).*	8.00	25.00	75.00

		GOOD	FINE	XF
S3364	**5 YÜAN** 1945. Blue. Irrigation system at r. Back brown. *(S/M #H180-25).*	7.00	20.00	62.50
S3364A	**5 YÜAN** 1945. Purple. Like #S3364. *(S/M #H180-25.5).*	—	—	—

		GOOD	FINE	XF
S3365	**5 YÜAN** 1945. Violet. Army bugler by Great Wall. Back green. *(S/M #H180-26).*	6.00	18.00	55.00
S3366	**5 YÜAN** 1945. Green. Planting rice. Back green. *(S/M #H180-27).*	8.00	25.00	75.00
S3367	**5 YÜAN** 1945. Green. Rural scene. Back violet. *(S/M #H180-30).*	8.00	25.00	75.00

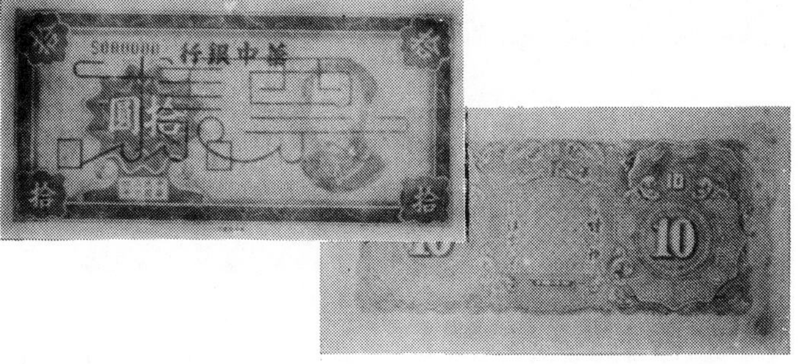

		GOOD	FINE	XF
S3368	**10 YÜAN** 1945. Red. Portr. Mao Tse-tung at r. Back green. *(S/M #H180-31).*	20.00	60.00	180.00
S3369	**20 YÜAN** 1945. Green. Plowing. *(S/M #H180-32).*	10.00	30.00	90.00

		GOOD	FINE	XF
S3370	**20 YÜAN** 1945. Green. Farm scene at r. Back yellow and m/c. *(S/M #H180-33).*	10.00	30.00	90.00

		GOOD	FINE	XF
S3371	**50 YÜAN** 1945. Violet. Ship and plane at r. Back blue; English. *(S/M #H180-34).*	8.00	25.00	75.00

		GOOD	FINE	XF
S3372	**50 YÜAN** 1945. Deep purple. Face like #S3371. Back blue-black; w/o English. *(S/M #H180-35).*	5.50	16.00	48.00

		GOOD	FINE	XF
S3373	**50 YÜAN** 1945. Dk. brown. Ship, turbine and steam passenger train at r. Back dk. blue, dk. brown and green. *(S/M #H180-36).*			
	a. Small 3mm serial #.	7.00	20.00	62.50
	b. Large 4mm serial #.	7.00	20.00	62.50
S3374	**50 YÜAN** 1945. Brown. Ships at dockside. Back blue. *(S/M #H180-37).*	8.00	25.00	75.00

		GOOD	FINE	XF
S3375	**100 YÜAN** 1945. Green. Great Wall. Back brown. Printer: HCBN. *(S/M #H180-40).*	7.00	20.00	62.50
S3375A	**100 YÜAN** 1945. Violet. Similar to #S3375. *(S/M #H180-40.5).*	8.00	25.00	75.00

S3376 100 YÜAN

	GOOD	FINE	XF
1945. Brown. Portr. Mao Tse-tung at r. *(S/M #H180-41).*	18.00	55.00	165.00

S3377 100 YÜAN

	GOOD	FINE	XF
1945. Green. Bugler by Great Wall. Back violet. *(S/M #H180-42).*			
a. Small serial #.	8.00	25.00	75.00
b. Large serial #.	8.00	25.00	75.00

S3378 100 YÜAN

1945. Green. City wall. Back violet. *(S/M #H180-43).*	8.00	25.00	75.00

1946 ISSUES

S3380 5 YÜAN

	GOOD	FINE	XF
1946. Red and blue. Bugler by Great Wall. Back blue. *(S/M #H180-50).*	7.00	20.00	62.50

S3381 5 YÜAN

1946. Blue and green. Like #S3380. Back violet. *(S/M #H180-51).*	7.00	20.00	62.50

S3382 5 YÜAN

1946. Violet and green. Like #S3380. Back green. *(S/M #H180-52).*	7.00	20.00	62.50

#S3383 Deleted.

S3384 20 YÜAN

1946. Green. Plowing. Back green. *(S/M #H180-54).*	7.00	20.00	62.50

S3385 20 YÜAN

	GOOD	FINE	XF
1946. Blue and green. Temple of Heaven at r. Pagoda at ctr. on back. *(S/M #H180-54.5).*	8.00	25.00	75.00

S3386 50 YÜAN

	GOOD	FINE	XF
1946. Brown. Bridge, pavillion w/tower in background at ctr r. *(S/M #H180-55).*			
a. Back green.	7.00	20.00	62.50
b. Back brown.	7.00	20.00	62.50

S3387 50 YÜAN

	GOOD	FINE	XF
1946. Violet. Pagoda and bridge. *(S/M #H180-56).*	8.00	25.00	75.00

S3388 100 YÜAN

1946. Violet. Great Wall. *(S/M #H180-56.5).*	8.00	25.00	75.00

S3389 200 YÜAN

	GOOD	FINE	XF
1946. Blue. Hillside pagoda at r. Back violet; steam passenger train at ctr. *(S/M #H180-57).*	8.00	25.00	75.00

S3390 200 YÜAN

	GOOD	FINE	XF
1946. Blue. Temple of Heaven at ctr. Back violet. *(S/M #H180-60).*	10.00	30.00	90.00

		Good	Fine	XF
S3391	**200 Yüan** 1946. Like #S3390 but green. Back brown. *(S/M #H180-61).*	10.00	30.00	90.00
S3392	**200 Yüan** 1946. Blue. Summer Palace. Back brown. *(S/M #H180-62).*	10.00	30.00	90.00

		Good	Fine	XF
S3393	**200 Yüan** 1946. Blue. Pagoda along river at r. Modern bldgs. along river at ctr. on back. *(S/M #H180-62.5).*	8.00	35.00	75.00
S3393A	**200 Yüan** 1946. Black. Like #S3392. Back dk. blue. *(S/M #H180-).*			
	a. White paper.	8.00	25.00	75.00
	b. Gray paper.	10.00	30.00	90.00

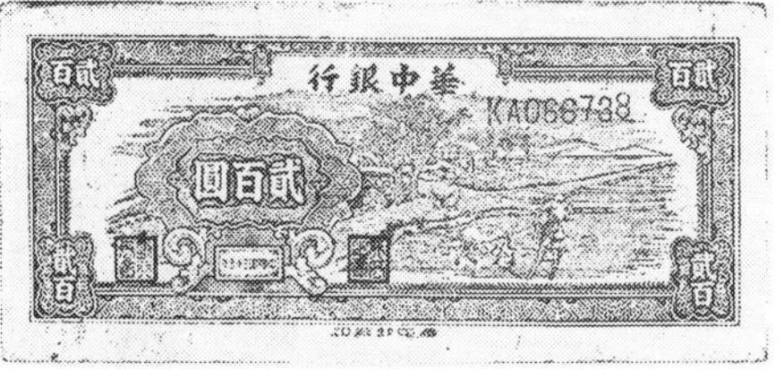

		Good	Fine	XF
S3393B	**200 Yüan** 1946. Orange. Peasant plowing w/ox at lower r. Back yellow-orange. *(S/M #H180-62.7).*	15.00	45.00	135.00

		Good	Fine	XF
S3394	**500 Yüan** 1946. Deep red. Steam passenger train, ship at r. Back dk. brown; sailing ship at r. *(S/M #H180-63).*	5.00	15.00	45.00

		Good	Fine	XF
S3394A	**500 Yüan** 1946. Deep red. Like #S3394A but back blue; w/value. *(S/M #H180-).*	10.00	30.00	90.00
S3395	**500 Yüan** 1946. Brown. Steam passenger train, ship at r. Back blue-black. *(S/M #H180-64).*	10.00	30.00	90.00

1947 Issue

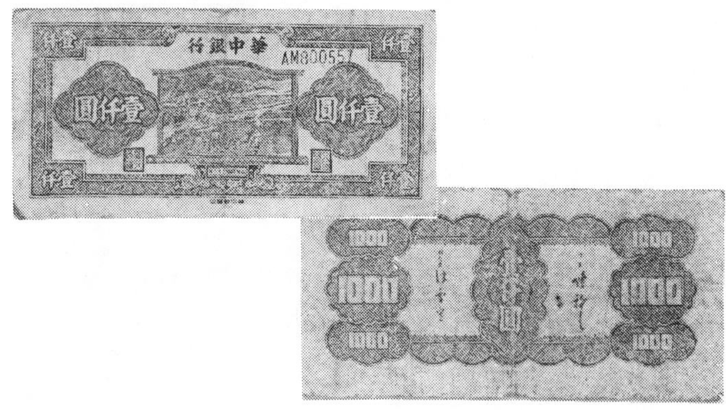

		Good	Fine	XF
S3397	**1000 Yüan** 1947. Brown. Peasant w/cows at ctr. Back blue-gray. *(S/M #H180-70).*			
	a. Regular serial #.	8.00	25.00	75.00
	b. Bold serial #.	8.00	25.00	75.00

1948 Issues

		Good	Fine	XF
S3399	**50 Yüan** 1948. Violet. Monument. *(S/M #H180-70.3).*	8.00	25.00	75.00
S3400	**100 Yüan** 1948. Bugler by Great Wall. *(S/M #H180-70.6).*	7.00	21.00	62.50

		Good	Fine	XF
S3401	**200 Yüan** 1948. Deep brown. Sawing logs at ctr. r. Back blue. *(S/M #H180-71).*	5.50	16.00	48.00
S3402	**200 Yüan** 1948. Blue. Wood sawing. *(S/M #H180-71.3).*	7.00	21.00	62.50
S3403	**200 Yüan** 1948. Violet. Temple. *(S/M #H180-71.6.*	7.00	21.00	62.50

		Good	Fine	XF
S3405	**500 Yüan** 1948. Blue. Great Wall at r. Back brown. *(S/M #H180-72).*	7.00	21.00	62.50

		Good	Fine	XF
S3406	**500 Yüan** 1948. Blue-black. Pagoda at ctr. Back brown. *(S/M #H180-73).*	7.00	21.00	62.50

		Good	Fine	XF
S3407	**1000 Yüan** 1948. Pale blue. Steam passenger train at r. Back green; ships dockside at ctr. *(S/M #H180-74).*	7.00	21.00	62.50

S3408 1000 YÜAN — 1948. Brown. Pagoda at l. ctr. Back green. *(S/M #H180-75).*

Good	Fine	XF
7.00	21.00	62.50

S3409 1000 YÜAN — 1948. Red. Windmill at ctr. r. Back green; sampans at ctr. *(S/M #H180-76).*

Good	Fine	XF
7.00	21.00	62.50

S3410 1000 YÜAN — 1948. Black. Hillside summer palace, pagoda along shoreline at ctr. r. Back brown. *(S/M #H180-77).*

Good	Fine	XF
7.00	21.00	62.50

S3411 2000 YÜAN — 1948. Brown and yellow. Hillside pagoda along shoreline at l. Back green. *(S/M #H180-80).*

Good	Fine	XF
4.00	12.50	37.50

S3412 2000 YÜAN — 1948. Blue. Sampan by house and bridge at ctr. *(S/M #H180-81).*

	Good	Fine	XF
a. 1 serial #.	6.00	18.00	55.00
b. 2 serial #.	8.00	25.00	75.00

S3413 2000 YÜAN — 1948. Green. Shrine. Back blue. *(S/M #H180-82).*

	Good	Fine	XF
a. Issued note.	7.00	21.00	62.50
s. Specimen.	—	Unc	80.00

S3414 2000 YÜAN — 1948. Red. Summer palace. Back blue. *(S/M #H180-83).*

Good	Fine	XF
8.00	25.00	75.00

S3415 2000 YÜAN — 1948. Brown on yellow unpt. Army bugler at l., Great Wall at l. and r. Back dk. green. *(S/M #H180-84).*

Good	Fine	XF
7.00	21.00	62.50

1949 ISSUES

S3416 5000 YÜAN — 1949. Brown. Minehead at r. Back green; temple at ctr. *(S/M #H180-90).*

Good	Fine	XF
6.00	18.00	55.00

S3417 5000 YÜAN — 1949. Brown on lt. green unpt. Ship at dockside at lower l. Back dk. green; cattle at ctr. *(S/M #H180-91).*

Good	Fine	XF
7.00	21.00	62.50

S3418 5000 YÜAN — 1949. Violet and green. Dump truck. Back blue. *(S/M #H180-92).*

Good	Fine	XF
10.00	30.00	90.00

HUAINAN BANK

行銀南淮

Huai Nan Yin Hang

1942 ISSUE

S3418B 10 YÜAN — 1942. House in woods at l. Birds over junk at l. on back. *(S/M #H194-13).*

Good	Fine	XF
—	—	—

1943 ISSUE

		GOOD	FINE	XF
S3418D	**5 YÜAN** 1943. Military observation post at r. *(S/M #H194-22).*	—	—	—

		GOOD	FINE	XF
S3418F	**10 YÜAN** 1943. Crowd rallied before speaker at r. *(S/M #H194-23).*	—	—	—

1944 ISSUES

		GOOD	FINE	XF
S3419	**1 CHIAO = 10 CENTS** 1944. Ox driven irrigation system at r. *(S/M #H194-31).*	—	—	—

		GOOD	FINE	XF
S3419C	**5 CHIAO = 50 CENTS** 1944. Worker, soldier, and peasant at ctr. *(S/M #H194-32).*	—	—	—
S3419E	**1 YÜAN** 1944. School class at l., farming and industrial scenes at r. *(S/M #H194-34).*	—	—	—

		GOOD	FINE	XF
S3419G	**5 YÜAN** 1944. Rural home at l. *(S/M #194-34).*	—	—	—

		GOOD	FINE	XF
S3419J	**10 YÜAN** 1944. Wmk: Mao Tse-tung at l. *(S/M #H194-35).*	—	—	—

		GOOD	FINE	XF
S3419L	**10 YÜAN** July 1944. Planting rice at r. *(S/M #H194-36).*	—	—	—

NORTHWEST ANHWEI SPECIAL DISTRICT SOVIET BANK

行銀埃維蘇區特地北西皖

Huan Hsi Pei Ti T'e Chü Su Wei Ai Yin Hang

1932 ISSUE

		GOOD	FINE	XF
S3421	**2 CHIAO** 1932. Portr. K. Marx at ctr. *(S/M #H195-1).*	57.50	175.00	525.00
#S3422 Deleted.				
S3423	**1 YÜAN** 1932. Black. Government bldg. at ctr. Back yellow; hammer and sickle in rays above top of globe at ctr. Printer: HHPC. *(S/M #H195-3).*	36.50	110.00	330.00

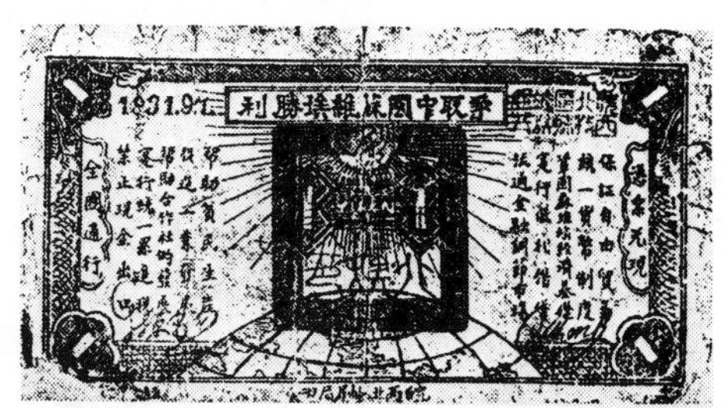

		GOOD	FINE	XF
S3423A	**1 YÜAN** 1932. Similar to #S3423 but reduced size. *(S/M #H195-4).*	36.50	110.00	330.00
S3423B	**1 YÜAN** 1932. Green and black. Government bldg. at ctr. Back green; K. Marx at lower l.; top of globe at lower r. *(S/M #H195-5).*	36.50	110.00	330.00
S3423C	**1 YÜAN** 1932. Green and brown. Like #S3423B. *(S/M #H195-6).*	36.50	110.00	330.00

1923 ISSUE

		GOOD	FINE	XF
S3423D	**5 YÜAN** 1923. Government bldg. at ctr. K. Marx at ctr. on back. *(S/M #H195-7).*	57.50	170.00	510.00

BANK OF REHHER SHEENG

行銀省河熱

Je Ho Sheng Yin Hang

1946 ISSUE

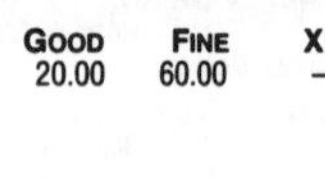

		GOOD	FINE	XF
S3424	**50 YÜAN** 1946. Black on lt. green. Cattle at l., farming at r. Back lt. blue-gray; Great Wall at ctr. *(S/M #J3-).*	20.00	60.00	—

		GOOD	FINE	XF
S3424A	**100 YÜAN** 1946. Red on lt. blue-green unpt. Steam passenger train at ctr. Back brown; rural scenes at l. and ctr. r. *(S/M #J3-).*	20.00	60.00	—

1947 ISSUES

		GOOD	FINE	XF
S3425	**10 YÜAN** 1947. Lt. red-brown. Modern bldgs. at l. Back brown. *(S/M #J3-).*	20.00	60.00	—

		GOOD	FINE	XF
S3425A	**20 YÜAN** 1947. Red on lt. yellow unpt. Rural village at ctr. Back brown; rural scene at ctr. *(S/M #J3-).*	20.00	60.00	—

		GOOD	FINE	XF
S3425B	**20 YÜAN** 1947. Dk. brown-violet on lt. yellow-green unpt. Pagoda, rural scene at ctr. Back purple; gazebo at ctr. *(S/M #J3-).*	20.00	60.00	—

		GOOD	FINE	XF
S3426	**50 YÜAN** 1947. Green. Great Wall at l. Back brown. *(S/M #J3-).*	20.00	60.00	—

		GOOD	FINE	XF
S3427	**100 YÜAN** 1947. Lilac on yellow unpt. Plowing w/oxen at l. Back gray. *(S/M #J3-1).*	8.00	25.00	75.00

		GOOD	FINE	XF
S3427A	**100 YÜAN** 1947. Brown-violet on yellow-green unpt. Rural village w/fortress gate at ctr. r. "18th special district" in Chinese at l. and r. Back lt. olive-green. *(S/M #J3-).*	15.00	45.00	100.00

S3427B 100 YÜAN

	Good	Fine	XF
1947. Similar to #S3427A but w/o "18th special district" at l. and r. *(S/M #J3-)*.	15.00	45.00	100.00

S3428 200 YÜAN

	Good	Fine	XF
1947. Gray on pink unpt. Gateway at l. Back red. *(S/M #J3-2)*.	15.00	45.00	—

NORTHEAST KIANGSI SOVIET BANK

行銀埃維蘇(省)北東贛

Kan Tung Pei (Sheng) Su Wei Ai Yin Hang

1932 ISSUE

S3433 5 CH'UAN

	Good	Fine	XF
1932. *(S/M #K13-1)*.	Reported Not Confirmed		

S3434 10 CENTS

	Good	Fine	XF
1932. Blue on red unpt. Flag on hemisphere at ctr. Back black on red unpt. *(S/M #K13-)*.	—	—	—

S3435 10 CENTS

	Good	Fine	XF
1932. Ovpt. on #S3468. *(S/M #K13-10)*.	Reported Not Confirmed		

S3437 50 CENTS

	Good	Fine	XF
1932. Red. Star, hammer and sickle. Back green. *(S/M #K13-11)*.	35.00	100.00	—

S3438 1 YÜAN

	Good	Fine	XF
1932. Ovpt. on #S3471. *(S/M #K13-20)*.	Reported Not Confirmed		

NORTHEAST KIANGSI SOVIET BANK

行銀北閩行銀埃維蘇(省)北東贛

Kan Tung Pei Sheng Su Wei Ai Yin Hang / Min Pei Yin Hang

NORTH FUKIEN BRANCH

1932 ISSUE

#S3440-S3440C hammer and sickle on star at ctr. Text, date and various hand stamps on back.

S3440 1 CHIAO

	Good	Fine	XF
Jan. 1932. *(S/M #K13.5-1)*.	—	—	—

S3440A 2 CHIAO

	Good	Fine	XF
Jan. 1932. Deep blue-green and red on yellow unpt. *(S/M #K13.5-2)*.			
a. Issued note.	—	—	—
r. Remainder w/o serial # filled in lower frame.	—	—	—

S3440B 5 CHIAO

	Good	Fine	XF
Jan. 1932. *(S/M #K13.5-3)*.	—	—	—

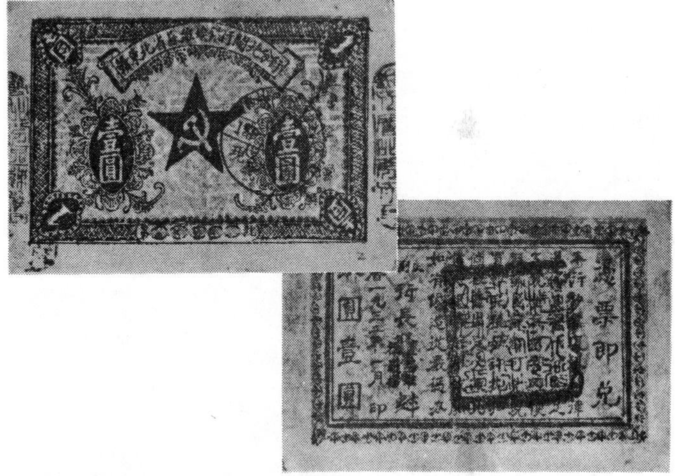

S3440C 1 YÜAN

	Good	Fine	XF
Jan. 1932. Black on red unpt. Lg. red hand stamped seal on back. *(S/M #K13.5-4)*.	—	—	—

KIANGSI, HUNAN, ANHWEI SOVIET WORKERS AND FARMERS BANK

行銀農工埃蘇皖豫贛

Kan Yü Huan Su Wei Ai Kung Nung Yin Hang

1932 ISSUE

S3441 1 YÜAN

	Good	Fine	XF
1932. *(S/M #K14-1)*.	Reported Not Confirmed		

BANK OF KUANTUNG

行銀東關

Kuan Tung Yin Hang

1948 ISSUE

#S3445-S3449 mountain lake at ctr. Ocean liner at ctr. on back.

		Good	Fine	XF
S3445	**1 Yüan** 9148. Orange. *(S/M #K20-1).*	10.00	30.00	90.00
S3446	**5 Yüan** 1948. Green and gray. *(S/M #K20-2).*	15.00	45.00	125.00

		Good	Fine	XF
S3447	**10 Yüan** 1948. Red and blue. Back red. *(S/M #K20-3).*	20.00	60.00	175.00
S3448	**50 Yüan** 1948. Violet and black. Back violet. *(S/M #K20-4).*	25.00	75.00	225.00

		Good	Fine	XF
S3449	**100 Yüan** 1948. Black on pale blue and lilac unpt. Mountain lake at l. Back black. *(S/M #K20-5).*	45.00	125.00	—

Bank of West Shantung

行銀西魯
Lu Hsi Yin Hang

1940 Issue

		Good	Fine	XF
S3450	**1 Chiao** 1940. Gazebo on hill at upper ctr. *(S/M #L24-0.2).*	45.00	125.00	—
S3451	**2 Chiao** 1940. Temple of Heaven at r. *(S/M #L24-0.4).*	45.00	125.00	—

		Good	Fine	XF
S3452	**5 Chiao** 1940. Brown. Farmer at ctr. Back ochre. *(S/M #L24-0.6).*	45.00	125.00	—
S3452A	**1 Yüan** 1940. Rural scenes at l. and r. *(S/M #L24-0.8).*	45.00	125.00	—
S3453	**20 Yüan** 1940. Blue and red. Bldg., mountains at l. Back orange. *(S/M #L24-1).*	50.00	150.00	—

1941 Issue

		Good	Fine	XF
S3454	**4 Fen** 1941. Rural scene at l. and r. House at ctr. on back. *(S/M #L24-3).*	25.00	75.00	—
S3454A	**5 Fen** 1941. Ship at l., truck at r. *(S/M #L24-4).*	30.00	85.00	—
S3454B	**20 Cents** 1941. Farmer at upper ctr. *(S/M #L24-5).*	30.00	85.00	—
S3454C	**25 Cents** 1941. Farmer plowing w/horse at l. *(S/M #L24-6).*	45.00	125.00	—
S3454D	**2 Yüan** 1941. Fortress at l., steam passenger train at r. *(S/M #L24-7).*	45.00	125.00	—

1942 Issue

		Good	Fine	XF
S3454E	**5 Yüan** 1942. *(S/M #L24-).*	25.00	75.00	—
S3454F	**10 Yüan** 1942. *(S/M #L24-).*	45.00	125.00	—
S3455	**20 Yüan** 1942. Green. Temple of Heaven at l., gazebo at r. Back brown. *(S/M #L24-10).*	50.00	150.00	—

1943 Issue

		Good	Fine	XF
S3456	**10 Yüan** 1943. Planting rice at ctr. Specimen. *(S/M #L24-12).*	—	—	—
S3456A	**50 Yüan** 1943. Brown. Bridge and lake at l. Back dk. green; pagoda at l. and r. *(S/M #L24-13).*	75.00	225.00	—
S3456B	**100 Yüan** 1943. Gateway at r. *(S/M #L24-14).*	50.00	150.00	—

		Good	Fine	XF
S3456C	**200 Yüan** 1943. Harvesting at ctr. Specimen. *(S/M #L24-15).*	—	—	—
S3456D	**500 Yüan** 1943. Plowing w/horse at l. Specimen. *(S/M #L24-16).*	—	—	—

1944 Issue

		Good	Fine	XF
S3456E	**10 Yüan** 1944. Temple of Heaven at l., tower at r. Specimen. *(S/M #L24-17).*	—	—	—
S3457	**100 Yüan** 1944. Blue and yellow. Steam passenger train at ctr. Back brown. *(S/M #L24-20).*	50.00	150.00	—

S3458 300 YÜAN | GOOD 25.00 | FINE 75.00 | XF —
1944. Temple of Heaven at upper ctr. Shoreline hillside village at ctr. on back. Vertical format. *(S/M #L24-22).*

S3459 500 YÜAN | — | — | —
1944. Ship at l., steam passenger train at r. Specimen. *(S/M #L24-25).*

1945 ISSUE

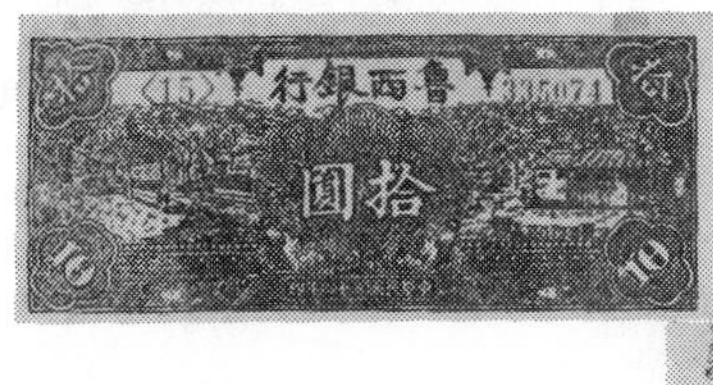

S3461 10 YÜAN | GOOD 50.00 | FINE 150.00 | XF —
1945. Green. Rural scene at l., bldg. at r. *(S/M #L24-30).*

S3462 25 YÜAN | 45.00 | 125.00 | —
1945. Hillside temple at r. *(S/M #L24-33).*

FUKIEN-CHEKIANG-KIANGSI SOVIET BANK

行銀埃維蘇省贛浙閩

Min Che Kan Sheng Su Wei Ai Yin Hang

ND ISSUE

S3465 1 CHIAO | GOOD 30.00 | FINE 90.00 | XF —
ND. Blue. Uniface. Crude hammer, sickle and star at ctr. *(S/M #M15-1).*

1932 ISSUE

S3468 1 CHIAO | GOOD 45.00 | FINE 125.00 | XF —
1932. Blue and red. Flag on hemisphere at ctr. Back red and black. *(S/M #M15-10).*

S3469 2 CHIAO | 45.00 | 125.00 | —
1932. Green. Back brown. *(S/M #M15-20).*

S3470 5 CHIAO | 45.00 | 125.00 | —
1932. Violet. Back green. *(S/M #M15-21).*

S3471 1 YÜAN | GOOD 50.00 | FINE 150.00 | XF —
1932. Red on yellow-green unpt. Flag and hemisphere. Back red on blue unpt. *(S/M #M15-30).*

NOTE: For #S3468 and S3471 w/additional ovpt. see #S3435 and #S3438.

1933 ISSUE

S3473 1 CHIAO | GOOD / FINE / XF: Reported Not Confirmed
1933. *(S/M #M15-40).*

S3476 1 YÜAN | 75.00 | — | —
1933. Flag and hemisphere. *(S/M #M15-50).*

S3478 10 YÜAN | 75.00 | — | —
1933. *(S/M #M15-51).*

1934 ISSUE

S3480 1 YÜAN | GOOD 100.00 | FINE 300.00 | XF —
1934. Green and red. Back blue and red. *(S/M #M15-60).*

FUKIEN-CHEKIANG-KIANGSI SOVIET BANK

行銀埃維蘇省贛浙閩行銀北閩

Min Che Kan Sheng Su Wei Ai Yin Hang / Min Pei Yin Hang

NORTH FUKIEN BRANCH

1934 ISSUE

#S3481-S3481B hammer and sickle on star at ctr. Text on back.

S3481 1 CHIAO | GOOD — | FINE — | XF —
Nov. 1934. *(S/M #M15.5-1).*

S3481A 2 CHIAO | GOOD — | FINE — | XF —
Nov. 1934. *(S/M #M15.5-2).*

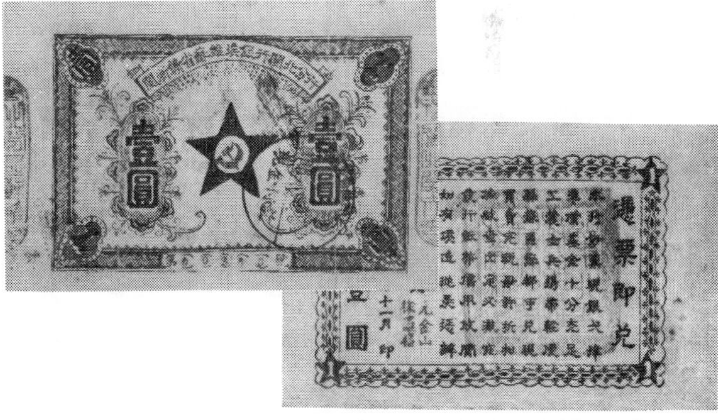

S3481B 1 YÜAN | GOOD — | FINE — | XF —
Nov. 1934. *(S/M #M15.5-4).*

FUKIEN-KWANGTUNG-KIANGSI BORDER AREA BANK

行銀區邊贛粵閩

Min Yüeh Kan Pien Chü Yin Hang

ND PROVISIONAL ISSUE

		Good	Fine	XF
S3482	**10 Yüan** ND (- old date 1949). Ovpt. on #S3489. *(S/M #M17-).*	8.00	25.00	75.00

NOTE: #S3482 is considered to be spurious by some authorities.

Southern Peoples Bank

行銀民人方南

Nan Fang Jen Min Yin Hang

1949 Issue

		Good	Fine	XF
S3483	**1 Chiao** 1949. Red and black. Ornamental frame around denomination at ctr. *(S/M #N5-).*	8.00	25.00	75.00

		Good	Fine	XF
S3483A	**1 Chiao** 1949. Modern municipal bldg. complex at ctr.	8.00	25.00	75.00
S3483B	**2 Chiao** 1949. Worker and farmer leaning on shield; modern municipal bldg. at l. *(S/M #N5-0.3).*	8.00	25.00	50.00
S3485	**5 Chiao** 1949. Red. Teahouse in woods at ctr. Back red; drying rice at ctr. *(S/M #N5-0.5).*	8.00	25.00	75.00

		Good	Fine	XF
S3486	**5 Chiao** 1949. Green. Worker and farmer leaning on shield, modern municipal bldg. at l. Back green; cows at ctr. *(S/M #N5-0.7).*	10.00	30.00	90.00

		Good	Fine	XF
S3487	**1 Yüan** 1949. Blue and green. Pagoda at r. Back blue. *(S/M #N5-1).*	8.00	25.00	—

		Good	Fine	XF
S3488	**5 Yüan** 1949. Violet. Gazebo at r. Back violet. *(S/M #N5-2).*	8.00	25.00	—

		Good	Fine	XF
S3489	**10 Yüan** 1949. Green. Gazebo at ctr. Back green. *(S/M #N5-3).*	.50	1.50	—

NOTE: For #S3489 w/additional red Chinese characters ovpt. see #S3482.

Inner Mongolia Peoples Bank

行銀民人古蒙內

Nei Mung Ku Jen Min Yin Hang

1948 Issue

		Good	Fine	XF
S3494	**200 Yüan** 1948. Black on blue unpt. Herdsman w/horses at ctr. Back purple; man w/ox drawn cart at ctr. *(S/M #N12-0.5).*	15.00	45.00	130.00

		Good	Fine	XF
S3495	**500 Yüan** 1948. Violet. Back green. *(S/M #N12-1).*	15.00	45.00	130.00
S3498	**2000 Yüan** 9148. Sheep. *(S/M #N12-).*	20.00	60.00	175.00

1949 Issue

		Good	Fine	XF
S3501	**100 Yüan** 1949. Like #S3494. *(S/M #N12-10).*	15.00	45.00	130.00

		GOOD	FINE	XF
S3502	**500 YÜAN** 1949. *(S/M #N12-11).*	Reported Not Confirmed		
S3503	**1000 YÜAN** 1949. *(S/M #N12-12).*	Reported Not Confirmed		
S3505	**5000 YÜAN** 1949. *(S/M #N12-13).*	Reported Not Confirmed		
S3506	**10,000 YÜAN** 1949. Red. Back brown. *(S/M #N12-14).*	20.00	60.00	175.00

BANK OF INNER MONGOLIA

行銀蒙內

Nei Mung Yin Hang

1947 ISSUE

		GOOD	FINE	XF
S3507	**200 YÜAN** 1947. Red on yellow unpt. Bank bldg. at r. Back blue-black. *(S/M #N12.5-6).*	35.00	100.00	250.00

		GOOD	FINE	XF
S3507A	**500 YÜAN** 1947. Steam passenger train at lower ctr. Monument at upper ctr. on back. *(S/M #N12.5-7).*	40.00	125.00	350.00

BANK OF INNER CHIANG

行銀省江嫩

Nen Chiang Sheng Yin Hang

1946 ISSUE

		GOOD	FINE	XF
S3507J	**5 YÜAN** 1946. Army machine gun crew at ctr. r. *(S/M #N12.7-5).*	—	—	—

		GOOD	FINE	XF
S3507K	**10 YÜAN** 1946. Peasant and mule by hut at ctr. *(S/M #N12.7-7).*	—	—	—

		GOOD	FINE	XF
S3507L	**10 YÜAN** 1946. Steam passenger train, bldgs. at r. *(S/M #N12.7-9).*	—	—	—

		GOOD	FINE	XF
S3507M	**10 YÜAN** 1946. Steam passenger train at r. *(S/M #N12.7-9).*	—	—	—

#S3507P-S3507R bank bldg. at ctr. on back.

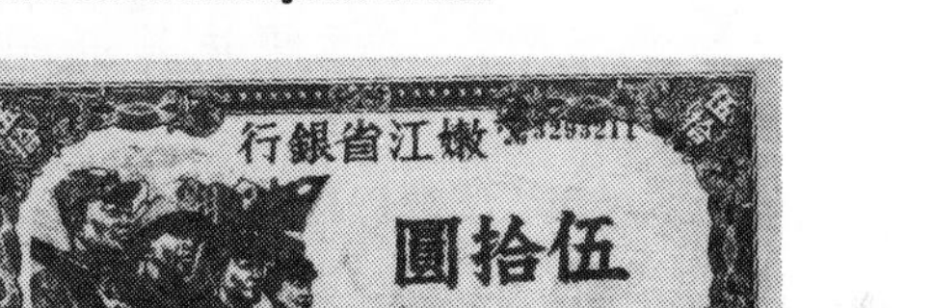

		GOOD	FINE	XF
S3507P	**50 YÜAN** 1946. Blue-black and yellow on lt. blue unpt. Soldiers at l. Back red-violet. Printer: Tung Pei Hifan. *(S/M #N12.7-13).*	8.00	25.00	75.00

#S3507Q-S3507R 2 soldiers at l.

		GOOD	FINE	XF
S3507Q	**100 YÜAN** 1946. 112 x 54mm. *(S/M #N12.7-14).*	—	—	—

		GOOD	FINE	XF
S3507R	**100 YÜAN** 1946. Deep blue-green on lt. green unpt. 150 x 69mm. *(S/M #N12.7-15).*	—	—	—

WEST HUPEI PEASANTS BANK

行銀民農西鄂

O Hsi Nung Min Yin Hang

1930 ISSUE

		GOOD	FINE	XF
S3508A	**1 CHIAO** 1930-1931. Red. Hammer and sickle on star at ctr. Back blue. *(S/M #04-0.2).*	—	—	—
S3508D	**1 YÜAN** 1930. Temple of Heaven at ctr. *(S/M #04-0.5).*	—	—	—

1931 ISSUES

		GOOD	FINE	XF
S3508F	**2 CHIAO** 1931. Tea house at ctr. *(S/M #04-1).*	—	—	—
S3508G	**2 CHIAO** 1931. *(S/M #04-2).*	—	—	—
S3508J	**1 YÜAN** 1931. Temple of Heaven at r. Rural hillside view at ctr. on back. *(S/M #04-5).*	—	—	—

NORTH HUPEH PEASANTS BANK

行銀民農北鄂

O Pei Nung Min Yin Hang

1931 ISSUE

#S3508P-S3508Q portr. N. Lenin at ctr.

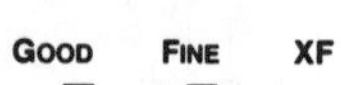

		GOOD	FINE	XF
S3508P	**5 CHIAO** 1931. *(S/M #05.5-11).*	—	—	

		GOOD	FINE	XF
S3508Q	**1 YÜAN** 1931. *(S/M #05.5-12).*	—	—	—

EAST HUPEI WORKERS AND PEASANTS BANK

行銀農工東鄂

O Tung Kung Nung Yin Hang

1932 ISSUE

		GOOD	FINE	XF
S3509	**1 CH'UAN** 1932. Brown. *(S/M #06-1).*	—	—	—

		GOOD	FINE	XF
S3510	**2 CH'UAN** 1932. Gray. City fortress gate at l. and r. *(S/M #06-2).*	—	—	—

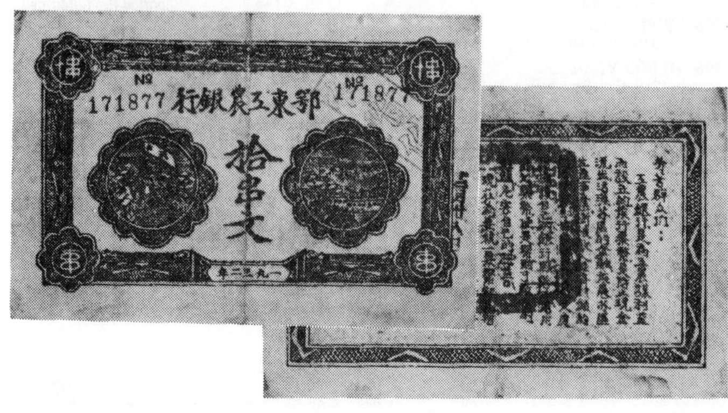

		GOOD	FINE	XF
S3512	**10 CH'UAN** 1932. Black. Bridge at l., and bldgs. at r. *(S/M #06-3).*	—	—	—

SOUTHEAST HUPEI WORKERS, PEASANTS AND SOLDIERS BANK

行銀兵農工南東鄂

O Tung Nan Kung Nung Ping Yin Hang

1931 ISSUE

		GOOD	FINE	XF
S3515	**500 CASH** 1931. *(S/M #07-0.3).*	50.00	125.00	—
S3517	**1 CH'UAN** 1931. Black. *(S/M #07-0.5).*	65.00	140.00	—
S3518	**2 CH'UAN** 1931. City gate. *(S/M #07-0.6).*	65.00	140.00	—
S3519 (S3525)	**5 CH'UAN** 1931. Black. Rural house in woods at ctr. Back green. *(S/M #07-0.7).*	120.00	300.00	—

#S3521 *Deleted.* See #S3526.

#S3522 *Deleted.* See #S3527.

1932 ISSUE

		GOOD	FINE	XF
S3524	**5 CH'UAN** 1932. Blue. *(S/M #07-0.9).*	65.00	140.00	—

SOUTHEAST HUPEI WORKERS AND PEASANTS BANK

行銀農工南東鄂

O Tung Nan Kung Nung Yin Hang

1932 ISSUE

		GOOD	FINE	XF
S3526	**200 CASH** 1932. Black. Village at ctr. Text on back. *(S/M #07-1).*	50.00	125.00	—

		GOOD	FINE	XF
S3527	**500 CASH** 1932. Blue and green. *(S/M #07-2).*	50.00	125.00	—

S3529 5 CH'UAN

1932. Dk. blue. Rural house in woods at ctr. Text on back w/lg. red hand stamped seal. *(S/M#07-10).*

	GOOD	FINE	XF
a. Issued note.	65.00	140.00	—
r. Remainder w/o serial # or lg. hand stamped seal on back.	40.00	100.00	—

HUPEI-HUNAN RECONSTRUCTION BANK

行銀設建豫鄂

O Yü Chien She Yin Hang

#S3531-S3537 *Deleted.*

HUPEI-HONAN-ANHWEI SOVIET BANK

行銀埃維蘇省皖豫鄂

O Yü Huan Sheng Su Wei Ai Yin Hang

1931 ISSUE

S3538 10 CHIAO

1931. *(S/M #O11-1).*

GOOD	FINE	XF
Reported Not Confirmed		

HUPEI-HONAN-ANHWEI PROVINCE SOVIET WORKERS & PEASANTS BANK

行銀農工埃維蘇省皖豫鄂

O Yü Huan Sheng Su Wei Ai Kung Neng Yin Hang

1923 ISSUE

S3539 2 CHIAO

ND. Portr. K. Marx at ctr. Upper hemisphere at ctr. on back. *(S/M #O11-2).*

GOOD	FINE	XF
50.00	150.00	400.00

S3540 5 CHIAO

1923. Government bldg. at ctr. Peasant, worker and soldier at ctr. on back. *(S/M #O11-3).*

GOOD	FINE	XF
30.00	100.00	250.00

1932 ISSUE

S3540A 5 CHIAO

1932. Dk. green on gray unpt. Pagoda at l., temple at r. Back red; peasant, worker and soldier at ctr. *(S/M #O11-4).*

GOOD	FINE	XF
40.00	120.00	—

S3540B 1 YÜAN

21.1.1932. Dk. green on lt. olive-green unpt. Government bldg. at ctr. Back lt. yellow-green; rural scene at ctr. w/bank name above in Chinese. *(S/M #O11-4).*

GOOD	FINE	XF
40.00	120.00	—

S3540C 1 YÜAN

1932. Similar to #S3540B but w/bank name in Russian text on back. *(S/M #O11-5).*

GOOD	FINE	XF
50.00	150.00	—

Bank of Bai Hai, Beei Hai Bank, Bo Xai Inxang, B. X. Inxang, Bank of Pei Hai Pei Hai Bank of China

行銀海北
Pei Hai Yin Hang

1938 ND Issue

		Good	Fine	XF
S3541	**1 Chiao** ND (1938). Blue on pink unpt. Rural bldg. w/fence in yard. Back red. *Chiaotung. (S/M #P21-0.1).*	5.00	20.00	60.00

		Good	Fine	XF
S3541A	**2 Chiao** ND (1938). Green. Rural bldg. w/courtyard at l. Back purple.			
	a. *Chiaotung. (S/M #P21-0.2a).*	11.00	33.00	100.00
	b. *Yeh Hsien. (S/M #P21-0.2b).*	11.00	33.00	100.00
S3542	**5 Chiao** ND (1938). Red. City gate at l. Back brown. *Chiaotung. (S/M #P21-0.3).*	13.00	40.00	120.00

		Good	Fine	XF
S3543	**1 Yüan** ND (1938). Red. Rural waterfront village at l. Ovpt: *Fan* at l. and r. Back brown. *(S/M #P21-0.4).*	17.00	50.00	150.00

1938 Issues

		Good	Fine	XF
S3543A	**5 Chiao** 1938. Blue. Bldg. at l. Back purple. *(S/M #P21-).*	13.00	40.00	120.00
S3543B	**5 Chiao** 1938. Similar to #S3543A. *Ch'ing-ho. (S/M #P21-).*	13.00	40.00	120.00

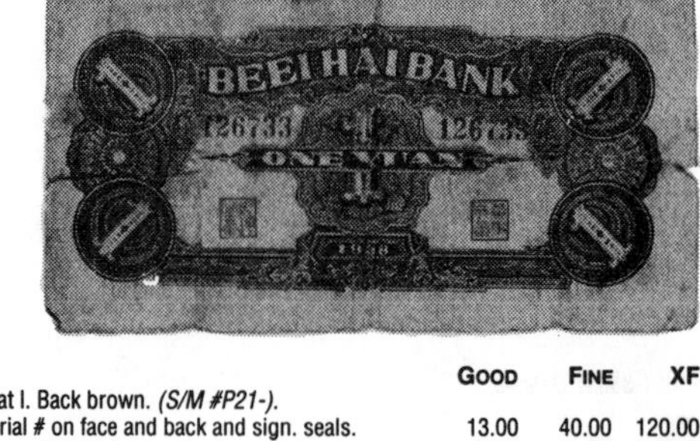

		Good	Fine	XF
S3543C	**1 Yüan** 1938. Red. Gateways at l. Back brown. *(S/M #P21-).*			
	a. Issued note w/serial # on face and back and sign. seals.	13.00	40.00	120.00
	b. *Nan.* W/o serial # or sign. seals.	13.00	40.00	120.00
	c. *Nanhai.* W/o serial # or sign. seals.	13.00	40.00	120.00
	d. *Tunghai.*	13.00	40.00	120.00
	e. *Yeh Hsien.* W/serial # and sign. seals.	13.00	40.00	120.00
	f. *Pei* at l. and r., w/serial # and sign. seals on face.	13.00	40.00	120.00

1940 Issues

		Good	Fine	XF
S3543E	**1 Chiao** 1940. Deep green. Peasant hoeing at r. Back yellow. *Ch'ingho. (S/M #P21-).*	11.00	33.00	100.00
S3543F	**2 Chiao** 1940. Blue. Back brown. *Ch'ingho. (S/M #P21-).*	11.00	33.00	100.00
S3544	**5 Yüan** 1940. Gateway at l.			
	a. *Sheng* at l. and r. *Chiaotung. (S/M #P21-0.6b).*	10.00	30.00	90.00
	s. *Jung* at l. and r. Specimen. *(S/M #P21-0.6a).*	—	Unc	100.00
S3544A	**5 Yüan** 1940. Blue. Back purple. *(S/M #P21-).*			
	a. W/o place name.	8.00	25.00	75.00
	b. *Chiaotung.*	10.00	30.00	90.00
	c. *Chi Lu Pian.*	10.00	30.00	90.00

		Good	Fine	XF
S3545	**10 Yüan** 1940. Red. Temple of Heaven at l., fortress gate at r. Shoreline cliffs, house and gazebo at ctr. on back. *(S/M #P21-0.7).*			
	a. Issued note.	10.00	30.00	90.00
	s. Specimen.	—	Unc	125.00

1941 Issues

#S3549 Deleted. See #S3551B.

		Good	Fine	XF
S3546	**1 Chiao** 1941. Brown. *Chi Lu Pien. (S/M #P21).*	10.00	30.00	90.00
S3548	**1 Yüan** 1941. Like #S3543 but w/date in ctr. of lower frame.			
	a. *Fa* at l. and r. *(S/M #P21-0.9a).*	10.00	30.00	90.00
	s. *Chan* at l. and r. *Giao Dung (Chiaotung).* Specimen. *(S/M #P21-0.9b).*	—	Unc	100.00

		Good	Fine	XF
S3550	**5 Yüan** 1941. Blue-gray. Junk at l., waterfront house at r. Gazebo at l., modern bldg. at r. on back. *GIAO DUNG (Chiaotung). (S/M #P21-2).*	13.00	40.00	120.00
S3550A	**5 Yüan** 1941. Green. Like #3550. *Giao Dung (Chioatung).* (twice) at l. and r. *(S/M #P21-).*	13.00	40.00	120.00

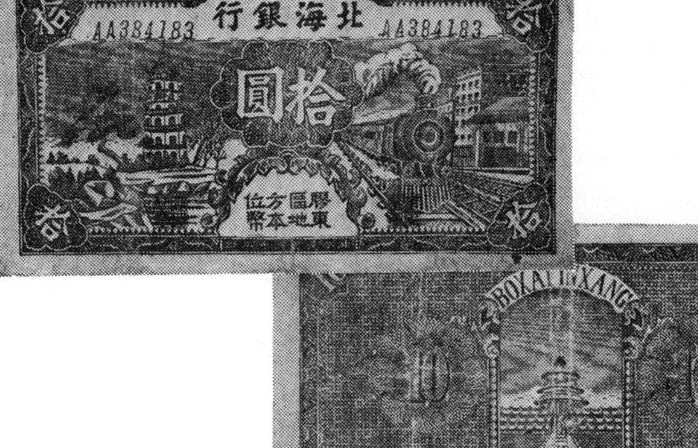

		Good	Fine	XF
S3550B (S3551)	**10 Yüan** 1941. Red. Pagoda at l., steam passenger train at r. Back red; Temple of Heaven at ctr. *(S/M #P21-3).*			
	a. *Giao Dung (Chiaotung).*	7.00	20.00	60.00
	b. As a w/ovpt. *Chien* at l. and r. *(S/M #P21-0.9a).*	7.00	20.00	60.00
	c. *Cing Xo (Ch'ingho).*	8.00	25.00	75.00
	s. Specimen. *(S/M #P21-0.9b).*	—	Unc	90.00

1942 Issues

		Good	Fine	XF
S3551	**2 Chiao** 1942. Green. City gate at l. Back olive-green. *Shantung. (S/M #P21-).*	7.00	20.00	60.00
S3551A	**5 Chiao** 1942. Green. Sheep. Back blue. *Chi Lu Pien. (S/M #P21-3.3).*	5.50	16.50	50.00
S3551B	**5 Chiao** 1942. Green. Lakeside park. *(S/M #P21-).*	5.00	15.00	45.00
S3551C	**5 Chiao** 1942. Dk. blue. Peasant hoeing at r. Back dk. brown. *Ching Ho. (S/M #P21-).*			
	a. *Kai* at l. in Chinese on face. *Kai* in script English at lower l. and r. on back.	—	—	—
	b. *Yüan* at l. in Chinese on face. *Yüan in script English at lower l. and r. on back.*	—	—	—

		Good	Fine	XF
S3551D	**5 Chiao** 1942. Dk. brown. Fortress gate at r. *Ch'ingho* at l., *Shantung* at r. *(S/M #P21-).*	—	—	—

		Good	Fine	XF
S3551F	**1 Yüan** 1942. Brown. Shepherd w/sheep. Back orange. *Chi Lu Pien. (S/M #P21-3.6).*	5.00	15.00	45.00

#S3552-S3552B rural waterfront village at l.

		Good	Fine	XF
S3552	**1 Yüan** 1942. Blue-black. Like #S3543 and S3548. Back brown.			
	a. W/o place name. Lg. date. *(S/M #P21-4a).*	2.50	7.50	22.50
	b. W/o place name. Sm. date. *(S/M #P21-4d).*	2.50	7.50	22.50
	s1. As b. Sm. date. Specimen. *(S/M #P21-0.4b).*	—	Unc	60.00
	s2. As b. Sm. date. *Chiaotung.* Specimen. *(S/M #P21-0.4c).*	—	Unc	60.00

		Good	Fine	XF
S3552A	**1 Yüan** 1942. Dk. green. Back dk. blue. *Chiaotung. (S/M #P21-5).*	7.00	20.00	60.00
S3552B	**1 Yüan** 1942. Red. Back red-brown. *(S/M #P21-).*	7.00	20.00	60.00
S3552C	**1 Yüan** 1942. Steam passenger train at ctr. *Shantung. (S/M #P21-).*	7.00	20.00	60.00

		Good	Fine	XF
S3553	**5 Yüan** 1942. Purple on lilac unpt. Modern ocean liner at ctr. Bank bldg. at ctr. *Chiaotung. (S/M #P21-).*	11.00	33.00	100.00

		Good	Fine	XF
S3553A	**10 Yüan** 1942. Bank bldg. at ctr. on back. Modern ocean liner at ctr. on back. *Chiaotung. (S/M #P21-7).*	8.00	25.00	75.00

		Good	Fine	XF
S3553B	**10 Yüan** 1942. Grayish green. Hillside view at l., mountain waterfall, stream at r. Back blue; temple at ctr., steam passenger train crossing bridge over river at r. *Shantung.* Specimen. *(S/M #P21-8).*			
	a. Issued note.	13.50	40.00	120.00
	s. Specimen.	—	Unc	90.00
S3553C	**10 Yüan** 1942. Like #S3553B. *Ch'ingho. (S/M #P21-).*	8.00	25.00	75.00
S3553F	**50 Yüan** 1942. *Chiaotung. (S/M #P21-).*	—	—	—

1943 Issues

		Good	Fine	XF
S3553J	**2 Chiao = 20 Cents** 1943. Blue-violet. Sampans at ctr. Back dk. brown. *Shantung. (S/M #P21-).*	8.00	25.00	75.00

		Good	Fine	XF
S3554	**5 Chiao = 50 Cents** 1943. Brown. Farmer plowing w/ox at r. Back green. *Shantung. (S/M #P21-9).*	8.00	25.00	75.00
S3554A	**5 Chiao = 50 Cents** 1943. Blue. Peasant spading. Back purple. *Ch'ingho. (S/M #P21-).*			
	a. Ovpt: *Yuan* at l. and r.	8.00	25.00	75.00
	b. Ovpt: *Kai* at l. and r.	8.00	25.00	75.00

		Good	Fine	XF
S3555	**1 Yüan** 1943. Brown. Pack mules at ctr. Back yellow. *(S/M #P21-10).*			
	a. *Shantung.* Block #.	7.00	20.00	60.00
	b. *Pohai.* Blue serial #.	7.00	20.00	60.00

		Good	Fine	XF
S3555A	**1 Yüan** 1943. Blue. Sampan at ctr. Farm scene at ctr. on back. (IPohai. (S/M #P21-10.3).	10.00	30.00	90.00

		Good	Fine	XF
S3555B	**1 Yüan** 1943. Rural scene at lower r. *Shantung. (S/M #P21-10.7).*	10.00	30.00	90.00

		Good	Fine	XF
S3555C	**1 Yüan** 1943. Red-brown. Steam passenger train at lower l., city gate at lower ctr. Back brown. *Luchung. (S/M #P21-).*	10.00	30.00	90.00
S3556	**5 Yüan** 1943. Violet and brown. Plowing. Back violet. *(S/M #P21-11).*	10.00	30.00	90.00

		Good	Fine	XF
S3556A	**5 Yüan** 1943. Purple. Peasant beside stream at ctr. Back purple and red; rural scene at ctr. *Pohai. (S/M #P21-11.3).*			
	a. Issued note.	10.00	30.00	90.00
	s. Specimen.	—	Unc	150.00

		GOOD	FINE	XF
S3556B	**5 YÜAN = GUINQUE (CINQUE) ARGENTENS** 1943. Peasants stacking harvest at l., peasant laboring at irrigation system at r. Construction scene at ctr. on back. *Pohai. (S/M #P21-11.7).*			
	a. Issued note.	40.00	120.00	—
	s. Specimen.	—	—	—
S3556C	**5 YÜAN** 1943. Red. Pavilion at ctr. *Luchung. (S/M #P21-).*	8.00	25.00	75.00
S3556D	**5 YÜAN** 1943. Blue. Like #S3556C. *Luchung. (S/M #P21-).*	8.00	25.00	75.00

		GOOD	FINE	XF
S3557	**10 YÜAN** 1943. Purple. Farming scene at l. and r. Back blue-green; farm scene at ctr. *Chiaotung. (S/M #P21-12a).*	8.00	25.00	75.00
S3557A	**10 YÜAN** 1943. Blue-gray. Similar to #S3557. *Chiaotung. (S/M #P21-12b).*			
	a. Back brown.	8.00	25.00	75.00
	b. Back purple.	8.00	25.00	75.00

		GOOD	FINE	XF
S3557B	**10 YÜAN = DECEM ARGENTENS** 1943. Multiple arch bridge at l., rural house at r. Peasants cultivating at ctr. on back. *Pohai.* Specimen. *(S/M #P21-12.5b).*	8.00	25.00	75.00
S3557C	**10 YÜAN** 1943. *Luchung. (S/M #P21-).*	8.00	25.00	75.00
S3557D	**10 YÜAN** 1943. Blue. Back orange. *Pinhai. (S/M #P21-).*	8.00	25.00	75.00

		GOOD	FINE	XF
S3557E	**10 YÜAN** 1943. Red on yellow unpt. Fortress gate at lower r. Back violet; rural houses at ctr. *Shantung. (S/M #P21-).*	—	—	—
S3557F	**50 YÜAN** 1943. Rural mountain scene at r. *Pinhai. (S/M #P21-).*	8.00	25.00	75.00
S3557G	**50 YÜAN** 1943. Harbor scene at r. *Luchung. (S/M #P21-).*	8.00	25.00	

		GOOD	FINE	XF
S3558	**100 YÜAN** 1943. Black. Trees along mountainous slopes at r. Back brown; *New democracy* and *Free Ching* as sign., *Pao* at l. and r. *Shantung.* 2 serial # varieties. *(S/M #P21-12.5).*	8.00	25.00	75.00
S3559	**100 YÜAN** 1943. Like #S3558 but green. *(S/M #P21-13).*	8.00	25.00	75.00

		GOOD	FINE	XF
S3560	**100 YÜAN** 1943. Red. Truck. Back red. *Shantung. (S/M #P21-14).*			
	a. Serial # at l. and r.	8.00	25.00	75.00
	b. Block letters at l., serial # at r.	8.00	25.00	75.00

1944 Issues

S3560B 5 Chiao = 50 Cents — Good / Fine / XF
1944. Dk. olive-green. Farm scene at l. *Pohai. (S/M #P21-17).* — 8.00 / 25.00 / 75.00

S3561 1 Yüan — Good / Fine / XF
1944. Farmer plowing w/horse at ctr. *Pohai. (S/M #P21-19).* — 8.00 / 25.00 / 75.00

S3562 1 Yüan — Good / Fine / XF
1944. Red-brown and red. Peasant w/cart at ctr. *Giao Dung (Chiaotung). (S/M #P21-20).*
a. Back brown-orange. — 8.00 / 25.00 / 75.00
b. Back blue-green. — 8.00 / 25.00 / 75.00

S3562A 5 Yüan — Good / Fine / XF
1944. Orange. Farm scene at l. Back ochre; steam passenger train, control tower at ctr. *Shantung. (S/M #P21-20.2).* — 11.00 / 33.00 / 100.00

S3563 5 Yüan — Good / Fine / XF
1944. Blue. Drawing water at r. Back brown. *Shantung. (S/M #P21-05).* — 8.00 / 25.00 / 75.00

S3563A 5 Yüan
1944. Red. Ship at l., steam passenger train at r. Back blue. *Nanlu. (S/M #P21-).* — 8.00 / 25.00 / 75.00

S3564 10 Yüan
1944. Red. Mountains, farm. Back red. *(S/M #P21-21).* — 10.00 / 30.00 / 90.00

#3565-S3565C houses by lake at ctr.

S3565 10 Yüan — Good / Fine / XF
1944. Blue. Back blue. *Luchung. (S/M #P21-22).* — 15.00 / 45.00 / 90.00

S3565A 10 Yüan
1944. Red. Back brown. *Shantung. (S/M #P21-).* — 10.00 / 30.00 / 90.00

S3565B 10 Yüan
1944. Blue-black (to gray). Back blue. *Shantung. (S/M #P21-).* — 10.00 / 30.00 / 110.00

S3565C 10 Yüan
1944. Blue-green. Like #S3565B. Back blue. *Shantung. (S/M #P21-).* — 12.00 / 36.00 / 110.00

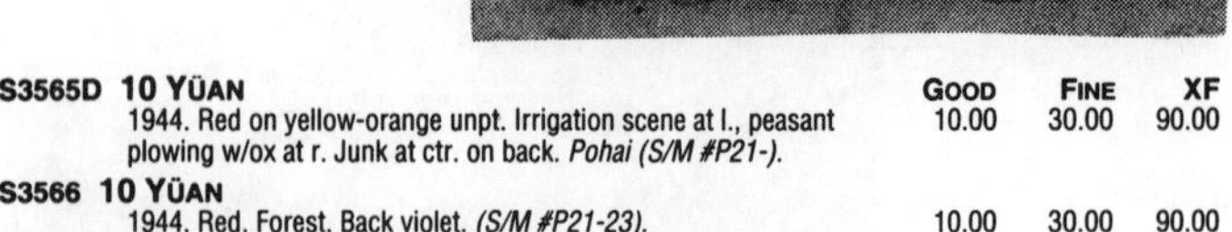

S3565D 10 Yüan — Good / Fine / XF
1944. Red on yellow-orange unpt. Irrigation scene at l., peasant plowing w/ox at r. Junk at ctr. on back. *Pohai (S/M #P21-).* — 10.00 / 30.00 / 90.00

S3566 10 Yüan
1944. Red. Forest. Back violet. *(S/M #P21-23).* — 10.00 / 30.00 / 90.00

S3566A 10 Yüan — Good / Fine / XF
1944. Green. Junk at l., peasant plowing w/ox at r. Back purple; farm at ctr. *Ch'ing ho. (S/M #P21-).* — 10.00 / 30.00 / 90.00

		Good	Fine	XF
S3567	**10 Yüan** 1944. Yellow. Rural mountain scene at ctr. Back green. *Shantung. (S/M #P21-24).*	10.00	30.00	90.00
S3567A	**10 Yüan** 1944. Red. Like #S3567. Back red. *Shantung. (S/M #P21-).*	10.00	30.00	90.00
S3568	**10 Yüan** 1944. Blue and green. Irrigation system. Back brown. *(S/M #P21-24.5).*	10.00	30.00	90.00
S3568A	**10 Yüan** 1944. Red and yellow. Like #S3568. Back brown. *(S/M #P21-24.6).*			
	a. Block letter and serial #.	10.00	30.00	90.00
	b. Serial # w/prefix letter.	10.00	40.00	80.00
S3569	**50 Yüan** 1944. Violet. Peasant winnowing rice at r. *Shantung. (S/M #P21-25).*			
	a. Back green.	11.00	33.00	100.00
	b. Back blue.	11.00	33.00	100.00
S3569A	**50 Yüan** 1944. Rural industries at ctr. *Pohai. (S/M #P21-26).*	11.00	33.00	100.00

		Good	Fine	XF
S3569B	**50 Yüan** 1944. Purple and green. Streamlined passenger train at ctr. Temple of Heaven at ctr. on back. *Chiaotung. (S/M #P21-28).*			
	a. Issued note.	11.00	33.00	100.00
	s. Specimen.	—	Unc	135.00
S3569C	**50 Yüan** 1944. Red and green. Peasant drawing water at l. *(S/M #P21-29).*			
	a. Dk. blue ovpt: *Chiaotung.*	11.00	33.00	100.00
	b. Red ovpt: *Shantung.*	11.00	33.00	100.00
S3570	**50 Yüan** 1944. Red on pale green. Similar to #3569C. Back olive-green. *(S/M #P21-30a).*	11.00	33.00	100.00

		Good	Fine	XF
S3570A	**50 Yüan** 1944. Orange on pale green. Like #S3570. Back brown. *(S/M #P21-30b).*	11.00	33.00	100.00

		Good	Fine	XF
S3571	**50 Yüan** 1944. Blue. Pagodas, hillside village at r. Back green; peasants hauling goods along rural trail at ctr. *Shantung. (S/M #P21-31).*	11.00	33.00	100.00

		Good	Fine	XF
S3572	**100 Yüan** 1944. Red. Truck at lower ctr. Back red. *Shantung. (S/M #P21-32).*	11.00	33.00	100.00
S3572A	**100 Yüan** 1944. Rice fields at ctr. Trees on back. *Chiaotung. (S/M #P21-).*	11.00	33.00	100.00
S3572B	**100 Yüan** 1944. Plowing w/water buffalo at r. *Pohai. (S/M #P21-).*	11.00	33.00	100.00
S3573	**200 Yüan** 1944. Red-orange. Peasant hoeing at ctr. 3 serial # varieties.			
	a. Issued note. *(S/M #P21-33a).*	11.00	33.00	100.00
	b. Black ovpt: *Shantung. (S/M #P21-33b).*	11.00	33.00	100.00
	c. Red-orange. *Shantung (S/M #P21-33c).*	11.00	33.00	100.00
	d. *Pohai. (S/M #P21-33d).*	11.00	33.00	100.00

		Good	Fine	XF
S3574	**200 Yüan** 1944. Black. Like #S3573b. Back blue. *Shantung. (S/M #P21-34).*	11.00	33.00	100.00

#S3575 Deleted. See #S3573C.

		Good	Fine	XF
S3576	**200 Yüan** 1944. Blue. Like #S3573c. Back green. *Pohai. (S/M #P21-36).*	11.00	33.00	100.00

1945 Issue

		Good	Fine	XF
S3577	**5 Chiao = 50 Cents** 1945. Red. Peasants cultivating, mountains in background. Back blue. *Chiaotung. (S/M #P21-37).*	10.00	30.00	90.00

		Good	Fine	XF
S3577A	**1 Yüan** 1945. Red-orange. Truck on rural highway at ctr. Back brown. *Shantung.*			
	a. Blue serial #. *(S/M #P21-38a).*	8.00	25.00	75.00
	b. Block letters. *(S/M #P21-38b).*	5.00	15.00	45.00

		Good	Fine	XF
S3578	**1 Yüan** 1945. Horsedrawn farm equipment at ctr. *Min* at l. and r. *Chiaotung.* *(S/M #P21-39).*	8.00	25.00	75.00

		Good	Fine	XF
S3578A	**2 Yüan** 1945. Red. Shrine at l. Back red. *Shantung. (S/M #P21-39.5).*	8.00	25.00	75.00
S3579	**5 Yüan** 1945. Green. Truck on rural road at ctr. Back green. *Shantung.* *(S/M #P21-40).*	10.00	30.00	90.00

		Good	Fine	XF
S3579A	**5 Yüan** 1945. Blue. Shrine at ctr. Back brown. *Shantung. (S/M #P21-40.5).*	8.00	25.00	75.00

		Good	Fine	XF
S3579B	**5 Yüan** 1945. Blue-gray. Drawing water at r. Back blue. *Shantung.* *(S/M #P21-).*	8.00	25.00	75.00
S3580	**10 Yüan** 1945. Red-orange. Peasant spearing in paddy at l. Back red. *Shantung.*			
	a. 2 serial #. Ovpt: *Ti. (S/M #P21-41a).*	8.00	25.00	75.00
	b. Serial # and block letters. *(S/M #P21-41b).*	5.50	16.50	50.00

NOTE: 12 different characters of control ovpt. have been recorded for #S3580.

		Good	Fine	XF
S3580A	**10 Yüan** 1945. Red. Farmer seated w/basket of corn cobs at l. Back green. *Chiaotung. (S/M #P21-41.3).*	8.00	25.00	75.00
S3580B	**10 Yüan** 1945. Red-orange. Rural scene at ctr. *Pohai. (S/M #P21-).*	8.00	25.00	75.00

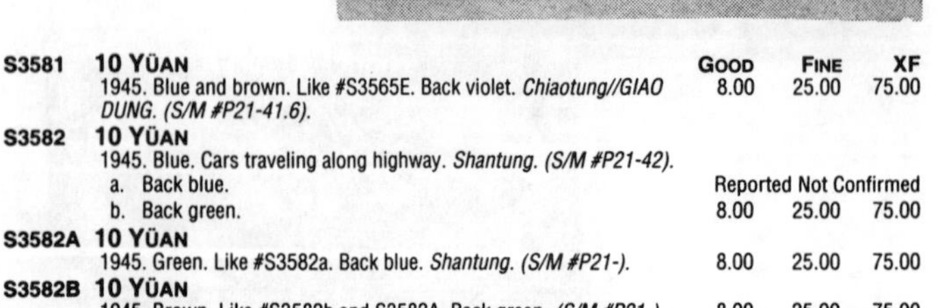

		Good	Fine	XF
S3581	**10 Yüan** 1945. Blue and brown. Like #S3565E. Back violet. *Chiaotung//GIAO DUNG. (S/M #P21-41.6).*	8.00	25.00	75.00
S3582	**10 Yüan** 1945. Blue. Cars traveling along highway. *Shantung. (S/M #P21-42).*			
	a. Back blue.	Reported Not Confirmed		
	b. Back green.	8.00	25.00	75.00
S3582A	**10 Yüan** 1945. Green. Like #S3582a. Back blue. *Shantung. (S/M #P21-).*	8.00	25.00	75.00
S3582B	**10 Yüan** 1945. Brown. Like #S3582b and S3582A. Back green. *(S/M #P21-).*	8.00	25.00	75.00
S3582C	**10 Yüan** 1945. Red. Winnowing rice at ctr. *Chiaotung. (S/M #P21).*	10.00	30.00	90.00
S3582D	**10 Yüan** 1945. Red. Trees by stream at ctr. *Pohai. (S/M #P21-).*	10.00	30.00	90.00

		Good	Fine	XF
S3583	**25 Yüan** 1945. Red. Planting rice at l., blue seals, serial # and block letter. Back blue. *Chiaotung//GIAO DUNG. (S/M #P21-42.3).*	10.00	30.00	90.00

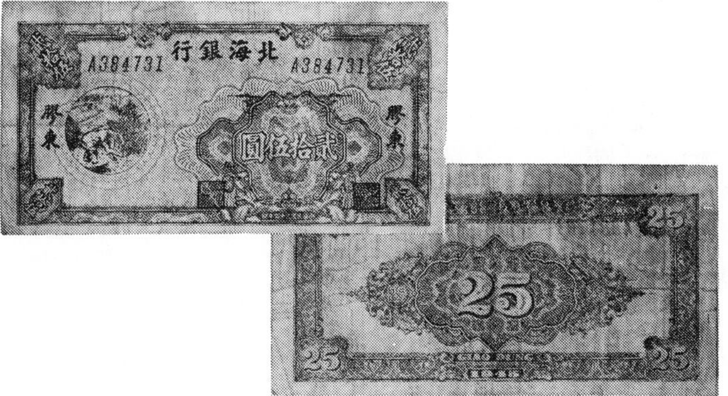

		Good	Fine	XF
S3583A	**25 Yüan** 1945. Blue on gray unpt. Like #S2583. Red seals and serial #. Back green. *Chiaotung//GIAO DUNG. (S/M #P21-42.6).*	10.00	30.00	90.00

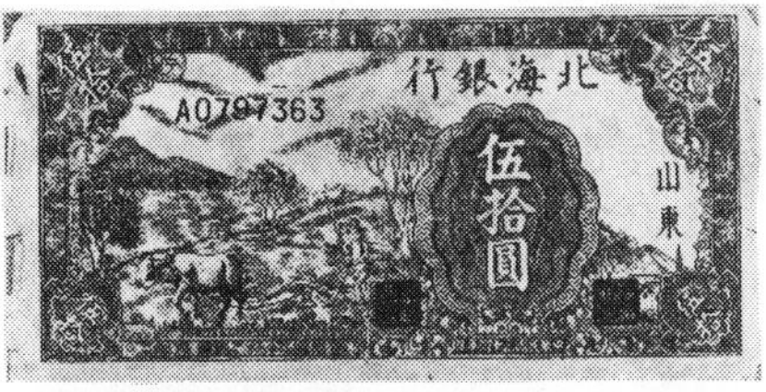

		Good	Fine	XF
S3584	**50 Yüan** 1945. Olive. Plowing w/water buffalo. Back red. *Shantung. (S/M #P21-43).*	10.00	30.00	90.00
S3584A	**50 Yüan** 1945. Brown. Like #S3584. Back red. *Shantung. (S/M #P21-).*	10.00	30.00	90.00

#S3585-S3586B terraced hillside at ctr.

		Good	Fine	XF
S3585	**50 Yüan** 1945. Violet. *Shantung. (S/M #P21-44).*	10.00	30.00	90.00
S3585A	**50 Yüan** 1945. Dk. blue. *Shantung. (S/M #P21-).*	10.00	30.00	90.00
S3586	**50 Yüan** 1945. Blue on tan unpt. Back green. *Shantung//SHAN DUNG. (S/M #P21-50).*	10.00	30.00	90.00
S3586A	**50 Yüan** 1945. Red. Back brown. *Shantung. (S/M #P21-).*	10.00	30.00	90.00
S3586B	**50 Yüan** 1945. Green on tan unpt. Back blue w/red bar across bank name Shantung//SHAN DUNG. *(S/M #P21-).*	10.00	30.00	90.00
S3587	**50 Yüan** 1945. Orange. Back red. *Shantung. (S/M #P21-46).*	10.00	30.00	90.00

		Good	Fine	XF
S3587A	**50 Yüan** 1945. Deep purple. Hillside village at l., *YWENTY FIFTY YUAN* (error) below. Back violet. *Shantung. (S/M #P21-).*	10.00	30.00	90.00
S3587B	**50 Yüan** 1945. Like #S3587A but value *YWENTY FIAE YIAM* (error). *(S/M #P21-).*	10.00	30.00	90.00
S3588	**50 Yüan** 1945. Violet. Winnowing rice. Back blue.			
	a. W/o place name. *(S/M #P21-51a).*	10.00	30.00	90.00
	b. *Shantung. (S/M #P21-51b).*	10.00	30.00	90.00
S3588A	**50 Yüan** 1945. Blue. Winnowing rice at ctr. Back purple. *Chiaotung//GIAO DUNG. (S/M #P21-).*	10.00	30.00	90.00

		Good	Fine	XF
S3588B	**50 Yüan** 1945. Red on pale yellow-orange unpt. Like #S3588A. Back red-brown; w/*New democracy* and *Free Ching* as sign. *Chiaotung//GIAO DUNG. (S/M #P21-).*	10.00	30.00	90.00

		Good	Fine	XF
S3589	**50 Yüan** 1945. Blue. Army bugler and two people at l., farming scene at r. Back red. *Shantung. (S/M #P21-52).*			
	a. Issued note.	10.00	30.00	90.00
	s. Specimen.	—	Unc	135.00
S3589A	**50 Yüan** 1945. Red-orange. Like #S3589. Back brown. *Shantung. (S/M #P52.5).*	10.00	30.00	90.00
S3590	**50 Yüan** 1945. Red. Farmer and worker. Back violet. *(S/M #P21-53).*	10.00	30.00	90.00

		Good	Fine	XF
S3591	**100 Yüan** 1945. Violet. Ship, steam passenger train at dockside. Back orange; w/*New democracy* and *Free Ching. Shantung. (S/M #P21-54).*	11.00	33.00	100.00
S3591A	**100 Yüan** 1945. Blue-black on pink unpt. Like #S3558. *Shantung. (S/M #P21-).*	10.00	30.00	90.00

S3591B 100 YÜAN — GOOD / FINE / XF
1945. Black. Hillside village at l. Similar to #S3587A and S3587B. Back deep olive-green; rural bldgs. at ctr. w/red *New democracy* and *Free Ching* as sign. *Shantung. (S/M #P21-).*

	GOOD	FINE	XF
a. Issued note.	11.00	33.00	100.00
s. Specimen.	—	Unc	135.00

		GOOD	FINE	XF
S3592	**100 YÜAN** 1945. Blue. Hillside. Back green. *Shantung. (S/M #P21-55).*	11.00	33.00	100.00
S3593	**100 YÜAN** 1945. Red. Ornamental design. Back brown. *Shantung. (S/M #P21-60).*	11.00	33.00	100.00
S3594	**100 YÜAN** 1945. Red. Peasant plowing w/water buffalo at r. Back red. *Chiaotung//GIAO DUNG. (S/M #P21-61).*	11.00	33.00	100.00
S3594A	**100 YÜAN** 1945. Brown on m/c unpt.er buffalo. Back brown. *Chiaotung. (S/M #P21-).*	11.00	33.00	100.00
S3594B	**100 YÜAN** 1945. Black and m/c. Like #S3594A. Back red-brown. *Chiaotung. (S/M #P21-).*	11.00	33.00	100.00
S3594C	**100 YÜAN** 1945. Purple and m/c. Cutting trees at l. Back red. *Pohai. (S/M #P21-).*	11.00	33.00	100.00

#S3595-S3596A ornamental design.

		GOOD	FINE	XF
S3595	**200 YÜAN** 1945. Blue. Back brown. *Shantung//SHAN DUNG. (S/M #P21-62).*	11.00	33.00	100.00
S3596	**200 YÜAN** 1945. Brown-violet on pink unpt. Back blue-gray. *Shantung. (S/M #P21-63).*	11.00	33.00	100.00
S3596A	**200 YÜAN** 1945. Purple on pink unpt. Back purple. *Shantung. (S/M #P21-).*	11.00	33.00	100.00
S3597	**200 YÜAN** 1945. Yellow. Mountain scene. Back blue. *(S/M #P21-64).*	11.00	33.00	100.00

1946 ISSUES

		GOOD	FINE	XF
S3599	**1 YÜAN** 1946. Red. Irrigation system. Back green. *(S/M #P21-71).*	8.00	25.00	75.00

		GOOD	FINE	XF
S3599A	**1 YÜAN** 1946. Red. Steam passenger train crossing bridge over river at r. Back red. *Shantung. (S/M #P21-).*	8.00	25.00	75.00
S3599B	**1 YÜAN** 1946. Red. Mountains at r. Back red. *Shantung. (S/M #P21-).*	8.00	25.00	75.00
S3602	**25 YÜAN** 1946. Red. Sheep. Back brown. *Shantung. (S/M #P21-71.5).*	8.00	25.00	75.00

#S3603-S3610A monument at ctr.

		GOOD	FINE	XF
S3603	**100 YÜAN** 1946. Brown. Back brown. *Shantung. (S/M #P21-72).*	8.00	25.00	75.00
S3604	**100 YÜAN** 1946. Brown. Back blue. *Shantung. (S/M #P21-73).*	8.00	25.00	75.00
S3605	**100 YÜAN** 1946. Blue on green unpt. Back green. *Shantung. (S/M #P21-74).*	8.00	25.00	75.00
S3606	**100 YÜAN** 1946. Blue. Back blue. *Shantung. (S/M #P21-74.5).*	8.00	25.00	75.00
S3607	**100 YÜAN** 1946. Black. Back brown. *Shantung. (S/M #P21-75).*	8.00	25.00	75.00
S3608	**100 YÜAN** 1946. Blue on pink unpt. Back green. *Shantung. (S/M #P21-80).*	8.00	25.00	75.00
S3609	**100 YÜAN** 1946. Red. Back brown. *Shantung. (S/M #P21-81).*	8.00	25.00	75.00
S3610	**100 YÜAN** 1946. Green. Back blue. *Shantung. (S/M #P21-82).*	8.00	25.00	75.00
S3610A	**100 YÜAN** 1946. Brown. Back green. *Shantung. (S/M #P21-).*	8.00	25.00	75.00

		GOOD	FINE	XF
S3611	**100 YÜAN** 1946. Green. Plowing w/ox at r. Back yellow. *Shantung. (S/M #P21-83).*	8.00	25.00	75.00

S3611A 100 YÜAN — GOOD / FINE / XF
1946. Dk. blue. Plowing w/water buffalo at r.; w/sign. *New democracy* and *Free Ching* on back. *Shantung. (S/M #P21-83.5).*

	GOOD	FINE	XF
a. Back brown.	8.00	25.00	75.00
b. Back purple.	8.00	25.00	75.00

		GOOD	FINE	XF
S3612	**200 YÜAN** 1946. Red. Mountain farm. Back red w/*TWENTY HUNDRED YUAN* (error). *(S/M #P21-84).*	16.00	50.00	120.00
S3613	**200 YÜAN** 1946. Red. Threshing at r. Back green. *Shantung. (S/M #P21-85).*	16.00	50.00	120.00

1947 ISSUES

		GOOD	FINE	XF
S3615	**50 YÜAN** 1947. Red. Back violet. *Shantung. (S/M #P21-90).*	11.00	33.00	100.00
S3618	**200 YÜAN** 1947. Brown. Threshing. Back brown. *Shantung. (S/M #P21-91).*	11.00	33.00	—

		GOOD	FINE	XF
S3620	**500 YÜAN** 1947. Blue. Truck on highway at ctr. Back brown. *Shantung.*			
	a. Serial # at l. Block letters at r. *(S/M #P21-92a).*	11.00	33.00	100.00
	b. Serial # at l., w/o block letters at r. *(S/M #P21-92b).*	11.00	33.00	100.00

		GOOD	FINE	XF
S3620A	**500 YÜAN** 1947. Blue. Radio station at r. Back brown. *Shantung. (S/M #P21-93).*	11.00	33.00	100.00
S3620B	**500 YÜAN** 1947. Brown and yellow. Gathering straw. Back blue. *Shantung. (S/M #P21-94).*	11.00	33.00	100.00

		GOOD	FINE	XF
S3620C	**500 YÜAN** 1947. Brown. Gathering straw at ctr. Back violet. *(S/M #P21-95).*			
	a. *Pohai.*	11.00	33.00	100.00
	b. *Shantung.*	11.00	33.00	100.00

		GOOD	FINE	XF
S3620D	**500 YÜAN** 1947. Brown on yellow unpt. Planting rice at r. Back blue. *Shantung. (S/M #P21-100).*	11.00	33.00	100.00

		GOOD	FINE	XF
S3620E	**500 YÜAN** 1947. Blue. Lakeside dock at ctr. Back brown. *Shantung. (S/M #P21-101).*	11.00	33.00	100.00

#S3620F *Deleted*. See #S3620.

1948 ISSUES

		GOOD	FINE	XF
S3621	**200 YÜAN** 1948. Red-orange. Farm tractor hauling wagons at r. Back blue. *Shantung. (S/M #P21-110).*	11.00	33.00	100.00

		GOOD	FINE	XF
S3622	**500 YÜAN** 1948. Brown. Cattle grazing at ctr. Back red. *Shantung. (S/M #P21-111).*	11.00	33.00	100.00

		GOOD	FINE	XF
S3622A	**500 YÜAN** 1948. Brown and yellow. Mountain temple at ctr. Back green. *Shantung. (S/M #P21-112).*	6.50	20.00	60.00

#S3622B-S3622D mountain temple at l.

		GOOD	FINE	XF
S3622B	**500 YÜAN** 1948. Gray. Back violet. *Shantung. (S/M #P21-113).*	11.00	33.00	100.00
S3622C	**500 YÜAN** 1948. Brown. Back green. *Shantung. (S/M #P21-113.3).*	11.00	33.00	100.00

		GOOD	FINE	XF
S3622D	**500 YÜAN** 1948. Blue. Back red. *Shantung. (S/M #P21-113.6).*	11.00	33.00	100.00
S3622E	**500 YÜAN** 1948. Brown. Factory. Back brown. *(S/M #P21-114).*	11.00	33.00	100.00
S3623	**500 YÜAN** 1948. Bugler along Great Wall at r. *Shantung. (S/M #P21-).*	11.00	33.00	100.00

		GOOD	FINE	XF
S3623A	**1000 YÜAN** 1948. Blue and green. Monument by modern city buildings at r. Back olive-green; steam passenger train at ctr. *Shantung. (S/M #P21-120).*	16.00	50.00	120.00
S3623B	**1000 YÜAN** 1948. Violet on m/c unpt. Portr. Mao Tse-tung. *(S/M #P21-).*	16.00	50.00	120.00
S3623C	**1000 YÜAN** 1948. Green and m/c. Farmer and worker. *(S/M #P21-).*	10.00	30.00	90.00
S3623D	**1000 YÜAN** 1948. Red and black. Pagoda at r. *Shantung. (S/M #P21-).*	10.00	30.00	90.00
S3623E	**1000 YÜAN** 1948. Black and green. Like #S3623H. *Shantung. (S/M #P21-).*	10.00	30.00	90.00

#S3623G-S3623J steam train at mine at l.

		GOOD	FINE	XF
S3623G	**1000 YÜAN** 1948. Brown and yellow. Back brown. *(S/M #P21-115).*	16.00	50.00	120.00
S3623H	**1000 YÜAN** 1948. Green on m/c unpt. *(S/M #P21-).*	16.00	50.00	120.00
S3623I	**1000 YÜAN** 1948. Black on m/c unpt. *(S/M #P21-).*	16.00	50.00	120.00
S3623J	**1000 YÜAN** 1948. Red on m/c unpt. *(S/M #P21-).*	16.00	50.00	120.00

		GOOD	FINE	XF
S3623K	**2000 YÜAN** 1948. Brown. Summer palace at r. Back red. *Shantung. (S/M #P21-121).*	16.00	50.00	120.00

		GOOD	FINE	XF
S3623L	**2000 YÜAN** 1948. Blue-black on yellow unpt. Army bugler along Great Wall at l. Back gray. *(S/M #P21-122).*	6.50	20.00	60.00
S3623M	**2000 YÜAN** 1948. Green. Factory. Back brown. *(S/M #P21-123).*	10.00	30.00	90.00

		GOOD	FINE	XF
S3623N	**2000 YÜAN** 1948. Blue. Ship at dockside at l. Back violet; junks at ctr. *(S/M #P21-124).*	16.00	50.00	120.00

P'ING CHIANG WORKERS AND FARMERS BANK

平江縣工農銀行

P'ing Chiang Hsien Kung Nung Yin Hang

1931 ISSUE

		GOOD	FINE	XF
S3624	**1 CHIAO** 1931. Blue. *(S/M #P47-1).*	—	—	—
S3625	**2 CHIAO** 1931. Green. *(S/M #P47-2).*	—	—	—

MAOJGUNGS LIUTUNGKYAN

陝甘寧邊區/貿易公司

Shan Kan Ning Pien Ch'ü / Mao I Kung Szu

1944 ISSUE

#S3630-S3632 vertical format.

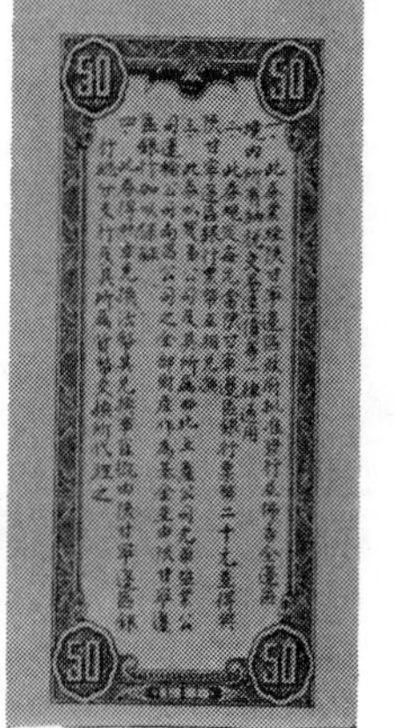

		GOOD	FINE	XF
S3630	**50 YÜAN** 1944. Blue and green. Back black. *(S/M #S31-1).*	11.00	33.00	100.00
S3631	**100 YÜAN** 1944. Violet and green. Back blue. *(S/M #S31-2).*	11.00	33.00	100.00
S3632	**200 YÜAN** 1944. Blue. Back blue. *(S/M #S31-3).*	11.00	33.00	100.00

1945 ISSUE

#S3635-S3640A vertical format.

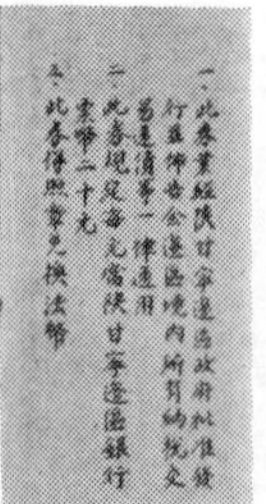

		GOOD	FINE	XF
S3635	**5 YÜAN** 1945. Green. Back black. *(S/M #S31-10).*	11.00	33.00	100.00
S3636	**10 YÜAN** 1945. Red. Back black. *(S/M #S31-11).*	11.00	33.00	100.00
S3637	**20 YÜAN** 1945. Black. Back black. *(S/M #S31-12).*	11.00	33.00	100.00
S3638	**50 YÜAN** 1945. Brown. Back brown. *(S/M #S31-13).*	13.00	40.00	120.00
S3639	**100 YÜAN** 1945. *(S/M #S31-14).*	Reported Not Confirmed		
S3640	**250 YÜAN** 1945. Brown on lt. green unpt. Back brown. *(S/M #S31-15).*	13.00	40.00	120.00

		GOOD	FINE	XF
S3640A	**500 YÜAN** 1945. Orange. Great Wall at upper ctr. *(S/M #S31-17).*	—	—	—

1946 Issues

#S3641-S3644 vertical format.

		Good	Fine	XF
S3641	**500 Yüan** 1946. Red. Back blue. *(S/M #S31-20).*	13.00	40.00	120.00

		Good	Fine	XF
S3642	**1000 Yüan** 1946. Blue. Back blue. *(S/M #S31-21).*	13.00	40.00	120.00

		Good	Fine	XF
S3643	**1000 Yüan** 1946. Lt. green. Factory at upper ctr.			
	a. Back grayish tan. *(S/M #S31-21.5a).*	13.00	40.00	120.00
	b. Back pale violet. *(S/M #S31-21.5b).*	13.00	40.00	120.00
S3644	**5000 Yüan** 1946. Orange. Back blue. *(S/M #S31-22).*	13.00	40.00	120.00

1947 Issues

#S3645-S3648 vertical format.

		Good	Fine	XF
S3645	**2000 Yüan** 1947. Black. Back blue. *(S/M #S31-30).*	13.00	40.00	120.00
S3646	**5000 Yüan** 1947. Violet. Gateway. Back blue. *(S/M #S31-31).*	13.00	40.00	120.00

		Good	Fine	XF
S3647	**5000 Yüan** 1947. Red. Like #S3646. Back blue. *(S/M #S31-32).*	13.00	40.00	120.00
S3648	**5000 Yüan** 1947. Brown. Like #S3646. Back blue. *(S/M #S31-33).*	13.00	40.00	120.00

Shaan Gan Ning Bianky Inxan(g)
Shensi-Kansu-Ninghsia Border Area Bank

陝甘寧邊區銀行

Shan Kan Ning Pien Ch'ü Yin Hang

1941 Issue

		Good	Fine	XF
S3651	**1 Chiao = 10 Cents** 1941. Brown. Rural scene w/pagoda on hill in distance. Back blue. Pink or buff paper. *(S/M #S32-1).*	10.00	30.00	90.00

		Good	Fine	XF
S3652	**2 Chiao = 20 Cents** 1941. Dk. blue. Sheep at ctr. Back brown. Pink or buff paper. *(S/M #S32-2).*	10.00	30.00	90.00

		Good	Fine	XF
S3655	**5 Yüan** 1941. Blue and yellow. City gate at ctr. r. Back violet. *(S/M #S32-11).*	10.00	40.00	120.00
S3656	**5 Yüan** 1941. Blue and violet. Rural scene. Back blue. *(S/M #S32-11.5).*	10.00	40.00	120.00

		Good	Fine	XF
S3656A	**10 Yüan** 1941. Blue-gray. Rural scene at ctr. *(S/M #S32-12).*	10.00	40.00	120.00

S3657 10 YÜAN

	GOOD	FINE	XF
1941. Violet. Government bldg at ctr. Back black and blue. *(S/M #S32-13).*	10.00	40.00	120.00

1942 ISSUE

S3658 50 YÜAN

	GOOD	FINE	XF
1942. Black. Like #S3657. Back violet. *(S/M #S32-20).*	10.00	40.00	120.00

S3659 100 YÜAN

	GOOD	FINE	XF
1942. Brown. Assembly hall. Back brown-violet; pagoda on hillside at ctr. *(S/M #S32-21).*			
a. Issued note.	10.00	40.00	120.00
b. Punched hole cancelled.	—	—	60.00

S3660 100 YÜAN

	GOOD	FINE	XF
1942. Like #S3657. *(S/M #S32-).*	10.00	40.00	120.00

1943 ISSUE

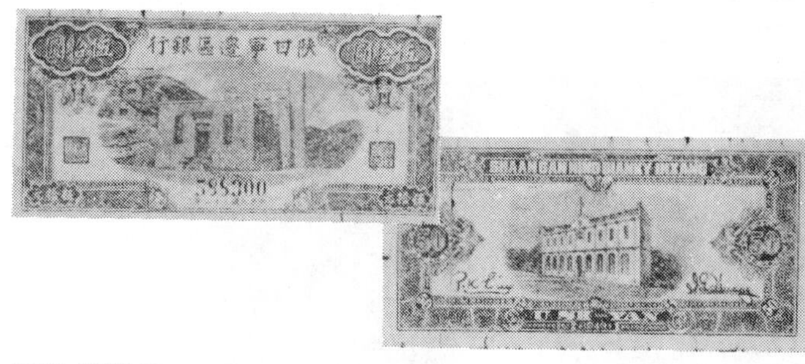

S3662 50 YÜAN

	GOOD	FINE	XF
1943. Blue-gray. Bldg. at ctr. Back brown-violet; bldg. at ctr. *(S/M #S32-).*	10.00	40.00	120.00

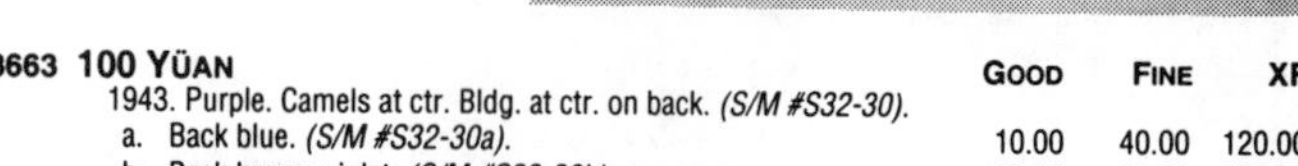

S3663 100 YÜAN

	GOOD	FINE	XF
1943. Purple. Camels at ctr. Bldg. at ctr. on back. *(S/M #S32-30).*			
a. Back blue. *(S/M #S32-30a).*	10.00	40.00	120.00
b. Back brown-violet. *(S/M #S32-30b).*	10.00	40.00	120.00

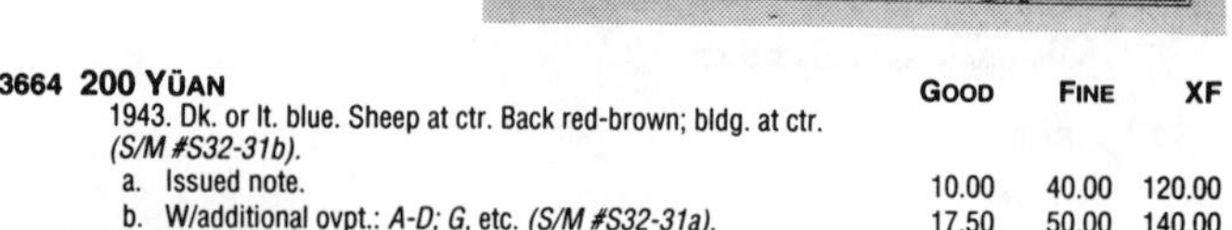

S3664 200 YÜAN

	GOOD	FINE	XF
1943. Dk. or lt. blue. Sheep at ctr. Back red-brown; bldg. at ctr. *(S/M #S32-31b).*			
a. Issued note.	10.00	40.00	120.00
b. W/additional ovpt.: *A-D; G*, etc. *(S/M #S32-31a).*	17.50	50.00	140.00

#S3665-S3667 Yenan Headquarters at ctr.

S3665 500 YÜAN

	GOOD	FINE	XF
1943. Red. *(S/M #S32-32b).*			
a. Additional letter ovpt.: *A; B; C* etc. *(S/M #S32-32a.).*	17.50	50.00	140.00

		GOOD	FINE	XF
S3666	**1000 YÜAN** 1943. Blue. Hillside pagoda at r. on back. *(S/M #S32-33).*			
	a. Lg. serial #.	20.00	60.00	—
	b. Sm. serial # w/prefix letters.	20.00	60.00	—
S3667	**5000 YÜAN** 1943. *(S/M #S32-34).*	25.00	75.00	—

1945 ISSUE

		GOOD	FINE	XF
S3668	**10 YÜAN** 1945. Great Wall at ctr. Remainder. *(S/M #S32-41).*	—	50.00	150.00

1946 ISSUE

		GOOD	FINE	XF
S3669	**10,000 YÜAN** 1946. Camels at ctr. on back. Specimen. *(S/M #S32-51).*	—	Unc	300.00
S3670	**50,000 YÜAN** 1946. Specimen. *(S/M #S32-55).*	—	Unc	400.00

BANK OF SHANGTONG

行銀黨上

Shang Tang Yin Hao

Later became part of the Chinan Bank.

1938 ISSUE

		GOOD	FINE	XF
S3671	**1 CHIAO = 10 CENTS** 1938. Purple on lt. green unpt. Rural railway station at l. Back purple; rural bldg. by bridge at ctr. *(S/M #S56.5-1).*	20.00	60.00	—

		GOOD	FINE	XF
S3672	**2 CHIAO = 20 CENTS** 1938. Rural scene at l. Bridge at ctr. on back. *(S/M #S56.5-2).*	20.00	60.00	—

		GOOD	FINE	XF
S3673	**5 CHIAO = 50 CENTS** 1938. Blue-gray. Bldg. at l. Back purple; ship at ctr. *(S/M #S56.5-3).*	20.00	60.00	—
S3674	**1 DOLLAR** 1938. Temple of Heaven at ctr. Bridge at ctr. on back. *(S/M #S56.5-4).*	20.00	60.00	—

		GOOD	FINE	XF
S3675	**5 DOLLARS** 1938. Red on pink unpt. Rural scene at ctr. Back red; rural bldg, by bridge at ctr. *(S/M #S56-5).*	25.00	75.00	—

SOVIET BANK (HOPEI-HONAN-ANHWEI SOVIET ECONOMIC COMMUNE)

行銀埃維蘇

Su Wei Ai Yin Hang

1932 ISSUE

		GOOD	FINE	XF
S3676	**2 TIAO** 1932. Brown-violet on blue-green unpt. Bldgs. at l. and r. Back blue-green; horseman w/flag at ctr. *(S/M #S84.5-12).*	33.00	100.00	250.00

		GOOD	FINE	XF
S3677	**2 TIAO** 1932. Brown-violet on blue-green unpt. Outline of Lenin at l., municipal bldg. at r. Back similar to #S3676. *(S/M #S84.5-14).*	33.00	100.00	250.00

TA CHIANG BANK / DAGIANG INXAN(G)

行銀江大
Ta Chiang Yin Hang

1942 ISSUE

		GOOD	FINE	XF
S3680	**5 CHIAO** 1942. Scenes at l. and r. *(S/M #T2-5).*	—	—	—

1944 ISSUES

		GOOD	FINE	XF
S3685	**1 CHIAO** 1944. Single arch stone bridge at ctr. People's Army in march on back. *(S/M #T2-11).*	—	—	—

		GOOD	FINE	XF
S3686	**1 CHIAO** 1944. Junks at l., lighthouse at r. People's supply column on back. *(S/M #T2-12).*	—	—	—

		GOOD	FINE	XF
S3687	**5 CHIAO** 1944. Teacher, doctor, soldier, peasant, and factory worker at ctr. Hoe, hammer, rifle, etc. on back. *(S/M #T2-14).*	—	—	—

		GOOD	FINE	XF
S3689	**2 YÜAN** 1944. Teacher, doctor, soldier, peasant and factory worker at l. ctr. Hammer, rifle, cycle, etc. on back.			
	a. Square sign. seals on face. *(S/M #T2-16a).*	—	—	—
	b. Square sign. seals on back. *(S/M #T2-16b).*	—	—	—

		GOOD	FINE	XF
S3690	**5 YÜAN** 1944. Single arch stone bridge at r. Peasant woman harvesting grain w/sickle at r. on back. *(S/M #T2-18).*	—	—	—

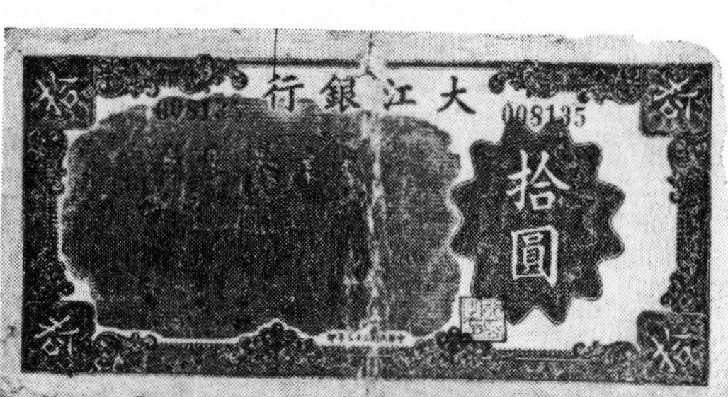

		GOOD	FINE	XF
S3691	**10 YÜAN** 1944. Teacher, doctor, etc. at l. ctr. *(S/M #T2-19).*	—	—	—

1945 ISSUES

		GOOD	FINE	XF
S3693	**5 CHIAO** 1945. Mountain scene at ctr. *S/M #T2-20).*	—	—	—

		GOOD	FINE	XF
S3694	**1 YÜAN** 1945. Single arch stone bridge at ctr. r. *(S/M #T2-21).*	—	—	—

S3695 1 YÜAN | GOOD — | FINE — | XF —
1945. People's Army in march at ctr. Vertical format. *(S/M #T2-22).*

S3696 1 YÜAN | GOOD — | FINE — | XF —
1945. Rural army sentry under tree, mountains in distance at l. *(S/M #T2-23).*

S3697 1 YÜAN | GOOD — | FINE — | XF —
1945. Rural bldgs., mountains in distance at l. *(S/M #T2-24).*

S3698 1 YÜAN | GOOD — | FINE — | XF —
1945. Teacher, doctor, etc. at l. ctr. Hammer, rifle, sickle, etc on back. *(S/M #T2-25).*

S3699 2 YÜAN | GOOD — | FINE — | XF —
1945. 2 peasants at ctr. *(S/M #T2-26).*

S3700 2 YÜAN | GOOD — | FINE — | XF —
1945. Soldiers raising flag in triumph at ctr. Vertical format. *(S/M #T2-27).*

S3701 2 YÜAN | GOOD — | FINE — | XF —
1945. Bldg., single arch bridge over river at l. *(S/M #T228).*

#S3702-S3704 vertical format.

#S3702

#S3703

S3702 2 YÜAN | GOOD — | FINE — | XF —
1945. Peasants harvesting grain at ctr. *(S/M #T2-29).*

S3703 2 YÜAN — — —
1945. People's Army marching from Great Wall at ctr. *(S/M #T2-30).*

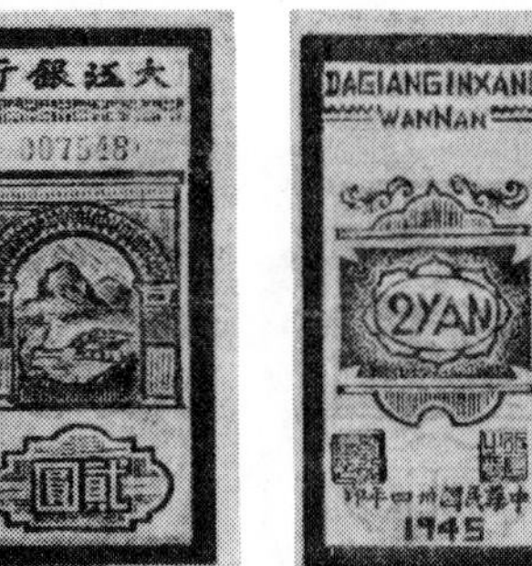

S3704 2 YÜAN | GOOD — | FINE — | XF —
1945. Rural bldg., mountains in background at ctr. *(S/M #T2-31).*

S3705 5 YÜAN | GOOD — | FINE — | XF —
1945. Lighthouse, junks at l. ctr. *(S/M #T2-41).*

S3706 5 YÜAN
1945. Rural scene, trees, mountains in background at ctr. r. *(S/M #T2-42).*

GOOD	FINE	XF
—	—	—

S3707 5 YÜAN
1945. Rural bldgs., peasant at ctr. r. *(S/M #T2-43).*

GOOD	FINE	XF
—	—	—

S3708 10 YÜAN
1945. Single arch stone bridge at ctr. r. *(S/M #T2-46).*

GOOD	FINE	XF
—	—	—

S3709 10 YÜAN
1945. Peasants plowing w/oxen at ctr. *(S/M #T2-47).*

GOOD	FINE	XF
—	—	—

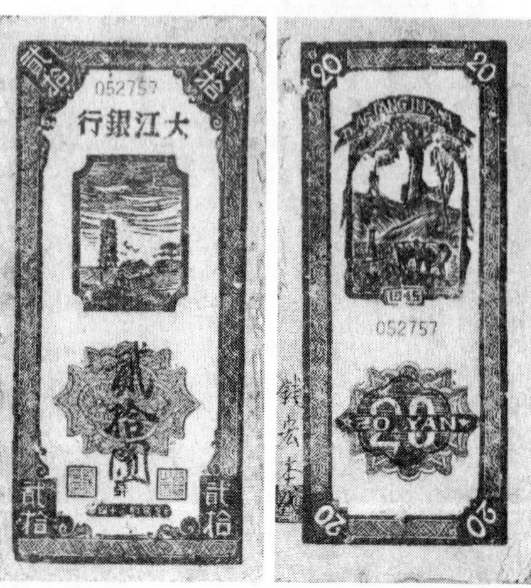

S3710 20 YÜAN
1945. Pagoda at ctr. Planting rice at ctr. on back. Vertical format. *(S/M #T2-450).*

GOOD	FINE	XF
—	—	—

EASTERN MONGOLIAN BANK

東蒙銀行
Tung Mung Yin Hang

1946 ISSUE

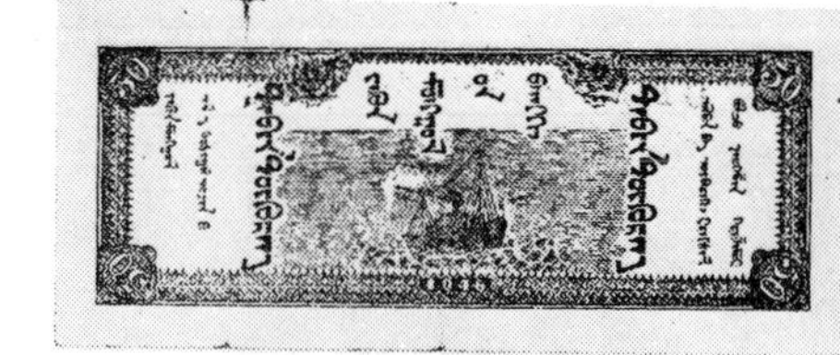

S3715 50 YÜAN
1946. Red on green unpt. Lakeside village at l. Back green; ship at ctr. *(S/M #T212.5-9).*

GOOD	FINE	XF
25.00	75.00	—

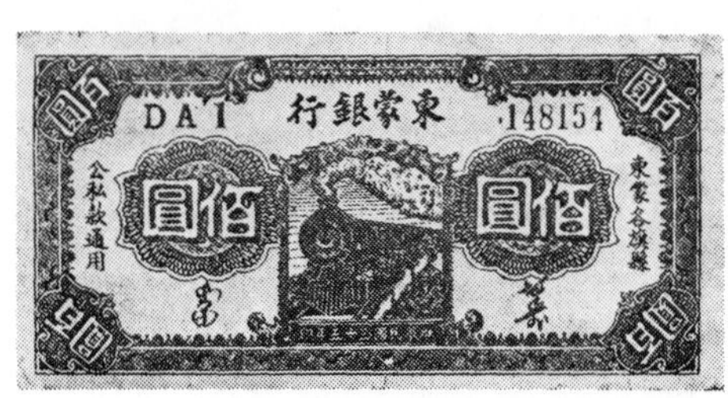

S3716 100 YÜAN
1946. Blue and yellow. Steam passenger train at ctr. Back red; modern municipal bldg. at ctr. *(S/M #T212.5-11).*

GOOD	FINE	XF
25.00	75.00	—

S3717 100 YÜAN
1946. Brown-violet. Gateway at ctr. Back green; monument at ctr. *(S/M #T212.5-14).*

GOOD	FINE	XF
25.00	75.00	—

KWANGSI-KWEICHOW-YUNNAN BORDER DISTRICT
DIAN-KIAN-GUI BIANKY

局易貿區邊桂黔滇

T'ien Ch'ien Kuei Pien Ch'ü Mao I Chü

1949 CIRCULATING NOTES (*LIU T'UNG CH'ÜAN*) ISSUE

S3719 1 YÜAN

	GOOD	FINE	XF
1949. Orange-brown. Mao Tse-tung at l., row of men at r. Back black; peasants and oxen at l. ctr. *(S/M #T125.5-11).*	30.00	90.00	200.00

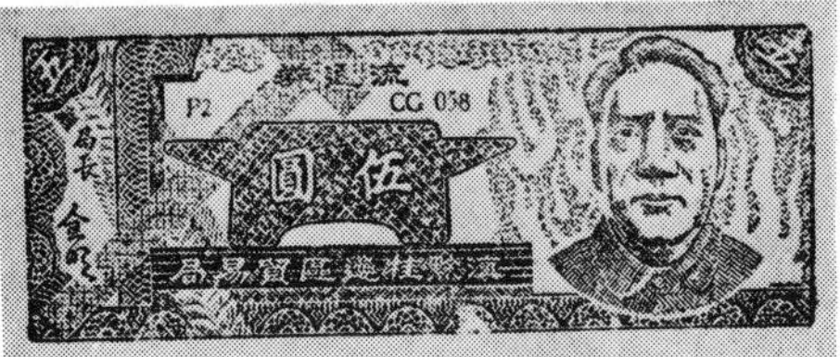

S3720 5 YÜAN

	GOOD	FINE	XF
ND (1949). Mao Tse-tung at r. Harvesting grain at ctr. r. on back. *(S/M #T125.5-12).*	30.00	90.00	200.00

NOTE: Similar wmkd. paper was used for some North Vietnamese issues.

BANK OF DUNG BAI
BANK OF DUNG PAI
TUNG PEI BANK OF CHINA

行銀北東

Tung Pei Yin Hang

1945 ISSUES

S3725 1 YÜAN

	GOOD	FINE	XF
1945. Red. Summer palace at l., Temple of Heaven at r. Back green. *(S/M #T213-1).*	5.00	15.00	45.00

S3726 5 YÜAN

	GOOD	FINE	XF
1945. Red. Farmer. Back green; village. *(S/M #T213-2).*	5.00	15.00	45.00

S3727 5 YÜAN

	GOOD	FINE	XF
1945. Red. Sawing logs at l. Small seascape at ctr. on back. *Liaotung. (S/M #T213-3).*			
a. *Liaotung* at upper ctr., control letter and # at l. and r., serial # at upper l. and r. Back black.	5.00	15.00	45.00
b. *Liaotung* at l. and r., control letter and # at upper l. and r. Back yellow-orange.	5.00	15.00	45.00

S3728 5 YÜAN

	GOOD	FINE	XF
1945. Red on lt. blue-green unpt. Horse and irrigation system. Back dk. olive-green; bldgs at ctr. *(S/M #T213-).*			
a. W/black serial # at upper r.	5.00	15.00	45.00
b. W/red block # at upper r.	5.00	15.00	45.00

S3729 10 YÜAN

	GOOD	FINE	XF
1945. Brown on pink unpt. Back red. *Liaotung. (S/M #T213-4).*			
a. Black. *Liaotung* at l. and r., serial # at upper l. and r., control letter and # at l. and r.	2.00	6.00	18.00
b. Red. *Liaotung* at l. and r., control letter at upper l., block # at upper r.	4.00	12.00	35.00

S3729A 10 YÜAN

	GOOD	FINE	XF
1945. Violet. Like #S3729. *Liaotung. (S/M #T213-).*	4.00	12.00	35.00

S3730 10 YÜAN

	GOOD	FINE	XF
1945. Blue. Plowing. Back violet; house at ctr. *(S/M #T213-5).*	5.00	15.00	45.00

		Good	Fine	XF
S3731	**50 Yüan** 1945. Red. Back red-brown; modern steamship at ctr. Blue serial # and block letters. *Liaotung. (S/M #T213-10).*	5.00	15.00	45.00
S3732	**50 Yüan** 1945. Red-brown. Like #S3671. Back red. Red block letters and serial #. *Liaotung. (S/M #T213-11).*	5.00	15.00	45.00
S3733	**100 Yüan** 1945. Yellow. Kitchen. Back red; flags. *(S/M #T213-12).*	7.00	20.00	60.00

		Good	Fine	XF
S3734	**100 Yüan** 1945. Dk. blue on red unpt. Gov't. bldg. at l. Back red. *(S/M #T213-14).*	7.00	20.00	60.00

1946 Issues

		Good	Fine	XF
S3735	**5 Chiao = 50 Cents** 1946. Pale olive-green. Boat dockside at r. Back pale blue. *(S/M #T213-16).*	7.00	20.00	60.00

		Good	Fine	XF
S3736	**1 Yüan** 1946. Red. Farmer plowing w/ox at r. Back orange. *Liaotung. (S/M #T213-18).*	3.00	9.00	25.00
S3737	**5 Yüan** 1946. Green. Ship. Back green. *Liaotung. (S/M #T213-20).*	5.00	15.00	45.00
S3738	**5 Yüan** 1946. Red. Plowing. Back green; village. *(S/M #T213-21).*	5.00	15.00	45.00

		Good	Fine	XF
S3739	**10 Yüan** 1946. Brown on lt. green unpt. Peasant operating irrigation system at r. Back grayish purple; Temple of Heaven at ctr. *(S/M #T213-21.3).*	7.00	20.00	60.00
S3739A	**10 Yüan** 1946. Brown. Face like #S3739. Back pale olive-green; lg. value *10* at ctr. *(S/M #T213-21.4).*	7.00	20.00	60.00

		Good	Fine	XF
S3740	**10 Yüan** 1946. Black on green unpt. Municipal bldg. at r. (w/national flag!). Back red-violet; Temple of Heaven at ctr. *Liaohsi. (S/M #T213-21.5).*	8.00	25.00	75.00
S3741	**50 Yüan** 1946. *(S/M #T213-21.7).*	8.00	25.00	75.00
S3742	**100 Yüan** 1946. Brown. Bldg. Back green. *Liaoshi. (S/M #T213-22).*	8.00	25.00	75.00

		Good	Fine	XF
S3743	**100 Yüan** 1946. Blue-gray on gray unpt. Steam passenger train at r. Back purple; municipal bldg. at ctr. *Liaohsi. (S/M #T213-24).*	8.00	25.00	75.00

		GOOD	FINE	XF
S3744	**100 YÜAN** 1946. Red-violet and black. Gazebo and boat at l. Back red. *Liaoshi. (S/M #T213-27).*	8.00	25.00	75.00

1947 ISSUE

		GOOD	FINE	XF
S3745	**10 YÜAN** 1947. Planting rice at r. Back violet.			
	a. Green unpt. *(S/M #T213-30).*	8.00	25.00	75.00
	b. Gray unpt.	8.00	25.00	75.00

		GOOD	FINE	XF
S3746	**50 YÜAN** 1947. Violet on lt. blue-green unpt. Soldier and peasant at l. ctr. Back red-violet. *S/M #T213-31).*	4.00	12.00	35.00
S3747	**100 YÜAN** 1947. Red on yellow unpt. w/blue serial #. Cultivating w/horses. Back brown. *(S/M #T213-32).*	8.00	25.00	75.00

		GOOD	FINE	XF
S3748	**100 YÜAN** 1947. Red on brown-orange unpt. Black serial #. Like #S3747 but back green. *(S/M #T213-33).*	5.00	15.00	45.00
S3749	**100 YÜAN** 1947. Red w/red serial #. Like #S3748 but back red. *(S/M #T213-34).*	5.00	15.00	45.00
S3750	**100 YÜAN** 1947. Red and yellow. Back brown. *(S/M #T213-40).*	5.00	15.00	45.00

		GOOD	FINE	XF
S3751	**200 YÜAN** 1947. Red and black on gray unpt. Steam passenger train at r. Back dk. blue; Temple of Heaven at ctr *Liaoshi. (S/M #T213-40.5).*	8.00	25.00	75.00

		GOOD	FINE	XF
S3752	**500 YÜAN** 1947. Blue on red unpt. Portr. Mao Tse-tung at r. Back red; bldg. at ctr. *(S/M #T213-41)*	8.00	25.00	75.00
S3753	**500 YÜAN** 1947. Red. Portr. Mao Tse-tung at l. Back violet. *(S/M #T213-42).*	8.00	25.00	75.00

		GOOD	FINE	XF
S3754	**500 YÜAN** 1947. Blue on lt. orange unpt. Portr. Mao Tse-tung at ctr. Back red; bldg. at ctr. *(S/M #T213-43).*	8.00	25.00	75.00

1948 ISSUES

		GOOD	FINE	XF
S3755	**250 YÜAN** 1948. Violet on red unpt. Soldier and farmer at l. ctr. Back red; bank bldg. at ctr. *(S/M #T213-50).*	7.00	20.00	60.00
S3756	**500 YÜAN** 1948. Green. Farmers and workers. Back red. *(S/M #T213-51).*	8.00	25.00	75.00
S3757	**1000 YÜAN** 1948. Brown on yellow-green unpt. Like #S3758. Back violet. *(S/M #T213-52).*	8.00	25.00	75.00

		GOOD	FINE	XF
S3758	**1000 YÜAN** 1948. Brown on ochre unpt. Farmer and worker at r. Back brown-violet; bank bldg. at ctr. *(S/M #T213-52.5).*	7.00	20.00	60.00

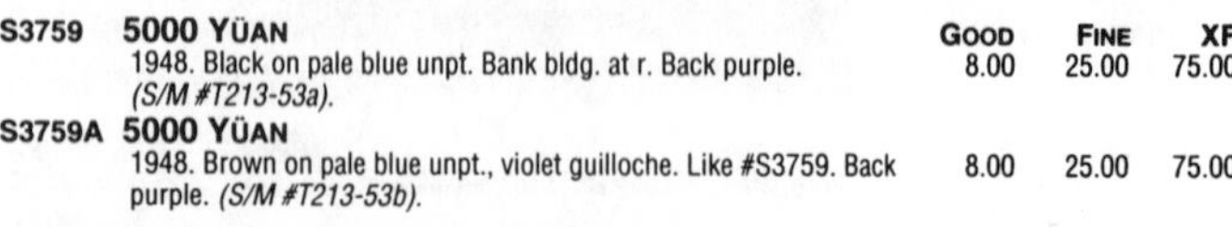

		GOOD	FINE	XF
S3759	**5000 YÜAN** 1948. Black on pale blue unpt. Bank bldg. at r. Back purple. *(S/M #T213-53a).*	8.00	25.00	75.00
S3759A	**5000 YÜAN** 1948. Brown on pale blue unpt., violet guilloche. Like #S3759. Back purple. *(S/M #T213-53b).*	8.00	25.00	75.00

		GOOD	FINE	XF
S3760	**10,000 YÜAN** 1948. Black and blue. Temple courtyard. Back violet; bank bldg. at ctr. *(S/M #T213-54).*	10.00	30.00	90.00

		GOOD	FINE	XF
S3761	**10,000 YÜAN** 1948. Blue-gray on brown-violet unpt. Like #S3760. *(S/M #T213-55).*	10.00	30.00	90.00
S3762	**10,000 YÜAN** 1948. Tower. *(S/M #T213-56).*	15.00	45.00	—

		GOOD	FINE	XF
S3763	**50,000 YÜAN** 1948. Gray-green on lt. blue unpt. Steam passenger train at l., ship at r. Back brown; bank bldg. at ctr. *(S/M #T213-57).*	15.00	45.00	—

1949 ISSUE

		GOOD	FINE	XF
S3764	**10,000 YÜAN** 1949. *(S/M #T213-58).*	Reported Not Confirmed		

		GOOD	FINE	XF
S3765	**100,000 YÜAN** 1949. Brown-violet, black and gray. Plowing w/horses at l., shoveling ore at r. Fortress gate at ctr on back. *(S/M #T213-59).*	25.00	75.00	—

1950 ISSUE

		VG	VF	UNC
S3766	**500 YÜAN** 1950. Dk. blue on lt. blue unpt. Cultivating w/tractor at r. Back blue-violet; bldg. at ctr. *(S/M #T213-60).*	5.00	15.00	45.00

1948 CIRCULATING CASHIER'S CHECKS ISSUE

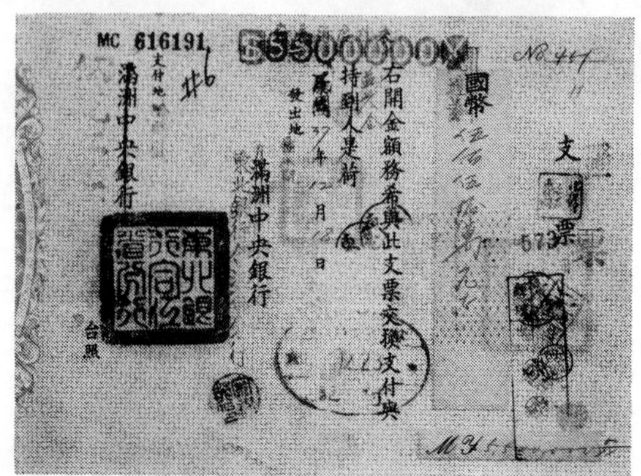

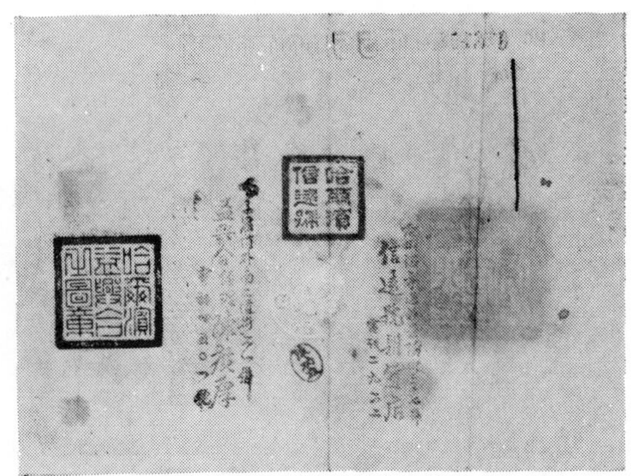

S3770 VARIOUS AMOUNTS

Dec. 1948. Black text and lg. red seal hand stamp on ochre unpt. Ovpt. in blue on Central Bank of Manchukuo cashier's check. *(S/M #T213-)*.

	GOOD	FINE	XF
a. 5,500,000 Dollars (18.12.1948).	15.00	45.00	110.00
b. 100,000,000 Dollars (28.12.1948).	15.00	45.00	110.00

GUANGXUA SHANGDIAN

延安光華商店

Yen An Kuang Hua Shang Tien

光華商店

Kuang Hua Shang Tien

1938 ISSUE

		GOOD	FINE	XF
S3775	**2 FEN = 2 CENTS** 1938. Dk. blue on red-orange unpt. Back black. *(S/M #Y3-1)*.	15.00	45.00	110.00
S3776	**5 FEN = 5 CENTS** 1938. Like #S3775. *(S/M #Y3-2)*.	15.00	45.00	110.00
S3777	**1 CHIAO = 10 CENTS** 1938. *(S/M #Y3-4)*.	15.00	45.00	110.00
S3778	**2 CHIAO = 20 CENTS** 1938. Rural village w/mountains in background. *(S/M #Y3-6)*.	15.00	45.00	110.00
S3779	**5 CHIAO = 50 CENTS** 1938. Black on lt. blue unpt. Gazebo at lower r. *(S/M #Y3-8)*.	15.00	45.00	110.00

1940 ISSUE

		GOOD	FINE	XF
S3780	**5 CHIAO = 50 CENTS** 1940. Red. Woman seated at l., sheep at r. Back dk. blue. *(S/M #Y3-10)*.	17.00	50.00	120.00

		GOOD	FINE	XF
S3781	**7 CHIAO 5 FEN = 75 CENTS** 1940. Brown. Rural scene at l. w/pagoda on hill in distance. Back blue. *(S/M #Y3-11)*.	20.00	60.00	140.00

MILITARY, 1912-30

The first military issues were soon released in the first year of the developing Republic as various parts of China were finally put under the control of the new Sun Yat-sen government. It wasn't very long after Yuan-Shi-K'ai became president that his plans to become emperor of China became obvious and that divided China's forces once again.

Throughout the following years military forces under war lords severely taxed the unresting populace in the areas under their control.

These military issues were soon followed by the many communist issues which were first released in the early 1930's and ceased in 1950 when the Chinese mainland became the Peoples Republic.

Certain military issues are also to be found listed under the Provincial section and once determined as strictly military in nature they will be moved to this section.

These listings are not virtually complete as new finds of this material are occasionally encountered.

For further information refer to *A Brief Illustrated History of Chinese Military Notes and Bonds* by S. P. Ting, Taipei, Taiwan (1981).

軍用鈔票 — Chün Yung Ch'ao P'iao

軍用手票 — Chün Yung Shou P'iao

NOTE: These phrases appear as overprints or in clauses used in principal heading on a number of notes. In most instances they are written horizontally but in some occasions they occur in two vertically written pairs.

Chen Wei, 3rd and 4th Army Corps
Treasury Notes (trans)
#S3791-S3796

鎮威軍第三四方面軍團兵站庫券

Chen Wei Chün Ti San Szu Fang Mien Chün T'uan Ping Chan K'u Ch'üan

Chihli Provincial Military
#S3803-S3807

直隸省軍用流通券

Chih Li Sheng Chün Yung Lin T'ung Ch'üan

Chihli-Shantung Military
#S3809-S3813

直魯省軍用券

Chih Lu Sheng Chün Yung Ch'üan

Republican Fukien Government Bank
#S3813A-S3813E

中華福建銀行

Chung Hua Fu Chien Yin Hang

Chinese National Pacification Army Notes
#S3814-S3816

中華民國靖國軍軍用鈔票

Chung Hua Min Kuo Ching Kuo Chün Chün Yung Ch'ao Piao

Republican China Military - Shanghai
#S3818-S3820

中華民國/軍用鈔票

Chung Hua Min Kuo / Chün Yung Ch'ao P'iao

Republican China Military - Nanking
#S3822

中華民國/南京軍用鈔票

Chung Hua Min Kuo / Nan Ching Chün Yung Ch'ao P'iao

Chinese Republic Army, Navy and Air Force Headquarters
#S3824-S3826

中華民國陸海空軍總司令部

Chung Hua Min Kuo Lu Hai K'ung Chün Tsung Szu Ling Pu

Chinese Republic Army, Navy and Air Force Sub-headquarters
#S3828-S3834

中華民國陸海空軍副總司令部

Chung Hua Min Kuo Lu Hai K'ung Chün Fu Tsung Szu Lin Pu

Kwangtung Republican Military Government
#S3836-S3839

中華民國粤省軍政府

Chung Hua Min Kuo Yüeh Sheng Chün Cheng Fu

Chinese Republican Military Bank-Anhwei
#S3841-S3842

中華銀行安徽

Chung Hua Yin Hang An Hui

Honan Province Treasury
#S3855

河南省金庫通券

Ho Nan Sheng Chin K'u T'ung Ch'üan

Honan Province
#S3857-S3859

河南省印

Ho Nan Sheng Yin

Bank of the Northwest
#S3861-S3889

西北銀行

Hsi Pei Yin Hang

Hunan Provincial Treasury
#S3892-S3896
券庫金省南湖
Hu Nan Sheng Chin K'u Ch'üan

Kiangse Bank of the Republic
#S3897-S3900B
行銀國民省贛
Kan (Sen) Sheng Min Kuo Yin Hang

Kansu (Military)
#3900D
號銀官肅甘
Kan Su Kuan Yin Hao

Kwangsi Military
#S3900F
票手用軍西廣
Kuang Hsi Chün Yung Shou P'iao

Kwangsi, Military (Provisional)
#S3900j-S3900M
票用軍時臨西廣
Kuang Ksi Lin Shih Chü Yung Piao

Kwangtung Provincial Treasury
#S3901-S3903
券庫金省東廣
Kuang Tung Sheng Chin K'u Ch'üan

Kweilin Regional Bank
#S3904 and S3906
行銀方地林桂
Kuei Lin Ti Fang Yin Hang

National Army (Circulating Notes)
#S3907-S3916
券通流融金軍民國
Kuo Min Chün Chin Jung Liu Tung Ch'üan

National Army Combined Headquarters
#S3818-S3920
票用軍部令司總軍聯軍民國
Kuo Min Chün Lien Chün Tsung Szu Ling Pu Chün Yung P'iao

National Revolutionary Army
#S3923-S3927
券需軍部令司總軍命革民國
Kuo Min Ke Ming Chün Tsung Szu Ling Pu Chün Hsü Ch'üan

Agricultural, Industrial and Commercial Trust Co., Ltd.
#S3928-S3930A
司公限有託信商工農
Nung Kung Shang Hsin Tok Yu Hsien Kung Szu

Provincial Army of Shantung
#S3931-S3941
票用軍省東山
Shan Tung Sheng Chün Yung P'iao

Local Bank of Szechuan (Szechuan Regional Bank)
#S3943-S3947
行銀方地川四
Szu Ch'uan Ti Fang Yin Hang

Ta Han Szechuan Military Government
#S3948
票銀用軍府政軍川四漢大
Ta Han Szu Ch'üan Chün Cheng Fu Chün Yung Yin P'iao

Yunnan-Kwangtung-Kwangsi United Army for Kiangsi Relief
#S3951-S3953
票用軍軍聯贛援桂粵滇
T'ien Yüeh Kuei Yüan Kan Lien Chün Chün Yung P'iao

Property Control Office Third and Fourth Route Army Headquarters
#S3955
處理管產財
Ts'ai Ch'an Kuan Li Ch'ü

Yunnan National Pacification Army
#S3958-S3960
券換兌行銀用軍軍國靖南雲
Yün Nan Ching Kuo Chün Chün Yung Yin Hang Tui Huan Ch'üan

Chen Wei, 3rd and 4th Army Corps Treasury Notes

券庫站兵團軍 面方 四三第 軍 威鎮
Chen Wei Chün Ti San Szu Fang Mien Chün T'uan Ping Chan K'u Ch'üan

1927 Issue

#S3791-S3793 rural scene at ctr. on back. Printer: BEPP.

		Good	Fine	XF
S3791	1927. Brown on m/c unpt. Houseboat in river at ctr. *(S/M #C42-0.3).*	50.00	125.00	—
S3792	1927. Olive-green on m/c unpt. Rural house at ctr. *(S/M #C42-0.6).*	100.00	250.00	—

		Good	Fine	XF
S3793	**5 Chiao = 50 Cents** 1927. Olive-green on m/c unpt. Pagoda at ctr. *(S/M #C42-1).*	300.00	500.00	—

		Good	Fine	XF
S3794	**1 Yüan** 1.5.1927. Blue on m/c unpt. Ship, boats at ctr. *(S/M #C42-10).*	—	—	—
S3795	**5 Yüan** 1.5.1927. Red-brown on m/c unpt. Proof. *(S/M #C42-11).*	—	—	—
S3796	**10 Yüan** 1.5.1927. Deep orange on m/c unpt. Proof. *(S/M #C42-12).*	—	—	—

Chihli Provincial Military

券通流用軍省隸直
Chih Li Sheng Chün Yung Liu T'ung Ch'üan

1920's ND Provisional Issue

#S3803-S3807 w/rectangular Chinese eight character ovpt. of new issuer's name at ctr. on Provincial Bank of Chihli.

		Good	Fine	XF
S3803	**1 Chiao = 10 Cents** ND (- old date 1926). Violet on brown and gray-green unpt. Ovpt. on #S1285. *(S/M #C161-1).*	10.00	25.00	75.00
S3804	**2 Chiao = 20 Cents** ND (- old date 1926). Blue-green on brown and violet unpt. Ovpt. on #S1286. *(S/M #C161-2).*	12.50	27.50	85.00
S3805	**1 Yüan** ND (- old date 1926). Violet on m/c unpt. Ovpt. on #S1288. *(S/M #C161-10).*	15.00	35.00	100.00

		GOOD	FINE	XF
S3806	**5 YÜAN** ND (- old date 1926). Blue-gray on m/c unpt. Ovpt. on #S1289a. *(S/M #C161-11).*	17.50	40.00	125.00
S3807	**10 YÜAN** ND (- old date 1926). Red on m/c unpt. Ovpt. on #S1290. *(S/M #C161-12).*	20.00	50.00	150.00

CHIHLI-SHANTUNG MILITARY

直魯省軍用券

Chih Lu Sheng Chün Yung Ch'üan

1920's ND PROVISIONAL ISSUE

#S3809-S3812A w/vertical Chinese six character ovpt. of new issuer's name on Market Stabilization Currency Bureau, Vol. 2.

		GOOD	FINE	XF
S3809	**1 CHIAO = 10 CENTS** ND (- old date 1.6.1923). Blue. Ovpt. on #616. *(S/M #C164-1).*	10.00	25.00	80.00
S3810	**2 CHIAO = 20 CENTS** ND (- old date 1.6.1923). Purple. Ovpt. on #617. *(S/M #C164-2).*	12.50	27.50	90.00

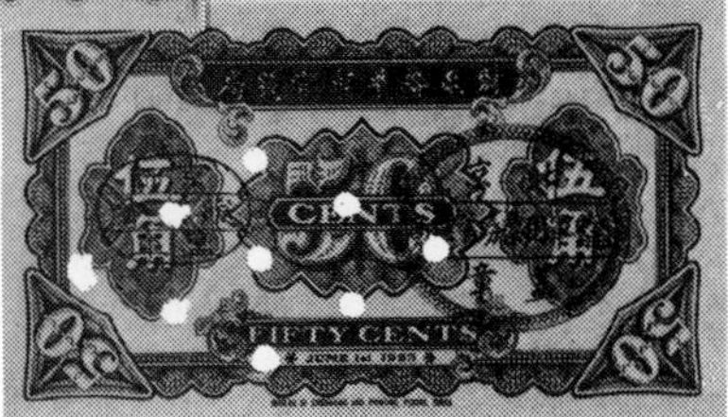

		GOOD	FINE	XF
S3811	**5 CHIAO = 50 CENTS** ND (- old date 1.6.1923). Green. Ovpt. on #618. *(S/M #C164-3).*			
	a. Issued note.	12.00	30.00	100.00
	b. Punched hole cancelled.	—	—	75.00

		GOOD	FINE	XF
S3812	**1 YÜAN** ND (- old date 15.8.1925). Green on m/c unpt. Ovpt. on #S2751b. *(S/M #C164-4).*	15.00	35.00	120.00
S3812A	**5 YÜAN** ND (- old date 15.8.1925). Blue on m/c unpt. Ovpt. on #S2752a. *(S/M #C164-5).*	25.00	50.00	165.00

REPUBLICAN FUKIEN GOVERNMENT BANK

中華福建銀行

Chung Hua Fu Chien Yin Hang

Issued for circulation in Fukien and Taiwan.

1912 ISSUE

#S3813A-S3813E w/o vignette.

		GOOD	FINE	XF
S3813A	**1 YÜAN** 1.4.1912. *(S/M #C255.5-1).*	—	—	—
S3813B	**2 YÜAN** 1.4.1912. Red orange on pale blue w/black text. Back pale green. *(S/M #C255.5-2).*	200.00	—	—
S3813C	**3 YÜAN** 1.4.1912. *(S/M #C255.5-3).*	—	—	—
S3813D	**5 YÜAN** 1.4.1912. *(S/M #C255.5-4).*	—	—	—
S3813E	**10 YÜAN** 1.4.1912. *(S/M #C255.5-5).*	—	—	—

CHINESE NATIONAL PACIFICATION ARMY NOTES

中華民國靖國軍軍用鈔票

Chung Hua Min Kuo Ching Kuo Chün Chün Yung Ch'ao P'iao

1912 ND ISSUE

#S3814-S3816 m/c, crossed flags at top ctr.

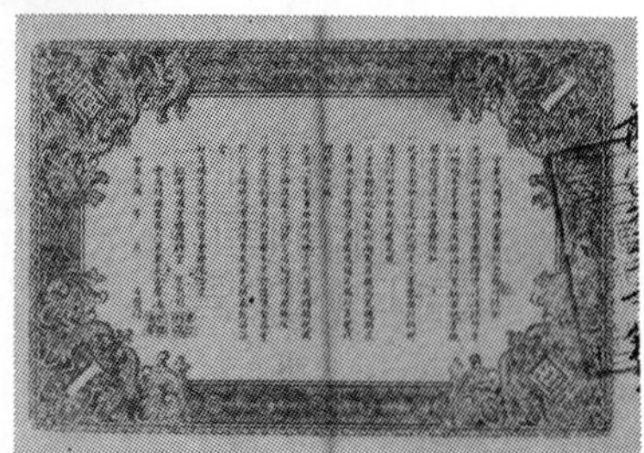

		GOOD	FINE	XF
S3814	**1 DOLLAR** ND (1912). Green w/black text. Back green. *(S/M #C263-1).*	10.00	25.00	75.00
S3815	**5 DOLLARS** ND (1912). Violet w/black text on violet unpt. Back violet. *(S/M #C263-2).*	25.00	75.00	175.00
S3816	**10 DOLLARS** ND (1912). *(S/M #C263-3).*	150.00	350.00	—

REPUBLICAN CHINA MILITARY - SHANGHAI

上海

中華民國/軍用鈔票

Chung Hua Min Kuo / Chün Yung Ch'ao P'iao

1912 ISSUE

#S3818-S3820 dated 9th moon 4609 from an archaic Chinese calendar.

NOTE: This issue was redeemed mostly by the Bank of China in Anwhei Province. Final redemption was made by "The Revolutionary Debts Committee" (RDC) in year 25 (1936).

		GOOD	FINE	XF
S3818	**1 DOLLAR** 4609 (1912). Black text on red-brown unpt. Back blue. *(S/M #C264-2a).*			
	a. Issued note.	100.00	250.00	—
	b. W/violet rectangular RDC redemption hand stamp.	100.00	250.00	—
S3819	**5 DOLLARS** 4609 (1912). Similar to #S3818 but black text on orange unpt. Back green. *(S/M #C264-3a).*			
	a. Issued note.	65.00	175.00	—
	b. W/violet rectangular RDC redemption hand stamp.	65.00	175.00	—

		Good	Fine	XF
S3820	**10 Dollars** 4609 (1912). Similar to #S3818 but black text on green unpt. Back brown. *(S/M #C264-4a).*			
	a. Issued note.	75.00	200.00	—

		Good	Fine	XF
	b. W/violet rectangular RDC redemption hand stamp.	75.00	200.00	—

Republican China Military - Nanking

中華民國/南京軍用鈔票

Chung Hua Min Kuo / Nan Ching Chün Yung Ch'ao P'iao

1912 Issue

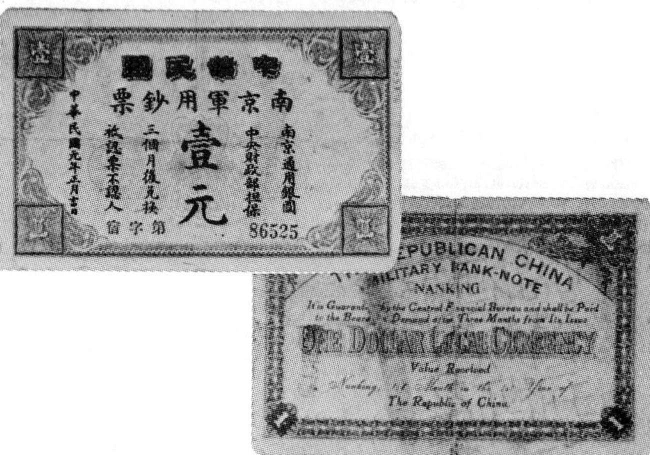

		Good	Fine	XF
S3822	**1 Dollar** 1912. Black text on brown unpt. Back green w/red seal hand stamp. *(S/M #-).*	125.00	300.00	750.00

Chinese Republic Army, Navy and Air Force Headquarters

中華民國陸海空軍總司令部

Chung Hua Min Kuo Lu Hai K'ung Chün Tsung Szu Ling Pu

1930 Issue

#S3824-S3826 printer: BEPP.

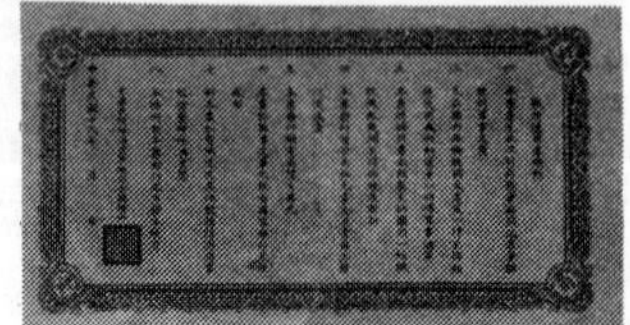

		Good	Fine	XF
S3824	**1 Chiao** 1930. Red-brown. Rural waterfront at ctr. *(S/M #C266-1).*	20.00	50.00	150.00

		Good	Fine	XF
S3825	**1 Yüan** 1930. Blue-gray. Gazebo at ctr. *(S/M #C266-10).*	20.00	50.00	150.00

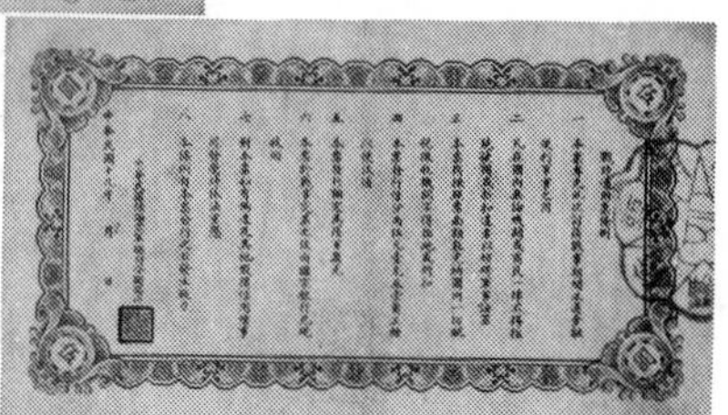

		Good	Fine	XF
S3826	**5 Yüan** 1930. Green. Gazebo at ctr. *(S/M #C266-11).*	25.00	75.00	200.00

Chinese Republic Army, Navy and Air Force Sub-Headquarters

中華民國陸海空軍副總司令部

Chung Hua Min Kuo Lu Hai K'ung Chün Fu Tsung Szu Lin Pu

1920's First ND Provisional Issue

#S3828-S3830 lg. rectangular black text ovpt. including new issuer's name on Provincial Bank of Kwangsi.

		Good	Fine	XF
S3828	**1 Yüan** ND (- old date Jan. 1926). *(S/M #C267-1).*			
	a. Ovpt. on #S2325e. (Nanning).	10.00	30.00	100.00
	b. Ovpt. on #S2325g. (Wuchow).	10.00	30.00	100.00

		Good	Fine	XF
S3829	**5 Yüan** ND (- old date Jan. 1926). *(S/M #C267-2).*			
	a. Ovpt. on #S2326e. (Nanning).	10.00	30.00	100.00
	b. Ovpt. on #S2326g. (Wuchow).	10.00	30.00	100.00

S3830 10 YÜAN

	GOOD	FINE	XF
ND (- old date Jan. 1926). *(S/M #C267-3).*			
a. Ovpt. on #S2327e. (Nanning).	15.00	40.00	130.00
b. Ovpt. on #S2327g. (Wuchow).	15.00	40.00	130.00

#S3831-S3834 lg. text ovpt. on Bank of the Northwest.

1920's Second ND Provisional Issue

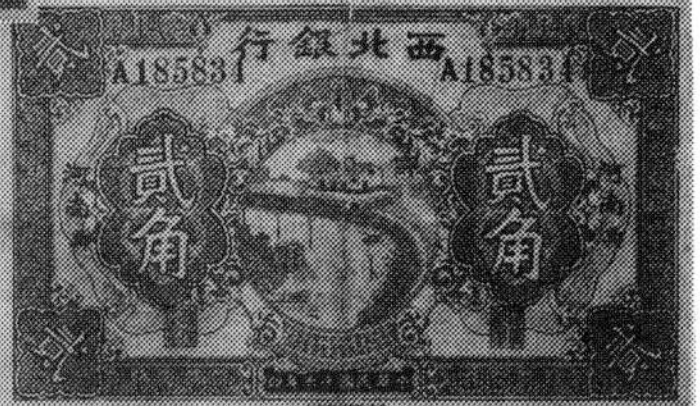

S3831 2 CHIAO = 20 CENTS

	GOOD	FINE	XF
ND (- old date 1928).			
a. Ovpt. on #S3886a. (Honan). *(S/M #C267-10a).*	10.00	25.00	75.00
b. Ovpt. on #S3886b. (Kaifeng). *(S/M #C267-10b).*	10.00	25.00	75.00
c. Ovpt. on #S3886c. (Taiyuan). *(S/M #C267-10c).*	10.00	25.00	75.00

S3832 1 YÜAN

	GOOD	FINE	XF
ND (- old date 1.8.1928). Ovpt. on #S3887f. (Honan). *(S/M #C267-20).*	15.00	30.00	90.00

S3833 5 YÜAN

	GOOD	FINE	XF
ND (- old date 1.8.1928). Ovpt. on #S3888b. (Honan). *(S/M #C267-21).*	12.00	30.00	90.00

S3834 10 YÜAN

	GOOD	FINE	XF
ND (- old date 1.8.1928). Ovpt. on #S3889b. (Honan). *(S/M #C267-22).*	15.00	40.00	120.00

Kwangtung Republican Military Government

中華民國粵省軍政府

Chung Hua Min Kuo Yüeh Sheng Chün Cheng Fu

1912 Issue

#S3836-S3839 bugles and swords at l., Hu Han Min at r. w/crossed flags at top ctr. Printer: CMPA.

S3836 5 CHIAO = 50 CENTS

	GOOD	FINE	XF
1912. Black and tan on lt. blue and orange unpt. Back blue w/black and blue-green text. *(S/M#C270-2).*	10.00	25.00	85.00

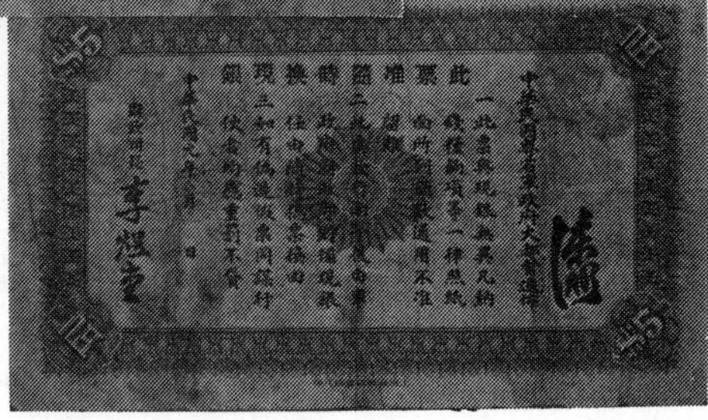

S3837 1 DOLLAR

	GOOD	FINE	XF
1912. Similar but red-brown frame. Back green w/black and red text. *(S/M #C270-10).*	12.00	30.00	100.00

S3838 2 DOLLARS

	GOOD	FINE	XF
1912. Similar but brown-violet frame. Back orange w/black and blue text. *(S/M #C270-11).*	15.00	35.00	120.00

S3839 5 DOLLARS

	GOOD	FINE	XF
1912. Similar but green frame. Back red-brown w/black and violet text. *(S/M #C270-12).*	20.00	45.00	150.00

Chinese Republican Military Bank - Anhwei

徽安行銀華中

Chung Hua Yin Hang An Hui

1912 Issue

#S3841-S3842 pagoda, village at ctr. Lion holding crossed flags on globe at ctr. on back. Various Chinese character ovpts.

		Good	Fine	XF
S3841	**1 Dollar** 1912. Black and green on red unpt. Back red on lt. blue unpt. *(S/M #C277-11).*	20.00	50.00	150.00

		Good	Fine	XF
S3842	**5 Dollars** 1912. Similar but back red on lt. green unpt. *(S/M #C277-12).*	35.00	100.00	300.00

Honan Province Treasury

券通庫金省南河

Ho Nan Sheng Chin K'u T'ung Ch'üan

1920's ND Provisional Issue

#S3855 ovpt. new issuer's name on Provincial Bank of Honan.

		VG	VF	Unc
S3855	**1 Yüan** ND (- old date 1921). Green. Lg. red square seal ovpt. on #S2985. *(S/M #H60-1).*	10.00	22.50	65.00

Honan Province

印省南河

Ho Nan Sheng Yin

1920's ND Provisional Issue

#S3857-S3859 rectangular seal stamp at l. Lg. square red seal ovpt. w/new issuer's name on back Provincial Bank of Honan.

		Good	Fine	XF
S3857	**1 Yüan** ND (- old date 1923). Red on m/c unpt. Ovpt. on #S1688a. (Honan). *(S/M #H61-1).*	15.00	40.00	125.00
S3858	**5 Yüan** ND (- old date 1923). Green on m/c unpt. Ovpt. on #S1689a. (Honan). *(S/M #H61-2).*	15.00	40.00	100.00

		Good	Fine	XF
S3859	**10 Yüan** ND (- old date 1923). Violet on m/c unpt. Ovpt. on #S1690a. (Honan). *(S/M #H61-3).*	15.00	40.00	125.00

Bank of the Northwest

1920's ND Provisional Issue

#S3861-S3863 ovpt. w/new issuer's name on Tsihar Hsing Yeh Bank.

		VG	VF	Unc
S3861	**1 Chiao = 10 Cents** ND (- old date 1924). Brown and blue. *(S/M #H77-1).*			
	a. Ovpt. on #S835a. (Peking).	10.00	30.00	100.00
	b. Ovpt. on #S835c. (Tulunnoerh).	10.00	30.00	100.00

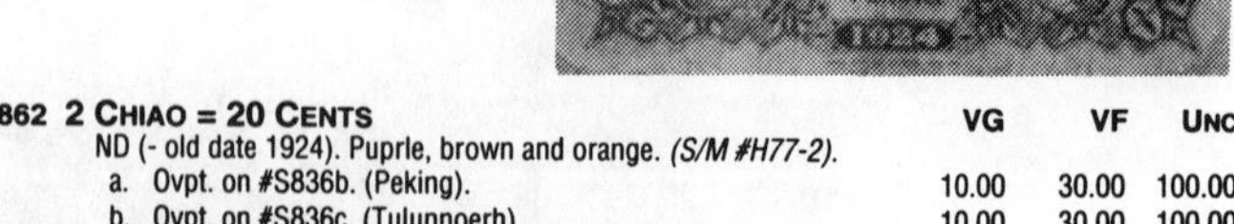

		VG	VF	Unc
S3862	**2 Chiao = 20 Cents** ND (- old date 1924). Puprle, brown and orange. *(S/M #H77-2).*			
	a. Ovpt. on #S836b. (Peking).	10.00	30.00	100.00
	b. Ovpt. on #S836c. (Tulunnoerh).	10.00	30.00	100.00

S3863 5 CHIAO = 50 CENTS

	VG	VF	UNC
ND (- old date 1924). Blue and brown. *(S/M #H77-3).*			
a. Ovpt. on #S837b. (Peking).	15.00	40.00	120.00
b. Ovpt. on #S837c. (Tulunnoerh).	15.00	40.00	120.00

1925 REGULAR ISSUES

#S3864-S3866 pagoda at ctr. Printer: BEPP.

S3864 10 COPPERS

	VG	VF	UNC
1.3.1925. Blue on red unpt. Back blue.			
a. *Kalgan. (S/M #H77-10a).*	5.00	15.00	50.00
b. Red ovpt: *Fengchen. (S/M #H77-10b).*	5.00	15.00	55.00
c. Black ovpt: *FENGCHEN. (S/M #H77-10c).*	5.00	15.00	55.00

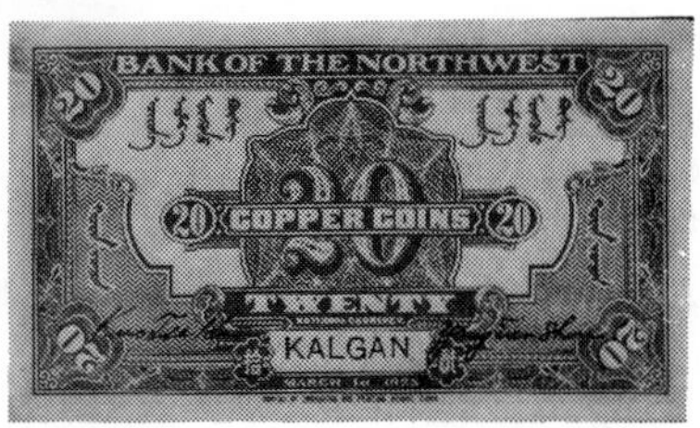

S3865 20 COPPERS

	VG	VF	UNC
1.3.1925. Brown on lt. green unpt. Back brown.			
a. *KALGAN. (S/M #H77-11a).*	5.00	15.00	40.00
b. *FENGCHEN. (S/M #H77-11b).*	5.00	17.50	50.00
c. *Fengchen/KALGAN. (S/M #H77-11c).*	5.00	15.00	40.00
d. *SUI YUAN. (S/M #H77-11d).*	10.00	30.00	90.00

S3866 50 COPPERS

	VG	VF	UNC
1.3.1925. Red on lt. blue unpt. Back red.			
a. *KALGAN. (S/M #H77-12a).*	7.00	20.00	60.00
b. *Fengchen/KALGAN. (S/M #H77-12b).*	7.00	20.00	70.00

	VG	VF	UNC
S3867 100 COPPERS 1.3.1925. Blue on lt. orange unpt. *KALGAN. (S/M #H77-12a).*	15.00	40.00	120.00
S3868 100 COPPERS 1.3.1925. Green on yellow unpt. *KALGAN. (S/M #H77-12b).*	15.00	40.00	120.00

#S3869-S3876 railroad track laying at l. Printer: BEPP.

	VG	VF	UNC
S3869 1 CHIAO = 10 CENTS 1.3.1925. Blue on yellow unpt. *KALGAN. (S/M #H77-20).*	5.00	15.00	50.00

S3870 2 CHIAO = 20 CENTS

	VG	VF	UNC
1.3.1925. Violet on lt. green unpt.			
a. *KALGAN. (S/M #H77-21a).*	5.00	15.00	50.00
b. *Fengchen/KALGAN. (S/M #H77-21b).*	5.00	15.00	50.00

S3871 1 YÜAN

	VG	VF	UNC
1.3.1925. Blue on lt. blue unpt.			
a. *FENGCHEN. (S/M #H77-30a).*	7.50	20.00	60.00
b. *JEHOL. (S/M #H77-30b).*	7.50	20.00	60.00
c. *KALGAN. (S/M #H77-30c).*	5.00	15.00	45.00
d. *Paotou. (S/M #H77-30d).*	10.00	30.00	90.00
e. *PEKING. (S/M #H77-30e).*	7.50	20.00	60.00
f. *SUI YUAN. (S/M #H77-30f).*	10.00	30.00	90.00
g. *TIENTSIN. (S/M #H77-30g).*	10.00	30.00	90.00
h. *TULUNNOERH. (S/M #H77-30h).*	10.00	30.00	90.00
i. *Fengchen/KALGAN. (S/M #H77-30i).*	7.50	20.00	60.00

S3872 1 YÜAN

	VG	VF	UNC
1.3.1925. Blue on lt. blue and m/c unpt. Like #S3871 but m/c guilloche added.			
a. *JEHOL. (S/M #H77-31a).*	8.00	20.00	70.00
b. *KALGAN. (S/M #H77-31b).*	8.00	20.00	70.00
c. *PEKING. (S/M #H77-31c).*	8.00	20.00	70.00
d. *TIENTSIN. (S/M #H77-31d).*	8.00	20.00	70.00
e. *HONAN. (S/M #H77-31e).*	8.00	20.00	70.00

S3873 5 Yüan

1.3.1925. Brown-orange on pale orange unpt.

	VG	VF	Unc
a. *FENGCHEN. (S/M #H77-32a).*	12.50	30.00	90.00
b. *JEHOL. (S/M #H77-32b).*	12.50	30.00	90.00
c. *KALGAN. (S/M #H77-32c).*	12.50	30.00	90.00
d. *PEKING. (S/M #H77-32d).*	12.50	30.00	90.00
e. *TIENTSIN. (S/M #H77-32e).*	12.50	30.00	90.00
f. *TULUNNOERH. (S/M #H77-32f).*	12.50	30.00	90.00
g. *PAOTOW. (S/M #H77-32g).*	15.00	40.00	120.00
h. *SUI YUAN. (S/M #H77-32h).*	15.00	40.00	120.00

S3874 5 Yüan

1.3.1925. Brown-orange on pale orange and m/c unpt. Like #S3873 but m/c guilloche added.

	VG	VF	Unc
a. *JEHOL. (S/M #H77-33a).*	12.50	30.00	90.00
b. *KALGAN. (S/M #H77-33b).*	12.50	30.00	90.00
c. *PEKING. (S/M #H77-33c).*	12.50	30.00	90.00
d. *SHENSI. (S/M #H77-33d).*	12.50	40.00	120.00
e. *HONAN. (S/M #H77-33e).*	15.00	40.00	120.00
f. *NING HSIA. (S/M #H77-33f).*	15.00	65.00	120.00

S3875 10 Yüan

1.3.1925. Green on lt. green unpt.

	VG	VF	Unc
a. *FENGCHEN. (S/M #H77-34a).*	15.00	35.00	100.00
b. *KALGAN. (S/M #H77-34b).*	15.00	35.00	100.00
c. *PEKING. (S/M #H77-34c).*	15.00	35.00	100.00
d. *TIENTSIN. (S/M #H77-34d).*	15.00	35.00	100.00
e. *TULUNNOERH. (S/M #H77-34e).*	17.50	40.00	125.00
f. *SUI YUAN. (S/M #H77-34f).*	17.50	40.00	125.00

A word on date ranges

Often date ranges or specific dates are listed. These have been observed or reported by our contributors. If a note is outside the published range, it only means that it is a newly reported date, and not necessarily worthy of a premium value.

S3876 10 Yüan

1.3.1925. Green on lt. green and m/c unpt. Like #S3874 but m/c guilloche added.

	VG	VF	Unc
a. *JEHOL. (S/M #H77-35a).*	17.50	40.00	125.00
b. *KALGAN. (S/M #H77-35b).*	17.50	40.00	125.00
c. *PEKING. (S/M #H77-35c).*	17.50	40.00	125.00

	VG	VF	Unc
d. *SHENSI. (S/M #H77-35c).*	15.00	40.00	125.00

	VG	VF	Unc
e. *HONAN. (S/M #H77-35d).*	15.00	40.00	125.00
f. *KANSU. (S/M #H77-35e).*	15.00	40.00	125.00

NOTE: #S3876d-f w/additional 2 Chinese character city (?) ovpt.

1926 Issue

		Good	Fine	XF
S3878	**1 Chiao = 10 Cents** 1926. Blue on red unpt. Pagoda on hillside at ctr. Back violet. *KALGAN. (S/M #H77-40).*	15.00	40.00	125.00
S3878A	**10 Cents** 1926. Blue on green and lt. orange unpt. Railroad station at ctr. Back black on green unpt. *SHENSI.*	—	—	—

		GOOD	FINE	XF
S3879	**2 CHIAO = 20 CENTS** 1926. Red on m/c unpt. Railroad station at ctr. Back brown. *KALGAN. (S/M #H77-41).*	17.50	47.50	150.00

1928 ISSUE

#S3881-S3884 troop oath taking at ctr. Great Wall at ctr. on back. Printer: BEPP.

		GOOD	FINE	XF
S3881	**10 COPPERS** 1.10.1928. Blue on orange unpt.			
	a. *LANCHOW. (S/M #H77-45a).*	15.00	35.00	85.00
	b. *KANSU. (S/M #H77-45b).*	15.00	35.00	85.00
S3882	**20 COPPERS** 1.10.1928. Blue on red unpt.			
	a. *LANCHOW. (S/M #H77-46a).*	15.00	35.00	85.00
	b. *KANSU. (S/M #H77-46b).*	15.00	35.00	85.00
	c. *SHENSI. (S/M #H77-46c).*	15.00	35.00	85.00
S3883	**50 COPPERS** 1.10.1928. Brown on blue unpt.			
	a. *LANCHOW. (S/M #H77-47a).*	15.00	35.00	85.00
	b. *KANSU. (S/M #H77-47b).*	15.00	35.00	85.00
S3884	**100 COPPERS** 1.10.1928. Red on green unpt.			
	a. *LANCHOW. (S/M #H77-48a).*	15.00	35.00	85.00
	b. *KANSU. (S/M #H77-48b).*	15.00	35.00	85.00

#S3885 and S3886 railroad station at ctr. Printer: HSPS.

		VG	VF	UNC
S3885	1928. Blue on m/c unpt. Back green.			
	a. *KALGAN. (S/M #H77-50a).*	15.00	40.00	100.00
	b. *KANSU. (S/M #H77-50b).*	15.00	40.00	100.00
S3886	1928. Red on m/c unpt. Back brown.			
	a. *HONAN. (S/M #H77-51a).*	15.00	40.00	100.00
	b. *KAIFENG. (S/M #H77-51b).*	20.00	50.00	120.00
	c. *TAIYUAN. (S/M #H77-51c).*	20.00	55.00	120.00
	d. *LANCHOW. (S/M #H77-51d).*	25.00	55.00	130.00
	e. *KANSU. (S/M #H77-51e).*	25.00	55.00	130.00

NOTE: For #S3885 and S3886 w/additional ovpt. see #S1443-S1444 and #S3831.

#S3887-S3889 troop oath taking at ctr. Great Wall at ctr. on back. *Honan // SHENSI*. Printer: BEPP.

		VG	VF	UNC
S3887	**1 YÜAN** 1.8.1928. Brown.	10.00	25.00	75.00
	a. *SHENSI. (S/M #H77-60a).*	10.00	25.00	75.00
	b. *Honan/SHENSI. (S/M #H77-60b).*	7.50	25.00	50.00
	c. *KANSU. (S/M #H77-60c).*	—	—	—
	d. *SHANTUNG. (S/M #H77-60d).*	10.00	25.00	75.00
	e. *Sian/SHENSI. (S/M #H77-60e).*	12.50	30.00	90.00
	f. *HONAN. (S/M #H77-60f).*	12.50	30.00	90.00
	g. *Kaifeng/HONAN. (S/M #H77-60f).*	12.50	30.00	90.00

		VG	VF	UNC
S3888	**5 YÜAN** 1.8.1928. Deep green. Back olive on lt. green unpt.			
	a. *Honan/SHENSI. (S/M #H77-61a).*	15.00	35.00	90.00
	b. *HONAN. (S/M #H77-61b).*	15.00	35.00	90.00
	c. *SHANTUNG. (S/M #H77-61c).*	15.00	35.00	90.00
	d. *SHENSI. (S/M #H77-61d).*	15.00	35.00	90.00
S3889	**10 YÜAN** 1.8.1928. Red-brown.			
	a. *Honan/SHENSI. (S/M #H77-62a).*	20.00	50.00	125.00
	b. *HONAN. (S/M #H77-62b).*	20.00	50.00	125.00
	c. *SHENSI. (S/M #H77-62c).*	20.00	50.00	125.00
	d. *SHANTUNG. (S/M #H77-62d).*	20.00	50.00	125.00

NOTE: For #S3887-S3889 w/additional ovpt. see #S1445-S1447, #S2681-S2683 and #S3832-S3834.

HUNAN PROVINCIAL TREASURY

湖南省金庫券

Hu Nan Sheng Chin K'u Ch'üan

1926 ISSUE

		VG	VF	UNC
S3892	**1 YÜAN** 1926. *(S/M #H162-1).*	25.00	75.00	175.00
S3893	**5 YÜAN** 1926. *(S/M #H162-2).*	30.00	90.00	200.00
S3894	**10 YÜAN** 1926. *(S/M #H162-3).*	40.00	100.00	250.00

1927 ISSUE

		VG	VF	UNC
S3896	**5 YÜAN** 1927. Violet on green unpt. *(S/M #H162-10).*	35.00	85.00	200.00

KIANGSE BANK OF THE REPUBLIC

贛省民國銀行

Kan (Sen) Sheng Min Kuo Yin Hang

1912 "CASH" ISSUE

#S3897-S3898 stylized birds facing at upper l. and r. w/various archaic objects in borders of vertical format.

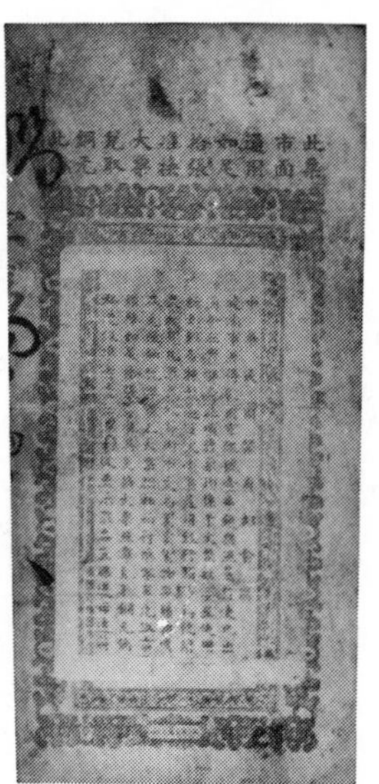

		GOOD	FINE	XF
S3897	**100 CASH** 4609 (1912). Blue green on yellow unpt. Back green. *(S/M #C97-0.5).*	300.00	600.00	—

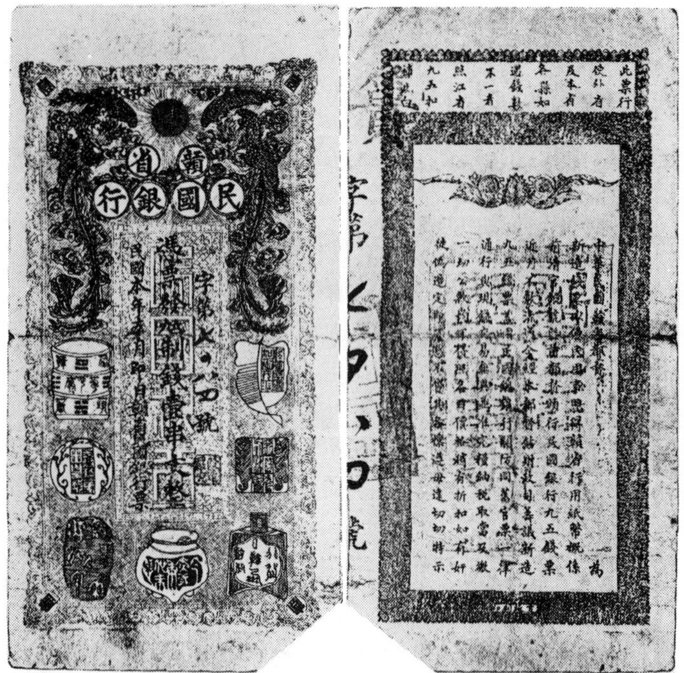

S3898 1 CH'UAN
1.1.1912. Blue and red on green unpt. Back green. *(S/M #C97-0.8).*

Good	Fine	XF
200.00	550.00	—

1912 "DOLLAR" ISSUE

#S3900-S3900B portr. Gen. Ma Yu-Pao at top ctr.

S3900 1 DOLLAR
1.1.1912. Black on blue unpt. Back green. *(S/M #C97-1).*

Good	Fine	XF
200.00	550.00	—

S3900A 5 DOLLARS
1.1.1912. *(S/M #C97-2).*
Reported Not Confirmed

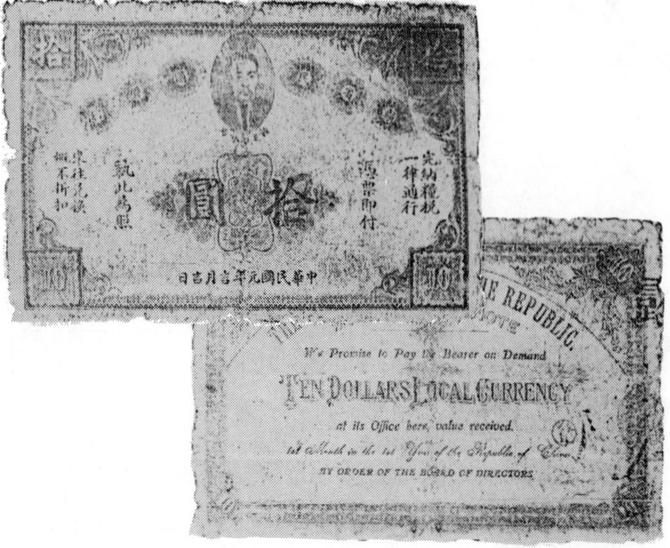

S3900B 10 DOLLARS
1.1.1912. Green. Back purple and black. *(S/M #C97-3).*

Good	Fine	XF
250.00	650.00	—

KANSU (MILITARY)

甘肅官銀號
Kan Su Kuan Yin Hao

1913 OFFICIAL NOTE ISSUE

S3900D 1000 CASH
(ca.1913). Brown and blue on m/c unpt. Facing phoenix above storks at l. and r. Remainder. *(S/M #K6.5-13).*

Good	Fine	XF
—	—	—

KWANGSI MILITARY

廣西軍用手票
Kuang Hsi Chün Yung Shou P'iao

1922 ISSUE

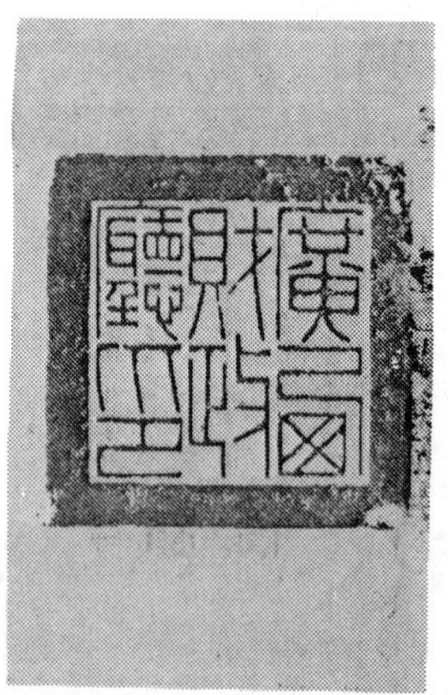

S3900F 1 YÜAN
May 1922.Green on orange unpt. w/black text. Uniface w/lg. square hand stamped seal on back. Vertical format. *(S/M #K30.5-11).*

Good	Fine	XF
10.00	25.00	75.00

KWANGSI MILITARY (PROVISIONAL)

廣西臨時軍用票
Kuang Hsi Lin Shih Chün Yung Piao

1922 ISSUE

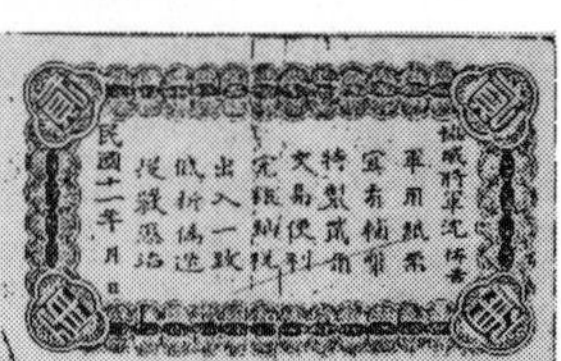

S3900J 2 CHIAO = 20 CENTS
1922. Antique steam passenger train at ctr. *(S/M #K31.5-10).*

Good	Fine	XF
50.00	150.00	—

S3900K 5 CHIAO = 50 CENTS
1922. Antique steam passenger train at l., waterfont village at r. *(S/M #K31.5-11).*

Good	Fine	XF
50.00	150.00	—

#S3900L and S3900M waterfront village at l., antique steam passenger train at r.

	Good	Fine	XF
S3900L 1 YÜAN 1922. Green on yellow unpt. Back violet. *(S/M #K31.5-12).*	50.00	150.00	—
S3900M 5 YÜAN 1922. *(S/M #K31.5-13).*	50.00	150.00	—

KWANGTUNG PROVINCIAL TREASURY

券庫金省東廣

Kuang Tung Sheng Chin K'u Ch'üan

1923 ISSUE

#S3901-S3903 truck and biplane at ctr. W/o imprint.

		GOOD	FINE	XF
S3901	**1 DOLLAR** 1923. Blue-green on lilac unpt. Back red-brown. *(S/M #K52-1).*	15.00	40.00	125.00
S3902	**5 DOLLARS** 1923. *(S/M #K52-2).*	20.00	50.00	150.00

		GOOD	FINE	XF
S3903	**10 DOLLARS** 1923. Green on tan unpt. Back green. *(S/M #K52-3).*	20.00	50.00	150.00

KWEILIN REGIONAL BANK

行銀方地林桂

Kuei Lin Ti Fang Yin Hang

1921-22 ISSUE

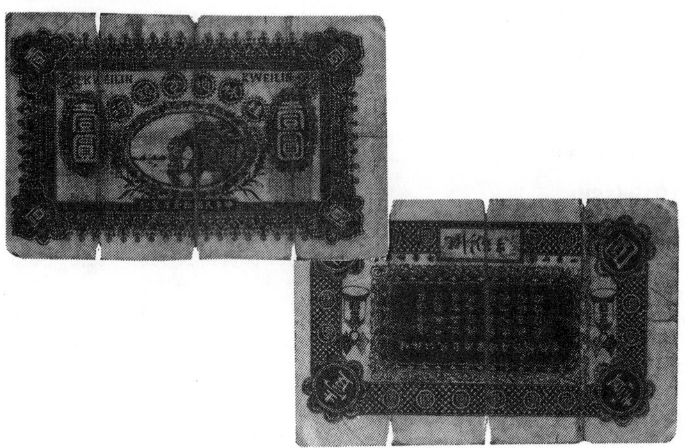

		GOOD	FINE	XF
S3904	**1 YÜAN** 1921. Black. Waterfront stone arch at ctr. *(S/M #K74.5-6.*	—	—	—

		GOOD	FINE	XF
S3906	**2 YÜAN** 1922. Flags at upper ctr. Boat at l., horseman at r. on back. *(S/M #K74.5-12).*	—	—	—

NOTE: Also see #S2363 and S2368.

NATIONAL ARMY

券通流融金軍民國

Kuo Min Chün Chin Jung Liu T'ung Ch'üan

1827 ND PROVISIONAL ISSUE

#S3907-S3909 rectangular ten character ovpt. of new issuer's name on Fu Chaing Bank of Shensi.

		GOOD	FINE	XF
S3907	ND (- old date 1927). Ovpt. on #S2608. *(S/M #K102-2).*	10.00	30.00	90.00

		GOOD	FINE	XF
S3908	**3 CHIAO = 30 CENTS** ND (- old date 1927). Ovpt. on #S2609. *(S/M #K102-4).*	17.50	40.00	120.00
S3909	**5 CHIAO = 50 CENTS** ND (- old date 1927). Ovpt. on #S2610. *(S/M #K102-5).*	20.00	42.50	130.00

1927 ISSUE

#S3910-S3911, S3913, S3915-S3916 pagoda at ctr. Printer: CHCC.

		GOOD	FINE	XF
S3910	**1 CHIAO = 10 CENTS** 1927. Orange on lt. green unpt. Back green. *(S/M #K102-1).*	10.00	30.00	90.00

		GOOD	FINE	XF
S3911	**2 CHIAO = 20 CENTS** 1927. Green on red unpt. Back orange. *(S/M #K102-3).*	10.00	30.00	90.00

		Good	Fine	XF
S3913	5 Chiao = 50 Cents 1927. Blue on yellow unpt. *(S/M #K102-5).*	15.00	35.00	100.00
S3914	1 Yüan 1927. Blue. Printer: SASO. *(S/M #K102-10).*	17.50	40.00	125.00

		Good	Fine	XF
S3915	2 Yüan 1927. Violet on orange unpt. Back lt. green. *(S/M #K102-11).*	50.00	150.00	—

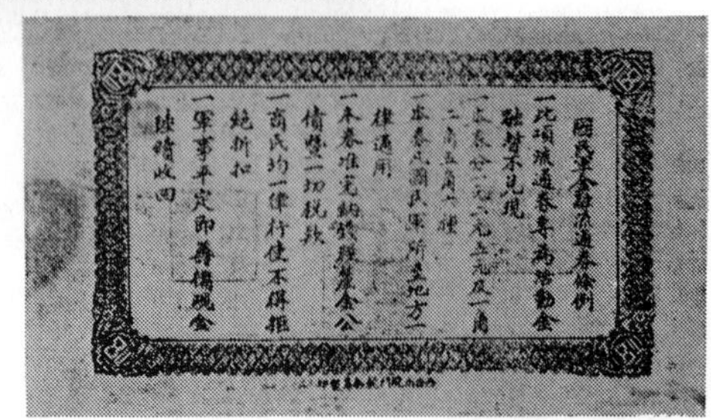

		Good	Fine	XF
S3916	5 Yüan 1927. Red on green unpt. Back blue. *(S/M #K102-12).*	20.00	65.00	200.00

National Army Combined Headquarters

國民軍聯軍總司令部軍用票

Kuo Min Chün Lien Chün Tsung Szu Ling Pu Chün Yung P'iao

1920's ND Provisional Issue

#S3918-S3920 w/square red nine character and twelve character text ovpts. on Fu Ching Bank of Shensi.

		Good	Fine	XF
S3918	1 Yüan ND (- old date 1922). Green. Ovpt. on #S2600. *(S/M #K103-1).*	20.00	50.00	150.00
S3919	5 Yüan ND (- old date 1922). Blue. Ovpt. on #S2600A. *(S/M #K103-2).*	20.00	50.00	150.00
S3920	10 Yüan ND (- old date 1922). Orange. Ovpt. on #S2600B. *(S/M #K103-3).*	25.00	70.00	200.00

National Revolutionary Army

國民革命軍總司令部軍需券

Kuo Min Ke Ming Chün Tsung Szu Ling Pu Chün Hsü Ch'üan

1926 Issue

#S3923-S3927 printer: TIPC.

#S3923 and S3924 two peasants, one w/axe, the other w/hoe at ctr. Chinese text on back.

		Good	Fine	XF
S3923	1 Chiao = 10 Cents Jan. 1926. Black on m/c unpt. Back brown. *(S/M #K104-1).*	15.00	35.00	100.00
S3924	2 Chiao = 20 Cents Jan. 1926. Blue on m/c unpt. Back violet. *(S/M #K104-2).*	17.50	40.00	130.00

		Good	Fine	XF
S3925	1 Yüan 1926. Black on m/c unpt. Back violet and green. *(S/M #K104-10).*	20.00	50.00	150.00

		Good	Fine	XF
S3926	5 Yüan 1926. Brown on green unpt. Back green and red. *(S/M #K104-11).*	22.50	60.00	175.00
S3927	10 Yüan 1926. *(S/M #K104-12).*	Reported Not Confirmed		

Agricultural, Industrial and Commercial Trust Co., Ltd.

農工商信託有限公司

Nung Kung Shang Hsin Tok Yu Ksien Kung Szu

Issued in Changchow.

1919 Issue

#S3928-S3930A SYS at ctr. W/o imprint.

		VG	VF	Unc
S3928	1 Chiao = 10 Cents ND (1919). Black and gray-green. Back blue-gray and dull purple on lt. blue unpt. *(S/M N22.3-1).*	25.00	60.00	100.00
S3929	2 Chiao = 20 Cents ND (1919). *(S/M #N22.3-2).*	30.00	75.00	125.00
S3930	5 Chiao = 50 Cents ND (1919). *(S/M #N22.3-3).*	35.00	90.00	150.00
S3930A	1 Dollar ND (1919). Blue-green and brown on red unpt. *(S/M #N22.3-4).*	45.00	110.00	185.00

PROVINCIAL ARMY OF SHANTUNG

票用軍省東山

Shan Tung Sheng Chün Yung P'iao

ND ISSUE

#S3931-S3933 gateway over railroad tracks at ctr. *RPOVINCIAL* (error) on back of #S3931 and #S3932. Printer: STPO.

		GOOD	FINE	XF
S3931	1 CHIAO = 10 CENTS ND. Red. *(S/M #S44-1).*	8.50	20.00	75.00
S3932	2 CHIAO = 20 CENTS ND. Green. *(S/M #S44-2).*	8.50	20.00	75.00
S3933	5 CHIAO = 50 CENTS ND. Violet. *(S/M #S44-3).*	10.00	30.00	90.00

		GOOD	FINE	XF
S3935	5 YÜAN ND. Brown on lt. green unpt. Face similar to #S3931. Back brown. *(S/M #S44-5).*	20.00	60.00	175.00

1926 ISSUE

#S3936-S3938 fortress on Great Wall at ctr. Printer: BEPP.

		GOOD	FINE	XF
S3936	1 CHIAO = 10 CENTS 1926. Blue. Back deep blue. *(S/M #S44-10).*	8.50	20.00	75.00
S3937	2 CHIAO = 20 CENTS 1926. Orange. *(S/M #S44-11).*	8.50	20.00	75.00

		GOOD	FINE	XF
S3938	5 CHIAO = 50 CENTS 1926. Violet. *(S/M #S44-12).*	8.50	20.00	75.00

#S3939-S3940 wooded roadway, gateway at ctr. Printer: BEPP.

		GOOD	FINE	XF
S3939	1 YÜAN 1.10.1926. Gray on m/c unpt. Back gray. *(S/M #S44-20).*	10.00	25.00	75.00

		GOOD	FINE	XF
S3940	5 YÜAN 1.10.1926. Red on m/c unpt. Back red. *(S/M #S44-21).*	15.00	40.00	100.00
S3941	10 YÜAN 1.10.1926. Green on m/c unpt. Back deep green. *(S/M #S44-22).*	20.00	50.00	150.00

LOCAL BANK OF SZECHUAN (SZECHUAN REGIONAL BANK)

行銀方地川四

Szu Ch'uan Ti Fang Yin Hang

1924 ISSUE

		GOOD FINE XF
S3943	1 DOLLAR 1924. *(S/M #S104-1).*	Reported Not Confirmed
S3944	5 DOLLARS 1924. *(S/M #S104-2).*	Reported Not Confirmed
S3945	10 DOLLARS 1924. *(S/M #S104-3).*	Reported Not Confirmed

1936 Issue

		Good	Fine	XF
S3946	**50 Cents** 1.10.1936. Hilltop pagoda above shoreline at upper ctr. *CHUNGKING.* *(S/M #S104-13).*	10.00	30.00	75.00
S3947	**1 Dollar** 1.10.1936. *(S/M #S104-14).*	—	—	—

Ta Han Szechuan Military Government

大漢四川軍政府軍用銀票

Ta Han Szu Chu'an Chün Cheng Fu Chün Yung Yin P'iao

1912 Issue

		Good	Fine	XF
S3948	**1 Yüan** 4609 (1912). Brown w/black text. Back blue. *(S/M #T14-1).*	—	—	—

Note: Illustration of #S3948 is considered a counterfeit by certain authorities. Modern replicas exist.

Yunnan-Kwangtung-Kwangsi United Army for Kiangsi Relief

滇粵桂援贛聯軍軍用票

T'ien Yüeh Kuei Yüan Kan Lien Chün Chün Yung P'iao

1916-17 Issue

#S3951-S3953 crossed m/c flags at top ctr.

		Good	Fine	XF
S3951	**1 Dollar** 1917. Lt. blue w/black text. *(S/M #T174-0.3).*			
	a. Issued note.	—	—	—
	r. Unissued remainder w/o sign.	25.00	60.00	200.00

		Good	Fine	XF
S3952	**5 Dollars** 1916. Lilac on yellow-orange unpt. w/black text. Unissued remainder w/o sign. *(S/M #T174-0.6).*	30.00	75.00	250.00

		Good	Fine	XF
S3953	**10 Dollars** 1916. Brown w/black text on yellow-orange unpt. *(S/M #T174-1).*			
	a. Issued note.	100.00	250.00	—
	r. Unsigned remainder.	45.00	110.00	300.00

Third and Fourth Route Army Headquarters Property Control Office

財產管理處

Ts'ai Ch'an Kuan Li Ch'ü

1918 Issue

		Good	Fine	XF
S3955	**5 Ch'uan** 1918. Black on yellow unpt. Back blue. *(S/M #T180-1).*	25.00	60.00	175.00

Yunnan National Pacification Army

雲南靖國軍軍用銀行兌換券

Yün Nan Ching Kuo Chün Chün Yung Yin Hang Tui Huan Ch'üan

1917 Issue

#S3958-S3960 printer: YMSO, Yunnan.

		Good	Fine	XF
S3958	**1 Yüan** 1917. Brown on green unpt. Back blue. *(S/M #Y66-1).*	40.00	120.00	—

S3959 5 YÜAN | GOOD | FINE | XF
1917. Green. Back violet. *(S/M #Y66-2).* | 40.00 | 120.00 | —

S3960 10 YÜAN | GOOD | FINE | XF
1917. Green. Back blue. *(S/M #Y66-3).* | 50.00 | 150.00 | —

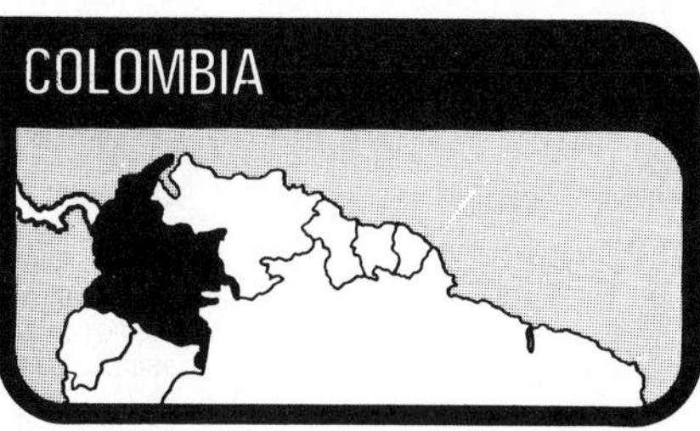

The Republic of Colombia, located in the northwestern corner of South America, has an area of 439,737 sq. mi. (1,138,914 sq. km.) and a population of 42.3 million. Capital: Bogotá. The economy is primarily agricultural with a mild, rich coffee the chief crop. Colombia has the world's largest platinum deposits and important reserves of coal, iron ore, petroleum and limestone; precious metals and emeralds are also mined. Coffee, crude oil, bananas, sugar, coal and flowers are exported.

The northern coast of present Colombia was one of the first parts of the American continent to be visited by Spanish navigators, and the site, at Darien in Panama, of the first permanent European settlement on the American mainland in 1510. New Granada, as Colombia was known until 1861, stemmed from the settlement of Santa Maria in 1525. New Granada was established as a Spanish Colony in 1549. Independence was declared in 1810, and secured in 1824. In 1819, Simón Bolívar united Colombia, Venezuela, Panama and Ecuador as the Republic of Greater Colombia. Venezuela withdrew from the Republic in 1829; Ecuador in 1830; and Panama in 1903.

MONETARY SYSTEM:

1 Real = 1 Decimo = 10 Centavos, 1870's
1 Peso = 10 Decimos = 10 Reales, 1880's
1 Peso = 100 Centavos 1993
1 Peso Oro = 100 Centavos to 1993

ARRANGEMENT

Listings for Colombia are divided into four major sections. The first contains regional or state issues issued from 1857 to 1885. The second lists all bank issues for the period 1869 to 1923. The third section consists of various government-sponsored issues from 1880 to 1919 and includes the revolution issue of 1900 under General Urribe. The fourth lists regional or state issues from 1898 to 1919.

The civil war period of 1899-1902 and the years of monetary chaos following are reflected in the many local printings and special overprint issues of the time. It is the plethora of such notes that caused the division of listings into the various sections as outlined above and as detailed below:

Section I, 1857-1885

STATES

BOLÍVAR

CAUCA

CUNDINAMARCA

PANAMÁ

SANTANDER

Section II, 1851-1923

BANKS

Banco de Pamplona, 1883-1884 . . . . . #S706-S714
Banco de Panamá, 1869 . . . . . #S721-S725
Banco de Circulación y Descuento de Perez y Planas, 1865 . . . . . #S726-S730
Banco Popular, 1877-1882 . . . . . #S736-S749
Banco Popular de Bolívar, 1883-1886 . . . . . #S756-S762
Banco Popular de Medellin, 1883-1899 . . . . . #S766-S778
Banco Popular de Soto, 188x . . . . . #S781-S783
Banco Prendario, 1881-1884 . . . . . #S788-S790
Banco Prendario de Soto, 1884 . . . . . #S796
Banco del Progreso, 1899 . . . . . #S801-S804
Banco de la República, 188x . . . . . #S807-S810A
Banco Republicano, 1899 . . . . . #S811-S813
Banco de Rio Hacha, 1883-1885 . . . . . #S816-S819A
Banco del Ruiz, 1905-1919 . . . . . #S821-S826
Banco de Santander, 1873-1900 . . . . . #S831-S835
Banco de Sogamoso, 1882 . . . . . #S841-S844
Banco de Sopetrán, 18xx . . . . . #S845-S846A
Banco de Sucre, 1913-1916 . . . . . #S847-S848
Banco del Sur, 1907-1908 . . . . . #S851-S854A
Banco de Tequendama, 1881 . . . . . #S856-S858
Banco del Tolima, 1882 . . . . . #S859
Banco de la Union, 1883 . . . . . #S861-S862
Banco Union, 1887-1888 . . . . . #S866-S869
Botero Arango e Hijos, 18xx . . . . . #S876
Caja de Propietarios, 188x . . . . . #S881-S886
G. de Caycedo & Ca., 1884 . . . . . #S886A
Central American Steam Navigation Co., 1851 . . . . . #S887-S890
Credito Caucano, 1919-1922 . . . . . #S891-S892
Exchange Bank of Colón, 1870 . . . . . #S896-S899
La Nueva Compañia Constructora, 188x . . . . . #S900
Señores Fernando Restrepo & Hijos, 1900 . . . . . #S900A
Restrepos y Compañia, 1884 . . . . . #S900B
Reyes Gonzales y Hermanos, ND . . . . . #S901-S906
Sociedád de Zancudo, 1882 . . . . . #S908-S909
Uribe e Hijos, 1871 . . . . . #S911-S915
José Maria Melguizo H. . . . . . #S916-S919
Vicente B. Villa e Hijos, 188x-1889 . . . . . #S921-S923

NOTE: Issues of the Banco Nacional de los Estados Unidos de Colombia (1881-1885) and Banco Nacional de la República de Colombia (1885-1900) are listed in Vol. 2.

Additionally, all government-sponsored issues formerly listed as Section III in Vol. I have been removed for later insertion into the next edition of Vol. 2. This includes all catalog numbers from #S931 through #S983.

Section III, 1898-1919

REGIONS OR STATES

ANTIOQUIA

Departamento de Antioquia, 1898-1901 . . . . . #S1001-S1024
Casa de Moneda de Medellin, 1919-1920 . . . . . #S1026-S1029
Tesoro del Departamento de Antioquia, 1901-1902 . . . . . #S1030-S1044
Gobierno Departamental, 1900-1903 . . . . . #S1051-S1115

BOLÍVAR

Departamento de Bolívar, 1900 . . . . . #S1121-S1124

MAGDALENA

Departamento del Magdalena, 1900 . . . . . #S1126-S1130
Gobernación del Magdalena, 1900 . . . . . #S1131-S1143

SANTANDER

Departamento de Santander, 1899-1900 . . . . . #S1151-S1154, #S1157-S1161
La Compañia Empresaria del Camino de Herradura de Bucaramanga á Sabana de Torres, 1887 . . . . . #S1156

TOLIMA

Departamento del Tolima, 1900-1919 . . . . . #S1166-S1191

Section IV

REGIONAL FERROCARRIL (RAILROAD) ISSUES, 188x-1912

Ferrocarril de Amaga, 191x . . . . . #S1401
Ferrocarril de Antioquía, 1893-1909 . . . . . #S1501, S1511, S1521
Ferrocarril de Cartagena, 1892 . . . . . #S1531
Ferrocarril del Cauca, 1897-1912 . . . . . #S1541-S1573
Ferrocaril de Cúcuta . . . . . #S1576
Ferrocarril de La Sabana, 1886 . . . . . #S1601
Ferrocarril de Santander, 188x-1893 . . . . . #S1621-S1651

Note: A great many notes of Colombia are either entirely hand dated or have dates filled in by hand. This accounts for the wide variation of issue dates in any given series.

SECTION I
STATE ISSUES, 1857-1885

BOLÍVAR
DEUDA PÚBLICA DEL DISTRITO DE CARTAJENA

1878 ISSUE

		Good	Fine	XF
S80	**5 PESOS** 1878. Red. Unsigned remainder.	100.00	200.00	350.00

DEUDA PÚBLICA DEL ESTADO

1870 ISSUE

		Good	Fine	XF
S90	**5 PESOS** 11.7.1870. Black on red unpt., lt. orange paper. Arms in border at l.	100.00	200.00	350.00

ESTADO SOBERANO DE BOLÍVAR

1877 FIRST ISSUE

		Good	Fine	XF
S101	**10 CENTAVOS = 1 REAL** 3.1877. Black. Man at l. Green seal. Back green; lg. numeral of value and arms at ctr. Perforated edges. Printer: HBNC.	25.00	75.00	150.00

		Good	Fine	XF
S102	**10 CENTAVOS = 1 REAL** 3.1877. Like #S101 except for red seal. Straight edges.	25.00	75.00	150.00

1877 SECOND ISSUE

#S103-S107 printer: CCBB.

		Good	Fine	XF
S103	**10 CENTAVOS = 1 REAL** 3.1877. Face like #S101. Red seal. Redesigned back; lg. numeral *10* at l. and r.	25.00	75.00	150.00

		Good	Fine	XF
S106	**1 PESO** 3.1877. Black on red unpt. Lg. and sm. ships at upper ctr. Back blue.	100.00	250.00	400.00

		Good	Fine	XF
S107	5 Pesos 3.1877. Black. Mining scene at ctr. Back yellow.	130.00	300.00	500.00

1883 First Issue

		Good	Fine	XF
S114	1 Peso 15.4.1883. Blue. Farm scenes and steam passenger train at upper ctr., arms at bottom ctr. Uniface. Local printer.	—	Rare	—

1883-85 Issue

#S123-S127 printer: HBNC.

		Good	Fine	XF
S123	50 Centavos 11.30.1883. Black on orange unpt. 3 girls at ctr.			
	a. Back orange. Proof.	—	—	200.00
	b. Back green.	50.00	125.00	200.00
	c. Back brown.	50.00	125.00	200.00

		Good	Fine	XF
S126	10 Pesos 9.11.1885. Black on orange unpt. Justice at l., steam passenger train at ctr. Back brown; hand sign. at ctr.			
	a. Issued note.	100.00	250.00	350.00
	s. Specimen.	—	—	—
S127	10 Pesos 188x. Black on green unpt. Like #S126. Specimen.	—	—	350.00

1885 Issues

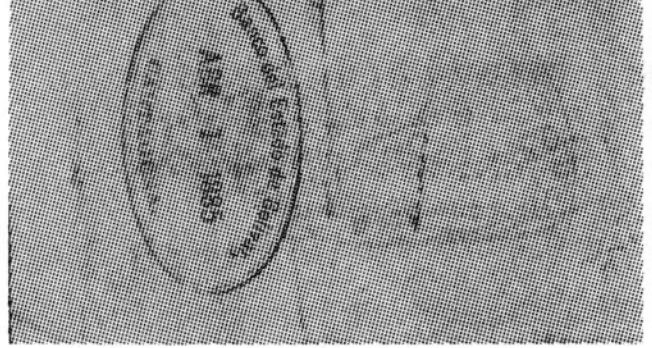

		Good	Fine	XF
S128	10 Centavos 3.1885; 5.1885. Red. Uniface. Oval hand stampings on back. Local printing.	100.00	250.00	450.00
S129	20 Centavos 3.1885. Blue.	100.00	250.00	450.00
S130	20 Centavos 5.1885. Black.	100.00	250.00	450.00

Cauca

Estado Soberano del Cauca

1879 Libranza al Portador Issue

Bill of Exchange to Bearer.

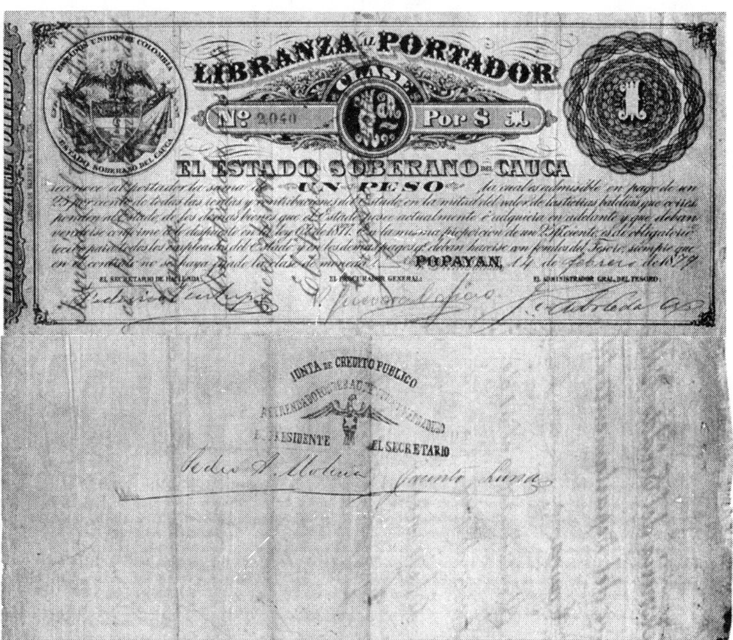

		Good	Fine	XF
S130A	1 Peso 14.2.1879. Black on lt. gray paper. Arms at upper l. "CLASE 1a" at ctr.			
	a. Unsigned remainder.	—	—	—
	b. Cancelled 31.1.1896 w/red handwritten text and name vertically in 7 lines on face.	—	—	—

#S131 issued under law #62 of 1877.

		Good	Fine	XF
S131	1 Peso 18xx. Black on gray paper. Arms at upper l. "CLASE 2d" at ctr. Uniface. Printer: Paredes & Ca., Bogotá.	50.00	100.00	175.00

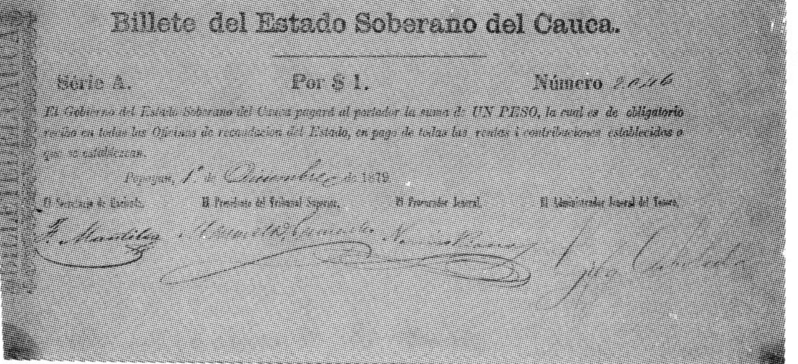

		Good	Fine	XF
S136	1 Peso 1.12.1879. Text printed on back of #S131. Series A.	60.00	125.00	200.00

1878 BILLETE FLOTANTE ISSUE

		GOOD	FINE	XF
S138	**100 PESOS** 17.3.1878. Black on brown paper. Eagle at upper ctr.	—	—	—

BILLETE DEL ESTADO

1882 VALE AL PORTADOR ISSUE

Promissory Note to Bearer.

#S141-S143 black. Arms at upper l., 3 hand sign. across bottom. White paper. *Clase 1a* or *2a* (1st or 2nd class). Some w/word *cinco* handwritten over *diez* in text (5% instead of 10%). Uniface, plain back or w/verification (varieties). Printer: D. Paredes, Bogotá.

		GOOD	FINE	XF
S141	**1 PESO** 1882.			
	a. 1st class. Usual verification on back in 3 straight lines w/o eagle. 18.2.1882; 15.4.1882.	25.00	50.00	100.00
	b. 2nd class. Lowered to 5%. W/o verification on back. 15.4.1882.	25.00	50.00	100.00

		GOOD	FINE	XF
S142	**5 PESOS** 1882.			
	a. 1st class. Usual verification as #S141a on back. 18.2.1882.	20.00	40.00	100.00
	b. 2nd class. Lowered to 5%. Usual verification on back. 15.4.1882.	20.00	40.00	100.00
S143	**10 PESOS** 1882.			
	a. 1st class. Usual verification on back. 18.2.1882; 15.4.1882.	30.00	50.00	100.00

	GOOD	FINE	XF
b. As a, but verification on back w/curved lines and eagle at ctr. 15.4.1882.	35.00	60.00	125.00
r. Unsigned remainder. 188x.	20.00	40.00	80.00

BONO FLOTANTE ISSUE

		GOOD	FINE	XF
S146	**5 PESOS** 18__. Black. Arms at ctr. Unsigned remainder.	—	—	—

CUNDINAMARCA

ESTADO DE CUNDINAMARCA

1857 VALE FLOTANTE DE 2A CLASE ISSUE

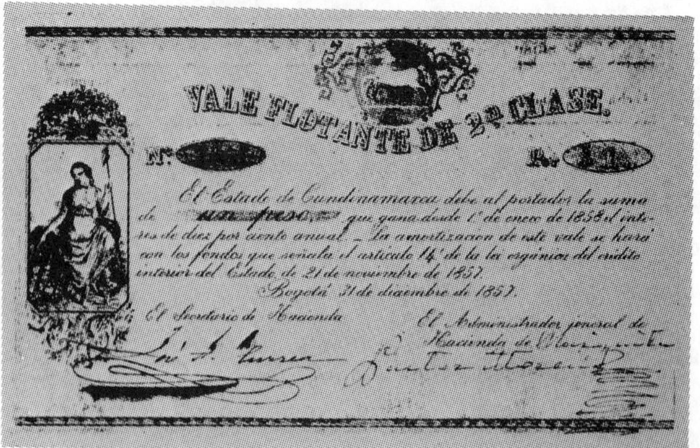

		GOOD	FINE	XF
S151	**1 PESO** 31.12.1857. Black on gray unpt. Seated Liberty at l., horse at top ctr. Back shows interest paid.	100.00	200.00	350.00

ESTADO SOBERANO DE CUNDINAMARCA

1869-70 VALES DE DEUDA FLOTANTE SIN INTERÉS ISSUE

Promissory Note of the Floating Debt Without Interest.

#S156-S158 black. Arms at ctr. Uniface. Printer: D. Paredes.

		Good	Fine	XF
S156	**1 Peso** 9.11.1869; 19.1.1870; 19.2.1870.	20.00	40.00	90.00
S157	**5 Pesos** 19.1.1870; 19.5.1870.	25.00	55.00	115.00
S158	**10 Pesos** 9.2.1870.	30.00	60.00	125.00

1871 Bono Flotante al 3% Anual (3% Annual Notes) Issue

#S161-S166 black. Eagle, arms, woman and tree at ctr. Uniface, P.O.C. Printer: D. Paredes.

		Good	Fine	XF
S161	**1 Peso** 27.4.1871; 29.4.1871; 12.5.1871. Violet unpt.	40.00	75.00	150.00
S162	**5 Pesos** 1871. Blue unpt.	50.00	100.00	190.00

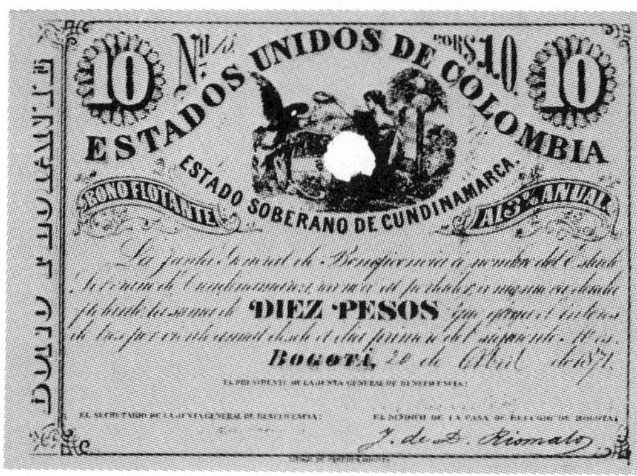

		Good	Fine	XF
S163	**10 Pesos** 20.4.1871; 29.4.1871; 12.5.1871. Gold unpt.	50.00	100.00	175.00
S165	**50 Pesos** 28.4.1871. Green unpt.	100.00	200.00	350.00
S166	**100 Pesos** 1871. Red unpt.	200.00	300.00	500.00

NOTE: #S161-S166 are always found w/hole at upper ctr. Dangerous forgeries exist.

1870 2% Monthly Bill Issue

		Good	Fine	XF
S170	**50 Pesos** 25.11.1870. Black on red unpt. Eagle and arms at upper ctr. P.O.C. Printer: D. Paredes.	50.00	125.00	300.00
S171	**100 Pesos** 187x. Black on blue unpt. Similar to #S170. Unsigned remainder.	200.00	300.00	500.00

1884 Billetes del Estado Issue

#S176-S178 uniface. Printer: D. Paredes.

		Good	Fine	XF
S176	**1 Peso** 10.1.1884; 3.3.1884; 30.5.1884. Black on blue unpt. Train station at upper l., arms in unpt. at ctr.	75.00	250.00	350.00

		Good	Fine	XF
S177	**5 Pesos** 14.2.1884. Black on orange unpt. Arms at upper l., steam passenger train at upper ctr.	95.00	300.00	450.00

		Good	Fine	XF
S178	**10 Pesos** 15.4.1884. Black on green unpt. Arms at l., man at r.	100.00	350.00	500.00

Panamá

Estado Soberano de Panamá

Treasury Bills

Law No. 17 of 1865 - Billetes de Tesoreria Issue

Treasury Bills.

#S186-S189 uniface. Printer: ABNC.

		Good	Fine	XF
S186	**1 Peso** 3.4.1866-20.12.1870. Black on blue unpt. Woman at lower l., boat and mountains in cartouche, standing allegorical woman and plants at ctr., Gen. T. Herrera at lower r.	250.00	500.00	900.00

S187 **2 PESOS**
12.10.1869; 2.5.1872. Black on green unpt. Gen. Herrera at lower l., ctr. design like #S186, standing allegorical woman and cornucopias at lower r.

GOOD	FINE	XF
275.00	700.00	1300.

S188 **3 PESOS**
3.4.1866-20.6.1873. Black on brown unpt. Like #S187 except for anchor at lower r.

GOOD	FINE	XF
300.00	600.00	1200.

S189 **10 PESOS**
3.4.1866. Black. Similar to #S187 but 2 girls at lower r.

GOOD	FINE	XF
400.00	750.00	1250.

LAW NO. 12 OF 27.1.1880

S194 **50 CENTAVOS**
L.1880. Black.

GOOD	FINE	XF
—	—	—

S195 **1 PESO**
L.1880. Black. Arms at ctr. on back.

GOOD	FINE	XF
—	Rare	—

NOTE: The 2 Pesos is reported, not confirmed.

ESTADO DE PANAMÁ

LAW OF 28.10.1861

Issue approved by General Buenaventura Correoso.

S196 **5 PESOS**
L.1861. Many vignettes around border of note including transportation, animals and allegorical figures.

GOOD	FINE	XF
—	Rare	—

S196A **10 PESOS**
L.1861. Reported Not Confirmed

S196B **15 PESOS**
L.1861. Reported Not Confirmed

DECREE OF 28.10.1875

S197 **5 PESOS**
D.1875. Black on green unpt. Woman at l. and r., ship at ctr.

GOOD	FINE	XF
—	Rare	—

SANTANDER

CONFEDERACIÓN GRANADINA

1859 ISSUE

S198 **10 PESOS**
7.10.1859. Handwritten denomination.

GOOD	FINE	XF
400.00	750.00	900.00

ESTADO DE SANTANDER

1855 TESORERIA JENERAL ISSUE

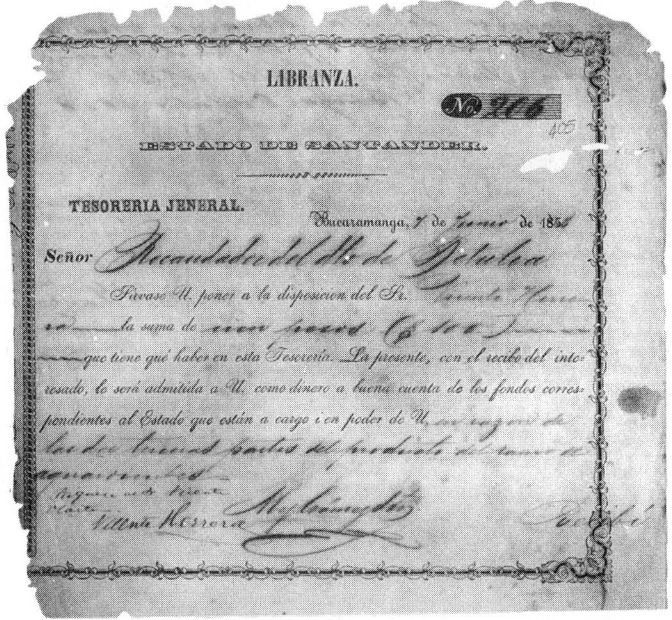
LIBRANZA.

ESTADO DE SANTANDER.

TESORERIA JENERAL. Bucaramanga, 7 de Junio de 1855

Señor Recaudador del dto de Betulia

Sírvase U. poner a la disposicion del Sr. [illegible] la suma de [illegible] que tiene qué haber en esta Tesorería. La presente, con el recibo del interesado, le será admitida a U. como dinero a buena cuenta de los fondos correspondientes al Estado que están a cargo i en poder de U. [illegible]

S201 VARIOUS AMOUNTS
7.6.1855. Black. Forms with amounts payable to individuals from the Treasury and usable as money.

	GOOD	FINE	XF
S201	—	—	—

LEY 37 OF 1879 - BILLETE DE TESORERIA

Issued at Socorro.

S204 1 PESO
14.4.1880. Black. Allegorical woman seated at lower l. Back green.

	GOOD	FINE	XF
S204	250.00	400.00	600.00

S205 2 PESOS
1.5.1880. Black. Eagle at lower l. Back green.

	GOOD	FINE	XF
S205	300.00	500.00	750.00

S206 3 PESOS
3.3.1880. Black. Eagle at lower l. Back sepia.

	GOOD	FINE	XF
S206	400.00	600.00	900.00

SECTION II
BANKS, 1851-1923

BANCO AMERICANO

Issued at Barranquilla.

1880'S ISSUE

S211 50 CENTAVOS
1.1.1883; 2.7.1886. Black. Seated Mercury at ctr. Uniface. Sign. on back. Printer: W&S.

	GOOD	FINE	XF
S211	—	Rare	—

S218 100 PESOS
2.7.1883. Black. Seated Britannia w/shield and tree at ctr. Printer: CS&E.

	GOOD	FINE	XF
S218	—	Rare	—

BANCO DE ANTIOQUIA

Issued at Medellin.

1870S-1900 ISSUE

S219 10 CENTAVOS
19.1.1900. Dk. blue on green unpt. Series A. Imprint: Tipografía Central - Medellín.

	GOOD	FINE	XF
S219	200.00	300.00	450.00

		GOOD	FINE	XF
S220	**1 PESO** 1.2.1885. Date finished by hand. Local print.	250.00	400.00	600.00

#S221-S224 printer: PBC.

		GOOD	FINE	XF
S221	**1 PESO** 1.12.1883; 2.7.1886. Green on orange unpt. Sailing ships at upper ctr.	40.00	100.00	250.00

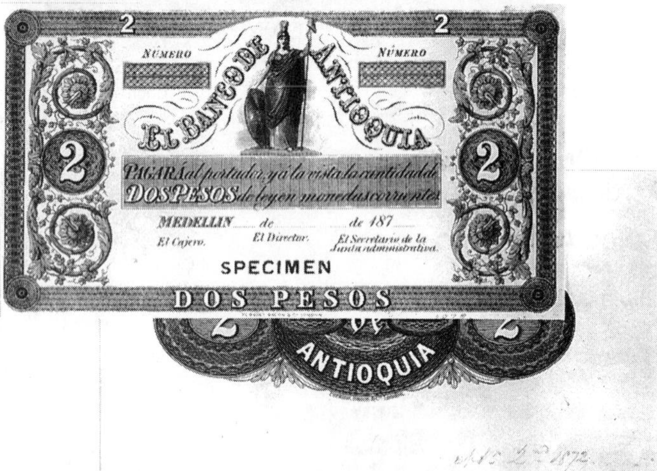

		GOOD	FINE	XF
S222	**2 PESOS** 187x. Black on red unpt. Standing Liberty w/shield and staff at top ctr.			
	p. Proof.	—	Unc	300.00
	s. Specimen.	—	—	—

		GOOD	FINE	XF
S223	**5 PESOS** 187x; 188x. Black on orange unpt. Sheep at ctr., small vignettes at each corner.			
	a. Issued note.	—	Rare	—

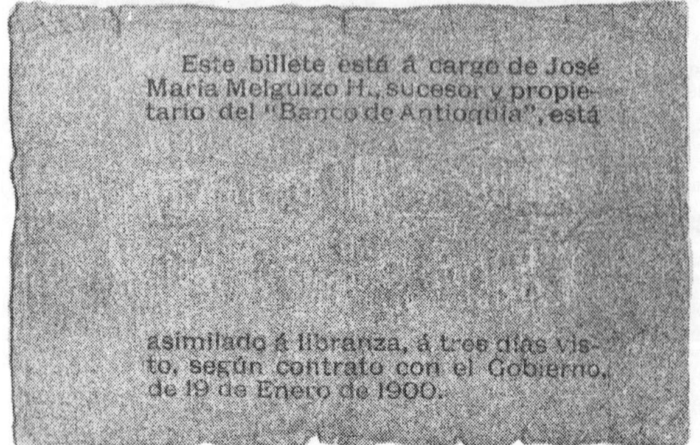

		GOOD	FINE	XF
	b. Ovpt. for José M. Melguizo on back. 19.1.1900.	300.00	500.00	800.00
	p. Proof.	—	Unc	300.00

		GOOD	FINE	XF
S224	**10 PESOS** 188x. Blue. Justice seated at top ctr. Proof.	—	Unc	300.00
S227	**100 PESOS** 18xx. Proof.	—	Unc	300.00

BANCO DE BARRANQUILLA

Issued at Barranquilla.

1871-86 ISSUE

#S231-S237 printer: ABNC.

		GOOD	FINE	XF
S231	**1 PESO** 10.11.1874. Black and tan. Horse and children at lower l., sailor at ctr., dog and safe at r. Back tan.			
	a. Issued note.	100.00	250.00	—
	b. Ovpt. 5 lines of text w/date 29.12.1899 on back.	60.00	175.00	—
	c. Like b. but w/oval black stamping on face and back: *PAGADERO EN BILLETES DEL BANCO NACIONAL.*	50.00	200.00	—
	p. Proof.	—	Unc	300.00

		GOOD	FINE	XF
S232	**2 PESOS** 1.3.1871; 1.7.1873; 1.7.1875; 1886. Black and green. Reclining allegorical woman w/sheaves and produce at ctr. Back green.			
	a. Issued note.	100.00	250.00	—
	b. Ovpt. like #S231b.	75.00	200.00	—
	p. Proof.	—	Unc	300.00
	s. Specimen w/serial # but w/o date or sign.	—	—	—

		GOOD	FINE	XF
S233	**5 PESOS** 12.5.1873; 6.10.1886. Black and orange. Woman w/fruit at lower l., large paddle wheel steamer at ctr., woman at lower r. Back orange.			
	a. Issued note.	—	Rare	—
	b. Ovpt. like #S231b.	100.00	250.00	—
	s. Specimen.	—	Unc	500.00

S234 10 Pesos

7.10.1876; 17.3.1877; 6.10.1881. Black on red-orange unpt. Woman w/tablet and child at l., Indian woman seated at upper ctr., woodcarver at lower r. Back red-orange.

	Good	Fine	XF
a. Issued note. *DIEZ* in orange letters under numeral at upper l.	—	Rare	—
b. Ovpt. like #S231b. *CIEN* in orange letters at l. (error).	125.00	275.00	—
p. Proof.	—	Unc	300.00

S235 20 Pesos

2.1872; 3.12.1873. Black and brown. Woman w/farm tools under tree at lower l., paddle wheel steamer and crocodile at ctr. Back brown.

	Good	Fine	XF
a. Issued note.	—	Rare	—
b. Ovpt. like #S231b.	—	—	—
p. Proof.	—	Unc	300.00

S236 50 Pesos

6.10.1886. Black and blue. Palm vignette at lower l., train at ctr., vignette of pine tree at lower r. Back blue.

	Good	Fine	XF
a. Issued note.	—	Rare	—
b. Ovpt. like #S231b.	—	—	—
s. Specimen.	—	—	—

S237 100 Pesos

	Good	Fine	XF
1.3.1871. Black on red-brown unpt. Arms at l., woman milking cows at ctr., 2 young girls at r. Back red-brown. Specimen.	—	Unc	500.00

NOTE: Some of #S231-S237 exist w/red ovpt: *PAGADERO EN MONEDA CORRIENTE* on face and/or back.

1900 Issues

Printer for most of these notes: Armenta and Prieto (A&P).

S241 10 Centavos

	Good	Fine	XF
3.9.1900. Black on green unpt. Arms at upper l. Back green. Series R.	10.00	20.00	45.00

S242 20 Centavos

	Good	Fine	XF
3.9.1900. Black on orange unpt. Back lt. orange. Series U.	4.00	8.00	20.00

S243 50 Centavos

	Good	Fine	XF
7.5.1900. Black. Sailing ship at r. Series L.	15.00	30.00	65.00

S244 50 Centavos

	Good	Fine	XF
3.9.1900. Brown on red unpt. Building "El Cuartel" at top l. ctr. Back blue; Bolívar at upper r. Series D.	8.00	20.00	50.00

S245 1 Peso

	Good	Fine	XF
8.3.1900; 10.3.1900.	10.00	25.00	60.00

S246 1 Peso

	Good	Fine	XF
1.5.1900.	10.00	25.00	60.00

S247 1 Peso

	Good	Fine	XF
7.5.1900. Blue on pink unpt. Arms at l., steam train leaving tunnel at r. Series J.	10.00	25.00	60.00

S248 1 Peso

	Good	Fine	XF
7.5.1900; 3.9.1900; 19.12.1900. Black on aqua unpt. Arms at l. Back aqua. Series Y.	8.00	20.00	50.00

		GOOD	FINE	XF
S249	**2 PESOS** 1.5.1900. Blue-green.	8.00	20.00	50.00
S250	**2 PESOS** 9.6.1900.	8.00	20.00	50.00

		GOOD	FINE	XF
S251	**2 PESOS** 1900. Black on green unpt. Theatre "Emiliano" at top ctr.			
	a. Series K. 7.5.1900.	8.00	25.00	60.00
	b. Series W. 3.9.1900.	8.00	25.00	60.00
	c. Series Z. 19.12.1900.	8.00	25.00	60.00

		GOOD	FINE	XF
S252	**5 PESOS** 3.4.1900. Blue on lt. yellow paper. Train at ctr. Series C. Printer: Imprenta Americana.	100.00	200.00	300.00

		GOOD	FINE	XF
S253	**5 PESOS** 12.6.1900. Brown on tan unpt. Long bridge at lower l., woman w/sailing ship in background at r. Series M.	20.00	65.00	150.00
S254	**10 PESOS** 10.3.1900.	150.00	250.00	400.00

		GOOD	FINE	XF
S254A	**10 PESOS** 5.4.1900. Eagle w/wings spread at upper ctr. Text and sign. on back. Series E.	200.00	350.00	500.00

		GOOD	FINE	XF
S255	**10 PESOS** 12.6.1900. Black and blue. Paddle wheel steamer at ctr. Series N.	20.00	65.00	150.00
S256	**10 PESOS** 1.7.1900; 3.9.1900.	20.00	65.00	150.00

		GOOD	FINE	XF
S257	**20 PESOS** 5.4.1900. Black on dk. orange paper. 2 women standing at l. Series G.	250.00	400.00	600.00

		GOOD	FINE	XF
S258	**20 PESOS** 3.9.1900. Brown on aqua unpt. Arms at upper l. Back aqua and brown. Series P; S.	25.00	100.00	250.00

		GOOD	FINE	XF
S259	**50 PESOS** 15.3.1900. Black on red unpt. Arms at l., paddle wheel steamer at ctr. Back brown w/black text. Series A.	30.00	120.00	275.00

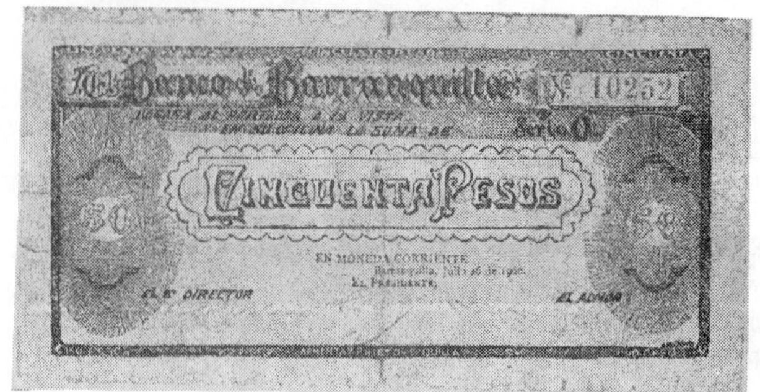

		GOOD	FINE	XF
S260	**50 PESOS** 14.7.1900, 22.7.1900, 26.7.1900, 3.9.1900. Black on pink, brown and bluish green unpt. Back brown and red. Series Q.	30.00	120.00	175.00

		Good	Fine	XF
S261	**100 Pesos** 5.3.1900; 15.3.1900. Black on yellow unpt. Arms at lower l., dog at ctr. Back green text and red vertical text ovpt. Series A.	50.00	150.00	200.00

		Good	Fine	XF
S262	**100 Pesos** 22.10.1900; 19.12.1900. Brown on green unpt. Government building at ctr. Back red; sailing ship at l., lighthouse at r. Black text ovpt. w/date at ctr. Series 3.	75.00	200.00	300.00

Banco de Bogotá

Issued at Bogotá.

1870's Issue

#S271-S277 partially engraved date and space for month and day to be filled in. Printer: PBC.

#S271-S275 w/o vignettes.

		Good	Fine	XF
S271	**1 Peso** 187x. Black. Red numerals.	—	Rare	—
S272	**2 Pesos** 187x. Blue. Orange numerals.	—	Rare	—
S273	**5 Pesos** 187x. Orange. Blue numerals.	—	Rare	—

		Good	Fine	XF
S274	**10 Pesos** 15.2.1875. Black. Sign. at ctr. on back.	—	Rare	—

NOTE: #S274 as listed is most likely a counterfeit.

		Good	Fine	XF
S275	**10 Pesos** 187x. Brown. Green numerals. Like #S274.	—	Rare	—
S276	**50 Pesos** 18xx. Black on green unpt. Seated woman at ctr. Back orange.	—	Rare	—
S277	**100 Pesos** 187x. Ship.	Reported Not Confirmed		

NOTE: All the above except #S274 are known issued only w/red seal ovpt: *Banco Nacional* and *30.10.1899* date in ovpt. on back. For listing see #S616-S620.

1873 Issue

#S281-S284 2 allegorical children w/barrel and bale at upper ctr. Fully engraved date. Printer: PBC.

		Good	Fine	XF
S281	**1 Peso** 1.5.1873. Black.	—	—	—
S282	**5 Pesos** 1.5.1873. Blue.	—	—	—
S283	**10 Pesos** 1.5.1873. Brown.	—	—	—
S284	**50 Pesos** 1.5.1873. Green.	—	—	—

NOTE: #S281-S284 are known in issued form only w/*Banco Nacional* ovpt. and *30.10.1899* date in ovpt. on back. For listing see #S621-S624.

1876 Issue

#S286-S287 date on back. Printer: D. Paredes, Bogotá.

		Good	Fine	XF
S286	**20 Centavos** 7.2.1876. Black. Allegorical woman at ctr. Back green.	200.00	300.00	400.00

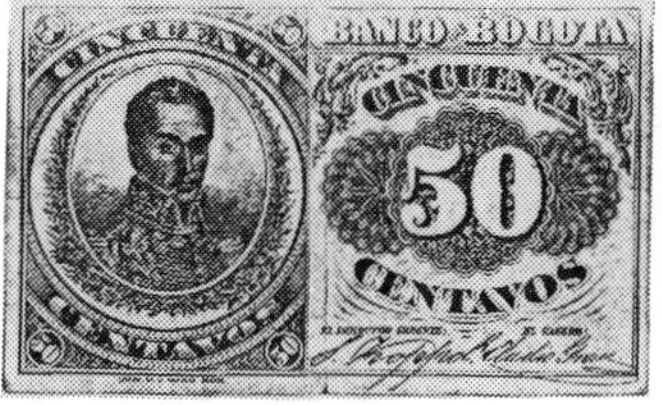

		Good	Fine	XF
S287	**50 Centavos** 7.2.1876. Black. Portr. Bolívar at l. Back blue.	250.00	400.00	600.00

1880 Issue

#S291-S295 printer: CCBB.

		Good	Fine	XF
S291	**5 Pesos** 1.1.1880. Black. Trees and shoreline w/boats at l., Bolívar at r. Series A. Proof.	—	—	—
S292	**5 Pesos** 27.11.1880. Black on pink unpt. Woman on shore and boats in water at l., Bolívar at r. Back blue-green. Series A.	—	—	—
S293	**10 Pesos** 18xx. Black on blue unpt. Waterfalls at l., Caldas at r. Back brown.	—	—	—
S294	**50 Pesos** 27.11.1880. Black on blue unpt. Officer at l., paddle wheel steamer *Francisco Montoya* at ctr. Back lt. brown.	—	—	—
S295	**100 Pesos** 18xx. Black on lt. red unpt. Pineapple trees and shoreline at ctr., man at r. Back dk. blue.	—	—	—

NOTE: #S292-S295 are known issued only w/red seal ovpt: *Banco Nacional* and *30.10.1899* date in ovpt. on back. For listing see #S627-S630.

1918 Cedula Hipotecaria Issue

		Good	Fine	XF
S296	**10 Pesos** 6.4.1918. Added text in red and *a la vista* blocked out on face of #S293.	200.00	350.00	550.00

LEY 7.2.1919 - CÉDULA HIPOTECARIA ISSUE

Mortgage Certificate.

#S297-S299 condor at l. Monument at ctr. on back. Printer: ABNC.

		Good	Fine	XF
S297	**1 PESO** 1.10.1919. Black on lt. red unpt. Back orange; Bolívar monument. Series X.			
	a. Issued note.	30.00	100.00	—
	p. Proof.	—	Unc	300.00
	s. Specimen.	—	—	—
S298	**5 PESOS** 19xx. Black on blue unpt. Back blue. Series Y.			
	a. Issued note.	100.00	250.00	—
	p. Proof.	—	Unc	300.00
	s. Specimen.	—	Unc	500.00
S299	**10 PESOS** 1.7.1919. Black on grayish brown unpt. Design like #S297. Back grayish brown. Series Z.			
	a. Issued note.	—	—	—
	p. Proof.	—	Unc	300.00
	s. Specimen.	—	Unc	500.00

BANCO DE BOLÍVAR

Issued at Cartagena.

1884 ISSUE

#S301-S303 printer: A. Macgregor, Liverpool and Manchester.

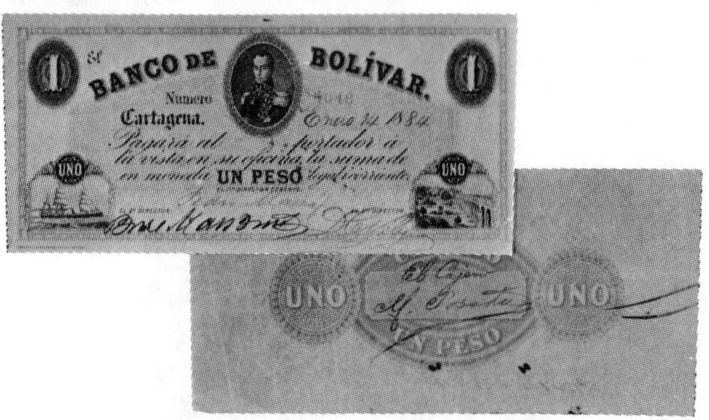

		Good	Fine	XF
S301	**1 PESO** 14.1.1884. Black on orange unpt. Sailing ship at lower l., portr. Bolívar at top ctr., bridge view at lower r. Back orange; hand sign. at ctr.			
	a. Issued note.	—	Rare	—
	r. Remainder.	—	—	—

		Good	Fine	XF
S303	**10 PESOS** 18xx. Black on red unpt. Bldgs. vignette at l. and r., portr. Bolívar at top ctr. Remainder.	—	Rare	—

BANCO DE BOYACÁ

Issued at Tunja.

1886 ISSUE

		Good	Fine	XF
S311	**50 CENTAVOS** 2.1886. Brown on pink unpt. Doorway and footbridge at ctr. Back orange.	200.00	300.00	400.00

		Good	Fine	XF
S314	**10 PESOS** 188x. Black w/red denomination and guilloche. Seated woman at top ctr. Uniface. Printer: Paredes.	—	Rare	—

BANCO DE BUGA

Prepared for issue at Buga.

1870's ISSUE

#S316-S320 uniface. Printer: D. Paredes, Bogotá.

		Good	Fine	XF
S316	**1 PESO** 187x. Black on red unpt. Arms at upper ctr.	—	Rare	—
S317	**5 PESOS** 187x. Black on brown unpt. Condor at ctr.	—	Rare	—
S318	**10 PESOS** 187x. Black on lt. blue-green unpt. Arms at l., cornucopia a ctr., 2 allegorical children at r.	—	Rare	—
S319	**20 PESOS** 187x. Black on orange unpt. 2 allegorical women w/eagle and value at ctr.	—	Rare	—
S320	**50 PESOS** 187x. Black on green unpt. 3 allegorical babies and value at ctr.	—	Rare	—

NOTE: #S316-S320 w/ovpt. for Banco del Estado 1900, see #S461-S465.

BANCO DE CALDAS

Issued at Manizales.

1910s ISSUE

#S325-S330 printer: ABNC.

#S325-S328 portr. Caldas at l.

		Good	Fine	XF
S325	**50 CENTAVOS** 191x. Black on m/c unpt. Back brown.			
	p. Proof.	—	Unc	175.00
	s. Specimen.	—	Unc	500.00

#S326-S330 l. sign. title: *EL GERENTE*.

		Good	Fine	XF
S326	**1 PESO** 17.5.1919; 1.7.1919. Black on green and m/c unpt. Back green.			
	a. 17.5.1919.	75.00	150.00	300.00
	b. 1.7.1919.	75.00	150.00	300.00
	c. Red oval ovpt: *CEDULA HIPOTECARIA* at r. on face; red curved ovpt: *CEDULA HIPOTECARIA DEL 2% AMORITIZABLE POR SORTEOS ANUALES* in 2 lines on back.	75.00	150.00	300.00
	p. Proof.	—	Unc	175.00
S327	**2 PESOS** 1.7.1919. Black on blue and m/c unpt. Back blue.	75.00	150.00	300.00
	a. Circular red ovpt: *CEDULA HIPOTECARIA...* (as #326c) at r.	75.00	175.00	300.00

S326 1 PESO

	GOOD	FINE	XF
p. Proof.	—	Unc	175.00

S328 5 PESOS

	GOOD	FINE	XF
1.7.1919. Black on orange and m/c unpt. Back dk. orange; ovpt: *CEDULA HIPOTECARIA...* (like #S326c) in red.	100.00	200.00	400.00

NOTE: #S327 and S328 exist w/o *CÉDULA HIPOTECARIA* as proofs or specimens.

S329 10 PESOS

191x. Black on m/c unpt. Portr. Caldas at ctr. Back orange.

	GOOD	FINE	XF
p. Proof.	—	Unc	300.00
s. Specimen.	—	Unc	300.00

S330 20 PESOS

191x. Black on m/c unpt. Portr. Caldas at upper r. Back brown.

	GOOD	FINE	XF
p. Proof.	—	Unc	300.00
s. Specimen.	—	Unc	300.00

S331 20 PESOS

	GOOD	FINE	XF
19xx (ca.1922). Black. Similar to #S330 but w/o m/c guilloche. L. sign. title: *EL PRESIDENTE.* Archive copy.	—	—	—

BANCO DE CARTAGENA

Issued at Cartagena.

1882 ISSUE

S336 10 CENTAVOS

	GOOD	FINE	XF
1.1.1882. Green. Dog atop safe at ctr.	15.00	40.00	85.00

S337 20 CENTAVOS

	GOOD	FINE	XF
1.1.1882. Blue. Woman.	50.00	100.00	200.00

S338 50 CENTAVOS

	GOOD	FINE	XF
1.1.1882. Blue. Liberty at upper l.	25.00	65.00	145.00

S339 1 PESO

	GOOD	FINE	XF
1.1.1882; 188x. Blue. Woman and wheel at ctr. Back blue-green.	50.00	120.00	200.00

S340 5 PESOS

	GOOD	FINE	XF
1.1.1882; 15.2.1887. Green. Palm trees along shoreline at l. Back blue.	100.00	250.00	350.00

1900 ISSUE

S344 50 CENTAVOS

	GOOD	FINE	XF
1900. Black on pink paper.	25.00	60.00	100.00

S345 1 PESO

10.3.1900. Black on red unpt. Back blue w/black text.

	GOOD	FINE	XF
a. Issued note.	12.50	30.00	85.00

	GOOD	FINE	XF
b. W/additional red ovpt. vertical text on back. 13.8.1903.	—	—	—

S346 2 PESOS

	GOOD	FINE	XF
10.3.1900.	100.00	200.00	300.00

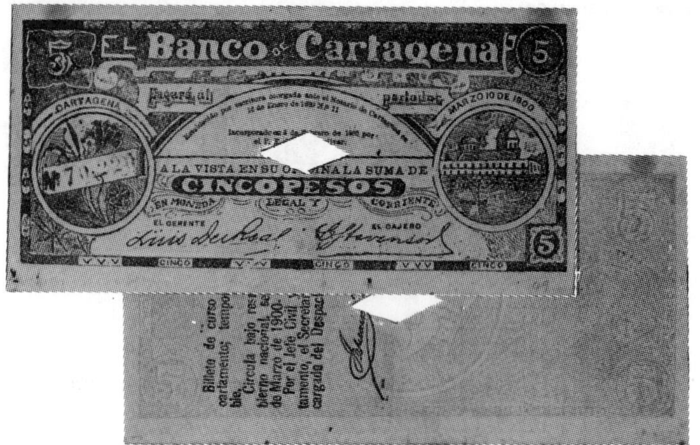

		Good	Fine	XF
S347	**5 Pesos** 10.3.1900. Black. Flowers at l. under serial #, bldg. near river at r. Back lt. green; seated woman and book at ctr. Black vertical text ovpt: *Billete de curso forzoso* at l.	15.00	60.00	125.00

		Good	Fine	XF
S348	**10 Pesos** 10.3.1900. Black on brown unpt. Seated Indian woman and tree at l. in circle. Back red; black vertical text ovpt. like #S347.			
	a. W/o series.	20.00	75.00	160.00
	b. Series A.	20.00	75.00	160.00
S349	**20 Pesos** 10.3.1900. Horseback rider.	100.00	200.00	300.00

		Good	Fine	XF
S350	**50 Pesos** 10.3.1900. Brown on yellow unpt. Monument of Bolívar on horseback in Cartagena at l. Back violet; arms at l., flower at r. Black vertical text ovpt. like #S347.	40.00	125.00	350.00

		Good	Fine	XF
S351	**100 Pesos** 10.3.1900. Black on red unpt. Lg. letters *CIEN* across face. Village view at ctr., eagle at r. Back blue w/black ovpt. text; 2 allegorical women at ctr.	60.00	175.00	350.00

		Good	Fine	XF
S351A	**100 Pesos** 10.3.1900. Like #S351 but w/o lg. *CIEN* across face.	—	—	—

Banco de la Provincia de Cartajena

1851 Issue

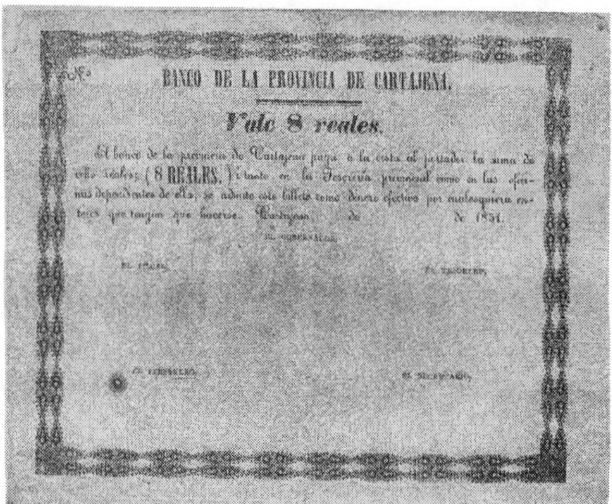

		Good	Fine	XF
S351B	**8 Reales** 1851. Black on orange paper. Unsigned remainder.	—	Rare	—

Banco del Cauca

Issued at Cali.

1870-86 Issue

		Good	Fine	XF
S352	**20 Centavos** 1884. Black on peach paper. Series G.	100.00	200.00	350.00

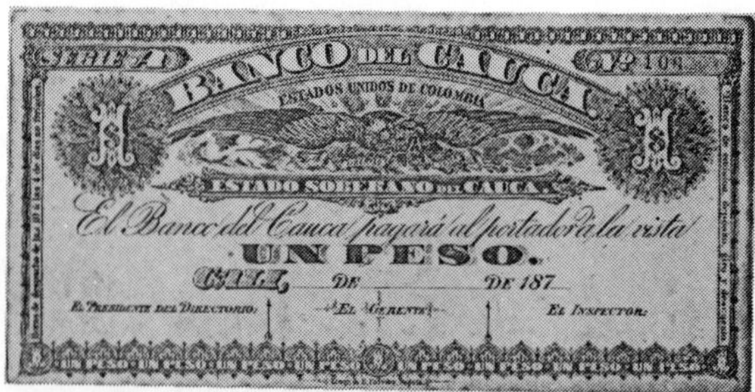

		Good	Fine	XF
S353	**1 Peso** 187x. Black. Eagle at upper ctr. Uniface. Printer: Lit. D. Paredes.	—	Rare	—

		Good	Fine	XF
S356	**20 Centavos** 1.5.1886. Black on red-orange unpt. Bolívar at l. Back brown. Series G. Printer: ABNC.			
	a. Issued note.	25.00	85.00	150.00
	p. Proof.	—	Unc	300.00

#S358-S360 arms at ctr. on back. Printer: ABNC.

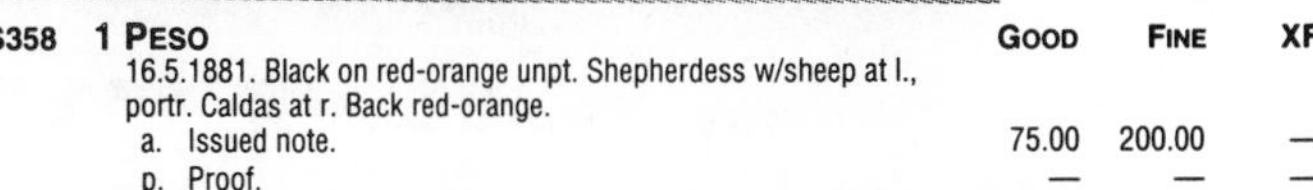

S358	1 PESO	GOOD	FINE	XF
	16.5.1881. Black on red-orange unpt. Shepherdess w/sheep at l., portr. Caldas at r. Back red-orange.			
	a. Issued note.	75.00	200.00	—
	p. Proof.	—	—	—

S359	5 PESOS	GOOD	FINE	XF
	16.5.1881. Black on gold unpt. Allegorical child w/fruit plate and sheaf at upper l., portr. man in uniform at upper ctr., allegorical woman and 2 children at lower r. Back orange.			
	a. Issued note.	125.00	275.00	500.00
	p. Proof.	—	Unc	300.00
	s. Specimen.	—	Unc	500.00

S360	10 PESOS	GOOD	FINE	XF
	16.5.1881. Black on blue unpt. Seated Indian woman at upper l., portr. Bolívar at r. Back blue Series C.			
	a. Issued note.	125.00	275.00	500.00
	p. Proof.	—	Unc	300.00

NOTE: For #S358-S360 w/notes ovpt. for Banco del Estado 1900, see #S471-S473.

BANCO CENTRAL

Issued at Bogotá.

1887-1907 ISSUE

#S366-S372 portr. Gen. R. Reyes at r. or ctr. Printer: ABNC.

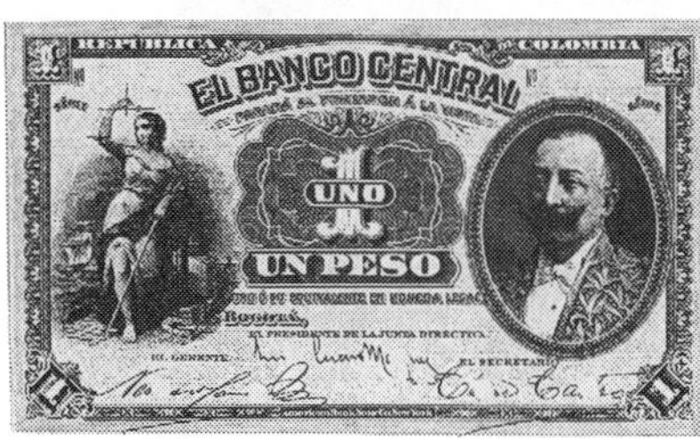

S366	1 PESO	GOOD	FINE	XF
	19.8.1887. Black on red-orange unpt. Standing Justice at l. Back red-orange; arms at ctr.			
	a. Issued note.	150.00	250.00	400.00
	p. Proof.	—	Unc	300.00
S367	1 PESO			
	17.7.1907; 15.9.1907. Like #S366 but round date stamping on back.	150.00	250.00	400.00

S368	5 PESOS	GOOD	FINE	XF
	ND (ca. 1900). Black and blue on green unpt. Allegorical woman and child at l. Back green; bldgs. at ctr.			
	p. Proof.	—	Unc	300.00
	r. Unsigned remainder.	—	Unc	300.00

S369	10 PESOS	GOOD	FINE	XF
	ND (ca.1900). Allegorical woman seated w/sheaf and sickle at l. Back brown; condor on mountain top at ctr. Proof.	—	Unc	300.00

NOTE: For #S366-S369 w/ovpt: *CÉDULA DE TESORERIA* and dated 1919 (formerly #S936-S938) see Vol. 2.

S370	25 PESOS	GOOD	FINE	XF
	ND (ca.1900). Black on red-brwon unpt. Allegorical woman and children at lower l. and r. Back red-brown; lumber barge at ctr. Proof.	—	Unc	300.00

S371	50 PESOS	GOOD	FINE	XF
	23.8.1907. Black on lt. red unpt. Allegorical woman and fallen man at l. Back red; bldg. at ctr.			
	a. Issued note.	—	Rare	—
	p. Proof.	—	Unc	400.00

		GOOD	FINE	XF
S372	**100 PESOS** 3.8.1907. Black on purple unpt. Allegorical woman w/globe and child at ctr. r. Back purple; 2 women at ctr.			
	a. Issued note.	—	Rare	—
	p. Proof.	—	Unc	500.00

BANCO DE CIPAQUIRÁ

Issued at Cipaquirá.

1882 ISSUE

#S376-S378 printer: D. Paredes, Bogotá.

		GOOD	FINE	XF
S376	**5 PESOS** 1.3.1882; 16.8.1882. Black on orange unpt. View of city at ctr. Back blue. Series A.			
	a. Issued note.	15.00	30.00	65.00
	b. Oval revalidation stamping w/date *Mayo - 86* at l. on face only.	15.00	30.00	65.00

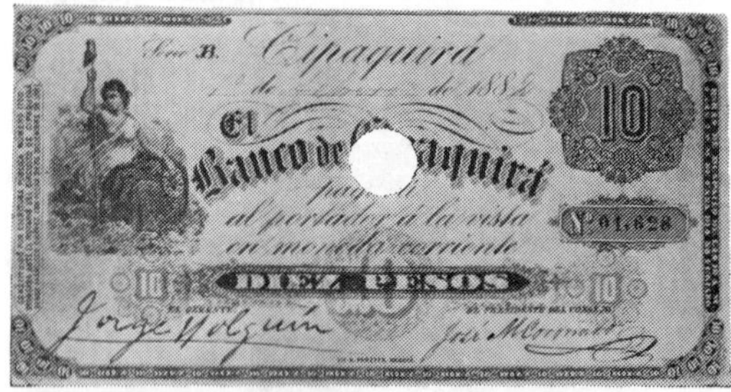

		GOOD	FINE	XF
S377	**10 PESOS** 1.2.1882. Black on aqua unpt. Woman seated w/staff of Liberty at l. Back red-brown. Series B.	20.00	35.00	70.00
S378	**50 PESOS** 29.8.1882. Black on green unpt.. Woman w/tablet and child at l. Back peach. Series C.	30.00	60.00	115.00

NOTE: #S376-S378 are generally found with punched hole cancellation at ctr.

BANCO DE COLOMBIA

Issued at Bogotá.

1875-81 ISSUE

#S382-S386 printer: CCBB.

		GOOD	FINE	XF
S382	**1 PESO** 1.4.1875. Black on aqua unpt. Girl w/shield and eagle at ctr. r. Uniface.	—	Rare	—

		GOOD	FINE	XF
S384	**10 PESOS** 20.7.1876. Black on lt. orange unpt. 2 girls w/sheaves at ctr. Back lt. orange.			
	a. Issued note.	—	Rare	—
	p. Proof.	—	—	—

		GOOD	FINE	XF
S385	**10 PESOS** 20.7.1876. Black. Blacksmith shop at upper l. Proof.	—	Rare	—

		GOOD	FINE	XF
S386	**20 PESOS** 20.7.1876. Black. Ships in harbor at ctr. Proof.	—	Rare	—

#S387-S388A printer: ABNC.

		GOOD	FINE	XF
S387	**50 PESOS** 15.12.1881. Black on brown unpt. Man w/pack animals at upper ctr. Back brown.			
	a. Issued note.	—	Rare	—
	p. Proof.	—	Unc	400.00
	s. Specimen.	—	Unc	450.00
S387A	**50 PESOS** 15.12.1881. Black on green unpt. Like #S387. Back green. Proof.	—	Unc	400.00

		GOOD	FINE	XF
S388	**100 PESOS** 15.12.1881. Black on orange unpt. Explorer landing in New World at upper ctr. Back orange.			
	p. Proof.	—	Unc	500.00
	s. Specimen.	—	—	—

		GOOD	FINE	XF
S388A	**100 PESOS** 15.12.1881. Black on red unpt. Like #S388. Back red. Specimen.	—	—	—

1918-19 CÉDULA HIPOTECARIA ISSUE

(Mortgage bill).

		GOOD	FINE	XF
S391	**50 CENTAVOS = 2 SHILLINGS** 1.7.1918; 1.9.1918. Green and red. Eagle at top ctr. Back green.	25.00	75.00	200.00
S392	**1 PESO = 4 SHILLINGS** 1.1.1919. Blue and red. Like #S391. Back blue.	30.00	100.00	225.00

		GOOD	FINE	XF
S397	**500 PESOS = 100 POUNDS** (ca.1919). Black, blue and red. Landing of Columbus at upper ctr., eagle in red at lower ctr. Blue-gray text on back. Specimen.	—	Rare	—

BANCO COLOMBIANO

A Guatemalan bank which had Colombian share capital. Some of its notes may have been in circulation also in Colombia. For a listing of notes from this bank see Guatemala #S121-S126.

BANCO DEL COMERCIO

Issued at Medellin.

1899 PROVISIONAL ISSUE

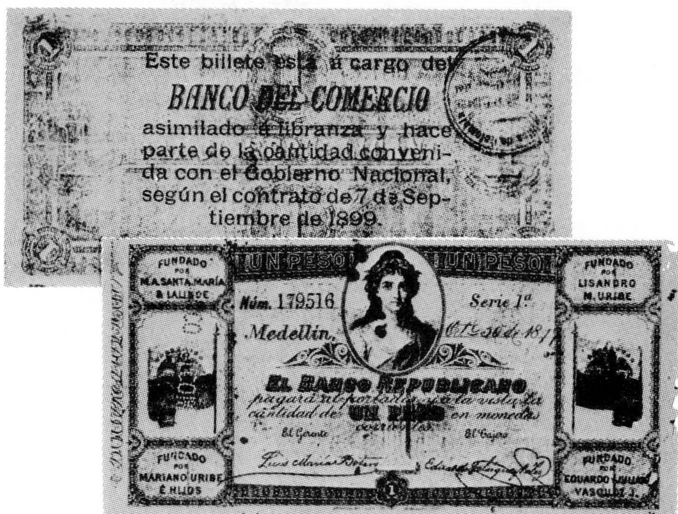

		GOOD	FINE	XF
S398	**1 PESO** 30.10.1899. New bank name ovpt. on back of Banco Republicano 1 Peso #S811.	—	Rare	—

1899 REGULAR ISSUE

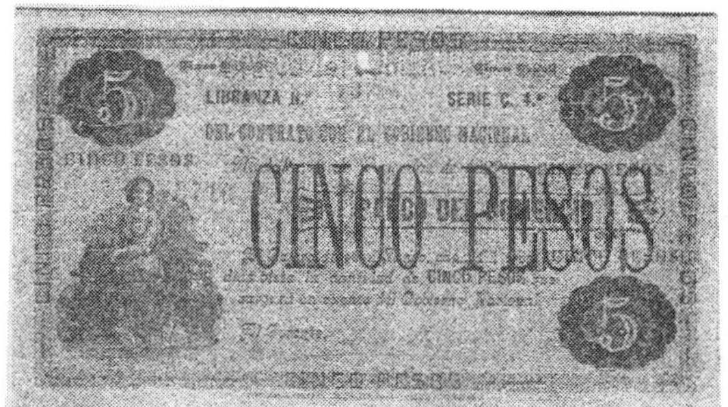

		GOOD	FINE	XF
S400	**5 PESOS** 8.12.1899. Black on green unpt. Similar to #S599.	200.00	350.00	500.00

		GOOD	FINE	XF
S401	**10 PESOS** 17.10.1899. Black and red on pink unpt. Similar to #S600. Printer: Tipografia Central Medellin.	300.00	450.00	600.00

BANCO DE CREDITO HIPOTECARIO

Issued at Bogotá.

1883 ISSUE

		GOOD	FINE	XF
S406	**5 PESOS** 1.4.1883. Black and brown. Back brownish red; lg. *X*'s at l. and r. Printer: D. Paredes.	300.00	450.00	600.00

BANCO DE CUNDINAMARCA

188X-1881 ISSUE

		GOOD	FINE	XF
S407	**50 CENTAVOS** 188x. Black on lt. brown unpt. Arms at upper r. Series D. Uniface. Unsigned remainder.	—	Rare	—
S408	**50 CENTAVOS** 188x. Arms at ctr. Uniface.	—	—	—
S411	**5 PESOS** 3.1.1881. Eagle.	—	—	—

BANCO DEL DEPARTAMENTO DE BOLÍVAR

Issued at Cartagena.

1885-88 ISSUE

#S421-S424 printer: HBNC.

		GOOD	FINE	XF
S421	**50 CENTAVOS** 1.3.1888. Black on orange unpt. People pouring water from jugs at ctr. Back orange.			
	a. Black ovpt: *Decreto No. 121 de 1895* and sign. at ctr. on back.	60.00	150.00	250.00
	p. Proof.	—	Unc	200.00

		GOOD	FINE	XF
S422	**1 PESO** 1.3.1888. Black on dk. orange unpt. Helmeted Athena at l., dog's head at r. Back dk. orange.			
	a. Black ovpt: *Decreto...1895* like #S421a, vertically at r. on back.	100.00	225.00	350.00
	p. Black on green unpt. Proof.	—	Unc	300.00

		GOOD	FINE	XF
S423	**5 PESOS** 1.3.1888. Black on blue unpt. Campsite w/barn and mountains in background at ctr. Back blue.			
	a. Black ovpt: *Decreto...1895* like #S422a.	150.00	325.00	500.00
	p. Proof.	—	Unc	300.00
S424	**10 PESOS** 9.11.1885. Bolívar; steam train.	Reported Not Confirmed		

NOTE: #S421-S423 are known issued only w/ovpt: *Decreto...1895*.

BANCO DUGAND

Issued at Barranquilla.

1919-22 ISSUE

#S426-S429 anchor and sun in circle at top ctr. Printer: ABNC.

		GOOD	FINE	XF
S426	**1 PESO** 20.2.1919. Black on gold unpt. Back gold. 200 x 108mm.	60.00	150.00	250.00
S427	**2 PESOS** 19xx (ca. 1919). Black on blue unpt. Back blue. 185 x 118mm. Archive copy only.	—	—	—
S428	**5 PESOS** ND (ca.1919). Black on red-orange unpt. Back red-orange. 185 x 118mm. Archive copy.	—	—	—

		GOOD	FINE	XF
S429	**1 PESO** 31.7.1921; 31.1.1922. Black on gold unpt. Similar to #S426. 150 x 75mm.			
	a. Issued note.	75.00	200.00	300.00
	s. Specimen.	—	Unc	400.00

BANCO DEL ESTADO DE BOLÍVAR

1885 ISSUE

		GOOD	FINE	XF
S430	**20 CENTAVOS** 6.1885. Black. Lg. value numeral at r.	—	Rare	—
S431	**20 CENTAVOS** 6.1885. Black. W/o value numeral at r.	—	Rare	—
S433	**1 PESO** 6.1885. Black. Arms at upper ctr.	—	Rare	—
S434	**5 PESOS** 11.20.1885. Dk. red. Arms at ctr.	—	Rare	—
S435	**10 PESOS** 11.20.1885. Dk. blue. Like #S435.	—	Rare	—
S435A	**100 PESOS** 6.1885. Black and red. Arms at ctr.	—	Rare	—

BANCO DEL ESTADO

Issued at Popayán.

1884 ISSUE

Issues w/heading *ESTADO SOBERANO DEL CAUCA*.

#S436-S443 arms w/condor at ctr. Uniface. Printer: D. Paredes.

		GOOD	FINE	XF
S436	**20 CENTAVOS** 1.3.1884. Black on blue unpt. Series A.	50.00	125.00	200.00
S437	**50 CENTAVOS** 1.3.1884. Black. Series B.	100.00	175.00	250.00
S438	**1 PESO** 1.3.1884. Black. Series C.	150.00	250.00	400.00
S439	**5 PESOS** 1.3.1884. Black and brown. Series D.	100.00	250.00	400.00

		GOOD	FINE	XF
S440	**10 PESOS** 1.3.1884. Black and red. Series E.	150.00	350.00	500.00
S441	**25 PESOS** 1.3.1884. Black. Series F.	200.00	400.00	600.00
S442	**50 PESOS** 1.3.1884. Black. Series G.	300.00	500.00	700.00
S443	**100 PESOS** 1.3.1884. Black. Series H.	400.00	600.00	850.00

1886 ISSUE

#S446-S452 printer: ABNC.

		GOOD	FINE	XF
S446	**10 CENTAVOS** 2.1.1886. Black on orange unpt. Helmeted woman at r. Back orange. Series A.	30.00	100.00	175.00

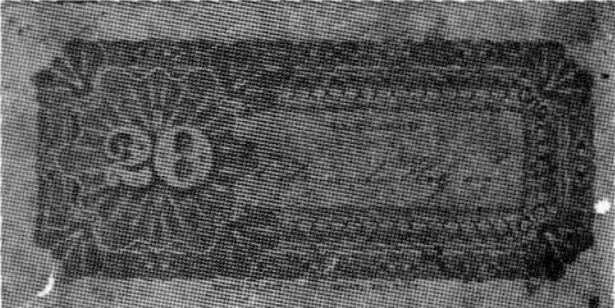

		Good	Fine	XF
S447	**20 Centavos** 2.1.1886. Black on brown unpt. Helmeted Athena at l. Back brown. Series B.	45.00	120.00	200.00

		Good	Fine	XF
S448	**50 Centavos** 2.1.1886. Black on green unpt. Man at l. Back green. green. Series C.	50.00	135.00	225.00

		Good	Fine	XF
S449	**1 Peso** 1.6.1887. Black on green and red-orange unpt. Portr. at l. and r., arms at ctr. Back red-orange. Series D.	45.00	120.00	200.00

		Good	Fine	XF
S450	**5 Pesos** 9.9.1886. Black on brown and blue unpt. Arms at l., portr. at r. and ctr. Back brown. Series E.	100.00	250.00	325.00

		Good	Fine	XF
S451	**10 Pesos** 21.4.1886. Black on green and red unpt. Portr. Bolívar at l., Raphael's *Angel* at ctr., standing woman at r. Back green. Series F.			
	a. Issued note.	125.00	300.00	425.00
	p. Proof.	—	Unc	500.00

		Good	Fine	XF
S452	**25 Pesos** 5.5.1882; 2.5.1886; 8.5.1886. Black on blue and orange unpt. Arms at l., reclining woman at ctr., portr. at r. Back blue. Series G.			
	a. Issued note.	300.00	550.00	750.00
	p. Proof.	—	Unc	400.00

1900 Provisional Issues

#S460-S465 ovpt. new bank name on Banco de Buga (#S316-S320). The entire back originally blank is now full of new text and 23.2.1900 date. Face also w/ovpt.

		Good	Fine	XF
S460	**1 Peso** 15.2.1900. Ovpt. on #S316.	—	Rare	—
S461	**1 Peso** 23.2.1900. Ovpt. on #S316.	—	Rare	—

		Good	Fine	XF
S462	**5 Pesos** 23.2.1900. Brown ovpt. on face of #S317. Back brown and black text and new date.	—	Rare	—

		Good	Fine	XF
S463	**10 Pesos** 23.2.1900. Red ovpt. on face of #S318. Back red and black text.	—	Rare	—

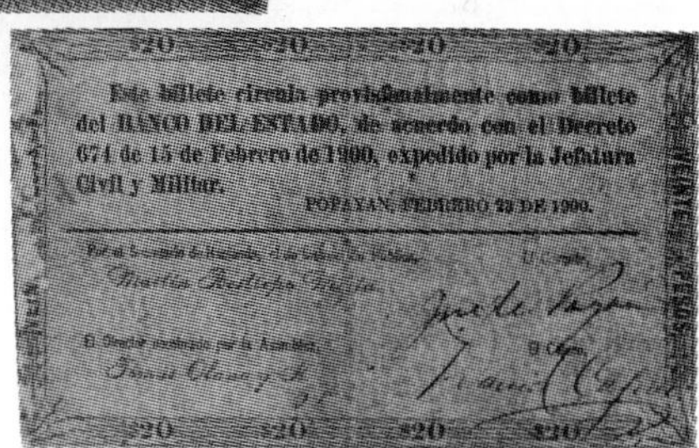

		Good	Fine	XF
S464	**20 Pesos** 23.2.1900. Green ovpt. on face of #S319. Back green and black text.	—	Rare	—

		Good	Fine	XF
S465	**50 Pesos** 23.2.1900. Red ovpt. on face of #S320. Back red and black text.	—	Rare	—

#S471-S473 ovpt. new bank name on Banco del Cauca notes (#S358-S360). New bank name ovpt. on face; several lines of black text and new date ovpt. on back.

		Good	Fine	XF
S471	1 Peso 23.2.1900. Black ovpt. on face and back of #S358.	60.00	150.00	250.00
S472	5 Pesos 23.2.1900. Ovpt. on #S359.	100.00	250.00	400.00

		Good	Fine	XF
S473	10 Pesos 23.2.1900. Red ovpt. on face, black text ovpt. on back of of #S360. Series C.	80.00	200.00	325.00

#S481-S483 locally printed notes dated 23.2.1900. Printer: Imp. del Depto.

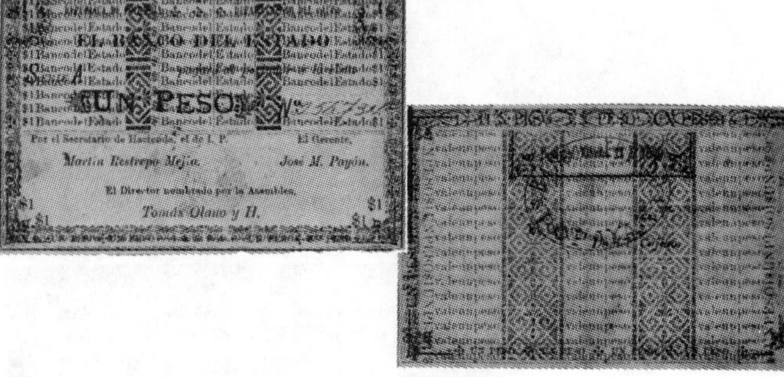

		Good	Fine	XF
S481	1 Peso 23.2.1900. Black on red unpt. Series A.			
	a. Printed names of officials.	30.00	75.00	125.00

		Good	Fine	XF
	b. Stamped sign. of officials.	30.00	75.00	125.00

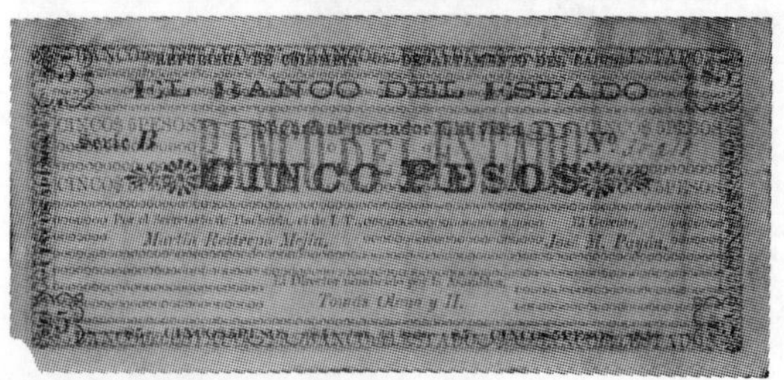

		Good	Fine	XF
S482	5 Pesos 23.2.1900. Black on red unpt. Series B.	30.00	75.00	125.00

		Good	Fine	XF
S483	10 Pesos 23.2.1900. Green on red unpt. Series C.	50.00	150.00	250.00

#S491-S496 dated 23.2.1900 on face and 21.6.1900 on back.

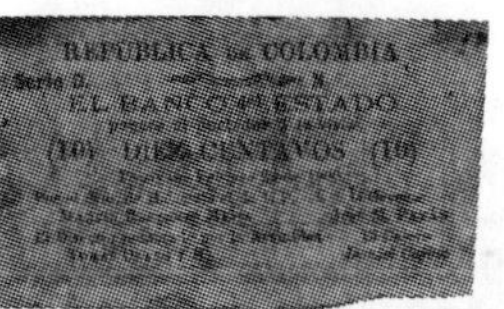

		Good	Fine	XF
S491	10 Centavos 23.2/21.6.1900. Black on blue unpt. Back blue. Series D.	15.00	40.00	75.00
S492	20 Centavos 23.2/21.6.1900. Black on blue unpt. Back blue. Series E.	20.00	50.00	90.00
S493	50 Centavos 23.2/21.6.1900. Black on red unpt. Arms at upper l. Series F.	30.00	75.00	125.00

		Good	Fine	XF
S494	1 Peso 23.2/21.6.1900. Black on yellow unpt. Arms w/flags at ctr. Back yellow. Series G.	30.00	75.00	125.00

#S495-S496 printer: Imp. Comercial, Cali.

		Good	Fine	XF
S495	5 Pesos 23.2/21.6.1900. Red on green unpt. Eagle at l., local arms at r. Back red. Series I.	15.00	60.00	125.00

		GOOD	FINE	XF
S496	10 PESOS 23.2/21.6.1900. Brown on gray unpt. Woman w/tablet at l., local arms at r. Back gray-brown. Series H.	40.00	125.00	250.00

1900 ISSUE

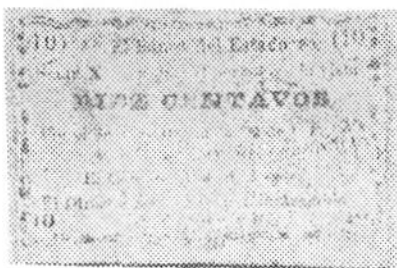

		GOOD	FINE	XF
S497	10 CENTAVOS 20.10.1900. Dk. red. Series X.	40.00	125.00	250.00
S499	50 CENTAVOS 20.10.1900. Lt. brown on blue paper. Series V.	40.00	125.00	250.00

1900 REGULAR ISSUE

#501-S506 most likely printed in the United States. Back design for all except #S501 have arms at l., date *1.10.1900* and printed sign. at r.

		VG	VF	UNC
S501	10 CENTAVOS 1.10.1900. Black on blue unpt. Bolívar at l. Back blue; sign. and date at l., arms at r. Series A.	1.00	2.50	5.00

		VG	VF	UNC
S502	20 CENTAVOS 1.10.1900. Black on brown unpt. Similar to #S501. Back brown; arms at l. Series B.			
	a. Issued note.	1.00	2.50	5.00
	b. Uniface w/blue bank stamping and handwritten #.	2.00	4.50	10.00

NOTE: Litho plates were found for #S501 and S502 (also others?). Reprints have been made.

		VG	VF	UNC
S503	50 CENTAVOS 1.10.1900. Black on orange unpt. A. J. de Sucre at l. Back orange. Series C. Blue or red serial #.	2.00	5.00	10.00

		VG	VF	UNC
S504	1 PESO 1.10.1900. Black on green unpt. Justice at l. Back green. Series D.			
	a. Printer: *Holden y Motley, Nueva York.*	2.00	5.00	10.00
	b. Printer: *W.L.H. Co., New York.*	3.00	6.00	12.00
	c. W/o printer's name, finished note w/serial #.	1.00	2.50	5.00
	d. Like c., but w/o serial #.	—	1.00	3.00
	e. Uniface print, face or back.	—	1.00	3.00
	f. Like b, but printer: *Hosford & Sons Ptg. Co. N.Y.*	2.00	5.00	10.00
	r. Like b, but w/o serial #. Remainder.	—	1.00	3.00

		VG	VF	UNC
S505	5 PESOS 1.10.1900. Black on orange unpt. Liberty w/pole and cap standing at l. Back orange. Series E.	1.00	2.50	5.00

		VG	VF	UNC
S506	10 PESOS 1.10.1900. Black on brown unpt. Arms, flags and seated woman at l. Back brown. Series F.	2.00	5.00	10.00

NOTE: #S501-S506 may be found as unfinished remainders w/o serial #.

BANCO HIPOTECARIO

Issued at Bogotá.

1881 ISSUE

#S511-S515 printer: ABNC.

		VG	VF	UNC
S511	5 PESOS 1.10.1881. Black on brown unpt. Seated woman w/sheaf w/farm in background at l., farmer plowing w/horses at r. Back brown. Series Y.			
	p. Proof.	—	Unc	300.00
	s. Specimen.	—	Unc	500.00

		VG	VF	UNC
S512	10 PESOS 1.10.1881. Black on green unpt. Seated woman w/sheep at l., 3 horse heads in circle at upper ctr. r. Back green. Series Z.			
	p. Proof.	—	Unc	300.00
	s. Specimen.	—	Unc	300.00
S514	50 PESOS 1.10.1881. Black on orange unpt. Sitting woman w/farm produce at l., basket of corn at r. Back orange. Series W.			
	p. Proof.	—	Unc	300.00
	s. Specimen.	—	Unc	300.00

A word on date ranges

Often date ranges or specific dates are listed. These have been observed or reported by our contributors. If a note is outside the published range, it only means that it is a newly reported date, and not necessarily worthy of a premium value.

S515 100 PESOS | VG | VF | UNC
1.10.1881. Black on blue unpt. Griffins at l. and r., farm implements and produce in background of portr., shepherdess w/sheep at ctr. Back blue. Series V.

	VG	VF	UNC
p. Proof.	—	Unc	300.00
s. Specimen.	—	Unc	500.00

NOTE: #S511-S515 are known issued only w/red seal ovpt. *Banco Nacional* and *30.10.1899* date in ovpt. on back. For listing see #S636-S640.

BANCO HIPOTECARIO DE LA MUTUALIDÁD

Issued at Bucaramanga.

LEY 24 DE 1905

#S516-S518 harvesting coffee beans at upper ctr.

	GOOD	FINE	XF
S516 50 CENTAVOS 1.1.1919. Black on deep blue, red and pale orange unpt. Agricultural scene at upper ctr. Back dk. brown on pale green unpt.; arms at ctr. Printer: Lit. J. L. Arango, Medellin.	150.00	250.00	400.00

#S517 and S518 printer: ABNC.

	GOOD	FINE	XF
S517 1 PESO ORO ND (ca.1919). Blue on yellow unpt. Similar to #S516. Back blue; arms at l. 6% interest-bearing note. Series A.			
a. Issued note.	150.00	250.00	400.00
s. Specimen.	—	Unc	500.00
S518 1 PESO ORO ND (ca.1921). Blue. Similar to S517 but w/o unpt. 4% interest-bearing note. Series A. Proof.	—	—	—

BANCO HIPOTECARIO DEL PACÍFICO

Issued at Cali.

1920-22 BONO BANCARIO ISSUE

#S521-S525 condor in flight at ctr. Printer: ABNC.

#S521-S523 w/solid bar ovpt. on text below denomination under condor at ctr. Ovpt: *Ley...* on back.

	GOOD	FINE	XF
S521 50 CENTAVOS 8.7.1920. Green on tan unpt. Back green.			
a. Issued note.	35.00	100.00	175.00
p. Proof w/o ovpt: *Ley...* on back.	—	Unc	300.00
s. Specimen.	—	Unc	300.00

	GOOD	FINE	XF
S522 1 PESO 1921. Green on lilac unpt. Back green. Series A.			
a. Issued note.	50.00	125.00	200.00
p. Proof w/o ovpt: *Ley...* on back.	—	Unc	300.00
s. Specimen.	—	Unc	300.00
S523 5 PESOS 2.1921. Black on red-orange unpt. Back red-orange.			
a. Issued note.	60.00	150.00	250.00
p. Proof w/o ovpt: *Ley...* on back.	—	Unc	300.00
s. Specimen.	—	Unc	300.00
S524 10 PESOS 19xx. Blue on olive unpt. Back orange.			
p. Proof.	—	Unc	300.00
s. Specimen.	—	Unc	400.00

	GOOD	FINE	XF
S525 20 PESOS 11.4.1922. Black on lt. brown and m/c unpt. Panel of interest markers at r. Back brown.			
a. Issued note. .	—	Rare	—
p. Proof. 19xx.	—	Unc	400.00

BANCO DE HONDA

1882 ISSUE

	GOOD	FINE	XF
S531 1 PESO 1882. Blue and black. Steam locomotive.	—	Rare	—
S532 5 PESOS 188x.	—	Rare	—
S533 10 PESOS 188x.	—	Rare	—

BANCO DEL HUILA

1921 PROVISIONAL BONO BONCARIO ISSUE

	GOOD	FINE	XF
S541 50 CENTAVOS 13.5.1921. Ovpt. on #S821.	45.00	135.00	200.00
S542 20 PESOS 9.6.1921. Ovpt. on #S825.	—	Rare	—

BANCO INDUSTRIAL

1883-1900 ISSUE

Issued at Manizales.

#S546-S548 printer: PBC.

		GOOD	FINE	XF
S546	**1 PESO** 20.1.1900. Blue. 2 allegorical women at upper ctr. Back orange.			
	a. Issued note.	150.00	250.00	400.00
	p. Proof.	—	Unc	200.00
S547	**5 PESOS** 188x; 20.1.1890. Orange on orange unpt. Back blue.	200.00	350.00	500.00
S548	**10 PESOS** 1883. Blue. Woman w/flowers.	300.00	450.00	700.00

LEY 24 DE 1905; 18 DE MAYO DE 1918 - CÉDULA HIPOTECARIA ISSUE

Issued at Cartagena.

#S551-S553 interest payable to 1934. Standing woman w/globe at l. Printer: ABNC.

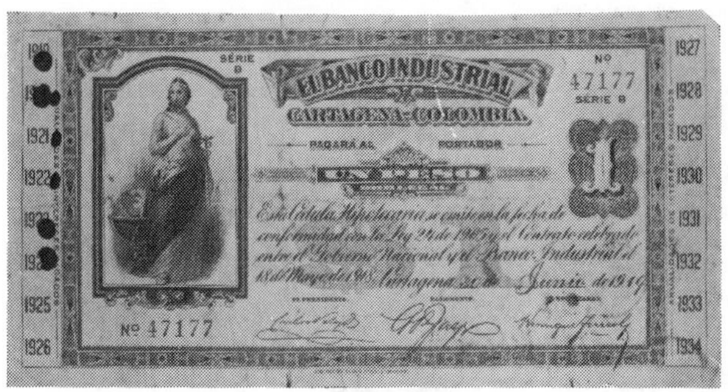

		GOOD	FINE	XF
S551	**1 PESO** 1.5.1919; 30.6.1919. Black and green. Back green.	40.00	150.00	225.00
S552	**2 PESOS** 1.1.1923. Black and orange. Like #S551. Back orange.			
	a. Issued note.	50.00	200.00	—
	p. Proof.	—	—	—
S553	**5 PESOS** 1.1.1923. Black and blue. Back blue.	—	Rare	—

1920S ISSUE

Issued at Cartagena.

#S554-S556 reduced size notes, 156 x 80mm. Similar to #S551-S553. Interest payaable to 1932. Printer: ABNC.

		GOOD	FINE	XF
S554	**1 PESO** ND. Black and green. Back green. Proof.	—	Unc	300.00
S555	**2 PESOS** ND. Black and red-orange. Back red-orange. Proof.	—	Unc	300.00
S556	**5 PESOS** ND. Black and blue. Back blue. Proof.	—	Unc	300.00
S558	**20 PESOS** ND (ca.1923). Black on brown unpt. Similar to #S556. Interest payable to 1968. Back brown. Archive copy.	—	—	—

BANCO INTERNACIONAL

Issued at Bogotá.

1884 ISSUE

#S561-S564 printer: ABNC.

		GOOD	FINE	XF
S561	**1 PESO** 15.12.1884. Black on green unpt. Cart w/oxen at ctr. Back green.			
	a. Issued note.	—	Rare	—
	s. Series A. Specimen.	—	Unc	500.00

		GOOD	FINE	XF
S562	**5 PESOS** 15.12.1884. Black on orange unpt. Portr. woman's head at l., allegorical woman w/safe, money and scales at ctr. r. Back orange.			
	p. Proof.	—	Unc	300.00
	s. Specimen.	—	Unc	300.00

		GOOD	FINE	XF
S563	**10 PESOS** 15.12.1884. Black on brown unpt. Justice seated at r. Back brown. Series C.			
	p. Proof.	—	Unc	300.00
	s. Specimen.	—	Unc	300.00

		GOOD	FINE	XF
S564	**50 PESOS** 15.12.1884. Black on orange unpt. 2 seated allegorical women at l., cherubs w/globe at ctr., 2 girls at r. Back orange. Series D.			
	p. Proof.	—	Unc	500.00

NOTE: #S561-S564 are known issued only w/red seal ovpt: *Banco Nacional* and *30.10.1899* date in ovpt. on back. For listing see #S646-S649.

BANCO LÓPEZ

Issued at Bogotá.

1921 PROVISIONAL BONO BANCARIO ISSUE

#S571 new bank name and other ovpt. on earlier notes of Banco del Ruiz.

		GOOD	FINE	XF
S571	**1 PESO** 9.6.1921. Black and green ovpt. on #S822.	45.00	135.00	250.00

1919 CÉDULA HIPOTECARIA ISSUES

#S575 and S576 ovpt. on earlier notes of Banco del Ruiz.

		GOOD	FINE	XF
S575	5 PESOS 1.5.1919. Dk. green ovpt. on #S823.			
	a. Issued note.	45.00	100.00	250.00
	b. Cancelled w/date perforations.	—	—	—
S576	10 PESOS 1.5.1919. Black ovpt. on #S824.	50.00	110.00	300.00

#S577-S580 on earlier notes of Banco del Sur.

		GOOD	FINE	XF
S577	1 PESO 1.5.1919. Ovpt. on #S851.	—	Rare	—
S578	5 PESOS 1.5.1919. Ovpt. on #S852.	—	Rare	—
S579	10 PESOS 1.5.1919. Ovpt. on #S853.	—	Rare	—
S580	25 PESOS 1.5.1919. Ovpt. on #S854.	—	Rare	—

BANCO DE MARQUEZ

Issued at Barranquilla.

1880S ISSUE

#S581-S586 printer: ABNC.

		GOOD	FINE	XF
S581	1 PESO 1.4.1883. Black on tan unpt. Shepherdess w/sheep at l., man at lower r. Back brown; hand sign. at ctr.			
	a. Issued note.	75.00	225.00	350.00
	p. Proof.	—	Unc	300.00
	s. Specimen.	—	Unc	300.00
S582	5 PESOS 188x. Black on green unpt. Man at l., seated woman w/flowers at ctr. r. Back green.			
	p. Proof.	—	Unc	300.00
	s. Specimen.	—	Unc	300.00

		GOOD	FINE	XF
S583	10 PESOS 188x. Black on orange unpt. Seated woman w/fruit at l., man at lower r. Back orange.			
	p. Proof.	—	Unc	300.00
	s. Specimen.	—	Unc	300.00

		GOOD	FINE	XF
S585	50 PESOS 188x. Black on gold unpt. Allegory of Art at l., condor at ctr., man at lower r. Back deep gold.			
	p. Proof.	—	Unc	300.00
	s. Specimen.	—	Unc	300.00

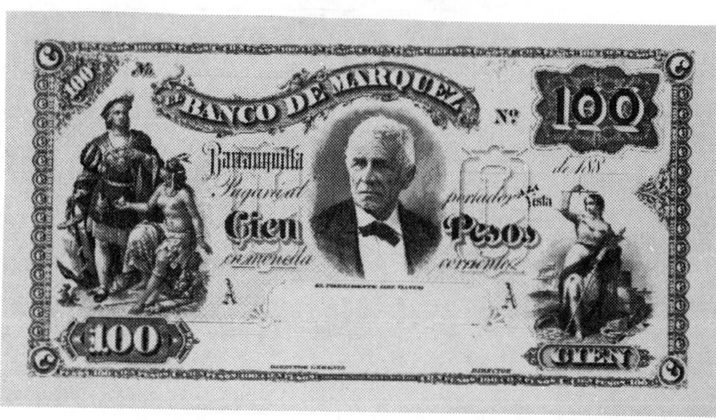

		GOOD	FINE	XF
S586	100 PESOS 188x (ca. 1882). Black on blue unpt. Columbus and Indian at l., man at ctr., Justice at r. Back blue.			
	p. Proof.	—	Unc	400.00
	s. Specimen.	—	Unc	500.00

NOTE: #S581-S586 are known issued only w/red seal ovpt: *Banco Nacional* and *30.10.1899* date on back. For listing see #S651-S655.

BANCO DE MEDELLIN

Issued at Medellin.

1895 ISSUE

#S591-S597 printer: BWC.

		GOOD	FINE	XF
S591	50 CENTAVOS 1.3.1895. Black on gold unpt. Portr. woman w/flag at l., beehives at top ctr., grapes at r. Back gold.	20.00	85.00	125.00

		GOOD	FINE	XF
S592	1 PESO 18xx. Black. Specimen.	—	—	—
S593	5 PESOS 18xx. Black. Specimen.	—	—	—
S594	10 PESOS 18xx. Black. Specimen.	—	—	—

		GOOD	FINE	XF
S597	100 PESOS 18xx. Black on orange and green unpt. Portr. woman w/flag at l., horses at top ctr., child w/pick at r. Back orange and green. Specimen.	—	—	—

1899 ISSUE

#S599 and S600 printer: Tipografia Central-Medellin.

		GOOD	FINE	XF
S599	**5 PESOS** 17.10.1899. Black. Seated woman w/hammer at lower l. Series C.	40.00	150.00	275.00

NOTE: For similar 5 Pesos see #S777.

		GOOD	FINE	XF
S600	**10 PESOS** 17.10.1899; 8.12.1899. Black on red-orange unpt. River scene w/church and trees at ctr. Back lilac. Series A1; A3.	25.00	100.00	225.00

1899 PROVISIONAL ISSUE

		GOOD	FINE	XF
S606	**1 PESO** 30.10.1899. Ovpt. new bank name and *7.9.1899* date in 7 lines of ovpt. on back of Banco Republicano #S811.	25.00	100.00	225.00
S607	**5 PESOS** 30.10.1899. Ovpt. as #S606 on back of Banco Republicano #S812.	—	Rare	—

		GOOD	FINE	XF
S608	**10 PESOS** 1899. Ovpt. as #S606 on back of Banco Republicano #S813.	—	Rare	—

BANCO MERCANTIL DE MEDELLIN

Issued at Medellin.

1870S ISSUE

		GOOD	FINE	XF
S611	**10 PESOS** 187x. Black on thin white paper. 2 seated allegorical women and casks at upper ctr. Uniface proof.	—	Rare	—

BANCO NACIONAL

PROVISIONAL ISSUES ONLY

All notes listed under this bank in this volume w/red seal ovpt: *BANCO NACIONAL* on face, and text ovpt. as follows: *ESTE BILLETE CIRCULA PROVISIONALMENTE COMO BILLETE DEL BANCO NACIONAL DE ACUERDO CON EL DECRETO NUMERO 517 DEL 30 DE OCTUBRE DE 1899 BOGOTÁ. OCTUBRE 30 DE 1899...* 3 printed sign. of members of the *Junta de Emisión*. There are variations in style of ovpt., but not content.

1899 PROVISIONAL ISSUES

#S616-S620 ovpt. on Banco de Bogotá notes, first issue (#S271-S276).

		GOOD	FINE	XF
S616	**1 PESO** 30.10.1899. Ovpt. on S271.	80.00	225.00	350.00
S617	**2 PESOS** 30.10.1899. Ovpt. on #S272.	80.00	225.00	350.00

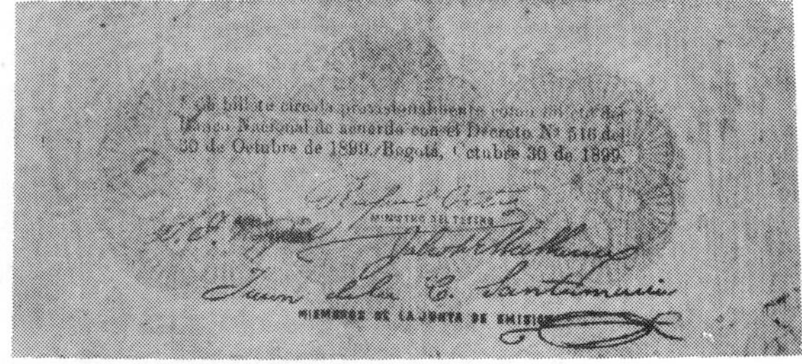

		GOOD	FINE	XF
S618	**5 PESOS** 30.10.1899. Ovpt. on #S273.	80.00	225.00	350.00
S619	**10 PESOS** 30.10.1899. Ovpt. on #S275.	90.00	275.00	350.00

		Good	Fine	XF
S620	**50 Pesos** 30.10.1899. Ovpt. on #S276.	—	Rare	—

#S621-S624 ovpt. on Banco de Bogotá notes, second issue (#S281-S284).

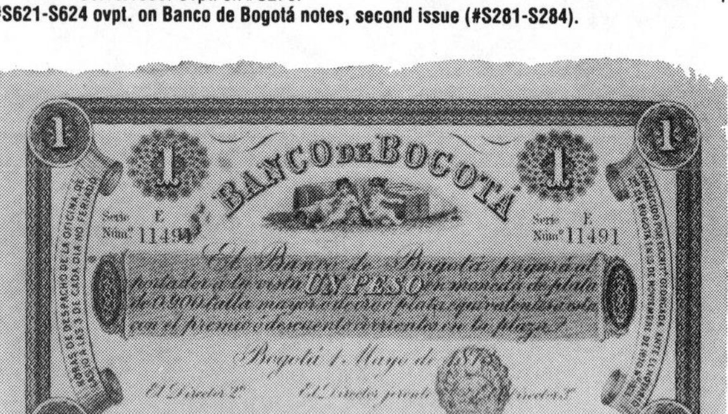

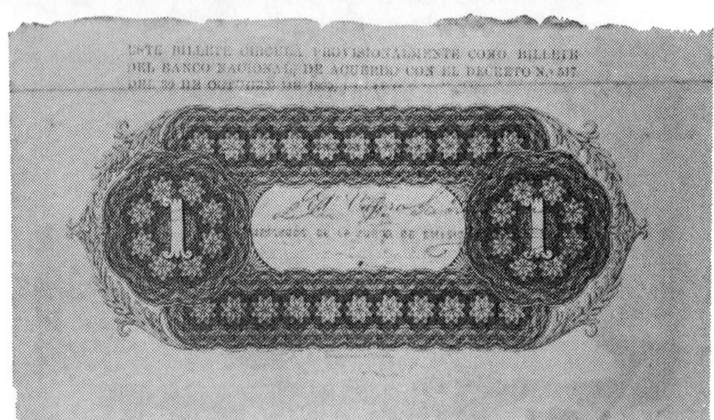

		Good	Fine	XF
S621	**1 Peso** 30.10.1899. Ovpt. on #S281.	75.00	200.00	325.00
S622	**5 Pesos** 30.10.1899. Ovpt. on #S282.	100.00	200.00	325.00
S623	**10 Pesos** 30.10.1899. Ovpt. on #S283.	150.00	250.00	400.00
S624	**50 Pesos** 30.10.1899. Ovpt. on #S284.	—	Rare	—

#S627-S630 ovpt. on Banco de Bogotá notes, third issue (#S292-S295).

		Good	Fine	XF
S627	**5 Pesos** 30.10.1899. Ovpt. on #S292.	75.00	200.00	325.00
S628	**10 Pesos** 30.10.1899. Ovpt. on #S293.	85.00	250.00	400.00

		Good	Fine	XF
S629	**50 Pesos** 30.10.1899. Ovpt. on #S294.	—	Rare	—

		Good	Fine	XF
S630	**100 Pesos** 30.10.1899. Ovpt. on #S295.	—	Rare	—

#S636-S640 ovpt. on Banco Hipotecario notes (#S511-S515).

		Good	Fine	XF
S636	**5 Pesos** 30.10.1899. Ovpt. on #S511.	80.00	225.00	350.00

S637 10 PESOS
30.10.1899. Ovpt. on #S512.

GOOD	FINE	XF
100.00	250.00	400.00

S639 50 PESOS
30.10.1899. Ovpt. on #S514.

GOOD	FINE	XF
—	Rare	—

S640 100 PESOS
30.10.1899. Ovpt. on #S515.

GOOD	FINE	XF
—	Rare	—

#S646-S649 ovpt. on Banco Internacional notes (#S561-S564).

S646 1 PESO
30.10.1899. Ovpt. on #S561.

GOOD	FINE	XF
75.00	175.00	300.00

S647 5 PESOS
30.10.1899. Ovpt. on #S562.

GOOD	FINE	XF
100.00	250.00	375.00

S648 10 PESOS
30.10.1899. Ovpt. on #S563.

GOOD	FINE	XF
100.00	250.00	375.00

S649 50 PESOS
30.10.1899. Ovpt. on #S564.

GOOD	FINE	XF
—	Rare	—

#S651-S655A ovpt. on Banco de Marquez notes (#S581-S585).

S651 1 PESO
30.10.1899. Ovpt. on #S581.

GOOD	FINE	XF
75.00	175.00	300.00

S652 5 PESOS
30.10.1899. Ovpt. on #S582.

GOOD	FINE	XF
90.00	250.00	400.00

S653 10 PESOS
30.10.1899. Ovpt. on #S583.

GOOD	FINE	XF
100.00	275.00	425.00

S655 50 PESOS
30.10.1899. Ovpt. on #S585.

GOOD	FINE	XF
—	Rare	—

S655A 100 PESOS
Reported Not Confirmed

#S656-S663 ovpt. on Banco Popular notes (#S736-S740, S747-S749).

		GOOD	FINE	XF
S656	50 CENTAVOS 30.10.1899. Ovpt. on #S736.	80.00	200.00	325.00

		GOOD	FINE	XF
S657	1 PESO 30.10.1899. Ovpt. on #S737.	100.00	250.00	400.00

		GOOD	FINE	XF
S658	5 PESOS 30.10.1899. Ovpt. on #S738.	100.00	250.00	400.00
S659	5 PESOS 30.10.1899. Ovpt. on #S739.	100.00	250.00	400.00

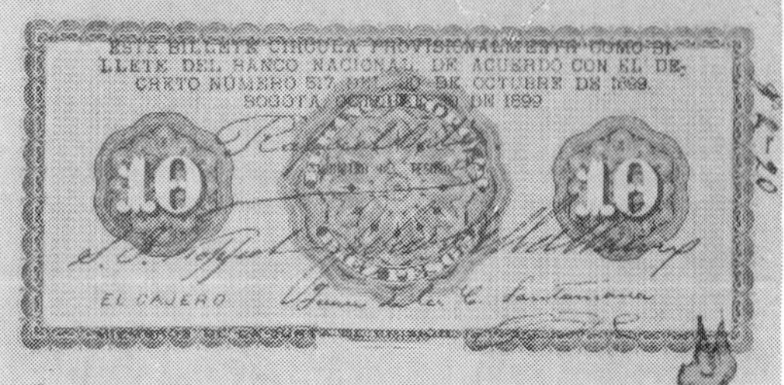

		GOOD	FINE	XF
S660	10 PESOS 30.10.1899. Ovpt. on #S740.	90.00	250.00	375.00

		GOOD	FINE	XF
S661	25 PESOS 30.10.1899. Ovpt. on #S747.	—	Rare	—
S662	50 PESOS 30.10.1899. Ovpt. on #S748.	—	Rare	—
S663	100 PESOS 30.10.1899. Ovpt. on #S749.	—	Rare	—

#S666 and S667 ovpt. on Banco de la Union notes (#S861-S862).

		GOOD	FINE	XF
S666	5 PESOS 30.10.1899. Ovpt. on #S861.	120.00	250.00	400.00

		GOOD	FINE	XF
S667	10 PESOS 30.10.1899. Ovpt. on #S862.	150.00	300.00	550.00

#S670 ovpt. on Banco Union note.

		GOOD	FINE	XF
S670	50 PESOS 30.10.1899. Ovpt. on #S869.	—	Rare	—

#S672-S677 ovpt. on Caja de Propietarios notes (#S881-S886).

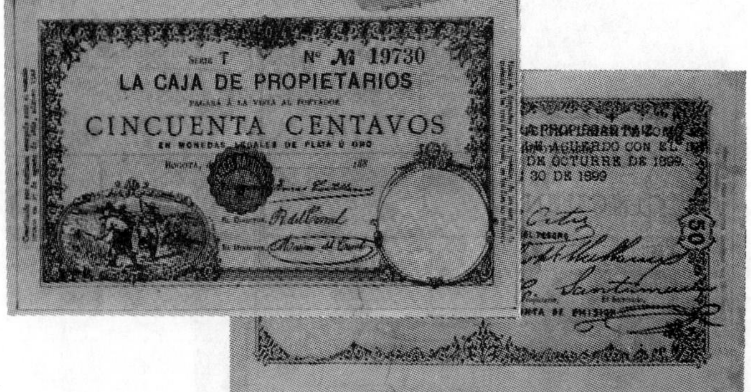

		GOOD	FINE	XF
S672	50 CENTAVOS 30.10.1899. Ovpt. on #S881.	60.00	150.00	250.00

		GOOD	FINE	XF
S673	**1 PESO** 30.10.1899. Ovpt. on #S882.	75.00	175.00	300.00

		GOOD	FINE	XF
S674	**2 PESOS** 30.10.1899. Ovpt. on #S883.	75.00	175.00	300.00

		GOOD	FINE	XF
S675	**5 PESOS** 30.10.1899. Ovpt. on #S884.	100.00	225.00	400.00

		GOOD	FINE	XF
S676	**10 PESOS** 30.10.1899. Ovpt. on #S885.	110.00	275.00	450.00

		GOOD	FINE	XF
S677	**20 PESOS** 30.10.1899. Ovpt. on #S886.	150.00	325.00	500.00

NOTE: All regularly prepared notes issued by the Banco Nacional 1881 to 1900 are listed in Vol. 2.

BANCO DEL NORTE

Issued at Socorro.

1882 ISSUE

#S681-S684 printer: D. Paredes.

		VG	VF	UNC
S681	**1 PESO** 1.1.1882. Black on brown unpt. Dog lying down at ctr. Back brown. Series A. Unsigned remainder.	3.50	7.50	17.50

		VG	VF	UNC
S682	**5 PESOS** 1.1.1882. Black on aqua unpt. Horses at upper l. Back aqua. Series B. Unsigned remainder.	3.50	7.50	17.50

		VG	VF	UNC
S683	**10 PESOS** 1.1.1882. Black on orange unpt. Early steam train by station at upper l. Back deep orange. Series C. Unsigned remainder.	5.00	15.00	37.50

		VG	VF	UNC
S684	**20 PESOS** 1.1.1882. Black on gold unpt. Portr. Gen. Santander at l. Back gold. Series D. Unsigned remainder.	4.00	10.00	22.50

BANCO DEL OCCIDENTE

Issued at Facatativa.

1882 ISSUE

#S691 and S692 printer: D. Paredes.

		VG	VF	UNC
S691	**5 PESOS** 1.5.1882. Steam locomotive.	—	Rare	—

		VG	VF	UNC
S692	**10 PESOS** 1.5.1882. Black on green unpt. Horses at upper ctr. Back orange. Series B.	—	Rare	—

BANCO DEL ORIENTE

Issued at Rionegro.

1884-1900 ISSUE

#S696-S701 meadow and mountain scene at upper ctr. Printer: PBC.

		GOOD	FINE	XF
S696	**50 CENTAVOS** 2.1.1900. Red-orange.	20.00	50.00	100.00

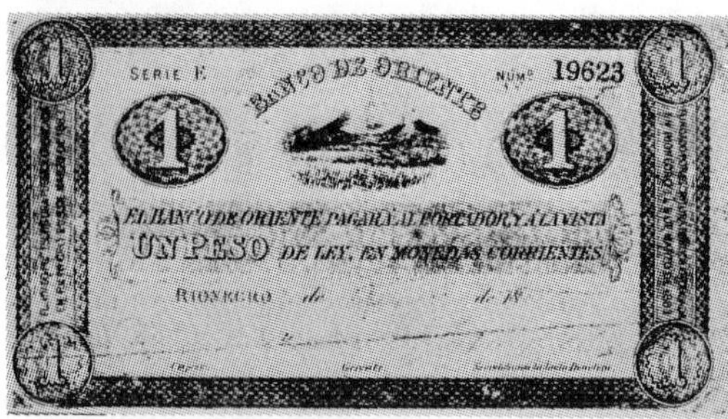

		GOOD	FINE	XF
S697	**1 PESO** 2.1.1900. Blue. Series E.	25.00	55.00	100.00
S698	**5 PESOS** 4.2.1884; 25.2.1887; 5.3.1900. Gold. Series I.	30.00	65.00	100.00

		GOOD	FINE	XF
S699	**10 PESOS** 22.2.1884; 5.3.1890; 5.3.1900. Green. Series O.	55.00	125.00	200.00

		GOOD	FINE	XF
S701	**100 PESOS** 5.7.1884; 5.3.1900. Lilac. Series U.	70.00	150.00	250.00

NOTE: A lg. hoard of this series was found several years ago in the bank archives.

BANCO DE PAMPLONA

Issued at Pamplona.

1883 ISSUE

		GOOD	FINE	XF
S706	**5 PESOS** 1.1.1883; 2.5.1883. Black on red unpt. Similar to #S378. Back red. Series B.	60.00	150.00	250.00

1883-84 ISSUE

#S711-S714 printer: BWC.

		GOOD	FINE	XF
S711	**1 PESO** 9.7.1883. Black on gold unpt. Portr. woman at upper ctr. Back gold. Series A.			
	a. Back w/o bank stamping.	7.00	20.00	50.00
	b. Back w/bank stamping.	7.00	20.00	50.00

		GOOD	FINE	XF
S712	**5 PESOS** 4.3.1884. Black on blue unpt. Portr. woman at upper ctr. Back blue. Series B.	100.00	250.00	400.00

S713 10 PESOS — GOOD 40.00 · FINE 120.00 · XF 250.00
21.1.1884; 4.3.1884; 19.5.1884. Black on green unpt. Bear at upper ctr. Back green. Series C.

S714 20 PESOS — GOOD 125.00 · FINE 250.00 · XF 500.00
21.1.1884; 4.3.1884. Black on red unpt. Leopard at upper ctr. Back red. Series D.

BANCO DE PANAMÁ

Formerly the Banco de Circulación y Descuento de Perez y Planas. Notes issued at Panamá w/vertical ovpt: *Administración general de Hacienda...* on back.

1869 ISSUE

#S721-S725 printer: ABNC.

S721 1 PESO — GOOD 175.00 · FINE 375.00 · XF 850.00
ND (ca. 1869). Black on green unpt. A. Planas at upper ctr. Red line ovpt. on sign. at lower r. Back green. Red text ovpt. vertically at r. (folio registry).

S722 5 PESOS — GOOD 350.00 · FINE 750.00 · XF 1250.
ND (ca. 1869). Black on brown unpt. Portr. A. Planas at l., globe between steamship and steam passenger train at ctr. r. Back blue; red ovpt. at r. like #S721.

S723 10 PESOS — GOOD — · FINE Rare · XF —
ND (ca.1869). Black on brown unpt. Similar to #S722. Back orange.

S724 20 PESOS — GOOD — · FINE Rare · XF —
ND (ca.1869). Black on orange unpt. Globe between steamship and steam passenger train at upper l. ctr., A. Planas at lower r. Back brown.

S725 50 PESOS — GOOD — · FINE Rare · XF —
ND (ca.1869). Black on tan unpt. A. Planas at lower l. and r., globe between steamship and steam passenger train at upper ctr. Back orange.

BANCO DE CIRCULACIÓN Y DESCUENTO DE PEREZ Y PLANAS

Later became the Banco de Panamá. Notes prepared for issue at Panamá.

1865 ISSUE

#S726-S730 design generally similar to #S722. Printer: ABNC.

S726 1 PESO — GOOD — · FINE Rare · XF —
ND (ca.1865). Black on brown unpt. Specimen.

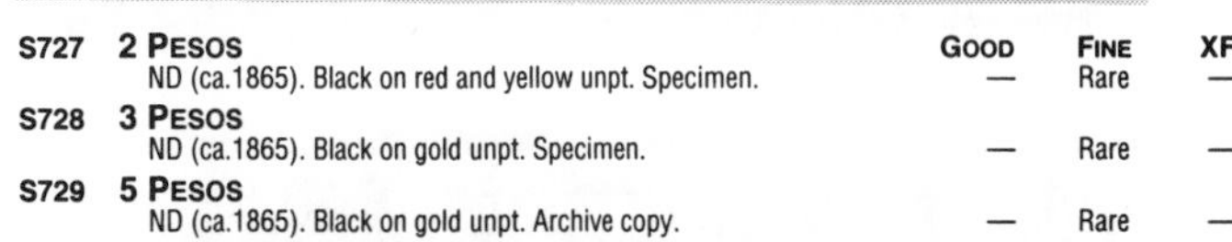

S727 2 PESOS — GOOD — · FINE Rare · XF —
ND (ca.1865). Black on red and yellow unpt. Specimen.

S728 3 PESOS — GOOD — · FINE Rare · XF —
ND (ca.1865). Black on gold unpt. Specimen.

S729 5 PESOS — GOOD — · FINE Rare · XF —
ND (ca.1865). Black on gold unpt. Archive copy.

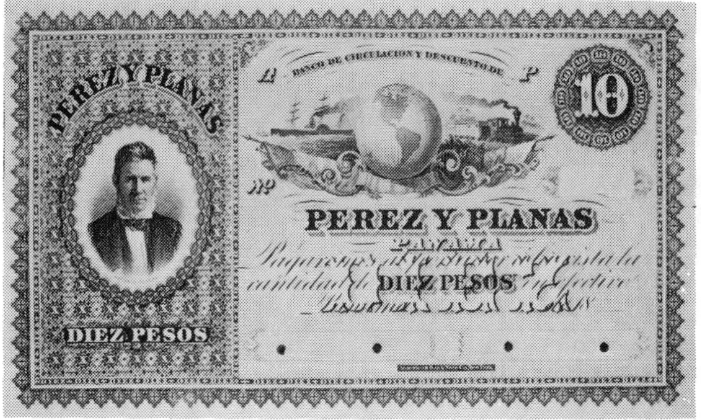

		Good	Fine	XF
S730	**10 Pesos** ND (ca.1865). Black on brown unpt. Specimen.	—	Rare	—

Banco Popular

Issued at Bogotá.

1877 Issue

#S736-S739 printer: D. Paredes.

		Good	Fine	XF
S736	**50 Centavos** 20.7.1877. Black on green unpt. Woman and globe vertically at l. Uniface. Series A.	—	—	
S737	**1 Peso** 20.7.1877. Black on orange unpt. Farmer plowing w/oxen at ctr. Back orange. Series B.	—	—	—
S738	**5 Pesos** 20.7.1877. Black on yellow unpt. Man and dog at ctr. Text under denomination at ctr. ends in *moneda de talla mayor.* Back yellow. Series C.	—	—	—
S739	**5 Pesos** 20.7.1877. Black on blue unpt. Like #S738, but text ends in ...*en moneda corriente.* Back blue.	—	—	—
S739A	**5 Pesos** 20.7.1877. Like #S739 but text w/o *En Moneda Corriente.* Series C.	—	—	—
S740	**10 Pesos** 20.7.1877. Black. 2 allegorical women, child and sheep at ctr. Back green. Printer: CCBB.	—	—	—
S743	**100 Pesos** 20.7.1877. Text similar to #S738.	—	—	—

1882 Issue

#S747-S749 printer: ABNC.

		Good	Fine	XF
S747	**25 Pesos** 1.1.1882. Black on brown unpt. Portr. 2 girls at l., seated woman w/llama at r. Back brown. Series D.	—	Rare	—

		Good	Fine	XF
S748	**50 Pesos** 1.1.1882. Black on green unpt. Family on log raft at upper l. ctr., cherub at lower r. Back green. Series E. Proof.	—	Unc	400.00

		Good	Fine	XF
S749	**100 Pesos** 1.1.1882. Black on gold unpt. Reclining allegorical woman w/book at l., portr. man at lower r. Back orange. Series F.			
	p. Proof.	—	Unc	400.00
	s. Specimen.	—	Unc	500.00

NOTE: #S736-S740, S748 and S749 are known in issued form only w/red ovpt: *Banco Nacional* and *30.10.1899* date in ovpt. on back. For listing see #S656-S663.

Banco Popular de Bolívar

Issued at Cartagena.

1883-86 Issue

#S756-S758 printer: Tip de Antonio Araujo.

		Good	Fine	XF
S756	**1 Peso** 20.2.1883. Black on lt. green and magenta unpt. Back gray.	—	Rare	—

		Good	Fine	XF
S757	**5 Pesos** 18xx. Black and blue on pink paper. Horse's head at lower r. Back blue.	—	Rare	—
S758	**10 Pesos** 18xx. Black and red on pink paper. Back red.	—	Rare	—

#S761 and S762 printer: ABNC.

		Good	Fine	XF
S761	**1 Peso** 11.4.1886. Black on orange unpt. Woman and horse at l., 2 horses and man leading mule train at r. Back orange.			
	a. Issued note.	—	Rare	—
	p. Proof.	—	—	—

		Good	Fine	XF
S762	**5 Pesos** 18xx. Black on blue unpt. 2 women at l., man and horses at r. Back blue.			
	p. Proof.	—	Unc	300.00
	r. Remainder w/sign.	200.00	—	—
	s. Specimen.	—	Unc	300.00

BANCO POPULAR DE MEDELLIN

Issued at Medellin.

1883-93 ISSUE

		GOOD	FINE	XF
S766	**20 CENTAVOS** 12.1893. Black and green on yellow unpt. Uniface.	—	—	—

#S770-S773 printer: ABNC.

		GOOD	FINE	XF
S770	**50 CENTAVOS** 31.12.1883. Black on lg. orange unpt. Gauchos roping steers at upper l., girl at upper ctr. r., farmer carrying sheaves at lower r. Back lt. orange. Series A.			
	a. Issued note.	—	—	—
	p. Proof.	—	Unc	300.00
	s. Specimen.	—	Unc	300.00

		GOOD	FINE	XF
S771	**1 PESO** 3.1885; 1.12.1893. Black on green unpt. Angel at upper l., farm implements and sheaf at upper r. ctr., allegorical woman w/torch at r. Back green. Series B.			
	p. Proof.	—	Unc	300.00
	s. Specimen.	—	Unc	300.00

		GOOD	FINE	XF
S772	**5 PESOS** 1.5.1883. Black and red-orange. Condor at l., woman w/sheaves and sheep at upper r. Back red-orange. Series C.			
	a. Issued note.	200.00	450.00	700.00
	p. Proof.	—	Unc	300.00
	s. Specimen.	—	Unc	300.00

		GOOD	FINE	XF
S773	**10 PESOS** 21.12.1883; 1.5.1885. Brown and black. Man watering horses at l., 2 cherubs and dog on safe at ctr., standing woman at r. Back brown. Series D.			
	a. Issued note.	190.00	350.00	650.00
	p. Proof.	—	Unc	300.00

1899 PROVISIONAL ISSUE

		GOOD	FINE	XF
S776	**1 PESO** 30.10.1899. Ovpt. new bank name and *7.9.1899* date in 6 lines of ovpt. at r. on face of Banco Republicano #S811. 2 or 3 hand stamps on back.	125.00	275.00	400.00

		GOOD	FINE	XF
S776A	**5 PESOS** 30.10.1899. Ovpt. new bank name and text in seven lines on back of #S812.	—	Rare	—

S777 5 PESOS — GOOD 90.00 · FINE 200.00 · XF 300.00
17.10.1899. Black on green unpt. Seated woman w/hammer at l. Back green. Series C1a. Printer: Tipografia Central, Medellin.

NOTE: For similar 5 Pesos see #S599.

S778 10 PESOS — GOOD — · FINE — · XF —
17.10.1899. Black and red. Tropical view at ctr.

BANCO POPULAR DE SOTO

Issued at Bucaramanga.

1880S ISSUE

#S781-S783 printer: ABNC.

S781 1 PESO
188x. Black on green unpt. Portr. man at ctr., seated allegorical woman w/money and scales at r. Back green.

		GOOD	FINE	XF
a.	Ovpt: *14.11.1900* date in 9 lines of text and 4 sign. on back.	90.00	225.00	350.00
p.	Proof.	—	Unc	300.00

S782 5 PESOS
188x. Black on red-brown unpt. Portr. man at l. ctr., seated Justice at r. Back red-brown.

		GOOD	FINE	XF
a.	Ovpt: *14.11.1900* like #S781a.	90.00	225.00	350.00
p.	Proof.	—	Unc	300.00

S783 10 PESOS
188x. Black on red unpt. Bust of Gen. Santander at l., Raphael's angel at ctr. r. Back red.

		GOOD	FINE	XF
a.	Ovpt: *14.11.1900* like #781a.	100.00	300.00	450.00
p.	Proof.	—	Unc	300.00

BANCO PRENDARIO

Issued at Bogotá.

1881-84 ISSUE

#S788-S790 uniface. Printer: D. Paredes.

S788 1 PESO
1881; 188x. Black on blue unpt. Workers at upper l.

		GOOD	FINE	XF
a.	Issued note.	—	Rare	—
r.	Unsigned remainder. Series A.	—	Rare	—

S790 10 PESOS — GOOD — · FINE Rare · XF —
1.6.1884. Black on brown unpt. Eagle at upper l., beehives at upper r. Series C.

BANCO PRENDARIO DE SOTO

Issued at Bucaramanga.

1884 ISSUE

S796 5 PESOS
1.1.1884. Black on orange unpt. Allegorical woman w/sheaf, beehive and sickle at ctr. Back purple text. Printer: D. Paredes.

		GOOD	FINE	XF
a.	Issued note.	10.00	20.00	45.00
b.	*14.11.1900* date in 9 lines of ovpt. like #S781a, also red outlined seal of the treasury of the Departamento de Santander at l.	80.00	175.00	250.00

NOTE: A large hoard was found of #S796a several years ago.

BANCO DEL PROGRESO

Issued at Medellin.

1883-99 ISSUE

S801 50 CENTAVOS — GOOD — · FINE Rare · XF —
10.12.1883; 22.11.1899. Black. Seated woman w/plants at ctr. Back blue.

S802 1 PESO — GOOD — · FINE Rare · XF —
22.11.1899. Black on red-brown unpt. 3 allegorical women at upper ctr. Back brown.

		Good	Fine	XF
S803	**5 Pesos** 1.2.1895. Black on green unpt. Allegorical woman and man w/wheat and tools at upper ctr. Back green.	—	Rare	—
S804	**10 Pesos** 17.10.1899. Scenery.	—	Rare	—

1899 Provisional Issue

		Good	Fine	XF
S805	**1 Peso** 1899. Ovpt. new bank name and date as on #S806 on back of #S811.	—	—	—
S806	**10 Pesos** 30.10.1899. Ovpt. new bank name and *7.9.1899* date in 7 lines of text on back of Banco Republicano #S813.	90.00	225.00	400.00

Banco de la República

188x Issue

#S807-S810A black and green. Not issued. Printer: HLBNC.

		Good	Fine	XF
S807	**1 Peso = 1 Dollar** 188x. Train crossing bridge at ctr. Triangular guilloches at upper corners.	—	Unc	250.00

		Good	Fine	XF
S807A	**1 Peso = 1 Dollar** 188x. Similar to #S807, but ornate round guilloches at upper corners. Cut cancelled.	—	Unc	250.00
S808	**2 Pesos = 2 Dollars** 188x. Train emerging from tunnel at lower ctr. Portr. Washington at ctr. on back.	—	Unc	250.00
S808A	**2 Pesos = 2 Dollars** 188x. Minerva reclining w/cherub at ctr. Back green.	—	Unc	250.00
S809	**5 Pesos = 5 Dollars** 188x. Portr. Washington at ctr.	—	Unc	250.00
S809A	**5 Pesos = 5 Dollars** 188x. Eagle at ctr. Punched hole cancelled.	—	Unc	250.00

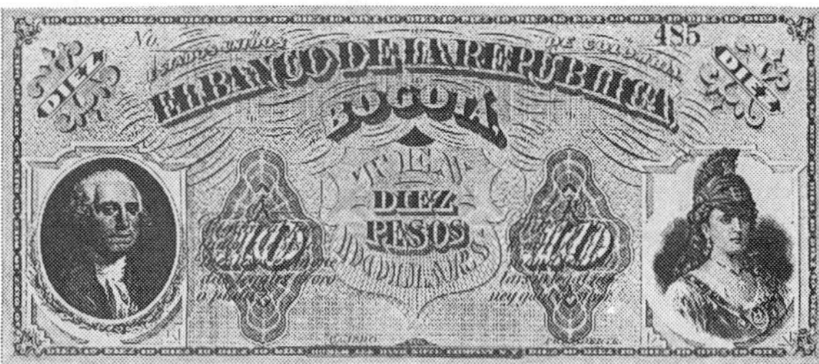

		Good	Fine	XF
S810	**10 Pesos = 10 Dollars** 188x. Portr. Washington at lower l., Minerva at lower r.	—	Unc	250.00
S810A	**10 Pesos = 10 Dollars** 188x. Woman standing at l. and r.	—	Unc	250.00

Banco Republicano

Issued at Medellin.

1899 Issue

#S811-S813 printer: BWC.

		Good	Fine	XF
S811	**1 Peso** 30.10.1899. Black on red unpt. Flags at l. and r., woman at ctr. Back red.	100.00	175.00	250.00

		Good	Fine	XF
S812	**5 Pesos** 30.10.1899. Black on red and orange unpt. Flag at l. and r., winged Mercury at upper ctr.			
	a. Issued note.	250.00	375.00	500.00
	s. Specimen.	—	Unc	300.00

		Good	Fine	XF
S813	**10 Pesos** 30.10.1899. Black and m/c on blue unpt. Flags at l. and r., cows at ctr. Back blue.	—	Rare	—

NOTE: Except for #S812, notes of the Banco Republicano are known in issued form only w/ovpt. of other bank names. See #S398, S606, S608, S776 and S806.

Banco de Rio Hacha

1883-85 Issue

		Good	Fine	XF
S816	**20 Centavos** 6.12.1885. Black on red-orange unpt. Portr. S. Bolívár at l., arms at lower r. Back red-orange. Series Y. Imprint: American Bank Note Co., New York. Litho. Specimen.	—	Rare	—

#S817-S819A printer: ABNC.

S817	50 CENTAVOS	GOOD	FINE	XF
	1.1.1883. Black on red-orange unpt. Arms at l., seated allegorical woman w/sheaf at ctr., portr. Bolívar at lower r. Back red-orange. Series A.			
	a. Issued note.	—	Rare	—
	p. Proof.	—	Unc	400.00
	s. Specimen.	—	Unc	400.00

S818	1 PESO	GOOD	FINE	XF
	1.1.1883. Black on lt. orange unpt. Portr. Bolívar at lower l., arms and allegorical woman w/plants at ctr., portr. Gen. A. Nariño at lower r. Back lt. orange. Series B.			
	a. Issued note.	—	Rare	—
	p. Proof.	—	Unc	550.00
	s. Specimen.	—	Unc	550.00

S819	5 PESOS	GOOD	FINE	XF
	1.1.1883. Black on brown unpt. Arms at l., Bolívar at ctr., woman w/wheel at r. Back brown. Series C.			
	p. Proof.	—	Unc	700.00
	s. Specimen.	—	Unc	700.00

S819A	10 PESOS	GOOD	FINE	XF
	1.1.1883. Black on green unpt. Portr. A. J. de Sucre at lower l., arms and woman w/caduceus and eagle at ctr., portr. S. Bolívar at lower r. Back green. Series D.			
	p. Proof.	—	Unc	1000.
	s. Specimen.	—	Unc	1000.

BANCO DEL RUIZ

Issued at Manizales.

1905 ISSUE

#S821-S826 prepared under Law 24 of 1905. Eagle and mountains in circle at ctr. Printer: ABNC.

S821	50 CENTAVOS	GOOD	FINE	XF
	L.1905. Brown on m/c unpt. Back brown.			
	p. Proof.	—	Unc	300.00
	s. Specimen.	—	Unc	300.00
S822	1 PESO			
	L.1905. Green on m/c unpt. Back green.			
	p. Proof.	—	Unc	300.00
	s. Specimen.	—	Unc	300.00
S823	5 PESOS			
	L.1905. Date 19.8.1919 on back. Red-orange on m/c unpt. Back orange.			
	a. Issued note. 1.8.1919.	—	Rare	—
	p. Proof.	—	Unc	300.00
	s. Specimen.	—	Unc	300.00
S824	10 PESOS			
	L.1905. Blue on m/c unpt. Back blue.			
	p. Proof.	—	Unc	300.00
	s. Specimen.	—	Unc	300.00

S825	20 PESOS	GOOD	FINE	XF
	L.1905. Black on m/c unpt. Panel of Interest markers at r. Back olive-green.			
	p. Proof.	—	Unc	300.00
	s. Specimen.	—	Unc	300.00
S826	50 PESOS			
	L.1905. Date 19.8.1919 on back.	—	Unc	300.00

NOTE: Except for #S823, #S821-S825 are known issued only w/new bank name ovpt. See Banco del Huila and Banco Lopez.

BANCO DE SANTANDER

Issued at Bucaramanga.

1873-1900 ISSUE

#S831-S835 printer: PBC.

S831 1 PESO

1.6.1873; 18.6.1883. Black. Star at ctr.

		GOOD	FINE	XF
a.	Issued note w/o ovpt.	—	Rare	—
b.	1.6.1873. W/ovpt: *Pagadero en moneda corriente.*	40.00	75.00	100.00

c.	Ovpt: *Decreto. 6.1.1900* date in 4 lines of ovpt. text on back. 4 sign. also part of ovpt. (sign. varieties).	3.50	10.00	25.00

S832 5 PESOS

1.6.1873; 6.1.1900. Blue. Woman seated near cross at ctr.

		GOOD	FINE	XF
a.	1.6.1873.	—	Rare	—
b.	Ovpt: *Decreto. 6.1.1900* like #S831c.	4.00	12.00	30.00

S833 10 PESOS

1.6.1873; 6.1.1900. Brown. Snake at upper ctr.

		GOOD	FINE	XF
a.	1.6.1873.	—	Rare	—
b.	Ovpt: *Decreto. 6.1.1900* like #S831c.	4.00	12.00	30.00

S834 20 PESOS

1.6.1873; 6.1.1900. Green. Mercury w/staff at upper ctr.

		GOOD	FINE	XF
a.	1.6.1873.	—	Rare	—
b.	Ovpt: *Decreto. 6.1.1900* like #S831c.	75.00	200.00	350.00

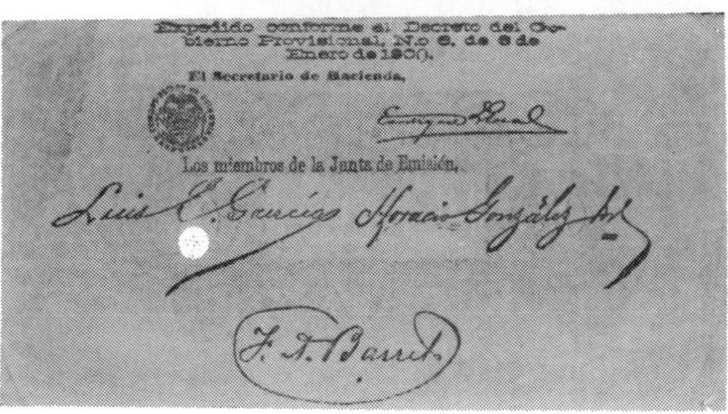

S835 50 PESOS

1.6.1873; 6.1.1900. Yellow.

		GOOD	FINE	XF
a.	1.6.1873.	—	Rare	—
b.	Ovpt: *Decreto. 6.1.1900* like #S831c.	25.00	150.00	225.00

NOTE: Most notes of #S831-S835 are known in issued form only w/*1900* date ovpt. on back.

BANCO DE SOGAMOSO

Issued at Sogamoso.

1882 ISSUE

#S841-S844 printer: D. Paredes.

S841 5 PESOS

	GOOD	FINE	XF
15.8.1882 (hand dated 22.10.1882 or 28.10.1882 at bottom ctr.). Black on green unpt. Horses at ctr. Back brown; hand sign. at ctr. Series A.	20.00	50.00	100.00

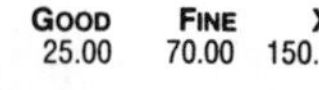

		Good	Fine	XF
S842	10 Pesos 15.8.1882 (hand dated 22.11.1882 at bottom ctr.). Black on red-orange unpt. Cows at water at upper ctr. Back blue-green; hand sign. at ctr. Series B.	25.00	70.00	150.00

		Good	Fine	XF
S843	50 Pesos 15.8.1882. Black on blue unpt. Like #S378 and #S706. Text under large numeral at r. ends in...*moneda de talla mayor.* Back red-orange; hand sign. at ctr. Series C.	30.00	60.00	125.00

		Good	Fine	XF
S844	50 Pesos 15.8.1882. Black on orange unpt. Like #S843 except for text under numeral at r. which ends...*moneda corriente.* Back blue. Series D. Unissued remainder.	20.00	50.00	100.00

NOTE: All sign. for #S841-S844 are forged.

Banco de Sopetrán

Issued at Antioquia.

ca.1880s Issue

#S845-S846A printer: BWC.

		Good	Fine	XF
S845	1 Peso 18xx. Black. Portr. woman at l., cow head at r. Specimen.	—	Rare	—
S846	5 Pesos 18xx. Black. Similar to #S845. Specimen.	—	Rare	—

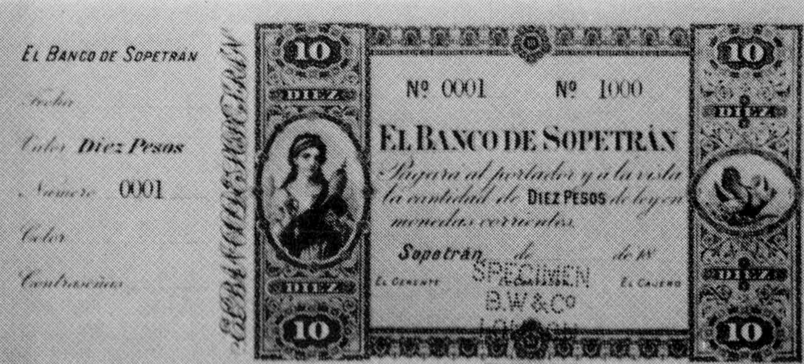

		Good	Fine	XF
S846A	10 Pesos 18xx. Black. Similar to #S845. Specimen, perforated B.W & Co/LONDON.	—	Rare	—

Banco de Sucre

Issued at Medellin.

1913 Issue

#S847 and S848 printer: Arango, Medellin.

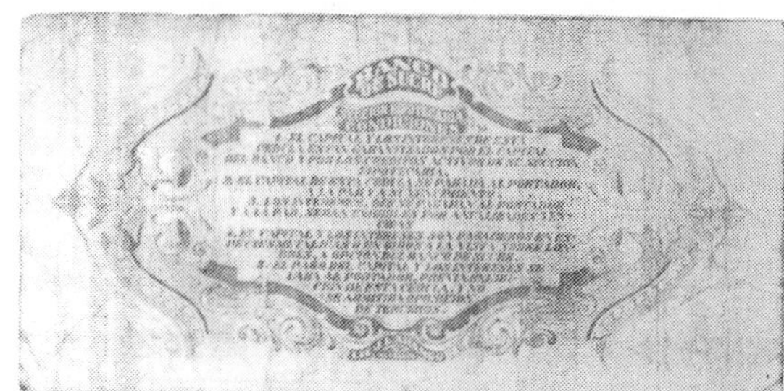

		Good	Fine	XF
S847	50 Centavos 20.5.1913; 20.5.1916. Black on green unpt. Portr. A. J. de Sucre at l. Text on back. Series A.	50.00	110.00	200.00

		Good	Fine	XF
S848	1 Peso 24.9.1913. Black on orange unpt. Allegorical woman at l., portr. A. J. de Sucre at r. Series A.	100.00	175.00	250.00

Banco del Sur

Issued at Pasto.

1907-08 Issue

#S851-S854A portr. Gen. A. Nariño at l., at r. or at ctr. Printer: ABNC.

		Good	Fine	XF
S851	1 Peso 25.8.1908. Black. Portr. at l. Back dk. green.	—	Rare	—

		Good	Fine	XF
S852	5 Pesos ND (ca.1907). Black. Portr. at l. Back dk. green.			
	a. Issued note.	—	Rare	—
	p. Proof.	—	Unc	400.00

		GOOD	FINE	XF
S853	10 PESOS ND (ca.1907). Black. Portr. at ctr. Back dk. green. Proof.	—	Unc	400.00
S854	25 PESOS ND (ca.1907). Black. Portr. at r. Back dk. green. Proof.	—	Unc	400.00

NOTE: #S851-S854 are also known w/ovpt. for Banco López. See #S577-S580.

		GOOD	FINE	XF
S854A	50 PESOS ND (ca.1907). Black. Back dk. green. Proof.	—	Unc	400.00

BANCO DE TEQUENDAMA

Issued at La Mesa.

1881 ISSUE

#S856-858 printer: D. Paredes.

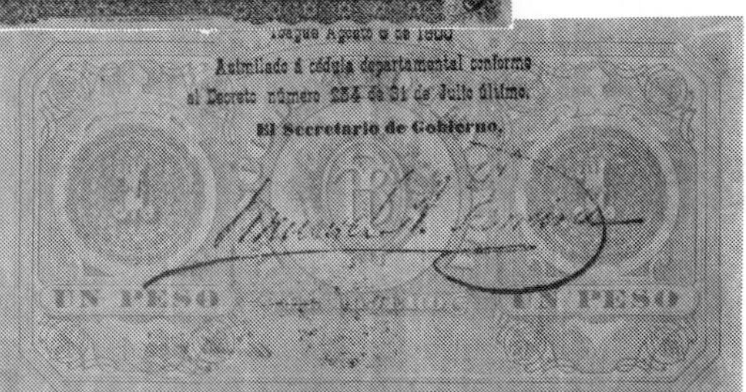

		GOOD	FINE	XF
S856	1 PESO 9.1881. Woman picking from bush at ctr. Back green.			
	a. Black on orange unpt.	—	Rare	—
	b. Black text and ovpt: *6.8.1900,* also purple stamped sign. across ctr. on back. Issued at Ibague.	—	Rare	—

		GOOD	FINE	XF
S858	10 PESOS 20.9.1881. Black on orange unpt. Bldgs. and factories at ctr. Back gray.	—	Rare	—

BANCO DEL TOLIMA

1882 ISSUE

		GOOD	FINE	XF
S859	10 PESOS 1882. Mountain lake w/Mt. Tolima in background. Neiva. Printer: D. Paredes.	—	Rare	—

BANCO DE LA UNION

Palau, Corrales & Compa. Issued at Bogotá.

1883 ISSUE

#S861 and S862 printer: ABNC.

		GOOD	FINE	XF
S861	5 PESOS 1.1.1883. Black on green unpt. Reclining woman leaning on cask at l., Raphael's angel at ctr., seated woman w/sheaf at r. Back green. Proof.	—	Unc	300.00

		GOOD	FINE	XF
S862	10 PESOS 1.1.1883. Black on orange unpt. Helmeted Athena at lower l., dog by boy on horseback at ctr. r. Back orange. Proof.	—	Unc	300.00

NOTE: #S861 and S862 are known in issued form only w/red seal ovpt: *Banco Nacional* and *30.10.1899* date in ovpt. on back. For listing see #S666 and S667.

BANCO UNION

Issued at Cartagena.

1887-88 ISSUE

#S866-S869 printer: ABNC.

		GOOD	FINE	XF
S866	1 PESO 15.4.1887; 5.1.1888. Black on lt. brown unpt. Child at l., sailing ship at ctr., Liberty at r. Back brown.			
	a. Issued note.	100.00	200.00	350.00
	b. Ovpt: *10.2.1900* date in horizontal 7-line text and sign. on back. Punched hole cancelled.	50.00	175.00	250.00
	p. Proof.	—	Unc	300.00

		GOOD	FINE	XF
S867	5 PESOS 5.1.1888. Black on blue unpt. Paddle wheel steamer at ctr., seated woman, numeral and sailing ship at r. Back purplish gray.			
	a. Issued note.	—	Rare	—
	b. Ovpt: *10.2.1900* on back like #S866a.	65.00	225.00	—
	c. Vertical red ovpt: *10.2.1900* at l. on back.	65.00	225.00	—
	p. Proof.	—	Unc	400.00

		Good	Fine	XF
S868	**10 Pesos** 22.2.1887. Black on blue unpt. Seated woman at l., sailing ship at ctr., seated allegorical woman w/vase at r. Back blue.			
	a. Issued note.	100.00	250.00	425.00
	b. Ovpt: *10.2.1900* like #S867b but on face at l.	100.00	250.00	425.00
	p. Proof.	—	Unc	400.00

		Good	Fine	XF
S869	**50 Pesos** 18xx. Black on pink unpt. Portr. shepherdess w/sheep at l., steam locomotive at ctr., seated woman at r. Back red. Proof.	—	Unc	400.00

NOTE: #S869 is known issued only w/red seal ovpt: *Banco Nacional* and *30.10.1899* date in ovpt. on back. For listing see #S670.

Botero Arango e Hijos

Prepared for issue at Medellin.

18xx Issue

		Good	Fine	XF
S876	**50 Centavos** 18xx. Black. Seated woman w/bale at ctr. Proof.	—	Rare	—

Caja de Propietarios

Issued at Bogotá.

1880s Issue

		Good	Fine	XF
S881	**50 Centavos** 188x. Lt. red. Farmers working in field at lower l.	—	—	—
S882	**1 Peso** 188x. Orange. Indian carrying box on back at l.	—	—	—
S883	**2 Pesos** 188x. Green. Woman carrying bags at l.	—	—	—
S884	**5 Pesos** 188x. Violet. Man carrying wide basket at l.	—	—	—
S885	**10 Pesos** 188x. Brown. Man w/loaded mules on mountain path at l.	—	—	—
S886	**20 Pesos** 188x. Blue. Monogram at l., cows and horses in oval at lower ctr.	—	—	—

NOTE: #S881-S886 are known issued only w/red seal ovpt: *Banco Nacional* and *30.10.1899* date in ovpt. on back. For listing see #S672-S677.

G. de Caycedo & Ca.

1884 Issue

		Good	Fine	XF
S886A	**25 Centavos** 1.1.1884. Black on blue unpt. Back blue. Printer: Howard y Jones, Grabadores, Londres.	—	Rare	—

Central American Steam Navigation Co.

Prepared for issue at Chagres.

1851 Issue

#S887-S890 black. Ship at upper l., eagle at ctr., Indian paddling canoe at upper r.

		Good	Fine	XF
S887	**1/2 Peso = 1/2 Dollar** 1.1.1851.	—	Rare	—

		Good	Fine	XF
S888	**1 Peso = 1 Dollar** 1.1.1851.	—	Rare	—
S889	**2 Pesos = 2 Dollars** 1.1.1851.	—	Rare	—
S890	**3 Pesos = 3 Dollars** 1.1.1851.	—	Rare	—

NOTE: #S888 has error *PESOS* in denomination.

Credito Caucano

Issued at Popayán.

1919-22 Cédula Hipotecario Issue

#S891 and S892 printer: ABNC.

		Good	Fine	XF
S891	**15 Pesos** 14.7.1922. Black on m/c unpt. 2 women at l. Back brown; town scene at l.			
	a. Issued note.	—	Rare	—
	p. Proof.	—	Unc	400.00
S892	**20 Pesos** ND (ca. 1919). Black on m/c unpt. Design like #S891. Back green. Proof.	—	Unc	400.00

Exchange Bank of Colón

Prepared for issue at Colón.

1870 Issue

#S896-S899 printer: CONB.

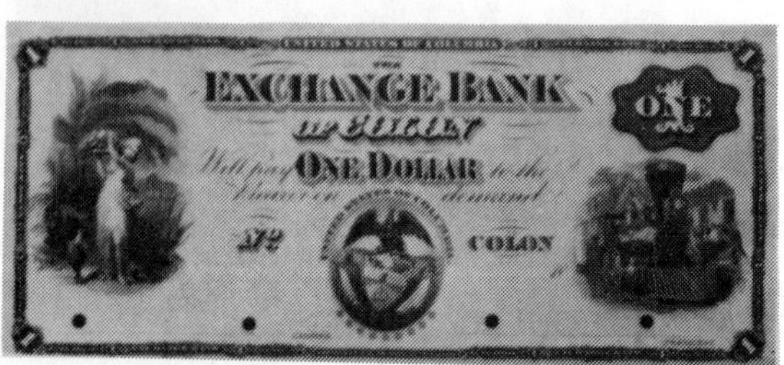

		Good	Fine	XF
S896	**1 Dollar** ND (ca. 1870). Black. Girl holding produce at l., arms at bottom ctr., steam locomotive at lower r.	—	Rare	—

		Good	Fine	XF
S897	**2 Dollars** ND (ca. 1870). Black. Arms at l., loading cotton bales at bottom ctr., steam train at lower r.	—	Rare	—

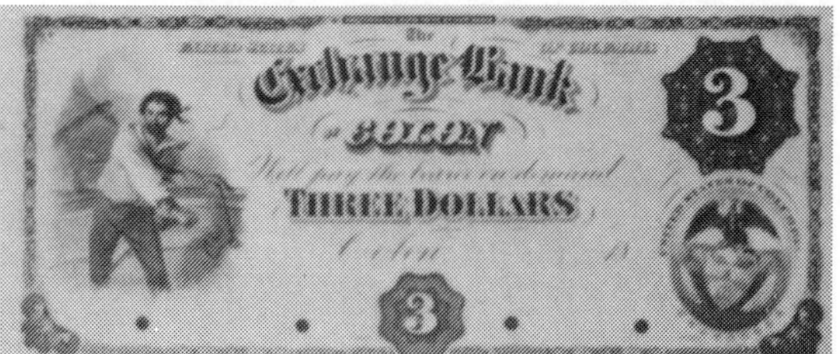

		Good	Fine	XF
S898	**3 Dollars** ND (ca. 1870). Black. Sailor at l., arms at lower r.	—	Rare	—

		Good	Fine	XF
S899	**5 Dollars** ND (ca. 1870). Black. Arms at upper l., paddle wheel steamboat at ctr.	—	Rare	—

NOTE: #S896-S899 are known only as unissued remainders.

La Nueva Compañia Constructora

1880s Issue

		Good	Fine	XF
S900	**5 Pesos** 188x. Black and blue. Bldg. at top ctr. Back blue. Imprint: Lit. de D. Paredes, Bogotá.	150.00	275.00	400.00

Señores Fernando Restrepo & Hijos

1900 Issue

		Good	Fine	XF
S900A	**50 Pesos** 19.5.1900. Black on lt. tan paper.	—	Rare	—

Restrepos y Compañia

1884 Issue

		Good	Fine	XF
S900B	**1 Peso** 5.6.1884. Blue. Seated Justice at upper ctr. Medellin issue. Printer: PBC.			
	a. Issued note.	—	—	—
	s. Specimen.	—	—	—

Reyes Gonzales y Hermanos

Issued at Bucaramanga.

1890s Billete Popular Issue

#S901-S906 printer: BWC (w/o imprint).

		Good	Fine	XF
S901	**1 Peso** ND. Oval purple stamping: *Tesorería General/ LEGITIMO/Bucaramanga.*	10.00	35.00	85.00

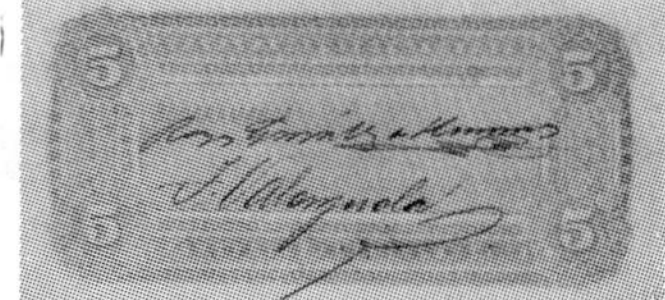

		Good	Fine	XF
S902	**5 Pesos** ND. Black on blue unpt. Hay in bunches at ctr. Back blue; 2 hand sign. Series B.	10.00	35.00	85.00
S903	**10 Pesos** ND. Black on yellow unpt. Fishing.			
	a. Issued note.	—	Rare	—
	b. Ovpt: *1900.*	Reported Not Confirmed		
S904	**20 Pesos** ND. Black on green unpt. Swans at ctr.	—	Rare	—
S905	**50 Pesos** ND. Black on lt. tan unpt. Steam train.	—	Rare	—
S906	**100 Pesos** ND. Black. Specimen.	—	Unc	400.00

Sociedád de Zancudo

Issued at Titiuli and Medellin.

1882 Issue

#S908 and S909 printer: ABNC.

		Good	Fine	XF
S908	**50 Centavos** ND (ca. 1882). Black on brown unpt. Miners at l., portr. Carlos C. Amador at r. Back red.			
	a. Issued note.	—	—	—
	p. Proof.	—	—	—

		Good	Fine	XF
S909	**1 Peso** ND (ca. 1882). Black on green unpt. 4 miners at l., portr. Carlos C. Amador at ctr. r. Back orange, green, blue and red.			
	a. Issued note.	—	—	—
	p. Proof.	—	—	—

URIBE E HIJOS

Issued at Bogotá.

1871 ISSUE

#S911-S915 printer: ABNC.

		GOOD	FINE	XF
S911	**1 PESO** 4.2.1871. Black on green unpt. 4 cherubs at l., cows at upper ctr., seated woman w/produce at lower r. Back green.	—	Rare	—

		GOOD	FINE	XF
S913	**5 PESOS** 187x. (ca.1871). Black on blue unpt. Gauchos roping steers at upper l., portr. young girl's head at upper ctr. r., farmer gathering hay at lower r. Back blue. Proof.	—	Rare	—

		GOOD	FINE	XF
S915	**20 PESOS** 5.2.1871. Black on brown unpt. Portr. young girl holding hen w/chicks at lower l., explorer landing in New World at upper ctr., portr. girl w/dog and puppies at lower r. Back orange.	—	Rare	—

JOSÉ MARÍA MELGUIZO H.

Successor to the Banco de Antioquia.

1900 ISSUE

		GOOD	FINE	XF
S916	**20 CENTAVOS** 19.1.1900. Black on green unpt. Series A2a. Printer: Tipografía Central Medellín.	—	—	—

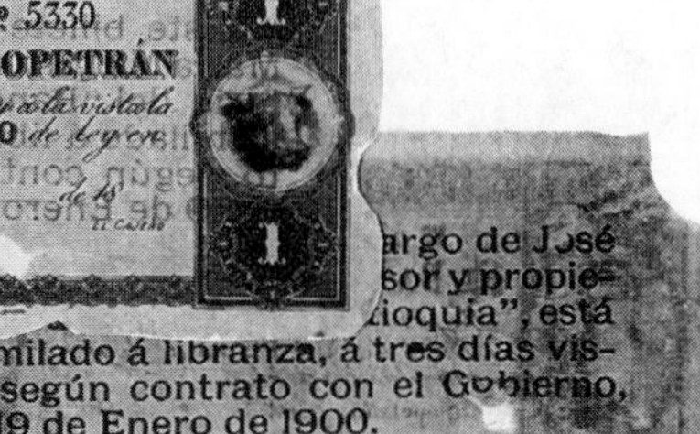

		GOOD	FINE	XF
S918	**1 PESO** 19.1.1900. Black ovpt. of new issuer's name and date in six lines on back of unissued #S845.	—	—	—
S919	**2 PESOS** 19.1.1900 (- old date 188_). Blue on dk. red unpt. New date ovpt. on type of #S222 but w/unissued date in 1880s.	—	—	—

VICENTE B. VILLA E HIJOS

Issued at Medellín.

1880S ISSUE

#S921-S923 printer: ABNC.

		GOOD	FINE	XF
S921	**1 PESO** 188x. Black on blue unpt. Man leading horse at l., allegorical woman w/sheep at ctr. r. Back blue. Series A.			
	p. Proof.	—	Unc	400.00
	r. Unsigned remainder.	—	—	—
	s. Specimen.	—	Unc	400.00
S922	**5 PESOS** 1.2.1885; 1.2.1889. Black on orange unpt. Seated woman at l., Raphael's angel at top ctr. r. Back brown. Series B.			
	a. Issued note.	100.00	275.00	400.00
	p. Proof.	—	Unc	400.00
	s. Specimen.	—	Unc	400.00

		Good	Fine	XF
S923	**10 Pesos** 188x. Black on green unpt. Man w/scythe at l., reclining woman at ctr. r. Back green. Series C.			
	a. Issued note.	100.00	275.00	400.00
	p. Proof.	—	Unc	400.00
	s. Specimen.	—	Unc	400.00

#S931 *Deleted*. See Vol. II #242.

#S936-S938 *Deleted*. See Vol. II #313-313B.

#S941 *Deleted*. See Vol. II #90.

#S943 and S946 *Deleted*. See Vol. II #308 and 309.

#S951-S955 *Deleted*. See Vol. II #312-312D.

#S960, S961 and S963 *Deleted*. See Vol. II #314-314B.

#S967 *Deleted*. See Vol. II #243.

#S971-S979 *Deleted*. See Vol. II #283-290.

#S980-S983 *Deleted*. See Vol. II #291-294.

Section III
Regional Issues, 1898-1919

Departamento de Antioquia

The following issues include notes w/ or w/o heading: *DEPARTAMENTO DE ANTIOQUIA* but issued at Medellin in 1900 and 1901.

1898 Issues

		Good	Fine	XF
S1001	**10 Pesos** 6.10.1898. Black on brown and red unpt. Seated Justice at l., steam locomotive at upper ctr. Back black on green unpt.; arms w/flags and condor at ctr. Series D. Imprint: Tip. Central.	65.00	150.00	275.00

Suministros Por Causa De Guerra Issue

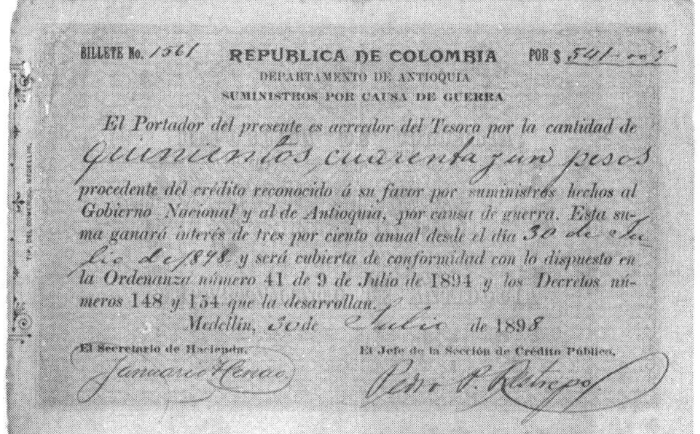

BILLETE No. 1561 REPUBLICA DE COLOMBIA POR $ 541

DEPARTAMENTO DE ANTIOQUIA

SUMINISTROS POR CAUSA DE GUERRA

El Portador del presente es acreedor del Tesoro por la cantidad de quinientos cuarenta y un pesos procedente del crédito reconocido á su favor por suministros hechos al Gobierno Nacional y al de Antioquia, por causa de guerra. Esta suma ganará interés de tres por ciento anual desde el dia 30 de Julio de 1898 y será cubierta de conformidad con lo dispuesto en la Ordenanza número 41 de 9 de Julio de 1894 y los Decretos números 148 y 154 que la desarrollan.

Medellin, 30 de Julio de 1898

El Secretario de Hacienda, Januario Henao — El Jefe de la Sección de Crédito Público, Pedro P. Restrepo

		Good	Fine	XF
S1003	**Various Amounts** 30.7.1898. Black. Printer: Tip Del Comercio, Medellin.	—	—	—

1899 Issue

		Good	Fine	XF
S1005	**5 Pesos** 6.1899.	100.00	175.00	300.00

1900 Issues

		Good	Fine	XF
S1011	**10 Centavos** 3.1900. Black on green unpt. Like #S1021. W/o series or imprint.			
	a. Back brown, w/o unpt.	8.00	25.00	70.00
	b. Back red on green unpt.	8.00	25.00	70.00
S1012	**10 Centavos** 3.1900. Black. Face like #S1011. W/o imprint.			
	a. Series II. Green unpt. on face and back.	7.00	20.00	60.00
	b. Series III, IV. Blue unpt. on face, brown unpt. on back.	7.00	20.00	60.00
S1012A	**10 Centavos** 9.1900. Black on pink unpt. Like #S1011. Series VI.	7.00	20.00	60.00

		Good	Fine	XF
S1013	**20 Centavos** 3.1900. Black. Back blue. W/o imprint.			
	a. Series V, VI. Brown unpt. on face. White paper.	8.00	25.00	70.00
	b. Series VII. W/o unpt. on face.	8.00	25.00	70.00
	c. Series VIII. Face like a. Back orange.	8.00	25.00	70.00
	d. Series V. Blue paper.	8.00	25.00	70.00

		Good	Fine	XF
S1014	**50 Centavos** 5.1900. Black on green unpt. Value *CINCO REALES* in unpt. across face. Series A1a; A2. Imprint: Tip. Central.	15.00	35.00	85.00

		Good	Fine	XF
S1015	**1 Peso** 5.1900. Black on orange unpt. Ox and man working the land at upper l. ctr., arms at bottom ctr. Back lt. brown. Series A.	15.00	40.00	100.00
S1017	**5 Pesos** 6.1900.	30.00	85.00	150.00

1901 Issues

		Good	Fine	XF
S1021	**10 Centavos** 1.1901. Black on violet unpt. Like #S1011. Back blue on violet unpt.			

		Good	Fine	XF
	a. Lt. tan paper. Series VII. Imprint: Imprenta Oficial.	5.00	10.00	45.00
	b. White paper. Series VII. Imprint like a.	5.00	10.00	45.00
	c. Lt. blue paper. Series VIII. Imprint like a.	5.00	10.00	45.00
	d. Lt. tan paper. Series VIII but no imprint.	3.00	8.00	35.00

		GOOD	FINE	XF
S1022	**20 CENTAVOS** Jan. 1901. Black. Series XI; X. Imprint: Imprenta Oficial.			
	a. Brown unpt., lt. tan paper. Back brown. Series X.	8.00	25.00	70.00
	b. Violet unpt., blue paper. Back violet. Series X.	8.00	25.00	70.00

#S1023 and S1024 imprint: Tipografia Central.

		GOOD	FINE	XF
S1023	**50 CENTAVOS** Feb. 1901. Black on lt. green unpt. Lg. numeral at l. Series A1.	25.00	50.00	100.00

		GOOD	FINE	XF
S1024	**1 PESO** March 1901. Black on yellow unpt. Lion at r.	10.00	35.00	85.00

CASA DE MONEDA DE MEDELLIN

1919-20 GOLD CERTIFICATES OF DEPOSIT

#S1026-S1029 seated woman w/flowers at ctr. on face, arms at lower ctr. on back. Printer: ABNC.

		GOOD	FINE	XF
S1026	**2 1/2 PESOS** 15.9.1919; 1.5.1920. Black on green and m/c unpt. Back green.			
	a. Issued note. 15.9.1919.	—	Rare	—
	p. Proof, w/ or w/o unpt.	—	Unc	500.00
	s. Specimen.	—	Unc	500.00
S1026A	**2 1/2 PESOS** 1.5.1920. Black. Like #S1026 but w/o unpt. Archive copy.	—	Rare	—
S1027	**5 PESOS** 15.9.1919. Black on brown and m/c unpt. Back brown.			
	a. Issued note.	—	Rare	—
	p. Proof.	—	Unc	500.00
	s. Specimen.	—	Unc	500.00

		GOOD	FINE	XF
S1028	**10 PESOS** 15.9.1919. Black on orange and m/c unpt. Back orange.			
	a. Issued note.	—	Rare	—
	p. Proof.	—	Unc	500.00
	s. Specimen.	—	Unc	500.00
S1029	**20 PESOS** 15.9.1919. Black on blue and m/c unpt. Back blue.			
	a. Issued note.	—	Rare	—
	p. Proof.	—	Unc	500.00
	s. Specimen.	—	Unc	500.00

NOTE: For notes w/ovpt: *BANCO DE LA REPUBLICA/BILLETE PROVISIONAL*, see Vol. 2, #351-354.

TESORO DEL DEPARTAMENTO DE ANTIOQUIA

#S1030-S1043 include notes w/heading: *Tesoro del Departamento de Antioquia* only. For notes w/heading: *Gobierno Departamental*, see #S1051-S1115.

1900 ISSUE

		GOOD	FINE	XF
S1029A	**1 PESO** 5.1900. Black on lt. red unpt., yellow paper. Ox and man working the land at upper ctr., arms below. Heading: TESORO DEPARTAMENTAL.	25.00	75.00	150.00

1901 ISSUES

#S1030-S1033 imprint: Imp. de La Verdad, Medellin.

		GOOD	FINE	XF
S1030	**50 CENTAVOS** Feb. 1901. Black. Arms at top ctr. Series F.	10.00	20.00	65.00

		GOOD	FINE	XF
S1031	**50 CENTAVOS** Feb. 1901. Black on yellow unpt. Similar to #S1030. Series G.	10.00	20.00	65.00

		GOOD	FINE	XF
S1032	**50 CENTAVOS** Dec. 1901. Black on pink paper. Open book at upper ctr. Series H.	10.00	30.00	85.00

DECRETO 203 DEL 25 DE MAYO DE 1900

		GOOD	FINE	XF
S1033	**1 PESO** March 1901. Black. Steam locomotive at top ctr. Bees at upper l. and r. on back. Series D.	25.00	75.00	150.00

1902 ISSUES

#S1035-S1044 printer: Imp. de La Verdad.

		GOOD	FINE	XF
S1035	**50 CENTAVOS** 6.1902. Black on pink unpt. Series L.	10.00	30.00	100.00

		GOOD	FINE	XF
S1036	**1 PESO** 9.1902. Black on blue unpt. Pink paper. Arms at ctr. Back red. Series F.	10.00	30.00	100.00

S1038 5 PESOS — GOOD 12.00 · FINE 40.00 · XF 125.00
6.1902. Black on deep pink unpt. Steam locomotive at upper ctr. Series N.

S1040 10 PESOS — GOOD 12.00 · FINE 40.00 · XF 125.00
7.1902. Black and red. Smaller sheaf and plow at upper ctr. Back gray-green. Series L.

S1041 10 PESOS — GOOD 12.00 · FINE 40.00 · XF 125.00
7.1902. Blue and black. Larger sheaf and plow at upper ctr. Lg. outlined: *DIEZ PESOS* in unpt. Back gray-green. Series Q.

S1042 10 PESOS — GOOD 12.00 · FINE 40.00 · XF 125.00
9.1902. Black on blue unpt. Like #S1041 but w/o *DIEZ PESOS* in unpt. Series V.

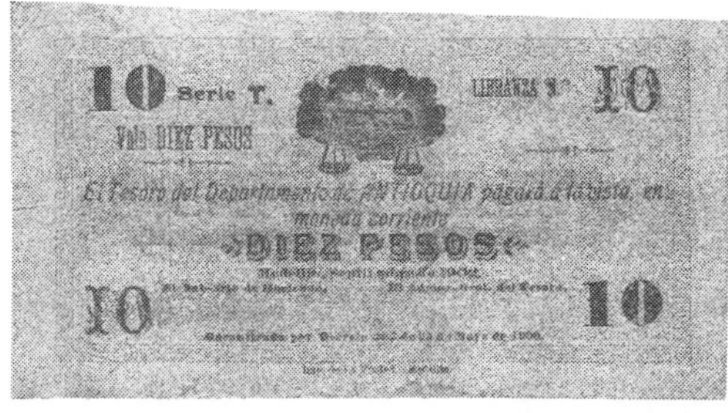

S1042A 10 PESOS — GOOD 12.00 · FINE 40.00 · XF 125.00
9.1902. Black on blue unpt., pink paper. Scale at upper ctr. Series T. Imprint: Imp. de La Verdad.

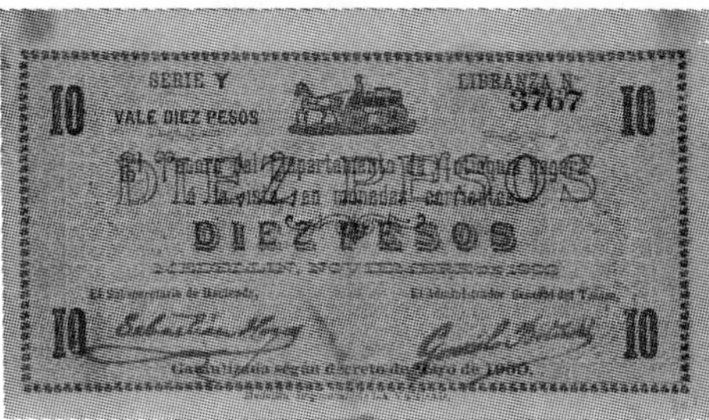

S1043 10 PESOS — GOOD 12.00 · FINE 40.00 · XF 125.00
11.1902. Black on greenish gray paper. Horse and wagon at upper ctr., lg. outlined: *DIEZ PESOS* like #S1041. Back blue-black. Series Y.

S1044 10 PESOS — GOOD 12.00 · FINE 40.00 · XF 125.00
11.1902. Black on blue unpt. Pink paper. Train at upper ctr. W/o lg. outlined: *DIEZ PESOS* in unpt. Like #S1043. Back blue. Series Z.

GOBIERNO DEPARTAMENTAL

#S1051-S1115 include notes w/heading: *Gobierno Departamental* regardless of any other kinds of headings they may or may not have.

1900 ISSUES

#S1051-S1052 printer: Tip. del Comercio.

S1051 50 CENTAVOS — GOOD 8.00 · FINE 25.00 · XF 70.00
6.1900. Black on tan unpt. Padlock at ctr. Series A.

S1052 50 CENTAVOS — GOOD 8.00 · FINE 25.00 · XF 70.00
9.1900. Black on orange unpt. Like #S1051. Series A; B.

S1053 50 CENTAVOS — GOOD 8.00 · FINE 25.00 · XF 70.00
11.1900. Black on orange unpt. Eagle at ctr. Back black on lilac. Series C. W/o imprint.

S1054 1 PESO — GOOD 6.00 · FINE 15.00 · XF 60.00
6.1900. Black on yellow paper. Train at ctr. Series B.2. Imprint: Tip. Central.

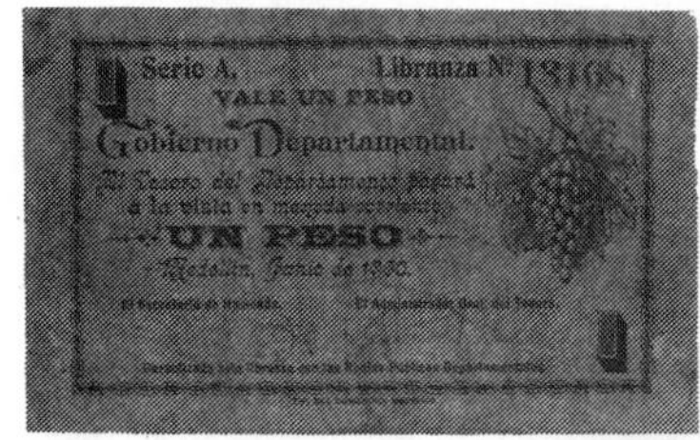

S1055 1 PESO — GOOD 6.00 · FINE 15.00 · XF 60.00
6.1900. Black on blue paper. Bunch of grapes at r. Back deep blue. Series A.

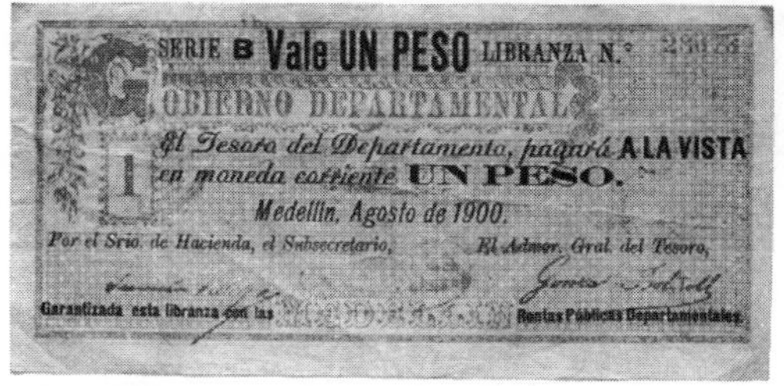

S1055A 1 PESO — GOOD — · FINE — · XF —
8.1900. Black on brown unpt. Series B.

S1056 1 PESO

	Good	Fine	XF
10.1900. Black on green unpt. Grapes at r. Series B. Imprint: Tip. del Comercio.	6.00	15.00	60.00

S1060 10 PESOS

	Good	Fine	XF
6.1900. Black on peach and red unpt. Paddle wheel steamboat at top ctr. Back brown. Imprint: Tip. Central. Series D2a.	10.00	35.00	95.00

#S1060A-S1062 printer: Tip. del Comercio.

S1060A 10 PESOS

	Good	Fine	XF
10.1900. Black on red unpt. Arms at upper ctr. Series L.	10.00	30.00	85.00

S1061 10 PESOS

	Good	Fine	XF
11.1900. Black on green unpt. Like #S1060A. Series F.	10.00	30.00	85.00

S1062 50 PESOS

	Good	Fine	XF
11.1900. Black on green and red unpt. Cow's head at l. Series A.	15.00	45.00	130.00

1901 ISSUES

S1062A 50 CENTAVOS

	Good	Fine	XF
1.1901. Black on red unpt. Eagle at upper ctr. Series D.	25.00	100.00	175.00

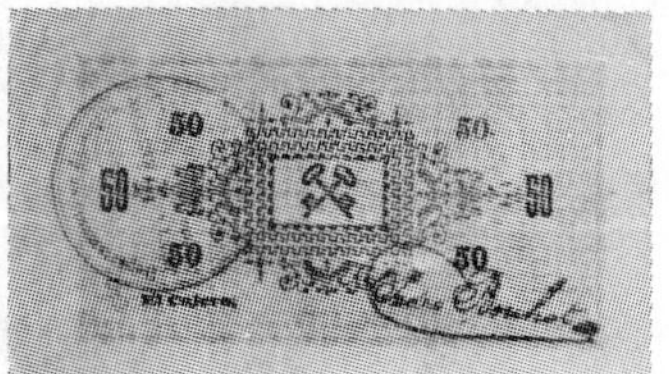

S1063 50 CENTAVOS

	Good	Fine	XF
2.1901. Like #S1051. Imprint: Tip. del Comercio. Series C.	8.00	25.00	70.00

S1063A 50 CENTAVOS

	Good	Fine	XF
4.1901. Black on brown unpt. Eagle at upper ctr. Series A. Imprint: Tipografía del Foto Club.	8.00	25.00	75.00

S1064 50 CENTAVOS

	Good	Fine	XF
7.1901; 12.1901. Black on orange unpt. Padlock at top ctr. Violet hand stamp: *Departamento de Antioquia/MEDELLIN* on back. Printer: Tip. del Comercio, Medellin. Series E.	20.00	60.00	100.00

S1064A 50 CENTAVOS

	Good	Fine	XF
12.1901. Black on red-brown unpt. Plow and sheaf at upper ctr. Series E. Imprint: Tipografía del Foto Club.	8.00	25.00	75.00

S1065 1 PESO

	Good	Fine	XF
1.1901. Black on red unpt. Train and hill at l., arms at ctr. Back green. Series A. Imprint: Lit. J. L. Arango, Medellin.	12.00	40.00	125.00

S1066 1 PESO

	Good	Fine	XF
1.1901. Black. Man (B. Franklin?) at upper l. Back red. Series B.	15.00	50.00	135.00

S1069 1 PESO

	Good	Fine	XF
1.1901. Black and red. Grapevine at l. Series E.	15.00	50.00	135.00

S1070 1 PESO

	Good	Fine	XF
1.1901. Black and green. Like #S1069. Grapevine at l. Back black on red-brown. Pink paper. Imprint: Imp. del Dpto. Series F.	12.00	40.00	125.00

		GOOD	FINE	XF
S1070A	**1 PESO** 1.1901. Black and blue. Like #S1069. Pink paper. Series O.	12.00	40.00	125.00

		GOOD	FINE	XF
S1071	**1 PESO** 1.1901. Black on red unpt. Arms at l. Back black on lilac unpt.; pink paper. Imprint: Lit. Oficial. Series H.	12.00	40.00	125.00

		GOOD	FINE	XF
S1071A	**1 PESO** 2.1901. Black. Portr. at upper l. Series B.	12.50	60.00	125.00
S1071B	**1 PESO** 3.1901. Black. Plow and sheaf at upper ctr. Imprint: Imp. de La Verdad - Medellin. Series A.	12.00	40.00	125.00

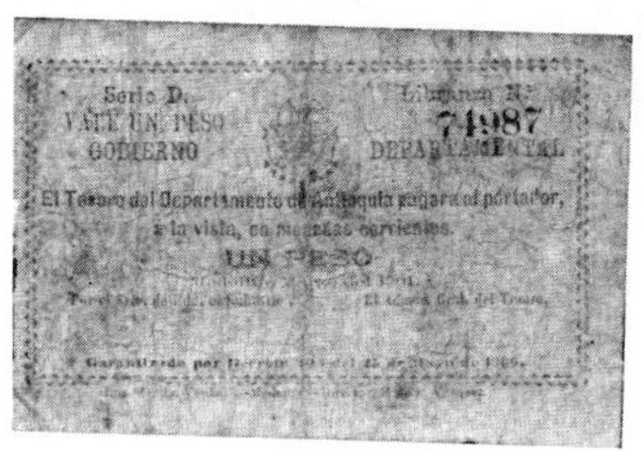

		GOOD	FINE	XF
S1072	**1 PESO** 3.1901. Black. Arms at ctr. Imprint: Imp. de La Verdad. Series D.	12.00	40.00	125.00
S1073	**1 PESO** 3.1901. Black on yellow unpt. Horse w/Indian runner leading. Red ovpt. on back. Series D.	12.00	40.00	125.00

		GOOD	FINE	XF
S1074	**1 PESO** 3.1901. Black. Steam locomotive at upper ctr. Series D. Imprint: Imp. de La Verdad.	12.50	40.00	125.00

		GOOD	FINE	XF
S1075	**1 PESO** 4.1901. Black on olive unpt. Sheaves and farm tools at upper l. Pink paper. Imprint: Tip. del Foto-Club. Series C.	12.00	40.00	125.00

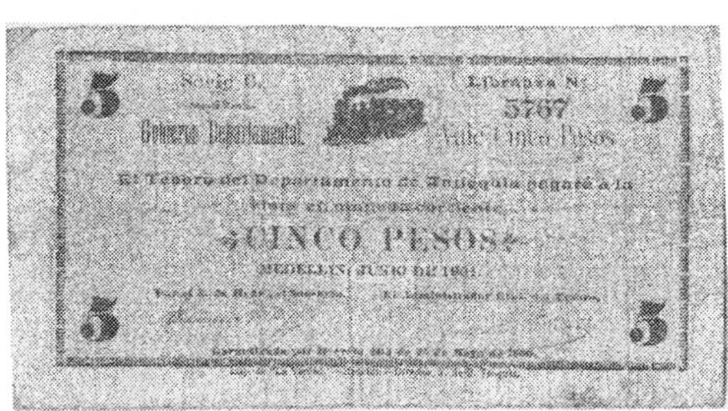

		GOOD	FINE	XF
S1076	**1 PESO** 1901. Black on green unpt. Like #S1056.			
	a. Series D; E. April 1901.	8.00	25.00	70.00
	b. Series G. July 1901.	8.00	25.00	70.00

#S1078 and S1080 printer: Imp. de La Verdad.

		GOOD	FINE	XF
S1078	**5 PESOS** 6.1901. Black on red unpt. Steam locomotive at upper ctr. Back red. Series C.	12.00	40.00	125.00

		GOOD	FINE	XF
S1080	**5 PESOS** 6.1901. Black on yellow unpt. Sheaf and plow at upper ctr. Series H.	12.00	40.00	125.00
S1082	**5 PESOS** 8.1901. Black on pink unpt. Similar to #S1080. Imprint: Tip. del Comercio. Series N.	12.00	40.00	125.00

#S1085-S1086 printer: Tip. del Foto-Club.

		GOOD	FINE	XF
S1085	**5 PESOS** 12.1901. Black on aqua unpt. Horse's head at upper ctr. Back black in inverted position. Lilac paper. Series A; B.	12.00	40.00	125.00
S1086	**5 PESOS** 12.1901. Black on deep pink unpt. Bull's head at upper ctr. Series B.	12.00	40.00	125.00

S1088 5 PESOS — GOOD / FINE / XF

12.1901. Black. Sheaf and farm tools at upper ctr. Imprint: Tip. del Comercio.

		Good	Fine	XF
a.	Blue and red unpt. Back blue. Series V.	12.00	40.00	125.00
b.	Aqua unpt. Pink paper. Series X.	12.00	45.00	140.00

S1092 10 PESOS — GOOD 15.00 / FINE 50.00 / XF 150.00

2.1901. Black on green and red unpt. Eagle and flag at upper ctr. Back blue. Imprint: Imp. de La Verdad. Series D.

S1093 10 PESOS — GOOD 15.00 / FINE 50.00 / XF 150.00

12.1901. Black on violet unpt. Plow and sheaf at upper ctr. Series H.

1902-03 ISSUES

#S1097-S1108 printer: Imp. Oficial.

S1097 20 CENTAVOS — GOOD 10.00 / FINE 40.00 / XF 100.00

7.1902. Series A.

S1103 5 PESOS — GOOD 12.00 / FINE 45.00 / XF 140.00

1.1902. Black and red on tan unpt., pink paper. Arms at ctr. Back black on purple unpt. Series B.

S1106 10 PESOS — GOOD 15.00 / FINE 50.00 / XF 150.00

3.1902. Black on lt. blue unpt. Arms at l. Back black on red unpt.; local arms at l. ctr. Series B.

S1108 20 PESOS — GOOD 15.00 / FINE 60.00 / XF 175.00

7.1902; 11.1902. Black on orange and green unpt. Arms at l. Back black on brown unpt. Series A.

S1109 20 PESOS — GOOD 15.00 / FINE 60.00 / XF 175.00

7.1902. Black on orange and green unpt. Woman standing and woman kneeling w/sheaf at l. Back green on orange unpt. Imprint: Imp. del Comercio. Series B and C.

S1112 50 PESOS — GOOD 12.00 / FINE 60.00 / XF 175.00

7.1902. Black on lilac and green unpt. White or lt. blue paper. Eagle and banner at l. Imprint: Imp. Oficial. Series A.

S1113 50 PESOS — GOOD 15.00 / FINE 60.00 / XF 175.00

9.1902. Black on lt. blue and brown unpt. Lt. blue paper. Woman w/casks, sheaf and sickle at l. Back blue on green unpt. Imprint: Tip. del Comercio. Series B.

S1115 50 PESOS — 15.00 / 60.00 / 175.00

4.1903. Woman. Imprint: Tip. del Comercio.

BOLÍVAR

DEPARTAMENTO DE BOLÍVAR

DECREE 10.7.1900

		GOOD	FINE	XF
S1120	**10 CENTAVOS** *D.1900.* Black. Cow at ctr.	—	Rare	—
S1121	**10 CENTAVOS** *D. 1900.* Arms.	—	Rare	—

		GOOD	FINE	XF
S1122	**20 CENTAVOS** *D. 1900.* Ship at ctr.	—	Rare	—

		GOOD	FINE	XF
S1123	**50 CENTAVOS** *D. 1900.* Black on green unpt. Arms at ctr. Back greenish gray. Issued at Lorica.	—	Rare	—

		GOOD	FINE	XF
S1124	**1 PESO** *D.1900.* Black on green unpt. Arms at ctr. Text at ctr. on back. Issued at Lorica. Series D.	—	Rare	—

MAGDALENA

DEPARTAMENTO DEL MAGDALENA

Issued at Riohacha.

1900 ISSUE

		GOOD	FINE	XF
S1126	**20 CENTAVOS** May 1900. Black. Arms at l. Issued at Riohacha. Series A.	—	Rare	—

		GOOD	FINE	XF
S1128	**1 PESO** 8.1900. Black. Ship at l.	—	Rare	—
S1128A	**1 PESO** 8.12.1900. Heading: *EMISION ESPECIAL.*	—	Rare	—
S1129	**5 PESOS** 6.1900. Black on yellow paper. Issued at Riohacha.	—	Rare	—

1900 ISSUE

		GOOD	FINE	XF
S1130	**10 PESOS** 6.1900. Black. Similar to #S1129.	—	Rare	—

GOBERNACIÓN DEL MAGDALENA

Issued at Santa Marta.

1900 FIRST ISSUE

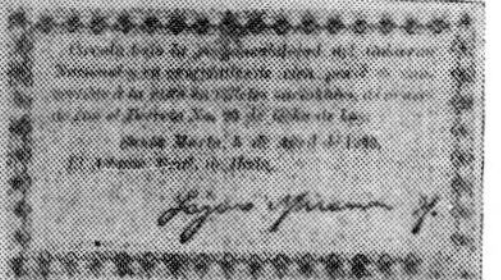

		GOOD	FINE	XF
S1131	**10 CENTAVOS** 5.4.1900. Black on lt. green unpt. 2 printed sign.	30.00	80.00	150.00

#S1132-S1134 on paper w/lt. blue lines, uniface, embossed seal at ctr., 1 stamped and 1 printed sign. No imprint.

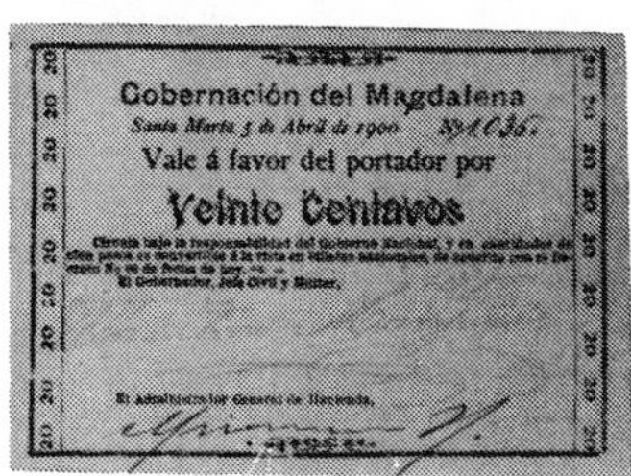

		GOOD	FINE	XF
S1132	**20 CENTAVOS** 5.4.1900. Black.	30.00	80.00	150.00
S1133	**50 CENTAVOS** 5.4.1900. Lt. red.	30.00	90.00	175.00
S1134	**1 PESO** 5.4.1900. Blue.	30.00	90.00	175.00

1900 SECOND ISSUES

#S1137-S1143 printer: Armenta and Prieto, Barranquilla. All notes w/printed sign. only.

		GOOD	FINE	XF
S1137	**10 CENTAVOS** 5.4.1900. Maroon-red. Crude print.	20.00	75.00	125.00
S1138	**10 CENTAVOS** 5.4.1900. Purple. Like #S1137.	20.00	75.00	125.00

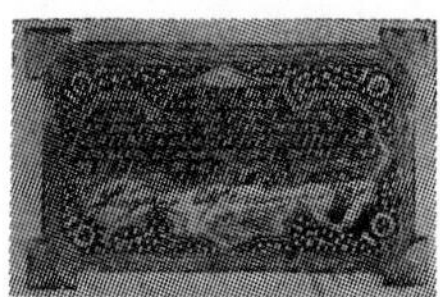

		GOOD	FINE	XF
S1139	**10 CENTAVOS** 5.4.1900. Blue. Like #S1137 w/o imprint.	20.00	75.00	125.00
S1140	**20 CENTAVOS** 5.4.1900. Black. Issued at Riohacha.	20.00	75.00	125.00

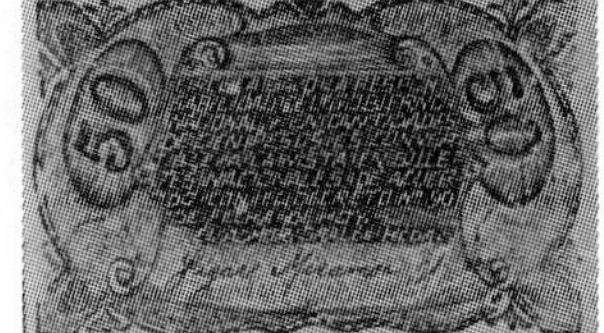

		GOOD	FINE	XF
S1141	**50 CENTAVOS** 5.4.1900. Green. Series G.	30.00	90.00	150.00

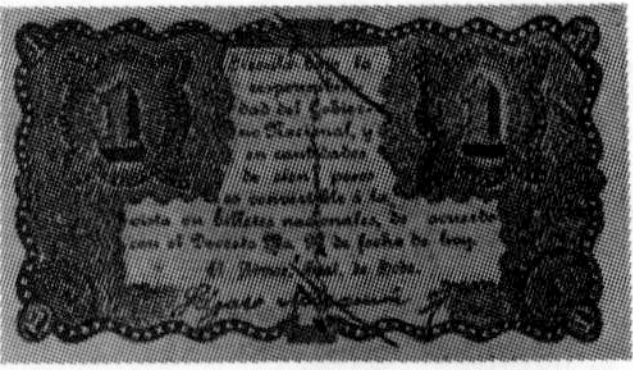

		GOOD	FINE	XF
S1142	**1 PESO** 5.4.1900. Black on lt. pink unpt. Sailing ship at r. Series H.	30.00	90.00	150.00
S1143	**1 PESO** 5.4.1900. Blue on lt. pink unpt. Like #S1142.	30.00	90.00	150.00

SANTANDER

DEPARTAMENTO DE SANTANDER

Issued at Bucaramanga.

1899 ISSUE

#S1151-S1154 printer: Tip. Mercantil.

		GOOD	FINE	XF
S1151	**20 CENTAVOS** 27.10.1899; 1.11.1899. Black on orange unpt. Horse's head at r. Text on back. Series AJ.	30.00	90.00	150.00

		GOOD	FINE	XF
S1152	**50 CENTAVOS** 1.11.1899. Blue on pink unpt. Palm at l. w/text: *DEPARTAMENTO NACIONAL DE SANTANDER* in unpt. across face. Back blue. Series B; C; F.	15.00	45.00	120.00

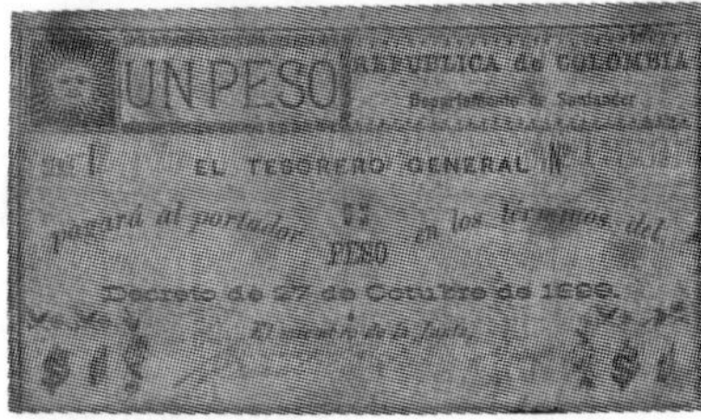

		GOOD	FINE	XF
S1153	**1 PESO** 1.11.1899. Black. Legend across face in unpt. like #S1152, rayed sun at upper l.			
	a. Series C. Green unpt. on face. Back green.	25.00	80.00	150.00
	b. Series I. Blue unpt. on face. Back blue.	25.00	80.00	150.00

		GOOD	FINE	XF
S1154	**5 PESOS** 1.11.1899. Black on pink unpt. Woman carrying branches at ctr. Back black. Series Z.	12.00	40.00	100.00

PROVINCIA DE OCAÑA

1900 ISSUE

		GOOD	FINE	XF
S1155	**1 PESO** 3.5.1900. Black. Arms at l. ctr.	—	Rare	—

LA COMPAÑIA EMPRESARIA DEL CAMINO DE HERRADURA DE BUCARAMANGA A SABANA DE TORRES

THE MANAGING COMPANY OF THE HORSESHOE ROAD FROM BUCARAMANGA TO SABANA DE TORRES

1887 ISSUE

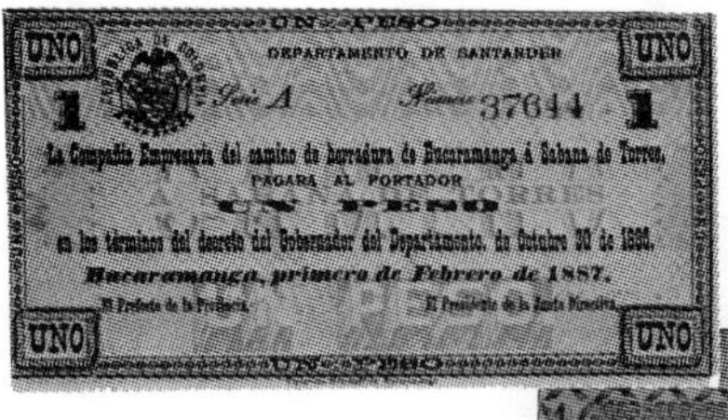
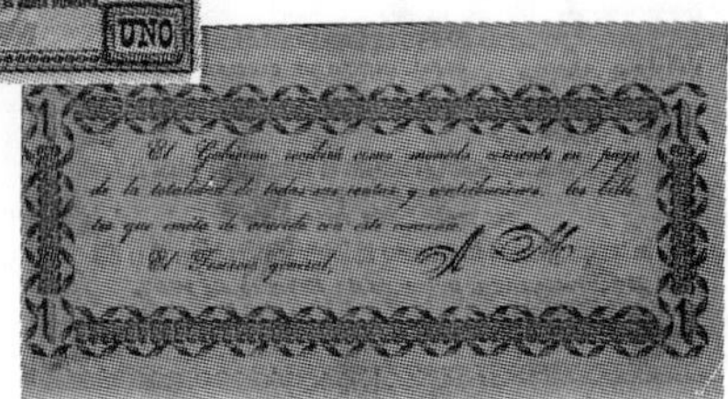

		GOOD	FINE	XF
S1156	**1 PESO** 1.2.1887. Black on green unpt. Arms at upper l. Printer: Tipografia Mercantil de Bucaramanga.	—	Rare	—

NOTE: #S1156 was fully acceptable as money through an agreement wth the government of the department.

DEPARTAMENTO DE SANTANDER (CONT.)

1900 ISSUES

#S1157-S1161 printer: Tip. Mercantil.

		GOOD	FINE	XF
S1157	**20 CENTAVOS** 1.4.1900. Black on yellow unpt. Small vase at upper l. Series A; D.	10.00	25.00	65.00

		GOOD	FINE	XF
S1158	**50 CENTAVOS** 1.4.1900. Black on yellow unpt. Small bldg. at upper l. Small vase at upper l. on back. Series C.	15.00	40.00	125.00

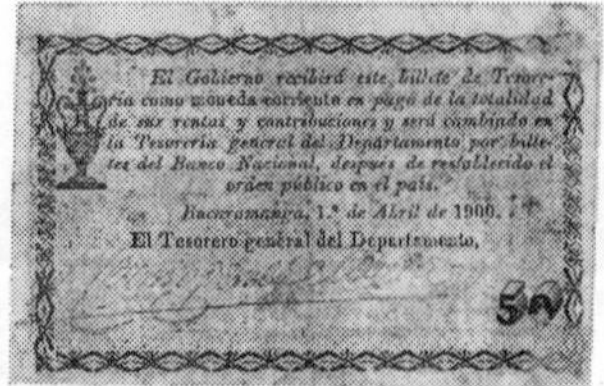

		GOOD	FINE	XF
S1158A	**50 CENTAVOS** 1.4.1900. Portr. of a woman at upper l., otherwise similar to S1158. Series L.	15.00	40.00	125.00

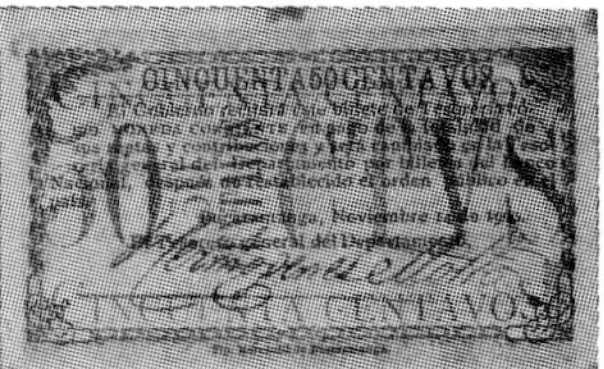

		Good	Fine	XF
S1159	**50 Centavos** 14.11.1900. Black on brown unpt. Series R; Y.	15.00	40.00	125.00

		Good	Fine	XF
S1160	**1 Peso** 14.11.1900. Black and green. Arms at l. Back green; date line.	25.00	85.00	200.00
S1161	**1 Peso** 11.1900. Black and green. Eagle on arms at l. Back green. Series A.	25.00	85.00	200.00

Tolima

Departamento del Tolima

Issued at Ibague and Neiva.

1900-19 Issue

		Good	Fine	XF
S1166	**10 Centavos** 2.7.1900.	—	Rare	—
S1167	**20 Centavos** 2.7.1900; 31.7.1900. Dk. blue on green unpt. Back green.	—	Rare	—
S1168	**50 Centavos**	—	Rare	—
S1169	**1 Peso** 2.7.1900.	—	Rare	—

		Good	Fine	XF
S1173	**1 Peso** 3.7.1900. Black on brown unpt. Back black. Series C.	20.00	75.00	125.00
S1176	**20 Pesos** 31.7.1900.	—	Rare	—
S1177	**20 Centavos** 10.6.1901. Black on brown unpt. Back black; sailing ships at ctr. Series B.	25.00	85.00	150.00
S1181	**1 Peso** 9.1902. Black on red unpt. Series D.	100.00	125.00	250.00
S1191	**1 Peso** 2.3.1919. Ovpt. on Banco Oriental note.	—	Rare	—

Section IV
Regional Ferrocarril (Railroad) Issues

Ferrocarril de Amaga

191x Issue

		Good	Fine	XF
S1401	**10 Pesos** 191x. Blue on yellow paper. Arms at upper ctr. Specimen.	—	Rare	—

Ferrocarril de Antioquía

1893 Issue

		Good	Fine	XF
S1501	**1000 Pesos** 1.4.1893. Black and brown on lt. blue unpt. Standing allegorical figure at l., redemption date of 1902 above. Series J. Imprint: Lit. de Villaveces. Printer's specimen.	—	Rare	—

		Good	Fine	XF
S1511	**50 Pesos** 5.1909. Blue. Train at upper l. ctr. Second series. Unsigned remainder.	—	Rare	—

1909 Issue

		Good	Fine	XF
S1521	**1 Peso** 5.1909. Black on orange and yellow unpt. Trains in mountains at upper l. Printer: Lit. Nacional. Specimen.	—	—	—

Ferrocarril de Cartagena

1892 Issue

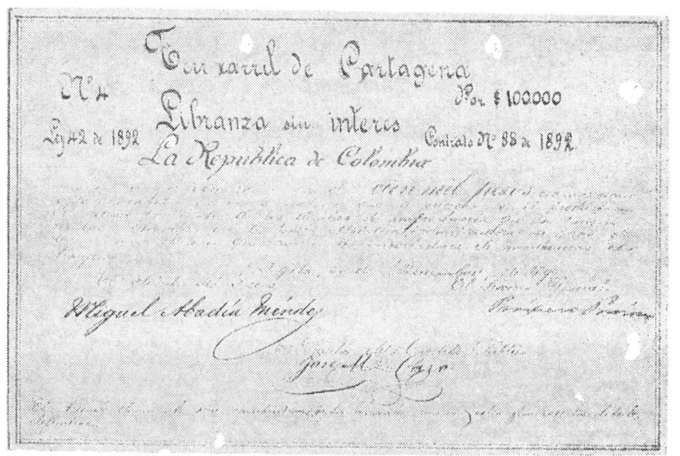

		Good	Fine	XF
S1531	**100,000 Pesos** 20.12.1892. Black.	250.00	400.00	600.00

FERROCARRIL DEL CAUCA

LAW OF 1896

		GOOD	FINE	XF
S1541	**1000 PESOS** 19xx. Black and purple on lt. blue unpt. Train at upper ctr. Unsigned remainder.	—	—	—

LAWS OF 1896; 1897

#S1551-S1555 tiny arms at upper corners. Printer: Villaveces.

		GOOD	FINE	XF
S1551	**10 PESOS** *L.1897.* Black on lilac unpt. Woman w/bird at upper l. Series B. Unsigned remainder.	250.00	400.00	600.00
S1551A	**20 PESOS** *L.1897.* Black on orange unpt. Eagle and arms at upper ctr. Unsigned remainder.	—	—	—
S1552	**50 PESOS** *L.1897.* Black on red-brown unpt. Series C. Unsigned remainder.	250.00	400.00	600.00

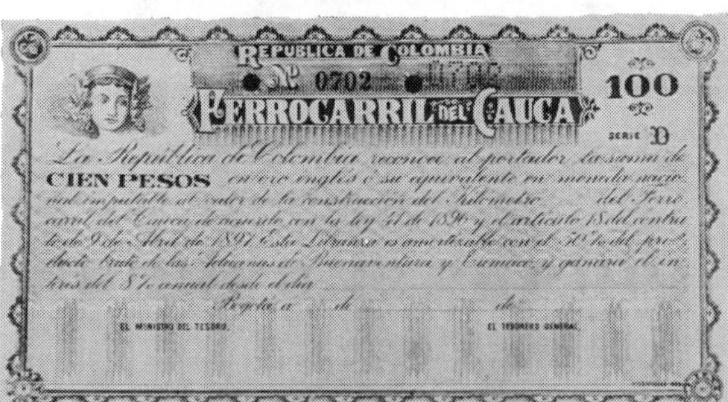

		GOOD	FINE	XF
S1553	**100 PESOS** *L.1897.* Black on lt. green unpt. Girl's head at upper l. Series D. Unsigned remainder.	250.00	400.00	600.00

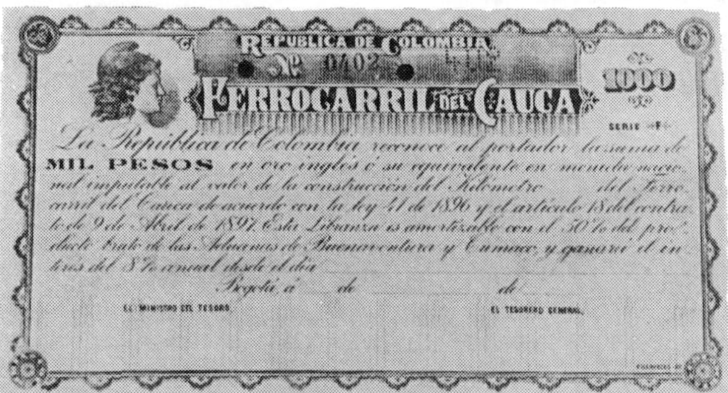

		GOOD	FINE	XF
S1555	**1000 PESOS** *L.1897.* Black on red unpt. Woman's head at upper l. Series F. Unsigned remainder.	300.00	500.00	700.00

Notice

Readers with unlisted dates, color or signature varieties are invited to submit photocopies of their notes to: Standard Catalog of World Paper Money, Krause Publications, 700 East State St. Iola WI 54990-0001 U.S.A. or by email: thernr@krause.com. Email submissions of material for possible inclusion need to be 100% jpeg attachments at 300 dpi.

1900S ISSUE

República de Colombia

N.º Por $1,000

Ferrocarril del Cauca

La República de Colombia reconoce al portador la suma de mil pesos en oro ó su equivalente en moneda nacional, imputable al valor del reconocimiento hecho por el Ministerio de Obras Públicas, de conformidad con el contrato celebrado por ese Despacho con el señor Ignacio Muñoz C. el 22 de Mayo próximo pasado. Esta libranza es amortizable con el cincuenta por ciento (50 %) del producto bruto de las Aduanas de Buenaventura y Tumaco, sin que devengue intereses.

Bogotá, de de 190

El Ministro de Hacienda y Tesoro,

El Administrador General de Hacienda Nacional,

		GOOD	FINE	XF
S1557	**1000 PESOS** 190x. Black. Printer: Eugenio Pardo.	—	—	—

1910 ISSUE

#S1558-S1562 arms at ctr. in unpt.

		GOOD	FINE	XF
S1558	**1 PESO** 3.1910. Black on yellow unpt. Specimen.	—	—	—
S1560	**10 PESOS** 3.1910. Black on brown unpt. Specimen.	—	—	—

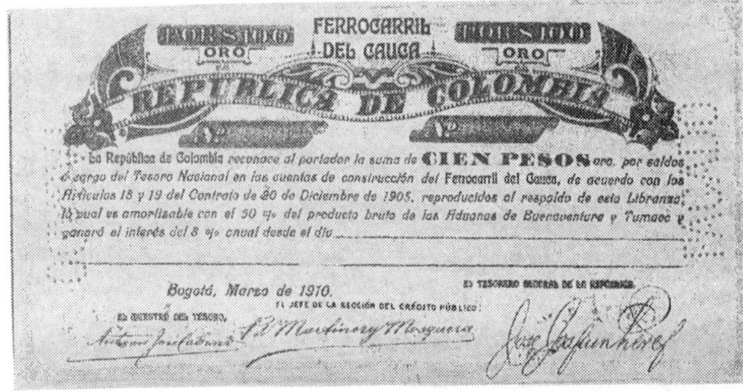

		GOOD	FINE	XF
S1561	**100 PESOS** 3.1910. Black on red unpt. Specimen.	250.00	400.00	600.00

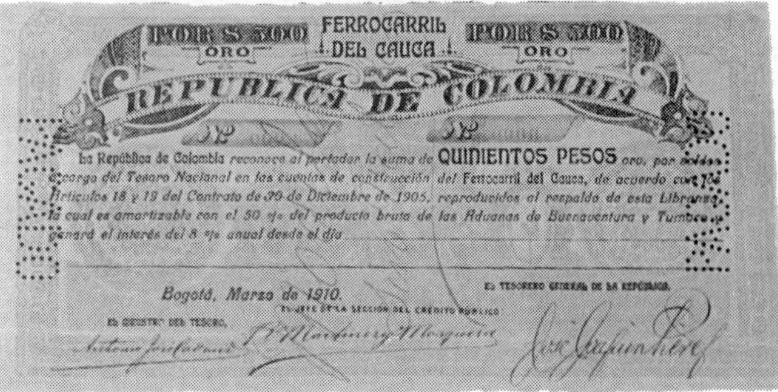

		GOOD	FINE	XF
S1562	**500 PESOS** 3.1910. Black on lt. blue unpt.			
	a. Back dk. red. Specimen.	—	—	—
	b. Back blue. Specimen.	—	—	—

1912 Issue

S1573 1000 Pesos
12.1912. Black on lt. lilac unpt. Specimen.

Good	Fine	XF
300.00	500.00	700.00

Ferrocarril de Cucuta

1886 Issue

Libranzas contra las Aduanas de la República.

(Ferrocarril de Cúcuta).

Número 154 Por $ 1,000.

Bogotá, 15 de Enero de 1886.

La República de Colombia reconoce al portador la suma de mil pesos ($1,000), la cual es admisible en la totalidad del producto de los derechos de importación que se recauden en las Aduanas de Barranquilla, Cartagena y Cúcuta.

El Secretario del Tesoro, El Tesorero General,

S1576 1000 Pesos
15.1.1886. Black.

Good	Fine	XF
—	—	—

Ferrocarril de La Sabana

1886 Issue

S1601 1 Peso
20.10.1886. Black and blue. Train at ctr., arms at lower ctr. Series B.
Imprint: Lit. de D. Paredes.

Good	Fine	XF
—	Rare	—

Ferrocarril de Santander

188x Issue

S1621 5 Pesos
188x. Blue and black. Steam locomotive at ctr.

Good	Fine	XF
100.00	200.00	300.00

S1625 100 Pesos
188x. Similar to #S1621.

Good	Fine	XF
150.00	300.00	450.00

1893 Issue

S1651 1000 Pesos
1.4.1893. Black on red unpt. Eagle at l., arms in unpt. at ctr. Series A.
Imprint: Villaveces.

Good	Fine	XF
—	Rare	—

The Republic of Costa Rica, located in southern Central America between Nicaragua and Panama, has an area of 19,575 sq. mi. (50,700 sq. km.) and a population of 3.8 million. Capital: San Jose. Agriculture predominates; coffee, bananas, beef and sugar contribute heavily to the country's export earnings.

Costa Rica was discovered by Christopher Columbus in 1502, during his last voyage to the new world, and was a colony of Spain from 1522 until independence in 1821. Columbus named the territory Nueva Cartago; the name Costa Rica wasn't generally employed until 1540. Bartholomew Columbus attempted to found the first settlement but was driven off by Indian attacks and the country wasn't pacified until 1530. Costa Rica was absorbed for two years (1821-23) into the Mexican Empire of Agustin de Iturbide. From 1823 to 1848 it was a constituent state of the Central American Republic (q.v.). It was established as a republic in 1848.

Constitution revisions followed in 1871 and 1948. In the early 1990's, Costa Rica was beset with economic problems.

MONETARY SYSTEM:

1 Colon = 100 Centimos

BANKS:

Banco Anglo-Costarricense .... #S108-S126
Banco Comercial de Costa Rica .... #S141-S150
Banco de Costa Rica .... #S151-S177
Banco Herediano .... #S181-S185
Banco Mercantil de Costa Rica .... #S201-S205
Banco Nacional de Costa Rica .... #S210-S217
Banco Rural de Credito Hipotecario de Costa Rica .... #S218-S218
Banco de la Union .... #S221-S227

RAILROAD:

Ferro Carril de Costa Rica .... #S231-S236

REPUBLIC

BANCO ANGLO-COSTARRICENSE

Established in 1863. For the centennial of its founding, in 1963, the bank issued special gray booklets with #S121-S124 attached. Notes had special ovpt on face: *MUESTRA SIN VALOR;* on back: *OBSEQUIO DEL BANCO ANGLO-COSTARRICENSE PRIMER CENTENARIO 1863-1963.* The booklets also contained stamps for the same event. In later years the bank prepared yellow booklets with the same notes attached (no stamps) as souvenirs. These had ovpt: *MUESTRA SIN VALOR* usually on the face but sometimes on the back, but no other ovpt. These booklets were given out, one to each employee, at special occasions.

OVERPRINT TYPES:

A. Sm. black *MUESTRA SIN VALOR* on face and *OBSEQUIO DEL BANCO ANGLO-COSTARRICENSE PRIMER CENTENARIO 1863-1963* on back.

B. Lg. black *MUESTRA SIN VALOR.*

C. Lg. red *MUESTRA SIN VALOR.*

1864 ISSUE

Peso System.

#S108-S111 portr. Qn. Victoria at top ctr. Wmk: Bank name, *SAN JOSE DE COSTA RICA* around value in frame. Printer: BWC.

		GOOD	FINE	XF
S107	**1 PESO** 1.1.1864.	—	Rare	—
S108	**10 PESOS** 1.1.1864. Ship at l.			
	a. Issued note.	—	Rare	—
	s. Specimen.	—	—	—

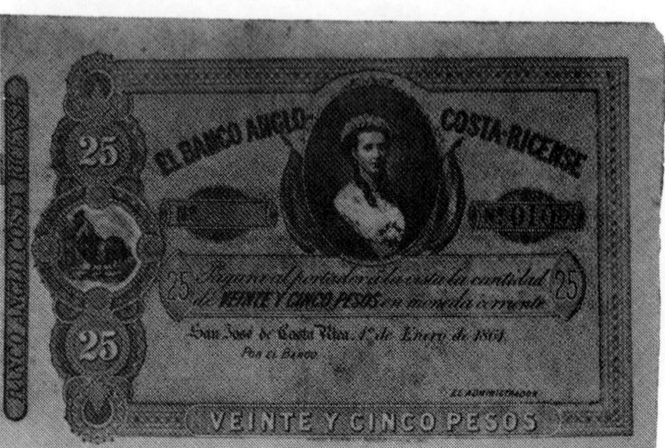

		GOOD	FINE	XF
S109	**25 PESOS** 1.1.1864. Rooster at l.			
	a. Issued note.	—	Rare	—
	r. Unsigned remainder.	—	—	—
	s. Specimen.	—	Rare	—
S110	**50 PESOS** 1.1.1864.	—	Rare	—
S111	**100 PESOS** 1.1.1864. Black and brown on green unpt. Bull at l. Orange paper.			
	a. Issued note.	—	Rare	—
	p. Proof.	—	Rare	—
	s. Specimen.	—	Rare	—
S111A	**100 PESOS** 3.12.1902. Like #S111 but w/text on back.	—	Rare	—

LAW OF 23.6.1917

Colon System.

		GOOD	FINE	XF
S121	**1 COLÓN** *L.1917.* Black on m/c unpt. Portr. man at ctr. Back green; seated Mercury at ctr. Printer: ABNC.			
	r. Unsigned remainder.	—	Unc	20.00
	s1. Specimen w/black ovpt., w/normal serial #. Type A.	—	10.00	30.00
	s2. Specimen w/black ovpt., w/normal serial #. Type B.	—	5.00	30.00
	s3. Specimen w/red ovpt., w/normal serial #. Type C.	—	5.00	30.00

NOTE: Remainders with spurious signatures are sometimes seen.

#S122-S123 arms at ctr. on back.

#S122-S124 printer: BWC.

		GOOD	FINE	XF
S122	**5 COLONES** 1.1.1903; 1.1.1904; 1.1.1911; 1.1.1917. Black on m/c unpt. Portr. J. M. Fernandez at upper ctr. Back brown. Series A.			
	a. Issued note.	—	Rare	—
	r. Unsigned remainder.	—	—	30.00
	s1. Specimen w/black ovpt., w/normal serial #. Type A.	—	20.00	75.00
	s2. Specimen w/black ovpt., w/normal serial #. Type B.	—	10.00	35.00
	s3. Specimen w/red ovpt., w/normal serial #. Type C.	—	10.00	30.00
	s4. Archive Specimen.	—	—	—

		GOOD	FINE	XF
S123	**10 COLONES** 1.1.1903; 1.1.1904; 1.1.1911; 1.1.1917. Black on m/c unpt. Portr. B. Carrillo at upper ctr. Back blue.			
	a. Issued note.	—	Rare	—
	r. Unsigned remainder.	—	Unc	40.00
	s1. Specimen w/black ovpt., w/normal serial #. Type A.	—	25.00	100.00
	s2. Specimen w/black ovpt., w/normal serial #. Type B.	—	10.00	35.00
	s3. Specimen w/red ovpt., w/normal serial #. Type C.	—	10.00	30.00
	s4. Archive Specimen.	—	—	—

		GOOD	FINE	XF
S124	**20 COLONES** 1.1.1909; 1.1.1911; 1.1.1917. Black on m/c unpt. Portr. man at l. Back brown and black; monument at ctr.			
	a. Issued note.	—	Rare	—
	r. Unsigned remainder.	—	Unc	60.00
	s1. Specimen w/black ovpt., w/normal serial #. Type A.	—	35.00	125.00
	s2. Specimen w/black ovpt., w/normal serial #. Type B.	—	15.00	40.00
	s3. Specimen w/red ovpt., w/normal serial #. Type C.	—	15.00	40.00
	s4. Archive Specimen.	—	—	—

Note: About 80% of the specimen examples of S121, S122, S123, S124 have staple holes in them as they were stapled into presentation booklets.

		GOOD	FINE	XF
S125	**50 COLONES** 1.1.1904-1.1.1917. Black on m/c unpt. Man at l.			
	a. Issued note.	—	Rare	—
	s. Specimen.	—	Rare	—
S126	**100 COLONES** 1.1.1904; 1.1.1906; 1.1.1907; 1.1.1912. Black on m/c unpt. Man at l.			
	a. Issued note.	—	Rare	—
	s. Specimen.	—	Rare	—

BANCO COMERCIAL DE COSTA RICA

1906-11 ISSUE

#S141-S145 Liberty head at ctr. on back. Printer: W&S.

		GOOD	FINE	XF
S141	**5 COLONES** 1.12.1906. Black on green and red unpt. Rural scene at l., banana plant at r. Back brown. Series A.			
	a. Issued note.	—	Rare	—
	s. Specimen.	—	—	—

		GOOD	FINE	XF
S142	**10 COLONES** 1.9.1911. Black on orange and pink unpt. Portr. man at l., village scene at ctr. Back red. Series B. Specimen.	—	Rare	—

		GOOD	FINE	XF
S144	**50 COLONES** ND. Black on orange unpt. Man at l., coffee workers at r. Back blue. Series A. Specimen .	—	Unc	450.00

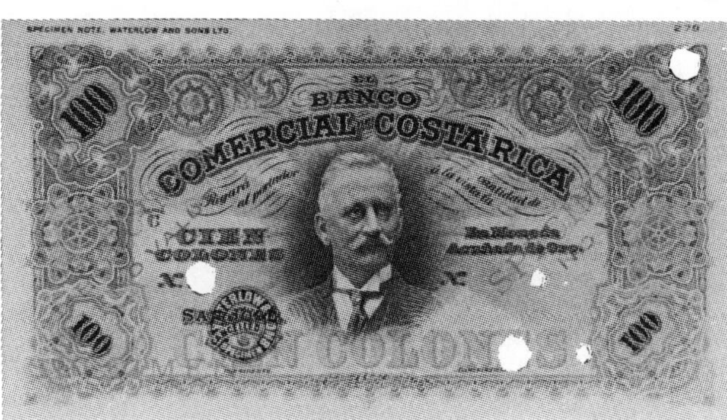

		GOOD	FINE	XF
S145	**100 COLONES** ND. Brown and black on green unpt. Man at ctr. Back blue; shore scenes at l. and r. Series C. Specimen.	—	Unc	550.00

1914 ISSUE

#S146-S150 National Theater at ctr. Printer: ABNC.

		GOOD	FINE	XF
S146	**5 COLONES** ND (ca.1914). Black on olive and blue unpt. Back black. Series B. Proof.	—	—	—

#S147-S150 Liberty at ctr. on back.

		GOOD	FINE	XF
S147	**10 COLONES** ND (ca.1914). Black on lt. orange and blue unpt. Back orange. Series E.			
	p. Proof.	—	—	—
	s. Specimen.	—	—	—
S148	**20 COLONES** ND (ca.1914). Black on yellow and orange unpt. Back blue. Series B.			
	p. Proof.	—	—	—
	s. Specimen.	—	—	—
S149	**50 COLONES** ND (ca.1914). Black on red and purple unpt. Back blue. Series D.			
	p. Proof.	—	—	—
	s. Specimen.	—	—	—
S150	**100 COLONES** ND (ca.1914). Black on purple and brown unpt. Back purple. Series H.			
	p. Proof.	—	—	—
	s. Specimen.	—	—	—

BANCO DE COSTA RICA

1895 ISSUE

Peso System.

#S151 and S152 arms at ctr. on back. Printer: W&S.

		GOOD	FINE	XF
S151	**1 PESO** 1.1.1895. Black on blue and orange unpt. Woman w/basket and cow at l., portr. woman at ctr., workers at r. Back blue. Series B.	75.00	250.00	600.00

		GOOD	FINE	XF
S152	**2 PESOS** 1.1.1895. Black on yellow unpt. Mythical charioteer at l., seated woman w/factory and ships behind at ctr. r. Back green. Series A.	—	—	—

1891-99 SERIES

#S163-S166 printer: ABNC.

		GOOD	FINE	XF
S163	**5 PESOS** 1.4.1899. Black on yellow and pale green unpt. Lion at ctr. Back deep olive-brown.			
	p. Proof.	—	—	—
	r1. Unsigned remainder.	—	Unc	50.00
	r2. Unsigned remainder w/curved red ovpt: *D. AVDO 1899* and lg. *5*.	—	Unc	75.00
	s. Specimen.	—	Unc	85.00

		GOOD	FINE	XF
S164	**10 PESOS** 1.4.1899. Black on red-orange and yellow unpt. American and Canadian Horseshoe Falls at Niagara at ctr. Back red-orange; woman's head at ctr.			
	p. Proof.	—	—	—
	r. Unsigned remainder.	—	Unc	75.00
	s. Specimen.	—	Unc	150.00
S165	**20 PESOS** 1.4.1899. Black on purple and m/c unpt. Ship at ctr. Back brown on m/c unpt.; portr. woman w/headdress at ctr.			
	p. Proof.	—	—	—
	r. Unsigned remainder.	—	Unc	100.00
	s. Specimen.	—	—	—
S166	**100 PESOS** 1.1.1891; 1.3.1897. Black on yellow and green unpt. Allegorical women at l., bank at r. Back brown.			
	p. Proof.	—	—	—
	s. Specimen.	—	—	—

1901 ISSUE

Colon System.

#S173-S177 bank bldg. at ctr. on back. Printer: ABNC.

		GOOD	FINE	XF
S173	**5 COLONES** 1.1.1901; 1.8.1908. Black on red, brown and green unpt. Seated woman w/farm and factory behind at ctr. Back red on violet, red-orange, brown and green unpt. Series A; C.			
	a. Issued note.	—	Rare	—
	b. Black circular overstamp: *SECRETARIA DE HACIENDA Y COMERCIO* on back.	—	—	—
	r. Unsigned remainder. Series C.	—	Unc	50.00

		GOOD	FINE	XF
S174	**10 COLONES** 1.1.1901; 1.7.1905. Black on green and m/c unpt. Steam passenger train at ctr. Back deep olive-green on green and m/c unpt.			
	a. Series A; B.	—	Rare	—
	r. Unsigned remainder. Series C.	—	Unc	60.00

S175 20 COLONES
1.1.1901. Black on brown and m/c unpt. Miners at ctr. Back dk. brown on blue and m/c unpt.

		GOOD	FINE	XF
p.	Proof. Series A.	—	—	—
r.	Unsigned remainder. Series D.	—	Unc	80.00
s.	Specimen. Series A.	—	—	—

S176 50 COLONES — GOOD — FINE — XF —
1.1.1901. Black on blue-green, brown and m/c unpt. Reclining allegorical woman at l. ctr. and ctr. r. Back blue-green and m/c. Series A. Specimen.

S177 100 COLONES
1.1.1901. Black on olive-green and m/c unpt. Portr. man at l. Back olive-green and m/c. Series A.

		GOOD	FINE	XF
p.	Proof.	—	—	—
s.	Specimen.	—	—	—

1906 ISSUE

S179 20 COLONES — GOOD — FINE Unc — XF 50.00
1.1.1906. Black and red on pink unpt. Soldier's monument at ctr. Back dk. brown; bank bldg. at ctr. Printer: W&S. Series C. Unsigned remainder.

> **A word on date ranges**
>
> Often date ranges or specific dates are listed. These have been observed or reported by our contributors. If a note is outside the published range, it only means that it is a newly reported date, and not necessarily worthy of a premium value.

BANCO HEREDIANO

1885; 1886 ISSUE

#S181-S185 winged figure at lower r. Issued at Heredía. Printer: ABNC litho.

S181 5 PESOS — GOOD — FINE — XF —
188x. Black on green unpt. Standing Commerce at l. Back green. Proof.

S182 10 PESOS
15.19.1885. Black on lt. orange unpt. Standing allegorical woman at l. Back lt. orange. Proof.

		GOOD	FINE	XF
a.	Issued note.	—	Rare	—
p.	Proof.	—	—	—

S183 25 PESOS
5.1886. Black on lt. brown unpt. Standing allegorical woman w/staff, shield and eagle at l. Back lt. brown.

		GOOD	FINE	XF
a.	Issued note.	—	Rare	—
p.	Proof.	—	—	—

S184 50 PESOS — — — —
188x. Black on red-orange unpt. 2 allegorical women w/fasces at l. Back red-orange. Proof.

S185 100 PESOS — — — —
188x. Black on blue unpt. Allegorical woman w/caduceus at l. Back blue. Proof.

BANCO MERCANTIL DE COSTA RICA

1909-16 ISSUE

#S201-S205 bald eagle at ctr. Woman at ctr. on back. Printer: ABNC.

S201 5 COLONES — GOOD 250.00 — FINE 650.00 — XF —
1.6.1910-1.7.1916. Black on m/c unpt. Back brown and green unpt.; seated woman w/book at ctr. Series A.

S202 10 COLONES
1.6.1910-1.8.1916. Black on m/c unpt. Back brown on m/c unpt; seated woman w/shield at ctr.

		GOOD	FINE	XF
a.	Series A. 1.6.1910-1.7.1916.	—	Rare	—
b.	Series B. 1.8.1916.	—	Rare	—

S203 20 COLONES
1.6.1910-1.7.1916. Black on blue and m/c unpt. Back green and m/c.

		GOOD	FINE	XF
a.	Issued note.	—	Rare	—
p.	Proof.	—	—	—
s.	Specimen.	—	—	—

S204 50 COLONES
1910-16. Black on brown and m/c unpt. Back dk. blue-gray on blue and brown unpt.

		GOOD	FINE	XF
a.	Series A. 1.6.1910-1.7.1916.	—	Rare	—
b.	Series B. 1.8.1916.	—	Rare	—
p.	Proof.	—	—	—
s.	Specimen.	—	—	—

		GOOD	FINE	XF
S205	**100 COLONES** 1.6.1910-1.7.1916. Black on orange and m/c unpt. Back olive-green on m/c unpt.			
	a. Issued note.	—	Rare	—
	p. Proof.	—	—	—
	s. Specimen.	—	—	—

BANCO NACIONAL DE COSTA RICA

Provisional issues consist of 4 diff. types of ovpt. found on various notes.

1858 ISSUE

#S210-S212 printer: Toppan, Carpenter and Co.

		GOOD	FINE	XF
S210	**2 PESOS** 1.6.1858. Red and black. Cherub at upper l., seated woman at ctr., portr. at l., arms at r. Uniface.	—	—	—
S211	**10 PESOS** 18xx. Black. Portr. man at upper l., men w/horses plowing field, woman at upper ctr. r., arms at r. Proof.	—	—	—

		GOOD	FINE	XF
S212	**20 PESOS** 18xx. Black and red. Portr. man at upper l., seated allegorical woman w/plow at ctr., arms at r. Uniface. Series A.	—	Rare	—

1878 ISSUE

#S214-S217 printer: ABNC.

		GOOD	FINE	XF
S214	**10 PESOS** 18xx (ca.1878); 1.1.1909. Black on orange unpt. Standing woman w/fasces by pedestal w/arms at l., portr. man at ctr., sailing ships at lower r. Back orange.	—	Rare	—
S215	**25 PESOS** 18xx (ca.1878). Black on green unpt. Shrub at l., arms w/2 seated women at ctr., man at r. Back green.			
	p. Proof.	—	—	—
	s. Specimen.	—	—	—
S216	**50 PESOS** 18xx (ca.1878). Black on blue unpt. Standing cherub and arms at l., man at ctr., standing cherub and ship at r. Back blue. Specimen.	—	—	—
S217	**100 PESOS** 18xx (ca.1878). Black on brown unpt. Ship, man and train across ctr., arms at lower r. Back brown.			
	p. Proof.	—	—	—
	s. Specimen.	—	—	—

NOTE: There was a provisional 1871 issue for the Banco Nacional in Ecuador using ovpt. notes of this bank. A 2 Peso note is thus listed - see Ecuador #S183. Other values may also exist; an issue was reported.

BANCO RURAL DE CREDITO HIPOTECARIO DE COSTA-RICA

1873 BEARER BOND ISSUE

		GOOD	FINE	XF
S218	**100 PESOS** 1.10.1873. Black.	300.00	550.00	850.00

BANCO DE LA UNION

1877 ISSUE

		GOOD	FINE	XF
S219	**100 PESOS** 1.11.1877. Black on deep yellow paper. C. Columbus w/flags at upper ctr. Uniface. Printer: Eden Fisher & Co., London.	—	Rare	—

NOTE: 25 and 50 Pesos values of this issue are reported to exist.

188X; 1887 ISSUE

#S221-S227 arms at ctr. on back. Printer: ABNC.

		GOOD	FINE	XF
S221	**1 PESO** 18xx; 21.10.1886; 1.7.1887; 1.5.1889. Black on blue and red unpt. Raphael's angel at upper ctr. w/cherubs at upper corners. Back blue. W/o series; Series A.	75.00	200.00	450.00

		GOOD	FINE	XF
S222	**2 PESOS** 18xx; 1.7.1887; 1.5.1889. Black on pink and green unpt. Eagle at upper ctr. Back green. Series A.	—	Rare	—

		Good	Fine	XF
S223	**5 Pesos** 18xx; 1.7.1887. Black on orange and blue unpt. Lion at upper ctr., griffins at l. and r. Back orange. Specimen.	—	—	—

		Good	Fine	XF
S224	**10 Pesos** 18xx; 1.7.1887. Black on red and green unpt. American and Canadian Horseshoe Falls at Niagara at upper ctr. Back red-orange. Specimen.	—	—	—

		Good	Fine	XF
S225	**25 Pesos** 18xx; 1.7.1887; 1.5.1889. Black on orange and blue unpt. Sailing ship at upper ctr. Back blue.			
	p. Proof.	—	—	—
	s. Specimen.	—	—	—
S226	**50 Pesos** 18xx; 1.7.1887; 1.5.1889. Black on orange and olive-green unpt. Train crossing bridge at ctr., facing locomotive at l. and r., small train at bottom ctr. Back olive-green.			
	p. Proof.	—	—	—
	s. Specimen.	—	—	—
S227	**100 Pesos** 18xx; 1.7.1887. Black on blue and orange unpt. Allegorical woman at ctr., allegorical heads at l. and r. Back brown.			
	p. Proof.	—	—	—
	s. Specimen.	—	—	—

Railroad

Ferro Carril de Costa Rica

1872 Issue

#S231-S235 black on brown unpt. Back green. Printer: ABNC.

		Good	Fine	XF
S231	**10 Centavos** 15.4.1872. Series A-E.	100.00	375.00	900.00
S232	**25 Centavos** 15.4.1872. Ship and mountains at ctr. Series A; B.	125.00	500.00	1200.

		Good	Fine	XF
S233	**50 Centavos** 15.4.1872. Ship and mountains at ctr. Series A; B.	150.00	600.00	1400.
S234	**1 Peso** 15.4.1872. Sailing ships at ctr., arms at lower r. Series A.	—	—	—
S235	**2 Pesos** 15.4.1872. Sailing ships and anchor at ctr. Series A.	—	—	—
S236	**5 Pesos** 15.4.1872. Steam train at l. ctr., arms at lower r. Series A.	—	—	—

NOTE: A complete set of #S231-S236 in issued form is known to exist.

The Republic of Croatia (Hrvatska), formerly a federal republic of the Socialist Federal Republic of Yugoslavia, has an area of 21,829 sq. mi. (56,538 sq. km.) and a population of 4.48 million. Capital: Zagreb.

Countless archeological sites witness the rich history of the area dating from Greek and Roman times, continuing uninterruptedly through the Middle Ages until today. An Independent state under the first Count Borna (about 800 AD), Croatia was proclaimed a kingdom under Tomislav in 925. In 1102 the country joined the personal union with Hungary, and by 1527 all Croatian lands were included in the Habsburg kingdom, staying in the union until 1918, when Croatia became part of the Yugoslav kingdom together with Slovenia and Serbia. In the past, Croats played a leading role in the wars against the Turks, the Antemuralis Christianitatis, and were renown soldiers in the Napoleonic army. From 1941 to 1945 Croatia was an independent military puppet state; from 1945 to 1991 it was part of the Socialist state of Yugoslavia. Croatia proclaimed its independence from Yugoslavia on Oct. 8, 1991.

Local Serbian forces supported by the Yugoslav Federal Army had developed a military stronghold and proclaimed an independent "SRPSKE KRAJINA" state in the area around Knin, located in southern Croatia. In August 1995 Croat forces overran this political-military enclave.

MONETARY SYSTEM:

Partisan - WWII

Oblasni Narod. Oslobod. Odbor Zagrebacke Oblasti

Zagreb Government Region

1943 ND Issue

#S101-S105 yellow-green and red. Star in sprays at ctr. within rectangular spray frame. Uniface.

		Good	Fine	XF
S101	**500 Kuna** ND (1943).	—	Rare	—

		Good	Fine	XF
S102	**1000 Kuna** ND (1943).	—	Rare	—
S103	**5000 Kuna** ND (1943).	—	Rare	—

		Good	Fine	XF
S104	10,000 Kuna ND (1943).	—	Rare	—
S105	50,000 Kuna ND (1943).	—	Rare	—

Zemaljsko Antifasisticko Vijece Hrvatske

Croatian Anti-Fascist Authority

1943 Issue

#S106-S110 brown, red and blue.

		Good	Fine	XF
S106	100 Dinara = 100 Kuna 15.1.1943. Series H-I/V.	—	Rare	—
S107	500 Dinara = 500 Kuna 15.1.1943. Series H-I/V.	—	Rare	—
S108	1000 Dinara = 1000 Kuna 15.1.1943. Series H-I/V.	—	Rare	—
S109	5000 Dinara = 5000 Kuna 15.1.1943. Series H-I/V.	—	Rare	—

		Good	Fine	XF
S110	10,000 Dinara = 10,000 Kuna 15.1.1943. Series H-I/V.	—	Rare	—

Zemaljsko Antifasisticko Vijece Narodnog Oslobodenja Hrvatske

Croatian Anti-Fascist Government Authority

1943 First Issue

Dinara/Kuna System.

#S111-S115 handwritten sign. w/o series.

		Good	Fine	XF
S111	100 Dinara = 100 Kuna 15.1.1943.	—	Rare	—

		Good	Fine	XF
S112	500 Dinara = 500 Kuna 15.1.1943.	—	Rare	—
S113	1000 Dinara = 1000 Kuna 15.1.1943.	—	Rare	—
S114	5000 Dinara = 5000 Kuna 15.1.1943.	—	Rare	—
S115	10,000 Dinara = 10,000 Kuna 15.1.1943.	—	Rare	—

1943 Second Issue

#S116-S121 red and lt. blue. Handwritten sign. Series H.

		Good	Fine	XF
S116	100 Dinara = 100 Kuna 15.1.1943.	—	Rare	—
S117	500 Dinara = 500 Kuna 15.1.1943.	—	Rare	—
S118	1000 Dinara = 1000 Kuna 15.1.1943.	—	Rare	—
S119	5000 Dinara = 5000 Kuna 15.1.1943.	—	Rare	—
S120	10,000 Dinara = 10,000 Kuna 15.1.1943.	—	Rare	—
S121	100,000 Dinara = 100,000 Kuna 15.1.1943.	—	Rare	—

1943 Third Issue

#S122-S127 yellow, red and gray-blue. Printed sign. W/o series.

		Good	Fine	XF
S122	100 Dinara = 100 Kuna 15.1.1943.	—	Rare	—
S123	500 Dinara = 500 Kuna 15.1.1943.	—	Rare	—
S124	1000 Dinara = 1000 Kuna 15.1.1943.	—	Rare	—
S125	5000 Dinara = 5000 Kuna 15.1.1943.	—	Rare	—
S126	10,000 Dinara = 10,000 Kuna 15.1.1943.	—	Rare	—
S127	100,000 Dinara = 100,000 Kuna 15.1.1943.	—	Rare	—

1943 Fourth Issue

#S128-S130 brown, blue and red. W/o sign. Series I/IV.

		Good	Fine	XF
S128	100 Dinara = 100 Kuna 15.1.1943.	—	Rare	—
S129	500 Dinara = 500 Kuna 15.1.1943.	—	Rare	—
S130	1000 Dinara = 1000 Kuna 15.1.1943.	—	Rare	—

1943 Fifth Issue

Lira System.

#S131-S133 red-lilac and violet. Series H and XXII - XXIX.

		Good	Fine	XF
S131	100 Lire 15.1.1943.	—	Rare	—
S132	500 Lire 15.1.1943.	—	Rare	—
S133	1000 Lire 15.1.1943.	—	Rare	—

#S134-S138 *Deleted.* See Bosnia & Herzegovina.

1813 Siege

Zara

Note: For previously listed #S140 refer to Italian States—Siege.

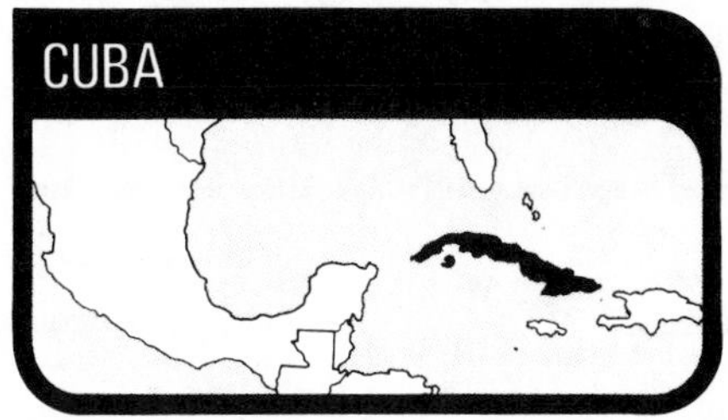

The Republic of Cuba, situated at the northern edge of the Caribbean Sea about 90 miles (145 km.) south of Florida, has an area of 44,218 sq. mi. (114,524 sq. km.) and a population of 11.2 million. Capital: Havana. The Cuban economy is based on the cultivation and refining of sugar, which provides 80 percent of export earnings.

Discovered by Columbus in 1492 and settled by Diego Velasquez in the early 1500s, Cuba remained a Spanish possession until 1898, except for a brief British occupancy in 1762-63. Cuban attempts to gain freedom were crushed, even while Spain was granting independence to its other American possessions. Ten years of warfare, 1868-78, between Spanish troops and Cuban rebels exacted guarantees of right which were never implemented. The final revolt, begun in 1895, evoked American sympathy, and with the aid of U.S. troops independence was proclaimed on May 20, 1902. Fulgencio Batista seized the government in 1952 and established a dictatorship. Opposition to Batista, led by Fidel Castro, drove him into exile on Jan. 1, 1959. A communist-type, 25-member collective leadership headed by Castro was inaugurated in March 1962.

MONETARY SYSTEM:

1 Peso = 100 Centavos

SPANISH ADMINISTRATION

EMPRESA DEL ACUEDUCTO DE CARDENAS

1870 ISSUE

		GOOD	FINE	XF
S112	**3 PESOS** Aug. 1870. Black. Reclining woman at top ctr., fountains at lower l. and lower r.			
	a. Issued note.	1500.	3000.	—
	r. Unsigned remainder. 187x.	300.00	600.00	1000.

NOTE: #S112 exists w/modern falsified sign.

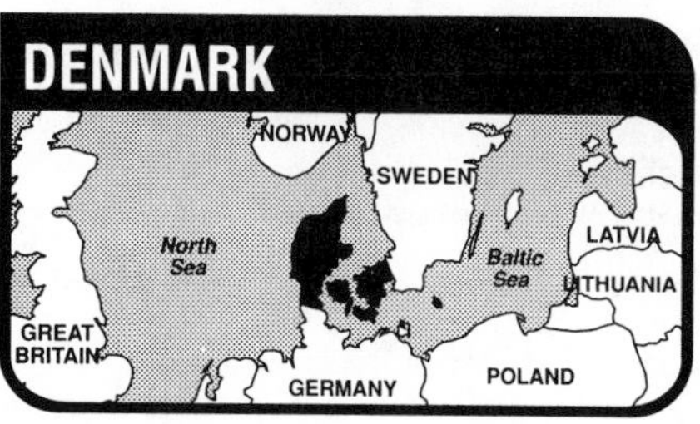

The Kingdom of Denmark, a constitutional monarchy located at the mouth of the Baltic Sea, has an area of 16,633 sq. mi. (43,069 sq. km.) and a population of 5.33 million. Capital: Copenhagen. Most of the country is arable. Agriculture, which used to employ the majority of the people, is now conducted by large farms served by cooperatives. The largest industries are food processing, iron and metal, and fishing. Machinery, meats (chiefly bacon), dairy products and chemicals are exported.

Denmark, a great power during the Viking period of the 9th-11th centuries, conducted raids on western Europe and England, and in the 11th century united England, Denmark and Norway under the rule of King Canute. Despite a struggle between the crown and the nobility (13th-14th centuries) which forced the king to grant a written constitution, Queen Margrethe (1353-1412) succeeded in uniting Denmark, Norway, Sweden, Finland and Greenland under the Danish crown, placing all of Scandinavia under the rule of Denmark. Sweden and Finland were lost in 1523, and an unwise alliance with Napoleon contributed to further dismembering of the empire and fostered a liberal movement which succeeded in making Denmark a constitutional monarchy in 1849.

The present decimal system of currency was introduced in 1874. As a result of a referendum held Sept. 28, 2000, the currency of the European Monetary Union, the Euro, will not be introduced in Denmark in the forseeable future.

RULERS:

Christian IX, 1863-1906
Frederik VIII, 1906-1912
Christian X, 1912-1947
Frederik IX, 1947-1972
Margrethe II, 1972-

MONETARY SYSTEM:

BANKS:

Aalborg Kreditbank	#S101-S120
Aarhus Kreditbank	#S121-S136
Dansk Købmandsbank	#S141-S145
Esbjerg Kreditbank	#S151-S184
Frederikshavn Kreditbank	#S191-S195
Hjørring Kreditbank	#S205-S215
Odense Kreditbank	#S221-S234
Randers Kreditbank	#S241-S286
Thisted Kreditbank	#S291-S296
Varde Kreditbank	#S301-S307
Vejle Kreditbank	#S311-S316

KINGDOM

AALBORG KREDITBANK

Established in 1894. Closed as the *Kreditbanken i Aalborg Hans Andersen* in 1918.

ND FIRST ISSUE

#S101 and S102 uniface.

		GOOD	FINE	XF
S101	**1 KRONE** ND. Black text. Yellow-gray paper.	30.00	90.00	200.00
S102	**5 KRONER** ND. Black text. Blue paper.	30.00	90.00	200.00

ND SECOND ISSUE

#S106-S110 vertical format. Uniface.

		GOOD	FINE	XF
S106	**10 ØRE** ND. Black and gray.	30.00	90.00	160.00
S107	**25 ØRE** ND. Black and green.	30.00	90.00	160.00
S108	**1 KRONE** ND. Red-brown.	30.00	90.00	160.00
S109	**5 KRONER** ND. Blue.	30.00	90.00	190.00
S110	**10 KRONER** ND. Yellow.	35.00	110.00	225.00

ND THIRD ISSUE

#S111-S115 local arms at upper l.

		GOOD	FINE	XF
S111	**10 ØRE** ND. Black and gray. Back gray.			
	a. Issued note.	30.00	90.00	200.00
	b. Violet hand stamp: *Serie A* on face at l. (Fourth Issue).	30.00	90.00	200.00
S112	**25 ØRE** ND. Black and green. Back black and gray.			
	a. Issued note.	30.00	90.00	200.00
	b. Violet hand stamp: *Serie A.* (Fourth Issue).	30.00	90.00	200.00
S113	**1 KRONE** ND. Brown. Back red-brown.	30.00	90.00	225.00

No.	Denomination	Good	Fine	XF
S114	5 Kroner ND. Lt. blue. Back dk. blue.	30.00	90.00	225.00
S115	10 Kroner ND. Yellow-green.	35.00	110.00	250.00

ND Provisional (Fifth) Issue

#S116-S120 ovpt. 3 lines of text on #S111-S115. Handwritten name on 2nd line and printed sign. at lower r.

No.	Denomination	Good	Fine	XF
S116	10 Øre ND. Ovpt. on #S111.	35.00	110.00	250.00
S117	25 Øre ND. Ovpt. on #S112.	35.00	110.00	250.00
S118	1 Krone ND. Ovpt. on #S113.	35.00	110.00	250.00
S119	5 Kroner ND. Ovpt. on #S114.	35.00	110.00	250.00
S120	10 Kroner ND. Ovpt. on #S115.	35.00	110.00	250.00

Aarhus Kreditbank

Established in 1894. Notes issued to 1.7.1914.

ND First Issue

#S121-S127 town view across top on face.

No.	Denomination	Good	Fine	XF
S121	10 Øre ND. Black and yellow-gray.	40.00	115.00	300.00
S122	25 Øre ND. Black and blue-gray.	40.00	115.00	300.00
S123	1 Krone ND. Black and red-brown.	60.00	135.00	325.00
S124	2 Kroner ND. Black and lt. green.	40.00	125.00	300.00
S125	5 Kroner ND. Black and gray-brown.	40.00	125.00	300.00
S126	10 Kroner ND. Black and yellow.	40.00	125.00	300.00
S127	25 Kroner ND. Black and lt. brown.	50.00	145.00	350.00

1902 Second Issue

#S131-S136 bank at ctr. on gray-green back.

No.	Denomination	Good	Fine	XF
S131	10 Øre 1902. Black and gray.	30.00	60.00	150.00
S132	25 Øre 1902. Like #S131.	40.00	100.00	300.00
S132A	50 Øre 1902. Lt. Purple.	—	Rare	—
S133	1 Krone 1902. Black and dk. green.	40.00	100.00	300.00

No.	Denomination	Good	Fine	XF
S134	2 Kroner 1902. Black and gray-green.	40.00	125.00	325.00
S135	5 Kroner 1902. Black and yellow.	40.00	125.00	325.00
S136	10 Kroner 1902. Black and lt. red.	40.00	125.00	325.00

Dansk Købmandsbank

Established in 1908; closed in 1909, bankrupt in 1910.

1908 Issue

#S141-S145 2 different local arms at upper and lower l.

No.	Denomination	Good	Fine	XF
S141	10 Øre 27.11.1908. Black and gray. Litra A.	30.00	60.00	150.00
S142	25 Øre 27.11.1908. Black and gray. Back black and red-brown. Litra B.	35.00	70.00	175.00
S143	1 Krone 27.11.1908. Black and gray. Back black and yellow. Litra C.	40.00	80.00	200.00
S144	2 Kroner 27.11.1908. Litra D.	Reported Not Confirmed		
S145	5 Kroner 27.11.1908. Litra E.	—	—	—

Esbjerg Kreditbank

Established in 1894; closed in 1898.

ND First Issue

#S151-S156 local arms in small tower at lower l. on face. Lions rampant at l. and r. of local arms at ctr. on back.

No.	Denomination	Good	Fine	XF
S151	10 Øre ND. Black and gray.	30.00	90.00	200.00
S152	25 Øre ND. Black on lt. blue unpt. Back lt. blue.	30.00	90.00	200.00

No.	Denomination	Good	Fine	XF
S153	1 Krone ND. Brown and peach. Back lt. peach.	25.00	70.00	175.00
S154	5 Kroner ND. Brown and red-brown. Back lt. brown.	25.00	70.00	175.00
S155	10 Kroner ND. Dk. and lt. brown. Back lt. brown.	100.00	225.00	—
S156	25 Kroner ND. Dk. and lt. green. Back lt. gray-green.	200.00	325.00	—

ND First Provisional Issue

#S161-S166 w/ovpt. 2 lines of text and 2 sign. on face of #S151-S156.

No.	Denomination	Good	Fine	XF
S161	10 Øre ND. Ovpt. on #S151.	25.00	70.00	175.00
S162	25 Øre ND. Ovpt. on #S152.	30.00	80.00	190.00
S163	1 Krone ND. Ovpt. on #S153.	30.00	90.00	200.00
S164	5 Kroner ND. Ovpt. on #S154.	30.00	100.00	225.00
S165	10 Kroner ND. Ovpt. on #S155.	40.00	150.00	275.00

No.	Denomination	Good	Fine	XF
S166	25 Kroner ND. Ovpt. on #S156.	40.00	150.00	350.00

ND Second Provisional Issue

#S171-S176 ovpt. on face like #S161-S166, and *VAREANVISNING* in lg. letters across back.

No.	Denomination	Good	Fine	XF
S171	10 Øre ND. Back ovpt. added to #S161.	30.00	90.00	200.00
S172	25 Øre ND. Back ovpt. added to #S162.	30.00	90.00	200.00
S173	1 Krone ND. Back ovpt. added to #S163.	30.00	90.00	200.00
S174	5 Kroner ND. Back ovpt. added to #S164.	30.00	90.00	200.00

No.	Denomination	Good	Fine	XF
S175	10 Kroner ND. Back ovpt. added to #S165.	40.00	110.00	250.00
S176	25 Kroner ND. Back ovpt. added to #S166.	45.00	130.00	275.00

ND FOURTH ISSUE

SERIES B

#S181-S184 sm. local arms at upper ctr. on face.

		Good	Fine	XF
S181	**10 ØRE** ND. Black on yellow-green unpt.	25.00	70.00	175.00
S182	**25 ØRE** ND. Brown on blue-gray unpt.	30.00	75.00	200.00

		Good	Fine	XF
S183	**1 KRONE** ND. Dk. blue on lt. red unpt.	30.00	90.00	200.00
S184	**5 KRONER** ND. Violet on gray unpt.	35.00	100.00	225.00

FREDERIKSHAVN KREDITBANK

ND ISSUE

#S191-S195 standing Mercury w/caduceus at l., round bldg. and town at ctr.

		Good	Fine	XF
S191	**10 ØRE** ND. Gray-brown. Back lt. gray.	25.00	70.00	175.00
S192	**25 ØRE** ND. Black and yellow. Back lt. yellow.	25.00	70.00	175.00
S193	**1 KRONE** ND. Brown and red-brown. Back lt. brown.	25.00	70.00	175.00
S194	**5 KRONER** ND. Blue-gray.	30.00	90.00	200.00
S195	**10 KRONER** ND. Green.	30.00	90.00	200.00

HJØRRING KREDITBANK

Established in 1894; closed in 1895.

1894 FIRST ISSUE

		Good	Fine	XF
S205	**25 KRONER** 10.11.1894. Blue-green w/black text. Back black text.	200.00	450.00	—

ND SECOND ISSUE

#S211-S215 standing queen above reclining king on checkerboard at l., school bldgs. at ctr.

		Good	Fine	XF
S211	**10 ØRE** ND. Gray and black.	30.00	100.00	225.00
S212	**25 ØRE** ND. Black and gray. Back lt. yellow.	40.00	110.00	250.00
S213	**1 KRONE** ND. Brown and red-brown.	40.00	110.00	250.00

		Good	Fine	XF
S214	**5 KRONER** ND. Lt. green and lt. blue. Back lt. blue.	40.00	125.00	300.00
S215	**10 KRONER** ND. Green. Back lt. green.	40.00	125.00	300.00

ODENSE KREDITBANK

Established in 1895; closed in 1898.

ND FIRST ISSUE

#S221-S227 local arms at ctr. on face. Top line on back: *Avers* at l. and serial # at r.

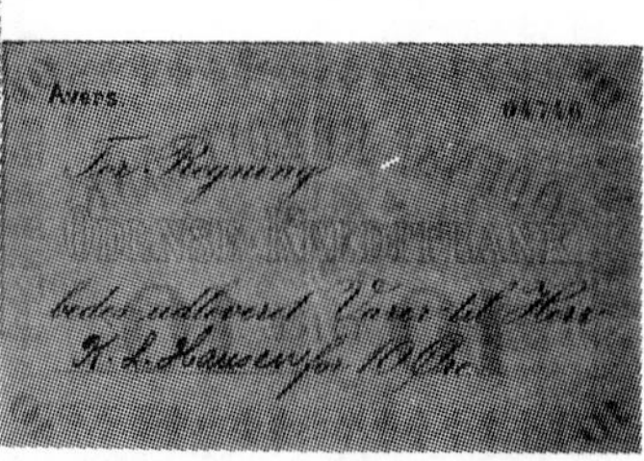

		Good	Fine	XF
S221	**10 ØRE** ND. Black and blue on lt. orange unpt. Back blue and black.	25.00	70.00	175.00
S222	**25 ØRE** ND. Like #S221.	30.00	90.00	200.00

		Good	Fine	XF
S223	**1 KRONE** ND. Black and orange on lt. blue unpt. Back orange and black.	25.00	70.00	175.00
S224	**2 KRONER** ND. Like #S223.	30.00	90.00	200.00
S225	**5 KRONER** ND. Like #S223.	30.00	90.00	250.00
S226	**20 KRONER** ND. Like #S223.	35.00	110.00	250.00
S227	**50 KRONER** ND. Like #S223.	50.00	145.00	275.00

ND SECOND ISSUE

#S233-S234 face like #S221-S227. Top line on back: *Avers* at ctr. and serial # at l. and at r.

		Good	Fine	XF
S233	**1 KRONE** ND. Like #S223.	30.00	90.00	200.00

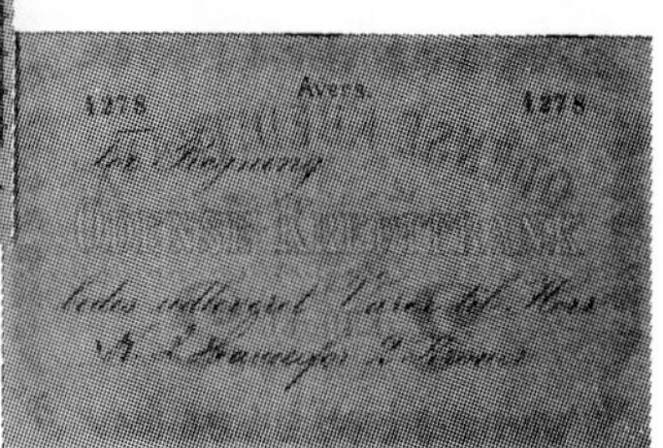

		Good	Fine	XF
S234	**2 KRONER** ND. Like #S224.	30.00	90.00	200.00

RANDERS KREDITBANK

Established in 1891; absorbed by Discontobank in 1927.

ND FIRST ISSUE

		Good	Fine	XF
S241	**10 KRONER** ND. Blue-gray w/black text. Back black text. (Not redeemable after 31.12.1892.)	35.00	110.00	250.00

ND; 1895 SECOND ISSUES

#S246-S265 local arms at upper l., town scene across upper ctr.

		Good	Fine	XF
S246	**10 ØRE** ND. Black and blue. Value: *10 ØRE* at lower ctr.	25.00	70.00	175.00
S247	**10 ØRE** ND. Like #S246 but added line of text: *har i Anl...* across ctr.	25.00	70.00	175.00
S248	**25 ØRE** ND. Dk. and lt. blue. Value: *25 ØRE* at lower ctr.	25.00	70.00	175.00
S249	**25 ØRE** ND. Added line of text like #S247.	30.00	100.00	200.00
S250	**1 KRONE** ND. Dk. and lt. red. Value: *EN KRONE* at lower ctr.	30.00	110.00	225.00
S251	**1 KRONE** ND. Added line of text like #S247.	30.00	110.00	225.00
S252	**2 KRONER** ND. Red. Value: *TO KRONER* at lower ctr.	30.00	110.00	225.00

		GOOD	FINE	XF
S253	**2 KRONER** ND. Added line of text like #S247.	30.00	110.00	225.00
S254	**2 KRONER** ND. Like #S253 but text printed on back.			
	a. Issued note.	30.00	110.00	225.00
	b. W/lg. date ovpt: *1895* at upper r. on face.	30.00	110.00	225.00
S255	**5 KRONER** ND. Brown. Back lt. brown. Value: *FEM KRONER* at lower ctr.	30.00	110.00	250.00
S256	**5 KRONER** ND. Added line of text like #S247.	30.00	110.00	250.00
S257	**5 KRONER** ND. Like #S256 but text printed on back. W/lg. date ovpt: *1895* at upper r. on face.	30.00	110.00	250.00
S258	**10 KRONER** ND. Blue-green. Back lt. blue-green. Value: *TI KRONER* at lower ctr.	30.00	125.00	300.00
S259	**10 KRONER** ND. Added line of text like #S247.	30.00	125.00	300.00
S260	**10 KRONER** ND. Like #S259 but text printed on back.			
	a. Issued note.	30.00	125.00	300.00
	b. W/lg. date ovpt: *1895* at upper r. on face.	30.00	125.00	300.00
S261	**20 KRONER** ND. Violet. Value: *20 KRONER* at lower ctr.	40.00	150.00	325.00
S262	**20 KRONER** ND. Added line of text like #S247.	40.00	150.00	325.00
S263	**20 KRONER** ND. Like #S262 but text printed on back.			
	a. Issued note.	40.00	150.00	325.00
	b. W/lg. date ovpt: *1895* at upper r. on face.	40.00	150.00	325.00
S264	**50 KRONER** ND. Gray-green. Text line like #S247.	60.00	250.00	500.00
S265	**50 KRONER** ND. Like #S264 but text printed on back.			
	a. Issued note.	50.00	175.00	450.00
	b. W/lg. date ovpt: *1895* at upper r. on face.	45.00	165.00	425.00

ND; 1895 THIRD ISSUE

#S271-S276 upper design like previous issue but value across lower face and some unpt. patterns are changed.

		GOOD	FINE	XF
S271	**10 ØRE** ND. Black and grayish blue. Similar to #S246 but w/value: *ØRE 10 ØRE* at lower ctr.	25.00	70.00	175.00

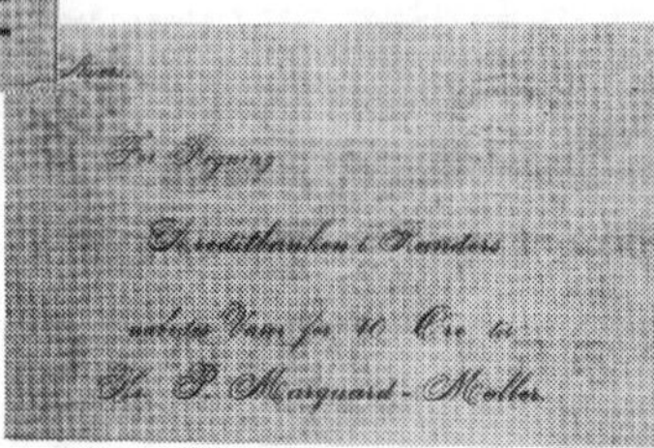

		GOOD	FINE	XF
S272	**10 ØRE** ND. Like #S271 but text printed on back.			
	a. Issued note.	25.00	70.00	175.00
	b. W/lg. date ovpt: *1895* at upper r. on face.	25.00	70.00	175.00
S273	**25 ØRE** ND. Blue and yellow on red unpt. Back green. Value: *ØRE 25 ØRE* at lower ctr.	30.00	100.00	200.00
S274	**25 ØRE** ND. Like #S273 but text printed on back.			
	a. Issued note.	30.00	100.00	200.00
	b. W/lg. date ovpt: *1895* at upper r. on face.	30.00	100.00	200.00
S275	**1 KRONE** ND. Red and green. Back green. Value: *KRONE 1 KRONE* at lower ctr.	30.00	100.00	200.00
S276	**1 KRONE** ND. Like #S275 but text printed on back.			
	a. Issued note.	30.00	100.00	200.00
	b. W/lg. date ovpt: *1895* at upper r. on face.	30.00	100.00	200.00

1896-1900 ISSUE

#S281-S283 similar to previous issue but w/scrollwork and some numeral changes, and the addition of 2 sign. at bottom on some notes. Each note is dated either on face or back.

		GOOD	FINE	XF
S281	**10 ØRE** 26.2.1896 (on back). Black, gray-green, and green. Sunburst in unpt. Black text on back.	25.00	70.00	175.00
S282	**25 ØRE** 1.3.1900. Black, lt. blue, and red. No rays in unpt. 2 sign. at bottom.	25.00	70.00	175.00
S283	**1 KRONE** ca.1900. Red, yellow, and green. 2 sign. at bottom.	30.00	75.00	190.00

#S284-S286 more ornately designed face w/larger and wider town view across upper ctr. and rising sun above.

		GOOD	FINE	XF
S284	**5 KRONER** 1.9.1897 (on back). Gray and brown.	30.00	100.00	200.00
S285	**10 KRONER** 1.9.1897 (on back). Blue.	35.00	110.00	250.00
S286	**50 KRONER** 1.7.1898 (on back). Red-brown.	40.00	150.00	325.00

THISTED KREDITBANK

Established in 1895; reportedly closed in 1924.

ND ISSUE

#S291-S293 local arms at ctr. r. on face.

		GOOD	FINE	XF
S291	**10 ØRE** ND. Blue-gray w/black text.	50.00	145.00	325.00
S292	**25 ØRE** ND. Gray w/black text.	55.00	215.00	350.00
S293	**1 KRONE** ND. Lt. red w/black text.	60.00	315.00	—
S294	**5 KRONER** ND. Gray-orange, black text.	—	—	—
S295	**10 KRONER** ND. Like #S294.	—	—	—
S296	**20 KRONER** ND. Gray-violet, black text.	—	—	—

VARDE KREDITBANK

ND PROVISIONAL ISSUE

#S301-S307 ovpt. new bank name *Kreditbanken Varde* on notes of the Randers Kreditbank.

		GOOD	FINE	XF
S301	**10 ØRE** ND. Ovpt. on #S271.	60.00	160.00	—
S302	**25 ØRE** ND. Ovpt. on #S273.	50.00	145.00	—
S303	**1 KRONE** ND. Ovpt. on #S275.	90.00	190.00	—
S304	**2 KRONER** ND. Ovpt. on #S253.	100.00	225.00	—
S305	**5 KRONER** ND. Ovpt. on #S256.	50.00	145.00	—
S306	**10 KRONER** ND. Ovpt. on #S259.	100.00	275.00	—
S307	**20 KRONER** ND. Ovpt. on #S262.	50.00	145.00	—

VEJLE KREDITBANK

Established in 1894.

ND ISSUE

#S311-S316 local arms at upper l. on face.

		GOOD	FINE	XF
S311	**10 ØRE** ND. Gray and black. Back lt. gray.	40.00	125.00	250.00
S312	**25 ØRE** ND. Lt. brown.	50.00	140.00	275.00
S313	**1 KRONE** ND. Green.	60.00	160.00	300.00
S314	**5 KRONER** ND.	Reported Not Confirmed		
S315	**10 KRONER** ND. Blue.	50.00	145.00	—
S316	**50 KRONER** ND.	Reported Not Confirmed		

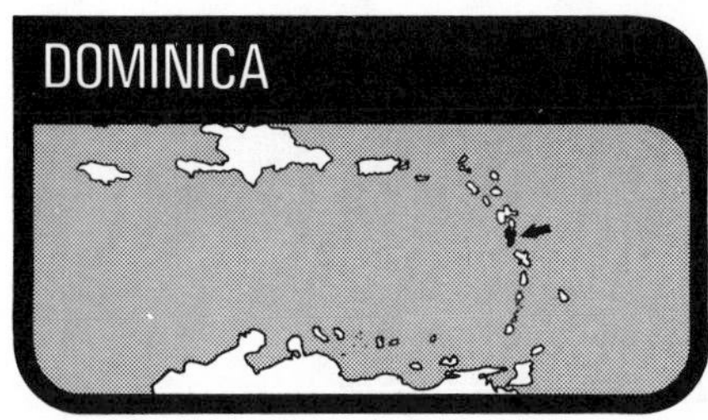

The commonwealth of Dominica, situated in the Lesser Antilles midway between Guadeloupe to the north and Martinique to the south, has an area of 290 sq. mi. (751 sq. km.) and a population of 77,000. Capital: Roseau.

Columbus discovered and named the island on Nov. 3, 1493. Spain neglected it and it was finally colonized by the French in 1632. The British drove the French from the island in 1756. Thereafter it changed hands between the French and British a dozen or more times before becoming permanently British in 1805. Throughout the greater part of its British history, Dominica was a presidency of the Leeward Islands. In 1940 its administration was transferred to the Windward Islands and it was established as a separate colony with considerable local autonomy.

RULERS:

British

MONETARY SYSTEM:

1 British West Indies Dollar = 4 Shillings 2 Pence
5 British West Indies Dollars = 1 Pound 10 Pence

BRITISH ADMINISTRATION

BARCLAYS BANK (DOMINION, COLONIAL AND OVERSEAS)

1926 PROVISIONAL ISSUE

		GOOD	FINE	XF
S101	**5 DOLLARS** 1926. Supported royal arms at ctr.	—	Rare	—

1937 PROVISIONAL ISSUE

#S101A and S102 ovpt: *ISSUED AT DOMINICA BRANCH* at l. and r. of ctr. Supported royal arms at r. Supported royal arms at ctr. on back. Printer: BWC.

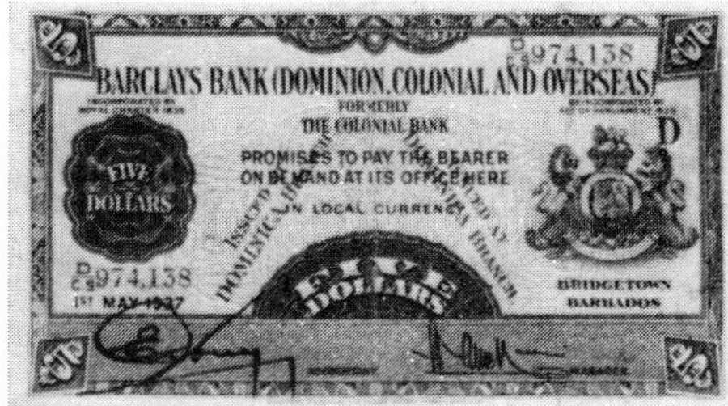

		GOOD	FINE	XF
S101A	**5 DOLLARS** 1.5.1937; 1.2.1941. Purple on m/c unpt. Lg. black *D* (Dominica) at upper r. on face. Issuing office Bridgetown, Barbados.	200.00	600.00	—

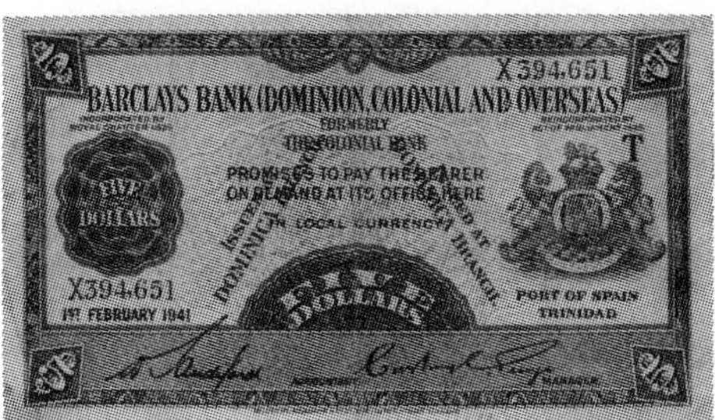

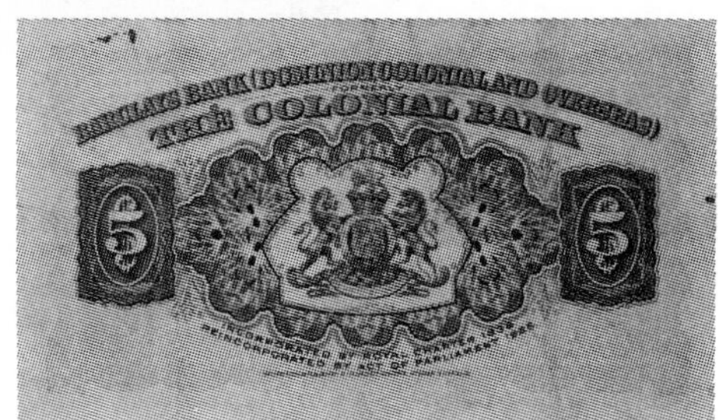

		GOOD	FINE	XF
S102	**5 DOLLARS** 1.5.1937; 1.2.1941. Purple on m/c unpt. Ovpt. on Trinidad #S102.	200.00	600.00	—

COLONIAL BANK

1900'S ISSUE

		GOOD	FINE	XF
S106	**5 DOLLARS** To 1926.	Reported Not Confirmed		

ROYAL BANK OF CANADA

Issuing office: Roseau, Dominica.

ND PROVISIONAL ISSUE

		GOOD	FINE	XF
S111	**5 DOLLARS = 1 POUND 10 PENCE** ND (- old date 2.1.1913). Black on green unpt. Ovpt: *DOMINICA* at l. and r. and *PAYABLE AT ROSEAU/DOMINICA* at ctr. on Canada #1378.			
	a. Issued note.	300.00	1000.	—
	s. Specimen.	—	Rare	—

1920 REGULAR ISSUE

#S112 and S113 w/text: *REDEEMABLE ONLY/IN/DOMINICA* at bottom ctr. Supported royal arms at ctr. on back.

		GOOD	FINE	XF
S112	**5 DOLLARS = 1 POUND 10 PENCE** 2.1.1920. Black on green unpt. Steamship at ctr. Back green.	300.00	750.00	—

1938 ISSUE

		GOOD	FINE	XF
S113	**5 DOLLARS = 1 POUND 10 PENCE** 3.1.1938. Black on green unpt. Similar to #S112 but smaller size. Printer: CBNC.			
	a. Issued note.	210.00	525.00	—
	p. Proof.	—	Unc	450.00

NOTE: For later issues see British East Caribbean Territories in Vol. 2 and East Caribbean States in Vol. 3.

The Dominican Republic, occupying the eastern two-thirds of the island of Hispañiola, has an area of 18,816 sq. mi. (48,734 sq. km.) and a population of 8.49 million. Capital: Santo Domingo. The agricultural economy produces sugar, coffee, tobacco and cocoa.

Columbus discovered Hispaniola in 1492, and named it *La Isla Espanola* - "the Spanish Island." Santo Domingo, the oldest white settlement in the Western Hemisphere, was the base from which Spain conducted its exploration of the New World. Later, French buccaneers settled the western third of Hispaniola, which in 1697 was ceded to France by Spain, and in 1804 became the Republic of Haiti - "mountainous country." At this time, the Spanish called their part of Hispaniola Santo Domingo, and the French called their part Saint-Domingue. In 1822, the Haitians conquered the entire island and held it until 1844, when Juan Pablo Duarte, the national hero of the Dominican Republic, drove them out of eastern Hispaniola and established an independent Dominican Republic. The republic returned voluntarily to Spanish dominion - after being rejected by France, Britain and the United States - from 1861 to 1865, when independence was restored.

Dictatorships and democratic rule was interspersed and from 1916 to 1924 it was occupied by the U.S. from 1930 to 1961, Rafael Trujillo was dictator. In the 1994 elections, a reform government gained power.

MONETARY SYSTEM:

1 Peso Oro = 100 Centavos Oro

REPUBLIC

BANCO DE LA COMPAÑIA DE CRÉDITO DE PUERTO PLATA

1880'S ISSUE

#S101-S107 Dominican arms on back. Printer: ABNC.

		GOOD	FINE	XF
S101	**25 CENTAVOS** 18xx. Black on green and brown unpt. Portr. Magellan at l. Back green.			
	r. Unsigned remainder.	5.00	15.00	50.00
	s. Specimen.	—	—	—

		GOOD	FINE	XF
S102	**50 CENTAVOS** 188x. Black on blue and gold unpt. Seated Indian woman at l. Back blue.			
	r. Unsigned remainder.	1.00	5.00	15.00
	s. Specimen.	—	—	—

		GOOD	FINE	XF
S103	**1 PESO** 188x. Black on red and green unpt. Portr. Magellan at l., seated woman w/jug at lower r. Back red.			
	r. Unsigned remainder.	4.00	12.00	50.00
	s. Specimen.	—	—	—

		GOOD	FINE	XF
S104	**2 PESOS** 188x. Black on blue and brown unpt. Reclining woman w/lamp sitting at l. Back blue.			
	r. Unsigned remainder.	8.00	25.00	90.00
	s. Specimen.	—	—	—

		GOOD	FINE	XF
S105	**5 PESOS** 188x. Black on lt. red and green unpt. Man seated at l., 2 sailors at lower r. Back lt. brown.			
	r. Unsigned remainder.	12.50	30.00	120.00
	s. Specimen.	—	—	—

		GOOD	FINE	XF
S106	**10 PESOS** 188x. Black on orange and blue unpt. Columbus in sight of land at l., Raphael's Angel at ctr., Mercury at r. Back dk. brown.			
	r. Unsigned remainder.	25.00	75.00	200.00
	s. Specimen.	—	—	—

		GOOD	FINE	XF
S107	**50 PESOS** 188x. Black on green and orange unpt. Sailor w/telescope and other marine implements at l., landing of Columbus at ctr., women w/spool at r. Back brown.			
	a. Issued note.	—	Rare	—
	p. Proof.	—	—	—
	s. Specimen.	—	—	—

1899 PROVISIONAL ISSUE

#S111-S112 red ovpt. of 6 lines of text: *REHABILITADO...* and 2 handwritten sign. at bottom. Date *21.7.1899* is included in ovpt. Back may have round purple hand stamping: *CONSTITUCIONAL...*

S111 25 CENTAVOS
21.7.1899. Ovpt. on #S101.

	GOOD	FINE	XF
S111	25.00	100.00	300.00

S112 50 CENTAVOS
21.7.1899. Ovpt. on #S102.

	GOOD	FINE	XF
S112	25.00	100.00	300.00

NOTE: Higher denominations ovpt. are reported but not confirmed.

BANCO NACIONAL DE SANTO DOMINGO

1869 ISSUE

#S119 and S120 printer: ABNC.

S119 25 CENTAVOS
ND (ca.1870). Green on black unpt. Portr. Lincoln at r. Face proof.

	GOOD	FINE	XF
S119	—	—	—

S120 50 CENTAVOS
ND (ca.1870). Green on black unpt. Portr. Washington at ctr. Face proof.

	GOOD	FINE	XF
S120	—	—	—

#S121-S125 back green; text at ctr. Printer: ABNC.

S121 1 PESO
1.12.1869. Black and dk. green on green unpt. Portr. Columbus at lower l., reclining woman w/globe at ctr., anchor at lower r.

	GOOD	FINE	XF
a. Issued note.	—	Rare	—
p. Proof.	—	—	—
r. Remainder, w/o serial #, punched hole cancelled.	—	—	—

S122 2 PESOS
1.12.1869. Black on green unpt. Sailor at l., woman seated at sugar cane press at r.

	GOOD	FINE	XF
a. Issued note.	—	Rare	—
p. Proof.	—	—	—

S123 5 PESOS
1.12.1869. Black on green unpt. Tree w/basket and other implements at l., dog and safe at ctr., woman at lower r. Proof.

	GOOD	FINE	XF
S123	—	—	—

S124 10 PESOS
1.12.1869. Black on green unpt. Ducks at l., explorer landing in new world at ctr., girl at r.

	GOOD	FINE	XF
S124	—	Rare	—

S125 20 PESOS
1.12.1869. Black on green unpt. Standing woman w/basket at l., allegorical woman w/staff and bird in foliage scene at ctr., man carrying sheaf at r. Proof.

	GOOD	FINE	XF
a. W/serial #. (Not issued).	—	Rare	—
p. Proof.	—	—	—

NOTE: Beware of remainders with spurious signatures.

1881 PROVISIONAL ISSUE

#S126 and S127 ovpt of seven lines of text on back w/sign. and title printed at bottom and vertically at l. and r. Date *21.12.1881* is included in ovpt.

	GOOD	FINE	XF
S126 1 PESO 21.12.1881. Ovpt. on back of #S121.	—	Rare	—
S127 2 PESOS 21.12.1881. Ovpt. on back of #S122.	—	Rare	—

NOTE: Higher denominations w/this provisional ovpt. are reported, not confirmed.

1889 ISSUE

#S129 and S130 printer: FBNC.

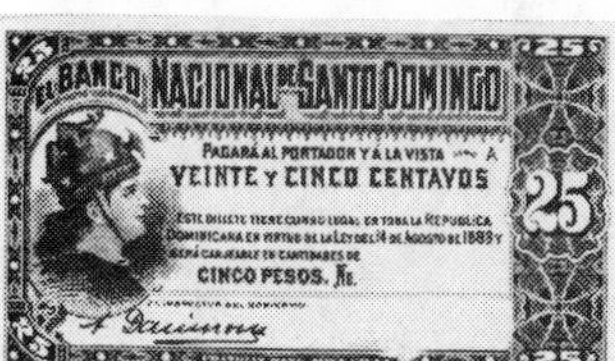

S129 25 CENTAVOS
L.14.8.1889. Black. Helmeted woman at l. Back black or orange. Proof.

	GOOD	FINE	XF
S129	—	—	—

		GOOD	FINE	XF
S130	**50 CENTAVOS** *L.14.8.1889.* Black. Portr. C. Columbus at l. Back black or green. Proof.	—	—	—

1889 ND ISSUE

#S131-S133 printer: FBNC.

		GOOD	FINE	XF
S131	**1 PESO** ND. Black on green unpt. Portr. Liberty at l., arms at r. Printed sign at r. Back green. Series C.			
	a. Issued note w/hand sign. at l., stamping at corner on back.	5.00	25.00	60.00
	r. Remainder w/o hand sign. at l. or stamping on back.	—	Unc	30.00

		GOOD	FINE	XF
S132	**2 PESOS** ND. Black on brown unpt. Arms at upper l., portr. C. Columbus at lower r. Back brown. Series D.			
	a. Issued note as #S131a.	8.00	45.00	100.00
	r. Remainder as #S131b.	—	Unc	60.00

		GOOD	FINE	XF
S133	**5 PESOS** ND. Black on olive unpt. Seated Liberty w/shield at l., arms at lower r. Back olive. Series E.	10.00	50.00	110.00

NOTE: #S132a and S133 often have small hole cancellations (3 to 4mm).

LAW OF 14.8.1889 - 1912 ISSUE

#S142-S147 arms at l. w/payable text: *PLATA MONEDA MEJICANA* (Silver Mexican Money). Printer: CS&E.

		GOOD	FINE	XF
S142	**2 PESOS** ND. Black on lt. green unpt. Portr. young woman at r. Back green. Series A.	95.00	225.00	—

		GOOD	FINE	XF
S143	**5 PESOS** ND. Black on red and green unpt. Portr. C. Columbus at upper ctr. Back red. Series B.	100.00	250.00	—

		GOOD	FINE	XF
S145	**25 PESOS** ND. Mercury standing by 2 seated women at l., arms at upper r. Unsigned remainder.	—	—	—

		GOOD	FINE	XF
S147	**100 PESOS** ND. Black on pink and blue unpt. Portr. C. Columbus at upper r. Back blue. Series D. Unsigned remainder.	40.00	100.00	225.00

1912 ISSUE

#S151-S157 notes in dual denominations. Back w/arms at ctr. Printer: ABNC.

		GOOD	FINE	XF
S151	**1 PESO = 1 DOLLAR** 31.1.1912. Black on blue and brown unpt. Seated allegorical woman at ctr. Back green.			
	p. Proof.	—	—	—
	s. Specimen, punched hole cancelled.	—	—	—

		GOOD	FINE	XF
S152	**2 PESOS = 2 DOLLARS** 31.1.1912. Black on orange and green unpt. Seated allegorical woman at r. Back red-orange. Proof.	—	—	—

		GOOD	FINE	XF
S153	**5 PESOS = 5 DOLLARS** 31.1.1912. Black on blue and brown unpt. Seated allegorical woman w/cherub supporters at ctr. Back blue-gray.			
	p. Proof.	—	—	—
	s. Specimen, punched hole cancelled.	—	—	—

		GOOD	FINE	XF
S154	**10 PESOS = 10 DOLLARS** 31.1.1912. Black on brown and purple unpt. Allegorical woman seated at ctr. Back brown. Proof.	—	—	—

		GOOD	FINE	XF
S155	**25 PESOS = 25 DOLLARS** 31.1.1912. Black on green and orange unpt. Seated allegorical woman w/globe at l. Back olive-green. Proof.	—	—	—

		GOOD	FINE	XF
S156	**50 PESOS = 50 DOLLARS** 31.1.1912. Black on purple and green unpt. Allegorical woman seated at ctr. Back purple. Proof.	—	—	—

		GOOD	FINE	XF
S157	**100 PESOS = 100 DOLLARS** 31.1.1912. Black on orange and green unpt. Allegorical woman seated at l. and r. of denomination numeral at ctr. Back orange.			
	p. Proof.	—	—	—
	s. Specimen, punched hole cancelled.	—	—	—

GOVERNMENT

1875-76 CRÉDITO PÚBLICO-DEUDA CONSOLIDADA ISSUE

Bond of Consolidated Public Debt.

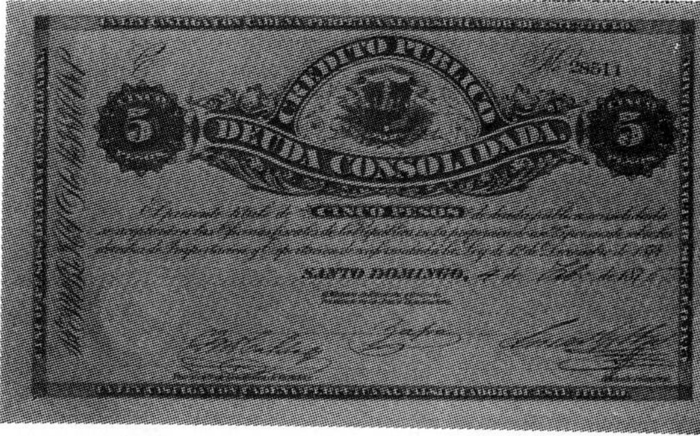

		GOOD	FINE	XF
S161	**5 PESOS** 1.6.1875; 4.2.1876. Red. Arms at ctr. Handwritten date. Uniface.	4.00	8.00	20.00
S162	**10 PESOS** 1.7.1875. Green. Like #S161.	10.00	20.00	45.00

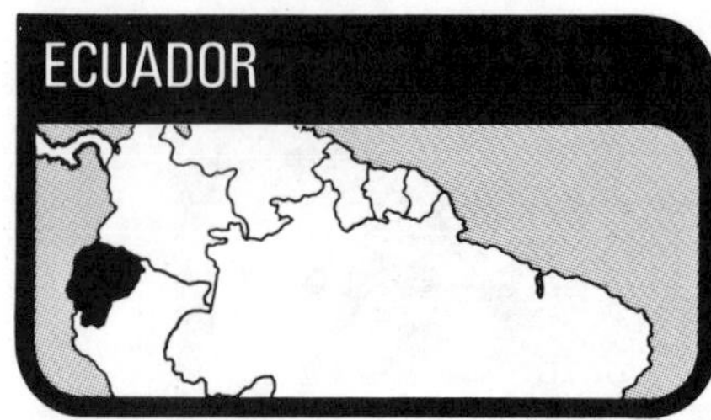

The Republic of Ecuador, located astride the equator on the Pacific coast of South America, has an area of 109,484 sq. mi. (283,561 sq. km.) and a population of 12.65 million. Capital: Quito. Agriculture is the mainstay of the economy but there are appreciable deposits of minerals and petroleum. It is the world's largest exporter of bananas and balsa wood. Coffee, cacao and shrimp are also valuable exports.

Ecuador was first sighted, 1526, by Bartolome Ruiz. Conquest was undertaken by Sebastian de Benalcazar who founded Quito in 1534. Ecuador was part of the province, later Vice-royalty, of Peru until 1739 when it became part of the Vice-royalty of New Granada. After two failed attempts to attain independence in 1810 and 1812, it successfully declared its independence in October 1820, and won final victory over Spanish forces May 24, 1822. Incorporated into the Gran Colombia confederacy, it loosened its ties in 1830 and regained full independence in 1835.

MONETARY SYSTEM:

1 Peso = 8 Reales
1 Peso = 100 Centavos
1 Sucre = 10 Decimos = 100 Centavos
1 Condor = 25 Sucres
1 USA Dollar = 25,000 Sucres (March 2001)

BANKS:

Banco Anglo-Ecuatoriano, 1885-88 .... #S91-S98
Banco del Azuay, 1914-24 .... #S101-S104
Banco de Circulación y Descuento de Manuel Antonio de Luzárraga, 1860-65 .. #S111-S116
Banco de Circulación y Descuento de Planas, Pérez & Obarrio, 1866-70 .... #S117-S119A
Banco Comercial y Agrícola, 1894-1926 .... #S120-S132A
Banco de Descuento, 1922-24 .... #S132B-S136
Banco del Ecuador, 1868-1926 .... #S137A-S164
Banco Internacional, 1884-95 .... #S171-S179A
Banco de Londres y Ecuador, ca. 1887 .... #S180-S182
Banco Nacional, 1871 .... #S183-S195A
Banco Particular de Descuento I Circulación de Guayaquil, 1861-70 .... #S196-S205
Banco del Pichincha, 1906-24 .... #S211-S227
Banco de Quito, 1869-85 .... #S231-S246
Banco Sur Americano, 1920 .... #S251-S254
Banco de La Unión, 1880-95 .... #S261-S271A
Compañia de Crédito Agrícola e Industrial, 1921 .... #S272-S274

GOVERNMENT

La Caja Central de Emisión y Amortización, 1926-27 .... #S280-S284

Banks

Banco Anglo-Ecuatoriano

Montecristi

1885-86 Issue

Peso System.

#S91-S94 condor on shield w/lion and unicorn supporters at ctr. on face. Mountain scene at ctr. on back. Originally printed for issue at Montecristi but actually issued w/ovpt: *GUAYAQUIL*. Printer: ABNC.

		Good	Fine	XF
S91	**1 Peso** 14.10.1885; 21.10.1885. Black on lt. brown unpt. W/text: *En Moneda Fuerte* on face. Back lt. brown.			
	p. Proof.	—	—	—
	s. Specimen.	—	—	—
S92	**1 Peso** 4.6.1886. Like #S91 but w/text: *En Moneda Corrieute* on face. Proof.	—	—	—

#S93 and S94 w/text: *en Moneda Fuerte* on face.

		Good	Fine	XF
S93	**5 Pesos** ca.1886. Black on orange unpt. Woman writing at r.			
	p. Back green. Proof.	—	—	—
	s. Back orange. Specimen.	—	—	—

		Good	Fine	XF
S94	**10 Pesos** ca.1886. Black on red-orange and green unpt. Watering horses at l.			
	p. Back blue. Proof.	—	—	—
	s. Back red-orange. Specimen.	—	—	—

Guayaquil

1885 Provisonal Issue

Sucre System.

		Good	Fine	XF
S95	**1 Sucre** 21.10.1885. Ovpt: *UN SUCRE* and *GUAYAQUIL* on #S91.	—	—	—

1886 Regular Issue

#S96-S98 similar to peso system. Guayaquil. *En Moneda Corriente* on face.

		Good	Fine	XF
S96	**1 Sucre** 1886. Similar to #S91.	—	—	—
S97	**5 Sucres** ca.1886. Similar to #S93. Back orange. Specimen.	—	—	—
S98	**10 Sucres** ca.1886. Similar to #S94, but back red-orange.			
	p. Proof.	—	—	—
	s. Specimen.	—	—	—

Banco del Azuay

1914-20 Issue

#S101-S104 printer: ABNC.

		Good	Fine	XF
S101	**1 Sucre** 24.4.1914; 1.12.1920; 17.12.1920; 8.7.1921. Black on blue and red unpt. Gil Ramírez Dávalos standing at l. Back green.	60.00	150.00	300.00

		Good	Fine	XF
S102	2 Sucres 6.3.1914; 16.3.1914; 16.6.1916; 1.12.1920. Black on orange and green unpt. 2 children w/bunches of string at ctr. Back dk. red.	70.00	160.00	325.00

		Good	Fine	XF
S103	5 Sucres 1.12.1920; 15.11.1924. Black on blue and pink unpt. Old fortress w/city behind at l., portr. Alonso de Mercadillo at r. Back brown.	100.00	350.00	—

		Good	Fine	XF
S104	10 Sucres 18.6.1917; 20.2.1920. Black on red and purple unpt. Portr. Diego de Almagro at l., Liberty monument at ctr., portr. Sebastián de Benalcázar at r. Back brown; ornamental head at ctr.			
	a. Issued note.	60.00	150.00	300.00
	p. Proof.	—	Unc	400.00

NOTE: Higher values (20, 50, 100, 500 and 1000 Sucres) are reported but not confirmed. Some dates may have capitalization amount ovpt. More information is needed.

NOTE: Some notes were issued w/ovpt: *CAJA CENTRAL DE EMISION Y AMORTIZACION*, see #S282A.

Banco de Circulación y Descuento de Manuel Antonio de Luzarraga

1860's Issue

		Good	Fine	XF
S111	1 Peso 1868. Black on orange unpt. Luzarraga at lower l., allegorical woman and plants at upper ctr., woman at lower r.			
	a. 1.10.1868.	—	Rare	—
	p. Proof. 18xx.	—	Unc	400.00

NOTE: #S111a was also issued by the Banco del Ecuador before its own notes were printed. See #S137A.

		Good	Fine	XF
S112	4 Pesos 186x. Black on blue unpt. Sailor at lower l., eagle at upper ctr. r. Proof.	—	Unc	400.00

		Good	Fine	XF
S113	4 Pesos 18xx; 31.12.1862. Black on brown unpt. Eagle at ctr. Proof.	—	Unc	400.00

		Good	Fine	XF
S113A	5 Pesos 186x. Black on red-orange unpt. Standing Justice at l., steamship at ctr. r. Proof.	—	Unc	400.00

		Good	Fine	XF
S114	5 Pesos 18xx. Black on yellow-orange unpt. Portr. girl at upper l., reclining woman w/tablet and child at upper ctr. r. Proof.	—	Unc	400.00

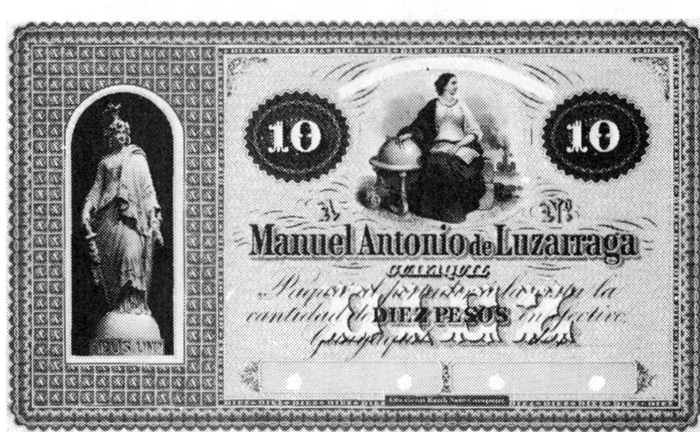

		Good	Fine	XF
S115	10 Pesos 18xx. Black on green unpt. Statue of Freedom at l., seated woman w/globe at upper ctr. r. Proof.	—	Unc	400.00
S116	20 Pesos 18xx. Black on brown unpt. Allegorical man wearing toga standing under tree at l., arms at r. Proof.	—	Unc	400.00

Note: For similar notes dated 1.10.1868 and counterstamped on back see #S137A-S137D.

Banco de Circulación y Descuento de Planas, Pérez & Obarrio

1867 Issue

#S117-S119A printer: CABB.

		Good	Fine	XF
S117	4 Reales 18xx (1867). Black on green unpt. Portr. young girl's head at ctr. Uniface. Proof, punched hole cancelled.	—	—	—
S117A	1 Peso 18xx (1867). Black on green unpt. Standing woman at l., girl's head at ctr. Archive copy.	—	—	—

		GOOD	FINE	XF
S118	**5 PESOS** 18xx (1867). Black on orange unpt. Cherub at upper l., seated sailor at ctr., woman w/numeral *V* at r. Proof, punched hole cancelled.	—	Rare	—
S119	**10 PESOS** 18xx (1867). Black on brown unpt. Girl's head at lower l. and r., horses at ctr.	—	Rare	—
S119A	**20 PESOS** 18xx (1867). Black on blue unpt. Tree, basket, sacks and shovel at l., allegorical woman holding sailing ship at upper ctr. Archive copy.	—	—	—

BANCO COMERCIAL Y AGRÍCOLA

1895 ISSUE

#S120-S130 issued at Guayaquil. Printer: ABNC.

		GOOD	FINE	XF
S120	**1 SUCRE** 1.10.1895; 1.7.1896. Similar to #S126, but *CAPITAL S/2,000,000* at r. border. Back green.	75.00	200.00	—
S121	**5 SUCRES** ND (ca.1895). Black on orange and yellow unpt. Similar to #S127, but *CAPITAL S/2,000,000* and minor plate differences. Back orange. Archive copy.	—	—	—
S122	**20 SUCRES** ND (ca.1895). Black on blue and yellow unpt. Similar to #S129, but *CAPITAL S/2,000,000.* Back blue; street view in town at r. Specimen or proof.	—	—	—

		GOOD	FINE	XF
S123	**100 SUCRES** ND (ca.1895). Black on lt. brown and yellow unpt. Similar to #S131, but *CAPITAL S/2,000,000.* Back brown; José Joaquín Olmedo monument at l.			
	p. Proof.	—	—	—
	s. Series L. Specimen.	—	—	—

		GOOD	FINE	XF
S124	**1000 SUCRES** ND (ca.1895). Black on red, orange and yellow unpt. Similar to #S132, but *CAPITAL S/2,000,000.* Back red-orange; monument w/man on horse at l. Series P. Specimen.	—	—	—

1897 ISSUE

		GOOD	FINE	XF
S125	**1 SUCRE** 1.1.1897 (date only in oval stamping at ctr. on back). Like #S120. Back dk. brown.	60.00	175.00	—

1903-22 ISSUE

		GOOD	FINE	XF
S126	**1 SUCRE** 1903-25. Black on green and yellow unpt. Reclining woman w/wheel and sheaf at l., portr. man at ctr., *CAPITAL S/5,000,000* at r. border. Back green.			
	a. 1.1.1903; 1.8.1905; 1.1.1907.	35.00	80.00	200.00
	b. 1.7.1910; 5.12.1911; 1.10.1913; 5.1.1916; 15.7.1917; 15.9.1917.	30.00	75.00	185.00
	c. 1.1.1920-17.1.1925.	25.00	55.00	160.00

		GOOD	FINE	XF
S127	**5 SUCRES** 1907-25. Black on orange and yellow unpt. Cherub w/fruit at l., portrs. 3 men at ctr. r., *CAPITAL S/5,000,000.* Back orange.			
	a. 1.1.1907.	75.00	200.00	—
	b. 15.1.1915-17.1.1925.	65.00	180.00	—

		GOOD	FINE	XF
S128	**10 SUCRES** 1907-25. Black on lt. brown unpt. Sailing ship at ctr., *CAPITAL S/5,000,000.* Back brown.			
	a. 1.1.1903; 1.1.1907.	75.00	225.00	—
	b. 5.1.1916-17.1.1925.	65.00	200.00	—

		GOOD	FINE	XF
S129	**20 SUCRES** 1.1.1907; 15.1.1915; 5.1.1916; 28.2.1923; 17.1.1925. Black on blue and yellow unpt. Threshing machine at r., *CAPITAL S/5,000,000.* Back blue; street view in town at r.	250.00	550.00	—

		GOOD	FINE	XF
S130	**50 SUCRES** 5.1.1916; 15.3.1916; 16.3.1918. Black on green unpt. Allegorical woman seated at ctr., *CAPITAL S/5,000,000.* Back dk. green.	—	—	—
S131	**100 SUCRES** 1.1.1922; 1.10.1922. Black on lt. brown and yellow unpt. Woman's head at upper l., woman seated at ctr. r. *CAPITAL S/5,000,000.* Back brown; Olmedo monument at l.	—	Rare	—
S131A	**500 SUCRES**		Reported Not Confirmed	
S132	**1000 SUCRES** 15.4.1907; 18.4.1916. Black on red, orange and yellow unpt. Woman seated w/fruit at l., Liberty at ctr. r. *CAPITAL S/5,000,000.* Back red-orange; monument w/man on horse at l.	—	Rare	—

19XX PROVISIONAL ISSUE

		GOOD	FINE	XF
S132A	**1 SUCRE** 19xx. Black bearer check form. Red value numeral and words at ctr., blue bank stamping at l. and r., red bank name and sign. title at lower r. Uniface.	—	—	—

BANCO DE DESCUENTO

1922 CÉDULA HIPOTECARIA ISSUE

S132B 5 SUCRES — Good — | Fine — | XF —
26.12.1922. Black on pale green paper. 4% interest-bearing note, with annual interest table on back. Printer: W&S (face). Local printer for back.

NOTE: #S132B was issued under the law of 6.8.1869.

S132C 5 SUCRES — Good — | Fine — | XF —
ND. Brown. Like #S132B. Uniface. Specimen.

1923-24 ISSUE

#S133-S136 printer: W&S.

S133 5 SUCRES — Good — | Fine — | XF —
13.11.1923; 13.12.1923; 5.3.1924. Black on blue and red unpt. Seated woman w/boy and produce at ctr. Back brown.

NOTE: For #S133 dated 1926 and ovpt: *CAJA CENTRAL...* see #S283.

S136 50 SUCRES — Good — | Fine — | XF —
30.1.1922; 23.10.1923. Green and pink. 3 allegorical seated women at ctr.

NOTE: For #S136 ovpt: *CAJA CENTRAL...* See #S287. Other denominations reported for this bank include 1, 10, 20, 100 and 1000 Sucres.

BANCO DEL ECUADOR

1868 PROVISIONAL ISSUE

#S137A-S137D ovpt. on notes of Banco de Circulación y Descuento de Manuel Antonio de Luzarraga.

		Good	Fine	XF
S137A 1 PESO	1.10.1868. Ovpt. on #S111.	—	—	—
S137B 4 PESOS	1.10.1868. Ovpt. on #S112.	—	—	—
S137C 5 PESOS	1.10.1868. Ovpt. on #S114.	—	—	—
S137D 10 PESOS	1.10.1868. Ovpt. on #S115.	—	—	—

1870'S ISSUE

Real/Peso System.

#S138-S139 printer: ABNC.

S138 2 REALES — Good — | Fine — | XF —
187x. Black on orange unpt. Sailor and anchor at l., woman at r.

S138A 2 REALES — Good — | Fine — | XF —
187x. Black on green unpt. Like #S138. Proof.

S139 4 REALES — Good — | Fine — | XF —
187x. Black on green unpt. 2 seated allegorical women at upper ctr. Back green. Proof.

		Good	Fine	XF
S141 1 PESO	15.12.1870; 21.12.1871; 7.6.1872; 1.10.1872. Brown and blue. Portr. Simón Bolívar at l., seated Minerva at r. Back orange, blue and brown.	—	Rare	—
S141A 1 PESO	1.10.1872. Black and red. Like #S141. Back green and violet.	—	Rare	—
S141B 10 PESOS	18xx. Violet and green. Portr. Simón Bolívar l. ctr., seated Minerva r. ctr. Back blue and brown. Proof.	—	Unc	500.00
S141C 10 PESOS	18xx. Brown and green. Similar to #S141B but for colors. Proof.	—	Unc	500.00
S141D 20 PESOS	18xx. Green and brown. Back brown and blue. Similar to #S141B. Proof.	—	Unc	600.00

1874 ISSUES

#S142-S164 printer: ABNC.

#S142-S143D originally issued w/hand stamps: *BANCO DEL ECUADOR and REPÚBLICA DEL ECUADOR-MINISTERIO DE HACIENDA* on back. Later issued w/only hand stamp: *MINISTERIO.*

		Good	Fine	XF
S142 1 PESO	2.1.1874. Black on green and orange unpt. 2 sailors at lower l., steam train at ctr., woman at lower r. Back orange. Series A.	75.00	275.00	—
S142B 1 PESO	2.1.1874. Black on salmon and green unpt. Like #S142. Back green. Series B. Archive copy.	—	—	—
S142C 1 PESO	2.1.1874. Black on magenta and brown unpt. Like #S142. Back magenta. Series C.	—	—	—

		Good	Fine	XF
S142D	**1 Peso** 2.1.1874. Black on red and green unpt. Like #S142. Back purple. Series D.	75.00	300.00	—
S143	**5 Pesos** 2.1.1874. Black on orange and olive unpt. Tree, shovel, basket and sacks at l., allegorical woman w/barrels and crate at ctr., allegorical woman w/cherub and produce at r. Back green. Series A. Archive copy.	—	—	—
S143B	**5 Pesos** 2.1.1874. Black on blue and orange unpt. Like #S143. Back salmon. Series B. Archive copy.	—	—	—

		Good	Fine	XF
S143C	**5 Pesos** 2.1.1874. Black on dk. green and lt. orange unpt. Like #S143. Back purple. Series C. Specimen, punched hole cancelled.	—	—	—
S143D	**5 Pesos** 2.1.1874. Black on orange and blue-gray unpt. Like #S143. Back red. Series D. Archive copy.	—	—	

1880; 1884 Issue

#S144-S145 issued w/hand stamp: *MINISTERIO DE HACIENDA.*

		Good	Fine	XF
S144	**1 Peso** 11.1880-26.5.1886. Black on blue and red unpt. Helmeted Minerva at l., woman w/cornucopia at ctr., Mercury at r. Back blue.	85.00	350.00	—
S145	**5 Pesos** 1.4.1884; 22.10.1884; 30.5.1887. Black on orange and green unpt. Local arms at l., reclining allegorical woman at ctr. Back brown.	—	—	—

NOTE: Denominations of 10, 20, 100 and 500 Pesos are reported for one or two full issues.

ND Provisional Issue

Sucre System.

#S147 and S148 new currency system values ovpt. on face in words at l. Each old peso from this bank equalled 80 centavos (80%) of the new sucre.

		Good	Fine	XF
S147	**80 Centavos on 1 Peso** ND (- old dates 1.2.1886; 22.3.1886; 26.5.1886). Ovpt. on #S144.	—	Rare	—

		Good	Fine	XF
S148	**4 Sucres on 5 Pesos** ND (- old dates 14.8.1885; 30.5.1887). Ovpt. on #S145.	—	Rare	—

1887-1926 Regular Issues

		Good	Fine	XF
S151	**1 Sucre** 1887-1901. Black on red and green unpt. Boy w/caduceus and fish at ctr. w/ship in background. Back green.			
	a. 13.7.1887-9.5.1894 handwritten dates. *CAPITAL S/1,200,000.*	50.00	125.00	—
	b. 1.9.1894. *CAPITAL S/2,000,000.*	40.00	180.00	—
	c. 1.10.1901 printed date. Also *CAPITAL S/2,000,000.*	25.00	75.00	275.00

		Good	Fine	XF
S152	**2 Sucres** 12.12.1901. Black on blue unpt. Ships at ctr. Back dk. blue.			
	a. *CAPITAL S/2,000,000.*	75.00	250.00	—
	b. *CAPITAL S/3,000,000.*	75.00	250.00	—
S152A	**2 Sucres** Like #S153. Back brown. Series C.	—	—	—
S153	**2 Sucres** 1.12.1907. Black on lt. orange unpt. Seated woman w/bales and caduceus at ctr. Back orange. Series E; J.	30.00	150.00	400.00
S154	**2 Sucres** 1.12.1907. Like #S153. Back olive. Series D.	30.00	150.00	400.00
S154A	**2 Sucres** Like #S153. Back green. Series F.	—	—	—
S155	**2 Sucres** 2.1.1911. Like #S153. Back blue. Series G.	30.00	150.00	400.00
S156	**2 Sucres** 2.1.1911. Like #S153. Back red-orange. Series H.	30.00	150.00	400.00
S156A	**2 Sucres** Like #S153. Back brown. Series J.	—	—	—

NOTE: #S152A, S154A and S156A data obtained from archive records.

		Good	Fine	XF
S157	**2 Sucres** 2.1.1911. Like #S153. Back red-brown. Series K.	30.00	150.00	400.00
S157A	**5 Sucres** 18xx (ca.1892). Black on orange, yellow and salmon unpt. Similar to #S158, but w/*CAPITAL S/2,000,000.* Back orange. Archive copy.	—	—	—
S157B	**5 Sucres** 18xx. Like #S157A, but back green.	—	—	—

		Good	Fine	XF
S158	**5 Sucres** 16.8.1899; 30.7.1919; 15.3.1926. Black on orange unpt. Sailor at l., portr. woman at l. ctr., seated allegorical woman w/2 children at r., *CAPITAL S/3,000,000.* Back green.			
	a. Issued note.	90.00	400.00	—
	p. Proof in black.	—	—	400.00

		GOOD	FINE	XF
S158A	**5 SUCRES** 19xx. Like #S158, but back red.	—	—	—

		GOOD	FINE	XF
S159	**10 SUCRES** 5.5.1902; 6.9.1912; 8.10.1920. Black on orange unpt. Woman w/board and child at l. Back orange; woman at ctr.	—	—	—

		GOOD	FINE	XF
S160	**20 SUCRES** 3.9.1898; 19xx. Black on green and brown unpt. Sailing ship at lower l., seated man shearing sheep at ctr., 2 standing men at lower r. Back brown.	—	—	—
S161	**50 SUCRES** 15.3.1926. Black on yellow and brown unpt. Ox-drawn cart at ctr. Back brown; ornamented head at ctr.	—	—	—
S161A	**100 SUCRES** 18xx. Black on blue and orange unpt. Similar to #S162, but w/*CAPITAL S/1,200,000*. Back orange. Proof.	—	—	—

		GOOD	FINE	XF
S162	**100 SUCRES** 15.3.1926. Black on blue and red unpt. Allegorical woman reclining at l., griffins at l. and ctr. r., horse's head at r. Back brown. *CAPITAL S/3,000,000.*			
	a. Issued note.	—	Rare	—
	s. Specimen.	—	—	—

		GOOD	FINE	XF
S163	**500 SUCRES** 18xx; 1911. Black on red and green unpt. Seated allegorical woman seated at upper l., allegorical woman holding ship at r. Back green. Specimen.	—	—	—
S164	**1000 SUCRES** 12.4.1926. Black on orange unpt. Allegorical woman at l. Back orange; Liberty at ctr.	—	—	—

ND ISSUE

		GOOD	FINE	XF
S167	**100 PESOS** 18xx. Green and red. Bolivar at l., seated figure at r. Remainder. Local printer.	—	—	—

BANCO INTERNACIONAL

1886-94 ISSUE

#S171-S179A printer: W&S.

		GOOD	FINE	XF
S171	**1 SUCRE** 17.5.1887 (stamped); 11.3.1889; 1.3.1891; 1.5.1891 (handwritten). Black on yellow unpt. Portr. Antonio José de Sucre at l., arms at r. Back blue. Narrow margins, 136 x 60mm.			
	a. Issued note.	75.00	200.00	—
	s. Specimen. Red back.	—	—	—

		GOOD	FINE	XF
S172	**1 SUCRE** 18xx; also 10.11.1892. Black on green unpt. Pink paper. Similar to #S171 but w/modified portr. details. Back brown. Wide margins, 152 x 71mm. Series B/A; G/A. Unissued remainder.	—	Unc	7.50
S173	**1 SUCRE** 10.11.1892. Like #S172 but white paper.	—	—	—
S174	**5 SUCRES** 1885-93. Black on pink unpt. J. J. Olmedo at l., arms at ctr.			
	a. Issued note. 14.2.1885; 5.11.1885; 6.6.1893.	—	—	—
	p. Proof.	—	—	—
S175	**10 SUCRES** 18xx; 6.6.1893. Vicente Rocafuerte at l., arms at r. Proof.	—	—	—
S176	**20 SUCRES** 2.6.1894. Arms at l.	—	—	—
S178	**100 SUCRES** 2.8.1893. Arms at l., Abdón Calderón at ctr.	—	—	—
S179	**500 SUCRES** 18xx. Blue and yellow. Standing Liberty w/pole at ctr., arms at lower r.	—	—	—

		GOOD	FINE	XF
S179A	**1000 SUCRES** 18xx. Black on yellow and orange unpt. Standing Simón Bolívar statue at l., arms w/cherub supporters at ctr. Proof.	—	—	—

BANCO DE LONDRES Y ECUADOR

1880'S ISSUE

#S180-S182 London arms at l., Ecuadorian arms at r. Printer: ABNC.

		GOOD	FINE	XF
S180	**1 SUCRE** 18xx (ca. 1887). Black on green unpt. Back green; Sucre Theater at ctr.			
	p. Proof.	—	—	—
	s. Series B. Specimen.	—	—	—

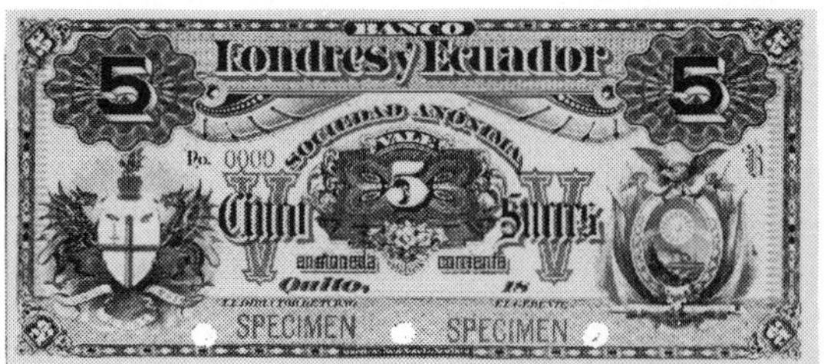

S181 5 SUCRES
18xx (ca.1887). Black on blue unpt. Back blue; National Palace at ctr.

	GOOD	FINE	XF
p. Proof.	—	—	—
s. Series A. Specimen.	—	—	—

S182 10 SUCRES
18xx (ca.1887). Black on orange unpt. Raphael's Angel at ctr. Back orange; road and town scene at ctr.

	GOOD	FINE	XF
p. Proof.	—	—	—
s. Specimen.	—	—	—

BANCO NACIONAL

1871 PROVISIONAL ISSUE

S183 2 PESOS
1.3.1871. Dk. green vertical ovpt. of bank name, city and issue date at l. on 1858 unissued Banco Nacional de Costa Rica note, #S210.

GOOD	FINE	XF
—	Rare	—

NOTE: Other similarly ovpt. values may exist.

1871 REGULAR ISSUE

Real/Peso System.

#S186-S195A printer: ABNC.

S186 2 REALES
187x. Black on brown unpt. Young girl at lower l. and cherub at lower r., arms at ctr. Back brown. Proof.

GOOD	FINE	XF
—	—	—

S187 4 REALES
187x. Liberty at lower l., head of girl at ctr., arms at lower r.

	GOOD	FINE	XF
p1. Black on green unpt. Proof.	—	—	—
p2. Black on blue unpt. Back blue. Proof.	—	—	—

S187A 4 REALES
187x. Black on blue unpt. Like #S187, but young Indian girl at upper ctr. Back blue. Archive copy.

GOOD	FINE	XF
—	—	—

S191 1 PESO
9.8.1871. Black on brown unpt. 4 cherubs holding denomination numeral at l., reclining allegorical woman at ctr., arms at lower r. Back brown.

GOOD	FINE	XF
—	—	—

S193 5 PESOS
187x. Black on green unpt. Arms at lower l., 5 cherubs holding denomination numeral at ctr., woman at lower r. Back green.

GOOD	FINE	XF
—	—	—

S194 10 PESOS
187x. Black on orange unpt. Arms at l., allegorical woman w/coins and marine implements at ctr., Justice at r. Back orange. Archive copy.

GOOD	FINE	XF
—	—	—

S195 20 PESOS
187x. Black on blue unpt. Boy w/staff and sheep at lower l., allegorical woman holding staff and bird w/foliage behind at ctr., arms at r. Back blue. Proof.

GOOD	FINE	XF
—	—	—

S195A 100 PESOS
187x. Black on purple unpt. Condor w/wings spread at l., arms at ctr., portr. woman's head at r. Back purple. Specimen.

GOOD	FINE	XF
—	—	—

A word on pricing

When a note is marked RARE in the price columns, this note seldom appears on the market, or few are known in private hands. When dashes are in the price column, means that the note has not traded on the open market recently and a definitive value could not accurately be determined. Rare does not always mean expensive. A dashed price does not mean expensive or rare.

BANCO PARTICULAR DE DESCUENTO I CIRCULACIÓN DE GUAYAQUIL

1862-66 ISSUES

Real/Peso System.

#S196-S197 printer: ABNC.

		GOOD	FINE	XF
S196	**2 REALES** 1.4.1865; 1.4.1866. Black on green unpt. Arms at ctr. Uniface.	90.00	—	—
S197	**4 REALES** 18xx. Black on green unpt. Arms at ctr. Uniface.			
	p. Proof.	—	—	—
	s. Series A. Specimen.	—	—	—
S198	**1 PESO** 1.6.1862. Black. Condor over arms at l., plants at r.	—	—	—
S199	**1 PESO** 5.9.1864.	—	—	—

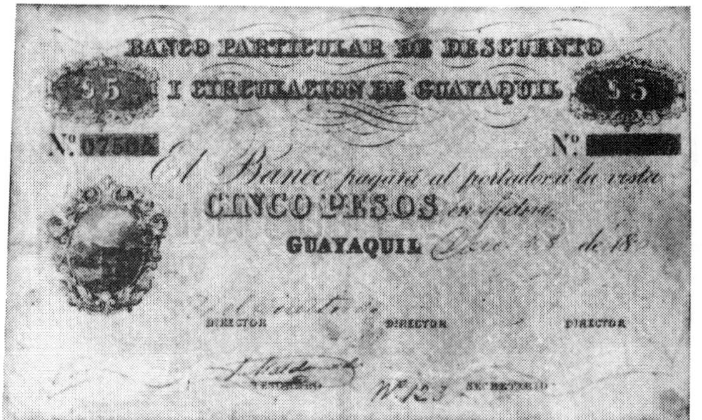

		GOOD	FINE	XF
S200	**5 PESOS** 23.12.1862. Boats along shoreline in ornate frame at l.	600.00	—	—

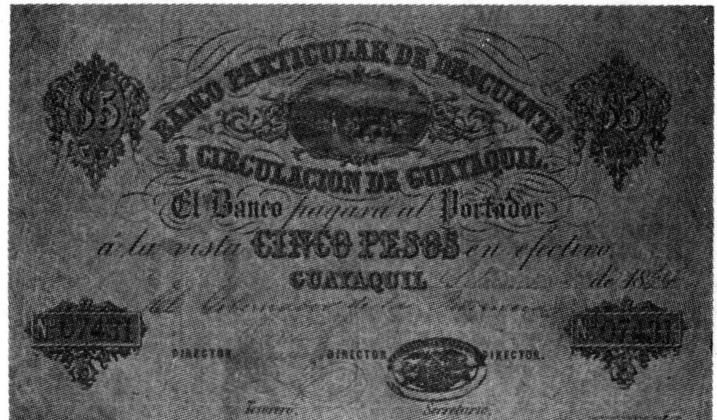

		GOOD	FINE	XF
S201	**5 PESOS** 5.9.1864. Black on brown unpt. Shoreline scene at upper ctr. Back red. Printer: Wm. Brown.	—	—	—

		GOOD	FINE	XF
S202	**10 PESOS** 23.12.1862. Black on brown unpt. Boats along shoreline in ornate frame at l.	—	—	—
S202A	**10 PESOS** 5.9.1864.	—	—	—
S203	**20 PESOS** 23.12.1862; 5.9.1864. Similar to #S202.	—	—	—
S204	**50 PESOS** 5.9.1864.	—	—	—
S205	**100 PESOS** 5.9.1864.	—	—	—

NOTE: An issue of compulsory acceptance notes using forms of the Banco Particular de Descuento y Circulación de Guayaquil is reported in denominations of 1, 5, 10, 20, 50 and 100 Pesos. Date is 23.12.1862.

BANCO DEL PICHINCHA

1907-08 ISSUE

Sucre System.

#S211-S214 printer: W&S.

#S212-S214 *Capital S/600,000.*

		GOOD	FINE	XF
S211	**1 SUCRE** 1907-10. Black and brown. Train at l., helmeted woman at ctr. r. Back green.			
	a. Ovpt: *Compania Anonima Capital S/600,000.* 15.4.1907-8.1.1908.	70.00	225.00	—
	b. Ovpt: *Capital S/845,000.* 31.1.1910; 18.2.1910; 21.11.1910	70.00	225.00	—
	c. ND. Blue and olive green. Back brown. Specimen.	—	—	—

		GOOD	FINE	XF
S212	**5 SUCRES** 1907; ND. Portr. Antonio José de Sucre at upper l., farmer plowing w/horses at ctr.			
	a. 29.5.1907.	—	—	—
	s. ND. Blue and pink. Back brown. Specimen.	—	—	—
S213	**10 SUCRES** 1908; ND. Seated woman w/shield at l.			
	a. 29.5.1907.	—	—	—
	s. ND. Brown and lilac. Back green.	—	—	—
S214	**20 SUCRES** ca.1907. Specimen.	—	—	—

NOTE: #S212-S214 w/Capital S845,000 are reported.

1912-15 ISSUES

#S220-S227 printer: ABNC.

		GOOD	FINE	XF
S220	**1 SUCRE** ND (ca.1912-14). Black on tan unpt. Like #S221. *CAPITAL S/1,000,000.*			
	a. Issued note.	—	—	—
	p. Proof.	—	—	—
S221	**1 SUCRE** 30.4.1914. Green. Portr. man at l. Back olive; reclining woman playing mandolin at ctr.	—	—	—

NOTE: For #S221 dated 1926 and ovpt: *CAJA CENTRAL...* See #S281.

NOTE: Capitalization amount for #S221 needs confirmation.

		GOOD	FINE	XF
S221A	**1 SUCRE** 20.11.1916; 4.1.1918. Black. Like #S221. *CAPITAL S/1,500,000.* Proof.	—	—	—

S222 1 SUCRE
1920-24. Black on brown unpt. Like #S221.

	GOOD	FINE	XF
a. 9.3.1920; 6.8.1920; 6.4.1921; 21.10.1921.	25.00	85.00	150.00
b. 2.1.1922; 3.4.1922; 5.4.1922; 18.5.1922; 23.5.1922; 7.11.1922; 17.11.1923; 17.12.1924; 19.12.1924.	20.00	75.00	175.00

S223 5 SUCRES
1912-20. Black on green unpt. Portr. man at ctr. Back green; woman and globe at ctr.

	GOOD	FINE	XF
a. 14.10.1912; 14.12.1912.	100.00	400.00	—
b. 8.1.1917; 9.3.1920; 6.8.1920.	100.00	400.00	—

S224 10 SUCRES
ND (ca.1912-14) - 1921. Black on orange and yellow unpt. Condor at r. Back orange; allegorical woman holding paddle, cherub at ctr.

	GOOD	FINE	XF
a. 15.10.1915; 8.1.1917; 7.2.1917.	—	—	—
b. 6.4.1921.	—	—	—
p. ND (ca.1912-14). *CAPITAL S/1,000,000.* Proof.	—	—	—

S225 20 SUCRES
ND (ca.1912-14) - 1921. Black on green unpt. Women at l. and r. of arms at l. ctr. Back blue; men w/oxen team at ctr.

	GOOD	FINE	XF
a. 9.3.1920; 6.8.1920; 19.11.1921.	—	—	—
p. ND (ca.1912-14). *CAPITAL S/1,000,000.* Proof.	—	—	—

S226 50 SUCRES
ND (ca.1912-14) - 1921. Black on gold and brown unpt. Allegorical woman seated w/globe and lute at l. ctr. Back green; Commerce seated w/condor and circular scene at ctr.

	GOOD	FINE	XF
a. 9.3.1920; 6.4.1921.	—	—	—
p. ND (ca.1912-14). *CAPITAL S/1,000,000.* Proof.	—	—	—

S227 100 SUCRES
ND (ca.1912-14) - 1922. Black on yellow and green unpt. Woman w/produce in sacks and barrels at ctr. r. Back brown.

	GOOD	FINE	XF
a. 9.3.1920; 9.11.1921; 19.11.1921; 2.1.1922.	—	—	—
p. ND (ca.1912-14). *CAPITAL S/1,000,000.* Proof.	—	—	—

NOTE: Higher values (500 and 1000 Sucres) are reported, not confirmed.

NOTE: Issues for 1912-14 have imprint or ovpt: *CAPITAL S/1,000,000;* from 1915-17 *CAPITAL S/1,500,000* (some w/*CAPITAL S/2,500,000);* from 1920-21 *CAPITAL S/3,000,000;* from 1922-24 *CAPITAL S/4,000,000.*

BANCO DE QUITO

1870s ND ISSUE

Real System.

S231 2 REALES
ND. Black on green unpt. Men w/water pitchers at fountain in town at l. Uniface; 2 stampigs on back. Printer: NBNC. Proof.

	GOOD	FINE	XF
	—	—	—

1874-78 ISSUE

Peso System.

S236 1 PESO
1.12.1874; 1.1.1875; 4.3.1875; 1.2.1878; 1.7.1878. Black on orange unpt. Portr. woman in shawl at l., arms at top ctr., portr. Indian at r. Back blue. Printer: CS&E.

	GOOD	FINE	XF
a. Issued note.	—	—	—
s. Specimen (unfinished date).	—	175.00	400.00

NOTE: Other denominations reported in this series include 2, 5, 10, 20, 50 and 100 Pesos.

1880 ISSUE

#S241-S245 printer: ABNC.

S241 1 PESO
2.1.1880. Horseman w/pack horse at upper l.

	GOOD	FINE	XF
a. Black on tan unpt. Back brown. Issued note.	—	—	—
p1. Black on orange unpt. Back blue. Proof.	—	—	—
p2. Black on pink unpt. Proof.	—	—	—

S242 5 PESOS
2.1.1880. Black on orange unpt. Woman w/sheaf and sickle seated at l., woman w/wheel seated at r. Back brown.

	GOOD	FINE	XF
p. Proof.	—	—	—
s. Specimen.	—	—	—

		GOOD	FINE	XF
S243	**10 PESOS** 2.1.1880. Black on blue unpt. Agriculture seated w/sheaf and sickle at l., woman w/spool at r. Back orange.			
	p. Proof.	—	—	—
	s. Specimen.	—	—	—

		GOOD	FINE	XF
S244	**20 PESOS** 2.1.1880. Black on green unpt. Seated woman at l., reclining woman and globe at ctr. r. Back red-orange.			
	p. Proof.	—	—	—
	s. Specimen.	—	—	—

		GOOD	FINE	XF
S245	**100 PESOS** 2.1.1880. Black on brown unpt. Standing Justice at l., arms at l. ctr., explorer landing at r. Back deep green.			
	p. Proof.	—	—	—
	s. Specimen.	—	—	—

1885 ISSUE

Sucre System.

		GOOD	FINE	XF
S246	**1 SUCRE** 1.1.1885. Black on brown unpt. Portr. Antonio José de Sucre at upper l., Raphael's Angel at upper ctr. r., arms at lower r. Back red-orange. Printer: ABNC.	—	—	—

NOTE: Other denominations reported in this series include 2, 5, 10, 20, 50 and 100 Sucres.

BANCO SUR AMERICANO

1920 ISSUE

		GOOD	FINE	XF
S251	**1 SUCRE** 2.1.1920. Black on orange unpt. Condor at l. Back brown; sailing ships at ctr.			
	a. Issued note.	—	—	—
	r. Remainder w/o serial # or sign.	—	Unc	1.00

		VG	VF	UNC
S252	**5 SUCRES** 2.1.1920. Black on yellow unpt. Christopher Columbus on ship deck in sight of land at l. Back blue; standing woman w/fasces at ctr.			
	a. Issued note.	—	—	—
	r. Remainder w/o serial # or sign.	3.00	6.00	15.00
S252A	**10 SUCRES** 2.1.1920.	—	—	—

		VG	VF	UNC
S253	**20 SUCRES** 2.1.1920. Black. Seated Christopher Columbus w/anchor, globe and arms at l. Back blue; men in rowboat heading towards shore at ctr. Remainder w/o serial # or sign.			
	a. Pink unpt.	.50	1.00	2.00
	b. W/o unpt.	.75	2.00	3.50
S253A	**50 SUCRES** 2.1.1920.	—	—	—

		VG	VF	UNC
S254	**100 SUCRES** 2.1.1920. Black on blue unpt. Woman standing on cornucopia and holding monogram scroll at l., woman and 2 children at ctr. Back slate-blue; crowd welcoming returing ships at ctr. Remainder.	.75	1.50	4.00

Banco de La Unión

1880's Issue

Peso System.

#S261-S271A printer: ABNC.

		Good	Fine	XF
S261	**1 Peso** 2.1.1882. Black on green unpt. Presidential palace at ctr., Mercury at r. Back green.			
	a. Issued note.	—	—	—
	p. Proof.	—	—	—

		Good	Fine	XF
S262	**5 Pesos** 18xx. Black on dk. orange unpt. Street scene at l., 2 cherubs at ctr. r. Back dk. orange. Proof.	—	—	—

		Good	Fine	XF
S263	**10 Pesos** 12.10.1887. Black on brown unpt. Cathedral at l., seated allegorical woman w/sheaves and sheep at upper ctr. r. Back brown. Proof.	—	—	—

		Good	Fine	XF
S264	**20 Pesos** 18xx. Black on blue unpt. San Francisco Church at ctr., woman at r. Back blue. Proof.	—	—	—

		Good	Fine	XF
S264A	**100 Pesos** 18xx. Black on orange unpt. Statue of Freedom at l., Jesuit church at ctr., ram at r. Back orange. Proof.	—	—	—

1887 Provisional Issue

Sucre System.

New value ovpt. on face of older issue.

		Good	Fine	XF
S265	**1 Sucre** 12.9.1887; 12.10.1887; 14.8.1893. Ovpt. at upper ctr. in red on face of #S261.	—	—	—
S266	**5 Sucres** (ca.1887.) Ovpt. on #S262.	—	—	—
S267	**10 Sucres** 12.10.1887. Ovpt. on #S263.	—	—	—

1893-94 Regular Issue

		Good	Fine	XF
S268	**1 Sucre** 12.4.1894; 27.5.1895; 27.12.1895. Like #S261.	—	—	—
S269	**5 Sucres** 14.8.1893; 28.6.1895. Like #S262.	—	—	—
S270	**10 Sucres** 18xx. Like #S263.	—	—	—
S271	**20 Sucres** 12.1.1893. Like #S264.	—	—	—
S271A	**100 Sucres** 18xx. Like #S264A. Proof.	—	—	—

Compañia de Crédito Agrícola e Industrial

1921 Issue

#S272-S274 printer: ABNC.

NOTE: For #S272 and #S274 dated 1926 w/ovpt: *CAJA CENTRAL. . .* see #S282 and S284.

		Good	Fine	XF
S272	**2 Sucres** 2.1.1921; 5.4.1921. Black on m/c unpt. Reclining allegorical woman w/globe (Commerce) at ctr. Back orange.	100.00	400.00	—

		Good	Fine	XF
S274	**10 Sucres** 5.4.1921. Black on m/c unpt. Allegorical man w/scythe and sheaf at l., allegorical woman holding ship at r. Back brown.	—	—	—

GOVERNMENT

LA CAJA CENTRAL DE EMISIÓN Y AMORTIZACIÓN

In February 1926, the Caja Central de Emisión y Amortización was established as a preliminary move towards the creation of the Banco Central del Ecuador. The main task of the Caja Central was the transferrance of notes and metallic reserves of the private banks. The Caja Central operated until August 12, 1927. Unissued notes of the private banks were ovpt. in the name of the Caja Central and the issuing place of Quito. Faces were ovpt. with medium large text across, either straight or at an angle, and in upper and lower case or all upper case letters. Backs were ovpt. in much larger letters at ctr. in curved or straight lines.

1926-27 ISSUE

		GOOD	FINE	XF
S280	**1000 SUCRES** 6.4.1927. Ovpt. on #S164.	—	—	—
S281	**1 SUCRE** 30.11.1926. Ovpt. on #S221A.	150.00	500.00	—
S282	**2 SUCRES** 30.11.1926; 19.1.1927. Ovpt. on #S272.	150.00	500.00	—

		GOOD	FINE	XF
S282A	**5 SUCRES** 19.1.1927. Ovpt. on #S103.	150.00	500.00	—

		GOOD	FINE	XF
S283	**5 SUCRES** 30.11.1926. Ovpt. on #S133.	150.00	500.00	—
S284	**10 SUCRES** 30.11.1926; 19.1.1927. Ovpt. on #S274.	150.00	500.00	—
S287	**50 SUCRES** 6.4.1927; 1.6.1927. Ovpt. on #S136.	—	—	—

EGYPT

The Arab Republic of Egypt, located on the northeastern corner of Africa, has an area of 386,650 sq. mi. (1,000,000 sq. km.) and a population of 68.12 million. Capital: Cairo. Although Egypt is an almost rainless expanse of desert, its economy is predominantly agricultural. Cotton, rice and petroleum are exported.

Egyptian history dates back to about 4000 B.C. when the empire was established by uniting the upper and lower kingdoms. Following its "Golden Age" (16th to 13th centuries B.C.), Egypt was conquered by Persia (525 B.C.) and Alexander the Great (332 B.C.). The Ptolemies ruled until the suicide of Cleopatra (30 B.C.) when Egypt became a Roman colony. Arab caliphs ruled Egypt from 641 to 1517, when the Turks took it for their Ottoman Empire. Turkish rule, interrupted by the occupation of Napoleon (1798-1801), became increasingly casual, permitting Great Britain to inject its influence by purchasing shares in the Suez Canal. British troops occupied Egypt in 1882, becoming the de facto rulers. On Dec. 14, 1914, Egypt was made a protectorate of Britain. British occupation ended on Feb. 28, 1922, when Egypt became a sovereign, independent kingdom. The monarchy was abolished and a republic proclaimed on June 18, 1952.

On Feb. 1, 1958, Egypt and Syria formed the United Arab Republic. Yemen joined on March 8 in an association known as the United Arab States. Syria withdrew from the United Arab Republic on Sept. 29, 1961, and on Dec. 26 Egypt dissolved its ties with Yemen in the United Arab States. On Sept. 2, 1971, Egypt shed the name United Arab Republic in favor of the Arab Republic of Egypt.

RULERS:

OTTOMAN
Abdul Mejid, AH1255-1277, 1839-1861AD
Abdul Aziz, AH1277-1293, 1861-1876AD
Abdul Hamid II, AH1293-1327, 1876-1909AD

MONETARY SYSTEM:

1 Piastre = 10 Ochr-El-Guerches
1 Pound = 100 Piastres, to 1916

REPLACEMENT NOTES:

Starting in 1969, 2 types exist. Earlier system uses a single Arabic letter as series prefix instead of normal number/letter prefix. Known notes: #42. Later system has the equivalent of English "200", "300" or "400" in front of a single Arabic series letter.

SIGNATURE VARIETIES

A. Elrefay, 1961-63A. Zendo, 1962-66
A. Abdel Hamid, 1967-70A. Zendo, 1972-75
M. Ibrahim, 1976-81A. Shalabi, 1981-84
A. Negm, 1985S. Hamed, 1986
I. N. Mohamad

OTTOMAN ADMINISTRATION

BANK OF EGYPT

Founded 1856, failed 1911.

Head office = London.

1850'S ISSUE

		GOOD	FINE	XF
S121	**1000 PIASTRES** 18xx. Pyramid between palm trees behind sphinx and supported arms at top ctr. Uniface specimen.	—	—	—

EL SALVADOR

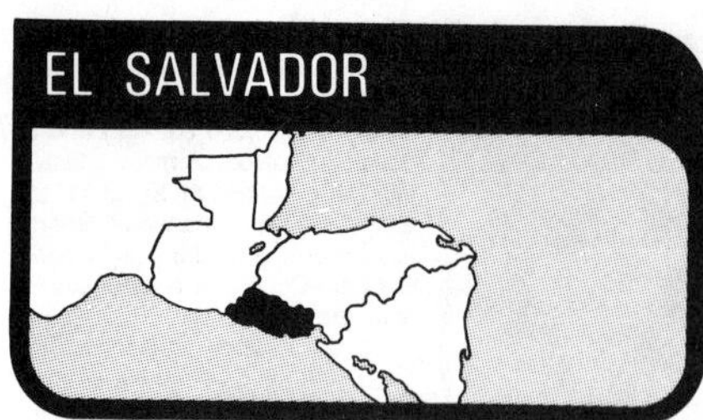

The Republic of El Salvador, a Central American country bordered by Guatemala, Honduras and the Pacific Ocean, has an area of 8,260 sq. mi. (21,041 sq. km.) and a population of 6.32 million. Capital: San Salvador. This most intensely cultivated country of Latin America produces coffee (the major crop), sugar and balsam for export. Gold, silver and other metals are largely unexploited.

The first Spanish attempt to subjugate the area was undertaken in 1523 by Pedro de Alvarado, Cortes' lieutenant. He was forced to retreat by superior Indian forces, but returned in 1525 and succeeded in bringing the region under control of the captaincy general of Guatemala, where it remained until 1821. In 1821, El Salvador and the other Central American provinces declared their independence from Spain. In 1823, the Federal Republic of Central America was formed by the five Central American States. When this federation was dissolved in 1829, El Salvador became an independent republic.

A twelve-year civil war was ended in 1992 with the signing of a UN sponsored Peace Accord. Free elections, with full participation of all political parties, were held in 1994 and 1997. Armando Calderón-Sol was elected as president in 1994 for a 5-year term.

On January 1, 2001, a monetary reform established the U.S. dollar as the accounting unit for all financial transactions, and fixed the exchange rate as 8.75 colones per dollar. In addition, the Central Reserve Bank has indicated that it will cease issuing coins and notes.

MONETARY SYSTEM:

1 Peso = 100 Centavos to 1919
1 Colón = 100 Centavos 1919-

COMMERCIAL BANKS:

Banco Agricola Comercial .... #S101-S113
Banco de Ahuachapám .... #S121-S126
Banco de Centro America y Londres .... #S131-S137
Banco Industrial del Salvador .... #S141-S145
Banco Internacional del Salvador .... #S151-S156
Banco Nacional del Salvador .... #S161-S166
Banco Occidental .... #S171-S199
Banco Salvadoreño .... #S201-S226

NOTE: Some commercial bank issues carry a validation ovpt. on the back, consisting of *TOMOSE RAZON* (or some form thereof), arms, city, date of issue and sign. The bank emissions which did not receive this back ovpt. were Banco Industrial, Banco Internacional and Banco de Centro America y Londres.

REPUBLIC

BANCO AGRICOLA COMERCIAL

Established in 1895; became part of the Banco Central de Reserva in 1934.

1890'S ISSUE

Peso System.

#S101-S107 printer: ABNC.

S101 1 PESO
189x-1917. Black on green and yellow unpt. 2 women kneeling, holding shield w/denomination at ctr. Back orange; stylized head of old man at ctr.

	Good	Fine	XF
a. 1.3.1904.	100.00	250.00	—
b. 25.2.1914-2.3.1917. Serial # varieties.	70.00	200.00	—
p. Proof. 189x.	—	—	—

S102 5 PESOS
189x-1904. Black on tan and green unpt. Seated woman w/sacks, caduceus and tablet at r. Back green.

	Good	Fine	XF
a. 1.3.1904.	—	—	—
p. Proof. 189x.	—	—	—

S103 10 PESOS
189x. Black on red-orange unpt. Seated woman w/caduceus at l. ctr., arms at ctr., seated woman w/scales at ctr. r. Back blue-black.

	Good	Fine	XF
a. Issued note.	—	—	—
p. Proof. 189x.	—	—	—
s. Specimen. 189x.	—	—	—

S104 25 PESOS
189x. Black on blue and yellow unpt. Sailing ship at upper l. ctr., allegorical woman w/sickle at r. Back dk. green; allegorical man at l. and r.

	Good	Fine	XF
a. Issued note.	—	—	—
p. Proof. 189x.	—	—	—
s. Specimen. 189x.	—	—	—

S105 100 PESOS
189x. Black on orange, yellow and pink unpt. Seated woman w/produce and parrot at ctr. Back red; arms at ctr.

	Good	Fine	XF
a. Issued note.	—	—	—
p. Proof. 189x.	—	—	—
s. Specimen. 189x.	—	—	—

1915 ISSUE

S106 50 PESOS
1.1.1915. Black on m/c unpt. Woman seated near globe at ctr. Back olive; arms at ctr.

	Good	Fine	XF
a. Issued note.	—	—	—
p. Proof. 189x.	—	—	—

		Good	Fine	XF
S107	**100 Pesos** 19xx. Black on m/c unpt. Cherub, seated woman and globe at ctr. Back orange; arms at ctr.			
	a. Issued note.	—	—	—
	p. Proof. 189x.	—	—	—

1922 Issues

Colón System.

#S108-S113 C. Columbus at ctr. on back. Printer: ABNC.

		Good	Fine	XF
S108	**1 Colón** 1.3.1922. Black on m/c unpt. Side view of bank at ctr. Back orange. Series A.			
	a. Issued note.	50.00	125.00	—
	p. Proof. ND.	—	—	—
	s. Specimen. ND.	—	—	—

		Good	Fine	XF
S109	**1 Colón** 1.3.1922. Black on m/c unpt. Front view of bank at ctr. Back orange. Series B.			
	a. Issued note.	90.00	250.00	—
	p. Proof. ND.	—	—	—
S110	**2 Colones** 1.3.1922. Black on m/c unpt. Like #S108. Back reddish brown.			
	a. Issued note.	90.00	275.00	—
	p. Proof.	—	—	—
S111	**5 Colones** 1.3.1922. Black on m/c unpt. Like #S108. Back green.	—	—	—
S112	**10 Colones** 1.3.1922. Black on m/c unpt. Like #S108. Back brown-black.			
	a. Issued note.	—	—	—
	p. Proof.	—	—	—

		Good	Fine	XF
S113	**25 Colones** 1.3.1922. Black on green and m/c unpt. Like #S109. Back blue.			
	a. Issued note.	—	—	—
	p. Proof.	—	—	—

Banco de Ahuachapam

Established in 1895.

1890's Issue

#S121-S126 were never released to circulation. Various denominations are known as specimens or proofs, as well as unissued remainders. Arms at ctr. on back. Printer: ABNC.

		Good	Fine	XF
S121	**1 Peso** 189x. Black on red-orange unpt. Portr. F. Morazan at l., ox-drawn cart at ctr. r. Back orange.			
	p. Proof.	—	—	—
	r. Unsigned remainder.	—	Unc	350.00

		Good	Fine	XF
S122	**2 Pesos** 189x. Black on pink, orange and yellow unpt. Women working at l. and r., portr. F. Morazan at ctr. Back red.			
	p. Proof.	—	Unc	350.00
	s. Specimen.	—	Unc	275.00

		Good	Fine	XF
S123	**5 Pesos** 189x. Black on lt. yellow and brown unpt. Woman kneeling w/globe at l. ctr. Back purple.			
	p. Proof.	—	Unc	400.00
	s. Specimen.	—	Unc	325.00

		Good	Fine	XF
S124	**10 Pesos** 189x. Black on pink, yellow and brown unpt. Woman seated w/children at r. Back brown; allegorical figures at l. and r. Proof.	—	Unc	400.00

S125 25 PESOS — GOOD | FINE | XF

189x. Black on green and yellow unpt. People gathered at watering place at l., locomotive at r. Back green; standing allegorical figures at l. and r.

	GOOD	FINE	XF
p. Proof.	—	—	—
s. Specimen.	—	Unc	400.00

S126 50 PESOS — GOOD | FINE | XF

189x. Black on blue and yellow unpt. Cow and calf at upper l., clasped hands at ctr. landscape at upper r. Back blue.

	GOOD	FINE	XF
p. Proof.	—	Unc	450.00
s. Specimen.	—	Unc	450.00

BANCO DE CENTRO AMERICA Y LONDRES

Originally known as the Banco de Nicaragua, Sucursal Salvador, it was later absorbed into El Banco Salvadoreño in 1902.

1895; 1897 ISSUE

#S131-S137 Columbus and standing Liberty w/flag on face, bank monogram at ctr. on back. Printer: W&S.

S131 1 PESO — GOOD | FINE | XF

1895; 8.2.1897; 30.6.1899. Black and brown on green unpt.Portr. C. Columbus at l., standing Liberty at r. — 150.00 | — | —

S132 5 PESOS — GOOD | FINE | XF

1895. Black on pink unpt. Standing Liberty at l., portr. C. Columbus at ctr. r. Back green. — — | — | —

S133 10 PESOS — GOOD | FINE | XF

1895. Black on green and pink unpt. Portr. C. Columbus at l., Liberty at ctr. Back red. — — | — | —

S134 50 PESOS

26.3.1897. Green and black on orange unpt. Portr C. Columbus at upper l., standing Liberty w/flag at ctr. Back blue.

	GOOD	FINE	XF
a. Issued note.	—	Rare	—
s. Specimen.	—	Rare	—

S135 100 PESOS

1895. Black on red and orange unpt. Portr. C. Columbus at upper l., Liberty at ctr. — — | — | —

1905 PROVISIONAL ISSUE

#S136 and S137 ovpt: *ORO* on #S131 and S132.

S136 1 PESO — GOOD | FINE | XF

1905. Like #S131 but ovpt: *ORO* in lg. letters vertically twice at l. and r., on face. — — | — | —

S137 5 PESOS — GOOD | FINE | XF

1905. Like #S132 but ovpt: *ORO* like #S136. — — | — | —

BANCO INDUSTRIAL DEL SALVADOR

Established in 1895; dissolved in 1906. Issued at Santa Ana.

1890'S ISSUE

#S141-S145 printer: ABNC.

S141 1 PESO — GOOD | FINE | XF

189x. Black on orange and yellow unpt. Ox cart loaded w/sugar cane at ctr., refinery in background. Back orange; coin-like design at ctr.

	GOOD	FINE	XF
a. Issued note.	—	—	—
p. Proof.	—	—	—
s. Specimen.	—	—	—

S142 5 PESOS — GOOD | FINE | XF

1.5.1896-15.1.1897. Black on green and red unpt. Woman w/fruit basket on her head at l., tree at r. Back green; obverse and reverse of coin-like design similar to Central American Republic coinage of the 1820's and 1830's.

	GOOD	FINE	XF
a. Issued note.	100.00	325.00	—
p. Proof.	—	—	—

S143 10 PESOS | GOOD | FINE | XF

15.4.1896; 15.8.1896; 15.11.1896; 15.1.1897. Black on blue and brown unpt. Coffee workers at l., bldg. at ctr., arms at r. Back ochre; coin-like design similar to #S142.

	GOOD	FINE	XF
a. Issued note.	175.00	—	—
p. Proof.	—	—	—
s. Specimen.	—	—	—

S144 25 PESOS | GOOD | FINE | XF

1.5.1896. Black on salmon and blue unpt. Church at l., ox cart at ctr., portr. Liberty at r. Back salmon; coin-like design at l., train at ctr. r.

	GOOD	FINE	XF
a. Issued note.	—	—	—
p. Proof.	—	—	—
s. Specimen.	—	—	—

S145 100 PESOS | GOOD | FINE | XF

1890; 1896. Black on lt. blue unpt. Seated allegorical woman at l. and r. of arms at ctr. Back lt. blue-gray; seated woman at l. and r. of obverse coin design at lower ctr.

	GOOD	FINE	XF
a. 3.4.1890; 8.4.1896. (Handwritten or hand stamped).	125.00	300.00	—
s. Specimen. 189x.	—	—	—

BANCO INTERNACIONAL DEL SALVADOR

Established in 1880; absorbed by El Banco Salvadoreño in 1898.

1880-90 ISSUE

#S151-S156 printer: Waterlow e Hijos (W&S).

		GOOD	FINE	XF
S151	**1 PESO** 1.12.1881; 1.6.1882. Black and gray. Seated allegorical woman holding shield w/arms at upper l. ctr. Back orange; 6 flags at ctr.	125.00	350.00	—
S152	**5 PESOS** 18xx. Seated allegorical woman holding shield w/arms at upper ctr. Back green; 6 flags at ctr.	—	—	—

		GOOD	FINE	XF
S153	**10 PESOS** 18xx. Black and gray. Seated allegorical woman holding shield w/arms at l. Back blue; 6 flags at ctr.	—	—	—

		GOOD	FINE	XF
S154	**25 PESOS** 18xx. Black and gray. Seated allegorical woman holding shield w/arms at upper l.	—	—	—

		GOOD	FINE	XF
S155	**100 PESOS** 1887; 1890; 1895. Black on rose and green unpt. Seated allegorical woman holding shield w/arms at upper ctr.	—	—	—

		GOOD	FINE	XF
S156	**500 PESOS** 1890; 1891; 1895. Black on green unpt. Mercury at l., seated allegorical woman holding shield w/arms at lower r.	—	—	—

BANCO NACIONAL DEL SALVADOR

Established in 1906; dissolved in 1913.

1906-08 ISSUE

#S161-S166 lg. denomination in guilloche at ctr. on face and back. Printer: W&S.

		GOOD	FINE	XF
S161	**1 PESO** 10.4.1908-6.2.1913. Black and red on rose unpt. Back red-orange or brownish red.			
	a. 1908. Serie B.	4.00	30.00	90.00
	b. 1909-13. Serie B.	4.00	30.00	90.00
S162	**5 PESOS** 18.9.1906-5.5.1913. Black and green on lt. red unpt. Back green.			
	a. 1906-07. Serie A. Handwritten sign.	3.00	20.00	75.00
	b. 1908. Serie A. Printed sign.	3.00	20.00	75.00
	c. 1909-13. Serie B. Printed sign.	3.00	20.00	75.00
S163	**10 PESOS** 15.2.1907-13.1.1911. Black and purple on brown unpt. Back lilac-brown.			
	a. 1907. Serie A. Handwritten sign.	6.00	45.00	110.00
	b. 1908-11. Serie A. Printed sign. Black ovpt. on back.	6.00	45.00	110.00
	c. 6.3.1908. Serie A. Printed sign. Red ovpt. on back.	6.00	45.00	110.00
S164	**25 PESOS** 20.4.1907-10.8.1911. Black and tan on lt. green unpt. Back lt. brown.	12.00	75.00	225.00

		GOOD	FINE	XF
S165	**50 PESOS** 15.2.1907-6.2.1913. Black and blue on pink unpt. Back blue.	20.00	90.00	275.00
S166	**100 PESOS** 20.4.1907-9.2.1912. Black and blue on tan unpt. Back blue.			
	a. 1907. Serie A. Handwritten sign.	35.00	125.00	300.00
	b. 1908-12. Serie A. Printed sign.	35.00	125.00	300.00

BANCO OCCIDENTAL

Established in 1899; dissolved in 1934.

1890-1914 ISSUES

Peso System.

#S171 and S172 printer: ABNC.

		GOOD	FINE	XF
S171	**1 PESO** 30.9.1899. Black on lt. green and yellow unpt. Cherub holding oval frame w/portr. woman at ctr. Back dk. green; woman's head at ctr. Middle sign. title: *DIRECTOR*. Sm. size, 136 x 55mm.			
	a. Series H.	50.00	175.00	—
	s. Specimen.	—	—	—

		GOOD	FINE	XF
S172	**1 PESO** Dec. 1910; Nov. 1912; Nov. 1914; 31.5.1917. Black on red unpt. Similar to #S171 but larger size, 170 x 70mm.			
	a. Back blue. Middle sign. title: *PRESIDENTE*.	70.00	200.00	—
	p. Back green. Middle sign. title: *DIRECTOR*. Proof.	—	—	—
	s. As a. Specimen, punched hole cancelled. ND. Series L.	—	Unc	200.00

#S173 and S174 printer: NYBNC.

		GOOD	FINE	XF
S173	**1 PESO** May 1914. Black on orange unpt. Horseman w/mountain and building in background at ctr. Back blue; stylized woman's head at ctr.	125.00	350.00	—
S174	**2 PESOS** 1.6.1913; Oct. 1913; July 1916; 1.6.1918. Black on lt. blue unpt. Like #S173. Back red-brown.			
	a. Issued note.	200.00	—	—
	s. July 1916. W/o Series, punched hole cancelled. Specimen.	—	—	—

#S175-S181 printer: ABNC.

		GOOD	FINE	XF
S175	**5 PESOS** 189x. Black on orange and yellow unpt. Standing Justice beside scene of presidential palace at l. Back orange; arms at ctr. (Not issued).			
	p. Proof.	—	Unc	250.00
	r. Unsigned remainder.	—	Unc	250.00

		GOOD	FINE	XF
S176	**5 PESOS** 1891-1915. Black on green unpt. Harvesting coffee at l., harbor scene at ctr. Back green; arms at ctr.			
	a1. Issued at Santa Ana. Middle sign. title: *DIRECTOR*. 10.8.1891; 20.3.1895.	—	Rare	—
	a2. Series A. 25.5.1905.	—	—	—
	b. San Salvador ovpt. for city of issue. Middle sign. title: *PRESIDENTE*. Series A. 31.1.1906.	100.00	—	—
	c. San Salvador. Series D. Dec. 1914; Jan. 1915.	100.00	—	—
	s. Series G. Proof. 189x.	—	—	—
	s. Series G. Specimen. 189x.	—	—	—

S177	**10 PESOS**	GOOD	FINE	XF
	1893-1917. Black on yellow and brown unpt. Steam locomotive at l., harbor scene at r. Back brown; arms at ctr.			
	a. Issued at Santa Ana. Middle sign. title: *DIRECTOR.* 1.7.1893; 25.5.1905.	—	—	—
	b. San Salvador ovpt. for city of issue. Middle sign. title: *PRESIDENTE.* 12.1917.	—	—	—
	p. Proof.	—	—	—
	s. Specimen. 189x.	—	—	—

S178	**25 PESOS**	GOOD	FINE	XF
	1890; 19xx. Black on orange and yellow unpt. Harbor scene at l. ctr., ship at r. Back orange; arms at ctr.			
	a. Issued at Santa Ana. Middle sign. title: *DIRECTOR.* 1.5.1890.	—	—	—
	b. Issued at San Salvador. Middle sign. title: *PRESIDENTE.* 19xx.	—	—	—
	s. Specimen. 189x.	—	—	—

S179	**50 PESOS**	GOOD	FINE	XF
	189x; ND (19xx). Bank at l., harbor scene at r. Arms at ctr. on back.			
	a. Black on orange and yellow unpt. Back orange. Issued at Santa Ana. Middle sign. title: *DIRECTOR.* 189x.	—	—	—
	b. Black on purple and yellow unpt. Back purple. Issued at San Salvador. Middle sign. title: *PRESIDENTE.* ND (19xx).	—	—	—
	p. Santa Ana. Proof. ND.	—	—	—
	s. Specimen.	—	—	—

S180	**100 PESOS**	GOOD	FINE	XF
	189x-1916. Black on olive and yellow unpt. Harbor scene at l., miners at lower r. Back olive; arms at ctr.			
	a. Issued at Santa Ana. Middle sign. title: *DIRECTOR.* 189x.	—	—	—
	b. Issued at San Salvador. Middle sign. title: *PRESIDENTE.* 19xx; Feb. 1916.	—	—	—
	c. Like b., but 19xx not in plate.	—	—	—
	p. Santa Ana. Proof. ND.	—	—	—
	s. Specimen.	—	—	—

S181	**500 PESOS**	GOOD	FINE	XF
	189x. Black on blue and yellow unpt. 2 seated allegorical women at l., harbor scene at r. Back blue; arms at ctr. Issued at Santa Ana. Middle sign. title: *DIRECTOR.*			
	p. Proof.	—	—	—
	s. Specimen.	—	—	—

1920-29 ISSUES

Colon System.

#S191-S199 portr. C. Columbus facing r. at ctr. on back. Printer: ABNC.

S191	**1 COLÓN**	GOOD	FINE	XF
	1.5.1920. Blue and m/c in plain white background. Woman at ctr. Back orange. Series A.			
	a. 2 printed sign., 1 hand sign. (at r.).	35.00	85.00	250.00
	b. 3 printed sign.	35.00	85.00	250.00

S192	**1 COLÓN**	GOOD	FINE	XF
	1.1.1929. Blue and m/c in m/c background. Similar to #S191 but different, larger guilloches and 3 printed sign. Series B.	20.00	70.00	200.00

S193	**2 COLONES**	GOOD	FINE	XF
	1.5.1920. Blue and m/c in plain white background. Seated allegorical woman at ctr. Back red-brown. Series A.			
	a. Issued note.	80.00	250.00	—
	p. Proof.	—	—	—
S194	**2 COLONES**			
	1926-29. Blue and m/c in m/c background. Similar to #S193 but different, larger guilloches.			
	a. Series B. 1.11.1926.	40.00	175.00	375.00
	b. Series C. 1.1.1929.	35.00	150.00	300.00
	s. Specimen.	—	—	—
S194A	**5 COLONES**			
	1.5.1920. Blue and m/c in plain white background. Seated allegorical woman w/globe at r. Back green. Series A in black.			
	p. Proof.	—	—	—
	s. Specimen.	—	—	—

		Good	Fine	XF
S195	**5 Colones** 1926-29. Blue and m/c in m/c background. Similar to #S194A but different, larger guilloches. Back green.			
	a. Series B. 1.11.1926.	70.00	300.00	—
	b. Series C. 1.1.1929.	60.00	250.00	—
	p. Proof.	—	—	—
	s. Series B. Specimen. 1.11.1926.	—	—	—

		Good	Fine	XF
S196	**10 Colones** 1.9.1925. Blue on m/c unpt. Seated allegorical woman w/globe at ctr. Back dk. brown. Series A in red.			
	p. Proof.	—	—	—
	s. Specimen.	—	—	—
S197	**25 Colones** 1.1.1929. Blue on m/c unpt. Seated allegorical woman w/globe at ctr. Back dk. blue. Series A.			
	a. Issued note.	—	—	—
	p. Proof.	—	—	—

		Good	Fine	XF
S198	**100 Colones** 1924-29. Blue on m/c unpt. Seated allegorical woman w/globe at l. Back olive-green.			
	a. Series A in red. 1.9.1924.	—	—	—
	b. Series B. 1.1.1929.	—	—	—
	p. Proof.	—	—	—
	s. Series A. Specimen.	—	—	—

		Good	Fine	XF
S199	**500 Colones** 1925-29. Blue on m/c unpt. Seated allegorical woman w/globe at ctr. Back dk. green.			
	a. Series A in red. 1.1.1925.	—	—	—
	b. Series B. 1.1.1929.	—	—	—
	c. As b. Cancelled, perforated *PAGADO.*	—	—	—
	p. Proof.	—	—	—
	s. Series A. Specimen.	—	—	—

Banco Salvadoreño

Established in 1885 as El Banco Particular de El Salvador; in 1891 the name was changed. It absorbed the Banco Internacional del Salvador in 1898 and Banco Centro Americano y Londres in 1902. It was dissolved in 1934.

1899-1913 Issues

Peso System.

#S201-S207 printer: ABNC.

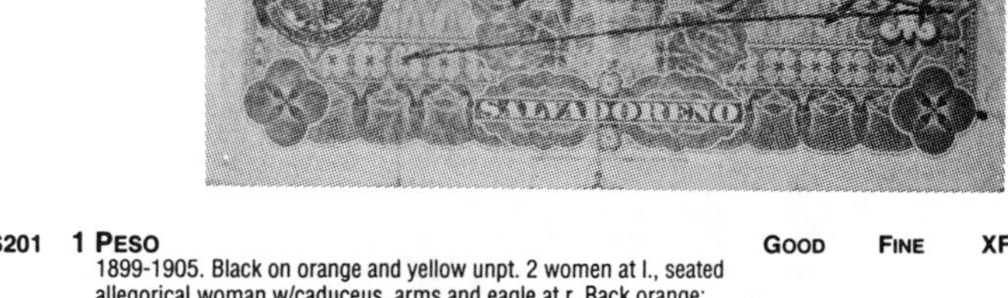

		Good	Fine	XF
S201	**1 Peso** 1899-1905. Black on orange and yellow unpt. 2 women at l., seated allegorical woman w/caduceus, arms and eagle at r. Back orange; stylized woman's head at ctr. Larger size, 192 x 85mm.			
	a. Series A. 14.1.1899; 1.7.1903; 8.1.1904.	75.00	—	—
	b. Series B. 1.10.1905; 1.12.1905.	65.00	150.00	325.00
	p. Proof.	—	—	—
	s. Series A. Specimen. 189x.	—	—	—

		Good	Fine	XF
S202	**1 Peso** 1913-19. Black on pink unpt. Like #S201 but reduced size and w/o eagle at r., 170 x 77mm.			
	a. Series C. 1.2.1913.	30.00	90.00	275.00
	b. Series D. 15.3.1914.	25.00	80.00	250.00
	c. Series E. 15.11.1914; 1.10.1915; 31.10.1916; 1.7.1918; 1.2.1919.	25.00	80.00	250.00

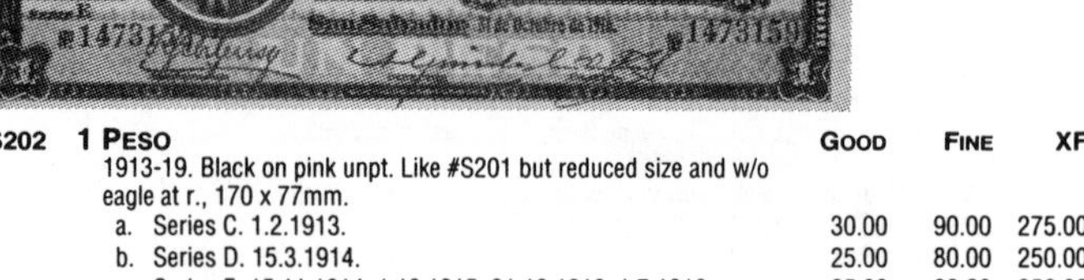

		Good	Fine	XF
S203	**5 Pesos** 189x-1916. Black on green unpt. Arms at l., seated woman w/quill pen and book near draped flags and cannon at r. Back green; cherub's head at top ctr.			
	a. Series A. 189x.	—	—	—
	b. Series B. 15.9.1913.	—	—	—
	c. Series C. 31.7.1916.	100.00	250.00	—
	p. Proof.	—	—	—
	s. Series A. Specimen. 189x.	—	—	—

	S204 10 PESOS	GOOD	FINE	XF
	189x; 15.1.1915; 15.7.1915; 1.7.1918. Black on yellow and purple unpt. Seated woman at l. and r. of value at upper l., seated woman at upper r. Back purple. Series A; B.			
a.	Issued note.	—	—	—
b.	Cancelled, perforated: *CANCELADO.*	—	—	—
p.	Proof.	—	—	—
s.	Specimen.	—	—	—

	S205 25 PESOS	GOOD	FINE	XF
	1893-1915. Black on brown and yellow unpt. Arms at l., seated woman w/book by globe at ctr. Back brown.			
a.	Series A. 4.7.1893.	—	—	—
b.	Series B. 15.7.1915.	—	—	—
p.	Proof.	—	—	—

	S206 100 PESOS	GOOD	FINE	XF
	189x; 15.9.1913. Black on blue and yellow unpt. Reclining woman at l., arms at upper ctr. r., seated woman at r. Back blue. Series A.			
a.	Issued note.	—	—	—
p.	Proof.	—	—	—

	S207 500 PESOS	GOOD	FINE	XF
	19xx. Black on yellow unpt. Minerva reclining w/lion at ctr. Back olive-green.			
a.	Issued note.	—	—	—
p.	Proof.	—	—	—

1913; 1914 ISSUE

#S208-S209 like previous issue. Printer: Carlos Parraga, San Salvador C.A.

	S208 1 PESO	GOOD	FINE	XF
	1.2.1913. Like #S202. Series C.	—	Rare	—

	S209 5 PESOS	GOOD	FINE	XF
	15.9.1913; 15.9.1914. Like #S203. Series B.			
a.	Issued note.	—	Rare	—
p.	Proof.	—	—	1200.

1920 ISSUE

Colón System.

#S211-S215 portr. C. Columbus facing l. at ctr. on back. Printer: ABNC.

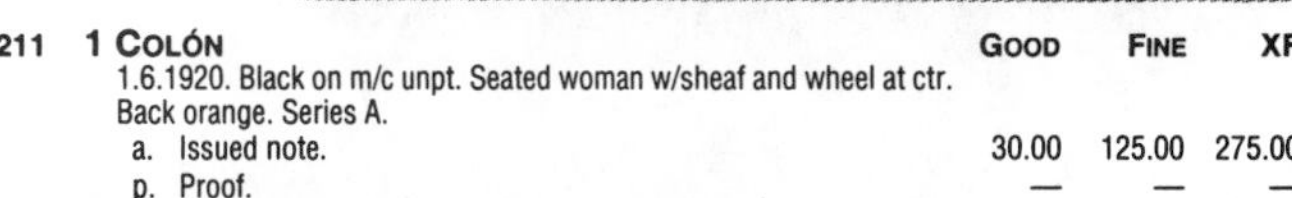

	S211 1 COLÓN	GOOD	FINE	XF
	1.6.1920. Black on m/c unpt. Seated woman w/sheaf and wheel at ctr. Back orange. Series A.			
a.	Issued note.	30.00	125.00	275.00
p.	Proof.	—	—	—

	S212 2 COLONES	GOOD	FINE	XF
	1.6.1920. Black on m/c unpt. Seated woman w/sheaf and wheel at l. ctr. Back red-brown. Series A.			
a.	Issued note.	70.00	250.00	—
p.	Proof.	—	—	—
	S213 5 COLONES			
	1.6.1920. Black on m/c unpt. Seated woman w/sheaf and wheel at l. ctr. Back green. Series A.			
a.	Issued note.	50.00	200.00	375.00
p.	Proof.	—	—	—

		GOOD	FINE	XF
S214	**10 COLONES** 1.6.1920. Black on m/c unpt. Seated woman w/sheaf and wheel at ctr. Back dk. brown. Series A.			
	a. Issued note.	300.00	1100.	—
	p. Proof. ND.	—	—	—
S215	**25 COLONES** 1.6.1920. Black on m/c unpt. Seated woman w/sheaf and wheel at ctr. Series A.	—	—	—

1924 ISSUE

#S221-S226 similar to #S211-S215. Printer: W&S.

		GOOD	FINE	XF
S221	**1 COLÓN** 1924-31. Black on red and blue unpt. Similar to #S211.			
	a. Series A. 1.11.1924.	25.00	90.00	250.00
	b. Series B. 1.1.1929.	20.00	80.00	225.00
	c. Series C. 1.1.1931; 1.10.1931.	20.00	80.00	225.00

		GOOD	FINE	XF
S222	**2 COLONES** 1.1.1924; 1.1.1929. Black on brown, green and m/c unpt. Back red-brown. Series A.			
	a. Issued note.	45.00	175.00	375.00
	b. Cancelled w/perforations.	—	—	—
S223	**5 COLONES** 1924-31. Black on m/c unpt. Similar to #S213.			
	a. Series A. 1.11.1924.	50.00	200.00	450.00
	b. Series B. 1.10.1931.	30.00	175.00	375.00
S224	**10 COLONES** 1924-31. Black on m/c unpt. Similar to #S214.			
	a. Series A. 1.11.1924.	—	—	—
	b. Series B. 1.10.1931.	—	—	—

		GOOD	FINE	XF
S225	**25 COLONES** 1.11.1924. Black on m/c unpt. Similar to #S215. Series A.	—	—	—

		GOOD	FINE	XF
S226	**100 COLONES** 1.11.1924; 1.1.1929. Black on orange and purple unpt. Back green. Series A.			
	a. Issued note.	—	—	—
	b. Cancelled w/perforations.	—	—	—

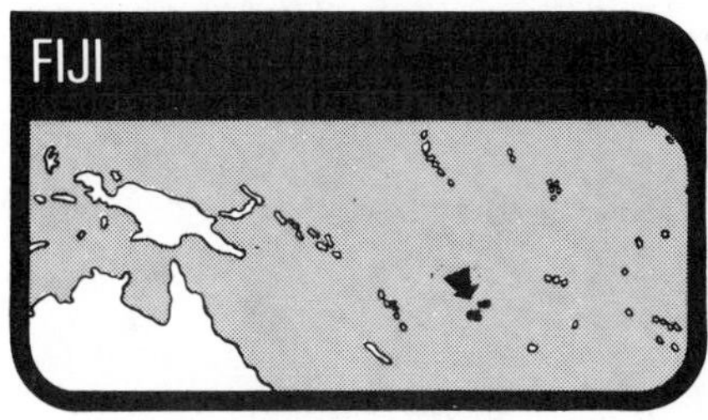

The self-declared republic of Fiji, an independent member of the British Commonwealth, consists of about 320 islands located in the southwestern Pacific 1,100 miles (1,770 km.) north of New Zealand. The islands have a combined area of 7,056 sq. mi. (18,274 sq. km.) and a population of 848,000. Capital: Suva, on the island of Viti Levu. Fiji's economy is based on agriculture and mining. Sugar, coconut products, manganese and gold are exported.

The Fiji Islands were discovered by Dutch navigator Abel Tasman in 1643 and visited by British naval captain James Cook in 1774. The first complete survey of the island was conducted by the United States in 1840. Settlement by missionaries from Tonga and traders attracted by the sandalwood trade began in 1835. Following a lengthy period of intertribal warfare, the islands were unconditionally and voluntarily ceded to Great Britain in 1874 by King Cakobau. The trading center was Levuka on the island of Ovalau which was also the capital under the British from 1874-82. Fiji became an independent nation on Oct 10, 1970, the 96th anniversary of the cession of the islands to Queen Victoria. It is a member of the Commonwealth of Nations.

RULERS:

British, 1874-

MONETARY SYSTEM:

1 Shilling = 12 Pence
1 Pound = 20 Shillings to 1969
1 Dollar = 100 Cents, 1969-

BRITISH ADMINISTRATION

BANK OF NEW ZEALAND

This bank began operations in Fiji on June 22, 1876 in Levuka when it took over the business of the Fiji Banking and Commercial Company Ltd. An agency in Suva opened in 1881. After Suva became the capital in 1882, the bank relocated its main Fiji office to that area.

1876 PROVISIONAL ISSUE

#S101-S104 Maoris at upper l., Kiwis at lower l. Printer: BWC. Design similar to third issue of Bank of New Zealand (listed under New Zealand) w/red handwritten: *LEVUKA* substituted for *BLENHEIM* or *NEW PLYMOUTH*. Hand stamped: *PAYABLE IN LEVUKA ONLY* at upper r.

		GOOD	FINE	XF
S101	**1 POUND** 18xx (ca. 1876). Black on green unpt. 180 x 112mm.	—	—	—
S102	**5 POUNDS** 18xx (ca. 1876). Black on brown unpt. 194 x 125mm.	—	—	—
S103	**10 POUNDS** 18xx (ca. 1876). Black on brown unpt. 191 x 119mm.	—	—	—
S104	**20 POUNDS** 18xx (ca. 1876). Black on blue unpt. 191 x 125mm.	—	—	—

1885 PROVISIONAL ISSUE

#S105-S108 Maoris at upper l., Kiwis at lower l. Printer: BWC. Design similar to third issue of Bank of New Zealand (listed under New Zealand) w/ovpt: *SUVA* on *BLENHEIM* or *NEW PLYMOUTH*. Hand stamped: *PAYABLE IN FIJI ONLY*.

		GOOD	FINE	XF
S105	**1 POUND** 18xx (ca. 1885); 1.7.1909. Back on green unpt. 180 x 112mm.	—	—	—
S106	**5 POUNDS** 18xx (ca. 1885). Black on brown unpt. 194 x 125mm.	—	—	—
S107	**10 POUNDS** 18xx (ca. 1885). Black on brown unpt. 191 x 119mm.	—	—	—
S108	**20 POUNDS** 18xx (ca. 1885). Black on blue unpt. 191 x 125mm.	—	—	—

1910 PROVISIONAL ISSUE

		GOOD	FINE	XF
S112	**20 POUNDS** 19xx (ca. 1910). Black on blue unpt. Maoris at upper l., Kiwis at lower l., w/ovpt: *SUVA* on *AUCKLAND*. Hand stamped: *PAYABLE IN FIJI ONLY*. Printer: BWC.	—	—	—

NOTE: Design similar to third issue of Bank of New Zealand (listed under New Zealand).

1918 PROVISIONAL ISSUE

		GOOD	FINE	XF
S116	**10 SHILLINGS** 19xx (ca. 1918 -old date 1917). Red on pink paper. 150 x 108mm.			
	a. Ovpt: SUVA.	—	—	—
	b. Ovpt: LEVUKA.	—	—	—

BANK OF NEW SOUTH WALES

1901 PROVISIONAL ISSUE

#S121 ovpt: *SUVA* on 1890-1910 issue w/vignette at upper ctr. Printer: CS&E.

		GOOD	FINE	XF
S121	**1 POUND** 19xx (ca. 1901). Black. 188 x 112mm.	—	—	—

FIJI BANKING AND COMMERCIAL COMPANY

1873 ISSUE

#S131-S135 issued ca. 1873-76. Denomination value in Fijian on back.

		GOOD	FINE	XF
S131	**1 DOLLAR** 1873. Black on green unpt. Vignette at ctr.	—	—	—
S132	**5 SHILLINGS** ND (ca.1873-76). Black.	—	—	—
S133	**10 SHILLINGS** ND (ca.1873-76). Green.	—	—	—
S134	**1 POUND** ND (ca.1873-76). Green.	—	—	—
S135	**5 POUNDS** ND (ca.1873-76). Blue.	—	—	—

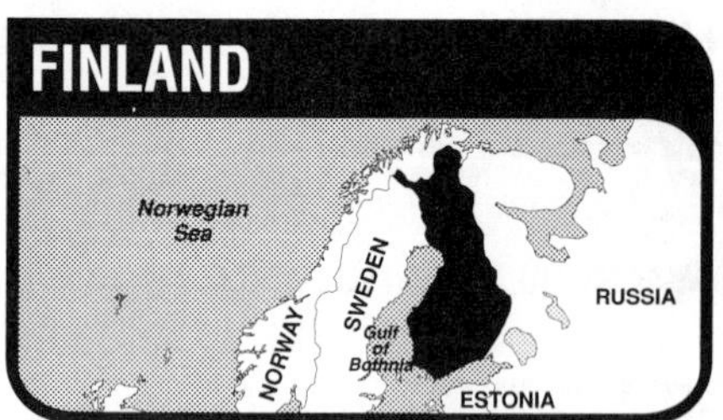

The Republic of Finland, the second most northerly state of the European continent, has an area of 130,120 sq. mi. (337,009 sq. km.) and a population of 5.18 million. Capital: Helsinki. Lumbering, shipbuilding, metal and woodworking are the leading industries. Paper, timber, wood pulp, plywood and metal products are exported.

The Finns, who probably originated in the Volga region of Russia, took Finland from the Lapps late in the 7th century. They were conquered in the 12th century by Eric IX of Sweden, and brought into contact with Western Christendom. In 1809, Sweden was invaded by Alexander I of Russia, and the peace terms gave Finland to Russia. It became a grand duchy within the Russian Empire until Dec. 6, 1917, when, shortly after the Bolshevik revolution, it declared its independence. After a brief but bitter civil war between the Russian sympathizers and Finnish nationalists in which the Whites (nationalists) were victorious, a new constitution was adopted, and on Dec. 6, 1917 Finland was established as a republic. In 1939 Soviet troops invaded Finland over disputed territorial concessions which were later granted in the peace treaty of 1940. When the Germans invaded Russia, Finland also became involved and in the Armistice of 1944 lost the Petsamo area also to the USSR.

RULERS:

Alexander II, 1855-1881
Alexander III, 1881-1894
Nicholas II, 1894-1917

MONETARY SYSTEM:

REGIONAL

FÖRENINGSBANKEN I FINLAND, SUOMEN YHDYSPANKKI UNION BANK OF FINLAND

1866 ISSUE

		GOOD	FINE	XF
S101	**15 MARKKAA** 1866. Lt. brown. Clasped hands in oval at ctr. on back.	1250.	2500.	—

		GOOD	FINE	XF
S102	**25 MARKKAA** 1866. Green. Beehive in oval at upper l. on back.	1100.	2200.	—
S103	**100 MARKKAA** 1866. Black. Mercury running at l. on back.	4000.	8000.	—

1882 ND ISSUE

#S104 and S105 printer: BWC.

		GOOD	FINE	XF
S104	**25 MARKKAA** ND (1882). Green. Portr. man wearing wolf's head fur skin on his head w/wolf at l.	450.00	900.00	—

		GOOD	FINE	XF
S105	**100 MARKKAA** ND (1882). Green and pink. Woman standing before starry sky at l.			
	a. Issued note.	1800.	3600.	—
	s. Specimen.	—	—	—

TAMPEREEN OSAKE PANKKI

1918 ISSUE

		GOOD	FINE	XF
S107	**10 MARKKAA** 1918. Black text on pink unpt. Uniface.	75.00	175.00	—

VAASAN OSAKE PANKKI / WASA AKTIE BANK

1918 ACCOUNT CHECKS ISSUE

#S111-S113 arms at lower ctr.

		VG	VF	UNC
S111	**25 MARKKAA** 1918. Lt. brown. Serial # prefix letters A; B or C.	25.00	100.00	275.00

		VG	VF	UNC
S112	**100 MARKKAA** 1918. Brown and tan.	35.00	125.00	375.00
S113	**500 MARKKAA** 1918.	800.00	1600.	3200.

NOTE: This and other banks in 1918 issued numerous emergency "notgeld" notes and checks in various denominations.

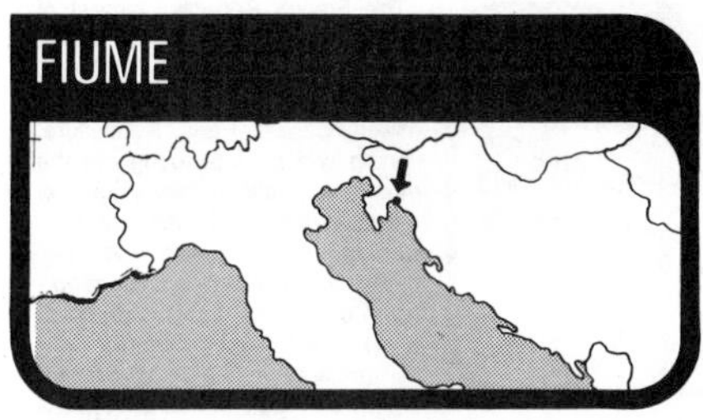

Fiume (Rijeka) is a major port and industrial center of Croatia, located on the Kvarner Gulf of the Adriatic Sea. The port was a primary base for the Yugoslav Navy.

By the 10th century, a recognizable settlement had developed at the present site of Fiume. It was incorporated into Austria in 1471, was made a free port in 1717, was united to Croatia in 1776, and was declared an autonomous city of the Austrian crown in 1770. The French occupied the city during 1809-14, after which it alternated under Austrian, Hungarian and Croatian rule until after World War I when set up as a free city. On September 1919, the Italian military commander D'Annunzio occupied Fiume with his troops, and he proclaimed the "Reggenza Italiana del Carnaro" and the Fiume free State, waiting for the annexation to Italy. Mussolini, who up to the time, had liked enterprise of Fiume, he was obliged by European diplomacy to change direction and, on January 1921 he sent regularly Italian troops to expell D'Annunzio from Fiume. Notes of Austro-Hungarian bank with Fiume overprint circulated since April 1919 up to February 1921. On January 1924, Mussolini proclaimed the Fiume's annexation to Italy. Occupied by the Germans during World War II, Fiume was liberated by the Yugoslavs in May, 1945 and transferred to Yugoslavia by the Italian Peace Treaty of 1947.

MONETARY SYSTEM:

1 Krone = 100 Heller

FREE STATE

CITTA DI FIUME

OVERPRINT VARIETIES:

Notes of the Austro-Hungarian Bank with one circular or one rectangular overprint. Examples with one circular and one rectangular ovpt. command up to a 25% premium.

Type I: Round hand stamp: *CITTA DI FIUME.*
Type II: Round machine ovpt: *CITTA DI FIUME.*
Type III: Round hand stamp: Savoyan Coat-of-arms
Type IV: 45 x 58mm. Rectangular ovpt: *INSTITUTO DI CREDITO CONSIGLIO NATIONALE, CITTA DI FIUME* around star

NOTE: Examples with ovpt. Type II became known to collectors in the 1950s.

1919/21 ISSUES

		Good	Fine	XF
S101	**1 KRONE** ND (1919/21- old date 1.12.1916). Red ovpt. on Austria #20.			
	a. Ovpt. Type I.	6.00	15.00	30.00
	b. Ovpt. Type II.	3.50	7.50	15.00
	c. Ovpt. Type III.	90.00	150.00	300.00
S102	**1 KRONE** ND (1919/21- old date 1.12.1916). Red ovpt. on Hungary #10. Serial # above 7000.			
	a. Ovpt. Type I.	11.00	25.00	50.00
	b. Ovpt. Type II.	6.00	12.50	25.00
	c. Ovpt. Type III.	120.00	200.00	400.00

		Good	Fine	XF
S103	**2 KRONEN** ND (1919/21- old date 5.8.1914). Blue ovpt. on Austria #17.			
	a. Ovpt. Type I.	12.50	25.00	50.00
	b. Ovpt. Type II.	6.00	12.50	25.00
	c. Ovpt. Type III.	120.00	200.00	400.00

		Good	Fine	XF
S104	**2 KRONEN** ND (1919/21- old date 1.3.1917). Red on gray unpt. Ovpt. on Austria #21.			
	a. Ovpt. Type I.	6.00	12.50	25.00
	b. Ovpt. Type II.	3.50	7.50	15.00
	c. Ovpt. Type III.	120.00	200.00	400.00

1920 ND ISSUES

		Good	Fine	XF
S105	**2 KRONEN** ND (1920- old date 1.3.1917). Red on gray unpt. Ovpt. on Hungary #11. Serial # above 7000.			
	a. Ovpt. Type I.	11.00	22.50	45.00
	b. Ovpt. Type II.	6.00	12.50	25.00
	c. Ovpt. Type III.	140.00	250.00	500.00
#S106	***Deleted.* (fabrication).**			
S107	**10 KRONEN** ND (1920- old date 2.1.1904). Blue-violet on red and green unpt. Ovpt. on Austria #9.			
	a. Ovpt. Type I.	25.00	50.00	100.00
	b. Ovpt. Type II.	11.00	22.50	45.00
	c. Ovpt. Type III.	180.00	350.00	700.00
	d. Ovpt. Type IV.	100.00	225.00	450.00

		Good	Fine	XF
S108	**10 KRONEN** ND (1920- old date 2.1.1915). Blue and green. Ovpt. on Austria #19.			
	a. Ovpt. Type I.	11.00	22.50	45.00
	b. Ovpt. Type II.	5.00	10.00	20.00
	c. Ovpt. Type III.	150.00	300.00	600.00
	d. Ovpt. Type IV.	80.00	160.00	350.00
S109	**20 KRONEN** ND (1920- old date 2.1.1907). Blue on red-brown and green unpt. Ovpt. on Austria #10.			
	a. Ovpt. Type I.	50.00	100.00	200.00
	b. Ovpt. Type II.	25.00	50.00	100.00
	c. Ovpt. Type III.	—	Rare	—
	d. Ovpt. Type IV.	200.00	400.00	800.00

		Good	Fine	XF
S110	**20 KRONEN** ND (1920- old date 2.1.1913). Blue on green and red unpt. Ovpt. on Austria #13.			
	a. Ovpt. Type I.	12.50	35.00	70.00
	b. Ovpt. Type II.	5.00	10.00	20.00
	c. Ovpt. Type III.	250.00	500.00	1000.
	d. Ovpt. Type IV.	75.00	150.00	300.00
S111	**20 KRONEN** ND (1920- old date 2.1.1913). Blue on green and red unpt. (II AUFLAGE). Ovpt. on Austria #14.			
	a. Ovpt. Type I.	11.00	25.00	50.00
	b. Ovpt. Type II.	5.00	15.00	30.00
	c. Ovpt. Type III.	250.00	500.00	1000.
	d. Ovpt. Type IV.	75.00	150.00	300.00

S112 50 KRONEN
ND (1920- old date 2.1.1902). Blue on rose unpt. Ovpt. on Austria #6.

	GOOD	FINE	XF
a. Ovpt. Type I.	80.00	160.00	350.00
b. Ovpt. Type II.	50.00	100.00	200.00
c. Ovpt. Type III.	—	Rare	—
d. Ovpt. Type IV.	180.00	350.00	700.00

S113 50 KRONEN
ND (1920- old date 2.1.1914). Blue and green. Ovpt. on Austria #15.

	GOOD	FINE	XF
a. Ovpt. Type I.	15.00	30.00	60.00
b. Ovpt. Type II.	5.00	10.00	20.00
c. Ovpt. Type III.	300.00	600.00	1200.
d. Ovpt. Type IV.	80.00	160.00	320.00

S114 100 KRONEN
ND (1920- old date 2.1.1910). Blue. Ovpt. on Austria #11.

	GOOD	FINE	XF
a. Ovpt. Type I.	200.00	400.00	800.00
b. Ovpt. Type II.	200.00	400.00	800.00
c. Ovpt. Type III.	—	Rare	—
d. Ovpt. Type IV.	350.00	700.00	1400.

S115 100 KRONEN
ND (1920- old date 2.1.1912). Green on red and blue unpt. Ovpt. on Austria #12.

	GOOD	FINE	XF
a. Ovpt. Type I.	15.00	40.00	80.00
b. Ovpt. Type II.	5.00	15.00	30.00
c. Ovpt. Type III.	—	Rare	—
d. Ovpt. Type IV.	80.00	160.00	320.00

S116 1000 KRONEN
ND (1920- old date 2.1.1902). Blue. Ovpt. on Austria #8.

	GOOD	FINE	XF
a. Ovpt. Type I.	18.00	40.00	80.00
b. Ovpt. Type II.	7.50	20.00	40.00
c. Ovpt. Type IV.	120.00	250.00	500.00

FRANCE

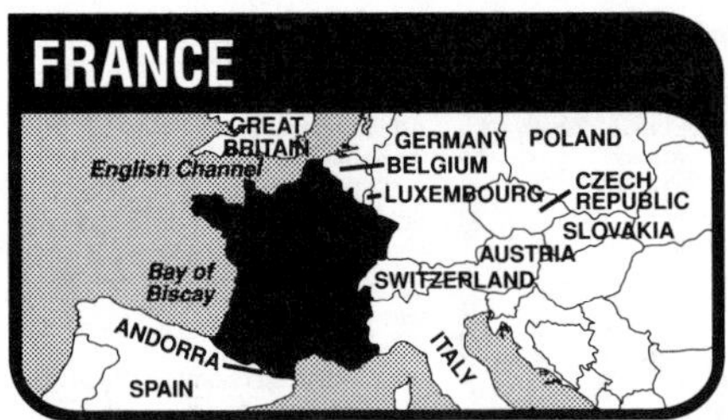

The French Republic, largest of the West European nations, has an area of 220,668 sq. mi. (547,026 sq. km.) and a population of 59.06 million. Capital: Paris. Agriculture, mining and manufacturing are the most important elements of France's diversified economy. Textiles and clothing, iron and steel products, machinery and transportation equipment, agricultural products and wine are exported.

France, the Gaul of ancient times, emerged from the Renaissance as a modern centralized national state which reached its zenith during the reign of Louis XIV (1643-1715) when it became an absolute monarchy and the foremost power in Europe. Although his reign marks the golden age of French culture, the domestic abuses and extravagance of Louis XIV plunged France into a series of costly wars. This, along with a system of special privileges granted the nobility and other favored groups, weakened the monarchy, brought France to bankruptcy - and laid the way for the French Revolution of 1789-94 that shook Europe and affected the whole world.

The monarchy was abolished and the First Republic formed in 1793. The new government fell in 1799 to a coup led by Napoleon Bonaparte who, after declaring himself First Consul for life, had himself proclaimed emperor of France and king of Italy. Napoleon's military victories made him master of much of Europe, but his disastrous Russian campaign of 1812 initiated a series of defeats that led to his abdication in 1814 and exile to the island of Elba. The monarchy was briefly restored under Louis XVIII. Napoleon returned to France in March 1815, but his efforts to regain power were totally crushed at the Battle of Waterloo. He was exiled to the island of St. Helena where he died in 1821.

The monarchy under Louis XVIII was again restored in 1815, but the ultrareactionary regime of Charles X (1824-30) was overthrown by a liberal revolution and Louis Philippe of Orleans replaced him as monarch. The monarchy was ousted by the Revolution of 1848 and the Second Republic proclaimed. Louis Napoleon Bonaparte (nephew of Napoleon I) was elected president of the Second Republic. He was proclaimed emperor in 1852. As Napoleon III, he gave France two decades of prosperity under a stable, autocratic regime, but led it to defeat in the Franco-Prussian War of 1870, after which the Third Republic was established.

The Third Republic endured until 1940 and ended with the capitulation of France to the swiftly maneuvering German forces. Marshal Henri Petain formed a puppet government that sued for peace and ruled unoccupied France from Vichy. Meanwhile, General Charles de Gaulle escaped to London where he formed a wartime government in exile and the Free French army. Charles de Gaulle's provisional exile government was officially recognized by the Allies after the liberation of Paris in 1944, and de Gaulle, who had been serving as head of the provisional government, was formally elected to that position. In October 1945, the people overwhelmingly rejected a return to the prewar government, thus paving the way for the formation of the Fourth Republic.

Charles de Gaulle was unanimously elected president of the Fourth Republic, but resigned in January 1946 when leftists withdrew their support. In actual operation, the Fourth Republic was remarkably like the Third, with the National Assembly the focus of power. The later years of the Fourth Republic were marked by a burst of industrial expansion unmatched in modern French history. The growth rate, however, was marred by a nagging inflationary trend that weakened the franc and undermined the competitive posture of France's export trade. This and the Algerian conflict led to the recall of de Gaulle to power, the adoption of a new constitution vesting strong powers in the executive, and establishment in 1958 of the current Fifth Republic.

RULERS:

Louis XIV, 1643-1715
Louis XV, 1715-74
Louis XVI, 1774-93
First Republic, 1793-94, L'An 2
Directory, 1795-99, L'An 4-7
Consulate, 1799-1803, L'An 8-11
Napoleon as Consul, 1799-1804
Napoleon I as Emperor, 1804-14
(First Restoration)
Louis XVIII, 1814-15
Napoleon I, 1815
(Second Restoration)
Louis XVIII, 1815-24
Charles X, 1824-30
Louis Philippe, 1830-48
Second Republic, 1848-52
Napoleon III, 1852-70

MONETARY SYSTEM:

1 Livre = 20 Sols (Sous)
1 Ecu = 6 Livres
1 Louis D'or = 4 Ecus to 1794
1 Franc = 10 Decimes = 100 Centimes, 1794-1960

FRENCH DENOMINATIONS

1 Un	13 Treize	125 Cent Vingt-Cinq
2 Deux	14 Quatorze	200 Deux Cents
3 Trois	15 Quinze	250 Deux Cent Cinquante
4 Quatre	16 Seize	300 Trois Cents
5 Cinq	20 Vingt	400 Quatre Cents
6 Six	25 Vingt-Cinq	500 Cinq Cents
7 Sept	30 Trente	750 Sept Cent Cinquante
8 Huit	40 Quarante	1000 Mille
9 Neuf	10 Cinquante	2000 Deux Mille
10 Dix	80 Quatre-Vingts	5000 Cinq Mille
11 Onze	90 Quatre-Vingt-Dix	10,000 Quatre-Vingt-Dix
12 Douze	100 Cent	

COMMERCIAL BANKS

Banque Rouennaise . . . . . #S188-S189
Banque Territoriale . . . . . #S201-S205
Banque de Toulouse . . . . . #S209-S215
Caisse de Commerce . . . . . #S218
Caisse de Comptes Courants . . . . . #S221-S222
Caisse d'Echange, Caen. . . . . . #S226
Caisse d'Echange, Orleans. . . . . . #S231-S233
Caisse d'Echange des Monnaies, Rouen . . . . . #S241-S246
Caisse d'Escompte du Commerce, Paris . . . . . #S253-S254
Comptoir Commercial, Paris . . . . . #S261-S265

SIEGE

Siege of Lyon . . . . . #S301-S304

COMMERCIAL BANKS

ACHILLE ADAM, BANQUIER

1800'S ISSUE

#S101-S102 view of ships in harbor at upper ctr.

		GOOD	FINE	XF
S101	**20 FRANCS** 18xx.	—	500.00	800.00

		GOOD	FINE	XF
S102	**100 FRANCS** 18xx. Like #S101.	—	750.00	1200.

BANQUE DE BORDEAUX

1818-48 ISSUE

		GOOD	FINE	XF
S103	**100 FRANCS** 18.3.1848. Black. Lt. yellow paper. 2 allegorical figures at l. w/flag, at r. w/trident; 2 women reclining at bottom, bank at ctr.	—	Rare	—
S104	**200 FRANCS** 18.3.1848. Black. Lt. green paper. Like #S103.	—	Rare	—
S105	**500 FRANCS** ND. Allegorical figures at l. and r., arms of Bordeaux at bottom.	—	Rare	—
S106	**500 FRANCS** 20.10.1825. Black. Ruby paper similar to parchment. Like #S103.	—	Rare	—
S107	**500 FRANCS** 10.8.1836; 9.5.1838; 20.6.1844. Black. Pink paper. Like #S106.	—	Rare	—

		GOOD	FINE	XF
S108	**1000 FRANCS** 1.7.1819-20.11.1846. Black. Like #S105.	—	Rare	—
S109	**1000 FRANCS** ND. Black. Like #S106.	—	Rare	—

BANQUE COMMERCIALE DU HAVRE

1800'S ISSUE

		GOOD	FINE	XF
S110	**100 FRANCS** 18xx. Unsigned remainder.	—	—	—

BANQUE DE DIJON

1839 ISSUE

		GOOD	FINE	XF
S111	**250 FRANCS** ND. Proof.	—	—	—
S112	**500 FRANCS** ND. Proof.	—	—	—
S113	**1000 FRANCS** ND. Proof.	—	—	—

NOTE: No examples of #S111-S113 are presently known.

BANQUE DU HAVRE

1837-48 ISSUE

		GOOD	FINE	XF
S121	**50 FRANCS** ND. Seated allegorical figure at l. and r. within frame, ships at bottom l., ctr. and r. Proof.	—	Rare	—
S122	**100 FRANCS** ND. Like #S121.	Reported Not Confirmed		
S123	**250 FRANCS** 15.2.1840. Black. Ruby paper. Like #S121.	—	Rare	—
S124	**250 FRANCS** 5.1.1840; 15.2.1840. Black.	—	Rare	—
S125	**500 FRANCS** ND (ca.1836). Man's head at l. and r. within frame, ships at bottom ctr.	—	Rare	—
S126	**500 FRANCS** 15.2.1840. Black. Gray-blue paper. Like #S121.	—	Rare	—

A word on pricing

When a note is marked RARE in the price columns, this note seldom appears on the market, or few are known in private hands. When dashes are in the price column, means that the note has not traded on the open market recently and a definitive value could not accurately be determined. Rare does not always mean expensive. A dashed price does not mean expensive or rare.

		Good	Fine	XF
S127	**1000 Francs** 24.12.1836. Black. Like #S125. Proof.	—	Rare	—

Banque de Lille

1836-48 Issue

		Good	Fine	XF
S131	**100 Francs** 27.3.1848. Black. Green paper. Bull's head at upper l., horse's head at upper r.	—	Rare	—
S132	**250 Francs** 1.2.1837. Black. Imprint at bottom: *Normand Fils Del.-Belhatte Sc.* Proof.	—	Rare	—
S133	**250 Francs** 23.2.1837. Black. Like #S132. Imprint at bottom: *Normand Fils Del.-Saunier Direcxit-Belhatte Sc.* Proof.	—	Rare	—
S134	**500 Francs** ND. Like #S131.	—	Rare	—
S135	**1000 Francs** 13.12.1838. Black. Like #S131. Proof.	—	Rare	—

Banque de Limoges, 1848

It is reported that the Banque de Limoges had proofs of notes printed in April of 1848. Denominations at first were from 20 to 1000 Francs, later including 5 and 10 Francs. No examples are presently confirmed.

Banque de Lyon

1835-48 Issue

		Good	Fine	XF
S141	**25 Francs** 20.3.1848. Black. Arms w/rampant lion at top ctr. Back blue.	—	Rare	—
S142	**100 Francs** 25.3.1848. Like #S141.	Reported Not Confirmed		

		Good	Fine	XF
S143	**250 Francs** 1836. Provisional issue Barre/Porret. Proof.	—	Unc	4000.

		Good	Fine	XF
S144	**250 Francs** 25.1.1839; 12.9.1839. Standing allegorical figures at l. and r., cherubs at bottom l. and r., arms at top ctr.	—	Unc	5000.
S145	**500 Francs** ND. Like #S144.	Reported Not Confirmed		
S146	**1000 Francs** 11.7.1844. 3 sign.	—	Rare	—

		Good	Fine	XF
S147	**1000 Francs** 1848. Like #S144. Imprint: *Louis Perrin impr.* at l., 2 sign.	—	Rare	—

BANQUE DE MARSEILLE

1836-48 ISSUE

		GOOD	FINE	XF
S151	**50 FRANCS** 22.3.1848. Black on green unpt. Paper texture like vellum. Seated allegorical figure at lower l. and r., old view of town at bottom ctr.	—	Rare	—
S152	**100 FRANCS** 25.3.1848. Like #S151.	—	Rare	—
S153	**250 FRANCS** 24.9.1836. Black. Proof.	—	Rare	—
S154	**250 FRANCS** 28.11.1838. Black. Ruby paper. Like #S151.	—	Rare	—

		GOOD	FINE	XF
S155	**500 FRANCS** 21.8.1839. Paper texture like vellum. Like #S151. Inscription at upper l. and r. in 2 circles.	—	Rare	—
S156	**500 FRANCS** 1848. Like #S151 but text at ctr. in circle.	Reported Not Confirmed		

		GOOD	FINE	XF
S157	**1000 FRANCS** 24.9.1836. Horse's head at bottom lower l. ctr. and bull's head at lower ctr. r. Proof.	—	Rare	—
S158	**1000 FRANCS** 1848. Like #S151.	Reported Not Confirmed		

BANQUE DE NANTES

1818-48 ISSUE

#S161-S163 imprint: ***Cornouailles Fecit.***

		GOOD	FINE	XF
S161	**250 FRANCS** Proof.	—	Rare	—
S162	**500 FRANCS** Proof.	—	Rare	—
S163	**1000 FRANCS** Proof.	—	Rare	—

NOTE: Only 3 proof examples are known for this bank.

BANQUE D'ORLÉANS

1838-48 ISSUE

		GOOD	FINE	XF
S171	**25 FRANCS** 1848.	—	Rare	—
S172	**100 FRANCS** 1848.	—	Rare	—

		GOOD	FINE	XF
S173	**250 FRANCS** 1.1.1839. Steam locomotives at bottom l., arms at top ctr., ship at bottom r.	—	Rare	—
S174	**500 FRANCS** 1.1.1839 (?).	—	Rare	—
S175	**1000 FRANCS** 1.1.1839 (?).	—	Rare	—

BANQUE DE ROUEN

1807-48 ISSUE

		GOOD	FINE	XF
S176	**50 FRANCS** 18.3.1848. Green. Ornate l. and r. border w/anchor, fruit, caduceus, cherubs, etc.			
	a. Issued note.	—	Rare	—
	b. Proof.	—	—	—
S177	**100 FRANCS** 1.4.1807. Black.	—	Rare	—

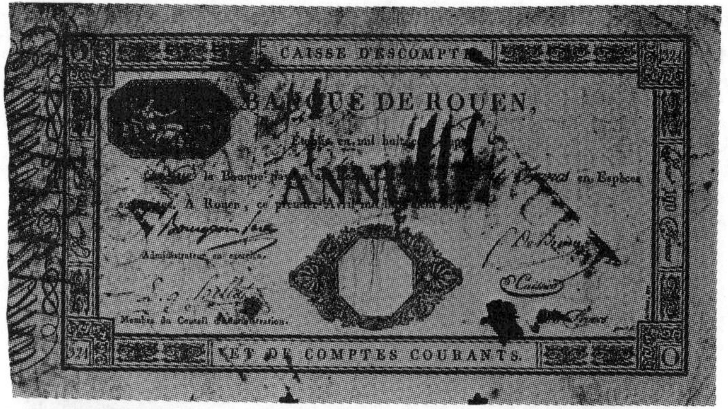

		Good	Fine	XF
S178	**100 Francs** 18.3.1848.	—	—	—
S179	**250 Francs** 22.8.1826; 2.9.1826. Text: *La loi punit de mort le contrefacteur.*	—	Rare	—

		Good	Fine	XF
S180	**250 Francs** 26.9.1826. Text: *Le contrefacteur est puni des travaux forces a perpetuite.*	—	Rare	—
S181	**500 Francs** 1.4.1807. Red.	3000.	4000.	—
S182	**500 Francs** ND (ca.1826). Like #S179.	—	Rare	—

		Good	Fine	XF
S183	**500 Francs** Red. Like #S180.	—	Rare	—
S184	**1000 Francs** ND (ca.1826). Like #S179.	—	Rare	—
S185	**1000 Francs** Like #S180.	—	Rare	—

		Good	Fine	XF
S186	**1000 Francs** 5.6.1842. standing allegorical woman at l. and r., 2 figures representing Seine and Ocean at bottom ctr. Designer: Barre. Proof.	—	Unc	5000.

Banque Rouennaise

1871 Issue

		Good	Fine	XF
S188	**5 Francs** 1871. Cut cancelled, hand stamped: *ANNULE.*	—	225.00	600.00
S189	**10 Francs** 1871. Like #S208. Cut cancelled, hand stamped: *ANNULE.*	—	225.00	600.00

Banque de Savoie

1851; 1859 Issue

For previously listed #S191-S197, see Italian States #S160-S166.

Banque Territoriale, Paris

1799-1803 Issues

		Good	Fine	XF
S201	**50 Francs** Black. Yellow paper.	—	—	—
S202	**100 Francs** Black. Green paper.	—	—	—
S203	**250 Francs** Black. Blue paper.	—	—	—

		Good	Fine	XF
S204	**500 Francs** Black. Pink paper.	—	—	2500.
S205	**1000 Francs** Black. White paper.	—	—	3000.

Banque de Toulouse

1838-48 Issue

		Good	Fine	XF
S209	**100 Francs** 20.3.1848. Red. 5 allegorical figures at bottom.	—	Rare	—
S210	**200 Francs** 20.3.1848. Blue. Like #S201.	—	Rare	—

		Good	Fine	XF
S211	**250 Francs** 1.2.1839. Black. Allegorical figures in border. Proof.	—	Rare	—
S212	**250 Francs** ND. Black. Like #S201.	—	Rare	—
S213	**500 Francs** ND. Like #S201.	Reported Not Confirmed		
S214	**500 Francs** ND. Like #S203.	—	Rare	—
S215	**1000 Francs** ND. Like #S201.	Reported Not Confirmed		

Caisse de Commerce, Paris

1792 Issue

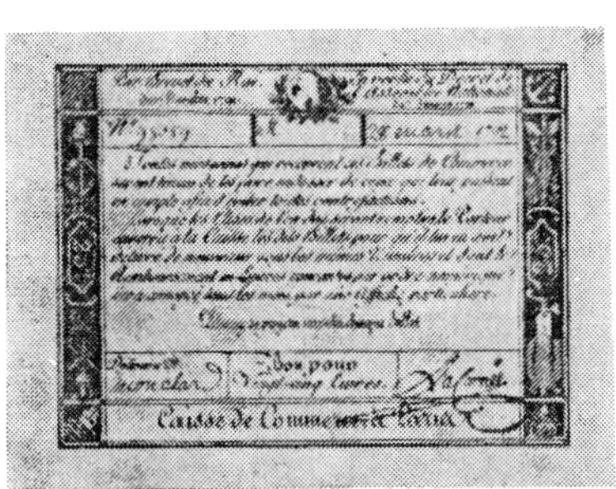

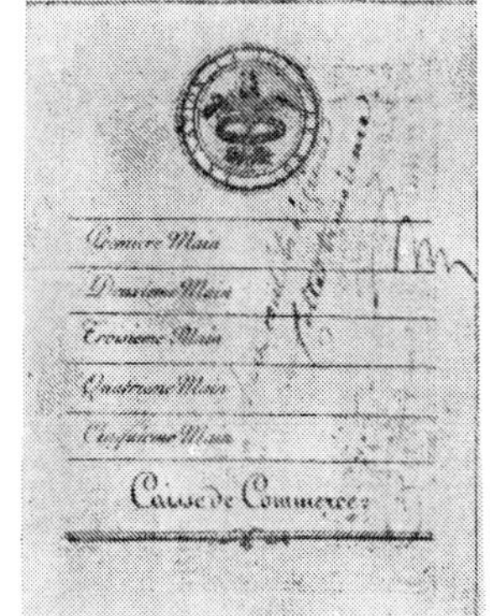

		Good	Fine	XF
S218	**25 Livres** 25.1.1792-28.3.1792. Black. Yellow paper. Handwritten dates w/handwritten sign. on face and back.	15.00	40.00	175.00

Caisse de Comptes Courants

1795 Issue

		Good	Fine	XF
S221	**500 Francs** AN4-AN8.	—	—	—
S222	**1000 Francs** AN4-AN8.	—	—	—

Caisse d'Echange, Caen

1800 Issue

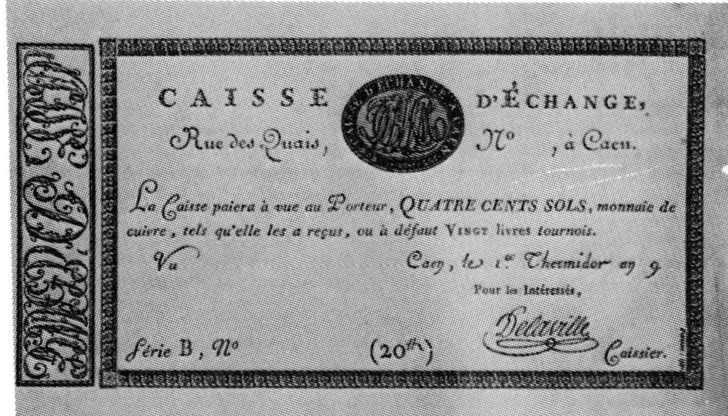

		Good	Fine	XF
S226	**400 Sols** AN9. Black. (Not issued).	—	75.00	175.00

Caisse d'Echange, Orléans

1801 Issue

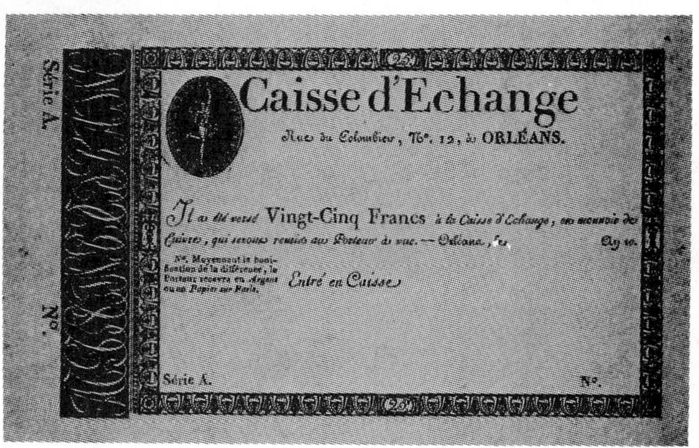

		Good	Fine	XF
S231	**25 Francs** AN10.			
	a. Issued note.	50.00	100.00	200.00
	r. Unissued remainder.	—	Unc	50.00
S232	**50 Francs** AN10.	60.00	120.00	240.00
S233	**100 Francs** AN10.	70.00	140.00	280.00

Caisse d'Echange des Monnaies, Paris

1798-1804 Issue

		Good	Fine	XF
S236	**12.50 Francs**	50.00	120.00	200.00
S237	**25 Francs**	50.00	120.00	200.00

Caisse d'Echange des Monnaies, Rouen

1797-1803 Issue

#S241, S245 and S246 angel at upper l.

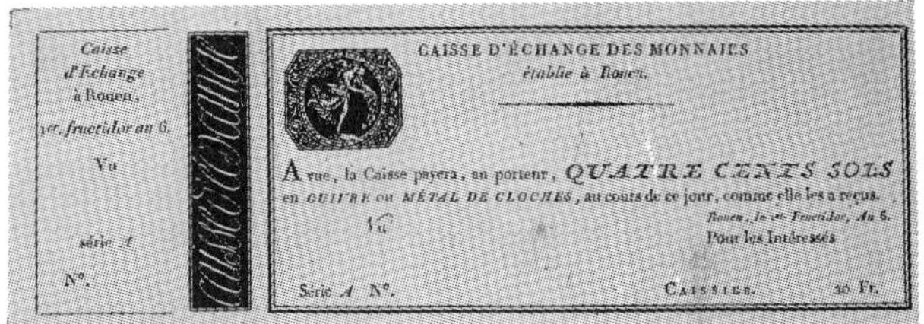

		Good	Fine	XF
S241	**400 Sols** 1 er Fructidor AN6. (Not issued).	—	90.00	225.00

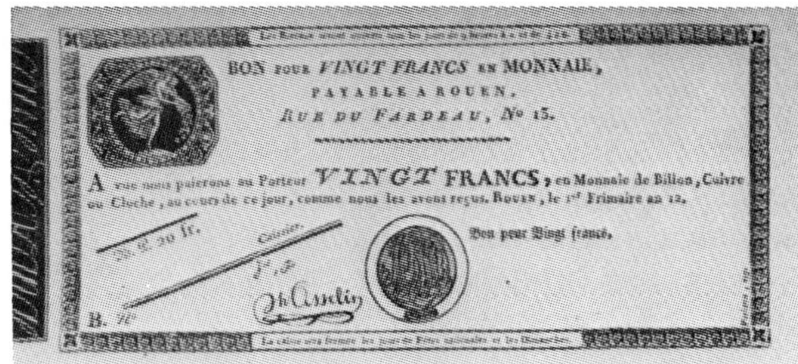

		Good	Fine	XF
S245	**20 Francs** AN10, 12.			
	a. Date: *1 er Frimaire AN 10.*	17.50	42.50	75.00
	b. Date: *1 er Frimaire AN 12.*	15.00	35.00	60.00

		Good	Fine	XF
S246	**100 Francs**			
	AN12.			
	a. Issued note.	17.50	42.50	75.00
	b. Cancelled, ovpt: *Annulé.*	12.50	30.00	50.00

Caisse d'Escompte du Commerce, Paris

1797-1803 Issue

		Good	Fine	XF
S253	**500 Francs**			
	24.11.1797-26.8.1803. Vignettes in corners, Mercury at bottom l. ctr., Ceres at bottom ctr. r.	—	2250.	4500.

		Good	Fine	XF
S254	**500 Francs**			
	AN6 and other dates. 2 allegorical figures sitting w/partial wreath at bottom ctr.	—	2250.	4500.

Comptoir Commercial, Paris

1800-03 Issue

		Good	Fine	XF
S261	**200 Francs**			
	1800-03.	—	—	—
S262	**250 Francs**			
	1800-03.	—	—	—
S263	**300 Francs**			
	1800-03.	—	—	—
S264	**500 Francs**			
	1800-03.	—	—	—
S265	**1000 Francs**			
	1800-03.	—	—	—

Factorerie du Commerce, Parris

Notes are reported ca. 1802, but denominations are unknown.

Societé Générale du Commerce, Rouen

Notes are reported, but denominations are unknown.

Siege

Siege of Lyon

Issued at Lyon in 1793 while the city was being beseiged by counterrevolutionary forces. The city was devastated during the fighting.

1793 ND Issue

#S301-S303 black. W/1 sign. at l. and embossed arms at r. Uniface.

		Good	Fine	XF
S301	**25 Sous**			
	ND (1793). Fleur-de-lis at corners, diamonds in border.	12.00	30.00	80.00
S302	**50 Sous**			
	ND (1793). Ornamented border. Off-white paper.	15.00	35.00	90.00

S#303

#S304

		Good	Fine	XF
S303	**5 Livres**			
	ND (1793). Plain border. White paper.	17.50	40.00	100.00
S304	**20 Livres**			
	ND (1793). Black. Border similar to #S301. W/2 sign. and 2 embossed arms. Cut cancelled.			
	a. Wmk: *Caise.*	25.00	60.00	180.00
	b. Wmk: *Patriotique.*	25.00	60.00	180.00
	c. Wmk: *De Lyon.*	25.00	60.00	180.00

NOTE: #S304 only one uncut example known.

Although the origin of the German Empire can be traced to the Treaty of Verdun, 843, that ceded Charlemagne's lands east of the Rhine to German Prince Louis, it was for centuries little more than a geographic expression, consisting of hundreds of effectively autonomous big and little states. Nominally the states owed their allegiance to the Holy Roman Emperor, who was also a German king, but as the emperors exhibited less and less concern for Germany the actual power devolved on the lords of the individual states. The fragmentation of the empire climaxed with the tragic denouement of the Thirty Years War, 1618-48, which devastated much of Germany, destroyed its agriculture and medieval commercial eminence and ended the attempt of the Hapsburgs to unify Germany. Deprived of administrative capacity by a lack of resources, the imperial authority became utterly powerless. At this time Germany contained an estimated 1,800 individual states, some with a population of as little as 300. The German Empire of recent history (the creation of Bismarck) was formed on April 14, 1871, when the King of Prussia became Emperor Wilhelm I of Germany. The new empire comprised four kingdoms, five grand duchies, 13 duchies and principalities, three free cities and the nonautonomous province of Alsace-Lorraine. Prior to the German unification in 1871 the various German States enjoyed varying degrees of political independence including the right to coin and issue money. Most of the paper currency issues of the German States from the middle of the 18th century until the unification are valued in thalers and gulden denominations with the gulden usually worth about half the thaler. There are a few exceptions such as the "Franken" valued notes of the Napoleonic Kingdom of Westphalia and the early "Pfund Banco" notes of the Prussian "Giro und Lehnbank."

After the unification many of these banks issued currency under the new mark system. These notes are listed in the Regional Bank listing which follows this section.

Bank notes of the German States prior to the unification in 1871, official government issues and local bank issues are listed together under the various states.

MONETARY SYSTEM:

Until 1871 the Mark (Marck) was a measure of weight.

North German States until 1837

2 Gulden = 1 Reichsthaler
1 Speciesthaler (before 1753)
1 Convention Thaler (after 1753)

North German States after 1837

30 Groschen = 1 Thaler
1 Vereinsthaler (after 1857)

South German States until 1837

120 Convention Kreuzer = 2 Convention Gulden = 1 Convention Thaler

ANHALT, DUCHY OF

HERZOGLICH ANHALTISCHE STAATSSCHULDENVERWALTUNG

ANHALT STATE INDEBTEDNESS ADMINISTRATION

1861-67 STATE TREASURY NOTES ISSUE

Issued for statewide circulation.

		GOOD	FINE	XF
S101	**1 THALER** 20.5.1861. Light green. Light brown on back. Wmk: II EIN THLER II. Printer: Gebr. Katz, Dessau. Sign. Funcke; Siebigk; Holzmann; Medicus.	300.00	600.00	1000.
S102	**1 THALER** 1.8.1866. Green. Light brown on back.			
	a. W/imprint and watermark.	300.00	600.00	1000.
	b. W/o imprint and w/o watermark.	300.00	600.00	1000.
S103	**1 THALER** 31.10.1867. Green. Light brown on back.	—	—	—

ANHALT-BERNBURG, DUCHY OF

The line died out in 1863, whereupon its territories were united with Anhalt-Dessau.

HERZOGLICH ANHALTISCHES STAATSMINISTERIUM

ANHALT STATE MINISTRY

1850 TREASURY BILLS ISSUE

#S107-S108 printer: Theodor Boesche, Berlin.

		GOOD	FINE	XF
S107	**1 THALER** 18.3.1850. Yellow brown. Pink on back. Wmk: A.I.B. Sign. Hempel; Krosigk; Ahlfeld.	300.00	600.00	1000.
S108	**5 THALER** 18.3.1850. Pink. Green on back. Wmk: A.5.B. Sign. Hempel; Krosigk; Ahlfeld.	350.00	700.00	1250.

1852-56 TREASURY BILLS ISSUE

		GOOD	FINE	XF
S109	**1 THALER** 5.2.1852.	—	—	—
S110	**25 THALER** 26.6.1856. Flesh colored. Light brown on back. Wmk: HERZOGLICH ANH.BERNBURG KASSENANWEISUNG. Sign. Schaetzell.	575.00	1350.	1850.

1859 ISSUE

		GOOD	FINE	XF
S111	**1 THALER** 25.7.1859. Black on green unpt. Monogram HAB as unpt. Wmk: HERZ ANH BERNB KASSENSCHEIN I THALER I. Printer: Theodor Boesche, Berlin. Sign. Schaetzell.	250.00	550.00	950.00

ANHALT-CÖTHEN, DUCHY OF

Anhalt-Cöthen was raised from a principality to a duchy when it entered the Confederation of the Rhine in 1807. In 1828 the main Anhalt-Cöthen line died out, whereupon the princes of Anhalt-Cöthen-Pless became the dukes of Anhalt-Cöthen. This line died out in 1847, whereupon its territories were jointly administered by Anhalt-Bernburg and Anhalt-Dessau. In 1863, after the Anhalt-Bernburg line died out, the three Anhalt duchies were united into one.

HERZOGL. ANHALT-CÖTHENSCHE KASSENSCHEIN

ANHALT-CÖTHEN TREASURY

1829 STATE TREASURY NOTES ISSUE

		GOOD	FINE	XF
S116	**1 THALER COURANT** 1.1.1829. Light green.	575.00	1350.	1850.
S117	**5 THALER COURANT** 1.1.1829.	—	—	—
S118	**10 THALER COURANT** 1.1.1829.	—	—	—

HERZOGL. ANHALT-CÖTHENSCHE STAATSSCHULDEN-COMMISSION

ANHALT-CÖTHEN STATE INDEBTEDNESS COMMISSION

1848 TREASURY NOTES ISSUE

Emergency issue during the Revolution of 1848.

		GOOD	FINE	XF
S121	**5 THALER** 1.5.1848. Black. Uniface.	350.00	700.00	1200.
S122	**1 THALER** 1.6.1848. Green.			
	a. W/imprint.	250.00	550.00	950.00
	b. W/o imprint.	300.00	600.00	1000.
S123	**5 THALER** 1.6.1848. Black on green unpt. Back printed.	300.00	600.00	1000.

ANHALT-CÖTHEN-BERNBURGER EISENBAHN-GESELLSCHAFT

ANHALT-CÖTHEN-BERNBURG RAILROAD COMPANY

In the 1840s a committee was formed to build a railroad line from Cöthen to Bernberg. The concession for this line was granted by the Duchy of Anhalt-Cöthen on June 3, 1844, and by the Duchy of Anhalt-Bernburg on August 16, 1844. It raised its capital through 500,000 thalers in common stock and 50,000 thalers in paper money. It opened to traffic on September 10, 1846. From 1846 until 1849 it was operated by the Magdenburg-Cöthen-Halle-Leipzig Railroad, and in 1849-50 by the Berlin-Anhalt Railroad. The Anhalt-Cöthen- Bernburg government took over the railroad in 1850 against a guaranteed interest payment of 2 1/2% on the common stock. In 1863 the reailroad was privatized by selling it to the Magdeburg-Halberstadt Railroad, which was agresively growing through acquisitions. Later acquisitions would be financed by the Berlin Disconto-Gesellschaft. The Magdeburg-Halberstadt Railroad took over the 2 1/2% interest guarantee. The Magdeburg-Halberstadt Railroad was taken over by the Prussian state on January 1, 1879. The Anhalt-Cöthen-Bernburg Railroad was a financial failure, even though it had a license to print money. Aside from the 2 1/2% interest guarantee, the shareholders never received any dividends.

1846 TREASURY NOTES ISSUE

		GOOD	FINE	XF
S126	**1 THALER** 2.3.1846. Light green. Face sign. Böttger; Friedheim; Hess; Jannasch; Steinthal. Back sign. Kersten; Braun. Printer: Eduard Haenel, Berlin.	350.00	700.00	1200.

1850-56 TREASURY NOTES ISSUE

		GOOD	FINE	XF
S127	**1 THALER** 20.2.1850. Black on green unpt.			
	a. W/wmk.	250.00	550.00	950.00
	b. W/o wmk. (forgery?).	—	—	—

		Good	Fine	XF
S128	**5 Thaler** 20.2.1850. Light green.	300.00	600.00	1000.
S129	**25 Thaler** 1.7.1856. Green on lt. green. Wmk: 25 CBEG 25. Printer: Albert Falckenberg, Magdeburg.	435.00	1000.	1500.

Anhalt-Dessau, Duchy of

The duchy absorbed Anhalt-Cöthen in 1847 and Anhalt-Bernberg in 1863. After uniting the three Anhalt lines, it called itself simply the "Duchy of Anhalt."

Herzoglich Anhalt-Dessauische Regierung

1849 State Treasury Notes Issue

		Good	Fine	XF
S131	**1 Thaler** 1.8.1849. Gray. Sign. Ploetz; Basedow.	250.00	550.00	950.00
S132	**5 Thaler** 1.8.1849. Coffee brown. Sign. Ploetz; Basedow.	350.00	700.00	1200.

1855 State Treasury Notes Issue

		Good	Fine	XF
S133	**10 Thaler** 1.10.1855. Light green. Green numbers on back. Sign. Basedow/Braunbehrens.	575.00	1350.	1850.

Anhalt-Dessauische Landesbank

In the 1840s Anhalt threatened to flood Prussia with bank notes, by creating a bank with the monstrous share capital of 200 million thalers. This "Anhalt-Prussian Bank war" led to the restructuring of the Preussische Bank. The bank commenced business with a much smaller capital on January 2, 1847. Under its first director, Nulandt, this bank launched many dubious companies, such as the Moldavian Bank in Jassy (now part of Romania). It had to be bailed out by the Duke of Anhalt after the Crisis of 1857; Nulandt resigned in 1858. His is the central signature on S134-137. Because of numerous forgeries, S134-135 had to be withdrawn from circulation in 1865. The bank abandoned its note-issuing privilege in 1876. In 1921 the bank entered an IG with the Allgemeine Deutsche Credit-Anstalt of Leipzig (ADCA). The bank merged into ADCA in 1932.

1847 Issue

Thaler System

		Good	Fine	XF
S134	**1 Thaler** 2.1.1847.	300.00	600.00	1000.

		Good	Fine	XF
S135	**5 Thaler** 2.1.1847.	435.00	1000.	1500.

1855 Issue

		Good	Fine	XF
S136	**10 Thaler** 1.6.1855.	575.00	1350.	1850.
S137	**50 Thaler** 1.6.1855.	—	—	—

1864 Issue

		Good	Fine	XF
S138	**1 Thaler** 2.1.1864. Green and lt. brown.	300.00	600.00	1000.

		Good	Fine	XF
S139	**5 Thaler** 2.1.1864.	435.00	1000.	1500.

1874 Issue

Mark System

		Good	Fine	XF
S140	**100 Mark** 1.7.1874. Printer: G&D.	500.00	950.00	1600.

Baden, Grand Duchy of

Grossh. Badische General-Staats-Casse

1849; 1854 Issue

#S141-143 printer: Hasper in Karlsruhe using plates prepared by C. Naumann in Frankfurt/Main.

		Good	Fine	XF
S141	**2 Gulden** 1.7.1849. Father Rhine at l., Danube at r., Badenia above. Sign. Fruttiger; Friderici.	95.00	275.00	425.00

		Good	Fine	XF
S142	**10 Gulden** 1.7.1849. Father Rhine at l., Danube at r. Badenia above. Sign. Fruttiger; Friderici.	350.00	700.00	1200.

		GOOD	FINE	XF
S143	**35 GULDEN** 1.7.1849. Father Rhine at l., Danube at r., Badenia above. Sign. Fruttiger; Friderici.	575.00	1350.	1850.
S144	**10 GULDEN** 1.7.1854. Printer: C. Naumann.	575.00	1350.	1850.
S145	**50 GULDEN** 1.7.1854. Printer: C. Naumann.	725.00	1650.	2500.

ALLGEMEINE VERSORGUNGSANSTALT

1870 STATE LOAN BANK TREASURY NOTES

An emergency issue of loan notes (Darlehenskassenscheinen) during the monetary stringency caused by the outbreak of the Franco-Prussian War.

		GOOD	FINE	XF
S148	**5 GULDEN** 30.7.1870.	575.00	1350.	1850.
S149	**10 GULDEN** 30.7.1870.	725.00	1650.	2500.

BADISCHE BANK

Refer to Regional Banks #S901-S915.

BAVARIA, KINGDOM OF

KGL. BAYER. STAATS-SCHULDENTILGUNGS-COMMISSION

1866 ISSUE

Issued to help pay for the costs of the Six Weeks War of 1866, and for the construction of state railroads. In July 1870 another 6 million gulden was issued to pay for the expenses of the Franco-Prussian War; this group is identical in all respects, including date to the 1866 issue. Printer: Dondorf & Naumann, Frankfurt/Main.

		GOOD	FINE	XF
S151	**2 GULDEN** 5.9.1866. Sign. Sutner; Bayer; Hegnenberg-Dux.	60.00	125.00	200.00

		GOOD	FINE	XF
S152	**5 GULDEN** 5.9.1866. Blue and black. Back blue and brown, Bavaria at ctr. Father Rhine at r. Sign. Sutner; Bayer; Hegnenberg-Dux.	60.00	125.00	200.00

		GOOD	FINE	XF
S153	**50 GULDEN** 5.9.1866. Sign. Sutner; Bayer; Hegnenberg-Dux.	575.00	1350.	1850.

BAYERISCHE HYPOTHEKEN-UND WECHSEL-BANK MÜNCHEN

MUNICH

Concession granted July 1, 1834; opened for business 1835. It is one of the oldest joint-stock banks in Germany. It transferred its right to issue bank notes to the Bayerische Notenbank in 1875. It merged with the Bayerische Vereins-Bank in July 1997 to form the Bayerische Hypo- und Vereins-Bank.

1836-39 ISSUE

Gulden System

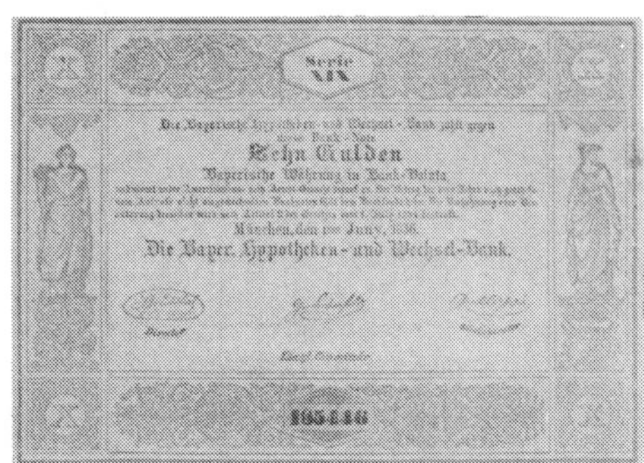

		GOOD	FINE	XF
S156	**10 GULDEN** 1.6.1836.	725.00	1650.	2500.

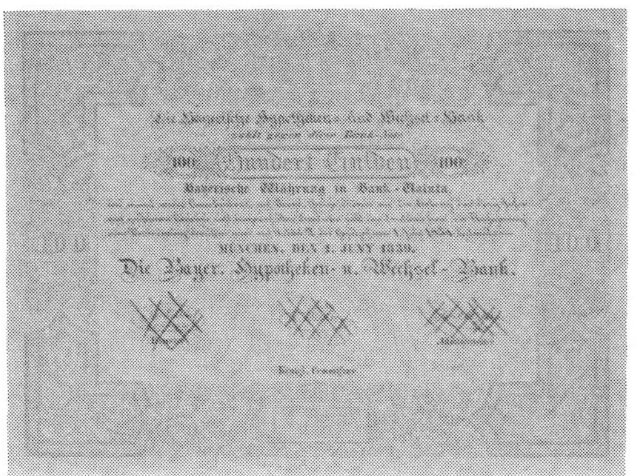

		GOOD	FINE	XF
S157	**100 GULDEN** 1.6.1839.	575.00	1350.	1850.

1841 ISSUE

		GOOD	FINE	XF
S158	**10 GULDEN** 1.5.1841.	435.00	1000.	1500.

1849 ISSUE

		GOOD	FINE	XF
S159	**10 GULDEN** 1.7.1849. Proof.	—	—	—

1850 ISSUE

		GOOD	FINE	XF
S160	**10 GULDEN** 1.7.1850. Red and black with blind embossing.	350.00	700.00	1200.
S161	**100 GULDEN** 16.9.1850.	575.00	1350.	1850.

1857 ISSUE

		GOOD	FINE	XF
S162	**35 GULDEN** 6.1.1857. Essay only.	—	—	—
S163	**10 GULDEN** 1.8.1857.	435.00	1000.	1500.

1865 ISSUE

		GOOD	FINE	XF
S164	**10 GULDEN** 1.7.1865. Woman and child at l. and r. Printer: G&D.	350.00	700.00	1200.

1870 ISSUE

		GOOD	FINE	XF
S165	**100 GULDEN** 1.10.1870. Printer: G&D.	725.00	1650.	2500.

1874 ISSUE

Mark System

		GOOD	FINE	XF
S166	**100 MARK** 1.7.1874. Printer: G&D.	—	—	—

BAYERISCHE NOTENBANK

Refer to Regional Banks, #S921-S943.

BRUNSWICK, DUCHY OF

HERZOGL. BRAUNSCHWEIG-LÜNEBURGISCHE LEIHHAUS-KOMMISSION

Founded as a state-owned pawn shop or *Mont de Piété* in 1765, and gradually developed into a state-owned bank. It abandoned its right to issue bank notes in 1875, and recalled all outstanding notes in for redemption on July 1, 1876. It changed its name to the Braunschweigische Staatsbank in 1919. On July 1, 1970, it merged with three other banks to form the Norddeutsche Landesbank Girozentrale.

1813 DEPOSIT NOTES ISSUE

Three-quarters of the issue was in 100-thaler notes.

		GOOD	FINE	XF
S171	**10 THALER** 1813. Deposit note.	—	—	—
S172	**20 THALER** 1813. Deposit note.	—	—	—
S173	**50 THALER** 1813. Deposit note.	—	—	—
S174	**100 THALER** 1813. Deposit note.	—	—	—

1842 DEPOSIT NOTES ISSUE

#S175-S177 printer: Gebr. Meyer, Braunschweig.

		GOOD	FINE	XF
S175	**1 THALER** 7.3.1842. W/o embossed stamp. Sign. Lastroy; Kybitz; Zimmerman.	435.00	1000.	1500.
S176	**5 THALER** 7.3.1842. W/o embossed stamp. Sign. Lastroy; Kybitz; Zimmerman.	575.00	1350.	1850.
S177	**20 THALER** 7.3.1842. W/o embossed stamp. Sign. Lastroy; Kybitz; Zimmerman.	575.00	1350.	1850.

1851 DEPOSIT NOTES ISSUE

#S178-S180 like #S175-177 but w/embossed stamp in upper r. corner w/horse, crown and initials *L.C.*

		GOOD	FINE	XF
S178	**1 THALER** 7.3.1842 (1851/52). Embossed stamp at upper r. Sign. Lastroy; Kybitz; Zimmerman.	575.00	1350.	1850.
S179	**5 THALER** 7.3.1842 (1851-52). Embossed stamp at upper r. Sign. Lastroy; Kybitz; Zimmerman.	—	—	—
S180	**20 THALER** 7.3.1842 (1851/52). Embossed stamp at upper r. Sign. Lastroy; Kybitz; Zimmerman.	—	—	—

HERZOGL. BRAUNSCHW.-LÜNEBURG. FINANZ-COLLEGIUM

1858 ISSUE

		GOOD	FINE	XF
S181	**1 THALER** 1.5.1858. Crowned arms at upper left. Stallion at ctr. on back. Sign. Thielau; Hantelmann; Kybitz; Zimmerman.	300.00	600.00	1000.
S182	**10 THALER** 1.5.1858. Sign. Thielau; Hantelmann; Kybitz; Zimmermann.	300.00	600.00	1000.

DARLEHNS-BANK, BRAUNSCHWEIG

BRUNSWICK

1848 ISSUE

An emergency issue of the Darlehnsbankscheinen, similar to the Prussian ones, during the Revolution of 1848. #S185 and S186 notes of the BRAUNSCHW.-LUNEBURG. LEIHHAUS-KOMMISSION w/red ovpt: *DARLEHNS-BANKSCHEIN, GESETZ V. 4.5.1848.*

Printer: Gebr. Meyer, Braunschweig.

		GOOD	FINE	XF
S185	**1 THALER** 4.5.1848. Red ovpt. on #S175. Sign. Lastroy; Kybitz; Zimmerman.	575.00	1350.	1850.
S186	**5 THALER** 4.5.1848. Red ovpt. on #S176. Sign. Lastroy; Kybitz; Zimmerman.	—	—	—

BRAUNSCHWEIGISCHE BANK

Founded 1853. The Brunswick lion on the ten-thaler notes was drawn by Wilhelm von Kaulbach. In 1871 it spun off an affiliate, the Braunschweigische Credit-Anstalt, to carry out the commercial banking activities which it could not do under the restrictions that applies to note-issuing banks. The Braunschweigische Bank refused to submit to the restrictions of the Imperial Law on bank notes of March 1875, so its bank note were good only within the Duchy of Brunswick, but not outside it. It abandoned its right to issue bank notes in 1905; it thereupon absorbed its commercial bank affiliate to form the Braunschweigische Bank und Kreditanstalt AG. In 1922 it entered an IG with the Allgemeine Deutsche Credit-Anstalt of Leipzig (ADCA). In March 1925, ADCA sold the controlling share packet to Braunschweigische Staatsbank, which concluded a new IG. In January 1929 the share packet was sold to Commerz- und Privatbank, which then absorbed the Braunschweigische Bank und Kreditanstalt; the Brunswick institution has a share capital of 5 million Reichsmarks. The Commerz- und Privatbank shortened its name to Commerzbank in March 1940. Temporarily dissolved after World War II, the Commerzbank AG was reconstituted in 1957.

1854 ISSUE

Thaler System

		GOOD	FINE	XF
S189	**10 THALER** 1.5.1854. Black. Printer: Vieweg, Braunschweig.	575.00	1350.	1850.

1856 ISSUE

		GOOD	FINE	XF
S190	**10 THALER** 1.6.1856. Black. Printer: Vieweg, Braunschweig.	725.00	1650.	2500.

1869 ISSUE

		GOOD	FINE	XF
S191	**10 THALER** 1.1.1869. Black on brown; bank at ctr. Lion wearing mural crown and holding sword above jars of money; agriculture at l., commerce at r. Printer: G&D.	300.00	600.00	1000.

1874 ISSUE

Mark System

		GOOD	FINE	XF
S192	**100 MARK** 1.7.1874. Printer G&D.	—	—	—

BREMEN, FREE AND HANSEATIC CITY OF

BREMER BANK

Concession granted by the Bremen Senate, January 31, 1856. It opened for business on July 1, 1856. Its founder and chairman of its administrative board was H. H. Meier, the founder of a leading German shipping line, Norddeutscher Lloyd; his signature appears on the notes. Before 1875, Bremen was the only German state on the gold standard. "Thaler Gold" is an imaginary money of account. The bank abandoned the right to issue bank notes in 1889. It merged into the Dresdner Bank in 1895. It then had a capital of 20 million marks. The Dresdner Bank has continued to use the "Bremer Bank" for some of its branches in that city. Temporarily dissolved after World War II, the Dresdner Bank AG was reconstituted in 1957.

1856 ISSUE

Gold Thaler System

		GOOD	FINE	XF
S196	**5 THALER GOLD** 1.10.1856. Sign. Meier; Renken.	575.00	1150.	1450.
S197	**10 THALER GOLD** 1.10.1856. Arms of Bremen at top ctr. Tyche holding kep and mappa on back. Sign. Meier; Renken.	575.00	1150.	1450.
S198	**25 THALER GOLD** 1.10.1856. Mercury (commerce) and mermaid (navigation) flanking arms of Bremen. Sign. Meier; Renken.	—	—	—
S199	**100 THALER GOLD** 1.10.1856.	—	—	—

1863 ISSUE

		GOOD	FINE	XF
S200	**10 THALER GOLD** 1.7.1863.	—	—	—
S201	**20 THALER GOLD** 1.7.1863.	—	—	—
S202	**50 THALER GOLD** 1.7.1863.	—	—	—
S203	**100 THALER GOLD** 1.12.1863.	—	—	—

1870 ISSUE

Courant Thaler System

#S204-S205 printer: G. Hunckel, Bremen.

		GOOD	FINE	XF
S204	**5 THALER COURANT** 14.2.1870. Sign. Meier; Renken.	575.00	1350.	1850.
S205	**10 THALER COURANT** 14.2.1870. Arms of Bremen at top ctr. Tyche holding key and mappa on back. Denomination printed in orange. Sign. Meier; Renken.	575.00	1350.	1850.

1872 ISSUE

Mark System

		GOOD	FINE	XF
S208	**20 MARK** 1.7.1872. Mercury (commerce) and mermaid (navigation) flank denomination in circle and wreath on back. Sign. Meier; Renken.	400.00	850.00	1350.

		GOOD	FINE	XF
S209	**100 MARK** 1.7.1872. Mercury (commerce) and mermaid (navigation) flank arms of Bremen on back. Sign. Meier; Renken.	600.00	1400.	1950.

FRANKFURT/MAIN, FREE CITY OF

RECHNEI-UND RENTENAMT

1826-54 ISSUE

		GOOD	FINE	XF
S211	**500 GULDEN** Black.			
	a. 1826-40. Printer: Andreas'sche Buchdruckerei.	—	—	—
	b. 1841-4.1848. Printer: Benjamin Krebs.	—	—	—
	c. 11.1848-1854. Printer: C. Krebs-Schmitt.	—	—	—

FRANKFURTER BANK

Founded 1854, to pre-empt the plans of the Bank für Handel und Industrie of Darmstadt (the Darmstädter Bank) to found a note-issuing bank on Frankfurt's doorstep. The Darmstädter Bank's plans resulted in the founding of the Bank für Süddeutschland in 1856. The Frankfurter Bank gave up its right to issue bank notes on March 26, 1901. It merged with the Berliner Handels-Gessellschaft to form the Berliner Handels-Gesellschaft und Frankfurter Bank, September 1, 1970. On June 5, 1975, it shortened its name to the Berliner Handels- und Frankfurter Bank. In May 1995 it shortened its name further to the BHF-BANK AG.

Printer for all issues: Dondorf & Naumann, Frankfurt/Main.

1855; 1870 ISSUE

Gulden System

		GOOD	FINE	XF
S214	**5 GULDEN** 1.1.1855. Brown and blue. Woman at l. and r. (Francofordia) cancelled.	300.00	600.00	1000.

		GOOD	FINE	XF
S215	**10 GULDEN** 1.1.1855.	300.00	600.00	1000.

		GOOD	FINE	XF
S216	**35 GULDEN** 1.1.1855. Brown and blue. Full-faced portrait of Francofordia at ctr., in profile above at l. and r.	575.00	1350.	1850.

		GOOD	FINE	XF
S217	**50 GULDEN** 1.1.1855. Like #S215.			
	a. Issued note.	575.00	1350.	1850.
	b. Punched hole cancelled.	400.00	800.00	1600.
S218	**100 GULDEN** 1.1.1855. Like #S215.	725.00	1650.	2500.

		GOOD	FINE	XF
S219	**500 GULDEN** 1.1.1855. Like #S215.			
	a. Issued note.	725.00	1650.	2500.
	b. Punched hole cancelled.	500.00	950.00	1650.
S220	**500 GULDEN** 25.7.1870. Deposit certificate.	725.00	1650.	2500.

1874 ISSUE

Mark System

		GOOD	FINE	XF
S223	**100 MARK** 1.1.1874.			

		GOOD	FINE	XF
	a. Issued note.	600.00	1400.	1950.

		GOOD	FINE	XF
	b. Punched hole cancelled.	425.00	1000.	1500.
S224	**500 MARK** 1.1.1874.			
	a. Issued note.	650.00	1500.	2200.
	b. Punched hole cancelled.	450.00	1050.	1550.
S225	**1000 MARK** 1.1.1874.			
	a. Issued note.	800.00	1750.	2750.
	b. Punched hole cancelled.	550.00	1300.	1750.

1890 ISSUE

		GOOD	FINE	XF
S226	**100 MARK** 1.8.1890.			
	a. Issued note.	800.00	1750.	2750.
	b. Punched hole cancelled.	550.00	1300.	1750.

		GOOD	FINE	XF
S227	**1000 MARK** 1.8.1890.			
	a. Issued note.	800.00	1750.	2750.
	b. Punched hole cancelled.	550.00	1300.	1750.

HAMBURG, FREE AND HANSEATIC CITY OF

NORDDEUTSCHE BANK

Founded 1856. In 1857 it printed up bills of exchange designed to circulate as bank notes, but they were not issued because of the crisis of 1857. In 1865 it again tried to issue these bills, but opposition of the Hamburg Diet and subsequent legislation restricting bank note issues by the North German Confederation meant the bills had a very limited circulation. The bills were payable three days after sight, which would make them "post notes" in the US banking system. The Norddeutsche Bank merged with Disconto-Gesellschaft, 1895, but continued to operate as a subsidiary under its own name. It ceased to operate independently when it merged into the Deutsche Bank und Disconto-Gesellschaft, October 1929, which shortened its name in 1937 to the Deutsche Bank. Temporarily dissolved after World War II, the Deutsche Bank AG was reconstituted in 1957.

1857 BILLS OF EXCHANGE ISSUE

Circulated as bank notes.

		GOOD	FINE	XF
S231	**10 THALER** 1857 (1865).	—	—	—
S232	**25 THALER** 1857 (1865).	—	—	—

HANNOVER, KINGDOM OF

MAGISTRAT DER KÖNIGL. RESIDENZSTADT

Since Hannover refused to submit to the terms of the Reichsbank law, after 1876 its notes were valid only within the cities of Hannover and Hildesheim. The city lost its right to issue bank notes in 1906.

1846 TREASURY NOTES ISSUE

Thaler System

		GOOD	FINE	XF
S235	**1 THALER** 7.12.1846.			
	a. Brown on yellowish paper.	300.00	600.00	1000.
	b. Black on yellowish paper.	300.00	600.00	1000.

		GOOD	FINE	XF
S236	**5 THALER** 7.12.1846.			
	a. Brown on reddish paper.	575.00	1350.	1850.
	b. Black on reddish paper.	575.00	1350.	1850.

1874 TREASURY NOTES ISSUE

Mark System

		GOOD	FINE	XF
S239	**100 MARK** ND (1874).			
	a. Blue.	800.00	1450.	2900.
	b. Green. Proof.	—	—	—

HANNOVERSCHE BANK

Concession granted July 22, 1856; opened for business January 2, 1857. It gave up the right to issue bank notes in 1889. The Deutsche Bank invested in it and concluded an IG in 1898, which later culminated in a complete merger into the Deutsche Bank. Temperoraily dissolved after World War II, the Deutsche Bank AGF was reconstituted in 1957.

1857 ISSUE

Thaler System

#S241-S244 Printer: G&D.

		GOOD	FINE	XF
S241	**10 THALER** 1.3.1857.	300.00	600.00	1000.

		GOOD	FINE	XF
S242	**20 THALER** 1.3.1857. Commerce and industry at l., agriculture at r. Arms at ctr., red *20* printed three times on back.	300.00	600.00	1000.
S243	**50 THALER** 1.3.1857.	575.00	1350.	1850.

		GOOD	FINE	XF
S244	**100 THALER** 1.3.1857.	575.00	1350.	1850.

1871 ISSUE

		GOOD	FINE	XF
S245	**10 THALER** 1.7.1871. Printer: G&D.	575.00	1350.	1850.

1874 ISSUE

Mark System

		GOOD	FINE	XF
S248	**100 MARK** 1.1.1874. Printer: G&D.	575.00	1350.	1850.

HESSE-DARMSTADT, GRAND DUCHY OF

GROSSHERZOGL. HESSISCHE STAATSSCHULDEN-TILGUNGSKASSE

1848 ISSUE

Printers: C. Naumann, Frankfurt/Main, and R.L. Venator, Darmstadt.

		GOOD	FINE	XF
S251	**1 GULDEN** 1.9.1848. Sign. Schenck; Hombergk.	300.00	600.00	1000.

		GOOD	FINE	XF
S252	**5 GULDEN** 1.9.1848. Sign. Schenck; Hombergk.	575.00	1350.	1850.
S253	**10 GULDEN** 1.9.1848. Sign. Schenck; Hombergk.	—	—	—
S254	**35 GULDEN** 1.9.1848. Sign. Schenck; Hombergk.	—	—	—
S255	**70 GULDEN** 1.9.1848. Sign. Schenck; Hombergk.	—	—	—

1852 ISSUE

#S256-S259 printers: C. Naumann, Frankfurt/Main, and R. L. Venator, Darmstadt.

		GOOD	FINE	XF
S256	**1 GULDEN** 28.2.1852. Sign. Eckhardt; Rabenau.	435.00	1000.	1500.
S257	**5 GULDEN** 28.2.1852. Sign. Eckhardt; Rabenau.	575.00	1350.	1850.

		Good	Fine	XF
S258	**10 Gulden** 28.2.1852. Sign. Eckhardt; Rabenau.	575.00	1350.	1850.
S259	**35 Gulden** 28.2.1852. Sign. Eckhardt; Rabenau.	—	—	—

1854 Issue

#S260-S262 printers: C. Naumann, Frankfurt/Main, and R. L. Venator, Darmstadt.

		Good	Fine	XF
S260	**1 Gulden** 11.11.1854. Sign. Eckhardt; Breidenbach.	300.00	600.00	1000.
S261	**5 Gulden** 11.11.1854. Sign. Eckhardt; Breidenbach.	—	—	—
S262	**10 Gulden** 11.11.1854. Sign. Eckhardt; Breidenbach.	575.00	1350.	1850.

1855 Issue

#S263-S266 printer: C.Naumann, Frankfurt/Main, and R. L. Venator, Darmstadt.

		Good	Fine	XF
S263	**1 Gulden** 1.11.1855. Sign. Eckhardt; Breidenbach.	435.00	1000.	1500.
S264	**5 Gulden** 1.11.1855. Sign. Eckhardt; Breidenbach.	575.00	1350.	1850.
S265	**10 Gulden** 1.11.1855. Sign. Eckhardt; Breidenbach.	575.00	1350.	1850.
S266	**35 Gulden** 1.11.1855. Sign. Eckhardt; Breidenbach.	—	—	—

1865 Issue

#S267-S270 printer: G&D.

		Good	Fine	XF
S267	**1 Gulden** 1.7.1865. Blue and black. Two medallions, Hassia at l., commerce, agriculture and industry at r. Orange unpt. on back. Sign. Eckhardt; Hesse.	235.00	500.00	800.00
S268	**5 Gulden** 1.7.1865. Sign. Eckhardt; Hesse.	300.00	600.00	1000.
S269	**10 Gulden** 1.7.1865. Sign. Eckhardt; Hesse.	575.00	1350.	1850.
S270	**50 Gulden** 1.7.1865. Sign. Eckhardt; Hesse.	725.00	1650.	2500.

Bank für Süddeutschland

Founded 1855. A note-issuing bank that was closely linked to the bank Für Handel und Industrie of Darmstadt (the Darmstädter Bank). It merged with the Darmstädter Bank in 1902 and abandoned its right to issue bank notes. The Darmstädter Bank merged to form the Darmstädter-Nationalbank, 1922 (Danat-Bank). The Danat-Bank's suspension of payments on July 13, 1931 commenced the German banking crisis. The government merged the Danat-Bank into the Dresdner Bank in 1932. Temporarily dissolved after World War II, the Dresdner Bank AG was reconstituted in 1957.

1856 Issue

Gulden Thaler System

#S276-S277 printer: C. Naumann, Frankfurt/Main

		Good	Fine	XF
S276	**10 Gulden** 1.7.1856.	575.00	1350.	1850.
S277	**10 Thaler** 1.7.1856.	575.00	1350.	1850.

#S278-S283 printer: Maximilian Frommann, Darmstadt

		Good	Fine	XF
S278	**25 Gulden** 1.12.1856.	725.00	1650.	2500.
S279	**50 Gulden** 1.12.1856.	725.00	1650.	2500.
S280	**100 Gulden** 1.12.1856.	725.00	1650.	2500.
S281	**25 Thaler** 1.12.1856.	725.00	1650.	2500.
S282	**50 Thaler** 1.12.1856.	725.00	1650.	2500.
S283	**100 Thaler** 1.12.1856.	725.00	1650.	2500.

1857 Issue

		Good	Fine	XF
S284	**10 Thaler** 21.3.1857. Printer: C. Naumann, Frankfurt/Main.	435.00	1000.	1500.

1870 Issue

		Good	Fine	XF
S285	**10 Gulden** 2.1.1870. Putti at lower l. and lower r. Tyche at ctr. on back. Printer: G&D.	435.00	1000.	1500.
S286	**25 Gulden** 2.1.1870. Printer: G&D.	575.00	1350.	1850.

1874 Issue

Mark System

		Good	Fine	XF
S287	**100 Mark** 1.1.1874. Printer: G&D.	600.00	1400.	1950.

Hesse-Homburg, Landgraviate of

Landgräflich Hessische Concessionirte Landesbank

Founded August 1854. Its opening was delayed because of the monetary stringency during the Crimean War, so it did not open for business until January 2, 1855. By 1900 the Frankfurt private bank of von Erlanger und Söhne had an IG with this bank. This IG then passed to the Dresdner Bank after the Dresdner Bank took over the Erlanger firm in 1904. The Landgräflich Hessische Concessionirte Landesbank merged into the Dresdner bank in 1929. Temporarily disolved after World War II, the Dresdner Bank AG was reconstituted in 1957.

1855 Issue

#S291-S292 Printer: C. Naumann, Frankfurt/Main

		GOOD	FINE	XF
S291	**5 GULDEN** 1.1.1855. Female profiles at l. and r., Same on back in mirror image.	300.00	600.00	1000.
S292	**10 GULDEN** 1.1.1855.	435.00	1000.	1500.

HESSE-CASSEL, ELECTORATE OF

KURFÜRSTLICH HESSISCHE DIREKTION DER HAUPT-STAATS-KASSE

1848 ISSUE

#S295-S297 printers: Dondorf, Frankfurt/Main and Theodor Fischer, Kassel

		GOOD	FINE	XF
S295	**1 THALER** 26.8.1848.	300.00	600.00	1000.
S296	**5 THALER** 26.8.1848.	435.00	1000.	1500.
S297	**20 THALER** 26.8.1848.	—	—	—

1849 ISSUE

#298-S300 printers: Dondorf, Frankfurt/Main and Theodor Fischer, Kassel

		GOOD	FINE	XF
S298	**1 THALER** 24.3.1849. Sign. Schotten; Stern; Schmerfeld.	235.00	500.00	800.00
S299	**5 THALER** 24.3.1849. Sign. Schotten; Stern; Schmerfeld.	—	—	—
S300	**20 THALER** 24.3.1849. Sign. Schotten; Stern; Schmerfeld.	—	—	—

In 1866 a new issue was being printed in 1866 at Giesecke & Devrient in Leipzig when the Prussian troops occupied the city. After the end of the war, when Hesse-Cassel was annexed by Prussia, the notes were entirely destroyed by Giesecke & Devrient.

KURHESSISCHE LEIH- UND COMMERZBANK, KASSEL

Established June 1721, it was one of the oldest banks in Germany. Little is known of its history because it was required to conduct its business with absolute secrecy. It collapsed during the crisis of 1859. Its notes were redeemed by the Electoral Hessian government in 1864 for half their face value.

1850 ISSUE

		GOOD	FINE	XF
S306	**1 THALER** 1.5.1850.	250.00	550.00	950.00

1855 ISSUE

		GOOD	FINE	XF
S307	**10 THALER** 1.5.1855. Putti representing commerce and industry at l. and r. Male portrait at l., Johann Gutenberg at r. on back. Printer: Theodor Fischer, Cassel.	150.00	300.00	550.00

LÜBECK, FREE AND HANSEATIC CITY OF

COMMERZ-BANK IN LÜBECK

COMMERCE BANK IN LÜBECK

Founded in 1856 as the Credit- und Verischerungsbank, Lübeck, with the assistance of the Allgemeine Deutsche Credit-Anstalt (ACDA). It opened for business on September 19, 1856. It lost money on its insurance business and had to carry out several capital reductions at the insistence of ADCA. Because of the losses, the 1858 note issue (S316-318) was never placed in circulation. After abandoning the insurance business, it changed its name to the Commerz-Bank in Lübeck on June 1, 1859. In 1871 it spun off an affiliate, the Lübecker Bank, to engage in commercial banking without the restrictions which were imposed on banks of issue. After the collapse of its Berlin redemption office in 1886, an extraordinary general meeting voted to surrender the note-issuing privilege. The Lübecker Bank was thereupon re-absorbed by the Commerzbank in Lübeck. In March 1940 the Berlin Commerz- und privatbank shortened its name to Commerzbank. To avoid confusion with the larger competitor, the Commerz-Bank in Lübeck changed its name to the Handelsbank in Lübeck in July 1940. It changed its name to the Deutsche Bank Lübeck AG on January 1, 1989. The Deutsche Bank AG owns nearly 94% of the shares.

1865 ISSUE

Thaler System

		GOOD	FINE	XF
S311	**10 THALER** 1.7.1865 (1866). Black on green unpt., Commerce and industry at l. and r. Back brown, bank name and denomination. Sign. Rehder; Crome; Possehl; Wolpmann; Borries.	60.00	150.00	350.00

No.	Description	Good	Fine	XF
S312	**20 Thaler** 1.7.1865 (1866). Back blue; bank name and denomination. Sign: Rehder; Crome; Posseh1; Wolpmann; Borries.	120.00	250.00	500.00
S313	**100 Thaler** 1.7.1865 (1866). Sign. Rehder; Crome; Posseh1; Wolpmann; Borries.	235.00	500.00	800.00

An issue of 1871, printed by H. G. Rahtgens in Lübeck, may exist.

1875 Issue

Mark system

No.	Description	Good	Fine	XF
S314	**100 Mark** 1.1.1875. Printer: G&D.	—	—	—

Credit-und Versicherungsbank, Lübeck

Credit and Insurance Bank

Founded 1856. It took over the business of the Privat-Disconto-und Darlehen-Kasse zu Lübeck. It abandoned the right to issue bank notes in 1875.

1858 Issue

#S316-S318 were never placed in circulation. Printer: G&D.

No.	Description	Good	Fine	XF
S316	**20 Thaler** 2.1.1858.	575.00	1350.	1850.
S317	**50 Thaler** 2.1.1858.	575.00	1350.	1850.
S318	**100 Thaler** 2.1.1858.	575.00	1350.	1850.

Lübecker Privatbank

Lübeck Private Bank

Founded 1856. It took over the business of the Privat-Disconto- und Darlehen-Kasse zu Lübeck. It abandoned the right to issue bank notes in 1875.

1856-57 Issue

Thaler System

No.	Description	Good	Fine	XF
S321	**10 Thaler** 2.1.1856.	—	—	—
S322	**20 Thaler** 2.1.1856.	—	—	—
S323	**100 Thaler** 2.1.1856.	—	—	—
S324	**200 Thaler** 2.1.1857.	—	—	—

1875 Issue

Mark System

No.	Description	Good	Fine	XF
S325	**100 Mark** 1.1.1875. Printer: G&D.	—	—	—

Note: #S325 was not placed into circulation.

Privat-Disconto-und Darlehen-Kasse zu Lübeck

Founded 1820. It was converted into the Lübecker Privatbank in 1856.

1819 Issue

No.	Description	Good	Fine	XF
S328	**100-1000 Mark Courant** (From 1819.)	—	—	—

Mecklenburg-Schwerin, Grand Duchy of

Renterei-Kassenscheine

1868-69 Issue

2% interest-bearing revenue office bills.

No.	Description	Good	Fine	XF
S331	**25 Thaler** 1868-69.	—	—	—
S332	**50 Thaler** 1868-69.	—	—	—
S333	**100 Thaler** 1868-69.	—	—	—

1870 Issue

No.	Description	Good	Fine	XF
S334	**10 Thaler** 1.6.1870. Sign. Müller.	575.00	1350.	1850.
S335	**25 Thaler** 1.6.1870. Sign. Müller.	575.00	1350.	1850.
S336	**50 Thaler** 1.6.1870. Sign. Müller.	575.00	1350.	1850.

Rostocker Bank

Bank of Rostock

Founded 1850. The bank abandoned the right to issue bank notes on July 11, 1877. In 1898 it tried to merge into another bank, but the shareholders blocked this out of Mecklenburg particularism. In April 1933 it was absorbed by the Mecklenburgische Depositen- und Wechselbank.

1850 Issue

Thaler System

No.	Description	Good	Fine	XF
S337	**10 Thaler** 1.7.1850.	—	—	—
S338	**20 Thaler** 1.7.1850.	—	—	—
S339	**50 Thaler** 1.7.1850.	—	—	—
S340	**100 Thaler** 1.7.1850.	—	—	—

1862 Issue

#S341-S344 printer: G&D.

No.	Description	Good	Fine	XF
S341	**10 Thaler** 1.3.1862.	575.00	1350.	1850.
S342	**20 Thaler** 1.3.1862.	575.00	1350.	1850.
S343	**50 Thaler** 1.3.1862.	575.00	1350.	1850.
S344	**100 Thaler** 1.3.1862.	575.00	1350.	1850.

1866 Issue

#S345-S348 printer: G&D.

No.	Description	Good	Fine	XF
S345	**10 Thaler** 28.7.1866.	—	—	—
S346	**20 Thaler** 28.7.1866.	—	—	—
S347	**50 Thaler** 28.7.1866.	—	—	—
S348	**100 Thaler** 28.7.1866.	—	—	—

1874 Issue

Mark System

No.	Description	Good	Fine	XF
S349	**100 Mark** 1.1.1874. Printer: G&D.	400.00	850.00	1350.

Mecklenburg-Strelitz, Grand Duchy of

Rentei-Cassenscheine

1866 Issue

No.	Description	Good	Fine	XF
S351	**5 Thaler** 1.6.1866. Sign. Voss; Engel.	725.00	1500.	2250.
S352	**10 Thaler** 1.6.1866. Sign. Voss; Engel.	—	—	—
S353	**25 Thaler** 1.6.1866. Sign. Voss; Engel.	—	—	—

1869 Issue

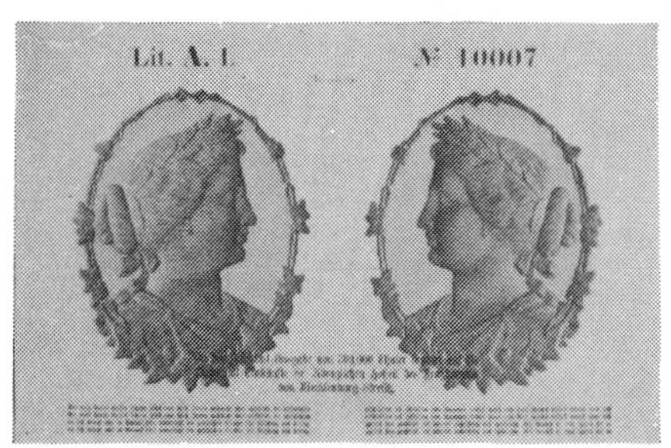

		GOOD	FINE	XF
S354	5 THALER 1.6.1869. Sign. Voss; Engel.	—	—	1150.
S355	10 THALER 1.6.1869. Sign. Voss; Engel.	—	—	1150.
S356	25 THALER 1.6.1869. Sign. Voss; Engel.	—	—	—

NASSAU, DUCHY OF

NASSAUISCHE LANDES-CREDIT-KASSE

NASSAU REGIONAL CREDIT OFFICE, WIESBADEN

A note-issuing institution set up in response to the demands of local business for a more elastic circulating medium. It was set up by a ducal decree on January 22, 1840. In 1849 its business was taken over by the Nassauische Landesbank.

1840 ISSUE

#S361-S362 printer: C. Naumann, Frankfurt/Main.

		GOOD	FINE	XF
S361	1 GULDEN 3.12.1840 (7.1841).	575.00	1350.	1850.

		GOOD	FINE	XF
S362	5 GULDEN 3.12.1840 (7.1841).	575.00	1350.	1850.

1841 ISSUE

#S363-S365 printer: C. Naumann, Frankfurt/Main.

		GOOD	FINE	XF
S363	1 GULDEN 15.6.1841.	575.00	1350.	1850.
S364	5 GULDEN 15.6.1841.	—	—	—
S365	25 GULDEN 15.6.1841.	—	—	—

1847 ISSUE

#366-S368 printer: C. Naumann, Frankfurt/Main.

		GOOD	FINE	XF
S366	1 GULDEN 12.8.1847.	300.00	600.00	1000.
S367	5 GULDEN 12.8.1847.	435.00	1000.	1500.
S368	25 GULDEN 12.8.1847.	575.00	1350.	1850.

1848 ISSUE

#S369-S370A printer: C. Naumann, Frankfurt/Main.

		GOOD	FINE	XF
S369	1 GULDEN 26.2.1848.	—	—	—
S370	5 GULDEN 26.2.1848.	—	—	—
S370A	25 GULDEN 26.2.1848.	—	—	—

NASSAUISCHE LANDESBANK, WIESBADEN

NASSAU REGIONAL BANK, WIESBADEN

Founded February 16, 1849. Opened for business, April 1, 1849. It was the legal successor to the Nassauische Landes-Credit-Kasse. After Prussia annexed Nassau in 1866, it cancelled the bank's right to issue bank notes and and redeemed them in exchange for Prussian treasury vouchers. On June 1, 1953, it merged with the Hessische Landesbak Girozentrale & Landeskreditkasse zu Kassel to form the Hessische Landesbank-Girozentrale. On July 1, 1992 this became the Landesbank Hessen-Thüringen Girozentrale.

1856-59 ISSUE

		GOOD	FINE	XF
S371	5 GULDEN 12.8.1856. Sign. Reuter; Brück; Rössler. Back sign. Weimar.	235.00	500.00	800.00
S372	25 GULDEN 12.8.1856. Sign. Reuter; Brück; Rössler. Back sign. Weimar.	575.00	1350.	1850.

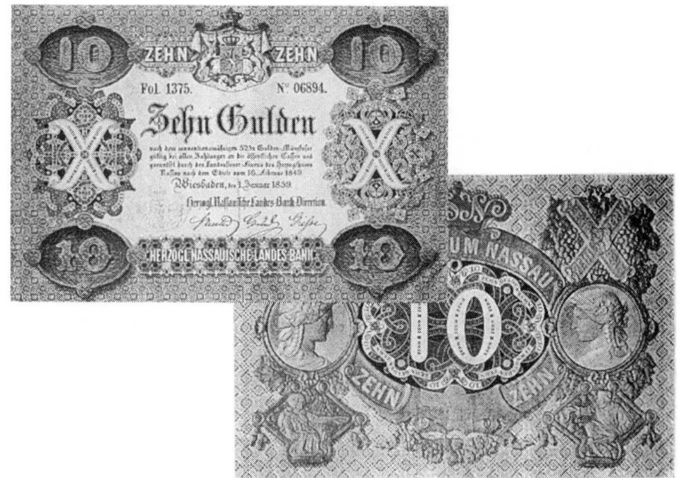

		GOOD	FINE	XF
S373	10 GULDEN 1.1.1859. Black. Back brown and blue. Sign. Reuter; Brück; Geisse. Printer: C. Naumann, Frankfurt/Main.	435.00	1000.	1500.

1865 ISSUE

		GOOD	FINE	XF
S374	5 GULDEN 24.7.1865. Sign. Hergenhahn; Langen; Wirth.	435.00	1000.	1500.
S375	50 GULDEN 24.7.1865. Sign. Hergenhahn; Langen; Wirth.	725.00	1650.	2500.

OLDENBURG, GRAND DUCHY OF

GROSSHERZOGL. OLDENBURG. STAATSMINISTERIUM

GRAND DUCHY OLDENBURG STATE MINISTRY

Since these notes were paid out by the Oldenburgische Landesbank, they could be considered bank notes rather than legal tender paper money.

1869 ISSUE

		GOOD	FINE	XF
S377	**5 THALER** 1.1.1869. Black on orange unpt. Themis holding mappa, fasces and shield at l., Commerce at r. Sign. Zedelius; Tebbenjohanns.	300.00	600.00	1000.

		GOOD	FINE	XF
S378	**10 THALER** 1.1.1869. Sign. Zedelius; Tebbenjohanns.	300.00	600.00	1000.

OLDENBURGISCHE LANDESBANK

OLDENBURG STATE BANK

Opened for business on January 15, 1869. In December 1875 it abandoned its note-issuing privilege. By 1900 the Frankfurt private bank of van Erlanger und Söhne had an IG with this bank. This IG then passed to the Dresdner Bank after the Dresdner bank took over the Erlanger firm in 1904. At that time the Oldenburgische Landesbank had a share capital of 3 million marks. It is still nominally independent, although the Dresdner Bank owns 63.1% of the shares.

1875 ISSUE

		GOOD	FINE	XF
S381	**100 MARK** 1.4.1875. Printer: Reichsdruckerei.	575.00	1350.	1850.

DEUTSCHE VOLKSBANK, EUTIN

GERMAN PEOPLES BANK, EUTIN

Founded August 1869 by Carl Baurmeister who issued shares with the very small par value of 20 thalers. He sold them to many people by promising them 10% dividends for the first year and 12-15% thereafter - a classic *Ponzi* scheme. The institution was supposed to be a small local institution to foster the saving habits of the working class. Most *Volksbanken* in Germany grew out of Schulze-Delitzsch's co-operative movement and have working class betterment as their primary object. Baurmeister issued paper money which he called deposit notes. He had the notes circulated by agents far out into the countryside. Baurmeister's fraudulent financial empire soon collapsed. Baurmeister was arrested and convicted of fraud and embezzlement in September 1872. He was sent to prison for two years and lost his civil rights for four. The notes of the Deutsche Volksbank of Eutin became worthless. The signature of the criminal Baurmeister appears at the lower right on the notes.

1870 DEPOSIT NOTES ISSUE

		GOOD	FINE	XF
S386	**10 THALER** 20.5.1870.	115.00	250.00	400.00
S387	**25 THALER** 20.5.1870.	100.00	220.00	350.00
S388	**50 THALER** 20.5.1870.	—	—	—
S389	**100 THALER** 20.5.1870.	—	—	—

PRUSSIA, KINGDOM OF

TRESORSCHEINE

Printed in 1804 by Hayn in the building of the Seehandlung on presses obtained from the Decker'sche Geheime Ober-Hofbuchdruckerei. The notes were issued in 1806, and were redeemable at any time into silver coin at the offices of the Bank of Prussia in Berlin, Breslau, Elbing, Königsberg, Stettin, Münster, Fürth and at the office of the Seehandlung in Warsaw. The latter two redemption offices indicate that at this period Prussian territory included Ansbach-Bayreuth (Franconia) and central Poland ("New Prussia").

1806 TREASURY NOTES ISSUE

		GOOD	FINE	XF
S391	**5 THALER** ND (1806). Sign. Schulenburg; Stein.	150.00	300.00	600.00
S392	**50 THALER** ND (1806). Sign. Schulenburg; Stein.	—	—	—
S393	**100 THALER** ND (1806). Sign. Schulenburg; Stein.	—	—	—
S394	**250 THALER** ND (1806). Sign. Schulenburg; Stein.	—	—	—

1809 TREASURY NOTES ISSUE

		GOOD	FINE	XF
S395	**1 THALER** ND (1809). Sign. Altenstein.			
	a. Ovpt: *REALISATIONS-COMPTOIR ZU BERLIN.*	100.00	220.00	350.00
	b. Ovpt: *REALISATIONS-COMPTOIR ZU BRESLAU.*	100.00	220.00	350.00

		GOOD	FINE	XF
	c. Ovpt: *REALISATIONS-COMPTOIR ZU KONIGSBERG.*	235.00	500.00	800.00

HAUPTVERWALTUNG DER STAATS-SCHULDEN

MAIN ADMINISTRATION OF GOVERNMENT DEBTS

The name of Prussian legal tender paper money was changed from *Tresor-Schein* to *Cassen-Anweisung* after lawyers for alleged counterfeiters in England convinced the English courts that *Schein* meant *Splendor* and that therefore their clients were not guilty of forging a monetary instrument. This legal decision explains why many German notes also bear the term *treasury bill* in English. Printers: Professor Frick (engraving) and Decker'sche Geheime Ober-Hofbuchdruckerei (letterpress).

1824 ISSUE

		GOOD	FINE	XF
S396	**1 THALER** 6.5.1824.	100.00	220.00	350.00

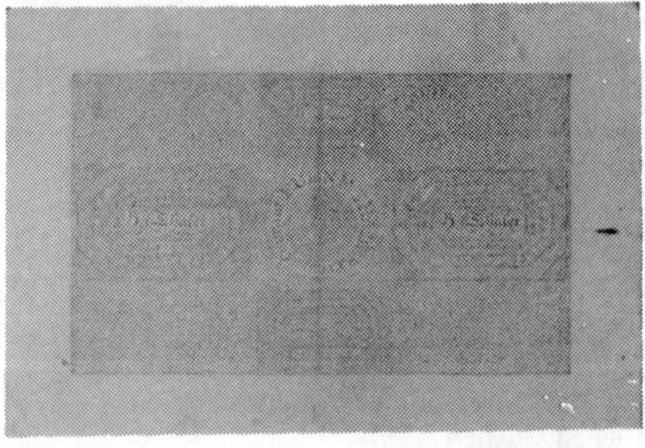

		GOOD	FINE	XF
S397	**5 THALER** 6.5.1824.	130.00	260.00	450.00
S398	**50 THALER** 6.5.1824.	—	—	—

1834 ISSUE

		GOOD	FINE	XF
S398A	**1 THALER COURANT** 1.1.1834. Black. Crowned and mantled arms with wildman supporters at upper ctr.	—	—	—

1835 ISSUE

		GOOD	FINE	XF
S399	**1 THALER** 2.1.1835.	110.00	220.00	350.00

		GOOD	FINE	XF
S400	**5 THALER** 2.1.1835.	235.00	500.00	800.00
S401	**50 THALER** 2.1.1835.	—	—	—
S402	**100 THALER** 2.1.1835.	—	—	—

		GOOD	FINE	XF
S403	**500 THALER** 2.1.1835. Proof.	—	—	—

1851 ISSUE

#S404-S408 printer: Preussische Staatsdruckerei.

		GOOD	FINE	XF
S404	**1 THALER** 2.11.1851. Sign. Natan; Köhler; Rolcke; Gamet. Printer: Preussische Staatsdruckerei.	110.00	220.00	350.00
S405	**5 THALER** 2.11.1851. Crowned and mantled arms w/wildman supporters. Oak and laurel branches at l. and r. Two putti flanking eagle on back. Sign. Natan; Köhler; Rolcke; Gamet.	235.00	500.00	800.00
S406	**10 THALER** 2.11.1851. Crowned shield in order collar flanked by two angels. Two seated angels flanking crowned monogram, denomination and order collar. Sign. Natan; Köhler; Rolcke; Gamet.	—	—	—
S407	**50 THALER** 2.11.1851. Eagle at l. standing on Roman helmet, all within oak wreath. Female seated on throne flanked by two youth standardbearers on back. Sign. Natan; Köhler; Rolcke; Gamet.	—	—	—
S408	**100 THALER** 2.11.1851. Crowned and mantled shield at left with wildman supporters. Two females seated on throne, two putti flanking on back. Sign. Natan; Köhler; Rolcke; Gamet.	—	—	—

1856 ISSUE

#S409-S410 printer: Preussische Staatsdruckerei.

		GOOD	FINE	XF
S409	**1 THALER** 15.12.1856. Black on blue, red, yellow, green and brown unpt. Sign. Natan; Gamet, Nobiling; Günther. Unpt. is a warning of the penalties for counterfeiting. Putti representing agriculture at l. and commerce at r. on back.	60.00	150.00	250.00

		GOOD	FINE	XF
S410	**5 THALER** 15.12.1856. Sign. Natan; Gamet; Nobiling; Günther.	85.00	175.00	275.00

1861 ISSUE

		GOOD	FINE	XF
S411	**1 THALER** 13.2.1861. Sign. Gamet; Günther; Löwe. Printer: Preussische Staatsdruckerei.	50.00	120.00	220.00

HAUPTVERWALTUNG DER DARLEHNSKASSEN

MAIN ADMINISTRATION OF STATE LOAN BANKS

Darlehenskassenscheinen **- loan notes - are a special emergency currency, invented by David Hansemann to provide liquidity during the revolution of 1848. They were issued to businessmen against up to three-quarters of the value of their inventories. The first Darlehenskasse opened in Berlin on May 29, 1848. They were issued during the liquidity crisis caused by the revolution of 1848-9, the wars of 1866, 1870 and 1914, and a flood in 1868. The issue of 1914 will be found in volume 2, General Issues.**

1848 ISSUE

		GOOD	FINE	XF
S416	**1 THALER** 15.4.1848. Black on yellow-brown unpt. Sign. Lamprecht; Rabe; Meyen; Woywod.	115.00	250.00	400.00
S417	**5 THALER** 15.4.1848. Black on gray unpt. Sign. Lamprecht; Rabe; Meyen; Woywod.	300.00	600.00	1000.

1866 ISSUE

Issued after the Prussian Landtag had been suspended. The ostensible reason was the mobilization of the Prussian Army and the Overend, Gurney crisis in Britain. It seemed more probable that this was one of Bismarck's methods of raising money when he was denied it during the Prussian Constitutional Conflict; hocking shares of the Cologne-Minden Railroad Company was another. When it re-assembled, the Landtag declared the issue illegal. The issue was legalized after the government asked the Landtag for an indemnity and the Landtag granted it. Printers: Preussische Staatsdruckerei, C. Ringer, and C. Schellenberg.

		GOOD	FINE	XF
S418	**1 THALER** 18/19.5.1866. Sign. Dechend; Scheller; Mendelssohn-Bartholdy; Böse. Control Commission: Costenoble; Conrad; Dehnicke.	115.00	250.00	400.00
S419	**5 THALER** 18/19.5.1866. Sign. Dechend; Scheller; Mendelssohn-Bartholdy; Böse. Control Commission: Costenoble; Conrad; Dehnicke.	300.00	600.00	1000.

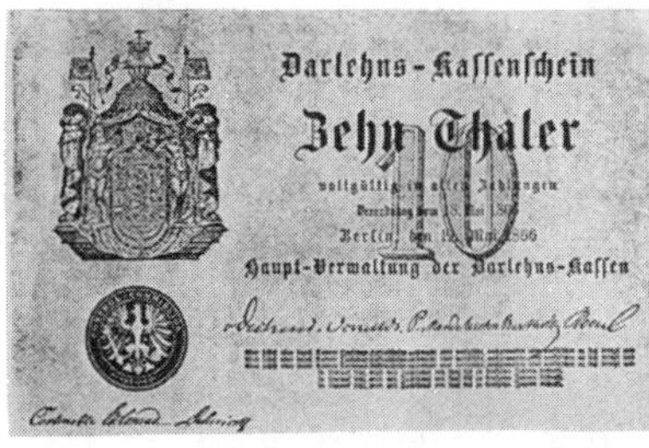

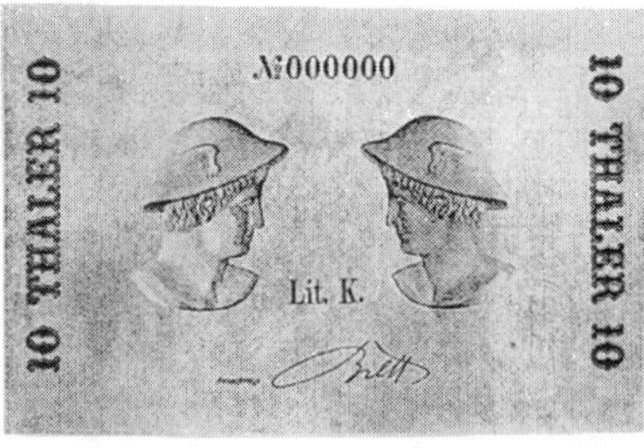

		GOOD	FINE	XF
S420	**10 THALER** 18/19.5.1866. Sign. Dechend; Scheller; Mendelssohn-Bartholdy; Böse. Control Commission: Costenoble; Conrad; Dehnicke.	435.00	1000.	1500.

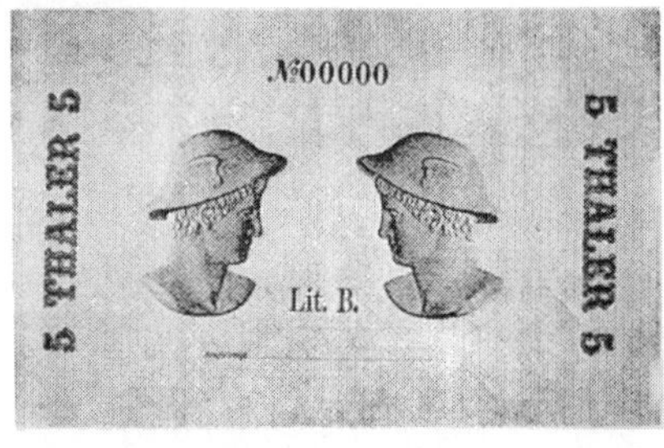

S421	**5 THALER** 2.1.1868. Sign. Wedell; Löwe; Meinecke.	435.00	1000.	1500.

1870 ISSUE

Issued at the outbreak of the Franco-Prussian War by Prussia on behalf of the North German Confederation. The arms of the North German Confederation are at upper left: a shield divided into three bars of sable, argent and gules. The North German Confederation became the German Empire on January 18, 1871 after Bavaria, Württemberg, Baden, and the southern portion of Hesse-Darmstadt agreed to join. Printer: Preussische Staatsdruckerei.

		GOOD	FINE	XF
S422	**5 THALER** 1.8.1870. Sign. Wedell; Löwe; Meinecke; Eck.	235.00	500.00	800.00

		GOOD	FINE	XF
S423	**10 THALER** 1.8.1870. Sign. Wedell; Löwe; Meinecke; Eck.	300.00	600.00	1000.

		GOOD	FINE	XF
S424	**25 THALER** 1.8.1870. Sign. Wedell; Löwe; Meinecke; Eck.	435.00	1000.	1500.

PRUSSIA, KINGDOM OF

KÖNIGLICHE GIRO-UND LEHNBANK

ROYAL ENDORSEMENT AND LOAN BANK

See Preussishe Bank.

PREUSSISHE BANK

BANK OF PRUSSIA

Founded June 17, 1765; opened for business October 1, 1765. Of the initial capital of 8 million thalers only 400,000 thalers was paid in, so that the bank soon collapsed. It was then reorganized and set up again on October 29, 1766. It was extensively reorganized on October 5, 1846 in response to the Prussia-Anhalt "bank war." The reorganized institution served as Prussia's central bank. As of January 1, 1876 it was converted into the Reichsbank and thereafter served as the central bank for all Germany; for its subsequent issues, see volume 2. From January 1, 1876 issues S454-456 were considered to be issues of the Reichsbank. Unlike the Seehandlung, the Preussische Bank had private shareholders.

1766-69 ISSUE

		GOOD	FINE	XF
S426	**10 PFUND BANCO** 29.10.1766.	—	—	—
S427	**20 PFUND BANCO** 29.10.1766.	—	—	—
S428	**100 PFUND BANCO** 29.10.1766.	—	—	—
S429	**500 PFUND BANCO** 29.10.1766.	—	—	—
S430	**1000 PFUND BANCO** 29.10.1766.	—	—	—
S431	**4 PFUND BANCO** 29.10.1766-69.	—	—	—
S432	**8 PFUND BANCO** 29.10.1766-69.	—	—	—

1774 ISSUE

		GOOD	FINE	XF
S433	**4 PFUND BANCO** 1774 (1793).	—	—	—
S433A	**8 PFUND BANCO** 1774 (1793).	—	—	—
S433B	**10 PFUND BANCO** 1774 (1793).	—	—	—
S433C	**20 PFUND BANCO** 1774 (1793).	—	—	—
S433D	**100 PFUND BANCO**	—	—	—
S433E	**500 PFUND BANCO** 1774 (1793).	—	—	—
S433F	**1000 PFUND BANCO** 1774 (1793).	—	—	—

BANKKASSENSCHEINE

BANK TREASURY NOTES

1798-1836 ISSUE

		GOOD	FINE	XF
S435	**100 THALER** 1798-1836.	—	—	—
S436	**200 THALER** 1798-1836.	—	—	—
S437	**300 THALER** 1798-1836.	—	—	—
S438	**500 THALER** 1798-1836.	—	—	—

1846 ISSUE

Thaler System

		GOOD	FINE	XF
S441	**25 THALER** 31.7.1846.	725.00	1650.	2500.
S442	**50 THALER** 31.7.1846.	725.00	1650.	2500.
S443	**100 THALER** 31.7.1846.	725.00	1650.	2500.
S444	**500 THALER** 31.7.1846.	—	—	—

1856-64 ISSUE

		GOOD	FINE	XF
S445	**10 THALER** 15.5.1856. W/o three-color back.	—	—	—
S446	**10 THALER** 15.5.1856. Three-color back.	575.00	1350.	1850.
S447	**25 THALER** 26.5.1857.	575.00	1350.	1850.
S448	**25 THALER** 26.11.1857. Proof.	575.00	1350.	1850.

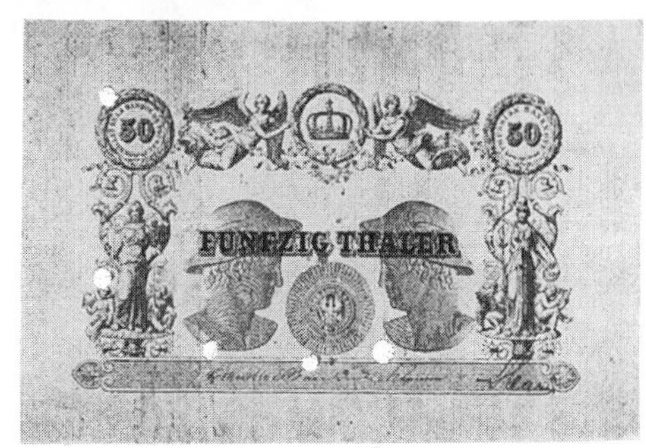

		GOOD	FINE	XF
S449	**50 THALER** 9.6.1860. Pink and brown. Images of Mercury in profile.	575.00	1350.	1850.
S450	**100 THALER** 19.12.1864.	575.00	1350.	1850.

1867-68 ISSUE

		GOOD	FINE	XF
S451	**10 THALER** 18.6.1867.	575.00	1350.	1850.
S452	**500 THALER** 5.12.1867.	875.00	1900.	2850.
S453	**25 THALER** 21.9.1868.	575.00	1350.	1850.

1874 ISSUE

Mark System

#S454-S456 printer: Reichsdruckerei.

		GOOD	FINE	XF
S454	**100 MARK** 1.5.1874.	575.00	1350.	1850.

		Good	Fine	XF
S455	500 Mark 1.5.1874.	650.00	1500.	2200.
S456	1000 Mark 1.5.1874.	750.00	1700.	2650.

Preussische Haupt-Bank

Prussian Main Bank, See Preussische Bank.

Kgl. Seehandlungsinstitut Berlin

Royal Institute of Maritime Commerce

The Seehandlung was established in 1772 to promote Prussia's overseas trade. It developed into a state-owned universal bank, eventually acknowledging this new role by changing its name to the Preussische Staatsbank (Seehandlung) in 1922. Unlike the Preussische Bank and, later, the Reichsbank, it had no private shareholders but was entirely owned by the Prussian state.

1820 ND Issue

		Good	Fine	XF
S461	100 Thaler ND (ca. 1820).	—	—	—
S462	500 Thaler ND (ca. 1820).	—	—	—

Städtische Bank, Breslau Silesia

State Bank, Breslau, Silesia

Founded June 10, 1848. King Frederick William IV granted the concession on the basis of a recommendation from the Prussian Finance Minister, David Hansemann. Its notes were still valid in 1892.

1848 Issue

Thaler System

		Good	Fine	XF
S466	1 Thaler 10.6.1848.	235.00	500.00	800.00
S467	5 Thaler 10.6.1848.	350.00	700.00	1200.
S468	25 Thaler 10.6.1848.	575.00	1350.	1850.
S469	50 Thaler 10.6.1848.	—	—	—

1863 Issue

		Good	Fine	XF
S470	10 Thaler 1.7.1863.	350.00	700.00	1200.
S471	20 Thaler 1.7.1863.	435.00	1000.	1500.

		Good	Fine	XF
S472	50 Thaler 1.7.1863. a. Issued note. b. Cancelled.	 575.00 —	 1350. —	 1850. —
S473	100 Thaler 1.7.1863.	725.00	1650.	2500.

1874 Issue

Mark System

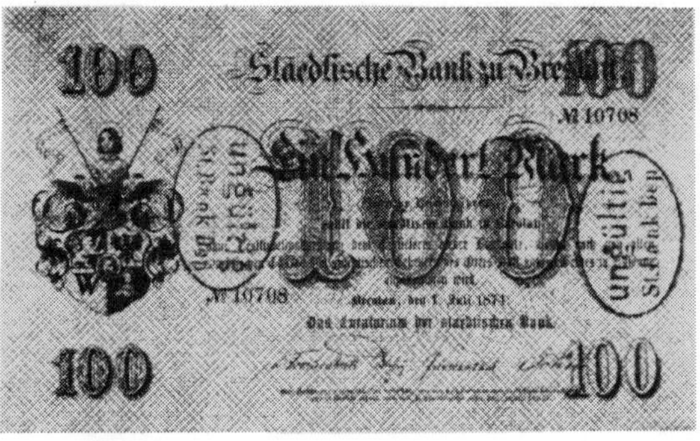

		Good	Fine	XF
S474	100 Mark 1.7.1874. a. Issued note. b. Cancelled.	 575.00 —	 1350. —	 1850. —

		Good	Fine	XF
S475	1000 Mark 1.7.1874.	725.00	1650.	2500.

KASSEN-VEREIN, BERLIN

TREASURY ASSOCIATION, BERLIN

This was a clearing house association set up on English and Dutch models, which issued clearing house certificates. These certificates has some monetary functions, but they were chiefly for interbank transactions. It was established by the Berlin banking house Gebr. Benecke, W. C. Benecke, August Friedrich Bloch, A. & F. Ewald, C. Heine, Meyer Jacobson, L. Lipke & Comp., Mendelssohn & Fränkel, D. J. Riess and Carl W. J. Schultz. The agreement was signed on April 18, 1823 and the treasury association opened for business on May 1, 1823. The driving force behind its creation was Joseph Mendelssohn of the house of Mendelssohn & Fränkel, which changed its name to Mendelssohn & Co. on January 1, 1828. Joseph Mendelssohn, one of the most briliant private bankers of the nineteenth century, was related to both Moses Mendelssohn, the philospher, and Felix Mendelssohn-Bartholdy, which shows that genius can take many forms. The Kassen-Verein became the Bank des Berliner Kassen-Vereins in 1850.

1825-33 ISSUE

		GOOD	FINE	XF
S481	1000 REICHSTHALER PREUSS. COUR. ND (ca. 1825).	—	—	—
S482	100 THALER ND (ca. 1825).	—	—	—
S483	200 THALER ND (1826-33).	—	—	—
S484	300 THALER ND (1826-33).	—	—	—
S485	500 THALER ND (1826-33).	—	—	—
S486	1000 THALER ND (1826-33).	—	—	—

1835 ISSUE

#S287-S488 bills payable at sight which circulated like bank notes. Dates from 1835.

		GOOD	FINE	XF
S487	100 THALER ca. 1835.	—	—	—

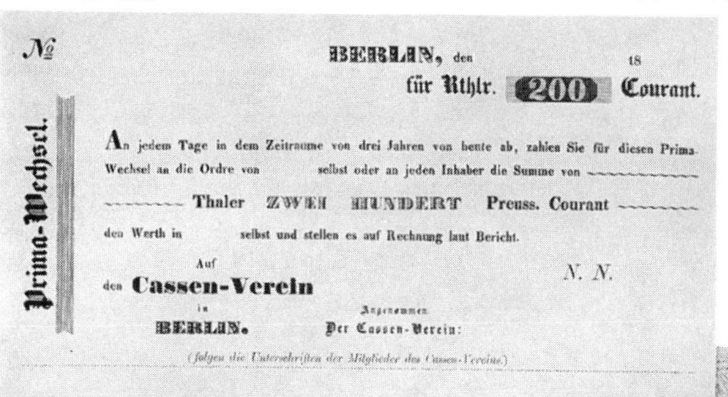

		GOOD	FINE	XF
S488	200 THALER ca. 1835. Black on red unpt. Back black on pink unpt.	—	—	—

BANK DES BERLINER KASSEN-VEREINS

BANK OF THE BERLIN TREASURY ASSOCIATION

Concession granted April 15, 1850. It opened for business in the old offices of the Kassen-Verein on October 1, 1850. This bank discounted the bills brought to it by the private bankers who were its members. Its membership comprised an *Almanach de Gotha* of the most eminent Berlin private banks of the time. Rival joint-stock banks, such as the Disconto-Gesellschaft, tended to be excluded from membership. The stork, with the motto *Ich wach,* (I watch) was the personal emblem of Joseph Mendelssohn, who died in November 1848, before he could see the founding of the bank des Berliner Kassen-Vereins, which had been largely his idea. The general meeting of the shareholders voted to abandon the note issuing privilege on December 28, 1875, effective as of April 1, 1876; the bank ceased to issue bank notes as of the end of 1875.

1850 FIRST ISSUE

		GOOD	FINE	XF
S491	10 THALER 1.10.1850.	—	—	—
S492	20 THALER 1.10.1850.	—	—	—
S493	50 THALER 1.10.1850.	—	—	—
S494	100 THALER 1.10.1850.	—	—	—
S495	200 THALER 1.10.1850.	—	—	—

1850 (1866) SECOND ISSUE

Differing slightly from first issue.

		GOOD	FINE	XF
S496	10 THALER 1.10.1850.	725.00	1650.	2500.

		GOOD	FINE	XF
S497	20 THALER 1.10.1850. Stork in medallion at l., Mercury at r. Back brown; large 20. Sign. Riess; Leo; Schmidt.	725.00	1650.	2500.
S498	50 THALER 1.10.1850.	—	—	—
S499	100 THALER 1.10.1850.	—	—	—
S500	200 THALER 1.10.1850.	—	—	—

KÖLNISCHE PRIVATBANK RHEINLAND

COLOGNE PRIVATE BANK

Concession granted October 10, 1855. In 1886 the bank gave up its right to issue bank notes; it ceased operations January 31, 1887 and was fully liquidated as of January 1, 1889.

1856 FIRST ISSUE

Thaler System

		GOOD	FINE	XF
S506	10 THALER 1.5.1856. No unpt.	575.00	1350.	1850.
S507	20 THALER 1.5.1856. No unpt.	575.00	1350.	1850.
S508	50 THALER 1.5.1856. No unpt.	575.00	1350.	1850.
S509	100 THALER 1.5.1856. No unpt.	575.00	1350.	1850.

1856 (1863) SECOND ISSUE

		GOOD	FINE	XF
S510	10 THALER 1.5.1856. Yellow-brown unpt.			
	a. Issued note.	300.00	600.00	1000.
	p. Face proof.	—	—	—

		GOOD	FINE	XF
S511	**20 THALER** 1.5.1856. Lt. green unpt.			
	a. Issued note.	300.00	600.00	1000.
	p. Face proof.	—	—	—
S512	**50 THALER** 1.5.1856. Pink unpt.			
	a. Issued note.	300.00	600.00	1000.
	p. Face proof.	—	—	—
S513	**100 THALER** 1.5.1856. Blue-green unpt.	435.00	1000.	1500.

1875 ISSUE

Mark System

		GOOD	FINE	XF
S514	**100 MARK** 6.3.1875.	—	—	—

COMMUNALSTÄNDISCHE BANK FUR DIE PREUSSISCHE OBERLAUSITZ GÖRLITZ

COMMUNAL PEOPLES BANK FOR PRUSSIAN OBERLAUSITZ, SILESIA

Opened for business August 1, 1866. It abandoned its right to issue bank notes as of January 1, 1876.

1866 ISSUE

Thaler System.

		GOOD	FINE	XF
S516	**10 THALER** 1.5.1866.	575.00	1350.	1850.
S517	**20 THALER** 1.5.1866.	575.00	1350.	1850.
S518	**50 THALER** 1.5.1866.	575.00	1350.	1850.
S519	**100 THALER** 1.5.1866.	575.00	1350.	1850.
S520	**200 THALER** 1.5.1866.	—	—	—

1874 ISSUE

Mark System.

		GOOD	FINE	XF
S521	**100 MARK** 31.3.1874.	—	—	—

WEST PREUSSEN
WEST PRUSSIA

DANZIGER PRIVAT-ACTIEN-BANK

Concession granted March 16, 1857. The bank opened for business on June 17, 1857. IN 1890 the Prussian government informed the bak that its right to issue banknotes would not be continued and the bank ceased to be a bank of issue on December 31. In 1933, when the Nazis won a majority in Danzig Volkstag, they changed the management. The new management compelled the Jewish directors to resign from its board. The bank's subsequent fate is unknown.

1857 ISSUE

Thaler System

#S522-S525 printer: G&D.

		GOOD	FINE	XF
S522	**10 THALER** 1.7.1857. Arms at ctr. 4 allegorical figures on back, representing from l. to r. the Vistula, Danzig, Mercury (Commerce) and the Baltic; Marienkirche at l. Sign. Normann; Frantzius; Schottler.	500.00	950.00	—
S523	**20 THALER** 1.7.1857.	—	—	—
S524	**50 THALER** 1.7.1857.	—	—	—
S525	**100 THALER** 1.7.1857.	900.00	—	—

1862-73 ISSUES

#S526-S531 printer: G&D.

		GOOD	FINE	XF
S526	**10 THALER** 1.9.1862. Arms at ctr. 4 allegoical figures on back, representing from l. to r. Visttula, Danzig, Mercury (Commerce) and the Baltic; Marienkirche at l. Sign. Normann; Frantzius; Schottler.	500.00	950.00	—
S527	**20 THALER** 2.1.1865.	600.00	1200.	—
S528	**50 THALER** 2.1.1865.	600.00	1200.	—

		GOOD	FINE	XF
S529	**100 THALER** 1.7.1867. Arms at l. Back like #S526.	900.00	—	—
S530	**100 THALER** 1.5.1871.	—	—	—
S531	**100 THALER** 1.3.1873.	900.00	—	—

1875 ISSUE

Mark System

		GOOD	FINE	XF
S532	**100 MARK** 1.6.1875.	—	Rare	—

1882 ISSUE

		GOOD	FINE	XF
S533	**100 MARK** 1.6.1882. Printer: Reichsdruckerei.	—	Rare	—

1887 ISSUE

		GOOD	FINE	XF
S534	**100 MARK** 1.6.1887. Arms w/lions at lower ctr. Back like #S522 but under arch. Sign. Mix; Damme; Langerfeldt; Steimmig; Rodenacker. Printer: Reichsdruckerei.	—	Rare	—

OSTPREUSSEN
EAST PRUSSIA

KÖNIGSBERGER PRIVATBANK

KÖNIGSBERG PRIVATE BANK

Concession granted October 13, 1856. In 1871, in accordance with a general meeting of the shareholders, the bank abandoned its right to issue notes and entered liquidation.

1857 ISSUE

		GOOD	FINE	XF
S535	10 THALER 1.4.1857.	—	—	—
S536	20 THALER 1.4.1857.	1150.	2000.	—
S537	50 THALER 1.4.1857.	—	—	—
S538	100 THALER 1.4.1857.	—	—	—

1866 ISSUE

		GOOD	FINE	XF
S539	10 THALER 13.10.1866. Arms at upper ctr. Head of man, either Neptune or River god Pregel, trident, anchor, rudder and seahorse below on back.	575.00	1350.	1850.
S540	20 THALER 13.10.1866.	1150.	2000.	—
S541	50 THALER 13.10.1866.	575.00	1350.	1850.
S542	100 THALER 13.10.1866.	725.00	1650.	2500.

KURMÄRKISCHE PRIVAT-BANK, BERLIN

PRIVATE BANK OF THE ELECTORALMARK, BERLIN

Probably a fraudulent, non-existent bank.

1860'S ISSUE

		GOOD	FINE	XF
S543	5 THALER 186x. Handwritten day, month and year.	725.00	1650.	2500.

MAGDEBURGER PRIVATBANK
PRUSSIAN PROVINCE OF SAXONY

PRIVATE BANK OF MAGDEBURG

Concession granted June 30, 1856, with a capital of a million thalers. Under the monetary reform of 1875, the Prussian government could withdraw the right to issue bank notes from banks of issue as of 1891. In 1890, the Prussian government informed the Magdeburger Privatbank that it planed to withdraw the right of issue. After ceasing to be a bank of issue, the Magdeburger Privatbank grew into one of the largest commercial banks in central Germany. In 1909, after acquiring a large bank in the Kingdom of Saxony, it changed its name to the Mitteldeutsche Privatebank AG. In 1920 it merged with the Commerz- und Privatbank, which shortened its name to Commerzbank, March 1940. Temporarily dissolved after World War II, the Commerzbank AG was reconstituted in 1957.

1856 ISSUE

Thaler System

		GOOD	FINE	XF
S544	10 THALER 30.6.1856.	—	—	—
S545	20 THALER 30.6.1856.	—	—	—
S546	50 THALER 30.6.1856.	—	—	—
S547	100 THALER 30.6.1856.	—	—	—

1866 ISSUE

		GOOD	FINE	XF
S548	10 THALER 1.7.1866.	725.00	1500.	2250.
S549	20 THALER 1.7.1866.	725.00	1500.	2250.
S550	50 THALER 1.7.1866.	725.00	1500.	2250.
S551	100 THALER 1.7.1866.	725.00	1500.	2250.

1874 ISSUE

Mark System

		GOOD	FINE	XF
S552	100 MARK 1.1.1874.	—	—	—

OWINSKER GENERAL-KASSE, OWINSK B. POSEN

GENERAL TREASURY OF OWINSK

1801 ISSUE

		GOOD	FINE	XF
S553	20 THALER 1801.	—	—	—

RITTERSCHAFTLICHE PRIVATBANK IN POMMERN, STETTIN

PRIVATE BANK OF KNIGHTHOOD IN POMMERANIA, STETTIN

Founded August 15, 1824; commenced business, January 10, 1825. Its notes refer to the Act of Parliament of 11 August 1803 because many of the counterfeits of the period were prepared in England. It soon got into trouble and its notes had to be withdrawn from circulation in 1834-35. To bail out the bank, the Prussian government issued its own paper money in exchange for the notes of the Ritterschaftliche Privatbank; the Prussian government notes are #S400.

1824-25 ISSUE

Thaler System

		GOOD	FINE	XF
S556	1 THALER ND (1824-25). View of Stettin on back. Sign. Bülow; Kleist; Bonin on back.	125.00	250.00	400.00
S557	5 THALER ND (1824-25).	235.00	500.00	800.00

1849 ISSUE

		GOOD	FINE	XF
S558	10 THALER 24.8.1849.	—	—	—
S559	20 THALER 24.8.1849.	—	—	—
S560	50 THALER 24.8.1849.	—	—	—
S561	100 THALER 24.8.1849.	—	—	—

1860 ISSUE

		GOOD	FINE	XF
S562	10 THALER 20.7.1860.	575.00	1350.	1850.
S563	20 THALER 20.7.1860.	—	—	—

		Good	Fine	XF
S564	**50 Thaler** 20.7.1860.	—	—	—
S565	**100 Thaler** 20.7.1860.	—	—	—

1869 Issue

		Good	Fine	XF
S566	**10 Thaler** 20.9.1869.	575.00	1350.	1850.
S567	**20 Thaler** 20.9.1869.	725.00	1650.	2500.
S568	**50 Thaler** 20.9.1869.	—	—	—
S569	**100 Thaler** 20.9.1869.	—	—	—

1874 Issue

Mark System

		Good	Fine	XF
S570	**100 Mark** 6.8.1874.			
	a. Issued note.	—	—	—
	p. Proof.	435.00	875.00	1350.

Provinzial-Actien Bank des Grossherzogthums Posen

Provincial Stock Bank of the Grand Duchy of Posen

Concession granted March 16, 1857. Its right to issue bank notes ended in 1890.

1857 Issue

Thaler System

#S571-S575 printer: G&D.

		Good	Fine	XF
S571	**10 Thaler** 1.12.1857.	435.00	1000.	1500.

		Good	Fine	XF
S572	**20 Thaler** 1.12.1857. Blue and black. Peace and commerce at l., agriculture at r.	575.00	1350.	1850.
S573	**50 Thaler** 1.12.1857.	725.00	1650.	2500.
S574	**100 Thaler** 1.12.1857.	725.00	1650.	2500.
S575	**200 Thaler** 1.12.1857.	725.00	1650.	2500.

1867 Issue

#S576-S579 printer: G&D.

		Good	Fine	XF
S576	**10 Thaler** 18.3.1867.	575.00	1350.	1850.
S577	**20 Thaler** 18.3.1867.	725.00	1650.	2500.
S578	**50 Thaler** 18.3.1867.	725.00	1650.	2500.
S579	**100 Thaler** 18.3.1867.	725.00	1650.	2500.

1874 Issue

Mark System

		Good	Fine	XF
S580	**100 Mark** 17.3.1874.	—	—	—
S581	**200 Mark** 17.3.1874.	—	—	—
S582	**500 Mark** 17.3.1874.	—	—	—

1883 Issue

		Good	Fine	XF
S583	**100 Mark** 17.3.1883.	—	—	—
S584	**200 Mark** 17.3.1883.	—	—	—
S585	**500 Mark** 17.3.1883.	—	—	—

Reuss Schleiz, Principality of Jüngere Linie

Kommission für die Verwaltung der Staatsschulden

Commission for the Administration of State Debts

1849 Issue

		Good	Fine	XF
S588	**1 Thaler** 27.3.1849. Sign. Semmel; Mayer; Hirt.	300.00	600.00	1000.

1860 Issue

		Good	Fine	XF
S589	**1 Thaler** 7.1.1860. Sign. Beulewitz; Glass.	235.00	500.00	800.00

1870 Issue

		Good	Fine	XF
S590	**1 Thaler** 4.7.1870. Black on green unpt. Arms at upper ctr. Arms at ctr. on back. Printer: G&D.	235.00	500.00	800.00

Geraer Bank

Concession granted November 13, 1855; opened for business January 15, 1856. The bank gave up its note-issuing privilege as of January 1, 1875. In 1891 a prominent stock market speculator seized control of this bank and the Weimarische Bank, merged the two banks and moved their domicile to Berlin. But the merged bank had to enter liquidation in 1894.

1856 Issue

Thaler System

#S594-S596 printer: G&D.

S594 10 THALER — 15.1.1856. Black and blue. Arms at ctr. Monument of angel crowning industry and agriculture on back.

S595 50 THALER — 15.1.1856.

S596 100 THALER — 15.1.1856.

		Good	Fine	XF
S594	10 Thaler	300.00	600.00	1000.
S595	50 Thaler	435.00	1000.	1500.
S596	100 Thaler	—	—	—

1874 ISSUE

Mark System

S597 100 MARK — 1.1.1874. Printer: G&D.

		Good	Fine	XF
S597	100 Mark	500.00	950.00	1600.

REUSS GREIZ, PRINCIPALITY OF ÄLTERE LINIE

KASSENSCHEINE

1858 TREASURY NOTES ISSUE

S601 1 THALER — 15.5.1858. Sign. Fritz; Raab; Bergner. Printer: Henning, Greiz.

		Good	Fine	XF
S601	1 Thaler	300.00	600.00	1000.

1863 TREASURY NOTES ISSUE

S602 1 THALER — 22.4.1863. Black and green. Sign. Geldern-Crispendorf; Kommerstädt; Bergner. Printer: Henning, Greiz.

		Good	Fine	XF
S602	1 Thaler	235.00	500.00	800.00

SAXONY, ELECTORATE OF

CHURFÜRSTL. SÄCHS. CASSEN-BILLETS

ROYAL ELECTORAL SAXON TREASURY BILLS

1772 ISSUE

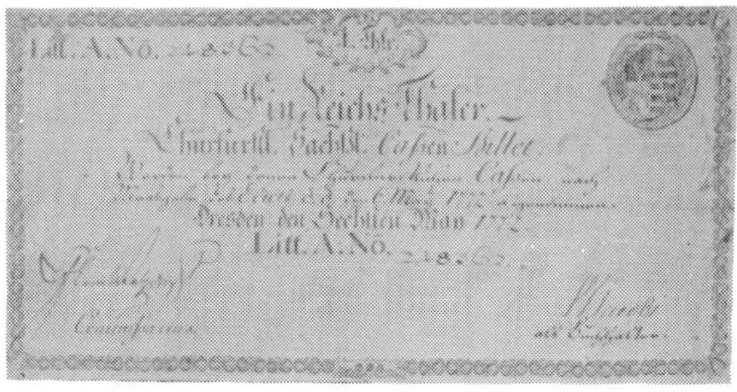

S606 1 REICHSTHALER — 6.5.1772.

		Good	Fine	XF
S606	1 Reichsthaler	235.00	500.00	800.00

S607 2 REICHSTHALER — 6.5.1772.

		Good	Fine	XF
S607	2 Reichsthaler	300.00	600.00	1000.

S608 5 REICHSTHALER — 6.5.1772.

S609 10 REICHSTHALER — 6.5.1772.

		Good	Fine	XF
S608	5 Reichsthaler	500.00	1000.	1600.
S609	10 Reichsthaler	—	—	—

		Good	Fine	XF
S610	50 Reichsthaler 6.5.1772.	—	—	—
S611	100 Reichsthaler 6.5.1772.	—	—	—

1804 Issue

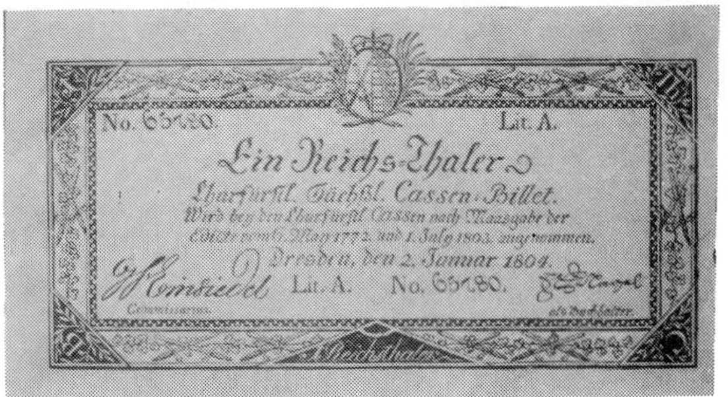

		Good	Fine	XF
S612	1 Reichsthaler 2.1.1804.			
	a. Sign. Einsiedel; Nagel.	115.00	250.00	425.00
	b. Sign. Einsiedel; Winkler.	115.00	250.00	425.00
	c. Sign. Leipziger; Nagel.	115.00	250.00	425.00
	d. Sign. Leipziger; Winkler.	115.00	250.00	425.00
	e. Sign. Richter; Nagel.	115.00	250.00	425.00
	f. Sign. Schönberg; Nagel.	115.00	250.00	425.00
	g. Sign. Watzdorf; Winkler.	115.00	250.00	425.00

		Good	Fine	XF
S613	2 Reichsthaler 2.1.1804.			
	a. Sign. Carlowitz; Winkler.	175.00	350.00	575.00
	b. Sign. Einsiedel; Winkler.	175.00	350.00	575.00
	c. Sign. Leipziger; Winkler.	175.00	350.00	575.00
	d. Sign. Richter; Nagel.	175.00	350.00	575.00
	e. Sign. Watzdorf; Einsiedel.	175.00	350.00	575.00
	f. Sign. Watzdorf; Nagel.	175.00	350.00	575.00
S614	5 Reichsthaler 2.1.1804.	300.00	600.00	950.00
S615	1, 2, 5 Reichsthaler Blank forms.	60.00	125.00	250.00

Saxony, Kingdom of

Königlich Sächsische Interims-Cassen-Scheine

Royal Saxon Treasury Notes

When Prussia annexed large parts of Saxony under the 1814 Treaty of Vienna, it also assumed part of the Saxon paper money obligation. The easiest way to do this was to have Prussia take over the entire sum of Lit. A Cassenbillets, which were all denominated 1 thaler. This lead to a shortage of 1 thaler notes. The temporary treasury notes of 1815 were issued as a remedy.

1815 Issue

		Good	Fine	XF
S616	1 Reichsthaler 18.12.1815.			
	a. Sign. Ferber; Rachel.	150.00	300.00	550.00
	b. Sign. Bünau; Rachel.	150.00	300.00	550.00
	c. Sign. Carlowitz; Rachel.	150.00	300.00	550.00
	d. Sign. Sahr; Rachel.	150.00	300.00	550.00

Königlich Sächsische Cassen Billets

Royal Saxon Treasury Bills

1818 Issue

		Good	Fine	XF
S617	1 Reichsthaler 1.10.1818. W/o red surcharge.			
	a. Sign. Bünau; Rachel.	115.00	250.00	425.00
	b. Sign. Carlowitz; Rachel.	115.00	250.00	425.00
	c. Sign. Ferber; Rachel.	115.00	250.00	425.00
S618	2 Reichsthaler 1.10.1818. W/o red surcharge.			
	a. Sign. Bünau; Rachel.	150.00	300.00	550.00
	b. Sign. Carlowitz; Rachel.	150.00	300.00	550.00
	c. Sign. Ferber; Rachel.	150.00	300.00	550.00
	d. Sign. Sahr; Rachel.	150.00	300.00	550.00

1834 Issue

Thaler Courant System.

		Good	Fine	XF
S619	1 Thaler Courant 1.10.1818 (30.7.1834). Black. One red surcharge: *1 Thlr. Cour.* on blue paper, which may appear as gray, gray-violet or violet colored.			
	a. Sign. Carlowitz; Rachel.	175.00	350.00	575.00
	b. Sign. Ferber; Rachel.	175.00	350.00	575.00
	c. Sign. Sahr; Rachel.	175.00	350.00	575.00
S620	2 Thaler Courant 1.10.1818 (30.7.1834). One red surcharge: *2 Thlr. Cour.* on blue paper, which may appear as gray, gray-violet or violet colored.			
	a. Sign. Bünau; Rachel.	200.00	400.00	700.00
	b. Sign. Carlowitz; Rachel.	200.00	400.00	700.00
	c. Sign. Sahr; Rachel.	200.00	400.00	700.00
S620A	1 Thaler Courant 1.10.1818 (1841). Two red surcharges: *I Thlr. Cour.* on white paper.			
	a. Sign. Bünau; Rachel.	—	—	—
	b. Sign. Carlowitz; Rachel.	—	—	—
S620B	2 Thaler Courant 1.10.1818 (1841). Two red surcharges: *2 Thlr. Cour.* on white paper.			
	a. Sign. Bünau; Rachel.	—	—	—
	b. Sign. Carlowitz; Rachel.	—	—	—
	c. Sign. Ferber; Rachel.	—	—	—

1840 Issue

Printer: J. B. Hirschfeld, Leipzig. The first printing was done in Dresden; most of Hirshfeld's personnel transferred there to perform it. Later printings were done in Leipzig.

		Good	Fine	XF
S621	1 Thaler 16.4.1840 (1.11.1842). Sign. Weissenbach; Hübler; Schmidt.	100.00	220.00	350.00
S622	5 Thaler 16.4.1840 (1.11.1842). Sign. Weissenbach; Hübler; Schmidt.	175.00	350.00	575.00

		Good	Fine	XF
S623	**10 THALER** 16.4.1840 (1.11.1842). Sign. Weissenbach; Hübler; Schmidt.	435.00	1000.	1500.

1855 ISSUE

1855 is the date of the law which authorized this issue; however, the 1 thaler note depicts a coin type which was not issued until 1857.

#S624-S627 values are for cancelled notes.

		Good	Fine	XF
S624	**1 THALER** 6.9.1855 (1857). Black on lt. brown paper. Obv. and rev. of imaginary thaler at l. and r. (based on thaler, KM 1192). Seated allegorical woman (Saxonia) at ctr., locomotive at r. on back. Sign. Weissenbach; Opelt; Pfotenhauer.	85.00	175.00	275.00

		Good	Fine	XF
S625	**5 THALER** 6.9.1855 (1857). Obv. and rev. of imaginary 5 thaler coin (based on thaler, KM 1192) at l. and r. Seated allegorical woman (Saxonia) at ctr., locomotive at r. on back. Sign. Weissenbach; Opelt; Pfotenhauer.	100.00	220.00	350.00
S626	**10 THALER** 6.9.1855 (1857) Sign. Weissenbach; Opelt; Pfotenhauer.	300.00	600.00	1000.
S627	**20 THALER** 6.9.1855 (1857). Sign. Weissenbach; Opelt; Pfotenhauer.	725.00	1650.	2500.
S628	**50 THALER** 6.9.1855 (1857). Sign. Weissenbach; Opelt; Pfotenhauer.	—	—	—

1867 ISSUE

#S629-S631 printer: G&D.

		Good	Fine	XF
S629	**1 THALER** 2.3.1867. Sign. Weissenbach; Roch; Pfotenhauer.	90.00	185.00	300.00
S630	**5 THALER** 2.3.1867. Sign. Weissenbach; Roch; Pfotenhauer.	100.00	220.00	350.00
S631	**10 THALER** 2.3.1867. Sign. Weissenbach; Roch; Pfotenhauer.	300.00	600.00	1000.

CHEMNITZER STADTBANK

CHEMNITZ CITY BANK

Concession granted May 25, 1848 to relieve the severe economic crisis of the late 1840s, after the Leipziger Bank refused to establish a branch in Chemnitz. The bank opened for business on April 1, 1849. The Reichsbank refused to renew the Chemnitzer Stadt-Bank's note-issuing privilege in 1890, so that its right to issue bank notes lapsed on January 1, 1891.

1848 CREDIT NOTE ISSUE

Thaler System

		Good	Fine	XF
S636	**1 THALER, 14-THALER-FUSS** 19.8.1848.	235.00	500.00	800.00
S637	**1 THALER, 30-THALER-FUSS** 19.8.1848.	235.00	500.00	800.00

1867 ISSUE

		Good	Fine	XF
S638	**1 THALER** 10.8.1867.	175.00	350.00	575.00

1874 ISSUE

Mark System

		Good	Fine	XF
S639	**100 MARK** 1.5.1874. Printer: G&D.	725.00	1650.	2500.

LANDSTÄNDISCHE HYPOTHEKENBANK FÜR DAS KÖNIGL. SÄCHS. MARKGRAFENTHUM OBERLAUSITZ, BAUTZEN

PEOPLES MORTGAGE BANK OF THE ROYAL SAXON MARGRAVIATE OBERLAUSITZ, BAUTZEN

Founded July 26, 1844. In 1857 it changed its name to the Landständische Bank des Königlichen Markgrafenthums Oberlausitz. Since the right to issue bank notes belonged not to the bank, but to the province of Upper Lusatia, it was not affected by the law of March 1875, but from 1876 onwards the notes were valid only in Saxony. The bank gave up its right to issue bank notes in 1906.

1850 ISSUE

		Good	Fine	XF
S641	**1 THALER** 15.11.1850.	—	—	—
S642	**5 THALER** 15.11.1850.	—	—	—

1860's Issue

Thaler System

		Good	Fine	XF
S646	5 Thaler 1860.	—	—	—
S647	10 Thaler 1861.	575.00	1350.	1850.

		Good	Fine	XF
S648	10 Thaler 10.10.1868.	575.00	1350.	1850.

1875 Issue

Mark System

		Good	Fine	XF
S649	100 Mark 1.1.1875. Printer: G&D.	725.00	1650.	2500.

Leipziger Bank

Bank of Leipzig

Founded July 1838; opened for business February 1839. It abandoned its right to issue bank notes on December 11, 1875. This bank collapsed spectacularly on June 25, 1901, because of its loans to the fraudulent Kassler Gesellschaft für Trebertrocknung.

1839 Issue

Thaler System

		Good	Fine	XF
S651	100 Thaler 11.3.1839.	—	—	—
S652	200 Thaler 11.3.1839.	—	—	—
S653	500 Thaler 11.3.1839.	—	—	—
S654	20 Thaler Konventionsfuss (1839).	—	—	—
S655	100 Thaler Konventionsfuss (1839).	—	—	—
S656	200 Thaler Konventionsfuss (1839).	—	—	—
S657	500 Thaler Konventionsfuss (1839).	—	—	—
S658	1000 Thaler Konventionsfuss (1839).	—	—	—
S659	100 Thaler 14-Thaler-Fuss	—	—	—
S660	500 Thaler 14-Thaler-Fuss	—	—	—

1843 Issue

		Good	Fine	XF
S661	50 Thaler 8.10.1843.	—	—	—

1845 Issue

		Good	Fine	XF
S662	20 Thaler 15.7.1845.	—	—	—

1855 Issue

		Good	Fine	XF
S663	20 Thaler 1.3.1855. Printer: G&D.	725.00	1600.	2250.

1860 Issue

		Good	Fine	XF
S664	50 Thaler 1.6.1860. Printer: G&D.	725.00	1600.	2250.
S665	100 Thaler 1.6.1860. Printer: G&D.	725.00	1600.	2250.

1864 Issue

		Good	Fine	XF
S666	10 Thaler 20.6.1864. Printer: G&D.	725.00	1600.	2250.

1866 Issue

		Good	Fine	XF
S667	10 Thaler 18.4.1866. Printer: G&D.	725.00	1600.	2250.

1874 Issue

Mark System

		Good	Fine	XF
S668	100 Mark 1.1.1874. Printer: G&D.	750.00	1600.	2250.

Leipziger Diskonto-Kasse

Leipzig Discount Bank, see Leipziger Kasen-Verein

Leipziger Kassenverein

Leipzig Treasury Association

The Leipziger Kassen-Verein was founded in 1824 to relieve the monetary stringency which tended to occur during the Leipzig Fair. The Kassen-Verein was so successful that it expanded its activities in 1827, using the name "Leipziger Diskonto-Kassa." The minimum size of its notes was 100 thalers. On March 19, 1867 it was given a regular note-issuing privilege, and was one of five Saxon banks of issue (the others being the Leipziger Bank, the Chemnitzer Stadtbank, the Landständische Bank in Bautzen and the Sächsische Bank zu Dresden). In 1890 it abandoned its right to issue notes and entered liquidation. Most of its business was transferred to the Leipziger Bank, which then failed in 1901.

1824 Currency Exchange Issue

		Good	Fine	XF
S671	100 Reichsthaler 1824.	—	—	—
S672	200 Reichsthaler 1824.	—	—	—
S673	500 Reichsthaler 1824.	—	—	—
S674	1000 Reichsthaler 1824.	—	—	—

1867 Issue

Thaler System

		Good	Fine	XF
S676	100 Thaler 1.5.1867.	—	—	—

1875 Issue

Mark System

		Good	Fine	XF
S677	500 Mark 31.3.1875. Printer: G&D.	—	—	—

Leipzig-Dresdner Eisenbahn-Compagnie

Eisenbahn-Cassa-Scheine

Leipzig-Dresden Railway Company

Railway Treasury Notes

The concession for the railroad was granted on May 6, 1835. Construction began in 1836; the entire railroad opened to traffic on April 7, 1839. Friedrich List (see Württembergische Notenbank, #S999), the theorist of German industrialization, was the major advocate of the railroad. Its management was in the hands of the industralist Gustav Harkort, brother of another economic theorist and advocate of German industralization, Friedrich Harkort. The railroad was one of the most profitable in Germany; its dividends peaked at 28 1/2% in 1868. The railroad was taken over by the Kingdom of Saxony on July 1, 1876. Per a declaration of June 27, 1876, the notes were to be considered Saxon state notes. The railroad gave up its right to issue notes in 1878.

1838-39 ISSUE

		GOOD	FINE	XF
S681	**1 THALER, 14-THALER-FUSS** ND (1838). Black on green colored paper. Back brown. 2 sign. Gustav Harkort at r.	150.00	300.00	550.00

1855 ISSUE

		GOOD	FINE	XF
S682	**1 THALER, 14-THALER-FUSS** ND (1855). *UMDRUCK VON 1855* on back.	150.00	300.00	550.00

1857 ISSUE

		GOOD	FINE	XF
S683	**1 THALER, 30-THALER-FUSS** ND (1857).	150.00	300.00	550.00

1870 ISSUE

		GOOD	FINE	XF
S684	**1 THALER, 30-THALER-FUSS** ND (1870). *UMDRUCK VON 1870* on back.	150.00	300.00	550.00

SÄCHSISCHE BANK ZU DRESDEN

Refer to Regional Banks #S946-S971.

SAXE-ALTENBURG, DUCHY OF

HERRSCHAFTL. FLOSS-KASSEN-BILLET FÜRSTL. KAMMER-HAUPTKASSE

GOVERNMENTAL FLOATING TREASURY BILL

ROYAL GOVERNMENT TREASURY

1785 ISSUE

		GOOD	FINE	XF
S686	**5 THALER** 15.12.1785. Hand dated.	875.00	1750.	3000.

KASSENSCHEINE

TREASURY NOTES

1848 ISSUE

		GOOD	FINE	XF
S688	**1 THALER** 16.7.1848 (1849). Sign. Bryogner; Meissner; Hempel; Reuter. Printer: J. B. Hirschfeld, Leipzig.	300.00	600.00	1000.

1858 ISSUE

		GOOD	FINE	XF
S689	**10 THALER** 11.11.1858. Sign. Geulebrück; Meissner; Gabelentz; Lingke. Printer: G&D.	435.00	1000.	1500.

SAXE-COBURG AND GOTHA, DUCHY OF

Although unified under one duke in 1826, Coburg and Gotha remained independent of each other in many respects. Coburg and Gotha each had their own Diet. In economic terms Gotha was in the orbit of Frankfurt/Main, Coburg in that of Nuremberg. This explains the separate issues of treasury vouchers for Coburg and Gotha.

GROSSHERZOGL. SACHISCHE KASSEN-ANWEISUNGEN

DUCAL TREASURY VOUCHERS

COBURG ISSUES

1849 ISSUE

#S691-S692. Plates by C. Naumann, printing by Dietz'sche Hofbuchdruckerei, Coburg.

		GOOD	FINE	XF
S691	**1 THALER** 22.1.1849. Sign. Hofmann; Braun; Scherzer.	435.00	1000.	1500.
S692	**5 THALER** 22.1.1849. Sign. Hofmann; Braun; Scherzer.	Reported Not Confirmed		

1870 ISSUE

#S693-S694 printer: G&D.

		GOOD	FINE	XF
S693	**1 THALER** 30.6.1870. Sign. Egidy; Westhäusser; Goebel.	300.00	600.00	1000.
S694	**5 THALER** 30.6.1870. Sign. Egidy; Westhäusser; Goebel.	Reported Not Confirmed		

PRIVATBANK ZU GOTHA

PRIVATE BANK OF GOTHA

Founded 1856; the founders included the Allgemeine Deutsche Credit-Anstalt (Acda) of Leipzig. The bank abandoned the note-issuing privilege in 1875. In 1877 Georg von Siemens of the Deutsche Bank obtained a seat on the board. In 1905 the Deutsche Bank acquired a share packet. The Privatbank zu Gotha merged into the Deutsche Bank in 1920. From October 1929 until 1937 the Deutsche Bank was called the Deutsche Bank und Disconto-Gesellschaft. Temporarily dissolved after World War II, the Deutsche Bank AG was reconstituted in 1957.

1857 ISSUE

Thaler System

		GOOD	FINE	XF
S701	**10 THALER** 2.1.1857.	—	—	—

		GOOD	FINE	XF
S702	20 THALER 2.1.1857.	575.00	1350.	1850.
S703	100 THALER 2.1.1857.	—	—	—

1874 ISSUE

Mark System

		GOOD	FINE	XF
S704	100 MARK 1.7.1874. Seated allegorical woman at l.	725.00	1650.	2500.

NOTE: Printer's proofs of higher denominations are valued at *XF $400.00*.

SAXE-GOTHA, DUCHY OF

HERZOGL. KASSEN ANWEISUNGEN IN SAXE-GOTHA

DUCAL TREASURY VOUCHERS

GOTHIC ISSUES

1847 ISSUE

#S706-S707 Printer: Haenels Hofbuchdruckerei, Magdeburg.

		GOOD	FINE	XF
S706	1 THALER 30.9.1847.	435.00	1000.	1500.
S707	5 THALER 30.9.1847.	575.00	1350.	1850.

1860 ISSUE

#S708-S709 printer: G&D.

		GOOD	FINE	XF
S708	1 THALER 12.7.1860. Sign. Hess; Grüzmüller; Thauget.	300.00	600.00	1000.
S709	5 THALER 12.7.1860. Sign. Hess; Grüzmüller; Thauget.	575.00	1350.	1850.

SAXE-MEININGEN, DUCHY OF

KASSENANWEISUNGEN

TREASURY VOUCHERS

1849 ISSUE

		GOOD	FINE	XF
S711	1 THALER 24.5.1849. Brown. Sign. Blomeyer; Trinks; Butler; Habersang. Printer: Haenel, Magdeburg.	115.00	250.00	400.00
S712	10 THALER 31.3.1856. Sign. Blomeyer; Trinks; Butler; Schaller.	350.00	700.00	1200.

MITTELDEUTSCHE CREDITBANK IN MEININGEN

MIDDLE GERMAN CREDIT BANK

Founded February 29, 1856 by a number of Frankfurt/Main private bankers, most notably Rudolph Sulzbach, who served as chairman of its supervisory board from 1867 until his death in 1904. After the law of March 14, 1875 tightened restrictions on banks of issue, the Mitteldeutsche Creditbank decided in an extraordinary general meeting of December 17, 1875, to abandon the note-issuing privilege. On June 30, 1876 it recalled the 10-thaler notes of 1857; these were not fully redeemed until ten years later, however. In January 1886 it moved its domicile from Meiningen to Frankfurt/Main. By 1900 it was considered one of the nine major German commercial banks; it is the only one which ever had the right to issue bank notes. It merged into the Commerz- und Privatbank in 1929. The Commerz- und Privatbank operated its Frankfurt branch under the name "Mitteldeutsche Creditbank" until 1940, when the entire bank changed its name to Commerzbank. The name Mitteldeutsche Creditbank was temporarily resurrected between June 1947 and September 1952, when it was used for the former Commerzbank branches in the state of Hesse. The various successor institutions re-merged into the Commerzbank AG in 1957.

1856 ISSUE

Thaler System

		GOOD	FINE	XF
S714	10 THALER 26.8.1856 (4.1857). Blue on brown unpt. Female portr. in medallion flanking seated knight holding shield and sword at ctr. Printers: B. Dondorf and C. Naumann's Druckerei, Frankfurt/Main.	435.00	1000.	1500.

1875 ISSUE

Mark System

		GOOD	FINE	XF
S715	100 MARK 2.1.1875. Printer: C. Naumann, Frankfurt/Main. Not placed in circulation.	725.00	1650.	2500.

SAXE-WEIMAR-EISENACH, GRAND DUCHY OF

GROSSHERZOGL. SÄCHSISCHE CASSEN ANWEISUNG

GRAND DUCAL TREASURY VOUCHER

1847 ISSUE

#S716-S717 printer: Haenels Hofbuchdruckerei, Magdeburg

		GOOD	FINE	XF
S716	1 THALER 27.8.1847. Sign. Meyer; Kühne; Horn.	300.00	600.00	1000.
S717	5 THALER 27.8.1847. Sign. Meyer; Krstl. Schaumburg-Lippischen Kassen-Anweisungen	435.00	1000.	1500.

CONTROL COMMISSION OF THE SCHAUMBURG-LIPPE TREASURY VOUCHERS

1857 ISSUE

		GOOD	FINE	XF
S733	**10 THALER** 2.1.1857. Black on yellow unpt. Angels at l. and r. Black and blue on back. Sign. Campe; Iffland.			
	a. Issued note.	235.00	500.00	800.00
	p. Proof.	—	—	350.00

NIEDERSÄCHSISCHE BANK, BÜCKEBURG

LOWER SAXONY BANK, BÜCKEBURG

Founded 1856. The bank abandoned the right to issue notes in 1875. It merged into the Dresdner Bank in 1899. At that time the share capital of the Niedersächsische Bank was six million marks. Temporarily dissolved after World War II, the Dresdner Bank AG was reconstituted in 1957.

1856 ISSUE

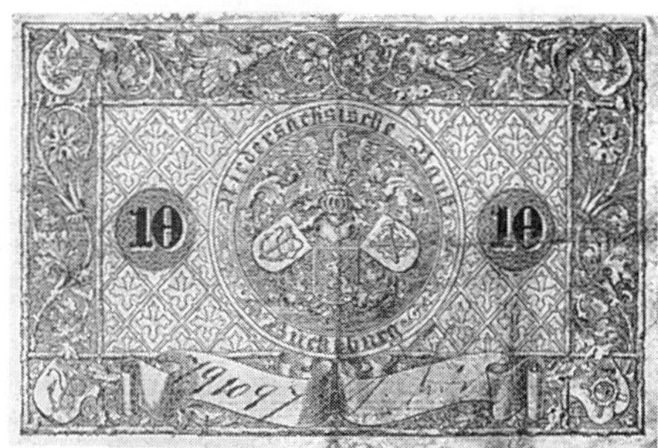

		GOOD	FINE	XF
S736	**10 THALER** 12.9.1856. Angels holding shields with emblems of manual and intellectual labor at l. and r. Arms at ctr. on back.	575.00	1350.	1850.

1865 ISSUE

		GOOD	FINE	XF
S737	**10 THALER** 28.6.1865. Printer: C. Naumann.	—	—	—

1874 ISSUE

		GOOD	FINE	XF
S738	**100 MARK** 1.1.1874. Printer: C. Naumann.	575.00	1350.	1850.

SCHLESWIG-HOLSTEIN, DUCHIES OF

Danish until 1864. An uprising against Danish rule occured 1848-1850; after a short period of Austro-Prussian military government in 1851, the duchies were restored to Denmark. After Austria and Prussia defeated Denmark in 1864, the duchies were under the military government of Austria and Prussia. Both duchies were annexed by Prussia in 1866.

OBERSTE ZIVILBEHÖRDE FÜR HOLSTEIN, KIEL

SUPREME CIVIL AUTHORITY FOR HOLSTEIN, KIEL

This is the civil authority which the Austro-Prussian committee for restoring order installed in the name of the local ruler (that is, the king of Denmark in his capacity as duke of Holstein) and at the command of the German Confederation. The duchy of Holstein was a member of the German Confederation, but the duchy of Schleswig was not.

1851 ISSUE

#S741-S743 printer: Köbner & Lehmkul, Altona.

		GOOD	FINE	XF
S741	**2 1/2 MARK** 17.7.1851.	150.00	300.00	550.00
S742	**10 MARK** 17.7.1851.	350.00	600.00	1000.
S743	**25 MARK** 17.7.1851.	750.00	1600.	2500.

SR. KÖNIGL. MAJESTÄT MINISTERIUM FÜR DIE HERZOGTÜMER HOLSTEIN UND LAUENBURG, KOPENHAGEN

HIS ROYAL MAJESTY'S MINISTRY FOR THE DUCHIES HOLSTEIN AND LAUENBURG, KOPENHAGEN

1854 ISSUE

		GOOD	FINE	XF
S746	**5 REICHSTHALER** 1.9.1854.	575.00	1350.	1850.
S747	**20 REICHSTHALER** 1.9.1854.	—	—	—

Königliches Finanz-Kollegium

Royal Financial Registry

Named only on notes of 1807 issue.

1807 Issue

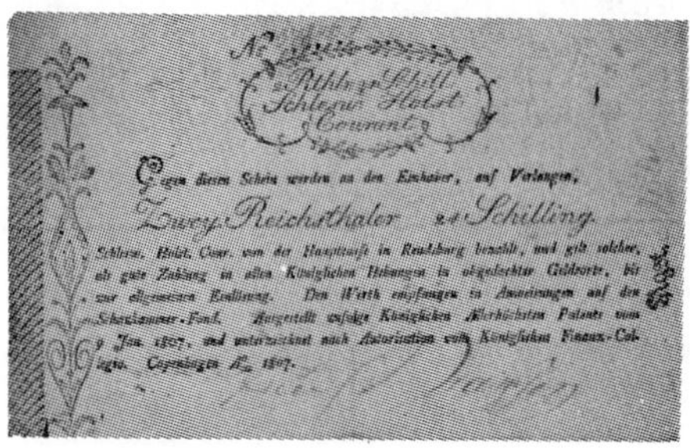

		Good	Fine	XF
S751	**2 Reichsthaler 24 Schilling** 9.1.1807. Kopenhagen, *Anweisung auf den Schatzkammer-Fond.*	300.00	600.00	1000.
S752	**20 Reichsthaler** 9.1.1807. Kopenhagen, *Anweisung auf die Einnahmen des Schatzkammer-Abtragsfonds.*	—	—	—

1808-15 Issue

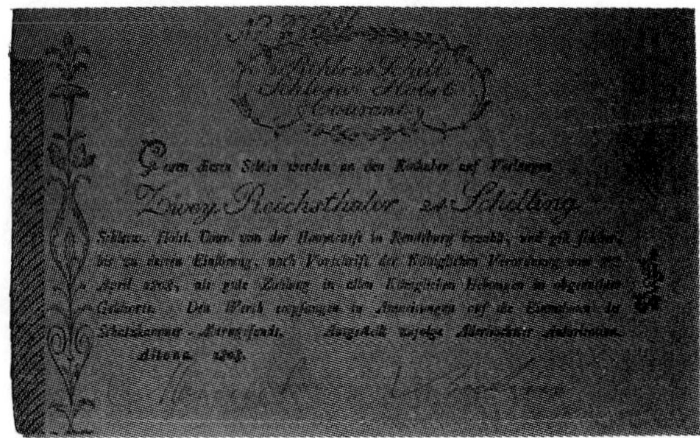

		Good	Fine	XF
S753	**2 Reichsthaler 24 Schilling** 8.4.1808. Altona, *Anweisung auf die Einnahmen des Schatzkammer-Abtragsfonds.*			
	a. Round embossed stamp.	115.00	250.00	400.00
	b. Octagonal embossed stamp.	235.00	500.00	800.00

		Good	Fine	XF
S754	**20 Reichsthaler** 8.4.1808. Altona.	575.00	1350.	1850.
S755	**5 Reichsthaler** 6.12.1815. Kopenhagen.	725.00	1650.	2250.

Schleswig-Holsteinische Species Bank in Altona

Schleswig-Holstein Specie Bank in Altona

Founded February 29, 1788. Until 1864 the king of Denmark was also the duke of Schleswig and the duke of Holstein. Schleswig-Holstein notes have more in common with Danish paper money than with German money. The first European paper money was invented in Scandinavia and Denmark used it extensively. As a neutral country Denmark prospered until 1807. In that year the British Royal navy destroyed the Danish fleet at Copenhagen, fearing that it fall into the hands of Napoleon. The Danes, understandably annoyed by this, went to war on the French side. Denmark financed its war with paper money. After Napoleon was defeated in Russia, his ally, Denmark, faced defeat as well and declared bankruptcy in 1813. Danish paper money became worthless. The Danish national bankruptcy of 1813 also ended the career of the Schleswig-Holsteinische Species Bank in Altona.

1787-1813 Issue

		Good	Fine	XF
S756	**8 Thaler Species = 10 Thaler Courant** 1787-1813.	575.00	1350.	1850.
S757	**20 Thaler Species = 25 Thaler Courant** 1787-1813.	575.00	1350.	1850.
S758	**40 Thaler Species = 50 Thaler Courant** 1787-1813.	725.00	1650.	2500.
S759	**80 Thaler Species = 100 Thaler Courant** 1787-1813.	725.00	1650.	2500.

1801 Issue

#S761-S767 serial letter A, B, C and D (redeemable in different years).

		Good	Fine	XF
S761	**5 Reichsthaler Schlesw.-Holst. Courant** 1801.	575.00	1350.	1850.

1802 Issue

		Good	Fine	XF
S762	**5 Reichsthaler Schlesw.-Holst. Courant** 1802.	575.00	1350.	1850.

1803 Issue

		Good	Fine	XF
S763	**5 Reichsthaler Schlesw.-Holst. Courant** 1803.	—	—	—

1810 Issue

		Good	Fine	XF
S764	**25 Reichsthaler** 1810.	—	—	—
S765	**50 Reichsthaler** 1810.	—	—	—
S766	**75 Reichsthaler** 1810.	—	—	—
S767	**100 Reichsthaler** 1810.	—	—	—

Schlesw. Holst. Kassen-Scheine

Provisional Government

A revolutionary government in rebellion against Danish rule, in office March 1848 until October 22, 1848, after the armistice at Malmö, Much of the paper money was issued in its name by the government which succeeded the provisional government.

1848 Issue

		Good	Fine	XF
S771	**1 Thaler = 2 1/2 Mark Courant** 31.7.1848. Sign. J. C. Ravit; H. W. Baudissin; M. Moltke; P. Lüders; Matthiessen; Tiedemann.	150.00	300.00	550.00

		Good	Fine	XF
S772	**4 Thaler = 10 Mark Courant** 31.7.1848. Sign. J. C. Ravit; H. W. Baudissin; M. Moltke; P. Lüders; Matthiessen; Tiedemann.	235.00	500.00	800.00
S773	**10 Thaler = 25 Mark Courant** 31.7.1848. Sign. J. C. Ravit; H. W. Baudissin; M. Moltke; P. Lüders; Matthiessen; Tiedemann.	435.00	1000.	1500.

Schleswig-Holstein, Statthalterschaft der Herzogtümer

Schleswig-Holstein, Governorship of the Duchies

1850, different values, are obligations.

Freiwillige Anleihe des Schleswig-Holst. Finanz-Departements

Voluntary Loan of the Schleswig-Holstein Finance Department

1863, 5 and 10 Thalers, are promissory notes.

Schwarzburg-Rudolstadt, Principality of

Kassenbillets

1848 Issue

		Good	Fine	XF
S776	**1 Thaler** 4.12.1848. Sign. Schwartz; Bamberg.			
	a. Edge light blue.	235.00	465.00	575.00
	b. Edge white.	235.00	465.00	575.00

1851-55 Issue

		Good	Fine	XF
S777	**1 Thaler** 30.5.1851. Count Albert VII at top, castles of Schwarzburg and Rudolstadt at l. and r. Pink unpt. on back. Sign. Schwartz; Bamberg. Wmk: SIR. Printer: Theodor Boesche, Berlin.	150.00	300.00	400.00
S778	**10 Thaler** 1.12.1855 (1.1856). Sign. Ketelhodt; Hercher; Bergmann.	435.00	875.00	1150.

Schwarzburg-Sondershausen, Principality of

Verwaltung des Kammerschulden-Tilgungsfonds

Administration of the Governmental Debt Redemption Treasury Assignments

1854-55 Issue

		Good	Fine	XF
S781	**1 Thaler** 11.3.1854. Themis holding scales and sword at l., arms at r. Numeral I on back. Sign. Cannabich; Gottschalck; Liebers.	300.00	600.00	1000.
S782	**5 Thaler** 11.3.1854. Sign. Cannabich; Gottschalck; Liebers.	—	—	—
S783	**10 Thaler** 20.12.1855. Sign. Cannabich; Gottschalck; Liebers.	—	—	—

1859 Issue

		Good	Fine	XF
S784	**1 Thaler** 25.10.1859. Sign. Cannabich; Huschke; Linke.	235.00	500.00	800.00

1866 Issue

		Good	Fine	XF
S785	**1 Thaler** 25.2.1866. Sign. Cannabich; Möller; Linke.	150.00	300.00	550.00

Thüringische Bank

Thuringian Bank

Founded 1856. The bank abandoned the right to issue notes when the Reichsbank was established in 1875. The bank was taken over and liquidated by the Dresdner Bank in 1878.

1856 Issue

		Good	Fine	XF
S788	**20 Thaler** 1.3.1856.	575.00	1350.	1850.

1870 Issue

		Good	Fine	XF
S789	**20 Thaler** 29.3.1870.	575.00	1350.	1850.

Waldeck, Principality of

Fürstl. Waldecksche Staatsschulden-Verwaltung

Royal Waldeck State Indebtedness Administration

1854 Issue

#S791-S792 printer: Dondorf & Naumann, Frankfurt/Main

		GOOD	FINE	XF
S791	1 THALER 13.11.1854. Sign. Schumacher; Steineck.	435.00	1000.	1500.
S792	10 THALER 13.11.1854.	575.00	1350.	1850.

WESTPHALIA, KINGDOM OF

OBLIGATIONEN DER REICHSSCHULDEN-AMORTISATIONS-CASSE

OBLIGATIONS OF THE IMPERIAL DEBT AMORTIZATIONS TREASURY

Different handwritten issue dates.

Strictly speaking #S796-S799 are bonds rather than paper money, and #S801-S811A are bond coupons rather than paper money.

DECREE OF OCTOBER 19, 1808

		GOOD	FINE	XF
S796	25 FRANKEN 19.10.1808. Black.	75.00	150.00	350.00
S797	50 FRANKEN 19.10.1808. Black.	75.00	150.00	350.00
S798	100 FRANKEN 19.10.1808. Black.	75.00	150.00	350.00
S799	200 FRANKEN 19.10.1808. Black.	75.00	150.00	350.00

VIERTELJÄRIGE ZINS-COUPONS

QUARTERLY INTEREST COUPONS TO THE OBLIGATIONS OF THE IMPERIAL DEBT AMORTIZATIONS TREASURY

Issued for 30.6.18xx or 31.12.18xx (printed), handwritten from (30.6.18)12 to (31.12.18)20; 2 different red sign. in facsimile, handwritten values. The red stamp is an acknowledgement of the obligation of the Prussian government after 1815.

1812-20 ISSUE

		GOOD	FINE	XF
S801	2 FRANKEN 1812-20. Black. W/o red stamp *F.W.*	20.00	40.00	75.00
S802	3 FRANKEN 1812-20. Black. W/o red stamp *F.W.*	20.00	40.00	75.00
S803	4 FRANKEN 1812-20. Black. W/o red stamp *F.W.*	20.00	40.00	75.00
S804	5 FRANKEN 1812-20. Black. W/o red stamp *F.W.*	20.00	40.00	75.00

		GOOD	FINE	XF
S805	6 FRANKEN 1812-20. Black. W/o red stamp *F.W.*	20.00	40.00	75.00
S806	10 FRANKEN 1812-20. Black. W/o red stamp *F.W.*	20.00	40.00	75.00
S807	2 FRANKEN 1812-20. Black. Red stamp *F.W.*	25.00	55.00	85.00
S808	3 FRANKEN 1812-20. Black. Red stamp *F.W.*	25.00	55.00	85.00
S809	4 FRANKEN 1812-20. Black. Red stamp *F.W.*	25.00	55.00	85.00
S810	5 FRANKEN 1812-20. Black. Red stamp *F.W.*	25.00	55.00	85.00
S811	6 FRANKEN 1812-20. Black. Red stamp *F.W.*	25.00	55.00	85.00
S811A	10 FRANKEN 1812-20. Black. Red stamp *F.W.*	25.00	55.00	85.00

1812 TREASURY NOTES ISSUE

		GOOD	FINE	XF
S812	20 FRANKEN 12.6.1812. Values handwritten.	100.00	160.00	275.00
S813	50 FRANKEN 12.6.1812. Values handwritten.	100.00	160.00	275.00
S814	100 FRANKEN 12.6.1812. Values handwritten.	100.00	160.00	275.00
S815	250 FRANKEN 12.6.1812. Values handwritten.	100.00	160.00	275.00
S816	20 FRANKEN 8.7.1812. Values printed.	125.00	250.00	400.00
S817	50 FRANKEN 8.7.1812. Values printed.	125.00	250.00	400.00

		GOOD	FINE	XF
S818	250 FRANKEN 8.7.1812. Values printed.	125.00	250.00	400.00

Issues of Westphalia were not intended to be legal tender for circulation and therefore cannot be considered paper money.

WÜRTTEMBERG, KINGDOM OF

KÖNIGL. STAATS-HAUPT-KASSE

ROYAL STATE TREASURY

1849 ISSUE

#S841-S843 printer: C. Naumann, Frankfurt/Main.

		GOOD	FINE	XF
S841	2 GULDEN 1.8.1849. Minerva at top; putti symbolizing agriculture and commerce at bottom. Sign. Herdegen; Schickhardt.	300.00	600.00	1000.
S842	10 GULDEN 1.8.1849. Sign. Herdegen; Schickhardt.	500.00	1000.	1600.
S843	35 GULDEN 1.8.1849. Sign. Herdegen; Schickhardt.	500.00	1000.	1600.

1858 ISSUE

#S844 printer: C. Naumann, Frankfurt/Main.

		GOOD	FINE	XF
S844	10 GULDEN 1.1.1858. Sign. Vogel; Schickhardt. Printer: C. Naumann, Frankfurt/Main.	500.00	1000.	1600.

1871 Issue

Printer: C. Naumann, Frankfurt/Main

		Good	Fine	XF
S845	10 Gulden 1.12.1871. Sign. Neuschler; Heider. Printer: C. Naumann, Frankfurt/Main.	500.00	1000.	1600.

Württembergischer Cassen-Verein von G. Müller und Genossen

Württemberg Treasury Association of G. Müller and Associates

When the outbreak of the Franco-Prussian War in July 1870 caused a monetary stringency, the leading banks in Württemberg issued their own paper money under the name of the "Württembergischer Cassen-Verein von G. Müller und Genossen." Müller was the chairman of the largest bank in Stuttgart, the Württembergische Vereinsbank. The Cassen-Verein became the Württembergische Notenbank the following September 1; and it opened for business on December 20, 1871. Its right to issue banknotes was ended by the law of December 1933, effective December 31, 1935. After abandoning the note issuing privilege in 1935, the bank changed its name to the Württembergische Bank. It merged on December 1, 1977 with the Badische Bank and the Handelsbank Heilbronn to form the Baden-Württembergische Bank.

1870 Issue

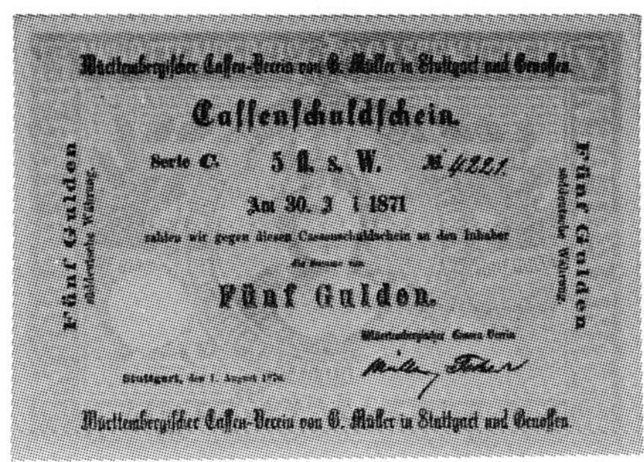

		Good	Fine	XF
S846	5 Gulden 1.8.1870. Punched.	75.00	150.00	275.00

Note: Interest bearing notes in higher denomination were also issued.

Württembergische Notenbank

See Regional Bank Issues #S975-S999.

Principalities

Fürstlich Anhalt-Cöthen-Plessner Rent-Kammer-Scheine

Princely Anhalt-Cöthen-Pless Governmental Interest Bearing Notes

1807-21 Issue

		Good	Fine	XF
S851	5 Silbergroschen 1807-21.	—	—	—
S852	10 Silbergroschen 1807-21.	300.00	600.00	1000.
S853	15 Silbergroschen 1807-21.	—	—	—
S854	1 Reichsthaler 1807-21.	—	—	—
S855	5 Reichsthaler 1807-21.	—	—	—
S856	10 Reichsthaler 1807-21.	—	—	—

Anhalt-Dessau, Herzogl. Anhalt-Dessauisches Steueramt

Anhalt-Dessau, Ducal Tax Bureau

1863 ND Issue

Dated by the use of the suffix "Dessau," which was not used after the absorption of Anhalt-Bernburg in 1863. Used during a period of shortage of copper money.

		Good	Fine	XF
S857	3 Pfennig ND (pre 1863). Red stamp: HERZ. ANH. DESSAU STEURAMT, DESSAU. Back handwritten: 3 PFENNIG. Cardboard.	—	—	—

Fürstl. Carolath-Beuthen'sche Kammer, Kassenanweisungen der Rent-Kasse

Princely Carolath-Beuthen Government Treasury Vouchers of the Revenue Fund

1830 Issue

		Good	Fine	XF
S858	1 Thaler Preuss. Courant 1.7.1830.			
	a. Issued note.	300.00	600.00	1000.
	p. Proof.	—	—	—

Fürst Pückler-Muskau in Muskau O.L., Schlesien

Treasury Vouchers

1826 ND Issue

		Good	Fine	XF
S859	1 Thaler ND (1826).	750.00	1600.	—
S860	5 Thaler ND (1826).	1000.	2000.	—

Solms-Hohensolms-Lich, Oberhessen, Fürst

A mediatized prince who sought to issue his own paper money to pay his own troops during the War of Liberation of 1813-15. The paper money and the troop contingent were both suppressed by the government of Hesse-Darmstadt.

1814 Issue

		Good	Fine	XF
S861	5 Thaler 1814.	—	—	—

Solms-Laubach, Oberhessen,Gräfl. Solms-Laubachische Kassenanweisungen

1847 Issue

#S862-S863 printer: C. Naumann, Frankfurt/Main.

		Good	Fine	XF
S862	1 Gulden 1847.	1000.	2000.	—
S863	5 Gulden 1847.	1000.	2000.	—

Stolberg-Rossla, Prov. Sachsen, Grafen

1706 Issue

An emergency issue when Electoral Saxon troops occupied the previously independent earldom in a *coup de main.*

		Good	Fine	XF
S864	3 Pfennig 1706.	—	—	—
S865	6 Pfennig 1706.	—	—	—
S866	1 Silbergroschen 1706.	—	—	—
S867	2 Silbergroschen 1706.	—	—	—
S868	6 Silbergroschen 1706.	—	—	—
S869	12 Silbergroschen 1706.	—	—	—

1813 Issue

Issued after the earldoms were liberated by Prussia; the small denominations were issued under a common law of the three Stolberg lines. Redeemed 1817.

		Good	Fine	XF
S870	3 Pfennig 11.1813.	—	—	—
S871	6 Pfennig 11.1813.	—	—	—
S872	1 Silbergroschen 11.1813.	—	—	—
S873	2 Silbergroschen 11.1813.	—	—	—
S874	6 Silbergroschen 11.1813.	—	—	—
S875	12 Silbergroschen 11.1813.	—	—	—

Stolberg-Stolberg, Prov. Sachsen, Grafen

1706 Issue

An emergency issue when Electroal Saxon troops occupied the previously independent earldom in a *coup de main.*

		Good	Fine	XF
S876	3 Pfennig 1706.	—	—	—
S877	6 Pfennig 1706.	—	—	—
S878	1 Silbergroschen 1706.	—	—	—
S879	2 Silbergroschen 1706.	—	—	—
S880	6 Silbergroschen 1706.	—	—	—
S881	12 Silbergroschen 1706.	—	—	—

1813 Issue

Issued after the earldoms were liberated by Prussia; the small denominations were issued under a common law of the three Stolberg lines. Redeemed 1817.

		Good	Fine	XF
S882	3 Pfennig 11.1813.	—	—	—
S883	6 Pfennig 11.1813.	—	—	—
S884	1 Silbergroschen 11.1813.	—	—	—
S885	2 Silbergroschen 11.1813.	—	—	—
S886	6 Silbergroschen 11.1813.	—	—	—
S887	12 Silbergroschen 11.1813.	—	—	—

Stolberg-Wernigerode, Prov. Sachsen, Grafen

Issued after the earldoms were liberated by Prussia; the small denominations were issued under a common law of the three Stolberg lines, the thaler notes were issued to pay the civil servants and to recruit a Werningerode Landwehr (militia of men between 35 and 45 years). Redeemed 1817.

1813 Issue

		Good	Fine	XF
S888	3 Pfennig 11.1813.	—	—	—
S889	6 Pfennig 11.1813.	—	—	—
S890	1 Silbergroschen 11.1813.	—	—	—
S891	2 Silbergroschen 11.1813.	—	—	—
S892	6 Silbergroschen 11.1813.	—	—	—
S893	12 Silbergroschen 11.1813.	—	—	—
S894	1 Thaler 11.1813.	—	—	—
S895	2 Thaler 11.1813.	—	—	—
S896	3 Thaler 11.1813.	—	—	—
S897	5 Thaler 11.1813.	—	—	—
S898	10 Thaler 11.1813.	—	—	—
S899	20 Thaler 11.1813.	—	—	—

Ysenburg-Büdingen, Oberhessen, Fürst

A mediatized prince who isued paper money to recruit his own troop contigent during the War of Liberation of 1813-15, but the issue of paper money and the recruitment of the troops were both quashed by the Hesse-Darmstadt government. The modern spelling is Isenburg.

1814 Issue

		Good	Fine	XF
S900	5 Thaler 1814.	—	—	—

Regional Banks

Notes issued by many banks during 1914-18 as well as those made during the inflation period by numerous states and banks are not included in this section. Only those from regional banks having had a history of issues over a number of years are included: Badische Bank, Bayerische Notenbank, Sächsische Bank and Württembergische Notenbank.

Baden

Badische Bank

Bank of Baden

Concession granted March 25, 1870. It opened for business January 1, 1871. Its right to issue bank notes was ended by the law of December 1933, effective December 31, 1935. It merged on December 1, 1977 with the Handelsbank Heilbronn and the Württembergische Bank to form the Baden-Württembergische Bank.

1870-74 Issue

#S901-S906 allegorical woman w/2 small angels at lower l. and r. on face, river god of the Rhine at l. and goddess of the river Neckar at r. on back. Printer: Naumann.

		Good	Fine	XF
S901	10 Gulden 1.12.1870. Black on gray and green unpt.	600.00	1000.	1600.

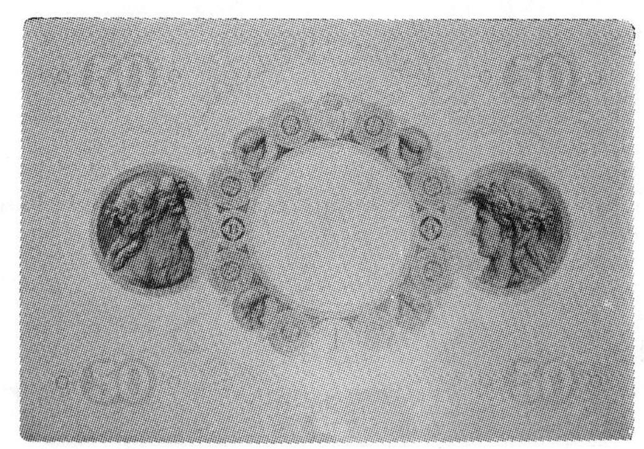

		Good	Fine	XF
S902	50 Gulden 1.7.1871. Black and blue on yellow-brown unpt.	850.00	1500.	2300.
S903	100 Mark 1.1.1874. Black and blue on yellow-brown unpt.	300.00	750.00	1450.

1890 Issue

Printer: Naumann.

		Good	Fine	XF
S904	100 Mark 1.1.1890. Black and blue on lt. blue unpt.	900.00	1600.	2400.

1902 Issue

Printer: Naumann.

		Good	Fine	XF
S905	100 Mark 1.10.1902. Black and blue on lt. blue unpt.	7.00	25.00	50.00

1907 Issue

Printer: Naumann.

		Good	Fine	XF
S906	100 Mark 1.1.1907. Black and blue on lt. blue unpt. Gray on lt. blue unpt. on back.			
	a. Printer: C. Naumann's Druckerei.	4.50	8.00	35.00
	b. W/o imprint.	3.00	9.00	30.00

1918-22 Issues

		VG	VF	Unc
S907	100 Mark 15.12.1918. Black on blue and blue-green unpt. Black on blue unpt. on back.	1.00	5.00	15.00

		VG	VF	UNC
S908	**500 MARK** 1.8.1922. Black-green on brown and gray unpt. Griffins and arms at ctr. Factory and field work on back.	1.00	5.00	15.00

		VG	VF	UNC
S909	**5000 MARK** 1.12.1922. Brown on violet and gold unpt. 2 lg. stylized griffins at ctr. Sm. scenes at corners, lg. allegorical scene at ctr. on back.	1.00	4.00	12.00

1923 ISSUE

		VG	VF	UNC
S910	**10,000 MARK** 1.4.1923. Lt. brown on blue and green unpt. 2 stylized griffins and arms at ctr. 2-faced head w/one facing l. and one facing r. at ctr. on back.	1.00	2.00	4.00

		VG	VF	UNC
S911	**500,000 MARK** 1.8.1923. Dk. brown on gray-brown and violet unpt. Man w/torch and hammer on back.	1.00	2.00	5.00
S912	**1 MILLION MARK** 7.8.1923. Black on violet unpt. Uniface.	1.00	2.00	4.00

		VG	VF	UNC
S913	**2 MILLIARDEN MARK** 25.9.1923. Dk. brown on gray-green unpt. Red ovpt: new denomination across 20 Millionen Mark on face and back.	1.00	2.50	6.00
S914	**100 MILLIARDEN MARK** 30.10.1923. Dk. brown on brown-violet and lt. blue unpt.	2.50	7.50	20.00

1924 ISSUE

		VG	VF	UNC
S915	**50 REICHSMARK** 11.10.1924. Dk. blue on brown and green unpt. Johann Peter Hebel at r.			
	a. Issued note.	300.00	500.00	1000.
	b. Cancelled, stamped: *Ungültig.*	40.00	100.00	250.00

BAVARIA

BAYERISCHE NOTENBANK

BAVARIAN NOTE ISSUING BANK

Founded in 1875 when the Bayerische Hypotheken- und Wechsel-Bank transfered to it the note-issuing right. The Bayerische Notenbank was in a certain sense a spinoff of the Bayerische Hypotheken- und Wechsel-Bank so that the latter could engage in commercial banking operations more freely than would be possible under the new Reichsbank law. The Commerzbank in Lübeck and the Braunschweigische Bank spun off similar affiliates, although in their cases the mother bank retained the note-issuing right and the spinoff was the commercial bank. The Bayerische Notenbank's note design continues that of the Bayerische Hypotheken- und Wechsel-Bank. It opened for business on November 3, 1875. Its right to issue bank notes was ended by the law of December 1933, effective December 31, 1935. The bank was liquidated; most of its personel and offices were taken over by the Bayerische Vereinsbank in 1969. The Bayerische Vereinsbank merged with the Bayerische Hypotheken- und Wechsel-Bank to form the Bayerische Hypo- und Vereins-Bank in 1997.

1875 ISSUE

Mark system

		VG	VF	UNC
S921	**100 MARK** 3.11.1875. Black on blue unpt. 2 seated allegorical figures w/child at l. and r., arms at bottom ctr. Printer: G&D. Made from the same plate as #S166.	325.00	600.00	1200.

1900 ISSUE

		VG	VF	UNC
S922	**100 MARK** 1.1.1900. Black on blue and m/c unpt. Like #S921. Printer: G&D.	2.00	5.00	12.00

1922 ISSUE

		VG	VF	UNC
S923	**100 MARK** 1.1.1922. Black on m/c unpt. Arms at r. on back.	.50	1.50	4.50

		VG	VF	UNC
S924	**1000 MARK** 1.10.1922. Blue-black on blue and brown unpt. Brown on lt. blue unpt. on back.	1.00	3.00	8.00
S925	**5000 MARK** 1.12.1922. M/c.	1.00	3.00	8.00

1923 FIRST ISSUE

		VG	VF	UNC
S926	**20,000 MARK** 1.3.1923. Dk. blue on blue and orange unpt. Arms at ctr. on back.	1.00	3.00	9.00

		VG	VF	UNC
S927	**50,000 MARK** 15.3.1923. Black on gray and m/c unpt. Blue on green and lt. brown unpt. on back.	1.00	3.00	9.00

		VG	VF	UNC
S928	**100,000 MARK** 15.6.1923. Black on green and red unpt. Back blue on lt. olive; griffins w/arms at l. and r., Bavaria Monument at Munich.	1.00	3.00	9.00

		VG	VF	UNC
S929	**1 MILLION MARK** 15.8.1923. Black and blue on tan and orange unpt. 2 stylized figures at ctr. Back blue and red; arms at ctr.	1.00	3.00	9.00

1923 SECOND ISSUE

		VG	VF	UNC
S930	**500,000 MARK** 18.8.1923. Dk. blue on violet and lilac unpt. Arms in unpt. on back.	1.00	3.00	9.00
S931	**1 MILLION MARK** 20.8.1923. Dk. brown on yellow and blue-green unpt. Blue-green on back.	1.00	3.00	9.00

		VG	VF	UNC
S932	**5 MILLIONEN MARK** 20.8.1923. Dk. brown on green and red-brown unpt. Back brown and red; arms at ctr.	1.50	4.00	12.00
S933	**25 MILLIONEN MARK** 20.8.1923. Blue and brown.	1.50	4.00	12.00

		VG	VF	UNC
S934	**50 MILLIONEN MARK** 20.8.1923. Black on lt. olive and red-brown unpt. Fruit baskets at l. and r. Arms on back.	1.50	4.00	12.00
S935	**10 MILLIONEN MARK** 1.9.1923. Blue and brown.	1.25	3.00	10.00

		VG	VF	UNC
S936	**1 MILLIARDE MARK** 1.10.1923. Dk. brown on violet unpt. Back violet.	1.50	4.00	12.00
S937	**5 MILLIARDEN MARK** 18.10.1923. Black on red, pink and gray-blue unpt. Uniface.	1.50	4.50	15.00
S938	**50 MILLIARDEN MARK** 24.10.1923. Dk. green.	2.00	7.50	25.00
S939	**500 MILLIARDEN MARK** ND (-old date 1.8.1923). M/c. Red-brown ovpt. New denomination on 100 Millionen Mark.	30.00	70.00	160.00

1924 ISSUE

Reichsmark System

		VG	VF	UNC
S940	**50 REICHSMARK** 30.8.1924. Brown-violet. Venetian woman by Albrecht Dürer. Like Federal Republic of Germany #18. Proof. (Not issued).	—	—	—
S941	**50 REICHSMARK** 11.10.1924. Green. Arms at upper r.	300.00	750.00	1400.
S942	**100 REICHSMARK** 11.10.1924. Blue. Arms on back.	250.00	600.00	1000.

1925 ISSUE

		VG	VF	UNC
S943	**50 REICHSMARK** 1.9.1925. Brown and green. Hieronymus Holzschuher (by Albrecht Dürer) at r.	250.00	600.00	1000.

SAXONY

SÄCHSISCHE BANK

BANK OF SAXONY

Founded July 18, 1865, by decree of King Johann. Its founders included the Jewish banker Carl Kaskel, who in 1872 would convert his private banking house into the Dresdner Bank. Issues of bank notes began January 21, 1866, in amounts from 10 to 500 thalers. Its right to issue bank notes was ended by the law of December 1933, effective December 31, 1935. By the 1930s a majority of its shares were in the hands of the Sächsische Staatsbank. From 1937 onwards the directorate of the two banks was identical.

1866 ISSUE

Thaler System

#S946-S949 portr. woman at l., Mercury at r. Printer: G&D.

		GOOD	FINE	XF
S946	**10 THALER** 15.1.1866.	800.00	1400.	—
S947	**20 THALER** 15.1.1866.	1000.	1600.	—
S948	**50 THALER** 15.1.1866.	—	—	—
S949	**100 THALER** 15.1.1866.	—	—	—

1874 ISSUE

Mark System

#S950 and S951 portr. woman at l., Mercury at r. Printer: G&D.

		VG	VF	UNC
S950	**100 MARK** 1.1.1874. Black on green and brown unpt. Back brown and gray on green unpt.	40.00	100.00	200.00
S951	**500 MARK** 1.1.1874. Black and brown on pink unpt.	Reported Not Confirmed		

1890; 1911 ISSUE

#S952 and S953 portr. woman at l., Mercury at r. Printer: G&D.

		VG	VF	UNC
S952	**100 MARK** 1890; 1911. Black on blue and brown unpt.			
	a. 15.6.1890.	8.00	25.00	75.00
	b. 2.1.1911.	3.00	10.00	25.00
S953	**500 MARK** 1890; 1911. Black on red-brown and blue unpt.			
	a. 15.6.1890.	30.00	80.00	175.00
	b. 2.1.1911.	7.00	20.00	60.00

1922 ISSUE

		VG	VF	UNC
S954	**500 MARK** 1.7.1922. Blue-black on blue, red and m/c unpt. Portr. woman at l., Mercury at r. Back dk. green and brown. Lithographed. Printer: G&D.			
	a. Back w/folio # at lower l., sign. at lower r.	1.00	3.00	12.00
	b. W/o folio # or sign. on back.	1.00	3.00	12.00
S955	**500 MARK** 12.9.1922. Blue on yellow unpt.	1.00	5.00	45.00

		VG	VF	UNC
S956	**1000 Mark** 12.9.1922. Dk. olive on lt. olive unpt.	1.00	6.00	45.00

1923 Issue

		VG	VF	UNC
S957	**5000 Mark** 12.3.1923. Black on blue-green and green unpt.	1.00	3.00	9.00
S958	**10,000 Mark** 1.3.1923. Green and pink.	1.00	2.50	10.00

		VG	VF	UNC
S959	**50,000 Mark** 25.7.1923. Blue-black on green and brown unpt. Back green on brown unpt.	1.00	3.00	9.00
S960	**100,000 Mark** 2.7.1923. Black on green and pink unpt. Back brown and green. Printer: G&D.	1.00	3.00	9.00

		VG	VF	UNC
S961	**500,000 Mark** 15.8.1923. Black on green, violet and blue unpt. Back black on green unpt.	.75	2.00	7.50
S962	**1 Million Mark** 18.8.1923. Brown and lt. blue.	.75	2.00	7.50

		VG	VF	UNC
S963	**2 Millionen Mark** 1.9.1923. Black on brown-olive unpt. Bridge at l. Back blue and lilac. Printer: Rommler & Jonas.	.75	2.00	7.50

		VG	VF	UNC
S964	**5 Millionen Mark** 12.8.1923. Dk. brown on peach and gray-green unpt. Printer: Stengel.	1.00	3.50	9.00
S965	**100 Millionen Mark** 1.10.1923. Blue-black on m/c unpt. Back red on blue unpt.	1.50	4.00	10.00
S966	**20 Milliarden Mark** 20.10.1923. Brown-violet and green.	4.00	10.00	45.00
S967	**100 Milliarden Mark** 20.10.1923. Brown-violet and lt. brown.	10.00	30.00	95.00

		VG	VF	UNC
S968	**1 Billion Mark** 15.11.1923. Green and olive.	30.00	80.00	175.00
S969	**10 Billionen Mark** 15.11.1923. Lilac and blue.	40.00	100.00	225.00

1924 Issue

Reichsmark System

		VG	VF	UNC
S970	**50 Reichsmark** 11.10.1924. Brown. Portr. Ludwig Richter (painter) at l.	275.00	550.00	1100.

		VG	VF	UNC
S971	**100 Reichsmark** 11.10.1924. Dk. blue and brown. Portr. Gotthold Ephraim Lessing (writer) at l.	300.00	600.00	1200.

Württemberg

Württembergische Notenbank

Württemberg Note Issuing Bank

1871 Issue

Gulden System

#S975 and S976 3 sm. cherubs at l. and r., arms at upper ctr. Printer: C. Naumann.

		Good	Fine	XF
S975	**10 Gulden** 15.11.1871.	800.00	1500.	—

		GOOD	FINE	XF
S976	**35 GULDEN** 15.11.1871. Back like #S975.	850.00	1500.	—

1874-75 ISSUE

Mark System

		GOOD	FINE	XF
S977	**100 MARK** 1874-75. Dk. brown on lt. brown and blue unpt. 3 sm. cherubs at l. and r., arms at upper ctr. Bank name in 2 lines. Printer: C. Naumann.			
	a. 1.1.1874.	500.00	900.00	1500.
	b. 1.1.1875.	—	—	—

1890 ISSUE

		GOOD	FINE	XF
S978	**100 MARK** 1.1.1890. Similar to #S977 but smaller size. Punched hole cancelled. Printer: Dondorf & Naumann.	350.00	700.00	1300.

1902; 1911 ISSUE

		VG	VF	UNC
S979	**100 MARK** 1902; 1911. Black on blue and lt. brown unpt. 3 sm. cherubs at l. and r., arms at upper ctr. Supported royal arms at ctr. on back. Printer: G&D.			
	a. 1.1.1902.	80.00	120.00	200.00
	b. 1.1.1911. Sign. Koerper; Steinhäuser.	4.50	8.00	15.00
	c. 1.1.1911. Sign. Koerper; Lotter.	4.50	8.00	15.00

1918 ISSUE

		VG	VF	UNC
S980	**100 MARK** 15.12.1918. Dk. green on olive-brown unpt. Undertype for #S991, w/o new value ovpt. Known only as Specimen w/ovpt: *Müsterdruck.*	—	400.00	750.00

1922 ISSUE

		VG	VF	UNC
S981	**1000 MARK** 1.9.1922. Blue on gray-violet unpt.	3.00	8.00	25.00

1923 FIRST ISSUE

		VG	VF	UNC
S982	**10,000 MARK** 20.2.1923. Blue-black on yellow-brown unpt. Back brown and blue.	1.00	3.00	8.00
S983	**20,000 MARK** 15.6.1923. Dk. green and red on lt. brown unpt. Ludwig Uhland at l. Back green on lt. brown unpt.; arms at top ctr.	.75	2.00	7.50

		VG	VF	UNC
S984	**50,000 MARK** 10.6.1923. Green and red-brown on lilac unpt. 2 deer and arms in unpt. on back.	.75	2.00	7.50
S985	**100,000 MARK** 15.6.1923. Dk. green and blue on brown unpt. Similar to #S984.	.75	2.00	7.50

		VG	VF	Unc
S986	**1 Million Mark** 15.6.1923. Blue-black and red-brown on brown unpt. Similar to #S984.	.75	2.00	7.50

		VG	VF	Unc
S987	**1 Million Mark** 1.8.1923. Black and red on orange unpt. Portr. Friedrich Schiller at upper ctr. Back brown and green; rising sun over hills at ctr.	.75	2.00	7.50
S988	**5 Millionen Mark** 1.8.1923. Black on red unpt. Brown arms in unpt. at ctr. on back.	1.00	3.00	9.00

		VG	VF	Unc
S989	**100 Millionen Mark** 1.8.1923. Black on dk. blue unpt. Similar to #S988; green arms on back.	1.50	4.00	12.00
S990	**10 Milliarden Mark** 15.10.1923.			
	a. Good until 30.11.1923.	2.50	7.50	20.00
	b. Good until 31.12.1923.	2.50	7.50	20.00

		VG	VF	Unc
S991	**50 Milliarden Mark** ND (1923-old date 15.12.1918). Ovpt. on 100 Mark, #S980.	7.50	20.00	50.00
S992	**500 Milliarden Mark** 20.11.1923. Black-brown on olive-brown and purple unpt. Back brown with black text; arms across ctr.	25.00	75.00	200.00

1923 Second Issue

Goldmark System

		VG	VF	Unc
S993	**4.20 Goldmark = 1 Dollar** 5.12.1923. (Not issued).	—	—	—

		VG	VF	Unc
S994	**21 Goldmark = 5 Dollars** 5.12.1923. (Not issued).	—	—	—
S995	**105 Goldmark = 25 Dollars** 5.12.1923. (Not issued).	—	—	—

1924 Issue

Reichsmark System

		VG	VF	Unc
S996	**50 Reichsmark** 11.10.1924. Brown. Portr. Johannes Kepler at l.	200.00	450.00	800.00
S997	**100 Reichsmark** 11.10.1924. Dk. blue. Portr. Jörg Syrlin der Ältere (wood carver) at r.	250.00	500.00	1000.

1925 Issue

		VG	VF	Unc
S998	**50 Reichsmark** 1.8.1925. Dk. brown and green. Portr. Christian Friedrich Daniel Schubart (port) at l.	275.00	550.00	1000.

1930 Issue

		VG	VF	Unc
S999	**50 Reichsmark** 1.10.1930. Dk. brown and dk. green. Portr. Friedrich List (economist) at l. (Not issued).	—	—	1200.

Germany, a nation of north-central Europe which from 1871 to 1945 was, successively, an empire, a republic and a totalitarian state, attained its territorial peak as an empire when it comprised a 208,780 sq. mi. (540,740 sq. km.) homeland and an overseas colonial empire.

As the power of the Roman Empire waned, several warlike tribes residing in northern Germany moved south and west, invading France, Belgium, England, Italy and Spain. In 800 AD the Frankish King Charlemagne, who ruled most of present-day France and Germany, was crowned Emperor of the Holy Roman Empire. Under his successors, this empire was divided into France in the West and Germany (including the Emperor's title) in the East. Over the centuries the German part developed into a loose federation of an estimated 1,800 German States that lasted until 1806. Modern Germany was formed from the eastern part of Charlemagne's empire.

After 1812, the German States were reduced to a federation of 32, of which Prussia was the strongest. In 1871, Prussian Chancellor Otto Von Bismarck united the German States into an empire ruled by Wilhelm I, the Prussian king. The empire initiated a colonial endeavor and became one of the world's greatest powers. Germany disintegrated as a result of World War I, and was reestablished as the Weimar Republic. The humiliation of defeat, economic depression, poverty and discontent gave rise to Adolf Hitler in 1933, who reconstituted Germany as the Third Reich and after initial diplomatic and military triumphs, led it to disaster in World War II. During the postwar era, the western provinces were occupied by the Allied forces while the eastern provinces were occupied and administered by the Soviet Union. East Germany and West Germany were established in 1949.

The post-WWII division of Germany ended on Oct. 3, 1990, when the German Democratic Republic (East Germany) ceased to exist and its five constituent provinces were formally admitted to the Federal Republic of Germany. An election held on Dec. 2, 1990 chose representatives to the united federal parliament (Bundestag), which then conducted its opening session in Berlin in the old Reichstag building. The Capital remained in Bonn until 1999.

MONETARY SYSTEM:

French Zone of Occupation, 1947

State Issues

Baden

1947 Fractional Currency Issue

#S1001-S1003 value at ctr. Arms at ctr. on back.

		VG	VF	UNC
S1001	**5 Pfennig**			
	1947. Brown and green.			
	a. *No.* w/series A; B; C.	1.00	6.00	20.00
	b. *Nr.* w/series A.	2.00	8.00	25.00

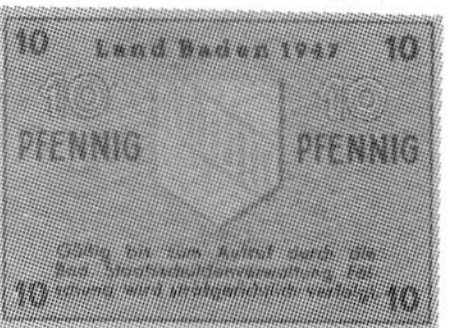

		VG	VF	UNC
S1002	**10 Pfennig**			
	1947. Blue and gray. Arms at l and r.			
	a. *No.* w/series A; B; C; D.	1.00	6.00	20.00
	b. *Nr.* w/series C; D.	2.00	12.00	25.00

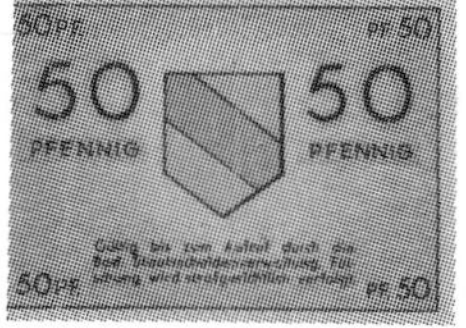

		VG	VF	UNC
S1003	**50 Pfennig**			
	1947. Red and yellow on orange unpt. Series A.	15.00	60.00	150.00

Rheinland-Pfalz

1947 Fractional Currency Issue

#S1004-S1006 wheat ears on face at ctr. Castle "Stolzenfels" and Rhine River on back.

		VG	VF	UNC
S1004	**5 Pfennig**			
	15.10.1947. Brown and violet-brown. Series A, B, C.	1.00	6.00	20.00
S1005	**10 Pfennig**			
	15.10.1947. Blue and blue-green. Series A-F.	1.00	6.00	20.00
S1006	**50 Pfennig**			
	15.10.1947. Lilac and red on olive-gray unpt. Series A.	10.00	25.00	60.00

Württemberg-Hohenzollern

1947 Fractional Currency Issue

		VG	VF	UNC
S1007	**5 Pfennig**			
	10.1947. Dk. and lt. brown. Castle Lichtenstein at ctr. on back. Series A-D have *No.* and no asterisk; series C and D are w/o *No.* and have asterisk.	1.00	4.00	15.00

		VG	VF	UNC
S1008	**10 Pfennig**			
	10.1947. Dk. and lt. blue. Castle at Sigmaringen on back. Series letters like #S1007.	1.00	4.00	15.00

		VG	VF	UNC
S1009	**50 Pfennig**			
	10.1947. Red and pink. Gateway to Castle Hohentübingen on back. Series A w/*No.*, or w/o *No.* and w/asterisk.	2.50	15.00	50.00

Note: The 10 and 50 Pfennig notes of the above issues circulated under the 1948 monetary reform with one-tenth of their former face value until 31.5.1949.

Railroads - Post WWI

Deutsche Reichsbahn Berlin (German Railroad)

Reichsverkehrsministerium

Ministry of Transport

Many notes have wmk. and serial # style variations. This is because so many different printers were used to meet the ever-increasing demand for more and more notes as the hyperinflation grew steadily worse.

All notes are listed in order by denomination. The German *Milliarde* = 1 Billion U.S.; the German *Billion* = 1 Trillion U.S.

1923 Issue

Mark System

#S1011-S1019 uniface.

#S1011-S1013 winged wheel at upper ctr.

		VG	VF	UNC
S1011	**1 Million Mark** 12.8.1923. Brown on orange unpt.	.20	.50	1.50

		VG	VF	UNC
S1012	**2 Millionen Mark** 20.8.1923. Brown on green and lilac-brown unpt.			
	a. Wmk: Interlaced squares.	.20	.50	1.50
	b. Wmk: Cups.	.25	.50	1.75
	c. Wmk: H-S-H.	.50	1.00	2.00
S1013	**5 Millionen Mark** 22.8.1923. Dk. brown on lilac and lt. green. Similar to #S1011.			
	a. Wmk: Stars and hexagons.	.20	.50	1.50
	b. Wmk: Interlaced squares.	.20	.50	1.50
	c. Wmk: Waves.	.20	.50	1.50
	d. Wmk: H-S-H.	.50	1.00	2.50

		VG	VF	UNC
S1014	**10 Millionen Mark** 2.9.1923. Black on lilac and lt. brown unpt. Winged wheel in unpt. Lt. green paper. Lt. green paper.	.20	.50	1.50

		VG	VF	UNC
S1015	**20 Millionen Mark** 18.9.1923. Green on lilac-brown and olive unpt. Steam locomotive in unpt. Lt. green paper.	.20	.50	1.50

		VG	VF	UNC
S1016	**50 Millionen Mark** 18.9.1923. Brown on green unpt. Steam locomotive in unpt. Lt. green paper.	.25	.50	1.75

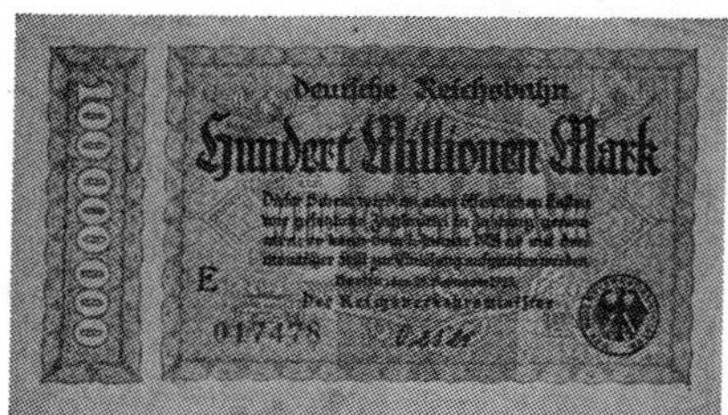

		VG	VF	UNC
S1017	**100 Millionen Mark** 25.9.1923. Black on brown and lt. violet unpt. Lt. green paper.			
	a. W/o black star near serial #.	.50	1.00	4.00
	b. Black star near serial #.	1.00	2.00	6.00

		VG	VF	UNC
S1018	**200 Millionen Mark** 10.10.1923. Black on lilac and lt. brown unpt. Similar to #S1014. Lt. green paper.	.50	1.00	4.00
S1019	**500 Millionen Mark** 10.10.1923. Black on gray-green and olive unpt. Like #S1018.	.75	1.25	4.00

		VG	VF	UNC
S1020	**1 Milliarde Mark** 18.10.1923. Black text on green and blue unpt. Steam locomotive in unpt. Back olive; City views of Cologne, Mainz at top; Steel works in Rheinhausen, Castle of Hambach at bottom; Pfalz of Caub in the Rhine at ctr. Lt. green paper.	.75	1.25	4.00

		VG	VF	UNC
S1021	**10 Milliarden Mark** 18.10.1923. Black text on violet unpt., pink paper. Steam locomotive in unpt.	1.00	2.00	6.00
S1022	**20 Milliarden Mark** 18.10.1923. Black text on dull brown-violet and dk. brown unpt. Similar to #S1020. Back dull brown-violet. Lt. green paper. W/or w/o serial #. Lt. green paper.	.50	1.00	4.00
S1023	**50 Milliarden Mark** 18.10.1923. Black text on brown unpt. Yellow paper. Like #S1020. Uniface.	1.50	3.00	9.00

		VG	VF	UNC
S1024	**100 MILLIARDEN MARK** 27.10.1923. Black on green unpt. Yellow paper. Uniface.	1.00	2.00	6.00
S1025	**200 MILLIARDEN MARK** 5.11.1923. Black on gray unpt. Pink paper. Winged wheel in unpt. Uniface.	1.50	3.00	9.00
S1026	**500 MILLIARDEN MARK** 3.11.1923. Brown on lilac unpt. Lt. green paper. Serial # at l. below or r. above.	1.50	3.00	9.00
S1027	**1 BILLION MARK** 27.10.1923. Black on brown and blue strips. 5 church views on back: Wittenberg, Ulm at top; Freiburg/Br., Danzig at bottom, Munich at ctr.	1.50	3.00	9.00

		VG	VF	UNC
S1028	**2 BILLIONEN MARK** 6.11.1923. Brown on lt. brown unpt. Yellow paper. Uniface.	1.50	3.00	9.00
S1029	**5 BILLIONEN MARK** 27.10.1923. Black on blue unpt. and strips. Uniface.	1.75	3.00	9.00

		VG	VF	UNC
S1030	**10 BILLIONEN MARK** 27.10.1923. Brown and pink and blue strips. Back deep orange; views of: Porta Nigra in Trier, fortress Ehrenbreitstein at top; Imperial palace in Goslar, castle in Nürnberg at bottom; War Memorial near Detmold (victory over the Romans) at ctr.	2.00	3.50	10.00
S1031	**20 BILLIONEN MARK** 5.11.1923. Black on olive unpt. Pink paper. Uniface.	2.00	4.00	12.00

WERTBESTÄNDIGE ANTEILSCHEINE

1923 ISSUE

Goldmark-Dollar System

#S1032-S1034 yellow paper. Uniface.

		VG	VF	UNC
S1032	**0.42 MARK GOLD = 1/10 DOLLAR** 23.10.1923. Black on brown unpt.	3.00	7.50	18.00
S1033	**1.05 MARK GOLD = 1/4 DOLLAR** 23.10.1923. Black on green unpt.	4.00	12.00	30.00
S1034	**2.10 MARK GOLD = 1/2 DOLLAR** 23.10.1923. Black on brown unpt.	6.00	25.00	55.00

WERTBESTÄNDIGE GELDSCHEINE

1923 ISSUE

#S1035-S1040 uniface.

		VG	VF	UNC
S1035	**0.42 MARK GOLD = 1/10 DOLLAR** 7.11.1923. Black on olive-brown unpt. Lg. value: *1/10* in unpt.	1.00	2.00	6.00
S1036	**1.05 MARK GOLD = 1/4 DOLLAR** 7.11.1923. Brown on lt. lilac unpt. Lg. value: *1/4 in unpt.*	2.00	5.00	15.00

		VG	VF	UNC
S1037	**2.10 MARK GOLD = 1/2 DOLLAR** 7.11.1923. Brown on lt. brown unpt. Lg. value *1/2* in unpt.	3.00	8.00	25.00

		VG	VF	UNC
S1038	**4.20 MARK GOLD = 1 DOLLAR** 7.11.1923. Red-brown on brown and olive unpt. Lg. value: *1* in unpt.	4.00	10.00	30.00
S1039	**8.40 MARK GOLD = 2 DOLLARS** 7.11.1923. Black on blue-gray unpt. Pink paper.	6.00	15.00	50.00
S1040	**21 MARK GOLD = 5 DOLLARS** 7.11.1923. Black on lilac-gray unpt. Pink paper.	10.00	25.00	70.00

REGIONAL RAILROADS - POST WWI

NOTE: For railroad notes w/*Deutsche Reichsbahn, Berlin* see #S1011-S1040.

REICHSVERKEHRSMINISTERIUM ZWEIGSTELLE BAYERN

MINISTRY OF TRANSPORT, BAVARIAN BRANCH

Issues for regional railroad offices of Augsburg, Ludwigshafen, Munich, Nürnberg.

1923 ISSUE

#S1101-S1105 w/2 cherubs at l. and r. of container w/letters at ctr.

		VG	VF	UNC
S1101	**1 MILLION MARK** 15.8.1923. Black on blue unpt. Arms w/steam train at ctr. on back. 2 sign. varieties.	.50	1.00	4.00
S1102	**5 MILLIONEN MARK** 15.8.1923. Dk. and lt. brown. Like #S1101.	.50	1.00	4.00
S1103	**10 MILLIONEN MARK** 15.8.1923. Dk. and lt. green. Like #S1101.	.50	1.00	4.00
S1104	**20 MILLIONEN MARK** 15.8.1923. Blue-violet and lilac. Like #S1101.	1.00	3.00	9.00

		VG	VF	UNC
S1105	**10 MILLIARDEN MARK** 26.10.1923. Deep purple on lt. tan unpt. Like #S1101.	1.00	3.00	10.00

		VG	VF	UNC
S1106	**50 MILLIARDEN MARK** 26.10.1923. Black on lt. brown and lt. green unpt. Color strip at r.	1.50	5.00	15.00
S1107	**50 MILLIARDEN MARK** 26.10.1923. Black on lt. tan and lt. green unpt. Uniface. Color strip at r.			
	a. Color strip lt. brown at top.	1.00	3.50	10.00
	b. Color strip lt. green at top.	1.00	3.50	10.00
S1107A	**100 MILLIARDEN MARK** 26.10.1923. Black on pink and gray.	1.50	4.00	12.50
S1108	**100 MILLIARDEN MARK** 26.10.1923. Green on gray-brown and olive green unpt.			
	a. *Münhen* instead of *München* in dateline. W/o imprint.	1.50	5.00	15.00
	b. Correct spelling *München* w/imprint. 2 wmk. varieties.	1.50	4.00	12.50
	c. Correct spelling but w/o imprint.	1.00	3.50	9.00
	d. Error like a., imprint *A. MEINDL, MÜNCHEN-PASING.*	1.50	4.00	12.50

		VG	VF	UNC
S1109	**500 MILLIARDEN MARK** 26.10.1923. Black.			
	a. Rose and lilac unpt.	2.50	7.00	20.00
	b. Additional gray-blue unpt.	1.50	5.00	15.00

		VG	VF	UNC
S1110	**1 BILLION MARK** 26.10.1923. Black on brown and blue unpt.			
	a. Brown unpt. at l., blue unpt. at r.	3.00	8.00	25.00
	b. Blue unpt. at l., brown unpt. at r.	3.00	8.00	25.00

REICHSBAHNDIREKTION ALTONA

REGIONAL RAILROAD OFFICE ALTONA

1923 ISSUE

#S1111-S1117 winged wheel in unpt. at upper ctr.

		VG	VF	UNC
S1111	**500,000 MARK** 8.8.1923. Dk. brown on gray unpt. 3 wmk. varieties.	.25	1.00	3.50
S1112	**1 MILLION MARK** 8.8.1923. Green on gray unpt. 2 wmk. varieties.	.25	1.00	3.50
S1113	**2 MILLIONEN MARK** 8.8.1923. Blue on gray unpt. 3 wmk. varieties.	.50	1.50	5.00
S1114	**5 MILLIONEN MARK** 8.8.1923. Purple on gray unpt.	.25	1.00	3.50

		VG	VF	UNC
S1115	**100 MILLIONEN MARK** 1.10.1923. Black on lilac unpt. Color strip at l.	.25	1.00	3.50
S1116	**200 MILLIONEN MARK** 1.10.1923. Purple on lilac unpt.	.25	1.00	3.50
S1117	**500 MILLIONEN MARK** 1.10.1923. Green on lilac unpt.	.50	1.25	3.50
S1118	**1 MILLIARDE MARK** 23.10.1923. Black on gray unpt.	.50	1.25	3.50
S1119	**5 MILLIARDEN MARK** 23.10.1923. Brown on gray unpt.	.50	1.25	3.50
S1120	**10 MILLIARDEN MARK** 23.10.1923. Blue on gray unpt.	.50	1.50	5.00

		VG	VF	UNC
S1121	**20 MILLIARDEN MARK** 23.10.1923. Brown on gray unpt.			
	a. W/wmk.	.50	1.50	5.00
	b. W/o wmk.	1.50	4.00	15.00
S1122	**50 MILLIARDEN MARK** 23.10.1923. Red on gray unpt.			
	a. Printer's monogram.	1.50	4.00	10.00
	b. Printer's name.	.50	1.50	5.00
S1123	**100 MILLIARDEN MARK** 23.10.1923. Green on gray unpt. 2 wmk. varieties.	.75	2.00	6.00
S1124	**500 MILLIARDEN MARK** 5.11.1923. Blue on gray unpt. 2 wmk. varieties.	.75	2.00	6.00

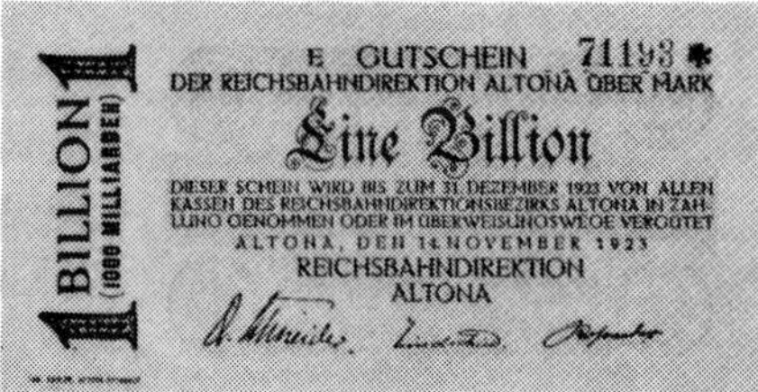

		VG	VF	UNC
S1125	**1 BILLION MARK** 14.11.1923. Purple on gray unpt.	1.50	4.00	9.00

REICHSBAHNDIREKTION BRESLAU

REGIONAL RAILROAD OFFICE BRESLAU

1923 ISSUES

#S1131-S1135 winged wheel at upper l.

		VG	VF	UNC
S1131	**500,000 MARK** 15.8.1923. Black on blue unpt.	1.00	2.50	7.50
S1132	**1 MILLION MARK** 15.8.1923. Black on green unpt.	.50	1.50	5.00
S1133	**2 MILLIONEN MARK** 15.8.1923. Black on red unpt.	.50	1.50	5.00
S1134	**5 MILLIONEN MARK** 15.8.1923. Black on brown-orange unpt.	1.00	2.50	7.50
S1135	**5 MILLIONEN MARK** 23.8.1923. Like #S1134. Series A.	1.00	3.00	9.00

#S1136 and S1137 winged wheel at ctr. on face. Lg. winged wheel at ctr. on back.

		VG	VF	UNC
S1136	**50 MILLIONEN MARK** 27.9.1923. Black on gray unpt.	.50	1.00	3.50

		VG	VF	UNC
S1137	**100 MILLIONEN MARK** 27.9.1923. Black on purple unpt.	.50	1.00	3.50

		VG	VF	UNC
S1138	**50 MILLIARDEN MARK** ND (- old date 23.8.1923). Red value ovpt. on unissued 2 Millionen Mark.	6.00	12.00	25.00

#S1139-S1141 winged wheel at upper ctr. Uniface.

		VG	VF	UNC
S1139	**50 MILLIARDEN MARK** 25.10.1923. Black on lt. brown and lilac unpt.	.75	2.00	6.00
S1140	**100 MILLIARDEN MARK** 25.10.1923. Black on gray-blue unpt.	.75	2.00	6.00
S1141	**500 MILLIARDEN MARK** 7.11.1923. Black on green and lt. brown unpt. 2 wmk. varieties.	1.50	5.00	15.00

REICHSBAHNDIREKTION CASSEL

REGIONAL RAILROAD OFFICE CASSEL

1923 FIRST ISSUE

#S1146-S1148 w/text at bottom: . . .*Eisenbahnkassen in Cassel*. . . w/*C* serial # prefix. Winged wheel in unpt. at l.

		VG	VF	UNC
S1146	**1 MILLION MARK** 10.8.1923. Black on green unpt.	1.50	5.00	15.00
S1147	**2 MILLIONEN MARK** 10.8.1923. Black on green unpt.	2.00	6.00	17.50
S1148	**5 MILLIONEN MARK** 10.8.1923. Black on lt. brown unpt.	6.00	12.00	30.00

1923 SECOND ISSUE

#S1149-S1151 w/text at bottom: . . .*Eisenbahnkassen in Göttingen*. . . w/*G* serial # prefix.

		VG	VF	UNC
S1149	**1 MILLION MARK** 10.8.1923. Like #S1146.	2.50	7.00	17.50
S1150	**2 MILLIONEN MARK** 10.8.1923. Like #S1147.	4.00	10.00	25.00
S1151	**5 MILLIONEN MARK** 10.8.1923. Like #S1148.	Reported Not Confirmed		

1923 THIRD ISSUE

#S1152-S1154 w/text at bottom: . . .*Eisenbahnkassen in Nordhausen und Sangerhausen*. . . w/*N* serial # prefix.

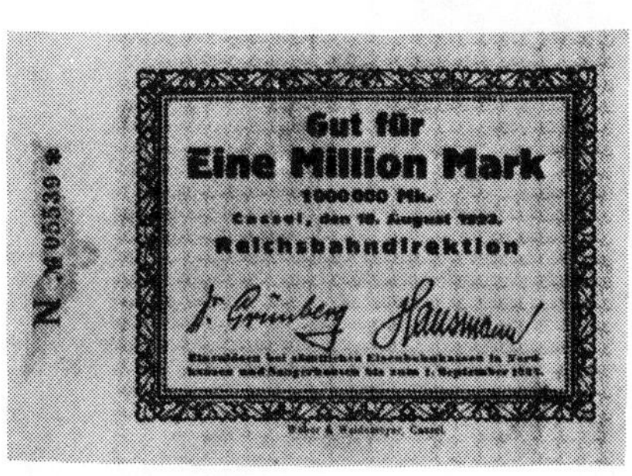

		VG	VF	UNC
S1152	**1 MILLION MARK** 10.8.1923. Like #S1146.	2.50	7.00	17.50
S1153	**2 MILLIONEN MARK** 10.8.1923. Like #S1147.	3.00	8.00	20.00
S1154	**5 MILLIONEN MARK** 10.8.1923. Like #S1148.	Reported Not Confirmed		

1923 FOURTH ISSUE

#S1155-S1157 w/text at bottom: . . .*Eisenbahnkassen in Paderborn*. . . w/*P* serial # prefix.

		VG	VF	UNC
S1155	**1 MILLION MARK** 10.8.1923. Like #S1146.	1.50	5.00	15.00
S1156	**2 MILLIONEN MARK** 10.8.1923. Like #S1147.	2.50	7.00	17.50
S1157	**5 MILLIONEN MARK** 10.8.1923. Like #S1148.	7.00	15.00	37.50

1923 FIFTH ISSUE

#S1158-S1162 w/text at bottom: . . .*Eisenbahnkassen des Reichsbahndirektionsbezirks Cassel*. . . w/*Ü* serial # prefix.

		VG	VF	UNC
S1158	**500,000 MARK** 10.8.1923. Black on lt. blue unpt.	.75	2.00	6.00
S1159	**1 MILLION MARK** 10.8.1923. Like #S1146.	.75	2.00	6.00
S1160	**2 MILLIONEN MARK** 10.8.1923. Like #S1147.	.50	1.50	5.00
S1161	**5 MILLIONEN MARK** 10.8.1923. Like #S1148.	.50	1.50	5.00
S1162	**10 MILLIONEN MARK** 10.8.1923. Black on purple unpt.	.75	2.00	6.00

1923 SIXTH ISSUE

#S1163-S1169 longer text at ctr. Winged wheel in unpt. at l.

		VG	VF	UNC
S1163	**10 MILLIARDEN MARK** 24.10.1923. Green.	1.00	2.50	7.50
S1164	**20 MILLIARDEN MARK** 24.10.1923. Brown.	1.00	2.50	7.50
S1165	**50 MILLIARDEN MARK** 24.10.1923. Blue.	1.00	3.00	9.00
S1166	**100 MILLIARDEN MARK** 24.10.1923. Black on yellow unpt.	1.00	3.50	10.00

		VG	VF	UNC
S1167	**500 MILLIARDEN MARK** 24.10.1923. Black on green unpt.	1.00	3.00	9.00
S1168	**1 BILLION MARK** 24.10.1923. Blue on brown-orange unpt.	1.50	4.00	10.00

		VG	VF	UNC
S1169	**5 BILLIONEN MARK** 24.10.1923. Black on red unpt.	1.50	5.00	15.00

REICHSBAHNDIREKTION DRESDEN

REGIONAL RAILROAD OFFICE DRESDEN

1923 ISSUE

		VG	VF	UNC
S1171	**500,000 MARK** 11.8.1923. Dk. brown on olive unpt. 2 wmk. varieties.	.40	1.00	3.50
S1172	**1 MILLION MARK** 11.8.1923. Red on gray unpt. Back red; eagle at ctr.	.40	1.00	3.50
S1173	**2 MILLIONEN MARK** 13.8.1923. Black and blue-gray on red-orange paper. Back red-orange.	1.00	2.50	7.50
S1174	**3 MILLIONEN MARK** 16.8.1923. Black and green on blue-gray paper. Back green.	1.00	2.50	7.50
S1175	**3 MILLIONEN MARK** 20.8.1923. Black and orange on green paper. Back orange.	1.00	2.50	7.50

		VG	VF	UNC
S1176	**5 MILLIONEN MARK** 21.8.1923. Black on blue-gray and orange unpt.	.40	1.00	3.50
S1177	**100 MILLIONEN MARK** 25.9.1923. Black on lt. green and lilac unpt.	1.00	2.50	7.50
S1178	**50 MILLIARDEN MARK** 26.10.1923. Black and red on blue-green unpt., dk. yellow paper.	1.00	3.00	9.00

		VG	VF	UNC
S1179	**100 MILLIARDEN MARK** 26.10.1923. Black on lt. blue, green and lt. orange unpt.	1.50	4.00	12.00
S1180	**500 MILLIARDEN MARK** 26.10.1923. Black on blue-gray, olive and red unpt. Similar to #S1179.	2.00	7.00	17.50
S1181	**10 BILLIONEN MARK** 22.11.1923. Green on lt. brown unpt.	—	Rare	—

NOTE: #S1181 only 1 example known.

REICHSBAHNDIREKTION ELBERFELD

REGIONAL RAILROAD OFFICE ELBERFELD

1923 ISSUES

#S1186 and S1187 in handwritten style.

		VG	VF	UNC
S1186	**1 MILLION MARK** 11.8.1923. Black.	1.50	5.00	15.00
S1187	**1 MILLION MARK** 11.8.1923. Red to red-brown.	1.00	3.50	9.00

		VG	VF	UNC
S1188	**2 MILLIONEN MARK** 16.8.1923. Green.	1.00	3.00	8.00
S1189	**2 MILLIONEN MARK** 16.8.1923. Blue.	1.00	3.50	9.00

		VG	VF	UNC
S1190	**5 MILLIONEN MARK** 17.8.1923. Blue on gray-green unpt. Winged wheel at upper ctr., bldg. at ctr. in unpt.	1.00	3.00	8.00

		VG	VF	UNC
S1191	**10 MILLIONEN MARK** 18.8.1923. Black on lilac and gray-green unpt. Eagle at l. and r. in unpt. Expiration date in text 30.9.1923.	1.00	3.00	8.00
S1192	**10 MILLIONEN MARK** 18.8.1923. Like #S1191 but w/o expiration date text.	1.00	3.00	8.00

		VG	VF	UNC
S1193	**50 MILLIARDEN MARK** 26.10.1923. Black on blue-green and blue-violet unpt.	1.50	4.00	10.00
S1194	**100 MILLIARDEN MARK** 2.11.1923. Green on lt. blue and pale yellow unpt.	2.50	7.00	17.50
S1195	**1 BILLION MARK** 14.11.1923. Lilac-brown on brown and olive unpt.	7.00	15.00	27.50

REICHSBAHNDIREKTION ERFURT

REGIONAL RAILROAD OFFICE ERFURT

1923 ISSUE

		VG	VF	UNC
S1201	**1 MILLION MARK** 12.8.1923. Black on green unpt. Winged wheel at each corner in unpt.	.75	2.00	6.00
S1202	**3 MILLIONEN MARK** 12.8.1923. Black on lilac-rose unpt. 2 winged wheels.	1.00	3.00	8.00
S1203	**5 MILLIONEN MARK** 12.8.1923. Black on lilac-blue unpt.	1.00	3.00	8.00
S1204	**10 MILLIONEN MARK** 12.8.1923. Black on greenish blue unpt.	.75	2.00	6.00

		VG	VF	UNC
S1205	**100 MILLIONEN MARK** 22.9.1923. Black on lilac-blue unpt. Winged wheel in unpt. at ctr.	1.00	3.00	8.00

		VG	VF	UNC
S1206	**500 MILLIONEN MARK** 22.9.1923. Black on green unpt.	1.00	3.50	9.00
S1207	**10 MILLIARDEN MARK** 20.10.1923. Blue on gray unpt. Winged wheel in unpt. at ctr.	1.50	4.00	10.00
S1208	**50 MILLIARDEN MARK** 20.10.1923. Black-green on gray-green unpt. Similar to #S1207.	1.50	4.00	10.00
S1209	**100 MILLIARDEN MARK** 26.10.1923. Black on orange unpt. 3 winged wheels in unpt. at ctr.	1.50	4.50	12.00
S1210	**500 MILLIARDEN MARK** 3.11.1923. Black on blue unpt.	2.50	7.00	17.50
S1211	**1 BILLION MARK** 3.11.1923. Black on green unpt.	8.50	19.00	45.00
S1212	**5 BILLIONEN MARK** 3.11.1923. Red on yellow unpt.	15.00	37.50	90.00

		VG	VF	UNC
S1213	**10 BILLIONEN MARK** 3.11.1923. Black on green unpt.	22.50	50.00	115.00

REICHSBAHNDIREKTION FRANKFURT AM MAIN

REGIONAL RAILROAD OFFICE FRANKFURT AM MAIN

1923 ISSUE

#S1216-S1218 gray ornament at l.

		VG	VF	UNC
S1216	**500,000 MARK** 10.8.1923. Gray and black.	.50	1.50	5.00
S1217	**1 MILLION MARK** 10.8.1923. Gray and black.	.50	1.50	5.00
S1218	**5 MILLIONEN MARK** 10.8.1923. Gray and black.	.50	1.50	5.00

		VG	VF	UNC
S1219	**10 MILLIONEN MARK** 1.9.1923. Dk. green on lt. green unpt. Eagle at corners in unpt.	.50	1.50	5.00
S1220	**20 MILLIONEN MARK** 1.9.1923. Dk. brown on yellow unpt. Like #S1219.	.50	1.50	5.00
S1221	**200 MILLIONEN MARK** 26.9.1923. Dk. brown on orange unpt. Like #S1219.	.50	1.75	6.00

#S1222-S1227 two wmk. varieties.

#S1222-S1224 winged wheel in unpt. at ctr.

		VG	VF	UNC
S1222	**20 MILLIARDEN MARK** 22.10.1923. Black on green unpt.	.75	2.00	6.00
S1223	**50 MILLIARDEN MARK** 22.10.1923. Dk. brown on purple unpt.	.75	2.00	6.00
S1224	**100 MILLIARDEN MARK** 22.10.1923. Dk. green on lilac-red unpt.	1.00	3.00	8.00

		VG	VF	UNC
S1225	**500 MILLIARDEN MARK** 22.10.1923. Dk. brown on gray-violet unpt. Winged wheel at lower ctr.	1.50	4.00	10.00

		VG	VF	UNC
S1226	**1 BILLION MARK** 2.11.1923. Black on orange unpt. Winged wheel at l. and r.	1.50	4.00	10.00

		VG	VF	UNC
S1227	**5 BILLIONEN MARK** 6.11.1923. Black on rose unpt. Winged wheel at upper ctr.	1.50	4.00	10.00
S1228	**10 BILLIONEN MARK** 6.11.1923. Dk. brown on brown unpt. Winged wheel at l. and r.	1.50	4.50	12.00

REICHSBAHNDIREKTION OSTEN IN FRANKFURT A.D. ODER

REGIONAL RAILROAD OFFICE IN THE EAST AT FRANKFURT A.D. ODER

1923 ISSUE

		VG	VF	UNC
S1231	**10 MILLIARDEN MARK** 27.10.1923. Dk. red on green unpt.	3.00	8.00	20.00
S1232	**20 MILLIARDEN MARK** 27.10.1923. Dk. green on green unpt.	2.50	7.00	17.50

		VG	VF	UNC
S1233	**50 MILLIARDEN MARK** 27.10.1923. Purple on green unpt.	2.00	6.00	17.50
S1234	**100 MILLIARDEN MARK** 3.11.1923. Blue on gray unpt.	6.00	12.50	35.00
S1235	**200 MILLIARDEN MARK** 3.11.1923. Brown on gray unpt.	7.00	15.00	37.50
S1236	**500 MILLIARDEN MARK** 14.11.1923. Black on yellow-brown unpt.	8.00	17.50	42.50

		VG	VF	UNC
S1237	**1 BILLION MARK** 14.11.1923. Black on lilac unpt.	35.00	75.00	90.00

REICHSBAHNDIREKTION HALLE (S.)

REGIONAL RAILROAD OFFICE HALLE (S.)

1923 ISSUE

		VG	VF	UNC
S1241	**500,000 MARK** ND (- good until 1.10.1923). Dk. green on lt. green unpt.	1.00	2.50	7.50
S1242	**1 MILLION MARK** ND. Like #S1241. Brown on rose unpt.	1.00	2.50	7.50
S1243	**100 MILLIONEN MARK** 26.9.1923. Black on brown unpt.	1.00	2.50	7.50

		VG	VF	UNC
S1244	**500 MILLIONEN MARK** 26.9.1923. Black on lt. blue unpt.	1.00	3.00	8.00
S1245	**10 MILLIARDEN MARK** 24.10.1923. Black on purple unpt.	1.00	3.50	9.00
S1246	**20 MILLIARDEN MARK** 24.10.1923. Black on gray unpt.	1.50	4.00	10.00
S1247	**50 MILLIARDEN MARK** 24.10.1923. Black on lt. green unpt.	1.50	4.50	12.00
S1248	**100 MILLIARDEN MARK** 2.11.1923. Purple on gray-violet unpt.	2.00	6.00	17.50
S1249	**500 MILLIARDEN MARK** 2.11.1923. Dk. brown on gray-blue unpt. 2 wmk. varieties.	2.00	6.00	17.50

		VG	VF	UNC
S1250	**1 BILLION MARK** 2.11.1923. Dk. brown on orange unpt.	4.00	10.00	25.00

REICHSBAHNDIREKTION HANNOVER

REGIONAL RAILROAD OFFICE HANNOVER

1923 ISSUE

		VG	VF	UNC
S1251	**100,000 MARK** 2.8.1923. Red on gray unpt. Winged wheel.	1.00	3.50	9.00

		VG	VF	UNC
S1252	**200,000 MARK** 29.7.1923. Gray on orange unpt.	2.50	7.00	17.50
S1253	**300,000 MARK** 2.8.1923. Purple on gray unpt.	1.50	4.50	12.00
S1254	**500,000 MARK** 2.8.1923. Blue on gray unpt. Winged wheel in unpt. at ctr.	.75	2.00	6.00
S1255	**1 MILLION MARK** 2.8.1923. Green on gray unpt.	.75	2.00	6.00
S1256	**20 MILLIARDEN MARK** 24.10.1923. Olive.			
	a. Gray unpt.	1.00	3.50	9.00
	b. Lt. blue unpt.	1.00	3.50	9.00
S1257	**50 MILLIARDEN MARK** 24.10.1923. Lilac-brown.			
	a. Gray unpt.	1.50	4.50	12.00
	b. Lt. blue unpt.	2.00	6.00	16.00
S1258	**100 MILLIARDEN MARK** 24.10.1923. Green on gray unpt.	1.50	4.50	12.00
S1259	**200 MILLIARDEN MARK** 24.10.1923. Lilac-brown on gray unpt.	1.50	5.00	15.00
S1260	**1 BILLION MARK** 24.10.1923.			
	a. Blue on gray and green unpt.	4.00	10.00	25.00
	b. Purple on gray and green unpt.	5.00	12.00	30.00
S1261	**2 BILLIONEN MARK** 24.10.1923. Blue on gray and green unpt.	7.00	15.00	37.50

REICHSBAHNDIREKTION KARLSRUHE

REGIONAL RAILROAD OFFICE KARLSRUHE

1923 ISSUES

#S1266-S1268 winged wheel at lower ctr. on back.

		VG	VF	UNC
S1266	**1 MILLION MARK** 10.8.1923. Dk. green on green unpt.	.50	1.50	5.00
S1267	**2 MILLIONEN MARK** 10.8.1923. Dk. brown on orange unpt.	.50	1.50	5.00

		VG	VF	UNC
S1268	**5 MILLIONEN MARK** 10.8.1923. Dk. purple on lilac unpt.	.50	1.50	5.00
S1269	**10 MILLIONEN MARK** 20.8.1923. Dk. gray on gray unpt. Women and children at ctr.	.50	1.75	6.00

		VG	VF	UNC
S1270	**20 MILLIONEN MARK** 20.8.1923. Red-violet on peach unpt. Like #S1269.	.50	1.75	5.00
S1271	**1 MILLIARD MARK** 20.8.1923. Dk. brown on brown unpt.	.75	2.00	7.00

		VG	VF	UNC
S1272	**100 MILLIARDEN MARK** 15.10.1923. Black on grayish blue unpt. Value: *Hundert*. Railroad bridge at Murg-Valley w/steam passenger train at ctr. Winged wheel at ctr. on back.	2.50	7.00	17.50

		VG	VF	UNC
S1273	**100 MILLIARDEN MARK** 15.10.1923. Like #S1272 but w/value: *Einhundert* in heading. 2 wmk. varieties.	1.00	3.00	8.00
S1274	**200 MILLIARDEN MARK** 15.10.1923. Dk. brown on lt. brown unpt. Like #S1273. First line *Gutschein*, second line *Deutsche Reichsbahn*.	1.50	4.00	10.00
S1275	**200 MILLIARDEN MARK** 15.10.1923. Like #S1274 but first line *Deutsche Reichsbahn* and second line *Gutschein*.	2.00	6.00	17.50
S1276	**500 MILLIARDEN MARK** 15.10.1923. Dk. green on lt. green unpt. Like #S1275.	1.00	3.50	9.00
S1277	**1 BILLION MARK** 15.10.1923. Blue on green unpt. Steam locomotive at ctr. Back lt. green; winged wheel ctr. 2 wmk. varieties.	1.50	4.00	10.00

		VG	VF	UNC
S1278	**10 BILLIONEN MARK** 15.10.1923. Dk. blue on blue-green unpt. Like #S1277.	2.00	6.00	17.50

		VG	VF	UNC
S1279	**5 BILLIONEN MARK** 15.11.1923. Black on gray-brown and blue unpt. Steam passenger trains at upper l. and r.	1.50	5.00	15.00

REICHSBAHNDIREKTION KÖLN

REGIONAL RAILROAD OFFICE COLOGNE

1923 FIRST ISSUE

Most notes have winged wheel at upper l. or r. on face, and at ctr. on back.

		VG	VF	UNC
S1280	**500,000 MARK** 11.8.1923. Used as undertype for #S1290. (Not issued).	—	—	—
S1281	**1 MILLION MARK** 11.8.1923. Black on lt. brown unpt.	1.50	4.00	10.00
S1282	**2 MILLIONEN MARK** 11.8.1923. Black on blue unpt.	1.50	4.00	10.00
S1283	**3 MILLIONEN MARK** 11.8.1923. Black on red unpt.	1.50	4.00	10.00

		VG	VF	UNC
S1284	**10 MILLIONEN MARK** 11.8.1923. Black on green unpt. 3 wmk varieties.	1.00	2.50	7.50
S1285	**20 MILLIONEN MARK** 11.8.1923. Black on purple unpt.	1.00	3.00	8.00

1923 SECOND ISSUE

		VG	VF	UNC
S1286	**10 MILLIONEN MARK** 2.9.1923. Black on green unpt.	1.00	3.00	8.00

		VG	VF	UNC
S1287	**20 MILLIONEN MARK** 2.9.1923. Brown-black on purple unpt.	1.00	3.00	8.00
S1288	**100 MILLIONEN MARK** 25.9.1923. Black on gray and red-orange unpt.	1.00	3.50	9.00
S1289	**500 MILLIONEN MARK** 10.10.1923. Black on blue-green and lilac unpt. 2 wmk. varieties.	1.00	3.50	9.00

		VG	VF	UNC
S1290	**1 MILLIARD MARK** ND (- old date 11.8.1923). Black on gray-green unpt. New denomination in words printed across face and back in carmine on unissued 500,000 Mark note #S1280. Locomotive on back.	1.00	3.00	8.00
S1291	**10 MILLIARDEN MARK** 18.10.1923. Black on orange and green unpt.	1.50	4.00	10.00
S1292	**100 MILLIARDEN MARK** 18.10.1923. Black on lt. brown and red unpt. 3 wmk. varieties.	5.00	12.00	30.00
S1293	**500 MILLIARDEN MARK** 18.10.1923. Black on green unpt. 2 wmk. varieties.	10.00	22.00	55.00
S1294	**1 BILLION MARK** 18.11.1923.	—	Rare	—
S1295	**5 BILLIONEN MARK** 18.11.1923. Blue on gray unpt.	—	Rare	—

REICHSBAHNDIREKTION KÖNIGSBERG/PR.

REGIONAL RAILROAD OFFICE KÖNIGSBERG/PRUSSIA

1923 FIRST ISSUE

		VG	VF	UNC
S1301	**1 MILLION MARK** 10.8.1923. Dk. blue.	2.50	7.00	17.50

1923 SECOND ISSUE

		VG	VF	UNC
S1302	**100,000 MARK** 18.8.1923. Brownish red.	3.00	8.00	20.00
S1303	**5 MILLIONEN MARK** 18.8.1923. Green.	4.00	10.00	25.00

		VG	VF	UNC
S1304	**20 MILLIARDEN MARK** ND (- old date 18.8.1923). Red ovpt. of new denomination in text across face of #S1303.	12.00	30.00	75.00
S1305	**50 MILLIARDEN MARK** 26.10.1923. Brown.	5.00	12.00	30.00
S1306	**100 MILLIARDEN MARK** 26.10.1923. Purple.	12.00	35.00	85.00

		VG	VF	UNC
S1307	**1 BILLION MARK** 5.11.1923. Dk. green on gray-green unpt. Steam locomotive at ctr. in unpt. 2 wmk. varieties.	25.00	55.00	140.00
S1308	**5 BILLIONEN MARK** 5.11.1923. 2 wmk. varieties.	—	Rare	—

REICHSBAHNDIREKTION MAGDEBURG

REGIONAL RAILROAD OFFICE MAGDEBURG

1923 ISSUE

		VG	VF	UNC
S1311	**500,000 MARK** 9.8.1923. Black and blue on green unpt.	1.00	3.00	8.00
S1312	**2 MILLIONEN MARK** 9.8.1923. Black and red on lt. brown unpt. 2 wmk. varieties.	.75	2.00	6.00

		VG	VF	UNC
S1313	**5 MILLIONEN MARK** 9.8.1923. Black and green on gray-blue unpt.	1.00	3.00	8.00

#S1314-S1317 winged wheel at ctr.

		VG	VF	UNC
S1314	**200 MILLIARDEN MARK** 29.10.1923. Black on lt. brown unpt.	2.00	6.00	17.50
S1315	**500 MILLIARDEN MARK** 14.11.1923. Black on purple unpt.	3.00	8.00	20.00
S1316	**1 BILLION MARK** 20.11.1923. Black on rose unpt.	4.00	10.00	25.00
S1317	**5 BILLIONEN MARK** 22.11.1923. Black on green unpt.	5.00	12.00	30.00

REICHSBAHNDIREKTION MÜNSTER/WESTF.

REGIONAL RAILROAD OFFICE MÜNSTER/WESTF.

1923 FIRST ISSUE

#S1321-S1335 winged wheel in unpt. at ctr.

		VG	VF	UNC
S1321	**1 MILLION MARK** 15.8.1923. Red on gray unpt.	1.50	4.00	10.00
S1322	**3 MILLIONEN MARK** 15.8.1923. Blue on gray unpt.	1.50	4.00	10.00
S1323	**5 MILLIONEN MARK** 15.8.1923. Purple on gray unpt.	1.50	4.00	10.00

1923 SECOND ISSUE

		VG	VF	UNC
S1323A	**1 MILLION MARK** 20.8.1923.	1.00	3.00	8.00
S1323B	**3 MILLIONEN MARK** 20.8.1923.	1.00	3.00	8.00
S1323C	**5 MILLIONEN MARK** 20.8.1923.	1.00	3.00	8.00
S1324	**1 MILLIARDE MARK** 25.10.1923.	Reported Not Confirmed		

#S1325-S1327 two wmk. varieties.

		VG	VF	UNC
S1325	**5 MILLIARDEN MARK** 25.10.1923. Brown-red on green unpt.	2.50	7.00	17.50
S1326	**10 MILLIARDEN MARK** 25.10.1923. Dk. green on green unpt.	1.50	5.00	15.00
S1327	**20 MILLIARDEN MARK** 25.10.1923. Dk. green on green unpt.	2.50	7.00	17.50

		VG	VF	UNC
S1328	**50 MILLIARDEN MARK** 25.10.1923. Dk. brown on green unpt. 3 wmk. varieties.	7.50	15.00	40.00
S1329	**100 MILLIARDEN MARK** 25.10.1923. Grayish purple on green unpt. 2 wmk. varieties.	2.50	7.00	17.50
S1330	**200 MILLIARDEN MARK** 25.10.1923. Lilac on green unpt.	4.00	10.00	25.00
S1331	**500 MILLIARDEN MARK** 25.10.1923.	Reported Not Confirmed		
S1332	**1 BILLION MARK** 25.10.1923. Blue on green unpt.	15.00	37.50	90.00
S1333	**2 BILLIONEN MARK** 25.10.1923.	Reported Not Confirmed		
S1334	**5 BILLIONEN MARK** 25.10.1923.	Reported Not Confirmed		
S1335	**10 BILLIONEN MARK** 25.10.1923.	Reported Not Confirmed		

REICHSBAHNDIREKTION OPPELN, OBERSCHLESISCHE EISENBAHNEN

REGIONAL RAILROAD OFFICE OPPELN, UPPER SILESIAN RAILROADS

1923 ISSUE

		VG	VF	UNC
S1341	**50,000 MARK** 16.8.1923. Brown. Eagle at l., winged wheel in unpt. at ctr.	2.50	7.00	17.50
S1342	**100,000 MARK** 16.8.1923. Green. Like #S1341.	4.00	10.00	25.00
S1343	**500,000 MARK** 16.8.1923. Rose. Like #S1341.	1.50	5.00	15.00

		VG	VF	UNC
S1344	**1 MILLION MARK** 16.8.1923. Dk. blue.	1.50	4.00	10.00
S1345	**500 MILLIONEN MARK** 27.9.1923. Olive green. Similar to #S1341.	2.50	7.00	17.50
S1346	**20 MILLIONEN MARK** 28.9.1923. Orange.	1.50	5.00	15.00
S1347	**50 MILLIONEN MARK** 28.9.1923. Blue.	2.50	7.00	17.50
S1348	**100 MILLIONEN MARK** 28.9.1923. Purple.	3.00	8.00	20.00
S1349	**10 MILLIARDEN MARK** 25.10.1923. Rose. Similar to #S1341.	2.50	7.00	17.50
S1350	**20 MILLIARDEN MARK** 25.10.1923. Gray-blue. Like #S1349.	3.00	8.00	20.00
S1351	**100 MILLIARDEN MARK** 25.10.1923. Blue.	4.00	10.00	25.00
S1352	**500 MILLIARDEN MARK** 25.10.1923. Lt. brown.	7.00	15.00	37.50
S1353	**1 BILLION MARK** 6.11.1923. Lilac. Similar to #S1341.	10.00	22.00	55.00
S1354	**5 BILLIONEN MARK** 13.11.1923. Orange. Similar to #S1341.	15.00	37.50	90.00

REICHSBAHNDIREKTION STETTIN

REGIONAL RAILROAD OFFICE STETTIN

1923 FIRST ISSUE

#S1356-S1358 printed in handwritten style.

		VG	VF	UNC
S1356	**500,000 MARK** 11.8.1923. Black.	7.00	15.00	37.50
S1357	**1 MILLION MARK** 11.8.1923. Black.	7.00	15.00	37.50
S1358	**3 MILLIONEN MARK** 11.8.1923. Black.	7.00	15.00	37.50

1923 SECOND ISSUE

#S1359-S1370 most notes have winged wheel at ctr. on face.

		VG	VF	UNC
S1359	**500,000 MARK** 20.8.1923. Black on green unpt.	1.50	5.00	15.00

		VG	VF	UNC
S1360	**1 MILLION MARK** 20.8.1923. Black on peach unpt.	3.00	8.00	20.00
S1361	**5 MILLIONEN MARK** 20.8.1923. Black on brown unpt.	2.50	7.00	17.50
S1362	**1 MILLIARDE MARK** 26.10.1923. Black on blue unpt.	3.00	8.00	20.00
S1363	**5 MILLIARDEN MARK** 26.10.1923. Black on lilac unpt.	4.00	10.00	25.00

#S1364-S1366 two wmk. varieties.

		VG	VF	UNC
S1364	**10 MILLIARDEN MARK** 26.10.1923. Black on green unpt.	4.00	10.00	25.00
S1365	**20 MILLIARDEN MARK** 26.10.1923. Black on brown unpt.	4.00	10.00	25.00
S1366	**50 MILLIARDEN MARK** 26.10.1923. Black on red-brown unpt.	4.00	10.00	27.50
S1367	**100 MILLIARDEN MARK** 26.10.1923. Black on green-gray unpt.	4.00	10.00	27.50

		VG	VF	UNC
S1368	**200 MILLIARDEN MARK** 5.11.1923. Dk. brown on lt. blue unpt.			
	a. White paper.	4.00	10.00	27.50
	b. Rose paper.	7.00	15.00	37.50
S1369	**500 MILLIARDEN MARK** 5.11.1923. Black on dk. brown unpt.			
	a. White paper.	8.50	20.00	45.00
	b. Rose paper.	10.00	22.00	55.00
S1370	**1 BILLION MARK** 5.11.1923. Black and red on lt. green unpt.	14.00	30.00	75.00

REICHSBAHNDIREKTION STUTTGART

REGIONAL RAILROAD OFFICE STUTTGART

1923 ISSUE

#S1371-S1380 winged wheel.

		VG	VF	UNC
S1371	**1 MILLION MARK** 13.8.1923. Brown on lt. brown unpt. Railroad Headquarter bldg. at Stuttgart.	.75	3.00	9.00
S1371A	**1 MILLION MARK** 21.8.1923. Similar to #S1371.	1.50	4.00	12.00

		VG	VF	UNC
S1372	**5 MILLIONEN MARK** 18.8.1923. Brown on lt. tan unpt. Eagle on back.			
	a. Red-brown.	1.00	4.00	12.00
	b. Brownish black.	1.00	4.00	12.00

		VG	VF	UNC
S1373	**50 MILLIONEN MARK** 26.9.1923. Black on blue-green unpt. Back green; steam locomotive at ctr.	.75	3.00	9.00

		VG	VF	UNC
S1374	**1 MILLIARDE MARK** 26.9.1923. Dk. brown on olive-brown unpt. Multiple arched railroad viaduct over the Neckar at Cannstadt on back.	1.00	3.00	9.00

		VG	VF	UNC
S1375	**20 MILLIARDEN MARK** 19.10.1923. Black on blue-gray unpt. Stuttgart railroad terminal on back.	1.00	3.00	9.00

		VG	VF	UNC
S1376	**50 MILLIARDEN MARK** 23.10.1923. Black on brown unpt. Interior of Stuttgart railroad terminal on back.	1.00	3.00	9.00

		VG	VF	UNC
S1377	**100 MILLIARDEN MARK** 23.10.1923. Black on gray unpt. Viaduct on back.	1.50	4.00	12.00
S1378	**500 MILLIARDEN MARK** 30.10.1923. Dk. brown on pale rose unpt. Steamship on back.	1.50	5.00	15.00

		VG	VF	UNC
S1379	**1 BILLION MARK** 5.11.1923. Dk. purple on dull orange unpt. Interior of Stuttgart railroad terminal on back.	1.50	5.00	15.00

		VG	VF	UNC
S1380	**5 BILLIONEN MARK** 9.11.1923. Dk. green on lt. green unpt. Steel railroad bridge on back.	2.00	6.00	17.50

SIEGE

COLBERG

Colberg was a Prussian fortress. During a siege by French forces in 1807 two issues of siege notes were made.

1807 FIRST *KOMMISSIONS-KUPON* ISSUE

#S1451-S1453 were authorized by a coinage commission, therefore the name. These notes are on cardboard, written entirely by hand, and bear 6 sign. Backs are hand stamped: *Kön. Preuss. Gouvernement zu Colberg*.

		GOOD	FINE	XF
S1451	**2 GROSCHEN** 1807. Black ink.	60.00	100.00	175.00

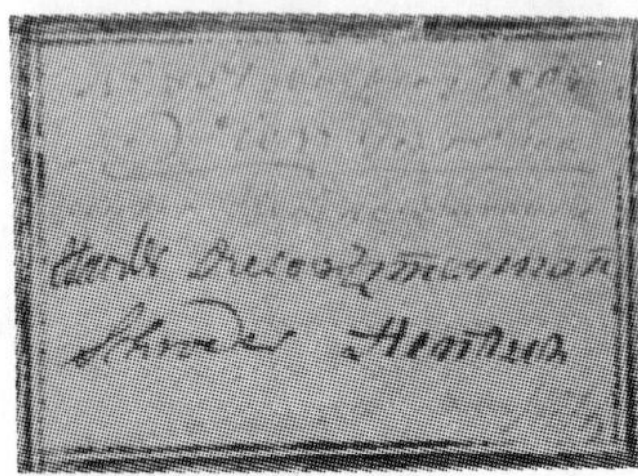

		GOOD	FINE	XF
S1452	**4 GROSCHEN** 1807. Blue ink.	60.00	100.00	175.00

		GOOD	FINE	XF
S1453	**8 GROSCHEN** 1807. Red ink.	75.00	150.00	225.00

1807 SECOND *MEINECKE-KUPONS* ISSUE

#S1454-S1456 are named after the Counselor for War and Crown Lands and bear only three sign. Otherwise they are like the previous issue.

		GOOD	FINE	XF
S1454	**2 GROSCHEN** 1807. Black ink. Like #S1451.	75.00	175.00	275.00
S1455	**4 GROSCHEN** 1807. Blue ink. Like #S1452.	75.00	175.00	275.00

		GOOD	FINE	XF
S1456	**8 GROSCHEN** 1807. Red ink. Like #S1453.	95.00	200.00	300.00

ERFURT

Erfurt, a city in Thuringia, was occupied by French forces. In 1813 Erfurt was besieged by advancing Prussian forces and an issue of siege notes was made by the French occupiers.

1813 ISSUE

#S1461-S1468 are printed in black on white paper. Uniface. Printer: Johann Immanuel Uckermann. Notes showing his name have it at lower ctr. r.

		GOOD	FINE	XF
S1461	**2 GROSCHEN** 1.11.1813. Flowered border, wheel design at upper ctr. and in embossed seal at r.			
	a. W/o imprint.	—	—	—
	b. W/imprint.	—	—	—

		GOOD	FINE	XF
S1462	**3 GROSCHEN** 1.11.1813. Similar to #S1461 but border has oval and diamond design.			
	a. W/o imprint.	—	—	—
	b. W/imprint.	—	—	—

		GOOD	FINE	XF
S1463	**4 GROSCHEN** 1.11.1813. Border at upper l. and r. has various symbolic designs, lower l. and r. have scenes of sunrise over city views.			
	a. W/o imprint.	—	—	—
	b. W/imprint.	—	—	—

S1464 8 Groschen	Good	Fine	XF
1.11.1813. Similar to #S1461 but border has design of leaves and branches.			
a. W/o imprint.	—	—	—
b. W/imprint.	—	—	—

S1465 12 Groschen	Good	Fine	XF
1.11.1813. Arms at upper ctr., ornamental border at top and bottom, wheel design at r.			
a. W/o imprint.	—	—	—
b. W/imprint.	—	—	—

S1466 1 Thaler	Good	Fine	XF
1.11.1813. Wheel design at upper ctr., anchors in lower border.			
a. W/o imprint.	—	—	—
b. W/imprint.	—	—	—

S1467 2 Thaler	Good	Fine	XF
1.11.1813. Arms at upper ctr., zigzag design in border.			
a. W/o imprint.	—	—	—
b. W/imprint.	—	—	—

S1468 5 Thaler	Good	Fine	XF
1.11.1813. Wheel design and branches at upper ctr., wheel design at r.			
a. W/o imprint.	—	—	—
b. W/imprint	—	—	—

MAINZ

MAYENCE

Mainz, a city in the Rhineland, was occupied by the French who were then besieged by the advancing Prussian army.

All notes are dated May 1793.

1793 First Issue

#S1471-S1474 handwritten value, sign., and w/stamping: *SIEGE DE MAYENCE* on backs of French assignats.

S1471 20 Sous	Good	Fine	XF
5.1793 (- old date 4.1.1792.) On back of 10 Sous #A53.	200.00	400.00	600.00

S1472 20 Livres	Good	Fine	XF
5.1793. (- old date 16.12.1791.) On back of 10 Livres #A51.	150.00	300.00	400.00
S1473 20 Livres			
5.1793. (- old date 24.10.1792.) On back of 10 Livres #A66.	—	—	—

S1474 50 Livres	Good	Fine	XF
5.1793. (- old date 24.10.1792.) On back of 25 Livres #A67.	200.00	400.00	600.00

1793 Second Issue

Regularly printed notes.

#S1475-S1477 w/o series letter. Uniface.

		GOOD	FINE	XF
S1475	**5 Sous** May 1793. Black. Red stamping in circle at l. 3 sign.			
	a. Hand sign.	90.00	175.00	350.00
	b. Printed sign.	50.00	100.00	175.00
	x. Error *écharger* instead of *échanger*.	300.00	400.00	700.00

		GOOD	FINE	XF
S1476	**10 Sous** May 1793. Like #S1475.			
	a. Hand sign.	90.00	200.00	350.00
	b. Printed sign.	50.00	100.00	175.00
	x. Error like #S1475x.	300.00	400.00	700.00

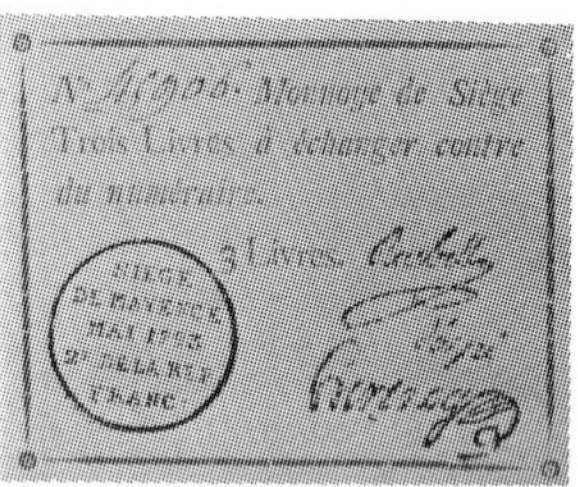

		GOOD	FINE	XF
S1477	**3 Livres** May 1793. Red. Black stamping at l. 3 sign.			
	a. Hand sign.	120.00	225.00	300.00
	b. Printed sign.	60.00	110.00	150.00
	x. Error like #S1475x.	300.00	400.00	500.00

#S1478-S1481 w/series letter, otherwise like previous issue.

		GOOD	FINE	XF
S1478	**5 Sous** May 1793. Like #S1475. Series A.			
	a. Issued note.	75.00	130.00	200.00
	x. Error like #S1475x.	300.00	400.00	500.00
S1479	**10 Sous** May 1793. Like #S1476. Series A.			
	a. Issued note.	75.00	130.00	175.00
	x. Error like #S1475x.	300.00	400.00	500.00

		GOOD	FINE	XF
S1480	**3 Livres** May 1793. Like #S1477. Series A.			
	a. Issued note.	75.00	130.00	175.00
	x. Error like #S1475x.	300.00	400.00	500.00

		GOOD	FINE	XF
S1481	**3 Livres** May 1793. Like #S1477. Series B.			
	a. Issued note.	100.00	200.00	300.00
	x. Error like #S1475x.	500.00	600.00	800.00

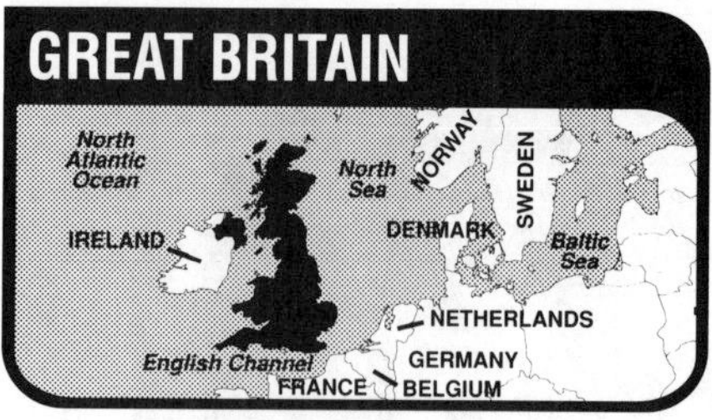

The United Kingdom of Great Britain and Northern Ireland, (including England, Scotland, Wales and Norhtern Ireland) is located off the northwest coast of the European continent, has an area of 94,227 sq. mi. (244,046 sq. km.), and a population of 59.45 million. Capital: London.

After the departure of the Romans, who brought Britain into an active relationship with Europe, Britain fell prey to invaders from Scandinavia and the Low Countries who drove the original Britons into Scotland and Wales, and established a profusion of kingdoms that finally united in the 11th century under the Danish King Canute. Norman rule, following the conquest of 1066, stimulated the development of those institutions which have since distinguished British life. Henry VIII (1509-47) turned Britain from continental adventuring and faced it to the sea - a decision that made Britain a world power during the reign of Elizabeth I (1558-1603). Strengthened by the Industrial Revolution and the defeat of Napoleon, 19th century Britain turned to the remote parts of the world and established a colonial empire of such extent and prosperity that the world has never seen its like. World Wars I and II sealed the fate of the Empire and relegated Britain to a lesser role in world affairs by draining her resources and inaugurating a worldwide movement toward national self-determination in her former colonies.

By the mid-20th century, most of the former British Empire had gained independence and had evolved into the Commonwealth of Nations. This association of equal and and autonomous states, set out to agree views and special relationships with one another (appointing High Commissioners rather than Ambassadors) for mutual benefit, trade interests, etc. The Commonwealth is presently (1999) composed of 54 member nations, including the United Kingdom. All recognize the monarch as Head of the Commonwealth; 16 continue to recognize Queen Elizabeth II as Head of State. In addition to the United Kingdom, they are: Antigua & Barbuda, Australia, The Bahamas, Barbados Belize, Canada, Grenada, Paupa New Guinea, St. Christopher & Nevis, St. Lucia, St. Vincent & the Grenadines, Solomon Islands.

RULERS:

Elizabeth II, 1952-

MONETARY SYSTEM:

1 Shilling = 12 Pence
1 Pound = 20 Shillings to 1971

PRIVATE AND COMMERCIAL JOINT STOCK BANKS

This series of note issues is very extensive, starting in the mid-18th century and extending into the earlier years of the 20th century. The history of these issues and their impact on the economic life of Great Britain is totally interwoven with the history of the country itself, and is a very complex story. There were literally hundreds of different banks, with the greatest concentration of note issues taking place during the first part of the 19th century. As centralization became stronger the need and influence of private note issues became less, until it finally ceased altogether.

In accordance with the Bank Charter Act of 1844, the number of issuing banks in England and Wales decreased considerably. In 1900 notes of the following banks were still in circulation.

Bank Name	Last Date of Issue
Ashford Bank, Pomfret, Burra & Co.	1902
Aylesbury Old Bank, Cobb Bartlett & Co.	1902
Banbury Bank, Gillet & Co.	1918
Banbury Old Bank, T.R. Cobb & Sons.	1902
Bank of Whitehaven Ltd.	1916
Bedford Bank, Thomas Barnard & Co.	1915
Bicester & Oxfordshire Bank - Tibb & Co.	1920
Bradford Banking Co. Ltd.	1910
Bradford Commercial Banking Co. Ltd.	1904
Buckingham Bank - Bartlett & Co.	1902
Cambridge & Cambridgeshire Bank Ltd. - Fosters	1904
Canterbury Bank, Hammand, Pumptre, Hilton, McMaster & Furley	1903
Carlisle & Cumberland Banking Co. Ltd.	1911
City Bank, Exeter - Milford, Snow & Co.	1901
Cumberland Union Banking Co. Ltd.	1901
Derby Bank, Samuel Smith & Co.	1902
East Riding Bank, Beckett & Co., York	1920
Exeter Bank - Sanders & Co.	1901
Faversham Bank, Hilton, Rigden & Rigden	1902
Halifax Commercial Banking Co., Ltd.	1919
Halifax & Huddersfield Union Bank Ltd.	1910
Hull & Kingston-upon-Hull, Samuel Smith	1902
Ipswich Bank, Bacon Cobbold & Co.	1904
Kington & Radnorshire Bank Ltd. - Davies, Banks & Co.	1910
Knaresborough & Claro Banking Co. Ltd.	1903
Lancaster Banking Co. Ltd.	1907
Leeds Bank, Beckett & Co. Leeds	1920
Leeds Union Bank, William Williams, Brown & Co.	1900
Leicestershire Banking Co., Ltd.	1900
Lincoln Bank, Smith, Ellison & Co.	1902
Lincoln & Lindsey Banking Co. Ltd.	1913
Llandovery & Llandilo Bank - David Jones & Co.	1909
Moore & Robinson, Notts Banking Co. Ltd.	1901
Naval Bank, Plymouth, Harris, Bulteel & Co.	1914
Newark Bank, Samuel Smith & Co.	1902
Newark & Sleaford Bank, Peacock, Wilson & Co.	1912
Newcastle upon Tyne Joint Stock Banking Co.	1908
Newmarket Bank, Hammand & Co.	1905
North & South Wales Bank Ltd.	1908
Nottingham Bank, Samuel Smith & Co.	1902
Nottingham & Nottingham Banking Co. Ltd.	1919
Oxford Old Bank, Parsons Thomson & Co.	1900
Oxfordshire Witney Bank, Gillett & Co.	1918
Pares' Leicestershire Banking Co. Ltd.	1902
Reading Bank, Simonds & Co.	1913
Richmond Bank, Yorkshire, Roper & Priestman	1902
Sheffield Banking Co. Ltd.	1905
Sheffield & Hallamshire Bank Ltd.	1913
Sheffield & Rotherham Joint Stock Banking Co. Ltd.	1907
Stamford, Spalding & Boston Banking Co. Ltd.	1907

Bank Name	Last Date of Issue
Stuckeys Banking Co. Ltd.	1909
Tring Bank & Chesham Bank, Thomos Butcher & Sons	1900
Uxbridge Old Bank - Woodbridge, Lacy, Hartland, Hibbert & Co.	1900
Wakefield & Barnsley Union Bank Ltd.	1906
Wallingford Bank, Hedges Wells & Co.	1905
Wellington, Somerset Bank, Fox, Fowler & Co.	1921
West Riding Bank, Leathern Tew & Co.	1906
West Riding Union Banking Co. Ltd.	1902
West Yorkshire Banking Co. Ltd.	1919
Whitehaven Joint Stock Banking Co. Ltd.	1908
Witts & Dorset Banking Co. Ltd.	1914
Worcester Old Bank, Berwick Lechmere & Co.	1905
Yarmouth, Norfolk & Suffolk Bank Ltd. - Lancons, Youell & Kemp	1901
York City & County Banking Co. Ltd.	1909
Yorkshire Banking Co. Ltd.	1901
York Union Banking Co. Ltd.	1902

NEWCASTLE UPON TYNE JOINT STOCK BANKING CO.

5 POUNDS 1.7.1840.

EXAMPLE OF A BRITISH PRIVATE AND JOINT STOCK BANK ISSUE

The Hellenic Republic of Greece is situated in southeastern Europe on the southern tip of the Balkan Peninsula. The republic includes many islands, the most important of which are Crete and the Ionian Islands. Greece (including islands) has an area of 50,949 sq. mi. (131,957 sq. km.) and a population of 10.6 million. Capital: Athens. Greece is still largely agricultural. Tobacco, cotton, fruit and wool are exported.

Greece, the Mother of Western civilization, attained the peak of its culture in the 5th century BC, when it contributed more to government, drama, art and architecture than any other people to this time. Greece fell under Roman domination in the 2nd and 1st centuries BC, becoming part of the Byzantine Empire until Constantinople fell to the Crusaders in 1202. With the fall of Constantinople to the Turks in 1453, Greece became part of the Ottoman Empire. Independence from Turkey was won with the revolution of 1821-27. In 1833, Greece was established as a monarchy, with sovereignty guaranteed by Britain, France and Russia. After a lengthy power struggle between the monarchist forces and democratic factions, Greece was proclaimed a republic in 1925. The monarchy was restored in 1935 and reconfirmed by a plebiscite in 1946. The Italians invaded Greece via Albania on Oct. 28, 1940 but were driven back well within the Albanian border. Germany began its invasion on April 6, 1941 and quickly overran the entire country, driving off a British Expeditionary force by the end of April. King George II and his new government went into exile. The German - Italian occupation of Greece lasted until Oct. 1944. On April 21, 1967, a military junta took control of the government and suspended the constitution. King Constantine II made an unsuccessful attempt against the junta in the fall of 1968 and consequently fled to Italy. The monarchy was formally abolished by plebiscite, Dec. 8, 1974, and Greece established as the "Hellenic Republic," the third republic in Greek history.

The island of Crete (Kreti), located 60 miles southeast of the Peloponnesus, was the center of a brilliant civilization that flourished before the advent of Greek culture. After being conquered by the Romans, Byzantines, Moslems and Venetians, Crete became part of the Turkish Empire in 1669. As a consequence of the Greek Revolution of the 1820s, it was ceded to Egypt. Egypt returned the island to the Turks in 1840, and they ceded it to Greece in 1913, after the Second Balkan War.

The Ionian Islands, situated in the Ionian Sea to the west of Greece, is the collective name for the islands of Corfu, Cephalonia, Zante, Santa Maura, Ithaca, Cthera and Paxo, with their minor dependencies. Before Britain acquired the islands, 1809-1814, they were at various times subject to the authority of Venice, France, Russia and Turkey. They remained under British control until their cession to Greece on March 29, 1864.

RULERS:

John Capodistrias, 1827-1831
Othon (Otto of Bavaria) 1832-1862
George I, 1863-1913
Constantine I, 1913-1923
George II, 1922-1923, 1935-1947

MONETARY SYSTEM:

1 Drachma = 100 Lepta, 1841-2001
1 Euro = 100 Cents, 2002-

DENOMINATIONS

1 - ΜΙΑ
2 - ΔΥΟ
5 - ΠΕΝΤΕ
10 - ΔΕΚΑ
20 - ΕΙΚΟΣΙ
25 - ΕΙΚΟΣΙΠΕΝΤΕ
50 - ΠΕΝΤΗΚΟΝΤΑ
100 - ΔΙΑΚΟΣΙΑ

REGIONAL

ΠΡΟΝΟΜΙΟΥΧΟΣ ΤΡΑΠΕΖΑ ΗΠΕΙΡΟΘΕΣΣΑΛΙΑΣ

PRIVILEGED BANK OF EPIRUS AND THESSALY

Founded in 1882; absorbed by the National Bank of Greece in 1899.

1882 ISSUE

#S101-S103 printer: G. Richard, Paris.

		Good	Fine	XF
S101	**10 DRACHMAI** 31.3.1882. Blue and brown. Woman holding torch, angel below at l., arms at r. Head at l. and r. on back.	—	Rare	—

		GOOD	FINE	XF
S102	**25 DRACHMAI** 31.3.1882. Blue and brown. 2 cherubs supporting arms at l., reclining woman w/lion at lower r. 3 allegorical figures at ctr. on back.	—	Rare	—
S103	**100 DRACHMAI** 31.3.1882. Lilac and brown. Arms and allegorical figure at l. Allegory of Justice and Law on back.	—	Rare	—

1885 ISSUE

#S104 and S105 portr. Alexander at l. on face, arms at ctr. on back (like #S145 and S146). Printer: BWC.

		GOOD	FINE	XF
S104	**1 DRACHMA** 21.12.1885. Brown on gray unpt. Back green.	60.00	175.00	450.00
S105	**2 DRACHMAI** 21.12.1885. Brown on blue and tan unpt. Portr. helmeted Athena at r. Back green.	65.00	200.00	500.00

#S106 and S107 dated 1885, issued 1897. Arms at ctr. on back (like #S147 and S148). Printer: BWC.

		GOOD	FINE	XF
S106	**1 DRACHMA** 21.12.1885 (issued 1897). Black on blue and brown unpt. Portr. helmeted Athena at l. Back green.	60.00	175.00	450.00
S107	**2 DRACHMAI** 21.12.1885 (issued 1897). Black on blue and brown unpt. Hermes at r. Back green.	65.00	200.00	500.00

NOTE: For notes similar to #S104-S107 but w/brown backs see #S145-S148; w/blue backs see Vol. II, #35-38.

1887-88 ISSUE

#S108 and S109 printer: G. Richard, Paris.

		GOOD	FINE	XF
S108	**25 DRACHMAI** 1.3.1887. Brown, green and blue. Arms at l., allegorical figures at r.	—	Rare	—

		GOOD	FINE	XF
S109	**100 DRACHMAI** 2.1.1888. Blue, brown and black. Supported arms at upper l., seated allegorical woman at lower r. 2 reclining figures at ctr. on back.	—	Rare	—

ΙΟΝΙΚΗ ΤΡΑΠΕΖΑ

IONIAN BANK

Founded in 1839.

ΚΕΦΑΛΛΗΝΙΑ

CEPHALONIA BRANCH

1840'S ISSUE

#S110-S113 Ionian Bank arms w/English and Greek flags at top ctr. on face. Printer: PB&P.

		GOOD	FINE	XF
S110	**10 SHILLINGS** 184x. Specimen.	—	Rare	—
S111	**1 POUND** 184x. Specimen.	—	Rare	—

		GOOD	FINE	XF
S112	**2 POUNDS** 184x. Specimen.	—	Rare	—
S113	**5 POUNDS** 184x. Specimen.	—	Rare	—

1843-44 ISSUE

#S114, S115 and S119 Ionian Bank arms w/English and Greek flags at top ctr. on face. Printer: PBC.

		GOOD	FINE	XF
S114	**2 COLONATA** 1843-69.	—	Rare	—

		GOOD	FINE	XF
S115	**5 COLONATA** 1844-69. Back blue.	—	Rare	—
S119	**100 COLONATA** 1844-69.	—	Rare	—

NOTE: Other denominations are reported, not confirmed.

ΚΕΡΚΥΡΑ

KERKYRA (CORFU) BRANCH

1840'S ISSUE

#S120-S123 Ionian Bank arms w/English and Greek flags at top ctr. on face. Printer: PB&P.

		GOOD	FINE	XF
S120	**10 SHILLINGS** 184x. Specimen.	—	Rare	—
S121	**1 POUND** 184x. Specimen.	—	Rare	—
S122	**2 POUNDS** 184x. Specimen.	—	Rare	—

		GOOD	FINE	XF
S123	**5 POUNDS** 184x. Specimen.	—	Rare	—

1843-44 ISSUE

#S124-S129 Ionian Bank arms w/English and Greek flags at top ctr. on face. Printer: PBC.

		GOOD	FINE	XF
S124	**2 COLONATA** 1843-69.	—	Rare	—
S125	**5 COLONATA** 1844-69.	—	Rare	—
S129	**100 COLONATA** 1844-69.	—	Rare	—

NOTE: Other denominations are reported, not confirmed.

ΖΑΚΥΝΘΟΣ

ZANTE BRANCH

1840'S ISSUE

#S130-S133 Ionian Bank arms w/English and Greek flags at top ctr. on face. Printer: PB&P.

		Good	Fine	XF
S130	**10 SHILLINGS** 184x. Specimen.	—	Rare	—
S131	**1 POUND** 184x. Specimen.	—	Rare	—

		Good	Fine	XF
S132	**2 POUNDS** 184x. Specimen.	—	Rare	—
S133	**5 POUNDS** 184x. Specimen.	—	Rare	—

1843-44 ISSUE

#S134, S135 and S139 Ionian Bank arms w/English and Greek flags at top ctr. on face. Printer: PBC.

		Good	Fine	XF
S134	**2 COLONATA** 1843-69.	—	Rare	—
S135	**5 COLONATA** 1844-69.	—	Rare	—
S139	**100 COLONATA** 1844-69.	—	Rare	—

NOTE: Other denominations are reported, not confirmed.

W/OUT BRANCH NAME

1876 ISSUE

#S140-S142 arms of Kg. George at upper l., Ionian Bank arms w/English and Greek flags at upper ctr. Bank name in French on back. Printer: PBC.

		Good	Fine	XF
S140	**10 NEW DRACHMAI** 1876-83. Black. Back brown and red.	—	Rare	—

		Good	Fine	XF
S141	**25 NEW DRACHMAI** 1876-83. Black on green unpt. Back blue.	—	Rare	—
S142	**100 NEW DRACHMAI** 1876-83. Black on blue unpt. Back green.	—	Rare	—

ΙΟΝΙΚΗ ΤΡΑΠΕΖΑ Λιμιτεδ

IONIAN BANK LIMITED

1883-1907 ISSUE

#S143 and S144 similar to previous issues except for addition of *LIMITED* in bank arms and under title at ctr., and [Greek] BAS. *EPITROPOS* (King's Commissioner) at bottom r. on face.

		Good	Fine	XF
S143	**10 NEW DRACHMAI** 1884-1907. Black. Similar to #S140.			
	a. Issue A. 27.12.1884. Printer: PBC.	—	Rare	—
	b. Issue B. 3.9.1895-10.9.1907. Printer: W&S.	—	Rare	—
S144	**25 NEW DRACHMAI** 1883. Similar to #S141.	—	Rare	—

1885 ISSUE

#S145 and S146 like #S104 and S105. Printer: BWC.

		Good	Fine	XF
S145	**1 DRACHMA** 21.12.1885. Black on blue and tan unpt. Back brown.	25.00	100.00	275.00

		Good	Fine	XF
S146	**2 DRACHMAI** 21.12.1885. Black on blue and tan unpt. Back brown.	30.00	125.00	375.00

#S147 and S148 like #S106 and S107. Printer: BWC. Issued 1897.

		Good	Fine	XF
S147	**1 Drachma** 21.12.1885. Black on blue and brown unpt. Back brown.	15.00	75.00	225.00

		Good	Fine	XF
S148	**2 Drachmai** 21.12.1885. Black on blue and brown unpt. Back brown.	20.00	100.00	275.00

NOTE: For notes similar to #S145-S148 but w/green backs see #S104-S107; w/blue backs see Vol. II, #34 and 35, #40 and 41, and also #301 and 302.

1888 Issue

#S149 and S150 arms of Kg. George at upper l., bank arms w/flags at upper ctr.

		Good	Fine	XF
S149	**25 Drachmai** 23.3.1889; 22.10.1894; 30.11.1898. Gray on yellow unpt. Athena at upper r. Back green. Printer: W&S.	—	—	—
S150	**100 Drachmai** 1888-99. Black on blue-green unpt. Back green. Printer: PBC.	—	—	—

1900 Issue

#S151 and S152 like #S149 and S150 except for unpt. and later dates.

		Good	Fine	XF
S151	**25 Drachmai** 1900-20. Blue-black on lt. orange unpt. Like #S149. Printer: W&S.	—	—	—

		Good	Fine	XF
S152	**100 Drachmai** 18.1.1903-1.3.1919. Black on blue unpt. Back green. Like #S150. Printer: PBC.	—	—	—

ΤΡΑΠΕΖΑ ΚΡΗΤΗΣ

Bank of Crete

Founded in 1899; merged with the National Bank in 1919.

1900-26 Issue

#S153 and S154 arms at upper ctr., portr. Kg. George at upper r. Printer: BWC.

		Good	Fine	XF
S153	**25 Drachmai** 2.1.1909-26.9.1915. Black on orange and green unpt. Sitting figure from ancient coin at l. Back green.	40.00	100.00	225.00

		Good	Fine	XF
S154	**100 Drachmai** 1900-17. Black on orange and green unpt. Head from ancient coin at l. Back blue.			
	a. 2.1.1900; 25.1.1901.	125.00	350.00	1000.
	b. 26.4.1914; 26.3.1915; 9.9.1916; 3.3.1917.	60.00	125.00	300.00

Partisan - WWII

ΠΟΛΙΤΙΚΗ ΕΠΙΤΡΟΠΗ ΕΘΝΙΚΗΣ ΑΠΕΛΕΥΘΕΡΩΣΗΣ

Civilian Committee of National Liberation

Issued by the Markos partisans. Notes may have any of eight different hand stamps of the individual regions on back. Denominations are given in okas of wheat (1 Oka = 2.82 pounds).

1944 Issue

#S161-S164 black on green and yellow unpt. Burning houses at l., standing soldier w/rifle at ctr., and farmers at r. Backs aqua and black. Hand stamp (if any) is on back.

		VG	VF	Unc
S161	**5 Oka** 5.6.1944.			
	a. Handwritten serial #.	20.00	55.00	125.00
	b. Stamped serial #.	20.00	55.00	125.00
	r. Remainder w/o serial #.	—	Unc	100.00

		VG	VF	UNC
S162	**25 OKA** 5.6.1944.			
	a. Handwritten serial #.	27.50	75.00	150.00
	b. Stamped serial #.	27.50	75.00	150.00

		VG	VF	UNC
S163	**100 OKA** 5.6.1944.			
	a. Handwritten serial #.	100.00	200.00	350.00
	b. Stamped serial #.	100.00	200.00	350.00
S164	**500 OKA** 5.6.1944. (Not issued).			
	a. Handwritten serial #.	—	Rare	—
	x. Ovpt: *ANAMNH TIKON.* (Souvenir Commemorative.)	—	—	—

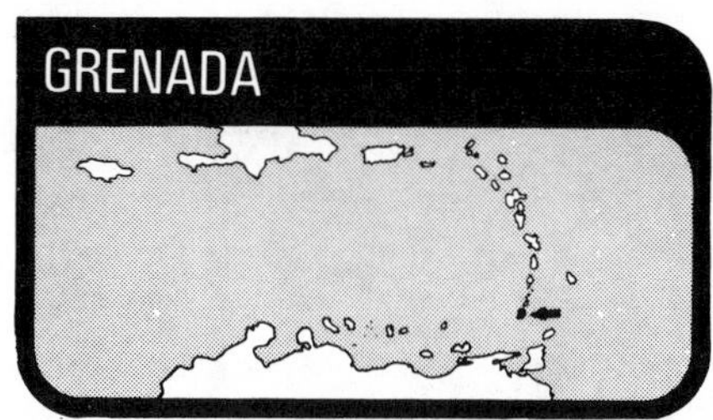

Grenada, located in the Windward islands of the Caribbean Sea 90 miles (145 km.) north of Trinidad, has (with Carriacou and Petit Martinique) an area of 133 sq. mi. (344 sq. km.) and a population of 99,700. Capital: St. George's. Grenada is the smallest independent nation in the Western Hemisphere.

Columbus discovered Grenada in 1498 during his third voyage to the Americas. Spain failed to colonize the island, and in 1627 granted it to the British who sold it to the French who colonized it in 1650. Grenada was captured by the British in 1763, retaken by the French in 1779, and finally ceded to the British in 1783. In 1958 Grenada joined the Federation of the West Indies, which was dissolved in 1962. In 1967, it became an internally self-governing British associated state. Full independence was attained on Feb. 4, 1974. Grenada is a member of the Commonwealth of Nations. The prime minister is the Head of Government.

RULERS:

British

MONETARY SYSTEM:

1 Shilling = 12 Pence
1 Pound = 20 Shillings to 1970
1 British West Indies Dollar = 4 Shillings-2 Pence

NOTE: For later issues see British East Caribbean Territories, Vol. II and East Caribbean States, Vol. III.

BANKS

BARCLAYS BANK (DOMINION, COLONIAL AND OVERSEAS)

1926 PROVISIONAL ISSUE

S106	**5 DOLLARS** 1.9.1926. Black on pink and blue-green unpt. Ovpt. *ISSUED AT GRENADA BRANCH* twice on face on Barbados #S101. Printer: BWC.	—	Rare	—

1937 PROVISIONAL ISSUE

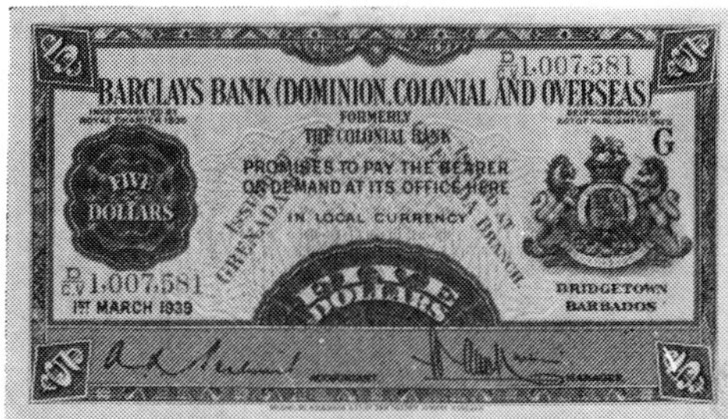

		GOOD	FINE	XF
S107	**5 DOLLARS** 1937-40. Purple on m/c unpt. Royal arms at r. Ovpt: *ISSUED AT GRENADA BRANCH* twice on face on Barbados #S111. Printer: BWC.			
	a. 1.5.1937.	175.00	500.00	1200.
	b. 1.3.1939.	165.00	475.00	1000.
	c. 1.3.1940.	160.00	450.00	900.00

1941 PROVISIONAL ISSUE

		GOOD	FINE	XF
S108	**5 DOLLARS** 1.2.1941. Purple on m/c unpt. Supported royal arms at r. Ovpt. on Trinidad #S102b.	160.00	450.00	900.00

COLONIAL BANK

1880S PROVISIONAL ISSUE

		GOOD	FINE	XF
S111	**5 DOLLARS** ND (ca. 1882-1912). Brown. Supported royal arms at upper ctr. Ovpt: *ISSUED AT GRENADA BRANCH* (twice) on Barbados #S141. Specimen.	—	Unc	4000.

1925 Provisional Issue

		Good	Fine	XF
S113	**5 Dollars** 1.1.1925. Black on pink unpt. Supported royal arms at upper ctr. Ovpt: *ISSUED AT GRENADA BRANCH* (twice) and lg. *G* at upper r. on Barbados #S151.			
	a. Issued note.	—	Rare	—
	s. Specimen.	—	Unc	1500.

Royal Bank of Canada

Issuing office St. George's, Grenada.

1909 Provisional Issue

#S116 blue ovpt: *GRENADA* vertically at l. and r., smaller vertical ovpt: *PAYABLE AT ST. GEORGE'S GRENADA* at ctr.

		Good	Fine	XF
S116	**5 Dollars = 1 Pound-10 Pence** 2.1.1909. Black on green and yellow unpt. Ovpt. on Canada #S1371. Specimen.	—	Unc	1500.

1920 Issue

		Good	Fine	XF
S117	**5 Dollars = 1 Pound-10 Pence** 2.1.1920. Black on green unpt. Steamship at ctr. Back green. Lg. size. Printer: ABNC. Specimen.			
	p. Proof.	—	Unc	500.00
	s. Specimen.	—	Unc	1250.

1938 Issue

		Good	Fine	XF
S118	**5 Dollars = 1 Pound-10 Pence** 3.1.1938. Similar to #S117 but reduced size. Printer: CBNC.			
	a. Issued note.	175.00	600.00	—
	p. Proof.	—	Unc	500.00

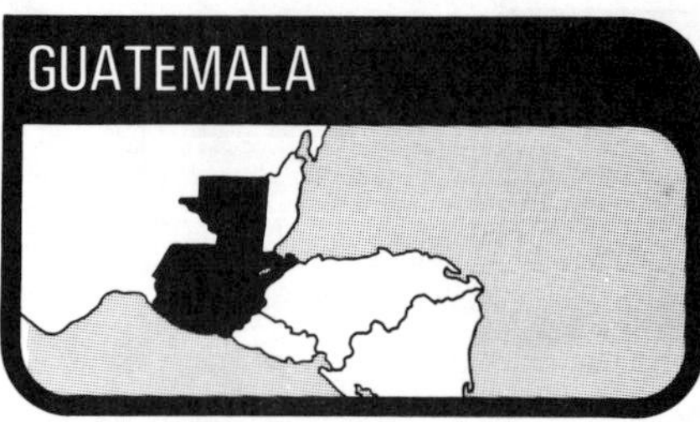

The Republic of Guatemala, the northernmost of the five Central American republics, has an area of 42,042 sq. mi. (108,889 sq. km.) and a population of 12.22 million. Capital: Guatemala City. The economy of Guatemala is heavily dependent on resources which are being developed. Coffee, cotton and bananas are exported.

Guatemala, once the site of the ancient Mayan civilization, was conquered by Pedro de Alvarado, the lieutenant of Cortes who undertook the conquest from Mexico. Skilled in strategy and cruelty, he progressed rapidly along the Pacific coastal lowlands to the highland plain of Quezaltenango where the decisive battle for Guatemala was fought. After routing the Mayan forces, he established the first capital of Guatemala in 1524.

Guatemala of the colonial period included all of Central America but Panama. Guatemala declared its independence of Spain in 1821 and was absorbed into the short-lived Mexican empire of Augustin Iturbide, 1822-23. From 1823 to 1839 Guatemala was a constituent state of the Central American Republic. Upon dissolution of the federation, Guatemala became an independent republic.

MONETARY SYSTEM:

1 Peso = 100 Centavos to 1924
1 Quetzal = 100 Centavos, 1924-

Availability of Early Bank Issues

A rising inflation from about 1900 to 1924 created a need for more and more bank notes to be listed. Their value decreased, higher denominations were introduced, and by the time of the 1924 currency reform it took 60 old pesos to equal 1 new quetzal. The Caja Reguladora reissued notes of 20 Pesos or more into the new system but all lower peso values ceased to circulate. Many notes of these earlier banks are still readily available today.

BANKS:

Banco Agricola Hipotecario .... #S101-S106
Banco Americano de Guatemala .... #S111-S120
Banco Colombiano .... #S121-S126
Banco Comercial de Guatemala .... #S131-S135
Banco de Guatemala .... #S141-S148
Banco Internacional de Guatemala .... #S151-S161
Banco Nacional de Guatemala .... #S166-S167
Banco de Occidente en Quezaltenango .... #S171-S183
Comite Bancario de Guatemala .... #S191-S193

GOVERNMENT

Tesorería Nacional de Guatemala .... #S201-S205

Banks

Banco Agricola Hipotecario

Founded in 1895. The former Banco Comercial de Guatemala.

1895-1926 Issue

#S101-S103, S105 and S106 red back, woman at ctr. Printer: W&S.

		Good	Fine	XF
S101	**1 Peso** 1895-1920. Black on pink and blue unpt. Seated woman w/caduceus at l., woman in winged chariot drawn by lions at ctr., girls w/sheep and cow at r.			
	a. 14.4.1895-26.3.1900.	7.50	20.00	85.00
	b. 26.3.1920; 30.6.1920.	2.50	10.00	40.00

		GOOD	FINE	XF
	c1. Black ovpt: *PAGADERO EN QUEZALTENANGO* in box on back. Date partially printed and filled in by hand. __de__de 189x.	—	—	—
	c2. Like c1, but w/printed date. 30.4.1895.	30.00	150.00	—

		GOOD	FINE	XF
	d1. *QUEZALTENANGO* lined out and ovpt: *GUATEMALA* on bottom of ovpt. in box on back. Date partially ovpt: *30... ABRIL... 5.*	—	—	—
	d2. Date entirely printed 6.4.1895; 30.4.1895.	—	—	—

		GOOD	FINE	XF
S102	**5 PESOS** 1895-1920. Black on red-orange and violet unpt. Woman w/winged cap at l., woman in winged chariot drawn by lions at ctr., man w/staff and seated woman at r.			
	a. Date partially ovpt: *5... ABRIL... 5.*	—	—	—
	b. Printed date. 5.4.1895; 2.7.1895.	15.00	50.00	225.00
	c. 1.8.1914; 1.6.1917; 30.6.1920.	6.00	20.00	80.00
	d. Ovpt. in box like #S101c. 5.4.1895.	—	—	—
	e. Altered ovpt. like #S101d. 2.7.1895.	—	45.00	200.00

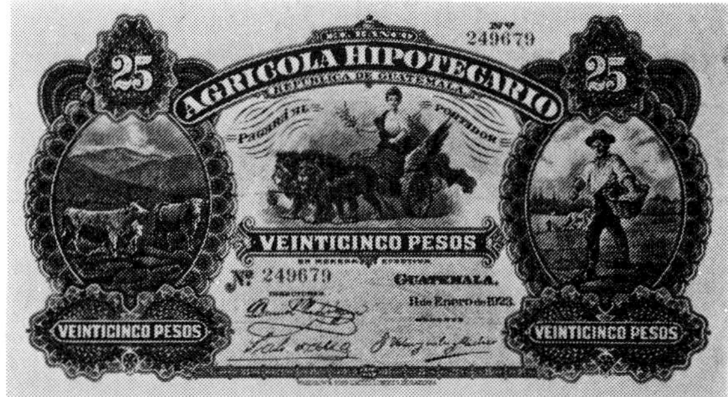

		GOOD	FINE	XF
S103	**25 PESOS** 1.8.1917; 11.1.1923. Black on red and violet unpt. Cattle at l., woman in winged chariot drawn by lions at ctr., farmer sowing at r.	10.00	50.00	200.00

		GOOD	FINE	XF
S104	**50 PESOS** 1917-26. Black on red, blue and olive unpt. Woman feeding bird at ctr. Back orange; Liberty at ctr. Printer: ABNC.			
	a. 1.8.1917.	12.50	50.00	150.00
	b. Caja Reguladora reissue, 2 sets of serial # (red and blue). 11.2.1924; 4.2.1926.	20.00	80.00	250.00

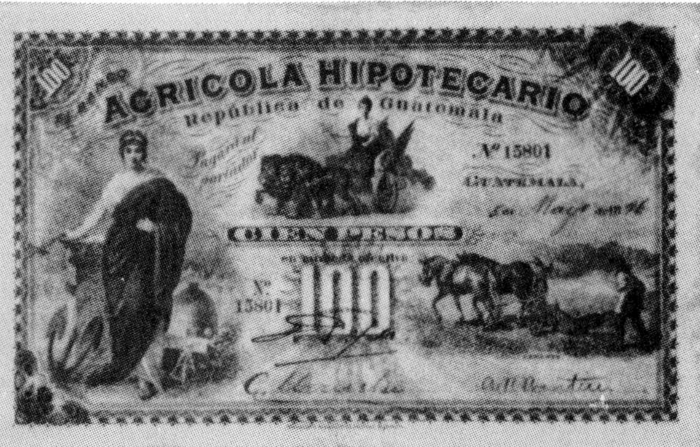

		GOOD	FINE	XF
S105	**100 PESOS** 1892-1926. Black on pink and blue unpt. Woman standing w/pedestal, anchor and beehive at l., woman in winged chariot drawn by lions at ctr., farmer plowing at r.			
	a. Handwritten sign. 8.5.1892-31.8.1915.	25.00	100.00	300.00
	b. Printed sign. 1.6.1917; 11.2.1924.	20.00	75.00	225.00
	c. Ovpt. in box like #S101c.	—	—	—

		GOOD	FINE	XF
	d. Date partially filled in by hand. *5... Marzo... 96.*	—	—	—
	e. Caja Reguladora reissue, 2 sets of serial #. 15.2.1926.	20.00	75.00	225.00

		GOOD	FINE	XF
S106	**500 PESOS** 1.6.1917. Black on m/c unpt. Man w/trident in chariot drawn by 3 horses at l. Woman in winged chariot drawn by lions at lower r.			
	a. Issued note.	—	Rare	—
	s. Specimen.	—	—	—

BANCO AMERICANO DE GUATEMALA

Founded in 1895.

1895-1926 ISSUES

#S111-S115 two seated women w/symbols of Agriculture and Commerce as face design, and arms of Guatemala at l., of the United States at r. Scene of three mountains overlooking village and train at ctr. on back. Printer: ABNC.

A word on date ranges

Often date ranges or specific dates are listed. These have been observed or reported by our contributors. If a note is outside the published range, it only means that it is a newly reported date, and not necessarily worthy of a premium value.

		GOOD	FINE	XF
S111	**1 PESO**			
	1895-1920. Black on gray unpt. Back red-orange. Series A.			
	a. 29.8.1895-30.4.1902.	6.00	20.00	75.00
	b. 2.11.1914-15.6.1920.	3.00	10.00	35.00
S112	**5 PESOS**			
	1897-1920. Black on gray unpt. Back brown. Series B.			
	a. 23.1.1897; 5.3.1897; 30.4.1902.	12.50	40.00	125.00
	b. 2.11.1914-15.6.1920.	6.00	20.00	75.00
S113	**25 PESOS**			
	2.11.1914-25.6.1918. Black on blue unpt. Back blue. Series C.	8.00	30.00	120.00

		GOOD	FINE	XF
S114	**100 PESOS**			
	1913-25. Black on gray and orange. unpt. Back brown. Series D.			
	a. 19.3.1913; 2.11.1914; 4.8.1915; 28.3.1922; 26.1.1923; 29.10.1924.	20.00	75.00	250.00
	b. Caja Reguladora reissue, 2 sets of red serial #. 14.1.1925	20.00	80.00	275.00
	s. Specimen.	—	—	—

		GOOD	FINE	XF
S115	**500 PESOS**			
	1895-1925. Black on orange unpt. Back orange. Series E.			
	a. 11.10.1895. Handwritten date at r.	—	—	—
	b. Date at r. 22.10.1917; 27.3.1920; 28.3.1922; 11.8.1922.	70.00	200.00	425.00
	c. Date at ctr. 26.1.1923; 14.1.1925.	70.00	200.00	425.00
	d. Caja Reguladora reissue, 2 sets of red serial #. ND.	90.00	225.00	—

#S116-S120 similar to #S111-S115. Backs are more darkly printed. Printer: W&S.

		GOOD	FINE	XF
S116	**1 PESO**			
	26.1.1923. Similar to #S111. Series C.	3.00	10.00	35.00

		GOOD	FINE	XF
S117	**5 PESOS**			
	22.5.1919; 15.5.1923. Similar to #S112. Series B; C.	6.00	20.00	75.00

		GOOD	FINE	XF
S118	**25 PESOS**			
	25.6.1918; 22.5.1919; 15.5.1923. Similar to #S113. Series B; C.	7.50	30.00	100.00
S119	**100 PESOS**			
	22.5.1919-14.1.1925. Black on lt. brown unpt. Similar to #S114. Series B; C.	17.50	75.00	200.00
S120	**500 PESOS**			
	4.2.1926; 15.2.1926. Similar to #S115. Series C. Caja Reguladora reissue, 2 sets of serial # (red and black).	75.00	225.00	500.00

BANCO COLOMBIANO

Founded in 1878. Notes from this bank are believed to have circulated in Colombia as well as Guatemala. Note issues were restricted and most were redeemed in silver, unlike the other bank notes in general use. Only 250,000 pesos was outstanding by 1923.

1879-1901 ISSUE

#S121-S126 standing soldier in armor w/shield and spear w/Liberty cap at l., sm. arms of Guatemala at ctr. l. and of Colombia at ctr. r. on face. Printer: BWC.

		GOOD	FINE	XF
S121	**1 PESO**			
	1879-1900. Black on green unpt. Ox-drawn cart at top ctr. Back green.			
	a. 17.10.1879. Sm. black serial #.	—	—	—
	b. 5.4.1900; 17.4.1900. Lg. black serial #.	12.00	50.00	125.00

		Good	Fine	XF
S122	**5 Pesos**			
	1884-1901. Black on reddish brown unpt. Cactus plants at top ctr. Back red-brown.			
	a. Black serial #. 16.5.1884; 16.3.1887.	—	—	—
	b. Red serial #. 19.9.1901; 21.9.1901; 23.9.1901.	17.50	75.00	225.00

		Good	Fine	XF
S123	**10 Pesos**			
	1887; 1901. Black on blue unpt. Boat loading at top ctr. Back blue.			
	a. 23.4.1887; 30.4.1887. Handsigned. Black serial #.	—	—	—
	b. 24.9.1901. Printed sign. Red serial #.	50.00	175.00	400.00
S124	**20 Pesos**			
	1890; 1901. Black on gold unpt. Farm work scene at top ctr. Back gold.			
	a. 12.7.1890. Handsigned. Black serial #.	—	—	—
	b. 25.9.1901. Printed sign. Black serial #.	125.00	400.00	—

		Good	Fine	XF
S125	**50 Pesos**			
	1885-1901. Black on lilac unpt. Harvest scene at top ctr. Back lilac.			
	a. Red serial #. 4.3.1885; 14.3.1885.	—	—	—
	b. Black serial #. 25.4.1889; 16.6.1890.	—	—	—
	c. Blue serial #. 25.9.1901.	100.00	350.00	—
S126	**100 Pesos**			
	28.2.1889. Black on red unpt. Cows at top ctr. Back red. Black serial #.	—	Rare	—

Banco Comercial de Guatemala

This bank became the Banco Agricola Hipotecario in 1895.

1890's Issue

#S131-S135 woman w/sheaf of wheat at l. Printer: IBNC.

		Good	Fine	XF
S131	**1 Peso**			
	1892-94. Black on blue unpt. Back brown and blue.			
	a. 1.11.1892; 15.11.1892; 15.2.1893. Hand dated.	150.00	400.00	—
	b. 31.3.1894. Printed date.	150.00	400.00	—
	p. Proof.	—	—	—

		Good	Fine	XF
S132	**5 Pesos**			
	31.12.1892; 31.3.1894. Black on green unpt. Back lt. brown and orange.			
	a. Issued note, hand dated.	—	—	—
	p. Proof.	—	—	—
S133	**25 Pesos**			
	189x. Similar to #S132 but larger size.			
	p. Proof.	—	—	—
	s. Specimen.	—	—	—
S134	**100 Pesos**			
	189x. Similar to #S132 but larger size. Proof.	—	—	—
S135	**500 Pesos**			
	189x. Similar to #S132 but larger size. Proof.	—	—	—

Banco de Guatemala

Established in 1895.

1895-1926 Issue

#S141, S143, and #S146-S148 black on blue unpt. Woman's head at lower l. and r. corners; arms between steam passenger trains at upper ctr. Printer for all except #S145: IBNC.

		Good	Fine	XF
S141	**1 Peso**			
	1895-1915. Back brown.			
	a. Sm.red serial #. 15.7.1895-25.6.1900.	5.00	20.00	60.00
	b. Lg. red serial #. 27.5.1914; 1.3.1915.	4.00	15.00	55.00

#S142 *Deleted*. See #S149.

		Good	Fine	XF
S143	**5 Pesos**			
	1895-1915. Back red-orange.			
	a. 15.7.1895.	—	—	—
	b. Sm. red serial # 15.6.1899-1.2.1905.	10.00	35.00	100.00
	c. Lg. red serial # 17.4.1914; 4.2.1915; 4.4.1915.	7.50	25.00	75.00

#S144 *Deleted*. See #S149A.

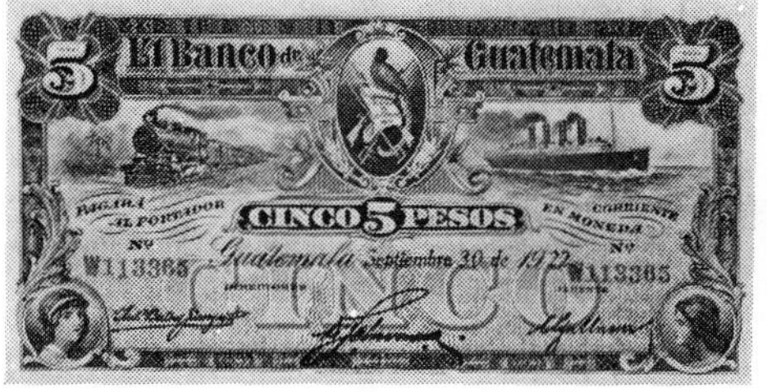

		GOOD	FINE	XF
S145	**5 PESOS** 30.9.1922. Black on blue unpt. Train at l., ship at r. of arms at ctr. Woman's head at lower corners. Back red-orange. Printer: W&S.	5.00	17.50	55.00
S146	**25 PESOS** 1905-25. Back olive.			
	a. 29.8.1905-26.2.1924.	15.00	55.00	150.00
	b. Caja Reguladora reissue, 2 sets of red serial #. 14.1.1925.	20.00	75.00	185.00
S147	**100 PESOS** 1895-1926. Back brown.			
	a. Handwritten date. 30.8.1895.	60.00	175.00	—
	b. 27.9.1895.	—	—	—
	c. 21.6.1907-14.2.1926.	20.00	75.00	185.00
	d. Caja Reguladora reissue, 2 sets of red serial #. 14.1.1925; 15.2.1926.	22.50	80.00	200.00

		GOOD	FINE	XF
S148	**500 PESOS** 1915-26. Back green.			
	a. 5.8.1915-4.2.1926.	55.00	200.00	400.00
	b. Caja Reguladora reissue, red and black serial #. 4.2.1926.	60.00	225.00	450.00
	c. Caja Reguladora reissue, black serial #. 15.2.1926.	60.00	225.00	450.00

QUEZALTENANGO

1895-1926 ISSUE

#S149-S149C w/added text: *SUCURSAL QUEZALTENANGO* at top on face and back.

		GOOD	FINE	XF
S149	**1 PESO** 1.9.1896-25.11.1897. Black on red-orange unpt. Like #S141 but w/branch name added on face and back. Back red-orange.	20.00	110.00	—
S149A	**5 PESOS** 10.9.1896; 17.9.1896; 29.9.1896. Black on red unpt. Like #S143 but w/branch name added on face and back. Back brown.	—	—	—
S149B	**25 PESOS** 17.9.1896. Like #S146 but w/branch name added on face and back.	—	—	—
S149C	**100 PESOS** 29.9.1896. Like #S147 but w/branch name added on face and back.	—	—	—

NOTE: The date 2.12.1897 is reported, not confirmed for #S149.

BANCO INTERNACIONAL DE GUATEMALA

Founded in 1877.

1878-1926 ISSUE

		GOOD	FINE	XF
S150	**1 PESO** (ca.1878). Green back proof. Printer: PBC.	—	—	—
S150A	**1 PESO** (ca.1878). Red back proof. Printer: PBC.	—	—	—

#S151-S161 hand holding eight flags as face design.

		GOOD	FINE	XF
S151	**1 PESO** 1879-99. Black on gray unpt. Sign. title: *JERENTE* below date. Back orange. Printer: NBNC.			
	a. Handwritten date. 7.1.1879; 25.4.1879.	100.00	300.00	—
	b. Stamped date. 30.6.1879.	40.00	150.00	—
	c. Partially printed date. 5.7.1893-20.12.1899. Also w/ABNC monogram.	6.00	20.00	55.00

		GOOD	FINE	XF
S152	**1 PESO** 1900-16. Black. Similar to #S151. Sign. title: GERENTE below date. Series 2. Printer: W&S.			
	a. 4 sign. 30.6.1900.	4.00	15.00	50.00
	b. 3 sign. across. 2.10.1916/1914.	3.00	12.50	45.00

		GOOD	FINE	XF
S153	**1 PESO** 1917-23. Black. Like #S151. Sign. title: *JERENTE* below date. Series 2A. Printer: NBNC.			
	a. 3 sign. across. 23.10.1917; 5.4.1920 (2 var.).	3.00	12.50	40.00
	b. 3 sign., 2 at l. and 1 at r. 18.5.1923.	3.00	12.50	40.00

		GOOD	FINE	XF
S154	**5 PESOS** 1885-1900. Black on gray unpt. Counterfoil at l. margin. Uniface. Printer: NBNC.			
	a. W/o ABNC monogram. 6.4.1885.	60.00	200.00	—
	b. ABNC monogram added. 8.1.1900.	50.00	175.00	—

		GOOD	FINE	XF
S155	**5 PESOS** 1900-16. Similar to #S154. Printed w/o counterfoil at l. Series 2. Back blue; bank at ctr. Printer: W&S.			
	a. 30.6.1900.	25.00	75.00	350.00
	b. 14.3.1913; 2.10.1916/1914.	15.00	50.00	175.00

		Good	Fine	XF
S156	**5 Pesos** 1917-23. Black on gray unpt. Similar to #S155. Series 2A. Back blue; steam passenger train at ctr. Printer: ABNC.			
	a. Handwritten sign. 23.10.1917.	8.00	30.00	95.00
	b. Printed sign. 5.4.1920; 18.5.1923.	7.00	25.00	90.00
S156A	**25 Pesos** 5.4.1895; 6.4.1895. Black on brown unpt. Counterfoil at l. margin. Uniface. Printer: NBNC.	—	—	—

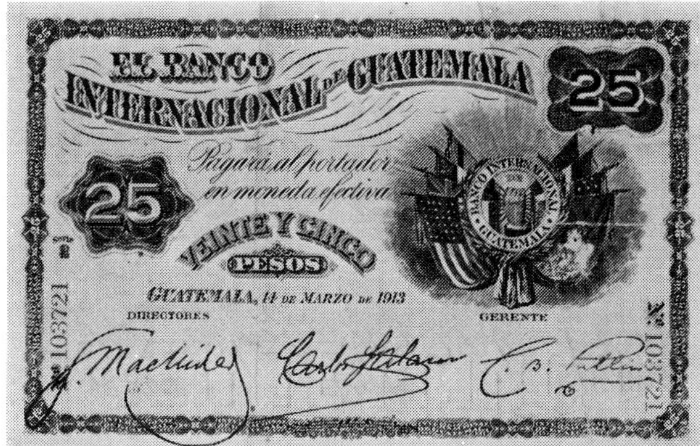

		Good	Fine	XF
S157	**25 Pesos** 1900-16. Black on brown unpt. Series 2. Back brown; bank at ctr. Printer: W&S.			
	a. 30.9.1907/1900; 14.3.1913; 2.10.1916/1914.	30.00	100.00	225.00
	p. Face and back proof. 30.9.1900.	—	Unc	75.00

		Good	Fine	XF
S158	**25 Pesos** 1917-25. Similar to #S157. Series 2A. Back brown; steam passenger train at ctr. Printer: ABNC.			
	a. Handwritten sign. 23.10.1917; 5.4.1920.	17.50	50.00	150.00
	b. Printed sign. 28.1.1925.	15.00	45.00	135.00

		Good	Fine	XF
S159	**100 Pesos** 18xx; 1909-14. Black on blue unpt. Back black, brown and blue. Printers: face, NBNC; back, ABNC.			
	a. 1.9.1909; 2.10.1914.	30.00	90.00	275.00
	p. Face and back proof. 18xx.	—	Unc	80.00

Notice

Readers with unlisted dates, color or signature varieties are invited to submit photocopies of their notes to: Standard Catalog of World Paper Money, Krause Publications, 700 East State St. Iola WI 54990-0001 U.S.A. or by email: thernr@krause.com. Email submissions of material for possible inclusion need to be 100% jpeg attachments at 300 dpi.

		Good	Fine	XF
S160	**100 Pesos** 1917-25. Similar to #S159 but smaller size. Series 2A. Printer: ABNC.			
	a. 23.10.1917-20.11.1922.	25.00	80.00	225.00
	b. Caja Reguladora reissue, 2 sets of serial #, red and black. 14.1.1925.	22.50	75.00	200.00
S160A	**500 Pesos** 18xx (ca.1890). Black on green unpt. Counterfoil at l. margin. Back green; steam passenger train at ctr. Printer: ABNC. Face and back proof.	—	Unc	85.00
S161	**500 Pesos** 1917-26. Similar to #S160A. Printer: ABNC.			
	a. 23.10.1917; 5.4.1920; 25.10.1920.	100.00	300.00	600.00
	b. Caja Reguladora reissue, black and red serial #. 4.2.1926.	100.00	300.00	600.00
	c. Caja Reguladora reissue. 15.2.1926.	100.00	300.00	600.00

Banco Nacional de Guatemala

Founded in 1874; liquidated in 1876.

1874 ND Issue

		Good	Fine	XF
S166	**1 Real** ND. Red. Green arms and black printed sign. on back. Local printing.	—	Rare	—

		Good	Fine	XF
S167	**1 Peso** ND. Black on red unpt. Seated allegorical woman at lower l. and at lower r., portr. Pres. J. Rufino Barrios at l., J. M. Samayoa at r. Back green. Printer: CCBB.	125.00	475.00	—

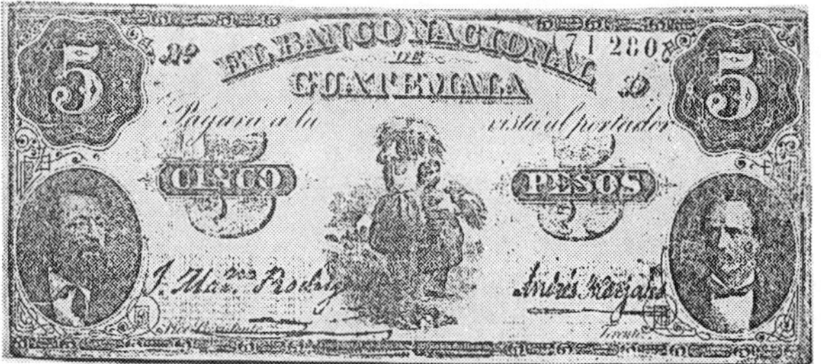

		Good	Fine	XF
S168	**5 Pesos** ND. Black. Portrs. Pres. J. R. Barrios at l., J. M. Samayoa at r., allegorical women w/sheaves at ctr.	—	—	—

		Good	Fine	XF
S169	**10 Pesos** ND. Black. Portrs. Pres. J. R. Barrios at top l., J. M. Samayoa at bottom l., standing allegorical woman w/tablet inscribed: *30 DE JUNIO DE 1871* at ctr.	—	—	—
S170	**20 Pesos** ND. Black. Portrs. Pres. J. R. Barrios and J. M. Samayoa at l. and r. ctr., allegorical woman at ctr.	—	—	—
S170A	**50 Pesos** ND. Black. Portrs. Pres. J. R. Barrios and J. M. Samayoa at l. and r. ctr., Indians at lower l., seated allegorical woman at lower r.	—	—	—
S170B	**100 Pesos** ND. Black. Portrs. Pres. J. R. Barrios at l., J. M. Samayoa at r., man w/horse at ctr.	—	—	—

Banco de Occidente en Quezaltenango

Founded in 1881.

1881-1926 Issue

		Good	Fine	XF
S171	**25 Centavos** 20.8.1881. Seated woman at l.	—	Rare	—

		Good	Fine	XF
S172	**50 Centavos** 15.8.1900; 20.12.1916. Black on pink unpt. Woman at l., green quetzal bird at ctr., standing woman w/basket on head w/other women harvesting at r. Back green; arms at ctr. Printer: W&S.	3.50	12.50	45.00

		Good	Fine	XF
S173	**1 Peso** 188x-1914. Black on green and m/c unpt. Arms at l., seated woman w/bales and caduceus at ctr., quetzal at r. Back green. Printer: ABNC.			
	a. 188x; 1890/8x. Hand sign at l. and r.	—	—	—
	b. Stamped date on printed line. 14.6.1899; 15.7.1899; 4.12.1899.	5.00	17.50	60.00
	c. Printed date. 1.7.1909; 1.8..1914.	3.00	10.00	35.00
	p. Proof. 188x.	—	—	—

#S174 *Deleted.* See #S184.

		Good	Fine	XF
S175	**1 Peso** 1900-21. Black. Portr. woman at l., sugar plantation at ctr. Back brown; arms at ctr. Printer: W&S.			
	a. Green and lilac unpt. 15.8.1900.	3.50	12.50	40.00
	b. Blue and green unpt. 20.12.1916; 9.6.1920; 2.11.1921.	2.50	10.00	30.00

		Good	Fine	XF
S176	**5 Pesos** 1890-1919. Black on m/c unpt. Arms at l., woman w/cogwheel and bales at ctr., quetzal at r. Back green. Printer: ABNC.			
	a. Handwritten date. 5.3.1890/188x; 24.10.1890; 1.6.1898.	15.00	55.00	—
	b. Printed date. 14.2.1903-2.6.1919.	4.00	15.00	65.00

		Good	Fine	XF
S177	**5 Pesos** 15.1.1918; 19.6.1920. Black on gray and orange unpt. Woman at l., Mercury at ctr. Back orange; arms at ctr. Printer: W&S.	6.00	15.00	60.00
S178	**5 Pesos** 2.11.1921. Black on gray and orange unpt. Like #S177. Back green. Smaller size. Printer: W&S.	7.00	20.00	75.00

		Good	Fine	XF
S179	**20 Pesos** 10.2.1903-18.10.1920. Black on m/c unpt. Arms at l., Liberty standing holding quetzal at ctr., quetzal at r. Back blue. Printer: ABNC.	8.00	30.00	95.00

S180 20 PESOS

	GOOD	FINE	XF
15.1.1918. Black on m/c unpt. Arms at l., seated woman w/caduceus at ctr. Back red; arms at ctr. Printer: W&S.	9.00	40.00	125.00

S181 20 PESOS

	GOOD	FINE	XF
1921-25. Black on m/c unpt. Similar to #S180 but smaller size. Back blue. Printer: W&S.			
a. 2.11.1921.	8.00	30.00	100.00
b. Caja Reguladora reissue, 2 sets of serial #. 14.1.1925 (old date lined out).	20.00	75.00	200.00

S182 100 PESOS

	GOOD	FINE	XF
1890-1920. Black on m/c unpt. Arms at l., coffee harvesting scene at ctr., quetzal at r. Back red-orange. Printer: ABNC.			
a. Handwritten date and sign. 29.4.1890; 25.5.1893; 15.8.1900; 22.5.1902.	25.00	85.00	225.00
b. Printed date and sign. 20.10.1902-18.10.1920.	17.50	70.00	200.00

S183 100 PESOS

	GOOD	FINE	XF
1921-26. Black on m/c unpt. Similar to #S182 but much smaller size. Printer: W&S.			
a. Printed date, red serial #. 2.11.1921.	22.50	80.00	225.00
b. Ovpt. date, black serial #. 10.10.1925; 18.1.1926.	20.00	70.00	200.00
c. Caja Reguladora reissue, 2 sets of serial #. 15.2.1926.	22.50	80.00	225.00

GUATEMALA CITY

1800'S ISSUE

S184 1 PESO

	GOOD	FINE	XF
16.7.1894. Black on blue and m/c unpt. Like #S173 but w/branch name added at top. Back blue; red vertical ovpt: *PAGADERO UNICAMENTE EN GUATEMALA* in box at ctr.	—	Rare	—

	GOOD	FINE	XF
S185 5 PESOS 18xx. Like #S176 but w/branch name added at top. Specimen.	—	—	—
S186 20 PESOS 18xx. Like #S179 but w/branch name added at top. Back orange. Proof.	—	—	—

S187 100 PESOS

	GOOD	FINE	XF
18xx. Like #S182 but w/branch name added at top.			
p. Proof.	—	—	—
s. Specimen.	—	—	—

COMITE BANCARIO DE GUATEMALA

Established in 1898, the Comite Bancario had as its aim the issuance of six million pesos in inconvertible currency. Though each bank had a representative on the Comite, the power was retained by the government. The notes were used in part to pay government debts to the banks along with other expenses. Notes issued by the Comite were declared legal tender and could not be refused as payment for any debts. By 1925 most had been withdrawn from circulation, with about one million pesos outstanding.

1899 ISSUE

#S191-S193 black on gray unpt. Steam ship at lower l., arms between seated Liberty and Justice at upper ctr., steam passenger train at lower r. Printer: HBNC (no imprint).

S191 1 PESO

	GOOD	FINE	XF
15.4.1899-3.8.1899. Back orange-brown.	12.50	60.00	250.00

		Good	Fine	XF
S192	5 Pesos 2.6.1899-13.7.1899. Back blue.	35.00	150.00	—

		Good	Fine	XF
S193	25 Pesos 2.6.1899; 15.6.1899; 22.6.1899; 3.7.1899; 6.7.1899; 13.7.1899. Back brown.	125.00	350.00	—

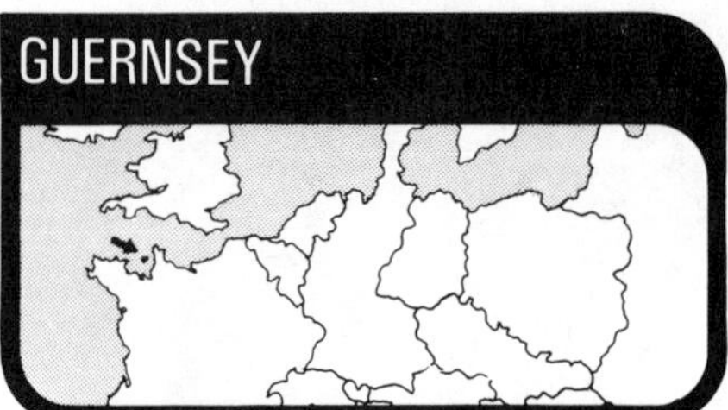

The Bailiwick of Guernsey, a British crown dependency located in the English Channel 30 miles (48 km.) west of Normandy, France, has an area of 30 sq. mi. (78 sq. km.), including the Isles of Alderney, Jethou, Herm, Brechou and Sark, and a population of 58,681. Capital: St. Peter Port. Agriculture and cattle breeding are the main occupations.

Militant monks from the Duchy of Normandy established the first permanent settlements on Guernsey prior to the Norman invasion of England, but the prevalence of prehistoric monuments suggests an earlier occupancy. The island, the only part of the Duchy of Normandy belonging to the British crown, has been a possession of Britain since the Norman Conquest of 1066. During the Anglo-French Wars, the harbors of Guernsey were employed in the building and outfitting of ships for the English privateers preying on French shipping. Guernsey is administered by its own laws and customs. Acts passed by the British Parliament are not applicable to Guernsey unless the island is specifically mentioned. During World War II, German troops occupied the island from 1940 to 1944.

RULERS:

British to 1940, 1944-

MONETARY SYSTEM:

1 Penny = 8 Doubles
1 Shilling = 12 Pence
1 Pound = 20 Shillings to 1971

British Administration

Guernsey Banking Co. Ltd.

Right of issue ceased in 1914, but the notes still circulated until the consolidation of the bank with the National Provincial Bank in 1924. Notes reportedly circulated from 1827-1924.

1861-1906 Issue

		Good	Fine	XF
S151	1 Pound 1861-87. Arms at upper l., ship at ctr., woman w/bales at upper r. w/title: *GUERNSEY BANKING COMPANY.* Printer: PBC.			
	a. Sign. titles: *MANAGER* and *CHAIRMAN.* 1.8.1887.	—	—	—
	s. Sign. title: *MANAGER.* Specimen. 22.8.1861.	—	—	—
S153	1 Pound 1.7.1906. Similar to #S151, but w/title: *GUERNSEY BANKING COMPANY LIMITED.* Sign. titles: *MANAGER* and *CHAIRMAN.* Printer: PBC.	—	—	—

NOTE: Issue dates of 25.9.1828, 1.5.1863, 1866, 1.12.1891 and 1.9.1903 are reported. Confirmation of full bank title and sign. title variety is needed.

Guernsey Commercial Banking Co. Ltd.

Right of issue ceased in 1914, but the notes still circulated until consolidation of the bank with the Westminster Bank Ltd. in 1924. Notes reportedly circulated from 1835-1923.

1886-1916 Issue

		Good	Fine	XF
S171	1 Pound 6.12.1886; 2.1.1906. Commerce seated at upper ctr. w/sailing ships in background. W/title: *GUERNSEY COMMERCIAL BANKING COMPANY.* 3 sign. Printer: PB&P.	—	Rare	—

NOTE: Issue dates of 2.12.1868 and 6.9.1869 are reported, not confirmed.

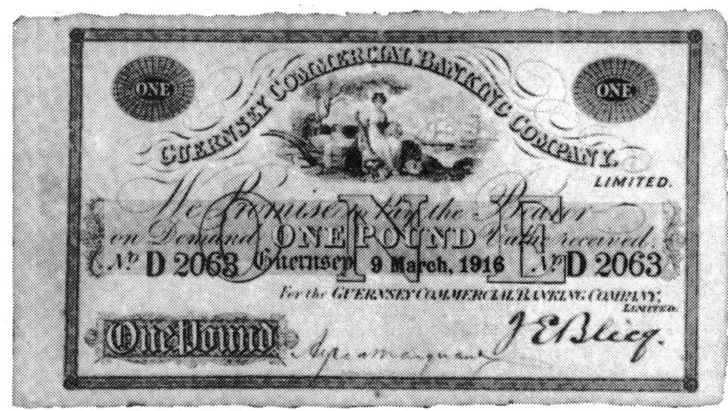

S173 **1 POUND** | GOOD | FINE | XF
9.3.1916. Similar to #S171, but w/title: *GUERNSEY COMMERIAL BANKING COMPANY LIMITED.* 2 sign.

	GOOD	FINE	XF
a. Issued note.	—	Rare	—
p. Proof. (ca.1913).	—	—	—

SOUTHERN DISTRICT BANKING COMPANY

GUERNSEY

1838 ISSUE

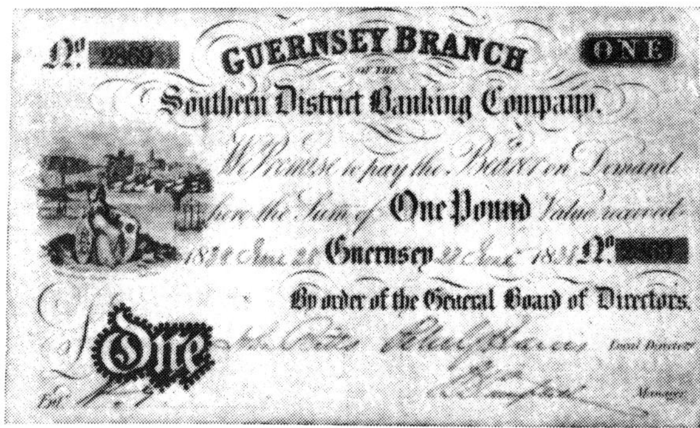

	GOOD	FINE	XF
S177 **1 POUND** 28.6.1838. Landscape at l.	—	2500.	—

REGIONAL

ISLE OF ALDERNEY

ALDERNEY COMMERCIAL BANK

1810 ISSUE

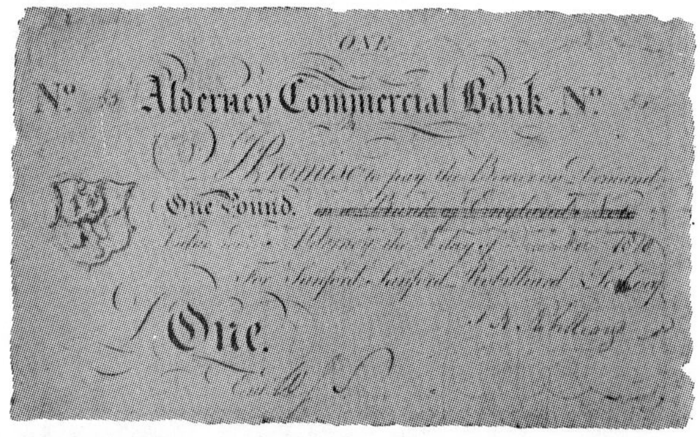

	GOOD	FINE	XF
S181 **1 POUND** 26.12.1810. Black. Arms at l.	—	—	2250.

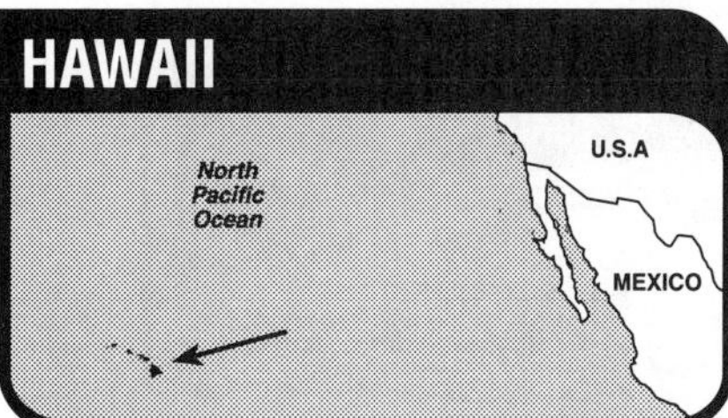

Hawaii consists of eight main islands and numerous smaller islands of coral and volcanic origin situated in the central Pacific Ocean 2,400 miles (3,862 km.) from San Francisco. The archipelago has an area of 6,471 sq. mi. (16,641 sq. km.) and a population of 1.1 million. Capital: Honolulu. The principal industries are tourism and agriculture. Cane sugar and pineapples are exported.

The islands, originally populated by Polynesians who traveled from the Society Islands, were discovered by British navigator Capt. James Cook in 1778. He named them the Sandwich Islands. King Kamehameha the Great united the islands under one kingdom (1795-1810) which endured until 1893 when Queen Liliuokalani, the gifted composer of "Aloha Oe" and other songs, was deposed and a provisional government established. This was followed by a republic which governed Hawaii until 1898 when it ceded itself to the United States. Hawaii was organized as a territory in 1900 and became the 50th state of the United States on Aug. 21, 1959.

RULERS

King Kalakaua, 1874-1891
Queen Liliuokalani, 1891-1893
Provisional Govt., 1893-1894
Republic, 1894-1898
Annexed to U.S., 1898-1900
Territory, 1900-1959

MONETARY SYSTEM

1 Dollar = 100 Cents

KINGDOM

BANK OF CLAUS SPRECKELS & CO.

1886-87 SILVER CERTIFICATE OF DEPOSIT ISSUE

#S101-S104 seated figure in rowboat at l. Hand cancelled by tearing off the signature at lower right on each note.

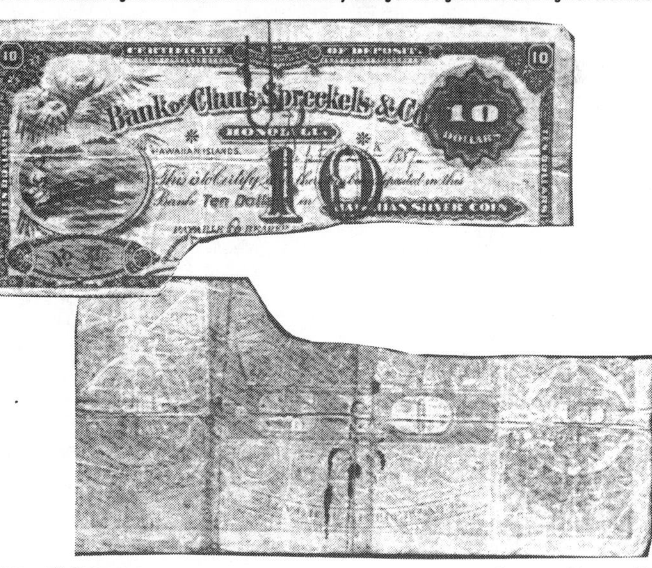

	GOOD	FINE	XF
S101 **10 DOLLARS** 24.9.1887. Purple. Back yellow.	—	Rare	—

	GOOD	FINE	XF
S102 **20 DOLLARS** 15.1.1887. Blue. Back red.	—	Rare	—

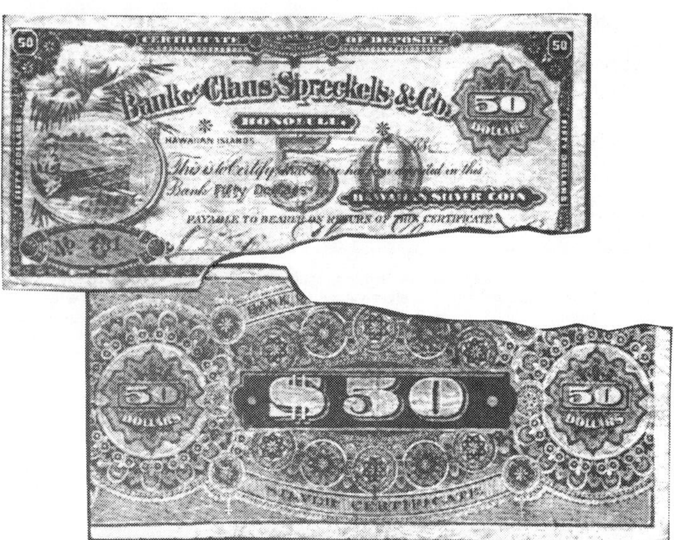

S103 50 DOLLARS — GOOD — FINE Rare — XF —
1.10.1886. Red. Back green.

S104 100 DOLLARS — GOOD — FINE Rare — XF —
1.10.1886. Green. Back blue.

NOTE: A single set of #S101-S104 was presented as a new discovery and sold at auction by Lyn F. Knight, Inc. at the 1997 Memphis Paper Money Show.

HONDURAS

The Republic of Honduras, situated in Central America between El Salvador, Nicaragua and Guatemala, has an area of 43,277 sq. mi. (112,088 sq. km.) and a population of 6.48 million. Capital: Tegucigalpa. Tourism, agriculture, mining (gold and silver), and logging are the chief industries. Bananas, timber and coffee are exported.

Honduras, a site of the ancient Mayan Empire, was claimed for Spain by Columbus in 1502, during his last voyage to the Americas. The first settlement was made by Cristobal de Olid under orders of Hernan Cortes, then in Mexico. The area, regarded as one of the most promising sources of gold and silver in the New World, was a part of the Captaincy General of Guatemala throughout the colonial period. After declaring its independence from Spain in 1821, Honduras fell briefly to the Mexican Empire of Agustin de Iturbide, and then joined the Central American Federation (1823-39). Upon dissolution of the federation, Honduras became an independent republic.

MONETARY SYSTEM:

I Peso = 100 Centavos, 1871-1926
1 Lempira = 100 Centavos, 1926-

BANKS:

Aguan Navigation and Improvement Company .... #S101-S107
Banco Atlantida .... #S111-S125
Banco Centro-Americano .... #S131-S139
Banco de Comercio .... #S141-S145
Banco Nacional de Honduras .... #S148
Banco Nacional Hondureño .... #S151-S159

REVOLUTION

Banco Territorial de Honduras .... #S161-S161A

REPUBLIC

Billete Aduanero (Customs Notes) .... #S162-S171

BANKS

AGUAN NAVIGATION AND IMPROVEMENT COMPANY

1886 ISSUE

#S101-S107 portr. Pres. Luis Bográn in civilian suit on face. Printer: HLBNC. All notes have green backs.

S101 50 CENTAVOS — GOOD 5.00 — FINE 15.00 — XF 75.00
25.6.1886. Black on red unpt. Portr. woman at l., portr. Pres. Bográn at ctr.

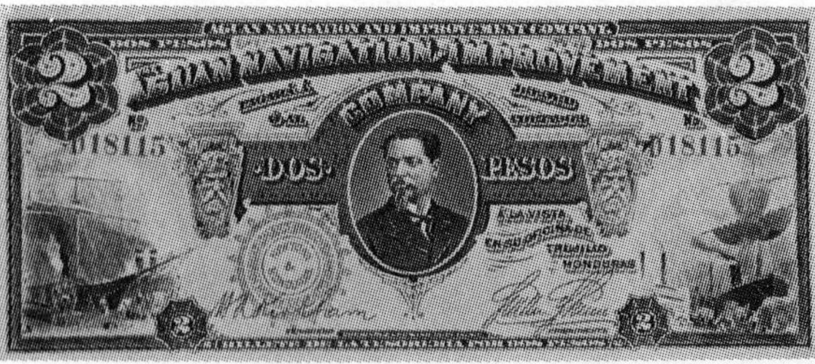

S103 2 PESOS — GOOD — FINE Rare — XF —
ND (1886). Black on yellow unpt. Sailing ship and steam passenger train at l., portr. Pres. Bográn at ctr., ship loading at r. Medallion of helmeted Minerva at upper ctr. on back.

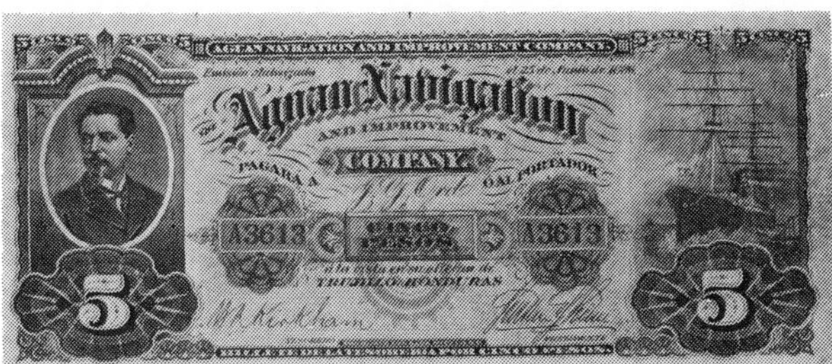

		GOOD	FINE	XF
S104	**5 PESOS** 25.6.1886. Black on gold unpt. Portr. Pres. Bográn at l., ship at r.	50.00	150.00	450.00

		GOOD	FINE	XF
S105	**10 PESOS** 25.6.1886. Black on red unpt. Portr. Pres. Bográn at upper l., ship at lower r.	75.00	225.00	550.00

		GOOD	FINE	XF
S107	**50 PESOS** 25.6.1886. Black on green unpt. Portr. Pres. Bográn at lower l., Justice seated between 2 children at ctr., paddle wheel steamer at lower r.	225.00	—	—

BANCO ATLANTIDA

1913-19 ISSUE

Peso System.

#S111-S115 printer: ABNC.

		GOOD	FINE	XF
S111	**1 PESO** 1.4.1913-14.1.1919. Black on green and brown unpt. Hope seated by seashore at ctr. Back green; arms at ctr.			
	a. Hand sign. 1.4.1913.	45.00	175.00	—
	b. Printed sign. 1.4.1913.	45.00	175.00	375.00

		GOOD	FINE	XF
	c. Ovpt: *Decree No. 11 of 14.1.1919* date in 5 lines of red text (in Spanish) on face.	125.00	350.00	—

		GOOD	FINE	XF
S113	**5 PESOS** 1.4.1913-14.1.1919. Black on blue unpt. Like #S111. Back blue.			
	a. Issued note.	—	Rare	—
	b. Ovpt: *Decree No. 11 of 14.1.1919* date like #S111c.	—	Rare	—
	p. Proof.	—	—	—

		GOOD	FINE	XF
S115	**20 PESOS** 1.4.1913. Black on orange and yellow unpt. Like #S111. Back orange. Proof.	—	—	—

NOTE: Other denominations are reported, not confirmed.

1932 ISSUE

Lempira System.

#S121-S125 printer: ABNC.

		GOOD	FINE	XF
S121	**1 LEMPIRA** 1932. Black on green and m/c unpt. Similar to #S111. Back olive-brown; arms at ctr.			
	a. Series A. L.h. sign. title: *PRESIDENTE*. 1.3.1932.	20.00	50.00	175.00
	b. Series A. L.h. sign. title: *VICE-PRESIDENTE*. 1.3.1932.	20.00	50.00	175.00
	c. Series B. 1.7.1932.	20.00	50.00	175.00
	s. Specimen.	—	—	—

S122 2 LEMPIRAS
1932. Black on blue, orange and m/c unpt. Helmeted woman protecting child at ctr. Back red; bank at ctr.

	GOOD	FINE	XF
a. Series A. 1.3.1932.	25.00	55.00	225.00
b. Series B. 1.7.1932.	25.00	55.00	225.00
s. Specimen.	—	—	—

S123 5 LEMPIRAS
1932-43. Black on pink, orange and m/c unpt. Similar to #S121. Back blue; arms at ctr.

	GOOD	FINE	XF
a. Series A. 1.3.1932.	30.00	75.00	275.00
b. Series B. L.h. sign. title: *PRESIDENTE*. 1.7.1932.	30.00	75.00	275.00
c. Series B. L.h. sign. title: *VICE-PRESIDENTE*. 1.7.1932.	30.00	75.00	275.00
d. Series C. L.h. sign. title: *VICE-PRESIDENTE*. 1.2.1943.	30.00	75.00	275.00
e. Series C. L.h. sign. title: *PRESIDENTE*. 1.2.1943.	30.00	75.00	275.00
s. Specimen.	—	—	—

S124 10 LEMPIRAS
1932-43. Black on m/c unpt. Seated woman and child at l. and r. Back brown; bank at ctr.

	GOOD	FINE	XF
a. Series A. 1.3.1932.	35.00	125.00	350.00
b. Series B. 1.7.1932.	35.00	125.00	350.00
c. Series C. L.h. sign. title: *PRESIDENTE*. 1.2.1943.	35.00	125.00	350.00
d. Series C. L.h. sign. title: *VICE-PRESIDENTE*. 1.2.1943.	35.00	125.00	350.00
s. Specimen.	—	—	—

S125 20 LEMPIRAS
1932-45. Black on green and m/c unpt. Woman reclining at ctr. Back green; arms at ctr.

	GOOD	FINE	XF
a. Series A. 1.3.1932.	40.00	175.00	—
b. Series B. 1.7.1932.	40.00	175.00	
c. Series C. 17.5.1945.	40.00	175.00	—
s. Specimen.	—	—	—

BANCO CENTRO-AMERICANO

1888 ISSUE

#S131-S137 printer: ABNC.

S131 1 PESO
30.11.1888. Black on brown and yellow unpt. Arms at l., woman at ctr. r. Back brown; griffins at l. and r.

	GOOD	FINE	XF
a. Issued note.	—	Rare	—
s. Specimen.	—	Rare	—

S132 2 PESOS
30.11.1888. Black on green and yellow unpt. Ship at upper l. and ctr., steam train at upper ctr. r., arms at r. Back green; figures at l. and r. Specimen.

GOOD	FINE	XF
—	—	—

S133 5 PESOS
30.11.1888. Black on orange and yellow unpt. Goats at l., arms at ctr., woman pouring water from pitcher at r. Back orange. Specimen.

GOOD	FINE	XF
—	—	—

S134 10 PESOS
30.11.1888. Black on blue and yellow unpt. Standing woman w/ship's wheel at l., ships at l. ctr., arms at r. Back blue. Specimen.

GOOD	FINE	XF
—	—	—

S135 20 PESOS
30.11.1888. Black on green and yellow unpt. Woman w/sheaf at upper l., arms at ctr., miners working at r. Back olive-green. Specimen.

GOOD	FINE	XF
—	—	—

		Good	Fine	XF
S136	**50 Pesos** 30.11.1888. Black on brown and yellow unpt. Allegorical woman w/3 children above arms at l., seated Indian at r. Back red-brown. Specimen.	—	—	—

		Good	Fine	XF
S137	**100 Pesos** 30.11.1888. Black on orange and yellow unpt. Seated woman at l., steer's head at ctr., arms at r. Back orange. Specimen.	—	—	—

1888 Emergency Issue

		Good	Fine	XF
S139	**1 Peso** 30.11.1888. Black on lt. brown paper. Arms handstamped at ctr. Back black. Tegucigalpa local printing.	—	—	—

Banco de Comercio

1915 Issue

#S141-S145 arms at ctr. on back. Printer: ABNC.

		Good	Fine	XF
S141	**1 Peso** 16.2.1915. Black on m/c unpt. Equestrian statue at l. Back green.	—	Rare	—

		Good	Fine	XF
S143	**5 Pesos** 16.2.1915. Black on m/c unpt. Equestrian statue at r. Back purple. Series A.	—	Rare	—
S144	**10 Pesos** 16.2.1915. Black on m/c unpt. Similar to #S141. Back blue.	—	Rare	—
S145	**20 Pesos** 16.2.1915. Black on m/c unpt. Similar to #S143. Back brown.			
	p. Proof.	—	—	—
	s. Specimen.	—	—	—

Banco Nacional de Honduras

1908 Issue

		Good	Fine	XF
S148	**5 Pesos** ND (ca. 1908). Black on green, orange and brown unpt. 2 standing allegorical women at r. Back green; arms at ctr. Printer: ABNC. Proof.	—	Unc	1000.

Banco Nacional Hondureño

Authorized to issue notes October 8, 1888.

1889 Issue

#S151-S159 printer: ABNC.

		Good	Fine	XF
S151	**10 Centavos** 1889. Black on yellow unpt. Liberty at r. Back brown.			
	a. Issued note.	125.00	500.00	—
	s. Specimen.	—	—	—

		Good	Fine	XF
S152	**25 Centavos** 1889. Black on green unpt. Miners at l. Back green.			
	a. Issued note.	125.00	500.00	—
	s. Specimen.	—	—	—

		Good	Fine	XF
S153	**50 Centavos** 1889. Black on orange unpt. Locomotive at l. Back orange.			
	a. Issued note.	200.00	850.00	—
	s. Specimen.	—	—	—

#S154-S159 portr. Pres. General Luis Bográn.

		Good	Fine	XF
S154	**1 Peso** 1889. Black on brown unpt. Woman seated at l., portr. Pres. Bográn at lower r. Back brown.			
	a. Issued note.	200.00	850.00	—
	s. Specimen.	—	—	—

		Good	Fine	XF
S155	**2 Pesos** 1889. Black on orange unpt. Standing sailor at l., supported portr. Pres. Bográn at ctr. Back orange.			
	a. Issued note.	250.00	950.00	—
	s. Specimen.	—	—	—

NOTE: #S154 and S155 sometimes w/hand stamp on back showing issue at San Pedro Sula branch.

		Good	Fine	XF
S156	5 PESOS 1889. Black on blue unpt. Seated allegorical woman at l., arms at ctr. r., portr. Pres. Bográn at r. Back blue.			
	a. Issued note.	—	Rare	—
	p. Proof.	—	—	—
	s. Specimen.	—	—	—
S157	10 PESOS 1889. Black on green unpt. Man at l., seated allegorical woman at upper ctr. Back green.			
	p. Proof.	—	—	—
	s. Specimen.	—	—	—

		Good	Fine	XF
S158	50 PESOS 1889. Black on orange unpt. Portr. Pres. Bográn l., reclining woman w/pitcher and lute at l. ctr. Back orange.			
	p. Proof.	—	—	—
	s. Specimen.	—	—	—

		Good	Fine	XF
S159	100 PESOS 1889. Black on red unpt. Seated allegorical woman at l. and r., portr. Pres. Bográn at upper ctr. Back red.			
	p. Proof.	—	—	—
	s. Specimen.	—	—	—

1935 REVOLUTION

BANCO TERRITORIAL DE HONDURAS

1935 ISSUE

		Good	Fine	XF
S161	1 LEMPIRA ND (ca.1935). Liberty at ctr. Arms at l., hill and town at ctr. on back. Revolution ovpt. at l. on back.	—	—	—
S161A	10 LEMPIRAS ND. Like #S161, but w/o revolution ovpt. on back.	—	—	—

REPÚBLICA DE HONDURAS

BILLETE ADUANERO

CUSTOMS NOTES

Issued and used for customs duty payments. Not payable in government offices.

DECREE OF 5.10.1927

Peso System.

#S162-S171 arms at l. Ornamental design on back. Printer: ABNC.

		Good	Fine	XF
S162	1 PESO 1928. Blue on lt. tan unpt. Back blue. Specimen or proof.	—	—	—
S163	2 PESOS 1928. Brown on lt. tan unpt. Back brown. Proof.	—	—	—
S164	5 PESOS 1928. Black on lilac unpt. Back olive-brown. Proof.	—	—	—
S165	10 PESOS 1928. Red on pink unpt. Back red. Proof.	—	—	—
S165A	50 PESOS 1928. Dk. green on lt. tan unpt. Back dk. green. Proof.	—	—	—
S165B	100 PESOS 1928. Orange on lt. tan unpt. Back orange. Proof.	—	—	—

DECRETO LEGISLATIVO NO. 72 DE MARZO DE 1937

Lempira system.

		Good	Fine	XF
S166	1 LEMPIRA 1937. Lt. blue on gray unpt. Back lt. blue. Series L.			
	a. Issued note.	10.00	20.00	60.00
	s. Specimen.	—	—	—
S167	2 LEMPIRAS 1937. Dk. brown on gray unpt. Back dk. brown. Series K.			
	a. Issued note.	10.00	22.50	60.00
	s. Specimen.	—	—	—
S168	5 LEMPIRAS 1937. Olive-green on lt. blue unpt. Back olive-green. Series J.			
	a. Issued note.	12.50	30.00	75.00
	b. Punched hole cancelled.	8.00	17.50	45.00
	s. Specimen.	—	—	—
S169	10 LEMPIRAS 1937. Red on gray unpt. Back red. Series I.			
	a. Issued note.	12.50	50.00	110.00
	s. Specimen.	—	—	—
S170	50 LEMPIRAS 1937. Green on gray unpt. Back green. Series H.			
	a. Issued note.	15.00	60.00	125.00
	b. Punched hole cancelled.	10.00	20.00	55.00
	s. Specimen.	—	—	—
S171	100 LEMPIRAS 1937. Gold on peach unpt. Back gold. Proof.	—	—	—

The Hungarian Republic, located in central Europe, has an area of 35,919 sq. mi. (93,030 sq. km.) and a population of 9.81 million. Capital: Budapest. The economy is based on agriculture and a rapidly expanding industrial sector. Machinery, chemicals, iron and steel, and fruits and vegetables are exported.

The ancient kingdom of Hungary, founded by the Magyars in the 9th century, expanded its greatest power and authority in the mid-14th century. After suffering repeated Turkish invasions, Hungary accepted Habsburg rule to escape Turkish occupation, regaining independence in 1867 with the Emperor of Austria as king of a dual Austro-Hungarian Empire.

MONETARY SYSTEM:

1 Forint = 100 Fillér 1946-
1 Forint (Florin) = 60 Krajczar

The first distinctly Hungarian money since 1526 came as a direct result of the Hungarian Independence War of 1848-49. Led by Lajos Kossuth, world famous patriot and president of the first Hungarian republic, the war was waged against the Austrian Habsburg dynasty, hereditary rulers of the country for centuries.

As the Austrian government would not supply currency to the insurrectionist Hungarian government, Kossuth as the first Minister of Finance quickly arranged for various monetary issues and later issued notes and receipts during his travels to raise funds for the continuation of the struggle.

AUSTRIAN ADMINISTRATION

Issues released in Hungary.

IPARMÜTÁRI ALAPITVÁNY JEGY

1847 ISSUE

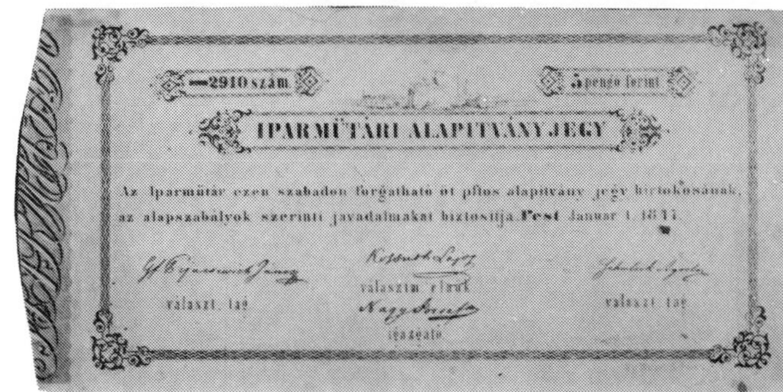

		GOOD	FINE	XF
S91	**5 PENGŐ FORINT** 1.1.1847. Kossuth sign. Black. Uniface.	—	—	—

KAMATOS UTALVÁNY

INTEREST-PAYING LEGAL TENDER TREASURY BILLS

1848 FIRST ISSUE

#S101-S103 larger size notes (232 x 130mm), w/different handwritten dates in 1848. Issued for a 6-month loan. Interest tables on backs.

		GOOD	FINE	XF
S101	**50 FORINT** 1848. Black on lt. blue unpt.	—	Rare	—
S102	**100 FORINT** 1848. Black on lt. brown unpt.	—	Rare	—
S103	**500 FORINT** 1848. Black on lt. gray unpt.	—	Rare	—

1848 SECOND ISSUE

#S104-S106 reduced size notes (185 x 130mm), different handwritten dates in 1848. Notes issued for 12-month loan and have coupons 47 x 130mm which were to be removed after six months. Interest tables on backs.

		GOOD	FINE	XF
S104	**50 FORINT** 1848. Black on yellow unpt.	—	Rare	—
S105	**100 FORINT** 1848. Black on pink unpt.	—	Rare	—
S106	**500 FORINT** 1848. Black on lt. gray unpt.	—	Rare	—

NOTE: Coupons were for values of 1 Fr 15 Kr (50 Forint), 2 Fr 30 Kr (100 Forint) and 12 Fr 30 Kr (500 Forint).

1848 THIRD ISSUE

#S107-S109 like previous issue but notes w/o coupons. 138 x 130mm.

		GOOD	FINE	XF
S107	**50 FORINT** 1848. Like #S104.	—	Rare	—
S108	**100 FORINT** 1848. Like #S105.	—	Rare	—

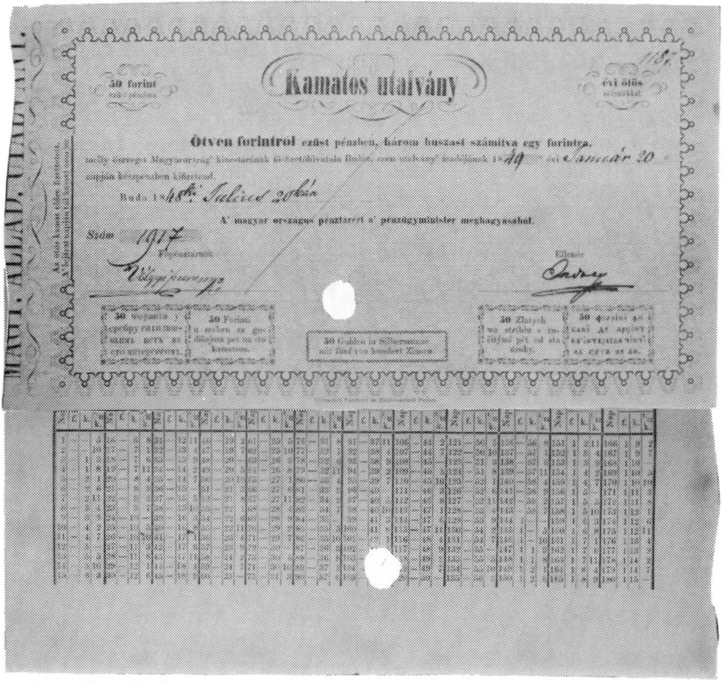

		GOOD	FINE	XF
S109	**500 FORINT** 1848. Like #S106.	—	Rare	—

MAGYAR KERESKEDELMI BANK

HUNGARIAN COMMERCIAL BANK

Notes redeemable in silver; 4 million in face value issued.

1848 ISSUE

#S111 and S112 printed sign. of Kossuth as Finance Minister, Ferenc Volgyi as Chief of State Treasury, and Janos Rogler as Bank Cashier.

		GOOD	FINE	XF
S111	**1 FORINT** ND (1848). Black on brown unpt. Arms in unpt. at bottom ctr. Back black text.	2.00	7.50	35.00

		GOOD	FINE	XF
S112	**2 FORINT** ND (1848). Black on lt. red unpt. Arms at bottom ctr. Back black text on green unpt.	1.75	6.00	35.00

PENZJEGY

STATE NOTES, FINANCE MINISTRY

Notes issued by the state to help finance the war effort.

1848 ISSUE

#S116-S118 printed sign. of Kossuth as Minister of Finance. No large heading at top of ctr. Penzjegy is in first line of small text under written out denomination.

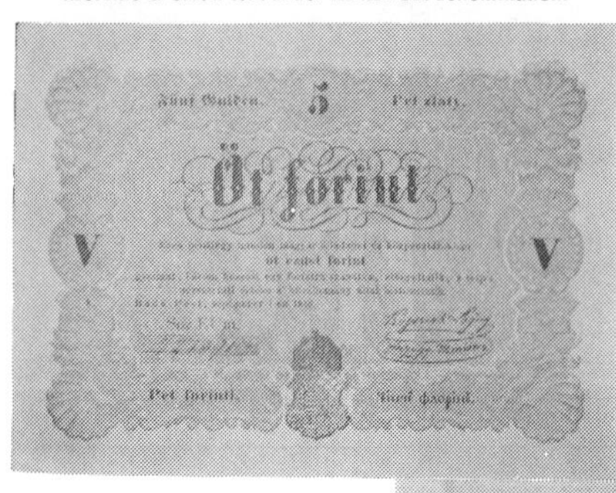

		GOOD	FINE	XF
S116	**5 FORINT**			
	1.9.1848. Gray unpt. Back green text on dk. pink unpt.			
	a. Red-brown face color.	2.00	6.00	30.00
	b. Brown face color.	2.00	6.00	30.00

		GOOD	FINE	XF
S117	**10 FORINT**			
	1.9.1848. Black on gray unpt. Arms at bottom ctr. Back black text on dull olive unpt.	3.00	10.00	45.00

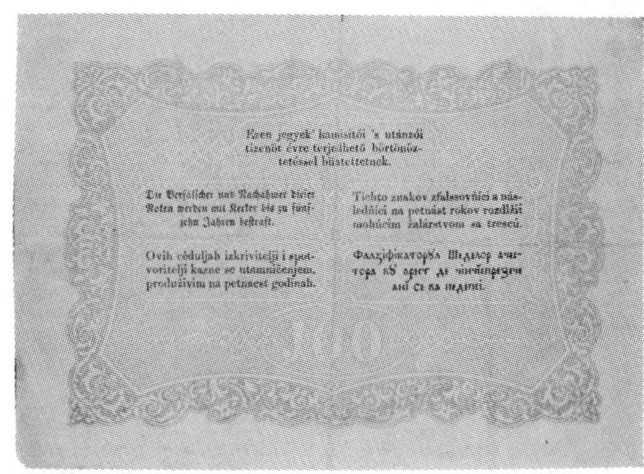

		GOOD	FINE	XF
S118	**100 FORINT**			
	1.9.1848. Black on gray unpt. Arms at top and woman at bottom ctr. Back black text on gray unpt.	30.00	85.00	225.00

KINCSTÁRI UTALVÁNY, ORSZAGOS HONVEDELMI BIZOTTMANY

STATE TREASURY NOTES, NATIONAL ARMY DEFENSE COMMITTEE

Issued to relieve a shortage of small coins in circulation.

1849 ISSUE

#S121 and S122 arms at bottom ctr. and printed sign. of Ferenc Volgyi as Chief of State Treasury.

		GOOD	FINE	XF
S121	**15 PENGŐ KRAJCZÁR**			
	1.1.1849. Black on red-brown or brown unpt. Back black text.	1.50	6.00	30.00

		GOOD	FINE	XF
S122	**30 PENGŐ KRAJCZÁR**			
	1.1.1849. Black on gray unpt. Back black text.	1.50	6.00	30.00

KINCSTÁRI UTALVÁNY

STATE TREASURY NOTE, FINANCE MINISTRY

Notes issued by the independent Hungarian state after its declaration of April 14, 1849. From this time forward the state arms deleted the royal crown on top.

1849 ISSUE

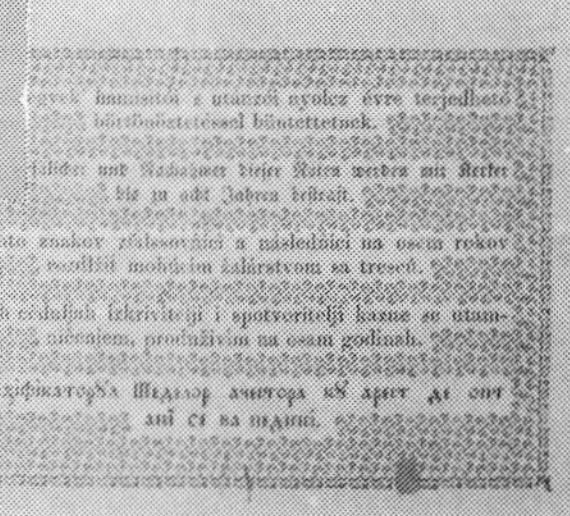

		GOOD	FINE	XF
S126	**2 PENGŐ FORINT** 1.7.1849. Black. Arms w/o crown at bottom ctr.			
	a. Sign. Kossuth and Ferenc Duschek as Governor of Hungary and Minister of Finance, respectively.	10.00	30.00	75.00
	b. Sign. Kossuth and Bertalan Szemere, Prime Minister.	—	Rare	—
S127	**10 PENGŐ FORINT** 1.7.1849. Black. Sign. Kossuth and Szemere.	—	Rare	—

NON-HUNGARIAN ISSUES

TURKEY

NYUGTATVÁNY RECEIPT

These national loan receipts were Lajos Kossuth's first fund-raising venture outside of Hungary. They were used while Kossuth was in Turkey in 1851.

1851 ISSUE

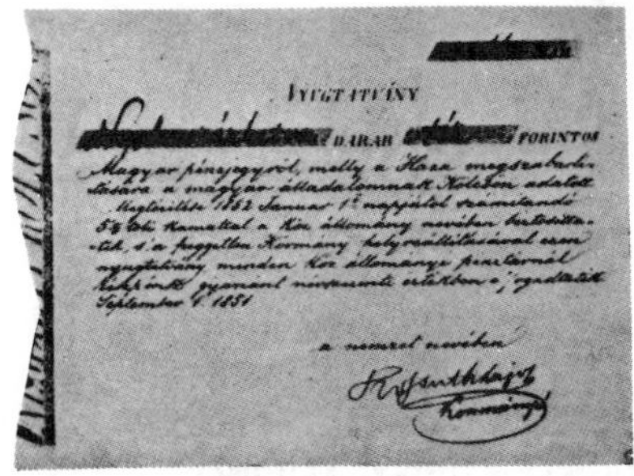

		GOOD	FINE	XF
S131	**VARIOUS AMOUNTS** 1.9.1851. Black. Counterfoil at l. margin.	—	—	—

UNITED STATES

HUNGARIAN FUND, NEW YORK

1852 ISSUE

#S136-S140 black. Thin white paper, English text. Uniface. Printer: Danforth, Bald and Co.

#S136-S138A printed sign. of L. Kossuth.

		VG	VF	UNC
S136	**1 DOLLAR** 2.2.1852. L. Kossuth at lower l., Hungaria w/sword over fallen crowned figure at ctr., Liberty at lower r. Arms at upper corners. Lg. *ONE* protector. Printed date. Letters A-C, A1-C1, A2-C2, A3-C3.			
	a. Issued note (w/serial #).	—	2.00	7.50
	b. Sheet of 3 subjects.	—	—	30.00
	r. Unissued remainder (w/o serial #).	—	—	5.00

		VG	VF	UNC
S137	**5 DOLLARS** 2.2.1852. L. Kossuth at lower l., arms at ctr., standing Liberty w/Hungarian shield at lower r. Handwritten date. Letter A.	5.00	15.00	60.00

		VG	VF	UNC
S137A	**5 DOLLARS** 2.2.1852. Black. Like #S137 but w/lg. *FIVE* protector. Printed date. Letter B.	5.00	15.00	60.00

		VG	VF	UNC
S138	**10 DOLLARS** 1.1.1852. Black. L. Kossuth at lower l., seated Liberty w/shield and 2 women at upper ctr., woman w/globe at r. Handwritten date. Letter A.	25.00	55.00	120.00

		VG	VF	UNC
S138A	**10 DOLLARS** 1.1.1852. Black. Like #S138 but w/lg. *TEN* protector. Printed date. Letter A.	25.00	55.00	120.00

#S139 and S140 have hand sign. and date.

		VG	VF	UNC
S139	**50 DOLLARS** 2.2.1852; 1.7.1852. Standing Liberty w/Hungarian shield and pole at lower l., portr. L. Kossuth at upper ctr., seated woman w/United States shield at r. Lg. *FIFTY* protector. Letters A; B.	150.00	300.00	—

		VG	VF	UNC
S140	**100 DOLLARS** 1.1.1852; 1.7.1852. Woman in flowing robe at l. and r. of portr. of L. Kossuth at upper ctr. Lg. *100* protector. Letter A.	175.00	325.00	—

PENZJEGY, PHILADELPHIA

FINANCE MINISTRY

1852 ND ISSUE

#S141-S143 printed sign. of L. Kossuth and printed in black on thin white paper, Hungarian text. Uniface. Printer: Toppan, Carpenter, Casilear and Co.

		VG	VF	UNC
S141	**1 FORINT** ND (1852). 3 standing women at l., Hungaria over fallen crowned figure in cartouche w/flags and cannon at ctr., woman w/pedestal at lower r. Letters A-H.			
	r1. Unissued remainder.	—	2.00	5.00
	r2. Sheet of 4 subjects.	—	—	25.00

		VG	VF	UNC
S142	**2 FORINT** ND (1852). Seated Justice w/scale at l., Liberty w/Hungarian shield and fasces at ctr., standing Athena at r. Letters A-H.			
	r1. Unissued remainder.	—	2.00	5.00
	r2. Sheet of 4 subjects.	—	—	25.00

		VG	VF	UNC
S143	**5 FORINT** ND (1852). Seated woman w/sickle at upper l., arm and hammer at ctr., beehive below, seated woman w/bales at upper r. Arms at lower l. and r. corners. Letters A-F.			
	r1. Unissued remainder.	—	1.50	6.00
	r2. Sheet of 3 subjects.	—	—	35.00

GREAT BRITAIN

PENZJEGY, LONDON

FINANCE MINISTRY

1860-61 ND ISSUE

#S146-S148 printed sign. of L. Kossuth "in the name of the nation." Uniface. Printed in London. Wmk: Arms, value and *RESURGO* (revolt against). No large heading at top or ctr. (similar to #S116-S118). Printer: Day and Son.

		VG	VF	UNC
S146	**1 FORINT** ND (1860-61). Black. Arms w/crown at bottom ctr.	—	Rare	—
S147	**2 FORINT** ND (1860-61). Red.	—	Rare	—
S148	**5 FORINT** ND (1860-61). Green.	—	Rare	—

NOTE: At the request of Austrian Emperor Franz Josef, #S146-S148 were confiscated by the British government, taken to the Bank of England, and burned. Only a very few were saved.

ITALY

KINCSTÁR UTALVÁNY/KINCSTÁR JEGY, TORINO

STATE TREASURY NOTES

1866 ISSUE

Plates for #S151-S153 were prepared by the sons of Lajos Kossuth and notes were printed in Torino, Italy in 1866. Denominations were in *garas* (= groats). No original notes exist; only reprints from the original plates are presently known.

		VG	VF	UNC
S151	**2 VALTO GARAS** 1.7.1866.	—	—	—

		VG	VF	UNC
S152	**10 VALTO GARAS** 1.7.1866.	—	—	—
S153	**1 FORINT** 1.7.1866.	—	—	—

SIEGE

ARAD

Austrian troops (General Berger c.d. Pleisse) besieged by Hungarians 1848-49.

1848-49 ND ISSUES

#S161-S163 w/K.K./F.z.A.

		GOOD	FINE	XF
S161	**1 KREUZER** ND. Round. 18mm.	—	—	—
S162	**3 KREUZER** ND. Round. 25mm.	—	—	—

		GOOD	FINE	XF
S163	**6 KREUZER** ND. Round. 34mm.	—	—	—
S164	**6 KREUZER** ND. Square. 35 x 20mm.	—	—	—

		GOOD	FINE	XF
S165	**6 KREUZER** ND. Square. 32 x 22mm.	—	—	—

		GOOD	FINE	XF
S166	10 KREUZER CONV. MÜNZ ND. Handwritten; sign. Saffran and Müller, 43 x 33mm.	80.00	100.00	—
S167	10 KREUZER ND. Handwritten and seal, sign. Saffran and Müller, 46 x 31mm.	80.00	100.00	—
S168	10 KREUZER ND. Printed, 61 x 41mm.	—	—	—
S169	18 KREUZER C. M. ND. 110 x 83mm.	—	—	—
S170	20 KREUZER ND. Sign. Alois.	—	—	—

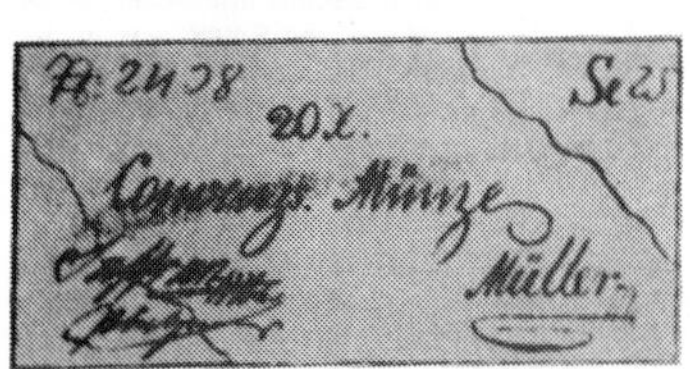

		GOOD	FINE	XF
S171	20 KREUZER CONVENZS. MÜNZE ND. Sign. Saffran and Müller, 65 x 30mm.	80.00	100.00	—
S172	1 GULDEN ND. Sign. Joh. Dietrich v. Hermannsthal.	—	—	—

		GOOD	FINE	XF
S173	1 GULDEN COVMÜZ ND. Sign. Saffran and Müller w/seal, 75 x 45mm.	80.00	100.00	—

		GOOD	FINE	XF
S174	5 GULDEN CO. MÜZ ND. Sign. Saffran and Müller, w/seal, 98 x 76mm. Value in Roman numeral.	80.00	100.00	—
S175	10 GULDEN CO. MÜZ ND. Sign. Saffran and Müller, w/seal, 83 x 102mm. Value in Arabic numerals.	80.00	100.00	—

1849 ISSUE

		GOOD	FINE	XF
S176	5 GULDEN CONV. FUSS 20.4.1849. 88 x 72mm. Value in Roman numeral.	80.00	100.00	—

		GOOD	FINE	XF
S177	10 GULDEN 20.4.1849. 87 x 103mm. Value in Roman numeral.	80.00	100.00	—

KOMÁROM

Hungarian army besieged by Austrians.

1849 FIRST ISSUE

		GOOD	FINE	XF
S179	1 KRAICZÁR ND (1849). 40 x 40mm.	—	—	—

		GOOD	FINE	XF
S180	2 KRAICZÁR ND (1849). Like #S179.	—	—	—

		GOOD	FINE	XF
S181	8 PENGÖ KRAJCZÁR 6.4.1849.	15.00	20.00	—

1849 SECOND ISSUE

#S182 and S183 different design variants. Forgeries exist.

		GOOD	FINE	XF
S182	5 PENGÖ KRAJCZÁR 13.7.1849. 3 varieties.	15.00	20.00	—
S183	10 PENGÖ KRAJCZÁR 13.7.1849. 3 varieties.	15.00	20.00	—

TEMESVÁR

Hungarian army besieged by Austrians (Haynau) in 1849.

1849 ISSUE

		GOOD	FINE	XF
S191	1 KREUZER W.W. ND. Sm. cardboard, 25 x 25mm.	—	—	—
S192	3 KREUZER W.W. ND. 54 x 34mm.	—	—	—
S193	6 KRAJCÁR C.M. 19.3.1849.	—	—	—
S194	8 KRAJCÁR C.M. 19.3.1849.	—	—	—

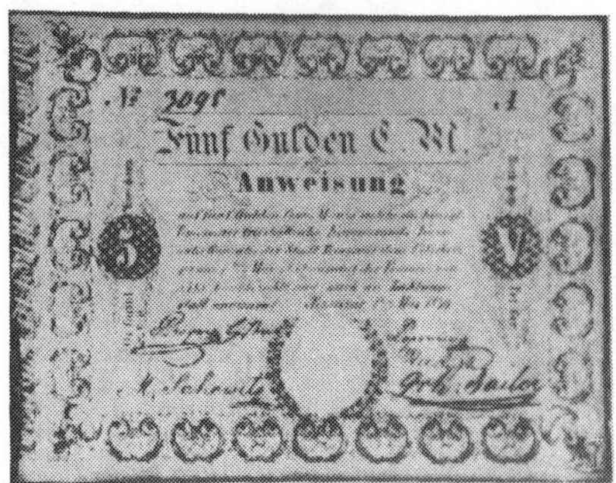

		Good	Fine	XF
S197	**5 Gulden C.M.** 1.5.1849. 130 x 85mm.			
	a. Issued note.	—	—	—
	b. Punched hole cancelled.	—	—	—

		Good	Fine	XF
S198	**10 Gulden C.M.** 1.5.1849. Like #S197.			
	a. Issued note.	—	—	—
	b. Punched hole cancelled.	—	—	—

INDIA-BRITISH

The civilization of India, which began about 2500 B.C., flourished under a succession of empires - notably those of Chandragupta, Asoka and the Mughals - until undermined in the 18th and 19th centuries by European colonial powers.

The Portuguese were the first to arrive, off Calicut in May 1498. It was not until 1612, after the Portuguese and Spanish power had begun to wane, that the British East India Company established its initial settlement at Surat. Britain could not have chosen a more propitious time. The northern Mogul Empire, the central girdle of petty states, and the southern Vijayanagar Empire were crumbling and ripe for foreign exploitation. By the end of the century, English traders were firmly established in Bombay, Madras, Calcutta and lesser places elsewhere, and Britain was implementing its announced policy to create such civil and military institutions as may be the foundation of secure English domination for all time. By 1757, following the successful conclusion of a war of colonial rivalry with France during which the military victories of Robert Clive, a young officer with the British East India Company, made him the most powerful man in India, the British were firmly settled in India as not only traders but as conquerors. During the next 60 years, the British East India Company acquired dominion over most of India by bribery and force, and governed it directly or through puppet princelings.

Because of the Sepoy Mutiny of 1857-58, a large scale mutiny among Indian soldiers of the Bengal army, control of the government of India was transferred from the East India Company to the British Crown in 1858. At this point in world history, India was the brightest jewel in the imperial diadem of the British lords of the earth, but even then a movement for greater Indian representation in government presaged the Indian Empire's twilight hour less than a century hence - it would pass into history on August 15, 1947.

All private bank issues ceased by 1862.

MONETARY SYSTEM:

1 Rupee = 16 Annas
1 Anna = 4 Pice
1 Pice = (Paisa) = 3 Pies

British Administration

Asiatic Bank

Founded 1804.

1800s Issue

#S5-8 India holding snake and mace seated w/tiger, mountains in background at upper l.

		Good	Fine	XF
S5	**5 Star Pagodas, 17.5 Arcot Rupees** 18xx. Black. Unsigned remainder.	400.00	2000.	4000.
S6	**10 Star Pagodas, 35 Arcot Rupees** 18xx. Black. Unsigned remainder.	400.00	2000.	4000.
S7	**100 Star Pagodas, 350 Arcot Rupees** 1.2.1820. Black.	400.00	2000.	4000.
S8	**500 Star Pagodas, 1750 Arcot Rupees** 18xx. Black. Unsigned remainder.	400.00	2000.	4000.

Bank of Bengal

In operation from 1809 to 1861.

1812 Issue

#S20 serial # at lower r. Cut signature examples are worth about 60% of listed values.

		Good	Fine	XF
S20	**20 Sicca Rupees** 13.9.1812-29.5.1819. Black.	400.00	750.00	1500.

1815-16 Issue

#S24-S25 serial # at upper l. and lower r. Cut signature examples are worth about 60% of quoted values.

		Good	Fine	XF
S24	**16 Sicca Rupees / 1 Gold Mohur** 7.9.1816-16.12.1820. Black.	400.00	750.00	1500.
S25	**500 Sicca Rupees** 13.7.1815-27.11.1820. Black.	400.00	750.00	1500.

1824-26 Issue

#S30-S36 Commerce seated at top ctr. value in Bengali, Persian and Kaithi above. Bank name in scroll on back. Cut signature examples are worth about 60% of quoted values.

		Good	Fine	XF
S30	**10 Sicca Rupees** 8.12.1824-11.7.1826. Black.	400.00	750.00	1500.
S31	**16 Sicca Rupees / 1 Gold Mohur** 6.4.1825. Black.	400.00	750.00	1500.
S32 (S97)	**50 Sicca Rupees** 4.12.1824-5.1.1828. Black.	400.00	750.00	1500.
S33	**100 Sicca Rupees** 27.10.1824-18.6.1829. Black.	400.00	750.00	1500.
S34 (S99)	**250 Sicca Rupees** 18xx. Proof w/ovpt: *SPECIMEN*. Uniface.	—	Unc	2000.
S35	**500 Sicca Rupees** 16.8.1824-31.12.1827. Black.	400.00	750.00	1500.

		Good	Fine	XF
S36 (S101)	**1000 Sicca Rupees** 16.1.1826; 2.2.1826. Black.			
	p. Proof w/ovpt: *SPECIMEN.*	—	Unc	2000.
	r. Remainder w/o sign.	—	Unc	750.00
	a. Issued note.	400.00	750.00	1500.

1827-29 Issue

#40-43 similar to #30-36 but with value added under r. serial #. Printer: P&H. Cut signzture examples are worth about 60% of quoted values.

		Good	Fine	XF
S40	**10 Sicca Rupees** 15.5.1828-28.10.1836. Black.	400.00	750.00	1500.
S41	**50 Sicca Rupees** 3.1.1828-27.2.1829. Black.	400.00	750.00	1500.
S42	**100 Sicca Rupees** 8.7.1829-18.1.1837. Black.	400.00	750.00	1500.
S43	**1000 Sicca Rupees** 21.3.1827; 1.4.1827. Black.	400.00	750.00	1500.

1828-33 Issue

#45-46 Commerce seated at top ctr., top border with Persian script, bottom with Kaithi. Bank name in center scroll on back. Printer: P&H. Cut signature examples are worth about 60% of quoted values.

		Good	Fine	XF
S45	**20 Sicca Rupees** 30.12.1828. Black.	400.00	750.00	1500.
S46	**25 Sicca Rupees** 20.1.1833. Black.	400.00	750.00	1500.

1828-34 Third Issue

#50-58 Commerce seated at upper ctr. Value in languages on back. Printer: P&B. Cut signature examples are worth about 60% of quoted values.

		Good	Fine	XF
S50	**10 Sicca Rupees** 31.10.1828-2.11.1835. Black.	400.00	750.00	1500.
S51	**16 Sicca Rupees / 1 Gold Mohur** 20.3.1833-28.8.1834. Black.	400.00	750.00	1500.
S52	**20 Sicca Rupees** 18.12.1833-2.1.1836. Black.	400.00	750.00	1500.
S53	**25 Sicca Rupees** 17.12.1833-2.1.1836. Black.	400.00	750.00	1500.
S54	**50 Sicca Rupees** 26.11.1829-26.1.1836. Black.	400.00	750.00	1500.
S55	**100 Sicca Rupees** 13.9.1832-23.10.1835. Black.	400.00	750.00	1500.
S56	**250 Sicca Rupees** 18.1.1834-12.11.1835. Black.	400.00	750.00	1500.
S57	**500 Sicca Rupees** 25.2.1832-14.3.1834. Black.	400.00	750.00	1500.
S58	**1000 Sicca Rupees** 12.5.1832-10.4.1835. Black.	400.00	750.00	1500.

1837-47 Issue

#S60-S66 Commerce seated at top ctr. Serial # handwritten. Printer: P&B. Cut signature examples are worth about 60% of quoted values.

		Good	Fine	XF
S60	**10 Company Rupees** 28.2.1842; 28.3.1842. Black.	400.00	750.00	1500.
S61	**15 Company Rupees** 28.2.1842-8.7.1845. Black.	400.00	750.00	1500.
S62	**20 Company Rupees** 22.9.1837; 25.1.1841. Black.	400.00	750.00	1500.
S63	**25 Company Rupees** 25.1.1841. Black.	400.00	750.00	1500.
S64	**50 Company Rupees** 8.11.1842; 20.12.1843. Black.	400.00	750.00	1500.
S65	**100 Company Rupees** 23.1.1841; 10.1.1842. Black.	400.00	750.00	1500.
S66	**500 Company Rupees** 3.12.1847. Black.	400.00	750.00	1500.

1840-53 Issue

#S70-S77 as #S60-S66 but serial # typescript. Printer: PBC. Cut signature examples are worth about 60% of quotedvalues.

		Good	Fine	XF
S70	**10 Company Rupees** 27.5.1852. Black.	400.00	750.00	1500.
S71	**15 Company Rupees** 3.5.1852-26.2.1857. Black.	400.00	750.00	1500.
S72 (S96)	**20 Company Rupees** 17.2.1840-9.10.1852. Black.	400.00	750.00	1500.
S73	**25 Company Rupees** 17.12.1842-20.3.1854. Black.	400.00	750.00	1500.
S74	**50 Company Rupees** 28.9.1852-18.11.1853. Black.	400.00	750.00	1500.
S75	**100 Company Rupees** 16.1.1852-10.11.1852. Black.	400.00	750.00	1500.
S76	**250 Company Rupees** 25.7.1845-10.5.1847. Black.	400.00	750.00	1500.
S77	**1000 Company Rupees** 15.4.1853. Black.	400.00	750.00	1500.

1853 Issue

#S80-88 Commerce seated at top ctr. W/o native scripts. Printer: PBC. Cut signature examples are worth about 60% of quoted values.

		Good	Fine	XF
S80	**10 Company Rupees** 15.4.1853-15.8.1855. Black.	400.00	750.00	1500.
S81	**15 Company Rupees** 15.4.1853-1.9.1855. Black.	400.00	750.00	1500.
S82	**20 Company Rupees** 15.4.1853. Black.	400.00	750.00	1500.
S83	**25 Company Rupees** 15.4.1853. Black.	400.00	750.00	1500.
S84	**50 Company Rupees** 15.4.1853. Black.	400.00	750.00	1500.
S85	**100 Company Rupees** 15.4.1853. Black.	400.00	750.00	1500.
S86	**250 Company Rupees** 15.4.1853. Black.	400.00	750.00	1500.
S87	**500 Company Rupees** 15.4.1853. Black.	400.00	750.00	1500.
S88	**1000 Company Rupees** 15.4.1853. Black.	400.00	750.00	1500.

1857 Issue

#S90-95 Justice and Commerce seated w/Britannia and lion at upper ctr. Large value in scroll on back.

		Good	Fine	XF
S90	**10 Rupees** 31.8.1857; 12.4.1859. Black on purple unpt. Back black and blue.	—	Rare	—
	a. Issued note.	400.00	750.00	1500.
	p. Proof ovpt: *SPECIMEN.*	—	Unc	2000.
S91 (S105)	**25 Rupees** 2.9.1857; 3.9.1857. Black on blue unpt. Back black and blue.			
	a. Issued note.	400.00	750.00	1500.
	p. Proof ovpt: *SPECIMEN.*	—	Unc	2000.
S92	**50 Rupees** 19.10.1857. Black on red unpt. Back black and blue.			
	a. Issued note.	400.00	750.00	1500.
	p. Proof ovpt: *SPECIMEN.*	—	Unc	2000.

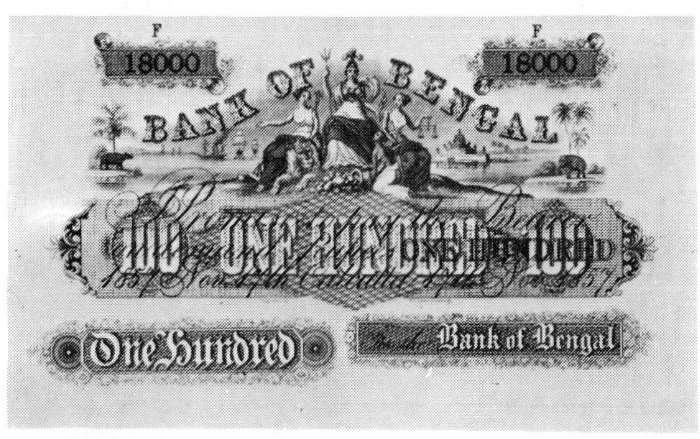

		Good	Fine	XF
S93 (S106)	**100 Rupees** 17.11.1857. Black on grene unpt. Back black and blue.			
	a. Issued note.	400.00	750.00	1500.
	p. Proof ovpt: *SPECIMEN.*	—	Unc	2000.
S94	**500 Rupees** 18.12.1857. Black on orange unpt. Back black and blue.			
	a. Issued note.	400.00	750.00	1500.
	p. Proof ovpt: *SPECIMEN.*	—	Unc	2000.

		Good	Fine	XF
S95 (S108)	**1000 Rupees** 27.1.1858. Black on red unpt. Back black and blue.			
	a. Issued note.	400.00	750.00	1500.
	p. Proof ovpt: *SPECIMEN.*	—	Unc	2000.

BANK OF BOMBAY

Operated from 1840-1861.

1846-54 ISSUE

#S100-S105 statues of standing Mountstuart Elphinstone at l., John Malcolm at r., starbursts at top and bottom ctr. Native legends in four border quadrants.

		GOOD	FINE	XF
S100 (S111)	**10 RUPEES** 5.1.1854-10.10.1856. Black.	400.00	1000.	2000.
S101	**15 RUPEES** 2.7.1849. Black.	400.00	1000.	2000.
S102 (S112)	**25 RUPEES** 18xx. Black.	400.00	1000.	2000.

		GOOD	FINE	XF
S103 (S113)	**50 RUPEES** 15.4.1846. Black.	400.00	1000.	2000.
S104 (S114)	**100 RUPEES** 2.9.1853.	400.00	1000.	2000.
S105	**10000 RUPEES** 18xx. Black. Proof ovpt: *SPECIMEN.*	—	Unc	2000.

1853-55 ISSUE

#S110-S113 native legends in two border quadrants.

		GOOD	FINE	XF
S110 (S116)	**10 RUPEES** 22.3.1853-1.11.1860. Black on brown or maroon unpt.			
	a. Issued note.	400.00	1000.	2000.
	p. Proof ovpt: *SPECIMEN.*	—	Unc	2000.
S111 (S117)	**25 RUPEES** 6.8.1855-18.11.1866. Black on pink unpt.			
	a. Issued note.	400.00	1000.	2000.
	p. Proof ovpt: *SPECIMEN.*	—	Unc	2000.

		GOOD	FINE	XF
S112 (S118)	**100 RUPEES** 1.1.1855; 10.8.1855. Black on brown unpt.			
	a. Issued note.	400.00	1000.	2000.
	p. Proof ovpt: *SPECIMEN.*	—	Unc	2000.
S113	**1000 RUPEES** 18xx. Black. Proof ovpt: *SPECIMEN.*	—	Unc	2000.

1859-60 ISSUE

		GOOD	FINE	XF
S115	**10 RUPEES** 1.11.1860. Black on brown unpt.			
	a. Issued note.	400.00	1000.	2000.
	p. Proof ovpt: *SPECIMEN.*	—	Unc	2000.
S116	**25 RUPEES** 29.9.1859. Black on rose unpt.	400.00	1000.	2000.
S117	**100 RUPEES** 29.9.1859. Black on green unpt.	400.00	1000.	2000.

BANK OF HINDOSTAN

Operated from 1770 to 1831.

1823-27 ISSUE

		GOOD	FINE	XF
S120	**4 SICCA RUPEES** 28.11.1823. Black on blue unpt.	400.00	1500.	3000.
S121	**16 SICCA RUPEES** 5.1.1827. Black on blue unpt.	500.00	2000.	4000.
S122	**20 SICCA RUPEES** 8.12.1823. Black on blue unpt.	500.00	2000.	4000.

1820S FIRST ISSUE

#S125-S129 tiger lying down at lower ctr. Printer: P&B. Unsigned remainders.

		GOOD	FINE	XF
S125	**50 SICCA RUPEES** 18xx. Black.	500.00	2000.	4000.

		GOOD	FINE	XF
S126	**100 SICCA RUPEES** 18xx. Black.	500.00	2000.	4000.

		Good	Fine	XF
S127	**250 Sicca Rupees** 18xx. Black.	500.00	2000.	4000.

		Good	Fine	XF
S128	**500 Sicca Rupees** 18xx. Black.	500.00	2000.	4000.
S129	**1000 Sicca Rupees** 18xx. Black.	500.00	2000.	4000.

1820s Second Issue

		Good	Fine	XF
S130	**4 Sicca Rupees** 18xx. Black on red unpt.	500.00	2000.	4000.

		Good	Fine	XF
S131 (S124)	**20 Sicca Rupees** 18xx. Black on red unpt.	500.00	2000.	4000.

1830s Issue

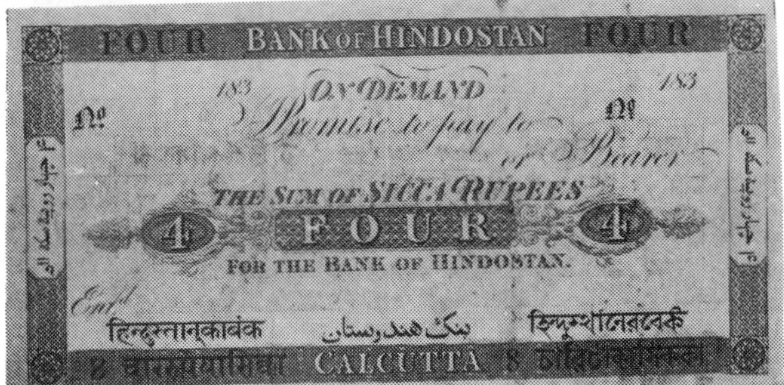

		Good	Fine	XF
S135 (S121)	**4 Sicca Rupees** 183x. Black.	150.00	750.00	2000.
S136 (S122)	**10 Sicca Rupees** 183x. Black.	400.00	1500.	3000.

		Good	Fine	XF
S137 (S123)	**16 Sicca Rupees** 183x. Black.	150.00	750.00	2000.

Bank of Madras

Operated from 1843 to 1861.

1845-49 Issue

		Good	Fine	XF
S140	**10 Rupees** 1.5.1845. Black.	400.00	2000.	4000.
S141	**20 Rupees** 24.7.1849. Black.	400.00	2000.	4000.
S142	**25 Rupees** 27.4.1849. Black.	400.00	2000.	4000.
S143	**50 Rupees** 10.4.1849. Black.	400.00	2000.	4000.
S144	**100 Rupees** 184x. Black.	400.00	2000.	4000.
S145	**500 Rupees** 1.4.1845. Black.	400.00	2000.	4000.
S146	**1000 Rupees** 2.1.1845. Black.	400.00	2000.	4000.
S147	**3000 Rupees** 184x. Black.	400.00	2000.	4000.

1849-61 Issue

		Good	Fine	XF
S149	**10 Rupees** 25.7.1861. Black.	400.00	2000.	4000.
S150	**15 Rupees** 1.4.1856; 4.4.1856. Black.	400.00	2000.	4000.
S151	**25 Rupees** 20.8.1849. Black.	400.00	2000.	4000.
S152	**50 Rupees** 20.7.1859. Black.	400.00	2000.	4000.
S153	**100 Rupees** 6.1.1860. Black.	400.00	2000.	4000.

Bank of Western India

Operated from 1842 to 1845.

1844 Issue

		Good	Fine	XF
S154	**5 Rupees** 1.5.1844. Black.	400.00	2000.	4000.

Calcutta Bank

Operated from 1824 to 1829.

1824-25 Issue

#S155-S160 allegorical figure of Agriculture seated at upper ctr. Bank name in scroll on back.

		Good	Fine	XF
S155 (S130)	**5 Sicca Rupees** 11.1.1824. Black.	300.00	1000.	2000.
S156 (S131)	**10 Sicca Rupees** 5.1.1825. Black.	300.00	1000.	2000.
S157	**20 Sicca Rupees** 18xx. Black.	300.00	1000.	2000.

		Good	Fine	XF
S158 (S135)	**500 Sicca Rupees** 18xx. Black.	300.00	1000.	2000.
S159	**1000 Sicca Rupees** 18xx. Black.	300.00	1000.	2000.
S160	**5000 Sicca Rupees** 18xx. Black.	300.00	1000.	2000.

Commercial Bank

Operated from 1819 to 1831.

1820s First Issue

#S166-S168 Britannia seated at upper l., Commerce and Mercury at upper ctr. r., Ganga statue at upper r. Calcutta issue. Persian script flanking central design.

		Good	Fine	XF
S166	**8 Sicca Rupees** 18xx. Black. Proof.	—	Unc	2000.

		Good	Fine	XF
S167 (S142)	**10 Sicca Rupees** 18xx. Black. Proof.	—	Unc	2000.
S168	**20 Sicca Rupees** 18xx. Black. Proof.	—	Unc	2000.

1820s Second Issue

#S170-S171 as #S166-S168 but w/o Persian script flanking.

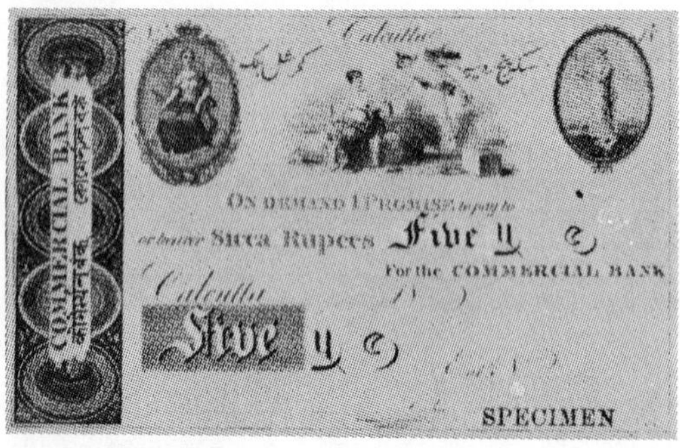

		Good	Fine	XF
S170 (S141)	**5 Sicca Rupees** 18xx. Black. Proof.	—	Unc	2000.
S171	**16 Sicca Rupees** 18xx. Black. Proof.	—	Unc	2000.

Commercial Bank of India

Operated from 1845 to 1866.

1845 Issue

		Good	Fine	XF
S175	**10 Rupees** 18xx. Black. Unsigned remainder.	400.00	2000.	4000.

Hindostan Bank

Probably an issue of the Bank of Hindostan, see #S120-S137.

1800s Issue

		Good	Fine	XF
S180	**5 Sicca Rupees** 18xx. Dk. brown on red unpt. Unissued remainder.	500.00	2500.	—

Madras Government Bank

Operated from 1806 to 1843.

1816-22 Issue

		Good	Fine	XF
S185	**2 Star Pagodas, 7 Rupees** 9.10.1816. Black.	400.00	2000.	4000.
S186	**5 Rupees** 24.5.1822. Black.	400.00	2000.	4000.

Oriental Bank

Operated in 1845.

1848 Issue

		Good	Fine	XF
S190	**5 Rupees** 184x. Unsigned remainder.	400.00	2000.	4000.
S191	**50 Rupees** 10.11.1845. Black.	400.00	2000.	4000.
S192	**500 Rupees** 184x. Black. Unsigned remainder.	400.00	2000.	4000.
S193	**1000 Rupees** 184x. Black. Unsigned remainder.	400.00	2000.	4000.

Union Bank

Operated from 1829 to 1848.

1840s Issue

		Good	Fine	XF
S195	**5 Rupees** 25.5.1847. Black. Elephant at l. and r. border.	400.00	2000.	4000.
S196	**10 Company Rupees** 18xx. Black. Elephant at l., tiger at r. border. Unissued remainder.	400.00	2000.	4000.
S197	**20 Company Rupees** 30.3.1841. Black. Snake at l. and r. border. Unsigned remainder.	400.00	2000.	4000.
S198 (S191)	**250 Company Rupees** 18xx. Black. Ganga standing at l., tiger at r. border.	400.00	2000.	4000.

World War II

Azad Hind Bank

Founded by Subhas Chandra Bose, the leader of the "Indian Freedom Movement" in Singapore.

#S181-S183 *Deleted*.

NOTE: Formerly listed #S181-S183 are political, possibly donation receipts.

Only four Native States ever prepared bank notes for issue - Jammu and Kashmir in 1876, Dhrangadhra and Hyderabad in 1918, and Kutch in 1946. Kutch never released its notes, while those of Jammu and Kashmir were recalled shortly afterward. Dhrangadhra's notes may have been used briefly. Only Hyderabad's issues enjoyed a lengthy circulation until their withdrawal about 1953.

As World War II progressed, the British Indian colonial coinage became in short supply, especially after the Japanese had invaded Burma and then the Imphal-Kohima-Manipur region of India in 1943-1944. A number of the Native States devised CASH COUPONS to meet the shortage - small ticket-like cardboards, some were prepared from postage or revenue stamp plates, others created with coin pictures, etc. Most were tightly controlled, as attested by their series letters and control numbers - and apparently very few were saved by the populace.

Except for small hoards of Bikaner, Bundi, Indergadh and Junagadh, few specimens have survived since their period of issue. India had few paper money collectors during World War II.

Other Indian state notes may exist.

For purposes of visual clarity, bank notes are shown in this section at 42% of actual size; cash coupons are shown at 65 to 70% of actual size; and stamp money at 100%.

PRINCELY STATES OF INDIA

Ambliara	Indergadh	Navanagar
Bajana	Jaipur	Nawalgarh
Balwan	Jaisalmir	Palitana
Bikaner	Jammu and Kashmir	Rajkot
Bundi	Jasdan	Ramgarh Raj
Chuda	Junagadh	Sailana
Dhar	Kutch	Sayala
Dhrangadhra	Mangrol	Sitamau
Dinajpur	Mengani	Tonk
Gondal	Muli	Vithalgadh
Hyderabad	Mysore	

MONETARY SYSTEM:

1 Paise (Pice) = 3 Pies
1 Anna = 4 Paisa
1 Rupee = 16 Annas

AMBLIARA

A small princely state located in the Sabar Kantha Agency of Western India with an area of 80 sq. mi. (207 sq. km.).

GOVERNMENT

ND ISSUE

		GOOD	FINE	XF
S201	1 PAISA (PICE) ND. Black text. Brown pressboard.	—	Unique	—

BAJANA

An estate located in the Western India States Agency between the Ranu of Kutch and Ahmadabad with an area of 183 sq. mi. (474 sq. km.).

GOVERNMENT

ND WWII CASH COUPON STAMP MONEY ISSUE

		GOOD	FINE	XF
S202	1 ANNA ND. Red. White pressboard. Purple sign. 48 x 33mm.	5.00	20.00	40.00

BALWAN

An estate located at the extreme northerly border of Kotah State wholly within the boundaries of the Indargarh *kotri*.

GOVERNMENT

ND WWII EMERGENCY CASH COUPONS ISSUE

		GOOD	FINE	XF
S206	1/4 ANNA ND. Black. Tan pressboard. 40 x 32mm.	3.50	10.00	18.00

		GOOD	FINE	XF
S207	1 ANNA ND. Dk. green. Tan pressboard. 31mm.	3.50	10.00	18.00

		GOOD	FINE	XF
S209	4 ANNAS ND. Red-brown. Tan pressboard. 31mm.	5.00	12.50	25.00

BIKANER

A state in the Rajputana Agency, with an area of 23,317 sq. mi. (60,407 sq. km.). Also called Bikanir.

GOVERNMENT

ND WWII EMERGENCY CASH COUPONS ISSUE

#S211-S214 oval hand stamp: *SADAR TREASURY-BIKANER* on back. Square pressboard.

		VG	VF	UNC
S211	1 PICE ND.	1.00	3.00	6.00

		VG	VF	UNC
S212	1 ANNA ND.	1.50	4.50	9.00

		VG	VF	UNC
S213	2 ANNAS ND.	3.00	7.50	15.00

		VG	VF	UNC
S214	4 ANNAS ND.	4.00	10.00	20.00

BUNDI

A state located in the Western Rajputana States Agency with an area of 21,200 sq. mi. (54,922 sq. km.).

GOVERNMENT

ND WWII EMERGENCY CASH COUPON STAMP MONEY ISSUE

#S221-S224 similar to postage or revenue stamps. Pressboard. Ovpt: *CASH COUPON* on face, control # on back.

		VG	VF	Unc
S221	**3 Pies = 1 Paisa (Pice)** ND. Violet. Maharaja between brahma bulls at ctr. English and Hindi denomination. Ovpt: *CASH COUPON BUNDI STATE.* 40 x 39 mm.	2.00	6.00	12.00

		VG	VF	Unc
S222	**1 Anna** ND. Red. Similar to #S221. 54 x 44mm.	2.00	6.00	12.00

		VG	VF	Unc
S224	**4 Annas** ND. Green. Court Fee stamp design.	4.00	12.00	25.00

Chuda

A small state located in the Western India States Agency between Ahmadabad and Rajkot with an area of 78 sq. mi. (202 sq. km.).

Government

ND WWII Emergency Cash Coupon Stamp Money Issue

#S226 and S227 portr. of *thakor.*

		VG	VF	Unc
S226	**1 Paisa** ND.	—	Rare	—
S227	**2 Paisa** ND.			
	a. Blue pressboard.	20.00	50.00	—
	b. Cream to lt. yellow pressboard.	30.00	75.00	—

Dhar

A state in the Southern States and Malwa Agency in Central India with an area of 1,800 sq. mi.

Dhar State Bank

ND WWII Emergency Cash Coupons Issue

		VG	VF	Unc
S231	**1 Pice** ND. Seal of Dhar State Bank at l. Pressboard.	8.00	20.00	35.00
S232	**1 Anna** ND. Like #S231. Sm. letters: *ONE ANNA.*	10.00	25.00	40.00

		VG	VF	Unc
S233	**1 Anna** ND. Like #S231. Lg. letters: *ONE ANNA* in English and Hindi.	8.00	20.00	35.00

Dhrangadhra

A small feudatory state located in Gujarat State with an area of 1,167 sq. mi. (3,023 sq. km.).

Jhalawad Bank

ND Circulating Checks Issue

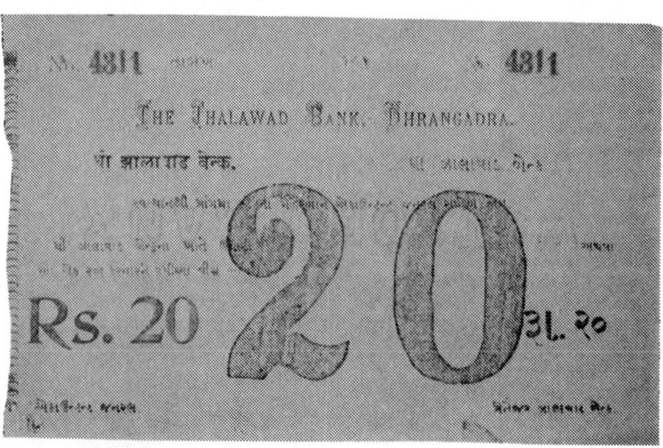

		Good	Fine	XF
S236	**20 Rupees** ND. Blue-gray. Lg. red value: *20.* Buff paper. Uniface.	3.00	8.00	20.00
S237	**50 Rupees** ND.	3.00	8.00	20.00
S238	**100 Rupees** ND.	3.00	8.00	20.00

		Good	Fine	XF
S239	**500 Rupees** ND. Like #S236.	4.00	10.00	30.00

1918 Treasury Notes Issue

#S241 and S244 black and red-brown. Numerals and text in Hindi w/3 handwritten sign. Wmk. native laid paper. Uniface.

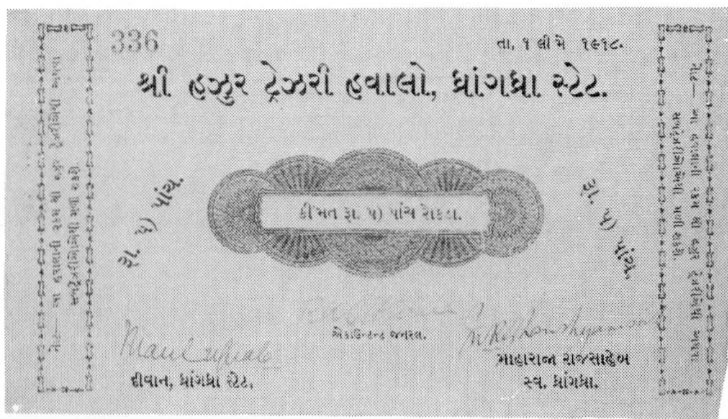

		Good	Fine	XF
S241	**5 Rupees** 1.5.1918.	7.50	15.00	25.00

A word on date ranges

Often date ranges or specific dates are listed. These have been observed or reported by our contributors. If a note is outside the published range, it only means that it is a newly reported date, and not necessarily worthy of a premium value.

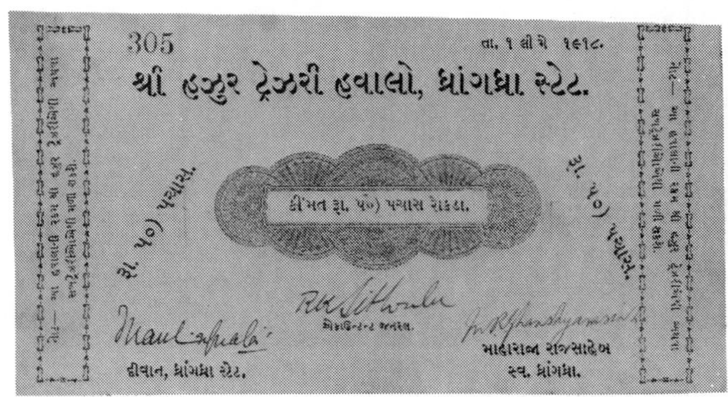

		GOOD	FINE	XF
S244	**50 RUPEES** 1.5.1918.	7.50	15.00	25.00

DINAJPUR

Previously listed 1 Pice and 1 Anna cash coupons have been determined to be fantasies.

GONDAL

A state in Kathiawar in the Western India States Agency with an area of 1,024 sq. mi. (2,653 sq. km.). These cash coupons also circulated in the neighboring states of Rajkot, Virpur and Jetpur.

GOVERNMENT

ND WWII CASH COUPONS ISSUE

		VG	VF	UNC
S251	**1 PAISO (PICE)** ND. Gujarati text: "Gondal State Stamp 1 Paiso". Lt. brown pressboard. Series T.	8.00	20.00	35.00

HYDERABAD

Largest of the Princely States located in south central India with an area of 82,313 sq. mi. Ruled by Muslim Nizams until invaded and annexed by India in 1948. Issued notes 1948-53 under British Indian rule.

Signature Varieties:

A. Sir Reginald R. Clancy, 1918-1919

B. Fakhr-ud-Din Ahmad, 1919-1920

C. Hyder Nawaz Jung, 1921-1936

D. Fakhr-Yar Jung, 1936-1938, 1940-1941

E. Mehdi Yar Jung, 1939

F. Ghulam Muhammad, 1941-1945

G. Liaquat Jung, 1945, 1946-1947

H. Zahed Husain, 1945-1946

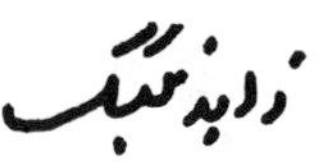

I. Zahed Jung, 1946

J. Moin Nawaz Jung, 1947-1948

K. D. R. Pradhan, 1948-1949

L. C.V.S. Rao, 1950

M. Dr. G. S. Melkote, 1950-1953

Dating:

Add 589 to the Fasli Era (FE) date for the corresponding AD date.

GOVERNMENT

NOTE: In 1932 a quantity of unissued but waterstained Hyderabad notes in 5, 10 and 100 Rupee denominations was recovered from the liner *S.S. Egypt* which sank in 1922 off the island of Ushant near Brest in northern France. Many of these were given a special stamping and sold as souvenirs.

1915-36 ISSUE

#S261-S267 printer: W&S.

		VG	VF	UNC
S261	**1 RUPEE** ND (1919). Black on peach unpt. Obverse of coin at upper l., reverse at upper r. Back lt. brown.	—	Rare	—

		GOOD	FINE	XF
S262	**1 RUPEE** ND (1919). Bicolored.	—	—	—

		GOOD	FINE	XF
S263	**5 RUPEES** FE 1331-47 (1920-36). Green. Five-1 Rupee coins on back.			
	a. Series IQ. W/o sign. Sea salvage note (most w/stamping), unissued. FE 1331 (1920).	40.00	—	—
	b. Series LX. Sign. C. FE 1337 (1926).	25.00	60.00	140.00
	c. Series MC. Sign. C. FE 1346 (1935).	20.00	50.00	125.00
	d. Series MD-ME. Sign. D. FE 1347 (1936).	20.00	50.00	125.00

		GOOD	FINE	XF
S264	**10 RUPEES** FE 1327 (1916). Yellow-brown and black on lilac unpt. Series AB. Sign. A.	75.00	150.00	300.00

A word on pricing

When a note is marked RARE in the price columns, this note seldom appears on the market, or few are known in private hands. When dashes are in the price column, means that the note has not traded on the open market recently and a definitive value could not accurately be determined. Rare does not always mean expensive. A dashed price does not mean expensive or rare.

S265 10 Rupees
FE 1331-47 (1920-36). Like #S264 but rectangular panel added for date on lower l. ctr. frame.

		Good	Fine	XF
a.	Series AI. W/o sign. Sea salvage note (most w/stamping), unissued. FE 1331 (1920).	40.00	—	—
b.	Series AN. Sign. C. FE 1333 (1922).	40.00	80.00	200.00
c.	Series ?. Sign. C. FE 1338 (1927).	35.00	70.00	175.00
d.	Series BK. Sign. C. FE 1339 (1928).	35.00	70.00	175.00
e.	Series BW. Sign. C. FE 1342 (1931).	35.00	70.00	175.00
f.	Series ?. Sign. C. FE 1344 (1933).	35.00	70.00	175.00
g.	Series CH. Sign. C. FE 1346 (1935).	35.00	70.00	175.00
h.	Series CZ. Sign. D. FE 1347 (1936).	40.00	80.00	200.00

S266 100 Rupees
FE 1331-39 (1920-28). Blue and black on tan unpt.

		Good	Fine	XF
a.	Series PS. W/o sign. Sea salvage note (most w/stamping), unissued. FE 1331 (1920).	50.00	—	—
b.	Series PY-PZ. Sign. C. FE 1339 (1928).	50.00	125.00	250.00
c.	Series QA. Sign. C.	50.00	125.00	250.00
d.	Series PT. Sign. C. FE 1334 (1923).	60.00	140.00	275.00

	Good	Fine	XF
S267 1000 Rupees FE 1340 (1929); 1341 (1930). Red and black on lt. green unpt. Series AA. Sign. C.	100.00	200.00	600.00

1939-53 Issue

#S271-S275 printer: Security Press, Nasik (w/o imprint).

S271 1 Rupee
ND (1939-46). Brown and m/c. Wording in 4 lines at ctr.= obverse and reverse of 1 Rupee coin at ctr. on back.

		VG	VF	Unc
a.	Series A. Sign. E. ND (1939).	2.50	7.50	17.50
b.	Series B-M. Sign. D. ND (1940-41).	2.50	7.50	17.50
c.	Series B-X. Sign. F, G. ND (1941-45).	2.50	7.50	17.50
d.	Series S-W. Sign. H. ND (1945-46).	2.50	7.50	17.50
e.	Series X-Y. Sign. I. ND (1946).	2.50	7.50	17.50

S272 1 Rupee
ND (1945-53). Similar to #S271 except that wording is in 2 lines at ctr. Series W-Z, AB-AQ.

		VG	VF	Unc
a.	Series Z, AB. Sign. G. ND (1946-47).	1.50	4.00	12.00
b.	Sign. H. ND (1945-46).	1.50	4.00	12.00
c.	Sign. I. ND (1946).	1.50	4.00	12.00
d.	Sign. J. ND (1947-48).	2.50	8.00	20.00
e.	Sign. K. ND (1948-49).	2.50	8.00	20.00
f.	Sign. L. ND (1950).	1.50	4.00	12.00
g.	Sign. M. ND (1950-53).	1.50	4.00	12.00

NOTE: #S271 and S272 issued from 1939-48 under Muslim rulers, 1948-53 under Indian occupation.

S273 5 Rupees
ND (1938-47). Green and m/c. Five 1 Rupee coins dated FE 1347 on back. Series MH-PX.

		VG	VF	Unc
a.	Sign. D. ND (1938; 1940-41).	4.50	12.50	40.00
b.	Sign. E. ND (1939).	4.50	12.50	40.00
c.	Sign. F. ND (1941-45).	4.50	12.50	40.00
d.	Sign. H. ND (1945-46).	4.50	12.50	40.00
e.	Sign. G. ND (1946-47).	4.50	12.50	40.00

S274 10 Rupees
ND (1938-47). Lt. brown and m/c. Series CP-JI.

		VG	VF	Unc
a.	Sign. D. ND (1938; 1940-41).	4.50	15.00	45.00
b.	Sign. E. ND (1939).	4.50	15.00	45.00
c.	Sign. F. ND (1941-45).	4.50	15.00	45.00
d.	Sign. H. ND (1945-46).	4.50	15.00	45.00
e.	Sign. G. ND (1946-47).	4.50	15.00	45.00

		VG	VF	UNC
S275	**100 RUPEES** ND (1939-45). Blue and m/c.			
	a. Series QC. Sign. D. ND (1938; 1940-41).	20.00	60.00	180.00
	b. Series QF; QH; QI. Sign. E. ND (1939).	20.00	60.00	180.00
	c. Series QN; QP. Sign. F. ND (1941-45).	20.00	60.00	180.00
	d. Series QS. Sign. G. ND (1945; 1946-47).	20.00	60.00	180.00
	e. Series QY. Sign. H. ND (1945-46).	20.00	60.00	180.00

INDERGADH

A state located in the northern tip of Kotah State now merged into Rajasthan with an area of 400 sq. mi. (109 sq. km.).

GOVERNMENT

1933-42 WWII EMERGENCY CASH COUPONS ISSUE

#S281 *Deleted.*

		VG	VF	UNC
S282	**1 ANNA** 1933 (1942). Reverse of 1 Anna coin of George V at ctr., control # at top.	2.00	5.00	10.00
S283	**2 ANNAS** 1939 (1942). Reverse of 2 Anna coin of George VI at ctr. Pressboard.	4.00	10.00	20.00

JAIPUR

Formerly listed #S291 is a 1935 dated 4 Annas dual portr. donation receipt from "Their Majesties' Silver Jubilee Fund."

JAISALMIR

A state located in the Western Raiputana States Residency with an area of 16,062 sq. mi. (41,611 sq. km.).

GOVERNMENT

ND WWII CASH COUPONS ISSUE

#S301-S303 Hindi text and Western control #. Thick pressboard.

		VG	VF	UNC
S301	**1/4 ANNA** ND.	—	Rare	—
S302	**1/2 ANNA** ND.	—	Rare	—
S303	**3/4 ANNA** ND.	—	Rare	—

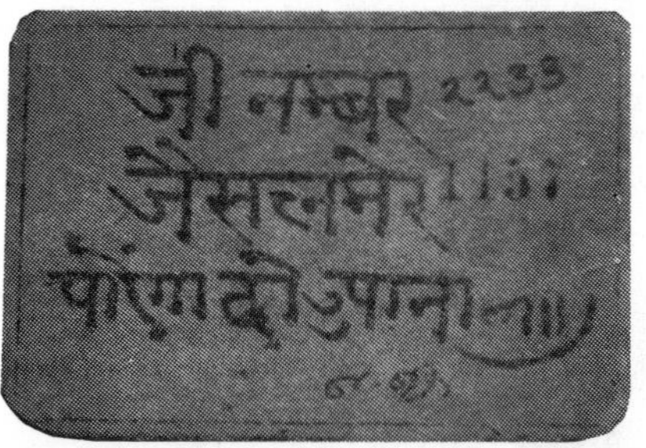

		VG	VF	UNC
S304	**1 3/4 ANNAS** ND. Different Hindi text and Western control #.	—	Rare	—
S305	**2 ANNAS** ND. Ovpt. on #S304.	—	Rare	—

JAMMU AND KASHMIR

A large state in the extreme north of India with an area of 85,885 sq. mi. (222,500 sq. km.). India and Pakistan are in continual dispute over control of the area. The two states had the same sovereign.

GOVERNMENT

1934 SRI KAR TEMPLE TOKENS ISSUE

#S311-S317 Hindi and Urdu script, radiant sunface at top ctr., Persian stamped seal of Jammu at lower ctr. Dated Vikrama Samvat 1934 (1876 AD).

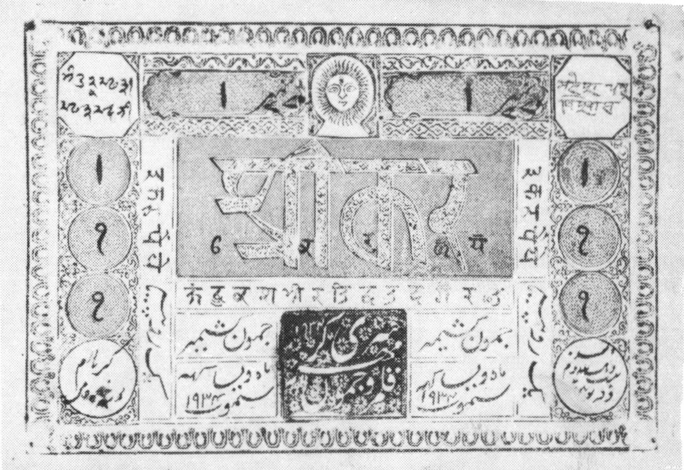

		VG	VF	UNC
S311	**1 RUPEE** VS 1934 (1876). Brown-orange.	—	Rare	—
S312	**2 RUPEES** VS 1934 (1876).	—	Rare	—
S313	**5 RUPEES** VS 1934 (1876).	—	Rare	—
S314	**10 RUPEES** VS 1934 (1876).	—	Rare	—
S315	**20 RUPEES** VS 1934 (1876).	—	Rare	—
S316	**50 RUPEES** VS 1934 (1876).	—	Rare	—

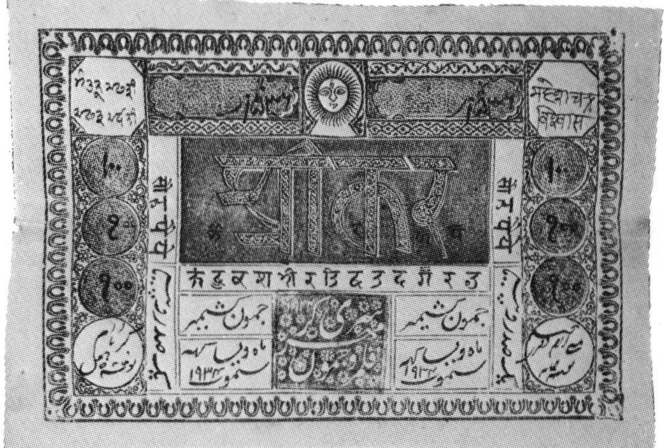

		VG	VF	UNC
S317	**100 RUPEES** VS 1934 (1876).	—	Rare	—

JASDAN

A state located in Western India States Agency with an area of 296 sq. mi. (767 sq. km.).

GOVERNMENT

1942 WWII EMERGENCY CASH COUPONS ISSUE

#S321 and S322 Gujarati legends.

		VG	VF	UNC
S321	**1 PICE** ND (1942). Lg. Gujarati numeral *1* and *LOT NO.* w/series letter at r., control # at r. margin. Lot No. G. Pressboard.	6.50	17.50	40.00

		VG	VF	UNC
S322	**1 ANNA** 1933 (1942). 1 Anna coin of Kg. George V at r. Lot No. B. Pressboard.	8.00	20.00	50.00

JUNAGADH

A state located in Kathiawar in the Western India States Agency with an area of 3,337 sq. mi. (8,645 sq. km.). It was also known as Soruth or Saurashtra. It gave its name to the Saurashtra Union in 1948 when India took control.

GOVERNMENT

1943 ND WWII CASH COUPONS ISSUE

#S331 *Deleted*.

NOTE: Previously listed #S331 1 Anna w/title: *JUNAGAD STETE* is a counterfeit.

#S332-S334 oval seal stamp: *JUNAGADH STATE*. Trimmed horizontally.

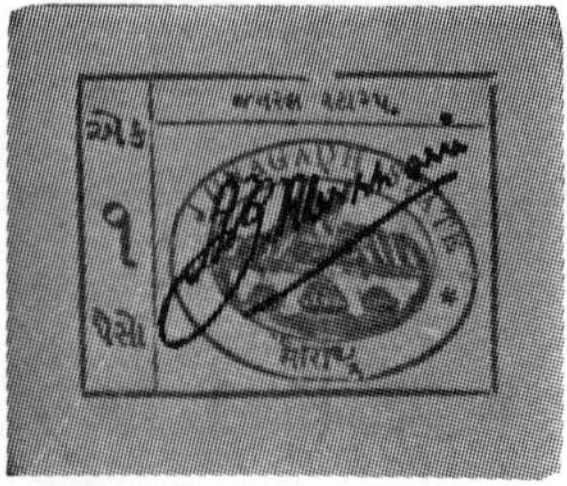

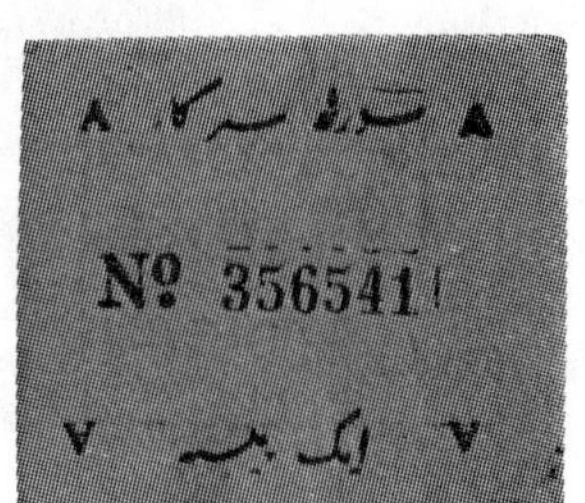

		VG	VF	UNC
S332	**1 PAISA** ND (1943). Green.	2.50	6.00	15.00

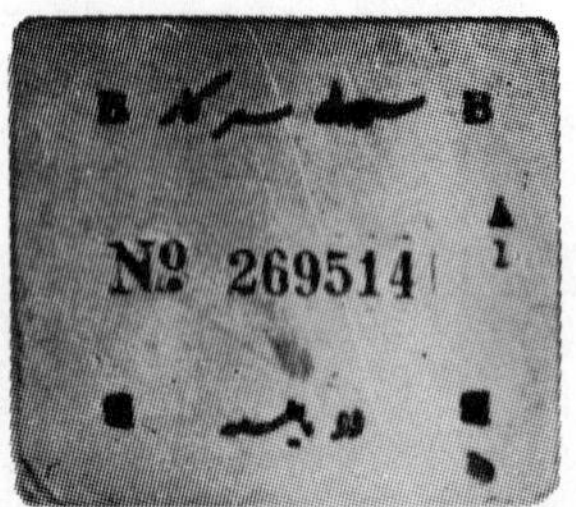

		VG	VF	UNC
S333	**2 PAISA** ND (1943). Red.	2.50	6.00	15.00

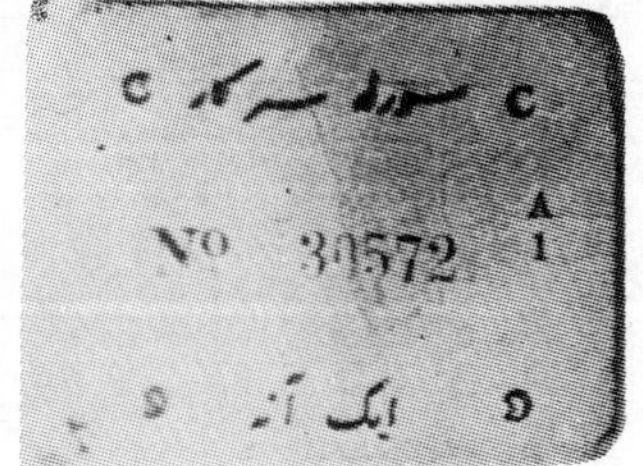

		VG	VF	UNC
S334	**1 ANNA** ND (1943). Violet.	3.00	8.00	20.00

KUTCH

GOVERNMENT

1946 ND ISSUE

#S341-S344 Maharajah Vijaya Rajji at r. Printer: W&S.

		VG	VF	UNC
S341	**25 KORIS** ND (1946). Specimen.	—	Rare	—
S342	**50 KORIS** ND (1946). Specimen.	—	Rare	—
S343	**100 KORIS** ND (1946). Specimen.	—	Rare	—

		VG	VF	UNC
S344	**500 KORIS** ND (1946). Specimen.	—	Rare	—

NOTE: Only a specimen set is known at this time.

MANGROL

A tiny state located in Kathiawar on the Arabian Sea coast, midway between Porbandar and Portuguese Diu with an area of 227 sq. mi. (588 sq. km.).

GOVERNMENT

ND WWII EMERGENCY CASH COUPON STAMP MONEY ISSUE

#S352 and S353 value in Gujarati and English on face. 5-digit control # and sign. Size: 50 x 50mm.

		VG	VF	UNC
S352	**1 PAISA (PICE)** ND. Pink pressboard.	5.00	12.00	25.00
S353	**2 PAISA (PICE)** ND. White pressboard.	8.00	20.00	40.00

		VG	VF	UNC
S354	**1 ANNA** ND. Gray-green pressboard.	5.00	12.00	25.00

MENGANI

A small state located in Kathiawar in Bombay Presidency, 15 miles south of Rajkot city with an area of 34 sq. mi. (88 sq. km.). The Talukdar paid an annual tribute to the British government and his affairs were looked after by a Kathiawar manager.

GOVERNMENT

ND WWII CASH COUPON STAMP MONEY ISSUE

#S361 revenue stamp printed on pressboard for use as cash coupons.

		VG	VF	UNC
S361	**1 PAISO** ND. Scroll below, cow at ctr. w/*MANGNI TALUKA* in English, and *STATE MENGNI TALUKA REVENUE STAMP, ONE PAISO* in Gujarati.	4.00	10.00	20.00

MULI

A small state located in the Western India States Agency with an area of 133 sq. mi. (344 sq. km.).

RULERS:

Harish Chandra Sinhji

GOVERNMENT

1943-45 WWII CASH COUPON STAMP MONEY ISSUE

#S371-S373 Sinhji at ctr.

		VG	VF	UNC
S371	**1 PAISA (PICE)** ca. 1943-45. Black pressboard.	2.00	5.00	10.00
S372	**2 PAISA (PICE)** ca. 1943-45. Lt. blue pressboard.	2.00	5.00	10.00
S373	**4 ANNAS** ca. 1943-45. Lt. brown pressboard.	3.00	7.50	15.00

MYSORE

Formerly listed #S381-S383 w/portr. of Maharaja at ctr. are donation receipts of the Imperial Indian Relief Fund.

NAVANAGAR

"Swasthan Nawanagar" (Navangar State) in Western India States Agency with an area of 3,791 sq. mi. (9,821 sq. km.).

GOVERNMENT

1943-44 WWII CASH COUPON STAMP MONEY ISSUE

#S391-S394 revenue stamps w/portr. of C. Maharaja Digvijaysingh at ctr. Pressboard. Perforated: *NS* (Navanagar State) w/Gujarati control # printed at top.

		VG	VF	UNC
S391	**2 PICE** 1943-44.	8.00	20.00	40.00
S392	**1 ANNA** 1943-44.	8.00	20.00	40.00

		VG	VF	UNC
S393	**2 ANNAS** 1943-44.	8.00	20.00	40.00
S394	**4 ANNAS** 1943-44.	8.00	20.00	40.00

NAWALGARH

A small city state located in Rajasthan.

GOVERNMENT

ND WWII EMERGENCY CASH COUPONS ISSUE

#S401-S405 embossed Indian numeral of value. Devnagri text on face. Hand stamped oval seal: *THIKANA OFFICE NAWALGARH* on back.

		VG	VF	UNC
S401	**1 PAISA (PICE)** ND. Dull brown pressboard.	4.00	10.00	25.00

		VG	VF	UNC
S402	**1 ANNA** ND. Cream pressboard.	4.00	10.00	25.00

		VG	VF	UNC
S403	**2 ANNAS** ND. Dull green pressboard.	4.00	10.00	25.00

		VG	VF	UNC
S404	**4 ANNAS** ND. Pink pressboard.	4.00	10.00	25.00

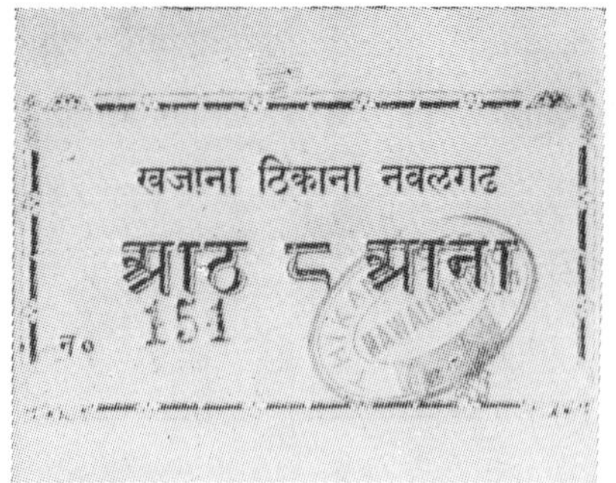

		VG	VF	UNC
S405	**8 ANNAS** ND. Lt. green pressboard. Uniface.	8.00	20.00	50.00

PALITANA

A small state in Kathiawar, Western India States Agency with an area of 300 sq. mi. (777 sq. km.). Joined Saurashtra Union in 1948.

GOVERNMENT

1943 WWII CASH COUPONS ISSUE

#S411-S413 Gujarati numeral of value within scroll printed over Palitana State arms. Western control # and hand sign.

		VG	VF	UNC
S411	**1 PAISA** 31.10.1943.	10.00	25.00	50.00
S412	**1/2 ANNA** 31.10.1943.	10.00	25.00	50.00
S413	**1 ANNA** 31.10.1943.	15.00	35.00	65.00

ND WWII CASH COUPON STAMP MONEY ISSUE

#S415-S420 revenue stamps printed on pressboard.

		VG	VF	UNC
S415	**1 PAISE** ND.	—	—	—
S416	**2 PAISA** ND.	—	—	—
S417	**1 ANNA** ND.	—	—	—
S418	**2 ANNAS** ND.	—	—	—
S419	**4 ANNAS** ND.	—	—	—
S420	**8 ANNAS** ND.	—	—	—

RAJKOT

A state in Kathiawar, Western India States Agency with an area of 344 sq. mi. (891 sq. km.). Joined Saurashtra Union in 1948.

GOVERNMENT

ND WWII EMERGENCY CASH COUPON STAMP MONEY ISSUE

#S421-S423 revenue stamps printed on pressboard.

		VG	VF	UNC
S421	**1 PICE** ND. Gray. 49 x 41mm.	4.00	10.00	25.00
S422	**2 PICE** ND. Green.	4.00	10.00	25.00
S423	**1 ANNA** ND. Red. Portr. ruler of Rajkot.	Reported Not Confirmed		

RAMGARH RAJ

Previously listed #S481 1 Anna is a fantasy (printed on post-WWII era postcards). A 1/2 Anna fantasy printed on different paper stock has recently been reported.

SAILANA

A small state located in Southern States and Malwa Agency with an area of 297 sq. mi. (769 sq. km.).

GOVERNMENT

ND WWII EMERGENCY CASH COUPON STAMP MONEY ISSUE

#S430 and S431 portr. Dileep Singh, Rajah.

		VG	VF	UNC
S430	**1 PAISA (PICE)** ND. Black. Rose pressboard	—	Rare	—

		VG	VF	UNC
S431	**1 ANNA** ND. Black and red. Maharaja at ctr.			
	a. Ovpt: *1 ANNA.*	3.50	10.00	22.50
	b. Ovpt: *ANNA.* (error).	30.00	75.00	150.00

NOTE: #S431b appears once in a full sheet of 16 examples.

#S432 *Deleted.*

SAYALA

A small state located in the Western India State Agency near Chuda with an area of 225 sq. mi. (583 sq. km.).

GOVERNMENT

ND WWII CASH COUPONS ISSUE

		VG	VF	UNC
S435	**1 PAISA (PICE)** ND. Black. Arms at l. Series D-F. Uniface.	1.00	3.00	9.00

SITAMAU

A small state located in Central India residency, in Mandsor district, with an area of 191 sq. mi. (495 sq. km.). Founded 1660. Merged w/India 1947.

GOVERNMENT

1942-43 WWII CASH COUPONS ISSUE

#S441-S443 have State seal on face, control #, date, value and sign. on back.

		VG	VF	UNC
S441	**1 ANNA** 1942-43.	—	Rare	—
S442	**2 ANNAS** 1942-43.	—	Rare	—
S443	**4 ANNAS** 1942-43.	—	Rare	—

TONK

The only Muslim-ruled state in Rajputana, Jaipur Residency with an area of 2,553 sq. mi. (6,614 sq. km.).

GOVERNMENT

1943 ND WWII CASH COUPONS ISSUE

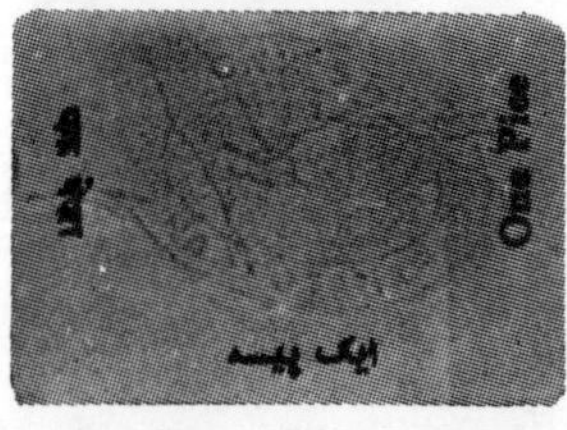

		GOOD	FINE	XF
S451	**1 PICE** ND (1943). Pressboard. Denomination in English, Hindi and Perso-Arabic.	12.00	30.00	—

		Good	Fine	XF
S453	4 Annas ND (1943).			
	a. *ANNAS 4.* Lg. letters: Control # on back.	25.00	65.00	125.00
	b. *ANNAS 4.* Sm. letters.	25.00	65.00	125.00

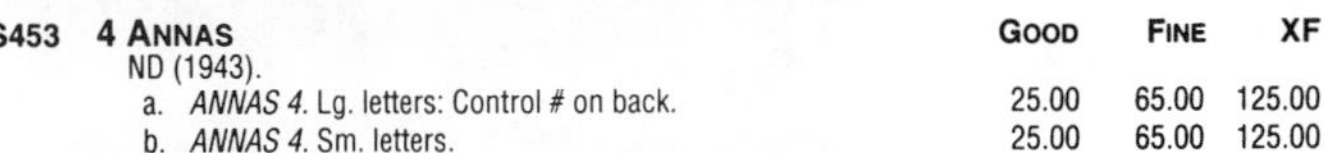

		Good	Fine	XF
S454	1 Pice ND (1943). Black pressboard. Tower at l.	25.00	55.00	—

		Good	Fine	XF
S455	1 Anna ND (1943). Minaret at l., airplanes at upper r. Blue pressboard.	25.00	55.00	—

1943 War Purposes Fund Issue

		VG	VF	Unc
S456	4 Annas ND (1943). Blue w/red text.	50.00	125.00	—

Vithalgadh

A small state in the Western India States Agency with an area of 56 sq. mi. (145 sq. km.).

Government

ND WWII Cash Coupon Stamp Money Issue

#S461 and S462 w/Gujarati script: *VITHALGADH* at ctr. and denomination across bottom, portr. Maharaja at ctr.

		VG	VF	Unc
S461	1 Anna ND.	7.50	17.50	35.00
S462	2 Annas ND.	7.50	17.50	35.00

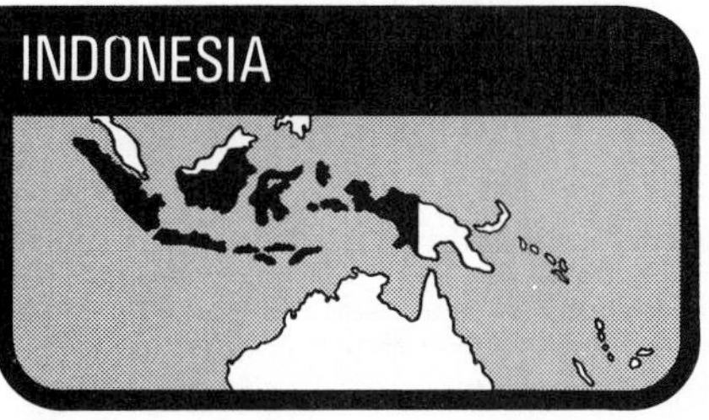

The Republic of Indonesia, the world's largest archipelago, extends for more than 3,000 miles (4,827 km.) along the equator from the mainland of southeast Asia to Australia. The 13,667 islands comprising the archipelago have a combined area of 735,268 sq. mi. (2,042,005 sq. km.) and a population of 202 million, including East Timor. Capital: Jakarta. Petroleum, timber, rubber and coffee are exported.

Had Columbus succeeded in reaching the fabled Spice Islands, he would have found advanced civilizations a millennium old, and temples still ranked among the finest examples of ancient art. During the opening centuries of the Christian era, the islands were influenced by Hindu priests and traders who spread their culture and religion. Moslem invasions began in the 13th century, fragmenting the island kingdoms into small states which were unable to resist Western colonial infiltration. Portuguese traders established posts in the 16th century, but they were soon outnumbered by the Dutch who arrived in 1602 and gradually asserted control over the islands comprising present-day Indonesia. Dutch dominance, interrupted by British incursions during the Napoleonic Wars, established the Netherlands East Indies as one of the richest colonial possessions in the world.

MONETARY SYSTEM:

1 Gulden = 100 Cents to 1948
1 Rupiah = 100 Sen, 1945-

INDONESIA, 1945-1950

Historical Introduction

After the Japanese surrender on August 14, 1945 (effective for Java and Sumatra on September 12), the Republic of Indonesia was proclaimed on August 17, 1945 by Sukarno and Dr. Mohammad Hatta. The Republic of Indonesia was not recognized by the Dutch who wanted to restore their colonial empire. During the Japanese occupation a well trained Indonesian army was formed as well as a cadre meant for a (puppet) government in the Japanese controlled Greater East Asian Co-prosperity Sphere.

The Indonesian nationalists took the opportunity given by the Japanese to prepare an independent Indonesia after the war. On March 6, 1946 the first Dutch troops landed on Java, and a state of siege was proclaimed by the Republic on June 7 for Java and on June 28 for Sumatra. Negotiations led to a cease-fire on February 15, but from July 21 until August 4, 1947 the Dutch launched the (first) attack on the Republic. Under international pressure the Dutch started negotiations and tried to form federal states in parts of the archipelago not under control of the Republic, outside Java and Sumatra. The Dutch wanted to set up a United States of Indonesia with the Republic as one of the states, under the Dutch Crown. This was unacceptable to the Indonesian nationalists.

A (second) Dutch attack on the regions held by the Republic was launched on December 18, 1948; by December 31 Java was occupied, and on January 5, 1949 Sumatra as well. The capital of the Republic (Jogjakarta, Central Java) was captured and the republican leaders, including Sukarno and Hatta, were carried off as prisoners to the island of Bangka. International pressure, especially from the Security Council of the United Nations, led to renewed negotiations and to the return of the republican leaders to Jogjakarta. A definitive cease-fire was proclaimed on August 3, 1949 and on December 27, 1949 the ex-colonial power formally transferred sovereignty to the new United States of Indonesia (Republik Indonesia Serikat).

During the period 1946-1949 The Republic of Indonesia issued (emergency) paper money for parts of Java and Sumatra (partly listed in Volume Two, Indonesia #13-30 and #33-35). The State Bank of Indonesia (Bank Negara Indonesia) was opened in Jogjakarta on August 17, 1946, and the first series of bank notes, dated Jakarta October 17, 1945, was issued on October 26, 1946 (Indonesia #13-20). Officially the rupiah had a gold par of 0.5 gram.

GENERAL INTRODUCTION

A. VARIATIONS

This listing does *not* include the wide range of variations in the emergency paper money, e.g.

COLOR: In most cases only the main colors are listed; green may vary from blue-green to yellow-green, red from dark stone red to red-orange, etc.

PAPER: White, brown, thin (rice paper), thick, with or w/o wmk., and even notebook paper are used for the notes.

UNDERPRINT (unpt.): Is sometimes clear, but mostly vague or almost absent.

NUMBERING: There is a wide range of combinations, 1 to 5 letters, 5 or 6 digits, square or round digits, differences in style of the letters (sans serif or not).

STAMPS or POSTMARKS: In most cases not listed as it is easy to produce hand stamped notes, and falsifications do exist.

B. COMMON WORDS FOUND ON INDONESIAN BANKNOTES

Tanda pembajaran jang sah	legal currency
Uang (or oeang *)	money
Uang kertas	paper money
Coupon penukaran	exchange coupon
Mandat pertahanan	defense mandate
Bon	coupon
Beredar	circulate
Berlaku	valid
Palsu	false
Tidak berlaku	not valid
Darurat	emergency
Istimewa	special
Ketetapan	decree
Gubernur	governor
Propinsi	Province
Sub-propinsi	Sub-province
Bupati	regent
Kabupaten	regency
Daerah	district, region
Kepala daerah	head of district/region
Kas negara	state treasury
Menteri keuangan	minister of finance
Djabatan keuangan	finance office
Residen	resident
Keresidenan	residency
Kewedanaan	district

NOTE: In January 1947 Indonesia changed the spelling "oe" to "u" because of the Dutch origin of the spelling "oe'. On notes the spelling is sometimes "oe" and sometimes "u", e.g. Boepati/Bupati, Keoeangan/Keuangan, Poeloeh/Puluh.

C. NUMBERS

1/2	setengah	40	empat puluh
1	satu	50	lima puluh
2 1/2	dua setengah	100	seratus
5	lima	250	dua ratus lima puluh
10	sepuluh	400	empat ratus
20	dua puluh	500	lima ratus
25	dua puluh lima	1000	seribu

D. ABBREVIATIONS

N.R.I. ....Negara Republik Indonesia (*negara* means state)
T.N.I. ....Tentara Negara Indonesia (*tentara* means army)

I. REGIONAL ISSUES REPUBLIC OF INDONESIA

A. JAVA

A1. Bodjonegoro .... #S61-S63
1. Djokjakarta (Jogjakarta) .... #S107-S111
1A. Kediri .... #S112-S113B
1B. Madiun .... #S113C-S114
2. Magelang .... #S116
2A. Patjitan .... #S118
3. Serang .... #S121-S125
4. Surakarta .... #S130-S134

B. SUMATRA

1. Asahan .... #S141-S154
1A. Barus .... #S157
2. Bengkoeloe (Bengkulu) .... #S161-S168
3. Bukit Barisan .... #S171
4. Bukittinggi (B. Tinggi) .... #S181-S195
4A. Issue for the Province of Sumatra .... #S181-S195
4B. Issue for the sub-province of South Sumatra .... #S201-S203
4C. Issue for East Sumatra .... #S211-S213
4D. Issue for West Sumatra .... #S221
4E. Issue for Aceh .... #S231-S232
4F. Issue for Djambi .... #S236
4G. Issue for Riau .... #S241
4H. Issue for Tapanuli .... #S251-S253
5. Djambi .... #S261-S269
6. Koealoeh Leidong (Kualuh Leidong) .... #S271-S279
7. Koetaradja (Kutaradja) .... #S281-S286
8. Kutatjane .... #S291-S293
9. Labuhan Batu .... #S301-S303
10. Labuhan Bilik .... #S308-S314
11. Langsa .... #S316-S317
11A. Lima Poeloeh .... #S318-S318A
11B. Membang Moeda .... #S319-S320B
12. Nias .... #S321-S325
12A. Pagar Alam .... #S327-S330
13. Palembang .... #S330A-S339
14. Panai .... #S341
14A. Pekanbaru .... #340
15. Pematang Siantar .... #S351-S354
15A. Pendopo .... #S354A-S355
16. Rantau Prapat .... #S361-S374
17. Tandjungkarang .... #S380-S388
18. Tapanoeli (Tapanuli) .... #S390-S398
19. Tigabinanga .... #S401-S403
20. Tjurup .... #S406
21. No place of issue; issue for the special military district of South Sumatra ... #S410-S412
22. No place of issue shown; issue in North Lampung for town of Kotabumi .... #S419-S421

REBELLIOUS MOVEMENTS AGAINST THE REPUBLIC OF INDONESIA

Movement/Region

JAVA

Pemerintah Negara Islam Indonesia .... #S431-S432

SUMATRA

Pemerintah Revolusioner Republik Indonesia (P.R.R.I.) .... #S461-S481

NORTH CELEBES

Piagan Perdjuangarn Semesta (Permesta) .... #S491-S501

SOUTH CELEBES

Republik Islam Indonesia .... #S510-S530

MOLUCCAS

Republik Maluku Selatan (R.M.S.) .... #S531

REPUBLIC REGIONALS

JAVA

BLITA

Town, East Java.

1948 ISSUE

		GOOD	FINE	XF
S50	**1 RUPIAH** 8.8.1948. Dk. blue.	—	—	—
S51	**5 RUPIAH** 8.8.1948. Red.	—	—	—

BODJONEGORO

East Java.

1948 ISSUE

#S61-S63 redeemable after 14.1.1949. Stamped sign. Brown packing paper. Uniface.

		GOOD	FINE	XF
S60	**1/2 RUPIAH** 15.11.1948.	—	—	—
S61	**1 RUPIAH** 15.11.1948. Black and red.	—	Rare	—
S62	**5 RUPIAH** 15.11.1948. Black and red.	—	Rare	—

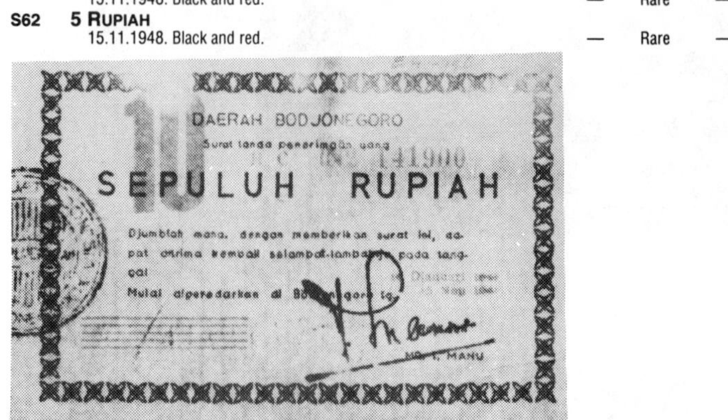

		GOOD	FINE	XF
S63	**10 RUPIAH** 15.11.1948. Black and red.	—	Rare	—

NOTE: Modern fakes have begun appearing on the market.

DJOKJAKARTA

JOGJAKARTA

Central Java.

1948 ISSUE

#S107-S109 signed by the Sultan of Jogjakarta, Hamengkubuwono IX. Central text: Daerah Istimewa Jogjakarta (Special region of Jogjakarta). Redeemable after 10.1.1949. Respective denomination unpt. Uniface.

		GOOD	FINE	XF
S107	**2 1/2 RUPIAH** 10.11.1948. Black on green unpt.			
	a. Stub at l.	—	Rare	—
	b. No stub at l.	—	Rare	—

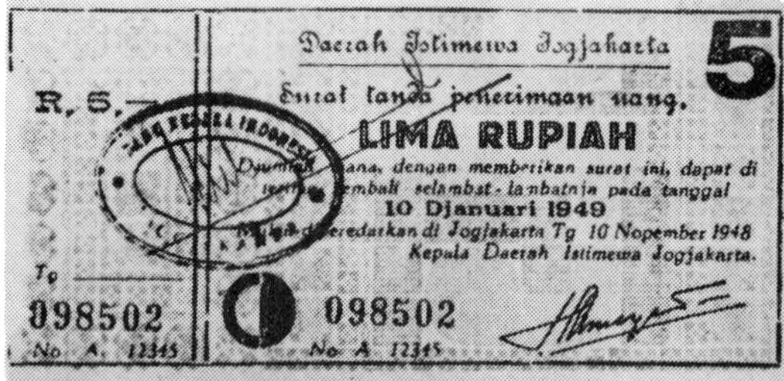

		GOOD	FINE	XF
S108	**5 RUPIAH** 10.11.1948. Black on green unpt.			
	a. Stub at l.	—	Rare	—
	b. No stub at l.	—	Rare	—
S109	**10 RUPIAH** 10.11.1948. Black on green unpt.	—	Rare	—

#S110 and S111 *Deleted.*

KEDIRI

Kediri City, Town, Residency, East Java.

1948 TOWN ISSUE

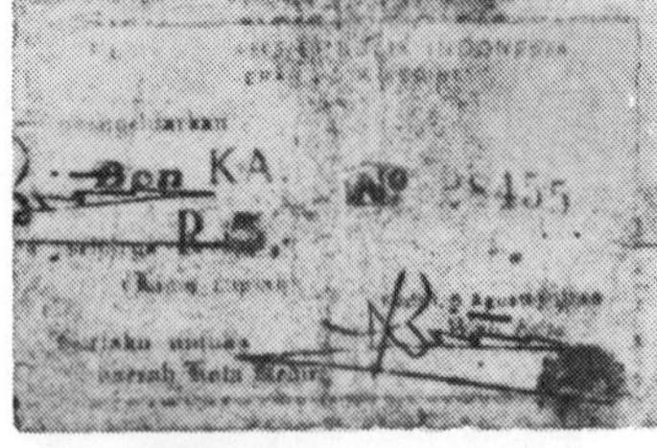

		GOOD	FINE	XF
S112	**5 RUPIAH** 5.8.1948. Red. Kediri. Uniface.	—	—	—

1948 RESIDENCE'S ISSUE

		Good	Fine	XF
S113	**2 1/2 Rupiah** 16.10.1948. Red. Kediri Residency. Uniface.	—	—	—
S113A	**5 Rupiah** 16.10.1948. Red. Kediri Residency. Uniface.	—	—	—
S113B	**10 Rupiah** 16.10.1948.	—	—	—

MADIUN

Town, East Java.

1948 City Issue

		Good	Fine	XF
S113C	**1/2 Rupiah** 1.9.1948. Uniface.	—	—	—
S113D	**1 Rupiah** 1.9.1948. Black. 1 red stripe.	—	—	—
S113E	**2 1/2 Rupiah** 1.9.1948. Black. 2 red stripes.	—	—	—
S113F (S113C)	**5 Rupiah** 1.9.1948. Black. 3 red stripes. Uniface.	—	—	—

		Good	Fine	XF
S114	**10 Rupiah** 1948. Black. Uniface.			
	a. 17.9.1948. 4 red vertical stripes.	—	—	—
	b. 1.11.1948. 4 red horizontal stripes.	—	—	—

MAGELANG

Kedu Residency, Central Java.

1948 Residency Issue

		Good	Fine	XF
S116	**2 1/2 Rupiah** 25.10.1948. Black and green. Landscape.	—	—	—
S117	**5 Rupiah** 25.10.1948.	—	—	—

MAGETAN

Magetan Regency, East Java.

1948 Issue

		Good	Fine	XF
S117A	**1 Rupiah** 17.9.1948. 1 vertical stripe.	—	—	—
S117B	**2 1/2 Rupiah** 17.9.1948. 2 vertical stripes.	—	—	—
S117C	**5 Rupiah** 17.9.1948. 3 vertical stripes.	—	—	—
S117D	**10 Rupiah** 17.9.1948. 4 vertical stripes.	—	—	—

PATJITAN

Patjitan Regency, District in East Java.

1947 ND Issue

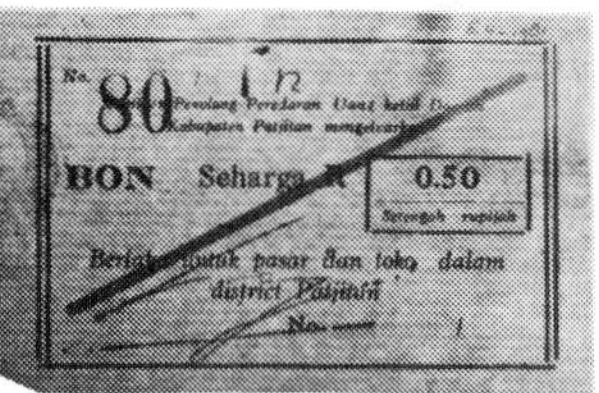

		Good	Fine	XF
S118	**1/2 Rupiah** ND (ca.1948). Uniface.	—	—	—
S118A	**1 Rupiah** ND(1948).	—	Rare	—
S118B	**5 Rupiah** ND(1948).	—	Rare	—
S118C	**10 Rupiah** ND(1948).	—	Rare	—

SEMARANG

Semarang Regency, Central Java.

1949 Issue

		Good	Fine	XF
S119	**25 Rupiah** 1.11.1949. Coconut tree at l.	—	—	—

SERANG

Banten Residency, West Java.

1947-48 Issue

#S121-S125 modern fakes exist of #S121-S125; made by the original printer's son.

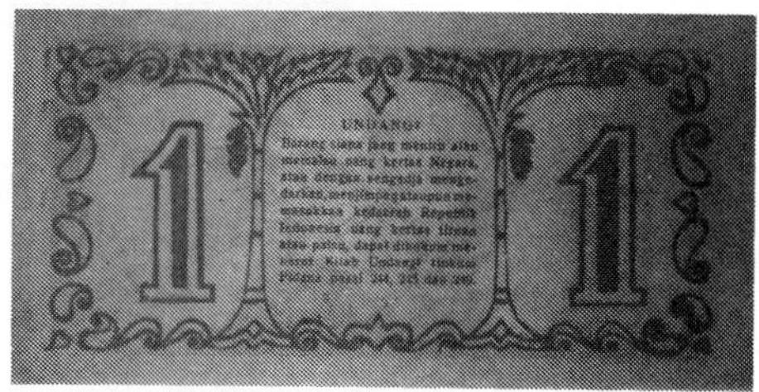

		Good	Fine	XF
S121	**1 Rupiah** 15.12.1947. Mauve and black. Rice and cotton stalks around gun, hammer and hoe.	10.00	30.00	60.00

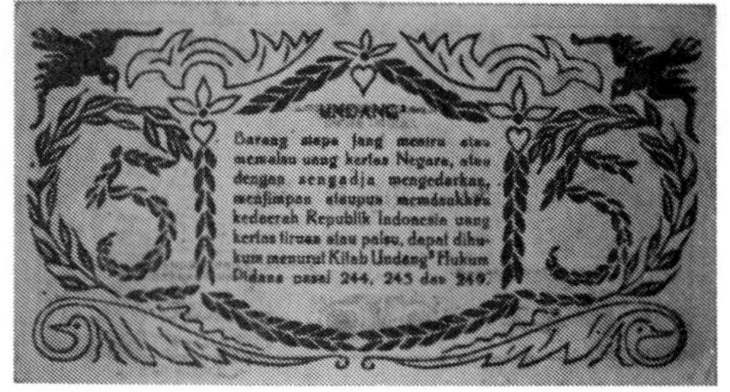

		Good	Fine	XF
S122	**5 Rupiah** 15.12.1947. Green and black. Ancient gate at ctr.	6.00	12.00	25.00

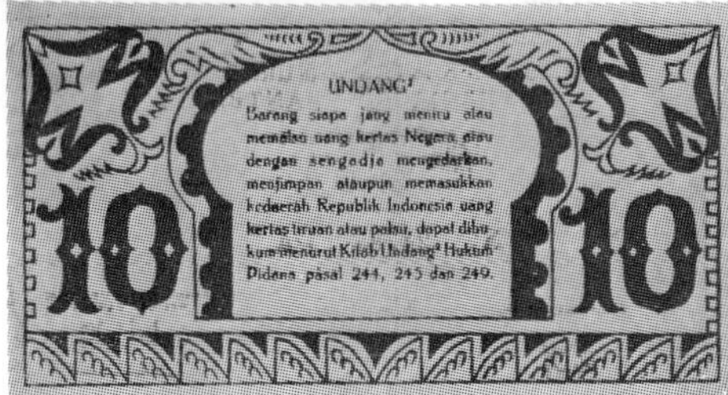

		Good	Fine	XF
S123	**10 Rupiah** 15.12.1947. Green and black on lt. green unpt. Minaret at ctr.	15.00	30.00	65.00

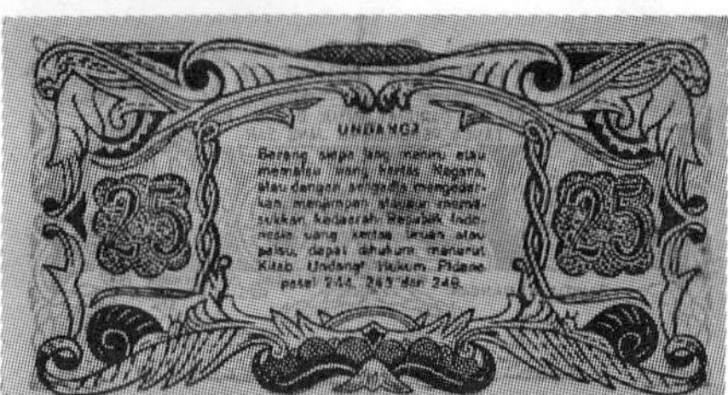

		Good	Fine	XF
S124	**25 Rupiah** 15.12.1947. Red to red-brown. Tower at l., gate at r.	3.00	5.00	12.50

		Good	Fine	XF
	a. Hand stamped: *palsu* (false) in black or blue.	2.00	5.00	10.00

NOTE: Contemporary fakes exist of #S124.

		Good	Fine	XF
S125	**50 Rupiah** 11.8.1948. Purple to red-violet and black. Tower at l., gate at r.	2.50	5.00	10.00

NOTE: Contemporary fakes exist of #S125.

Surakarta

City/Residency in Central Java. Brown packing paper.

1948-49 City Issues

		Good	Fine	XF
S130	**1 Rupiah** 1.11.1948. Black and red. Uniface. Torch at lower ctr.	—	—	—
S131	**2 1/2 Rupiah** 1.11.1948. Black and red. Lamp at lower ctr.	—	Rare	—

		Good	Fine	XF
S132	**5 Rupiah** 1.11.1948. Black and red. Lg. value: *5* at r. Uniface. Like #S131.	—	—	—
S132A	**5 Rupiah** 1.11.1949. Black on red. Ember at lower ctr.	—	—	—
S133	**10 Rupiah** 1.11.1949. Fighting lion and buffalo at lower ctr.			
	a. Black.	—	Rare	—
	b. Yellow.	—	Rare	—
S134	**25 Rupiah** 1.11.1949. Temple at lower ctr.			
	a. Black.	—	—	—
	b. Blue.	—	—	—

NOTE: Modern fakes exist of #S130, S132, S132A.

Tjlpu

Town, East Java.

1948 Issue

		Good	Fine	XF
S135	**1 Rupee** 17.8.1948. Legendary figure and serpent at l.	—	—	—
S135A	**5 Rupee** 17.8.1948. Legendary figure at upper l., dove in ctr.	—	—	—

Sumatra

Asahan

Asahan Regency, Northeast Sumatra.

Central text: *Bon - Pemerintau Negara Republik Indonesia, Kabupaten Asahan* (Coupon - Government of the State Republic of Indonesia, Asahan regency).

1947 Issues

#S141-S150 hand stamps on back.

		Good	Fine	XF
S141	**10 Sen** 21.8.1947. Value in circle.			
	a. Purple.	—	—	—
	b. Black.	—	—	—
	c. Sepia.	—	—	—
S142	**50 Sen** 21.8.1947. Value in circles.			
	a. Red-brown.	—	—	—
	b. Green.	300.00	—	—

		Good	Fine	XF
S143	**1 Rupiah** 21.8.1947. Black. Value in circles.			
	a. Black.	300.00	—	—
	b. Sepia.	—	—	—
S144	**2 1/2 Rupiah** 21.8.1947. Purple. Value in circles.			
	a. Purple.	—	—	—
	b. Green.	—	—	—
	c. Black.	—	—	—

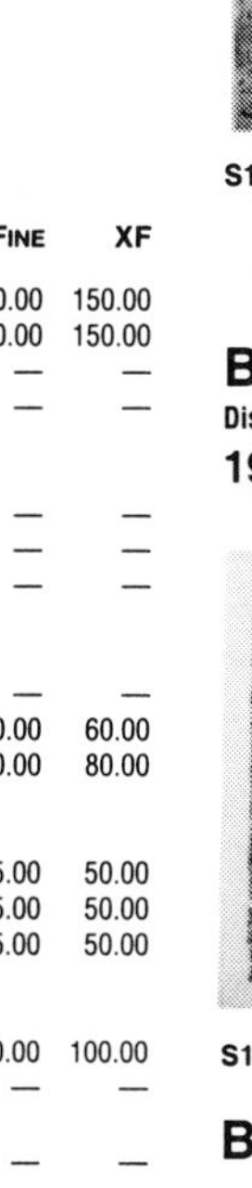

		Good	Fine	XF
S145	**5 Rupiah** 21.8.1947.			
	a. Black.	30.00	60.00	150.00
	b. Red-brown.	30.00	60.00	150.00
	c. Grey-purple.	—	—	—
	d. Green.	—	—	—
S146	**10 Rupiah** 21.8.1947. Banana tree at r.			
	a. Purple.	—	—	—
	b. Red.	—	—	—
	c. Black.	—	—	—
S147	**25 Rupiah** 21.8.1947. Coconut trees at r.			
	a. Black.	—	—	—
	b. Brown.	15.00	30.00	60.00
	c. Green.	20.00	40.00	80.00
S148	**50 Rupiah** 21.8.1947. Coconut trees at l. and r.			
	a. Brown.	10.00	25.00	50.00
	b. Red.	10.00	25.00	50.00
	c. Black.	10.00	25.00	50.00
S149	**100 Rupiah** 21.8.1947. Landscape at l., flowers at r.			
	a. Green.	25.00	50.00	100.00
	b. Black.	—	—	—
S150	**2500 Rupiah** 21.8.1947. Brown-red. Landscape at l., flowers at r.	—	—	—

1948 Issues

#S150A-S150D hand stamps on back.

		Good	Fine	XF
S150A	**1000 Rupiah** 12.2.1948. Black.	—	—	—
S150B	**2500 Rupiah** 27.2.1948.			
	a. Red.	—	—	—
	b. Black.	—	—	—
	c. Purple, blue, green.	—	—	—
S150C (S150A)	**5000 Rupiah** 1948.			
	a. Red.	—	—	—
	b. Blue.	—	—	—
S150D	**20,000 Rupiah** 3.3.1948.			
	a. Black.	—	—	—
	b. Blue.	—	—	—

1947 Issues

#S151-S154 hand stamps on back.

		Good	Fine	XF
S151	**100,000 Rupiah** 21.8.1947. Green.	30.00	60.00	110.00

		Good	Fine	XF
S152	**100,000 Rupiah** 7.2.1948.			
	a. Purple.	—	—	—
	b. Green.	—	—	—
	c. Black.	—	—	—
S153	**100,000 Rupiah** 7.2.1948. Green.	—	—	—

		Good	Fine	XF
S154	**250,000 Rupiah** 7.2.1948. Flower at lower ctr.			
	a. Green (Test).	—	—	—
	b. Blush.	—	—	—
	c. Blue-green.	—	—	—

Barus

District in Northwest Sumatra.

1948 Issue

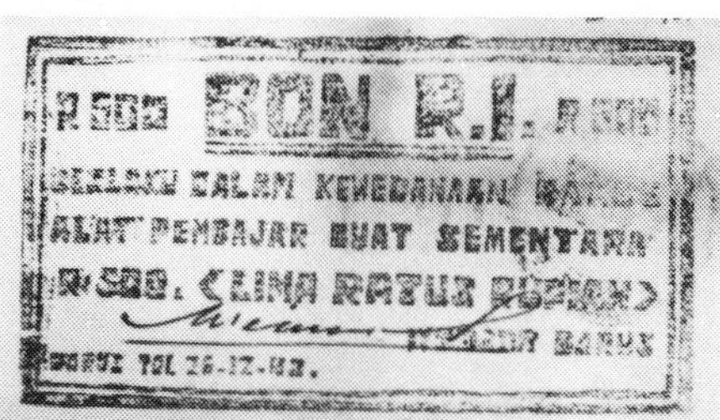

		Good	Fine	XF
S157	**500 Rupiah** 26.12.1948.	—	—	—

Bengkoeloe

Bengkulu

Residency, Southwest Sumatra.

1947 Issue

#S161-S165 seal and printed sign., handwritten initials. *MANDAT P(anitia) M(akanan) R(akjat) Kas Negara di Bengkoeloe* (Mandate Committee for people's food - state treasury Bengkulu).

		Good	Fine	XF
S161	**50 Rupiah** 1.6.1947. Red on purple unpt.	20.00	30.00	75.00

		Good	Fine	XF
S162	**100 Rupiah** 1.6.1947. Green on yellow unpt.	15.00	25.00	60.00

		Good	Fine	XF
S163	**250 Rupiah**			
	1.6.1947. Red on yellow unpt.	10.00	25.00	50.00

		Good	Fine	XF
S164	**500 Rupiah**			
	1.6.1947. Black on pink unpt.			
	a. Denomination w/thin type *ROEPIAH DJEPANG* 41 1/2mm long.	8.50	12.50	31.00

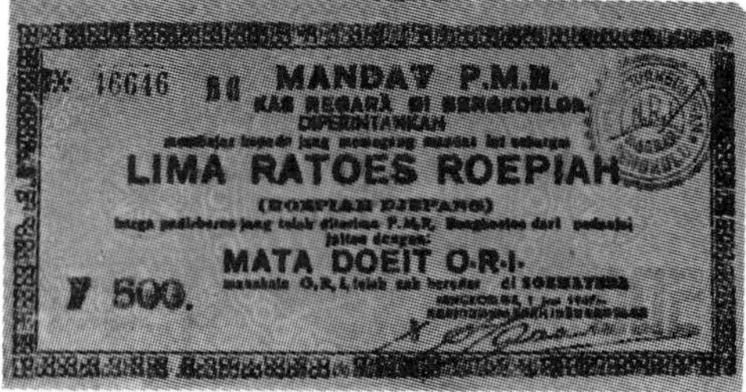

	b. Denomination w/thick serif type: *ROEPIAH DJEPANG* 48mm long.	8.00	12.00	35.00

		Good	Fine	XF
S165	**1000 Rupiah**			
	1.6.1947. Dk. brown to violet on green unpt. W/ or w/o unpt.			
	a. Blue seal, sign. and serial #.	6.00	12.00	25.00
	b. Red seal, sign. and serial #.	6.00	10.00	20.00
	c. Black seal, sign. and serial #.	8.00	12.00	20.00

1947 Sub-Province Issue

#S166-S168 red seal and sign. printed, w/o initials.

		Good	Fine	XF
S166	**1 Rupiah**			
	1.12.1947. Green. Nurse at r.	6.00	15.00	25.00

		Good	Fine	XF
S167	**5 Rupiah**			
	1.12.1947. Brown-violet. Coast scene at upper ctr.	10.00	20.00	45.00

		Good	Fine	XF
S168	**10 Rupiah**			
	1.12.1947. Blue. Country scene at l. and ctr.	7.00	15.00	30.00

Bukit Barisan

Military Governorship of South Sumatra Region.

1949 Issue

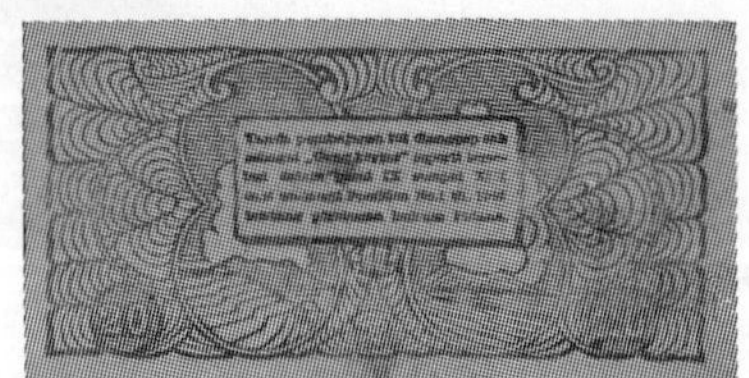

		Good	Fine	XF
S171	**20 Rupiah**			
	1.5.1949. Mounted lancer at l., buffalo at ctr.			
	a. Dk. green.	15.00	30.00	50.00
	b. Red-brown.	12.00	20.00	40.00

BUKITTINGGI

B. TINGGI

Provincial capital & municipality, West Sumatra.

PROPINSI SUMATERA
PROVINCE OF SUMATERA

1947 FIRST ISSUE

#S181-S195 central text: *Propinsi Sumatera* (Province of Sumatra).

		GOOD	FINE	XF
S181	**1/2 RUPIAH** 17.8.1947. Dk. red-brown. Religious houses.	6.00	12.00	25.00

		GOOD	FINE	XF
S182	**1 RUPIAH** 17.8.1947. Red-brown. Sukarno at l.	3.00	9.00	18.00

		GOOD	FINE	XF
S183	**2 1/2 RUPIAH** 17.8.1947. Red-brown on tan unpt. Portr. Sukarno at l.	10.00	25.00	60.00

		GOOD	FINE	XF
S184	**5 RUPIAH** 17.8.1947. Blue on lt. blue to green unpt. Sukarno at l., Borobudur temple at r.	3.00	8.00	15.00

		GOOD	FINE	XF
S185	**10 RUPIAH** 17.8.1947. Mountain scenery at l. falls at r.	3.00	8.00	15.00

		GOOD	FINE	XF
S186	**25 RUPIAH** 17.8.1947. Green. Sukarno at ctr.	20.00	40.00	60.00

1947 SECOND ISSUE

		GOOD	FINE	XF
S187	**2 1/2 RUPIAH** 17.12.1947. Mauve on yellow-green unpt. Woman at r.			
	a. W/serial #.	3.00	7.50	15.00
	b. W/block letters only.	3.00	6.00	15.50

1948 FIRST ISSUE

		GOOD	FINE	XF
S188	**1 RUPIAH** 1.1.1948. Brown.			
	a. Blue unpt. w/2 serial #.	4.00	7.00	16.00
	b. W/o unpt. w/1 serial #.	—	—	—

S189	5 RUPIAH	GOOD	FINE	XF
	1.1.1948. Green. Rising sun behind mountains at l.			
	a. 2 serial #.	1.50	4.00	12.00
	b. 1 serial #.	1.50	4.00	12.00

S190	10 RUPIAH	GOOD	FINE	XF
	1.1.1948. Rice stalks at l., coconut at r.			
	a. Purple on yellow unpt.	1.50	4.00	12.00
	b. Blue on green unpt.	1.50	4.00	12.00
	c. Blue, w/o unpt.	1.50	4.00	12.00

S191	25 RUPIAH	GOOD	FINE	XF
	17.1.1948. Transports at l.			
	a. Red (color variations from orange to brown-violet).	2.00	5.00	10.00
	b. Green.	3.00	6.00	15.00
	c. Blue, w/o unpt. Black serial #.	6.00	11.00	20.00
	d. Black, w/o unpt. Red serial #.	4.00	8.00	15.00
	e. As a. Printed on tissue paper.	5.00	10.00	20.00

NOTE: For #S191a, d, 184, 189, 192 w/*segel-inflasi R5* (inflation stamp) see #S410a-b.

1948 SECOND ISSUE

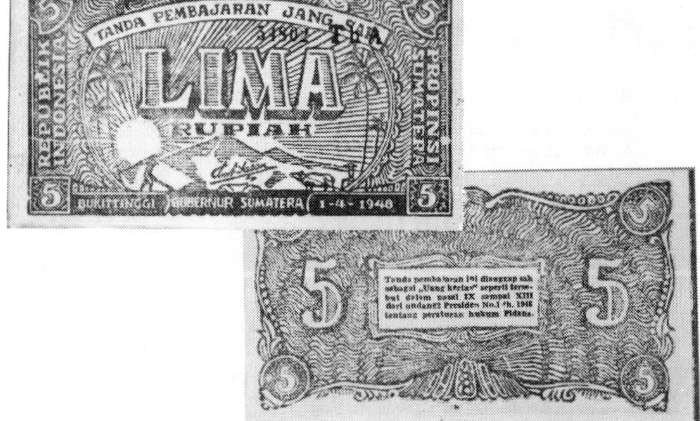

S192	5 RUPIAH	GOOD	FINE	XF
	1.4.1948. Rising sun behind mountains. Like #S189.			
	a. Green, red serial #.	2.00	5.00	11.00
	b. Brown on yellow unpt. Black serial #.	1.50	4.00	10.00
	c. Brown, red serial #. W/o unpt.	1.50	4.00	10.00

S193	10 RUPIAH	GOOD	FINE	XF
	1.4.1948. Like #S190.			
	a. Dk. green on yellow unpt.	1.50	3.00	8.00
	b. Lt. green.	1.50	3.00	8.00

S194	50 RUPIAH	GOOD	FINE	XF
	1.4.1948. Factory at l.; refinery at r.			
	a. Dk. brown on yellow unpt.	3.00	8.00	15.00
	b. Lt. brown to red-brown, w/o unpt.	3.00	8.00	15.00
	c. Green on yellow unpt.	8.00	12.00	25.00

NOTE: For #S194 w/text ovpt. (1949) see #S412.

S195	100 RUPIAH	GOOD	FINE	XF
	17.4.1948.			
	a. Green on pink unpt.	17.50	30.00	55.00
	b. Brown-red, w/o unpt.	10.00	25.00	45.00
	c. Black, w/o unpt., handwritten serial #. (Printed in Djambi).	17.50	30.00	55.00

SUMATERA SELATAN
SOUTH SUMATERA

1948 ISSUE

#S201-S203 central text: ***Berlaku untuk sub propinsi Sumatera Selatan*** **(Valid in the sub-province of South Sumatera).**

		GOOD	FINE	XF
S201	**1 RUPIAH** 1.1.1948. Green.	3.00	6.00	12.00

		GOOD	FINE	XF
S202	**2 1/2 RUPIAH** 1.1.1948. Red on yellow unpt.	2.00	4.00	8.00

		GOOD	FINE	XF
S203	**10 RUPIAH** 1.1.1948. Lt. blue to dk. blue. Temple at r.	2.50	6.00	11.00

NOTE: All notes are signed by the Governor of Sumatra, Teuku A. M. Hassan.

SUMATERA TIMUR
EAST SUMATERA

A Residency.

1948 ISSUE

#S211-S213 central text: ***Sumatera Timur*** **(East Sumatera).**

		GOOD	FINE	XF
S211	**10 SEN** 1.1.1948. Lilac on gray unpt.	—	—	—
S212	**1/2 RUPIAH** 1.1.1948. Purple on gray unpt.	—	—	—

		GOOD	FINE	XF
S213	**5 RUPIAH** 1.1.1948. Blue on gray unpt. Lake at ctr.	10.00	25.00	45.00

NOTE: All notes are signed by the Governor of Sumatra, Teuku A. M. Hassan.

SUMATERA BARAT
WEST SUMATERA

1948 ISSUE

#S221 central text: ***Berlaku untuk daerah S. Barat*** **(Valid for the of West Sumatra region).**

		GOOD	FINE	XF
S221	**10 RUPIAH** 17.1.1948. Blue. Imam Bonjol at l., traditional houses at r.	10.00	25.00	45.00

NOTE: All notes are signed by the Governor of Sumatra, Teuku A. M. Hassan.

ATJEH
ATCHEH

A Residency in the northern tip of Sumatra.

1948 ISSUE

#S231 and S232 central text: ***Berlaku untuk daerah Atjeh*** **(Valid for the Atcheh region).**

		GOOD	FINE	XF
S231	**10 RUPIAH** 1.1.1948. Blue. Great Mosque at r.	10.00	25.00	45.00

		GOOD	FINE	XF
S232	**25 RUPIAH** 1.1.1948. Terraced rice field at l.			
	a. Green on yellow unpt.	20.00	40.00	60.00
	b. Blue on yellow unpt.	25.00	45.00	65.00
	c. Brown.	20.00	40.00	60.00

NOTE: All notes are signed by the Governor of Sumatra, Teuku A. M. Hassan.

DJAMBI

A Residency in Central Sumatra.

1947 ISSUE

#S236 central text: ***Berlaku untuk daerah Djambi*** **(Valid for the Djambi region).**

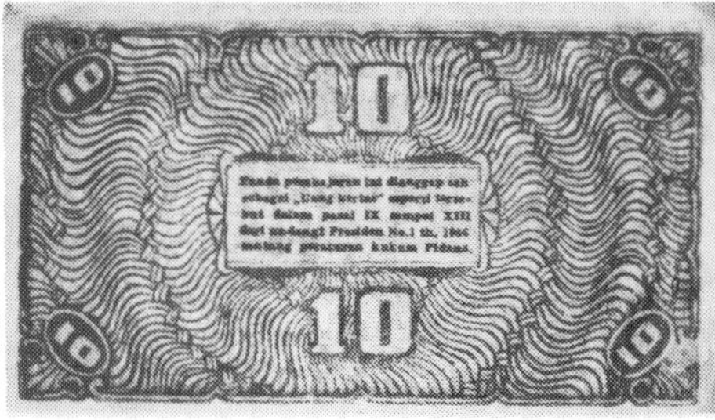

		Good	Fine	XF
S236	**10 Rupiah** 17.12.1947. Blue on green unpt. Ships at l.	10.00	25.00	45.00

NOTE: All notes are signed by the Governor of Sumatra, Teuku A. M. Hassan.

Riau

1947 Issue

#S241 central text: *Berlaku untuk daerah Riau* (Valid in the Riau region).

		Good	Fine	XF
S241	**5 Rupiah** 17.12.1947. Female dancer at l.			
	a. Dk. brown, dk. brown-green unpt.	10.00	25.00	45.00
	b. Green.	20.00	40.00	65.00

NOTE: All notes are signed by the Governor of Sumatra, Teuku A. M. Hassan.

Tapanoeli

Tapanuli

A Residency in Northern Sumatra.

1948 Issue

#S251 central text: *Berlaku buat daerah Tapanuli* (Valid for the Tapanuli region).

		Good	Fine	XF
S251	**5 Rupiah** 1.1.1948. Dk. Blue. Toba lake at ctr.	10.00	25.00	45.00

#S252 and S253 *Deleted.*

NOTE: Notes are signed by the Governor of Sumatra, Teuku A. M. Hassan.

Djambi

Residency in Southeast Sumatra.

1947 Issues

#S261-S263B w/handwritten # and hand stamped sign.

		Good	Fine	XF
S261	**1/2 Rupiah** 1947. Red.			
	a. 24.10.1947.	17.50	32.50	50.00
	b. 28.11.1947.	17.50	32.50	50.00

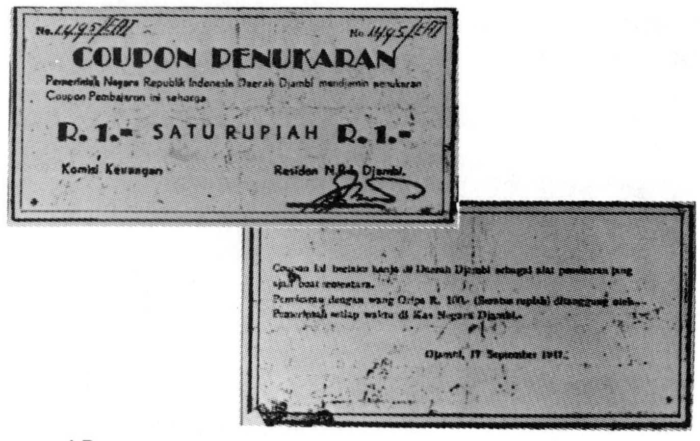

		Good	Fine	XF
S262	**1 Rupiah** 17.9.1947. Black.			
	a. L.h. sign. title: *a/n Ketua Muda D.P.R.*	15.00	30.00	50.00
	b. L.h. sign. title: *Ketua Muda D.P.R.*	15.00	30.00	50.00
	c. L.h. sign. title: *Komisi Keuangan.*	15.00	30.00	50.00

		Good	Fine	XF
S263	**2 1/2 Rupiah** Red.			
	a. 24.10.1947.	15.00	25.00	45.00
	b. 28.11.1947.	15.00	25.00	45.00
S263A	**5 Rupiah** 17.11.1947. Black.	—	—	—

		Good	Fine	XF
S263B	**10 Rupiah** 17.11.1947. Black.	—	—	—

1947; 1948 Issue

#S263C-S269 w/printed # and sign., also stamped letters.

		Good	Fine	XF
S263C	**1 Rupiah** Blue on lt. green unpt.			
	a. 31.3.1948.	17.50	30.00	50.00
	b. 1.4.1948.	17.50	30.00	50.00

S264 2 1/2 RUPIAH
1947. Similar to #S267.

	GOOD	FINE	XF
a. 27.12.1917. Red on yellow unpt.	7.50	15.00	30.00
b. 20.15.1947.	3.00	8.00	15.00

S265 5 RUPIAH
1947; 1948. Red on yellow unpt.

	GOOD	FINE	XF
a. 27.12.1947.	11.00	16.00	26.00
b. 31.3.1948.	7.50	12.00	25.00

S266 10 RUPIAH
1947; 1948. Red on pale red unpt.

	GOOD	FINE	XF
a. 27.12.1947.	12.50	25.00	40.00
b. 31.3.1948.	12.50	25.00	40.00

1948 ISSUE

S268 5 RUPIAH

	GOOD	FINE	XF
20.5.1948. Lt. green on yellow unpt.	6.00	15.00	30.00

S269 25 RUPIAH

	GOOD	FINE	XF
20.5.1948. Brown-red on blue-green unpt.	17.00	27.00	42.00

NOTE: #S270-S279, formerly listed here, see #S319-S319L.

KOETARADJA

KUTARADJA

A. Capital of the Atcheh residency 1945-49.

B. Capital of the Province of North Sumatra 1949-51.

1947-48 ISSUE

#S281-S284A *Keresidenan Atjeh* (Atcheh residency).

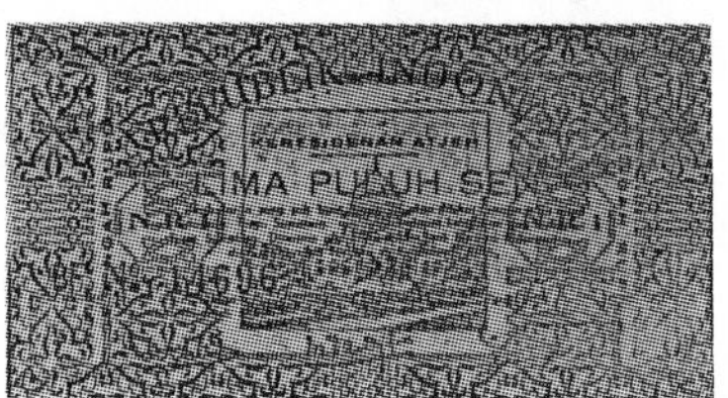

S281 1/2 RUPIAH

	GOOD	FINE	XF
15.9.1947. Black on yellow. Great Mosque at ctr.	10.00	20.00	40.00

S282 1 RUPIAH

	GOOD	FINE	XF
15.9.1947. Black on pink.	7.50	15.00	30.00

S283 2 1/2 RUPIAH

	GOOD	FINE	XF
15.9.1947. Black on green.	7.50	18.00	35.00

S283A 2 1/2 RUPIAH

1.12.1947. Brown. Scenery in ctr.	—	—	—

S283B 5 RUPIAH

1.12.1947. Dk. blue. 5 in circles.	—	—	—

S283C 10 RUPIAH
(S284A)

	GOOD	FINE	XF
1.12.1947. Black. 10 in circles.	—	Rare	—

S284 5 RUPIAH

15.1.1948. Black on green. Sukarno at l.	—	Rare	—

1949 Issues

#S285-S286 central text: *Daerah Sumatera Utara* (District of North Sumatra).

		Good	Fine	XF
S285	**250 Rupiah** 1.3.1949. Blue on yellow unpt. Atchenese dagger at r. 160 x 84mm.	7.50	25.00	50.00

		Good	Fine	XF
S286	**250 Rupiah** 1.3.1949. Black on purple unpt. Atchenese dagger. 120 x 63mm.	6.00	12.50	30.00

Kutatjane

A town in the Acech Residency.

1948 Issue

#S291-S293 are of Res(imen) I Div(ision) X of the Tentara Negara Indonesia (National Army of Indonesia), Southeast Atcheh.

		Good	Fine	XF
S291	**1 Rupiah** 1948. Black on yellow unpt. Guns.	—	—	—
S292	**5 Rupiah** 1948. Black. Soldiers.	—	—	—
S293	**10 Rupiah** 1948. Black on red unpt. Landscape.	—	—	—

NOTE: Former #S301-S303 are the same as #S361, S362 and S370.

Laboehan Bilore

1948 Issue

		Good	Fine	XF
S306	**5 Rupiah** 23.12.1947.	—	—	—
S307	**10 Rupiah** 23.12.1947.	—	—	—

Labuhan Bilik

District in Northeast Sumatra.

1948 Issues

		Good	Fine	XF
S308	**25 Rupiah** 23.12.1948. Black.	—	—	—

		Good	Fine	XF
S309	**100 Rupiah** 19.1.1948. *100* in block l. and r.			
	a. Black.	—	—	—
	b. Green.	—	—	—
S310	**100 Rupiah** 5.2.1948. Like #S309.			
	a. Blue.	—	—	—
	b. Red-brown.	—	—	—

		Good	Fine	XF
S311	**100 Rupiah** 14.2.1948. Coastal scenery at l. and r.	—	—	—
S311A	**10,000 Rupiah** 24.2.1948. Red.	—	—	—

		Good	Fine	XF
S311B	**50,000 Rupiah** 6.3.1948.	—	—	—
S312	**100,000 Rupiah** 24.2.1948. Red.	—	—	—
S312A	**250,000 Rupiah** 25.3.1948. Orange.	—	—	—
S313	**500,000 Rupiah** 9.4.1948. Black.	—	—	—

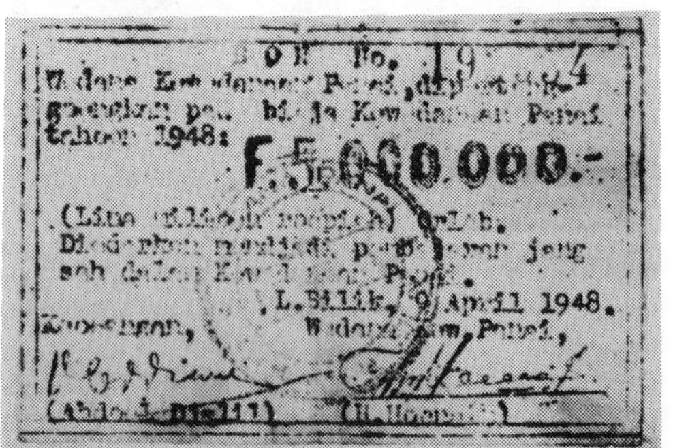

		Good	Fine	XF
S313A	**5,000,000 Rupiah** 9.4.1948.	—	—	—
S313B	**25,000,000 Rupiah** 7.5.1948. Similar to #S313A.	—	—	—
S314	**25,000,000 Rupiah** 7.5.1948. Black.	—	—	—

Langsa

Defensive quarter of East Atcheh, Northeast Sumatra.

1949 Issue

		Good	Fine	XF
S316	**100 Rupiah** 2.1.1949. Red.			
	a. W/o signature.	—	—	—
	b. W/ signatures.	—	—	—

		Good	Fine	XF
S317	**250 Rupiah** 2.1.1949.			
	a. Black.	35.00	105.00	175.00
	b. Green.	35.00	105.00	175.00

NOTE: Modern fakes of #S316, S317 w/coarse paper exist.

Small district previously a kingdom located in Northeast Sumatra. Bon Sementara (Provisional Coupons).

1947 ISSUE

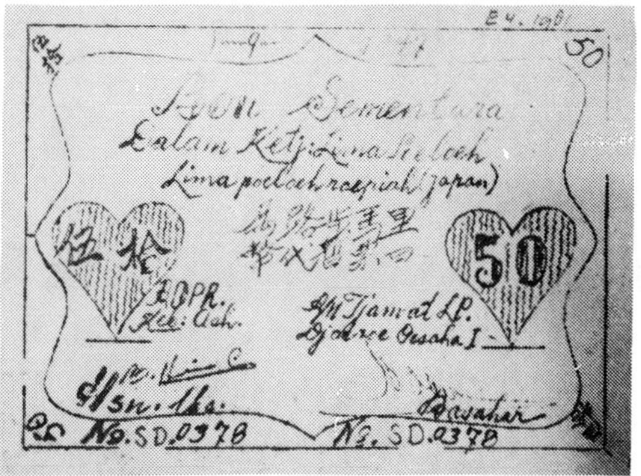

		GOOD	FINE	XF
S318	**50 RUPIAH** 1.9.1947. Red. Value in heart-shaped guilloche at l. and r. Blue hand stamp on back.	—	Rare	—

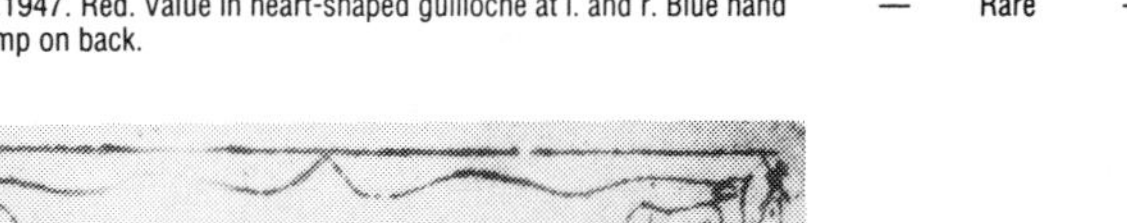

		GOOD	FINE	XF
S318A	**100 RUPIAH** 1.9.1947; 10.9.1947. Red. Value in diamond design at ctr.	—	Rare	—

MEMBANG MOEDA (M. MUDA)

Capital of Kocaloch Leidong District.

1947-48 ISSUES

		GOOD	FINE	XF
S319A	**50 RUPIAH** 1.9.1947. Black.	—	—	—

		GOOD	FINE	XF
S319B (S319)	**100 RUPIAH** 1.9.1947. Red.	—	—	—
S319C	**250 RUPIAH** 10.1947. Green. 2 lines of trees at l. or r.	—	—	—

		GOOD	FINE	XF
S319D	**1000 RUPIAH** 10.12.1947. Red-brown. Coconut tree at l. and r.	—	—	—

		GOOD	FINE	XF
S319E (S319A)	**2500 RUPIAH** 1.1.1948. Dk. brown. Lightning at l. and r.	—	—	—
S319F (S319B)	**5000 RUPIAH** 15.1.1948. Brown. Mountain scene at l. and r.	—	—	—
S319G	**10,000 RUPIAH** 20.1.1948. Brown. Lighthouse at l. and r. Palms at l. and r.	—	—	—

		GOOD	FINE	XF
S319H	**10,000 RUPIAH** 10.2.1948. Brown. Tree at l. and r.	—	—	—
S319I	**25,000 RUPIAH** 22.2.1948. Brown. Trees at l. and r.	—	—	—
S319J	**50,000 RUPIAH** 3.3.1948. Green. Floral design.	—	—	—
S319K (S319H)	**250,000 RUPIAH** 15.2.1948 Green. Value in floral design.	—	—	—

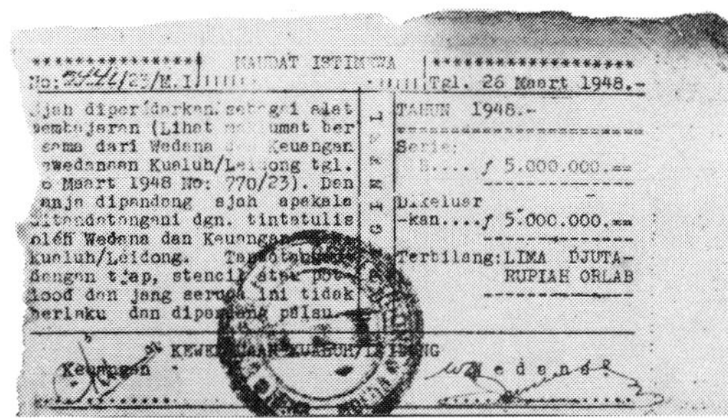

		GOOD	FINE	XF
S320	**5,000,000 RUPIAH** 26.3.1948. Black. Full text.	—	—	—
S320A	**10,000,000 RUPIAH** 5.4.1948. Black. Similar to #S320.	—	—	—
S320B	**10,000,000 RUPIAH** 12.4.1948.			
	a. Full text 8 x 17cm.	—	—	—
	b. Short text 6 x 11.5cm.	—	Rare	—

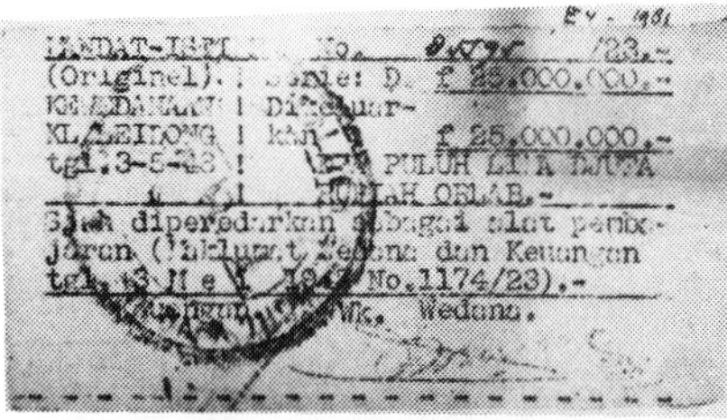

		GOOD	FINE	XF
S320C (S320B)	**25,000,000 RUPIAH** 3.5.1948. Black.	—	—	—

NIAS

Nias Regency, an island northwest of Sumatra.

1947-49 ISSUES

#S321-S324 central text: ***Alat pembajar berlaku dalam Kabupaten Nias*** **(Legal tender valid in the Nias regency).**

		GOOD	FINE	XF
S321	**1 RUPIAH** 25.9.1947. Black on yellow unpt.	—	—	—
S321A	**100 RUPIAH** 20.12.1948. Black.	—	—	—
S321B	**200 RUPIAH** 20.12.1948. Black on yellow, leaves all around.	—	—	—

#S322 ***Deleted.***

		Good	Fine	XF
S323	**500 Rupiah**			
	5.1.1949. Leaves all around.			
	a. Black on green.	10.00	30.00	60.00
	b. Black on orange unpt.	20.00	40.00	60.00
	c. Black on lt. blue.	10.00	20.00	40.00
S324	**500 Rupiah**			
	7.1.1949. Green.	7.50	25.00	50.00

		Good	Fine	XF
S325	**500 Rupiah**			
	12.11.1949. Black on lt. blue unpt.	—	—	—

P. Alam

Pagar Alam

Town in South Sumatra.

1947 Issue

		Good	Fine	XF
S326	**10 Rupiah**			
	12.17.1947. Black. Eagle on mountain at l.	—	—	—

		Good	Fine	XF
S327	**50 Rupiah**			
	17.12.1947. Red. Eagle on mountain at lower ctr. Uniface.	—	—	—
S328	**100 Rupiah**			
	17.12.1947. Blue. Eagle on mountain at ctr.	—	—	—

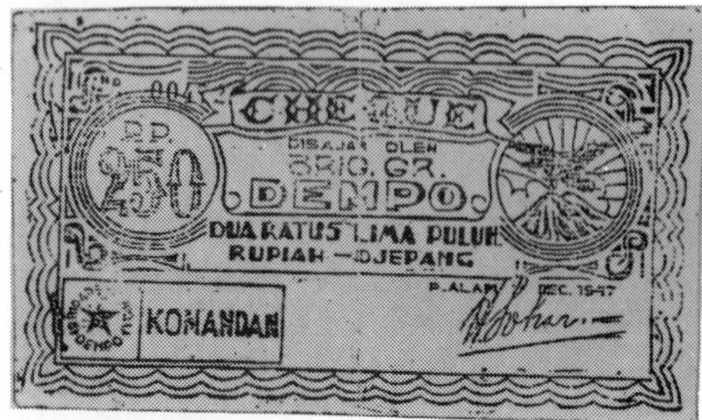

		Good	Fine	XF
S329	**250 Rupiah**			
	17.12.1947. Black. Eagle on mountain at r.	—	—	—
S330	**1000 Rupiah**			
	17.12.1947. Red. Eagle and mountain at l. ctr.	—	—	—

Palembang

Palembang Residency, Southeast Sumatra.

1947 Issues

#S331-S335 central text: *Mandat D(ewan) P(ertahanan) D(aerah) P(alembang)* (Mandate Board of Defense District of Palembang).

		Good	Fine	XF
S331 (S330A)	**50 Rupiah**			
	1.8.1947. Flag in circle at l. and r.			
	a. Blue.	—	—	—
	b. Green.	—	—	—

		Good	Fine	XF
S332	**250 Rupiah**			
	1.8.1947. Red.	7.50	25.00	50.00

		Good	Fine	XF
S333	**500 Rupiah**			
	1.8.1947. Green on brown.	—	—	—

		Good	Fine	XF
S334	**1000 Rupiah**			
	1.8.1947. Blue. *1000* in 4 corners. Value at l., blue seal.	3.00	8.00	20.00

		Good	Fine	XF
S335	**1000 Rupiah**			
	1.8.1947. Blue to blue-green on lt. green unpt. Value at l., blue seal.			
	a. Blue.	5.00	8.00	20.00
	b. Blue. Uniface.	6.00	9.00	20.00
	c. Green.	8.00	12.00	25.00
	d. Green. Uniface.	8.00	12.00	25.00

1949 First Issue

#S336 and S337 text: ***Cheque Keresidenan Palembang*****. Palembang.**

		Good	Fine	XF
S336	**10 Rupiah** 17.4.1949. Gray. Rice field. Uniface.	7.50	25.00	50.00

		Good	Fine	XF
S337	**50 Rupiah** 17.4.1949. Coconut tree at l. Uniface.			
	a. Black.	7.50	25.00	50.00
	b. Green.	6.00	17.50	45.00

1949 Second Issue

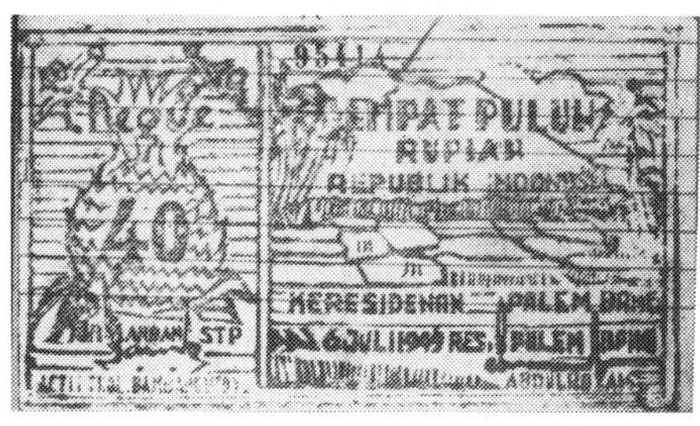

		Good	Fine	XF
S338	**40 Rupiah** 6.7.1949. Pineapple at l. Text: *Cheque Keresidenan Palembang.* Uniface.			
	a. Red.	7.50	25.00	50.00
	b. Green.	12.00	25.00	50.00
	c. Orange.	8.00	20.00	40.00
	d. Dk. brown.	10.00	25.00	50.00
S339	**50 Rupiah** 18.11.1949. Leaves and candle.			
	a. Blue.	—	—	—
	b. Black.	—	—	—

Pekanbaru

Capital of Riau Residency, Central Sumatra.

1940 Exchange Coupon Issue

		Good	Fine	XF
S342	**1 Rupiah** 1.7.1940. Green.	—	—	—

Pematang Siantar

Capital of Sumatra Province, later replaced by Bukuttinggi.

1947 Issue

#S351-S354 central text: ***Propinsi Soematera*** **(Province of Sumatra).**

		Good	Fine	XF
S351	**1 Rupiah** 31.3.1947. Dk. red on blue unpt. Portr. Sukarno at l., volcano at r.	5.00	9.00	20.00

		Good	Fine	XF
S352	**5 Rupiah** 31.3.1947. Sukarno at l.			
	a. Green on yellow unpt.	4.00	8.00	17.50
	b. Blue on red unpt.	6.00	12.50	25.00

		Good	Fine	XF
S353	**10 Rupiah** 31.3.1947. Sukarno at l.			
	a. Deep purple on pink unpt.	3.00	6.00	20.00
	b. Green on lt. green unpt.	4.00	8.00	22.50
	x. Blue-violet on lilac unpt. (Counterfeit).	—	—	—

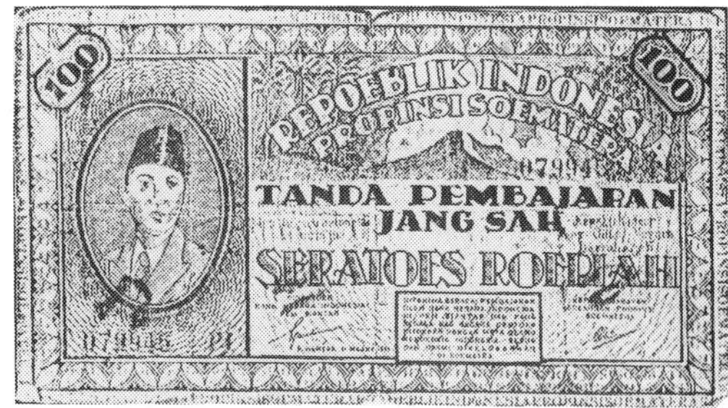

		Good	Fine	XF
S354	**100 Rupiah** 31.3.1947. Sukarno at l.			
	a. Lilac on yellow and lt. blue unpt.	10.00	25.00	60.00
	b. Violet on yellow and lt. blue unpt.	10.00	25.00	60.00

NOTE: Modern fakes of #S345 exists (prefix CN).

Pendopo

Capital of Lintang IV Lowang District, South Sumatra.

1949 Issue

		Good	Fine	XF
S354A	**10 Rupiah** 17.1.1949. Black. Uniface.	—	—	—

		Good	Fine	XF
S355	**25 Rupiah** 17.1.1949. Uniface.			
	a. Red.	—	—	—
	b. Black.	—	—	—

NOTE: For #S355 w/inflation strip, see #S411C.

RANTAU PRAPAT

Labuhan Batu Regency, Northeast Sumatra.

1947-48 ISSUES

#S361-S374 central text: *Kaboepaten Laboean Batoe, Rantau Prapat* (Labuan Batu regency, Rantauprapat). Mimeographed.

		Good	Fine	XF
S361	**2 1/2 Rupiah** ND(1947). Value in ctr.	—	—	—
S361A	**5 Rupiah** ND(1947). Black. Value in ctr.	—	—	—
S362	**10 Rupiah** ND(1947). Value in ctr.	—	—	—
S363	**50 Rupiah** ND(1947). Black. Value in ctr.	—	—	—

		Good	Fine	XF
S364	**100 Rupiah** ND(1947).			
	a. Red.	15.00	30.00	60.00
	b. Black.	15.00	30.00	60.00
S364A	**500 Rupiah** ND(1947). Red. Value in upper & lower block.	—	—	—

		Good	Fine	XF
S364B	**1000 Rupiah** 29.11.1947; 4.12.1947. Blue. Value on 3 blocks.	—	—	—
S365	**2500 Rupiah** 22.12.1947-10.1.1948. Value in 2 blocks and lozenge.			
	a. Red-violet.	—	—	—
	b. Red.	—	—	—
	c. Black.	—	—	—

		Good	Fine	XF
S366	**5000 Rupiah** 9.1.1948-5.3.1948. Value in l. and r. circle.			
	a. Blue.	—	—	—
	b. Black.	—	—	—

		Good	Fine	XF
S367	**10,000 Rupiah** 3.2.1948-21.2.1948. Coconut tree at upper ctr., banana tree at upper r.			
	a. Blue.	—	—	—
	b. Black.	—	—	—
S367A	**10,000 Rupiah** 6.2.1948-21.2.1948. Value within three conjoined circles.			
	a. Blue.	—	—	—
	b. Black.	—	—	—
S368	**25,000 Rupiah** 1948. Leaves at l., value at ctr.			
	a. Black.	—	—	—
	b. Blue.	—	—	—

		Good	Fine	XF
S369	**50,000 Rupiah** 23.2.1948-17.3.1948. Leaves at l.			
	a. Blue.	—	—	—
	b. Black.	—	—	—

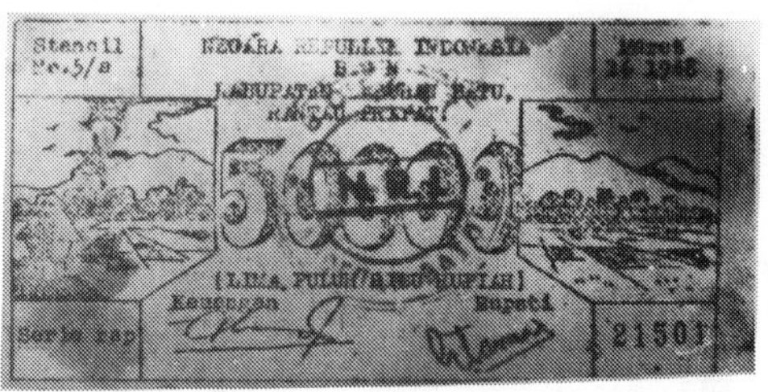

		Good	Fine	XF
S369A	**50,000 Rupiah** 16.3.1948. Mountain scenes at l. and r.	—	—	—
S370	**250,000 Rupiah** 18.3.1948-24.3.1948. Palm tree at l., mountain scene at r.			
	a. Blue.	—	—	—
	b. Red.	—	—	—
	c. Black.	—	—	—

		Good	Fine	XF
S370A	**250,000 Rupiah** 10.3.1948-26.3.1948. Black. Trees at l. and r.	—	—	—
S370B	**250,000 Rupiah** 1.4.1948. Black. Value in ctr. square.	—	—	—
S370C	**250,000 Rupiah** 3.4.1948.	—	—	—
S370D	**250,000 Rupiah** 6.4.1948.	—	—	—
S370E	**250,000 Rupiah** ND(1948). Green. Value in ctr. square.	—	—	—

		Good	Fine	XF
S371	**5,000,000 Rupiah** 9.21.1948-24.4.1948. Black. Trees at ctr.			
	a. Black.	—	—	—
	b. Blue.	—	—	—
	c. Orange.	—	—	—

	GOOD	FINE	XF
S371A 5,000,000 RUPIAH 14.4.1948. Black. Value in ctr. block.	—	—	—

	GOOD	FINE	XF
S372 25,000,000 RUPIAH 9.4.1948-8.5.1948. Mountains at lower ctr.			
a. Red.	—	—	—
b. Brown.	—	—	—
c. Black.	—	—	—
d. Green.	—	—	—

	GOOD	FINE	XF
S374 25,000,000 RUPIAH 12.5.1948. Black.	—	—	—

TANDJUNGKARANG

Capital of the Lampung Residency, South Sumatra.

1947 ISSUES

#S380-S381 central text: *Mandat Pertahanan Daerah Lampung* (Defense Mandate of Lampung Region).

	GOOD	FINE	XF
S380 25 RUPIAH 15.11.1947. Black w/red seal, 1 red and 1 black sign.	15.00	30.00	60.00

	GOOD	FINE	XF
S381 25 RUPIAH 15.11.1947. Orange and black w/violet seal, 1 blue and 1 black sign. Like #S380 but w/floral unpt.	18.00	35.00	75.00

1948 FIRST ISSUE

#S382-S383 w/one handwritten initial each. Central text: *Mandat Pertahanan Keresidenan Lampung* (Defense Mandate Lampung Residency).

	GOOD	FINE	XF
S382 50 RUPIAH 15.1.1948. Black. Dagger at l.			
a. Red seal.	10.00	20.00	50.00
b. Black seal.	10.00	20.00	50.00
c. Blue seal.	15.00	25.00	60.00

	GOOD	FINE	XF
S383 100 RUPIAH 15.1.1948. Black. Female at l.			
a. Red seal.	15.00	30.00	60.00
b. Black seal.	15.00	30.00	60.00
c. Blue seal.	20.00	35.00	65.00

1948 SECOND ISSUE

#S384-S388 central text: *Republik Indonesia, Propinsi Sumatera, Keresidenan Lampung* (Republic of Indonesia, Province of Sumatera, Lampung Residency).

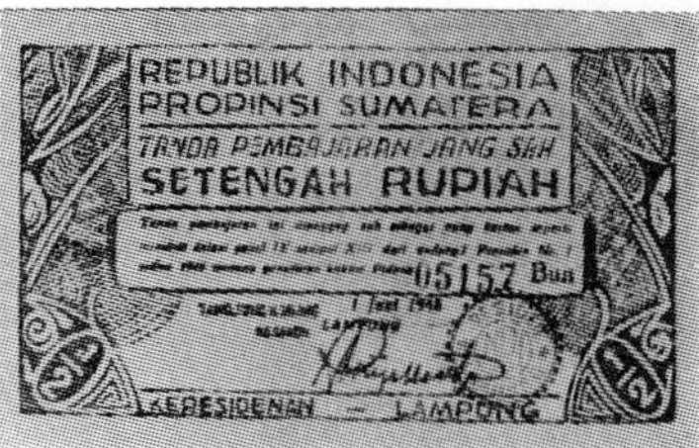

	GOOD	FINE	XF
S384 1/2 RUPIAH 1.6.1948. Gray-green. Uniface.			
a. Red seal, red serial #.	3.00	8.00	20.00
b. Black seal, black serial #.	3.00	8.00	20.00

S385 1 RUPIAH

1.6.1948. Dk. purple. Uniface.

	GOOD	FINE	XF
a. Blue seal.	3.00	9.00	20.00
b. Black seal.	2.50	5.00	12.50
c. Red seal.	2.00	4.00	10.00

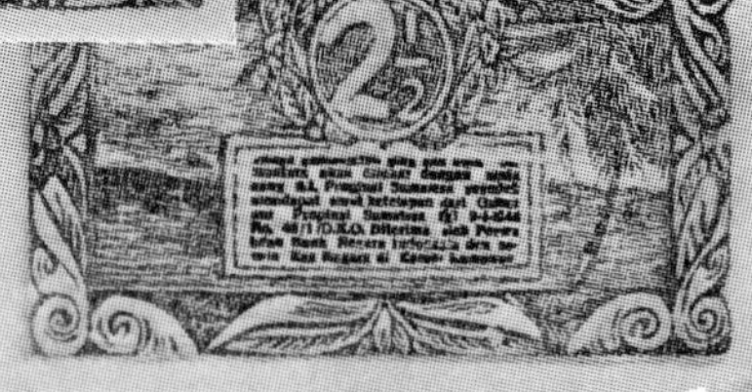

S386 2 1/2 RUPIAH

1.6.1948.

	GOOD	FINE	XF
a. Red.	2.00	5.00	10.00
b. Pink.	2.50	6.00	10.00

S387 5 RUPIAH

1.6.1948. Black. Industry at l., trees at r.

	GOOD	FINE	XF
a. Red seal, red serial #.	3.00	8.00	15.00
b. Black seal, black serial #.	3.00	8.00	15.00

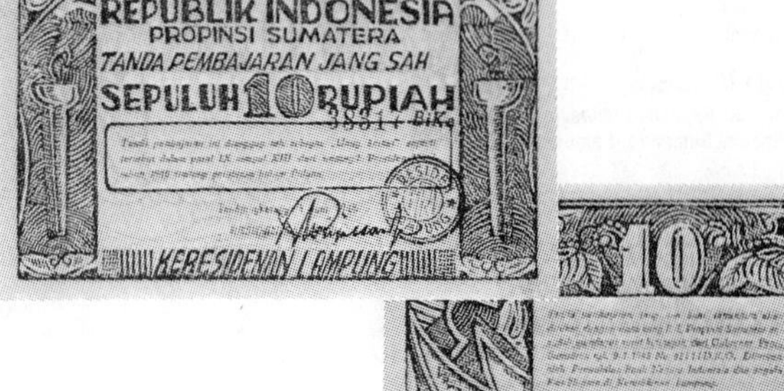

S388 10 RUPIAH

1.6.1948. Black. Dagger at l. and r.

	GOOD	FINE	XF
a. Red seal, red serial #.	3.00	8.00	17.00
b. Black seal, black serial #.	3.00	8.00	17.00

TAPANOELI

TAPANULI DISTRICT

Tapanuli Residency, North Sumatra.

All notes bear one handwritten sign. on face and four or five stamped sign. (in blue) on back. The following charts show the known sign.

SIGNATURES

1.	2.	3.	4.
5.	6.	7.	8.
9.	10.	11.	12.
13.	14.	15.	16.
17.	18.	19.	20.
21.	22.		

a	b	c	d

1947-48 ISSUES

#S390-S398 central text: ***Alat pembajar berlakoe dalam daerah Tapanoeli*** **(Legal tender valid in the district Tapanuli).**

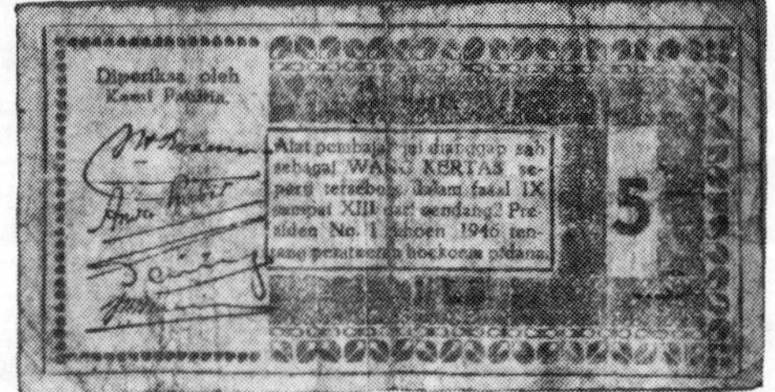

S390 5 RUPIAH

8.8.1947. Black on red. *Harga R 5.*

GOOD	FINE	XF
12.50	25.00	55.00

		Good	Fine	XF
S391	**10 Rupiah** 8.9.1947. Black on pink unpt. Central text: *Harga R 10.*	25.00	40.00	86.00

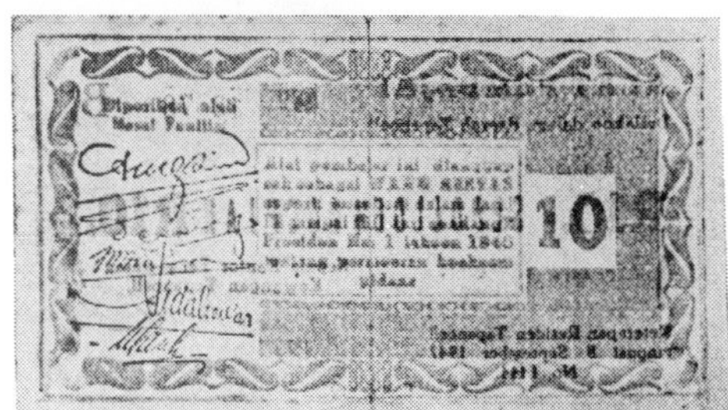

		Good	Fine	XF
S392	**10 Rupiah** 8.9.1947. Black on red unpt. Central text: *R 10.*	20.00	30.00	60.00

#S393 Deleted.

		Good	Fine	XF
S394	**25 Rupiah** 18.11.1947. Black on pink. Central text: *Harga R 25.*	15.00	35.00	75.00

		Good	Fine	XF
S395	**25 Rupiah** 18.11.1947. Central text: *R 25.*	7.50	20.00	50.00

		Good	Fine	XF
S396	**50 Rupiah** 28.4.1948. Black on pink.			
	a. Number of decree *464* (lower l. corner).	12.50	27.50	60.00
	b. Number of decree *646* (lower l. corner).	10.00	25.00	55.00

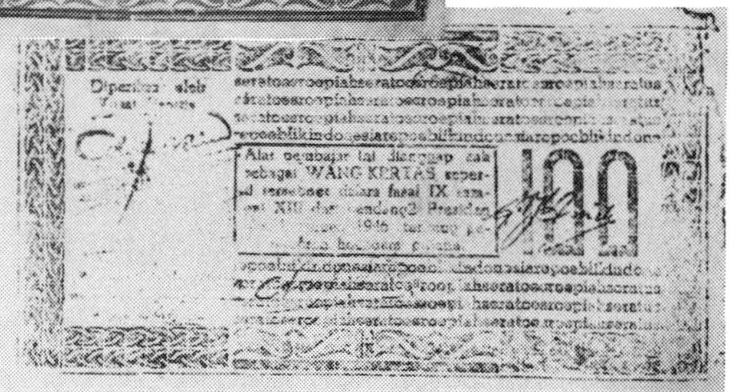

		Good	Fine	XF
S397	**100 Rupiah** 11.10.1948.			
	a. Black on lt. red.	12.50	30.00	65.00
	b. Black on green.	15.00	35.00	70.00
	c. Black on yellow-green.	12.50	30.00	65.00

		Good	Fine	XF
S398	**200 Rupiah** 23.11.1948. Black on green.			
	a. Green unpt.	20.00	45.00	90.00
	b. Yellow unpt.	15.00	40.00	85.00

TIGABINANGA

Karo Regency, north of Lake Toba, North Sumatera.

1947-49 ISSUE

		Good	Fine	XF
S399	**50 Rupiah** 17.9.1947. Black. Typewritten.	—	—	—
S400	**100 Rupiah** 3.11.1947. Black. Typewritten.	—	—	—

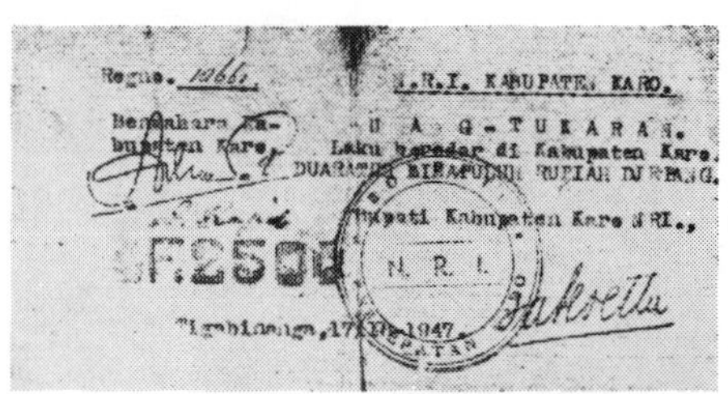

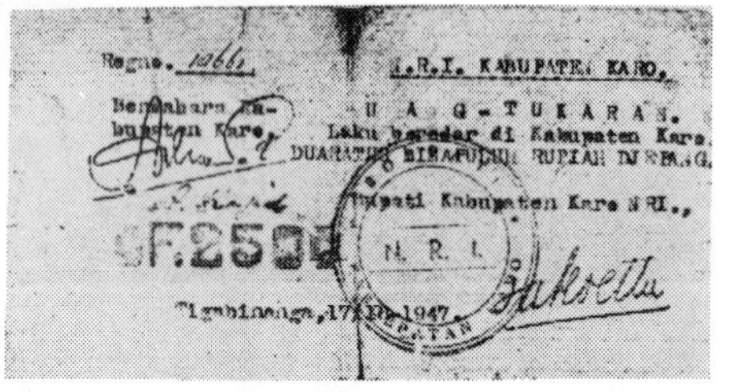

S401 250 RUPIAH
17.9.1947; 17.10.1947; 20.11.1947. Black. Typewritten.

	GOOD	FINE	XF
	—	—	—

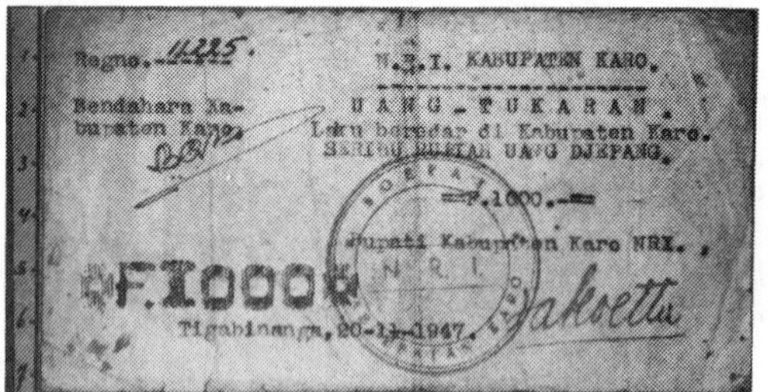

S402 1000 RUPIAH
20.11.1947.

	GOOD	FINE	XF
a. Red.	—	—	—
b. Blue.	—	—	—
c. Black.	—	—	—

NOTE: Modern fakes of #S401-S402 exist.

#S403 *Deleted.*

TJURUP

CURUP

Capital of South Sumatra Province.

1949 ISSUE

S406 40 RUPIAH
17.1.1949. Purple on yellow unpt. Soldier w/rifle at r.

	GOOD	FINE	XF
	3.00	10.00	25.00

A word on date ranges

Often date ranges or specific dates are listed. These have been observed or reported by our contributors. If a note is outside the published range, it only means that it is a newly reported date, and not necessarily worthy of a premium value.

DAERAH MILITER ISTIMEWA SUMATERA SELATAN

SPECIAL MILITARY REGION OF SOUTH SUMATRA

No place of issue shown.

1949 ND PROVISIONAL ISSUE

S410 5 RUPIAH
ND (1949). Yellow.

	GOOD	FINE	XF
a. Adhesive stamp on #S189.	5.00	10.00	20.00
b. Adhesive stamp on #S192.	5.00	10.00	20.00
c. Adhesive stamp on #S352.	5.00	10.00	20.00
d. Adhesive stamp on #S387.	—	—	—

#S411 w/inflation stamp 25 rupiah 1949.

S411 25 RUPIAH
ND (1949 -old date 17.1.1948). Red or yellow unpt.

	GOOD	FINE	XF
a. Adhesive stamp on #S191a.	2.00	8.00	15.00
b. Adhesive stamp on #S191d.	2.00	8.00	15.00
c. Adhesive stamp on #S355.	—	—	—

#S412 w/long ovpt. 1949. Red ovpt. w/ornamental border and serial #.

S412 50 RUPIAH
ND (1949 -old date 1.4.1948). Back ovpt. text on #S194.

	GOOD	FINE	XF
	4.00	10.00	25.00

NOTE: The military governor of South Sumatra called in all notes of 5 and 25 rupiah and for every two notes one was returned w/stamp in an attempt to control inflation.

KOTABUMI

Capital of North Lampung regency, Southern Sumatra.

No place of issue shown.

1949 ISSUE

#S419-S421 notes w/title *LAMPUNG UTARA* (North Lampung) w/postmark of issuing place.

S419 10 RUPIAH
1949. Green. Rising sun at l.

	GOOD	FINE	XF
	—	—	—

		Good	Fine	XF
S421	**50 Rupiah** 1949.			
	a. Purple. (ca.1949).	5.00	12.00	25.00
	b. Black. 4.5.1949.	2.00	8.00	15.00
	c. Blue. 15.4.1949.	5.00	12.00	25.00

NOTE: Modern counterfeits exist of #S421b.

Rebellious Movements

Pemerintah Negara Islam Indonesia (PNII)

Government of the Islamic State of Indonesia

Islamic fundamentalist rebellion led by S. M. Kartosuwiryo of the Darul Islam who proclaimed the PNNI on August 7, 1949 at Tjisampah, West Java.

Tjirebon, West Java

1949 Issue

#S431 place of issue Karesidenan Tjirebon (Tjirebon residency).

		Good	Fine	XF
S431	**5 Rupiah** 10.10.1949.	—	—	—

ND Issue

#S432 place of issue Daerah Tjirebon (Tjirebon district).

		Good	Fine	XF
S432	**5 Rupiah** ND. Similar to #S431.	—	—	—

Pemerintah Revolusioner Republik Indonesia (PRRI)

Revolutionary Government of the Republic Indonesia

The PRRI was declared February 15, 1958 at Padang in Central Sumatra by military governors dissatisfied with the central government in Jakarta spending the foreign exchange (earned by their provinces) on Java island and not distributing it to the exporting provinces.

The top rebel commander was Col. Ahmed Husein who signed the current Indonesian bank notes as *Land Forces Commander, Buffalo Division* (Angkatan Darat Panglima, Divisi Banteng) as well as Col. Barlian, the Territorial Commander South Sumatra, Palembang. He signed: *Komando Koordinasi Sumatra Selatan.* They were joined in December 1957 by Sjafruddin Prawiranegara, at that time Governor of the central bank (Bank Indonesia) and previously Minister of Finance and Head of the Government in Exile under Soekarno. He signed current Indonesian banknotes as Minister of Finance of PRRI (Menteri Keuangan). His signature also appears on the three banknote issues of the PRRI, although he was by then Prime Minister of the PRRI.

Notes of 5 to 100 Rupiah were also overstamped, but not signed, by military district heads. They used their official seal, a PRRI stamp.

Officially the rebellion was put down by military action which started on February 21, 1958, but although the major towns were captured by May 22, 1958 the PRRI managed to continue in the mountains for at least 18 months more. Later the RPI was proclaimed at Bonjol as the successor to the PRRI in 1960.

A wide range of ovpt. and sign. exists. The following examples are indicative.

SIGNATURES

a. Sjafruddin Prawiranegara (handwritten)

b. Ahmed Husein (handwritten or stamped)

c. Nawawi (handwritten)

d. Nainggolan (handwritten)

Examples of PRRI ovpt. notes:

2 ovpt. and sign. a.

1 ovpt. and sign. b.

2 ovpt. and sign. c.

2 ovpt., no sign.

Ovpt: *TIDAK BERLAKU* (g.) on PRRI ovpt. a.

PRRI ovpt. are found on the following notes listed in Volume II: the 1946 series of De Javasche Bank, Indonesia #1-9; the 1950 Republik Indonesia Serikat issue, #36-37; the 1952 Republik Indonesia issue #42-48.

OVERPRINTS (colors black or blue)

a. Rectangular ovpt., different measurements, w/ and w/o frame: *Alat Pembajaran Jang Sah/Menurut U(ndang). U(ndang). Darurat PRRI No. 8 Th. 1959* (Instrument of legal tender/in accordance with PRRI emergency law No. 8, year 1959)
b. Rectangular ovpt: *Alat Pembajaran Jang Sah PRRI;* different measurements, etc. (Instrument of legal tender PRRI)
c. Oval ovpt: *Pemerintah Revolusioner Republik Indonesia/Komando Koordinasi Sumatera Selatan,* sign. Barlian. (PRRI/Coordinating Commander South Sumatra)
d. Oval ovpt: *Pemerintah Revolusioner Republik Indonesia/Menteri Keuangan,* w/ or w/o sign. Sjafruddin Prawiranegara. (PRRI/Minister of Finance)
e. Round ovpt: *Angkatan Darat Kom. S(umatra). T(engah). Divisi Banteng/Panglima,* w/ or w/o sign. Ahmed Hussein. (Land Forces Commander Central Sumatra, Buffalo Division)
f. Various town and district seals.
g. Stamp *TIDAK BERLAKU* (not valid) used by the Indonesian officials for the notes they captured.
h. Round ovpt: Provisional Revolutionary Republic Indonesia/Mentoru Pertanian. Sign. Nainggolan.

NOTE: No market valuations are quoted for the overstamped PRRI notes as it is easy to falsify these types of overstamps. Dangerous falsifications exist.

1959 LOCAL ISSUE

#S461-S464 locally printed notes, w/engraved wooden blocks.

		GOOD	FINE	XF
S461	**1 RUPIAH** 9.1959. Green. Native houses at lower l. No serial #. (Not issued).	—	—	—

		GOOD	FINE	XF
S462	**5 RUPIAH** 9.1959. Dk. blue on yellow unpt. Batek house at l., Atchente dagger at r.	1.50	4.00	10.00

		GOOD	FINE	XF
S463	**25 RUPIAH** 9.1959. Red on yellow unpt. Torpgan house at lower l., boat at r.	1.50	4.00	10.00

		GOOD	FINE	XF
S464	**100 RUPIAH** 9.1959. Brown on lt. brown unpt. Minangkabau house of lower l., Mt. Merapi at r.	3.00	7.50	25.00

1959 BELGIAN ISSUE

#S470-S475 reportedly to have been printed in Belgium. Not issued for use by the Free Atcheh Movement.

		GOOD	FINE	XF
S470	**1 RUPIAH** ND (ca.1959).	—	—	—
S471	**5 RUPIAH** ND (ca.1959). Purple.	—	20.00	40.00
S472	**10 RUPIAH** ND (ca.1959). Green.	—	20.00	40.00
S473	**50 RUPIAH** ND (ca.1959). Dk. brown.	—	23.00	45.00
S474	**100 RUPIAH** ND (ca.1959). Red-brown.	—	25.00	50.00

		GOOD	FINE	XF
S475	**1000 RUPIAH** ND (ca.1959). Blue-green.	—	—	80.00

1960 ISSUE

#S481 local PRRI issue of Bonabulu.

		GOOD	FINE	XF
S481	**100 RUPIAH** 1.1.1960. Red. Tin of rice. Uniface.	—	—	—

PIAGAM PERDJUANGAN SEMESTA (PERMESTA)

TOTAL REVOLUTIONARY CHARTER

The PRRI rebellion of Central Sumatra was joined by military governors in other provinces. In Manado, North Celebes (Sulawesi) Col. Joop F. Warouw led the rebellion in 1958-60.

1958 ISSUE

		GOOD	FINE	XF
S491	**5 RUPIAH** 1958. Black on blue.	25.00	50.00	100.00

S492 10 RUPIAH

	GOOD	FINE	XF
1958. Red on black.	22.00	45.00	85.00

S493 25 RUPIAH

	GOOD	FINE	XF
1958. Black on red.	10.00	25.00	45.00

S494 50 RUPIAH

	GOOD	FINE	XF
1958. Gray-green on yellow.	15.00	30.00	60.00

S495 100 RUPIAH

	GOOD	FINE	XF
1958. Red on yellow.	7.50	20.00	40.00

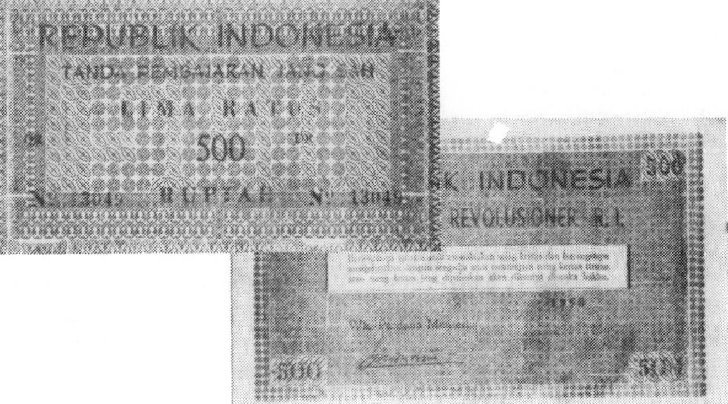

S495A 500 RUPIAH

	GOOD	FINE	XF
1958. Blue on pink.	10.00	20.00	40.00

S496 1000 RUPIAH

	GOOD	FINE	XF
1958. Red and green on yellow.	20.00	50.00	100.00

1959 ISSUE

S497 100 RUPIAH

	GOOD	FINE	XF
1959. Red.	12.00	30.00	60.00

S498 250 RUPIAH

1959. Reported Not Confirmed

S499 500 RUPIAH

	GOOD	FINE	XF
1959. Black and green on purple.	15.00	30.00	60.00

S500 1000 RUPIAH

	GOOD	FINE	XF
1959. Black and yellow on green.	20.00	40.00	80.00

S501 5000 RUPIAH

	GOOD	FINE	XF
1959. Black on green.	17.50	40.00	80.00

1953-65 Rebellion

At the beginning of 1952 Lt. Col. Kahar Muzakkar, in charge of government operations against the rebellious Republic of the South Moluccas (RMS), placed himself under the orders of the Imam S. M. Kartosuwiryo as commander in South Sulawesi (Celebes). On August 7, 1953 he proclaimed Sulawesi and adjacent territories to be part of the Islamic State. See also PNII.

Republik Islam Indonesia (RII)

Islamic Republic of Indonesia

OVERPRINTS

A. One sign. ovpt:
Republik Islam Indonesia Ketua P.U.S. RII-Bg: Timur.
(Sign. B. Baranti)

B. Two sign. ovpt:
Same as A., but added:
Gubernur Militer RII-BG: Timur.
(Sign. Muzakker)

Translation of the two sign. ovpt:
Islamic Republic of Indonesia Chairman, Provisional General Government, Islamic Republic of Indonesia, East Indonesian region. (Usman Balo).
Military governor, Islamic Republic of Indonesia, East Indonesian region. (Kahar Muzakkar).

1953-65 Provisional ND Gulden Issue

#S510-S516 genuine overprints on notes:

		Good	Fine	XF
S510	**1/2 Gulden** ND. 1 sign. ovpt. on N.I. #122.	2.50	5.00	10.00

		Good	Fine	XF
S511	**1 Gulden** ND. 1 sign. ovpt. Colors: purple, black, green, red, red-orange, pink, red-purple. Ovpt. on back, face or both back and face on N.I. #123c.	2.00	4.00	8.00
S512	**5 Gulden** ND. 2 sign. ovpt. Colors: purple, black, red, orange on N.I. #124c.	3.00	6.00	12.00

		Good	Fine	XF
S513	**10 Gulden** ND. 2 sign. ovpt. Colors: purple, black, green, red, blue, orange. Ovpt. on back or face on N.I. #125c.	2.50	5.00	10.00

1953-65 Genuine Ovpt. Provisional ND Roepiah Issue

		Good	Fine	XF
S514	**10 Roepiah** ND. 2 sign. ovpt. Colors: purple, black, red, blue, grey on N.I. #131.	2.00	4.00	8.00

		Good	Fine	XF
S515	**10 Roepiah** ND. 2 sign. ovpt. Colors:. purple, black on falsification of N.I.#131 (not known w/o ovpt.).	3.00	6.00	12.00

1953-65 Genuine Ovpt. Provisional ND Dollar Issue

		Good	Fine	XF
S516	**10 Dollars** ND. Ovpt. colors: black, blue, gray on Malaya #M7c.	4.00	8.00	15.00

1953-65 Modern False Ovpt. Provisional ND Gulden Issue

#S521-S530 modern false overprints on notes:

		Good	Fine	XF
S521	**1/2 Gulden** ND. Ovpt. on N.I. #122b.	—	—	—

		Good	Fine	XF
S522	**1 Gulden** ND. Ovpt. on N.I. #123c.	—	—	—
S523	**5 Gulden** ND. Ovpt. on N.I. #124c.	—	—	—
S524	**10 Gulden** ND. Ovpt. on N.I. #125c.	—	—	—

1953-65 False Ovpt. Provisional ND Roepiah Issue

		Good	Fine	XF
S525	**1/2 Roepiah** ND. Ovpt. on N.I. #128.	—	—	—
S526	**1 Roepiah** ND. Ovpt. on N.I. #129.	—	—	—
S527	**5 Roepiah** ND. Ovpt. on N.I. #130.	—	—	—
S528	**10 Roepiah** ND. Ovpt. on N.I. #131.	—	—	—

		Good	Fine	XF
S529	**100 Roepiah** ND. Ovpt. on N.I. #132.	—	—	—

1953-65 False Ovpt. Provisional ND Dollar Issue

		Good	Fine	XF
S530	**10 Dollars** ND. Ovpt. on Malaya #M7c.	—	—	—

NOTE: The above exist w/either black, red or lilac ovpt.

1950-66 REBELLION

In July 1950 the RMS government ordered an ovpt. on notes of the Dutch East Indies in circulation at that time. The oval ovpt. bears the sign. of Mr. G. G. H. Apituley, Secretary of the Ministry of Finance of the RMS.

REPUBLIK MALUKU SELATAN (RMS)

REPUBLIC OF THE SOUTH MOLUCCAS

Oval 70 x 42mm.

1950-66 DUTCH OVPT. ISSUE

Bar-type ovpt. (see example illus.) as well as oval ovpt. from the island of Saparua are not recognized as genuine by the RMS government-in-exile.

NOTE: No market valuations are quoted for the RMS notes as it is easy to falsify this type of overstamp.

		GOOD	FINE	XF
S531	**VARIOUS DENOMINATIONS** Ovpt. colors: mainly red and blue. Ovpt. on back, often upside down.	—	—	—

NOTE: Dangerous falsifications exist.

Former province of northwestern Iran. In 1938 it was divided into Eastern and Western Azerbaijan. In November of 1945 a Communist-led revolt broke out against the central government of Iran. On December 15 an autonomous republic was proclaimed. It lasted until December 11, 1946 when troops of the Iranian central government reoccupied the territory.

MONETARY SYSTEM:
1 Toman = 10 Krans

IRANIAN AZERBAIJAN

AUTONOMOUS GOVERNMENT

1946 ISSUE

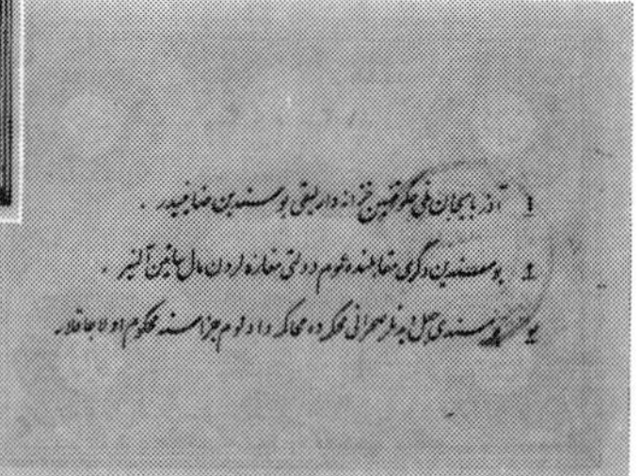

		VG	VF	UNC
S101	**5 KRANS** AH1324 (1946). Red on olive unpt. w/hand stamp on face. Persian text on back.	5.00	12.00	30.00

#S102-S106 ornate guilloches. Persian text on back w/perforated denomination numerals at upper ctr.

		VG	VF	UNC
S102	**1 TOMAN** AH1324 (1946). Violet on gray unpt.			
	a. W/hand stamp on face. Sm. or lg. sign.	5.00	12.00	30.00
	b. W/o hand stamp.	5.00	12.00	30.00

		VG	VF	UNC
S103	**2 TOMANS** AH1324 (1946). Blue on gray unpt.			
	a. W/hand stamp on face.	7.50	20.00	40.00
	b. W/o hand stamp.	7.50	20.00	40.00
S104	**5 TOMANS** AH1324 (1946). Green on gray unpt.			
	a. W/hand stamp on face.	12.50	27.50	50.00
	b. W/o hand stamp.	10.00	22.50	42.50
S105	**10 TOMANS** AH1324 (1946). Red on gray unpt.			
	a. W/hand stamp on face.	10.00	22.50	42.50
	b. W/o hand stamp.	12.50	27.50	50.00
S106	**50 TOMANS** AH1324 (1946). Blue on gray unpt.			
	a. W/hand stamp, handwritten sign.	12.50	30.00	65.00
	b. W/hand stamp, stamped sign.	10.00	27.50	55.00
	r. W/o hand stamp or perforated denomination numeral. Remainder.	4.00	10.00	22.50

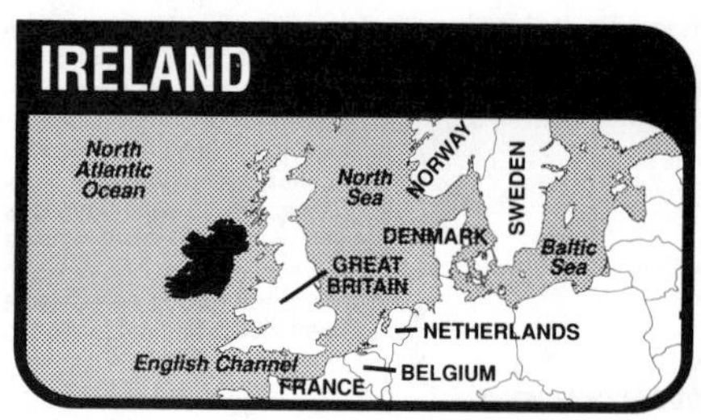

Ireland, the island located in the Atlantic Ocean west of Great Britain, was settled by dark and swarthy Celts from Gaul about 400 BC, but eventually they became known for their red hair and light complexions after frequent Viking invasions. The Celts assimilated the native Erainn and Picts and established a Gaelic civilization. After the arrival of St. Patrick in 432 AD, Ireland evolved into a center of Latin learning which sent missionaries to Europe and possibly North America. In 1154, Pope Adrian IV gave all of Ireland to English King Henry II to administer as a Papal fief. Because of the enactment of anti-Catholic laws and the awarding of vast tracts of Irish land to Protestant absentee landowners, English control did not become reasonably absolute until 1800 when England and Ireland became the "United Kingdom of Great Britain and Ireland". Religious freedom was restored to the Irish in 1829, but agitation for political autonomy continued until the Irish Free State was established as a dominion on Dec. 6, 1921 while Northern Ireland remained within the United Kingdom.

RULERS:

British to 1921

MONETARY SYSTEM:

1 Shilling = 12 Pence
1 Pound = 20 Shillings to 1971
1 Guinea = 21 Shillings

PRIVATE BANKS:

At present there is no comprehensive listing of the early private bank notes issued in Ireland. It is believed there were about 100 banks which issued circulating notes during the earlier part of the 19th century. A random selection of those early notes is included in this section.

- Agricultural and Commercial Bank of Ireland, Carrick-on-Suir, Enniscorthy, Tralee, etc. (46 branches), (1834-1841)
- Ball, Benjamin & Co., Dublin (1810-1888)
- Bank of Limerick, Limerick
- Belfast Bank (1787-1797) Ewing & Co.
- Belfast Bank (1808-1827) Gordon & Co., later Batt & Co.
- Belfast Commercial Bank (1809-1827) Tennent & Co.
- Beresford & Co., Dublin (1794-1810)
- Callan Bank, Callan, County Kilkenny (1801-1807) Michael Hearn
- Clonmel Bank, Clonmel, County Tipperary (1800-1820) Watson & Co.
- Clonmel Bank, Clonmel, County Tipperary (ca. 1720-1820) Bagwell & Co. leter Riall & Co.
- Cork Bank, Cork (1799-1820) Roche Brothers
- Fermoy Bank, Fermoy, County Cork (1800-1816) John Anderson & Co.
- Finlay & Co., Dublin (1754-1829)
- Galway Bank, Galway
- Gibbons & Williams, Dublin
- Hannyngton, Thomas, Dungannon, County Tyrone & Dublin (1804-1816)
- Kilkenny Bank, Kilkenny (1800-1820)
- Lighton, Needham & Shaw, Dublin (1799-1805)
- Limerick Bank (1801-1825) Rocke Brothers
- Lurgan Bank, The, Lurgan, County Armagh (1804-1820) Brownlow & Co. later Malcolmson & Co.
- Malahide Bank or Silver Bank, Malahide, County Dublin (1803-1804) Talbot & Co.
- Mallow Bank, Mallow, County Cork (1813)
- Moylan, Denis, Cork (1813)
- Newenham's Bank, Cork (1800-1825)
- Northern Bank, Belfast (1809-1824) Montgomery & Co. later Orr & Co.
- O'Neile's Bank, Waterford
- Provident Bank of Ireland (1837-1840)
- Ross Bank, Ross
- Ross Island Mine, Killarney (1804-ca.1819)
- Shaw & Co., Dublin (1805-1836)
- Southern Bank of Ireland
- Tipperary Bank (1803-ca.1830)
- Tuam Bank, Tuam (1804-1814) French & Co.
- Waterford Bank, Waterford
- Williams & Finn, Kilkenny & Dublin (1800-1806)
- Youghall Bank, Youghall (ca.1800-1810) George & Richard Giles

Agricultural and Commercial Bank of Ireland 30 SHILLINGS 1.2.1839

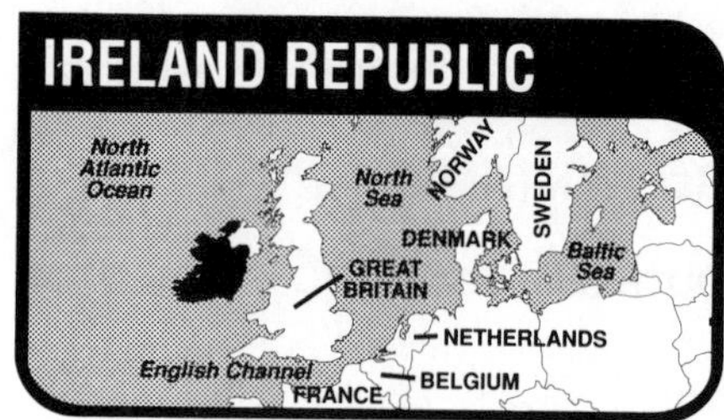

The Republic of Ireland, occupying five-sixths of the island of Ireland located in the Atlantic Ocean west of Great Britain, has an area of 27,136 sq. mi. (70,283 sq. km.) and a population of 3.71 million. Capital: Dublin.

The Fenian Brotherhood was organized in 1858 and consisted of Irish emigrants embittered by British attitude and policy towards Ireland. The leader of the group was John O'Mahoney. The Brotherhood sought Irish independence through pressure and embarassment tactics, perpetrating a number of raids in Canada mostly during the 1860s and 1870s. Though such activities proved largely unsuccessful, the movement continued until World War I when it became part of a newer group with similar aims, the Sinn Fein.

RULERS:

British to 1921

MONETARY SYSTEM:

1 Shilling = 12 Pence
1 Pound = 20 Shillings to 1971
1 Dollar = 100 Cents

IRELAND (EIRE)

IRISH REPUBLIC

1866-67 NATIONAL PROMISSORY BONDS ISSUE

National promissory bonds or notes in various denominations were printed in several series during 1866-67. Only those pieces most resembling paper currency are included in this listing. There are a number of other bond issues but they are outside the scope of this catalog.

#S101-S104 fully or partially printed dates. Printer: CONB.

		GOOD	FINE	XF
S101	**5 DOLLARS** 17.3.1866. Black. Standing allegorical woman at l., portr. of man at lower r. Uniface.	25.00	80.00	200.00

REPUBLIC OF IRELAND

1866-67 ISSUE

#S102-S104 black on green unpt. Eagle perched on sword and flag on mountain peak at upper ctr. Back green.

		GOOD	FINE	XF
S102	**10 DOLLARS** 1866-1919. Portr. of men at lower l. and r. Two *10* protectors in unpt. at lower l. ctr. and lower ctr. r.			
	a. Original issue 1866-67.	20.00	75.00	200.00
	b. Reissue Jan. 1919.	75.00	175.00	—

S103 **20 DOLLARS** — 1866-67. Similar to #S102 but different portr. at lower l. and r.

GOOD	FINE	XF
40.00	125.00	325.00

S104 **50 DOLLARS** — 1866-67. Similar to #S103 but different portr. at lower l. and r. Lg. *FIFTY* protector in unpt. at lower ctr.

GOOD	FINE	XF
50.00	200.00	425.00

S105 **100 DOLLARS** — 1866-67. Reported Not Confirmed

S106 **500 DOLLARS** — 1866-67. Reported Not Confirmed

The Isle of Man, a dependency of the British Crown located in the Irish Sea equidistant from Ireland, Scotland and England, has an area of 227 sq. mi. (588 sq. km.) and a population of 71,714. Capital: Douglas. Agriculture, dairy farming, fishing and tourism are the chief industries. The prevalence of prehistoric artifacts and monuments on the island gives evidence that its mild, almost sub-tropical climate was enjoyed by mankind before the dawn of history. Vikings came to the Isle of Man during the 9th century and remained until ejected by Scotland in 1266. The island came under the protection of the English Crown in 1288, and in 1406 was granted, in perpetuity, to the Earls of Derby. In 1736 it was inherited by the Duke of Atholl. Rights and title were purchased from the Duke of Atholl in 1765 by the British Crown; the remaining privileges of the Atholl family were transferred to the crown in 1829. The Sovereign of the United Kingdom (currently Queen Elizabeth II) holds the title Lord of Man. The Isle of Man is ruled by its own legislative council and the House of Keys, one of the oldest legislative assemblies in the world. Acts of Parliament passed in London do not affect the island unless it is specifically mentioned.

United Kingdom bank notes and coinage circulate concurrently with Isle of Man money as legal tender.

RULERS:

British

MONETARY SYSTEM:

1 Pound = 20 Shillings to 1971
1 Guinea = 1 Pound 1 Shilling

BANKS:

Castle Rushen .... #S111
Douglas & Isle of Man Bank (Dumbell's) .... #S121-S122
Douglas & Isle of Man Bank (Holmes') .... #S121-S122
Dumbell's Banking Co. Ltd. .... #S141-S143

PRIVATE BANKS

CASTLE RUSHEN

1790S ISSUE

S111 **1 GUINEA = 1 POUND 1 SHILLING** — 179x. Black. Crowned arms at l., castle at upper ctr. Uniface. Unsigned remainder.

GOOD	FINE	XF
—	—	—

DOUGLAS & ISLE OF MAN BANK (DUMBELL'S)

1854-65 ISSUE

S121 **1 POUND** — 1854-65. 2 allegorical women w/child, farm tools, sheep below at l., crowned shield w/triskeles w/lion and unicorn as supports at top ctr. 2 sign. at lower r.

	GOOD	FINE	XF
a. Issued note.	750.00	1500.	—
r. Unsigned remainder.	—	—	—

1865-74 Issue

S122 1 Pound

	Good	Fine	XF
1865-74. Like #S121a but 3 sign. at lower r.	125.00	275.00	600.00

Douglas & Isle of Man Bank (Holmes')

1844 Issue

S131 1 Pound

	Good	Fine	XF
1.1.1844. Black. Harbor scene at upper ctr. r. Ships and Isle arms on back.	30.00	70.00	—

NOTE: Although the two banks listed above bear the same title, they were actually run by different individuals.

Dumbell's Banking Co. Ltd.

1874-75 Provisional Issue

S141 1 Pound

	Good	Fine	XF
1874-75. Ovpt. new bank name on #S122.	200.00	450.00	—

1875-99 Issue

S142 1 Pound

	Good	Fine	XF
1875-78. Lion, triskeles and unicorn above bank name at top ctr.	250.00	550.00	—

S143 1 Pound

21.12.1891; 7.8.1885; 21.5.1897; 4.11.1899. Lion and unicorn supporting crowned shield w/triskeles below bank name at upper ctr.

	Good	Fine	XF
a. Issued note.	300.00	700.00	—
r. Remainder w/o date.	175.00	375.00	700.00

ITALIAN STATES
VENETIA
LOMBARDY
Gorzia
Palmanova
Trieste
Milan
Mantua
Venice
Turin
Belgiojoso
Parma
PIEDMONT
Reggio
Bologna
LIGURIA
Modena
Emilia
Gerioa
Lucca
Pisa
Florence
Castelfidardo
GRAND DUCHY OF TUSCANY
PAPAL STATES
Adraidic Sea
CORSICA
Rome
KINGDOM OF TWO SICILIES
Naples
SARDINIA
Tyrrhenian Sea
Palermo
ISLE OF SICILY
AFRICA (Ottoman)
REPUBLICS
Palmanova
Gorzia
Trieste
Milan
Venice
Turin
Mantua
Reggio
Parma
Bologna
Gerioa
Emilia
Lucca
Pisa
Florence
Castelfidardo
Adraidic Sea
CORSICA
Rome
Naples
Tyrrhenian Sea
SARDINIA
Palermo
ISLE OF SICILY
KEY
CISALPINE REPUBLIC
CISPADINE REPUBLIC
KINGDOM OF NAPOLEON
KINGDOM OF SARDINIA
Maccagno
SAVOY
Messerano
Milan
Desana
Retegno
Castiglione
Venice
Trieste
Solferino
Casale
Turin
MONFERRATO
Mantua
Piacenza
Bossolo
Sabbioneta
Vergagni
Mirandola
Guastalla
Ferrara
Bardi
Parma
Correggio
PIEDMONT
Rovegno
Ronco
Modena
Genoa
Bologna
Loana
Adriatic Sea
Tresana
Massa
Florence
Urbino
Lucca
Pisa
Livorno
Ancona
TUSCANY
Piombino
Seventeenth Century
PAPAL STATES
Tyrrhenian Sea

From the fall of Rome until modern times, "Italy," a 700 mile-long peninsula, was little more than a geographical expression. Although nominally included in the Empire of Charlemagne and the Holy Roman Empire, it was in reality divided into a number of independent states and kingdoms presided over by wealthy families, soldiers of fortune or hereditary rulers. The 19th century unification movement fostered by Mazzini, Garibaldi and Cavour attained fruition in 1860-70 with the creation of the Kingdom of Italy and the installation of Victor Emanuele, House of Savoy, as King.

MONETARY SYSTEM:
1 Lira = 100 Centesimi

ANTICHI STATI ITALIANI - OLD ITALIAN STATES

REGNO D'ITALIA - KINGDOM OF ITALY

REGNO DI SARDEGNA
KINGDOM OF SARDINIA

Victor Amadeus II, duke of Savoy, after acquiring Sardinia by means of the Treaty of the Hague, in 1720 transformed into a kingdom the state that Berthold had made a county in 999 starting from the region of Moriana in Savoy; at the beginning of 1400, Victor Amadeus VIII had transformed this county into a dukedom. From then on the House of Savoy directed its expansionist interests towards the Italian regions to the point of becoming the interpreter and guide the movements of the Risorgimento determined to create an Italian state. The Kingdom of Sardinia had a short life, only 141 years; in fact, it was transformed into the Kingdom of Italy on March 17, 1866, when Victor Emmanuele II was reigning.

The succession of sovereigns:

Vittorio Amadeo II, 1720-1730
Carlo Emanuele III, 1730-1773
Vittorio Amadeo III, 1773-1796
Carlo Emanuele IV, 1796-1902
Vittorio Emanuele I, 1802-1821
Carlo Felice, 1821-1831
Carlo Alberto, 1831-1849
Vittorio Emanuele II, 1849-1861 later King of Italy

REGIE FINANZE-TORINO

1746 ISSUE

#S101-S105 printed in black on heavy handmade white-creamed colored paper w/wmk.

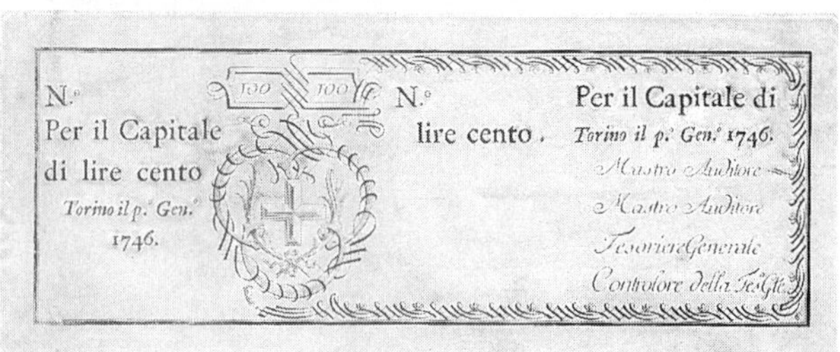

		Good	Fine	XF
S101	**100 LIRE** 1.1.1746.			
	a. Issued note.	1000.	1800.	3500.
	r. Remainder.	—	—	500.00
S102	**200 LIRE** 1.1.1746.			
	a. Issued note.	1000.	1800.	3500.
	r. Remainder.	—	—	500.00
S103	**500 LIRE** 1.1.1746.	—	Rare	—
S104	**1000 LIRE** 1.1.1746.	—	—	5000.

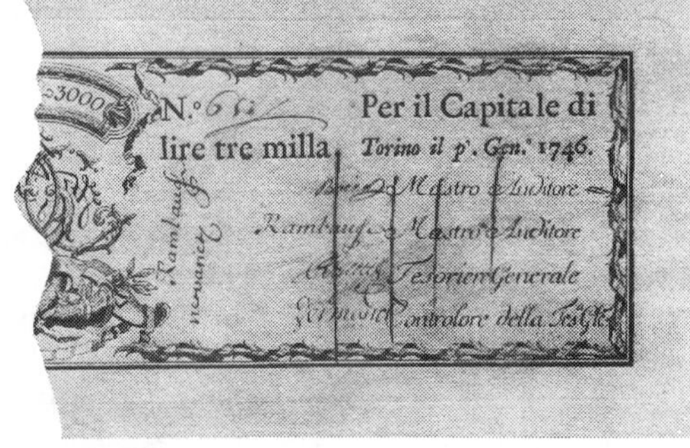

		Good	Fine	XF
S105	**3000 LIRE** 1.1.1746.	—	—	10,000.

1750 ISSUE

#S106 and S107 printed in black on heavy handmade white-creamed colored paper w/wmk.

		Good	Fine	XF
S106	**100 LIRE** 1.1.1750.	—	Rare	—
S107	**200 LIRE** 1.1.1750.	—	Rare	—

1756 ISSUE

#S108 and S109 printed in black on heavy handmade white-creamed colored paper w/wmk.

		Good	Fine	XF
S108	**50 LIRE** 1.8.1756.	—	Rare	—
S109	**100 LIRE** 1.8.1756.	—	Rare	—

1760 ISSUE

#S110 and S111 printed in black on heavy handmade white-creamed colored paper w/wmk.

		Good	Fine	XF
S110	**50 LIRE** 1.4.1760.	—	Unknown	—
S111	**100 LIRE** 1.4.1760.	—	Unknown	—

1765 ISSUE

#S112 and S113 printed in black on heavy handmade white-creamed colored paper w/wmk.

S112 50 LIRE
1.1.1765.

	GOOD	FINE	XF
a. Issued note.	—	Rare	—
r. Remainder.	—	—	500.00

S113 100 LIRE
1.1.1765.

	GOOD	FINE	XF
a. Issued note.	—	Rare	—
r. Remainder.	—	—	500.00

1774 ISSUE

#S114-S117 printed in black on heavy handmade white-creamed colored paper w/wmk.

	GOOD	FINE	XF
S114 50 LIRE 25.2.1774. Ovpt. new date on #S112.	—	Rare	—
S115 50 LIRE 1.4.1774. Like #S112.	—	Rare	—
S116 100 LIRE 25.2.1774. Ovpt. new date on #S113.	—	Rare	—
S117 100 LIRE 1.4.1774; 1.10.1776. Like #S113.	—	Rare	—

1781; 1794 ISSUE

#S118 and S119 printed on tinted paper.

S118 50 LIRE
1.6.1781; 1.7.1786; 1.10.1792; 1.6.1794; 1.10.1794.

	GOOD	FINE	XF
a. Issued note.	20.00	40.00	100.00
r. Remainder, 1794.	—	—	—

	GOOD	FINE	XF
S119 100 LIRE 1.6.1781.	—	Rare	—

1785 ISSUE

#S120 printed in black on heavy handmade white-creamed colored paper w/wmk.

	GOOD	FINE	XF
S120 100 LIRE 1.7.1785.	250.00	450.00	800.00
S121 200 LIRE 1.7.1785.	150.00	300.00	600.00

1786 ISSUE

#S122-S123 printed in black on heavy handmade white-creamed colored paper w/wmk.

S122 100 LIRE
1.7.1786; 1.10.1792; 15.5.1794; remainder, 1794.

	GOOD	FINE	XF
a. Issued note.	60.00	140.00	280.00
r. Remainder. 1794.	—	—	—

	GOOD	FINE	XF
S123 200 LIRE 1.7.1786; 1.10.1792.	250.00	500.00	800.00

1792; 1794 ISSUE

#S124-S128 printed in black on heavy handmade white-creamed colored paper w/wmk., except for 10 and 15 Lire, printed in color.

	GOOD	FINE	XF
S124 10 LIRE 1.4.1793; 1.6.1794; 1.10.1794. Blue paper.	200.00	500.00	1000.
S125 15 LIRE 1.4.1793; 1.6.1794; 1.10.1794. Amaranth paper.	—	Rare	—

S126 25 LIRE
1.10.1792; 1.6.1794; 1.10.1794.

	GOOD	FINE	XF
a. Issued note.	20.00	40.00	100.00
r. Remainder. 1792-94.	—	—	—

	GOOD	FINE	XF
S127 300 LIRE 1.4.1793.	150.00	400.00	900.00

	GOOD	FINE	XF
S128 600 LIRE 1.4.1793.	260.00	600.00	1500.

1796 ISSUE

#S129 and S130 printed in black on heavy handmade white-creamed colored paper w/wmk.

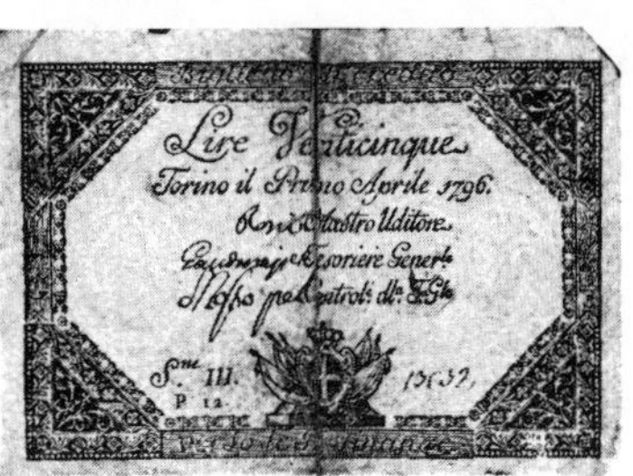

	GOOD	FINE	XF
S129 25 LIRE 1.4.1796.	20.00	40.00	100.00

S130 50 LIRE
1.4.1796.

	GOOD	FINE	XF
a. Issued note.	30.00	60.00	140.00
r. Remainder.	—	—	—

1799 Issue

#S131-S133 printed in black on heavy handmade white-creamed colored paper w/wmk.

		Good	Fine	XF
S131	**50 Lire** 1.9.1799. Seated allegorical woman holding portr. man at l.	25.00	50.00	120.00

		Good	Fine	XF
S132	**100 Lire** 1.9.1799. Seated allegorical woman at l., angel at r.	35.00	80.00	200.00

		Good	Fine	XF
S133	**200 Lire** 1.9.1799. Bust on pedestal at l., standing Mercury at r.	40.00	120.00	280.00

Special Issues for Sardinia

Restricted for circulation only on the island.

1780 Issue

		Good	Fine	XF
S134	**50 Lire** 1.7.1780. Black. Crowned arms at l.			
	a. Issued note. W/o counterfoil.	—	Rare	—
	r. Remainder w/counterfoil.	—	250.00	—

1781 Issue

		Good	Fine	XF
S135	**5 Scudi** 1.7.1781. Black. Vertical format.			
	a. Issued note.	—	Rare	—
	r. Remainder w/counterfoil.	—	—	2000.

Monte di San Secondo

1794; 1800 Issues

Issue to replace the Regie Finanze notes..

		Good	Fine	XF
S140	**500 Lire** 1794-1800. Bull in crowned oval.	—	Rare	—
S141	**1000 Lire** 1794-1800. Bull in crowned oval.	—	Rare	—

Repubblica Cisalpina - Nazione Piemontese

1800 Issue

This issue was withdrawn from circulation after three months.

		Good	Fine	XF
S145	**50 Lire** 11.9.1800.	—	Rare	—
S146	**250 Lire** 11.9.1800.	—	—	—
S147	**500 Lire** 11.9.1800.	—	—	—
S148	**1000 Lire** 11.9.1800.	—	—	—

Banca di Genova

Founded in 1844. Merged with Banca di Torino to form Banca Nazionale Stati Sardi.

1848; 1849 Issue

		Good	Fine	XF
S150	**100 Lire** 13.9.1848; 26.10.1849. Red. Genoa arms at top, Janus at bottom, value across ctr. Uniface.	—	Rare	—

#S151-S153 Columbus in medallion w/Industry and Abundance allegories at l., Janus in medallion w/Commerce and Science allegories at r., Genoa arms at top ctr. Uniface.

		Good	Fine	XF
S151	**250 Lire** 22.12.1848. Green.	—	Rare	—
S152	**500 Lire** 13.9.1848. Yellow.	—	Rare	—
S153	**1000 Lire** 7.9.1848. Black.	—	Rare	—

Banca di Torino

Founded 1847. This bank merged with Banca di Genova to form Banca Nazionale negli Stati Sardi.

1849 Issue

#S155-S157 standing figures at l. and at r., arms of Turin at top ctr. Uniface.

		Good	Fine	XF
S155	**200 Lire** 15.9.1849. Blue.	—	Rare	—
S156	**500 Lire** 15.9.1849. Black. Cream paper.	—	Rare	—

		Good	Fine	XF
S157	**1000 Lire** 15.9.1849. Black.	—	Rare	—

Banca di Savoia

Savoia region, where the bank was established in 1851, was part of the Sardinia Kingdom. In 1860 it was ceded to France and stopped issuing bank notes.

#S160-S166 were previously listed in France as #S191-S197.

1851 Issue

		Good	Fine	XF
S160	**50 Livres** 1.12.1851. Black on gray unpt. Man at l. and r.	—	Rare	—
S161	**100 Livres** 1.12.1851. Black.			
	a. Pink unpt.	—	Rare	—
	b. W/o unpt.	—	Rare	—
S162	**250 Livres** 1.12.1851. Black.			
	a. Green unpt.	—	Rare	—
	b. W/o unpt.	—	Rare	—

		GOOD	FINE	XF
S163	**500 LIVRES** 1.12.1851. Black.			
	a. Orange unpt.	—	Rare	—
	b. W/o unpt.	—	Rare	—
S164	**1000 LIVRES** 1.12.1851. Black.	—	Rare	—

1859 ISSUE

		GOOD	FINE	XF
S165	**20 LIVRES** 1.7.1859. Black. Yellow paper. Arms at top ctr.	2500.	3500.	—
S166	**50 LIVRES** 1.7.1859. Black. Value: *50* at l. and r.	—	Rare	—

BANCA NAZIONALE NEGLI STATI SARDI

Founded in 1849 w/merger of Banca di Genova and Banca di Torino. Until 1859, notes were only circulated in Sardinia Kingdom. After the transformation to Kingdom of Italy, notes were eventually accepted all over Italy. All notes printed in France.

1851; 1857 ISSUE

#S170-S175 crowned arms of Genoa and Turin between reclining gods at top ctr., portr. C. Columbus in medallion at bottom ctr., ornamental border. Uniface.

		GOOD	FINE	XF
S170	**20 LIRE** 8.1.1857-30.10.1867. Black. Yellow paper.	180.00	500.00	1000.
S171	**50 LIRE** 8.1.1857-23.1.1867. Black. White paper.	250.00	650.00	1400.
S172	**100 LIRE** 1.7.1851-17.1.1872. Black. Red paper.	80.00	200.00	500.00

		GOOD	FINE	XF
S173	**250 LIRE** 1.7.1851-19.7.1871. Black. Green paper.	240.00	600.00	1200.
S174	**500 LIRE** 1.7.1851-17.1.1872. Black. Cream paper.	500.00	1400.	3000.
S175	**1000 LIRE** 1.7.1851-19.7.1871. Black. White paper.	—	Rare	—

LOMBARDO - VENETO

Comprised of the northern Italy duchies of Milan and Mantua and the Venetian Republic, which were absorbed by the Kingdom of Napoleon in 1805. After Napoleon fell in 1815, they were awarded by Austria and incorporated as Kingdom of Lombardy-Venice. This kingdom ceased after the conquest of Lombardy in 1859, and the conquest of Venetian territory in 1866, by the King of Italy, Vittorio Emanuele II.

BANCO GIRO DI VENEZIA

1798 ISSUE

#S181-S184 crowned double-headed Austro-Hungarian imperial eagle top ctr. San Marco (Venice symbol) at bottom ctr. Uniface, black on white paper w/wmk.

		VG	VF	UNC
S181	**10 DUCATI** 1.10.1798.	10.00	30.00	80.00
S182	**50 DUCATI** 1.10.1798.	10.00	40.00	160.00

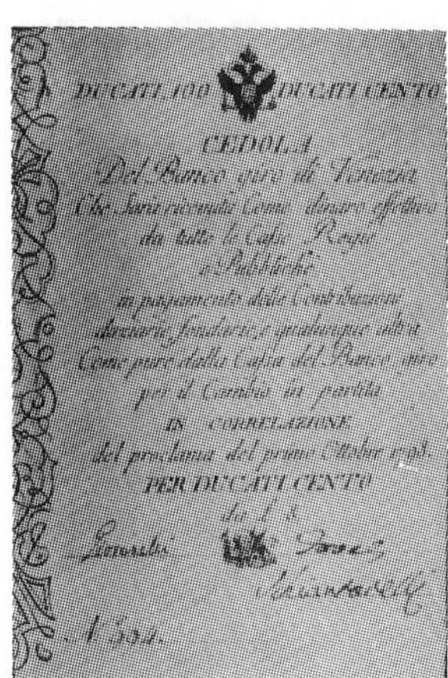

		VG	VF	UNC
S183	**100 DUCATI** 1.10.1798.	10.00	30.00	100.00
S184	**500 DUCATI** 1.10.1798.	Reported Not Confirmed		

VENETIAN REPUBLIC - MONETA PATRIOTTICA

Issued by Banca Nazionale di Venezia.

1848 ISSUE

#S185-S188 black. White paper w/ or w/o wmk. Uniface. W/o bank name indicated. Orange seal of Venice on back, w/ or w/o handwritten sign.

		VG	VF	UNC
S185	**1 LIRA** 1848. Ornamental border w/winged horses, flowers.	1.00	3.00	12.00

		VG	VF	UNC
S186	**2 LIRE** 1848. Seated Neptune at l., Justice at r.	1.00	4.00	15.00

		VG	VF	UNC
S187	**3 LIRE** 1848. Two cherubs at ctr., coat-of-arms of Venice and Milan at upper l. and r.	1.00	3.00	12.00

		VG	VF	UNC
S188	**5 LIRE** 1848. Coat-of-arms of Venice and Milan at upper l. and r.	1.00	3.00	12.00

#S189 and S190 black on pink unpt. White paper w/o wmk. Bank name around *S. Marco* Lion in embossed seal.

		VG	VF	UNC
S189	**50 LIRE** 1848. Allegorical figures, coat-of-arms of Venice at lower l., Milan at top r.	10.00	40.00	150.00

		VG	VF	UNC
S190	**100 LIRE** 1848. Coat-of-arms of Venice at top ctr., Milan at bottom ctr.	5.00	20.00	70.00

VENETIAN REPUBLIC - MONETA DEL COMUNE

1848; 1849 ISSUE

#S191-S194 black and gray. White paper. Uniface. Banca Nazionale di Venezia name around *S. Marco* Lion in embossed seal. Orange seal of Venice on front of #S191 and on back of #S192-S196.

		GOOD	FINE	XF
S191	**50 CENTESIMI** 1849.			
	a. Issued note (=1 Lira).	250.00	600.00	1400.
	b. Cut l. or r. half (= 50 centesimi).	30.00	80.00	200.00

NOTE: #S191 was printed w/the possibility to be cut in half and used as fifty centesimi, while whole it was worth 1 lira.

		GOOD	FINE	XF
S192	**1 LIRA** 1848. Coat-of-arms of Venice and Milan at bottom l. and r.	20.00	60.00	140.00

		GOOD	FINE	XF
S193	**3 LIRE** 1848. Winged Mercury head at top ctr., 2 arms at upper ctr., 2 winged horses below, ornamental border.	40.00	120.00	280.00
S194	**5 LIRE** 1848. Mercury and Industry at lower ctr., Venetian and Milan coat-of-arms at l.	100.00	300.00	900.00
S195	**50 LIRE** 1849. Green. Ornamental geometric border. White thin paper.	—	Rare	—
S196	**100 LIRE** 1849. Red. Standing allegorical *Italia* at l. w/white lance and shield representing Venice, Milan coat-of-arms in l. hand.	—	Rare	—

REGNO LOMBARDO-VENETO - VIGLIETTO DEL TESORO

1849 ISSUE

#S197-S199 2 embossed seals of the Milan Administration w/crowned double-headed Austro-Hungarian imperial eagle. Uniface. Wmk. paper.

		GOOD	FINE	XF
S197	**5 LIRE** 1.4.1849. Black on lt. cream unpt.	100.00	300.00	800.00
S198	**10 LIRE** 1.4.1849. Black on rose unpt.	200.00	500.00	1400.
S199	**15 LIRE** 1.4.1849. Black on lt. green unpt.	250.00	700.00	1800.

#S200-S204 prospectus of interest on back.

		GOOD	FINE	XF
S200	**30 LIRE** 1.4.1849. Grey on lt. green unpt.	500.00	1200.	—
S201	**60 LIRE** 1.4.1849. Blue on lt. azure unpt.	—	Rare	—
S202	**120 LIRE** 1.4.1849.	—	Rare	—
S203	**600 LIRE** 1.4.1849.	—	Unknown	—
S204	**1200 LIRE** 1.4.1849.	—	Unknown	—
S205	**2400 LIRE** 1.4.1849.	—	Unknown	—

NOTE: #S202-S205 only green formulare known.

CITTA' DI FIUME

Municipal provisional issue to make up for lack of coins after Kossuth revolution and Austrian intervention.

1848-50 ISSUE

#S206-S210 uniface. White paper.

1 Austrian Florin = 60 Carantani

		GOOD	FINE	XF
S206	**3 CARANTANI** 8.5.1849. Red.	150.00	400.00	1000.
S207	**3 CARANTANI** 1.5.1850. Black.	180.00	450.00	1000.
S208	**5 CARANTANI** 17.10.1848. Red.	150.00	400.00	1000.
S209	**5 CARANTANI** 1.5.1850. Blue-green.	150.00	400.00	1000.
S210	**10 CARANTANI** 17.10.1848. Red.	180.00	500.00	1200.

MONTE LOMBARDO-VENETO - VAGLIA

Issued in Verona.

1859 ISSUE

#S211-S214 black. White paper w/wmk: *KKCK*. Uniface.

		GOOD	FINE	XF
S211	**1 FIORINO** 15.6.1859. Female allegories at bottom ctr., crowned Austro-Hungarian imperial eagle at top ctr.	100.00	250.00	1800.
S212	**5 FIORINI** 15.6.1859. 2 allegories at l. and r., crowned Austro-Hungarian imperial eagle at bottom ctr.	250.00	700.00	1800.
S213	**10 FIORINI** 15.6.1859. 2 allegories at l. and r., crowned Austro-Hungarian imperial eagle at bottom ctr.	500.00	1200.	2800.
S214	**100 FIORINI** 15.6.1859. 2 allegories at l. and r., crowned Austro-Hungarian imperial eagle at bottom ctr.	—	Rare	—
S215	**1000 FIORINI** 15.6.1859. Many allegories in the borders, crowned Austro-Hungarian eagle at bottom ctr.	—	Rare	—

I. R. MONTE VENETO

Forced loan certificates were issued 1st September, 1866 and they were withdrawn from circulation after one month with the advent of the Peace of Vienna (3 October). The Venetian territory was ceded to the Italian Kingdom.

1866 ISSUE

#S216-S218 issued in Treviso, Udine and Verona.

		GOOD	FINE	XF
S216	**1 FIORINO** 1.9.1866. Country woman at l., workman at r., crowned Austro-Hungarian imperial eagle at top ctr.	—	Rare	—
S217	**10 FIORINI** 1.9.1866. Farmer at l. and country woman at r., crowned Austro-Hungarian imperial eagle at bottom ctr.	—	Rare	—
S218	**100 FIORINI** 1.9.1866. 2 angels standing at l. and r., 2 angels flying at top ctr., crowned Austro-Hungarian imperial eagle at bottom ctr.	—	Unique	—

SIEGES

MANTOVA

Austrians besieged by French forces.

1796 ISSUE

#S221-S229 black w/2 red seals w/crowned Austro-Hungarian imperial eagle. Uniface. White paper.

		GOOD	FINE	XF
S221	**10 SOLDI** 6.10.1796.	—	Rare	—
S222	**1 LIRA** 6.10.1796.	—	Rare	—

		Good	Fine	XF
S223	**3 Lire** 6.10.1796.	80.00	200.00	450.00
S224	**6 Lire** 6.10.1796.	100.00	250.00	650.00
S225	**9 Lire** 6.10.1796.	200.00	600.00	1400.
S226	**12 Lire** 6.10.1796.	500.00	1200.	2800.

		Good	Fine	XF
S227	**18 Lire** 6.10.1796.	700.00	1600.	3800.
S228	**45 Lire** 6.10.1796.	—	Unique	—
S229	**135 Lire** 6.10.1796.	—	Unknown	—

Zara

Napoleonic garrison besieged by Austrian forces.

1813 ND Issue

#S231 and S232 black w/brown-red seal. White paper. Exchange rate indicated w/Venetian Lira.

		Good	Fine	XF
S231	**1 Franc** ND (1813).	—	Unique	—
S232	**2 Francs** ND (1813).	—	Rare	—

Palmanova, 1814

Napoleonic garrison besieged by Austrian forces, 1813-14.

1814 Issue

#S233 and S236 handwritten w/black seal. Issued notes have blue seal w/French imperial eagle and serial #. Laid paper. Uniface.

		Good	Fine	XF
S233	**2 Lire** 1814.	—	Unique	—
S234	**5 Lire** 1814. Remainder.	—	—	2000.
S235	**10 Lire** 1814.	—	Unknown	—
S236	**25 Lire** 1814.	—	Unknown	—

Osoppo

After the Milan and Venice insurrections, the Italian Patriots took command of Osoppo fortress in March 1848. Since April, Austrian forces began to lay siege to the Osoppo fortress where the Patriots held out for 7 months before they capitulated on 12 October.

1848 ND Issue

#S237-S243 handwritten, w/3 rectangular black seals and partial circular black seal in upper l. corner.

		Good	Fine	XF
S237	**50 Centesimi** ND (1848).	—	Rare	—

		VG	VF	Unc
S238	**1 Lira** ND (1848).	500.00	1100.	2200.
S239	**2 Lire** ND (1848).	550.00	1200.	2400.
S240	**3 Lire** ND (1848).	600.00	1400.	2800.
S241	**6 Lire** ND (1848).	800.00	2000.	—
S242	**50 Lire** ND (1848).	—	Rare	—
S243	**100 Lire** ND (1848).	—	Rare	—

Palmanova, 1848

After the Milan and Venice insurrections, Italian Patriots took command of Palmanova fortress and they held out against the Austrian forces for 3 months up to June 24, 1848.

1848 Issue

#S244 and S245 black w/hand sign. Heavy white wmk. paper.

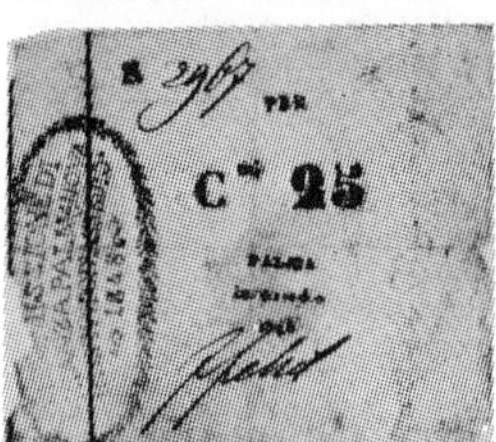

		VG	VF	Unc
S244	**25 Centesimi** 1848.	60.00	200.00	600.00

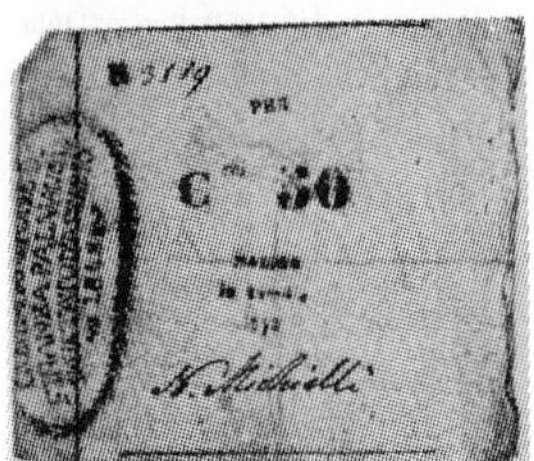

		VG	VF	Unc
S245	**50 Centesimi** 1848.	40.00	160.00	500.00

#S246-S249 black text, value in red, date in green w/4 hand sign. Heavy white wmk. paper.

		Good	Fine	XF
S246	**1 Lira** 1848.			
	a. Value word printed.	25.00	100.00	275.00
	b. Value word handwritten.	—	—	—

		VG	VF	Unc
S247	**2 Lire** 1848.	25.00	100.00	275.00
S248	**3 Lire** 1848.	30.00	120.00	300.00
S249	**6 Lire** 1848.	60.00	250.00	450.00

Principato di Lucca e Piombino
Princedom of Lucca and Piombino

The Grand Duchy of Lucca and the Princedom of Piombino had during the centuries independent histories. The former was a republic from the 15th century and remained as such until the Napoleonic conquest. The latter was variously ruled or occupied by the Appiani first and then by the Buoncompagni from whom Napoleon took it away. On March 18, 1805 Napoleon united the two small states and granted them to his sister Elisa Bonaparte Baciocchi as a French principality. This new small state had a short life: with the fall of Napoleon, it joined the Grand Duchy of Tuscany.

BANCA DI LUCCA

These notes were printed in France but were never issued.

1813 ND ISSUE

#S261-S263 black. Brown thin paper w/wmk.

		VG	VF	UNC
S261	50 SOLDI ND (ca.1813).		Reported Not Confirmed	
S262	5 LIRE ND (ca.1813).		Reported Not Confirmed	
S263	30 LIRE ND (ca.1813).	—	Rare	—

GRANDUCATO DI TOSCANA
GRAND DUCHY OF TUSCANY

The Medici family ruled the State from 1421 to 1737, when, as a consequence of the Spanish succession war, Tuscany fell under the Austrian influence with the Lorena House. This influence lasted until 1860, when the Grand Duchy joined the Kingdom of Italy. After the accession of Napoleon, from 1809 to 1814, the Grand Duchy was united to France and, after Napoleon's fall, underwent the indirect rule of Austria before joining the Kingdom of Italy.

The last Granduchi:

Ferdinando III, 1790-1801
and for a second period, 1814-1824
Leopoldo II, 1824-1859
Ferdinando II, 1859-1860

From 1817 up until 1856, the following Granducal Banks issued paper money:
Cassa di Sconto de Firenze
Banca di Sconto di Firenze
Banca di Sconto di Livorno
Banca di Siena
Banca di Arezzo
Banca di Pisa
Banca di Lucca

In 1857, all these banks merged to form Banca Nazionale Toscana and in 1859, this institute issued bank notes in the amount of nearly 10 million Lire. Until today, not one of the many different notes issued during the Granducal period is known to exist in proof or specimen form. For this reason, we decided not to list any of these issues until when, eventually, some may turn up.

BANCA D. P. ADAMI & C.

Issued in Livorno.

1859 ISSUE

#S291 and S292 black. Heavy grease-proof paper. Embossed seal. 2 circular black seals on back.

		VG	VF	UNC
S291	100 LIRE 1.3.1859.	140.00	300.00	900.00
S292	500 LIRE 1.3.1859.	80.00	200.00	450.00

STATO PONTIFICIO
PAPAL STATES

During many centuries prior to the formation of the unified Kingdom of Italy, Italy was divided into numerous independent papal and ducal states. The Popes held temporal sovereignty over an area in central Italy comprising some 17,000 sq. mi. (44,030 sq. km.) including the city of Rome. At the time of the general unification of Italy under the Kingdom of Sardinia, 1861, the papal dominions beyond Rome were acquired by that kingdom, diminishing the Pope's sovereignty to Rome and its environs. In 1870, while France's opposition to papal dispossession was neutralized by its war with Prussia, the Italian army seized weakly defended Rome and made it the capital of Italy, thereby abrogating the last vestige of papal temporal power. In 1871, the Italian Parliament enacted the Law of Guarantees, which guaranteed a special status for the Vatican area, and spiritual freedom and a generous income for the Pope. Pope Pius IX and his successors adamantly refused to acknowledge the validity of these laws, and voluntarily "imprisoned" themselves in the Vatican. The impasse between State and Church lasted until the signing of the Lateran Treaty, Feb. 11, 1929, by which Italy recognized the sovereignty and independence of the new Vatican City state.

Papal States have now been integrated into Italian States under the heading Stato Pontificio - Papal States (#S301-S708). Numbers in parenthesis refer to "old" Papal States listings in the 7th edition.

PONTIFFS:

Clement XIII, 1758-1769
Sede Vacante, Feb. 2 - May 19, 1769
Clement XIV, 1769-1774
Sede Vacante, Sept. 22, 1774 - Feb. 15, 1775
Pius VI (Sextus), 1775-1799
Pius VII, 1800-1823
Sede Vacante, Aug. 20 - Sept. 28, 1823
Leo XII, 1823-1829
Sede Vacante, Feb. 10 - Mar. 31, 1829
Pius VIII, 1829-1830
Sede Vacante, Nov. 30, 1830 - Feb. 2, 1831
Gregory XVI, 1831-1846
Sede Vacante, June 1-16, 1846
Pius IX, 1846-1878

MONETARY SYSTEM:

100 Bajocchi = 1 Scudo
30 Paoli = 1 Doppia

S. MONTE DELLA PIETA' DI ROMA

S. Monte Della Pieta' di Roma first printed issue appeared on November 15, 1785. Later, 15 more releases were issued with these dates: 6/12/85; 9/1/86; 21/6/86; 12/12/86; 12/6/87; 7/1/88; 15/1/88; 1/7/90; 9/7/90; 1/2/92; 25/2/95; 22/9/95; 1/8/96; 1/5/97; 1/8/97. Not all issues include all denominations, as an example, the first issue was limited to 5 up to 10 Scudi, the second enclosed only the denominations between 11 and 18 Scudi, on June 21, 1796 and June 12, 1787 only the 9 Scudi denomination was issued and on July 1, 1790 only the 24 Scudi was put into circulation. First five issues do not have printed value on back.

1785-95 ISSUE

#S301 and S302 135 x 100mm.

		GOOD	FINE	XF
S301	3 SCUDI 14.9.1795.	15.00	40.00	120.00
S302	4 SCUDI 14.9.1795.	15.00	40.00	120.00

#S303-S376 black. White wmk. paper. 200 x 145mm.

		GOOD	FINE	XF
S303	5 SCUDI 1785-97.	8.00	24.00	70.00
S304	6 SCUDI 1785-97.	8.00	24.00	70.00
S305	7 SCUDI 1785-97.	8.00	24.00	70.00
S306	8 SCUDI 1785-97.	8.00	24.00	70.00
S307	9 SCUDI 1785-97.	8.00	24.00	70.00
S308	10 SCUDI 1785-97.	8.00	24.00	70.00
S309	11 SCUDI 1785-97.	8.00	24.00	70.00

		GOOD	FINE	XF
S310	12 SCUDI 1785-97.	8.00	24.00	70.00
S311	13 SCUDI 1785-97.	8.00	24.00	70.00
S312	14 SCUDI 1785-92.	8.00	24.00	70.00
S313	15 SCUDI 1785-97.	8.00	24.00	70.00
S314	16 SCUDI 1785-92.	9.00	25.00	80.00
S315	17 SCUDI 1785-92.	9.00	25.00	80.00
S316	18 SCUDI 1785-95.	9.00	25.00	80.00
S317	19 SCUDI 1786-97.	9.00	25.00	80.00
S318	20 SCUDI 1786-97.	9.00	25.00	80.00
S319	21 SCUDI 1786-97.	9.00	25.00	80.00
S320	22 SCUDI 1786-97.	9.00	25.00	80.00
S321	23 SCUDI 1786-97.	9.00	25.00	80.00
S322	24 SCUDI 1786-97.	9.00	25.00	80.00
S323	25 SCUDI 1786-97.	9.00	25.00	80.00
S324	26 SCUDI 1786-97.	9.00	25.00	80.00
S325	27 SCUDI 1786-97.	9.00	25.00	80.00
S326	28 SCUDI 1786-97.	9.00	25.00	80.00
S327	29 SCUDI 1786-97.	9.00	25.00	80.00
S328	30 SCUDI 1786-97.	9.00	25.00	80.00

		Good	Fine	XF
S329	**31 Scudi** 1786-97.	10.00	30.00	90.00
S330	**32 Scudi** 1786-97.	10.00	30.00	90.00
S331	**33 Scudi** 1786-97.	10.00	30.00	90.00
S332	**34 Scudi** 1786-97.	10.00	30.00	90.00
S333	**35 Scudi** 1786-97.	10.00	30.00	90.00
S334	**36 Scudi** 1786-97.	10.00	30.00	90.00
S335	**37 Scudi** 1786-97.	10.00	30.00	90.00
S336	**38 Scudi** 1786-97.	10.00	30.00	90.00
S337	**39 Scudi** 1786-97.	10.00	30.00	90.00
S338	**40 Scudi** 1786-97.	10.00	30.00	90.00
S339	**41 Scudi** 1786-97.	10.00	30.00	90.00

		Good	Fine	XF
S340	**42 Scudi** 1786-97.	10.00	30.00	90.00
S341	**43 Scudi** 1786-97.	10.00	30.00	90.00
S342	**44 Scudi** 1786-97.	10.00	30.00	90.00
S343	**45 Scudi** 1786-97.	10.00	30.00	90.00
S344	**46 Scudi** 1786-97.	10.00	30.00	90.00
S345	**47 Scudi** 1786-97.	10.00	30.00	90.00
S346	**48 Scudi** 1786-97.	10.00	30.00	90.00
S347	**49 Scudi** 1786-97.	10.00	30.00	90.00
S348	**50 Scudi** 1786-97.	10.00	30.00	90.00
S349	**55 Scudi** 1786-97.	12.00	35.00	100.00
S350	**60 Scudi** 1786-97.	12.00	35.00	100.00
S351	**65 Scudi** 1786-97.	14.00	40.00	120.00
S352	**70 Scudi** 1786-97.	14.00	40.00	120.00
S353	**75 Scudi** 1786-97.	16.00	50.00	140.00
S354	**80 Scudi** 1786-97.	16.00	50.00	140.00
S355	**85 Scudi** 1786-97.	16.00	50.00	140.00
S356	**90 Scudi** 1786-97.	16.00	50.00	140.00

		Good	Fine	XF
S357	**95 Scudi** 1786-97.	16.00	50.00	140.00
S358	**100 Scudi** 1786-97.	20.00	60.00	180.00
S359	**110 Scudi** 1788-95.	100.00	300.00	900.00
S360	**120 Scudi** 1788-95.	100.00	300.00	900.00
S361	**130 Scudi** 1788.	100.00	300.00	900.00
S362	**140 Scudi** 1788.	100.00	300.00	900.00
S363	**150 Scudi** 1788-92.	60.00	200.00	600.00
S364	**200 Scudi** 1788-92.	60.00	200.00	600.00
S365	**250 Scudi** 1788-92.	100.00	300.00	900.00
S366	**300 Scudi** 1788-92.	80.00	240.00	700.00
S367	**350 Scudi** 1788.	120.00	350.00	1000.
S368	**400 Scudi** 1788.	120.00	350.00	1000.
S369	**450 Scudi** 1788.	—	Rare	—
S370	**500 Scudi** 1788.	80.00	240.00	700.00
S371	**600 Scudi** 1788.	—	Rare	—
S372	**700 Scudi** 1788.	—	Rare	—
S373	**800 Scudi** 1788.	150.00	450.00	1200.
S374	**900 Scudi** 1788.	120.00	350.00	1000.

		Good	Fine	XF
S375	**1000 Scudi** 1788-97.	180.00	350.00	1400.
S376	**1500 Scudi** 1788.	250.00	800.00	2200.

NOTE: During First Roman Republic, some S. Monte Della Pietà notes were ovpt. by the Republican Municipal Administration with the seal of about 20 different towns, to ratify the validity of circulation. All the Republican validated notes are rare, and in comparison with the normal notes, a price increase up to double the value for common seals and up to five times for rarer seals.

Banco di S. Spirito di Roma

First Banco di Santo Spirito printed note was issued in Rome on January 7, 1786 and each day, until January 13, the issues continued day by day without stopping. After this, the issue was interrupted for ten years until the last two on February 29 and March 1, 1796.

1786; 1795 Issue

#S377 and S378 black. White wmk. paper. 135 x 100mm.

		Good	Fine	XF
S377	**3 Scudi** 15.9.1795.	15.00	40.00	120.00
S378	**4 Scudi** 15.9.1795.	15.00	40.00	120.00

#S379-S519 black. White wmk. paper. 200 x 145mm.

		Good	Fine	XF
S379	**5 Scudi** 1786-96.	10.00	30.00	90.00
S380	**6 Scudi** 1786-96.	10.00	30.00	90.00

		Good	Fine	XF
S381	7 Scudi 786-96.	10.00	30.00	90.00
S382	8 Scudi 1786-96.	10.00	30.00	90.00
S383	9 Scudi 1786-96.	10.00	30.00	90.00
S384	10 Scudi 1786-96.	10.00	30.00	90.00
S385	11 Scudi 1786-96.	10.00	30.00	90.00
S386	12 Scudi 1786-96.	10.00	30.00	90.00
S387	13 Scudi 1786-96.	10.00	30.00	90.00
S388	14 Scudi 1786-96.	10.00	30.00	90.00
S389	15 Scudi 1786-96.	10.00	30.00	90.00
S390	16 Scudi 1786-96.	12.00	35.00	100.00
S391	17 Scudi 1786-96.	12.00	35.00	100.00
S392	18 Scudi 1786-96.	12.00	35.00	100.00
S393	19 Scudi 1786-96.	12.00	35.00	100.00
S394	20 Scudi 1786-96.	12.00	35.00	100.00

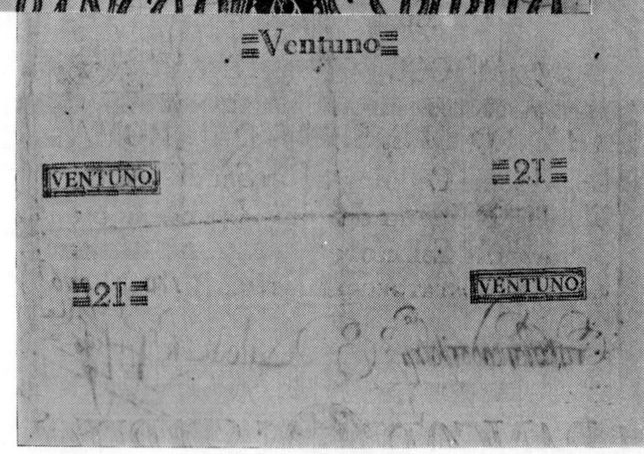

		Good	Fine	XF
S395	21 Scudi 1786-96.	12.00	35.00	100.00
S396	22 Scudi 1786-96.	12.00	35.00	100.00
S397	23 Scudi 1786-96.	14.00	40.00	120.00
S398	24 Scudi 1786-96.	14.00	40.00	120.00
S399	25 Scudi 1786-96.	14.00	40.00	120.00
S400	26 Scudi 1786-96.	14.00	40.00	120.00
S401	27 Scudi 1786-96.	14.00	40.00	120.00
S402	28 Scudi 1786-96.	14.00	40.00	120.00
S403	29 Scudi 1786-96.	14.00	40.00	120.00
S404	30 Scudi 1786-96.	14.00	40.00	120.00
S405	31 Scudi 1786-96.	15.00	45.00	140.00

		Good	Fine	XF
S406	32 Scudi 1786-96.	15.00	45.00	140.00
S407	33 Scudi 1786-96.	15.00	45.00	140.00
S408	34 Scudi 1786-96.	15.00	45.00	140.00
S409	35 Scudi 1786-96.	15.00	45.00	140.00
S410	36 Scudi 1786-96.	18.00	35.00	160.00
S411	37 Scudi 1786-96.	18.00	35.00	160.00
S412	38 Scudi 1786-96.	18.00	35.00	160.00
S413	39 Scudi 1786-96.	18.00	35.00	160.00
S414	40 Scudi 1786-96.	18.00	35.00	160.00
S415	41 Scudi 1786-96.	18.00	35.00	160.00
S416	42 Scudi 1786-96.	30.00	90.00	280.00
S417	43 Scudi 1786-96.	25.00	75.00	200.00
S418	44 Scudi 1786-96.	25.00	75.00	200.00
S419	45 Scudi 1786-96.	20.00	60.00	180.00
S420	46 Scudi 1786-96.	20.00	60.00	180.00
S421	47 Scudi 1786-96.	20.00	60.00	180.00
S422	48 Scudi 1786-96.	20.00	60.00	180.00
S423	49 Scudi 1786-96.	20.00	60.00	180.00
S424	50 Scudi 1786-96.	25.00	75.00	200.00
S425	51 Scudi 1786-96.	30.00	90.00	280.00
S426	52 Scudi 1786-96.	35.00	100.00	300.00
S427	53 Scudi 1786-96.	35.00	100.00	300.00
S428	54 Scudi 1786-96.	35.00	100.00	300.00
S429	55 Scudi 1786-96.	35.00	100.00	300.00
S430	56 Scudi 1786-96.	35.00	100.00	300.00
S431	57 Scudi 1786-96.	35.00	100.00	300.00
S432	58 Scudi 1786-96.	35.00	100.00	300.00
S433	59 Scudi 1786-96.	35.00	100.00	300.00
S434	60 Scudi 1786-96.	35.00	100.00	300.00
S435	61 Scudi 1786-96.	40.00	120.00	350.00
S436	62 Scudi 1786-96.	40.00	120.00	350.00
S437	63 Scudi 1786-96.	40.00	120.00	350.00
S438	64 Scudi 1786-96.	40.00	120.00	350.00
S439	65 Scudi 1786-96.	40.00	120.00	350.00
S440	66 Scudi 1786-96.	40.00	120.00	350.00
S441	67 Scudi 1786-96.	40.00	120.00	350.00
S442	68 Scudi 1786-96.	40.00	120.00	350.00
S443	69 Scudi 1786-96.	40.00	120.00	350.00
S444	70 Scudi 1786-96.	40.00	120.00	350.00
S445	71 Scudi 1786-96.	50.00	150.00	450.00
S446	72 Scudi 1786-96.	50.00	150.00	450.00
S447	73 Scudi 1786-96.	50.00	150.00	450.00
S448	74 Scudi 1786-96.	50.00	150.00	450.00
S449	75 Scudi 1786-96.	50.00	150.00	450.00
S450	76 Scudi 1786-96.	50.00	150.00	450.00
S451	77 Scudi 1786-96.	50.00	150.00	450.00
S452	78 Scudi 1786-96.	50.00	150.00	450.00
S453	79 Scudi 1786-96.	50.00	150.00	450.00

#	Denomination	Good	Fine	XF
S454	80 Scudi 1786-96.	50.00	150.00	450.00
S455	81 Scudi 1786-96.	50.00	150.00	450.00
S456	82 Scudi 1786-96.	50.00	150.00	450.00
S457	83 Scudi 1786-96.	50.00	150.00	450.00
S458	84 Scudi 1786-96.	50.00	150.00	450.00
S459	85 Scudi 1786-96.	50.00	150.00	450.00
S460	86 Scudi 1786-96.	50.00	150.00	450.00
S461	87 Scudi 1786-96.	50.00	150.00	450.00
S462	88 Scudi 1786-96.	50.00	150.00	450.00

#	Denomination	Good	Fine	XF
S463	89 Scudi 1786-96.	40.00	120.00	350.00
S464	90 Scudi 1786-96.	35.00	100.00	300.00
S465	91 Scudi 1786-96.	50.00	150.00	450.00
S466	92 Scudi 1786-96.	50.00	150.00	450.00
S467	93 Scudi 1786-96.	50.00	150.00	450.00
S468	94 Scudi 1786-96.	50.00	150.00	450.00
S469	95 Scudi 1786-96.	50.00	150.00	450.00
S470	96 Scudi 1786-96.	50.00	150.00	450.00
S471	97 Scudi 1786-96.	50.00	150.00	450.00
S472	98 Scudi 1786-96.	50.00	150.00	450.00
S473	99 Scudi 1786-96.	40.00	120.00	350.00
S474	100 Scudi 1786-96.	45.00	130.00	400.00
S475	105 Scudi 1786-96.	60.00	180.00	500.00
S476	110 Scudi 1786-96.	60.00	180.00	500.00
S477	115 Scudi 1786-96.	60.00	180.00	500.00
S478	120 Scudi 1786-96.	60.00	180.00	500.00
S479	125 Scudi 1786-96.	60.00	180.00	500.00
S480	130 Scudi 1786-96.	60.00	180.00	500.00
S481	135 Scudi 1786-96.	60.00	180.00	500.00
S482	140 Scudi 1786-96.	60.00	180.00	500.00
S483	145 Scudi 1786-96.	60.00	180.00	500.00
S484	150 Scudi 1786-96.	60.00	180.00	500.00
S485	155 Scudi 1786-96.	60.00	180.00	500.00
S486	160 Scudi 1786-96.	60.00	180.00	500.00
S487	165 Scudi 1786-96.	60.00	180.00	500.00
S488	170 Scudi 1786-96.	60.00	180.00	500.00

#	Denomination	Good	Fine	XF
S489	175 Scudi 1786-96.	60.00	180.00	500.00
S490	180 Scudi 1786-96.	60.00	180.00	500.00
S491	185 Scudi 1786-96.	60.00	180.00	500.00
S492	190 Scudi 1786-96.	60.00	180.00	500.00
S493	195 Scudi 1786-96.	60.00	180.00	500.00
S494	200 Scudi 1786-96.	60.00	180.00	500.00
S495	210 Scudi 1786-96.	70.00	200.00	600.00
S496	220 Scudi 1786-96.	70.00	200.00	600.00
S497	230 Scudi 1786-96.	70.00	200.00	600.00
S498	240 Scudi 1786-96.	70.00	200.00	600.00
S499	250 Scudi 1786-96.	70.00	200.00	600.00
S500	260 Scudi 1786-96.	70.00	200.00	600.00
S501	270 Scudi 1786-96.	70.00	200.00	600.00
S502	280 Scudi 1786-96.	70.00	200.00	600.00
S503	290 Scudi 1786-96.	70.00	200.00	600.00
S504	300 Scudi 1786-96.	70.00	200.00	600.00
S505	320 Scudi 1786-96.	80.00	240.00	700.00
S506	340 Scudi 1786-96.	80.00	240.00	700.00
S507	360 Scudi 1786-96.	80.00	240.00	700.00
S508	380 Scudi 1786-96.	80.00	240.00	700.00
S509	400 Scudi 1786-96.	80.00	240.00	700.00
S510	450 Scudi 1786-96.	120.00	350.00	1000.
S511	500 Scudi 1786-96.	120.00	350.00	1000.
S512	600 Scudi 1786-96.	—	Rare	—
S513	700 Scudi 1786-96.	—	Rare	—
S514	800 Scudi 1786-96.	—	Rare	—
S515	900 Scudi 1786-96.	—	Rare	—
S516	1000 Scudi 1786-96.	—	Rare	—
S517	1500 Scudi 1786-96.	—	Rare	—
S518	2000 Scudi 1786-96.	— Unknown		—
S519	3000 Scudi 1786-96.	— Unknown		—

NOTE: During First Roman Republic, some Banco Di S. Spirito notes were ovpt. by the Republican Municipal Administration with the seal of about 15 different towns, to ratify the validity of circulation. All the Republican validated notes are rare and, in comparison with the normal notes, prices increase up to double the value for common seals and up to five times for rarer seals.

PRIMA REPUBBLICA ROMANA

Banco di S. Spirito

1798 Issue

#S521-S525 black. White wmk. paper. Various handwriten dates. Republican seal at top l. and r.

#	Denomination	VG	VF	Unc
S521	25 Bajocchi 8.6.1798-5.8.1798.			
	a. Value in words.	15.00	30.00	120.00
	b. Value in numerals.	25.00	50.00	200.00
S522	40 Bajocchi 5.8.1798-27.8.1798.	15.00	30.00	120.00

		VG	VF	Unc
S523	**50 Bajocchi** 23.6.1798-4.9.1798.			
	a. Value in words.	12.00	25.00	100.00
	b. Value in numerals.	20.00	40.00	150.00
S524	**60 Bajocchi** 3.7.1798-4.8.1798.	20.00	40.00	160.00
S525	**10 Paoli = 100 Bajocchi** 3.7.1798-4.9.1798.	10.00	25.00	100.00

Monte di Pieta'

1798 Issue

#S526-S530 black. White wmk. paper. Various handwritten dates. Republican seal at top l. and r.

		VG	VF	Unc
S526	**25 Bajocchi** 11.6.1798-30.10.1798.			
	a. Value in words.	15.00	30.00	120.00
	b. Value in numerals.	20.00	40.00	160.00
S527	**40 Bajocchi** 11.8.1798-4.9.1798.	15.00	30.00	100.00

		VG	VF	Unc
S528	**50 Bajocchi** 3.7.1798-4.9.1798.			
	a. Value in words.	10.00	20.00	80.00
	b. Value in numerals.	15.00	30.00	100.00
S529	**60 Bajocchi** 6.8.1798-4.9.1798.	15.00	30.00	100.00
S530	**10 Paoli = 100 Bajocchi** 6.7.1798-4.9.1798.	10.00	20.00	80.00

Assegnati - Assignats

1798 Issue

#S531-S540 black. Value printed. Black seal on back. White wmk. paper.

		VG	VF	Unc
S531	**3 Bajocchi** ANNO 7 (1798).	25.00	80.00	200.00
S532	**5 Bajocchi** ANNO 7 (1798).	150.00	400.00	1200.
S533	**10 Bajocchi = 1 Paolo** ANNO 7 (1798).	120.00	300.00	800.00
S534	**1 1/2 Paoli** ANNO 7 (1798).	15.00	40.00	80.00
S535	**2 Paoli** ANNO 7 (1798).	25.00	80.00	180.00
S536	**2 1/2 Paoli** ANNO 7 (1798).	25.00	70.00	160.00

		VG	VF	Unc
S537	**7 Paoli** ANNO 7 (1798).	10.00	25.00	60.00
S538	**8 Paoli** ANNO 7 (1798).	10.00	25.00	60.00
S539	**9 Paoli** ANNO 7 (1798).	10.00	25.00	60.00
S540	**10 Paoli** ANNO 7 (1798).			

		VG	VF	Unc
	a. Value in triangle on back.	5.00	15.00	40.00
	b. Value in circle on back.	5.00	15.00	40.00

		VG	VF	Unc
	c. Value in square on back.	5.00	15.00	40.00
	d. Value in rhombus on back.	5.00	15.00	40.00

Banca Romana

Founded in Rome in 1826, the bank was authorized in 1834 to issue bank notes until 1849. It opened two branches in Bologna and in Ancona. In 1851 it merged into Banca Dello Stato Pontificio.

1834; 1849 Issue

#S551-S555 seal w/*Banca Romana* and value on back. White wmk. paper.

		Good	Fine	XF
S551	**5 Scudi** 1835-49. Light gray. Fortune at l. and r.	800.00	1800.	2800.
S552	**10 Scudi** 1835-49. Light brick red. Tevere allegory at top l. and r.	—	Rare	—

		Good	Fine	XF
S553	**20 Scudi** 1834-49. Orange. Allegorical figure all around in oval.	—	Rare	—
S554	**50 Scudi** 1834-49. Blue on azure unpt. Allegory all around in oval.	—	Rare	—
S555	**100 Scudi** 1834-49. Gray on white. Allegorical figure all around.	—	Rare	—

Buoni del Tesoro

1848 Issue

#S556-S562 embossed seal. 2-1/2 seals on front and red seal on back. Paper w/wmk.

		Good	Fine	XF
S556	**1 Scudo** 1848. Brown, rose on creme unpt.	—	Rare	—
S557	**2 Scudi** 1848. Deep gray on yellow unpt.	150.00	300.00	500.00
S558	**5 Scudi** 1848. Gray-olive. White paper.	250.00	600.00	1000.
S559	**10 Scudi** 1848. Gray-green. Green paper.	500.00	1400.	2500.
S560	**20 Scudi** 1848.	Reported Not Confirmed		
S561	**50 Scudi** 1848.	Reported Not Confirmed		
S562	**100 Scudi** 1848. Red on rose unpt.	—	Rare	—

Legazione di Bologna - Boni Provinciali

1848; 1849 Provisional Issue

#S563-S568 deep blue. Lt. blue paper w/wmk.

		Good	Fine	XF
S563	**5 Scudi** 14.8.1848; 3.1.1849.	—	Rare	—
S564	**10 Scudi** 14.8.1848; 3.1.1849. Black on blue.	—	Rare	—
S565	**20 Scudi** 14.8.1848; 3.1.1849.	—	Rare	—

		Good	Fine	XF
S566	**30 Scudi** 3.1.1849.	—	Rare	—
S567	**50 Scudi** 14.8.1848; 3.1.1849.	—	Rare	—
S568	**100 Scudi** 14.8.1848.	—	Rare	—

SECONDA REPUBBLICA ROMANA

Boni Centrali

1849 Issue

#S571-S583 Republican eagle at top ctr., embossed seal w/Republican eagle.

		Good	Fine	XF
S571	**10 Bajocchi** 1849. Black. White paper.	25.00	100.00	250.00
S572	**16 Bajocchi** 1849. Black on gray unpt.	25.00	100.00	250.00

		Good	Fine	XF
S573	**24 Bajocchi** 1849. Black. Yellow paper.	20.00	100.00	250.00
S574	**24 Bajocchi** 1849. Black. Yellow paper. New typology.	—	Rare	—
S575	**32 Bajocchi** 1849. Blue on azure unpt.	100.00	300.00	600.00
S576	**40 Bajocchi** 1849. Black on green unpt.	100.00	300.00	600.00
S577	**1 Scudo** 1849. Slate on gray unpt.	80.00	260.00	450.00
S578	**2 Scudi** 1849. Slate on gray unpt.	100.00	300.00	650.00
S579	**5 Scudi** 1849. Slate. White paper.	200.00	800.00	1500.

		Good	Fine	XF
S580	**10 Scudi** 1849. Olive on green unpt.	—	Rare	—
S581	**20 Scudi** 1849. Slate. White paper.	—	Rare	—
S582	**50 Scudi** 1849. Slate on light azure-green unpt.	—	Rare	—
S583	**100 Scudi** 1849.	Reported Not Confirmed		

Boni Provinciali

Ancona

1849 Issue

#S584-S591 black. Several stampings on back. White paper.

		Good	Fine	XF
S584	**5 Bajocchi** 10.6.1849.	250.00	600.00	1000.
S585	**5+5 Bajocchi** 1849.			
	a. Issued note (= 10 Bajocchi).	200.00	500.00	800.00
	b. Cut l. or r. half (= 5 Bajocchi).	80.00	200.00	325.00

		Good	Fine	XF
S586	**10 Bajocchi** 1849.	250.00	600.00	1000.
S587	**20 Bajocchi** 1849.	—	Rare	—
S588	**25 Bajocchi** 1849.	—	Rare	—
S589	**30 Bajocchi** 1849.	—	Rare	—
S590	**40 Bajocchi** 1849.	280.00	700.00	1200.
S591	**50 Bajocchi** 1849.	—	Rare	—

Ascoli

ND Issue

		Good	Fine	XF
S592	**1 1/2 Bajocchi** ND. Green paper.	Reported Not Confirmed		
S593	**3 Bajocchi** ND. Blue paper.	Reported Not Confirmed		
S594	**5 Bajocchi** ND. Creme paper.	Reported Not Confirmed		
S595	**10 Bajocchi** ND. White paper.	Reported Not Confirmed		
S596	**20 Bajocchi** ND. Yellow paper.	Reported Not Confirmed		
S597	**30 Bajocchi** ND. Rose paper.	Reported Not Confirmed		
S598	**50 Bajocchi** ND. White paper.	Reported Not Confirmed		

BOLOGNA

ORDINANCE OF MARCH 7, 1849

#S599-S604 black w/embossed seal. Blue seal on back.

		Good	Fine	XF
S599	**5 Bajocchi** *L. 1849.* Blue paper.	50.00	150.00	300.00
S600	**10 Bajocchi** *L. 1849.* White paper.	50.00	150.00	300.00
S601	**20 Bajocchi** *L. 1849.* Orange paper.	60.00	180.00	400.00

		Good	Fine	XF
S602	**1/2 Scudo** *L. 1849.* Black on creme unpt. White paper.	120.00	380.00	800.00
S603	**1 Scudo** *L. 1849.* Black on rose unpt. White paper.	200.00	600.00	1200.
S604	**2 1/2 Scudi** *L. 1849.* Black. White paper.	—	Rare	—

CIVITAVECCHIA

1849 ISSUE

		Good	Fine	XF
S605	**10 Bajocchi** 14.5.1849.	Reported Not Confirmed		
S606	**20 Bajocchi** 14.5.1849. Black. Red paper.	—	Rare	—
S607	**30 Bajocchi** 14.5.1849.	Reported Not Confirmed		
S608	**50 Bajocchi** 14.5.1849. Black. Yellow paper.	—	Rare	—
S609	**1 Scudo** 14.5.1849. Black. Green paper.	—	Rare	—

FORLI

1849 ISSUE

#S611-S613 black, embossed seal w/different seals on face and back.

		Good	Fine	XF
S611	**5 Bajocchi** 14.4.1849. White paper.	—	Rare	—

		Good	Fine	XF
S612	**20 Bajocchi** 14.4.1849. Rose paper.	—	Rare	—
S613	**1 Scudo** 14.4.1849. White paper.	—	Rare	—

FROSINONE

ND ISSUE

		Good	Fine	XF
S614	**5 Bajocchi** ND. Blue w/blue seal on face. Red seal on back. White paper.	—	Rare	—

PERUGIA

ND ISSUE

		Good	Fine	XF
S620	**5 Bajocchi** ND. Slate. Creme paper.	—	Rare	—

RIETI

ND ISSUE

		Good	Fine	XF
S621	**6 Bajocchi** ND. Black w/red seal. White paper.	—	Rare	—
S622	**14 Bajocchi** ND. Black w/red and black seals. White paper.	—	Rare	—
S623	**35 Bajocchi** ND. Black w/red and black seals. Creme paper.	—	Rare	—

BONI COMUNALI

ALBANO

ND ISSUE

#S631-S633 black.

		Good	Fine	XF
S631	**5 Bajocchi** ND. White paper.	—	Rare	—
S632	**7 1/2 Bajocchi** ND. Creme paper.	—	Rare	—
S633	**12 1/2 Bajocchi** ND. Yellow paper.	—	Rare	—

ARSOLI

ND ISSUE

#S634-S636 black.

		Good	Fine	XF
S634	**3 Bajocchi** ND. Lt. green paper.	—	Rare	—

		Good	Fine	XF
S635	**5 Bajocchi** ND. Lt. azure paper.	—	Rare	—
S636	**10 Bajocchi** ND. Lt. green paper.	—	Rare	—

MONSANVITO

ND ISSUE

		Good	Fine	XF
S641	**2 1/2 Bajocchi** ND. Black. White paper.	—	Unique	—

PESARO

ND ISSUE

#S642-S648 white paper.

		Good	Fine	XF
S642	**5 Bajocchi** ND. Blue and black.	—	Rare	—
S643	**10 Bajocchi** ND. Blue w/red seal. Back blue.	—	Rare	—
S644	**20 Bajocchi** ND. Blue w/red seal. Back blue.	—	Rare	—
S645	**50 Bajocchi** ND. Blue w/red seal. Back blue.	—	Rare	—
S646	**1 Scudo** ND. Red w/black seal. Two seals on back.	—	Rare	—
S647	**2 Scudi** ND. Red w/black seal. Two seals on back.	—	Rare	—
S648	**5 Scudi** ND. Orange w/seal. Two seals on back.	—	Rare	—

COMMISSARIATO PONTIFICIO PER LE 4 LEGAZIONI-BOLOGNA

On June 1849, while Rome was still under the Republican Government, Bologna was under the control of the Papal Restoration.

1849 ISSUE

		GOOD	FINE	XF
S651	**20 BAJOCCHI** 1.6.1849. Black w/embossed seal. Two seals on back. White paper.	60.00	180.00	300.00

BONI DEL TESORO IN SOSTITUZIONE

1849 ISSUE

#S652-S657 full seal w/2 partial circular seals at upper and lower l. Red seal on back. Wmk. paper.

		GOOD	FINE	XF
S652	**1 SCUDO** 3.8.1849. Slate. Gray-azure paper.	120.00	300.00	800.00
S653	**2 SCUDO** 3.8.1849. Slate. Yellow paper.	—	Rare	—

		GOOD	FINE	XF
S654	**5 SCUDI** 3.8.1849. Slate. Creme paper.	200.00	600.00	1500.

		GOOD	FINE	XF
S655	**10 SCUDI** 3.8.1849. Slate. Green-yellow paper.	—	Rare	—
S656	**20 SCUDI** 3.8.1849. Olive on lt. green unpt.	—	Rare	—
S657	**50 SCUDI** 3.8.1849. Slate on deep green unpt.	120.00	280.00	600.00

BONI DEL TESORO IN SURROGAZIONE

1851 ISSUE

#S658-S663 blue seal. Red seal on back. Wmk. paper.

		GOOD	FINE	XF
S658	**1 SCUDO** 10.6.1851. Red on rose unpt.	200.00	600.00	1000.

		GOOD	FINE	XF
S659	**5 SCUDI** 10.6.1851. Red on azure unpt.	400.00	1200.	2000.
S660	**10 SCUDI** 10.6.1851. Blue-green on azure unpt.	—	Rare	—
S661	**20 SCUDI** 10.6.1851.		Reported Not Confirmed	
S662	**50 SCUDI** 10.6.1851.		Reported Not Confirmed	
S663	**100 SCUDI** 10.6.1851.		Reported Not Confirmed	

BANCO DI SANTO SPIRITO

Issued in order to withdraw earlier Papal State issues. Circulated 1855-58, eventually all being exchanged for silver coinage.

1855; 1858 ISSUE

		GOOD	FINE	XF
S665	**20 SCUDI** 1855-58. Black on blue unpt. w/black seal at lower ctr.	—	Unique	—

BANCA PONTIFICIA PER LE 4 LEGAZIONI

Merged into Banca Nazionale Negli Stati Sardi in 1851.

1855 ND PROVISIONAL ISSUE

#S671-S674 ovpt: *BIGLIETTO PROVVISORIO/DELLA BANCA DI BOLOGNA PER LE 4 LEGAZIONI/PAGABILE IN BOLOGNA* on notes of Banca Dello Stato Pontificio.

		GOOD	FINE	XF
S671	**10 SCUDI** ND (1855- old date 1853). Ovpt. on #S692.			
	a. Issued note.	—	Rare	—
	r. Remainder.	—	—	140.00
S672	**20 SCUDI** ND (1855- old date 1853). Ovpt. on #S694.			
	a. Issued note.	—	Rare	—
	r. Remainder.	—	—	220.00
S673	**50 SCUDI** ND (1855- old date 1853). Ovpt. on #S695.		Reported Not Confirmed	
S674	**100 SCUDI** ND (1855- old date 1853). Ovpt. on #S696.		Reported Not Confirmed	

BANCA DELLO STATO PONTIFICIO

Founded 1850 and approved on 1851 with the absorption of Banca Romana including also Ancona and Bologna branches. During the first two years of its existence, the bank used old bank notes of absorbed Banca Romana.

1851-52 ND PROVISIONAL ISSUE

#S681-S685 ovpt: *Biglietto Provvisorio della Banca della Stato Pontificio* on back.

		GOOD	FINE	XF
S681	**5 SCUDI** ND (1851-52- old dates 1835-49). Ovpt. on #S551.	—	Rare	—
S682	**10 SCUDI** ND (1851-52- old dates 1835-49). Ovpt. on #S552.	—	Rare	—
S683	**20 SCUDI** ND (1851-52- old dates 1834-49). Ovpt. on #S553.	—	Rare	—

		Good	Fine	XF
S684	**50 Scudi** ND (1851-52- old dates 1834-49). Ovpt. on #S554.	—	Rare	—
S685	**100 Scudi** ND (1851-52- old dates 1834-49). Ovpt. on #S555.	—	Rare	—

Banca Dello Stato Pontificio - Regular Issue

1853-61 ND Issue

		Good	Fine	XF
S686	**1 Scudo** ND (1853). Black. White paper.	200.00	600.00	1200.
S687	**1 Scudo** 1866; 1867. Blue. Italian lire denomination on back. White paper.	160.00	500.00	900.00
S688	**2 Scudi** ND (1856). Blue. White paper.	Reported Not Confirmed		
S689	**5 Scudi** ND (1853). Azure. White paper.	240.00	750.00	1200.
S690	**5 Scudi** ND (1861). Female head at l. and at r., allegorical figure around.	—	Rare	—
S691	**5 Scudi** 1866; 1867. Red. Allegorical figure all around in oval.	—	Rare	—
S692	**10 Scudi** ND (1853). Female head at l. and at r., allegorical figure around.	—	Rare	—
S693	**10 Scudi** ND (1859).	Reported Not Confirmed		

		Good	Fine	XF
S694	**20 Scudi** (1853). Green. Allegorical figures all around in oval.	—	Rare	—
S695	**50 Scudi** (1853). Yellow. Allegorical figures all around in oval.	Reported Not Confirmed		
S696	**100 Scudi** (1853). Red. Allegorical figures all around in oval.	Reported Not Confirmed		

Banca Dello Stato Pontificio

After the unification of Italy in 1861, Papal State territory was limited at the town of Rome. In 1867, Banca Dello Stato Pontificio decided to issue bank notes in Italian Lire, and they circulated up to 1870 when Rome was invaded by Italian troops, and the bank was incorporated by Banca Nazionale Negli Stati Sardi.

1867 Italian Lire Issue

#S701-S708 wmk. white paper.

		Good	Fine	XF
S701	**5 Lire** 1867-70. Black and blue. Woman's head on back.	—	Rare	—
S702	**10 Lire** 1867-70. Blue. Woman with headpiece at l.	—	Rare	—
S703	**20 Lire** 1867-70. Allegorical women at l. and at r.	—	Rare	—
S704	**50 Lire** 1867-70. Agriculture at l. and Industry at r.	—	Rare	—
S705	**100 Lire** 1867-70. Allegorical women standing at l. and at r.	—	Rare	—
S706	**200 Lire** 1867-70. Two columns at l. and at r. w/allegorical figures.	—	Rare	—
S707	**500 Lire** 1867-70. Seated allegorical figures at l. and at r., allegories below.	—	Rare	—
S708	**1000 Lire** 1867-70. Six allegories including Industry and Agriculture.	—	Rare	—

Regno Delle Due Sicilie
Kingdom of the Two Sicilies

The Kingdom was formally created in 1816 from the ashes of the Napoleonic empire; but the history of the two regions continually crosses starting from the 12th century with Roger II, followed by the Angevin occupation in 1266, the Aragonese one in 1442, the very short French one during the first years of 1500. In 1905 the two areas became provinces of the Spanish monarchy ruled by a viceroy. After a short Austrian occupation subsequent to the Treaty of Utrecht (1713), the two provinces returned to the Spanish influence with the Bourbon of Spain until the Napoleonic occupation and the Rule of Joachim Murat.

The succession of sovereigns.:
Ferdinando I, 1816-1825
Francesco I, 1825-1830
Ferdinando II, 1830-1859
Francesco II, 1859-1861

Governo Provvisorio di Sicilia

Issue during the regency of Ruggero Settimo, January 12, 1848 to April 23, 1849.

1849 Issue

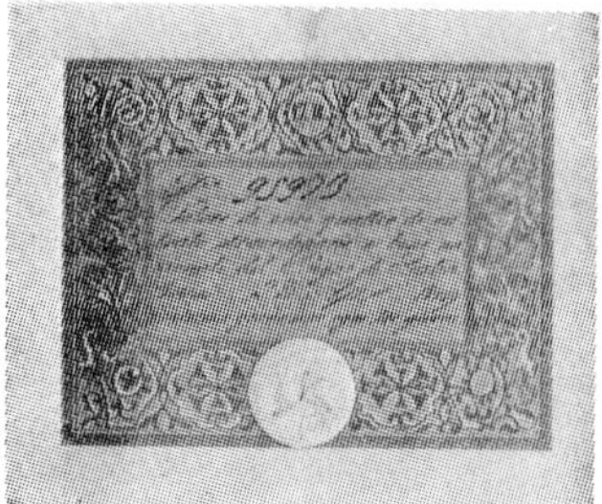

		Good	Fine	XF
S711	**4 Oncia** 23.4.1849. Gray and hazel.	220.00	600.00	1000.

REGNO D'ITALIA

From the fall of the Roman empire until last century, Italy was divided into many independent states and kingdoms, and some of them were sometimes occupied by other European States. The *Risorgimento* unification movement, fostered by Cavour, Garibaldi and Mazzini, with the help of England and France, attained fruition in 1860-70 with the creation of the Kingdom of Italy (March 1861) and the installation of Victor Emanuele II, King of Sardinia, as King of Italy.

Government Banks

Banca Nazionale nel Regno d'Italia

Because of a serious shortage of coins, and awaiting this release of new paper money, the Italian administration decided to put into circulation revenue stamps normally affixed to bills of exchange. The circulation of these stamps began in June 1866 and they were controlled by Banca Nazionale.

1866 ND Provisional Marca da Bollo Stamp Issue

#S721-S723 portr. Kg. Victor Emanuele II, w/bar ovpt. across *DA BOLLA.*

		Good	Fine	XF
S721	**5 Lire** ND (1866).	100.00	250.00	400.00

#S721

#722

		Good	Fine	XF
S722	**10 Lire** ND (1866).	200.00	450.00	750.00
S723	**15 Lire** ND (1866).	—	Rare	—

1866-96 Regular Issues

		Good	Fine	XF
S731	**1 Lira** 20.1.1869; 17.7.1872; 15.1.1873. Black on green unpt. Head at lower l. and r., date in circles at lower ctr. Portrs. Cavour and Manin at upper and lower l., Columbus and Dante at upper and lower r. on back	3.00	10.00	50.00

		Good	Fine	XF
S732	**2 Lire** 25.7.1866; 22.1.1868. Black. Count Cavour at ctr. Back green; date at top.	4.00	12.50	65.00

S733 5 LIRE — GOOD 60.00 · FINE 200.00 · XF 800.00
29.8.1866. Black. Head of Italia at upper l. White paper.

S734 5 LIRE — GOOD 4.00 · FINE 12.00 · XF 70.00
30.10.1867; 15.1.1873. Black on blue unpt. Portrs. Cavour at upper l., Columbus at upper r., heads at lower l. and r. Back black on olive unpt.

S735 10 LIRE — GOOD 200.00 · FINE 800.00 · XF 1800.
19.5.1866. Dk. blue. Victor Emanuele II at upper ctr.

S736 10 LIRE — GOOD 5.00 · FINE 20.00 · XF 125.00
16.5.1866-28.9.1870. Black. Count Cavour at lower l., supported royal arms at upper ctr., Columbus at lower r. Back blue; date at top, text at ctr.

S737 10 LIRE — GOOD 5.00 · FINE 20.00 · XF 125.00
17.7.1872. Black on peach and green unpt. Similar to #S212. Back blue and black; portr. Italia at ctr.

S738 25 LIRE — GOOD 80.00 · FINE 250.00 · XF 800.00
25.7.1866; 30.10.1867; 22.7.1868. Black. Red paper.

S739 25 LIRE — GOOD 60.00 · FINE 200.00 · XF 650.00
24.1.1883-20.7.1892. Dk. blue on orange unpt. 3 cherubs at lower ctr., seated woman w/fasces and cornucopia at r., arms at top ctr. Back blue; bust of Italia at ctr., head at each corner.

S740 40 LIRE — GOOD — · FINE Rare · XF —
25.7.1866. Black. Olive paper.

S741 50 LIRE — GOOD 40.00 · FINE 150.00 · XF 500.00
1874-24.6.1895. Blue. Arms at upper ctr., portr. Italia at l., seated Justice at bottom ctr. Anchor between 2 medallion portraits at ctr. on back. Ivory paper.

S742 100 LIRE — GOOD 35.00 · FINE 130.00 · XF 450.00
15.1.1873-18.5.1896. Black. Rose paper.

S743 250 LIRE — GOOD 350.00 · FINE 1200. · XF 3000.
15.1.1873. Black. Lt. green paper.

S744 500 LIRE — GOOD 150.00 · FINE 550.00 · XF 1400.
17.7.1872-24.6.1895. Black. Yellow paper.

S745 1000 LIRE — GOOD — · FINE Rare · XF —
17.7.1872; 15.1.1873. Black. White paper.

S746 1000 LIRE — GOOD 350.00 · FINE 1200. · XF 2400.
16.1.1878-18.5.1896. Yellow-brown. Cherubs at sides, allegorical figures of Industry and Agriculture seated at bottom ctr., arms at top ctr. Bust of Italia on back. Lt. blue paper.

BANCA NAZIONALE TOSCANA

As mentioned under the Granducato di Toscana, this bank was founded in 1857, issued bank notes up to 1859. None of these have survived. The following listings are only of the bank note issues after the establishment of the Kingdom of Italy.

1859-73 ISSUES

S751 50 CENTESIMI — GOOD 5.00 · FINE 12.00 · XF 50.00
1873. Black on orange unpt. Back orange; facing heads of Italia at ctr.

S752 1 LIRA — GOOD 8.00 · FINE 20.00 · XF 80.00
1873. Black. Back green; head of Italia at ctr.

S753 2 LIRE — GOOD 25.00 · FINE 70.00 · XF 250.00
1873. Black on red unpt. Portr. Dante at l. Back red; similar to #S262.

S754 5 LIRE — GOOD 80.00 · FINE 250.00 · XF 900.00
1873. Black on purple unpt. Similar to #S263. Back purple; 4 heads of Italia.

S755 10 LIRE — GOOD 120.00 · FINE 500.00 · XF 1600.
1873. Black on red unpt. Similar to #S753. Back red; 2 facing heads of Italia at ctr.

S756 20 LIRE — GOOD 100.00 · FINE 400.00 · XF 1200.
19.5.1866; 17.7.1866. Black on green paper.

#	Description	Good	Fine	XF
S757	**20 Lire** 3.9.1872. Black on peach unpt. Back red-orange and green; Italia at ctr.	200.00	800.00	2000.
S758	**25 Lire** 1883. Red and green on red-orange unpt.	120.00	400.00	1200.
S759	**50 Lire** 19.5.1866; 4.7.1866; 17.7.1866. Black on pink paper. Like #S246.	130.00	450.00	1400.
S760	**50 Lire** 1872. Black on rose unpt. Italia at l., Dente at r. Back red-orange and brown.	180.00	650.00	1800.
S761	**50 Lire** 23.12.1883. Blue-green on gray.	100.00	400.00	1000.
S762	**100 Lire** 19.5.1866; 17.7.1866.	—	Rare	—
S763	**100 Lire** 2.1.1865.	Reported Not Confirmed		

#	Description	Good	Fine	XF
S764	**100 Lire** 9.9.1869-23.12.1883. Black on violet unpt. Back violet. Tan paper.	100.00	400.00	1000.
S765	**200 Lire** 2.1.1865.	Reported Not Confirmed		
S766	**200 Lire** 9.9.1869; 18.8.1870. Black on green unpt. Back green. Lt. blue paper.	300.00	1500.	3600.
S767	**500 Lire** 2.1.1865.	Reported Not Confirmed		

#	Description	Good	Fine	XF
S768	**500 Lire** 9.9.1869; 18.8.1870. Black on orange unpt. Back orange. Yellow paper.	—	Rare	—
S769	**1000 Lire** 2.1.1865.	Reported Not Confirmed		
S770	**1000 Lire** 9.9.1869; 18.8.1870. Black on blue and lt. tan unpt. Back orange.	—	Rare	—

Banca Toscana di Credito

Founded in 1860, the bank started operations in 1863. In 1893 the bank merged into Banca d'Italia.

1864-80 Issue

#	Description	Good	Fine	XF
S771	**20 Lire** 30.6.1866. Black. Yellow paper. Uniface.	130.00	450.00	1400.

#S772-S782 printer: BWC.

#	Description	Good	Fine	XF
S772	**20 Lire** 1.1.1873; 17.9.1876. Black. Italia head in oval at l., yellow paper. Back peach on white paper.	—	Rare	—
S773	**50 Lire** 2.1.1864; 1.7.1874. Similar to 20 Lire, #S772.	—	Rare	—
S774	**50 Lire** 2.1.1880. Similar to #S773 but larger size.	—	Rare	—
S775	**100 Lire** 2.1.1864; 1.7.1874. Similar to 20 Lire, #S772.	—	Rare	—
S776	**100 Lire** 2.1.1880. Similar to #S775 but larger size.	800.00	2500.	6000.
S777	**200 Lire** 2.1.1864. Similar to 20 Lire, #S772.	—	Rare	—
S778	**200 Lire** 2.1.1880. Similar to #S777 but larger size.	—	Rare	—
S779	**500 Lire** 2.1.1868; 1.7.1874. Black. Arms on back. Peach paper.	—	Rare	—
S780	**500 Lire** 2.1.1880. Similar to #S779 but larger size.	—	Rare	—
S781	**1000 Lire** 2.1.1864. Proof.	—	Unique	—
S782	**5000 Lire** 2.1.1864. (2 known.)	—	Rare	—

Banca Romana

During 1870, after the military occupation of Rome by the Kingdom of Italy forces, Banca Dello Stato Pontificio became Banca Romana and issued bank notes until 1890. In 1891, because of serious administrative irregularities, the bank was put under the court of justice control. In 1893 Banca Romana was absorbed by Bank of Italy.

1872; 1890 Issue

#S791 and S792 printer: BWC. Backs have varying numbers of heads of Italia/Roma, some w/multiple arms.

		VG	VF	Unc
S791	**50 Centesimi** 1872. Black on violet unpt. Italia at r. 1 head on back at l.	12.00	30.00	140.00
S792	**1 Lira** 1872. Black on brown unpt. Italia at l. 1 head on back at ctr.	15.00	40.00	150.00

#S793-S795 printer: A.B.C.

#S272A

#S273

#	Description	Good	Fine	XF
S793	**2 Lire** ND. Cameo portr. woman at upper ctr. Proof.	—	—	—
S794	**5 Lire** 1872. Black on orange unpt. Italia at lower l., wolf w/twins at bottom ctr., arms at r. Back green; no heads.	100.00	400.00	1200.

#	Description	Good	Fine	XF
S795	**10 Lire** 1872. Black on green unpt. Similar to #S273. Back brown; no heads.	80.00	350.00	1000.

#S796-S802 backs have varying numbers of heads of Italia/Roma, some also have multiple arms.

#	Description	Good	Fine	XF
S796	**20 Lire** 1872. Brown on orange unpt. Italia at l., Roma at r. Back green; 3 heads.	—	Rare	—
S797	**25 Lire** 1883. Black on orange unpt. Like #S281. Back red.	40.00	160.00	450.00

#	Description	Good	Fine	XF
S798	**50 Lire** 1872; 1890. Black on green unpt. Portr. Italia and arms at upper l., wolf w/twins at ctr., portr. Roma and arms at upper r. Back brown; 6 heads. Yellow paper.	30.00	140.00	350.00

#S799-S802 Italia at l., arms at upper ctr., wolf w/twins at lower ctr., Roma at r.

#	Description	Good	Fine	XF
S799	**100 Lire** 1872-90. Blue on green unpt. Back green; 6 heads. Yellow paper.	165.00	420.00	—

		GOOD	FINE	XF
S800	**200 LIRE** 1872-90. Blue on orange unpt. Back red; 6 heads. Lt. green paper.	200.00	800.00	2400.
S801	**500 LIRE** 1872-90. Blue on orange unpt. Back green; 7 heads, 8 arms. Cream paper.	350.00	1500.	—
S802	**1000 LIRE** 1872-90. Blue on brown unpt. Cream paper. Back red; 10 heads, 8 arms.	600.00	—	—

BANCO DI NAPOLI

Banco di Napoli denominations appear on handwritten *FEDI DI CREDITO* since 1861, but the Bank was officially recognized on 1866. After 1866, the bank issued *FEDI DI CREDITO* (cash receipts) and after 1877 introduced bank notes. During 1926, the Banco di Napoli lost the privilege to issue bank notes.

1866 FEDI DI CREDITO - PROVISIONAL CASH RECEIPT ISSUE

#S811-S814 embossed seal. White wmk. paper. Uniface.

		GOOD	FINE	XF
S811	**1 LIRA** 1866; 1867. Red.	80.00	350.00	1000.
S812	**2 LIRE** 1867. Green.	80.00	350.00	1000.
S813	**5 LIRE** 1866-67. Blue.	100.00	450.00	1200.
S814	**10 LIRE** 1866. Black.	100.00	450.00	1200.

1867-70 FEDI DI CREDITO - REGULAR CASH RECEIPT ISSUES

		GOOD	FINE	XF
S815	**50 CENTESIMI** 1868; 1873. Black. White thin paper.	10.00	30.00	100.00

		GOOD	FINE	XF
S816	**1 LIRA** 3.9.1868. Black. Red thin paper.	90.00	300.00	1000.

		GOOD	FINE	XF
S817	**1 LIRA** 1.1.1867; 1.6.1867. Black on lt. blue unpt. 3 sign. Back lt. blue.	70.00	250.00	800.00
S818	**1 LIRA** 1.7.1867-1.12.1867. Like #S997 but w/2 sign.	60.00	220.00	650.00
S819	**1 LIRA** 1.5.1869. Black on blue unpt.	90.00	300.00	1000.

		GOOD	FINE	XF
S820	**1 LIRA** 1.10.1870; 1.5.1874. Black on blue unpt.	12.00	40.00	150.00
S821	**2 LIRE** ND (1867). Black on green unpt. White paper.	80.00	280.00	900.00
S822	**5 LIRE** ND (1867). Black on red-rose unpt.	100.00	400.00	1200.
S823	**5 LIRE** 1868. Black on rose unpt.	90.00	300.00	1000.

		GOOD	FINE	XF
S824	**5 LIRE** 1.5.1869. Black on lt. rose unpt. Back maroon.	90.00	300.00	1000.

		GOOD	FINE	XF
S825	**5 LIRE** 1870-73. Black on brown unpt. Back brown.	40.00	200.00	500.00

#S826-S835 horse at l. and at r.

		GOOD	FINE	XF
S826	**10 LIRE** ND (1867). Black on green unpt. 3 sign.	—	Rare	—
S827	**10 LIRE** 1868-69. Black on lt. green unpt.	120.00	600.00	1600.
S828	**10 LIRE** 1870-72. Brown and blue.	—	Rare	—

		GOOD	FINE	XF
S829	**20 LIRE** ND (1867). Black on lt. red unpt.	—	Rare	—
S830	**20 LIRE** 1868. Black on red unpt.	—	Rare	—
S831	**20 LIRE** 1869-72. Black on rose unpt.	—	Rare	—
S832	**50 LIRE** ND (1867). Black on rose unpt.	—	Rare	—

		Good	Fine	XF
S833	**50 Lire** 1868. Black on lt. rose unpt.	—	Rare	—
S834	**50 Lire** 1869-76. Black on red unpt.	—	Rare	—

		Good	Fine	XF
S835	**100 Lire** ND (1867). Green and rose.	—	Rare	—
S836	**100 Lire** 1868. Lt. green and rose.	—	Rare	—

		Good	Fine	XF
S837	**100 Lire** 1869; 1872. Black, green and blue on peach unpt. 2 female heads at l. and reverse image at r. Back green.	—	Rare	—

		Good	Fine	XF
S838	**250 Lire** 1.7.1867. Black on green, yellow and red-brown unpt. Portr. Italia at l. and reverse image at r. Back gray-green. Yellow paper.	—	Unique	—
S839	**250 Lire** 1.11.1869. Black on yellow and blue unpt. Portr. L. da Vinci at l., portr. Art at r.	—	Rare	—
S840	**500 Lire** 1.7.1867. Black on lt. green and rose-brown unpt. Italia at l. and r.	—	Rare	—
S841	**500 Lire** 1.11.1869-1.11.1870. Black on green and red-brown unpt. Italia at l. and at r.	—	Rare	—
S842	**1000 Lire** 1.11.1869-1.11.1870. Green and brown. Portr. Galileo at l., portr. Flavo Gioia at r. Horse at each corner of ctr. design. Back red. Proof.	—	Rare	—

1877-1905 Regular Bank Notes Issues

		Good	Fine	XF
S843	**25 Lire** 1.8.1883. Black and brown. Portr. Cavour at l. Back brown; 2 Mercury heads.	150.00	500.00	1400.

		Good	Fine	XF
S844	**50 Lire** 29.1.1877-1.6.1879. Black on red unpt. Horse at l. and r. Back red and green. Printer: BWC.	200.00	600.00	2000.

		Good	Fine	XF
S845	**50 Lire** 6.9.1881. Brown and black. Portrs. Galileo at l., G. Manna at r. Back brown.	60.00	200.00	700.00

		Good	Fine	XF
S846	**50 Lire** 1896; 1903. Green. Industry w/caduceus and book at r. Back violet and green; Mercury at l. and r. on back.	50.00	150.00	550.00

		VG	VF	Unc
S847	**100 Lire** 29.1.1877; 18.8.1880. Brown on blue-cream unpt. Portr. woman at l., mirror image at r. Back purple and green. Printer: BWC.	200.00	800.00	2000.

S848 100 LIRE | VG | VF | UNC
6.9.1881. Green and black. Portrs. L. Da Vinci at l., Kg. Vittorio Emanuele II at r. Back green. | 100.00 | 260.00 | 800.00

S849 100 LIRE | GOOD | FINE | XF
30.6.1896; 22.10.1903. Black on red-brown unpt. Agriculture w/sickle and corn at r. Back brown and red; woman at l. and r. | 80.00 | 240.00 | 700.00

S850 200 LIRE
1877; 1883. Black on red rose unpt. Portr. L. da Vinci at l., woman at r. Back dk. green. Red paper. Printer: BWC. | — | Rare | —

S851 500 LIRE | GOOD | FINE | XF
1877; 1885. Black on blue unpt. Portr. Italia at l. and reverse image at r. Back green and blue-violet. | 350.00 | 1000. | 3000.

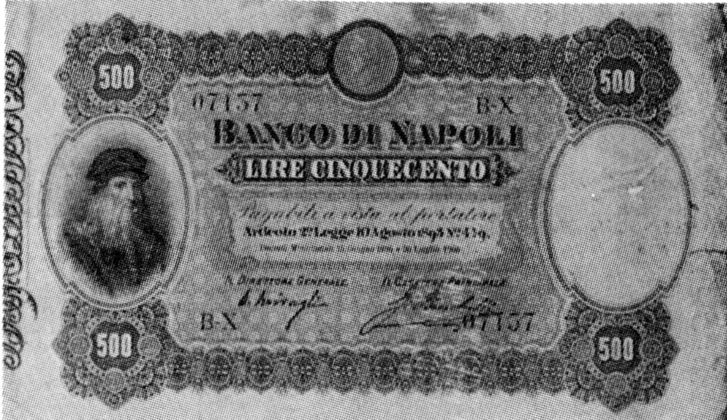

S852 500 LIRE | GOOD | FINE | XF
1896; 1905. Black on rose and yellow unpt. Portr. L. da Vinci at l. Back green-violet. | 400.00 | 1400. | —

S853 1000 LIRE | GOOD | FINE | XF
1877; 1885. Black on rose and creme unpt. Portr. Galileo at l., F. Gioia at r. Back green and red. | 600.00 | 1800. | —

S854 1000 LIRE
2.3.1896; 22.10.1903. Black on violet-brown unpt. Portr. Galileo at l., horse at each corner of ctr. design. | — | Rare | —

1908-21 ISSUES

S855 25 LIRE | VG | VF | UNC
17.8.1918; 4.6.1919. Black on gray and blue unpt. Arms at l. Back green-gray. | 100.00 | 300.00 | 800.00

S856 50 LIRE | VG | VF | UNC
1909-21. Black on blue-gray unpt. Portr. S. Rosa at lower l. Back dk. blue; portr. Minerva at lower r. | 30.00 | 90.00 | 200.00

S857 100 LIRE | VG | VF | UNC
1908-21. Black on blue unpt. Portr. T. Tasso at l. Back red-brown; classic head of Platone/Dionysius at r. | 40.00 | 100.00 | 280.00

		VG	VF	UNC
S858	**500 LIRE** 1909-21. Black on green-gray unpt. Portr. G. Filangieri at l. Back brown; Medusa at r.	60.00	180.00	650.00

		VG	VF	UNC
S859	**1000 LIRE** 1909; 1921. Black on lilac and gray unpt. Portr. G. Vico at l. Back dk. green; head of Heraclea at r.	80.00	250.00	800.00

BANCO DI SICILIA

The name Banco di Sicilia appeared unofficially on Fedi di Credito notes issued in Palermo since 1849. Since 1850 this bank was a branch of Banco Delle Due Sicilie based in Napoli. By Decree on May 1, 1866, Banco di Sicilia became the institute of issue. In 1926, the Banco di Sicilia lost the privilege to issue bank notes.

BANCO REGIO

1866 POLIZZINI DI CASSA PROVISIONAL ISSUE

#S861-S868 w/embossed seal. Wmk. paper. Uniface.

		GOOD	FINE	XF
S861	**2 LIRE** 1866. Red and black.			
	a. White paper.	250.00	900.00	—
	b. Blue paper.	280.00	1000.	—
S862	**3 LIRE** 1866.			
	a. White paper.	350.00	1200.	—
	b. Lt. blue paper.	—	Rare	—
S863	**5 LIRE** 1866.			
	a. White paper.	280.00	1000.	—
	b. Lt. blue paper.	—	Rare	—
S864	**6 LIRE** 1866.			
	a. White paper.	—	Rare	—
	b. Lt. blue paper.	—	Rare	—
S865	**7 LIRE** 1866. Black.			
	a. White paper.	—	Rare	—
	b. Lt. blue paper.	—	Rare	—
S866	**8 LIRE** 1866.			
	a. White paper.	—	Rare	—
	b. Lt. blue paper.	—	Rare	—
S867	**9 LIRE** 1866. Black.			
	a. White paper.	—	Rare	—
	b. Lt. blue paper.	—	Rare	—
S868	**10 LIRE** 1866.			
	a. White paper.	350.00	—	—
	b. Lt. blue paper.	—	Rare	—

1866 TESORERIA PROVINCIALE DI PALERMO PROVISIONAL ISSUE

#S869-S871 w/black seal *Cassa di Palermo Ore e Argento*. Wmk. paper. Uniface.

		GOOD	FINE	XF
S869	**2 LIRE** 1866. Green and black.			
	a. White paper.	250.00	900.00	—
	b. Lt. blue paper.	—	Rare	—
S870	**5 LIRE** 1866. Green and black.			
	a. White paper.	300.00	1200.	—
	b. Lt. blue paper.	—	Rare	—
S871	**10 LIRE** 1866.			
	a. White paper.	220.00	650.00	1500.
	b. Lt. blue paper.	—	Rare	—

The name Banco di Sicilia appeared unofficially on Fedi di Credito notes issued in Palermo since 1849. Since 1850 this bank was a branch of Banco Delle Due Sicilie based in Napoli. By Decree on May 1, 1866, Banco di Sicilia became the institute of issue. In 1926, the Banco di Sicilia lost the privilege to issue bank notes.

1866 FEDI DI CREDITO PROVISIONAL ISSUE

#S872-S874 black. W/printed seal *Cassa oro e argento di Palermo* and embossed seal. White wmk. paper.

		GOOD	FINE	XF
S872	**2 LIRE** 1866; 1867.	320.00	—	—
S873	**3 LIRE** 1866; 1867.	350.00	—	—
S874	**5 LIRE** 1866; 1867.	280.00	—	—

1867; 1868 POLIZZINI DI CASSA PROVISIONAL ISSUE

#S875-S877 blue-green. W/embossed seal. White wmk. paper.

		GOOD	FINE	XF
S875	**2 LIRE** 1867.			
	a. Palermo branch.	280.00	—	—
	b. Messina branch.	—	Rare	—
S876	**3 LIRE** 1867-69.	—	Rare	—

		GOOD	FINE	XF
S877	**5 LIRE** 1868.	—	Rare	—

1868 FEDI DI CREDITO ISSUE

		GOOD	FINE	XF
S878	**1 LIRA** 3.9.1868. Black on blue unpt. Ceres Agriculture at l., portr. Italia at lower r. Back blue; arms of Savoy at ctr.	250.00	700.00	2000.

1870; 1876 FEDI DI CREDITO ISSUE

#S879-S888 red seal w/bank arms at top ctr. Printer: BWC (w/o imprint).

		GOOD	FINE	XF
S879	**1 LIRA** 27.4.1870. Black on blue unpt. Back blue.	50.00	100.00	250.00

		Good	Fine	XF
S880	**2 Lire** 24.7.1870. Dk. blue on orange unpt. Back orange.	70.00	180.00	400.00

		Good	Fine	XF
S881	**5 Lire** 24.7.1870. Black on blue unpt. Back blue.	200.00	600.00	1800.

#S882-S886 bank arms at top ctr., three-leg design (triquetra) at l. and r. on back. Printer: BWC (w/o imprint).

		Good	Fine	XF
S882	**10 Lire** 24.7.1870. Black on tan unpt. Back tan.	200.00	600.00	1800.

		Good	Fine	XF
S883	**20 Lire** 27.4.1870. Dk. blue on orange and green unpt. Back green.	—	Rare	—

#S884-S886 state arms at upper ctr.

		Good	Fine	XF
S884	**50 Lire** 24.7.1870; 2.1.1875. Black on green and rose unpt. Back red.	100.00	350.00	900.00
S885	**100 Lire** 27.4.1870; 2.1.1875. Black on tan unpt. Back tan.	150.00	500.00	1300.

		Good	Fine	XF
S886	**200 Lire** 1870; 1876. Black on azure and peach unpt. Back blue-green.	280.00	850.00	2500.
S887	**500 Lire** 1870; 1876. Black on brown unpt. Neptune at l., Italia at r. Back brown.	500.00	1400.	3000.

		Good	Fine	XF
S888	**1000 Lire** 1870; 1876. Brown on azure and creme unpt. Back brown on azure unpt.	—	Rare	—

1879; 1892 Bank Notes Issues

		Good	Fine	XF
S889	**25 Lire** 17.5.1883; 25.2.1891. Black and blue on tan unpt. Neptune at l. Back tan with Italia head at ctr. Printer: BWC.	220.00	600.00	1500.

#S890-S894 red seal with bank arms at top ctr. Printer: BWC (w/o imprint).

		Good	Fine	XF
S890	**50 Lire** 11.4.1879; 5.7.1892. Black and green on rose unpt. Back red and green.	260.00	800.00	2200.
S891	**100 Lire** 11.4.1879; 5.7.1892. Black and red on creme unpt. Back tan.	160.00	500.00	1200.
S892	**200 Lire** 23.9.1879. Black and azure on creme unpt. Back orange and green.	—	Rare	—
S893	**500 Lire** 1879; 1892. Black and brown on blue unpt. Neptune at l., portr. Italia at r. Back brown and blue.	—	Rare	—

		Good	Fine	XF
S894	**1000 Lire** 1879; 1892. Black and green on red unpt. Neptune at l., portr. Italia at r. Back green and red.	—	Rare	—

1896; 1920 Issues

#S895-S899 red medallic head of Italia seal at bottom ctr. Neptune statue at l. Back seven classic heads in circle at ctr. Imprint: *STADERINI* (vertical imprint at l.).

		Good	Fine	XF
S895	**25 Lire** 21.2.1918; 6.8.1918. Black and olive on lilac unpt. Back red-brown.	30.00	90.00	280.00

#S896-S899 backs w/seven heads in circle at ctr. and triquetra at r.

		Good	Fine	XF
S896	**50 Lire** 1897; 1915. Black and brown on creme unpt. Back gray and rose.	15.00	50.00	180.00

		Good	Fine	XF
S897	**100 Lire** 1896; 1915. Black and gray-blue on lt. gray unpt. Back blue and gray.	20.00	80.00	260.00
S898	**500 Lire** 1897; 1919. Black and blue on brown unpt. Back brown.	90.00	280.00	750.00
S899	**1000 Lire** 1897; 1920. Black and brown on gray unpt. Back azure.	120.00	350.00	850.00

Credito Agrario
Agrarian Credit Banks and Associations

Cassa di Risparmio di Bologna

1871; 1887 Issue

#S901-S904 wmk. paper. Printer: BWC.

		Good	Fine	XF
S901	**30 Lire** 5.3.1871. Black on creme unpt. Re head at l. Back m/c.			
	a. Issued note.	Reported Not Confirmed		
	s. Specimen.	—	—	1000.
S902	**40 Lire** 5.3.1871. Black on red unpt. Back m/c.			
	a. Issued note.	Reported Not Confirmed		
	s. Specimen.	—	—	1200.

		Good	Fine	XF
S903	**50 Lire** 5.3.1871. Black on rose unpt. Head of I. Malvasia at l. Back m/c.			
	a. Issued note.	Reported Not Confirmed		
	s. Specimen.	—	—	1000.

		Good	Fine	XF
S904	**100 Lire** 1874; 1887. Black on red unpt. Head of P. Crescenzio at l. Back m/c.			
	a. Issued note.	—	Rare	—
	s. Specimen.	—	—	1200.

Banca Agricola Nazionale

1870 Issue

#S905-S910 bust of Italia at upper ctr. Two women reclining w/crowned shield below. Printer: BWC.

		Good	Fine	XF
S905	**30 Lire** 1.6.1870. Black and rose.			
	a. Issued note.	Reported Not Confirmed		
	s. Specimen.	—	—	1000.
S906	**40 Lire** 1.6.1870. Black on green unpt.			
	a. Issued note.	Reported Not Confirmed		
	s. Specimen.	—	—	1200.
S907	**50 Lire** 1.6.1870. Black and brown.			
	a. Issued note.	Reported Not Confirmed		
	s. Specimen.	—	—	1000.
S908	**100 Lire** 1.6.1870. Black and red.			
	a. Issued note.	Reported Not Confirmed		
	s. Specimen.	—	—	1000.
S909	**250 Lire** 1.6.1870. Black on brown unpt.			
	a. Issued note.	Reported Not Confirmed		
	s. Specimen.	—	—	1000.
S910	**500 Lire** 1.6.1870. Black and azure on rose unpt.			
	a. Issued note.	Reported Not Confirmed		
	s. Specimen.	—	—	1500.
S911	**1000 Lire** 1.6.1870. Black and lt. amaranth.			
	a. Issued note.	Reported Not Confirmed		
	s. Specimen.	—	Rare	—

Monte dei Paschi di Siena

1870; 1898 Issue

#S911-S916 portr. Abate at l., allegorical cherub at r. Printer: BWC.

		Good	Fine	XF
S912	**30 Lire** 1870; 1898. Black and yellow on creme unpt. Back green.	—	Rare	—
S913	**40 Lire** 1870; 1876. Black and violet. Back brown.			
	a. Issued note.	Reported Not Confirmed		
	s. Specimen.	—	—	—

		Good	Fine	XF
S914	**50 Lire** 1870; 1898. Black on rose unpt. Back red.			
	a. Issued note.	—	Rare	—
	s. Specimen.	—	—	—
S915	**100 Lire** 1870; 1898. Black and amaranth on yellow. Back brown.			
	a. Issued note.	—	Rare	—
	s. Specimen.	—	—	—

		Good	Fine	XF
S916	**200 Lire** 1870; 1898. Black on red and blue unpt. Back red.	—	Rare	—
S917	**500 Lire** 1870; 1898.	Reported Not Confirmed		

A word on pricing

When a note is marked RARE in the price columns, this note seldom appears on the market, or few are known in private hands. When dashes are in the price column, means that the note has not traded on the open market recently and a definitive value could not accurately be determined. Rare does not always mean expensive. A dashed price does not mean expensive or rare.

BIGLIETTI CONSORZIALE

For previously listed #S491-S499, refer to Vol. II.

BIGLIETTI GIA' CONSORZIALE

For previously listed #S501-S508, refer to Vol. II.

BANCA GENERALE DI ROMA

1880; 1892 ISSUE

#S918 and S919 two children w/bunch of grapes at l., Italia head at r., she-wolf w/twins at lower ctr. White paper. Printer: BWC.

		GOOD	FINE	XF
S918	**30 LIRE** 1880; 1892. Black. Back blue.	200.00	600.00	1200.
S919	**50 LIRE** 1880; 1892. Black. Back blue.	—	Rare	—

BANCA AGRARIA COMMERCIALE DI FOGGIA

1882 ISSUE

		GOOD	FINE	XF
S920	**30 LIRE** 2.6.1882. Black on azure and rose unpt. Allegorical child w/plow at l., agricultural wagon at l. Printer: BWC.	—	Rare	—

BANCA AGRICOLA SARDA

1871; 1880 ISSUE

#S921-S923 portr. E. d'Arborea at l., portr. Priore at r. Profile head of Italia at l. and mirror image at r. on back. Printer: BWC.

		GOOD	FINE	XF
S921	**30 LIRE** 1871-80. Black. Lilac paper.			
	a. Florence. 10.2.1871.	20.00	80.00	300.00
	b. Rome. 1.9.1875.	18.00	70.00	250.00
	c. Oristano. 1870; 1.1.1878; 1880.	8.00	35.00	110.00
S922	**50 LIRE** 10.12.1871. Black and green. Back green. White paper.	100.00	280.00	800.00
S923	**100 LIRE** 15.1.1872. Dk. blue and green. Back green. White paper.	—	Rare	—

		GOOD	FINE	XF
S924	**250 LIRE** 1.11.1872. Black. Portr. E. d'Arborea at lower ctr. Back green. Green paper.			
	a. Issued note.	Reported Not Confirmed		
	b. Specimen.	—	—	—

CREDITO AGRICOLO INDUSTRIALE SARDO

1874; 1884 ISSUE

#S925-S928 portr. helmeted Roman warrior at l., various agricultural allegories at r. Printer: BWC.

		GOOD	FINE	XF
S925	**30 LIRE** 1.3.1874. Black and brown w/red seal. Back brown.	2.00	8.00	30.00
S926	**30 LIRE** 1.1.1884. Black and green on green unpt. w/red seal. Back green.	200.00	600.00	1800.

		GOOD	FINE	XF
S927	**50 LIRE** 1.1.1874. Black and brown, blue *50* protector at ctr., w/red seal. Back brown.	8.00	20.00	90.00

		GOOD	FINE	XF
S928	**100 LIRE** 1.1.1874. Black on brown unpt. w/red seal.	20.00	60.00	200.00

COMMERCIAL BANKS - ABUSIVE ISSUES

BANCA DEL POPOLO

Founded in Florence in 1865, because of a large unauthorized issue of paper money, the business of this bank has developed considerably and in a few years it has opened nearly 100 branches in Italy. In 1871 this bank had an extensive and abusive circulation of notes for the amount of nearly 5,000,000 Lire.

1866; 1871 ISSUE

#S941-S945 2 reclining allegories flanking crowned shield at top ctr., various coats-of-arms at l. and at r., bust of Italia at bottom ctr.

		GOOD	FINE	XF
S941	**10 LIRE** 23.11.1867. Black, brown and red. White paper.	—	Rare	—
S942	**20 LIRE** 2.9.1867. Black. White paper.	—	Rare	—

		Good	Fine	XF
S943	**30 Lire** 1866; 1871. Black on brown unpt.	—	Rare	—
S944	**50 Lire** 1866; 1871. Black on yellow-green unpt. Similar to #S943.	—	Rare	—
S945	**100 Lire** 1866; 1871. Black on lt. green unpt. Similar to #S943.	—	Rare	—

Monte dei Paschi di Siena

Before this institution issued regular *Buoni Agrari* #S911-S916, it issued unauthorized *Buoni di Cassa*.

1866; 1871 Issue

		Good	Fine	XF
S951	**10 Lire** 1866; 1869. Black on blue-violet paper.			
	a. Issued note.	—	Rare	—
	r. Remainder.	—	—	250.00
S952	**25 Lire** 1866; 1869.	Reported Not Confirmed		
S953	**50 Lire** 1866; 1871. Black. Rose paper.			
	a. Issued note.	—	Rare	—
	b. Punched hole cancelled.	—	—	400.00
S954	**100 Lire** 1866; 1871.	Reported Not Confirmed		
S955	**200 Lire** 1866; 1871.	—	Rare	—

Banca di Valdinievole in Pescia

Founded in 1870, this bank issued an abusive amount of notes that circulated only in Lucca province, and after a few years of activity it was absorbed by Monte dei Paschi di Siena.

1871 ND Issue

		Good	Fine	XF
S961	**20 Lire** ND (ca.1871). Black and green on brown unpt. Back brown.			
	a. Issued note.	—	Rare	—
	r. Remainder.	—	—	200.00
S962	**50 Lire** ND.	Reported Not Confirmed		
S963	**100 Lire** ND.	Reported Not Confirmed		

Banca Italo - Germanica

Founded at the end of 1871, the bank immediately started to issue *certificati di deposito*.

1871; 1872 Issue

#S971-S978 black. White paper. Printer: BWC.

		Good	Fine	XF
S971	**5 Lire** 1871; 1872. Heads of Italia and Germania at r. on face and back. Back red and green.			
	a. Issued note.	—	Rare	—
	r. Remainder.	—	—	600.00

		Good	Fine	XF
S972	**10 Lire** 1871; 1872. Tevere bridge at l., Main bridge at r. Back green, red and blue.			
	a. Issued note.	—	Rare	—
	r. Remainder.	—	—	600.00
S973	**20 Lire** 1871; 1872. Black. Hadrian's tomb at l., castle at r. Back blue and violet.			
	a. Issued note.	—	Rare	—
	r. Remainder.	—	—	500.00
S974	**50 Lire** 1871; 1872. Castle at l., Ducal palace of Venice at r. Prospectus of interest on back.			
	a. Issued note.	—	Rare	—
	r. Remainder.	—	—	700.00
S975	**100 Lire** 1871; 1872. Standing Italia w/shield and baton at l. Prospectus of interest on back.			
	a. Issued note.	—	Rare	—
	r. Remainder.	—	—	700.00

		Good	Fine	XF
S976	**250 Lire** 1871; 1872. Standing Italia w/books and shield at l. Prospectus of interest on back.			
	a. Issued note.	—	Rare	—
	r. Remainder.	—	—	800.00
	s. Specimen.	—	—	—
S977	**500 Lire** 1871; 1872. Black. Germania w/shield and spear at l. Prospectus of interest on back.			
	a. Issued note.	—	Rare	—
	r. Remainder.	—	—	800.00

		Good	Fine	XF
S978	**1000 Lire** 1871; 1872. Germania and Italia w/four cherubs at l. Prospectus of interest on back.			
	a. Issued note.	—	Rare	—
	r. Remainder.	—	—	700.00
	s. Specimen.	—	—	—

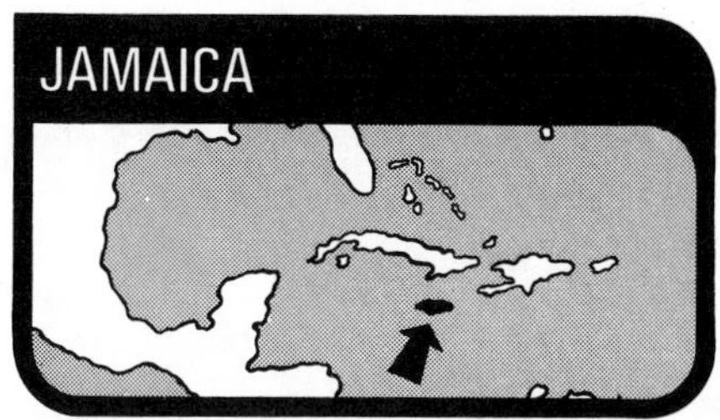

Jamaica, a member of the British Commonwealth situated in the Caribbean Sea 90 miles south of Cuba, has an area of 4,232 sq. mi. (10,991 sq. km.) and a population of 2.59 million. Capital: Kingston. The economy is founded chiefly on mining, tourism and agriculture. Alumina, bauxite, sugar, rum and molasses are exported.

Jamaica was discovered by Columbus on May 3, 1494, and settled by Spain in 1509. The island was captured in 1655 by a British naval force under the command of Admiral William Penn, and ceded to Britain by the Treaty of Madrid in 1670. For more than 150 years, the Jamaican economy of sugar, slaves and piracy was one of the most prosperous in the New World. Dissension between the property-oriented island legislature and the home government prompted Parliament to establish a crown colony government for Jamaica in 1866. From 1958 to 1961 Jamaica was a member of the West Indies Federation, withdrawing when Jamaican voters rejected the association. The colony attained independence on Aug. 6, 1962.

RULERS:
British

MONETARY SYSTEM:
1 Shilling = 12 Pence
1 Pound = 20 Shillings to 1969

BRITISH ADMINISTRATION

ISLAND TREASURY

Issued by the Receiver General and Commissioners of Public Accounts.

1822 ISSUE

		GOOD	FINE	XF
S101	**5 POUNDS** 12.1822.	—	—	—
S102	**10 POUNDS** 12.1822.	—	—	—
S103	**20 POUNDS** 12.1822.	—	—	—
S104	**50 POUNDS** 12.1822.	—	—	—
S105	**100 POUNDS** 12.1822. Proof.	—	—	—

1840'S ISSUE

		GOOD	FINE	XF
S106	**1 POUND** 184x.	—	—	—

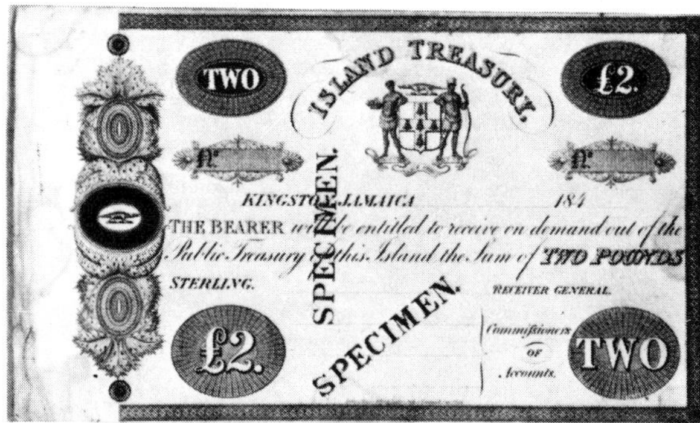

		GOOD	FINE	XF
S107	**2 POUNDS** 184x. Arms at upper ctr. Specimen.	—	—	—
S108	**3 POUNDS** 184x.	—	—	—
S109	**4 POUNDS** 184x.	—	—	—
S110	**10 POUNDS** 184x.	—	—	—
S111	**50 POUNDS** 184x.	—	—	—
S112	**100 POUNDS** 184x.	—	—	—

NOTE: Only printer's proofs for #S106-S112 are known.

BANK OF JAMAICA

Founded in 1836 and taken over by the Colonial Bank in 1864. This private bank has no relation to the modern Bank of Jamaica of today. Printer: PB.

1830'S ISSUE

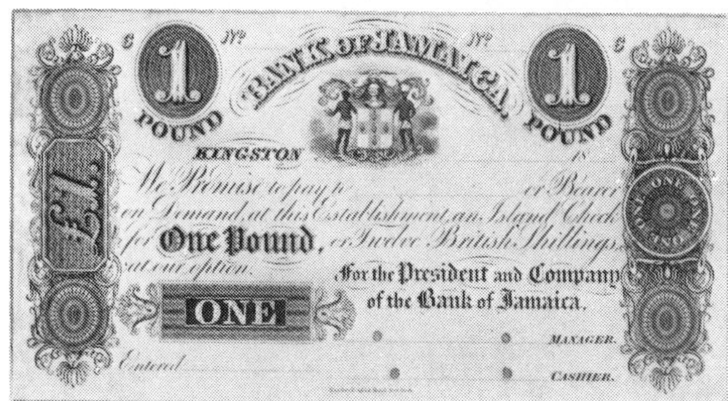

		GOOD	FINE	XF
S121	**1 POUND** 18xx. Arms at upper ctr. Proof, punched hole cancelled.	—	Unc	3000.
S122	**2 POUNDS** 18xx. Like #S121.	—	—	—
S123	**4 POUNDS** 18xx.	—	—	—
S124	**10 POUNDS** 18xx.	—	—	—

NOTE: Only printer's proofs for #S121-S124 are known. Other denominations may exist.

BANK OF NOVA SCOTIA

Established in Jamaica in 1889; did not issue notes until 1900. Kingston office.

1900; 1919-20 ISSUE

#S131 and S132 printer: ABNC.

		GOOD	FINE	XF
S131	**1 POUND** 1900; 1919-20. Black on green and pale yellow unpt. Value between woman w/helmet and sword at l.; woman w/palm branch and wreath at r. Back green.			
	a. Sign. J. Y. Payzant. 2.1.1919.	—	Rare	—
	p. Proof.	—	—	—
	s. Specimen.	—	—	—

		GOOD	FINE	XF
S132	**5 POUNDS** 1900; 1920. Black on orange and pale yellow unpt. 2 women w/scroll and book at ctr. Back brown.			
	a. Sign. J. Y. Payzant. 2.1.1900.	—	Rare	—
	b. Sign. C. Archibald. 2.1.1920.	300.00	800.00	—
	p. Proof.	—	—	—

1930 ISSUE

		GOOD	FINE	XF
S139	**1 POUND**			
	2.1.1930. Black on green, yellow, and blue unpt. Woman seated among produce at ctr. Back green. 2 sign. varieties. Printer: CBNC.	125.00	350.00	—

BARCLAYS BANK (DOMINION, COLONIAL AND OVERSEAS)

Formerly the Colonial Bank; began issuing notes in Jamaica in 1926. Kingston office.

1926-35 ISSUE

#S141-S143 arms at ctr. Serial # prefix C. Hand signed. Printer: BWC.

		GOOD	FINE	XF
S141	**1 POUND**			
	1926-35. Black on orange unpt.			
	a. 1.9.1926; 15.12.1927; 1.6.1929.	350.00	800.00	—
	b. 1.4.1932; 1.2.1934; 1.1.1935.	300.00	750.00	—
	s. Specimen.	—	Unc	600.00
S142	**5 POUNDS**			
	1.9.1926. Black on yellow unpt.	—	Rare	—
S143	**10 POUNDS**			
	1.9.1926. Black on green unpt.	—	Rare	—

1937; 1940 ISSUE

#S146-S148 arms at r. Serial # prefix D. Printer: BWC.

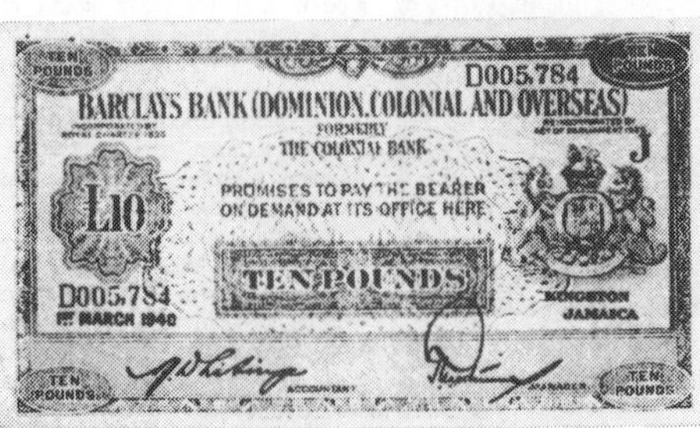

		GOOD	FINE	XF
S146	**1 POUND**			
	1937-41. Black on red unpt.			
	a. 1.1.1937.	250.00	750.00	—
	b. 1.5.1937.	225.00	675.00	—
	c. 1.2.1938.	200.00	600.00	—
	d. 1.3.1939.	—	—	—
	e. 1.2.1941.	185.00	550.00	—
S147	**5 POUNDS**			
	1.3.1940. Black on orange unpt.	750.00	1750.	—

		GOOD	FINE	XF
S148	**10 POUNDS**			
	1937-40. Black on blue and mauve unpt.			
	a. 1.1.1937.	500.00	1000.	—
	b. 1.5.1937.	400.00	800.00	—
	c. 1.3.1940.	100.00	300.00	850.00

CANADIAN BANK OF COMMERCE

Established in Jamaica in 1920. Kingston office.

1921 ISSUE

#S151 and S152 Mercury at ctr. w/allegorical women at l. and r. of bank arms at ctr. on back.

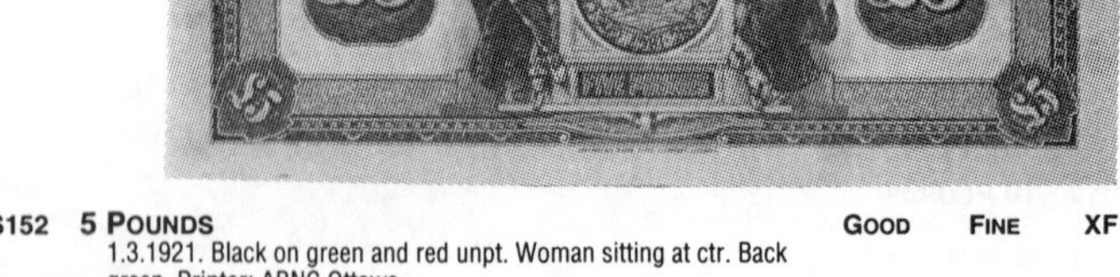

		GOOD	FINE	XF
S151	**1 POUND**			
	1.3.1921. Black on orange unpt. 3 allegorical figures at ctr. Back brown. No letter designation. Printer: ABNC.			
	a. Issued note.	—	—	—
	p. Proof.	—	—	—
S151A	**1 POUND**			
	1.3.1921. Like #S151, but letter designation *B* on face. Printer: CBN.	—	—	—

		GOOD	FINE	XF
S152	**5 POUNDS**			
	1.3.1921. Black on green and red unpt. Woman sitting at ctr. Back green. Printer: ABNC Ottawa.			
	a. Issued note.	—	—	—
	p. Proof.	—	—	—

1938 ISSUE

#S156 and S157 Mercury and allegorical woman at l. and r. of bank arms at ctr. on back.

		Good	Fine	XF
S156	**1 Pound** 1.6.1938. Black on orange unpt. Similar to #S151A. Back brown. Printer: CBN. Reduced size.	—	—	—

		Good	Fine	XF
S157	**5 Pounds** 1.6.1938. Black. Like #S152. Specimen.	—	Unc	1000.

NOTE: #S157 was prepared for issue, but all were withheld from circulation and destroyed.

Colonial Bank

Founded in 1836; later became Barclays Bank (Dominion, Colonial and Overseas). Kingston office.

1840's Issue

#S161 and S162 arms at upper ctr.

S161 1 Pound 5 Shillings Sterling = 6 Dollars or 2 Pounds 1 Shilling 8 Pence

	Good	Fine	XF
10.3.1840. (ca.1838-83).	—	Rare	—

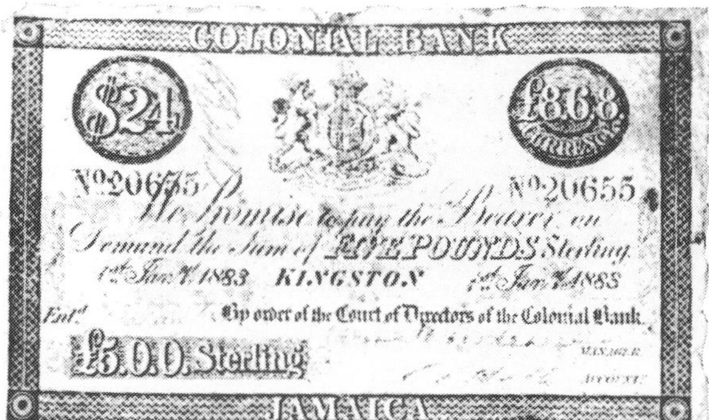

S162 5 Pounds Sterling = 24 Dollars or 8 Pounds 6 Shillings 8Pence

	Good	Fine	XF
ca.1838-1.1.1883.	—	Rare	—

1885 Issue

		Good	Fine	XF
S171	**1 Pound** 1.1.1885; 1.1.1896; 1.10.1898; 1.10.1902. Black. Supported royal arms at upper ctr. Printer: PBC.	900.00	2250.	—

1907 Issue

Issued after 1900. Notes have serial # prefix A.

#S181-S183 supported royal arms at upper ctr. w/lg. curved *COLONIAL BANK* in ornate unpt.

		Good	Fine	XF
S181	**1 Pound** 1.1.1907; 1.5.1912. Black on orange unpt.	—	Rare	—
S182	**5 Pounds** 1907. Black on yellow unpt.	—	Rare	—

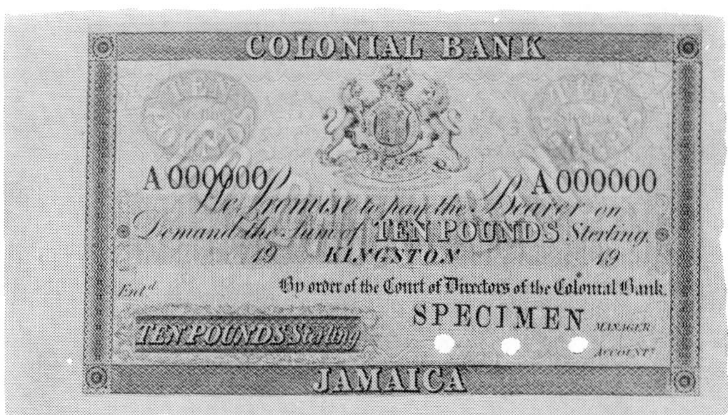

		Good	Fine	XF
S183	**10 Pounds** 1907. Black on green and orange unpt.	—	Rare	—

1917-20 Issue

#S191-S193 supported royal arms at upper ctr. W/serial # prefix B and lg. *J* (Jamaica) at upper r.

		Good	Fine	XF
S191	**1 Pound** 1.11.1917; 1.4.1925.			
	a. Issued note.	750.00	2000.	—
	s. Specimen.	—	Unc	1500.
S192	**5 Pounds** 1.11.1920.			
	a. Issued note.	—	—	—
	s. Specimen.	—	Unc	2000.
S193	**10 Pounds** 1.6.1919; 1.4.1925.	—	Rare	—

A word on pricing

When a note is marked RARE in the price columns, this note seldom appears on the market, or few are known in private hands. When dashes are in the price column, means that the note has not traded on the open market recently and a definitive value could not accurately be determined. Rare does not always mean expensive. A dashed price does not mean expensive or rare.

LONDON AND COLONIAL BANK LIMITED

Founded in 1864, ceased operations in 1865. Kingston office.

1800'S ISSUE

		GOOD	FINE	XF
S201	**10 SHILLINGS** 18xx. Seated allegory of Commerce at upper ctr. Printer: Batho. Remainder.	—	—	2000.

PLANTERS BANK

Founded in 1839, ceased operations in 1848. Kingston office.

1839 ISSUE

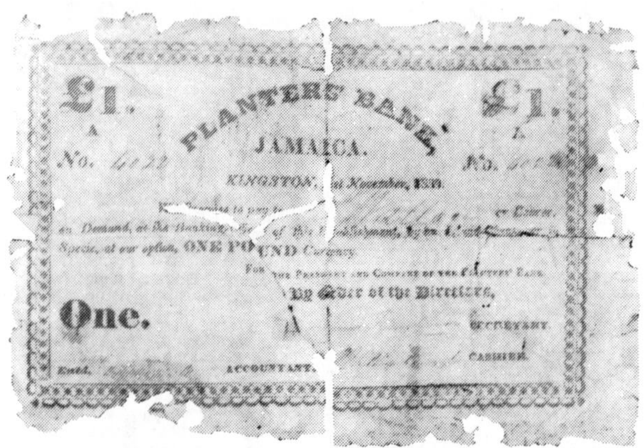

		GOOD	FINE	XF
S206	**1 POUND** 1.11.1839. Blue.	—	Rare	—

1844 ISSUE

#S211-S215 black. Uniface. Printer: John Scott, Glasgow.

		GOOD	FINE	XF
S211	**1 POUND** 1.9.1844. Seated Britannia w/lion, sailing ships in background at l., farmers w/cows at upper ctr., seated woman w/produce, sailing ship in background at r.			
	a. Issued note.	—	Rare	—
	r. Unsigned remainder.	500.00	900.00	—

		GOOD	FINE	XF
S212	**3 POUNDS** (ca.1844). Seated Britannia w/lion and sailing ships in ornate border at l., 2 allegorical figures w/ship at upper ctr.			
	a. Issued note.	—	Rare	—
	r. Unsigned remainder.	—	Rare	—

		GOOD	FINE	XF
S213	**5 POUNDS** (ca.1844). 2 allegorical figures at upper ctr. w/sailing ship at l., plantation at r.			
	a. Issued note.	—	Rare	—
	r. Unsigned remainder.	800.00	1500.	—

		GOOD	FINE	XF
S214	**10 POUNDS** 18xx. Horseman, dockyard at l., seated Britannia w/shield and lion at upper ctr., trader checking goods at r.	—	—	—
S215	**50 POUNDS** Proof.	—	Rare	—
S216	**100 POUNDS** Proof.	—	Rare	—

ROYAL BANK OF CANADA

Established in Jamaica in 1911. Kingston office.

1911 ISSUE

#S221 and S222 arms at ctr. on back. Larger size notes. Printer: ABNC.

		GOOD	FINE	XF
S221	**1 POUND** 2.1.1911. Black on green and pale yellow unpt. Woman seated w/lyre and model ship at r. Back green.			
	a. Issued note.	400.00	1000.	—
	p. Proof w/o plate letter A or sign.	—	—	—
	r. Proof w/plate letter A and sign. H. S. Holt.	—	—	—

		GOOD	FINE	XF
S222	**5 POUNDS** 2.1.1911. Black on red-orange and lt. green unpt. Seated woman at l. Back brown. Proof.	—	Unc	750.00

1938 ISSUE

#S226 and S227 arms at ctr. on back. Smaller size notes. Printer: CBNC.

		GOOD	FINE	XF
S226	**1 POUND** 3.1.1938. Similar to #S221.			
	a. Issued note.	500.00	—	—
	p. Proof.	—	—	—

		GOOD	FINE	XF
S227	**5 POUNDS** 3.1.1938. Similar to #S222. Proof.			
	a. Issued note.	—	Rare	—
	p. Proof.	—	—	—

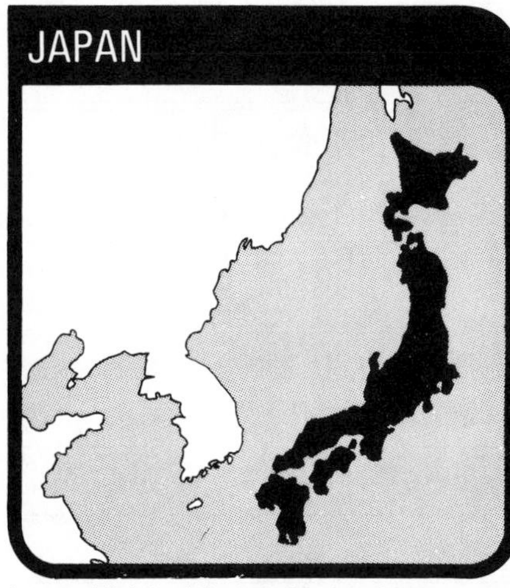

Japan, a constitutional monarchy situated off the east coast of Asia, has an area of 145,856 sq. mi. (377,819 sq. km.) and a population of 127.13 million. Capital: Tokyo. Japan, one of the three major industrial nations of the free world, exports machinery, motor vehicles, textiles and chemicals.

Founded (so legend holds) in 660 BC by a direct descendant of the Sun Goddess, the country was first brought into contact with the west by a storm-blown Portuguese ship in 1542. European traders and missionaries proceeded to enlarge the contact until the Shogunate, sensing a military threat in the foreign presence, expelled all foreigners and severed relations with the outside world in the 17th century. (Except for one Dutch outpost in Nagasaki.) After contact was reestablished by Commodore Perry of the U.S. Navy in 1854, Japan rapidly industrialized, abolished the Shogunate and established a parliamentary form of government, and by the end of the 19th century achieved the status of a modern economic and military power. A series of wars with China and Russia, and participation with the Allies in World War I, enlarged Japan territorially but brought its interests into conflict with the Far Eastern interests of the United States and Britain, causing it to align with the Axis powers for the pursuit of World War II. After its defeat in World War II, Japan renounced military aggression as a political instrument, established democratic self-government, and quickly reasserted its position as an economic world power.

RULERS:

Mutsuhito (Meiji), Years 1-45, (1868-1912) 明治
Yoshihito (Taisho), 1912-1926
Hirohito (Showa), 1926-1989
Akihito (Heisei), 1989-

MONETARY SYSTEM:

1 Shu = 1000-1750 Mon (copper or iron "cash" coins)
1 Bu (fun) = 4 Shu
1 Ryo = 4 Bu to 1870
1 Sen = 10 Rin
1 Yen = 100 Sen, 1870-

MONETARY UNITS:

1 Monme = 3.75 grams
1 Kanme = 1000 Monme
1 Kanmon = 1000 Mon

両 Ryo 匁 Monme 朱 Shu 分 Bu 文 Mon

圓 or 圓 or 円 Yen 銭 Sen 厘 Rin

METALS

金 Gold (Kin) 銀 Silver (Gin) 銅 Copper (Zeni)

REVALIDATION SEAL OVERPRINT:

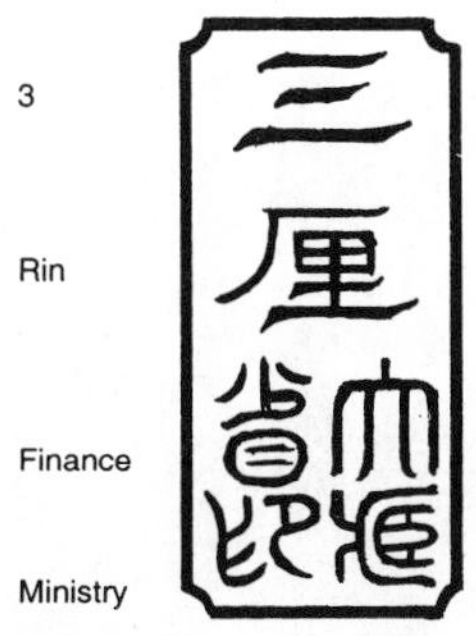

NUMERICAL

A - CONVENTIONAL

B - FORMAL

NUMERALS

NUMBER	CONVENTIONAL	FORMAL
1	一	壹 or 弌
2	二	弍 or 貳
3	三	叁 弎
4	四	肆
5	五	伍
6	六	陸
7	七	柒
8	八	捌
9	九	玖
10	十	拾
20	十 二 or 廿	拾貳
25	五 十 二 or 五廿	伍拾貳
30	十 三 or 卅	拾叁
100	百 一	佰壹
1,000	千 一	仟壹
10,000	萬 一 or 万	萬壹
100,000	萬 十 or 万十	萬拾
1,000,000	萬百一	萬佰壹

NOTE: This table has been adapted from *Chinese Bank Notes* by Ward Smith and Brian Matravers.

HAN-SATSU TYPES:

"Hansatsu" was issued in various colors and sizes of paper, some with various parts dyed in other colors to help the illiterate be aware of the denomination. Those illustrated are but a mere sampling of the extensive number of varieties issued.

Sendai Clan. 1 Kire (Bu), gold

Kochi Clan. 1 Kanme, silver

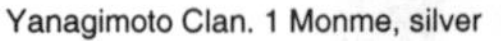

Yanagimoto Clan. 1 Monme, silver

Takatsuka. 1 Shu, gold (personal note)

GOVERNMENT

OIN-SATSU

During the transition from numerous issues to one uniform currency (the Shin-Shihei notes), the Finance Ministry agents and some local officials found it expedient to revalue various old hansatsu still in circulation to relieve the shortage of small coins. In 1872 this was done on a local basis with notes worth less than 5 sen which were then hand stamped in red with their new "official" valuation and returned into circulation. Since many were finally redeemed and destroyed by the treasury, the Oin-Satsu remain rather scarce today.

See introduction for facsimile of this ovpt.

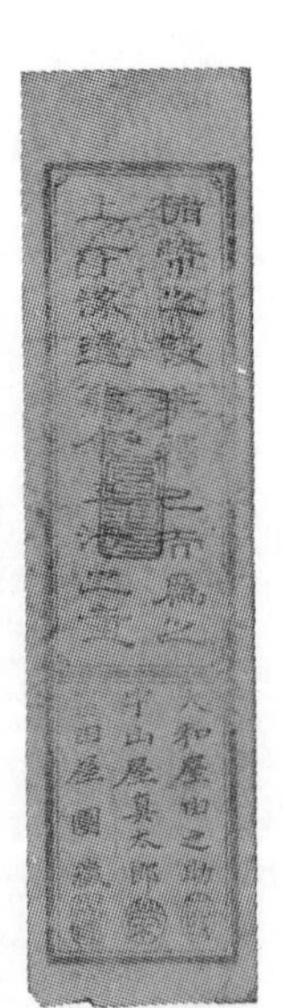

Mori-han (clan) w/ovpt: 3 Rin on 100 Mon

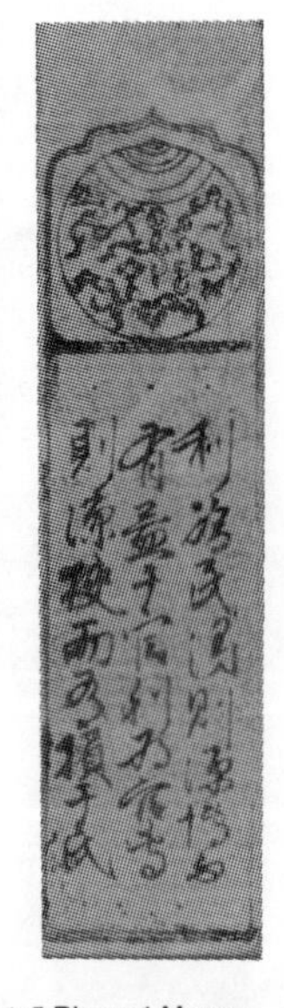

Matsue-han (clan) w/ovpt: 5 Rin on 1 Monme

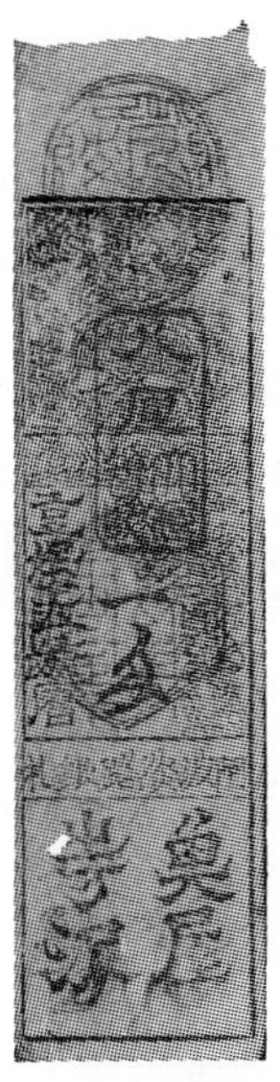

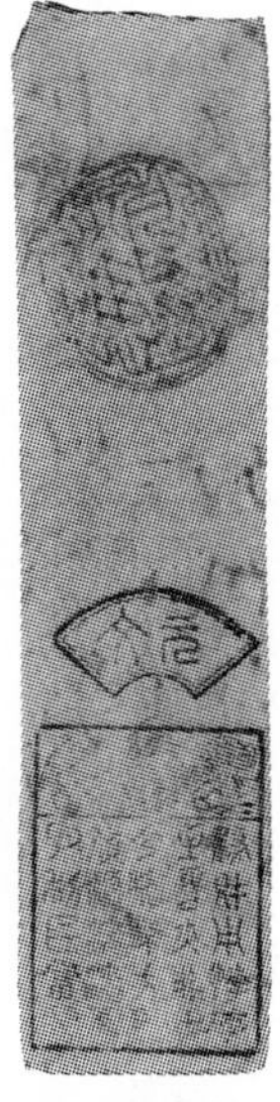

Tokushima-han w/ovpt: 8 Rin on 1 Monme

Toba-han (clan) w/ovpt: 1 Sen 3 Rin on 1 Monme

1872 ND Provisional Issue

		Good	Fine	XF
S101	1 Rin ND (1872).	4.00	10.00	20.00
S102	2 Rin ND (1872).	4.00	10.00	20.00
S103	3 Rin ND (1872).	4.00	10.00	20.00
S104	4 Rin ND (1872).	4.00	10.00	20.00
S105	5 Rin ND (1872).	4.00	10.00	20.00
S106	6 Rin ND (1872).	5.00	12.00	24.00
S107	7 Rin ND (1872).	5.00	12.00	24.00
S108	8 Rin ND (1872).	5.00	12.00	24.00
S109	9 Rin ND (1872).	5.00	12.00	24.00
S110	1 Sen ND (1872).	5.00	12.00	24.00
S112	1 Sen 2 Rin ND (1872).	6.00	15.00	30.00
S113	1 Sen 3 Rin ND (1872).	6.00	15.00	30.00
S114	1 Sen 4 Rin ND (1872).	6.00	15.00	30.00
S115	1 Sen 5 Rin ND (1872).	6.00	15.00	30.00
S116	1 Sen 6 Rin ND (1872).	6.00	15.00	30.00
S117	1 Sen 7 Rin ND (1872).	6.00	15.00	30.00
S118	1 Sen 8 Rin ND (1872).	6.00	15.00	30.00
S119	1 Sen 9 Rin ND (1872).	6.00	15.00	30.00
S120	2 Sen ND (1872).	6.00	15.00	32.00
S121	2 Sen 1 Rin ND (1872).	7.00	17.50	35.00
S124	2 Sen 4 Rin ND (1872).	7.00	17.50	35.00
S125	2 Sen 5 Rin ND (1872).	7.00	17.50	35.00
S126	2 Sen 6 Rin ND (1872).	7.00	17.50	35.00
S127	2 Sen 7 Rin ND (1872).	7.00	17.50	35.00
S129	2 Sen 9 Rin ND (1872).	7.00	17.50	35.00
S130	3 Sen ND (1872).	7.00	17.50	35.00
S131	3 Sen 1 Rin ND (1872).	8.00	20.00	40.00
S132	3 Sen 2 Rin ND (1872).	8.00	20.00	40.00
S133	3 Sen 3 Rin ND (1872).	8.00	20.00	40.00
S135	3 Sen 5 Rin ND (1872).	8.00	20.00	40.00
S138	3 Sen 8 Rin ND (1872).	8.00	20.00	40.00
S139	3 Sen 9 Rin ND (1872).	8.00	20.00	40.00
S140	4 Sen ND (1872).	10.00	25.00	50.00
S142	4 Sen 2 Rin ND (1872).	12.50	30.00	60.00
S145	4 Sen 5 Rin ND (1872).	12.50	30.00	60.00
S148	4 Sen 8 Rin ND (1872).	12.50	30.00	60.00

NOTE: The market valuations for Oin-satsu are for the more common varieties of the basic Han-satsu.

Government

Edo - Yokohama Bakafu (Shogunate)

Tokyo

1867 Gold Note Issue

		Good	Fine	XF
S150	1 Ryo Yr. 3 Keio (1867).	600.00	1250.	1500.
S151	5 Ryo Yr. 3 Keio (1867).	750.00	1500.	2000.
S152	10 Ryo Yr. 3 Keio (1867).	750.00	1500.	2000.

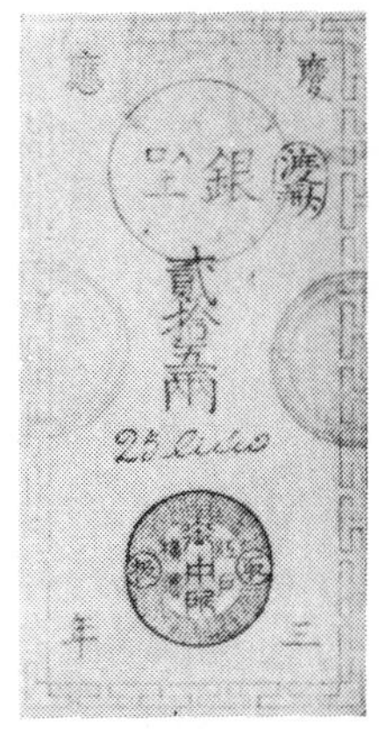

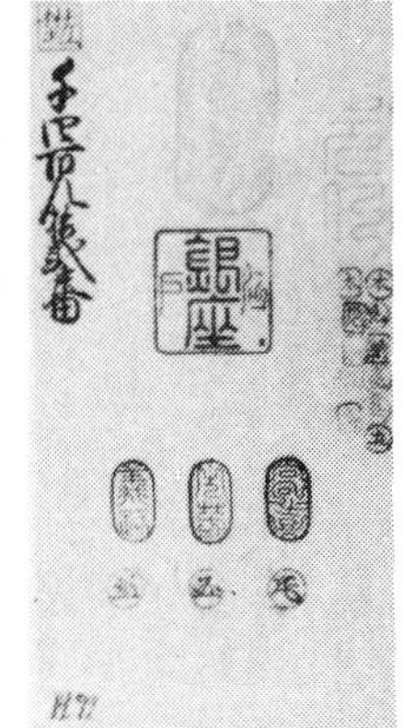

		Good	Fine	XF
S153	25 Ryo Yr. 3 Keio (1867).	1250.	2000.	2500.

Edo & Eight Provinces of the Kanto

1867 Gold Note Issue

		Good	Fine	XF
S154	1 Ryo Yr. 3 Keio (1867).	600.00	1250.	1500.
S155	25 Ryo Yr. 3 Keio (1867).	750.00	1500.	2000.
S156	50 Ryo Yr. 3 Keio (1867).	1000.	1750.	2250.

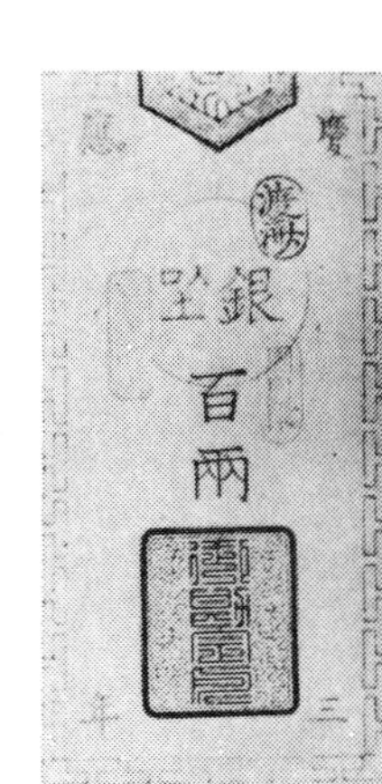

		Good	Fine	XF
S157	100 Ryo Yr. 3 Keio (1867).	1250.	2000.	2500.
S158	200 Ryo Yr. 3 Keio (1867).	1500.	2500.	3000.

HYOGO PORT-DEVELOPMENT

KOBE

1867 ISSUE

#S159

#S160

#S161

		GOOD	FINE	XF
S159	1 FUN Yr. 3 Keio (1867). Black.	12.00	20.00	30.00
S160	2 FUN Yr. 3 Keio (1867). Black.	12.00	20.00	30.00
S161	1 RYO Yr. 3 Keio (1867). Black.	25.00	40.00	60.00

DAJOKAN-SATSU

Cabinet

1868 GOLD NOTE ISSUE

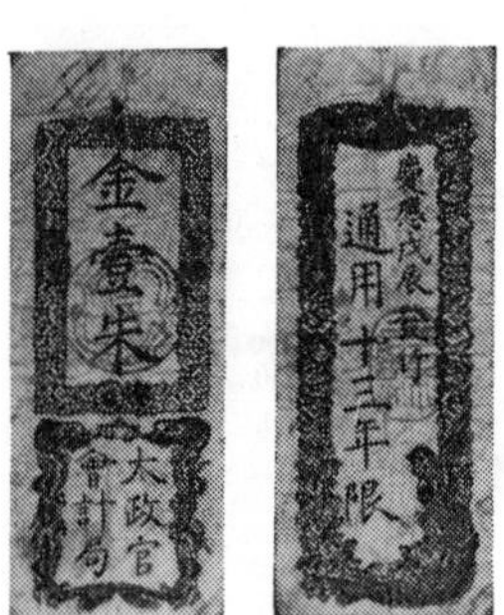

#S162

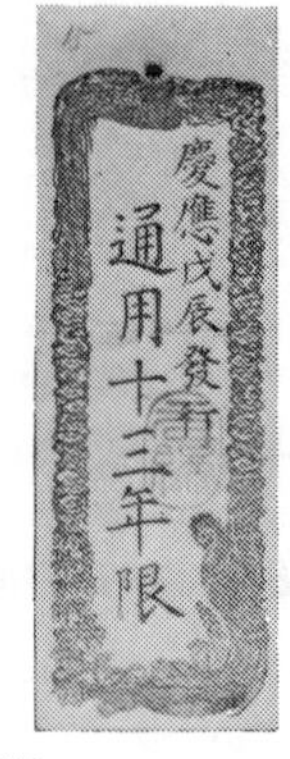

#S163

		GOOD	FINE	XF
S162	1 SHU Yr. 4 Keio (1868).	7.50	17.50	25.00
S163	1 BU Yr. 4 Keio (1868).	7.50	17.50	25.00

#S164

#S165

#S166

		GOOD	FINE	XF
S164	1 RYO Yr. 4 Keio (1868).	17.50	35.00	50.00
S165	5 RYO Yr. 4 Keio (1868).	60.00	125.00	200.00
S166	10 RYO Yr. 4 Keio (1868).	85.00	175.00	250.00

MINBUSHO-SATSU

Civil Department

1869 GOLD NOTE ISSUE

#S167-S170 two facing dragons at bottom. Dragon at bottom on back.

#S167

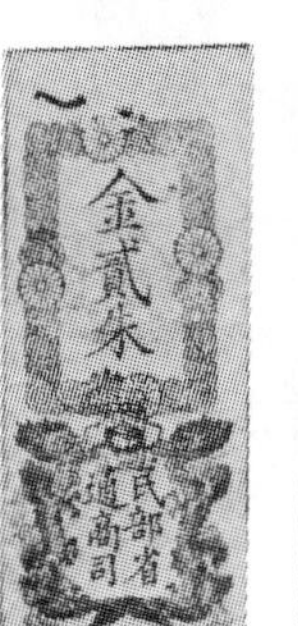
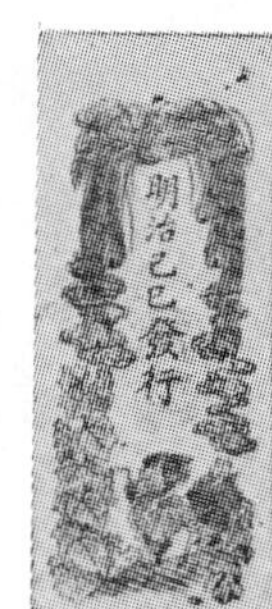

#S168

		GOOD	FINE	XF
S167	1 SHU Yr. 2 Meiji (1869). Black.	15.00	30.00	45.00
S168	2 SHU Yr. 2 Meiji (1869). Black.	12.00	25.00	35.00

#S169

#S170

		GOOD	FINE	XF
S169	1 BU Yr. 2 Meiji (1869). Black.	15.00	30.00	45.00
S170	2 BU Yr. 2 Meiji (1869). Black.	17.50	40.00	60.00

OKURASHO DAKAN SHOKEN

Finance Ministry

1871 CONVERTIBLE GOLD NOTE ISSUE

#S171-S173 w/blue-gray adhesive stamp affixed on back w/impressed oval vermilion seal.

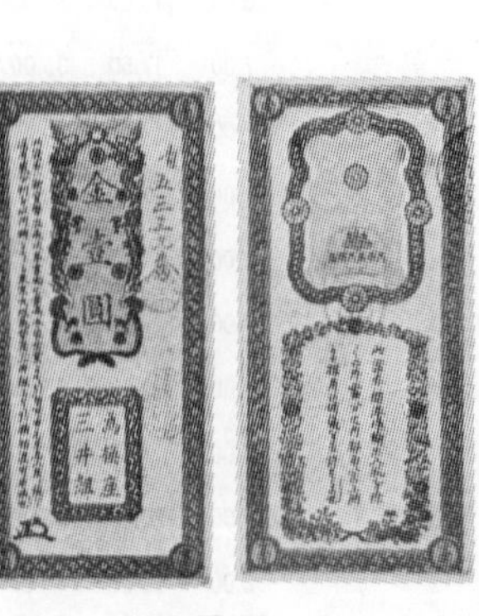

#S171

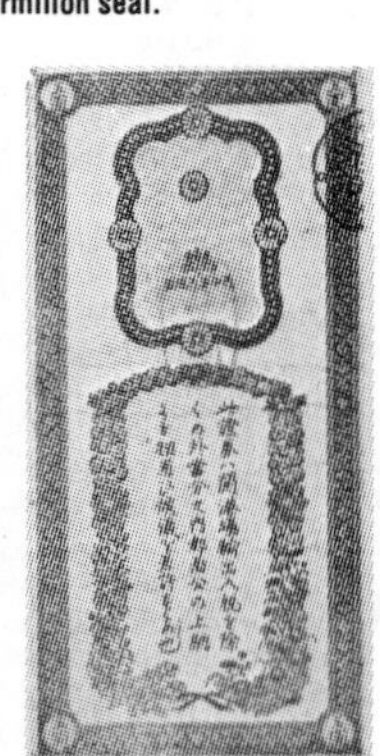

#S172

		GOOD	FINE	XF
S171	1 YEN ND (1871).	125.00	250.00	400.00
S172	5 YEN ND (1871).	450.00	1000.	1750.
S173	10 YEN ND (1871).	900.00	1500.	2000.

KAITAKUSHI DAKAN SHOKEN

Development Office

1872 CONVERTIBLE NOTE ISSUE

#S174-S179 w/blue-gray adhesive stamp affixed on back w/impressed oval vermilion seal of denomination; like #S171-S173 but w/circular red seal of the development office on face. Higher denominations may also have a black ovpt. of the denomination.

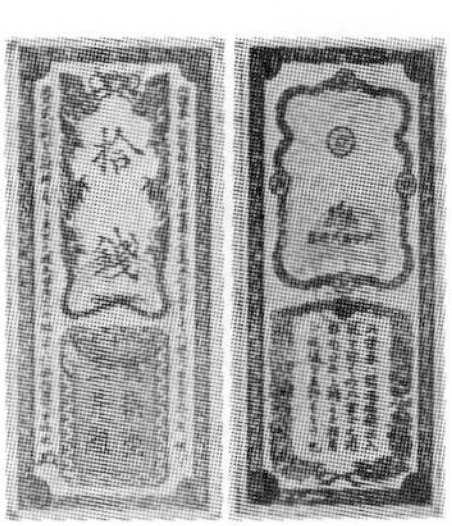

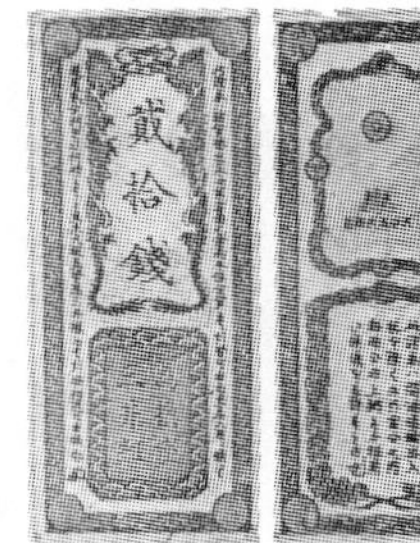

#S174 #S175

		GOOD	FINE	XF
S174	**10 SEN** ND (1872). Black.	17.50	40.00	60.00
S175	**20 SEN** ND (1872). Black.	27.50	60.00	100.00

#S176 #S177

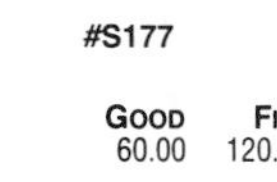

		GOOD	FINE	XF
S176	**50 SEN** ND (1872). Black.	60.00	120.00	175.00
S177	**1 YEN** ND (1872). Black.	200.00	500.00	750.00
S178	**5 YEN** ND (1872). Black.	—	Rare	—
S179	**10 YEN** ND (1872). Black.	—	Rare	—

EXCHANGE BANKS

TOKYO KAWASE KAISHA

Some Exchange banknotes are distinguishable only by the seal of each office.

TOKYO

1869 SILVER NOTE ISSUE

		GOOD	FINE	XF
S180	**3 MOMME 7 FUN 5 RIN** ND (1869). Black.	7.50	17.50	25.00

1869 MULTI-OFFICE GOLD NOTE ISSUE

#S181 and S182 crane superimposed over rising sun at top, sailboat at bottom. Turtle at bottom on back.

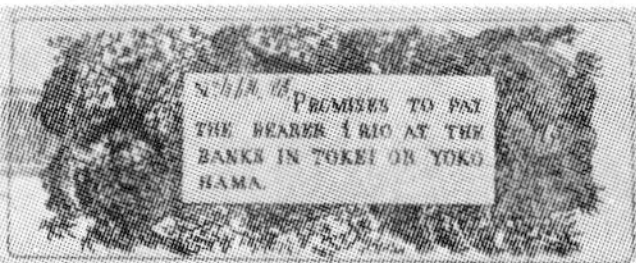

		GOOD	FINE	XF
S181	**1 RYO** ND (1869). Black.			
	a. Red 2 character oval ovpt: *Tokyo.*	85.00	175.00	250.00
	b. Red 2 character rectangular ovpt: *Yokohama.*	165.00	350.00	500.00
	c. Red 2 character square ovpt: *Niigata.*	—	Rare	—

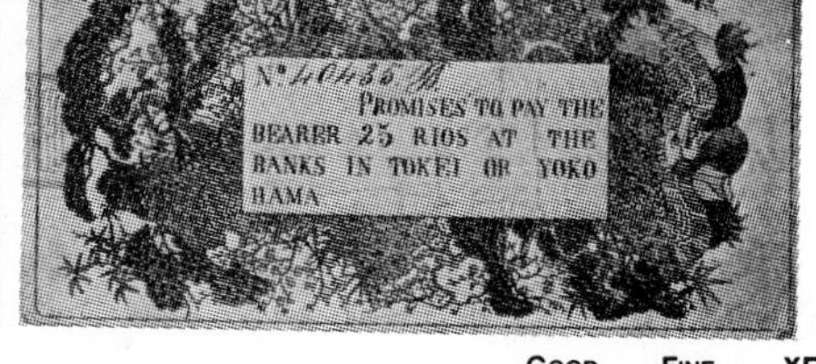

		GOOD	FINE	XF
S182	**25 RYO** ND (1869). Black.			
	a. Red 2 character oval ovpt: *Tokyo.*	350.00	800.00	1250.
	b. Red 2 character rectangular ovpt: *Yokohama.*	—	Rare	—
	c. Red 2 character square ovpt: *Niigata.*	—	Rare	—
	d. Violet 2 character oval ovpt: *Kobe.*	—	Rare	—

KYOTO

1869 COPPER NOTE ISSUE

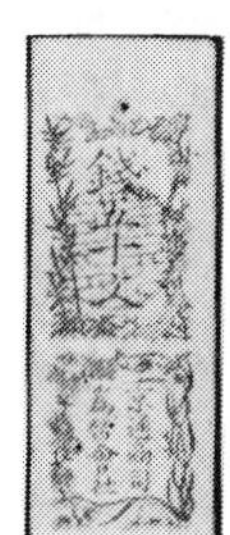

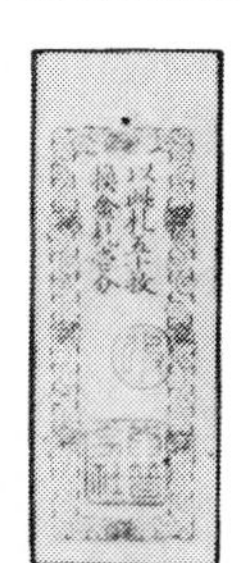

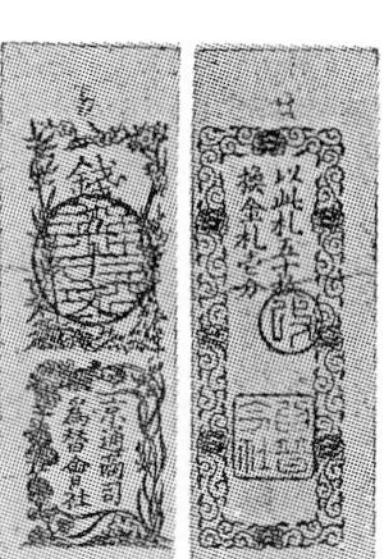

#S183 #S184

		GOOD	FINE	XF
S183	**50 MON** ND (1869). Black.	10.00	17.50	25.00
S184	**100 MON** ND (1869). Black.	12.50	20.00	30.00

A word on pricing

When a note is marked RARE in the price columns, this note seldom appears on the market, or few are known in private hands. When dashes are in the price column, means that the note has not traded on the open market recently and a definitive value could not accurately be determined. Rare does not always mean expensive. A dashed price does not mean expensive or rare.

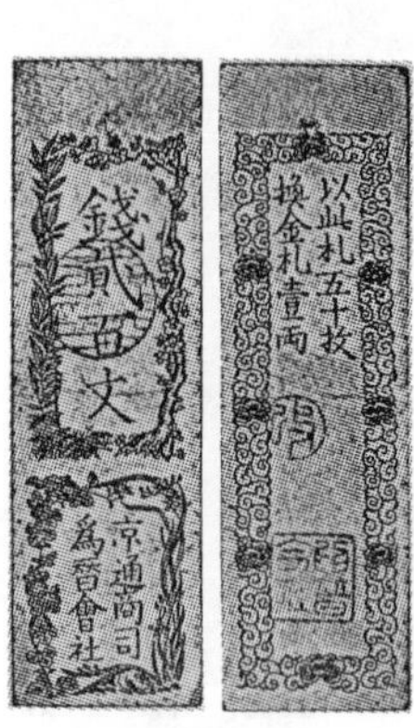
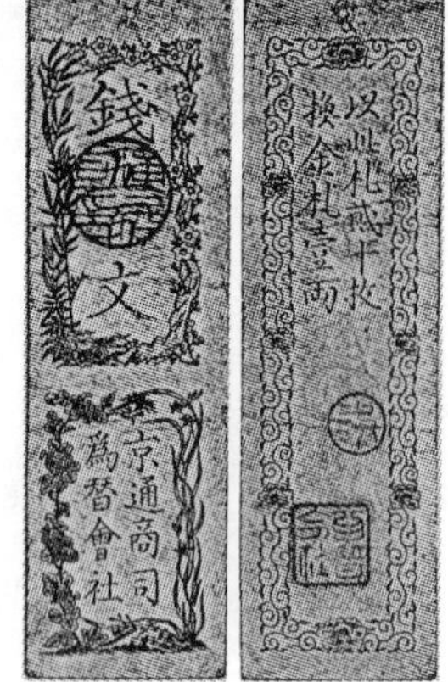

#S185 #S186

		Good	Fine	XF
S185	**200 Mon** ND (1869). Black.	17.50	35.00	50.00
S186	**500 Mon** ND (1869). Black.	30.00	60.00	80.00

Osaka

1869 Copper Note Issue

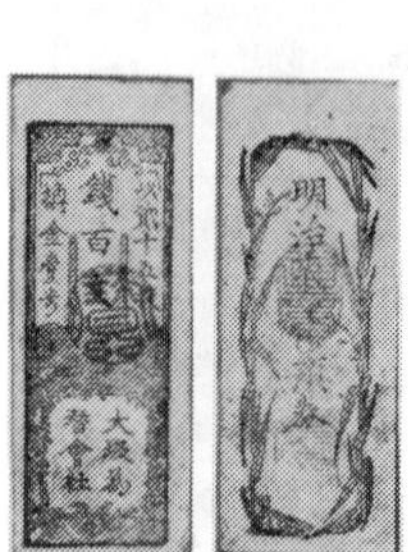

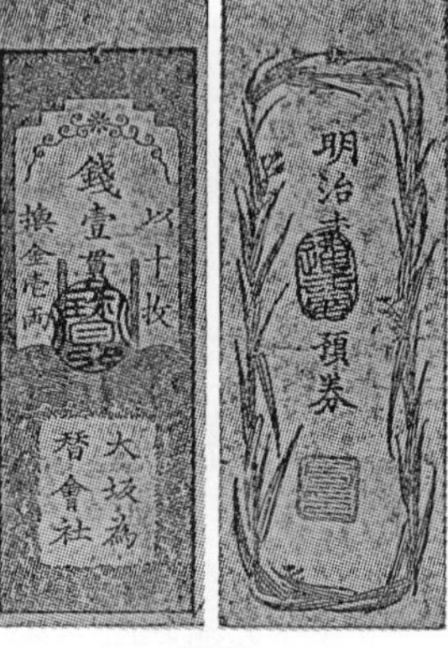

#S187 #S188 #S190

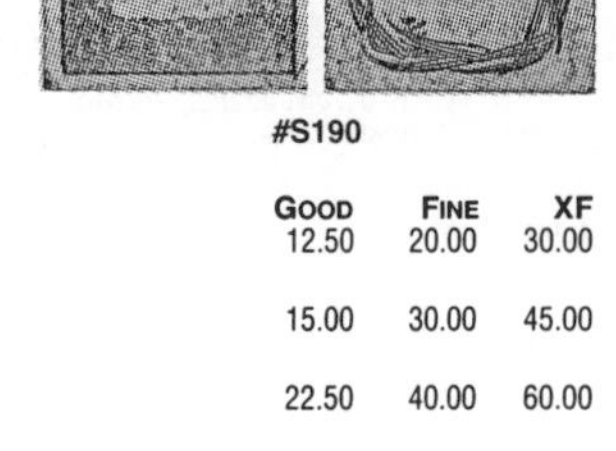

		Good	Fine	XF
S187	**100 Mon** Yr. 2 Meiji (1869). Black.	12.50	20.00	30.00
S188	**200 Mon** Yr. 2 Meiji (1869). Black.	15.00	30.00	45.00
S189	**500 Mon** Yr. 2 Meiji (1869). Black.	22.50	40.00	60.00
S190	**1 Kan Mon = 1000 Mon** Yr. 2 Meiji (1869). Black.	125.00	250.00	400.00

1869 Multi-Office Gold Note Issue

#S191a #S192

		Good	Fine	XF
S191	**1 Ryo** ND (1869). Black.			
	a. Red 1 character circular ovpt: *Kyoto.*	55.00	110.00	150.00
	b. Red 2 character oval ovpt: *Otsu.*	125.00	200.00	300.00
	c. Red 2 character fundo ovpt: *Tsuruga.*	175.00	300.00	500.00
S192	**1 Ryo** ND (1869). Black. Saikyo *(Kyoto).*	125.00	225.00	300.00

Hikone

1870 Issue

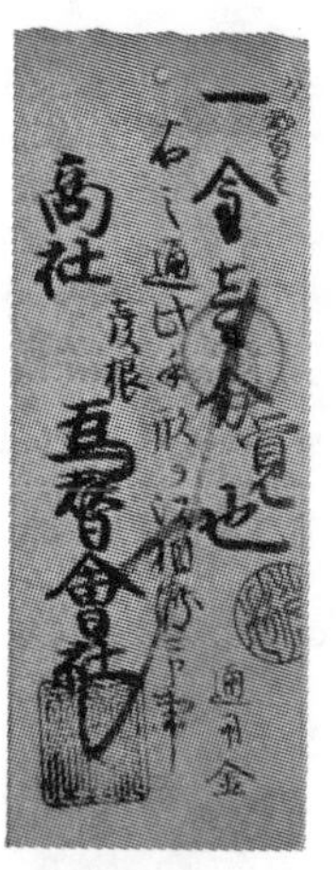

#S193 #S194 #S195

		Good	Fine	XF
S193	**1 Bu** Yr. 3 Meiji (1870). Black.	175.00	350.00	500.00
S194	**2 Bu** Yr. 3 Meiji (1870). Black.	175.00	350.00	500.00
S195	**1 Ryo** Yr. 3 Meiji (1870). Black.	175.00	350.00	500.00

Matsuzaka

1870 Issue

		Good	Fine	XF
S195A	**1 Ryo** Yr. 3 Meiji (1870). Black.	—	Rare	—

Osaka

1870 Foreign Silver Note Issue

#S196-S202 photographic print of Osaka Exchange Office glued w/impressed oval seal at bottom.

		Good	Fine	XF
S196	**25 Mexican Dollars** Yr. 3 Meiji (1870).	—	Rare	—
S197	**50 Mexican Dollars** Yr. 3 Meiji (1870).	—	Rare	—

1869 Gold Note Issue

		Good	Fine	XF
S198	**1 Ryo** Yr. 2 Meiji (1869). Black.	125.00	200.00	400.00
S199	**5 Ryo** Yr. 2 Meiji (1869). Black.	400.00	800.00	1500.
S200	**10 Ryo** Yr. 2 Meiji (1869). Black.	—	Rare	—

		GOOD	FINE	XF
S201	**50 RYO** Yr. 2 Meiji (1869). Black.	—	Rare	—

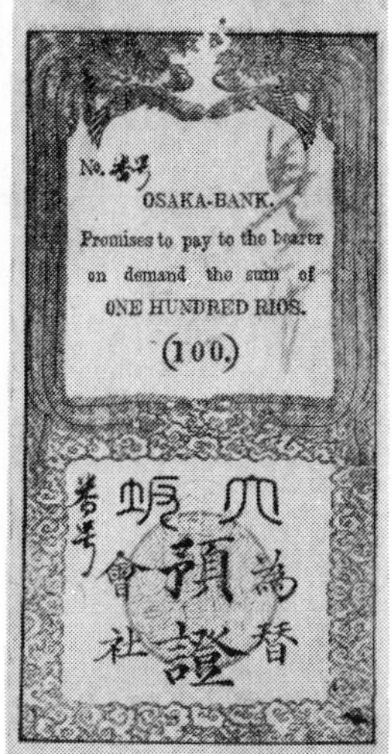

		GOOD	FINE	XF
S202	**100 RYO** Yr. 2 Meiji (1869). Black.	—	Rare	—

YOKOHAMA

1870 FOREIGN SILVER NOTE ISSUE

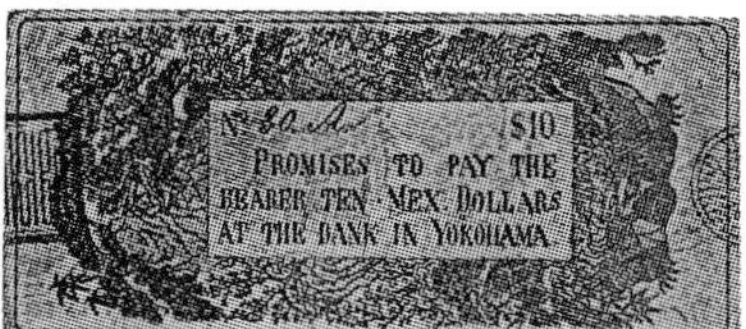

		GOOD	FINE	XF
S203	**10 MEX(ICAN) DOLLARS** ND (1870). Black.	—	Rare	—
S204	**100 MEX(ICAN) DOLLARS** ND (1870). Black.	—	Rare	—

1872 LOCAL CURRENCY - FOREIGN SILVER NOTE ISSUE

#S205-S211 Mt. Fuji in frame of two facing dragons at top ctr. Back two dragon frame. Printer: PBC.

		GOOD	FINE	XF
S205	**5 DOLLARS** Yr. 5 Meiji (1872). Black.	—	Rare	—

		GOOD	FINE	XF
S206	**10 DOLLARS** Yr. 5 Meiji (1872). Blue.	—	Rare	—
S207	**20 DOLLARS** Yr. 5 Meiji (1872). Maroon.	—	Rare	—
S208	**50 DOLLARS** Yr. 5 Meiji (1872). Green.	—	Rare	—
S209	**100 DOLLARS** Yr. 5 Meiji (1872). Blue. Back black.	—	Rare	—
S210	**500 DOLLARS** Yr. 5 Meiji (1872). Blue.	—	Rare	—
S211	**1000 DOLLARS** Yr. 5 Meiji (1872). Green. Back black.	—	Rare	—

NOTE: #S205-S211 exist in black as proofs.

FOREIGN BANKS

CENTRAL BANK OF WESTERN INDIA

YOKOHAMA

1866 ISSUE

		GOOD	FINE	XF
S224	**25 DOLLARS** 9.2.1866. Seated Justice w/scale at l., ship and palm trees in background. Printer: Batho Sprague & Co.			
	a. Issued note, hand cancelled.	—	Rare	—
	r. Remainder.	—	Rare	—

NOTE: Other denominations may have been prepared.

CHARTERED MERCANTILE BANK OF INDIA, LONDON & CHINA

YOKOHAMA

1860'S ISSUE

#S228-S231 printer: PBC.

		Good	Fine	XF
S228	**5 Dollars** May 1866. Black on blue unpt. Back black.	—	Rare	—
S229	**10 Dollars** 18xx.	—	—	—
S230	**50 Dollars** 18xx.	—	—	—
S231	**100 Dollars** 18xx.	—	—	—

NOTE: #S228-S231 exist as specimens in the collection of HK & SBC Ltd. Other denominations are suspected, not confirmed.

Commercial Bank Corporation of India & the East

Yokohama

1866 Issue

		Good	Fine	XF
S235	**10 Dollars** 3.2.1866.	—	—	—

NOTE: One issued note is known. Other denominations may have been prepared.

Hong Kong & Shanghai Banking Corporation

Hiogo

Opened in 1869.

1870's Issue

#S240-S244 printer: BLF.

#S239 *Deleted.*

		Good	Fine	XF
S240	**5 Dollars** 18xx. Green on brown unpt. Specimen.	—	—	—
S241	**10 Dollars** 18xx. Blue on brown unpt. Specimen.	—	—	—

#S242 *Deleted.*

		Good	Fine	XF
S243	**50 Dollars** 18xx. Violet on brown unpt. Specimen.	—	—	—

NOTE: Color trials w/modified unpt. exist for #S243.

		Good	Fine	XF
S244	**100 Dollars** 18xx.	—	—	—

Yokohama

Opened May 1866.

1866 Provisional Issue

#S246-S250 ovpt: *YOKOHAMA, JAPAN* and *YOKOHAMA* on Hong Kong notes. Printer: Ashby & Co.

#S245 *Deleted.*

		Good	Fine	XF
S246	**5 Dollars** 2.7.1866. Black on blue unpt. Back green.	—	—	—
S247	**10 Dollars** 18xx.	Reported Not Confirmed		
S248	**25 Dollars** 2.7.1866. Gray. Back orange.	—	—	—
S249	**50 Dollars** 18xx.	Reported Not Confirmed		
S250	**100 Dollars** 18xx.	Reported Not Confirmed		

1870's Issue

#S252-S256 black on red unpt. Bank arms at top ctr. w/*YOKOHAMA* in frame. Printer: Ashby & Co.

#S251 *Deleted.*

		Good	Fine	XF
S252	**5 Dollars** 18xx. Specimen.	—	—	—
S253	**10 Dollars** 18xx. Specimen.	—	—	—
S254	**25 Dollars** 18xx. Specimen.	—	—	—
S255	**50 Dollars** 18xx.			
	a. Issued note.	—	—	—
	s. Specimen.	—	—	—
S256	**100 Dollars** 18xx. Specimen.	—	—	—

		Good	Fine	XF
S257	**500 Dollars** 18xx. Back green. Specimen.	—	—	—

New Oriental Bank Corporation Ltd.

Yokohama

1886 Issue

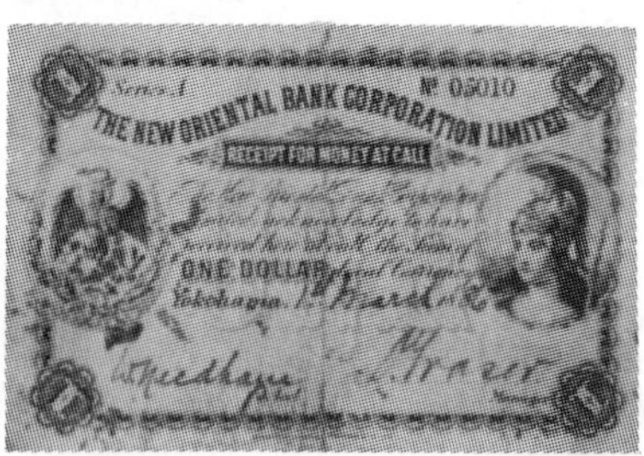

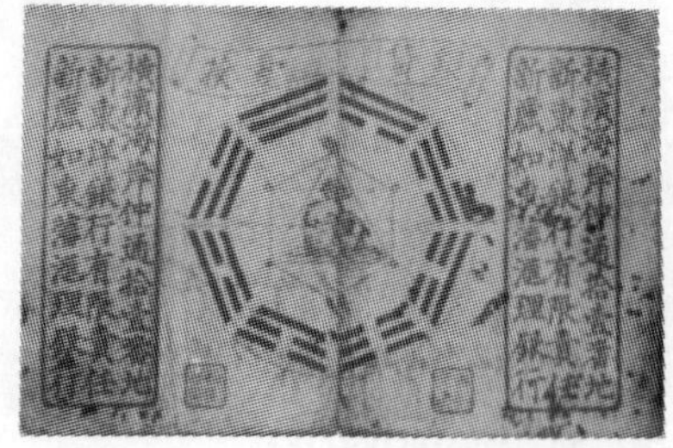

		Good	Fine	XF
S260	**1 Dollar** 1.1.1886; 1.3.1886. Black on pink unpt. Mexican eagle at l., portr. Minerva at r. Octagonal "tri-grams" at ctr. on back.			
	a. Issued note.	750.00	2250.	—
	s. Specimen.	—	Unc	4000.

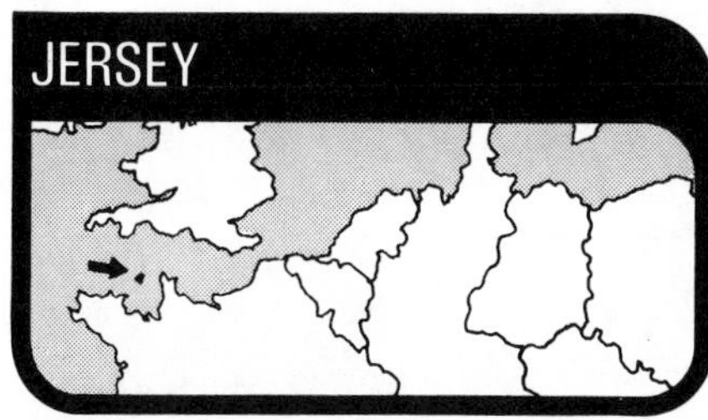

The Bailiwick of Jersey, a British Crown dependency located in the English Channel 12 miles (19 km.) west of Normandy, France, has an area of 45 sq. mi. (117 sq. km.) and a population of 90,000. Capital: St. Helier. The economy is based on agriculture and cattle breeding - the importation of cattle is prohibited to protect the purity of the island's world-famous strain of milk cows.

Jersey was occupied by Neanderthal man 100,000 years B.C., and by Iberians of 2000 B.C. who left their chamber tombs in the island's granite cliffs. Roman legions almost certainly visited the island although they left no evidence of settlement. The country folk of Jersey still speak an archaic form of Norman-French, lingering evidence of the Norman annexation of the island in 933 B.C. Jersey was annexed to England in 1206, 140 years after the Norman Conquest. The dependency is administered by its own laws and customs; laws enacted by the British Parliament do not apply to Jersey unless it is specifically mentioned. During World War II, German troops occupied the island from 1940 until 1944.

United Kingdom bank notes and coinage circulate concurrently with Jersey money as legal tender.

RULERS:
British

MONETARY SYSTEM:
1 Shilling = 12 Pence
1 Pound = 20 Shillings to 1971

BANKS AND CHURCHES

PARISHES

From 1816 to 1941, only two notes circulated as government issues: a 5 Pound 1840 Bearer Bond (see #A1 in Volume 2) and a 1 Pound 1874 Harbour Committee note. Some States politicians were bankers who apparently wanted fiscal control to remain with their banks. Eventually, over 100 banks, parishes and individuals became note issuers. Notes were often issued for road-building and other public works. Bank and parish issues sometimes became intertwined with those of private companies. The notes catalogued here are church, parish or bank issues which seemed to serve the general public in some capacity.

BANKS AND CHURCHES

Issued to defray expenses of building the Masonic Temple.

BIBLE CHRISTIAN CHURCH

Royal Crescent, Jersey.

1872 ND ISSUE

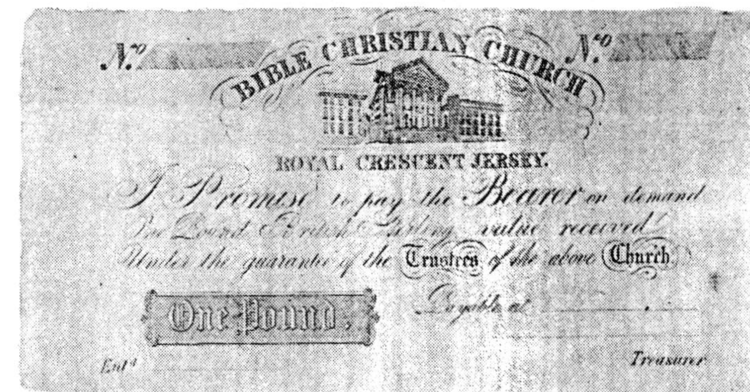

		Good	Fine	XF
S121	**1 POUND** ND (ca.1872-84). Green. Bldg. w/marble-columned facade at top ctr. Uniface. Remainder.	—	—	80.00

BIBLE CHRISTIAN SOCIETY

ND ISSUE

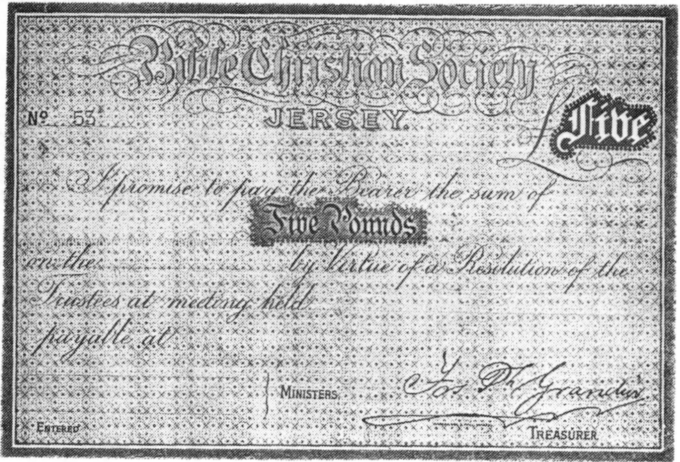

		Good	Fine	XF
S126	**5 POUNDS** ND. Black text. Tan paper. Remainder.	—	—	—

ESPLANADE

St. Helier. Issued to pay for the construction of a line of Quays under guarantee of the States.

1858 ISSUE

		Good	Fine	XF
S136	**1 POUND** 1858. Farm at upper l., street scene at upper ctr., arms at upper r.	—	850.00	—

INTERNATIONAL BANK

St. Heliers, Jersey.

1865 ISSUE

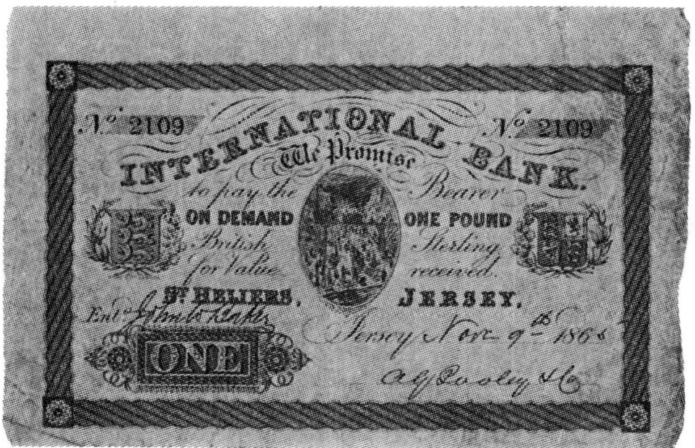

		Good	Fine	XF
S161	**1 POUND** 9.11.1865. Black. Arms at l. and r., construction scene at ctr. Uniface. Printer; Rowe Co., London.	40.00	80.00	160.00

JERSEY AGRICULTURAL ASSOCIATION, TRINITY BANK

1835 ISSUE

		GOOD	FINE	XF
S166	1 POUND 20.10.1835. Farm tools at upper ctr.	—	Rare	—

JERSEY MERCANTILE UNION BANK

Established in 1834.

1850'S ISSUE

		GOOD	FINE	XF
S208	1 POUND 18xx. Black. Harbor scene at upper l., arms at upper ctr., 3 allegorical figures at upper r., *BRITISH STERLING* in bottom frame. Back blue-gray. Printer: CS&E. Specimen.	—	—	—

1860'S ISSUE

		GOOD	FINE	XF
S213	1 POUND 1.1.1864. Black. Similar to #S208 but date within central panel, *ESTABLISHED IN 1834* in bottom frame.	650.00	1350.	—

NOTE: A similar issue exists drawn on this bank by Le Bailly, Deslandes & Co.

A word on pricing

When a note is marked RARE in the price columns, this note seldom appears on the market, or few are known in private hands. When dashes are in the price column, means that the note has not traded on the open market recently and a definitive value could not accurately be determined. Rare does not always mean expensive. A dashed price does not mean expensive or rare.

MASONIC TEMPLE COMPANY, LIMITED

Issued to defray expenses of building the Masonic Temple.

1866 ISSUE

		GOOD	FINE	XF
S226	1 POUND 1.1.1866. Bldg. at upper l., arms at upper r.	—	Rare	—

NOTE: Poor quality reprints of an 1844 date exist.

TOWN VINGTAINE OF ST. HELIER

1830'S ISSUE

		GOOD	FINE	XF
S236	1 POUND 10.5.1834. Shield and shore scene at l.	—	—	—
S238	1 POUND 18xx. Like #S241 but uniface.	—	—	—

1850'S ISSUE

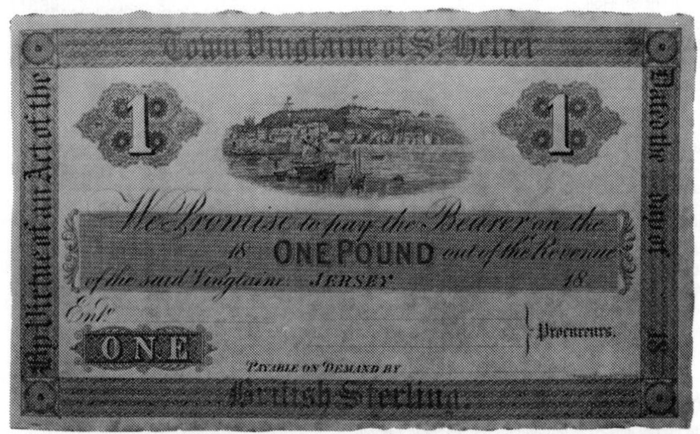

		GOOD	FINE	XF
S241	1 POUND 18xx. Gray and orange. Harbor and town at upper ctr. Printer: PBC. Remainder.	—	—	90.00

VINGTAINE DU MONT AU PRETRE

1838 ISSUE

		GOOD	FINE	XF
S292	1 POUND 7.12.1838.	—	—	—

WESLEYAN METHODIST COUNTRY CHAPELS BANK

1835-50 ISSUE

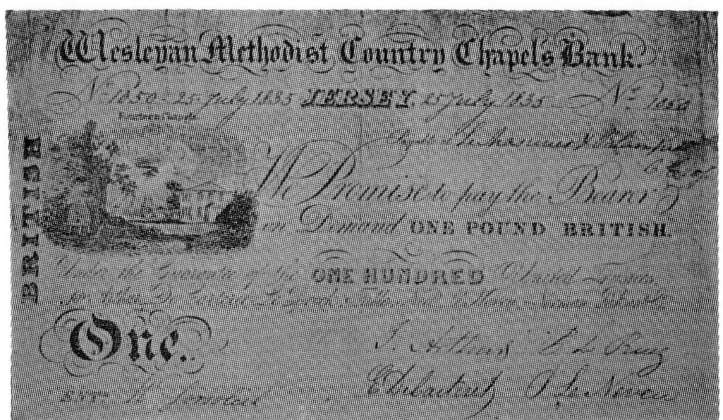

		GOOD	FINE	XF
S301	1 POUND 25.7.1835; 1850. Beehive and chapels at l.	—	Rare	—

NOTE: Blue printings appearing as proofs without dates may be reprints.

PARISHES

PARISH OF ST. BRELADE

1859; 1886 ISSUE

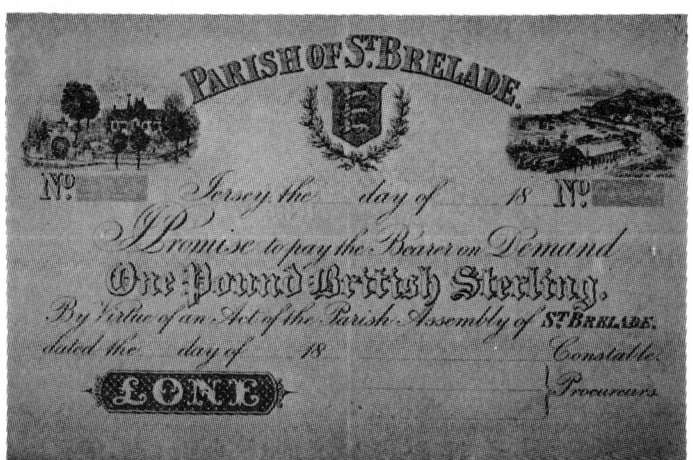

		GOOD	FINE	XF
S306	1 POUND 7.10.1859; 12.2.1886. Church and grounds at upper l., seacoast road w/hill at upper r.	50.00	85.00	150.00

ST. CLEMENT'S PARISH BANK

1800'S ISSUE

		GOOD	FINE	XF
S308	1 POUND 18xx. Black. Arms at upper l., church bldg. at upper r. Remainder.	—	—	—

PARISH OF ST. HELIER

1835 ISSUE

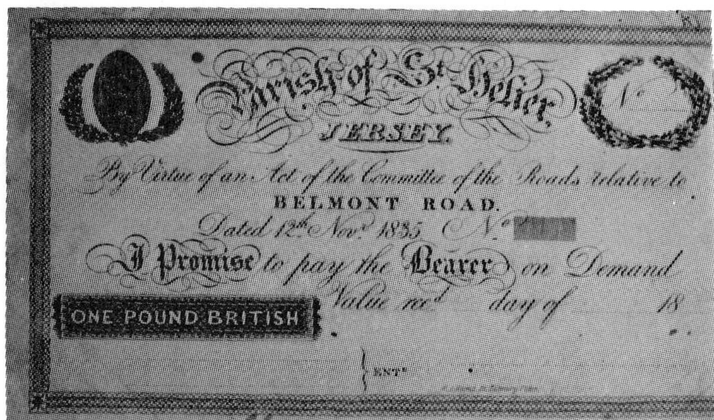

		GOOD	FINE	XF
S311	1 POUND *L.12.11.1835.* Arms at upper l. Belmont road issue.	—	Rare	—

TOWN AND PARISH OF ST. HELIER

1858 ISSUE

		GOOD	FINE	XF
S316	1 POUND 25.9.1858. Trees and bldg. at upper ctr., arms at r. Printer: PBC. Proof.	—	Rare	—

NOTE: Several other Parish of St. Helier issues are reported in association with various public works.

ST. JOHN'S BANK

1800'S ISSUE

		VG	VF	UNC
S318	1 POUND 18xx. Black. Church bldg. at l., old town view at top ctr. Remainder.	—	—	—

NOTE: A collectors reprint (250) was produced dated 1982.

ST. MARTIN'S PARISH BANK

1897 ISSUE

		GOOD	FINE	XF
S320	1 POUND 18xx. Similar to #S321, but w/o frame border. Uniface.	—	—	

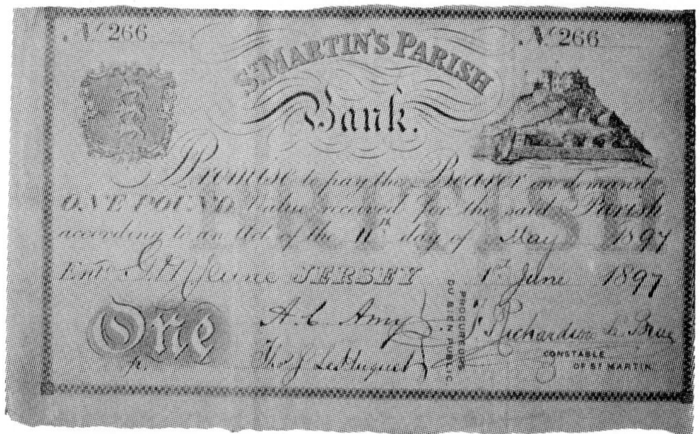

		GOOD	FINE	XF
S321	1 POUND 1.6.1897. Arms at upper l., castle on hill at r.	—	Rare	—

NOTE: The date 1831 is reported for a St. Martin's Parish Bank note. Confirmation is needed.

ST. MARY'S PAROCHIAL BANK

1850'S ISSUE

		GOOD	FINE	XF
S326	1 POUND 18xx. Arms at l. and r., church at ctr. Plain blue paper.	—	—	75.00
S327	1 POUND 18xx. Like #S326 but brown-black. Plain white paper. Proof.	—	—	95.00
S328	1 POUND 18xx. Like #S326 but black. White paper wmk: *Island of Jersey* and Jersey shield of arms. Proof.	—	—	95.00

NOTE: Other varieties are reported, not confirmed.

St. Peter's Parochial Bank

1830's Issue

		Good	Fine	XF
S331	**1 Pound** 18xx. House w/trees at upper l., church at upper r.			
	a. Ovpt: *BEAUMONT ROAD* upper ctr.	—	Rare	—
	r. Unsigned remainder.	—	Rare	—

NOTE: Reported colors for #S331 are black or orange. A variety dated 1827 w/inscription: *bon pour un louis* is reported, not confirmed.

St. Peter's Valley Road

1828 Issue

		Good	Fine	XF
S336	**1 Pound** 1.1.1828. House and horses at l.	—	Rare	—

Parish of St. Peter

1890's Issue

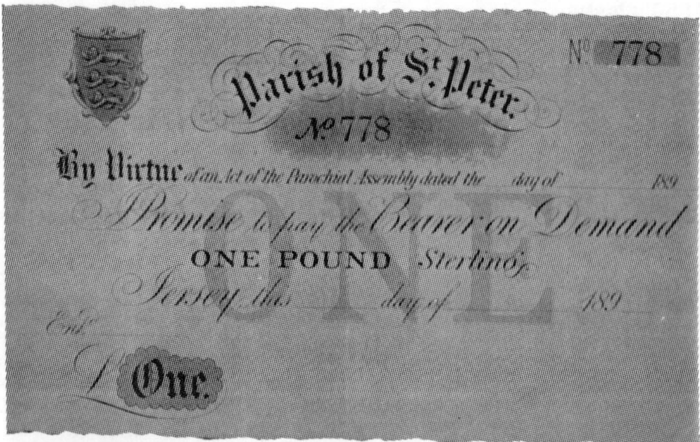

		Good	Fine	XF
S341	**1 Pound** 189x. Arms at upper l.			
	a. Blue unpt. and back.	—	Rare	—
	b. Brown unpt.	—	Rare	—

Parish of St. Saviour

St. Saviour's Bank

1832 Issue

		Good	Fine	XF
S346	**1 Pound** 12.5.1832. Church at upper l., arms and lion at upper r.	50.00	100.00	200.00

Parish of Trinity

1836 Issue

		Good	Fine	XF
S350	**1 Pound** 1836. Proof.	—	—	—

NOTE: Issued for paving of the Rozel Road and for other public works.

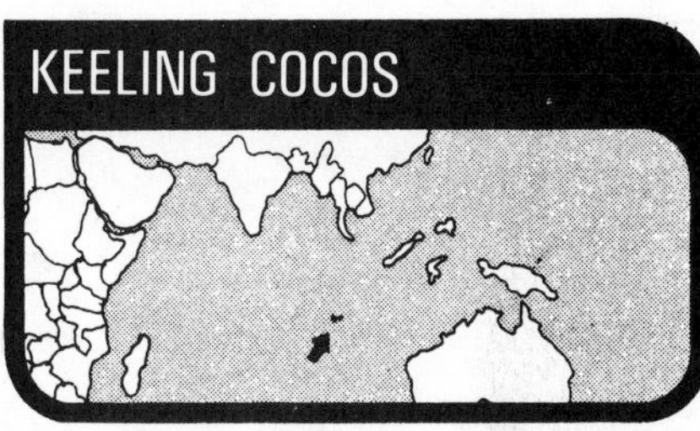

Keeling Cocos Islands are a group of 27 small coral islands located in the Indian Ocean. Discovered by Captain Keeling of the East India Company in 1609, they became a British protectorate in 1857. The islands were successfully administered from Ceylon from 1878, the Straits Settlements from 1886, and the Crown Colony of Singapore from 1903. However, the real administration was vested in the hands of the Clunies-Ross family, who established themselves in the islands in about 1827. In 1955 the administration of the islands was transferred from the United Kingdom to Australia on the understanding that the Clunies-Ross family would retain their ownership of their property although the islanders have been given the opportunity to acquire Australian citizenship. In July 1978 the Australian Government announced that it had arranged to buy the islands from Mr. John Clunies-Ross, thus ending the grant of territory in perpetuity by Queen Victoria.

RULERS:

British since 1857

MONETARY SYSTEM:

1 Rupee = 100 Cents

BRITISH ADMINISTRATION

COCOS

1887-88 ISSUE

#S101-S104 w/title: *COCOS* at top. Hand dated and signed by J. C. Ross. Embossed seal at ctr. Sheepskin. Uniface.

		GOOD	FINE	XF
S101	**1/4 RUPEE** 1887-88.	—	Rare	—
S102	**1/2 RUPEE** 24.7.1888.	—	Rare	—

		GOOD	FINE	XF
S103	**1 RUPEE** 1888.	—	Rare	—

		GOOD	FINE	XF
S104	**2 RUPEES** 1888.	—	Rare	—

KEELING COCOS ISLANDS

1888 ISSUE

#S111-S116 w/title: *KEELING COCOS ISLANDS* by arms at top ctr. Embossed seal at ctr. Hand signed by J. C. Ross, hand dated from 1888. Sheepskin. Uniface.

		GOOD	FINE	XF
S111	**1/4 RUPEE** 1888.	600.00	1000.	—

		GOOD	FINE	XF
S112	**1/2 RUPEE** 1888.	300.00	500.00	—
S113	**1 RUPEE** 1888.	300.00	500.00	—
S114	**2 RUPEES** 1888.	300.00	500.00	—
S115	**3 RUPEES** 1888.	300.00	500.00	—
S116	**5 RUPEES** 1888.	300.00	500.00	—

1897 ISSUE

#S117-S122 black. Arms at top ctr. Handwritten serial # and sign. of G. Clunies Ross. Paper. Uniface.

		GOOD	FINE	XF
S117	**1/4 RUPEE** 1897.	125.00	200.00	350.00

		GOOD	FINE	XF
S118	**1/2 RUPEE** 1897.	125.00	200.00	350.00

		GOOD	FINE	XF
S119	**1 RUPEE** 1897.	125.00	200.00	350.00
S120	**2 RUPEES** 1897.	125.00	200.00	350.00
S121	**3 RUPEES** 1897.	125.00	200.00	350.00
S122	**5 RUPEES** 1897.	125.00	200.00	350.00

1902 ISSUE

#S123-S128 black. Arms at top ctr. Printed sign. of G. Clunies Ross. Paper. Uniface.

		VG	VF	UNC
S123	**1/10 RUPEE** 1902.	—	22.00	40.00

		VG	VF	UNC
S124	**1/4 RUPEE** 1902.	—	22.00	40.00
S125	**1/2 RUPEE** 1902.	—	22.00	40.00

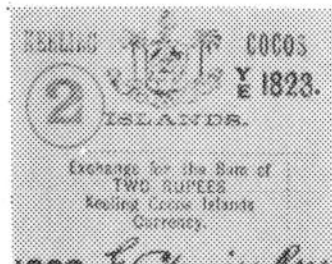

		VG	VF	UNC
S126	**1 RUPEE** 1902.	—	25.00	50.00

		VG	VF	UNC
S127	**2 RUPEES** 1902.	—	25.00	50.00
S128	**5 RUPEES** 1902.	—	22.00	55.00

NOTE: A sizeable group from the 1902 issue was made available on the market in recent years.

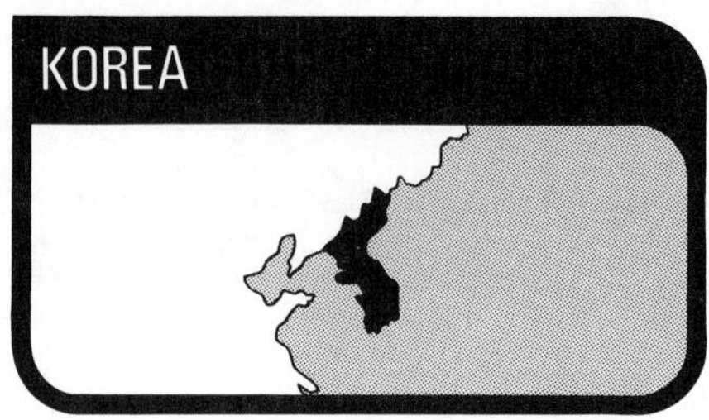

Korea,"Land of the Morning Calm", occupies a mountainous peninsula in northeast Asia bounded by Manchuria, the Yellow Sea and the Sea of Japan. According to legend, the first Korean dynasty, that of the House of Tangun, ruled from 2333 BC to 1122 BC. It was followed by the dynasty of Kija, a Chinese scholar, which continued until 193 BC and brought a high civilization to Korea. The first recorded period in the history of Korea, the Period of the Three Kingdoms, lasted from 57 BC to 935 AD and achieved the first political unification on the peninsula. The Kingdom of Koryo, from which Korea derived its name, was founded in 935 and continued until 1392, when it was superseded by the Yi dynasty of King Yi, Sung Kye which was to last until the Japanese annexation in 1910.

At the end of the 16th century Korea was invaded and occupied for 7 years by Japan, and from 1627 until the late 19th century it was a semi-independent tributary of China. Japan replaced China as the predominant foreign influence at the end of the Sino-Japanese War (1894-95), only to find its position threatened by Russian influence from 1896 to 1904. The Russian threat was eliminated by the Russo-Japanese War (1904-05) and in 1905 Japan established a direct protectorate over Korea. On Aug. 22, 1910, the last Korean ruler signed the treaty that annexed Korea to Japan as a government general in the Japanese Empire. Japanese suzerainty was maintained until the end of World War II.

RULERS:

Yi Hyong (Kojong), 1864-1897
as Kwangmu, 1897-1907
Yung Hi, 1907-1910

MONETARY SYSTEM:

1 Yang = 100 Fun
1 Whan = 5 Yang to 1902
1 Won = 100 Chon 1902-
1 Yen = 100 Sen

MONETARY UNITS:

Fun
Mun
Yang, Niang
Chon
Won
Hwan

MONETARY UNITS:

文 Mun

Yang

Kingdom

Keijo-Pusan Railway Company

1900 Issue

#S101-S104 steam train at upper ctr. Backs orange. Vertical format.

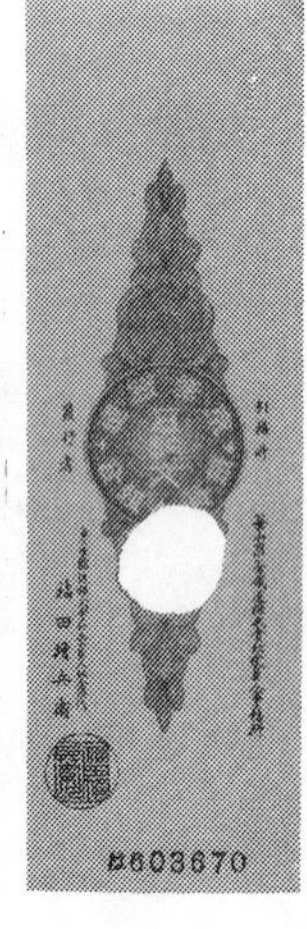

		Good	Fine	XF
S101	**50 Mun** 1900. Blue on lt. blue unpt.			
	a. Issued note.	—	—	—
	b. Punched hole cancelled.	50.00	175.00	375.00
S102	**100 Mun** 1900. Brown on lt. tan unpt.			
	a. Issued note.	—	Rare	—
	b. Punched hole cancelled.	50.00	175.00	375.00
S103	**300 Mun** 1900.		Reported Not Confirmed	
S104	**500 Mun** 1900. Orange on lt. tan unpt.			
	a. Issued note.	—	Rare	—
	b. Punched hole cancelled.	55.00	200.00	400.00

Seoul Exchange Office

ND Issue

		Good	Fine	XF
S115	**100 Corean Dollars** ND. Brown w/black text on green unpt. Back black and ochre w/blue, green and black text.	—	—	—

Kuang Tong Company

ND Issue

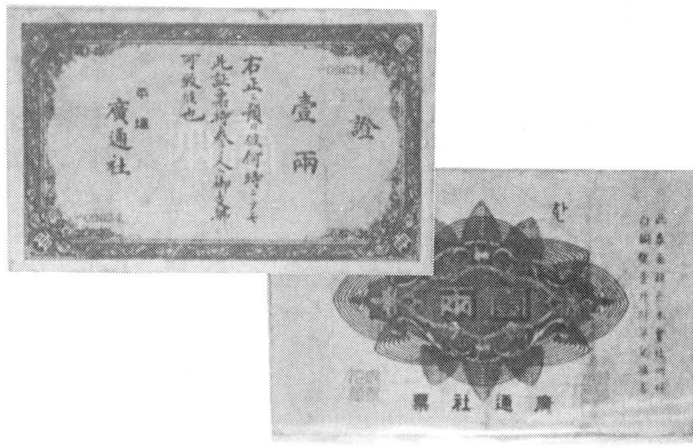

		Good	Fine	XF
S121	**1 Yang** ND. Black on pale blue-green unpt. Back dk. blue.	—	—	—

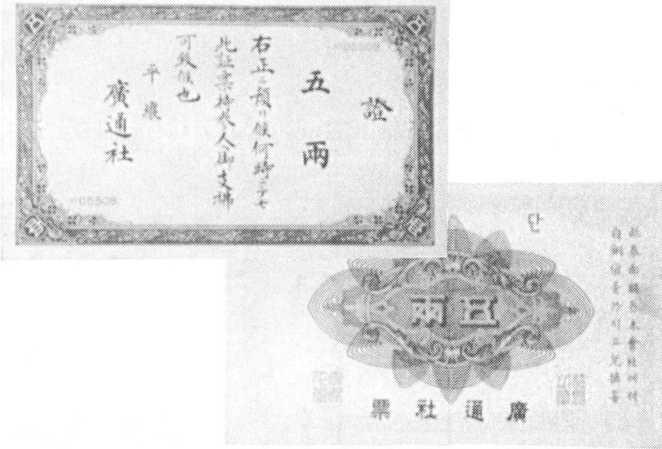

		Good	Fine	XF
S122	**5 Yang** ND. Black on pale yellow unpt. Back dk. green.	—	—	—

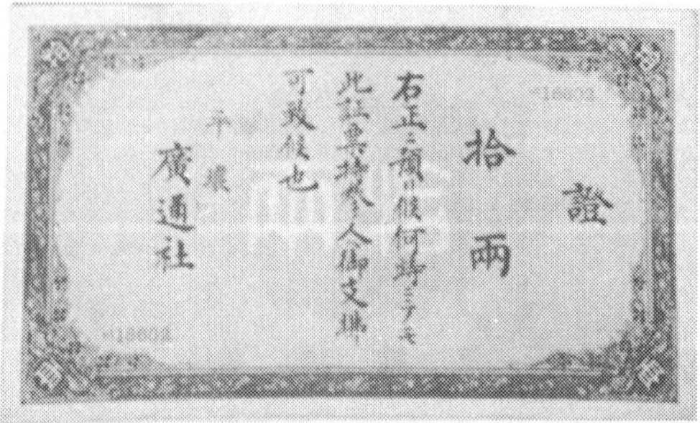

		GOOD	FINE	XF
S123	**10 YANG** ND. Black on pale blue unpt. Back red-brown.	—	—	—

KUANG TUNG CHON HIANG

KUANG TUNG CASH BANK

ND ISSUE

		GOOD	FINE	XF
S133	**10 YANG** ND.	—	—	—

TONG SUN TAI HOA

ND ISSUE

#S141-S145 denominations given in Yang Yopchon.

		GOOD	FINE	XF
S141	**25 YANG** ND.	—	—	—

		GOOD	FINE	XF
S142	**50 YANG** ND. Black and orange on blue unpt. Back pale blue.	—	—	—
S143	**100 YANG** ND.	—	—	—
S144	**500 YANG** ND.	—	—	—

		GOOD	FINE	XF
S145	**1000 YANG**	—	—	—
S151	**10,000 MUN**	—	—	—

CHINDO BANK

SHOTOKU CHOSEN GINKO

Reported issuer.

ND ISSUE

#S171-S177 denominations given in Yang Yopchon.

		GOOD	FINE	XF
S171	**1 YANG** ND.	—	—	—

		GOOD	FINE	XF
S173	**10 YANG** ND. Black on plae green unpt. Back brown.	—	—	—

		GOOD	FINE	XF
S174	**50 YANG** ND. Black on ochre unpt. Back ochre.	—	—	—

		GOOD	FINE	XF
S175	**100 YANG** ND. Black on pale purple unpt. Back pale green.	—	—	—

		GOOD	FINE	XF
S176	**500 YANG** ND.	—	—	—
S177	**1000 YANG** ND.	—	—	—

NOTE: No relation to Chosen Ginko listed in Vol. 2.

Lagos

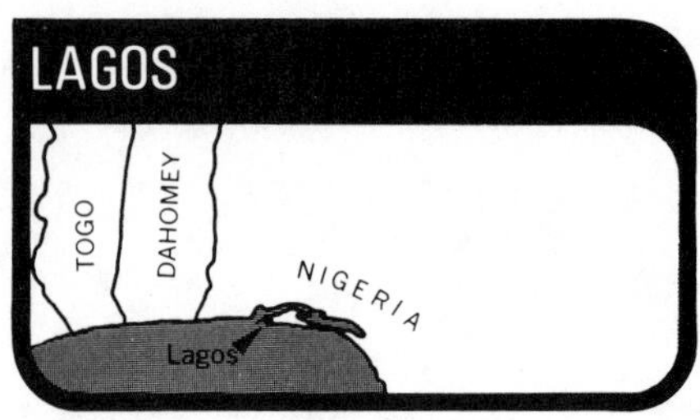

After centuries of self-determination, followed by various colonial occupations, Lagos (so named by the Portuguese because of its many lakes and lagoons) fell under British rule in 1861. The British administered Lagos at first from Sierra Leone, then as part of the Gold Coast. Lagos became a separate colony from 1886 to 1906; it was then conjoined with southern Nigeria. Lagos became the capital of Nigeria in 1960 and is located in the southwestern part of the country.

British Administration

African Banking Corporation Ltd.

Established in August 1891. Became the Bank of British West Africa a little over a year later.

1891 Issue

#S101 and S102 printer: BWC. Specimens perforated: *SPECIMEN B.W. & CO/LONDON.*

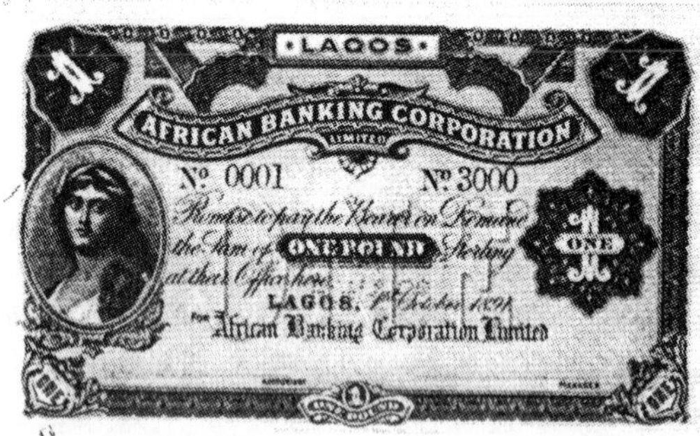

		VG	VF	Unc
S101	**1 Pound** 1.10.1891. Black and green. Portr. woman at l. Back green.			
	a. Issued note.	—	—	—
	s. Specimen.	—	—	1250.

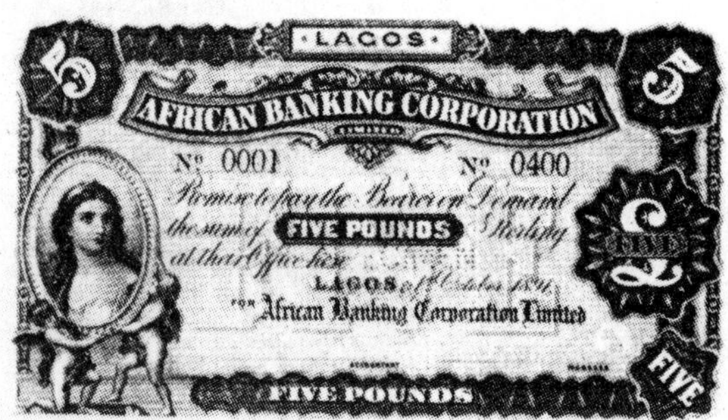

		VG	VF	Unc
S102	**5 Pounds** 1.10.1891. Black and brown. Portr. woman supported by 2 cherubs at l. Back brown.			
	a. Issued note.	—	—	—
	s. Specimen.	—	—	1250.

Bank of British West Africa Limited

1890s Issue

		VG	VF	Unc
S111	**5 Pounds** 189x. Beehive at upper l., man in headdress at lower r. Printer: BWC. Proof.	—	—	—

Liberia

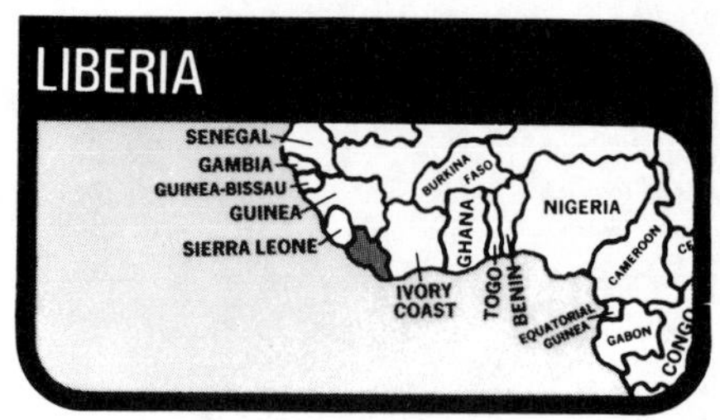

The Republic of Liberia, located on the southern side of the west African bulge between Sierra Leone and the Ivory Coast, has an area of 38,250 sq. mi. (111,369 sq. km.) and a population of 3.26 million. Capital: Monrovia. The major industries are agriculture, mining and lumbering. Iron ore, diamonds, rubber, coffee and cocoa are exported.

The Liberian coast was explored and chartered by Portuguese navigator Pedro de Cintra in 1461. For the following three centuries Portuguese traders visited the area regularly to trade for gold, slaves and pepper. The modern country of Liberia, Africa's first republic, was settled in 1822 by the American Colonization Society as a homeland for American freed slaves, with the U.S. government furnishing funds and assisting in negotiations for procurement of land from the indigenous chiefs. The various settlements united in 1839 to form the Commonwealth of Liberia, and in 1847 established the country as a republic with a constitution modeled after that of the United States.

Notes were issued from 1857 through 1880; thereafter the introduction of dollar notes of the United States took place. U.S. money was declared legal tender in Liberia in 1943, replacing British West African currencies. Not until 1989 was a distinctive Liberian currency again issued.

MONETARY SYSTEM:

1 Dollar = 100 Cents

United States Administration

American Colonization Society

1840's Issue

#S101-S103 printer: UBS&H/DU.

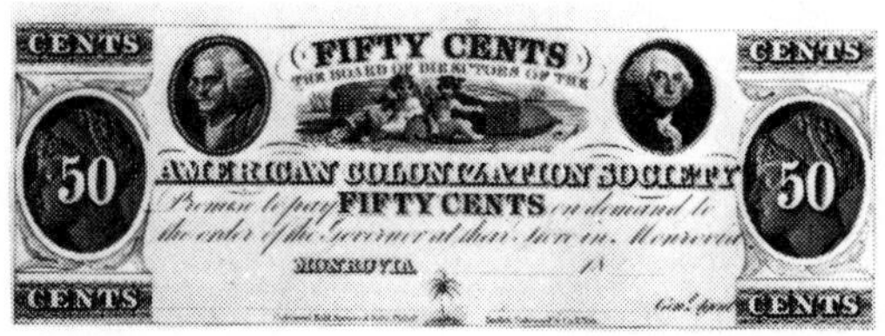

		Good	Fine	XF
S101	**50 Cents** 18xx. Black. Portr. B. Franklin at upper l., 2 cherubs w/barrel and bale at upper ctr., portr. G. Washington at upper r. Proof.	—	—	—

		Good	Fine	XF
S102	**1 Dollar** 1840. Black. 2 seated allegorical children writing and reading at top ctr.	—	—	—

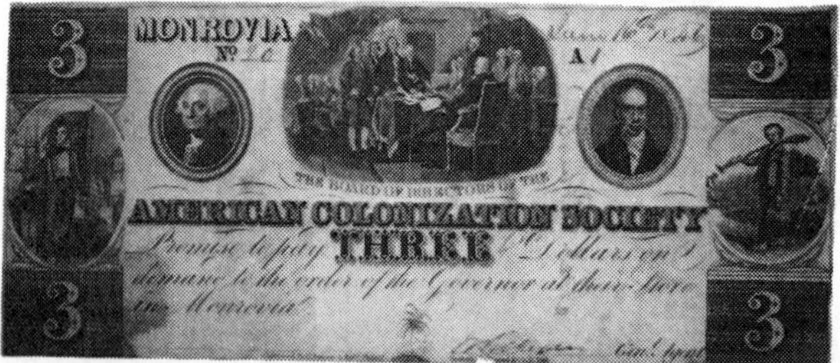

		Good	Fine	XF
S103	**3 Dollars** 16.6.1846. Black. Boy w/flag at far l., portr. G. Washington at upper l., signing of Declaration of Independence at ctr., portr. man at upper r., boy w/shovel at far r.	—	—	—

Colonial Agent, Monrovia

1834 Issue

		Good	Fine	XF
S106	**5 Cents** 4.7.1834. Wild pig at ctr. w/text: *The Colonial Agent promises to pay to the bearer, on demand, five cents.*	—	—	—
S107	**10 Cents** 4.7.1834. Sheep at ctr. w/text: *The Colonial Agent. . . ten cents.*	125.00	275.00	600.00

S108 25 CENTS — GOOD 150.00 · FINE 350.00 · XF 750.00
4.7.1834. Cow at ctr. w/text: *The Colonial Agent . . . twenty-five cents.*

MARYLAND STATE COLONIZATION SOCIETY

1837 ISSUE

#S111-S115 black and golden brown. W/text: *This. . . will be received for (value) at the government store, in Harper, Maryland in Liberia, Africa, in payment for goods.* Pink paper.

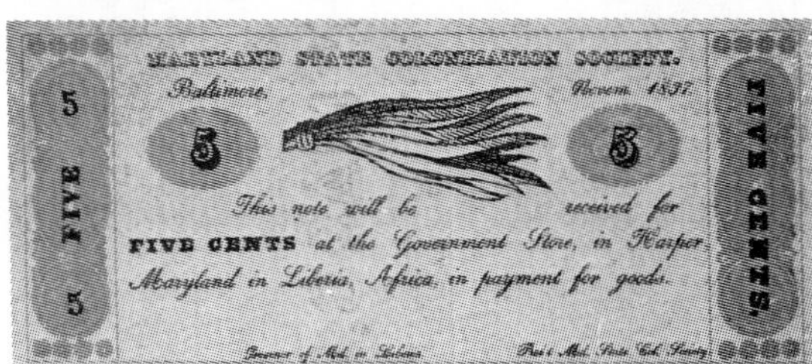

S111	5 CENTS	VG	VF	UNC
	Novem. 1837. Tobacco leaves at upper ctr.			
	a. Issued note.	—	—	—
	rp. Reprint w/wmk: 1883....	—	—	250.00

S112	10 CENTS	VG	VF	UNC
	November 1837. Rooster at upper ctr.			
	a. Issued note.	—	—	—
	rp. Reprint w/wmk: 1883....	—	—	250.00

S113	25 CENTS	VG	VF	UNC
	November 1837. Duck at upper ctr.			
	a. Issued note.	—	—	—
	rp. Reprint w/wmk: 1883....	—	—	250.00

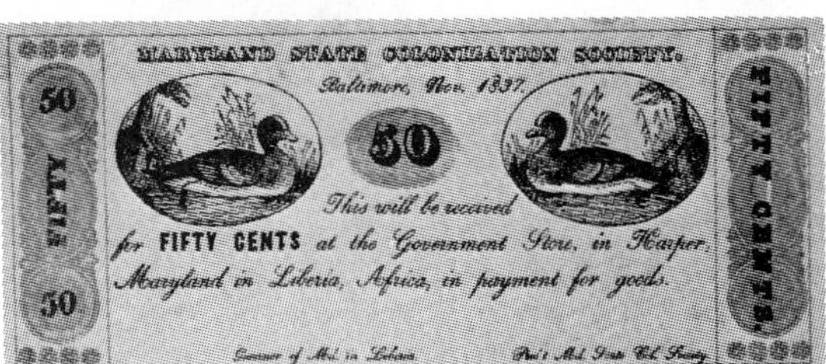

S114	50 CENTS	VG	VF	UNC
	Nov. 1837. Facing ducks at upper l. and r.			
	a. Issued note.	—	—	—
	rp. Reprint w/wmk: 1883....	—	—	250.00

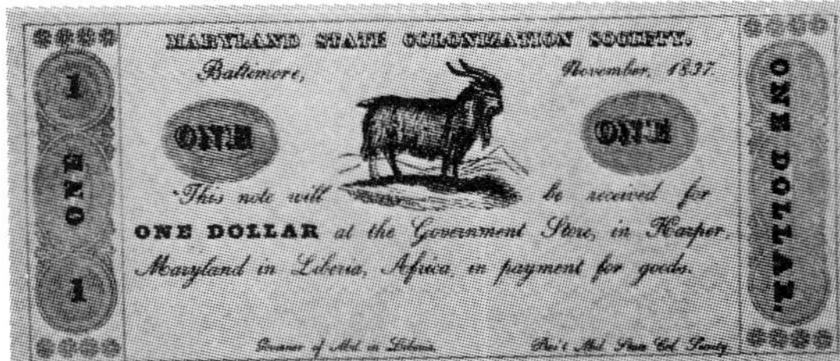

S115	1 DOLLAR	VG	VF	UNC
	November, 1837. Goat at top ctr.			
	a. Issued note.	—	—	—
	rp. Reprint w/wmk: 1883....	—	—	250.00

NOTE: The total issued of #S111-S115 was only $1,450 in full face value. All, or nearly all, were redeemed. In 1885, 100 notes of each denomination were reprinted and the plates destroyed. Reprints, issued in sheets, were not signed. Reprints are on paper bearing wmk. containing 1883 date.

The Macao R.A.E.M., a former Portuguese overseas province located in the South China Sea 35 miles (56 km.) southwest of Hong Kong, consists of the peninsula and the islands of Taipa and Coloane. It has an area of 14 sq. mi. (21.45 sq. km.) and a population of 415,850. Capital: Macao. The economy is based on tourism, gambling, commerce and gold trading - Macao is one of the few entirely free markets for gold in the world. Cement, textiles, vegetable oils and metal products are exported.

Established by the Portuguese in 1557, Macao is the oldest European settlement in the Far East. The Chinese, while agreeing to Portuguese settlement, did not recognize Portuguese sovereign rights and the Portuguese remained largely under control of the Chinese until 1849, when the Portuguese abolished the Chinese custom house and declared the independence of the port. The Manchu government formally recognized the Portuguese right to *perpetual occupation* of Macao in 1887. In March 1940 the Japanese army demanded recognition of the nearby "puppet" government at Changshan. In Sept. 1943 they demanded installation of their "advisors" in lieu of a military occupation.

Macao became a special administrative area known as Macao R.A.E.M under The Peoples Republic of China on December 20, 1999.

RULERS:

Portuguese from 1849-1999

MONETARY SYSTEM:

1 Dollar = 100 Cents
1 Pataca = 100 Avos

DATING

Most notes were issued in the year of the Chinese Republic but occasionally the old Chinese lunar calendar was used. These dates are listed as "CD". Refer to China-introduction for Cyclical Date Chart.

DATE CHART

Cyclical Dates

	庚	辛	壬	癸	甲	乙	丙	丁	戊	己
戌	1850 1910		1862 1922		1874 1934		1886 1946		1838 1898	
亥		1851 1911		1863 1923		1875 1935		1887 1947		1839 1899
子	1840 1900		1852 1912		1864 1924		1876 1936		1888 1948	
丑		1841 1901		1853 1913		1865 1925		1877 1937		1889 1949
寅	1830 1890		1842 1902		1854 1914		1866 1926		1878 1938	
卯		1831 1891		1843 1903		1855 1915		1867 1927		1879 1939
辰	1880 1940		1832 1892		1844 1904		1856 1916		1868 1928	
巳		1881 1941		1833 1893		1845 1905		1857 1917		1869 1929
午	1870 1930		1882 1942		1834 1894		1846 1906		1858 1918	
未		1871 1931		1883 1943		1835 1895		1847 1907		1859 1919
申	1860 1920		1872 1932		1884 1944		1836 1896		1848 1908	
酉		1861 1921		1873 1933		1885 1945		1837 1897		1849 1909

PRIVATE BANKS

During the 1920's and early 1930's the private banks of Macao issued various circulating checks in dollars to facilitate trade with Chinese firms. These apparently circulated freely along with the Pataca issues of the Banco Nacional Ultramarino which quite obviously were in short supply. Most examples known have appropriate colonial revenue adhesive stamps affixed as found on bills of exchange and private checks. The additional large brush strokes or marks obliterating the denomination indicates the sum has been paid. A similar circulating check was issued in 1944 by the Tai Fong Cambista.

PORTUGUESE ADMINISTRATION

CHAN TUNG CHENG BANK

1934 ISSUE

S92	10 DOLLARS	GOOD	FINE	XF
	1934. Black on pink unpt. Back red; gov't. bldg. at ctr. Printer: HKPP.	100.00	250.00	600.00

CHEE CHEONG BANK

1934 INTEREST BEARING NOTES ISSUE

S101	100 DOLLARS	GOOD	FINE	XF
	1934.	50.00	150.00	—

		Good	Fine	XF
S102	**200 Dollars** 1934.	55.00	160.00	—
S103	**800 Dollars** 1934.	60.00	180.00	—

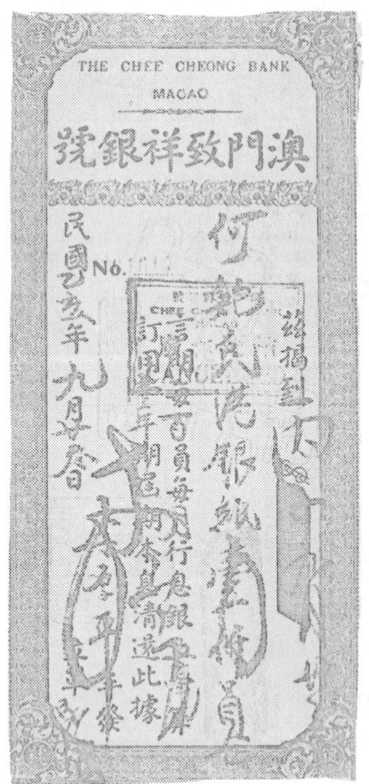

		Good	Fine	XF
S104	**1000 Dollars** 23.7.1934. Maroon on yellow unpt. Back red text. Vertical format.	75.00	200.00	—

Foo Hang Bank

1937 Issue

		Good	Fine	XF
S105	**10 Dollars** 1937. Blue on pale green unpt. Back red; gov't. bldg. at ctr.	50.00	125.00	350.00

Fu Quei Cambista

1933 Cashier's Checks Issue

		Good	Fine	XF
S106	**50 Dollars** 1933. Green on lt. ochre unpt. Back red; pagoda at ctr. Vertical//horizontal format.	135.00	350.00	—

Hang Hing Bank

1931 Issue

		Good	Fine	XF
S107	**50 Dollars** 23.1.1931. Green on yellow-green unpt. 2 cherubs holding shield at top. Back red-brown.	100.00	250.00	—

Kwong Yuen Bank

1924; 1925 Cashier's Checks Issue

#S108-S110 vertical format.

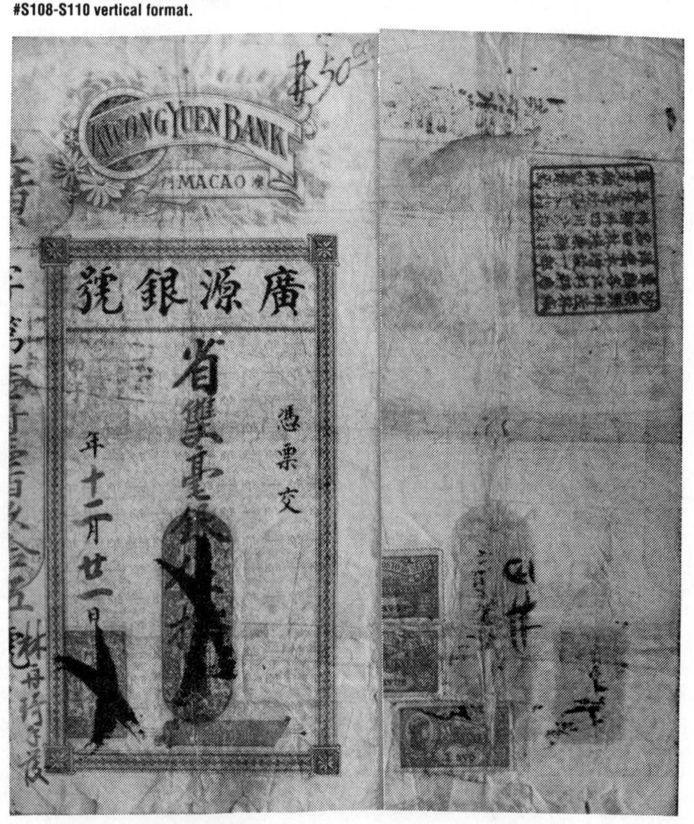

		Good	Fine	XF
S108	**50 Dollars** 27.11.1924; 21.12.1924. Green on yellow unpt. Uniface.	100.00	250.00	—
S109	**100 Dollars** 23.2.1925; 1.10.1930. Uniface.	100.00	250.00	—
S110	**200 Dollars** 17.10.1924; 23.2.1925. Uniface.	135.00	350.00	—

1932 Cashier's Checks Issue

#S111 and S112 vertical format.

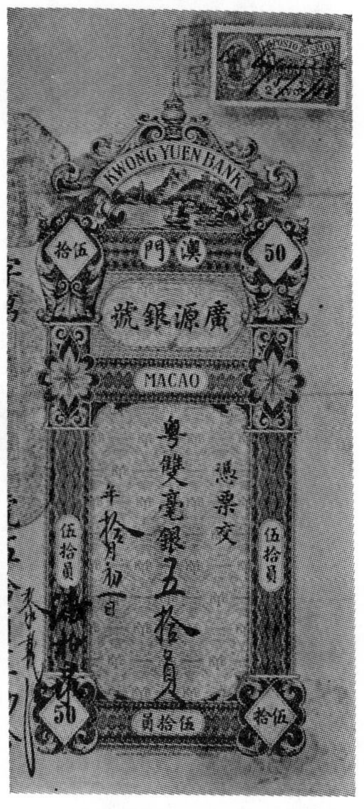

		Good	Fine	XF
S111	**50 Dollars** 1.9.1932; 1.10.1932. Brown-violet on lt. green unpt. Shoreline view at upper ctr. Uniface.	90.00	200.00	—
S112	**100 Dollars** CD 1.9.1932. Red. Uniface.	90.00	200.00	—

Lee Yuen

1931 Cashier's Checks Issue

		Good	Fine	XF
S116	**10 Dollars** 1.4.1931. Vertical format.	150.00	400.00	—

Pao Shin Bank

1927 Cashier's Checks Issue

		Good	Fine	XF
S121	**10 Dollars** CD 1.11.1927. Brown-violet on olive-green unpt. Uniface. Vertical format.	150.00	400.00	—

Po Wing Bank, Macao

1928 Cashier's Checks Issue

		Good	Fine	XF
S126	**1 Dollar**	Reported Not Confirmed		
S127	**5 Dollars**	Reported Not Confirmed		

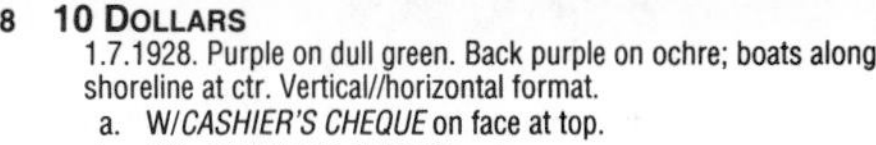

		Good	Fine	XF
S128	**10 Dollars** 1.7.1928. Purple on dull green. Back purple on ochre; boats along shoreline at ctr. Vertical//horizontal format.			
	a. W/*CASHIER'S CHEQUE* on face at top.	100.00	250.00	—
	b. W/o *CASHIER'S CHEQUE* on face.	100.00	250.00	—

BANCO POU-SENG

POU-SENG BANK

1926 CASHIER'S CHECKS ISSUE

		GOOD	FINE	XF
S131	**100 DOLLARS** 3.1.1926. Black on ochre and lt. blue unpt. Back dull brown; arch at ctr. Vertical format.	150.00	400.00	—
S132	**100 DOLLARS** 17.3.1926. Dk. green on yellow unpt. Back purple on yellow unpt.; bank at ctr.	160.00	450.00	—

SHING SHUN BANK, MACAO

1931 CASHIER'S CHECKS ISSUE

#S136-S139 printer: YPFC.

		GOOD	FINE	XF
S136	**1 DOLLAR** ND (1931).	100.00	250.00	—
S137	**5 DOLLARS** ND (1931).	100.00	275.00	—

		GOOD	FINE	XF
S138	**10 DOLLARS** 26.2.1931. Brown and lt. brown. Back red; sampan at ctr. Vertical//horizontal format.	100.00	275.00	—
S139	**50 DOLLARS** 6.2.1931. Green. Back brown. Like #S138.	135.00	375.00	—

SHUN WOO BANK

ND CASHIER'S CHECKS ISSUE

		GOOD	FINE	XF
S141	**10 DOLLARS** ND. Violet and green.	150.00	400.00	—

SUM YICK BANK

1944 CASHIER'S CHECKS ISSUE

		GOOD	FINE	XF
S146	**50 DOLLARS** ND. Blue. Back purple; bldg. at ctr. Vertical//horizontal format.	150.00	400.00	—

TAI FONG CAMBISTA

ND ISSUE

		GOOD	FINE	XF
S148	**50 DOLLARS** ND. Red and orange, w/blue center guilloche, on peach unpt.	75.00	—	—

1944 CASHIER'S CHECKS ISSUE

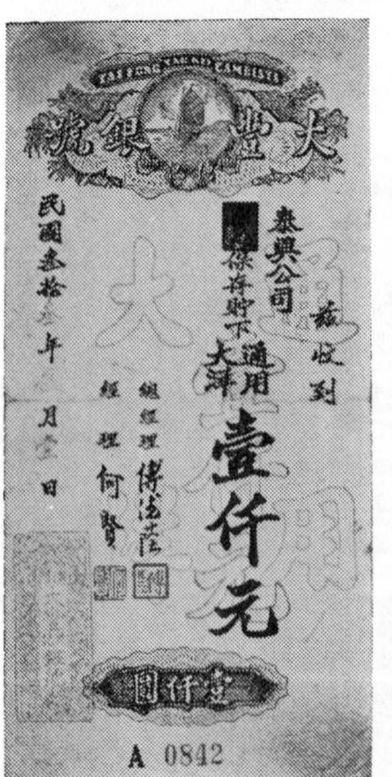

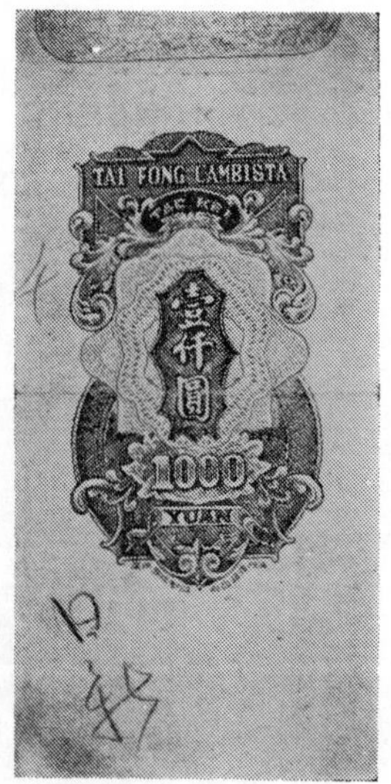

		VG	VF	UNC
S151	**1000 YUAN** 1.5.1944. Brown and lilac on yellow unpt. Sampan at top ctr. Back black and lilac. Vertical format.	50.00	125.00	350.00

TAI SENG BANK

1930 CASHIER'S CHECKS ISSUE

		GOOD	FINE	XF
S156	**10 DOLLARS** 1.7.1930. Violet on ochre unpt. Back blue-gray on tan unpt.; steam locomotive at lower l. Vertical//horizontal format.	150.00	400.00	—

TONG TAK IÜN KEL CAMBISTA

1944 CASHIER'S CHECKS ISSUE

		GOOD	FINE	XF
S161	**5000 YUAN** 7.5.1944. Brown on green and gold unpt. Back brown on yellow unpt. Vertical format.	100.00	250.00	—

BANCO VUI HANG

1923 CASHIER'S CHECKS ISSUE

		GOOD	FINE	XF
S171	**10 PATACAS** 1923. Gray. Back dull green; steamship at ctr. Vertical//horizontal format.	150.00	400.00	—

YICK KEE BANK

1927 CASHIER'S CHECKS ISSUE

		GOOD	FINE	XF
S176	**10 DOLLARS** 20.9.1927. Olive-green on orange unpt. Back red-brown. Vertical//horizontal format.	90.00	225.00	—

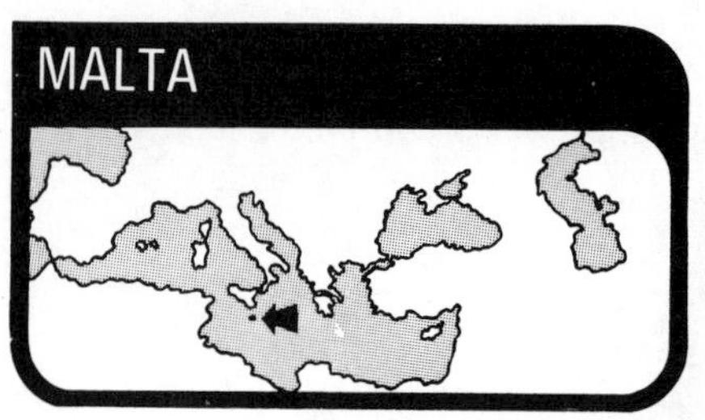

The Republic of Malta, an independent parliamentary democracy within the British Commonwealth, is situated in the Mediterranean Sea between Sicily and North Africa. With the islands of Gozo and Comino, Malta has an area of 122 sq. mi. (316 sq. km.) and a population of 379,000. Capital: Valletta. With the islands of Gozo (Ghawdex), Comino, Cominetto and Filfla, Malta has no proven mineral resources, an agriculture insufficient to its needs and a small but expanding, manufacturing facility. Clothing, textile yarns and fabrics, and knitted wear are exported.

For more than 3,500 years Malta was ruled, in succession, by Phoenicians, Carthaginians, Romans, Arabs, Normans, the Knights of Malta, France and Britain. Napoleon seized Malta by treachery in 1798. The French were ousted by a Maltese insurrection assisted by Britain, and in 1814, Malta, of its own free will, became part of the British Empire. The island was awarded the George Cross for conspicuous corrage during World War II. Malta obtained full independence in September 1964, electing to remain within the Commonwealth with Elizabeth II as Head of State as Queen of Malta.

RULERS:

British to 1974

MONETARY SYSTEM:

1 Lira = 100 Centesimi

1 Scudo = 2 1/2 Lire = 20 British Old Pence to 1857

BRITISH ADMINISTRATION

ANGLO-EGYPTIAN BANKING COMPANY, LTD.

1866 ISSUE

#S101-S105 black. Portr. Grand Master La Valette at l., arms below. Pink paper. Printer: BWC.

		Good	Fine	XF
S101	**10 SHILLINGS** 1.10.1866.	—	Rare	—
S102	**1 POUND** 1.10.1866.	—	Rare	—
S103	**5 POUNDS** 1.10.1866.	—	Rare	—
S104	**10 POUNDS** 1.10.1866.	—	Rare	—

		Good	Fine	XF
S105	**20 POUNDS** 1.10.1866.	—	Rare	—

BANCO ANGLO MALTESE

NOTE: These notes were in use into the 1920's.

1880S ISSUE

#S111-S116 black. St. George slaying dragon at upper l.

		Good	Fine	XF
S111	**1 POUND** 1.10.1888.	—	Rare	—
S112	**5 POUNDS** 18xx.	—	Rare	—
S113	**10 POUNDS** 18xx.	—	Rare	—
S114	**20 POUNDS** 18xx.	—	Rare	—
S115	**30 POUNDS** 18xx.	—	Rare	—

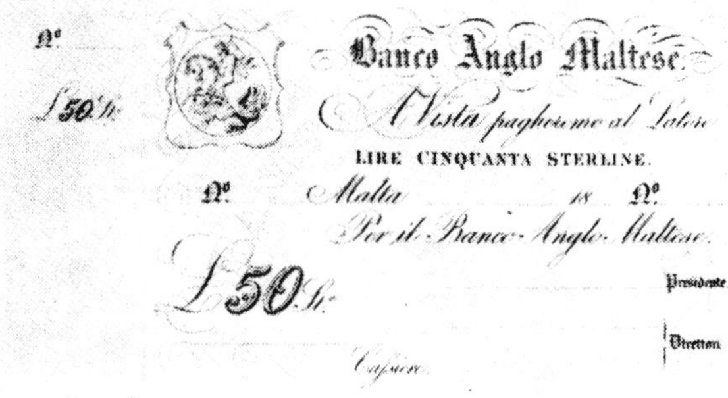

		Good	Fine	XF
S116	**50 POUNDS** 18xx.	—	Rare	—

BANCO DI MALTA

Notes of this bank were withdrawn from circulation by 1886.

1812 ISSUE

#S121-S133 black. St. Paul in oval frame at upper l. Printer: A. Oaby, London.

		Good	Fine	XF
S121	**5 SCUDI** 1812.	—	Rare	—

		Good	Fine	XF
S122	**10 SCUDI** 1812.	—	Rare	—
S123	**20 SCUDI** 1812.	—	Rare	—
S124	**30 SCUDI** 1812.	—	Rare	—
S125	**40 SCUDI** 1812.	—	Rare	—
S126	**100 SCUDI** 1812.	—	Rare	—
S127	**100 SCUDI** 1812.	—	Rare	—
S128	**150 SCUDI** 1812.	—	Rare	—
S129	**200 SCUDI** 1812.	—	Rare	—
S130	**250 SCUDI** 1812.	—	Rare	—
S131	**300 SCUDI** 1812.	—	Rare	—
S132	**500 SCUDI** 1812.	—	Rare	—
S133	**1000 SCUDI** 1812.	—	Rare	—

ND FIRST ISSUE

#S141-S153 black. W/o vignette. Different format than S121-S133.

		Good	Fine	XF
S141	**5 SCUDI** 18xx.	—	Rare	—
S142	**10 SCUDI** 18xx.	—	Rare	—
S143	**20 SCUDI** 18xx.	—	Rare	—
S144	**30 SCUDI** 18xx.	—	Rare	—
S145	**40 SCUDI** 18xx.	—	Rare	—

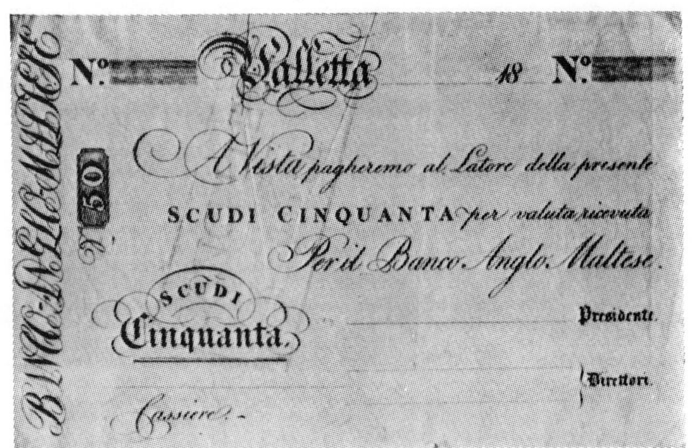

		GOOD	FINE	XF
S146	**50 SCUDI** 18xx.	—	Rare	—
S147	**100 SCUDI** 18xx.	—	Rare	—
S148	**150 SCUDI** 18xx.	—	Rare	—
S149	**200 SCUDI** 18xx.	—	Rare	—
S150	**250 SCUDI** 18xx.	—	Rare	—
S151	**300 SCUDI** 18xx.	—	Rare	—
S152	**500 SCUDI** 18xx.	—	Rare	—
S153	**1000 SCUDI** 18xx.	—	Rare	—

ND SECOND ISSUE

#S161-S165 like first issue but printer: Batho & Co., London. Denominations in sterling lire.

		GOOD	FINE	XF
S161	**5 LIRE** 18xx.	—	—	75.00

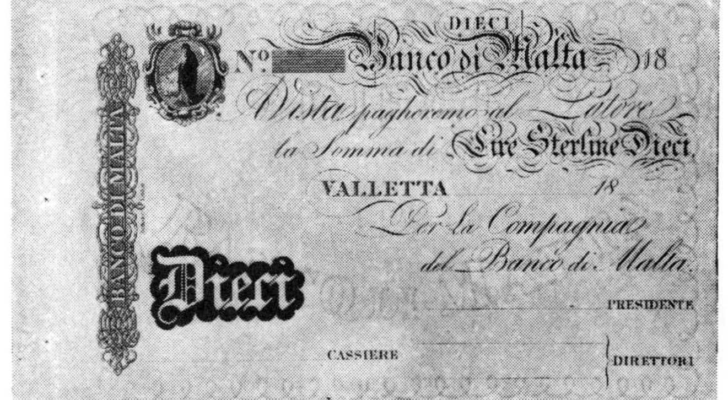

		GOOD	FINE	XF
S162	**10 LIRE** 18xx.	—	—	75.00
S163	**20 LIRE** 18xx.	—	—	100.00
S164	**50 LIRE** 18xx.	—	—	100.00
S165	**100 LIRE** 18xx.	—	—	125.00

NOTE: #S161-S165 are encountered in sets of remainders.

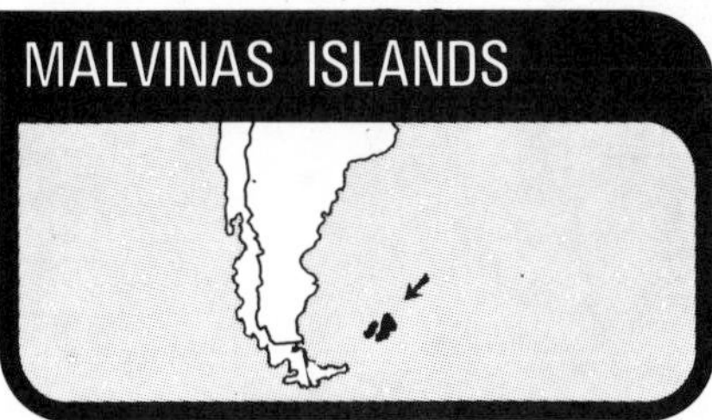

Malvinas Islands, generally known as the Colony of the Falkland Islands and Dependencies, a British colony located in the South Atlantic about 500 miles northeast of Cape Horn, has an area of 4,700 sq. mi. (12,173 sq. km.). East Falkland and West Falkland, South Georgia, and South Sandwich are the dependencies and are the largest of the 200 islands. Capital: Port Stanley.

The Malvinas were discovered by British navigator John Davis (Davys) in 1592. French navigator Louis de Bougainville established the first settlement, at Port Louis, in 1764. The following year Capt. John Byron claimed the islands for Britain and left a small party at Saunders Islands. Spain later forced the French and British to abandon their settlements but did not implement its claim to the islands. In 1829 the Republic of Buenos Aires, which claimed to have inherited the Spanish rights, sent Louis Vernet to develop a colony on the island. In 1831 he seized three American sailing vessels, whereupon the men of the corvette, *U.S.S. Lexington,* destroyed his settlement and proclaimed the Malvinas to be *free of all governance.* Britain, which had never renounced its claim, then re-established its settlement in 1833. Argentine military forces invaded the Falkland Islands on April 2, 1982 which resulted in a confrontation of war; these occupation forces surrendered to the British between June 14-15, 1982. In April 1990 the Argentine Congress declared the Falkland and other British-held South Atlantic islands all part of the new Argentine province of Tierra del Fuego.

RULERS:

British

REPUBLIC OF BUENOS AIRES REGIONAL

ISLA DE MALVINAS

Issued by Luis Vernet.

1924 ISSUE

#S101-S104 black. Uniface.

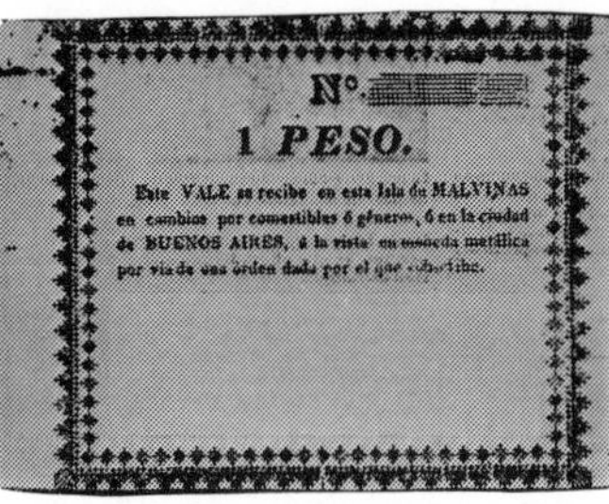

		GOOD	FINE	XF
S101	**1 PESO** ND. (ca.1824-29). Unsigned remainder.	—	—	—

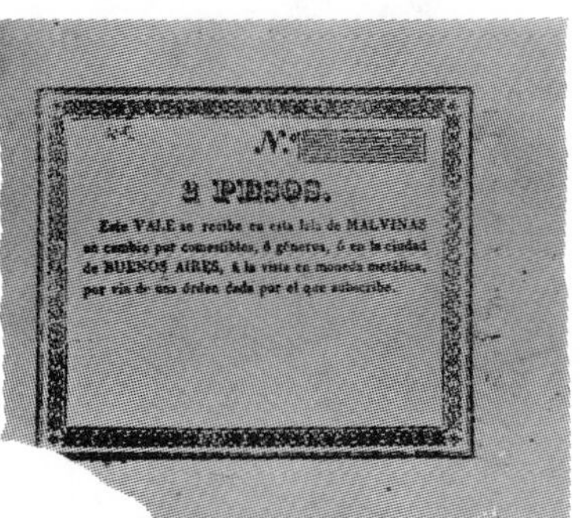

		GOOD	FINE	XF
S102	**2 PESOS** ND. (ca.1824-29). Unsigned remainder.	—	Rare	—

VALE CINCO PESOS. 5
QUE SE RECIBIRÁ EN ESTA
ISLA DE MALVINAS,
En cambio de efectos por el que subscribe.

		GOOD	FINE	XF
S103	**5 PESOS** ND. (ca.1824-29). Unsigned remainder.	—	Rare	—

S104 10 PESOS
ND. (ca.1824-29). Farmer w/plow at top ctr.

GOOD	FINE	XF
—	Rare	—

MAURITIUS

The island of Mauritius, a member of the British Commonwealth located in the Indian Ocean 500 miles (805 km.) east of Madagascar, has an area of 790 sq. mi. (2,045 sq. km.) and a population of 1.18 million. Capital: Port Louis. Sugar provides 90 percent of the export revenue.

Cartographic evidence indicates that Arabs and Malays arrived at Mauritius during the Middle Ages. Domingo Fernandez, a Portuguese navigator, visited the island in the early 16th century, but Portugal made no attempt at settlement. The Dutch took possession, and named the island, in 1598. Their colony failed to prosper and was abandoned in 1710. France claimed Mauritius in 1715 and developed a strong and prosperous colony that endured until the island was captured by the British in 1810, during the Napoleonic Wars. British possession was confirmed by the Treaty of Paris, 1814. Mauritius became independent on March 12, 1968, with Elizabeth II as Head of State as Queen of Mauritius. Mauritius became a Republic on March 12, 1992, with a President as Head of State.

RULERS:
British

MONETARY SYSTEM:
1 Shilling = 12 Pence
1 Crown = 5 Shillings
1 Pound = 4 Crowns
1 Pound = 5 Dollars to 1948
1 Rupee = 100 Cents, 1848-
1 Crown = 10 Mauritius Livres

BRITISH ADMINISTRATION

COLONIAL BANK OF MAURITIUS BOURBON & DEPENDENCIES

1810'S ISSUE

#S103 and S105 Britannia seated in ornate frame at upper l.

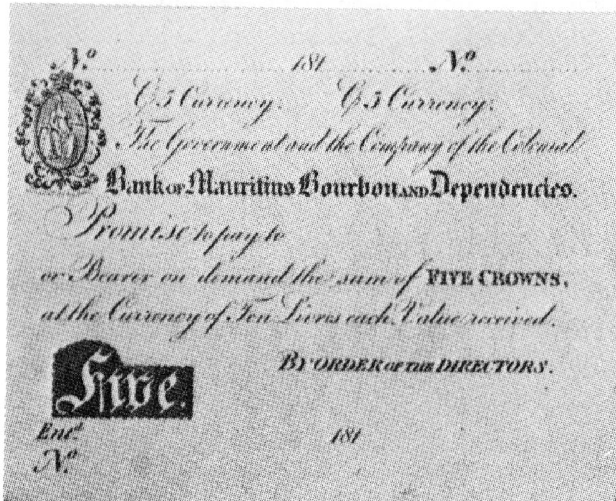

S103 5 CROWNS
181x. Black. Unsigned remainder.

GOOD	FINE	XF
—	—	850.00

S105 20 CROWNS
181x. Black uniface. Unsigned remainder.

GOOD	FINE	XF
—	—	1200.

MAURITIUS BANK

1830-35 ISSUE

S111 10 DOLLARS
1830-35.

GOOD	FINE	XF
—	—	—

		GOOD	FINE	XF
S112	**15 DOLLARS** 1830-35.	—	—	—
S113	**20 DOLLARS** 1830-35.	—	—	—
S114	**100 DOLLARS** 1830-35.	—	—	—
S115	**200 DOLLARS** 1830-35.	—	—	—

MAURITIUS COMMERCIAL BANK

1838-40 ISSUES

Dollar System.

#S121-S129 various date and sign. varieties.

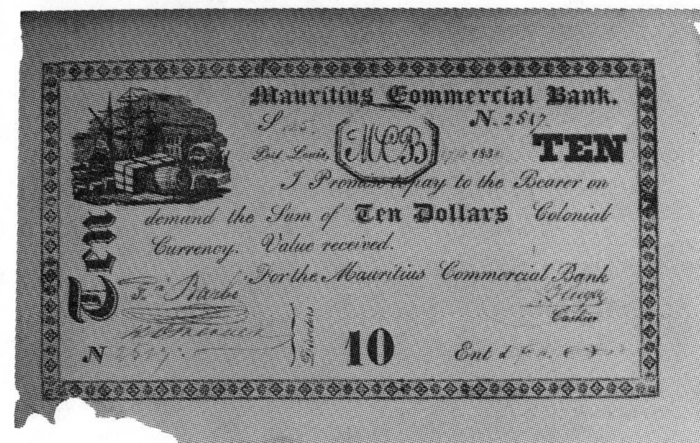

		GOOD	FINE	XF
S121	**10 DOLLARS** 27.8.1838. Blue-black. Sailing ship, barrel and bales dockside at upper l.	600.00	1500.	3000.

		GOOD	FINE	XF
S122	**10 DOLLARS** 16.4.1839; 2.3.1843. Black. Waterfront scene at ctr. Back orange.			
	a. Issued note.	20.00	40.00	85.00
	r. Remainder w/o sign. 2.3.1843.	12.00	25.00	60.00
S123	**15 DOLLARS** 27.8.1838. Blue-black.	35.00	100.00	225.00

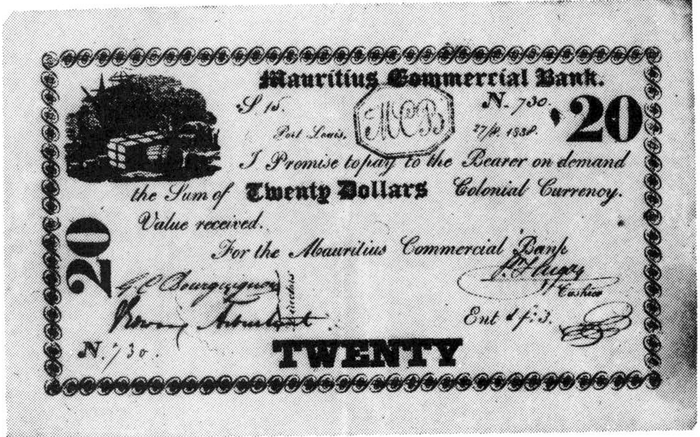

		GOOD	FINE	XF
S124	**20 DOLLARS** 27.8.1838. Black. Sailing ship, barrel and bales dockside at upper l.	375.00	850.00	—

		GOOD	FINE	XF
S125	**20 DOLLARS** 8.2.1839-18.10.1839. Black. Similar to #S122. Uniface.	30.00	65.00	150.00
S126	**50 DOLLARS** 16.1.1840; 5.5.1840. Black. Like #S125.	30.00	100.00	225.00
S127	**100 DOLLARS** 4.4.1839; 5.4.1839; 8.4.1839; 9.4.1839; 14.9.1841. Black. Like #S125.	65.00	200.00	500.00
S128	**200 DOLLARS** 2.4.1839; 3.4.1839; 7.4.1839; 9.4.1839.	100.00	250.00	750.00
S129	**500 DOLLARS** 28.6.1839; 25.7.1839.	175.00	450.00	1000.
S130	**1000 DOLLARS** 7.8.1839; 7.11.1839.	300.00	850.00	2000.

ND ISSUE

Rupee System.

		GOOD	FINE	XF
S136	**50 RUPEES** (Not issued).	—	Unc	750.00

ORIENTAL BANK CORPORATION

1858 ISSUE

#S141 and S142 printer: PBC.

		GOOD	FINE	XF
S141	**1 POUND = 5 DOLLARS** 11.12.1858. Supported royal arms, ornate border. Specimen.	—	Unc	2250.

		GOOD	FINE	XF
S142	**5 POUNDS = 25 POUNDS** Similar to #S141. Specimen.	—	Unc	2800.

The United States of Mexico, located immediately south of the United States, has an area of 1,222,612 sq. mi. (1,967,183 sq. km.) and a population of 98.88 million. Capital: Mexico City. The economy is based on agriculture, manufacturing and mining. Cotton, sugar, coffee and shrimp are exported.

Mexico was the site of highly advanced Indian civilizations 1,500 years before conquistador Hernando Cortes conquered the wealthy Aztec empire of Montezuma, 1519-1521, and founded a Spanish colony which lasted for nearly 300 years. During the Spanish period, Mexico, then called New Spain, stretched from Guatemala to the present states of Wyoming and California, its present northern boundary having been established by the secession of Texas (1836) and the war of 1846-1848 with the United States.

Independence from Spain was declared by Father Miguel Hidalgo on Sept. 16, 1810, Mexican Independence Day, and was achieved by General Agustin de Iturbide in 1821. Iturbide became emperor in 1822 but was deposed when a republic was established a year later. For more than half a century following the birth of the republic, the political scene of Mexico was characterized by turmoil which saw two emperors (including the unfortunate Maximilian), several dictators and an average of one new government every nine months passing swiftly from obscurity to oblivion. The land, social, economic and labor reforms promulgated by the Reform Constitution of Feb. 5, 1917 established the basis for a sustained economic development and participative democracy that have made Mexico one of the most politically stable countries of modern Latin America.

MONETARY SYSTEM:

1 Peso = 100 Centavos, 1863-
1 Escudo = 16 Reales to 1897

COMMERCIAL BANKS:

Banco Comercial de Chihuahua (Chihuahua) .... #S124-S131B
Banco de Aguascalientes (Aguascalientes) .... #S101-S107
Banco de Campeche (Campeche) .... #S108-S112
Banco de Chiapas (Chiapas) .... #S113-S115
Banco de Chihuahua (Chihuahua) .... #S115A-S123
Banco de Coahuila (Coahuila) .... #S195-S204
Banco de Durango (Durango) .... #S272-S281
Banco de Empleados (Distrito Federal) .... #S204A-S204F
Banco de Guanajuato (Guanajuato) .... #S287-S297
Banco de Guerrero (Guerrero) .... #S298-S303
Banco de Hidalgo (Hidalgo) .... #S304-S310
Banco de Hidalgo, Parral (Chihuahua) .... #S138-S142
Banco de Jalisco (Jalisco) .... #S312-S328
Banco de Londres y México (Distrito Federal) .... #S232-S241
Banco de Londres México y Sud America (Distrito Federal) .... #S216-S230
Banco de Michoacán (Michoacán) .... #S338-S344
Banco de Morelos (Morelos) .... #S345-S351
Banco de Nuevo León (Nuevo León) .... #S358-S365
Banco de Oaxaca (Oaxaca) .... #S371-S375
Banco de Patricio Milmo (Nuevo León) .... #S366-S370
Banco de Querétaro S.A.(Querétaro) .... #S390-S398
Banco de San Ignacio (Sinaloa) .... #S415-S418
Banco de San Luis Potosí (San Luis Potosí) .... #S399-S407
Banco de Santa Eulalia (Chihuahua) .... #S187-S193
Banco de Sonora (Sonora) .... #S419-S423
Banco de Tabasco (Tabasco) .... #S424-S428
Banco de Tamaulipas (Tamaulipas) .... #S429-S436
Banco de Veracruz (Veracruz) .... #S436A
Banco de Zacatecas (Zacatecas) .... #S474-S481
Banco del Estado de Chihuahua (Chihuahua) .... #S131C-S137
Banco del Estado de Durango (Durango) .... #S284-S286
Banco del Estado de Mexico (México) .... #S329-S337
Banco Industrial de México, Sociedád Anónima (Distrito Federal) .... #S205-S206
Banco Internacional e Hipotecario de México (Distrito Federal) .... #S207-S215A
Banco Mejicano (Chihuahua) .... #S143-S149A
Banco Mercantil de Monterrey (Nuevo León) .... #S352-S357
Banco Mercantil de Veracruz (Veracruz) .... #S437-S444
Banco Mercantil de Yucatán (Yucatán) .... #S445-S457A
Banco Mercantil Mexicano (Distrito Federal) .... #S242-S248
Banco Mexicano (Chihuahua) .... #S150-S159
Banco Minero (Chihuahua) .... #S160-S171
Banco Minero Chihuahuense (Chihuahua) .... #S172-S182
Banco Minero de Chihuahua (Chihuahua) .... #S183-S186
Banco Nacional de Mexico (Distrito Federal) .... #S254-S263
Banco Nacional Mexicano (Distrito Federal) .... #S249-S253B
Banco Occidental de Mexico (Sinaloa) .... #S408-S414
Banco Oriental de México (Pueblo) .... #S376-S389
Banco Peninsular Mexicano (Yucatán) .... #S458-S465
Banco Yucateco (Yucatán) .... #S466-S473

GOVERNMENT

Crédito del Estado de Tamaulipas (Tamaulipas) .... #S428A-S428G
Ejército Nacional (Jalisco) .... #S311-S311A

PAWN SHOP

Nacional Monte de Piedad (Distrito Federal) .... #S264-S271

NOTE: Catalog numbers in ( ) are cross references to *The Complete Encyclopedia of Mexican Paper Money* by Duane Douglas, Claudio Verrey & Alberto Hidalgo ©1982 Krause Publications.

AGUASCALIENTES

BANCO DE AGUASCALIENTES

1902-10 ISSUE

#S101-S107 gypsy woman on back. Printer: ABNC.

		GOOD	FINE	XF
S101	**5 PESOS** 1902-10. Black on green unpt. Portr. P. J. G. Rojas at l., Church of San Marcos at r. Back green.			
	a. Series A. 1.10.1902. *(BK-AGU-1).*	35.00	80.00	—
	b. Series B. 19.11.1906. *(BK-AGU-2).*	30.00	70.00	—
	c. Series C. 1.7.1910. *(BK-AGU-3).*	25.00	60.00	—
	d. Ovpt: *GUADALAJARA.* 15.4.1903/1.10.1902. *(BK-AGU-4).*	80.00	130.00	—
	p. Proof. W/o series. ND.	—	Unc	250.00
	s1. Specimen. Series B. ND.	—	Unc	200.00
	s2. Specimen. Series C. 1.7.1910.	—	Unc	250.00
S102	**10 PESOS** 1902-10. Black on yellow and brown unpt. Church at l., man w/ox-cart at r. Back brown.			
	a. Series A. 1.10.1902; 3.4.1903; 14.10.1903; *(BK-AGU-7).*	35.00	80.00	—
	b. Series B. 19.11.1906; 1.5.1907. *(BK-AGU-8).*	30.00	70.00	150.00
	c. Series C. 1.7.1910. *(BK-AGU-9).*	25.00	60.00	125.00
	d. Ovpt: *GUADALAJARA.* 30.11.1904/14.10.1903; 25.5.1903/3.4.1905. *(BK-AGU-10).*	50.00	100.00	—
	p. Proof.	—	Unc	300.00
	s. Specimen. Series B. 1.7.1910.	—	Unc	200.00

		GOOD	FINE	XF
S103	**20 PESOS** 1902-07. Black on orange unpt. Church at l., seated Ceres (Goddess of Agriculture) at r. Back orange.			
	a. Series A. 1.10.1902. *(BK-AGU-12).*	80.00	170.00	—
	b. Series B. 19.11.1906; 1.5.1907. *(BK-AGU-13).*	90.00	180.00	350.00
	c. Red ovpt: *GUADALAJARA.* 1.10.1903/1.10.1902; 15.5.1905/1.10.1902. *(BK-AGU-14).*	80.00	170.00	—
	d. Black ovpt: *GUADALAJARA.* 15.4.1903/1.10.1902. *(BK-AGU-15).*	80.00	170.00	—
	e. Ovpt: *SUCURSAL EN GUADALAJARA.* 19.11.1906. *(BK-AGU-16).*	80.00	170.00	—
	s. Specimen. Series B. ND.	—	Unc	350.00

		GOOD	FINE	XF
S104	**50 PESOS** 1902-07. Black on blue and yellow unpt. Church at ctr., horsedrawn plow at l., men gathering wood at r. Back blue.			
	a. Series A. 1.10.1902-14.10.1903. *(BK-AGU-18).*	400.00	800.00	—
	b. Series B. 1.5.1907. *(BK-AGU-19).*	300.00	600.00	—
	c. Ovpt: *GUADALAJARA.* 3.4.1903/25.5.1903; 14.10.1903/1.9.1905. *(BK-AGU-20).*	400.00	800.00	—

		GOOD	FINE	XF
S105	**100 PESOS** 1902-07. Black on yellow and pink unpt. Church at l., portr. Flora (Goddess of Flowers and Gardens) at r. Back red.			
	a. Series A. 14.10.1902; 3.4.1903; 14.10.1903. *(BK-AGU-22).*	400.00	650.00	—
	b. Series B. 1.5.1907. *(BK-AGU-23).*	400.00	600.00	1000.
	c. Ovpt: *GUADALAJARA.* 15.8.1904/14.10.1903. *(BK-AGU-24).*	400.00	700.00	—

		GOOD	FINE	XF
S106	**500 PESOS** 1.10.1902. Black on yellow and olive-green unpt. Church at l., farmer plowing w/oxen at r. Back olive-green. Series A.			
	a. Issued note.	3500.	5000.	—
	r. Unsigned remainder.	—	—	—

		GOOD	FINE	XF
S107	**1000 PESOS** 19xx (ca.1902). Black on orange unpt. Church at l., portr. P. J. G. Rojas at r. Back orange. Series A.			
	p. Proof.	—	—	—
	s. Specimen.	—	—	—

CAMPECHE

BANCO DE CAMPECHE

1903-09 ISSUE

#S108-S112 scene of village landscape on back. Printer: ABNC.

		GOOD	FINE	XF
S108	**5 PESOS** 1.7.1903-09. Black on green unpt. State arms at l. ctr., Nike (Victory) and Irene (Peace) at r. Back green. Series A. *(BK-CAM-1).*			
	a. Issued note.	1500.	2500.	—
	p. Proof.	—	Unc	1000.
	s. Specimen.	—	Unc	1000.

		GOOD	FINE	XF
S109	**10 PESOS** 1.7.1903-ca.1906. Black on orange and yellow unpt. Themis (Goddess of Justice) at l., State arms at ctr. Back red. Series B. *(BK-CAM-3).*			
	a. Issued note.	2500.	3500.	—
	p. Proof.	—	Unc	1250.
	s. Specimen.	—	Unc	1250.
S110	**20 PESOS** 1.7.1903; 1.7.1909. Black on blue and yellow unpt. State arms at l., ship at r. Back blue-gray. Series C. *(BK-CAM-4).*			
	a. Issued note.	2500.	3500.	—
	b. Ovpt: *SURCUSAL EN MÉRIDA.* 2.7.1906/1.7.1903. *(BK-CAM-5).*	2500.	3500.	—
	p. Proof.	—	Unc	1750.
	s. Specimen,	—	Unc	1750.

		GOOD	FINE	XF
S111	**50 PESOS** 19xx (ca.1903-06). Black on brown and yellow unpt. State arms at l., lion at ctr. Back brown. Series D. *(BK-CAM-7).*			
	p. Proof.	—	Unc	2000.
	s. Specimen.	—	Unc	2000.

		GOOD	FINE	XF
S112	**100 PESOS** 19xx (ca.1903-06). Black on olive-green and yellow unpt. State arms at l., standing allegorical woman w/sword and shield at r. Back olive-green. *(BK-CAM-8).*			
	p. Proof.	—	—	—
	s. Specimen.	—	—	—

CHIAPAS

BANCO DE CHIAPAS

1901-06 ISSUE

#S113-S115 printer: ABNC.

S113 5 PESOS
12.2.1902. Black on green and yellow unpt. Portr. man at l. Back green; crop workers at ctr. Series A. *(BK-CHIP-1).*

	GOOD	FINE	XF
a. Issued note.	1500.	2100.	3000.
p. Proof.	—	Unc	1200.
s. Specimen.	—	Unc	1200.

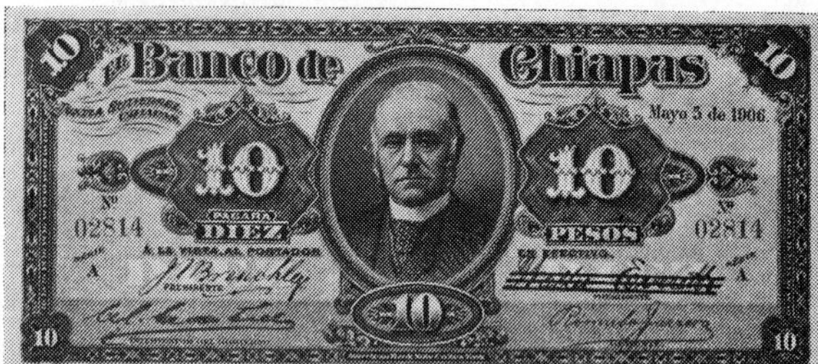

S114 10 PESOS
12.2.1902; 5.5.1906; 4.4.1909. Black on orange unpt. Portr. man at ctr. Back orange; man w/ox-cart at ctr. Series A. *(BK-CHIP-3).*

	GOOD	FINE	XF
a. Issued note.	1500.	2100.	3000.
p. Proof.	—	Unc	1500.
s. Specimen.	—	Unc	1500.

S115 20 PESOS
ND (ca.1901-06). Black on blue and yellow unpt. 3 Indians at l. Back blue-gray; men leading oxen team at ctr. *(BK-CHIP-5).*

	GOOD	FINE	XF
p. Proof.	—	—	—
s. Specimen.	—	—	—

CHIHUAHUA

BANCO DE CHIHUAHUA

1874-89 ISSUE

#S115A-S117 printer: NBNC.

S115A 25 CENTAVOS
1876. Black. Allegorical woman w/sheaves and beehive at ctr. Back brown; 2 beehives at ctr. Series C. Proof.

GOOD	FINE	XF
—	—	—

S116 50 CENTAVOS
1875. Black. Basket of corn at l., Themis (Goddess of Justice) at r. Back blue. Series B. *(BK-CHI-1).*

GOOD	FINE	XF
400.00	700.00	1200.

S117 1 PESO
1874. Black. Harvest at lower l., horsemen at ctr., woman w/flowers at lower r. Back green. Series A. *(BK-CHI-2).*

GOOD	FINE	XF
600.00	900.00	1500.

#S118-S123 printer: ABNC.

S118 25 CENTAVOS
1889. Black on yellow unpt. Woman w/children at r. Back green. Series A. *(BK-CHI-3).*

	GOOD	FINE	XF
a. Issued note.	75.00	350.00	—
p. Proof.	—	Unc	250.00
s. Specimen.	—	Unc	250.00

S119 50 CENTAVOS
1889. Black on yellow-green unpt. Woman w/fruit at l. Back blue. Series A. *(BK-CHI-6).*

	GOOD	FINE	XF
a. Issued note.	125.00	500.00	—
p. Proof.	—	Unc	350.00
s. Specimen.	—	Unc	350.00

S120 1 PESO
1889. Black on yellow and brown unpt. Woman at l., man w/child at r. Back brown; dog on safe at ctr.

	GOOD	FINE	XF
a. Issued note. *(BK-CHI-8).*	450.00	700.00	—
b. Ovpt: *BANCO MINERO DE CHIHUAHUA* and *Creel Hernan.* *(BK-CHI-9).*	500.00	800.00	—
p. Proof.	—	Unc	500.00
s. Specimen.	—	Unc	500.00

S121 5 PESOS
1889. Black on orange and yellow unpt. Woman w/flowers at l., Minerva (Goddess of Science, Art and War) at ctr. r. Back green; cattle at pond in ctr. Series A. *(BK-CHI-9a).*

	GOOD	FINE	XF
p. Proof.	—	—	—
s. Specimen.	—	—	—

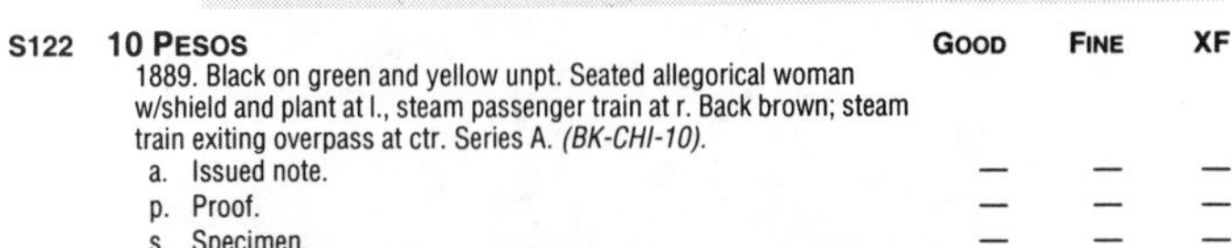

S122 10 Pesos

1889. Black on green and yellow unpt. Seated allegorical woman w/shield and plant at l., steam passenger train at r. Back brown; steam train exiting overpass at ctr. Series A. *(BK-CHI-10).*

	Good	Fine	XF
a. Issued note.	—	—	—
p. Proof.	—	—	—
s. Specimen.	—	—	—

S123 20 Pesos

1889. Black on blue and yellow unpt. Reclining allegorical woman at l., Irene (Goddess of Peace) w/child at r. Back blue; ships at ctr. Series A. *(BK-CHI-11).*

	Good	Fine	XF
p. Proof.	—	—	—
s. Specimen.	—	—	—

Banco Comercial de Chihuahua

1889-99 Issue

#S124-S131B printer: ABNC.

S124 25 Centavos

1889. Black on orange unpt. Portr. Hidalgo at ctr. Back blue; Raphael's Angel at ctr. Series A. *(BK-CHI-135).*

	Good	Fine	XF
a. Issued note.	65.00	150.00	300.00
p. Proof.	—	Unc	250.00
s. Specimen.	—	Unc	250.00

S125 50 Centavos

1889. Black on yellow unpt. Hidalgo at l., steam locomotive at r. Back green; miner at l. Series A. *(BK-CHI-137).*

	Good	Fine	XF
a. Issued note.	80.00	300.00	600.00
p. Proof.	—	Unc	250.00
s. Specimen.	—	Unc	250.00

S126 1 Peso

1889. Black on orange and yellow unpt. Hidalgo at l., cow w/calf at r. Back red; men and horses at ctr. Series A. *(BK-CHI-138).*

	Good	Fine	XF
a. Issued note.	175.00	400.00	800.00
p. Proof.	—	Unc	350.00
s. Specimen.	—	Unc	350.00

#S127-S131B seated Mercury on back.

S127 5 Pesos

1889. Black on brown and yellow unpt. Portr. Hidalgo at l., young Mercury w/caduceus and fish at r. Text: *EN MONEDA DE PLATA DEL CUÑO MEXICANO* at lower l. Middle sign. title: *DIRECTOR.* Series A. *(BK-CHI-139).*

	Good	Fine	XF
a. Issued note.	300.00	600.00	—
p. Proof.	—	Unc	800.00
s. Specimen.	—	Unc	800.00

S127A 5 Pesos

1898. Like #S127, but w/text: *A LA PAR, EN EFECTIVO* at lower l. Middle sign. title: *GERENTE.* Back brown.

	Good	Fine	XF
a. Issued note. 5.2.1898. Series B.	300.00	600.00	—
b. Ovpt: *GÓMEZ PALACIO.* 20.5.1898-15.6.1898. *(BK-CHI-140).*	300.00	600.00	—
p. Proof. 1898. Series D.	—	Unc	800.00
s. Specimen. 1898. Series D.	—	Unc	800.00

S128 10 Pesos

1889. Black on blue and yellow unpt. Portr. Hidalgo at ctr. l., workers at r. Text: *EN MONEDA DE PLATA DEL CUÑO MEXICANO* at lower l. ctr. Middle sign. title: *DIRECTOR.* Back blue. Series A. *(BK-CHI-142).*

	Good	Fine	XF
a. Issued note.	300.00	600.00	—
b. Ovpt: *GÓMEZ PALACIO.* 20.10.1898. *(BK-CHI-140).*	300.00	600.00	—
p. Proof.	—	Unc	800.00
s. Specimen.	—	Unc	800.00

S128A 10 Pesos

1898-99. Like #S128, but w/text: *A LA PAR, EN EFECTIVO* at lower l. ctr. Middle sign. title: *GERENTE.* Back blue.

	Good	Fine	XF
a. Issued note.	300.00	600.00	—
p. Proof.	—	Unc	800.00
s. Specimen.	—	Unc	800.00

S129 20 Pesos

1889. Black on orange and yellow unpt. Portr. Hidalgo at l., sheep at ctr., woman w/bow and arrows at r. Text: *EN MONEDA DE PLATA DEL CUÑO MEXICANO* at lower ctr. Middle sign. title: *DIRECTOR.* Back orange. Series A.

	Good	Fine	XF
p. Proof.	—	Unc	1000.
s. Specimen.	—	Unc	1000.

S129A 20 Pesos

1898-99. Like #S129, but w/text: *A LA PAR, EN EFECTIVO* at lower ctr. Middle sign. title: *GERENTE.* Back orange. Series B. Hand signed & issued.

	Good	Fine	XF
a. Ovpt: *GÓMEZ PALACIO.* 19.8.1899/1898; 19.19.1899. *(BK-CHI-144).*	400.00	750.00	1200.
p. Proof.	—	Unc	1000.
s. Specimen.	—	Unc	1000.

S130 50 Pesos

1889. Black on green and yellow unpt. Hidalgo at ctr., C. Columbus w/Indian maiden at r. Text: *EN MONEDA DE PLATA DEL CUÑO MEXICANO* at lower l. Middle sign. title: *DIRECTOR.* Back green. Series A. *(BK-CHI-145).*

	Good	Fine	XF
p. Proof.	—	Unc	800.00
s. Specimen.	—	Unc	800.00

S130A 50 Pesos

1898-99. Like #S130, but w/text: *A LA PAR, EN EFECTIVO* at lower l. Middle sign. title: *GERENTE.* Back green.

		Good	Fine	XF
a.	Ovpt: *GÓMEZ PALACIO.* 1.5.1898; 20.10.1898. Series B. *(BK-CHI-146).*	300.00	600.00	—
s.	Specimen. 1898. Series B; 1899. Series C.	—	Unc	800.00

S131 100 Pesos

1899. Black on orange and yellow unpt. Steam passenger train through mountain pass at l., portr. Hidalgo at ctr., miner at r. Text: *EN MONEDA DE PLATA DEL CUÑO MEXICANO* at lower ctr. Sign. title: *DIRECTOR* at r. Back red-orange. Series A.

		Good	Fine	XF
p.	Proof.	—	Unc	1500.
s.	Specimen.	—	Unc	1500.

S131A 100 Pesos

1898-99. Black on orange and yellow unpt. Similar to #S131, but w/text: *A LA PAR, EN EFECTIVO* at lower ctr. Sign. title: *GERENTE* at r. Back red-orange.

		Good	Fine	XF
a.	Ovpt: *GÓMEZ PALACIO.* 20.10.1898. 19.8.1899/1898. Series B. *(BK-CHI-147).*	1000.	1500.	—
s.	Specimen. 1898. Series B; 1899. Series C.	—	Unc	1500.

S131B 500 Pesos

1889. Black on brown and yellow unpt. Standing Liberty at l., allegorical woman holding cherub at ctr., portr. Hidalgo at r. Text: *EN MONEDA DE PLATA DEL CUÑO MEXICANO* at lower ctr. Middle sign. title: *DIRECTOR.* Back brown and black. Series A.

		Good	Fine	XF
p.	Proof.	—	—	—
s.	Specimen.	—	—	—

Banco del Estado de Chihuahua

Notes were issued by revolutionary forces in Chihuahua. All have only one printed sign. at ctr., none at l. or r.

Decree of 12.12.1913

#S131C-S137 black on m/c unpt. Back orange; national arms at ctr. Printer: ABNC. Series A.

S131C 1 Peso

D.1913 (ca.1915). Loggers at ctr. Not issued.

		VG	VF	Unc
p.	Proof.	—	—	—
s.	Specimen.	—	—	—

S132 5 Pesos

D.1913. Miner w/drill at ctr. *(BK-CHI-148).*

		VG	VF	Unc
a.	Issued note w/1 sign.	1.50	4.00	10.00
b.	Uncut sheet of four. *(BK-CHI-148A).*	—	Unc	150.00
p.	Proof.	—	Unc	75.00
s.	Specimen.	—	Unc	75.00

S133 10 Pesos

D.1913. Cowboy herding cattle at ctr. *(BK-CHI-149).*

		VG	VF	Unc
a.	Issued note w/1 sign.	1.50	4.00	10.00
b.	Uncut sheet of four. *(BK-CHI-149A).*	—	Unc	150.00
p.	Proof.	—	Unc	75.00
s.	Specimen.	—	Unc	75.00

S134 20 Pesos

D.1913. Harvesting scene at ctr. *(BK-CHI-150).*

		VG	VF	Unc
a.	Issued note w/1 sign.	2.00	5.00	15.00
p.	Proof.	—	Unc	75.00
s.	Specimen.	—	Unc	75.00

S135 50 Pesos

D.1913. Steam passenger train by station at ctr. *(BK-CHI-151).*

		VG	VF	Unc
a.	Issued note w/1 sign.	5.00	20.00	85.00
b.	Uncut sheet of 4. *(BK-CHI-151A).*	—	Unc	150.00
p.	Proof.	—	Unc	100.00
s.	Specimen.	—	Unc	100.00

S136 100 Pesos

D.1913. Ceres (Goddess of Agriculture), Goddess Juno, and Industry at ctr. *(BK-CHI-153).*

		VG	VF	Unc
a.	Issued note w/1 sign.	12.00	30.00	85.00
p.	Proof.	—	Unc	150.00
s.	Specimen.	—	Unc	150.00

S137 500 Pesos

D.1913. Women w/young boys representing "Work" & "Knowledge" at ctr. *(BK-CHI-154).*

		VG	VF	Unc
a.	Issued note w/1 sign.	20.00	60.00	150.00
p.	Proof.	—	Unc	200.00
s.	Specimen.	—	Unc	200.00

EL BANCO DE HIDALGO, PARRAL

1883 ISSUE

#S138-S142 printer: HLBNC.

		GOOD	FINE	XF
S138	**25 CENTAVOS** 1883. Black on blue unpt. Portr. Hidalgo at l. Back brown. Series A. *(BK-CHI-125).*			
	a. Issued note.	400.00	800.00	1200.
	p. Proof.	—	—	—
S139	**50 CENTAVOS** 1883. Portr. Hidalgo at lower ctr. Series A.			
	a. Black on red-orange unpt. *(BK-CHI-126).*	400.00	800.00	—
	p. Proof. Black on green unpt. Back green. *(BK-CHI-127).*	—	—	—

		GOOD	FINE	XF
S140	**1 PESO** 1883. Black on brown unpt. Portr. Hidalgo at ctr., cherubs at l. and r. in unpt. Back green. Series A.			
	a. Black on brown unpt. *(BK-CHI-128).*	800.00	1200.	—
	p. Proof. Black on green unpt. Back green. *(BK-CHI-129).*	—	—	—
	s. Specimen. *(BK-CHI-130).*	—	—	—

		GOOD	FINE	XF
S141	**5 PESOS** 1883. Black on green unpt. Portr. Hidalgo at upper l., steam passenger train at lower r. Back green. Series A.			
	p. Proof.	—	Unc	1600.
	s. Specimen. *(BK-CHI-131).*	—	—	—

		GOOD	FINE	XF
S142	**10 PESOS** 1883. Black on green unpt. Mining scenes at lower l., portr. Hidalgo at upper r. Back green. Series A.			
	p. Proof. *(BK-CHI-134).*	—	—	—
	s. Specimen. *(BK-CHI-133).*	—	—	—

BANCO MEJICANO

1878 ISSUE

#S143-S145 printer: NBNC.

		GOOD	FINE	XF
S143	**25 CENTAVOS** 1878. Black on blue unpt. Shepherdess holding lamb w/sheep at l., plow and sheaf at r. Back dk. orange; plow and sheaf at ctr.			
	a. Issued note. *(BK-CHI-22).*	7.00	15.00	50.00
	p. Proof.	—	Unc	100.00
	r. Remainder w/o serial #. *(BK-CHI-23).*	—	8.00	20.00
	s. Specimen.	—	Unc	100.00

		GOOD	FINE	XF
S144	**50 CENTAVOS** 1878. Black on white with pale orange unpt. Man plowing at l., Irene (Goddess of Peace) at r. Back blue.			
	a. Issued note. *(BK-CHI-25).*	80.00	150.00	300.00
	b. Lg. red ovpt: *BATOPILAS.*	100.00	200.00	—
	p. Proof.	—	Unc	250.00
	s. Specimen.	—	Unc	250.00

		GOOD	FINE	XF
S145	**1 PESO** 1878. Black on green-orange unpt. Agriculture work at ctr. Back brown; National arms at ctr. Series A-E. *(BK-CHI-27).*	150.00	400.00	—

1883 ISSUE

#S146-S149A printer: ABNC.

		GOOD	FINE	XF
S146	**1 PESO** 1883. Black on tan unpt. Steam train by station at ctr. Back tan. Series A. *(BK-CHI-28)*			
	a. Issued note.	350.00	900.00	1500.
	p. Proof.	—	Unc	800.00
	s. Specimen.	—	—	—

		GOOD	FINE	XF
S147	**2 PESOS** 1883. Black on green unpt. Helmeted Athena at l., 2 prospectors at r. Back green. Series B.			
	p. Proof.	—	—	—
	s. Specimen.	—	—	—

		GOOD	FINE	XF
S148	**5 PESOS** 1883. Black on blue unpt. Woman harvesting wheat at l., horses heads at upper ctr., standing Themis (Goddess of Justice) at r. Back blue. Series C. *(BK-CHI-29).*	1500.	3000.	—

		Good	Fine	XF
S149	**10 Pesos** 1883. Black on orange unpt. Town square scene at l., Ceres (Goddess of Agriculture) at ctr., market scene at r. Back orange. Series D. Punched hole cancelled. *(BK-CHI-30).*	1500.	3000.	—

		Good	Fine	XF
S149A	**20 Pesos** 1883. Black on brown unpt. Man plowing field w/palm trees in background at l., village scene w/people, water fountain, and bldgs. at r. Back brown. Series E.			
	p. Proof.	—	—	—
	s. Specimen.	—	—	—

Banco Mexicano

1888 Issue

		Good	Fine	XF
S150	**25 Semillas (seeds)** 1888. Black. Eagle in unpt. *(BK-CHI-31).*	125.00	250.00	—

#S151-S159 series A. Printer: ABNC.

		Good	Fine	XF
S151	**25 Centavos** 1888. Black on yellow unpt. Farmer w/sheaf at l. Back brown; Indian at ctr. *(BK-CHI-32).*			
	a. Issued note.	12.50	50.00	130.00
	p. Proof.	—	Unc	160.00
	s. Specimen.	—	Unc	160.00

		Good	Fine	XF
S152	**50 Centavos** 1888. Black on yellow unpt. 2 goats at r. Back orange; steam locomotive at ctr. *(BK-CHI-35).*			
	a. Issued note.	150.00	450.00	750.00
	p. Proof.	—	Unc	500.00
	s. Specimen.	—	Unc	500.00
S153	**1 Peso** 1888. Black on yellow and orange unpt. Woman w/chickens at l., Cleo (Muse of History) at r. Back brown: cow's head at ctr. Series A. *(BK-CHI-37).*			
	a. Issued note.	100.00	375.00	650.00
	p. Proof.	—	Unc	500.00
	s. Specimen.	—	Unc	500.00

		Good	Fine	XF
S154	**2 Pesos** 1888. Black on brown and yellow unpt. Columbus in sight of land at l., Indian w/feather headdress at lower r. Back dk. red; girl and horse at ctr.			
	a. Issued note. *(BK-CHI-39).*	1500.	2500.	—
	p. Proof.	—	—	—
	s. Specimen.	—	—	—

		Good	Fine	XF
S155	**5 Pesos** 1888. Black on green unpt. Cleo (Muse of History) at ctr. Back olive-green; woman's head at ctr.			
	a. Issued note. *(BK-CHI-41).*	1750.	2500.	—
	b. Back proof. *(BK-CHI-41A).*	—	Unc	100.00
	p. Proof.	—	—	—
	s. Specimen.	—	—	—

#S156-S159 church at ctr. on back.

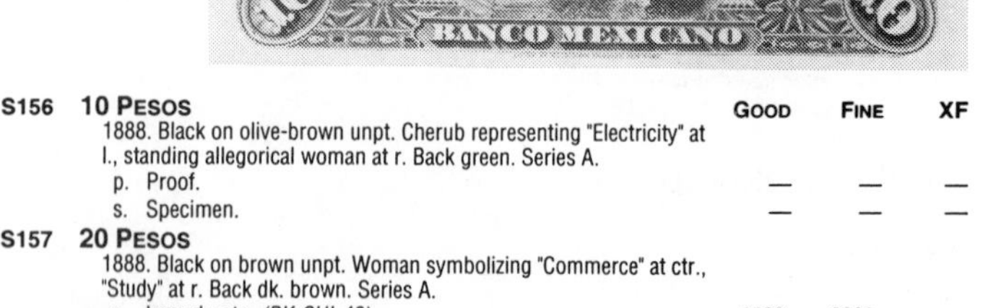

		Good	Fine	XF
S156	**10 Pesos** 1888. Black on olive-brown unpt. Cherub representing "Electricity" at l., standing allegorical woman at r. Back green. Series A.			
	p. Proof.	—	—	—
	s. Specimen.	—	—	—
S157	**20 Pesos** 1888. Black on brown unpt. Woman symbolizing "Commerce" at ctr., "Study" at r. Back dk. brown. Series A.			
	a. Issued note. *(BK-CHI-43).*	1500.	2000.	—
	p. Proof.	—	—	—
	s. Specimen.	—	—	—

S158 50 PESOS

1886; 1888. Black on orange and yellow unpt. Dog at lower l. w/bldg. in background, young Jupiter at r. Back red-brown. Series A.

	GOOD	FINE	XF
a. Issued note. *(BK-CHI-45).*	2000.	3000.	—
p. Proof.	—	—	—
s. Specimen.	—	—	—

S159 100 PESOS

1888. Black on yellow-green unpt. Farmer plowing at l. ctr., man shearing sheep at r. Back blue. Series A.

	GOOD	FINE	XF
a. Issued note. *(BK-CHI-47).*	1500.	2500.	—
p. Proof.	—	—	—
s. Specimen.	—	—	—

BANCO MINERO

1888-1914 ISSUE

#S160-S171 printer: ABNC.

S160 25 CENTAVOS

1888. Black on brown unpt. Seated woman w/quill and book at r. Text: *EN MONEDA DE PLATA DEL CUÑO MEXICANO.* Back orange; seated woman w/sheep at ctr. *(BK-CHI-67).*

	GOOD	FINE	XF
a. Issued note. Series A-C.	50.00	150.00	300.00
p. Proof. Series A.	—	Unc	275.00
s. Specimen. Series A.	—	Unc	275.00

S161 50 CENTAVOS

1888. Black on pink unpt. Women w/shawl at l., Minerva (Goddess of Science, Art and War) at r. Text: *EN MONEDA DE PLATA DEL CUÑO MEXICANO.* Back brown; Filia (Goddess of Friendship) at ctr. Series A. *(BK-CHI-70).*

	GOOD	FINE	XF
a. Issued note.	40.00	100.00	250.00
p. Proof.	—	Unc	275.00
s. Specimen.	—	Unc	275.00

S162 1 PESO

1888-1914. Black on green unpt. Seated Indian symbolizing Ambition at l., seated woman representing Legality at r. Text: *EN MONEDA DE PLATA DEL CUÑO MEXICANO.* Back green; Banco Minero at ctr.

	GOOD	FINE	XF
a. Series A. 1888. *(BK-CHI-72).*	35.00	100.00	175.00
b. Series B. 1888. *(BK-CHI-73).*	25.00	80.00	—
c. Series C. 1895. *(BK-CHI-74).*	20.00	40.00	—
d. Series A-D. Reissued 23.4.1914; 24.4.1914. *(BK-CHI-75).*	2.00	6.00	12.00
e. Series E. 7.7.1914.	2.00	6.00	12.00
f. Series F1-F10. 22.6.1914; 7.7.1914. *(BK-CHI-75).*	2.00	6.00	12.00
g. Series G1-G10. 22.6.1914; 7.7.1914. *(BK-CHI-75).*	2.00	6.00	12.00
p. Proof. Series A. 1888.	—	Unc	275.00
s1. Specimen. Series B. 1888.	—	Unc	200.00
s2. Specimen. Series C. 1895.	—	Unc	150.00
s3. Specimen. Series E; F1; F2.	—	Unc	75.00
s4. Specimen. W/o series. ND.	—	Unc	75.00

S163 5 PESOS

1888-97. Black on orange and yellow unpt. Themis (Goddess of Justice) at l., Euthenia (Goddess of Plenty) at r. Text: *EN MONEDA DE PLATA DEL CUÑO MEXICANO.* Back blue; allegorical woman w/safe and coins at l., miners at ctr.

	GOOD	FINE	XF
a. Series A. 1888. *(BK-CHI-77).*	50.00	100.00	—
b. Series B. 1895. *(BK-CHI-78).*	20.00	40.00	—
c. Series A. 1896. *(BK-CHI-79).*	20.00	40.00	—
d. Series B. 1897. *(BK-CHI-80).*	10.00	20.00	—
p. Proof. Series A. 1888.	—	Unc	250.00
s1. Specimen. Series A. 1888.	—	Unc	250.00
s2. Specimen. Series A52.	—	Unc	250.00
s3. Specimen. Series B.	—	Unc	200.00

S163A 5 PESOS

1898-1914. Like #S163 but w/text: *A LA PAR EN EFECTIVO.*

	GOOD	FINE	XF
a. Seriec C. 1898-1899. *(BK-CHI-81).*	5.00	10.00	—
f. Series D. 3.5.1900/1899. *(BK-CHI-82).*	5.00	10.00	—
g. 12.11.1901; 20.1.1902-1909. *(BK-CHI-83).*	4.00	10.00	27.50
h. 16.3.1910-1.8.1914. *(BK-CHI-84).*	2.00	6.00	18.00
i. Ovpt: *CHIHUAHUA.* 11.9.1903/1903-31.5.1911/1911. *(BK-CHI-85).*	4.00	10.00	27.50
j. Ovpt: *GÓMEZ PALACIO.* 16.7.1900/1899; 1901. *(BK-CHI-86).*	20.00	60.00	—
k. Ovpt: *HERMOSILLO.* 3.3.1903; 24.8.1903; 25.8.1903. *(BK-CHI-87).*	15.00	50.00	—
l. Ovpt: *HERMOSILLO/CHIHUAHUA.* 3.4.1903/1904; 3.3.1905/1903/1904. *(BK-CHI-88).*	15.00	50.00	—
s1. Specimen. Series C; E.	—	Unc	100.00
s2. Specimen. Series D; F1; F2.	—	Unc	75.00
s3. Specimen. Series H4; J3; O3; R3; U50; U51; Y32.	—	Unc	150.00
s4. Specimen. Series H. 1902; L. 1903; P. 1904.	—	Unc	250.00
s5. Specimen. W/o series. 1903; 1906-07.	—	Unc	150.00
s6. Specimen. W/o series. ND.	—	Unc	75.00

S164 10 PESOS

1888. Black on orange and yellow unpt. Portr. Minerva (Goddess of Science, Art and War) at l., Banco Minero at ctr. Text: *en moneda de plata del cuño mexicano.* Back brown; cattle and sheep at ctr.

	GOOD	FINE	XF
p. Proof. Series A. 1888.	—	Unc	175.00
s. Specimen. Series A. 1888.	—	Unc	175.00

S164A 10 PESOS

1897-1914. Like #S164 but w/text: *a la par en efectivo.*

	GOOD	FINE	XF
a. Series B. 1897. *(BK-CHI-91).*	20.00	40.00	—
b. 1898. *(BK-CHI-92).*	10.00	20.00	—

	Good	Fine	XF
c. 20.3.1900-1.8.1914. *(BK-CHI-93).*	4.00	10.00	30.00
d. Ovpt: *CHIHUAHUA.* 13.4.1903/1903-21.11.1912/ 1912. *(BK-CHI-94).*	6.00	12.00	35.00
e. Ovpt: *GÓMEZ PALACIO.* 20.3.1900.	30.00	70.00	—
f. Ovpt: *HERMOSILLO/CHIHUAHUA.* 21.8.1903/1903. *(BK-CHI-96).*	20.00	50.00	—
p1. Proof. Series B; C.	—	Unc	150.00
p2. Proof. W/o series. ND.	—	Unc	100.00
s1. Specimen. Series B.	—	Unc	150.00
s2. Specimen. Series A26-A28; E4; J3; L3; L4; O; U25.	—	Unc	125.00
s3. Specimen. Series F; w/o series. 1903; 1906.	—	Unc	150.00
s4. Specimen. W/o series. ND.	—	Unc	100.00

S165 20 Pesos
1888. Black on orange and yellow unpt. Seated Ceres (Goddess of Agriculture) w/child at l., public water well scene at r. Text: *EN MONEDA DE PLATA DEL CUÑO MEXICANO.* Back red; steam locomotive at ctr.

	Good	Fine	XF
a. Issued note. *(BK-CHI-99).*	80.00	150.00	—
p. Proof. Series A.	—	Unc	250.00
s. Specimen. Series A.	—	Unc	250.00

S165A 20 Pesos
1898-1908. Like #S165 but w/text: *a la par en efectivo* and curved *CHIHUAHUA 1903.*

	Good	Fine	XF
a. 20.3.1900-25.7.1914. *(BK-CHI-100).*	12.00	20.00	60.00
b. Ovpt: *CHIHUAHUA.* 9.7.1906/1906/1903. Series C. 24.12.1908/1908/1903. Series E. 4.12.1908/1908/1903. *(BK-CHI-101).*	15.00	30.00	75.00
c. Ovpt: *GÓMEZ PALACIO/CHIHUAHUA.* 9.7.1906/1903. *(BK-CHI-102).*	50.00	100.00	—
p. Proof. W/o series. ND.	—	Unc	200.00
s1. Specimen. Series C. 1903.	—	Unc	200.00

S165B 20 Pesos
1910-14. Like #S165A but *CHIHUAHUA* in straight line.

	Good	Fine	XF
a. Series F; H. 27.1.1910.	10.00	25.00	60.00
b. Series R. 30.12.1912.	10.00	25.00	60.00
c. Series W. 24.3.1913.	10.00	25.00	60.00
d. Series J.10. 21.4.1914; 3.7.1914.	10.00	25.00	60.00
e. Series N.11. 7.7.1914.	10.00	25.00	60.00
s1. Specimen. Series A10; D12; E11; S-V.	—	Unc	175.00
s2. Specimen. W/o series. ND.	—	Unc	200.00

S166 50 Pesos
1888-97. Black on yellow and blue unpt. Banco Minero at ctr., Urania (Muse of Astrology) at r. Text: *EN MONEDA DE PLATA DEL CUÑO MEXICANO.* Back blue; seated Indian w/hatchet at ctr.

	Good	Fine	XF
p. Proof. Series A. 1888.	—	Unc	400.00
s. Specimen. Series A. 1888.	—	Unc	400.00

S166A 50 Pesos
1900-14. Like #S166 but w/text: *A LA PAR EN EFECTIVO.*

	Good	Fine	XF
a. 1898-17.7.1914. *(BK-CHI-106).*	80.00	150.00	500.00
b. Ovpt: *GÓMEZ PALACIO.* 26.6.1900/1899-20.2.1907/1903. *(BK-CHI-109).*	150.00	225.00	—
c. Ovpt: *CHIHUAHUA.* 6.2.1902/1901-30.12.1912/ 1913. *(BK-CHI-108).*	80.00	150.00	—
p1. Proof. Series A. ND; 1903.	—	Unc	375.00
p2. Proof. W/o series. ND.	—	Unc	300.00
s1. Specimen. Series A. ND; 1903.	—	Unc	375.00
s2. Specimen. Series B-D; F; N; O; T7.	—	Unc	300.00
s3. Specimen. Series A8.	—	Unc	275.00
s4. Specimen. W/o series. ND.	—	Unc	300.00

S167 100 Pesos
1888; 1897; 5.5.1899. Black on yellow and olive unpt. Cherubs at lower l., woman in canoe at ctr., cow w/calf at lower r. Text: *EN MONEDA DE PLATA DEL CUÑO MEXICANO.* Back olive-green; 3 children at l.

	Good	Fine	XF
a. Series B. 1888. *(BK-CHI-111).*	150.00	300.00	—
p. Proof. Series A. 1888.	—	Unc	500.00
s1. Specimen. Series A. 1888.	—	Unc	500.00
s2. Specimen. Series E.	—	Unc	375.00

S168 100 Pesos
1899-1914. Like #S167 but w/text: *A LA PAR EN EFECTIVO.*

	Good	Fine	XF
a. 5.5.1899-21.4.1914. *(BK-CHI-112-113).*	70.00	125.00	—
b. Ovpt: *CHIHUAHUA.* 31.4.1903/1899-1912/5.12.1911. Series P. *(BK-CHI-114).*	80.00	150.00	300.00
c. Ovpt: *SUC. DEL BANCO MINERO.* 16.7.1908; 26.8.1907/1907/1903. *(BK-CHI-115).*	100.00	175.00	—
d. Ovpt: *GÓMEZ PALACIO.* 16.6.1900; 23.4.1908-28.4.1908/ 11.11.1898. *(BK-CHI-116).*	250.00	400.00	—
e. Ovpt: *HERMOSILLO/CHIHUAHUA.*; 3.3.1903/8.4.1908/1903; 3.3.1903/16.3.19-/1903. *(BK-CHI-117).*	110.00	225.00	—
p1. Proof. Series A.	—	Unc	500.00
p2. Proof. W/o series. ND.	—	Unc	400.00
s1. Specimen. Series A5; A6; A7; C. 1898.	—	Unc	500.00
s2. Specimen. Series E; F. 1902; O; P; R; X.	—	Unc	375.00
s3. Specimen. W/o series. ND; 1902; 1903.	—	Unc	375.00

S169 1000 Pesos
1888-1914. Black on m/c unpt. 185 x 85mm. Reclining woman at l. ctr. Back black on m/c unpt.; woman at ctr.

	Good	Fine	XF
a. Ovpt: *CHIHUAHUA.* 10.7.1908/1908/1904. *(BK-CHI-119).*	3500.	—	—
b. 1909. Archive copy.	—	—	—
s1. Specimen. 1902.	—	—	—
s2. Specimen. Series J.2; N.1. ND (1914).	—	—	—

NOTE: For #S162-S169, more reports of specific dates from 1888-1914 are needed to augment these listings.

S169A 1000 Pesos

	Good	Fine	XF
ND (ca.1908). Black on green wnpt. Allegorical woman holding book and boy at at l., allegorical woman holding scythe and fruit w/boy at r. Back green. Proof. (Not issued).	—	—	—

1910 Commemorative Issue

#S170-S171 100th Anniversary of Independence ovpt. on face. Back red, white and green (National colors).

S170 5 Pesos
1910. Black on brown and yellow unpt. Ovpt: *1810-CENTENARIO-1910* on face of #S163. Text around coin design at ctr. on back. Series T3. *(BK-CHI-90).*

	Good	Fine	XF
a. Issued note.	85.00	250.00	—
p. Proof.	—	Unc	750.00
s. Specimen.	—	Unc	750.00

S171 10 Pesos
1910. Black on orange unpt. Ovpt: *1810-CENTENARIO-1910* on face on #S164. Commemorative text around coin design at ctr. on back. *(BK-CHI-98).*

	Good	Fine	XF
a. Issued note.	75.00	200.00	500.00
p. Proof.	—	Unc	750.00
s. Specimen. Series U3; V3.	—	Unc	750.00

Banco Minero Chihuahuense

Later became Banco Minero de Chihuahua.

1880-87 Issue

#S172-S176 printer: ABNC.

S172 25 Centavos
1880. Black on salmon unpt. Miners working at l. Back deep blue. Series A.

	Good	Fine	XF
a. *(BK-CHI-52).* 1880.	30.00	75.00	150.00
b. Ovpt: 1882. *(BK-CHI-52a).*	60.00	150.00	—
c. Ovpt: 1883. *(BK-CHI-52a).*	—	—	—
d. Ovpt: *BATOPILAS.* (4 different varieties known). 1880. *(BK-CHI-53).*	70.00	150.00	—
e. Ovpt: *ADMOR. GRAL. DE RENTAS, 1880* w/additional sign.	125.00	—	—
p. 1880. Proof.	—	Unc	250.00
s. 1880. Specimen.	—	Unc	250.00

		Good	Fine	XF
S173	**50 Centavos** 1880-ca.1887. Black on orange unpt. Minerva (Goddess of Science, Art and War) at ctr. Back brown.			
	a. Series A. 1880. *(BK-CHI-57).*	75.00	200.00	350.00
	b. Ovpt: 1882.	—	—	—
	p1. Proof. Series A. 1880.	—	Unc	300.00
	p2. Proof. Series B. 1880 (ca.1887).	—	Unc	250.00
	s1. Specimen. Series A. 1880.	—	Unc	300.00
	s2. Specimen. Series B. 1880.	—	Unc	250.00
S174	**1 Peso** 1880. Black on green unpt. Symbolic figure of Fertility at ctr. Back green. Series A.			
	a. Handwritten sign. 1880. *(BK-CHI-60).*	70.00	150.00	250.00
	b. Red ovpt: *1882/1880.* Printed sign. *(BK-CHI-61).*	70.00	150.00	250.00

	Good	Fine	XF
c. Red vertical ovpt: *VALE POR PESOS FUERTES A LA PAR* twice on face. *(BK-CHI-).*	120.00	250.00	—

	Good	Fine	XF
d. Red vertical ovpt. similar to c. Lg. text: *VALE PESOS FUERTES A LA PAR* added across face. *(BK-CHI-63.)*	120.00	250.00	—
p. Proof.	—	—	350.00
r. Unsigned remainder. *(BK-CHI-62).*	75.00	150.00	250.00
s. Specimen.	—	Unc	350.00

		Good	Fine	XF
S175	**1 Peso** 1880; 1882. Black on tan unpt. Like #S174. Back brown. Series A. Red ovpt: *VALE POR PESOS FUERTES A LA PAR* across face. *(BK-CHI-64).*			
	a. 1880.	120.00	250.00	450.00
	b. 1882/1880.	—	—	—
	p. Proof. 1880.	—	Unc	450.00
	s. Specimen. 1880.	—	Unc	450.00
S176	**1 Peso** 1880. Black on pink unpt. Like #S174. Back red-orange. Series B. *(BK-CHI-65).*			
	a. Issued note.	200.00	500.00	1000.
	p. Proof.	—	Unc	750.00
	s. Specimen.	—	Unc	750.00
S180	**5 Centavos** 1884. Black. *APRIL 16, 1884* in inked seal. *(BK-CHI-49).*	50.00	100.00	175.00
S181	**10 Centavos** 1884. *April 15, 1884* in inked seal. Value: *DIEZ CENTAVOS* in thin letters. *(BK-CHI-50).*	60.00	120.00	200.00

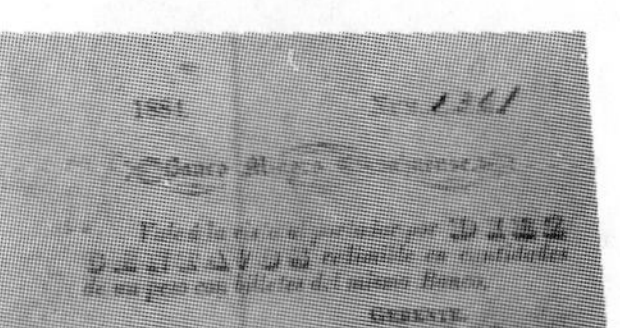

		Good	Fine	XF
S182	**10 Centavos** 1884. *April 15, 1884* in inked seal. *DIEZ CENTAVOS* in thick letters. *(BK-CHI-51).*	60.00	120.00	200.00

Banco Minero de Chihuahua

1914 Issue

		Good	Fine	XF
S183	**50 Centavos** 1914. Black on green-yellow unpt. W/o pictorial design. Back brown. Printer: Eduardo I. Aguilar. *(BK-CHI-121).*	150.00	300.00	450.00

		Good	Fine	XF
S184	**2 Pesos** 7.2.1914-5.9.1914. Black on pink unpt. Mining scene at ctr. Back red; Minero Bank at ctr. Printer: AB&PC. *(BK-CHI-122).*	3.00	10.00	30.00

		Good	Fine	XF
S185	**5 Pesos** 19.5.1914-9.6.1914. Black on tan unpt. Euthenia (Goddess of Plenty) by beehive at l., portr. young woman at top ctr r. Back brown; national arms at ctr. Printer: B&S. *(BK-CHI-123).*	3.00	10.00	30.00

		Good	Fine	XF
S186	**10 Pesos** 9.5.1914-24.6.1914. Black on green unpt. Polyhymnia (Muse of Lyrical Poetry) at r. Back green; national arms at ctr. Printer: B&S. *(BK-CHI-124).*	3.00	10.00	25.00

Banco de Santa Eulalia

1875-84 Issue

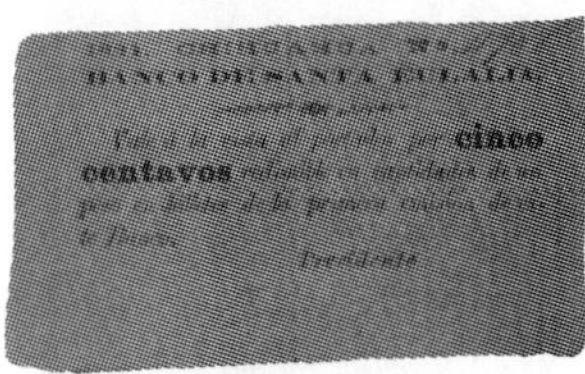
#S187

#S188

S187 5 Centavos
1884. *(BK-CHI-12).*

	Good	Fine	XF
1884. *(BK-CHI-12).*	50.00	100.00	175.00

S188 10 Centavos

	Good	Fine	XF
1884. *(BK-CHI-13).*	75.00	180.00	250.00

#S189-S193 printer: ABNC.

S189 25 Centavos
1875 (ca.1875-82). Black on pale-orange unpt. Woman's head at lower l. and r., steam locomotive at ctr. Back brown.

	Good	Fine	XF
a. Series A; B. *(BK-CHI-14).*	60.00	200.00	400.00
p. Proof. Series A.	—	Unc	300.00
s. Specimen. Series A.	—	Unc	300.00

S190 50 Centavos
1875 (ca.1875-82). Black on orange unpt. Man w/wool pack at l., miners at r. Back orange.

	Good	Fine	XF
a. Series A; B. *(BK-CHI-16).*	60.00	200.00	400.00
p. Proof. Series A.	—	Unc	400.00
s. Specimen. Series A.	—	Unc	400.00

NOTE: For #S189 and S190, on Series A the sign. on the r. is handsigned; for Series B, the sign. on the r. is printed.

S191 1 Peso
1875 (ca.1875-82). Black on tan and green unpt. Herdsman at l., train at r. Back tan.

	Good	Fine	XF
a. Series A; B. *(BK-CHI-18).*	150.00	400.00	700.00
p. Proof. Series A.	—	Unc	500.00
s. Specimen. Series A.	—	Unc	500.00

S192 5 Pesos
1882. Black on orange unpt. Helmeted allegorical man representing "Electricity" and allegorical woman w/wings at ctr. Back green; five 8 reales coins at ctr. Series C.

	Good	Fine	XF
p. Proof. Series A.	—	—	—
s. Specimen. Series A.	—	—	—

S193 10 Pesos
1882-83. Black on pink unpt. Euthenia (Goddess of Plenty) at l., cherub at r. Back blue; ten 8 reales coins, 5 at l., 5 at r.

	Good	Fine	XF
a. Series C. *(BK-CHI-20).*	1500.	—	—
p. Proof. Series C.	—	Unc	500.00

NOTE: The following text was prepared as an ovpt. on #S189-S193 ca.1884-86: *BANCO DE SANTA EULALIA PAGARÁ A LA VISTA EL VALOR DE ESTE BILLETE EN PLATA A LA PAR. 1884.* This ovpt. was made in two styles: the first in black, the second in blue. No examples are known.

Coahuila

Banco de Coahuila

1898-1914 Issue

#S195-S201 portr. Arizpe at l., portr. Cepeda at r. Printer: ABNC.

S195 5 Pesos
1898-1914. Black on lt. green unpt. Ceres (Goddess of Agriculture) at l. Back green; allegorical woman representing Commerce at ctr.

	Good	Fine	XF
a. Series E. 15.1.1898; 16.5.1898.	20.00	50.00	—
b. Series E. 5.3.1900-5.5.1912.	10.00	25.00	65.00
c. Series E. 15.2.1914. *(BK-COA-5).*	8.00	15.00	55.00
p. Proof. W/o series. ND.	—	Unc	100.00
s. Specimen. W/o series. ND.	—	Unc	100.00

S196 10 Pesos
1898-1914. Black on tan unpt. Woman representing Work at r. Back brown; cowboy herding cattle at ctr.

	Good	Fine	XF
a. Series S. 3.3.1898; 16.5.1898; 5.5.1902. *(BK-COA-8).*	20.00	50.00	—
b. Series S. 5.3.1900; 15.11.1900; 15.9.1909. *(BK-COA-9).*	15.00	35.00	80.00
c. Series S. 15.2.1914. *(BK-COA-10).*	10.00	20.00	70.00
d. Ovpt: *Torreon.* Series S. 3.3.1898.	30.00	70.00	—
p. Proof. W/o series. ND.	—	Unc	100.00
s. Specimen. W/o series. ND.	—	Unc	100.00

S197 20 Pesos
1898-1914. Black on orange unpt. Woman representing Wisdom at l., sheep at r. Back orange; sheep and country landscape at ctr., train by station at ctr.

	Good	Fine	XF
a. Series C. 3.3.1898; 16.5.1898. *(BK-COA-15).*	50.00	100.00	—
b. Series C. 5.3.1900; 15.11.900. *(BK-COA-17).*	35.00	70.00	—
c. Series C. 15.9.1909; 7.6.1910; 5.2.1914. *(BK-COA-17).*	25.00	50.00	100.00
d. Ovpt: *Torreon.* Series C. 3.3.1898. *(BK-COA-18).*	60.00	120.00	—
p. Proof. W/o series. ND.	—	Unc	150.00
s. Specimen. W/o series. ND.	—	Unc	150.00

		GOOD	FINE	XF
S198	**50 PESOS** 1898-1914. Black on green unpt. Standing Minerva w/shield at r. Back blue; steam passenger train by station at ctr.			
	a. Series R. 3.3.1898; 16.5.1898;5.3.1900. *(BK-COA-20).*	125.00	250.00	—
	b. Series R. 7.6.1910; 5.5.1912; 5.2.1914; w/2 sign. varieties. *(BK-COA-21).*	100.00	200.00	350.00
	c. Ovpt: *Torreon.* Series R. 3.3.1898.*(BK-COA-22).*	150.00	300.00	—
	p. W/o series. ND. Proof.	—	Unc	250.00
	s. W/o series. ND. Specimen.	—	Unc	250.00
S199	**100 PESOS** 1898-1914. Black on orange and yellow unpt. Filia (Goddess of Friendship) at r. Back orange; woman at ctr.			
	a. Series I. 3.2.1898. *(BK-COA-24).*	350.00	700.00	—
	b. Series I. 5.3.1900; 15.9.1909. *(BK-COA-25).*	300.00	550.00	—
	c. Series I. 7.6.1910; 5.5.1912. *(BK-COA-26).*	300.00	500.00	1000.
	p. Proof. W/o series. ND.	—	Unc	500.00
	s. Specimen. W/o series. ND.	—	Unc	500.00

NOTE: For #S195-S199, reports of specific dates from 1898-1914 are needed to augment these listings.

		GOOD	FINE	XF
S200	**500 PESOS** 1897-98. Black on olive-green and yellow unpt. Woman w/basket on head at l., palm tree at r. Back olive-green; Minerva (Goddess of Science, Art and War) at l., woman at r.			
	a. Series T-1. 16.5.1898. *(BK-COA-28).*	2000.	3000.	—
	b. Ovpt: *Torreon.* Series T. 3.2.1898. *(BK-COA-29).*	2000.	3000.	—
	p. Proof. W/o series. ND.	—	—	—
	s. Specimen. W/o series. ND.	—	—	—
S201	**1000 PESOS** 1897-98. Black on purple and yellow unpt. Art and Literature at r. Back purple; sheep and cattle. *(BK-COA-31).*			
	p. Proof. W/o series. ND.	—	—	—
	s. Specimen. W/o series. ND.	—	—	—

#S202-S203 portr. Arizpe at l., portr. Cepeda at r. Printer: AB&PC.

S202	**1 PESO** 2.4.1914; 15.7.1914. Black on green unpt. Back green; Coahuila Bank at ctr. Series U. *(BK-COA-1).*	8.00	25.00	70.00

		GOOD	FINE	XF
S203	**2 PESOS** 2.4.1914; 14.7.1914. Black on orange unpt. Back red; Coahuila Bank at ctr. Series N. *(BK-COA-2).*	5.00	20.00	65.00

		GOOD	FINE	XF
S204	**10 PESOS** 15.2.1914; 1.5.1914. Black on lt. green unpt. Polyhymnia (Muse of Lyrical Poetry) at r. Back olive-green; national arms at ctr. Printer: B & S. Series S. *(BK-COA-13).*	4.00	10.00	30.00

DISTRITO FEDERAL - MÉXICO CITY

BANCO DE EMPLEADOS

1800'S ISSUE

#S204A-S204F various vignettes at l. and r. Printer: BWC. (Not issued).

		GOOD	FINE	XF
S204A	**5 PESOS FUERTES** 18xx. Portr. woman at l., national arms at r. Specimen.	—	—	—
S204B	**10 PESOS FUERTES** 18xx. National arms at l., woman at r. Specimen.	—	—	—

		GOOD	FINE	XF
S204C	**20 PESOS FUERTES** 18xx. Portr. woman at l. and r., national arms at upper ctr. Specimen.	—	—	—
S204D	**50 PESOS FUERTES** 18xx. Boy kneeling at bookcase at l., national arms at r. Specimen.	—	—	—

		GOOD	FINE	XF
S204E	**100 PESOS FUERTES** 18xx. Palace at l., portr. woman at r., national arms at upper ctr. Specimen.	—	—	—

		GOOD	FINE	XF
S204F	**500 PESOS FUERTES** 18xx. Boy kneeling at bookcase at l., palace at r., national arms at upper ctr. Specimen.	—	—	—

BANCO INDUSTRIAL DE MÉXICO, SOCIEDAD ANÓNIMA

1898 ISSUE

#S205 and S206 maritime Progress and Industry at l.

		GOOD	FINE	XF
S205	**50 CENTAVOS** 6.3.1898. *(BK-DF-379).*	250.00	400.00	650.00

		GOOD	FINE	XF
S206	**100 CENTAVOS** 6.3.1898. *(BK-DF-380).*	—	Unc	1000.

BANCO INTERNACIONAL E HIPOTECARIO DE MÉXICO

1800'S ISSUE

#S207-S215 printer: ABNC. (Not issued).

		GOOD	FINE	XF
S207	**1 PESO** 18xx (ca.1889). Black on blue and yellow unpt. standing allegorical woman w/flags at l. ctr., portr. M. Lerdo de Tejada at r. Back blue; Indian at ctr. *(BK-DF-360).*			
	p. Proof.	—	Unc	500.00
	s. Specimen.	—	—	—

		GOOD	FINE	XF
S208	**2 PESOS** 18xx (ca.1889). Black on green and yellow unpt. Portr. 2 women at l., 2 children seated at r. Back brown; Indian at ctr. *(BK-DF-362).*			
	p. Proof.	—	—	—
	s. Specimen.	—	—	—

		GOOD	FINE	XF
S209	**5 PESOS** 18xx (ca.1889). Black on olive and yellow unpt. Standing woman at l., steam passenger train at ctr. Back olive; Aztec calendar superimposed on five 8 reales coins at ctr. *(BK-DF-364).*			
	p. Proof.	—	—	—
	s. Specimen.	—	Unc	500.00

		GOOD	FINE	XF
S210	**10 PESOS** 18xx (ca.1889). Black on brown and yellow unpt. Crop worker at l., portr. woman w/cherub supporters at r. Back green; steam passenger train at ctr. *(BK-DF-366).*			
	p. Proof.	—	—	—
	s. Specimen.	—	—	—

		GOOD	FINE	XF
S211	**20 PESOS** 18xx (ca.1889). Black on orange and yellow unpt. Child supporting shield w/value flanked by allegorical women at l. and r. at ctr. Back orange; woman w/sheep at ctr. *(BK-DF-368).*			
	p. Proof.	—	—	—
	s. Specimen.	—	—	—

		GOOD	FINE	XF
S212	**50 PESOS** 18xx (ca.1889). Black on brown and yellow unpt. Seated Indian w/bow and arrow at l., rural vista at ctr. r. Back brown; steer's head at ctr. *(BK-DF-370).*			
	p. Proof.	—	Unc	700.00
	s. Specimen.	—	—	—

		GOOD	FINE	XF
S213	**100 PESOS** 18xx (ca.1889). Black on blue and yellow unpt. Boy seated playing guitar on mule at l., 2 children seated at r. Back blue-black; cattle wading at ctr. *(BK-DF-372).*			
	p. Proof.	—	Unc	800.00
	s. Specimen.	—	—	—

S214 500 PESOS — GOOD | FINE | XF

18xx (ca.1889). Black on orange and yellow unpt. Fleet of ships at l., young man at r. Back black and orange; woman at l. *(BK-DF-374).*

	GOOD	FINE	XF
p. Proof.	—	Unc	1000.
s. Specimen.	—	—	—

S215 1000 PESOS — GOOD | FINE | XF

18xx (ca.1889). Black on green and yellow unpt. Cleo (Muse of History) at ctr. r. Back black and green; allegorical woman w/globe and child at ctr. *(BK-DF-375).*

	GOOD	FINE	XF
p. Proof. 18xx.	—	—	—
s. Specimen. 18xx.	—	—	—

1914 GOLD CERTIFICATE OF DEPOSIT ISSUE

S215A 1000 GRAMS — GOOD | FINE | XF

ND (ca.1914). Black on green and yellow unpt. National arms and seated Justice wearing crown and holding key at l. Back orange; bldg. at upper ctr. Series A. Printer: ABNC. Specimen. *(BKDF-378).* — — —

BANCO DE LONDRES MÉXICO Y SUD AMERICA

1867-78 ISSUE

S216 5 PESOS — GOOD | FINE | XF

15.11.1867. Pale orange unpt. Man on horseback at l., British crowned supported arms at upper ctr., Cathedral of Mexico at r. Uniface. *(BK-DF-1).* — — —

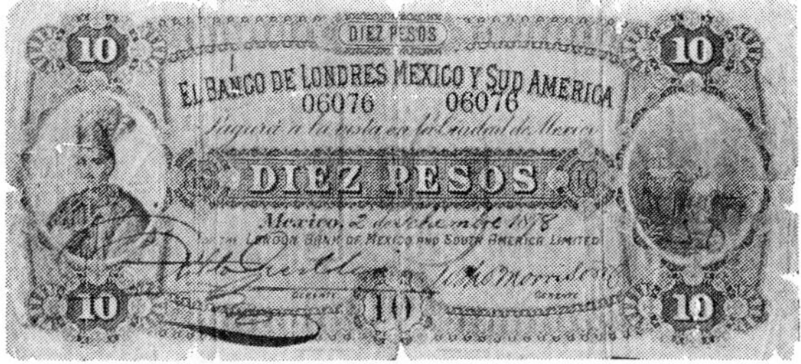

S217 10 PESOS — GOOD | FINE | XF

2.9.1878. Portr. Montezuma at l., donkey w/cart at r. Printer: BWC. *(BK-DF-2).* 5000. — —

1800'S TEXT VARIETIES ISSUES

Type I: No branch name engraved.

Type II: Payable at Distrito Federal.

#S220-S223B printer: ABNC.

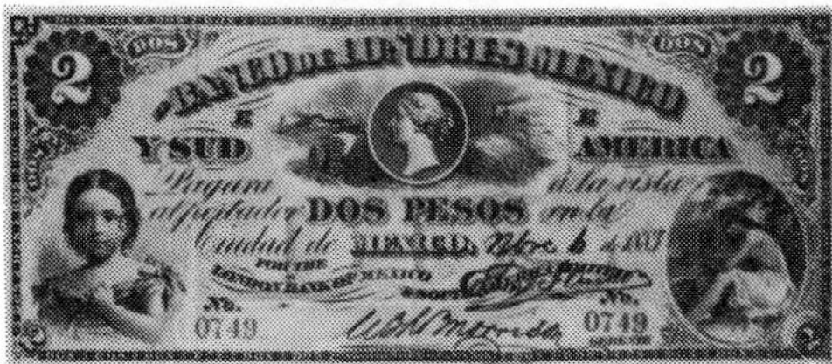

S220 2 PESOS — GOOD | FINE | XF

6.11.1883. Black on green and orange unpt. Young girl at lower l., Portr. Qn. Victoria at upper ctr., woman w/child at lower r. Back blue. Series A-F. Text Type II. *(BK-DF-3).* 1800. 3000. 5000.

#S221-S223B man w/boy and horses at upper ctr. on face.

S221 20 PESOS — GOOD | FINE | XF

18xx (ca.1868-81). Education at upper l., men w/telescope at lower r. Text Type II. *(BK-DF-5).*

	GOOD	FINE	XF
p1. Proof. 18xx (ca.1868). Black on blue unpt. Series A.	—	Unc	2500.

	GOOD	FINE	XF
p2. Proof. 18xx (ca.1874-81). Black on blue and brown unpt. Back blue. Series B.	—	Unc	2500.
s. Specimen. Series B.	—	—	—

S222 50 PESOS — GOOD | FINE | XF

18xx (ca.1868-81). Young sailor at lower l., woman kneeling at lower r. Text Type II. Series A. *(BK-DF-6).*

	GOOD	FINE	XF
p1. Proof. 18xx (ca.1868). Black on brown unpt.	—	Unc	3000.
p2. Proof. 18xx (ca.1874-81). Black on brown and blue unpt. Back blue.	—	Unc	3000.
s. Specimen.	—	—	—

S223 100 PESOS — GOOD | FINE | XF

18xx (ca.1866-81). Girl w/dog at lower l., seated allegorical woman w/cherub at lower r. Back blue. Series A. *(BK-DF-7).*

	GOOD	FINE	XF
p1. Proof. 18xx (ca.1866). Black on green unpt. Text Type I.	—	Unc	3000.
p2. Proof. 18xx (ca.1868-81). Black on green and orange unpt. Text Type II.	—	Unc	3000.
s. Specimen.	—	—	—

	GOOD	FINE	XF
S223A 500 PESOS 18xx (ca.1866-79). Anchor at lower l., chickens at lower r. Back blue. Series A.			
p1. Proof. 18xx (ca.1866). Black on green unpt. Text Type I.	—	Unc	4000.
p2. Proof. 18xx (ca.1868-79). Black on green and orange unpt. Text Type II.	—	Unc	4000.
s. Specimen.	—	—	—

	GOOD	FINE	XF
S223B 1000 PESOS 18xx (ca.1866-75). Two women at l., woman w/fruit at r. Back blue. Series A.			
p1. Proof. 18xx (ca.1866). Black on green unpt. Text Type I.	—	—	—
p2. Proof. 18xx (ca.1868-75). Black on green and orange unpt. Text Type II.	—	—	—

#S224-S230 portr. B. Juárez at l., national arms at upper ctr. Printer: BWC.

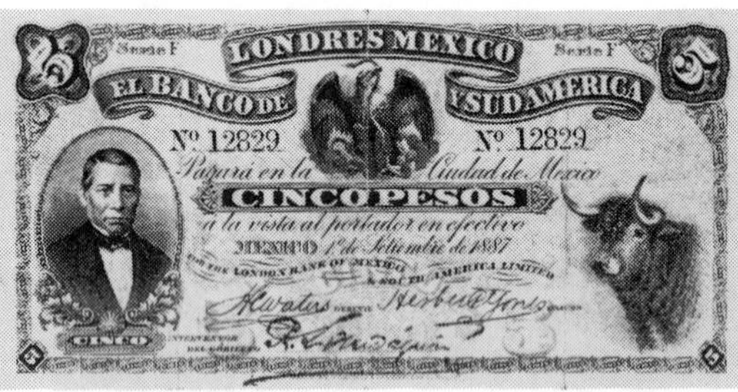

	GOOD	FINE	XF
S224 5 PESOS 1887-89. Black on green unpt. Bull's head at lower r. Back green; bldg. and landscape at ctr.			
a. Series F. 1.9.1887. *(BK-DF-9).*	3000.	4000.	—
b. Ovpt: *Puebla.* Series F. 1.2.1889. *(BK-DF-10).*	3000.	4000.	—
c. Ovpt: *Veracruz.* Series F. 1.9.1887. *(BK-DF-11).*	3000.	4000.	—

	GOOD	FINE	XF
S225 10 PESOS 1.5.1889. Horse at r. Ovpt: *GUANAJUATO.* Series E. *(BK-DF-13).*	—	5000.	—

	GOOD	FINE	XF
S226 10 PESOS 18xx. Woman w/bunch of grapes at lower r. Series E. Proof. *(BK-DF-14).*	—	Unc	1100.

	GOOD	FINE	XF
S227 20 PESOS 1887. Black on pale blue unpt. Dog's head at lower r. Back blue; bldg. and landscape at ctr.			
a. Series D. 1.9.1887. *(BK-DF-15).*	3500.	4500.	—
b. Ovpt: *Puebla.* Series D. 1.9.1887. *(BK-DF-16).*	3500.	4500.	—

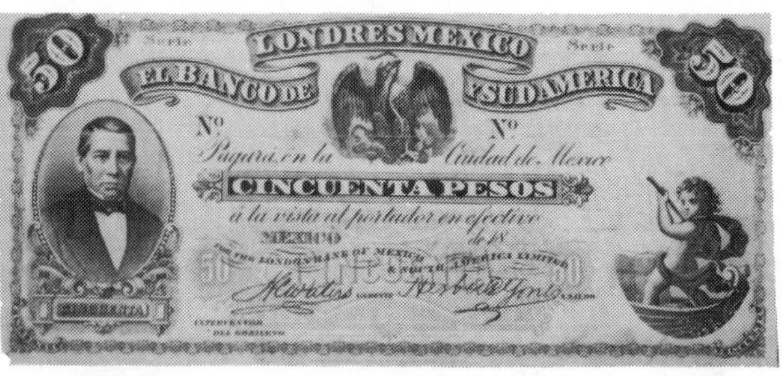

	GOOD	FINE	XF
S228 50 PESOS 18xx. Young boy in boat at r. Series C. Proof. *(BK-DF-17).*	—	Unc	1600.
S229 100 PESOS 18xx. 3 children at r. Series B. Proof. *(BK-DF-18).*	—	Unc	1600.

	GOOD	FINE	XF
S230 500 PESOS 18xx. Mercury seated at r. Back dk. green; palace and landscape at ctr. Series A. *(BK-DF-19).*			
p1. Face proof.	—	Unc	1500.
p2. Back proof ovpt: *SPECIMEN.*	—	Unc	1000.

BANCO DE LONDRES Y MÉXICO

1889-1914 ISSUE

#S233-S237 national arms on back.

#S233-S239 printer: ABNC.

	GOOD	FINE	XF
S232 1 PESO ND. W/o pictorial design. Proof.	—	—	—

	GOOD	FINE	XF
S233 5 PESOS 1889-1913. Black on green and yellow unpt. Portr. B. Juárez at l., Chastity at r. Back green.			
a. Center sign. title: *Cajero.* Series A. 9.1.1891; 15.5.1893. *(BK-DF-25).*	15.00	40.00	—
b. Center sign. title: *Consejero* Series B. 2.1.1894-2.7.1897. *(BK-DF-26).*	5.00	10.00	—
c. Series C. 1.1.1902; D. 1.5.1906; E. 1.7.1909. *(BK-DF-27).*	2.50	6.00	20.00
d. Series E. 1.7.1910; F. 2.1.1912; G. 2.1.1913; H. 1.10.1913; I. 1.10.1913. *(BK-DF-28).*	2.50	6.00	20.00
e. Ovpt: *AGUASCALIENTES.* 1.5.1906; 1.7.1910. *(BK-DF-31).*	6.00	12.00	—
f. Ovpt: *DURANGO.* 1.1.1902; 1.5.1906; 1.7.1910. *(DK-DF-32).*	10.00	20.00	—
g. Ovpt: *GUADALAJARA.* 1.5.1906; 2.1.1912; 2.1.1913. *(BK-DF-33).*	6.00	12.00	25.00
h. Ovpt: *GUADALAJARA* and *COCULA.* 1.5.1906. *(BK-DF-34).*	15.00	25.00	—
i. Ovpt: *GUANAJUATO.* 1.7.1897; 1.7.1909; 1.7.1910. *(BK-DF-35).*	8.00	15.00	—

		Good	Fine	XF
j.	Ovpt: *LERDO.* 1.7.1897. *(BK-DF-36).*	10.00	20.00	—
k.	Ovpt: *MAZATLÁN.* 1.7.1897; 1.5.1906. *(BK-DF-37).*	10.00	20.00	—
l.	Ovpt: *MONTERREY.* 1.7.1897; 1.5.1906; 2.1.1912. *(BK-DF-38).*	8.00	15.00	35.00
m.	Ovpt: *MORELIA.* 1.7.1897; 1.7.1909; 1.7.1910. *(BK-DF-39).*	6.00	12.00	—
n.	Ovpt: *PUEBLA.* 1.7.1889 (printed date). (BK-DF-40).	30.00	60.00	90.00
o.	Ovpt: *PUEBLA.* 1.7.1897. *(BK-DF-41).*	6.00	12.00	—
p.	Ovpt: *QUERÉTARO.* 15.5.1893-2.1.1913. *(BK-DF-42).*	6.00	12.00	25.00
q.	Ovpt: *SAN LUIS POTOSÍ.* 1.9.1894-2.1.1913. *(BK-DF-43).*	6.00	12.00	25.00
r.	Ovpt: *TORREÓN.* 1.1.1902-1.7.1910. *(BK-DF-44).*	8.00	15.00	35.00
s.	Ovpt: *VERACRUZ.* 16.6.189x-2.1.1913. *(BK-DF-45).*	6.00	12.00	25.00
p.	Proof. Series A. 189x.	—	Unc	100.00
s.	Specimen. Series A. 1.7.1889.	—	Unc	100.00

S234 10 PESOS
1889-1913. Black on brown and yellow unpt. Portr. B. Juárez at l., miners at ctr. and at r. Back dk. brown.

		Good	Fine	XF
a.	Center sign. title: *Cajero.* Series A. 1.7.1889. (printed date). *(BK-DF-46).*	25.00	50.00	—
b.	Series A. 1.9.1891-22.2.1897. *(BK-DF-47).*	10.00	20.00	—
c.	Center sign. title: *Consejero.* Series B. 1.7.1897. *(BK-DF-48).*	3.00	8.00	25.00
d.	Series C. 1.1.1902; D. 1.5.1906; E. 1.7.1909; 1.7.1910; F. 2.1.1912. *(BK-DF-49).*	2.50	6.00	20.00
e.	Series G. 2.1.1913; H. 1.10.1913; I. 1.10.1913. *(BK-DF-50).*	2.50	6.00	20.00
f.	Ovpt: *AGUASCALIENTES.* 1.1.1902; 1.5.1906; 1.7.1910. *(BK-DF-52).*	6.00	12.00	—
g.	Ovpt: *DURANGO.* 1.1.1902; 1.5.1906; 1.7.1910. *(BK-DF-53).*	6.00	12.00	25.00
h.	Ovpt: *GUADALAJARA.* 1.7.1889.	20.00	50.00	—
i.	Ovpt: *GUADALAJARA.* 1.1.1902; 2.1.1912; 2.1.1913. *(BK-DF-55).*	8.00	15.00	—
j.	Ovpt: *GUANAJUATO.* 1.7.1897-1.7.1910. *(BK-DF-56).*	8.00	15.00	—
k.	Ovpt: *LERDO.* 1.7.1897. *(BK-DF-57).*	10.00	20.00	—
l.	Ovpt: *MAZATLÁN.* 1.7.1897. *(BK-DF-58).*	10.00	20.00	—
m.	Ovpt: *MONTERREY.* 1.7.1897; 1.1.1902; 2.1.1912. *(BK-DF-59).*	8.00	15.00	—
n.	Ovpt: *MORELIA.* 1.7.1897; 1.7.1909; 1.7.1910. *(BK-DF-60).*	6.00	12.00	—
o.	Ovpt: *PUEBLA.* 1.7.1889. *(BK-DF-61).*	30.00	60.00	—
p.	Ovpt: *PUEBLA.* 1.7.1897. *(BK-DF-62).*	6.00	12.00	—
q.	Ovpt: *QUERÉTARO.* 1.7.1897-1.7.1910. *(BK-DF-63).*	6.00	12.00	—
r.	Ovpt: *SAN LUIS POTOSÍ. 1.9.1897; 1.9.1891; 1.1.1902; 2.1.1912; 2.1.1913. (BK-DF-64).*	6.00	12.00	25.00
s.	Ovpt: *TORREÓN.* 1.7.1897; 1.9.1891; 1.1.1902; 1.7.1909; 1.7.1910. *(BK-DF-65).*	8.00	15.00	—
t.	Ovpt: *VERACRUZ.* 1.7.1889. *(BK-DF-66.)*	25.00	50.00	—
u.	Ovpt: *VERACRUZ.* 1.1.1902; 2.1.1912; 2.1.1913. *(BK-DF-67).*	12.00	25.00	50.00
p.	Proof. Series A. 189x.	—	Unc	125.00
s.	Specimen. Series A. 1.7.1889.	—	Unc	125.00

S235 20 PESOS
1889-1913. Black on orange-brown and yellow unpt. Portr. B. Juárez at l., Friar Bartolome de las Casas at ctr. Back brown.

		Good	Fine	XF
a.	Center sign. title: *Cajero.* Series A. 1.7.1889 (printed date); 1.9.1891; 2.1.1894. *(BK-DF-68).*	15.00	40.00	—
b.	Series A. 1.9.1891-22.2.1897. *(BK-DF-69).*	10.00	20.00	—
c.	Center sign. title: *Consejero.* Series B. 1.7.1897; C. 1.1.1902. *(BK-DF-70).*	5.00	10.00	—
d.	Series D. 1.7.1910; E. 2.1.1913; F. 2.1.1913; G. 1.10.1913; H. 1.10.1913. *(BK-DF-71).*	5.00	10.00	25.00
e.	Ovpt: *AGUASCALIENTES.* 1.1.1902. *(BK-DF-73).*	20.00	40.00	—
f.	Ovpt: *COCULA.* 1.1.1902. *(BK-DF-74).*	20.00	40.00	—
g.	Ovpt: *DURANGO.* 1.1.1902; 1.7.1910. *(BK-DF-75).*	20.00	40.00	—
h.	Ovpt: *GUADALAJARA.* 1.7..1897; 2.1.1912; 2.1.1913. *(BK-DF-76).*	15.00	30.00	—
i.	Ovpt: *GUANAJUATO.* 1.7.1889; 1.7.1897; 1.7.1910. *(BK-DF-77).*	20.00	40.00	—
j.	Ovpt: *LERDO.* 1.7.1897. *(BK-DF-78).*	20.00	40.00	—
k.	Ovpt: *MAZATLAN.* 1.7.1897. *(BK-DF-79).*	20.00	40.00	—
l.	Ovpt: *MONTERREY.* 1.7.1897; 2.1.1912. *(BK-DF-80).*	20.00	40.00	—
m.	Ovpt: *MORELIA.* 1.7.1897; 1.7.1910. *(BK-DF-81).*	20.00	40.00	—
n.	Ovpt: *PUEBLA.* 1.7.1897; 1.7.1889. *(BK-DF-82).*	15.00	30.00	60.00
o.	Ovpt: *QUERÉTARO.* 1.7.1897; 1.7.1910. *(BK-DF-83).*	20.00	40.00	—
p.	Ovpt: *SAN LUIS POTOSÍ.* 1.7.1897; 1.9.1891; x.1.1893 - hand-written date; 1.7.1910; 2.1.1912. *(BK-DF-84).*	15.00	30.00	60.00
q.	Ovpt: *TORREÓN.* 1.1.1902; 1.7.1910. *(BK-DF-85).*	20.00	40.00	—
r.	Ovpt: *VERACRUZ.* 9.1.1891. *(BK-DF-86).*	20.00	40.00	—
p.	Proof. Series A. 189x.	—	Unc	125.00
s.	Specimen. Series A. 1.7.1889.	—	Unc	125.00

S236 50 PESOS
1889-1913. Black on blue and yellow unpt. Portr. B. Juárez at l., cowboy w/longhorns at r. Back blue.

		Good	Fine	XF
a.	Center sign. title: *Cajero.* Series A. 1.7.1889 (printed date). *(BK-DF-87).*	70.00	125.00	—
b.	Series A. 1.9.1891-22.2.1897. *(BK-DF-88).*	30.00	50.00	—
c.	Center sign. title: *Consejero.* Series B. 1.7.1897. *(BK-DF-89).*	25.00	50.00	—
d.	Series C. 1.1.1902. *(BK-DF-90).*	25.00	50.00	—
e.	Series D. 1.7.1910; E. 2.1.1912. *(BK-DF-91).*	25.00	50.00	—
f.	Series F. 2.1.1913; G. 1.10.1913.	20.00	35.00	70.00
g.	Series H. 1.10.1913. *(BK-DF-93).*	20.00	35.00	70.00
h.	Ovpt: *AGUASCALIENTES.* 1.1.1902. *(BK-DF-95).*	40.00	70.00	—
i.	Ovpt: *DURANGO.* 1.1.1902. *(BK-DF-96).*	30.00	50.00	—
j.	Ovpt: *GUADALAJARA.* 1.9.1891; 1.7.1897; 2.1.1912. *(BK-DF-97).*	40.00	70.00	—
k.	Ovpt: *GUANAJUATO.* 1.7.1889; 1.7.1897. *(BK-DF-98).*	40.00	70.00	—
l.	Ovpt: *LERDO.* 1.7.1897. *(BK-DF-99).*	50.00	100.00	—
m.	Ovpt: *MONTERREY.* 1.7.1897. *(BK-DF-100).*	40.00	70.00	—
n.	Ovpt: *MORELIA.* 1.7.1897. *(BK-DF-101).*	40.00	70.00	—
o.	Ovpt: *PUEBLA.* 1.7.1889; 1.7.1897; 2.7.1897. *(BK-DF-102).*	30.00	50.00	—
p.	Ovpt: *QUERÉTARO.* 1.7.1897; 1.7.1910. *(BK-DF-103).*	40.00	70.00	—
q.	Ovpt: *SAN LUIS POTOSÍ.* 9.1.1891-2.1.1912. *(BK-DF-104).*	30.00	50.00	100.00
r.	Ovpt: *TORREÓN.* 1.1.1902; 1.7.1910. *(BK-DF-105).*	40.00	70.00	120.00
s.	Ovpt: *MAZATLAN.* 3.8.1897.	40.00	70.00	—
p.	Proof. Series A. 189x.	—	Unc	200.00
s.	Specimen. Series A. 1.7.1889.	—	Unc	200.00

S237 100 PESOS
1889-1913. Black on orange and yellow unpt. Cattle at l., portr. B. Juárez at ctr., men w/horses at r. Back orange and black.

		Good	Fine	XF
a.	Center sign. title: *Cajero.* Series A. 1.7.1889 (printed date). *(BK-DF-106).*	70.00	150.00	—
b.	Series A. 1.9.1891; 19.9.1891; 1.8.1896. *(BK-DF-107).*	40.00	100.00	—
c.	Center sign. title: *Consejero.* Series B. 1.7.1897. *(BK-DF-108).*	30.00	80.00	—
d.	Series C. 1.1.1902; D. 1.7.1910; E. 2.1.1912. *(BK-DF-109).*	25.00	70.00	—
e.	Series F. 2.1.1913; G. 1.10.1913; H. 1.10.1913. *(BK-DF-110).*	25.00	70.00	—
f.	Ovpt: *AGUASCALIENTES.* 1.1.1902. *(BK-DF-112).*	70.00	120.00	—
g.	Ovpt: *DURANGO.* 1.1.1902.	50.00	100.00	—
h.	Ovpt: *GUANAJUATO.* 1.7.1897. *(BK-DF-114).*	70.00	100.00	—
i.	Ovpt. and needle punched: *MAZATLAN.* 1.7.1897. *(BK-DF-115).*	70.00	100.00	—
j.	Ovpt: *MONTERREY.* 1.7.1897.	50.00	100.00	—
k.	Ovpt: *QUERÉTARO.* 1.7.1897.	50.00	120.00	—
l.	Ovpt: *SAN LUIS POTOSÍ.* 1.7.1897; 1.7.1910. *(BK-DF-118).*	50.00	100.00	175.00
m.	Ovpt: *TORREON.* Series C. 1.1.1902.	50.00	100.00	—
p.	Proof. Series A. 189x.	—	Unc	300.00
s.	Specimen. Series A. 1.7.1889.	—	Unc	300.00

S238 500 Pesos | Good | Fine | XF

1889-1913. Black on yellow and olive unpt. Pride of lions at ctr., portr. B. Juárez at r. Back olive-green; men walking horses at ctr.

	Good	Fine	XF
a. Center sign. title: *Consejero.* Series B. 1.7.1897; C. 10.1.1903; E. 1.7.1909; 1.10.1910; F. 1.5.1911; G. 1.10.1913; H. 19.10.1913. *(BK-DF-119).*	450.00	800.00	—
b. Ovpt: *DURANGO.* 10.1.1903. *(BK-DF-121).*	500.00	900.00	—
p. Proof. Center sign. title: *Cajero.* Series A. 189x.	—	Unc	500.00
s. Specimen. Series A. 1.7.1889.	—	Unc	500.00

S239 1000 Pesos

1889-1913. Black on orange and yellow unpt. Seated Wisdom at l. ctr., portr. B. Juárez at r. Back black and orange; train at ctr.

	Good	Fine	XF
a. Center sign title: *Consejero.* Series B. 1.7.1897; E. 1.7.1909; F. 1.5.1911; G. 1.10.1913. *(BK-DF-122).*	700.00	1000.	1750.
p. Proof. Center sign. title: *Cajero.* Series A. 189x.	—	Unc	1200.
s. Specimen. Series A. 1.7.1889.	—	Unc	1200.

#S240 and S241 printer: B&S.

	Good	Fine	XF
S240 1 Peso 14.2.1914. Black on orange unpt. Seated Justice and Peace at r. Back brown. *(BK-DF-20).*	3.00	8.00	30.00

	Good	Fine	XF
S241 2 Pesos 14.2.1914. Black on orange unpt. Seated Faith and Happiness at l. Back green. *(BK-DF-22).*	3.00	8.00	30.00

NOTE: For #S233-S239, reports of specific dates from 1889-1913 are needed to augment these listings. Series A.

Banco Mercantil Méxicano

1882 Text Varieties Issue

Type I: Payable at *CIUDAD DE MÉXICO*.

Type II: Payable at various branches w/*Ciudad de. . .* engraved.

#S242-S248 monument to C. Columbus on back. Printer: ABNC. Series A.

S242 1 Peso

1882. Black on salmon unpt. Standing Irene (Goddess of Peace) at l., Mercury at lower r. Back dk. green; 8 Reales coin at l. and r.

	Good	Fine	XF
a. 1.10.1882; 1.3.1883. Text Type I. *(BK-DF-131).*	1200.	2000.	—
b. Ovpt: *SAN LUIS POTOSÍ.* 1.6.1882; 1.12.1882. Text Type II. *(BK-DF-132).*	1200.	2000.	—
c. Ovpt: *VERACRUZ.* 1.3.1883; 1.7.1883. Text Type II. *(BK-DF-133).*	1200.	2000.	—
p. Proof.	—	Unc	1200.
s. Specimen.	—	Unc	1200.

S243 5 Pesos

1882. Black on orange unpt. Sailing ships at l., Raphael's Angel at ctr., woman w/spool at r. Back dk. green. *(BK-DF-134).*

	Good	Fine	XF
a. Ovpt: *QUERÉTARO.* 1.6.1882. Text Type II.	2500.	—	—
p. Proof.	—	Unc	1600.
s. Specimen.	—	Unc	1600.

S244 10 Pesos

1882. Black on green unpt. Anchor at l., allegorical woman w/sheaf and tools at r. Back red. *(BK-DF-136).*

	Good	Fine	XF
a. 1.6.1882. Text Type I.	2500.	—	—
p. Proof.	—	Unc	2000.
s. Specimen.	—	Unc	2000.

S245 20 Pesos

1882. Black on blue unpt. Portr. shepherdess w/sheep at l., allegorical woman w/marine implements at lower r. Back brown. *(BK-DF-137).*

	Good	Fine	XF
a. Ovpt: *GUANAJUATO.* 1.6.1882. Text Type II.	2500.	—	—
p. Proof.	—	Unc	2000.
s. Specimen.	—	Unc	2000.

		GOOD	FINE	XF
S246	**50 PESOS** 18xx. Black on orange unpt. Farm implements at upper l., sailing ship at ctr., seated Justice w/sword and flag at r. Back blue.			
	p. Proof. Series A.	—	Unc	2500.
	s. Specimen.	—	Unc	2500.

		GOOD	FINE	XF
S247	**100 PESOS** 18xx. Black on brown unpt. Reclining allegorical woman at l. ctr., woman writing at r. Back green.			
	p. Proof. Series A.	—	Unc	2500.
	s. Specimen.	—	Unc	2500.

		GOOD	FINE	XF
S247A	**500 PESOS** 18xx. Black on olive unpt. Indian woman holding plant at l., allegorical woman leaning on crate at r. Back red-brown.			
	p. Proof.	—	Unc	3000.
	s. Specimen.	—	Unc	3000.

		GOOD	FINE	XF
S248	**1000 PESOS** 18xx. Black on brown unpt. Steam train at l., woman holding pitcher at ctr., ships at r. Back orange. *(BK-DF-138).*			
	p. Proof.	—	Unc	3000.
	s. Specimen.	—	Unc	3000.

BANCO NACIONAL MEXICANO

1882 ISSUE

#S249-S253B printer: ABNC.

#S249-S251, S253-S253B reverse design of 8 reales coin on back.

#S249-S251 national arms at ctr. on face.

		GOOD	FINE	XF
S249	**1 PESO** 1882. Black on green unpt. Back blue.			
	a. 1.7.1882; 10.7.1882; 31.10.1882. *(BK-DF-124).*	1800.	4500.	—
	b. Ovpt. and needle punched: *SAN LUIS POTOSÍ.* 10.7.1882.	1800.	4500.	—
	c. Ovpt. and needle punched: *VERACRUZ.* 31.10.1882. *(BK-DF-125).*	1800.	4500.	—
	p. Proof.	—	Unc	2000.
	s. Specimen.	—	—	—
S250	**2 PESOS** 1882. Black on lt. green unpt. Back red-brown.			
	a. 1882. *(BK-DF-126).*	2000.	5000.	—
	b. Ovpt. and needle punched: *VERACRUZ.* 1882. *(BK-DF-126).*	2000.	5000.	—
	p. Proof.	—	Unc	2000.
	s. Specimen.	—	—	—
S251	**5 PESOS** 18xx. Black on lt. green unpt. Back orange.			
	p. Proof.	—	—	—
	s. Specimen.	—	—	—

#S252-S253B national arms at l.

		GOOD	FINE	XF
S252	**10 PESOS** 10.2.1882. Black on lt. brown unpt. Back green. *(BK-DF-128).*			
	a. Issued note.	2750.	5500.	—
	p. Proof.	—	—	—
	s. Specimen.	—	—	—
S252A	**20 PESOS** 18xx. Black on lt. brown unpt. Back dk. brown.			
	p. Proof.	—	—	—
	s. Specimen.	—	—	—
S252B	**50 PESOS** 18xx. Black on lt. brown unpt. Back orange.			
	p. Proof.	—	—	—
	s. Specimen.	—	—	—
S253	**100 PESOS** 23.2.1882. Black on gray unpt. Back brown.			
	a. Issued note.	3250.	6500.	—
	p. Proof.	—	—	—
	s. Specimen.	—	—	—
S253A	**500 PESO** 18xx. Black on gray unpt. Back red.			
	p. Proof.	—	—	—
	s. Specimen.	—	—	—

		GOOD	FINE	XF
S253B	**1000 PESOS** 18xx. Black on olive-brown unpt. National arms at l. Back blue.			
	p. Proof.	—	—	—
	s. Specimen.	—	—	—

BANCO NACIONAL DE MÉXICO

1885-1913 ISSUE

#S254-S263 printer: ABNC. Many city ovpt. are usually encountered with the same city name needle punched also.

		GOOD	FINE	XF
S254	**50 CENTAVOS** ND (ca.1914). Black on green unpt. C. Columbus in sight of land at l. Back brown; 50 centavos coin at l. and ctr. r. (Not issued). *(BK-DF-139).*			
	p. Proof.	—	Unc	500.00
	s. Specimen.	—	Unc	500.00

		Good	Fine	XF
S255	**1 Peso** 1885-1913. Black on green and yellow unpt. Portr. M. García Teruel at l., steam locomotive at ctr. Back green; 8 reales coin at l. and ctr. r.			
	a. 1.1.1885. *(BK-DF-141).*	70.00	225.00	—
	b. 6.12.1913. *(BK-DF-142).*	2.00	4.00	10.00
	c. Ovpt: *CHIHUAHUA.* 1.1.1885; 1.1.1888; 1.1.1889; 1.5.1889. *(BK-DF-144).*	20.00	50.00	100.00
	d. Ovpt: *CHIHUAHUA.* Ovpt. on back: *Pagadero en Mexicoo y en todas las Sucursales sin descuento.* 1.5.1889. *(BK-DF-145).*	12.00	30.00	70.00
	e. Ovpt: *DURANGO.* 1.12.1890. *(BK-DF-146).*	60.00	130.00	—
	f. Ovpt: *GUADALAJARA.* 1.1.1885. *(BK-DF-147).*	40.00	90.00	175.00
	g. Ovpt: *MONTERREY.* 1.12.1889; 1.8.1890. *(BK-DF-148).*	60.00	130.00	—
	h. Ovpt: *OAXACA.* 1.1.1888; 1.8.1890. *(BK-DF-149).*	60.00	130.00	—
	i. Ovpt: *SAN LUIS POTOSÍ.* 1.1.1885. *(BK-DF-150).*	35.00	80.00	—
	j. Ovpt: *VERACRUZ.* 1.1.1885; 1.1.1887. *(BK-DF-151).*	20.00	60.00	—
	k. Ovpt: *PAGADERO EN PUEBLA,* perforated: *PUEBLA.* 1.1.1885.	120.00	350.00	—
	p1. Proof. 188x.	—	Unc	250.00
	p2. Proof. ND.	—	Unc	75.00
	s1. Specimen. 188x.	—	Unc	250.00
	s2. Specimen. ND.	—	Unc	75.00

		Good	Fine	XF
S256	**2 Pesos** 1885-1913. Black on yellow and orange unpt. Portr. M. García Teruel at l., prospectors at r. Back orange; national arms at ctr.			
	a. 6.12.1913. *(BK-DF-152).*	3.50	10.00	25.00
	b. Ovpt: *CHIHUAHUA.* 1.1.1885. *(BK-DF-154).*	40.00	100.00	—
	c. Ovpt: *CHIHUAHUA* and needle punched: *E. CHIHUAHUA.* 1.1.1885. *(BK-DF-155).*	50.00	120.00	—
	d. Ovpt: *GUADALAJARA.* 1.1.1885. *(BK-DF-156).*	70.00	150.00	—
	e. Ovpt: *GUANAJUATO.* 1.1.1885. *(BK-DF-157).*	70.00	150.00	—
	f. Ovpt: *SAN LUIS POTOSÍ.* 1.1.1885. *(BK-DF-158).*	70.00	120.00	—
	g. Ovpt: *VERACRUZ.* 1.1.1885. *(BK-DF-159).*	50.00	120.00	—
	p1. Proof. 188x.	—	Unc	250.00
	p2. Proof. ND.	—	Unc	75.00
	s1. Specimen. 188x.	—	Unc	250.00
	s2. Specimen. ND.	—	Unc	75.00

		Good	Fine	XF
S257	**5 Pesos** 1885-1913. Black on yellow and brown unpt. Allegorical symbol of Study at l., portr. M. García Teruel at r. Back brown; C. Columbus discovering America at ctr.			
	a. 1.1.1885; 1.1.1888; 1.10.1889; 1.12.1890. *(BK-DF-160).*	20.00	60.00	—
	b. 1.8.1895; 8.8.1896; 26.7.1897. *(BK-DF-161).*	6.00	15.00	30.00
	c. 1.7.1901-6.12.1913. *(BK-DF-162).*	2.00	4.00	10.00
	d. Ovpt: *ACAPULCO.* 1.10.1906. *(BK-DF-166).*	15.00	30.00	—
	e. Ovpt: *AGUASCALIENTES.* 1.12.1902. *(BK-DF-167).*	10.00	20.00	40.00
	f. Ovpt: *AUTLÁN, JAL.* 1.8.1905. *(BK-DF-168).*	10.00	20.00	—
	g. Ovpt: *BRAVOS, Chilpancingo.* 1.12.1902. *(BK-DF-169).*	10.00	20.00	40.00
	h. Ovpt: *CAMPECHE.* 1.10.1906. *(BK-DF-170).*	8.00	15.00	30.00
	i. Ovpt: *CHIHUAHUA.* 1.4.1902. *(BK-DF-172).*	15.00	30.00	—
	j. Ovpt: *C. GUZMÁN, JAL.* 1.8.1905. *(BK-DF-171).*	10.00	20.00	—
	k. Ovpt: *C. JUÁREZ.* 1.8.1905. *(BK-DF-174).*	10.00	20.00	—
	l. Ovpt: *CIUDAD VICTORIA.* 1.8.1905. *(BK-DF-173).*	8.00	15.00	—
	m. Ovpt: *COLIMA.* 1.42.1902; 1.12.1902. *(BK-DF-175).*	12.50	25.00	—
	n. Ovpt: *CÓRDOBA.* 1.3.1910. *(BK-DF-176).*	6.00	15.00	30.00
	o. Ovpt: *CUERNAVACA.* 1.8.1905. *(BK-DF-17).*	12.00	20.00	40.00
	p. Ovpt: *DURANGO.* 1.4.1902. *(BK-DF-178).*	12.00	25.00	—
	q. Ovpt: *GUADALAJARA.* 1.4.1902. *(BK-DF-179).*	15.00	30.00	—
	r. Ovpt: *GUAYMAS.* 1.12.1902. *(BK-DF-180).*	10.00	20.00	—
	s. Ovpt: *HERMOSILLO, SON.* 1.10.1906. *(BK-DF-181).*	12.00	25.00	40.00
	t. Ovpt: *IRAPUATO.* 1.10.1906. *(BK-DF-182).*	10.00	20.00	—
	u. Ovpt: *LAGOS.* 1.7.1905; 1.8.1905. *(BK-DF-183).*	10.00	20.00	—
	v. Ovpt: *LA PIEDAD.* 1.8.1905. *(BK-DF-184).*	15.00	30.00	—
	w. Ovpt: *LERMA/PACHUCA.* ND. *(BK-DF-185).*	15.00	30.00	—
	x. Ovpt: *MATEHUALA.* 1.4.1902. *(BK-DF-186).*	12.00	25.00	—
	y. Ovpt: *MAZATLÁN.* 1.4.1902. *(BK-DF-187).*	12.00	25.00	—
	z. Ovpt: *MÉRIDA.* 1.4.1902. *(BK-DF-188).*	12.00	25.00	—
	aa. Ovpt: *MONCLOVA.* 1.8.1905.*(BK-DF-189).*	12.00	25.00	—
	ab. Ovpt: *MONTERREY.* and needle punched: 1.12.1890. *(BK-DF-190).*	12.00	25.00	—
	ac. Ovpt: *MONTERREY.* 1.4.1902. *(BK-DF-191).*	12.00	25.00	—
	ad. Ovpt: *MORELIA.* 1.12.1902. *(BK-DF-192).*	15.00	30.00	—
	ae. Ovpt: *PACHUCA..* 1.8.1905. *(BK-DF-1193).*	6.00	15.00	30.00
	af. Ovpt: *PUEBLA.* 1.4.1902. *(BK-DF-194).*	15.00	30.00	—
	ag. Ovpt: *PURUANDIRO.* 1.8.1905. *(BK-DF-195).*	10.00	20.00	—
	ah. Ovpt: *QUERÉTARO.* 1.7.1905; 1.8.1905; 1.10.1906. *(BK-DF-196).*	10.00	20.00	—
	ai. Ovpt: *RIOVERDE.* 1.8.1905. *(BK-DF-197).*	12.00	25.00	40.00
	aj. Ovpt: *S. ANDRÉS TUSTLA.* 1.8.1905. *(BK-DF-198).*	12.00	25.00	—
	ak. Ovpt: *SAN LUIS POTOSÍ.* 1.4.1902. *(BK-DF-199).*	10.00	20.00	35.00
	al. Ovpt: *SOMBRERETE.* 1.3.1910. *(BK-DF-200).*	12.00	25.00	40.00
	am.Ovpt: *TANTOYUCA.* 1.12.1902; 1.8.1905. *(BK-DF-201).*	12.00	25.00	40.00
	an. Ovpt: *TAPACHULA.* 1.1.1908. *(BK-DF-202).*	10.00	20.00	—
	ao. Ovpt: *TEHUACÁN.* 1.9.1909. *(BK-DF-203).*	15.00	40.00	—
	ap. Ovpt: *TEPIC.* 1.8.1905. *(BK-DF-204).*	15.00	40.00	—
	aq. Ovpt: *TEZIUTLÁN.* 1.12.1902; 1.7.1901. *(BK-DF-205).*	15.00	40.00	—
	ar. Ovpt: *TLALTENANGO.* 1.10.1906. *(BK-DF-206).*	12.00	25.00	—
	as. Ovpt: *TOLUCA.* 1.12.1902. *(BK-DF-207).*	8.00	18.00	—
	at. Ovpt: *TORREON.* 1.12.1902. *(BK-DF-208).*	15.00	30.00	—
	au. Ovpt: *TULANCINGO.* 1.10.1906. *(BK-DF-209).*	15.00	40.00	—
	av. Ovpt: *TUXLA GUTIÉRREZ.* 1.8.1905. *(BK-DF-210).*	10.00	20.00	—
	aw. Ovpt: *URUAPÁN MICH.* 1.8.1905. *(BK-DF-211).*	15.00	40.00	—
	ax. Ovpt: *VERACRUZ.* 1.4.1902. *(BK-DF-212).*	12.00	25.00	—
	ay. Ovpt: *XALAPA.* 1.8.1905. *(BK-DF-213).*	12.00	25.00	—
	az. Ovpt: *PAGADERO EN ZACATECAS.* 1.12.1890; 1.4.1902. *(BK-DF-214).*	10.00	20.00	—
	ba. Ovpt: *PAGADERO IN TAMPICO.* 1.4.1902.	15.00	30.00	—
	p1. Proof. 188x.	—	Unc	200.00
	p2. Proof. ND.	—	Unc	75.00
	r. ND. Remainder w/ovpt: *BILLETE SIN VALOR.* *(BK-DF0220).* 1.8.1905. *(BK-DF-164).*	—	Unc	10.00
	s1. Specimen. 188x; 189x.	—	Unc	200.00
	s2. Specimen. ND.	—	Unc	75.00

		Good	Fine	XF
S258	**10 Pesos** 1885-1913. Black on yellow and blue unpt. Portr. M. García Teruel at l. Euthenia (Goddess of Plenty) at ctr. r. Back blue; National Bank of Mexico at ctr.			
	a. 1.1.1885. *(BK-DF-215).*	35.00	70.00	—
	b. 1.12.1886; 1.1.1887; 1.1.1888. *(BK-DF-216).*	15.00	30.00	—
	c. 1.10.1889-26.7.1897. *BK-DF-217).*	4.00	15.00	50.00
	d. 1.7.1901-1.1.1908. *(BK-DF-218).*	2.50	6.00	25.00
	e. 1.9.1909-6.12.1913. *(BK-DF-219).*	2.50	6.00	25.00
	f. Ovpt: *ACAPULCO.* 1.10.1906. *(BK-DF-222).*	15.00	30.00	—
	g. Ovpt: *AGUASCALIENTES.* 1.12.1902. *(BK-DF-223).*	20.00	40.00	—
	h. Ovpt: *AUTLÁN, JAL.* 1.8.1905. *(BK-DF-224).*	15.00	30.00	—
	i. Ovpt: *BRAVOS CHILPANCINGO.* 1.12.1902. *(BK-DF-225).*	10.00	20.00	—
	j. Ovpt: *CAMPECHE.* 1.10.1906. *(BK-DF-226).*	6.00	15.00	30.00
	k. Ovpt: *CHIHUAHUA.* 1.4.1902. *(BK-DF-228).*	15.00	30.00	—
	l. Ovpt: *C. GUZMÁN, JAL.* 1.8.1905. *(BK-DF-227).*	10.00	20.00	—
	m. Ovpt: *C. JUÁREZ.* 1.8.1905. *(BK-DF-230).*	10.00	20.00	—
	n. Ovpt: *CIUDAD VICTORIA.* 1.8.1905. *(BK-DF-229).*	15.00	30.00	—
	o. Ovpt: *COLIMA.* 1.12.1902. *(BK-DF-231).*	10.00	20.00	—
	p. Ovpt: *CÓRDOBA.* 1.3.1911. *(BK-DF-232).*	6.00	15.00	30.00
	q. Ovpt: *CUERNAVACA.* 1.8.1905. *(BK-DF-233).*	10.00	20.00	40.00
	r. Ovpt: *DURANGO.* 1.4.1902. *(BK-DF-234).*	20.00	40.00	—
	s. Ovpt: *GUADALAJARA.* 1.5.1889. *(BK-DF-235).*	25.00	50.00	—
	t. Ovpt: *GUANAJUATO.* 1.5.1889. *(BK-DF-236).*	25.00	50.00	—
	u. Ovpt: *GUAYMAS.* 1.12.1902. *(BK-DF-237).*	15.00	30.00	—
	v. Ovpt: *HERMOSILLO, SON.* 1.10.1906; 1.4.1902. *(BK-DF-238).*	15.00	30.00	—
	w. Ovpt: *HUAUCHINANGO, PUE.* 1.3.1911. *(BK-DF-239).*	25.00	50.00	—
	x. Ovpt: *RAPUATO.* 1.10.1906. *(BK-DF-240).*	25.00	50.00	—
	y. Ovpt: *LAGOS.* 1.12.1902. *(BK-DF-241).*	10.00	20.00	—
	z. Ovpt: *LA PIEDAD.* 1.8.1905. *(BK-DF-242).*	10.00	20.00	—

	Good	Fine	XF
aa. Ovpt: *MATEHUALA* (Agencia en). 26.7.1897. *(BK-DF-243).*	35.00	60.00	—
ab. Ovpt: *MAZATLÁN.* 1.5.1889. *(BK-DF-244).*	25.00	40.00	—
ac. Ovpt: *MÉRIDA.* 4.6.1889. *(BK-DF-245).*	25.00	20.00	—
ad. Ovpt: *MONCLOVA, COAH.* 1.8.1905; 1.7.1901. *(BK-DF-246).*	25.00	30.00	—
ae. Ovpt: *MONTERREY.* 1.4.1902. *(BK-DF-247).*	25.00	30.00	—
af. Ovpt. and needle punched: *MONTERREY.* 1.12.1890. *(BK-DF-248).*	25.00	50.00	—
ag. Ovpt: *OAXACA.* 1.10.1889; 1.8.1890; 1.4.1902. *(BK-DF-249).*	25.00	50.00	—
ah. Ovpt: *PACHUCA.* 1.12.1902. *(BK-DF-250).*	6.00	15.00	30.00
ai. Ovpt: *PUEBLA.* 1.4.1902. *(BK-DF-251).*	15.00	30.00	—
aj. Ovpt: *QUERÉTARO.* 1.8.1905; 1.1.1902. *(BK-DF-252).*	10.00	20.00	—
ak. Ovpt: *RIO VERDE.* 1.8.1905. *(BK-DF-253).*	15.00	30.00	—
al. Ovpt: *S. ANDRÉS TUXTLA.* 1.8.1905. *(BK-DF-254).*	6.00	15.00	30.00
am. Ovpt: *SOMBRERETE.* 1.3.1910. *(BK-DF-255).*	15.00	30.00	—
an. Ovpt: *TABASCO.* 1.4.1902. *(BK-DF-256).*	15.00	30.00	—
ao. Ovpt: *TAMPICO.* 1.4.1902. *(BK-DF-257).*	15.00	30.00	—
ap. Ovpt: *TANTOYUCA.* 1.10.1906. *(BK-DF-258).*	15.00	30.00	—
aq. Ovpt: *TEHUACÁN.* 1.3.1910. *(BK-DF-259).*	10.00	20.00	—
ar. Ovpt: *TEPIC.* 1.8.1905. *(BK-DF-260).*	15.00	30.00	—
as. Ovpt: *TEZIUTLÁN.* 26.7.1897; 1.7.1901. *(BK-DF-261).*	15.00	30.00	—
at. Ovpt: *TLALTENANGO.* 1.10.1906. *(BK-DF-262).*	15.00	30.00	—
au. Ovpt: *TOLUCA.* 1.12.1902. *(BK-DF-263).*	10.00	20.00	—
av. Ovpt: *TORREON.* 1.12.1902. *(BK-DF-264).*	10.00	20.00	—
aw. Ovpt: *TULANCINGO.* 1.10.1906. *(BK-DF-265).*	15.00	30.00	—
ax. ND. Remainder w/ovpt: *BILLETE SIN VALOR.* 1.8.1905. *(BK-DF-220).*	—	Unc	10.00
p1. Proof. 188x.	—	Unc	200.00
p2. Proof. ND.	—	Unc	75.00
s1. Specimen. 188x.	—	Unc	200.00
s2. Specimen. ND.	—	Unc	75.00

S259 20 Pesos

1885-1913. Black on green and ochre unpt. Portr. M. García Teruel at l., cowboys rounding up cattle at r. Back green; monument at ctr.

	Good	Fine	XF
a. 1.1.1887. *(BK-DF-271).*	20.00	50.00	—
b. 1.12.1890; 26.7.1897. *(BK-DF-272).*	12.50	30.00	—
c. 1.7.1901-1.1.1908. *(BK-DF-273).*	5.00	12.00	—
d. 1.9.1909-15.9.1913. *(BK-DF-274).*	4.00	10.00	30.00
e. Ovpt: *ACAPULCO.* 1.10.1906. *(BK-DF-277).*	30.00	60.00	—
f. Ovpt: *AUTLÁN, JAL.* 1.8.1905. *(BK-DF-278).*	15.00	30.00	—
g. Ovpt: *CHIHUAHUA.* 1.4.1902. *(BK-DF-280).*	30.00	60.00	—
h. Ovpt: *C. GUZMÁN JAL.* 1.8.1905. *(BK-DF-279).*	30.00	60.00	—
i. Ovpt: *CIUDAD VICTORIA.* 1.8.1905. *(BK-DF-281).*	30.00	60.00	—
j. Ovpt: *COLIMA.* 1.4.1902; 1.12.1902. *(BK-DF-282).*	30.00	60.00	—
k. Ovpt: *CÓRDOBA.* 1.3.1911. *(BK-DF-283).*	15.00	30.00	—
l. Ovpt: *CUERNAVACA.* 1.8.1905. *(BK-DF-284).*	30.00	60.00	—
m. Ovpt: *DURANGO.* 15.10.1890/188x. *(BK-DF-285).*	35.00	70.00	—
n. Ovpt: *GUANAJUATO.* 1.5.1889. *(BK-DF-286).*	30.00	60.00	—
o. Ovpt: *GUAYMAS.* 1.12.1902. *(BK-DF-287).*	30.00	60.00	—
p. Ovpt: *HERMOSILLO SON.* 1.10.1906. *(BK-DF-288).*	30.00	60.00	—
q. Ovpt: *IRAPUATO.* 1.10.1906.	30.00	60.00	—
r. Ovpt: *LA PIEDAD.* 1.8.1905. *(BK-DF-289).*	30.00	60.00	—
s. Ovpt: *MAZATLÁN.* 1.5.1889. *(BK-DF-291).*	30.00	60.00	—
t. Ovpt. and needle punched: *MÉRIDA.* 4.6.1889. *(BK-DF-292).*	30.00	60.00	—
u. Ovpt: *MÉRIDA.* 1.4.1902. *(BK-DF-293).*	15.00	30.00	—
v. Ovpt: *MONCLOVA, COAH.* 1.8.1905. *(BK-DF-294).*	30.00	60.00	—
w. Ovpt: *MONTERREY.* 1.4.1902. *(BK-DF-295).*	30.00	60.00	—
x. Ovpt: *NUEVO LAREDO.* 26.7.1897; 1.7.1901. *(BK-DF-296).*	30.00	60.00	—
y. Ovpt: *PUEBLA.* 1.1.1887. *(BK-DF-297).*	30.00	60.00	—
z. Ovpt: *PUEBLA.* 1.4.1902. *(BK-DF-298).*	30.00	60.00	—
aa. Ovpt: *PURUANDIRO.* 1.8.1905. *(BK-DF-299).*	25.00	60.00	—
ab. Ovpt: *RIO VERDE.* 1.8.1905. *(BK-DF-30).*	15.00	30.00	50.00
ac. Ovpt: *SALTILLO.* 1.4.1902. *(BK-DF-301).*	30.00	60.00	—
ad. Ovpt: *TABASCO.* 1.4.1902. *(BK-DF-302).*	30.00	60.00	—
ae. Ovpt: *TAMPICO.* 1.4.1902. *(BK-DF-303).*	30.00	60.00	—
af. Ovpt: *TEHUACÁN.* 1.3.1910. *(BK-DF-304).*	30.00	60.00	—
ag. Ovpt: *TEPIC.* 1.8.1905. *(BK-DF-305).*	30.00	60.00	—
ah. Ovpt: *TLALTENANGO.* 1.10.1906.. *(BK-DF-306).*	30.00	60.00	—
ai. Ovpt: *TORREON.* 1.12.1902. *(BK-DF-307).*	30.00	60.00	—
aj. Ovpt: *TULANCINGO.* 1.10.1906. *(BK-DF-308).*	30.00	60.00	—
ak. Ovpt: *TUXTLA GUTIÉRREZ.* 1.8.1905. *(BK-DF-309).*	30.00	60.00	—
al. Ovpt: *URUAPAN, MICH.* 1.8.1905. *(BK-DF-310).*	30.00	60.00	—
am. Ovpt: *VERACRUZ.* 1.4.1902. *(BK-DF-311).*	30.00	60.00	—
an. Ovpt. and needle punched: *ZACATECAS.* 1.12.1890. 188x. *(BK-DF-312).*	35.00	70.00	—
ao. Ovpt: *ZACATECAS.*. 1.4.1902. *(BK-DF-313).*	30.00	60.00	—
ap. Ovpt: *AGUASCALIENTES.* 1.7.1901. *(BK-DF-277A).*	30.00	60.00	—
aq. Ovpt: *BRAVOS.* 1.12.1902. *(BK-DF-278A).*	30.00	60.00	—
ar. Ovpt: *CIUDAD JUAREZ.* 1.8.1905. *(BK-DF-280A).*	30.00	60.00	—
as. Ovpt. and needle punched: *PAGADERO EN.* *(BK-DF-297A).*	30.00	60.00	—
at. Branch ovpt: *QUERETARO.* 1.8.1905. *(BK-DF-299A).*	30.00	60.00	—
au. Ovpt: *SAN ANDRES TUXTLA.* 1.8.1905. *(BK-DF-301A).*	30.00	60.00	—
av. Ovpt: *TANTOYUCA.* 1.6.1906. *(BK-DF-303A).*	30.00	60.00	—
aw. Branch ovpt: *VERACRUZ.* 1.1.1885.	125.00	200.00	—
p1. Proof. 188x.	—	Unc	200.00

	Good	Fine	XF
p2. Proof. ND.	—	Unc	75.00
r. ND. Remainder w/ovpt: *BILLETE SIN VALOR.* *(BK-DF-275).*	—	Unc	22.50
s1. Specimen. 188x.	—	Unc	200.00
s2. Specimen. ND.	—	Unc	75.00

S260 50 Pesos

1885-1913. Black on yellow and and brown unpt. Filia (Symbol of Friendship) at l., portr. M. García Tereul at r. Back brown; church and street scene at ctr.

	Good	Fine	XF
a. 1.1.1885. *(BK-DF-314).*	60.00	120.00	—
b. 1.12.1890; 26.7.1897. *(BK-DF-315).*	20.00	35.00	—
c. 1.7.1901-1.1.1908. *(BK-DF-316).*	15.00	25.00	—
d. 1.9.1909-5.11.1913. *(BK-DF-317).*	10.00	22.00	60.00
e. Ovpt: *CUERNAVACA.* 1.12.1902; 1.8.1905. *(BK-DF-320).*	50.00	100.00	—
f. Ovpt: *GUAYMAS.* 1.12.1902. *(BK-DF-321).*	50.00	100.00	—
g. Ovpt: *MAZATLÁN.* 1.7.1901. *(BK-DF-322).*	50.00	100.00	—
h. Ovpt. and needle punched: *MERIDA.* 1.5.1889. *(BK-DF-323).*	60.00	120.00	—
i. Ovpt. and needle punched: *MERIDA.* 1.4.1902. *(BK-DF-324).*	50.00	100.00	—
j. Ovpt: *MONTERREY.* 1.8.1890. *(BK-DF-325).*	60.00	120.00	—
k. Ovpt: *PURUANDIRO.* 1.8.1905. *(BK-DF-326).*	50.00	100.00	—
l. Ovpt: *S. ANDRÉS TUXTLA.* 1.12.1902. *(BK-DF-327).*	50.00	100.00	—
m. Ovpt: *SOMBRERETE.* 1.3.1910. *(BK-DF-328).*	50.00	100.00	—
n. Ovpt: *TABASCO.* 1.7.1901. *(BK-DF-320).*	50.00	100.00	—
o. Ovpt. and needle punched: *ZACATECAS.* 1.12.1890. *(BK-DF-330).*	60.00	120.00	—
p. Ovpt: *PAGADERO EN VERACRUZ.* 1.4.1902.	—	—	—
q. Ovpt: *PUEBLA.* 1.12.1890.	—	—	—
p1. Proof. 188x.	—	Unc	250.00
p2. Proof. ND.	—	Unc	100.00
r. ND. Remainder w/ovpt: *BILLETE SIN VALOR.* *(BK-DF-318).*	—	Unc	40.00
s. Ovpt: *TUXTLA GUTIÉRREZ.* 1.8.1905. *(BK-DF-229A).*	—	—	—
t. Ovpt: *VERACRUZ.* 1.4.1902. *(BK-DF-329b).*	—	—	—
s1. Specimen. 188x.	—	Unc	250.00
s2. Specimen. ND.	—	Unc	100.00

S261 100 Pesos

1885-1911. Black on yellow and brown unpt. Portr. M. García Teruel at l. ctr., Themis (Goddess of Justice) at r. Back blue-gray; eagle w/wings spread eye to eye w/snake at ctr.

	Good	Fine	XF
a. 1.1.1885; 1.6.1886. *(BK-DF-331).*	75.00	140.00	—
b. 1.1.1888. *(BK-DF-332).*	70.00	130.00	—
c. 1.12.1890/1888-1.12.1902. *(BK-DF-334).*	50.00	80.00	—
d. 1.1.1908-1.3.1911. *(BK-DF-334).*	30.00	60.00	175.00
e. Ovpt: *CAMPECHE.* 1.10.1906. *(BK-DF-338).*	70.00	130.00	—
f. Ovpt. and needle punched: *GUANAJUATO.* 1.1.1885. *(BK-DF-339).*	75.00	140.00	—
g. Ovpt: *MATEHUALA.* 5.11.1901. *(BK-DF-340).*	70.00	130.00	—

		Good	Fine	XF
	h. Ovpt. and needle punched: *MERIDA.* 1.1.1888. *(BK-DF-341).*	75.00	140.00	—
	i. Ovpt: *MORELIA.* 1.12.1902. *(BK-DF-342).*	70.00	130.00	—
	j. Ovpt: *QUERETARO.* 1.12.1902. *(BK-DF-343).*	70.00	130.00	—
	k. Ovpt: *SAN ANDRÉS TUXTLA.* 1.1.1902. *(BK-DF-344).*	70.00	130.00	—
	l. Ovpt: *TUXTLA GUTIÉRREZ.* 1.12.1902. *(BK-DF-345).*	70.00	130.00	—
	m. Ovpt: *VERACRUZ.* 1.1.1885; 1.1.1888. *(BK-DF-346).*	75.00	140.00	—
	n. Ovpt: *VERACRUZ.* Ovpt. and needle punched: *VERACRUZ.* 1.3.188x. 1.1.1885; 1.1.1888. *(BK-DF-346). (BK-DF-347).*	75.00	75.00	140.00
	o. Ovpt. and needle punched: *ZACATECAS.* 1.12.1890. *(BK-DF-348).*	75.00	140.00	—
	p. Ovpt: *CUERNAVACA.* 1.12.1902. *(BK-DF-338A).*	70.00	140.00	—
	q. Ovpt: *TABASCO.* 5.11.1901. *(BK-DF-344A).*	70.00	130.00	—
	p1. Proof. 188x.	—	Unc	300.00
	p2. Proof. ND.			
	r. ND. Remainder w/ovpt: *BILLETE SIN VALOR. (BK-DF-335).*	—	Unc	50.00
	s1. Specimen. 188x.	—	Unc	300.00
	s2. Specimen. ND.	—	Unc	175.00
S261A	**100 PESOS** 19xx (ca.1913). Black on blue, green and brown unpt. Arms at r. Back green; bldg at ctr. Proof.	—	—	—

		Good	Fine	XF
S262	**500 PESOS** 1885-1913. Black on yellow and orange unpt. Cleo (Muse of History) at l., portr. M. García Teruel at ctr., Urania at r. Back orange and black; herdsmen and wild horses at ctr.			
	a. Series A. 1.1.1885. *(BK-DF-349).*	400.00	800.00	—
	b. 26.7.1897-11.12.1913. *(BK-DF-350).*	300.00	600.00	1000.
	c. Ovpt: *MONTERREY.* 12.8.188x. *(BK-DF-351).*	350.00	700.00	—
	p1. Proof 188x.	—	Unc	650.00
	p2. Proof. ND.	—	Unc	250.00
	r. ND. Remainder w/ovpt: *BILLETE SIN VALOR* on face or back. *(BK-DF-352).*	—	Unc	100.00
	s1. Specimen. 188x.	—	Unc	650.00
	s2. Specimen. 189x.	—	Unc	600.00
	s3. Specimen. ND.	—	Unc	250.00

		Good	Fine	XF
S263	**1000 PESOS** 1885-1913. Black on m/c unpt. Portr. M. García Teruel at l., symbolization of Riches at r. Back red-orange and black; reclining woman w/water jug at ctr.			
	a. 25.10.1888-1.4.1913. *(BK-DF-355).*	450.00	850.00	—
	p1. Proof. 188x.	—	Unc	750.00
	p2. Proof. ND.	—	Unc	300.00
	r. ND. Remainder w/ovpt: *BILLETE SIN VALOR* on face or back. *(BK-DF-356).*	—	Unc	150.00
	s1. Specimen. 188x.	—	Unc	750.00
	s2. Specimen. 189x.	—	Unc	650.00
	s3. Specimen. ND.	—	Unc	300.00

NOTE: For #S258-S263, reports of specific dates from 1885-1913 are needed to augment these listings.

NATIONAL PAWN SHOP

NACIONAL MONTE DE PIEDAD

1880-81 CERTIFICATES ISSUE

#S264-S271 Monte de Piedad bldg. at ctr. on back. Printer: ABNC.

		Good	Fine	XF
S264	**1 PESO** 12.7.1880-15.10.1881. Black on green unpt. Portr. P. Romero de Terreros at l., shepherdess w/sheep at r. Back brown. Series A. *(PR-DF-22).*			
	a. Issued certificate.	120.00	250.00	—
	p. Proof.	—	—	—
	r1. Remainder w/o counterfoil.	—	Unc	25.00
	r2. Remainder w/counterfoil. *(PR-DF-24).*	—	Unc	35.00
	s. Specimen.	—	—	—

		Good	Fine	XF
S265	**5 PESOS** 12.7.1880; 17.1.1881. Black on green unpt. Portr. P. Romero de Terreros at l., locomotive at upper r. Back brown. Series A. *(PR-DF-27).*			
	a. Issued certificate.	200.00	450.00	—
	p. Proof.	—	—	—
	r1. Remainder w/o counterfoil. Series A. *(PR-DF-28).*	—	Unc	30.00
	r2. Remainder w/counterfoil. *(PR-DF-29).*	—	Unc	45.00
	s. Specimen.	—	—	—

		Good	Fine	XF
S266	**10 PESOS** 188x. Black on brown unpt. Deer at upper l. ctr., portr. P. Romero de Terreros at lower r. Back blue. Series A.			
	p. Proof.	—	—	—
	r1. Remainder w/o counterfoil. *(PR-DF-32).*	—	Unc	40.00
	r2. Remainder w/counterfoil. *(PR-DF-33).*	—	Unc	45.00
	s. Specimen.	—	—	—

S267 20 PESOS

188x. Black on brown unpt. Portr. P. Romero de Terreros at l. ctr., farm produce at lower r. Back blue.

	GOOD	FINE	XF
p. Proof.	—	—	—
r1. Remainder w/o counterfoil. *(PR-DF-36).*	—	Unc	60.00
r2. Remainder w/counterfoil. *(PR-DF-37).*	—	Unc	65.00
s. Specimen.	—	—	—

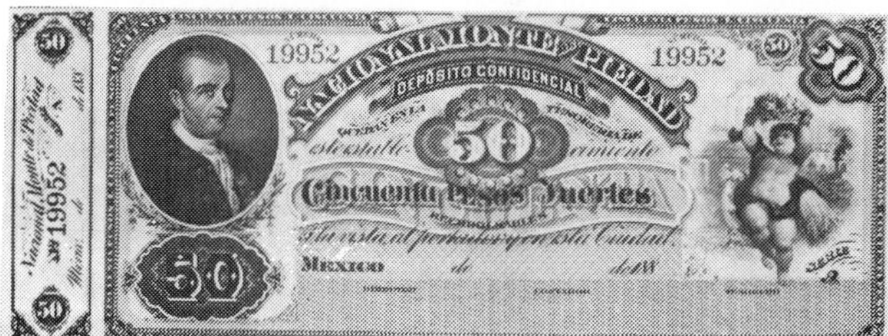

S268 50 PESOS

188x. Black on brown unpt. Portr. P. Romero de Terreros at upper l., cherub holding sheaf of grain at r. Back blue.

	GOOD	FINE	XF
p. Proof.	—	—	—
r1. Remainder w/o counterfoil. *(PR-DF-40).*	—	Unc	90.00
r2. Remainder w/counterfoil. *(PR-DF-41).*	—	Unc	100.00
s. Specimen.	—	—	—

S269 100 PESOS

188x. Black on orange unpt. Seated Agriculture at l., portr. P. Romero de Terreros at ctr., horse's head at r. Back green.

	GOOD	FINE	XF
p. Proof.	—	—	—
r1. Remainder w/o counterfoil. *(PR-DF-44).*	—	Unc	125.00
r2. Remainder w/counterfoil. *(PR-DF-45).*	—	Unc	175.00
s. Specimen.	—	—	—

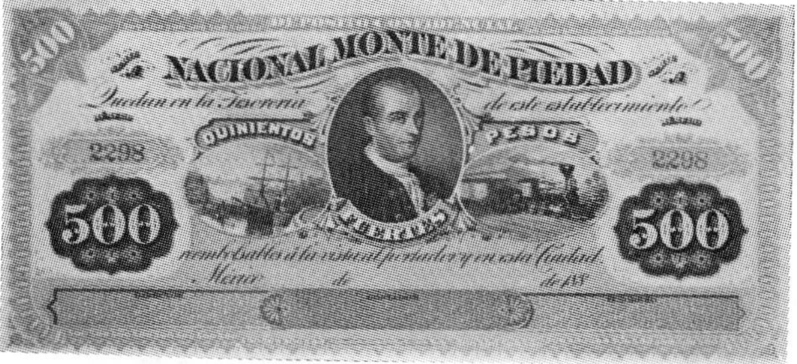

S270 500 PESOS

188x. Black on orange unpt. Sailing ship at l. ctr., portr. P. Romero de Terreros at ctr., steam locomotive at ctr. r. Back green.

	GOOD	FINE	XF
p. Proof.	—	—	—
r1. Remainder w/o counterfoil. *(PR-DF-48).*	—	Unc	175.00
r2. Remainder w/counterfoil. *(PR-DF-49).*	—	Unc	225.00
s. Specimen.	—	—	—

S271 1000 PESOS

188x. Black on orange unpt. Market scene at lower l., portr. P. Romero de Terreros at ctr., Wisdom at lower r. Back green.

	GOOD	FINE	XF
p. Proof.	—	—	—
r1. Remainder w/o counterfoil. *(PR-DF-52).*	—	Unc	200.00
r2. Remainder w/counterfoil. *(PR-DF-53).*	—	Unc	250.00
s. Specimen.	—	—	—

DURANGO

BANCO DE DURANGO

1891 ISSUE

#S272-S278 printer: ABNC.

S272 1 PESO

1891-1901. Black on blue and yellow unpt. Liberty and Harmony flanking shield at l. ctr., Back blue; allegorical woman's head at ctr.

	GOOD	FINE	XF
a. Series A. 15.6.1891; 1.9.1892. *(BK-DUR-5).*	100.00	180.00	—
b. Series B. 30.6.1893. *(BK-DUR-5).*	100.00	180.00	—
c. W/o bank seals; 3.3.1901. *(BK-DUR-6).*	80.00	150.00	—
p. Proof. Series A.	—	Unc	250.00
r. Remainder. ND. Series C. *(BK-DUR-7).*	4.00	12.00	30.00
s1. Specimen. Series A-C.	—	Unc	100.00
s2. Specimen. Series G. 1914.	—	Unc	100.00

S273 5 PESOS

1891-1913. Black on red-orange and yellow unpt. Miners at ctr., seated Irene (Goddess of Peace) at r. Text: *PAGARÁ A LA VISTA. . .* at upper l. Serial # at r. only. Back red-orange.

	GOOD	FINE	XF
a. Series D. 1.1.1900. *(BK-DUR-11).*	15.00	40.00	—
b. Series E. 11.5.1903. *(BK-DUR-12).*	12.50	35.00	—
c. Series F. 5.9.1906; 10.5.1907; 1.1.1910. *(BK-DUR-12).*	12.50	35.00	—
d. Series G. 18.6.1913. *(BK-DUR-13).*	10.00	30.00	65.00
e. Ovpt: *PAGADERO EN GÓMEZ PALACIO.* Series E. 11.5.1903.	30.00	90.00	—
f. Series B. 30.6.1893. *(BK-DUR-10A).*	40.00	100.00	—
p1. Proof. Series A.	—	Unc	250.00
p2. Proof. W/o series.	—	Unc	75.00
s1. Specimen. Series A.	—	Unc	250.00
s2. Specimen. Series B.	—	Unc	300.00
s3. Specimen. W/o series; series D; G.	—	Unc	75.00
s4. Specimen. Series E.	—	Unc	150.00

S273A 5 PESOS

ND (ca.1914). Similar to #S273, but w/text: *PAGARÁ A LA VISTA . . .* at lower ctr. Serial # at l. and r. Series J.

	GOOD	FINE	XF
p. Proof.	—	Unc	175.00
s. Specimen.	—	Unc	175.00

S274 10 PESOS

1891-1914. Black on orange and yellow unpt. Cathedral of Durango at l., farmer mowing at r. Back orange.

	GOOD	FINE	XF
a. Series B. 15.6.1891; 30.6.1893; 1.8.1896. *(BK-DUR-18).*	30.00	80.00	—
b. Series D. 1.1.1900. *(BK-DUR-19).*	15.00	40.00	—
c. Series E. 11.5.1903; F. 5.9.1906; 10.5.1907; 1.1.1910. *(BK-DUR-20).*	12.50	35.00	65.00
d. Series G. 18.6.1913; J. March 1914. *(BK-DUR-21).*	12.50	35.00	65.00
e. Ovpt: *PAGADERO EN GÓMEZ PALACIO.* Series E. 11.5.1903. *(BK-DUR-22).*	30.00	75.00	—
p1. Proof. Series A.	—	Unc	300.00
p2. Proof. W/o series.	—	Unc	75.00
s1. Specimen. Series A.	—	Unc	300.00
s2. Specimen. Series B; D; E; G; J.	—	Unc	100.00
s3. Specimen. Series C.	—	Unc	200.00
s4. Specimen. W/o series.	—	Unc	75.00

S275 20 PESOS

1891-1914. Black on brown and yellow unpt. Steam passenger train traveling through prairie w/mountain in distance at l. ctr., Harvest at r. Back sepia.

		GOOD	FINE	XF
a.	Series C. 1.8.1896. *(BK-DUR-25).*	40.00	90.00	—
b.	Series D. 1.1.1900; E. 11.5.1903; F. 11.11.1903; 10.5.1907; 1.11.1910. *(BK-DUR-26).*	25.00	55.00	115.00
c.	Series H. 1.3.1914; J, March 1914. *(BK-DUR-27).*	20.00	50.00	105.00
d.	Ovpt: *PAGADERO EN GÓMEZ PALACIO.* 11.5.1903. *(BK-DUR-28).*	50.00	110.00	—
p1.	Proof. Series A.	—	Unc	300.00
p2.	Proof. W/o series.	—	Unc	125.00
s1.	Specimen. Series A.	—	Unc	300.00
s2.	Specimen. W/o series; series C-E; H; J.	—	Unc	125.00

S276 50 PESOS

1891-1907. Black on green and yellow unpt. Mercury reclining on fish at l., seated Liberty w/eagle and and child at r. Back green; 50 printed 3 times, allegorical figure at l. and ctr. r. 184 x 87mm.

		GOOD	FINE	XF
a.	Series A. 1.6.1891. *(BK-DUR-30).*	150.00	450.00	—
b.	Series C. 1.8.1896; D. 1.1.1900; E. 11.5.1903; F. 10.5.1907; 30.6.1907. *(BK-DUR-31).*	125.00	300.00	600.00
p.	Proof. Series A.	—	Unc	500.00

S276A 50 PESOS

1913-14. Similar to #S276, but 176 x 83mm and 50 printed 5 times on back.

		GOOD	FINE	XF
a.	Series G. 18.6.1913; J. Feb. 1914; H. 1.3.1914. *(BK-DUR-32).*	85.00	160.00	300.00
p.	Proof. W/o series.	—	Unc	300.00
s1.	Specimen. Series G.	—	Unc	350.00
s2.	Specimen. Series H; J.	—	Unc	250.00

S277 100 PESOS

1888-1907. Black on brown and yellow unpt. Ship at upper l. ctr., seated Justice at r. Back brown. 189 x 86mm.

		GOOD	FINE	XF
a.	Series D. 1.1.1900; F. 5.9.1906; 30.6.1907. *(BK-DUR-34).*	400.00	1000.	1850.
s.	Specimen. Series A. 1888; B. ND.	—	Unc	750.00

S277A 100 PESOS

1913-14. Similar to #S277, but 168 x 78mm and different denomination guilloches.

		GOOD	FINE	XF
a.	Series H. 18.6.1913; J. Feb. 1914. *(BK-DUR-35).*	150.00	350.00	700.00
p.	Proof. W/o series. ND.	—	Unc	400.00
s.	Specimen. W/o series; series J. ND.	—	Unc	400.00

S278 500 PESOS

	GOOD	FINE	XF
ND (ca.1914). Black on yellow and green unpt. Bank of Durango at ctr. Back blue-gray. Series A. *(BK-DUR-36).* (Not issued).	10.00	30.00	85.00

NOTE: For #S272-S277A, reports of specific dates from 1891-1914 are needed to augment these listings.

1914 ISSUE

#S280 and S281 printer: B&S.

S280 5 PESOS

	GOOD	FINE	XF
23.5.1914. Black on tan unpt. Ceres at l. Back brown. Series E.S.P. *(BK-DUR-16).*	3.00	12.00	50.00

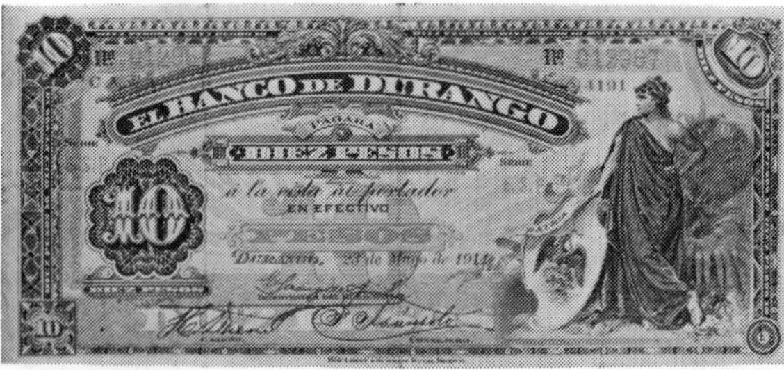

S281 10 PESOS

	GOOD	FINE	XF
23.5.1914. Green and black. Polyhymnia (Muse of Lyrical Poetry) at r. Back green. Series E.S.P. *(BK-DUR-24).*	3.00	12.00	50.00

BANCO DEL ESTADO DE DURANGO

1882 ISSUE

#S284-S286 portr. M. Hidalgo at l. Printer: H. S. Crocker & Co., S.F.

S284 25 CENTAVOS

5.1.1882.

		GOOD	FINE	XF
a.	Issued note. *(BK-DUR-1).*	200.00	400.00	650.00
r.	Remainder. *(BK-DUR-2).*	150.00	300.00	500.00

S285 50 CENTAVOS

	GOOD	FINE	XF
5.1.1882. Black on white. *(BK-DUR-3).*	200.00	400.00	650.00

S286 1 PESO

	GOOD	FINE	XF
5.1.1882. Black on white. Steam passenger train at r. Back green. Remainder. *(BK-DUR-4).*	150.00	300.00	650.00

GUANAJUATO

BANCO DE GUANAJUATO

1913 ISSUE

#S287 and S288, S291 and S293 state arms at ctr. on back.

#S287-S295 printer: ABNC.

S287 1 PESO

1913-14. Black on yellow unpt. Seated Alethia (Truth) at ctr. Back olive-green.

	GOOD	FINE	XF
a. Series A. 3.12.1913; B. 3.12.1913. *(BK-GUA-1).*	5.00	15.00	40.00
b. Series C. 26.6.1914; 10.7.1914; 20.7.1914.	5.00	15.00	40.00
p. Proof. W/o series. ND.	—	Unc	50.00
s. Specimen. Series B; C. 19xx. *(BK-GUA-2s).*	—	Unc	50.00

S288 2 PESOS

1913-14. Black on blue and brown unpt. Eudemonia (Happiness) at r. Back blue.

	GOOD	FINE	XF
a. Series A and B. 3.12.1913; B and C. 1.6.1914. *(BK-GUA-3).*	4.00	15.00	40.00
p. Proof. W/o series. ND.	—	Unc	65.00
r. Unsigned remainder. ND. *(BK-GUA-4).*	7.50	20.00	45.00
s. Specimen. Series B; C. 19xx. *(BK-GUA-5s).*	—	Unc	65.00

S289 5 PESOS

1900-14. Black on green unpt. Portr. M. Doblado at l. Back green.

	GOOD	FINE	XF
a. Series A. 15.10.1900; 30.10.1900; 29.10.1901. *(BK-GUA-6).*	10.00	25.00	—
b. Series B. 14.10.1902; 9.12.1902.	7.50	20.00	60.00
c. Series C. 1.3.1903-6.7.1910. *(BK-GUA-7).*	10.00	20.00	60.00
d. Series D. 30.1.1914; E. 20.7.1914. *(BK-GUA-8).*	15.00	35.00	60.00
e. Ovpt: *IRAPUATO.* Series A, 30.11.1900. *(BK-GUA-9).*	20.00	70.00	—
p. Proof. W/o series. ND.	—	Unc	80.00
s. Specimen. Series E. 19xx. *(BK-GUA-10s).*	—	Unc	80.00

NOTE: For #S289, reports of specific dates from 1903-10 are needed to augment this listing. A note dated ca.1912 is reported in archive records. No examples are known.

S290 10 PESOS

1900-14. Black on red-orange and pale yellow-green unpt. State arms at l., Eros at ctr. r. Back red-orange.

	GOOD	FINE	XF
a. Series A. 15.10.1900; 29.10.1901. *(BK-GUA-11).*	12.00	30.00	—
b. Series B. 8.9.1902; 9.12.1902; C. 19.9.1907; 3.8.1909; 6.7.1910. *(BK-GIA-12).*	10.00	20.00	60.00
c. Series D. 12.4.1911; 30.1.1914; E. 26.6.1914; 10.7.1914; 20.7.1914. *(BK-GUA-13).*	6.00	15.00	40.00
d. Ovpt: *IRAPUATO.* Series A. 15.10.1900; B. 14.10.1902. *(BK-GUA-14).*	20.00	70.00	—
p. Proof. W/o series. ND.	—	Unc	100.00
s. Specimen. Series B; C; E; F. 19xx. *(BK-GUA-15s).*	—	Unc	100.00

S291 20 PESOS

1900-14. Black on blue and yellow unpt. Woman's head at l., woman holding flowers at r. Back blue-gray.

	GOOD	FINE	XF
a. Series A. 15.10.1900. *(BK-GUA-16).*	25.00	80.00	—
b. Series A. 20.3.1902; 8.9.1902; 14.10.1902; B. 1.3.1903; 3.8.1909. *(BK-GUA-17).*	20.00	75.00	—
c. Series B. 3.5.1912. *(BK-GUA-18).*	20.00	65.00	130.00
d. Ovpt: *IRAPUATO. Series A. 15.10.1900. (BK-GUA-19).*	50.00	100.00	—
e. Series C. 30.1.1914; E; F. 20.7.1914.	20.00	65.00	130.00
p. Proof. W/o series. ND.	—	Unc	150.00
s. Specimen. Series D. 19xx. *(BK-GUA-20s).*	—	Unc	250.00

S292 50 PESOS

1901-14. Black on olive-green and yellow unpt. State arms at r. Back dk. green.

	GOOD	FINE	XF
a. Series A. 1.8.1901; 29.10.1901; 14.10.1902. *(BK-GUA-21).*	150.00	300.00	—
b. Series B. 3.8.1909; B; C. 3.5.1912; B; D. 30.1.1914; E. 1.6.1914. *(BK-GUA-22).*	125.00	250.00	450.00
p. Proof. W/o series. ND.	—	Unc	300.00
r. Remainder. Series F. ND. *(BK-GUA-23).*	—	Unc	250.00

S293 100 Pesos
1900-14. Black on red and yellow unpt. Miner holding pick and lamp at ctr. Back red.

		Good	Fine	XF
a.	Series A. 15.10.1900; 1.8.1901; B. 1.3.1903. *(BK-GUA-25).*	250.00	450.00	—
b.	Series B. 1.12.1909; 30.1.1912; C. 1.3.1913; B; D. 30.1.1914; B; D; E. 1.6.1914; 20.7.1914. *(BK-GUA-26).*	350.00	—	700.00
p.	Proof. W/o series. ND.	—	Unc	500.00
s.	Specimen. Series D. 19xx.	—	Unc	500.00

S294 500 Pesos
(ca.1900-14). Black on brown and yellow unpt. State arms at l., portr. M. Doblado at r. Back brown; Minerva (Goddess of Science, Art and War) at ctr.

		Good	Fine	XF
a.	Series C. 1.12.1909; 1.4.1914; 20.7.1914. *(BK-GUA-28).*	1250.	2500.	—
p1.	Proof. Series A. 19xx (ca.1900).	—	—	—
p2.	Proof. W/o series. ND.	—	Unc	1500.

S295 1000 Pesos
(ca.1900-14). Black on purple and yellow unpt. Portr. M. Doblado at l., State arms at r. Back purple.

		Good	Fine	XF
a.	Series E. 20.7.1914. *(BK-GUA-32).*	—	4000.	—
p.	Proof. Series A. 19xx (ca.1900).	—	—	—

NOTE: For #S294 and S295, reports of specific dates are needed to augment these listings.

1914 Issue

#S296 and S297 national arms at ctr. on back. Series G. Printer: B&S.

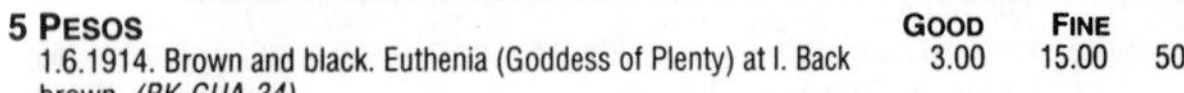

		Good	Fine	XF
S296	**5 Pesos** 1.6.1914. Brown and black. Euthenia (Goddess of Plenty) at l. Back brown. *(BK-GUA-34).*	3.00	15.00	50.00

		Good	Fine	XF
S297	**10 Pesos** 1.6.1914. Green, yellow and black. Polyhymnia (Muse of Lyrical Poetry) at r. *(BK-GUA-35).*	3.00	15.00	50.00

Guerrero

Banco de Guerrero

1906-14 Issue

#S298-S303 port of Acapulco on back. Printer: ABNC.

S298 5 Pesos
1906-14. Black on green unpt. Young girl w/fruit basket at ctr. Back green.

		Good	Fine	XF
a.	Series A. 5.5.1906. *(BK-GUE-1).*	60.00	120.00	—
b.	Series A. 6.2.1914. *(BK-GUE-2).*	50.00	100.00	225.00
c.	Series B. 19xx (ca.1914). Perforated: *AMORTIZADO. (BK-GUE-3).*	—	Unc	7.50
p.	Proof. W/o series. 190x.	—	Unc	140.00
s1.	Specimen. Series A. 190x.	—	Unc	140.00
s2.	Specimen. Series B. 19xx.	—	Unc	75.00
s3.	Specimen. W/o series. ND.	—	Unc	75.00

S299 10 Pesos
(ca.1906-14). Black on brown and green unpt. Portr. V. G. Saldana at ctr. Back blue.

		Good	Fine	XF
a.	Series A. 5.5.1906. *(BK-GUE-6).*	75.00	140.00	275.00
b.	Series B. 19xx (ca.1914). Perforated: *AMORTIZADO. (BK-GUE-7).*	—	Unc	7.50
p.	Proof. W/o series. 190x.	—	Unc	150.00
s1.	Specimen. Series A. 190x.	—	Unc	150.00
s2.	Specimen. Series B. 19xx.	—	Unc	75.00
s3.	Specimen. W/o series. ND.	—	Unc	100.00

		GOOD	FINE	XF
S300	**20 PESOS**			
	(ca.1906-14). Black on green unpt. Miners working at ctr. Back blue-gray.			
	a. Series A. 5.5.1906. *(BK-GUE-9).*	100.00	200.00	425.00
	b. Series B. 19xx (ca.1914). Perforated: *AMORTIZADO. (BK-GUE-10).*	—	Unc	9.00
	p. Proof. W/o series. 190x.	—	Unc	200.00
	s1. Specimen. Series A. 190x.	—	Unc	200.00
	s2. Specimen. Series B. 19xx.	—	Unc	100.00
	s3. Specimen. W/o series. ND.	—	Unc	100.00

NOTE: For #S299 and S300, confirmation is needed for the 1914 date as issued notes.

		GOOD	FINE	XF
S301	**50 PESOS**			
	1906-14. Black on green unpt. Portr. V. G. Saldana at l. Back dk. red.			
	a. Series A. 5.5.1906. *(BK-GUE-12).*	100.00	200.00	—
	b. Series A. Jan. 1914; 15.1.1914. *(BK-GUE-13).*	65.00	150.00	250.00
	c. Series B. 21.4.1914. *(BK-GUE-13).*	65.00	150.00	250.00
	d. Series B. 19xx (ca.1914). Perforated: *AMORTIZADO. (BK-GUE-14).*	—	Unc	30.00
	p. Proof. W/o series. 190x.	—	Unc	250.00
	s1. Specimen. Series A. 190x.	—	Unc	250.00
	s2. Specimen. Series B. 19xx.	—	Unc	125.00
	s3. Specimen. W/o series. ND.	—	Unc	125.00

		GOOD	FINE	XF
S302	**100 PESOS**			
	1906-14. Black on brown unpt. Cathedral of Taxco at ctr. r. Back brown.			
	a. Series A. 5.5.1906. *(BK-GUE-16).*	600.00	1200.	—
	b. Series A. 15.1.1914. *(BK-GUE-17).*	600.00	1000.	1850.
	c. Series B. 28.5.1908. Perforated: *AMORTIZADO. (BK-GUE-18).*	—	Unc	30.00
	p. Proof. W/o series. 190x.	—	Unc	700.00
	s1. Specimen. Series A. 190x.	—	Unc	700.00
	s2. Specimen. Series B. 190x.	—	Unc	250.00

		GOOD	FINE	XF
S303	**500 PESOS**			
	190x (ca.1904). Black on orange and yellow unpt. Ships at l. ctr. Back orange. Series A. *(BK-GUE-20).*			
	p. Proof.	—	—	—
	s. Specimen.	—	—	—

HIDALGO

BANCO DE HIDALGO

1902-14 ISSUE

#S304-S310 printer: ABNC.

		GOOD	FINE	XF
S304	**1 PESO**			
	1914. Black on blue and yellow unpt. Mining scene at ctr. Back blue-gray; Hidalgo at ctr.			
	a. Series A. 5.5.1914. *(BK-HID-1).*	4.00	10.00	17.50
	b. Series A. 19xx. Perforated: *AMORTIZADO. (BK-HID-2).*	—	Unc	4.50
	p. Proof. W/o series. ND.	—	Unc	100.00
	s. Specimen. Series A. ND.	—	Unc	75.00

#S305-S309 city view of Pachuca at ctr. on back.

		GOOD	FINE	XF
S305	**5 PESOS**			
	1902-14. Black on orange and pale green unpt. Monument to Miguel Hidalgo at l., miners at r. Back orange.			
	a. Series A. 23.9.1902. *(BK-HID-4).*	7.50	18.00	—
	b. Series B. 1.12.1913. *(BK-HID-5).*	5.00	15.00	30.00
	c. Series C. 21.4.1914. *(BK-HID-6).*	5.00	15.00	30.00
	d. Series C. 19xx. Perforated: *AMORTIZADO. (BK-HID-7).*	—	Unc	7.50
	p1. Face proof. W/o series. 190x.	—	Unc	120.00
	p2. Back proof.	—	Unc	75.00
	s. Specimen.	—	Unc	75.00

		GOOD	FINE	XF
S306	**10 PESOS**			
	1902-14. Black on green and yellow unpt. Miners at l. and r., portr. Juan C. Doria at ctr. Back green.			
	a. Series A. 23.9.1902; 1.11.1902; 6.6.1906. *(BK-HID-10).*	25.00	75.00	—
	b. Series A. 1.9.1910: B. 21.4.1914. *(BK-HID-11).*	20.00	60.00	110.00
	c. Series B. 19xx. Perforated: *AMORTIZADO. (BK-HID-12).*	—	Unc	10.00
	d. Ovpt: *TULANCINGO* on back; Series A. 1.11.1902; 23.9.1902. *(BK-HID-13).*	40.00	100.00	—
	p. Proof. W/o series. 190x.	—	Unc	150.00
	s. Specimen. Series A; B. 190x.	—	Unc	125.00

		GOOD	FINE	XF
S307	**20 PESOS**			
	1902-10. Black on brown and yellow unpt. Monument to M. Hidalgo at l., factory at ctr. r. Back brown.			
	a. Series A. 23.9.1902; 1.11.1902; 6.6.1903. *(BK-HID-15).*	30.00	80.00	140.00
	b. Series A. 1.9.1910; 23.11.1910; B. 21.4.1914. *(BK-HID-16).*	20.00	60.00	100.00
	c. Series A. 1.9.1910. Perforated: *AMORTIZADO.* W/3 sign. *(BK-HID-17).*	15.00	30.00	50.00
	d. Series A. 1.9.1910. Perforated: *AMORTIZADO.* W/ 2 sign. *(BK-HID-18).*	—	Unc	40.00
	e. Ovpt: *TULANCINGO* on back. Series A. 6.6.1903. *(BK-HID-21).*	40.00	100.00	—
	p. Proof. W/o series. 190x.	—	Unc	200.00

	Good	Fine	XF
r1. Unsigned remainder w/back seals. Series A. 1.9.1910. Perforated: *AMORTIZADO. (BK-HID-19).*	—	Unc	22.00
r2. Unsigned remainder. Series B. 19xx. Perforated: *AMORTIZADO. (BK-HID-20).*	—	Unc	20.00
s1. Specimen. Series A. 190x.	—	Unc	150.00
s2. Specimen. Series B. 190x.	—	Unc	100.00

S308 50 PESOS	Good	Fine	XF
1902-14. Black on blue and ochre unpt. Portr. P. Romero de Terreros at l., mining scene at r. Back dk. blue on blue unpt.			
a. Series A. 23.9.1902-1.9.1910. *(BK-HID-23).*	100.00	225.00	—
p. Proof. W/o series. 190x.	—	Unc	250.00
r. Unsigned remainder. Series B. 19xx. Perforated: *AMORTIZADO. (BK-HID-24).*	—	Unc	37.50
s. Specimen. W/o series. 19xx.	—	Unc	175.00

NOTE: For #S308, confirmation is needed for the 1914 date as an issued note.

S309 100 PESOS	Good	Fine	XF
1904-14. Black on yellow and olive-green unpt. Monument to M. Hidalgo at l., portr. Juan C. Doria at r. Back olive-green. Series A-C.			
a. 16.7.1904; 1.1.1914; 21.4.1914. *(BK-HID-26).*	—	—	—
b. Series A. 2.4.1903.	600.00	1250.	—
p. Proof. W/o series. 190x.	—	Unc	850.00
s. Specimen. Series A; B. 190x.	—	Unc	750.00

NOTE: For #S309, a note dated ca.1910 is reported in archive records. No examples are known.

S310 500 PESOS	Good	Fine	XF
ca.1906; 1914. Black on red amd yellow unpt. Portr. M. Hidalgo at l., miners working at ctr. r. Back red; bank at ctr.			
a. Series B. 22.1.1914.	—	—	—
p. Proof. 190x (ca.1906).	—	—	—
s. Specimen. 190x (ca.1906).	—	—	—

JALISCO

EJÉRCITO NACIONAL

Issued at Ciudad Guzmán.

1864 BONO ISSUE

#S311 and S311A black text. Arms at upper l. Blue-gray paper.

	Good	Fine	XF
S311 25 PESOS 25.5.1864. *(PR-JAL-11).*	150.00	400.00	—
S311A 50 PESOS 25.5.1864. *(PR-JAL-12).*	150.00	400.00	—

BANCO DE JALISCO

1900-14 FIRST ISSUE

#S312-S319 city view of Guadalajara at ctr. on back. Printer: BWC.

S312 50 CENTAVOS	Good	Fine	XF
1914. Pink and black. Woman's head at l., horses's head at r. Back orange and pink. W/ or w/o date.			
a. 1.5.1914. *(BK-JAL-1).*	10.00	45.00	120.00
r. Remainder. 1.5.1914. *(BK-JAL-3).*	—	Unc	100.00

S313 1 PESO	Good	Fine	XF
20.1.1914/18xx. Black and blue. Dog's head at l., Ceres (Goddess of Agriculture) at ctr., ram at r. Back green and blue. *(BK-JAL-4).*	10.00	45.00	120.00

S314 5 PESOS	Good	Fine	XF
5.9.1900. Portr. Eleutheria (Goddess of Liberty) at l., portr. Mercury (God of Commerce) at r. Series A. *(BK-JAL-6).*			
a. Issued note.	1000.	1750.	—
b. Ovpt: *COLIMA. (BK-JAL-7).*	1100.	2000.	—
c. Ovpt: *TEPIC/COLIMA. (BK-JAL-8).*	1100.	2000.	—

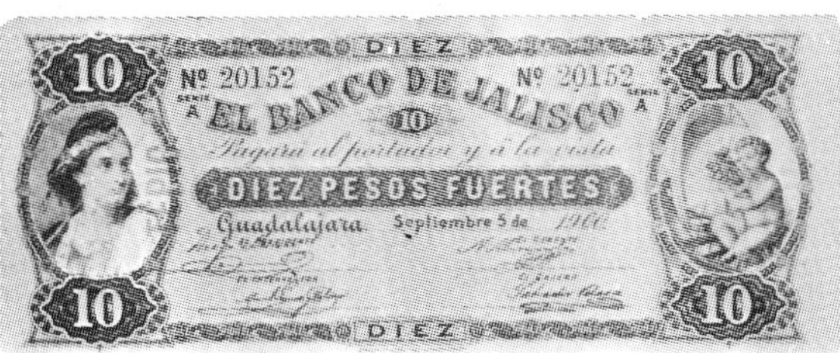

		GOOD	FINE	XF
S315	**10 PESOS** 1898-1900. Yellow and green unpt. Portr. Eleutheria (Goddess of Liberty) at l., child on sailboat at r. Back green and yellow. Series A.			
	a. 28.11.1898; 5.9.1900. *(BK-JAL-9).*	500.00	1200.	—
	b. Ovpt: *TEPIC.* 5.9.1900. *(BK-JAL-10).*	600.00	1500.	—
	c. Ovpt: *TEPIC/COLIMA.* 5.9.1900. *(BK-JAL-11).*	600.00	1500.	—

		GOOD	FINE	XF
S316	**20 PESOS** 20.5.1900. Portr. Polyhymnia (Muse of Lyrical Poetry) at l., herd of cattle at r. Series A. *(BK-JAL-12).*	2000.	3750.	—

		GOOD	FINE	XF
S317	**50 PESOS** 28.11.1898; 3.12.1900. Portr. Chloris (Goddess of Flowers) at l., allegory of Spring at r. Series A. *(BK-JAL-13).*	2000.	3750.	—

		GOOD	FINE	XF
S318	**100 PESOS** 1.3.1900. Portr. Minerva (Goddess of Science, Art and War) at l., oxen drawing hay wagon at r. Series A. *(BK-JAL-14).*	2000.	3750.	—

		GOOD	FINE	XF
S319	**500 PESOS** 18xx. Red, green and black. Boy at l., steam locomotive at r.			
	p. Proof.	—	—	—
	s. Specimen.	—	—	—

1900-14 SECOND ISSUE

#S320-S327 city view of Guadalajara at ctr. on back. Printer: ABNC.

		GOOD	FINE	XF
S320	**5 PESOS** 1902-14. Black on green and yellow unpt. State arms at l. Back green.			
	a. Series A. 1.8.1902; B. 1.2.1903; 5.5.1903. *(BK-JAL-16).*	10.00	30.00	—
	b. Series C. 15.10.1908; 15.12.1908; D. 1.2.1910. *(BK-JAL-17).*	10.00	30.00	—
	c. Series E. 5.1.1911; F. 26.3.1914. *(BK-JAL-18).*	10.00	30.00	55.00
	d. Ovpt: *TEPIC.* Series B. 1.2.1903; 5.5.1903. *(BK-JAL-19).*	15.00	50.00	—
	e. Ovpt: *ZAMORA.* Series A. 1.8.1902; Series B. 1.2.1903. *(BK-JAL-20).*	15.00	50.00	—
	f. Ovpt: *ZAPOTLÁN.* Series A. 10.9.1902. *(BK-JAL-21).*	15.00	50.00	—
	p. 19xx. Proof.	—	Unc	75.00
	s. Specimen.	—	Unc	75.00

		GOOD	FINE	XF
S321	**10 PESOS** 1902-14. Black on orange unpt. State arms at l., woman and child at lower r. Back orange.			
	a. Series A. 1.2.1903. *(BK-JAL-25).*	15.00	40.00	—
	b. Series B. 25.3.1908; D. 1.2.1910. *(BK-JAL-26).*	15.00	40.00	80.00
	c. Series E. 5.1.1911; 1.2.1911; F. 26.3.1914. *(BK-JAL-27).*	15.00	40.00	80.00
	d. Ovpt: *TEPIC.* Series A. 1.2.1903. *(BK-JAL-28).*	20.00	60.00	—
	e. Ovpt: *ZAMORA.* Series A. 10.9.1902; 1.2.1903. *(BK-JAL-29).*	20.00	60.00	—
	p. Proof. 19xx.	—	Unc	120.00
	s. Specimen.	—	Unc	120.00

		GOOD	FINE	XF
S322	**20 PESOS** 1902-14. Black on blue unpt. State arms at l., symbolic figure of Clemency at r. Back blue.			
	a. Series A. 10.9.1902; 5.5.1902. *(BK-JAL-31).*	40.00	90.00	—
	b. Series B. 12.3.1907; D. 1.2.1910. *(BK-JAL-32).*	40.00	90.00	—
	c. Series E; F. 26.3.1914. *(BK-JAL-33).*	40.00	90.00	175.00
	p1. Face proof. Green and black, mounted on card. *(BK-JAL-33A).*	—	Unc	100.00
	p2. Proof. 19xx.	—	Unc	150.00
	s. Specimen.	—	Unc	150.00

		GOOD	FINE	XF
S323	**50 PESOS** (ca.1902-14). Black on olive-green and yellow unpt. State arms at l., ceramic workers and their wares at r. Back olive-green.			
	a. 25.3.1908. *(BK-JAL-35).*	250.00	450.00	—
	b. Series A. 16.7.1909; B. 16.7.1909; E. 1.1.1911; F. 26.3.1914. *(BK-JAL-36).*	200.00	350.00	600.00
	p. Proof. 19xx. (ca.1902).	—	Unc	450.00
	s. Specimen.	—	Unc	450.00

S324 100 Pesos
(ca.1902-09). Black on brown and yellow unpt. State arms at l. ctr., men and burros at r. Back brown.

	Good	Fine	XF
a. Series B. 16.7.1909. *(BK-JAL-38).*	1500.	3000.	—
p. Proof. 19xx (ca.1902).	—	—	—
s. Specimen.	—	—	—

S325 100 Pesos
1.2.1910; 5.1.1911. Black on green and purple unpt. Portr. Eleutheria (Goddess of Liberty) at l., State arms at r. Back purple. Series D; E.

	Good	Fine	XF
a. Issued note. *(BK-JAL-39).*	300.00	600.00	1250.
p. Proof.	—	—	—
s. Specimen. *(BK-JAL-39s).*	—	—	—

S326 500 Pesos
1.2.1910; 5.1.1911. Black on pink, green and brown unpt. Reclining woman at l. state arms at ctr. r. Back blue-gray. Series D; E.

	Good	Fine	XF
a. Issued note. *(BK-JAL-41).*	1500.	3000.	—
p. Proof.	—	—	—
s. Specimen. *(BK-JAL-42s).*	—	—	—

NOTE: For #S325 and S326, a note dated ca.1914 is listed in archive records. No examples are known.

S327 1000 Pesos
19xx (ca.1909-14). Black on brown, purple and blue unpt. Seated allegorical woman holding globe at l., state arms at r. Back red.

	Good	Fine	XF
p. Proof.	—	—	—
s. Specimen. *(BK-JAL-43s).*	—	—	—

1914 ND Issue

S328 5 Pesos
ND. Green. State arms at l. Series B. Printer: NBNC. Unsigned remainder. *(BK-JAL-44).*

Good	Fine	XF
325.00	700.00	—

México (Estado de)

Banco del Estado de Mexico

1897-1914 Issue

#S329-S337 steam passenger train traveling through mountain pass at ctr. on back.

#S329-S335 printer: ABNC.

S329 5 Pesos
1897-1912. Black on yellow and brown unpt. Nike (Victory) at l., national arms at l. ctr., Polyhymnia (Muse of Lyrical Poetry) at r. Back brown.

	Good	Fine	XF
a. Series A. 5.11.1897; 18.7.1898; 2.4.1899. Series A. Sign. title: *DIRECTOR GERENTE* at r. *(BK-MEX-3).*	20.00	50.00	—
b. Series B. 26.8.1901; 29.10.1902. Series A & B. Sign. title: *CAJERO* at r. *(BK-MEX-4).*	15.00	40.00	100.00
c. Series B. 19.11.1907-22.10.1912. *(BK-MEX-5).*	15.00	40.00	100.00
d. Ovpt: *MORELIA.* 21.10.1908; 22.10.1912. *(BK-MEX-6).*	15.00	70.00	—
p1. Proof. W/o series. 189x.	—	Unc	125.00
p2. Proof. Series A. ND.	—	Unc	175.00
s1. Specimen. W/o series. 189x.	—	Unc	175.00
s2. Specimen. W/o series. ND.	—	Unc	125.00
s3. Specimen. Series B. ND.	—	Unc	125.00

#S330-S332, S335 national arms at r.

S330 10 Pesos
1898-1912. Black on green and yellow unpt. Woman at l. Back green; allegorical man at l. and r.

	Good	Fine	XF
a. Series A. 1.1.1898; 18.7.1898; 2.4.1899. Sign. title: *DIRECTOR GERENTE* at r. *(BK-MEX-9).*	20.00	60.00	125.00
b. Series B. 26.8.1901-5.11.1909. Sign. title: *CAJERO* at r. *(BK-MEX-10).*	15.00	40.00	100.00
c. Series B. 16.7.1910; 1.7.1911; 22.10.1912. *(BK-MEX-11).*	15.00	40.00	100.00
d. Ovpt: *MORELIA.* 19.11.1907; 2.10.1908; x.11.1910. *(BK-MEX-12).*	20.00	70.00	—
p. Proof. W/o series. 189x.	—	Unc	150.00
s. Specimen. W/o series. 189x.	—	Unc	150.00

S331 20 PESOS

1898-1912. Black on orange and yellow unpt. Nike (Victory) at ctr. Back orange.

		GOOD	FINE	XF
a.	Series A. 1.1.1898; 18.7.1898; 22.9.1899; 5.2.1900. Sign. title: *DIRECTOR GERENTE* at r. *(BK-MEX-14).*	50.00	140.00	—
b.	Series B. 26.8.1901-25.11.1905. Sign. title: *CAJERO* at r. *(BK-MEX-15).*	40.00	110.00	—
c.	Series B. 2.4.1909-22.10.1912. *(BK-MEX-16).*	40.00	110.00	225.00
d.	Ovpt: *MORELIA.* 26.8.1901; 25.11.1905; 22.10.1912. *(BK-MEX-17).*	60.00	150.00	—
p.	Proof. W/o series. 189x.	—	Unc	275.00
s.	Specimen. W/o series. 189x.	—	Unc	275.00

S332 50 PESOS

1898-1912. Black on yellow and olive unpt. Urania (Astronomy) at l. Back brown.

		GOOD	FINE	XF
a.	Series A. 1.1.1898; 18.7.1898; 5.2.1900. Sign. title: *DIRECTOR GERENTE* at r. *(BK-MEX-19).*	200.00	450.00	—
b.	Series B. 26.8.1901; 25.11.1905. Sign. title: *CAJERO* at r. *(BK-MEX-20).*	150.00	350.00	—
c.	Series B. 1.7.1911; 22.10.1912. *(BK-MEX-21).*	125.00	300.00	—
d.	Ovpt: *MORELIA.* 1.7.1911. *(BK-MEX-22).*	200.00	500.00	—
p.	Proof. W/o series. 189x.	—	Unc	750.00
s.	Specimen. W/o series. 189x.	—	Unc	750.00

#S333 and S334 national arms at ctr.

S333 100 PESOS

1898-1911. Black on blue and yellow unpt. Ship at l., seated Ceres (Goddess of Agriculture) at r. Back blue.

		GOOD	FINE	XF
a.	Series A. 1.1.1898; 18.7.1898; 5.2.1900. Sign. title: *DIRECTOR GERENTE* at r. *(BK-MEX-24).*	400.00	800.00	—
b.	Series B. 25.8.1901/189x; 25.11.1905. Sign. title: *CAJERO* at r. *(BK-MEX-25).*	350.00	700.00	—
c.	Series B. 1.7.1911; 22.10.1912. *(BK-MEX-26).*	300.00	500.00	950.00
p.	Proof. W/o series. 189x.	—	Unc	750.00
s.	Specimen. W/o series. 189x.	—	Unc	750.00

S334 500 PESOS

(ca.1897-1911). Black on red-orange and yellow unpt. Wisdom seated at l. ctr., Study seated at ctr. r. Sign. title: *DIRECTOR GERENTE* at r. Back red. *(BK-MEX-28).*

		GOOD	FINE	XF
a.	Series B. 1.7.1911.	2000.	4000.	—
p.	Proof. W/o series. 189x (ca.1897).	—	—	—
s.	Specimen. W/o series. 189x (ca.1897).	—	—	—

S335 1000 PESOS

(ca. 1897-1900). Black on blue and yellow unpt. Eleutheria (Liberty) at l. ctr. Sign. title: *DIRECTOR GERENTE* at r. Back dk. blue. *(BK-MEX-30).*

		GOOD	FINE	XF
a.	Series A. 6.2.1900.	3500.	—	—
p.	Proof. W/o series. 189x (ca.1897).	—	—	—
s.	Specimen. W/o series. 189x (ca.1897).	—	—	—

1914 ISSUE

#S336 and S337 portr. M. Hidalgo at ctr. Printer: AB&PC.

		GOOD	FINE	XF
S336	**1 PESO** 9.2.1914. Black on green unpt. Back green. Series C.D., E.F. *(BK-MEX-1).*	3.00	15.00	50.00
S337	**2 PESOS** 9.2.1914. Orange and black. Back red. Series NO, PQ. *(BK-MEX-2).*	2.50	12.00	45.00

MICHOACÁN

BANCO DE MICHOACÁN

1903 ISSUE

#S338-S344 cathedral at ctr. on back. Printer: ABNC.

S338 5 PESOS

5.1.1903; 6.8.1903. Black on green and yellow unpt. Portr. José M. Morelos Pavón at l., lion at ctr., Eros (God of Love) at r. Back green. Series A. *(BK-MIC-1).*

		GOOD	FINE	XF
a.	Issued note.	900.00	1500.	2250.
b.	Ovpt: *MOROLEÓN.* 6.8.1903. *(BK-MIC-2).*	900.00	1500.	—
c.	Ovpt: *PURUANDIRO.* 5.1.1903. *(BK-MIC-3).*	900.00	1500.	—
d.	Ovpt: *ALAMBARO.* ND. *(BK-MIC-4).*	900.00	1500.	—
p.	Proof.	—	Unc	800.00
s.	Specimen.	—	Unc	800.00

		Good	Fine	XF
S339	**10 Pesos** 5.1.1903; 6.8.1903. Black on orange and yellow unpt. Man carrying water jug at l. Back orange. Series A. *(BK-MIC-7).*			
	a. Issued note.	1000.	1750.	—
	b. Ovpt: *COTIJA.* 6.8.1903. *(BK-MIC-8).*	1000.	1750.	—
	c. Ovpt: *MOROLEÓN.* 5.1.1903. *(BK-MIC-9).*	1000.	1750.	—
	d. Ovpt: *PURUANDIRO.* 5.1.1903. *(BK-MIC-10).*	1000.	1750.	—
	p. Proof.	—	Unc	1200.
	s. Specimen.	—	Unc	1200.

		Good	Fine	XF
S340	**20 Pesos** 5.1.1903. Black on blue and yellow unpt. Portr. José Michelena at ctr. Back blue-gray. Series A. *(BK-MIC-12).*			
	a. Issued note.	1500.	3000.	—
	p. Proof.	—	Unc	1750.
	s. Specimen.	—	Unc	1750.

		Good	Fine	XF
S341	**50 Pesos** 6.2.1903. Black on brown and yellow unpt. Women w/young boys representing work and knowledge at l. Back brown. Series A. *(BK-MIC-14).*			
	a. Issued note.	3500.	—	—
	p. Proof.	—	—	—
	s. Specimen.	—	—	—

		Good	Fine	XF
S342	**100 Pesos** 16.2.1903. Black on olive-green and yellow unpt. Portr. Vasco de Quiroga at ctr. Back olive-green. Series A. *(BK-MIC-16).*			
	a. Issued note.	3500.	—	—
	p. Proof.	—	—	—
	s. Specimen.	—	—	—
S343	**500 Pesos** 19xx (ca.1906). Black on red and yellow unpt. Man w/farm tool at l. Back brown.			
	p. Proof.	—	—	—
	s. Specimen.	—	—	—

		Good	Fine	XF
S344	**1000 Pesos** 19xx (ca. 1906). Black on purple and yellow unpt. Farmer beside wagon at ctr. Back purple.			
	p. Proof.	—	—	—
	s. Specimen.	—	—	—

MORELOS

BANCO DE MORELOS

1903 ISSUE

#S345-S350 printer: ABNC.

		Good	Fine	XF
S345	**5 Pesos** 1903-10. Black on green unpt. Horse at l., Flora (Goddess of Flowers and Gardens) at r. Back green.			
	a. 25.3.1903-20.12.1904. *(BK-MOR-2).*	25.00	70.00	—
	b. Series C. 11.2.1910. *(BK-MOR-3).*	20.00	60.00	—
	c. Ovpt: *ACAPULCO.* 14.8.1903. *(BK-MOR-4).*	30.00	80.00	—
	p. Proof. W/o series. ND.	—	Unc	150.00
	s. Specimen. Series C. ND.	—	Unc	150.00

		Good	Fine	XF
S346	**10 Pesos** 1903-10. Black on brown unpt. Seated Eratus and woman at l., standing Urania (Astronomy) at r. Back brown; allegorical woman's head at ctr.			
	a. Series A; E. 25.3.1903-20.12.1904. *(BK-MOR-7).*	25.00	75.00	—
	b. Series A; E. 11.2.1910. *(BK-MOR-8).*	20.00	60.00	125.00
	c. Ovpt: *ACAPULCO.* 14.8.1903. *(BK-MOR-9).*	30.00	80.00	—
	p. Proof. W/o series. ND.	—	Unc	150.00
	s. Specimen. Series E. ND.	—	Unc	150.00

		Good	Fine	XF
S347	**20 Pesos** 1903-10. Black on blue unpt. Filia (Friendship) and Faith at l., seated woman holding national arms next to lion at r. Back blue-black.			
	a. Series A; D. 3.6.1903; 14.8.1903; 29.10.1903; 20.12.1904. *(BK-MOR-011).*	45.00	120.00	—
	b. Series D. 11.2.1910. *(BK-MOR-12).*	40.00	100.00	—
	c. Ovpt: *ACAPULCO.* 14.8.1903. *(BK-MOR-13).*	50.00	140.00	—
	p. Proof. W/o series. ND.	—	Unc	250.00
	s. Specimen.	—	—	—

		Good	Fine	XF
S348	**50 Pesos** 1903-10. Black on blue unpt. Seated Fertility w/children at ctr. Back blue.			
	a. 3.6.1903; 14.8.1903; 29.10.1903. *(BK-MOR-15).*	85.00	170.00	—
	b. Series A; F. 11.2.1910. *(BK-MOR-16).*	75.00	150.00	300.00
	p. Proof. W/o series. ND.	—	Unc	350.00
	s. Specimen.	—	—	—

S349 100 PESOS
1903-10. Black on red unpt. Themis (Justice) and child at l., portr. Jose M. Morelos at ctr. r. Back red; allegorical woman's head at ctr.

	Good	Fine	XF
a. Series A; G. 3.6.1903-20.12.1904. *(BK-MOR-18).*	400.00	1250.	—
b. Series A. ND (ca.1903). Specimen or proof.	—	—	—
p. Proof. W/o series. ND.	—	Unc	800.00
s. Specimen. Series A.	—	—	—

	Good	Fine	XF
S350 500 PESOS ND (ca.1902). Black on olive-green unpt. Lion facing l. at ctr. Back olive-green; lion's head at ctr. Series B. Specimen or proof. *(BK-MOR-20).*	—	—	—

1914 ISSUE

	Good	Fine	XF
S351 1 PESO 31.7.1914. Portr. Jose M. Morelos y Pavon at l., woman (Abundance) at r. Printer: E.I.A. *(BK-MOR-1).*	—	800.00	—

NUEVO LEÓN

BANCO MERCANTIL DE MONTERREY

1900-11 ISSUE

#S352-S357 city of Monterrey at ctr. on back. Printer: ABNC.

S352 5 PESOS
1900. Black on green and yellow unpt. Portr. M. Escobedo at l., ore loading platform at ctr. Text: *EN MONEDA DE PLATA.* Middle sign. title: *PRESIDENTE.* Back green. *(BK-NUE-39).*

	Good	Fine	XF
a. Series E. 2.4.1900; 15.8.1900.	100.00	—	—

S352A 5 PESOS
1906; 1911. Like #S352 but w/text: *EN MONEDA CORRIENTE.* Middle sign. title: *CONSEJERO. (BK-NUE-40).*

	Good	Fine	XF
a. 23.10.1906.	50.00	100.00	—
b. Series L; N. 27.7.1911. *(BK-NUE-41).*	40.00	90.00	150.00
p. Proof. Series A. 19xx.	—	—	—
s. Specimen. Series A. 19xx.	—	—	—

S353 10 PESOS
1900. Black on brown and yellow unpt. Railroad depot at l., portr. M. Escobedo at ctr. r. Text; *EN MONEDA DE PLATA.* Middle sign. title: *PRESIDENTE.* Back brown. *(BK-NUE-44).*

	Good	Fine	XF
a. Series K; M. 2.4.1900; 15.8.1900.	80.00	160.00	—
b. Ovpt: *LINARES.* Series M. 2.4.1900; 15.8.1900. *(BK-NUE-47).*	125.00	250.00	—
p. Proof. Series H. 19xx.	—	—	—
s. Specimen. Series H. 19xx.	—	—	—

S353A 10 PESOS
1906; 1911. Like #S353 but w/text: *EN MONEDA CORRIENTE.* Middle sign. title: *CONSEJERO. (BK-NUE-45).*

	Good	Fine	XF
a. 23.10.1906.	80.00	160.00	—
b. Series R. 27.7.1911.	60.00	120.00	225.00

S354 20 PESOS
1900. Black on olive-green unpt. Portr. M. Escobedo at l., cathedral at r. Text: *EN MONEDA DE PLATA.* Middle sign. title: *PRESIDENTE.* Back olive-green. *(BK-NUE-49).*

	Good	Fine	XF
a. Series P. 15.8.1900.	200.00	300.00	—
p. Proof. Series R. 19xx.	—	—	—
s. Specimen. Series R. 19xx.	—	—	—

	Good	Fine	XF
S354A 20 PESOS 6.3.1907. Like #S354 but w/text: *EN MONEDA CORRIENTE.* Middle sign. title: *CONSEJERO.* Series S. *(BK-NUE-50).*	225.00	425.00	600.00

S355 50 PESOS
1900. Black on red-orange unpt. Portr. M. Escobedo at l., theater bldg. at r. Text: *EN MONEDA DE PLATA.* Middle sign. title: *PRESIDENTE.* Back orange. *(BK-NUE-52).*

	Good	Fine	XF
a. Series S. 2.4.1900; 6.3.1902.	—	—	—
b. Series T; U; V. 15.8.1900.	350.00	650.00	—

	Good	Fine	XF
S355A 50 PESOS (ca.1906). Like #S355 but w/text: *EN MONEDA CORRIENTE.* Middle sign. title: *CONSEJERO.* ND. Specimen.	—	—	—
S356 100 PESOS 2.4.1900-6.3.1907. Black on blue and yellow unpt. Portr. M. Escobedo at l., bldg. at ctr. Text: *EN MONEDA DE PLATA* Middle sign. title: *PRESIDENTE.* Series W. Back blue-black. *(BK-NUE-54).*	1000.	2250.	—

S356A 100 PESOS
6.3.1907. Like #S356 but w/text: *EN MONEDA CORRIENTE;* middle sign. title: *CONSEJERO.* Series Z.

	Good	Fine	XF
p. Proof.	—	—	—
s. Specimen.	—	—	—

		Good	Fine	XF
S357	**500 Pesos** 19xx. Black on red and yellow unpt. Portr. M. Escobedo at l., lg. bldg. at ctr. r. Text: *EN MONEDA DE PLATA.* Middle sign. title: *PRESIDENTE.* Back red. Series Z. *(BK-NUE-55s).*	—	—	—
S357A	**500 Pesos** (ca.1907). Like #S357 but w/text: *EN MONEDA CORRIENTE;* middle sign. title: *CONSEJERO.*			
	p. Proof.	—	—	—
	s. Specimen.	—	—	—

Banco de Nuevo León

1893-1914 Issue

		Good	Fine	XF
S358	**50 Centavos** ND. I. Zaragoza at r. W/o sign. Essay. *(BK-NUE-6).*	—	—	800.00

#S359-S365 state seal at ctr. on back. Printer: ABNC.

		Good	Fine	XF
S359	**1 Peso** 1892-1914. Black on yellow and brown unpt. Portr. I. Zaragoza at l., Minerva (Goddess of Science, Art and War) at ctr., beehives at r. Back brown. *(BK-NUE-7).*			
	a. 12.1.1892; 15.1.1893; 5.2.1893; 5.5.1893; 1893- ca.1913. R.h. sign. title: *EL CAJERO.*	100.00	175.00	300.00
	b. Perforated: *CANCELADO.* 5.2.1914. *(BK-NUE-8).*	—	60.00	100.00
	c. Issues w/needle punched cancel: *CANCELADO.* 1.1.1913. *(BK-NUE-7A).*	75.00	150.00	275.00
	s. Specimen. (ca.1913-14). R.h. sign. title: *EL GERENTE.*	—	—	—

		Good	Fine	XF
S360	**5 Pesos** 1892-1912. Black on green and yellow unpt. Jaguar at l. ctr., portr. I. Zaragoza at r. Back green.			
	a. Series G. 1.12.1892; 15.5.1895; 4.7.1897. R.h. sign. title: *EL CAJERO. (BK-NUE-11).*	60.00	125.00	—
	b. 25.9.1900/18xx-5.2.1903/19xx. R.h. sign. title: *EL GERENTE. (BK-NUE-12).*	22.50	60.00	—
	c. Series G. 20.2.1907; 1.1.1910-15.5.1912. *(BK-NUE-13).*	20.00	50.00	120.00
	d. Perforated: *CANCELADO.* ND. *(BK-NUE-14).*	—	—	100.00
	e. Ovpt: *ALLENDE.* 25.9.1900/18xx.	70.00	125.00	—
	f. 1.1.1913. *(BK-NUE-14A).*	—	—	100.00

		Good	Fine	XF
S361	**10 Pesos** 1895-1913. Black on orange and yellow unpt. Seated Euthenia (Goddess of Plenty) at l., portr. I. Zaragoza at ctr., seated Themis (Goddess of Justice) at r. Back orange.			
	a. 1.1.1895; 15.7.1896/2.2.1896; 4.7.1897; 2.4.1900. R.h. sign. title: *EL CAJERO. (BK-NUE-17).*	60.00	150.00	—
	b. 14.7.1900-16.10.1909. R.h. sign. title: *EL GERENTE. (BK-NUE-18).*	50.00	125.00	—
	c. Series L. 16.9.1910-1.1.1913. *(BK-NUE-19).*	45.00	80.00	170.00
	d. Perforated: *CANCELADO.* 1.1.1913. W/ or w/o date. *(BK-NUE-21).*	—	—	100.00
	e. Ovpt: *TORREÓN, COAH.* 14.7.1900. *(BK-NUE-20).*	75.00	175.00	—

		Good	Fine	XF
S362	**20 Pesos** 1894-1912. Black on blue and yellow unpt. Progress at l. ctr., portr. I. Zaragoza at r. Back blue.			
	a. 5.5.1893; 5.2.1894; 2.4.1896; 4.7.1897; 18.10.1897; 25.9.1900; 25.3.1904. R.h. sign. title: *EL CAJERO. (BK-NUE-23).*	175.00	400.00	—
	b. 27.11.1906; 21.11.1908. R.h. sign. title: *EL GERENTE. (BK-NUE-24).*	150.00	350.00	—
	c. Series A. 1.1.1910-15.5.1912. *(BK-NUE-25).*	125.00	300.00	550.00
	d. Perforated: *CANCELADO.* ND. *(BK-NUE-26).*	—	—	100.00
	e. 1.1.1913. *(BK-NUE-26A).*	—	—	—

		Good	Fine	XF
S363	**50 Pesos** 1893-1913. Black on yellow and olive-green unpt. Woman standing at l., portr. I. Zaragoza at top l. ctr., Nike (Victory) at r. Back olive-green.			
	a. 5.5.1893; 18.10.1897. R.h. sign. title: *EL CAJERO. (BK-NUE-28).*	275.00	600.00	—
	b. 5.5.1893; 14.7.1900. R.h. sign. title: *EL GERENTE. (BK-NUE-28).*	275.00	600.00	—
	c. 19.9.1907; 1.1.1911; 5.2.1912; 15.5.1912. *(BK-NUE-29).*	250.00	500.00	750.00
	d. Perforated: *CANCELADO.* 1.1.1913. *(BK-NUE-30).*	70.00	125.00	175.00
	s. Specimen. 18xx (ca.1899). R.h. sign. title: *EL GERENTE.*	—	—	—

		Good	Fine	XF
S364	**100 Pesos** 1893-1913. Black on orange, yellow and pink unpt. Terpichore (Muse of Dance) at l., river scene w/mountain in background at ctr., portr. I. Zaragoza at r. Back red.			
	a. 5.2.1893. R.h. sign. title: *EL CAJERO. (BK-NUE-33).*	400.00	850.00	—
	b. 25.9.1900/18xx; 15.9.1904. R.h sign title: *EL GERENTE. (BK-NUE-33).*	400.00	850.00	—
	c. Series I. 5.5.1910; 16.9.1910; 1.1.1911; 5.2.1912; 15.5.1912. *(BK-NUE-34).*	350.00	600.00	800.00
	d. Perforated: *CANCELADO.* 1.1.1913. *(BK-NUE-35).*	—	—	250.00

		Good	Fine	XF
S365	**500 Pesos** (ca.1893-1.1.1913). Black on yellow and brown unpt. Portr. I. Zaragoza at l., city view at ctr. r., griffin at r. Back dk. brown.			
	a. Perforated: *CANCELADO.* 1.1.1913. *(BK-NUE-37).*	—	—	—
	s1. Specimen. 18xx. R.h. sign. title: *EL CAJERO.*	—	—	—
	s2. Specimen. 18xx. R.h. sign. title: *EL GERENTE.*	—	—	—
	s3. Specimen. 19xx.	—	—	—

NOTE: For #S360-S365, reports of specific dates from 1893-1913 are needed to augment these listings.

BANCO DE PATRICIO MILMO

1800'S ISSUE

#S366-S370 vaquero on horseback at ctr. Printer: KBNC.

		GOOD	FINE	XF
S366	**5 PESOS** 18xx. Unsigned remainder. *(BK-NUE-1).*	—	Unc	700.00
S367	**10 PESOS** 18xx. Unsigned remainder. *(BK-NUE-2).*	—	Unc	700.00
S368	**20 PESOS** 18xx. Unsigned remainder. *(BK-NUE-3).*	—	Unc	900.00
S369	**50 PESOS** 18xx. Unsigned remainder. *(BK-NUE-4).*	—	Unc	900.00

		GOOD	FINE	XF
S370	**100 PESOS** 18xx. Unsigned remainder. *(BK-NUE-5).*	—	Unc	900.00

OAXACA

BANCO DE OAXACA

1903-07 ISSUE

#S371-S375 Tehuana at ctr. on back. Printer: ABNC.

		GOOD	FINE	XF
S371	**5 PESOS** 1903-07. Black on green and yellow unpt. Monument to B. Juarez at lower l., seated Homonea (Harmony) at ctr. Back green. *(BK-OAX-1).*			
	a. Series B; C. 10.3.1903-1.7.1907.	225.00	600.00	1250.
	p. Proof. W/o series. ND.	—	Unc	750.00
	s. Specimen. Series D or w/o series. ND.	—	—	—

		GOOD	FINE	XF
S372	**10 PESOS** 10.3.1903-21.3.1907. Black on orange and yellow unpt. Juno (Goddess of Roman Mythology) at l. Back orange.			
	a. Series E; J. *(BK-OAX-3).*	700.00	1200.	2000.
	p. Proof. W/o series. ND.	—	Unc	900.00
	s. Specimen.	—	—	—

		GOOD	FINE	XF
S373	**20 PESOS** 1903-05. Black on red and yellow unpt. Beauty at ctr. Back red. Series F.			
	a. 23.5.1903; 2.4.1905. *(BK-OAX-5).*	1200.	1800.	2500.
	b. Ovpt: *ISTMO.* 2.4.1905. *(BK-OAX-6).*	1200.	1800.	2500.
	p. Proof. W/o series. ND.	—	Unc	1800.
	s. Specimen.	—	—	—

		GOOD	FINE	XF
S374	**50 PESOS** 10.3.1903. Black on olive-green unpt. Monument to B. Juarez at l. Back olive-green.			
	a. Series G. *(BK-OAX-9).*	2000.	3500.	4500.
	p. Proof.	—	—	—
	s. Specimen.	—	—	—
S375	**100 PESOS** ND (ca.1903). Black on yellow and brown unpt. Monument to B. Juarez at ctr. Back brown.			
	p. Proof. W/o series. ND.	—	—	—
	s. Specimen. Series H.	—	—	—

PUEBLA

BANCO ORIENTAL DE MÉXICO

1913 ND ISSUE

#S376-S377 Banco Oriental de México at ctr. State arms at ctr. on back. Printer: AB&PC.

		GOOD	FINE	XF
S376	**5 PESOS** ND (1913).			
	a. W/printed sign. Face proof. *(BK-PUE-23).*	—	—	—
	x. Inverted 10 Peso guilloche. Face proof. *(BK-PUE-24).*	—	350.00	500.00

		Good	Fine	XF
S377	**10 Pesos** ND (1914). Proof. *(BK-PUE-33).*	250.00	350.00	500.00

1914 ND Issue

#S378-S387 printer: ABNC.

		Good	Fine	XF
S378	**50 Centavos** ND (ca.1914). Black on bright green unpt. Portr. E de Antunáno at l. Back green; Aztec calendar at ctr. *(BK-PUE-1).*			
	p. Proof.	—	Unc	500.00
	s. Specimen.	—	Unc	500.00
S379	**1 Peso** ND (ca.1914). Black on purple, orange and blue unpt. Bank bldg. at l. Back orange; Indian woman at ctr. *(BK-PUE-4).*			
	p. Proof.	—	Unc	700.00
	s. Specimen.	—	Unc	700.00
S380	**2 Pesos** ND (ca.1914). Black on red, orange, and m/c unpt. Bank bldg. at ctr. Back red; Indian woman at ctr. *(BK-PUE-7).*			
	p. Proof.	—	Unc	800.00
	s. Specimen.	—	Unc	800.00

1900-10 Issue

#S381-S387 state arms at ctr. on back.

		Good	Fine	XF
S381	**5 Pesos** 1900-14. Black on orange and yellow unpt. Portr. Estebán de Antunáno at l., Cathedral of Puebla at r. Back orange.			
	a. 1.3.1900; 12.3.1900; 15.3.1900. *(BK-PUE-8).*	5.00	20.00	—
	b. 1.5.1901; 30.6.1901; 1.9.1909. *(BK-PUE-9).*	3.00	10.00	35.00
	c. 3.2.1910-24.4.1914. *(BK-PUE-10).*	2.00	6.00	15.00
	d. ND. *(BK-PUE-11).*	4.00	12.00	25.00
	e. Ovpt: *ATLIXCO.* 15.3.1900. *(BK-PUE-14).*	15.00	40.00	—
	f. Ovpt: *HUAJUAPAM.* 3.2.1910. *(BK-PUE-15).*	10.00	25.00	—
	g. Ovpt: *JUCHITAN.* 3.2.1910. *(BK-PUE-16).*	10.00	25.00	—
	h. Ovpt: *OAXACA.* 1.5.1901. *(BK-PUE-17).*	15.00	35.00	—
	i. Ovpt: *SANTA ANA.* 3.2.1910. *(BK-PUE-18).*	12.50	30.00	—
	j. Ovpt: *TEHUACÁN.* 15.3.1900; 30.6.1901. *(BK-PUE-19).*	12.50	30.00	—
	k. Ovpt: *TEHUÁNTEPEC.* 3.2.1910. *(BK-PUE-20).*	10.00	25.00	—
	l. Ovpt: *TEZIUTLÁN.* 15.3.1900. *(BK-PUE-21).*	12.50	30.00	—
	m. Ovpt: *TLAXCALA.* 3.2.1910. *(BK-PUE-22).*	10.00	25.00	—
	p. Proof. W/o series. ND.	—	Unc	100.00
	s. Specimen. W/o series. ND.	—	Unc	75.00

Notice

Readers with unlisted dates, color or signature varieties are invited to submit photocopies of their notes to: Standard Catalog of World Paper Money, Krause Publications, 700 East State St. Iola WI 54990-0001 U.S.A. or by email: thernr@krause.com. Email submissions of material for possible inclusion need to be 100% jpeg attachments at 300 dpi.

		Good	Fine	XF
S382	**10 Pesos** 1900-14. Black on olive-green unpt. Portr. Estebán de Antunáno at l., city of Puebla at r. Back dk. green.			
	a. 23.5.1900; 1.5.1900; 30.6.1901. *(BK-PUE-25).*	4.00	15.00	40.00
	b. 1.5.1901xxx1.9.1909. *(BK-PUE-26).*	3.00	10.00	30.00
	c. 3.2.1910-22.4.1914. *(BK-PUE-27).*	2.00	8.00	20.00
	d. Ovpt: *ATLIXCO.* 13.5.1900. *(BK-PUE-29).*	20.00	50.00	—
	e. Ovpt: *OAXACA.* 1.5.1901. *(BK-PUE-30).*	20.00	50.00	—
	f. Ovpt: *TEHUACÁN.* 30.6.1901. *(BK-PUE-31).*	15.00	40.00	—
	g. Ovpt: *TEZIUTLÁN.* 23.5.1900; 1.6.1901; 30.6.1901. *(BK-PUE-32).*	15.00	40.00	—
	p. Proof. W/o series.	—	Unc	100.00
	s. Specimen. W/o series.	—	Unc	75.00

		Good	Fine	XF
S383	**20 Pesos** 1900-14. Black on brown unpt. Monument of Liberty at l., portr. Estebán de Antunáno at r. Back brown.			
	a. 30.6.2900. *(BK-PUE-35).*	7.50	20.00	50.00
	b. 1.5.1901; 12.6.1901; 1.9.1909. *(BK-PUE-36).*	7.50	20.00	—
	c. 1.9.1909-1.4.1914. *(BK-PUE-37).*	5.00	15.00	45.00
	d. Ovpt: *OAXACA.* 1.5.1901. *(BK-PUE-39).*	20.00	60.00	—
	e. Ovpt: *TEHUACÁN.* 12/1.6.1901; 30.6.1901. *(BK-PUE-40).*	20.00	60.00	—
	f. Ovpt: *TEZIUTLÁN.* 12/1.6.1901; 30.6.1901. *(BK-PUE-41).*	20.00	60.00	—
	p. Proof. W/o series. ND.	—	Unc	150.00
	s. Specimen. W/o series. ND.	—	Unc	75.00

		Good	Fine	XF
S384	**50 Pesos** 1900-14. Black on green unpt. Portr. Estebán de Antunáno at l., Euterpe (Music) at r. Back green.			
	a. 30.6.1900. *(BK-PUE-42).*	10.00	20.00	50.00
	b. 1.5.1901-1.9.1909. *(BK-PUE-43).*	10.00	20.00	50.00
	c. 3.1.1914; 12.1.1914; 14.3.1914; 1.4.1914. *(BK-PUE-44).*	5.00	15.00	45.00
	d. Ovpt: *OAXACA.* 1.5.1901; 12/1.6.1901. *(BK-PUE-45).*	20.00	60.00	—
	e. Ovpt: *TEHUACAN.* 2.3.1903. *(BK-PUE-45A).*	—	—	—
	p. Proof. W/o series. ND.	—	Unc	125.00
	s. Specimen. W/o series. ND.	—	Unc	100.00

S385 100 PESOS	GOOD	FINE	XF
1901-14. Black on red unpt. Portr. Estebá de Antunáno at l., Government Palace at ctr. Back red.			
a. 11.6.1900; 12.6.1901; 30.6.1901. *(BK-PUE-47).*	20.00	40.00	90.00
b. 1.9.1909. *(BK-PUE-48).*	18.00	35.00	70.00
c. 3.2.1910; 3.1.1914; 10.3.1914. *(BK-PUE-49).*	15.00	30.00	60.00
d. ND. W/o sign. of *Gerente. (BK-PUE-50).*	15.00	30.00	60.00
e. Ovpt: *ATLIXCO.* ND. *(BK-PUE-52).*	35.00	70.00	—
f. Ovpt: *TEZIUTLÁN.* 30.6.1901. *(BK-PUE-53).*	35.00	70.00	—
g. Ovpt: *TEHUACAN.* 11.6.1901. *(BK-PUE-52a).*	50.00	100.00	—
p. Proof. W/o series. ND.	—	Unc	175.00
s. Specimen. W/o series. ND.	—	Unc	150.00

S386 500 PESOS	GOOD	FINE	XF
1901-14. Black on blue and yellow unpt. Minerva and Irene (Reason leading Force) at l., portr. Estebán de Antunáno at r. Back dk. blue.			
a. 30.6.1901. *(BK-PUE-54).*	275.00	500.00	—
b. 1.4.1914; 3.1.1914; 14.2.1914. *(BK-PUE-55).*	200.00	400.00	650.00
p1. Face proof. *(BK-PUE-55a).*	—	—	300.00
p2. Proof. W/o series. ND.	—	Unc	500.00
s. Specimen. W/o series. ND.	—	Unc	500.00

S387 1000 PESOS	GOOD	FINE	XF
1901-14. Black on orange and yellow unpt. Sailor at l., portr. Estebán de Antunáno at ctr., Ceres (Goddess of Agriculture) at r. Back orange.			
a. 30.6.1901. *(BK-PUE-57).*	400.00	850.00	—
b. 17.6.1913-1.4.1914. *(BK-PUE-58).*	500.00	900.00	1250.
p. Proof. W/o series. ND.	—	Unc	1000.
s. Specimen. W/o series. ND.	—	Unc	1000.

NOTE: For #S383-S387, reports of specific dates from 1900-14 are needed to augment these listings.

1914 ISSUE

#S388-S389 state arms at ctr. on back. Printer: AB&PC.

S388 1 PESO	GOOD	FINE	XF
1914. Black, green and yellow. Monogram at l., Fort Loreto at ctr. r. Back olive-green.			
a. Circular seals on face. 12.1.1914-28.4.1914. *(BK-PUE-2).*	1.00	3.00	10.00
b. Square seals on face. 1.4.1914; 22.4.1914. *(BK-PUE-3).*	1.00	4.00	12.00

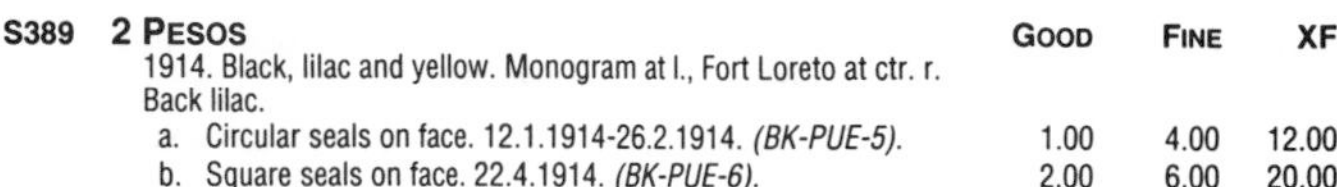

S389 2 PESOS	GOOD	FINE	XF
1914. Black, lilac and yellow. Monogram at l., Fort Loreto at ctr. r. Back lilac.			
a. Circular seals on face. 12.1.1914-26.2.1914. *(BK-PUE-5).*	1.00	4.00	12.00
b. Square seals on face. 22.4.1914. *(BK-PUE-6).*	2.00	6.00	20.00

QUERÉTARO

BANCO DE QUERÉTARO S.A.

1903-14 ISSUE

#S390-S396 steam passenger train traveling below aqueduct at ctr. on back. Printer: ABNC.

S390 5 PESOS	GOOD	FINE	XF
1903-14. Black on green unpt. Ox-cart at l., state arms at ctr. r. Back green. Series A.			
a. 30.7.1903; 4.1.1905; 1.11.1905; 15.1.1906. *(BK-QUE-3).*	15.00	30.00	—
b. New sign. ovpt. at l. and at ctr. 10.4.1914. *(BK-QUE-4).*	10.00	20.00	50.00
c. Ovpt: *IRAPUATO.* 30.7.1903; 15.1.1906. *(BK-QUE-6).*	15.00	30.00	—
p. Proof. W/o series. ND.	—	Unc	150.00
s. Specimen.	—	Unc	150.00

S391 10 PESOS	GOOD	FINE	XF
1903-14. Black on brown unpt. Portr. Guadalupe Obregón (as a child) at l., state arms at r. Back dk. brown. Series A.			
a. 1.11.1895; 15.1.1906. *(BK-QUE-7).*	15.00	30.00	—
b. New sign. ovpt. at l. and at ctr. 10.4.1914. *(BK-QUE-8).*	10.00	20.00	50.00
c. Ovpt: *IRAPUATO.* 30.7.1903; 15.1.1906. *(BK-QUE-10).*	15.00	30.00	—
p. Proof. W/o series; Series A. ND.	—	Unc	175.00
s. Specimen. ND.	—	—	—

S392 20 PESOS	GOOD	FINE	XF
1903-14. Black on orange unpt. Man carrying water jugs at l., portr. J. A. U. Arana at r. Back brown. Series A.			
a. 30.7.1903; 1.11.1905. *(BK-QUE-11).*	70.00	140.00	—
b. 15.4.1914. *(BK-QUE-12).*	80.00	160.00	300.00
c. Ovpt: *IRAPUATO.* 30.7.1903. *(BK-QUE-14).*	70.00	140.00	—
p. Proof. W/o series. ND.	—	Unc	450.00
s. Specimen.	—	—	—

S393	50 PESOS	GOOD	FINE	XF
	1903-14. Black on blue and yellow unpt. Portr. J. O. Domínguez at l., state arms at r. Back blue. Series A.			
	a. 30.7.1903; 1.11.1905; 15.1.1906. *(BK-QUE-15).*	250.00	425.00	—
	b. 15.4.1914. *(BK-QUE-16).*	200.00	350.00	600.00
	c. Ovpt: *IRAPUATO.* 30.7.1903. *(BK-QUE-18).*	300.00	500.00	—
	p. Proof. W/o series. ND.	—	Unc	600.00
	s. Specimen.	—	—	—

S394	100 PESOS	GOOD	FINE	XF
	1903-10. Black on red unpt. standing Eleutheria (Liberty) at l., state arms at r. Back dk. red. Series A; B.			
	a. 30.7.1903; 1.9.1910. *(BK-QUE-19).*	400.00	700.00	1000.
	b. Ovpt: *IRAPUATO.* 30.7.1903; 15.1.1906. *(BK-QUE-21).*	500.00	800.00	1100.
	s. Specimen.	—	Unc	1000.

S395	500 PESOS	GOOD	FINE	XF
	1903-10. Black on olive-green unpt. Portr. J. A. U. Arana at l., Minerva (Goddess of Science, Art and War) at r. Back dk. green. Series A.			
	a. 30.7.1903; 1.9.1910. *(BK-QUE-22).*	1000.	1750.	2750.
	b. Ovpt: *IRAPUATO.* 30.7.1903. *(BK-QUE-23).*	1250.	2000.	—
	s. Specimen.	—	Unc	1500.
S396	**1000 PESOS**			
	ND (ca.1903-09). Black on red unpt. J. O. Domínguez at l., state arms at r. Back orange. Series A. *(BK-QUE-25).*			
	p. Proof.	—	—	—
	s. Specimen.	—	—	—

1914 ISSUE

#S397 and S398 national arms at ctr. Printer: AB&PC.

S397	1 PESO	GOOD	FINE	XF
	1914. Blue and black. State arms at l., man w/pack mule at r. Back blue.			
	a. Series A. 1.1.1914. *(BK-QUE-1).*	7.50	30.00	65.00
	b. Series B. 15.2.1914. *(BK-QUE-1).*	7.50	30.00	65.00
	c. Series C. 15.4.1914. *(BK-QUE-1).*	7.50	30.00	65.00

S398	2 PESOS	GOOD	FINE	XF
	1914. Orange and yellow unpt. State arms at l., seated Indian at ctr. r., ox-cart at r. Back red-orange.			
	a. Series A. 1.1.1914. *(BK-QUE-2).*	10.00	35.00	75.00
	b. Series B. 15.2.1914. *(BK-QUE-2).*	10.00	35.00	75.00

SAN LUIS POTOSÍ

BANCO DE SAN LUIS POTOSÍ

1897-98 ISSUE

#S399-S405 state arms on face. Printer: ABNC.

#S399-S403, S405 national arms at ctr. on back.

S399	5 PESOS	GOOD	FINE	XF
	1898-1913. Black on green and yellow unpt. Portr. Mariano Arista at l. Back green.			
	a. Series A. 20.7.1898. *(BK-SAN-3).*	35.00	90.00	—
	b. Series A. 6.8.1900; 18.2.1901; 10.3.1903. *(BK-SAN-4).*	30.00	80.00	—
	c. Series B. 10.3.1903; 8.11.1911; C. 15.10.1913. *(BK-SAN-5).*	25.00	70.00	150.00
	d. Ovpt: *CELAYA.* 1.9.1898. *(BK-SAN-7).*	40.00	90.00	—
	e. Ovpt: *LEÓN.* 28.2.1898. *(BK-SAN-8).*	40.00	100.00	—
	p. Proof. Series A. ND.	—	Unc	150.00
	s. Specimen. Series. A. ND.	—	Unc	150.00

S400	10 PESOS	GOOD	FINE	XF
	1897-1913. Black on brown unpt. Eleutheria (Liberty) at l., Ceres (Agriculture) at r. Back brown.			
	a. Series A. 4.11.1897; 9.11.1897; 20.11.1897; 11.12.1897; 28.2.1898; 12.8.1898. *(BK-SAN-9).*	45.00	100.00	200.00
	b. Series A; B. 18.2.1901; B. 10.3.1903. *(BK-SAN-10).*	30.00	60.00	—
	c. Series C. 15.10.1913. *(BK-SAN-11).*	35.00	70.00	150.00
	d. Ovpt: *CELAYA.* 10.2.1900; 1.4.1900. *(BK-SAN-13).*	40.00	90.00	—
	e. Ovpt: *LEÓN.* 12.8.1898; 28.2.1898. *(BK-SAN-14).*	40.00	90.00	—
	p. Proof. Series A. ND.	—	Unc	175.00
	s. Specimen. Series A. ND.	—	Unc	175.00

S401	20 PESOS	GOOD	FINE	XF
	1897-1913. Black on orange and yellow unpt. Faith at r. Back orange.			
	a. Series A. 20.12.1897; 10.6.1898; 26.11.1899. *(BK-SAN-15).*	40.00	80.00	—
	b. Series A. 18.1.1898; 28.2.1898; B. 26.11.1899; 18.12.1899; 28.12.1899; 18.2.1901. *(BK-SAN-16).*	35.00	70.00	—
	c. Series B. 18.2.1911; 8.11.1911; C. 15.10.1913. *(BK-SAN-17).*	25.00	50.00	150.00
	d. Ovpt: *CELAYA.* 1.9.1899; 18.2.1901. *(BK-SAN-19).*	40.00	90.00	—
	e. Ovpt: *LEÓN.* 28.2.1898-18.2.1901. *(BK-SAN-20).*	35.00	80.00	—
	p. Proof. Series A. ND.	—	Unc	200.00
	s. Specimen. Series A. ND.	—	Unc	200.00

S402 50 PESOS

1898-1913. Black on blue unpt. Tyche (Fortune) w/Pluto at ctr. Back blue.

	Good	Fine	XF
a. Series A. 18.5.1898; 1.2.1899; B. 18.2.1901. *(BK-SAN-21).*	150.00	350.00	—
b. Series B. 8.11.1911; C. 15.10.1913. *(BK-SAN-22).*	125.00	300.00	—
c. Ovpt: *CELAYA.* 18.2.1901. *(BK-SAN-24).*	150.00	350.00	—
d. Ovpt: *LEÓN.* 26.5.1898. *(BK-SAN-25).*	150.00	350.00	—
p. Proof. Series A. ND.	—	Unc	500.00
s. Speciman. Series A. ND.	—	Unc	500.00

S403 100 PESOS

(ca.1897-1913). Black on yellow, orange and red unpt. Commerce at r. Back red.

	Good	Fine	XF
a. Series A. 1.6.1899. *(BK-SAN-26).*	300.00	500.00	—
b. Series B. 18.2.1901; 6.12.1909. *(BK-SAN-27).*	250.00	450.00	800.00
c. Ovpt: *LEÓN.* 8.12.1898. *(BK-SAN-29).*	350.00	550.00	—
p. Proof. Series A. ND.	—	Unc	800.00
s1. Specimen. Series A. ND.	—	Unc	800.00
s2. Specimen. Series C. ND.	—	Unc	800.00

S404 500 PESOS

1897-1913. Black on olive-green unpt. Mining scene at r. Back olive-green; national arms at l.

	Good	Fine	XF
a. Series A. 21.6.1900. *(BK-SAN-30).*	1000.	2000.	—
b. Series B. 18.2.1901. *(BK-SAN-30).*	1000.	2000.	—
p. Proof. Series A. ND.	—	Unc	1500.
s1. Specimen. Series A. ND.	—	Unc	1500.
s2. Specimen. Series C. ND.	—	Unc	1500.

S405 1000 PESOS

ND (ca.1897-1913). Black on orange and yellow unpt. Portr. Mariano Arista at ctr. Back orange. *(BK-SAN-32s).*

	Good	Fine	XF
p. Proof. Series A. ND.	—	Unc	1750.
s1. Specimen. Series A. ND.	—	Unc	1750.
s2. Specimen. Series B. ND.	—	—	—
s3. Specimen. Series C. ND.	—	—	—

1914 ISSUE

#S406 and S407 state arms at ctr. r., bank bldg. at l. on face. National arms at ctr. on back. Series D. Printer: AB&PC.

S406 1 PESO

15.2.1914. Orange and black. Back red. *(BK-SAN-1).*

	Good	Fine	XF
	5.00	20.00	50.00

S407 2 PESOS

15.2.1914. Green and black. Back green. *(BK-SAN-2).*

	Good	Fine	XF
	5.00	20.00	50.00

SINALOA

BANCO OCCIDENTAL DE MÉXICO

1898-1913 ISSUE

#S408-S414 port of Mazatlán at ctr. on back. Printer: ABNC.

S408 5 PESOS

1898-1913. Black on orange and yellow unpt. Portr. woman at l., cattle trail scene w/train in background at ctr. Back red-orange.

	Good	Fine	XF
a. 26.9.1898. *(BK-SIN-4).*	25.00	80.00	—
b. Series E. 1.5.1900; 1.8.1900. *(BK-SIN-5).*	18.00	60.00	—
c. Series K. 15.1.1904; L; M. 1.3.1904; P. 5.5.1906. *(BK-SIN-6).*	15.00	45.00	125.00
d. Series R. W/o sign. of *Gerente;* 1.1.1913 *(BK-SIN-7).*	15.00	40.00	80.00
e. Ovpt: *COLIMA.* 1.8.1900. *(BK-SIN-9).*	60.00	100.00	—
f. Ovpt: *GUAYMAS.* 15.3.1900. *(BK-SIN-9A).*	60.00	100.00	—

S409 10 PESOS

1900-13. Black on green unpt. Portr. woman at l., train at ctr. Back green.

	Good	Fine	XF
a. Series M; R. 1.4.1900-1.3.1904. *(BK-SIN-10).*	20.00	60.00	120.00
b. Series R. 16.10.1909. *(BK-SIN-11).*	18.00	40.00	80.00
c. 1.1.1913. *(BK-SIN-12).*	20.00	60.00	120.00
d. Ovpt: *COLIMA.* Series F. 1.8.1900. *(BK-SIN-14).*	25.00	75.00	180.00
e. Ovpt: *GUAYMAS.* 15.3.1900. *(BK-SIN-15).*	30.00	90.00	—

		Good	Fine	XF
S410	**20 Pesos** 1900-13. Black on brown unpt. Sailor standing at l. and r., portr. woman at ctr. Back brown.			
	a. Series D. 15.3.1900; 1.4.1900; E. 1.5.1900; G. 1.9.1900; 15.10.1900; N. 1.3.1904. *(BK-SIN-16).*	200.00	350.00	650.00
	b. 1.1.1913. *(BK-SIN-17).*	225.00	400.00	700.00
	c. Ovpt: *PAGADERO EN COLIMA*. Series G. 1.8.1900; 15.10.1900. *(BK-SIN-19).*	200.00	350.00	—
	d. Ovpt: *PAGADERO EN GUAYMAS*. 1.12.1900. *(BK-SIN-20).*	200.00	350.00	—

		Good	Fine	XF
S411	**50 Pesos** 1898-1904. Black on blue and yellow unpt. Standing Themis (Justice) at l., portr. woman at ctr., Zephyr (Wind and Youth) at r. Back blue.			
	a. Series B. 1.1.1900; G. 1.9.1900; N. 1.3.1904. *(BK-SIN-1).*	600.00	1200.	—
	b. Ovpt: *PAGADERO EN CULIACÁN*. 25.10.1898. *(BK-SIN-24).*	600.00	1200.	—
	c. Ovpt: *PAGADERO EN GUAYMAS*. Series C. 15.3.1900. *(BK-SIN-25).*	550.00	900.00	—
	d. Ovpt: *COLIMA*. Series H. 15.10.1900. *(BK-SIN-26).*	550.00	900.00	—

		Good	Fine	XF
S412	**100 Pesos** 1900. Black on red and yellow unpt. Cherubs at l. and r. supporting portr. of woman at l. ctr. Back red.			
	a. Series C. 1.1.1900; D. 1.4.1900; G. 1.9.1900; H. 15.10.1900; I. 1.12.1900. *(BK-SIN-27).*	400.00	700.00	—
	b. Ovpt: *PAGADERO EN GUAYMAS*. Series C. 15.3.1900. *(BK-SIN-29).*	450.00	850.00	—
	c. Ovpt: *PAGADERO EN COLIMA*. ND; 15.10.1900; *(BK-SIN-30).*	450.00	850.00	—

NOTE: For #S409-S412, notes dated ca.1898 are reported in archive records. No issued examples are known.

S413	**500 Pesos** ND (ca. 1900). Black on olive-green unpt. Woman at l., Aztec calendar at r. ctr. Back olive-green.			
	p. Proof.	—	—	—
	s. Specimen. *(BK-SIN-31s).*	—	—	—

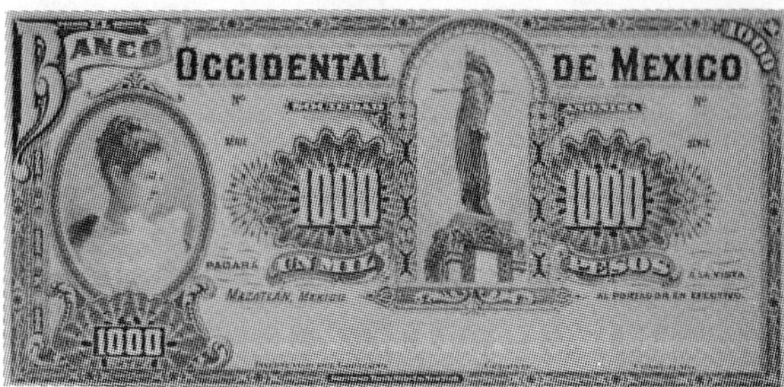

		Good	Fine	XF
S414	**1000 Pesos** ND (ca.1900). Black on brown unpt. Portr. woman at l., monument to Cuauhtémoc at ctr. Back dk. brown.			
	p. Proof. *(BK-SIN-32).*	—	—	—
	s. Specimen. *(BK-SIN-33s).*	—	—	—

Banco de San Ignacio (Ignatio)

1878 Issue

#S415-S418 printer: S. C. Toof & Co. Lith., Memphis, TN.

		Good	Fine	XF
S415	**Dos (2) Reales** 1878. Black. Woman at ctr. Back green; man at ctr. *(BK-SIN-1).*	12.50	30.00	60.00
S416	**Quatro (4) Reales** 1878.	Reported Not Confirmed		

		Good	Fine	XF
S417	**1 Peso** 1878. Black. Woman hugging child at upper l. Back green; dog's head at ctr. Series A. *(BK-SIN-2).*	60.00	200.00	—

		Good	Fine	XF
S418	**5 Pesos** 1878. Farm family w/horse and wagon at l. Steam train by station at ctr. on back. Series A. *(BK-SIN-3).*	200.00	400.00	—

Sonora

Banco de Sonora

1897-1911 Issue

#S419-S423 printer: ABNC.

S419 5 PESOS

1897-1911. Black on brown and yellow unpt. Portr. Hortensia C. Vélez at l., young Eros at l. ctr., Minerva (Goddess of Science, Art and War) at r. Back brown.

		GOOD	FINE	XF
a.	Series B. 4.4.1898; 1.8.1899. *(BK-SON-1).*	40.00	100.00	—
b.	1.7.1901-24.11.1909. *(BK-SON-2).*	10.00	45.00	—
c.	Series CK. 2.1.1911. *(BK-SON-3).*	7.50	30.00	75.00
d.	Ovpt: *CHIHUAHUA.* 1.7.1903/1902. *(BK-SON-4).*	40.00	100.00	—
p.	Proof. Series E. 1.7.1902. Back dk. brown w/brown unpt.	—	—	—
r.	Unissued remainder. Series DI; DN; DU; DZ. (ND). *(BK-SON-5).*	—	5.00	10.00
s.	Specimen.	—	—	—

S420 10 PESOS

1897-1911. Black on green and yellow unpt. Portr. Hortensia C. Vélez at l., cowboys and cattle scene at r. Back green.

		GOOD	FINE	XF
a.	1.9.1899; 1.11.1899. *(BK-SON-7).*	40.00	110.00	—
b.	Grill unpt. on back w/printed sign. 1.7.1902-14.8.1906/1.1.1906; 24.11.1909. *(BK-SON-8).*	20.00	70.00	—
c.	Series DD; DJ. 2.1.1911. *(BK-SON-9).*	2.00	6.00	15.00
d.	Ovpt: *CHIHUAHUA.* 1.7.1903/2. *(BK-SON-10).*	40.00	110.00	—
p.	Proof. Series B. 1.7.1902. Back dk. green w/green unpt.	—	—	—
r.	Unissued remainder. Series DL; DM; DO; DT; DQ; DU. (ND). *(BK-SON-11).*	—	6.00	15.00
s.	Specimen. Series B. 1.7.1902.	—	—	—

NOTE: Backs for #S419 and S420 *EL* in bank title (ca.1897-99). Later dates w/o *EL* on back.

S421 20 PESOS

1897-1911. Black on orange and yellow unpt. Reclining Agua (Water) at l., portr. Hortensia C. Vélez at r. Back orange.

		GOOD	FINE	XF
a.	1.6.1899. *(BK-SON-12).*	50.00	125.00	—
b.	1.7.1901-24.11.1909. *(BK-SON-13).*	40.00	90.00	—
c.	Series DL; DP; DR; DS. 2.1.1911. *(BK-SON-14).*	30.00	80.00	150.00
p.	Proof. Series B. 1.7.1902. Back dk. orange w/orange unpt.	—	—	—
r.	Unissued remainder. Series DT; DU; DV. ND. *(BK-SON-15).*	—	6.00	15.00
s.	Specimen. Series B. 1.7.1902.	—	—	—

S422 50 PESOS

1899-1911. Black on green and yellow unpt. Men working at l., portr. H. C. Vélez at r. Back blue-gray; head of allegorical woman at ctr.

		GOOD	FINE	XF
a.	Series CF. 1.12.1899. *(BK-SON-16).*	85.00	175.00	—
b.	Printed sign. Grill unpt. on back. 1.7.1901-24.11.1909. *(BK-SON-17).*	70.00	150.00	—
c.	Series CF. 2.1.1911. *(BK-SON-18).*	60.00	130.00	200.00
p.	Proof. Series M. 1.7.1902. Back blue-black w/blue-gray unpt.	—	—	—
r.	Remainder. Series DP-DT; DW; DX. (ND). *(BK-SON-19).*	—	7.50	25.00
s.	Specimen. Series M. 1.7.1902.	—	—	—

S423 100 PESOS

1898-1911. Black on olive-brown and yellow unpt. Portr. Hortensia C. Vélez at l., sailing ships at ctr. Back olive-brown.

		GOOD	FINE	XF
a.	Series CP. 1.11.1898. *(BK-SON-20).*	300.00	450.00	—
b.	Grill unpt. on back. 1.7.1903/1902-1.1.1906. *(BK-SON-21).*	250.00	375.00	—
c.	Series CL; CP. 2.1.1911. *(BK-SON-22).*	225.00	350.00	500.00
p.	Proof. Series D. 1.7.1902. Back olive-green w/lt. olive unpt.	—	—	—
r.	Remainder. Series DR; DT; DW; DX; DZ. (ND). *(BK-SON-23).*	—	15.00	30.00
s.	Specimen. Series D. 1.7.1902.	—	—	—

NOTE: For #S419-S423, reports of specific dates from 1897-1911 are needed to augment these listings.

TABASCO

BANCO DE TABASCO

1901-03 ISSUE

#S424-S428 Villahermosa on the Grijalva River at ctr. on back. Printer: ABNC.

S424 5 PESOS

1901-03. Black on green and yellow unpt. State arms at l., Marina "La Malinche" at r. Back green.

		GOOD	FINE	XF
a.	1.1.1901; 15.10.1901; 19.9.1903. *(BK-TAB-1).*	20.00	75.00	200.00
b.	Needle punched: *LAGUNA.* 19.9.1903. *(BK-TAB-2).*	100.00	200.00	—
c.	Ovpt: *PICHUCALCO.* 19.9.1903. *(BK-TAB-3).*	25.00	65.00	200.00

S425 10 PESOS

1901-03. Black on orange and yellow unpt. Government Palace at r. Back orange.

		GOOD	FINE	XF
a.	1.1.1901; 15.10.1901; 19.9.1903. *(BK-TAB-5).*	45.00	90.00	200.00
b.	Ovpt: *PICHUCALCO.* 19.9.1903. *(BK-TAB-6).*	65.00	130.00	250.00
c.	Needle punched: *LAGUNA.* 19.3.1903. *(BK-TAB-7).*	100.00	200.00	—

S426 20 PESOS

	GOOD	FINE	XF
1.1.1901. Black on blue and yellow unpt. Lumberjacks cutting trees at l. Back blue. Series A. *(BK-TAB-9).*	800.00	1400.	—

S427 50 Pesos

	Good	Fine	XF
1.1.1901. Black on olive-green unpt. Vaquero herding cattle at l., workers picking fruits at r. Back greenish brown. Series A. *(BK-TAB-11).*	400.00	1100.	—

S428 100 Pesos

	Good	Fine	XF
1.1.1901. Black on red and yellow unpt. Palm tree at l., harvesting of sugar cane at ctr. r. Back red. Series A. *(BK-TAB-13).*	1000.	1750.	2750.

Tamaulipas

Crédito del Estado de Tamaulipas

Issued by order of Governor Servando Canales. Most notes of this series show traces of glue at right edge and/or bear small punched hole cancellation.

1876 Emergency Issue

#S428A-S428G oval black seals: *gobierno del estado* above eagle and *SECRETARIO DEL GOBIERNO DE TAMAULIPAS.*

S428A 12 1/2 Centavos = Un Real

	Good	Fine	XF
1876. Violet.	18.00	30.00	60.00

S428B 25 Centavos = 4 Reales

	Good	Fine	XF
1876. Violet.	7.50	15.00	35.00

S428C 50 Centavos

	Good	Fine	XF
1876. Gray on pale lilac paper.	7.50	15.00	35.00

S428D 1 Peso

	Good	Fine	XF
1876. Pale brown.	9.00	20.00	45.00

S428E 5 Pesos

	Good	Fine	XF
1876. Gray-blue.	15.00	35.00	70.00

S428F 10 Pesos

	Good	Fine	XF
1876. Pale brown.	15.00	35.00	70.00

S428G 25 Pesos

	Good	Fine	XF
1876. Pale brown.	15.00	35.00	70.00

Banco de Tamaulipas

1902 Issue

#S429-S435 dogs at shoreline, man in canoe at ctr. on back. Printer: ABNC.

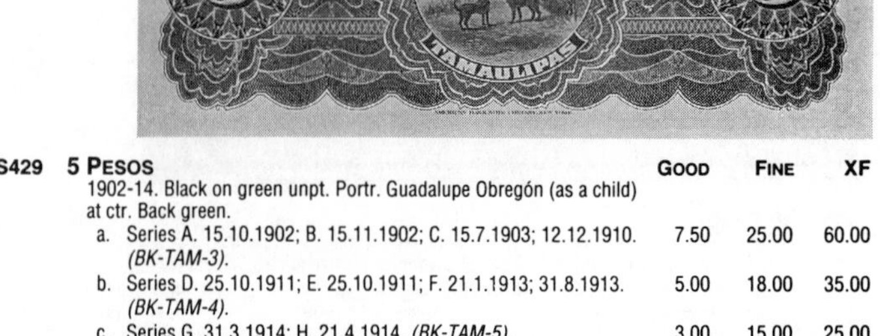

S429 5 Pesos

1902-14. Black on green unpt. Portr. Guadalupe Obregón (as a child) at ctr. Back green.

	Good	Fine	XF
a. Series A. 15.10.1902; B. 15.11.1902; C. 15.7.1903; 12.12.1910. *(BK-TAM-3).*	7.50	25.00	60.00
b. Series D. 25.10.1911; E. 25.10.1911; F. 21.1.1913; 31.8.1913. *(BK-TAM-4).*	5.00	18.00	35.00
c. Series G. 31.3.1914; H. 21.4.1914. *(BK-TAM-5).*	3.00	15.00	25.00
d. Series H. (ND). *(BK-TAM-7)*	—	—	6.00
p. Proof.	—	—	—
r. Unsigned remainder. Series G; H. 31.3.1914. *(BK-TAM-6).*	—	—	8.00
s. Specimen.	—	—	—

S430 10 PESOS

1902-14. Black on orange and lt. green unpt. Cattle at ctr. Back orange.

		GOOD	FINE	XF
a.	Series A. 15.10.1902; C. 15.7.1903. *(BK-TAM-10).*	20.00	50.00	—
b.	Series D. 12.12.1910; E. 25.10.1911; F. 31.8.1913; 10.1.1914. *(BK-TAM-11).*	15.00	30.00	60.00
c.	Series H. (ND). *(BK-TAM-12).*	—	—	12.00
p.	Proof.	—	—	—
s1.	Specimen. Series B. 190x.	—	—	—
s2.	Specimen. Series D. 190x.	—	—	—
s3.	Specimen. Series G. 31.3.1914.	—	—	—

S431 20 PESOS

1902-14. Black on blue and lt. green unpt. Train at ctr. Back blue.

		GOOD	FINE	XF
a.	Series A. 15.10.1902; C. 15.7.1903. *(BK-TAM-14).*	70.00	150.00	—
b.	Series D. 12.12.1910; F. 31.8.1913. *(BK-TAM-15).*	50.00	100.00	160.00
c.	Series H. 21.4.1914. *(BK-TAM-15).*	50.00	100.00	160.00
d.	Series H. (ND). *(BK-TAM-17).*	5.00	15.00	30.00
p.	Proof.	—	—	—
r.	Unsigned remainder. Series G. 31.3.1914. *(BK-TAM-16).*	10.00	18.00	35.00
s.	Specimen. Series D. 190x.	—	—	—

S432 50 PESOS

1902-14. Black on brown and yellow unpt. Commerce at ctr. Back brown.

		GOOD	FINE	XF
a.	Series A. 15.10.1902; C. 15.7.1903. *(BK-TAM-18).*	250.00	400.00	—
b.	Series D. 12.12.1910; F. 10.1.1914. *(BK-TAM-19).*	200.00	350.00	550.00
c.	Series H. 21.4.1914. *(BK-TAM-19).*	200.00	350.00	550.00
d.	Series H. (ND). *(BK-TAM-21).*	20.00	35.00	60.00
p.	Proof.	—	—	—
r.	Unsigned remainder. Series G. 31.3.1914. *(BK-TAM-20).*	25.00	40.00	70.00
s.	Specimen.	—	—	—

S433 100 PESOS

1902-14. Black on olive-green unpt. Sailing ships at ctr. Back dk. green.

		GOOD	FINE	XF
a.	Series B. 15.10.1902; C. 15.7.1903. *(BK-TAM-23).*	300.00	600.00	—
b.	Series D. 12.12.1910. *(BK-TAM-24).*	200.00	450.00	—
c.	Series F. 10.1.1914. *(BK-TAM-24).*	250.00	500.00	1000.
p.	Proof. Series A. 190x (ca.1902).	—	—	—
r1.	Remainder. Series G. 31.3.1914. *(BK-TAM-26).*	15.00	25.00	45.00
r2.	Remainder. Series H. (ND). *(BK-TAM-27).*	15.00	25.00	45.00
s1.	Specimen. Series A. 190x.	—	—	—
s2.	Specimen. Series D. 190x (ca.1903).	—	—	—
s3.	Specimen. ND (ca.1912).	—	—	—

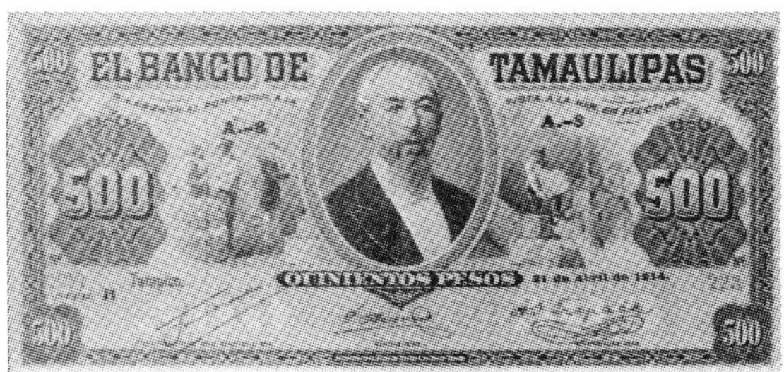

S434 500 PESOS

(ca.1902-14). Black on red and yellow unpt. Workers at docks at l., portr. Juan de la Garza at ctr. Back red.

		GOOD	FINE	XF
a.	Series H. 21.4.1914. *(BK-TAM-29).*	—	2000.	—
p.	Proof. Series A. 190x (ca.1902).	—	—	—
r.	Unsigned remainder. Series G. 31.3.1914. *(BK-TAM-30).*	200.00	500.00	950.00
s1.	Specimen. Series A. 190x (ca.1903).	—	—	—
s2.	Specimen. Series C. 190x (ca.1903).	—	—	—
s3.	Specimen. W/o series. ND.	—	—	—

S435 1000 PESOS

(ca.1902-14). Black on olive-brown unpt. Representing Work and Wisdom at l. ctr., Allegory of Triumph at ctr. r. Back brown.

		GOOD	FINE	XF
a.	Series B. 15.10.1902. *(BK-TAM-32).*	2000.	3250.	—
p.	Proof. Series A. 190x (ca.1902).	—	—	—
r.	Unsigned remainder. Series G. 31.3.1914. *(BK-TAM-33).*	400.00	850.00	—
s1.	Specimen. Series A. 190x.	—	—	—
s2.	Specimen. Series D. 190x (ca.1903).	—	—	—
s3.	Specimen. W/o series. ND.	—	—	—

1914 ISSUE

		GOOD	FINE	XF
S436	**1 PESO** 15.2.1914. Black on orange unpt. Oil rigs, storage tanks, steam freight train and tanker ship at upper ctr. Back red; standing Mercury on dock, sailing ship and fortress in background at ctr. Series 1A:1J; 1A:1P. 2 sign. varieties. Printer: AB&PC. *(BK-TAM-1).*	4.00	25.00	70.00

VERACRUZ

EL BANCO DE VERACRUZ

1890 ISSUE

		GOOD	FINE	XF
S436A	**1 PESO FUERTE** 1.9.1890. Portr. Prosperity at lower l., national arms at r. Series A. Printer: BWC.	—	—	—

BANCO MERCANTIL DE VERACRUZ

1898-1910 ISSUE

#S437-S444 harbor of Veracruz on back. Printer: ABNC.

		GOOD	FINE	XF
S437	**5 PESOS** 1898-1910. Black on green and yellow unpt. Eudemonia (Happiness) at ctr. Back green; blue stamp and red seal.			
	a. 15.3.1898. *(BK-VER-1).*	10.00	45.00	—
	b. 20.2.1902-8.11.1905. *(BK-VER-2).*	10.00	45.00	125.00
	c. 13.4.1910. *(BK-VER-3).*	8.00	35.00	110.00
	d. Ovpt: *ORIZABA.* 14.4.1904. *(BK-VER-5).*	15.00	50.00	—
	e. Ovpt: *ANDRÉS TUXTLA* 15.7.1905. *(BK-VER-6).*	15.00	50.00	—
	f. Ovpt: *XALAPA.* 14.4.1904. *(BK-VER-7).*	15.00	50.00	—
	p. Proof. W/o series. ND.	—	Unc	120.00
	s. Specimen. W/o series. ND.	—	Unc	120.00

		GOOD	FINE	XF
S438	**10 PESOS** 15.3.1898. Black on brown and yellow unpt. steam passenger train at l., sugar cane harvest at ctr., pine tree at r. Back brown. *(BK-VER-8).*			
	a. Issued note.	1500.	3000.	—
	p. Proof. W/o series. ND.	—	Unc	1800.
	s. Specimen. W/o series. ND.	—	Unc	1800.

		GOOD	FINE	XF
S439	**10 PESOS** 1900-14. Black on brown and yellow unpt. Portr. Miguel Lerdo de Tejada at l. Back blue.			
	a. 2.4.1900. *(BK-VER-9).*	40.00	100.00	—
	b. 31.8.1903-8.11.1905. *(BK-VER-10).*	15.00	40.00	80.00
	c. 13.4.1910; 20.4.1914. *(BK-VER-11).*	10.00	25.00	70.00
	d. Ovpt: *ORIZABA.* 14.4.1904. *(BK-VER-13).*	15.00	50.00	—
	e. Ovpt: *XALAPA.* 14.4.1904. *(BK-VER-15).*	15.00	50.00	100.00
	f. Ovpt: *S. ANDRÉS TUXTLA. 15.7.1905. (BK-VER-14).*	15.00	50.00	—
	p. Proof. W/o series. ND.	—	Unc	150.00
	s. Specimen. W/o series. ND.	—	Unc	150.00

		GOOD	FINE	XF
S440	**20 PESOS** 1898-1905. Black on olive-green and yellow unpt. Seated woman w/fruit at ctr. Back olive-green; orange stamp and blue seal.			
	a. 15.3.1898. *(BK-VER-16).*	50.00	130.00	—
	b. 20.2.1902-8.2.1905. *(BK-VER-17).*	45.00	120.00	—
	c. Ovpt: *ORIZABA.* 14.4.1904. *(BK-VER-19).*	50.00	120.00	225.00
	d. Ovpt: *XALAPA.* 14.4.1904. *(BK-VER-20).*	50.00	120.00	225.00
	p. Proof. W/o series. ND.	—	Unc	240.00
	s. Specimen. W/o series. ND.	—	Unc	240.00

		GOOD	FINE	XF
S441	**50 PESOS** 1898-1905. Black on orange and yellow unpt. Sailing ships at ctr. Back orange.			
	a. 15.3.1898. *(BK-VER-21).*	100.00	250.00	—
	b. 31.8.1903; 8.11.1905. *(BK-VER-22).*	100.00	225.00	500.00
	c. Ovpt: *S. ANDRÉS TUXTLA.* 15.7.1905. *(BK-VER-24).*	130.00	250.00	—
	d. Ovpt: *ORIZABA.* 14.4.1904.	100.00	250.00	—
	p. Proof. W/o series. ND.	—	Unc	600.00
	s. Specimen. W/o series. ND.	—	Unc	600.00

S442 100 PESOS

(ca.1898-1914). Black on blue and yellow unpt. Horsemen and steam passenger train at ctr. Back blue-gray; green stamp and blue seal.

	GOOD	FINE	XF
a. 15.3.1898. *(BK-VER-25).*	275.00	600.00	1000.
b. 20.2.1902-15.7.1905; 8.11.1905. *(BK-VER-26).*	250.00	550.00	—
d. Ovpt: *ORIZABA.* 14.4.1904. *(BK-VER-29).*	275.00	600.00	—
e. Ovpt: *XALAPA.* 14.4.1904. *(BK-VER-30).*	275.00	600.00	—
p. Proof. W/o series. ND.	—	Unc	900.00
r. Unissued remainder. Perforated: *PAGADO;* ND. *(BK-VER-27).*	125.00	300.00	—
s. Specimen. W/o series. ND.	—	Unc	900.00

S443 500 PESOS

15.3.1898. Black on orange and yellow unpt. Sailing ships at ctr, steam train at upper r. Back red. *(BK-VER-31).*

	GOOD	FINE	XF
a. Issued note.	750.00	1500.	2500.
p. Proof. W/o series. ND.	—	Unc	1500.
s. Specimen. W/o series. ND.	—	Unc	1500.

S444 1000 PESOS

(ca.1898-1914). Black on yellow and purple unpt. Group of horsemen at l. Back purple. *(BK-VER-33).*

	GOOD	FINE	XF
a. 15.3.1898.	1600.	2750.	—
p. Proof. W/o series. ND.	—	—	—
s. Specimen. W/o series. ND.	—	—	—

NOTE: For #S437-S444, reports of specific dates from 1898-1914 are needed to augment these listings.

YUCATÁN

BANCO MERCANTIL DE YUCATÁN

1890-92 ISSUE

#S445-S452 printer: HLBNC.

S445 1 PESO

	GOOD	FINE	XF
1.2.1892. Green on orange unpt. Locomotive at l., seated Industry at r. at r. Back green. *(BK-YUC-31).*	300.00	650.00	1000.

S446 5 PESOS

	GOOD	FINE	XF
1890. Black on blue and brown unpt. Eleutheria (Liberty) at l., ship dockside at ctr. r. Back blue; helmeted man's head at ctr. Proof. *(BK-YUC-34).*	—	—	—

S447 10 PESOS

	GOOD	FINE	XF
1890. Black on blue and orange unpt. Woman at l., national arms at ctr. r. Back blue. Proof. *(BK-YUC-39).*	—	—	—

S448 20 PESOS

	GOOD	FINE	XF
1890. Black on brown and blue unpt. Indian warrior at l., Minerva (Goddess of Science, Art and War) at r. Back brown. Proof. *(BK-YUC-43).*	—	—	—

S449 50 PESOS

9.4.1890. Dog's head at l., reclining Urania (Goddess of Astronomy) at r. Back brown; steam locomotive at ctr. *(BK-YUC-46).*

	GOOD	FINE	XF
a. Issued note.	1500.	2500.	—
p. Proof. 189x.	—	—	—

S450 100 PESOS — GOOD — FINE — XF

30.6.1893. Seated Irene (Goddess of Peace) at l., portr. M. Hidalgo at r. Back green. — — —

S451 500 PESOS — GOOD — FINE — XF

189x. Seated woman w/anchor, sailing ships in background at l., dog's head at r. Back orange; national arms at l. Proof. *(BK-YUC-58).* — — —

S452 1000 PESOS — GOOD — FINE — XF

1890. Steam train crossing viaduct bridge w/merchants below at l., Euthenia (Plenty) overlooking the harvest at r. Back blue; helmeted man at lower l. and r. ctr., national arms at ctr. Proof. *(BK-YUC-61).* — — —

NOTE: For #S446-S452, an issue with the printed date *189x* was reportedly made. Only #S449 and S451 have been confirmed with this style so far.

1897-1900 ISSUE

#S452A-S457A printer: ABNC.

S452A 5 PESOS — GOOD — FINE — XF

30.8.1897. Black on green and yellow unpt. Allegorical woman reading, recining on sacks and barrels at ctr. Back green. Series B. *(BK-YUC-36).* — 1500. — —

S453 5 PESOS

	GOOD	FINE	XF
1898-ca.1903. Black on green and yellow unpt. Similar to to #S452A, but w/text: *A LA PAR* added at l. Back green.			
p. Proof. Series C. 1898.	—	Unc	1500.
s1. Specimen. Series D. 1899.	—	—	—
s2. Specimen. Series G. Dec.190x.	—	—	—
s3. Specimen. Series H. 190x (ca.1903).	—	—	—
s4. Specimen. Series C. 1898.	—	—	—

S454 10 PESOS

	GOOD	FINE	XF
1900-04. Black on blue and yellow unpt. Victory, Work and Effort by beehive at l. Back blue-gray.			
a. Series H. Perforated: *CANCELADO;* 28.5.1904. *(BK-YUC-41).*	10.00	20.00	45.00
p. Proof. W/o series. ND.	—	Unc	150.00
s. Specimen. Series G. Dec.190x.	—	Unc	80.00

S455 50 PESOS

	GOOD	FINE	XF
1897. Black on orange, yellow and brown unpt. Similar to #S456, but *PORTADOR EN DINERO* at upper ctr. r.			
p1. Proof. W/o series. ND.	—	Unc	600.00
p2. Proof. Series B. 1897.	—	Unc	800.00
s. Specimen. Series G. Dec.190x.	—	—	—

S456 50 PESOS

	GOOD	FINE	XF
1898-1904. Black on orange, yellow and brown unpt. Gypsy woman at l., Eleutheria (Liberty) at r. *PORTADOR* above denomination numeral at upper ctr., *A LA PAR* added at upper ctr. r. Back brown.			
a. Series C. 28.6.1898; 18.11.1899; 1.5.1900. *(BK-YUC-49).*	150.00	300.00	—
p1. Proof. W/o series. ND.	—	—	—
p2. Proof. Series B. 1897.	—	—	—
s1. Specimen. Series D. 1899.	—	—	—
s2. Specimen. Series E. 1900.	—	—	—
s3. Specimen. Series G. Dec.190x.	—	—	—
s4. Specimen. Series H. 190x (ca.1903).	—	—	—

S457 100 PESOS

	GOOD	FINE	XF
1900-04. Black on olive-brown unpt. Columbus and his men sighting land at l., Faith and Friendship at r. Back olive-brown.			
a. Series G. 1900. *(BK-YUC-55).*	800.00	1500.	—
b. Series B. 10.11.1900; 10.12.1900; 28.3.1904.	350.00	700.00	—
p1. Proof. W/o series. ND.	—	Unc	1000.
p2. Proof. Series G. Dec.190x.	—	Unc	1000.
s. Specimen. Series G. 1900.	—	—	—

		GOOD	FINE	XF
S457A	**500 PESOS**			
	(ca.1900-04). Black on yellow and purple unpt. Allegorical woman and child w/books at l. Back purple; women's head at ctr.			
	p1. Proof. W/o series. ND.	—	—	—
	p2. Proof. Series G. Dec.190x.	—	—	—
	s1. Specimen. Series F. 1900.	—	—	—
	s2. Specimen. Series H. 190x.	—	—	—

NOTE: For #S452A-S457A, reports of specific dates from 1897-1904 are needed to augment these listings.

BANCO PENINSULAR MEXICANO

1893-1901 PROVISIONAL ISSUES

#S458-S460 ovpt. new bank name on notes of the Banco Yucateco.

		GOOD	FINE	XF
S458	**5 PESOS**			
	29.6.1901; 1.10.1903. Ovpt. on #S467.			
	a. 29.6.1901; 1.10.1903. *(BK-YUC-7).*	12.00	25.00	65.00
	b. Ovpt: *SUCURSAL DE CÁRMEN* and perforated: *CAMPECHE;* 1.10.1903. *(BK-YUC-9).*	17.50	40.00	—
	c. Purple handstamp: *SUCURSAL EN CÁRMEN* and perforated: *LAGUNA, CAMPECHE.* ND *(BK-YUC-9).*	40.00	80.00	—
	r. Remainder. W/o series. 2 sign. handwritten.	50.00	—	—

		GOOD	FINE	XF
S459	**10 PESOS**			
	1897-1903. Ovpt. on #S468. *(BK-YUC-14).*			
	a. Perforated: *CAMPECHE.* 1.11.1897; 6.10.1898. *(BK-YUC-15).*	15.00	45.00	—
	b. Ovpt: *Sucursal de Campeche* and perforated: *CAMPECHE.* 9.8.1898; 6.10.1898. *(BK-YUC-16).*	20.00	55.00	—
	c. Ovpt: *Sucursal en Cármen, Campeche* and perforated: *LAGUNA.* ND. *(BK-YUC-17).*	40.00	80.00	—
	d. W/o branch ovpt. Handwritten date. 1.8.1897; 7.1.1899; 29.6.1901.	40.00	80.00	—
	e. W/o branch ovpt. Engraved date. 1.10.1903.	20.00	55.00	—

		GOOD	FINE	XF
S460	**20 PESOS**			
	1895-1902. Ovpt. on #S469.			
	a. 11.9.1895-11.11.1902. *(BK-YUC-21).*	17.50	50.00	—
	b. Ovpt: *Sucursal en Campeche* and perforated: *CAMPECHE.* 1.11.1897; 10.5.1898; 7.6.1898. *(BK-YUC-22).*	30.00	75.00	—

#S461-S463 ovpt. new bank name on notes of the Banco Mercantil de Yucatán.

		GOOD	FINE	XF
S461	**50 PESOS**			
	19.6.1898-16.4.1904. Ovpt. on #S456. *(BK-YUC-51).*	90.00	250.00	—

		GOOD	FINE	XF
S462	**100 PESOS**			
	30.6.1893. Ovpt. on #S450. *(BK-YUC-52).*	1500.	2500.	—

		GOOD	FINE	XF
S463	**100 PESOS**			
	10.11.1900; 17.11.1900; 10.12.1900; 28.3.1904. Ovpt. on #S457 *(BK-YUC-57).*	350.00	700.00	—

1913-14 ISSUES

		GOOD	FINE	XF
S464	**1 PESO**			
	30.11.1913. Black on yellow and orange unpt. Indian woman at l., sailing ship at r. Back green. Printer: AB&PC. Series A.			
	a. Handwritten sign. at l. *(BK-YUC-63).*	6.00	17.50	—
	b. Printed sign. at l. *(BK-YUC-64).*	2.00	6.00	15.00
	p. Proof.	—	—	—
	s. Specimen.	—	—	—
S464A	**1 PESO**			
	1913. Similar to #S464. Printer: ABNC. Proof.	—	—	—

		GOOD	FINE	XF
S465	**5 PESOS**			
	1.4.1914. Black on yellow and orange unpt. Steam locomotive at l., dock workers at r. Back orange; allegorical figures at l. and ctr. r. Printer: ABNC. Series A.			
	a. Issued note.	1.00	3.00	8.00
	p. Proof. W/o series. 189x.	—	Unc	475.00
	s1. Specimen. W/o series. 189x.	—	Unc	350.00
	s2. Specimen. Series A. 19xx.	—	Unc	100.00

Banco Yucateco

1889-1903 Issue

#S466-S473 printer: ABNC.

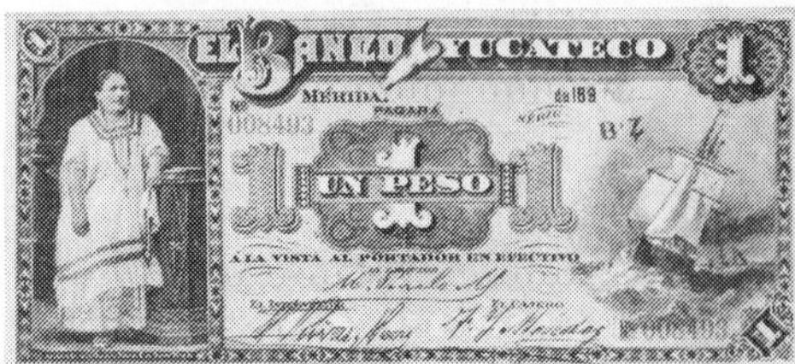

		Good	Fine	XF
S466	**1 Peso**			
	1.11.1891; 1.1.1892. Black on brown-yellow unpt. Indian woman at l., sailing ship at r. Back olive-green. Series BZ. *(BK-YUC-1).*			
	a. Issued note.	125.00	250.00	—
	p. Proof. W/o series. 189x.	—	Unc	450.00
	s. Specimen.	—	Unc	350.00

		Good	Fine	XF
S467	**5 Pesos**			
	(ca.1890-1903). Black on red-orange and yellow unpt. Steam locomotive at l., men working dockside at r. Back red-orange; allegorical figures at l. and ctr. r.			
	a. 5.1.1899. *(BK-YUC-4).*	50.00	100.00	—
	b. Series TA. 29.6.1901. *(BK-YUC-4).*	50.00	100.00	—
	c. Series HC. 1.10.1903. *(BK-YUC-4).*	50.00	100.00	—
	d. Ovpt: *Sucursal de Campeche* and perforated: *CAMPECHE.* 9.8.1897; 2.12.1901; 1.10.1903. *(BK-YUC-6).*	30.00	60.00	—
	p. Proof. W/o series. 189x (ca.1890).	—	Unc	150.00
	s1. Specimen. W/o series. 189x.	—	Unc	125.00
	s2. Specimen. Series TM. 189x (ca.1898).	—	—	—
	s3. Specimen. Series OO. 1xxx (ca.1899).	—	—	—
	s4. Specimen. Series MGT. 19xx (ca.1903).	—	—	—

		Good	Fine	XF
S468	**10 Pesos**			
	ca.1890-1903. Black on green and yellow unpt. Power and Riches in Commerce at l., man feeding horse at r. Back dk. green.			
	a. 13.10.1900; 1.11.1900; 29.6.1901; 28.9.1901. *(BK-YUC-10).*	20.00	40.00	80.00
	b. Perforated: *CAMPECHE.* 189x; 6.10.1898. *(BK-YUC-12).*	30.00	70.00	—
	c. Ovpt: *Sucursal de Campeche* and perforated: *CAMPECHE.* 6.8.1898; 9.8.1898; 23.9.1899. *(BK-YUC-13).*	35.00	70.00	—
	p. Proof. 189x (ca.1890).	—	Unc	175.00
	s1. Specimen. W/o series. 189x.	—	Unc	150.00
	s2. Specimen. Series LA. 189x (ca.1898).	—	—	—
	s3. Specimen. Series EC. 1xxx (ca.1899).	—	—	—
	s4. Specimen. Series CA. 1xxx (ca.1900).	—	—	—
	s5. Specimen. Series MH. 1xxx (ca.1903).	—	—	—
S469	**20 Pesos**			
	ca.1890-1903. Black on blue and yellow unpt. Faith at l. ctr, seated woman w/sheaf and water jug at r. Back blue. *(BK-YUC-18).*			
	a. 1897-1902.	30.00	60.00	100.00
	b. Ovpt: *Sucursal en Campeche* and perforated: *CAMPECHE.* 1.11.1897; 7.6.1898. *(BK-YUC-20).*	45.00	100.00	—
	p1. Proof. W/o series. 189x (ca.1890).	—	Unc	200.00
	p2. Proof. W/o series. 190x.	—	Unc	200.00
	p3. Proof. Series YU. 190x (ca.1900).	—	—	—
	s1. Specimen. W/o series. 189x.	—	Unc	200.00
	s2. Specimen. Series OM. 189x (ca.1898).	—	—	—
	s3. Specimen. Series AT. 1xxx (ca.1898).	—	—	—
	s4. Specimen. Series YU. 190x (ca.1900).	—	—	—
	s5. Specimen. Series MGG. 190x (ca.1903).	—	—	—

		Good	Fine	XF
S470	**50 Pesos**			
	(ca.1890-1903). Black on red-brown and yellow unpt. Sailing ship at l., reclining woman at r. Back brown. *(BK-YUC-23).*			
	a. 24.5.1898; 24.7.1899.	1000.	1750.	—
	p. Proof. W/o series. 189x (ca.1890).	—	Unc	750.00
	s1. Specimen. W/o series. 189x.	—	Unc	600.00
	s2. Specimen. Series RC. 189x (ca.1898).	—	—	—
	s3. Specimen. Series UC. 1xxx (ca.1899).	—	Unc	600.00
	s4. Specimen. Series DE. 1xxx (ca.1900).	—	—	—
	s5. Specimen. Series JDC. 1xxx (ca.1903).	—	—	—

		Good	Fine	XF
S471	**100 Pesos**			
	(ca.1890-1903). Black on orange and yellow unpt. Helmsman at wheel at l., Indian woman in canoe at ctr. r. Back orange. *(BK-YUC-25).*			
	a. Series MGT. 29.5.1902; 16.3.1903.	1500.	2250.	3000.
	p. Proof. W/o series. 189x (ca.1890).	—	Unc	850.00
	s1. Specimen. W/o series. 189x.	—	Unc	700.00
	s2. Specimen. Series AR. 189x (ca.1898).	—	—	—
	s3. Specimen. Series OY. 1xxx (ca.1899).	—	—	—
	s4. Specimen. Series DA. 1xxx (ca.1900).	—	—	—
	s5. Specimen. Series JDC. 1xxx (ca.1903).	—	—	—

		Good	Fine	XF
S472	**500 Pesos**			
	(ca.1890-1903). Black on brown and gold unpt. Electricity at l. ctr., ships at r. Back black and brown; allegorical animals at l. and ctr. r., profile of Minerva (Goddess of Science, Art and War) at ctr. *(BK-YUC-27).*			
	a. 1.5.1889; 7.10.1897.	—	—	—
	p. Proof. W/o series. 189x (ca.1890).	—	Unc	1750.
	s1. Specimen. W/o series. 189x.	—	—	—
	s2. Specimen. Series NC. 1xxx (ca.1899).	—	—	—
	s3. Specimen. Series RI. 1xxx (ca.1900).	—	—	—
	s4. Specimen. Series CC. 1xxx (ca.1902).	—	—	—
	s5. Specimen. Series JIL. 1xxx (ca.1903).	—	—	—

S473	1000 PESOS	GOOD	FINE	XF
	(ca.1890-1903). Black on olive-green, red and orange unpt. Chastity at l., seated woman w/shield and plant at r. Back black and red; allegorical woman representing Art at ctr. *(BK-YUC-29).*			
	a. Series BA, ca.1891.	—	3500.	—
	p. Proof. W/o series. 189x (ca.1890).	—	Unc	2000.
	s1. Specimen. W/o series. 189x.	—	—	—
	s2. Specimen. Series ME. 1xxx (ca.1900).	—	—	—
	s3. Specimen. Series NEP. 1xxx (ca.1902).	—	—	—
	s4. Specimen. Series PD. 1xxx (ca.1903).	—	—	—

NOTE: For #S467-S473, reports of specific dates from 1889-1903 are needed to augment these listings.

ZACATECAS

BANCO DE ZACATECAS

1891 ISSUE

#S474-S480 printer: ABNC.

#S474-S476 village landscape on back.

S474	1 PESO	GOOD	FINE	XF
	8.12.1891. Black on orange and yellow unpt. Young girl at l, portr. F. G. Salinas at r. Back orange. Series A. *(BK-ZAC-1).*			
	a. Issued note.	600.00	1500.	—
	p. Proof.	—	—	—
	s. Specimen.	—	—	—

S475	5 PESOS	GOOD	FINE	XF
	1891-1914. Black on green and yellow unpt. Farmer plowing at l., portr. F. G. Salinas at r. Back green.			
	a. Series A. 8.12.1891. *(BK-ZAC-4).*	20.00	60.00	—
	b. Series H. 20.6.1896; 15.8.1900. *(BK-ZAC-5).*	10.00	30.00	—
	c. Series K. 2.3.1906: L. 18.11.1908; M. 22.9.1909. *(BK-ZAC-6).*	7.50	20.00	—
	d. Series N. 1.11.1912; 1.11.913; Ñ. 15.2.1914: O. 15.5.1914. *(BK-ZAC-11).*	5.00	15.00	50.00
	e. *AGUASCALIENTES.* 2.3.1906. *(BK-ZAC-11).*	30.00	70.00	—
	f. Ovpt: *LAGOS.* 2.3.1906. *(BK-ZAC-11).*	30.00	70.00	—
	p. Proof.	—	—	—
	r. Remainder. W/o sign. or series. ND.	—	Unc	15.00
	s. Specimen.	—	—	—

S476	10 PESOS	GOOD	FINE	XF
	1891-1914. Black on brown and yellow unpt. Panoramic view of factory at l., portr. F. G. Salinas at ctr. Back brown.			
	a. Series A. 8.12.1891. *(BK-ZAC-13).*	30.00	80.00	—
	b. 15.8.1900. Series K. 2.3.1906; 8.11.1908; Series M. 22.9.1909. *(BK-ZAC-14).*	20.00	45.00	—
	c. Series N. 1.11.1912; 15.2.1914. *(BK-ZAC-15).*	15.00	35.00	100.00

		GOOD	FINE	XF
	d. Ovpt: *AGUASCALIENTES.* 1.3.1906. *(BK-ZAC-18).*	40.00	90.00	—
	e. Ovpt: *LAGOS.* 2.3.1906. *(BK-ZAC-19).*	40.00	90.00	—
	p. Proof.	—	—	—
	r. Remainder. W/o sign. or series. ND. *(BK-ZAC-16).*	—	Unc	17.50
	s. Specimen.	—	—	—

#S477-S478 street scene on back.

S477	20 PESOS	GOOD	FINE	XF
	1891-1914. Black on orange and yellow unpt. 2 women at l., Industry and Commerce at ctr., portr. F. G. Salinas at r. Back orange.			
	a. Series B. 20.12.1891; 15.5.1895; 8.7.1897; 1.7.1899. *(BK-ZAC-20).*	250.00	400.00	—
	b. 15.8.1900; 18.11.1908. *(BK-ZAC-21).*	225.00	375.00	—
	c. Series N. 1.11.1912; Ñ 15.2.1914. *(BK-ZAC-22).*	200.00	350.00	550.00
	p. Proof.	—	—	—
	s. Specimen.	—	—	—

S478	50 PESOS	GOOD	FINE	XF
	(ca.1891-1912). Black on blue and green unpt. Farmer w/scythe at l., young girl feeding cow at ctr., portr. F. G. Salinas at r. Back blue.			
	a. 7.8.1897; 1.11.1898; 1.7.1899. *(BK-ZAC-24).*	250.00	400.00	—
	b. Series H. 15.8.1900. *(BK-ZAC-25).*	225.00	375.00	—
	c. Series K. 2.3.1906.	—	—	—
	d. Series N. 1.11.1912. *(BK-ZAC-26).*	200.00	350.00	550.00
	e. Ovpt: *LAGOS.* 2.3.1906. *(BK-ZAC-30).*	260.00	425.00	—
	p. Proof. 1xxx (ca.1891).	—	—	—
	r. Remainder. *(BK-ZAC-27).*	—	40.00	75.00
	s. Specimen.	—	—	—

	S479 100 PESOS	GOOD	FINE	XF
	1891-1912. Black on red, orange and yellow unpt. Apollo w/harp at l., portr. F. G. Salinas at ctr., young girl at r. Back red; miners at ctr.			
a.	Series B. 20.12.1891. *(BK-ZAC-31).*	600.00	1000.	—
b.	Series E. 7.8.1897; F. 15.11.1898. *(BK-ZAC-31).*	600.00	1000.	—
c.	Series H. 15.8.1900; I, 5.5.1903. *(BK-ZAC-32).*	550.00	900.00	—
d.	Series N. 1.11.1912. *(BK-ZAC-32).*	550.00	900.00	—
p.	Proof.	—	—	—
r.	Remainder. ND. *(BK-ZAC-33).*	—	30.00	60.00
s.	Specimen.	—	—	—

	S480 500 PESOS	GOOD	FINE	XF
	(ca.1891-1906). Black on brown and yellow unpt. Industrial Progress at l., portr. F. G. Salinas at r. Back brown and black; allegorical woman w/eagle at ctr. r., head of allegorical woman at r.			
a.	Series G. 1.7.1899. *(BK-ZAC-35).*	2000.	3250.	—
b.	2.3.1906. *(BK-ZAC-35).*	2000.	3250.	—
p.	Proof. 1xxx (ca.1891).	—	—	—
r.	Remainder. ND. *(BK-ZAC-36).*	100.00	200.00	350.00
s.	Specimen. 1xxx.	—	—	—

NOTE: For #S475-S480, reports of specific dates from 1891-1914 are needed to augment these listings.

NOTE: For #S480, a note dated ca.1913 is reported in archive records. No examples are known.

1914 ISSUE

	S481 1 PESO	GOOD	FINE	XF
	1914. Red and yellow or gray. Monument at ctr. Back proof. Printer: E.I.A. *(BK-ZAC-3).*	—	Unc	350.00

The Mexican independence movement is of interest and concern to collectors because of the warfare-induced activity of local and state mints, which began with the Sept. 15, 1810 march on the capital led by Father Miguel Hidalgo, a well-intentioned man of imagination and courage who proved to be an inept organizer and leader. Hidalgo was captured and executed within 10 months. His revolution, led by such as Morelos, Guerrero and Iturbide, continued and culminated in Mexican independence in 1821. Turbulent years followed. From 1821 to 1867 there were two emperors, several dictators, and enough presidents to provide a change of government on the average of once every nine months. Porfirio Diaz, who had the longest tenure of any dictator in Latin American history, seized power in 1876 and did not relinquish it until 1911.

The final phase of Mexico's lengthy revolutionary period began in 1910 and lasted through the adoption of a liberal constitution and the election of a new congress in 1917. The 1910-17 revolution was agrarian in character and intended to destroy the regime of Díaz and to make Mexico economically and diplomatically independent. The republic experienced a state of upheaval that saw most of the leading figures of the revolution (Villa, Carranza, Obregón, Zapata, Calles) fighting each other at one time or another. Carranza eventually emerged as the most powerful figure of the early revolution. As de facto president in 1916, he convened a constitutional convention which produced a constitution in which the aims of the revolution were formalized.

MONETARY SYSTEM

1 Peso = 100 Centavos

REVOLUTION

1910-17

Issues of state, regional, municipal and military authorities

Administración General de Rentas del Estado (Guanajuato) .... #S772-S773
Administración General de Rentas del Estado (Querétaro) .... #S985A
Ayuntamiento de 1915, Iguala (Guerrero) .... #S790-S808
Banco de Coahuila/Banco de la Laguna (Coahuila) .... #S563-S569
Banco de Coahuila/Banco Nacional de México (Coahuila) .... #S570-S572
Banco Español Refaccionario S.A./Banco Oriental de México (Puebla) .... #S964-S967
Banco de la Laguna/Banco de Coahuila (Coahuila) .... #S579-S591
Banco de la Laguna/Banco de Londres y México (Coahuila) .... #S592-S596A
Banco de la Laguna/Banco Minero (Coahuila) .... #S597-S602
Banco de Londres y México/Deutsch-Sudamerikanische Bank (Berlin) (Coahuila) .... #S603-S606
Banco de Londres y México/Banco de la Laguna (Coahuila) .... #S607-S608
Banco de Londres y México/Banco Nacional de México (Coahuila) .... #S609-S612
Banco Minero/Banco de la Laguna, Gómez Palacio (Durango) .... #S762-S766
Banco Nacional de México/Banco de Coahuila (Coahuila) .... #S613-S614
Banco Nacional de México/Deutsch-Sudamerikanische Bank (Berlin) (Coahuila) .... #S615-S617
Banco Nacional de México/Banco de Londres y México .... #S618-S621
Banco Revolucionario de Guerrero .... #S785-S789
Bonos al Portador, Durango .... #S717-S723
Brigada Azuara (Hidalgo) .... #S828-S830
Brigada Serdan .... S#984B-C
La Caja de Ahorros de la R.M., S.A. (Chihuahua) .... #S542-S544
La Caja de la Brigada CABALLERO, Tampico (Tamaulipas) .... #S1083-S1084
Circulación Forzosa en el Estado de Morelos, Cuernavaca .... #S899-S902
La Comisión Reguladora del Comercio de Zacatecas .... #S1139-S1142
Comisión Reguladora del Mercado de Henequén y la Tesorería General del Estado (Yucatan) .... #S1120-S1127
Compañiá Real del Monte y Pachuca/Bank of Montreal (Hidalgo) .... #S831-S839
Cuartel General del Ejército Constitucionalista de la Sierra Norte de Puebla .... #S985
Cuerpo de Ejército del Noreste (Nuevo Leon) .... #S940-S941
Cuerpo de EJE?rcito del Noroeste, Tepic (Nayarit) .... #S916-S917B
Deutsch-Sudamerikanische Bank (Berlin)/Banco de Londres y México (Coahuila. ....)#S573-S575
Deutsch-Sudamerikanische Bank (Berlin)/Banco Nacional de México (Coahuila) .... #S576-S578
Dirección General de Rentas del Estado, Cuernavaca (Morelos) .... #S903-S905
La Dirección General de Rentas del Estado, Guadalajara (Jalisco) .... #S844-S856
Distrito de Matamoros (Puebla) .... #S972-S984A
Distrito de Morelos (Tlaxcala) .... #S1085-S1087
División Almazán, Huajuapán (Oaxaca) .... #S942
División del Bravo, Monterrey (Nuevo Leon) .... #S935-S939
Ejército Constitucionalista (San Luis Potosí) .... #S986-S989
Ejército Constitucionalista Uruapán (Michoacán) .... #S898
Ejército Constitucionalista, División del Norte, Torreón (Coahuila) .... #S652-S654
Ejército Constitucionalista, División de Occidente, Guadalajara (Jalisco) .... #S860-S862
Ejército Constitucionalista de México (Chihuahua) .... #S523-S526
Ejército Constitucionalista de México, Tampico (Tamaulipas) .... #S1082
Ejército Constitucionalista, Parras (Coahuila) .... #S638-S641
Ejército Constitucionalista del Sur (Guerrero) .... #S809-S812
Ejército Libertador de Guerrero, Chilpancingo .... #S812A
Ejército Revolucionario de Guerrero .... #S813-S816
Estado de Aguascalientes - Tesorería Municipal (Aguascalientes) .... #S501-S503
El Estado de Chihuahua (Chihuahua) .... #S527-S538
El Estado de Coahuila .... #S655-S659
El Estado de Durango .... #S724-S753
El Estado de Durango, San José de la Boca .... #S768
El Estado de Durango, Topia .... #S769-S770

El Estado de Jalisco .... #S873-S875
El Estado Libre y Soberano de Colima .... #S662-S663
Estado Libre y Soberano de México .... #S877-S882
El Estado Libre y Soberano de Sinaloa .... #S1041-S1048
El Estado de Michoacán de Ocampo .... #S883
Estado de Sinaloa, Culiacán .... #S1000-S1004
Estado de Sinaloa, Mazatlán .... #S1005-S1008
El Estado de Sinaloa, San Blas .... #S1026-S1040
El Estado de Sonora, Hermosillo .... #S1062-S1078
Gobierno Constitucionalista, Brigada Morales y Molina (Guerrero) .... #S817-S824
Gobierno Constitucionalista del Estado de Durango .... #S754-S758
Gobierno Constitucionalista del Estado Libre y Soberano del Veracruz, Liave .... #S1091-S1096
Gobierno Constitucionalista de Mexico, La Paz (Baja, California) .... #S504-S508
Gobierno Constitucionalista de Mexico, Monclova (Coahuila) .... #S625-S635
Gobierno Constitucionalista de México, República (Distrito Federal) .... #S681-S684
Gobierno Constitucionalista Provisional de Chihuahua (Chihuahua) .... #S539-S540
Gobierno Constitucionalista, República Méxicana (Distrito Federal) .... #S685-S689
Gobierno Constitucionalista Territorio de la Baja, Cfa., La Paz la Jefatura Politica (Baja, California) .... #S509-S522
El Gobierno Constitucionalista del Territorio de Tepic y del Estado de Sinaloa, Rosario .... #S1009-S1014
Gobierno Constitucionalista de Yucatán, Tesorería General .... #S1128-S1133
Gobierno Convencionista, Cuernavaca (Morelos) .... #S906-S908
Gobierno Convencionista de México (Morelos) .... #S909-S912
Gobierno Convencionista de Mexico (Toluca) .... #S882
Gobierno del Estado de Colima .... #S660-S661
Gobierno del Estado de Durango .... #S759-S761
Gobierno Federal de la República Mexicana (Distrito Federal) .... #S690-S696
Gobierno de Nuevo León, Monterrey .... #S934
Gobierno Preconstitucional del Estado de Oaxaca .... #S950-S951
Gobierno Provisional de México, (Distrito Federal) México .... #S701-S712
Gobierno Provisional de México, República (Distrito Federal) .... #S697-S700
Gobierno Provisional de México, Veracruz .... #S1097-S1115
Gobierno Provisional de Michoacán .... #S884-S887
Gobierno Provisional de Zacatecas .... #S1143-S1145
Jefatura de Armas - M.S. González, Muzquiz (Coahuila) .... #S637
Jefatura de Armas, Morelia (Michoacán) .... #S888-S893
Jefatura de Armas, Yautepec (Morelos) .... #S913-S915
Jefatura de Hacienda en el Estado (Chihuahua) .... #S541
Jefatura de Hacienda en el Estado Jalisco .... #S875A
La Jefatura de Hacienda, Guaymas (Sonora) .... #S1055-S1057
La Jefatura Municipal, Guanaceví (Durango) .... #S767
Jefe de la Columna Territorio de Tepic (Nayarit) .... #S920-S928
Jefe de la División de Occidente (Jalisco) .... #S876
Jefe Político del Territorio (Nayarit) .... #S918-S919
Junta Comercial, Chalchicomula (Puebla) .... #S968-S969
Municipio de San Pedro (Coahuila) .... #S648-S651
Obligación Provisional del Erario Federal (Distrito Federal) .... #S713-S716
La Pagaduría del Cuerpo de Ejército del Noroeste (Jalisco) .... #S863-S867
La Pagaduría General de la Brigada Avila, Jérez (Zacatecas) .... #S1146-S1147
Pagaduría General de la Brigada de Sinaloa, San Blas .... #S1049-S1054
La Pagaduría Gral. del Cuerpo de Ejército del Noroeste (Jalisco) .... #S868-S872
La Pagaduría Gral. de la Brigada de Sinaloa .... #S1015-S1021
La Tesorería de la Federación, Guaymas (Sonora) .... #S1058-S1061
La Tesorería de la Federación, Saltillo (Coahuila) .... #S642-S647
Tesorería General del Estado (Chihuahua) .... #S548-S561
La Tesorería General del Estado de Colima .... #S664-S680
Tesorería General del Estado - Transitorio (Chihuahua) .... #S545-S547
Tesorería General del Estado (Guanajuato) .... #S774-S784
La Tesorería General del Estado de Oaxaca .... #S948-S949
La Tesorería General del Estado de Oaxaca, Oaxaca de Juárez .... #S952-S960
La Tesorería General del Estado de Sinaloa .... #S1022-S1025
La Tesorería General del Estado de Tabasco, San Juan Batista .... #S1079-S1081
Tesorería General Territorio de Tepic (Nayarit) .... #S929-S933
La Tesorería General, Tliaxiaco (Oaxaca) .... #S963
Tesorería General del Estado de Veracruz Llave .... #S1116-S1119
Tesorería de la Junta Comercial de Chalchicomula (Puebla) .... #S970-S971
La Tesorería Municipal de C. Jimínez (Chihuahua) .... #S562
Tesorería Municipal, Municipio de Matamoros (Coahuila) .... #S622-S624
Tesorería Municipal, Monclova (Coahuila) .... #S636
La Tesorería Municipal, Pátcuaro (Michoacán) .... #S894-S895
Tesorería Municipal, Puruandiro (Michoacán) .... #S896-S897
La Tesorería Municipal de esta Ciudad Tliaxcala .... #S1088-S1090
La Tesorería Provisional del Comercio, Huajuapán (Oaxaca) .... #S943-S947
Tesorería Provisional, Tamazola (Oaxaca) .... #S961-S962

AGUASCALIENTES

ESTADO DE AGUASCALIENTES TESORERÍA MUNICIPAL

ND ISSUE

#S501-S503 eagle at ctr.

		GOOD	FINE	XF
S501	**5 CENTAVOS** ND. Black. Brown/green pasteboard. *(SI-AGU-1).*	7.00	15.00	35.00
S502	**10 CENTAVOS** ND. Black. Violet/green pasteboard. *(SI-AGU-2).*	7.00	15.00	35.00
S503	**20 CENTAVOS** ND. Black. Red/green pasteboard. *(SI-AGU-3).*	8.00	17.50	37.50

BAJA CALIFORNIA

GOBIERNO CONSTITUCIONALISTA DE MÉXICO, LA PAZ

ND ISSUE

#S504-S507 eagle at ctr.

		GOOD	FINE	XF
S504	**5 CENTAVOS** ND. Black on pale green pasteboard. *(MI-BAJ-1).*	15.00	30.00	—

		GOOD	FINE	XF
S505	**10 CENTAVOS** ND. Black. Pasteboard. *(MI-BAJ-2).*	15.00	30.00	—
S506	**20 CENTAVOS** ND. Black on gray pasteboard. *(MI-BAJ-3).*	15.00	30.00	—
S507	**50 CENTAVOS** ND. Black on red, pink pasteboard. *(MI-BAJ-4).*	16.50	33.00	—

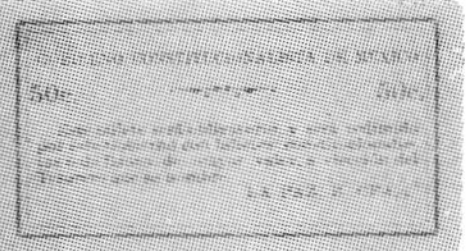

		GOOD	FINE	XF
S508	**50 CENTAVOS** ND. Black. *(MI-BAJ-5).*			
	a. Red pasteboard.	17.50	35.00	—
	b. Gray pasteboard.	17.50	35.00	—
	c. Salmon pasteboard.	17.50	35.00	—

GOBIERNO CONSTITUCIONALISTA TERRITORIO DE LA BAJA CFA, LAPAZ LA JEFATURA POLITICA

1914 ISSUE

#S509-S512 violet circular seal *JEFATURA POLITICA DEL DISTRITO DE LA DAJA CALIFORNIA * LA PAZ ** on face or back.

		GOOD	FINE	XF
S509	**5 PESOS** 21.8.1914. Black. Gray pasteboard. *(MI-BAJ-6).*	17.50	35.00	70.00
S510	**5 PESOS** 21.8.1914. Black. Green pasteboard.			
	a. Issued note. *(MI-BAJ-7).*	20.00	40.00	—
	b. Ovpt: *DISTRITO DE MAZATLAN. RETIRADO DE LA CIRCULACION* (withdrawn from circulation). *(MI-BAJ-8).*	—	—	—

		GOOD	FINE	XF
S511	**10 PESOS** 21.8.1914. Black. Maroon pasteboard. *(MI-BAJ-9).*	22.50	45.00	90.00
S512	**20 PESOS** 21.8.1914. Black. Lt. pink thin paper. Wmk: *REGIST... (MI-BAJ-10).*	20.00	40.00	80.00

CHIAPAS

GOBIERNO PRECONSTITUCIONAL - CAJA DE CAMBIO

1914 ISSUE

#S513-S516 national arms at l.

		GOOD	FINE	XF
S513	**5 CENTAVOS** 28.12.1914. Black on tan pasteboard, 53 x 30mm. Series A. *(SI-CHIP-1).*	8.00	25.00	50.00
S514	**10 CENTAVOS** 28.12.1914. Black on blue pasteboard, 53 x 30mm. Series B. *(SI-CHIP-3).*	8.00	25.00	50.00
S515	**20 CENTAVOS** 28.12.1914. Blue on white pasteboard, 53 x 30mm. Series C. *(SI-CHIP-5).*	17.50	35.00	—

		GOOD	FINE	XF
S516	**50 CENTAVOS** 28.12.1914. Orange on cream pasteboard, 53 x 31mm. Series D. *(SI-CHIP-7).*	17.50	35.00	—

1915 ISSUE

#S517-S520 national arms at l.

		GOOD	FINE	XF
S517	**5 CENTAVOS** 12.5.1915. Black on blue pasteboard. Series A. *(SI-CHIP-2).*	7.00	17.50	35.00

		GOOD	FINE	XF
S518	**10 CENTAVOS** 12.5.1915. Black on orange pasteboard. Series B. *(SI-CHIP-4).*	12.50	27.50	45.00

		GOOD	FINE	XF
S519	**20 CENTAVOS** 12.5.1915. Black on cream pasteboard. Series C. *(SI-CHIP-6).*	12.50	27.50	45.00

		GOOD	FINE	XF
S520	**50 CENTAVOS** 12.5.1915. Black on brown pasteboard, 50 x 29mm. Series D. *(SI-CHIP-8).*			
	a. Issued note.	7.00	17.50	35.00
	b. W/o serial # & back seal. 12.5.1915.	20.00	37.50	55.00

		GOOD	FINE	XF
S521	**1 PESO** ND. Portr. J. Carranza at l., Aztec calendar stone at r. Series A. *(SI-CHIP-9).*	40.00	110.00	175.00

		GOOD	FINE	XF
S522	**2 PESOS** ND. Portr. B. Dominguez at l., Aztec calendar stone at r. Series A. *(SI-CHIP-10).*	35.00	85.00	145.00

CHIHUAHUA

EJÉRCITO CONSTITUCIONALISTA DE MÉXICO

As its name indicates, this series of notes was issued by the Constitutionalist Army in Chihuahua by Decree of February 12, 1914 with the date of issue March 30, 1914. These notes are also found with validations which are listed according to approximate scarcity from the more common to scarcer. No notes are known with more than one validation in this series.

VALIDATION HAND STAMPS:

1. JEFATURA POLITICA DEL DISTRITO NORTE DE LA BAJA CALIFORNIA, ENSENADA.
2. ADUANA MARITIMA DE GUAYMAS, ADMINISTRACIÓN.
3. IMPRESORA DE BILLETES, VERACRUZ, RESELLO.
4. TESORERÍA GENERAL DEL ESTADO DE SONORA, HERMOSILLO.
5. JEFATURA DE HDA., GUADALAJARA.
6. DISTRITO DE GUAYMAS, RIO YAQUI, SONORA.
7. SECRETARIA DE HACIENDA.
8. DEUDA NACIONAL, 4A, DEMARCACION D.F.
9. CANANEA - PRESIDENCIA MUNICIPAL DE CANANEA - SONORA, MEX.
10. FUERZAS DEL ESTADO DE SONORA - DETALL GENERAL.
11. REPUBLICA MEXICANA, LA PAZ, B.C.
12. ADUANA MARITIMA DE NOGALES - ADMINISTRACIÓN.
13. JEFATURA DE HACIENDA, ESTADO DE SONORA.
14. JEFATURA POLITICA DEL DISTRITO NORTE, ENSENADA (plus date).

DECREE OF FEBRUARY 12, 1914

#S523-S526 national coat-of-arms at ctr. Liberty cap and rays at ctr. on back.

		GOOD	FINE	XF
S523	**1 PESO** 30.3.1914. Black on pink unpt. Series A.			
	a. Issued note. *(MI-CHI-68).*	.75	2.50	7.50

		GOOD	FINE	XF
	b. Ovpt: *MICHOACAN DE OCAMPO. TESORERIA GENERAL, RETIRADO* in purple, red, green or black. *(MI-CHI-69).*	10.00	25.00	—
	c. Ovpt: *HACIENDA DE SAN JOAQUIN, 1916. (MI-CHI-70).*	12.00	35.00	—
	d. As b. w/*VILA HIDALGO.*	10.00	35.00	—
S524	**5 PESOS** 30.3.1914. Black on green unpt. Series B. *(MI-CHI-71).*	.75	2.00	5.00
S525	**10 PESOS** 30.3.1914. Black on lilac unpt. Series C. *(MI-CHI-72).*			
	a. Black seal.	2.00	5.00	10.00
	b. Brown seal.	2.00	5.00	10.00
S526	**20 PESOS** 30.3.1914. Black on orange unpt. Series D. *(MI-CHI-73).*	2.00	6.00	15.00

EL ESTADO DE CHIHUAHUA

This series is an authentic revolutionary issue and is commonly referred to in Spanish as the *Dos Caritas* series (two little faces or two portraits). As in the case of Villa's "bedsheets," despite the fact that these notes bear the name of the State of Chihuahua, they are true revolutionary issues as they were issued by military decree as specified by the face legend: *Conforme al Decreto Militar de Fecha 10 de Febrero de 1914.*

The 10, 20 and 50 peso denominations are known with two handwritten signatures, and one printed center signature. All denominations exist with all three printed signatures, except the 50 pesos which always has two handwritten signatures and one printed signature.

A large variety of validations exist in this series on denominations of 5, 10, 20 and 50 pesos. The 50 peso notes with a validation are quite scarce. Normally, only one validation appears on each note. However, a few are known with two. As in the case of Villa's "bedsheets," these validations were applied in order to authorize the free circulation of these notes within a given area or state and frequently indicated in the validation itself who the new issuing authorities were.

The following listing indicates the known validations according to their approximate scarcity, beginning with the most common and ending with the scarcest. Initialed signatures over or next to the control letters on the back are quite common on notes bearing a back validation.

A few early 50 peso notes are known with a black State of Chihuahua seal and black control letters.

The early issues of this series bear circular seals on the face or back and in some cases control letters on the face. These seals appear in a single color on each denomination. That is, on the 50 centavos this face seal is green, on the 1 peso it is blue, on the 5 pesos it is purple, on the 10 pesos it is black, and later becomes dark blue. The face seal does not seem to exist on the 20 and 50 peso denominations. However, both early denominations have a red scalloped hacienda seal and red control letters on the back as well as a black hand stamped treasury seal. All the early types change in the late issues, as observed in the next paragraph.

The late issues of this series bear the seal as well as control letters on the back of all denominations. Again, colors are fairly consistent: the 50 centavos seal is red on #S528 and blue on #S527. The 1 peso back seal and control letters are also red. The 5 peso seal and letters are black; the 50 pesos are red; the 20 pesos are black, and the 50 pesos back scalloped hacienda seal and control letters are purple or, less frequently, they may be red. Within this later type, a state treasury seal containing a large eagle was used first and then it was changed for a scalloped version containing a smaller eagle.

Many, though not all, of the late issues bear a date at the center of the back. The date will usually appear in the same color ink as the seal and control letters, and though it seems to be typewritten at first glance, it was really printed together with the seal and control letters in a type face very similat to that of a typewriter. Known dates are quite numerous and appear on all denominations of the late series, though not on all notes of each denomination. The back seal normally appears at the left, the date at the center, and the control letters at the right of each note, though it appears on the face of #S527 and at the right back of #S528. The control letters are normally found in a horizontal position, though once in a while they may be seen in a vertical position.

VALIDATION HAND STAMPS:

1. FUERZAS DEL ESTADO DE SONORA - DETALL GENERAL.
2. TESORERÍA GENERAL DE ESTADO DE SONORA HERMOSILLO.
3. JEFATURA DE HACIENDA EN EL ESTADO - GUADALAJARA, JAL.
4. ADUANA MARITIMA DE GUAYMAS, ADMINISTRACIÓN.
5. PRESIDENCIA MUNICIPAL DE CANANEA - SONORA, MEXICO.
6. DISTRITO DE GUAYMAS, RIO YAQUI, SONORA.
7. SECRETARIA PARTICULAR DEL GOBERNADOR DEL ESTADO DE SONORA.
8. ADUANA FRONTERIZA DE NOGALES, SON. - ADMINISTRACIÓN.
9. JEFATURA DE ARMAS - SALTILLO, COAH.
10. EJÉRCITO CONSTITUCIONALISTA - DIVISION DE OCCIDENTE PAGADURÍA GENERAL.
11. BANCO DEL ESTADO DE CHIH. - DURANGO, DGO. (handwritten signature: M. Arrieta).
12. AYUNTAMIENTO DEL ESTADO DE COAHUILA, SALTILLO.
13. ADMINISTRACIÓN PRINCIPAL DEL TIMBRE - DURANGO.
14. DISTRITO DE CULIACAN - COMANDANCIA MILITAR.
15. TESORERÍA GENERAL DEL ESTADO, MOCTEZUMA, SONORA.
16. TESORERÍA MUNICIPAL DE COCORITA.
17. LA PAZ, B.C. (eagle aboe).
18. EJÉRCITO CONSTITUCIONALISTA PAGADURIA GENERAL BRIGADA MORELOS w/additional sign. *el Pag. Gral* at r. on face.

DECRETO 10.2.1914

		VG	VF	UNC
S527	**50 CENTAVOS** Various dates in 1915. Blue. Back green; national arms at ctr. *(MI-CHI-37)*.			
	a. Issued note.	.75	2.00	5.00
	b. Inverted Treasury seal in back.	4.00	12.50	25.00

		VG	VF	UNC
S528	**50 CENTAVOS** *D. 1914*. Various dates in 1915. Green and black. Back green; national arms at ctr. Series U.			
	a. Circular black treasury and scalloped red state seals; lg. sign. at l. and r. *(MI-CHI-38)*.	1.00	3.00	7.50
	b. Scalloped red seal; sm. sign. at l. and r. Circular black treasury seal on back. *(MI-CHI-39)*.	.75	2.50	6.00

		VG	VF	UNC
	c. Sm. sign. at l. and r. Circular red treasury seal and horizontal control letters on back. *(MI-CHI-40)*.	.75	2.00	5.00

		VG	VF	UNC
	d. Sm. sign. at l. and r. Vertical scalloped red treasury seal and control letters on back. *(MI-CHI-41)*.	1.00	3.00	6.00

		VG	VF	UNC
	e. Like c, but w/date below control letters on back. 20.4.1915; 1.6.1915.	.75	2.50	5.00
	f. Violet ovpt: *FALSO* on c.	2.50	7.50	15.00
	g. Sm. sign. at l. and r. Back w/o seal or control letters. *(MI-CHI-43)*.	1.00	3.00	6.00
	h. W/o serial # or seals. *(MI-CHI-)*.	3.50	10.00	20.00

#S529-S538 portr. F. I. Madero at l., portr. Gov. A. González at r. Capitol bldg. at ctr. on back.

		VG	VF	UNC
S529	**1 PESO** *D. 1914*. Blue and black. Back blue. Series A.			
	a. Lg. printed sign. Red scalloped state seal. Black or blue-black circular treasury seal on back. *(MI-CHI-44)*.	2.50	7.50	15.00
	b. Sm. printed sign. Red scalloped treasury seal on back. *(MI-CHI-46)*.	1.00	3.00	6.00
	c. Like a, but w/date at ctr. on back. 5.10.1915; 10.7.1915.	.75	2.00	5.00
	d. W/o serial # or sign. at l. and r. *(MI-CHI-45)*.	5.00	10.00	20.00
	e. Scalloped red seal on face, circular black or blue-black seal on back.	1.50	4.50	9.00
	f. Red circular treasury seal on back.	1.50	4.50	9.00
	g. Red scalloped treasury seal and control letters on back.	.75	2.50	5.00
	x. Error: Ovpt. inverted.	—	—	—
S530	**1 PESO** June 1915. Like #S529 but w/sm. printed sign. Series L.			
	a. Circular red treasury seal on back. *(MI-CHI-47)*.	.75	2.00	5.00
	b. Scalloped red treasury seal on back.	.75	2.00	5.00
	c. Red seal on blank back. *MI-CHI-48)*.	7.00	20.00	40.00
	d. Like a, but w/date at ctr. on back. 11.1.1915.	.75	1.50	5.00
	e. Like b, but w/date at ctr. on back. 20.6.1915-10.11.1915.	.75	1.50	5.00
S531	**5 PESOS** *D. 1914*. Black on pink unpt. Back red.			
	a. Lg. sign. at l. and r. Blue scalloped state seal. Black circular treasury seal on back. *(MI-CHI-49)*.	3.00	9.00	17.50
	b. W/o blue scalloped state seal on face.	3.00	9.00	17.50
	c. Sm. sign. *(MI-CHI-50)*.	2.50	7.50	15.00
	d. Black scalloped treasury seal on back.	2.50	7.50	15.00
	e. W/o treasury seal, sign., date or serial #. *(MI-CHI-51)*.	8.00	25.00	50.00
	f. Black circular seal on back.	2.00	6.00	10.00
	g. W/lg. printed sign. and rubber stamp seal on back. *(MI-CHI-51a)*.	2.00	6.00	—

		VG	VF	UNC
S532	**5 PESOS** Jan. 1915. Like #S531. Series H.			
	a. Black scalloped treasury seal on back. *(MI-CHI-52)*.	2.00	6.00	12.00
	b. Black scalloped seal on blank back. *(MI-CHI-53)*.	12.50	25.00	50.00
	c. Blue scalloped treasury seal on back. *(MI-CHI-54)*.	.75	2.00	5.00
	d. Blue scalloped treasury seal on blank back. *(MI-CHI-55)*.	12.50	25.00	50.00
	e. Like #S532b w/date at ctr. on back. 1.6.1915; 10.6.1915.	.75	2.00	5.00

		VG	VF	Unc
S532A	**5 Pesos** June 1915. Like #S532. Series M. Date at ctr. on back. 1.6.1915-11.1.1915.	.75	2.00	5.00

		VG	VF	Unc
S533	**10 Pesos** *D. 1914.* Black on yellow-orange unpt. Back green. Series D.			
	a. 2 handwritten sign. at l. and r. Black circular treasury seal on back. *(MI-CHI-56).*	8.00	25.00	50.00

		VG	VF	Unc
	b. Dk. blue circular treasury seal and 2 dk. blue sm. printed sign. at l. and r. *(MI-CHI-57).*	4.00	12.50	25.00
	c. Sm. black printed sign. at l. and r. Red circular treasury seal on back. *(MI-CHI-58).*	2.00	6.00	12.00
	d. Red circular treasury seal on blank back. *(MI-CHI-58a).*	12.50	25.00	50.00
	e. Black scalloped treasury seal on back. *(MI-CHI-58b).*	2.00	6.00	12.00
	f. Ovpt: *FALSO* on d.	3.00	10.00	20.00
	g. Red scalloped treasury seal on back. *(MI-CHI-59).*	1.00	3.00	6.00
	h. W/o sign. W/seal on back.	12.50	25.00	50.00
	i. W/o sign. W/o seal on back. (Counterfeit).	4.00	12.00	20.00
	x1. Error: Ovpt. inverted.	—	—	—
	x2. Error: Ovpt. on face.	—	—	—
S534	**10 Pesos** Jan. 1915. Like #S533. Series J.			
	a. Red circular treasury seal on back.	1.00	3.00	6.00
	b. Red scalloped treasury seal on back. *(MI-CHI-59).*	.75	2.00	5.00
	c. Red scalloped treasury seal on blank back. *(MI-CHI-60).*	10.00	20.00	40.00

		VG	VF	Unc
S535	**10 Pesos** June 1915. Like #S534. Series N. *(MI-CHI-61).*			
	a. W/o date at ctr. on back.	.75	2.00	5.00
	b. W/ date at ctr. on back. 20.8.1915; 9.10.1915.	.75	2.00	5.00
	c. Red scalloped treasury seal on blank back. *(MI-CHI-62).*	10.00	20.00	40.00

		VG	VF	Unc
S536	**20 Pesos** *D. 1914.* Brown and black. 2 handwritten sign. Back brown. Series E.			
	a. Black circular treasury seal and red scalloped state seal on back. *(MI-CHI-63).*	6.50	20.00	40.00
	b. Sm. black printed sign. Circular black treasury seal on back.	.75	2.00	4.00
	c. Circular red seal on back.	1.50	4.00	8.00

		VG	VF	Unc
S537	**20 Pesos** Jan. 1915. Like #S536 but w/sm. printed sign. Series K.			
	a. Black scalloped treasury seal on back. *(MI-CHI-64).*	1.75	5.00	10.00
	b. W/ date on back. 27.3.1915-20.7.1915.	.75	2.00	4.00
	c. W/o seal on back.	3.50	10.00	20.00
	d. Black scalloped treasury seal on blank back. *(MI-CHI-65).*	5.00	15.00	30.00
	e. Black circular treasury seal on back.	2.00	6.00	12.00

		VG	VF	Unc
	f. Inverted black scalloped treasury seal, date and block letters on back.	10.00	30.00	60.00

		VG	VF	Unc
S538	**50 Pesos** *D. 1914.* Green and black. 2 handwritten sign. Back yellow to orange. Series F. *(MI-CHI-66).*			
	a. Violet circular treasury seal on back.	1.50	4.50	9.00
	b. Violet scalloped treasury seal on back.	2.50	7.50	15.00
	c. Red scalloped treasury seal on back.	2.50	7.50	15.00
	d. Red scalloped state and black circular treasury seal on back.	3.00	9.00	18.00
	e. Black circular treasury seal on back.	3.00	9.00	18.00
	f. Violet scalloped treasury seal on blank back.	5.00	15.00	30.00
	r. Remainder w/o serial #, l. and r. sign. or seal on back. *(MI-CHI-67).*	5.00	15.00	30.00

Gobierno Constitucionalista Provisional de Chihuahua

1916 Issue

#S539 and S540 national arms at upper ctr.

		Good	Fine	XF
S539	**10 Centavos** 1916. Green pasteboard. *(MI-CHI-1).*	2.00	6.00	15.00

		GOOD	FINE	XF
S540	**20 CENTAVOS** 1916. Brown to yellow-black on green unpt. *(MI-CHI-2).*	2.00	6.00	15.00

JEFATURA DE HACIENDA EN EL ESTADO DE CHIHUAHUA

1913 ISSUE

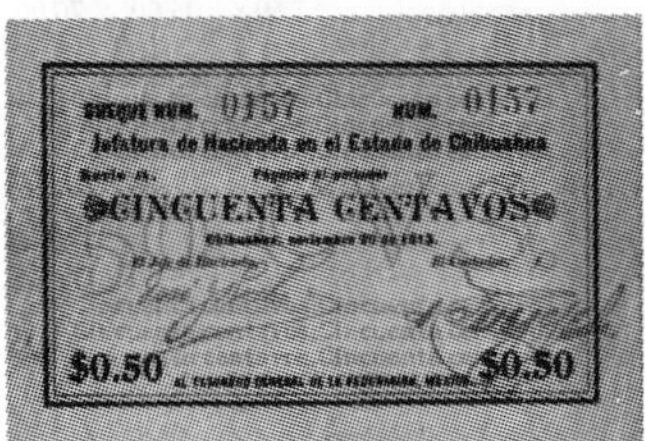

		GOOD	FINE	XF
S541	**50 CENTAVOS** 20.11.1913. Black on pink unpt. *(SI-CHI-4).*	45.00	100.00	250.00

LA CAJA DE AHORROS DE LA R.M., S.A.

1913 ISSUE

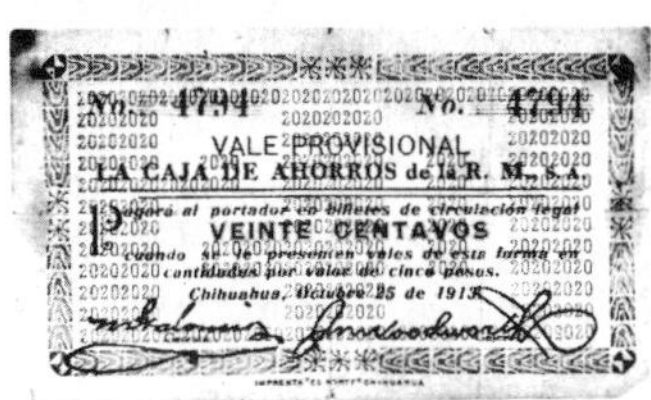

		GOOD	FINE	XF
S542	**20 CENTAVOS** 25.10.1913. Black on yellow unpt. *(PI-CHI-1).*	12.50	25.00	50.00

		GOOD	FINE	XF
S543	**50 CENTAVOS** 25.10.1913. Black on green unpt. Like #S542. *(PI-CHI-2).*	12.50	25.00	50.00

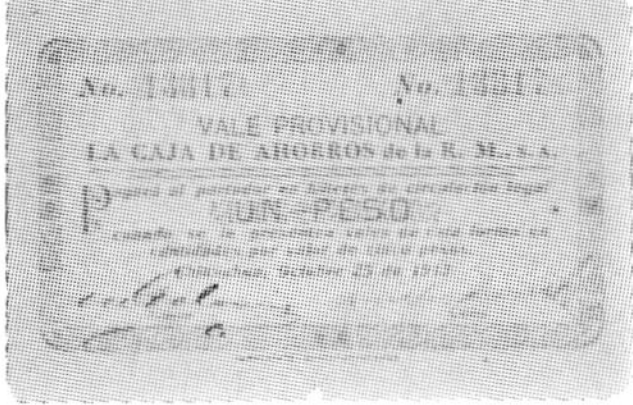

		GOOD	FINE	XF
S544	**1 PESO** 25.10.1913. Black on orange unpt. Like #S542. *(PI-CHI-3).*	12.50	25.00	50.00

TESORERÍA GENERAL DEL ESTADO - TRANSITORIO

ND ISSUE

#S545-S547 circular hand stamp: *TESORERÍA GENERAL DEL ESTADO CHIHUAHUA.*

		GOOD	FINE	XF
S545	**5 CENTAVOS** ND. Green. maroon pasteboard. Series A; B. *(SI-CHI-1).*	3.00	6.00	12.00

		GOOD	FINE	XF
S546	**5 CENTAVOS** ND. Green. orange pasteboard. Series A. *(SI-CHI-2).*	3.00	6.00	12.00
S546A	**5 CENTAVOS** ND. Green. White pasteboard. Series B. *(SI-CHI-3).*	2.50	7.50	15.00
S546B	**5 CENTAVOS** ND. Green on red pasteboard. Series B. *(SI-CHI-3A).*	3.00	9.00	18.00
S546C	**5 CENTAVOS** ND. Green on white pasteboard w/o *D* before and after *5. (SI-CHI-).*	4.00	8.00	12.00

		GOOD	FINE	XF
S547	**5 CENTAVOS** ND. Black on red-violet. *(SI-CHI-3B).*	3.00	9.00	18.00

TESORERÍA GENERAL DEL ESTADO

GENERAL STATE TREASURY

Printed by the State Print Shop of Chihuahua. Despite their title of the General Treasury of the State, these notes also bear the name of General Francisco Villa, and they were used to pay Villa's troops. This is the series commonly referred to as "Villa's bedsheets" (Sabanas de Villa). Multiple overprints exist on faces and backs of denominations from 5 through 100 pesos. Most of these overprints are either state, political or military which were effected with the prime purpose of giving official authorization in order that these notes could legally circulate within the entity or geographical area indicated by the overprint in question. The following list indicates those overprints. The following are listed with the most common ones first and working towards the scarcest.

REVALIDATION HAND STAMPS:

1. JEFATURA DE HACIENDA EN EL ESTADO, GUADALAJARA, JAL., around the state coat-of-arms.
2. PAGADURÍA GENERAL, TORREON, COAH, above the legend *ESTE BILLETE ES DE CIRCULACIÓN FORZOSA POR SER AUTENTICO.*
3. JEFATURA DE HACIENDA EN EL ESTADO DE JALISCO, GUADALAJARA.
4. TESORERÍA GENERAL DEL ESTADO, CHIHUAHUA.
5. JEFATURA DE HACIENDA EN EL ESTADO, JALISCO (sm.).
6. JEFATURA DE HACIENDA EN EL ESTADO, JALISCO (lg.).
7. RENTA DEL TIMBRE PRINCIPAL DE NUEVO LEON.
8. JEFATURA POLITICA DEL DISTRITO NORTE, ENSENADA (and date).
9. DIRECCIÓN GENERAL DE RENTAS DEL ESTADO, DURANGO.
10. GOBIERNO CONSTITUCIONALISTA, PRESIDENCIA MUNICIPAL, LEON, GTO. (GUANAJUATO).
11. INSPECCION GENERAL DE POLICIA -TOLUCA - MEXICO.
12. EJÉRCITO CONSTITUCIONALISTA, JEFATURA DE ARMAS DE SAN PEDRO, COAH.
13. PREFECTURA REGIONAL DEL PARTIDO DE LA CAPITAL, SAN LUIS POTOSI.
14. EJÉRCITO CONSTITUCIONALISTA, BRIGADA ROBLES, COMANDANCIA.
15. RECAUDACION DE RENTAS, H. DEL PARRAL, CHIH.
16. JEFATURA DE HACIENDA, EN EL ESTADO DE MICHOACÁN, MORELIA.
17. JEFATURA DE ARMAS, TULANCINGO, HGO. (HIDALGO).
18. REVALIDADO, DOLORES, HIDALGO, GTO. (GUANAJUATO).
19. RECAUDACION DE RENTAS DE CIUDAD JUAREZ.
20. PRESIDENCIA MUNICIPAL DE PARRAS DE LA FUENTE, COAHUILA.
21. F.F.C.C. CONSTITUCIONALISTAS DE MEXICO, TORREON, COAH.
22. CUERPO DEL EJÉRCITO DEL NORTE, 2o. REGIMIENTO DE INFANTERIA, CUARTEL GENERAL.
23. JEFATURA POLITICA DEL PARTIDO DE SAN JUAN DEL RIO, QRO. (QUERETARO).
24. ADMINISTRACIÓN PRINCIPAL DEL TIMBRE, DURANGO.
25. BATALION DE ZAPADORES, HIDALGO.
26. LAGOS DE MORENO. PRESIDENCIA MUNICIPAL. JAL.
27. CIUDAD GUZMAN, JEFATURA DE HACIENDA EN EL ESTADO, JAL.
28. JEFATURA POLITICA DEL TERRITORIO DE TEPIC.
29. JEFATURA SUPERIOR DE HACIENDA, GUANAJUATO.
30. JEFATURA DE ARMAS, ENCARNACION DE DIAZ, JAL. (JALISCO).
31. TESORERIA MUNICIPAL, SILAO, GTO. (GUANAJUATO).
32. REVALIDADO DECRETO DE 17 DE DICIEMBRE DE 1914. PAGADURIA GENERAL DE LA COLUMNA DE OPERACIONES, MICHOACÁN.
33. GOBIERNO CONSTITUCIONALISTA. DURANGO.
34. EJÉRCITO CONSTITUCIONALISTA. MORELOS.
35. ADMON. PRAL. DEL TIMBRE. DURANGO. ESTE BILLETE ES DE CIRCULACIÓN FORZOZA POR SER AUTENTICO.
36. SECRETARIA DE GOBIERNO. AGUASCALIENTES.
37. REVALIDADO (eagle at center).
38. EJÉRCITO CONSTITUCIONALISTA. ESTADO DE GUANAJUATO.
39. BRIGADA MALPICA.
40. ADMINISTRACIÓN PRINCIPAL DEL TIMBRE, COLIMA.
41. PAGADURIA GENERAL. . .BRIGADA M. CHAO. . .?

NOTE: Some of the above overprints are followed by additional handwritten sign. Up to five different overprints have been found on a single note. Any combination of the overprints listed may be found. A large number of different combinations are known to exist.

SEALS:

A. *ESTADO LIBRE Y SOBERANO DE CHIHUAHUA. TESORERÍA GENERAL*
B. *TESORERIA GENERAL DEL ESTADO CHIHUAHA.*

IMPRINTS:

A. Imp. del Gobierno.
B. Imp. del Gobierno Chih.
C. Imp. del Gobierno. Chihuahua.

1913 ISSUE

		GOOD	FINE	XF
S548	**5 CENTAVOS** 10.12.1913. Black and yellow. Series A, 92 x 69mm. *(MI-CHI-3).*	125.00	200.00	350.00

		GOOD	FINE	XF
S549	**10 CENTAVOS** 10.12.1913. Black and pink. 102 x 68mm. Straight text: *TESORERÍA. .* .Series A. *(MI-CHI-4).*	180.00	300.00	600.00

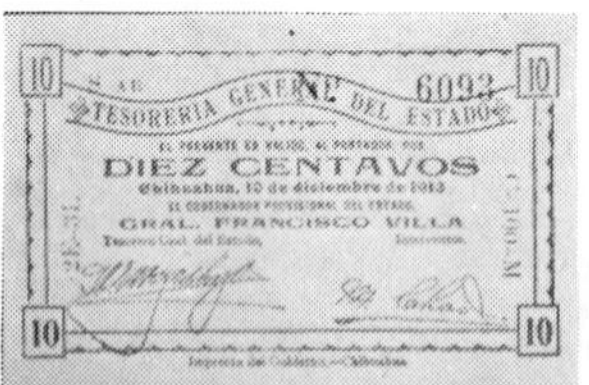

		GOOD	FINE	XF
S550	**10 CENTAVOS** 10.12.1913. Curved text: *TESORERÍA. . .(MI-CHI-5).*	.75	3.00	5.00

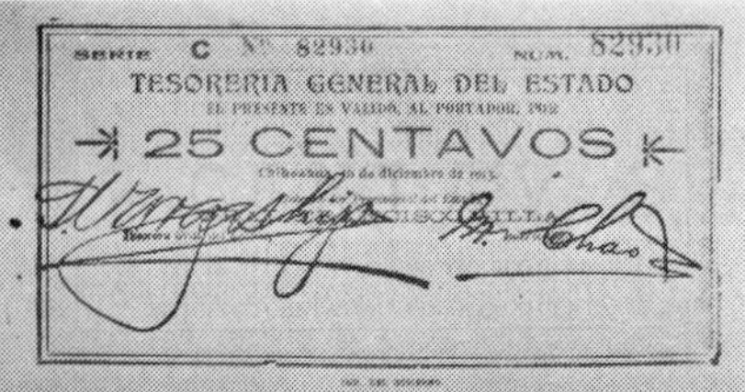

		GOOD	FINE	XF
S551	**25 CENTAVOS** 10.12.1913. Black on pink unpt. Lg. or sm. sign. Series C. *(MI-CHI-6).*			
	a. Lg. seal on back. Imp. A.	15.00	30.00	60.00
	b. Imp. B. *(MI-CHI-7).*	2.00	6.00	12.00
	c. Sm. black treasury seal on back. Series H.	2.00	6.00	12.00
	d. Lg. black seal on back. Imp. C. *(MI-CHI-8).*	.75	2.00	4.00
	e. Sm. black seal on back. Imp. C. Series N; BB. *(MI-CHI-9).*	.75	2.00	4.00
	f. Ovpt: *Revalidado por Decreto del 17 de Diciembre de 1914. (MI-CHI-10).*	5.00	15.00	30.00
	g. Sm. red seal on back. *(MI-CHI-11).*	.75	2.00	4.00
	h. Sm. blue seal on back. *(MI-CHI-12).*	1.00	3.00	6.00
	i. Sm. green seal on back. *(MI-CHI-13).*	1.25	3.75	7.50

		GOOD	FINE	XF
	j. Red circular treasury seal type B, red vertical date at upper l., w/o NUM. at upper r. Series CC; DD. 7.12.(19)15; 7.21.(19)15. *(MI-CHI-14).*	.75	2.25	4.50

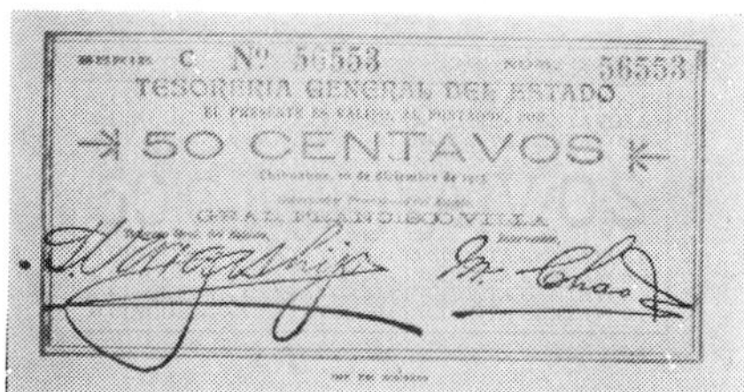

		GOOD	FINE	XF
S552	**50 CENTAVOS** 10.12.1913. Black. *(MI-CHI-15).*			
	a. Imp. B.	25.00	50.00	100.00
	b. Imp. C. Series D; G. *(MI-CHI-16).*	17.50	35.00	70.00
	c. Blue on lt. brown unpt. Imp. A. *(MI-CHI-16A).*	15.00	30.00	60.00
	d. Imp. C. Ovpt: *Revalidado por Decreto de 17 de Diciembre de 1914* .	17.50	35.00	70.00

		GOOD	FINE	XF
S553	**1 PESO** 10.12.1913. Black on green unpt. *(MI-CHI-17).*			
	a. Series A; C-F.	6.00	17.50	35.00
	b. Imp. C. Series B; D; G-J; L; P; Q; T; U. *(MI-CHI-18).*	3.00	12.00	25.00
	c. Imp. A. Series A; C. *(MI-CHI-18A).*	10.00	20.00	40.00
	d. Imp C. Ovpt: *Revalidado por Decreto de 17 de Diciembre de 1914. (MI-CHI-19).*	6.00	17.50	35.00
	e. Imp. C. Hand stamped: *FALSO.*	6.00	17.50	35.00
	f. Imp C. Wmk: *Oldham...* Series O.	6.00	17.50	35.00
S553A	**5 PESOS** 10.12.1913. Black on brown unpt. 2 handwritten sign. Uniface w/o imprint. Series A.	10.00	20.00	40.00

		GOOD	FINE	XF
S554	**5 PESOS** 10.12.1913. Black on brown unpt. Imp. B. Series A-D.			
	a. Handwritten sign. *(MI-CHI-20a).*	20.00	60.00	—
	b. Printed sign. *(MI-CHI-20).*	2.00	6.00	12.00
	c. Ovpt: *Revalidado por Decreto de 17 de Diciembre de 1914. (MI-CHI-21).*	3.00	10.00	20.00
	d. Violet hand stamped:	2.50	7.50	15.00
	e. *Goberñado* (error) for *Goberñador. (MI-CHI-21a).*	2.50	7.50	15.00

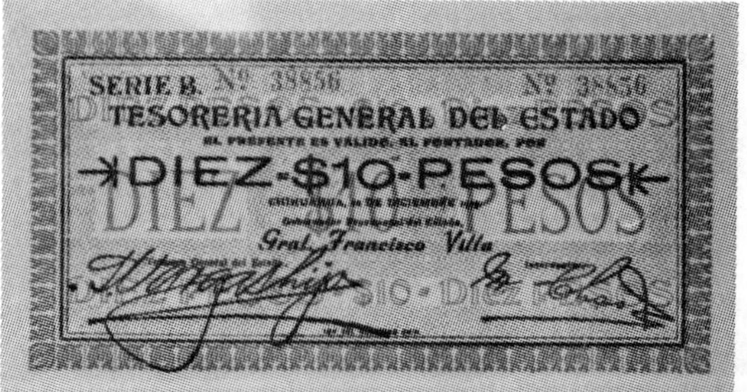

		GOOD	FINE	XF
S555	**10 PESOS** 10.12.1913. Black on blue, gray or blue-green unpt. Imp. B. Series A; B.			
	a. Issued note. Violet seal A on back. *(MI-CHI-22).*	1.50	4.50	10.00
	b. Ovpt: *Revalidado por Decreto de 17 de Diciembre de 1914. (MI-CHI-23).*	3.00	10.00	20.00
	c. Ovpt: *FALSO* on genuine note. *(MI-CHI-24).*	2.00	6.00	12.00

		GOOD	FINE	XF
S556	**20 PESOS** 10.12.1913. Black on pale green unpt. Seal A on back. Imp. B. Series A. *(MI-CHI-25).*			
	a. Issued note.	3.00	10.00	20.00
	b. Ovpt: *Revalidado por Decreto de 17 de Diciembre de 1914. (MI-CHI-27).*	4.00	12.50	25.00
	c. Ovpt: *FALSO* on genuine note. *(MI-CHI-26).*	3.50	12.00	22.00
	x. Error: *VIENTE* instead of *VEINTE. (MI-CHI-28).*	175.00	350.00	600.00

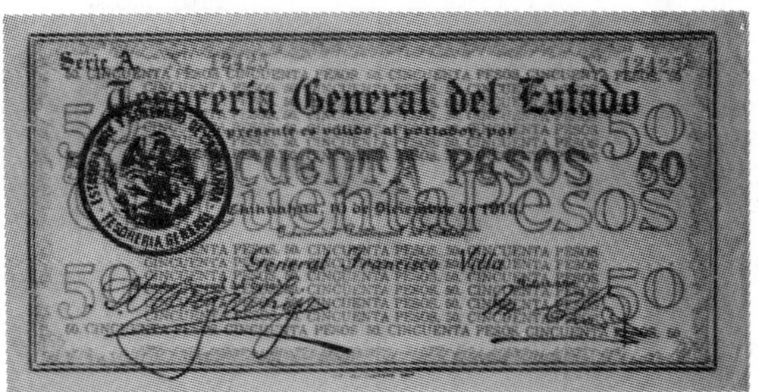

		GOOD	FINE	XF
S557	**50 PESOS** 10.12.1913. Black on green unpt. Imp. B. Series A.			
	a. 2 handwritten sign. *(MI-CHI-30).*	20.00	40.00	80.00
	b. 2 printed sign. *(MI-CHI-29).*	20.00	40.00	80.00
	c. Ovpt: *Revalidado por Decreto de 17 de Diciembre de 1914. (MI-CHI-31).*	20.00	40.00	80.00

		GOOD	FINE	XF
S558	**100 PESOS** 10.12.1913. Black on red unpt. Imp. B. Series A.			
	a. 2 handwritten sign. *(MI-CHI-33).*	37.50	75.00	150.00
	b. 2 printed sign. *(MI-CHI-32).*	30.00	60.00	120.00
	c. Ovpt: *Revalidado por Decreto de 17 de Diciembre de 1914.*	30.00	60.00	120.00

#S559-S561 ovpt: ***República Mexicana-Ejército Libertador-Comandancia; Estado Libre y Soberano de Chihuahua-Tesorería General; República Mexicana-Ejército Libertador-Brigada Pacheco-Detall*** **on back.**

		GOOD	FINE	XF
S559	**1 PESO** 10.12.1913. Black on blue unpt. *(MI-CHI-34).*	115.00	350.00	700.00

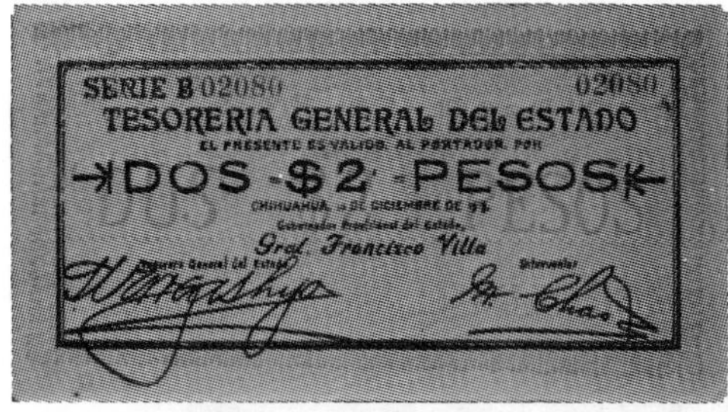

		GOOD	FINE	XF
S560	**2 PESOS** 10.12.1913. Black on blue unpt. W/o imprint. Series B.			
	a. Issued note. *(MI-CHI-35).*	125.00	250.00	500.00
	b. Additional ovpt: *Brigada Malpica* on back.	150.00	300.00	—
S561	**10 PESOS** 10.12.1913. Black on blue unpt. W/o imprint. Series B. *(MI-CHI-36).*	75.00	150.00	—

LA TESORERÍA MUNICIPAL DE C. JIMÉNEZ

1915 ISSUE

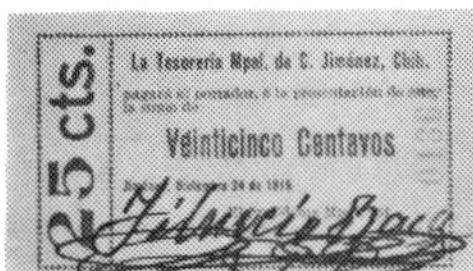

		GOOD	FINE	XF
S562	**25 CENTAVOS** 24.12.1915. Black. *(SI-CHI-5).*	12.50	30.00	65.00

COAHUILA

BANK ON BANK CHECKS

These checks were issued by the banks of Torreón, Coahuila, payable to the bearer in Mexico City once the railroad was reopened. They were cleverly devised by the local bank executives when under pressure by General Francisco Villa who demanded cash to pay his troops. Thus, these bank on bank checks became legal tender and the bank executives met a dire commitment.

There are 2 series; A and B. Some of these notes bear the ovpt: *FALSO;* however, they are all genuine. The name of the issuing bank appears at the lower right and the name of the bank upon which the check is drawn appears at the center above. Thus, the following listings express the former over the latter. All these pieces are handsigned except the 1 and 2 pesos, Banco de la Laguna/Banco de Coahuila.

BANCO DE COAHUILA/BANCO DE LA LAGUNA (REFACCIONARIO)

1913 ISSUE

#S563-S566 printer: Tip. C. Mountauriol.

		GOOD	FINE	XF
S563	**1 PESO** 7.10.1913. Black on green unpt. Series A. *(MI-COA-20).*	15.00	30.00	—

		GOOD	FINE	XF
S564	**5 PESOS** 7.10.1913. Black. Series A. *(MI-COA-21).*	12.50	25.00	—
S565	**10 PESOS** 7.10.1913. Green. Series A. *(MI-COA-22).*	15.00	30.00	—
S566	**20 PESOS** 7.10.1913. Red. Series A.			
	a. Issued note. *(MI-COA-23).*	15.00	30.00	—
	b. Ovpt: *San Luis Potosi. (MI-COA-24).*	30.00	60.00	—

1914 Issue

#S567-S569 printer: Tip. Valdez.

		Good	Fine	XF
S567	5 Pesos 5.2.1914. Black. Series B. *(MI-COA-25).*	17.50	35.00	—
S568	10 Pesos 5.2.1914. Green. Series B. *(MI-COA-26).*	17.50	35.00	—

		Good	Fine	XF
S569	20 Pesos 5.2.1914. Red. Series B.			
	a. Issued note. *(MI-COA-27).*	35.00	—	—
	b. Ovpt: *Guadalajara. (MI-COA-28).*	35.00	—	—

Banco de Coahuila/Banco Nacional de México

1913 Issue

#S570-S572 printer: Tip. C. Mountauriol.

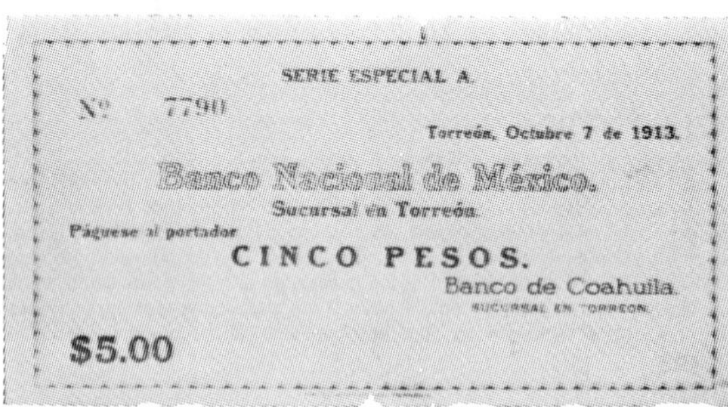

		Good	Fine	XF
S570	5 Pesos 7.10.1913. Black. Series A. *(MI-COA-29).*	15.00	30.00	—
S571	10 Pesos 7.10.1913. Green. Series A. *(MI-COA-30).*	15.00	30.00	—
S572	20 Pesos 7.10.1913. Red. Series A. *(MI-COA-31).*	15.00	30.00	—

Deutsch-Sudamerikanische Bank (Berlin) / Banco de Londres y México

1913 Issue

#S573-S575 printer: Tip. C. Mountauriol.

		Good	Fine	XF
S573	5 Pesos 7.10.1913. Black. Series A.			
	a. Issued note. *(MI-COA-32).*	37.50	75.00	150.00
	b. Cancellation: *Banco Germanico (Sucursal Mexico) Pagado. (MI-COA-33).*	65.00	130.00	—
S574	10 Pesos 7.10.1913. Green. Series A.			
	a. Issued note. *(MI-COA-34).*	50.00	100.00	200.00
	b. Perforated: *CANCELADO. (MI-COA-35).*	75.00	150.00	—
S575	20 Pesos 7.10.1913. Red. Series A.			
	a. Issued note. *(MI-COA-36).*	60.00	125.00	250.00
	b. Perforated: *CANCELADO. (MI-COA-37).*	90.00	180.00	—

Deutsch-Sudamerikanische Bank (Berlin) / Banco Nacional de México

1913 Issue

#S576-S578 w/o imprint.

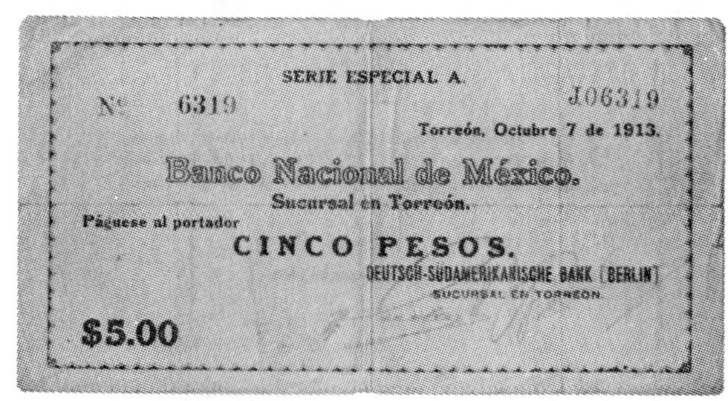

		Good	Fine	XF
S576	5 Pesos 7.10.1913. Black. Series A.			
	a. Issued note. *(MI-COA-38).*	37.50	75.00	125.00
	b. Perforated: *CANCELADO. (MI-COA-39).*	65.00	130.00	—
S577	10 Pesos 7.10.1913. Green. Series A.			
	a. Issued note. *(MI-COA-40).*	50.00	100.00	165.00
	b. Perforated: *CANCELADO. (MI-COA-41).*	75.00	150.00	—
S578	20 Pesos 7.10.1913. Red. Series A.			
	a. Issued note. *(MI-COA-42).*	65.00	135.00	225.00
	b. Perforated: *CANCELADO. (MI-COA-43).*	100.00	200.00	—

Banco de la Laguna (Refaccionario) / Banco de Coahuila

1913 Issues

#S579-S584 printer: Tip. C. Mountauriol.

		Good	Fine	XF
S579	1 Peso 7.10.1913. Black on green unpt. Series A. *(MI-COA-44).*	15.00	30.00	—
S580	5 Pesos 7.10.1913. Black. Series A. *(MI-COA-45).*	12.50	25.00	—

		Good	Fine	XF
S581	10 Pesos 7.10.1913. Green. Series A.			
	a. Issued note. *(MI-COA-46).*	17.50	35.00	—
	b. Hand stamped: *FALSO (MI-COA-47).*	10.00	20.00	—
S582	20 Pesos 7.10.1913. Red. Series A.			
	a. Issued note. *(MI-COA-48).*	12.50	25.00	50.00
	b. Hand stamped: *FALSO. (MI-COA-49).*	10.00	20.00	—

		GOOD	FINE	XF
S583	**50 PESOS** 18.12.1913. Blue thick paper. Series A.			
	a. Issued note. *(MI-COA-50).*	30.00	60.00	100.00
	b. Hand stamped: *FALSO. (MI-COA-50a).*	30.00	60.00	100.00
S584	**50 PESOS** 18.12.1913. Thin blue paper. Series A. *(MI-COA-51).*	37.50	75.00	125.00

1914 ISSUES

#S585-S587 printer: Tip. C. Mountauriol, Torreón.

		GOOD	FINE	XF
S585	**1 PESO** 5.1.1914. Black on blue-green unpt. Hand stamped sign. Series B. *(MI-COA-52).*	7.50	17.50	35.00

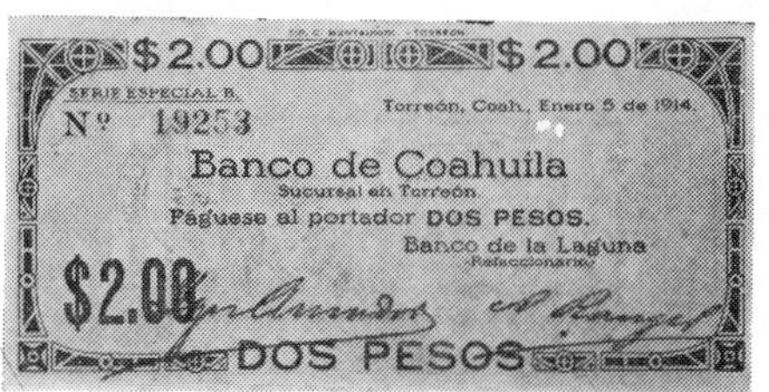

		GOOD	FINE	XF
S586	**2 PESOS** 5.1.1914. Black on green unpt. Hand stamped sign. Series B. *(MI-COA-53).*	7.50	17.50	35.00
S587	**5 PESOS** 5.1.1914. Black. Like #S580. Series B.			
	a. Issued note. *(MI-COA-55).*	22.50	45.00	—
	b. Ovpt: *GUADALAJARA. (MI-COA-56).*	22.50	45.00	—

#S588-S591 printer: Tip. S. de la Peña.

		GOOD	FINE	XF
S588	**5 PESOS** 5.1.1914. Black. Series B. *(MI-COA-54).*	15.00	30.00	—

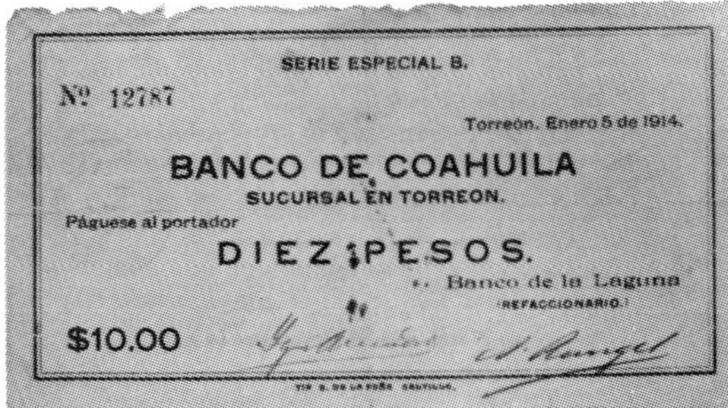

		GOOD	FINE	XF
S589	**10 PESOS** 5.1.1914. Blue. Series B. *(MI-COA-57).*	18.00	35.00	—
S590	**20 PESOS** 5.1.1914. Sepia. Series B. *(MI-COA-58).*	18.00	35.00	—
S591	**50 PESOS** 5.1.1914. Series B. *(MI-COA-59).*	45.00	90.00	—

A word on pricing

When a note is marked RARE in the price columns, this note seldom appears on the market, or few are known in private hands. When dashes are in the price column, means that the note has not traded on the open market recently and a definitive value could not accurately be determined. Rare does not always mean expensive. A dashed price does not mean expensive or rare.

BANCO DE LA LAGUNA (REFACCIONARIO) / BANCO DE LONDRES YMÉXICO

1913 ISSUE

#S592 and S593 w/o imprint.

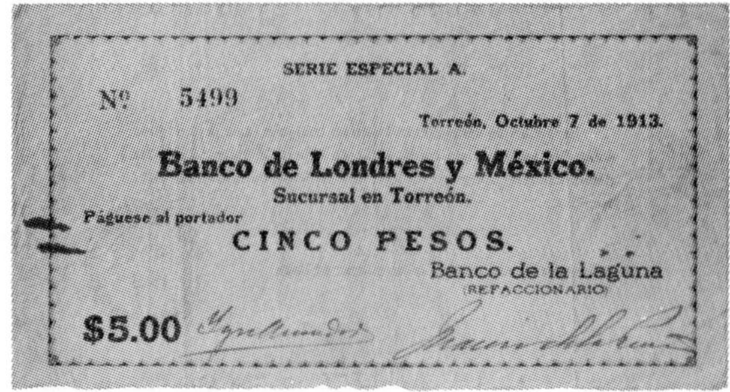

		GOOD	FINE	XF
S592	**5 PESOS** 7.10.1913. Black. Series A.			
	a. Issued note. *(MI-COA-60).*	15.00	30.00	—
	b. Hand stamped: *FALSO. (MI-COA-61).*	10.00	20.00	—

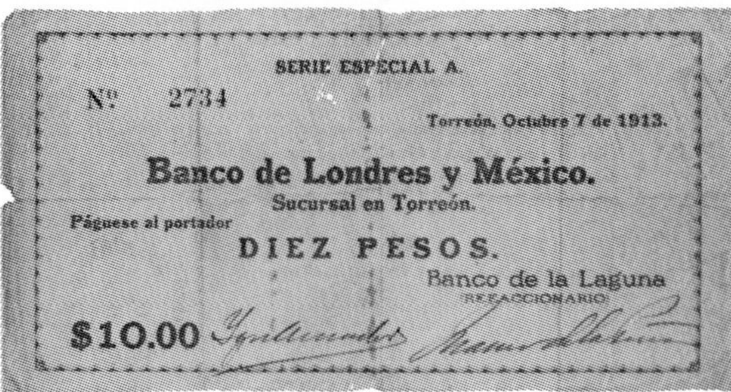

		GOOD	FINE	XF
S593	**10 PESOS** 7.10.1913. Green. Series A.			
	a. Issued note. *(MI-COA-62).*	15.00	30.00	—
	b. Hand stamped: *FALSO. (MI-COA-63).*	10.00	20.00	—
	c. Hand stamped: *CANCELADO. (MI-COA-63A).*	18.00	36.00	—

#S594-S596A printer: Tip. C. Mountauriol, Torreón. Wmk: *OLD HAMPSHIRE BOND.*

		GOOD	FINE	XF
S594	**5 PESOS** 7.10.1913.	Reported Not Confirmed		
S595	**10 PESOS** 7.10.1913. Green.			
	a. Issued note.	17.50	35.00	—
	b. Lg. violet hand stamp: *CANCELADO.*	17.50	35.00	—
	c. Lg. black hand stamp: *CANCELADO.*	17.50	35.00	—
	d. Blue rectangular outlined hand stamp: *CANCELADO/MEXICO.*	17.50	35.00	—
	e. Perforated: *AMORTIZADO.*	17.50	35.00	—
	f. Sm. violet hand stamp: *CANCELADO.*	17.50	35.00	—

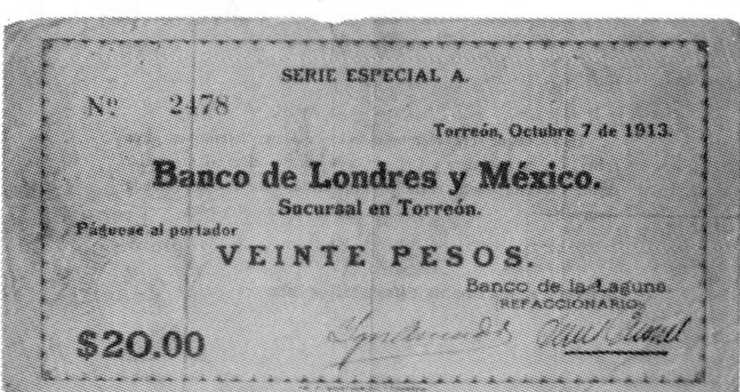

		GOOD	FINE	XF
S596	**20 PESOS** 7.10.1913. Red. Series A.			
	a. Issued note. *(MI-COA-64).*	22.50	45.00	—
	b. Hand stamped: *FALSO. (MI-COA-65).*	22.50	45.00	—
S596A	**50 PESOS** 7.10.1913.	Reported Not Confirmed		

BANCO DE LA LAGUNA (REFACCIONARIO) /BANCO MINERO

1913 ISSUE

#S597-S602 printer: Tip. C. Mountauriol.

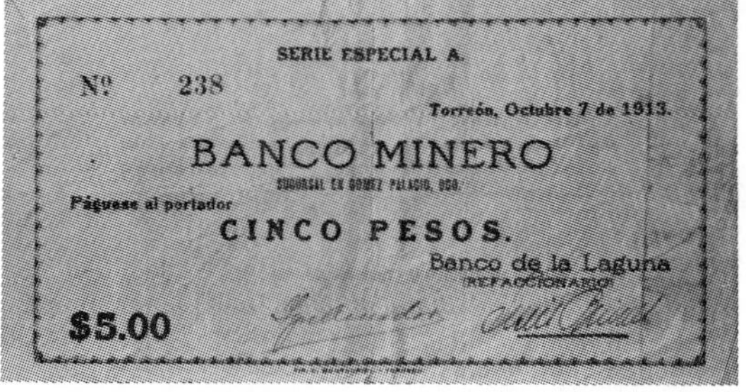

		Good	Fine	XF
S597	**5 Pesos** 7.10.1913. Black. Sm. text: *SUCURSAL . . .* Series A. *(MI-COA-66).*	15.00	30.00	—

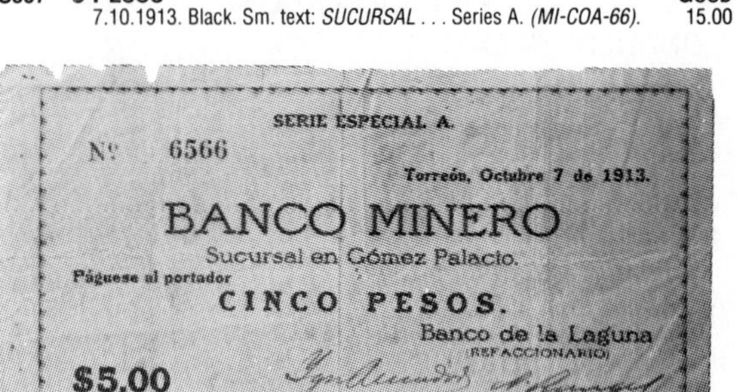

		Good	Fine	XF
S598	**5 Pesos** 7.10.1913. Lg. text: *SUCURSAL . . .* Series A. *(MI-COA-67).*	17.50	35.00	—
S599	**10 Pesos** 7.10.1913. Green. Series A.			

		Good	Fine	XF
	a. Issued note. *(MI-COA-68).*	7.50	35.00	—
	b. Hand stamped: *FALSO. (MI-COA-69).*	10.00	20.00	—

		Good	Fine	XF
S600	**20 Pesos** 7.10.1913. Red. Sm. text: *SUCURSAL. . .* Series A. *(MI-COA-70).*	7.50	35.00	—
S601	**20 Pesos** 7.10.1913. Red. Lg. text: *SUCURSAL. . .* Series A.			
	a. Issued note. *(MI-COA-71).*	7.50	35.00	—
	b. Hand stamped: *FALSO. (MI-COA-72).*	12.50	25.00	—
S602	**50 Pesos** 18.12.1913. Blue. Series A.			
	a. Issued note. *(MI-COA-73).*	45.00	90.00	—
	b. Hand stamped: *CANCELADO.*	30.00	60.00	—

Banco de Londres y México / Deutsch-Sudamerikanische Bank (Berlin)

1913 Issue

#S603-S605 w/o imprint.

		Good	Fine	XF
S603	**5 Pesos** 7.10.1913. Black. Series A. *(MI-COA-74).*	37.50	75.00	150.00
S603A	**5 Pesos** 7.10.1913. Black. Similar to #S603 but w/*Torreón* and date centered.	37.50	75.00	150.00
S604	**10 Pesos** 7.10.1913. Green. Series A. *(MI-COA-75).*	50.00	100.00	175.00
S605	**20 Pesos** 7.10.1913. Red. Series A. *(MI-COA-76).*	60.00	120.00	225.00
S606	**20 Pesos** 7.10.1913. Red. Torreón and date at ctr. Both serial # printed. Series A. Printer: Mountauriol, Torreon. *(MI-COA-77).*	75.00	150.00	275.00

Banco de Londres y México / Banco de la Laguna (Refaccionario)

1913 Issue

#S607 and S608 printer: Tip. C. Mountauriol.

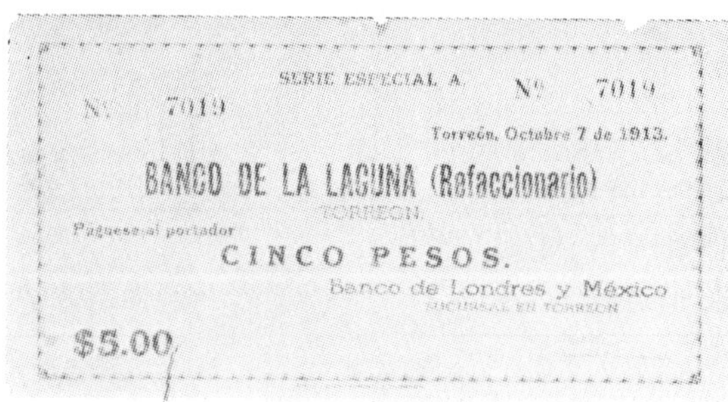

		Good	Fine	XF
S607	**5 Pesos** 7.10.1913. Series A. *(MI-COA-78).*	37.50	75.00	—
S608	**10 Pesos** 7.10.1913. Green. Series A.			
	a. Issued note. *(MI-COA-79).*	45.00	90.00	—
	b. Hand stamped: *CANCELADO. (MI-COA-80).*	45.00	90.00	—

Banco de Londres y México / Banco Nacional de México

1913 Issue

#S609-S612 printer: Tip. C. Mountauriol.

		Good	Fine	XF
S609	**1 Peso** 7.10.1913. Black on green unpt. Series A. *(MI-COA-81).*	22.50	45.00	—

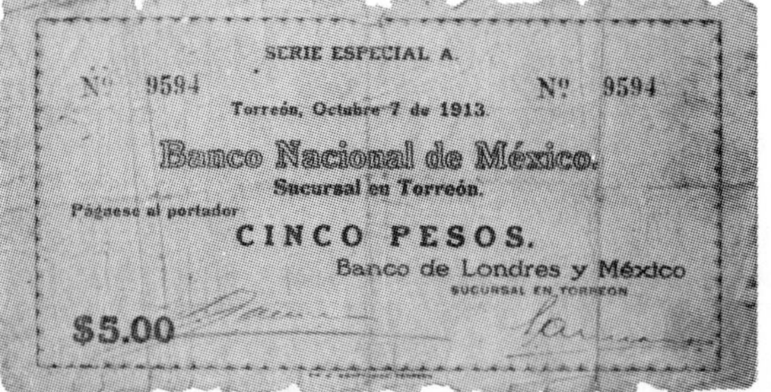

		Good	Fine	XF
S610	**5 Pesos** 7.10.1913. Black. Series A. *(MI-COA-82).*	22.50	45.00	—

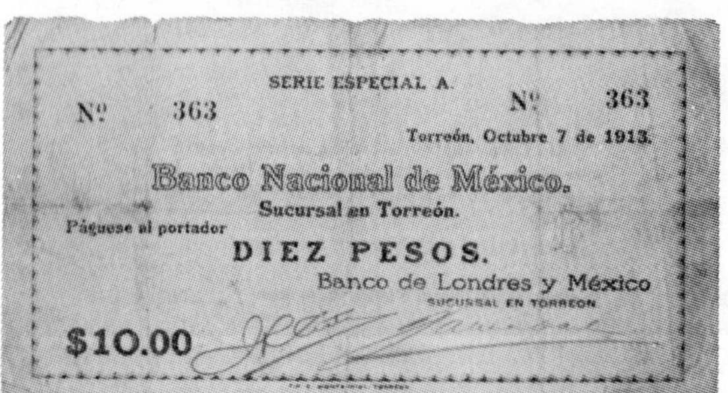

		Good	Fine	XF
S611	**10 Pesos** 7.10.1913. Series A. *(MI-COA-83).*	30.00	60.00	—
S612	**20 Pesos** 7.10.1913. Series A. *(MI-COA-84).*	30.00	60.00	—

BANCO NACIONAL DE MÉXICO /BBANCO DE COAHUILA

1913 ISSUE

#S613 and S614 w/o imprint.

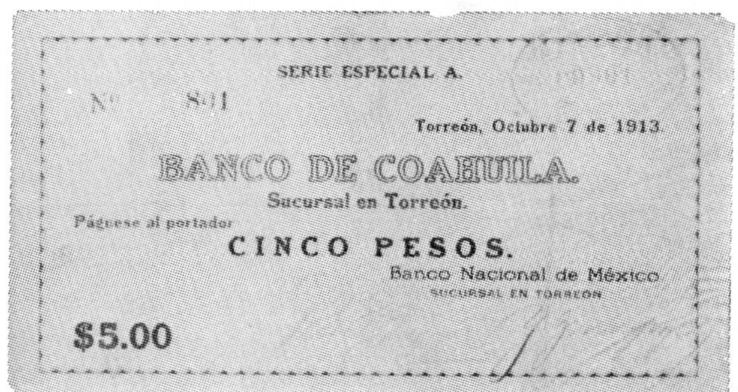

		GOOD	FINE	XF
S613	**5 PESOS** 7.10.1913. Black. Series A. *(MI-COA-85).*	22.50	45.00	—
S614	**10 PESOS** 7.10.1913. Green. Series A. *(MI-COA-86).*	12.50	25.00	50.00

BANCO NACIONAL DE MÉXICO / DEUTSCH-SUDAMERIKANISCHE BANK (BERLIN)

1913 ISSUE

#S615-S617 printer: Tip. C. Mountauriol.

		GOOD	FINE	XF
S615	**5 PESOS** 7.10.1913. Black. Series A. *(MI-COA-87).*	37.50	75.00	150.00
S616	**10 PESOS** 7.10.1913. Series A. *(MI-COA-88).*	50.00	100.00	175.00
S617	**20 PESOS** 7.10.1913. Series A. *(MI-COA-89).*	60.00	120.00	225.00

BANCO NACIONAL DE MÉXICO /

BANCO DE LONDRES Y MÉXICO

1913 ISSUE

#S618-S621 printer: Tip. C. Mountauriol.

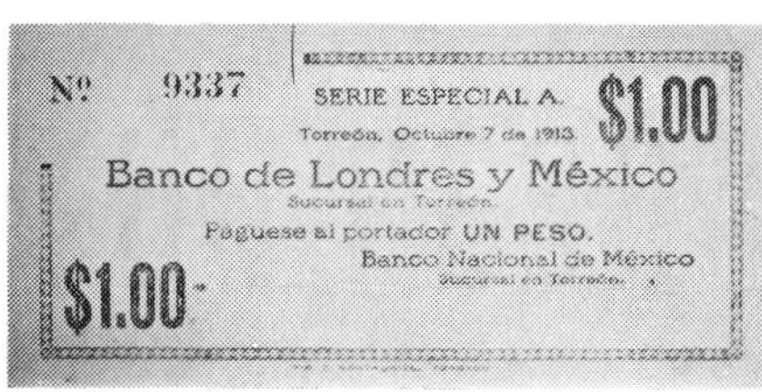

		GOOD	FINE	XF
S618	**1 PESO** 7.10.1913. Series A. *(MI-COA-90).*	20.00	45.00	—

		GOOD	FINE	XF
S619	**5 PESOS** 7.10.1913. Series A. *(MI-COA-91).*	20.00	60.00	—

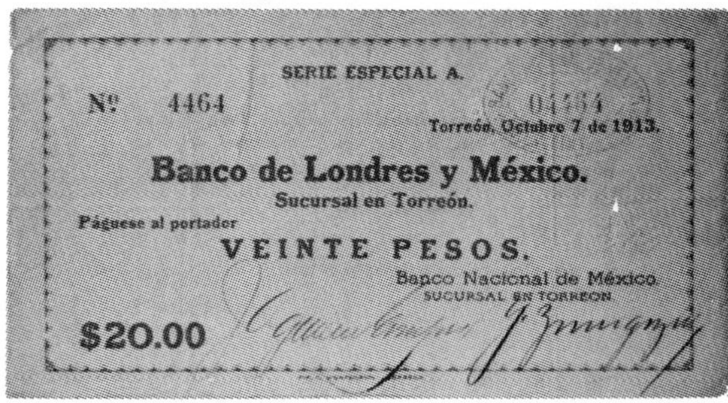

		GOOD	FINE	XF
S620	**10 PESOS** 7.10.1913. Green. Series A.			
	a. Issued note. *(MI-COA-92).*	12.50	25.00	50.00
	b. Ovpt: *EL CHEQUE LEJITIMO DEL CONTENIDO DE ESTE FUE PAGADO. (MI-COA-93).*	12.50	25.00	50.00
	c. Hand stamped: *CANCELADO.*	10.00	20.00	40.00

		GOOD	FINE	XF
S621	**20 PESOS** 7.10.1913. Red. Series A.			
	a. Issued note. *(MI-COA-94).*	12.50	25.00	50.00
	b. Ovpt: *EL CHEQUE LEJITIMO DEL CONTENIDO DE ESTE FUE PAGADO. (MI-COA-95).*	12.50	25.00	50.00

TESORERÍA MUNICIPAL, MUNICIPIO DE MATAMOROS

ND ISSUE

		GOOD	FINE	XF
S622	**5 CENTAVOS** ND. Black. Cream pasteboard. *(SI-COA-1).*	5.00	15.00	30.00
S623	**10 CENTAVOS** ND. Red. Cream pasteboard. Series A. *(SI-COA-2).*	5.00	15.00	30.00

		GOOD	FINE	XF
S624	**20 CENTAVOS** ND. Blue. Cream pasteboard. Series A. *(SI-COA-3).*	5.00	15.00	30.00

GOBIERNO CONSTITUCIONALISTA DE MÉXICO, MONCLOVA

DECREE OF APRIL 26, 1913

This was the first issue of paper money emitted by revolutionary forces and consequently, the first military issue of the revolution. These notes were issued by General Venustiano Carranza's forces when they were fighting against those of President Victoriano Huerta.

VALIDATION HAND STAMPS:

1. REVALIDADO POR DECRETO DE 17 DE DICIEMBRE DE 1914.
2. DIVISION DEL NORTE, EJERCITO CONSTITUCIONALISTA, JEFATURA DE ARMAS.
3. PREFECTURA DEL DISTRITO DE NAZAS - ESTADO DE COAHUILA, MEXICO.
4. TESORERIA GENERAL DEL ESTADO DE SONORA, HERMOSILLO.
5. RENTA DEL TIMBRE, PRINCIPAL DE NUEVO LEON.
6. JEFATURA POLITICAL DEL DISTRITO NORTE, ENSENADA.
7. PRESIDENCIA MUNICIPAL DE CANANEA, SONORA, MEX.
8. LA PAZ, B.C. (eagle above).
9. RECAUDACION DE RENTAS DEL DISTRITO DE MAZATLAN. RETIRADO DE LA CIRCULACION.
10. BRIGADA CARRASCO, 3A, DIVISION.

		GOOD	FINE	XF
S625	**1 PESO** 28.5.1913. Black. Back green w/circular red seal. Series A.			
	a. Sm. sign. at r.	4.00	15.00	37.50
	b. As a. W/ovpt: *REVALIDADO/POR DECRETO DE 17 DE DICEMBRE DE 1914.*	6.50	20.00	40.00
	c. Lg. printed sign. at r.	1.00	3.50	10.00
	d. As c. W/ovpt: *REVALIDADO/POR DECRETO DE 17 DE DICIEMBRE DE 1914.*	1.50	5.00	15.00

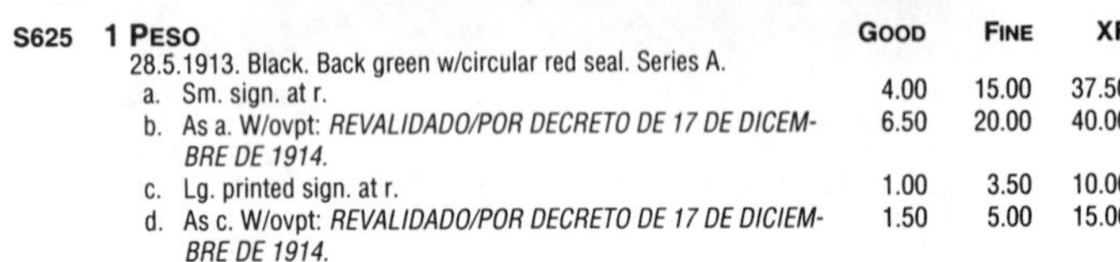

		GOOD	FINE	XF
S626	**1 PESO** 28.5.1913. Like #S625 but w/different guilloches around numerals. Series A. *(MI-COA-1).*	1.00	3.00	9.00

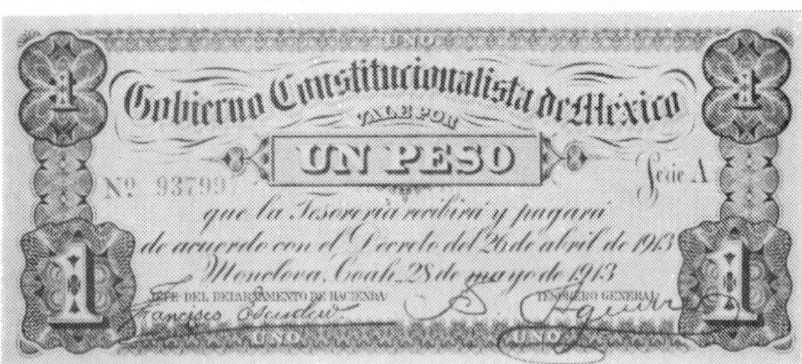

		GOOD	FINE	XF
S627	**5 PESOS** 28.5.1913. Black. Narrow *5's* in corners. Back green; narrow *5's* at l. and r. Series B. *(MI-COA-2).*	6.00	18.00	35.00

		GOOD	FINE	XF
S628	**5 PESOS** 28.5.1913. Black. Lg. *5's* in lower corners, sm. *5's* in upper corners. Series B. Back green.			
	a. Sm. sign at r.	1.00	2.50	7.50
	b. As a. W/ovpt: *REVALIDADO/POR DECRETO DE 17 DE DICIEMBRE DE 1914.*	1.00	4.00	12.00
	c. Lg. sign. at r. *(MI-COA-3).*	1.00	2.50	7.50

		GOOD	FINE	XF
S629	**10 PESOS** 28.5.1913. Black. Back green. Poor quality printing. Lg: *DIEZ* at upper l. and r. on back. Series C. *(MI-COA-4).*	3.00	12.00	25.00

		GOOD	FINE	XF
S630	**10 PESOS** 28.5.1913. Like #S629 but w/narrow 0's in 10's. Back green; sm. *DIEZ* at upper l. and r. on back. Series C.	3.00	12.00	25.00

		GOOD	FINE	XF
S631	**10 PESOS** 28.5.1913. Like #S629 but better quality printing. *(MI-COA-5).*	2.00	5.00	12.00

		Good	Fine	XF
S632	**20 Pesos**			
	28.5.1913. Black. *VIENTE* (error) in upper and lower borders. Series D.			
	a. Sm. sign. at r. *(MI-COA-6).*	3.00	7.00	15.00
	b. As a. W/ovpt: *REVALIDADO/POR DECRETO DE 17 DE DICIEMBRE DE 1914* on a.	3.00	7.00	15.00
	c. Lg. sign. at r.	3.00	7.00	15.00
	d. As c. W/ovpt: *REVALIDADO/POR DECRETO DE 17 DE DICIEMBRE DE 1914* on c.	3.00	7.00	15.00

		Good	Fine	XF
S633	**20 Pesos**			
	28.5.1913. Like #S629 but w/retouched 20's at lower l. and r. and *VEINTE* corrected in borders. Back green. Series D. *(MI-COA-7).*	—	—	—

NOTE: Serial #'s have been recorded for #S632 both above and below #S633. The crude appearance of the *20's* at lower l. and r. similar to the *10's* on #S630 may prove the claims of earlier catalogers of a spurious issue.

		Good	Fine	XF
S634	**50 Pesos**			
	28.5.1913. Black. Back orange. Series E.			
	a. 1 handwritten and 1 printed sign. *(MI-COA-8).*	10.00	20.00	40.00
	b. 2 printed sign. *(MI-COA-9).*	20.00	40.00	80.00

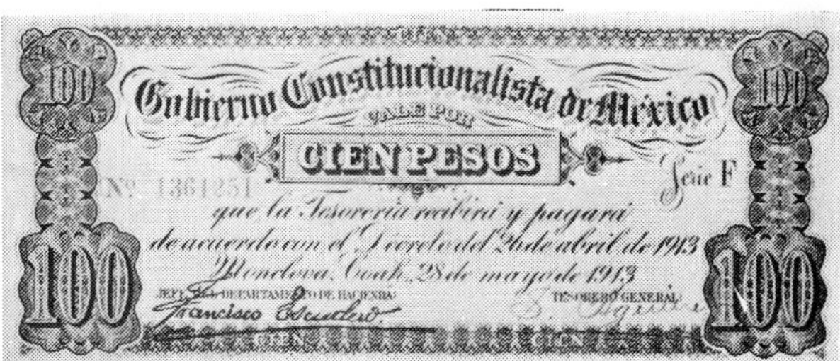

		Good	Fine	XF
S635	**100 Pesos**			
	28.5.1913. Black. Back orange. Series F.			
	a. 2 handwritten sign. *(MI-COA-10).*	15.00	30.00	60.00
	b. 1 handwritten and 1 printed sign. *(MI-COA-11).*	20.00	40.00	80.00
	c. W/o sign.	25.00	50.00	100.00

Tesorería Municipal, Monclova

1914 ND Issue

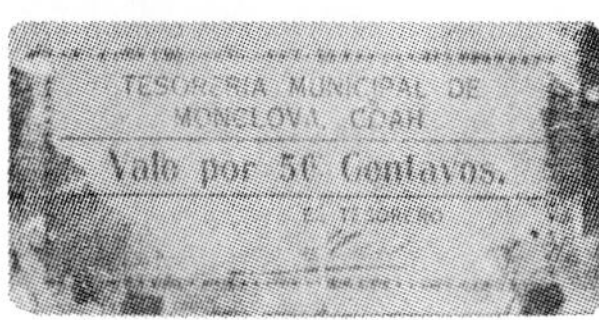

		Good	Fine	XF
S636	**5 Centavos**			
	ND. Green pasteboard. *(SI-COA-4).*	30.00	60.00	—

Jefatura de Armas - M.S. González, Muzquiz

1914 Issue

		Good	Fine	XF
S637	**50 Centavos**			
	18.5.1914. *(MI-COA-12).*	25.00	50.00	—

Ejército Constitucionalista, Parras

1914 Issue

#S638-S641 hand stamped sign. of Roberto Rivas.

		Good	Fine	XF
S638	**25 Centavos**			
	30.4.1914. Black on yellow unpt.			
	a. Issued note. *(MI-COA-13).*	37.50	75.00	—
	b. Hand stamped: *AMORTIZADO.*	30.00	60.00	—
S639	**50 Centavos**			
	30.4.1914. Green on yellow unpt. *(MI-COA-14).*	37.50	75.00	—

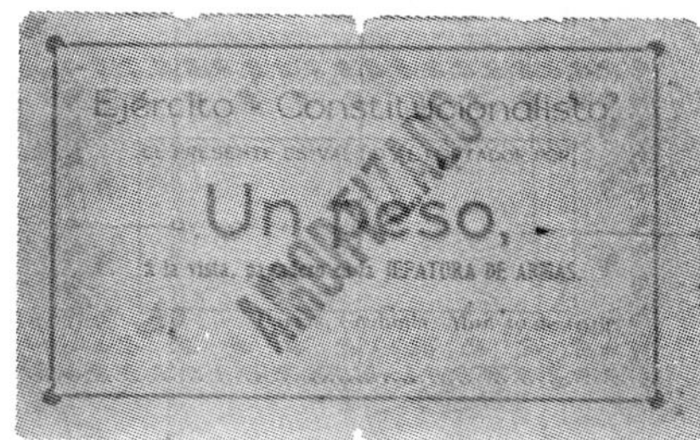

		Good	Fine	XF
S640	**1 Peso**			
	30.4.1914. Orange on gray unpt.			
	a. Issued note. *(MI-COA-15).*	37.50	75.00	—
	b. Hand stamped: *AMORTIZADO.*	30.00	60.00	—

		Good	Fine	XF
S641	**5 Pesos**			
	30.4.1914. Black on yellow and pink unpt., thin paper.			
	a. Issued note. *(MI-COA-16).*	45.00	100.00	—
	b. Hand stamped: *AMORTIZADO.*	37.50	75.00	—

La Tesorería de la Federación, Saltillo

Validation Hand Stamps:

The following hand stamps are known on 50 centavos, 1 and 2 peso denominations.

1. JEFATURA DE HACIENDA, COAHUILA (round).
2. JEFATURA DE HACIENDA, COAHUILA (oval).
3. JEFATURA DE ARMAS, COAHUILA.
4. GOBIERNO DEL ESTADO DE COAHUILA. SALTILLO, COAH.
5. ADMON. PRAL. DE RENTAS SAN LUIS POTOSI.

1914 ISSUE

#S642-S647 national arms at ctr.

		GOOD	FINE	XF
S642	**10 CENTAVOS** 27.1.1914. Black on pale pink unpt. Series F. *(SI-COA-5).*	1.00	3.00	7.00
S643	**25 CENTAVOS** 27.1.1914. Black on yellow unpt. Back brown. Series E. *(SI-COA-6).*	10.00	30.00	60.00
S644	**50 CENTAVOS** 27.1.1914. Black on dull purple unpt. Back dull purple. Series D-B; D-E; D-G. *(SI-COA-7).*	1.00	3.00	4.50
S645	**1 PESO** 27.1.1914. Black on pale blue unpt. Series B; C. *(SI-COA-8).*	1.00	2.75	4.00

		GOOD	FINE	XF
S646	**2 PESOS** 27.1.1914. Black on pale green unpt. Series C. *(SI-COA-9).*	1.00	3.00	4.50
S647	**5 PESOS** 27.1.1914. Black on pink unpt. Back red. Series A. *(SI-COA-10).*	1.25	4.00	12.00

MUNICIPIO DE SAN PEDRO

1916 ISSUE

		GOOD	FINE	XF
S648	**5 CENTAVOS** 1916. Gray pasteboard. Series A. *(SI-COA-11).*	5.00	10.00	30.00
S649	**10 CENTAVOS** 1916. Green pasteboard. Like #S648. Series D. *(SI-COA-12).*	5.00	10.00	30.00
S650	**25 CENTAVOS** 1916. Pasteboard. Like #S648. *(SI-COA-13).*	6.00	18.00	35.00
S651	**50 CENTAVOS** 1916. Orange pasteboard. Like #S648. *(SI-COA-14).*	6.00	18.00	35.00

EJÉRCITO CONSTITUCIONALISTA - DIVISIÓN DEL NORTE, TORREÓN
GENERAL FRANCISCO"PANCHO" VILLA

The back legend on these notes stipulates that they are redeemable in multiples of 5 pesos for checks pertaining to the bank over bank series issues at Torreón, Coahuila and Gómez Palacio. General Francisco Villa ordered this series to be printed when he was still under Venustiano Carranza's orders.

1913 ISSUE

#S652-S654 national arms at ctr.

		GOOD	FINE	XF
S652	**5 CENTAVOS** 20.11.1913. *(MI-COA-17).*	25.00	50.00	100.00
S653	**50 CENTAVOS** 20.11.1913. *(MI-COA-18).*	25.00	50.00	100.00

		GOOD	FINE	XF
S654	**1 PESO** 20.11.1913. Blue. *(MI-COA-19).*	25.00	50.00	100.00

EL ESTADO DE COAHUILA

DECREE OF SEPTEMBER 1, 1914

Translation of back text: "This Emission is Authorized by the First Chief of the Constitutionalist Army, in Charge of the Executive Power of the Nation."

		GOOD	FINE	XF
S655	**50 CENTAVOS** *D.1914.* Series A. *(MI-COA-96).*	125.00	250.00	400.00

		GOOD	FINE	XF
S656	**1 PESO** *D.1914.* Seated Justice at l. Series B. *(MMI-COA-97).*	125.00	250.00	400.00

		GOOD	FINE	XF
S657	**5 PESOS** *D.1914.* Black on brown unpt. Standing Justice at l. Series C. *(MI-COA-98).*	100.00	200.00	350.00

		GOOD	FINE	XF
S658	**10 PESOS** *D.1914.* Black on green unpt. Seated Justice at l. Series D. *(MI-COA-97).*	100.00	200.00	350.00
S659	**20 PESOS** *D.1914.* Like #S657. Series E. *(MI-COA-100).*	125.00	250.00	400.00

COLIMA

GOBIERNO DEL ESTADO DE COLIMA

ND ISSUE

#S660 and S661 palm tree at l. ctr., national arms at ctr. on back.

		GOOD	FINE	XF
S660	**5 CENTAVOS** ND. Black. Gray pasteboard. *(SI-COL-20).*	12.50	25.00	50.00

		GOOD	FINE	XF
S661	**10 CENTAVOS** ND. Red. Gray pasteboard. *(SI-COL-21).*	12.50	25.00	50.00

EL ESTADO LIBRE Y SOBERANO DE COLIMA

ND ISSUE

#S662 and S663 arms at l., national arms at ctr. Printer: Imprenta Franco Mexicana, S.A.

		GOOD	FINE	XF
S662	**50 CENTAVOS** ND. Remainder. (Not issued). *(SI-COL-16).*	90.00	180.00	—

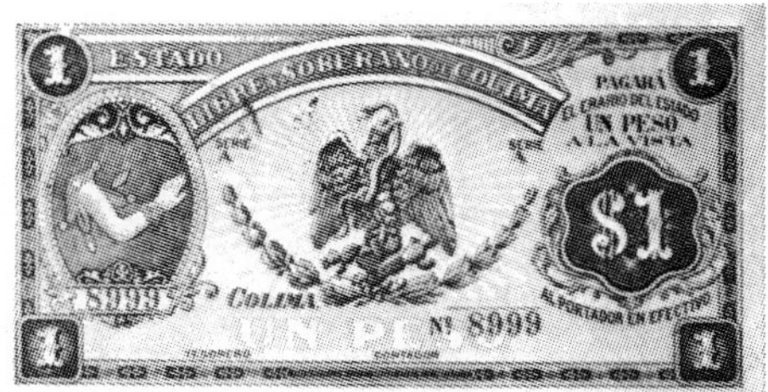

S663	**1 Peso**	**Good**	**Fine**	**XF**
	ND. Black on green unpt. *(SI-COL-17)*.			
	a. Issued note. *(SI-COL-17A)*.	100.00	130.00	—
	r. Remainder.	75.00	150.00	250.00

La Tesorería General del Estado de Colima

ND Issue

S664	**5 Centavos**	**Good**	**Fine**	**XF**
	ND. Blue pasteboard. National arms at ctr. *(SI-COL-18)*.	12.50	25.00	40.00
S665	**10 Centavos**			
	ND. Brown pasteboard. Like #s664. *(SI-COL-19)*.	12.50	25.00	50.00

Decree No. 117 of April 22, 1914

S666	**10 Centavos**	**Good**	**Fine**	**XF**
	June 1914. Orange on cream. Series A. *(SI-COL-1)*.	30.00	50.00	85.00

S667	**50 Centavos**	**Good**	**Fine**	**XF**
	June 1914. Green on orange unpt. National arms at upper ctr. *(SI-COL-2)*.	30.00	50.00	85.00

S668	**1 Peso**	**Good**	**Fine**	**XF**
	June 1914. Blue on brown unpt. *(SI-COL-3)*.	22.50	45.00	70.00

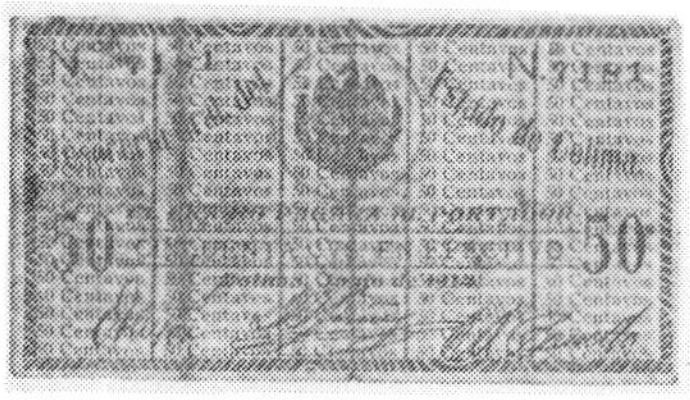

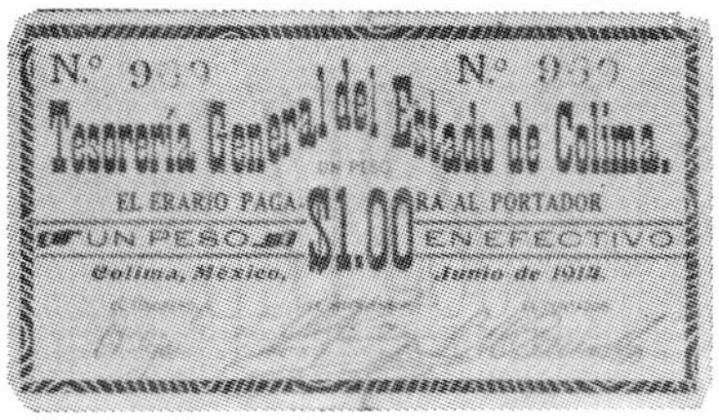

Decree of July 22, 1914

S669	**10 Centavos**	**Good**	**Fine**	**XF**
	22.7.1914. *(SI-COL-4)*.	37.50	75.00	—

S670	**20 Centavos**	**Good**	**Fine**	**XF**
	22.7.1914. Black on orange unpt. Volcanoes, palm trees at r. Series B. *(SI-COL-5)*.	37.50	75.00	110.00

S671	**50 Centavos**	**Good**	**Fine**	**XF**
	22.7.1914. Black on blue unpt. Like #S670. Series B. *(SI-COL-6)*.	20.00	50.00	80.00

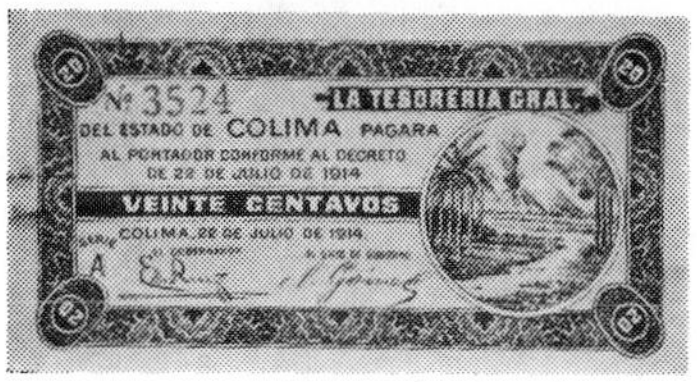

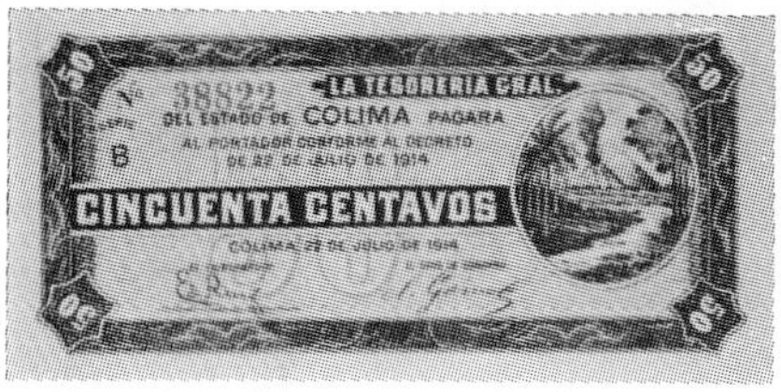

Decree of January 18, 1915

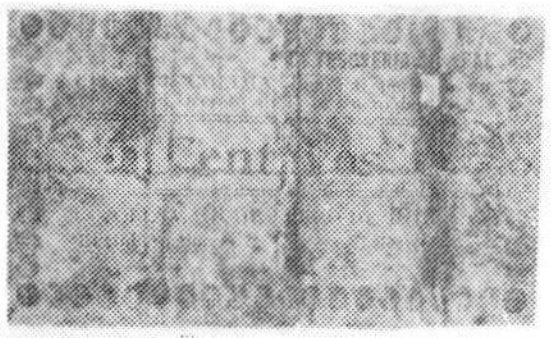

S672	**5 Centavos**	**Good**	**Fine**	**XF**
	18.1.1915. Blue. *(SI-COL-7)*.	45.00	90.00	—
S673	**10 Centavos**			
	18.1.1915. *(SI-COL-8)*.	60.00	120.00	—

S674	**20 Centavos**	**Good**	**Fine**	**XF**
	18.1.1915. Series A. *(SI-COL-9)*.	37.50	75.00	125.00

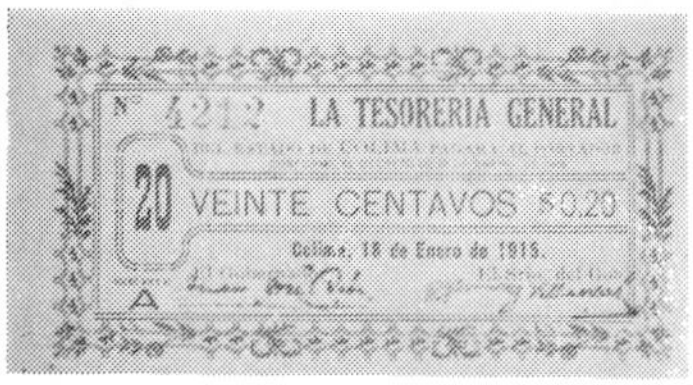

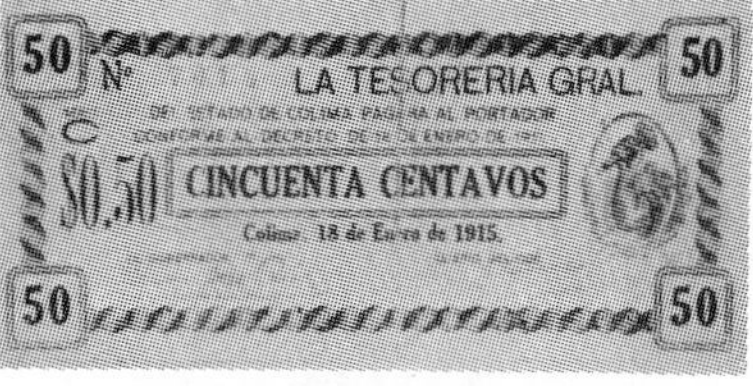

S675	**50 Centavos**	**Good**	**Fine**	**XF**
	18.1.1915. Arm and hammer at r. Series C. *(SI-COL-10)*.	37.50	75.00	125.00

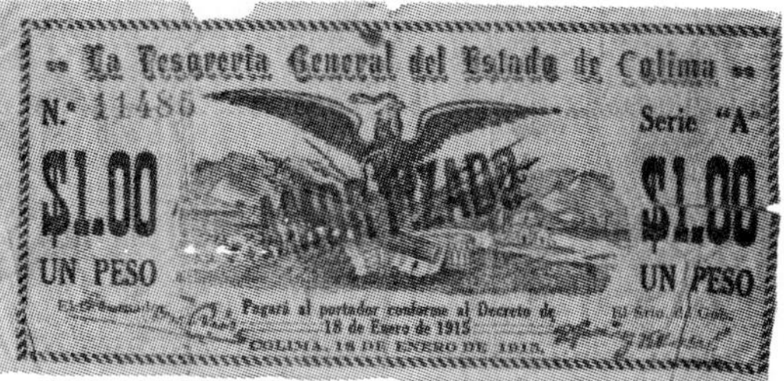

S676	**1 Peso**	**Good**	**Fine**	**XF**
	18.1.1915. Blue on pink unpt. National arms at ctr. Series A.			
	a. Issued note. *(SI-COL-11)*.	45.00	90.00	—
	b. Ovpt: *AMORTIZADO*.	45.00	90.00	—

Decree of June 4, 1915

#S677-S680 printer: Lit. de J. M. Iguiniz Guada.

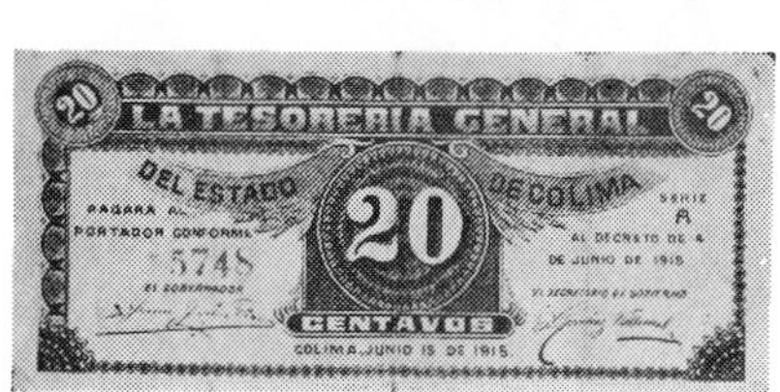

S677	**20 Centavos**	**Good**	**Fine**	**XF**
	15.6.1915. Black. Series A. *(SI-COL-12)*.	12.00	25.00	55.00

		Good	Fine	XF
S678	**50 Centavos** 15.6.1915. Black on lt. green unpt. Series B. *(SI-COL-13).*	12.00	25.00	55.00

		Good	Fine	XF
S679	**1 Peso** 15.6.1915. Black on brown unpt. Gvmt. bldg. at ctr. Series C. *(SI-COL-14).*	17.50	35.00	75.00

		Good	Fine	XF
S680	**5 Pesos** 15.6.1915. Black on brown unpt. Like #S679. Series C. *(SI-COL-15).*	50.00	110.00	—

Distrito Federal

Gobierno Constitucionalista de México, República

ND Transitorio Issue

Small cardboard notes.

#S681-S684 standing Justice at ctr. Hand stamped *GMC* monogram. National arms at ctr. on back.

		Good	Fine	XF
S681	**5 Centavos** ND. Orange pasteboard. Eagle's head to l. *(MI-DF-67).*	.50	1.00	1.50
S682	**5 Centavos** ND. Pink pasteboard. Eagle's head to r.			
	a. Issued note. *(MI-DF-68).*	1.00	1.00	1.50
	b. Ovpt: *C. I. JUAREZ. (MI-DF-69).*	1.00	2.00	4.00
	c. Ovpt: *Durango. (MI-DF-70).*	1.00	2.00	4.00
	d. Ovpt. *PARRAL. (MI-DF-71).*	1.00	3.00	9.00
	e. Ovpt: *NOGALES.*	1.50	4.00	12.00
S683	**10 Centavos** ND. Dk. blue pasteboard. Like #S681.			
	a. Issued note. *(MI-DF-72).*	.75	2.00	6.00
	b. Ovpt: *NOGALES.*	1.00	3.00	9.00
S684	**10 Centavos** ND. Lt. blue pasteboard. Like #S682.			
	a. Issued note. *(MI-DF-73).*	.50	1.25	2.50
	b. Ovpt: *C. JUAREZ (MI-DF-74).*	.50	1.25	3.00
	c. Ovpt: *Durango.*	.50	1.25	3.00
	d. Ovpt: *MATAMOROS.*	1.00	3.00	9.00

Gobierno Constitucionalista, República Mexicana

Decree of July 21, 1915 - "Infalsificables" Issue

#S685-S689 printer: ABNC.

		Good	Fine	XF
S685	**5 Pesos** *D.1915.* Black, green, and m/c. Monument to Cuauhtémoc at l. Back green. Series C.			
	a. Issued note. *(SI-DF-5).*	.75	1.50	4.50
	p. Proof.	—	Unc	60.00
	s. Specimen.	—	Unc	60.00

		Good	Fine	XF
S686	**10 Pesos** *D.1915.* Black, blue, and m/c. Portr. J. M. Morelos y Pavón at ctr. Back blue. Series I.			
	a. Issued note.*(SI-DF-6).*	.50	1.00	4.00
	p. Proof.	—	Unc	75.00
	s. Specimen.	—	Unc	75.00

		Good	Fine	XF
S687	**20 Pesos** *D.1915.* Black, pale orange and m/c. Monument to Juárez at l. Back orange. Series X.			
	a. Issued note. *(SI-DF-7).*	1.50	3.50	10.00
	p. Proof.	—	Unc	85.00
	s. Specimen.	—	Unc	85.00

		Good	Fine	XF
S688	**50 Pesos** *D.1915.* Black, tan, and m/c. Courtyard at ctr. brown. Series E.			
	a. Issued note. *(SI-DF-8).*	7.00	15.00	50.00
	p. Proof.	—	Unc	100.00
	s. Specimen.	—	Unc	100.00

		GOOD	FINE	XF
S689	**100 PESOS** *D.1915.* Black, pale green, and m/c. Indigenous ruins at ctr. Back olive-green. Series M.			
	a. Issued note. *(SI-DP-9).*	6.00	12.50	35.00
	p. Proof.	—	Unc	125.00
	s. Specimen.	—	Unc	125.00

GOBIERNO FEDERAL DE LA REPÚBLICA MEXICANA

The following is a special group of proofs, unknown as issued notes, which were prepared by the Federal Government of the Mexican Republic to be circulated as legal tender throughout the entire nation. Consequently, in the strict sense of the word, they are not State "Issues of the Mexican Revolution" but are listed as such because they were to be issued in the Federal District (Mexico City).

1915 ISSUE

#S690-S696 national arms at ctr. Printer: ABNC.

		VG	VF	UNC
S690	**1 PESO** 1.8.1915. Black on green unpt. Proof. *(SI-DF-18).*	—	—	150.00
S691	**2 PESOS** 1.8.1915. Black on orange unpt. Proof. *(SI-DF-19).*	—	—	150.00
S692	**5 PESOS** 1.8.1915. Black on green unpt. Proof. *(SI-DF-20).*	—	—	150.00
S693	**10 PESOS** 1.8.1915. Black on tan unpt. Proof. *(SI-DF-21).*	—	—	175.00
S694	**20 PESOS** 1.8.1915. Black on olive-green unpt. Proof. *(SI-DF-22).*	—	—	175.00
S695	**50 PESOS** 1.8.1915. Black on tan unpt. Proof. *(SI-DF-23).*	—	—	200.00

		VG	VF	UNC
S696	**100 PESOS** 1.8.1915. Black on tan unpt. Proof. *(SI-DF-24).*	—	—	225.00

GOBIERNO PROVISIONAL DE MÉXICO, REPÚBLICA

The period between August 15, 1914 and June 4, 1916 is known as the Constitutionalist Party paper money period because, despite the fact that other types of paper money were in circulation, the dominant issues were those of General Venustiano Carranza's Constitutionalist Government. On August 18, 1914 Carranza entered Mexico City to take charge and establish the first revolutionary administration whose control would be at a national level. On September 19, 1914, Carranza decreed that an interior debt of 130,000,000 pesos was to be created by means of paper currency. The bills were issued in denominations of 1, 5, 10, 20, 50 and 100 pesos series lettered A, B, C, D, E and F respectively. The new bills were declared compulsory circulation, to be accepted at face value in all types of payments and transactions. A certain amount of this new issu was used to retire from circulation previous Constitutionalist Government issues. On September 28, 1914, Carranza decreed that the issue of fractional money, created by decree of March 4, 1914, was to be increased by 3,000,000 pesos, by means of *cartones,* small pasteboard notes in the following amounts: 1,000,000 pesos of the 5 centavos denomination, 1,000,000 pesos of the 10 centavos denomination, and 1,000,000 pesos in the 20 centavos denomination.

During the first days of December of 1914, due to pressure from the Conventionist Government, Carranza decided to move the capital of the Constitutionalist Government to Veracruz. The newly formed Conventionist Government set up its headquarters in Mexico City at this time and, on December 13, 1914, decreed the issuance of *REVALIDADO* notes. That is, Carranza's *Gobierno Provisional de Mexico* notes in denominations of 1, 5, 10, 20, 50 and 100 pesos were overprinted with bold type in red ink with the following legend: *REVALIDADO - Por Decreto de 17 de Diciembre de 1914* (Revalidated - by Decree of December 17, 1914).

It is believed that the Conventionist Government ordered the printing of *Gobierno Provisional de México* issues at Yecapixtla, Morelos with the overprint, *REVALIDADO.* The difference between these notes and the Mexico City issues is that the paper used is much thinner than the normal issues. The design and printing is also much more crude. That is, the 5 peso note of the normal issue is of a much higher quality engraving and printing than the Yecapixtla issue. However, the 10 peso note differs only in regard to the paper, which is much thinner in the Yecapixtla issue, but the quality of engraving is much the same as the normal issue. They are both quite crude.

Resellos (overprints) of diverse types and nature are abundant on notes of the *Gobierno Provisional de Mexico* series. Municipal, state, federal and military resellos are known, and they normally appear in very low grades (Fair). In order to indicate that these issues should be accepted in local areas, municipalities and within a given state, they were handstamped with seals pertaining to the corresponding local authorities. These resellos also served as a guarantee of the authenticity of the notes. It is also common to find these notes with either overprint of *FALSO* or *NULO* but many of these notes are genuine despite these overprints.

1914 ND ISSUE

		VG	VF	UNC
S697	**5 CENTAVOS** ND. Deep orange or yellow-orange pasteboard. Seated Justice at ctr. National arms at l. on back. Brown or red ovpt: *V. (MI-DF-1).*	.50	1.00	2.00

		VG	VF	UNC
S698	**10 CENTAVOS** ND. Gray or blue pasteboard. Standing Justice at l. National arms at ctr. on back. Ovpt: *X. (MI-DF-2).*	.50	1.00	2.00

		VG	VF	UNC
S699	**20 CENTAVOS** ND. Gray pasteboard. Liberty at l. National arms at ctr. on back. *(MI-DF-3).*	.50	1.00	2.00

1914 ISSUE

		VG	VF	UNC
S700	**20 CENTAVOS** 1914. Lt. brown pasteboard. Justice at ctr. National arms at ctr. on back. Series U; Y. *(MI-DF-4).*	.50	1.25	3.00

GOBIERNO PROVISIONAL DE MÉXICO, MEXICO CITY

DECRETO 19.9.1914; 1914 ISSUE

#S701-S708 seated Liberty at l., national arms w/Popocatepetl and Ixtaccihuatl (volcanoes) in background at ctr.

		GOOD	FINE	XF
S701	**1 PESO** 20.10.1914. Black on tan unpt. Back brown. Series A.			
	a. Issued note. *(MI-DF-5).*	1.50	5.00	12.00
	b. Ovpt: *REVALIDADO/por decreto 17.... w/serial # on face. (MI-DF-6).*	.75	2.00	4.00
	c. W/o serial # or seals on back. *(MI-DF-7).*	5.00	15.00	30.00
	d. Back blank. *(MI-DF-8).*	15.00	30.00	65.00
	e. Ovpt: *ATOYAC, AGENCIA DEL TIMBRE. (MI-DF-10).*	4.00	12.00	25.00
	f. Ovpt: *ADMON. PRINCIPAL DEL TIMBRE, GUADALAJARA. (MI-DF-11.*	2.00	6.00	12.00
	g. Ovpt: *ADMON. PRINCIPAL DEL TIMBRE, REVALIDADO, SAN LUIS POTOSI. (MI-DF-12).*	2.00	6.00	12.00
	h. Ovpt: *ADMINISTRACION SUBALTERNA DEL TIMBRE, CIUDAD GUZMAN. (MI-DF-13).*	2.00	6.00	12.00
	i. Ovpt: *ADMINISTRACION SUBALTERNA DEL TIMBRE, COCULA. (MI-DF-14).*	4.00	12.00	25.00
	j. Ovpt: *AGENCIA DEL TIMBRE, SAN GABRIEL. (MI-DF-15).*	4.00	12.00	25.00
	k. Ovpt: *AGENCIA DEL TIMBRE, SAYULA. (MI-DF-16).*	4.00	12.00	25.00
	l. Ovpt: *AGENCIA DEL TIMBRE, ZACOALCO. (MI-DF-17).*	4.00	12.00	25.00
	m. Ovpt: *DEPARTAMENTO DE HACIENDA, MARZO 15, 1915, ZAMORA. (MI-DF-18).*	3.00	10.00	20.00
	n. Ovpt: *REPUBLICA MEXICANA, SECRETARIA DE HACIENDA, REVALIDADO. (MI-DF-19).*	4.00	12.00	25.00

		GOOD	FINE	XF
o.	Ovpt: *REVALIDADO POR ORDEN DEL DEPARTAMENTO DE HACIENDA, CELAYA, MARZO DE 1915. (MI-DF-20).*	3.00	10.00	20.00
p.	Ovpt: *REVALIDADO/POR DECRETO, SAN MIGUEL DE ALLENDE. (MI-DF-21).*	4.00	12.00	25.00
q.	Ovpt: *REVALIDADO CONFORME A LA CIRCULAR DE HACIENDA DE 17 DE FEBRERO DE 1915, SAN MARCOS. (MI-DF-22).*	5.00	15.00	30.00
r.	Ovpt: *TEOCUITATLAN. (MI-DF-23).*	4.00	12.00	25.00
s.	Ovpt: *TAMAZULA, AGENCIA DEL TIMBRE. (MI-DF-24).*	3.00	10.00	20.00
t.	Ovpt: *PAGADURIA GENERAL DE LA OFICINA DE OPERACIONES 15 MARZO DE 1915, MICHOACAN. (MI-DF-25).*	5.00	15.00	30.00
u.	Ovpt: *ADMON. SUBALTERNA DEL TIMBRE, TAPALPA. (MI-DF-26).*	4.00	12.00	25.00
v.	Ovpt: *AGENCIA DEL TIMBRE, 9o CANTON, TUXPAN. (MI-DF-27).*	4.00	12.00	25.00
w.	Ovpt: *REVALIDADO POR ACUERDO DEL DEPARTAMENTO DE HACIENDA, QUERETARO. (MI-DF-28).*	3.00	9.00	20.00
x.	Ovpt: *SECRETARIA DE HACIENDA, VERACRUZ.*	3.00	9.00	20.00
y.	Face proof. *(MI-DF-9).*	—	Unc	75.00

S702 5 PESOS
20.10.1914. Black on lt. green unpt. Back green. Series B.

		GOOD	FINE	XF
a.	Issued note. *(MI-DF-29).*	1.00	3.00	6.00
b.	Ovpt: *REVALIDADO/por decreto 17.... (MI-DF-30).*	.75	2.00	4.00
c.	Back blank. *(MI-DF-32).*	12.00	35.00	70.00
d.	Ovpt: *ADMINISTRACION PRINCIPAL DEL TIMBRE, REVALIDADO, SAN LUIS POTOSI. (MI-DF-33).*	4.00	12.00	25.00
e.	Ovpt: *REVALIDADO POR ACUERDO DEL DEPARTAMENTO DE HACIENDA. AGUASCALIENTES, ENERO 1915. (MI-DF-34).*	4.00	12.00	25.00
f.	Ovpt: *REVALIDADO ACUERDO DEL DEPARTAMENTO DE HACIENDA, CHIHUAHUA. (MI-DF-35).*	6.00	20.00	35.00
g.	Ovpt: *REVALIDADO POR ACUERDO DEL DEPARTAMENTO DE HACIENDA, SAN LUIS POTOSI. (MI-DF-36).*	4.00	12.00	25.00
h.	Ovpt:*REVALIDADO POR ACUERDO DEL DEPARTAMENTO DE HACIENDA, CELAYA. (MI-DF-37).*	4.00	12.00	25.00
i.	Ovpt: *ADMINISTRACION PRAL. DEL TIMBRE LEON, GTO. (MI-DF-38).*	4.00	12.00	25.00
j.	Ovpt: *QUERETARO REVALIDADO POR ACUERDO DEL DEPARTAMENTO DE HACIENDA. (MI-DF-39).*	6.00	20.00	35.00
k.	Ovpt: *ADMON. PRINCIPAL DEL TIMBRE, CHIHUAHUA. (MI-DF-40).*	6.00	20.00	35.00
l.	Ovpt: *AGENCIA DEL TIMBRE, ZACOALCO. (MI-DF-41).*	6.00	20.00	35.00

		GOOD	FINE	XF
S703 5 PESOS	20.10.1914. Like #S702 but thin paper. Series B. *(MI-DF-31).*	1.50	5.00	10.00
S704 10 PESOS	20.10.1914. Black on brown unpt. Ovpt: *REVALIDADO/por decreto 17....* Series C. *(MI-DF-42).*	.75	2.00	4.00
S705 20 PESOS	20.10.1914. Black on brown unpt. Lower text at r.: *EL S. S. encargado de la Sria, de Hacienda.* Ovpt: *REVALIDADO/por decreto 17....* Series D. *(MI-DF-45).*	.75	2.00	4.00

		GOOD	FINE	XF
S706 20 PESOS	20.10.1914. Like #S705 but lower text at r.: *El OM encarga de la Sria, de Hacienda.* Ovpt: *REVALIDADO por decreto 17....* Series D. *(MI-DF-46).*	2.00	4.00	6.00

S707 50 PESOS
20.10.1914. Black on lt. blue unpt. Series E.

		GOOD	FINE	XF
a.	Issued note. *(MI-DF-47).*	3.50	10.00	25.00
b.	W/o date, sign., serial #, series letters or seals on back. *(MI-DF-48).*	10.00	30.00	60.00
c.	W/o date, sign. or serial #; w/seals on back. *(MI-DF-49).*	10.00	30.00	60.00
d.	Back blank. *(MI-DF-50).*	20.00	60.00	120.00

		GOOD	FINE	XF
e.	Ovpt: *REVALIDADO/por decreto 17.... (MI-DF-51).*	.75	2.00	4.00
f.	Ovpt: *REVALIDADO/por decreto 17....*, w/o sign. or date; w/seals on back. *(MI-DF-52).*	20.00	60.00	—
g.	Ovpt: *PAGADURIA GENERAL, TORREÓN, COAH. (MI-DF-53).*	4.00	12.00	25.00
h.	Ovpt: Needle punch perforation: *TAMPICO. (MI-DF-54).*	3.00	10.00	20.00
i.	Ovpt: *ADM. PRINCIPAL DEL TIMBRE GUADALAJARA* around eagle. *(MI-DF-55).*	4.00	12.00	25.00
j.	Ovpt: *ADM. PRAL. DEL TIMBRE, GUADALAJARA. (MI-DF-56).*	1.50	5.00	10.00
k.	Ovpt: *REVALIDADO. Reynosa* sign. at r. 20.10.1914. *(MI-DF-51A).*	6.00	12.00	20.00
l.	Ovpt: *ADMINISTRACIÓN de ARENTAS, URUAPAN, MICH. (MI-DF-56A).* 20.10.1914.	6.00	10.00	—

S708 100 PESOS
28.9.1914. Black on red-brown to pink unpt. Series F.

		GOOD	FINE	XF
a.	Issued note. *(MI-DF-57).*	1.00	3.00	6.00
b.	Ovpt: *REVALIDADO/por decreto 17.... (MI-DF-58).*	.75	2.00	4.00
c.	Ovpt: *REVALIDADO/por decreto 17....*w/o sign. or date, w/seals on back. *(MI-DF-60).*	20.00	60.00	—
d.	Ovpt: *ESTADO DE MICHOACAN, REVALIDADO CONFORME AL DECRETO DE ENERO DE 1915. (MI-DF-62).*	6.00	20.00	35.00
e.	Ovpt: *REPUBLICA MEXICANA, BUENAVISTA, GUERRERO. (MI-DF-63).*	6.50	20.00	40.00
f.	Ovpt: *ADM. PRINCIPAL DEL TIMBRE, GUADALAJARA*, around eagle. *(MI-DF-64).*	4.00	12.00	25.00
g.	Ovpt: *TESORERIA MUNICIPAL, PARRAL, CHIHUAHUA. (MI-DF-65).*	6.50	20.00	40.00
h.	Ovpt: *ADM. PRAL. DEL TIMBRE, GUADALAJARA. (MI-DF-66).*	1.00	4.00	10.00
x.	Error: *SEPT. 1914*, lacking day of month in date. *(MI-DF-61).*	6.00	20.00	35.00

NOTE: Also see #S875A and S876 under Jalisco for more ovpt. varieties.

DECREE OF APRIL 3, 1916

#S709-S712 printer: Oficina de Gobierno México.

		VG	VF	UNC
S709 1 PESO	1.5.1916. Black and green. Statue of C. Columbus at l., national arms w/Popocatepetl and Ixtaccihuatl (volcanoes) in background at l. ctr., Toltec stone head at lower r. Back blue. Series A-U. *(SI-DF-10).*	.75	2.00	4.00

S710 1 PESO
5.1.1916. Black. Statue of C. Columbus at l., Aztec throne at l. ctr., Toltec stone head at lower r. Back brown. Series J.

		VG	VF	UNC
a.	Issued note. *(SI-DF-15).*	1.00	3.00	6.00
p1.	Face proof. *(SI-DF-13).*	—	—	—
p2.	Back proof. *(SI-DF-14).*	—	—	—

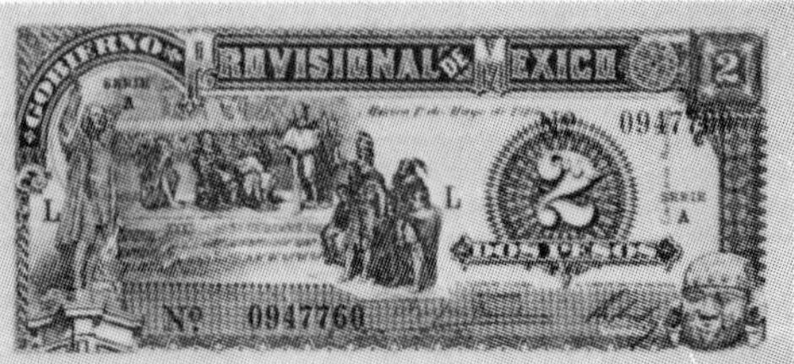

S711 2 PESOS
5.1.1916. Black. Like #S710. Vertical text at r.: *Circulación Provisional.*

		VG	VF	UNC
a.	Series A; B. *(SI-DF-12).*	.75	2.00	4.00
b.	Series B w/inverted B at upper l.	—	—	—

		VG	VF	UNC
S712	**2 PESOS** 5.1.1916. Like #S711 but w/o vertical legend at r. Series Z.			
	a. Issued note. *(SI-DF-16).*	.75	2.00	4.00
	p1. Gray proof. *(SI-DF-17).*	—	—	—
	p2. Sepia proof.	—	—	—
	p3. Green proof.	—	—	—

OBLIGACIÓN PROVISIONAL DEL ERARIO FEDERAL

The following validation is known to exist on notes of this series: *EJÉRCITO CONSTITUCIONALISTA. DIVISION DEL NORTE BRIGADA ROBLES.*

1914 FEDERAL TREASURY BONDS ISSUE

#S713-S716 national arms at l. Printer: Oficina Impresora de Estampillas.

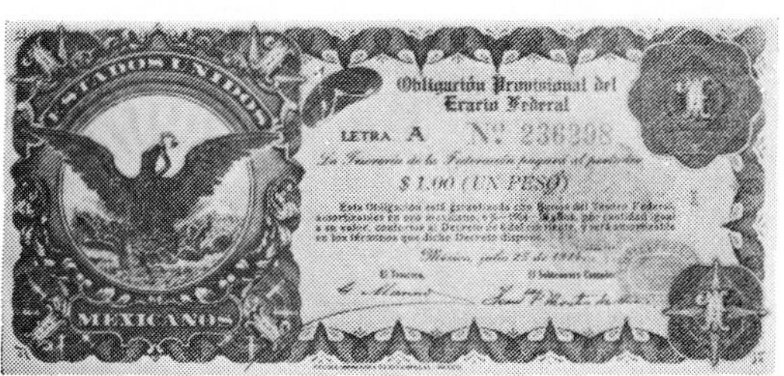

		VG	VF	UNC
S713	**1 PESO** 25.7.1914. Black on pale green unpt. Back green. Series A. *(SI-DF-1).*	1.00	3.00	10.00
S713A	**5 PESOS** 25.7.1914. Dk. green-black on lt. blue unpt. Back blue. Series B. *(SI-DF-2).*	1.00	3.00	10.00
S714	**5 PESOS** 25.7.1914. Black on pale blue unpt. Back blue. Series B.	.75	2.00	4.00
S715	**25 PESOS** 25.7.1914. Black on pink unpt. Back violet. Series C. *(SI-DF-3).*	2.00	6.00	15.00
S716	**50 PESOS** 25.7.1914. Black on pale orange unpt. Back orange. Series D. *(SI-DF-4).*	1.00	3.00	6.00

DURANGO

BONOS AL PORTADOR, DURANGO

1913 FIRST ISSUE

		GOOD	FINE	XF
S717	**20 CENTAVOS** Aug. 1913. Black on brown unpt. *(SI-DUR-1).*	20.00	40.00	85.00
S718	**50 CENTAVOS** Aug. 1913. Black on green unpt. Like #S717. *(SI-DUR-2).*	6.00	18.00	35.00
S719	**1 PESO** Aug. 1913. Black on yellow unpt. Like #S717. *(SI-DUR-3).*	4.50	12.00	30.00
S720	**5 PESOS** Aug. 1913. Black on red unpt. Like #S717. *(SI-DUR-4).*	6.00	18.00	40.00

1913 SECOND ISSUE

		GOOD	FINE	XF
S721	**20 CENTAVOS** 3.10.1913. Black on brown unpt. Like #S717. *(SI-DUR-5).*	6.00	18.00	35.00

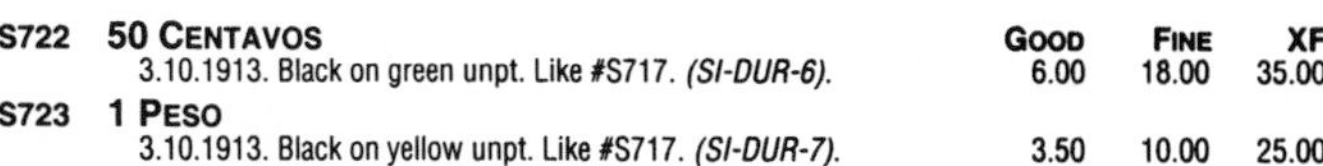

		GOOD	FINE	XF
S722	**50 CENTAVOS** 3.10.1913. Black on green unpt. Like #S717. *(SI-DUR-6).*	6.00	18.00	35.00
S723	**1 PESO** 3.10.1913. Black on yellow unpt. Like #S717. *(SI-DUR-7).*	3.50	10.00	25.00

ESTADO DE DURANGO

1913 ISSUES

		GOOD	FINE	XF
S724	**10 CENTAVOS** Dec. 1913. Red and black on lt. blue unpt. Series A. *(SI-DUR-8).*	10.00	20.00	45.00

		GOOD	FINE	XF
S725	**50 CENTAVOS** Dec. 1913. Black and red on green unpt. Series A.			
	a. Issued note. *(SI-DUR-9).*	10.00	20.00	45.00
	b. Ovpt: *AMORTIZADO. (SI-DUR-10).*	6.00	18.00	35.00

		GOOD	FINE	XF
S726	**1 PESO** Dec. 1913. Black and red on yellow unpt. Series A; B.			
	a. Issued note. *(SI-DUR-11).*	10.00	20.00	45.00
	b. Ovpt: *AMORTIZADO. (SI-DUR-12).*	6.00	18.00	35.00

		GOOD	FINE	XF
S727	**5 PESOS** Dec. 1913. Black on orange unpt. Series A. *(SI-DUR-13).*	6.00	18.00	35.00

		GOOD	FINE	XF
S728	**5 PESOS** Dec. 1913. Black on brown unpt. Series A. *(SI-DUR-14).*	10.00	20.00	45.00

1914 ISSUES

#S729-S733 standing Liberty w/flag at l.

	GOOD	FINE	XF
S729 50 CENTAVOS Jan. 1914. Black. Back red. W/o Series, Series A ;B.			
a. Issued note. *(SI-DUR-15).*	.75	2.00	7.50
b. Ovpt: *Revalidado por Decreto . . .(SI-DUR-16).*	3.00	10.00	20.00
S730 1 PESO Jan. 1914. Black on brown-orange unpt. Denomination: *UN PESO* upside down in upper and lower borders. Back green.			
a. Issued note. *(SI-DUR-17).*	1.50	4.50	10.00
b. Ovpt: *Revalidado por Decreto . . .(SI-DUR-18).*	3.00	10.00	22.50

	GOOD	FINE	XF
S731 1 PESO Jan. 1914. Black on brown-orange unpt. Back green. Like #S729 but *UN PESO* normal in upper and lower borders. Series F-J.			
a. Issued note. *(SI-DUR-19).*	.50	1.50	5.00
b. Ovpt: *Revalidado por Decreto . . .(SI-DUR-20).*	2.50	7.50	17.50
c. Ovpt: *Jefatura de Hacienda en el Estados de Jalisco. (SI-DUR-19a).*	2.50	7.50	17.50

	GOOD	FINE	XF
S732 5 PESOS Jan. 1914. Black on red unpt. Back blue-gray. 3 sign. Series B-D.			
a. Issued note. *(SI-DUR-21).*	.75	2.00	6.00
b. Circular ovpt: *Distrito De Culiacán Comandancia Militar. (SI-DUR-21A).*	2.50	8.00	17.50
c. Ovpt: *Revalidado por Decreto . . .(SI-DUR-21).*	.50	1.50	5.00

	GOOD	FINE	XF
S733 5 PESOS Jan. 1914. Like #S729 but 1 sign.			
a. Issued note. *(SI-DUR-23).*	4.00	12.50	30.00
b. Ovpt: *Revalidado por Decreto . . .(SI-DUR-25).*	3.00	10.00	22.50
c. Ovpt: *Jefatura Politica del Distrito Norte, Ensenada. (SI-DUR-22).*	4.00	12.50	30.00
d. Ovpt: *Jefatura en el Estado-Jalisco. (SI-DUR-24).*	4.00	12.50	30.00

#S734 and S735 printer: TIP.DORADOR.DGO.

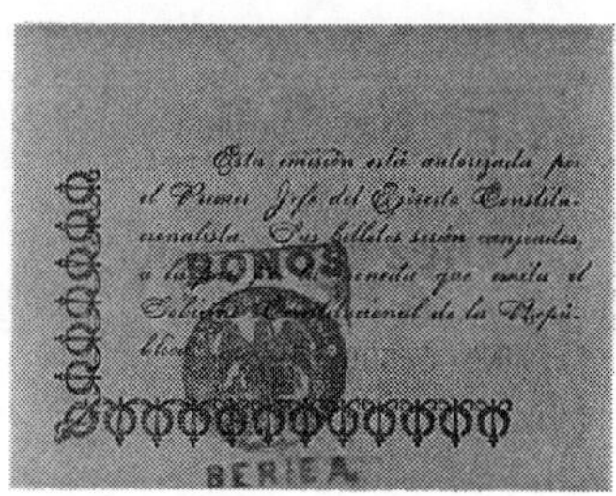

	GOOD	FINE	XF
S734 10 CENTAVOS March 1914. Black and red-orange on pale blue-gray unpt. Series B. *(SI-DUR-26).*			
a. Issued note.	5.00	15.00	30.00
b. Violet handstamp seal w/ *BONOS/eagle/SERIE A.*	—	—	—

	GOOD	FINE	XF
S735 50 CENTAVOS March 1914. Black and orange on pale green unpt. Series C. *(SI-DUR-27).*	5.00	15.00	35.00

	GOOD	FINE	XF
S736 5 PESOS Aug. 1914. Black on pink unpt. Like #S732. Series E; F.			
a. Issued note. *(SI-DUR-28).*	1.50	4.00	15.00
b. Ovpt: *Revalidado por Decreto . . .(SI-DUR-29).*	3.50	10.00	22.50
c. Ovpt: *Leon, Gto. (SI-DUR-30).*	6.00	18.00	40.00
d. Ovpt: *AMORTIZADO. (SI-DUR-31).*	3.00	10.00	20.00
e. Ovpt: two black seals on back.	3.00	10.00	20.00

	GOOD	FINE	XF
S737 50 PESOS Aug. 1914. Black on brown unpt. Like #S732. Series A. *(SI-DUR-32).*	5.00	20.00	40.00

DECREE OF DECEMBER 12, 1913

	GOOD	FINE	XF
S738 1 PESO Oct. 1914. Black on lt. orange unpt. National arms at ctr. r. Series L; M. *(SI-DUR-33).*	1.75	5.00	10.00

		GOOD	FINE	XF
S739	**50 CENTAVOS** Dec. 1914. Black on pale blue unpt. Back blue and green. Series C; D; E. *(SI-DUR-34).*	1.25	3.50	7.50

#S740-S743 standing Liberty w/flag at l.

		GOOD	FINE	XF
S740	**50 CENTAVOS** 31.12.1914. Black. Back brown. Series F. *(SI-DUR-35).*	5.00	15.00	30.00

		GOOD	FINE	XF
S741	**1 PESO** 31.12.1914. Black on pale brown unpt. Back maroon. Series F. *(SI-DUR-36).*	2.00	6.00	12.00

		GOOD	FINE	XF
S742	**5 PESOS** 31.12.1914. Black on blue paper. Series F. *(SI-DUR-37).*	3.00	10.00	20.00

		GOOD	FINE	XF
S743	**10 PESOS** 31.12.1914. Black on blue. Back green. Series F. *(SI-DUR-38).*	15.00	35.00	65.00

DECREE OF DECEMBER 12, 1913; 1915 ISSUE

#S750-S752 national arms at ctr. r.

		GOOD	FINE	XF
S744	**1 PESO** Jan. 1915. Like #S738. Series N. *(SI-DUR-39).*	1.75	5.00	10.00

		GOOD	FINE	XF
S745	**2 PESOS** Feb. 1915. Seated Justice at l. Punched hole cancellation. Series A. *(SI-DUR-40).*	3.00	10.00	20.00

		GOOD	FINE	XF
S746	**5 PESOS** Aug. 1915. Black. Like #S745. Back blue. Series A.			

		GOOD	FINE	XF
	a. Issued note. *(SI-DUR-42).*	15.00	35.00	65.00
	b. Ovpt: *Revalidado, Octubre, 1915 . . .* on back. *(SI-DUR-43).*	2.50	8.00	17.50

		GOOD	FINE	XF
S747	**25 CENTAVOS** ND. Black. Back pink; National arms at ctr. W/o series; Series A. *(SI-DUR-44).*	1.00	3.00	8.00

		GOOD	FINE	XF
S748	**25 CENTAVOS** ND. Portr. Gen. J. E. Garciá at ctr. Back proof. *(SI-DUR-45).*	—	Unc	225.00

		GOOD	FINE	XF
S749	**50 CENTAVOS** Sept. 1915. Black on pale blue unpt. Back blue; like #S747. Series F. *(SI-DUR-46).*	1.00	3.00	7.00
S750	**2 PESOS** Sept. 1915. Black. Series A. *(SI-DUR-47).*	2.00	6.00	15.00

		Good	Fine	XF
S751	**5 Pesos** Sept. 1915. Black. W/o seals, w/black serial #. Back blue. *(SI-DUR-48).*	3.00	10.00	20.00
S752	**5 Pesos** Sept. 1915. Black. Red seals, red serial #. Like #S751. Back blue. *(SI-DUR-49).*	1.50	5.00	10.00

		Good	Fine	XF
S753	**10 Pesos** Oct. 1915. Pale orange. Seated Justice at l. Back brown. Series A. *(SI-DUR-50).*	3.50	10.00	20.00

Gobierno Constitucionalista del Estado de Durango

1914 Issue

		VG	VF	Unc
S754	**5 Pesos** Dec. 1914. Black on cream. Back with hand stamped seal, hand signed. *(SI-DUR-51).*	25.00	75.00	—
S755	**10 Pesos** Dec. 1914. Black on cream. Printed sign. *(SI-DUR-52).*	25.00	75.00	—

1915 Issue

		VG	VF	Unc
S756	**5 Pesos** March 1915. Black on cream. Hand stamped seal on back. *(SI-DUR-53).*			
	a. Denomination in upper border.	20.00	50.00	75.00
	b. Denomination in upper and lower border.	20.00	50.00	75.00

		VG	VF	Unc
S757	**10 Pesos** March 1915. Black on cream. W/o denomination in border. *(SI-DUR-54).*	30.00	60.00	100.00

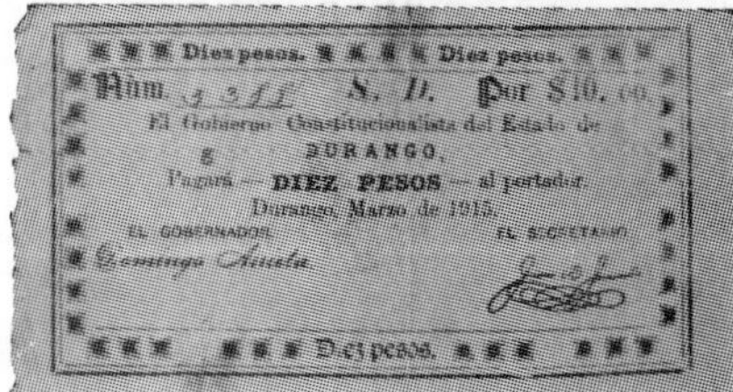

		VG	VF	Unc
S758	**10 Pesos** March 1915. Denomination in border 3 times. *(SI-DUR-55).*	30.00	60.00	100.00

Gobierno del Estado de Durango

ND Issue

#S759-S761 Indian head at ctr. Farmer plowing w/oxen on back.

		Good	Fine	XF
S759	**5 Centavos** ND. Orange pasteboard. Series A. *(SI-DUR-56).*	2.00	8.00	17.50

		Good	Fine	XF
S760	**10 Centavos** ND. Gray pasteboard. Series A. *(SI-DUR-57).*	2.00	8.00	17.50
S761	**20 Centavos** ND. Brown pasteboard. Series A. *(SI-DUR-58).*	3.00	10.00	20.00

Banco Minero/Banco de la Laguna, Gómez Palacio

The issuing bank appears in small letters at bottom and the receiving bank appears in lg. letters at top. These notes are military issues because they were created to pay revolutionary troops. They are the same type of issue as the bank over bank series cataloged under Coahuila.

1913 Issue

		Good	Fine	Unc
S762	**5 Pesos** 7.10.1913. Red. Series A. *(MI-DUR-4).*	30.00	60.00	—
S763	**5 Pesos** 7.10.1913. Black. Series A. *(MI-DUR-5).*	30.00	60.00	—
S764	**10 Pesos** 7.10.1913. Black. Series A. *(MI-DUR-6).*	37.50	75.00	—
S765	**20 Pesos** 7.10.1913. Red. Series A. *(MI-DUR-7).*	60.00	120.00	—
S766	**50 Pesos** 7.10.1913. Series A. *(MI-DUR-8).*	85.00	170.00	—

La Jefatura Municipal, Guanaceví

1913 Issue

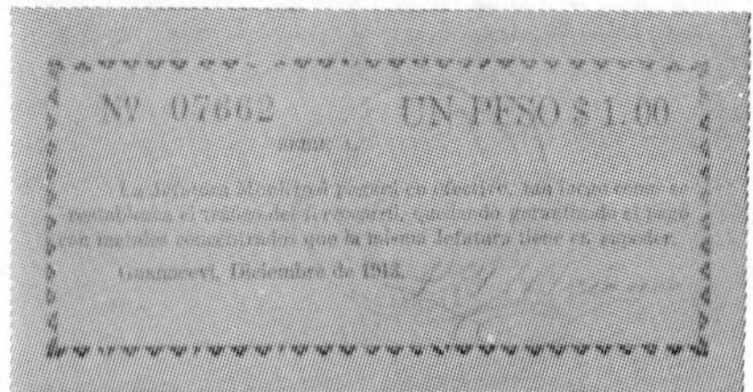

		Good	Fine	Unc
S767	**1 Peso** Dec. 1913. Series A. *(SI-DUR-59).*	45.00	90.00	—

El Estado de Durango, San José de la Boca

1914 Issue

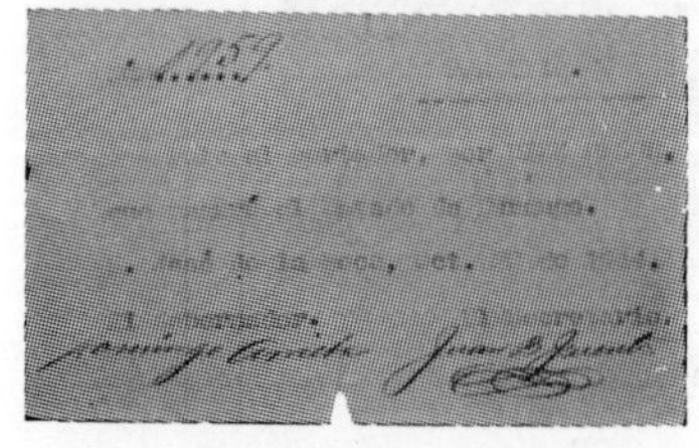

		Good	Fine	Unc
S768	**10 Pesos** 22.10.1914. Typewritten voucher signed by Gov. D. Arrieta. *(SI-DUR-62)*.	37.50	75.00	—

El Estado de Durango, Topia

1914 Issue

		Good	Fine	Unc
S769	**1 Peso** Dec. 1914. Black on white. 109 x 73mm. *(SI-DUR-63)*.	45.00	90.00	—

1915 Issue

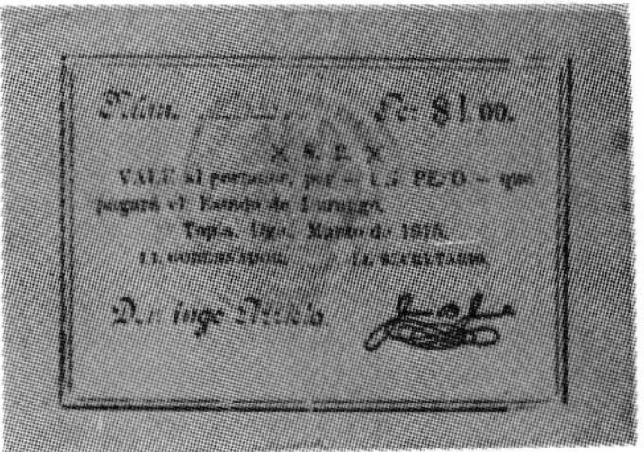

		Good	Fine	XF
S770	**1 Peso** March 1915. Black. 114 x 76mm. *(SI-DUR-64)*.	37.50	75.00	125.00

Guanajuato

Administración General de Rentas del Estado

ND Issue

		Good	Fine	XF
S771	**10 Centavos** ND. Red on tan. Vertical format on back, state of arms at ctr. *(SI-GUA-58)*.	5.00	15.00	30.00

#S772 and S773 statue of man at l. State arms at ctr. on back.

		Good	Fine	XF
S772	**50 Centavos** ND. Black. Series A. *(SI-GUA-59)*.	4.00	12.00	24.00

		Good	Fine	XF
S773	**50 Centavos** ND. Violet. Series G. *(SI-GUA-60)*.	4.00	12.00	24.00

Tesorería General del Estado

ND Bonos de Circulación Obligatoria Issue

#S774-S779 mining scene at upper ctr. Name of original issuer is blocked out and *Tesorería General del Estado* is printed below. Originally printed for Guanajuato in 1883. Printer: Kendall Bank Note Co., New York.

		Good	Fine	XF
S774	**5 Centavos** ND. Orange. *(SI-GUA-52)*.	4.50	10.00	20.00
S775	**10 Centavos** ND. Green. *(SI-GUA-53)*.	5.00	12.00	22.50
S776	**20 Centavos** ND. Blue. *(SI-GUA-54)*.	4.50	10.00	20.00
S777	**30 Centavos** ND. Brown. *(SI-GUA-55)*.	6.00	15.00	50.00
S778	**40 Centavos** ND. Sepia. *(SI-GUA-56)*.	7.00	20.00	40.00

		Good	Fine	XF
S779	**50 Centavos** ND. Black. *(SI-GUA-57)*.	6.00	15.00	40.00

1914 First Bonos Issue

#S780 and S781 state arms at l.

		Good	Fine	XF
S780	**50 Centavos** 6.1.1914. Black on blue unpt. *(SI-GUA-47)*.	25.00	50.00	85.00
S781	**1 Peso** 6.1.1914. Like #S780. *(SI-GUA-48)*.	45.00	90.00	—

1914 Second Bonos Issue

#S782-S784 state arms at l.

		Good	Fine	XF
S782	**25 Centavos** 16.4.1914. *(SI-GUA-49)*.	60.00	120.00	—
S783	**50 Centavos** 16.4.1914. Green. *(SI-GUA-50)*.	60.00	120.00	—
S784	**1 Peso** 16.4.1914. *(SI-GUA-51)*.	25.00	50.00	90.00

Guerrero

Banco Revolucionario de Guerrero

Decree of October 6, 1914

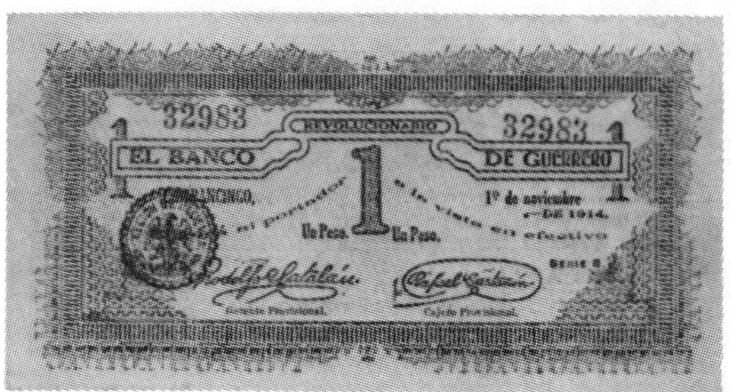

		Good	Fine	XF
S785	**1 Peso** 1.1.1914. Black on lt. blue unpt. Sunburst State seal at ctr. on back. Series B.			
	a. Issued note. *(SI-GUE-6).*	37.50	75.00	150.00
	b. Perforated cancellation. *(SI-GUE-7).*	25.00	50.00	85.00

		Good	Fine	XF
S786	**2 Pesos** 1.12.1914. Red. Steam passenger train at ctr. Series A.			
	a. Issued note. 65 x 38mm. *(SI-GUE-8).*	90.00	200.00	350.00
	r. Remainder w/o serial # and seal. *(SI-GUE-9).*	120.00	275.00	425.00

		Good	Fine	XF
S787	**5 Pesos** 6.10.1914. Blue. Boys at ctr. on back. Series A.			
	a. Black printed sign. *(SI-GUE-10).*	80.00	175.00	300.00
	b. Red printed sign. *(SI-GUE-11).*	100.00	200.00	—

		Good	Fine	XF
S788	**10 Pesos** 20.10.1914. Black. M. Hidalgo y Costilla at upper l. ctr. Series A. *(SI-GUE-12).*	375.00	750.00	—

		Good	Fine	XF
S789	**20 Pesos** 20.10.1914. Black. Series A. *(SI-GUE-13).*	150.00	300.00	600.00

Ayuntamiento de 1915, Iguala

1915 Issue

#S790-S808 national arms on back.

		Good	Fine	XF
S790	**2 Centavos** 1915. Brown. Straight line border. 62 x 41mm. *(SI-GUE-34).*	5.00	17.50	—
S790A	**2 Centavos** 1915. W/o border. 60 x 38mm. *(SI-GUE-34A).*	5.00	17.50	—
S790B	**2 Centavos** 1915. Pink ornate border. 60 x 40mm. *(SI-GUE-34B).*	5.00	17.50	—
S791	**3 Centavos** 1915. Brown. Straight line border. 59 x 39mm. *(SI-GUE-35).*	5.00	17.50	—

		Good	Fine	XF
S792	**3 Centavos** 1915. Ornate border on brown pasteboard. 64 x 42mm. *(SI-GUE-36).*	5.00	17.50	—
S793	**4 Centavos** 1915. Brown. Straight line border. 58 x 40mm. *(SI-GUE-37).*	5.00	17.50	—
S794	**4 Centavos** 1915. Brown. W/o border. *(SI-GUE-38).*	5.00	17.50	—
S795	**4 Centavos** 1915. Ornate border. *(SI-GUE-39).*	5.00	17.50	—
S796	**5 Centavos** 1915. Brown. Straight line border. 61 x 41mm. *(SI-GUE-40).*	5.00	17.50	—
S797	**5 Centavos** 1915. Brown. W/o border. *(SI-GUE-41).*	5.00	17.50	—
S798	**10 Centavos** 1915. Brown. Straight line border. 66 x 42mm. *(SI-GUE-42).*	3.00	10.00	—

No.	Description	Good	Fine	XF
S799	**10 Centavos** 1915. Brown. W/o border. *(SI-GUE-43).*	5.00	15.00	—
S800	**10 Centavos** 1915. White pasteboard. Ornate border. 61 x 41mm. *(SI-GUE-44).*	4.00	12.00	—
S801	**20 Centavos** 1915. Red-brown pasteboard. Straight line border. *(SI-GUE-45).*	5.00	15.00	—
S802	**20 Centavos** 1915. Red-brown pasteboard. W/o border. 63 x 41mm. *(SI-GUE-46).*	5.00	15.00	—
S803	**20 Centavos** 1915. Black. Ornate border. 59 x 43mm.			
	a. Pink/white pasteboard. *(SI-GUE-47).*	5.00	15.00	30.00
	b. Blue pasteboard.	5.00	15.00	30.00
	c. White pasteboard.	5.00	15.00	30.00
S804	**25 Centavos** 1915. Black. Straight line border. 60 x 42mm.			
	a. White-salmon pasteboard. *(SI-GUE-48).*	7.50	17.50	35.00
	b. Orange pasteboard.	7.50	17.50	35.00
	c. Violet pasteboard.	7.50	17.50	35.00
	d. Brown pasteboard.	7.50	17.50	35.00
S805	**25 Centavos** 1915. Black. White-salmon pasteboard. Red, ornate border. 61 x 42mm. *(SI-GUE-49).*	2.50	7.50	15.00

No.	Description	Good	Fine	XF
S806	**50 Centavos** 1915. Black. White pasteboard. Straight line border. 69 x 42mm. *(SI-GUE-50).*	3.00	9.00	18.00
S807	**50 Centavos** 1915. Black. Ornate border.			
	a. White pasteboard. *(SI-GUE-51).*	2.50	7.50	15.00
	b. Green pasteboard.	2.50	7.50	15.00
	c. Brown pasteboard.	2.50	7.50	15.00
	d. Red pasteboard.	2.50	7.50	15.00
	e. Pink paper.	2.50	7.50	15.00
	f. Orange pasteboard.	2.50	7.50	15.00
	g. Gray pasteboard.	2.50	7.50	15.00
	h. Lilac pasteboard.	2.50	7.50	15.00

No.	Description	Good	Fine	XF
S808	**1 Peso** 1915. Black. Ornate border. 60 x 43mm.			
	a. Blue pasteboard. *(SI-GUE-53).*	1.50	4.50	10.00
	b. Brown pasteboard.	1.50	4.50	10.00
	c. Gray paper.	1.50	4.50	10.00
	d. Buff pasteboard. W/green hand stamp *MUNICIPAL IGUALA* on face. Serial # on back.	1.50	4.50	10.00

Ejército Constitucionalista del Sur

ND Issue

#S809-S812 national arms at ctr.

No.	Description	Good	Fine	XF
S809	**5 Centavos** ND. Black. Pasteboard. *(MI-GUE-14).*	25.00	55.00	90.00

No.	Description	Good	Fine	XF
S810	**10 Centavos** ND. Black. Pasteboard. *(MI-GUE-15).*	25.00	55.00	90.00
S811	**50 Centavos** ND. Black. Cream pasteboard. *(MI-GUE-16).*	17.50	35.00	—

No.	Description	Good	Fine	XF
S812	**1 Peso** ND. 75 x 42mm.			
	a. Orange pasteboard. *(MI-GUE-17).*	17.50	35.00	—
	b. Yellow pasteboard.	17.50	35.00	—
	c. Blue pasteboard.	17.50	35.00	—
	d. Violet pasteboard.	17.50	35.00	—
	e. Ovpt: *AMORTIZADO. (MI-GUE-18).*	15.00	30.00	—
	f. Cream pasteboard.	15.00	30.00	—

Ejército Libertador de Guerrero, Chilpancingo

Decree of October 6, 1914

No.	Description	Good	Fine	XF
S812A	**1 Peso** *D.6.10.1914.* Black. Arms at ctr. Series A. *(MI-GUE-5).*	400.00	650.00	—

Ejército Revolucionario de Guerrero

ND Issue

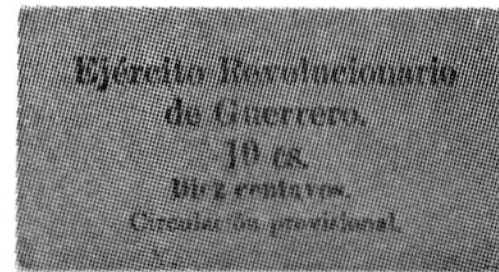

No.	Description	Good	Fine	XF
S813	**10 Centavos** ND. Black. White pasteboard. *(MI-GUE-29).*	17.50	35.00	55.00

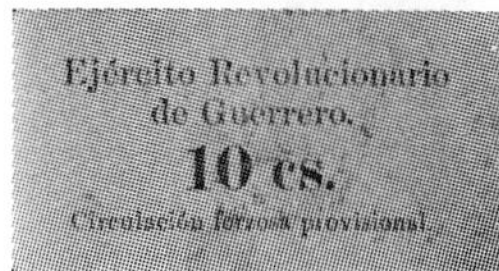

No.	Description	Good	Fine	XF
S814	**10 Centavos** ND. Black. Gray pasteboard. *(MI-GUE-30).*	9.00	20.00	35.00
S815	**20 Centavos** ND. Black. Pink or white pasteboard. *(MI-GUE-31).*	12.50	27.50	55.00
S816	**50 Centavos** ND. Black. Tan pasteboard. 80 x 41mm. *(MI-GUE-32).*	12.50	27.50	55.00

Gobierno Constitucionalista, Brigada Morales y Molina

ND Issue

No.	Description	Good	Fine	XF
S817	**10 Centavos** ND. Black. Red pasteboard. *(MI-GUE-33).*	9.00	20.00	35.00

		Good	Fine	XF
S818	**20 Centavos**			
	ND. Black. Orange pasteboard.			
	a. Issued note. *(MI-GUE-34).*	9.00	20.00	35.00
	b. Ovpt: *AMORTIZADO.*	9.00	20.00	35.00

		Good	Fine	XF
S819	**50 Centavos**			
	ND. Black.			
	a. Cream pasteboard. *(MI-GUE-35).*	3.00	12.00	25.00
	b. Pink pasteboard.	3.00	12.00	25.00
	c. Red pasteboard.	3.00	12.00	25.00
	d. Green pasteboard.	3.00	12.00	25.00
	e. White pasteboard.	3.00	12.00	25.00

		Good	Fine	XF
S820	**1 Peso**			
	ND. Black. National arms at ctr.			
	a. White pasteboard. *(MI-GUE-36).*	3.00	12.00	25.00
	b. Blue pasteboard.	3.00	12.00	25.00

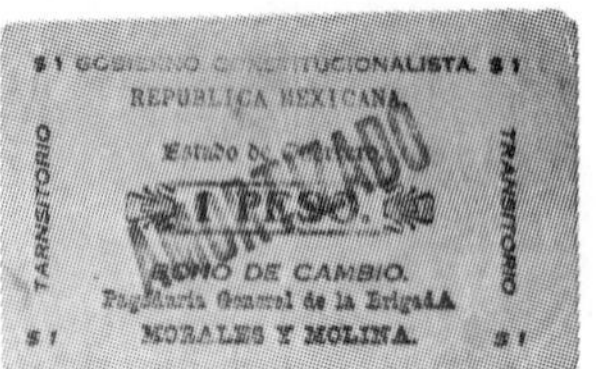

		Good	Fine	XF
S821	**1 Peso**			
	ND. Black. Tan pasteboard. Sign: *Morales y Molina* handwritten on back.			
	a. Issued note. *(MI-GUE-37).*	4.00	15.00	30.00
	b. Ovpt: *AMORTIZADO.*	4.00	15.00	30.00

#S822-S824 national arms at ctr.

		Good	Fine	XF
S822	**1 Peso**			
	ND. Black on tan unpt. *(MI-GUE-38).*	3.00	9.00	17.50

		Good	Fine	XF
S823	**5 Pesos**			
	ND. Black.			
	a. Deep pink unpt. *(MI-GUE-39).*	6.00	20.00	40.00
	b. Pale salmon unpt.	6.00	20.00	40.00

		Good	Fine	XF
S824	**10 Pesos**			
	ND. Gray.			
	a. Issued note. *(MI-GUE-40).*	12.50	27.50	55.00
	b. Ovpt: *AMORTIZADO.*	12.50	27.50	55.00

Hidalgo

Brigada Azuara

1915 Issue

		Good	Fine	XF
S825	**50 Centavos**			
	12.1.1915. Black. 106 x 56mm. *(MI-HID-1).*	25.00	60.00	125.00
S826	**1 Peso**			
	12.1.1915. Black. *(MI-HID-2).*	25.00	60.00	125.00

		Good	Fine	XF
S827	**1 Peso**			
	20.1.1915. Black on brown. Series A. *(MI-HID-3).*	30.00	70.00	140.00

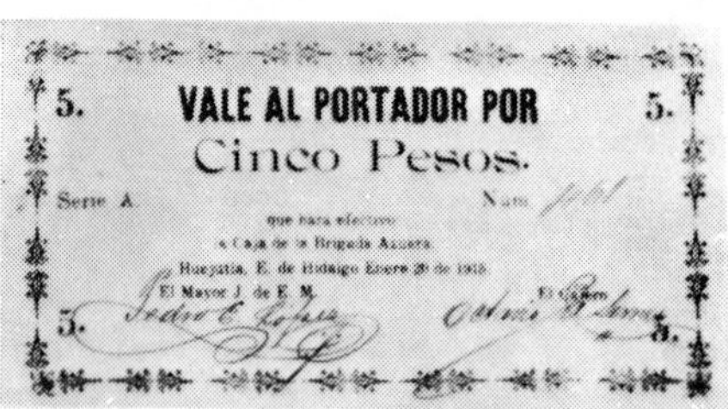

		Good	Fine	XF
S828	**5 Pesos**			
	20.1.1915. Black. Series A. *(MI-HID-4).*	30.00	70.00	140.00

		Good	Fine	XF
S829	**50 Centavos**			
	ND. Blue on white unpt. 138 x 75mm. *(MI-HID-5).*	75.00	150.00	—
S830	**1 Peso**			
	ND. *(MI-HID-6).*	75.00	150.00	—

Compañiá Real del Monte y Pachuca / Bank of Montreal

1915 First Issue

#S831-S833 hand signed adhesive fiscal stamp and hand stamped seal on back.

		Good	Fine	XF
S831	**5 Pesos**			
	28.5.1915. Black on pale tan unpt. Series L. *(PI-HID-58).*	275.00	500.00	—

		Good	Fine	XF
S832	**10 Pesos** 28.5.1915. Black on pale green unpt. Series N. *(PI-HID-59).*	275.00	500.00	—
S833	**20 Pesos** 28.5.1915. Black. Series M. *(PI-HID-60).*	275.00	500.00	—

1915 Second Issue

#S834-S839 hand signed adhesive fiscal stamp and hand stamped seal on back. Various handwritten dates.

		Good	Fine	XF
S834	**1 Peso** 1915. Green. *(PI-HID-61).*			
	a. Various dates. Series A.	15.00	25.00	—
	b. ND. Series A.	10.00	20.00	40.00
S835	**2 1/2 Pesos** 1915. Yellow. Series E. *(PI-HID-62).*	100.00	200.00	350.00
S836	**5 Pesos** 1915. Green. Series B. *(PI-HID-63).*	45.00	90.00	—
S837	**5 Pesos** 1915. Blue. Series B. *(PI-HID-64).*	20.00	45.00	75.00
S838	**10 Pesos** 1915. Cream. Series C. *(PI-HID-66).*	35.00	75.00	125.00
S839	**20 Pesos** 1915. Pink. Series D. *(SI-HID-67).*	50.00	100.00	165.00

Estado Libre y Soberano de Hidalgo

1915 Issue

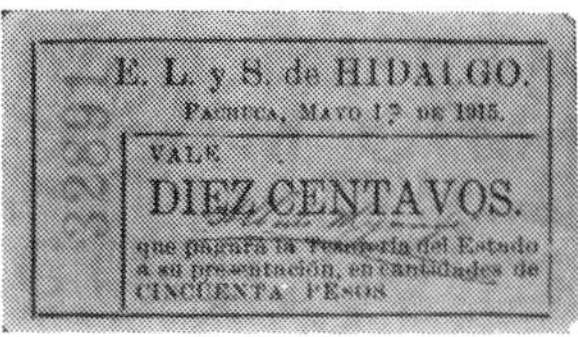

		Good	Fine	XF
S840	**10 Centavos** 1.5.1915. Black on pink pasteboard. Series E. *(SI-HID-2).*	2.00	8.00	15.00
S841	**20 Centavos** 1.5.1915. Pasteboard. *(SI-HID-3).*	15.00	30.00	—
S842	**25 Centavos** 1.5.1915. Black on pale green unpt. Pasteboard. Series C. *(SI-HID-4).*	4.00	12.00	25.00
S843	**50 Centavos** 1.5.1915. Black on pale green unpt. Pasteboard. Series B; G. *(SI-HID-5).*	2.00	8.00	15.00

Jalisco

La Dirección General de Rentas del Estado, Guadalajara

Decree No. 2 of June 18, 1914

#S844 amd S845 national arms at ctr. on back.

		Good	Fine	XF
S844	**5 Centavos** 19.7.1914. Black on pale orange unpt. Series A.			
	a. Issued note. *(SI-JAL-12).*	5.00	15.00	30.00
	b. W/o serial #; perforated: *PAGADO. (SI-JAL-13).*	—	—	30.00
S845	**10 Centavos** 19.7.1914. Black on pale blue unpt. Series A.			
	a. Issued note. *(SI-JAL-14).*	5.50	17.50	35.00
	b. W/o serial #; perforated: *PAGADO. (SI-JAL-15).*	—	—	27.50

		Good	Fine	XF
S846	**20 Centavos** 19.7.1914. Black on pink unpt. Series A.			
	a. Issued note. *(SI-JAL-16).*	6.50	20.00	40.00
	b. W/o serial #; perforated: *PAGADO. (SI-JAL-17).*	—	—	45.00

		Good	Fine	XF
S847	**50 Centavos** 19.7.1914. Black on lt. blue unpt. Men at l. Series B.			
	a. Issued note. *(SI-JAL-18).*	6.50	20.00	40.00
	b. W/o serial #; perforated: *PAGADO. (SI-JAL-19).*	—	—	45.00

Decree No. 12 of August 11, 1914

		Good	Fine	XF
S848	**5 Centavos** 15.8.1914. Sepia and green. State arms at ctr. in unpt. Series B.			
	a. Issued note. *(SI-JAL-20).*	2.00	6.00	15.00
	b. W/o serial #; perforated: *PAGADO. (SI-JAL-21).*	—	—	17.50

		Good	Fine	XF
S849	**10 Centavos** 15.8.1914. Black and brown. National arms at ctr. on back. Series B.			
	a. Issued note. *(SI-JAL-22).*	10.00	20.00	35.00
	b. W/o serial #; perforated: *PAGADO. (SI-JAL-23).*	—	—	30.00

		Good	Fine	XF
S850	**20 Centavos** 15.8.1914. Black on pink. State arms at ctr. on back. Series B.			
	a. Issued note. *(SI-JAL-24).*	3.00	9.00	18.00
	b. W/o serial #; perforated: *PAGADO. (SI-JAL-25).*	—	—	22.50

		Good	Fine	XF
S851	**50 Centavos** 15.8.1914. Black on sepia. Series C.			
	a. Issued note. *(SI-JAL-26).*	2.50	7.50	15.00
	b. W/o serial #; perforated: *PAGADO. (SI-JAL-27).*	—	—	22.50

		GOOD	FINE	XF
S852	**5 CENTAVOS** 30.10.1914. Black and green. State arms at ctr. in unpt. Series C. *(SI-JAL-28).*	3.00	9.00	18.00
S853	**10 CENTAVOS** 30.10.1914. Black and brown. State arms at ctr. in unpt. Series C. *(SI-JAL-29).*	12.00	20.00	35.00

		GOOD	FINE	XF
S854	**20 CENTAVOS** 30.10.1914. Black on pink unpt. State arms at ctr. on back. Series C. *(SI-JAL-30).*	4.00	12.00	25.00
S855	**50 CENTAVOS** 30.10.1914. Black on sepia. Series D. *(SI-JAL-31).*	1.50	5.00	10.00

DECREE NO. 59 OF FEBRUARY 1, 1915

		GOOD	FINE	XF
S856	**50 CENTAVOS** 1.2.1915. Black on sepia. Series E. *(SI-JAL-32).*	3.00	6.00	12.00

DECREE NO. 65 OF MAY 29, 1915

		GOOD	FINE	XF
S857	**5 CENTAVOS** 8.6.1915. Brown and green. State arms at ctr. in unpt. Series E.			
	a. Issued note. *(SI-JAL-33).*	1.50	4.50	9.00
	b. Decree No. 64 (error). *(SI-JAL-34).*	6.00	20.00	40.00

		GOOD	FINE	XF
S858	**20 CENTAVOS** 8.6.1915. Black on pink unpt. State arms at ctr. on back. Series F. *(SI-JAL-35).*	1.50	4.50	9.00

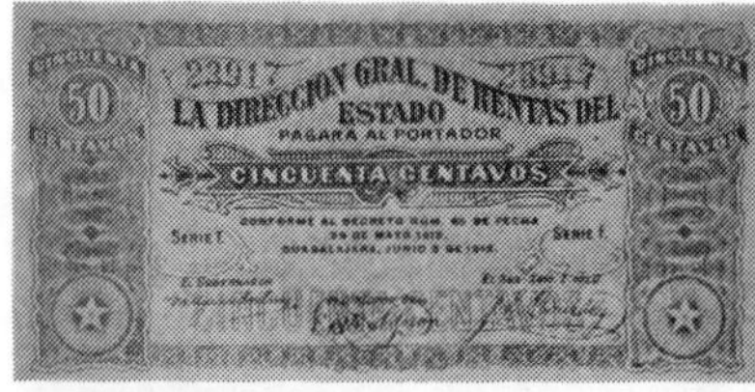

		GOOD	FINE	XF
S859	**50 CENTAVOS** 8.6.1915. Black on dull red-brown unpt. Back green. Series F. *(SI-JAL-36).*	1.50	4.50	9.00

EJÉRCITO CONSTITUCIONALISTA, DIVISIÓN DE OCCIDENTE, GUADALAJARA

1915 ISSUE

#S860-S862 portr. Ramón Corona at l., Government bldg. at r.

		VG	VF	UNC
S860	**1 PESO** 20.1.1915. Black on pink unpt. Series A. *(MI-JAL-22).*	1.50	5.00	10.00
S861	**5 PESOS** 20.1.1915. Brown on blue unpt. Back green. Series A. *(MI-JAL-23).*	2.00	6.00	12.00
S862	**10 PESOS** 20.1.1915. Brown on pale green unpt. Series A. *(MI-JAL-24).*	5.00	15.00	30.00

LA PAGADURÍÁ DEL CUERPODE EJÉRCITO DEL NOROESTE

1914 ISSUE

		GOOD	FINE	XF
S863	**50 CENTAVOS** 1.8.1914. Black on orange unpt. Series C. *(MI-JAL-10).*	15.00	40.00	85.00

		GOOD	FINE	XF
S864	**1 PESO** 1.8.1914. Black on green unpt. Series C. *(MI-JAL-11).*	25.00	50.00	85.00

#S865-S867 F. I. Madero at l., Liberty at r.

		GOOD	FINE	XF
S865	**5 PESOS** 1914; 1915. Black on rose unpt. Back deep blue; field artillery troops w/cannon at ctr., arms at l. and r.			
	a. Issued note. Series C. 1.8.1914. *(MI-JAL-12).*	17.50	35.00	60.00
	r. Remainder w/o serial #. Series D. 1.5.1915. *(MI-JAL-13).*	30.00	60.00	—
S866	**10 PESOS** 1.8.1914. Black on orange unpt. Series C. *(MI-JAL-14).*	20.00	50.00	85.00
S867	**20 PESOS** 1.8.1914. Black on green unpt. Series C. *(MI-JAL-15).*	30.00	60.00	100.00

LA PAGADURÍÁ GRAL. DEL CUERPO DE EJÉRCITO DEL NOROESTE

1915 ISSUE

#S868-S872 sign. General Serrano.

		GOOD	FINE	XF
S868	**50 CENTAVOS** 1.5.1915. Black on pale orange unpt. Series D; E. *(MI-JAL-16).*	2.50	7.50	15.00

		GOOD	FINE	XF
S869	**1 PESO** 1.5.1915. Black on green unpt. Series D. *(MI-JAL-17).*	5.00	15.00	30.00

#S870-S872 F. I. Madero at l., Liberty at r.

		GOOD	FINE	XF
S870	**5 PESOS** 1.5.1915. Black on pink unpt. Soldiers and cannon at ctr. on back. Paper and cardboard. Series D.			
	a. Issued note. *(MI-JAL-18).*	2.50	7.50	15.00
	b. W/o serial #. *(MI-JAL-19).*	3.00	9.00	18.00
S871	**10 PESOS** 1.5.1915. Black on yellow and green unpt. Back red; arms at l., soldiers w/cannon at ctr. Series D. *(MI-JAL-20).*			
	a. Issued note.	7.00	15.00	35.00
	r. Remainder w/o serial #.	7.00	15.00	35.00
S872	**20 PESOS** 1.5.1915. Black on olive green unpt. Series D. *(MI-JAL-21).*	17.50	30.00	60.00

ESTADO DE JALISCO

ND ISSUE

#S873-S875 national arms at ctr. on back.

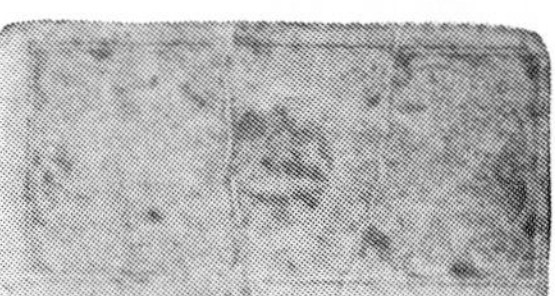

		GOOD	FINE	XF
S873	**5 CENTAVOS** ND. Blue pasteboard. *(SI-JAL-9).*	1.50	5.00	10.00

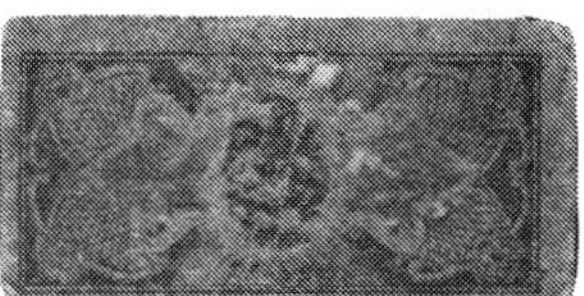

		GOOD	FINE	XF
S874	**10 CENTAVOS** ND. Purple pasteboard. Series F. *(SI-JAL-10).*	1.50	5.00	10.00

		GOOD	FINE	XF
S875	**20 CENTAVOS** ND. Red.			
	a. Blue pasteboard. *(SI-JAL-11).*	1.50	5.00	10.00
	b. Green pasteboard.	1.50	5.00	10.00

JEFATURA DE HACIENDA EN EL ESTADO JALISCO

1915 ISSUE

		GOOD	FINE	XF
S875A	**50 PESOS** 22.2.1915. Like #S876, similar ovpt. on face. Back ovpt. text in circle, also 5 lines of text and date. Issued at Guadalajara.	12.50	50.00	—

JEFE DE LA DIVISIÓN DE OCCIDENTE

1915 ISSUE

These are #S707 notes lacking date, signatures and serial letters and bearing a lg. red face ovpt: *Circulá-Forzosamente este Billete con la sola Firma del Subscrito, por carecer de las ordinarias. Guadalajara, Enero 28, 1915. El Gral. Jefe de la Division de Occidente.* (May this Bill be of compulsory circulation with the lone signature appearing below, because the ordinary ones are unavailable. Guadalajara, January 28, 1915. Commander General of the Western Division). Signed by M. M. Diéguez.

		GOOD	FINE	XF
S876	**50 PESOS** 28.1.1915. Seated Liberty at l., national arms at ctr.			
	a. Ovpt: *RETIRADO* on face and back. *(MI-JAL-25).*	12.50	50.00	80.00
	b. W/seal on back: *Jefatura de Hacienda en el Estado. Jalisco. Autorizado. . . Febrero 22 de 1915.* ovpt: *RETIRADO* on face and back.	30.00	75.00	—
	c. Like a. but w/o *RETIRADO* on face or back.	—	—	—

MÉXICO (ESTADO DE)

ESTADO LIBRE Y SOBERANO DE MÉXICO, TOLUCA

DECREE NO. 4 OF MARCH 1, 1915

		GOOD	FINE	XF
S877	**5 CENTAVOS** 1.3.1915. Stamped coin-like gray pasteboard.			
	a. W/o dot after: *TOLUCA.*	15.00	35.00	65.00
	b. W/dot after: *TOLUCA.*	15.00	35.00	65.00

#S878 and S879 eagle on pedestal at l.

		VG	VF	UNC
S878	**20 CENTAVOS** 1.3.1915. Brown on blue unpt. Series A. *(SI-MEX-9).*	1.00	3.00	6.00
S879	**50 CENTAVOS** 1.3.1915. Blue on pale orange pasteboard or paper. Series A; B; C; D; F. *(SI-MEX-10).*	1.75	5.00	10.00

#S880 and S881 monument of C. Columbus at ctr.

		VG	VF	UNC
S880	**1 PESO** 1.3.1915. Black on green and tan unpt. Back blue. Series A. *(SI-MEX-11).*	4.00	12.00	30.00
S881	**1 PESO** 1.3.1915. Blue. Series B-F. *(SI-MEX-12).*	.75	2.00	4.50

GOBIERNO CONVENCIONISTA DE MÉXICO, TOLUCA

1915 ISSUE

		VG	VF	UNC
S882	**50 CENTAVOS** 16.8.1915. Black on yellow unpt. Justice at l. Back purple; coin at ctr. Series A. *(SI-MEX-7).*	.75	2.00	4.00

MICHOACÁN

EL ESTADO DE MICHOACÁN DE OCAMPO, MORELIA

MILITARY DECREE OF FEBRUARY 5, 1915

		VG	VF	UNC
S883	**10 PESOS** 5.2.1915. Brown-violet on pink unpt. W/printed sign. Black or blue serial #. Back blue-green; arms at upper ctr., red circular Treasury seal. Wmk: Titanic Bond.			
	a. Issued note. *(MI-MIC-8).*	1.25	3.50	7.00
	b. W/o serial #. *(MI-MIC-9).*	1.50	5.00	15.00
	c. Ovpt: *Comandancia Militar, La Union, Gro. (MI-MIC-10).*	1.50	5.00	—
	d. W/o unpt.	1.50	5.00	—
	e. W/serial # and w/o unpt.	1.50	5.00	—

GOBIERNO PROVISIONAL DE MICHOACÁN

1915 ND TRANSITORIO ISSUE

#S884-S887 Melchor Ocampo at ctr. National arms at ctr. on back. Sign. varieties.

		GOOD	FINE	XF
S884	**5 CENTAVOS** ND (1915). Black. Pink pasteboard. Series O. *(SI-MIC-9).*	3.50	10.00	20.00
S885	**10 CENTAVOS** ND (1915). Green. Brown pasteboard. Series N. *(SI-MIC-10).*	2.50	8.00	17.50
S886	**20 CENTAVOS** ND (1915). Violet. Brown pasteboard. Series E. *(SI-MIC-11).*	2.50	8.00	17.50
S887	**50 CENTAVOS** ND (1915). Red-orange. White pasteboard.			

	GOOD	FINE	XF
a. Issued note. Series A; D; E. *(SI-MIC-12).*	1.50	5.00	10.00

	GOOD	FINE	XF
b. Circular ovpt: *Cuerpo de Ejercito del Norte* and various dates ca.1915.	3.00	10.00	20.00
c. Oval ovpt: *Angangueo.* Series B. *(SI-MIC-14).*	7.50	15.00	30.00

A word on date ranges

Often date ranges or specific dates are listed. These have been observed or reported by our contributors. If a note is outside the published range, it only means that it is a newly reported date, and not necessarily worthy of a premium value.

JEFATURA DE ARMAS, MORELIA

1915 ISSUE

		GOOD	FINE	XF
S888	**1 CENTAVO** July 1915. *(MI-MIC-2).*	9.00	18.00	35.00

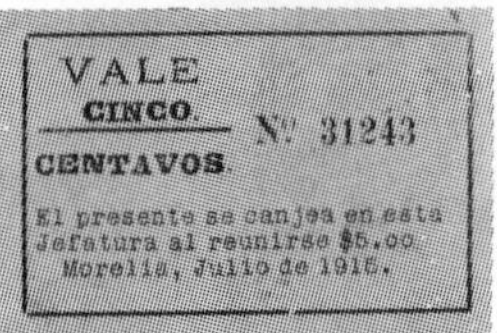

		GOOD	FINE	XF
S889	**5 CENTAVOS** July 1915. *(MI-MIC-3).*	5.00	15.00	30.00

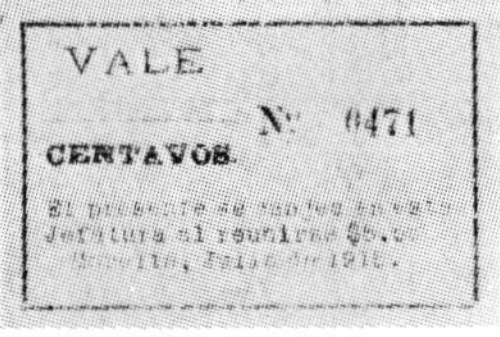

		GOOD	FINE	XF
S890	**5 CENTAVOS** July 1915. *(MI-MIC-4).*	5.00	15.00	30.00
S891	**10 CENTAVOS** July 1915. *(MI-MIC-5).*			
	a. Paper.	5.00	15.00	30.00
	b. Pasteboard.	5.00	15.00	30.00

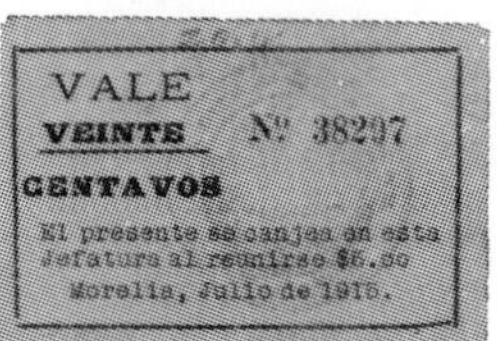

		GOOD	FINE	XF
S892	**20 CENTAVOS** July 1915. *(MI-MIC-6).*	8.00	18.00	30.00
S893	**50 CENTAVOS** July 1915. *(MI-MIC-7).*	8.00	18.00	30.00

LA TESORERÍA MUNICIPAL, PÁTZCUARO

1915 ISSUE

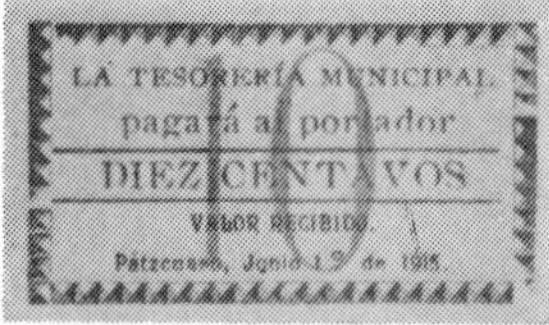

		GOOD	FINE	XF
S894	**10 CENTAVOS** 1.6.1915. Black and red. Yellow pasteboard. *(SI-MIC-15).*	7.50	15.00	30.00
S895	**20 CENTAVOS** 1.6.1915. Brown and red. White pasteboard. *(SI-MIC-16).*	9.00	18.00	35.00

TESORERÍA MUNICIPAL, PURUANDIRO

1915 ISSUE

		GOOD	FINE	XF
S896	**5 CENTAVOS** (ca.1915). Brown paper. Various dates. Series A. *(SI-MIC-17).*	10.00	20.00	—

		GOOD	FINE	XF
S897	**10 CENTAVOS** (ca.1915). Brown paper. Various dates. Series A. *(SI-MIC-18).*	10.00	20.00	—

EJÉRCITO CONSTITUCIONALISTA, URUAPÁN

1914 ISSUE

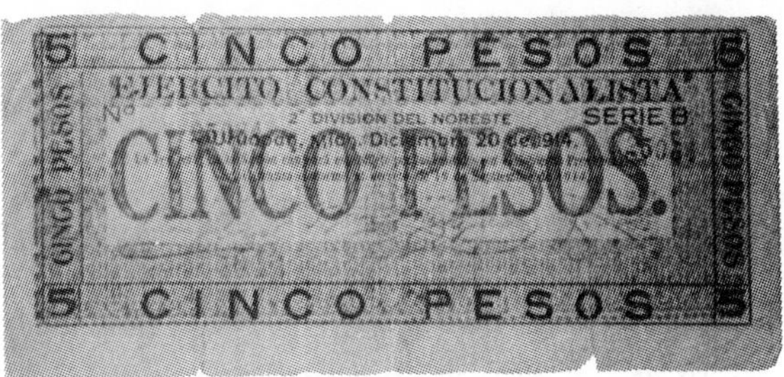

		Good	Fine	XF
S898	**5 Pesos** 20.12.1914. Black on green unpt. Series B. *(SI-MIC-20).*	7.50	15.00	40.00

MORELOS

CIRCULACIÓN FORZOSA EN EL ESTADO DE MORELOS, CUERNAVACA

ND ISSUE

		Good	Fine	XF
S899	**10 Centavos** ND. Pasteboard. *(SI-MOR-23).*	10.00	30.00	—

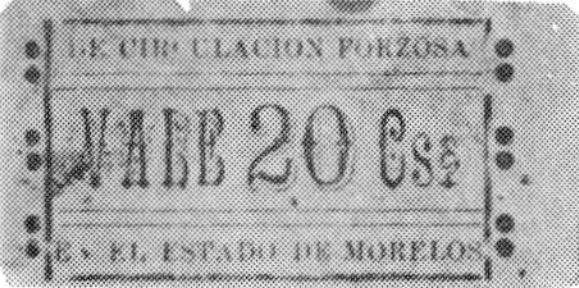

		Good	Fine	XF
S900	**20 Centavos** ND. Brown pasteboard. 55 x 30mm. *(SI-MOR-24).*	3.50	10.00	20.00

		Good	Fine	XF
S901	**1 Peso** ND. Gray pasteboard. 60 x 28mm. *(SI-MOR-25).*	7.50	30.00	—

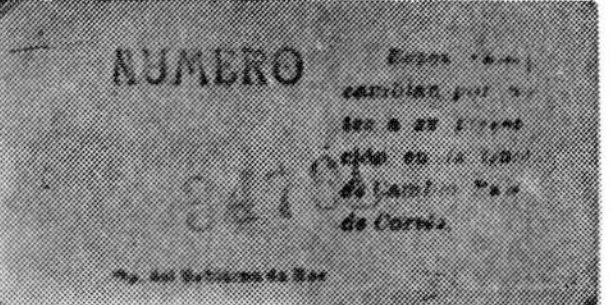

		Good	Fine	XF
S902	**1 Peso** ND. Black. 55 x 30mm. *(SI-MOR-26).*			
	a. Gray paper.	.50	2.50	5.00
	b. Brown paper.	.50	2.50	5.00
	c. Pink paper.	.50	2.50	5.00
	d. Orange paper.	.50	2.50	5.00
	e. Maroon paper.	.50	2.50	5.00
	f. White paper.	.50	2.50	5.00

DIRECCIÓN GENERAL DE RENTAS DEL ESTADO, CUERNAVACA

1914 ISSUE

		Good	Fine	XF
S903	**10 Centavos** June 1914. Green. 105 x 50mm. *(SI-MOR-7).*	10.00	30.00	60.00
S904	**20 Centavos** June 1914. Red. 105 x 50mm. *(SI-MOR-8).*	10.00	30.00	60.00

		Good	Fine	XF
S905	**50 Centavos** 28.7.1914. Black. 105 x 50mm. *(SI-MOR-9).*	10.00	30.00	60.00

GOBIERNO CONVENCIONISTA, CUERNAVACA

1915 TRANSITORIO ISSUE

		Good	Fine	XF
S906	**5 Centavos** 1915. Pink pasteboard. 55 x 30mm. *(SI-MOR-10).*	7.50	15.00	30.00

		Good	Fine	XF
S907	**10 Centavos** 1915. Yellow pasteboard. Sunface at ctr. on back. Series B. *(SI-MOR-11).*	7.50	15.00	30.00
S908	**20 Centavos** 1915. Red pasteboard. Like #S907. Series A. 56 x 30mm. *(SI-MOR-12).*	2.50	7.50	15.00

GOBIERNO CONVENCIONISTA DE MÉXICO

DECREE OF OCTOBER 1, 1915

		Good	Fine	XF
S909	**5 Pesos** 12.10.1915. Black on tan unpt. Justice at l.			
	a. Issued note, printed top to top. *(SI-MOR-16).*	1.50	4.50	9.00
	b. Inverted back.	20.00	60.00	120.00

DECREE OF DECEMBER 27, 1915

		Good	Fine	XF
S910	**50 Centavos** ND. Yellow. Farmer and laborer at ctr. Red seal on back. *(SI-MOR-13).*	12.50	25.00	60.00
S911	**50 Centavos** ND. Red. 115 x 68mm. *(SI-MOR-14).*	10.00	30.00	70.00

DECREE OF JANUARY 10, 1916

		Good	Fine	XF
S912	**2 Pesos** *D.1916.* Black on green unpt. Woman at r. *(SI-MOR-15).*	.75	2.00	4.00

JEFATURA DE ARMAS, YAUTEPEC

1915 ISSUE

		Good	Fine	XF
S913	**5 Centavos** Jan. 1915. White pasteboard. 67 x 42mm. *(MI-MOR-4).*	6.00	20.00	40.00
S914	**10 Centavos** Jan. 1915. Green pasteboard. 68 x 42mm. Series R. *(MI-MOR-5).*	6.00	20.00	40.00
S915	**20 Centavos** Jan. 1915. Violet pasteboard. 70 x 44mm. Series C. *(MI-MOR-6).*	6.00	20.00	40.00

Nayarit

Cuerpo de Ejército del Noroeste, Tepic
Army of the Northwest

1914 Issue

#S916-S917B national arms at upper l. Denomination and monogram on back.

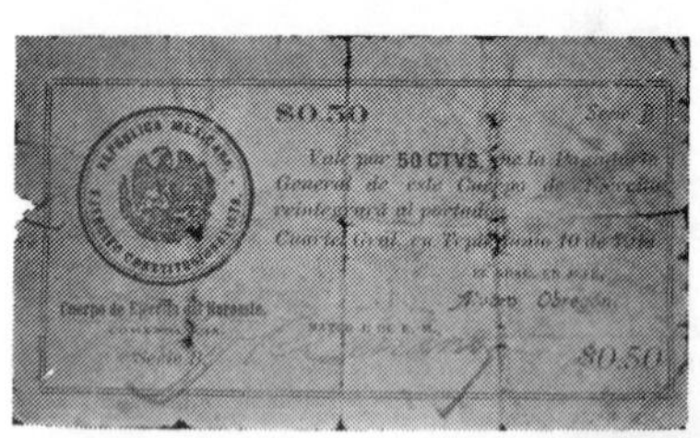

		Good	Fine	XF
S916	**50 Centavos** 10.6.1914. Blue. Series D. *(MI-NAY-3).*	6.00	20.00	45.00

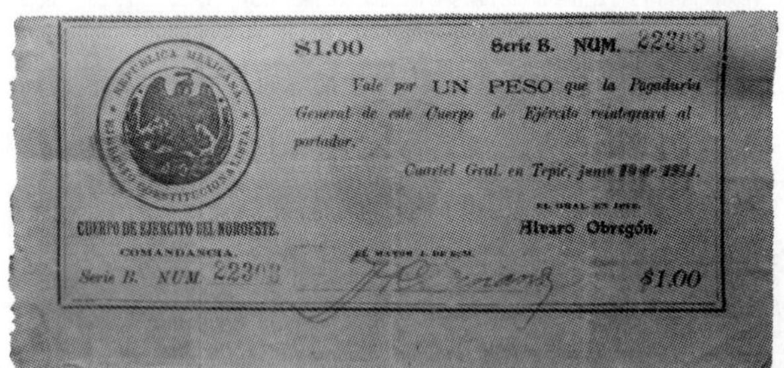

		Good	Fine	XF
S917	**1 Peso** 10.6.1914. Series B. *(MI-NAY-4).*	45.00	75.00	150.00
S917B	**10 Pesos** 10.6.1914. Red. Similar to #S917. Series B. *(MI-NAY-4).*	55.00	90.00	175.00

Gobierno Constitucionalista, Territorio de Tepic

Gral. Rafael Buelna.

1913 Issue

		Good	Fine	XF
S917F	**10 Pesos** Nov. 1913. *(MI-NAY-4A).*	—	—	—

Jefe Político del Territorio

Gral. Juan Carrasco.

ND Issue

#S918 and S919 ovpt: *Gral Juan Carrasco.*

		Good	Fine	XF
S918	**5 Centavos** ND. 70 x 40mm. *(SI-NAY-29).*			
	a. Red pasteboard.	15.00	30.00	—
	b. Pink pasteboard.	15.00	30.00	—
	c. Green pasteboard.	15.00	30.00	—

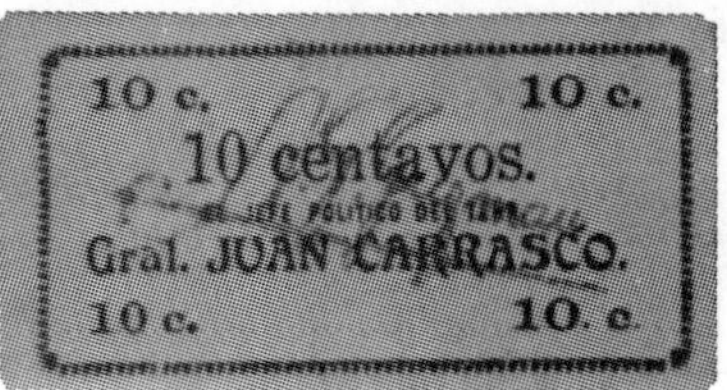

		Good	Fine	XF
S919	**10 Centavos** ND. 71 x 34mm. *(SI-NAY-30).*			
	a. Lilac pasteboard.	15.00	30.00	—
	b. Gray pasteboard.	15.00	30.00	—
	c. Blue pasteboard.	15.00	30.00	—
	d. Pink pasteboard.	15.00	30.00	—

Jefe de la Columna, Territorio de Tepic

Gral. Rafael Buelna.

1915 Issue

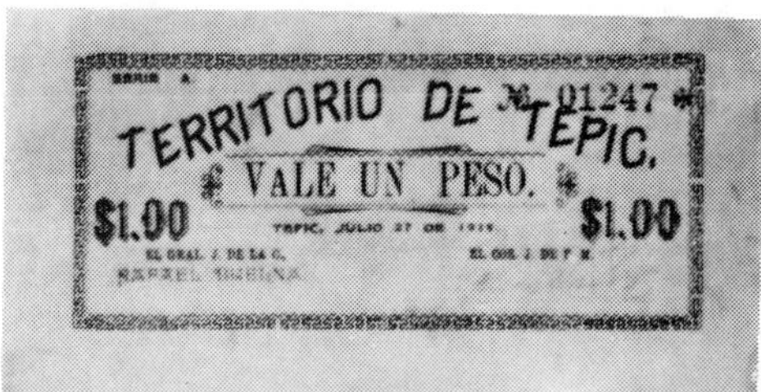

		Good	Fine	XF
S920	**1 Peso** 27.7.1915. Black on pink unpt. Series A. *(SI-NAY-5).*	30.00	60.00	120.00

ND Issues

		Good	Fine	XF
S921	**5 Centavos** ND. Green. 85 x 42mm. *(SI-NAY-20).*	9.00	18.00	35.00

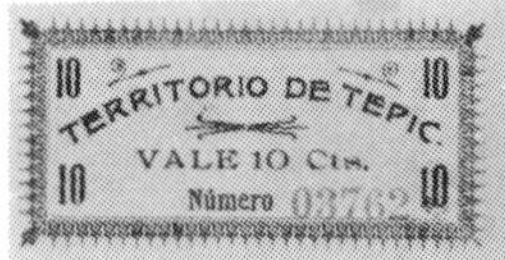

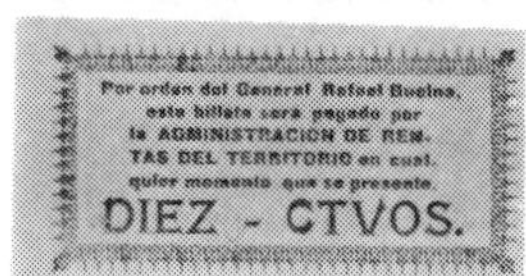

		Good	Fine	XF
S922	**10 Centavos** ND. Yellow. 87 x 42mm. *(SI-NAY-21).*	4.00	12.00	25.00
S923	**20 Centavos** ND. Gray pasteboard. *(SI-MAY-23).*	4.00	12.00	25.00

		Good	Fine	XF
S924	**50 Centavos** ND. Black. 88 x 50mm. *(SI-NAY-24).*	12.50	25.00	50.00

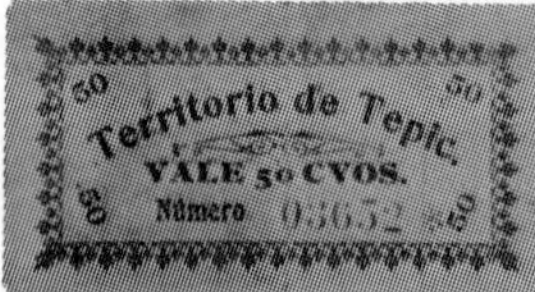

		Good	Fine	XF
S925	**50 Centavos** ND. *(SI-NAY-25).*	12.50	25.00	50.00
S926	**50 Centavos** ND. *(SI-NAY-26).*	12.50	25.00	50.00
S927	**50 Centavos** ND. Brown. 92 x 55mm. *(SI-NAY-27).*	3.00	10.00	20.00

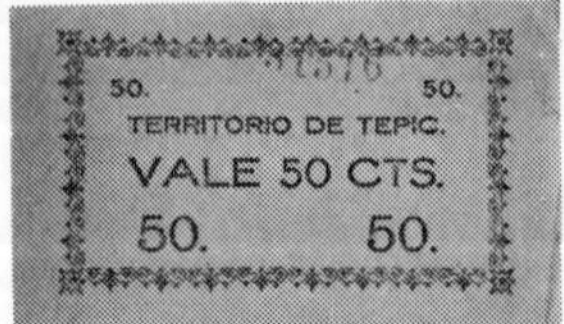

		Good	Fine	XF
S928	**50 Centavos** ND. 92 x 55mm. Inc. diagonal ovpt: *STAL MEXI. (SI-NAY-28).*	3.00	10.00	20.00
S928A	**50 Centavos** ND. Ornamental border face and back.	3.00	10.00	20.00

TESORERÍA GENERAL, TERRITORIO DE TEPIC

ND ISSUE

		GOOD	FINE	XF
S929	**5 CENTAVOS** ND. Pale blue. *(SI-NAY-15)*.	15.00	30.00	—

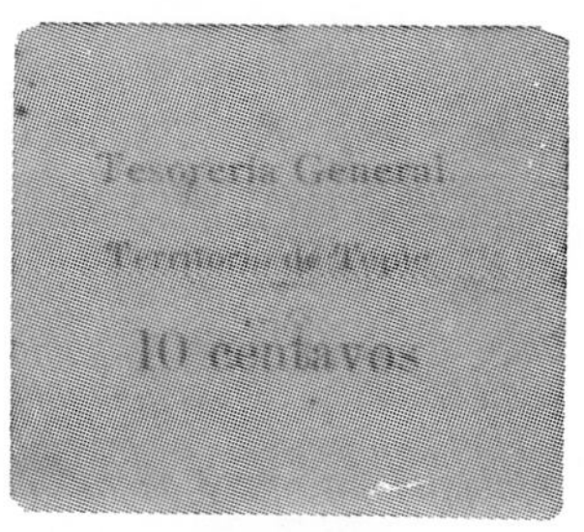

		GOOD	FINE	XF
S930	**10 CENTAVOS** ND. Pale blue. *(SI-NAY-16)*.	15.00	30.00	—
S931	**20 CENTAVOS** ND. Pale blue. *(SI-NAY-17)*.	15.00	30.00	—
S932	**50 CENTAVOS** ND. Pale blue. *(SI-NAY-18)*.	15.00	30.00	—

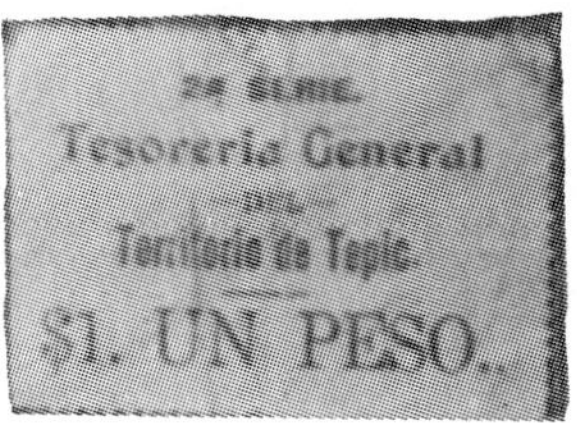

		GOOD	FINE	XF
S933	**1 PESO** ND. Pale blue. *(SI-NAY-19)*.	15.00	30.00	—

NUEVO LEÓN

GOBIERNO DE NUEVO LEÓN, MONTERREY

1914 ISSUE

		GOOD	FINE	XF
S934	**1 CENTAVO** 1914. Black on lt. green unpt. Violet monogram stamping. Pasteboard. 53 x 30mm. *(SI-NUE-3)*.	1.00	4.00	9.00

DIVISIÓN DEL BRAVO, MONTERREY

1914 ISSUE

#S935-S939 national arms at ctr. The symmetrical back design is usually the same color w/some shade varieties as the unpt. of the face. The 1, 2 and 5 peso denominations bear 3 circular printed seals on back. The 10 and 50 centavos are w/o seals.

VALIDATION HAND STAMPS:

1. JEFATURA DE HACIENDA, MONTERREY, N.I.
2. EJERCITO NACIONAL, DIVISION DEL BRAVO.
3. GOBIERNO DE ESTADO LIBRE Y SOBERANO DE NUEVO LEON.

		GOOD	FINE	XF
S935	**10 CENTAVOS** 8.1.1914. Black on blue or green unpt. Series E; F. *(MI-NUE-1)*.	2.50	7.50	17.50

		GOOD	FINE	XF
S936	**50 CENTAVOS** 8.1.1914. Black on blue unpt.			
	a. Lg. sign. at ctr. Series D. *(MI-NUE-2)*.	1.00	3.00	6.00
	b. Hand stamped: *DIVISION DEL BRAVO/JEFATURA DE ARMAS DE N. LAREDO * CUARTEL GENERAL * around eagle ovpt. (MI-NUE-3)*.	3.00	9.00	—
	c. Sm. sign. at ctr. Series D-A; D-B; D-C; D-D; D-E; E-B.	1.00	3.00	6.00

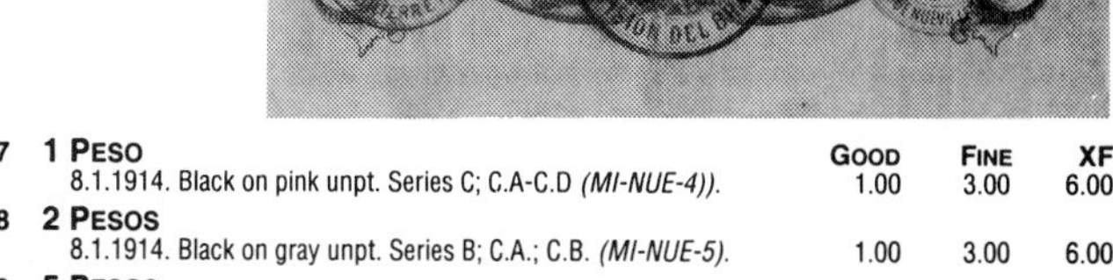

		GOOD	FINE	XF
S937	**1 PESO** 8.1.1914. Black on pink unpt. Series C; C.A-C.D *(MI-NUE-4))*.	1.00	3.00	6.00
S938	**2 PESOS** 8.1.1914. Black on gray unpt. Series B; C.A.; C.B. *(MI-NUE-5)*.	1.00	3.00	6.00
S939	**5 PESOS** 8.1.1914. Black on brown unpt. Series A. *(MI-NUE-6)*.	2.50	7.50	17.50

UNDETERMINED ORIGIN

CUERPO DE EJÉRCITO DEL NOROESTE

ND ISSUE

#S940 and S941 Constitutionalist Army seal on face, handwritten sign.

		GOOD	FINE	XF
S940	**1 PESO** ND. Green. Series B.			
	a. Regular paper. *(MI-NUE-10)*.	20.00	45.00	70.00
	b. Tan ledger paper.	20.00	45.00	70.00

		GOOD	FINE	XF
S941	**5 PESOS** ND. Green. Series A.			
	a. Issued note. *(MI-NUE-11)*.	30.00	60.00	100.00
	b. Ovpt: *AMORTIZADO*.	30.00	60.00	100.00
	r. Remainder, w/o Army seal. Printed sign. Series B. *(MI-NUE-12)*.	25.00	55.00	90.00

OAXACA

DIVISIÓN ALMAZÁN, HUAJUAPÁN

1916 ISSUE

		GOOD	FINE	XF
S942	**1 PESO** 1.4.1916. Black. Seated woman at l., national arms at ctr. Series A. *(MI-OAX-1).*	45.00	90.00	175.00

LA TESORERÍA PROVISIONAL DEL COMERCIO, HUAJUAPÁN

1915 ISSUE

		GOOD	FINE	XF
S943	**5 CENTAVOS** 19.10.1915. Black. 60 x 40mm. *(PI-OAX-12).*	4.00	12.00	25.00
S944	**10 CENTAVOS** ND. Black. 60 x 40mm. *(PI-OAX-13).*	5.00	15.00	30.00
S945	**20 CENTAVOS** ND. Black. 60 x 40mm. *(PI-OAX-14).*	5.00	15.00	30.00

		GOOD	FINE	XF
S946	**50 CENTAVOS** 18.9.1915; 10.5.1915. Black. 60 x 40 mm. *(PI-OAX-15).*	4.00	12.00	25.00

		GOOD	FINE	XF
S947	**1 PESO** 18.9.1915. Black. 60 x 40mm. *(PI-OAX-16).*	5.00	15.00	30.00

LA TESORERÍA GENERAL DEL ESTADO DE OAXACA, NOCHIXTLÁN

1916 ISSUE

#S948 and S949 national arms at l. M. Hidalgo at l. on back.

		GOOD	FINE	XF
S948	**1 PESO** 15.3.1916. Black. Series A1. *(SI-OAX-4).*			
	a. W/o sign.	10.00	20.00	—
	b. Stamped sign. at l., w/o sign. at r.	1.00	3.00	6.00

		GOOD	FINE	XF
S949	**5 PESOS** 15.3.1916. Black. Series O.			
	a. Stamped violet sign. at l., handwritten sign. at r. *(SI-OAX-5).*	4.00	12.00	25.00
	b. 2 stamped violet or blue sign. *(SI-OAX-6).*	.75	2.00	4.00
	r. Remainder. *(SI-OAX-6a).*	1.65	5.00	10.00

GOBIERNO PRECONSTITUCIONAL DEL ESTADO DE OAXACA

DECREE OF APRIL 1, 1916

		GOOD	FINE	XF
S950	**50 CENTAVOS** 1.4.1916. Blue. White pasteboard. 55 x 32mm. *(SI-OAX-26).*	4.00	12.00	25.00
S951	**50 CENTAVOS** 1.4.1916. Blue. Maroon pasteboard. 55 x 32mm. *(SI-OAX-27).*	4.00	12.00	25.00

LA TESORERÍA GENERAL DEL ESTADO DE OAXACA, OAXACA DE JUÁREZ

All denominations of this series display great variety except the 5 centavo note. Ledger paper was commonly used on the 1 through 50 peso notes. There are varieties in the way the name of the printer Julián S. Soto, Oaxaca appears. There are many date changes, color varieties and errors. Progressive proofs exist.

1914 ISSUE

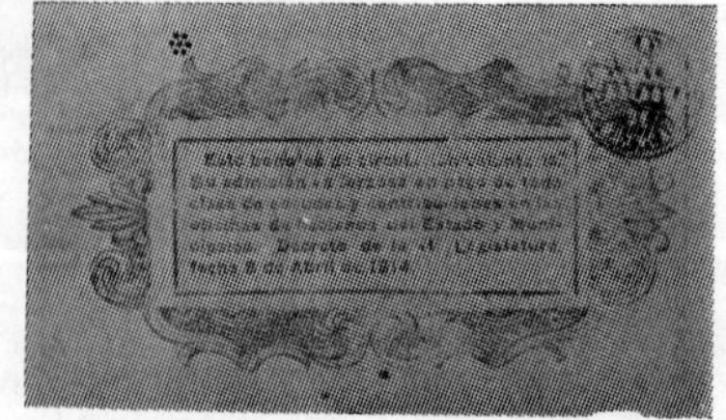

		GOOD	FINE	XF
S952	**5 CENTAVOS** 8.4.1914; May 1914. Black on pink unpt. *(SI-OAX-7).*	30.00	50.00	100.00

DECREES OF 19.2.1915; 10.7.1915; 8.11.1915; 12.1.1916; 18.1.1916

#S953-S955 wreathed head of woman at upper l. Lg. portr. of B. Juárez at l. on back.

		GOOD	FINE	XF
S953	**1 PESO** Various dates ca.1915. Green and red on yellow to ochre and yellow-green to olive-green unpt.			
	a. Series A; D; E; J; P; R; U; Z. *(SI-OAX-8).*	.50	1.50	3.00
	b. Small bust of Juarez.	1.00	3.00	6.00
	c. Blue paper. Series I. 15.11.1915. *(SI-OAX-10).*	1.50	4.00	8.00
	d. Ledger paper. Series A. 3.9.1915.	10.00	30.00	60.00
	e. As d. Series P. 10.8.1915.	10.00	30.00	60.00

		GOOD	FINE	XF
	x. Error: *NU PESO* instead of *UN PESO.* Series P. 24.9.1915. *(SI-OAX-9).*	100.00	350.00	—

		GOOD	FINE	XF
S954	**5 PESOS** Various dates ca.1915-16. Blue and green on orange and yellow unpt. Series A; D; E; I; J; R; U; Y; Z. *(SI-OAX-11).*	.50	1.50	3.00

		GOOD	FINE	XF
S955	**5 PESOS** Various dates ca.1915. Like #S954 but upper serial # above series letter. Sm. portr. Juárez at l. on back. Series J; Z. *(SI-OAX-12).*	2.50	8.00	17.50

		GOOD	FINE	XF
S956	**5 PESOS** ND (ca.1915). Hidalgo at ctr. on back. Back proof. *(SI-OAX-13).*	75.00	150.00	—

#S957-S959 wreathed head of woman at l. Portr. B. Juárez at r. on back.

		GOOD	FINE	XF
S957	**10 PESOS** Various dates ca.1915-16. Blue, maroon, brown, gray, gold on pink unpt.			
	a. Issued note. Series A; D; W; X. *(SI-OAX-14).*	3.50	7.50	15.00
	b. Blue paper. Series A; I. 15.11.1915. *(SI-OAX-15).*	3.50	7.50	15.00
S958	**10 PESOS** Various dates ca.1915. Purple.			
	a. Issued note. *(SI-OAX-16).*	1.50	5.00	10.00
	x. Error: w/o unpt. on back. *(SI-OAX-17).*	5.00	15.00	30.00

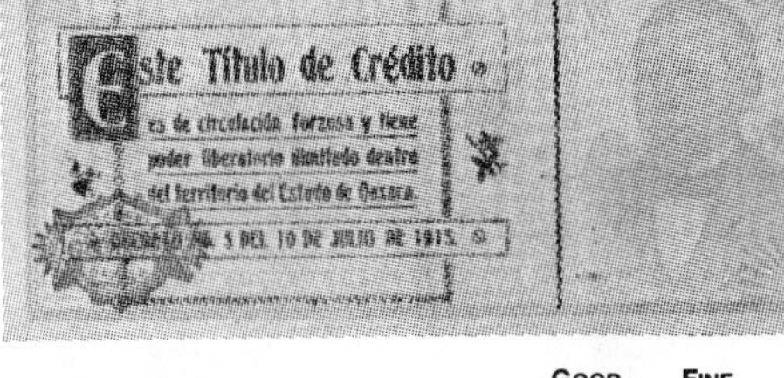

		GOOD	FINE	XF
S959	**20 PESOS** Various dates ca.1915. Green and brown.			
	a. Oil cloth. Series D. *(SI-OAX-19).*	3.50	10.00	20.00
	b. Paper on cloth. Series D; P. *(SI-OAX-20).*	3.50	10.00	20.00
	c. Paper. Series Z. *(SI-OAX-21).*	15.00	35.00	60.00
	d. Paper on cloth. Series Z. *(SI-OAX-21a).*	22.50	45.00	75.00

		GOOD	FINE	XF
S960	**50 PESOS** 10.11.1915. Red, orange and blue. Wreathed head of woman at l. Portr. B. Juárez at l. on back. Series LA; LI. *(SI-OAX-22).*	7.50	15.00	30.00

TESORERÍA PROVISIONAL, TAMAZOLA

1915 ISSUE

		GOOD	FINE	XF
S961	**20 CENTAVOS** 20.7.1915. Pasteboard. Like #S962. *(SI-OAX-28).*	12.50	25.00	—

		GOOD	FINE	XF
S962	**25 CENTAVOS** 20.7.1915. Pasteboard. 54 x 46mm. *(SI-OAX-29).*	12.50	25.00	—

LA TESORERÍA GENERAL, TLAXIACO

DECREE OF JUNE 24, 1916

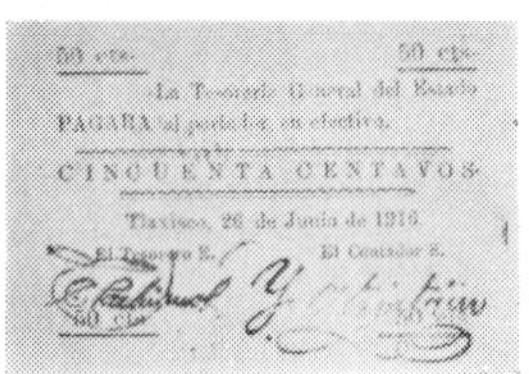

		GOOD	FINE	XF
S963	**50 CENTAVOS** 26.6.1916. Lt. brown thin pasteboard. 83 x 55mm. Series F. *(SI-OAX-30).*			
	a. Issued note.	1.00	3.00	6.00
	r. Remainder w/o handstamped seal on back.	—	—	—

PUEBLA

BANCO ESPAÑOL REFACCIONARIO S.A. / BANCO ORIENTAL DE MÉXICO

1914 ISSUE

#S964-S967 checks payable to bearer w/printed denominations.

		GOOD	FINE	XF
S964	**5 CENTAVOS** 1.7.1914. Blue and brown. 128 x 57mm. *(PI-PUE-10).*	12.50	25.00	42.50
S965	**10 CENTAVOS** 1.7.1914. Brown. *(PI-PUE-11).*	12.50	25.00	42.50
S966	**20 CENTAVOS** 1.7.1914. Brown. *(PI-PUE-12).*	12.50	25.00	42.50
S967	**50 CENTAVOS** 1.7.1914. Black and red on pink paper. Back red. *(PI-PUE-13).*	17.50	35.00	55.00

JUNTA COMERCIAL, CHALCHICOMULA

ND ISSUE

#S968 and S969 coin at l.

		GOOD	FINE	XF
S968	**10 CENTAVOS** ND. Green. Cream pasteboard. 63 x 32mm. *(PI-PUE-6).*	5.00	15.00	30.00
S969	**20 CENTAVOS** ND. Blue. Cream pasteboard. 64 x 32mm. *(PI-PUE-7).*	5.00	15.00	30.00

TESORERÍA DE LA JUNTA COMERCIAL DE CHALCHICOMULA

ND ISSUE

		GOOD	FINE	XF
S970	**50 CENTAVOS** ND. Green and black. Cream paper. *(PI-PUE-2).*	30.00	50.00	100.00
S971	**1 PESO** ND. Brown and black. Cream paper.			
	a. Issued note. *(PI-PUE-3).*	40.00	80.00	150.00
	b. Ovpt: *Revalidado Cincuenta Centavos Papel Infalsificable. (PI-PUE-5).*	30.00	60.00	125.00

DISTRITO DE MATAMOROS

ND ISSUE

#S972-S977 ornate borders face and back.

		GOOD	FINE	XF
S972	**2 CENTAVOS** ND. Violet pasteboard. 55 x 35mm. Series C. *(SI-PUE-13).*	4.00	12.50	25.00
S973	**5 CENTAVOS** ND. Orange pasteboard. 55 x 35mm. *(SI-PUE-14).*	4.00	12.00	25.00
S974	**10 CENTAVOS** ND. Pasteboard. 55 x 35mm. Series B. *(SI-PUE-15).*	4.00	12.00	25.00
S975	**20 CENTAVOS** ND. Green. Yellow pasteboard. 55 x 35mm. Series B; C. *(SI-PUE-16).*	4.00	12.00	25.00
S976	**25 CENTAVOS** ND. Purple pasteboard. 55 x 35mm. Series A-C. *(SI-PUE-17).*	4.00	12.00	25.00

		GOOD	FINE	XF
S977	**50 CENTAVOS** ND. Green pasteboard. 55 x 35mm. Series B. *(SI-PUE-18).*	4.00	12.00	25.00

#S978 ***Deleted.*** **See #S984A.**

#S979-S984A straight line borders on face and back.

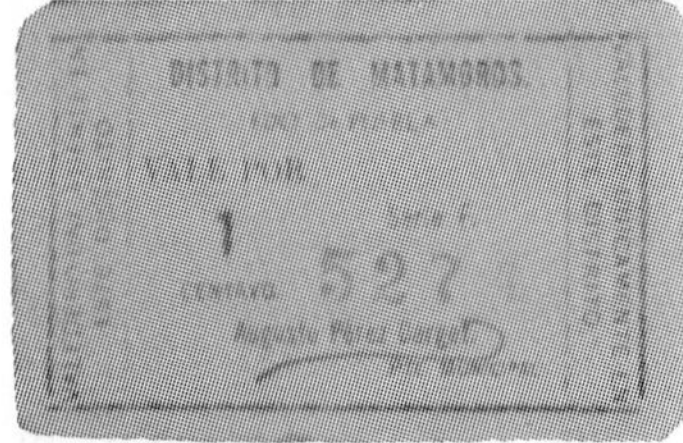

		GOOD	FINE	XF
S979	**1 CENTAVO** ND. Dull yellow, pasteboard. Series F. *(SI-PUE-20).*	4.00	12.50	25.00
S980	**2 CENTAVOS** ND. Gold, tan pasteboard. 65 x 42mm. Series E. *(SI-PUE-21).*	4.00	12.00	25.00
S981	**5 CENTAVOS** ND. Salmon pasteboard. Series D. *(SI-PUE-22).*	4.00	12.00	25.00
S982	**10 CENTAVOS** ND. Pink pasteboard. 65 x 42 mm. Series A. *(SI-PUE-23).*	4.00	12.00	25.00
S983	**20 CENTAVOS** ND. Yellow pasteboard. 65 x 42 mm. Series A. *(SI-PUE-24).*	4.00	12.00	25.00

		GOOD	FINE	XF
S984	**50 CENTAVOS** ND. 65 x 42mm. Series A. *(SI-PUE-25).*			
	a. Lt. green pasteboard.	4.00	12.00	25.00
	b. ND. Gray-type variety pasteboard.	4.00	12.00	25.00
S984A	**1 PESO** ND. White pasteboard. 55 x 35mm. Series B; C. *(SI-PUE-19).*	5.00	15.00	30.00

BRIGADA SERDAN

1914-15 ISSUE

		GOOD	FINE	XF
S984B	50 CENTAVOS 5.12.1914. Black on lt. gold unpt. Arms at ctr. Back aqua. Series A.	—	—	—
S984C	50 CENTAVOS 14.3.1915. Black on green unpt. Arms at ctr.	—	—	—

CUARTEL GENERAL DEL EJÉRCITO CONSTITUCIONALISTA DE LA SIERRA NORTE DE PUEBLA

ND ISSUE

		GOOD	FINE	XF
S985	5 CENTAVOS ND. *(SI-PUE-20).*	15.00	35.00	60.00

QUERETARO

LA ADMINISTRACION GENERAL DE RENTAS DEL ESTADO

1924 ISSUE

		GOOD	FINE	XF
S985A	2 PESOS 1924. Black on blue security paper. Arms in red at ctr. on back.	20.00	50.00	90.00

SAN LUIS POTOSÍ

EJÉRCITO CONSTITUCIONALISTA

ND ISSUE

#S986-S989 Liberty w/flags at ctr.

		GOOD	FINE	XF
S986	5 CENTAVOS ND. Orange. Red pasteboard. *(MI-SAN-4).*	4.00	12.00	25.00
S987	10 CENTAVOS ND. Blue. White pasteboard. *(MI-SAN-5).*	4.00	12.00	25.00
S988	20 CENTAVOS ND. Blue. Gray pasteboard. *(MI-SAN-6).*	4.00	12.00	25.00
S989	50 CENTAVOS ND. Yellow. Orange pasteboard. *(MI-SAN-7).*	1.50	5.00	10.00

SINALOA

EJÉRCITO CONSTITUCIONALISTA, CUERPO DE EJÉRCITO DEL NOROESTE, CULIACÁN

CONSTITUTIONALIST ARMY OF THE NORTHWEST

1914 ISSUE

#S990-S993 national arms at l. Printed sign. of Alvaro Obregon and handwritten sign. of Francisco Serrano.

		GOOD	FINE	XF
S990	5 PESOS 23.4.1914. Black. *(MI-SIN-1).*	17.50	35.00	—
S991	10 PESOS 23.4.1914. Black. *(MI-SIN-2).*	20.00	50.00	—
S992	20 PESOS 23.4.1914. Black. *(MI-SIN-3).*	20.00	50.00	—
S993	50 PESOS 23.4.1914. Black. *(MI-SIN-4).*	20.00	50.00	—

1914 COMANDANCIA ISSUE

#S994-S999 national arms at l. Seal on back.

		GOOD	FINE	XF
S994	50 CENTAVOS 1.5.1914. *(MI-SIN-5).*	25.00	60.00	—
S995	1 PESO 1.5.1914. Brown.			
	a. Issued note. *(MI-SIN-6).*	20.00	50.00	—
	b. Ovpt: *AMORTIZADO. (MI-SIN-7).*	20.00	50.00	—

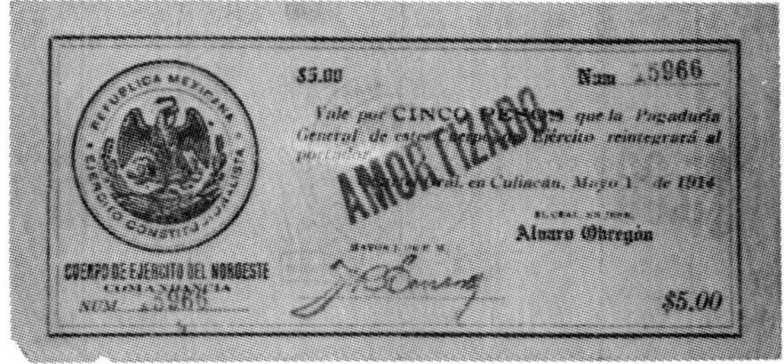

		GOOD	FINE	XF
S996	5 PESOS 1.5.1914. Black.			
	a. Issued note. *(MI-SIN-8).*	10.00	20.00	50.00
	b. Ovpt: *AMORTIZADO. (MI-SIN-9).*	10.00	20.00	50.00
S997	10 PESOS 1.5.1914. Orange. *(MI-SIN-10).*	10.00	20.00	50.00
S998	20 PESOS 1.5.1914. Dk. pink. *(MI-SIN-11).*	12.50	25.00	60.00

		GOOD	FINE	XF
S999	50 PESOS 1.5.1914. Blue.			
	a. Issued note. *(MI-SIN-12).*	12.50	25.00	60.00
	b. Ovpt: *AMORTIZADO. (MI-SIN-13).*	12.50	25.00	60.00

ESTADO DE SINALOA, CULIACÁN

DECREE NO. 17 OF DECEMBER 13, 1913

#S1000-S1002 national arms at l. Printed sign. of Felipe Riveros and José G. Heredia.

		GOOD	FINE	XF
S1000	1 PESO 13.12.1913. Orange. Series C. Ovpt: *AMORTIZADO. (SI-SIN-1).*	5.00	20.00	40.00

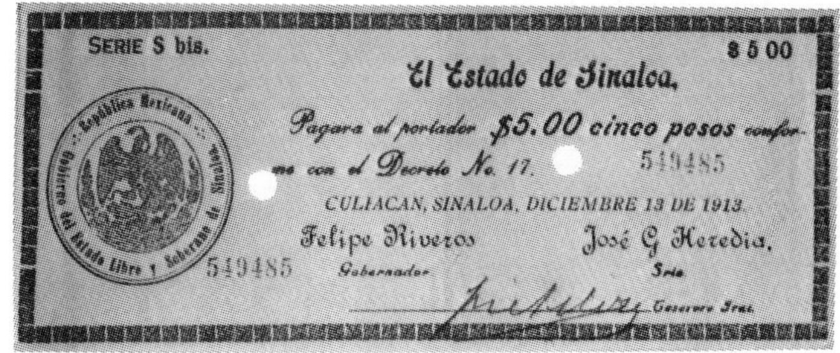

		GOOD	FINE	XF
S1001	5 PESOS 13.12.1913. Blue. Series G; P; S; W; Y. *(SI-SIN-2).*	4.00	17.50	35.00
S1002	10 PESOS 13.12.1913. Black. Series L; T; U. *(SI-SIN-3).*	5.00	17.50	35.00

DECREE NO. 2 OF APRIL 15, 1915

#S1003 and S1004 national arms at ctr.

		GOOD	FINE	XF
S1003	5 CENTAVOS 15.4.1915. Brown pasteboard. 50 x 30mm. *(SI-SIN-4).*	4.00	15.00	30.00

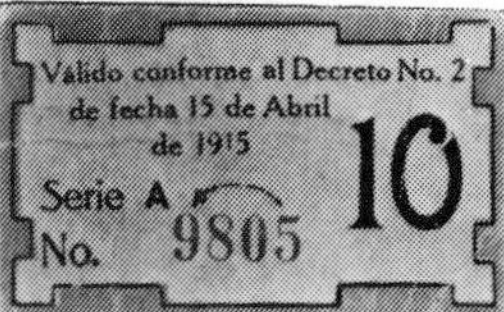

		GOOD	FINE	XF
S1004	10 CENTAVOS 15.4.1915. Green pasteboard. 50 x 30mm. Series A. *(SI-SIN-5).*	4.00	15.00	30.00

ESTADO DE SINALOA, MAZATLÁN

1916 FIRST ISSUE

#S1005 and S1006 seated Mercury w/globe at ctr.

		GOOD	FINE	XF
S1005	1 PESO 1.7.1916. Dk. blue and gray. Series A. Red text on back, green unpt. *(SI-SIN-10).*	20.00	45.00	100.00
S1006	2 PESOS 1.7.1916. Brown and gray. Series B. Blue text on back, green unpt. *(SI-SIN-12).*	20.00	50.00	110.00

1916 SECOND ISSUE

#S1007 and S1008 seated Mercury w/globe at ctr.

		GOOD	FINE	XF
S1007	1 PESO 15.8.1916. Purple and gray. *(SI-SIN-11).*	20.00	45.00	100.00
S1008	2 PESOS 15.8.1916. Purple and gray on white. *(SI-SIN-13).*	37.50	75.00	—

EL GOBIERNO CONSTITUCIONALISTA DEL TERRITORIO DE TEPIC YDEL ESTADO DE SINALOA, ROSARIO

1913 ISSUE

#S1009-S1014 handwritten sign., uniface.

		GOOD	FINE	XF
S1009	10 CENTAVOS Oct. 1913. Black on brown unpt. 145 x 86 mm. Series A. *(MI-SIN-23).*	60.00	125.00	—
S1010	20 CENTAVOS Oct. 1913. Series A. *(MI-SAN-24).*	60.00	125.00	—
S1011	50 CENTAVOS Oct. 1913. Series C. *(MI-SIN-25).*	60.00	125.00	—

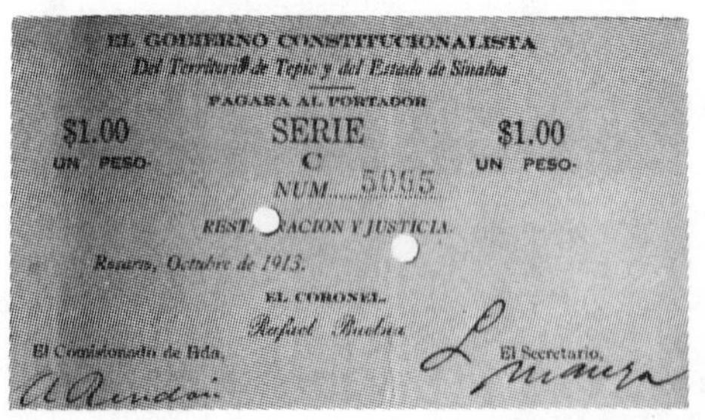

		GOOD	FINE	XF
S1012	1 PESO Oct. 1913. Black on brown. 153 x 83 mm. Series C. *(MI-SIN-26).*	40.00	80.00	—
S1013	5 PESOS Oct. 1913. Series C. *(MI-SIN-27).*	60.00	125.00	—
S1014	20 PESOS Oct. 1913. Series C. *(MI-SIN-28).*	60.00	125.00	—

A word on pricing

When a note is marked RARE in the price columns, this note seldom appears on the market, or few are known in private hands. When dashes are in the price column, means that the note has not traded on the open market recently and a definitive value could not accurately be determined. Rare does not always mean expensive. A dashed price does not mean expensive or rare.

LA PAGADURÍA GRAL. DE LA BRIGADA DE SINALOA

LAW OF 19 AUGUST 1914

#S1015-S1021 national arms at upper ctr. Printer: Imprenta Moderna-Mazatlan.

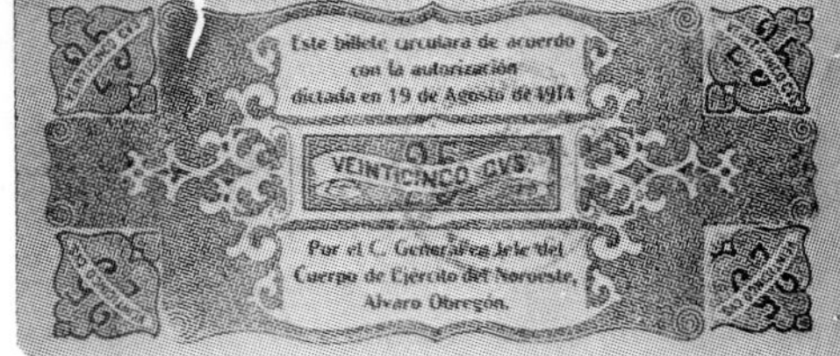

		GOOD	FINE	XF
S1015	25 CENTAVOS 21.8.1914. Black. Series A. *(MI-SIN-15).*	15.00	30.00	60.00

		GOOD	FINE	XF
S1016	50 CENTAVOS 21.8.1914. Black. Series A.			
	a. Issued note. *(MI-SIN-16).*	17.50	35.00	—
	b. Ovpt: *AMORTIZADO. (MI-SIN-17).*	15.00	30.00	—
S1017	1 PESO 21.8.1914.Black on pink unpt. Series A-C.			
	a. Issued note. *(MI-SIN-18).*	1.50	5.00	12.00
	b. Ovpt. for Mazatlan and *Retirado de la Circulacion.*	1.50	5.00	12.00
	c. Ovpt: *JEFATURA DE HACIENDA MAZATLAN.*	1.50	5.00	12.00
S1018	5 PESOS 21.8.1914. Blue on orange unpt. Series A-C. *(MI-SIN-19).*	2.00	6.00	15.00
S1019	10 PESOS 21.8.1914. Red on pale blue unpt. Series A; C. *(MI-SIN-20).*	3.50	10.00	20.00
S1020	20 PESOS 21.8.1914. Blue. Series A; B. *(MI-SIN-21).*	10.00	30.00	60.00

		GOOD	FINE	XF
S1021	50 PESOS 21.8.1914. Orange and black on lt. green unpt. Series A. *(MI-SIN-22).*	10.00	30.00	60.00

LA TESORERÍA GENERAL DEL ESTADO DE SINALOA

1914 ISSUE

#S1022-S1025 national arms on back.

		GOOD	FINE	XF
S1022	**10 CENTAVOS**			
	25.2.1914. Green. Series C. *(SI-SIN-6)*.	3.00	9.00	17.50
S1023	**20 CENTAVOS**			
	25.2.1914. Blue-green. Series B. *(SI-SIN-7)*.	3.00	9.00	17.50
S1024	**50 CENTAVOS**			
	25.2.1914. Black on pale orange unpt. Series A. *(SI-SIN-8)*.	2.00	6.00	12.00

		GOOD	FINE	XF
S1025	**50 CENTAVOS**			
	10.4.1914. Black on pale orange unpt. Series B. *(SI-SIN-9)*.	1.50	4.50	9.00

ESTADO DE SINALOA, SAN BLAS

DECREE NO. 3 OF JULY 13, 1913

#S1026-S1030 national arms at l. Printed sign. of Felipe Riveros and Felipe Dassart and two handwritten sign.

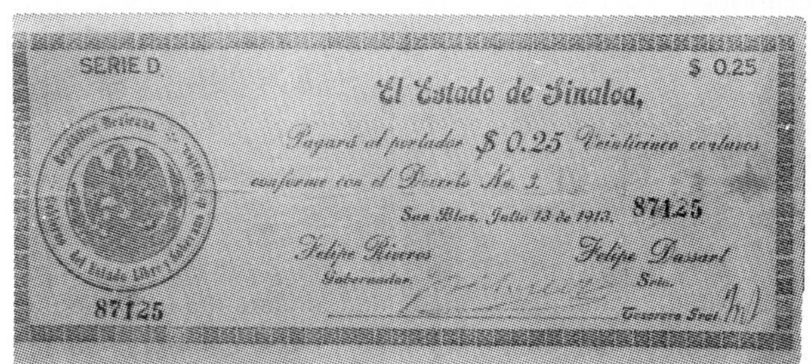

		GOOD	FINE	XF
S1026	**25 CENTAVOS**			
	13.7.1913. Black. Series O. *(SI-SIN-14)*.	25.00	50.00	—
S1027	**50 CENTAVOS**			
	13.7.1913. Black. Series D.			
	a. Issued note. *(SI-SIN-15)*.	20.00	45.00	—
	b. Ovpt: *AMORTIZADO*. *(SI-SIN-16)*.	15.00	35.00	—

		GOOD	FINE	XF
S1028	**1 PESO**			
	13.7.1913. Orange on cream. Series R. *(SI-SIN-17)*.	25.00	50.00	—
S1029	**5 PESOS**			
	13.7.1913. Blue on cream. Series C. *(SI-SIN-18)*.	20.00	55.00	—
S1030	**10 PESOS**			
	13.7.1913. Series C. *(SI-SIN-19)*.	20.00	45.00	—

DECREE NO. 11 OF SEPTEMBER 15, 1913

#S1031-S1035 national arms at l. Printed sign. of Felipe Riveros and Fidencio E. Schmidt and two handwritten sign.

		GOOD	FINE	XF
S1031	**25 CENTAVOS**			
	15.9.1913. Black. Series F. *(SI-SIN-20)*.	15.00	35.00	—

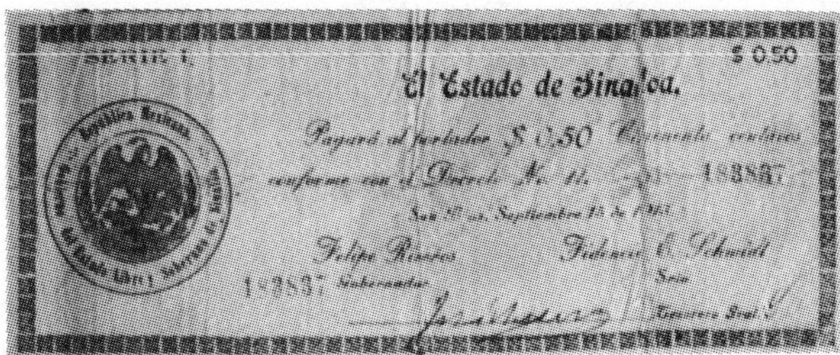

		GOOD	FINE	XF
S1032	**50 CENTAVOS**			
	15.9.1913. Series I. *(SI-SIN-21)*.	15.00	40.00	—
S1033	**1 PESO**			
	15.9.1913. *(SI-SIN-22)*.	15.00	40.00	—

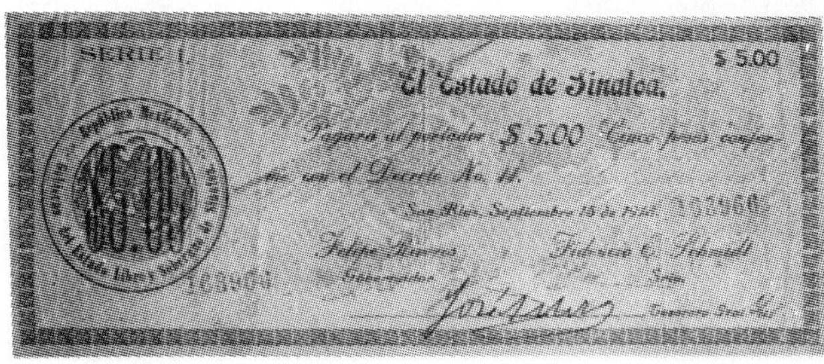

		GOOD	FINE	XF
S1034	**5 PESOS**			
	15.9.1913. Blue on pale orange unpt. Series I. *(SI-SIN-23)*.	15.00	40.00	—
S1035	**10 PESOS**			
	15.9.1913. Series G. *(SI-SIN-24)*.	15.00	40.00	—

DECREE NO. 14 OF OCTOBER 23, 1913

#S1036-S1039 national arms at l. Printed sign. of Felipe Riveros and Fidencio E. Schmidt, and one or two handwritten sign.

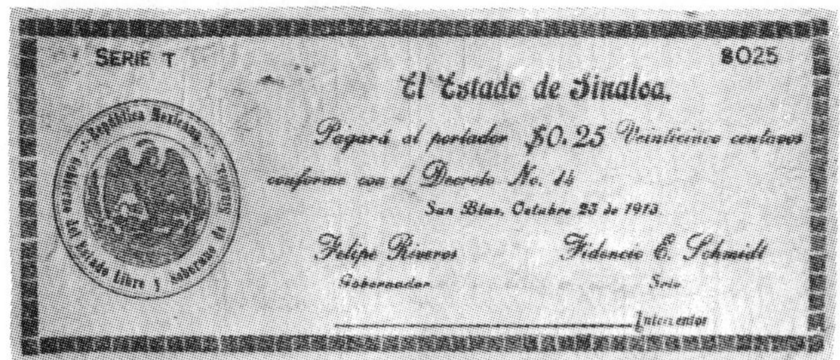

		GOOD	FINE	XF
S1036	**25 CENTAVOS**			
	23.10.1913. Black.			
	a. Sign. title: *Interventor*. Series T. *(SI-SIN-25)*.	12.50	25.00	45.00
	b. Sign. title: *Tesoreria Gral.* Series N. *(SI-SIN-26)*.	12.50	25.00	45.00

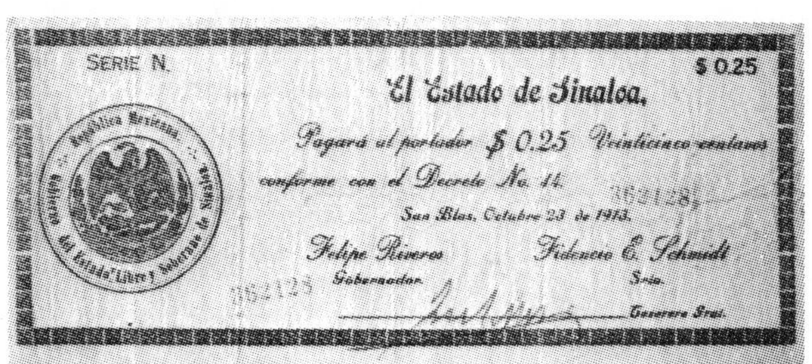

		GOOD	FINE	XF
S1037	**50 CENTAVOS**			
	23.10.1913. Black.			
	a. Sign. title: *Interventor*. *(SI-SIN-27)*.	25.00	50.00	—
	b. Sign. title: *Tesoreria Gral.* Series Y. *(SI-SIN-28)*.	12.00	25.00	40.00
S1038	**1 PESO**			
	23.10.1913. Orange on cream. sign. title: *Tesoreria Gral.* Series Z. *(SI-SIN-29)*.	12.00	25.00	40.00
S1039	**5 PESOS**			
	23.10.1913. Blue and brown on red unpt. Sign. title: *Tessoreria Gral.* Series V. *(SI-SIN-30)*.	12.00	25.00	40.00
S1040	**10 PESOS**			
	23.10.1913. Black on green unpt. Series U. *(SI-SIN-31)*.	12.00	25.00	40.00

EL ESTADO LIBRE Y SOBERANO DE SINALOA

DECREE OF FEBRUARY 22, 1915

#S1041-S1048 portr. B. Juárez at l., portr. F. I. Madero at r. Circular violet treasury handstamp on back. Printer: Britton & Rey, San Francisco, California.

		VG	VF	UNC
S1041	**25 CENTAVOS**			
	D.1915. Black on tan unpt. Back lt. green. Series A; C; D; F; H; I. *(SI-SIN-32)*.	1.00	3.50	9.00

		VG	VF	UNC
S1042	**50 CENTAVOS** *D.1915.* Black on lt. blue unpt. Back orange. Series A; C-J. *(SI-SIN-33).*	1.00	3.50	9.00
S1043	**1 PESO** *D.1915.* Black on pale purple unpt. Back tan. Series A-J.			
	a. W/blue circular treasury seal of Sinaloa on back. Series A; B; C. *(SI-SIN-34).*	1.00	3.50	11.00
	b. Typewritten ovpt. on back: *Esta Emisión se cangeará en su oportunidad por emisión constitucionalista. P. O. del Gral. J.D.E.M.* and handwritten sign of R. Dominguez. *(SI-SIN-35).*	10.00	20.00	—
	c. W/o blue circular treasury seal of *SINALOA* on back. Series B; D; E; F; G; H; I; J.	1.00	3.00	9.00
S1044	**5 PESOS** *D.1915.* Black on pale yellow-orange unpt. Back dull red.			
	a. 2 printed sign. Series A; C; D; E; G; H; J. *(SI-SIN-36).*	1.50	4.00	12.00

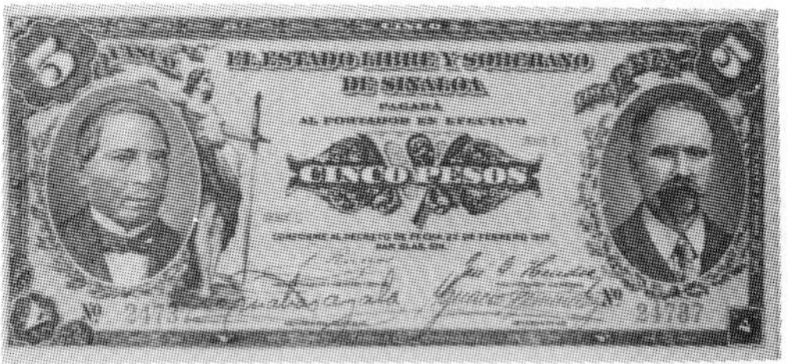

		VG	VF	UNC
	b. 2 printed sign. and 2 handwritten sign. Treasury ovpt: *SINALOA* at r. on back. Series A; C; D; E; G; J. *(SI-SIN-37).*	6.00	15.00	—
	c. Handwriting on back: *Este billete . . . P.O. del Gral. J.D.E.M.* and handwritten sign. of R. Dominguez. Series H. *(SI-SIN-38).*	10.00	20.00	—
	r. Unsigned remainder. Series F.	2.50	5.00	12.00

NOTE: #S1044a Series H exists w/printed narrow serial # and handstamped wide serial #.

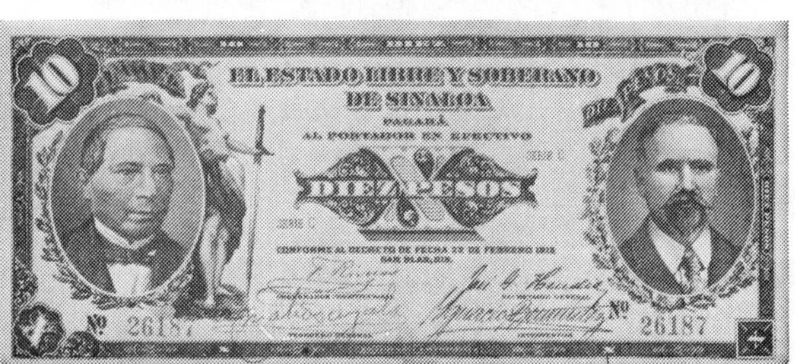

		VG	VF	UNC
S1045	**10 PESOS** *D.1915.* Black on pale green unpt. Back deep blue.			
	a. 2 printed sign. *(SI-SIN-39).*	1.50	5.00	15.00
	b. 2 printed sign. and 2 handwritten sign. Treasury ovpt: *SINALOA* at r. on back. Series A; C; D; E. *(SI-SIN-40).*	6.00	15.00	—
	c. Typewritten ovpt: *Esta emisión se cangerá en su oportunidad por emisión constitucionalista. P. O. del Gral. J.D.E.M.* and handwritten sign. of R. Dominguez on back. *(SI-SIN-41).*	10.00	20.00	—
	r. Unsigned remainder. Series F. Punch hole cancelled.	3.00	10.00	20.00

#S1046-S1048 w/4 printed sign. w/2 additional blue control # sideways.

		VG	VF	UNC
S1046	**20 PESOS** *D.1915.* Black on yellow unpt. Back deep olive-green. 4 sign. Series E; F; G; J. *(SI-SIN-42).*	7.50	15.00	30.00
S1047	**50 PESOS** *D.1915.* Black on brown and yellow unpt. Back dull purple. Series D; E; I. *(SI-SIN-43).*			
	a. Issued note.	7.50	15.00	30.00
	r. Remainder, w/o serial #. Punch hole cancelled.	4.00	10.00	20.00
S1048	**100 PESOS** *D.1915.* Black on pink unpt. Back lt. brown. Series O. *(SI-SIN-44).*	37.50	75.00	125.00

PAGADURÍA GENERAL DE LA BRIGADA DE SINALOA, SAN BLAS

DECREE OF SEPTEMBER 15, 1913

		GOOD	FINE	XF
S1049	**25 CENTAVOS** 1913. *(MI-SIN-29).*	25.00	50.00	—
S1050	**50 CENTAVOS** 1913. *(MI-SIN-30).*	20.00	40.00	—
S1051	**1 PESO** 1913. *(MI-SIN-31).*	25.00	50.00	—
S1052	**5 PESOS** 1913. *(MI-SIN-32).*	25.00	50.00	—

DECREE OF OCTOBER 15, 1913

		GOOD	FINE	XF
S1053	**50 CENTAVOS** ND. *(MI-SIN-33).*	25.00	50.00	—
S1054	**1 PESO** ND. *(MI-SIN-34).*	25.00	50.00	—

MÉXICO (ESTADO DE)

1914 ISSUE

		GOOD	FINE	XF
S1055	**10 CENTAVOS** 1.4.1914. Black on orange unpt. Uniface. Series G. *(SI-SON-8).*	10.00	20.00	—

SONORA

LA JEFATURA DE HACIENDA, GUAYMAS

1914 ISSUE

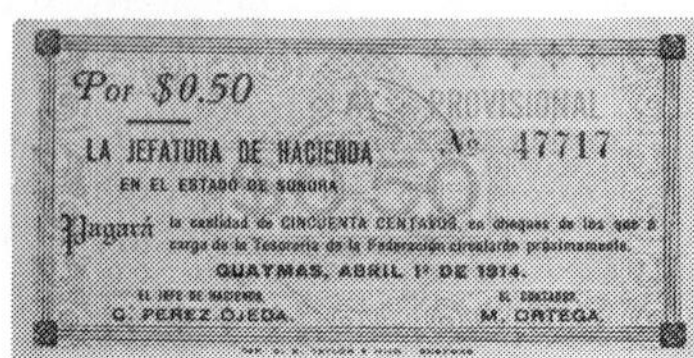

		GOOD	FINE	XF
S1056	**50 CENTAVOS** 1.4.1914. Black on green unpt. Uniface.			
	a. Issued note. *(SI-SON-9a).*	1.50	4.00	12.00
	b. *"A"* before *PROVISIONAL* in unpt. *(SI-SON-9A).*	3.00	6.00	20.00
S1057	**1 PESO** 1.4.1914. Black on brown unpt.			
	a. Issued note. *(SI-SON-10).*	1.50	4.00	12.00
	b. *"A"* before *PROVISIONAL* in unpt. *(SI-SON-10A).*	3.00	6.00	20.00
	c. Handstamped seal *Division del Yaqui, General en Jefe. (SI-SON-10B).*	3.00	6.00	20.00

LA TESORERÍA DE LA FEDERACIÓN, GUAYMAS

LAW OF SEPTEMBER 6, 1913

#S1058-S1061 national arms at upper r. Harbor scene at ctr. on back. W/ or w/o stamped sign. or revalidation hand stamps on back.

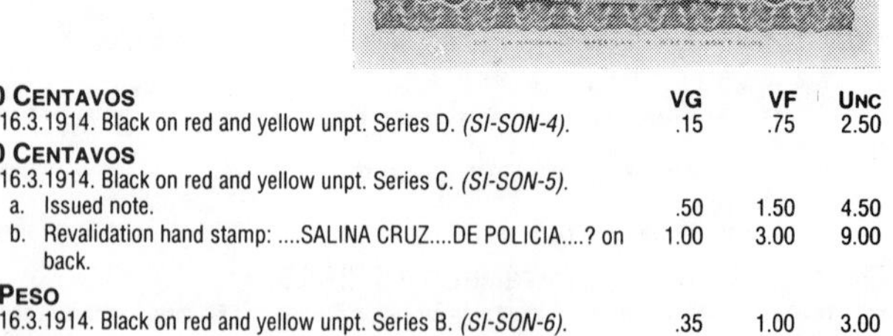

		VG	VF	UNC
S1058	**10 CENTAVOS** 16.3.1914. Black on red and yellow unpt. Series D. *(SI-SON-4).*	.15	.75	2.50
S1059	**50 CENTAVOS** 16.3.1914. Black on red and yellow unpt. Series C. *(SI-SON-5).*			
	a. Issued note.	.50	1.50	4.50
	b. Revalidation hand stamp: ....SALINA CRUZ....DE POLICIA....? on back.	1.00	3.00	9.00
S1060	**1 PESO** 16.3.1914. Black on red and yellow unpt. Series B. *(SI-SON-6).*	.35	1.00	3.00
S1061	**2 PESOS** 16.3.1914. Black on red and yellow unpt. Series A. *(SI-SON-7).*	.35	1.00	3.00

EL ESTADO DE SONORA, HERMOSILLO

DECREES NO. 13 OF AUGUST 27, 1913 AND NO. 40 OF FEBRUARY 12, 1914

VALIDATION HAND STAMPS:

Different series, w/ or w/o seals. The 5 and 10 peso notes are hand signed. This series bears resellos on the 5 and 10 peso denominations as follows:

1. DISTRITO DE GUAYMAS, RIO YAQUI, SONORA.
2. FUERZAS DEL ESTADO DE SONORA, DETALL, GENERAL.
3. ADUANA MARITIMA DE GUAYMAS, ADMINISTRACION.
4. EJÉRCITO CONSTITUCIONALISTA - COMANDANCIA
5. ADUANA FRONTERIZA DE NOGALES, SON. IADMINISTRACIONI FEB 14 1915. MILITAR, LA PAZ, B. CFA.

#S1062 and S1063 state seal at upper l.

		VG	VF	UNC
S1062	**5 CENTAVOS** *L.1913-14.* Black on pale green unpt. *(SI-SON-11).*	6.00	12.00	20.00
S1063	**10 CENTAVOS** *L.1913-14.* Black on red unpt. Similar to #S1062. *(SI-SON-12).*	15.00	30.00	50.00

DECREE NO. 13 OF AUGUST 27, 1913

#S1064-S1068 printer: Imp. del Estado.

#S1064 and S1065 state seal at upper l. w/2 sign. varieties.

A. W/o series. W/sign. *Augustín Lewels* w/title: *EL. CONT. E. DE LA TRIA. GRAL.*
B. Series 1-4. W/sign. *Carlos E. Randall* w/title: *EL TESORERO GENERAL.*

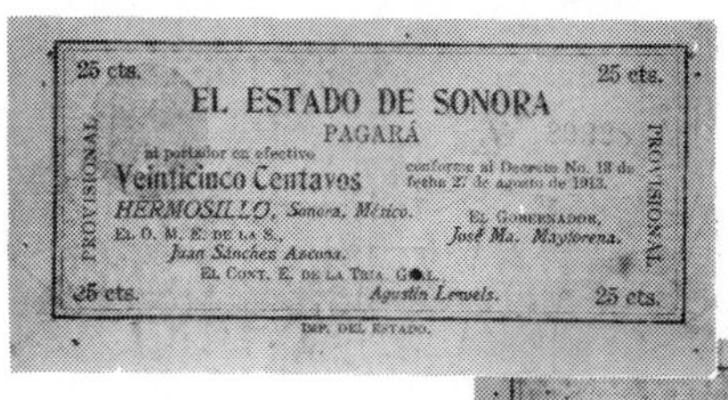

		GOOD	FINE	XF
S1064	**25 CENTAVOS** *L.1913.* Black on brown unpt. Back brown and green.			
	a. Face plate 117 x 50mm. W/o series. Sign. A. Back plate 118 x 50mm. W/35mm gov't seal. *(SI-SON-).*	17.50	35.00	60.00
	b. W/o series. *(SI-SON-13).*	15.00	30.00	50.00
	c. Series 2.	15.00	30.00	50.00
	d. Series 3.	15.00	30.00	50.00

		GOOD	FINE	XF
	e. Face plate 122 x 53mm. Series 4. Sign. B. Back plate 121 x 53mm. W/39mm gov't seal. *(SI-SON-13).*	15.00	30.00	50.00
	r. Remainder. Series 4. W/o oval seal or serial #. *(SI-SON-16).*	5.00	12.00	20.00
S1065	**50 CENTAVOS** *L.1913.* Black on green unpt. Back green.			
	a. W/o series. Sign. A. *(SI-SON-).*	17.50	35.00	60.00
	b. Series 2-4. Sign. B. *(SI-SON-15).*	15.00	30.00	50.00

		GOOD	FINE	XF
	r. Remainder. Series 4. W/o oval seal or serial #. *(SI-SON-16).*	5.00	12.00	20.00

		GOOD	FINE	XF
S1066	**1 PESO** *L.1913.* Black on pale yellow-orange unpt. w/blue-gray oval seal.			
	a. W/o series. Handwritten sign. *(SI-SON-17).*	2.00	6.00	12.00
	b. Series 2. W/38mm govt. seal.			
	c. Series 3. Sign. B. W/35mm or 38mm gov't. seal. *(SI-SON-17).*	2.00	6.00	12.00
	d. Series 4. Sign. B. W/38mm gov't. seal. *(SI-SON-17).*	2.00	6.00	12.00
	r. Remainder. Series 4. W/o oval seal or serial #. *(SI-SON-18).*	5.00	12.00	20.00

		GOOD	FINE	XF
S1067	**5 PESOS** *L.1913.* Black on pale blue unpt.			
	a. W/o series. Sign. A. *(SI-SON-19).*	5.00	12.00	20.00
	b. Series 2. Sign. B. W/35mm gov't. seal. *(SI-SON-19).*	5.00	12.00	20.00
	c. Series 3 or 4. W/35mm gov't. seal. Red 4th sign. title: *INTERVENTOR* at lower l. *(SI-SON-19).*	5.00	12.00	20.00

		GOOD	FINE	XF
	d. Series 4. W/38mm seal. Red 4th sign. title: *INTERVENTOR* at lower l. *(SI-SON-19).*	5.00	12.00	20.00

S1068 10 PESOS	GOOD	FINE	XF
L.1913. Black on pink unpt., handwritten sign.			
a. W/o series, sign. A. *(SI-SON-).*	9.00	17.50	30.00
b. Series 1. *(SI-SON-20).*	7.50	15.00	25.00
c. Series 2. Sign. B. W/35mm gov't. seal. *(SI-SON-20).*	7.50	15.00	25.00

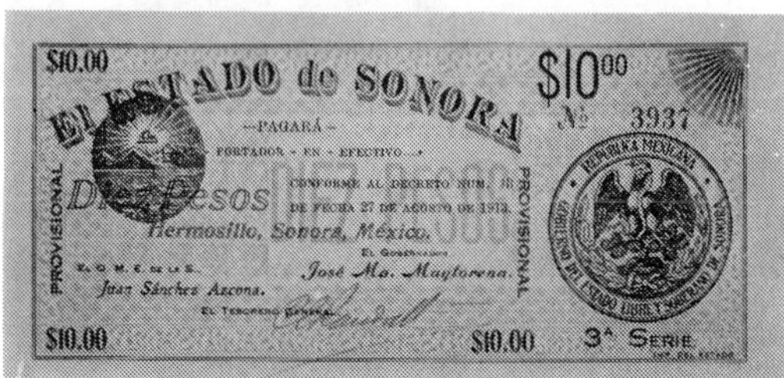

d. Series 2; 3. Sign. B. W/38mm gov't. seal. *(SI-SON-20).*	4.00	9.00	15.00
e. Series 4. W/35mm gov't. seal. 4th sign. title: *INTERVENTOR* at r. *(SI-SON-20).*	4.00	9.00	15.00

f. Series 4. W/38mm gov't. seal. 4th sign. title: *INTERVENTOR* at r. *(SI-SON-20).*	7.50	15.00	25.00

NOTE: #S1068d Series 2 also exists w/*PROVSIONAL* or *PROVIISIONAL* (errors) at l.

DECREE NO. 13 OF AUGUST 27, 1913

#S1069-S1076 portr. F. I. Madero at l., portr. J. M. Pino Suárez at r. Printer: ABNC.

	VG	VF	UNC
S1069 25 CENTAVOS 1.1.1915. Black. Printed sign. Back green. Series A-J. *(SI-SON-21).*	.50	1.00	3.00
S1070 50 CENTAVOS 1.1.1915. Black. Printed sign. Series A-J. *(SI-SON-22).*	.50	1.00	3.00
S1071 1 PESO 1.1.1915. Black on pale yellow unpt. Printed sign. Series B; C; D-I. *(SI-SON-23).*	.50	1.50	4.50
S1072 5 PESOS 1.1.1915. Black on pale blue unpt. Printed sign. Series C-L. *(SI-SON-24).*	.50	1.50	4.50
S1073 10 PESOS 1.1.1915. Black on pink unpt. Printed sign. Series A-J. *(SI-SON-25).*	1.00	3.00	9.00

S1074 20 PESOS	VG	VF	UNC
1.3.1915. Black on pale green unpt.			
a. 2 printed and 2 handwritten sign.	5.00	15.00	30.00
r. Remainder w/2 printed sign. Series L; M; N. *(SI-SON-26).*	4.00	12.00	25.00
s. Specimen, perforated hole cancelled. Series N.	—	—	250.00
S1075 50 PESOS			
1.3.1915. Black on lilac unpt.			
a. 2 printed and 2 handwritten sign.	37.50	75.00	150.00
r. Remainder w/2 printed sign. Series L; N. *(SI-SON-27).*	30.00	60.00	120.00
S1076 100 PESOS			
1.3.1915. Black on pale pink and blue unpt.			
a. 2 printed and 2 handwritten sign.	30.00	60.00	120.00
r. Remainder w/2 printed sign. Series L-N. *(SI-SON-28).*	25.00	50.00	100.00

DECREE NO. 70 OF APRIL 16, 1915

S1077 5 CENTAVOS	VG	VF	UNC
D.1915. Black on pink unpt. Back red.			
a. Issued note. *(SI-SON-29).*	3.00	6.00	12.00
b. W/o seal or serial #. *(SI-SON-30).*	1.50	3.00	6.00

S1078 10 CENTAVOS	VG	VF	UNC
D.1915. Black on blue unpt.			
a. Issued note. *(SI-SON-31).*	2.50	5.00	10.00
a. W/o seal or serial #. *(SI-SON-32).*	1.50	3.00	6.00

TABASCO

LA TESORERÍA GENERAL DEL ESTADO DE TABASCO, SAN JUAN BAUTISTA

1914 ISSUE

	GOOD	FINE	XF
S1078A 20 CENTAVOS 22.5.1914. Series J; S. *(SI-TAB-4).*	80.00	160.00	—
S1078B 50 CENTAVOS 22.5.1914. *(SI-TAB-5).*	80.00	160.00	—

DECREE OF MARCH 22, 1915

	GOOD	FINE	XF
S1079 20 CENTAVOS Mar. 1915. Black on pink or blue unpt. Series D. *(SI-TAB-6).*	17.50	35.00	60.00
S1080 50 CENTAVOS Mar. 1915. Black on gray. *50* at ctr. Series F. *(SI-TAB-7).*	24.00	48.00	80.00
S1081 50 CENTAVOS Mar. 1915. Black. *50* at each side. Series J. *(SI-TAB-8).*	22.50	45.00	75.00

TAMAULIPAS

EJÉRCITO CONSTITUCIONALISTA DE MÉXICO, TAMPICO

1914 ISSUE

		Good	Fine	XF
S1082	**20 Pesos** 6.7.1914. Black on pink unpt. National arms at l. Series B.			
	a. Issued note. *(MI-TAM-6).*	50.00	100.00	—
	b. Ovpt: *AMORTIZADO. (MI-TAM-7).*	40.00	80.00	—

La Caja de la Brigada Caballero, Tampico

1914 Issue

		Good	Fine	XF
S1083	**50 Centavos** 6.6.1914. Black on green unpt. Back dk. blue; eagle at ctr. Series A.			

		Good	Fine	XF
	a. Issued note. *(MI-TAM-3).*	75.00	175.00	—
	b. Ovpt: *AMORTIZADO. (MI-TAM-4).*	60.00	150.00	—

		Good	Fine	XF
S1084	**1 Peso** 6.6.1914. Green unpt. Back blue; small eagle in oval at ctr. Series A. *(MI-TAM-5).*	60.00	150.00	250.00

Tlaxcala

Distrito de Morelos

ND Issue

		Good	Fine	XF
S1085	**5 Centavos** ND. Red and black on dk. blue unpt. Ceres (Goddess of Agriculture) seated w/plow at l. ctr. Series A. *(SI-TLA-1).*	—	—	450.00

		Good	Fine	XF
S1086	**20 Centavos** ND. Green and blue on cream. Girl w/cattle at l. ctr. Series A. *(SI-TLA-2).*	—	—	450.00

		Good	Fine	XF
S1087	**50 Centavos** ND. Dk. brown pasteboard. Locomotive at ctr. Series A. *(SI-TLA-3).*	—	—	450.00

La Tesorería Municipal de Ciudad Tlaxcala

1914 Issue

		Good	Fine	XF
S1088	**5 Centavos** 1.10.1914. *(SI-TLA-4).*	75.00	150.00	250.00

		Good	Fine	XF
S1089	**10 Centavos** 25.8.1914. *(SI-TLA-5).*	75.00	150.00	—

		Good	Fine	XF
S1090	**20 Centavos** 1.10.1914. *(SI-TLA-6).*	75.00	150.00	—

Veracruz

Gobierno Constitucionalista del Estado Libre y Soberano de Veracruz-Llave

ND First Issue

		VG	VF	Unc
S1091	**5 Centavos** ND. Pink pasteboard. Portr. F. Madero at ctr. Arms at ctr. on back. Series B; F. *(MI-VER-8).*	2.00	4.00	8.00

		VG	VF	Unc
S1092	**10 Centavos** ND. Blue pasteboard. Portr. B. Juárez at ctr. Arms at ctr. on back. Series K. *(MI-VER-9).*	2.00	4.00	8.00

		VG	VF	Unc
S1093	**20 Centavos** ND. Yellow pasteboard. Portr. M. Hidalgo at ctr. Arms at ctr. on back. Series S. *(MI-VER-10).*	2.00	4.00	8.00

ND SECOND ISSUE

		VG	VF	UNC
S1094	**5 CENTAVOS** ND. Pink pasteboard. Portr. F. Madero at ctr. Arms at ctr. on back. *(MI-VER-11).*	1.00	3.00	5.00

		VG	VF	UNC
S1095	**10 CENTAVOS** ND. Blue pasteboard. Portr. B. Juárez at r. Arms at ctr. on back. *(MI-VER-12).*	1.00	3.00	5.00

		VG	VF	UNC
S1096	**20 CENTAVOS** ND. Yellow pasteboard. Portr. M. Hidalgo at ctr. Arms at ctr. on back. *(MI-VER-13).*	1.00	3.00	5.00

GOBIERNO PROVISIONAL DE MÉXICO, VERACRUZ

The following series of notes pertains to those issued by Venustiano Carranza when he retreated from Mexico City during the first days of December, 1914, due to pressure from the Conventionist Government and established the capital of his Constitucionalist Government in Veracruz (see Distrito Federal listings).

DECREE OF 19.9.1914

#S1097-S1115 seated Liberty at l., national arms w/Popocatepetl and Ixtaccihuatl (volcanoes) in background at ctr. Peso coins at ctr. on back.

		GOOD	FINE	XF
S1097	**1 PESO** 1.12.1914. Brown on pale green unpt. Small number *1's* in corners. Series A. *(MI-VER-14).*	25.00	50.00	—
S1098	**1 PESO** 1.12.1914. Black on lt. brown unpt. Flat base *1's* w/rhombus in corners. Series A.			
	a. Issued note. *(MI-VER-15).*	1.25	4.00	12.00
	b. Ovpt: *Michoacán de Ocampo, Retirado.*	1.75	5.00	15.00

		GOOD	FINE	XF
S1099	**1 PESO** 1.12.1914. Black on lt. brown unpt. Flat base *1's* on both sides. Series A. *(MI-VER-16).*	.75	2.50	7.50
S1100	**1 PESO** 1.12.1914. Black on lt. brown unpt. Flat base *1's* on face and curved *1's* on back. Series A *(MI-VER-17).*	1.75	5.00	15.00

		GOOD	FINE	XF
S1101	**1 PESO** 5.2.1915. Black on ochre unpt. Curved based *1's* in corners. Series A.			
	a. Issued note. *(MI-VER-18).*	.50	1.00	2.25
	b. Ovpt: *Michoacán de Ocampo, Tesorería General/Retirado (MI-VER-23).*	1.00	3.00	9.00
	c. Blank back w/seal. *(MI-VER-21).*	4.00	12.00	35.00

		GOOD	FINE	XF
	d. Ovpt: *Administración de Rentas de Jalapa/Retirado de la Circulación. (MI-VER-).*	2.00	6.00	17.50
	e. Ovpt: *Retirado de la Circulación. (MI-VER-18).*	1.00	4.00	8.00
	f. Vertical ovpt: *VERACRUZ* at l. and r.	—	—	—

		GOOD	FINE	XF
S1102	**2 PESOS** 5.2.1915. Brown. Straight based *2's* in denomination. Series G.			
	a. Tan unpt. *(MI-VER-24).*	2.50	7.50	22.50
	b. Yellow-brown unpt. *(MI-VER-25).*	12.50	25.00	50.00
	c. Straight based *2's* in denomination. Green unpt. *(MI-VER-26).*	25.00	50.00	—
	d. Ovpt: *Ret. de la Circulación. (MI-VER-29).*	1.25	4.00	12.00
	e. Ovpt: *Michoacán de Ocampo Tesorería General Retirado. (MI-VER-30).*	2.00	6.00	17.50

		GOOD	FINE	XF
S1103	**2 PESOS** 5.2.1915. Black on yellow unpt. Curved based *2's* in denomination. Back lt. blue-green. Series G.			
	a. Issued note. *(MI-VER-27).*	.50	1.00	2.25
	b. Back blank w/seal. *(MI-VER-28).*	12.50	25.00	50.00

		GOOD	FINE	XF
S1104	**5 PESOS** 1.12.1914. Dk. green unpt. Lg. *5's* in denomination on back. Series B.			
	a. Issued note. *(MI-VER-31).*	.50	1.00	2.25
	b. Ovpt: *Yucatán, GOBIERNO Constitucionalista. (MI-VER-33).*	10.00	20.00	—
	c. Ovpt: *Jefatura de Hacienda Queretaro. (MI-VER-34).*	1.75	5.00	15.00
	d. Ovpt: *Ga. Jefatura de Hda. Guadalajara. (MI-VER-35).*	1.75	5.00	15.00
S1105	**5 PESOS** 1.12.1914. Sm. *5's* in denomination on back. Series B.			
	a. Issued note. *(MI-VER-32).*	1.25	4.00	12.00
	b. Ovpt: *Yucatán, GOBIERNO Constitucionalista. (MI-VER-33).*	10.00	20.00	—
	c. Ovpt: *Jefatura de Hacienda Querétaro. (MI-VER-34).*	1.75	5.00	15.00
	d. Ovpt: *Ga. Jefatura de Hda Guadalajara. (MI-VER-35).*	1.75	5.00	15.00
S1106	**10 PESOS** 1.12.1914. Black on brown and yellow unpt. Sm. *10* at r. Series C. *(MI-VER-36).*	30.00	60.00	—

S1107 10 PESOS

		GOOD	FINE	XF
	1.12.1914. Back brown. Lg. *10* at r. Series C.			
a.	*C* or *D* serial # suffix. *(MI-VER-37).*	.50	1.00	2.25
b.	4 punched hole cancellation and purple hand stamp: *CANCELADO* on a.	.50	1.00	2.25

S1108 10 PESOS

		GOOD	FINE	XF
	1.12.1914. Back purple. Series C.			
a.	Issued note. *(MI-VER-38).*	.75	2.00	6.00
b.	Ovpt: *Gto. Jefatura Superior de Hacienda - Estado de Guanajuato. (MI-VER-39).*	1.75	5.00	15.00
c.	Ovpt: *Yucatán, GOBIERNO Constitucionalista. (MI-VER-40).*	1.00	3.00	9.00
d.	Ovpt: *Toluca. (MI-VER-41).*	2.50	8.00	25.00
e.	Ovpt: *Jefatura de Hacienda, Querétaro. (MI-VER-42).*	1.75	5.00	15.00
f.	Ovpt: *Ga Jefatura de Hda Guadalajara. (MI-VER-43).*	.75	2.00	6.00
g.	Ovpt: *Tabasco, Jefatura de Hacienda - Resellado. (MI-VER-44).*	2.00	6.00	17.50
h.	Ovpt: *Mich. de Ocampo, Jefatura de Hacienda - Resellado. (MI-VER-45).*	2.00	6.00	17.50
i.	Ovpt: *Mich. de Ocampo Tesorería General Retirado.*	2.00	6.00	17.50

S1109 20 PESOS

	GOOD	FINE	XF
1.12.1914. Straight based *2's* in corners. Series D. *(MI-VER-46).*	30.00	60.00	100.00

S1110 20 PESOS

		GOOD	FINE	XF
	1.12.1914. Deep gray on dull olive-brown unpt. w/*VEINTE PESOS* repeated. Curved based *2's* in corners. Back blue-gray. Printer: México Oficina del Gobierno. Series D.			
a.	Olive unpt. *(MI-VER-47).*	.25	.75	2.25
b.	Brown unpt. in pattern w/o wording.	1.65	5.00	15.00
c.	Ovpt: *Ebano, S.L.P.* (series) *C//Rgto. de Cab. Gral. José Cavazos.*	2.50	7.50	22.50

S1111 20 PESOS

		GOOD	FINE	XF
	1.12.1914. Black on brown and yellow unpt. Semi-straight based *2's* in corners. Back blue. Printer: Oficina del Gobierno. Series D.			
a.	Issued note. *(MI-VER-48).*	.50	1.50	4.50
b.	Ovpt: *Yucatán, GOBIERNO Constitucionalista. (MI-VER-51).*	1.75	5.00	15.00
c.	Ovpt: *Campeche, Eduardo Morales. (MI-VER-52).*	1.75	5.00	15.00
d.	Ovpt: *Jefatura Superior de Hacienda. Estado de Guanajuato. (MI-VER-53).*	1.75	5.00	15.00
e.	Ovpt: *Jfra. de Hda. Guadlajara. (MI-VER-54).*	2.50	8.00	25.00
f.	Ovpt: *Michoacán de Ocampo, Tesorería General Retirado. (MI-VER-55).*	2.50	8.00	25.00
g.	Ovpt: *Michoacán de Ocampo, Amortizado. (MI-VER-56).*	12.00	25.00	50.00
h.	Ovpt: *Jefatura de Hacienda, Querétaro. (MI-VER-57).*	2.50	8.00	25.00

S1112 20 PESOS

		GOOD	FINE	XF
	1.12.1914. Semi-straight based *2's* in corners. Green unpt. Blue back. Series D.			
a.	Issued note. *(MI-VER-49).*	1.75	5.00	15.00
b.	Ovpt: *Yucatán, GOBIERNO Constitucionalista. (MI-VER-51).*	1.75	5.00	15.00
c.	Ovpt: *Campeche, Eduardo Morales. (MI-VER-52).*	1.75	5.00	15.00
d.	Ovpt: *Jefatura Superior de Hacienda. Estado de Guanajuato. (MI-VER-53).*	1.75	5.00	15.00
e.	Ovpt: *Jfra. de Hda. Guadalajara. (MI-VER-54).*	3.00	9.00	27.00
f.	Ovpt: *Michoacán de Ocampo, Retirado. (MI-VER-55).*	3.00	9.00	27.00
g.	Ovpt: *Michoacán de Ocampo, Amortizado. (MI-VER-56).*	12.00	24.00	—
h.	Ovpt: *Jefatura de Hacienda, Querétaro. (MI-VER-57).*	2.00	6.00	18.00

S1113 20 PESOS

		GOOD	FINE	XF
	1.12.1914. Semi-straight *2's*. Pink back. Series D.			
a.	Issued note. *(MI-VER-50).*	2.00	6.00	18.00
b.	Ovpt: *Yucatán, GOBIERNO Constitucionalista. (MI-VER-51).*	1.75	5.00	15.00
c.	Ovpt: *Campeche, Eduardo Morales. (MI-VER-52).*	1.75	5.00	15.00
d.	Ovpt: *Jefatura Superior de Hacienda. Estado de Guanajuato. (MI-VER-53).*	1.75	5.00	15.00
e.	Ovpt: *Jfra. de Hda. Guadalajara. (MI-VER-54).*	3.00	9.00	27.00
f.	Ovpt: *Michoacán de Ocampo, Retirado. (MI-VER-55).*	3.00	9.00	27.00
g.	Ovpt: *Michoacán de Ocampo, Amortizado. (MI-VER-56).*	12.00	25.00	—
h.	Ovpt: *Jefatura de Hacienda, Querétaro. (MI-VER-57).*	2.00	6.00	17.50

S1114 50 PESOS

		GOOD	FINE	XF
	1.12.1914. Series E.			
a.	Issued note. *(MI-VER-58).*	1.00	3.00	9.00
b.	Ovpt: *Yucatán. Gobierno Constitucionalista. (MI-VER-61).*	3.00	9.00	27.00
c.	Ovpt: *Jefatura de Hda. Guadalajara. (MI-VER-62).*	12.00	24.00	—
r.	W/o date, sign. or series. *(MI-VER-59).*	25.00	50.00	—

S1115 100 PESOS

		GOOD	FINE	XF
	1.12.1914. Series E: F.			
a.	Series E. *(MI-VER-63).*	.50	1.50	4.50
b.	Ovpt: *Yucatán, GOBIERNO Constitucionalista. (MI-VER-66).*	1.00	3.00	9.00
c.	Series F. *(MI-VER-65).*	1.75	5.00	15.00
d.	As c. Ovpt: *Yucatán. (MI-VER-67).*	7.50	15.00	—
e.	W/o date, sign. and series. Back w/o seals. *(MI-VER-64).*	17.50	35.00	70.00
f.	As c. Ovpt: *TEZIUTLAN.*	5.00	12.50	—

TESORERÍA GENERAL DEL ESTADO DE VERACRUZ LLAVE

DECREE OF JUNE 1, 1915

#S1116-S1119 national arms at lower ctr.

		GOOD	FINE	XF
S1116	**1 PESO** ND. Series A. *(SI-VER-9).*	45.00	90.00	—
S1117	**5 PESOS** ND. Series A. *(SI-VER-10).*	45.00	90.00	—
S1118	**10 PESOS** ND. Series A. *(SI-VER-11).*	55.00	110.00	—
S1119	**20 PESOS** ND. Pasteboard. Series A. *(SI-VER-12).*	65.00	135.00	225.00

Yucatán

Comisión Reguladora del Mercado de Henequén y la Tesorería General del Estado

1914 First Issue

#S1120 and S1121 crowned state arms at l., sisal harvesting at r. National arms at ctr. on back.

S1120 20 Centavos	Good	Fine	XF
27.7.1914. Brown. Back blue. *(PI-YUC-5).*			
a. Needle punched *CAMPECHE.* Series A.	2.50	8.00	25.00
b. Series A; B; e; F; G; H; I; J.	2.50	8.00	25.00

S1121 50 Centavos	Good	Fine	XF
27.7.1914. Black on orange, pink and yellow unpt. Back pink. Series A; C; F; G; H; I; J; K; M; N; O; P.			
a. Issued note. *(PI-YUC-6).*	1.50	5.00	15.00

	Good	Fine	XF
b. Black ovpt: *ORO NACIONAL* on back. *(PI-YUC-7).*	17.50	35.00	60.00
c. As b. w/red-violet hand stamp: *JEFATURA DE HACIENDA MERIDA RESELLADO.*	30.00	60.00	100.00

1914 Second Issue

S1122 1 Peso	Good	Fine	XF
20.11.1914. Black, green and pink. Yucatan woman at l., worker at r. Back brown; coin at ctr. Series A.			
a. Needle punched *CAMPECHE* vertically at r. *(PI-YUC-8A). (PI-YUC-8).*	2.50	8.00	25.00
b. W/o needle punched *CAMPECHE. (PI-YUC-8).*	32.50	65.00	—

S1123 5 Pesos	Good	Fine	XF
20.11.1914. Black and green. National arms at l. ctr. Back green. Series A.			
a. Issued note. *(PI-YUC-10).*	2.50	8.00	25.00
b. Red ovpt: *ORO NACIONAL* on back. *(PI-YUC-11).*	37.50	75.00	—

S1124 20 Pesos	Good	Fine	XF
20.11.1914. Black on yellow and brown. Government bldg. at l., sisal harvesting at r. Back blue. Series B; C; D.			
a. Issued note. *(PI-YUC-12).*	1.50	4.50	9.00

	Good	Fine	XF
b. Ovpt: *ORO NACIONAL* on back. *(PI-YUC-13).*	65.00	130.00	—

	Good	Fine	XF
c. Red ovpt: *Resellado por la Comisión Reguladora del Mercado de Henequén. Mérida, April 25, 1915* on back. *(PI-YUC-14).*	3.00	6.50	15.00

1915 Issue

S1125 100 Pesos	Good	Fine	XF
1.3.1915. Black on orange and yellow unpt. Portr. M. Hidalgo at l. Back brown-violet; gateway at ctr. Series A; B; G. *(PI-YUC-15).*	2.00	6.00	20.00

Bono de Caja, Mérida

1916 Issue

S1126 20 Pesos	Good	Fine	XF
9.5.1916. Green unpt. Bldg. at ctr. Back gold. Series F.			
a. Issued note. *(PI-YUC-17).*	225.00	500.00	850.00
r. Remainder w/o seal. *(PI-YUC-17A).*	120.00	275.00	500.00

DECREE NO. 536 OF MAY 9, 1916

		GOOD	FINE	XF
S1127	**100 PESOS** 9.5.1916. Brown on tan unpt. Portr. B. Juárez above national arms at ctr. National arms at ctr. on back. Series G. *(PI-YUC-19).*	150.00	400.00	—

GOBIERNO CONSTITUCIONALISTA DE YUCATÁN, TESORERÍA GENERAL

ND ISSUE

#S1128-S1130 state arms at ctr. on back.

		GOOD	FINE	XF
S1128	**1 CENTAVO** ND. Gray or pink pasteboard. 50 x 27mm. *(SI-YUC-10).*	3.00	9.00	27.00

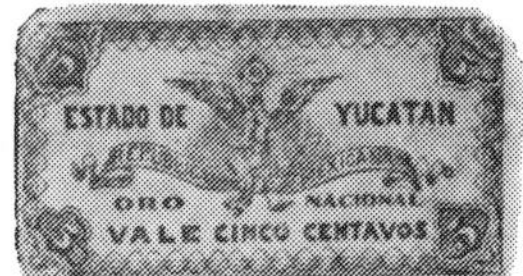

		GOOD	FINE	XF
S1129	**5 CENTAVOS** ND. Red or pink pasteboard. 50 x 27mm. *(SI-YUC-11).*	1.75	5.00	15.00

		GOOD	FINE	XF
S1130	**10 CENTAVOS** ND. Cream pasteboard. 50 x 27 mm. *(SI-YUC-12).*	1.75	5.00	15.00

ND TRANSITORIO ISSUE

#S1131-S1133 national arms at ctr. on back.

		GOOD	FINE	XF
S1131	**5 CENTAVOS** ND. Red pasteboard. 52 x 30mm. *(SI-YUC-13).*	1.00	3.00	9.00

		GOOD	FINE	XF
S1132	**10 CENTAVOS** ND. Gray pasteboard. 52 x 30mm. *(SI-YUC-14).*	1.00	3.00	9.00
S1133	**20 CENTAVOS** ND. Lt. brown pasteboard. 52 x 30mm. *(SI-YUC-15).*	1.00	4.00	12.00

TESORERÍA GENERAL DEL ESTADO

DECREE NO. 550 OF MAY 23, 1916

		GOOD	FINE	XF
S1134	**50 CENTAVOS** 26.5.1916. Brown on orange unpt. Palm tree and hut at ctr. Back pale gold; figures at ctr. *(SI-YUC-1).*	3.50	15.00	60.00

		GOOD	FINE	XF
S1135	**1 PESO** 23.5.1916. Dk. brown. Bldg. at ctr. Back green; Maya ruins at ctr. Series A. *(SI-YUC-2).*	2.00	6.00	15.00

		GOOD	FINE	XF
S1136	**2 PESOS** 23.5.1916. Dk. brown on green unpt. Portr. Maya Indian at ctr. Back blue. Series B. *(SI-YUC-4).*	1.00	4.00	10.00

DECREE NO. 559 OF MAY 22, 1916

		GOOD	FINE	XF
S1137	**5 PESOS** 22.5.1916. Seated Euthenia (Goddess of Plenty) at l. *(SI-YUC-5).*	20.00	40.00	75.00

		GOOD	FINE	XF
S1138	**10 PESOS** 22.5.1916. Portr. F. Madero at ctr. National arms at ctr. on back. Series D. *(SI-YUC-7).*	4.00	12.00	35.00

ZACATECAS

LA COMISIÓN REGULADORA DEL COMERCIO DE ZACATECAS

ND ISSUE

		GOOD	FINE	XF
S1139	**10 CENTAVOS** ND. Brown pasteboard. Ovpt: *INFALSIFICABLE.*	3.00	9.00	27.00

		Good	Fine	XF
S1140	**20 Centavos** ND. Pasteboard.	5.00	12.50	37.50

		Good	Fine	XF
S1141	**50 Centavos** ND. Pasteboard.	5.00	12.50	37.50
S1142	**1 Peso** ND. Gray pasteboard. Ovpt: *INFALSIFICABLE.*	5.00	12.50	37.50

Gobierno Provisional de Zacatecas

ND Issue

		VG	VF	Unc
S1143	**5 Centavos** ND. Black on pink pasteboard. Arms at ctr.	1.00	2.00	3.00

		VG	VF	Unc
S1144	**10 Centavos** ND. Black on gray pasteboard.	.75	2.00	6.00

		VG	VF	Unc
S1145	**20 Centavos** ND. Black on lt. brown pasteboard.	2.00	6.00	17.50

La Pagaduría General de la Brigada Avila, Jérez

1915 Issue

		Good	Fine	XF
S1146	**25 Centavos** 15.8.1915. Ledger paper. Series R. *(MI-ZAC-1).*	35.00	75.00	150.00

		Good	Fine	XF
S1147	**50 Centavos** 15.8.1915. Ledger paper. Series R. *(MI-ZAC-2).*	35.00	75.00	150.00

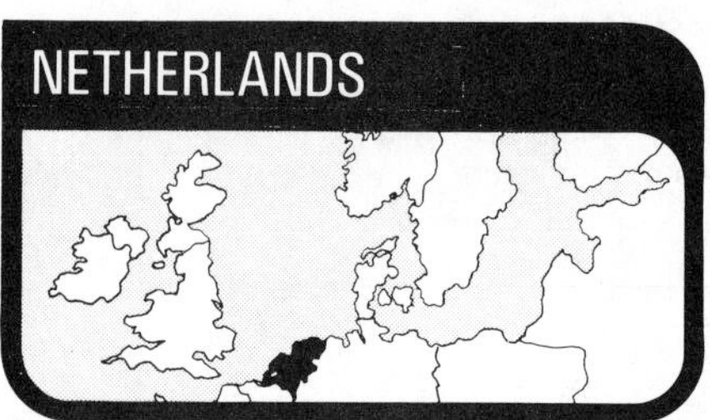

The Kingdom of the Netherlands, a country of western Europe fronting on the North Sea and bordered by Belgium and Germany, has an area of 15,770 sq. mi. (40,844 sq. km.) and a population of 15.87 million. Capital: Amsterdam, but the seat of government is at The Hague. The economy is based on dairy farming and a variety of industrial activities. Chemicals, yarns and fabrics, and meat products are exported.

After being a part of Charlemagne's empire in the 8th and 9th centuries, the Netherlands came under the control of Burgundy and the Austrian Hapsburgs, and finally were subjected to Spanish domination in the 16th century. Led by William of Orange, the Dutch revolted against Spain in 1568. The seven northern provinces formed the Union of Utrecht and declared their independence in 1581, becoming the Republic of the United Netherlands. In the following century, the "Golden Age" of Dutch history, the Netherlands became a great sea and colonial power, a patron of the arts and a refuge for the persecuted. In 1814, all the provinces of Holland and Belgium were merged into the Kingdom of the United Netherlands under William I. The Belgians withdrew in 1830 to form their own kingdom, the last substantial change in the configuration of European Netherlands. German forces invaded in 1940 and the royal family fled to England where a government in exile was formed. German High Commissioner Arthur Seyss-Inquart was placed in command until 1945 when the arrival of Allied military forces ended the occupation. Reigning since 1948, in 1981 Queen Juliana abdicated in favor of her daughter, Beatrix.

RULERS:

Spanish, until 1581
Juliana, 1948-1981

MONETARY SYSTEM:

1 Gulden = 20 Stuivers
1 Gulden = 100 Cents, to 2001

Siege

Leyden

Besieged by Spanish forces in 1574. Coinage dies were used to make these pieces which were stamped out of pressed paper from prayer books. Exist w/ or w/o countermark of a lion in small oval.

1574 Issue

		Good	Fine	XF
S101	**5 Stuiver** 1574. Crowned lion w/shield and sword. Legend: *PUGNO PRO PATRIA* (I fight for my country). Legend on back: *LUGDUNUM BATAVORUM.* 30mm.			
	a. W/o countermark.	—	200.00	425.00
	b. W/countermark.	—	225.00	500.00
S102	**14 Stuiver** 1574.	—	—	—
S103	**16 Stuiver** 1574.	—	—	—
S104	**18 Stuiver** 1574.	—	—	—
S105	**20 Stuiver** 1574. Crowned lion w/Liberty hat on lance. Legend: *HAEC LIBERTATIS ERGO* (This is sustained in behalf of Liberty). Legend on back: *GODT BEHOEDE LEYDEN.* 37mm.	—	—	—

		Good	Fine	XF
S106	**20 Stuiver** 1574. Crowned lion w/standard. Legend on back: *GOD BEHOEDE LEYDEN* (May God protect Leyden) around city arms.			
	a. W/o countermark.	—	—	—
	b. W/countermark.	—	—	—

		GOOD	FINE	XF
S107	**28 STUIVER** 1574. Lion w/shield and sword. Legend on back: *GOTT BEHOEDE LEYDEN* within wreath border.	—	—	—

		GOOD	FINE	XF
S108	**30 STUIVER** 1574. Lion w/sword and shield, crown above. Legend: *HAEC LIBERTATIS ERG.* Legend on back: *GOTT BEHOEDE LEYDEN* above city arms.			
	a. W/o countermark.	—	—	—
	b. W/countermark.	—	—	—

Netherlands Indies (now Indonesia) comprised Sumatra and adjacent islands, Java with Madura, Borneo (except for Sabah, Sarawak and Brunei), Celebes with Sangir and Talaud Islands, and the Moluccas and Lesser Sunda Islands east of Java (excepting the Portuguese half of Timor and the Portuguese enclave of Oe-Cusse). Netherlands New Guinea (now Irian Jaya) was ceded to Indonesia in 1962. The Dutch colonial holdings formed an archipelago of more than 13,667 islands spread across 3,000 miles (4,824 km.) in southeast Asia. The area is rich in oil, rubber, timber and tin.

Portuguese traders established posts in the East Indies in the 16th century, but they were soon outnumbered by the Dutch VOC (United East India Company) who arrived in 1602 and gradually established themselves as the dominant colonial power. Dutch dominance, interrupted by British incursions during the Napoleonic Wars, established the Netherlands Indies as one of the richest colonial possessions in the world.

RULERS:

United East India Company, 1602-1799
Batavian Republic, 1799-1806
Louis Napoleon, King of Holland, 1806-1811
British Administration, 1811-1816
Kingdom of the Netherlands, 1816-1942

MONETARY SYSTEM:

Dutch:
1 Rijksdaalder = 48 Stuivers = 0.60 Ducatoon
1 Gulden = 120 Duits = 100 Cents 1854-
British:
1 Spanish Dollar = 66 Stuivers
1 Java Rupee = 30 Stuivers

DUTCH ADMINISTRATION

VERENIGDE OOSTINDISCHE COMPAGNIE

UNITED EAST INDIA COMPANY

1703 CREDIT LETTER ISSUES

		GOOD	FINE	XF
S50	**5 RIJKSDAALDERS** 15.10.1703.	—	Rare	—
S51	**10 RIJKSDAALDERS** 15.10.1703.	—	Rare	—
S52	**15 RIJKSDAALDERS** 15.10.1703.	—	Rare	—
S53	**20 RIJKSDAALDERS** 15.10.1703.	—	Rare	—
S54	**50 RIJKSDAALDERS** 15.10.1703.	—	Rare	—

1704 CREDIT LETTER ISSUES

		GOOD	FINE	XF
S55	**15 RIJKSDAALDERS** 1704.	—	Rare	—

1795 CREDIT LETTER ISSUES

		GOOD	FINE	XF
S56	**1 RIJKSDAALDER** 26.4.1796.	—	Rare	—
S57	**5 RIJKSDAALDERS** 29.12.1795.	—	Rare	—
S58	**10 RIJKSDAALDERS** 29.12.1795.	—	Rare	—
S59	**15 RIJKSDAALDERS** 29.12.1795.	—	Rare	—

1796 CREDIT LETTER ISSUES

		GOOD	FINE	XF
S60	**1 RIJKSDAALDER** 2.4.1799.	—	Rare	—
S61	**5 RIJKSDAALDERS** 2.4.1799.	—	Rare	—
S62	**15 RIJKSDAALDERS** 2.4.1799.	—	Rare	—

1782 BATAVIA ISSUE

#S101-S108 brown ribbed paper. Dutch and Malay-Arabic text.

		GOOD	FINE	XF
S101	**25 RIJKSDAALDERS** 27.12.1782.	—	Rare	—
S102	**50 RIJKSDAALDERS** 27.12.1782.	—	Rare	—
S103	**100 RIJKSDAALDERS** 27.12.1782.	—	Rare	—
S104	**200 RIJKSDAALDERS** 27.12.1782.	—	Rare	—
S105	**300 RIJKSDAALDERS** 27.12.1782.	—	Rare	—
S106	**400 RIJKSDAALDERS** 27.12.1782.	—	Rare	—
S107	**500 RIJKSDAALDERS** 27.12.1782.	—	Rare	—
S108	**1000 RIJKSDAALDERS** 27.12.1782.	—	Rare	—

Former #S111-S120 have been re-listed as S126-S135.

1805 Amboina Issue

		Good	Fine	XF
S120	50 Rijksdaalders 30.4.1805.	—	Rare	—

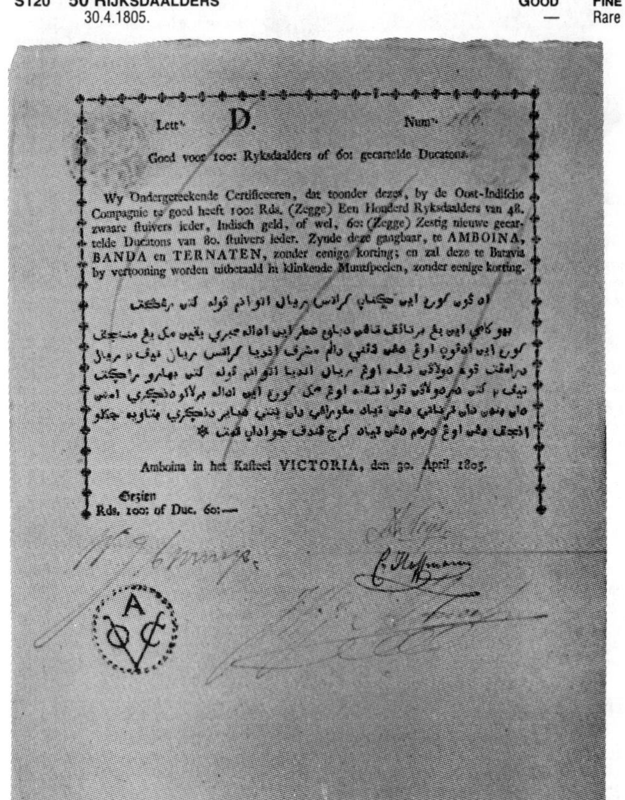

		Good	Fine	XF
S121	100 Rijksdaalders 30.4.1805.	—	Rare	—
S122	100 Rijksdaalders Handwritten text and value.	—	Rare	—
S123	200 Rijksdaalders 30.4.1805.	—	Rare	—
S124	500 Rijksdaalders 30.4.1805.	—	Rare	—
S125	1000 Rijksdaalders 30.4.1805.	—	Rare	—

1809 Amboina Issue

		Good	Fine	XF
S126	5 Rijksdaalders 29.3.1809 (- old date 27.7.1808).	—	Rare	—
S127	10 Rijksdaalders 29.3.1809 (- old date 27.7.1808).	—	Rare	—

1805 Amboina Issue

		Good	Fine	XF
S128	20 Rijksdaalders 29.3.1809 (- old date 27.7.1808).	—	Rare	—

Gouvernement General

1807-09 Issue

#S131-S133 hand stamp: *V.E.I.C.* in bale mark.

		Good	Fine	XF
S129	2 Rijksdaalders 13.3.1809.	125.00	350.00	850.00
S130	5 Rijksdaalders 27.3.1807.	—	Rare	—

1811 Lentemmand Issue

		Good	Fine	XF
S131	2 Rijksdaalders 1811.	—	Rare	—
S132	3 Rijksdaalders 1811.	—	Rare	—
S133	5 Rijksdaalders 1811.	—	Rare	—
S134	10 Rijksdaalders 1811.	—	Rare	—
S135	15 Rijksdaalders 1811.	—	Rare	—

Batavian Republic

Bataviaasch Bank Van Leening

Batavian Bank of Loan

1803 Mortgage Letters Issue

		Good	Fine	XF
S139	15 Rijksdaalders — — —			

(S135) 1803. Java issue.

#S136-S140 are deleted, as they have been determined to be the same as #S121-S125.

Kingdom of Holland and French Empire

Government

1807-11 Provisional Issue

#S140A-S143 w/various dates: Batavian, 1807-11; Amboina, 1808-09; Banda, 1808; Ternaten, 1808-09. Circular hand stamp: *LN* monogram.

		Good	Fine	XF
S140A	1/2 Rijksdaalder 1807-11.	—	Rare	—
S141	1 Rijksdaalder 1807-11.	—	Rare	—

		Good	Fine	XF
S142	2 Rijksdaalders 1807-11.	—	Rare	—

		Good	Fine	XF
S143	3 Rijksdaalders 1807-11.	—	Rare	—

British Administration

Government

1812 Issue

		Good	Fine	XF
S146	1 Spanish Dollar 1.5.1812.	—	—	—
S147	2 Spanish Dollars 1.5.1812.	—	—	—
S148	3 Spanish Dollars 1.5.1812.	—	—	—

1814 Issue

		Good	Fine	XF
S149	5 Java Rupees Oct. 1814. Lombard Bank.	—	—	—
S150	15 Java Rupees 7.4.1814.	—	—	—

Note: For previously listed #S151-S166 refer to Volume II.

REGIONAL - FRENCH INFLUENCE

JAVA

GOVERNMENT

1810 ISSUE

#S171-S176 Dutch text on upper part, Malay-Arabic text on lower part. Circular hand stamp: *LN* monogram *1810* on face and back. Uniface.

		GOOD	FINE	XF
S171	**100 RIJKSDAALDERS** 1810.	—	Rare	—

		GOOD	FINE	XF
S172	**200 RIJKSDAALDERS** 1810.	—	Rare	—
S173	**300 RIJKSDAALDERS** 1810.	—	Rare	—
S174	**400 RIJKSDAALDERS** 1810.	—	Rare	—
S175	**500 RIJKSDAALDERS** 1810.	—	Rare	—
S176	**1000 RIJKSDAALDERS** 1810.	—	Rare	—

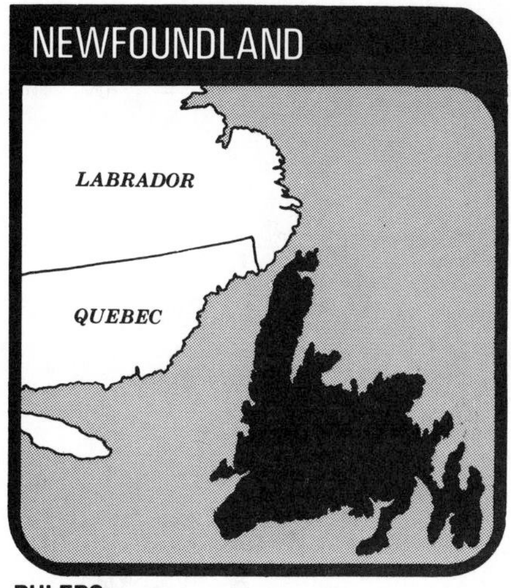

John Cabot, who visited Newfoundland in 1497, is given the title of discoverer although it is likely that Vikings visited its shore on their various trips to the west. Early settlement efforts were made by the British involving such men as Sir Humphrey Gilbert, John Guy and Sir George Calvert. There was much dispute between the French and the British for the island and its fishing rights. Awarded to England by the Treaty of Utrecht of 1713. Granted first governor in 1728. Adequate local government did not develop until the mid 1800s. Made a British colony in 1934 and became a province of Canada (along with Labrador) in 1949.

RULERS:
British

MONETARY SYSTEM:
1 Pound = 4 Dollars = 20 Shillings
1 Dollar = 100 Cents

CHARTERED BANKS

COMMERCIAL BANK OF NEWFOUNDLAND

1857-58 ISSUE

Pound Sterling System.

#S101-S104 seated Commerce at ctr. Uniface. Printer: PBC.

		GOOD	FINE	XF
S101	**1 POUND** 25.8.1857; 20.10.1858. Black. Uniface. Printer: PBC.			
	a. Issued note.	1000.	3000.	—
	p. Proof. 18xx.	—	Unc	400.00
S102	**5 POUNDS** 18xx. Black. Proof.	—	Unc	400.00
S103	**10 POUNDS** 18xx. Black. Proof.	—	Unc	400.00
S104	**20 POUNDS** 18xx. Black. Proof.	—	Unc	400.00

1865-67 ISSUE

Pound Sterling/Dollar System.

#S106-S108 seal in oval at l., seated Commerce at ctr., codfish in oval at r. Uniface. 2 sign. spaces at l. Printer: PBC.

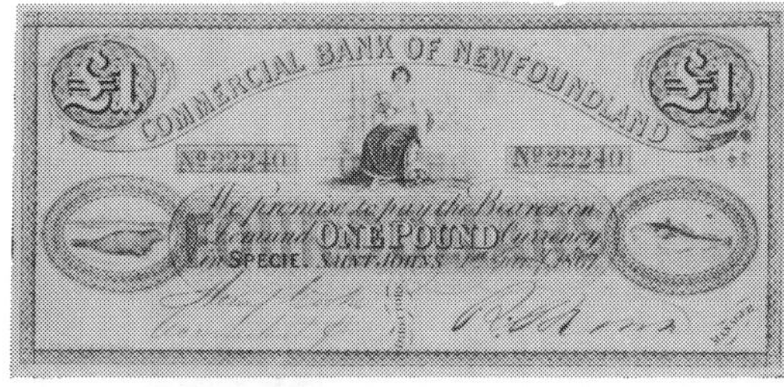

		GOOD	FINE	XF
S106	**1 POUND/4 DOLLARS** 1.1.1867. Black on blue unpt.	500.00	1250.	—
S107	**5 POUNDS/20 DOLLARS** 1.1.1867. Black on red-brown unpt.	500.00	1250.	—

		GOOD	FINE	XF
S108	**10 POUNDS/40 DOLLARS** 1865; 1.1.1867. Black on green unpt.	800.00	2000.	—

1874 ISSUE

#S109-S110 one sign. space at l.

		GOOD	FINE	XF
S109	**1 POUND/4 DOLLARS** 1874-84. Like #S106.			
	a. 1.1.1874; 1.3.1882.	500.00	1250.	—
	b. 1.7.1884.	450.00	1100.	—

		Good	Fine	XF
S110	**5 Pounds/20 Dollars**			
	1874; 1885. Like #S107, but different guilloche at ctr.			
	a. 1.1.1874.	450.00	1500.	—
	p. Proof. 1.7.1885.	—	Unc	700.00

1881 Issue

Dollar System.

		Good	Fine	XF
S111	**2 Dollars**			
	1881-84. Black. Seal at l., codfish at r. Back blue. Printer: PBC.			
	a. 1.1.1881; 1882.	400.00	1000.	—
	b. 1.7.1884.	350.00	850.00	—

1888 Issue

#S112-S117 seated Commerce at upper or top ctr. Printer: BABNC.

		VG	VF	Unc
S112	**2 Dollars**			
	3.1.1888. Black on orange unpt. Sailor at lower l., fisherman at lower r. Back green.	125.00	600.00	—

#S113-S117 black on green unpt. Back green.

		VG	VF	Unc
S113	**2 Dollars**			
	3.1.1888. Like #S112.	250.00	1000.	—

		VG	VF	Unc
S114	**5 Dollars**			
	3.1.1888. Sailor at lower l., seals at r.	125.00	600.00	—

		VG	VF	Unc
S115	**10 Dollars**			
	3.1.1888. Portr. Qn. Victoria at lower l., sailor at lower r.			
	a. Issued note.	350.00	1000.	—
	b. Redemption ovpt: *2 DOLLARS.*	—	—	—

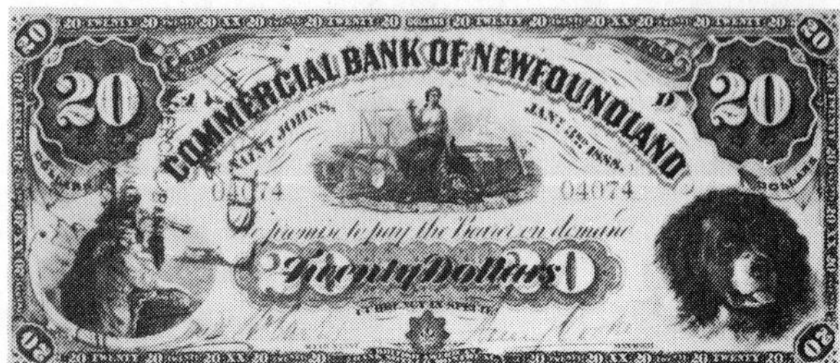

		VG	VF	Unc
S116	**20 Dollars**			
	3.1.1888. Man, woman and telescope at lower l., dog's head at lower r.	600.00	950.00	—

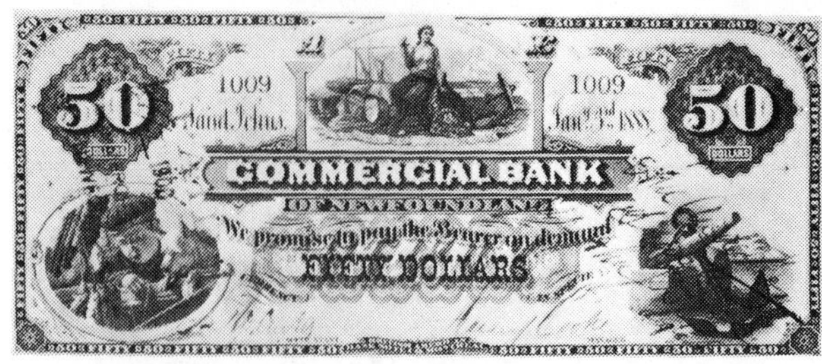

		VG	VF	Unc
S117	**50 Dollars**			
	3.1.1888. Boy and dog at lower l., anchor at lower r.	—	Rare	—

Union Bank of Newfoundland

1854 Issue

#S118-S120 sailing ship at upper ctr. Printer: PBC.

		Good	Fine	XF
S118	**1 Pound**			
	1854-55. Black.			
	a. Red word protector. Back red. 18.5.1854.	1125.	2800.	—
	b. Green word protector. Back green. 1.3.1855.	1125.	2800.	—
S118A	**2 Pounds**			
	18xx. Black. Proof.	—	Unc	400.00

		Good	Fine	XF
S119	**5 Pounds**			
	18xx. Black. Proof w/ovpt: *SPECIMEN.*	—	Unc	400.00
S120	**10 Pounds**			
	18xx. Black. Proof w/ovpt: *SPECIMEN.*	—	Unc	400.00

1865 Issue

#S121-S123 portr. Qn. Victoria at lower l., sailing ship "Fishing Smack" at upper ctr. Uniface. Printer: ABNC.

		VG	VF	Unc
S121	**1 Pound**			
	1865-80. Black on green unpt. Seal at r.			
	a. Partially engraved date. 1.5.1865.	600.00	1750.	—
	b. Fully engraved date. 1.3.1867; 1.9.1877.	500.00	1200.	—
	c. 1.5.1880.	350.00	700.00	2250.
S122	**5 Pounds**			
	1865-83. Brown on blue unpt. Similar to #S121, but codfish at r.			
	a. Partially engraved date. 2.10.1865; 3.4.1876; 1.10.1881.	900.00	2000.	—
	b. Fully engraved date. 1.8.1883.	700.00	1500.	—

NOTE: #S122 sometimes encountered w/handstamped guarantee of $16.

		VG	VF	Unc
S123	**10 Pounds**			
	2.10.1865; 3.4.1876; 1.10.1881. Blue on red unpt. Partially engraved date. Similar to #S122.	—	Rare	—

NOTE: #S123 sometimes encountered w/handstamped guarantee of $32.

1882; 1889 ISSUE

#S124-S128 printer: ABNC.

		VG	VF	UNC
S124	**2 DOLLARS** 1.5.1882. Black on green unpt. Codfish at lower l., portr. J. Smith at ctr., dog and safe at lower r. Back green.	275.00	950.00	1800.

		VG	VF	UNC
S125	**5 DOLLARS** 1.5.1889. Black on green and yellow unpt. Sailing ship at l., steamship at ctr. r. Back green; cattle in pond at ctr.	425.00	1500.	3750.

		VG	VF	UNC
S126	**10 DOLLARS** 1.5.1889. Black on orange and yellow unpt. Dog's head at lower l., sailing ship "Sealing" at ctr., sailors at r. Back orange; woman and safe at ctr.	400.00	1200.	2000.

		VG	VF	UNC
S127	**20 DOLLARS** 1.5.1889. Black on blue and yellow unpt. Steam locomotive at l. and r. w/value superimposed, steam locomotive at ctr. Back blue; steam locomotive at ctr.	425.00	1000.	2500.
S128	**50 DOLLARS** 1.5.1889. Black on brown and yellow unpt. Allegorical woman at l. and r., bank at ctr. Back brown; dog by safe at ctr.	—	Rare	—

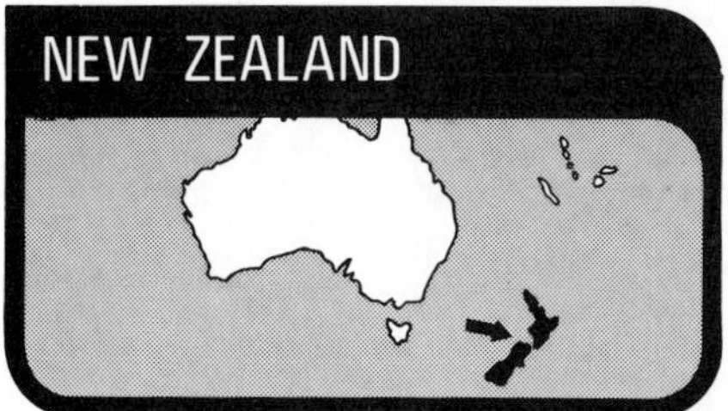

New Zealand, a parliamentary state located in the southwestern Pacific 1,250 miles (2,011 km.) east of Australia, has an area of 103,736 sq. mi. (269,056 sq. km.) and a population of 3.8 million. Capital: Wellington. Wool, meat, dairy products and some manufactured items are exported.

New Zealand was discovered and named by Dutch navigator Abel Tasman in 1642, and explored by British navigator Capt. James Cook who surveyed it in 1769 and annexed the land to Great Britain. The British government disavowed the annexation and for the next 70 years the only white settlers to arrive were adventurers attracted by the prospects of lumbering, sealing and whaling. Great Britain annexed the land in 1840 by treaty with the native chiefs and made it a dependency of New South Wales. The colony was granted self-government in 1852, a ministerial form of government in 1856, and full dominion status on Sept. 26, 1907. Full internal and external autonomy, which New Zealand had in effect possessed for many years, was formally extended in 1947. New Zealand is a member of the Commonwealth of Nations. Elizabeth II is Head of State as Queen of New Zealand.

RULERS:

British

MONETARY SYSTEM:

1 Shilling = 12 Pence
1 Pound = 20 Shillings to 1967

BANKS:

Bank of Aotearoa, ca.1880 .... #S101
Bank of Auckland, 1864-67 .... #S106-S108
Bank of Australasia, 1863-1934 .... #S111-S136
Bank of New South Wales, 1844-1934 .... #S139-S165
Bank of New Zealand, 1861-1934 .... #S171-S240
Bank of Otago Ltd., 1863-74 .... #S241-S243
Colonial Bank of Issue, 1850-56 .... #S246-S247
Colonial Bank of New Zealand, 1874-95 .... #S251-S270
Commercial Bank of Australia, 1912-34 .... #S270A-S286
Commercial Bank of New Zealand Limited, 1865-66 .... #S288-S290
National Bank of New Zealand, 1873-1934 .... #S291-S321
New Zealand Banking Company, 1840-45 .... #S326-S327
New Zealand Banking Corporation, Ltd., 1863-66 .... #S331
Oriental Bank Corporation, 1857-61 .... #S333-S335A
Otago Banking Company, 1851 .... #S336-S338
Union Bank of Australia, 1840-1934 .... #S341-S376
??Union Bank of Australia Limited, 1905-23 .... #S361-S376

OFFICES OF ISSUE:

(a) - not named	(i) - Nelson
(b) - Auckland, Auckland & Wellington	(j) - Picton
(c) - Christchurch	(k) - Sydney
(e) - Dunedin	(l) - Wanganui
(f) - Invercargill	(m) - Wellington
(g) - Lyttelton	(y) - Auckland, Wanganui & Dunedin
(h) - Napier, Napier or Wellington	(z) - Unknown

BRITISH ADMINISTRATION

BANK OF AOTEAROA

An institution under the reign of Maori chief Tawhiao (appears on a number of later New Zealand notes).

1894 ISSUE

		GOOD	FINE	XF
S101	**1 PAUNA (POUND)** 1894. Black and red. Lg. *N* at ctr.	—	—	—

BANK OF AUCKLAND

Established in 1864.

1864 ISSUE

		GOOD	FINE	XF
S104	**1 POUND** 18xx; 7.3.1865. Black. Bank name at top.	—	Rare	—

1865 ISSUE

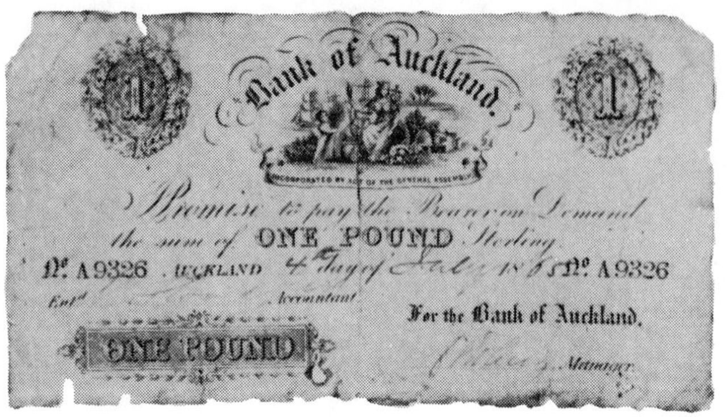

		GOOD	FINE	XF
S106	**1 POUND** 4.7.1865; 17.8.1866. Black. Seated woman w/symbols of commerce at upper ctr., ships in background. Printer: CS&E.	—	Rare	—
S108	**10 POUNDS** ND. Similar to #S106.			
	p1. Back orange. Proof.	—	Unc	650.00
	p2. Back black. Proof.	—	Unc	650.00

BANK OF AUSTRALASIA

Established on January 26, 1864. Merged with the Union Bank in 1951 to form the Australia and New Zealand Banking Group. Notes issued from 1863-1934.

1863 ISSUE

#S109-S110 arms at upper ctr. Uniface.

		GOOD	FINE	XF
S109	**1 POUND** 1863.	—	—	—
S109A	**5 POUNDS** 1863.	Reported Not Confirmed		
S110	**10 POUNDS** 1863.	—	—	—
S110A	**20 POUNDS** 1863.	Reported Not Confirmed		

1863-76 ISSUE

#S111-S115 black on green ctr., two seated women at upper ctr., arms at upper l. inner guilloche, Numeral *1* in inner guilloche at upper r. Designs in all corner guilloches. Promissory text may vary according to office of issue. Uniface. Printer: PBC.

		GOOD	FINE	XF
S111	**1 POUND** (ca.1863-86).			
	b. Auckland. 14.7.1863.	—	—	—
	c. Christchurch. 13.10.1868; 13.12.1873; 13.7.1875.	—	—	—
	e. Dunedin. 11.10.18xx (ca.1867).	—	—	—
	m. Wellington. 13.4.1874.	—	—	—
S112	**5 POUNDS** (ca.1864-86).			
	c. Christchurch. 13.6.1870; 13.12.1870.	—	—	—
	e. Dunedin. 11.10.1864.	—	—	—
S113	**10 POUNDS** (ca.1863-86).			
	b. Auckland. ND (ca.1867).	—	—	—
	c. Christchurch. ND (ca.1863).	—	—	—
	e. Dunedin. ND (ca.1867).	—	—	—
	h. Napier or Wellington. 6.1875.	—	—	—

		GOOD	FINE	XF
S114	**20 POUNDS** (ca.1863-76).			
	c. Christchurch. ND.	—	—	—
	h. Napier. ND.	—	—	—
S115	**50 POUNDS** (ca.1863-76).	—	—	—

1877-1923 ISSUE

#S116 similar to previous issue.

		GOOD	FINE	XF
S116	**10 SHILLINGS** 1.6.1918-2.6.1923. Wellington. Orange on blue unpt.	—	—	—

#S117-S121 similar to above, but value spelled out in inner guilloche at upper right. Value numeral in each corner guilloche. Uniface.

		GOOD	FINE	XF
S117	**1 POUND** 1885-1923. Black on purple and green unpt. Arms in upper l. guilloche.			
	m. Wellington. 2.1.1911-1923.	—	—	—
	z. Office of issue unknown. 1907; 1.7.1915.	—	—	—

		GOOD	FINE	XF
S118	**5 POUNDS** 1907-21. Black on blue and orange unpt.			
	m. Wellington. 5.2.1917-5.8.1921.	—	—	—
	z. Office of issue unknown. 1907.	—	—	—
S119	**10 POUNDS** 1902-21. Black on brown and blue unpt.			
	c. Christchurch. 13.9.1902.	—	—	—
	m. Wellington. 13.9.1912-14.3.1921.	—	—	—
	z. Office of issue unknown. 1906.	—	—	—
S120	**20 POUNDS** (ca.1877-1923).	—	—	—
S121	**50 POUNDS** 1888-1921. Black on red and brown unpt.			
	c. Christchurch. 17.10.1890; 18.4.1898; 18.4.1904.	—	Rare	—
	e. Dunedin. 17.4.1906.	—	Rare	—
	m. Wellington. 17.10.1888; 17.4.1913; 18.10.1921.	—	Rare	—
	z. Office of issue unknown. 1903.	—	—	—

1923-32 ISSUES

#S131-S136 similar to #S116-S121 but reduced size, 179 x 89mm. Printer: PBC except #S133.

		GOOD	FINE	XF
S131	**10 SHILLINGS** 1924-2.6.1931. Orange on blue unpt.	175.00	500.00	800.00

		GOOD	FINE	XF
S132	**1 POUND** 1.7.1923-1.7.1931. Black on purple and green unpt. Serial # varieties.	175.00	500.00	700.00
S133	**1 POUND** 19.7.1932. Similar to #S132. Printer: TDLR.	175.00	500.00	700.00
S134	**5 POUNDS** 5.2.1925-1931. Black on blue and orange unpt.	200.00	600.00	900.00
S135	**10 POUNDS** 12.3.1927; 10.9.1927. Black on brown and blue unpt.	250.00	500.00	—
S136	**50 POUNDS** (ca.1923-24). Black on red and green unpt.	400.00	—	—

BANK OF NEW SOUTH WALES

Established in Sydney in 1817. Took over the Oriental Bank Corporation in 1861. Formed part of the Westpac Banking Corporation in 1981.

1840S ISSUE

		GOOD	FINE	XF
S139	**1 POUND** 24.10.1844. Black. Seated figure at ctr.	—	—	—

1861; 1862 ISSUE

#S141-S144 profile of Qn. Victoria at upper l., seated Commerce at upper ctr., ships in background. Various offices of issue. Printer: CS&E.

		GOOD	FINE	XF
S141	**1 POUND** 30.7.1861; 1.6.1866; 15.5.1867. Gray and black.	—	—	—
S142	**5 POUNDS** 30.7.1861. Blue.	—	—	—
S143	**10 POUNDS** 30.7.1861. Brown.	—	—	—
S144	**20 POUNDS** 1.10.1862. Lt. green.	—	—	—

1870 ISSUE

#S146-S149 similar to #S141-S144 except that value word replaces Victoria at upper l. *NEW ZEALAND* at upper and lower borders.

		GOOD	FINE	XF
S146	**1 POUND** (ca.1870-90). Black. Back red.			
	b. Auckland. 18xx.	—	—	—
	c. Christchurch. 18xx.	—	—	—
	e. Dunedin. 18xx.	—	—	—
	i. Nelson. 18xx.	—	—	—
	l. Wanganui. 18xx.	—	—	—
	m. Wellington. 18xx.	—	—	—

		GOOD	FINE	XF
S147	**5 POUNDS** (ca.1870-90). Blue.			
	a. Office of issue not named. ND. Specimen.	—	—	—
	b. Auckland. 18xx.	—	—	—
	c. Christchurch. 18xx. Specimen.	—	—	—
	e. Dunedin. 18xx.	—	—	—
	l. Wanganui. 18xx.	—	—	—
	m. Wellington. 18xx. Specimen.	—	—	—
	y. Auckland, Wanganui and Dunedin. 18xx.	—	—	—
S148	**10 POUNDS** (ca.1870-90). Brown. Back red.	—	—	—
S149	**20 POUNDS** (ca.1870-90). Lt. green. Back red.			
	e. Dunedin. 18xx. Specimen.	—	Unc	500.00

1890-1922 ISSUES

#S151-S159 similar to #S146-S149 but different vignette of seated Commerce at upper ctr. *BANK OF NEW SOUTH WALES* in top and bottom margin.

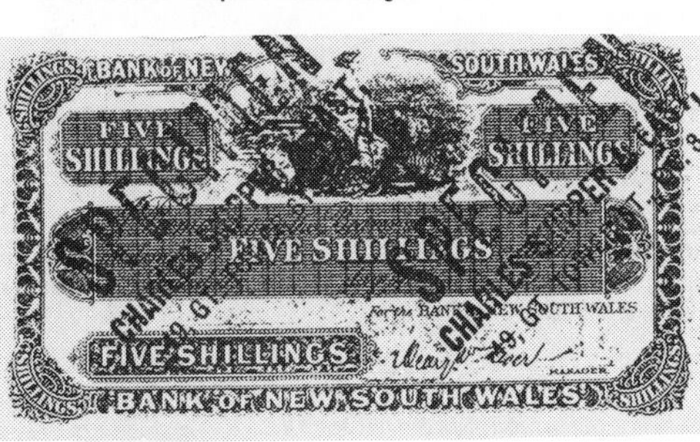

		GOOD	FINE	XF
S150	**5 SHILLINGS** 19xx. Seated Commerce at upper ctr. Bank name at top separated by vignette. Specimen.	—	—	—
S151	**10 SHILLINGS** 1918. Orange and brown. Value: *10/-* over *SHILLINGS* at upper l. and r.	—	—	—
S152	**10 SHILLINGS** 1.9.1919; 1921. Like #S151 but value: *TEN SHILLINGS* at upper l. and r. Circular designs in corners on back.	—	—	—
S153	**10 SHILLINGS** 1922. Similar to #S152, but bank name at top separated by vignette. Oval designs in corners on back. Smaller size.	—	—	—

		GOOD	FINE	XF
S154	**1 POUND** (ca.1890-1923). Black. Back red.			
	a. Office of issue not named. 1.7.1915. Specimen.	—	—	—
	e. Dunedin. Specimen.	—	—	—
	m. Wellington. 1.5.1914; 1.2.1917; 1.11.1918.	—	—	—
	z. Office of issue unknown. 1.1.1891; 1.7.1892; 1.10.1908-14.	—	—	—

NOTE: A specimen of #S154 has been reported with date 1.10.1914, and subsequent hand dates of 1.2.1915 and 1.4.1918. Office of issue unknown.

		GOOD	FINE	XF
S155	**5 POUNDS** (ca.1890-1923). Black and green.			
	m. Wellington. 1.8.1914; 1.8.1921.	—	—	—
	z. Office of issue unknown. 5.2.1921.	—	—	—
S156	**10 POUNDS** ND (ca.1890-1923). Brown. Back red.			
	a. Office of issue not named. 19xx.	—	—	—
	m. Wellington. 1.4.1922.	—	—	—
	z. Office of issue unknown. 1.3.1918.	—	—	—
S157	**20 POUNDS** (ca.1890-1923). Lt. green.			
	a. Office of issue not named. 19xx. Specimen.	—	—	—
	z. Office of issue unknown. 1890-1923.	—	—	—
S158	**50 POUNDS** (ca.1914-23). Vermilion.			
	a. Office of issue not named. 19xx.	—	—	—
	z. Office of issue unknown. 1.4.1914.	—	—	—
S159	**100 POUNDS** (ca.1914-23). Black.			
	a. Office of issue not named. 19xx.	—	—	—
	z. Office of issue unknown. 1.11.1914.	—	—	—

1923; 1924 ISSUE

#S161-S165 similar to previous issues. Bank title in full in ornate borders at top and bottom. Reduced size, 179 x 89mm. Printer: CS&E.

		GOOD	FINE	XF
S161	**10 SHILLINGS** 1.1.1924-1.18.1933. Orange and brown.	—	—	—

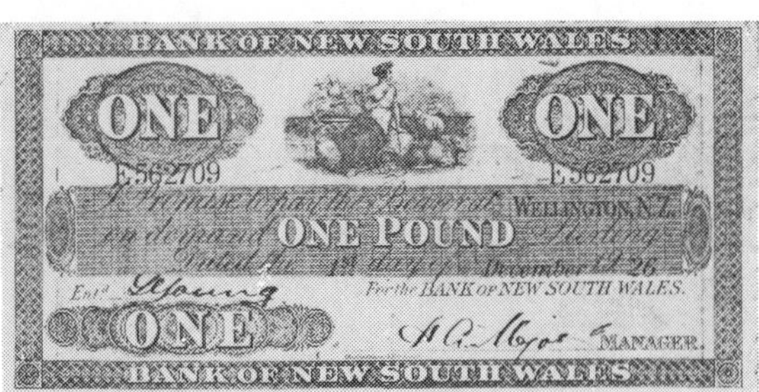

		Good	Fine	XF
S162	**1 Pound** 1.1.1924; 1.12.1926; 1.9.1931; 1.2.1932. Purple-brown.	—	—	—
S163	**5 Pounds** 1.8.1924; 1.3.1926; 1929; 1.19.1931; 1.12.1932. Blue. Back green.	—	—	—
S164	**10 Pounds** (ca.1923-34). Brown. Specimen.	—	—	—
S165	**20 Pounds** (ca.1923-34). Lt. green. Specimen.	—	—	—

NOTE: For the above issue (#S161-S165), it is believed that the office of issue is Wellington only.

BANK OF NEW ZEALAND

Established in 1861. This institution became the second largest note issuer for Australia. In 1945, the government obtained sole control of this bank.

1861 EMERGENCY ISSUE

		Good	Fine	XF
S171	**1 Pound** 1861. Lithograph on plain paper. Dunedin office only. Printer: B.N.Z.	—	—	—

NOTE: No examples of #S171 are presently known to exist.

1861 ISSUE

#S176 and S177 royal arms at top ctr. Uniface. Printer: W. Moffit & Co., Sydney.

		Good	Fine	XF
S176	**1 Pound** 186x; 1862. Black.			
	f. Invercargill.	—	—	—
	i. Nelson. 13.1.1862.	—	—	—
S177	**5 Pounds** 1861; 1862. Black.			
	b. Auckland.	—	—	—

1862 ISSUE

#S181-S184 similar to #S176-S177. Printer: PBC.

		Good	Fine	XF
S181	**1 Pound** (ca.1862-70). Black.			
	b. Auckland. 18xx. Specimen.	—	—	—
	i. Nelson.	—	—	—

		Good	Fine	XF
S182	**5 Pounds** (ca.1862). Blue.			
	b. Auckland. 18xx. Specimen.	—	—	—
	f. Invercargill. 18xx. Specimen.	—	—	—
	j. Picton. 18xx. Specimen.	—	—	—
S183	**10 Pounds** (ca.1862). Green.	—	—	—
S184	**20 Pounds** (ca.1862). Orange.			
	g. Lyttelton.	—	—	—

1870; 1873 ISSUE

#S191-S196 w/two Maoris at top l., two kiwis in rural scene at bottom l. Printer: BWC.

		Good	Fine	XF
S191	**1 Pound** 1.12.1870; 1.4.1884-90. Gray and green.	—	—	—

		Good	Fine	XF
S192	**5 Pounds** (ca.1870-1916). Gray and brown.			
	m. Wellington. 1.1.1913; 19xx.	—	—	—

		Good	Fine	XF
S193	**10 Pounds** (ca.1870-1916). Dk. gray and dk. brown.			
	m. Wellington. 1.12.1908; 19xx.	—	—	—

A word on date ranges

Often date ranges or specific dates are listed. These have been observed or reported by our contributors. If a note is outside the published range, it only means that it is a newly reported date, and not necessarily worthy of a premium value.

S194	**20 POUNDS**	**GOOD**	**FINE**	**XF**
	(ca.1870-1926). Gray and blue-green.			
	m. Wellington. 1.8.1924.	200.00	650.00	—

S195	**50 POUNDS**	**GOOD**	**FINE**	**XF**
	(ca.1870-1929). Green and mauve.			
	e. Dunedin. 18xx. Specimen.	—	—	—

S196	**100 POUNDS**	**GOOD**	**FINE**	**XF**
	(ca.1873-1929). Brown and red.			
	b. Auckland. 18xx. Specimen.	—	—	—
	k. Sydney. 18xx. Specimen.	—	—	—
	m. Wellington. 19xx. Specimen.	—	—	—

NOTE: It is reported that #S194-S196 were issued in 1929. Confirmation is needed.

1880's ISSUE

#S200-S202 printer: BWC.

S201	**1 POUND**	**GOOD**	**FINE**	**XF**
	18xx. Portr. man at l. and r.; animals at top l. and r. Proof.			
	a. Red and green unpt.	—	Unc	350.00
	b. Blue and yellow unpt.	—	Unc	350.00

1889 ISSUE

S202	**1 POUND**	**GOOD**	**FINE**	**XF**
	1889; 1891; 1.3.1898. Black, green and brown. Portr. woman at l., 2 Maoris at r., animals at top l. and r., rural scenes at bottom. River scene at ctr. on back.	700.00	2000.	—

1898 ISSUE

S206	**1 POUND**	**GOOD**	**FINE**	**XF**
	7.11.1898; 1.4.1900; 1.12.1900; 1.4.1901; 1.10.1901; 1.5.1902. Black and gray. Woman w/cherub, sheep and kiwi at l., arms at upper ctr. River w/palms at l., bank arms at ctr., Maori standing and kneeling at r. on back.	350.00	650.00	—

1901 Issue

		Good	Fine	XF
S212	**1 Pound** 1.10.1901; 1.12.1912-1918. Black. Like #S191, but w/continuous unpt. and letter preceding serial #. Printer: BWC.	600.00	900.00	—
S213	**1000 Pounds** Bank transactions only.	—	—	—

1916; 1920 Provisional Issue

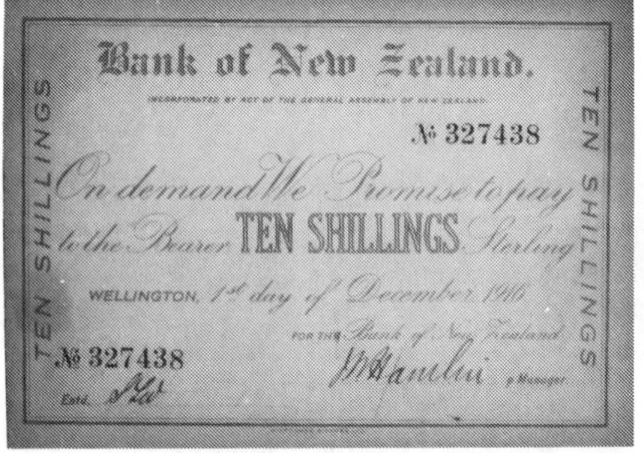

		Good	Fine	XF
S215	**10 Shillings** 1916-18. Red on pink paper. Issued at Wellington. Uniface. Printer: Whitcombe & Tombs.			
	a. Various dates handwritten or stamped w/o printer's name.	750.00	2000.	—
	b. W/o printer's name. 1.8.1916.	750.00	2000.	—
	c. Printer's name. 1.8.1916.	700.00	1800.	—
	d. Like c. 1.12.1916; 1.3.1918.	700.00	1800.	—

1916-21 Regular Issues

#S222-S229 printer: BWC.

		Good	Fine	XF
S221	**5 Shillings** 1.3.1920. Black on red unpt. *5/-* in blue. Men at lower l., 2 kiwis in rural scene at lower r. Printer: Whitcombe & Tombs. (Not issued.)	—	—	—

		Good	Fine	XF
S222	**10 Shillings** 1.4.1917. M/c. 2 Maoris at l., 2 kiwis in rural scene at r. Back brown.	750.00	1800.	—

		Good	Fine	XF
S223	**10 Shillings** 1.10.1917; 1.10.1918; (ca.1918-20). M/c. Similar to #S222. *10 SHILLINGS* deleted from top l. and r. corners. (Applies to #500,001 and above.)	750.00	2000.	—

NOTE: Other full dates of #S223 should be reported.

		Good	Fine	XF
S224	**10 Shillings** 1.4.1920-24. M/c. Text and figures removed from back.	1000.	1950.	—

		Good	Fine	XF
S225	**1 Pound** 1.10.1916; 1.10.1919; 1.4.1920-21. M/c. Similar to #S222.	300.00	700.00	—
S226	**1 Pound** 1.4.1920-1.4.1924. M/c. Similar to #S222. All text and figures removed from back.	350.00	800.00	—

		Good	Fine	XF
S227	**5 Pounds** 1.10.1917; 1.10.1918; (ca.1918-21). Blue on pink and green unpt. 2 kiwis in rural scene at lower l., 2 Maoris at lower r. Back brown on gray unpt.	600.00	1000.	—

NOTE: Other full dates of #S227 should be reported.

		Good	Fine	XF
S228	**5 Pounds** 1.4.1921; 1.10.1921; 1.10.1922; 1.4.1923. M/c. Similar to #S227. All text and figures removed from back.	450.00	850.00	—

		Good	Fine	XF
S229	**10 Pounds** 1.10.1916; (ca.1916-21). M/c. Similar to #S227.	475.00	750.00	—
S230	**10 Pounds** 1.10.1919; 1.10.1920; 1.10.1921; (ca.1921-23). M/c. Similar to #S227. All text and figures removed from back.	475.00	750.00	—

1924-29 Issues

#S231-S238 reduced size, 179 x 89mm. Printer: BWC.

		Good	Fine	XF
S231	**10 Shillings** (ca.1924-27). Yellow and m/c. Portr. Maori Kg. Tawhiao at r.	150.00	375.00	—

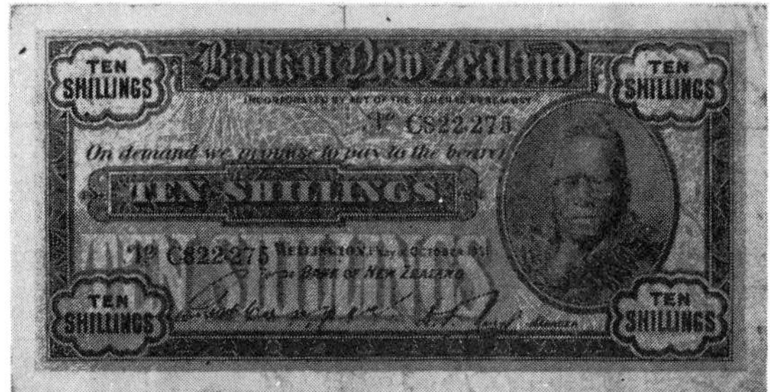

		Good	Fine	XF
S232	**10 Shillings** (ca.1927-34). Like #S231 but £1/2 deleted from corners on face. (Applies to #A500,001 and above.)	150.00	375.00	—

NOTE: 1.10.1931 is the only full date confirmed for #S232. Other full dates should be reported.

		Good	Fine	XF
S233	**1 Pound** 1.10.1924; 1.10.1925-27. Violet and m/c. Portr. Kg. Tawhiao at ctr. Bank name arched.	100.00	250.00	450.00

		Good	Fine	XF
S234	**1 Pound** 1.10.1926; (ca.1926-34). Violet and m/c. Like #S233 but bank name in straight line.	100.00	225.00	450.00

		Good	Fine	XF
S235	**5 Pounds** 1.10.1924; 1.10.1925; 1.10.1927; 1.10.1928. Blue and m/c. Portr. Kg. Tawhiao at l. Bank name arched.	125.00	250.00	—
S235A	**5 Pounds** 1.10.1926; 1.10.1928; 1.10.1929; (ca.1929-34). Like #S235 but bank name in straight line.	175.00	300.00	—

		Good	Fine	XF
S237	**10 Pounds** 14.8.1924; 1.10.1924; 1.10.1926; 1.10.1927; 1.10.1928; (ca.1928-34). Brown. Like #S233.	275.00	600.00	—
S238	**20 Pounds** 1.10.1926; (ca.1926-34). Green. Portr. Kg. Tawhiao at r.	—	—	—
S239	**50 Pounds** 24.5.1929; (ca.1929-34). Pink. Portr. Kg. Tawhiao at r.	—	—	—
S240	**100 Pounds** 24.5.1929; 1.10.1929; (ca.1929-34). Olive. Portr. Kg. Tawhiao at r.	—	—	—

NOTE: For #S231-S240, more full dates are needed for confirmation. Various color shades may exist.

Bank of Otago Ltd.

Established in Dunedin in 1863. Taken over by the National Bank in 1873. Issued in Dunedin only.

1864-68 Issue

#S241-S243 Britannia w/flag at l. Bank name in oval guilloche on back. W/ or w/o prefix letter in serial #. Printer: Batho & Co.

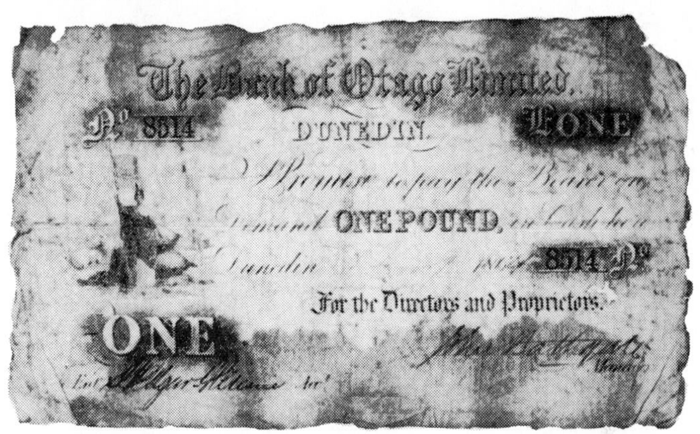

		Good	Fine	XF
S241	**1 Pound** 1.1.1864; 17.4.1867; 21.1.1872; 19.1.1878. Black and blue.	—	—	—
S242	**5 Pounds** 3.1.1866; 2.5.1868. Black.	—	Rare	—
S243	**10 Pounds** 10.3.1868.	—	Rare	—
S244	**20 Pounds** (ca.1863-73).		Reported Not Confirmed	

Colonial Bank of Issue

Established on October 16, 1847 by Governor Sir George Grey. This bank was founded to prevent further issuance of private notes. The bank closed in 1856. Printer: PB&P.

1850's Issue

		Good	Fine	XF
S246	**1 Pound** (ca.1850-56). Brown. Royal arms at top ctr. 3 different value statements in 3 corners on face. Uniface.			
	b. Auckland. Specimen.	—	—	—
	m. Wellington. Specimen.	—	—	—
S247	**5 Pounds** (ca.1850-56). Orange. Like #S246.			
	e. Dunedin.	—	—	—
	m. Wellington. Specimen.	—	—	—

Colonial Bank of New Zealand

Established in 1874. This bank was one of the smaller issuers, and was purchased by the Bank of New Zealand in 1895.

1874 First Issue

		Good	Fine	XF
S251	**1 Pound** 1874. Brown. Woman at upper ctr. Uniface. Printer: Fergusson & Mitchell.	—	Rare	—

1874 Second Issue

		Good	Fine	XF
S256	**1 Pound** (ca.1874). Black. Two women at upper ctr.	—	—	—

1875 Issue

#S262-S266 allegorical woman flanked by sailors w/implements and beehive at upper ctr. Serial # varieties. Printer: PBC.

		GOOD	FINE	XF
S262	**1 POUND** (ca.1875-90). Blue and yellow.			
	b. Auckland. 187x.	—	—	—
	c. Christchurch. 187x.	—	—	—
	e. Dunedin.	—	—	—
	h. Napier. Proof.	—	—	—
	m. Wellington. Proof.	—	—	—

		GOOD	FINE	XF
S263	**5 POUNDS** (ca.1875-90).			
	b. Auckland. 187x.	—	—	—
	c. Christchurch. 187x. Specimen.	—	—	—
	e. Dunedin.	—	—	—
	h. Napier. Proof.	—	—	—
S264	**10 POUNDS** (ca.1875-90).	—	—	—
	b. Auckland. 187x.	—	—	—
	e. Dunedin.	—	—	—
	h. Napier. Proof.	—	—	—

		GOOD	FINE	XF
S265	**20 POUNDS** (ca.1875-90).			
	a. Auckland. 187x.	—	—	—
	c. Christchurch. 187x.	—	—	—
	e. Dunedin. Proof.	—	—	—
	h. Napier. Proof.	—	—	—
S266	**50 POUNDS** (ca.1875-90).			
	h. Napier. Proof.	—	—	—

1880's ISSUE

#S267-S270 shield w/bank monogram flanked by two women at upper ctr., ships in background. Portrs. l. and r., bldg. at ctr. on back. Printer: BWC.

		GOOD	FINE	XF
S267	**1 POUND** 1.3.1889-95. Black and orange.			
	e. Dunedin.	—	—	—
S268	**5 POUNDS** (ca.1889-95). Proof.	—	—	—
S269	**10 POUNDS** 1.5.18xx (ca.1889-95). Allegorical head at l. and r., tower bldg. at ctr. on back.			
	e. Dunedin. 1.5.18xx. Specimen.	—	—	—
	p. Proof.	—	—	—

		GOOD	FINE	XF
S269A	**20 POUNDS** 1.6.18xx (ca.1889-95).			
	e. Dunedin. 1.6.18xx. Specimen.	—	—	—
	p. Proof.	—	—	—
S270	**50 POUNDS** 1.7.18xx. Brown on blue and yellow-orange unpt.			
	e. Dunedin. 1.7.18xx. Unsigned remainder.	—	—	—

NOTE: Wellington office issue may exist for #S267-S270.

COMMERCIAL BANK OF AUSTRALIA

Established in Melbourne in 1866 for use in Australia. This became the smallest issuing bank in New Zealand. All notes were issued from Wellington.

1914-19 ISSUE

#S270A-S275 seated woman w/globe and caduceus. Printer: Sands (w/o imprint).

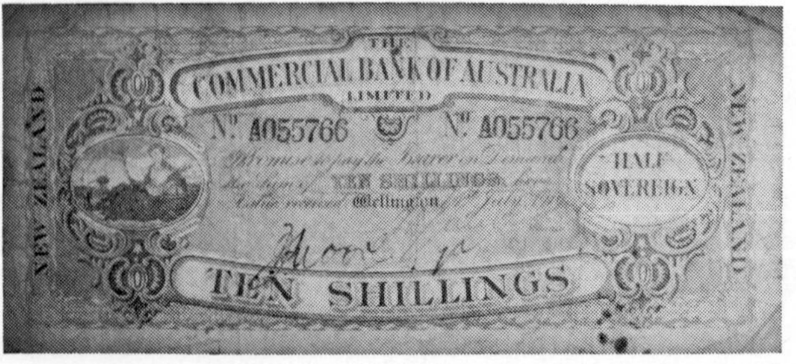

		GOOD	FINE	XF
S270A	**10 SHILLINGS** 14.4.1917; 1.7.1919. Yellow and green. Seated woman at l.	—	—	—

		Good	Fine	XF
S271	**1 Pound** 1914; 1.1.1915; 1917; 1.1.1919. Purple. Seated woman at ctr. Facing female head at l. and r. on back.	350.00	650.00	—
S272	**5 Pounds** 18.8.1914; 1916. Blue.	475.00	700.00	—
S273	**10 Pounds** 12.7.1914; 1915. Brown.	350.00	—	—
S274	**50 Pounds** (ca.1914-19). Red.	—	—	—
S275	**100 Pounds** (ca.1914-19). Green.	—	—	—
S276	**1000 Pounds** (ca.1914-19). Bank transactions only.	—	—	—

1917-19 Issue

#S277-S280B reclining Industry at l. Printer: W&S.

		Good	Fine	XF
S277	**10 Shillings** 1919; 1.1.1923. Yellow	300.00	600.00	—
S278	**1 Pound** 1.1.1919; (ca.1919-24). Purple.	—	—	—
S279	**5 Pounds** 1917; (ca.1919-24). Blue.	—	—	—
S280	**10 Pounds** (ca.1919-24). Brown.	—	—	—
S280A	**50 Pounds** (ca.1919-24). Red.	Reported Not Confirmed		
S280B	**100 Pounds** (ca.1919-24). Green.	Reported Not Confirmed		

1926 Issue

#S281-S286 similar to #S277-S280B, but smaller size. Printer: W&S.

		Good	Fine	XF
S281	**10 Shillings** 1.1.1926-1.1.1930. Yellow and orange.	300.00	450.00	—

		Good	Fine	XF
S282	**1 Pound** 1.1.1926; 1.1.1927; 1.1.1928; 1930. Purple.	250.00	500.00	—
S283	**5 Pounds** 1.1.1926. Blue.	300.00	600.00	—
S284	**10 Pounds** 1926. Brown.	—	—	—
S285	**50 Pounds** 1926. Red.	—	—	—
S286	**100 Pounds** 19xx. (ca.1924-34). Green.	—	—	—

Commercial Bank of New Zealand Limited

Established in 1863 in Loon. Issuance stopped in May 1866.

1865 Issue

#S288-S289B printer: PBC.

		Good	Fine	XF
S288	**1 Pound** 2.1.1865. Arms at top ctr. Dunedin.	—	—	—
S289	**5 Pounds** (ca.1865-66). Specimen.	—	—	—
S289A	**10 Pounds** (ca.1865-66). Specimen.	—	—	—
S289B	**20 Pounds** (ca.1865-66). Specimen.	—	—	—
S289C	**50 Pounds** 2.1.1865. Arms at top ctr. Dunedin. Specimen.	—	—	—
S290	**100 Pounds** (ca.1865-66). Specimen.	—	—	—

National Bank of New Zealand

Established in Loon in 1872. Took over the Bank of Otago the following year, and eventually became part of the Lloyds Insurance Group.

1873 Issue

#S291-S295 arms w/crowned lion and unicorn facing r. No line below bank name. Uniface. Printer: PBC.

		Good	Fine	XF
S291	**1 Pound** ND (ca.1873-77). Gray.			
	a. Office of issue not named. Specimen.	—	—	—
	b. Auckland. Specimen.	—	—	—
	e. Dunedin. Specimen.	—	—	—
S292	**5 Pounds** ND (ca.1873-77). Blue.			
	a. Office of issue not named. Specimen.	—	—	—
	b. Auckland.	—	—	—
S293	**10 Pounds** ND (ca.1873-77). Green.			
	a. Office of issue not named. Specimen.	—	—	—
	b. Auckland.	—	—	—
S294	**20 Pounds** ND (ca.1873-77). Green.			
	a. Office of issue not named. Specimen.	—	—	—
	c. Christchurch.	—	—	—

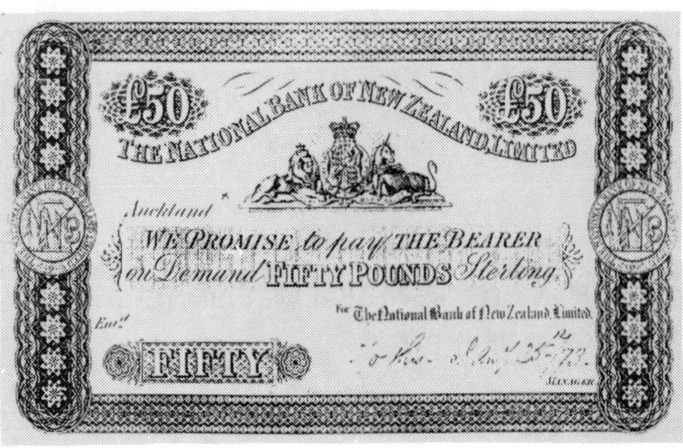

		GOOD	FINE	XF
S295	**50 POUNDS**			
	ND (ca.1873-77). Orange.			
	b. Auckland.	—	—	—

1877 ISSUE

#S296-S300 similar to #S291-S295, but w/incorporation text line under bank title. Larger size. Printer: PBC.

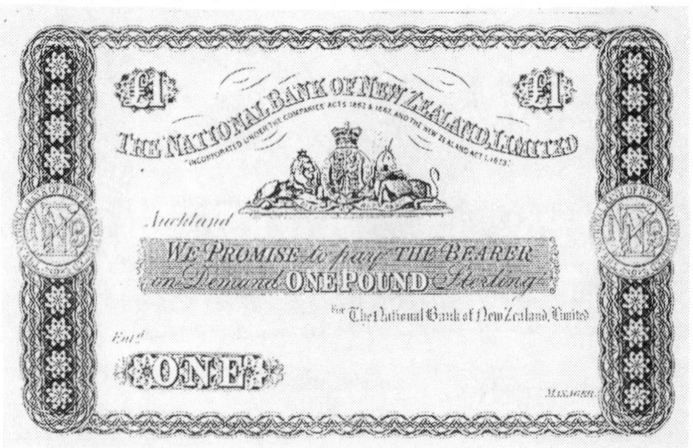

		GOOD	FINE	XF
S296	**1 POUND**			
	ND (ca.1877-1894). Gray and green.			
	b. Auckland.	—	—	—
	c. Christchurch. 18xx.	—	—	—
S297	**5 POUNDS**			
	ND (ca.1877-1894). Blue and dk. brown.			
	e. Dunedin. 18xx.	—	—	—
S298	**10 POUNDS**			
	ND (ca.1877-1894). Brown and green.	—	—	—
S299	**20 POUNDS**			
	ND (ca.1877-1894). Green and orange.	—	—	—
S300	**50 POUNDS**			
	ND (ca.1877-1894). Pink and dk. blue.	—	—	—

1894 ISSUE

#S301-S305 larger arms w/lion facing slightly r. and unicorn facing l. w/o denomination unpt. at ctr. Colors like previous issue. Printer: PBC.

		GOOD	FINE	XF
S301	**1 POUND**			
	(ca.1894-1910).			
	b. Auckland. 18xx.	—	—	—
	e. Dunedin. 18xx.	—	—	—
	m. Wellington. 18xx.	—	—	—
S302	**5 POUNDS**			
	(ca.1894-1910).			
	b. Auckland. 18xx.	—	—	—
	c. Christchurch. 18xx.	—	—	—
	m. Wellington. 18xx.	—	—	—
S303	**10 POUNDS**			
	(ca.1894-1910).			
	b. Auckland. 19xx.	—	—	—
	c. Christchurch. 19xx.	—	—	—
	e. Dunedin. 18xx.	—	—	—
	m. Wellington. 19xx.	—	—	—
S304	**20 POUNDS**			
	(ca.1894-1910).			
	b. Auckland. 18xx.	—	—	—
	c. Christchurch. 19xx.	—	—	—
	e. Dunedin. 18xx.	—	—	—
	m. Wellington. 19xx; 1.1.1912.	—	—	—
S305	**50 POUNDS**			
	(ca.1894-1910).			
	b. Auckland. 18xx.	—	—	—
	c. Christchurch. 18xx.	—	—	—
	e. Dunedin. 18xx.	—	—	—
	m. Wellington. 18xx; 19xx.	—	—	—

1910-22 ISSUE

#S306-S311 larger arms. Wellington Office (other offices need confirmation).

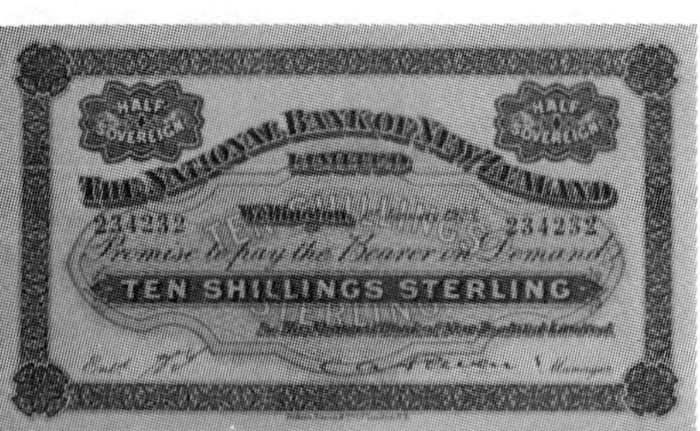

		GOOD	FINE	XF
S306	**10 SHILLINGS**			
	2.1.1922; 1.1.1923. Gray and green.	300.00	600.00	—

NOTE: #S306 may be dated from 1917-24. Full dates other than those listed need confirmation.

#S307-S311 denomination unpt. at ctr.

		GOOD	FINE	XF
S307	**1 POUND**			
	1.1.1910-1.1.1917; 1.1.1921; 1.1.1923. Gray.	300.00	500.00	—

		GOOD	FINE	XF
S308	**5 POUNDS**			
	1.1.1916; 1.1.1919; 1.1.1923. Blue	325.00	750.00	—

		GOOD	FINE	XF
S309	**10 POUNDS** 1.6.1910; 1.1.1912. Brown.	250.00	800.00	—
S310	**20 POUNDS** 1.1.1912; 1.6.1916. Green.	—	—	—
S311	**50 POUNDS** Pink.	—	—	—

NOTE: For #S307-S311, notes may be dated from ca.1910-24. Full dates other than those listed need confirmation.

1925; 1926 ISSUE

#S316-S321 are smaller size and have bank name in double lined capital letters. Wellington office.

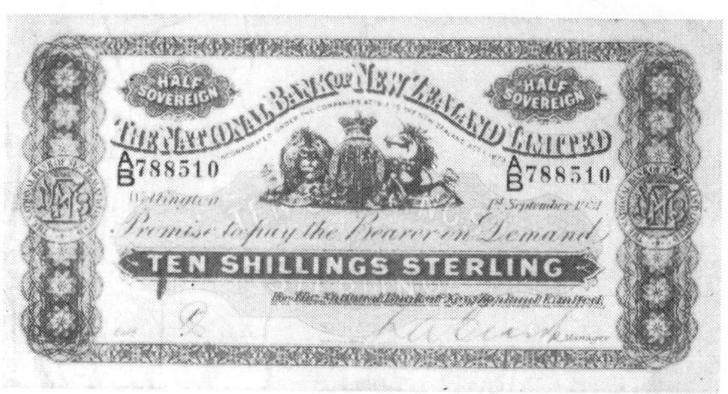

		GOOD	FINE	XF
S316	**10 SHILLINGS** 1.1.1925; 1.6.1926; 1.7.1929; 1.7.1933. Orange and purple. Uniface.	275.00	400.00	—
S317	**1 POUND** 1.1.1925; 1.6.1925; 1.6.1926; 1.7.1929; 1.8.1930. Purple and dk. brown. Uniface.	250.00	400.00	—
S318	**5 POUNDS** 1.6.1926. Blue and dk. brown. Back blue.	350.00	700.00	—

		GOOD	FINE	XF
S319	**10 POUNDS** 1.6.1925; 1.6.1926. Brown and dk. green. Back brown.	400.00	1000.	—
S320	**20 POUNDS** (ca.1925-30). Green and orange. Back green.	—	—	—
S321	**50 POUNDS** (ca.1925-30). Pink and dk. blue. Back pink.	—	—	—

NOTE: For #S316-S321, notes may be dated from ca.1924-34. Full dates other than those listed need confirmation.

NEW ZEALAND BANKING COMPANY

Established in 1840, it quickly became short of funds. No notes are presently known.

1840 ISSUE

		GOOD	FINE	XF
S326	**1 POUND** (ca.1840-45). Black. Britannia at upper l.	—	—	—
S327	**5 POUNDS** (ca.1840-45). Black. Like #S326.	—	—	—

NEW ZEALAND BANKING CORPORATION, LTD.

Reported issuer during 1863-66.

1885 ISSUE

		GOOD	FINE	XF
S331	**1 POUND** 2.1.1865. Black frame. Uniface. (Not issued.)	—	—	—

ORIENTAL BANK CORPORATION

Established in 1857. Purchased by Bank of New South Wales in 1861.

1857 ISSUE

#S333-S335A arms at upper ctr. Printer: PBC.

		GOOD	FINE	XF
S333	**1 POUND** (ca.1857-61). Black.			
	a. Issued note. Wellington. 1.1.1857.	—	Rare	—
	s. Specimen. Auckland.	—	—	—

		GOOD	FINE	XF
S334	**5 POUNDS** (ca.1857-61). Lt. brown. Auckland. Specimen.	—	—	—
S335	**10 DOLLARS** (ca.1857-61).	Reported Not Confirmed		
S335A	**20 POUNDS** (ca. 1857-61). Auckland. Specimen.	—	—	—

OTAGO BANKING COMPANY

1851 ISSUE

#S336-S338 Scottish arms at top ctr.

		GOOD	FINE	XF
S336	**10 SHILLINGS** (ca.1851). Blue. (Not issued.)	—	—	—

		GOOD	FINE	XF
S337	**1 POUND** (ca.1851). Black. (Not issued.)	300.00	—	—
S338	**5 POUNDS** (ca.1851). Black and blue. (Not issued.)	350.00	—	—

UNION BANK OF AUSTRALIA

Established in 1837, this bank issued New Zealand's first bank notes. Became part of the Australia and New Zealand Banking Group in 1951.

1840 ISSUE

		GOOD	FINE	XF
S341	**1 POUND** 24.3.1840; 30.5.1842. Black. Enthroned Qn. Victoria at upper l., Britannia and ships at top ctr. Uniface. Printer: PBC.	—	Rare	—

NOTE: 2, 5, 10 and 20 Pound values are reported, not confirmed.

1852 ISSUE

#S346-S349 Qn. Victoria at upper l., ship at ctr. Date handwritten. Uniface. Printer: PBC.

		GOOD	FINE	XF
S346	**1 POUND** 1.3.1859; 1.4.186x. Green and pink. Christchurch.	—	—	—
S347	**5 POUNDS** (ca.1852-60). Black.	—	—	—
S348	**10 POUNDS** (ca.1852-60). Black.	—	—	—
S349	**20 POUNDS** (ca.1852-60.). Specimen.	—	—	—

1861 ISSUE

#S351-S353 like previous issue. Partial date printed. Uniface.

		GOOD	FINE	XF
S351	**1 POUND** 1866. Green and pink.	—	—	—
S352	**5 POUNDS** (ca.1861-78). Black.	—	—	—

		GOOD	FINE	XF
S353	**10 POUNDS** (ca.1861-78). Black.			
	m. Wellington. 1.3.186x.	—	—	—
	s. Napier. Specimen. 18xx.	—	—	—

1878 ISSUE

#S356-S359 LIMITED added below, and back design initiated. Printer: PBC.

		GOOD	FINE	XF
S356	**1 POUND** (ca.1878-1904). Black w/green ovpt. Britannia seated w/symbols of commerce, lion and kangaroo at top ctr.			
	a. W/o printer's name. 1878; 1.4.1882; 1892; 1896.	—	—	—
	b. W/printer's name. 1900; 1903.	—	—	—
S357	**5 POUNDS** (ca.1878-1904). Black.	—	—	—
S358	**10 POUNDS** (ca.1878-1904). Black.	—	—	—
S359	**20 POUNDS** (ca.1878-1904). Gray. Back brown.	—	—	—

1905; 1920 ISSUE

#S361-S366 Wellington office. Printer: W&S.

		GOOD	FINE	XF
S361	**10 SHILLINGS** 1.3.1920; (ca.1920-23). Blue on red unpt. Portr. Qn. Victoria at lower l., Britannia seated w/symbols of commerce, lion and kangaroo at ctr.	300.00	600.00	—

		GOOD	FINE	XF
S362	**1 POUND** 1.3.1905; (ca.1905-23). Black, dk. green and red. Portr. Qn. Victoria at l., Britannia and symbols of commerce at top ctr.			
	a. Plain margins.	300.00	600.00	—
	b. *NEW ZEALAND* added in upper and lower margins.	300.00	600.00	—

		GOOD	FINE	XF
S363	**5 POUNDS** 1.3.1905; (ca.1905-23). Black on green unpt. Portr. Qn. Victoria at top ctr., Britannia and symbols of commerce at lower r.			
	a. Plain margins.	450.00	875.00	—
	b. *NEW ZEALAND* added in margins.	450.00	900.00	—
S364	**10 POUNDS** (ca.1905-24). Black and orange.	325.00	650.00	—
S365	**20 POUNDS** (ca.1905-23). Black on lt. blue unpt. Qn. Victoria at lower r.			
	a. Plain margins.	—	—	—
	b. *NEW ZEALAND* added in margins.	—	—	—

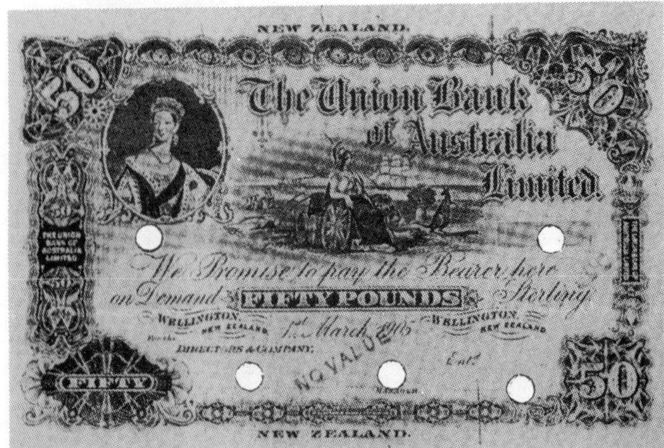

		GOOD	FINE	XF
S366	**50 POUNDS** 1.3.1905. Black. Qn. Victoria at upper l., Britannia seated w/symbols of commerce at ctr.			
	a. Plain margins.	—	—	—
	b. *NEW ZEALAND* added in margins.	—	—	—
	p. Proof.	—	Unc	750.00

NOTE: #S362-S366, only the 1905 date has been confirmed. Other dates need confirmation.

1923 ISSUE

#S371-S376 smaller size. Wellington office. Printer: W&S.

		GOOD	FINE	XF
S371	**10 SHILLINGS** 1.10.1923. Orange on green unpt. Portr. Qn. Victoria at lower l., Britannia and symbols of commerce at ctr. Back orange.			
	a. Text: W/*STERLING.*	250.00	500.00	—
	b. W/o *STERLING.*	250.00	500.00	—

		GOOD	FINE	XF
S372	**1 POUND** 1.10.1923. Mauve and green. Portr. Qn. Victoria at l., Britannia and symbols of commerce at top ctr.			
	a. Issued note.	250.00	550.00	—
	s. Specimen.	—	—	1000.

		GOOD	FINE	XF
S373	**5 POUNDS** 1.10.1923. Blue and pink. Portr. Qn. Victoria at top ctr., Britannia and symbols of commerce at lower r.	400.00	800.00	—
S374	**10 POUNDS** 1923. Brown and green. Qn. Victoria at r.	400.00	—	—
S375	**20 POUNDS** 1923. Qn. Victoria at lower r.	—	—	—

NOTE: #S371-S375, only the 1923 date has been confirmed. Other dates need to be reported.

		GOOD	FINE	XF
S376	**50 POUNDS** (ca.1923). Red. Qn. Victoria.	—	—	—

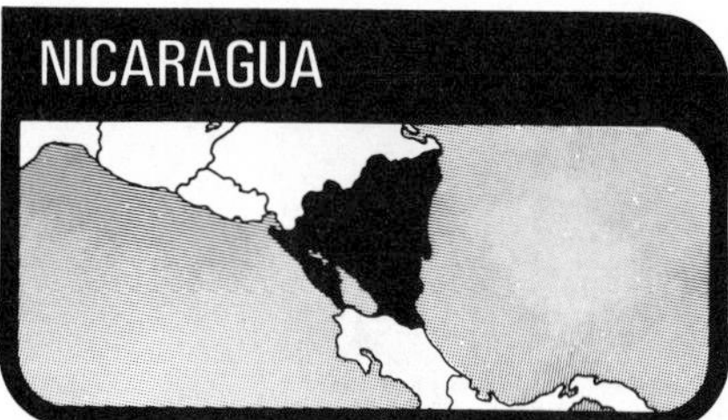

The Republic of Nicaragua, situated in Central America between Honduras and Costa Rica, has an area of 50,193 sq. mi (130,000 sq. km.) and a population of 4.69 million. Capital: Managua. Agriculture, mining (gold and silver) and hardwood logging are the principal industries. Cotton, meat, coffee, tobacco and sugar are exported.

Columbus sighted the coast of Nicaragua in 1502 during the course of his last voyage of discovery. It was first visited in 1522 by conquistadors from Panama, under command of Gonzalez Davila. After the first settlements were established in 1524 at Granada and Leon, Nicaragua was incorporated, for administrative purpose, in the Captaincy General of Guatemala, which included every Central American state but Panama. The Captaincy General declared its independence from Spain on Sept. 15, 1821. The next year Nicaragua united with the Mexican Empire of Agustin de Iturbide, then in 1823 with the Central American Republic. When the federation was dissolved, Nicaragua declared itself an independent republic in 1838.

MONETARY SYSTEM:

1 Peso = 100 Centavos to 1912

BANKS

#S101 and S102 *Deleted.* See #S131-S132.

BANCO AGRICOLA-MERCANTIL

Founded on 6.11.1888; failed in 1890.

1888 ISSUE

#S106-S112 printer: ABNC.

		GOOD	FINE	XF
S106	**50 CENTAVOS** 6.11.1888. Black. Animals feeding at l. Lithograph.			
	a. Issued note.	—	—	—
	s. Specimen.	—	—	—

		GOOD	FINE	XF
S107	**1 PESO** 6.11.1888. Black on orange unpt. Sitting child w/lyre at l., woman and sheep at top ctr., cow's head at r. Back red.			
	a. Issued note.	—	—	—
	r. Unsigned remainder.	—	—	—
	s. Specimen.	—	—	—

		Good	Fine	XF
S108	5 Pesos 6.11.1888. Black on yellow-green and brown unpt. Seated woman at l., rural farm scene at ctr. Back brown.			
	a. Issued note.	—	—	—
	s. Specimen.	—	—	—

#S109 *Deleted.*

NOTE: For #S107 and S108 w/ovpt: *TESORERIA GENERAL* see #A14 and A15 in Volume 2.

		Good	Fine	XF
S110	25 Pesos 6.11.1888. Black on green and blue unpt. Seated woman at l., woman w/farm produce at ctr., farm animals at lower r. Back blue. Specimen.	—	—	—

		Good	Fine	XF
S111	50 Pesos 6.11.1888. Black on blue, yellow and green unpt. Sailor at l., reclining woman at ctr. Back green.			
	a. Issued note.	—	—	—
	r. Unsigned remainder w/serial #.	—	—	—
	s. Specimen.	—	—	—

		Good	Fine	XF
S112	100 Pesos 6.11.1888. Black on yellow and tan unpt. Cow's head at l. ctr. Seated Mercury at r. w/ship in background. Back brown.			
	a. Issued note.	—	—	—
	r. Unsigned remainder w/serial #.	—	—	—
	s. Specimen.	—	—	—

Banco de Centro America y Londres

#S115 and S119 printer: W&S.

1889 Issue

		Good	Fine	XF
S115	1 Peso 18xx. C. Columbus at l., standing Liberty w/flag at r. Bank monogram at ctr. on back.	—	Rare	—
S119	100 Pesos 18xx. Specimen.	—	Rare	—

Banco de Nicaragua

1889; 1890 Issue

#S121-S126 printer: W&S.

		Good	Fine	XF
S121	50 Centavos 17.9.1890; 22.12.1893. Brown on yellow unpt. Standing Liberty w/flag at l., arms at ctr. r. Back blue.	80.00	300.00	650.00

		GOOD	FINE	XF
S122	**1 PESO** 8.11.1889; 27.4.1891; 24.8.1891; 27.8.1891; 22.12.1893. Brown and black on gold unpt. Portr. Medina at l., standing Liberty w/flag at r. Back dull red.	150.00	400.00	950.00

		GOOD	FINE	XF
S123	**5 PESOS** 18xx. Standing Liberty w/flag at l., portr. E. Carazo at ctr.			
	a. Issued note.	—	—	—
	s. Specimen.	—	—	—

		GOOD	FINE	XF
S124	**10 PESOS** 18xx. Black on brown and gold unpt. Portr. Pres. A. Cardenas at l., standing Liberty w/flag at ctr. Back green; arms.			
	a. Issued note.	—	—	—
	s. Specimen.	—	—	—
S125	**50 PESOS** 18xx. Portr. J. Zavala at ctr.	—	—	—
S126	**100 PESOS** 18xx.	Reported Not Confirmed		

MILITARY

WILLIAM WALKER MILITARY SCRIPT

A notaphilic oddity of Nicaragua, which might rank with the Papel Moneda of El Salvador, is the "Military Script" of William Walker, one time President of Nicaragua. Walker, a United States citizen, achieved a degree of fame in 1855 when he and a group of followers captured the city of Granada on behalf of a Nicaraguan political interest group. Walker, however, soon established himself as the real power in Nicaraguan politics and made peace with certain opposition groups. Though in control of the country, his domination was short-lived as a result of Commodore Cornelius Vanderbilt's sponsorship of Walker's overthrow in response to restriction placed on transit of the Isthmus. Vanderbilt was part owner of a company which had previously had the right of transit. Walker made several attempts to invade Central America again, only to be apprehended by the British who turned him over to authorities in Honduras in 1860 where he was promptly executed.

While President of Nicaragua, Walker issued "Military Script" to his followers as payment for services rendered. While not technically money because the issues were not declared to be legal tender for all debts public and private, the notes did serve as a form of near money. All specimens are believed to be quite scarce and of considerable historical significance.

SIGNATURE VARIETIES

1. F.(ermin) Ferrer
2. M.(anual) Carrascosa
3. Wm. K. Rogers

Notice

Readers with unlisted dates, color or signature varieties are invited to submit photocopies of their notes to: Standard Catalog of World Paper Money, Krause Publications, 700 East State St. Iola WI 54990-0001 U.S.A. or by email: thernr@krause.com. Email submissions of material for possible inclusion need to be 100% jpeg attachments at 300 dpi.

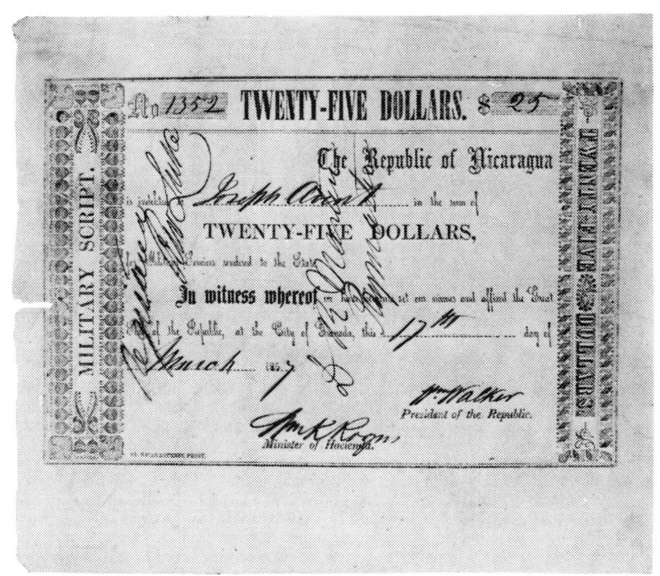

1856 ISSUE

#S131 and S132 soft paper w/dry seal of the Republic at lower l. ctr.

		GOOD	FINE	XF
S131	**25 DOLLARS** 29.7.1856; 20.2.1857; 17.3.1857.	800.00	1500.	3500.

NOTE: #S131 w/sign. 3 in XF sold at Smythe auction 6/98 for $8,250.

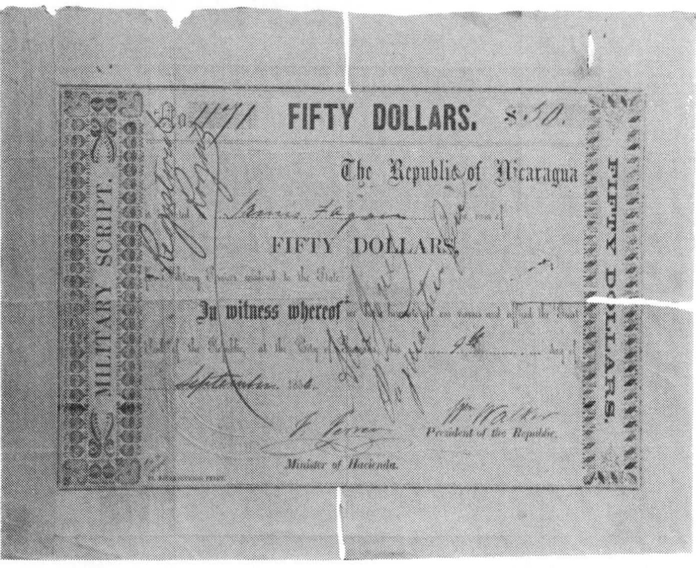

		GOOD	FINE	XF
S132	**50 DOLLARS** 31.10.1856.	1500.	3000.	5000.

Papua New Guinea, an independent member of the British Commonwealth, occupies the eastern half of the island of New Guinea. It lies north of Australia near the equator and borders on West Irian. The country, which includes nearby Bismarck Archipelago, Buka and Bougainville, has an area of 176,280 sq. mi. (461,691 sq. km.) and a population of 4.81 million who are divided into more than 1,000 separate tribes speaking more than 700 mutually unintelligible languages. Capital: Port Moresby. The economy is agricultural, and exports include copra, rubber, cocoa, coffee, tea, gold and copper.

New Guinea, the world's largest island after Greenland, was discovered by Spanish navigator Jorge de Menezes, who landed on the northwest shore in 1527. European interests, attracted by exaggerated estimates of the resources of the area, resulted in the island being claimed in whole or part by Spain, the Netherlands, Great Britain and Germany.

Papua (formerly British New Guinea), situated in the southeastern part of the island of New Guinea, has an area of 90,540 sq. mi. (234,499 sq. km.) and a population of 740,000. It was temporarily annexed by Queensland in 1883 and by the British Crown in 1888. Papua came under control of the Australian Commonwealth in 1901 and became the Territory of Papua in 1906. Japan invaded New Guinea and Papua early in 1942, but Australian control was restored before the end of the year in Papua and in 1945 in New Guinea.

In 1884 Germany annexed the area known as German New Guinea (also Neu-Guinea or Kaiser Wilhelmsland) comprising the northern section of eastern New Guinea, and granted its administration and development to the New-Guinea Compagnie. Administration reverted to Germany in 1889 following the failure of the company to exercise adequate administration. While a German protectorate, German New Guinea had an area of 92,159 sq. mi. (238,692 sq. km.) and a population of about 250,000. Capital: Herbertshohe, later named Rabaul. Copra was the chief crop. Australian troops occupied German New Guinea in Aug. 1914, shortly after Great Britain declared war on Germany. It was mandated to Australia by the League of Nations in 1920 and known as the Territory of New Guinea. The territory was invaded and occupied by Japan in 1942. Following the Japanese surrender, it came under U.N. trusteeship, Dec. 13, 1946, with Australia as the administering power.

The Papua and New Guinea Act, 1949, provided for the government of Papua and New Guinea as one administrative unit. On Dec. 1, 1973, Papua New Guinea became self-governing with Australia retaining responsibility for defense and foreign affairs. Full independence was achieved on Sept. 16, 1975 and Papua New Guinea is now a member of the Commonwealth of Nations. The Queen of England is Chief of State.

RULERS:

British

MONETARY SYSTEM:

1 Shilling = 12 Pence
1 Crown = 5 Shillings
1 Pound = 4 Crowns

Territory of Papua

Bank of New South Wales

Port Moresby

1910 Issue

		Good	Fine	XF
S111	**1 Pound** 1.5.1910; 1.6.1910. Black. Seated allegorical woman holding caduceus by sheep w/sailing ship in background at top ctr. Printer: CS&E.	—	—	—
S112	**5 Pounds** (ca.1910).	Reported Not Confirmed		
S113	**10 Pounds** (ca.1910).	Reported Not Confirmed		

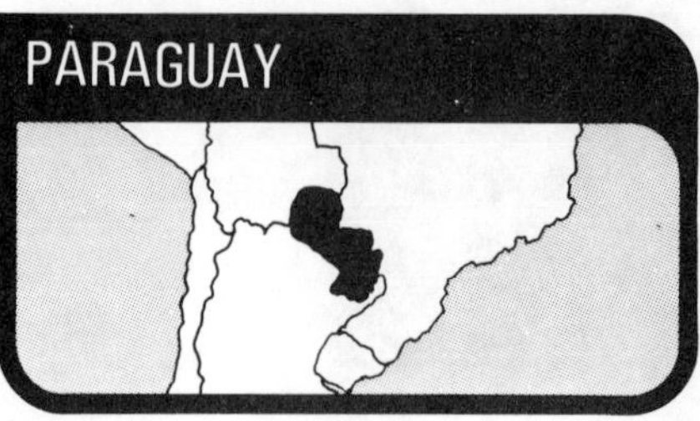

The Republic of Paraguay, a landlocked country in the heart of South America surrounded by Argentina, Bolivia and Brazil, has an area of 157,042 sq. mi. (406,752 sq. km.) and a population of 5.5 million, 95 percent of whom are of mixed Spanish and Indian descent. Capital: Asunción. The country is predominantly agrarian, with no important mineral deposits or oil reserves. Meat, timber, oilseeds, tobacco and cotton account for 70 percent of Paraguay's export revenue.

Paraguay was first visited by Alejo Garcia, a shipwrecked Spaniard, in 1520. The interior was explored by Sebastian Cabot in 1526 and 1529, when he sailed up the Paraná and Paraguay Rivers. Asunción, which would become the center of a province embracing much of southern South America, was established by the Spanish explorer Juan de Salazar on Aug. 15, 1537. For a century and a half the history of Paraguay was largely the history of the agricultural colonies established by the Jesuits in the south and east to Christianize the Indians. In 1811, following the outbreak of the South American wars of independence, Paraguayan patriots overthrew the local Spanish authorities and proclaimed their country's independence.

MONETARY SYSTEM:

1 Peso = 100 Centavos to 1870
1 Guaraní = 100 Céntimos, 1944-

Banks

Banco de Comercio

1886 Issues

#S102-S104 printer: Stiller y Laass, Buenos Aires.

#S105-S110 printer: G&D.

S102	**1 1/2 Pesos** 6.3.1866. Steam locomotive at l. Series A.	—	Rare	—

S103	**2 Pesos** 6.3.1886. Black on brown unpt. Railroad depot at ctr. r. Back brown; arms at ctr. Series B.	—	Rare	—
S104	**5 Pesos** 6.3.1886. Black on orange unpt. Bldg. w/tower at l.	—	Rare	—

NOTE: Other denominations are reported, not confirmed.

		VG	VF	Unc
S105	**1 1/2 Pesos** 6.3.1886. Brown on lt. blue unpt. Passenger train at ctr. Face proof.	—	—	700.00
S106	**2 Pesos** 6.3.1886. Black and red on lt. green unpt. Govt. bldg. at upper l. Face proof.	—	—	700.00
S107	**5 Pesos** 6.3.1886. Black and brown on lt. green unpt. Govt. bldg. at upper r. Back brown on blue unpt. Proof.	—	—	800.00
S108	**10 Pesos** 6.3.1886. Black on blue and orange unpt. Portr. man at l., plantation scene at ctr. r. Back brown and violet; arms at ctr. Proof.	—	—	1000.
S109	**20 Pesos** 6.3.1886. Black on lt. orange and blue unpt. Portr. man at upper r., workers building native huts at lower ctr. Face proof.	—	—	900.00
S110	**50 Pesos** 6.3.1886. Black on red and purple unpt. River scene at ctr., portr. man at r. Proof.	—	—	900.00

Banco del Paraguay

1879-82 Issue

Pesos Fuertes System.

#S111-S114 black. Uniface. Printer: Litografia Nacional, Buenos Aires.

S111 5 CENTAVOS

1879; 1882. Deer running at ctr.	GOOD	FINE	XF
a. 1.1.1879.	—	—	—
b. 1.1.1882.	—	—	—

S112 10 CENTAVOS

1879; 1882. Cows at ctr.	GOOD	FINE	XF
a. 1.1.1879.	—	—	—
b. 1.1.1882.	—	—	—

S113 20 CENTAVOS

1879; 1882. Fox at ctr.	GOOD	FINE	XF
a. 1.1.1879.	—	—	—
b. 1.1.1882.	—	—	—

S114 50 CENTAVOS

1879; 1882. Green numeral *50* at ctr. Lion under tree at r.	GOOD	FINE	XF
a. 1.1.1879.	—	—	—
b. 1.1.1882.	—	—	—

S119 20 PESOS

1.1.1882. Dog's head at lower l., horses at upper ctr. Printer: Litografía Nacional, Buenos Aires.	—	—	—

1882 ISSUE

#S121-S129 printer: ABNC.

#S121-S124 uniface.

S121 5 CENTAVOS

1.1.1882. Black on blue unpt. Dog's head at r.	GOOD	FINE	XF
a. Issued note.	25.00	75.00	175.00
p. Proof.	—	—	—

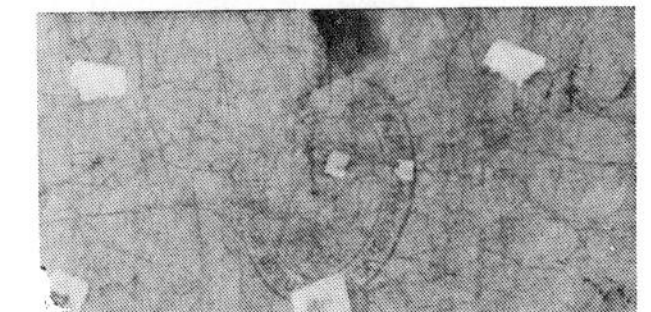

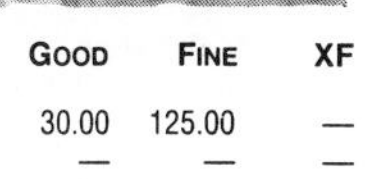

S122 10 CENTAVOS

1.1.1882. Black on gold unpt. Bull at l.	GOOD	FINE	XF
a. Issued note.	30.00	125.00	—
p. Proof.	—	—	—

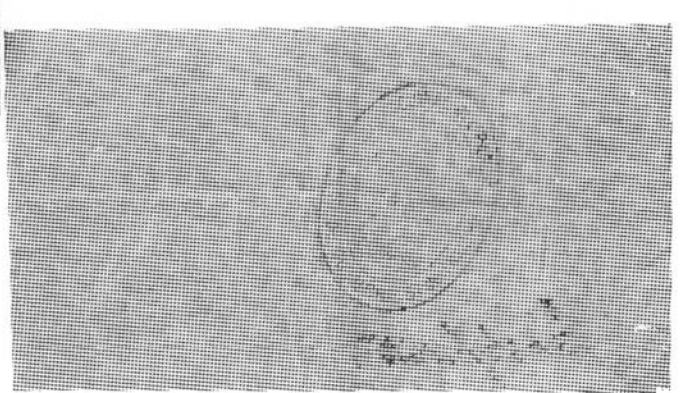

S123 20 CENTAVOS

1.1.1882. Black on brown unpt. Jaguar at ctr.	GOOD	FINE	XF
a. Issued note.	40.00	150.00	—
p. Proof.	—	—	—

S124 50 CENTAVOS

1.1.1882. Black on red unpt. Horse at l. under tree, value between griffens at ctr. r.	GOOD	FINE	XF
a. Issued note.	50.00	175.00	—
p. Proof.	—	—	—

S125 1 PESO

1.1.1882. Black on brown unpt. Steam locomotive at upper l., young woman at lower r. Back brown.	GOOD	FINE	XF
p. Proof.	—	—	—
s. Specimen.	—	—	—

S126 2 PESOS

1.1.1882. Black on green unpt. Steam passenger train at ctr. Back green.	GOOD	FINE	XF
a. Issued note.	—	—	—
p. Proof.	—	—	—

S127 5 PESOS

1.1.1882. Black on red unpt. Arms at l., crowned woman at r. Back orange.	GOOD	FINE	XF
p. Proof.	—	—	—
s. Specimen.	—	—	—

		GOOD	FINE	XF
S128	10 PESOS 1.1.1882. Black on olive-green unpt. Sailing ship at ctr. r. Back olive-green.			
	p. Proof.	—	—	—
	s. Specimen.	—	—	—

		GOOD	FINE	XF
S129	20 PESOS 1.1.1882. Black on lilac unpt. Ships at l. ctr., woman at r. Back purple.			
	p. Proof.	—	—	—
	s. Specimen.	—	—	—

BANCO NACIONAL DEL PARAGUAY

1886 ISSUE

#S141-S152 Law of 31.10.1883 but later issue date. Similar to #S121-S129. Printer: ABNC.

#S141-S144 uniface.

		GOOD	FINE	XF
S141	5 CENTAVOS 1.1.1886. Similar to #S121.	3.00	15.00	50.00

		GOOD	FINE	XF
S142	10 CENTAVOS 1.1.1886. Similar to #S122.	5.00	25.00	70.00
S143	20 CENTAVOS 1.1.1886. Black on pink unpt. Similar to #S123.	7.50	30.00	85.00
S144	50 CENTAVOS 1.1.1886. Black on brown unpt. Similar to #S124.	10.00	35.00	95.00

		GOOD	FINE	XF
S145	1 PESO 1.1.1886. Similar to #S125.	20.00	50.00	120.00

		GOOD	FINE	XF
S146	2 PESOS 1.1.1886. Similar to #S126.	—	—	—
S147	5 PESOS 1.1.1886.	Reported Not Confirmed		
S148	10 PESOS 1.1.1886.	Reported Not Confirmed		
S149	20 PESOS 1.1.1886. Similar to #S129. Series B. Proof.	—	—	—
S150	50 PESOS 1.1.1886. Black on green and red unpt. Man at l., arms at ctr., allegorical woman w/globe and pitcher at r. Back orange; woman w/spool at ctr. Series A. Proof.	—	—	—

		GOOD	FINE	XF
S151	100 PESOS 1.1.1886. Black on orange and blue unpt. Liberty standing at l., arms at ctr., portr. Gen. Bernardino Caballero at r. Back blue; woman writing at ctr. Series A.			
	a. Issued note.	—	Rare	—
	p. Proof.	—	—	—

		GOOD	FINE	XF
S152	200 PESOS 1.1.1886. Black on green and red unpt. Portr. Gen. Escobar at l., horses at upper ctr., arms at r. Back brown; steam passenger trains in terminal. Series A. Proof.	—	—	—

BANCO DEL PARAGUAY Y RIO DE LA PLATA

1889 ISSUE

#S161-S168 printer: ABNC.

		GOOD	FINE	XF
S161	**1 PESO - 25 CENTAVOS** 26.12.1889. Black on green unpt. Seated woman w/safe at l., arms at r. Back green.	30.00	125.00	375.00

		GOOD	FINE	XF
S162	**2 PESOS** 26.12.1889. Black on blue and yellow unpt. Portr. H. Ponzini at l., arms at r. Back blue.	50.00	175.00	450.00

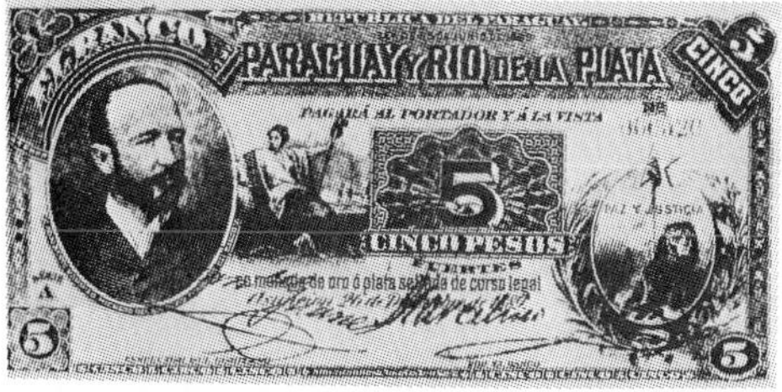

		GOOD	FINE	XF
S163	**5 PESOS** 26.12.1889. Black on brown unpt. Portr. A. Schmied at l., seated woman at l. ctr., arms at r. Back brown.	—	—	—

		GOOD	FINE	XF
S164	**10 PESOS** 26.12.1889. Black on brown unpt. Hope at the Seashore at l., arms at ctr., portr. Higinio Uriarte at r. Back brown; figures at l. and ctr. r. Proof.	—	—	—

		GOOD	FINE	XF
S165	**20 PESOS** 26.12.1889. Black on orange and yellow unpt. Arms at l., allegorical woman and child at ctr., portr. J. A. Meza at r. Back orange.			
	a. Purple ovpt.	125.00	400.00	—
	b. W/o ovpt.	125.00	400.00	—
	p. Proof.	—	—	—

		GOOD	FINE	XF
S166	**50 PESOS** 26.12.1889. Black on yellow and brown unpt. Portr. Gen. Bernardino Caballero at l., seated Agriculture at upper ctr., arms at r. Back dk. brown; Indian woman paddling at ctr. Proof.	—	—	—

		GOOD	FINE	XF
S167	**100 PESOS** 26.12.1889. Black on green and yellow unpt. Portr. T. Dugan at l., allegorical child and fish at ctr., arms at lower r. Back green; viaduct at l. ctr., steam train at ctr. r. Proof.	—	—	—

		GOOD	FINE	XF
S168	**200 PESOS** 26.12.1889. Black on orange and gold unpt. Portr. Gen. Escobar at l., woman and child at ctr., arms at r. Back orange; 2 women at ctr. Proof.	—	Rare	—

#S171 and S172 printer: CSABB.

		GOOD	FINE	XF
S171	**1 PESO - 25 CENTAVOS** 20.12.1889. Portr. Higinio Uriarte at l., arms at r.	—	Rare	—

		GOOD	FINE	XF
S172	2 PESOS 20.12.1889. Black on brown unpt. Portr. A. Schmied at l. Back green; arms at ctr.	—	Rare	—

ARGENTINE OCCUPATION

Issued by Argentine military authority for occupation of Paraguay 1870. Uniface. Printer: Lit. San Martin, Buenos Aires.

LEZICA Y LANÚS

ARMY SUPPLIES

1870'S ISSUE

Pesos Fuertes System.

		GOOD	FINE	XF
S181	50 CENTIMOS 187x. Black on dk. blue paper. Arms at l., dog on strongbox at ctr.	—	Unc	65.00
S182	1 PESO 1.3.1870. Arms at upper ctr.	—	Rare	—

#S184 and S185 blue hand stamp: *PROVEEDURA/DEL/EJERCITO* on face.

		GOOD	FINE	XF
S184	5 PESOS 1.3.1870. Blue and black. Arms at upper l., 2 women seated at upper ctr. Blue hand stamp over arms.	400.00	500.00	—

		GOOD	FINE	XF
S185	10 PESOS 1.3.1870. Black and blue-green on dk. pink paper. Woman at l., arms at upper ctr. Blue hand stamp over arms.	400.00	500.00	—

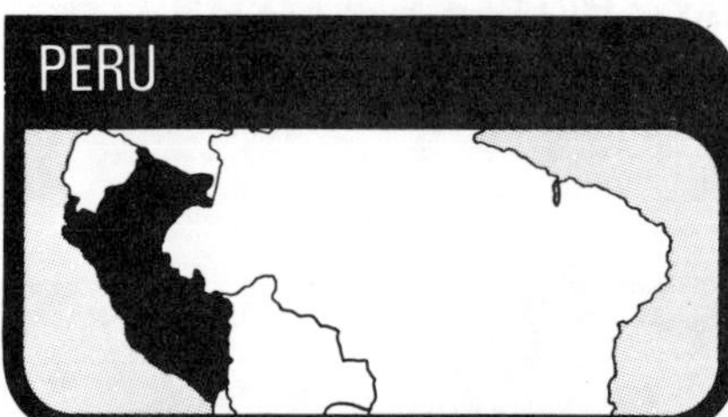

The Republic of Perú, located on the Pacific coast of South America, has an area of 496,222 sq. mi. (1,285,216 sq. km.) and a population of 25.66 million. Capital: Lima. The diversified economy includes mining, fishing and agriculture. Fish meal, copper, sugar, zinc and iron ore are exported.

Once part of a great Inca Empire that reached from northern Ecuador to central Chile, Perú was conquered in 1531-33 by Francisco Pizarro. Desirable as the richest of the Spanish viceroyalties, it was torn by warfare between avaricious Spaniards until the arrival in 1569 of Francisco de Toledo, who initiated 2 1/2 centuries of efficient colonial rule which made Lima the most aristocratic colonial capital and the stronghold of Spain's South American possessions. José de San Martín of Argentina proclaimed Perú's independence on July 28, 1821; Simón Bolívar of Venezuela secured it in Dec. of 1824 when he defeated the last Spanish army in South America. After several futile attempts to re-establish its South American empire, Spain recognized Perú's independence in 1879.

MONETARY SYSTEM:

1 Sol = 1 Sol de Oro = 100 Centavos, 1879-1985
1 Libra = 10 Soles
1 Sol = 100 Centavos (10 Dineros)

BANKS:

BANKS

BANCO ANGLO-PERUANO

Founded in 1873; ceased operations in 1877.

1875 FIRST ISSUE

#S101-S103 English and Peruvian arms at ctr. on back. Printer: CNBB/NBNC.

		GOOD	FINE	XF
S101	20 CENTAVOS 1.7.1875. Black.			
	a. Back green.	—	—	—
	b. Back orange.	—	—	—

		GOOD	FINE	XF
S101A	40 CENTAVOS 1.7.1875. Black on brown unpt. Back brown.			
	a. Issued note.	—	—	—
	p. Proof.	—	—	—

S101B 50 CENTAVOS
1.7.1875. Black on blue unpt. Back blue.

GOOD	FINE	XF
—	—	—

1875 SECOND ISSUE

S102 40 CENTAVOS
1.7.1875. Black on yellow-orange unpt. Back brown-orange. Sign R. J. Jameson at r. Proof.

GOOD	FINE	XF
—	—	—

S103 50 CENTAVOS
1.7.1875. Black on dk. brown unpt. Back dk. brown. Sign. R. J. Jameson at r. Proof.

GOOD	FINE	XF
—	—	—

S103A 1 SOL
ca. 1875. Brown. Bank monogram at ctr. Back proof.

GOOD	FINE	XF
—	—	—

1874-75 ISSUE

#S104-S108 printer: Dondorf & Naumann, Frankfurt a/M.

S104 1 SOL
1.9.1874. Green. Mercury on globe at r.

GOOD	FINE	XF
—	Rare	—

S105 5 SOLES
17.3.1875. Brown. Similar to #S104.

GOOD	FINE	XF
—	Rare	—

S106 10 SOLES
1.9.1874. Blue. Cherubs at bottom ctr.

GOOD	FINE	XF
—	Rare	—

		GOOD	FINE	XF
S107	**20 SOLES** 1.9.1874; 17.3.1875. Brown. Woman and cherubs at l.	—	Rare	—
S108	**100 SOLES** 187x. Green. Similar to #S107.	—	Rare	—

BANCO DE AREQUIPA

Founded in 1871.

1870'S ISSUE

#S111-S112 printer: Abele y Ca., Lima.

S111 20 CENTAVOS
ND. Black and red. Man and llama w/city view in back at ctr.

GOOD	FINE	XF
—	—	—

S112 40 CENTAVOS
ND. Blue. Similar to #S111.

GOOD	FINE	XF
—	—	—

#S116-S124 printer: CNBB.

#S116-S118 seated woman w/safe and shield at ctr.; city, train and mountain in background.

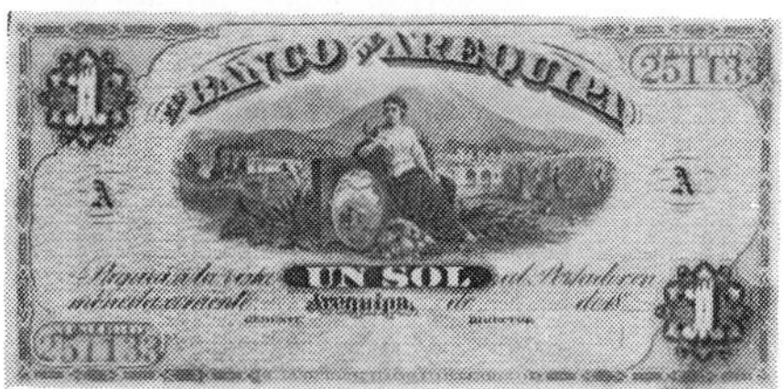

S116 40 CENTAVOS
1.10.1874. Black on green unpt. Back green.

VG	VF	UNC
5.00	20.00	65.00

		VG	VF	UNC
S117	**1 SOL** 18xx. Black on green unpt. Similar to #S116. Back green.	5.00	20.00	65.00
S118	**2 SOLES** 18xx. Black on orange unpt. Similar to #S116. Back orange.	8.00	25.00	75.00

S119 5 SOLES
187x. Black on brown unpt. Similar to #S116 but cow at l., wheat at r. Back brown.

VG	VF	UNC
20.00	60.00	150.00

		VG	VF	UNC
S120	**10 SOLES** 187x. Black on brown unpt. Similar to #S116 but man at l., roosters at r. Back brown.	35.00	125.00	—

		VG	VF	UNC
S121	**20 SOLES** 187x. Black on brown unpt. Similar to #S116 but ducks at l., train at r.	—	—	—

		VG	VF	UNC
S122	**50 SOLES** 187x. Black on brown unpt. Similar to #S116 but basket of corn at l., sheep at r.	—	—	—

		VG	VF	UNC
S123	**100 SOLES** 187x. Black on red unpt. Similar to #S116 but man at l., anchor at r.	—	—	—

		VG	VF	UNC
S124	**500 SOLES** 1.8.1872. Black on yellow unpt. Similar to #S116 but sailing ship at l., scroll at r.	—	—	—

BANCO DE LA COMPAÑIA GENERAL DEL PERÚ

None of these notes were issued under the name of this bank. #S131, S132 and S134 were later issued by the government of Nicolas Pierola with ovpt. in fractions of the Inca.

1873 ISSUE

#S131-S134 colors and printers: face, black and green, NBNC; back, green, ABNC. Proofs, punched hole cancelled.

		GOOD	FINE	XF
S131	**1 SOL** 1873. Portr. J. Galvez between sailing ship and steam train at upper l., steam train at lower ctr. Steam train on back.			
	p. Proof.	—	—	—
	r. Unissued remainder.	—	—	—
S132	**5 SOLES** 1873. Man w/horses and mule train at upper ctr., train below. Laureated J. Galvez at r. Man w/llamas at l., steam train at r. on back.	—	—	—

		GOOD	FINE	XF
S133	**20 SOLES** 1873. Portr. J. Galvez at l., woman seated at ctr., train below. Steam train at ctr. on back.	—	—	—

		GOOD	FINE	XF
S134	**100 SOLES** 1873. Woman in feather headdress w/sword and lion at l., laureated portr. J. Galvez at l. ctr., train below. Steam train at l., man w/llamas at r. on back.	—	—	—

NOTE: For #S131, S132 and S134 ovpt. in Incas as issued in 1881, see Volume II, #11-13.

BANCO DE LA EMANCIPACIÓN

PAPER-MONEY AUXILIARY BANK

Founded in 1822, closed in 1823.

Created by José de San Martín in order to obtain funds to alleviate economic strain caused by the independence movement.

1822 ISSUE

#S141

#S142

#S143

		GOOD	FINE	XF
S141	**2 REALES** 1822. Black.	—	Rare	—
S142	**4 REALES** 1822. Black.	—	Rare	—
S143	**1 PESO = 8 REALES** 5.1822. Black.	—	Rare	—

BANCO DEL EMISIÓN DEL CERRO

Founded in 1872; issued banknotes in small denominations (possibly ovpt. on larger values). None are known at this time.

1870'S ISSUE

		GOOD	FINE	XF
S151	**1 DINERO = 1/10 SOL**	Reported Not Confirmed		
S153	**1/2 SOL**	Reported Not Confirmed		

BANCO GARANTIZADOR

Founded in 1872.

1876 ISSUE

#S161-S168 printer: NBNC.

		GOOD	FINE	XF
S161	**10 CENTAVOS** 1.9.1876. Black on green unpt. Helmeted Minerva at l. Back green.	100.00	350.00	—

		GOOD	FINE	XF
S162	**20 CENTAVOS** 1.9.1876. Black on brown unpt. Woman and fruit at upper ctr. Back brown.	100.00	350.00	—

		GOOD	FINE	XF
S163	**40 CENTAVOS** 1.9.1876. Black on red-orange unpt. Eagle at ctr. Back orange.	120.00	400.00	—

#S164-S168 fully printed, or partially printed and stamped date.

		GOOD	FINE	XF
S164	**1 SOL** 1.9.1876. Black and blue. Farm family at ctr. Back blue; 2 men at ctr.	100.00	350.00	—

		GOOD	FINE	XF
S165	**2 SOLES** 1.9.1876. Black and orange. Woman sitting w/bale at ctr. Back orange.	90.00	350.00	—

		GOOD	FINE	XF
S166	**5 SOLES** 1.9.1876. Black and brown. Lg. ornaments at l. and r., portr. girl at upper ctr. Back brown.	100.00	375.00	—

		GOOD	FINE	XF
S167	**10 SOLES** 1.9.1876. Black and green. Portr. 3 girls at upper ctr.	—	—	—

		GOOD	FINE	XF
S168	**50 SOLES** 1.9.1876. Black and green. Cherub w/fruit at lower l., 3 allegorical women at upper ctr., cotton at lower r. Street scene of bank facade on vertical back.			
	a. Issued note.	—	Rare	—
	s. Specimen.	—	—	—

BANCO LA PROVIDENCIA

Founded in 1862, this was Peru's first private bank. Its first notes were issued under the name *La Providencia Sociedad Anonima General del Peru.*

1863 FIRST ISSUE

Peso System.

#S191-S195 black. Woman and child at upper l., cornucopias and caduceus at lower r. Uniface.

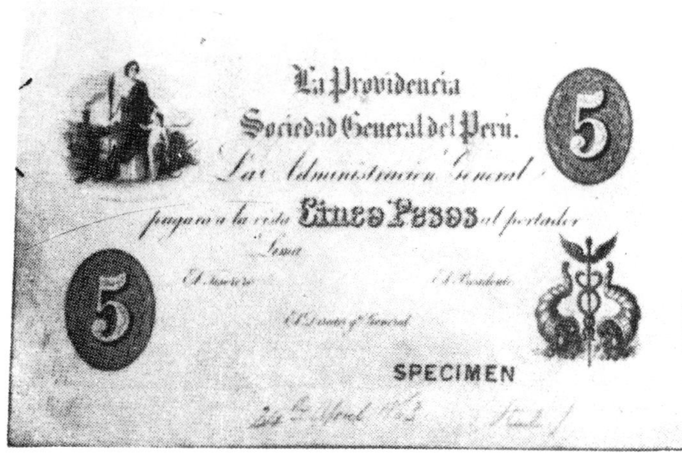

		GOOD	FINE	XF
S191	**5 PESOS** 18xx-(7.1863).	—	Rare	—
S192	**25 PESOS** 31.12.1863.	—	Rare	—
S193	**50 PESOS** 31.12.1863.	—	Rare	—
S194	**100 PESOS** 31.12.1863.	—	Rare	—
S195	**500 PESOS** 31.12.1863.	—	Rare	—

1863 Second Issue

#S201-S204 like #S192-S195 but w/lg. denomination word added in color at ctr. in unpt.

		Good	Fine	XF
S201	**25 Pesos** 31.12.1863. Lg. denomination word in red.	—	Rare	—

		Good	Fine	XF
S202	**50 Pesos** 31.12.1863. Lg. denomination word in blue.	—	Rare	—
S203	**100 Pesos** 31.12.1863. Lg. denomination word in yellow.	—	Rare	—
S204	**500 Pesos** 31.12.1863. Lg. denomination word in green.	—	Rare	—

1864 Issue

Sol System.

#S209-S214 similar to #S191-S195 but center design guilloche is more ornate and has word plus numerals at either side. They also express value in soles as well as pesos in special text near lower ctr.

		Good	Fine	XF
S209	**5 Soles** 30.6.1864.	—	Rare	—
S211	**20 Soles = 25 Pesos** 30.6.1864. Yellow protector.	—	Rare	—

		Good	Fine	XF
S212	**40 Soles = 50 Pesos** 30.6.1864. Red protector.	—	Rare	—

		Good	Fine	XF
S213	**80 Soles = 100 Pesos** 30.6.1864. Green protector.	—	Rare	—
S214	**200 Soles = 250 Pesos** 30.6.1864. Yellow protector.	—	Rare	—

#S221 and S222 printer: NBNC.

		Good	Fine	XF
S221	**4 Soles** 1869. Black and red. Woman standing at l., rayed head at ctr., anchor at r.	—	Rare	—

		Good	Fine	XF
S222	**8 Soles** 1869. Black and red. 2 men at l., sailing ship at ctr., cotton at r.	—	Rare	—

1867-77 Issue

#S226-S236 printer: ABNC.

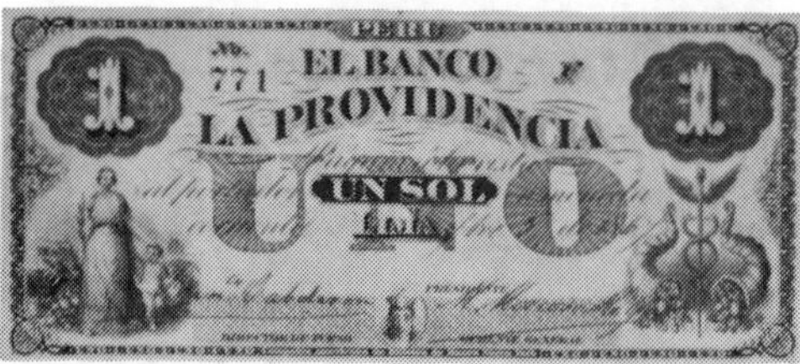

		Good	Fine	XF
S226	**1/2 Sol** 18xx. Black on green unpt. Cornucopias and caduceus at ctr. Back green.	95.00	300.00	—

#S227-S231 llamas on back.

		Good	Fine	XF
S227	**1 Sol** 5.4.1867; 10.11.1872. Black on green unpt. Woman and child at l., 2 cornucopias and caduceus at r. Back green.	100.00	300.00	—
S228	**2 Soles** 2.8.1867; 17.4.1868; 1.1.1875. Black on green unpt. Similar to #S227. Back brown.	—	Rare	—

NOTE: According to archive records, two back color varieties exist for #S227 and S228.

		Good	Fine	XF
S229	**4 Soles** 1.1.1875. Black on green unpt. Similar to #S227, but lg. star ovpt. at upper ctr. r.	90.00	250.00	—
S230	**5 Soles** 1877. Black on green unpt. Similar to #S229.	—	Rare	—
S231	**10 Soles** 1877. Black on green unpt. Similar to #S229.	—	Rare	—

S232 20 SOLES — Good: — | Fine: Rare | XF: —
20.7.1877. Black on green unpt. Similar to #S229 but man w/llamas added at ctr.

S233 50 SOLES — Good: — | Fine: Rare | XF: —
20.7.1877. Black on green unpt. Similar to #S232.

S234 100 SOLES — Good: — | Fine: Rare | XF: —
20.7.1877. Black on green unpt. Similar to #S232.

S235 500 SOLES — Good: — | Fine: Rare | XF: —
18xx. Black on green unpt. Similar to #S232.

S236 1000 SOLES — Good: — | Fine: Rare | XF: —
20.7.1877. Black on green unpt. Similar to #S232.

BANCO DE LIMA

Founded in 1869; operated from 1870 to 1878.

1870-76 ISSUE

#S241-S246 printer: CNBB.

S241 1 SOL — Good: — | Fine: — | XF: —
1.7.1870; 1.11.1875. Black on orange unpt. Indian woman w/sword and flag standing at l., mountain view at ctr., llamas at r. Back deep orange.

S242 4 SOLES
1.1.1870 (hand stamped or handwritten dates). Black on green unpt. Girls at lower l., 2 women and shield at upper l., train and shield at r. Back blue-green.

	Good	Fine	XF
a. Issued note.	150.00	—	—
p. Proof.	—	—	—

S243 8 SOLES — Good: — | Fine: Rare | XF: —
1.1.1870; 1.2.1876. Black on blue unpt. 3 girls at lower l., 2 women and sunface at lower r. Back blue.

S244 20 SOLES — Good: — | Fine: Rare | XF: —
1.11.1875. Black on blue unpt. Sailing ship at l., seated woman w/produce and shield at upper ctr., Mercury at lower r. Back lt. blue.

S245 80 SOLES — Good: — | Fine: Rare | XF: —
1.1.1871. Black on brown unpt. Liberty w/constitution at l., steamship at r. Back brown.

S246 400 SOLES — Good: — | Fine: Rare | XF: —
1.9.1875. Black on yellow unpt. Sitting woman at lower l., harbor scene at ctr., angel and scroll at lower r.

BANCO DE LONDRES Y SUD AMERICA

Established in 1863; shortly thereafter became Banco de Londres Mexico y Sud America.

1800's ISSUE

#S251-S257 black. Standing woman by beehive w/sailing ship in background at upper l., crowned royal arms at upper ctr., standing woman in cornfield at lower r. Printer: PBC.

		GOOD	FINE	XF
S251	**5 PESOS** 18xx.	—	Rare	—
S253	**25 PESOS** 18xx.	—	Rare	—
S255	**100 PESOS** 18xx.	—	Rare	—

		GOOD	FINE	XF
S257	**1000 PESOS** 18xx.	—	Rare	—

BANCO DE LONDRES MEXICO Y SUD AMERICA

Formerly the Banco de Londres y Sud America.

1860's ISSUE

Peso System.

#S261-S267 like #S251-S257 except for bank name change.

		GOOD	FINE	XF
S261	**5 PESOS** 18xx.	—	Rare	—
S263	**25 PESOS** 18xx.	—	Rare	—
S265	**100 PESOS** 18xx.	—	Rare	—
S267	**1000 PESOS** 18xx.	—	Rare	—

1866-72 ISSUES

Sol System.

#S271-S278 dates filled in by hand. Back blue. Printer: ABNC.

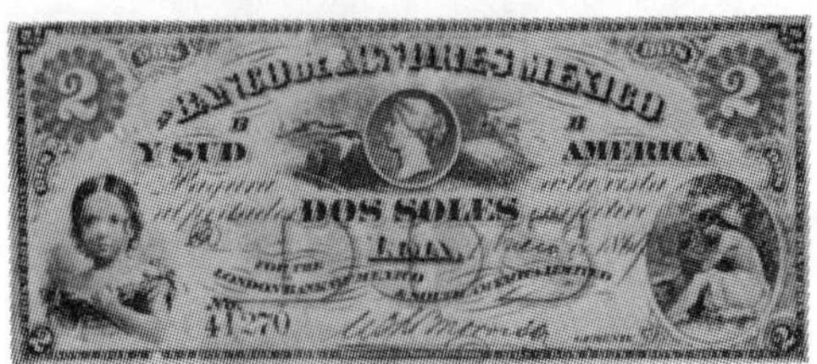

		GOOD	FINE	XF
S271	**2 SOLES** 1.1.1866. Black on orange unpt. Girl at lower l., portr. Qn. Victoria at ctr., woman w/child at lower r.	—	Rare	—
S272	**5 SOLES** 1866; 1.3.1870. Black on green unpt. 2 girls at lower 1., 2 seated women and English shield at ctr., woman at r.	—	Rare	—
S273	**5 SOLES** 1.3.1870. Black on red unpt. Like #S272.	—	Rare	—

		GOOD	FINE	XF
S274	**10 SOLES** 1.1.1866. Black on red unpt. Woman holding rabbit at lower l., boys and mule train at top ctr., Shield w/flags w/portr. Qn. Victoria at lower r.	—	Rare	—

		GOOD	FINE	XF
S275	**25 SOLES** 1.10.1871. Black on red unpt. Boys and mule train at upper l., girl holding dog at lower r.	—	Rare	—

		GOOD	FINE	XF
S276	**100 SOLES** 1.6.1872; 1.1.1875. Black on green unpt. Sailors at lower l., 2 women and Peruvian shield at upper ctr., 2 horses at lower r.	—	Rare	—

		GOOD	FINE	XF
S277	**500 SOLES** 18xx. Black on green unpt. 2 girls at lower l., lion and reclining woman w/portr. Qn. Victoria at upper ctr., helmeted figure at r.	—	Rare	—

		GOOD	FINE	XF
S278	**1000 SOLES** 18xx. Black on green unpt. 2 girls w/sheaves at lower l., 2 women seated at upper ctr., shield w/flags w/portr. Qn. Victoria at lower r.	—	Rare	—

1871 ISSUE

#S281-S284 printer: TDLR.

		GOOD	FINE	XF
S281	**1 SOL** 20.9.1871. Blue. Woman's head at l.	—	Rare	—

		GOOD	FINE	XF
S282	**2 SOLES** 20.9.1871. Purple. Woman's head at lower ctr.	—	Rare	—

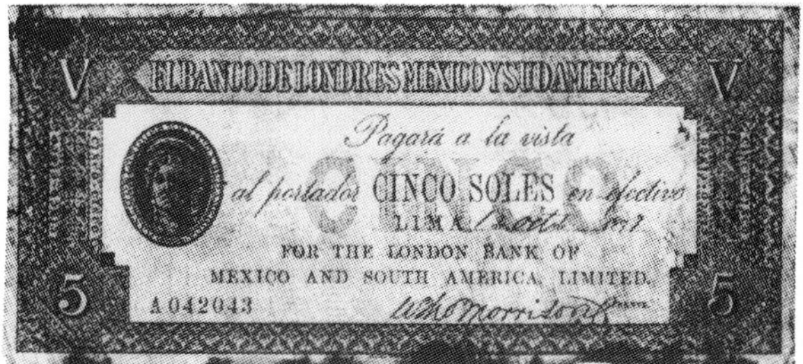

		GOOD	FINE	XF
S283	**5 SOLES** 1.10.1871. Green. Woman's head at l.	—	Rare	—

		GOOD	FINE	XF
S284	**10 SOLES** 1.10.1871. Yellow. Woman's head at upper ctr.	—	Rare	—

1873-74 ISSUE

#S291-S298 printer: ABNC.

		GOOD	FINE	XF
S291	**1 SOL** 1.1.1873. Blue. People w/horse at lower l., arms at upper ctr., laureated woman at lower r.	—	Rare	—

#S292-S297 designs like #S271 and S272, S274-S276. Printed date.

		GOOD	FINE	XF
S292	**2 SOLES** 1.1.1873. Blue. Like #S271.	—	Rare	—

		GOOD	FINE	XF
S293	**5 SOLES** 1.1.1873. Black on brown and green unpt. Like #S272.			
	a. Issued note.	—	Rare	—
	s. Specimen.	—	—	—
S294	**5 SOLES** 1.1.1873. Brown and blue. Like #S293.	—	Rare	—
S295	**10 SOLES** 1.1.1873. Lt. brown on gray unpt. Like #S274. Back blue.	—	Rare	—
S295A	**10 SOLES** 18xx (ca.1872). Black on brown and green unpt. Like #S295. Archive copy.	—	—	—
S296	**25 SOLES** 18xx (ca.1874). Brown on blue unpt. Like #S275. Archive copy.	—	—	—
S297	**100 SOLES** 18xx (ca.1874). Green on brown unpt. Like #S276. Archive copy.	—	—	—
S298	**500 SOLES** 18xx (ca.1874). Reported in archive records, not confirmed.	—	—	—

BANCO NACIONAL DEL PERÚ

Began operations in 1872.

1873 FIRST FRACTIONAL ISSUE

#S301 and S302 sign. titles: *DIRECTOR* and *GERENTE*. Printer: ABNC.

S301 20 CENTAVOS

	GOOD	FINE	XF
1.1.1873. Black on blue unpt. Woman at ctr. Back blue.	15.00	50.00	175.00

S302 40 CENTAVOS

	GOOD	FINE	XF
1.1.1873. Black on green unpt. Girl w/necklace at ctr. Back green.	20.00	75.00	200.00

1873 SECOND FRACTIONAL ISSUE

#S303-S304 sign. titles: *GERENTE* and *GERENTE*. Printer: ABNC.

S303 10 CENTAVOS

	GOOD	FINE	XF
1.1.1873. Black on green unpt. Girl at ctr. Back green.	10.00	40.00	125.00

#S303A-S305 like previous issue.

S303A 20 CENTAVOS

	GOOD	FINE	XF
1.1.1873. Black on blue unpt. Like #S301.	40.00	125.00	350.00

S304 20 CENTAVOS

	GOOD	FINE	XF
1.1.1873. Black on orange unpt. Like #S301. Series A. Back orange.	20.00	65.00	175.00

S305 40 CENTAVOS

	GOOD	FINE	XF
1.1.1873. Black on peach unpt. Like #S302. Series A. Back peach. Sign. titles combined read: *LOS GERENTES*.	30.00	90.00	250.00

1871-73 ISSUE

#S311-S318 engraved partial date 18xx. Printer: ABNC.

#S311-S313 sign. titles: *DIRECTOR* and *DIRECTOR*. Printed sign. on #S311 and S312; printed or hand sign. on #S313.

S311 1 SOL

	GOOD	FINE	XF
1871-76. Black on green and red-brown unpt. Young man standing at l., Indian woman at ctr., reclining woman at lower r. Back red-brown; cow head at ctr.			
a. Issued note. 15.9.1871; 1.9.1872; 10.9.1875; 10.9.1876.	60.00	200.00	—

	GOOD	FINE	XF
b. Inverted branch ovpt: *EN YQUIQUE* on face. 15.11.1872.	200.00	—	—

S312 2 SOLES

	GOOD	FINE	XF
1.9.1872; 10.9.1875; 5.5.1876. Black on red and green unpt. Boy w/sheep at l., Indian woman w/child at ctr., cows at r. Back green; goat head at l. and r.	60.00	200.00	—

S313 5 SOLES

	GOOD	FINE	XF
187x. Black on gold and blue unpt. Cherub at upper l., man on mule at ctr., girl at r. Back blue; 2 women, cherubs and denomination numeral at ctr.	150.00	—	—

#S314 sign. titles: *GERENTE* and *GERENTE*.

S314 10 SOLES

	GOOD	FINE	XF
1.9.1872; 1.1.1874. Black on orange unpt. 2 women at upper l., woman and 3 cherubs at ctr., 2 girls at lower r. Back green; dog head at ctr.	—	—	—

#S315-S318 sign. titles: *GERENTE, DIRECTOR, GERENTE*. Printed sign. on #S311-S312.

S315 20 SOLES
187x. Black on blue unpt. Man at upper l., men loading llamas at ctr., dog and safe at lower r. Back red; men and horses at ctr. Specimen.

GOOD	FINE	XF
—	—	—

S316 50 SOLES
187x. Black on green unpt. 2 girls w/sheaves at upper l., Spanish man and Indian woman at ctr., portr. woman at lower r. Back brown; men leading horses at ctr.

	GOOD	FINE	XF
p. Proof.	—	—	—
s. Specimen.	—	—	—

S317 100 SOLES
10.9.1873; 10.9.1875; 10.11.1875. Black on orange and gray unpt. Dog at upper l., man roping steer at ctr., girl at r. Back brown; like #S327.

GOOD	FINE	XF
—	—	—

NOTE: #S314-S317 back colors come from archive copies and may not be those used for issued notes.

S318 500 SOLES
15.6.1874. Black on orange unpt. Woman at upper l., standing Liberty w/sword and fasces at ctr., Indian man at r. Back like #S327.

	GOOD	FINE	XF
a. Issued note.	—	—	—
p. Proof.	—	—	—

1877 PROVISIONAL ISSUE

#S321-S328 face designs like previous issue. All have black oval ovpt: *EMISION PAGADERA POR EL GOBIERNO 1877* (payable by the government) on back for #S321-S325 and on face for #S327-328. All notes have printed date and sign.

#S321-S323 sign. titles: *GERENTE* and *GERENTE*.

S321 1 SOL
10.9.1877. Black on green and red unpt. Like #S311. Back brown; 1 Sol coin at ctr. under black ovpt.

GOOD	FINE	XF
5.00	15.00	70.00

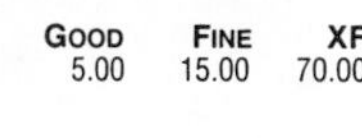

S322 2 SOLES
10.9.1877. Black on red and green unpt. Like #S312. Back green; 1 Sol coin at l. and r.

	GOOD	FINE	XF
a. Issued note.	7.50	25.00	90.00
b. Black w/ovpt: *COMISION DE SUBSIDIOS AREQUIPA 1881* in circle at l. and r. on back.	40.00	100.00	—
p. Proof.	—	—	—

S323 5 SOLES
10.9.1877. Black on gold and blue unpt. Like #S313. Back blue; dog and safe at ctr. under black ovpt.

GOOD	FINE	XF
5.00	15.00	70.00

S324 10 SOLES
10.9.1877. Reported Not Confirmed

#S325-S328 add *DIRECTOR*. Printer: ABNC.

S325 20 SOLES
10.9.1877. Black on blue unpt. Like #S315. Back orange; farm scene under black ovpt.

GOOD	FINE	XF
—	—	—

S326 50 SOLES
10.9.1877. Reported Not Confirmed

S327 100 SOLES
10.9.1877. Black on orange and gray unpt. Like #S317. Back black and brown; funeral of Atahualpa scene at ctr.

GOOD	FINE	XF
—	Rare	—

S328 500 SOLES
10.9.1877. Black on orange unpt. Like #S318.

GOOD	FINE	XF
—	Rare	—

TACNA

100,000 soles was authorized to be printed for issue by the Tacna branch of the Banco Nacional, and 500,000 soles for the Iquique (spelled Yquique on the notes) branch. Neither branch actually issued any of these notes, though each had a series prepared in new designs and various denominations.

1870S ISSUE

#S331-S335 printer: ABNC.

		GOOD	FINE	XF
S331	**1 SOL** 187x. Green and orange. Indian woman and child at ctr. Proof.	—	—	—

		GOOD	FINE	XF
S332	**2 SOLES** 187x. Green and orange. Men loading llamas at lower l., Indian man at lower r. Proof.	—	—	—

		GOOD	FINE	XF
S333	**5 SOLES** 187x. Yellow and blue. Indian woman at lower l., men loading llamas at ctr., young girl at r. Proof.	—	—	—

		GOOD	FINE	XF
S334	**20 SOLES** 187x. Green. Indian woman and child at lower l., field workers harvesting at ctr., young girl at lower r. Proof.	—	—	—

		GOOD	FINE	XF
S335	**100 SOLES** 187x. Brown. Woman w/3 cherubs at l., cattle at ctr., Indian woman at lower r. Back blue. Archive copy.	—	—	—

YQUIQUE

1870S ISSUE

#S341-S345 printer: ABNC.

		GOOD	FINE	XF
S341	**1 SOL** 187x. Orange and red. Running horse at upper ctr., Indian man at lower r. Back like #S321. Proof.	—	—	—

		GOOD	FINE	XF
S342	**2 SOLES** 187x. Green and red. Indian woman at l., reclining woman w/produce at upper ctr. Back like #S322. Proof.	—	—	—

		GOOD	FINE	XF
S343	**5 SOLES** 187x. Red and orange. Man, woman and child near boat and anchor at ctr. Back like #S323. Proof.	—	—	—

		GOOD	FINE	XF
S344	**20 SOLES** 187x. Black and red. Arms at ctr., w/scenes of boats, mountains and llamas in background. Woman milking cows in farm scene on back. Proof.	—	—	—
S345	**100 SOLES** 187x. Black on pinkish red unpt. Sailor and marine implements at ctr. Back green; like #S327. Archive copy.	—	—	—

BANCO DEL PERÚ

Founded in 1863.

1864-69 ISSUES

Peso System.

#S351-S355 radiant sunface at r.

		GOOD	FINE	XF
S351	**5 PESOS** 15.6.1864. Black on green unpt. Lg. denomination numeral at l., seated woman and shield at upper l. ctr., worker at r. Back green. Printers: face, CNBB; back, CABB.	—	—	—

#S352-S355 printers: face, CABB; back, CNBB.

		GOOD	FINE	XF
S352	**10 PESOS** 15.6.1869. Black on red and green unpt. Liberty seated at l., woman and shield at upper ctr.	—	—	—

		GOOD	FINE	XF
S353	**100 PESOS** 15.12.1864; 5.1.1867. Black on green and brown unpt. Similar to #S352 but different women at l.			
	a. Issued note.	—	—	—
	p. Proof.	—	—	—
	s. Specimen.	—	—	—

		GOOD	FINE	XF
S354	**500 PESOS** 1.7.1867. Black on green and brown unpt. Similar to #S352 but woman and ornate shield at l.	—	Rare	—

		GOOD	FINE	XF
S355	**1000 PESOS** 18xx. Black on green and red unpt. Woman and shield at l., Indian and sailor at upper ctr. Uniface. Proof.	—	Rare	—

1864-77 ISSUE

Sol System.

#S361-S368 different combinations of printers for face and back.

		GOOD	FINE	XF
S361	**1 SOL** 2.11.1864. Black on green unpt. Radiant sunface at ctr. Back green; pillar w/names at ctr. Printers: face, ABNC; back, CNBB.			
	a. Issued note. Series J.	35.00	100.00	300.00
	p. Proof.	—	—	—

		GOOD	FINE	XF
S362	**2 SOLES** 1.5.1869; 1.5.1871; 1.12.1873. Black on green unpt. Woman's head at upper l., sm. radiant woman's head at ctr. Back green; radiant woman's head at lower l. Printers: face, CNBB; back, CONB.	40.00	175.00	—

NOTE: All examples seen of #S362 exist w/varieties of black text: *a la vista y en moneda corriente hoy* (at sight in current money today) ovpt. in curved line near ctr.

		GOOD	FINE	XF
S363	**4 SOLES** 1871-73. Black on green unpt. Radiant woman's head at l., woman at r. Back green; Liberty at l. Printers: face, CNBB; back, CONB.			
	a. 1.5.1871. W/o round black stamping at l. on face.	40.00	175.00	—
	b. 1.12.1873. Round black stamping: *CIRCULACION AUTORIZADA POR EL GOBIERNO* (arms ctr.) at l. on face.	—	—	—

NOTE: All examples seen of #S363 varieties of black text ovpt. similar to that on #S362 except that the word hoy (today) is deleted at the end.

		GOOD	FINE	XF
S364	**4 SOLES** 1.1.1874. Black on green unpt. Bank monogram at l. Back green; bank monogram at ctr. Printer: NBNC.			
	a. Round black stamping like #S363b, at l. on face and at r. on back.	20.00	100.00	300.00
	b. No round black stamping but oval ovpt: *EMISION PAGADERA . . .* like #S321-S325 at ctr. on back.	20.00	100.00	300.00

		GOOD	FINE	XF
S365	**10 SOLES** 1.1.1874. Black on orange unpt. Similar to #S364. Back brown; black ovpt. like #S364b at ctr.	175.00	—	—

		GOOD	FINE	XF
S366	**20 SOLES** 186x. Black and brown on gold unpt. 2 reclining women w/wreath on pillar at ctr., sm. faces around border. Back brown on gold unpt.; radiant sunface at ctr. Printer: NBNC.	—	Rare	—

Note: Trial prints in about six different colors of #366 are known.

		GOOD	FINE	XF
S367	**20 SOLES** 1.12.1877. Black on green unpt. Woman wearing plumes at l., radiant woman's head at ctr. Back black on orange unpt.; woman at ctr. Black ovpt. like #S364b at ctr. Printers: face, CNBB; back, CONB.	350.00	—	—

		GOOD	FINE	XF
S368	**100 SOLES** 1.12.1877; 1.5.1878. Black on green unpt. Radiant woman's head at l., woman at ctr. w/men and ship in background. Printers: face, CNBB; back, CONB.	—	Rare	—

BANCO DE PIURA

Founded in 1873.

1873-78 ISSUE

#S371-S374 boy and woman at lower l., worker gathering cotton at lower r. Printer: G&D.

		GOOD	FINE	XF
S371	**1 SOL** 1.12.1873. Black on green unpt.	—	Rare	—

		GOOD	FINE	XF
S372	**5 SOLES** 20.10.1878. Black on red unpt.	—	Rare	—

		GOOD	FINE	XF
S373	**10 SOLES** 31.1.1875. Black on blue unpt.	—	Rare	—

		GOOD	FINE	XF
S374	**20 SOLES** 30.12.1874; 1.1.1875. Black on brown unpt.	—	Rare	—

BANCO DE TACNA

Operated from 1872 to 1921 under Peruvian and Chilean governments.

1870'S ISSUE

#S381-S387 printer: CNBB/NBNC.

		GOOD	FINE	XF
S381	**1/2 SOL** (18xx). Black. Farm animals at upper l. Back black and green; cow head at ctr.			
	a. Issued note.	—	Rare	—
	r. Unsigned remainder.	—	Unc	30.00

		GOOD	FINE	XF
S382	**1 SOL** (18xx). Black on brown unpt. Girl's head at upper l. and lower r., steam train on rural bridge at ctr. Back brown.			
	a. Issued note.	—	Rare	—
	r. Unsigned remainder.	—	Unc	20.00

		GOOD	FINE	XF
S383	**2 SOLES** (18xx). Black and brown. Steam passenger train at upper l. ctr., woman w/child at lower r.	150.00	350.00	—

		GOOD	FINE	XF
S384	**5 SOLES** (18xx). Black and green. Standing woman at l., llamas w/men at ctr. Back green.			
	a. Issued note.	—	Rare	—
	r. Unsigned remainder.	—	Unc	25.00

		GOOD	FINE	XF
S385	**10 SOLES** (18xx). Black and blue. Fruit and basket at lower l., miners at lower ctr., woman and cornucopia at lower r. Back blue.			
	a. Issued note.	—	—	—
	r. Unsigned remainder.	—	40.00	85.00

		GOOD	FINE	XF
S386	**50 SOLES** (18xx). Black and yellow. Woman seated w/gear and tools at l. Unsigned remainder.	—	Rare	—

		GOOD	FINE	XF
S387	**100 SOLES** (18xx). Black. Woman holding sm. pitcher at ctr. Proof.	—	Rare	—

1886 ND CHILEAN OCCUPATION ISSUE

After the war between Peru and Chile, the area including Tacna was occupied by Chilean forces. The Banco de Tacna was reorganized under the laws of Chile in 1884, and notes were authorized to be issued.

Three notes w/provisional ovpt. are known from the Chilean epoch.

		GOOD	FINE	XF
S391	**1 SOL** ND. Ovpt: *EN QUINTOS DE BOLIVIANO A LA PAR* in 2 lines across face of #S382.	—	Rare	—
S392	**1 PESO ON 1 SOL** 1.4.1886. Vertical brown ovpt. in 3 Lines at l. ctr: *TACNA* (date) *CINCO QUINTOS BOLIVIANOS POR PESO O SU EQEQUIVALENTE EN MONEDA CORRIENTE.*	—	Rare	—

		GOOD	FINE	XF
S394	**10 SOLES** 1.4.1886. Vertical ovpt: *CINCO QUINTOS BOLIVIANOS POR PESO O SU EQUIVALENTE EN MONEDA CORRIENTE* in 2 lines at l., Chilean Casa de Moneda round stamping at r., word *SOLES* cut out at upper ctr. Ovpt. on #S385.	—	Rare	—

Note: For reported 1 Peso issue of Banco de Tacna under Chilean occupation see Chili #S441.

Notice

Readers with unlisted dates, color or signature varieties are invited to submit photocopies of their notes to: Standard Catalog of World Paper Money, Krause Publications, 700 East State St. Iola WI 54990-0001 U.S.A. or by email: thernr@krause.com. Email submissions of material for possible inclusion need to be 100% jpeg attachments at 300 dpi.

BANCO DE TRUJILLO

Founded in 1871.

1872-74 ISSUE

#S401-S406 printer: ABNC.

#S401-S404 hand dated.

		GOOD	FINE	XF
S401	**50 CENTAVOS** 1.8.1872. Black on orange unpt. Dog at ctr. Curved sign. title: *GERENTE*, 1 sign. Back orange.			
	a. Issued note.	30.00	—	—
	r. Unsigned remainder.	—	Unc	40.00

NOTE: For 1876 issue of #S401, see #S413.

		GOOD	FINE	XF
S402	**1 SOL** 1.5.1872. Black on blue and green unpt. Sitting woman w/sheaf and sickle at lower l., arms at top ctr., young boy at lower r.	—	Rare	—

NOTE: For 1876 issue of #S402, see #S414.

		GOOD	FINE	XF
S403	**5 SOLES** 1.6.1874. Black on green unpt. Dog at lower l., man and woman watering horses at upper ctr., woman at lower r.			
	a. Issued note.	—	Rare	—
	p. Proof.	—	—	—

		GOOD	FINE	XF
S404	**10 SOLES** 1.1.1872. Black on red unpt. Seated woman w/scale at l., winged woman blowing trumpet w/globe and eagle at ctr., woman at r.	—	Rare	—
S405	**50 SOLES** 18xx (ca.1871). Black on orange unpt. Justice at l., explorer landing at ctr., farmer w/sheep at r. Back orange. Archive copy.	—	—	—
S406	**100 SOLES** 18xx (ca.1871). Black on blue unpt. Liberty w/shield and flag at l., mythical bird holding bank arms at upper ctr., reclining allegorical figure w/globe at r. Back brown. Archive copy.	—	—	—

1876 ISSUE

#S411-S414 printed date. Printer: ABNC.

		GOOD	FINE	XF
S411	**10 CENTAVOS** 1.5.1876. Black on blue unpt. Woman at ctr. Back blue.	45.00	150.00	—

		GOOD	FINE	XF
S412	**20 CENTAVOS** 1.5.1876. Black on green unpt. Helmeted Minerva at l., Mercury at r.			
	a. Issued note.	45.00	150.00	—
	s. Specimen.	—	—	—
S413	**50 CENTAVOS** 1.5.1876. Black on orange unpt. Like #S401. Sign. title: *GERENTE* twice and in straight line. 2 sign.			
	a. Issued note.	45.00	150.00	—
	s. Specimen.	—	—	—

		GOOD	FINE	XF
S414	**1 SOL** 1.5.1876. Like #S402. Proof.	—	—	—

BANCO DEL VALLE DE CHICAMA

Established in 1873.

1800'S ISSUE

#S421-S425 circulated w/o date or sign. being written in. Printer: ABNC.

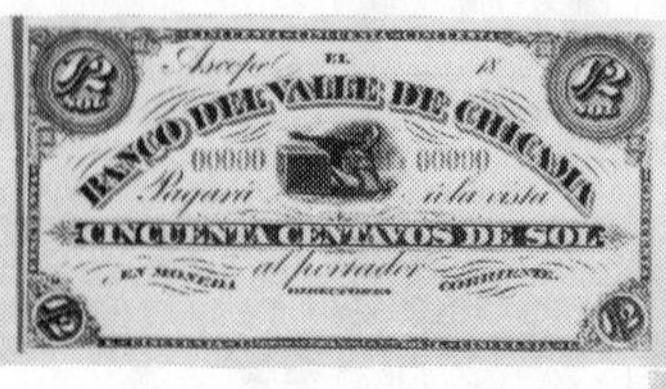

		GOOD	FINE	XF
S421	**20 CENTAVOS = 1/5 SOL** 18xx. Black. Farmer w/sheaf and plow at upper ctr. Back brown.	20.00	50.00	125.00

		GOOD	FINE	XF
S422	**50 CENTAVOS = 1/2 SOL** 18xx. Black. Dog at ctr. Back brown.	25.00	60.00	150.00

S423 1 SOL | GOOD | FINE | XF

18xx. Black on orange unpt. Portr. young woman's head at lower l. and r., standing woman w/tablet and column at ctr. Back orange.

	GOOD	FINE	XF
p. Proof.	—	—	—
r. Unsigned remainder.	40.00	100.00	—

S424 5 SOLES

18xx. Black on green unpt. Sitting woman w/sheaf and sickle at lower l., beehive at lower r.

	GOOD	FINE	XF
p. Proof.	—	—	—
r. Unsigned remainder.	60.00	150.00	—

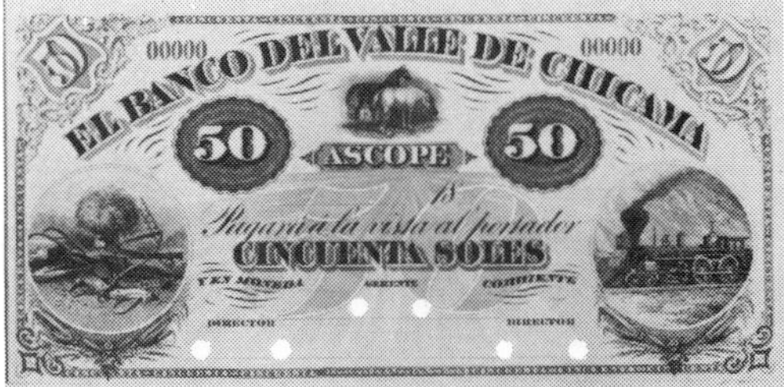

S425 50 SOLES

18xx. Black on blue unpt. Plow, farming tools at lower l., 2 horses at upper ctr., steam locomotive at lower r.

	GOOD	FINE	XF
p. Proof.	—	—	—
r. Unsigned remainder.	75.00	200.00	—

COMPAÑIA DE OBRAS PÚBLICAS Y FOMENTO DEL PERÚ

Founded by Henry (Enrique) Meiggs in order to help finance his grandiose construction plans for railroads. Meiggs' printed sign. appears on all these notes.

1876 ISSUE

#S441-S449 printed date. Printer: CNBB/NBNC.

S441 10 CENTAVOS

	GOOD	FINE	XF
4.7.1876. Black on blue unpt. Seated woman w/shield at l. Back blue.	10.00	35.00	100.00

S442 20 CENTAVOS

	GOOD	FINE	XF
4.7.1876. Black on green unpt. Steam train on high trestle at l. Back green.	12.00	50.00	150.00

S443 40 CENTAVOS

4.7.1876. Black on brown unpt. Street scene w/steam passenger train on viaduct at l. Back brown.

	GOOD	FINE	XF
a. Issued note.	25.00	150.00	—
p. Proof.	—	—	—

S444 1 SOL

4.7.1876. Black on green unpt. Steam train at ctr. Back green.

	GOOD	FINE	XF
a. Issued note.	25.00	150.00	—
b. Oval black ovpt: *EMISION PAGADERA...* like #S321-S325 on back.	20.00	80.00	200.00

S445 5 SOLES

4.7.1876. Black on brown unpt. Steam train on rural bridge at ctr. Back brown.

	GOOD	FINE	XF
a. Issued note.	25.00	150.00	—
b. Oval black ovpt. like #S444b on back.	20.00	80.00	—

S446 10 SOLES

4.7.1876. Black on orange unpt. Worker viewing train emerging from tunnel at ctr. Back orange.

	GOOD	FINE	XF
a. Issued note.	25.00	150.00	—
b. Oval black ovpt. like #S444b on back.	25.00	150.00	—
p. Proof.	—	—	—

S447 20 SOLES

4.7.1876. Black on gold unpt. Reclining woman pouring water from jug and holding lute at l. Back gold.

	GOOD	FINE	XF
a. Oval black ovpt. like #S444b on back.	50.00	300.00	—
p. Proof.	—	—	—

		Good	Fine	XF
S448	50 Soles 4.7.1876. Black on blue unpt. Seated woman at l., steam train under archway at r. Back blue.			
	a. Issued note.	—	Rare	—
	b. Oval black ovpt. like #S444b on back.	—	Rare	—
	p. Proof.	—	—	—

		Good	Fine	XF
S449	100 Soles 4.7.1876. Black on brown unpt. Steam locomotive at upper l. Back brown. Series A.			
	a. Oval black ovpt. like #S444b on back.	200.00	—	—
	p. Proof.	—	—	—

NOTE: Though dated 4.7.1876 the above issue was not released until February 1877.

Pawn Shops

Monte de Piedad de Callao

No background information is available on this proposed issue.

1800's Issue

#S552-S554 printer: ABNC.

		Good	Fine	XF
S552	1 Sol 18xx. Black on green unpt. Allegorical woman at l., man, woman and child near shoreline at ctr., sailor at r. Back red. Archive copy.	—	—	—
S553	2 Soles 18xx. Black on green unpt. Woman and marine implements at l., man and boy in marine scene at r. Back brown. Archive copy.	—	—	—

		Good	Fine	XF
S554	5 Soles 18xx. Black on green unpt. Woman sitting w/scale at l., girl at ctr., man seated and man w/spyglass at r. Uniface specimen.	—	—	—

NOTE: Blue back for #S554 is known only from archive copy.

		Good	Fine	XF
S555	5 Soles 18xx. Black on brown unpt. Similar to #S554 except that girl at ctr. is different.	—	—	—

Monte de Piedad de Lima

1870's Issue

		Good	Fine	XF
S564	4 Soles 187x. Black on green unpt. Mother w/child at l., Abundance reclining w/cornucopia at upper ctr., arms at lower r. Back green. Printer: ABNC.	150.00	450.00	—

Revolution

Iquitos Revolution

Guillermo Cervantes

Issued at Loreto.

1921 Cheque Provisional Issue

#S601-S607 printer: El Oriente.

#S601-S604 Indian facing l. at ctr. Backs in black.

		Good	Fine	XF
S601	10 Centavos on 1 Sol 1.10.1921. Black w/brown ovpt.	1.50	4.50	10.00

		Good	Fine	XF
S602	20 Centavos on 1 Sol 1.10.1921. Black w/dk. red ovpt.	1.50	4.50	10.00
S603	50 Centavos on 1 Sol 1.10.1921. Black w/green ovpt.	2.50	9.00	20.00

		Good	Fine	XF
S604	1 Sol 1.10.1921. Black on red-brown paper. Seated woman w/staff and scale on back.	1.50	4.50	10.00

		Good	Fine	XF
S605	1/2 Libra 1.10.1921. Black on blue unpt. Indian facing r. at ctr. Back blue; arms at ctr.	2.00	8.00	15.00

		Good	Fine	XF
S606	1 Libra 1.10.1921. Black on red unpt. Angel w/wreath and branch at l. Back red; arms at ctr.			
	a. W/o series or embossed seal.	3.00	10.00	25.00
	b. Embossed seal at l. Series B.	4.00	12.00	30.00

		Good	Fine	XF
S607	**5 Libras** 1.10.1921. Dk. blue on yellow unpt. Rider in uniform on horseback at ctr. Back yellow; soldiers at ctr.	8.00	20.00	45.00

The Republic of the Philippines, an archipelago in the western Pacific 500 miles (805 km.) from the southeast coast of Asia, has an area of 115,830 sq. mi. (300,000 sq. km.) and a population of 75.04 million. Capital: Manila. The economy of the 7,000-island group is based on agriculture, forestry and fishing. Timber, coconut products, sugar and hemp are exported.

Migration to the Philippines began about 30,000 years ago when land bridges connected the islands with Borneo and Sumatra. Ferdinand Magellan claimed the islands for Spain in 1521. The first permanent settlement was established by Miguel de Legazpi at Cebu in April of 1565; Manila was established in 1572. A British expedition captured Manila and occupied the Spanish colony in Oct. of 1762, but it was returned to Spain by the treaty of Paris, 1763. Spain held the Philippines amid a growing movement of Filipino nationalism until 1898 when they were ceded to the United States at the end of the Spanish-American War. The Filipinos then fought unsuccessfully against the United States to maintain their independent Republic proclaimed by Emilio Aguinaldo. The country became a self-governing Commonwealth of the United States in 1935, and attained independence as the Republic of the Philippines on July 4, 1946. During World War II the Japanese had set up a puppet republic, but this quasi-government failed to achieve worldwide recognition. The occupation lasted from late 1941 to 1945. Ferdinand Marcos lost to Corazón Aquino in elections of 1986. Marcos then fled the country. In 1992 Fidel Ramos was elected president. He was succeeded in 1998 by Joseph E. Estrada.

MONETARY SYSTEM:

1 Peso = 100 Centavos to 1967
1 Piso = 100 Sentimos, 1967-

PROVINCES

Abra	Capiz	Marinduque	Rizal
Agusan	Cavite	Masbate	Romblon
Albay	Cebu	Mindoro	Samar
Antique	Cotabato	Misamis Occidental	Sorsogon
Bataan	Davao	Misamis Oriental	Sulu
Batanes	Ilocos Norte	Mountain Province	Surigao
Batangas	Ilocos Sur	Negros Occidental	Tarlac
Bohol	Iloilo	Negros Oriental	Tayabas
Bukidnon	Isabela	Nueva Ecija	Zambales
Bulacan	La Union	Nueva Vizcaya	Zamboanga
Cagayan	Laguna	Palawan	
Camarines Norte	Lanao	Pampanga	
Camarines Sur	Leyte	Pangasinan	

Each *Province* was governed by a *Provincial Board* consisting of the *Governor* and two elected *Board Members*. The Provincial Treasurer, Provincial Auditor and *Provincial Fiscal* (equivalent of an Attorney General) were appointed by the national government. They could be, and often were, transferred from one province to another.

CHARTERED CITIES

Manila	Davao (1936)
Baguio	Iloilo (1936)
Bacolod (1938)	Quezon (1939)
Cavite (1940)	San Pablo (1940)
Cebu (1936)	Tagatay (1938)
Dansalan (1940)	Zamboanga (1936)

WWII EMERGENCY & GUERRILLA CURRENCY

INTRODUCTION

The outbreak of war in December 1941 brought about a vast increase in Philippine military and governmental expenditures. This in turn resulted in a critical shortage of coins and small denomination bank notes. The situation was further aggravated when Commonwealth President Manuel L. Quezon decreed an advance of three months' salary to all government employees. In effect this was a bonus, as all employees remaining at their posts were to receive their regular salary also.

Provincial treasuries, regional banks and commercial enterprises were all dependent upon Manila for their currency supplies. The deteriorating military situation soon made this impossible.

To provide the desperately needed currency - including fractional notes for small change - President Quezon created Currency Committees which were authorized to print *emergency currency.*

Provincial treasuries were soon called upon to pay for Commonwealth expenditures, and to ensure an adequate money supply. President Quezon authorized provincial governments to print currency if such could not be obtained from currency committees already established. Even before such authorization, some provinces had, of necessity, resorted to the use of couponized checks.

All *emergency currency* issued under Presidential authority had the same validity as regular Philippine currency and was legal tender throughout the entire Philippines, regardless of where it was printed. Exchange rate was to stay at 2 to 1; 2 Pesos = 1 U.S. dollar.

There came into being two separate areas, the occupied and the unoccupied or free. In the occupied area only regular Philippine bank notes and Japanese military currency was permitted to circulate. In free areas (excluding Luzon and Cebu) Japanese military currency was prohibited and *emergency currency,* outlawed by the Japanese, continued in circulation.

To finance the free civil governments and the guerrilla military forces, currency was issued under various authority. Some was issued under military authority, and some under authority granted by President Quezon prior to his departure from the Philippines. But the majority of it was printed by currency committees appointed by President Quezon via radio from Washington.

This post-surrender currency is often referred to as guerrilla currency. However, all issues under presidential authority were officially designated by President Quezon as *emergency currency.* In theory it had the same validity as regular Philippine currency. In practice, such was not the case. Although there was some inter-island acceptance, these currencies circulated primarily in the area of issuance, or in adjacent areas. Nor did the currency ever achieve acceptance on a par with regular Philippine bank notes despite penalties for discrimination against it. The prolific amount printed in some areas such as Panay (Iloilo currency) and Negros (Montelibano currency) resulted in successive depreciation until the notes were actually worth but a tenth of their face value. Although not as severe, similar depreciation took place in other areas.

The emergency and guerrilla notes listed in this catalog consist only of the major issues of a regional or provincial nature. There are, in addition, numerous issues by local and municipal authority primarily to provide small change and which had only local circulation.

PAPER

Almost every type of available paper was used in one place or another. These included bond (often commercially wmk.), laid, manila, brown, ledger, old documents, cloth (actually cloth-reinforced paper), and *Bais.* Bais paper was manufactured as a side product by the Bais Sugar Central in Negros Oriental Province. The paper varies in thickness but is distinguished by a wmk. of parallel bars widely spaced. Clarity of this wmk. varies from almost indiscernible to so pronounced that it actually weakens the paper. Depending on how the paper was fed into the presses, the wmk. may be either vertical or horizontal.

COUNTERFEITS

Known counterfeits are listed, but others undoubtedly exist and may turn up as collectors become better informed. Actually, counterfeiting was a very minor problem considering the adverse conditions under which these currencies were produced. The collector need have little concern about being stuck with a counterfeit. Except for three notes, counterfeits are far scarcer than their genuine counterparts and are eagerly sought by the specialist. It should be emphasized that the listed counterfeits were produced during the war for circulation. There are no known modern fakes of any currency listed in this section.

Most counterfeits are easily identified as the majority were produced under even more adverse conditions than the genuine. In most cases counterfeiters did not have numbering machines, thus many counterfeits are readily identifiable by the crudeness of serial number. In other cases counterfeiters made glaring mistakes. The most difficult to identify are counterfeits of the 5 and 10 Pesos notes of Bohol. A few of these are of even better production than the genuine, including serial numbers. Even so, the majority of them are identifiable as they have the wrong countersignatures for corresponding serial number blocks.

Two counterfeits of Mindanao (cat. #S488X2 and S528X) are very common, but easily identified. None of them ever saw use in Mindanao. They were produced in the Manila area for the black market when the Japanese military Peso had depreciated so much (1000 to 1) that *any* other form of currency was preferable.

The 100 Pesos counterfeit of Iloilo (cat. #S322X1) was produced in large quantities. Even so, it has about the same numismatic value as the genuine, except that the counterfeit is more readily available in AU or Unc. All other counterfeits command a premium over the genuine, and many of them are in the *scarce* to *rare* category.

Counterfeiting in Bohol was so rampant that it must have been a major wartime occupation. However, there are so many different counterfeits of 5 and 10 Pesos notes, and genuine notes are so common, that even here the counterfeit is far scarcer than the genuine.

REDEMPTION

by the Japanese Puppet Government

It was not until Japan invaded Cebu and Panay in April 1942 that they were confronted with *emergency currency* printed on instructions from President Quezon. The Japanese Commander-in-Chief declared these currencies to be *enemy Military notes* having *no monetary value whatsoever.*

From a military viewpoint the ordinance made good sense. On both Cebu and Panay the USAFFE had withdrawn to mountain strongholds capable of sustaining prolonged resistence. By declaring the *emergency* notes worthless the Japanese hoped to prevent the USAFFE from purchasing food and other supplies.

But with the USAFFE surrender and Japanese occupation of the Visayan and Mindanao provinces, the ordinance became a white elephant. Regular Philippine coins and currency had disappeared from circulation and *emergency* notes had become the sole medium of exchange. Prohibiting use of these notes would have destroyed what little vitality remained in the badly damaged economy. Apparently the Japanese realized this, as they made little effort to enforce the ordinance.

The circulation of emergency notes became an increasing embarrassment to the Japanese. Not only was it in violation of their military laws, but a constant reminder of their failure to discredit the former regime. Even worse, *emergency* notes were an obstacle to the circulation of their own military currency. Some way had to be found to remove the offending notes from circulation.

The obvious solution was to redeem the notes, but for the Japanese to do so would be an even greater embarrassment. The dilemma was resolved by having the puppet government do it for them. As the puppet government was bereft of funds, the Japanese generously arranged to lend it the money to do so.

On March 14, 1943 Jorge B. Vargas, Chairman of the *Philippine Executive Commission,* issued executive orders under which redemption of *emergency* currency would take place. The announcement received elaborate coverage in the news media with lavish praise to the Japanese for their unselfish generosity. This was followed up by an enormous propaganda campaign designed to ensure the success of the undertaking.

Only *printed* notes, issued prior to surrender, were eligible for redemption. Notes produced by mimeograph were not.

Before notes could be redeemed they first had to be registered. A June 30, 1943 deadline was set for registration, after which the amount could be computed and necessary funds sent from Manila for redemption.

Provincial Treasurers, as well as Municipal Treasurers in the larger towns, were provided with rubber stamps for the purpose. Other treasurers did countersigning by pen or typewriter.

After notes were registered (countersigned) they were returned to the owner until funds arrived for redemption. For various reasons, many notes properly registered (countersigned) were never presented for redemption. The collector may find numerous different examples, particularly the notes of Mountain Province.

Regulations required that after redemption, each note was to be stamped PAID in black on the face. Regulations also required that each note be stamped with *suitable Japanese characters.* The redeemed notes were then sent to Manila for final counting and destruction.

Apparently the requirement for stamping in Japanese was generally ignored, as only the provinces of Lanao and Leyte seem to have done so. Stampings applied in Lanao are illustrated in the catalog listing for that province (cat. #S381-S383). The Leyte stamping is illustrated below. A rough translation is *officially acknowledged.*

Despite the fanfare and propaganda which accompanied the registration period, final results were disappointing. The Japanese were furious and put pressure on their puppet government.

The disappointing results were concealed. It was announced instead that it was most successful, but as not everyone had been able to take advantage of the generosity of the Japanese, the period for redemption was being extended - in some provinces for six months, in others *until further notice.* The period between registration and redemption was shortened, and in some cases eliminated. Puppet officials toured the provinces urging people to turn in all notes remaining in their possession. The propaganda campaign continued until March 30, 1944 when it was finally terminated.

The success of the campaign can be judged by giving actual results for two provinces where it was carried out most vigorously. Leyte: 242,748.65 redeemed out of a total in circulation of 2,065,410.00. Negros Occidental: 443,781.55 redeemed out of a total in circulation of 4,660,980.

AKLAN

Refer to Capiz Military Issue (#S204-S209).

APAYAO

One of five semi-autonomous sub-provinces which, during WWII, comprised the Mountain Province.

Following the surrender on May 6, 1942 of all USAFFE forces, provincial officials of Mountain Province subsequently surrendered to the Japanese. In the remote sub-province of Apayao, the surrender orders were ignored. Deputy Governor Milton Ayochok assumed, *for the duration of the emergency,* authority to print emergency currency which President Quezon had previously given to the Mountain Province.

On September 11, 1942 the Apayao Provincial Board adopted *Resolution No. 4,* authorizing the printing of emergency currency to provide funds for fiscal year 1942-1943. A Currency Committee was formed composed of Deputy Governor Ayochok as Chairman, with Deputy Treasurer M. Medina and Deputy Auditor F. A. Enciso as Members.

The *first issue* of Apayao notes was printed from hand-carved plates at Kabugao in late 1942. A total of 102,495 pesos was issued. (Note: The fourth issue of Cagayan notes was also printed at Kabugao during the same period which accounts for the similarity between the two issues.)

A *second issue* of Apayao notes was produced by mimeograph in 1943 after Japanese military forces had driven the Provincial Government to a remote area. On April 1, 1943, Governor Ayochok was captured by the Japanese. He was among those killed in a mass execution of officials and civilians at Ripang in mid-1943. Subsequently the Japanese also captured the official records of the Currency Committee, so no information survives as to quantity printed. It would appear from recorded serial numbers that this second issue equalled, and possibly even exceeded, that of the first issue.

APAYAO LEGAL TENDER NOTES

Printed in a variety of colors and shades on an even greater variety of paper.

1942 ND ISSUE

#S101-S107 eagle w/wings outstretched at ctr. on face and back.

		Good	Fine	XF
S101	**5 CENTAVOS** ND. Green (shades). Serial # for #S101 and S102: 00,011 to 08,110.	1.00	2.00	4.00
S102	**5 CENTAVOS** ND. Slate blue (shades).	1.00	2.50	6.00

		Good	Fine	XF
S103	**10 CENTAVOS** ND. Lavender. Serial # for #S103 and S104: 00,011 to 08,210.	1.00	3.00	8.00
S104	**10 CENTAVOS** ND. Lt. brown.	1.00	2.00	4.00
S105	**20 CENTAVOS** ND. Olive-green (shades). Serial #: 00,011 to 07,110.	1.00	2.00	4.00

#S106 *Deleted.* See #S105.

		Good	Fine	XF
S107	**50 CENTAVOS** ND. Brown (shades). Serial #00,011 to 07,510.			
	a. Issued note.	.50	1.00	4.00
	x. Counterfeit. Crude serial #.	—	—	—

#S109-S115 arms in orange, and black text on back.

#S109-S117 Philippine arms at ctr. on face.

Border styles #S109-S111:

TYPE I: coarse lines in shading.

TYPE II: fine lines in shading.

Top and bottom border areas show these differences.

		Good	Fine	XF
S109	**1 PESO** ND. Purple. Type I borders. Tree at l. on back. Serial #00,011 to 00,408 plus some mixed w/#S110.			
	a. White paper.	4.00	7.50	15.00
	b. Manila paper.	4.00	7.50	15.00
S110	**1 PESO** ND. Buff. Type I borders. Serial #00,426 to 03,248.			
	a. White paper.	1.00	3.00	5.00
	b. Manila paper.	2.00	4.00	9.00

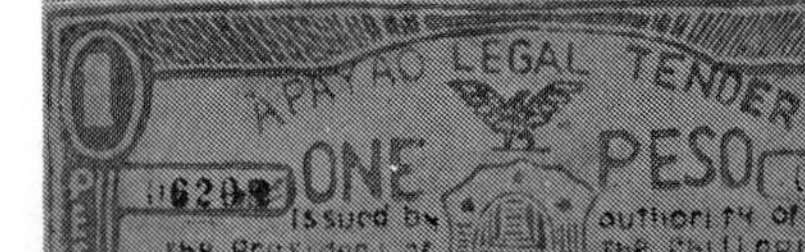

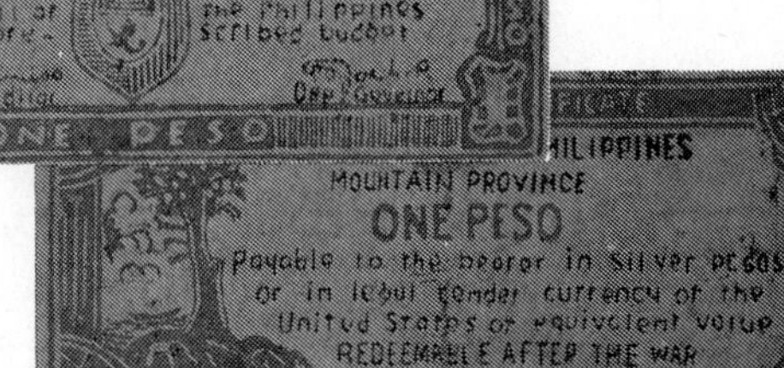

		Good	Fine	XF
S111	**1 PESO** ND. Buff. Type II borders. Serial #03,324 to 08,710.			
	a. White paper.	2.00	4.00	9.00
	b. Manila paper.	1.00	3.00	5.00

Lettering styles #S112-S113:

TYPE I: *TWO PESOS* at ctr. and bottom in thick letters.

TYPE II: *TWO PESOS* at ctr. and bottom in thin letters.

		Good	Fine	XF
S112	**2 Pesos** ND. Green. Type I denomination words. Serial #00,011 to 03,005. White paper.	1.00	2.50	5.00
S113	**2 Pesos** ND. Green. Type II denomination words. Serial #04,812 to 08,410. Manila paper.	1.00	2.50	5.00

NOTE: Serial # 03,006 to 04,811 are Types I and II lettering mixed.

		Good	Fine	XF
S114	**5 Pesos** ND. Maroon. Serial # for #S114 and S115: 00,011 to 06,110. Statue at l. on back.			
	a. White paper.	2.50	5.00	9.00
	b. Manila paper.	2.00	3.00	6.00
S115	**5 Pesos** ND. Lt. brown (shades).			
	a. White paper.	1.50	2.50	6.00
	b. Manila paper.	1.50	2.50	6.00
S116	**10 Pesos** ND. Dk. red-brown. Arms on face and text on back in green. Sunrise over terraced hill at l. on back. Serial # for #S116 and S117: 00,011 to 04,110.	4.00	9.00	15.00
S117	**10 Pesos** ND. Lt. brown (shades).	2.50	7.50	12.50

Emergency Script of the Philippines

1943 ND Issue

#S121-S127 all Series A. Serial # are estimates. Mimeographed in sheets of ten and/or twelve on a different color paper for each denomination. More than one stencil was prepared for some denominations, resulting in numerous minor varieties due to typing mistakes in spacing, alignment and spelling.

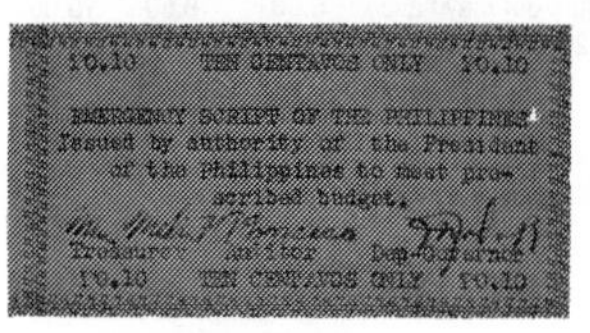

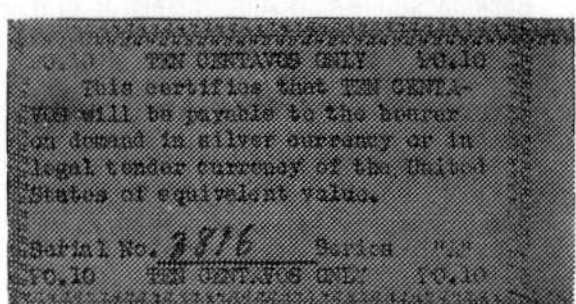

		Good	Fine	XF
S121	**10 Centavos** ND. Yellow paper. Serial #1 to 8,853.	1.00	3.00	6.00
S122	**20 Centavos** ND. Dull rose paper. Serial #1 to 10,813.	1.00	3.00	6.00
S123	**50 Centavos** ND. White paper. Serial #1 to 8,955.	1.00	3.00	6.00
S124	**1 Peso** ND. Pale buff paper. Serial #1 to 8,912.	1.00	3.00	6.00
S125	**2 Pesos** ND. Green paper (shades). Serial #1 to 5,446.	1.00	5.00	8.00
S126	**5 Pesos** ND. Salmon paper. Serial #1 to 9,671.	1.50	5.00	10.00
S127	**10 Pesos** ND. Gray-blue paper. Serial #1 to 2,330.	2.00	6.00	15.00

NOTE: #S121-S127 have no indication of origin except for sign. which carry over from the previous issue.

NOTE: Many Apayao notes were printed on paper which had previously been stamped in purple:

FOR OFFICIAL USE ONLY

MOUNTAIN PROVINCE

Bohol

On May 22, 1942 Japanese occupation forces established garrisons at Tagbilaran, the capital, and Guindulman where they operated manganese mines.

On January 9, 1943 guerrilla officers and unsurrendered provincial officials established a free provincial government with Conrado D. Marapao as Governor. Eventually its jurisdiction was established over 34 of the 36 municipalities.

Just prior to the surrender, President Quezon had authorized Bohol to issue 150,000 pesos in emergency currency. This authority was the basis for printing currency to finance the free government and guerrilla force. The Currency Board consisted of Prov. Auditor Dalmatio Ramos as Chairman, with Prov. Fiscal Jose C. Borromeo and Acting Prov. Treasurer Doroteo Toledo as Members.

In June, 1943 radio contact was established with President Quezon who authorized an additional 200,000 pesos. In September President Quezon authorized an additional 1,000,000 pesos. The printing took place at the Municipality of Carmen. Notes were printed in gray-black to intense black on manila paper of varying thickness, except for a few hundred notes on white paper. Serial numbers were applied in two different styles of type. As an anti-counterfeiting measure, various arrangements of countersignatures were applied on the back. Nearly three times the authorized amount was printed, and of this 3,710,789.55 pesos officially issued, when printing was abruptly halted by the Japanese.

On June 24, 1944 large Japanese forces landed at seven different places. At Carmen they captured Auditor Ramos and Fiscal Borromeo along with printing press, plates and tens of thousands of pesos in finished and partly printed currency. These notes were soon in circulation.

When redemption took place after the war the notes captured by the Japanese were specifically excluded from redemption. Thus many of them may be found with pen inscription *excess, fallen,* or *fallen to Japanese* as well as COUNTERFEIT rubber stamped.

Somehow, quantities of 5 Pesos notes (serial # 203,572 to 208,764) and 10 Pesos notes (serial # 192,555 to 208,741) were saved from capture. These were officially issued even though most of them did not have proper countersignatures.

Counterfeiting began shortly after the notes were issued and soon became rampant. Counterfeits of the 50 Centavos and 1 Peso *SERIES 1942* are rare, but the 5 and 10 Pesos notes were extensively counterfeited, and there are numerous varieties of each, ranging from crude to excellent. Many may be identified by crude serial numbers. Most may be identified because of the fake countersignatures not coinciding with the correct ones for a particular serial number group. Not only were Bohol notes counterfeited, but also those of Mindanao and Misamis Occidental, and possibly notes of Iloilo and Cebu.

Commonwealth of The Philippines

1942 Series - Official Issue

#S131-S134 Commonwealth arms at lower r. Printed in black.

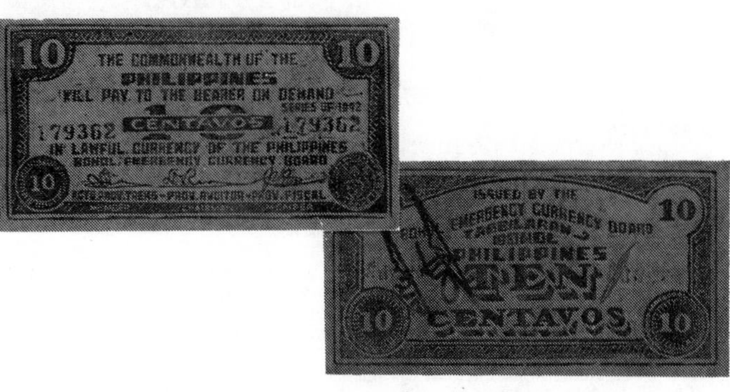

		Good	Fine	XF
S131	**10 Centavos** 1942. Serial #1 to 203,258. Countersigned back.			
	a. Back: pen sign. Treas., initials Aud. and Fiscal (serial #1 to 1100).	4.00	10.00	—
	b. Back: facsimile sign. all 3 Members (serial #1101 to 4300).	2.00	5.00	8.50
	c. Back: pen sign. Treas. and Aud., facsimile sign. Fiscal (serial #4301 to 5300).	2.00	5.00	8.50
	d. Back: pen initial one Member, facsimile sign. 2 Members (serial #5301 to 203,258).	.25	.50	1.00
S132	**25 Centavos** 1942. No engraver's initials at lower l. corner. Countersigned back. Serial #1 to 206,200.			
	a. Back: pen sign. Aud., initials Treas. and Fiscal (serial #1 to 1100).	4.00	10.00	—
	b. Back: pen initial Treas., facsimile sign. Aud. and Fiscal (serial #1101 to 3500; 4501 to 21,700; 22,701 to 27,700; 28,601 to 37,700).	1.00	2.00	3.50
	c. Back: pen initial Treas., w/o facsimile sign. (Serial #3601 to 4400).	2.00	5.00	8.50
	d. Back: facsimile sign. Aud. and Fiscal, w/o pen sign. (serial #28,201 to 28,300).	—	—	—
	e. Back: pen initial Treas., facsimile sign. Aud. and Fiscal (serial #38,301 to 47,500).	1.00	2.00	3.50
	f. Back: like "e" except pen initial of Clerk (serial #47,701 to 206,200).	.25	.50	1.00

		Good	Fine	XF
S133	**25 Centavos** 1942. Engraver's initials *F. D.* at lower l. corner on face. Back like #S132f. Serial #206,301 to 397,687.	.25	.50	1.00
S134	**50 Centavos** 1942. Serial #1 to 401,388. Countersigned back.			
	a. Back: pen sign. or initials of each Member (serial #1 to 1100).	4.00	10.00	—
	b. Back: facsimile sign. of each Member (serial #1101 to 4300).	2.00	5.00	8.50
	c. Back: pen initials Treas. and Aud., facsimile sign. Fiscal (serial #4301 to 4700).	2.00	5.00	8.50
	d. Back: pen initial one Member, sm. facsimile sign. Treas. and Fiscal.	.25	.50	1.00
	e. Back: like "d" except lg. facsimile sign. (serial # for #S134d and e, 4801 to 401,388).	.25	.50	1.00
	x. Counterfeit.	—	—	—

#S135-S137 black. Lg. Commonwealth arms at r.

		Good	Fine	XF
S135	**1 Peso** 1942. Serial #1 to 80,553. Countersigned back.			
	a. Back: pen sign. all 3 Members (serial #1 to 400; 701 to 900; 1101 to 4300).	4.00	10.00	—
	b. Back: facsimile sign. all 3 Members (serial #501 to 600; 901 to 1000).	—	—	—
	c. Back: pen sign. Treas. and Aud., facsimile sign. Fiscal (serial #1001 to 1100).	2.00	5.00	8.50
	d. Back: pen sign. Fiscal, facsimile sign. Treas. and Aud. (serial #401 to 500; 601 to 700).	—	—	—
	e. Back: pen sign. Aud., facsmile sign. Treas. and Fiscal (serial #4301 to 80,553).	.25	.75	1.50
	x. Counterfeit.	—	—	—

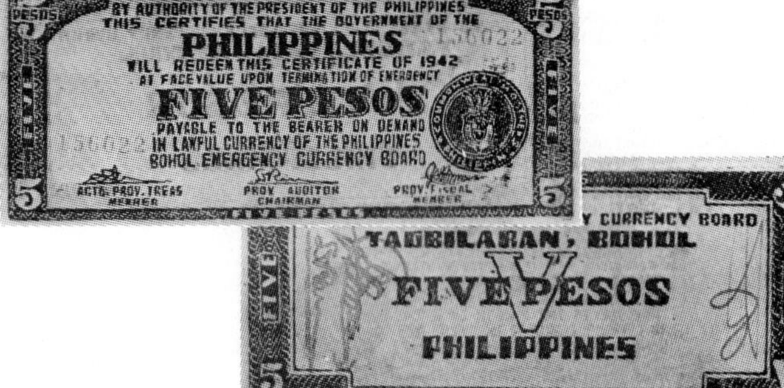

		GOOD	FINE	XF
S136	**5 PESOS** 1942. Serial #1 to 195,574 and 203,572 to 208,764. Countersigned back.			
	a. Back: pen sign. Treas., small facsimile sign. Aud. and Fiscal (serial #1 to 22,000).	.50	1.00	2.00
	b. Back: like "a" but w/o pen sign. (serial # included in "a".	—	—	—
	c. Back: pen sign. Treas., facsimile sign. Treas. and Aud. (serial #106,701 to 107,700).	—	—	—
	d. Back: pen sign. Treas., large facsimile sign. Aud. and Fiscal (serial # groups 22,001 to 96,700; 98,901 to 106,700; 108,201 to 122,900; 125,001 to 127,000; 128,901 to 131,000; 133,301 to 133,700; 135,401 to 144,500; 146,301 to 147,400; 149,601 to 167,100; 172,901 to 185,800; 187,751 to 195,574; 203,572 to 205,300).	.25	.50	1.00
	e. Back: pen sign. Aud., facsimile sign. Aud. and Fiscal (serial #96,701 to 98,900).	1.00	2.00	4.00
	f. Back: pen sign. Fiscal, facsimile sign. Aud. and Fiscal (serial # groups 122,901 to 125,000; 127,001 to 128,900; 131,101 to 133,300; 133,901 to 135,400; 144,501 to 146,300; 147,401 to 149,400; 167,101 to 172,900; 185,801 to 187,750).	.25	.50	1.00
	g. Back: facsimile sign. Aud. and Fiscal, w/o pen sign. (serial #205,301 to 208,764).	.75	1.50	2.50
	h. White paper. Countersign. and serial # in with "d".	1.50	3.00	6.00
	i. White paper. Countersign. and serial # in with "f".	2.00	5.00	8.50
	x. Counterfeit. Numerous varieties.	6.00	10.00	15.00

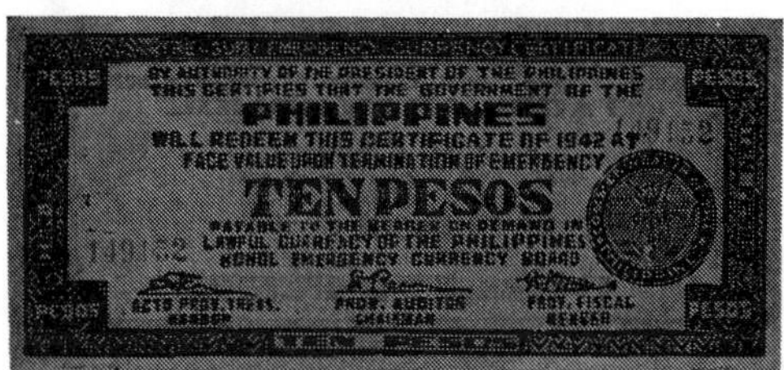

		GOOD	FINE	XF
S137	**10 PESOS** 1942. Serial #1 to 185,462 and 192,555 to 208,741. Countersigned back.			
	a. Back: pen sign. all 3 Members (serial #1 to 62,700).	1.00	2.00	3.50
	b. Back: pen sign. Aud. and Fiscal only (serial # included in "a").	—	—	—
	c. Back: pen sign. Treas. and Fiscal, facsimile sign. Aud. (serial #62,701 to 98,800).	1.00	2.00	3.50
	d. Back: pen sign. Treas. and Fiscal only (serial # included in "c").	—	—	—
	e. Back: pen sign. 1 Member, facsimile sign. Aud. (serial #98,901 to 158,000).	.50	1.00	2.00
	f. Back: pen sign. Treas. only (serial # included in "e").	—	—	—
	g. Back: pen sign. Treas. on 1 end, facsimile sign. Treas. and Fiscal together at opposite end (serial #158,001 to 159,000 and 161,000 to 185,462).	.50	1.00	2.00
	h. White paper. Countersign. and serial # in with "g".	2.00	5.00	8.50
	i. Back: w/o countersign. (serial # 192,555 to 195,500).	1.00	2.00	3.50
	j. Back: facsimile sign. Aud. and Fiscal (serial #195,501 to 208,741).	1.00	2.00	3.50
	x. Counterfeit. Numerous varieties.	6.00	10.00	15.00

1943 SERIES - OFFICIAL ISSUE

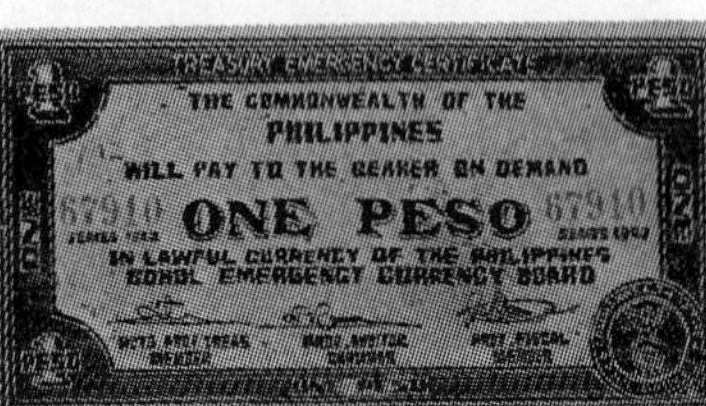

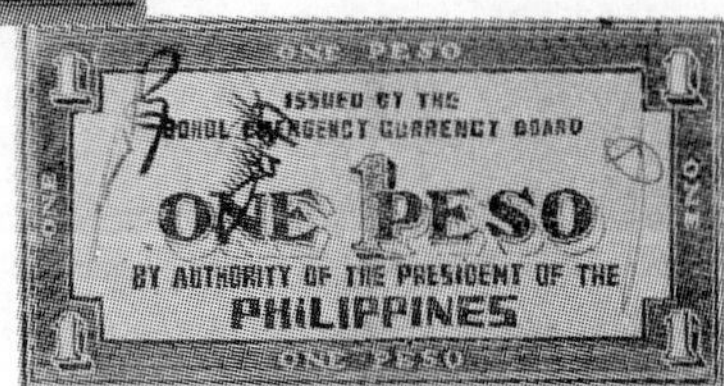

		GOOD	FINE	XF
S138	**1 PESO** 1943. Black. No engraver's initials on seal at lower r. Serial #1 to 87,900 (approx.). Back: pen initial Aud., facsimile sign. Treas. and Fiscal.	.50	1.00	2.00

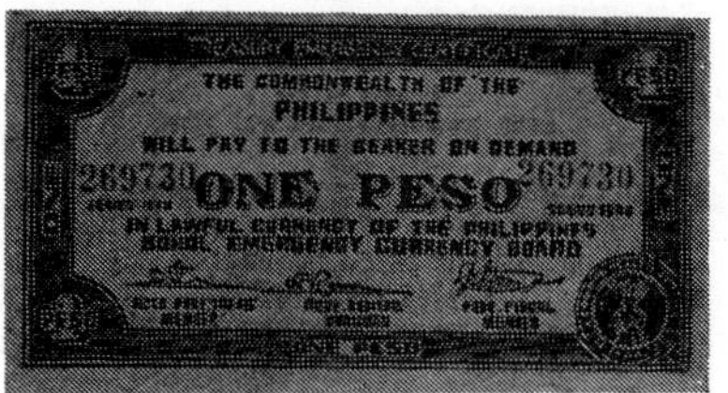

		GOOD	FINE	XF
S139	**1 PESO** 1943. Engraver's initials F. D. on seal at lower r. Serial # (approx.) 88,001 to 279,485. Countersigned back.			
	a. Back: pen initial Aud., facsimile sign. Treas. and Fiscal (serial # groups 88,001 to 97,500; 125,601 to 126,600; 127,901 to 128,600).	.25	.50	1.00
	b. Back: pen sign. of Clerk, facsimile sign. Treas. and Fiscal (serial # groups 98,401 to 125,300; 127,001 to 127,800; 129,001 to 279,485).	.25	.50	1.00

1942 SERIES - ILLEGAL ISSUE

Captured by Japanese.

		GOOD	FINE	XF
S141	**25 CENTAVOS** 1942. Like #S133. Serial #397,688 upwards.	—	—	—
S142	**50 CENTAVOS** 1942. Like #S134. Serial #401,389 upwards.	—	—	—
S143	**5 PESOS** 1942. Like #S136. Serial #195,575 to 203,571 and 208,765 upwards.			
	a. Back: pen sign. Fiscal, facsimile sign. Aud. and Fiscal (serial #195,575 to 198,500).	—	—	—
	b. Back: pen sign. Treas., facsimile sign. Aud. and Fiscal (serial #200,701 to 203,571).	—	—	—
	c. Back: facsimile sign. Aud. and Fiscal. W/o pen sign. but may have a forged sign. (serial #198,501 to 200,600 and 208,765 upwards).	—	—	—
S144	**10 PESOS** 1942. Like #S137. Serial #185,463 to 192,554 and 208,742 upwards.			
	a. Back: pen sign. Treas., facsimile sign. Aud. and Fiscal (serial #185,463 to 190,800).	5.00	8.50	15.00
	b. White paper. Countersign. and serial # in with "a".	5.00	8.50	15.00
	c. Back: facsimile sign. Aud. and Fiscal. W/o pen sign. but may have a forged sign. (serial #191,801 to 192,554 and 208,742 to approx. 212,000).	5.00	8.50	15.00
	d. Face: w/o serial #, but has false serial # applied w/captured numbering machine, Serial # always very faint, and ranges from around 220,000 up to 800,000. Back like "c".	—	—	—

1943 SERIES - ILLEGAL ISSUE

Captured by Japanese.

		GOOD	FINE	XF
S145	**1 PESO** 1943. Like #S139. Serial #279,486 upwards.			
	a. Back: pen sign. of Clerk, facsimile sign. Treas. and Fiscal.	3.50	8.00	14.00
	b. Back: facsimile sign. Aud. and Fiscal only. W/o pen sign. but may have a forged sign. of a Board Member.	—	—	—

BUKIDNON

(GRINSTEAD ISSUE, 109TH DIV. USFIP)

Refer to Mindanao Military Issues.

CAGAYAN

The Japanese *Tanaka Detachment* landed at Aparri and Gonzaga on December 10, 1941 and occupied the capital, Tuguegarao, and its adjacent airfield on December 12.

Provincial Governor Marcelo Adduru hastily evacuated the entire provincial government to the municipality of Tuao where the provincial government continued to function despite its isolation. One of the major problems confronting it was in paying for necessary expenditures. The small amount of ready cash was quickly exhausted, and soon also the supply of Treasury checks. On January 1, 1942 the Provincial Board created a Currency Board to devise ways to overcome the currency shortage. This Currency Board issued four distinct types of currency.

The *first issue* utilized postal money order forms, the serial numbers of which were recorded. Originally, some odd denominations were issued. But as this did not provide an adequate circulating medium, subsequent issues were produced in standard currency denominations.

When the available supply of money order forms was exhausted, a *second issue* of currency was provided by utilizing the stock of Internal Revenue stamps affixed to mimeographed forms. The Peso denominations are dated Tuao, Cag. Jan. 1, 1942 although all were issued much later. Specimen notes, with *Sample* written in the space normally occupied by the revenue stamp, were distributed to Municipalities to be posted in public places to acquaint people with this new form of currency.

When the supply of revenue stamps ran out, a *third issue* was created by imprinting a facsimile *WAR BILL* stamp on the mimeographed forms. When the Provincial Fiscal voiced the opinion that this might be misconstrued as counterfeiting Commonwealth revenue stamps, printing came to a halt, with only a small quantity of 50 Centavos notes having been issued.

A *fourth issue* was prepared by printing currency from hand-engraved plates made of lead obtained from old auto batteries. While this issue was being printed radio contact was established with President Quezon who officially approved the actions of the Currency Board.

Increased Japanese military activity forced the provincial government to move from Tuao to Magabubong, a *barrio* of the Municipality of Rizal. Later it became necessary to leave Cagayan province entirely, and the provincial government was re-established at Kabugao in the sub-province of Apayao. The *fourth issue* of currency may have been undertaken originally at Tuao, but the majority was printed at the later locations.

1942 ND FIRST ISSUE

Prepared by utilizing postal money order forms. While a few were in odd denominations most were in standard currency values. Denominations issued are not presently known, but records disclose that 130,699.70 pesos were issued. As the large size money orders were inconvenient, most of them were subsequently redeemed and cancelled, being replaced by subsequent issues.

CURRENCY BOARD

1942 ND SECOND ISSUE

Mimeographed on various colors of paper. Notes were folded and glued together, with silk threads between folds. An Internal Revenue stamp of equivalent value was affixed on the left side of each note, which was then serially numbered and embossed with the official seal of the provincial government. Sample notes, without revenue stamp or seal, were distributed to municipal treasurers to be posted in public places. Official records give a total of 64,658.70 pesos issued, but 5 Pesos notes are known with serial numbers far beyond those listed on the records. Serial # shown for the 5 Pesos therefore represent the highest reported.

Typewritten fakes are known with forged sign. in India ink and typewritten 6-digit serial numbers. These have genuine Internal Revenue adhesive stamps affixed.

Notes of 10 Centavos through 50 Centavos are undated and indicate payment *after the war in Gold Coin of Equivalent Value.*

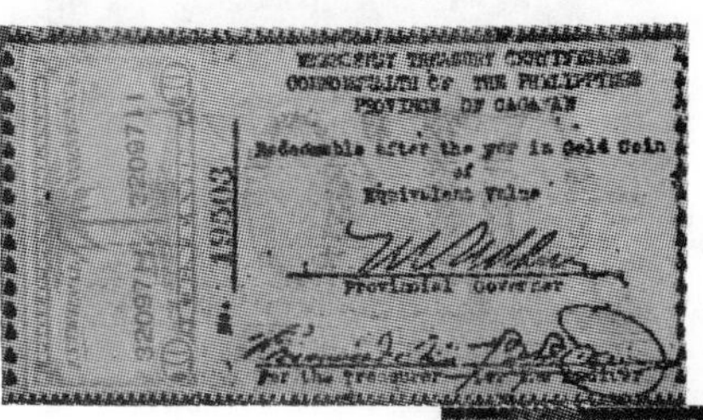

		GOOD	FINE	XF
S161	**10 CENTAVOS** ND (1942). Cream paper.			
	a. Yellow-green stamp. Serial #18,001 to 19,569.	22.50	50.00	100.00
	x. Error; correct stamp, and *0.10* stamped on back, on 20 Centavos form.	—	—	—
S162	**20 CENTAVOS** ND (1942). Lt. brown paper. Orange-yellow stamp. Serial #16,001 to 17,299.	25.00	60.00	—
S163	**50 CENTAVOS** ND (1942).			
	a. Cream paper. Greenish gold stamp. Serial # 14,001 to 15,256.	30.00	65.00	—
	x. Error; correct stamp, and *0..50* stamped on back, on 20 Centavos form.	—	—	—

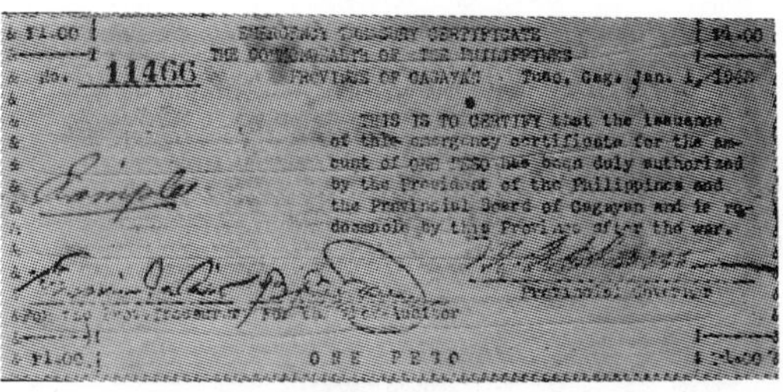

		GOOD	FINE	XF
S164	**1 PESO** 1942. White paper. Lt. brown stamp.			
	a. Serial #10,001 to 11,465.	30.00	65.00	100.00
	s. Handwritten: *Sample.*	—	—	—
S165	**2 PESOS** 1942. White paper. Red stamp.			
	a. Serial #20,001 to 21, 474.	30.00	65.00	100.00
	s. Handwritten: *Sample.*	—	—	—

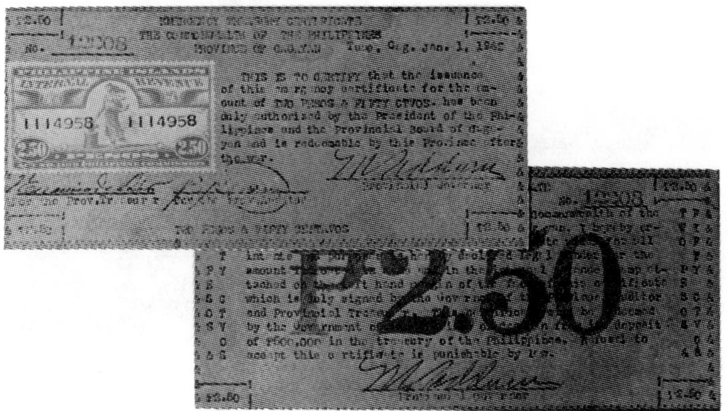

		GOOD	FINE	XF
S166	**2.50 PESOS** 1942. Gold paper. Salmon stamp. Serial #12,001 to 12,514.	40.00	85.00	200.00

		GOOD	FINE	XF
S167	**4 PESOS** 1942. Blue paper. Dk. blue stamp.			
	a. Serial #13,001 to 13,891.	30.00	70.00	150.00
	s. Handwritten: *Sample.*	—	—	—
	x. Counterfeit.	—	—	—
S168	**5 PESOS** 1942. Buff paper. Dk. blue stamp.			
	a. Serial #80,001 to (approx.) 82,995.	25.00	50.00	90.00
	s. Handwritten: *Sample.*	—	—	—
	x. Counterfeit.	—	—	—
S169	**10 PESOS** 1942. Dull rose paper. Green stamp.			
	a. Serial #10,001 to 10,852.	25.00	60.00	125.00
	s. Handwritten: *Sample.*	—	—	—
	x. Counterfeit.	—	—	—
S170	**20 PESOS** 1942. Dk. green paper. Orange-yellow stamp.			
	a. Serial #90,001 to 90,669.	35.00	75.00	175.00
	s. Handwritten: *Sample.*	—	—	—
	x. Counterfeit.	—	—	—

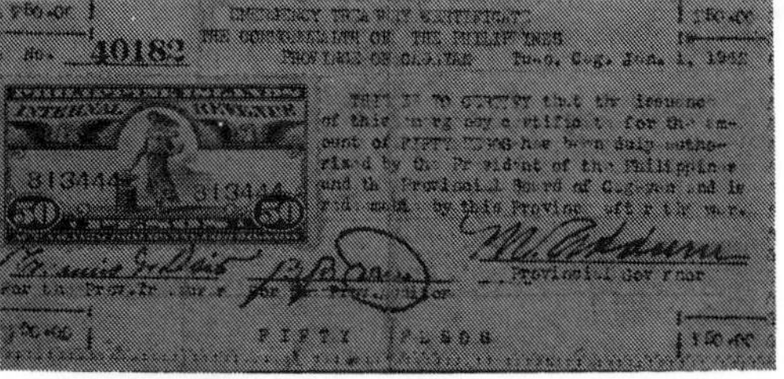

		GOOD	FINE	XF
S171	**50 PESOS** 1942. Pale green paper. Orange stamp.			
	a. Serial #40,001 to 40,337.	40.00	85.00	200.00
	b. Handwritten: *Sample.*	—	—	—
S172	**200 PESOS** 1942. Salmon paper. Dk. brown stamp. Serial # 11,001 to 11,046.	1000.	2000.	—

NOTE: #S161-S163 state redemption in gold coin and are not dated. There is no 100 Pesos denomination in this issue because no revenue stamps of that value were on hand.

1942 ND THIRD ISSUE

Facsimile *WAR BILL* stamp imprinted at l. Only one denomination was issued, and in a quantity of 212 pesos.

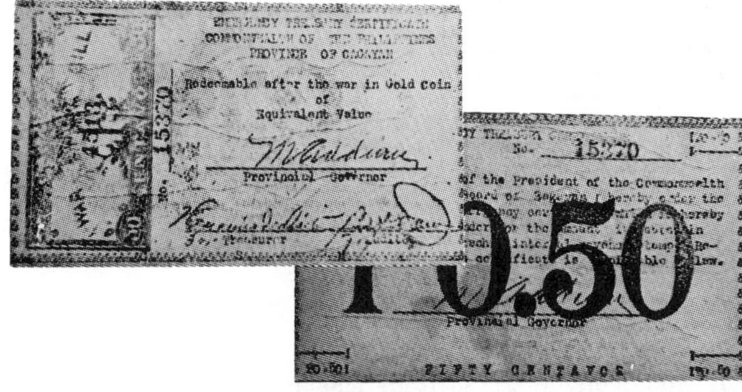

		GOOD	FINE	XF
S173	**50 CENTAVOS** ND. Cream paper. Purple stamp at l. Serial #15,257 to 15,680.	75.00	175.00	—

1942 ND FOURTH ISSUE

Printed from hand-engraved lead plates. Ink ranges from duplicator ink to diluted house paint, resulting in considerable variation of color. The Centavo notes were nearly all printed on manila paper of various grades and thicknesses. Larger size centavo notes were printed first, and reduction in size was to conserve paper. Serial numbers for small size centavo notes commenced where numbers for the large size terminated, and with the 50 centavos notes also filled in a large block of numbers skipped in numbering the larger size notes.

Lowest and highest serial numbers given are from official records. The numbers for minor varieties are given as guides. Numbering gaps, in this case, result from intermixture of varieties.

Known counterfeits are listed. Most may be easily identified by their crude serial numbers. Many small size centavo counterfeits have serial numbers used only on the genuine larger size centavo notes.

#S174-S176 small hut and trees at ctr. on face and back. Large size, 116 x 63mm.

		Good	Fine	XF
S174	**10 Centavos** ND. Purple. Serial #0001 to 4265.			
	a. Black text and names.	2.50	6.00	10.00
	b. Green text and names.	2.50	6.00	10.00
S175	**20 Centavos** ND. Green. Serial #0001 to 7790.	5.00	12.50	30.00
S176	**50 Centavos** ND. Brown. Green or black text. Serial # 0101 to 14,279; 23,030 to 24,588.			
	a. W/o wmk.	2.50	7.50	12.50
	b. Commercially wmk. paper.	5.00	12.50	15.00
	x. Counterfeit.	—	—	—

#S177-S185 similar to #S174-S176. Small size, 77 x 43mm.

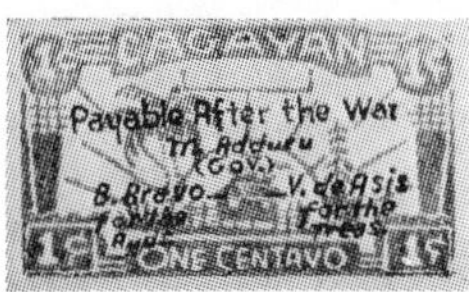

		Good	Fine	XF
S177	**1 Centavo** ND. Brown. Serial #0001 to 2600.	—	—	—
S178	**5 Centavos** ND. Green. Serial #0001 to 36,300.			
	a. Black text.	.25	.50	1.00
	b. Red text.	1.00	2.00	4.00
S179	**10 Centavos** ND. Purple. Serial # on back 4307 to 9393.			
	a. Issued note.	1.00	2.00	4.00
	x. Counterfeit.	—	—	—
S180	**10 Centavos** ND. Purple. Serial # on face 9419 to 64,600.			
	a. Issued note.	.25	.50	1.00
	x1. Counterfeit.	—	—	—
S180A	**10 Centavos** ND. Purple. Back brown.	—	—	—
S181	**10 Centavos** ND. Brown. Serial # mixed with #S180.	4.00	7.50	12.50
S182	**20 Centavos** ND. Green. Serial # on back 7816 to 11,896.	1.00	2.00	4.00

		Good	Fine	XF
S183	**20 Centavos** ND. Green. Serial # on face 11,981 to 65,000.			
	a. Black text.	.50	1.00	2.00
	b. Red text.	.75	1.50	3.00
	x. Counterfeit.	—	—	—
S184	**50 Centavos** ND. Brown. Serial # on back 14,303 to 15,299.	1.00	2.00	4.00
S185	**50 Centavos** ND. Brown. Serial # on face 15,471 to 22,963; 24,706 to 63,700.			
	a. Issued note.	.25	.50	1.00
	x. Counterfeit.	—	—	—

ND Emergency Peso Certificate Issue

#S186-S194 eagle at ctr. on face. 157 x 67mm.

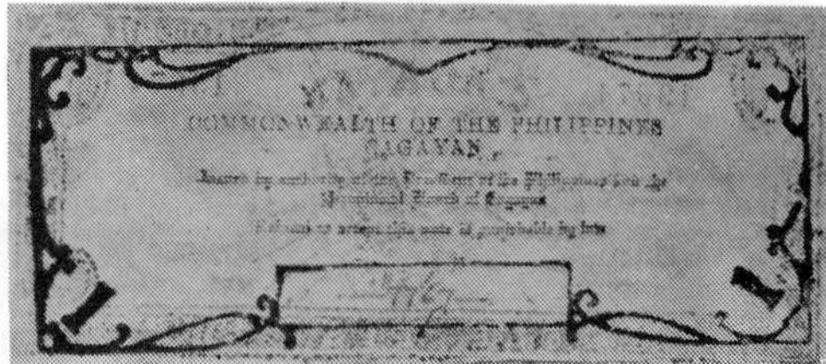

		Good	Fine	XF
S186	**1 Peso** ND. Purple. White laid paper. No upper corner numerals or words *ONE PESO* at bottom on back. Serial #0101 to 21,000.			
	a. Black text face and back.	1.50	4.00	7.50
	b. Green text face and back.	1.50	4.00	7.50

		Good	Fine	XF
S187	**1 Peso** ND. Purple. Manila paper. New back plate; 1 at upper corners, *ONE PESO* at bottom. Serial #26,000 to 65,700.	.75	1.50	4.00
S188	**1 Peso** ND. Green. Eagle in brown. Like #S187. Manila paper. Serial #65,800 to 92,300.	.50	1.00	2.50

		Good	Fine	XF
S189	**2 Pesos** ND. Green. Eagle in brown. Manila paper. Lg. dashes under top border. Farmer plowing at ctr. on back. Serial #0201 to 23,290.	.75	1.50	3.50
S190	**2 Pesos** ND. Similar to #S189 but sm. dashes under top border. Serial #23,330 to 64,800.	.75	1.50	3.00

		Good	Fine	XF
S190A	**2 Pesos** ND. Like #S190 but w/*TWO PESO* (error) at ctr. Serial # in w/#S190.	8.00	20.00	40.00

		Good	Fine	XF
S191	**5 Pesos** ND. Brown (shades). Back w/numeral *5* at upper corners, w/o vignette under text at ctr.			
	a. White laid paper. Black or green text. Serial #00501 to 28,400.	1.00	2.00	4.00
	b. Manila paper. Black or green text. Serial #31,000 to 42,700.	.75	1.50	3.00
	x. Counterfeit.	—	—	—

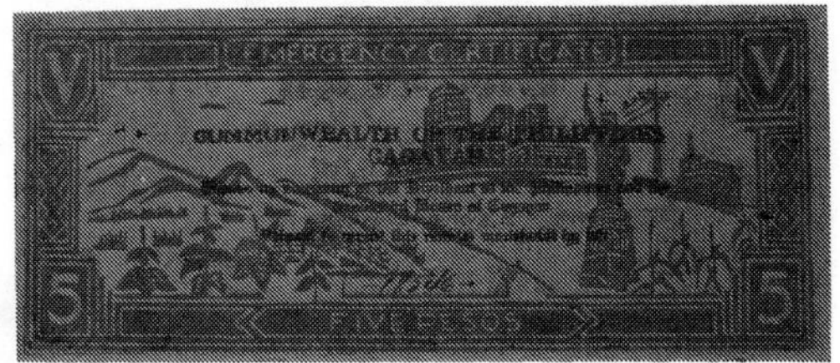

		Good	Fine	XF
S192	**5 Pesos** ND. Brown w/green text. Manila paper. Face like #S191. Back w/Roman Numeral *V* at upper corners. Hills, plants, bldgs. and Statue of Liberty under text across ctr. Serial #43,200 to 58,700.	1.00	2.00	4.00

		Good	Fine	XF
S193	**20 Pesos** ND. Green w/black text. *TWENTY PESOS* at bottom. No vignette across ctr. on back. White laid paper. Serial #2001 to 7300.			
	a. Issued note.	6.00	15.00	25.00
	x. Counterfeit.	—	—	—

		Good	Fine	XF
S194	**20 Pesos** ND. Green w/black text. Eagle in red-brown. *EMERGENCY CERTIFICATE* at bottom. Mt. Mayon and native scenes across ctr. on back. Serial #7400 to 11,698.			
	a. White paper w/o wmk.	4.00	10.00	20.00
	b. Commercially wmk. paper.	6.00	15.00	25.00

NOTE: The Second and Fourth Cagayan Issues are known w/3-line rubber stamping *Registered/Countersigned/Prov. Troas. (Troas, not Treas.)* with dates from August through October, 1945. The Fourth Issue may also be found ovpt. in purple with ¢ and $ symbols.

Capiz

In 1941 the island of Panay was divided into three provinces: Antique, Capiz and Iloilo. When the Japanese occupied Panay, the provincial officials of Antique and Capiz remained in office as Japanese puppets.

In Iloilo, however, Provincial Governor Tomas Confessor never surrendered. On August 13, 1942 he issued a *Proclamation* establishing his authority over the *free* areas of both Antique and Capiz in a government of *Free Panay*. To head the free government in the Capiz area, Confessor appointed Cornelio Villareal as *Supervising Deputy Governor*.

In 1943 Supervising Deputy Governor Villareal authorized the issuance of small denomination notes to provide small change. A Currency Committee was named consisting of Deputy Provincial Treasurer Severino Gonzales as Chairman, with Deputy Provincial Auditor Miguel Reynaldo and Deputy Provincial Fiscal Roman Martinez as Members.

The issue consisted of two denominations, backed up by large denomination Iloilo emergency notes held in the Provincial Treasury. The 50 Centavos notes were printed on manila paper. The 1 Peso notes were printed on leftover 1941 electoral census forms. The facsimile signature of Treasurer Gonzales is stamped on the back.

Some 500,000 pesos were reportedly issued, but that figure seems grossly exaggerated.

Currency Committee

Emergency Loose Change of 1943 Provincial Issue

		Good	Fine	XF
S201	**50 Centavos** 1943. Manila paper.			
	a. Issued note.	20.00	40.00	—
	x1. Counterfeit.	—	—	—

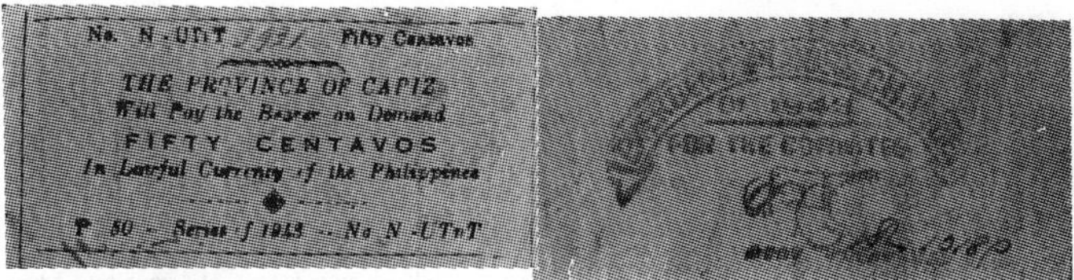

		Good	Fine	XF
S201A	**50 Centavos** 1943. Like #S201 but w/*COMMITEE* (error) on back.	20.00	45.00	—

		Good	Fine	XF
S202	**1 Peso** 1943. White paper.			
	a. Issued note.	20.00	45.00	—
	x1. Counterfeit.	—	—	—

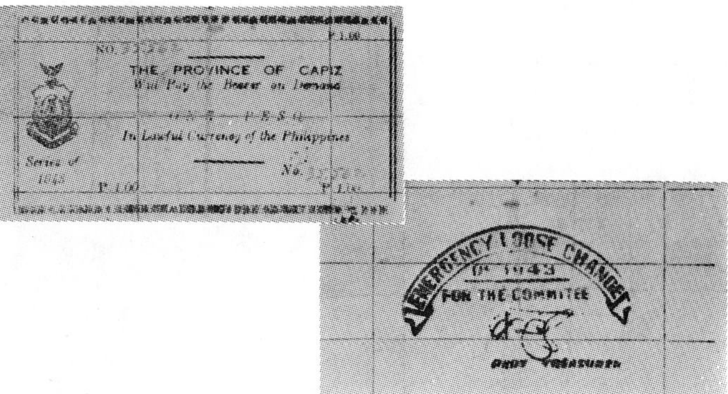

		Good	Fine	XF
S202A	**1 Peso** 1943. Like #S202 but w/*COMMITEE* (error) on back.	17.50	40.00	—

Aklan Military

Maj. Pedro Yatar, commanding the 2nd Battalion, 64th Infantry Regiment, printed 100,000 pesos in low denomination notes to provide small change in the Aklan area of Capiz. The notes were distributed to Municipal Treasurers who were required to keep on deposit an equivalent amount in large denomination Iloilo emergency notes. The notes were printed in sheets, and the shortage of type resulted in variations in border ornaments and text on each denomination. Of the six denominations issued, not all are presently known to collectors. The Aklan area of Capiz later became a separate province in 1956.

1942 Emergency Bills Issue

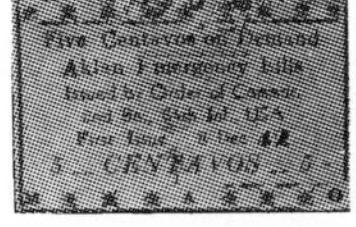

		Good	Fine	XF
S204	**5 Centavos** 1942. Thick manila paper. *First Issue, 8 Dec. 42.* 100,000 notes.	60.00	100.00	—
S205	**10 Centavos** 3.12.1942. 100,000 notes.			
	a. Denomination 15mm long.	75.00	—	—
	b. Denomination 30mm long.	75.00	—	—
	c. Denomination in italics.	75.00	—	—
S206	**20 Centavos** 50,000 notes.			
	a. Value *20* in italics.	75.00	—	—
	b. Value *20* regular type.	75.00	—	—
	c. Value *20* at l. larger than at r.	75.00	—	—
S207	**50 Centavos** 50,000 notes.	75.00	—	—

		Good	Fine	XF
S208	**1 Peso** 2.2.1943. Blue. Coarse white paper. 25,000 notes.	75.00	125.00	—
S209	**2 Pesos** 12,500 notes.	—	Rare	—

CEBU

Cebu Currency Committee

The Cebu Currency Committee was created by President Quezon in a telegram dated December 29, 1941. Simeon C. Miranda, Acting Manager of the Cebu Branch of the Philippine National Bank, was designated Chairman, with Provincial Auditor Roman T. del Bando and Provincial Fiscal Feliberto Imperial Reyes as Members.

The first notes produced were of 1 Peso denomination, printed in blue on white bond paper. By mid-February 1942, one million notes had been printed. By then stocks of paper had been obtained, primarily from the Bais Cellulose factory in Negros Oriental, and printing of the other denominations, in black, was undertaken. The centavo notes were printed on a thick yellow paper. Each of the peso denominations had an underprinting in a different color. Officially, printing ended in late March, by which time a total of 11,005,000 pesos had been printed and turned over to the Philippine National Bank for distribution.

For reasons never explained, Chairman Miranda had an additional 550,000 pesos printed in 5 and 20 Pesos notes, without the knowledge of the other Committee Members. On April 8, he turned the entire amount over to two USAFFE officers. When the Japanese invaded Cebu two days later, the currency was secretly hidden to prevent its capture. Later on, the Cebu guerrillas retrieved it and used it to finance their operations. Since no currency was printed in Cebu after the surrender, as was done in other areas, these notes may be regarded as a guerrilla issue.

Most counterfeits are poorly done, none as good as the genuine. Serial numbers are often crude, sometimes faded to illegibility, and many of them have numbers far beyond the genuine.

PHILIPPINE NATIONAL BANK - CEBU

1941 OFFICIAL EMERGENCY CIRCULATING NOTE ISSUE

#S211-S214 bank arms at ctr. on face. Yellow paper.

		GOOD	FINE	XF
S211	**5 CENTAVOS** 1941. Like #S301. Serial #1 to 100,000.	1.00	2.50	6.00
S212	**10 CENTAVOS** 1941. Like #S302. Serial #1 to 50,000.	1.00	3.00	8.00
S213	**20 CENTAVOS** 1941. Like #S303. Serial #1 to 100,000.	1.00	2.50	6.00
S214	**50 CENTAVOS** 1941. Like #S304. Serial #1 to 50,000.	1.00	3.00	8.00

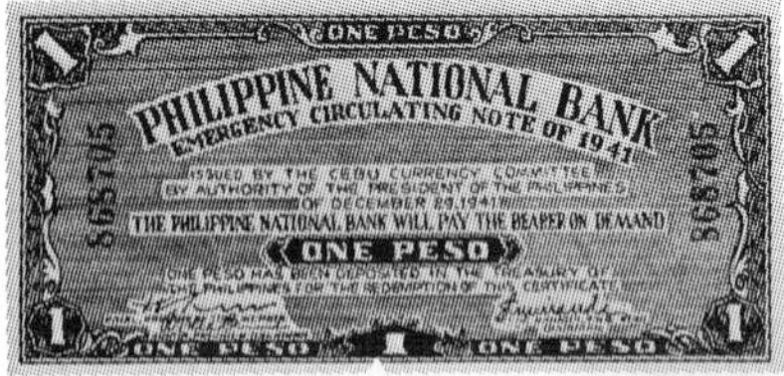

		GOOD	FINE	XF
S215	**1 PESO** 1941. Blue. Lt. orange back. White bond paper. Serial #1 to 1,000,000.	.10	.25	1.25

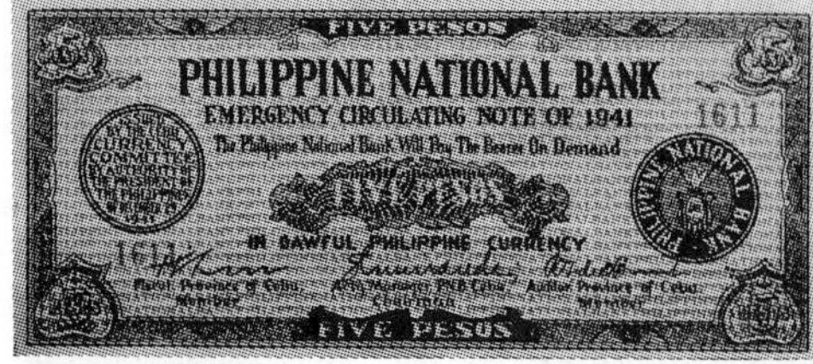

		GOOD	FINE	XF
S216	**5 PESOS** 1941. Black on green unpt. Wmk: Vertical bars. Serial #1 to 180,000.	1.00	2.50	7.00

		GOOD	FINE	XF
S217	**10 PESOS** 1941. Black on yellow unpt. Serial #1 to 300,000.			
	a. W/o wmk. Serial #1 to approx. 75,000.	.50	1.25	2.50
	b. Bais paper. Wmk: Vertical bars. Serial # approx. 75,001 upwards.	.50	1.25	2.50
	x1. Printed counterfeit. Two varieties known.	—	—	—
	x2. Hand-drawn counterfeit, quality from crude to excellent.	—	—	—
S218	**20 PESOS** 1941. Black on orange unpt. Bais paper. Wmk: Vertical bars. Serial #1 to 302,500.			
	a. Issued note.	.50	1.25	2.50
	x1. Printed counterfeit.	—	—	—
	x2. Hand-drawn counterfeit.	—	—	—

1941 CEBU GUERRILLA ISSUE

		GOOD	FINE	XF
S219	**5 PESOS** 1941. Like #S216. Serial #180,001 to 200,000.	7.50	15.00	25.00
S220	**20 PESOS** 1941. Like #S218. Serial #302,501 to 325,000.	4.00	8.00	15.00

CEBU EMERGENCY CURRENCY BOARD

TREASURY EMERGENCY CURRENCY CERTIFICATES

From February 20-22, 1942 a Conference of Provincial Treasurers convened by President Quezon was held at Bacolod, Negros Occidental. Concern was expressed that the multiplicity of emergency currency issues was creating confusion and distrust. A *Resolution* was adopted which called for creation of a single Currency Board to print emergency currency for all the provinces of the Visayan islands and Mindanao.

As a result of this *Resolution* the Cebu Emergency Currency Board was created by President Quezon in a telegram dated March 1, which designated Acting Provincial Auditor Roman T. del Bando as Chairman, with Acting Provincial Treasurer Pedro Elizalde and Cebu City Treasurer Rosalio D. Macrohon as Members. Twenty million pesos was authorized and instructions specified that all notes were to be countersigned by each Board Member.

Printing of 20 Pesos notes got underway as soon as plates could be prepared, followed by the 10, 5 and 2 Pesos denominations. Centavo notes were planned but never got past the design stage. Some of the first 20 Pesos notes issued were countersigned in pen, but the enormous amount of work involved necessitated use of facsimile signature stamps which could be applied by each Member's representative.

Printing was brought to a halt with the Japanese invasion of Cebu during the early morning hours of April 10, 1942. Until then no 2 Pesos notes had been completely printed. None of the 5 Pesos notes had been countersigned, and many of the 10 and 20 Pesos notes also lacked countersignatures. Of the 3,650,000 pesos printed, only 865,000 pesos had been issued.

That same morning as the Japanese rapidly approached, the Currency Board began destroying the unissued currency. Notes were piled behind the capital building, gasoline poured over them, and they were then set afire.

At the last minute, however, 19,500 Pesos were set aside for use by the Cebu Provincial Government. This consisted of 500 notes each of the 5, 10 and 20 Pesos denominations, each serially numbered from 1-500, plus 200 10 Pesos notes serially numbered 30,601-30,800.

The 5 and 10 Pesos notes numbered 1-500 had not been countersigned, and thus became the only notes officially issued without countersignatures.

As soon as the fire was blazing, the Board Members hastily departed, leaving behind three Constabulary soldiers to guard the burning notes. As soon as the officials left, the soldiers followed suit. Before the Japanese arrived, spectators to the scene scattered the fire and retrieved bundles of currency which were not burned at all, or had only the outer edges singed. Thousands of pesos thus reached circulation illegally.

1942 SERIES - OFFICIAL ISSUE

#S221-S222 no countersign. on back.

		GOOD	FINE	XF
S221	**5 PESOS** 1942. Black on brown unpt. Serial #1 to 500.	—	—	—

		GOOD	FINE	XF
S222	**10 PESOS** 1942. Black on green or aqua unpt. Quezon at upper l. Serial #1 to 500.	—	—	—

#S223-S224 three countersign on back. Like #S222.

		GOOD	FINE	XF
S223	**10 PESOS** 1942. Serial #501 to 6000 and 30,601 to 30,800.	12.00	30.00	60.00

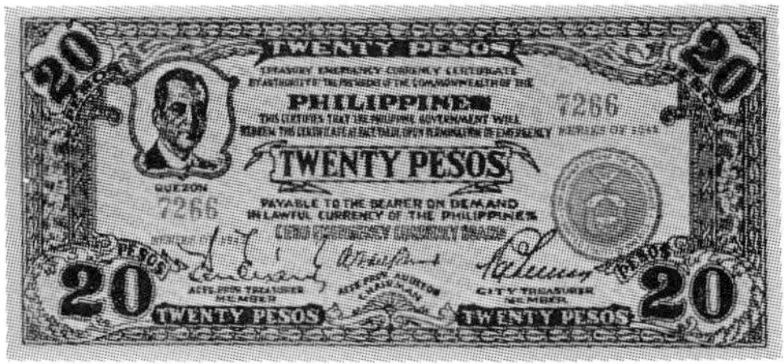

		GOOD	FINE	XF
S224	**20 PESOS** 1942. Black on orange unpt. Serial #1 to 41,000.			
	a. Pen countersign. of all 3 Board Members.	8.00	20.00	45.00
	b. Pen countersign. of del Bando and Macrohon, facsmiile sign. Elizalde.	20.00	45.00	70.00
	c. Facsimile sign. of all 3 Board Members.	2.00	4.00	8.00

1942 ILLEGAL ISSUE

		GOOD	FINE	XF
S226	**5 PESOS** 1942. W/o countersign. Like #S221. Serial #501 upwards.	—	—	—
S227	**10 PESOS** 1942. Serial #6001 to 30,600 and 30,801 upwards.			
	a. W/countersign. Like #S223.	20.00	40.00	65.00
	b. W/o countersign. Like #S222.	—	—	—
S228	**20 PESOS** 1942. Serial #41,000 upwards.			
	a. W/countersign. Like #S224.	4.00	7.50	15.00
	b. W/o countersign.	—	—	—

NOTE: As all legally issued 20 pesos had countersign., many of the looted notes which were w/o them had forged sign. applied in India ink.

COTABATO

In legislation dealing with redemption of wartime emergency notes, introduced into the First Session of the Third Congress of the Republic of the Philippines, there is specifically mentioned an issue by the *Provincial Government of Free Cotabato,* described as *of doubtful authority.*

Nothing further is known regarding this issue of emergency currency.

CULION LEPER COLONY

The Culion Leper colony was administered by the Commonwealth Bureau of Health. Normal monthly expenditure was about 25,000 pesos, most of which was obtained directly from Manila. The outbreak of the war effectively severed source of supply.

Funds on hand were nearly exhausted in meeting the December 1941 payroll. The special Culion coinage was reissued, but was only a stop-gap measure. In late January 1942 at a public meeting a proposal was adopted to issue local scrip. A Currency Committee was formed consisting of Dr. H. W. Wade, Medical Director of the Leonard Wood Memorial, as Chairman, with Acting Chief Pathologist Jose O. Nolasco and Disbursing Officer Julio Lisboa as Members.

The scrip was mimeographed on pink paper for centavo denominations and blue paper for peso denominations. The Bureau of Health stamping was applied on the back in blue. Notes were dipped in paraffin for durability.

Even so, the scrip was accepted with reluctance, and an appeal was made to President Quezon who telegraphed on February 9, 1942: *IF NECESSARY ISSUE NOTES FOR PAYMENT OF SALARIES AND OTHER EXPENSES. THESE NOTES WILL BE REDEEMED BY GOVERNMENT LATER.*

A total of 144,485 pesos was printed, but only 92,130 pesos placed in circulation. When Japanese military scrip arrived at the end of July 1942, use of Culion scrip was officially prohibited.

1942 FIRST ISSUE

#S241-S247 w/o typed Presidential authority on back.

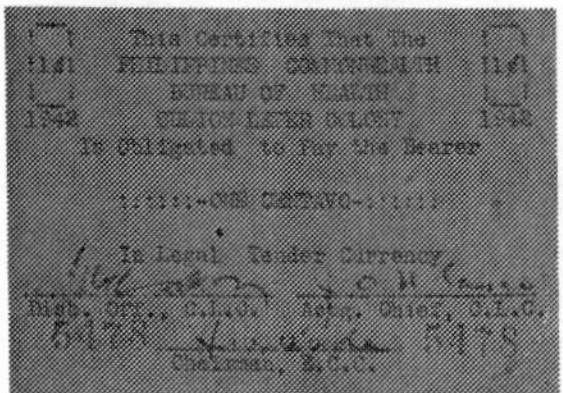

		GOOD	FINE	XF
S241	**1 CENTAVO** 1942. Serial #1 to 20,800.	30.00	55.00	75.00
S242	**5 CENTAVOS** 1942. Serial #1 to 18,400.	35.00	60.00	80.00
S243	**20 CENTAVOS** 1942. Serial #1 to 16,800.	40.00	70.00	100.00
S244	**50 CENTAVOS** 1942. Serial #1 to 16,000.			
	a. Issued note.	40.00	70.00	100.00

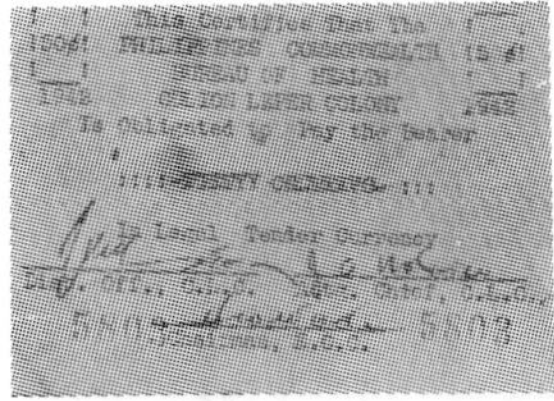

		GOOD	FINE	XF
	x. Error; *FIFTY CENTAVOS* typed over *TWENTY CENTAVOS.*	—	—	—

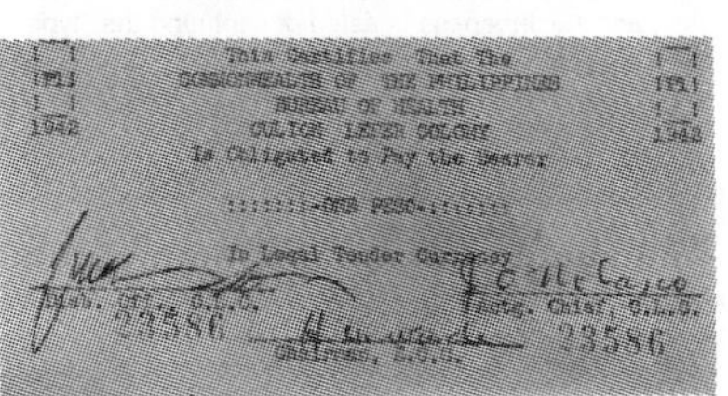

		GOOD	FINE	XF
S245	**1 PESO** 1942. Serial #1 to 16,999; 23,000 to 23,999; 34,000 to 34,999; 45,000 to 46,000.	40.00	70.00	110.00
S246	**5 PESOS** 1942. Serial #1 to 14,400.	50.00	100.00	180.00
S247	**20 PESOS** 1942. Serial #1 to 2000.	—	—	—

1942 SECOND ISSUE

#S251-S253 w/typed Presidential authority on back.

After the telegram from President Quezon was received, an additional clause citing Presidential authority was typewritten on the back. The following denominations are known, but there may be others. Serial #'s are included in the previous listing.

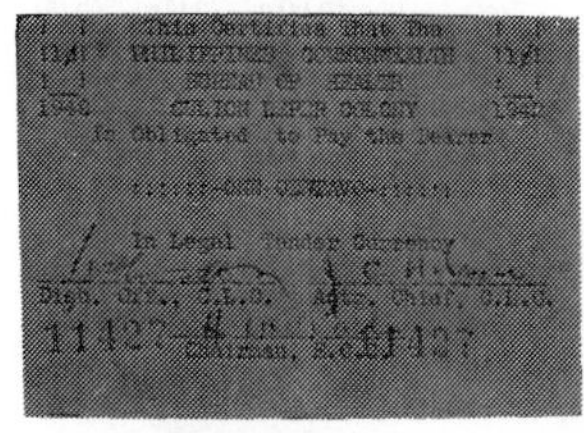

		GOOD	FINE	XF
S251	**1 CENTAVO** 1942. Like #S241.	40.00	70.00	100.00
S252	**5 CENTAVOS** 1942. Like #S242.	45.00	75.00	110.00
S253	**20 CENTAVOS** 1942. Like #S243.	50.00	80.00	135.00

NOTE: 10,000 pesos in Culion scrip was loaned to, and issued by, the Municipality of Coron on Palawan. It is possible that such notes were stamped for identification. At any rate, Culion notes without the typewritten Presidential authority are known with the following facsimile signature stamped on the back:

ILOCOS NORTE

The Japanese *Kanno Detachment* landed at Vigan, Ilocos Sur on December 10, 1941. Warned of advancing Japanese forces, Governor Roque B. Ablan hastily transferred the provincial government to Ma-an-anteng, a *barrio* of Solsona. Despite a Treasury bereft of funds, his personal popularity was such that all officials and employees loyally remained at their spots.

In early March, Gov. Ablan radioed President Quezon requesting 100,000 pesos be dropped by plane. Quezon replied the next day and authorized Gov. Ablan to issue emergency notes for authorized expenditures.

On returning to Ilocos Norte Gov. Ablan called a meeting of the Provincial Board on March 15, which adopted a *Resolution* creating a Currency Committee with authorization to print 500,000 pesos in emergency currency. President Quezon was notified of this, and in a reply radioed April 21, he not only gave his approval, but alloted an additional 50,000 pesos for a relief fund. Of the authorized amount, 519,865.55 pesos were actually printed and placed in circulation.

The Currency Committee consisted of Gov. Ablan as Chairman, with Provincial Treasurer Baldomero Perez and Provincial Auditor Roman O. Moreno as members.

Notes were mimeographed as that was the only form of printing available. The original issue was handsigned by each Committee Member. On subsequent issues signatures were printed along with the text. Notes were printed in sheets of two, with face and back for each taking 1/4 sheet. After printing they were cut apart, folded and glued together. When two notes of the same denomination were printed on the same sheet, differences occurred because of typing mistakes and alignment. Some of these differences are of major importance (but are not differentiated in this listing); their existence will be noted as text varieties.

Each note had the denomination overprinted in purple. There are variations. On centavo notes some had a zero between peso symbol and decimal point, others did not. The size of type used for the ovpt. also varied, and will be referred to as:

Small ovpt. = 20 mm. high; Large ovpt. = 25 mm. high.

Specific amounts and denominations to be printed were authorized from time to time. Dates on the notes are dates of such authorization - delivery was later, in some cases much later. The last delivery was August 9, 1942 and even then was not complete. Printing was halted by Japanese military action.

Series refers only to subsequent authorizations of a specific denomination. They were intended to be in sequence, as were serial numbers. This did not work out too well in practice because of difficulties under which the notes were printed. For example: There were no 20 Centavos and 100 Pesos notes in the original authorization. When these were subsequently authorized the 20 Pesos was correctly inscribed *First Series* but the 100 Pesos was mistakenly inscribed *Second Series.* And in the case of 5 Pesos notes, the *Third Series* was inadvertently omitted. As for serial numbers, there were several instances of duplication as well as skipped numbers. And the final delivery of 20 Centavos notes was accidentally omitted from the records, so quantity and serial numbers can only be estimated.

After the USAFFE surrender, the Japanese dropped leaflets urging Gov. Ablan to surrender, promising he could remain in office. This only strengthened Gov. Ablan's determination to fight on. The enraged Japanese sent large forces to destroy the free government and capture its leader. Realizing that Ilocos Norte emergency notes were a vital part of Gov. Ablan's resistance, the notes were outlawed, and torture and death were meted out to those found with them in their possession. Still the notes continued to circulate clandestinely.

Time after time the Japanese thought they had Gov. Ablan cornered, but always he eluded them. On January 28, 1943 he barely escaped, and the Japanese boasted of capturing the "typewriter" with which the notes were printed.

Gov. Ablan's fate remains a mystery, despite a substantial reward offered by the Commonwealth government in 1945 for any information concerning him.

On February 13, 1945 Laoag was liberated by the guerrilla *15th Infantry,* USAFIP-North Luzon. The next day a *Military Provisional Government* was organized. One of the first acts of this government was to authorize the circulation of Governor Ablan's war notes. Because of counterfeiting, the notes were called in for verification, after which they were stamped *REGISTERED.* Approximately 430,000 pesos were stamped. In June, 1945 all notes were called in to be replaced by VICTORY currency. Redeemed notes were stamped *PAID.*

Counterfeits are easily identifiable as the typewriter used to cut the stencil did not have a symbol for *peso,* so the letter *P* was used, especially in the corner value tablets. Most counterfeits observed also have fake *REGISTERED* stampings.

Catalog values are for notes which were *REGISTERED.* Notes which remain as originally issued, without the stamping, are valued considerably higher. Redeemed notes stamped *PAID* are valued about half or less of listed values.

PROVINCE OF ILOCOS NORTE

The following listings are by date, regardless of series designations.

1942 FIRST EMERGENCY TREASURY CERTIFICATES ISSUE

#S261-S269 dated March 1942. No Series. Handsigned. White paper. Typewritten serial #.

		GOOD	FINE	XF
S261	**5 CENTAVOS** 1942. Lg. ovpt. Serial #1 to 720.	15.00	25.00	75.00
S262	**10 CENTAVOS** 1942. Lg. ovpt. Serial #1 to 655.	15.00	25.00	75.00
S263	**50 CENTAVOS** 1942. Sm. ovpt. Serial #1 to 910.	15.00	25.00	75.00
S264	**1 PESO** 1942. Lg. ovpt. Serial #1 to 537.	15.00	25.00	75.00

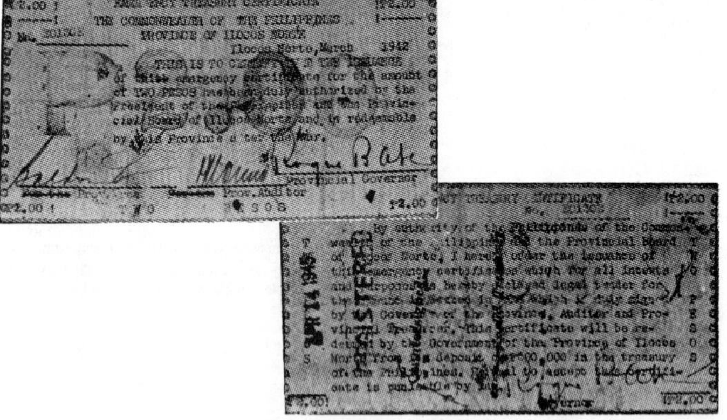

		GOOD	FINE	XF
S265	**2 PESOS** 1942. Lg. ovpt. Serial #1 to 540.	15.00	30.00	80.00
S266	**5 PESOS** 1942. Lg. ovpt. Serial #1 to 627.	15.00	30.00	80.00
S267	**10 PESOS** 1942. Lg. ovpt. Serial #1 to 620.	15.00	30.00	80.00
S268	**20 PESOS** 1942. Sm. ovpt. Serial #1 to 900.	15.00	30.00	80.00

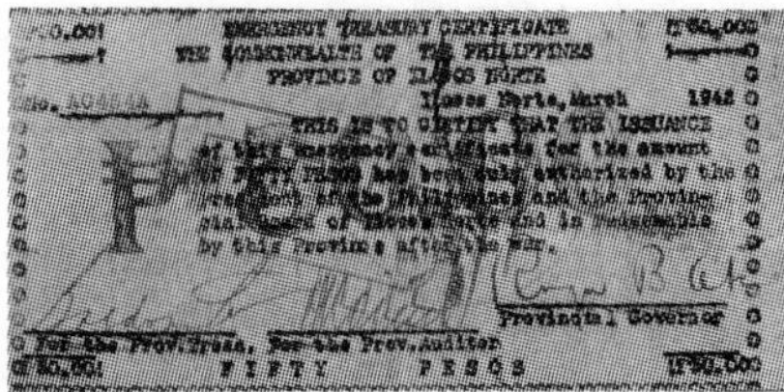

		GOOD	FINE	XF
S269	**50 PESOS** 1942. Sm. ovpt. Serial #1 to 465.	—	—	—

1942 SECOND EMERGENCY TREASURY CERTIFICATES ISSUE

#S270-S276 dated April 1, 1942. Second Series. Printed sign. White paper. Typewritten serial #.

		GOOD	FINE	XF
S270	**1 PESO** 1.4.1942. Sm. ovpt. Serial #538 to 2753. 2 text varieties, 5 or 6 lines of text on face.	15.00	22.50	55.00
S271	**2 PESOS** 1.4.1942. Sm. ovpt. Serial #541 to 5331. 3 text varieties of last line on back: *punishable by law, able by law, ble by law.*	15.00	25.00	60.00
S272	**5 PESOS** 1.4.1942. Sm. ovpt. Serial #628 to 2682.	15.00	25.00	60.00

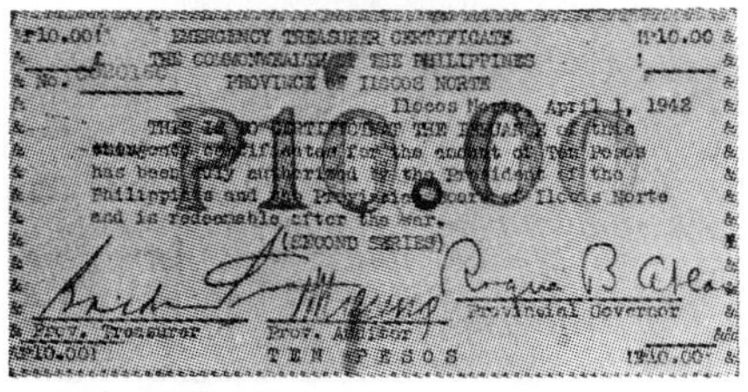

		GOOD	FINE	XF
S273	**10 PESOS** 1.4.1942. Sm. ovpt. Serial #621 to 2540.	15.00	25.00	60.00
S274	**20 PESOS** 1.4.1942. Sm. ovpt. Serial #901 to 2327.	15.00	25.00	60.00
S275	**50 PESOS** 1.4.1942. Sm. ovpt. Serial #466 to 956.			
	a. Issued note.	30.00	75.00	
	x. Counterfeit. Dated *March 1942* but inscribed *SECOND SERIES.*	—	—	—
S276	**100 PESOS** 1.4.1942. Sm. ovpt. Serial #1 to 477.			
	a. Issued note.	—	—	—
	x1. Counterfeit. Dated *March 3, 1942,* inscribed *FIRST SERIES.*	—	—	—
	x2. Counterfeit. Dated *March 1942,* inscribed *SECOND SERIES.*	—	—	—
	x3. Counterfeit. Dated *April 15, 1942,* inscribed *THIRD SERIES.*	—	—	—

1942 THIRD EMERGENCY TREASURY CERTIFICATES ISSUE

#S277-S281 April 15, 1942. Third Series. White paper. Typewritten serial #.

		GOOD	FINE	XF
S277	**1 PESO** 15.4.1942. Sm. ovpt. Serial #2754 to 8124. Two text varieties, title at right *Provincial Governor* or *Provincial Board* (typing error).	15.00	25.00	60.00
S278E	**2 PESOS** 15.4.1942. Sm. ovpt. Error; *P2.00* purple ovpt. on 50 Pesos #S281 mimeographed form.	—	—	—

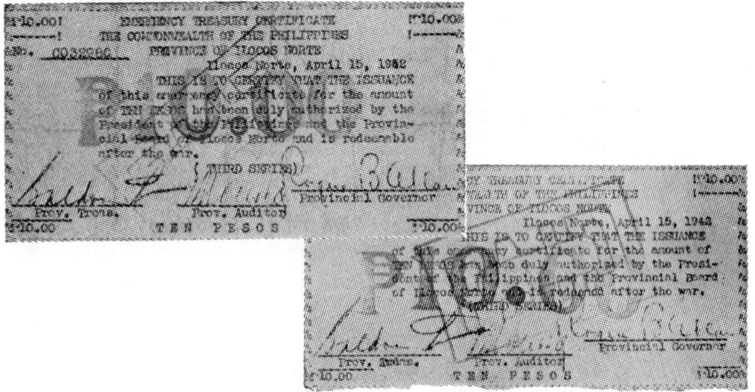

		GOOD	FINE	XF
S279	**10 PESOS** 15.4.1942. Sm. ovpt. Serial #2541 to 4384 in black or red. Two text varieties, 5 or 6 lines of text on face.			
	a. Issued note.	15.00	25.00	60.00
	x. Counterfeit. Correctly dated but inscribed *FOURTH SERIES.*	—	—	—
S280	**20 PESOS** 15.4.1942. Sm. ovpt. Serial #2328 to 3457.	15.00	25.00	60.00
S281	**50 PESOS** 15.4.1942. Sm. ovpt. Serial #957 to 2212. Two text varieties of last line on back *punishable by law or nisable by law.*			
	a. Issued note.	20.00	50.00	100.00
	x. Counterfeit. Dated *April, 1942* (no day), inscribed *THIRD SERIES.*	—	—	—

1942 FOURTH EMERGENCY TREASURY CERTIFICATES ISSUE

#S282-S283 May 4, 1942. Fourth Series. White paper.

		GOOD	FINE	XF
S282	**5 PESOS** 4.5.1942. Sm. ovpt. typewritten serial #1328 to 5333. Two text varieties of last line on face: *after the war* or *ter the war.*	15.00	25.00	60.00

NOTE: Serial #1328 to 2682 for #S282 mistakenly duplicated those of April 1 printing.

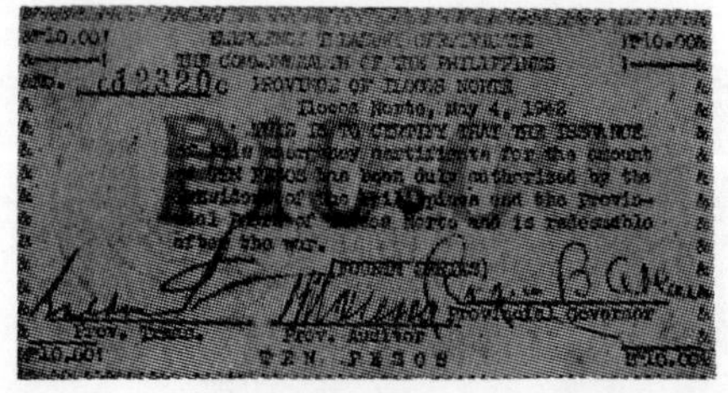

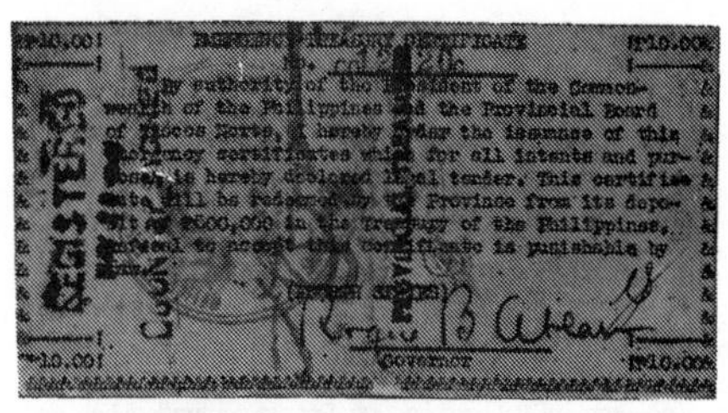

		GOOD	FINE	XF
S283	**10 PESOS** 4.5.1942. Sm. ovpt. Serial #4385 to 12,772. Two text varieties of last line back: *able by law* or *law.*			
	a. Typewritten serial #4385 to 9400.	15.00	25.00	60.00
	b. Printed serial #9401 to 9971 in purple.	15.00	25.00	60.00
	c. Printed serial #9972 to 12,772 in black.	15.00	25.00	60.00

#S284 May 12, 1942. Fourth Series.

		GOOD	FINE	XF
S284	**1 PESO** 12.5.1942. Sm. ovpt. Serial #8125 to 18,144 (est.). Two text varieties of last line on back: 6 words or 1 word.			
	a. White paper. Typewritten serial #8125 to 12,633.	15.00	25.00	50.00
	b. Manila paper. Printed serial #12,634 to 13,400.	15.00	25.00	60.00
	c. White paper. Printed serial #13,401 to 18,144 (est.).	15.00	25.00	50.00

#S285-S288 two text varieties of last line on back: *nisable by law* or *law.*

#S285 and S286 May 15, 1942. Second Series.

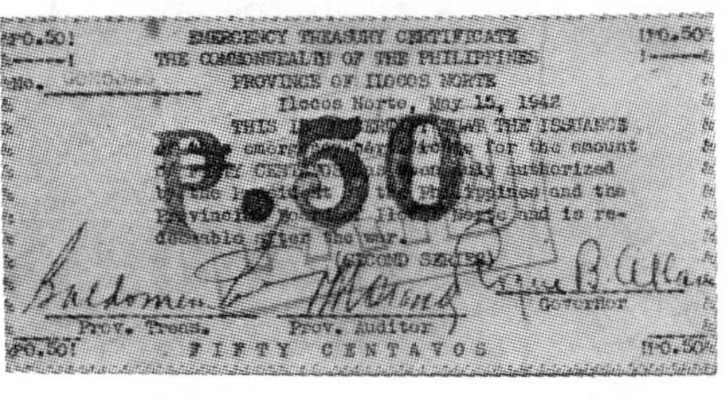

		GOOD	FINE	XF
S285	**50 CENTAVOS** 15.5.1942. Sm. *P.50* ovpt. Typewritten serial #911 to 3679.	15.00	25.00	50.00
S286	**50 CENTAVOS** 15.5.1942. Sm. *P0.50* ovpt. Printed serial #3680 to 11,414 (est.).			
	a. Manila paper. Serial #3680 to 7748 and 10,341 to 11,414.	15.00	25.00	50.00
	b. White paper. Serial #7749 to 10,340.	15.00	25.00	50.00

1942 VARIOUS SERIES EMERGENCY TREASURY CERTIFICATES ISSUE

#S287-S294 May 20, 1942.

		GOOD	FINE	XF
S287	**5 CENTAVOS** 20.5.1942. Sm. *P.05* ovpt. Second Series. Manila paper. Serial # 721 to 4100.			
	a. Typewritten serial # 721 to 1900.	15.00	25.00	60.00
	b. Printed serial # 1901 to 4100.	15.00	25.00	50.00
S288	**5 CENTAVOS** 20.5.1942. Lg. *P.05* ovpt. Second Series. Manila paper. Serial #4101 to 6457.	15.00	40.00	70.00

#S289-S293 two text varieties of last line on face: *deemable after the war* or *after the war.*

		GOOD	FINE	XF
S289	**10 CENTAVOS** 20.5.1942. Sm. *P.10* ovpt. Second Series. Manila paper. Serial #656 to 2000.	15.00	25.00	50.00
S290	**10 CENTAVOS** 20.5.1942. Sm. *P0.10* ovpt. Second Series. Manila paper. Serial #2001 to 2100 and 2616 to 3542 (approx.).	15.00	25.00	50.00
S291	**10 CENTAVOS** 20.5.1942. Lg. *P0.10* ovpt. Second Series. Serial #3575 (approx.) to 6667.			
	a. Manila paper. Serial #3575 to 4823.	15.00	40.00	70.00
	b. White paper. Serial #4824 to 6667.	15.00	25.00	50.00

NOTE: Serial #2101-2600 are #S290 and S291 intermixed.

		GOOD	FINE	XF
S292	**20 CENTAVOS** 20.5.1942. Sm. *P.20* ovpt. First Series. Manila paper. Typewritten serial #1 to 2950. Two varieties: w/ or w/o value in box at upper r. corner.	15.00	25.00	50.00

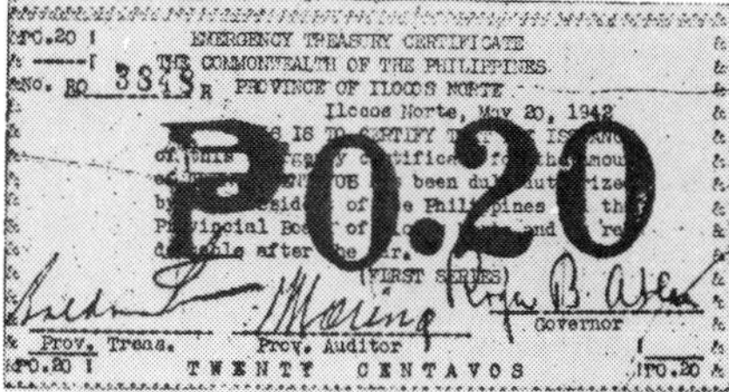

		GOOD	FINE	XF
S293	**20 CENTAVOS** 20.5.1942. Lg. *P0.20* ovpt. First Series. White paper. Printed serial #2951 to 8760. Two varieties: w/ or w/o value in box at upper r. corner.	15.00	25.00	50.00
S294	**5 PESOS** 20.5.1942. Sm. ovpt. Fifth Series. Manila paper. Printed serial # in purple or black 5334 to 8400. Two text varieties.	15.00	25.00	50.00

JUNE 6, 1942 ISSUE

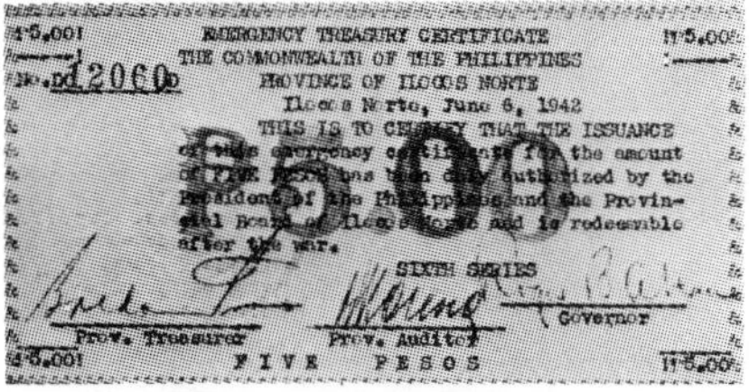

		GOOD	FINE	XF
S295	**5 PESOS** 6.6.1942. Sixth Series. Lt. manila paper. Serial #9755 to 15,600 (approx.). Two text varieties.			
	a. W/2 zeroes after decimal point.	15.00	25.00	50.00
	b. W/o 2 zeroes after decimal point.	—	—	—

JUNE 15, 1942 ISSUE

At this point the originally authorized amount of 500,000 Pesos was exhausted, although the amount had not yet been completely printed. The following authorization was therefore based on the 50,000 pesos President Quezon had authorized for civilian relief. This is reflected in the back text of #S296 and S297 stating that redemption will be by the Commonwealth Government.

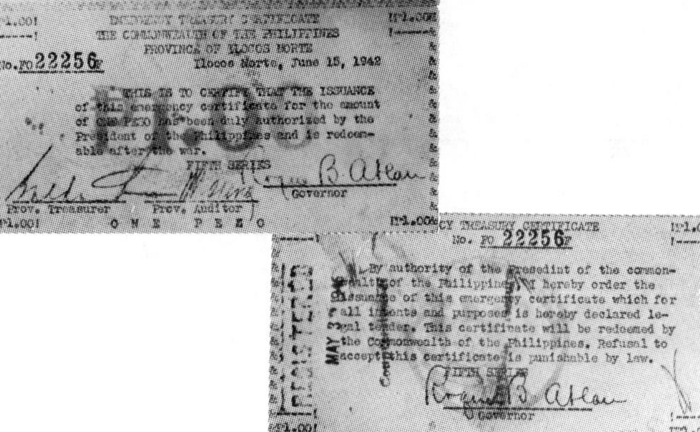

		GOOD	FINE	XF
S296	**1 PESO** 15.6.1942. Fifth Series. Serial #18,164 (approx.) to 29,397. Two text varieties of first line on back: *President* or *Presedint* (error).	15.00	25.00	50.00
S297	**5 PESOS** 15.6.1942. Seventh Series. Serial # 15,601 (approx.) to 23,347. Two text varieties of last line on back: 8 or 4 words.	15.00	25.00	50.00

ILOILO

PRE-SURRENDER ISSUE

The Iloilo Currency Committee was created by President Quezon in a telegram dated December 29, 1941. Cenon S. Cervantes, Manager of the Iloilo Branch of the Philippine National Bank, was named Chairman, with Provincial Auditor Bartolome Fernandez and Provincial Fiscal Jose Quisumbing as Members. They were authorized to print 100,000 pesos in fractional and 1 peso notes to provide change to ease the coin shortage.

But the shortage of small denomination currency notes was equally acute. The Committee, therefore, went ahead with preparations to print denominations from 5 centavos to 10 pesos. La Defensa Press in Iloilo City was engaged to do the printing.

On January 27, 1942 printing of 10 pesos notes began and by February 3, ten thousand notes had been printed, the full amount authorized. All of these notes were handsigned by each Committee Member. All subsequent printings would have facsimile signatures.

The Committee telegraphed President Quezon requesting that the amount authorized be increased to 3,000,000 pesos. When no reply was received, the committee, on its own initiative, decided to continue printing due to the urgency of the situation.

Printing of 10 pesos notes was resumed, and that of the 1 peso began. La Editorial Press in Bilibagan, a *barrio* of Santa Barbara, was engaged to print 2 and 5 pesos notes. It was March before printing of centavo notes was undertaken.

In the meantime President Quezon had arrived in Panay, and not only commended the Committee for its initiative, but increased the authorized amount to 5,000,000 pesos. Later, in a telegram dated March 14, Quezon informed Chairman Cervantes, *YOU ARE AUTHORIZED TO PRINT ALL THE CURRENCY NEEDED BY THE ARMY IN PANAY.*

Printing operations came to a halt with the Japanese invasion of Iloilo on April 16, 1942. A total of 6,551,450 pesos had been turned over to the Iloilo Branch of the Philippine National Bank. 20 Centavos notes are known with serial numbers higher than officially recorded. Apparently the Japanese invasion prevented final delivery, and how these notes reached circulation is not known.

Shortly after the notes were issued there were reports of identical serial numbers being found on both the 2 and 10 pesos denominations. The notes were identical except that one would be less clearly printed and have poorer serial numbers. This leads to the possibility that poorly printed and rejected sheets were pilfered, serially numbered outside the plant, and placed in circulation.

There are several varieties of counterfeit 10 pesos notes. Most of these were produced during the occupation. One type, with very crude serial numbers, circulated widely in Bohol and may have been produced there.

All the counterfeits can be identified by the inferior quality of serial numbers.

PHILIPPINE NATIONAL BANK - ILOILO

1941 EMERGENCY CIRCULATING NOTE ISSUE

Pre-Surrender Issue.

#S301-S304 ornamental borders.

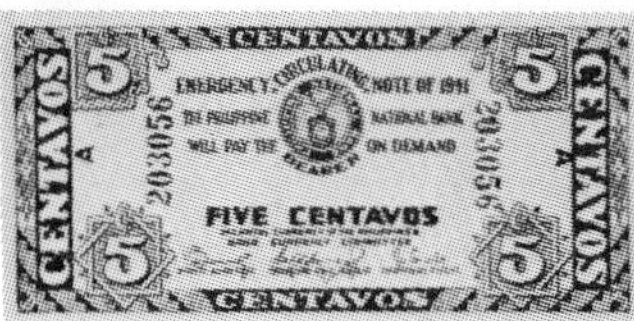

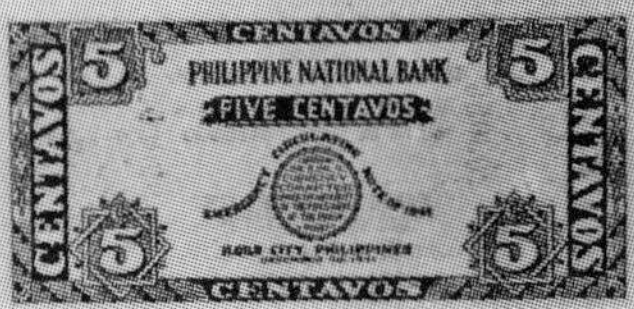

		GOOD	FINE	XF
S301	**5 CENTAVOS** 1941. Green. Like #S211. Serial #1 to 297,000.	1.00	4.00	9.00
S302	**10 CENTAVOS** 1941. Blue. Like #S212. Serial #1 to 259,000.	1.00	5.00	10.00
S303	**20 CENTAVOS** 1941. Red. Like #S213. Serial #: official, 1 to 281,000; estimated, 1 to 285,000.	1.00	4.00	9.00
S304	**50 CENTAVOS** 1941. Yellow. Like #S214. Serial #1 to 181,000.	1.50	6.00	15.00

NOTE: Orange to brown colored 50 Centavos notes are color changelings, a result of oxidation.

#S305-S309 eagle in lg. *V* at ctr.

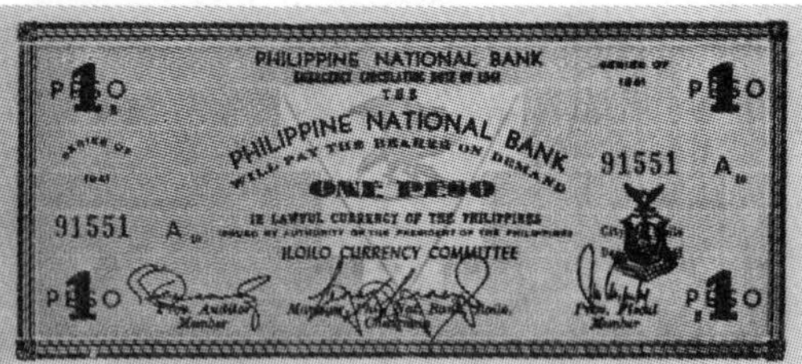

		GOOD	FINE	XF
S305	**1 PESO** 1941. Black on green unpt. Eagle facing r. Serial #1 to 240,000.	2.00	8.00	15.00
S306	**2 PESOS** 1941. Black on blue unpt. Eagle's wings spread. Serial #1 to 942,000.			
	a. Issued note.	1.00	3.00	8.00
	x. Counterfeit.	—	—	—

		GOOD	FINE	XF
S307	**5 PESOS** 1941. Black on red unpt. Eagle like #S306. *THE* in bank title.	1.00	2.00	5.00
S307A	**5 PESOS** 1941. Like #S307 but w/o *THE* in bank title.	3.00	8.00	20.00

NOTE: Serial #1 - 220,000 are #S307. Serial #220,001-268,000 are #S307 and #S307A intermixed.

		GOOD	FINE	XF
S308	**10 PESOS** 1941. Black on brown unpt. Handsigned. Eagle like #S305. Serial #1 to 10,000.	15.00	30.00	65.00
S309	**10 PESOS** 1941. Like #S308 but printed sign. Serial #10,001 to 290,000.			
	a. Issued note.	1.00	2.00	5.00
	x1. Counterfeit. Corner numerals thicker than genuine.	10.00	15.00	25.00
	x2. Counterfeit. Corner numerals thinner than genuine.	10.00	15.00	25.00

POST-SURRENDER ISSUES

The Japanese invasion of Panay on April 16, 1942 found USAFFE forces and the provincial government of Iloilo under Government Tomas Confessor well prepared. The USAFFE withdrew to mountain redoubts, and the Iloilo provincial government evacuated to a previously designated area.

These carefully laid plans of the USAFFE came to naught with the unconditional surrender by Gen. Wainwright. Reluctantly Col. Christie obeyed the orders to surrender. But many of his officers, led by Lt. Col. Macario Peralta, refused, as did the greater portion of the USAFFE.

Col. Peralta immediately set about organizing the unsurrendered soldiers into a guerrilla force. As the provincial governments of both Antique and Capiz had become Japanese puppets, he suggested that Governor Confessor extend his jurisdiction over the free areas of those two provinces. This was done by a *Proclamation* issued on August 13. Later, the province of Romblon was included, and thus was born the *Government of Free Panay* and *Romblon.* Col. Peralta also set out to bring under his own command the other Visayan Islands in what he called the *IV Philippine Corps.*

As both the civil government and the military command were in desperate need of funds, a conference was called on November 15. Auditor Fernandez, a Member of the now inoperative Iloilo Currency Committee, called attention to President Quezon's final message to that Committee, which was *to print all the currency needed by the Army in Panay.*

As the situation was urgent, it was agreed that this was sufficient authority to resume printing of currency. As Chairman Cervantes was in Japanese hands, his Assistant manager, Juan Buenafe, was appointed to replace him on this reconstituted Second Iloilo Currency Committee.

Two press sites in widely separated areas were set up - the DIALOSA press to print currency for the army, the VILLALON press for the civil government. Printing operations got underway January 1, 1943. The Dialosa printing was in new designs, while the Villalon printing retained those of the presurrender printing. Both were dated *Series of 1942.*

In December 1942, Col. Peralta established radio contact with Gen. MacArthur in Australia. In a message dated January 13, 1943, MacArthur authorized Peralta to *issue a reasonable amount of military script.* This was the only time MacArthur authorized the printing of any type of currency, and he no doubt regretted it later. Since preparations were already well advanced for printing notes on *The Philippine National Bank,* it was decided to continue with these, rather than change to a military issue.

Through MacArthur, President Quezon was notified of the actions taken in regard to printing currency. Quezon granted approval, but specified that Peralta was to receive only such amount as was *specifically authorized by Gen. MacArthur.*

On receipt of this authority, the Villalon printing was changed to *Series of 1943* and extended to a wider range of denominations.

On February 28, 1943 the Dialosa press had been forced to shut down through lack of printing supplies, and Peralta's demands for currency from the Villalon press steadily increased. Confessor sent him everything not needed by the provincial government. It wasn't enough. Peralta demanded it all, and sent a company of soldiers to enforce the demand. Deputy Governor Juan Griño, commanding the Provincial Guard at the press site, refused to be cowed. Bloodshed was narrowly averted. As tension increased Griño stopped printing, dismantled the press and told Peralta to "come and get it." While the army was moving it to a new location they were ambushed by the Japanese who captured the press.

On October 17, 1943 the Dialosa press resumed printing for the army. To increase production Peralta instituted two 12-hour shifts and added a 100 pesos denomination. The 1942 date continued in use, and although both Auditor Fernandez and Fiscal Quisumbing had surrendered to the Japanese the currency continued to bear their signatures.

Relations between Governor Confessor and Col. Peralta had steadily worsened. Thus when Confessor appointed Abelardo Apartado and Eduardo Hibionada to replace the surrendered officials, Peralta substituted his own appointees in the radio message to President Quezon requesting confirmation. Unaware of the deception, Quezon approved Peralta's nominees designating Aniceto Belisario as Acting Provincial Fiscal and Demetrio G. Vinson as Acting Provincial Auditor. Confessor considered their appointments null and void. There thus came into being two sets of officials, one set loyal to Confessor, the other to Peralta.

The acute lack of small change caused Governor Confessor to take affairs into his own hands. In an *Executive Order* dated March 2, 1944 he directed Deputy Governor Juan Griño, who was concurrently Acting Provincial Treasurer, to print small denomination notes of 10, 20 and 50 centavos. The notes were to be backed up by large denomination notes held in the Provincial Treasury. In addition to Griño's signature, these notes also have the signature of Eduardo Hibionada who was Confessor's appointee as Acting Provincial Auditor.

By then Peralta had come to consider the printing of currency to be his exclusive privilege. Ignoring the fact that such denominations were badly needed, he ordered the army to *confiscate the notes and to suppress their circulation.* While no 10 centavos notes were printed, there were over half a million 50 centavos and 20,000 20 centavos notes placed in circulation. Considering their scarcity today, Peralta's orders must have been effectively carried out.

In mid-September 1944 the Dialosa press began printing a new issue of currency, with small denominations. These notes are dated *Series of 1944* and have facsimile signatures of Peralta's best of officials.

Printing of currency ceased December 5, 1944 on orders of President Osmeña. By then a total of 43,511,033 pesos had been printed. Peralta alone had printed three times the amount authorized for his use by Gen. MacArthur.

An enormous amount of counterfeits reached circulation. The majority were of 20 and 100 pesos denominations.

1942 EMERGENCY CIRCULATING NOTE ISSUE

First Dialosa Printing

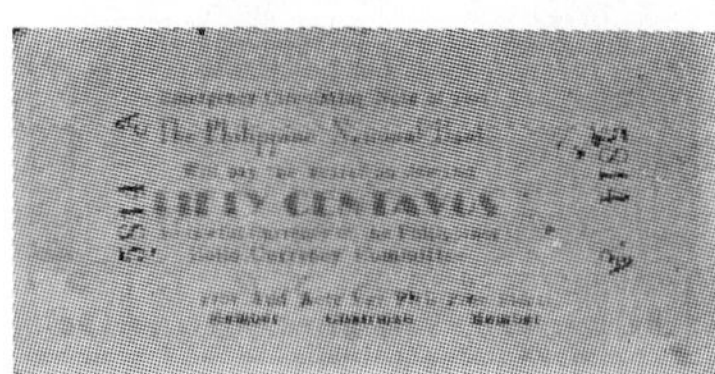

		GOOD	FINE	XF
S311	**50 CENTAVOS** 1942. Yellow w/green text. Serial #1 to 6466.	10.00	25.00	60.00

		GOOD	FINE	XF
S312	**2 PESOS** 1942. Dk. blue w/brown text. Filipino *tao* at l. Serial #1 to 5000.	15.00	60.00	130.00

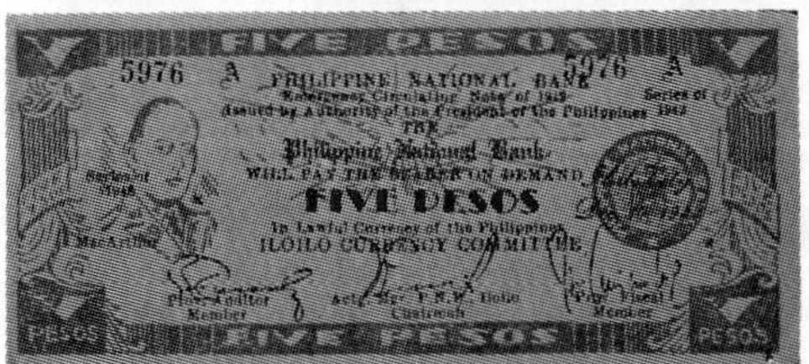

		GOOD	FINE	XF
S313	**5 PESOS** 1942. Dk. red w/black text. MacArthur at l., eagle at ctr. Serial #1 to 24,800.			
	a. Issued note.	3.50	7.50	15.00
	x1. Counterfeit. Portr. better than genuine.	—	—	—
	x2. Counterfeit. Very crude portr.	—	—	—
S314	**10 PESOS** 1942. Brown w/black text. Quezon at l. Serial #1 to 1850.	5.00	10.00	30.00

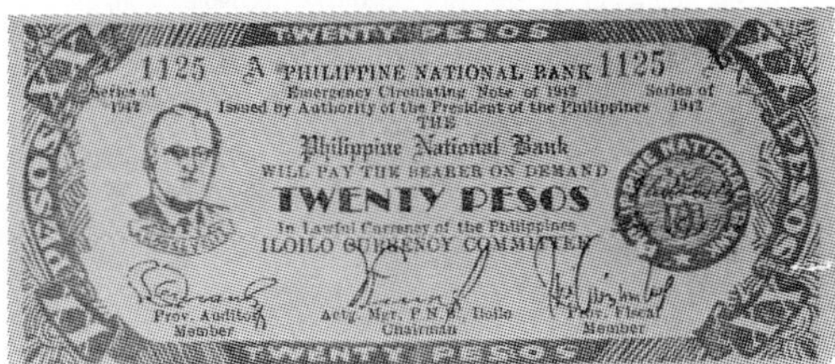

		GOOD	FINE	XF
S315	**20 PESOS** 1942. Green w/black text. Roosevelt at l. Serial #1 to 55,200.			
	a. Issued note.	1.50	3.00	6.00
	x1. Counterfeit. Portr. better than genuine.	—	—	—
	x2. Counterfeit. Crude portr.	—	—	—

Second Dialosa Printing

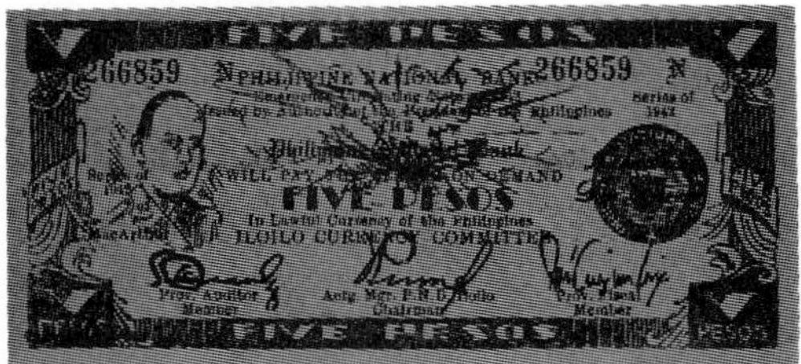

		GOOD	FINE	XF
S316	**5 PESOS** 1942. Dull salmon-red w/black text. Like #S313. Serial #24.801 to 294,000.	1.00	2.50	5.00

		GOOD	FINE	XF
S317	**10 PESOS** 1942. Brown w/black text. Like #S314. Serial #1851 to 421,000.			
	a. Dk. brown, serial # to 296,000.	1.00	2.50	5.00
	b. Lt. brown, very high serial # (for example 395,222).	1.00	2.50	5.00
S318	**20 PESOS** 1942. Green w/black text. Like #S315. Standing woman w/hammer and Mt. Mayon design (as on Philippine silver coins) at ctr. on back. Serial #55,201 to 998,000. 4 plates used.			
	a. Issued note.	.50	1.50	3.50

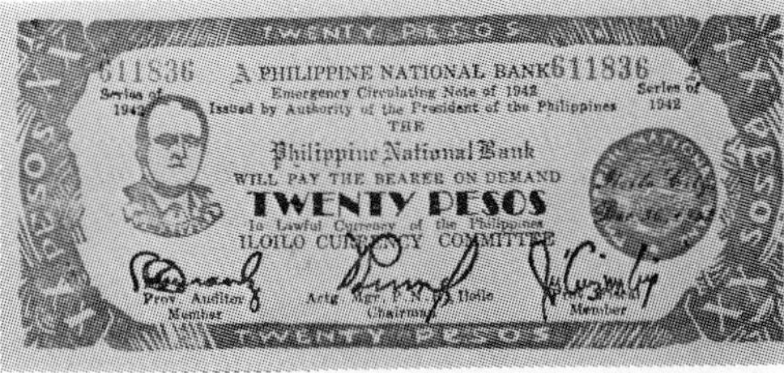

		GOOD	FINE	XF
	x. Counterfeit. Misspelling *ROOSAVELT* (w/*A*) under portr.	4.00	6.00	10.00

		GOOD	FINE	XF
S322	**100 PESOS** 1942. Yellow-orange w/black text. Mt. Mayon at l. Ribbon directly above drapes *over* bar. Serial #1 to 23,000 and 229,001 to 300,000.			
	a. Issued note.	2.50	6.00	10.00

GENUINE
Ribbon drapes over the bar.

COUNTERFEIT
Ribbon is pierced by the bar.
All 5-digit serial #s.

		GOOD	FINE	XF
	x1. Counterfeit. Ribbon above Mt. Mayon is pierced by bar. 5-digit serial #.	2.00	4.00	7.50
	x2. Counterfeit. Different type. 6-digit serial #.	—	—	—

Villalon Printing

#S324 and S325 eagle and *V* design of some 1941 notes.

		GOOD	FINE	XF
S324	**1 PESO** 1942. Black on green unpt. Similar to #S305 but eagle w/wings spread. Serial #1 to 75,000.	5.00	12.00	30.00
S325	**5 PESOS** 1942. Black on red unpt. Similar to #S307. Serial #1 to 30,000.	4.00	10.00	25.00

1943 EMERGENCY CIRCULATING NOTE ISSUE

Villalon Printing

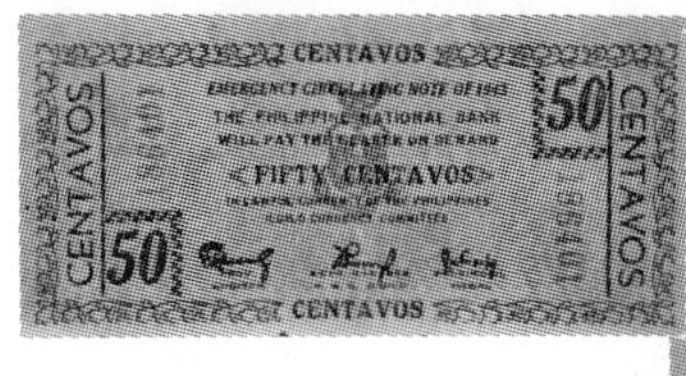

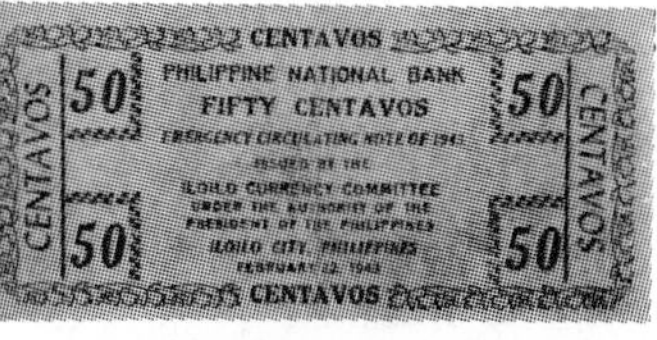

		GOOD	FINE	XF
S326	**50 CENTAVOS** 1943. Black w/red arms at ctr. Serial #1 to 200,000.	4.00	10.00	25.00
S327	**2 PESOS** 1943. Black on blue unpt. Similar to #S306. Serial #1 to 37,400.	2.50	5.00	15.00
S328	**5 PESOS** 1943. Black on red to violet unpt. Like #S325. Serial #1 to 455,000.			
	a. White paper.	2.00	4.00	10.00
	b. Yellow paper.	3.00	5.00	12.00
	x. Counterfeit.	—	—	—

NOTE: 5 Pesos notes w/serial #363,001 to 367,000 and 367,501 to 368,000 were reported stolen and officially prohibited from circulating.

		GOOD	FINE	XF
S329	**10 PESOS** 1943. Black on brown unpt. Like #S328. Serial #1 to 200,000.			
	a. White paper.	1.00	2.50	6.00
	b. Yellow paper.	2.00	4.00	10.00
S330	**20 PESOS** 1943. Black on green unpt. Like #S328. Serial #1 to 5000.	25.00	85.00	—

		Good	Fine	XF
S331	**50 Pesos** 1943. Black on mauve unpt. Like #S328. Serial #1 to 20,000.	7.50	15.00	40.00

1944 Treasury Certificate Issue

		Good	Fine	XF
S332	**20 Centavos** 1944. Serial #000,001 to 020,000.	—	Rare	—
S334	**50 Centavos** 1944. Initials *smc, pav* and *mvb* in upper l., upper r., and lower r. corners respectively. Serial #00,001 to (approx.) 160,000.	5.00	15.00	30.00

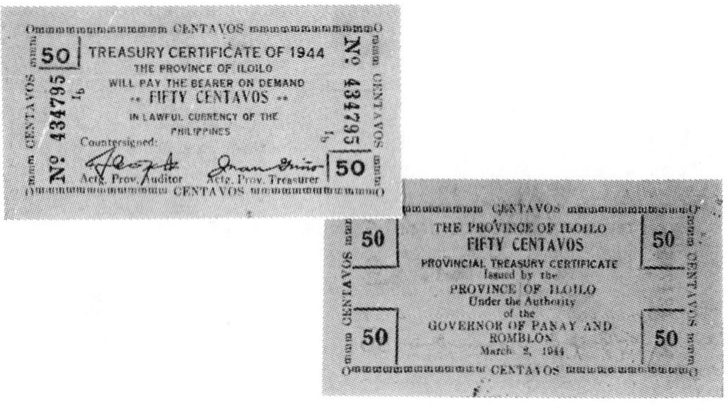

		Good	Fine	XF
S335	**50 Centavos** 1944. Like #S334 but no initials at corners. Serial # (approx.) 165,001 to 539,980.	5.00	15.00	30.00
S337	**50 Centavos** 1944. *SPECIAL MUNICIPALITY OF SIBUYAN ROMBLON PHILS* stamped on back.	20.00	40.00	65.00

1944 Emergency Circulating Note Issue

Dialosa Printing

		Good	Fine	XF
S338	**50 Centavos** 1944. Black w/red arms at ctr. Serial #1 to 150,000.			
	a. Plain paper.	.50	2.00	5.00
	b. Wmk. paper.	—	—	—
S339	**1 Peso** 1944. Black w/red arms at ctr. Serial #1 to 500,000.	.50	2.00	5.00
S340	**2 Pesos** 1944. Black w/red arms at ctr. Serial #1 to 494,000.			
	a. Issued note.	.50	2.00	5.00
	x. Counterfeit.	—	—	—
S341	**5 Pesos** 1944. Dull salmon-red w/black text. Like #S316. Serial #1 to 206,000.	.50	2.00	5.00

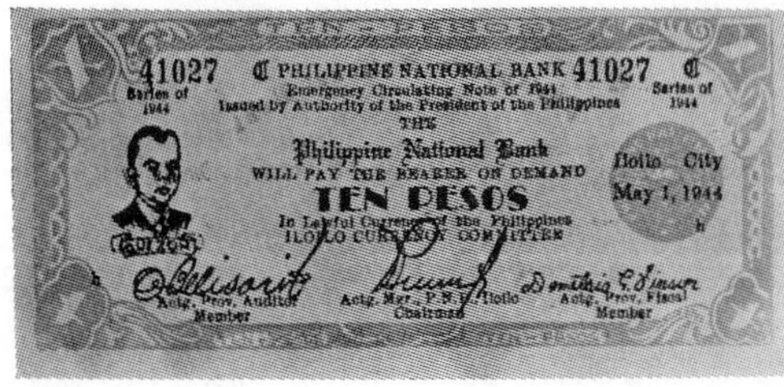

		Good	Fine	XF
S342	**10 Pesos** 1944. Brown w/black text. Like #S317. Serial #1 to 263,000.	.50	1.50	3.00

Isabela

There is but little factual information on these emergency notes. They were reportedly authorized by President Quezon in a radio message in early March 1942. The Currency Board was composed of Provincial Governor Gabriel R. Visaya as Chairman, with Provincial Treasurer Sisenando Silvestre and Provincial Auditor Francisco Malig as Members. A total of 182,377.10 pesos was officially reported as issued.

There were two issues, both mimeographed on manila paper. A rather crude handmade seal was stamped on the back which reads *Isabela Province Treasury.* The value was applied by a checkwriter obtained from the Isabela Agency of the Philippine National Bank. Notes were serially numbered on the back by pen or colored pencil.

First Issue: Early issues had the denomination by checkwriter only. This soon caused confusion as wear from circulation often made the value illegible. To correct this, later issues had the value stamped on the back with a crude handmade rubber stamp.

Second Issue: In order to eliminate confusion as to the value of the notes, this issue had denominations in numerals on the face, as well as with checkwriter. Early issues had pen signatures as before, but later issues had signatures rubber stamped.

Province of Isabela

1942 ND First Emergency Legal Tender Issue

#S351-S354 w/o numerals of value on face.

		Good	Fine	XF
S351	**1 Peso** ND (1942).			
	a. W/o denomination stamped on back.	20.00	60.00	—
	b. Denomination stamped on back.	20.00	60.00	—
S352	**5 Pesos** ND (1942).			
	a. W/o denomination stamped on back.	20.00	60.00	—
	b. Denomination stamped on back.	20.00	60.00	—
S353	**10 Pesos** ND (1942).			
	a. W/o denomination stamped on back.	20.00	60.00	—
	b. Denomination stamped on back.	20.00	60.00	—

		Good	Fine	XF
S354	**20 Pesos** ND (1942).			
	a. W/o denomination stamped on back.	20.00	60.00	—
	b. Denomination stamped on back.	20.00	60.00	—

1942 ND Second Emergency Legal Tender Issue

#S361-S367 numerals of value on face.

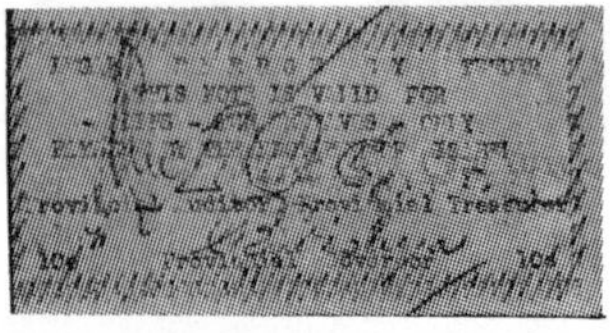

		Good	Fine	XF
S361	**10 Centavos** ND (1942).	—	—	—
S362	**20 Centavos** ND (1942).	—	—	—
S364	**1 Peso** ND (1942).	—	—	—
S365	**2 Pesos** ND (1942).	—	—	—

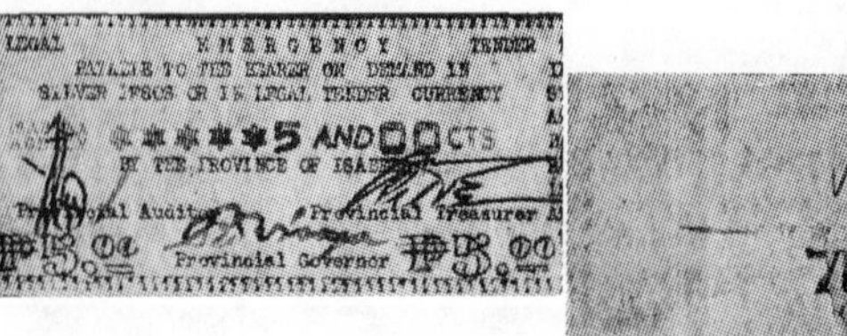

		Good	Fine	XF
S366	**5 Pesos** ND (1942).	—	—	—
S367	**10 Pesos** ND (1942).	—	—	—

KKKK

Refer to Masbate #S461-S462.

LANAO

PRE-SURRENDER ISSUE

The Lanao Currency Committee was authorized by President Quezon in a telegram relayed through Gen. Sharp in the latter part of January, 1942. The amount authorized to be printed was up to two-thirds of the Province's unencumbered bank deposits.

The Committee consisted of Provincial Treasurer Pedro Encarnacion as Chairman, with Provincial Auditor Fortunato Alabagan and Provincial Fiscal Francisco A. Obach as Members. Printing ended in March, when the (first) Mindanao Emergency Currency Board began printing currency for the Mindanao provinces. No information is available regarding quantities and serial numbers because records were destroyed during the war. After the war Treasurer Encarnacion estimated that 80,000 pesos had been issued.

PHILIPPINE NATIONAL BANK - LANAO

1942 EMERGENCY CIRCULATING NOTES ISSUE

There are two types of Lanao currency:

TYPE I: With *titles* of Committee Members.

TYPE II: With *names* of Committee Members.

		GOOD	FINE	XF
S372	**20 CENTAVOS** 1942. Type I. Facsimile sign. stamped in blue. Manila paper.	25.00	60.00	—
S374	**50 CENTAVOS** 1942. Type I. Handsigned. Yellow paper.	20.00	50.00	—
S376	**50 CENTAVOS** 1942. Type I. Printed sign. Yellow paper.	20.00	50.00	—
S377	**1 PESO** 1942. Type I. Handsigned. White paper.	20.00	50.00	—
S378	**1 PESO** 1942. Type II. Handsigned. White paper.			
	a. Issued note.	25.00	60.00	—
	x1. Counterfeit. Typewritten.	—	—	—
	x2. Counterfeit. Crudely printed.	—	—	—

		GOOD	FINE	XF
S380	**2 PESOS** 1942. Type I. Green. Printed sign. White paper. Back blue; Moro stringed musical instrument called a *kotivapi* in red across ctr.	25.00	50.00	—

1942 SPURIOUS ISSUE

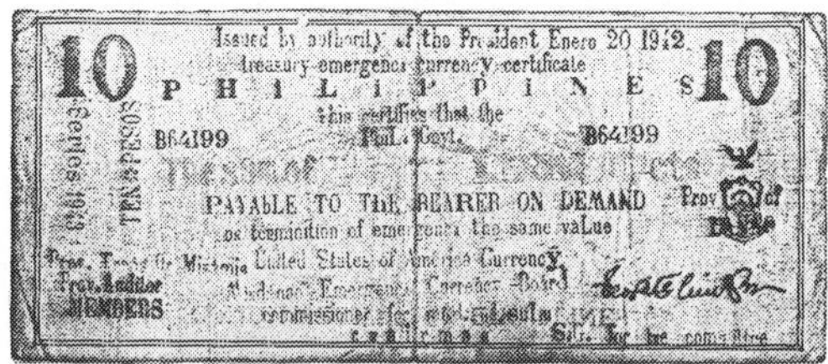

		GOOD	FINE	XF
S380X	**10 PESOS** 1.20.1942. Spurious note.	—	—	—

NOTE: A 10 Pesos note dated "Enero 20, 1942" is completely spurious. It is mentioned here not only to acquaint collectors with its true status but also as an example of the confusion brought about by the numerous types and varieties of currency being issued which resulted in an entirely bogus issue being placed in circulation.

FREE LANAO PROVISIONAL GOVERNMENT

On October 8, 1944 the guerrilla 108th Division (10th Military District) liberated Dansalan, capital of Lanao Province. They captured the puppet provincial officials and the puppet Treasury. In the Treasury they found 62,000 pesos in pre-surrender emergency currency which had been redeemed by the puppet administration. The notes had been stamped in Japanese as required for redemption.

Due to the shortage of currency, Col. Fertig, commanding the 10th Military District (Mindanao), authorized the Provincial Treasurer of the Free Lanao Provincial Government to use the notes for necessary expenditures.

Three different Japanese stampings are presently known, but other types may exist. Along with the Japanese stampings are countersignatures of the Provincial or Municipal treasurers to whom the notes were presented for redemption.

Inasmuch as all pre-surrender emergency currency was eligible for redemption (except mimeographed notes), the variety which could theoretically have been redeemed is extensive. However, the following are those most likely to have been redeemed:

Letter Indication	Note Type	Catalog #
a.	2 Pesos Mindanao 1942	S471
b.	5 Pesos as above	S472
c.	10 Pesos as above	S473
d.	20 Pesos as above	S474
e.	1 Peso Cebu 1941	S215
f.	5 Pesos as above	S216
g.	10 Pesos as above	S217
h.	20 Pesos as above	S218
i.	10 Pesos Cebu 1942	S223
j.	20 Pesos as above	S224

As these notes were not eligible for postwar redemption, efforts were made to erase or remove the markings. Thus, finding notes with legible markings is very difficult.

Only those notes positively identified have been listed.

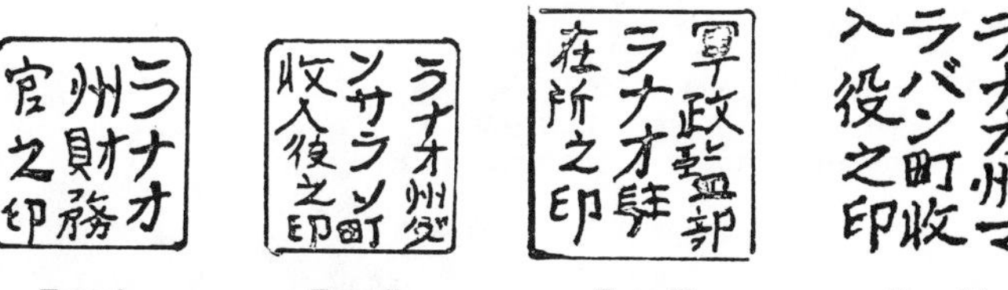

Type I Type II Type III Type IV

There are two different hand stamps on each note: (A) In English by the puppet Treasurer to whom they were presented for redemption and (B) by the Japanese "advisor" of that office. Generally they were applied in red to red-violet on the back, but Type III has Treasurer's counterstamping on the face. The notes generally have additional stampings in black *PAID*.

Type I	(A) Countersigned, 1943, Provincial Treasurer, Dansalan, Lanao.
	(B) Seal of Lanao Province Comptroller.
Type II	(A) Countersigned, 1943, Deputy Mun, and Provl. Treasurer, Dansalan, Lanao.
	(B) Seal of Treasurer, Dansalan City, Lanao Province.
Type III	(A) (B) Countersigned in pen, 1943, Deputy Treasurer, Iligan, Lanao.
	(B) Seal of Military Government Headquarters Stationed in Lanao.
	(B) (A) Counterstamped in black, 1943, Deputy Treasurer, Iligan, Lanao.
	(B) Same as Type III A.
Type IV	(A) Countersigned, 1943, Deputy Provl. Treasurer, Malabang, Lanao.
	(B)Seal of Treasurer of Malabang (town), Lanao Province.

1942 OVPT. ISSUE

		GOOD	FINE	XF
S381	**TYPE I OVPT. ON:**			
	c. 10 Pesos Mindanao 1942, #S473.	—	—	—
	e. 1 Peso Cebu 1941, #S215.	—	—	—
	f. 5 Pesos Cebu 1941, #S216.	—	—	—
	h. 20 Pesos Cebu 1941, #S218.	—	—	—
S382	**TYPE II OVPT. ON:**			
	a. 2 Pesos Mindanao 1942, #S471.	—	—	—
	c. 10 Pesos Mindanao 1942, #S473.	—	—	—
	e. 1 Peso Cebu 1941, #S215.	—	—	—
	d. 20 Pesos Mindanao 1942, #S474.	—	—	—
	f. 5 Pesos Cebu 1941, #S216.	—	—	—
	h. 20 Pesos Cebu 1941, #S218.	—	—	—
S383	**TYPE III A OVPT. ON:**			
	h. 20 Pesos Cebu 1941, #S218.	—	—	—
S383A	**TYPE III B OVPT. ON:**			
	c. 10 Pesos Mindanao, 1942, #S473.	—	—	—
	h. 20 Pesos Cebu 1941, #S218.	—	—	—
S384	**TYPE IV OVPT. ON:**			
	b. 5 Pesos Mindanao 1942, #S472.	—	—	—
	h. 20 Pesos Cebu 1941, #S218.	—	—	—

LEYTE

SERIES 1942

During the first part of 1942, Leyte was able to obtain adequate currency supplies from Cebu. But Cebu currency became increasingly hard to get, especially in smaller denominations.

With the Japanese invasion of Cebu on April 10, 1942, it was obvious that no more currency could be obtained from that source. At a special session of the Provincial Board on April 13, *Resolution No. 487* was adopted which created an Emergency Currency Board which was requested *to print as early as possible* notes to the value of 1,000,000 pesos. The amount was later increased to 2,000,000 pesos.

The Currency Board was composed of Provincial Auditor Alberto Santa Cruz as Chairman, with Provincial Treasurer Ildefonso D. Jiminez and Provincial Fiscal Quintin Paredes, Jr. as Members.

The printing took place in the Municipality of San Miguel. 5 Centavos notes were printed on thin blue paper, all other denominations on white paper. All denominations but the 1 Peso had an underprinting which occurs in two types:

Type I. Leyte Emergency Currency Board (repeated), upper and lower case.

Type II. LEYTE EMERGENCY CURRENCY BOARD (repeated), upper case only.

Printing ceased the afternoon of May 23, and all unfinished notes plus 4,000 pesos in finished 10 and 20 pesos notes were incinerated.

A total of 627,861.60 pesos had been printed. Records disclose the quantity for each denomination, but not the serial numbers. As notes are known with serial numbers higher than the quantity printed, it would appear that notes were numbered in blocks and that numbers assigned to some blocks were not used.

LEYTE EMERGENCY CURRENCY BOARD

1942 TREASURY EMERGENCY CERTIFICATE ISSUE

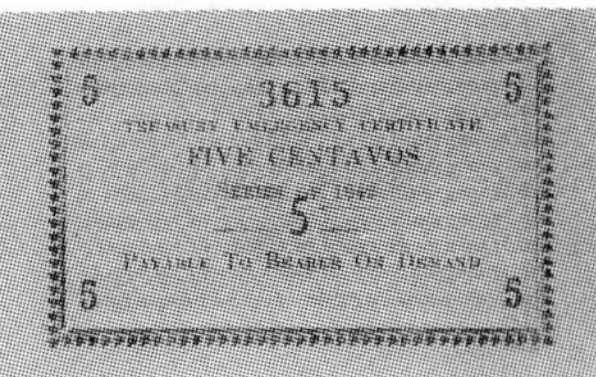

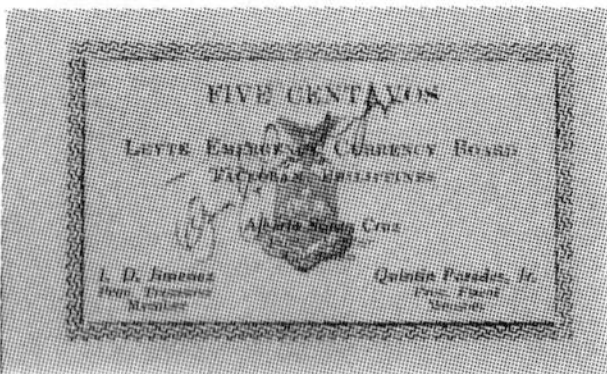

		GOOD	FINE	XF
S391	**5 CENTAVOS** 1942. Black on lt. blue paper. Red arms at ctr. on back. 34,932 notes.			
	a. Type I unpt. in yellow.	10.00	15.00	35.00
	b. Type II unpt. in yellow.	10.00	15.00	35.00

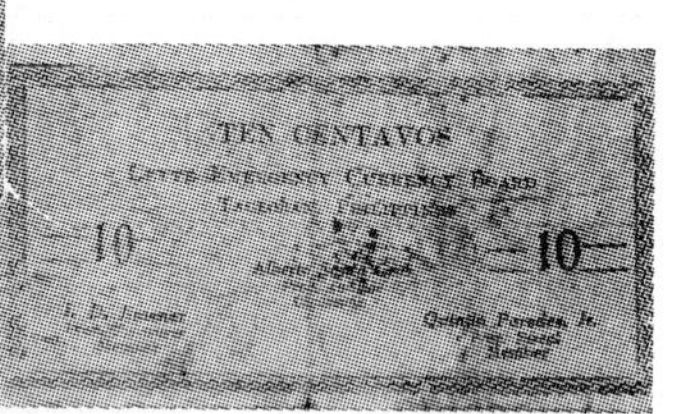

		GOOD	FINE	XF
S392	**10 CENTAVOS** 1942. Green. Red arms at ctr. Type I unpt. 9,750 notes.	50.00	100.00	—

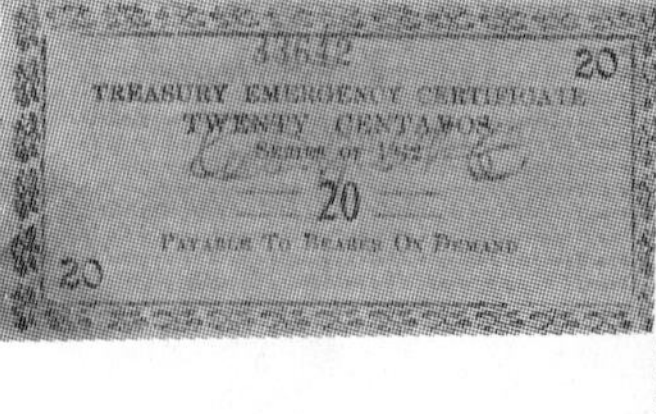

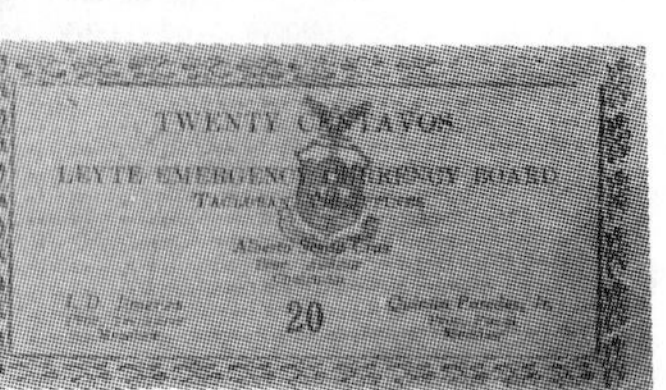

		GOOD	FINE	XF
S393	**20 CENTAVOS** 1942. Blue. Red arms at ctr. Type I unpt. in yellow. 8,100 notes.	20.00	50.00	—

		GOOD	FINE	XF
S394	**1 PESO** April 1942. Green. Orange arms at ctr. Filipino plowing w/carabao at l. Series A. 50,500 notes.	5.00	10.00	25.00

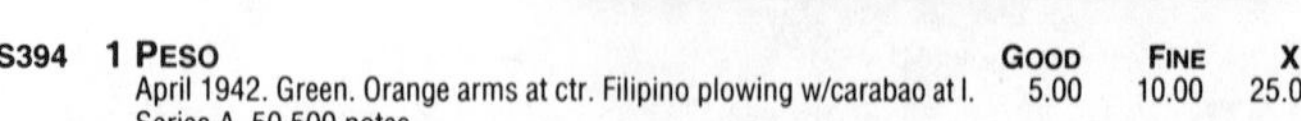

1942 TREASURY EMERGENCY CURRENCY CERTIFICATE ISSUE

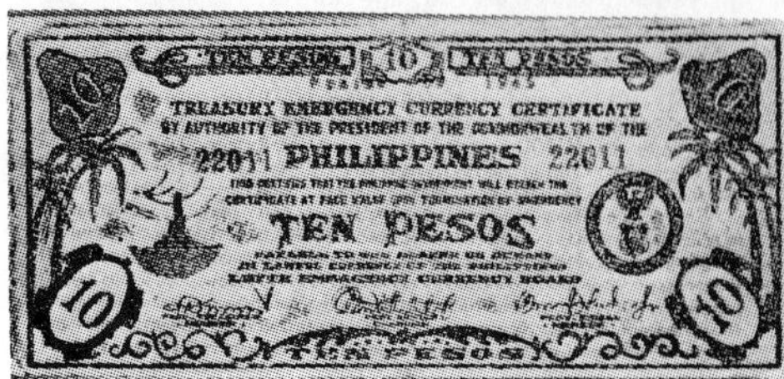

		GOOD	FINE	XF
S395	**10 PESOS** 1942. Black. Palm and Rizal Monument at l., seal and palm at r. 44,054 notes.			
	a. Type I unpt. in yellow on face only.	7.50	15.00	35.00
	b. Type I unpt. in yellow on face and back.	7.50	15.00	35.00
	c. Type II unpt. in yellow on face only.	10.00	20.00	40.00

		GOOD	FINE	XF
S396	**20 PESOS** 1942. Blue. Filipinos cultivating rice at l., arms at r. Unpt. in yellow. 6,300 notes.			
	a. Type I unpt. on face only.	25.00	85.00	—
	b. Type I unpt. on face and back.	25.00	85.00	—

SERIES 1943

Japanese occupation forces arrived in Leyte on May 24, 1942, setting up garrisons at Tacloban (the capital) and Ormoc.

Of the 1,800 USAFFE troops in Leyte, less than one third surrendered.

As the Japanese began to hunt down unsurrendered USAFFE soldiers, small bands of ex-USAFFE began to ambush Japanese patrols. In northern and western Leyte four major groups came into being, two of which were loosely affiliated with Col. Peralta's *IV Philippine Corps* (see Iloilo). There were also numerous smaller groups, particularly in southern Leyte. Several attempts at unification met with failure.

Lt. Col. Ruperto K. Kangleon who was released from the Butuan prison camp was approached by leaders of some of the smaller guerrilla groups who suggested that he should take over command to put an end to the rivalry among them. About this time liaison officers arrived from Mindanao who assured Kangleon of the support of "Gen." Fertig (see Mindanao). In early 1943 Kangleon set about the task of bringing all Leyte guerrilla groups under his personal command.

As in other areas, there was a desperate lack of money to finance operations. When Kangleon was informed that only 600,000 pesos of an authorized 2,000,000 pesos had been printed prior to surrender, he saw it as a solution to the problem. As currency was being printed in Mindanao, Kangleon sought Fertig's advice on how to go about it. Fertig promptly sent Lt. Iliff D. Richardson (former P.T. boat commander) to Leyte with full details, including samples of the Mindanao money, but cautioned that printing currency was a *civil,* not a *military,* function.

Acting on the advice, Kangleon set up a *Free Leyte Provisional Government* on July 19, 1943, with orders to begin printing currency immediately. On July 26 the Provincial Board created a new Leyte Currency Board composed of Provincial Auditor Enrique Potente as Chairman, with Provincial Treasurer Proceso Kadavero and Provincial Fiscal Filemon Saavedra as Members.

Lt. Richardson was assigned to get printing operations underway. There was no printing press available, or any type of printing supplies. A single hand-carved printing plate was made for the face and back of each denomination, along with seals and facsimile signatures. Ink was made from "RIT" dye, a product used in dying cloth. Notes were stamped by hand, one side at a time, on precut paper. The first delivery of the "new" Leyte currency was on August 24.

In the meantime Kangleon had radioed President Quezon (through Fertig) details regarding the new government, the Currency Board, and requesting authorization to print the unissued portion of the previous authorization. On September 27, Fertig notified Kangleon that Quezon had granted his approval.

Printing came to a halt on December 8, 1943, at which time 1,023,000 pesos had been printed. On that day the Japanese invaded Leyte with a large force, quickly occupying the larger towns. It was not until July, 1944 that printing of currency could be resumed. This second printing resumed where the previous one had left off, with the same wooden plates and cuts, except that the color of 2 Pesos note was changed to blue. As printing continued some plates began to show signs of wear, and new plates of a new design were made of rubber. The first to be replaced was the face for the 2 Pesos note. Later, new plates were made of rubber for both face and back of the 1 Peso note. Final delivery of the authorized 1,400,000 pesos was made on August 22, 1944.

But this did not end the printing. Col. Kangleon was dissatisfied with nearly half of the 20 Pesos notes, which he described as "heavy" and "rough finish." In *Executive Order No. 11* he ordered 150,060 pesos destroyed, to be replaced by smaller denomination notes from 20 Centavos to 5 Pesos.

This third printing began in September 1944. As the wood plates of both 20 and 50 centavos denominations were worn, new plates were made of rubber in a new design. Later on the 5 Pesos plates also needed replacing and new rubber plates were made for this denomination also. Final delivery of the third printing was October 7, 1944.

Two weeks later, October 20, 1944, American liberation forces landed in Leyte. President Osmeña immediately ordered that further issuance of the "new" Leyte currency notes be stopped. There were 131,260 pesos in the Provincial Treasury, plus another 168,459.80 in the hands of guerrilla finance officers. The combined total of 299,719.80 pesos was incinerated on January 17, 1945. Thus, most of the 20 and 50 Centavos notes printed from the rubber plates were destroyed and it is equally likely that all, or nearly all, of the rubber plate printings of 5 Pesos notes were also destroyed.

Official records do not disclose either serial numbers or quantities printed from the wood as opposed to the rubber plates. Serial numbers in the following listing are therefore estimates.

1943 SERIES FIRST ISSUE

#S403-S410 printed from wood plates. All are *Plate A.*

#S403-S405 Commonwealth arms at ctr.

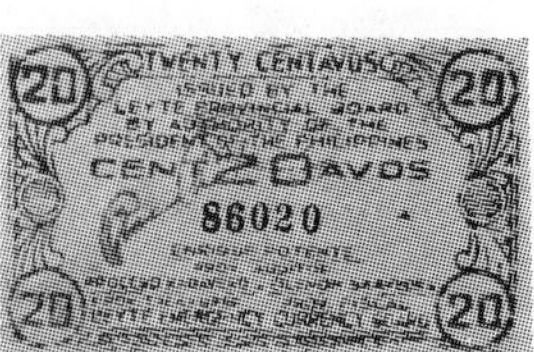

		GOOD	FINE	XF
S403	**20 CENTAVOS** 1943. Arms and sign. (on back) in red, purple or brown. Serial #00,101 to 99,100.			
	a. Issued note.	5.00	7.50	15.00
	x. *ERROR:* Inverted back.	—	—	—

S404 50 CENTAVOS

	GOOD	FINE	XF
1943. Arms and sign. (on back) in red or purple. Serial #00,101 to 159,100.			
a. Issued note.	5.00	7.50	15.00
x. Counterfeit.	—	—	—

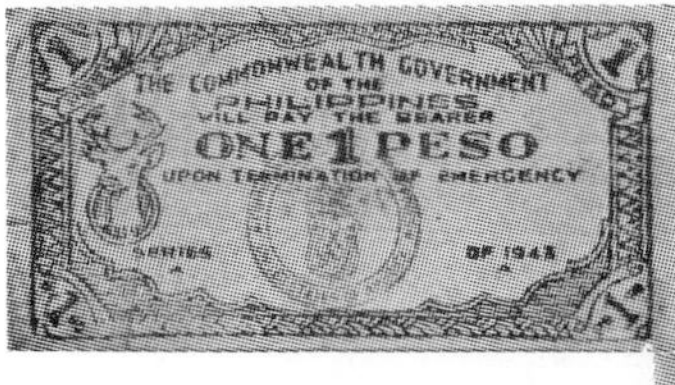

S405 1 PESO

	GOOD	FINE	XF
1943. Black. Arms and sign. (on back) in red, purple or brown. Serial #00,101 to 120,700.	5.00	10.00	25.00

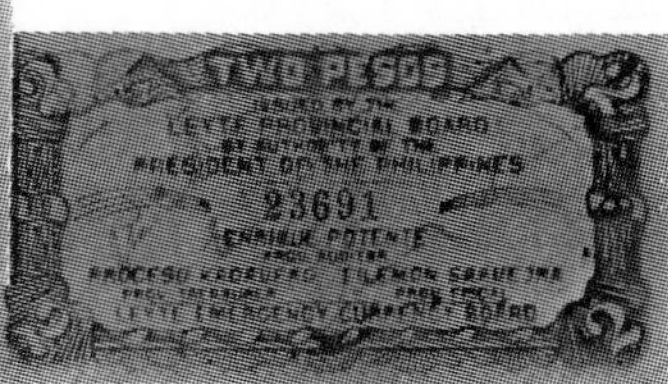

S406 2 PESOS

	GOOD	FINE	XF
1943. Black. Carabao head at l., red arms at r. Serial #00,101 to 41,000.			
a. Issued note.	5.00	10.00	25.00
x. Counterfeit (the carabao is smiling!).	—	—	—

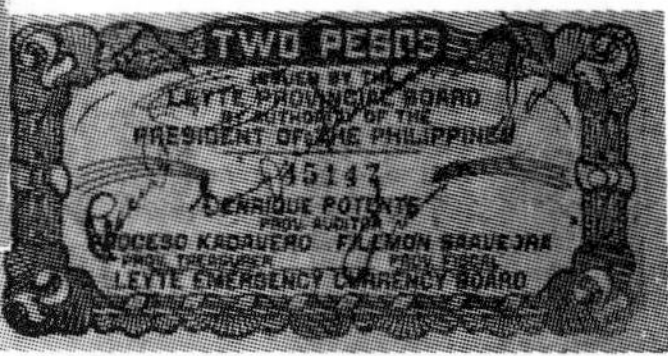

S407 2 PESOS

	GOOD	FINE	XF
1943. Blue. Like #S406. Red or purple seal at r. Smaller size serial # on back. Serial #42,001 to 50,000.	20.00	45.00	—

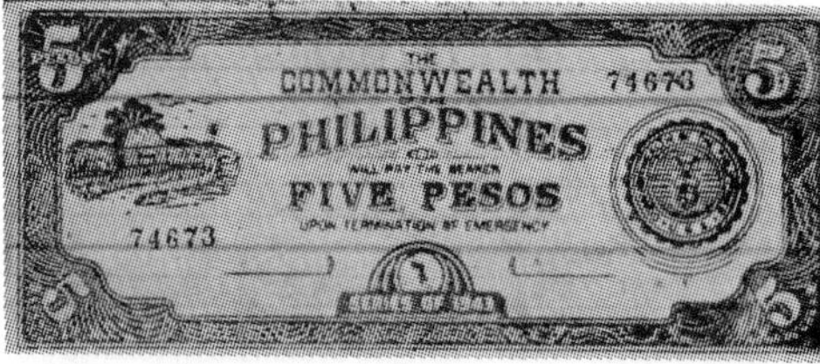

S408 5 PESOS

	GOOD	FINE	XF
Brown. Native village at l., seal in plate at r. Back green. Serial #0101 to 88,000.			
a. Thin to medium thick white paper.	10.00	25.00	45.00
b. Ruled ledger paper.	10.00	20.00	—
c. Dk. brown paper.	10.00	20.00	—

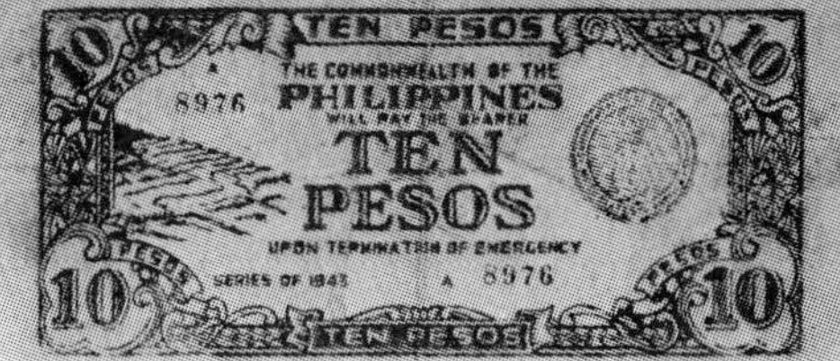

S409 10 PESOS

	GOOD	FINE	XF
1943. Black. Rice terraces at l., red seal at r. Back red. Serial #101 to 24,300.			
a. White paper.	15.00	30.00	75.00
b. Ruled ledger paper.	—	—	—
x. Counterfeit.	—	—	—

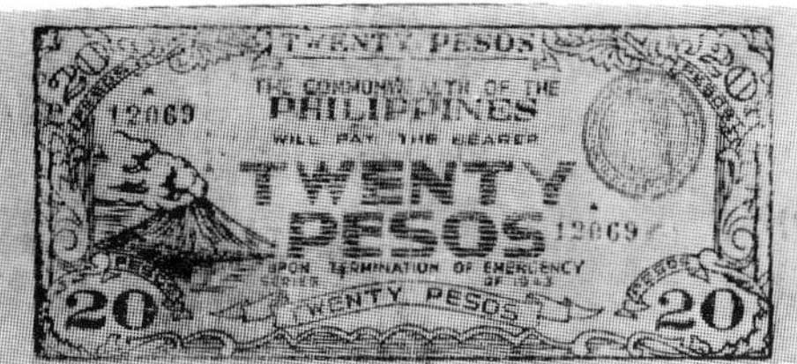

S410 20 PESOS

	GOOD	FINE	XF
1943. Black on yellow unpt. Red or maroon serial # and seal. Mt. Mayon at l. Back lt. blue-green. Serial #101 to 16,000.	22.50	75.00	—

NOTE: Serial # of 20 Pesos notes destroyed by orders of Col. Kangleon are as follows: 1401 to 4400; 4601 to 6600; 7501 to 8600; 13,201 to 14,600; also 3 individual notes (12,903, 12,912, 12,913).

1943 SERIES SECOND ISSUE

#S411-S415 printed from rubber plates.

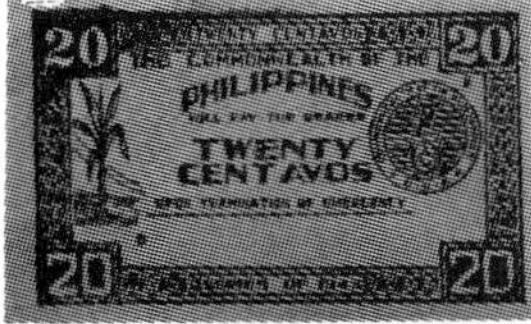

S411 20 CENTAVOS

	GOOD	FINE	XF
1943. Olive-green. Banana tree at l., seal in plate at r. Plate B. Serial #99,101 to 121,900.			
a. Issued note.	15.00	45.00	90.00
r. Remainder w/o serial #.	—	—	—

S412 50 CENTAVOS

	GOOD	FINE	XF
1943. Rust-brown. Palm tree at l., seal in plate at r. Plate B. Serial #159,101 to 199,500.			
a. Issued note.	15.00	45.00	90.00
r. Remainder w/o serial #.	—	—	—

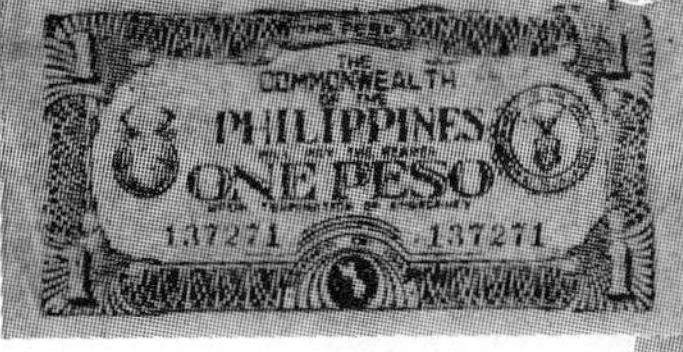

S413 1 PESO

	GOOD	FINE	XF
1943. Purple on pink paper. Antelope head at l., seal in plate at r. Plate B. Serial #121,001 to 180,300.	15.00	25.00	50.00

S414 2 PESOS

	GOOD	FINE	XF
1943. Blue. Carabao head at l., purple printed seal at r. Plate A2 (face only). Back like #S407. Serial #51,001 to 101,600.	15.00	25.00	50.00

NOTE: #S414 face is from rubber plate; back is from wood plate.

S415 5 PESOS

	GOOD	FINE	XF
1943. Plate B. Serial #88,001 to 96,400.	—	—	—

NOTE: No examples of #S415 are known at this time.

1943 Military Issue

One of the first to organize a successful guerrilla movement on Leyte was Capt. Glicerio I. Erfe, the highest ranking unsurrendered USAFFE officer on the island. His organization was designated USAFFE-ALL (USAFFE At Large Leyte) in the Abuyog - Burauan - Dulag - La Paz area.

He was among the first to attempt unification by bringing other guerrilla groups into an organization called the *11th Leyte Guerrilla Warfare Division, IX Philippine Corps*. Each guerrilla group became part of this organization and assigned to its respective area of control. To ensure a minimum of friction, the overall command would be exercised by a *Guerrilla War Tribunal* in which Capt. Erfe would serve as an "advisor."

Here also, the matter of money to finance the organization was a major problem. At a conference called by the Guerrilla War Tribunal on March 1, 1943 the matter of finance was discussed. Capt. Erfe informed the Tribunal he had received a communication from Col. Peralta in Panay who had sent along a copy of a radio message in which Gen. MacArthur had authorized the issuance of "military script." The Tribunal was also informed that prior to the surrender Leyte had been given authority to print 2,000,000 pesos in emergency notes, and that only 600,000 of this had actually been printed.

After considerable debate a *Resolution* was drafted which was approved by everyone present, part of which stated:

"We who are gathered here deem it necessary and indispensable to continue the printing of Emergency Currency notes under previous authority to make effective our resistance."

A Currency Board was formed which was composed of the *President* of the *Guerrilla War Tribunal,* Galicano Enerlan, with GHQ Auditor Ramon L. Mercado and the Finance and Disbursing officers (unnamed) as Members. A goal of June 1, 1943 was set for issuing the currency.

After numerous delays the essential equipment and materials were collected, and printing began in June 1943.

At this point Col. Kangleon decided to act. Even though Capt. Erfe had offered to place his USAFFE-ALL under Kangleon's command, some of the other guerrilla units in the *11th Division* had not. If these organizations obtained funds to finance their operations, Kangleon's goal of unification under his own command would be enormously difficult, if not impossible. By secretly promising one of Erfe's commanders with promotion in his own organization, Kangleon arranged for him to kidnap Cap. Erfe and some of the Currency Board Members, who were then thrown into Kangleon's military stoackade. With Erfe removed from the scene, the organization he had formed was broken up and Kangleon was able to move in.

In September 1943, Capt. Erfe and Auditor Mercado were belatedly charged by Col. Kangleon with *"printing and circulated money without authority."* The ironic aspect is that shortly after arranging for Capt. Erfe's kidnapping, Col. Kangleon would order the printing of currency for his own use, using the same "authority" that Capt. Erfe had used - the unissued portion of the pre-surrender authorization of 2,000,000 pesos.

Capt. Erfe was released on bail in October. He was captured by the Japanese in February 1944 and subsequently executed.

No reliable information is available regarding currency printed under authority of the Guerrilla War Tribunal, and no such notes are presently known to numismatists.

LUZON

LUZON USAFFE GUERRILLA ARMY FORCE

Walter Mickey Cushing was a mining engineer and part owner of the Rainbow gold mining properties in Abra Province. He was the first to organize a guerrilla force, for which he used his mine employees. The first recorded guerrilla action took place on New Year's Day, 1942. His exploits brought him to the attention of Col. John P. Horan, Commanding Officer of the *43rd Infantry, Philippine Scouts,* operating in Mountain Province. He was commissioned a Major by Col. Horan and given authority to organize guerrilla forces in Abra and the Ilocos Provinces. Cushing's guerrillas had no formal designation until after the fall of Bataan, at which time it was designated the *121st Infantry* by Gen. Wainwright.

Maj. Cushing died by his own hand on September 19, 1942 after being badly wounded in a Japanese ambush. He preferred death to surrender and saved his last cartridge for himself. His guerrilla operations had already made him a legend in northern Luzon, and even the Japanese paid him honor for the manner in which he died.

Little is known about the currency issued by Major Cushing. The notes were probably printed by Saint Mary the Virgin Mission press in Sagada, Mountain Province, which also printed the Mountain Province notes and was the only press in north Luzon capable of doing such printing. There is no way to confirm this as the press and records were destroyed during the war. There reportedly were 2,385,154 pesos issued, but the accuracy of this figure is questionable.

1942 ISSUE

Dated Feb. 22, 1942. Portr. of President Roosevelt at l., "Keep 'Em Flying" symbol of the Army Air Force at r. Facsimile sign. of Maj. Walter M. Cushing and Capt. W. H. Stephens. Embossed seal at ctr.

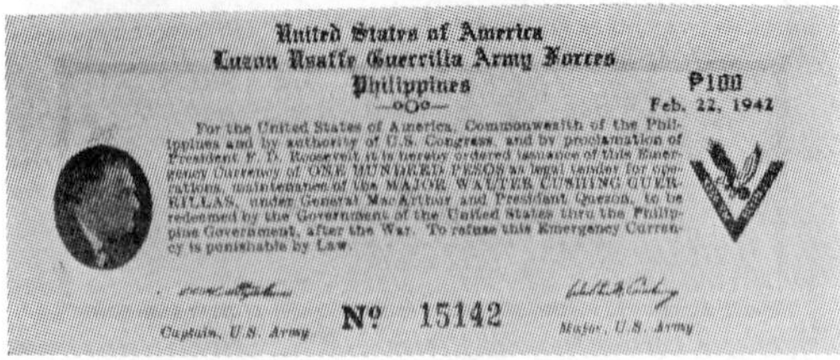

		GOOD	FINE	XF
S421	**100 PESOS** 1942. Black on pink paper.	15.00	35.00	75.00
S422	**500 PESOS** 1942. Black on pink paper.	40.00	75.00	125.00

MARKING'S GUERRILLAS

The Marking Guerrillas were organized by Marcos V. Agustin, using the *nom-de-guerre* Agustin V. Marking. He was given a commission in the Sierra Madre mountains by Maj. Russell D. Barros (91st Inf., P.A.) and authorized to organize a guerrilla unit. Starting with nothing, he began to build what eventually became one of the larger guerrilla organizations in Luzon. In mid-1942 he was joined by Ms. Yay Panlillo, a former newspaper reporter and U.S. Army Intelligence agent.

Their organization was among the first to accept the leadership of Col. Hugh Straughn, a retired Army officer who was trying to unify guerrillas in an alliance he called *Fil-American Irregular Troops (FAIT).*

Straughn was captured by the Japanese on August 5, 1943 and subsequently executed. As a result his organization broke up and the Markings pursued an independent course, eventually expanding into several provinces.

As records of the Marking currency were destroyed during the war, the following is based on reports written from memory by Ms. Panlillo in 1947.

The first Marking currency was printed by mimeograph in October 1942 under authority of Col. Hugh Straughn. Straughn reportedly authorized an issue of 10,000 pesos stating he would redeem it from his own pocket if necessary. Far more was issued than was authorized, as Panlillo estimated a total of 50,000 pesos.

The second issue was prepared in July or August 1943, in blue from engraved plates. The text states *Advised by Col. Hugh Straughn.* As Col. Straughn was captured shortly after that, some of these notes had his name x'd out by typewriter, and that of *Gen. W. W. Fertig* typed in. The *Gen. Fertig* referred to Col. W. W. Fertig in Mindanao, whose intelligence agents had briefly contacted the Markings.

The third issue differs from the second only in that new plates were made which substituted Gen. Fertig's name for Col. Straughn.

Panlillo estimated the total for the combined second and third issue at 25,000 pesos. However, she also mentions that large quantities were captured by the Japanese. (A small quantity of third issue notes, without the thumbprints, came on the numismatic market in 1979. It is quite possible that these are some the Japanese captured.)

The fourth issue was orginally called *exchange notes* and was given in exchange for cash contributions in Japanese military notes. Later, the notes were called *liberty bonds* and sold for their face value in military notes. At present only a 1,000 Pesos denomination is known, but other denominations were sold. As the amount was filled in by hand, there could be numerous different denominations. As the value of Japanese military notes steadily depreciated, Panlillo estimates the amount issued as not less than one million or more than three million pesos.

All Marking's notes which were issued bore inked thumbprints of Col. Marking, Col. Enrique Zulaybar and Yay Panlillo. Enrique Zulaybar was the *nom-de-guerre* of Lt. Col. Ruperto Batora, commanding officer of the Marking II Corps. He was later killed by the Japanese.

Only notes which have been confirmed are listed.

ND FIRST ISSUE

Mimeographed in October 1942.

		GOOD	FINE	XF
S427	**5 PESOS** ND.	—	—	—

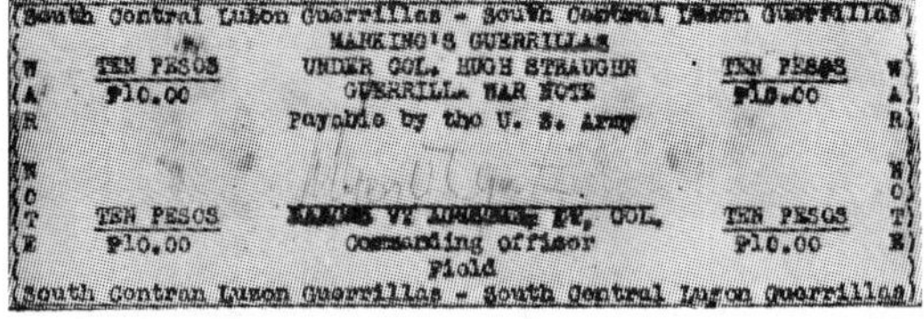

		GOOD	FINE	XF
S428	**10 PESOS** ND.	—	—	—

SECOND ISSUE

Printed in blue. *Advised by Col. Hugh Straughn.* No examples known.

ND THIRD ISSUE

Printed in blue. *Advised by Gen. W. W. Fertig.*

		GOOD	FINE	XF
S438	**10 PESOS** ND. W/o inked thumbprints. Remainder.	—	—	—

ND FOURTH ISSUE

Exchange notes.

		GOOD	FINE	XF
S443	**1000 PESOS** ND. Lt. blue. *Col. Hugh Straughn* x'd out and *Gen. W. W. Fertig* typed in. Tree and mountain at l., U.S. and Philippine flags at ctr., huts and trees at r. Lg. *V* at ctr. on back.	—	Rare	—

PRESIDENT QUEZON'S OWN GUERRILLAS (PQOG)

The PQOG was one of the larger guerrilla units in Central Luzon, organized and commanded by Col. Vicente Umali, prewar Mayor of Tiaong, Tayabas. The *II Corps* was the *Propaganda Section* of the PQOG under command of Lt. Col. Benedicto S. Valenzona. Its membership was made up of prominent prewar newspaper journalists and artists. Among other activities it published the underground newspaper *Liberator* which was distributed in Manila under the very noses of the Japanese. The first issue came out in July 1944 and continued up to the liberation.

No information is available regarding currency printed by the PQOG II Corps, and only one denomination is presently known.

ND EMERGENCY CERTIFICATE ISSUE

		GOOD	FINE	XF
S448	**100 PESOS** ND. Black on pink paper. Mimeographed. Guerrilla fighter on hill at ctr. PQOG and eagle w/Philippine arms in unpt. and on back. Facsimile sign. of Lt. Col. Benedicto S. Valenzona.	—	—	—

MASBATE

MASBATE CONSOLIDATED MINING CO.

PRE-SURRENDER ISSUES

This firm normally received currency for its monthly payrolls from the home office in Manila. With transportation disrupted by the war it became impossible to do so. Mine Superintendent Barney Faust received instructions by radio to print token notes to meet the 1941 year-end payroll.

On December 15, 1941 the Philippine National Assembly passed a bill conferring *additional* extraordinary powers on President Quezon. Using this authority President Quezon issued an *Executive Order* on December 20 which suspended *Commonwealth Act No. 303* which had previously prohibited payment of wages by token notes or company chits. This action was taken to enable commercial firms cut off from normal currency supplies, such as mines and sugar centrals, to meet their year-end payrolls by means of token notes.

The Masbate Consolidated Mining Co. is the only firm presently known to have issued token notes under this authority. The notes were used to meet the December payroll. These notes are therefore not only the first emergency currency issued under Presidential authority, but the only ones actually issued in 1941. They probably also rank first in being the shortest-lived issue.

On January 2, 1942 a Philippine Constabulary officer phoned Mine Manager Barney Faust and told him the Japanese were invading Masbate, and ordered all Americans to evacuate. It was a hoax. As soon as the American staff and engineers left, the mine was looted. The loot was enormous, some 600,000 pesos in gold bullion alone, plus another half million pesos worth of warehouse supplies, 200,000 pesos in stores, all the office equipment as well as furniture and personal property from staff housing. Unissued - and unsigned - token notes were reported to have been scattered on the floor of the looted Paymaster's office.

Because of the looting the mine ceased operations. When operations resumed after the war the token notes were honored by Masbate Consolidated Mining Co.

The MCMC token notes were printed by hectograph, a duplicating process by which copies are made from a sheet of gelatin. The notes were printed with two facsimile signatures. One is of Office Manager Reginald W. Verney (an Englishman), the other of I. J. Rebutoc, Chief Clerk under Verney and not the *Paymaster* as stated on the notes. Each note was serially numbered and signed in pen by Mine Manager Barney Faust before being issued. A reported 10,000 pesos were printed, but it is not known how much of this was actually issued.

1941 ND TOKEN NOTES ISSUE

#S451-S453 printed in green. Series A.

		GOOD	FINE	XF
S451	**50 CENTAVOS** ND (1941).	—	Rare	—
S452	**1 PESO** ND (1941).	—	Rare	—

		GOOD	FINE	XF
S453	**5 PESOS** ND (1941).	—	Rare	—

PROVINCE OF MASBATE

All official records concerning this currency were destroyed when the capital building was burned during the war. According to a postwar report by Governor Pecson, authority for printing the currency was a *Resolution* passed by the Provincial Board after receiving telegraphic instructions from President Quezon at the end of December, 1941.

The Currency Committee consisted of Provincial Governor Mateo S. Pecson as Chairman, with Provincial Treasurer Jose Recife and Provincial Auditor Ceferino Loreña as Members. A maximum of 80,000 pesos was authorized, of which 40,000 pesos was printed. Only 33,000 pesos were placed in circulation. The balance was destroyed sometime in 1943 on orders of the Japanese.

The notes were mimeographed in sheets of three. The 50 Centavos, 1 Peso and 2 Pesos denominations were printed with one stencil. The second stencil contained two 5 Pesos notes and one 10 Pesos note. They are stamped on the back with the Provincial Auditor's *Received* stamp dated Jan. 15, 1942.

1942 EMERGENCY TREASURY CERTIFICATES ISSUE

Serial numbers are estimates.

		GOOD	FINE	XF
S456	**50 CENTAVOS** 15.1.1942. White paper. Serial #1 to 4000.	—	—	—
S457	**1 PESO** 15.1.1942. White paper. Serial #1 to 4000.	20.00	40.00	70.00
S458	**2 PESOS** 15.1.1942. White paper. Serial #1 to 4000.	—	—	—

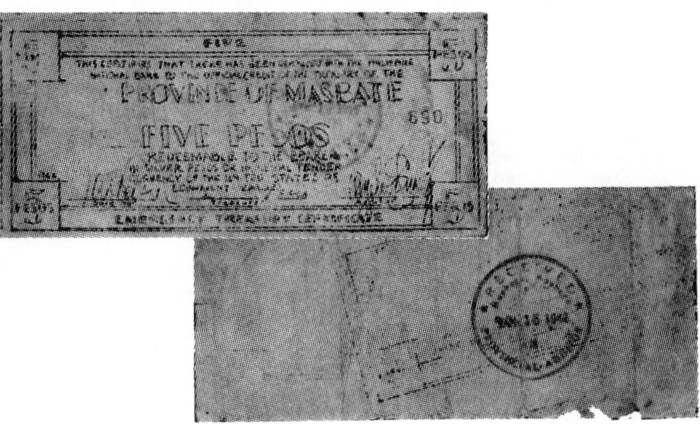

		GOOD	FINE	XF
S459	**5 PESOS** 15.1.1942. Cream to yellow paper. Serial #1 to 2600.	—	—	—
S460	**10 PESOS** 15.1.1942. Cream to yellow paper. Serial #1 to 1300.	—	—	—

POST-SURRENDER ISSUES

KKKK KATIPUNAN SA KALUWASAN SANG KA-ANAKAN SANG KAPUPUD-AN

The *Army of the Free People,* as it was called, was a guerrilla organization formed in 1942 by Jesus Azarraga, using the *nom-de-guerre* Capt. Juan Villaojada. Assisted by two brothers he built up a force of about 400 men which operated in the Milagros area.

Rumors that this was a communist group reached Col. Peralta in Panay. Using this as a pretext, Peralta sent an expedition in 1943 under Maj. Vincente A. Tansiongco to wipe out the Communists and take control of Masbate.

This proved to be a more formidable task than anticipated. On January 23, 1944, Maj. Tansiongco arranged a meeting with the Japanese garrison officers and arranged a "truce" whereby they would not molest each other.

This enabled Maj. Tansiongco to concentrate his entire force against the Villaojada guerrillas. In February 1944 he succeeded, driving the few survivors deep into the mountains. Peralta's control of Masbate, however, was short lived. (See "Free" Masbate.)

ND LOOSE CHANGE ISSUE

		GOOD	FINE	XF
S461	**50 CENTAVOS** ND. Slate black on orange unpt. Red KKKK seal at l., 2 guerrilla fighters w/flag at r. Back brown; crossed rifle, knife and gear at ctr., black ovpt: *FIFTY CENTAVOS.* Ruled ledger paper.	75.00	125.00	175.00

		GOOD	FINE	XF
S462	**1 PESO** ND. Black. Red KKKK seal at r. Back orange; like #S461. Thin lt. manila paper.	75.00	125.00	175.00

FREE MASBATE

Capt. Manuel P. Donato had organized a small guerrilla unit on Masbate in 1942. Relations with the Villaojada unit had been cordial (see KKKK) but in 1943 Capt. Donato went to Panay to seek backing from Col. Peralta. He returned to Masbate as Executive Officer under Maj. Tansiongco whom Peralta sent to liquidate the Villaojada guerrillas.

In July 1944, Capt. Donato led a revolt against the command of Maj. Tansiongco after which a conference of guerrilla officers was called on July 18. A *Resolution* was adopted severing all connections between Masbate and Col. Peralta's command in Panay.

A *Free Masbate Provincial Government* was organized and at the inaugural meeting on October 9, 1944, the Provincial Board adopted a *Resolution* creating a Currency Committee to print emergency notes.

The Currency Committee was composed of Acting Provincial Governor Severo Castillo as Chairman, with Acting Provincial Treasurer Francisco Dimatara and Acting Provincial Auditor Ceferino Loreña as Members.

The committee was authorized to print and issue 40,000 pesos in notes of 50 Centavos, 1, 5, 10 and 20 Pesos denominations. Authority for this currency was based on the pre-surrender authorization to print 80,000 pesos and of which only 40,000 had been printed.

No information is available as to whether such currency was printed or issued.

MINDANAO

MINDANAO EMERGENCY CURRENCY BOARD

When the Cebu Emergency Currency Board was established on March 1, 1942 it was hoped that this Board would be able to print all the currency required by the provinces in Mindanao and the Visayan islands. However, it soon became apparent that this goal was unrealistic so an additional Board was established to print currency for the provinces of Mindanao.

The Mindanao Emergency Currency Board was officially created at Dansalan, Lanao on March 16, 1942. Teopisto Guingona, Commissioner of Mindanao and Sulu, was appointed Chairman, with Ubaldo D. Laya, Provincial Treasurer of Misamis Oriental, and Fortunato Alabagan, Provincial Auditor of Lanao, as Members.

Printing plates were made in Cebu City of the same design as those of the Cebu Board. Lt. Samuel J. Wilson (USNR) was assigned to transport printing presses and plates to Dansalan and to supervise the printing.

Printing operations got underway immediately but were brought to a halt on May 1, 1942 as a result of the Japanese invasion of Mindanao. Records of this Board state that 1,769,690 pesos were officially issued. The figure for the 2 Pesos denomination is 40,000 pesos with serial numbers 0001 to 20,000.

However, on the night of May 1, finished but uncut sheets of 2 Pesos notes, unfinished sheets of all four denominations and such printing equipment as could be carried was hastily moved to Siwagat. On May 4 this was again moved to Tamparan where the next day the finished sheets of the 2 Pesos notes, serially numbered 20,001 to 90,000, were cut; all unfinished sheets were destroyed.

These 2 Pesos notes were turned over to Mr. Donato Ducusin, Provincial Treasurer of Sulu, who was serving as Secretary of the Mindanao Emergency Currency Board. Mr. Ducusin was reportedly murdered by Moros a few days later, and it is not known how these notes reached circulation. Adding them to the official figures, we get a total of 1,909,690 pesos as having reached circulation.

All notes were printed on Bais paper.

1942 EMERGENCY CURRENCY CERTIFICATE ISSUE

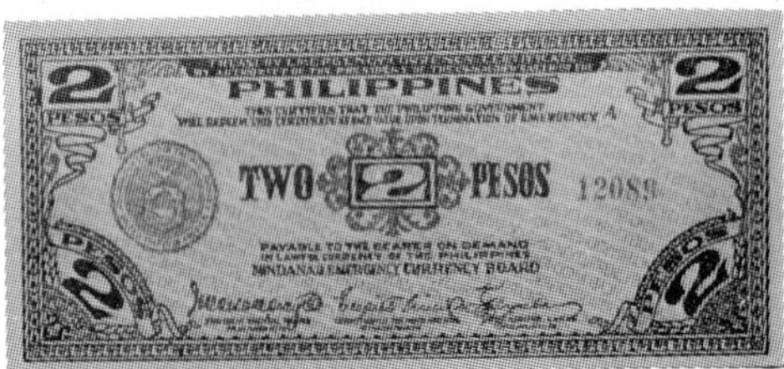

		GOOD	FINE	XF
S471	**2 PESOS** 1942. Black on blue unpt. Serial #0001 to 90,000.	1.00	5.00	7.50

		GOOD	FINE	XF
S472	**5 PESOS** 1942. Blue on green unpt. Tan unpt. on back. Serial #0001 to 76,338.	2.00	5.00	12.50

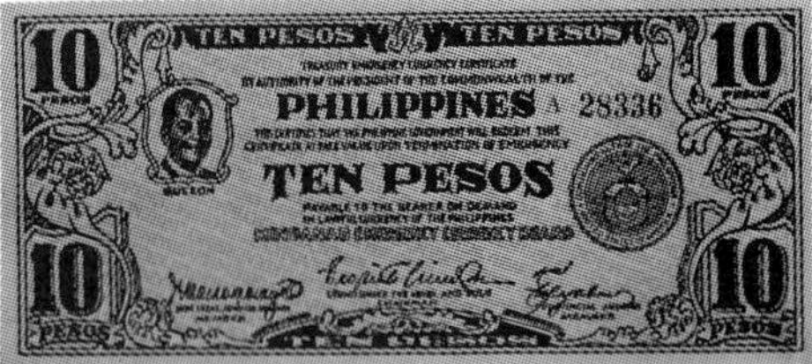

		GOOD	FINE	XF
S473	**10 PESOS** 1942. Black on reddish brown unpt. Quezon at l. Serial #0001 to 29,000.	2.00	5.00	12.50
S474	**20 PESOS** 1942. Black on green unpt. Similar to #S473. Serial #0001 to 52,900.	2.50	5.00	12.00

SECOND MINDANAO EMERGENCY CURRENCY BOARD

Japanese invasion forces landed in 1942 and quickly broke through the defenses of the poorly equipped and mostly untrained USAFFE forces.

In obedience to Gen. Wainwright's orders, Gen. William F. Sharp surrendered the Visayan-Mindanao Force on May 10, but it was not until May 27 that the final surrender took place in Mindanao. In the meantime thousands of soldiers took to the hills.

In Lanao, Lt. Col. Wendell W. Fertig began uniting the guerrillas under his command. In September he proclaimed the establishment of the *United States Forces in the Philippines*, (USFIP) *Mindanao-Sulu Command*, with his assumed rank of Brigadier General. Lanao, Misamis Occidental and the northern part of Zamboanga were under his command with *Free* provincial governments functioning, but it would require another year before all of Mindanao was united under his command and free provincial governments could be established in other provinces.

One of the major problems confronting *Gen.* Fertig was the matter of money with which to finance both the military force and civil governments. This was temporarily solved when Fertig learned that the Misamis Occidental Currency Committee had issued only a fraction of the currency it had been authorized to print. In December 1942 Fertig ordered the Committee to print the unissued balance of the authorized amount (see Misamis Occidental, Second Printing).

In February 1943 Fertig established radio contact with Gen. MacArthur in Australia, and was designated by MacArthur as Commanding Officer of the *10th Military District* (Mindanao and Sulu), with the rank of Lieutenant Colonel.

In the meantime, Lt. *Sam* Wilson, supervisor of the pre-surrender printing of currency by the Mindanao Emergency Currency Board, had joined Fertig and told him that this Board also had printed only a part of its authorized amount. Fertig promptly radioed MacArthur of his intentions to reconstitute this Board with new members (original members had surrendered) and resume printing currency under authority previously granted by President Quezon. MacArthur passed the message on to President Quezon in Washington, who promptly granted his approval. Thus, the *second* Mindanao Emergency Currency Board came into being.

The new Board consisted of Judge Florentino Saguin as Chairman, with Misamis Occidental Provincial Treasurer Filomena D. Pacana and Provincial Auditor Ireneo Barbasa as Members.

Maj. Sam Wilson (guerrilla rank) was assigned to get printing operations underway. Wood border cuts were made for the face of the 2 Pesos note, and for both face and back of the 10 and 20 Pesos notes. The 5 Pesos notes were printed from the same border cuts previously made for the Misamis Occidental printing (#S578). Other denominations were printed entirely from metal type.

Printing operations began on April 5, 1943 at the Rozito Z. Bacarro press in the *barrio* of Matugas, Municipality of Jiminez, Misamis Occidental. On June 26, the Japanese invaded Misamis Occidental. At the press site thousands of pesos in partly printed currency were burned. The presses were dismantled and hidden in the hills along with printing supplies. At Oroquieta, Treasurer Pacana hastily packed 702,619.30 pesos into sacks and evacuated to the hills.

Driven out of Misamis Occidental, Col. Fertig relocated his headquarters in the *barrio* Liangan, Municipality of Kolumbugan, Lanao Province. As currency supplies dwindled, Fertig requested that the printing be done in Australia. MacArthur rejected the proposal. Printing supplies, yes; printed currency, no.

Maj. Sam Wilson was assigned the difficult task of getting the presses to Liangan. It took ten days to move the heavy presses from their hiding place in the hills down to the coast. They were moved by *banca* across Iligan Bay at night to avoid Japanese naval patrols. Printing resumed at Liangan on September 6, and ended November 1, 1943 when supplies ran out.

As Japanese activity increased in the Lanao area, Fertig moved his headquarters to Esperanza in Agusan province. The presses were moved by water transport along the coast and then up the Agusan River.

In the meantime the cargo submarine USS NARWHAL had delivered 90 tons of supplies at Nasipit. Among the supplies were 30 boxes of paper, 27 cans of ink and dryer, and 84 metal plates made in Australia for printing currency.

Printing resumed at Esperanza on December 13, 1943 using the metal plates. As no metal plates had been made for either the 5 Centavos or 20 Pesos denominations, these were printed from the same metal type and wood border cuts as previously. Printing ended on January 23, 1944 when supplies ran out.

Once again stepped up Japanese military activity necessitated moving the presses to a safer area. In early February they were moved up the river to Loreto, Agusan. Printing finally got underway on March 18, 1944 after more supplies were delivered by USS NARWHAL.

The Japanese garrisoned Butuan, Agusan, using it as a base of operations and almost daily planes bombed the towns along the river. Esperanza was reduced to rubble, and on July 5, 1944 Loreto was bombed. As further attacks were expected, the presses were dismantled and hidden, and press personnel evacuated to a safer area.

It was October before the Japanese attack abated enough to allow the press personnel to return to Loreto. Printing resumed on November 4, 1944 but was halted in mid-November on instructions from Col. Fertig.

Immediately after printing had ceased at Loreto in July, Sam Wilson and two printing technicians left there, carrying with them some of the printing plates. They hiked over mountains to the coast of Misamis Oriental where they obtained transportation by banca along the coast to Dipolog, Zamboanga. The trip took the greater part of two months.

At Dipolog, arrangements were made for use of a small press owned by the Rev. Angel Soto. Printing resumed at the *barrio* of Tingkugas on September 14, and continued until October 6, 1944 when paper supplies ran out.

It was not until February 27, 1945, after new paper supplies had been brought in by submarine, that printing operations were resumed at the *barrio* Estaka. On March 8, 1945 the first American liberation forces landed at the guerrilla-held airfield at Dipolog. Military operations placed the press site in jeopardy, so printing was stopped to permit the press to be moved to a safer location.

Printing resumed at the *barrio* of Calamba, Municipality of Plaridel, Misamis Occidental on April 1, 1945. Printing operations ceased on April 22, on orders of Col. Fertig, thus ending the printing of currency by the second Mindanao Emergency Currency Board.

Meanwhile, back at Loreto in Agusan province, printing operations had resumed on January 2, 1945. As there was only a small stock of paper on hand it was soon exhausted and printing ended on January 5. This printing is mentioned last, as these were the only notes dated *Series 1945*.

A total of 23,613,415 pesos was printed by the second Mindanao Emergency Currency Board.

COUNTERSIGNERS OF MINDANAO NOTES:

Provincial Auditor

F.D. Pacana | I. Barbasa with title | I. Barbasa

L.J. Oteyza | Gabriel Cuerpo

Crispin Pangalinan | Armando Ala

Pedro G. Perez | Leoncio Mendoza

Pedro Dagandan

Vicente D. Roa

1943 First Treasury Emergency Currency Certificate Issue

(Matugas, Misamis Occ., April 5 to June 25, 1943)

All notes were printed on thin to very thick manila paper. Originally it was intended that all centavo notes be initialed by a representative of each Board member, and that all peso notes be countersigned on the back by a member of the Board. The enormous amount of work this entailed soon resulted in a *Resolution* which halted the initialing, and authorized additional personnel to do the countersigning. When this occurred, no 50 Centavos or 1 Peso notes had been printed. Apparently there was confusion regarding the countersigning of 1 Peso notes, perhaps because of their smaller size, and only a portion were countersigned. Later on, four thousand 5 Pesos notes were officially issued without countersignatures due to the urgent need for currency.

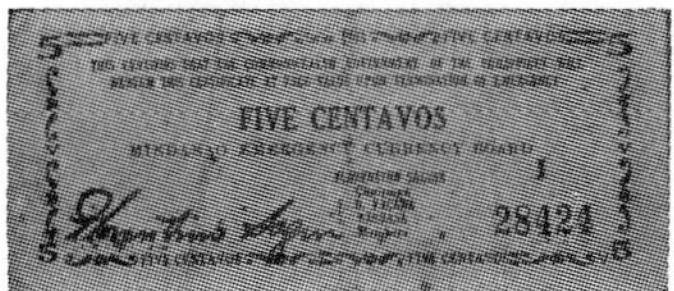

		Good	Fine	XF
S481	**5 Centavos** 1943. Series *I*. Serial #00,001 to 62,400.			
	a. Initials. Serial #00,001 to 08,000.	—	—	—
	b. W/o initials. Serial #08,001 to 62,400.	4.00	9.00	25.00

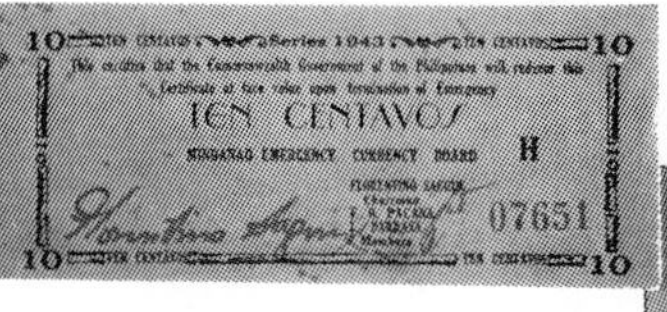

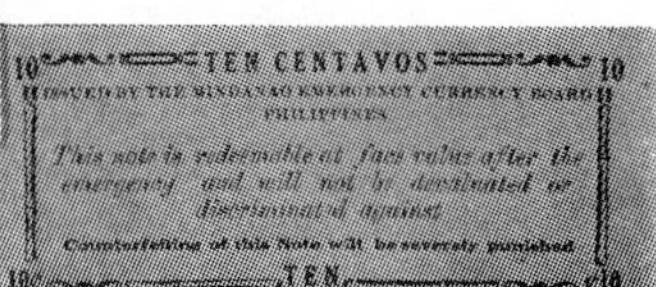

		Good	Fine	XF
S482	**10 Centavos** 1943. Series *H*. Serial #00,001 to 68,000.			
	a. Initials. Serial #00,001 to 08,000.	—	—	—
	b. W/o initials. Serial #08,001 to 68,000.	4.00	9.00	25.00
S483	**20 Centavos** 1943. Series *G*. Serial #00,001 to 68,000.			
	a. Initials. Serial #00,001 to 08,000.	—	—	—
	b. W/o initials. Serial #08,001 to 68,000.	4.00	9.00	25.00
S484	**50 Centavos** 1943. Series *F*. Serial #00,001 to 60,000. *SERIES OF 1943.*	5.00	12.00	30.00
S485	**1 Peso** 1943. Series *E*. Serial #00,001 to 60,000.			
	a. Countersign. Crispin Pangalinan.	—	—	—
	b. Countersign. Armando Ala.	—	—	—
	c. Countersign. Pedro G. Perez.	—	—	—
	d. Countersign. Pedro Dagandan.	—	—	—
	e. Countersign. Vicente D. Roa.	—	—	—
	f. W/o countersign.	3.00	9.00	25.00

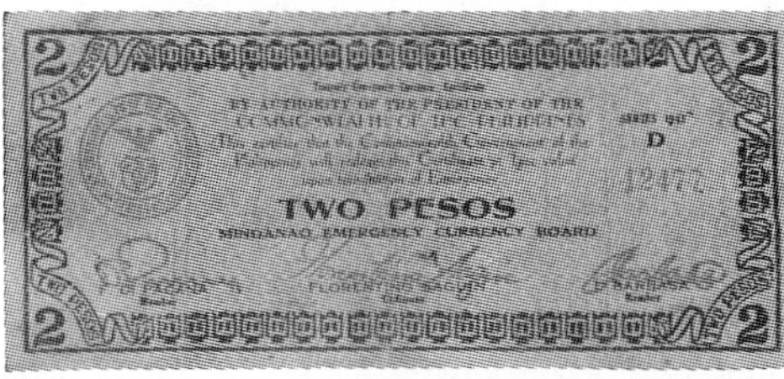

		Good	Fine	XF
S486	**2 Pesos** 1943. Series *D*. Serial #0,001 to 84,000.			
	a. Countersign. F. D. Pacana.	—	—	—
	b. Countersign. I. Barbasa, w/o stamped title.	—	—	—
	c. Countersign. L. J. Oteyza.	—	—	—
	d. Countersign. Gabriel Cuerpo.	3.50	7.00	12.00
	e. Countersign. Armando Ala.	2.00	4.00	10.00
	f. Countersign. Pedro G. Perez.	2.00	4.00	10.00

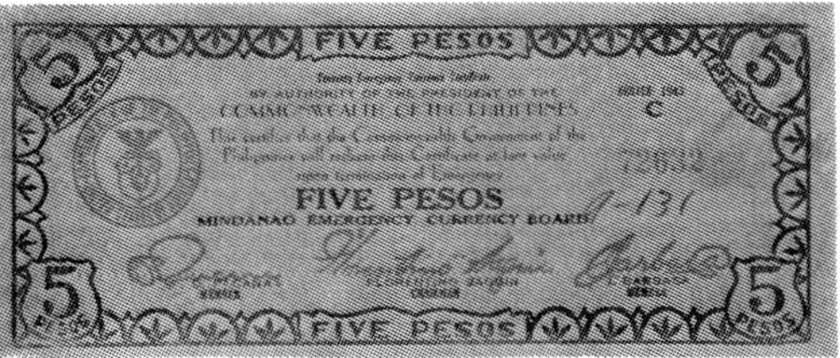

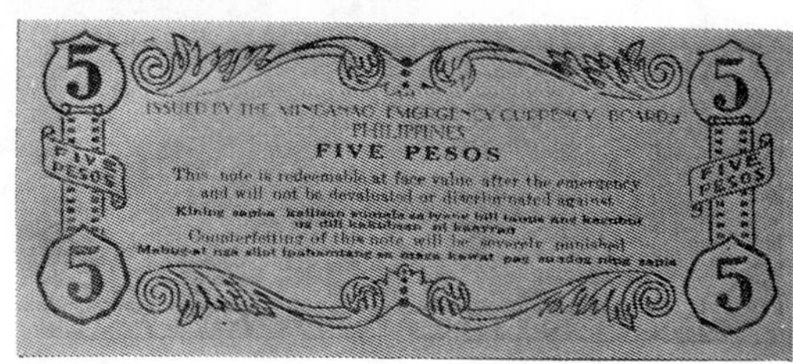

		Good	Fine	XF
S487	**5 Pesos** 1943. Series *C*. Second *E* in *EMERGENCY* on back is a *C* w/line at ctr. Serial #0,001 to 92,000.			
	a. Countersign. F. D. Pacana.	2.50	7.50	12.00
	b. Countersign. I. Barbasa, w/o stamped title.	2.50	7.50	12.00
	c. Countersign. L. J. Oteyza.	1.50	5.00	10.00
	d. Countersign. Gabriel Cuerpo.	1.00	2.50	6.00
	e. Countersign. Leoncio Mendoza. Serial #89,001 to 90,000.	—	—	—
	f. Countersign. Pedro Dagandan. Serial #90,001 to 92,000.	—	—	—
	g. W/o countersign. Serial #69,001 to 73,000.	—	—	—

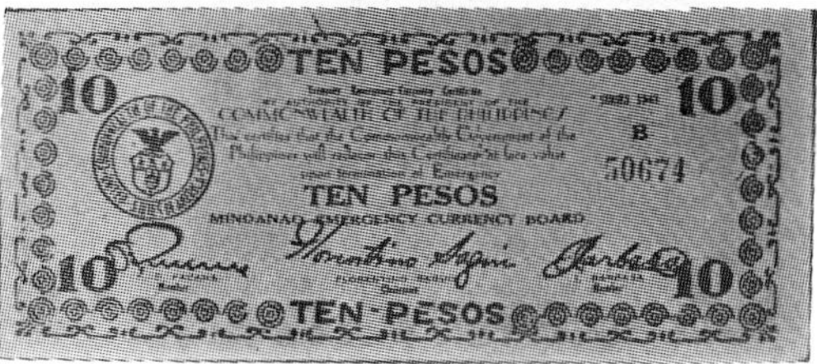

		Good	Fine	XF
S488	**10 Pesos** 1943. Series *B*. Serial #0,001 to 82,000.			
	a. Countersign. F. D. Pacana.	1.50	3.00	6.00
	b. Countersign. I. Barbasa, w/stamped title.	2.50	5.00	8.00
	c. Countersign. I. Barbasa, w/o stamped title.	3.00	6.00	10.00
	d. Countersign. L. J. Oteyza.	1.50	3.00	6.00
	e. Countersign. Gabriel Cuerpo.	2.50	5.00	8.00

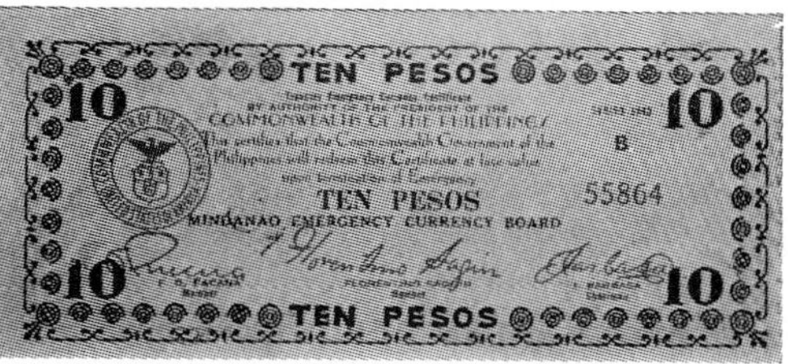

	Good	Fine	XF
x1. Counterfeit. Misspelling *Chariman* in title. Forged countersign. I. Barbasa on back.	3.00	7.50	22.50

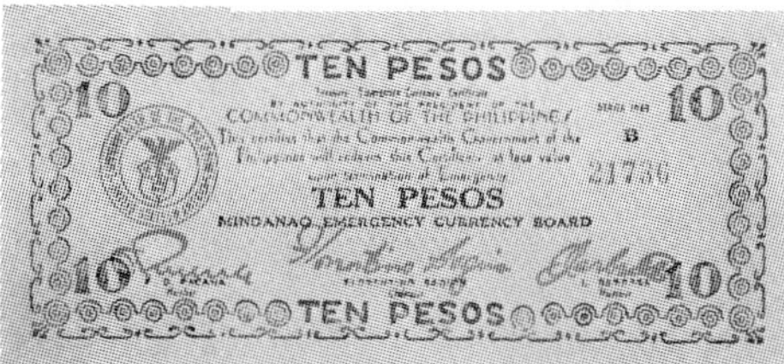

	Good	Fine	XF
x2. Counterfeit. Top ornaments connected; w/o countersign.	.30	.50	1.00

NOTE: #S488x1 was produced in Bohol. Few if any reached Mindanao.

NOTE: #S488x2 was produced in the Manila area for the *black market* when Japanese military notes had depreciated to the point that any other currency was preferable.

		Good	Fine	XF
S489	**20 Pesos** 1943. Series *A*. Serial #00,001 to 58,000.			
	a. Countersign. F. D. Pacana.	1.00	3.00	6.00
	b. Countersign. I. Barbasa, w/o stamped title.	2.00	5.00	8.00
	c. Countersign. L. J. Oteyza.	2.00	5.00	8.00
	d. Countersign. Gabriel Cuerpo.	2.50	6.00	12.00
	x. Counterfeit. Crude printing.	—	—	—

NOTE: #S489 w/serial # 45,001 to 47,000 were officially reported lost *due to enemy action*.

1943 Second Treasury Emergency Currency Certificate Issue

(Liangan, Lanao, September 6 to November 1, 1943)

#S491-S495 were printed on manila paper.

#S496-S499 were printed on white bond paper (delivered by submarine), some of which has commercial wmks. Linen Bond or PREMIER BOND. Border cuts for #S497 had somehow been misplaced, so new cuts were made which differ slightly from the previous ones. To avoid duplication of serial numbers the Series letters were doubled. Countersigning was dispensed with.

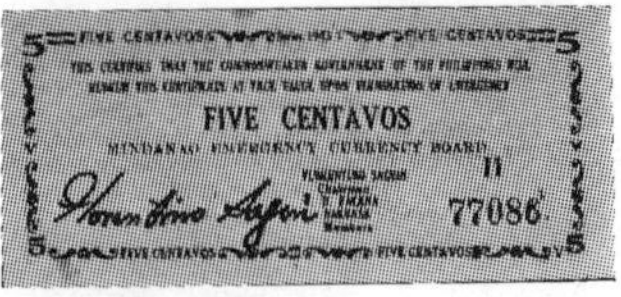

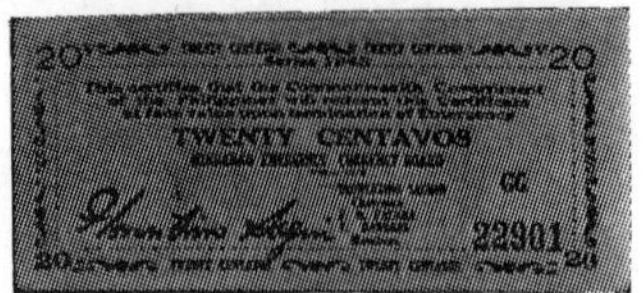

		Good	Fine	XF
S491	**5 Centavos** 1943. Series *II*. Serial #00,001 to 84,000.	2.00	5.00	12.00
S492	**10 Centavos** 1943. Series *HH*. Serial # 00,001 to 84,000.	2.00	5.00	12.00
S493	**20 Centavos** 1943. Series *GG*. Serial # 00,001 to 84,000.	2.00	5.00	12.00

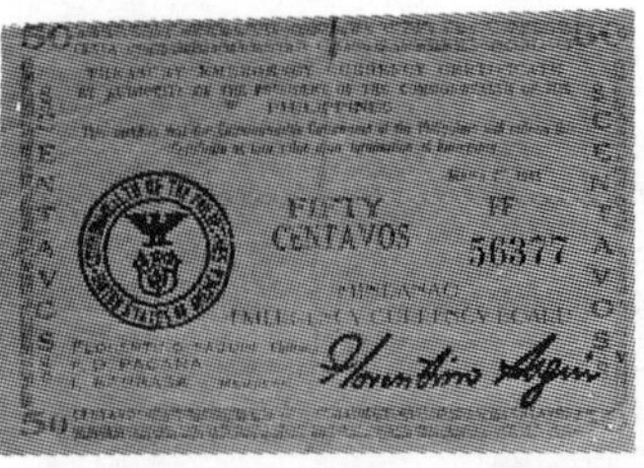

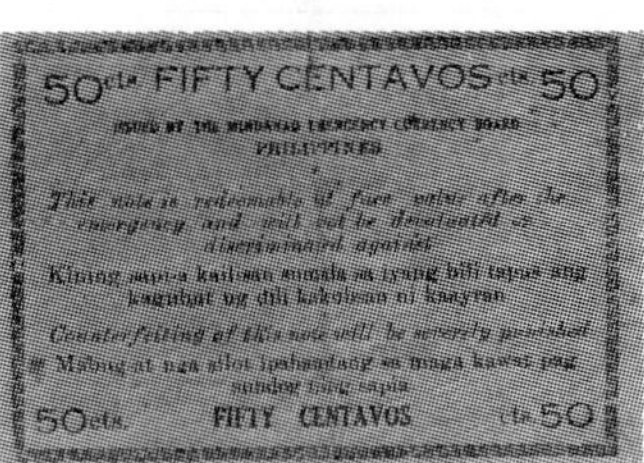

		Good	Fine	XF
S494	**50 Centavos** 1943. Series *FF*. Serial #00,001 to 84,000. *SERIES OF 1943.*	2.00	6.00	15.00
S495	**1 Peso** 1943. Series *EE*. Serial #00,001 to 84,000.	2.00	6.00	15.00

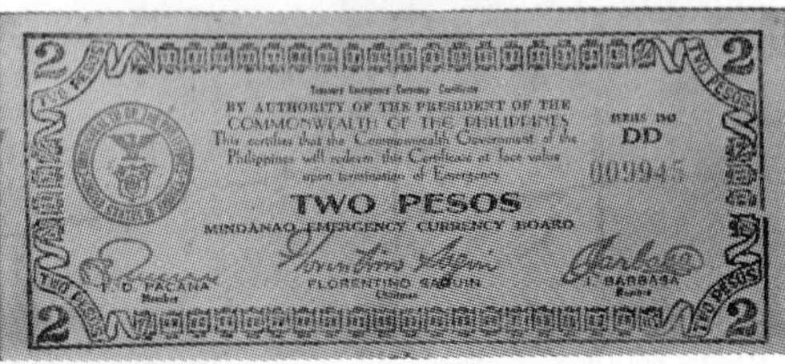

		Good	Fine	XF
S496	**2 Pesos** 1943. Series *DD*. Serial #000,001 to 010,100; 10,101 to 68,000.	.50	1.50	3.50
S497	**5 Pesos** 1943. Series *CC*. Second *E* in *EMERGENCY* like #S487. Serial #000,001 to 010,100; 10,101 to 68,000.	1.00	2.50	5.00
S498	**10 Pesos** 1943. Series *BB*. Serial #000,001 to 010,100; 10,101 to 68,000.	.50	2.00	4.00
S499	**20 Pesos** 1943. Series *AA*. Serial #00,001 to 69,000.			
	a. Issued note.	2.00	5.00	7.50
	x. Counterfeit.	—	—	—

NOTE: #S496-S499 all started with 6-digit serial # but later went to 5 digits to conserve ink.

1943 Third Treasury Emergency Currency Certificate Issue

(Esperanza, Agusan, Dec. 13, 1943 to Jan. 23, 1944)

#S502-S508 printed from metal plates brought in by USS NARWHAL, #S501 and S509 from previous type and wood border cuts. All notes printed on white paper delivered with the plates. Paper ranged from ordinary book to bond paper. Some of the bond paper has commercial PREMIER BOND wmk. Serial numbers continued from where the Second printing left off.

		Good	Fine	XF
S501	**5 Centavos** 1943. Series *II*. Serial #84,001 to 117,200.	2.50	5.00	10.00

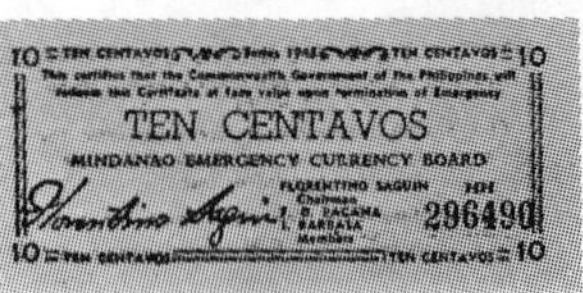

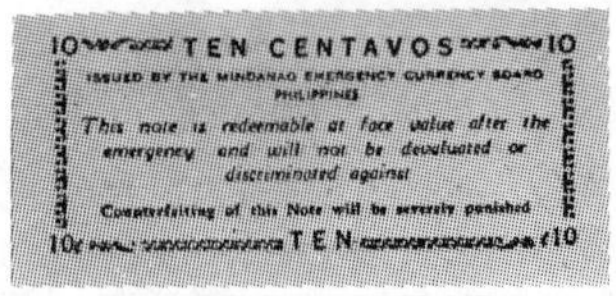

		Good	Fine	XF
S502	**10 Centavos** 1943. Series *HH*. Serial #84,001 to 323,100.	1.00	2.50	6.00

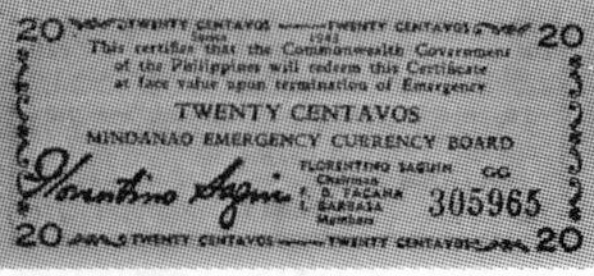

		Good	Fine	XF
S503	**20 Centavos** 1943. Series *GG*. Serial #84,001 to 340,800.	1.00	2.50	6.00
S504	**50 Centavos** 1943. Series *FF*. Serial #84,001 to 286,900.	1.00	2.50	6.00

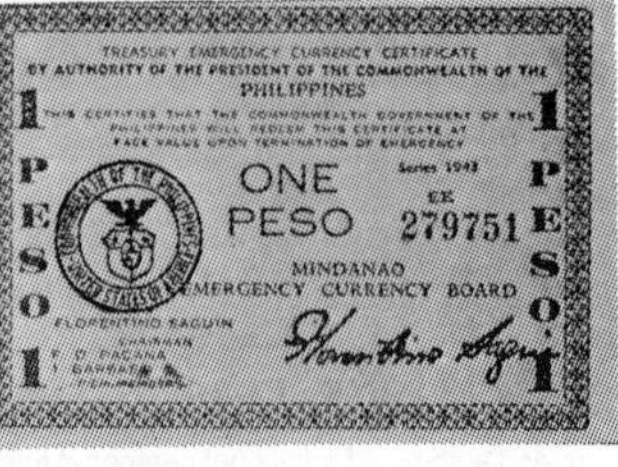

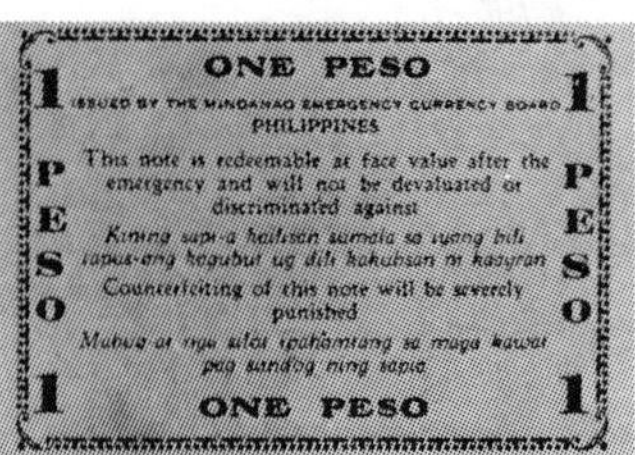

		Good	Fine	XF
S505	**1 Peso** 1943. Series *EE*. Serial #84,001 to 421,300.	1.00	2.00	3.50
S506	**2 Pesos** 1943. Series *DD*. Serial #68,001 to 275,100.	1.00	2.00	3.50
S507	**5 Pesos** 1943. Series *CC*. Second *E* in *EMERGENCY* on back is a *C*. Serial #68,001 to 299,400.	1.00	2.00	3.00
S508	**10 Pesos** 1943. Series *BB*. Serial #68,001 to 296,400.			
	a. Series *BB* wide.	1.00	2.50	3.50
	b. Series *BB* narrow.	2.50	5.00	8.00

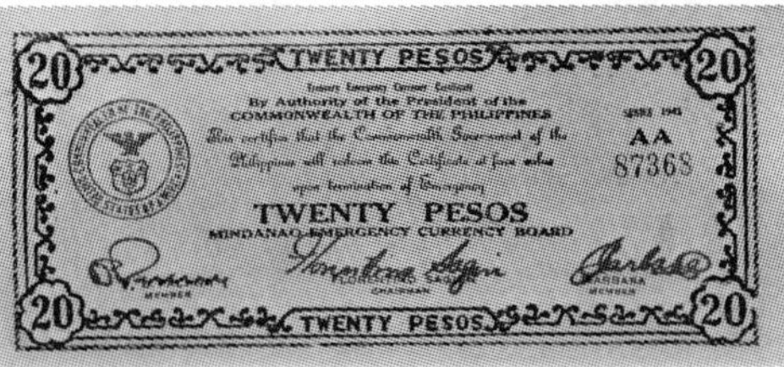

		Good	Fine	XF
S509	**20 Pesos** 1943. Series *AA*. Serial #69,001 to 98,400.	1.00	2.00	4.00

1943 Illegal Issues

10 Pesos notes amounting to 203,000 pesos were lost due to enemy action. They soon turned up in circulation but were officially outlawed and declared worthless.

		Good	Fine	XF
S510	**10 Pesos** 1943. Like #S508. Serial numbers: 172,701 to 173,400; 174,801 to 176,200; 176,901 to 183,900; 184,601 to 186,000; 186,701 to 189,500; 191,601 to 195,100; 195,801 to 196,500; 197,901 to 198,600; 201,401 to 202,100; 222,401 to 223,100; 225,901 to 226,600.	—	—	—

1943 Fourth Treasury Emergency Currency Certificate Issue

(Loreto, Agusan, March 18 to July 5, 1944 and November 4 to 15, 1944)

Printed from the same paper stock as the Third printing, so some may also be found with commercial wmk. *PREMIER BOND*. As this printing showed the change in date from 1943 to 1944, serial numbers started over again and with single series letters.

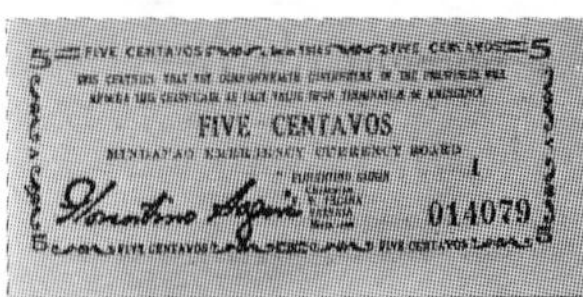

		Good	Fine	XF
S511	**5 Centavos** 1944. Series *I*. Serial #00,001 to 015,800.	4.00	8.00	15.00

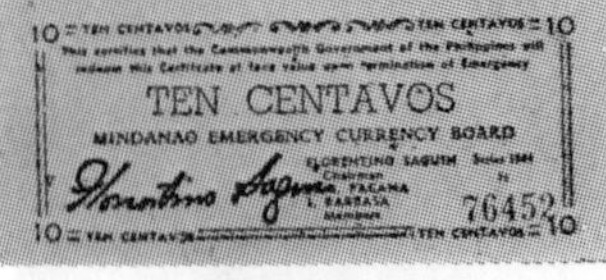

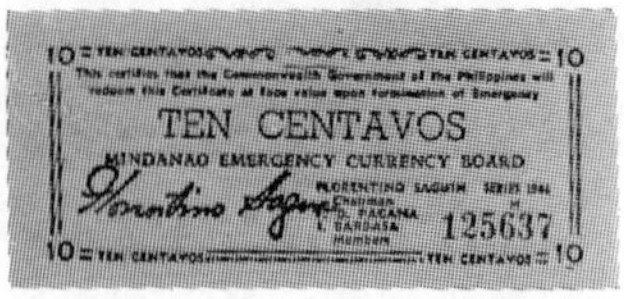

		Good	Fine	XF
S512	**10 Centavos** 1944. Series *H*. Serial #0,001 to 140,000.			
	a. *Series 1944* (upper and lower case).	2.00	4.00	7.00
	b. *SERIES 1944* (all upper case).	2.50	5.00	9.00

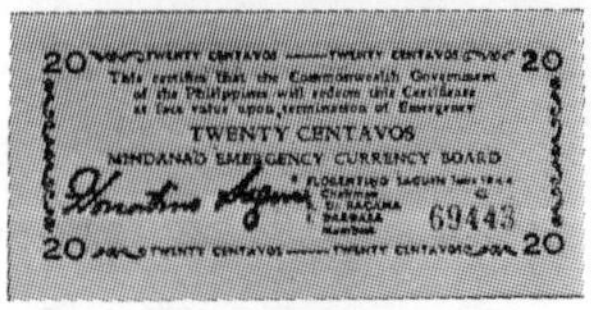

		Good	Fine	XF
S513	**20 Centavos** 1944. Series *G*. Serial #00,001 to 117,600. Date at r.			
	a. *Series 1944.*	1.50	5.00	9.00
	b. *SERIES 1944.*	—	—	—

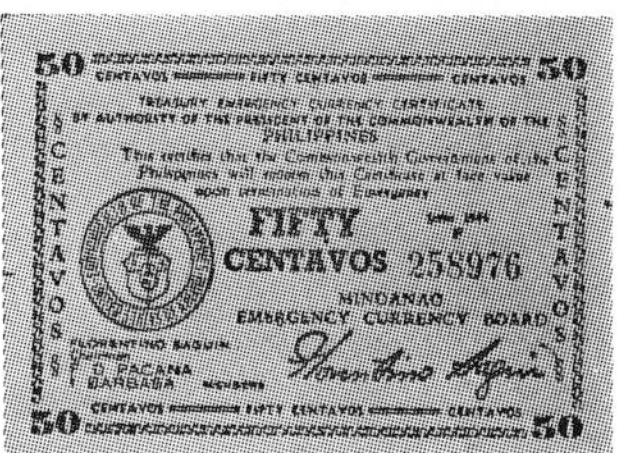

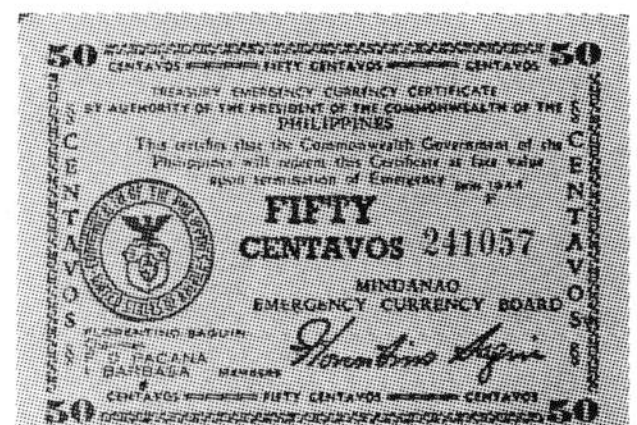

		Good	Fine	XF
S514	**50 Centavos** 1944. Series *F*. Serial #00,001 to 285,700.			
	a. *Series 1944* is 10mm. long (narrow date).	.50	1.50	3.00
	b. *Series 1944* is 12mm. long (wide date).	1.00	2.50	5.00

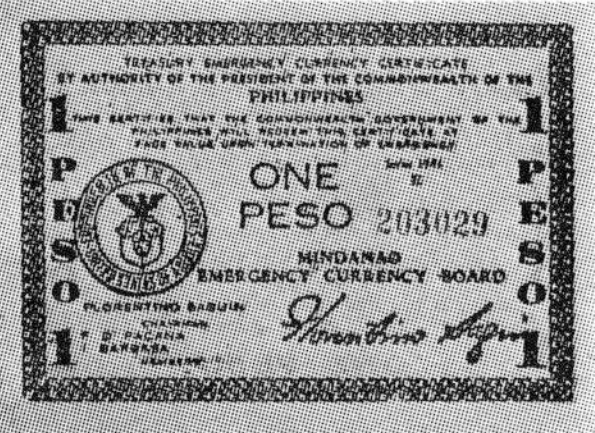

		Good	Fine	XF
S515	**1 Peso** 1944. Series *E*. Serial #00,001 to 273,300.	.50	1.50	3.00

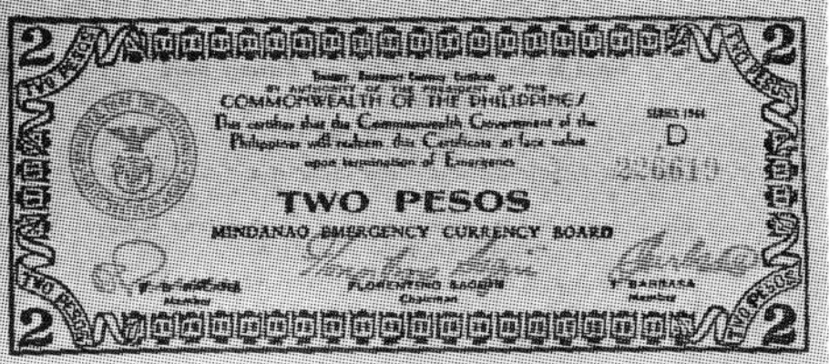

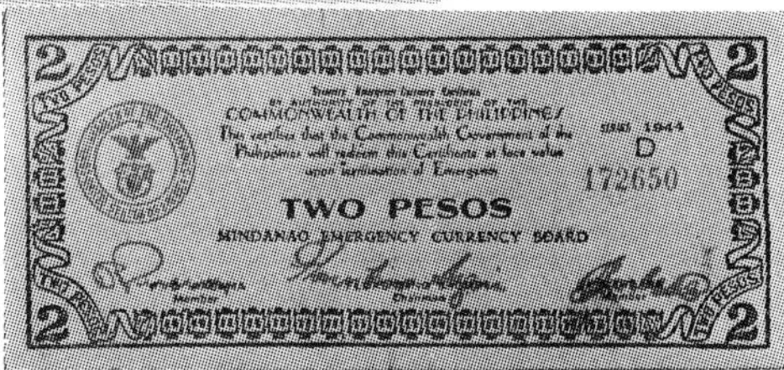

		Good	Fine	XF
S516	**2 Pesos** 1944. Series *D*. Serial #00,001 to 263,200.			
	a. *SERIES 1944* is 11 1/2mm. long (narrow date).	.50	1.50	3.00
	b. *SERIES 1944* is 17mm. long (wide date).	1.00	3.00	5.00

		Good	Fine	XF
S517	**5 Pesos** 1944. Series *C*. *EMERGENCY* on back like #S507. Serial #00,001 to 259,200.			
	a. *SERIES 1944* is 11 1/2mm. long (narrow date).	.50	1.50	3.00
	b. *SERIES 1944* is 15mm. long (wide date).	.50	1.50	3.00
S518	**10 Pesos** 1944. Series *B*. Serial #00,001 to 170,700.			
	a. *SERIES 1944* is 11mm. long (narrow date).	.50	1.50	3.00
	b. *SERIES 1944* is 15mm. long (wide date).	1.00	2.00	4.00

1944 Treasury Emergency Currency Certificate Issue

Printing took place in three different locations:
(1) Tingkugas, Zamboanga, September 14 to October 6, 1944.
(2) Estaka, Dipolog, Zamboanga, February 27 to March 25, 1945.
(3) Calamba, Plaridel, Misamis Occidental, April 1 to 22, 1945.
All notes printed on white paper.

		Good	Fine	XF
S521	**20 Centavos** 1944. No Series letter. Date at top. Serial # 00,001 to 15,000.	5.00	10.00	25.00

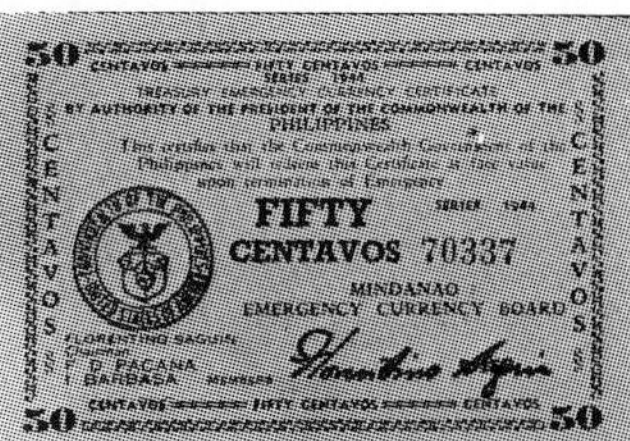

		Good	Fine	XF
S522	**50 Centavos** 1944. Date at top and at ctr. r.			
	a. No Series letter. Serial #00,001 to 44,900.	2.00	4.00	6.00
	b. *Series 5*. Serial #44,901 to 71,800.	2.00	5.00	8.00

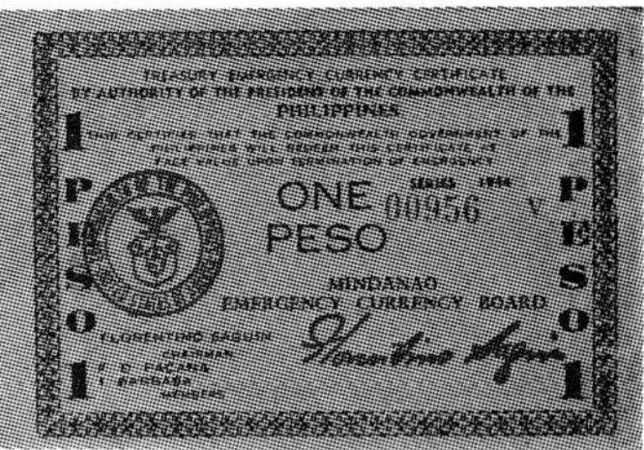

		Good	Fine	XF
S523	**1 Peso** 1944.			
	a. No Series letter. *Series 1944*. Serial # (for "a" and "b"): 00,001 to 99,000.	2.00	4.00	6.00
	b. No Series letter. *SERIES 1944*.	1.00	3.00	5.00
	c. Series *V*. Serial #00,001 to 19,300.	2.50	6.00	10.00
	d. Series *V5*. Serial #19,301 to 57,700.	1.00	4.00	7.00

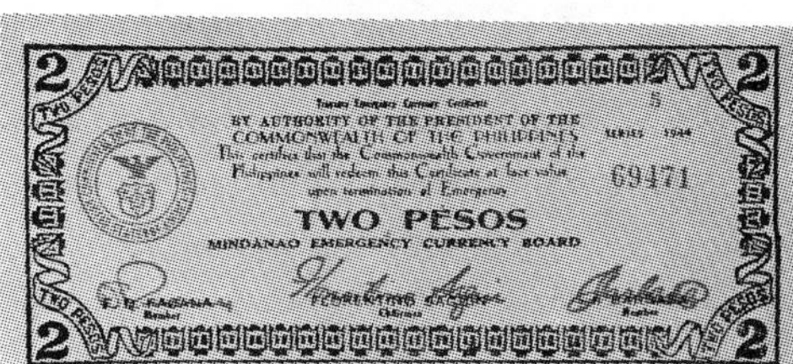

		Good	Fine	XF
S524	**2 Pesos** 1944.			
	a. No Series letter. Serial #00,001 to 32,200.	1.50	3.00	5.00
	b. Series *5*. Serial #32,201 to 88,600.	1.50	3.00	6.00

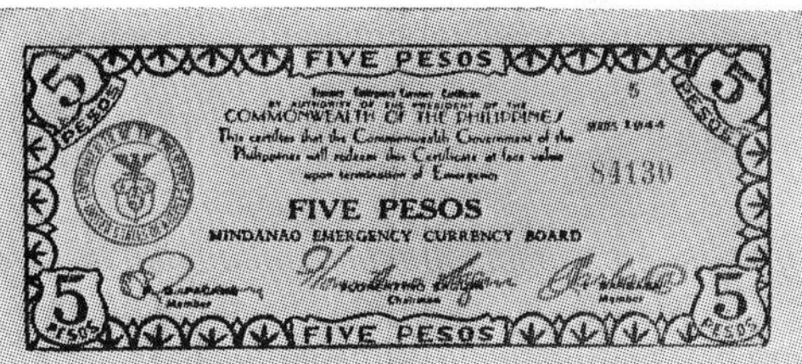

		Good	Fine	XF
S525	**5 Pesos** 1944. Type I. Wide date.			
	a. No Series letter. Type I and Type II mixed in serial #00,001 to 69,000.	.50	1.00	2.50
	b. Series *5*. Type I and Type II mixed in serial #69,001 to 99,000.	1.00	3.00	8.00
	c. Series *T*. Serial #00,001 to 07,100.	5.00	12.00	17.50

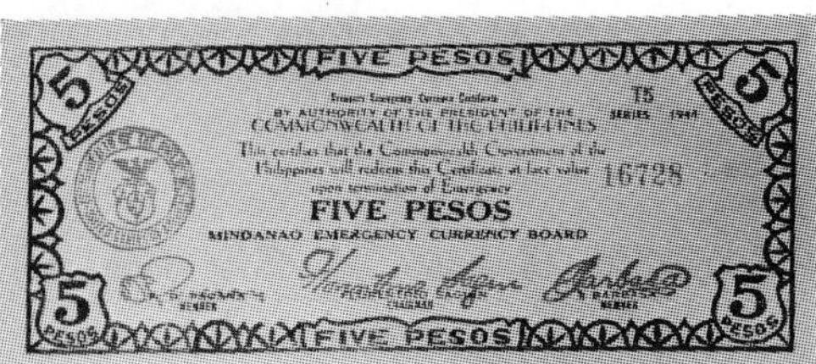

		GOOD	FINE	XF
S526	**5 PESOS**			
	1944. Type II.			
	a. No Series letter. Type I and Type II mixed in serial #00,001 to 69,000.	.50	1.00	2.50
	b. Series *5*. Type I and Type II mixed in serial #69,001 to 99,000.	1.00	2.50	8.00
	c. Series *T5*. Serial #07,101 to 39,600.	1.50	3.00	6.00

NOTE: For #S525-S526, Type I has a 2 1/2 circular ornaments in r. border and was printed from a metal plate made in Australia. Type II has 3 circular ornaments in r. border and was printed from the wooden plate previously used at Liangan.

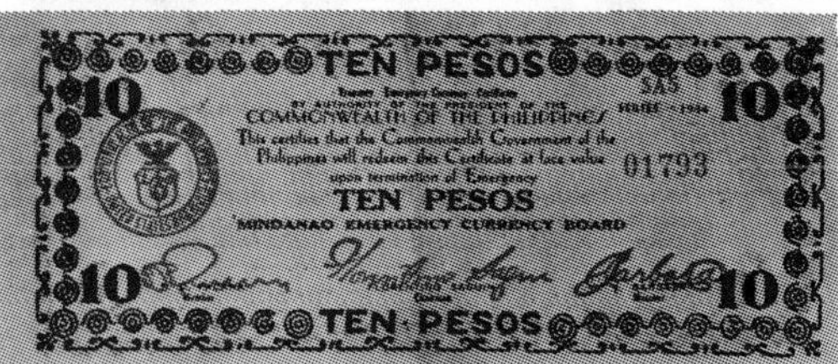

		GOOD	FINE	XF
S527	**10 PESOS**			
	1944.			
	a. *Series 1944*. No Series letter. Serial #00,001 to 92,000.	2.00	4.00	7.00
	b. *SERIES 1944*. No Series letter. Serial # included in "a".	1.00	2.00	4.00
	c. Series *5*. Serial #92,001 to 99,000.	2.00	4.00	7.00
	d. Series *S*. Serial #00,001 to 16,600.	1.00	2.50	5.00
	e. Series *S5*. Serial #16,601 to 99,000.	.50	1.50	3.00
	f. Series *SA5*. Serial #00,001 to 04,200.	5.00	7.50	12.50

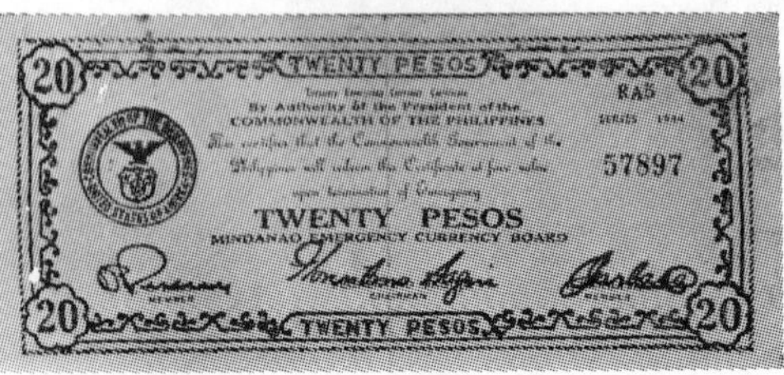

		GOOD	FINE	XF
S528	**20 PESOS**			
	1944.			
	a. No Series letter. Serial #00,001 to 99,000.	1.00	2.00	3.00
	b. Series *R*. Serial #00,001 to 25,700.	1.00	2.50	4.50
	c. Series *R5*. Serial #25,701 to 99,000.	.50	1.50	3.00
	d. Series *RA5*. Serial #00,001 to 70,300.	.50	1.50	3.00

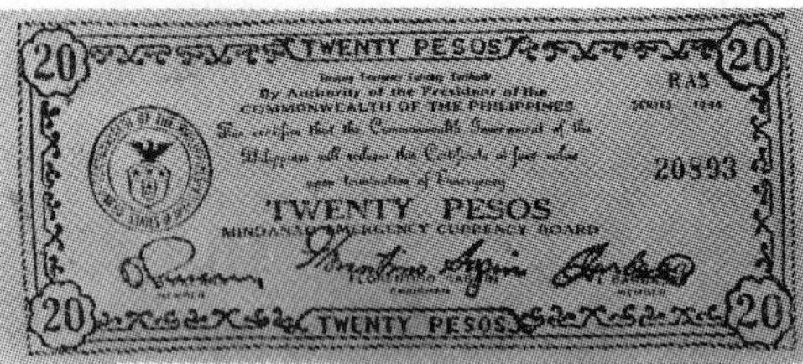

		GOOD	FINE	XF
	x. Counterfeit. Series *RA5*. Companion piece to #S488x2.	.25	.50	1.00

NOTE: For #S528 the *R* of *RA5* is slightly wider on serial # 00,001 to 36,300 than the others.

1945 TREASURY EMERGENCY CURRENCY CERTIFICATE ISSUE

(Loreto, Agusan, January 2 to 5, 1945)

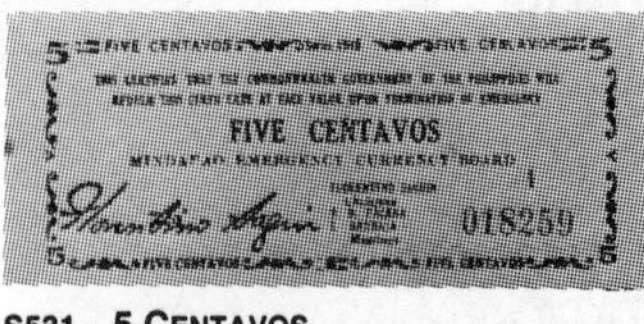

		GOOD	FINE	XF
S531	**5 CENTAVOS**			
	1945. Series *I*. Serial #000,001 to 024,900.	5.00	12.00	25.00
S532	**10 CENTAVOS**			
	1945. Series *H*. Serial #000,001 to 041,900.			
	a. *Series 1945*.	4.00	10.00	15.00
	b. *SERIES 1945*.	5.00	10.00	20.00
S533	**20 CENTAVOS**			
	1945. Series *G*. Serial #000,001 to 044,900.	4.00	10.00	15.00

		GOOD	FINE	XF
S534	**50 CENTAVOS**			
	1945. Series *F*. Serial #000,001 to 056,200.	1.00	4.00	8.00
S535	**1 PESO**			
	1945. Series *E*. Serial #000,001 to 028,200.	1.00	4.00	8.00
S536	**2 PESOS**			
	1945. Series *D*. Serial #000,001 to 056,000.	.50	2.50	5.00
S537	**5 PESOS**			
	1945. Series *C*. *EMERGENCY* on back like #S507. Serial #000,001 to 046,100.	.50	2.50	5.00

		GOOD	FINE	XF
S538	**10 PESOS**			
	1945. Series *B*. Serial #000,001 to 038,100.	.50	3.00	7.00

BUKIDNON PROVINCE

109TH DIVISION USFIP, SERIES 1944

1944 NEGOTIABLE RECEIPT

This was a temporary issue in Bukidnon Province necessitated when a shipment of Mindanao (MECB) currency was captured by the Japanese. The notes were called in and redeemed when a new supply of Mindanao currency was received.

Notes were mimeographed on white paper. They are embossed with notarial seal of Maj. Ignacio Cruz at left, and parish seal of St. Joseph Mission of Talakag at right. The back has stamped facsimile signature of the Division commander, Lt. Col. James R. Grinstead, and pen signature of Maj. Cruz, Division Quartermaster. Around 200,000 pesos were issued.

		GOOD	FINE	XF
S546	**5 PESOS**			
	1944.	—	Rare	—

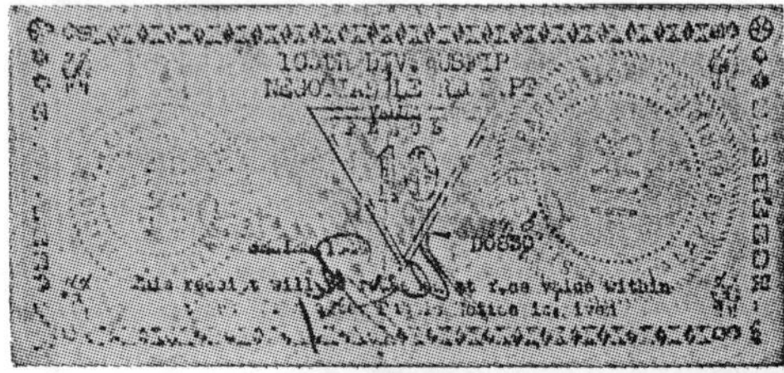

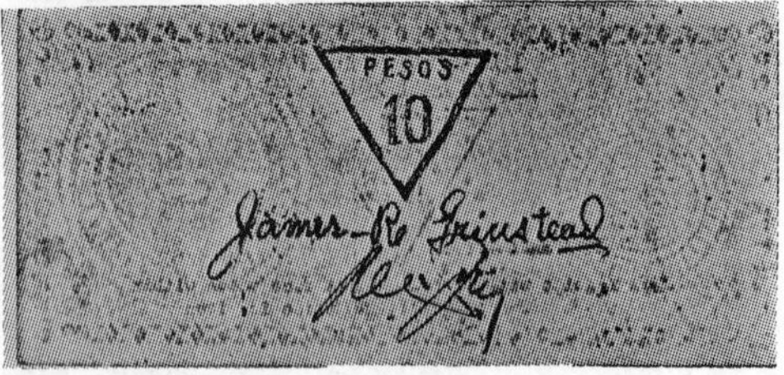

		GOOD	FINE	XF
S547	**10 PESOS**			
	1944.	—	Rare	—

		GOOD	FINE	XF
S548	**20 PESOS**			
	1944.	—	Rare	—

116TH INFANTRY REGIMENT USFIP, 1943-44

1943-44 ISSUE

This currency was issued by Maj. Herbert C. Page, Commanding Officer of the 116th Inf. Regt., on authority of Col. Wendell W. Fertig, commanding the 10th Military District.

Notes were printed by mimeograph and handsigned by Maj. Page. They also have stamped facsimile signature of Deputy Provincial Treasurer Cecilio Ferolin.

A total of 131,470.80 pesos was placed in circulation. The notes were called in for redemption in November, 1944 when a supply of Mindanao (MECB) currency was received.

		Good	Fine	XF
S551	5 CENTAVOS Serial # E1 to E535.	—	—	—
S552	10 CENTAVOS Serial # D1 to D3339.	—	—	—

		Good	Fine	XF
S553	20 CENTAVOS Serial # C1 to C2564.	—	—	—
S554	50 CENTAVOS Serial # B1 to B2029.	—	—	—
S555	1 PESO Serial # A1 to A17,526.	—	—	—
S556	2 PESOS Serial # AA1 to AA13,778.	—	—	—
S557	5 PESOS Serial # AAA1 to AAA865 and V866 to V15,143.	—	—	—
S558	10 PESOS Serial # X1 to X885.	—	—	—

MISAMIS OCCIDENTAL

FIRST PRINTING

The Misamis Occidental Currency Committee was created in March, 1942. It was composed of Provincial Treasurer Filomena D. Pacana as Chairman, with Provincial Auditor Ireneo Barbasa and Provincial Fiscal Ramon O. Nolasco as Members. The amount authorized was up to two-thirds of the province's unencumbered bank deposits.

Printing was done by Rozito Z. Baccaro at Matugas, Jiminez. Although authorization amounted to over a million pesos, only 75,000 pesos were printed when they ran out of paper.

PHILIPPINE NATIONAL BANK - MISAMIS OCCIDENTAL

1942 FIRST EMERGENCY CIRCULATING NOTE ISSUE

#S571 and S572 white paper. Handsigned.

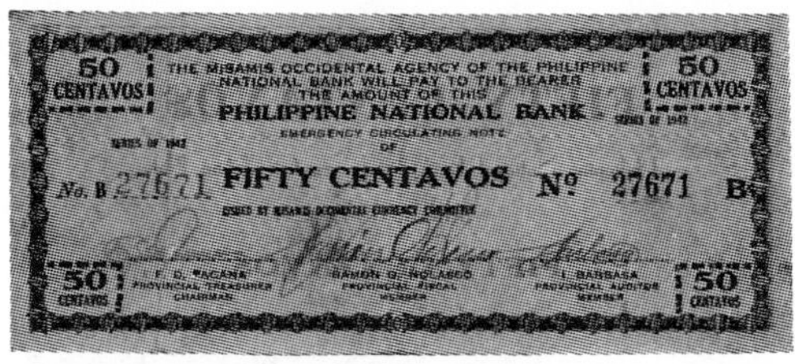

		Good	Fine	XF
S571	50 CENTAVOS 1942. Orange. Serial #00,001 to 30,000.	7.50	15.00	50.00
S572	1 PESO 1942. Black. Inverted back. Serial #00,001 to 60,000.			
	a. Issued note.	7.50	15.00	50.00
	x. Counterfeit.	—	—	—

1942 SECOND EMERGENCY CIRCULATING NOTE ISSUE

On December 8, 1942 *Brig.* Gen. Wendell W. Fertig, *Mindanao-Sulu Command, USFIP,* ordered the Misamis Occidental Currency Committee to resume printing currency up to the amount authorized prior to surrender.

Facsimile signature cuts were carved from hardwood for all denominations, along with border cuts, seal and portr. of President Quezon for the 5 Pesos note. Metal type was used elsewhere. Notes were again printed by Rozito Z. Baccaro at Matugas, Jiminez. Printing ended in mid-January 1943 when the authorized amount had been printed.

A total of 945,000 pesos was printed, of which 925,956.30 was placed in circulation. A Japanese bombing attack on the capital building in Oroquieta on December 26, 1942 destroyed 3,000 of the 50 Centavos notes (serial # 147,001 to 150,000) and 3,500 of the 5 Pesos notes (serial # 00,001 to 03,500). An additional 43.70 pesos in misprinted notes were incinerated.

The 2 Pesos counterfeits are crude and easily detected. There are at least three different 5 Pesos counterfeits, most of them produced and circulated in Bohol. All the counterfeits have crude serial numbers, often illegible.

#S573-S578 black print on manila paper.

		Good	Fine	XF
S573	10 CENTAVOS 1942. Inverted back. Serial #0001 to 100,000.	10.00	20.00	50.00

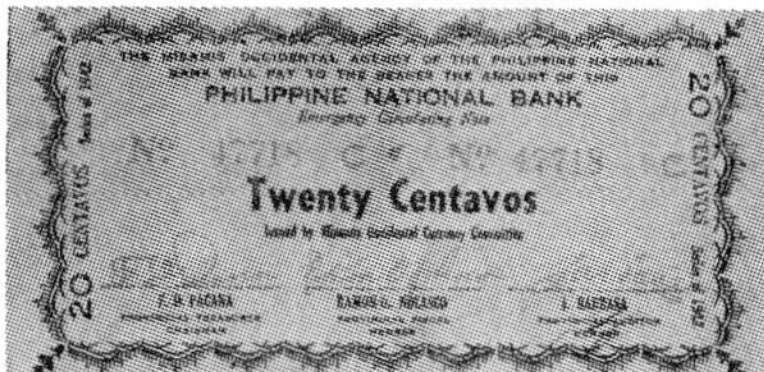

		Good	Fine	XF
S574	20 CENTAVOS 1942. Serial #0001 to 100,000.	7.50	17.50	45.00

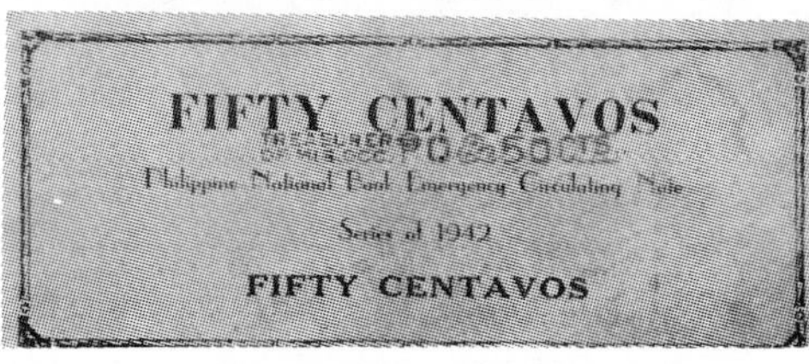

		Good	Fine	XF
S575	50 CENTAVOS 1942. Back has value written w/check protector. Serial #30,001 to 140,000.			
	a. Check protector in blue and red. Serial #30,001 to (approx.) 71,700.	3.00	10.00	20.00
	b. Check protector in blue. Serial # (approx.) 74,101 to 140,000.	2.00	7.50	15.00

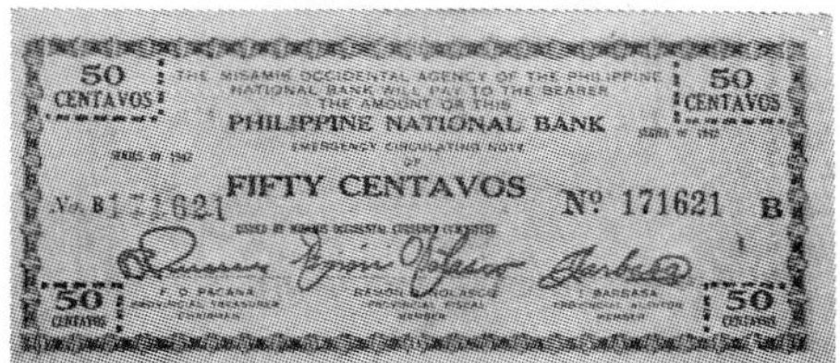

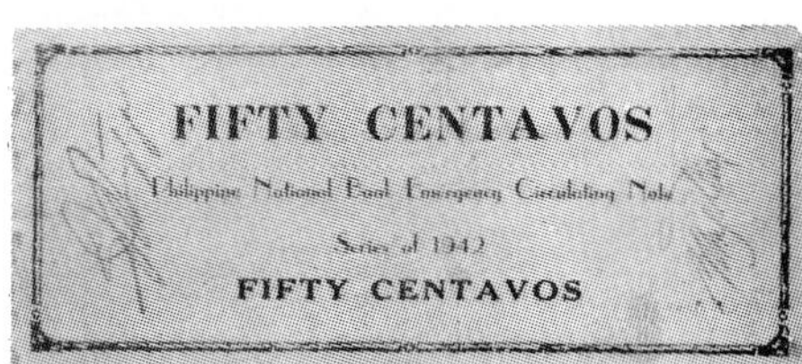

		Good	Fine	XF
S576	50 CENTAVOS 1942. Back is countersign. in pen. Serial #140,001 to 260,000.			
	a. Countersign. L.J. Oteyza at l., Gabriel Cuerpo at r. Serial #140,001 to 181,000.	2.00	7.00	12.50
	b. Countersign. at ctr. by L. J. Oteyza. Serial #: 181,001 to 190,000; 200,001 to 210,000; 220,001 to 230,000; 240,001 250,000.	2.00	7.00	12.50
	c. Countersign at ctr. by Gabriel Cuerpo. Serial #: 190,001 to 200,000; 210,001 to 220,000; 230,001 to 240,000; 250,001 to 260,000.	2.00	7.00	12.50

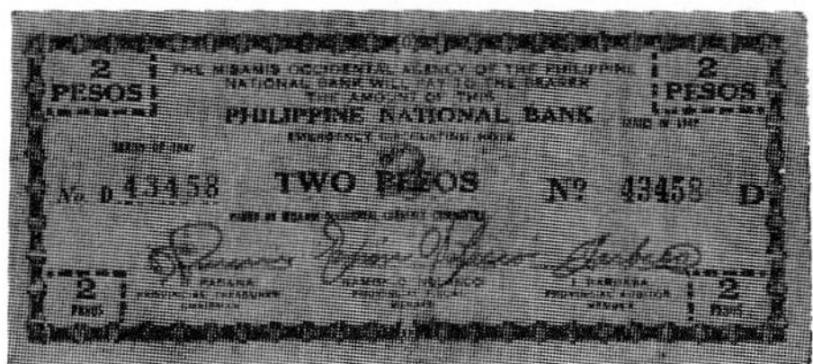

		Good	Fine	XF
S577	2 PESOS 1942. Arms at ctr. on back. Serial #00,001 to 100,000.			
	a. Issued note.	2.00	7.00	12.50
	x. Counterfeit.	—	—	—

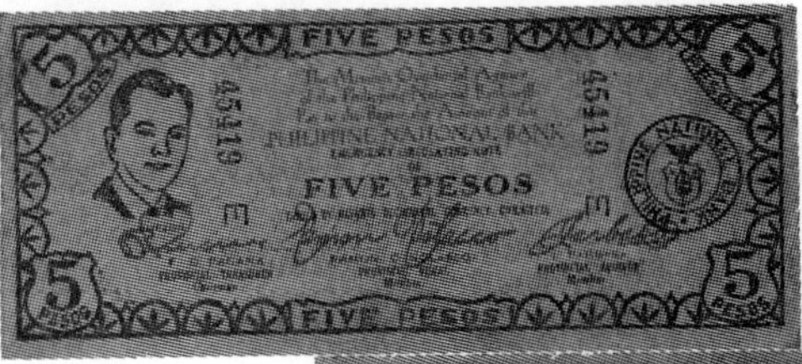

		Good	Fine	XF
S578	**5 Pesos** 1942. Quezon at l., seal in red at r. Arms at ctr. on back. Countersign. in pen on back. Seriial #00,001 to 120,000.			
	a. Countersign. I. Barbasa at l., F. D. Pacana at r. Serial #00,001 to 60,000.	2.00	6.00	10.00
	b. Countersign. at ctr. by I. Barbasa. Serial # 60,001 to 70,000; 80,001 to 90,000; 100,001 to 110,000.	2.00	6.00	10.00
	c. Countersign. at ctr. by F. D. Pacana. Serial #70,001 to 80,000; 90,001 to 100,000; 110,001 to to 120,000.	2.00	6.00	10.00
	x. Counterfeit.	—	—	—

Misamis Oriental

Misamis Oriental emergency currency was issued under authority of President Quezon, December 29, 1941. All records were lost during the war so the exact text of the message or amount authorized is not known. However, Treasurer Laya reported the total amount issued as being less than that authorized.

The Oriental Misamis Currency Committee was composed of Provincial Treasurer Ubaldo D. Laya as Chairman, with Provincial Auditor Agapito Flores and Provincial Fiscal Antonio Tann Yacapin as Members.

There were two issues. The first, Series of 1941, amounted to 10,000 pesos and was printed in January 1942. The second, Series of 1942, amounted to 34,000 pesos and was printed in March 1942 in response to the urgent need for currency.

Both issues were printed on white bond paper, some of which is commercially watermarked. All notes were handsigned by the Committee. All have inverted backs.

Oriental Misamis Agency - Philippine National Bank

1941 Emergency Circulating Note - Series A Issue

#S581-S584 black print.

		Good	Fine	XF
S581	**10 Centavos** 1941. Serial #0001 to 20,000.	—	—	—
S582	**20 Centavos** 1941. Serial #0001 to 10,000.	—	—	—
S583	**50 Centavos** 1941. Serial #0001 to 6,000.	—	—	—
S584	**1 Peso** 1941. Serial #0001 to 3,000.	—	—	—

1942 Emergency Circulating Note - Series B Issue

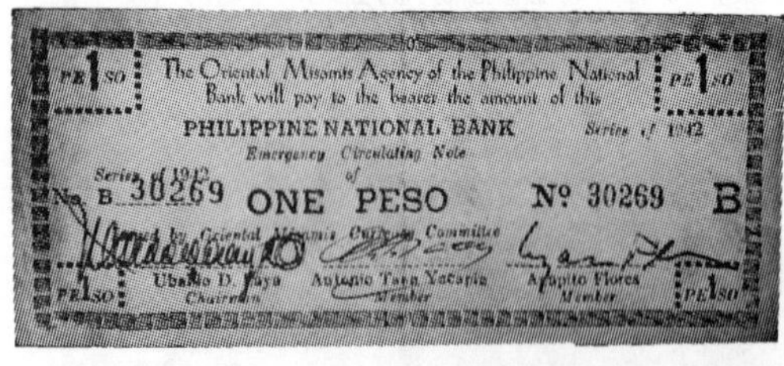

		Good	Fine	XF
S585	**1 Peso** 1942. Black. Serial #0001 to 34,000.	30.00	80.00	—

Mountain Province

The Japanese 14th Army began landing at Lingayen Gulf on December 22, 1941. Gen. MacArthur ordered USAFFE forces to withdraw to Bataan, but the rapid Japanese advance cut the lines of retreat of many units. When the 43rd Infantry crossed the Cordillera Mountains it found Japanese tanks blocking further withdrawal. Col. John P. Horan decided to take the remnants of this unit to Mountain Province to engage in guerrilla warfare.

The Japanese advance had also isolated the provincial government at Bontoc. The Provincial Treasurer was able to meet financial obligations by issuing checks, but it was obvious the supply of checks would soon run out.

On January 24, 1942 the Provincial Board adopted *Resolution No. 5* which established a Currency Committee, in accordance with instructions by President Quezon, with authority to print 300,000 pesos in emergency currency.

The Currency Committee consisted of Acting Provincial Governor Roque Perido as Chairman, with Assistant Provincial Treasurer Ambrosio Vallejo and Provincial Auditor Lupo Guzman as Members (President Quezon's instructions had designated the Provincial Treasurer as a Member of the Committee, but since he was absent from the province he could not serve although his name does appear on the currency.)

The Committee arranged for currency printing by the Mission Press at Saint Mary the Virgin Mission in Sagada, with delivery by the end of the month. This first printing actually amounted to 96,070.35 pesos.

In late January 1942 as the Japanese approached Bontoc, the provincial government moved to Lubuagan. The Japanese occupied Bontoc on February 2, but were forced to withdraw south later.

The provincial government returned to Bontoc and a second printing of currency got underway. The Provincial Board by *Resolution No. 6* increased the authorized amount to 500,000 pesos.

With the fall of Bataan the Japanese were able to redeploy large forces for mopping up operations and the provincial government once again moved to Lubuagan. The Currency Committee destroyed just under 200,000 pesos of currency which had not yet been turned over to the Treasury. The provincial government then evacuated Lubuagan for a remote area.

Of the 500,000 pesos authorized, 307,902.90 pesos were delivered to the Provincial Treasury. Of this amount 265,756.90 pesos were placed in circulation. The balance of 42,146 pesos remained unissued in the Treasury until it was looted during an American bombing attack on March 16, 1945.

Mountain Province Emergency Board

Resolution No. 5, Series 1942 First Issue

#S591-S594 black on thin white paper, facsimile stamped sign. All serial # data is approximate.

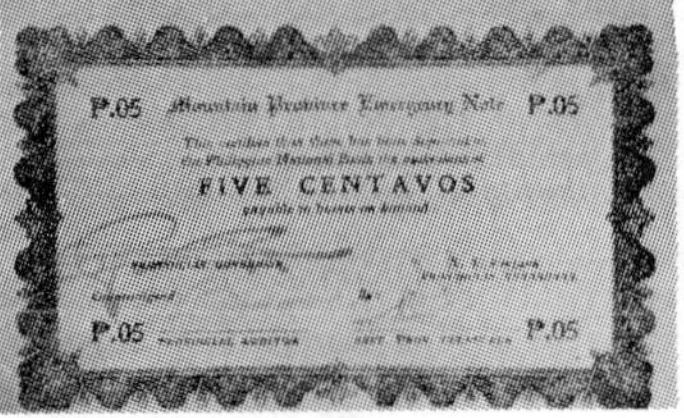

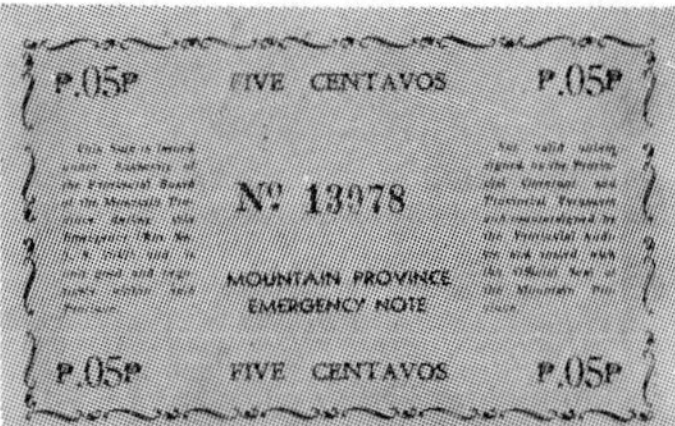

		Good	Fine	XF
S591	**5 Centavos** 1942. Serial #0,001 to 22,353 (approx.).	.50	1.00	2.50
S592	**10 Centavos** 1942. Serial #0,001 to 39,163 (approx.).	.50	1.00	3.00
S593	**20 Centavos** 1942. Serial #0,001 to 9,587 (approx.).	.50	1.00	2.50
S594	**50 Centavos** 1942. Serial #0,001 to 39,262 (approx.).			
	a. First 2 lines of text equal in length.	.50	1.00	3.00
	b. First line longer than second.	1.00	2.00	4.00

#S595-S598 black on white bond paper, handsigned. Some have commercial wmk: *HAMMERMILL BOND*. Redemption clause payable to bearer on demand.

#S595-S597 lg. size heading.

		Good	Fine	XF
S595	**1 Peso** 1942. Back red to brownish red. Serial #0,001 to 40,508 (approx.).			
	a. First 2 lines of text equal in length.	.75	1.50	4.00
	b. First line longer than second.	1.00	2.00	5.00

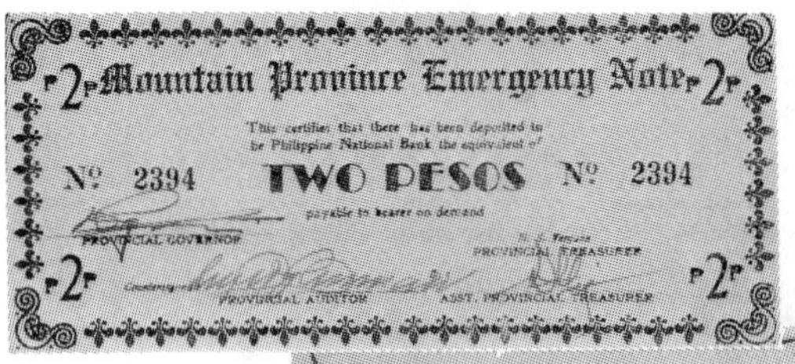

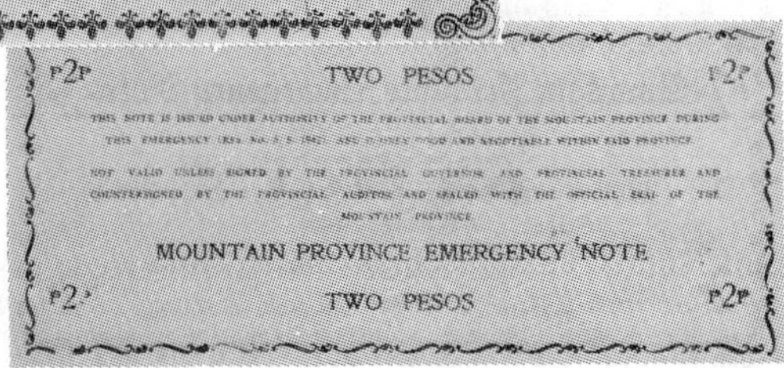

		Good	Fine	XF
S596	**2 Pesos** 1942. Back blue. Serial #0,001 to 9,956 (approx.).			
	a. First 2 lines of text equal in length.	1.50	3.00	6.00
	b. First line longer than second.	1.50	3.00	6.00
S597	**5 Pesos** 1942. Back yellow. Serial #0,001 to 1,387 (approx.).	4.00	10.00	17.50

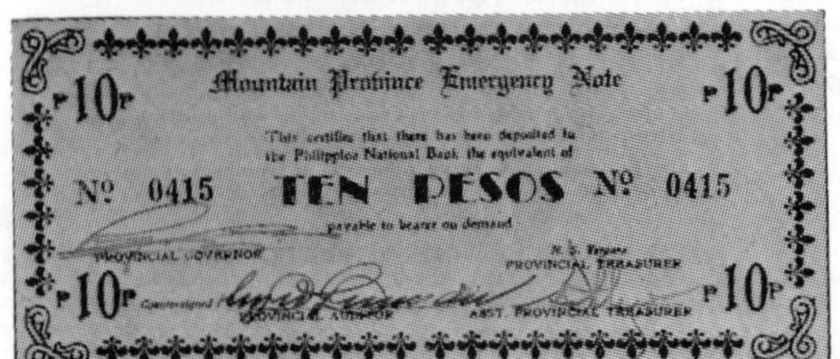

		Good	Fine	XF
S598	**10 Pesos** 1942. Smaller size heading like Second Issue. Back brown. Serial #0,001 to 0,999 (approx.).	4.00	10.00	17.50

Resolution No. 5, ND Second Issue

#S601-S604 w/o Resolution date on back. Smaller size heading (like #S598). Series A. Black on manila paper. Stamped facsimile sign. Longer redemption clause, *Redeemable in the Currency of the Philippine Commonwealth after this Emergency*. All serial # data is approximate.

		Good	Fine	XF
S601	**1 Peso** ND. Back red to brownish red. Serial #41,065 to 60,952 (approx.).	.75	1.50	4.00
S602	**2 Pesos** ND. Back blue. Serial #10,945 to 24,857 (approx.).	.75	1.75	5.00
S603	**5 Pesos** ND. Back yellow. Serial #2,122 to 16,944 (approx.).	1.00	3.00	7.50
S604	**10 Pesos** ND. Back brown. Serial #1,094 to 8,409 (approx.).			
	a. Issued note.	2.00	5.00	10.00
	x. Error; inverted back.	—	—	—

NOTE: Many Mountain Province notes may be found with various countersigning applied when notes were presented for redemption during the Japanese occupation. Those also marked *PAID* are from 3,000 such pesos looted from the Treasury during the bombing attack in 1945.

Negros Occidental

Negros Occidental Currency Committee - Philippine National Bank

This Currency Committee was created by President Quezon and composed of Jose V. Buenaventura, Manager of the Bacolod branch of the Philippine National Bank, as Chairman, with Acting Provincial Auditor Ceferino Ramos and Provincial Fiscal Francisco Arellano as Members.

Two issues of Emergency currency printed by this Committee were turned over to the Philippine National Bank for distribution.

First Issue: The telegram creating this Committee authorized 100,000 pesos to be printed in denominations of 1, 5 and 10 Pesos. In a telegram sent the next day, President Quezon increased the authorization to 500,000 pesos. Of the authorized amount, 475,000 pesos were issued. For some reason, 25,000 pesos in 5 Pesos notes (serial # 35,001 - 40,000) were never printed.

Second Issue: Acting on a petition of the Committee, President Quezon authorized an additional 1,000,000 pesos. The next day he visited Bacolod, met with the Committee and increased the amount to 7,000,000 pesos. Two days later he authorized a total of 14,500,000 pesos in emergency currency to be printed for Negros Occidental. As this included 6,448,771 pesos allocated to the Negros Occidental Provincial Currency Committee, the final authorization amounted to 8,051,229 pesos.

Of the authorized amount, 1,425,000 had been printed. There were 19,456.30 pesos in unissued currency remaining in the vault when Bacolod was occupied by Japanese forces.

1941 First Emergency Circulating Note Issue

Printed by Filma Press on white bond paper, some of which has commercial wmk. Some 5 Pesos notes have *HAMMERMILL BOND* wmk. and some 10 Pesos notes have wmk: *LANCASTER BOND.* Notes were handsigned until sign. cuts could be delivered from Cebu City. Lg. numeral at l., arms at r.

		Good	Fine	XF
S611	**1 Peso** 1941. Black on green unpt. Handsigned Serial #1 to 30,000.			
	a. Handsigned Buenaventura.	7.50	15.00	—
	b. Handsigned Ramos	10.00	22.50	—
	c. Handsigned Arellano.	7.50	17.50	—

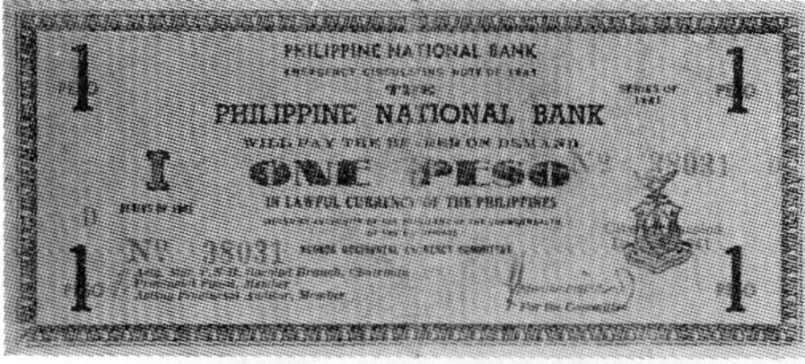

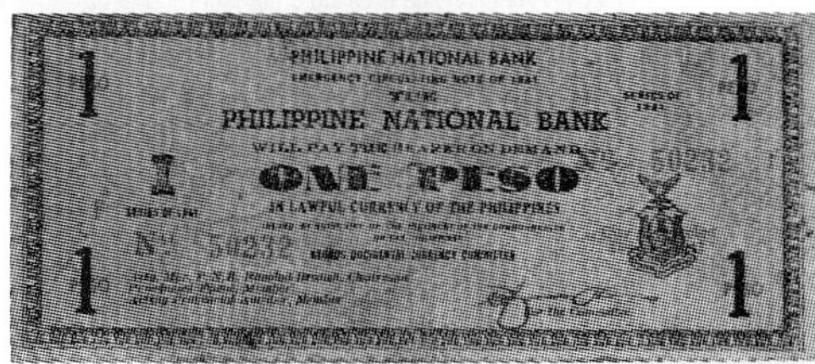

		Good	Fine	XF
S612	**1 Peso** 1941. Like #S611 but printed sign. Serial #30,001 to 100,000.			
	a. Sign. Buenaventura.	2.50	7.50	20.00
	b. Sign. Ramos.	3.50	10.00	25.00
	c. Sign. Arellano.	3.50	10.00	25.00

#S613-S617 plate differences:

TYPE I - face, solid *5* in top corners. Back text: *December 29 and 30, 1941.*

Type II - face, shaded *5* in top corners. Back w/o date.

Type III - face, shaded *5* like Type II. Back text like Type I w/dates.

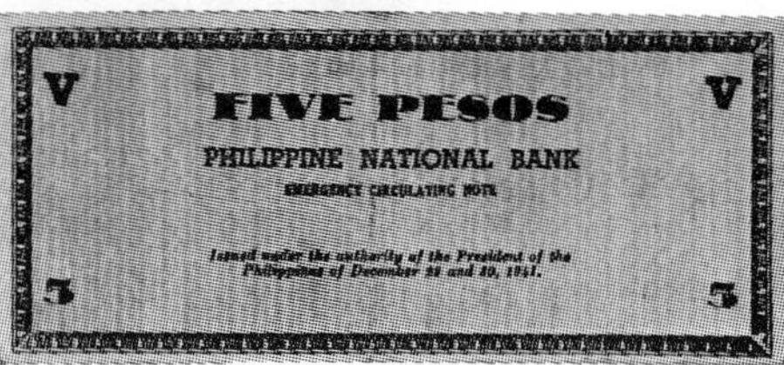

		Good	Fine	XF
S613	**5 Pesos** 1941. Type I. Black on orange unpt. Handsigned. Serial #1 to 5,000.	7.50	15.00	32.50

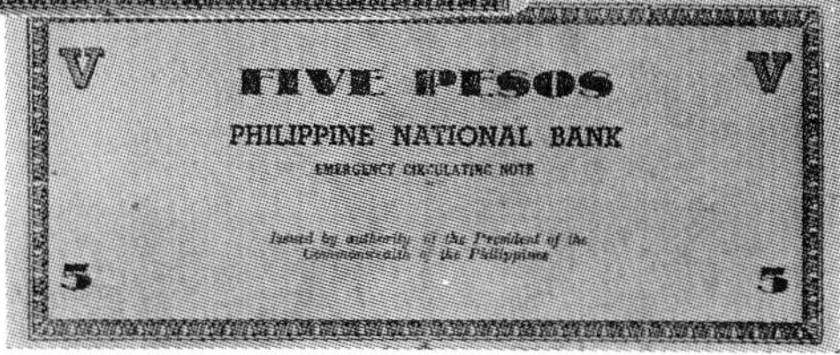

		Good	Fine	XF
S614	**5 Pesos** 1941. Type II. Handsigned. Serial #5,001 to 10,000 and 15,001 to 20,000.	5.00	12.00	25.00
S615	**5 Pesos** 1941. Type III. Handsigned. Serial #10,001 to 15,000.	7.50	15.00	32.50
S616	**5 Pesos** 1941. Type II. Printed sign. Serial #25,001 to 30,000.	7.50	15.00	32.50

		Good	Fine	XF
S617	**5 Pesos** 1941. Type III. Printed sign. Serial #20,001 to 25,000 and 30,001 to 35,000.	5.00	12.50	25.00

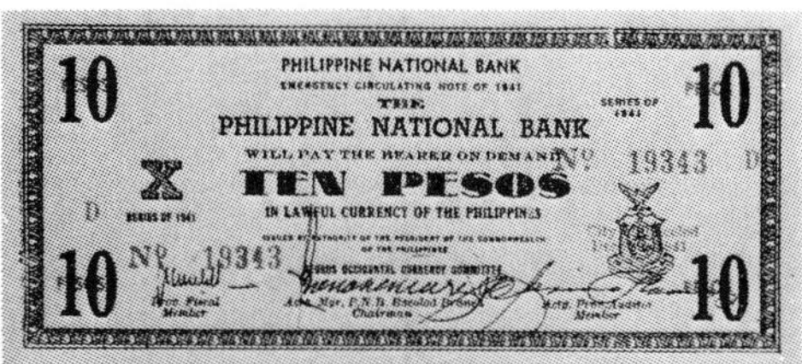

		Good	Fine	XF
S618	**10 Pesos** 1941. Black on lt. yellow unpt. Handsigned. Numeral *X* on back is 6mm high. Serial # for this and #S619: 1 to 20,000.	3.00	7.00	15.00
S619	**10 Pesos** 1941. Handsigned. Numeral *X* on back is 7-1/2mm high. Serial # mixed w/those for #S618.	3.00	7.00	15.00

1941 Second Emergency Circulating Note Issue

#S621-S627 printed by Filma Press. Centavo notes on colored paper, 1 and 2 Pesos and most 10 Pesos on Bais paper, the 5 Pesos and part of the 10 Pesos on white bond paper (some commercial wmk: *(LANCASTER BOND).*

#S621-S623 arms at ctr. on back.

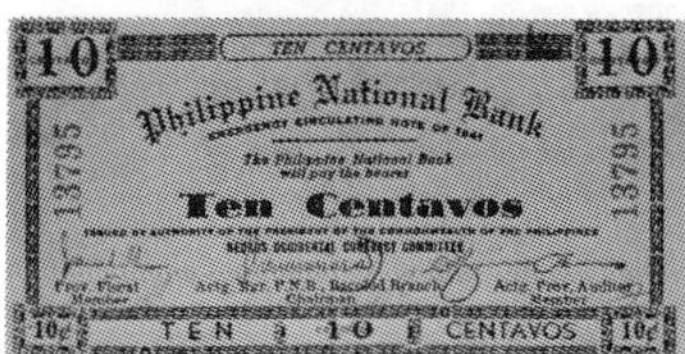

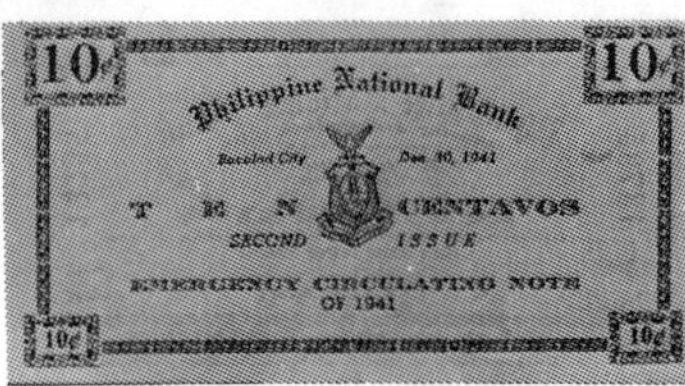

		Good	Fine	XF
S621	**10 Centavos**			
	1941. Serial #1 to 37,500.			
	a. Pink paper.	15.00	30.00	50.00
	b. White paper.	—	—	—
	x. Error: *Philipipne* in heading.	22.50	40.00	—
S622	**20 Centavos**			
	1941. Serial #1 to 37,500.			
	a. Blue paper.	15.00	30.00	50.00
	b. White paper.	20.00	35.00	—
	x. Error: *Philipipne* in heading.	15.00	35.00	—
S623	**50 Centavos**			
	1941. Yellow paper. Serial #1 to 25,000.			
	a. Issued note.	15.00	30.00	—
	x. Error: *Philipipne* in heading.	20.00	40.00	—

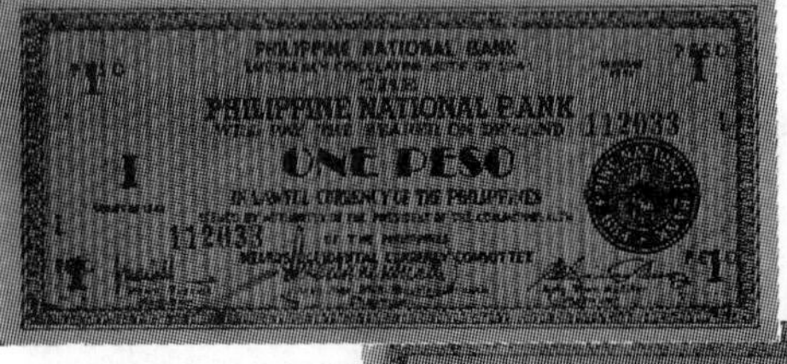

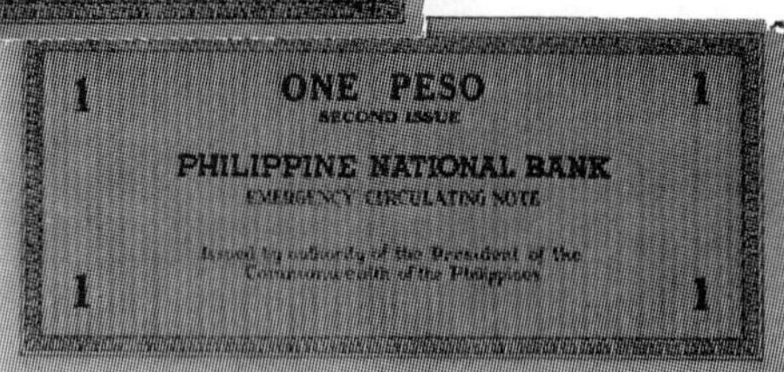

		Good	Fine	XF
S624	**1 Peso**			
	1941. Black on green unpt. Bais paper. Serial #100,001 to 195,000.			
	a. *PESO* (in red) at lower l. is 7mm long. Serial #100,001 to (approx.) 148,826.	2.00	4.00	15.00
	b. *PESO* at lower l. is 10mm long. Serial # (approx.) 151,586 to 195,000.	2.00	4.00	15.00
S625	**2 Pesos**			
	1941. Black on blue unpt. Bais paper. Serial #1 to 65,000.			
	a. Issued note.	3.00	6.00	17.50
	x. Counterfeit.	—	—	—
S626	**5 Pesos**			
	1941. Black on orange unpt. White bond paper. Serial #40,001 to 106,000.			
	a. Issued note.	1.50	3.50	12.50
	x. Counterfeit.	—	—	—
S627	**10 Pesos**			
	1941. Black on yellow unpt. Serial #20,001 to 104,500.			
	a. Bond paper. Serial #20,001 to 50,000.	2.50	5.00	15.00
	b. Bais paper. Serial #50,001 to 104,500.	1.50	3.00	12.50
	x. Counterfeit.	—	—	—

Commonwealth of the Philippines

January 13, 1942 Couponized Check Issue

By January 1942 the shortage of small denomination currency was so acute that the Provincial Treasury experienced difficulty in paying government employees, and salaried personnel found it difficult to cash their paychecks. To alleviate this situation the Provincial Board, on January 13, 1942, authorized the Provincial Treasurer to issue *couponized checks* in small denominations. They were made payable to bearer and were drawn on the deposits of the provincial government in the Philippine National Bank.

The *couponized checks* were printed by Nalco Press on white bond paper. They have printed facsimile signatures of Provincial Treasurer Nicolas Encarnacion and Acting Provincial Auditor Ceferino Ramos. Originally the centavo notes were of the same size and design as the peso notes, but this resulted in confusion when they were placed in circulation. To correct this, the centavo notes were altered in design and printed in a smaller size.

When President Quezon authorized the provincial government to print emergency currency on January 20, further printing of these checks became unnecessary.

#S629 and S630 larger size (same size as #S634-S639).

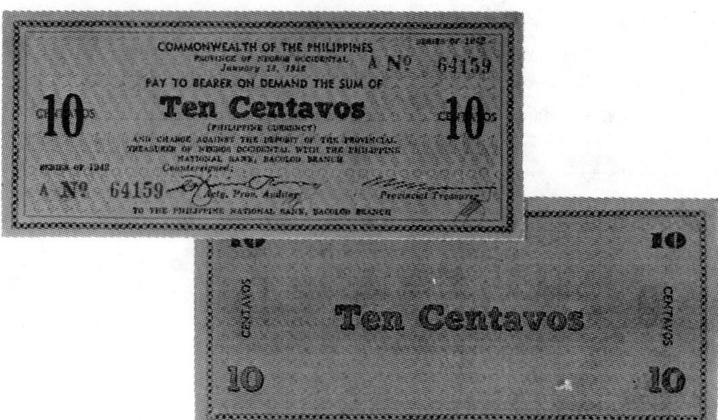

		Good	Fine	XF
S629	**10 Centavos**			
	13.1.1942. Green unpt. Serial # for this and #S631: 1 to 150,000.	10.00	25.00	—
S630	**20 Centavos**			
	13.1.1942. Dk. yellow unpt. Lower numerals on back are 6mm high. Serial # for this and #S632: 1 to 75,000.	20.00	45.00	—
S630A	**20 Centavos**			
	13.1.1942. Like #S630, but lower numerals on back are 7-1/2mm high.	15.00	40.00	—

#S631-S633 reduced size.

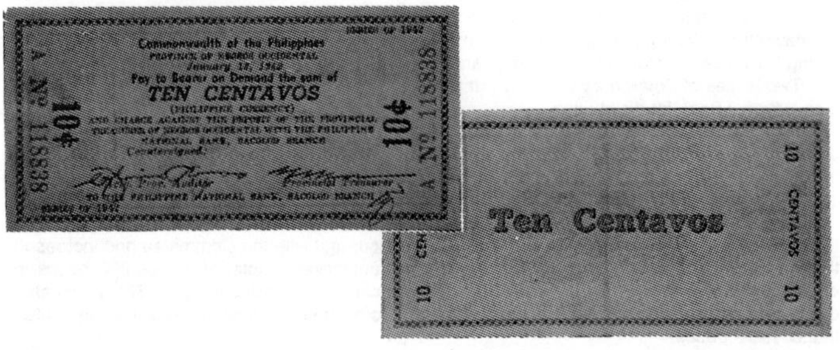

		Good	Fine	XF
S631	**10 Centavos**			
	13.1.1942. Dk. yellow unpt. Serial # included w/S629.	7.50	15.00	—
S632	**20 Centavos**			
	13.1.1942. Dk. yellow unpt. Serial # included w/S630.	10.00	20.00	—
S633	**50 Centavos**			
	13.1.1942. Dk. yellow unpt. Serial # 1 to 40,000.	10.00	20.00	—

#S634-S639 larger size (same as #S629-S630).

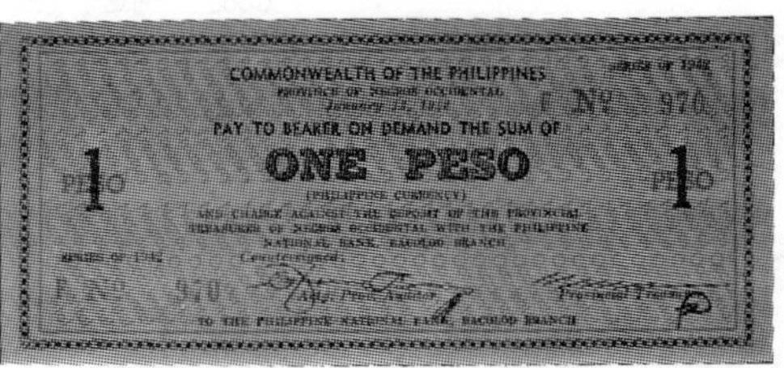

		Good	Fine	XF
S634	**1 Peso**			
	13.1.1942. Brown unpt. Serial #1 to 50,000.	8.00	25.00	—
S635	**2 Pesos**			
	13.1.1942. Dk. yellow unpt. Lower numerals on back are 6mm high. Serial # for this and #S636: 1 to 50,000.	3.00	9.00	25.00
S636	**2 Pesos**			
	13.1.1942. Lower numerals on back are 7-1/2mm high. Serial # included w/S635.	3.50	10.00	30.00
S637	**5 Pesos**			
	13.1.1942. Dk. yellow unpt. Back numerals like #S635. Serial #1 to 10,000.	3.50	10.00	30.00
S638	**5 Pesos**			
	13.1.1942. Back numerals like #S636. Serial #10,001 to 20,000.	3.50	10.00	30.00
S639	**10 Pesos**			
	13.1.1942. Orange unpt. Serial #1 to 20,000.	6.50	25.00	50.00

Negros Occidental Provincial Currency Committee

This Committee was created by President Quezon and was composed of Provincial Treasurer Nicolas Encarnacion as Chairman, with Acting Provincial Auditor Ceferino Ramos and Provincial Fiscal Francisco Arellano as Members.

No specific amount was stated, the authorization being for sufficient currency to *pay salaries of employees and government laborers.* In the latter part of February, 1942 when President Quezon visited Bacolod, the total amount to be issued was set at 6,448,771 pesos.

The currency printed by this Committee was turned over to the Provincial Treasurer for distribution. Printing was by Nalco Press on white paper. A total of 4,825,350 pesos was delivered prior to the arrival of Japanese occupation forces. All but 150,000 pesos had been placed in circulation. The unissued notes remained in the Philippine National Bank vault until liberation when they were destroyed when the bank building was burned in March 1945.

Just prior to the Japanese arrival, three sacks of currency were taken from Nalco Press by Treasurer Encarnacion when he evacuated to the mountains. The currency amounted to 86,250 pesos in 5 Pesos notes serially numbered 341,851 to 359,100.

In July 1942 Encarnacion surrendered to the Japanese, turning over to them 26,250 pesos of the 5 Pesos notes. These were incinerated on Japanese orders. What happend to the other 60,000 pesos was never explained.

1942 Emergency Circulating Note Issue

#S640-S645 sm. red Commonwealth arms at r.

		Good	Fine	XF
S640	**5 Centavos** 1942. Bluish or purple. Sign. Encarnacion. Serial # for this and #S641: 1 to 600,000.			
	a. Bond paper.	1.00	3.50	7.00
	b. Bais paper.	1.00	3.50	7.00
S641	**5 Centavos** 1942. Sign. Ramos. Serial # included in #S640.	1.00	3.50	7.00
S642	**10 Centavos** 1942. Brown. Back black. Sign. Encarnacion. Serial # for this and #S643: 1 to 100,500.	3.00	10.00	15.00
S643	**10 Centavos** 1942. Sign. Ramos. Serial # included in #S642.			
	a. Bond paper.	3.00	10.00	15.00
	b. Bais paper.	3.00	10.00	15.00

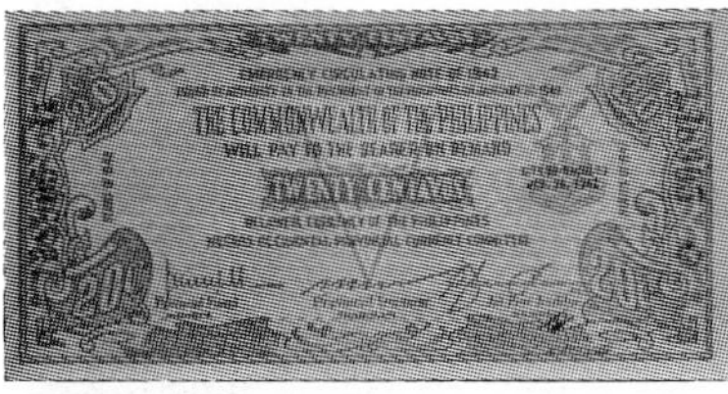

		Good	Fine	XF
S644	**20 Centavos** 1942. Green. Lg. *V* at ctr. Back black. Bond paper. Serial #1 to 501,500.	3.50	12.00	25.00
S645	**50 Centavos** 1942. Black on green unpt. Similar to #S644. Back green. Bond paper. Serial #1 to 20,500.	5.00	15.00	40.00

#S646-S650 Quezon at l., red or pale red-orange Commonwealth seal at r. Lg. *V* at ctr. on back.

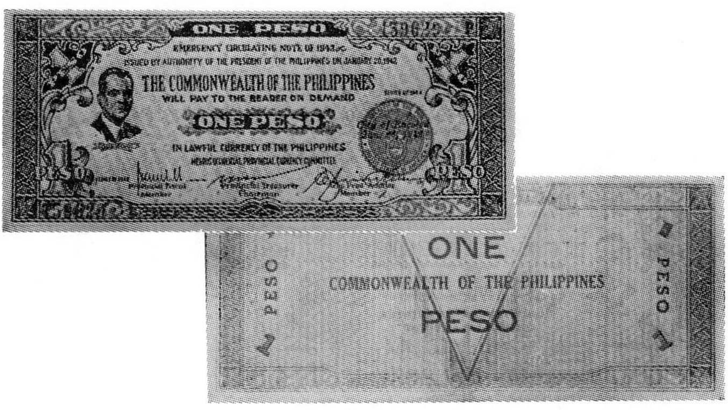

		Good	Fine	XF
S646	**1 Peso** 1942. Black on orange unpt. words. Back red. Bond paper. Serial #1 to 402,000.			
	a. *PESOS* at l. and r. on back facing in.	.50	2.50	5.00
	b. *PESOS* at l. and r. on back facing out.	.50	2.50	5.00
S647A	**2 Pesos** 1942. Blue on blue unpt. Bond paper. Serial #1 to (approx.) 250,000.	.50	2.00	4.00
S647B	**2 Pesos** 1942. Purple on purple unpt. Bais paper. Serial # (approx.) 275,001 to 678,000.	.50	2.00	4.00
S648	**5 Pesos** 1942. Black on yellow unpt. Back yellow. Serial #1 to 341,850.			
	a. Bond paper. Serial #1 to (approx.) 240,000.	.50	2.00	4.00
	b. Bais paper. Serial # (approx.) 244,001 to 341,850.	.50	2.00	4.00
S649	**10 Pesos** 1942. Black on brown unpt. Back brown. Serial #1 to 120,750.			
	a. Bond paper. *PESOS* at l. and r. on back facing in. Serial #1 to (approx.) 58,000.	.50	1.50	4.00
	b. Bond paper. *PESOS* at l. and r. on back facing out. Serial # included in "a".	.50	1.50	4.00
	c. Bais paper. *PESOS* at l. and r. on back facing in. Serial # (approx.) 60,001 to 120,000.	.50	1.50	4.00
	d. Bais paper. *PESOS* at l. and r. on back facing out. Serial # included in "c".	.50	2.50	6.00

#S650 unofficially issued.

		Good	Fine	XF
S650	**5 Pesos** 1942. Like #S648. Serial #341,851 to 359,100.	—	—	—

Negros Oriental

Pre-Surrender Issue 1942

In December 1941 coins almost disappeared from circulation. The situation got so bad that Silliman University issued campus scrip to pay student employees and to make change at campus dining halls and bookstores. While valid only on campus, such was the need for small change that it was readily accepted elsewhere. By the end of January, 1942, small denominations of currency also became scarce.

On February 10, 1942 the Provincial Board adopted *Resolution No. 124* which authorized the printing of *couponized checks* in the amount of 300,000 pesos to be charged against deposits of the Provincial Treasurer in the Bacolod branch of the Philippine National Bank. The Provincial Treasurer and Auditor were assigned to see to the printing and issuance of the *checks.*

The *checks* were printed by Silliman University press, and have stamped facsimile signatures of Provincial Treasurer Vicente Avila and Provincial Auditor Nicolas Ybanez. A total of 50,900 pesos was issued.

Commonwealth of the Philippines

1942 Couponized Check Issue

#S651-S653 dk. brown on lt. manila paper; green backs.

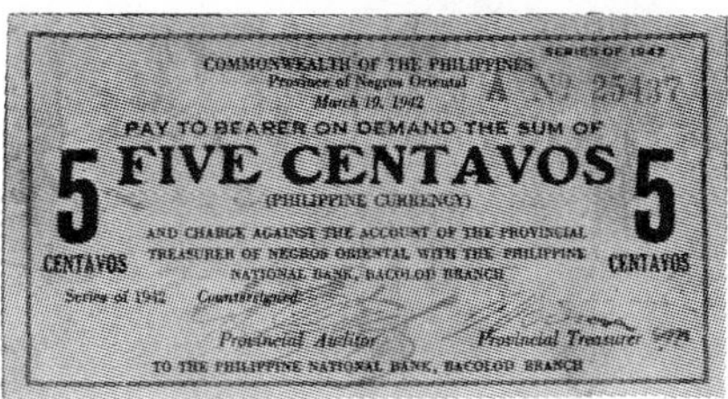

		Good	Fine	XF
S651	**5 Centavos** 19.3.1942. Serial #1 to 34,000.			
	a. Manila paper.	10.00	25.00	50.00
	b. Bais paper.	17.50	35.00	75.00
S652	**10 Centavos** 19.3.1942. Serial #1 to 34,000.	10.00	25.00	—
S653	**20 Centavos** 19.3.1942. Serial #1 to 34,000.	17.50	35.00	—

#S654-S655 blue on white Bais paper; orange backs.

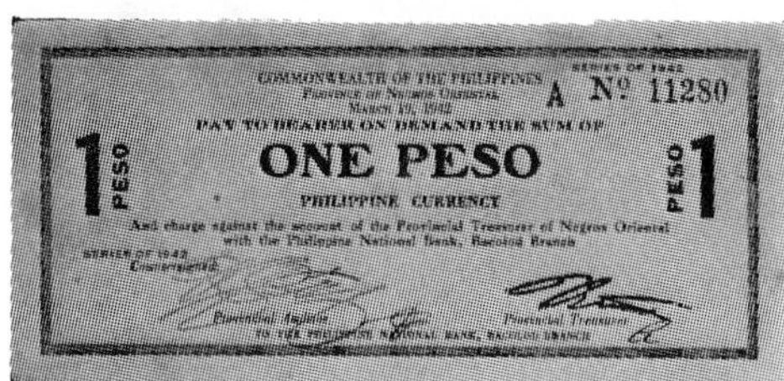

		VG	VF	Unc
S654	**1 Peso** 19.3.1942. Serial #1 to 13,000.			
	a. Blue ink.	7.50	20.00	50.00
	b. Gray ink.	7.50	20.00	50.00
S655	**2 Pesos** 19.3.1942. Serial #1 to 13,000.			
	a. Blue ink.	7.50	20.00	50.00
	b. Gray ink.	7.50	20.00	50.00

March 12, 1942 Spurious Issue

A 20 Pesos note, Province of Negros Oriental, with a March 12, 1942 date is spurious. No such denomination was *officially* authorized or issued.

It is listed here not only to acquaint numismatists with its true status, but also as an example of the confusion caused by the numerous types and varieties of emergency currency being issued, which apparently resulted in an entirely bogus issue being accepted.

		Good	Fine	XF
S656x	**20 Pesos** 12.3.1942. (Spurious note.)	—	—	—

Negros Oriental Currency Committee Issue

While this would ostensibly appear to be a provincial issue, in actuality it was a military issue to finance the ambitions of one man - Lt. Col. Gabriel R. Gador.

At the outbreak of the war, Lt. Col. Gador commanded the 7th Military District (Negros island). In January 1942, Gador was transferred to the staff of Gen. Sharp in Mindanao. When Gen. Sharp surrendered, Gador escaped to Negros Oriental where he hid out in the mountains, scorning any involvement in the early struggle to organize guerrillas.

But as the guerrillas became better organized, Gador suddenly decided to take over. On January 27, 1943 he issued *General Order No. 1* proclaiming himself to be the Commanding Officer of not only Negros, but of all the Visayan islands, with the rank of Major General. This only served to further disrupt attempts at guerrilla unification in Negros.

On May 14, 1943, General MacArthur appointed Maj. Jesus Villamor, who had previously arrived in Negros by submarine, as Commanding Officer of the 7th Military District. In order to set up a formal command structure, Villamor called a meeting at his headquarters of all the guerrilla leaders. Hoping to smooth unification, Villamor appointed Gador as his Executive Officer.

Gador's participation did not last long. When the Japanese landed a force near the headquarters area on June 26, Gador fled in the night.

Returning to his mountain hideout, Gador created his own Provincial Government of Negros Oriental, designating former Provincial Board member Albert Furbeyre as Acting Governor. This was apparently in defiance of President Quezon's appointment of Alfredo Montelibano as Governor of Free Negros. As Montelibano was printing currency, Gador decided he would do the same.

On September 19, 1943 the Provincial Board of Gador's newly created government passed *Resolutions No. 1 and 2* which (a) created a Negros Oriental Currency Committee and, (b) authorized it to issue 200,000 pesos in 5 Pesos notes.

The Currency Committee was composed of Acting Provincial Treasurer Jacinto Valente as Chairman, with Acting Provincial Auditor Nicasio Villarin and Acting Provincial Fiscal Vicente Paras as Members. They in turn met and passed *Resolutions No. 1 and 2* which (a) fixed design and text of the new currency, and (b) delegated to Governor Furbeyre sole authority for printing and issuing it.

The notes were printed at Payabon, Municipality of Manjuyod, the location of Col. Gador's headquarters. Printing ceased and the *government* became defunct with the coup d'etat on December 8, 1943.

Acting Governor Furbeyre reported that "50,000 pesos *more or less*" had been printed, a rather vague figure. At any rate, 42,000 pesos were serially numbered. In 1944, the now defunct Currency Committee reported to Governor Montelibano an additional 23,000 pesos which were not numbered. On October 25, 1944, 22,500 pesos of this was incinerated. The remaining 500 pesos were marked *Non-Negotiable, for Specimen Only* and sent to Governor Montelibano as *samples.* Since notes without serial numbers have turned up, it would appear that not all of these were destroyed, and that some may have reached circulation.

1942 Emergency Circulating Note Issue

Negros Oriental Currency Committee. Series of 1942. Printed in black from wood cuts on white paper, 42,000 pesos serially numbered, the quantity without serial numbers being unknown.

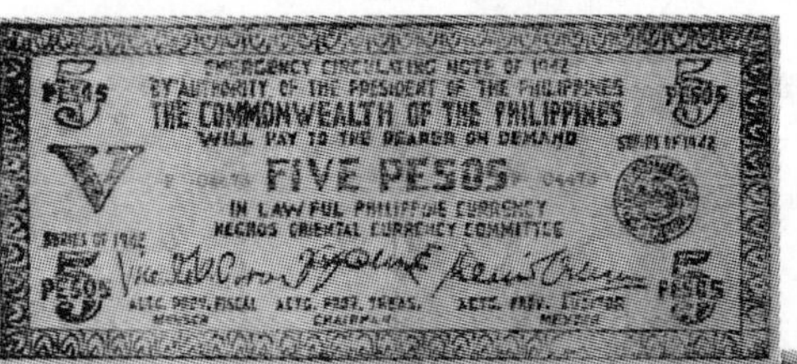

		Good	Fine	XF
S658	**5 Pesos** 1942. Serial #D00501 to D02900; E02901 to E03900; F03901 to F05100; H01300 to H05100.			
	a. Regular paper.	7.50	15.00	40.00
	b. Bais paper.	10.00	22.50	50.00
S659	**5 Pesos** 1942. W/o serial #.	—	—	—
	x. Error. Printed on face only. No serial #.	—	—	—

Island Of Negros

Negros Emergency Currency Board

At the time of the USAFFE surrender, Negros island was divided into five military sectors, each garrisoned by an infantry battalion. Two battalion commanders, Majors Salvador Abcede and Ernesto S. Mata, flatly refused to obey the surrender orders. Instead, they withdrew into the mountains and disbanded their units. The other three battalion commanders obeyed orders and surrendered, but the majority of their men didn't. They became an army of small guerrilla bands desperately in search of leadership.

In southern Negros Occidental the guerrilla groups united under command of Maj. Salvador Abcede, while those in the north united under Maj. Ernesto S. Mata. They made contact with Col. Peralta in Panay and affiliated with his *IV Philippine Corps.* Peralta designated their combined units as the *72nd Division* with Abcede as Commanding Officer and Mata as Chief of Staff. Both were promoted to Lieutenant Colonel rank.

Silliman University Professor Henry Roy Bell suddenly found himself leader of a guerrilla movement. His former ROTC students had even posted notices in the lowland towns, *report immediately to Mr. Bell in the mountains.* Bell finally located an unsurrendered officer, Maj. Placido A. Ausejo, to take over military command while he devoted his efforts to organization, supply and civil affairs. As this area was dependent upon Mindanao for a large part of its food supply, they affiliated with the *Mindanao-Sulu Command* of Col. Fertig, who promptly sent 10,000 pesos in Mindanao currency to aid in their finance.

In northern Negros Oriental, Lt. Col. Gabriel Gador proclaimed himself supreme commander of all Negros with the assumed rank of Major General.

On the night of January 14, 1943, the submarine USS GUDGEON surfaced off Catmon Point and landed the first *Penetration Party* under command of Maj. Jesus Villamor whose mission was to set up an intelligence network in the Philippines.

Villamor's next step was to establish a civil government by appointing Alfredo Montelibano, former Mayor of Bacolod, as Governor of *Free Negros.* This appointment was confirmed by President Quezon on June 9, 1943 when he designated Montelibano Governor of the *Province of Negros,* consisting of Negros Occidental, Negros Oriental and the sub-province of Sequijor.

To finance the new government, Governor Montelibano borrowed 700,000 pesos from wealthy plantation owners until permission could be obtained from President Quezon to print emergency currency.

Since the Members of pre-surrender currency committees were all in Japanese controlled cities, President Quezon on July 11, 1943 created the Negros Emergency Currency Board composed of the following officials of the newly organized government: Governor Alfredo Montelibano as Chairman, with Acting Provincial Treasurer Pedro Elizalde and Provincial Auditor Alfredo Benedicto as Members.

The Currency Board had not been authorized to print any currency, but Montelibano recommended: *One hundred thousand monthly needs of Civil Government, fifty thousand monthly to be used for redemption of mutilated notes, and one million pesos for a revolving fund, army is asking one million monthly.*

Quezon immediately approved the recommendations but stipulated the amount for the army as being subject to MacArthur's approval. Despite numerous requests, MacArthur would not commit any specified amount. And after liberation MacArthur would deny any responsibility for redemption of currency on the grounds that he had not given his approval.

Printing got underway on September 18, 1943 in a secret location near Pagnatangan. Except for signature cuts and seals, all printing was done from standard metal type. On May 31, 1944 a second press press was set up at Tolong. This press printed only 1 Peso notes (#S668-S671). Also, on June 1, 1944 Acting Provincial Auditor Nicasio Villarin replaced Benedicto as a Member of the Currency Board, but for the balance of 1944 all notes continued to be printed with Benedicto's signature. The 1945 series has Villarin's signature.

Almost any type of paper available was used for printing. The greater portion of it was derived from commercially manufactured brown paper bags. The white paper used at Tolong was brought in by submarine.

Printing operations ended on May 8, 1945. By that time the astounding total of 40,128,539 pesos had been printed, of which all but 8,346,000 had been issued. Unissued notes were ordered destroyed.

There are several varieties of seals, used indiscriminately. There are also variations in the type set-up for dates. Numerous different clerks were employed in the task of initialing each note after it was printed. In giving serial numbers only those reported as having been issued are included, with mention where necessary of those reportedly destroyed.

ALPHABETICAL/NUMERICAL DESIGNATIONS

Each note has a combined letter-number combination, such as A1, B4, E3 etc. Where possible serial # are given for each of these combinations; at times the printing was not consecutive and various letter-number combinations cannot be definitively separated.

The alphabetical/numerical series designation with respective serial # range is given in two methods, of which the following are examples:

a. Serial # 0001 to 200,000 B1-B4;

b. B1-B4 serial # 0001 to 200,000.

For example *a.,* the B1-B4 series are not in consecutive order, but mixed. Thus, serial # 0001 might well be B4 or B2.

For example *b.,* the B1-B4 series groups were printed in equal quantity and in consecutive order. Thus B1 = serial # 0001 to 50,000; B2 = serial # 50,001 to 100,000; B3 = serial # 100,001 to 150,000; and B4 = serial # 150,001 to 200,000.

1943 Treasury Emergency Currency Certificate Issue

#S661-S664 green Commonwealth seal at r.

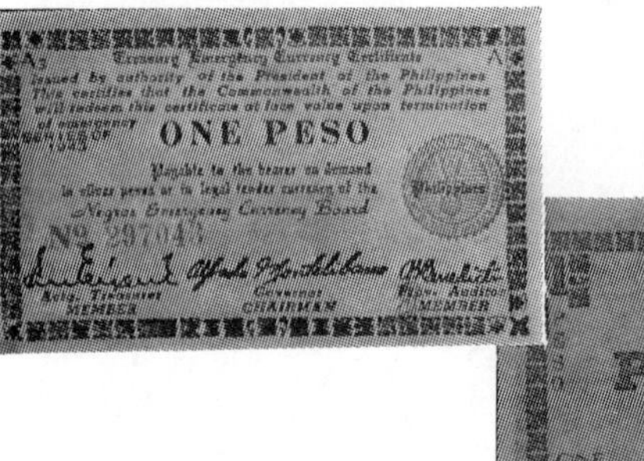

		Good	Fine	XF
S661	**1 Peso** 1943. Red. Back green. Serial #1 to 403,600 A1-A3; B1 1,001 to 21,700; 1751 to 280,000 C1-C4.			
	a. Yellow paper. Normal or small 3 in date.	.50	1.00	2.00
	b. Manila paper. Normal or small 3 in date.	.50	1.00	2.00
	c. Gray paper.	1.00	3.00	5.00
S662	**5 Pesos** 1943. Black. Back green. White paper. Serial #1 to 150,000 A1-A4; 1,001 to 88,370 B1-B4. Normal or small 3 in date.	1.00	2.00	3.50
S663	**10 Pesos** 1943. Black.			
	a. White paper. Serial # 1 to 138,280 A1-A4: 1,001 to 239,000 B1-B4. Normal or small 3 in date.	.50	1.00	2.00
	x. Counterfeit, brown paper.	—	—	—
S664	**20 Pesos** 1943. Black. White paper. Serial #1 to 60,000 A1-A3.	1.00	2.00	4.00
S665	**50 Pesos** 1943. Black. Orange seal at r. Back orange. White paper. Serial #A1-A2 1 to 40,000. Countersign. on back by Treasurer and Auditor.	9.50	15.00	25.00

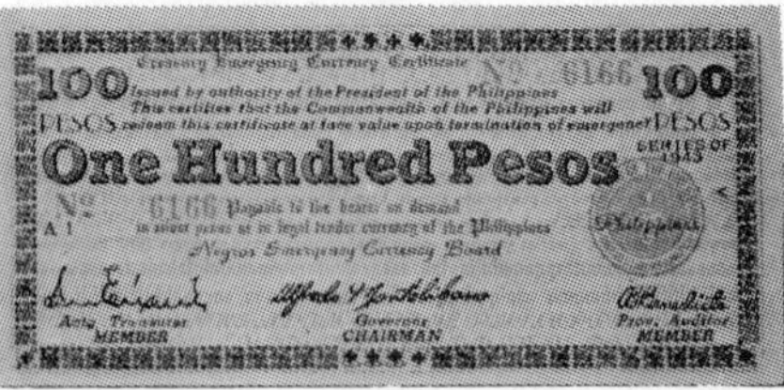

		Good	Fine	XF
S666	**100 Pesos** 1943. Black. Like #S665. Serial #1 to 15,100 A1-A2 (#15,100 to 20,965 not issued). Countersign. on back by Gov. Montelibano.	15.00	25.00	50.00

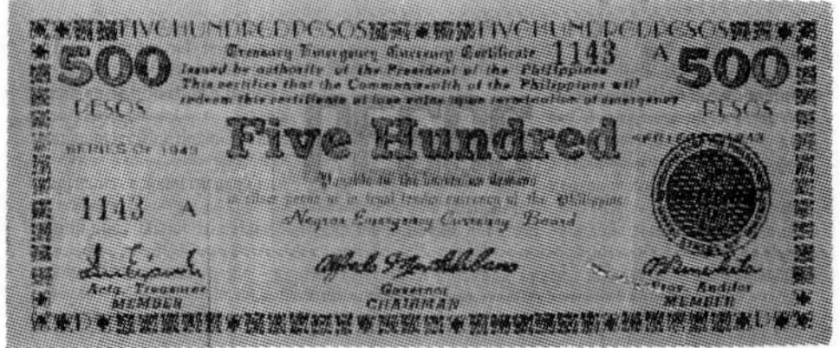

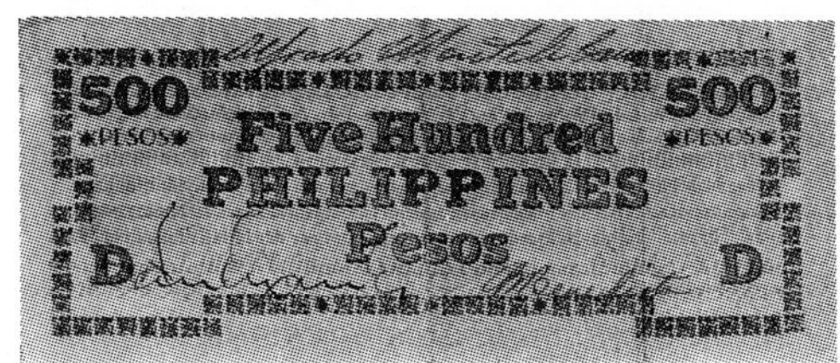

S667 500 PESOS

1943. Blue on yellow unpt. Red seal at r. Green numerals at corners, also large words across ctr. Back blue on yellow unpt. White paper. Serial #A1 1 to 1,700 (#1,701 to 4,240 not issued). Countersign. on back by all 3 Members.

	GOOD	FINE	XF
a. Montelibano sign. at bottom.	50.00	85.00	160.00
b. Montelibano sign. at top.	30.00	60.00	125.00
c. Watermaked paper.	50.00	—	—

1944 TREASURY EMERGENCY CURRENCY CERTIFICATE ISSUE

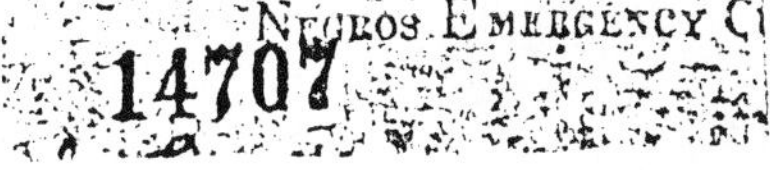

Serial # w/o A

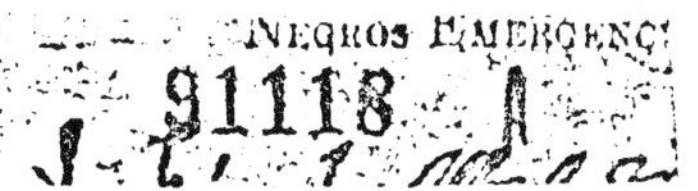

Crude A Suffix

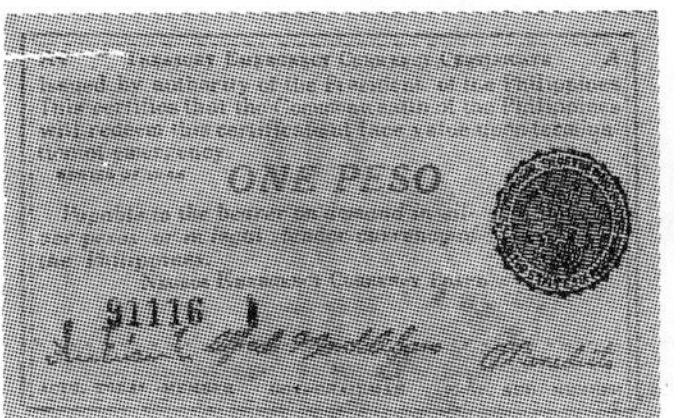

S668 1 PESO

1944. Blue text, red-orange seal and serial #. Back red-brown. White paper.

	GOOD	FINE	XF
a. Normal serial #; A1-A4 0,001 to 80,000.	.50	1.00	2.00
b. Serial # w/crude narrow *A* suffix. Serial #A1-A4 0,001A to 120,000A.	.50	1.00	2.00

S669 1 PESO

1944. Blue text, black seal and serial #. Back slate black. White paper. Serial # included in #S668. — — —

S670 1 PESO

1944. Black text, blue seal and serial #. Back blue. White paper. Serial #B1-B4 0,001 to 100,000. .75 1.50 3.00

S671 1 PESO

1944. Black text, seal and serial #. Back slate black. White paper. Serial # included in #S670. — — —

	GOOD	FINE	XF
S672 1 PESO 1944. Brown paper (varieties). Red text, green seal and serial #. Back dk. green. Serial #D1-D4 0,001 to 100,000; E1-E3 0,001 to 60,000; F1-F4 0,001 to 60,000; G1-G3 0,001 to 60,000.	.50	1.00	1.50
S673 1 PESO 1944. Like #S672 but different border ornaments at top l. and r. Serial #H1-H4 0,001 to 200,000.	2.00	3.00	5.00
S674 5 PESOS 1944. Black. Green seal and serial #. Back dk. green. Brown paper (varieties). Serial #C1-C4 0,001 to 200,000.	1.00	2.00	3.50
S675 5 PESOS 1944. Green. Red seal and serial #. Back red. Brown paper (varieties). Serial #D1-D4 0,001 to 200,000.	1.00	2.00	3.50

Notice

Readers with unlisted dates, color or signature varieties are invited to submit photocopies of their notes to: Standard Catalog of World Paper Money, Krause Publications, 700 East State St. Iola WI 54990-0001 U.S.A. or by email: thernr@krause.com. Email submissions of material for possible inclusion need to be 100% jpeg attachments at 300 dpi.

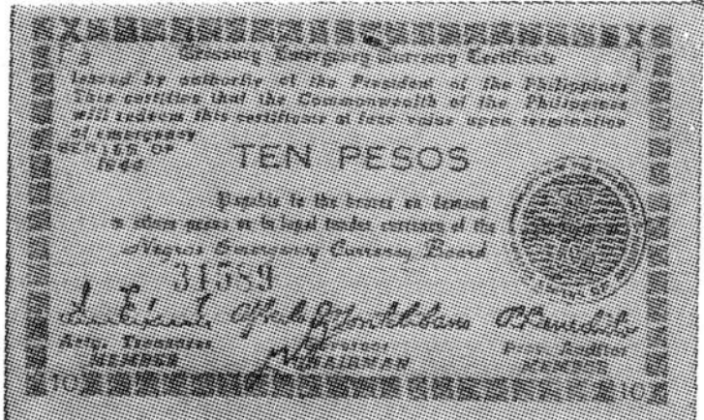

S676 10 PESOS

1944. Black. Green seal and serial #. Smaller words *TEN PESOS* at ctr., letters 4mm tall. Brown paper (varieties). Serial #C1-C4 0,001 to 200,000; D1-D4 0,001 to 100,000; E1-E4 0,001 to 100,000; F1-F4 0,001 to 100,000.

	GOOD	FINE	XF
a. Issued note.	.50	1.00	2.00
x1. Counterfeit, ornate serial # 4mm high.	—	—	—
x2. Counterfeit, like x1 but plain serial # 5mm high.	—	—	—

S677 10 PESOS

1944. Black. Like #S676 except that words *TEN PESOS* at ctr. are larger, 5mm tall. Serial #G1-G4 0,001 to 100,000; H1-H4 0,001 to 100,000; I1-I4 0,001 to 100,000.

	GOOD	FINE	XF
a. Issued note.	.50	1.00	2.00
x. Counterfeit, lg. *TEN PESOS* but series *D2* which occurs only on genuine notes with small *TEN PESOS*, #S676.	—	—	—

S678 20 PESOS

1944. Black. Green seal and serial #. White paper. Serial #B1-B3 1 to 57,000. 1.00 2.00 4.00

S679 20 PESOS

1944. Like #S678 but pink paper. Serial #1 to 24,600 C1-C3. 1.50 3.00 5.00

S680 20 PESOS

1944. Like #S678 but brown paper (varieties). Serial #0,001 to 249,300 D1-D3.

	GOOD	FINE	XF
a. Issued note.	.75	1.50	3.00
x. Counterfeit, brown paper but series *B1* which occurs only on genuine notes of white paper, #S678.	—	—	—

1945 TREASURY EMERGENCY CURRENCY CERTIFICATE ISSUE

	GOOD	FINE	XF
S681 1 PESO 1945. Red. Green seal and serial #. Back dk. green. Brown paper. Serial # I1-I4 0,001 to 100,000; J1-J4 0,001 to 100,000.	1.00	2.00	4.00
S683 10 PESOS 1945. Black. Green seal and serial #. Brown paper. Serial # J1-J4 0,001 to 199,000 (#199,001 to 200,000 not issued).	2.50	5.00	9.00

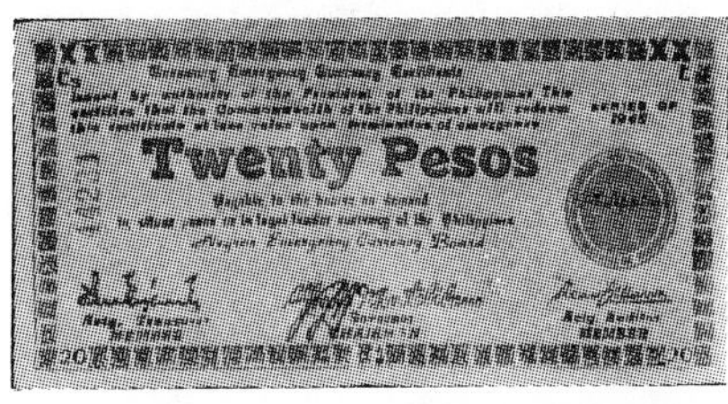

	GOOD	FINE	XF
S684 20 PESOS 1945. Dk. green. Red seal and serial #. Brown paper. Serial #E1-E3 0,001 to 46,000 (#46,001 to 51,000 not issued).	4.00	7.50	17.50
S685 20 PESOS 1945. Dk. green. Red seal and serial #. White paper. Serial #G1 1,001 to 3,000 (#G1-G3 3,001 to 75,000 not issued). Serial #I1 0,001 to 4,000 (#I1-I3 4,001 to 75,000 not issued). Serial #J1 0,001 to 1,000 (#J1-J3 1,001 to 75,000 not issued).	5.00	10.00	20.00

NOTE: 20 Pesos notes serial # F1-F3 0,001 to 75,000 not issued. 20 Pesos notes serial # H1-H3 0,001 to 75,000 not issued. In addition, some 140,000 1 Peso notes printed at the Tolong press were not issued.

FREE NEGROS MILITARY CURRENCY COMMITTEE

Bearer Checks on the Cebu Branch of the PNB.

These checks were issued by Pedro Elizalde in his official capacity as *Agent for the Treasurer of the Philippines*.

Prior to the Japanese invasion of Cebu, Elizalde was concurrently Acting Provincial Treasurer of Cebu, *Agent for the Treasurer of the Philippines*, and a Member of the Cebu Emergency Currency Board. As *Agent* he had been given authority by President Quezon to advance funds to the Army against deposits in the Cebu branch of the Philippine National Bank, even incurring overdrafts up to 200,000 pesos if necessary.

When the Japanese invaded Cebu, Treasurer Elizalde moved all of his official papers to the Municipality of Catmon where it was intended to relocate the provincial government. When Provincial Governor Hillario Abellana decided to discontinue governmental functions, Treasurer Elizalde left Cebu and moved to Cadiz, Negros Occidental.

At Cadiz, Elizalde issued checks to unsurrendered Army officers, under the authority he held as *Agent for the Treasurer of the Philippines*. As these checks were made out to individual officers, they required proper endorsement each time they changed hands.

In order for the checks to change hands more readily and to *circulate as currency,* Elizalde issued his remaining checks in round figures and made them payable to bearer. A total of 360,180 pesos was issued in checks in denominations from 10 to 5,000 Pesos. The quantity of each denomination is given in parentheses.

ND Issue

		Good	Fine	XF
S691	10 Pesos (30).	—	—	—
S692	20 Pesos (74).	—	—	—
S693	30 Pesos (25).	—	—	—
S694	40 Pesos (5).	—	—	—
S695	50 Pesos (70).	—	—	—
S696	100 Pesos (152).	—	—	—
S697	150 Pesos (1).	—	—	—
S698	200 Pesos (114).	—	—	—
S699	300 Pesos (1).	—	—	—
S700	500 Pesos (78).	—	—	—
S701	1,000 Pesos (35).	—	—	—
S702	2,000 Pesos (45).	—	—	—
S703	2,500 Pesos (1).	—	—	—
S704	3,000 Pesos (10).	—	—	—
S705	4,000 Pesos (1).	—	—	—
S706	5,000 Pesos (23).	—	—	—

NOTE: Elizalde's support of the Negros guerrilla movements, from the very beginning, was recognized by Governor Montelibano who appointed him Acting Provincial Treasurer of the *Free Negros* government and a Member of the Negros Emergency Currency Board. Elizalde personally supervised printing of Free Negros emergency currency printed by this Board.

IV Philippine Corps

On May 9, 1942 Col. Roger Hillsman, commanding USAFFE forces in Negros, ordered all units to surrender. Only one of five battalions complied.

The unsurrendered rank and file began the guerrilla movements. At the urging of these groups both Abcede and Mata accepted command of guerrillas in southern and northern Negros.

Meanwhile, over in Panay, Col. Peralta was organizing a *IV Philippine Corps.* When Abcede and Mata affiliated their organizations with his, both were given promotions and their joint units were designated the 72nd Infantry.

On January 17, 1943 Gen. MacArthur authorized him to issue *"a reasonable amount of military script."* Peralta lost no time in passing on the good news and authorized Col. Abcede to issue 500,000 pesos in Negros. Later the amount was increased to 5,000,000 pesos.

In Special Order No. 11, dated March 2, 1943, Col. Abcede set up the *Free Negros Military Currency Committee* composed of Lt. Col. Ernesto S. Mata as Chairman, with Division Finance Officer Lt. Agustin Paraiso and Ass't. Div. Finance Officer Lt. Liberato Montañez as Members. The first notes printed bear the designation *IV Philippine Corps,* and were printed under the first authorization of 500,000 pesos.

Gen. MacArthur ordered Col. Peralta to dissolve his IV Philippine Corps and restrict his command to Panay. Peralta was a bit slower in disseminating this information, but Negros was finally informed. So the second printing, while issued under Peralta's 5,000,000 authorization, had the designation changed to *7th Military District.*

Printing was ordered stopped by Maj. Jesus Villamor, who was appointed Commanding Officer of the 7th Military District by Gen. MacArthur. By then a total of 824,450 pesos had been printed, and all but 1,213 pesos put in circulation.

1943 Military Script Issue

Army of the United States of America

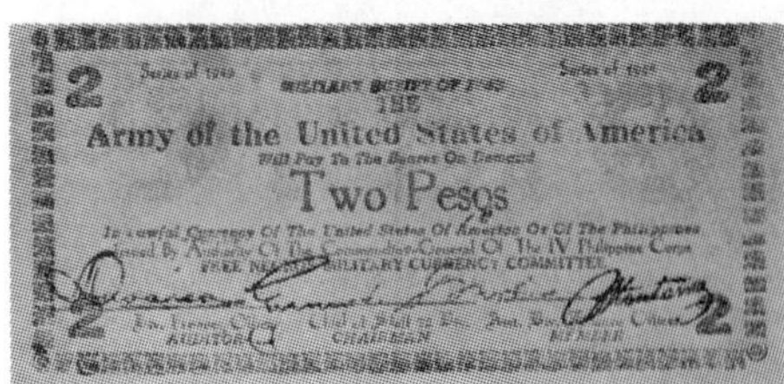

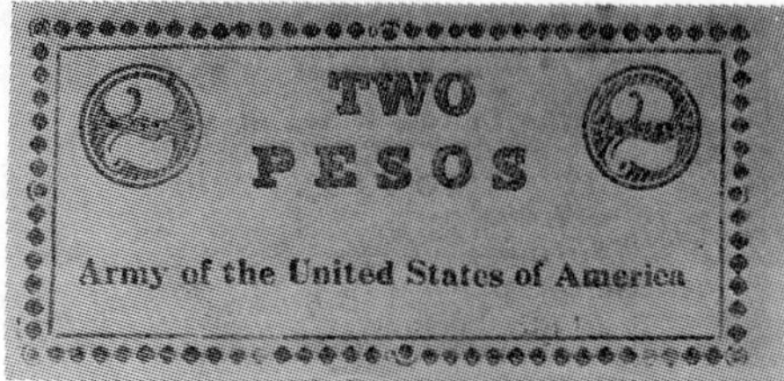

		Good	Fine	XF
S711	2 Pesos 1943. Black on brown paper. Serial #10,001 to 50,796. Frame on back is 133 x 53mm, top of *TWO* is 7mm below top frame line.	7.50	20.00	—
S711A	2 Pesos 1943. Like #S711, but back frame is 126 x 52mm. Top of *TWO* is 4mm below top frame line.	9.00	25.00	—

		Good	Fine	XF
S712	5 Pesos 1943. Brown w/black text. Woman standing at l. looking towards a smoking volcano, sun behind. Back lt. orange. Serial #10,001 to 29,213.	12.50	30.00	—

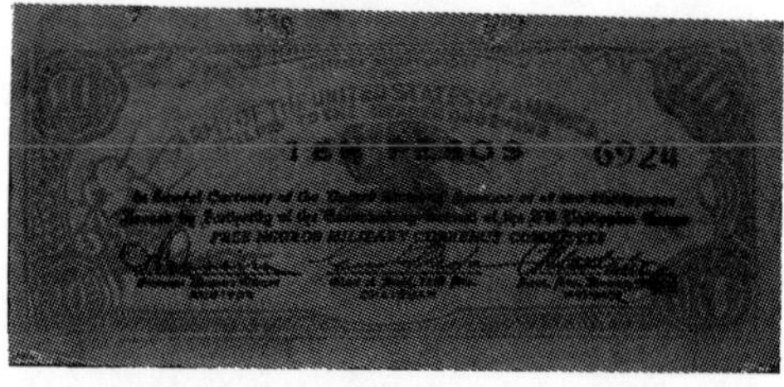

		Good	Fine	XF
S713	10 Pesos 1943. Pale brown w/black text. Cannon w/man behind at l., eagle at ctr. Serial #1,001 to 21,835.	15.00	40.00	—

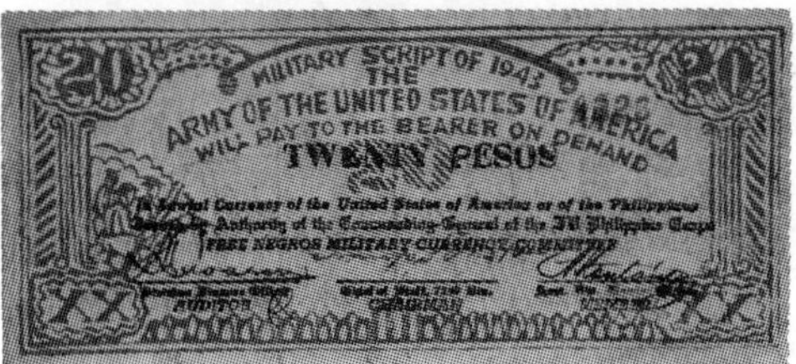

		Good	Fine	XF
S714	20 Pesos 1943. Green w/black text. Armed guerrillas at l. Back brown; standing woman holding hammer on anvil at ctr. Serial #1,001 to 6,064.	17.50	55.00	—

1943 7th Military District Issue

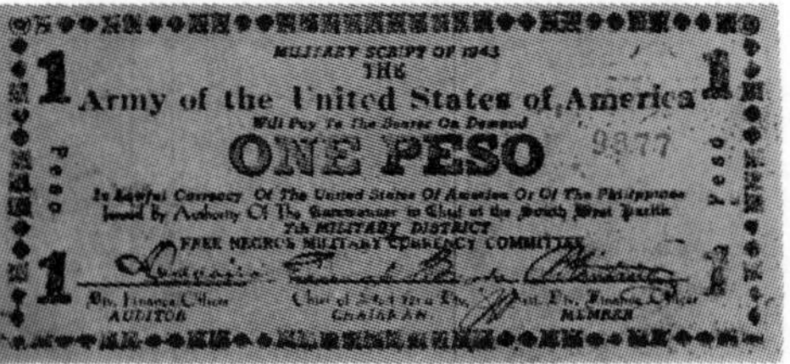

		Good	Fine	XF
S715	1 Peso 1943. Black. Back greenish slate. Serial #1,001 to 41,756.	7.50	20.00	50.00

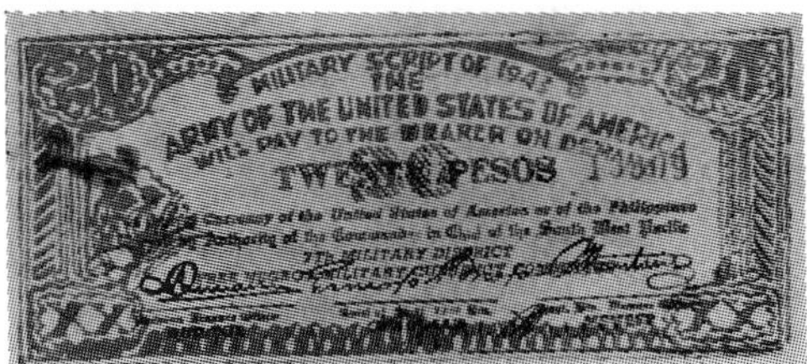

		GOOD	FINE	XF
S716	**20 PESOS** 1943. Like #S714 except for changes in authorization text. Serial #6,065 to 19,805.			
	a. Issued note.	12.50	35.00	—
	x. Counterfeit.	—	—	—

U.S. FORCES IN THE PHILIPPINES - LOCAL MILITARY

It was the original intention of the Negros Emergency Currency Board to print denominations as small as 1 Centavo. However, the urgent need for currency to finance both the *Free Negros* government and the military forces necessitated printing larger denominations. The smallest value printed was 1 Peso, and even these were in short supply.

Therefore, the Provincial Board of *Free Negros* authorized military units to print notes in fractional and 1 Peso denominations for local use. Units doing so were required to hold on deposit an equivalent value in what had become known as *Montelibano* money.

Just how many of the numerous military units issued notes under this authority may never be known, or for that matter, the denominations they issued. Many had a very limited circulation, and were later redeemed by the unit which issued them. We can give here only a brief mention of the major military units.

The overall command was, of course, the *7th Military District.* Originally it was under command of Maj. Jesus Villamor, who was succeeded on July 23, 1943 by Lt. Col. Salvador Abcede.

The 7th Military District was in turn originally divided into four Sectors: the *North Negros Sector,* the *Central Negros Sector,* the *East Negros Sector,* and the *South Negros Sector.*

After the coup d'etat against Col. Gador by Lt. Col. Julian C. Aspilla on December 8, 1943 those units formerly under Gador were designated the *Special District Headquarters Troops.*

In June 1944 the North Negros Sector was further divided into two sectors designated *Northwest Negros Sector* and *Northeast Negros Sector.*

The major sectors were further divided into sub-sectors, with their respective command posts. Most of these were given alphabetical designations. For example, the Northwest Sector was divided into sub-sectors A, C, D, E and G. The Northeast Sector was divided into sub-sectors B, I, H, X. Sub-sectors of the other areas are not presently known.

The following local military issues are presently known.

7TH MILITARY DISTRICT

#S724 was further designated: Negotiable within *Free Kabankalan-Tolong-Dumaguete-Bais Area.* Stamped facsimile sign. of Lt. Col. Salvador Abcede, Commanding Officer of the 7th Military District. (Kabankalan was in the Central Negros Sector, the other three Municipalities in the South Negros Sector.)

1944 ISSUE

		GOOD	FINE	XF
S724	**50 CENTAVOS** 1944. Black. (1/100 of a 50-Peso Montelibano note.)	—	—	—

CENTRAL NEGROS SECTOR

1944 EMERGENCY CHIT ISSUE

#S743 and S744 sign. of Sector Commander Maj. Abenir D. Bornales.

		GOOD	FINE	XF
S743	**20 CENTAVOS** 1944. Brown paper.	—	Rare	—

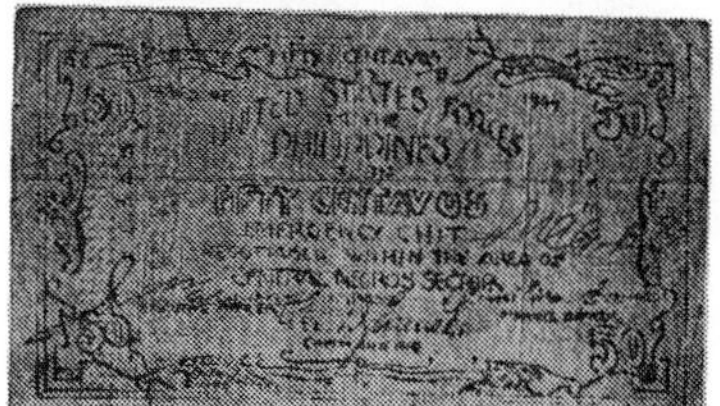

		GOOD	FINE	XF
S744	**50 CENTAVOS** 1944. Brown paper.	—	Rare	—

SPDHQT (SPECIAL DISTRICT HEADQUARTERS TROOPS)

1944 CERTIFICATE ISSUE

#S759 embossed seal of Notary Public Juez de Paz, of Manjuyod.

		GOOD	FINE	XF
S759	**50 CENTAVOS** 1944. Black on pink paper. Uniface.	—	Rare	—

CPW AREA (COMMAND POST W - SECTOR NOT KNOWN)

ND CIRCULATING CHIT ISSUE

#S784 and S785 pink paper.

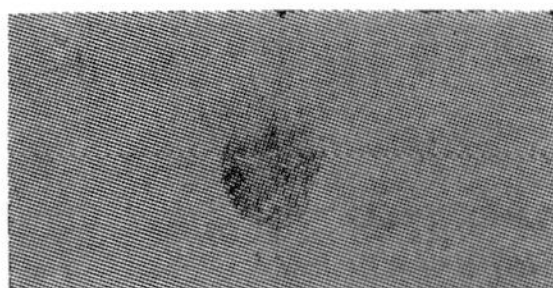

		GOOD	FINE	XF
S784	**50 CENTAVOS** ND. Mimeographed. Inked fingerprint on back.	—	Rare	—
S785	**1 PESO** ND. Like #S784.	—	Rare	—

NUEVA VIZCAYA

With the Japanese occupation of Manila on January 2, 1942 the provincial governments in Luzon could no longer obtain currency supplies.

On January 17, 1942 the Provincial Governor of Nueva Vizcaya received a message from President Quezon stating: *Impossible to send you money. . .you are authorized to issue chips* (chits).

In April, an Emergency Currency Board was formed, composed of Governor Demetrio Quirino as Chairman, with Acting Provincial Treasurer Rodrigo Acosta and Provincial Auditor Cirilo Torralba as Members.

Three denominations were procuded by mimeograph, the signatures of Board Members being cut on the stencil. After some notes had been issued it was decided to apply an embossed seal as an anti-counterfeiting measure. Later printings had the seal embossed on the stencil.

A total of 45,098.20 pesos was issued. Printing ceased after the unconditional surrender of all USAFFE forces on May 7, 1942.

PROVINCIAL GOVERNMENT OF NUEVA VIZCAYA

ND ISSUE

		GOOD	FINE	XF
S791	**20 CENTAVOS** ND. White laid paper.			
	a. W/o embossed seal. Serial #0001 to (approx.) 3,200.	30.00	50.00	75.00
	b. Embossed seal of Justice of the Peace. Serial # (approx.) 3,201 to (approx.) 4,900.	30.00	50.00	75.00
S792	**20 CENTAVOS** ND. White laid paper. Mimeo. seal of Justice of the Peace. Serial # (approx.) 10,100 to 16,121.	20.00	45.00	—

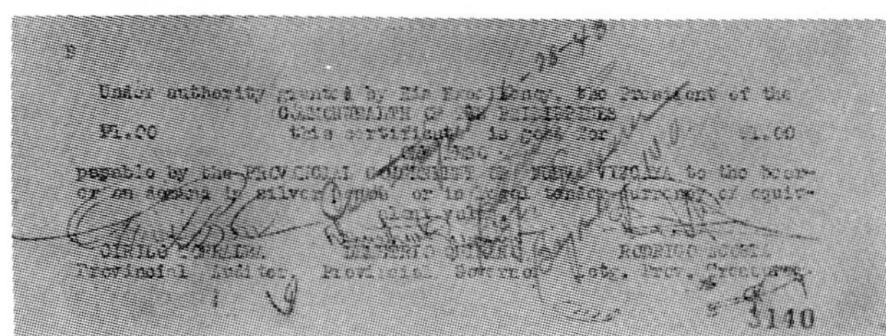

		GOOD	FINE	XF
S793	**1 PESO** ND. Yellow paper.			
	a. Embossed seal of Provincial Auditor. Serial #1 to (approx.) 5,100.	20.00	45.00	70.00
	b. W/o embossed seal. Serial # (approx.) 5,200 to (approx.) 11,500.	20.00	45.00	70.00
	c. Embossed seal of Justice of the Peace. Serial # (approx.) 13,400 to (approx.) 14,000.	20.00	45.00	70.00

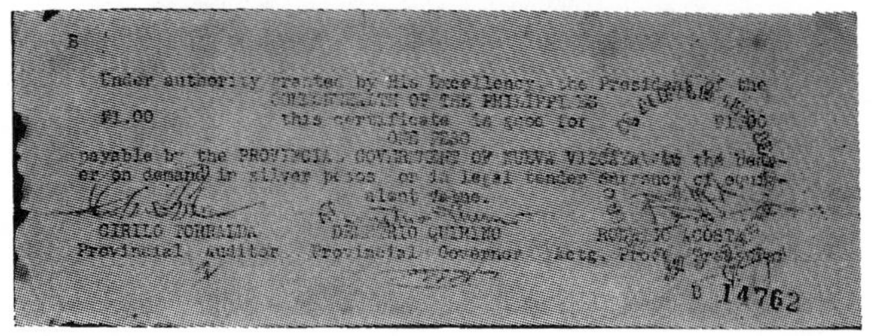

		Good	Fine	XF
S794	**1 Peso** ND. Yellow paper. Mimeo. seal of Justice of the Peace. Serial # (approx.) 14,762 to 25,134.	20.00	45.00	—
S795	**5 Pesos** ND. White bond paper. Serial #0001 to 3,348.			
	a. Embossed seal of Provincial Auditor. Serial #0001 to (approx.) 1,400.	30.00	50.00	75.00
	b. Embossed seal of Justice of the Peace. Serial # (approx.) 2,000 to 3,348.	30.00	50.00	75.00

NOTE: In July 1943 the puppet Philippine Executive Commission authorized redemption of pre-surrender emergency notes, but specifically excluded any notes printed by mimeograph. Even though this excluded the notes of Nueva Vizcaya, Governor Quirino ordered them accepted for registration in the vain hope they would be included. Thus, many of these notes may be found countersigned in red pen on the face, or with a circular *RECEIVED* date stamp in purple on the back. Catalog values are for notes as originally issued. Countersigned notes are worth only about half as much.

PALAWAN

On May 14, 1942 Governor Gaudencio Abordo called a public meeting at Mentes which was attended by all available prominent citizens, the armed forces and government officials. A *Resolution* was unanimously adopted which stated that *no officials or employees of Palawan shall surrender to the enemy.*

Despite Japanese occupation of Puerto Princesa on May 18, 1942 the provincial government continued to function at Caramay. The various guerrilla groups which sprang up throughout Palawan were organized into the *Palawan Special Battalion* financed by the provincial government.

Up to late 1942 the provincial government was able to meet financial obligations by means of checks and postal money orders. But the scarcity of a circulating medium became so serious that on December 10, 1942 the Provincial Board adopted *Resolution No. 53* which created a Currency Board with authorization to print 20,000 pesos in scrip to be exchanged for *checks, warrants, and other papers of value.*

This Resolution provided for notes of fractional and small denomination currency in specified amounts. Unfortunately the shortage of paper prevented its accomplishment. Subsequent Resolutions Nos. 5, 20, and 22 in 1943 amended this provision by providing for substitution of 5 Pesos notes in place of smaller denominations. Even so, 19,640 pesos was the total issue.

On March 16, 1943 *Resolution No. 24* authorized printing of an additional 50,000 pesos to be used by the provincial government to meet operational expenses. As before, fractional and 1 Peso denominations were planned, but the shortage of paper prevented them from being printed, and only 46,000 pesos were actually issued.

On May 3, 1943 the Provincial Board adopted *Resolution No. 56* which authorized an additional 60,000 pesos to meet governmental expenses. This was made retroactive to April 30 which resulted in two different dates appearing on notes printed under this authorization. The shortage of paper prevented the printing of small denominations called for, and only 10 and 20 Pesos notes could be issued.

On May 1, 1944 *Resolution No. 1* amended the previous *Resolution* to increase the authorized amount to *such amounts as may be deemed necessary from time to time to meet operational expenses.*

All currency printed under Resolutions No. 24 and No. 56, Series of 1943, and Resolution No. 1, Series of 1944 were to be charged against provincial funds deposited in the Philippine National Bank.

The Currency Committee was composed of Governor Gaudencio Abordo as Chairman, with Provincial Treasurer Pedro Cecilia and Provincial Auditor Angel Paguia as Members. On February 2, 1945 Auditor Paguia was captured by the Japanese. On February 19, Mauricio Reynosa was appointed temporary Auditor in his place.

All notes were handsigned by each Committee member, and in addition have the embossed seal of the provincial government. Printing ended on February 28, 1945 at which time a total of 343,088 pesos had been printed and 311,648 placed in circulation.

It was estimated that about 5,000 pesos of counterfeit notes were placed in circulation. The counterfeiters were arrested and held for trial until liberation.

PROVINCE ISSUES UNDER PROVINCIAL AUTHORITY

1942 CIRCULATING PAPER BILL ISSUE

RESOLUTION NO. 53, SERIES 1942 DECEMBER 10, 1942

#S801-S805 white paper. Typewritten in pica or elite type. Uniface.

		Good	Fine	XF
S801	**10 Centavos** 10.12.1942. Serial #1 to 400.	—	—	—
S802	**50 Centavos** 10.12.1942. Serial #1 to 200.	—	—	—
S803	**1 Peso** 10.12.1942. Serial #1 to 500.	—	—	—
S804	**2 Pesos** 10.12.1942. Serial #1 to 2,000.	—	—	—

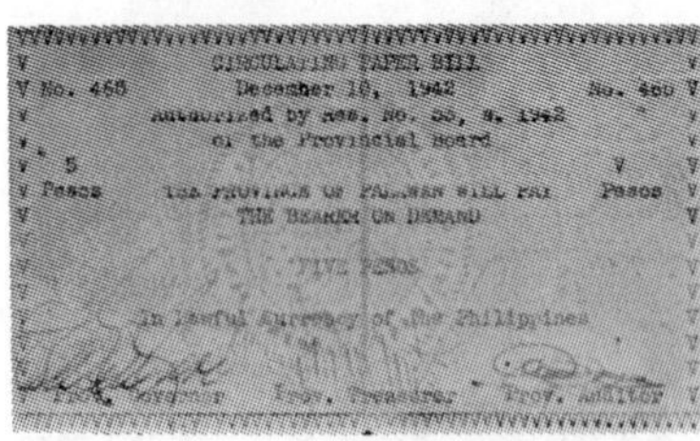

		Good	Fine	XF
S805	**5 Pesos** 10.12.1942. Serial #1 to 1,900.	—	—	—

1943 FIRST CIRCULATING PAPER BILL ISSUE

RESOLUTION NO. 5, SERIES 1943. JANUARY 23, 1943

#S806 typewritten. White paper. Uniface.

		Good	Fine	XF
S806	**5 Pesos** 23.1.1943. Serial #1,901 to 2,500.	—	—	—

1943 SECOND CIRCULATING PAPER BILL ISSUE

RESOLUTION NO. 20, SERIES 1943. FEBRUARY 25, 1943

#S807 typewritten. White paper. Uniface.

		Good	Fine	XF
S807	**5 Pesos** 25.2.1943. Serial #2,501 to 2,900.	—	—	—

1943 THIRD CIRCULATING PAPER BILL ISSUE

RESOLUTION NO. 22, SERIES 1943. MARCH 15, 1943

#S808 typewritten. White paper. Uniface.

		Good	Fine	XF
S808	**5 Pesos** 15.3.1943. Serial #2,901 to 3,000.	—	—	—

1943 FOURTH CIRCULATING PAPER BILL ISSUE

RESOLUTION NO. 24, SERIES 1943. MARCH 15, 1943

#S809-S812 mimeographed. White paper.

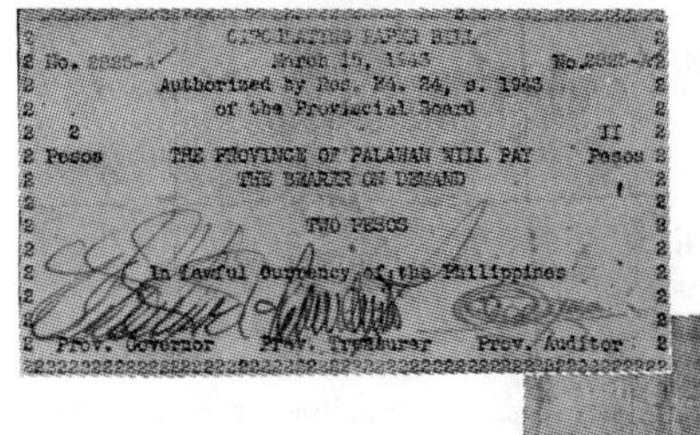

		Good	Fine	XF
S809	**2 Pesos** 15.3.1943. Serial #1A to 3,000A. Back: Numeral *2* is 47mm high.	—	—	—
S810	**5 Pesos** 15.3.1943. Serial #1-A to 2,000-A. Back: Numeral *5* is 47mm high.	—	—	—
S811	**10 Pesos** 15.3.1943. Serial #1-A to 2,000-A. Back: *P10* is 19-1/2mm high.	—	—	—
S812	**20 Pesos** 15.3.1943. Serial #1-A to 500-A. Back: *P20* is 19-1/2mm high.	—	—	—

1943 FIFTH CIRCULATING PAPER BILL ISSUE

RESOLUTION NO. 56, SERIES 1943. APRIL 30, 1943

#S813 and S814 mimeographed.

		Good	Fine	XF
S813	**10 Pesos** 30.4.1943. Back: *P10* is 19-1/2mm high. Serial # (for #S813 and S815): 1-B to 1,500-B.	—	—	—
S814	**20 Pesos** 30.4.1943. Back: *P20* is 19-1/2mm high. Serial # (for #S814 and S816): 1-B to 1,000-B.	—	—	—

1943 SIXTH CIRCULATING PAPER BILL ISSUE

RESOLUTION NO. 56, SERIES 1943. MAY 3, 1943

#S815 and S816 mimeographed.

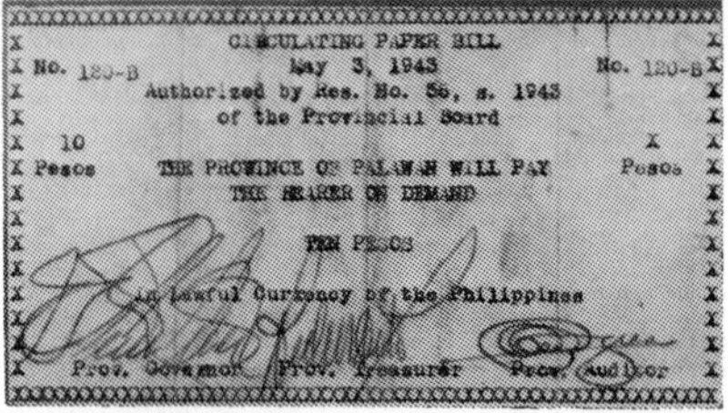

		Good	Fine	XF
S815	**10 Pesos** 3.5.1943. Back: *P10* is 19 1/2mm high. Serial # mixed w/#S813.			
	a. Graph paper.	—	—	—
	b. White paper.	—	—	—
	x. Counterfeit. Typewritten. Graph or white paper. Back: *P10* is 23mm high.	—	—	—
S816	**20 Pesos** 3.5.1943. Back: *P20* is 19-1/2mm high. Serial # mixed w/#S814.			
	a. Issued note.	—	—	—
	x. Counterfeit. Typewritten. Back: *P20* is 23mm high.	—	—	—

1943 SEVENTH CIRCULATING PAPER BILL ISSUE

RESOLUTION NO. 56, SERIES 1943 *AS AMENDED*

#S817 and S818 mimeographed. Sign. of Provincial Auditor Paguia.

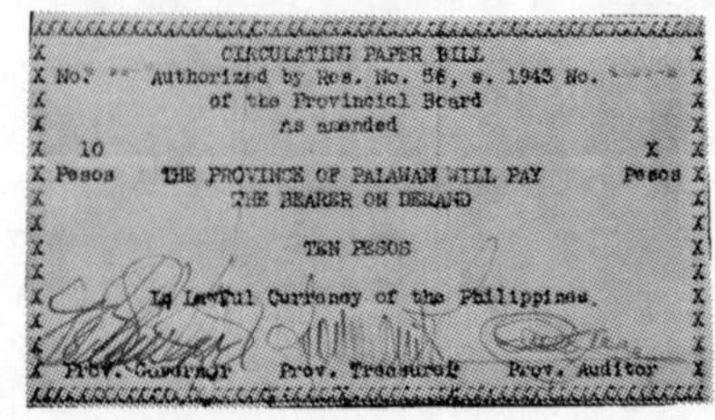

S817 10 PESOS — GOOD FINE XF
1943. Back: *P10* is 19-1/2mm high. Serial # (for #S817, S819, S820): 1,501-B to 7,126-B.
- a. White paper. — — —
- b. Manila paper. — — —
- c. Blue paper. — — —
- d. Ledger or document paper. — — —

S818 20 PESOS
1943. Back: *P20* is 19-1/2mm high. Serial # (for #S818, S821, S822): 1,001-B to 8,716-B.
- a. White paper. — — —

1943 EIGHTH CIRCULATING PAPER BILL ISSUE

RESOLUTION NO. 56, SERIES 1943 *AS AMENDED*

#S819-S822 mimeographed. Sign. of Provincial Auditor Reynosa.

S819 10 PESOS — GOOD FINE XF
1943. Uniface. Serial # mixed w/#S817 and S820.
- a. White paper. — — —
- b. Brown paper. — — —

S820 10 PESOS
1943. Like #S819. Back: *P10* is 19-1/2mm high. Serial # mixed w/S817 and S819.
- b. Brown paper. — — —

S821 20 PESOS
1943. Back: *P20* is 19-1/2mm high. Serial # mixed w/S818 and S822.
- a. White paper. — — —
- b. Brown paper. — — —
- c. Ledger or document paper. — — —

S822 20 PESOS
1943. Like #S821. Uniface. Serial # mixed w/S818 and S821.
- a. White paper. — — —

NOTE: 20 Pesos notes serial # 8,717-B to 10,288-B were not issued.

MUNICIPAL ISSUES UNDER PROVINCIAL AUTHORITY

OFFICIAL REPORT:

Due to the shortage of printing materials such as paper, ink, etc., and the impending dangers of sending funds to the different municipalities and districts, the Provincial Board of Palawan, by Resolution No. 18, Series 1942, authorized the municipalities and districts to print local scrips in amounts as may be authorized by the Provincial Board for their operational expenses and to make available in scrips, too, funds allotted to them for relief work projects and such amounts to cover salaries of national and provincial officials and employees stationed in the different municipalities and districts as well as to far out guerrilla units.

Gaudencio Abordo, governor of Palawan, October 12, 1945.

Resolution No. 18, Series 1943, authorized Municipalities and Municipal Districts to issue notes *authorized by competent authority.* Resolutions passed by Municipal Councils constituted *competent authority,* thus all notes issued by authority of Municipal Councils were *provincially authorized,* and were so regarded by Governor Abordo. However, only those which *specifically* refer to provincial authority are included in this listing.

AGUTAYA

All notes were issued under authority of *Resolution No. 18, Series 1943,* of the Provincial Board. Unless otherwise stated, all notes have printed serial numbers. A total of 21,950.63 pesos were issued.

Only notes definitely confirmed are listed.

Actg. Mun. Mayor:	S. Pablico
Municipal Treasurer:	Feliciano Cadiaon
Municipal Councilor:	Marciana Z. Cabristante

MAY 13, 1943 CIRCULATING PAPER BILL ISSUE

#S830-S837 typewritten, with carbon copies. Rose paper. Handsigned.

S830 10 CENTAVOS — GOOD FINE XF
13.5.1943. — — —

S833 1 PESO
13.5.1943. *P1* on back. — — —

S834 1 PESO
13.5.1943. *ONE 1 PESO* on back. — — —

S835 2 PESOS
13.5.1943. *P2* on back. — — —
- a. Typewritten serial #. — — —
- b. Printed serial #. — — —

S837 5 PESOS
13.5.1943. *P5* on back. — — —

#S840-S843 hectograph printing in purple. Rose paper. Printed sign. Stamped denomination on back.

S840 20 CENTAVOS
13.5.1943. — — —

S842 1 PESO
13.5.1943. — — —

S843 2 PESOS
13.5.1943. — — —

#S846 and S849 hectograph printing in purple. Green paper. Printed sign. Stamped denomination on back.

S846 20 CENTAVOS
13.5.1943. — — —

S849 2 PESOS
13.5.1943. — — —

JUNE 2, 1943 FIRST CIRCULATING PAPER BILL ISSUE

#S852-S856 typewritten, with carbon copies. Handsigned. Manila paper. Stamped denomination on back.

S852 20 CENTAVOS — GOOD FINE XF
2.6.1943. — — —

S854 1 PESO
2.6.1943. — — —

S855 2 PESOS — GOOD FINE XF
2.6.1943. — — —

S856 5 PESOS
2.6.1943. — — —

JUNE 2, 1943 SECOND CIRCULATING PAPER BILL ISSUE

#S858-S864 new Municipal Mayor: Segundo Raguin. Typewritten, with carbon copies. Handsigned. Stamped denomination on back.

S858 10 CENTAVOS — GOOD FINE XF
2.6.1943.
- a. Manila paper. — — —
- b. White document paper. — — —

S859 20 CENTAVOS
2.6.1943.
- a. Manila paper. — — —

S861 1 PESO
2.6.1943.
- a. Manila paper. — — —
- b. White document paper. — — —

S862 2 PESOS
2.6.1943.
- a. Manila paper. — — —
- b. White document paper. — — —

S863 5 PESOS
2.6.1943.
- a. Manila paper. — — —
- b. White document paper. — — —

S864 10 PESOS
2.6.1943.
- b. White document paper. — — —

JULY 2, 1943 CIRCULATING PAPER BILL ISSUE

#S867 typewritten, with carbon copies. Handsigned.

S867 5 PESOS — GOOD FINE XF
2.7.1943. Manila paper. Stamped denomination on back. — — —

AUGUST 4, 1943 CIRCULATING PAPER BILL ISSUE

#S870 typewritten, with carbon copies. Handsigned.

S870 2 PESOS — GOOD FINE XF
4.8.1943. Manila paper. Stamped denomination on back. — — —

SEPTEMBER 30, 1943 CIRCULATING PAPER BILL ISSUE

#S873-S876 typewritten, with carbon copies. Handsigned.

S873 1 CENTAVO — GOOD FINE XF
30.9.1943. Manila paper. *ONE 01 CENTAVO* on back. — — —

S874 1 CENTAVO
30.9.1943. Manila paper. *ONE 1 CENTAVO* on back. — — —

S876 5 CENTAVOS
30.9.1943. *FIVE 5 CENTAVOS* on back.
- a. Manila paper.
- b. White document paper. — — —

#S877-S884 stamped denomination on back.

S877 10 CENTAVOS
30.9.1943.
- a. Manila paper. — — —
- b. White document paper. — — —

S878 20 CENTAVOS
30.9.1943.
- a. Manila paper. — — —
- x. Error. Border composed of repeated *V* instead of *H*. — — —

S879 50 CENTAVOS
30.9.1943.
- a. Manila paper. — — —

S880 1 PESO — GOOD FINE XF
30.9.1943.
- a. Manila paper. — — —
- b. White document paper. — — —

		GOOD	FINE	XF
S881	**2 PESOS** 30.9.1943.			
	a. Manila paper.	—	—	—
	b. White document paper.	—	—	—
S883	**5 PESOS** 30.9.1943.			
	a. Manila paper.	—	—	—
	b. White document paper.	—	—	—
S884	**10 PESOS** 30.9.1943.			
	b. White document paper.	—	—	—

ND CIRCULATING PAPER BILL ISSUE

#S887 typewritten, with carbon copies. Handsigned.

		GOOD	FINE	XF
S887	**10 PESOS** ND. White document paper. Stamped denomination on back.	—	—	—

BACUIT

Municipal Mayor: Francisco Abrina Bobis, Sr.
Municipal Treasurer: Bernardo Ola Dangan
Municipal Councilor: Agustin Sabarez Seastres

The Municipality of Bacuit reported a total issue of 14,139.60 pesos. The portion that specified Provincial authority is not known, but it must have been relatively small as only one denomination is presently known.

CIRCULATING PAPER BILL

RESOLUTION NO. 20, SERIES OF 1944, OF THE PROVINCIAL BOARD

#S893 typewritten. White bond paper. Handsigned.

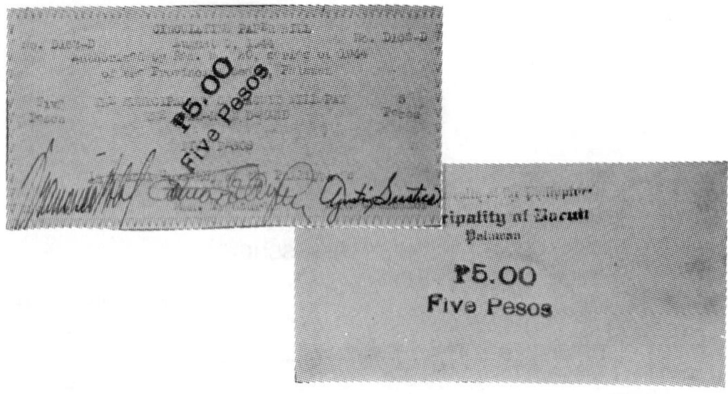

		GOOD	FINE	XF
S893	**5 PESOS** 9.8.1944. Municipal stamping and denomination on back.	—	—	—

BALABAC

Municipal Mayor: Matias Vicente
Municipal Treasurer: Sofronio Aban
Member: Clodualdo Masangkay

The Municipality of Balabac reported a total issue of 3,417 pesos.

RESOLUTIONS NO. 18 AND 19, SERIES 1943 OF THE PROVINCIAL BOARD. FEBRUARY 25, 1943

#S900-S904 typewritten. White bond paper. Handsigned. Embossed seal of Justice of the Peace.

		GOOD	FINE	XF
S900	**50 CENTAVOS** 25.2.1943.	—	—	—
S901	**1 PESO** 25.2.1943. Initial for first names of Members.			
	a. Top 2 lines in lower case letters.	—	—	—
S902	**1 PESO** 25.2.1943. First names of Members spelled out.			
	b. Top 2 lines in upper case letters.	—	—	—

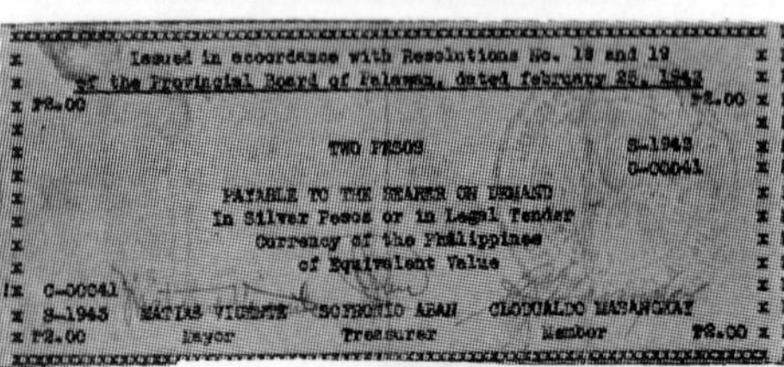

		GOOD	FINE	XF
S904	**2 PESOS** 25.2.1943. First names of Members spelled out.			
	a. Top 2 lines in lower case letters.	—	—	—
	b. Top 2 lines in upper case letters.	—	—	—

BROOKE'S POINT

Chairman: Municipal District Treasurer Eduardo A. Villapa
Member: Municipal District Mayor Saturnino C. Moreno
Alternate and Member: Justice of the Peace Modesto Rodriguez
Member: District Surveyor Paulino Apostol

The original Currency Committee was composed of the Treasurer, Mayor and District Surveyor. Justice of the Peace Rodriguez, commander of the local guerrilla Bolo Battalion, originally served as an alternate because of the poor health of the Mayor, and sometimes signed notes on the Mayor's behalf. When Mayor Moreno died on September 16, 1944, Justice Rodriguez became a full member of the Committee.

Printing of the scrip was a one man operation done entirely by Treasurer Villapa under trying circumstances in what time he could spare from his regular duties as Treasurer and many additional duties (such as Procurement Officer for the Bolo Battalion and the Municipal District). Printing was done partly at his office, partly at his evacuation home some 17 km. distant, where he often printed far into the night. Due to the urgent need for notes almost as soon as authorization arrived, Villapa would stockpile notes which needed only the addition of the *authority*. This accounts for notes being dated earlier or later than the date of authorization, and also for the unissued remainders. While some stockpiled notes were signed in advance by one or both of the two Members, the final signature by Chairman Villapa was not affixed until notes were to be placed in circulation. All unissued remainders bearing any signature were destroyed, so while remainders do exist, they do not have signatures.

The scarcity of paper resulted in almost anything available being utilized - white bond paper, manila wrapping paper, brown paper bags, etc. Those notes described as being printed on cloth were printed on cloth-backed map paper from the Surveyor's office.

All notes were printed by typewriter and carbon paper, and were handsigned by Committee members. Backs have rubber stampings of Treasurer's office, and sometimes a hand with pointing finger. A total of 86,507.60 pesos was issued.

CIRCULATING PAPER BILLS

RESOLUTION NO. 18, SERIES 1943 OF THE PROVINCIAL BOARD

NOTES DATED SEPTEMBER 24, 1943

#S913-S917 typewritten with (a) original copies, (b) black carbon copies. Centavo notes were signed by Justice of the Peace, peso notes by the Mayor.

		GOOD	FINE	XF
S913	**50 CENTAVOS** 19.4.1943. Manila paper.	—	—	—
S914	**1 PESO** 19.4.1943. White bond paper.	—	—	—

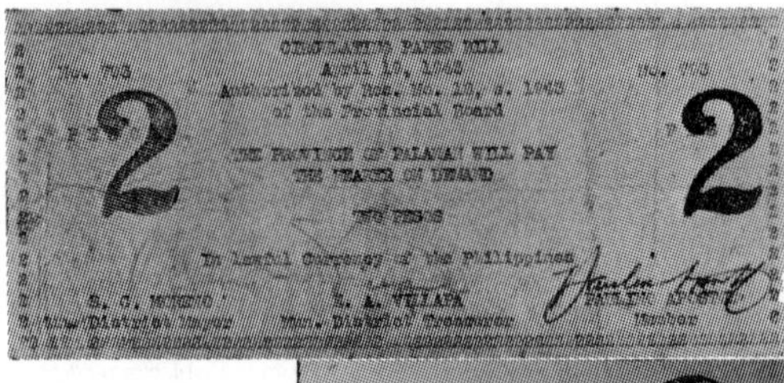

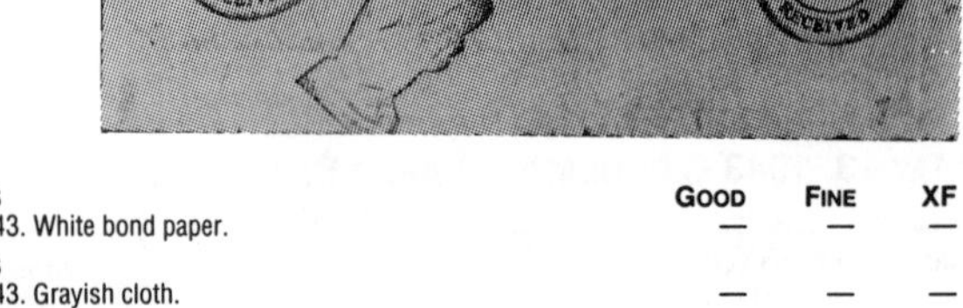

		GOOD	FINE	XF
S915	**2 PESOS** 19.4.1943. White bond paper.	—	—	—
S916	**5 PESOS** 19.4.1943. Grayish cloth.	—	—	—
S917	**10 PESOS** 19.4.1943. Grayish cloth.	—	—	—

RESOLUTION NO. 33, SERIES 1943 OF THE PROVINCIAL BOARD

NOTES DATED SEPTEMBER 24, 1943

#S920-S928 typewritten with (a) original, (b) black carbon, and (c) blue carbon copies. Sizes given are approximate, and may vary several mm.

		GOOD	FINE	XF
S920	**20 CENTAVOS** 24.9.1943. White paper.	—	—	—
S921	**50 CENTAVOS** 24.9.1943. White paper.	—	—	—
S922	**1 PESO** 24.9.1943. Numeral *1* is 25mm high. 133 x 63 mm.			
	a. White paper.	—	—	—
	b. Bluish green paper.	—	—	—

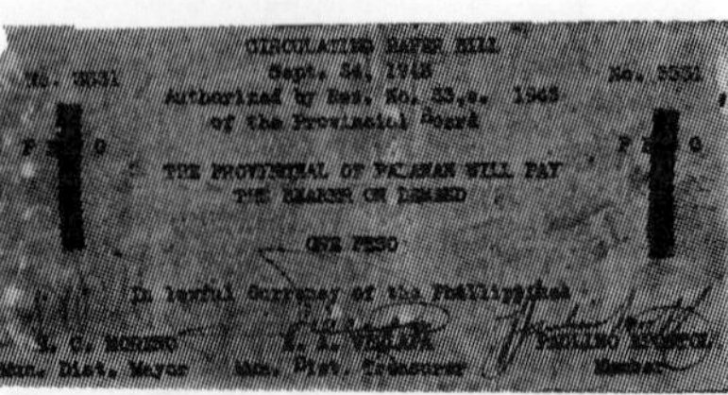

		GOOD	FINE	XF
S923	**1 PESO** 24.9.1943. Numeral *1* is 33mm high. 133 x 63 mm.			
	b. Bluish green paper.	—	—	—

		GOOD	FINE	XF
S924	**1 PESO** 24.9.1943. White paper. 115 x 63mm.	—	—	—
S925	**2 PESOS** 24.9.1943. White paper. 133 x 63mm.	—	—	—
S926	**2 PESOS** 24.9.1943. White document paper. 115 x 63mm.	—	—	—
S928	**5 PESOS** 24.9.1943. Brown paper. 115 x 63mm.	—	—	—

AUTHORIZED LETTER P.T. (PROV. TREAS.) OF NOV. 6, 1943.

NOTES DATED MAY 27, 1944

#S931-S933 typewritten with (a) original, (b) black carbon, and (c) blue carbon copies.

		GOOD	FINE	XF
S931	**1 PESO** 27.5.1944. Manila paper.	—	—	—
S932	**2 PESOS** 27.5.1944. Manila paper.	—	—	—
S933	**5 PESOS** 27.5.1944. Manila paper.	—	—	—

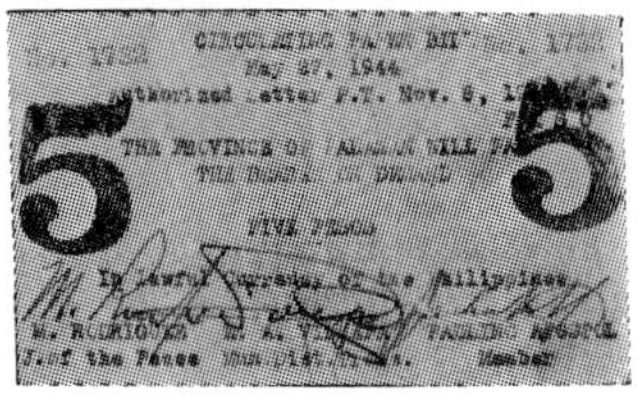

AUTHORIZED LETTER P.T. (PROV. TREAS.) OF MAY 9, 1944.

NOTES DATED MAY 29, 1944

#S935-S940 typewritten with (a) original, (b) black carbon, and (c) blue carbon copies.

		GOOD	FINE	XF
S935	**20 CENTAVOS** 29.5.1944.	—	—	—
S936	**1 PESO** 29.5.1944. Manila paper.	—	—	—
S937	**2 PESOS** 29.5.1944. Manila paper.	—	—	—
S938	**5 PESOS** 29.5.1944. Manila paper.	—	—	—
S940	**20 PESOS** 29.5.1944.	—	—	—

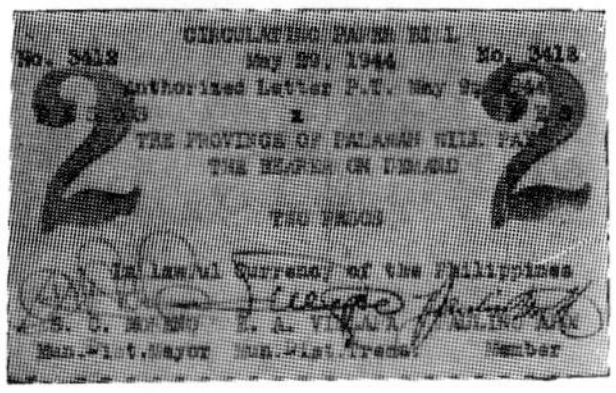

SEPTEMBER 22, 1944 ISSUE

		GOOD	FINE	XF
S945	**20 PESOS** 22.9.1944. Manila paper.	—	—	—

AUTHORIZED LETTER P.T. (PROV. TREAS.) OF OCTOBER 23, 1944

#S948-S955 typewritten with black carbon copies.

		GOOD	FINE	XF
S948	**2 PESOS** May 27, 1944. Unsigned remainder. Brown paper.	—	—	—
S949	**2 PESOS** Jan. 2, 1945. Unsigned remainder. Brown paper.	—	—	—
S950	**5 PESOS** May 27, 1944. Brown paper.	—	—	—
S952	**10 PESOS** May 27, 1944. Brown paper.	—	—	—
S955	**20 PESOS** Jan. 2, 1945. Manila or brown paper.	—	—	—

RESOLUTION NO. 5, SERIES 1944 OF THE PROVINCIAL BOARD

NOTES DATED 1945

#S956-S958 typewritten with black carbon copies. Brown paper.

		GOOD	FINE	XF
S956	**5 PESOS** 1.3.1945. Unsigned remainder.	—	—	—
S957	**5 PESOS** 1.4.1945. Unsigned remainder.	—	—	—
S958	**10 PESOS** 1.3.1945. Unsigned remainder.	—	—	—

CAGAYANCILLO

A total of 17,627.50 pesos was issued, but none are presently known which cite provincial authority.

CORON

A total of 11,260 pesos was issued, but none are presently known which cite provincial authority.

CUYO

Municipal Mayor:	Pedro Ponce de Leon
Acting Municipal Mayor:	Francisco Soto
Municipal Treasurer:	Antero Gabo
Justice of the Peace:	N. Feliciano

Francisco Soto served as Acting Mayor from May 1943 to some time in 1944, during Mayor Ponce de Leon's absence from Cuyo. His name appears only on notes printed under *Resolution No. 43, Series 1943* (#S980-S982).

All notes were printed by mimeograph on white document paper. Denomination is stamped on back along with stamping of the Treasurer's office. A total of 32,600 pesos was issued under Provincial authorization.

CIRCULATING PAPER BILLS

RESOLUTION NO. 18, SERIES 1943 OF THE PROVINCIAL BOARD

AUTHORIZATION 7,600 PESOS FOR PUBLIC WORKS

#S971-S973 mimeographed sign, printed serial #.

		GOOD	FINE	XF
S971	**1 PESO** 1943. Serial #1 to 950.	—	—	—
S972	**2 PESOS** 1943. Serial #1 to 950.	—	—	—
S973	**5 PESOS** 1943. Serial #1 to 950.	—	—	—

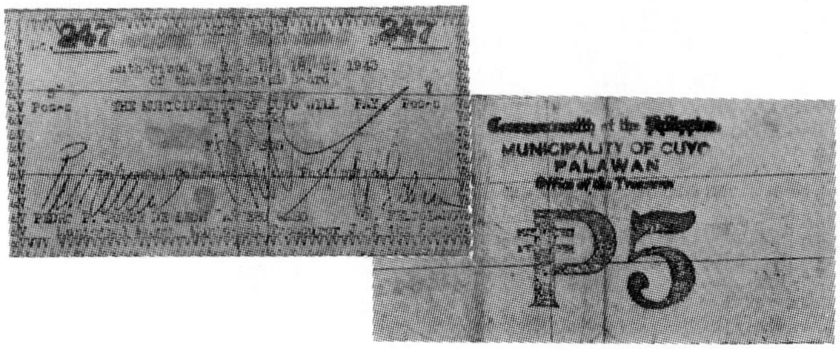

RESOLUTION NO. 18, SERIES 1943 OF THE PROVINCIAL BOARD

AUTHORIZATION 5,000 PESOS FOR TEACHER'S SALARIES

#S974-S976 handsigned. Typewritten serial #.

		GOOD	FINE	XF
S974	**1 PESO** 1943. Serial #951-A to 1,575-A.	—	—	—
S975	**2 PESOS** 1943. Serial # 951-A to 1,575-A.	—	—	—
S976	**5 PESOS** 1943. Serial #951-A to 1,575-A.	—	—	—

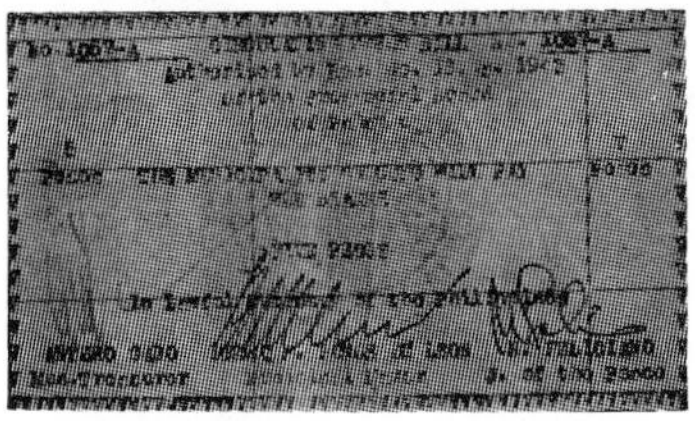

RESOLUTION NO. 42, SERIES 1943 OF THE PROVINCIAL BOARD

AUTHORIZATION 3,000 PESOS FOR CIVILIAN RELIEF

#S977-S979 handsigned. Typewritten serial #.

		GOOD	FINE	XF
S977	**1 PESO** 1943. Serial #1 to 375.	—	—	—
S978	**2 PESOS** 1943. Serial #1 to 375.	—	—	—
S979	**5 PESOS** 1943. Serial #1 to 375.	—	—	—

RESOLUTION NO. 43, SERIES 1943 OF THE PROVINCIAL BOARD

AUTHORIZATION 3,000 PESOS ADDITIONAL FOR CIVILIAN RELIEF

#S980-S982 mimeographed sign. Printed serial #.

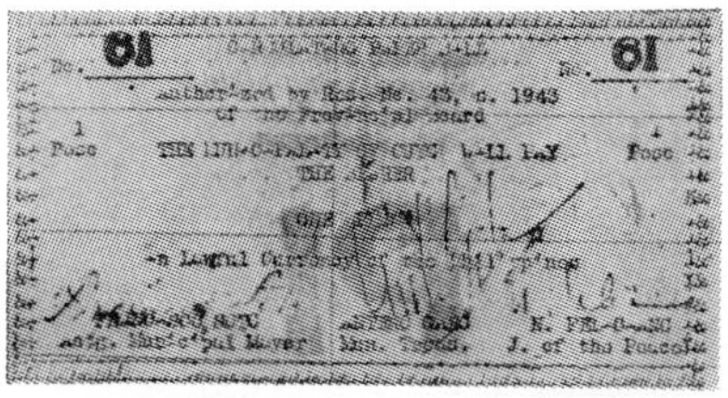

		GOOD	FINE	XF
S980	**1 PESO** 1943. Serial #1 to 375.	—	—	—
S981	**2 PESOS** 1943. Serial #1 to 375.	—	—	—
S982	**5 PESOS** 1943. Serial #1 to 375.	—	—	—

RESOLUTION NO. 5, SERIES 1944 OF THE PROVINCIAL BOARD

AUTHORIZATION 3,000 PESOS FOR FISCAL YEAR 1944-45

#S983-S985 mimeographed sign. Printed serial #.

		GOOD	FINE	XF
S983	**1 PESO** 1944. Serial #1 to 375.	—	—	—

		GOOD	FINE	XF
S984	**2 PESOS** 1944. Serial #1 to 375.	—	—	—
S985	**5 PESOS** 1944. Serial #1 to 375.	—	—	—

RESOLUTION NO. 16, SERIES 1944 OF THE PROVINCIAL BOARD

AUTHORIZATION 6,000 PESOS FOR SALARIES OF TEACHERS

#S986-S988 mimeographed sign. Printed serial #.

		GOOD	FINE	XF
S986	**1 PESO** 1944. Serial #1 to 750.	—	—	—
S987	**2 PESOS** 1944. Serial #1 to 750.	—	—	—

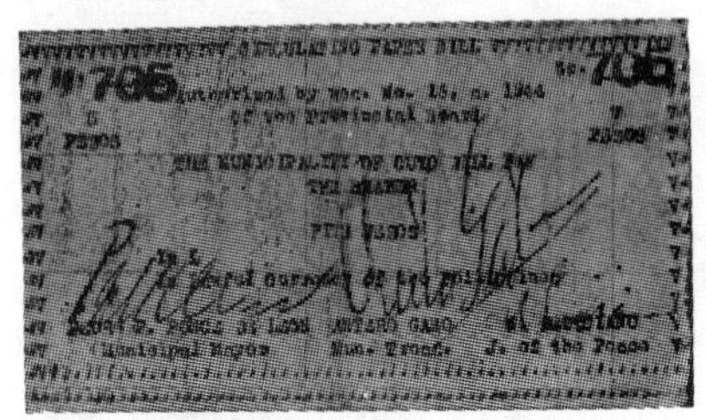

		GOOD	FINE	XF
S988	**5 PESOS** 1944. Serial #1 to 750.	—	—	—

RESOLUTION NO. 29, SERIES 1944 OF THE PROVINCIAL BOARD

AUTHORIZATION 5,000 PESOS FOR USE BY THE PROVINCE

#S989-S991 mimeographed sign. Printed serial #.

		GOOD	FINE	XF
S989	**1 PESO** 1944. Serial #1 to 625.	—	—	—
S990	**2 PESOS** 1944. Serial #1 to 625.	—	—	—
S991	**5 PESOS** 1944. Serial #1 to 625.	—	—	—

DUMARAN

Municipal Mayor: Segundo Blanco
Municipal Treasurer: Eustaquio P. Gacot
Justice of the Peace: Generoso P. Gorja

A total of 21,500 pesos was issued by Dumaran, which includes issues under both municipal and provincial authority. Only the following listed notes are presently known to have been issued under provincial authority.

CIRCULATING PAPER BILLS

AUTHORIZED BY THE GOVERNOR OF PALAWAN

DATED NOVEMBER 9, 1943

#S998 mimeographed. Embossed seal of Justice of the Peace. Typewritten serial #.

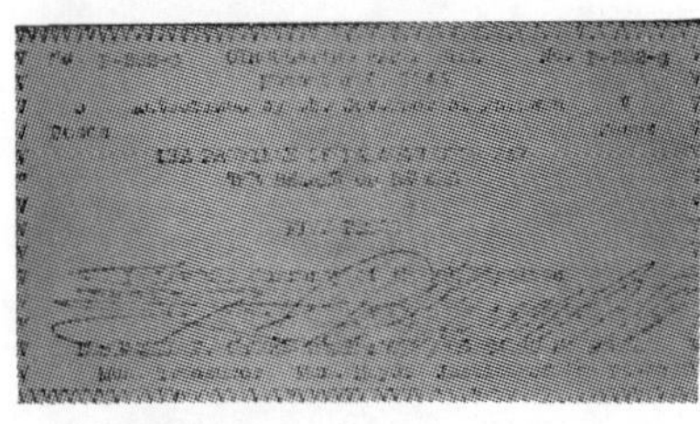

		GOOD	FINE	XF
S998	**5 PESOS** 9.11.1943. *P5* on back. a. White bond paper. b. Manila paper.	 — —	 — —	 — —

RESOLUTION NO. 20, SERIES 1944 OF THE PROVINCIAL BOARD

#S1008 typewritten, w/black carbon copies. Hand signed. Embossed seal of Justice of the Peace.

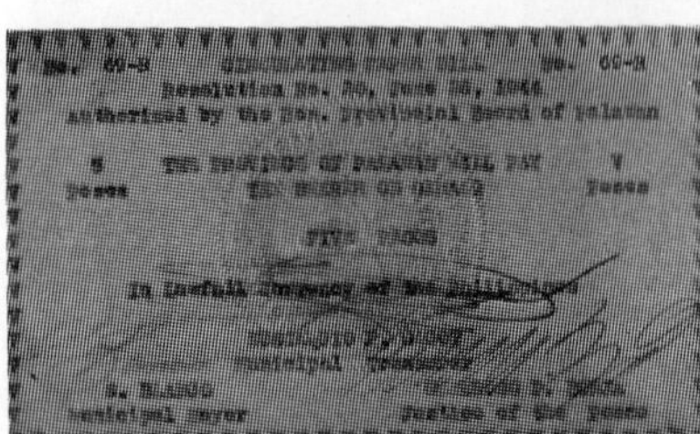

		GOOD	FINE	XF
S1008	**5 PESOS** 26.6.1944. *P5* on back.	—	—	—

NOTE: Neither #S998 nor #S1008 mention Dumaran by name in the text. Only through embossed seals and names of signers can these be ascribed to Dumaran.

PUERTO PRINCESA

Municipal Mayor: Teodoro Malate
Municipal Treasurer: Raymundo Buncag
Municipal Councilor: A. del Oglon (?)

The total issue was small - only 3,890 pesos, and only the 10 Pesos denomination is known.

CIRCULATING PAPER BILLS

RESOLUTION NO. 5, SERIES 1944 OF THE PROVINCIAL BOARD

DATED AUGUST 24, 1944

#S1012 and S1014 manila paper.

		GOOD	FINE	XF
S1012	**10 PESOS** 24.8.1944. Uniface. Typewritten, 134 x 60mm. Handsigned.	—	—	—

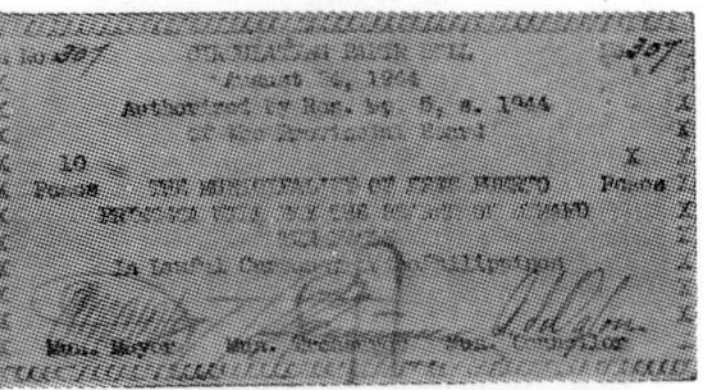

		GOOD	FINE	XF
S1014	**10 PESOS** 24.8.1944. Uniface. Mimeograhped, 115 x 60mm. Handsigned. Pen serial #.	—	—	—

TAYTAY

Municipal Mayor: Francisco H. Alli
Municipal Treasurer: Crispin H. Grande

A total of 29,003.74 pesos was issued, but this included issues under municipal authority.

SMALL CIRCULATING PAPER BILLS

RESOLUTION NO. 18, SERIES 1943 OF THE PROVINCIAL BOARD

DATED APRIL 10, 1943

#S1022 smaller, 128 x 68mm. Typewritten (pica type) w/carbon copies. White paper.

		GOOD	FINE	XF
S1022	**2 PESOS** 10.14.1943. *P2* on back.	—	—	—

LARGE CIRCULATING PAPER BILLS

RESOLUTION NO. 18, SERIES 1943 OF THE PROVINCIAL BOARD

DATED APRIL 10, 1943

#S1026-S1030 larger, 148 x 68mm. Typewritten (elite type) w/carbon copies. White paper.

		GOOD	FINE	XF
S1026	**1 PESO** 10.4.1943. *P1* on back.	—	—	—

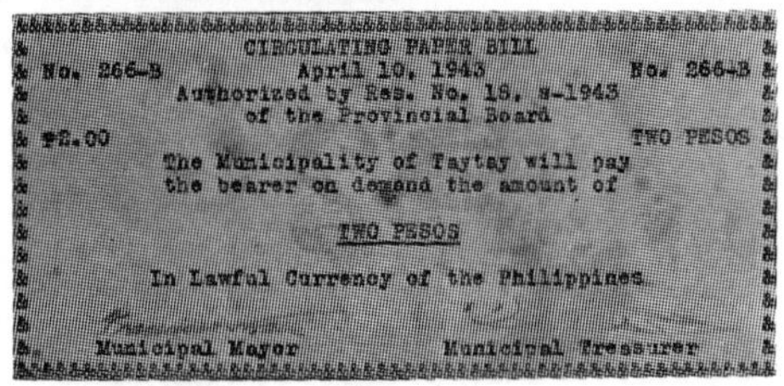

		GOOD	FINE	XF
S1027	**2 PESOS** 10.4.1943. *P2* on back.	—	—	—
S1028	**5 PESOS** 10.4.1943. *P5* on back.	—	—	—
S1030	**20 PESOS** 10.4.1943. *P20* on back.	—	—	—

CIRCULATING PAPER BILLS

RESOLUTION NO. 20, SERIES 1944 OF THE PROVINCIAL BOARD

DATED SEPTEMBER 20, 1944

#S1042-S1045 217 x 68mm. Typewritten (pica type) w/carbon copies. Manila paper.

Municipal Mayor: Francisco H. Alli
Municipal Treasurer: Julio Arzaga
Municipal Councilor: Alejandro Sarabia

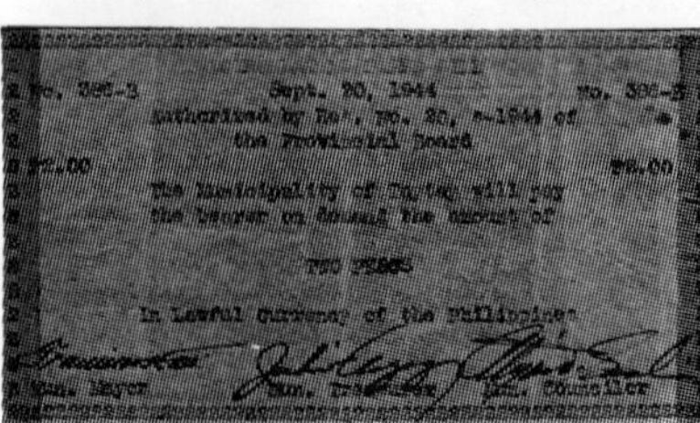

		GOOD	FINE	XF
S1042	**2 PESOS** 20.9.1944. *P2* on back.	—	—	—
S1044	**10 PESOS** 20.9.1944. *P10* on back.	—	—	—
S1045	**20 PESOS** 20.9.1944. *P20* on back.	—	—	—

ROMBLON

The *Province of Romblon* designation on these notes no doubt refers to area of circulation rather than any provincial authority. There was no provincial government in Romblon even prior to the war. The provincial government had been abolished on June 8, 1941 by Commonwealth Act No. 581. To govern the province four *Special Municipalities* were created - Maghali, Romblon, Sibuyan and Tablas.

During the war, the province came under Tomas Confessor's government of *Free Panay and Romblon* (see Iloilo), and what government existed on a provincial level was under a *Supervising Deputy Governor* appointed by Gov. Confessor.

ND FIRST ISSUE

#S1061-S1065 mimeographed on manila paper. Each denomination has a crudely drawn head of an animal on the face. Serial # is on back, along with different combinations of stamped facsimile sign. Quantity issued is not known, but serial # indicate an amount in excess of 25,000 pesos.

	GOOD	FINE	XF
S1061 1 CENTAVO ND. Pig head at ctr., palm tree at either side of head.	—	—	—

	GOOD	FINE	XF
S1062 5 CENTAVOS ND. Ox head at ctr., palm trees like #S1061.	—	—	—

	GOOD	FINE	XF
S1063 10 CENTAVOS ND. Carabao head at ctr., palm trees like #S1061.	—	—	—

	GOOD	FINE	XF
S1064 20 CENTAVOS ND. Horse head at ctr. facing l., lg. leaf at l. and r.	—	—	—

	GOOD	FINE	XF
S1065 50 CENTAVOS ND. Dog head at ctr. facing r., decorative border.	—	—	—

ND SECOND ISSUE

#S1075 and S1076 ornamental design. Printed in purple. Printed sign. on face, serial # on back. White paper.

	GOOD	FINE	XF
S1075 50 CENTAVOS ND.	—	—	—

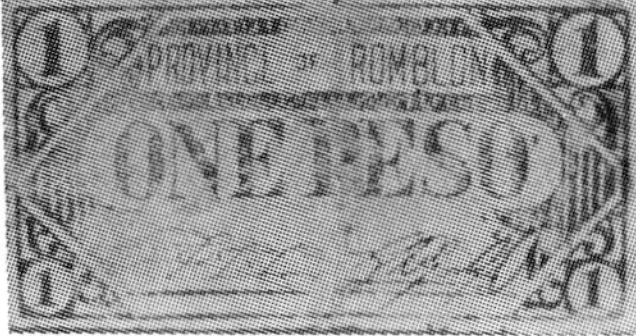

	GOOD	FINE	XF
S1076 1 PESO ND.	—	—	—

SAMAR

At the time of the USAFFE surrender, Samar was garrisoned by little more than three Constabulary Companies under Col. Theodore M. Cornell, Commanding Officer of the 9th Military District (Leyte and Samar). Col. Cornell surrendered on Leyte with perhaps 50 officers and 20 enlisted men. The rest of his command, including the USAFFE forces in Samar, took to the hills or returned home.

From unsurrendered Constabulary soldiers and civilian volunteers small guerrilla units were organized which eventually merged into four main groups.

In the Santa Rita-Zumarraga area in western Samar, former governor Pedro Arteche, with assumed rank of Brigadier General, set up his own separate state, even appointing ministers of Cabinet rank. He was captured by, or surrendered to, the Japanese in early 1944 and his *state* broke up.

Basey was under control of Capt. Luciana Abila. His facsimile signature appears on the back of scrip issued by Basey for local circulation.

Balangiga, Guiuan, Salcedo and Pambujan Sur formed the Southern Samar Sector under command of Manuel Valley. Scrip issued by these four Municipalities would appear to be military issues, but in actuality were authorized by the respective Municipal Councils and circulated only in the Municipality where issued.

All the northern part of Samar was under command of Capt. Pedro V. Merritt, an unsurrendered Army officer. In December 1942 Merritt created a Military Currency Committee which issued 1 and 2 Pesos notes, backed up by Treasury checks, to provide a circulating medium.

In mid-1943 Merritt organized a military government. To support both his guerrilla organization and the military government, the Free Samar Currency *Committee* was organized to print currency. Backing was once again Treasury checks.

On December 1, 1943, Merritt appointed a Free Samar Provincial Government which in turn created the Free Samar Currency *Board* which issued emergency currency. Notes printed by these three committees or boards circulated throughout all of Samar and were subsequently officially recognized and accepted for postwar redemption.

Currency authorized by the Free Samar Currency Committee and Board was printed by the Rev. Alejandro Froilan who personally carved the border cuts from hardwood. Printing ink and two cuts of the Commonwealth seal were obtained from the Printing Department of the puppet government in Manila, through the assistance of Mr. Serafin Marabut, an official in that government. Paper was obtained by commandeering all paper bags in stores and groceries, and also using official forms from municipal buildings.

In early 1944, the Japanese invaded Samar with large forces. Realizing that the currency being produced by Rev. Froilan was the backbone of guerrilla operations, the Japanese posted a 100,000 peso reward for his head. During all of 1944 the printing section under Rev. Froilan became a mobile operation, constantly moving from place to place to avoid capture by the Japanese.

The Samar guerrilla groups, hard pressed by the Japanese, finally agreed to unite under command of anyone designated by Gen. MacArthur. On October 4, 1944 MacArthur appointed Lt. Col. Charles M. Smith, then in Samar on an intelligence mission, as Commanding Officer of the Samar Area Command.

USAFFE CURRENCY BOARD

In order to provide *cash* to pay his soldiers and to purchase supplies, Capt. Pedro V. Merritt created the USAFFE (Samar) Currency Board composed of himself and Lt. Pedro M. Bautista, his Finance Officer. A total of 70,000 pesos in 1 and 2 Pesos notes was authorized; Treasury checks totaling 70,829.50 pesos were the backing for these notes.

The notes were, originally, mimeographed on postal money order forms obtained from 19 different post offices. Each money order form bore two sets of numbers: the post office number, and the serial number of the money order. By separating the money order forms into two portions, two notes could be printed with identical numbers. The smaller portion was used for 1 Peso notes, the larger portion for 2 Pesos notes. The money order forms came in two colors, pink for peso money orders, and yellow for dollar money orders.

When the available supply of money order forms was exhausted, an additional printing took place on manila paper.

This committee was officially dissolved on August 15, 1943, by which time 37,230 pesos had been printed.

ND FIRST ISSUE

#S1081-S1084 mimeographed on Postal Money Order forms.

	GOOD	FINE	XF
S1081 1 PESO ND. Pink money order form. *ONE PESO* on back.	—	—	—
S1082 1 PESO ND. Yellow money order form. *ONE PESO* on back.	—	—	—

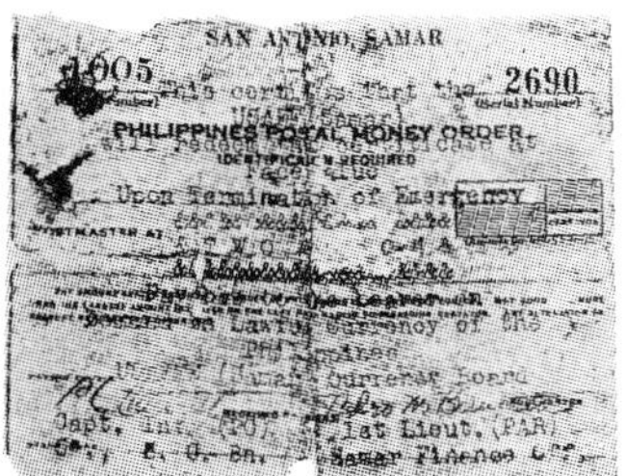

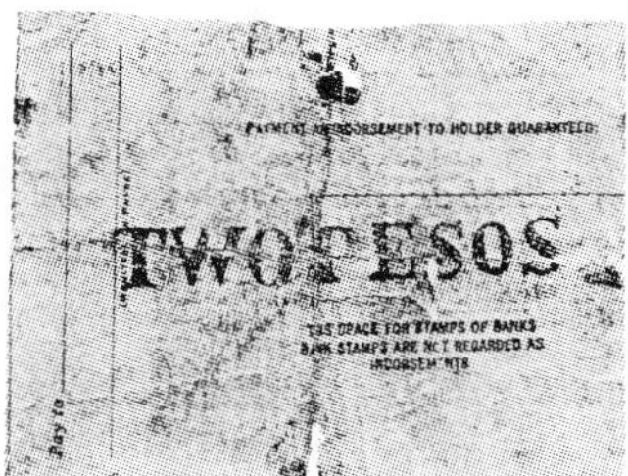

	GOOD	FINE	XF
S1083 2 PESOS ND. Pink money order form. *TWO PESOS* on back.	—	—	—
S1084 2 PESOS ND. Yellow money order form. *TWO PESOS* on back.	—	—	—

ND SECOND ISSUE

#S1085 and S1086 mimeographed on manila paper.

	GOOD	FINE	XF
S1085 1 PESO ND. *ONE PESO* on back. Serial #00001 to 01,100.	—	—	—
S1086 2 PESOS ND. *TWO PESOS* on back. Serial #00001 to 01,100.	—	—	—

FREE SAMAR CURRENCY COMMITTEE

The Free Samar Currency Committee was appointed by Capt. Pedro V. Merritt on July 5, 1943.

The Committee was composed of Deputy Military Governor Vicente A. Dira as Chairman, with Assistant Chief of Staff Lt. Pedro Bautista and Military Auditor Pedro Rama as Members.

A total of 428,900 pesos was authorized, and backing consisted of checks, money orders and vouchers borrowed from Municipal Treasurers. Final delivery from the press was on December 29, 1943, by which time 280,000 pesos of the authorized amount hand been printed.

1943 TREASURY EMERGENCY CURRENCY CERTIFICATE ISSUE

AUSA Free Samar 1943

Printed from metal type, wood border cuts and facsimile sign. Stamped facsimile sign. of Chairman Dira and Auditor Rama on back.

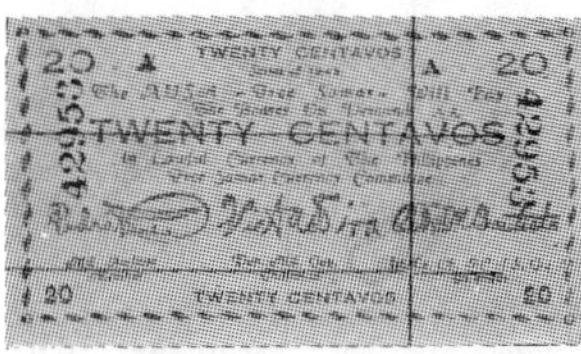

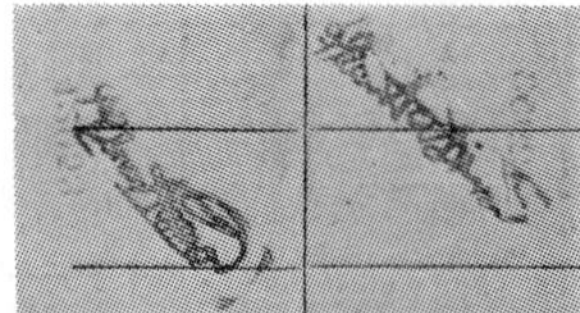

		Good	Fine	XF
S1090	**20 Centavos**			
	1943. Facsimile sign. stamped in purple on back. Serial #A0001 to A50,000.			
	a. White document paper.	8.00	17.50	35.00
	b. Off-white document or ledger paper.	8.00	17.50	35.00
	c. Manila document paper.	10.00	20.00	45.00
S1091	**50 Centavos**			
	1943. *SERIES OF 1943* in 2 lines at top. Stamped sign. in black on back. Serial #A0001 to A20,000.			
	a. White paper.	17.50	35.00	—
	b. Brown paper.	17.50	35.00	—

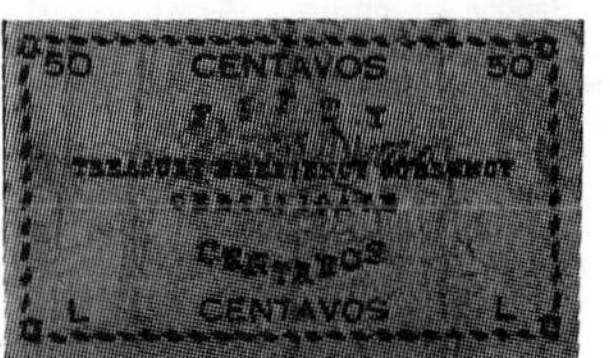

		Good	Fine	XF
S1092	**50 Centavos**			
	1943. *Series of 1943* in 1 line at top. Stamped sign. in black on back. Manila or brown paper. Serial # B0001 to B20,000.	12.50	25.00	50.00
S1093	**50 Centavos**			
	1943. *Series of 1943* in 1 line. Inverted border. Stamped sign. in purple on back. Manila or brown paper. Serial #C0001 to C20,000.	15.00	30.00	—

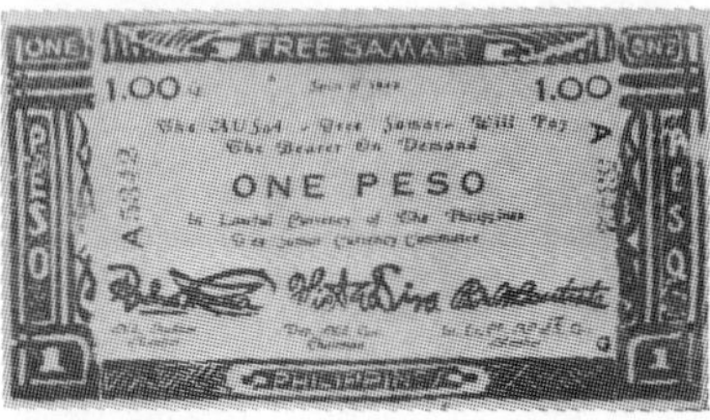

		Good	Fine	XF
S1094	**1 Peso**			
	1943. Neat *FREE SAMAR* 3mm high. Lg. facsimile sign. stamped in black on back. Manila or brown paper. Serial #A0001 to A10,000.	7.50	15.00	—
S1095	**1 Peso**			
	1943. Crude *FREE SAMAR* 2mm high. Sm. facsimile sign. stamped in purple on back. Manila or brown paper. Serial #B0001 to B10,000; C0001 to C10,000; D0001 to D10,000; E0001 to E10,000.	7.50	15.00	25.00
S1096	**2 Pesos**			
	1943. *FREE SAMAR* 2mm high. Manila or brown paper. Serial #A0001 to (approx.) A5,200.			
	a. Lg. facsimile sign. on back. Serial #0001 to (approx.) 4,900.	12.50	25.00	—
	b. Sm. facsimile sign. on back. Serial # (approx.) 5,000 to 5,200.	—	—	—

		Good	Fine	XF
S1097	**2 Pesos**			
	1943. *FREE SAMAR* 3 1/2mm high. Sm. purple facsimile sign. on back. Thin to thick brown paper. Serial # (approx.) A5,201 to A10,000; B0001 to B10,000.	10.00	20.00	45.00
S1098	**5 Pesos**			
	1943. *FREE SAMAR* 4mm high. Lg. facsimile sign. in black on back. White paper. Serial #A0001 to (approx.) A1,000.	—	—	—

		Good	Fine	XF
S1099	**5 Pesos**			
	1943. *FREE SAMAR* 2mm high. Lg. sign. as #S1098. Manila or brown paper. Serial # (approx.) A2,300 to A10,000; B0001 to B10,000; C0001 to (approx.) C4,000.	7.50	17.50	35.00
S1100	**5 Pesos**			
	1943. Crude *FREE SAMAR* 3mm high. Sm. purple facsimile sign. on back. Manila or brown paper. Serial # (approx.) C4,300 to C10,000.	10.00	20.00	—

NOTE: Some denominations may be found with serial # either 3-1/2 or 4mm high.

Free Samar Currency Board

Administrative Order No. 4, issued by Maj. Pedro V. Merritt on December 1, 1943 appointed Gregorio B. Abogado as Governor of Free Samar, with instructions to form a civil government. The *Provincial Government of Free Samar* was formally organized on December 12. At the first meeting of the Provincial Board on December 14 a Free Samar Currency Board was appointed with authority to print 500,000 pesos.

The Currency Board was composed of Provincial Auditor Escolastico G. Chicano as Chairman, with Provincial Treasurer Mateo C. Taala and Provincial Fiscal Valeriano del Valle as Members.

In April, 1942 President Quezon had authorized the Province of Samar to print emergency currency up to the amount of the Province's unencumbered deposits in the Philippine National Bank, said deposits amounting to 1,300,000 pesos. A Currency Board was in fact created, consisting of the (then) Provincial Auditor, Treasurer and Fiscal, but the surrender of the USAFFE occurred before any notes could be printed. This authority was the basis for printing emergency currency by this, the third, board.

On April 20, 1944 the Provincial Board by *Resolution No. 8* increased the authorized amount to 1,000,000 pesos. Later, by *Resolution No. 9* the Provincial Board again increased the amount authorized by another 500,000 pesos. As this exceeded Presidential authorization by 200,000 pesos, the excess was to be charged to the U.S. Army for financing the Samar Combat Intelligence Unit organized per instructions of Gen. MacArthur.

Printing ceased on September 30, 1944, by which time 1,411,000 pesos had been printed.

1943 Treasury Emergency Currency Certificate Issue

Printed from metal type, wood border and facsimile sign. cuts. Cuts for the Commonwealth seal were secretly obtained from the Bureau of Printing in Manila. On 10 and 20 Centavos notes seal and serial numbers are in purple, on other denominations both are in red. Facsimile sign. of all three Members were also stamped in purple on the back.

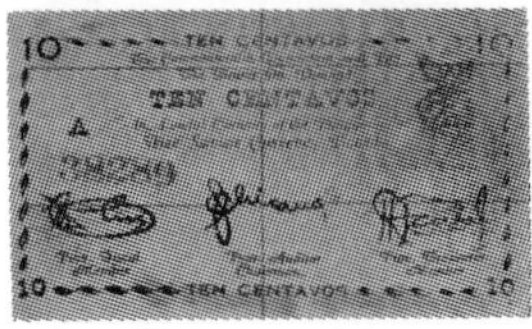

		Good	Fine	XF
S1101	**10 Centavos**			
	1943. Denomination in black on back. Serial # for S1101 and S1102: A 0,001 to 60,000.			
	a. White document paper.	10.00	17.50	37.50
	b. Off-white document paper.	10.00	17.50	37.50
	c. Manila paper.	10.00	17.50	37.50
S1102	**10 Centavos**			
	1943. Denomination in purple on back. Serial # mixed with #S1101. Off-white paper.	—	—	—

		Good	Fine	XF
S1103	**20 Centavos**			
	1943. Denomination in black on back. Serial #A 0,001 to 50,000.			
	a. White document paper.	6.00	12.00	25.00
	b. Manila paper.	6.00	12.00	25.00
	x. Error; denomination omitted from back.	—	—	—

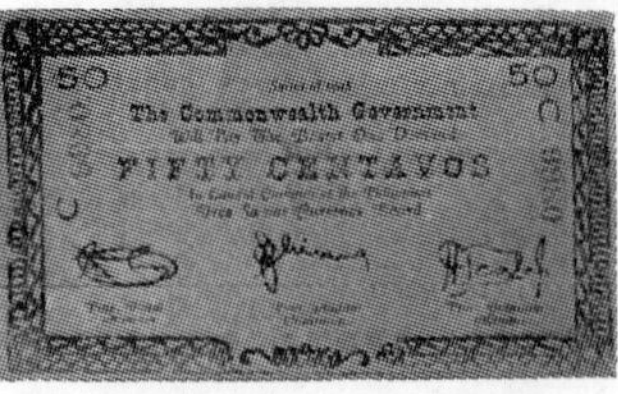

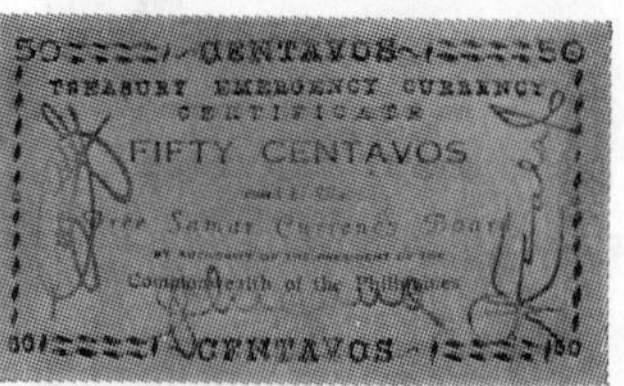

		Good	Fine	XF
S1105	**50 Centavos**			
	1943. Manila paper. Serial #A 0,001 to 20,000; B 0,001 to 20,000; C 0,001 to 20,000.	6.00	12.00	25.00
S1106	**1 Peso**			
	1943. Manila or brown paper. Serial #A 0,001 to 10,000; B 0,001 to 10,000; C 0,001 to 10,000; D 0,001 to 10,000; E 0,001 to 10,000.	6.00	12.00	25.00
S1107	**2 Pesos**			
	1943. Neat border plate. Manila paper. Serial #A 0,001 to 10,000; B 0,001 to 10,000; C 0,001 to (approx.) 8,000.	6.00	12.00	25.00
S1108	**2 Pesos**			
	1943. Worn border plate, blurred printing. Manila paper. Serial #C (approx.) 8,001 to 10,000; D 0,001 to 10,000.	6.00	12.00	25.00

		Good	Fine	XF
S1109	**2 Pesos** 1943. New, neat border plate. Manila paper. Serial #E 0,001 to 10,000.	5.00	10.00	20.00

		Good	Fine	XF
S1110	**5 Pesos** 1943. *FIVE PESOS* at top 3mm high. Manila paper. Serial # (series A, low numbers).	—	—	—

		Good	Fine	XF
S1111	**5 Pesos** 1943. Worn plate, blurred printing. Border line above *PESOS* at top slopes downward. Manila or brown paper. Serial # (series A, high numbers; series B, low numbers).	8.00	15.00	—
S1112	**5 Pesos** 1943. Badly worn plate, blurred printing. Line above *PESOS* at top is horizontal. Manila or brown paper. Serial # (series B, high numbers).	—	—	—

NOTE: On #S1110-S1112 serial # A 0,001 to 10,000; B 0,001 to 10,000.

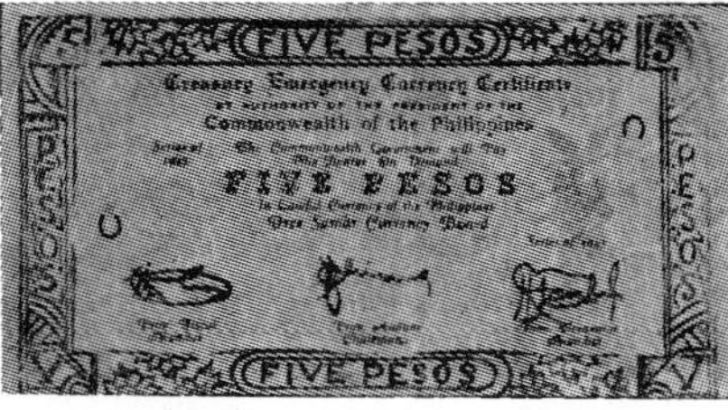

		Good	Fine	XF
S1113	**5 Pesos** 1943. New, neat border plate. *FIVE PESOS* at top is 3 3/4mm high. Serial #C 0,001 to 10,000; D 0,001 to 10,000; E 0,001 to 10,000.			
	a. White paper.	8.00	15.00	—
	b. Manila paper.	8.00	15.00	—

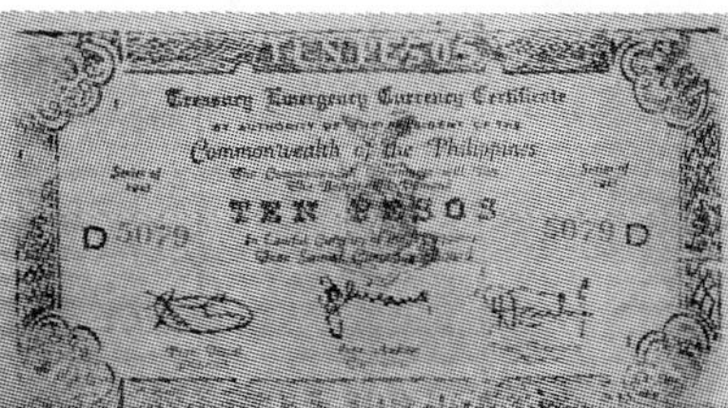

		Good	Fine	XF
S1114	**10 Pesos** 1943. Brown paper. Winged *X* at ctr. on back. Serial #A 0,001 to 10,000; B 0,001 to 10,000; C 0,001 to 10,000; D 0,001 to 10,000; E 0,001 to 10,000.	7.50	15.00	25.00

NOTE: Serial # on all denominations may be either 3-1/2 or 4mm high. They are not listed as sub-varieties because those printed in red are often faded to the point of illegibility.

1944 Issue

#S1116-S1120 face like #S1106-S1114.

		Good	Fine	XF
S1116	**1 Peso** 1944. Manila or brown paper. New back design. Serial #F 0,001 to 10,000.	7.50	15.00	35.00

		Good	Fine	XF
S1117	**2 Pesos** 1944. Manila or brown paper. New back design. Serial #F 0,001 to 10,000; G 0,001 to 10,000; H 0,001 to 10,000; I 0,001 to 10,000; J 0,001 to 10,000.	7.50	15.00	25.00
S1118	**5 Pesos** 1944. White paper. Serial #F 0,001 to 10,000.	7.50	15.00	35.00
S1119	**10 Pesos** 1944. Brown paper. Serial #F 0,001 to 6,000.	10.00	22.50	50.00

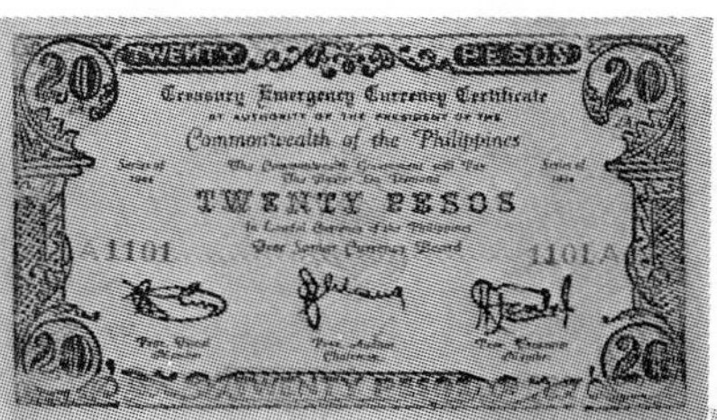

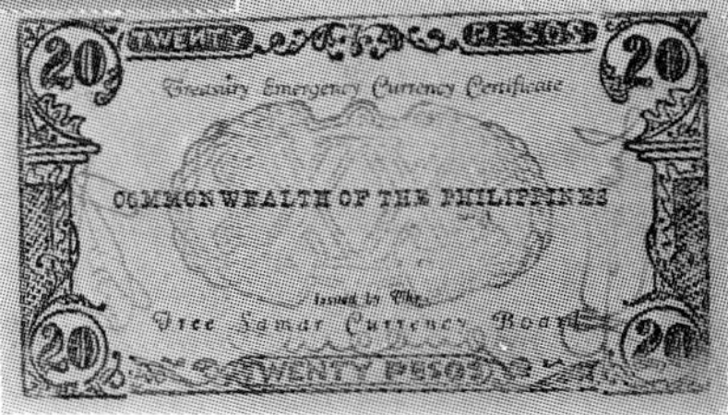

		Good	Fine	XF
S1120	**20 Pesos** 1944. Denominational guilloche in red on back. White paper. Serial #A 0,001 to 10,000; B 0,001 to 2,500.	8.00	20.00	45.00

Sulu and British North Borneo

The hereditary lands of the *Sultanate of Sulu* comprised all of British North Borneo and part of Sarawak. This was recognized by the British government through a treaty in 1880 under which a stipend of 5,000 pounds was paid annually to the Sultan of Sulu. This continued up to the death of Sultan Madji Mohammad Jamal-ul Kiram II on June 7, 1936 who left no direct heir. The resultant rivalry for the Sultanate by various factions led by *Datus* and *Hajis* was never resolved.

In March 1938 President Quezon appointed *Datu* Ombra Amilbangsa Governor of Sulu. In the November 1941 elections Sultan (courtesy title) Ombra was elected to the Philippine Senate. To fill the vacant office of Governor, President Quezon on December 4, 1941 appointed Maj. Alejandro Suarez Acting Governor and, concurrently, Inspector of Constabulary for the Province of Sulu.

On December 24, 1941 the Japanese *Sakaguchi Detachment* landed in Kaunayan, Jolo island. Led by Maj. Suarez, the Jolo Constabulary unit inflicted heavy losses on the invaders before being forced to withdraw into the hills.

Maj. Suarez went to Zamboanga hoping to procure arms and supplies, but instead, was ordered to Lanao Province to serve on the Staff of Gen. Guy O. Fort, with a promotion to Lieutenant Colonel. He surrendered with Gen. Fort on May 30, 1942.

After escaping, on February 9, 1943 Col. Suarez assumed command of guerrilla forces in eastern Jolo, Siasi and Tawi Tawi, locating his headquarters in Bato Bato. These units became part of Col. Fertig's *Mindanao-Sulu Command* (later redesignated the *10th Military District)* known as the *125th Division.*

In the Jesselton area of British North Borneo, Dr. Albert I. N. Kwok had secretly organized an underground movement of Overseas Chinese. As trade between North Borneo and the Sulu islands continued despite Japanese occupation, Dr. Kwok soon learned of the Sulu guerrillas. In April 1943 he visited Col. Suarez and was commissioned a lieutenant in the *Mindanao-Sulu Command.* Returning to North Borneo, he organized what became known as the Kinabalu Guerrillas.

The Overseas Chinese in North Borneo contributed generously to the Sulu guerrillas, sending quinine and other badly needed medicines as well as tens of thousands of dollars in British North Borneo currency. This currency circulated freely in Sulu, along with 20,000 pesos in Mindanao currency sent by Col. Fertig.

In mid-1943, intelligence agents sent by Gen. MacArthur arrived with radio transmitters and set up coast-watcher stations in the Sulu islands and North Borneo. Their reports of Japanese shipping enabled U.S. submarines to take a heavy toll of Japanese shipping, and the area was considered of such importance that in February 1944 the Sulu islands were separated from Col. Fertig's command by Gen. MacArthur who appointed Col. Suarez Commanding Officer of the *Sulu Area Command.*

FREE SULU PROVINCIAL GOVERNMENT

One of the most important activities of the *125th Infantry* was the establishment of a Free Sulu government. The Free Government was given the mission to procure and store food supplies and *to print emergency currency to finance the activities of the military forces and the civil government of Sulu.*

As far as is presently known, no currency was printed for the purpose of financing the Sulu guerrillas. It is quite possible that the currency referred to was the low denomination notes printed to provide small change.

Two such issues are known. Both were authorized by Colonel (and Acting Governor) Suarez, and were backed up by an equivalent amount of large denomination notes held in a special *Trust Fund* by the Finance Officer of the *125th Infantry Division.* This *Trust Fund* was used to redeem the notes after the war.

1943 TUBIG-INDANGAN ISSUE

Mimeographed on white paper. Dated Tubig-Indangan, Sulu April 26, 1943. Notes have both mimeographed and pen signature of Harun Alibasa, Treasurer.

		Good	Fine	XF
S1132	**2 CENTAVOS** 26.4.1943. *2¢* on back.	—	Rare	—

125TH INFANTRY REGIMENT

1943 EMERGENCY MONEY ISSUE

#S1141-S1145 mimeographed on white paper. Stamped with crude cut of an eagle. Mimeographed sign. of Col. Suarez. Pen sign. of Regimental Finance Officer and Auditor. Two different dates presently known.

		Good	Fine	XF
S1141	**5 CENTAVOS** July 1943. *5* on back.	—	Rare	—
S1143	**20 CENTAVOS** July 1943. *20* on back.	—	Rare	—
S1144	**50 CENTAVOS** Dec. 1943. *50* on back.	—	Rare	—
S1145	**1 PESO** Dec. 1943. *P1.00* on back.	—	Rare	—

ZAMBOANGA

ZAMBOANGA CITY ISSUES

This is one of twelve Cities in the Philippines. In population around 132,000, but in land area one of the largest Cities in the world as its Charter included a good portion of the Zamboanga peninsula, the island of Basilan, and numerous smaller islands. It was also the capital of Zamboanga Province.

In early 1942, the shortage of currency necessitated issuance of *couponized checks.* There were four simultaneous issues; two by banks, and one each by the city and province. That all were provincially authorized is evident from their common design, and that all have the embossed "Official Seal" of the Provincial "Treasury," although it is often barely discernible.

Printed uniface on white paper, made payable to "bearer" and void 90 days after the blue stamped date of issue, each note is perforated on the left edge which permitted separation from its counterfoil. Stamped dates range from February 5 to April 30, 1942.

The latter date is intriguing because the City was invaded by the Japanese on March 2, 1942. They occupied the harbor area, the Poblacion, and presumably also the banks where the *couponized checks* had to be presented for payment.

1942 SERIES A ISSUE

#S1161-S1165 signed by Cashier Rafael Paredes, Sr. *for* Manager, and by Accountant Mateo Paulino, of Philippine National Bank.

		Good	Fine	XF
S1161	**50 CENTAVOS** 1942. Green.	—	—	—
S1162	**1 PESO** 1942. Red.	—	—	—
S1163	**2 PESOS** 1942. Blue.	—	—	—
S1164	**5 PESOS** 1942. Black.	—	—	—

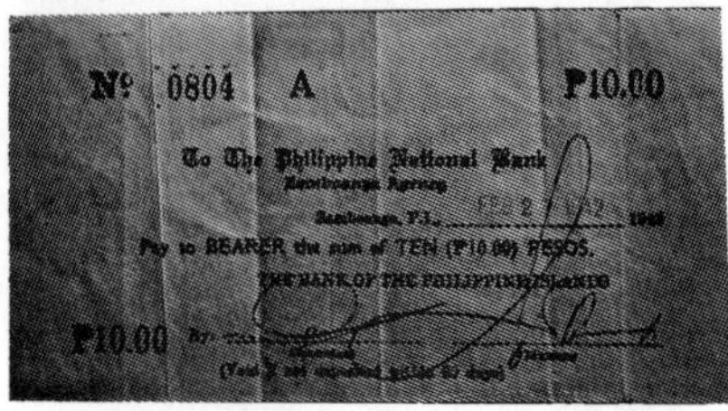

		Good	Fine	XF
S1165	**10 PESOS** 1942. Black.	—	—	—

1942 SERIES B ISSUE

#S1166-S1170 signed by Assistant City Treasurer L. R. Barinaca and City Auditor Jose G. Concepcion.

		Good	Fine	XF
S1166	**50 CENTAVOS** 1942. Green.	—	—	—
S1167	**1 PESO** 1942. Red.	—	—	—
S1168	**2 PESOS** 1942. Blue.	—	—	—
S1169	**5 PESOS** 1942. Black.	—	—	—
S1170	**10 PESOS** 1942. Black.	Reported Not Confirmed		

1942 SERIES C ISSUE

#S1171-S1175 signed by Cashier, and either *by* or *for* Agent of Bank of the Philippine Islands.

		Good	Fine	XF
S1171	**50 CENTAVOS** 1942. Green.			
	a. Signed by Cashier and Agent.	25.00	—	—
	b. Signed by Cashier and *for* Agent.	25.00	—	—

		Good	Fine	XF
S1172	**1 PESO** 1942. Red.			
	b. Signed by Cashier and *for* Agent.	—	—	—
S1173	**2 PESOS** 1942. Blue.			
	b. Signed by Cashier and *for* Agent.	—	—	—
S1174	**5 PESOS** 1942. Black.			
	a. Signed by Cashier and Agent.	—	—	—
	b. Signed by Cashier and *for* Agent.	—	—	—
S1175	**10 PESOS** 1942. Black.	Reported Not Confirmed		

1942 SERIES D ISSUE

#S1176-S1180 two different date stamps used, 3-1/2mm high and 5mm high.

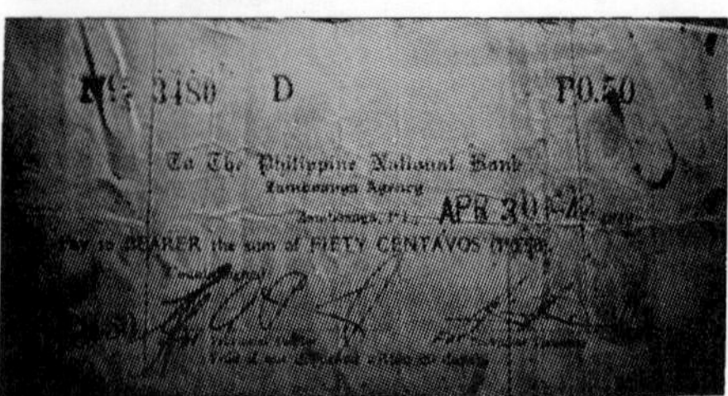

		Good	Fine	XF
S1176	**50 CENTAVOS** 1942. Green.			
	a. Signed by Provincial Treasurer Lazaro J. Agapito, and *for* Provincial Auditor. Serial #0,001 to (approx.) 0.812.	—	—	—
	b. Signed *for* Provincial Treasurer stamped facsimile sign. in violet of Provincial Auditor. (Only #1001 seen).	—	—	—
	c. Signed *for* Provincial Treasurer, and *for* Provincial Auditor. Serial # (approx.) 1,398 upward.	—	—	—
S1177	**1 PESO** 1942. Red.			
	c. Signed *for* Prov. Treasurer, and *for* Prov. Auditor.	—	—	—

		GOOD	FINE	XF
S1178	**2 PESOS**			
	1942. Blue.			
	c. Signed *for* Prov. Treasurer, and *for* Prov. Auditor.	—	—	—
S1179	**5 PESOS**			
	1942. Black.			
	c. Signed *for* Prov. Treasurer, and *for* Prov. Auditor.	—	—	—
S1180	**10 PESOS**			
	1942. Black.	Reported Not Confirmed		

ZAMBOANGA PROVINCE ISSUE

Following the Japanese invasion of Zamboanga City on March 2, 1942, the provincial government was transferred to the Municipality of Dipolog in the northern part of the province.

A telegram from Gen. Roxas, Secretary to President Quezon, dated April 8, 1942 authorized the Provincial Treasurer to advance whatever funds were necessary for continued operation of local governments. Cash for this purpose was to be obtained from the Mindanao Emergency Currency Board if possible, but *otherwise to be printed locally.*

In early May 1942, the Provincial Board passed a *Resolution* creating a Currency Committee which was composed of Provincial Treasurer Lazaro J. Alfabeto as Chairman, with Acting Provincial Governor Felipe B. Azcuna and Acting Provincial Auditor Ireneo Barbasa as Members. This Committee functioned from May 21 to June 15, 1942.

Notes were printed by the Rev. Angel Soto on a small hand press. A total of 44,000 pesos was issued.

PHILIPPINE NATIONAL BANK - ZAMBOANGA

1942 EMERGENCY CIRCULATING NOTE ISSUE

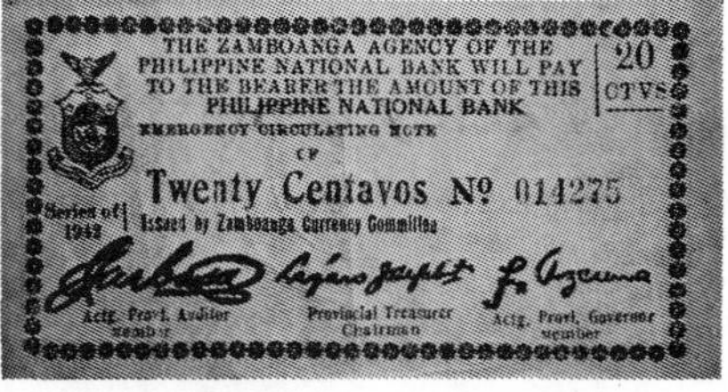

		GOOD	FINE	XF
S1181	**20 CENTAVOS**			
	1942. Manila paper. Serial #000,001 to 020,000.	—	—	—
S1182	**50 CENTAVOS**			
	1942. Manila paper. Serial #000,001 to 020,000.	45.00	85.00	—

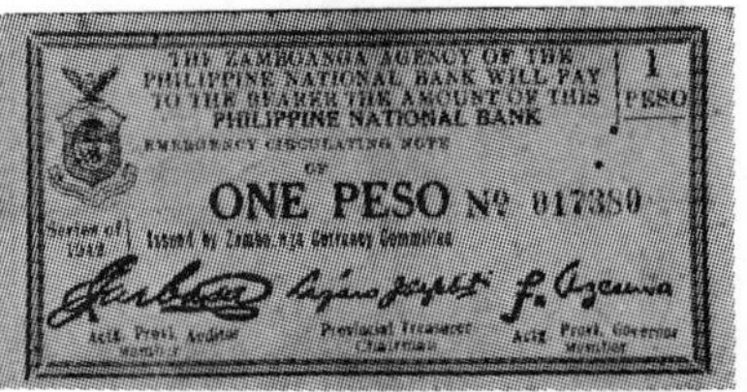

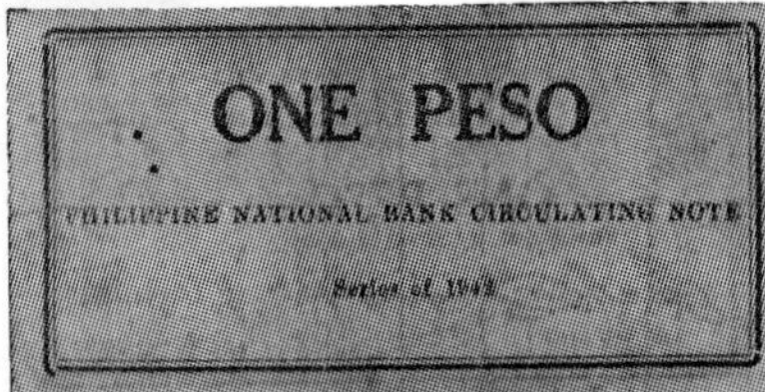

		GOOD	FINE	XF
S1183	**1 PESO**			
	1942. White paper. Serial #000,001 to 030,000.			
	a. *"Porvl."* Governor (misspelling). Highest Serial # seen - 000457.	—	—	—
	b. Corrected spelling. Lowest Serial # seen - 001257.	45.00	85.00	125.00
	x. Counterfeit.	—	—	—

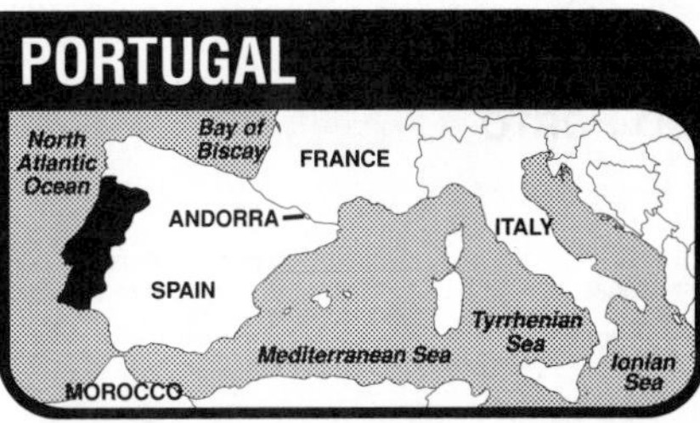

The Portuguese Republic, located in the western part of the Iberian Peninsula in southwestern Europe, has an area of 35,553 sq. mi. (91,905 sq. km.) and a population of 9.79 million. Capital: Lisbon. Portugal's economy is based on agriculture and a small but expanding industrial sector. Textiles, machinery, chemicals, wine and cork are exported.

After centuries of domination by Romans, Visigoths and Moors, Portugal emerged in the 12th century as an independent kingdom financially and philosophically prepared for the great period of exploration that would follow. Attuned to the inspiration of Prince Henry the Navigator (1394-1460), Portugal's daring explorers of the 14th and 15th centuries roamed the world's oceans from Brazil to Japan in an unprecedented burst of energy and endeavor that culminated in 1494 with Portugal laying claim to half the transoceanic world. Unfortunately for the fortunes of the tiny kingdom, the Portuguese proved to be inept colonizers. Less than a century after Portugal laid claim to half the world, English, French and Dutch trading companies had seized the lion's share of the world's colonies and commerce, and Portugal's place as an imperial power was lost forever. The Príncipe).

MONETARY SYSTEM:

1 Escudo = 100 Centavos, 1910-

BANKS

TREASURY FOR COMMODITIES

PUBLIC UTILITIES

BANKS

BANCO ALLIANÇA

1870'S ISSUE

#S141-S145 arms at l. Printer: Nissen and Parker, London.

		GOOD	FINE	XF
S141	**10,000 REIS**			
	18xx (ca.1870). Red-brown.	—	—	—
S142	**20,000 REIS**			
	18xx (ca.1870). Lt. red-brown. Unissued remainder.	—	—	—
S143	**20,000 REIS**			
	18xx. Blue. Like #S142.	—	—	—
S144	**50,000 REIS**			
	2.1.1873. Blue.	—	—	—
S145	**100,000 REIS**			
	18xx (ca.1870). Orange. Unissued remainder.	—	—	—

BANCO COMMERCIAL DE BRAGA

1870'S ISSUE

		GOOD	FINE	XF
S151	**20,000 REIS** 18xx. Black and orange. 4 cartouches and statue in counterfoil area at l.	—	—	—

BANCO COMMERCIAL DO PORTO

1830'S ISSUE

		GOOD	FINE	XF
S161	**10,000 REIS** 18xx. Black. Diamond-shaped inner border.	—	—	—
S162	**20,000 REIS** 18xx. Neptune at ctr.	—	—	—

		GOOD	FINE	XF
S163	**50,000 REIS** 4.4.1837. Blue. Ornate octagonal-shaped inner border, lg. leaves at upper corners.			
	a. Issued note.	—	—	—
	b. Handwritten cancellation.	—	—	—
S164	**100,000 REIS** 18xx. Mercury at ctr.	—	—	—

1859 ISSUE

		GOOD	FINE	XF
S165	**10,000 REIS** 31.12.1859. Helmeted Greek warrior w/shield in counterfoil area at l., bldg. at ctr.	—	—	—
S166	**50,000 REIS** 31.12.1859. Helmeted Greek warrior w/shield in counterfoil area at l., lg. bldg. at ctr. Printer: BWC.	—	—	—

BANCO DE GUIMARÃES

1873; 1891 ISSUE

#S171-S174 arms in counterfoil area at l.

		GOOD	FINE	XF
S171	**5000 REIS** 1.6.1891. Black on blue-green paper.	—	—	—

		GOOD	FINE	XF
S172	**10,000 REIS** 1.6.1891. Black.	—	—	—
S173	**20,000 REIS** 4.11.1873. Black on yellow paper.	—	—	—
S174	**50,000 REIS** 4.11.1873. Green.	—	—	—

BANCO INDUSTRIAL DO PORTO

1800'S ISSUE

		GOOD	FINE	XF
S181	**10,000 REIS** 18xx. Green and orange. Bldg. at upper ctr. Unissued remainder.	—	—	—
S182	**20,000 REIS** 18xx. Brown and purple. Sailing ships at upper ctr.	—	—	—

BANCO DE LISBOA

BANK OF LISBON

Founded in 1822.

MONETARY SYSTEM:

1 Moeda = 4800 Reis

1820-46 ISSUES

#S191-S193 oval inner borders.

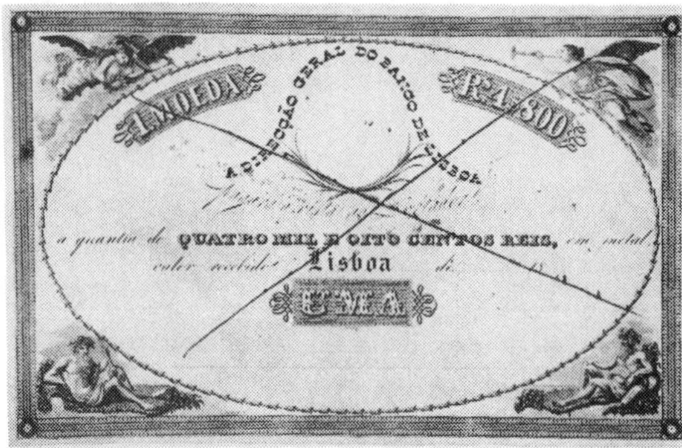

		GOOD	FINE	XF
S191	**1 MOEDA = 4800 REIS** 18xx. Black. Allegorical vignette at each corner.	—	—	—
S192	**1 MOEDA = 4800 REIS** 6.9.1839. Black. Allegorical vignette at each corner, and more embellishments in text over ctr.	—	—	—

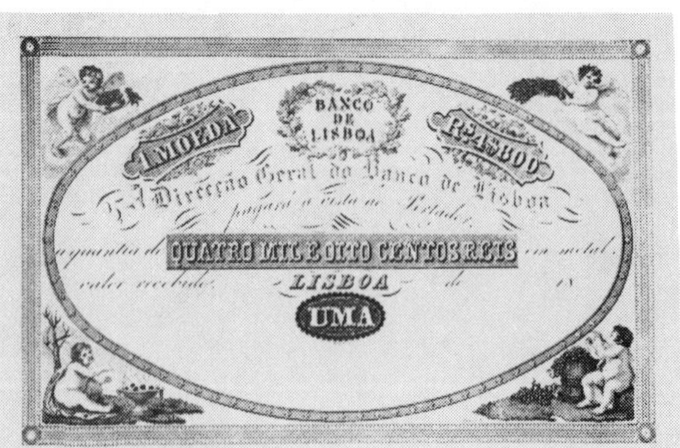

		GOOD	FINE	XF
S193	**1 MOEDA = 4800 REIS** 18xx. Black. Similar style to #S192, but 4 different vignettes at corners.	—	—	—
S194	**1 MOEDA = 4800 REIS** 19.5.1843. Black. Elongated octagonal inner border, 4 different vignettes at corners.	—	—	—
S195	**1 MOEDA = 4800 REIS** 1.5.1846. Black. Elongated octagonal inner border w/thin eagle at upper ctr., standing allegorical woman at each corner.	—	—	—
S196	**4 MOEDAS = 19,200 REIS** 1822. Black. Justice standing at lower ctr.	—	—	—

		GOOD	FINE	XF
S197	**4 MOEDAS = 19,200 REIS** 1822. Black. Woman w/barrel at upper l.	—	—	—

		GOOD	FINE	XF
S198	**4 MOEDAS = 19,200 REIS** 1822. Allegorical winged woman w/ribbon at upper l.	—	—	—
S199	**4 MOEDAS = 19,200 REIS** 1824. Black. Cherub w/long ribbon of flowers across top.	—	—	—

		GOOD	FINE	XF
S200	**4 MOEDAS = 19,200 REIS** 20.11.1824. Black. Winged cherub at upper l.	—	—	—
S201	**4 MOEDAS = 19,200 REIS** 16.11.1825. Winged Mercury at upper l.	—	—	—

		GOOD	FINE	XF
S202	**4 MOEDAS = 19,200 REIS** 12.8.1836. Allegorical figure w/torch at upper l., cherub w/cornucopia at lower ctr.	—	—	—
S203	**4 MOEDAS = 19,200 REIS** 18xx. Black. Chapel at upper l.	—	—	—

		GOOD	FINE	XF
S204	**4 MOEDAS = 19,200 REIS** 31.3.1840. Allegorical figure w/barrel and bale at upper l.	—	—	—

		GOOD	FINE	XF
S205	**4 MOEDAS = 19,200 REIS** 26.3.1841. Black. Helmeted woman w/trident at upper l.	—	—	—
S206	**4 MOEDAS = 19,200 REIS** 18xx. Black. Woman in circle at upper l.	—	—	—
S207	**10 MOEDAS = 48,000 REIS** 4.8.1822. Bird at upper l.	—	—	—

		GOOD	FINE	XF
S208	**10 MOEDAS = 48,000 REIS** 1822. Value in wreath at upper l.	—	—	—
S209	**10 MOEDAS = 48,000 REIS** 1824. Seated allegorical woman w/shield at upper ctr.	—	—	—
S210	**10 MOEDAS = 48,000 REIS** 17.11.1825. 2 allegorical figures w/cherub above at upper ctr.	—	—	—

		GOOD	FINE	XF
S211	**10 MOEDAS = 48,000 REIS** 4.12.1838. Seated Neptune at ctr.	—	—	—

		GOOD	FINE	XF
S212	**10 MOEDAS = 48,000 REIS** 21.4.1839. 3 allegorical figures and cherub at ctr.	—	—	—

		GOOD	FINE	XF
S213	**10 MOEDAS = 48,000 REIS** 18xx. Neptune w/other figures and sea horses at ctr., value in curved lines w/cornucopias at upper l. and r.	—	—	—
S214	**10 MOEDAS = 48,000 REIS** 18xx. Similar to #S213, but value in straight line at upper corners.	—	—	—
S215	**10 MOEDAS = 48,000 REIS** 21.1.1845. Scarred trees w/church behind *(Invicta Serra Do Pilar)* at ctr.	—	—	—
S216	**10 MOEDAS = 48,000 REIS** 18xx. Lg. bldg. w/people at ctr.	—	—	—

		GOOD	FINE	XF
S217	**20 MOEDAS = 96,000 REIS** 182x. Allegorical woman w/crown and caduceus at lower l. ctr.	—	—	—

		GOOD	FINE	XF
S218	**20 MOEDAS = 96,000 REIS** 1822. Angel w/cherubs at upper l.	—	—	—
S219	**20 MOEDAS = 96,000 REIS** 1825. 2 allegorical figures at upper ctr.	—	—	—
S220	**20 MOEDAS = 96,000 REIS** 16.3.1833. 3 cherubs w/barrels and bales at upper ctr.	—	—	—

		GOOD	FINE	XF
S221	**50 MOEDAS = 240,000 REIS** 1825. Cherubs w/barrels and bales at ctr.	—	—	—

		GOOD	FINE	XF
S222	**100 MOEDAS = 480,000 REIS** 1825. Neptune seated at ctr.	—	—	—

1840'S LOW DENOMINATION ISSUES

		GOOD	FINE	XF
S223	**1200 REIS** 18xx. Allegorical women w/crowned shield at upper ctr.	—	—	—

		GOOD	FINE	XF
S224	**1200 REIS** 10.12.1846; 12.12.1846; 1.10.1847. Black. Cherub at upper l. and r., helmeted soldier at lower l., old man at lower r.	400.00	—	—

		Good	Fine	XF
S225	**1200 Reis** 18xx. Standing figure in each corner.	—	—	—

1830's Cobre Ou Bronze Issues

		Good	Fine	XF
S226	**4 Moedas = 19,200 Reis** 183x. Red. Allegorical figure w/box and cornucopia at upper l.	—	—	—

		Good	Fine	XF
S227	**4 Moedas = 19,200 Reis** 18xx. Red. Seated figure w/shield at ctr.	—	—	—
S228	**4 Moedas = 19,200 Reis** 18xx. Red. 2 winged cherubs at ctr.	—	—	—

		Good	Fine	XF
S229	**4 Moedas = 19,200 Reis** 18xx. Red. Helmeted woman w/spear and shield at ctr.	—	—	—
S230	**4 Moedas = 19,200 Reis** 4.10.1845. Blue. 3 allegorical women at ctr.	—	—	—

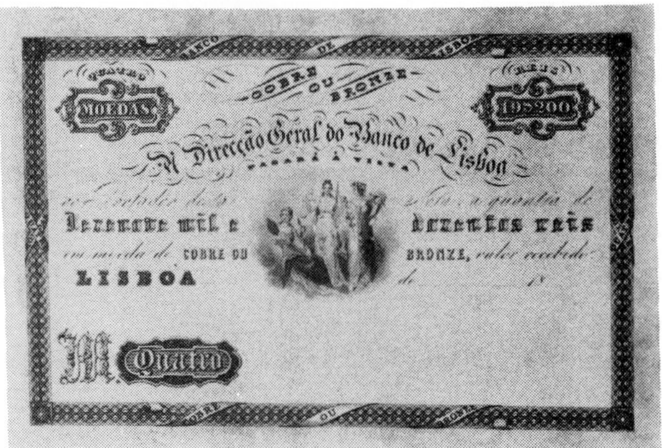

		Good	Fine	XF
S231	**4 Moedas = 19,200 Reis** 18xx. Red. Like #S230.	—	—	—
S232	**4 Moedas = 19,200 Reis** 18xx. Black. Like #S230.	—	—	—

		Good	Fine	XF
S233	**10 Moedas = 48,000 Reis** 183x. Blue. 2 allegorical figures w/sm. monument and bank name at ctr.	—	—	—
S234	**10 Moedas = 48,000 Reis** 183x. Black. 2 cherubs w/coin cornucopia at upper r.	—	—	—

		Good	Fine	XF
S235	**2400 Reis** *D.19.11.1846.* Crowned arms w/barrel, plants and anchor at upper ctr.	—	—	—
S236	**1 Moeda = 4800 Reis** 5.12.1837. Blue. Value at lower l. and upper r.	—	—	—
S237	**1 Moeda = 4800 Reis** 16.2.1841. Blue. Similar to #S236, but many stylistic changes.	—	—	—
S238	**1 Moeda = 4800 Reis** 18.3.1842. Blue. Reclining women vertically at l., 2 cherubs w/bales at upper ctr.	—	—	—

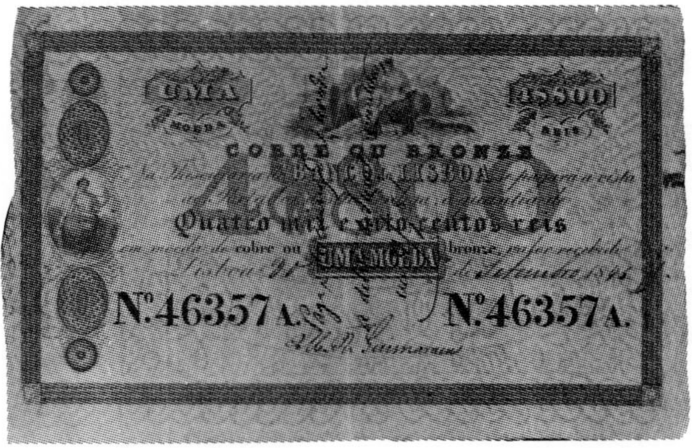

		Good	Fine	XF
S239	**1 Moeda = 4800 Reis** 30.9.1845. Blue. Seated Justice at l., 2 allegorical women w/beehive, barrels and bales at upper ctr.	—	—	—
S240	**1 Moeda = 4800 Reis** 18xx. Blue. Winged allegorical woman at l., 3 allegorical women at upper ctr.	—	—	—

1833 ND Circulating Bearer Checks Issue

#S246-S248 COBRE AU BRONZE - PAYABLE TO BEARER.

		Good	Fine	XF
S246	**9600 Reis** ND.	—	—	—
S247	**14,400 Reis** 2.3.1833.	—	—	—
S248	**10 Moedas = 48,000 Reis** ND. Cherub at l.	—	—	—

Banco Mercantil Portuense

1830's Issue

		Good	Fine	XF
S251	**9000 Reis** 18xx. Green.	—	—	—
S252	**18,000 Reis** 18xx. Black.	—	—	—

1859-85 Issue

#S253-S258 arms in medallion at l.

		Good	Fine	XF
S253	**50,000 Reis** 15.11.1859. Red and black.	—	—	—
S254	**100,000 Reis** 20.8.1863. Green.	—	—	—
S255	**10,000 Reis** 31.1.1885. Black on green paper. Back red-brown.	—	—	—
S256	**20,000 Reis** 31.1.1885. Black on pink paper. Back red-brown.	—	—	—
S257	**50,000 Reis** 7.2.1885. Blue. Back red-brown.	—	—	—

		Good	Fine	XF
S258	**100,000 Reis** 2.3.1885. Black. Back green.	—	—	—

Banco do Minho

1874; 1887 Issue

#S261-S265 various scenes in five ornate cartouches in counterfoil area at l.

		Good	Fine	XF
S261	**2500 Reis** 1.4.1887. Black and green on yellowish paper. Back brown.	—	—	—
S262	**5000 Reis** 1.7.1874. Black and blue on pink paper. Back blue.	—	—	—
S263	**10,000 Reis** 1.4.1887. Black and red on dk. blue paper. Back black.	—	—	—
S264	**20,000 Reis** 1.4.1887. Black and blue. Back black.	—	—	—
S265	**50,000 Reis** 1.4.1887. Blue and orange. Back orange.	—	—	—

Banco Uniáo do Porto

1886-88 Issue

		Good	Fine	XF
S271	**10,000 Reis** 18xx. Blue. Hands clasping at top ctr.	—	—	—

#S272-S275 arms in counterfoil area at l.

		Good	Fine	XF
S272	**10,000 Reis** 2.5.1888. Black on yellow paper.	—	—	—
S273	**20,000 Reis** 2.5.1888. Black and blue.	—	—	—
S274	**50,000 Reis** 18xx. Green.	—	—	—
S275	**100,000 Reis** 7.6.1886. Red.	—	—	—

Treasury For Commodities

Contracto do Sabão

Contract for Soap

1840's Issue

		Good	Fine	XF
S281	**1 Moeda = 4800 Reis** 18xx. 2 cherubs at upper ctr.	—	—	—

Contracto do Tabaco

Contract for Tobacco

1840's Issue

		Good	Fine	XF
S291	**1 Moeda = 4800 Reis** 18xx. Allegorical woman w/barrels blowing trumpet at upper ctr.	—	—	—
S292	**1 Moeda = 4800 Reis** 18xx. 2 cherubs at ctr.	—	—	—

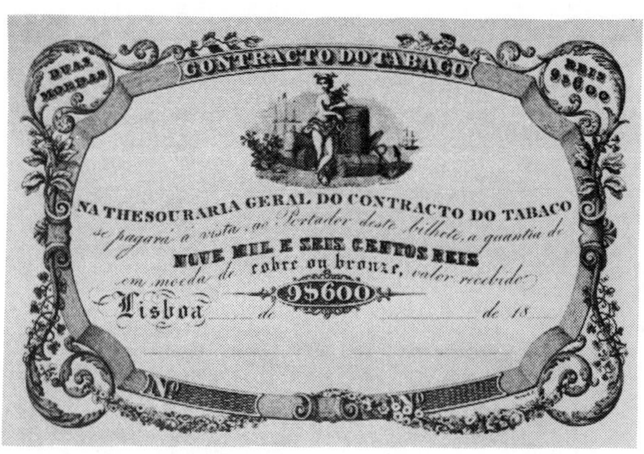

		Good	Fine	XF
S293	**9600 Reis** 18xx. Mercury w/barrel at upper ctr.	—	—	—

Public Utilities

A Empreza de Estrada de Lisboa Ao Porto

Road Construction Lisbon to Porto

1840's Issue

		Good	Fine	XF
S301	**1 Moeda = 4800 Reis** 184x. Woman w/plant, boxes and ships at upper ctr.	—	—	—

Nova Companhia Utilidade Pública

New Public Utilities Company

1877-89 Issue

#S311-S315 boat and animals in river at upper ctr.

		Good	Fine	XF
S311	**5000 Reis** 15.1.1877. Red.	—	—	—
S312	**10,000 Reis** 20.4.1889. Black and blue. Factory row in vertical silhouette at l. Back blue.	—	—	—
S313	**20,000 Reis** 1.5.1888. Black and green. Lumberyard vertically at l. Back green.	—	—	—
S314	**50,000 Reis** 15.1.1877. Black. Back purple.	—	—	—
S315	**100,000 Reis** 15.1.1877. Black and red. Back red.	—	—	—

The Commonwealth of Puerto Rico, the easternmost island of the Greater Antilles in the West Indies, has an area of 3,435 sq. mi. (9,104 sq. km.) and a population of 3.3 million. Capital: San Juan. The commonwealth has its own constitution and elects its own governor. Its people are citizens of the United States, liable to the draft - but not to federal taxation. The chief industries of Puerto Rico are manufacturing, agriculture, and tourism. Manufactured goods, cement, dairy and livestock products, sugar, rum, and coffee are exported, mainly to the United States.

Puerto Rico ("Rich Port") was discovered by Columbus who landed on the island and took possession for Spain on Oct. 19, 1493 - the only time Columbus set foot on the soil of what is now a possession of the United States. The first settlement, Caparra, was established by Ponce de Leon in 1508. The early years of the colony were not promising. Considerable gold was found, but the supply was soon exhausted. Efforts to enslave the Indians caused violent reprisals. Hurricanes destroyed crops and homes. French, Dutch, and English freebooters burned the towns. Puerto Rico remained a Spanish possession until 1898, when it was ceded to the United States following the Spanish-American War. Puerto Ricans were granted a measure of self-government and U.S. citizenship in 1917. Effective July 25, 1952, a Congressional resolution elevated Puerto Rico to the status of a free commonwealth associated with the United States.

Vieque (or Crab Island), located to the east of Puerto Rico, is the largest of the Commonwealth's major offshore islands. The others are Culebra, a naval station to the east, and Mona to the west.

RULERS:

Spanish, 1493-1898 United States of America, 1898-present

MONETARY SYSTEM:

1 Peso = 5 Pesetas = 100 Centavos to 1898
1 Dollar = 100 Cents, 1898-

SPANISH ADMINISTRATION

COMPAÑIA DE LOS FERRO-CARRILES DE PUERTO RICO

PUERTO RICO RAILROAD COMPANY

1880 ND ISSUE

		VG	VF	UNC
S101	**5 PESOS** ND (ca.1880). Black on orange unpt. Steam passenger train at l. Back blue. Printer: CS&E.			
	a. Issued note.	500.00	1500.	—
	s1. Specimen.	—	—	1500.
	s2. Specimen. W/o pinholes.	—	—	—

Note: Color proofs are known, but more information is needed.

LA CAJA DE AHORROS DE PONCE

SAVINGS BANK OF PONCE

ND ISSUE

		VG	VF	UNC
S107	**3 PESOS** ND. Black on blue unpt. Similar to #S110.	—	Rare	—

		VG	VF	UNC
S110	**50 PESOS** ND. Black on red unpt. Minerva seated at top ctr.	—	Rare	—

U.S.A. NATIONAL BANKS

FIRST NATIONAL BANK OF PORTO RICO AT SAN JUAN

This bank was in operation from 1902 until its placement in voluntary liquidation September 8, 1911. Less than fifteen surviving notes are known.

CHARTER #6484 - THIRD CHARTER PERIOD 1902-22

#S121-S124 black w/red seal at lower r. Back green; w/o dates *1902-1908*.

		VG	VF	UNC
S121	**10 DOLLARS** 1902. Portr. W. McKinley at l.	—	Rare	—
S122	**20 DOLLARS** 1902. H. McCulloch at l.	—	Rare	—
S123	**50 DOLLARS** 1902. Portr. J. Sherman at l.	—	Rare	—

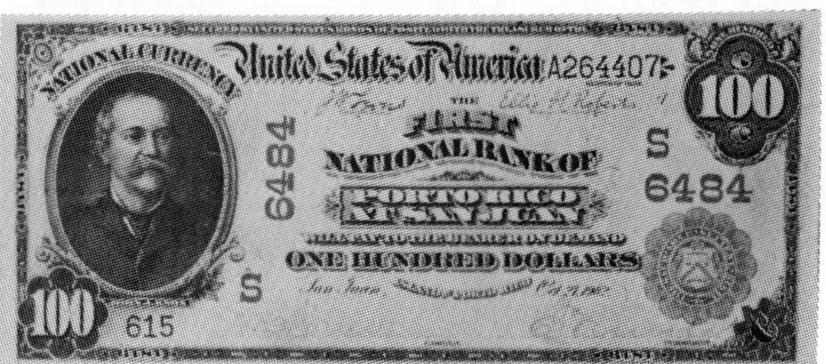

		VG	VF	UNC
S124	**100 DOLLARS** 27.10.1902. Portr. J. J. Knox at l.	—	Unique	—

1902-08 ISSUE

#S125-S128 black w/blue seal at lower r. Like previous issue. Back green; w/dates *1902-1908*.

		VG	VF	UNC
S125	**10 DOLLARS** 27.10.1902. Portr. W. McKinley at l.	—	Rare	—
S126	**20 DOLLARS** ND (ca.1908). H. McCulloch at l.	—	Rare	—
S127	**50 DOLLARS** ND (ca.1908). Portr. J. Sherman at l.	—	Unknown	—
S128	**100 DOLLARS** ND (ca.1908). Portr. J. J. Knox at l.	—	Unknown	—

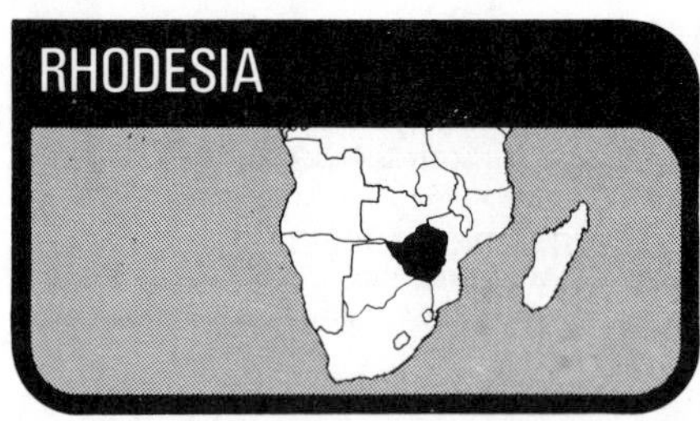

The "Republic of" Rhodesia (never recognized by the British government and was referred to as Southern Rhodesia, now Zimbabwe) located in the east-central part of southern Africa, has an area of 150,804 sq. mi. (390,580 sq. km.) and a population of 9.9 million. Capital: Harare. The economy is based on agriculture and mining. Tobacco, sugar, asbestos, copper and chrome ore and coal are exported.

The Rhodesian area, the habitat of paleolithic man, contains extensive evidence of earlier civilizations, notably the world-famous ruins of Zimbabwe, a gold-trading center that flourished about the 14th or 15th century AD. The Portuguese of the 16th century were the first Europeans to attempt to develop south-central Africa, but it remained for Cecil Rhodes and the British South Africa Co. to open the hinterlands. Rhodes obtained a concession for mineral rights from local chiefs in 1888 and administered his African empire (named Southern Rhodesia in 1895) through the British South Africa Co. until 1923, when the British government annexed the area after the white settlers voted for existence as a separate entity, rather than for incorporation into the Union of South Africa.

RULERS:

British to 1970 (1980)

MONETARY SYSTEM:

1 Shilling = 12 Pence
1 Pound = 20 Shillings

BRITISH ADMINISTRATION

AFRICAN BANKING CORPORATION

Established 1891 in South Africa, in Rhodesia ca.1892. Absorbed by Standard Bank in 1921.

BULAWAYO

1896 ISSUE

		GOOD	FINE	XF
S101	**10 SHILLINGS** ND. Proof.	—	—	—

#S102-S105B map of Africa at ctr. on back. Payable at Cape Town. Printer: BWC.

		GOOD	FINE	XF
S102	**1 POUND** ND (ca.1896). Allegorical woman's portr. at l. Specimen.	—	—	—
S103	**5 POUNDS** ND (ca.1896). Cherubs holding allegorical woman's portrait at l. Specimen.	—	—	—
S104	**10 POUNDS** ND (ca.1896). Prince standing at l. Specimen.	—	—	—

		GOOD	FINE	XF
S105	**20 POUNDS** ND (ca.1896). *Africa* w/shield at l. Specimen.	—	—	—

		GOOD	FINE	XF
S105A	**100 POUNDS** ND (ca.1896). Allegorical woman w/shield of Africa and lion at l. Specimen.	—	—	—

1920 ISSUE

		GOOD	FINE	XF
S105B	**1 POUND** ND (ca.1920). Springbok at upper ctr. Specimen.	—	—	—

BANK OF AFRICA LIMITED

1901 ISSUE

#S106 ovpt: *RHODESIA ISSUE* on Durban note.

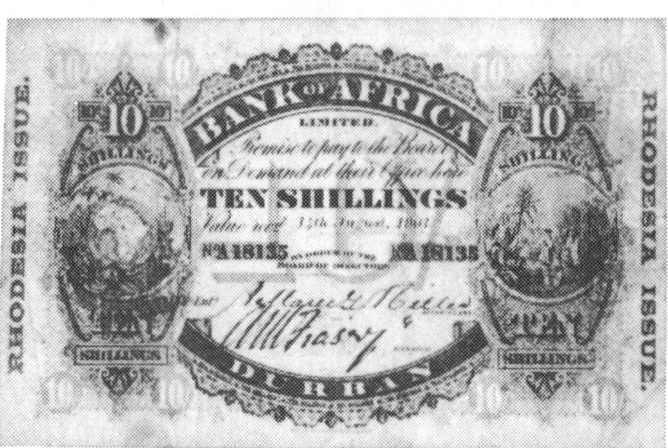

		GOOD	FINE	XF
S106	**10 SHILLINGS** 1901. Black on olive unpt. Map of Africa in cartouche at l., field workers in cartouche at r. Red ovpt. at sides. Back purple. Printer: W&S.			
	a. Lg. letters ovpt: *RHODESIA ISSUE* at sides. 10.8.1901.	—	Rare	—
	b. Sm. letters ovpt. at sides. 14.8.1901.	—	Rare	—

BARCLAYS BANK (DOMINION, COLONIAL AND OVERSEAS)

SALISBURY

1926 ISSUE

#S111-S113 seated woman w/sheep at l., Victoria Falls at r. Lion resting at bottom ctr. on back. Various date and sign. varieties. Ovpt. *RHODESIAN ISSUE* at upper margin. Printer: W&S.

		GOOD	FINE	XF
S111	**10 SHILLINGS** 1.9.1926; 2.1.1928; 1.10.1931; 1.1.1936; 1.8.1938. Red and m/c.			
	a. Issued note.	150.00	750.00	1250.
	s. Punched hole specimen.	—	—	—

		GOOD	FINE	XF
S112	**1 POUND** 1.9.1926; 1.12.1930; 1.6.1936; 1.9.1937. Blue and m/c.			
	a. Issued note.	175.00	400.00	850.00
	s. Punched hole specimen.	—	—	—
S113	**5 POUNDS** 1.9.1926. Green and m/c.			
	a. Issued note.	—	—	—
	s. Punched hole specimen.	—	—	—

NATIONAL BANK OF SOUTH AFRICA LIMITED

SALISBURY

1921 PROVISIONAL ISSUE

#S119 ovpt: *RHODESIAN ISSUE* in upper margin. Printer: W&S.

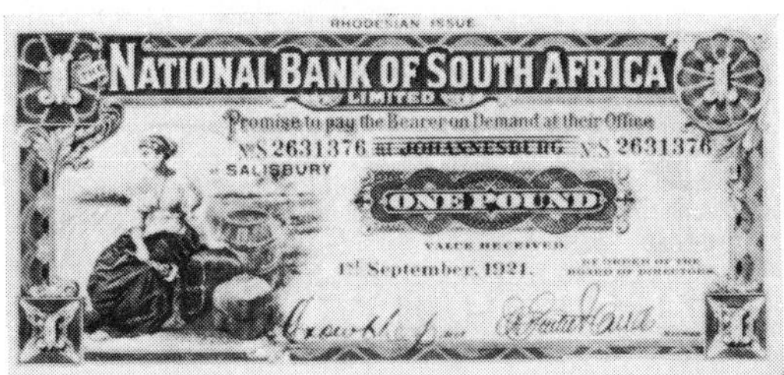

		GOOD	FINE	XF
S119	**1 POUND** ND (- old date 1.9.1921). Ovpt. on South Africa #S572.	300.00	650.00	1500.

1922 REGULAR ISSUE

#S121-S123 ovpt: *RHODESIAN ISSUE* in upper margin. Printer: W&S.

		GOOD	FINE	XF
S121	**10 SHILLINGS** 1.7.1922. Green on red-orange unpt. Child w/cornucopia at l. Back blue-gray; head at ctr.			
	a. Issued note.	300.00	750.00	1350.
	s. Punched hole specimen.	—	—	—
S122	**1 POUND** 1.7.1922. Black and yellow. Seated woman at l., w/Victoria Falls in background.	300.00	650.00	1200.

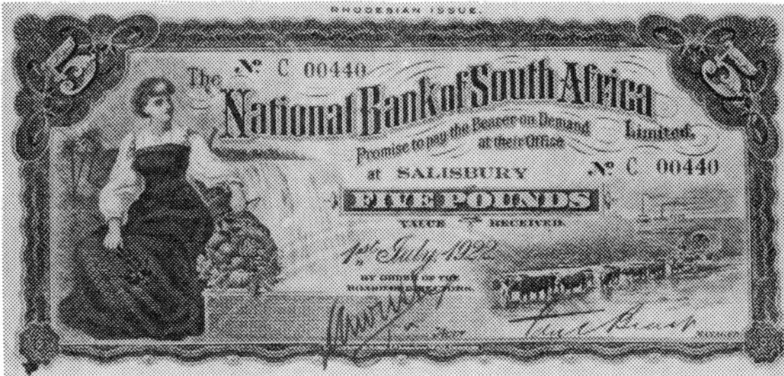

		GOOD	FINE	XF
S123	**5 POUNDS** 1.7.1922. Blue, yellow and orange. Seated woman w/cornucopia at l., Victoria Falls in background at l., cattle and wagon crossing stream at lower r. Portr. woman at ctr. on back.	—	—	—

STANDARD BANK OF SOUTH AFRICA

SALISBURY

1896 PROVISIONAL ISSUE

#S132-S134 ovpt. on Durban Branch issues, South Africa.

		GOOD	FINE	XF
S132	**1 POUND** 27.8.1896.	—	Rare	—
S133	**5 POUNDS** 27.8.1896.	—	Rare	—
S134	**10 POUNDS** 27.8.1896. (Not issued.)	—	Rare	—

1911 ISSUE

#S138-S148 various date and sign. varieties. Ovpt: *RHODESIAN ISSUE* at upper margin. Printer: W&S.

		GOOD	FINE	XF
S138	**5 POUNDS** 1.8.1911; 13.12.1911; 8.7.1912; 1.5.1913. Black on yellow unpt. Standing Britannia w/flag and shield at l.	—	—	—

NOTE: The earlier 1911 note may be unique.

1916 ISSUE

		GOOD	FINE	XF
S139	**5 POUNDS** 1916-17. Red. Statue of Van Riebeeck at l., standing Britannia w/flag and shield at r.			
	a. Issued note. 1.1.1917.	300.00	900.00	2000.
	s. Specimen. 1.12.1916.	—	—	—

1917-33 ISSUE

		GOOD	FINE	XF
S146	**10 SHILLINGS** 1917-38. Black, green and orange. Statue of J. Van Riebeeck at l., *R* script letter at ctr., standing Britannia w/flag at r. Back green.			
	a. 1.7.1917; 1.3.1920; 22.6.1925; 2.1.1928; 31.1.1930.	200.00	550.00	1250.
	b. 3.12.1932; 17.11.1933; 4.4.1936; 5.4.1938.	125.00	350.00	800.00

1925; 1933 Issue

		Good	Fine	XF
S147	**1 Pound** 30.6.1925; 30.9.1927; 30.6.1928-3.12.1937; 1938. Brown, green and m/c. Standing Britannia w/flag and shield at l. Back brown and black.	100.00	275.00	650.00
S148	**5 Pounds** 17.11.1933. Blue, black and m/c. View of Johannesburg and bank.	—	—	—

Listings For:

REPUBLICA ROMANA, see Italian States-Papal States

RUSSIA

Russia, (formerly the central power of the Union of Soviet Socialist Republics and now of the Commonwealth of Independent States) occupying the northern part of Asia and the far eastern part of Europe, has an area of 8,649,538 sq. mi. (17,075,450 sq. km.) and a population of 146.2 million. Capital: Moscow. Exports include machinery, iron and steel, crude oil, timber and nonferrous metals.

The first Russian dynasty was founded in Novgorod by the Viking Rurik in 862 AD. Under Yaroslav the Wise (1019-54) the subsequent Kievan state became one of the great commercial and cultural centers of Europe before falling to the Mongols of the Batu Khan, 13th century, who ruled Russia until late in the 15th century when Ivan III threw off the Mongol yoke. The Russian Empire was enlarged and solidified during the reigns of Ivan the Terrible, Peter the Great and Catherine the Great, and by 1881 extended to the Pacific and into Central Asia.

Assignats, the first government paper money of the Russian Empire, were introduced in 1769, and gave way to State Credit Notes in 1843. Russia was put on the gold standard in 1897 and reformed its currency at that time.

All pre-1898 notes were destroyed as they were turned in to the Treasury, accounting for their uniform scarcity today.

The last Russian Czar, Nicholas II (1894-1917), was deposed by the provisional government under Prince Lvov and later Alexander Kerensky during the military defeat in World War I. This government rapidly lost ground to the Bolshevik wing of the Socialist Democratic Labor Party which attained power following the Bolshevik Revolution. During the Russian Civil War (1917-1922) many regional governments, national states and armies in the field were formed which issued their own paper money (see Vol. I).

After the victory of the Red armies, many of these areas became federal republics of the Russian Socialist Federal Soviet Republic (РСфСР), or autonomous soviet republics which united on Dec. 30, 1922, to form the Union of Soviet Socialist Republics (СССР). Beginning with the downfall of the communist government in Poland, other European countries occupied since WW II, began democratic elections that spread into Russia itself, leaving the remaining states united in a newly founded Commonwealth of Independent States (C.I.S.). The USSR Supreme Soviet voted a formal end to the treaty of union signed in 1922 and dissolved itself.

RULERS:

Catherine II (the Great), 1762-1796
Paul I, 1796-1801
Alexander I, 1801-1825
Nicholas I, 1825-1855
Alexander II, 1855-1881
Alexander III, 1881-1894
Nicholas II, 1894-1917

MONETARY SYSTEM:

1 Ruble = 100 Kopeks, until 1997

(Some other areas where notes are listed in this volume had local currencies.)

MONETARY UNITS

KOPEK	КОП., КОПЪИКА, КОПЕЙКА
KOPEKS	КОПЬЕКЬ., КОП., КОПЕЕК
RUBLE	РУБЛЬ
RUBLES	РУБЛЕИ
CHERVONETS	ЧЕРВОНЕЦ
CHERVONTSA (plural)	ЧЕРВОНЦА
KARBOVANETS	КАРБОВАНЕЦ(RUS), КАРБОВАНЕЦЬ(UKR)
KARBOVANTSIV (pl.)	КАРБОВАНЦІВ
HRYVEN	ГРИВЕНЬ
SHAGIV	ШАГІВ

CYRILLIC ALPHABET

А	а	А	а	A	С	с	С	с	S
Б	б	Б	б	B	Т	т	Т	т	T
В	в	В	в	V	У	у	У	у	U
Г	г	Г	г	G	Ф	ф	Ф	ф	F
Д	д	Д	д	D	Х	х	Х	х	Kh
Е	е	Е	е	ye	Ц	ц	Ц	ц	C(ts)
Ё	ё	Ё	ё	yo	Ч	ч	Ч	ч	ch
Ж	ж	Ж	ж	zh	Ш	ш	Ш	ш	sh
З	з	З	з	Z	Щ	щ	Щ	щ	shch
И	и	И	и	I	Ъ*)	ъ*)	—	ъ	'
Й	й	Й	й	J	Ы	ы	—	ы	
К	к	К	к, к	K	Ь**)	ь**)	—	ь	'
Л	л	Л	л	L	Э		Э		E
М	м	М	м	M	Ю	ю	Ю	ю	yu
Н	н	Н	н	N	Я	я	Я	я	ya
О	о	О	о	O	І	і	І	і	I
П	п	П	п	P	Ѣ	ѣ	Ѣ	ѣ	ye
Р	р	Р	р	R					

*) "hard", and **) "soft" signs; both soundless. і and ѣ were dropped in 1918.

DENOMINATIONS

1	ОДИН, ОДИНЪ or ОДНА
2	ДВА or ДВЕ
3	ТРИ
5	ПЯТЬ
10	ДЕСЯТЬ
20	ДВАДЦАТЬ
25	ДВАДЦАТЬ ПЯТЬ
30	ТРИДЦАТЬ
40	СОРОК or СОРОКЪ
50	ПЯТЬДЕСЯТ or ПЯТЬДЕСЯТЪ
60	ШЕСТЬДЕСЯТ or ЩЕСТЬДЕСЯТЬ
100	СТО
250	ДВЬСТИ ПЯТЪДЕСЯТЪ or ДВЕСТИ ПЯТЪДЕСЯТ
500	ПЯТЬСОТ or ПЯТЬСОТЪ
1,000	ТЫСЯЧА
5,000	ПЯТЬ ТЫСЯЧ or ТЫСЯЧЪ
10,000	ДЕСЯТЬ ТЫСЯЧ or ТЫСЯЧЪ
15,000	ПЯТНАДЦАТЬ ТЫСЯЧ or ТЫСЯЧЬ
25,000	ДВАДЦАТЬ ПЯТЬ ТЫСЯЧ
50,000	ПЯТЬ ДЕСЯТ ТЫСЯЧ or ПЯТЬСОТ
100,000	СТО ТЫСЯЧ or ТЫСЯЧЪ
250,000	ДВЬСТИ ПЯТЬДЕСЯТ ТЫСЯЧ
500,000	ПЯТЬ СОТЪ ТЫСЯЧ or ПЯТЬСОТ
1,000,000	ОДИН МИЛЛИОН or МИЛЛИОНЪ
5,000,000	ПЯТЬ МИЛЛИОНОВ

REGIONAL ISSUES

SECTION BREAKDOWN AND IDENTIFICATION LIST

Regional issues of Russia in this catalog are arranged on a geographic basis from north to south, west to east. A number of major locally circulating issues are included as well.

Shown with the breakdown of each section are some of the Russian headings to assist in locating listed issues. Insofar as possible these headings are given exactly as they appear on the notes, regardless of grammatical construction.

NORTH RUSSIA

ГОСУДАРСТВЕННЬИ БАНКЪ АРХАНГЕЛЬСКОЕ ОТДѢЛЕНІЕМЪ
Archangel Government (Red and White Regimes) . . . . . #S101-S108
МУРМАНСК НА ФИНАНСОВЫЙ ОТДѢЛ.
Murmansk Soviet (Red and White Regimes) . . . . . #S111-S118
5% КРАТКОСРОЧНОЕ ОБЯЗАТЕЛЬСТВО ВЕРХОВНАГО
УПРАВЛЕНІЯ СѢВЕРНОЙ ОБЛАСТИ. . . . . #S121-S125
5% КРАТКОСРОЧНОЕ ОБЯЗАТЕЛЬСТВО ВРЕМЕННАГО
ПРАВИТЕЛЬСТВА СѢВЕРНОЙ ОБЛАСТИ
Government of the North Region . . . . . #S126-S129
СѢВЕРНАЯ РОССІЯ
North Russia . . . . . #S131-S186
ОЛОНЕЦКОЙ ГУБЕРНІЙ
Olonets Government . . . . . #S191-S195

NORTHWEST RUSSIA

ПОЛЕВОЕ КАЗНАЧЕИЧТВО СѢВЕРОЗАПАДНАГО ФРОНТА
Field Treasury, Northwest Front (Gen. Yudenich). . . . . #S201-S210
КРЕДИТНЫЙ БИЛЕТЪ ПСКОВСКАГО ОБЛАСТНОГО КАЗНАЧЕЙСТВА
Pskov Regional Government (Gen. Vandamm) . . . . . #S211-S213
ОТДѢЛЬНЫИ КОРПУСЪ СѢВЕРНОЙ АРМІИ. ГЕН. РОДЗЯНКО
Special Corps of the North Army (Gen. Rodzianko) . . . . . #S216-S222
ЗАПАДНАЯ ДОБРОВОЛЬУЕСКАЯ АРМІЯ , ПОЛК АВАЛОВ - БЕРМОНДТЪ
Independent West Army (Col. Avalov-Bermondt) . . . . . #S226-S230
ПАРТИ ЗАНСКИЙ ОТРЯД ПОЛК БУЛАК - БАЛАХОВИЧА
Partisan Detachment of Lt. Col. Bulak-Balakhovich . . . . . #S231
КРОНШТАДТСКАЯ РЕСПУБЛИКА
Kronstadt Republic (naval mutineers) . . . . . #S232-S235
МОГИЛЕВЧКАЯ ГУБЕРІЯ
Mogilev Region . . . . . #S236-S240A

WHITE RUSSIA

СЛУЦКОЕ УѢЗДНОЕ ЗЕМСТВО.
Slutsk Zemstvo Issue. . . . . #S241-S244

UKRAINE

УКРАЙНСКАЯ СОЦ (ИАЛИСТИУЕСКАЯ) СОВЕТ. РЕСПУБЛ. (МКА)
Ukrainian Socialist Soviet Republic . . . . . #S293-S304
ЕЛИСАБЕТГРАДСК (СКОЕ) ОТДѢЛЕНІЯ ГОСУДАРСТВЕННАГО БАНКА
Elizabetgrad Branch Government Bank . . . . . #S323-S323B
ЕЛИСАБЕТГРАДСКАГО ОТДѢЛЕНІЯ НАРОДНАГО БАНКА
Elizabetgrad Branch Peoples Bank . . . . . #S324-S325
ВСЕУКРАЇНЬСКИЙ КООПЕРАТИВНИЙ БАНК
Ukrainian Cooperative Bank, Kiev. . . . . #S326-S328
УКРАЙНЬСКА ПОВСТАНСКА АРМІЯ (УКРАЇНСЬКА ПОВСТАНСЬКА АРМІЯ)
Ukrainian Revolutionary Army (Post-WW II) . . . . . #S330
РАЗМѢННАИ МАРКА Г. ОДЕССЫ
РАЗМѢННЫИ БИЛЕТЪ Г. ОДЕССЫ
Odessa . . . . . #S331-S338
ЖИТОМИР
Zhitomir. . . . . #S341-S363
РОЗМІННИЙ БІЛЕТ МІСТА ЖИТОМИРА
Municipal Receipts. . . . . #S341-S343
РАЗМЕНИЫЙ БИЛЕТ НАРОДНОГО БАНКА
National Bank . . . . . #S344-S346
АЗОВСКО-ДОНСКОЙ КОММЕРУЕСКІЙ БАНКЪ
ЖИТОМИРСКОЕ ОТДѢЛЕНІЕ
Azov-Don Commercial Bank, Zhitomir Branch . . . . . #S351-S356
ЖИТОМИРСКОЕ ОТДѢЛЕНІЕ ГОСУДАРСТВЕНН. БАНКА
Zhitomir Branch, Government Bank . . . . . #S361-S363
СОЕДИНЕННЫЙ БАНКЪ ЖИТОМИРСКОЕ ОТДѢЛЕНІЕ
Zhitomir Branch Soednenni Bank . . . . . #S364-S364D
КРЫМСКОЕ КРАЕВОЕ ПРАВИТЕЛЬСТВО
ОБЯЗАТЕЛСТВО КРЫМСКАГО КРАЕВОГО КАЗНАЧЕЙСТВА
Crimea Territorial Government (Gen. Sulkevich). . . . . #S366-S372
Provisional Government of Workers and Peasants. . . . . #S375
УПРАВЛЕНІЕ УПОЛНОМОЧ. ПО ПРОД. ХЕСР. ГУБ. ВРЕМЕННАЯ КВИТАНЧІЯ
Kherson Government Plenipotentiary for Food . . . . . #S376-S380

SOUTH RUSSIA

5% КРАТКОСРОЧНОЕ ОЬЯЗАТЕЛЬСТВО ВСЕВЕЛИКАГО ВОЙСКА ДОНСКОГО
Don Cossack Government. . . . . #S381-S404
ГЛАВНОЕКОМАНДОВАНІЕ ВООРУЖЕННЫМИ
СИЛАМИ НА ЮГѢ РОССІЙ
South Russia, High Command of the Armed Forces (Generals Denikin and Wrangel)
ВЫПУЩЕНЪ (or А) РОСТОВСКОЙ (УД) ГОСУДАРСТВЕННАГО БАНКА
Rostov Branch Government Bank . . . . . #S406-S419
ВИЛЕТЪ ГОСУДАРСТВЕННАГО КАЗНАЧЕЙСТВА
Government Treasury Notes . . . . . #S420-S434
ГОСУДАРСТВО РОССІЙСКОЕ
Russian Government. . . . . #S435-S440
АСТРАХАНСКАГО КАЗНАЧЕЙСТВА
Astrakhan Region . . . . . #S441-S446

NORTH CAUCASUS

СЕВЕРО КАВКАЗСКАЯ СОЦИАЛИСТИЧЕСКАЯ СОВЕТСКАЯ РЕСПУЬЛИКА
КРАЕВОГО ИСПОЛНИТ. КОМИТЕТА СОВЕТОВ
North Caucasian Soviet Socialist Republic . . . . . #S447-S448
ВРЕМЭН.-ЕНТР. УПРАВЛ. ОТДВЛЕНІЙ НАРОДНАГО БАНКА
Provisional Central Administration of the Branch of the National Bank. . . . . #S451-S453
СЕВ. КАВКАЗА
Area Executive Committee of the N. Caucasian Soviet Republic . . . . . #S456-S460
СЕВЕРО-КАВКАЗСКИЙ ЭМИРАТ
North Caucasian Emirate. . . . . #S461-S478
АРМАВИРСКАГО ОТДѢЛЕНІЯ ГОСУДАРСТВЕННАГО БАНКА
Armavir Branch Government Bank . . . . . #S479A-S479K
КУБАНСКАГО КРАЕВОГО ПРАВИТЕЛЬСТВА
Kuban Territorial Government . . . . . #S481-S488
КУБАНСКАЯ РЕСПУБЛИКА
Kuban Soviet Republic . . . . . #S491-S494
ЕКАТЕРИНОДАРСКОГО ОТДЕЛЕНИЯ ГОСУДАРСТВЕННАГО БАНКА
Ekaterinodar Branch Government Bank . . . . . #S494A-S497
ГОСУДАРСТВЕННАГО БАНКА ЕКАТЕРИНОДАРСКОЕ ОТДѢЛЕНІЕ
ГАРАНТИРОВАННЫЙ ЧЕКЪ
Guaranteed Check, Government Bank Ekaterinodar Branch . . . . . #S498A-S498E
МИНЕРАЛЬНЫЕ ВОДЫ
Mineralnyie Vodyi District . . . . . #S501-S520
ГОСУДАРЧТВЕННЫЙ БАНКЪ СТАВРОПОЛСКОЕ ОТДѢЛЕНІЕ
Stavropol Branch Government Bank. . . . . #S520A-S520H
ТЕРСКО-ДАГЕСТАНСКАЯ ОБЛАСТЬ
Terek-Daghestan Territory. . . . . #S521-S528
ТЕРСКОЙ РЕСПУБЛИКИЙ (ТЕРСК РЕСП.)
Terek Republic. . . . . #S529-S538
ВРЕМЕНН. РАЗМѢННЫЙ ЗНАКЪ
Black Sea Peasant Militia (Voronovich). . . . . #S539-S544
(ПИАТИГОРСК-) БАТАЛПАЩИНСК КАЗНАЧ.
Piatigorsk-Batalpashchinsk Company of the Independent Army
(Col. A. Shkuro) . . . . . #S551-S565
ТЕРСКОЕ КАЗНАЧЬЕ ВОЙСКО
Terek Cossack Command (Col. Bicherakov). . . . . #S566-S568
КОМАНДОВАНІЕ КРАСНОЙ АРМІИ. ТЕРСКОЙ ОБЛАСТИ
Terek District Command of the Red Army. . . . . #S569-S570
ВОЛЖСКО-КАМСКІЙ КОММЕРЧЕСКІЙ БАНКЪ
Volga-Kama Commercial Bank-Grozny. . . . . #S571-S573
РУССКО-АЗІАТСКИЙ БАНКЪ
Russo-Asiatic Bank . . . . . #S576-S579
АЗОВЧКО-ДОНЧКОЙ КОММЕРЧЕЧКІИ БАНКЪ
Azov-Don Commercial Bank . . . . . #S581-S584
ВОНЫ СОЧИНСКАГО ГОРОДСКОГО УПРАВЛЕНІЯ
Sochi (City) . . . . . #S585-S585H
ЧЕРНОМОРСКАЯ ЖЕЛЕЗНАЯ ДОРОГА
Black Sea Railroad . . . . . #S586-S591
ОБЩЕСТВА ВЛАДИКАВКАЗСКОЙ ЖЕЛЬЗНОЙ ДОРОГИ

Vladikavkaz Railroad Company ... #S593-S599
ВЛАДИКАВКАЗСКОЕ ОТДѢЛЕНІЕ ГОСУДАРСТВЕННАГО БАНКА
Vladikavkaz Branch Government Bank ... #S600A-S600D

TRANSCAUCASIA

ЗАКАВКАЗСКАГО КОМИССАРІАТА
Transcaucasian Commissariat ... #S601-S607
ФЕДЕРАЦИЯ СОВ. СОЦ. РЕСПУБЛИК ЗАКАВКАЗЬЯ С.Ф.С.Р.
Federation of Soviet Socialist Republics of Transcaucasia ... #S611-S631
Transcaucasian Socialist Federal Soviet Republic ... #S632-S639
УПРАВЛЕИЕ ЖЕЛЕЗНЫХ ДОРОГ, С.С.Р. ЗАКАВКАЗЬЯ.
Transcaucasian S.S.R. Railroad ... #S641-S645
СОЦИАЛИСТИЧЕСКАЯ СОВЕТСКАЯ РЕСПУБЛИКА АРМЕНИИ
(or АРМЕНИЯ)
Armenian Socialist Soviet Republic ... #S678-S687
АЛЕКСАНДРОПОЛСКІЙ ГОРОДСК ОБЩЕСТВЕНН БАНКЪ
Alexandropol Bank Issues ... #S691-S692
Shirak Government Corporation Bank ... $S693-S698
АЗЕРБАЙДЖАНСКАЯ СОЦ. СОВОТ. РЕСПУБЛИКА
Azerbaijan Socialist Soviet Republic ... #S709-S720
БАКИНСКАЯ ГОРОДСКАЯ УПРАВА СОВѢТЪ БАКИНСКАГО
ГОРОДСКОГО ХОЗЯИСТВА
Baku City Administration ... #S731-S733
БАТУМСКАГО КАЗНАЧЕЙСТВА
Batum Treasury ... #S736-S745
ГРУЗИНСКАЯ СОЦ . СОВЕТСКАЯ РЕСПУБЛИКА
ОБЯЗАТЕЛЬСТВО НАРОДНАГО БАНКА С.С.Р. ГРУЗИН.
Georgia Socialist Soviet Republic ... #S761-S769

SIBERIA AND URALS

САМАРСКАЯ ДИРЕКТОРИЯ
Samara Directory (Komuch) ... #S771-S812
СИБИРСКАГО ВРЕМЕННАГО ПРАВИТЕЛЬСТВА
5% КРАТКОСОРОЧНОЕ ОБЯЗАТЕЛЬСТВО
ГОСУДАРСТВЕННАГО КАЗНАЧЕЙСТВА СИБИРИ
Siberian Provisional Government ... #S816-S825
СИБИРСКАГО ВРЕМЕННАГО ПРАВИТЕЛЬСТВА
5% КРАТКОСРОЧНОЕ ОБЯЗАТЕЛЬСТВО ГОСУДАРСТВЕННАГО КАЗНАЧЕЙСТВА
ГОСУДАРСТВЕННЫЙ КРЕДИТНЫЙ БИЛЕТЪ
БИЛЕТЪ ГОСУДАРСТВЕННЫЙ ВНУТРЕННІИ 4-1/2% ВЫЙГРЫЩНЫЙ
ЗАЕМЪ 1917 ГОДА
Provisional Siberian Government (Kolchak) ... #S826-S878
ИРК. ОТД. ГОС.Б
Irkutsk Branch, Government Bank ... #S881-S892
УПОЛНОМОЧЕННЫЙ МИНИСТРА СНАБЖЕНІЯ И ПРОДОВОЛЬСТВІЯ ПО
ХАБАРОВСКОМУ РАЙОНУ
Minister Representative Plenipotentiary for Provisions for Khabarovsk District ... #S896-S898
РОССИЙСКОЙ СОЦИАЛИСТИЧЕСКОЙ ФЕДЕРАТИВНАЯ СОВЕТСКАЯ РЕСПУБЛИКА
БИЛЕТЪ ГОСУДАРСТВЕННЫИ ВНУТРЕННІЙ 4-1/2% ВЫЙГРЫЩНЫЙ ЗАЕМЪ
Siberian Revolution Committee ... #S899-S904
ЧРЕЗВЫЧАЙНО-УПОЛНОМОЧЕННЫЙ ПРИКАМСКАГО РАЙОНА
Urals and Kama Region ... #S906-S919
РАБОЧЕЕ И КРЕСТЬЯНСКОЕ ПРАВИТЕЛЬСТВО ЕКАТЕРИНБУРГСКОЕ ОТДЕЛЕНИЕ
ГОСУДАРСТВЕННАГО БАНКА
Soviet of the Urals Region, Ekaterinburg Branch Government Bank ... #S921-S923
УРАЛСКАГО КАЗАЧЬЯГО БОЙСКА
Urals Cossack Region ... #S926-S953
УРАЛЬСКОЕ ОТД. Г. Б.
Uralsk Branch, State Bank ... #S956-S958
ПРАВИТЕЛЬСТВО ЦЕНТРОСИБИРИ СИБИРСКИЙ
Government of Central Siberia ... #S961
АКМОЛИНСКОЙ ОБЛАСТИ
Akmolinsk Region Revolutionary Committee ... #S962-S964
КРАСНОЯРСК. ЕНИС. Г. О-БО
Krasnoyarsk ... #S966-S971
ОРЕНБУРГСКАГО ОТДѢЛИНІЯ ГОСУДАРСТВЕННАГО БАНКА
Orenburg Branch Government Bank ... #S976-S983
ПЕРМСКАГО ГОРОДСКОГО ОБЩЕСТВА
Perm City Association ... #S986-S993

RUSSIAN CENTRAL ASIA

Bukhara, Soviet Peoples Republic ... #S1026-S1054
Khwarezm Peoples Soviet Republic ... #S1076-S1114
СЕМИРЕЧЕНСКАЯ ОБЛАСТЬ ДЕНЕЖНЫИ ЗНАКЪ ВРЕМЕНН.
РАЗМѢНН. ЗНАКЪ
Semireche Region ... #S1116-S1133
ЗАКАСПІЙСКАГО ВРЕМЕННАГО ПРАВИТЕЛЬСТВА
Transcaspian Provisional Administration
АСХАБАДСКАГО ОТДѢЛЕНІЯ ГОСУДАРСТВЕННАГО БАНКА
Government Bank, Askhabod Branch ... #S1136
ЗАКАСПІЙСКАГО НАРОДНАГО БАНКА
Transcaspian National Bank ... #S1139
АСХАБАДСКАГО ОТДѢЛЕНІЯ НАРОДНАГО БАНКА
National Bank, Askhabad Branch ... #S1141-S1146
ОБЯЗАТЕЛЬСТВО ВЕЛИКОБРИТАНСКОЙ ВОЕННОЙ МИССІЙ
Great Britain Government Military Mission (British Maj. Gen. Malleson) ... #S1148
ТУРКЕСТАНСКІЙ КРАЙ ТАШКЕТСКАГО ОТДѢЛЕНІЯ ГОСУДАРСТВЕННАГО
БАНКА
Turkestan District Tashkent Branch Government Bank ... #S1151-S1175

EAST SIBERIA

ДАЛЬНЕВОСТОЧНЫЙ СОВЕТ. НАРОДНЫХ КОМИССАРОВ
Baikalia - Far Eastern Soviet of Peoples Commissars ... #S1181-S1183
ПРАВИТЕЛЬСТВО РОССІЙСКОЙ ВОСТОЧНОЙ ОКРАЙНЫ
ГОСУДАРСТВЕННЫЙ БАНКЪ ЧИТИНСКОЕ ОТДѢЛЕНІЕ
Government of the Russian Eastern Border Regions ... #S1186-S1188
СИБИРСКАГО ВРЕМЕННАГО ПРАВИТЕЛЬСТВА
Siberian Provisional Administration ... #S1189-S1194
ВРЕМЕННАЯ ЗЕМСКАЯ ВЛАСТЬ ПРИБАЙКАЛЬЯ
Provisional Power of the Pribaikal Region ... #S1196-S1197
ДАЛЬНЕ-ВОСТОЧНОЙ РЕСПУБЛИКИ
Far Eastern Republic ... #S1201-S1215
АМУРСКИЙ ОБЛАСТНОЙ КОММИТЕТ
Amur Region Executive Committee ... #S1216-S1220
АМУРСКОЕ ОБЛАСТНОЕ ЗЕМСТВО
Amur Region Zemstvo ... #S1221-S1224
АМУРЧКІЙ ОБЛАСТНОЙ КРЕДИТНЫЙ СОЮЗЪ
ХАБАРОВСКІЙ КООПЕРАТИВ БАНКЪ
Amur Region Credit Union-Habarovsk Cooperative Bank ... #S1224A-S1224D
ХАБАРОВСКОЕ ОТДѢЛЕНІЕ ГОСУДАРСТВЕННАГО БАНКА
Habarovsk Branch Government Bank ... #S1225A-S1225W
ЗЕМЧКИЙ ПРИАМУРСКИЙ КРАЙ
Rural Priamur Province (Gen. Dietrichs) ... #S1226-S1227
ОРГАНИЗАЦІЯ КАЗЕННЫХЬ С.-Х. СКЛАДОВЬ
Nikolsk-Ussuriisk ... #S1231-S1237
РАЗМѢННЫЙ ЗНАКЪ ГОСУДАРСТВЕННЫЙ КРЕДИТНЫЙ БИЛЕТЪ
Far East Provisional Government ... #S1241-S1249
АМУРСКОЕ ОТДЕЛЕНИЕ ЖЕЛѢЗНОД ДОРОГИ
Amur Railroad ... #S1251-S1253
ВЛАДИВОСТОКСКАГО ОТДѢЛЕНІЯ ГОСУДАРСТВЕННАГО БАНКА
Vladivostok ... #S1254
ВЛАДИВОСТОКСКАЯ КОНТОРА ГОСУДАРСТВЕННАГО БАНКА
Vladivostok Office Government Bank ... #S1255A-S1255C
ИНДОКИТАЙСКІЙ БАНКЪ
Vladivostok - Banque de L'Indochine ... #S1256-S1259
БЛАГОВЫЩЕНСКАГО ОТДѢЛЕНІЯ ГОЧУДАРСТВЕННАГО БАНКА
Blagoveshchensk Branch Government Bank ... #S1259A-S1259H
АЛТАЙСКИЙ ГУБЕРНСКИЙ СОЮЗ
Altai ... #S1260-S1268
БАРНАУЛЬСКАГО ОТДѢЛЕНІЯ ГОСУДАРСТВЕННАГО БАНКА
Barnaul Branch Government Bank ... #S1268-S1268A
БАРНАУЛЬСКАГО ОТДѢЛЕНІЯ НАРОДНАГО БАНКА
Barnaul Branch Peoples Bank ... #S1268B-S1268F
БІЙСКАГО ОТДѢЛЕНІЯ ГОСУДАРСТВЕННАГО БАНКА
Biisk Branch Government Bank ... #S1269A-A1269D
КАМЧАТСКІЙ ОБЛАСТНОЙ КОМИТЕТЪ (КАМЧАТСКІЙ)
Kamchatka Region Committee ... #S1270
КАМЧАТСКИЙ ОБЛАСТНОЙ СОВЕТ. НАРОДНАГО ХОЗЯИСТВА
Kamchatka Provincial National Economic (Org). ... #S1271-S1274
САХАЛИНСКАЯ ОБЛАСТИ
Sakhalin Province ... #S1275
САХАЛИНСКИЙ ОБЛАСТНОИ НАРОДНО РЕВОЛЮЦИОННЫЙ КОМИТЕТ
Sakhalih Provincial National Revolutionary Committee ... #S1276-S1282
ТОМСКОЕ ОТДѢЛЕНІЕ ГОСУДАРСТВЕННАГО БАНКА
Tomsk Branch Government Bank ... #S1283-S1284
НИКОЛАЕВСКАГО НА АМУРТ ОТД. ГОС . БАНКА
Nikolaevsk-on-Amur Government Bank ... #S1286-S1288
НИКОЛАЕВСКАГО НА АМУРЕ ГОСУДАРСТВЕННОГО БАНКА Р.С.ф.С .Р.
Nikolaevsk-on-Amur Government Bank ... #S1291-S1293
ПЕРЕВОДНОЕ ПИСЬМО ПРИЙСКОВ.
УПРАВЛЕН АМГУНСКАЯ ЗОЛОТО ПРОМЫЩЛЕННАЯ КОМПАНІЯ
Amgun Gold Company ... #S1296-S1300
ЯКУТЧКАЯ АВТОНОМНАЯ СОЦИАЛ. СОВЕТ. РЕСПУБЛИКА
Yakutia ... #S1301-S1302
НАРОДНЫЙ КОМИССАРИАТ ТОРГ. И ПРОМЫШЛЕННОСТИ
National Commissariat of Commercial Manufacturing ... #S1306-S1313

KEY RUSSIAN WORDS & PHRASES

БИЛЕТЪ ... #S1117
БИЛЕТЪ ГОСУДАРСТВЕННАГО КАЗНАЧЕЙСТВА .. #S420-S427, S432-S434, S799-S784
БОНА ... #S1276-S1282
ВОНЫ ... #S585-S591
ВРЕММЕННЫЙ БОН ... #S234-S235A
ВРЕММЕННЫЙ КРЕДИТНЫЙ БИЛЕТЪ ... #S441-S445, S1162-S1175
ВРЕММЕННЫЙ ОБЯЗАГЕЛЬСТВО ... #S1268A
ВРЕММЕННЫЙ РАЗМѢННЫЙ ЗНАКЪ ... #S539-S544
ГАРАНТИРОВАННЫЙ ЧЕКЪ ... #S551-S565
ГОСУДАРСТВ. ВНУГРЕНН. 5% ЗАЕМЪ ... #S771-S776
ГОСУДАРСТВЕННЫЙ КРЕДИТНЫЙ БИЛЕТЪ ... #S871-S878, S1208,
... S1213-S1214, S1245-S1249
ДЕНЕЖНЫЙ ЗНАКЪ ... #S201-S210, S294, S370-S372, S408-S419, S456-S460,
... S611-S639, S687, S976-S983, S1116, S1139, S1161,
... S1259A-S1259H
ЗЗАЕМНЫЙ БИЛЕТЪ ... #S593-S599
ЗНАК ДЕРЖАВНОІ СКАРБНИЦІ ... #S293
КАЗНАЧЕЙСКІЙ ЗНАКЪ ... #S435-S440, S816-S818, S826-S828, S1189-S1194
КРАТКОСРОЧНАЯ БОНА ... #S241-S244
5% КРАТКОСРОЧНОЕ ОБЯЗАТЕЛЬСТВО ... #S121-S129, S381-S404, S821-S825,
... S831-S870A
6% КРАТКОСРОЧНОЕ ОБЯЗАТЕЛЬСТВО ... #S431
(as above but without the 5 or 6%) ... #S807-S812
КРЕДИТНЫЙ БИЛЕТЪ ... #S191-S195, S211, S471-S477, S961, S1118-S1133,
... S1201-S1204, S1207, S1209-S1212
КРЕДИТНЫЙ ЗНАК ... #S1271-S1274
ОБЯЗАТЕЛСТВО БОН ... #S766-S769
ОБЛИГАЦІЯ ВНУТРЕНН. ЗАЙМА ... #S777-S778
ОБЛИГАЦІЯ 5 1/2% ВОЕННАГО КР. ЗАЙМА ... #S785-S797, S906-S915
ОБЛИГАЦІЯ ЗАЙМА СВОБОДЫ ... #S798-S806, #S916-S919
РАСУЕТНЫЙ ЗНАКЪ ... #S641-S645, S1205-S1206, S1226-S1227, S1301-S1302
РАЗМѢННІЙ БИЛЕТЪ ... #S236-S240A, S323-S325A, S334-S338, S344-S347,
... S1216-S1220, S1291-S1293
РАЗМѢННІЙ ЗНАКЪ ... #S461-S469, S501-S520, S529-S535, S1241-S1244
РАЗМѢННІЙ ЧЕКЪ ... #S966-S971
РАЗМЉННЫЙ ДЕНЕЖНЫЙ ЗНАКЪ ... #S736-S745, S1136, S1141-S1146, S1151-S1157
ТАЛОН ... #S1261-S1268
ЧЕКЪ ... #S326-S328, S571-S573, S576-S584, #S691-S692,
... S1254, S1269A-S1269D, S1286-S1288

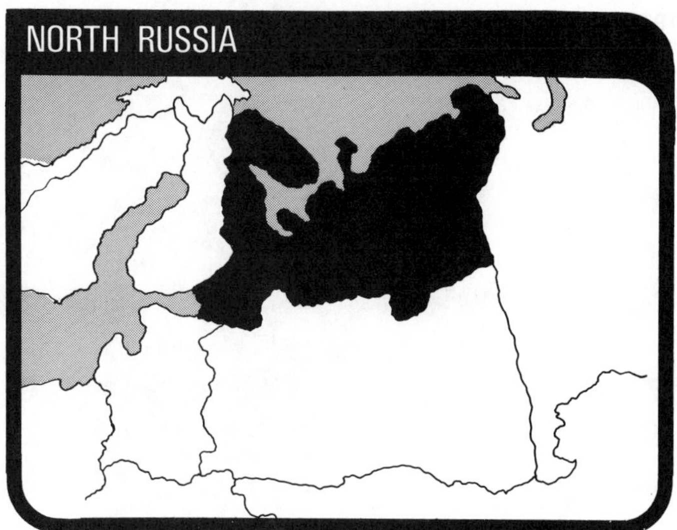

GOVERNMENTS

- Archangel Government (Red and White Regimes)
- Murmansk Soviet (Red and White Regimes)
- Government of the North Region (North Russia)
- Olonets Government

ARCHANGEL GOVERNMENT

ГОСУДАРСТВЕННЫЙ БАНКЪ
Government Bank - Red Regime
АРХАНГЕЛЬСКОЕ ОТДѢЛЕНIЕМЪ
Archangel

Issues of the Archangel Government Soviet before the August 1918 landings of Allied troops at Archangel, Bakaritza and Onega.

1918 ND ISSUE

		GOOD	FINE	XF
S101	**3 RUBLES** ND (1918). Green and black. Fasces at l. and r. of lg. *3* at upper ctr.			
	a. Issued note.	2.50	6.00	15.00
	x. Misprint: face w/o black text printing.	10.00	20.00	35.00
S102	**5 RUBLES** ND (1918). Gray-blue and black.	3.50	9.00	20.00
S103	**10 RUBLES** ND (1918). Red-brown and black.			
	a. Issued note.	8.50	16.00	30.00
	x. Misprint: face w/o black text printing.	12.00	22.50	37.50

		GOOD	FINE	XF
S104	**25 RUBLES** ND (1918). Black on blue-gray unpt. Polar bear at lower l., walrus at lower r.	7.50	17.50	32.50

ГОСУДАРСТВЕННЫЙ БАНКЪ
Government Bank - White Regime
АРХАНГЕЛЬСКОЕ ОТДѢЛЕНIЕМЪ
Archangel

1918 PROVISIONAL ISSUE

#S106-S108 issues of the Red regime w/validation ovpt. on back by the White regime. Ovpt. sign. of A. Faddeyev.

		GOOD	FINE	XF
S106	**3 RUBLES** ND (1918). Green. Red ovpt. on back #S101.	8.50	20.00	45.00
S107	**10 RUBLES** ND (1918). Red-brown. Black ovpt. on back #S103.	7.50	17.50	40.00
S108	**25 RUBLES** ND (1918). Gray-blue. Red ovpt. on a back #S104.	7.00	15.00	35.00

МУРМАНСК MURMANSK

STATE BANK - RED REGIME

Checks of the Archangel Branch of the State Bank bearing a round stamp reading: МУРМАНСКИ ФИНАНСОВЫИ ОТДѢЛ

ARCHANGEL

1918 CHECK ISSUE

		GOOD	FINE	XF
S111	**3 RUBLES** ND (1918).	50.00	100.00	—
S112	**10 RUBLES** ND (1918).	40.00	70.00	—
S113	**25 RUBLES** ND (1918).	30.00	60.00	—

STATE BANK - WHITE REGIME

Red regime issues w/registration ovpt. on back. Issued after June 27, 1918.

ARCHANGEL

1918 ND ISSUE

		GOOD	FINE	XF
S116	**3 RUBLES** ND (1918).	15.00	45.00	—
S117	**10 RUBLES** ND (1918).	12.00	40.00	—
S118	**25 RUBLES** ND (1918).	10.00	35.00	—

GOVERNMENT OF THE NORTH REGION

Socialist-Bourgeois government 1918-1920 under Chairman Nikolai Chaikovskii and later under General Eugene Miller. It was supported throughout much of its life by British, American and French troops. The area fell to the Reds in Feb. 1920, after Allied troops had withdrawn.

ВЕРХОВНАГО УПРАВЛЕНIЯ СѢВЕРНОЙ ОБЛАСТИ

1918 5% КРАТКОСРОЧНОЕ ОБЯЗАТЕЛЬСТВО
DEBENTURE BONDS ISSUE

		GOOD	FINE	XF
S121	**100 RUBLES** 15.8.1918. Yellow.	12.50	27.50	45.00

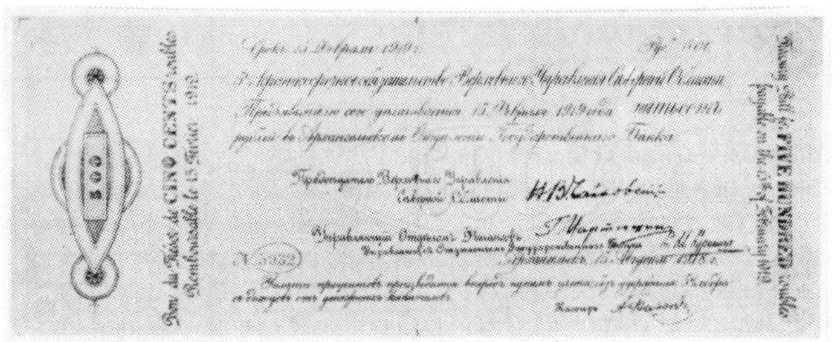

		GOOD	FINE	XF
S122	**500 RUBLES** 15.8.1918. Blue.	15.00	32.50	60.00

		Good	Fine	XF
S123	**1000 Rubles** 15.8.1918. Red.	27.50	55.00	90.00
S124	**5000 Rubles** 15.8.1918.	45.00	90.00	150.00
S125	**10,000 Rubles** 15.8.1918.	55.00	110.00	190.00

ВРЕМЕННАГО ПРАВИТЕЛЬСТВА СѢВЕРНОЙ ОБЛАСТИ

1918 5% КРАТКОСРОЧНОЕ ОБЯЗАТЕЛЬСТВО Debenture Bonds Issue

Notes exist both w/ or w/o И after ФИНАНСОВЪ. This type appeared in Oct. 1918.

		Good	Fine	XF
S126	**50 Rubles** 15.8.1918. Green.	4.00	8.00	20.00
S127	**100 Rubles** 15.8.1918.			
	a. W/И.	10.00	20.00	40.00
	b. W/o И.	4.00	8.00	20.00
S128	**500 Rubles** 15.8.1918. Blue.			
	a. W/green or black serial #. W/И.	10.00	20.00	40.00
	b. W/o И.	5.00	10.00	25.00

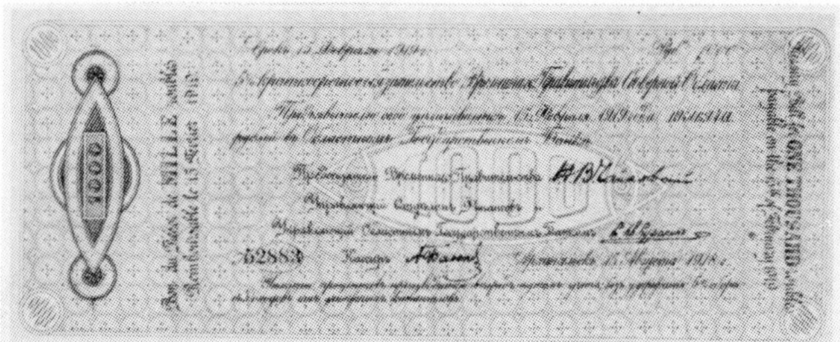

		Good	Fine	XF
S129	**1000 Rubles** 15.8.1918. Red.			
	a. W/И.	10.00	20.00	40.00
	b. W/o I.	5.00	10.00	25.00

NOTE: #S121-S129 signed by N. V. Chaikovskii, K. Kurakin and A. Faddeyev. #S121-S124 also bear a fourth sign.

СѢВЕРНАЯ РОССИЯ North Russia

Chaikovskii Government

#S131-S150 were printed in England, and issued in Northern Russia from Dec., 1918, on Barclays Bank to support the the Chaikovskii government. Similar in style to Imperial all but the Small Change notes state on their face they are payable at the rate of 40 rubles to the pound sterling. The larger notes bear the sign. of K. Kurakin and Thomas Harvey. Some of the notes have a double headed eagle crowned, and some of these have the monarchist device covered by overprinting.

1919 ND Small Change Notes Issue

#S131-S134 like Czarist notes #28, #30 and #31 (in Vol. 2) but w/title: СѢВЕРНАЯ РОССІЯ.

		Good	Fine	XF
S131	**10 Kopeks** ND (1919). Green on peach unpt.	1.00	4.00	9.00
S132	**20 Kopeks** ND (1919). Brown on green unpt.	1.00	4.00	9.00

		Good	Fine	XF
S133	**50 Kopeks** ND (1919). Blue on yellow unpt. Eagle w/crown at upper ctr.	.75	3.00	7.50
S134	**50 Kopeks** ND (1919). Eagle w/o crown.	6.00	15.00	40.00

1918 First Issue

#S135-S138 like Czarist issues but w/title: СѢВЕРНАЯ РОССІЯ. Eagle w/crown. W/sign. title: ЧЛЕНЪ ГОСУДАРСТВЕННОЙ ЭМИССІОННОЙ КАССЫ on back.

		Good	Fine	XF
S135	**5 Rubles** 1918. Blue-green. Also known w/o stamp on back.	8.00	20.00	40.00
S136	**10 Rubles** 1918. Red and green.	8.00	20.00	40.00
S137	**25 Rubles** 1918. Pink and green.	15.00	37.50	70.00

		Good	Fine	XF
S138	**100 Rubles** 1918. Brown, red and green.	50.00	100.00	250.00

1918 Second Issue

#S139-S143 like #S135-S138 but w/sign. title: ЧЛЕНЪ ГОРОДСКОЙ ЭМИСІОННОЙ КАССЫ on back.

		Good	Fine	XF
S139	**5 Rubles** 1918. Blue-green.	8.00	20.00	40.00

		Good	Fine	XF
S140	**10 Rubles** 1918. Black on lt. red and green unpt.	8.00	20.00	40.00

		Good	Fine	XF
S141	**25 Rubles** 1918. Pink and green.			
	a. Eagle ovpt.	15.00	37.50	70.00
	b. Eagle w/o ovpt.	20.00	40.00	75.00
S142	**100 Rubles** 1918. Brown, red and green. Back black.	50.00	100.00	250.00
S143	**500 Rubles** 1918.	90.00	270.00	450.00

1919 Issue

#S144-S150 like #1 and #9-14 (in Vol. 2) but text reads: СЪВЕРНАЯ РОССІЯ. Eagle w/o crown.

		Good	Fine	XF
S144	**1 Ruble** 1919. Blue on red-brown unpt. Back red-brown.	3.00	8.00	15.00

		Good	Fine	XF
S145	**3 Rubles** 1919. Black on green and m/c unpt.	3.00	8.00	15.00
S146	**5 Rubles** 1919. Black on blue and lt. orange unpt.	4.00	10.00	20.00
S147	**10 Rubles** 1919. Similar to #S140.	6.00	15.00	30.00

		Good	Fine	XF
S148	**25 Rubles** 1919. Rose and green.	10.00	25.00	60.00
S149	**100 Rubles** 1919. Brown, red and green.	50.00	150.00	350.00
S150	**500 Rubles** 1919.	75.00	250.00	550.00

1919 ГВСО Revalidated Notes Issue

Notes of the Czarist and the Provisional Governments w/perforation: ГВСО. The perforation is frequently forged. Issued from April 14, 1919. Reference # in listings are to notes in Vol. 2.

		Good	Fine	XF
S151	**50 Kopeks** ND (1919). Blue on yellow unpt. Perforation on #31.	.50	1.00	2.00
S152	**1 Ruble** ND (1919 -old date 1898). Blue on red-brown unpt. Perforation on #1.	.75	1.25	4.00

		Good	Fine	XF
S153	**1 Ruble** ND (1919 -old date 1898). Blue on brown unpt. Perforation on #15.	.25	.50	2.00
S154	**3 Rubles** ND (1919 -old date 1905). Black on green and m/c unpt. Perforation on #9.	1.00	2.00	4.00
S155	**5 Rubles** ND (1919 -old date 1898). Blue on m/c unpt. Perforation on #3.	10.00	30.00	100.00
S156	**5 Rubles** ND (1919 -old date 1909). Blue-black on m/c unpt. Perforation on #10.	.25	.50	2.00
S157	**5 Rubles** ND (1919 -old date 1909). Blue-black on m/c unpt. Perforation on #35.	.75	2.00	4.00
S158	**10 Rubles** ND (1919 - old date 1898). Red on m/c unpt. Perforation on #4.	15.00	60.00	—
S159	**10 Rubles** ND (1919 -old date 1909). Deep olive-green on green and red unpt. Perforation on #11.	.50	1.00	2.00
S160	**20 Rubles** ND (1919). Brown on red-brown unpt. Perforation on #41.	.25	.50	2.00
S161	**20 Rubles** ND (1919 -old date 1917). Black on yellow unpt. Perforation on #77.	3.00	7.50	15.00
S162	**25 Rubles** ND (1919 -old date 1909). Red and blue on m/c unpt. Perforation on #12.	1.00	4.00	6.00

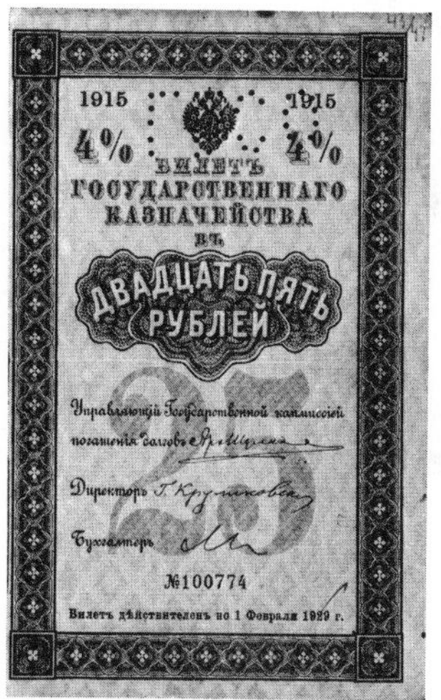

		Good	Fine	XF
S163	**25 Rubles** ND (1919 -old date 1915). Green on violet unpt. Perforation on #48.	1.00	4.00	6.00
S164	**40 Rubles** ND (1919). Red on green unpt. Perforation on #42.	.25	.50	2.00
S165	**40 Rubles** ND (1919 -old date 1917). Black. Perforation on #78.	1.50	5.00	15.00
S166	**50 Rubles** ND (1919 -old date 1899). Black on m/c unpt. Perforation on #8.	2.00	6.00	17.00
S167	**50 Rubles** ND (1919 -old date 1909). Brown on green unpt. Perforation on #49.	2.00	7.00	20.00
S168	**50 Rubles** ND (1919 -old date 1914). Brown on green unpt. Perforation on #52.	2.00	7.00	20.00
S169	**50 Rubles** ND (1919 -old date 1915). Brown on green unpt. Perforation on #53.	2.00	7.00	20.00
S170	**50 Rubles** ND (1919 -old date 1917). Black on green unpt. Perforation on #79.	2.00	7.00	20.00
S171	**100 Rubles** ND (1919 -old date 1898). Black on tan and m/c unpt. Perforation on #5.	10.00	30.00	100.00

		Good	Fine	XF
S172	**100 Rubles** ND (1919 -old date 1910). Lt. brown. Perforation on #13.	1.00	4.00	6.00
S173	**100 Rubles** ND (1919 -old date 1913). Black on pink unpt. Perforation on #56.	2.00	5.00	12.00
S174	**100 Rubles** ND (1919 -old date 1914). Black on pink unpt. Perforation on #57.	2.00	5.00	12.00
S175	**100 Rubles** ND (1919 -old date 1915). Black on pink unpt. Perforation on #58.	2.00	5.00	12.00
S176	**100 Rubles** ND (1919 -old date 1917). Black on brown unpt. Perforation on #80.	2.00	5.00	12.00
S177	**250 Rubles** ND (1919 -old date 1917). Black on lilac unpt. Perforation on #36.	.50	1.00	5.00
S178	**500 Rubles** ND (1919 -old date 1898). Black on m/c unpt. Perforation on #6.	20.00	50.00	150.00
S179	**500 Rubles** ND (1919 -old date 1912). Green on m/c unpt. Perforation on #14.	1.50	5.00	10.00
S180	**500 Rubles** ND (1919 -old date 1915). Black on blue unpt. Perforation on #59.	2.00	5.00	12.00
S181	**500 Rubles** ND (1919 -old date 1916). Black on blue unpt. Perforation on #60.	2.00	5.00	12.00
S182	**1000 Rubles** ND (1919 -old dates 1916; 1917). Lilac-brown. Perforation on #61-63.	2.50	8.00	15.00
S183	**1000 Rubles** ND (1919 -old date 1917). Dk. brown on green unpt. Perforation on #37.	1.00	3.00	5.00

		Good	Fine	XF
S184	**5000 Rubles** ND (1919 -old dates 1916; 1917). Orange. Perforation on #64.	3.00	8.00	17.50
S185	**10,000 Rubles** ND (1919 -old dates 1916; 1917). Red. Perforation on #65-67.	3.00	8.00	20.00
S186	**100,000 Rubles** ND (1919 -old dates 1916; 1917). Perforation on #73.	10.00	30.00	60.00

OLONETS GOVERNMENT

ОЛОНЕЦКОЙ ГУБЕРНІЙ

Soviet government set up in 1918 w/capital at Petrozavodsk (Finnish Petrikoi). The short-lived regime printed only proofs of their intended note issue.

1918 КРЕДИТНЫЙ БИЛЕТЬ CREDIT NOTE ISSUE

#S191-S195 arms at upper ctr.

		Good	Fine	XF
S191	**1 Ruble** 1918. Yellow. 133 x 80mm. Proof.	—	Rare	—
S192	**5 Rubles** 1918. Blue. Proof.	—	Rare	—
S193	**10 Rubles** 1918. Rose. Proof.	—	Rare	—
S194	**25 Rubles** 1918. Olive-gray. Proof.	—	Rare	—
S195	**100 Rubles** 1918. Brown. 157 x 96mm. Proof.	—	Rare	—

MILITARY

- Northwest Front (Gen. N. N. Yudenich)
- Pskov Regional Government (Maj. Gen. Vandamm)
- Special Corps of the North Army (Gen. Rodzianko)
- Independent West Army (Col. Avalov-Bermondt)
- Partisan Company of Lt. Col. Bulak-Balakhovich
- Kronstadt Republic (Naval Mutineers)
- Mogilev Region
- Slutsk (White)

ПОЛЕВОЕ КАЗНАЧЕЙСТВО СѢВЕРОЗАПАДНАГО ФРОНТА
Field Treasury, Northwest Front

General N. N. Yudenich

1919 ДЕНЕЖНЫЙ ЗНАКЪ CURRENCY TOKENS ISSUE

In May and October, 1919, Yudenich's White army made two unsuccessful attempts to penetrate from Estonia into Petrograd. His elegant notes come in three series - w/o prefix letter and w/A or Б before the serial #. The back of each note shows an uncrowned double eagle and the Peter the Great Monument.

Each note bears two signatures: Yudenich, commander in chief, general of infantry, and St. Lianozov, manager of finance department. Notes were offset printed in Stockholm, Sweden by Centraltryckeriet. Yudenich disbanded his army on Jan. 22, 1920.

		VG	VF	Unc
S201	**25 Kopeks** 1919. Black on lt. green unpt.	.75	2.25	4.50

		VG	VF	Unc
S202	**50 Kopeks** 1919. Black on gray unpt.	.75	2.25	5.00
S203	**1 Ruble** 1919. Dk. green on lt. green unpt.	1.00	3.50	6.00
S204	**3 Rubles** 1919. Green on rose unpt.			
	a. Serial # w/o letters (first issue).	1.50	4.00	8.00
	b. Serial # prefix: A (second issue).	1.00	3.50	7.50

		VG	VF	Unc
S205	**5 Rubles** 1919. Black on blue unpt.			
	a. Like #S204a.	1.50	4.00	7.50
	b. Like #S204b.	1.00	3.00	7.00
S206	**10 Rubles** 1919. Brown on lt. green unpt.			
	a. Like #S204a. (first issue).	1.00	3.50	5.00
	b. Like #S204b. (second issue).	1.50	4.00	7.00
	c. Serial # prefix: Б (third issue).	1.50	5.00	12.50

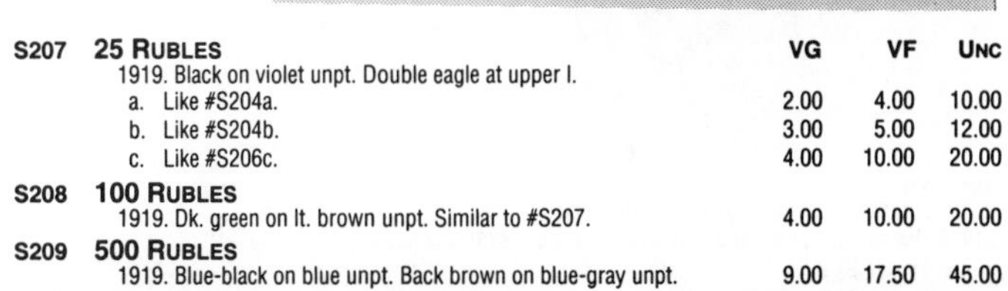

		VG	VF	UNC
S207	**25 RUBLES** 1919. Black on violet unpt. Double eagle at upper l.			
	a. Like #S204a.	2.00	4.00	10.00
	b. Like #S204b.	3.00	5.00	12.00
	c. Like #S206c.	4.00	10.00	20.00
S208	**100 RUBLES** 1919. Dk. green on lt. brown unpt. Similar to #S207.	4.00	10.00	20.00
S209	**500 RUBLES** 1919. Blue-black on blue unpt. Back brown on blue-gray unpt.	9.00	17.50	45.00

		VG	VF	UNC
S210	**1000 RUBLES** 1919. Black-green on lt. brown unpt. Flags and shields around value at l., double eagle at r. Back brown on lilac unpt.	8.00	15.00	40.00

ПСКОВСКАГО ОБЛАСТНОГО КАЗНАЧЕЙСТВА
Pskov Regional Government Treasury

Regional issue of notes in the Pskov (Pleskau) area by the White army under General Vandamm.

1918 КРЕДИТНЫЙ БИЛЕТЪ TREASURY CREDIT NOTES ISSUE

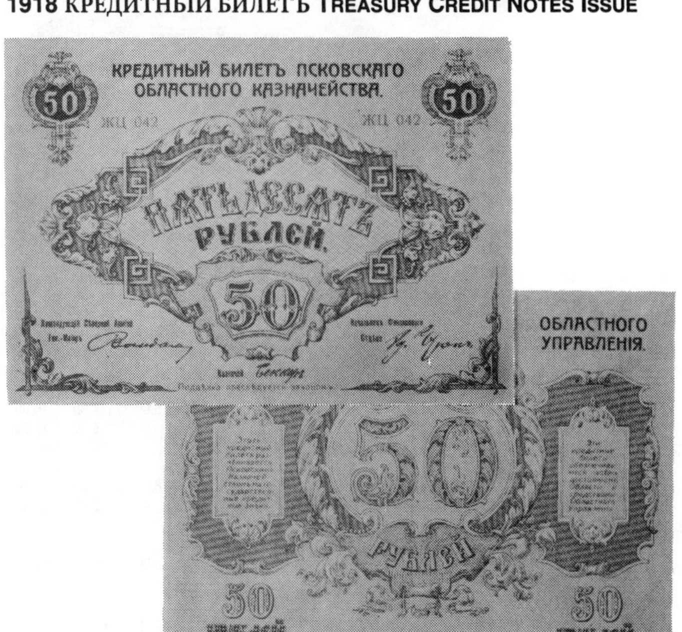

		VG	VF	UNC
S211	**50 RUBLES** 2.11.1918. Dull green and red. Back blue and red on green unpt. Autograph sign. of Major General Vandamm, commander of the North Army, and a financial officer and treasurer.	12.00	25.00	60.00

1918 PSKOV BANK SMALL CHANGE NOTES ISSUE

Three sign. In 1918 there were also Pskov bonds pressed into use as currency. Not connected with Gen. Vandamm's army, as that organization was not activated until Oct. 12, 1918.

		VG	VF	UNC
S212	**1 RUBLE** 15.3.1918. Orange.	5.00	12.00	35.00
S213	**5 RUBLES** 15.3.1918. Blue and brown.	7.50	17.50	50.00

ОТДѢЛЬНЫЙ КОРПУСЪ СѢВЕРНОИ АРМІИ, ГЕН. РОДЗЯНКО
Special Corps of Northern Army under Gen. Rodzianko

The letters OKCA appear on the postage notes, abbreviation for the Russian words for *Special Corps Northern Army.* There are other postage stamps of OKCA, but only the 50-kopek stamp was printed on cardboard for currency use.

1919 STAMP MONEY ISSUE

		VG	VF	UNC
S216	**50 KOPEKS** ND (1919). Lt. green. Postage stamp, both sides printed.	50.00	100.00	150.00

Original size

		VG	VF	UNC
S217	**50 KOPEKS** ND (1919). Lt. green.			
	a. Face only of #S216.	5.00	10.00	25.00
	b. Back only of #S216.	5.00	10.00	25.00
S218	**50 KOPEKS** ND (1919). Dk. green.			
	a. Face only of #S216.	6.00	12.50	30.00
	b. Back only of #S216.	6.00	12.50	30.00

1919 NOTES ISSUE

		VG	VF	UNC
S219	**1 RUBLE** 1919. Brown on yellow.	2.50	5.00	10.00
S220	**3 RUBLES** 1919. Green.	3.50	7.00	15.00
S221	**5 RUBLES** 1919. Blue.	10.00	15.00	30.00

		VG	VF	UNC
S222	**10 RUBLES** 1919. Red.	4.00	8.00	17.50

ЗАПАДНАЯ ДОБРОВОЛЬЧЕСКАЯ АРМІЯ, ПОЛК АВАЛОВ-БЕРМОНДТЪ
Independent West Army under Colonel Avalov-Bermondt

Bermondt, the self-styled Prince Avalov, raised a mixed force of Russian volunteers and German regulars in the Baltic area to move against the Bolsheviks in West Russia. His force was defeated by the Latvian army in October, 1919. The 1, 5, and 10 mark notes were printed in Jelgava (Mitau); the 50 mark note was printed in Berlin. Signatures on the notes are Avalov-Bermondt, colonel, commander-in-chief of the army; Engelhardt, manager of state economic dept. of the army.

1919 KASSENSCHEINE (TREASURY NOTES) ISSUE

#S226-S228 arms at upper ctr. Face in Russian, back in German.

		VG	VF	UNC
S226	**1 MARK** 10.10.1919. Black on pale blue, red, and gray lines in unpt. Back dk. blue on lt. blue.			
	a. Embossed seal at lower l.	1.50	3.00	7.50
	b. No embossed seal.	1.50	3.00	7.50
S227	**5 MARK** 10.10.1919. Black on pale blue, red, and gray lines in unpt. Back red on pink unpt.			
	a. Embossed seal at lower l.	1.50	4.00	10.00
	b. No embossed seal.	1.50	4.00	10.00
S228	**10 MARK** 10.10.1919. Black. Back brown on pale blue unpt., green paper.			
	a. Face on green paper w/fine lines horizontally in unpt. w/embossed seal at lower l.	8.00	25.00	60.00
	b. Face on white paper w/o unpt. Seal as above.	3.50	10.00	25.00
	c. W/o embossed seal, unpt. as a.	10.00	30.00	75.00
	d. W/o embossed seal unpt. as b.	4.50	12.00	30.00

NOTE: Unfinished sheets of #S228 (printed on one side only) were used to print Latvian postage stamps in 1920.

#S229 *Deleted*. See #S228.

		VG	VF	UNC
S230	**50 MARK** 10.10.1919. Black. Arms at l. Back gray-green on brown unpt.			
	a. Stamped imprint.	5.00	20.00	65.00
	b. W/o stamped imprint.	4.00	15.00	55.00

ПАРТИЗАНСКИЙ ОТРЯД ПОЛК БУЛАК-БАЛАХОВИЧА
Partisan Detachment of Lt.Col. Bulak-Balakhovich

1919 ND ISSUE

		VG	VF	UNC
S231	**40 RUBLES** ND (1919).	—	Rare	—

КРОНШТАДТСКАЯ РЕСПУБЛИКА
Kronstadt Republic

1917 ND ВРЕМЕННЫЙ БОН PROVISIONAL *BONS* OR NOTES ISSUE

#S234 and S235 were apparently intended for issue by the short-lived Kronstadt Republic, a Bolshevik state declared by naval mutineers at the Kronstadt naval fortress outside Petrograd in 1917, which collapsed along with the Bolshevik coup against the Provisional government July 16-18, 1917.

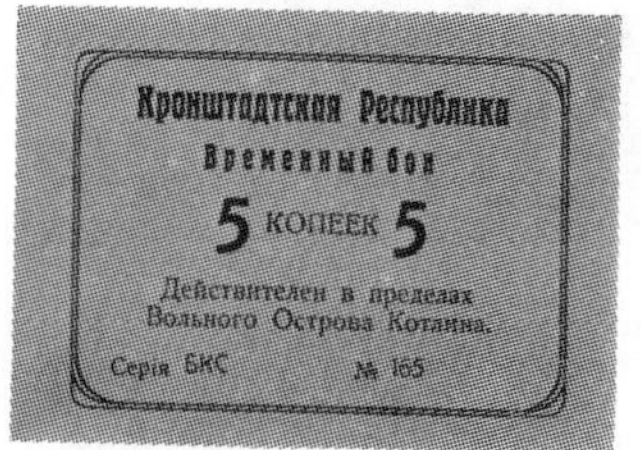

		VG	VF	UNC
S234	**5 KOPEK** ND (1917). Black text on bright red unpt. 99 x 70mm. Seriya БКС.	—	—	45.00

		VG	VF	UNC
S235	**10 KOPEK** ND (1917). Like #S234 but Seriya ВТР.	—	—	45.00

NOTE: Some authorities question the authenticity of #S234 and S235.

S235A	**10 KOPEK** ND (1917). Like #S235 but off-white paper, and reduced in size.	—	—	150.00

МОГИЛЕВСКОЙ ГУБЕРНIИ
Mogilev Region

1918 РАЗМѢННЫЙ БИЛЕТЪ EXCHANGE NOTES ISSUE

#S236-A240A eagle w/outstretched wings and holding scroll w/arms at lower l., 3 volcanos w/center erupting at lower r. Russian text on back for all except #S237.

		GOOD	FINE	XF
S236	**1 RUBLE** 1918. Blue.			
	a. Issued note w/serial # on lower back.	8.00	17.50	45.00
	r. Remainder w/o serial #.	—	6.00	12.00

		GOOD	FINE	XF
S237	**3 RUBLEI** Black on blue paper. Back w/text in Polish.			
	a. Issued note w/serial # on back.	8.00	17.50	45.00
	r. Remainder w/o serial # on back.	—	6.00	12.50
	x. Error w/inverted back.	20.00	40.00	75.00
S238	**5 RUBLEI** 1918. Black on blue paper.			
	a. Issued note w/serial # on back.	8.00	17.50	45.00
	r. Remainder w/o serial #.	—	8.00	17.50
S239	**10 RUBLEI** 1918.			
	a. Issued note w/serial # on back.	8.00	17.50	45.00
	r. Remainder w/o serial #.	—	9.00	20.00
S240	**25 RUBLEI** 1918. Black on blue paper.			
	a. Issued note w/serial # on back.	9.00	25.00	50.00
	r. Remainder w/o serial #.	—	12.50	27.50
S240A	**100 RUBLEI** 1918. (Not issued.)	10.00	25.00	50.00

СЛУЦКОЕ УѢЗДНОЕ ЗЕМСТВО
Slutsk (White Russia) Zemstvo

Zemstvos were cooperatives formed under the Empire, some of which survived into the Soviet period. Slutsk was in Minsk Guberniya (White Russia).

1918 КРАТКОСРОЧНАЯ БОНА
DEBENTURE *BONS* OR NOTES ISSUE

#S241-S244 w/handstamp at l.

		GOOD	FINE	XF
S241	**1 RUBLE** 1918. Black on red-brown unpt. 4 sign.	4.00	15.00	40.00
S242	**3 RUBLES** 1918. Black on green unpt.			
	a. Normal unpt.	4.00	15.00	40.00
	x. Error w/reversed unpt.	7.50	17.50	45.00

		GOOD	FINE	XF
S243	**5 RUBLES** 1918. Black on blue unpt.	4.00	15.00	40.00
S244	**10 RUBLES** 1918. Black on red unpt.	5.00	20.00	50.00

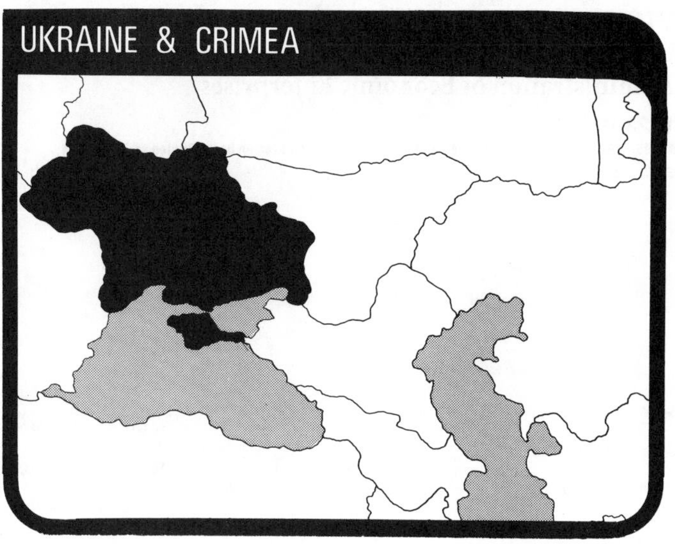

ISSUES OF:

- Ukrainian Socialist Soviet Republic
- Administration of Economic Enterprises
- Elizabetgrad Branch, Government Bank
- Elizabetgrad Branch, Peoples Bank
- Revolutionary Army of Insurgent Ukraine (Makhno)
- Ukrainian Cooperative Bank, Kiev (Kyiv)
- Ukrainian Revolutionary Army (Post-WW II)
- Odessa City
- Zhitomir City
- Zhitomir Branch, Soednenni Bank
- Crimea Territorial Government (Gen. Sulkevich)
- Provisional Govt. of Workers and Peasants
- Kherson Government Territory Plenipotentiary for Food

UKRAINIAN PEOPLES REPUBLIC

NOTE: For previously listed #S251-S292, see Vol. 2, Ukraine #1-41.

УКРАИНСКОЙ СОЦ. СОВЕТ. РЕСПУБЛ.

1920 ND ЗНАК ДЕРЖАВНОЙ СКАРБНИЦІ ISSUE

		VG	VF	UNC
S293	**10 KARBOVANETS** ND (1920). Red-brown. Wmk: Spades, white paper and w/block #.	8.00	15.00	40.00

1919 (1920) ДЕНЕЖНЫЙ ЗНАК CURRENCY TOKEN ISSUE

		VG	VF	UNC
S294	**50 KARBOVANETS** 1919 (1920). Workers w/hammer at l., factory in background. Proofs only.			
	a. Green.	—	Rare	—
	b. Lt. blue.	—	Rare	—
	c. Violet.	—	Rare	—
	d. Brown.	—	Rare	—

УПРАВЛЕНИЕ ХОЗЯЙСТВЕН. ПРЕДПРЕЯТИЯМИ ВУЦИК.
Administration of Economic Enterprises

1923 ISSUE

#S295-S299 green and blue on face, w/mark of denomination lilac on back. Printed script serial #.

		VG	VF	UNC
S295	**5 KOPEKS** 1923.	18.00	30.00	60.00

		VG	VF	UNC
S296	**10 KOPEKS** 1923.	18.00	30.00	60.00
S297	**25 KOPEKS** 1923.	18.00	35.00	70.00
S298	**50 KOPEKS** 1923.	20.00	40.00	80.00

		VG	VF	UNC
S299	**1 RUBLE** 1923.	30.00	50.00	95.00
S300	**3 RUBLES** 1923.	32.50	52.50	100.00
S301	**5 RUBLES** 1923.	35.00	60.00	140.00
S302	**10 RUBLES** 1923.	32.50	70.00	175.00
S303	**25 RUBLES** 1923.	60.00	140.00	300.00
S304	**50 RUBLES** 1923.	100.00	200.00	500.00

GERMAN OCCUPATION - WWII

NOTE: For previously listed #S305-S320, see Vol. 2, Ukraine #42-57.

ГОСУДАРСТВЕННАГО БАНКА
Government Bank

ЕЛИСАВЕТГРАСКОЕ ОТДЪЛ
Elizabetgrad

1918 РАЗМѢННЫЙ БИЛЕТЪ EXCHANGE NOTES ISSUE

		GOOD	FINE	XF
S323	**1 RUBLE** 1918. Black on brown unpt. Double-headed eagle at l., arms at r. Back dull orange; double-headed eagle at ctr.	4.00	10.00	20.00
S323A	**3 RUBLEI** 1918. Black-green. Eagle w/outstretched wings and holding scroll w/arms at lower l., laureated woman's head at lower r.	3.00	7.50	15.00

		GOOD	FINE	XF
S323B	**10 RUBLEI** 1918. Black-green on salmon unpt. Like #S323A.			
	a. Issued note w/serial # at r.	6.00	15.00	30.00
	r. Remainder w/o serial #.	2.50	7.00	15.00

НАРОДНАГО БАНКА
NATIONAL BANK
ЕЛИСАБЕТГРАДСКАГО ОТДѢЛЕНІЯ
ELIZABETGRAD

1919 РАЗМѢННІЙ БИЛЕТЪ EXCHANGE NOTES ISSUE

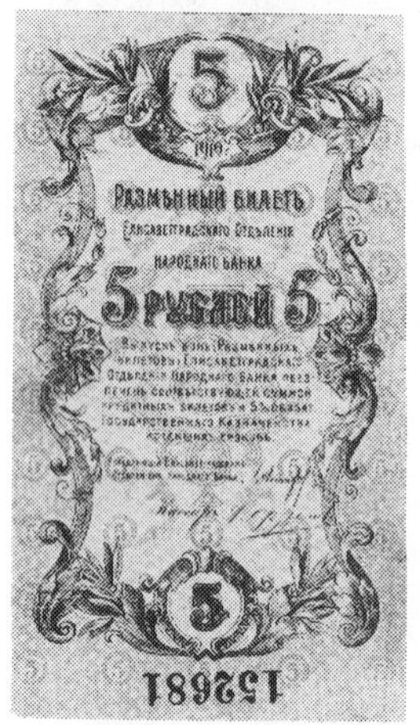

		GOOD	FINE	XF
S324	**5 RUBLEI** 1919. Dk. blue on lt. blue unpt. Ornate border. Back dk. blue on lt. green unpt. Vertical format.	2.50	7.00	15.00

		GOOD	FINE	XF
S324A	**25 RUBLEI** 1919. Black on red and green unpt. Back green.			
	a. W/o series.	2.50	5.00	10.00
	b. W/series.	2.50	5.00	10.00

1920 РАЗМѢННІЙ БИЛЕТЪ EXCHANGE NOTES ISSUE

		Good	Fine	XF
S325	**50 RUBLEI**			
	1920. Black on lt. brown and lt. green unpt. Back black on brown unpt.			
	a. W/o series.	4.00	10.00	20.00
	b. W/series.	2.00	5.00	10.00
S325A	**50 RUBLEI**			
	1920. Black on brown and green unpt. Back black on green unpt.			
	a. W/o series.	4.00	10.00	20.00
	b. W/series.	2.00	5.00	10.00

1ST REVOLUTIONARY ARMY OF INSURGENT UKRAINE

Partisan overprints supposedly made on notes of the Denikin Armies by partisan leader N. Makhno at Gulyai-Pole in Ekaterinoslav Guberniya. It is also possible that Makhno could have made some ovpt. for propaganda reasons while he was in exile in Paris. However, all examples on the market are bogus and in Unc. or nearly new condition. These began to appear in January 1980.

ВСЕУКРАЇНСЬКИЙ КООПЕРАТИВНИЙ БАНК

UKRAINIAN COOPERATIVE BANK, KIEV UKRAINBANK

1924 ЧЕК CIRCULATING CHECKS ISSUE

		VG	VF	Unc
S326	**1 KARBOVANETS**			
	1924. Brown.	10.00	25.00	55.00
S327	**3 KARBOVANTSI**			
	1924. Green.	8.00	15.00	40.00

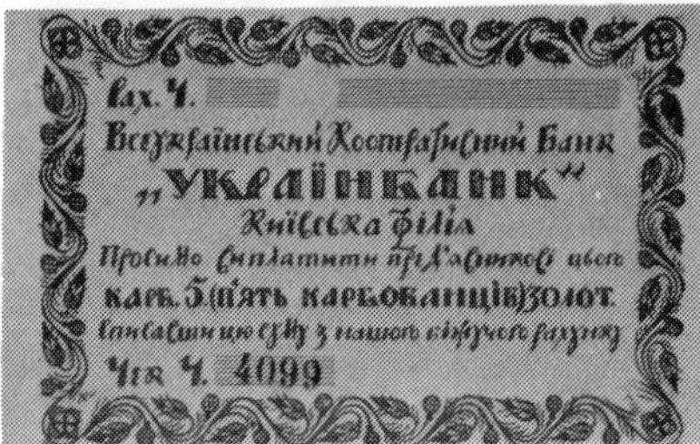

		VG	VF	Unc
S328	**5 KARBOVANTSIV**			
	1924. Blue.	10.00	22.50	50.00

POST WWII

УКРАИНЬСКА ПОВСТАНСКА АРМІЯ УПА-UPA (УКРАЇНСЬКА ПОВСТАНСЬКА АРМІЯ)

UkrainianRevolutionary Army

Anti-Nazi, anti-Communist Ukrainian nationalist forces, organized in 1942 and led by Gen. Roman Shukhevych 1944-1950. Its *bons* were donation receipts, but the 5-karbovanez is a circulating note. There are related *bons* issued by other Ukrainian groups - OUN, UHVR and ABN - from 1945 to 1949.

1946 ND ISSUE

		VG	VF	Unc
S330	**5 KARBOVANETS**			
(S322)	ND (1946). Brown, violet and m/c. Soldier at machine gun and soldier w/hand grenade.	—	Rare	—

ОДЕССА Odessa City

1917 РАЗМѢННАЯ МАРКА POSTAGE STAMP MONEY ISSUE

#S331

#S332

		VG	VF	Unc
S331	**15 KOPEKS**			
	ND (1917). Brown.	1.50	4.50	10.00
S332	**20 KOPEKS**			
	ND (1917). Green.	1.50	4.50	10.00

		VG	VF	Unc
S333	**50 KOPEKS**			
	ND (1917). Black and dk. blue on brown unpt. Arms at upper ctr. Wreath on back.	1.00	3.50	7.50

1917; 1918 РАЗМѢННЫИЙ БИЛЕТБ Г. ОДЕССЫ EXCHANGE NOTES OF ODESSA AREA ISSUE

Many varieties of color, paper and serial #.

		VG	VF	Unc
S334	**3 RUBLES**			
	1917. Dk. green. Double eagle w/arms at l., Mercury at lower r. Bldg. in unpt. on back.	1.00	2.00	5.00
S335	**5 RUBLES**			
	1917. Blue. Similar to #S334.	1.00	2.50	6.00

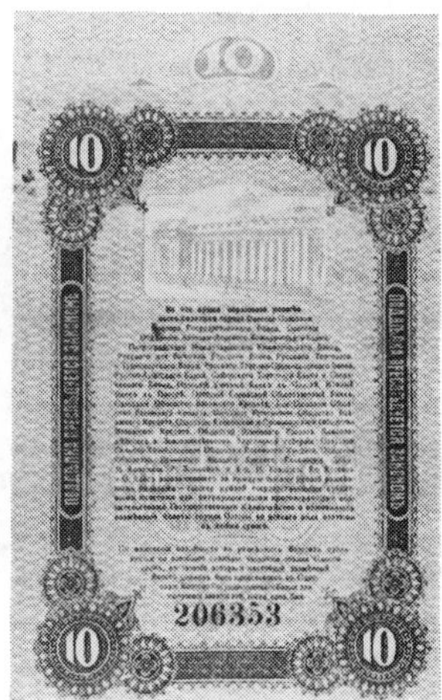

		VG	VF	UNC
S336	**10 RUBLES** 1917. Dk. green on pale green and lt. red unpt. Double eagle w/arms at upper ctr. Back dk. brown on pale orange-brown unpt; bldg. facade at upper ctr.	1.50	4.00	10.00

		VG	VF	UNC
S337	**25 RUBLES** 1917. Black on dull green and pink unpt. Double eagle at upper l. and r., arms at upper ctr. Back black and deep green on tan unpt.; bldg. at l. and at r., arms at upper ctr.			
	a. Wmk: Waves.	1.50	4.00	10.00
	b. W/o wmk. Bldg. unpt, columns at l.	1.00	3.50	10.00
	c. Bldg. unpt., columns at r.	1.00	3.50	10.00
S338	**50 RUBLES** 1918. Green and blue. Similar to #S337.	7.00	15.00	40.00

NOTE: #S331-S338 were circulating from 1917-20 in the southwestern part of the Ukraine.

ЖИТОМИР Zhytomyr City

As with the Odessa city notes, the Zhytomyr issues circulated throughout much of the Ukraine, especially in the central regions.

1918 РОЗМІННИЙ БІЛЕТ МІСТА ЖИТОМИРА MUNICIPAL RECEIPTS ISSUE

		GOOD	FINE	XF
S341	**1 KARBOVANETS** 1918. Black on tan unpt.	2.50	7.50	20.00
S342	**3 KARBOVANTSI** 1918. Green unpt. Like #S343.	1.50	4.00	10.00

		GOOD	FINE	XF
S343	**5 KARBOVANTSIV** 1918. Blue.			
	a. Black serial #.	2.50	5.00	12.50
	b. Red serial #.	2.50	5.00	12.50

НАРОДНОГО БАНКА

NATIONAL BANK

1919-20 РАЗМЕННЫЙ БИЛЕТ TREASURY NOTES ISSUE

		GOOD	FINE	XF
S344	**50 RUBLES** 1919. Black on lt. brown unpt.	2.00	4.00	10.00
S345	**75 RUBLES** 1919. Black on blue-green unpt.	2.00	4.00	10.00
S346	**100 RUBLES** 1919. Black on reddish brown unpt.	1.50	3.00	9.00

		GOOD	FINE	XF
S347	**250 RUBLES** 1920. Blue on green unpt.	2.00	4.00	10.00

АЗОВСКО-ДОНСКОЙ КОММЕРЧЕСКІЙ БАНКЪ Azov-Don Commercial Bank

ЖИТОМИРСКОЕ ОТДѢЛЕНІЕ

Zhytomyr

Circulating bearer checks issued by bank branches in Zhytomyr.

1918 CIRCULATING BEARER CHECKS ISSUE

Eleven different issues of checks dated from 27.1.1918 through 10.5.1920. Values are for the commonest variety of each denomination.

		GOOD	FINE	XF
S351	**25 RUBLES** 8.4.1918-4.5.1918.	2.50	8.00	20.00
S352	**50 RUBLES** 27.1.1918-4.5.1918 (4 types).	3.00	9.00	25.00
S353	**60 RUBLES** 27.1.1918-6.3.1918.	—	Rare	—
S354	**100 RUBLES** 27.1.1918-12.12.1919.	2.50	7.00	20.00
S355	**200 RUBLES** 27.1.1918-18.4.1918 (4 types).	2.50	7.00	20.00
S356	**250 RUBLES** 20.4.1918-12.12.1919.	2.50	7.00	20.00

		GOOD	FINE	XF
S357	**300 RUBLES** 14.3.1918-12.12.1919 (4 types).	2.50	7.50	25.00
S358	**500 RUBLES** 27.1.1918-12.12.1919 (6 types).	2.50	7.50	25.00
S359	**1000 RUBLES** 14.3.1918-10.5.1920 (9 types).	2.50	7.50	25.00

ГОСУДАРСТВЕНН. БАНКА
Government Bank

ЖИТОМИРСКОЕ ОТДѢЛЕНІЕ
Zhytomyr

1918-1919 CIRCULATING BEARER CHECKS ISSUE

Seven different issues of checks from 13.2.1918 to 5.4.1919.

		GOOD	FINE	XF
S361	**25 RUBLES** 26.3.1918-5.4.1919 (3 diff.).	3.00	10.00	25.00
S362	**50 RUBLES** 13.2.1918-5.4.1919 (7 diff.).	2.50	8.00	20.00
S363	**100 RUBLES** 13.2.1918-29.4.1918 (4 diff.).	6.00	20.00	50.00

NOTE: Circulating checks also were issued at Zhitomir by the Union Bank, Vzaimnago Credit Company and a cooperative. Details not available.

СОЕДИНЕННЫЙ БАНКЪ

SOEDNENNI BANK

ЖИТОМИРСКОЕ ОТДѢЛЕНІЕ

ZHYTOMYR

1918 ISSUE

		GOOD	FINE	XF
S364	**40 RUBLEI** 26.3.1918.	—	Rare	—
S364A	**50 RUBLEI** 26.3.1918.	20.00	50.00	120.00

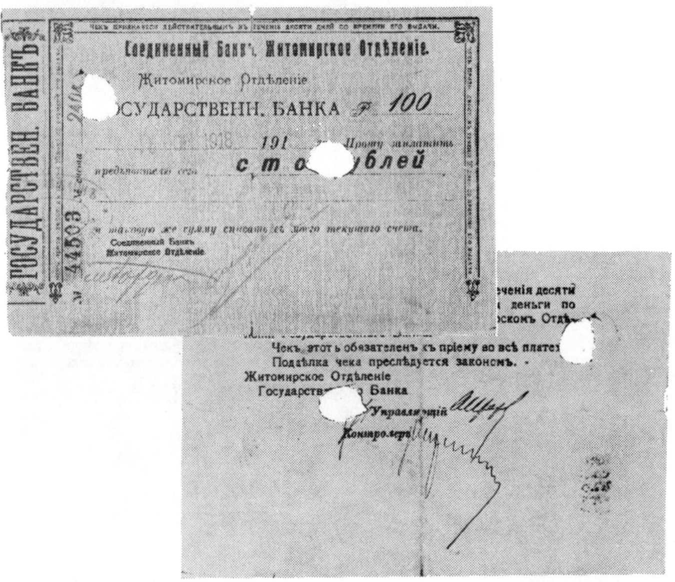

		GOOD	FINE	XF
S364B	**100 RUBLEI** 15.6.1918. Black on green unpt. Black text on back. Punched hole cancelled w/2 holes.	6.00	15.00	30.00
S364C	**200 RUBLEI** 1918-19.	8.00	20.00	40.00
S364D	**500 RUBLEI** 11.4.1918.	25.00	60.00	120.00

КРЫМСКОЕ КРАЕВОЕ ПРАВИТЕЛЬСТВО
Crimea Territorial Government

Gen. Sulkevich.

1918 ОБЯЗАТЕЛЬСТВО КРЫМСКАГО КРАЕВОГО КАЗНАЧЕЙСТВА
OBLIGATION OFTHE CRIMEA AREA TREASURY ISSUE

#S366-S368 black on green unpt. Double eagle at upper l. Uniface.

		GOOD	FINE	XF
S366	**500 RUBLES** 1.9.1918.	10.00	30.00	100.00

		GOOD	FINE	XF
S367	**1000 RUBLES** 1.9.1918.	10.00	30.00	100.00
S368	**5000 RUBLES** 1.9.1918.			
	a. Issued note.	60.00	150.00	350.00
	b. W/o serial #.	—	—	100.00

1918 МАРКА POSTAGE STAMP MONEY ISSUE

		GOOD	FINE	XF
S369	**50 KOPEKS** ND (1918). Brown. Double eagle at ctr. on face, at upper ctr. on back. Vertical format.	3.00	8.00	20.00

1918 ДЕНЕЖНЫЙ ЗНАКЪ CURRENCY TOKENS ISSUE

		GOOD	FINE	XF
S370	**5 RUBLES** 1918. Blue and brown. Map of the Crimea on back.			
	a. Serial # 3 1/2mm wide.	2.00	5.00	15.00
	b. Serial # 3 1/2-6mm (Soviet issue of 1920).	1.50	5.00	20.00
S371	**10 RUBLES** 1918. Red and brown. Map of the Crimea on back.			
	a. Serial # 3mm wide.	4.00	8.00	17.50
	b. Serial # 3 1/2-6mm (Soviet issue of 1920).	2.50	4.50	12.50

		Good	Fine	XF
S372	**25 Rubles** 1918. Green and lilac. Map of the Crimea on back.			
	a. Serial # 3mm high.	3.00	5.00	20.00
	b. Serial # 3 1/2-6mm. (Soviet issue of 1920).	1.50	3.00	12.00

Provisional Government of Workers and Peasants

1919 Issue

		Good	Fine	XF
S375	**250 Rubles** 1919. Back blank. (Not issued).	—	—	—

УПРАВЛЕНІЕ УПОЛНОМОЧ. ПО ПРОД. ХЕРС. ГУБ.
Plenipotentiary for Food of the Government Territory of Kherson

1919 ОДЕССА ВРЕМЕННАЯ КВИТАНЦІЯ
Odessa Provisional Receipts Issue

		Good	Fine	XF
S376	**25 Rubles** 10.10.1919. Blue and red on brown paper.	10.00	20.00	60.00
S377	**50 Rubles** 10.10.1919. Blue and red on green paper.	10.00	20.00	50.00

		Good	Fine	XF
S378	**100 Rubles** 10.10.1919. Blue and red on brown paper.	10.00	20.00	50.00
S379	**250 Rubles** 10.10.1919. Blue and red on green paper.	10.00	20.00	50.00
S380	**500 Rubles** 10.10.1919. Blue and red on brown paper.	12.00	25.00	60.00

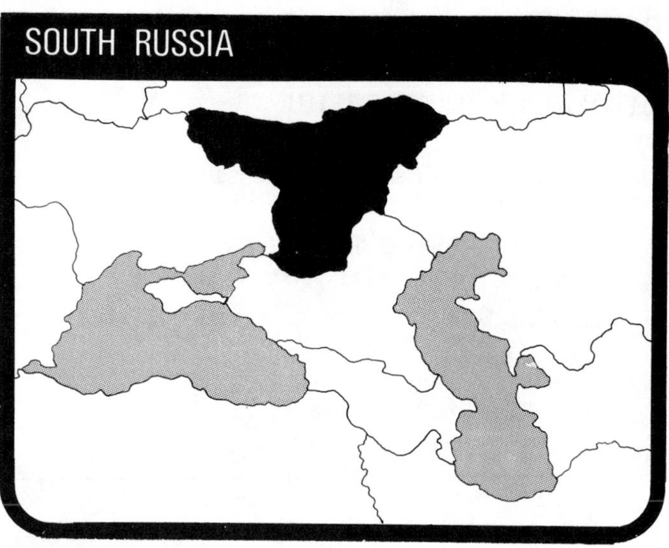

Government
Don Cossack Government

Military
High Command of the Armed Forces in South Russia (Generals Denikin and Wrangel)

ВСЕВЕЛИКАГО ВОЙСКА ДОНСКОГО
Don Cossack Military Government

5% КРАТКОСРОЧНОЕ ОБЯЗАТЕЛЬСТВО
Debenture Bonds Issue

Valuations are for filled out notes. Blank notes must be valued much lower. All notes red-brown and olive; on back acceptances of the State Bank branches in:

H = Novocherkassk НОВОЧЕРКАССК
T = Taganrog ТАГАНРОГ
P = Rostov РОСТОВ

Astrakhan

1 ЯНВАРЯ 1919 Issue

		Good	Fine	XF
S381	**500 Rubles** 1.1.1919. Novocherkassk.	8.00	20.00	40.00
S382	**1000 Rubles** 1.1.1919. Novocherkassk.	8.00	20.00	40.00
S383	**5000 Rubles** 1.1.1919. Novocherkassk.	10.00	25.00	65.00

		Good	Fine	XF
S384	**10,000 Rubles** 1.1.1919. Novocherkassk.	20.00	50.00	200.00
S385	**25,000 Rubles** 1.1.1919. Novocherkassk.	40.00	80.00	350.00
S386	**50,000 Rubles** 1.1.1919. Novocherkassk.	50.00	150.00	550.00

1 АПРѢЛЯ 1919 Issue

		Good	Fine	XF
S387	**500 Rubles** 1.4.1919.			
	a. Novocherkassk.	2.00	8.00	25.00
	b. Taganrog.	8.00	20.00	40.00

		Good	Fine	XF
S388	**1000 Rubles** 1.4.1919.			
	a. Novocherkassk.	7.00	15.00	35.00
	b. Taganrog.	12.00	25.00	55.00
	c. Rostov.	—	—	—
S389	**5000 Rubles** 1.4.1919.			
	a. Novocherkassk.	8.00	20.00	55.00
	b. Taganrog.	30.00	65.00	125.00
	c. Rostov.	—	—	—
S390	**10,000 Rubles** 1.4.1919.			
	a. Novocherkassk.	75.00	225.00	500.00
	b. Taganrog.	75.00	225.00	500.00
S391	**25,000 Rubles** 1.4.1919.			
	a. Novocherkassk.	45.00	125.00	350.00
	b. Rostov.	—	—	—
S392	**50,000 Rubles** 1.4.1919. Novocherkassk.	120.00	300.00	650.00

1 ИЮЛЯ 1919 Issue

		Good	Fine	XF
S393	**500 Rubles** 1.7.1919.			
	a. Novocherkassk.	1.00	4.00	17.50
	b. Taganrog.	2.00	5.00	22.50
S394	**1000 Rubles** 1.7.1919.			
	a. Novocherkassk.	2.00	5.00	25.00
	b. Taganrog.	2.50	6.00	27.50
S395	**5000 Rubles** 1.7.1919.			
	a. Novocherkassk.	3.00	8.00	27.50
	b. Taganrog.	3.00	8.00	27.50
S396	**10,000 Rubles** 1.7.1919.			
	a. Novocherkassk.	10.00	25.00	75.00
	b. Taganrog.	15.00	40.00	100.00
S397	**25,000 Rubles** 1.7.1919.			
	a. Novocherkassk.	15.00	45.00	125.00
	b. Taganrog.	75.00	150.00	350.00
S398	**50,000 Rubles** 1.7.1919.			
	a. Novocherkassk.	100.00	250.00	575.00
	b. Taganrog.	—	—	—

1 ОКТЯБРЯ 1919 Issue

		Good	Fine	XF
S399	**500 Rubles** 1.10.1919.			
	a. Novocherkassk.	1.50	4.50	17.50
	b. Taganrog.	3.00	8.00	27.50
S400	**1000 Rubles** 1.10.1919.			
	a. Novocherkassk.	2.50	6.00	25.00
	b. Taganrog.	2.00	5.00	20.00
S401	**5000 Rubles** 1.10.1919.			
	a. Novocherkassk.	7.00	15.00	40.00
	b. Taganrog.	4.00	12.00	40.00
S402	**10,000 Rubles** 1.10.1919.			
	a. Novocherkassk.	10.00	25.00	75.00
	b. Taganrog.	10.00	25.00	75.00

		Good	Fine	XF
S403	**25,000 Rubles** 1.10.1919. Taganrog.	30.00	100.00	200.00
S404	**50,000 Rubles** 1.10.1919. Taganrog. Swastika in the unpt. Misprint; back inverted.	75.00	150.00	400.00

A word on date ranges

Often date ranges or specific dates are listed. These have been observed or reported by our contributors. If a note is outside the published range, it only means that it is a newly reported date, and not necessarily worthy of a premium value.

ГОСУДАРСТВЕННЫЙ БАНК

Government Bank

ВЫМУЩЕН (or A) РОСТОВСКОЙ НА. ДОНУ КОНТОРОЙ

Rostov

General Anton I. Denikin, 1918-20.
General Baron Peter Wrangel, 1920.
#S408-S427 the initial letter of the control # identifies the place of issue. For example, a note numbered Я-060 was issued at Simferopol; one numbered Б-022 was issued at Rostov, etc.

A = Rostov, except:
A = Feodosiya on 3R. Pick #S409.
A = Novorossisk on 1000R. Pick #S424.
A = Feodosiya on all 1920 issues.
A = Ekaterinodar on 50R. Pick #S416.

Б = Rostov	У = Feodosiya
В = Novorossisk	Я = Simferopol
К = Novorossisk	О = Odessa
Л = Kiev	

1918 ND РАЗМѢННАЯ МАРКА Postage Stamp Money Issue

		VG	VF	Unc
S406	**20 Kopeks** ND (1918). Green on thin cardboard. Ermak at ctr. Printed text and eagle in black on back.	5.00	15.00	35.00

1918 ND Small Change Notes Issue

		VG	VF	Unc
S407	**50 Kopeks** ND (1918). Black and gray on lt. brown unpt. Gen. Platov on back.	1.00	3.00	7.00

1918 ДЕНЕЖНЫЙ ЗНАКЪ Currency Tokens Issue

Many color shades and print varieties.

		VG	VF	Unc
S408	**1 Ruble** 1918. Black and blue on brown unpt. Double eagle at upper ctr. Back brown on tan unpt.			
	a. White, thin paper - B.	.50	1.50	5.00
	b. Yellow, thick paper - A.	.50	1.50	5.00

		VG	VF	UNC
S409	**3 RUBLES** 1918. Black and green on orange unpt. Double eagle at upper ctr. Back green on yellow unpt.			
	a. White, thin paper w/o wmk. - А; К.	.50	2.25	6.00
	b. Gray, thin paper w/o wmk. - Л.	.75	3.50	9.00
	c. Yellow, thick paper w/o wmk. - А.	.50	2.25	6.00
	d. Wmk: Monogram - А.	1.00	3.00	10.00

		VG	VF	UNC
S410	**5 RUBLES** 1918. Black and blue on peach unpt. Double eagle at upper ctr.			
	a. W/o wmk: - А.	.75	2.00	7.00
	b. Wmk: Monogram - А.	.75	2.00	7.00

		VG	VF	UNC
S411	**10 RUBLES** 1918. Red-brown on lt. green unpt. Double eagle at upper ctr.			
	a. W/o wmk: - А.	.50	2.00	6.00
	b. Wmk: Monogram - А.	.40	1.50	5.00
	c. Wmk: Horizontal lines - А.	.40	1.50	6.00

		VG	VF	UNC
S412	**25 RUBLES** 1918. Black and green on brown unpt. Woman w/sword at l. Standing figure at l. and r. on back.			
	a. W/o wmk: - А.	.40	1.50	6.00
	b. Wmk: Monogram - А; К.	.40	1.50	6.00
	c. Wmk: Horizontal lines - А.	.40	1.50	6.00

		VG	VF	UNC
S413	**100 RUBLES** 1918. Dk. brown and gray-blue. Portr. helmeted Ermak supported by seated woman - А.	.40	1.50	5.00
S414	**250 RUBLES** 1918. Black and green on red-brown unpt. Women seated at l. and r., Cossack Gen. Platov in uniform at l. ctr. Back black on green and lt. red unpt. Eagle at upper ctr.			
	a. White paper w/o wmk. - А.	.75	2.75	6.00
	b. Yellowish paper w/o wmk. - А.	.75	2.75	6.00
	c. Wmk: Monogram - А.	.75	2.75	6.00
S415	**500 RUBLES** 1918. Black on green and tan unpt. Small double eagle at upper l. Allegory of Russia seated at l. on back.			
	a. White paper w/o wmk. - А.	.75	2.00	7.00
	b. Yellowish paper w/o wmk. - А. Serial # or control # (like ВА-91).	.75	2.00	5.00
	c. Wmk: Monogram - А; Б; В.	1.00	2.50	7.00
	d. Laid paper - АМ.	1.00	2.50	7.00

1919 ДЕНЕЖНЫЙ ЗНАКЪ CURRENCY TOKENS ISSUE

		VG	VF	UNC
S416	**50 RUBLES** 1919. Brown and blue on gray unpt. Woman w/flag on back. W/ or w/o wmk.			
	a. Wmk: Monogram *A* - А.	.30	1.25	4.00
	b. W/o wmk: - Б.	.30	1.25	4.00
S417	**100 RUBLES** 1919. Black on brown and m/c unpt. Double eagle at upper l. Back black on brown unpt.; warrior in armor w/standard at r., monument w/2 warriors behind.			
	a. W/o wmk. - У.	.40	1.50	5.00
	b. Wmk: Monogram - А.	.40	1.50	5.00

Notice

Readers with unlisted dates, color or signature varieties are invited to submit photocopies of their notes to: Standard Catalog of World Paper Money, Krause Publications, 700 East State St. Iola WI 54990-0001 U.S.A. or by email: thernr@krause.com. Email submissions of material for possible inclusion need to be 100% jpeg attachments at 300 dpi.

		VG	VF	UNC
S418	**1000 RUBLES** 1919. Black on blue, lt. green and pink unpt. Double eagle at upper ctr. Back dk. blue on gray unpt.; allegory of Russia at ctr., bldgs. w/spires at lower l. and r.			
	a. W/o wmk. - *У*.	.40	1.50	4.00
	b. Wmk: Monogram - А; Б; В; Я.	.40	1.50	4.00
	c. Wmk: Mosaic - Я.	.40	1.50	4.00

		VG	VF	UNC
S419	**5000 RUBLES** 1919. Dk. brown on orange, green and lt. brown unpt. Double eagle at upper l., head of Mercury at upper ctr. Back green on brown and orange unpt. St. George w/shield, flag and snake at l., eagle at upper ctr.			
	a. W/o wmk. - У. Series #.	.40	1.75	4.50
	b. Gray paper w/o wmk. - У. Serial #.	.50	1.75	5.00
	c. Wmk: Monogram - А.	.40	1.50	4.00
	d. Wmk: Mosaic - Я.	.40	1.50	4.00

ГЛАВНАГОКОМАНДОВАНІЯ ВООРУЖЕННЫМИ СИЛАМИ НА ЮГЉ РОССІЙ
High Command of the Armed Forces of South Russia

1919 БИЛЕТЪ ГОСУДАРСТВЕННАГО КАЗНАЧЕЙСТВА
GOVERNMENT TREASURY NOTES ISSUE

Issued by General Wrangel. All have monument w/cross honoring the millenium of Russia on back.

		VG	VF	UNC
S420	**3 RUBLES** 1919. Green.			
	a. W/o wmk. - А.	7.50	25.00	55.00
	b. Wmk: Mosaic - А.	.50	2.00	7.00

		VG	VF	UNC
S421	**10 RUBLES** 1919. Black on red-brown unpt. Double eagle at upper ctr. Memorial w/2 warriors on back.			
	a. W/o wmk. - У.	.40	1.50	6.00
	b. Wmk: Wavy lines - У.	.40	1.50	6.00
S422	**50 RUBLES** 1919. Black on olive-brown unpt. Woman w/2 children at l. Back black on lt. blue and olive-brown unpt.			
	a. Wmk: Lines - К; О.	.40	1.50	6.00
	b. Wmk: Spades - О; У.	.40	1.50	6.00
	c. W/o wmk. - К.	.40	1.50	6.00
	x. Error w/back only. Wmk: Lines.	—	—	10.00

		VG	VF	UNC
S423	**200 RUBLES** 1919. Black on brown and gray-violet unpt. Double eagle at upper ctr. Back brown on tan unpt.; equestrian statue and soldiers standing in front at ctr. Mosiac - А; Я.	1.00	2.50	7.00

		VG	VF	UNC
S424	**1000 RUBLES** 1919. M/c. Bell at l., St. George and dragon at r. Color variations of unpt. and top ribbon from lt. yellow to wine-red.			
	a. W/o wmk. 3 serial # varieties - А; Б; В; О.	1.50	5.00	15.00
	b. Wmk: Mosaic - Б II В - 023; Я.	1.50	5.00	17.50

		VG	VF	Unc
S425	**10,000 Rubles**			
	1919. Brown on green and dull orange unpt. Double eagle at upper ctr. Woman seated w/lance at l., woman seated w/sword at r. on back. Color shade variants. Various series.			
	a. Wmk: Mosaic - А; Я.	.75	2.00	5.00
	b. W/o wmk. - Я.	.75	2.00	5.00

1920 БИЛЕТЪ ГОСУДАРСТВЕННАГО КАЗНАЧЕЙСТВА Government Treasury Notes Issue

Issued by General Wrangel. All have double eagle at upper ctr. on face, monument w/cross honoring the millenium of Russia on back.

		VG	VF	Unc
S426	**5 Rubles**			
	1920. Blue-green.			
	a. Printed on both sides. - А.	—	Rare	—
	b. Printed on back only.	—	15.00	35.00
	c. Printed on face only.	—	15.00	35.00

		VG	VF	Unc
S427	**25,000 Rubles**			
	1920. Gray-blue and brown. (Unfinished printing). - А.	6.00	15.00	45.00

1920 6% КРАТК. ОБЯЗАТЕЛЬСТВО ГОСУД. КАЗНАЧЕЙСТВА Debenture Bonds Issue

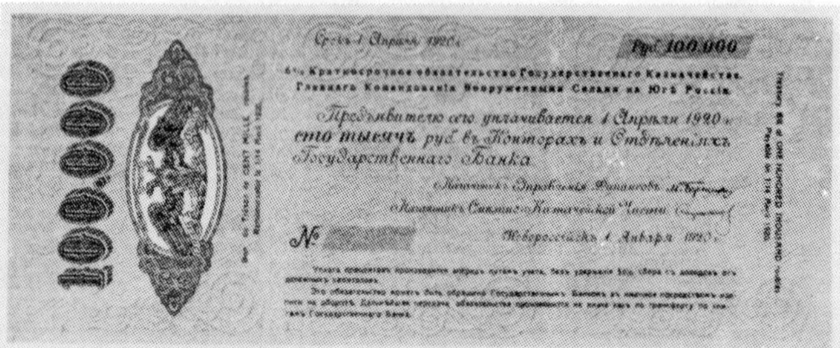

		VG	VF	Unc
S431	**100,000 Rubles**			
	1.1.1920. Brown on red-brown.			
	a. Date Line (СРОК) 1. IV.	—	Rare	—
	b. Date Line (СРОК) 15. VIII.	—	Rare	—
	c. Date Line (СРОК) 15. XI.	25.00	75.00	200.00

1920 БИЛЕТЪ ГОСУДАРСТВЕННАГО КАЗНАЧЕЙСТВА Government Treasury Notes Issue

Issued by General Wrangel. All have double eagle at upper ctr. on face, monument w/cross honoring the millenium of Russia on back.

		VG	VF	Unc
S432	**100 Rubles**			
	1920. Red-brown.			
	a. Wmk: Stars.	1.00	3.00	8.00
	b. Wmk: Wavy lines.	.50	2.00	6.00
	c. Wmk: Mosaic.	.25	.75	1.75
S433	**250 Rubles**			
	1920. Lilac-brown.			
	a. Brown paper, wmk: Spades.	1.00	4.00	9.00
	b. White paper, wmk: Mosaic.	.25	.50	1.50
S434	**500 Rubles**			
	1920. Blue or greenish color.	.25	.75	1.75

NOTE: These notes were also ovpt. for use by Russian Forces trapped in a section of the Ottoman Empire in the early 1920's. More information is needed.

ГОСУДАРСТВО РОССІЙСКОЕ
Russian Government

1920 КАЗНАЧЕИСКІЙ ЗНАКЪ Treasury Tokens Issue

#S435-S438 British printing by W&S, but never issued due to the Nov. 1920 evacuation of Sevastopol.

		VG	VF	Unc
S435	**1 Ruble**			
	1920.	—	—	—
S436	**3 Rubles**			
	1920.	—	—	—
S437	**5 Rubles**			
	1920. Blue.	—	—	—

		VG	VF	Unc
S438	**50 Rubles**			
	ND (1920). Blue on yellow. Helmeted woman's head at upper l. Eagle on back.	2.50	6.00	15.00

1919 КАЗНАЧЕИСКІЙ ЗНАКЪ Treasury Tokens Issue

#S439 and S440 British printing by W&S, but never issued due to the Nov. 1920 evacuation of Sevastopol.

		VG	VF	Unc
S439	**100 Rubles**			
	1919. Brown on green. Helmeted woman's head at l. on back. Serial letters in the plate or printed w/serial #.			
	a. Black serial #.	3.00	8.00	20.00
	b. Brown serial #.	3.00	8.00	20.00

		VG	VF	Unc
S440	**500 Rubles**			
	1919. Green on orange unpt. St. George on horseback at lower l. ctr., lion head at upper ctr. Helmeted woman's head at ctr. on back.			
	a. Black serial #.	3.00	8.00	20.00
	b. Green serial #.	3.00	8.00	20.00

АСТРАХАНСКАТО КАЗНАЧЕЙСТВА
Astrakhan Region

1918 ВРЕМЕННЫЙ КРЕДИТНЫЙ БИЛЕТЪ
PROVISIONAL CREDIT NOTES ISSUE

		GOOD	FINE	XF
S441	**1 RUBLE** 1918. Dk. blue on brown unpt. Double-headed eagle at ctr. Back brown.	3.00	8.50	27.50

		GOOD	FINE	XF
S442	**3 RUBLEI** 1918. Black on lt. olive green unpt. Double-headed eagle at upper ctr. on back.	3.00	8.50	27.50
S443	**5 RUBLEI** 1918. Dk. blue on salmon unpt. Similar to #S441.	4.50	15.00	32.50
S444	**10 RUBLEI** 1918. Brown on red-brown unpt. Like #S443. Back green on red and green unpt.	5.00	17.50	40.00

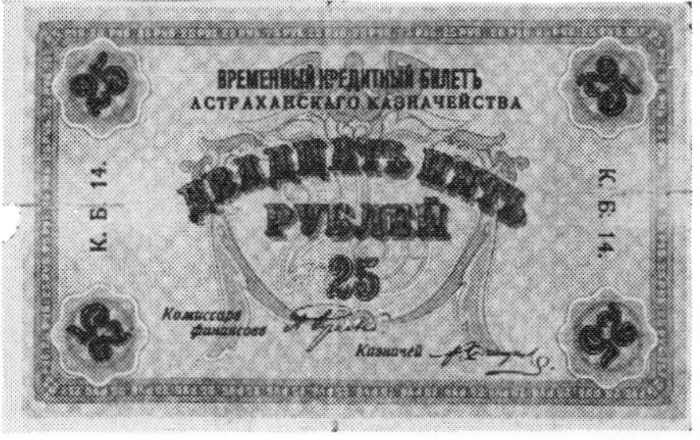

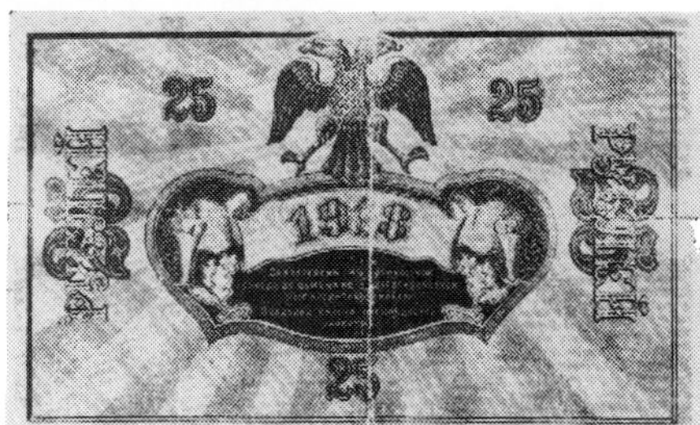

		GOOD	FINE	XF
S445	**25 RUBLEI** 1918. Dk. blue on green and pink unpt. Back brown on green unpt.; double-headed eagle at upper ctr.	7.50	25.00	60.00

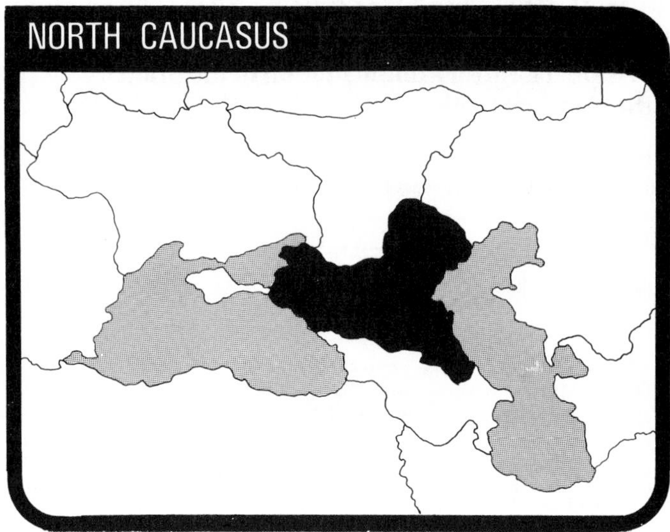

GOVERNMENTS

- North Caucasian Socialist Soviet Republic
- North Caucasian Emirate (Imam Usun-Khadzhi)
- Armavir Branch
- Kuban Territorial Government
- Kuban Soviet Republic
- Ekaterinodar Branch
- Mineralnyie Vodyi District
- Stavropol Branch
- Terek-Daghestan Territory (Imam Gozinskii)
- Terek Republic

MILITARY

- Black Sea Peasant Militia (Chief of Staff Voronovich)
- North Caucasus Volunteer Revolutionary Army
- Piatigorsk-Batalpashchinsk Company of the Independent Army (Col. A. Shkuro)
- Terek Cossack Command (Col. Bicherakov)
- Terek District Command of the Red Army (Partisan Gikalo)

BANKS

- Grozny
- Sochi (City)

RAILROADS

- Black Sea Railroad
- Vladikavkaz Railroad Company

СЕВЕРО КАВКАЗСКАЯ СОЦИАЛИСТИЧЕСКАЯ СОВЕТСКАЯ РЕСПУБЛИКА
North Caucasian Socialist Soviet Republic

1918 ISSUE

		GOOD	FINE	XF
S447	**10 RUBLES** 1918. Black on red and yellow unpt. Sickles and corn.			
	a. Text on face: ОВЩЕГОСУДАР ...ОГО.	5.00	10.00	35.00
	b. Text on face: ОБЩЕГООУДАР ...АГО.	5.00	10.00	35.00
S448	**25 RUBLES** 1918. Black on lilac and yellow unpt. Sickles and corn.			
	a. Text on face: ОВЩЕГОСУДАР ...ОГО.	5.00	10.00	35.00
	b. Text on face: ОБЩЕГООУДАР...АГО.	5.00	10.00	35.00

ВРЕМЕН. ЦЕНТРААЬНАГО УПРАВЛ. ОТДЕАЕНИЯМИ НАРОД. БАНКА
Provisional Central Administration of the Branch of the National Bank

1918 ISSUE

#S451-S453 printed on bills of exchange paper. Purple text on back.

		GOOD	FINE	XF
S451	**25 RUBLES** 1918. Black on blue-green unpt.	4.50	15.00	40.00
S452	**50 RUBLES** 1918. Black on yellow-brown unpt.	4.50	15.00	40.00
S453	**100 RUBLES** 1918. Black on green unpt.	4.50	15.00	40.00

#S454-S455 ***Deleted*****, see #S447a and S448.**

КРАЕВОГО ИСПОЛНИТ. КОМИТЕТА СОВЕТОВ СЕВ. КАВКАЗА
Area Executive Committee of the North Caucasian Soviet Republic

1918 ДЕНЕЖНЫЙ ЗНАК CURRENCY TOKENS ISSUE

		GOOD	FINE	XF
S456	**5 RUBLES** 1918. Blue and pink.	5.00	12.50	50.00

		GOOD	FINE	XF
S457	**50 RUBLES** 1918. Green.	5.00	12.50	50.00
S458	**100 RUBLES** 1918. Brown.	5.00	12.50	50.00
S459	**250 RUBLES** 1918. Black on lt. green and brown unpt.	5.00	12.50	50.00

		GOOD	FINE	XF
S460	**500 RUBLES** 1918. M/c.	12.50	35.00	80.00

СЕВЕРО-КАВКАЗСКИЙ ЭМИРАТ
North Caucasian Emirate

This state, an amalgam of the Muslim nationalities of North Caucasus, was set up in 1919 after the defeat of the Reds by Denikin's armies of South Russia. The state was crushed by Red forces in March, 1920.

Notes of Soviet Terek and North Caucasia w/the stamp of Imam Usun-Khadzhi or Vizier Kyamil Khan.

1919 ND РАЗМѢННЫЙ ЗНАКБEXCHANGE TOKENS ISSUE

		GOOD	FINE	XF
S461	**50 RUBLES** ND (1919). Like #S534b w/circular stamp of Vizier.	40.00	80.00	125.00
S462	**50 RUBLES** ND (1919). Like #S534a w/circular stamp of Vizier.	10.00	20.00	50.00
S463	**100 RUBLES** ND (1919). Like #S535 w/oval imprint of ring of Imam.	40.00	80.00	125.00
S464	**100 RUBLES** ND (1919). Like #S535 w/oval imprint of ring of the Imam and circular stamp of Vizier.	20.00	50.00	80.00

		GOOD	FINE	XF
S465	**100 RUBLES** ND (1919). Like #S535 w/round stamp of Vizier. Handwritten date and text.	40.00	80.00	125.00
S466	**100 RUBLES** ND (1919). Like #S535 w/round stamp of Vizier. W/o handwritten date and text.	15.00	40.00	70.00
S467	**100 RUBLES** ND (1919). Like #S458 w/round stamp of Vizier. Handwritten date and text.	60.00	125.00	175.00
S468	**100 RUBLES** ND (1919). Like #S458 w/round stamp of Vizier. W/o handwritten date and text.	60.00	125.00	175.00
S469	**500 RUBLES** ND (1919). Like #S460 w/round stamp of Vizier. Handwritten date and text.	60.00	125.00	175.00

AH1338/1919 КРЕДИТНЫЙ БИЛЕТЪ CREDIT NOTES/BILLET DE CREDIT ISSUE

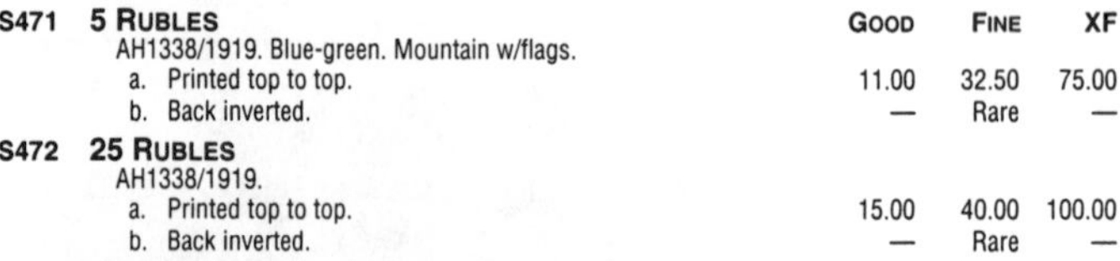

		GOOD	FINE	XF
S471	**5 RUBLES** AH1338/1919. Blue-green. Mountain w/flags.			
	a. Printed top to top.	11.00	32.50	75.00
	b. Back inverted.	—	Rare	—
S472	**25 RUBLES** AH1338/1919.			
	a. Printed top to top.	15.00	40.00	100.00
	b. Back inverted.	—	Rare	—

		GOOD	FINE	XF
S473	**50 RUBLES** 1919. Scales at ctr. Flag on mountain at l. on back.			
	a. Printed top to top.	15.00	40.00	100.00
	b. Back inverted.	—	Rare	—

		Good	Fine	XF
S474	**100 Rubles** AH1338/1919. Black on lt. green and lt. brown unpt. Similar to #S473. Mountain and flag on back.			
	a. No text below Arabic numeral of value in unpt. on back.	5.00	20.00	60.00
	b. Like "a" but w/Arabic text.	6.00	25.00	75.00
	c. Like "a" but back inverted.	—	Rare	—

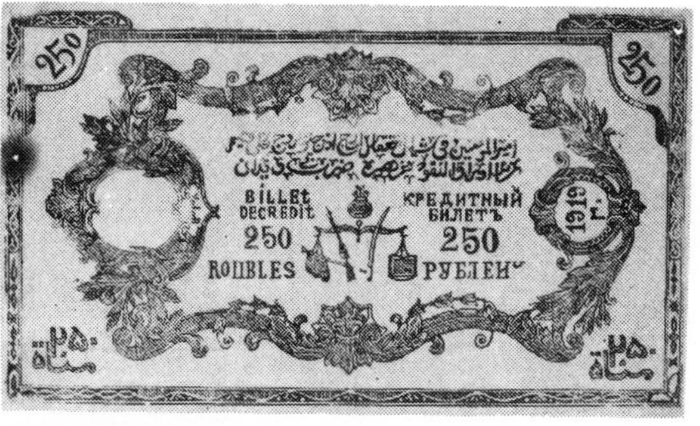

		Good	Fine	XF
S475	**250 Rubles** AH1338/1919. Black on green unpt. Lg. arms.			
	a. Printed top to top.	8.00	25.00	75.00
	b. Back inverted.	—	Rare	—
S476	**250 Rubles** AH1338/1919. Lt. blue. Small arms.			
	a. Printed top to top.	8.00	25.00	75.00
	b. Back inverted.	—	Rare	—

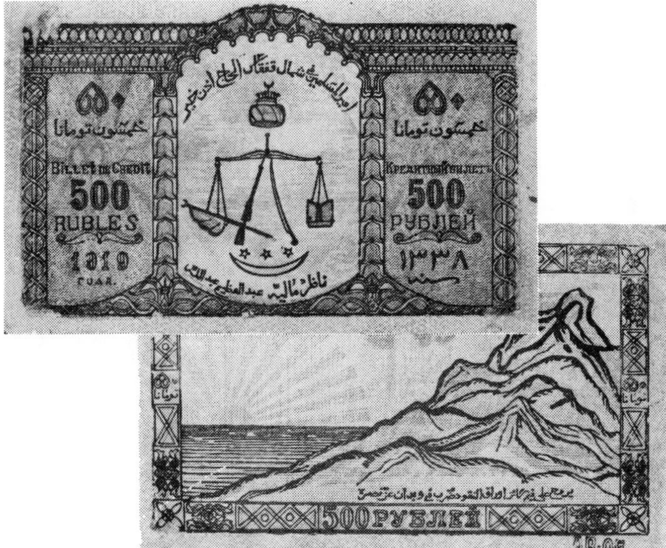

		Good	Fine	XF
S477	**500 Rubles** AH1338/1919. Black on blue and lt. brown unpt. Mountains and sea w/setting sun on back.			
	a. Printed top to top.	8.00	25.00	75.00
	b. Back inverted.	—	Rare	—

#S478 Deleted.

ГОСУДАРСТВЕННАГО БАНКА
Government Bank

АРМАВИРСКАГО ОТДѢЛЕНІЯ
Armavir

1918 Issue

#S479A-S479K w/various dates in 1918. Different bank stampings across bottom. Back black text, red circular stamping at lower l.

		Good	Fine	XF
S479A	**3 Rublya** 18.6; 1.12.1918. Black on green unpt.	3.50	8.00	15.00
S479B	**5 Rublei** 18.6; 1.12.1918. Black on blue unpt.	3.50	8.00	15.00

		Good	Fine	XF
S479C	**10 Rublei** 1.7.; 21.8.; 1.12.1918. Black on red unpt.	2.50	6.00	10.00
S479D	**25 Rublei** 8.6.; 1.7.; 1.12.1918. Black on olive green unpt.	2.50	6.00	10.00
S479E	**40 Rublei** 1.7.; 1.12.1918.	3.50	8.00	15.00
S479F	**50 Rublei** 1.7.1918.	20.00	50.00	100.00
S479G	**100 Rublei** 1.7.1918.	25.00	60.00	120.00

		Good	Fine	XF
S479H	**150 Rublei** 18.6.; 1.7.; 1.12.1918. Black on brown unpt.	2.50	6.00	10.00
S479I	**200 Rublei** 1.7.1918.	20.00	55.00	110.00
S479J	**300 Rublei** 1.7.; 1.12.1918.			
	a. Date w/correct numerals.	20.00	35.00	60.00
	x. Error w/issue of 1.7. but date 1928.	6.00	15.00	35.00
S479K	**500 Rublei** 1.7.1918.	—	—	—

КУБАНСКАГО КРАЕВОГО ПРАВИТЕЛЬСТВА
Kuban Territorial Government

Some of these notes were not in circulation. The 50-kopek and 250-ruble notes circulated.

1918 Bank Issue

		VG	VF	Unc
S481	**50 Kopeks** Ekaterinodar Branch.	6.00	15.00	40.00

1918; 1920 Territorial Issue

		VG	VF	Unc
S482	**5 Rubles** 15.3.1918.	—	—	—
S483	**3 Rubles** 25.3.1918.	—	—	—
S484	**5 Rubles** 25.3.1918.	—	—	—
S485	**10 Rubles** 25.3.1918.	—	—	—
S486	**20 Rubles** 25.3.1918.	—	—	—
S487	**100 Rubles** 25.3.1918.	—	—	—

		VG	VF	Unc
S488	**250 Rubles**			
	1.3.1920. Green.			
	a. Text on back: АПРЬЛЯ	6.00	15.00	40.00
	b. Text on back: АЛРЬЛЯ	6.00	15.00	40.00

КУБАНСКАЯ РЕСПУБЛИКА
Kuban Soviet Republic

1918 ND State Loan Notes Issue

#S491-S494 Russian notes #77-80 (in Vol. 2) w/square stamp.

		VG	VF	Unc
S491	**20 Rubles** ND (1918).	6.00	15.00	40.00
S492	**40 Rubles** ND (1918).	6.00	15.00	40.00
S493	**50 Rubles** ND (1918).	5.00	12.50	40.00
S494	**100 Rubles** ND (1918).	5.00	12.50	40.00

ГОСУДАРСТВЕННОГО БАНКА
Government Bank

ЕКАТЕРИНОДАРСКОГО ОТДЕЛЕНИЯ
Ekaterinodar

1918 ND Issue

		VG	VF	Unc
S494A	**50 Kopeks** ND (ca.1918). Blue on tan unpt. Lg. denomination numeral at ctr. on face and back.	.50	1.00	2.50

1918 State Bank Vouchers Issue

		VG	VF	Unc
S495	**10 Rubles**			
	1918. Blue on brown.			
	a. Retention money 25,000 Rubles.	4.00	10.00	22.50
	b. Retention money 50,000 Rubles.	4.00	10.00	22.50
	c. Retention money 100,000 Rubles.	4.00	10.00	22.50

#S496-S497 are printed on Bill of Exchange paper bearing a wmk. and m/c printed imperial revenue stamp at l.

		VG	VF	Unc
S496	**50 Rubles**			
	ND (1918). Black, red, blue, green, and lt. brown. Uniface. Colored guilloche (ornament) at l.			
	a. Perforation.	3.00	9.00	20.00
	b. W/o perforation.	4.00	10.00	22.50
S497	**100 Rubles** ND (1918). Like #S496a.	5.00	17.50	40.00

NOTE: #S496 and S497 state they are issued by the Ekaterinodar Branch of the State Bank for the North Caucasus Soviet Socialist Republic. See #S451-S460.

1918 ГАРАНТИРОВАННЫЙ ЧЕКЪ Guaranteed Checks Issue

#S498A-S498E w/ or w/o stamping of various banks. Handwritten dates in 1918. Uniface.

		Good	Fine	XF
S498A	**50 Rublei**			
	1918. Black and brown on blue unpt.			
	a. Issued note.	2.50	5.00	10.00
	b. Punched hole cancelled.	2.00	4.00	8.00
S498B	**100 Rublei**			
	1918. Black and brown on gold unpt.			
	a. Issued note.	2.50	5.00	10.00
	b. Punched hole cancelled..	2.00	4.00	8.00
S498C	**200 Rublei**			
	1918. Black and brown on tan unpt.			
	a. Issued note.	2.50	5.00	10.00
	b. Punched hole cancelled.	2.00	4.00	8.00
S498D	**300 Rublei** 1918. Black and brown on lt. green unpt. Punched hole canceled.	2.50	6.00	12.00
S498E	**500 Rublei** 1918. Black and brown on olive-green and yellow unpt. Punched hole canceled.	2.50	6.00	12.00

МИНЕРАЛЬНЫЕ ВОДЫ
Mineralnyie Vodyi District

United issues of the independent cities of Pyatigorsk and Kislovodsk for the Mineral Waters District of the North Caucasus, 1917-19.

1917 First РАЗМѢННЫЙ ЗНАКЪ Exchange Tokens Issue, Letter А, 1917

		Good	Fine	XF
S501	**1 Ruble** 1917.	5.00	15.00	35.00
S502	**3 Rubles** 1917.	5.00	15.00	35.00
S503	**5 Rubles** 1917.	6.00	17.50	45.00
S504	**10 Rubles** 1917.	6.00	17.50	45.00
S505	**25 Rubles** 1917.	10.00	30.00	75.00
S506	**100 Rubles** 1917. Brown, rose and green.	15.00	50.00	150.00

1918 Second РАЗМѢННЫЙ ЗНАКЪ Exchange Tokens Issue, Letter Б, 1918

		Good	Fine	XF
S507	**1 Ruble** 1918. Black on orange unpt. Arms at l. Back orange.	1.50	5.00	12.00
S508	**3 Rubles** 1918. Black on green and maroon unpt. Back green.	2.00	6.00	15.00
S509	**5 Rubles** 1918. Black on blue unpt. Back blue.	2.00	6.00	15.00

		Good	Fine	XF
S510	**10 Rubles** 1918. Black on red unpt. Back brown on red unpt.	2.00	6.00	15.00
S511	**25 Rubles** 1918. Black on olive-green unpt.	5.00	20.00	45.00
S512	**25 Rubles** 1918. Lt. violet.	5.00	20.00	45.00

		Good	Fine	XF
S512G	**50 Rubles** 1918.	10.00	45.00	100.00

1919 THIRD РАЗМѢННЫЙ ЗНАКЪ EXCHANGE TOKENS ISSUE, LETTER B, 1919

		Good	Fine	XF
S513	**50 Kopeks** ND (1919). Dk. blue on orange unpt.	1.25	3.50	8.00
S514	**1 Ruble** 1919.	1.25	3.50	8.00
S515	**3 Rubles** 1919.	1.25	3.50	8.00
S516	**5 Rubles** 1919.	1.25	3.50	8.00
S517	**10 Rubles** 1919.	4.00	10.00	25.00
S518	**25 Rubles** 1919. Brown and yellow.	4.00	10.00	25.00
S519	**50 Rubles** 1919.	4.00	15.00	35.00
S520	**100 Rubles** 1919.	15.00	45.00	125.00

ГОСУДАРСТВЕННЫЙ БАНКЪ
Government Bank

СТАВРОПОЛЬСКОЕ ОТДѢЛЕНІЕ
Stavropol

1918-19 ISSUE

		Good	Fine	XF
S520A	**1 Ruble** 1.5.1918.	2.50	6.00	12.50
S520B	**3 Rublya** 1.2.1919. Black and green text and numerals on lt. green unpt.	2.50	6.00	12.50
S520C	**5 Rublei** 15.5.1918. Black and red text and numerals on green unpt.	3.50	10.00	20.00

		Good	Fine	XF
S520D	**10 Rublei** 15.5.1918. Black and red text and numerals on lt. red unpt.	4.50	12.00	25.00
S520E	**25 Rublei** 1.5.1918.	40.00	100.00	225.00
S520F	**50 Rublei** 1.5.1918.	50.00	125.00	275.00

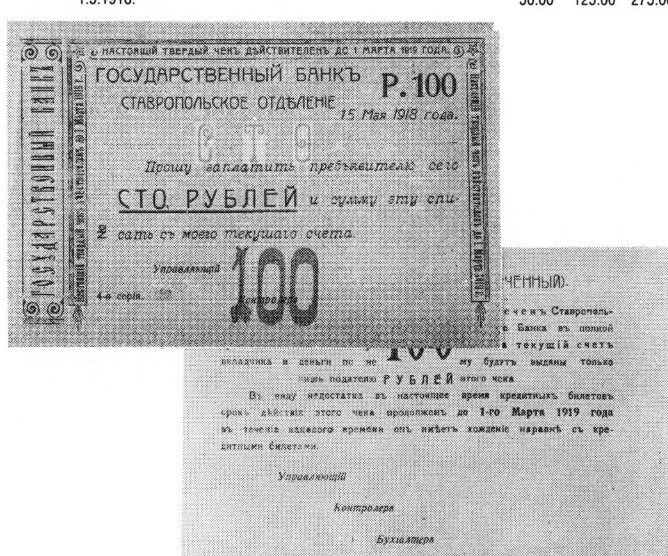

		Good	Fine	XF
S520G	**100 Rublei** 1.5.1918. Black on green unpt.	7.00	15.00	35.00
S520H	**250 Rublei** 1.5.1918.	5.00	12.00	25.00

ТЕРСКО-ДАГЕСТАНСКАЯ ОБЛАСТЬ
Terek-Daghestan Territory

Affixed check stamps for savings banks, paper on back printed.

a. H in the date narrow, no full-stop after 1918, issue Imam Gozinskii.

b. H in the date wide, full-stop after 1918, issued by the Soviet People's Commissariat.

1918 ISSUE

		Good	Fine	XF
S521	**25 Kopeks** 25.1.1918.	3.50	9.00	27.50
S522	**50 Kopeks** 25.1.1918.	3.50	9.00	27.50
S523	**1 Ruble** 25.1.1918. Yellow unpt.	3.50	9.00	27.50
S524	**3 Rubles** 25.1.1918.Green unpt.			
	a. Issued note.	4.50	12.00	35.00
	e. Error: БИЛЕТЕМИ.	9.00	22.00	45.00
S525	**5 Rubles** 25.1.1918.	3.50	9.00	27.50

		Good	Fine	XF
S526	**10 Rubles** 25.1.1918. Black on red unpt.	4.00	10.00	30.00
S527	**25 Rubles** 25.1.1918. Black on brown unpt.	3.00	8.00	25.00
S528	**100 Rubles** 25.1.1918. Black on blue unpt.	6.00	15.00	30.00

ТЕРСКОИ РЕСПУБЛИКИЙ
Terek Republic

1918 РАЗМѢННЫЙ ЗНАКЪEXCHANGE TOKENS ISSUE

		Good	Fine	XF
S529	**1 Ruble** 1918. Black on brown unpt. Double headed eagle within mantle at ctr. Back brown.	4.00	12.00	25.00

		Good	Fine	XF
S530	**3 Rubles** 1918. Black on green unpt. Like #S529. Back brown on green unpt.	5.00	15.00	30.00

		Good	Fine	XF
S531	**5 Rubles** 1918. Blue on gray unpt. Double headed eagle at upper ctr.			
	a. Printed top on top.	6.00	17.50	40.00
	x. Error w/back inverted.	10.00	25.00	60.00

		Good	Fine	XF
S532	**10 Rubles** 1918. Black on red unpt.	4.00	12.00	25.00
S533	**25 Rubles** 1918. Black on blue-green unpt.	6.00	17.50	40.00

		Good	Fine	XF
S534	**50 Rubles** 1918. Black on orange and tan unpt. Sunburst at ctr. Back brown on green unpt.			
	a. Brown printing on face.	5.00	15.00	30.00
	b. Black printing on face.	6.00	17.50	35.00

		Good	Fine	XF
S535	**100 Rubles** 1918.			
	a. Brown on red-brown unpt.	5.00	15.00	30.00
	b. Brown on lt. yellow-brown unpt.	6.00	17.50	35.00

1918; 1919 ND Postage Stamp Money Issue

Cardboard w/double-headed eagle at ctr. Text on back.

		Good	Fine	XF
S536	**10 Kopeks** ND (1918). Blue.	8.00	20.00	50.00

		Good	Fine	XF
S537	**15 Kopeks** ND (1918). Brown.	8.00	20.00	50.00
S538	**20 Kopeks** ND (1919). Green.	8.00	20.00	50.00

Black Sea Peasant Militia

1920 ВРЕМЕНН. РАЗМѢННЫЙ ЗНАКЪ Provisional Exchange Tokens Issue

		Good	Fine	XF
S539	**10 Rubles** 1.4.1920.	—	Rare	—
S540	**25 Rubles** 1.4.1920.	—	Rare	—
S541	**25 Rubles** 1920.	10.00	20.00	50.00
S542	**100 Rubles** 1920. Lg. numerals.	15.00	30.00	70.00
S543	**100 Rubles** 1920. Sm. numerals.	17.50	35.00	75.00

		Good	Fine	XF
S544	**250 Rubles** 1920. Black on lt. brown paper. Proof.	—	Rare	—

NOTE: Modern forgeries of #S544 are becoming available.

КИСЛОВОДСКОЕ ОТДѢЛЕНІЕ

Kislovodsk Branch

ГОСУДАРСТВЕННАГО БАНКА

Government Bank

ПИАТИГОРСК-БАТАЛПАЩИНСК КАЗНАЧ. Piatigorsk-Batalpashchinsk Company, Independent Army

Col. A. Shkuro

1918 ГАРАНТИРОВАННЫЙ ЧЕКЪ Guaranteed Checks Issue

#S551-S558 double eagle at upper ctr. Stamp on back: БАТАЛПАЩИНСК КАЗНАЧ.

		Good	Fine	XF
S551	**3 Rubles** 1918.	15.00	35.00	75.00
S552	**5 Rubles** 1918.	17.50	45.00	90.00

		Good	Fine	XF
S553	**10 Rubles** 1918.	35.00	90.00	185.00

		Good	Fine	XF
S554	**25 Rubles** 1918.	50.00	130.00	275.00
S555	**50 Rubles** 1918.	—	Rare	—

		Good	Fine	XF
S556	**75 Rubles** 1918.	—	Rare	—

		Good	Fine	XF
S557	**100 Rubles** 1918.	—	Rare	—
S558	**500 Rubles** 1918.	—	Rare	—

1918 Issue

#S559-S565 double eagle at upper ctr. Stamp on back: КИСЛОВОДСК ОТД. ГОС. Б.

		Good	Fine	XF
S559	**3 Rubles** 1918.	20.00	50.00	125.00
S560	**5 Rubles** 1918.	30.00	80.00	180.00
S561	**50 Rubles** 1918.	—	Rare	—
S562	**100 Rubles** 1918.	—	Rare	—

		Good	Fine	XF
S563	**200 Rubles** 1918.	—	Rare	—

1919 Issue

		Good	Fine	XF
S564	**20 Rubles** 1919.	—	Rare	—

		Good	Fine	XF
S565	**40 Rubles** 1919. Varieties.	—	Rare	—

ТЕРСКОЕ КАЗАЧЬЕ ВОИСКО
Terek Cossack Command

Col. Lazar Bicherakov

1918 Issue

		Good	Fine	XF
S566	**100 Rubles** 19.7.1918.	—	Rare	—
S567	**500 Rubles** 19.7.1918.	—	Rare	—
S568	**1000 Rubles** 19.7.1918.	—	Rare	—

КОМАНДОВАНІЕ КРАСНОЙ АРМІИ ТЕРСКОЙ ОБЛАСТИ
Terek District Command of the Red Army

Partisan Gikalo

1918 Issue

Hand stamp on Terek note #S528a: КОМ. КРАСН. АРМІЙ ТЕРСК. ОБЛ.

		Good	Fine	XF
S569	**100 Rubles** 1918. Black stamp.	20.00	50.00	100.00
S570	**100 Rubles** 1918. Violet stamp.	25.00	60.00	110.00

Grozny (City)

ВОЛЖСКО-КАМСКІЙ КОММЕРЧЕСКІЙ БАНКЪ
Volga-Kama Commercial Bank

Grozny

Circulating bearer checks w/issue dates stamped on back, from 24.1.1918 to 6.6.1918. Grozny was in Terek Oblast.

1918 ЧЕКЪ Circulating Bearer Checks Issue

		Good	Fine	XF
S571	**3 Rubles** 1918. Black.	5.00	12.00	35.00
S571A	**5 Rubles** 1918. Black.	7.50	20.00	50.00

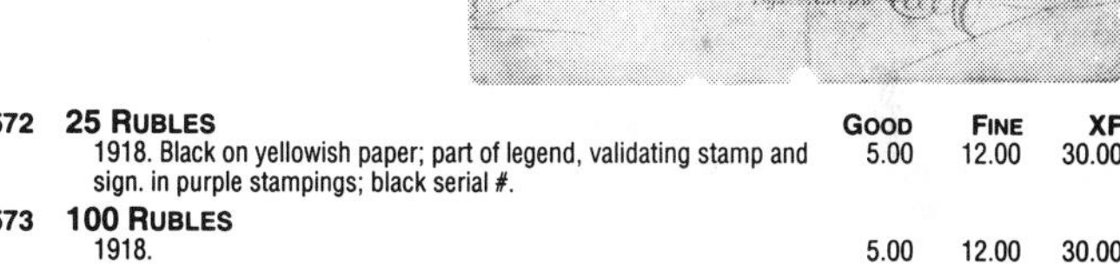

		Good	Fine	XF
S572	**25 Rubles** 1918. Black on yellowish paper; part of legend, validating stamp and sign. in purple stampings; black serial #.	5.00	12.00	30.00
S573	**100 Rubles** 1918.	5.00	12.00	30.00

РУССКО-АЗІАТСКІЙ БАНКЪ
Russo-Asiatic Bank

Grozny

1918 ЧЕКЪ Circulating Bearer Checks Issue

#S576-S579 circulating bearer checks 27.1.1918 to 9.3.1918.

		Good	Fine	XF
S576	**3 Rubles** 1918.	—	Rare	—
S577	**5 Rubles** 1918.	25.00	60.00	125.00
S578	**25 Rubles** 1918.	25.00	60.00	125.00
S579	**100 Rubles** 1918.	—	Rare	—

АЗОВСКО-ДОНСКОЙ КОММЕРЧЕСКІЙ БАНКЪ
Azov-Don Commercial Bank

Grozny

1918 ЧЕКЪ Circulating Bearer Checks Issue

#S581-S584 circulating bearer checks 5.2.1918 to 8.9.1918. Perforation and ovpt. varieties.

		Good	Fine	XF
S581	**3 Rubles** 1918.	6.00	15.00	—
S582	**5 Rubles** 1918.	6.00	15.00	—
S583	**25 Rubles** 1918.	5.00	10.00	—

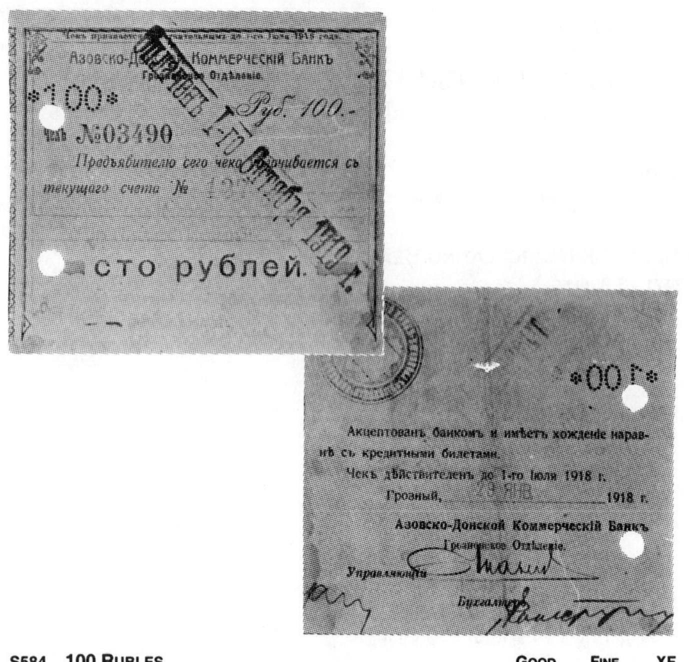

		Good	Fine	XF
S584	**100 Rubles** 1918.	6.00	15.00	—

Sochi (City)

ВОНЫ СОЧИНСКАГО ГОРОДСКОГО УПРАВЛЕНІЯ
Bons of the Sochi City Administration

1919 ND ВОНЫ Bons (Vouchers) Third Issue

		Good	Fine	XF
S585	**1 Ruble** ND (1919). Blue on lt. brown unpt.	4.00	9.00	20.00
S585A	**3 Rublei** 1919. Black on gray-green unpt.	4.00	9.00	20.00
S585B	**5 Rublei** 1919. Blue on gray unpt.	3.00	6.00	15.00
S585C	**10 Rublei** 1919. Black on lt. brown unpt.	4.00	8.00	17.50

1919 ВОНЫ Bons (Vouchers) Third Issue

		Good	Fine	XF
S585D	**25 Rublei** 1919. Black on tan unpt.	4.00	8.00	17.50
S585E	**50 Rublei** 1919. Deep blue on blue unpt.	2.00	4.00	9.00
S585F	**50 Rublei** 1919. Deep blue on gray unpt.	2.00	4.00	9.00
S585G	**100 Rublei** 1919. Dk. brown and orange on lt. orange-brown unpt.	20.00	45.00	100.00
S585H	**250 Rublei** 1919. Blue and orange on olive-gray unpt.	12.50	27.50	55.00

ЧЕРНОМОРСКАЯ ЖЕЛЕЗНАЯ ДОРОГА
Black Sea Railroad

1918 ВОНЫ Bons (Vouchers) Issue

		Good	Fine	XF
S586	**1 Ruble** 1918. Yellow unpt.	10.00	20.00	100.00
S587	**3 Rubles** 1918. Green unpt.	10.00	20.00	100.00
S588	**5 Rubles** 1918. Blue unpt.	12.00	25.00	150.00
S589	**10 Rubles** 1918.	15.00	30.00	250.00
S590	**25 Rubles** 1918.	15.00	30.00	125.00
S591	**50 Rubles** 1918. Blue on green.	—	—	300.00

ОБЩЕСТВА ВЛАДИКАВКАЗСКОЙ ЖЕЛЬЗНОЙ or КЕЛЕЗИОЙ ДОРОГИ
Vladikavkaz Railroad Company

1918 ЗАЕМНЫЙ БИЛЕТЪ
5.4% Interest-bearing Loan Notes Issue

#S593-S599 w/Caucasus map on back showing railroad's main line from Rostov-on-the-Don to Petrovsk and Baku on the Caspian Sea.

		VG	VF	Unc
S593	**50 Rubles** 1.9.1918. Black on lt. blue, buff and lt. green unpt. Winged gear at lower l., steam locomotive below partly robed woman at r.	5.00	15.00	27.50

		VG	VF	Unc
S594	**100 Rubles** 1.9.1918. Black on lt. blue and lt. brown unpt. Steam passenger train at upper l.	6.00	17.50	35.00

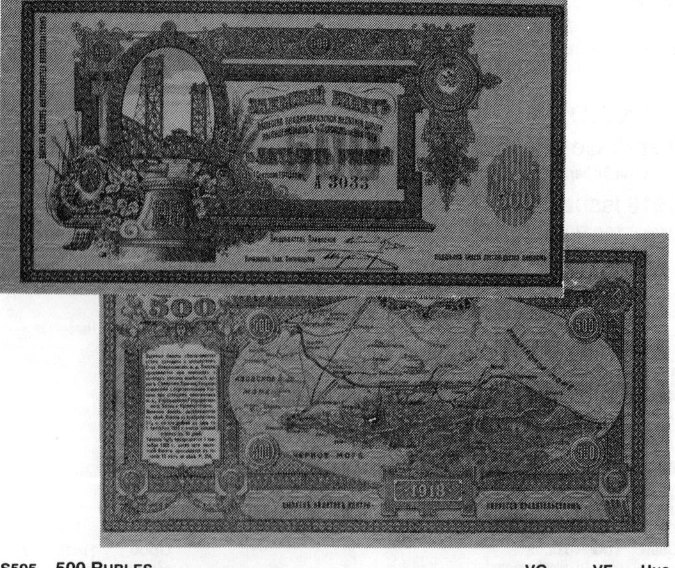

		VG	VF	Unc
S595	**500 Rubles** 1.9.1918. Black on green, gray and lt. blue unpt. Railroad bridge at upper l.	8.00	20.00	40.00

		VG	VF	UNC
S596	**1000 RUBLES** 1.9.1918. Black on lt. maroon and lt. blue unpt. Bldg. atop mountainous scene at lower r.	10.00	22.50	45.00

1919 ЗАЕМНЫЙ БИЛЕТЪ
5.4% INTEREST-BEARING LOAN NOTES ISSUE

		VG	VF	UNC
S597	**1000 RUBLES** 1.9.1919. Proof only.	—	Rare	—

		GOOD	FINE	XF
S598	**5000 RUBLES** 1.9.1919. Black on blue and salmon unpt. Railroad bridge w/central span lifted on uprights at lower l.	55.00	120.00	300.00
S599	**10,000 RUBLES** 1.9.1919. Blue-gray on lt. brown unpt. Steam train at lower ctr.	90.00	225.00	650.00

ГОСУДАРСТВЕННАГО БАНКА
Government Bank
ВЛАДИКАВКАЗСКОЕ ОТДѢЛЕНІЙ
Vladikavkaz

1920 ND ISSUE

#S599A-S600D black text on blue unpt., red denomination. W/o filled in date or sign. on face. Perforated w/number and "Г.Б." (for Government Bank). Black text w/2 sign. on back.

		GOOD	FINE	XF
S599A	**1 RUBLE** ND (1910- old date 191x).	—	—	—
S599B	**3 RUBLEI** ND (1920- old date 191x).	—	—	—

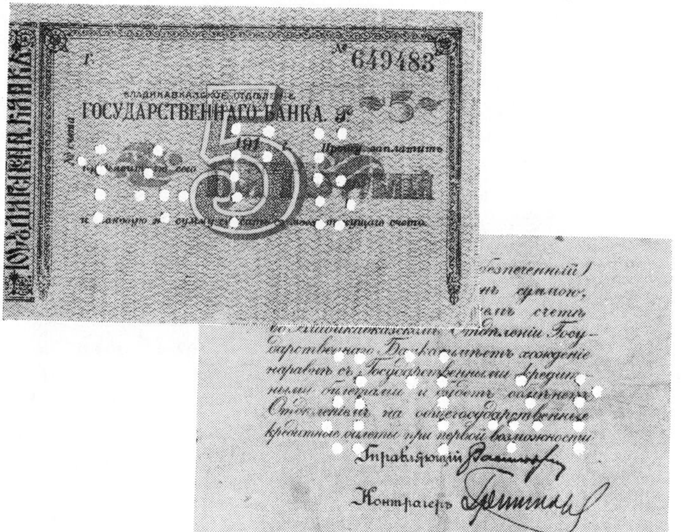

		GOOD	FINE	XF
S600A	**5 RUBLEI** ND (1920- old date 191x).	5.00	12.00	25.00
S600B	**10 RUBLEI** ND (1920- old date 191x).	5.00	12.00	25.00
S600C	**25 RUBLEI** ND (1920- old date 191x).	15.00	40.00	85.00
S600D	**50 RUBLEI** ND (1920- old date 191x).	25.00	60.00	120.00

GOVERNMENTS

Transcaucasian Commissariat
Federation of Socialist Soviet Republics of Transcaucasia
Armenian Socialist Soviet Republic
Alexandropol
Azerbaijan Socialist Soviet Republic
Baku
Batum (British Occupation)
Georgian Socialist Soviet Republic

RAILROAD

Transcaucasian S.S.R. Railroad

ЗАКАВКАЗСКАГО КОМИССАРІАТА
Transcaucasian Commissariat

On Nov. 24, 1917, the Armenians, Georgians and Turkic Azerbaijani peoples declared their independence of the central government, forming this federation. It broke up into the national republics of Armenia, Georgia and Azerbaijan the next year, on May 26, 1918. These notes continued to circulate, however.

1918 ISSUE

All notes w/ or w/o oil-varnish wetting (patterns in the unpt.). Paper varieties.

		VG	VF	UNC
S601	**1 RUBLE** 1918. Blue on lt. tan unpt.	1.50	2.50	6.50
S602	**3 RUBLES** 1918. Black on green unpt.	1.00	2.00	5.00

		VG	VF	UNC
S603	**5 RUBLES** 1918. Blue on gray unpt.			
	a. Wmk.	2.00	4.00	7.00
	b. W/o wmk.	2.00	4.00	7.00
S604	**10 RUBLES** 1918. Red-brown or maroon on olive unpt.	2.00	4.00	7.00
S605	**50 RUBLES** 1918. Black on blue-gray unpt.	2.50	5.00	12.00

NOTE: Partial sheets or strips of #S601-S605 are found on occasion.

		VG	VF	UNC
S606	**100 RUBLES** 1918. Black on brown and tan unpt.	2.50	5.00	12.00

		VG	VF	UNC
S607	**250 RUBLES** 1918. Gray-olive on pale lilac unpt. Back brown and blue.			
	a. Thin paper.	4.00	7.50	15.00
	b. Thick paper, crude printing.	4.00	7.50	15.00

ФЕД. С. С. Р. ЗАКАВКАЗЬЯ
Federation of Socialist Soviet Republics of Transcaucasia

1923 FIRST ДЕНЕЖНЫЙ ЗНАК CURRENCY TOKENS ISSUE

#S611-S622 bldg. w/flag at ctr. on face, arms at ctr. on back. Flourishes in frame border face in one direction on back.

		VG	VF	UNC
S611	**1000 RUBLES** 1923. Black-green on yellow-brown unpt.	1.75	4.00	8.50
S612	**5000 RUBLES** 1923. Blue on lilac-brown unpt.	2.00	4.50	9.00
S613	**10,000 RUBLES** 1923. Red-brown on gray unpt.	2.00	4.50	10.00
S614	**10,000 RUBLES** 1923. Dk. purple on red-violet unpt.	4.00	7.50	15.00
S615	**25,000 RUBLES** 1923. Black on brown unpt.	1.25	3.00	6.50

		VG	VF	UNC
S616	**50,000 RUBLES** 1923. Black on green unpt.			
	a. Wmk: Stars.	4.50	10.00	18.00
	b. W/o wmk.	1.00	2.50	6.00
S617	**100,000 RUBLES** 1923. Brown on red-brown unpt.			
	a. Wmk: Stars.	4.50	10.00	18.00
	b. W/o wmk.	1.00	3.00	6.50
S618	**250,000 RUBLES** Black on green unpt.			
	a. Normal print.	4.00	10.00	18.00
	b. Misprint: back inverted.	6.00	12.00	25.00
S619	**500,000 RUBLES** 1923. Purple on lt. blue unpt.			
	a. Wmk: Stars.	2.50	6.00	12.50
	b. W/o wmk.	1.00	3.00	6.50
S620	**1,000,000 RUBLES** 1923. Brown on violet unpt.			
	a. Wmk: Stars.	1.75	5.00	10.00
	b. W/o wmk.	1.00	3.00	7.00
S621	**5,000,000 RUBLES** 1923. Dk. brown on green and lilac unpt.	1.75	5.00	10.00
S622	**10,000,000 RUBLES** 1923. Black on blue, green, yell	2.50	6.00	12.50

1923 SECOND ДЕНЕЖНЫЙ ЗНАК CURRENCY TOKENS ISSUE

#S623-S631 like #S612-S622. Flourishes in frame border face l. and r. on back.

		VG	VF	UNC
S623	**5000 RUBLES** 1923.	1.00	3.00	6.50
S624	**10,000 RUBLES** 1923.	1.00	3.50	7.00
S625	**50,000 RUBLES** 1923.	1.00	4.00	8.00
S626	**100,000 RUBLES** 1923.	1.00	4.00	8.00
S627	**250,000 RUBLES** 1923.	1.00	4.00	8.00
S628	**500,000 RUBLES** 1923.	1.50	4.50	9.00
S629	**1,000,000 RUBLES** 1923.	1.50	4.50	9.00
S630	**5,000,000 RUBLES** 1923.	1.50	4.50	9.00
S631	**10,000,000 RUBLES** 1923.	2.50	6.00	10.00

З.С.ф.С.Р.

Transcaucasian Socialist Federal Soviet Republic

1924 ДЕНЕЖНЫЙ ЗНАК CURRENCY TOKENS ISSUE

#S632-S634 similar to #S623-S631.

		VG	VF	UNC
S632	**25,000,000 RUBLES** 1924. Black on gray unpt.			
	a. Wmk: Stars.	2.50	6.00	10.00
	b. W/o wmk.	2.50	6.00	10.00
	x. Error: w/back inverted.	6.00	12.00	22.50

		VG	VF	UNC
S633	**50,000,000 RUBLES** 1924. Black on gray-violet unpt.	4.00	8.00	20.00
S634	**50,000,000 RUBLES** 1924. Horizontal format. Printed back only.	25.00	100.00	300.00

		VG	VF	UNC
S635	**75,000,000 RUBLES** 1924. Black on brown unpt. Oil derrick on back.			
	a. Wmk: Lg. stars.	5.00	12.00	30.00
	b. W/o wmk.	4.00	10.00	25.00

		VG	VF	UNC
S636	**100,000,000 RUBLES** 1924. Brown on green unpt. Like #S632.	6.00	15.00	32.50
S637	**250,000,000 RUBLES** 1924. Brown on tan unpt. Similar to #S635. Back green on tan unpt.	9.00	20.00	42.50

		VG	VF	UNC
S638	**1 MILLIARD (= BILLION) RUBLES** 1924. Lilac. Woman seated w/fruit and wheat on green back.			
	a. Black-green on green and lilac unpt.	15.00	30.00	65.00
	b. Brown on tan and lilac unpt.	17.50	35.00	70.00
	c. Olive on olive and lilac unpt.	17.50	35.00	70.00
S639	**10 MILLIARDE RUBLES** 1924. Black on lilac and green unpt.	22.50	50.00	125.00

Notice

Readers with unlisted dates, color or signature varieties are invited to submit photocopies of their notes to: Standard Catalog of World Paper Money, Krause Publications, 700 East State St. Iola WI 54990-0001 U.S.A. or by email: thernr@krause.com. Email submissions of material for possible inclusion need to be 100% jpeg attachments at 300 dpi.

УПРАВЛЕНИЕ ЖЕЛЕЗНЫХ ДОРОГ С.С.Р. ЗАКАВКАЗЬЯ
Transcaucasian S.S.R.R. Railroad

1920 ND РАСЧЕТНЫЙ ЗНАК EXCHANGE TOKENS ISSUE

		VG	VF	UNC
S641	**5000 RUBLES** ND (1920). Black on yellow unpt.	2.00	4.00	10.00
S642	**10,000 RUBLES** ND (1920). Black on blue unpt.	2.00	4.00	10.00
S643	**25,000 RUBLES** ND (1920). Black on green unpt.	2.50	5.00	12.00
S644	**50,000 RUBLES** ND (1920). Black on red unpt.	2.50	5.00	12.00
S645	**100,000 RUBLES** ND (1920). Black on purple unpt.	3.00	6.00	15.00

РЕСПУБЛИКА АРМЕНИИ (orАРМЕНИЯ)
Armenia - Autonomous Republic

NOTE: For previously listed #S646-S677 see Vol. 2, Armenia #1-32.

СОЦИАЛИСТИЧЕСКАЯ СОВЕТСКАЯ РЕСПУБЛИКА АРМЕНИИ
Armenian Socialist Soviet Republic

1919; 1921; 1922 ISSUES

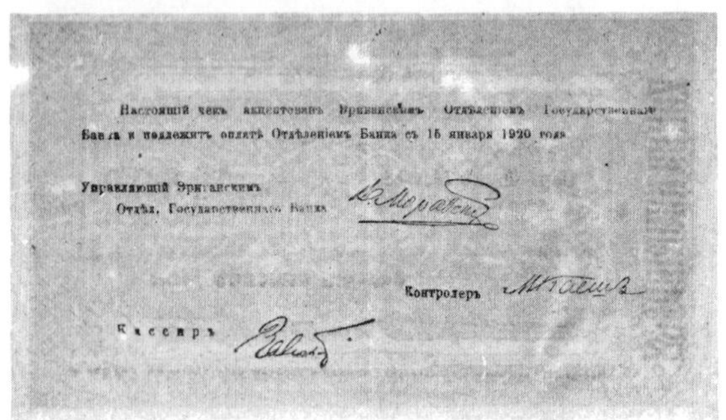

		GOOD	FINE	XF
S678	**10,000 RUBLES** Aug. 1919. Lt. green. Like #S674 but sign. on back in in facsimile print. НОЯБРЯ.	4.00	10.00	25.00

		GOOD	FINE	XF
S679	**5000 RUBLES** 1921. Blue on gray unpt. Arms at ctr. on back.	3.00	9.00	20.00
S680	**10,000 RUBLES** 1921. Arms at top ctr.			
	a. Rose paper. Wmk.	3.00	9.00	20.00
	b. Rose to brown paper. W/o wmk.	3.00	9.00	20.00
	c. Lilac paper. W/o wmk.	4.00	10.00	25.00
	d. Trial printing in green.	—	—	100.00

		GOOD	FINE	XF
S681	**25,000 RUBLES** 1922. Blue. Arms at ctr.			
	a. Wmk.	6.00	15.00	30.00
	b. W/o wmk.	6.00	15.00	30.00
S682	**100,000 RUBLES** 1922. Gray-green on yellow-brown unpt. Arms at upper r.	4.00	10.00	25.00
S683	**500,000 RUBLES** 1922. Trial printing of back only.	—	Rare	—

		GOOD	FINE	XF
S684	**1,000,000 RUBLES** 1922. Red. Arms at ctr. on back.	8.00	20.00	50.00

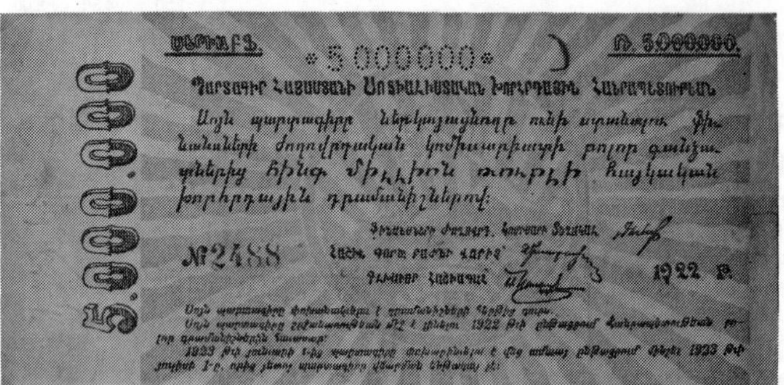

		GOOD	FINE	XF
S685	**5,000,000 RUBLES** 1922. Black on gray-olive.			
	a. Wmk.	10.00	25.00	60.00
	b. W/o wmk.	10.00	25.00	60.00

		GOOD	FINE	XF
S686	**5,000,000 RUBLES** 1922. Blue-green on lt. green.	10.00	25.00	60.00

1923 ДЕНЕЖНЫЙ ЗНАКЪ CURRENCY TOKENS ISSUE

		VG	VF	UNC
S687	**1 CHERVONETZ** 1923. Blue, lt. brown and green. Landscape and mountains in background on back. (Not issued).	—	100.00	200.00

Series letters A; AB and ABG (all Armenian) are known; the illustrated specimen is AB (panels at upper l. and r. of face side).

ALEXANDROPOL (CITY, ARMENIA)

NOTE: Now called Leninakan. It was in Brivansk Guberniya in Czarist and Independence periods.

ALEXANDROPOL

АЛЕКСАНДРОПОЛСКІЙ ГОРОДСК. ОБЖЕСТВЕНН. БАНКЪ
Alexandropol Government Corporation Bank

1919 BEARER ЧЕКЪ CHECKS ISSUE

White regime.

		VG	VF	UNC
S691	**25 RUBLES** Oct. to Dec. 1919.	—	Rare	—
S692	**50 RUBLES** Oct. to Dec. 1919.	—	Rare	—

SHIRAK

SHIRAK GOVERNMENT CORPORATION BANK

1920-21 ND ISSUE

Soviet regime.

#S693-S698 text in Armenian. Paper, text, and wmk. varieties. Stamped sign. Purple stamping on back.

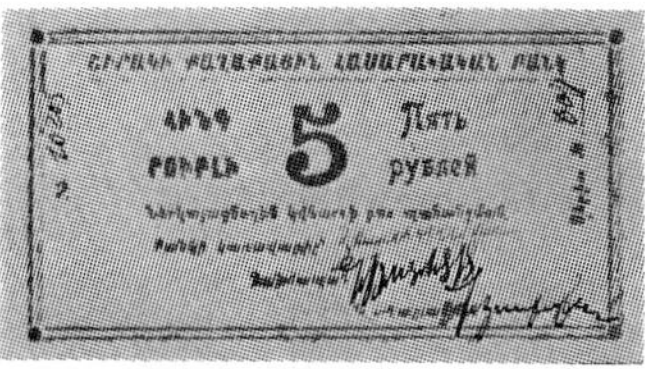

		GOOD	FINE	XF
S693	**5 RUBLES** ND (1920-21). Gray.	12.00	30.00	80.00
S694	**10 RUBLES** ND (1920-21). Gray.	15.00	35.00	90.00
S695	**20 RUBLES** ND (1920-21). Gray.	15.00	35.00	90.00
S696	**25 RUBLES** ND (1920-21). Gray.	25.00	60.00	150.00
S697	**50 RUBLES** ND (1920-21). Gray.	25.00	60.00	150.00
S698	**100 RUBLES** ND (1920-21). Gray.	40.00	100.00	225.00

АЗЕРБАЙДЖАНСКАЯ РЕСПУБЛИКА
AZERBAIJAN, AUTONOMOUS REPUBLIC

NOTE: For previously listed #S701-S708 see Vol. 2, Azerbaijan #1-8.

АЗЕРБАЙДЖАНСКАЯ СОЦИАЛИСТИЧЕСКАЯ СОБЕТСКАЯ РЕСПУБЛИКА
Azerbaijan Socialist Soviet Republic

1920 ND ISSUE

		GOOD	FINE	XF
S709	**5 RUBLES** ND (1920). Worker and farmer. Back black on purple unpt; factory.			
	a. Black on yellow unpt.	2.50	7.00	15.00
	b. Black on orange unpt.	5.00	12.00	30.00

		GOOD	FINE	XF
S710	**100 RUBLES** ND (1920). Olive and violet. Railway train.	2.50	7.00	15.00

1920-23 ISSUE

		GOOD	FINE	XF
S711	**1000 RUBLES** 1920. Black on green and red unpt. Arms at upper l. and r. 167 x 107mm.			
	a. Issued note.	3.50	8.00	17.50
	p. Proof print in gray and lt. blue.	—	—	60.00

		GOOD	FINE	XF
S712	**1000 RUBLES** 1920. Like #S711. 107 x 66mm.	3.50	8.00	17.50

		GOOD	FINE	XF
S713	**5000 RUBLES** 1921. Dk. brown on m/c unpt. Worker at l., arms at ctr., farmer seated at r. Back black on blue and brown unpt.	4.00	9.00	20.00

		GOOD	FINE	XF
S714	**10,000 RUBLES** 1921. Black on rose and green unpt. Worker and farmer standing at ctr., arms behind. Back black on brown unpt; bldgs. at l. and r.	4.00	10.00	25.00

		Good	Fine	XF
S715	**25,000 Rubles** 1921. Black on brown and gray unpt.			
	a. W/o wmk.	4.00	10.00	25.00
	b. Wmk.	4.00	10.00	25.00
S716	**50,000 Rubles** 1921. Black on gray-green and brown unpt. Standing figures at l. and r., arms at ctr.	4.00	10.00	25.00

		Good	Fine	XF
S717	**100,000 Rubles** 1922. Black. Arms at ctr. on back.			
	a. Violet unpt. W/o wmk.	2.50	7.50	17.50
	b. Blue unpt. W/o wmk.	4.00	10.00	25.00
	c. Wmk.	5.00	12.00	27.50
S718	**250,000 Rubles** 1922. Brown on blue unpt.	2.50	7.50	17.50

		Good	Fine	XF
S719	**1,000,000 Rubles** 1922. Red on pink unpt.			
	a. Issued note.	3.50	10.00	22.50
	b. W/o pink unpt. on back.	—	—	—
	c. Dk. red. Wmk: *BANK URANIA.*	—	—	—
S720	**5,000,000 Rubles** 1923. Green on olive and dull red unpt. Arms at upper ctr. Lilac in unpt. on back.	5.00	12.00	30.00

БАКУ Baku

Notes of the city government of Baku, which were accepted all over Azerbaijan. All notes incorporate the city arms of *Three Flames.*

Baku was under Bolshevik control January to July 31, 1918. Then under British to Sept. 14, 1918; Turks to Oct. 30, 1918; British again from Nov. 14, 1918.

БАКИНСКАЯ ГОРОДСКАЯ УПРАВА
Baku City Management

1918 Issue

		Good	Fine	XF
S721	**1 Ruble** 1918. Blue on brown unpt. Back brown.	2.00	5.00	20.00
S722	**3 Rubles** 2918. Brown on orange and lt. green unpt. Back green.	2.00	5.00	20.00
S723	**5 Rubles** 1918. Blue on green and red unpt. Back blue-gray.	2.00	5.00	20.00

		Good	Fine	XF
S724	**10 Rubles** 1918. Dk. blue and red on lilac unpt. Back pale red.	2.00	5.00	20.00

		Good	Fine	XF
S725	**25 Rubles** 1918. Black on purple and lt. brown unpt. Back brown on green unpt.	3.00	6.00	22.50

1918 ND Postage Stamp "Style" Money Issue

#S726-S728 arms at upper ctr.

		Good	Fine	XF
S726	**5 Kopeks** ND (1918). Green.	1.00	4.00	10.00
S727	**15 Kopeks** ND (1918). Brown.	1.00	4.00	10.00
S728	**50 Kopeks** ND. Black on reddish brown unpt.			
	a. Perforated.	2.00	5.00	12.00
	b. Imperforate.	2.00	5.00	12.00

СОВѢТЪ БАКИНСКАГО ГОРОДСКОГО ХОЗЯЙСТВА
Soviet Baku City Adminstration

1918 Issue

		Good	Fine	XF
S731	**10 Rubles** 1918. Brown on red and lt. brown unpt. Seated Mercury at l. Arms on back at ctr. in unpt. W/ or w/o series IV-VIII.	2.00	6.00	17.50

		GOOD	FINE	XF
S732	**25 RUBLES** 1918. Black and red on violet unpt. Mercury and worker at lower l., arms above. Back black on violet unpt.	2.00	6.00	17.50

		GOOD	FINE	XF
S733	**50 RUBLES** 1918. Black on lt. brown and lt blue unpt. Arms above oil derricks, sailing ship w/anchor, gear, crates and cornucopiae below at l. Serial # and letter on face or on back.			
	a. W/o series.	3.00	7.50	20.00
	b. Series V-VIII.	3.00	7.50	20.00

NOTE: Minor plate and color shade varieties exist between Series V and VI.

BATUM (BRITISH OCCUPATION)

British occupation lasted Dec. 27, 1918 to June 4, 1920.

БАТУМСКАГО КАЗНАЧЕИСТВА
Batum Treasury

1919 ND; 1919 РАЗМѢННЫЙ ДЕНЕЖНЫЙ ЗНАКЪ EXCHANGE CURRENCY TOKENS ISSUE

		GOOD	FINE	XF
S736	**1 RUBLE** ND (April 1919). Orange-yellow Tree. Uniface. 31 x 48mm.	4.00	10.00	25.00
S737	**3 RUBLES** ND (April 1919). Green. Tree. Uniface. 31 x 48mm.	4.00	10.00	25.00

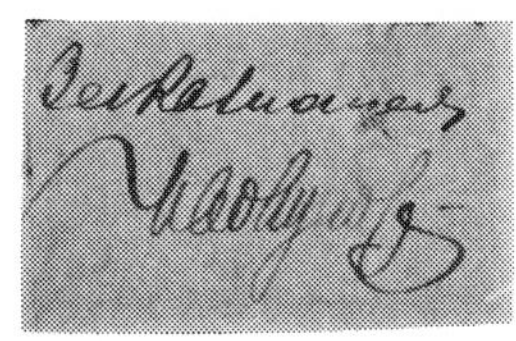

		GOOD	FINE	XF
S738	**5 RUBLES** ND (April 1919). Tree. Sign. on back. 31 x 48mm.	4.00	10.00	25.00
S739	**5 RUBLES** 1919. Like #S738 but perforated date *1919* is across ctr.	—	—	—
S740	**10 RUBLES** ND (April 1919). Tree. Sign. on back. 31 x 48mm.	4.50	12.50	30.00
S741	**10 RUBLES** 1919. Perforated date.	—	—	—
S742	**25 RUBLES** ND (April 1919). Brown. Tree. Sign. on back. 31 x 48mm.	8.00	25.00	40.00
S743	**25 RUBLES** 1919. Brown. Tree. Uniface. Like #S742 but perforated date *1919* is vertically at ctr.	—	—	—
S744	**50 RUBLES** ND (April 1919). Tree. Sign. on back. 31 x 48mm.	9.00	27.50	45.00
S745	**50 RUBLES** 1919. Perforated date.	—	—	—

GEORGIA, AUTONOMOUS REPUBLIC

ГРУЗИНСКОИ РЕСПУБЛИКИ ОБЯЗАТЕЛЬСТВО КАЗНАЧЕИСТВА
GEORGIAN REPUBLIC TREASURY OBLIGATIONS

NOTE: For previously listed #S746-S760 see Vol. 2, Georgia #1-15.

ГРУЗИНСКАЯ СОЦ. СОВЕТСКАЯ РЕСПУБЛИКА
Georgian Socialist Soviet Republic

1921 ISSUE

		GOOD	FINE	XF
S761	**5000 RUBLES** 1921. Lilac to brown. Bldg. w/flag at ctr. Like #15, Vol. 2. but margin circles around corner numerals are ringed twice at each side.			
	a. Thick paper.	1.50	3.50	7.00
	b. Thin paper, black printing.	3.00	6.00	12.50
	c. Thin paper, blue printing.	1.50	3.50	7.50
	d. Misprint: unpt. inverted.	6.00	8.00	15.00

		GOOD	FINE	XF
S762	**10,000 RUBLES** 1922. Bldg. w/flags. Arms at ctr. on back.			
	a. Green back.	2.50	5.00	10.00
	b. Lt. blue back.	3.00	6.00	12.50
	c. Red back.	4.00	7.00	15.00
	d. Misprint: unpt. inverted.	5.00	8.00	17.50

1922 ND ACCOUNTING SCRIP ISSUE

		GOOD	FINE	XF
S765	**50,000 RUBLES** ND (ca.1922). Red; same design face and back.	3.00	6.00	15.00

НАРОДНАГО БАНКА С.С.Р. ГРУЗИН
Banque Nationale de Georgie

1922 ОБЯЗАТЕЛЬСТВО БОН DEBENTURE BONDS ISSUE

		GOOD	FINE	XF
S766	**100,000 RUBLES** 31.5.1922.	7.00	17.50	37.50
S767	**500,000 RUBLES** 31.5.1922. Black and brown on lt. green and orange unpt. Back lt. green.	8.00	20.00	40.00

		GOOD	FINE	XF
S768	**1,000,000 RUBLES** 31.5.1922. Face like #S767. Back gray.	12.00	30.00	55.00
S769	**5,000,000 RUBLES** 31.5.1922.	18.00	45.00	85.00

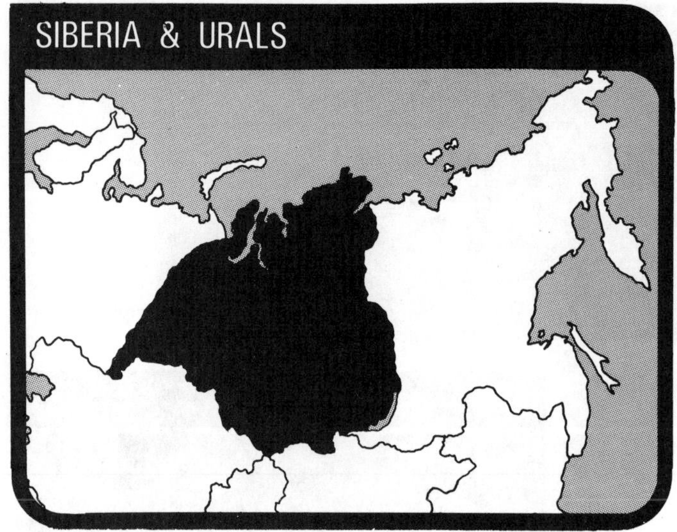

Issues of:

- Samara Directory (Komuch)
- Siberian Provisional Government
- Provisional Russian Government (Kolchak)
- Minister Representative Plenipotentiary for Provisions for Khabarovsk District
- Siberian Revolution Committee
- Urals and Kama Region
- Soviet of the Urals Region
- Urals Cossack Region
- Uralsk Branch, Government Bank
- Government of Central Siberia
- Akmolinsk Region Revolutionary Committee
- Krasnoyarsk
- Orenburg
- Perm

САМАРСКАЯ ДИРЕКТОРИЯ
Samara Directory (Komuch)

Socialist regime, claiming succession to the Provisional (Kerensky) government; known as the Komuch. In late 1918 it merged with the Siberian Provisional Government to form the All-Russian Provisional Government.

RUSSIAN DEBENTURES W/DIFFERENT STAMPS AND PERFORATIONS.

1918 ND FIRST ГОСУДАРСТБ. ВНУТРЕНН. 5% ЗАЕМЪ 1905 Г. PROVISIONAL GOVERNMENT LOAN OBLIGATIONS ISSUE

		GOOD	FINE	XF
S771	100 RUBLES ND (1918).	12.00	30.00	—
S772	1000 RUBLES ND (1918).	17.50	40.00	—

1918 ND SECOND ГОСУДАРСТВ. ВТОРОЙ ВНУТР. 5% ЗАЕМЬ 1905 Г. PROVISIONAL GOVERNMENT LOAN OBLIGATIONS ISSUE

		GOOD	FINE	XF
S773	100 RUBLES ND (1918).	12.00	30.00	—
S774	200 RUBLES ND (1918).	15.00	35.00	—
S775	500 RUBLES ND (1918).	17.50	40.00	—
S776	1000 RUBLES ND (1918).	25.00	60.00	—

1918 ND ОБЛИГАЦIЯ ВНУТРЕНН. ЗАЙМА 1914 Г. PROVISIONAL LOAN OBLIGATION ISSUE

		GOOD	FINE	XF
S777	100 RUBLES ND (1918).	10.00	25.00	—
S778	1000 RUBLES ND (1918).	20.00	50.00	—

1914-15 БИЛЕТЪ ГОСУДАРСТВЕННАГО КАЗНАЧЕЙСТВА GOVERNMENT TREASURY NOTE ISSUE

		GOOD	FINE	XF
S779	50 RUBLES 1914.	8.00	20.00	—
S780	100 RUBLES 1914.	10.00	25.00	—
S781	25 RUBLES 1915.	8.00	20.00	—
S782	50 RUBLES 1915.	8.00	20.00	—
S783	100 RUBLES 1915.	12.00	30.00	—
S784	500 RUBLES 1915.	17.50	40.00	—

1915 ОБЛИГАЦIЯ 5-1/2% ВОЕННАГО КР. ЗАЙМА MILITARY DEBENTURE LOAN OBLIGATION ISSUE

		GOOD	FINE	XF
S785	50 RUBLES 1915.	8.00	20.00	—
S786	100 RUBLES 1915.	8.00	20.00	—
S787	500 RUBLES 1915.	12.00	30.00	—
S788	1000 RUBLES 1915.	12.00	30.00	—
S789	5000 RUBLES 1915.	17.50	40.00	—
S790	10,000 RUBLES 1915.	25.00	60.00	—

1916 ОБЛИГАЦIЯ 5-1/2% ВОЕННАГО КР. ЗАЙМА MILITARY DEBENTURE LOAN OBLIGATION ISSUE

		GOOD	FINE	XF
S791	50 RUBLES 1916.	8.00	20.00	—
S792	100 RUBLES 1916.	8.00	20.00	—
S793	500 RUBLES 1916.	8.00	20.00	—
S794	1000 RUBLES 1916.	10.00	25.00	—
S795	5000 RUBLES 1916.	17.50	40.00	—
S796	10,000 RUBLES 1916.	30.00	80.00	—
S797	25,000 RUBLES 1916.	50.00	120.00	—

1917 ОБЛИГАЦIЯ ЗАЙМА СВОБОДЫ 1917 Г. FREEDOM LOAN OBLIGATION ISSUE

		GOOD	FINE	XF
S798	20 RUBLES 1917.	8.00	20.00	—
S799	40 RUBLES 1917.	8.00	20.00	—
S800	50 RUBLES 1917.	8.00	20.00	—
S801	100 RUBLES 1917.	8.00	20.00	—
S802	500 RUBLES 1917.	10.00	25.00	—
S803	1000 RUBLES 1917.	17.50	40.00	—
S804	5000 RUBLES 1917.	25.00	60.00	—
S805	10,000 RUBLES 1917.	30.00	80.00	—
S806	25,000 RUBLES 1917.	40.00	100.00	—

1918 КРАТКОСРОЧНОЕ ОБЯЗАТЕЛЬСТВО BILLS OF EXCHANGE ISSUE

#S807-S812 black on green unpt. M/c guilloche at l.

		GOOD	FINE	XF
S807	50 RUBLES 1918.	10.00	20.00	—
S808	100 RUBLES 1918.	10.00	20.00	—
S809	250 RUBLES 1918.	12.00	25.00	—

		GOOD	FINE	XF
S810	500 RUBLES 1918.	15.00	40.00	—
S811	1000 RUBLES 1918.	15.00	40.00	—
S812	5000 RUBLES 1918.	25.00	65.00	—

СИБИРСКАГО ВРЕМЕННАГО ПРАВИТЕЛЬСТВА
Siberian Provisional Administration (First)

Conservative White regime at Omsk, under Premier P. V. Vologodskii. After merging with the Samara Directory (Komuch), it gave way on Nov. 18, 1918 to Kolchak's dictatorship.

1918 КАЗНАЧЕЙСКІЙ ЗНАКЪ
TREASURY TOKEN CURRENCY ISSUE

		VG	VF	UNC
S816	**1 RUBLE** 1918. Black on lt. brown unpt. Double headed eagle at l. and r. Arms on back.	.25	1.00	3.00
S817	**5 RUBLES** 1918. Black on blue unpt. Double-headed eagle in wreath between 2 torches at l. and r. Arms on back.	.25	1.00	3.00
S818	**10 RUBLES** 1918. Black on red unpt. Like #S817. Thick or thin paper.	.25	1.00	3.50

1918 ГОСУДАРСТВЕННАГО КАЗНАЧЕЙСТВА СИБИРИ 5% КРАТКОСРОЧНОЕ ОБЯЗАТЕЛЬСТВО
SIBERIAN GOVERNMENT DEBENTURE OBLIGATIONS ISSUE

		GOOD	FINE	XF
S821	**500 RUBLES** 1.10.1918. Violet on olive unpt.	2.00	5.00	9.00
S822	**1000 RUBLES** 1.10.1918. Red-brown on green unpt.	4.00	10.00	20.00
S823	**5000 RUBLES** 1.10.1918. Brown on yellow unpt.	7.00	15.00	35.00

		GOOD	FINE	XF
S824	**500 RUBLES** 1.11.1918. Violet on olive unpt.	2.00	5.00	10.00
S825	**5000 RUBLES** 1.11.1918. Brown on yellow unpt.	4.00	10.00	20.00

СИБИРСКАГО ВРЕМЕННАГО ПРАВИТЕЛЬСТВА
Provisional Siberian Administration (Second)

ADMIRAL ALEKSANDR KOLCHAK, SUPREME RULER

Kolchak, war minister in the Directory, became dictator of Siberia and theoretical head of all White armies on Nov. 18, 1918, following a Cossack coup in Omsk led by Ataman Krasilnikov and supported by British troops under Col. Ward. On Nov. 14, 1919, the Bolsheviki captured Omsk and Kolchak fled toward Irkutsk. He was captured, and shot by the Reds on Feb. 7, 1920, aged 46. Much of the Kolchak paper money was printed by the Czech Legion, which controlled the Trans-Siberian Railroad, on Japanese rice paper.

1918-19; 1919 ND КАЗНАЧЕИСКИЙ ЗНАКЪ
TREASURY TOKEN CURRENCY ISSUE

		GOOD	FINE	XF
S826	**300 RUBLES** 1918. Black on blue unpt. Double-headed eagle at l. and r. Back dk. brown on lt. brown unpt. Arms at ctr.	1.00	4.00	8.50

		GOOD	FINE	XF
S827	**3 RUBLES** 1919. Black on green unpt. Double-headed eagle at l. and r. Back green.	.25	1.00	3.50

		GOOD	FINE	XF
S828	**50 KOPEKS** ND (1919). Orange. Double-headed eagle on back. No sign. Printer: ABNC (w/o imprint).	.25	1.00	2.00

NOTE: For #S828 w/sign. see #S1244.

1918-20 5% КРАТКОСРОЧНОЕ ОБЯЗАТЕЛЬСТВО ГОСУДАРСТВЕННАГО КАЗНАЧЕИСТВА
5% GOVERNMENT DEBENTURE OBLIGATIONS

1. ДЕК. 1918 ISSUE

Apparently 2 or more printers made this series of notes as there are significant variations in serial #, type style, prefix letter, etc.

		GOOD	FINE	XF
S831	**500 RUBLES** 1.12.1918. Violet on olive unpt.	1.00	4.00	8.00
S832	**1000 RUBLES** 1.12.1918. Lt. brown on green and orange unpt.	1.00	4.00	8.00

		GOOD	FINE	XF
S833	**5000 RUBLES** 1.12.1918. Brown on yellow-brown unpt.	2.00	6.00	10.00

1. ЯНВАРЯ 1919 ISSUE

		GOOD	FINE	XF
S834	**25 RUBLES** 1.1.1919. Black on blue unpt.			
	a. Sixth line: ДИРЕКТОРЪ ОТДѢЛА. Unpt. lg. flowers.	1.00	4.00	8.00
	b. Like a., but unpt. sm. flowers.	.50	2.00	4.00
	c. Sixth line: ДИРЕКУОРЪ ДЕПАРТАМЕНТА.	1.50	5.00	10.00
S835	**50 RUBLES** 1.1.1919. Black on green unpt.			
	a. Like #S834a.	1.50	5.00	10.00
	b. Like #S834b.	.50	2.00	4.00
	c. Like #S834c.	2.00	6.00	12.00

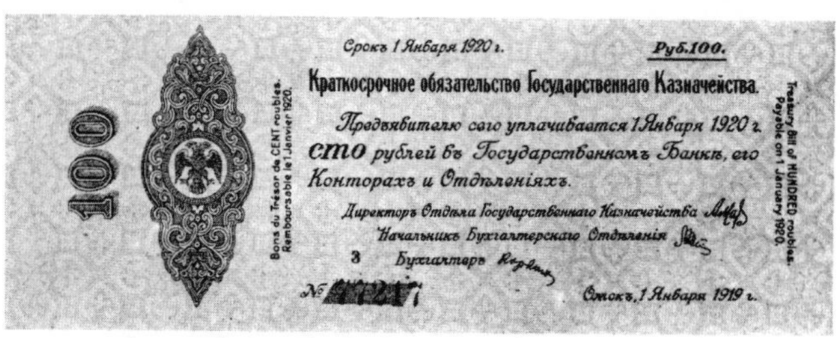

		GOOD	FINE	XF
S836	**100 RUBLES** 1.1.1919. Blue on blue-violet unpt.			
	a. Second line: 5% КРАТКОС...	2.00	6.00	12.00
	b. Second line: КРАТКОС...	2.00	6.00	12.00
	c. Error; like a., but *Januari* ЯНБАПЬ misspelling at r.	3.50	8.00	15.00

No.	Denomination	Good	Fine	XF
S837	**250 Rubles** 1.1.1919. Brown on orange unpt.	1.00	4.00	8.00
S838	**500 Rubles** 1.1.1919. Gray-violet on green unpt.	1.00	4.00	8.00
S839	**1000 Rubles** 1.1.1919. Red-brown on green unpt.	.50	2.00	4.00

1. ФЕВРАЛЯ 1919 ISSUE

No.	Denomination	Good	Fine	XF
S840	**25 Rubles** 1.2.1919. Black on blue unpt.			
	a. Sixth line: ДИРЕКТОРЪ ОТДѢЛА. W/ or w/o wmk.	.30	1.50	3.00
	b. Sixth line: ДИРЕКТОРЪ ДЕПАРТАМЕНТА.	.50	2.00	6.00
S841	**50 Rubles** 1.2.1919. Black on green unpt.			
	a. Like #S840a.	1.50	5.00	10.00
	b. Like #S840b.	.25	1.00	2.00
S842	**250 Rubles** 1.2.1919. Brown on orange unpt.	.25	1.00	2.00
S843	**500 Rubles** 1.2.1919. Gray-violet on olive unpt.	.25	1.00	2.00
S844	**1000 Rubles** 1.2.1919. Red-brown on green unpt.	.30	1.50	3.00
S845	**5000 Rubles** 1.2.1919. Brown on yellow unpt.	1.50	5.00	10.00

1. МАРТА 1919 ISSUE

No.	Denomination	Good	Fine	XF
S846	**25 Rubles** 1.3.1919. Black on blue unpt.	.25	1.00	2.00

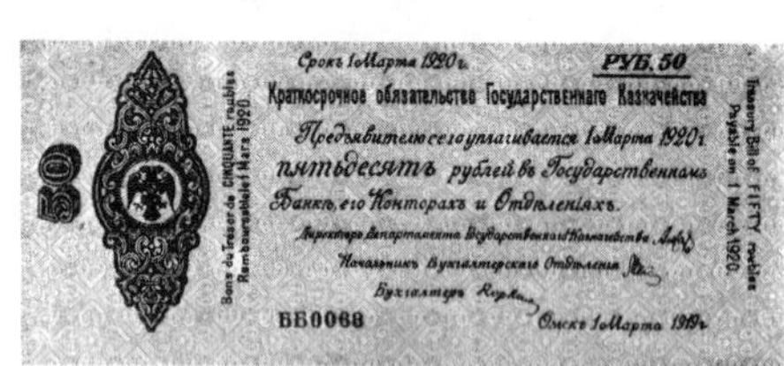

No.	Denomination	Good	Fine	XF
S847	**50 Rubles** 1.3.1919. Black on green unpt.	.25	1.00	2.00
S848	**250 Rubles** 1.3.1919. Brown on orange unpt.	.30	1.50	3.00
S849	**500 Rubles** 1.3.1919. Gray-violet on olive unpt.			
	a. Sixth line: ДИРЕКТОРЪ ОТДѢЛА.	.30	1.50	3.00
	b. Sixth line: ДИРЕКТОРЪ ДЕПАРТАМЕНТА.	.30	1.50	3.00
S850	**1000 Rubles** 1.3.1919. Red-brown on green unpt.			
	a. Like #S849a.	.40	2.00	4.00
	b. Like #S849b.	.30	1.50	3.00

1. АПРѢЛЯ 1919 ISSUE

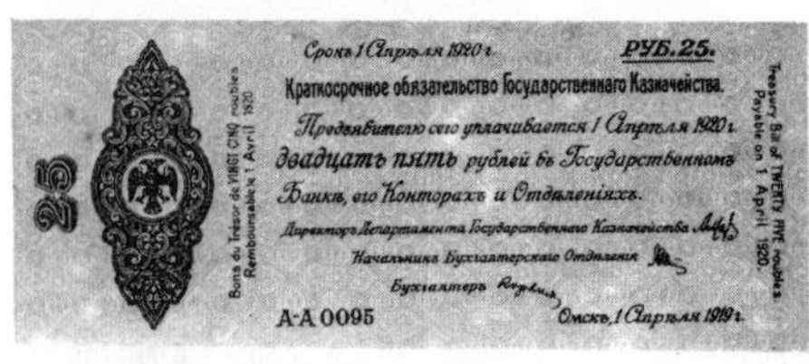

No.	Denomination	Good	Fine	XF
S851	**25 Rubles** 1.4.1919. Black on blue unpt.	.30	1.50	3.00
S852	**50 Rubles** 1.4.1919. Black on green unpt.	.25	1.00	2.00
S853	**250 Rubles** 1.4.1919. Brown on orange unpt.	.30	1.50	3.00
S854	**500 Rubles** 1.4.1919. Gray-violet on olive unpt.			
	a. Like #S849a.	.40	2.00	4.00
	b. Like #S849b.	.40	2.00	4.00

1. МАЯ 1919 ISSUE

No.	Denomination	Good	Fine	XF
S855	**25 Rubles** 1.5.1919. Black on blue unpt.			
	a. Vertical format note: *Remboursable le Mai 1920* at I.	.25	1.00	2.00
	b. Vertical format note: *Remboursable le I. Mai 1920* at I.	.40	2.00	4.00
S856	**50 Rubles** 1.5.1919. Black on green unpt.			
	a. Like #S855a.	.25	1.00	2.00
	b. Like #S855b, only as a forgery.	2.00	5.00	10.00
S857	**250 Rubles** 1.5.1919. Brown on orange unpt.	.30	1.50	3.00
S858	**500 Rubles** 1.5.1919. Gray-violet on green-yellow unpt.	.40	2.00	4.00

1. ІЮНЯ 1919 ISSUE

No.	Denomination	Good	Fine	XF
S859	**25 Rubles** 1.6.1919. Black on blue unpt.			
	a. Sixth line: ГОСУДАРСТВЪ.	.25	1.00	2.00
	b. Sixth line:. ГОСУДАРСТВЕННАГО.	.25	1.00	2.00
S860	**50 Rubles** 1.6.1919. Black on green unpt.	.25	1.00	2.00
S861	**250 Rubles** 1.6.1919. Brown on orange unpt.	.40	2.00	4.00
S862	**500 Rubles** 1.6.1919. Gray-violet on green unpt.	.25	1.00	2.00
S863	**1000 Rubles** 1.6.1919. Red-brown on green unpt.	.40	2.00	4.00

1. ІЮЛЯ 1919 ISSUE

No.	Denomination	Good	Fine	XF
S864	**25 Rubles** 1.7.1919. Black on blue unpt.	.30	1.50	3.00
S865	**50 Rubles** 1.7.1919. Black on green unpt.			
	a. Sixth line like #S859a.	.30	1.50	3.00
	b. Sixth line like #S859b.	.30	1.50	3.00
S866	**250 Rubles** 1.7.1919. Brown on orange unpt.			
	a. Sixth line 115mm.	.30	1.50	3.00
	b. Sixth line 85mm.	.40	2.00	4.00
S867	**500 Rubles** 1.7.1919. Gray-violet on green unpt.	.40	2.00	4.00

1. ОКТЯБРЯ 1919 (1920) ISSUE

No.	Denomination	Good	Fine	XF
S867B	**50 Rubles** 1.10.1919 (1920). Black on green unpt.	4.00	7.00	15.00
S868	**250 Rubles** 1.10.1919 (1920). Brown on orange unpt.	5.00	8.00	18.00
S869	**1000 Rubles** 1.10.1919 (1920). Red-brown on yellow unpt.	6.00	10.00	35.00
S870	**5000 Rubles** 1.10.1919 (1920). Brown on yellow-brown unpt.	7.00	12.00	25.00

NOTE: #S867B-S870 on wmk. paper. Wmk: Uncrowned double-headed eagle inside diamond pattern.

1. ЯНВАРЯ 1920 ISSUE

Issued in Vladivostok.

No.	Denomination	Good	Fine	XF
S870A	**5000 Rubles** 1.1.1920. Black on green unpt. Back blue; w/o design. (Printer: ABNC).			
	a. Issued note.	—	Rare	—
	p. Proof.	—	Unc	500.00
	s. Specimen.	—	Unc	800.00

1919-20 ГОСУДАРСТВЕННЫЙ КРЕДИТНЫЙ БИЛЕТЪ GOVERNMENT CREDIT NOTES ISSUE

#S871-S878 different proof-prints w/eagle of the Provisional Government and St. George. (Not issued.)

		VG	VF	Unc
S871	**1 Ruble** 1919.	—	—	600.00
S872	**3 Rubles** 1919.	—	—	600.00
S873	**5 Rubles** 1919.	—	—	600.00
S874	**10 Rubles** 1919.	—	—	600.00
S875	**25 Rubles** 1919.	—	—	600.00
S876	**100 Rubles** 1919.	—	—	600.00
S877	**1000 Rubles** 1919.	—	—	600.00
S878	**5000 Rubles** 1920.	—	Rare	—

ГОСУДАРСТВЕННИЙ БАНК
Government Bank

ИРК. ОТД.

Irkutsk

1917 БИЛЕТЪ ГОСУДАРСТВЕННЫЙ ВНУТРЕННІЙ. 4-1/2% ВЫИГРЫШНЫЙ ЗАЕМЪ
COMMITTEE SAVINGS LOAN NOTES ISSUE

Public bonds and coupons used as currency. Different places of issue are hand stamped at lower l. of bonds, thus: ИРК. ОТД. ГОЧ. Б.

#S881-S892 printer: ABNC.

#S881-S884 brown and black. Back brown.

		VG	VF	UNC
S881	**290 RUBLES** 1917 (1919). Woman w/child, sword and shield at top ctr. Public loan w/20 coupons.	10.00	25.00	60.00

		VG	VF	UNC
S882	**200 RUBLES** 1917 (1919). Like #S881 but w/o coupons.	4.00	10.00	25.00
S883	**90 RUBLES** 1917 (1919). Sheet of 20 coupons from #S881.	3.00	7.50	17.50
S884	**4 RUBLES 50 KOPEKS** 1917 (1919). Single coupon of #S881.	.25	.50	1.00

#S885-S888 green and black. Back green.

		VG	VF	UNC
S885	**290 RUBLES** 1917 (1919). Woman w/child, sword and shield. Public loan w/20 coupons.	7.50	20.00	40.00
S886	**200 RUBLES** 1917 (1919). Like #S885 but w/o coupons.	3.00	7.50	17.50
S887	**90 RUBLES** 1917 (1919). Sheet of 20 coupons from #S885.	2.00	6.00	15.00

		VG	VF	UNC
S888	**4 RUBLES 50 KOPEKS** 1917 (1919). Single coupon of #S885.	.25	.50	1.00

#S889-S892 orange and black. Back orange.

		VG	VF	UNC
S889	**290 RUBLES** 1917 (1919). Woman w/child, sword and shield at top. Public loan w/20 coupons.	5.00	12.00	22.50
S890	**200 RUBLES** 1917 (1919). Like #S889 but w/o coupons.	4.00	10.00	22.50
S891	**90 RUBLES** 1917 (1919). Sheet of 20 coupons from #S889.	3.00	7.50	17.50
S892	**4 RUBLES 50 KOPEKS** 1917 (1919). Single coupon from #S889.	.25	.50	1.00

УПОЛНОМОЧЕННЫЙ МИНИСТРА СНАБЖЕНІЯ И ПРОДОВОЛЬСТВІЯ ПО ХАБАРОВСКОМУ РАЙОНУ
Minister RepresentativePlenipotentiary for Provisions for Khabarovsk District

1919 ISSUE

		VG	VF	UNC
S896	**3 RUBLES** 1919. Black on green unpt.	6.00	15.00	40.00

		VG	VF	UNC
S897	**5 RUBLES** 1919. Black on blue unpt.	7.50	25.00	50.00
S898	**10 RUBLES** 1919.	7.50	25.00	50.00

РОССИЙСКАЯ СОЦИАЛИСТИЧЕСКАЯ ФЕДЕРАТИВНАЯ СОВЕТСКАЯ РЕСПУБЛИКА
Siberian Revolution Committee

Bolshevik successors to Kolchak, headquarters at Irkutsk.

1917 БИЛЕТЪ ГОСУД. ВНУТРЕНН. 4-1/2% ВЫЙГР. ЗАЕМЪ
PROVISIONAL GOVERNMENT SAVINGS LOAN NOTES ISSUE

#S899-S904 Kolchak notes w/ovpt. of R.S.F.S.R. text.

		VG	VF	UNC
S899	**200 RUBLES** 1920 (-old date 1917). Brown. Blue ovpt. of text, arms and date on #S882.	5.00	12.00	37.50
S900	**90 RUBLES** ND(1920). Blue ovpt. on #S883.	8.00	25.00	50.00
S901	**4 RUBLES 50 KOPEKS** ND(1920). Brown. Blue ovpt. on #S884.	1.50	3.50	7.50
S902	**200 RUBLES** 1920 (-old date 1917). Blue. Woman w/child, sword and shield at top. Red ovpt. as on #S899.	7.50	20.00	40.00
S903	**90 RUBLES** ND(1920). Blue. Sheet of 20 coupons from #S902 w/red ovpt.	8.00	25.00	50.00

		VG	VF	UNC
S904	**4 RUBLES 50 KOPEKS** ND(1920). Single coupon from #S903 w/red ovpt.	1.50	3.50	7.50

URALS & KAMA REGION

ЧРЕЗВЫЧАЙНО-УПОЛНОМОЧЕННЫЙ ПРИКАМСКАГО РАЙОНА
Plenipotentiary Extraordinary for the Kama Region

1915 ОБЛ. 5-1/2% ВОЕНН. КР. ЗАЙМОВ.
MILITARY DEBENTURE LOAN OBLIGATION ISSUE

#S906-S915 stamps on Russian public bonds and w/perforation 256 ЧУПР.

		VG	VF	UNC
S906	**50 RUBLES** 1915.	8.00	20.00	—
S907	**100 RUBLES** 1915.	8.00	20.00	—
S908	**500 RUBLES** 1915.	8.00	20.00	—
S909	**1000 RUBLES** 1915.	10.00	25.00	—
S910	**5000 RUBLES** 1915.	12.00	30.00	—

1916 ОБЛ. 5-1/2% ВОЕНН. КР. ЗАЙМОВ.
MILITARY DEBENTURE LOAN OBLIGATION ISSUE

		VG	VF	UNC
S911	**50 RUBLES** 1916.	6.00	15.00	—
S912	**100 RUBLES** 1916.	6.00	15.00	—
S913	**500 RUBLES** 1916.	8.00	20.00	—
S914	**1000 RUBLES** 1916.	8.00	20.00	—
S915	**5000 RUBLES** 1916.	10.00	25.00	—

1918 ND ОБЛ. ЗАЙМА СВОБОДЫ 1917
FREEDOM LOAN OBLIGATION ISSUE

		VG	VF	UNC
S916	**500 RUBLES** ND (1918).	15.00	35.00	—
S917	**1000 RUBLES** ND (1918).	17.50	40.00	—
S918	**5000 RUBLES** ND (1918).	20.00	50.00	—
S919	**10,000 RUBLES** ND (1918).	40.00	100.00	—

SOVIET OF THE URALS REGION

РАБОЧЕЕ И КРЕСТЬЯНСКОЕ ПРАВИТЕЛЬСТВО
Workers and Christians Administration

РОССИЙСКОЙ СОЦИАЛИСТИЧЕСКОЙ ФЕДЕР-АТИВНОЙ РЕСПУБЛИКИ СОВЕТОВ or СОВЕТСКОЙ РЕСПУБЛИКИ)
Russian Socialist Federated Soviet Republic

ГОСУДАРСТВЕННЫЙ БАНК
Government Bank

ЕКАТЕРИНБУРГСКОЕ ОТДЕЛЕНИЕ
Ekaterinburg

1918 ISSUE

These notes have always held a grim fascination for collectors because their issuers also ordered the murder of Czar Nicholas II and the entire imperial family on July 16, 1918 at the *House of Special Purpose* (home of merchant N. N. Ipatiev) in Ekaterinburg. A combined Czech Legion - White Army force captured the city July 24, 1918, ending the Urals Region Soviet.

		GOOD	FINE	XF
S920	**50 KOPEKS** 21.10.1918. Blue on gold unpt. Double headed eagle at upper ctr. Black text on back.	10.00	30.00	—

		GOOD	FINE	XF
S921	**1 RUBLE** 1918. Blue-black on yellow or orange unpt. Circular ornament w/agricultural implements on back.			
	a. W/o stamp.	2.50	7.50	25.00
	b. W/stamp (different kinds).	5.00	15.00	40.00

		GOOD	FINE	XF
S922	**5 RUBLES** 1918. Blue. Vertical format. Arms at upper ctr., soldier and sailor at bottom ctr. on back.			
	a. W/o stamp.	10.00	30.00	100.00
	b. W/stamp (different kinds).	12.50	35.00	120.00
	c. Commemorative ovpt. in 8 lines of vertical red German and 9 lines of Russian text for German Communist Karl Liebknecht.	—	Rare	—
S923	**100 RUBLES** 1918. Only printed half-finished face proof. (Not issued.)	—	Rare	—

URALS COSSACK REGION

УРАЛЬСКАГО КАЗАЧЬЯГО ВОЙСКА
Urals Cossack Territory

GEN. TOLSTOV

The Ural Cossacks, under their ataman, Gen. Tolstov, drove the Bolsheviks out of Uralsk and set up their own military government on March 29, 1918. Bolshevik forces retook the area in late 1918.

1918 МАРТА Г. 6% ОБЯЗАТЕЛЬСТВО OBLIGATION ISSUE

M/c guilloche at l., varieties in the denomination numerals.

		GOOD	FINE	XF
S926	**50 RUBLES** 1918.	17.50	40.00	—
S926A	**50 RUBLES** 1918.	—	—	—

		GOOD	FINE	XF
S927	**100 RUBLES** 1918.	17.50	40.00	—
S928	**200 RUBLES** 1918.	17.50	45.00	—
S929	**300 RUBLES** 1918.	20.00	75.00	—
S930	**400 RUBLES** 1918.	—	—	—
S931	**500 RUBLES** 1918.	—	—	—
S932	**600 RUBLES** 1918.	—	—	—
S933	**700 RUBLES** 1918.	—	—	—
S934	**800 RUBLES** 1918.	—	—	—
S935	**900 RUBLES** 1918.	—	—	—
S936	**1000 RUBLES** 1918.	—	—	—
S937	**1500 RUBLES** 1918.	—	—	—
S938	**2000 RUBLES** 1918.	—	—	—
S939	**3000 RUBLES** 1918.	—	—	—

1918 6% Г. КУПОНЪ 6% ОБЯЗАТЕЛЬСТВА

COUPON OBLIGATION ISSUE

		GOOD	FINE	XF
S940	**75 KOPEKS** 1918.	10.00	25.00	—
S941	**1 RUBLE 50 KOPEKS** 1918.	10.00	25.00	—
S942	**3 RUBLES** 1918.	10.00	25.00	—
S943	**4 RUBLES 50 KOPEKS** 1918.	10.00	30.00	—
S944	**6 RUBLES** 1918.	12.00	40.00	—
S945	**7 RUBLES 50 KOPEKS** 1918.	12.00	40.00	—
S946	**9 RUBLES** 1918.	15.00	50.00	—
S947	**10 RUBLES 50 KOPEKS** 1918.	15.00	50.00	—
S948	**12 RUBLES** 1918.	20.00	55.00	—
S949	**13 RUBLES 50 KOPEKS** 1918.	22.00	60.00	—
S950	**15 RUBLES** 1918.	25.00	75.00	—
S951	**22 RUBLES 50 KOPEKS** 1918.	30.00	95.00	—
S952	**30 RUBLES** 1918.	40.00	150.00	—
S953	**45 RUBLES** 1918.	40.00	150.00	—

ГОСУДАРСТВЕННЫЙ БАНК
Government Bank

УРАЛЬСКОЕ ОТД. Г. Б.Uralsk

1918 ND ПОЧТОВАЯ МАРКА POSTAGE STAMP MONEY ISSUE

Postage stamps of Czarist Russia on heavy paper, w/printing on back:

ИМѢЕТЬ ХОЖДЕ-
НІЕ НАРАВНѢСЪ
ДЕНЕЖНЫМИ
ЗНАКАМИ
УРАЛЬСКОЕ
ОТД. Г. Б.

		GOOD	FINE	XF
S956	**1 RUBLE** ND (1918). Brown, lt. brown and orange stamp. Black text on back.	12.00	30.00	70.00

Original size

		GOOD	FINE	XF
S957	**5 RUBLES** ND (1918). Blue, lt. blue and yellow stamp. Black text on back.	12.00	30.00	70.00
S958	**10 RUBLES** ND (1918). Red. Black text on back.	15.00	35.00	75.00

ПРАВИТЕЛЬСТВО ЦЕНТРОСИБИРИ. СИБИРСКИЙ
Government of Central Siberia

CHAIRMAN VASILY V. YAKOVLEV

Yakovlev was the last jailer of Czar Nicholas and his family at Tobolsk. After he delivered the imperial family to their executioners at Ekaterinburg, he deserted to the Whites and set up a government about Sept., 1918.

1918 КРЕДИТНЫЙ БИЛЕТЪ CREDIT NOTES ISSUE

		GOOD	FINE	XF
S961	**50 RUBLES** 1918. Blue on pink to brown unpt. Tools under value at l. Double-headed eagle at l. on back, factory and worker at r.			
	a. W/o stamp.	8.00	20.00	45.00
	b. Stamping and ovpt. from different State Bank branches.	8.00	20.00	45.00

NOTE: Forgeries exist of #S961b.

АКМОЛИНСКОЙ ОБЛАСТИ Akmolinsk Region Revolutionary Committee

Ovpt. on 5% Kolchak bonds with:

ПО ПОСТАНОВЛЕНИЮ
РЕВКОМА ИМЕЕТ ХОЖДЕНИЕ В ПРЕДЕЛАХ АКМОЛИНСКОЙ
ОБЛАСТИ НАРАВНЕ СДЕНЕЖНЫМИ
ЗНАКАМИ Р.С.Ф.С.Р.
ПО НОМИНАЛЬНОЙ СТОИМОСТИ

1919 ND ISSUE

		VG	VF	UNC
S962	**250 RUBLES** ND (1919).	30.00	60.00	—
S963	**500 RUBLES** ND (1919).	30.00	60.00	—
S964	**1000 RUBLES** ND (1919).	30.00	80.00	—

ГОСУДАРСТВЕННЫЙ БАНК
Government Bank

КИСЛОБОДСК. ОТДЕЛЕНИЕ
Kislovodsk

ND ЧЕК CHECKS ISSUE

		VG	VF	UNC
S965	**25 RUBLES** ND.	4.00	10.00	25.00
S965A	**50 RUBLES** ND.	4.00	10.00	25.00
S965B	**100 RUBLES** ND.	5.00	15.00	45.00

NOTE: #S965-S965B series varieties.

НАРОДНОГО БАНКА Р.С.ф.С.Р.
National Bank R.S.F.S.R.

КИСЛОВОДСКОЕ ОТДЕЛЕНИЕ
Kislovodsk

ND ЧЕК CHECKS ISSUE

		VG	VF	UNC
S965C	**50 RUBLES** ND. Black. Tan paper. 2 hand sign. Handstamped circular purple seal.	4.00	10.00	25.00
S965D	**100 RUBLES** ND.	4.00	10.00	25.00
S965E	**250 RUBLES** ND.	5.00	15.00	45.00

КРАСНОЯРСК. ЕНИС. Г. О-БО
Krasnoyarsk Territory

1919 РАЗМѢННЫЙ ЧЕКЪ EXCHANGE CHECKS ISSUE

		VG	VF	UNC
S966	**1 RUBLE** 1919. Brown w/black text.			
	a. W/o series.	4.00	10.00	30.00
	b. Series A.	4.00	10.00	30.00
S967	**3 RUBLES** 1919.			
	a. W/o series.	2.00	8.00	20.00
	b. Series A.	2.00	8.00	20.00
S968	**5 RUBLES** 1919.			
	a. W/o series.	2.00	8.00	20.00
	b. Series A.	2.00	8.00	20.00
S969	**10 RUBLES** 1919. Red w/black text. Back red.			
	a. W/o series.	1.75	6.00	15.00
	b. Series A.	1.00	3.00	10.00
	c. Series Ъ, В, or Г.	1.00	3.00	10.00

		VG	VF	UNC
S970	**25 RUBLES**			
	1919. Black on purple and gray unpt. Back purple.			
	a. W/o series.	4.00	10.00	30.00
	b. Series A.	1.50	4.00	12.00
	c. Series Ъ, В, or Г.	1.50	4.00	12.00
S971	**50 RUBLES**			
	1919. W/o series.	10.00	25.00	60.00

ГОСУДАРСТВЕННЬИЙ БАНК
Government Bank

ОРЕНБУРГСКАГО ОТДѢЛЕНІЯ
Orenburg

1917 ДЕНЕЖНЫЙ ЗНАКЪ CURRENCY TOKENS ISSUE

		GOOD	FINE	XF
S976	**5 RUBLES**			
	1917.	3.50	10.00	25.00

		GOOD	FINE	XF
S977	**25 RUBLES**			
	1917. Black on lt. red unpt. Arms at upper l.	2.00	6.00	20.00

		GOOD	FINE	XF
S978	**100 RUBLES**			
	1917. Black on orange unpt. Arms at ctr.	1.50	6.00	18.00

NOTE: #S976 and #978 have variations.

1918 ДЕНЕЖНЫЙ ЗНАКЪ CURRENCY TOKENS ISSUE

		VG	VF	UNC
S979	**1 RUBLE**			
	1918. Black on tan unpt. Arms at upper l.	1.50	6.00	15.00
S980	**3 RUBLES**			
	1918. Black on green unpt. Arms at l.	1.50	6.00	15.00

NOTE: #S980 has variations.

		VG	VF	UNC
S981	**25 RUBLES**			
	1918.	1.50	6.00	15.00
S982	**100 RUBLES**			
	1918. Black on rose unpt. Arms.	1.50	6.00	15.00

		VG	VF	UNC
S983	**500 RUBLES**			
	1918. Black on red unpt. Woman and boy at l. 2 youths at l. on back.	5.00	12.50	35.00

ПЕРМСКАГО ГОРОДСКОГО ОБЩЕСТВА
Perm City Association

1917 ISSUE

#S986-S990 ornate flower design w/bear in arms at ctr. Text on back.

		VG	VF	UNC
S986	**100 RUBLES**			
	1917. Dk. brown on tan paper.			
	a. Issued note w/sign.	30.00	65.00	150.00
	r. Remainder.	—	40.00	100.00
S987	**300 RUBLES**			
	1917. Blue on lt. green unpt.			
	a. Issued note w/sign.	40.00	70.00	175.00
	r. Remainder.	—	45.00	110.00

		VG	VF	UNC
S988	**500 RUBLES**			
	1917. Blue on lilac unpt., gray paper.			
	a. Issued note w/sign.	45.00	100.00	225.00
	r. Remainder.	—	50.00	125.00
S989	**1000 RUBLES**			
	1917. Red on lt. red unpt., pink paper.			
	a. Issued note w/sign.	50.00	125.00	250.00
	r. Remainder.	—	60.00	140.00
S990	**5000 RUBLES**			
	1917.			
	a. Issued note w/sign.	70.00	160.00	350.00
	r. Remainder.	—	75.00	175.00

NOTE: Some authorities believe all supposedly issued notes of #S986-S990 are falsely signed and filled in.

#S991-S993 *Deleted.*

RUSSIAN CENTRAL ASIA

GOVERNMENTS

Bukhara Soviet Peoples Republic
Khorezmian Peoples Soviet Republic
Semireche Region
Transcaspian Provisional Government

BANKS

Transcaspian State Bank
Ashkhabad Branch, State Bank
Turkestan District (Tashkent)

MILITARY

Great Britain Government Military Mission (British Maj. Gen. Malleson)

BUKHARA, EMIRATE

NOTE: For previously listed #S1001-S1024 see Vol. 2 - Uzbekistan #1-24.

BUKHARA SOVIET PEOPLES REPUBLIC

All notes w/Persian script, only denominations (subsequently dates) also in Russian; printing, color and paper varieties.

AH1339/1920 TENGAS ISSUE

Sign. #S1026-S1028

		GOOD	FINE	XF
S1026	**50 TENGAS** AH 1339 (1920).	12.00	27.50	—
S1027	**100 TENGAS** AH 1339 (1920).	12.00	27.50	—
S1028	**200 TENGAS** AH 1339 (1920).	15.00	35.00	—

Sign. #S1029-S1034

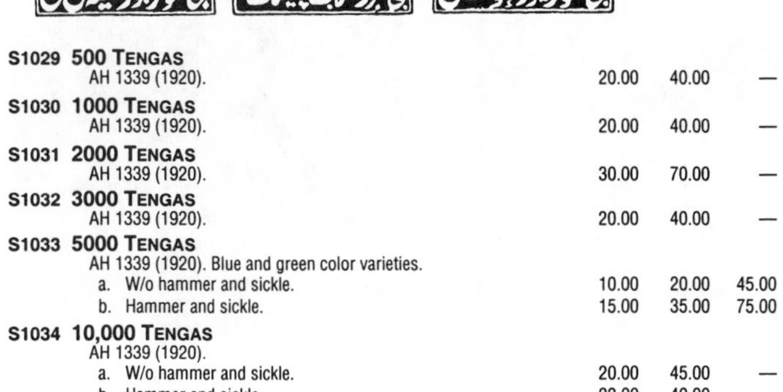

		GOOD	FINE	XF
S1029	**500 TENGAS** AH 1339 (1920).	20.00	40.00	—
S1030	**1000 TENGAS** AH 1339 (1920).	20.00	40.00	—
S1031	**2000 TENGAS** AH 1339 (1920).	30.00	70.00	—
S1032	**3000 TENGAS** AH 1339 (1920).	20.00	40.00	—
S1033	**5000 TENGAS** AH 1339 (1920). Blue and green color varieties.			
	a. W/o hammer and sickle.	10.00	20.00	45.00
	b. Hammer and sickle.	15.00	35.00	75.00
S1034	**10,000 TENGAS** AH 1339 (1920).			
	a. W/o hammer and sickle.	20.00	45.00	—
	b. Hammer and sickle.	22.00	40.00	—

1920-23 RUBLE ISSUES

Sign. #S1035-S1036

		GOOD	FINE	XF
S1035	**50 RUBLES** AH 1339 (1920). Red-brown to yellow. Paper smooth or ribbed.	9.00	17.50	30.00

		GOOD	FINE	XF
S1036	**100 RUBLES** AH 1339 (1920). Dk. brown and blue. Paper smooth or ribbed.	9.00	17.50	30.00

Sign. #S1037-S1041A

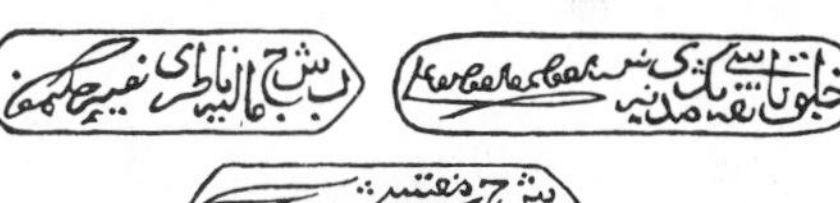

S1037	**3000 RUBLES** 1920.	15.00	35.00	—

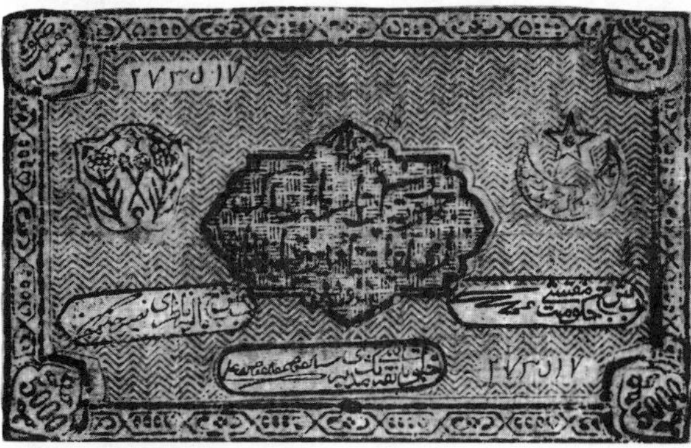

		GOOD	FINE	XF
S1038	**5000 RUBLES** 1920. Red-brown and green.	25.00	50.00	—
S1039	**10,000 RUBLES** 1920. Paper smooth or ribbed. W/ or w/o wmk.	40.00	75.00	—

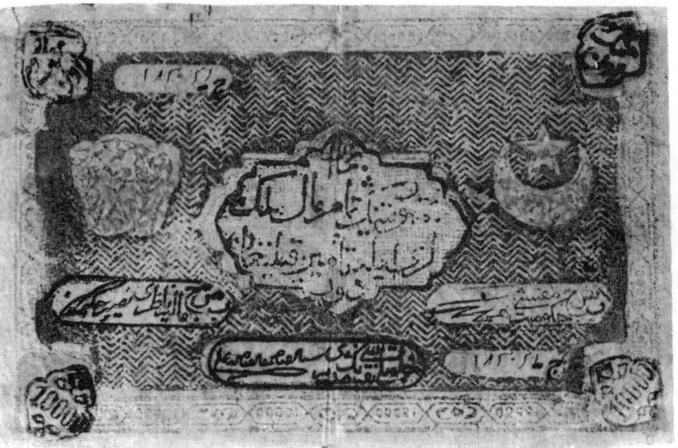

		GOOD	FINE	XF
S1040	**10,000 RUBLES** 1921. Dk. brown. Paper smooth or ribbed. W/ or w/o wmk.	40.00	70.00	110.00

		GOOD	FINE	XF
S1040A	**10,000 RUBLES** 1922.	25.00	45.00	75.00

		GOOD	FINE	XF
S1041	**20,000 RUBLES** 1921. Brown and green over orange unpt. on both sides. 218 x 119mm. Arabic legends, typically primitive printing quality. Ribbed or plain paper w/o wmk. Sign. as on #S1040.	25.00	45.00	75.00
S1041A	**20,000 RUBLES** 1923. Similar to #S1041.	30.00	65.00	100.00

Sign. #S1042

		GOOD	FINE	XF
S1042	**20,000 RUBLES** 1922. Green and pink.	35.00	70.00	120.00

1922 FIRST RUBLE ISSUE

Sign. #S1043-S1050

		VG	VF	UNC
S1043	**10 RUBLES** 1922. Green.	30.00	50.00	—
S1044	**25 RUBLES** 1922. Brown.	12.00	18.00	40.00
S1045	**100 RUBLES** 1922. Pink.	12.00	18.00	40.00

1922 SECOND RUBLE ISSUE

		VG	VF	UNC
S1046	**1 RUBLE** 1922. Yellow-brown.	12.00	18.00	40.00

		VG	VF	UNC
S1047	**5 RUBLES** 1922. Blue.	12.00	18.00	—
S1048	**10 RUBLES** 1922. Green-blue.	12.00	18.00	—
S1049	**25 RUBLES** 1922. Dk. brown.	12.00	18.00	—

		VG	VF	UNC
S1050	**100 RUBLES** 1922. Red-brown. W/ or w/o wmk.	12.50	22.50	—

Sign. #S1051-S1054

		VG	VF	UNC
S1051	**1000 RUBLES** 1922. Violet.	20.00	35.00	65.00
S1052	**2500 RUBLES** 1922. Blue. W/ or w/o wmk.	16.00	30.00	60.00

		VG	VF	UNC
S1053	**5000 RUBLES** 1922. Red-brown to pink. W/ or w/o wmk.	17.50	32.50	75.00

		VG	VF	UNC
S1054	**5000 RUBLES/5 NEW RUBLES** 1922. Red. White and yellowish paper.	15.00	30.00	60.00

KHIVA (KHOREZM), KHANATE OF THE PADISHAH

Note: For previously listed #S1056-S1073 see Vol. 2 - Uzbekistan #25-42.

KHOREZMIAN PEOPLES SOVIET REPUBLIC

NOTE: Many printing, paper and color varieties.

1920 FIRST ISSUE

Sign. #S1076-S1078

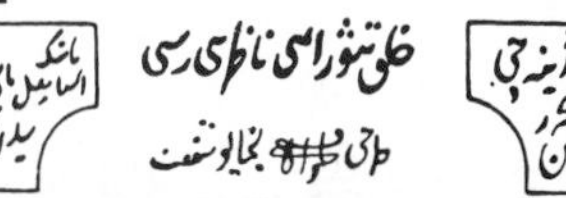

		GOOD	FINE	XF
S1076	**250 RUBLES** 1920. Paper ribbed, smooth or lined.	110.00	155.00	—

		GOOD	FINE	XF
S1077	**500 RUBLES** 1920. Red-brown on green. Silk. Lg. or sm. star on back. *1920* sm. or lg.	90.00	140.00	—

		GOOD	FINE	XF
S1078	**1000 RUBLES** 1920. Violet or blue, red-brown and dk. blue on blue. Silk.	90.00	140.00	250.00

Sign. #S1079-S1081

1920 SECOND ISSUE

Sign. #S1079-S1081

		GOOD	FINE	XF
S1079	**250 RUBLES** 1920. Paper smooth or ribbed.	70.00	100.00	—
S1080	**500 RUBLES** 1920. Silk note.	90.00	135.00	—
S1081	**1000 RUBLES** 1920. Red-brown and black on lt. blue. Silk note.	110.00	185.00	—

Sign. #S1082 similar to #S1076-S1078.

		GOOD	FINE	XF
S1082	**750 RUBLES** 1920. Paper lined or w/o lines.	100.00	170.00	—

Sign. #S1083-S1085 similar to #S1079-S1081.

		GOOD	FINE	XF
S1083	**750 RUBLES** 1920. Paper lined or w/o lines.	110.00	170.00	—

1921 FIRST ISSUE

		GOOD	FINE	XF
S1084	**2000 RUBLES** 1921. Frame in different colors.	100.00	160.00	—

		GOOD	FINE	XF
S1085	**5000 RUBLES** 1921. Black, red and green. Silk note.	110.00	185.00	—

Sign. #S1086-S1090

1921 SECOND ISSUE

		GOOD	FINE	XF
S1086	**750 RUBLES** 1921. Paper lined, w/o lines or checkered.	120.00	200.00	—
S1087	**1000 RUBLES** 1921. Silk note.	300.00	500.00	—
S1088	**2000 RUBLES** 1921. Silk note.	175.00	300.00	—
S1089	**5000 RUBLES** 1921. Silk note. Red, green and black.	140.00	225.00	—
S1090	**10,000 RUBLES** 1921. Paper lined or w/o lines.	65.00	100.00	—

Sign. #S1091-S1092

Sign. #S1093-S1094

Individual notes also w/extension stamp.

AH1339/1921 ISSUE

		GOOD	FINE	XF
S1091	**5000 RUBLES** AH 1339 (1921). Silk note.	90.00	135.00	—
S1092	**10,000 RUBLES** AH 1339 (1921). Paper lined or w/o lines.	40.00	70.00	—
S1093	**25,000 RUBLES** AH 1339 (1921). Paper note.	50.00	85.00	—

AH1340/1921 ISSUE

		GOOD	FINE	XF
S1094	**10,000 RUBLES** AH 1340 (1921). Paper lined or w/o lines.	37.50	65.00	—

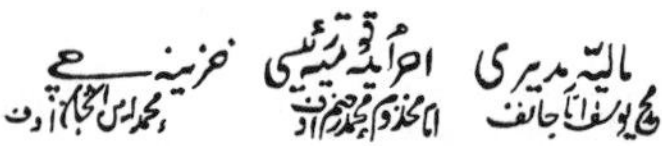

Sign. #S1095

1921 Third Issue

		Good	Fine	XF
S1095	**5000 Rubles** 1921. Paper note.	100.00	155.00	—

Sign. #S1096-S1097

AH1340/1922 Issue

		Good	Fine	XF
S1096	**10,000 Rubles** AH 1340 (1921).	20.00	35.00	—

		Good	Fine	XF
S1097	**25,000 Rubles** AH 1340 (1921). White or gray paper. W/or w/o wmk.			
	a. Issued note. Printed top to top.	20.00	50.00	—
	x. Error w/inverted back.	30.00	80.00	—

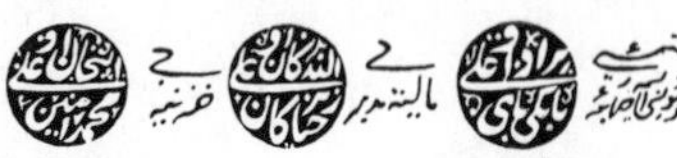

Sign. #S1098

1921 Fourth Issue

		Good	Fine	XF
S1098	**10,000 Rubles** 1921. Paper lined or w/o lines.	17.50	35.00	—

Sign. #S1099

		Good	Fine	XF
S1099	**25,000 Rubles** 1921. White or gray paper. W/o W/or w/o wmk.	15.00	27.50	—

Sign. #S1100

1922 First Issue

		Good	Fine	XF
S1100	**3 = 30,000 Rubles** 1922. Paper lined or w/o lines, w/or w/o wmk.	15.00	27.50	—

Sign. #S1101

		Good	Fine	XF
S1101	**5 = 50,000 Rubles** 1922. White or gray paper, lined or w/o lines.	12.50	25.00	—

Sign. #S1102

		Good	Fine	XF
S1102	**10 = 100,000 Rubles** 1922. Paper lined or w/o lines, w/or w/o wmk.	15.00	27.50	—

1922 Second Issue

		Good	Fine	XF
S1103	**3 Rubles** 1922. Paper lined or w/o lines.	30.00	60.00	—
S1104	**5 Rubles** 1922. Paper lined or w/o lines.	60.00	100.00	—

Sign. #S1105

		Good	Fine	XF
S1105	**1 = 10,000 Rubles** 1922. Paper smooth, ribbed lines or w/o lines, w/or w/o wmk.	25.00	50.00	—

Sign. #S1106

		Good	Fine	XF
S1106	**10 = 100,000 Rubles** 1922. Paper lined or w/o lines.	17.50	32.50	—

Sign. #S1107

1922 THIRD ISSUE

		GOOD	FINE	XF
S1107	**25 RUBLES** 1922.	15.00	27.50	—

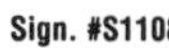

Sign. #S1108

S1108	**20 RUBLES** 1922. Blue and green print. Paper lined or w/o lines.	12.00	22.50	—

Sign. #S1109 similar to #S1107.

		GOOD	FINE	XF
S1109	**25 RUBLES** 1922. Blue or black print.	12.00	22.50	—

Sign. #S1110

S1110	**100 RUBLES** 1922. W/or w/o wmk.	12.00	22.50	—

Sign. #S1111

1923 ISSUE

		GOOD	FINE	XF
S1111	**50 RUBLES** 1923. White or yellowish paper.	40.00	70.00	—

Sign. #S1112-S1114 similar to #S1110.

S1112	**100 RUBLES** 1923. Paper lined or w/o lines, w/or w/o wmk.	50.00	80.00	—

		GOOD	FINE	XF
S1113	**500 RUBLES** 1923. W/or w/o wmk.	40.00	70.00	—
S1114	**1000 RUBLES** 1923.	40.00	70.00	120.00

СЕМИРЕЧЕНСКАЯ ОБЛАСТЬ
Semireche Region

1918 ND ДЕНЕЖНЫЙ ЗНАКЪ-ВРЕМЕНН. РАЗМѢНН. ЗНАКЪ

CURRENCY TOKENS - PROVISIONAL EXCHANGE TOKENS ISSUE

		GOOD	FINE	XF
S1116	**5 RUBLES** ND (1918). Blue or black print.			
	a. Unpt. sm. crosses.	10.00	25.00	50.00
	b. Unpt. points.	8.00	20.00	40.00

1918 БИЛЕТЪ NOTE ISSUE

		GOOD	FINE	XF
S1117	**50 KOPEKS** 1918. Yellow or orange.	8.50	15.00	30.00

1918 ND; 1918 КРЕДИТНЫЙ БИЛЕТЪ CREDIT NOTES ISSUE

Sign. name: ВОЕННЫЙ КОМИССАРЪ

		GOOD	FINE	XF
S1118	**1 RUBLE** ND (1918). Brown.	12.50	30.00	65.00

		GOOD	FINE	XF
S1119	**3 RUBLES** 1918. Black on green unpt. Worker w/hammer at l., opium poppies at ctr. Differences in text and in numerals on back.	8.50	20.00	60.00

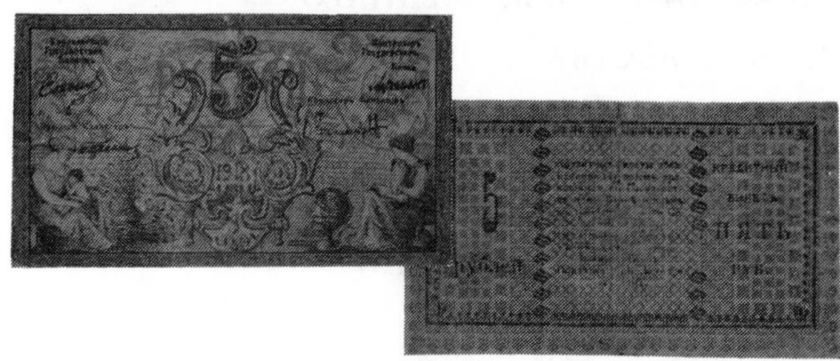

		GOOD	FINE	XF
S1120	**5 RUBLES** 1918. Black on blue-gray unpt. Woman and child at l., woman and globe at r. W/or w/o serial #.	7.50	17.50	50.00

		GOOD	FINE	XF
S1121	**10 RUBLES** ND (1918). Black on lt. orange unpt.	10.00	25.00	75.00
S1122	**25 RUBLES** ND (1918). Black on brown unpt. Arms on back.	15.00	30.00	85.00
S1123	**50 RUBLES** ND (1918). Lt. green.	25.00	55.00	115.00
S1124	**100 RUBLES** ND (1918). Brown on lt. brown unpt. Back brown and dull orange; seated figure w/2 winged cherubs at lower ctr. on archway, city scene at l., farm scene at r.	30.00	65.00	135.00
S1125	**250 RUBLES** ND (1918).	35.00	100.00	210.00

1918 КРЕДИТНЫЙ БИЛЕТЪ CREDIT NOTES ISSUE

Sign. name: ПРЕД. ОБЛ. or ПРЭД. ОБ. ИСП. КОМ.

		GOOD	FINE	XF
S1126	**10 RUBLES** 1918.	7.00	17.50	45.00
S1127	**25 RUBLES** 1918.	10.00	25.00	60.00

		Good	Fine	XF
S1128	**100 RUBLES** 1918.	30.00	70.00	150.00
S1129	**250 RUBLES** 1918. Brown and green.	20.00	50.00	110.00

1919 КРЕДИТНЫЙ БИЛЕТЪ CREDIT NOTES ISSUE

		Good	Fine	XF
S1130	**50 RUBLES** 1919.	35.00	75.00	175.00
S1131	**100 RUBLES** 1919.	6.00	17.00	37.50

		Good	Fine	XF
S1132	**250 RUBLES** 1919.			
	a. Brown.	12.00	25.00	55.00
	b. Dk. blue.	7.50	17.50	40.00
S1133	**500 RUBLES** 1919.			
	a. Brown.	12.00	25.00	55.00
	b. Black.	7.50	17.50	40.00

TRANSCASPIAN REGION

ЗАКАСПІЙСКАГО ВРЕМЕННАГО ПРАВИТЕЛЬСТВА

TRANSCASPIAN PROVISIONAL ADMINISTRATION

ГОСУДАРСТВЕННАГО БАНКА
Government Bank

АСХАБАДСКАГО ОТДѢЛЕНІЯ
Ashkhabad

1919 РАЗМѢННЫЙ ДЕНЕЖНЫЙ ЗНАКЪ
EXCHANGE CURRENCY TOKENS ISSUE

		Good	Fine	XF
S1136	**10 RUBLES** 1919. Red and brown. Arms at ctr. (tiger), eagle at l. and r. (Not issued).	6.00	12.00	30.00

ЗАКАСПІЙСКАГО НАРОДНАГО БАНКА
Transcaspian National Bank

1919 ДЕНЕЖНЫЙ ЗНАКЪ CURRENCY NOTES ISSUE

		Good	Fine	XF
S1139	**500 RUBLES** 1919. Green on lt. brown unpt. Arms (tiger) at l. on back, above double headed eagle.	5.00	18.00	40.00

НАРОДНАГО БАНКА
National Bank

АСХАБАДСКАГО ОТДѢЛЕНІЯ
Ashkhabad

1919 РАЗМѢННЫЙ ДЕНЕЖНЫЙ ЗНАКЪ
EXCHANGE CURRENCY TOKENS ISSUE

		Good	Fine	XF
S1141	**5 RUBLES** 1919. Black on green unpt. Arms at ctr.	2.00	6.00	15.00
S1142	**10 RUBLES** 1919. Black on red unpt.	3.00	8.00	18.00

		Good	Fine	XF
S1143	**25 RUBLES** 1919. Black on blue unpt.	2.50	7.00	20.00
S1144	**50 RUBLES** 1919. Black.			
	a. Green unpt.	3.00	9.00	22.50
	b. Blue unpt.	2.00	6.00	15.00
S1145	**100 RUBLES** 1919. Black on yellow unpt.	2.00	6.00	15.00

		Good	Fine	XF
S1146	**250 RUBLES** 1919. Black on violet unpt. W/or w/o bank stamp.	2.00	6.00	15.00

ОБЯЗАТЕЛЬСТВО ВЕЛИКОБРИТАНСКОЙ ВОЕННОЙ МИССІИ
Great Britain Government Military Mission

1918-19 BRITISH MILITARY INTERVENTION ISSUE

Issued by Major General Malleson. Several major varieties.

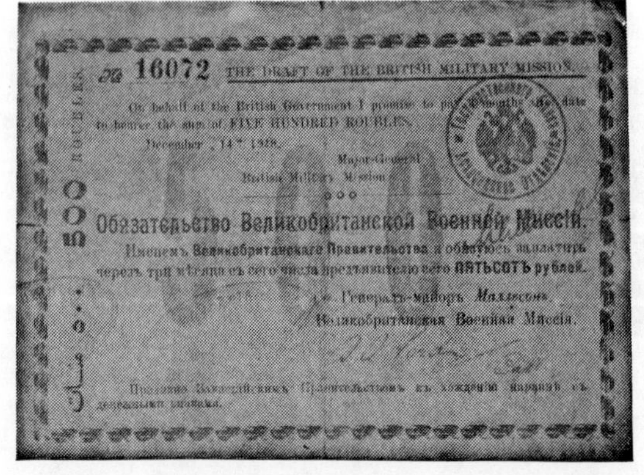

		GOOD	FINE	XF
S1148	**500 RUBLES** Dec. 1918. Different hand stamped numerals of the day.			
	a. Issued note.	300.00	700.00	—
	b. W/o unpt.	300.00	700.00	—
	c. Green unpt. w/*3 months.*	300.00	700.00	—
	d. Green unpt. w/*6 months.*	300.00	700.00	—
	x. Error w/*BOUBLES.*	300.00	700.00	—
S1149	**500 RUBLES** 14.1.1919. Black on green paper. Value in dull red unpt. at ctr.	300.00	700.00	—

ТУРКЕСТАНСКІЙ КРАЙ

TURKESTAN DISTRICT

ГОСУДАРСТВЕННАГО БАНКА
Government Bank

ТАШКЕНТСКАГО ОТДѢЛЕНІЯ
Tashkent

1918 РАЗМѢННЫЙ ДЕНЕЖНЫЙ ЗНАКЪ EXCHANGE CURRENCY TOKENS ISSUE

		VG	VF	UNC
S1151	**1 RUBLE** 1918. Blue on brown unpt.	2.00	5.00	15.00
S1152	**3 RUBLES** 1918. Dk. green on green unpt.	2.50	6.00	17.50

#S1153-S1155 have bust of woman at upper ctr.

		VG	VF	UNC
S1153	**5 RUBLES** 1918. Blue on blue unpt.	5.00	10.00	25.00
S1154	**10 RUBLES** 1918. Black on red and green unpt.	4.00	8.50	17.50

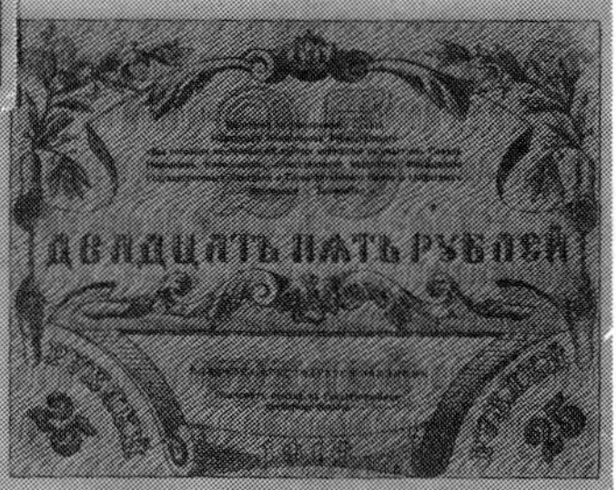

		VG	VF	UNC
S1155	**25 RUBLES** 1918. Black on lilac and green unpt.	6.00	15.00	40.00
S1156	**50 RUBLES** 1918. Black on blue unpt. Double headed eagle w/five arms at ctr. Town view on back.	3.50	7.50	18.00

		VG	VF	UNC
S1157	**100 RUBLES** 1918. Black on yellow-brown unpt. Face like #S1156. Double eagle at l. on back.	5.00	10.00	25.00

ТУРКЕСТАНСКАГО КРАЯ Turkestan District

1918 ДЕНЕЖНЫЙ ЗНАКЪ CURRENCY TOKENS ISSUE

		VG	VF	UNC
S1161	**50 KOPEKS** ND (1918). Blue. Arms w/hammer and sickle (Not issued). Also in sheets of 20 pieces.	2.00	5.00	10.00

1918 ВРЕМЕННЫЙ КРЕДИТНЫЙ БИЛЕТЪ PROVISIONAL CREDIT NOTES ISSUE

#S1162-S1170 like Tashkent #S1151-S1157. Sign., paper and color varieties.

		VG	VF	UNC
S1162	**1 RUBLE** 1918. Blue on brown unpt.	1.00	3.00	10.00
S1163	**3 RUBLES** 1918. Dk. green on green unpt.	1.00	3.00	10.00

		VG	VF	UNC
S1164	**5 RUBLES** 1918. Blue on blue unpt.			
	a. Black print.	3.00	6.00	15.00
	b. Dk. blue print.	3.00	6.00	15.00
S1165	**10 RUBLES** 1918. Red and green unpt.			
	a. Black print.	3.00	6.00	15.00
	b. Dk. blue print.	3.00	6.00	15.00
S1166	**25 RUBLES** 1918. Black or blue on lilac and green unpt.	3.00	6.00	15.00

		VG	VF	UNC
S1167	**50 RUBLES** 1918. Black on blue unpt.	4.00	9.00	20.00

		VG	VF	UNC
S1168	**100 RUBLES** 1918. Black on yellow-brown unpt.	4.00	10.00	20.00
S1169	**50 RUBLES** 1919. Black on blue unpt. Like #S1167.	4.00	10.00	20.00

		VG	VF	UNC
S1170	**100 RUBLES** 1919. Black or blue on brown to red-brown unpt. Like #S1168. W/or w/o wmk.	5.00	15.00	30.00

		GOOD	FINE	XF
S1171	**250 RUBLES** 1919. Brown. Ornament w/two torches, gun and hammer at l. Arms at ctr. on back. W/ or w/o wmk. Paper and color varieties.			
	a. Green unpt.	10.00	25.00	50.00
	b. Blue unpt.	10.00	25.00	50.00

		VG	VF	UNC
S1172	**500 RUBLES** 1919. Blue on red-brown unpt. Arms w/hammer and sickle at upper ctr. Vertical format. W/ or w/o wmk. Paper and color varieties.	9.50	25.00	55.00
S1173	**1000 RUBLES** 1920. Black on brown unpt. Arms w/hammer and sickle at l. on back. W/or w/o wmk. Paper and color varieties.	7.50	17.50	45.00
S1174	**5000 RUBLES** 1920. Blue and red. Arms w/hammer and sickle at ctr. on back.	8.00	20.00	50.00

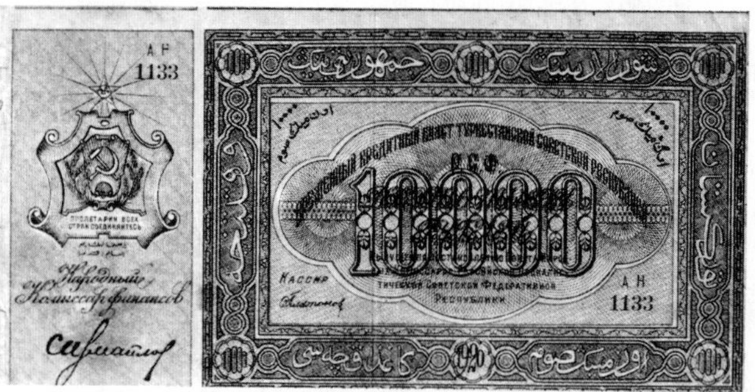

		VG	VF	UNC
S1175	**10,000 RUBLES** 1920. Red and green. Arms w/hammer and sickle at l. Blacksmith seated w/hammer and anvil at l. on back.	20.00	50.00	115.00

BAIKALIA

- Far Eastern Soviet of People's Commissars
- Government of the Russian Eastern Border Regions
- Provisional Power of the Pribaikal Region
- Far Eastern Republic

MARITIME AREA

- Amur Region Executive Committee
- Amur Region Zemstvo
- Amur Region Credit Union
- Habarovsk Branch Government Bank
- Rural Priamur Province
- Nikolsk-Ussuriisk
- Far East Provisional Government
- Amur Railroad
- Vladivostok
- Vladivostok Office Government Bank
- Vladivostok - Bank de L'Indochine
- Blagoveschchensk Bank
- Blagoveshchensk Branch Government Bank

OUTLYING REGIONS

- Altai
- Barnaul Branch Government Bank
- Barnaul Branch Peoples Bank
- Biisk Branch Government Bank
- Kamchatka
- Sakhalin
- Tomsk Branch Government Bank
- Nikolaevsk-on-Amur
- Yakutia

BAIKALIA

ДАЛЬНЕВОСТОЧНЫЙ СОВЕТ НАРОДНЫХ КОМИССАРОВ

Far Eastern Soviet of the Peoples Commissars

Chairman Krasnoshchekov

1918 ISSUE

		GOOD	FINE	XF
S1181	**10 RUBLES** 1918. Black on pink unpt. Globe at ctr. Back green; workers and farmers.			
	a. W/o hand stamp.	15.00	35.00	60.00
	b. Hand stamp of Kolchak Government.	12.00	25.00	50.00
S1182	**25 RUBLES** 1918. Like #S1181.			
	a. W/o hand stamp.	15.00	35.00	60.00
	b. Hand stamp of Kolchak Government.	15.00	35.00	60.00
S1183	**50 RUBLES** 1918. Like #S1181.			
	a. W/o hand stamp.	17.50	45.00	125.00
	b. Hand stamp of Kolchak Government.	15.00	40.00	100.00

NOTE: #S1181-S1183 bear sign. of Chairman Krasnoshchekov, commissar of finance T. Kalmanevich, and Fugalevich, director of the Khabarovsk branch of the State Bank. In all, 307,560 R10 notes were issued, 122,639 R25 notes, and 105,101 R50 notes.

ПРАВИТЕЛЬСТВО РОССІЙСКОЙ ВОСТОЧНОЙ ОКРАИНЫ

GOVERNMENT OF THE RUSSIAN EASTERN BORDER REGIONS

Ataman Grigori Semenov

ГОСУДАРСТВЕННАГО БАНКА
Government Bank

ЧИТИНСКОЕ ОТДѢЛЕНІЕ
Chita

1920 ISSUE

		VG	VF	UNC
S1186	**50 RUBLES** 1920. Blue. Winter landscape on back. Proof.	—	—	—

		VG	VF	UNC
S1187	**100 RUBLES** 1920. Black. Flowers below double-headed eagle.			
	a. Frame consisting of lines on back. Proof.	—	—	—
	b. Frame consisting of sm. cubes.	5.00	10.00	20.00

		VG	VF	UNC
S1188	**500 RUBLES** 1920. Arms (double-headed eagle) w/flowers at ctr.			
	a. Blue.	5.00	10.00	22.50
	b. Green. (Many shade varieties).	4.00	9.00	20.00

СИБИРСКАГО ВРЕМЕННАГО ПРАВИТЕЛЬСТВА
Siberian Provisional Administration

1920 КАЗНАЧЕЙСКІЙ ЗНАКЪ TREASURY TOKENS ISSUE

		VG	VF	UNC
S1189	**25 RUBLES** 1920. W/or w/o pink unpt. W/or w/o wmk.	30.00	60.00	250.00
S1190	**50 RUBLES** 1920. Green. (Many varieties).	40.00	70.00	250.00

		VG	VF	UNC
S1191	**100 RUBLES** 1920.			
	a. Brown. W/or w/o wmk.	25.00	50.00	150.00
	b. Dk. green.	25.00	50.00	150.00

		VG	VF	UNC
S1192	**500 RUBLES** 1920. Green unpt. Woman w/sword at l. on back w/double-headed eagle at ctr.	10.00	20.00	50.00
S1193	**1000 RUBLES** 1920. Woman wearing helmet seated w/sword and shield at l.			
	a. Pink and green.	30.00	65.00	200.00
	b. Yellow and brown.	30.00	65.00	200.00
S1194	**5000 RUBLES** 1920. Green on yellow unpt. Double-headed eagle w/maltese cross at ctr.			
	a. Printed on both sides.	—	—	—
	b. Uniface print.	—	—	700.00

ВРЕМЕННАЯ ЗЕМСКАЯ ВЛАСТЬ ПРИБАЙКАЛЬЯ
Provisional Power of the Pribaikal Region

1918 (1920) ISSUE

		VG	VF	UNC
S1196	**25 RUBLES** 1918 (1920). Black on dk. blue unpt. Woman seated at ctr. W/o sign. Red ovpt. on back of #S1248.	8.00	15.00	40.00

		VG	VF	UNC
S1197	**100 RUBLES** 1918 (1920). Black on brown unpt. Woman seated w/fruit at ctr. W/o sign. Blue ovpt. on back of #S1249.	9.00	17.50	45.00

NOTE: For #S1196 and S1197 issued w/o Pribaikal ovpt. see Russia #40 and 42 in Vol. 2.

ДАЛЬНЕ-ВОСТОЧНОЙ РЕСПУБЛИКИ
Far Eastern Republic

Capital at Verkhne-Udinsk, later at Chita. Organized April 6, 1920. Annexed to Russia Nov. 19, 1922.

1920 FIRST КРЕДИТНЫЙ БИЛЕТ CREDIT NOTES ISSUE

1920 Credit Notes

		VG	VF	UNC
S1201	**1 RUBLE** 1920. Dk. blue on tan unpt. Wheat pickaxe and anchor at upper ctr. Back brown.	1.00	4.00	9.00

		VG	VF	UNC
S1202	**3 RUBLES** 1920. Dk. green. Like #S1201.	1.00	4.00	9.00

		VG	VF	UNC
S1203	**5 RUBLES** 1920. Blue. Wheat, pickaxe and anchor at ctr.	1.00	4.00	9.00
S1204	**10 RUBLES** 1920. Red on pink paper. Wheat, pickaxe and anchor at ctr. on back.	.75	3.50	8.00

1920 РАСЧЕТНЫЙ ЗНАК - TOKEN CURRENCY ISSUE

		VG	VF	UNC
S1205	**25 RUBLES** 1920. Black on green unpt. Violet back; wheat, pickaxe and anchor at ctr.	1.00	4.00	9.00
S1206	**50 RUBLES** 1920. Black on red-brown unpt. Back green.	1.50	5.00	10.00

1920 SECOND КРЕДИТНЫЙ БИЛЕТ CREDIT NOTES ISSUE

		VG	VF	UNC
S1207	**500 RUBLES** 1920. Brown on tan unpt. Bear and fox at ctr. in outdoor scene w/mountains. Back blue; ships and boat.	4.00	9.00	20.00

1920 ГОСУДАРСТВЕННЫЙ КРЕДИТИЫЙ БИЛЕТ GOVERNMENT CREDIT NOTES ISSUE

		VG	VF	UNC
S1208	**1000 RUBLES** 1920. Black-green on green unpt. Plow at ctr., sea and mountains in background. Back brown; man w/scythe, wheat sheaves and arms at ctr.	4.50	10.00	25.00

1920 THIRD КРЕДИТНЫЙ БИЛЕТ CREDIT NOTES ISSUE

#S1209-S1211 similar to #S1201-S1203 but larger size. Single or double-sided proof prints.

		VG	VF	UNC
S1209	**1 RUBLE** 1920.	—	—	250.00
S1210	**3 RUBLES** 1920.	—	—	250.00
S1211	**5 RUBLES** 1920.	—	—	250.00
S1212	**10 RUBLES** 1920.	—	—	250.00

1918 ГОСУДАРСТВЕННЫЙ КРЕДИТНЫЙ БИЛЕТЪ Government Credit Notes Provisional Issue

#S1213 and S1214 ovpt: ДАЛЬНЕ-ВОСТОЧНАЯ РЕСПУБЛИКА.

		VG	VF	Unc
S1213	**25 Rubles** 1918 (1921). Red, bronze-colored ovpt. or red and bronze colored circular ovpt. on back of #S1248.	15.00	25.00	55.00
S1214	**100 Rubles** 1918 (1921). Red, bronze-colored or red and bronze-colored ovpt. on back of #S1249.	18.00	30.00	65.00

NOTE: It is not known wheather #S1213 or S1214 are official or private issues.

1920 БАНКОВЫЙ БИЛЕТ Gold Kopek Bank Notes Issue

#S1215A-S1215C not issued.

S1215A

S1215B

		VG	VF	Unc
S1215A	**5 Kopeks** 1922.	—	—	500.00
S1215B	**10 Kopeks** 1922.	—	—	500.00

		VG	VF	Unc
S1215C	**20 Kopeks** 1922.	—	—	500.00

Maritime Area

АМУРСКІЙ ОБЛАСТНОЙ КОММИТЕТ
Amur Region Executive Committee

Chairman Mukhin

1918 РАЗМѢННЫЙ БИЛЕТЪ Exchange Notes Issue

#S1216-S1220 arms w/three stars at top.

		VG	VF	Unc
S1216	**5 Rubles** 1918. Blue.			
	a. W/o hand stamp.	5.00	12.00	22.50
	b. Various hand stamps of the Kolchak Government.	5.00	9.00	20.00
S1217	**10 Rubles** 1918.			
	a. W/o hand stamp.	15.00	25.00	50.00
	b. Various hand stamps of the Kolchak Government.	10.00	17.50	37.50

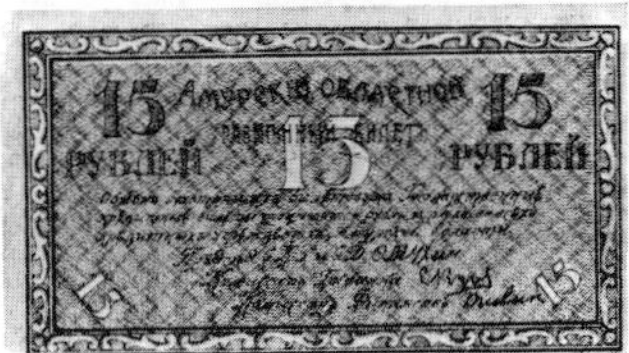

		VG	VF	Unc
S1218	**15 Rubles** 1918. Brown on green.			
	a. W/o hand stamp.	6.00	12.00	25.00
	b. Various hand stamps of the Kolchak Government.	5.00	10.00	20.00
S1219	**25 Rubles** 1918.			
	a. W/o hand stamp.	20.00	40.00	85.00
	b. Various hand stamps of the Kolchak Government.	15.00	35.00	65.00
S1220	**100 Rubles** 1918.			
	a. W/o hand stamp.	6.00	12.00	25.00
	b. Various hand stamps of the Kolchak government.	5.00	10.00	20.00

АМУРСКОЕ ОБЛАСТНОЕ ЗЕМСТВО
Amur Region Zemstvo

1917 Stamp "Type" Notes Issue

#S1221-S1224 arms w/three stars at top.

		VG	VF	Unc
S1221	**50 Kopeks** 1917 (1919). Brown and yellow.	5.00	9.00	17.50
S1222	**1 Ruble** 1917 (1919). Brown.	4.00	7.50	12.50
S1223	**3 Rubles** 1917 (1919). Green.	4.00	7.50	12.50

		VG	VF	Unc
S1224	**5 Rubles** 1917 (1919). Blue.	4.50	8.50	15.00

АМУРСКІЙ ОБЛАСТНОЙ КРЕДИТНЫЙ СОЮЗЪ
Amur Region Credit Union
ХАБАРОВСКІЙ КООПЕРАТИВ БАНКЪ
Habarovsk Cooperative Bank

1919 Issue

#S1224-S1224D w/ or w/o round bank stamping at l. on face or at ctr. on back. Text on ornate oval at ctr. on back. Sunrise over farm scene w/trees at upper ctr. on back.

		VG	VF	Unc
S1224A	**1 Ruble** 1919. Black on orange unpt.			
	a. Soyuz Bank hand stamp.	5.00	12.50	20.00
	b. Cooperative Bank hand stamp.	10.00	25.00	40.00
	r. W/o stamp. Remainder.	3.00	7.50	17.50
S1224B	**3 Rublya** 1919. Black on green unpt.			
	a. Soyuz Bank hand stamp.	4.00	8.00	15.00
	b. Cooperative Bank hand stamp.	4.00	8.00	15.00
	r. W/o stamp. Remainder.	3.00	7.50	17.50
S1224C	**5 Rublei** 1919. Black on blue unpt.			
	a. Soyuz Bank hand stamp.	4.00	8.00	15.00
	b. Cooperative Bank hand stamp.	4.00	8.00	15.00
	r. W/o hand stamp. Remainder.	3.00	7.50	17.50
S1224D	**10 Rublei** 1919. Black on lt. red unpt.			
	a. Soyuz Bank hand stamp.	5.00	10.00	17.50
	b. Cooperative Bank hand stamp.	5.00	10.00	20.00
	r. W/o hand stamp. Remainder.	3.00	7.50	17.50

ГОСУДАРСТВЕННАГО БАНКА
Government Bank
ХАБАРОВСКОЕ ОТДѢЛЕНІЕ
Habarovsk

1918 ЯНВАРЬ-МАРТ Issue

#S1225A-S1225V combine several issues dated from Jan.-Mar. 1918. Black text on blue frame, or on blue or green unpt. Back stamped w/maroon text and red round seal. All w/hand dating over 190x to 191x.

		Good	Fine	XF
S1225A	**5 Rublei** 1918.	4.00	10.00	20.00
S1225B	**10 Rublei** 1918.	4.00	10.00	20.00
S1225C	**15 Rublei** 1918.	4.00	10.00	20.00
S1225D	**20 Rubeli** 1918.	4.00	10.00	20.00

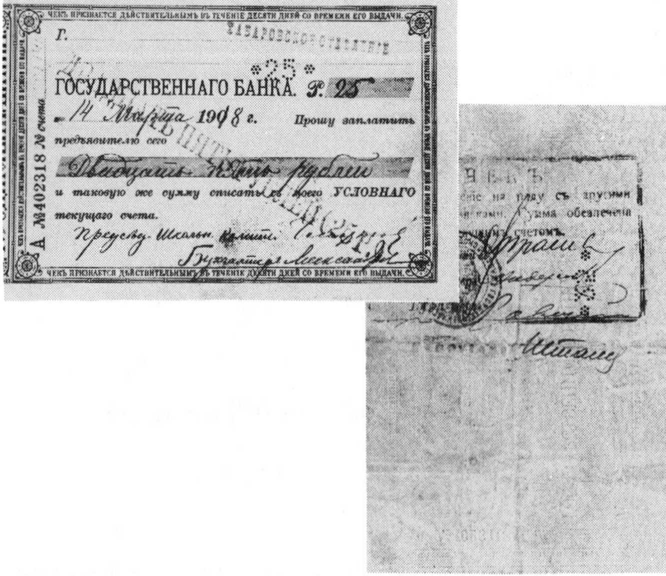

		Good	Fine	XF
S1225E	**25 Rublei** 1918.	4.00	12.00	22.50
S1225F	**30 Rublei** 1918.	5.00	12.50	30.00
S1225G	**40 Rublei** 1918.	4.00	12.00	22.50
S1225H	**45 Rublei** 1918.	12.50	30.00	60.00
S1225I	**50 Rublei** 1918.	4.00	10.00	20.00
S1225J	**55 Rublei** 1918.	10.00	25.00	50.00
S1225K	**60 Rublei** 1918.	7.50	15.00	35.00
S1225L	**75 Rublei** 1918.	5.00	12.00	22.50

		Good	Fine	XF
S1225M	**80 Rublei** 1918.	10.00	25.00	50.00
S1225N	**100 Rublei** 1918.	4.00	10.00	20.00
S1225P	**125 Rublei** 1918.	8.00	20.00	40.00
S1225Q	**140 Rublei** 1918.	10.00	25.00	50.00
S1225R	**150 Rublei** 1918.	8.00	20.00	40.00
S1225S	**170 Rublei** 1918.	—	Rare	—
S1225T	**200 Rublei** 1918.	10.00	25.00	50.00
S1225U	**250 Rublei** 1918.	10.00	25.00	50.00
S1225V	**3000 Rubeli** 1918.	—	Rare	—

1918 АВГУСТ-ДЕКАБРЬ Issue

		Good	Fine	XF
S1225W	**100 Rublei** 1918. Black text on lt. green unpt. Denomination stamped diagonally in purple. Back like previous issue.	3.00	8.50	20.00

Priamur Province

Gen. Milo K. Dietrichs

This was a monarchist Japanese-supported government established by the Czech General Dietrichs at Nikolaevsk-on-Amur on May 26, 1921. It lasted until mid-1922.

ЗЕМСКИЙ ПРИАМУРСКИЙ КРАЙ
Rural Priamur Province

1921 ND РАЗМѢННЫЙ ЗНАКЪ Exchange Tokens Issue

		Good	Fine	XF
S1226	**1 Kopek** ND (1921). Black on lt. tan unpt. Back blue.	2.00	6.00	15.00

		Good	Fine	XF
S1227	**5 Kopeks** ND (1921). Black on blue unpt. Back blue.	3.00	10.00	25.00

Nikolsk-Ussuriisk

ОРГАНИЗАЦІЯ КАЗЕННЫХЪ С.-Х. СКЛАДОВЪ
Organization of Farmers Depots

Japanese-sponsored organization. Notes printed in Tokyo. All have plowing scene at ctr.

1919 ND Issue

		Good	Fine	XF
S1231	**1 Ruble** ND (1919). Brown.	8.00	22.50	50.00
S1232	**3 Rubles** ND (1919). Green.	7.00	20.00	45.00
S1233	**5 Rubles** ND (1919). Blue.	12.00	30.00	65.00
S1234	**10 Rubles** ND (1919). Red.	12.00	30.00	65.00
S1235	**20 Rubles** ND (1919). Orange.	12.00	30.00	65.00

		Good	Fine	XF
S1236	**40 Rubles** ND (1919). Violet.	15.00	40.00	85.00
S1237	**100 Rubles** ND (1919). Brown.	15.00	40.00	85.00

Far East Provisional Government - Priamur Region

Chairman Medvyedev

Government set up in 1920 by the Allied occupying powers, the local Red authorities, and the disparate White elements. Its authority extended only through the maritime Province, capital Vladivostok. The notes were issued for the currency reform of June 5, 1920, utilizing stocks of ABNC-printed money (50-kopeks, 25-rubles and 100-rubles) and specially printed new notes. The chairman was a Chicago attorney, Medvyedev.

1918-19 РАЗМѢННЫЙ ЗНАКЪ Exchange Tokens Issue

		Good	Fine	XF
S1241	**5 Kopeks** 1918 (1920). Black on gold unpt. Double-headed eagle at top ctr.	3.00	7.00	15.00

		Good	Fine	XF
S1242	**10 Kopeks** 1918 (1920). Brown on orange unpt. Double-headed eagle at ctr. Back orange.	3.00	7.00	15.00
S1243	**30 Kopeks** 1918 (1920). Black on green unpt. Double-headed eagle at ctr. Back green.	3.00	7.00	15.00

		Good	Fine	XF
S1244	**50 Kopeks** 1919 (1920). Orange. American printing w/2 black sign.	.75	1.50	3.50

NOTE: For #S1244 w/o sign. see #S828.

1920 ГОСУДАРСТВЕННЫЙ КРЕДИТНЫЙ БИЛЕТЪ Government Credit Notes Issue

		Good	Fine	XF
S1245	**1 Ruble** 1920. Blue on brown unpt. Ship, steam locomotive, houses at ctr. Back brown.	2.00	6.00	12.50

		Good	Fine	XF
S1246	**5 Rubles** 1920. Black on green and pink unpt. Double-headed eagle at l., arms at r. steam locomotive in front of tunnel entrance at l. on back.	4.00	10.00	30.00

		Good	Fine	XF
S1247	**10 Rubles** 1920. Black on green and pink unpt. Sheafs of grain w/fruits and shield at ctr. Back red; double-headed eagle at ctr.	3.00	8.00	20.00

		Good	Fine	XF
S1248	**25 Rubles** 1918 (1920). Black on dk. blue unpt. Commerce seated at ctr. w/2 sign. on face and on back on Russia #38 (in Vol. 2).	3.00	8.00	20.00

		Good	Fine	XF
S1249	**100 Rubles** 1918 (1920). Black on brown unpt. Agriculture seated w/fruit at ctr. w/2 sign. on face and back on Russia #40 (in Vol. 2).	3.00	8.00	20.00

NOTE: For #S1248 and S1249 w/red or blue circular ovpt. on back; see #S1196 and S1197. Also see #S1213 and #S1214 for notes w/red or bronze ovpt. on back.

АМУРСКОИ ЖЕЛѢЗНОИ ДОРОГИ
Amur Railroad

This rail line was partly opened 1914 and completed 1916. The notes were to pay advances to workers in a time of scarcity of currency.

1919 General Committee - Cartes d'Avances Issue

		Good	Fine	XF
S1251	**1 Ruble** 1919. Red-brown. 100 x 73mm.	8.00	20.00	55.00
S1252	**3 Rubles** 1919. Blue.	10.00	25.00	65.00
S1253	**5 Rubles** 1919. Green.	12.50	30.00	75.00

ГОСУДАРСТВЕННАГО БАНКА
Government Bank

ВЛАДИВОСТОКСКАГО ОТДѢЛЕНІЙ
Vladivostok

1920 ЧЕК Checks Issue

		Good	Fine	XF
S1254	**1000 Rubles** 1.4.1920. Dk. blue. Uniface.	10.00	25.00	55.00

NOTE: See also #S867-S870.

ВЛАДИВОСТОКСКАЯ КОНТОРА ГОСУДАРСТВЕННАГО БАНКА
Vladivostok Office Government Bank

192x Issue

#S1255A-S1255C not signed, dated or issued. Black text face and back. Notes may or may not have a hole cancellation.

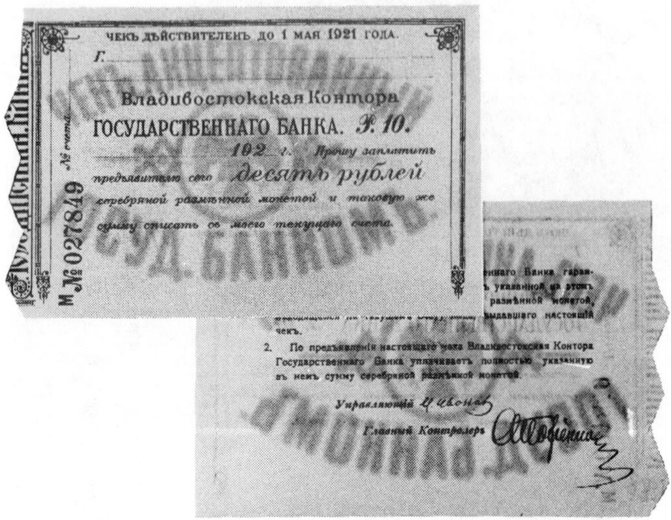

		Good	Fine	XF
S1255A	**10 Rublei** 192x. Green unpt.	—	10.00	25.00
S1255B	**25 Rublei** 192x. Lt. tan paper.	—	10.00	25.00
S1255C	**100 Rublei** 192x. Lt. brown paper.	—	10.00	25.00

ИНДО-
КИТАЙСКІЙ БАНКЪ
Banque de L' Indo-Chine

Vladivostok

1919 Issue

#S1256-S1259 proposed Allied issue. Portr. of Marianne wearing Liberty cap at ctr. Text in Russian and French. The exchange rate on the notes is 1 Ruble = 60 French Centimes. Printer: ABNC. Specimen or proof only. (Not issued).

		VG	VF	Unc
S1256	**5 Rubles** 12.2.1919. Blue on m/c unpt. Back blue. Series A.	—	—	—
S1257	**25 Rubles** 12.2.1919. Green on m/c unpt. Back green. Series A; B.	—	—	—
S1258	**100 Rubles** 12.2.1919. Brown on m/c unpt. Back brown. Series A.	—	—	—
S1259	**500 Rubles** 12.2.1919. Dk. brown on m/c unpt. Back dk. brown. Series A.	—	—	—

Blagoveshchensk

ГОСУДАРСТВЕННАГО БАНКА
Government Bank

БЛАГОВѢЩЕНСКАГО ОТДѢЛЕНІЯ
Blagoveshchensk

Issues by the White regime of Ataman Grigori Semenov and his irregular Cossack, Mongol and bandit force after their expulsion from Chita in the Transbaikal province. Semenov laid claim to the *All-Russian Government* because Admiral Kolchak, before his execution by the Reds on Feb. 1920, had appointed him commander-in-chief of White forces in Siberia. Semenov was backed militarily by the Japanese.

In Jan. 1921 a White Russian and Mongol force under Baron Ungem von Sternberg, deputy to Semenov, seized Urga in Outer Mongolia from its Chinese garrison. Sternberg was ousted from Urga by Red forces of the Far Eastern Republic (Chita) by June 1921, leading to the July 7 declaration of a Mongolian People's Revolutionary Government.

After the withdrawal of other Allied units from Vladivostok in the spring of 1920, the Japanese kept Cossack and other White units in garrison cities such as Blagoveshchensk, Nikolaevsk on Amur, Nikolsk-Ussuriisk, etc. The Japanese themselves withdrew from Siberia in Oct. 1922.

1920 ДЕНЕЖНЫЙ ЗНАКЪ Currency Notes Issue

#S1259A-S1259C and S1259E cross over double-headed eagle at ctr.

		Good	Fine	XF
S1259A	100 Rubles 1920. Black on orange unpt. Larger size, 167 x 105mm.	3.00	8.00	20.00
S1259B	500 Rubles 1920. Black on lilac unpt.	3.50	10.00	25.00

		Good	Fine	XF
S1259C	1000 Rubles 1920. Black-brown on green unpt. Back blue on brown unpt.			
	a. Black serial #.	1.50	5.00	12.00
	b. Seriya 2, red serial #.	1.50	4.00	10.00

		Good	Fine	XF
S1259D	3000 Rubles 1920. Black on dull orange unpt. Double-headed eagle w/o cross. Reduced size, 107 x 65mm.			
	a. Control # on back.	5.00	10.00	25.00
	b. Control # and series on face.	2.00	6.00	15.00
S1259E	5000 Rubles 1920. Black on blue unpt.	1.50	5.00	12.50

A word on pricing

When a note is marked RARE in the price columns, this note seldom appears on the market, or few are known in private hands. When dashes are in the price column, means that the note has not traded on the open market recently and a definitive value could not accurately be determined. Rare does not always mean expensive. A dashed price does not mean expensive or rare.

1919-20 Issue

#S1259F-S1259H black text on pink paper. Purple stamped text w/date filled in on back, also round stamped seal.

		Good	Fine	XF
S1259F	500 Rublei 1919.	12.00	30.00	60.00
S1259G	1000 Rublei 1919.	12.00	30.00	60.00

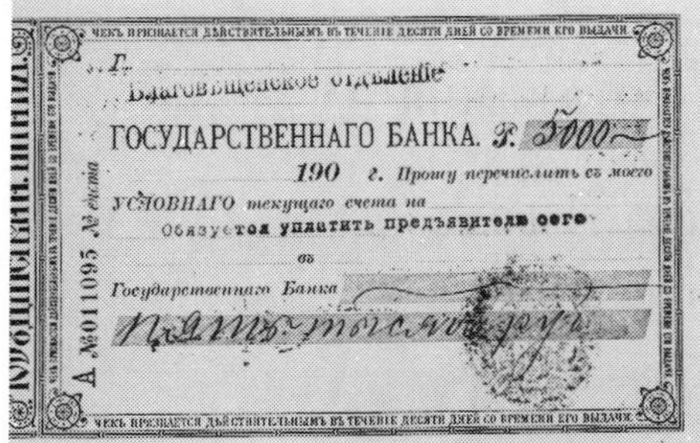

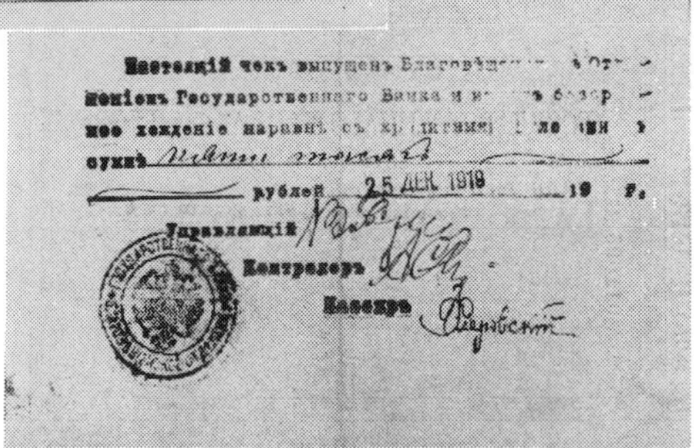

		Good	Fine	XF
S1259H	5000 Rublei 1919-20.	12.00	30.00	60.00

Outlying Regions

АЛТАЙ Altai
Committee of Nationalities of Altai

1919 Issue

		Good	Fine	XF
S1260	30 Rubles 1919. Proof.	—	—	200.00

АЛТАЙСКИЙ ГУБЕРНСКИЙ СОЮЗ
Altai Government Union

1920's ND ТАЛОН Talons Issue

All w/circular hand stamp at l. 3 or 4 edges perforated. Uniface.

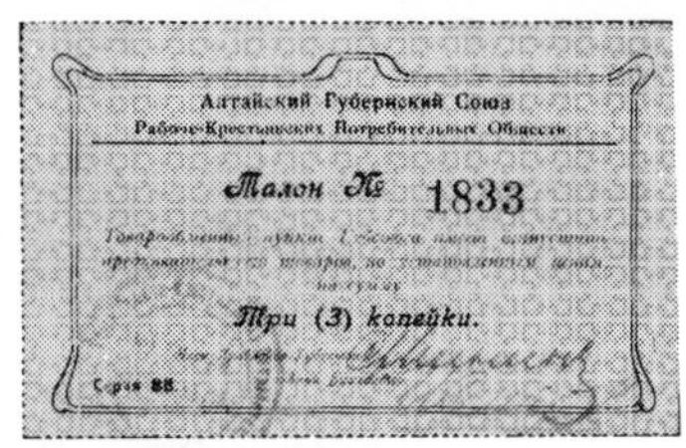

		VG	VF	Unc
S1261	1 Kopek ND (1923?). Black on brown unpt.	8.50	17.50	40.00
S1262	3 Kopeks ND. Black on lt. green unpt.	8.50	17.50	40.00
S1263	5 Kopeks ND. Black on green unpt.	8.50	17.50	40.00
S1264	10 Kopeks ND. Black on gray unpt.	8.50	17.50	40.00

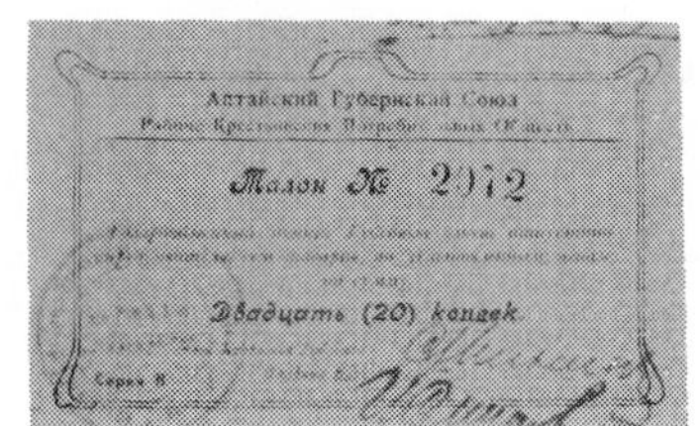

		VG	VF	Unc
S1265	20 Kopeks ND. Black on red unpt.	8.50	17.50	40.00
S1265A	50 Kopeks ND. Black on pink unpt.	10.00	25.00	55.00
S1266	1 Ruble ND.	8.50	17.50	40.00

		VG	VF	UNC
S1267	**5 RUBLES** ND.	9.00	20.00	45.00
S1268	**10 RUBLES** ND.	9.00	20.00	45.00

ГОСУДАРСТВЕННАГО БАНКА
Government Bank

БАРНАУЛЬСКАГО ОТДѢЛЕНІЯ
Barnaul

1920 ВРЕМЕННОЕ ОБЯЗАТЕЛЬСТВО

PROVISIONAL OBLIGATIONS ISSUE

		GOOD	FINE	XF
S1268A	**1000 RUBLEI** 1.2.1920/191x. Black on gray unpt. Lg. oval red stamping on back for branch.	5.00	12.00	25.00

НАРОДНАГО БАНКА
National Bank

БАРНАУЛЬСКАГО ОТДѢЛЕНІЯ

Barnaul

1918 ND ISSUE

		GOOD	FINE	XF
S1268B	**20 RUBLEI** ND (1918).	10.00	25.00	50.00
S1268C	**40 RUBLEI** ND (1918).	10.00	25.00	50.00
S1268D	**50 RUBLEI** ND (1918).	7.00	15.00	30.00
S1268E	**100 RUBLEI** ND (1918).	7.00	15.00	30.00
S1268F	**500 RUBLEI** ND (1918).	12.00	22.50	45.00

ГОСУДАРСТВЕННАГО БАНКА
Government Bank

БІЙСКАГО ОТДѢЛЕНІЯ
Biisk

1920 ND ЧЕКЪ CHECKS ISSUE

#S1269A-S1269B w/o red ovpt: РСфСР.

		GOOD	FINE	XF
S1269A	**250 RUBLEI** ND (1920). Dk. brown on lt. tan paper. Dk. brown text in 6 lines on back.	5.00	15.00	35.00
S1269B	**1000 RUBLEI** ND (1920). Black text on pink unpt. Black text on back.	4.00	12.00	25.00

#S1269C-S1269D as previous issue but w/red ovpt: РСфСРin diagonal rectangle across face.

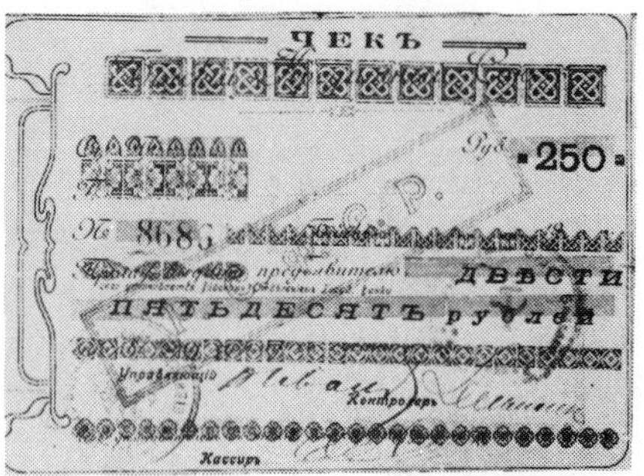

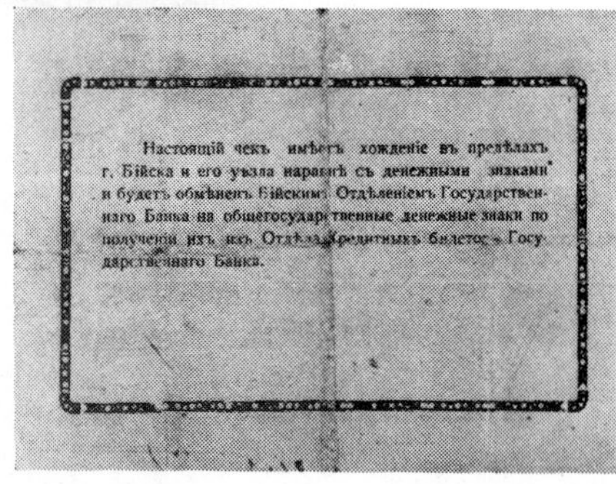

		GOOD	FINE	XF
S1269C	**250 RUBLEI** ND (1920).			
	a. W/o city and branch bank title across upper ctr.	5.00	15.00	35.00

	GOOD	FINE	XF
b. W/city and branch bank title across upper ctr., also other text changes.	4.00	12.00	25.00

		GOOD	FINE	XF
S1269D	**1000 RUBLEI** ND (1920).	4.00	12.00	25.00

KAMCHATKA

КАМЧАТСКIИ ОБЛАСТНОЙ КОМИТЕТЪ
Kamchatka Region Committee

1915 ND ISSUE

		GOOD	FINE	XF
S1270	**100 RUBLES** ND(-old date 1915). 35mm black hand stamp w/committee name around two-headed eagle on Russia #58, Vol. 2.	3.50	8.00	15.00

КАМЧАТСКИЙ ОБЛАСТНОИ СОВЕТ НАРОДНАГО ХОЗЯИСТВА
Kamchatka Provincial National Economic (Org.)

1920 КРЕДИТНЫЙ ЗНАК CREDIT TOKEN CURRENCY ISSUE

		GOOD	FINE	XF
S1271	**100 RUBLES** 1920. Blue on lt. brown unpt. Crowned arms at ctr. (3 volcanos).	12.50	40.00	100.00

		GOOD	FINE	XF
S1272	**250 RUBLES** 1920. Blue on red unpt. Crowned arms at ctr.	12.50	40.00	100.00
S1273	**500 RUBLES** 1920. Blue paper. Crowned arms at ctr. Red-brown back.	20.00	60.00	150.00
S1274	**1000 RUBLES** 1920. Black and red on blue unpt.	15.00	50.00	125.00

САХАЛИНСКОЙ ОБЛАСТИ
Sakhalin Province

1918 КРЕДИТНЫЙ БИЛЕТЪ CREDIT NOTES ISSUE

		GOOD	FINE	XF
S1275	**1000 RUBLES** 1918.			
	a. W/*1000* in corners on back.	20.00	75.00	200.00
	b. W/o *1000* in corners on back.	30.00	100.00	250.00

САХАЛИНСКИЙ ОБЛАСТНОЙ НАРОДНО РЕВОЛЮЦИОННЫЙ КОМИТЕТ
Sakhalin Provincial National Revolutionary Committee

1920 БОНА BONS ISSUE

#S1276-S1282 blue.

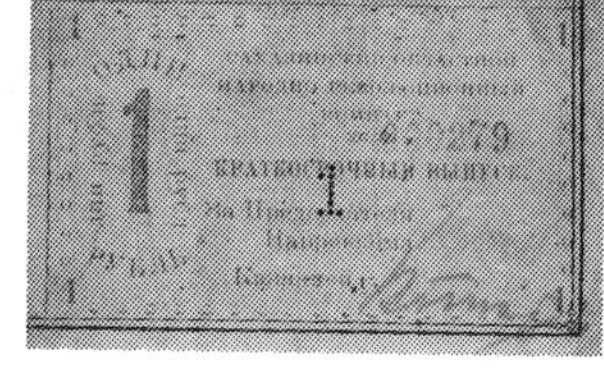

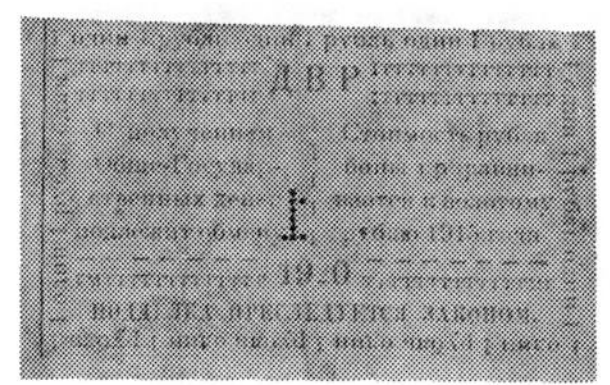

		GOOD	FINE	XF
S1276	**1 RUBLE** 1920.	40.00	40.00	300.00
S1277	**3 RUBLES** 1920.	40.00	60.00	300.00
S1278	**5 RUBLES** 1920.	40.00	100.00	300.00
S1279	**10 RUBLES** 1920.	40.00	100.00	300.00
S1280	**25 RUBLES** 1920.	50.00	125.00	350.00
S1281	**50 RUBLES** 1920.	75.00	200.00	600.00
S1282	**100 RUBLES** 1920.	125.00	275.00	750.00

ГОСУДАРСТВЕННАГО БАНКА
Government Bank

ТОМСКОЕ ОТДѢЛЕНІЕ
Tomsk

1918 ISSUE

		GOOD	FINE	XF
S1283	**100 RUBLEI** 1918. Black on orange-brown unpt. Uniface.	5.00	12.00	25.00
S1284	**500 RUBLEI** 1918.	6.00	15.00	30.00

NIKOLAEVSK ON AMUR

This port city was under Allied occupation beginning in mid-1918, continuing under Japanese bayonets until Oct. 25,1922, long after the Americans and British had pulled out. The city had a large Japanese civilian population in this period.

НИКОЛАЕВСКОГО НА АМУРЕ
Nikolaevsk-on-Amur

1918 ЧЕКЪ CHECKS ISSUE

		GOOD	FINE	XF
S1286	**5 RUBLES** 1918.	15.00	30.00	90.00
S1287	**25 RUBLES** 1918.	12.50	25.00	75.00
S1288	**100 RUBLES** 1918. Black on brown unpt.	12.50	25.00	75.00

НИКОЛАЕВСКОГО НА АМУРЕ ГОСУДАРСТВЕННОГО БАНКА Р.С.ф.Р. or Р.ф.С.Р.
Nikolaevsk-on-Amur Branch Government Bank, R.S.F.R. or R.F.S.R.

1920 РАЗМЕННЫЙ БИЛЕТ EXCHANGE NOTES ISSUE

		VG	VF	UNC
S1291	**250 RUBLES** 1920. Black on red-brown unpt.	6.00	14.00	30.00

		VG	VF	UNC
S1292	**500 RUBLES** 1920. Black on blue unpt.	8.00	17.50	40.00
S1293	**1000 RUBLES** 1920. Black on green unpt.			
	a. White paper.	10.00	22.50	50.00
	b. Lt. green paper.	10.00	22.50	50.00
	c. Lt. blue paper.	10.00	22.50	50.00
	d. Yellowish paper.	12.00	27.50	60.00

ПЕРЕВОДНОЕ ПИСЬМО ПРИЙСКОВ. УПРАВЛЕН. АМГУНСКАЯ ЗОЛОТО ПРОМЫЩЛЕННАЯ КОМПАНІЯ
Amgun Gold Company

1920 ISSUE

		VG	VF	UNC
S1296	**50 RUBLES** 20.4.1920.	50.00	125.00	300.00
S1297	**100 RUBLES** 20.4.1920.	50.00	125.00	300.00
S1298	**250 RUBLES** 20.4.1920.	50.00	125.00	300.00
S1299	**500 RUBLES** 20.4.1920.	50.00	125.00	300.00
S1300	**1000 RUBLES** 20.4.1920.	50.00	125.00	300.00

YAKUTIA

ЯКУТСКАЯ АВТОНОМНАЯ СОЦИАЛ. СОВЕТ РЕСПУБЛИКА
Yakut Autonomous Socialist Soviet Republic

1921 РАСЧЕТНЫЙ ЗНАК EXCHANGE TOKENS ISSUE

		VG	VF	UNC
S1301	**500 RUBLES** 1921 (1922). Russia #111 (Vol. 2) w/stamp.	—	—	—
S1302	**1000 RUBLES** 1921 (1922). Russia #112 (Vol. 2) w/stamp.	—	—	—

НАРОДНЫИ КОМИССАРИАТ ТОРГ. И ПРОМЫЩЛЕННОСТЍ

NATIONAL COMMISSARIAT OF COMMERCIAL MANUFACTURING

Market values are for cancelled notes.

1923 ISSUE

		VG	VF	UNC
S1306	**3 RUBLES** 1923. Black and blue on green unpt.	—	—	—
S1307	**5 RUBLES** 1923.	—	—	—
S1308	**10 RUBLES** 1923.	—	—	—

NOTE: Market values are for cancelled notes.

1924 ISSUE

		VG	VF	UNC
S1309	**1 RUBLE** 1924.	—	—	—
S1310	**3 RUBLES** 1924.	—	—	—
S1311	**5 RUBLES** 1924.	—	—	—
S1312	**10 RUBLES** 1924.	—	—	—
S1313	**25 RUBLES** 1924.	—	—	—

NOTE: Market values are for cancelled notes.

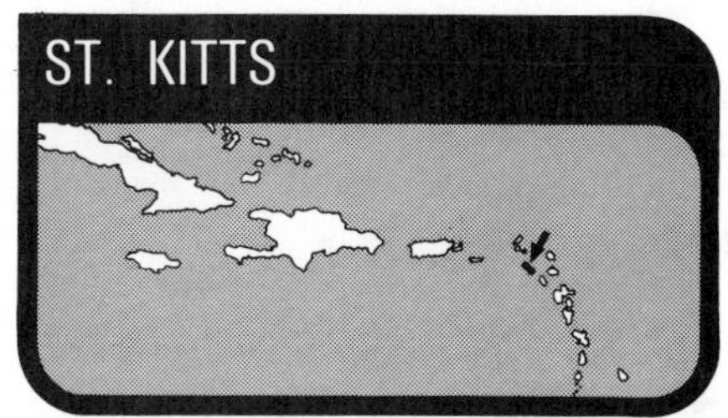

St. Kitts (St. Christopher), a West Indian island located in the Leeward Islands southeast of Puerto Rico, is the principal component of a British associated state composed of the islands of St. Kitts, Nevis, and Anguilla. The associated state has an area of 104 sq. mi. (269 sq. km.) Capital: Basseterre, St. Kitts.

St. Kitts was discovered by Columbus in 1493 and was settled by Thomas Warner, an Englishman, in 1623. The island was ceded to the British by the Treaty of Utrecht, 1713. France protested British occupancy, and on three occasions between 1666 and 1782 seized the island and held it for short periods.

RULERS:
British

MONETARY SYSTEM:
1 Dollar = 100 Cents

BRITISH ADMINISTRATION

BARCLAYS BANK (DOMINION, COLONIAL AND OVERSEAS)

1926 PROVISIONAL ISSUE

#S101-S106 original office: Bridgetown, Barbados w/ovpt: *ISSUED AT ST. KITTS BRANCH* at l. and r. of ctr. and lg. *K* at upper r. Printer: BWC.

#S101 *Deleted.* See #S111.

		GOOD	FINE	XF
S104	5 DOLLARS 1.9.1926. Black on pink and blue-green unpt. Crowned supported royal arms at ctr. Ovpt: Lg. *K* at upper r. Back green.	600.00	1750.	—

1937 ISSUE

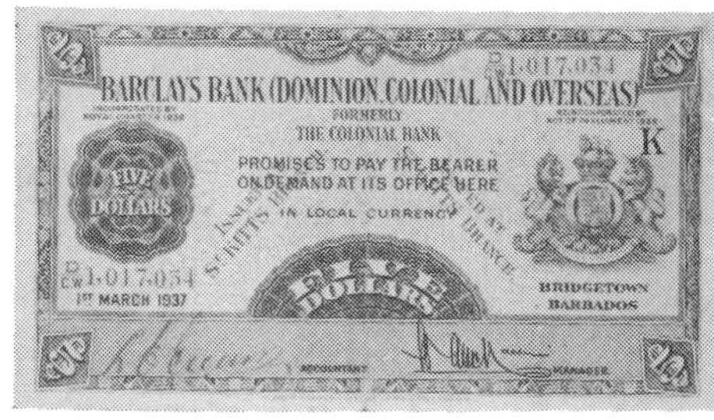

		GOOD	FINE	XF
S106	5 DOLLARS 1937; 1940. Purple on m/c unpt. Crowned supported royal arms at r. Ovpt: Lg. *K* at upper r.			
	a. Issued note. 1.3.1937; 1.5.1937.	250.00	600.00	1500.
	s. Specimen. 1.3.1940.	—	Unc	850.00

COLONIAL BANK

1900'S PROVISIONAL ISSUE

		GOOD	FINE	XF
S111	5 DOLLARS To 1926. Black. Arms at upper ctr. Ovpt: *ISSUED AT ST. KITTS BRANCH.*	2000.	4500.	—

ROYAL BANK OF CANADA

Issued at Basseterre.

1913 PROVISIONAL ISSUE

#S116 ovpt: *ST. KITTS* vertically at l. and r., smaller vertical ovpt: *PAYABLE AT BASSETERRE, ST. KITTS* at l. ctr. on regular Canadian issue.

		GOOD	FINE	XF
S116	5 DOLLARS 2.1.1913. Black on green unpt. Ovpt: on Canada #S1378. Printer: ABNC.	—	Rare	—

1920 ISSUE

		GOOD	FINE	XF
S121	5 DOLLARS = 1 POUND - 10 PENCE 2.1.1920. Black on green unpt. Steampship at ctr. Back green. Lg. size note. Printer: ABNC.			
	a. Issued note.	750.00	2250.	—
	p. Proof.	—	Unc	1500.
	s. Specimen.	—	Unc	1500.

1938 ISSUE

		GOOD	FINE	XF
S126	5 DOLLARS = 1 POUND - 10 PENCE 3.1.1938. Similar to #S121 but reduced size.			
	a. Issued note.	300.00	850.00	1500.
	p. Proof.	—	Unc	1000.
	s. Specimen.	—	Unc	1000.

Saint Lucia, an independent island nation located in the Windward Islands of the West Indies between St. Vincent and Martinique, has an area of 238 sq. mi. (616 sq. km). Capital: Castries.

St. Lucia was discovered by Columbus in 1502. The first attempts at settlements undertaken by the British in 1605 and 1638 were frustrated by sickness and the determined hostility of the fierce Carib inhabitants. The French settled it in 1650 and made a treaty with the indigenous population. Until 1814, when the island became a definite British possession, it was the scene of a continuous conflict between the British and French which saw the island change loyalty on at least 14 occasions.

RULERS:
British

MONETARY SYSTEM:
1 Pound = 20 Shillings
1 Dollar = 100 Cents

BRITISH ADMINISTRATION

BARCLAYS BANK (DOMINION, COLONIAL AND OVERSEAS)

1926 PROVISIONAL ISSUES

#S106 and S107 printer: BWC.

		Good	Fine	XF
S106	**5 DOLLARS** 1.9.1926. Brown and green. Crowned supported royal arms at ctr. Office of issue: Bridgetown, Barbados. Ovpt: *ISSUED AT ST. LUCIA BRANCH* and lg. *L*.	700.00	2250.	—
S107	**5 DOLLARS** 1.9.1926. Like #S106. Office of issue: Castries, St. Lucia.	1000.	2750.	—

1937 ISSUE

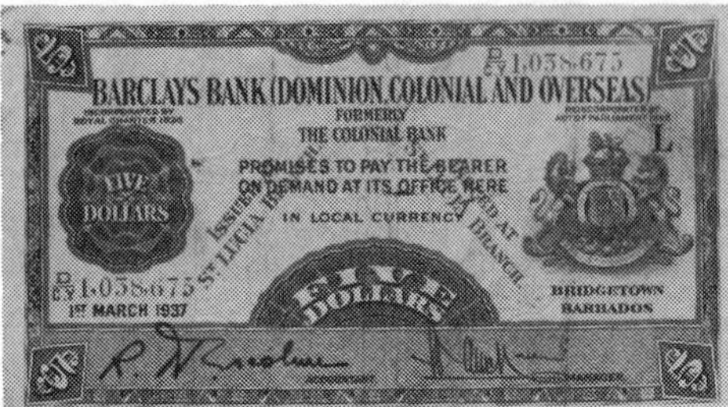

		Good	Fine	XF
S111	**5 DOLLARS** 1937-41. Purple on m/c unpt. Crowned supported royal arms at r. Office of issue: Bridgetown, Barbados. Ovpt: *ISSUED AT ST. LUCIA BRANCH* twice at ctr., and lg. *L*. Printer: BWC.			
	a. Issued note. 1.3.1937; 1.5.1937; 1.3.1940; 1.2.1941.	450.00	1750.	—
	s. Specimen. 1.2.1941.	—	Unc	1000.

COLONIAL BANK

1900'S ISSUE

		Good	Fine	XF
S116	**5 DOLLARS** To 1926.	—	Rare	—

ROYAL BANK OF CANADA

1900'S ISSUE

		Good	Fine	XF
S121	**5 DOLLARS = 1 POUND - 10 PENCE** 2.1.1920. Black on green unpt. Steamship at ctr. Back green. Printer: ABNC.	1000.	3500.	5500.

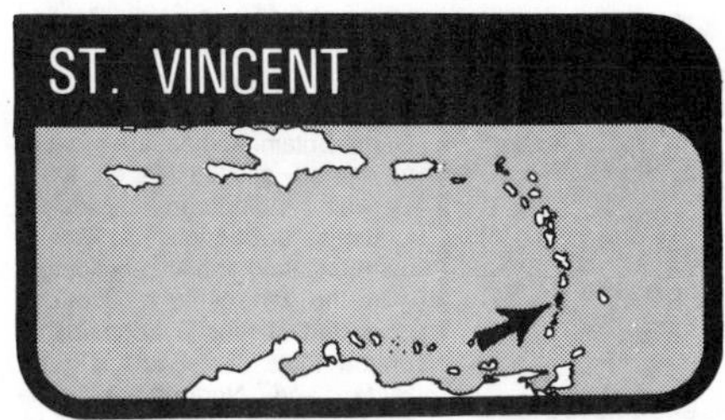

The State of St. Vincent, a British associated state located in the Windward Islands of the West Indies west of Barbados and south of St. Lucia, has an area of 150 sq. mi. (388 sq. km.). Capital: Kingstown.

St. Vincent was discovered by Columbus on Jan. 22, 1498, and was left undisturbed for more than a century. The British began colonization early in the 18th century, against bitter and prolonged Carib resistance. The island was taken by the French in 1779, but restored to the British in 1783, by the Treaty of Paris.

RULERS:

British

MONETARY SYSTEM:

1 Dollar = 100 Cents

BRITISH ADMINISTRATION

BARCLAYS BANK (DOMINION, COLONIAL AND OVERSEAS)

1926 PROVISIONAL ISSUE

#S101 and S106 ovpt: *ISSUED AT ST. VINCENT BRANCH* twice, at l. and r. of ctr. Printer: BWC.

		GOOD	FINE	XF
S101	**5 DOLLARS** 1.9.1926; 1.6.1929. Black on pink and blue-green unpt. Crowned supported royal arms at ctr. Issuing office: Bridgetown, Barbados. Ovpt: Lg. *V* at upper r. Back green.	450.00	1500.	—

1939 ISSUE

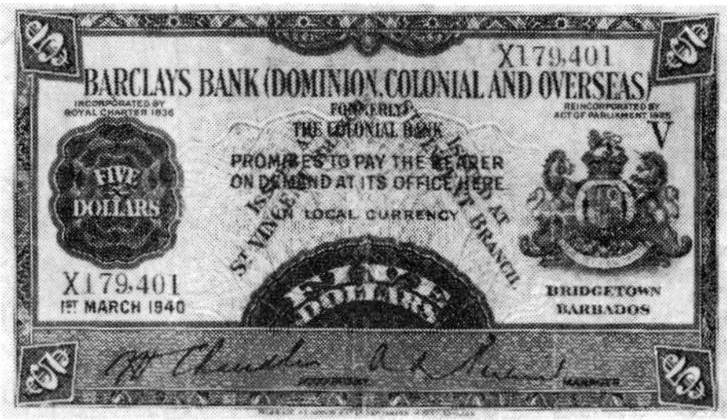

		GOOD	FINE	XF
S106	**5 DOLLARS** 1939-41. Purple on m/c unpt. Crowned supported royal arms at r. Ovpt: Lg. *V* at upper r.			
	a. Issuing office: Bridgetown, Barbados. 1.3.1940.	300.00	750.00	1500.

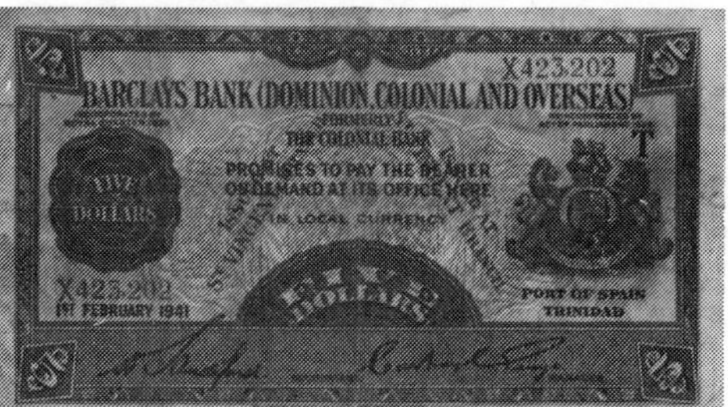

		GOOD	FINE	XF
	b. Issuing office: Port of Spain, Trinidad. Ovpt: Lg. *T* at upper r. 1.3.1939; 1.2.1941.	250.00	700.00	1500.

COLONIAL BANK

1882 PROVISIONAL ISSUE

#S111 Bridgetown, Barbados office. Ovpt: *Issued at ST. VINCENT Branch* twice, at l. and r. of ctr.

		GOOD	FINE	XF
S111	**5 DOLLARS** 1.7.1882. Black. Crowned supported royal arms at upper ctr.	1500.	5000.	—

1917 ISSUE

#S115 Bridgetown, Barbados office. Ovpt: *Issued at ST. VINCENT Branch* twice, at l. and r. of ctr.

		GOOD	FINE	XF
S115	**5 DOLLARS** 1.2.1917. Black on orange unpt. Crowned supported royal arms at upper ctr. Ovpt: Lg. *S V* at upper r. Specimen.	—	Unc	2000.

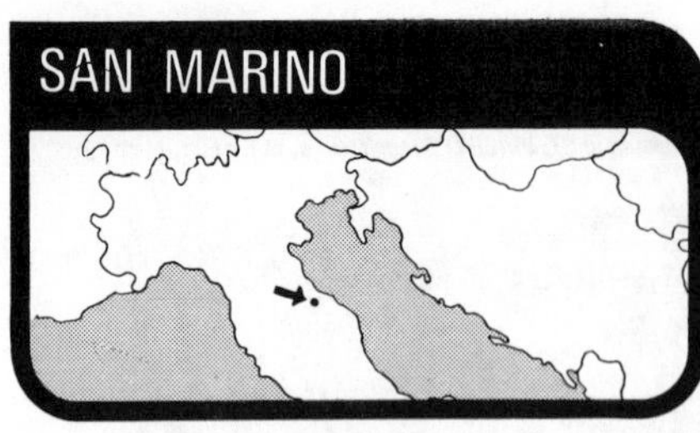

The Republic of San Marino, the oldest and smallest republic in the world, is located in north central Italy entirely surrounded by the Province of Emilia - Romagna. It has an area of 24 sq. mi. (62 sq. km.) Capital: San Marino.

According to tradition, San Marino was founded about 350 A.D. by a Christian stonecutter as a refuge against religious persecution. While gradually acquiring the institutions of an independent state, it avoided the factional fights of the middle ages and except for a brief period in fief to Cesare Borgia, retained its freedom despite attacks on its sovereignty by the Papacy, the lords of Rimini, Napoleon and Mussolini. In 1862 San Marino established a customs union with, and put itself under the protection of, Italy. A Communist - Socialist coalition controlled the government for 12 years after World War II. The Christian Democratic Party has been the core of government since 1957.

San Marino does not issue its own paper money although it has issued coins since 1864. The notes issued in 1976 are emergency small denomination issues prompted by a coin shortage. Similar pieces were issued in 1944 and 1966.

MONETARY SYSTEM:

1 Lira = 100 Centesimi

REPUBLIC

CASSA DI RISPARMIO DELLA REPUBBLICA DI SAN MARINO

1976 EMERGENCY ISSUE

		VG	VF	UNC
S101	**150 LIRE** 5.4.1976. Arms in lt. brown unpt.	2.00	5.00	15.00

San Marino, 6 5 Aprile 1976 £ —200—
CASSA DI RISPARMIO DELLA REPUBBLICA DI SAN MARINO
A vista la Cassa di Risparmio della Rep. di S. Marino
pagherà al Sig. PORTATORE DEL PRESENTE ASSEGNO
Lire DUECENTO
Questo assegno può circolare
solo nella Repubblica di San Marino
N° 230759

		VG	VF	UNC
S102	**200 LIRE** 5.4.1976. Arms in lt. green unpt.	2.00	5.00	15.00

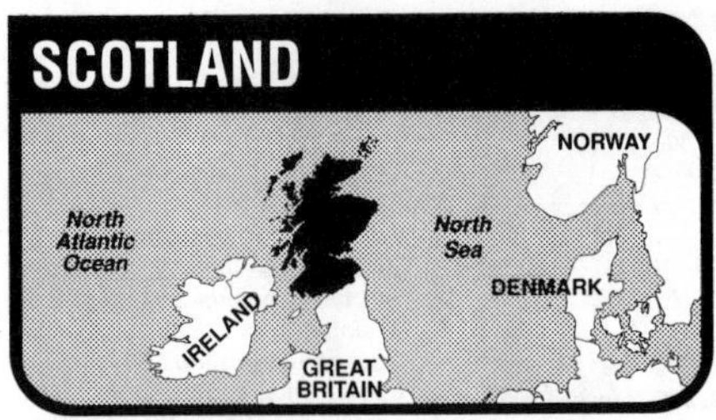

Scotland, a part of the United Kingdom of Great Britain and Northern Ireland, consists of the northern part of the island of Great Britain. It has an area of 30,414 sq. mi. (78,772 sq. km.). Capital: Edinburgh. Principal industries are agriculture, fishing, manufacturing and ship-building.

In the 5th century, Scotland consisted of four kingdoms; that of the Picts, the Scots, Strathclyde, and Northumbria. The Scottish kingdom was united by Malcolm II (1005-34), but its ruler was forced to payo homage to the English crown in 1174. Scotland won independence under Robert Bruce at Bannockburn in 1314 and was ruled by the house of Stuart from 1371 to 1688. The personal union of the kingdoms of England and Scotland was achieved in 1603 by the accession of King James VI of Scotland as James I of England. Scotland was united with England by Parliamentary act in 1707.

RULERS:

British

MONETARY SYSTEM:

1 Shilling = 12 Pence
1 Guinea = 21 Shillings
1 Pound = 20 Shillings to 1971
1 Pound = 20 Shillings to 1971

NOTE ON LISTINGS

Listings for Scotland in Volume I are comprised of selected obsolete bank issues formerly in Volume II, and they go back to the beginning of each bank.

COMMERCIAL BANKS:

British Linen Company. . . . . #S141-S179
Commercial Banking Company of Scotland . . . . . #S281-S290
Commercial Bank of Scotland . . . . . #S291-S309
Commercial Bank of Scotland Ltd. . . . . . #S310-S336
North of Scotland Banking Company. . . . . #S611-S619
North of Scotland Bank Ltd.. . . . . #S620-S624
North of Scotland & Town & County Bank Ltd. . . . . #S625-S632
North of Scotland Bank Ltd.. . . . . #S633-S647
Union Bank of Scotland . . . . . #S776-S798
Union Bank of Scotland Ltd. . . . . . #S799-S819

PRIVATE BANKS:

The following listing of private banks in Scotland that either issued notes or had notes prepared was furnished by James Douglas, author of *Scottish Banknotes* published in 1975. This catalog was a pioneering effort in reporting what was available, although incomplete, to the author at that time.Aberdeen Commercial Banking Company, 1778-1833
Arbroath Banking Company, 1825-44
Ayrshire Banking Company, 1830-48
Banking Company in Aberdeen, 1767-1849
Caithness Banking Company, 1812-25
Caledonian Banking Company Limited, 1838-1907
Central Bank of Scotland, 1834-68
City of Glascow Bank, 1839-79
Cupar Banking Company, 1802-11
Douglas Heron & Company, 1769-73
Dumfries Commercial Bank, 1804-08
Dundee Banking Company, 1763-1864
Dundee Commercial Bank, 1825-38
Dundee New Bank, 1802-38
Dundee Union Bank, 1809-44
East Lothian Banking Company, 1810-22
Eastern Bank of Scotland, 1838-63
Edinburgh and Glasgow Bank, 1844-58
Edinburgh and Leith Bank, 1839-44
Falkirk Banking Company, 1782-1825
Falkirk Union Banking Company, 1803-16
Fife Banking Company, 1802-29
William Forbes, James Hunter & Co., 1773-1838
Galloway Banking Company, 1806-21
Glasgow and Ship Bank, 1836-43
Glasgow Arms Bank, 1750-93
Glasgow Bank Company, 1809-36
Glasgow Joint Stock Bank, 1840-44
Glasgow Union Banking Company, 1830-43
Greenock Bank Company, 1785-1843
Greenock Union Bank, 1840-44
Hunters & Company, 1773-1843
Kilmarnock Bank, 1802-21
Leith Banking Company, 1793-1842
Montrose Bank, 1814-29
North British Bank, 1844
North of Scotland Banking Company, 1836-82
Paisley Banking Company, 1783-1836
Paisley Commercial Banking Company, 1838-44
Paisley Union Banking Company, 1788-1838
Perth Banking Company, 1787-1857
Perth Union Bank, 1810-36
Renfrewshire Banking Company, 1802-42
Shetland Bank, 1821-42
Ship Bank, 1750-1836
Southern Bank of Scotland, 1838-40
Stirling Banking Company, 1777-1826
Stirling Merchant Banking Company, 1784-1813
Stornoway Bank (J. Stewart McKenzie), 1823-26
Thistle Bank, 1761-1836
Town and County Bank, 1825-1908
Western Bank of Scotland, 1832-5

COMMERCIAL BANKS

BRITISH LINEN COMPANY

Later became the British Linen Bank. Absorbed by the Bank of Scotland in 1971. Early notes black. Uniface.

1747 ISSUE

#S141-S144 w/text: *for value received in goods. Payable without interest.*

		GOOD	FINE	XF
S141	**5 POUNDS** (ca.1747).	—	—	—
S142	**10 POUNDS** (ca.1747).	—	—	—
S143	**20 POUNDS** (ca.1747).	—	—	—
S144	**100 POUNDS** (ca.1747). Interest-bearing, payable after 3 months.	—	—	—

1750 ISSUE

#S145-S148 w/text: *for value received in goods.*

		GOOD	FINE	XF
S145	**10 SHILLINGS** (ca.1750).	—	—	—
S146	**1 POUND** (ca.1750).	—	—	—

1754 ISSUE

		GOOD	FINE	XF
S147	**20 SHILLINGS** (ca.1754). Seated woman w/sailing ship behind at upper l.	—	—	—

1763 ISSUE

		GOOD	FINE	XF
S148	**5 POUNDS** (ca.1763). Bank emblem in ornate frame at upper l.	—	—	—

1768 ISSUE

		GOOD	FINE	XF
S149	**1 GUINEA** 5.4.1768. Bank emblem at upper ctr., panel of thistles across top. Words from text: *in goods* deleted.	—	—	—

1770 ISSUE

		GOOD	FINE	XF
S150	**1 GUINEA** 6.9.1770. Similar to #S149.	—	—	—

1780 ISSUE

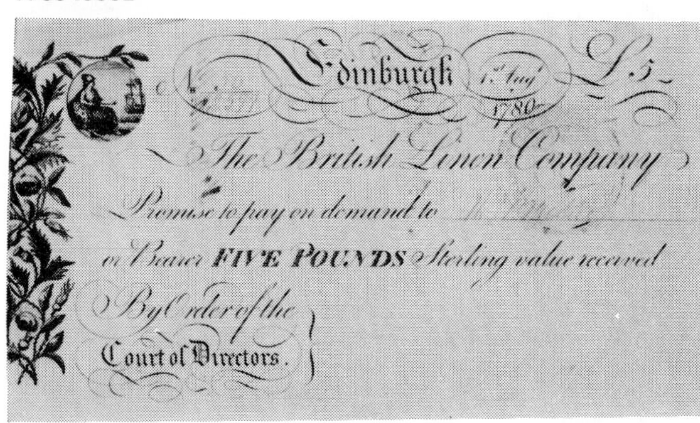

		GOOD	FINE	XF
S151	**5 POUNDS** 1.8.1780. Emblem of Pallas at upper l., vertical panel of thistles and roses at l.	700.00	1400.	—

1797 ISSUE

		GOOD	FINE	XF
S152	**5 SHILLINGS** 31.3.1797. Bank emblem at upper l.	—	—	—

1808 ISSUE

		GOOD	FINE	XF
S153	**1 GUINEA** Oct. 1808. Bank emblem at upper l., panel of thistle and rose motif across top.	300.00	650.00	—

1811 ISSUE

		GOOD	FINE	XF
S154	**20 SHILLINGS** (ca.1811). Bank emblem at l.			
	a. Issued note.	300.00	650.00	—
	x. Contemporary forgery. 30.5.1811.	—	—	—

1815 ISSUE

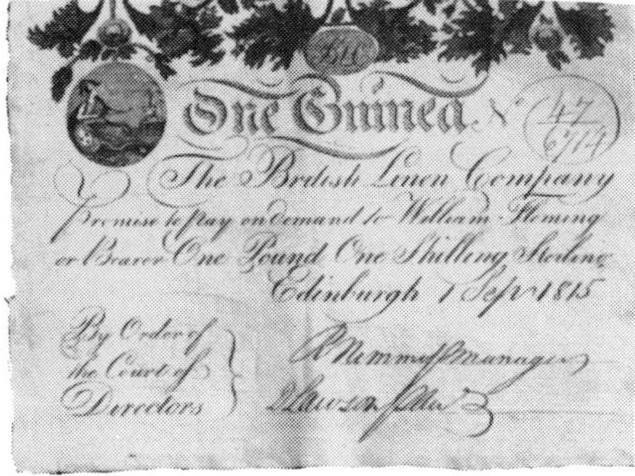

		GOOD	FINE	XF
S155	**1 GUINEA** 1.9.1815; 1.9.1819. Similar to #S153 but oval panel at top w/letters: *BLC* instead of date.			
	a. Issued note.	400.00	850.00	—
	x. Contemporary forgery. 1.9.1815.	—	—	—

1821 ISSUE

		GOOD	FINE	XF
S156	**20 SHILLINGS** (ca.1821). Bank emblem at upper ctr.			
	a. Issued note.	400.00	850.00	—
	x. Contemporary forgery. 18.5.1825.	—	—	—
S157	**1 GUINEA** (ca.1821). 2 seated women at upper ctr., vertical panel of thistles at l.	400.00	850.00	—
S158	**5 POUNDS** (ca.1821). Vertical panel of roses and thistles at l., small vignette of bank emblem at upper l.	450.00	1250.	—
S158A	**20 POUNDS** (ca.1821). Similar to #S158.	—	—	—
S158B	**100 POUNDS** (ca.1821). Similar to #S158.	—	—	—

1822 ISSUE

#S159-S164 black. Made from steel engraved plates by Perkins Fairman & Heath (later Perkins Bacon & Co.). Crowned supported royal arms at upper ctr., seated Britannia with spear, shield and lion in vertical panel at l. Uniface.

		GOOD	FINE	XF
S159	**1 POUND** (ca.1822).			
	a. Issued note.	300.00	650.00	—
	x. Contemporary forgeries. 2.11.1826; 1.5.1828; 1.3.1829.	—	—	—
S160	**1 GUINEA** (ca.1822).	300.00	650.00	—
S161	**5 POUNDS** (ca.1822).	300.00	650.00	—
S162	**10 POUNDS** (ca.1822).	400.00	1000.	—
S163	**20 POUNDS** (ca.1822).	400.00	1000.	—
S164	**100 POUNDS** (ca.1822).	—	—	—

1861 ISSUE

#S165-S169 blue and red. Similar to #S159-S164 but printed in blue, w/lg. red letters: *B.L.Co.* added as an anti-counterfeiting device. First issue dated 1.9.1860 but not issued until 1861.

		GOOD	FINE	XF
S165	**1 POUND** (ca.1861); 1.8.1863.	250.00	600.00	—
S166	**5 POUNDS** (ca.1861).	300.00	650.00	—
S167	**10 POUNDS** (ca.1861).	350.00	750.00	—
S168	**20 POUNDS** (ca.1861).	400.00	1000.	—
S169	**100 POUNDS** (ca.1861).	—	—	—

1871 ISSUE

#S170-S174 blue and red. Similar to #S165-S169 but different promissory text at ctr.

		GOOD	FINE	XF
S170	1 POUND (ca.1871); 1891-1904.			
	a. 10.9.1891.	100.00	325.00	—
	b. 12.11.1900; 1.2.1901; 9.8.1902; 31.5.1904.	125.00	350.00	—
S171	5 POUNDS (ca.1871); 14.10.1901.	300.00	650.00	—
S172	10 POUNDS (ca.1871).	350.00	750.00	—

		GOOD	FINE	XF
S173	20 POUNDS (ca.1871); 31.8.1901.	400.00	1000.	—

		GOOD	FINE	XF
S174	100 POUNDS (ca.1871); 1.10.1901. Remainder.	—	—	350.00

1905 ISSUE

#S175-S179 blue w/lg. red: *B. L. Co.* Similar to #S170-S174. Printer: W&S.

		GOOD	FINE	XF
S175	1 POUND 28.2.1905; 30.3.1906.	200.00	500.00	1250.
S176	5 POUNDS 8.3.1905; 1.6.1905; 14.4.1906; 4.2.1907. Like #S175.	200.00	500.00	1250.
S177	10 POUNDS 15.4.1905. Like #S175.	—	Rare	—
S178	20 POUNDS 7.6.1905; 20.3.1906. Like #S175.	—	Rare	—
S179	100 POUNDS 14.2.1905; 18.3.1905; 3.8.1905; 30.9.1905; 5.10.1905; 23.11.1905. Like #S175.	—	Rare	—

BRITISH LINEN BANK

For previously listed #S181-S196 refer to Vol. II.
For previously listed #S197-S205 refer to Vol. III.

COMMERCIAL BANKING COMPANY OF SCOTLAND / COMMERCIAL BANK OF SCOTLAND

Most early issues printed in black. Uniface.

1810 ISSUE

		GOOD	FINE	XF
S281	1 POUND (ca.1810). Sm. vignette of Edinburgh Castle at upper ctr.			
	a. Issued note.	—	—	—
	x. Contemporary forgery.	—	—	—

NOTE: 5, 20 and 100 Pounds notes are also reported, but none appear to have survived.

1818 ISSUE

		GOOD	FINE	XF
S285	1 GUINEA 1.10.1818. Similar to #S281.	400.00	1000.	—

		GOOD	FINE	XF
S286	1 POUND (ca.1818); 1.5.1826. Larger vignette of Edinburgh Castle at upper l.			
	a. Payable to Edwd. Robertson.	450.00	1250.	—
	b. Payable to Robert Paul (from 1823).	450.00	1250.	—
	c. Ornamental frame ovpt. (1825).	450.00	1250.	—
	x. Contemporary forgery.	—	—	—
S287	5 POUNDS (ca.1820).	400.00	1200.	—

NOTE: The 5 Pounds was probably not issued until after 1820. 20 and 100 Pound notes are presumed to have been issued, but no record exists.

1826 ISSUE

		GOOD	FINE	XF
S289	1 POUND (ca.1826). Edinburgh Castle flanked by medallions. Engraved by W. H. Lizars.	—	—	—

1827 ISSUE

		GOOD	FINE	XF
S290	1 POUND (ca.1827). Edinburgh Castle flanked by medallions, the l. w/Kg. George IV and the r. w/allegorical figure of Caledonia. At bottom is medallion w/allegory of Commerce. Printed revenue stamp on back. Printer: Perkins & Heath (later Perkins Bacon & Co.).	400.00	1000.	—

COMMERCIAL BANK OF SCOTLAND

The bank received its Royal Charter in 1832, and printing plates were modified.

1832 ISSUE

		GOOD	FINE	XF
S291	1 POUND (ca.1832-44). Similar to #S290 but portr. of Kg. William IV.			
	a. Payable to Robert Paul (1832).	400.00	1000.	—
	b. Payable to J. S. Cunningham; partly printed # (1835).	400.00	1000.	—
	c. Entire serial # printed (1844).	400.00	1000.	—

1833 ISSUE

#S292 and S293 from plates by W. H. Lizars. Kg. William IV at l., Edinburgh Castle at upper ctr. Printed revenue stamp on back.

		GOOD	FINE	XF
S292	5 POUNDS 2.6.1835.	2500.	5000.	—
S293	10 POUNDS (ca.1833). Additional portr. in design.	—	—	—

1848 ISSUE

		GOOD	FINE	XF
S294	1 POUND (ca.1848). Qn. Victoria at l., arms at ctr., Prince Albert at r. Bank at bottom. Elaborate design w/revenue stamp on back. Plate by W. H. Lizars.	400.00	1000.	—

1850 ISSUE

#S295-S299 from steel plates by W. H. Lizars. Allegorical classic figures at upper ctr., portrs. of Qn. Victoria and Prince Albert as before. Bank at bottom. Printed revenue stamp on back. Printed serial #, hand dated.

		GOOD	FINE	XF
S295	1 POUND (ca.1850).	300.00	650.00	—
S296	5 POUNDS (ca.1850).	400.00	1000.	—

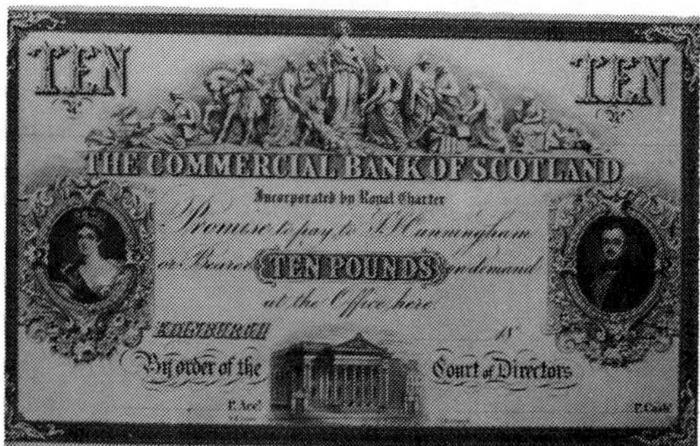

		GOOD	FINE	XF
S297	10 POUNDS (ca.1850).	400.00	1000.	—
S298	20 POUNDS (ca.1850).	400.00	1000.	—
S299	100 POUNDS (ca.1850).	—	—	—

1856 ISSUE

#S300-S304 similar to #S295-S299 but w/o royal portrs. No printed revenue stamp on back. Printer: PBC.

		GOOD	FINE	XF
S300	1 POUND (ca.1856).	300.00	650.00	—
S301	5 POUNDS (ca.1856).	400.00	1000.	—
S302	10 POUNDS (ca.1856).	400.00	1000.	—
S303	20 POUNDS (ca.1856).	400.00	1000.	—
S304	100 POUNDS (ca.1856).	—	—	—

1860 ISSUE

#S305-S309 blue w/lithographic overlay of protector across ctr. in red. Like #S300-S304.

		GOOD	FINE	XF
S305	1 POUND (ca.1860); 1.11.1864.	300.00	650.00	—
S306	5 POUNDS (ca.1860).	300.00	650.00	—
S307	10 POUNDS (ca.1860).	400.00	1000.	—
S308	20 POUNDS (ca.1860).	400.00	1000.	—
S309	100 POUNDS (ca.1860).	—	—	—

COMMERCIAL BANK OF SCOTLAND LIMITED

Because the principle of limited liability was assumed in 1882, the bank name was modified to include *LIMITED* in its title.

1882 ISSUE

#S310-S314 blue and red. Similar to #S305-S309.

		GOOD	FINE	XF
S310	1 POUND (ca.1882).			
	a. Serial # in red.	—	—	—
	b. Serial # in black.	300.00	600.00	—
S311	5 POUNDS (ca.1882).	300.00	650.00	—
S312	10 POUNDS (ca.1882).	400.00	1000.	—
S313	20 POUNDS (ca.1882).	400.00	1000.	—

		GOOD	FINE	XF
S314	100 POUNDS (ca.1882); 3.1.1887.	—	—	—

1886; 1887 ISSUE

#S315-S318 blue on buff unpt. Allegorical figures on face. Back green; bank bldg. at ctr. Printer: BWC.

		GOOD	FINE	XF
S315	1 POUND 1886-1906.			
	a. Handsigned. Imprint: Bradbury Wilkinson & Co. 1.7.1886-2.1.1892.	250.00	550.00	—
	b. Printed sign. of Accountant. Imprint: Bradbury Wilkinson & Co. Ltd. 2.1.1892-4.1.1906.	250.00	550.00	—

		Good	Fine	XF
S316	**5 Pounds** 3.1.1887-2.1.1906.	300.00	650.00	—
S317	**20 Pounds** 3.1.1887-4.1.1906.	400.00	1000.	—
S318	**100 Pounds** 3.1.1887-2.1.1907.	—	—	—

1907; 1908 Issue

#S319-S322 blue on buff unpt. Printer: BWC.

		Good	Fine	XF
S319	**1 Pound** 2.1.1907; 2.1.1908. Bldgs. at l. and r., group of allegorical figures at bottom.	150.00	375.00	800.00
S320	**5 Pounds** 2.1.1908. Like #S319.	400.00	1000.	2250.
S321	**20 Pounds** 2.1.1907. Like #S319.	—	Rare	—
S322	**100 Pounds** 2.1.1907. Like #S319.	—	Rare	—

1908-10 Issue

#S323-S326 similar to previous issue but oval frame around bldgs. at l. and r.

		Good	Fine	XF
S323	**1 Pound** 1909-23. Similar to #S319.			
	a. Printed sign. of *ACCOUNTANT*, handsigned on behalf of the *CASHIER*. 2.1.1909-2.1.1914.	75.00	225.00	500.00
	b. Printed sign. of *ACCOUNTANT* and *CASHIER. 2.1.1914-2.1.1923.*	50.00	150.00	350.00

		Good	Fine	XF
S324	**5 Pounds** 2.1.1909-2.1.1923. Like #S323.	150.00	350.00	650.00
S325	**20 Pounds** 3.1.1910-2.1.1923. Like #S323.	175.00	400.00	850.00
S326	**100 Pounds** 2.1.1908-2.1.1923. Like #S323.	350.00	750.00	—

1924 Issue

		VG	VF	Unc
S327	**1 Pound** 31.10.1924; 31.10.1925; 1.11.1926. Blue on yellow and orange. Portr. John Pitcairn at bottom.	50.00	175.00	400.00
S328	**5 Pounds** 1924-44. Like #S327.			
	a. Printed sign. of *ACCOUNTANT* and handsigned on behalf of the *MANAGER*. 31.10.1924-1.11.1926.	50.00	175.00	400.00
	b. Printed sign. of *CASHIER* and *GENERAL MANAGER*. 1.12.1928-1.12.1944.	30.00	100.00	250.00
S329	**20 Pounds** 1924-43. Like #S327.			
	a. Printed sign. of *ACCOUNTANT* and handsigned on behalf of the *MANAGER*. 31.10.1924; 1.5.1925.	100.00	350.00	750.00
	b. Printed sign. of *CASHIER* and *GENERAL MANAGER*. 1.5.1928-4.1.1943.	50.00	175.00	400.00
S330	**100 Pounds** 1924-43. Like #S327.			
	a. Printed sign. of *ACCOUNTANT* and handsigned on behalf of the *MANAGER*. 31.10.1924; 1.12.1928.	300.00	800.00	—
	b. Printed sign. of *CASHIER* and *GENERAL MANAGER*. 30.9.1937; 1.8.1940; 2.1.1943.	250.00	600.00	—

1927 Issue

#S331-S335 printer: W&S.

		VG	VF	Unc
S331	**1 Pound** 1.12.1927-2.12.1944. Blue on yellow and orange. Like #S327 but 150 x 85mm.			
	a. Sign. titles: *ACCOUNTANT* and *CASHIER*. 1.12.1927-4.5.1939.	10.00	35.00	85.00
	b. Sign. titles: *CHIEF ACCOUNTANT* and *CASHIER*. 6.8.1940-2.12.1944.	7.50	25.00	60.00

1947 Issue

		VG	VF	Unc
S332	**1 Pound** 2.1.1947-2.1.1953. Lilac. Lord Cockburn at r.	7.50	25.00	60.00

		VG	VF	UNC
S333	**5 POUNDS** 2.1.1947-2.1.1958. Violet. Lord Cockburn at upper ctr. Bank bldg. at ctr., people at l. and r. on back.	20.00	60.00	150.00
S334	**20 POUNDS** 2.1.1947-2.1.1958. Blue. Lord Cockburn at upper ctr. Back like #S333.	40.00	100.00	300.00
S335	**100 POUNDS** 2.1.1947; 3.1.1951; 2.1.1953. Green. Lord Cockburn at upper ctr. Back like #S333.	250.00	550.00	1250.

1954 ISSUE

		VG	VF	UNC
S336	**1 POUND** 2.1.1954-1.7.1958. Blue. Like #S332.	7.50	25.00	60.00

NATIONAL BANK OF SCOTLAND

Previously listed #S541-S555 is now in Vol. II.

NATIONAL BANK OF SCOTLAND LIMITED

Previously listed #S556-S576 is now in Vol. II.

NATIONAL COMMERCIAL BANK OF SCOTLAND LIMITED

Previously listed #S591-S594 is now in Vol. II.
For previously listed #S595-S601 refer to Vol. III.

NORTH OF SCOTLAND BANKING COMPANY

1836 ISSUE

#S611-S613 black. Kings College, Aberdeen, at upper ctr., seated allegorical woman at l., standing allegorical woman at r. Hand dated and numbered. Uniface. Printer: W. H. Lizars.

		GOOD	FINE	XF
S611	**1 POUND** (ca.1836).	400.00	1000.	—
S612	**5 POUNDS** (ca.1836).	400.00	1000.	—

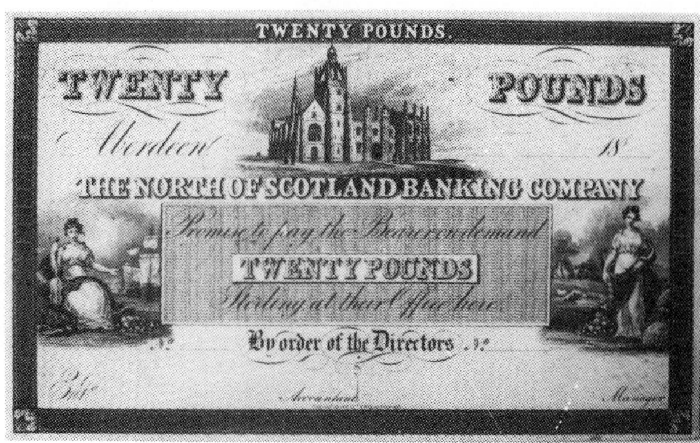

		GOOD	FINE	XF
S613	**20 POUNDS** (ca.1836).	—	—	—

1863 ISSUE

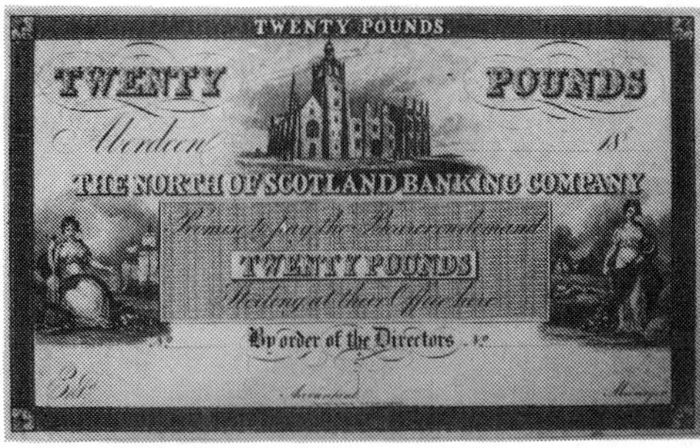

		GOOD	FINE	XF
S614	**5 POUNDS** (ca.1863). Similar to #S612 but modified frame includes text: *ESTABLISHED 1836 INCORPORATED 1862.*			
	a. Black.	300.00	650.00	—
	b. Black w/red protector: *FIVE* across face.	300.00	650.00	—

1865 ISSUE

#S615-S618 black w/red protector. Sm. arms at lower ctr. Back blue. Printer: W. & A. K. Johnston.

		GOOD	FINE	XF
S615	**1 POUND** (ca.1865). Kings College at upper ctr.	300.00	650.00	—
S616	**5 POUNDS** (ca.1865). Similar to #S614.	300.00	650.00	—
S617	**20 POUNDS** (ca.1865). Similar to #S613 w/added panel of text like #S616.	400.00	1000.	—
S618	**100 POUNDS** (ca.1865). Similar to #S617.	—	—	—

1871 ISSUE

		GOOD	FINE	XF
S619	**1 POUND** 29.9.1871. Black w/green denomination panel across ctr. Similar to #S615. Printer: PBC.	300.00	650.00	—

NORTH OF SCOTLAND BANK LTD.

1882 ISSUE

#S620-S624 w/new title. Similar to previous issues. Printer: W. & A. K. Johnston.

		Good	Fine	XF
S620	**1 POUND** (ca.1882); 1.10.1903; 1.8.1907. Similar to #S619.	300.00	650.00	—
S621	**5 POUNDS** (ca.1882). Similar to #S616.	300.00	650.00	—
S622	**10 POUNDS** (ca.1882). Similar to #S616.	300.00	650.00	—
S623	**20 POUNDS** (ca.1882). Similar to #S617.	400.00	1000.	—
S624	**100 POUNDS** (ca.1882). Similar to #S618.	—	—	—

NORTH OF SCOTLAND & TOWN & COUNTY BANK LTD.

Formerly the North of Scotland Bank Ltd; later in 1923 it reverted to North of Scotland Bank Ltd. In 1950 it amalgamated with the Clydesdale Bank.

1908 PROVISIONAL ISSUE

New bank name ovpt. on North of Scotland Bank Ltd. notes.

		Good	Fine	XF
S625	**1 POUND** ND (ca.1908-old date 1.8.1907).	300.00	650.00	1350.
S626	**5 POUNDS** ND (ca.1908).	—	Rare	—
S627	**20 POUNDS** ND (ca.1908).	—	Rare	—
S628	**100 POUNDS** ND (ca.1908).	—	Rare	—

1909; 1910 ISSUE

#S629-S632 Marischal College at top ctr.

		Good	Fine	XF
S629	**1 POUND** 1.3.1910-1.3.1918. Blue and green on yellow unpt.	50.00	175.00	400.00
S630	**5 POUNDS** 1909-18. Blue and green on yellow unpt.	150.00	350.00	750.00
S631	**20 POUNDS** 1909-18. Purple and green on yellow unpt.	450.00	—	—
S632	**100 POUNDS** 1909-18. Brown and green on yellow unpt.	—	Rare	—

NORTH OF SCOTLAND BANK LIMITED

1923 PROVISIONAL ISSUE

		Good	Fine	XF
S633	**1 POUND** ND (ca.1923). Ovpt. on #S629.			
	a. Hand stamped ovpt.	100.00	250.00	550.00
	b. Printed ovpt.	85.00	200.00	450.00
S634	**5 POUNDS** ND (ca.1923). Hand stamped ovpt. on #S630.	150.00	350.00	750.00
S635	**20 POUNDS** ND (ca.1923). Hand stamped ovpt. on #S631.	250.00	—	—
S636	**100 POUNDS** ND (ca.1923). Hand stamped ovpt. on #S632.	—	Rare	—

1924-35 ISSUES

#S637 *Deleted.*

		VG	VF	Unc
S638	**1 POUND** 1924; 1926. Blue and green on yellow unpt. Reduced size.			
	a. Printed sign. of *GENERAL MANAGER* and handsigned on behalf of the *ACCOUNTANT.* 1.3.1924; 1.3.1926.	25.00	65.00	150.00
	b. As a. but printed sign. of *ACCOUNTANT.* 1.3.1926.	60.00	150.00	350.00

		VG	VF	UNC
S639	**1 POUND** 1.3.1928; 1.3.1932; 1.3.1935. Blue and green on yellow unpt. *1* instead of £1 at l. and r. of bldg. at top.	10.00	40.00	100.00

		VG	VF	UNC
S640	**5 POUNDS** 1.3.1928-1.3.1934. Brown and green on yellow unpt. Like #S630.	40.00	175.00	450.00
S641	**20 POUNDS** 1928-1.3.1930; 1.3.1934. Brown, purple and olive-green on ochre unpt. Like #S631.	125.00	400.00	1000.
S642	**100 POUNDS** 1928-34 (1.3.1930 confirmed). Brown on lt. blue, green and orange unpt. Like #S632.	300.00	750.00	—

#S643 Deleted.

1938 ISSUE

		VG	VF	UNC
S644	**1 POUND** 1.7.1938-1.7.1949. Blue and green on yellow unpt.	7.50	30.00	85.00
S645	**5 POUNDS** 1938-1.7.1949. Red.	20.00	50.00	125.00

		VG	VF	UNC
S646	**20 POUNDS** 1938-1.7.1949. Green.	50.00	125.00	300.00
S647	**100 POUNDS** 1938-49.	200.00	500.00	1250.

UNION BANK OF SCOTLAND

1843 ISSUE

#S776-S780 black. Names of four constituent banks in border. Uniface. Printer: W. H. Lizars.

		GOOD	FINE	XF
S776	**1 POUND** 1.7.1843. Equestrian statue at upper l. and r., allegorical women at lower l. and r.	—	—	—
S777	**5 POUNDS** (ca.1843). Similar to #S776 but different allegorical figures.	—	—	—
S778	**10 POUNDS** (ca.1843). 3 allegorical figures at upper ctr., equestrian statues at lower l. and r.	—	—	—
S779	**20 POUNDS** (ca.1843). Front view of 2 equestrian statues at upper l. and r., allegorical figures at lower l. and r.	—	—	—
S780	**100 POUNDS** (ca.1843). Sm. portr. of Qn. Victoria w/2 allegorical women at ctr., front view of 2 equestrian statues at lower l. and r.	—	—	—

NOTE: #S776-S779 payable at Edinburgh, #S780 payable at Glasgow.

1846 ISSUE

#S781-S784 two more bank names added to border for a total of six, otherwise like previous issue.

		GOOD	FINE	XF
S781	**1 POUND** (ca.1846).	—	—	—
S782	**5 POUNDS** (ca.1846).	—	—	—
S782A	**10 POUNDS** (ca.1846).	—	—	—
S783	**20 POUNDS** (ca.1846).	—	—	—
S784	**100 POUNDS** (ca.1846).	—	—	—

NOTE: #S781-S782A, S784 payable at Edinburgh, #S783 payable at Glasgow.

1850 ISSUE

		GOOD	FINE	XF
S785	**1 POUND** (ca.1850). Additional bank name added to border for total of 7, otherwise similar to #S781.	—	—	—

#S786-S789 equestrian statue of William of Orange at upper ctr. Vertical panel at l. contains names of six constituent banks in ovals. Circular panel on back. Printer: PB&P.

		GOOD	FINE	XF
S786	**5 POUNDS** (ca.1850).	—	—	—
S787	**10 POUNDS** (ca.1850).	—	—	—
S788	**20 POUNDS** (ca.1850).	—	—	—
S789	**100 POUNDS** (ca.1850).	—	—	—

1855 ISSUE

		GOOD	FINE	XF
S790	**1 POUND** (ca.1855). Similar to #S785 but back printed in blue w/equestrian statue design.	400.00	1000.	—

1863 ISSUE

#S791-S792D added text: *Incorporated by Act of Parliament*.

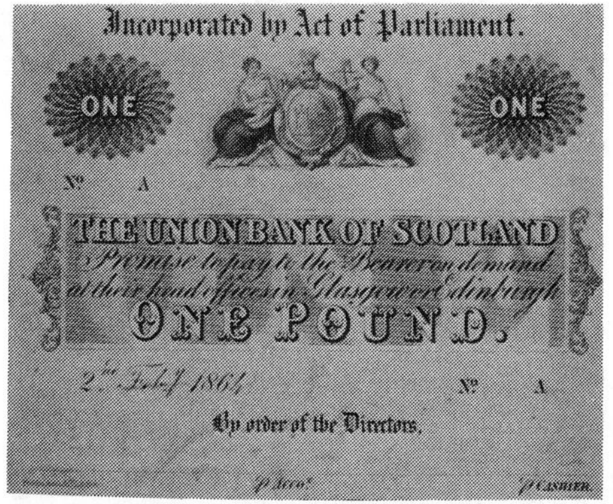

		GOOD	FINE	XF
S791	**1 POUND** (ca.1863-65) 2.2.1864. Blue. Arms of bank flanked by panels w/value. *ONE* in lg. letters across legend panel in green. Printer: PBC.			
	a. Issued note.	400.00	1000.	—
	x. Contemporary forgery. 1.11.1865.	—	—	—
S792	**5 POUNDS** 1.5.1863. Black. Imprint: W. & A. K. Johnston. Specimen.	—	—	—

1866 ISSUE

		GOOD	FINE	XF
S792A	**5 POUNDS** 2.11.1866. Black. Similar to #S791. Proof.	—	—	—
S792D	**100 POUNDS** 2.11.1866. Black. Similar to #S791. Proof.	—	—	—

1867 ISSUE

#S793-S797 black w/green protector. Bank arms flanked by value panels at upper ctr. Equestrian statues of William of Orange at lower l. and Charles II at lower r. Printed dates and serial #. Printer: PBC.

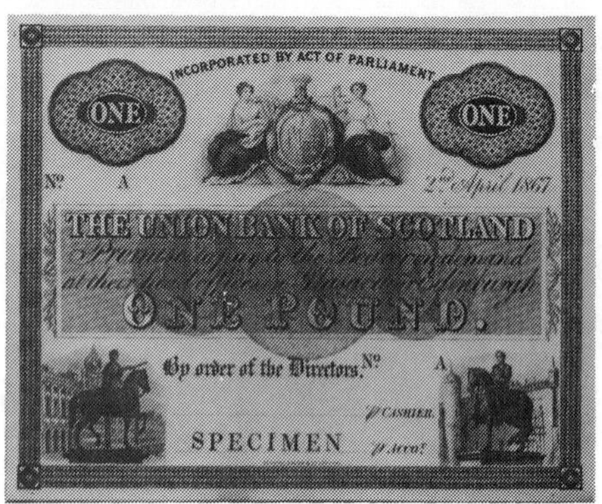

		Good	Fine	XF
S793	**1 POUND**			
	2.4.1867.			
	a. Issued note.	400.00	1000.	—
	s. Specimen.	—	Unc	250.00
S794	**5 POUNDS**			
	2.4.1867. Specimen.	—	Unc	350.00
S795	**10 POUNDS**			
	2.4.1867. Specimen.	—	Unc	350.00

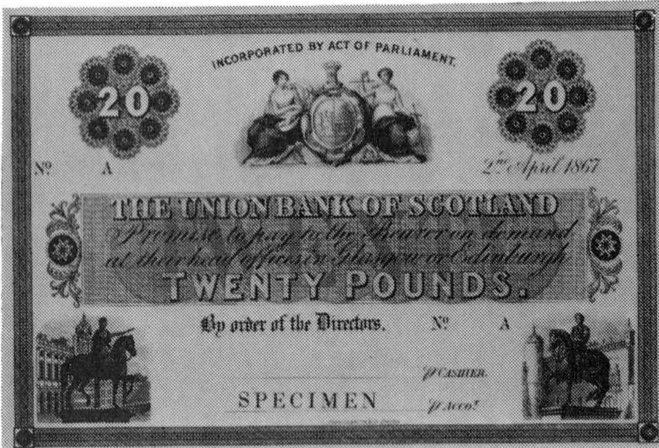

		Good	Fine	XF
S796	**20 POUNDS**			
	2.4.1867. Specimen.	—	Unc	400.00

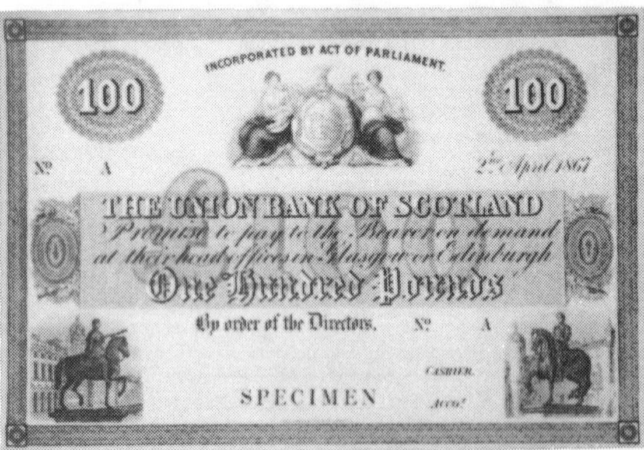

		Good	Fine	XF
S797	**100 POUNDS**			
	2.4.1867. Specimen.	—	Unc	400.00

1872 ISSUE

		Good	Fine	XF
S798	**100 POUNDS**			
	(ca.1872). Similar to #S797 but curved bank title at top, and other sm. differences in design. Printer: PBC.	—	—	—

UNION BANK OF SCOTLAND LTD.

Upon assuming limited liability in 1882, the bank name was changed to include the word *LIMITED.*

1882-93 ISSUE

#S799-S803 similar to previous issue but modified plates for altered bank name. Denomination wording across face in dk. red.

		Good	Fine	XF
S799	**1 POUND**			
	15.4.1882-29.8.1902. Handwritten sign. w/title: *ACCOUNTANT*. Back blue.			
	a. Issued note.	300.00	650.00	—
	s. Specimen.	—	Unc	250.00

		Good	Fine	XF
S800	**5 POUNDS**			
	(ca.1882-1905).			
	a. Issued note.	400.00	1000.	—
	s. Specimen. 3.4.1893.	—	Unc	250.00
S801	**10 POUNDS**			
	1893. Specimen.	—	Unc	250.00
S802	**20 POUNDS**			
	2.4.1891. Specimen.	—	Unc	300.00

		Good	Fine	XF
S803	**100 POUNDS**			
	2.4.1891; 7.4.1905. Specimen.	—	Unc	400.00

1903 ISSUE

		Good	Fine	XF
S804	**1 POUND**			
	10.3.1903; 3.5.1904. Like #S799 but printed sign. of *ACCOUNTANT*.	300.00	650.00	—

1905-06 ISSUE

#S805-S815 equestrian statues at lower l. and r., arms at top ctr. flanked by 2 allegorical women at l. and r.

#S805-S809 blue on red unpt. Value at ctr. Back blue. Printer: W&S.

		Good	Fine	XF
S805	**1 POUND**			
	6.4.1905-10.12.1920.	85.00	200.00	500.00
S806	**5 POUNDS**			
	25.2.1905-18.8.1920.	200.00	450.00	850.00
S807	**10 POUNDS**			
	4.4.1905; 15.10.1913; 23.3.1917; 28.2.1918; 6.8.1920.	350.00	750.00	1500.
S808	**20 POUNDS**			
	31.3.1905-4.6.1920.	350.00	750.00	1500.
S809	**100 POUNDS**			
	7.4.1905; 27.3.1906; 4.11.1913; 9.11.1915; 2.4.1919.	—	Rare	—

1921-23 ISSUE

#S810-S815 unpt. in the form of a sunburst printed in orange and red. Printer: W&S.

		VG	VF	Unc
S810	**1 POUND**			
	1.10.1921; 2.11.1923. Blue. Printed sign. of *GENERAL MANAGER* and *CASHIER*.	100.00	350.00	750.00

		VG	VF	UNC
S811	**5 POUNDS** 1921-49. Blue.			
	a. Printed sign. of *GENERAL MANAGER* and handsigned on behalf of the *CASHIER*. 5.4.1921; 4.5.1923.	75.00	175.00	400.00
	b. As a. but w/printed sign. of the *CASHIER*. 4.8.1923; 5.4.1926; 15.1.1927.	60.00	150.00	350.00
	c. Printed sign. of *GENERAL MANAGER* and *CHIEF ACCOUNTANT*. 6.7.1928-18.5.1936	40.00	100.00	250.00
	d. Printed sign. of *GENERAL MANAGER* and *CASHIER*. 18.8.1937-3.5.1949.	30.00	80.00	200.00
S812	**10 POUNDS** 3.8.1923-8.7.1935. Blue.			
	a. Printed sign. of *GENERAL MANAGER* and handsigned on behalf of the *CASHIER*. 3.8.1923.	100.00	350.00	750.00
	b. Printed sign. of *GENERAL MANAGER* and *CHIEF ACCOUNTANT*. 4.7.1928; 8.12.1933; 8.7.1935.	90.00	300.00	650.00

		VG	VF	UNC
S813	**20 POUNDS** 1923-47. Blue.			
	a. Handsigned on behalf of the *GENERAL MANAGER* and the *CASHIER*. 2.8.1923; 3.7.1928; 2.8.1932; 5.9.1933; 2.10.1934; 14.8.1935.	90.00	300.00	650.00
	b. Handsigned on behalf of the *GENERAL MANAGER* and the *CHIEF ACCOUNTANT*. 31.5.1937; 30.3.1938; 30.11.1938; 3.1.1939; 1.6.1940; 2.1.1942.	75.00	175.00	400.00
	c. Printed sign. of the *GENERAL MANAGER* and the *CASHIER*. 30.4.1942; 1.2.1943; 10.7.1944; 2.12.1946; 1.9.1947.	60.00	150.00	350.00
S814	**100 POUNDS** 1923-47. Blue.			
	a. Handsigned on behalf of the *GENERAL MANAGER* and the *CASHIER*. 1.8.1923; 1.3.1939; 2.1.1942.	250.00	500.00	1250.
	b. Handsigned on behalf of the *GENERAL MANAGER* and the *CHIEF ACCOUNTANT*. 30.6.1928; 10.4.1931; 10.8.1931; 1.12.1933; 20.5.1936.	225.00	450.00	900.00
	c. Printed sign. of the *GENERAL MANAGER* and the *CHIEF ACCOUNTANT*. 18.2.1947.	225.00	400.00	850.00

1924 ISSUE

		VG	VF	UNC
S815	**1 POUND** 1924-48. Blue, red, orange and yellow. Reduced size.			
	a. Printed sign. of *GENERAL MANAGER* and *CASHIER*. 2.6.1924; 4.1.1926; 3.10.1927.	20.00	60.00	175.00
	b. Printed sign. of *GENERAL MANAGER* and *CHIEF ACCOUNTANT*. 2.1.1929-31.3.1936.	15.00	50.00	125.00
	c. Printed sign. of *GENERAL MANAGER* and *CASHIER*. 12.2.1937-1.6.1948.	12.50	40.00	100.00

1949-50 ISSUE

#S816-S819 blue on red, orange and yellow unpt. Arms at l., sailboat at r. Industrial and shipping scene on back. Printer: W&S.

		VG	VF	UNC
S816	**1 POUND** 1949-54.			
	a. Sign. of J. A. Morrison. 1.3.1949-1.9.1953.	10.00	25.00	75.00
	b. Sign. of Sir W. Watson. 1.6.1954.	20.00	60.00	175.00

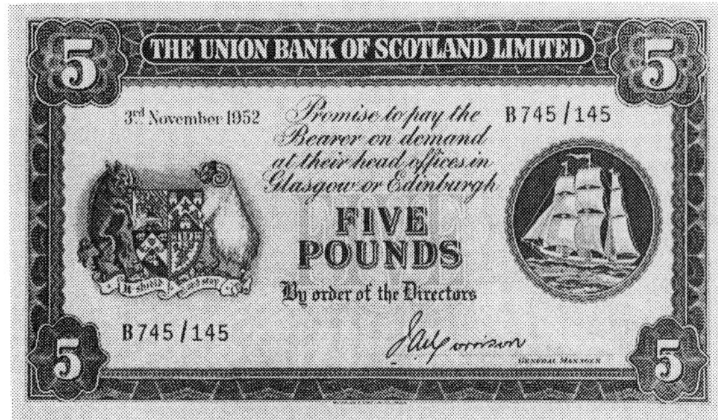

		VG	VF	UNC
S817	**5 POUNDS** 1950-54.			
	a. Sign. of J. A. Morrison. 17.7.1950-1.10.1953.	20.00	60.00	175.00
	b. Sign. of Sir W. Watson. 2.4.1954.	85.00	200.00	550.00
S818	**20 POUNDS** 1.9.1950-1.5.1953.	50.00	150.00	400.00
S819	**100 POUNDS** 1950-54.			
	a. Sign. of J. A. Morrison. 9.10.1950; 10.3.1952.	225.00	450.00	900.00
	b. Sign. of Sir W. Watson. 1.10.1954. (100 notes issued).	—	Rare	—

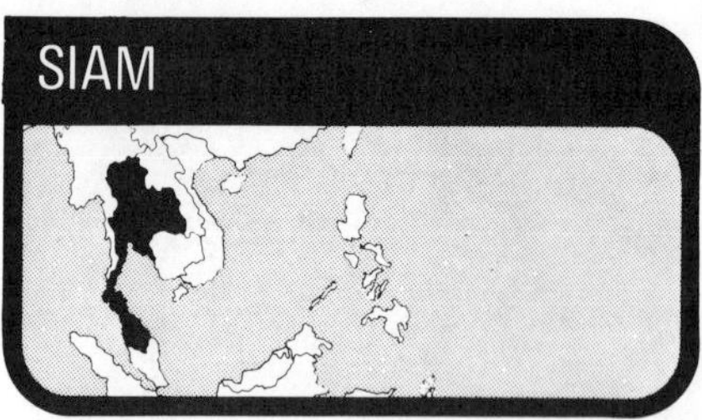

Siam (now the Kingdom of Thailand), a constitutional monarchy located in the center of mainland southeast Asia between Burma and Laos, has an area of 198,457 sq. mi. (514,000 sq. km). Capital: Bangkok.

The history of Siam, the only country in south and southeast Asia that was never colonized by a European power, dates from the 6th century AD when tribes of the Thai stock migrated into the area from the Asiatic continent, a process that accelerated with the Mongol invasion of China in the 13th century. After 400 years of sporadic warfare with the neighboring Burmese, King Taksin won the last battle in 1767. He founded a new capital, Dhonburi, on the west bank of Chao Praya River. King Rama I moved the capital to Bangkok in 1782.

The Thai were introduced to the Western world by the Portuguese, who were followed by the Dutch, British and French. Rama III of the present ruling dynasty negotiated a treaty of friendship and commerce with Britain in 1826, and in 1896 the independece of the kingdom was guaranteed by an Anglo-French accord.

RULERS:

Rama V (Phra Maha Chulalongkorn), 1868-1910
Rama VI (Vajiravudh), 1910-1925
Rama VII (Prajadhipok), 1925-1935
Rama VIII (Ananda Mahidol), 1935-1946
Rama IX (Bhumiphol Adulyadej), 1946-

MONETARY SYSTEM:

1 (Tical) Baht = 100 Satang

KINGDOM

BANQUE DE L'INDOCHINE

BANGKOK

DÉCRETS DES 21.1.1875 ET 20.2.1898

#S101-S104 Chinese and Thai language text on back. No issued notes known.

S101	**5 TICALS** 19.12.1898. Blue-green. Oriental woman holding bamboo staff seated below France seated holding caduceus at l. Specimen.	—	Rare	—
S102	**20 TICALS** 6.12.1898. Brown. Neptune reclining holding trident at lower l. Specimen.	—	Rare	—
S103	**80 TICALS** 7.11.1898. Blue. Elephant at l. and r., two reclining women w/animals at lower ctr. Specimen.	—	Rare	—
S104	**100 TICALS** 31.2.1898. Red. Vasco da Gama at l., sailing ships at lower ctr., Polynesian man w/paddle by dragon boat at r. Specimen.	—	Rare	—

CHARTERED BANK OF INDIA, AUSTRALIA AND CHINA

BANGKOK

1898 ISSUE

#S111-S117 crowned supported royal arms at top ctr. Stamped dates. Thai language text on back. Printer: WWS.

		GOOD	FINE	XF
S111	**1 TICAL** 1.9.1898. Black on purple unpt. Back green.	1500.	3000.	—
S112	**5 TICALS** 1898; 1.9.1899. Blue, pink and red.	—	6500.	—
S113	**10 TICALS** (ca.1898). Brown, pink and blue.	—	Rare	—
S114	**20 TICALS** (ca.1898). Green, pink and orange.	—	Rare	—
S115	**40 TICALS** (ca.1898). Orange, pink and green.	—	Rare	—

		GOOD	FINE	XF
S116	**80 TICALS** 1.5.1898. Gray, pink and brown.	—	Rare	—
S117	**400 TICALS** (ca.1898). Red, pink and mauve.	—	Rare	—

HONGKONG AND SHANGHAI BANKING CORPORATION

BANGKOK

1889-99 ISSUE

#S121-S127 crowned supported royal arms at top ctr. Hand dated. Thai language text on back. Printer: BFL.

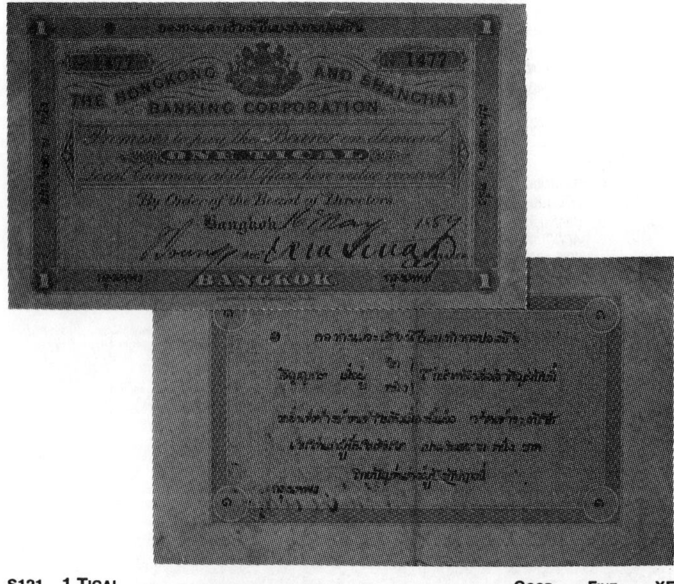

		GOOD	FINE	XF
S121	**1 TICAL** 16.5.1889; 1.7.1890; 1.8.1891; 1.8.1901. Orange on gray unpt.	2200.	4750.	—

NOTE: The 1.7.1890 date is known w/additional 4 Chinese character ovpt. of denomination in l. and r. margins.

		Good	Fine	XF
S122	**5 TICALS** 15.11.1897. Green on pink unpt. Back red-orange. Perforated: *CANCELLED.*			
	r1. Remainder w/ 1 sign.	—	Rare	—
	r2. Remainder w/ 1 sign. w/Chinese character ovpt.	—	Rare	—
S123	**10 TICALS** 6.2.1899. Blue on lt. red ovpt. Back red-orange. Remainder perforated: *CANCELLED.*	—	Rare	—
S124	**40 TICALS** 18xx. Brown on lt. blue ovpt. Back red-orange. Remainder perforated: *CANCELLED.*	—	Rare	—
S125	**80 TICALS** 18xx. Lilac on yellow-orange unpt. Back red-orange. Remainder perforated: *CANCELLED.*	—	Rare	—
S126	**100 TICALS** 18xx. Pink-red on lt. blue ovpt. Back red-orange. Remainder perforated: *CANCELLED.*			
	r1. W/o Chinese character ovpt.	—	Rare	—
	r2. (ca.1891) w/Chinese character ovpt.	—	Rare	—
S127	**400 TICALS** 18xx. Red and green. Ovpt. Back red-orange. Remainder perforated: *CANCELLED.*			
	r1. W/o Chinese character ovpt.	—	Rare	—
	r2. W/ Chinese character ovpt. (ca.1891).	—	Rare	—

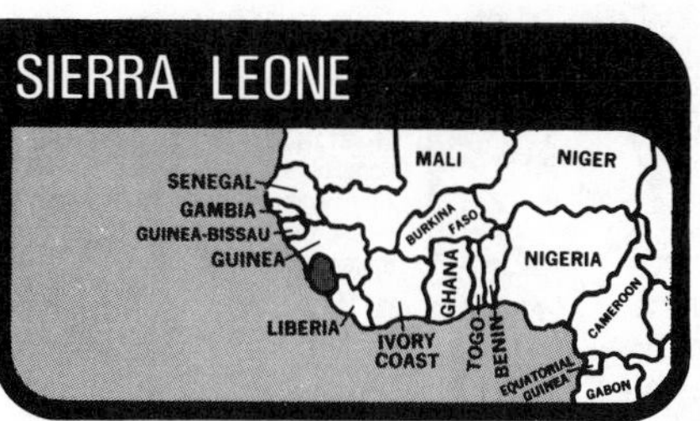

The Republic of Sierra Leone, a British Commonwealth nation located in western Africa between Guinea and Liberia, has an area of 27,699 sq. mi. (71,740 sq. km.) and a population of 4.87 million. Capital: Freetown. The economy is predominantly agricultural but mining contributes significantly to export revenues. Diamonds, iron ore, palm kernels, cocoa and coffee are exported.

The coast of Sierra Leone was first visited by Portuguese and British slavers in the 15th and 16th centuries. The first settlement at Freetown was established in 1787 as a refuge for freed slaves within the British Empire, runaway slaves from the United States and blacks discharged from the British armed forces. The first settlers were virtually wiped out by tribal attacks and disease. The colony was re-established under the auspices of the Sierra Leone Company and transferred to the British Crown in 1907. The interior region was secured and established as a protectorate in 1896. Sierra Leone became independent within the Commonwealth on April 27, 1961, and adopted a republican constitution ten years later. It is a member of the Commonwealth of Nations. The president is Chief of State and Head of Government.

RULERS:
British to 1971

MONETARY SYSTEM:
1 Pound = 20 Shillings

REPUBLIC

COMMERCIAL BANK OF SIERRA LEONE

1865 ISSUE

		Good	Fine	XF
S106	**1 POUND** 12.9.1865. Black. Animals, trees at upper l. Uniface.	2500.	4000.	—

SIERRA LEONE

FREE TOWN

1800'S ISSUE

		Good	Fine	XF
S111	**1 POUND** 18xx. Black. *CHARLES HEDDLE* across ctr. Uniface.			
	a. White paper.	—	Unc	5000.
	b. Green paper.	—	Unc	5000.

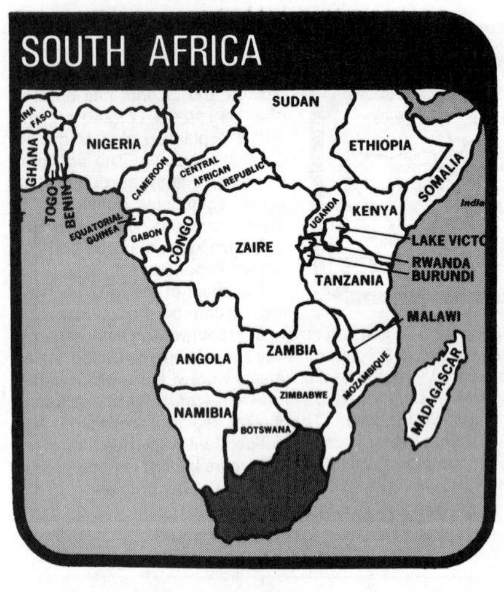

The Republic of South Africa, located at the southern tip of Africa, has an area, including the enclave of Walvis Bay, of 472,359 sq. mi. (1,221,040 sq. km.) and a population of 46.26 million. Capital: Administrative, Pretoria; Legislative, Cape Town; Judicial, Bloemfontein. Manufacturing, mining and agriculture are the principal industries. Exports include wool, diamonds, gold and metallic ores.

Portuguese navigator Bartholomeu Diaz became the first European to sight the region of South Africa when he rounded the Cape of Good Hope in 1488, but throughout the 16th century the only white men to come ashore were the survivors of ships wrecked while attempting the stormy Cape passage. The first permanent settlement was established by Jan van Riebeeck of the Dutch East India Company in 1652. In subsequent decades additional Dutch, Germans and Huguenot refugees from France settled in the Cape area to form the Afrikaner segment of today's population.

Great Britain captured the Cape colony in 1795, and again in 1806, receiving permanent title in 1814. To escape British political rule and cultural dominance, many Afrikaner farmers (Boers) migrated northward (the Great Trek) beginning in 1836, and established the independent Boer republics of the Transvaal (the South African Republic, Zuid-Afrikaansche Republiek) in 1852, and the Orange Free State in 1854. British political intrigues against the two republics, coupled with the discovery of diamonds and gold in the Boer-settled regions, led to the bitter Boer Wars (1880-1881, 1899-1902) and the incorporation of the Boer republics into the British Empire.

On May 31, 1910, the two former Boer republics (Transvaal and Orange Free State) were joined with the British colonies of Cape of Good Hope and Natal to form the Union of South Africa, a dominion of the British Empire. In 1934 the Union achieved status as a sovereign state within the British Empire. Political integration of the various colonies did not still the conflict between the Afrikaners and the English-speaking groups, which continued to have a significant impact on political developments. A resurgence of Afrikaner nationalism in the 1940s and 1950s led to a referendum in the white community authorizing the relinquishment of dominion status and the establishment of a republic. The decision took effect on May 31, 1961. The Republic of South Africa withdrew from the British Commonwealth in Oct., 1961. The apartheid era ended on April 27, 1994 with the first democratic election for all people of South Africa. Nelson Mandela was inaugurated as president on May 10, 1994. South Africa was readmitted to the Commonwealth of Nations.

South African currency carries inscriptions in both Afrikaans and English.

RULERS:

British to 1961

MONETARY SYSTEM:

1 Shilling = 12 Pence
1 Pound = 20 Shillings to 1961
1 Rand = 100 Cents (= 10 Shillings), 1961-

The major areas comprising this section are covered individually according to the following outline:

CAPE OF GOOD HOPE

Many notes issued at Cape Town.

IMPERIAL BANKS:

London and South African Bank .... #S106-S108
Oriental Bank Corporation .... #S110-S115
Standard Bank of British South Africa .... #S116-S117

COMMERCIAL BANKS:

Agricultural Bank of Queenstown .... #S121
Bank of South Africa .... #S131-S146
Beaufort Bank .... #S151
British Kaffrarian Bank .... #S156-S157
Cape Commercial Bank .... #S161-S163
Cape of Good Hope Bank .... #S171-S179
Colesburg Bank .... #S180-S182
Commercial Bank of Port Elizabeth .... #S191
Fort Beaufort & Victoria Bank .... #S196-S198
Frontier Commercial & Agricultural Bank .... #S201-S202
George Divisional Bank .... #S211
Graaf Reinet Bank .... #S216-S217
Kaffrarian Colonial Bank .... #S221
Malmesbury Agricultural & Commercial Bank .... #S226
Montagu Bank .... #S231
Paarl Bank .... #S236
Port Elizabeth Bank .... #S241-S243
Queenstown Bank .... #S251-S253
Somerset East Bank .... #S256-S258
South African Bank .... #S261-S263
South African Central Bank .... #S271
Stellenbosch Bank .... #S276
Stellenbosch District Bank .... #S281
Swellendam Bank .... #S286
Wellington Bank .... #S291
Western Province Bank .... #S296
Worcester Commercial Bank .... #S301

CAPE UNIFORM BANKNOTES:

African Banking Corporation Limited .... #S321-S325
Bank of Africa Limited .... #S331-S335
National Bank of South Africa Limited .... #S341-S345
Standard Bank of South Africa Limited .... #S351-S355

GRIQUALAND

Government of New Griqualand .... #S361

NATAL

Many notes issued at Durban.

IMPERIAL BANKS:

African Banking Corporation Limited .... #S367-S370
Bank of Africa Limited .... #S381-S382
National Bank of South Africa Limited .... #S391-S395
Oriental Bank Corporation .... #S397
Standard Bank of British South Africa Limited .... #S401-S402
Standard Bank of South Africa Limited .... #S406-S425

COMMERCIAL BANKS:

Colonial Bank of Natal .... #S431-S433
Commercial and Agricultural Bank of Natal .... #S436
Durban Bank .... #S440-S444
London and Natal Bank .... #S451-S454
Natal Bank Limited .... #S462-S469

ORANGE RIVER COLONY/ORANGE FREE STATE

Many notes issued at Bloemfontein.

IMPERIAL BANKS:

African Banking Corporation Limited .... #S471-S474
Bank of Africa Limited .... #S482-S485
National Bank of South Africa Limited .... #S491-S495
Standard Bank of South Africa Limited .... #S498-S505

COMMERCIAL BANKS:

Bloemfontein Bank .... #S507-S513
Fauresmith Bank .... #S521-S527
Nationale Bank van den Oranje Vrystaat .... #S531
National Bank of the Orange River Colony Limited .... #S537-S540
Orange Free State Government .... #S541-S549

TRANSVAAL

Many notes issued at Pretoria and Johannesburg.

IMPERIAL BANKS:

African Banking Corporation Limited .... #S551-S556
Bank of Africa Limited .... #S562-S566
National Bank of South Africa Limited .... #S571-S578
Standard Bank of British South Africa Limited .... #S579-S582
Standard Bank of South Africa Limited .... #S583-S589

PRIVATE BANKS:

Cape of Good Hope Bank .... #S597
Cape Commercial Bank .... #S601-S602
Natal Bank Limited .... #S613-S615
Nederlandsche Bank & Crediet Vereeniging voor Zuid-Afrika .... #S621-S624
Nederlandsche Bank voor Zuid-Afrika/Netherlands Bank of South Africa .... #S625-S636

BOER WAR ISSUES

BECHUANALAND

Siege of Mafeking .... #S651-S655

MATABELELAND

Marshall Hole, Bulawayo .... #S661-S670

NAMAQUALAND

Siege of O'okiep .... #S676-S678

ORANGE FREE STATE

Postal Money Orders .... #S681-S689

ORANGE RIVER COLONY

Siege of Koffyfontein .... #S691

TRANSVAAL (Z.A.R.)

Postal Money Orders .... #S701-S709

UPINGTON

Upington Border Scouts Issue .... #S711-S715

CAPE OF GOOD HOPE

Imperial Banks

LONDON AND SOUTH AFRICAN BANK

Operated in the Cape from 1861 to 1877. Issuing office: Port Elizabeth.

1874 ISSUE

S106 5 POUNDS — GOOD / FINE / XF

6.3.1874; 18.3.1874; 28.4.1874; 8.5.1874. Black on purple unpt. Qn. Victoria at upper l., arms at ctr. Back black, valve engraving. Printer: William Brown & Co.

	GOOD	FINE	XF
a. Issued note.	200.00	400.00	—
b. Hand stamped: *CANCELLED.*	—	—	—

S107 10 POUNDS

Reported Not Confirmed

ORIENTAL BANK CORPORATION

Operated from 1873 to 1879. Taken over by the Bank of Africa.

KIMBERLEY - PORT ELIZABETH

1878 PROVISIONAL ISSUE

		GOOD	FINE	XF
S110	**5 POUNDS** 1.7.1878. Black and blue. Arms at upper ctr. Dual ovpt.: *KIMBERLEY ISSUE PORT ELIZABETH* on face. Printer: PBC.	—	Rare	—

CAPE TOWN

1876 ISSUE

#S111-S112 printer: PBC.

		GOOD	FINE	XF
S111	**10 POUNDS** (ca.1876). Black. Crowned supported royal arms at upper ctr. Proof.	—	—	—
S112	**20 POUNDS** (ca.1876). Black. Like #S111. Proof.	—	—	—

PORT ELIZABETH

1873 ISSUE

#S113 and S114 crowned supported royal arms at upper ctr. Printer: PBC.

		GOOD	FINE	XF
S113	**5 POUNDS** (ca.1873). Black. Like #S112. Proof. Hand stamped: *Specimen.*	—	—	—
S114	**20 POUNDS** (ca.1873). Black. Like #S112. Proof. Hand stamped: *Specimen.*	—	—	—

Notice

Readers with unlisted dates, color or signature varieties are invited to submit photocopies of their notes to: Standard Catalog of World Paper Money, Krause Publications, 700 East State St. Iola WI 54990-0001 U.S.A. or by email: thernr@krause.com. Email submissions of material for possible inclusion need to be 100% jpeg attachments at 300 dpi.

1878 ISSUE

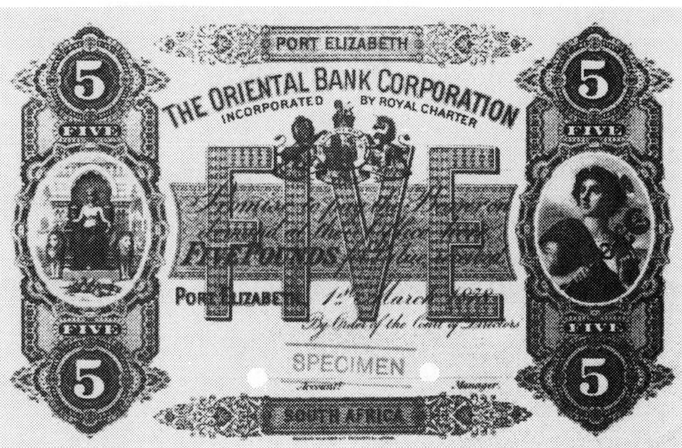

		GOOD	FINE	XF
S115	**5 POUNDS** 1.3.1878. Black on green unpt. Crowned supported royal arms at upper ctr., seated Britannia at l., Mercury at r. Printer: BWC. Proof.	—	—	—

STANDARD BANK OF BRITISH SOUTH AFRICA LIMITED

Began operations in 1863. Later became the Standard Bank of South Africa Limited. Issuing office: Cape Town.

BURGERSDORP

1864 ISSUE

		GOOD	FINE	XF
S116	**5 POUNDS** 16.3.1864. Britannia standing w/flag and shield at l.	—	Rare	—

MIDDELBURG

1864 ISSUE

		GOOD	FINE	XF
S117	**5 POUNDS** 4.2.1864. Black. Local print.	—	—	—

PIETERMARITZBURG

1865 ISSUE

		GOOD	FINE	XF
S119	**5 POUNDS** (ca.1865). Blue on lt. red unpt. Standing Britannia at l. w/flag by sheep, bales and anchor. Perforated: *CANCELLED.* Specimen. Printer: W & S.	—	—	—

CAPE OF GOOD HOPE

Commercial Banks

AGRICULTURAL BANK OF QUEENSTOWN

Operated from 1862 to 1872.

1862 ISSUE

		GOOD	FINE	XF
S121	**4 POUNDS** 18xx.	—	Rare	—

BANK OF SOUTH AFRICA

This bank did not open. Notes were printed but not issued.

1830'S ISSUE

#S131-S146 lion at bottom ctr. Printer: William Congreve.

		GOOD	FINE	XF
S131	**2 SKILLINGS** 18xx. Black and blue.	—	Rare	—

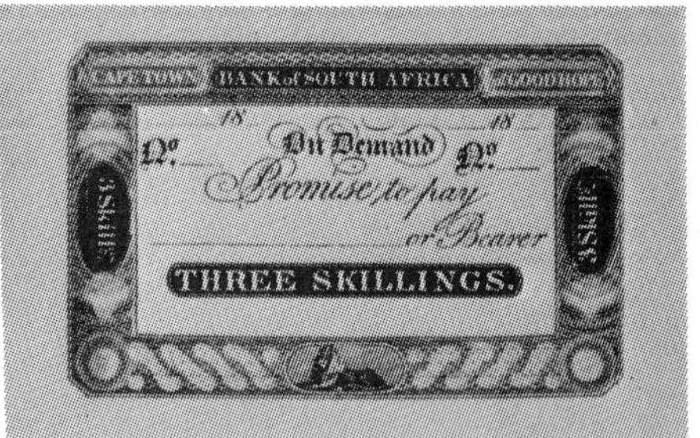

		GOOD	FINE	XF
S132	**3 SKILLINGS** 18xx. Black and green.	—	Rare	—
S133	**4 SKILLINGS** 18xx. Black and red.	—	Rare	—
S134	**1 RIX DOLLAR** 18xx. Black and orange.	—	Rare	—

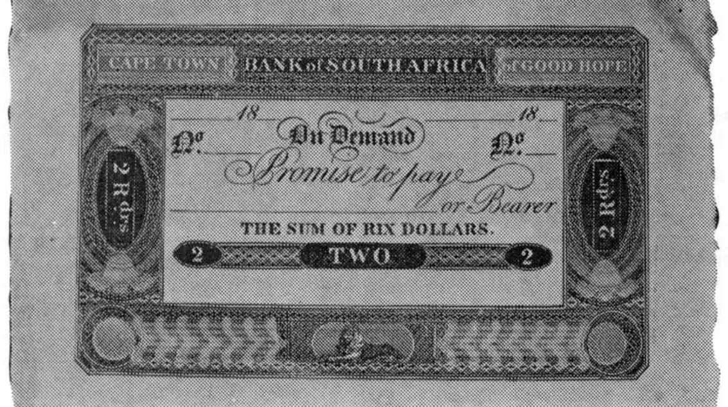

		GOOD	FINE	XF
S135	**2 RIX DOLLARS** 18xx. Black and orange.	—	Rare	—
S136	**3 RIX DOLLARS** 18xx.	—	Rare	—

		GOOD	FINE	XF
S145	**400 RIX DOLLARS** 18xx. Red and green.	—	Rare	—
S146	**500 RIX DOLLARS** 18xx. Magenta and orange.	—	Rare	—

BEAUFORT BANK

Operated from 1854 to 1864.

1854 ISSUE

		GOOD	FINE	XF
S151	**5 POUNDS** 18xx.	—	Rare	—

BRITISH KAFFRARIAN BANK

Operated from 1858 to 1863.

1800'S ISSUE

		GOOD	FINE	XF
S156	**5 POUNDS** 18xx.	—	Rare	—

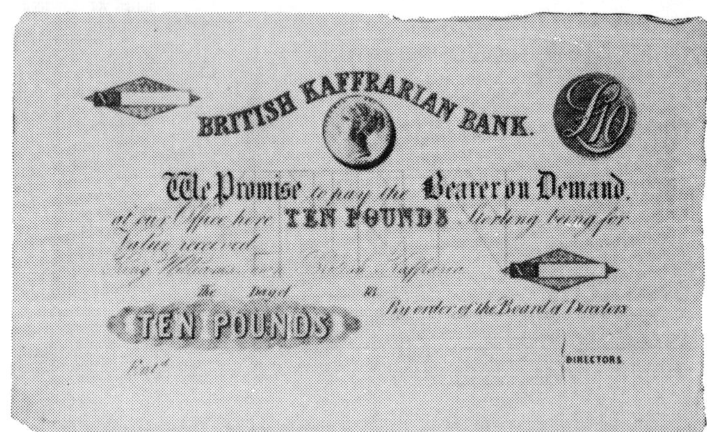

		GOOD	FINE	XF
S157	**10 POUNDS** 18xx. Qn. Victoria medallion at upper ctr.	200.00	400.00	—

CAPE COMMERCIAL BANK

Operated from 1854 to 1862.

1854 ISSUE

		GOOD	FINE	XF
S161	**5 POUNDS** 18xx.	—	Rare	—
S162	**10 POUNDS** 18xx.	—	Rare	—

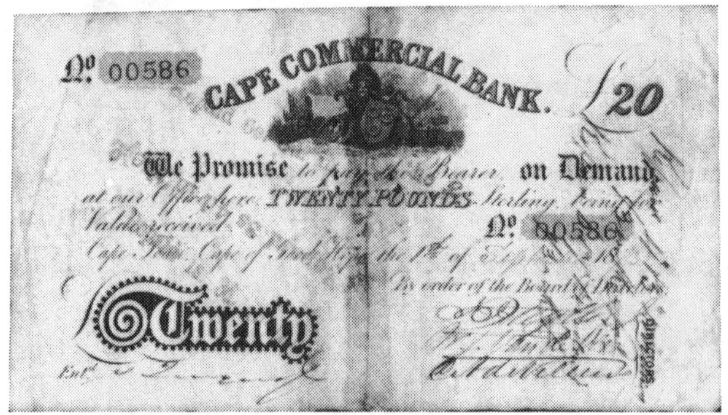

		GOOD	FINE	XF
S163	**20 POUNDS** 1.9.1873. Black. Arms at upper ctr.	—	Rare	—

CAPE OF GOOD HOPE BANK (FIRST)

There were actually two different banking organizations of the same name, but operating at different times. The first group tried to organize in the 1820's but did not succeed. Bank notes in a single denomination were printed but not issued. The second bank did succeed in opening.

1828 ISSUE

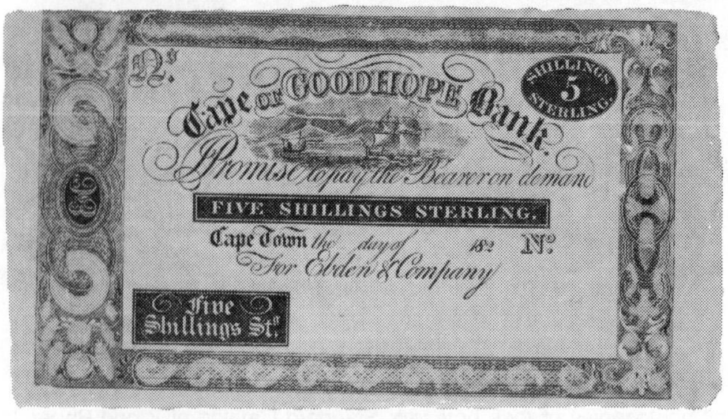

		GOOD	FINE	XF
S171	**5 SHILLINGS** 3.6.1828. Black and blue. Sailing ships at upper ctr. Remainder.	—	Unc	175.00

CAPE OF GOOD HOPE BANK (SECOND)

Operated from 1837 to 1890.

CAPE TOWN

1800S ISSUE

		GOOD	FINE	XF
S175	**1 POUND** 18xx. Specimen.	—	—	—

NOTE: For #S175 w/ovpt: *KLERKSDORP ISSUE* see #S591.

		GOOD	FINE	XF
S176	**5 POUNDS** 18xx. Specimen.	—	—	—
S177	**10 POUNDS** 18xx. Specimen.	—	—	—

		GOOD	FINE	XF
S178	**20 POUNDS** 1.10.1886. Black on blue and brown unpt. Woman standing at l. Printer: BWC.			
	a. Issued note.	—	Rare	—
	s. Specimen.	—	—	—

JOHANNESBURG

PROVISIONAL ISSUE

		GOOD	FINE	XF
S179	**5 POUNDS** 2.12.1889. Like #S176 but *CAPE TOWN* crossed out, *JOHANNESBURG* beneath lower name. *JOHANNESBURG ISSUE* at upper r. in red.	—	Rare	—

COLESBURG BANK

Operated from 1861 to 1863.

1861-62 ISSUE

		GOOD	FINE	XF
S180	**5 POUNDS** 24.10.1861. Black. Arms at upper ctr. Printer: Saul Solomon & Co.	—	Rare	—
S181	**4 POUNDS** 30.1.1862. Black. Horse, hay and cow at ctr. Printer: William Brown & Co.	—	Rare	—
S182	**5 POUNDS** 25.1.1862. Similar to #S181.	—	Rare	—

COMMERCIAL BANK OF PORT ELIZABETH

Operated from 1853 to 1863.

1854-60 ISSUE

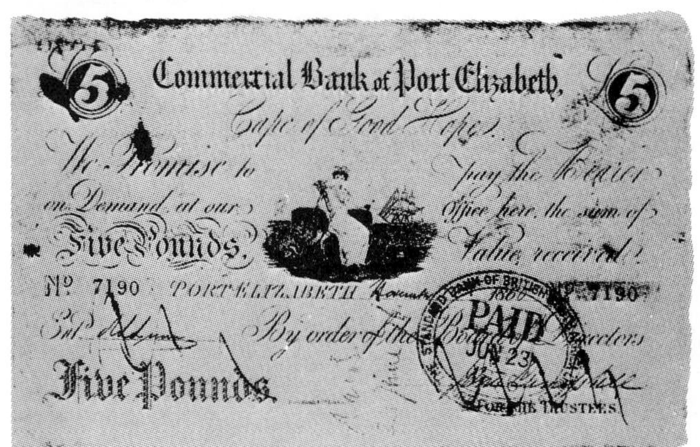

		GOOD	FINE	XF
S191	**5 POUNDS** 21.12.1854; 23.11.1857; 10.11.1860. Black. Seated woman w/bales and sailing ship in background at ctr. Printer: Rowe, Rentigh & Co., London.	—	Rare	—

FORT BEAUFORT & VICTORIA BANK

Operated from 1860 to 1873.

1860'S ISSUE

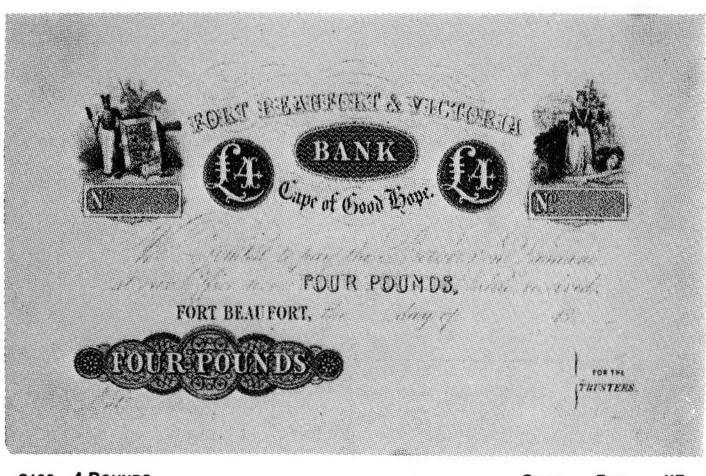

		GOOD	FINE	XF
S196	**4 POUNDS** 18xx. Soldier by lg. shield at upper l., crowned woman at upper r.	—	Rare	—
S197	**5 POUNDS** 18xx.	—	Rare	—
S198	**10 POUNDS** 18xx. Value flanking central bank name.	—	Rare	—

FRONTIER COMMERCIAL & AGRICULTURAL BANK

Operated from 1847 to 1869.

1863 ISSUE

		GOOD	FINE	XF
S201	**5 POUNDS** 18xx.	—	Rare	—

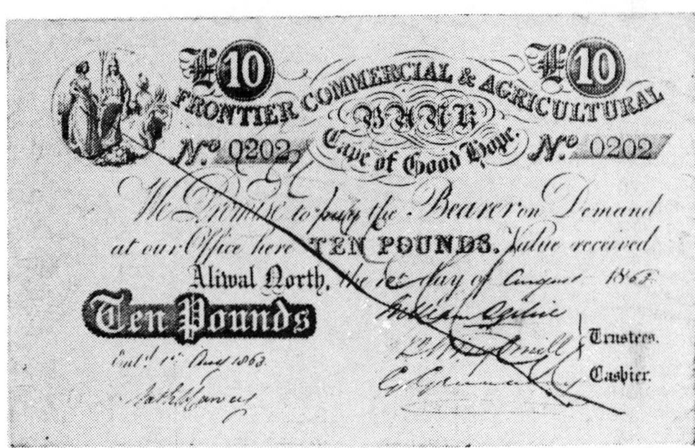

		GOOD	FINE	XF
S202	**10 POUNDS** 1.8.1863. Black. Seated Britannia w/2 allegorical women at upper l. Printer: William Brown & Co.	300.00	600.00	—

GEORGE DIVISIONAL BANK

Operated from 1860 to 1869.

1862 ISSUE

		GOOD	FINE	XF
S211	**5 POUNDS** 1862. Woman's portr. at l. and r.	—	Rare	—

GRAAF REINET BANK

Operated from 1848 to 1878.

1860'S ISSUE

		GOOD	FINE	XF
S216	**5 POUNDS** 18xx.	—	Rare	—
S217	**10 POUNDS** 18xx. Black. Printer: Royston & Brown.	—	Rare	—

KAFFRARIAN COLONIAL BANK

Operated from 1862 to 1891.

1800'S ISSUE

		GOOD	FINE	XF
S221	**5 POUNDS** 18xx. Black. Allegorical woman w/shield at ctr. Printer: William Brown & Co.	—	Rare	—

MALMESBURY AGRICULTURAL & COMMERCIAL BANK

Operated from 1862 to 1878.

1860'S ISSUE

		GOOD	FINE	XF
S226	**5 POUNDS** 18xx.	—	Rare	—

MONTAGU BANK

Operated from 1861 to 1868.

1860's ISSUE

		GOOD	FINE	XF
S231	**5 POUNDS** 18xx. Black on green unpt. Portr. of man at upper l., town and mountains at upper ctr. Printer: William Brown & Co. Remainder.	—	Unc	40.00

PAARL BANK

Operated from 1852 to 1890.

1873-74 ISSUE

		GOOD	FINE	XF
S236	**5 POUNDS** 4.8.1873; 27.8.1874. Workers and cherubs at sides, seated Britannia at upper ctr. Printer: Nissen, Parker & Arnold.	—	Rare	—

PORT ELIZABETH BANK

Operated from 1846 to 1873. Printer: PBC.

1850's-70's ISSUE

		GOOD	FINE	XF
S241	**5 POUNDS** 18xx; 1872. Black. Woman standing at l.			
	a. 1.1.1872.	—	Rare	—
	s. Hand stamped: *SPECIMEN.* 18xx.	—	—	—
S242	**10 POUNDS** 18xx; 1871. Black. Standing female at upper ctr.			
	a. 19.10.1871.	—	Rare	—
	s. Hand stamped: *SPECIMEN.* 18xx.	—	—	—
S243	**20 POUNDS** 18xx; 1857. Black. Standing Perote at ctr.			
	a. 1857.	—	Rare	—
	s. Hand stamped: *SPECIMEN.* 18xx.	—	—	—

QUEENSTOWN BANK

Operated from 1859 to 1873.

1860's ISSUE

#S251-S253 printer: WB&Co.

		GOOD	FINE	XF
S251	**4 POUNDS** 25.4.1870. Black. Similar to #S253.	—	Rare	—
S252	**5 POUNDS** 18xx. Black. Similar to #S253. Proof.	—	—	—

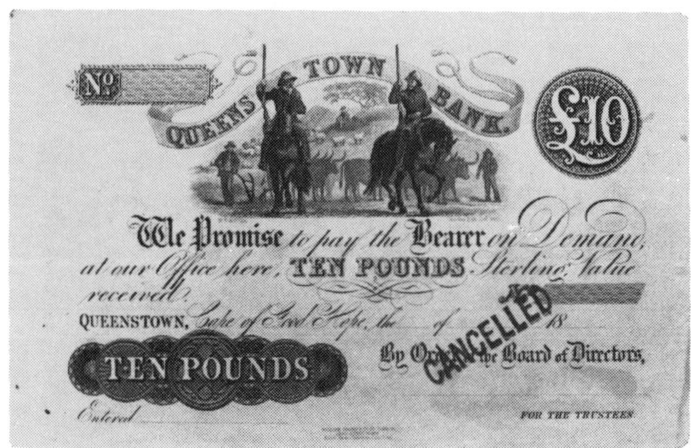

		GOOD	FINE	XF
S253	**10 POUNDS** 18xx. (ca.1859). Black. 2 horseback troopers at ctr., sheep, cattle and farmers in background.			
	p1. Proof.	—	—	—
	p2. Proof. Hand stamped: *CANCELLED.*	—	—	—

SOMERSET EAST BANK

Operated from 1860 to 1877.

1860's ISSUE

		GOOD	FINE	XF
S256	**4 POUNDS** 18xx.	—	Rare	—

		GOOD	FINE	XF
S257	**5 POUNDS** 25.11.1867; 29.11.1867. Black. Crowned supported royal arms at upper ctr. Printer: Nissen and Parker.	—	Rare	—
S258	**10 POUNDS** 18xx. Black. Arms at ctr. Printer: J. A. Crew Engr.	—	Rare	—

SOUTH AFRICAN BANK

Operated from 1838 to 1886.

1881 ISSUE

		GOOD	FINE	XF
S261	**5 POUNDS** (ca.1881).	—	Rare	—

		Good	Fine	XF
S262	**10 Pounds** 9.2.1881. Arms at upper ctr. Printer: William Brown & Co.	—	Rare	—
S263	**20 Pounds** 7.2.1881. Similar to #S262.	—	Rare	—

South African Central Bank

Operated from 1854 to 1873.

1850's Issue

		Good	Fine	XF
S271	**5 Pounds** Black. Printer: Roberts, Cape Town.	—	Rare	—

Stellenbosch Bank

Operated from 1854 to 1877.

1860's Issue

		Good	Fine	XF
S276	**5 Pounds** Allegorical figure at lower l. and r., arms at ctr.	—	Rare	—

Stellenbosch District Bank

Operated from 1882 to the present. Note issues ceased in 1892.

1860's Issue

		Good	Fine	XF
S281	**5 Pounds** 18xx. Black. Similar to #S276. Printer: Saul Solomon & Co.	—	Rare	—

Swellendam Bank

Operated from 1852 to 1877.

1860's Issue

		Good	Fine	XF
S286	**5 Pounds** 18xx. Black. Bank arms at upper ctr. Printer: C. J. Roberts S.C.	—	Rare	—

NOTE: #S286 is not to be confused with the commonly seen Barry and Nephews 5 Pound note which also mentions Swellendam as its place of issue. The Barry and Nephews note is a private issue, easily encountered as an uncirculated, unissued remainder at about $30.00 retail.

Wellington Bank

Operated from 1857 to 1890.

1888 Issue

		Good	Fine	XF
S291	**5 Pounds** 21.5.1888; 11.9.1888. Black. Anchor at l., Wellington medallion at upper ctr., rake and shovel at r. Printer: Saul Solomon & Co.	—	Rare	—

Western Province Bank

Operated from 1847 to 1891.

1880's Issue

		Good	Fine	XF
S296	**5 Pounds** 188x. Black and green. Bldg. at l., mountain scene at ctr. Printers: Barry Arnold, Cape Town; William Brown & Co.	—	Rare	—

Worcester Commercial Bank

Operated from 1850 to 1892.

1860's Issue

		Good	Fine	XF
S301	**5 Pounds** 18xx.	—	Rare	—

Cape Uniform Banknotes

From 1891 to 1920 a group of four banks used banknotes uniform in design except for the name of the bank. These notes are known as Cape Uniform Banknotes. The four banks are: African Banking Corporation, Bank of Africa Limited, National Bank of South Africa Limited, and Standard Bank of South Africa Limited.

#S321-S355 arms at ctr. An example of the form all banks used is shown:

Note form for Uniform Banknotes supplied by the Cape government.

African Banking Corporation Limited

1892-1917 Uniform Issue

		Good	Fine	XF
S321	**10 Shillings** 1917-1920. Black and red on yellow unpt.	—	Rare	—

		Good	Fine	XF
S322	**1 Pound** 1892-1920.Black w/orange text on yellow unpt.			
	a. Issued note.	—	Rare	—
	b. Perforated: *CANCELLED*. 27.2.1918.	200.00	350.00	—
S323	**5 Pounds** 1892-1920. Green and red on tan unpt. Back green.	—	Rare	—
S324	**10 Pounds** 1892-1900. Red and green on tan unpt. Back red.	—	Rare	—
S325	**20 Pounds** 1892-1920. Blue and red on tan unpt. Back blue.	—	Rare	—

Bank of Africa Limited

1892-1917 Uniform Issue

		Good	Fine	XF
S331	**10 Shillings** 1917-1920.	—	Rare	—
S332	**1 Pound** 1892-1920.	—	Rare	—

		Good	Fine	XF
S333	**5 Pounds** 1892-1920. Green w/red text on pink unpt.	—	Rare	—
S334	**10 Pounds** 1892-1920.	—	Rare	—
S335	**20 Pounds** 1892-1920.	—	Rare	—

National Bank of South Africa Limited

Issuing Office: Cape Town.

1892-1917 Uniform Issue

		Good	Fine	XF
S341	**10 Shillings** 1917-1920. Brown w/blue text on green unpt. Back brown.			
	a. 18.8.1919; 19.3.1920.	—	Rare	—
	b. Perforated: *CANCELLED*.	—	—	—

		Good	Fine	XF
S342	**1 Pound** 1892-1920. Black, w/red and blue text on yellow unpt. Back dk. gray.			
	a. 5.4.1918.	—	Rare	—
	b. Perforated: *CANCELLED.* 27.2.1918.	240.00	400.00	—

		Good	Fine	XF
S343	**5 Pounds** 1892-1920. Green w/red text on pink unpt. Back green.			
	a. 29.3.1917.	—	Rare	—
	b. Perforated: *CANCELLED.*	275.00	450.00	—
S344	**10 Pounds** 1892-1920. Red and green on tan unpt. Back red.			
	a. Issued note.	—	Rare	—
	b. Perforated: *CANCELLED.*	325.00	550.00	—
S345	**20 Pounds** 1892-1920.	—	Rare	—

Standard Bank of South Africa Limited

1892-1917 Uniform Issue

		Good	Fine	XF
S351	**10 Shillings** 1917-1920.	—	Rare	—

		Good	Fine	XF
S352	**1 Pound** 16.11.1891-1920. Blue and yellow.	—	Rare	—
S353	**5 Pounds** 1892-1920.	—	Rare	—

		Good	Fine	XF
S354	**10 Pounds** 1892-1920. Red and green on tan unpt. Back red.			
	a. Issued note.	—	Rare	—
	b. Perforated: *CANCELLED.*	275.00	450.00	—
S355	**20 Pounds** 1892-1920. Blue and red on tan unpt.	—	Rare	—

Griqualand

Government of New Griqualand

Plans were made to issue a series of notes, but only the 1 Pound denomination was printed. (Not issued).

1868 Issue

		Good	Fine	XF
S361	**1 Pond (= 1 Pound)** 1.1.1868. Black on blue unpt. Arms at upper ctr. Uniface. Printer: Saul Solomon & Co.			
	r1. Remainder.	—	Rare	—
	r2. Remainder, cut cancelled.	550.00	950.00	—

Natal

Imperial Banks

Many notes issued at Durban.

African Banking Corporation Limited

Established in 1891. Taken over by the Standard Bank in 1920.

1890's Issue

#S367-S370 Durban issue. Printer: BWC.

		Good	Fine	XF
S367	**1 Pound** 189x. Portr. woman at l. Specimen.	—	—	—
S368	**5 Pounds** 189x. Portr. woman at l. Specimen.	—	—	—

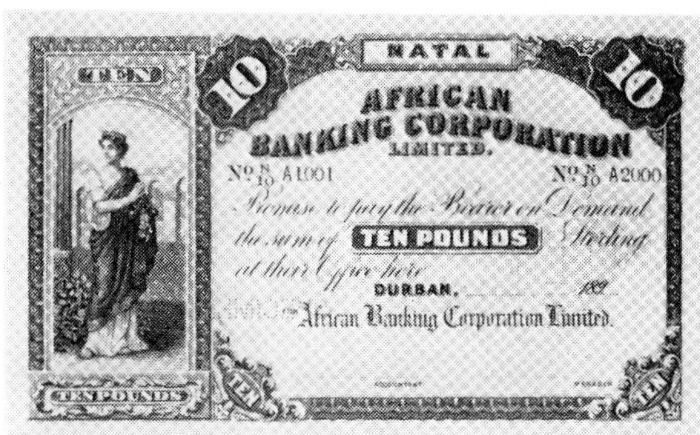

		GOOD	FINE	XF
S369	**10 POUNDS** 189x. Standing allegorical woman at l. Specimen.	—	—	—
S370	**20 POUNDS** 189x. Woman holding shield at l. Specimen.	—	—	—

BANK OF AFRICA LIMITED

Established in 1879; the Durban branch opened in 1880.

1890'S ISSUE

		GOOD	FINE	XF
S381	**10 SHILLINGS** Before 1900.	Reported Not Confirmed		

1900'S ISSUE

		GOOD	FINE	XF
S382	**10 SHILLINGS** After 1900. Black on olive unpt. Map of Africa at l., field workers at r. Back purple. Printer: W&S.	—	Rare	—

NATIONAL BANK OF SOUTH AFRICA LIMITED

The Natal branch began in 1896. Became part of Barclays Bank (Dominion, Colonial and Overseas) in 1926.

1900-14 ISSUE

#S391-S395 Ovpt: *NATAL ISSUE* at top border. Printer: W&S.

		GOOD	FINE	XF
S391	**10 SHILLINGS** 1900-20. Green and orange. Cherub holding cornucopia at lower l. Springbok at ctr. on back.	175.00	450.00	—

		GOOD	FINE	XF
S392	**1 POUND** 1.5.1900; 1.9.1919; 1.5.1920. Black on lt. red unpt. Seated woman w/bale and barrel at l. Back dk. green; map of Africa.	250.00	600.00	—

		GOOD	FINE	XF
S393	**5 POUNDS** 1.9.1914; 1.9.1915. Seated woman w/cornucopia w/Victoria Falls in background at l., cows and wagon at r.	300.00	750.00	—
S395	**20 POUNDS** 1900-20.	—	Rare	—

ORIENTAL BANK CORPORATION

Issuing Office: Pietermaritzburg.

1877 ISSUE

		GOOD	FINE	XF
S397	**1 POUND** (ca.1877). Black. Arms at upper ctr. Punched hole cancelled. Proof.	—	—	—

STANDARD BANK OF BRITISH SOUTH AFRICA LIMITED

Established in 1863, its first branch was located in Durban.

1873 ISSUE

		GOOD	FINE	XF
S402	**1 POUND** 14.4.1873. Blue on red unpt. Unpt. of lg. *ONE.* Standing Britannia w/flag and shield at upper ctr. Handwritten: *CANCELLED.* Printer: WWS.	250.00	550.00	—

STANDARD BANK OF SOUTH AFRICA LIMITED

Formerly the Standard Bank of British South Africa Limited.

DURBAN

1889 ISSUE

#S406-S410 standing Britannia w/flag and shield at upper ctr.

#S406 and S407 printer: WWS.

		GOOD	FINE	XF
S406 (S401)	**10 SHILLINGS** 1.5.1889. Orange on blue unpt. Back green.	200.00	500.00	—

		Good	Fine	XF
S407	**1 Pound** 1.3.1889. Similar to #S402 but unpt. of sunburst in gold and *ONE* twice in red. Back green; bank monogram.			
	a. Issued note.	200.00	500.00	—
	p1. Black and red unpt. Uniface. Proof.	—	—	—
	p2. Back uniface. Proof.	—	—	—

		Good	Fine	XF
S410 (S406)	**20 Pounds** 18xx. Black. Standing Britannia w/flag and shield at ctr. Back lt. brown; Athena head at ctr. Punched hole cancelled.	—	—	—

1896 Issue

#S411-S412 printer: William Brown.

		Good	Fine	XF
S411	**10 Shillings** 1.10.1896. Black on orange unpt. Similar to #S412. Back green.	125.00	275.00	600.00

		Good	Fine	XF
S412	**1 Pound** 1.10.1896. Green.	125.00	300.00	700.00

1900 Issue

#S421-S425 ovpt: *NATAL ISSUE* in top border. Printer: W&S.

		Good	Fine	XF
S421	**10 Shillings** 1900-20.	750.00	2000.	—

		Good	Fine	XF
S422	**1 Pound** 1900-20. Black and brown. Standing Britannia w/flag and shield at l. Woman at ctr. on back.			
	a. Issued note. 1.7.1918.	100.00	300.00	—
	s. Specimen.	—	Unc	250.00

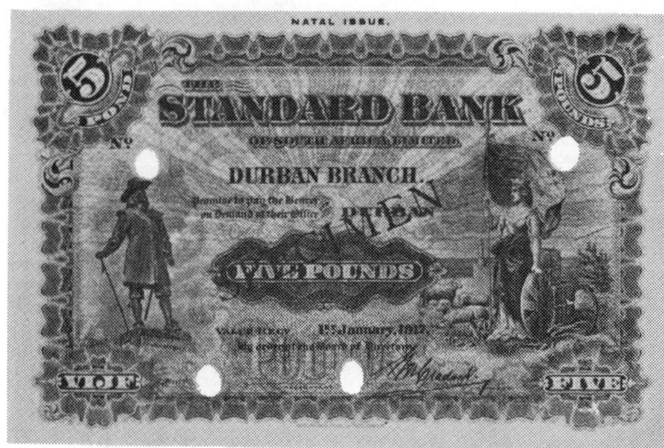

		Good	Fine	XF
S423	**5 Pounds** 1900-20. Statue of Van Riebeeck at l., standing Britannia w/flag and shield at r.			
	a. Issued note. 1.7.1918.	175.00	500.00	—
	s. Specimen.	—	Unc	350.00
S425	**20 Pounds** 1900-20 (1.1.1919). Black on yellow and green unpt. Similar to #S423.	275.00	650.00	—

Natal

Commercial Banks

Colonial Bank of Natal

Established in Pietermaritzburg; operated from 1862 to 1868.

1862-64 Issue

#S431-S433 black. Sm. cow, letters: *CBN* on bales of wool, corn and wheat at top ctr. Uniface. Printer: Saul Solomon & Co., Cape Town.

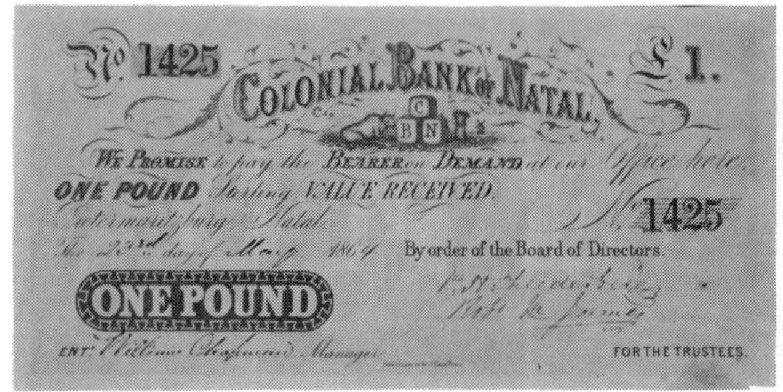

		Good	Fine	XF
S431	**1 Pound** 1.5.1862; 23.5.1864. Lt. blue unpt.	—	Rare	—

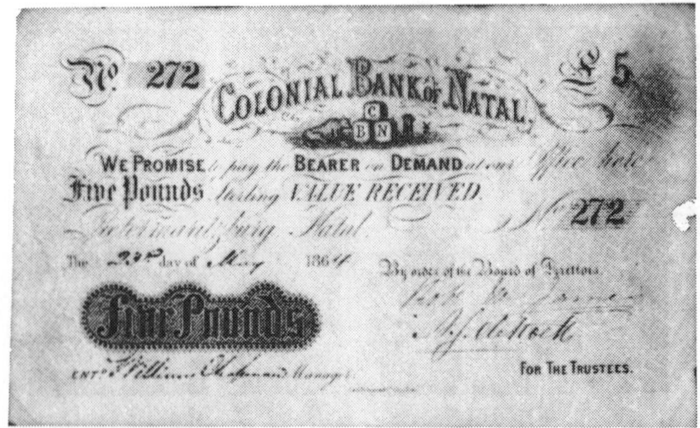

		Good	Fine	XF
S432	**5 Pounds** 9.6.1862; 23.5.1864. Lt. brown unpt.	300.00	500.00	—
S433	**10 Pounds** 9.6.1862. Lt. brown unpt.	—	Rare	—

Commercial and Agricultural Bank of Natal

Operated from 1860-67.

1860's Issue

		Good	Fine	XF
S436	**1 Pound** 186x. Black and lt. blue. Coast scene at upper ctr. Printer: Nissen & Parker, London.	—	Rare	—

Durban Bank

Operated from 1862 to 1877; reorganized as the London and Natal Bank in 1864, but never opened under this name. The Durban Bank was then reestablished.

1860-70's Issue

#S441-S444 Atlas carrying world at upper l., dock scene at the Point Railway Station at upper ctr. Black print, uniface. Printer: Nissen & Parker, London.

		Good	Fine	XF
S440	**10 Shillings** 187x. Black. Arms at upper l., animals and shields at upper ctr. Printer: G. Waterston and Son.	—	—	—

		Good	Fine	XF
S441	**1 Pound** 186x (ca.1864). Blue. Office: *Durban* or *DURBAN, NATAL* at ctr. Sign. title: *ACCOUNTANT*. Back lt. gray; value in floral rectangle. Wmk: *DURBAN BANK*.	—	Rare	—
S442	**5 Pounds** 1862; 1864.			
	a. Sign. title: *CHIEF CLERK*. 3.11.1862.	—	Rare	—
	b. Sign. title: *ACCOUNTANT*. 12.4.1864.	—	Rare	—
S443	**10 Pounds** 186x (ca.1862). Sign. title: *CHIEF CLERK*.	—	Rare	—

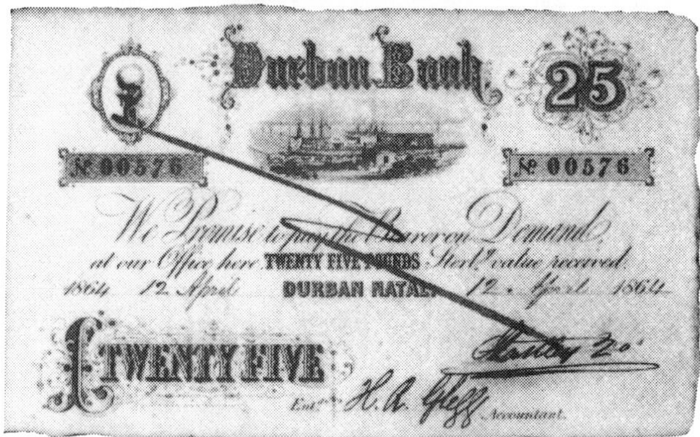

		Good	Fine	XF
S444	**25 Pounds** 186x; 1864.			
	a. Sign. title: *CHIEF CLERK*. 186x.	—	Rare	—
	b. Sign. title: *ACCOUNTANT*. Pen cancelled. 12.4.1864.	—	—	300.00

London and Natal Bank

This was a planned bank that never opened though notes in several denominations were prepared. Originated from the Durban Bank.

1864 Issue

#S451-S454 shield at upper l., shields, produce, and animals at ctr. Printer: Waterston & Son, Edinburgh.

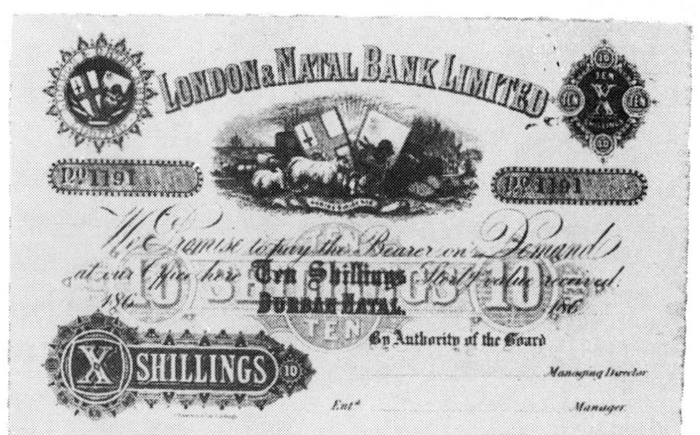

		Good	Fine	XF
S451	**10 Shillings** 186x. Black on red unpt. Remainder w/serial #.	—	Rare	—
S452	**1 Pound** 186x. Black on green unpt.	—	Rare	—
S453	**5 Pounds** 186x. Black on dk. brown unpt.	—	Rare	—
S454	**10 Pounds** 186x. Black on blue unpt. Remainder w/o serial #.	—	Rare	—

Natal Bank Limited

Operated from 1854 to 1914, when it was taken over by the National Bank of South Africa.

1850's Issue

		Good	Fine	XF
S462	**1 Pound** 1852. Black. Arms at upper ctr. Printer: Jeremiah Cullingworth, Durban.	—	—	—

#S462A-S464 printer: CS&E.

		Good	Fine	XF
S462A	**5 Pounds** 18xx. Black on lt. red and lt. blue unpt. Bldg. at l. and r., crowned supported royal arms at upper ctr. Back black and lt. red; portr. of Victoria and value.			
	a. Issued note.	—	Rare	—
	p1. Perforated: *SPECIMEN*. Proof.	—	—	—
	p2. Orange back. Uniface. Proof.	—	—	—
	s1. Black back. Uniface. Perforated: *SPECIMEN*.	—	—	—
	s2. Perforated: *SPECIMEN*.	—	—	—

		Good	Fine	XF
S463	**10 Pounds** 18xx. Black on orange and yellow unpt. Similar to #S462A. Back red and yellow; 2 portr. of Qn. Victoria and value.			
	a. Issued note.	—	Rare	—
	p. Back uniface. Proof.	—	—	—
	s. Perforated: *SPECIMEN*.	—	Unc	300.00
S464	**20 Pounds** 18xx. Black on green and orange unpt. Similar to #S462A. Back green and orange; similar to #S463.			
	a. Issued note.	—	Rare	—
	s1. Face w/o unpt. Uniface. Perforated: *SPECIMEN*.	—	—	—
	s2. Perforated: *CANCELLED* and *SPECIMEN*.	—	—	—

18xx; 1906 Issue

		Good	Fine	XF
S466	**1 Pound** 1.11.1906. Black on brownish gray unpt. 2 seated women and shield at ctr. Back black. Printer: W&S.	—	Rare	—
S467	**5 Pounds** 18xx. Similar to #S466.	—	—	—
S468	**10 Pounds** 18xx. Similar to #S466. Specimen.	—	Unc	500.00
S469	**20 Pounds** 18xx. Similar to #S466. Printer: BWC. Specimen.	—	Unc	500.00

NOTE: A 10 Shillings denomination is reported. 10 and 20 Pound denominations ca.1900-20 are also reported.

Orange Free State

Imperial Banks

Many notes issued at Bloemfontein.

African Banking Corporation Limited

1900-20 Issue

#S471 and S472 printer: BWC.

		Good	Fine	XF
S471	**10 Shillings** 1900-20. Blue on m/c unpt. Deer grazing at upper ctr. Back green and purple; map of Africa at ctr.	250.00	650.00	—
S472	**1 Pound** 12.5.1920. Brown. Arms at l. and r., deer grazing at ctr.	250.00	650.00	—
S473	**5 Pounds** 191x. Similar to #S472.	—	Rare	—
S474	**10 Pounds** 1900-20. Similar to #S472.	—	Rare	—

Bank of Africa Limited

#S482-S485 printer: W&S.

1900-20 Issue

		Good	Fine	XF
S482	**1 Pound** 18xx. Winburg branch. Specimen.	—	300.00	—
S484	**10 Pounds** 1900-20. Pink and black.	—	Rare	—
S485	**20 Pounds** 1900-20. Black and yellow.	—	Rare	—

National Bank of South Africa Limited

1900-20 Issue

#S491-S495 ovpt: *ORANGE FREE STATE ISSUE* at top border. Printer: W&S.

		Good	Fine	XF
S491	**10 Shillings** 1900-20. Green and red. Like #S391.	—	Rare	—
S492	**1 Pound** 1900-20.	—	Rare	—

		Good	Fine	XF
S493	**5 Pounds** 1900-20. Seated woman w/cornucopia w/Victoria Falls in background at l., cows and wagon at r.	—	Rare	—
S494	**10 Pounds** 3.1.1918. Wagon and cattle at lower l., seated woman w/cornucopia at ctr. Perforated: *CANCELLED.*	—	—	—
S495	**20 Pounds** 1900-20.	—	Rare	—

Standard Bank of South Africa Limited

Bloemfontein

1900s Issue

		Good	Fine	XF
S498	**5 Pounds** 19xx. Orange on tan unpt. Standing Britannia w/flag at l. Back orange. Specimen.	—	—	—

#S501-S504 ovpt: *ORANGE FREE STATE ISSUE* at top border. Printer: W&S.

		Good	Fine	XF
S501	**10 Shillings** 1900-20. Statue of Van Riebeeck at l., standing Britannia w/flag and shield at r.			
	a. Issued note.	—	Rare	—
	s. Specimen.	—	—	—
S502	**1 Pound** Before 1900.	—	Rare	—
S503	**5 Pounds** 1900-20.	—	Rare	—
S504	**10 Pounds** 1900-20.	—	Rare	—

#S505 smaller size. Printer: W&S.

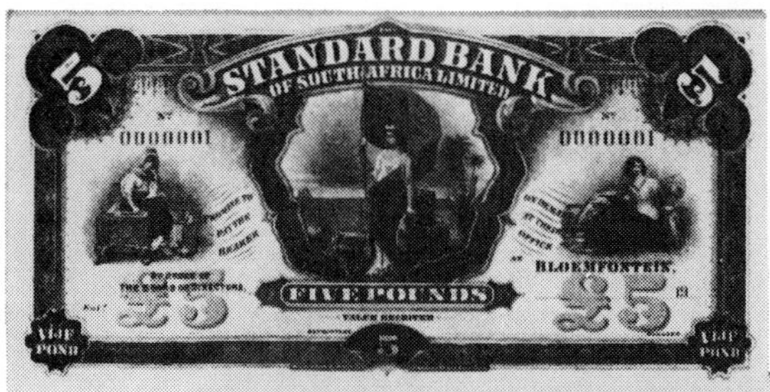

		Good	Fine	XF
S505	**5 Pounds** Black on orange unpt. Female seated w/foul at l.; standing Britannia w/flag at ctr.; female seated w/wheel and wheat at r. Back orange; female portr. at ctr.	—	—	—

ORANGE FREE STATE

Commercial Banks

BLOEMFONTEIN BANK

Operated from 1862 to 1877.

1867-74 Issue

#S507

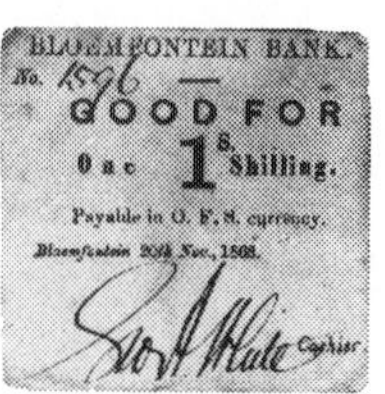

#S507A

#S508

		Good	Fine	XF
S507	**6 Pence** ND. Black on heavy green paper.	—	Rare	—
S507A	**1 Shilling** 20.11.1868. Black on heavy cream paper.	—	Rare	—
S508	**1 Shilling - 6 Pence** 2.9.1867; 16.4.1874. Printed on heavy paper.	50.00	125.00	275.00
S509	**2 Shillings - 6 Pence** 1870.	50.00	125.00	275.00
S510	**5 Shillings** (ca.1870).	60.00	150.00	300.00
S511	**1 Pound** 18xx.	Reported Not Confirmed		
S512	**5 Pounds** 1876. Black.	250.00	500.00	—
S513	**10 Pounds** 30.12.1874. Black.	200.00	500.00	—

FAURESMITH BANK

Operated at first only from 1863 to 1864. Later reestablished and operated from 1873 to 1875.

1863 Issue

#S521 and S522 printer: Saul Solomon & Co.

		Good	Fine	XF
S521	**1 Pound** 1863. Red.	—	Rare	—

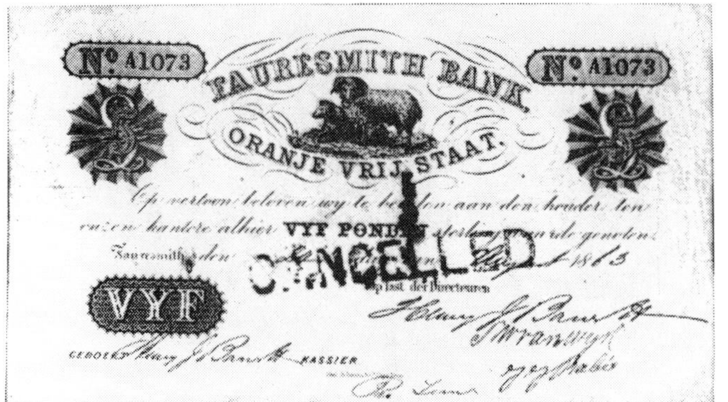

		Good	Fine	XF
S522	**5 Pounds** 24.8.1863. Black. Sheep at upper ctr. Hand stamped: *CANCELLED.*	250.00	500.00	—

1873-74 Issue

#S526 and S527 printer: William Brown & Co.

		Good	Fine	XF
S526	**1 Pound** 18.3.1873.	—	Rare	—
S527	**5 Pounds** 14.10.1874.	—	Rare	—

NATIONALE BANK VAN DEN ORANJE VRYSTAAT BEPERKT

Operated from 1877 to 1900. Became the National Bank of the Orange River Colony in 1900.

1860-92 Issue

		Good	Fine	XF
S531	**1 Pound** 9.7.1860; 21.7.1891; 24.6.1892. Black on brown unpt. Uniface. Printer: William Brown Co.	—	Rare	—

NATIONAL BANK OF THE ORANGE RIVER COLONY, LIMITED

Issued notes after change of name in 1900 from the previously listed bank. Operated to 1910.

1900-10 Issue

#S537-S540 printer: William Brown & Co.

		Good	Fine	XF
S537	**1 Pound** (ca.1900-1910). Black and yellow.	—	Rare	—

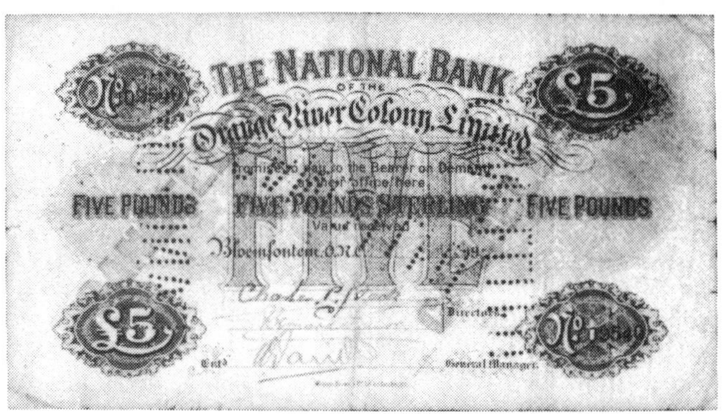

		Good	Fine	XF
S538	**5 Pounds** 1900-10. Black and blue. Cancelled.	450.00	900.00	—
S539	**10 Pounds** 1900-10. Black on gray and red unpt.			
	a. Issued note. 1.11.1902.	—	Rare	—
	b. Hand stamped: *CANCELLED:* perforated: *CANCELLED.*	—	—	—
S540	**20 Pounds** 1900-10. Black, blue and green.	—	Rare	—

A word on date ranges

Often date ranges or specific dates are listed. These have been observed or reported by our contributors. If a note is outside the published range, it only means that it is a newly reported date, and not necessarily worthy of a premium value.

ORANGE VRYSTAAT

ORANGE FREE STATE GOVERNMENT

1865 ISSUE

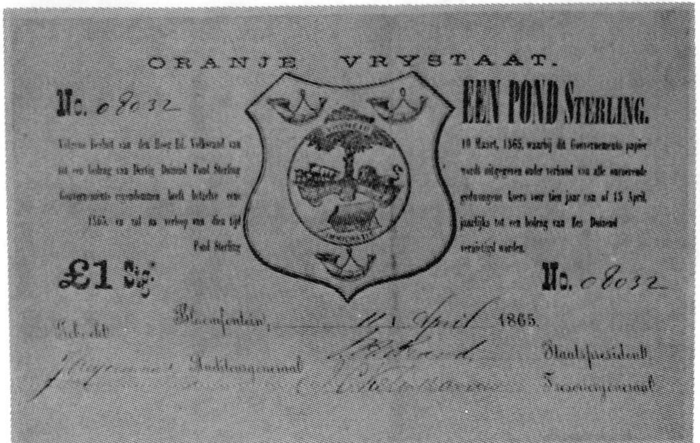

		Good	Fine	XF
S541	**1 POUND** 11.4.1865. Arms at ctr.	—	Rare	—
S542	**5 POUNDS** 1865.	—	Rare	—
S543	**10 POUNDS** 1865.	—	Rare	—
S544	**20 POUNDS** 1865.	—	Rare	—

1866 ISSUE

#S546-S549 printer: William Brown & Co.

		Good	Fine	XF
S546	**1 POUND** 26.7.1867. Arms at upper ctr.	—	Rare	—
S547	**5 POUNDS** 1866.	—	Rare	—
S548	**10 POUNDS** 1866.	—	Rare	—
S549	**20 POUNDS** 1866.	—	Rare	—

TRANSVAAL

Imperial Banks

Many notes issued in Pretoria or Johannesburg.

AFRICAN BANKING CORPORATION LIMITED

1900-20 ISSUE

#S551-S556 printer: BWC.

		Good	Fine	XF
S551	**10 SHILLINGS** 1900-20. Blue on m/c unpt. Like #S471.	—	Rare	—

		Good	Fine	XF
S552	**1 POUND** 1900-19. Green on pink unpt. Portr. woman at l. Map of Africa on back.	—	Rare	—

		Good	Fine	XF
S553	**1 POUND** 9.7.1920. Violet. Deer grazing at ctr.			
	a. Issued note.	—	Rare	—
	s. Specimen.	—	Unc	500.00
S554	**5 POUNDS** 1900-20.	—	Rare	—
S555	**10 POUNDS** 1900-20.	—	Rare	—
S556	**20 POUNDS** 189x. Red and black. Woman holding shield at l.	—	Rare	—

BANK OF AFRICA LIMITED

1870's-1920 ISSUE

#S562-S566 map of Africa at l. Printer: W&S.

		Good	Fine	XF
S562	**10 SHILLINGS** 18xx. Back green; value in ornate engraving. Specimen.	—	—	—
S563	**1 POUND** 18xx. Back green; value in ornate engraving. Specimen.	—	—	—
S564	**5 POUNDS** 18xx-1920. Black on blue unpt. Train at r.			
	a. Issued note.	—	Rare	—
	s. Specimen. 18xx.	—	—	—

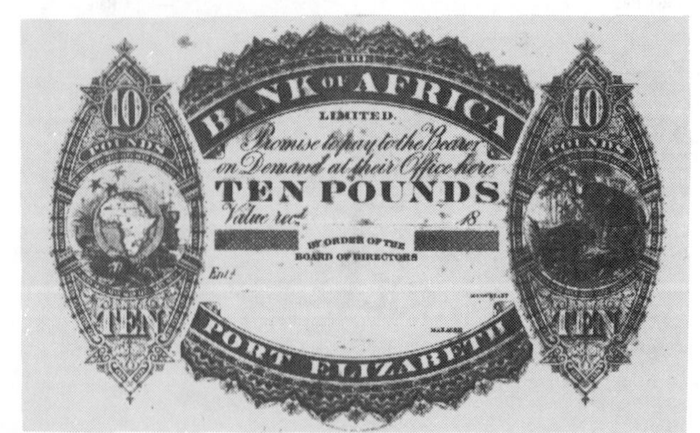

		Good	Fine	XF
S565	**10 Pounds** 18xx-1920. Black and pink. Elephant and hippopotamus at r.			
	a. Issued note.	—	Rare	—
	s. Specimen. 18xx.	—	—	—

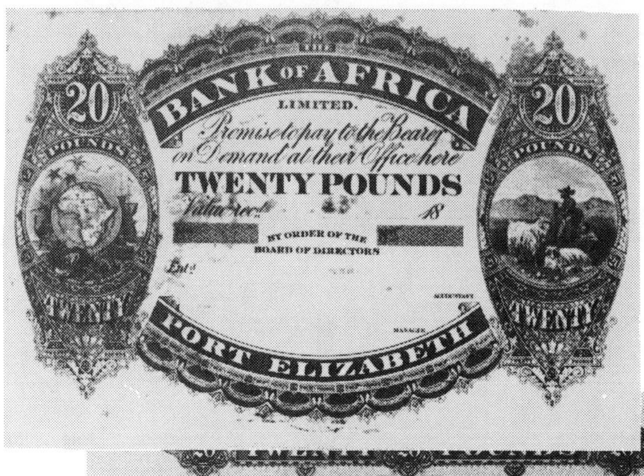

		Good	Fine	XF
S566	**20 Pounds** 18xx-1920. Black and yellow. Men and mountain goats at r. Back brown; value in ornate engraving.			
	a. Issued note.	—	Rare	—
	s. Specimen. 18xx.	—	—	—

National Bank of South Africa Limited

1900's Issue

#S571, S572 and #S576-S578 printer: W&S.

		Good	Fine	XF
S571	**10 Shillings** 1.9.1921. Green and red. Like #S391. Ovpt: *TRANSVAAL ISSUE* at top margin.	250.00	500.00	—

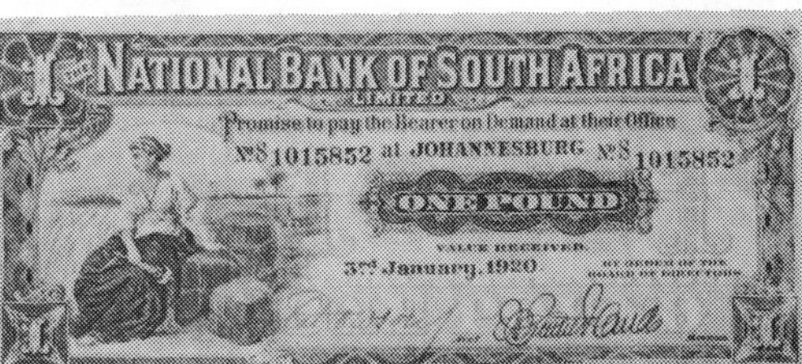

		Good	Fine	XF
S572	**1 Pound** 3.1.1920; 1.5.1920. Like #S392.	200.00	350.00	—
S573	**5 Pounds** 1.12.1900. Lg. denomination at l., bank monogram at upper ctr.	—	Rare	—

#S574 and S575 printer CS&E. Wmk. of value.

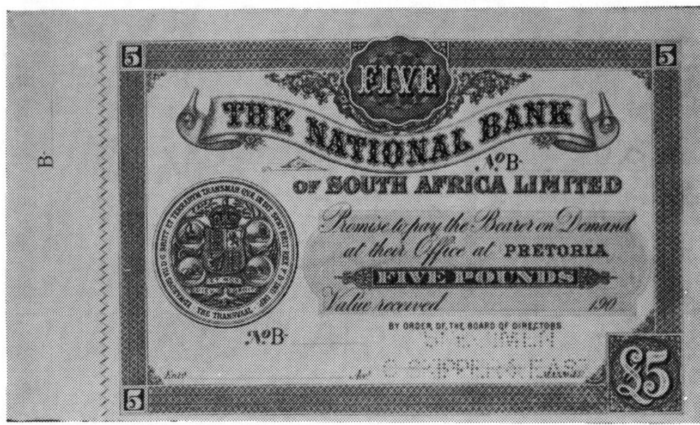

		Good	Fine	XF
S574	**5 Pounds** ND. Black on red unpt. Similar to #S573 but seal at l., *FIVE* in oval at top ctr., serial # at lower l. Back red.			
	r. Remainder.	500.00	800.00	—
	s. Specimen perforated *SPECIMEN/C. SKIPPER & EAST.*	—	—	—

		Good	Fine	XF
S575	**5 Pounds** 190x. Black on red and blue unpt. Seal at lower l., serial # at upper l. and r. Back red. Smaller size note. Remainder perforated: *CANCELLED.*	500.00	800.00	—
S576	**5 Pounds** 1.9.1919. Like #S393.	—	Rare	—

		Good	Fine	XF
S577	**10 Pounds** 1902. Black on green unpt. Monogram at l. and top ctr. Back green.			
	a. Hand stamped: *CANCELLED.* 1.10.1902.	—	—	—
	r. Remainder. 190x.	—	—	—

A word on date ranges

Often date ranges or specific dates are listed. These have been observed or reported by our contributors. If a note is outside the published range, it only means that it is a newly reported date, and not necessarily worthy of a premium value.

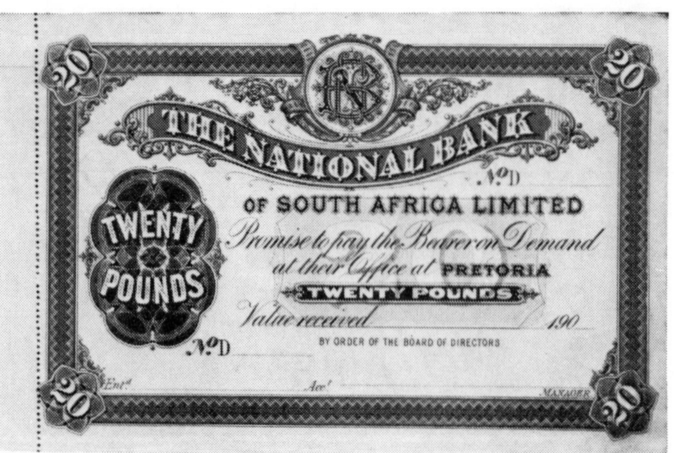

		GOOD	FINE	XF
S578	**20 POUNDS** 1900-1920. Monogram at top ctr. Proof.	—	Rare	—

STANDARD BANK OF BRITISH SOUTH AFRICA LIMITED

Later became the Standard Bank of South Africa Limited.

1870's ISSUE

#S579-S582 printer: W&S (w/o imprint or office of issue).

		GOOD	FINE	XF
S579	**4 POUNDS** 18xx. Black. Standing Britannia at l. w/flag by sheep, bales and anchor. Engraved border.			
	p1. Face w/o unpt. Proof.	—	—	—
	p2. Back uniface. Proof.	—	—	—

		GOOD	FINE	XF
S580	**5 POUNDS** 18xx. Black on gold unpt. Similar to #S579. Back red; lg. value.			
	p1. Black face w/o unpt. Proof. Perforated: *CANCELLED*.	—	—	—
	p2. Red back. Uniface. Proof.	—	—	—

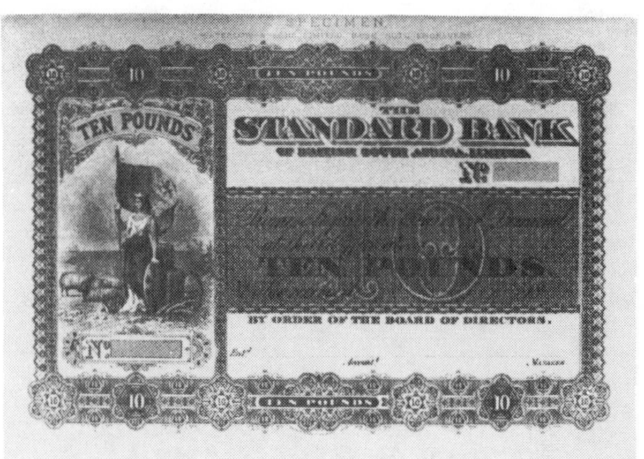

		GOOD	FINE	XF
S581	**10 POUNDS** 18xx. Black. Similar to #S579. Back red; lg. value in scroll.			
	p1. Black face w/o unpt. Uniface. Proof.	—	—	—
	p2. Red back. Uniface. Proof.	—	—	—

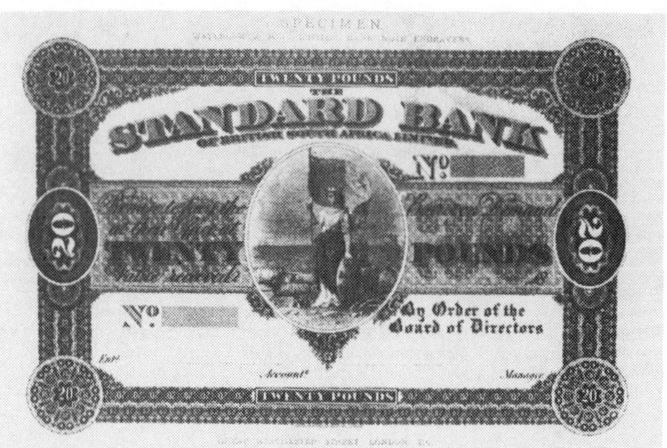

		GOOD	FINE	XF
S582	**20 POUNDS** 18xx. Black. Similar to #S579 except standing Britannia is at ctr. Back lt. brown; Athena head at ctr.			
	p1. Black face w/o unpt. Uniface. Proof.	—	—	—
	p2. Lt. brown back. Uniface. Proof.	—	—	—

STANDARD BANK OF SOUTH AFRICA LIMITED

Formerly the Standard Bank of British South Africa Limited.

1890's ISSUE

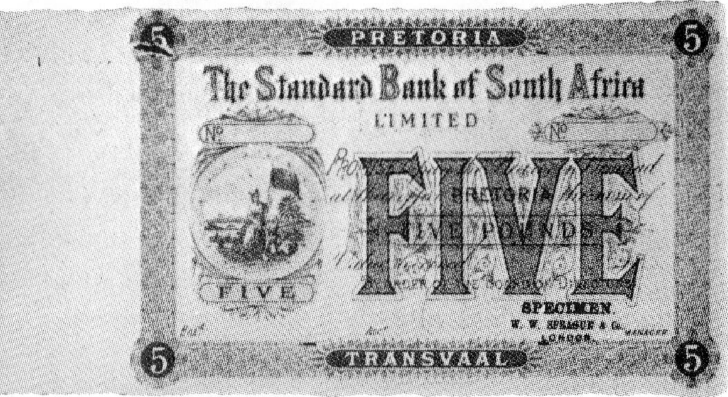

		GOOD	FINE	XF
S583	**5 POUNDS** 18xx. Blue w/purple *FIVE*. Seated woman w/flag and shield at l. Back green. Printer: WWS. Specimen.	—	Rare	—

1896 Issue

		Good	Fine	XF
S583B	**5 Pounds** 18xx. Like #S580.	—	—	—

1900 Issue

		Good	Fine	XF
S584	**20 Pounds** 1.1.1896. Black on blue and yellow unpt. Standing Britannia w/flag and shield at ctr.	—	Rare	—

#S585-S589 ovpt: *TRANSVAAL ISSUE* in top border. Printer: W&S.

		Good	Fine	XF
S585	**10 Shillings** 1900-20. Like #S501.			
	a. Issued note.	250.00	450.00	—
	s1. Ovpt: *Specimen*, punched hole cancelled.	—	—	—
	s2. Specimen w/o markings.	—	—	—

		Good	Fine	XF
S586	**1 Pound** 1900-20. Black and brown. Like #S422.			
	a. Issued note.	200.00	350.00	—
	s. Specimen.	—	—	—
S587	**5 Pounds** 1900-20. Similar to #S589.	—	Rare	—
S588	**10 Pounds** 1900-20. Similar to #S589.	—	Rare	—

		Good	Fine	XF
S589	**20 Pounds** 1900-1.7.1919. Red and green. Statue of Van Riebeeck at l., standing Britannia w/flag and shield at r. ctr. Back red and black; allegorical woman at ctr. between Cape Town and Johannesburg branch bank offices.	—	Rare	—

Transvaal

Private Banks

Cape of Good Hope Bank

Operated beginning 1885.

1888 Provisional Issue

		Good	Fine	XF
S597	**1 Pound** 1.9.1888. Standing woman at l. Ovpt: *KLERKSDORP ISSUE* at lower l. and upper r.	—	Rare	—

Cape Commercial Bank

Began operations in 1873.

1870's Issue

		Good	Fine	XF
S601	**1 Pound** 18xx.	—	Rare	—
S602	**5 Pounds** 18xx.	—	Rare	—

Natal Bank Limited

Operated beginning 1885.

1900-20 Issue

		Good	Fine	XF
S613	**5 Pounds** 1900-20.	—	Rare	—
S614	**10 Pounds** 1900-20.	—	Rare	—
S615	**20 Pounds** 1900-20. 2 seated women and shield at upper ctr.	—	Rare	—

Nederlandsche Bank & Crediet-Vereeniging voor Zuid-Afrika

Began operations in 1888. Later became the Nederlandsche Bank voor Zuid-Afrika, and is still in operation.

1890 Issue

#S621-S624 printer: JEZ.

		Good	Fine	XF
S621	**1 Pound** 12.4.1890. Black. Man standing w/rifle and flag at l.	—	Rare	—
S622	**5 Pounds** 14.4.1890. Lilac. Similar to #S621.	—	Rare	—
S623	**10 Pounds** 18xx.	—	Rare	—
S624	**20 Pounds** 26.4.1890. Black. Similar to #S621.	—	Rare	—

NEDERLANDSCHE BANK VOOR ZUID-AFRIKA

NETHERLANDS BANK OF SOUTH-AFRICA

Formerly the Nederlandsche Bank & Crediet-Vereeniging voor Zuid-Afrika.

1888 ISSUE

#S625-S628 Kingdom of the Netherlands arms at lower l., Zuid-Afrikaansche Republiek arms at lower r. Crowned lion supporting Netherlands arms at l. ctr., Zuid-Afrikaansche Republiek arms at ctr. r. on back. Issuing office: Pretoria.

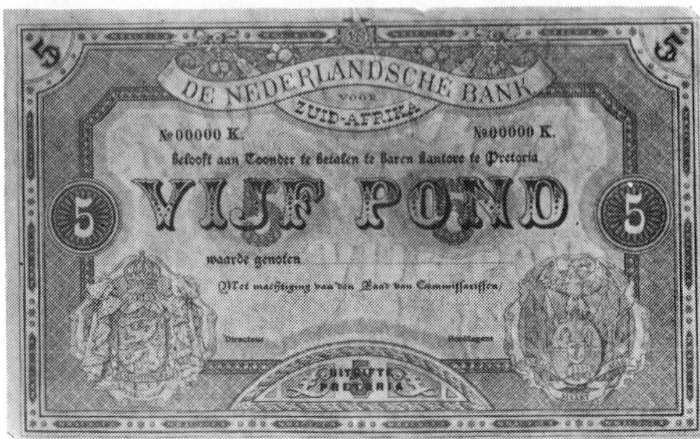

		GOOD	FINE	XF
S625	**5 POND** (ca.1888). Orange. Afrikaans text. Back orange and brown.	—	Rare	—

		GOOD	FINE	XF
S626	**5 POUNDS** (ca.1888). Similar to #S625 but English text.	—	Rare	—

		GOOD	FINE	XF
S627	**10 POND** 1888. Black on blue unpt. Afrikaans text.	—	Rare	—
S628	**10 POUNDS** (ca.1888). Similar to #S627 but English text.	—	Rare	—

#S629-S634 South African arms at upper ctr. Printer: J. H. Bussy, Amsterdam, Holland.

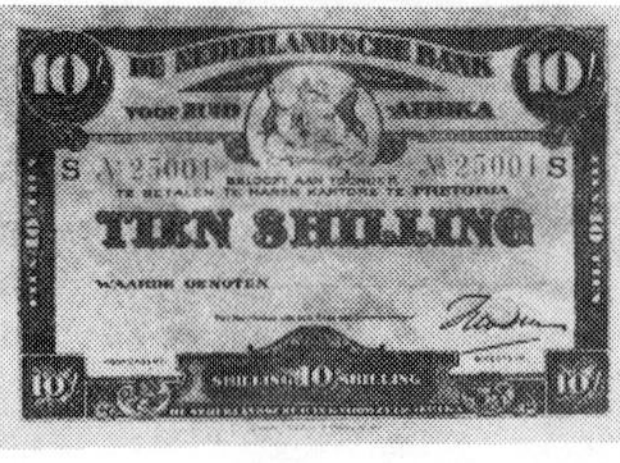

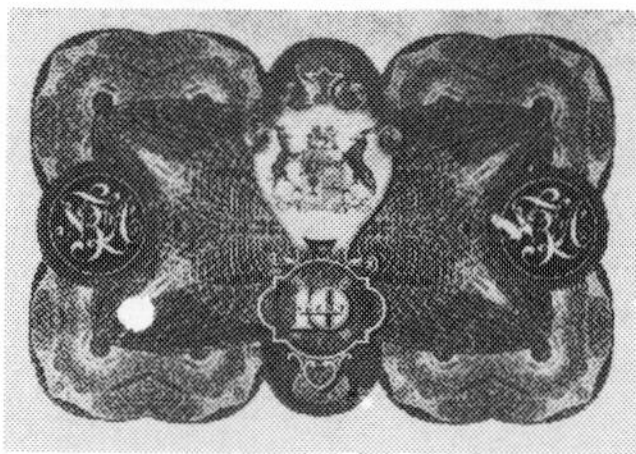

		GOOD	FINE	XF
S629	**10 SHILLING** To 1920. Brown. Afrikaans text. Arms at upper ctr. Bank monogram at l. and r. on back. Specimen w/punched hole cancellation.	—	Rare	—

		GOOD	FINE	XF
S630	**10 SHILLINGS** 14.12.1920. Similar to #S629 but English text.	—	Rare	—
S631	**1 POND** To 1920. Afrikaans text.	—	Rare	—
S632	**1 POUND** To 1920. Similar to #S631 but English text.	—	Rare	—

#S633-S636 arms at l., bank monogram at r. on back.

		GOOD	FINE	XF
S633	**5 POND** To 1920. Black. Afrikaans text. Specimen w/punched star hole cancellation.	—	Rare	—

		GOOD	FINE	XF
S634	**5 POUNDS** To 1920. Similar to #S633 but English text. Specimen w/punched star hole cancellation.	—	Rare	—
S635	**10 POND** To 1920. Brown. Afrikaans text. Specimen w/punched star hole cancellation.	—	Rare	—

		Good	Fine	XF
S636	**10 Pounds** To 1920. Similar to #S635 but English text. Specimen w/punched star hole cancellation.	—	Rare	—

Boer War

Bechuanaland

Siege of Mafeking

On October 11, 1899 war broke out between the Dutch settlers (Boers) and British settlers. Boer forces seized much of a railway line running from Vryburg, Cape Province, to Bechuanaland, and besieged the town of Mafeking. The commander of the Mafeking garrison was Col. R. S. S. Baden-Powell of later Boy Scout fame. During January to March 1900 he authorized an issue of emergency paper money in various denominations on the Standard Bank. All notes were to bear a blind embossed 1 penny revenue stamp of the Bechuanaland Protectorate, but not all received this embossing. The siege was lifted after 217 days, on May 18, 1900.

The 1, 2 and 3 Shillings notes were printed on ruled notebook paper or railway stationery. Better paper was used for the 10 Shillings and 1 Pound notes. Col. Baden-Powell himself designed the 1 Pound note which was photographically produced.

1900 Issue

#S651-S654 royal arms at top ctr. Printer: Townshend and Son.

		Good	Fine	XF
S651	**1 Shilling** 1.1900; 2.1900. Blue w/green value.	50.00	85.00	175.00
S652	**2 Shillings** 1.1900; 2.1900. Blue w/brown value.	60.00	100.00	200.00

NOTE: #S651 and S652 dated 3.1900 were printed but not issued. Several essays and unadopted designs for these notes are known.

		Good	Fine	XF
S653	**3 Shillings** 1.1900. Blue w/red value.	200.00	400.00	800.00

		Good	Fine	XF
S654	**10 Shillings** 3.1900. Green. Man w/firearms at l., man w/cannon at r.			
	a. Misspelled *Commaning* (letter d left out).	95.00	175.00	300.00
	b. Corrected *Commanding.*	50.00	130.00	230.00

		Good	Fine	XF
S655	**1 Pound** 3.1900. Blue. Baden-Powell standing by flag, cannon *"WOLF"* w/kneeling woman and two soldiers, all at ctr.	250.00	500.00	900.00

Matabeleland

Marshall Hole

Postage Stamp Money, Bulawayo

This issue consists of small cards upon which are affixed various adhesive stamps of the British South Africa Company to indicate face value. The stamped sign. of H. Marshall Hole appears on the back along with printed text. These cards were issued in October 1900 as small change during the Boer War.

POSTAGE STAMP VARIETIES:

Type A Type B Type C Type D

TYPE A: Ribbons curl over hind legs of supporters.
TYPE B: Ribbons curl between hind legs of supporters.
TYPES C & D: Smaller size, modified designs.

HAND STAMP VARIETIES:

TYPE I: *ADMINSTRATOR'S * OFFICE BULAWAYO* in violet oval frame.
TYPE II: *ADMINISTRATOR'S OFFICE* in violet oval frame.

1900 Issue

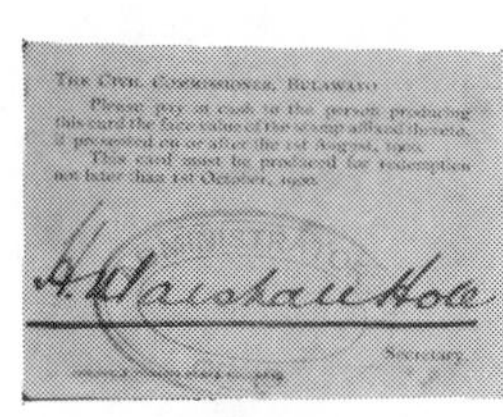

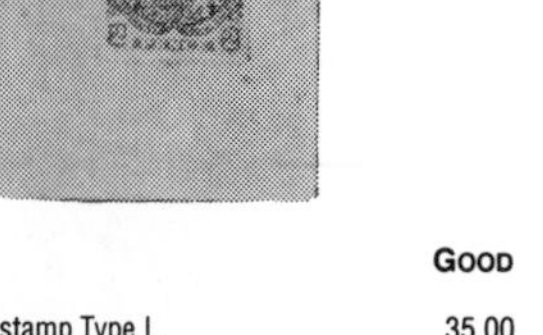

		Good	Fine	XF
S661	**2 Pence** 1.8.1900.			
	a. Adhesive stamp Type A; hand stamp Type I.	35.00	75.00	135.00
	b. Adhesive stamp Type A; hand stamp Type II.	35.00	75.00	135.00
	c. Adhesive stamp Type B; hand stamp Type I.	35.00	75.00	135.00
	d. Adhesive stamp Type B; hand stamp Type II.	35.00	75.00	135.00

		GOOD	FINE	XF
S662	**3 PENCE** 1.8.1900.			
	a. Adhesive stamp Type A; hand stamp Type I.	38.00	85.00	145.00
	b. Adhesive stamp Type A; hand stamp Type II.	38.00	85.00	145.00
	c. Adhesive stamp Type B; hand stamp Type I.	38.00	85.00	145.00
	d. Adhesive stamp Type B; hand stamp Type II.	38.00	85.00	145.00
S663	**4 PENCE** 1.8.1900.			
	a. Adhesive stamp Type A; hand stamp Type I.	40.00	95.00	155.00
	b. Adhesive stamp Type A; hand stamp Type II.	40.00	95.00	155.00
	c. Adhesive stamp Type B; hand stamp Type I.	40.00	95.00	155.00
	d. Adhesive stamp Type B; hand stamp Type II.	40.00	95.00	155.00

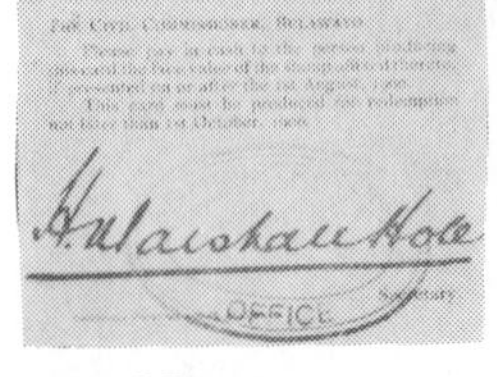

		GOOD	FINE	XF
S664	**6 PENCE** 1.8.1900.			
	a. Adhesive stamp Type A; hand stamp Type I.	45.00	110.00	165.00
	b. Adhesive stamp Type A; hand stamp Type II.	45.00	110.00	165.00
	c. Adhesive stamp Type B; hand stamp Type I.	45.00	110.00	165.00
	d. Adhesive stamp Type B; hand stamp Type II.	45.00	110.00	165.00
	e. Adhesive stamp Type C; hand stamp Type I.	45.00	110.00	165.00
	f. Adhesive stamp Type C; hand stamp Type II.	45.00	110.00	165.00
S665	**1 SHILLING** 1.8.1900.			
	a. Adhesive stamp Type A; hand stamp Type I.	50.00	125.00	200.00
	b. Adhesive stamp Type A; hand stamp Type II.	50.00	125.00	200.00
	c. Adhesive stamp Type D; hand stamp Type I.	50.00	125.00	200.00
	d. Adhesive stamp Type D; hand stamp Type II.	50.00	125.00	200.00
S666	**2 SHILLINGS** 1.8.1900.			
	a. Adhesive stamp Type A; hand stamp Type I.	65.00	135.00	225.00
	b. Adhesive stamp Type A; hand stamp Type II.	65.00	135.00	225.00

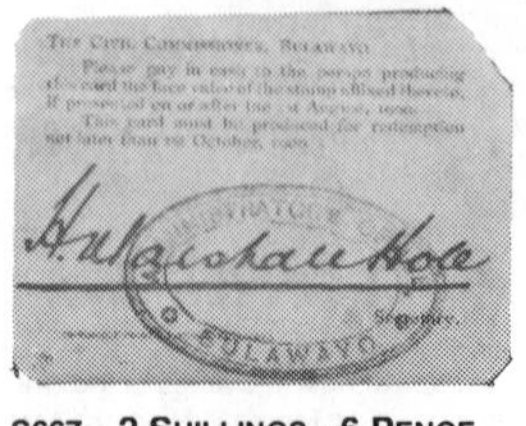

		GOOD	FINE	XF
S667	**2 SHILLINGS - 6 PENCE** 1.8.1900.			
	a. Adhesive stamp Type A; hand stamp Type I.	75.00	150.00	250.00
	b. Adhesive stamp Type A; hand stamp Type II.	75.00	150.00	250.00
S668	**4 SHILLINGS** 1.8.1900. Adhesive stamp Type A; oval hand stamp Type I.	400.00	650.00	1100.
S669	**5 SHILLINGS** 1.8.1900. Adhesive stamp Type A; oval hand stamp Type I.	350.00	600.00	1050.
S670	**10 SHILLINGS** 1.8.1900.			
	a. Adhesive stamp Type A; hand stamp Type I.	400.00	750.00	1500.
	b. Adhesive stamp Type A; hand stamp Type II.	400.00	750.00	1500.

NAMAQUALAND

SIEGE OF O'OKIEP

O'okiep lies 75 miles inland on a rail line from Port Nolloth. In the 1890s it was the center of the Cape Copper Mining Company. During 1902 the Boers laid siege to the area. Typewritten siege notes were issued briefly.

1902 ISSUE

		GOOD	FINE	XF
S676	**10 SHILLINGS** 5.1902.	—	Rare	—
S677	**1 POUND** 5.1902.	—	Rare	—

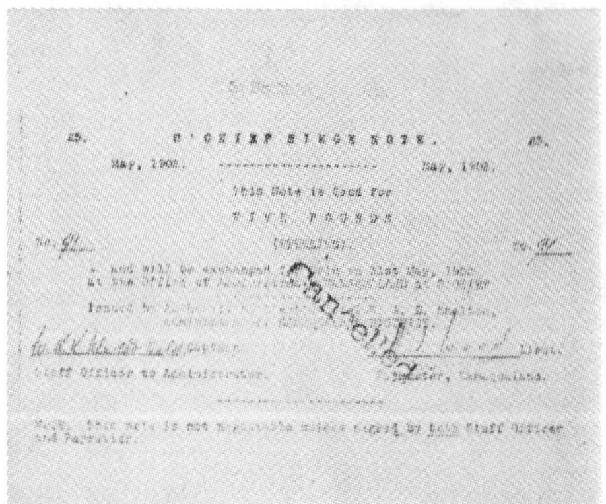

O'OKIEP SIEGE NOTE.

May, 1902. May, 1902.

This Note is Good for

FIVE POUNDS

(STERLING).

Staff Officer to Administrator. Paymaster, Namaqualand.

Cancelled

		GOOD	FINE	XF
S678	**5 POUNDS** 5.1902.	—	Rare	—

ORANGE FREE STATE

POST OFFICE

1900 "POST NOOT" POST NOTES ISSUE

#S681-S689 blank postal note forms used as currency during the Boer War.

		GOOD	FINE	XF
S681	**1 SHILLING** 1900.	15.00	30.00	60.00
S682	**2 SHILLINGS - 6 PENCE** 1900.	15.00	30.00	60.00
S683	**5 SHILLINGS** 1900.	15.00	30.00	60.00
S684	**7 SHILLINGS - 6 PENCE** 1900.	15.00	30.00	60.00
S685	**10 SHILLINGS** 1900.	18.00	35.00	65.00
S686	**12 SHILLINGS - 6 PENCE** 1900.	20.00	40.00	75.00
S687	**15 SHILLINGS** 1900.	20.00	40.00	75.00
S688	**17 SHILLINGS - 6 PENCE** 1900.	25.00	50.00	85.00

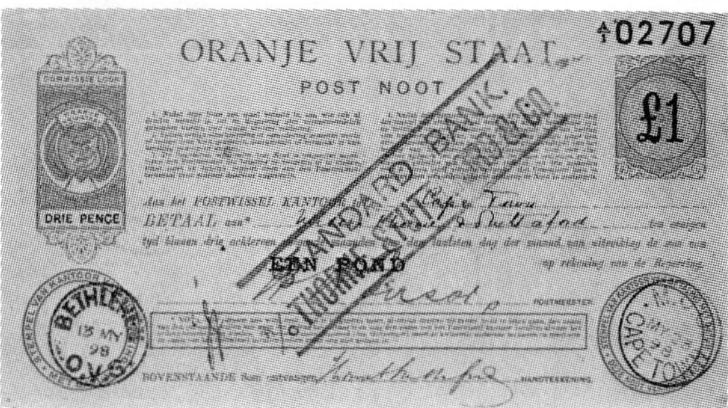

		GOOD	FINE	XF
S689	**1 POUND** 1900.	30.00	60.00	90.00

NOTE: Cancelled postal orders are worth about 1/2 of the values shown.

ORANGE RIVER COLONY

SIEGE OF KOFFYFONTEIN

Koffyfontein is a small diamond-mining town near Kimberley. During the war the British forces under Major Robertson were besieged. Only the single denomination of 5 pounds is known to have been issued during the siege.

1901 ISSUE

		GOOD	FINE	XF
S691	**5 POUNDS** 1.1.1901. British flag at l., lg. numeral at r.	—	Rare	—

TRANSVAAL (Z.A.R.)

POST OFFICE

1900 POSTAL MONEY ORDER ISSUE

#S701-S709 blank postal note forms used as currency during the war.

		GOOD	FINE	XF
S701	**1 SHILLING** 1900.	15.00	30.00	60.00
S702	**2 SHILLINGS - 6 PENCE** 1900.	15.00	30.00	60.00
S703	**5 SHILLINGS** 1900.	15.00	30.00	60.00
S704	**7 SHILLINGS - 6 PENCE** 1900.	15.00	30.00	60.00
S705	**10 SHILLINGS** 1900.	18.00	35.00	65.00
S706	**12 SHILLINGS - 6 PENCE** 1900.	20.00	40.00	75.00
S707	**15 SHILLINGS** 1900.	20.00	40.00	75.00
S708	**17 SHILLINGS - 6 PENCE** 1900.	25.00	50.00	85.00
S709	**1 POUND** 1900.	30.00	60.00	90.00

NOTE: Cancelled postal orders are worth about 1/2 of the values shown.

UPINGTON

UPINGTON BORDER SCOUTS

The Upington Border Scouts ran short of money because of the war. In the absence of paper supplies, notes were handwritten w/hand stamp: Issued By/Paymaster. B.S. Upington and border scouts' seal on different kinds of cloth (unbleached calico and khaki) and handsigned by Major Birkbeck O.C. These were issued during 1902.

1902 ISSUE

#S711-S715 are hand dated from the first of February-April 1902. Emblem of the Border Scouts at l.

		GOOD	FINE	XF
S711	**2 SHILLINGS** 1.3.1902.			
	a. Issued note.	—	Rare	—
	b. Hand stamped: *CANCELLED BY PAYMENT.*	—	Rare	—
S712	**5 SHILLINGS** 1902.			
	a. Issued note.	—	Rare	—
	b. Hand stamped: *CANCELLED BY PAYMENT.*	—	Rare	—
S713	**10 SHILLINGS** 1902.			
	a. Issued note.	—	Rare	—
	b. Hand stamped: *CANCELLED BY PAYMENT.*	—	Rare	—
S714	**1 POUND** 1.2.1902.			
	a. Issued note.	—	Rare	—
	b. Hand stamped: *CANCELLED BY PAYMENT.*	—	Rare	—

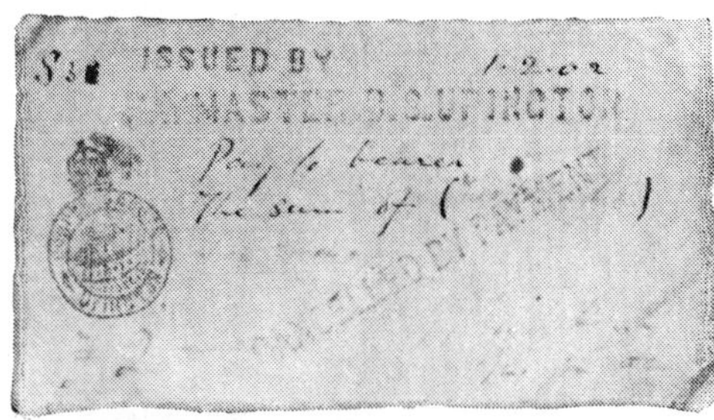

		GOOD	FINE	XF
S715	**2 POUNDS** 1902.			
	a. Issued note.	—	Rare	—
	b. Hand stamped: *CANCELLED BY PAYMENT.*	—	1000.	—

The Spanish State, forming the greater part of the Iberian Peninsula of southwest Europe, has an area of 194,884 sq. mi. (504,750 sq. km.) and a population of 40.5 million including the Balearic and the Canary Islands. Capital: Madrid. The economy is based on agriculture, industry and tourism. Machinery, fruit, vegetables and chemicals are exported.

It is not known when man first came to the Iberian Peninsula - the Altamira caves off the Cantabrian coast approximately 50 miles west of Santander were fashioned in Paleolithic times. Spain was a battleground for centuries before it became a united nation, fought for by Phoenicians, Carthaginians, Greeks, Celts, Romans, Vandals, Visigoths and Moors. Ferdinand and Isabella destroyed the last Moorish stronghold in 1492, freeing the national energy and resources for the era of discovery and colonization that would make Spain the most powerful country in Europe during the 16th century. After the destruction of the Spanish Armada, 1588, Spain never again played a major role in European politics. Napoleonic France ruled Spain between 1808 and 1814. The monarchy was restored in 1814 and continued, interrupted by the short-lived republic of 1873-74, until the exile of Alfonso XIII in 1931, when the Second Republic was established. A bloody civil war ensued in 1936, and Francisco Franco established himself as ruler of fascist Spain after his forces, aided by the Italians and especially the Germans, defeated the Republican forces.

The monarchy was reconstituted in 1947 under the regency of General Francisco Franco, the king designate to be crowned after Franco's death. Franco died on Nov. 30, 1975. Two days after his passing, Juan Carlos de Borbón, the grandson of Alfonso XIII, was proclaimed King of Spain.

RULERS:

Ferdinand VII, 1808-1833
Isabella II, 1833-1868
Amadeo I, 1871-1873
Regency, 1874
Alfonso XII, 1875-1885
Alfonso XIII, 1886-1931
2nd Republic and Civil War, 1932-1936
Francisco Franco, regent, 1937-1975
Juan Carlos I, 1975-

MONETARY SYSTEM:

1 Peseta = 100 Centimos 1874-2001

COMMERCIAL BANKS:

NOTE: The Assignado Imperial issues are known to be fantasies.

COMMERCIAL BANKS

ARAMBURU HERMANOS

CADIZ ISSUE

S151	**500 REALES DE VELLON** 18xx. Black on brown and green unpt. Allegorical man w/lions, 2 pillars behind, at upper ctr. Back green; head at l. and r. Printer: BWC. Unsigned remainder.	—	Unc	125.00

BANCO BALEAR

1864 ISSUE

		GOOD	FINE	XF
S201	**100 REALES DE VELLON** 186x.	—	—	—
S202	**200 REALES DE VELLON** 186x.	—	—	—
S203	**500 REALES DE VELLON** 186x.	—	—	—
S204	**1000 REALES DE VELLON** 186x.	—	—	—

		Good	Fine	XF
S205	**2000 Reales De Vellon** 1864. 2 seated allegorical women flanking arms at upper ctr. Series E.	—	—	—
S206	**4000 Reales De Vellon** 186x.	—	—	—

Banco de Barcelona

NOTE: Reprints are on specially wmk. paper.

1845 Issue

		Good	Fine	XF
S211	**250 Pesos** 184x.			
	a. Issued note.	—	—	—
	b. Reprint. (1894).	—	—	—

1840's Issue

		Good	Fine	XF
S221	**5 Pesos** 184x.	—	—	—
S222	**10 Pesos** 184x.	—	—	—
S223	**25 Pesos** 184x.	—	—	—
S224	**50 Pesos** 184x.	—	—	—
S225	**100 Pesos** 184x.	—	—	—
S226	**200 Pesos** 184x.			
	a. Issued note.	—	—	—
	b. Reprint. (1894).	—	—	—

1859 Issue

		Good	Fine	XF
S231	**5 Pesos** 18xx.	—	—	—
S232	**10 Pesos** 18xx.	—	—	—
S233	**25 Pesos** 18xx.	—	—	—
S234	**50 Pesos** 18xx.	—	—	—
S235	**100 Pesos** 18xx.	—	—	—
S236	**200 Pesos** 18xx.			
	a. Issued note.	—	—	—
	b. Reprint. (1894).	—	—	—

1868 Issue

#S241-S246 crowned woman at l., woman w/shield at r.

		Good	Fine	XF
S241	**5 Pesos** 18xx. Series A.			
	a. Issued note.	—	—	—
	b. Reprint. (1894).	—	—	—
S242	**10 Pesos** 18xx. Series B.	—	—	—
S243	**25 Pesos** 18xx. Series C.	—	—	—
S244	**50 Pesos** 18xx. Series D.	—	—	—

		Good	Fine	XF
S245	**100 Pesos** 18xx. Series E.	—	—	—
S246	**200 Pesos** 18xx. Series F.	—	—	—

Banco de Bilbao

Issued from 1857 to about 1873.

1859 Issue

		Good	Fine	XF
S251	**100 Reales De Vellon** 1.9.1859. Crowned arms at upper ctr. Series F.	—	—	—

NOTE: Facsimiles exist of #S251 and similar designs for denominations of 200, 500, 1000 and 2000 Reales de Vellon produced for stockholder's books in 1932 which were printed on normal paper.

		Good	Fine	XF
S252	**200 Reales De Vellon** 18xx. Series E.	—	—	—

		Good	Fine	XF
S253	**500 Reales De Vellon** 1.9.1859. Cherub at l. and r., seated allegorical woman holding staff and shield, sailing ship in background at ctr. Series D.	—	—	—
S254	**1000 Reales De Vellon** 18xx. Like #S253. Series C.	—	—	—

		Good	Fine	XF
S255	**2000 Reales De Vellon** 1.9.1859. Like #S253. Series B.	—	—	—

		GOOD	FINE	XF
S256	**4000 REALES DE VELLON** 18xx. Gateway to mine at l., sailing ship and seated allegorical woman holding staff and shield at ctr., smelting at r. Head at l. and r. on back. Series A.	—	—	—

BANCO DE BURGOS

1864 ISSUE

		GOOD	FINE	XF
S261	**100 REALES DE VELLON** 1864.	—	—	—
S262	**200 REALES DE VELLON** 1864.	—	—	—
S263	**500 REALES DE VELLON** 1864.	—	—	—
S264	**1000 REALES DE VELLON** 1864.	—	—	—
S265	**2000 REALES DE VELLON** 1864.	—	—	—
S266	**4000 REALES DE VELLON** 1864.	—	—	—

BANCO DE CÁDIZ

1847 ISSUE

#S271-S296 black. Hercules w/two lions between pillars at top ctr.

#S271-S286 dates filled in by hand.

#S271-S276 w/o red unpt. at ctr.

		GOOD	FINE	XF
S271	**100 REALES DE VELLON** 18xx. Green paper.	50.00	125.00	—
S272	**200 REALES DE VELLON** 18xx. Blue paper.	80.00	150.00	—

		GOOD	FINE	XF
S273	**500 REALES DE VELLON** 1.8.1851. Brown paper.	50.00	125.00	225.00
S274	**1000 REALES DE VELLON** 18xx. Yellow paper.	65.00	125.00	—
S275	**2000 REALES DE VELLON** 18xx. Rose paper.	125.00	—	—

		GOOD	FINE	XF
S276	**4000 REALES DE VELLON** 18xx. White paper.	75.00	140.00	—

186X ISSUE

#S281-S286 red unpt. at ctr.

		GOOD	FINE	XF
S281	**100 REALES DE VELLON** 1.8.186x. Green paper.	40.00	100.00	185.00
S282	**200 REALES DE VELLON** 18xx. Blue paper.	75.00	145.00	—
S283	**500 REALES DE VELLON** 18xx. Brown paper.	80.00	150.00	—
S284	**1000 REALES DE VELLON** 18xx. Yellow paper.	80.00	150.00	—
S285	**2000 REALES DE VELLON** 18xx. Rose paper.	80.00	150.00	—
S286	**4000 REALES DE VELLON** 18xx. White paper.	80.00	150.00	—

1863 ND ISSUE

		GOOD	FINE	XF
S291	**100 REALES DE VELLON** ND. Green paper, orange unpt. at ctr.	30.00	85.00	150.00

		Good	Fine	XF
S292	**200 Reales De Vellon** ND. Blue paper.	125.00	—	—
S293	**500 Reales De Vellon** ND. Brown paper.	60.00	120.00	—

		Good	Fine	XF
S294	**1000 Reales De Vellon** ND. Yellow paper.	80.00	150.00	—
S295	**2000 Reales De Vellon** ND. Rose paper.	60.00	120.00	—

		Good	Fine	XF
S296	**4000 Reales De Vellon** ND. White paper, lt. green unpt. at ctr.	65.00	185.00	—

Banco de la Coruña

1857 Issue

		Good	Fine	XF
S301	**100 Reales De Vellon** 18xx.	—	—	—
S302	**200 Reales De Vellon** 18xx.	—	—	—
S303	**500 Reales De Vellon** 18xx.	—	—	—
S304	**1000 Reales De Vellon** 18xx.	—	—	—
S305	**2000 Reales De Vellon** 18xx.	—	—	—
S306	**4000 Reales De Vellon** 18xx.	—	—	—

Banco de Emisión y Descuentos de Santiago

1800's Issue

		Good	Fine	XF
S308	**200 Reales De Vellon** 18xx. Standing allegorical woman holding staff and shield, foliage in background at upper ctr. r. Series B.	—	—	—

Banco de Jerez de la Frontera

1800's Issue

		Good	Fine	XF
S311	**100 Reales De Vellon** 18xx.	—	—	—
S312	**200 Reales De Vellon** 18xx.	—	—	—
S313	**500 Reales De Vellon** 18xx.	—	—	—
S314	**1000 Reales De Vellon** 18xx.	—	—	—
S315	**2000 Reales De Vellon** 18xx.	—	—	—
S316	**4000 Reales De Vellon** 18xx.	—	—	—

Banco de Málaga

1860 Issue

#S321-S326 seated woman w/cornucopia at upper ctr.

		Good	Fine	XF
S321	**100 Reales De Vellon** 18xx.	80.00	175.00	—
S322	**200 Reales De Vellon** 18xx.	125.00	—	—
S323	**500 Reales De Vellon** 18xx.	—	—	—
S324	**1000 Reales De Vellon** 18xx.	—	—	—

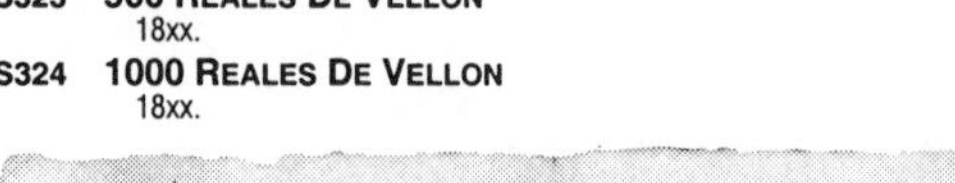

		Good	Fine	XF
S325	**2000 Reales De Vellon** 18xx.			
	a. Issued note.	—	—	—
	b. Punched hole cancelled.	500.00	1000.	—
S326	**4000 Reales De Vellon** 18xx.	—	—	—

1865 ND Issue

#S331-S336 similar to #S321-S326 but more ornate m/c printing.

		Good	Fine	XF
S331	**100 Reales De Vellon** ND.	150.00	400.00	—
S332	**200 Reales De Vellon** ND.	—	—	—
S333	**500 Reales De Vellon** ND.	—	—	—
S334	**1000 Reales De Vellon** ND.	—	—	—
S335	**2000 Reales De Vellon** ND.	—	—	—
S336	**4000 Reales De Vellon** ND.	—	—	—

Banco de Oviedo

1864 Issue

		Good	Fine	XF
S341	**100 Reales De Vellon** 186x.	—	—	—
S342	**200 Reales De Vellon** 186x.	—	—	—
S343	**500 Reales De Vellon** 186x.	—	—	—
S344	**1000 Reales De Vellon** 186x.	—	—	—
S345	**2000 Reales De Vellon** 186x.	—	—	—
S346	**4000 Reales De Vellon** 186x.	—	—	—

Banco de Palencia

1864 Issue

		Good	Fine	XF
S351	**100 Reales De Vellon** 186x.	—	—	—
S352	**200 Reales De Vellon** 186x.	—	—	—
S353	**500 Reales De Vellon** 186x.	—	—	—
S354	**1000 Reales De Vellon** 186x.	—	—	—
S355	**2000 Reales De Vellon** 186x.	—	—	—
S356	**4000 Reales De Vellon** 186x.	—	—	—

Banco de Pamplona

1863 Issue

		Good	Fine	XF
S361	**100 Reales De Vellon** 186x.	—	—	—
S362	**200 Reales De Vellon** 186x.	—	—	—
S363	**500 Reales De Vellon** 186x.	—	—	—
S364	**1000 Reales De Vellon** 186x.	—	—	—
S365	**2000 Reales De Vellon** 186x.	—	—	—
S366	**4000 Reales De Vellon** 186x.	—	—	—

Banco de Reus

1862 Issue

		Good	Fine	XF
S371	**100 Reales De Vellon** 186x.	—	—	—
S372	**200 Reales De Vellon** 186x.	—	—	—
S373	**500 Reales De Vellon** 186x.	—	—	—
S374	**1000 Reales De Vellon** 186x.	—	—	—
S375	**2000 Reales De Vellon** 186x.	—	—	—
S376	**4000 Reales De Vellon** 186x.	—	—	—

1870s Issue

		Good	Fine	XF
S380	**2000 Reales De Vellon** 187x. Black. Arms at upper ctr., standing figures at l. and r. Series B.	—	—	—

Banco de San Sebastián

1862 Issue

		Good	Fine	XF
S381	**100 Reales De Vellon** 186x.	—	—	—
S382	**200 Reales De Vellon** 186x.	—	—	—
S383	**500 Reales De Vellon** 186x.	—	—	—
S384	**1000 Reales De Vellon** 186x.	—	—	—
S385	**2000 Reales De Vellon** 186x.	—	—	—
S386	**4000 Reales De Vellon** 186x.	—	—	—

Banco de Santander

1857 Issue

#S391-S396 flags and sailing ship at upper ctr.

		Good	Fine	XF
S391	**100 Reales De Vellon** 18xx.	—	—	—
S392	**200 Reales De Vellon** 18xx.	—	—	—
S393	**500 Reales De Vellon** 1.5.1861. Black on pink unpt. Series C.	—	—	—
S394	**1000 Reales De Vellon** 18xx.	—	—	—
S395	**2000 Reales De Vellon** 18xx.	—	—	—
S396	**4000 Reales De Vellon** 18xx.	—	—	—

Banco de Santiago

1864 Issue

		Good	Fine	XF
S401	**100 Reales De Vellon** 186x.	—	—	—
S402	**200 Reales De Vellon** 186x.	—	—	—
S403	**500 Reales De Vellon** 186x.	—	—	—
S404	**1000 Reales De Vellon** 186x.	—	—	—
S405	**2000 Reales De Vellon** 186x.	—	—	—
S406	**4000 Reales De Vellon** 186x.	—	—	—

Banco de Sevilla

1857 Issue

#S411-S416 arms at ctr.

		Good	Fine	XF
S411	**100 Reales De Vellon** 185x.	—	—	—
S412	**200 Reales De Vellon** 185x.	—	—	—
S413	**500 Reales De Vellon** 185x.	—	—	—
S414	**1000 Reales De Vellon** 185x.	—	—	—
S415	**2000 Reales De Vellon** 185x.	—	—	—
S416	**4000 Reales De Vellon** 185x.	—	—	—

Banco de Tarragona

1864 Issue

		Good	Fine	XF
S421	**100 Reales De Vellon** 186x.	—	—	—
S422	**200 Reales De Vellon** 186x.	—	—	—
S423	**500 Reales De Vellon** 186x.	—	—	—
S424	**1000 Reales De Vellon** 186x.	—	—	—
S425	**2000 Reales De Vellon** 186x.	—	—	—
S426	**4000 Reales De Vellon** 186x.	—	—	—

Banco de Valladolid

Liquidated in 1886.

1857 Issue

#S431-S436 double arms at upper ctr.

		Good	Fine	XF
S431	**100 Reales De Vellon** 1.8.1857. Series A.	—	—	—
S432	**200 Reales De Vellon** 1.8.1857. Series B.	—	—	—

		GOOD	FINE	XF
S433	**500 REALES DE VELLON** 1.8.1857. Series C.			
	a. Issued note.	—	—	—

		GOOD	FINE	XF
	b. W/liquidation hand stamp.	675.00	1350.	2250.
S434	**1000 REALES DE VELLON** 1.8.1857. Lilac and black. Series D.	—	—	—
S435	**2000 REALES DE VELLON** 1.8.1857. Series E.	—	—	—
S436	**4000 REALES DE VELLON** 1.8.1857. Series F.	—	—	—

BANCO DE VITORIA

1860 ND ISSUE

#S441-S446 arms at upper l., ctr. and r.

		GOOD	FINE	XF
S441	**100 REALES DE VELLON** 186x.	—	—	—
S442	**200 REALES DE VELLON** 186x.	—	—	—
S443	**500 REALES DE VELLON** 186x.	—	—	—
S444	**1000 REALES DE VELLON** 186x.	—	—	—
S445	**2000 REALES DE VELLON** 186x.	—	—	—
S446	**4000 REALES DE VELLON** 186x.	—	—	—

BANCO DE ZARAGOZA

1857 ISSUE

#S451-S456 crowned double arms at upper ctr.

		GOOD	FINE	XF
S451	**100 REALES DE VELLON** 14.5.1857.			
	a. Issued note.	—	—	—
	b. Punched hole cancelled.	80.00	150.00	—

		GOOD	FINE	XF
S452	**200 REALES DE VELLON** 14.5.1857. Series B.			
	a. Issued note.	—	—	—
	b. Punched hole cancelled.	90.00	160.00	—

		GOOD	FINE	XF
S453	**500 REALES DE VELLON** 14.5.1857. Series B.			
	a. Issued note.	—	—	—
	b. Punched hole cancelled.	75.00	140.00	—
S454	**1000 REALES DE VELLON** 14.5.1857.	—	—	—

		Good	Fine	XF
S455	**2000 Reales De Vellon** 14.5.1857. Series E. Remainder.	80.00	150.00	—
S456	**4000 Reales De Vellon** 14.5.1857.	—	—	—

With the end of the Spanish-American War (1898) and the loss of her empire, Spain drifted into chaotic times. Stung by their defeats in Cuba, the army blamed the socialists for what they considered to be mismanagement at home. Additional political complications were derived from the successful Russian Revolution which gave impetus to an already thriving socialist party and trade union movement. Finally, King Alfonso XIII committed the fatal mistake of encouraging a reckless general to start a campaign in Morocco that ended in the virtual extermination of the Spanish army. Fearing that the inevitable parliamentary investigation would incriminate the crown, he offered no objection when General Primo de Rivera seized the government and established himself as dictator in 1926. Rivera fell from power in 1930, and the government was taken over by an alliance of Liberals and Socialists who tried to separate the Church and State, take the army out of politics, and introduce effective labor and agrarian reforms despite numerous strikes and street riots. The election of 1936 brought to power a coalition of Socialists, Liberals and Communists, to the dismay of the traditionalists and landowners.

A number of right-wing generals, including a young and clever Francisco Franco, began preparations for a military coup which erupted into a civil war in July of 1936. The destructive conflict, in which more than a million died, lasted three years. During the struggle, areas under control of both the Nationalist (rebels) and the Republican (Loyalists) issued currency that whatever extent the political and military situation permitted. The war ended in defeat for the Loyalists when Madrid fell to Franco on March 29, 1939.

Poor reproductions have surfaced with tell-tale characteristics such as printed creases, folds, altered serial # areas etc.

MONETARY SYSTEM

1 Peseta = 100 Centimos

BANCO DE ESPAÑA, BILBAO

1936 ISSUE

The name of the issuing bank was hand stamped at lower right on the 5 Pesetas notes and imprinted on the 25, 50 and 100 Pesetas notes. The following banks and a bank pawn shop issued notes:

a. Banco de Bilbao
b. Banco Central de Bilbao
c. Banco del Comercio de Bilbao
d. Banco Guipuzcoano
e. Banco Hispano Americano
f. Banco Urquijo Vascongado
g. Banco de Vizcaya (9 varieties of hand stamps)
h. Caja de Ahorros Vizcaína (2 varieties of hand stamps)
i. Caja de Ahorros y Monte de Piedad Municipal de Bilbao

#S551-S554 uniface.

		VG	VF	Unc
S551	**5 Pesetas** 30.8.1936. Red on olive. Hand stamps: a-i.			
	a. Serial # at upper ctr. 2 serial # varieties. Denomination at upper r.	5.00	20.00	50.00
	b. Prefix serial letter A at upper r. Denomination at upper ctr.	5.00	20.00	50.00

#S552-S554 various hand stamped dates.

		VG	VF	Unc
S552	**25 Pesetas** 1.9.1936-13.3.1937. Brown-violet. Local bank imprints: a-i.	7.50	25.00	60.00
S553	**50 Pesetas** 1.9.1936-17.3.1937. Green on olive. Local bank imprints: a-i.	10.00	30.00	75.00
S554	**100 Pesetas** 1.9.1936; 28.10.1936; 9.1.1937; 6.3.1937. Blue on olive. Local bank imprints: a-i.	12.50	40.00	90.00

1937 ISSUE

This series has designs on back.

The name of the issuing bank was imprinted at lower right. The following banks and a pawn shop issued notes.

a. Banco de Bilbao
b. Banco del Comercio
c. Banco Guipuzcoano
d. Banco Hispano Americano
e. Banco Urquijo Vascongado
f. Banco de Vizcaya
g. Caja de Ahorros Vizcaína
h. Caja de Ahorros y Monte de Piedad Municipal de Bilbao
i. Banco Central

Market valuations indicated are for the more commonly encountered issues. Some of the scarcer issues are #S561c; S562g; S563d and e, and S564g.

		VG	VF	UNC
S561	**5 PESETAS** 1.1.1937. Green. Shepherd w/herd and tree on back. Local bank imprints: a; c; d; e; f; g; h.	1.00	3.50	8.00

		VG	VF	UNC
S562	**10 PESETAS** 1.1.1937. Brown. Entrance to a bldg. on back. Local bank imprints: a; f; g; h.	1.50	4.50	10.00

		VG	VF	UNC
S563	**25 PESETAS** 1.1.1937. Brown. Forge on back. Local bank imprints: b; d; e; g.	1.75	5.00	12.00

		VG	VF	UNC
S564	**50 PESETAS** 1.1.1937. Blue. Worker on back. Local bank imprints: a; f; g; h.	2.00	7.00	15.00

		VG	VF	UNC
S565	**100 PESETAS** 1.1.1937. Green. Farmer plowing w/2 oxen on back. Local bank imprints: a; f; h.	5.00	12.50	35.00

		VG	VF	UNC
S566	**500 PESETAS** 1.1.1937. Gray-brown. Port on back.			
	a. Local bank imprints: a-i.	10.00	20.00	50.00
	b. W/o local bank imprint.	—	—	—

		VG	VF	UNC
S567	**1000 PESETAS** 1.1.1937. Lilac. Factory plant on back.			
	a. Local bank imprints: a-i.	10.00	30.00	80.00
	b. W/o local bank imprint.	—	—	—

BANCO DE ESPAÑA, GIJÓN

1936 ISSUE

		VG	VF	UNC
S571	**5 PESETAS** 5.11.1936. Pink with brown. Diagonal stripe.	5.00	20.00	—
S572	**10 PESETAS** 5.11.1936. Pink with green. Diagonal stripe.	7.50	30.00	—

		VG	VF	UNC
S573	**25 PESETAS** 5.11.1936. Pink with blue. Diagonal stripe.	10.00	35.00	—
S574	**50 PESETAS** 5.11.1936. Green with yellow. Diagonal stripe.	12.50	40.00	—

		VG	VF	UNC
S575	**100 PESETAS** 5.11.1936. Green with red-brown. Diagonal stripe.	20.00	50.00	—

1937 ISSUE

		VG	VF	UNC
S579	**50 PESETAS** Sept., 1937. Blue. Worker in factory plant on back.	—	—	—

		VG	VF	UNC
S580	**100 PESETAS** Sept., 1937. Blue on lt. brown. 2 farmers working on back.	3.00	8.00	15.00

BANCO DE ESPAÑA, SANTANDER

1936 ISSUE

Issued by different banks whose name appears imprinted at lower right. The following banks and a pawn shop issued notes:

a. Banco de Bilbao-Santander
b. Banco Español de Crédito
c. Banco Hispano Americano
d. Banco Mercantil
e. Banco de Santander
f. Monte de Piedad

		VG	VF	UNC
S581	**5 PESETAS** 1.11.1936. Gray. Local bank or pawn shop imprints: a-f.	3.00	10.00	25.00
S582	**10 PESETAS** 1.11.1936. Gray. Local bank or pawn shop imprints: a-f.	5.00	15.00	35.00
S583	**25 PESETAS** 1.11.1936. Gray. Local bank or pawn shop imprints: a-f.	7.50	17.50	40.00

		VG	VF	UNC
S584	**50 PESETAS** 1.11.1936. Gray. Local bank or pawn shop imprints: a-f.	10.00	22.50	50.00
S585	**100 PESETAS** 1.11.1936. Gray. Local bank or pawn shop imprints: a-f.	12.50	27.50	60.00

GENERALITAT DE CATALUNYA

1936 ISSUE

		VG	VF	UNC
S591	**2.50 PESSETES** 25.9.1936. Gray-green. Worker and factory on back.			
	a. Red serial #.	10.00	30.00	—
	b. Black serial #.	10.00	30.00	—

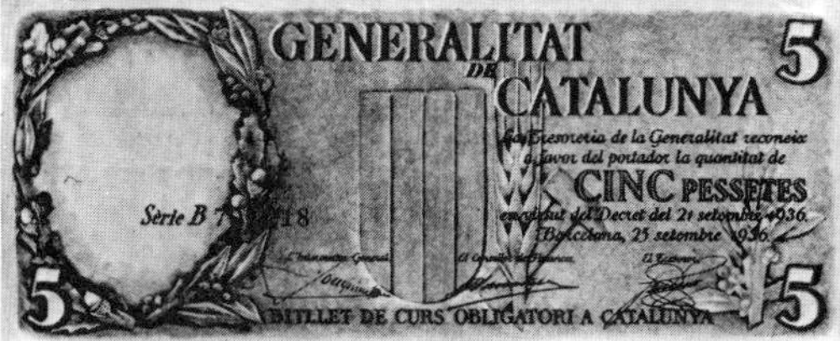

		VG	VF	UNC
S592	**5 PESSETES** 25.9.1936. Brown. Rifles at ctr. on back, worker at l., farmer at r.	12.50	37.50	—
S593	**10 PESSETES** 25.9.1936. Green. Fishing boats on back.	22.50	70.00	—

NOTE: There are primitively produced notes in denominations of 10, 25, 50, 500, 1000 Pesetas, stamped, date hand typewritten and printed heading: *GENERALITAT DE CATALUNYA* which are believed to be forgeries produced for collectors.

CONSEJO DE ASTURIAS Y LEÓN

1936 ISSUE

		VG	VF	UNC
S601	**25 CENTIMOS** ND (ca.1936). Gray-violet and blue. Working in the port on back.	.75	2.00	4.00
S602	**40 CENTIMOS** ND (ca.1936). Brown-violet and green. Working in the port on back.	1.00	2.50	5.00
S603	**50 CENTIMOS** ND (ca.1936). Blue and violet. Blacksmith on back.	1.25	3.00	6.00

		VG	VF	UNC
S604	**1 PESETA** ND (ca.1936). Red-brown and yellow. Seated woman w/lion at l.	1.25	4.00	10.00
S605	**2 PESETAS** ND (ca.1936). Gray-olive and red. Seated woman w/lion at l.	2.25	5.00	12.00

Straits Settlements is a former British crown colony on the south and west coast of Malay Peninsula consisting of Malacca, Penang, Singapore, Labuan (Borneo), Cocos Island and Christmas Island. Cocos Island, Christmas Island and Labuan were placed under control of the Governor of Straits Settlements in 1886.

The colony was united under one government as a presidency of India in 1826, was incorporated under Bengal in 1830, and was removed from control of the Indian government and placed under direct British control in 1867. Japanese forces occupied the colony in 1941-45.

RULERS:
British

MONETARY SYSTEM:
1 Dollar = 100 Cents

BRITISH ADMINISTRATION

ASIATIC BANKING CORPORATION

SINGAPORE

The Singapore branch opened in 1862, and issued its first bank notes in 1864. This bank closed during a financial crisis in 1866.

1862 ISSUE

#S75-S79 arms at ctr. 210 x 132mm. Printer: Smith Elder & Company, Engravers, London. Unsigned remainders.

		GOOD	FINE	XF
S75	**10 DOLLARS** 18xx. Pink and black.	—	—	—
S76	**25 DOLLARS** 18xx. Orange and black.	—	—	—
S77	**50 DOLLARS** 18xx. Mauve and black.	—	—	—
S78	**100 DOLLARS** 18xx. Green and black.	—	—	—

		GOOD	FINE	XF
S79	**500 DOLLARS** 18xx. Blue and black.	—	—	—

CHARTERED BANK OF INDIA, AUSTRALIA AND CHINA

PENANG

This branch opened in 1875, issuing notes until 1907.

1875 ISSUE

#S101-S106 various date and sign. varieties. Crowned supported arms at upper ctr. Printer: WWS.

		GOOD	FINE	XF
S101	**5 DOLLARS** 18xx. Dk. black w/deep yellow *FIVE* protector.	—	Rare	—.

		GOOD	FINE	XF
S102	**10 DOLLARS** 18xx. Blue w/green *TEN* protector.	—	Rare	—
S103	**20 DOLLARS** 18xx. Orange and blue.	—	Rare	—
S104	**50 DOLLARS** 18xx. Brown w/magenta protector.	—	Rare	—
S105	**100 DOLLARS** 18xx. Green and red-orange.	—	Rare	—
S106	**500 DOLLARS** 18xx. Orange and brown.	—	Rare	—

NOTE: A $25 denomination is reported, not confirmed.

SINGAPORE

This branch opened on February 19, 1859, and began issuing bank notes in 1861. Such notes were issued as needed until 1903.

1861 ISSUE

#S111-S117 various date and sign. varieties. Crowned supported arms at upper ctr. Printer: WWS.

		GOOD	FINE	XF
S111	**5 DOLLARS** 1.1.1890; 26.3.1890; 1.9.1893. Black w/deep yellow *FIVE* protector.	—	Rare	—

		GOOD	FINE	XF
S112	**10 DOLLARS** 25.5.1895. Blue w/green *TEN* protector.	—	Rare	—
S113	**20 DOLLARS** 18xx. Yellow and mauve.	—	Rare	—
S115	**50 DOLLARS** 18xx. Brown w/magenta protector.	—	Rare	—
S116	**100 DOLLARS** 18xx. Green and brown.	—	Rare	—

CHARTERED MERCANTILE BANK OF INDIA, LONDON AND CHINA

MALACCA

This branch was authorized to issue bank notes in 1881; it ceased issuing notes in 1889.

1881 ISSUE

#S121-S127 crowned supported English arms at upper ctr. Various date and sign. varieties. Printer: PBC.

		GOOD	FINE	XF
S121	**5 DOLLARS** 1.5.1886. Dk. blue on lt. blue unpt.	—	Rare	—

		GOOD	FINE	XF
S122	**10 DOLLARS** 2.1.1882; 2.1.1884. Blue w/ornate red *TEN* protector. Cancelled.	—	Rare	—
#S123	***Deleted.***			
S124	**25 DOLLARS** 18xx. Brown and black.	—	Rare	—
S125	**50 DOLLARS** 18xx. Green.	—	Rare	—
S126	**100 DOLLARS** 18xx. Black.	—	Rare	—
S127	**500 DOLLARS** 18xx. Orange and brown.	—	Rare	—

PENANG

This branch opened in 1860, and issued notes from December 31, 1861 until February of 1889.

1861 ISSUE

#S131-S137 crowned supported English arms at upper ctr. Various date and sign. varieties. Printer: PBC.

		GOOD	FINE	XF
S131	**5 DOLLARS** 2.1.1884; 2.12.1887. Blue on lt. blue unpt.	—	Rare	—
S132	**10 DOLLARS** 18xx. Blue w/ornate red *TEN* protector.	—	Rare	—
#S133	***Deleted.***			
S134	**25 DOLLARS** 18xx. Brown and black.	—	Rare	—
S135	**50 DOLLARS** 18xx. Green.	—	Rare	—
S136	**100 DOLLARS** 18xx. Black.	—	Rare	—
S137	**500 DOLLARS** 18xx. Orange and brown.	Reported Not Confirmed		

SINGAPORE

This branch began operations on September 12, 1855. $5, $10, $50 and $100 were first issued in 1861. Notes were issued with various dates and signatures up to July, 1892. Proofs of a $50, $100 and $500 from plates prepared after a Royal Charter allowed the word *CHARTERED* to be added to the bank name are known. That word was placed above the old name of the bank on these proofs.

1861 ISSUE

		Good	Fine	XF
S138	**50 DOLLARS** 18xx. Seated allegorical woman w/lion, crowned shield, tree at ctr. Proof.	—	—	—
S139	**100 DOLLARS** 18xx. Proof.	—	—	—
S140	**500 DOLLARS** 18xx. Dk. brown. Proof.	—	—	—

#S141-S147 crowned royal arms at upper ctr. Printer: WWS.

		Good	Fine	XF
S141	**5 DOLLARS** 19xx. Blue and black.	—	Rare	—
S142	**10 DOLLARS** 19xx. Blue w/red *TEN* protector.	—	Rare	—

#S143 Deleted.

		Good	Fine	XF
S144	**25 DOLLARS** (ca.1862). Brown.	—	Rare	—
S145	**50 DOLLARS** 18xx. Green.	—	Rare	—
S146	**100 DOLLARS** 19xx.	—	Rare	—
S147	**500 DOLLARS** (ca.1864). Brown w/ornate blue *FIVE HUNDRED* protector.	—	Rare	—

HONGKONG AND SHANGHAI BANKING CORPORATION

PENANG

This branch opened in 1884, and was given permission to issue bank notes in 1892. Issue dates run from January 1, 1893 to September 28, 1909.

1893 ISSUE

#S151-S157 crowned supported arms at upper ctr., lg. *PENANG* in unpt. Ornate arms at ctr. on back. Various date and sign. varieties. Printer: Metchim & Son, London.

		Good	Fine	XF
S151	**5 DOLLARS** 1.9.1893. Lt. green. Punched hole cancelled: *PAID.*	—	Rare	—
S152	**10 DOLLARS** 18xx. Blue.	—	Rare	—
S153	**20 DOLLARS** 18xx. Blue-green.	—	Rare	—
S154	**25 DOLLARS** 18xx. Brown.	—	Rare	—
S155	**50 DOLLARS** 18xx. Violet.	—	Rare	—
S156	**100 DOLLARS** 18xx. Red-orange.	—	Rare	—
S157	**500 DOLLARS** 18xx. Red.	—	Rare	—

SINGAPORE

This branch was opened in 1877, issuing its first bank notes on December 1, 1881. Various dates and signatures were used until September 28, 1909.

1881 FIRST ISSUE

#S161-S167 crowned supported arms at upper ctr. w/denomination protectors. Ornate arms at ctr. on back. Printer: Metchim & Son, London.

		Good	Fine	XF
S161	**5 DOLLARS** 1.1.1894. Green.	4250.	6600.	8750.

		Good	Fine	XF
S162	**10 DOLLARS** 18xx. Blue.	4000.	7000.	12,500.

#S163 Deleted.

		Good	Fine	XF
S164	**25 DOLLARS** 18xx. Brown.	—	Rare	—
S165	**50 DOLLARS** 18xx. Violet.	—	Rare	—
S166	**100 DOLLARS** 18xx. Red-orange w/dk. blue $100-$100 protector.	—	Rare	—
S167	**500 DOLLARS** 18xx. Red.	—	Rare	—

1881 SECOND ISSUE

#S169-S174 arms at upper ctr. Lg. guilloche as protector.

		VG	Fine	VF
S169	**5 DOLLARS** 18xx. Green.	—	Rare	—
S170	**10 DOLLARS** 18xx. Blue.	—	Rare	—
S171	**25 DOLLARS** 18xx. Blue-green.	—	Rare	—
S172	**50 DOLLARS** 18xx. Violet.	—	Rare	—
S173	**100 DOLLARS** 18xx. Red-orange.	—	Rare	—
S174	**500 DOLLARS** 18xx. Red.	—	Rare	—

NEW ORIENTAL BANK CORPORATION, LIMITED

Formed in 1884 after the collapse of the Oriental Bank Corporation. It also later failed in 1892.

SINGAPORE

1884 ISSUE

		VG	Fine	VF
S181	**1 DOLLAR** 18xx. Arms of Mexico at l., woman's head at r. Printer: BWC. Specimen.	—	Rare	—

NORTH WESTERN BANK OF INDIA

Established at Singapore in late 1855; closed 1859.

SINGAPORE

1830'S ISSUE

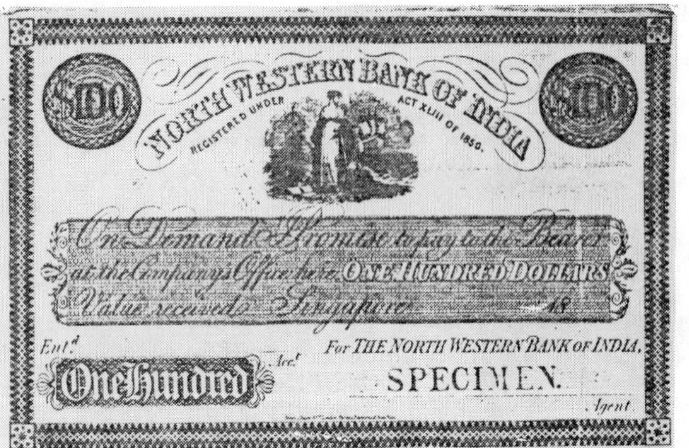

		VG	FINE	VF
S196	**100 DOLLARS** Woman standing by beehive at top ctr. Specimen.	—	Rare	—

NOTE: The single known example of #S196 is unissued. Other denominations are reported, not confirmed.

ORIENTAL BANK

Later became the Oriental Bank Corporation.

SINGAPORE

1849 ISSUE

		GOOD	FINE	XF
S201	**5 DOLLARS** 31.5.1849.	—	—	—
S205	**100 DOLLARS** 31.5.1849.	—	—	—

NOTE: No notes are known.

ORIENTAL BANK CORPORATION

Formerly the Oriental Bank. New name took effect in 1851; the bank failed in 1883. A single cut proof of the $100 denomination is known.

SINGAPORE

1851 ISSUE

		GOOD	FINE	XF
S215	**100 DOLLARS** 1851.	—	—	—

UNION BANK OF CALCUTTA

Opened in December 1840. Closed a few years later.

SINGAPORE

1840'S ISSUE

		GOOD	FINE	XF
S225	**100 SPANISH DOLLARS** 184x. Printer: Smith, Elder & Co., Cornhill, London, England.	—	Rare	—

NOTE: Other denominations are reported, not confirmed.

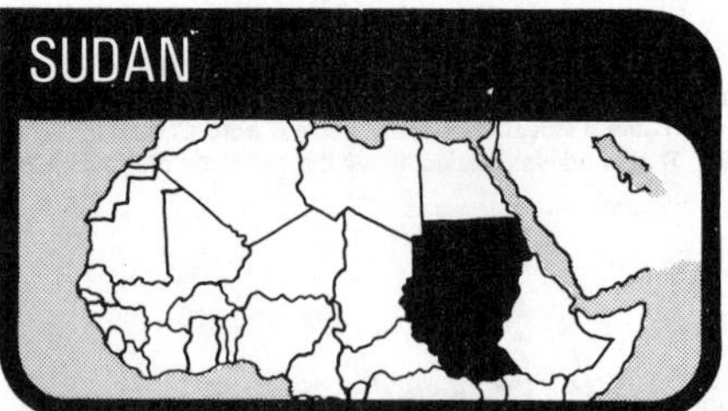

The Democratic Republic of the Sudan, located in northeast Africa on the Red Sea between Egypt and Ethiopia, has an area of 967,500 sq. mi. (2,505,810 sq. km.) and a population of 29.82 million. Capital: Khartoum. Agriculture and livestock raising are the chief occupations. Cotton, gum arabic and peanuts are exported.

The Sudan, site of the powerful Nubian kingdom of Roman times, was a collection of small independent states from the 14th century until 1820-22 when it was conquered and united by Mohammed Ali, Pasha of Egypt. Egyptian forces were driven from the area during the Mahdist revolt, 1881-98, but the Sudan was retaken by Anglo-Egyptian expeditions, 1896-98, and established as an Anglo-Egyptian condominium in 1899. Britain supplied the administrative apparatus and personnel, but the appearance of joint Anglo-Egyptian administration was continued until Jan. 9, 1954, when the first Sudanese self-government parliament was inaugurated.

RULERS:

British, 1899-1954

SIEGE OF KHARTOUM, 1884

In 1881, Mohammed Ahmed, a boat builder from Dongola, incensed at Egyptian brutality and mismanagement of the Sudan, announced that he was the *ruler of righteousness* who would wipe out the British and Egyptian forces. He proclaimed himself the *Mahdi* - the reincarnation of the Prophet. With that he began fighting against Egyptian forces sent in against him, and in 1883 wiped out two large groups.

With Egypt bankrupt and Prime Minister Gladstone opposed to colonial adventures, the Egyptians were ordered to evacuate the Sudan. To supervise these arrangements he sent General Charles George Gordon - "Chinese" Gordon of earlier Taiping fame - to Khartoum. Gordon saw this as an opportunity to wrest some action from Gladstone by forcing an army to be sent in to suppress the rebellion, thus saving the Sudan from falling into the hands of slave traders and Muslim fanatics. Gordon then locked himself up in Khartoum to create siege conditions against himself, however, the Mahdi was reluctant to storm the city, but Gladstone was equally reluctant to send any troops to fight the Mahdi's forces. British reinforcements at Aswan were ordered to stay put, and Gordon was again ordered to leave while he controlled the Nile. Still Gordon refused! Public clamor to end this stalemate finally did force Gladstone to order the British force to move in from Aswan, and this in turn forced the reluctant Mahdi to attack Khartoum. The city was carried by storm and Gordon slain on January 26, 1885 after a siege of almost a year.

During the siege period Gordon needed money with which to pay his troops and cover the expenses. He caused these notes to be issued and declared he was "personally responsible for the liquidation and anyone can bring action against me, in my individual capacity, to recover the money." It is thought that around £168,500 sterling was issued in face value. A large number of notes were destroyed immediately after the end of the siege. Controversy about their redemption lasted for years. It is estimated that only 3-4,000 notes of all denominations escaped destruction. The majority of the notes carry a hectographic reproduction of General Gordon's signature but there are some which have a hand signature claimed to be that of Gordon himself.

Determining denominations is very difficult unless one studies the upper frame of the note. The different designs seen there indicate denomination. Some notes are stamped *RESTITUE PAR LA COMMISSION DES INDEMNITES DU SOUDAN* on the back.

1884 FIRST SUDAN PIASTRE ISSUE

#S101-S111 w/sign. and seal of General Gordon. All notes are dated 25.4.1884 in Arabic.

#S101

#S102

		GOOD	FINE	XF
S101	**1 PIASTRE** 1884.	3000.	4000.	6000.
S102	**5 PIASTRES** 1884. Half-moon design going up at ctr.	350.00	500.00	750.00

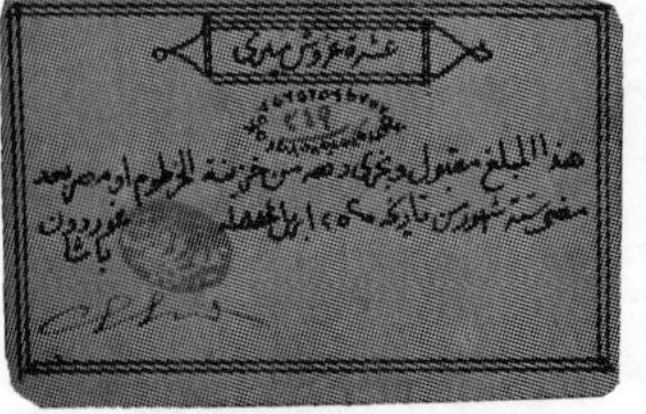

#S103

#S104

		GOOD	FINE	XF
S103	**10 PIASTRES** 1884. Oval design consisting of circles and angles at ctr.	150.00	350.00	600.00
S104	**20 PIASTRES** 1884. Half-moon design going down at ctr.	125.00	175.00	300.00

#S105

#S106

		Good	Fine	XF
S105	**100 Piastres** 1884. Longer oval design of wavy line and dots at ctr.	100.00	150.00	250.00
S106	**500 Piastres** 1884. Circle w/sawteeth at ctr.	150.00	225.00	500.00

#S107

#S108

		Good	Fine	XF
S107	**1000 Piastres** 1884. More evenly oval design of circles and lines at ctr.	150.00	250.00	650.00
S108	**2000 Piastres** 1884. Rectangle w/sawteeth design at ctr.	200.00	400.00	900.00

#S109

#S110

		Good	Fine	XF
S109	**2500 Piastres** 1884. Plain half-moon going up w/a smaller semicircular line coming down through it at ctr.	100.00	150.00	250.00
S110	**5000 Piastres** 1884. Diamond design at ctr.	125.00	175.00	300.00

1884 Egyptian Pound Issue

		Good	Fine	XF
S111	**50 Egyptian Pounds** 1884. Diamond design at ctr.	2000.	3000.	4500.

1884 British Pound Issue

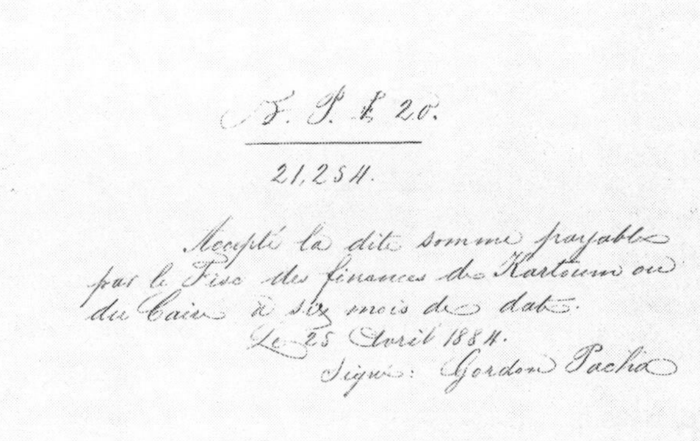

B. P. £ 20.

21,254.

Accepté la dite somme payable par le Fisc des finances de Kartoum ou du Caire à six mois de date.
Le 25 Avril 1884.
Signé: Gordon Pacha

		Good	Fine	XF
S112	**20 Pounds** 25.4.1884. 125 x 200mm. French text: B.P £20 with serial number 21,254 below. Payable in six months and signed, Gordon Pacha.	—	4500.	—

1884 Second Sudan Piastre Issue

		Good	Fine	XF
S113	**100 Piastres** 1.8.1884. 87 x 63mm, regular card stock. Similar to earlier issues, but with a later date and with the denomination 100 added to the border design.	—	6000.	—

The Kingdom of Sweden, a limited constitutional monarchy located in northern Europe between Norway and Finland, has an area of 173,732 sq. mi. (449,964 sq. km.) and a population of 8.9 million. Capital: Stockholm. Mining, lumbering and a specialized machine industry dominate the economy. Machinery, paper, iron and steel, motor vehicles and wood pulp are exported.

Sweden was founded as a Christian stronghold by Olaf Skottkonung late in the 10th century. After conquering Finland late in the 13th century, Sweden, together with Norway, came under the rule of Denmark, 1397-1523, in an association known as the Union of Kalmar. Modern Sweden had its beginning in 1523 when Gustavus Vasa drove the Danes out of Sweden and was himself chosen king. Under Gustavus Adolphus II and Carl XII, Sweden was one of the great powers of 17th century Europe - until Carl invaded Russia, 1708, and was defeated at the Battle of Pultowa in June 1709. Early in the 18th century, a coalition of Russia, Poland and Denmark took away Sweden's Baltic empire and in 1809 Sweden was forced to cede Finland to Russia. Norway was ceded to Sweden by the Treaty of Kiel in January 1814. The Norwegians resisted for a time but later signed the Act of Union at the Convention of Moss in August 1814. The Union was dissolved in 1905 and Norway became independent.

RULERS:

Carl XIV John, 1818-1844
Oscar I, 1844-1859
Carl XV, 1859-1872
Oscar II, 1872-1907
Gustaf V, 1907-1950
Gustaf VI Adolf, 1950-1973

MONETARY SYSTEM:

1 Krona = 100 Öre

MONETARY ABBREVIATIONS

DALER SMT. = Daler Silvermynt
DALER KMT. = Daler Kopparmynt
RKD. SP. = Riksdaler Specie
RKD. BC. = Riksdaler Banco
RKD. RMT. = Riksdaler Riksmynt
SK. SP = Skillingar Specie
SK. BC. = Skillingar Banco

NOTE ON VALUES: Indicated values apply only to uncancelled examples. Notes with cancellations are worth up to 50% less.

SWEDISH PRINTERS

C. A. Broling .... CAB
AB Jacob Bagges .... JB
Per Axel Nyman .... PAN
Carl Axel Nyman .... CAN

PRIVATE BANKS

Bohus Läns Enskilda Bank .... #S101-S108
Boras Enskilda Bank .... #S111-S120
Christianstads Enskilda Bank .... #S121-S134
Christinehamns Enskilda Bank, see Enskilda Banken i Christinehamn
Enskilda Banken i Christinehamn .... #S141-S149
Enskilda Banken i Wenersborg .... #S151-S159
Enskilda Banken i Orebro, see Privat Banken i Orebro
Enskilda Industribanken i Norrköping .... #S161-S164
Gefleborgs Enskilda Bank, see Gefleborgs Läns Enskilda Bank
Gefleborgs Läns Enskilda Bank .... #S171-S182
Gotlands Enskilda Bank .... #S191-S199
Götheborgs Enskilda Bank, see Götheborgs Privat Bank
Götheborgs Privat Bank .... #S201-S231
Hallands Enskilda Bank .... #S241-S252
Helsinglands Enskilda Bank .... #S261-S267
Hernösands Enskilda Bank .... #S271-S279
Kalmar Enskilda Bank .... #S281-S291
Kopparbergs Enskilda Bank, see Stora Kopparbergs Läns och Bergslags Enskilda Bank
Malmö Enskilda Bank .... #S301-S304
Mälare-Provinsernas Enskilda Bank .... #S311-S333
Norrbottens Enskilda Bank .... #S341-S343
Norrköpings Enskilda Bank .... #S351-S366
Öscarhamns Enskilda Bank .... #S371-S374
Privat Banken i Örebro .... #S381-S404
Skaraborgs Läns Enskilda Bank .... #S411-S421
Skånska Enskilda Bank, see Skånska Priwat-Banken
Skåska Privat-Banken, see Skånska Priwat-Banken
Skånska Priwat-Banken .... #S431-S464
Smalands Enskilda Bank, see Smalands Privat Bank
Smalands Privat Bank .... #S471-S499
Stockholms Enskilda Bank .... #S501-S514
Stora Kopperbergs Läns och Bergslags Enskilda Bank .... #S521-S572
Sundsvalls Enskilda Bank .... #S581-S595
Södermanlands Enskilda Bank .... #S601-S611
Uplands Enskilda Bank .... #S621-S629
Wadstena Enskilda Bank .... #S631-S642
Wermlands Enskilda Bank, see Wermlands Provincial-Bank
Wermlands Provincial-Bank .... #S651-S690
Westerbottens Enskilda Bank .... #S701-S710
Örebro Enskilda Bank, see Privat Banken i Örebro
Öst-Göta Bank .... #S711-S739

NOTE: Numerous deletions and the combining numbering changes in this section from the previous edition.

Republic

Bohus Läns Enskilda Bank

Notes issued to 15.10.1901.

1869-70 Issue

#S101-S104 Mercury standing at l. Printer: JB.

		Good	Fine	XF
S101	5 Riksdaler 1869.	100.00	200.00	500.00
S102	10 Riksdaler 1869.	125.00	250.00	600.00
S103	50 Riksdaler 1870.	—	—	—
S104	100 Riksdaler 1870.	—	—	—

1879 Issue

#S105-S108 laureated woman at l., crowned arms at r.

		Good	Fine	XF
S105	10 Kronor 1879. Printer: JB.	100.00	200.00	500.00
S106	10 Kronor 1879. Printer: BWC.	100.00	200.00	500.00

#S107-S108 printer: BWC.

		Good	Fine	XF
S107	50 Kronor 1879.	—	—	—
S108	100 Kronor 1879.	—	—	—

Boras Enskilda Bank

Notes issued to 1.11.1902.

1866 Issue

#S111-S113 seated allegorical woman w/wheels and town in background at upper ctr. Printer: JB.

		Good	Fine	XF
S111	5 Riksdaler 1866.	75.00	150.00	300.00
S112	10 Riksdaler 1866.	90.00	175.00	350.00
S113	50 Riksdaler 1866.	—	—	—

1876 Issue

#S114-S117 like previous issue. Notes in Kronor. Printer: JB.

		Good	Fine	XF
S114	5 Kronor 1876.	60.00	125.00	250.00
S115	10 Kronor 1876.	75.00	150.00	300.00
S116	50 Kronor 1876.	—	—	—
S117	100 Kronor 1876.	—	—	—

1894 Issue

#S118-120 Kg. Gustav II Adolf standing at lower l., allegorical woman as previous issue at upper ctr. Portr. of Gustav II Adolf at ctr. on back. Printer: JB.

		Good	Fine	XF
S118	10 Kronor 1894.	—	—	—
S119	50 Kronor 1894.	—	—	—
S120	100 Kronor 1894.	—	—	—

Christianstads Enskilda Bank

Notes issued to 1.8.1901.

1865 First Issue

#S121-S124 arms of Kg. Christian IV at upper ctr. Printer: PAN.

		Good	Fine	XF
S121	5 Riksdaler 1865.	75.00	150.00	300.00
S122	10 Riksdaler 1865.	75.00	150.00	300.00
S123	50 Riksdaler 1865.	90.00	175.00	350.00
S124	100 Riksdaler 1865.	90.00	175.00	350.00

1865 Second Issue

#S125-S126 like previous issue. Printer: JB.

		Good	Fine	XF
S125	5 Riksdaler 1865.	—	—	—
S126	10 Riksdaler 1865.	—	—	—

1875 First Issue

#S127-S130 similar to previous issue. Notes in Kronor. Printer: JB.

		Good	Fine	XF
S127	5 Kronor 1875.	60.00	125.00	300.00
S128	10 Kronor 1875.	75.00	150.00	300.00
S129	50 Kronor 1875.	75.00	150.00	300.00
S130	100 Kronor 1875.	—	—	—

1875 Second Issue

#S131-S134 Kg. Christian IV of Denmark at l., arms at r. Printer: BWC.

		Good	Fine	XF
S131	10 Kronor 1875; 1894.	75.00	150.00	300.00

		Good	Fine	XF
S132	50 Kronor 1875; 1894. Portr. Kg. Christian IV at upper ctr., arms at lower ctr.	—	—	—
S133	100 Kronor 1875; 1894.	—	—	—

A word on date ranges

Often date ranges or specific dates are listed. These have been observed or reported by our contributors. If a note is outside the published range, it only means that it is a newly reported date, and not necessarily worthy of a premium value.

		Good	Fine	XF
S134	500 Kronor 1875; 1894.	—	—	—

Enskilda Banken i Christinehamn

Notes issued to 5.10.1901. Later became Christinehamns Enskilda Bank.

1866 Issue

#S141-S144 city arms at upper ctr. Printer: PAN.

		Good	Fine	XF
S141	5 Riksdaler 1866.	75.00	150.00	300.00
S142	10 Riksdaler 1866.	90.00	175.00	350.00
S143	50 Riksdaler 1866.	—	—	—
S144	100 Riksdaler 1866.	—	—	—

Christinehamms Enskilda Bank

Formerly the Enskilda Banken i. Christinehamn.

1876 Issue

#S145-S148 new bank name. Like previous issue. Notes in Kronor. Printer: PAN.

		Good	Fine	XF
S145	5 Kronor 1876.	60.00	125.00	300.00
S146	10 Kronor 1876.	75.00	150.00	300.00
S147	50 Kronor 1876.	—	—	—
S148	100 Kronor 1876.	—	—	—

1884 Issue

		Good	Fine	XF
S149	10 Kronor 1884. Portr. woman at lower l., city arms at top ctr., eagle at lower r.	75.00	150.00	300.00

Enskilda Banken i Wenersborg

Notes issued to 1.11.1902.

1865 Issue

#S151-S154 city arms at upper ctr. Printer: JB.

		Good	Fine	XF
S151	5 Riksdaler 1865.	100.00	200.00	500.00
S152	10 Riksdaler 1865.	125.00	250.00	600.00
S153	50 Riksdaler 1865.	—	—	—
S154	100 Riksdaler 1865.	—	—	—

1874 Issue

#S155 and S156 like previous issue. Notes in Kronor. Printer: JB.

		Good	Fine	XF
S155	5 Kronor 1874.	85.00	175.00	400.00
S156	100 Kronor 1874.	—	—	—

1879 Issue

#S157-S159 printer: BWC.

		Good	Fine	XF
S157	10 Kronor 1879. Arms at l. and r., woman at ctr.	100.00	200.00	500.00

#S158 and S159 arms at l. and r., bldg. at top ctr., woman at bottom ctr.

#	Denomination	Good	Fine	XF
S158	**50 Kronor** 1879.	—	—	—
S159	**100 Kronor** 1879.	—	—	—

Enskilda Industribanken i Norrköping

Notes issued to 30.12.1869.

1865 Issue

#S161-S164 printer: PAN.

#	Denomination	Good	Fine	XF
S161	**5 Riksdaler** 1865. Ceres at l., Mercury at r.	100.00	200.00	500.00
S162	**10 Riksdaler** 1865. Like #S161.	125.00	250.00	600.00
S163	**50 Riksdaler** 1865. Ceres and Mercury at upper l. and r. ctr.	—	—	—
S164	**100 Riksdaler** 1865. Like #S163.	—	—	—

Gefleborgs Läns Enskilda Bank

Notes issued to 1.5.1903. After 1875 the name changed to Geflebörgs Enskilda Bank.

1865-66 Issue

#S171-S175 double arms at upper ctr. Printer: PAN.

#	Denomination	Good	Fine	XF
S171	**5 Riksdaler** 1865.	75.00	150.00	300.00
S172	**10 Riksdaler** 1865.	90.00	175.00	350.00
S173	**50 Riksdaler** 1865.	—	—	—
S174	**100 Riksdaler** 1865.	—	—	—
S175	**500 Riksdaler** 1866.	—	—	—

Gefleborgs Enskilda Bank

Formerly the Gefleborgs Läns Enskilda Bank.

1875 First Issue

#S176-S179 single arms at upper ctr. Printer: PAN.

#	Denomination	Good	Fine	XF
S176	**5 Kronor** 1875.	60.00	125.00	300.00
S177	**10 Kronor** 1875.	75.00	150.00	300.00
S178	**50 Kronor** 1875.	75.00	150.00	300.00
S179	**100 Kronor** 1875.	—	—	—

1875 Second Issue

#S180-S182 printer: BWC.

#	Denomination	Good	Fine	XF
S180	**10 Kronor** 1875. Allegorical woman at l., arms at r.	—	—	—
S181	**50 Kronor** 1875. Arms at l. and r., allegorical woman at upper ctr.	—	—	—
S182	**100 Kronor** 1875. Like #S181.	—	—	—

Gotlands Enskilda Bank

Notes issued to 15.12.1902.

1869 Issue

#S191-S194 arms at upper ctr. Printer: JB.

#	Denomination	Good	Fine	XF
S191	**5 Riksdaler** 1869.	75.00	150.00	300.00
S192	**10 Riksdaler** 1869.	90.00	175.00	350.00
S193	**50 Riksdaler** 1869.	—	—	—
S194	**100 Riksdaler** 1869.	—	—	—

1879 Issue

#S195-S198 like previous issue. Notes in Kronor. Printer: JB.

#	Denomination	Good	Fine	XF
S195	**5 Kronor** 1879.	60.00	125.00	300.00
S196	**10 Kronor** 1879.	75.00	150.00	300.00
S197	**50 Kronor** 1879.	—	—	—
S198	**100 Kronor** 1879.	—	—	—

1893 Issue

#	Denomination	Good	Fine	XF
S199	**10 Kronor** 1893. Arms at l., portr. woman at r. Printer: BWC.	75.00	150.00	300.00

Götheborgs Privat Bank

Notes issued to 15.10.1901. After 1858 the name changed to Götheborgs Enskilda Bank.

1848 Issue

#S201-S205 arms w/two cherubs at upper ctr. Printer: CAB.

#	Denomination	Good	Fine	XF
S201	**3 1/3 Riksdaler Banco** 1848.	—	—	—
S202	**6 2/3 Riksdaler Banco** 1848.	—	—	—
S203	**10 Riksdaler Banco** 1848.	—	—	—
S204	**50 Riksdaler Banco** 1848.	—	—	—
S205	**100 Riksdaler Banco** 1848.	—	—	—

1852 Issue

#S206-S207 like previous issue. Printer: JB.

#	Denomination	Good	Fine	XF
S206	**3 1/3 Riksdaler Banco** 1852.	—	—	—
S207	**10 Riksdaler Banco** 1852.	—	—	—

Götheborgs Enskilda Bank

Formerly the Götheborgs Privat Bank.

1858 First Issue

#S208-S210 printer: BWC.

#	Denomination	Good	Fine	XF
S208	**5 Riksdaler** 1858. 2 allegorical women and arms at upper ctr.	75.00	150.00	300.00
S209	**100 Riksdaler** 1858. City scene w/arms above at upper ctr.	90.00	175.00	350.00
S210	**500 Riksdaler** 1858. Similar to #S209.	—	—	—

1858 Second Issue

#S211-S213 printer: JB.

#	Denomination	Good	Fine	XF
S211	**10 Riksdaler** 1858; 1866. Arms at upper ctr.	—	—	—
S212	**50 Riksdaler** 1858. City scene w/arms above at upper ctr.	—	—	—
S213	**100 Riksdaler** 1858. Similar to #S212.			
	a. Issued note.	—	—	—
	p. Proof.	—	—	—

1868 ISSUE

#S215-S219 like previous issue. Printer: PAN.

		GOOD	FINE	XF
S215	**5 RIKSDALER** 1868.	75.00	150.00	300.00
S216	**10 RIKSDALER** 1868.	90.00	175.00	350.00
S217	**50 RIKSDALER** 1868.	—	—	—
S218	**100 RIKSDALER** 1868.	—	—	—
S219	**500 RIKSDALER** 1868.	—	—	—

1873 ISSUE

#S220-S223 like previous issue. Printer: JB.

		GOOD	FINE	XF
S220	**5 RIKSDALER** 1873.	75.00	150.00	300.00
S221	**10 RIKSDALER** 1873.	90.00	175.00	350.00
S222	**50 RIKSDALER** 1873.	—	—	—
S223	**100 RIKSDALER** 1873.	—	—	—

1877-78 ISSUE

#S224-S227 new rendition of arms at upper ctr. Printer: JB.

		GOOD	FINE	XF
S224	**5 KRONOR** 1877.	60.00	125.00	300.00
S225	**10 KRONOR** 1877.	75.00	150.00	300.00
S226	**50 KRONOR** 1878.	—	—	—
S227	**100 KRONOR** 1878.	—	—	—

1878-82 ISSUE

#S228-S231 Kg. Gustav II Adolf at l., city arms at r. Printer: BWC.

		GOOD	FINE	XF
S227A	**500 KRONOR** 1878.	—	—	—
S228	**500 KRONOR** 1879; 1894.	75.00	150.00	300.00
S229	**50 KRONOR** 1882.	75.00	150.00	300.00

		GOOD	FINE	XF
S230	**100 KRONOR** 1882.	—	—	—

#S231 *Deleted*. See #S227A.

HALLANDS ENSKILDA BANK

Notes issued to 15.7.1902.

1857 ISSUE

#S241-S244 city arms at upper ctr. Printer: JB.

		GOOD	FINE	XF
S241	**5 RIKSDALER** 1857; 1867.	75.00	150.00	300.00
S242	**10 RIKSDALER** 1857; 1867.	90.00	175.00	350.00
S243	**50 RIKSDALER** 1857; 1867.	—	—	—
S244	**100 RIKSDALER** 1857; 1867.	—	—	—

1877 ISSUE

#S249-S252 like previous issue. Notes in Kronor. Printer: JB.

		GOOD	FINE	XF
S249	**5 KRONOR** 1877.	60.00	125.00	300.00
S250	**10 KRONOR** 1877; 1888; 1894.	75.00	150.00	300.00
S251	**50 KRONOR** 1877; 1888.	—	—	—
S252	**100 KRONOR** 1877; 1888.	—	—	—

HELSINGLANDS ENSKILDA BANK

Notes issued to 1.5.1903.

1874 ISSUE

#S261-S264 city arms at upper ctr. Printer: JB.

		GOOD	FINE	XF
S261	**5 KRONOR** 1874.	60.00	125.00	300.00
S262	**10 KRONOR** 1874.	75.00	150.00	300.00
S263	**50 KRONOR** 1874.	—	—	—
S264	**100 KRONOR** 1874.	—	—	—

1879 ISSUE

#S265-S267 helmeted Minerva at l., city arms at r. Printer: BWC.

		GOOD	FINE	XF
S265	**10 KRONOR** 1879.	75.00	150.00	300.00

		GOOD	FINE	XF
S266	**50 KRONOR** 1879.	—	—	—
S267	**100 KRONOR** 1879.	—	—	—

HERNÖSANDS ENSKILDA BANK

Notes issued to 1.8.1903.

1870 ISSUE

#S271-S273 city arms at upper ctr. Printer: JB.

		GOOD	FINE	XF
S271	**5 RIKSDALER** 1870.	75.00	150.00	300.00
S272	**10 RIKSDALER** 1870.	90.00	175.00	350.00
S273	**50 RIKSDALER** 1870.	—	—	—

1874 ISSUE

#S274-S275 like previous issue. Notes in Kronor. Printer: JB.

		GOOD	FINE	XF
S274	**5 KRONOR** 1874.	60.00	125.00	300.00
S275	**10 KRONOR** 1874.	75.00	150.00	300.00

1880 ISSUE

		GOOD	FINE	XF
S276	**10 KRONOR** 1880. Arms at l. and r., Mercury at ctr.	75.00	150.00	300.00
S277	**50 KRONOR** 1880. Woman at l., arms at upper and lower ctr., Mercury at r. Square format.	—	—	—

		Good	Fine	XF
S278	**100 Kronor** 1880. Like #S277.	—	—	—

1892 Issue

		Good	Fine	XF
S279	**10 Kronor** 1892. Portr. woman at l., two arms at r. Printer: BWC.	75.00	150.00	300.00

Kalmar Enskilda Bank

Notes issued to 1.1.1902.

1867 Issue

#S281-S284 printer: JB.

		Good	Fine	XF
S281	**5 Kronor** 1867. Double arms at l.	75.00	150.00	300.00
S282	**10 Kronor** 1867. Like #S281.	90.00	175.00	350.00
S283	**50 Kronor** 1867. Double arms at upper ctr. Square format.	—	—	—
S284	**100 Kronor** 1867. Like #S283.	—	—	—

1877 Issue

#S285-S288 Mercury at l., double arms at upper ctr., Ceres at r. Printer: JB.

		Good	Fine	XF
S285	**5 Kronor** 1877.	60.00	125.00	300.00
S286	**10 Kronor** 1877.	75.00	150.00	300.00
S287	**50 Kronor** 1877.	—	—	—
S288	**100 Kronor** 1877.	—	—	—

1894 Issue

#S289-S291 Qn. Margareta at l., castle view at upper ctr. r., arms at r. Printer: BWC.

		Good	Fine	XF
S289	**10 Kronor** 1894; 1898. Sailboat at l. on back.	75.00	150.00	300.00
S290	**50 Kronor** 1894.	—	—	—
S291	**100 Kronor** 1894; 1897.	—	—	—

Malmö Enskilda Bank

Notes issued to 31.12.1868.

1865 Issue

#S301-S304 city arms at upper ctr. Printer: JB.

		Good	Fine	XF
S301	**5 Riksdaler** 1865.	75.00	150.00	300.00
S302	**10 Riksdaler** 1865.	90.00	175.00	350.00
S303	**50 Riksdaler** 1865.	—	—	—
S304	**100 Riksdaler** 1865.	—	—	—

Mälare-Provinsernas Enskilda Bank

Notes issued to 31.12.1902.

1847 Issue

#S311 and S312 crowned supported royal arms at top ctr. Printer: CAB.

		Good	Fine	XF
S311	**3 1/3 Riksdaler Banco** 1.10.1847.	—	—	—

		Good	Fine	XF
S312	**6 Riksdaler Banco** 1.10.1847.	—	—	—

#S313 and S314 crowned supported royal arms w/bldgs. in background at upper ctr. Printer: CAB.

		Good	Fine	XF
S313	**33 1/3 Riksdaler Banco** 1.10.1847.	—	—	—
S314	**50 Riksdaler Banco** 1.10.1847.	—	—	—

1856 ISSUE

#S315-S319 similar to previous issue. Printer: Bradbury & Evans.

		GOOD	FINE	XF
S315	5 RIKSDALER 1856.	75.00	150.00	300.00
S316	10 RIKSDALER 1856.	90.00	175.00	350.00
S317	50 RIKSDALER 1856.	—	—	—
S318	100 RIKSDALER 1856.	—	—	—
S319	500 RIKSDALER 1856.	—	—	—

1863 ISSUE

#S320 and S321 similar to previous issue. Printer: JB.

		GOOD	FINE	XF
S320	5 RIKSDALER 1863.	75.00	150.00	300.00
S321	10 RIKSDALER 1863.	90.00	175.00	350.00

1867 ISSUE

#S322-S326 similar to previous issue. Printer: JB.

		GOOD	FINE	XF
S322	5 RIKSDALER 1867.	75.00	150.00	300.00
S323	10 RIKSDALER 1867.	90.00	175.00	350.00
S324	50 RIKSDALER 1867.	—	—	—
S325	100 RIKSDALER 1867.	—	—	—
S326	500 RIKSDALER 1867.	—	—	—

1875 ISSUE

#S327-S330 similar to previous issue. Notes in Kronor. Printer: JB.

		GOOD	FINE	XF
S327	5 KRONOR 1875.	60.00	125.00	300.00

		GOOD	FINE	XF
S328	10 KRONOR 1875. Crowned supported royal arms at top ctr. Litt. K.	75.00	150.00	300.00
S329	50 KRONOR 1875.	—	—	—
S330	100 KRONOR 1875.	—	—	—

1894 ISSUE

#S331-S333 Ceres and Mercury at l., arms at r. Portr. A. Oxenstierna at ctr. on back. Printer: BWC.

		GOOD	FINE	XF
S331	10 KRONOR 1894.	75.00	150.00	300.00
S332	50 KRONOR 1894.	—	—	—

		GOOD	FINE	XF
S333	100 KRONOR 1894.	—	—	—

NORRBOTTENS ENSKILDA BANK

Notes issued to 15.1.1903.

1893 ISSUE

#S341-S343 printer: BWC.

		GOOD	FINE	XF
S341	10 KRONOR 1893. Mercury and arms at r.	100.00	200.00	500.00
S342	50 KRONOR 1893. Cherub w/city arms and woman holding sword at l.	—	—	—

		GOOD	FINE	XF
S343	100 KRONOR 1893. Like #S342.	—	—	—

NORRKÖPINGS ENSKILDA BANK

Notes issued to 1.8.1902.

1857 ISSUE

#S351-S355 city arms at upper ctr. Printer: JB.

		GOOD	FINE	XF
S351	5 RIKSDALER 1857; 1867.	75.00	150.00	300.00
S352	10 RIKSDALER 1857.	90.00	175.00	350.00
S353	50 RIKSDALER 1857.	—	—	—
S354	100 RIKSDALER 1857.	—	—	—
S355	500 RIKSDALER 1857.	—	—	—

1867 ISSUE

#S357-S360 similar to previous issue. Printer: JB.

		GOOD	FINE	XF
S357	5 RIKSDALER 1867.	75.00	150.00	300.00
S358	10 RIKSDALER 1867.	90.00	175.00	350.00

		Good	Fine	XF
S359	**50 Riksdaler** 1867.	—	—	—
S360	**100 Riksdaler** 1867.	—	—	—

1877 Issue

#S361-S362 like previous issue. Notes in Kronor. Printer: JB.

		Good	Fine	XF
S361	**5 Kronor** 1877.	60.00	125.00	300.00
S362	**10 Kronor** 1877.	75.00	150.00	300.00

#S363 and S364 head at l. and r. on back. Printer: BWC.

		Good	Fine	XF
S363	**50 Kronor** 1877. Woman w/spool at l., arms at upper ctr. and r.	—	—	—

		Good	Fine	XF
S364	**100 Kronor** 1877. Arms at l. and r., woman w/spool at upper ctr.	—	—	—
S365	**500 Kronor** 1877. City arms at upper ctr. Rectangular format. Printer: JB.			

1887 Issue

		Good	Fine	XF
S366	**10 Kronor** 1887. Arms at l. and r., woman w/spool at ctr. Printer: BWC.	75.00	150.00	300.00

Oscarshamns Enskilda Bank

Notes issued to 31.12.1889.

1877 Issue

#S371-S374 standing woman w/arms of Kg. Oscar I in design. Printer: JB.

		Good	Fine	XF
S371	**5 Kronor** 1877. Woman and arms at l.	85.00	175.00	400.00
S372	**10 Kronor** 1877. Like #S371.	100.00	200.00	500.00
S373	**50 Kronor** 1877. Woman and arms at upper ctr. Square format.	—	—	—
S374	**100 Kronor** 1877. Like #S373.	—	—	—

Privat Banken i Örebro

After 1847 it became Enskilda Banken Örebro; later it became the Örebro Enskilda Bank.

1837-47 Issue

#S381-S385 two torches crossed at upper ctr. Printer: CAB.

		Good	Fine	XF
S381	**2 Riksdaler Schillingar** 1837.	—	—	—
S382	**3 Riksdaler Banco** 1837.	—	—	—
S383	**3 1/3 Riksdaler Schillingar** 1.12.1847.	—	—	—
S384	**10 Riksdaler Schillingar** 1837.	—	—	—
S385	**50 Riksdaler Schillingar** 1840.	—	—	—

Enskilda Banken Örebro

Formerly the Privat Banken i Örebro and after 1857 became the Örebro Enskilda Bank.

1847 Issue

#S386-S389 ornate design w/o vignette. Printer: CAB.

		Good	Fine	XF
S386	**3 1/3 Riksdaler Banco** 15.12.1847.	—	—	—
S387	**6 2/3 Riksdaler Banco** 1847.	—	—	—
S388	**10 Riksdaler Banco** 1847.	—	—	—
S389	**50 Riksdaler Banco** 1847.	—	—	—

Örebro Enskilda Bank

Formerly the Privat Banken i Örebro and the Enskilda Banken Örebro. Notes issued to 1.8.1902.

1857 Issue

#S390-S393 printer: JB.

		Good	Fine	XF
S390	**5 Riksdaler** 1857; 1867. Staff of Mercury and cornucopia at upper ctr.	75.00	150.00	300.00
S391	**10 Riksdaler** 1857; 1867. Like #S390.	90.00	175.00	350.00
S392	**50 Riksdaler** 1857; 1867. Mercury w/produce and industrial implements at upper ctr. Square format.	—	—	—
S393	**100 Riksdaler** 1857; 1867. Like #S392.	—	—	—

1876 Issue

#S398-S401 printer: JB.

		Good	Fine	XF
S398	**5 Kronor** 1876. Arms w/2 figures at upper ctr.	60.00	125.00	300.00
S399	**10 Kronor** 1876. Like #S398.	75.00	150.00	300.00
S400	**50 Kronor** 1876. Arms w/o figures at upper ctr. Square format.	—	—	—

		Good	Fine	XF
S401	**100 Kronor** 1876. Like #S400.	—	—	—

1882-93 Issue

#S402 and S403 statue of Carl Gustav at l., city arms at r. Printer: W&S.

No.	Denomination	Good	Fine	XF
S402	**10 Kronor** 1882. Litt. C.	75.00	150.00	300.00
S403	**10 Kronor** 1893.	75.00	150.00	300.00

1896 Issue

No.	Denomination	Good	Fine	XF
S404	**10 Kronor** 1896. Statue of Carl Gustav at l., city arms at upper ctr. Castle on back. Printer: JB.	75.00	150.00	300.00

Skaraborgs Läns Enskilda Bank

Notes issued to 1.11.1902.

1865 Issue

#S411-S414 printer: PAN.

No.	Denomination	Good	Fine	XF
S411	**5 Riksdaler** 1865. Single arms at each corner, triple arms at upper ctr.	100.00	200.00	500.00
S412	**10 Riksdaler** 1865. Like #S411.	125.00	250.00	600.00
S413	**50 Riksdaler** 1865. Arms like #S411, but 2 reclining figures added at lower ctr. Square format.	—	—	—
S414	**100 Riksdaler** 1865. Like #S413.	—	—	—

1875 Issue

#S415-S418 Mercury w/city arms at l. Printer: JB.

No.	Denomination	Good	Fine	XF
S415	**5 Kronor** 1875.	85.00	175.00	400.00
S416	**10 Kronor** 1875.	100.00	200.00	500.00
S417	**50 Kronor** 1875.	—	—	—
S418	**100 Kronor** 1875.	—	—	—

1888 Issue

#S419-S421 statue at l., arms at r. Printer: BWC.

No.	Denomination	Good	Fine	XF
S419	**10 Kronor** 1888. Standing man at l. Litt. E.	100.00	200.00	500.00
S420	**50 Kronor** 1888.	—	—	—
S421	**100 Kronor** 1888.	—	—	—

Skånska Priwat-Banken

After 1841 the name became Skånska Privat-Banken; it later became the Skånes Enskilda Bank.

1831 Issue

No.	Denomination	Good	Fine	XF
S431	**20 Riksdaler Banco** 1831. Assignationer.	—	—	—

1830's Issue

#S432-S435 are Depositionsbevis. Arms of Ystad at upper ctr. Printer: J. O. Ostberg, Ystad.

No.	Denomination	Good	Fine	XF
S432	**2 Riksdaler Schillingar** 183x.	—	—	—
S433	**3 Riksdaler Banco** 183x.	—	—	—
S434	**5 Riksdaler Banco** 183x.	—	—	—
S435	**10 Riksdaler Banco** 183x.	—	—	—

Skånska Privat-Banken

Formerly the Skånska Priwat-Banken. Later to become the Skånes Enskilda Bank.

1841 Issue

#S436-S441 staff of Mercury at l., city arms at r. Printer: CAB.

No.	Denomination	Good	Fine	XF
S436	**2 Riksdaler Schillingar** 1841.	—	—	—
S437	**3 Riksdaler Banco** 1841.	—	—	—
S438	**6 2/3 Riksdaler Banco** 1841.	—	—	—
S439	**10 Riksdaler Banco** 1841.	—	—	—
S440	**25 Riksdaler Banco** 1841.	—	—	—
S441	**100 Riksdaler Banco** 1841.	—	—	—

1847 Issue

#S442-S447 city arms at upper ctr. Printer: CAB (to 1851); afterwards, JB.

No.	Denomination	Good	Fine	XF
S442	**3 1/3 Riksdaler Banco** 1847.	—	—	—
S443	**6 2/3 Riksdaler Banco** 1847.	—	—	—
S444	**10 Riksdaler Banco** 1847.	—	—	—
S445	**25 Riksdaler Banco** 1847.	—	—	—
S446	**50 Riksdaler Banco** 1847.	—	—	—
S447	**100 Riksdaler Banco** 1847.	—	—	—

Skånes Enskilda Bank

Formerly the Skånska Priwat-Banken and the Skånska Privat-Banken. Notes issued to 1.8.1901.

1857-66 Issue

#S448-S452 crowned city arms at upper ctr. Printer: JB.

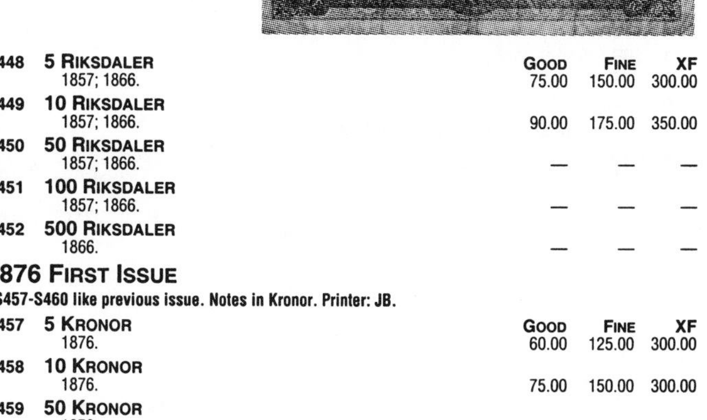

No.	Denomination	Good	Fine	XF
S448	**5 Riksdaler** 1857; 1866.	75.00	150.00	300.00
S449	**10 Riksdaler** 1857; 1866.	90.00	175.00	350.00
S450	**50 Riksdaler** 1857; 1866.	—	—	—
S451	**100 Riksdaler** 1857; 1866.	—	—	—
S452	**500 Riksdaler** 1866.	—	—	—

1876 First Issue

#S457-S460 like previous issue. Notes in Kronor. Printer: JB.

No.	Denomination	Good	Fine	XF
S457	**5 Kronor** 1876.	60.00	125.00	300.00
S458	**10 Kronor** 1876.	75.00	150.00	300.00
S459	**50 Kronor** 1876.	—	—	—
S460	**100 Kronor** 1876.	—	—	—

1876 SECOND ISSUE

#S461-S464 printer: BWC.

		Good	Fine	XF
S461	10 KRONOR 1876; 1894. Ceres at l., city arms at r.	—	—	—

#S462-S464 Mercury at l., Ceres at r., city arms at upper ctr.

		Good	Fine	XF
S462	50 KRONOR 1876.	—	—	—
S463	100 KRONOR 1876.	—	—	—

		Good	Fine	XF
S464	1000 KRONOR 1876.	—	—	—

SMALANDS PRIVAT BANK

Later became the Smalands Enskilda Bank.

1837 ISSUE

#S471-S476 triple arms of three cities at upper ctr. Printer: CAB.

		Good	Fine	XF
S471	2 RIKSDALER SCHILLINGAR 1837; 1842.	—	—	—
S472	2 2/3 RIKSDALER BANCO 1837.	—	—	—
S473	3 RIKSDALER BANCO 1837; 1842.	—	—	—
S474	3 1/3 RIKSDALER BANCO 1837.	—	—	—
S475	10 RIKSDALER BANCO 1837.	—	—	—
S476	50 RIKSDALER BANCO 1837.	—	—	—

1847-48 ISSUE

#S477-S481 quadruple arms of 4 cities at upper ctr. Printer: CAB.

		Good	Fine	XF
S477	2 RIKSDALER SCHILLINGAR 1847.	—	—	—
S478	3 1/3 RIKSDALER BANCO 1847; 1848.	—	—	—
S479	6 2/3 RIKSDALER BANCO 1848.	—	—	—
S480	10 RIKSDALER BANCO 1848.	—	—	—
S481	50 RIKSDALER BANCO 1848.	—	—	—

SMALANDS ENSKILDA BANK

Formerly the Smalands Privat Bank.

1857 ISSUE

#S485-S488 Mercury w/implements at upper ctr. Printer: JB.

		Good	Fine	XF
S485	5 RIKSDALER 1857.	75.00	150.00	300.00
S486	10 RIKSDALER 1857.	90.00	175.00	350.00
S487	50 RIKSDALER 1857.	—	—	—
S488	100 RIKSDALER 1857.	—	—	—

1867 ISSUE

#S489 and S490 triple arms at upper ctr. Printer: PAN.

		Good	Fine	XF
S489	5 RIKSDALER 1867.	75.00	150.00	300.00
S490	10 RIKSDALER 1867.	90.00	175.00	350.00

#S491 and S492 single arms at l., upper ctr., and r. Printer: PAN.

		Good	Fine	XF
S491	50 RIKSDALER 1867.	—	—	—
S492	100 RIKSDALER 1867.	—	—	—

1877 ISSUE

#S493-S496 crowned arms at upper ctr. Printer: JB.

		Good	Fine	XF
S493	5 KRONOR 1877.	60.00	125.00	300.00
S494	10 KRONOR 1877.	75.00	150.00	300.00
S495	50 KRONOR 1877.	—	—	—
S496	100 KRONOR 1877.	—	—	—

1894 ISSUE

#S497-S499 helmeted woman w/sword and shield at l., Smaland arms at upper ctr. Portr. of C. van Linné on back. Printer: BWC.

		Good	Fine	XF
S497	10 KRONOR 1894.	75.00	150.00	300.00
S498	50 KRONOR 1894.	—	—	—

		Good	Fine	XF
S499	100 KRONOR 1894.	—	—	—

STOCKHOLMS ENSKILDA BANK

Notes issued to 15.7.1902.

1856 ISSUE

#S501-S503 Stockholm arms (w/portr.) at upper ctr. Printer: PAN.

		Good	Fine	XF
S501	5 RIKSDALER 1856; 1860.	75.00	150.00	300.00
S502	10 RIKSDALER 1856; 1860.	90.00	175.00	350.00
S503	50 RIKSDALER 1856; 1865.	—	—	—

1872 ISSUE

		Good	Fine	XF
S507	100 RIKSDALER 1872. Black on dk. green unpt. Allegorical woman w/shield and lion at lower l., city scene w/bridge at upper ctr., St. Eric at r. *STOCKHOLM* slanted letters. Back brown. Printer: NBNC.	—	—	—

1876 First Issue

#S508-S510 like 1856 issue. Notes in Kronor. Printer: JB.

		Good	Fine	XF
S508	**5 Kronor** 1876.			
	a. *STOCKHOLM* in tall letters.	60.00	125.00	300.00
	b. *STOCKHOLM* in slanted letters.	60.00	125.00	300.00
S509	**10 Kronor** 1876.			
	a. *STOCKHOLM* in tall letters.	60.00	125.00	300.00
	b. *STOCKHOLM* in slanted letters.	60.00	125.00	300.00
S510	**50 Kronor** 1876.	—	—	—

1876 Second Issue

#S511, S512 and S514 printer: BWC.

		Good	Fine	XF
S511	**10 Kronor** 1876. Crowned St. Eric at ctr.	75.00	150.00	300.00

#S512-S514 standing woman w/sword and lion at l., bridge and bldgs. at upper ctr., portr. Kg. at r.

		Good	Fine	XF
S512	**50 Kronor** 1876.	—	—	—
S513	**100 Kronor** 1876. Printer: NBNC.	—	—	—

		Good	Fine	XF
S514	**1000 Kronor** 1876.	—	—	—

Stora Kopparbergs Läns och Bergslags Enskilda Bank

Later became Kopparbergs Enskilda Bank.

1836 Issue

#S521-S524 latticework design at upper ctr. Square format. Printer: CAB.

		Good	Fine	XF
S521	**2 Riksdaler Schillingar** 1836; 1837; 1838; 1839; 1841; 1842; 1845.	—	—	—
S522	**3 Riksdaler Banco** 1836; 1837; 1838; 1839; 1841; 1842; 1845.	—	—	—
S523	**6 2/3 Riksdaler Banco** 1836; 1837; 1838; 1839; 1841; 1842; 1845; 1847.	—	—	—
S524	**10 Riksdaler Banco** 1836; 1837; 1838; 1839; 1841; 1842; 1845; 1847.	—	—	—

1848 Issue

#S551-S555 similar to previous issue. Printer: CAB (to 1851); afterwards, JB.

		Good	Fine	XF
S551	**4 Riksdaler Banco** 1848; 2.1.1852.	—	—	—
S552	**6 2/3 Riksdaler Banco** 1848; 1856.	—	—	—
S553	**10 Riksdaler Banco** 1848.	—	—	—
S554	**33 1/2 Riksdaler Banco** 1848.	—	—	—
S555	**50 Riksdaler Banco** 1848.	—	—	—

Kopparbergs Enskilda Bank

Formerly the Stora Kopparbergs Läns och Bergslags Enskilda Bank.

1858 Issue

#S559-S561 similar to previous issue. Printer: PAN.

		Good	Fine	XF
S558	**5 Riksdaler** 1858; 1868.	75.00	150.00	300.00
S559	**10 Riksdaler** 1858; 1868.	90.00	175.00	350.00
S560	**50 Riksdaler** 1858; 1868.	—	—	—
S561	**100 Riksdaler** 1858; 1868.	—	—	—

1878 Issue

#S566-S569 latticework design in wreath at upper ctr. Printer: JB.

		Good	Fine	XF
S566	**5 Kronor** 1878. Arms at upper ctr.	60.00	125.00	300.00
S567	**10 Kronor** 1878.	75.00	150.00	300.00
S568	**50 Kronor** 1878.	—	—	—
S569	**100 Kronor** 1878.	—	—	—

1894 Issue

#S570-S572 Kg. Gustav Vasa at l. Printer: BWC.

No.	Denomination	Good	Fine	XF
S570	10 Kronor 1894.	75.00	150.00	300.00
S571	50 Kronor 1894.	—	—	—
S572	100 Kronor 1894.	—	—	—

Sundsvalls Enskilda Bank

Notes issued to 1.8.1903.

1865 Issue

#S581-S585 arms of Sundsvall at upper ctr. Printer: PAN.

No.	Denomination	Good	Fine	XF
S581	5 Riksdaler 1865.	100.00	200.00	500.00
S582	10 Riksdaler 1865.	125.00	250.00	600.00

#S583-S585 standing figures of Mercury and Neptune w/arms.

No.	Denomination	Good	Fine	XF
S583	50 Riksdaler 1865.	—	—	—
S584	100 Riksdaler 1865.	—	—	—
S585	500 Riksdaler 1865.	—	—	—

1875 First Issue

#S586-S588 seated allegorical woman w/helmeted shield and holding wreath at upper ctr. Printer: JB.

No.	Denomination	Good	Fine	XF
S586	5 Kronor 1875.	85.00	175.00	400.00
S587	10 Kronor 1875.	100.00	200.00	500.00
S588	100 Kronor 1875.	—	—	—

1875 Second Issue

#S589-S591 woman on face (position varies). Printer: BWC.

No.	Denomination	Good	Fine	XF
S589	10 Kronor 1875. Woman at ctr.	—	—	—
S590	50 Kronor 1875. Woman at l.	—	—	—
S591	100 Kronor 1875.	—	—	—

1894-1900 Issues

No.	Denomination	Good	Fine	XF
S592	10 Kronor 1898. Like #S587. Printer: JB.	—	—	—

#S593-S595 like second 1875 issue. Printer: BWC.

No.	Denomination	Good	Fine	XF
S593	10 Kronor 1900; 1901; 1902.	—	—	—
S594	50 Kronor 1897.	—	—	—
S595	100 Kronor 1894; 1898; 1902.	100.00	200.00	500.00

Södermanlands Enskilda Bank

Notes issued to 1.8.1902.

1867 Issue

#S601-S604 crowned arms of Södermanland at upper ctr. Printer: PAN.

No.	Denomination	Good	Fine	XF
S601	5 Riksdaler 1867.	75.00	150.00	300.00
S602	10 Riksdaler 1867.	90.00	175.00	350.00
S603	50 Riksdaler 1867.	—	—	—
S604	100 Riksdaler 1867.	—	—	—

1877 Issue

#S605-S608 like previous issue. Notes in Kronor. Printer: PAN.

No.	Denomination	Good	Fine	XF
S605	5 Kronor 1877.	60.00	125.00	300.00
S606	10 Kronor 1877.	75.00	150.00	300.00
S607	50 Kronor 1877.	—	—	—
S608	100 Kronor 1877.	—	—	—

#S609-S610 like previous issue. Printer: JB.

No.	Denomination	Good	Fine	XF
S609	10 Kronor 1882; 1888; 1898.	75.00	150.00	300.00
S610	100 Kronor 1897; 1898.	—	—	—

Uplands Enskilda Bank

Notes issued to 1.1.1903.

1865 Issue

#S621-S624 crowned arms at upper ctr. Printer: JB.

No.	Denomination	Good	Fine	XF
S621	5 Riksdaler 1865.	75.00	150.00	300.00
S622	10 Riksdaler 1865.	90.00	175.00	350.00
S623	50 Riksdaler 1865.	—	—	—
S624	100 Riksdaler 1865.	—	—	—

1874 First Issue

#S625 and S626 like previous issue. Notes in Kronor. Printer: JB.

No.	Denomination	Good	Fine	XF
S625	5 Kronor 1874. Like #S621.	60.00	125.00	300.00
S626	10 Kronor 1874. Like #S622.	75.00	150.00	300.00

1874 Second Issue

#S627-S629 statue of B. Fogelberg at l. Printer: BWC.

No.	Denomination	Good	Fine	XF
S627	10 Kronor 1874.			
	a. W/o *I Guldmynt* text at ctr.	75.00	150.00	300.00
	b. W/*I Guldmynt* text at ctr.	—	—	—
S628	50 Kronor 1874. Town scene at upper ctr., arms at r. Square format.	—	—	—

No.	Denomination	Good	Fine	XF
S629	100 Kronor 1874. Like #S628.	—	—	—

WADSTENA ENSKILDA BANK

Notes issued to 23.8.1881.

1857 ISSUE

#S631-S634 crowned arms of Wadstena at upper ctr. Printer: JB.

		GOOD	FINE	XF
S631	**5 RIKSDALER** 1857.	100.00	200.00	500.00
S632	**10 RIKSDALER** 1857.	125.00	250.00	600.00
S633	**50 RIKSDALER** 1857.	—	—	—
S634	**100 RIKSDALER** 1857.	—	—	—

1867 ISSUE

#S635-S638 like previous issue. Printer: JB.

		GOOD	FINE	XF
S635	**5 RIKSDALER** 1867.	100.00	200.00	500.00
S636	**10 RIKSDALER** 1867.	125.00	250.00	600.00
S637	**50 RIKSDALER** 1867.	—	—	—
S638	**100 RIKSDALER** 1867.	—	—	—

1877 ISSUE

#S639-S642 crowned arms of Wadstena at upper ctr. Printer: JB.

		GOOD	FINE	XF
S639	**5 KRONOR** 1877.	85.00	175.00	400.00
S640	**10 KRONOR** 1877.	100.00	200.00	500.00
S641	**50 KRONOR** 1877. Mercury at l. ctr., woman at r. ctr. Square format.	—	—	—
S642	**100 KRONOR** 1877. Like #S641.	—	—	—

WERMLANDS PROVINCIAL-BANK

After 1857 it became the Wermlands Enskilda Bank.

1833 ISSUE

#S651-S654 crowned eagle w/outstretched wings at upper ctr. Notes hand dated. Printer: CAB.

		GOOD	FINE	XF
S651	**2 RIKSDALER SCHILLINGAR** 18xx (1833-43).	—	—	—
S652	**3 RIKSDALER BANCO** 18xx (1833-43).	—	—	—
S653	**5 RIKSDALER BANCO** 18xx (1833-43).	—	—	—
S654	**10 RIKSDALER BANCO** 18xx (1833-43).	—	—	—

1843-47 ISSUE

#S655-S659 city arms at l. and r., crowned eagle at upper ctr. Printer: CAB.

		GOOD	FINE	XF
S655	**2 RIKSDALER SCHILLINGAR** 184x (1843-47).	—	—	—
S656	**3 1/3 RIKSDALER BANCO** 184x (1843-47).	—	—	—
S657	**6 2/3 RIKSDALER BANCO** 184x (1843-47).	—	—	—
S658	**10 RIKSDALER BANCO** 184x (1843-47).	—	—	—
S659	**50 RIKSDALER BANCO** 184x (1843-47).	—	—	—

1848 ISSUE

#S660-S664 like previous issue. Printer: CAB.

		GOOD	FINE	XF
S660	**3 1/3 RIKSDALER BANCO** 1848; 1851.	—	—	—
S661	**5 RIKSDALER BANCO** 1848; 1951.	—	—	—
S662	**6 2/3 RIKSDALER BANCO** 1848; 1851.	—	—	—
S663	**10 RIKSDALER BANCO** 1848; 1851.	—	—	—
S664	**50 RIKSDALER BANCO** 184x.	—	—	—

1852 ISSUE

#S666-S669 like previous issue. Printer: JB.

		GOOD	FINE	XF
S666	**3 1/3 RIKSDALER BANCO** 1852; 1853; 1855.	—	—	—
S667	**5 RIKSDALER BANCO** 1852; 1853; 1855.	—	—	—
S668	**6 2/3 RIKSDALER BANCO** 1852; 1853; 1855.	—	—	—
S669	**10 RIKSDALER BANCO** 1852; 1853; 1855.	—	—	—

WERMLANDS ENSKILDA BANK

Formerly the Wermlands Provincial-Bank. Notes issued to 15.10.1901.

1857 ISSUE

#S682-S686 new bank name. Crowned eagle w/outstretched wings at upper ctr. Printer: JB.

		GOOD	FINE	XF
S682	**5 RIKSDALER** 1857.	75.00	150.00	300.00

		GOOD	FINE	XF
S683	**10 RIKSDALER** 1857.	90.00	175.00	350.00
S684	**50 RIKSDALER** 1857.	—	—	—
S685	**100 RIKSDALER** 1857.	—	—	—
S686	**500 RIKSDALER** 1857.	—	—	—

1875 ISSUE

#S687-S690 like previous issue. Notes in Kroner. Printer: JB.

		GOOD	FINE	XF
S687	**5 KRONOR** 1875.	60.00	125.00	250.00

		GOOD	FINE	XF
S688	**10 KRONOR** 1875; 1891. Black and pink.	75.00	150.00	300.00
S689	**50 KRONOR** 1875.	—	—	—
S690	**100 KRONOR** 1875.	—	—	—

WESTERBOTTENS ENSKILDA BANK

Notes issued to 1.1.1899.

1866 ISSUE

#S701-S703 arms of Lappland (wildman) at upper ctr. Printer: JB.

		GOOD	FINE	XF
S701	**5 RIKSDALER** 1866.	75.00	150.00	300.00
S702	**10 RIKSDALER** 1866.	90.00	175.00	350.00
S703	**50 RIKSDALER** 1866.	—	—	—

1876 ISSUE

#S704-S707 like previous issue. Notes in Kronor. Printer: JB.

		GOOD	FINE	XF
S704	**5 KRONOR** 1876.	60.00	125.00	300.00

		GOOD	FINE	XF
S705	**10 KRONOR** 1876.	75.00	150.00	300.00

		Good	Fine	XF
S706	**50 Kronor** 1876.	—	—	—
S707	**100 Kronor** 1876.	—	—	—

1881-83 Issue

#S708-S710 printer: BWC.

		Good	Fine	XF
S708	**10 Kronor** 1881. Portr. Qn. Christina at l., arms at r. Head at ctr. on back.	—	—	—
S709	**50 Kronor** 1883. Arms at l. and r., Qn. Christina at upper ctr.	—	—	—

		Good	Fine	XF
S710	**100 Kronor** 1883. Like #S709.	—	—	—

Öst-Göta Bank

After 1847 the bank name is Östgöta Enskilda Bank; later changed to Östergötlands Enskilda Bank.

1837 Issue

#S711-S716 crowned arms of Östergötland at upper ctr. Notes hand dated. Printer: CAB.

		Good	Fine	XF
S711	**2 Riksdaler Schillingar** 183x (1837-47).	—	—	—
S712	**3 Riksdaler Banco** 183x (1837-47).	—	—	—
S713	**3 1/3 Riksdaler Banco** 183x (1837-47).	—	—	—
S714	**10 Riksdaler Banco** 183x (1837-47); 1839. Black on green paper.	—	—	—
S715	**50 Riksdaler Banco** 183x (1837-47).	—	—	—
S716	**100 Riksdaler Banco** 183x (1837-47).	—	—	—

Östgöta Enskilda Bank

Formerly the Öst-Göta Bank, later to be the Östergötlands Enskilda Bank.

1847 Issue

#S717-S723 new bank name. Like previous issue. Some notes hand dated. Printer: CAB.

		Good	Fine	XF
S717	**3 1/3 Riksdaler Banco** 1847.	—	—	—
S718	**6 2/3 Riksdaler Banco** 1847.	—	—	—
S719	**10 Riksdaler Banco** 1847.	—	—	—
S720	**33 1/3 Riksdaler Banco** 18xx or 184x (1847-57).	—	—	—
S721	**50 Riksdaler Banco** 18xx or 184x (1847-57).	—	—	—
S722	**66 2/3 Riksdaler Banco** 18xx or 184x (1847-57).	—	—	—
S723	**100 Riksdaler Banco** 18xx or 184x (1847-57).	—	—	—

Östergötlands Enskilda Bank

Formerly the Öst-Göta Bank and the Östgöta Enskilda Bank. Notes issued to 1.8.1902.

1857 Issue

#S724-S727 newer bank name. Like previous issue. Printer: JB.

		Good	Fine	XF
S724	**5 Riksdaler** 1857; 1867.	75.00	150.00	300.00
S725	**10 Riksdaler** 1857; 1867.	90.00	175.00	350.00
S726	**50 Riksdaler** 1857; 1867.	—	—	—
S727	**100 Riksdaler** 1857; 1867.	—	—	—

1877 Issue

#S732-S735 like previous issue, but in Kronor. Printer: JB.

		Good	Fine	XF
S732	**5 Kronor** 1877.	60.00	125.00	300.00
S733	**10 Kronor** 1877; 1888.	75.00	150.00	300.00
S734	**50 Kronor** 1877.	—	—	—
S735	**100 Kronor** 1877.	—	—	—

1894 Issue

#S737-S739 two allegorical woman w/lion at l., crowned arms at upper ctr. Printer: BWC.

		Good	Fine	XF
S737	**10 Kronor** 1894.	75.00	150.00	300.00
S738	**50 Kronor** 1894.	—	—	—
S739	**100 Kronor** 1894.	—	—	—

The Swiss Confederation, located in central Europe north of Italy and south of Germany, has an area of 15,941 sq. mi. (41,290 sq. km.) and a population of 7.41 million. Capital: Berne. The economy centers about a well developed manufacturing industry, however the most important economic factor is services (banks and insurance).

Switzerland, the habitat of lake dwellers in prehistoric times, was peopled by the Celtic Helvetians when Julius Caesar made it a part of the Roman Empire in 58 BC. After the decline of Rome, Switzerland was invaded by Teutonic tribes who established small temporal holdings which, in the Middle Ages, became a federation of fiefs of the Holy Roman Empire. As a nation, Switzerland originated in 1291 when the districts of Nidwalden, Schwyz and Uri united to defeat Austria and attain independence as the Swiss Confederation. After acquiring new cantons in the 14th century, Switzerland was made independent from the Holy Roman Empire by the 1648 Treaty of Westphalia. The revolutionary armies of Napoleonic France occupied Switzerland and set up the Helvetian Republic, 1798-1803. After the fall of Napoleon, the Congress of Vienna, 1815, recognized the independence of Switzerland and guaranteed its neutrality. The Swiss Constitutions of 1848, 1874, and 1999 established a union modeled upon that of the United States.

MONETARY SYSTEM:

1 Franc (Franken) = 10 Batzen = 100 Centimes (Rappen)
Plural: Francs, Franchi or Franken.

This section contains listings of cantonal and private banks arranged according to city or area of issue. The following outline indicates where to locate the banks:

AARGAU
Aargauische Bank ..... #S101-S111

APPENZELL
Appenzell-Ausserhodische Kantonalbank ..... #S112-S117
Innerhodische Kantonalbank ..... #S118-S119

BASEL

CANTON
Basellandschaftliche Kantonalbank ..... #S121-S132

CITY
Bank in Basel ..... #S133-S149
Basler Kantonalbank ..... #S150-S153
Passavant & Co. ..... #S154

BERNE
Deposito-Cassa der Stadt Bern ..... #S156-S157
Eidgenössische Bank ..... #S161-S172
Kantonalbank von Bern ..... #S181-S207
Marcuard & Co. ..... #S209

FRIBOURG
Banque Cantonale Fribourgeoise ..... #S210-S227
Banque de l'Etat de Fribourg ..... #S228-S230
Banque Populaire de la Gruyère ..... #S231-S239
Caisse d'Amortissement de la Dette Publique à Fribourg ..... #S241-S249
Caisse Hypothècaire de Canton de Fribourg ..... #S251-S253
Crèdit Agricole et Industriel de la Broye ..... #S261-S266
Crèdit Gruyèrien ..... #S271-S274

GENEVA
Banque de Genève ..... #S281-S289
Banque du Commerce de Genève ..... #S291-S305
Banque Gènèrale Suisse ..... #S307-S308
B.F. Bonna ..... #S309
Caisse d'Escompte de Genève ..... #S311
Hentsch & Cie. ..... #S316
Lombard, Odier & Cie. ..... #S321

GLARUS
Bank in Glarus ..... #S326-S332
Leih-Cassa Glarus ..... #S341-S343
Glarner Kantonalbank ..... #S346-S348

GRAUBÜNDEN
Bank für Graubünden ..... #S351-S357
Graubündner Kantonalbank ..... #S361-S368

LUCERNE
Bank in Luzern ..... #S371-S391
Luzerner Kantonalbank ..... #S392-S395
Kantonal-Spar-und Leihkasse Luzern ..... #S396-S400

NEUCHATEL
Banque Cantonale Neuchâteloise ..... #S401-S412
Bank Commerciale Neuchâteloise ..... #S413-S415
Banque de Fred: Perret & Co. ..... #S416
Banque de Dépôt et d'Émission ..... #S417-S418
Union Horlogère ..... #S419

NIDWALDEN
Spar-und Leihkasse des Kantons Unterwalden nid dem Wald ..... #S421-S424
Kantonale Spar-und Leihkasse von Nidwalden ..... #S425-S426

OBWALDEN
Obwaldner Kantonalbank ..... #S427-S428

ST.GALLEN
Bank in St. Gallen ..... #S431-S453
Leih-und Sparkasse des Seebezirks ..... #S454
St. Gallische Kantonalbank ..... #S455-S462
Toggenburger Bank ..... #S463-S471

SCHAFFHAUSEN
Bank in Schaffhausen ..... #S473-S479
Schaffhauser Kantonalbank ..... #S480-S482

SCHWYZ
Kantonalbank Schwyz ..... #S483-S486

SOLOTHURN
Solothurner Kantonalbank ..... #S487-S490
Solothurnische Bank ..... #S491-S505

THURGAU
Thurgauische Hypothekenbank ..... #S506-S514
Thurgauische Kantonalbank ..... #S515-S521

TICINO
Banca Cantonale Ticinese ..... #S522-S532
Banca della Svizzera Italiana ..... #S533-S542
Banca Popolare di Lugano ..... #S543-S545
Credito Ticinese ..... #S546-S548

URI
Ersparniss-Cassa des Kantons Uri ..... #S549-S552

VAUD
Banque Cantonale Vaudoise ..... #S553-S569
Banque Populaire de la Broye ..... #S571-S572
Philippe Genton ..... #S574
Felix Marcel ..... #S576

WALLIS
Banque Cantonale du Valais ..... #S581-S585
Caisse Hypothecaire & de Crédit du Valais ..... #S586-S586B

ZUG
Zuger Kantonalbank ..... #S587-S589

ZÜRICH
Bank in Zürich ..... #S591-S610
Zürcher Kantonalbank ..... #S611-S625

CONCORDAT NOTE VARIETIES 1883-1906

German language: *in gesezlicher Baarschaft* to 1892 (50-1000 Fr.)
in gesetzlicher Barschaft 1893-1906

Serial #: small, narrow: to 1893 (50, 100 Fr.)
wide: 1894-1906

Series: *SERIE* written out: first issue, 50 Fr. to 1888, 100 Fr. to 1886, 500 Fr. to 1890, 1000 Fr. to 1883.
Ser. abbreviated: later issues, 50 Fr. from 1890, 100 Fr. from 1888, 500 Fr. from 1890, 1000 Fr. from 1892.

CANTONS

AARGAU

AARGAUISCHE BANK

Founded in 1854; note-issuing privilege terminated in 1910.

1856-57 ISSUE

#S101-S103 Castles Lenzburg and Homburg, entrance to a mine, and arms surrounded by children.

		Good	Fine	XF
S101	**20 Fr.** 1856. Yellow paper.	—	—	—
S102	**50 Fr.** 1856. Blue paper.	—	—	—
S103	**100 Fr.** 1856. White paper.	—	—	—
S104	**500 Fr.** 1857. Pink paper.	—	—	—

1873 ISSUE

#S105-S107 heads of woman and Hermes.

		Good	Fine	XF
S105	**50 Fr.** 1873.	—	—	—
S106	**100 Fr.** 1873.	—	—	—
S107	**500 Fr.** 1873.	—	—	—

1883-1910 CONCORDAT ISSUE

Many note-issuing banks used uniform designs for their issues from about 1883-1910. The basic format for all notes shows standing Helvetia at l. leaning on shield, cherub at lower r. on face, head at l. and r. on back.

		Good	Fine	XF
S108	**50 Fr.** 1883-1910.	—	—	—
S109	**100 Fr.** 1883-1910.	—	—	—
S110	**500 Fr.** 1883-1910.	—	—	—
S111	**1000 Fr.** 1883-1910.	—	—	—

APPENZELL (AUSSERRHODEN)

AUSSERHODISCHE KANTONALBANK, HERISAU

Founded in 1877; note-issuing privilege terminated in 1910.

1877 ISSUE

#S112-S114 wagon w/cloth in front of factory at l., farm family at farmhouse w/trough at r. Cantonal arms on back. Printer: Dondorf & Naumann, Frankfurt a.M.

No.	Denomination	Good	Fine	XF
S112	**50 FR.** 1877. Black on orange unpt.	—	—	—

No.	Denomination	Good	Fine	XF
S113	**100 FR.** 1.9.1877. Black on blue-green unpt.	—	—	—
S114	**500 FR.** 1877. Black on red unpt.	—	—	—

1883-1910 CONCORDAT ISSUE

#S115-S117 like #S108-S110.

No.	Denomination	Good	Fine	XF
S115	**50 FR.** 1883-1910.	—	—	—
S116	**100 FR.** 1883-1910.	—	—	—
S117	**500 FR.** 1883-1910.	—	—	—

INNERHODISCHE KANTONALBANK

Founded in 1900; note-issuing privilege terminated in 1910.

1901-10 CONCORDAT ISSUE

#S118 and S119 like #S108 and S109.

No.	Denomination	Good	Fine	XF
S118	**50 FR.** 1901-1910.	—	—	—
S119	**100 FR.** 1901-1910.	—	—	—

BASEL (CANTON)

BASELLANDSCHAFTLICHE KANTONALBANK, LIESTAL

Founded in 1864; note-issuing privilege terminated in 1910.

1867 ISSUE

No.	Denomination	Good	Fine	XF
S121	**20 FR.** 1867.	—	—	—
S122	**50 FR.** 1867.	—	—	—
S123	**100 FR.** 1867.	—	—	—
S124	**500 FR.** 1867.	—	—	—

1871 ISSUE

#S125-S128 cantonal arms, mountains and hills w/cattle grazing, farm equipment and farm scenes, blacksmith at anvil, train, and angel w/cornucopia. Text on back: *Banque Cantonale Liestal*.

No.	Denomination	Good	Fine	XF
S125	**20 FR.** 1871.	—	—	—
S126	**50 FR.** 1871.	—	—	—
S127	**100 FR.** 1871.	—	—	—
S128	**500 FR.** 1871.	—	—	—

1883-1910 CONCORDAT ISSUE

#S129-S132 like #S108-S111.

No.	Denomination	Good	Fine	XF
S129	**50 FR.** 1883-1910.	—	—	—
S130	**100 FR.** 1883-1910.	—	—	—
S131	**500 FR.** 1883-1910.	—	—	—
S132	**1000 FR.** 1883-1910.	—	—	—

BASEL (CITY)

BANK IN BASEL

Founded in 1844; note-issuing privilege terminated in 1907.

1845 ISSUE

#S133-S134 River Rhine and woman w/Basel arms above.

No.	Denomination	Good	Fine	XF
S133	**100 FR. (20 FÜNFFRANKENTALER)** 1845. Yellow paper.	—	—	—
S134	**500 FR. (100 FÜNFFRANKENTALER)** 1845. White paper.	—	—	—

1847 ISSUE

No.	Denomination	Good	Fine	XF
S135	**100 FR.** 1847. Similar to #S133 but different paper.	—	—	—
S136	**500 FR.** 1847. Similar to #S134 but different paper.	—	—	—

1852 ISSUE

No.	Denomination	Good	Fine	XF
S137	**100 FR.** 1852.	—	—	—
S138	**500 FR.** 1852.	—	—	—
S139	**1000 FR.** 1854. Interest-bearing state note. Printer: OFZ.	—	—	—

1856 ISSUE

#S140 and S141 like #S137 and S138 but w/stamping: *ODER WERTH IN GOLDSORTEN IM FRANZ. MÜNZFUSS*.

No.	Denomination	Good	Fine	XF
S140	**100 FR.** 1856.	—	—	—
S141	**500 FR.** 1856.	—	—	—

1873-74 ISSUE

#S141C-S145B Swiss cross, woman's head, and two boys carrying shields.

No.	Denomination	Good	Fine	XF
S141C	**1000 FR.** 1.12.1873.	—	—	—
S142	**100 FR.** 1874.	—	—	—
S143	**500 FR.** 1874.	—	—	—
S144	**1000 FR.** 1874.	—	—	—

NOTE: #S144 was issued together with the Bank in Zürich, Bank in St. Gallen and the Kantonalbank von Bern.

1876 ISSUE

No.	Denomination	Good	Fine	XF
S145	**50 FR.** 1876.	—	—	—

NOTE: #S145 was issued together with the Kantonalbank von Bern.

No.	Denomination	Good	Fine	XF
S145B	**500 FR.** 1876.	—	—	—

1883-1907 CONCORDAT ISSUE

#S146-S149 like #S108-S111.

		GOOD	FINE	XF
S146	**50 FR.** 1883-1907.	800.00	1400.	—
S147	**100 FR.** 1883-1907.	1400.	2000.	—
S148	**500 FR.** 1883-1907.	—	—	—
S149	**1000 FR.** 1883-1907.	—	—	—

BASLER KANTONALBANK

Founded in 1899; note-issuing privilege terminated in 1910.

1900-10 CONCORDAT ISSUE

#S150-S153 like #S108-S111.

		GOOD	FINE	XF
S150	**50 FR.** 1900-1910.	—	—	—
S151	**100 FR.** 1900-1910.	—	—	—
S152	**500 FR.** 1900-1910.	—	—	—
S153	**1000 FR.** 1900-1910.	—	—	—

PASSAVANT & CO., BASEL

1840 ISSUE

		GOOD	FINE	XF
S154	**100 FR.** ca.1840.	—	—	—

NOTE: #S154 was made to replace the former letters of credit.

BERNE

DEPOSITO-CASSA DER STADT BERN

Founded in 1825; note-issuing privilege terminated in 1867.

1825-32 ISSUE

		GOOD	FINE	XF
S156	**500 FR.** Alter Währung 1825. Gut-Schein. Yellow paper.	—	—	—
S157	**100 FÜNFFRANKENTALER** 1832.			
	a. Issued note.	—	—	—
	r. Remainder.	—	Unc	1200.

EIDGENÖSSISCHE BANK, BERN

Founded in 1863; note-issuing privilege terminated in 1882.

1864 ISSUE

#S161-S162 allegorical figures of Fortune and Industry, also Swiss cross.

		GOOD	FINE	XF
S161	**50 FR.** 1864. Blue.	—	—	—
S162	**100 FR.** 1864.	—	—	—
S163	**500 FR.** 1864.	—	—	—

1873 ISSUE

#S164-S166 like previous three notes but w/hand stamping: *COMPTOIR ZÜRICH*.

		GOOD	FINE	XF
S164	**50 FR.** 1873. Like #S161.	—	—	—
S165	**100 FR.** 1873. Like #S162.	—	—	—
S166	**500 FR.** 1873. Like #S163.	—	—	—
S167	**50 FR.** 19.12.1873.	—	—	—
S168	**100 FR.** 19.12.1873.	—	—	—
S169	**500 FR.** 19.12.1873.	—	—	—

#S170-S172 like previous three notes but w/hand stamping: *COMPTOIR LUZERN*.

		GOOD	FINE	XF
S170	**50 FR.** 19.12.1873. Like #S167.	—	—	—
S171	**100 FR.** 19.12.1873. Like #S168.	—	—	—
S172	**500 FR.** 19.12.1873. Like #S169.	—	—	—

KANTONALBANK VON BERN

Founded in 1833; note-issuing privilege terminated in 1910.

1834-47 ISSUE

#S181-S182 stub, arms of Bern, and vines.

		GOOD	FINE	XF
S181	**10 FÜNFFRANKENTALER** 1834. Yellow paper.	—	—	—
S182	**20 FÜNFFRANKENTALER** 1834. Yellow paper.	—	—	—
S183	**100 FÜNFFRANKENTALER** 1838.	—	—	—
S184	**1 FÜNFFRANKENTALER** 1847. Issued as welfare assistance for poor watchmakers.	—	—	—

1852 ISSUE

		GOOD	FINE	XF
S185	**50 FR.** 1852.	—	—	—
S186	**100 FR.** 1852.	—	—	—
S187	**500 FR.** 1852.	—	—	—

1852-60 ISSUE

#S188-S190 like previous three notes but w/hand stamping: *IN GOLD ODER SILBER*.

		GOOD	FINE	XF
S188	**50 FR.** 1852. Like #S185.	—	—	—
S189	**100 FR.** 1852. Like #S186.	—	—	—
S190	**500 FR.** 1852. Like #S187.	—	—	—
S191	**50 FR.** 1860.	—	—	—
S192	**100 FR.** 1860.	—	—	—
S193	**500 FR.** 1860.	—	—	—

1860-62 ISSUE

#S194-S196 like previous three notes but w/hand stamping: *IN GOLD ODER SILBER*.

		GOOD	FINE	XF
S194	**50 FR.** 1860. Like #S191.	—	—	—
S195	**100 FR.** 1860. Like #S192.	—	—	—
S196	**500 FR.** 1860. Like #S193.	—	—	—
S197	**20 FR.** 1862. German text.	—	—	—
S198	**20 FR.** 1862. French text.	—	—	—

1862-74 ISSUE

#S199-S200 like previous two notes but w/hand stamping: *IN GOLD ODER SILBER*.

		GOOD	FINE	XF
S199	**20 FR.** 1862. Like #S197.	—	—	—
S200	**20 FR.** 1862. Like #S198.	—	—	—
S201	**1000 FR.** 1874.			

NOTE: #S201 was issued together with the Bank in Basel, Bank in Zürich, and the Bank in St. Gallen.

1876 ISSUE

		GOOD	FINE	XF
S202	**100 FR.** 1876.	—	—	—

1877 ISSUE

#S203 and S204 similar to #S145 and S145B.

		GOOD	FINE	XF
S203	**50 FR.** 1877.	—	—	—
S204	**500 FR.** 1877.	—	—	—

1883-1910 CONCORDAT ISSUE

#S205-S207 like #S108-S110.

		GOOD	FINE	XF
S205	**50 FR.** 1883-1910.	—	—	—
S206	**100 FR.** 1883-1910.	1400.	2000.	—
S207	**500 FR.** 1883-1910.	—	—	—

MARCUARD & CO., BERN

Note-issuing privilege terminated in 1833.

1830 ISSUE

		GOOD	FINE	XF
S209	**50 FR. ALTER WÄHRUNG** 1830.	—	—	—

NOTE: #S209 was issued to replace checks and letters of credit.

FRIBOURG

BANQUE CANTONALE FRIBOURGEOISE

Founded in 1850; note-issuing privilege terminated in 1910.

1851 ISSUE

#S210-S217 printed on low quality white paper.

		GOOD	FINE	XF
S210	**5 FR.** 1851.	—	—	—
S211	**10 FR.** 1851.	—	—	—
S212	**25 FR.** 1851.	—	—	—
S213	**50 FR.** 1851.	—	—	—
S214	**100 FR.** 1851.	—	—	—
S215	**200 FR.** 1851.	—	—	—
S216	**500 FR.** 1851.	—	—	—

1853 ISSUE

		GOOD	FINE	XF
S217	**500 FR.** 1853. Tinted paper.	—	—	—

1855-78 ISSUE

#S218-S220 plow drawn by two horses, Alps, bridges over a river, rope bridge near Fribourg, and castles of Gruyères and Estavayer.

		GOOD	FINE	XF
S218	**20 FR.** 1855. Green paper.	—	—	—
S219	**100 FR.** 1855. Pink paper.	—	—	—
S220	**500 FR.** 1855. White paper.	—	—	—
S221	**5 FR.** 1861.	—	—	—
S222	**10 FR.** 1861. Brown unpt.	—	—	—
S223	**50 FR.** 1878. Similar to #S218-S220.	—	—	—

1884-1910 CONCORDAT ISSUE

#S224-S227 like #S108-S111.

		GOOD	FINE	XF
S224	**50 FR.** 1884-1910.	—	—	—
S225	**100 FR.** 1884-1910.	—	—	—
S226	**500 FR.** 1884-1910.	—	—	—
S227	**1000 FR.** 1884-1910.	—	—	—

BANQUE DE L'ETAT DE FRIBOURG

Founded in 1893; note-issuing privilege terminated in 1910.

1893-1910 CONCORDAT ISSUE

#S228-S230 like #S108-S110.

		GOOD	FINE	XF
S228	**50 FR.** 1893-1910.	—	—	—
S229	**100 FR.** 1893-1910.	—	—	—
S230	**500 FR.** 1893-1910.	—	—	—

BANQUE POPULAIRE DE LA GRUYÈRE, BULLE

Founded in 1853; note-issuing privilege terminated in 1890.

1857-66 ISSUE

#S231-S234 beehive w/angels, view of Bulle near globe, palette, waterwheel, sheaves and thresher, wine barrel and anchor on face. Two girls on back. Blurred printing.

		GOOD	FINE	XF
S231	**10 FR.** 1857. Violet paper.	—	—	—
S232	**20 FR.** 1857. Violet paper.	—	—	—
S233	**50 FR.** 1866.	—	—	—

1874 ISSUE

#S234-S236 beehive w/angels, view of Bulle near globe, palette, waterwheel, sheaves and thresher, wine barrel and anchor on face. Two girls on back. Finer, sharper printing.

		GOOD	FINE	XF
S234	**20 FR.** 1874. Violet paper.	—	—	—
S235	**50 FR.** 1874. Blue on white paper.	—	—	—
S236	**100 FR.** 1874. Red on white paper.	—	—	—

1883-90 CONCORDAT ISSUE

#S237-S239 like #S108-S110.

		GOOD	FINE	XF
S237	**50 FR.** 1883-1890.	—	—	—
S238	**100 FR.** 1883-1890.	—	—	—
S239	**500 FR.** 1883-1890.	—	—	—

CAISSE D'AMORTISSEMENT DE LA DETTE PUBLIQUE ÀFRIBOURG

Founded in 1867. Merged with Banque de l'Etat de Fribourg in 1893.

DECRET DU 15.5.1874

#S241-S243 seated girl writing on tablet at l., view of Fribourg, the Alps, along bottom, seated girl w/sheep at r. Circular bank seal w/Fribourg shield at ctr. Flanked by value scrolls on back. Printer: J. J. Hofer, Zürich.

		GOOD	FINE	XF
S241	**20 FR.** *D.1874.* Black w/red-brown text, border and counterfoil. Back red-brown.	—	—	—

		GOOD	FINE	XF
S242	**50 FR.** *D.1874.* Black w/green text, border and counterfoil. Back green.	—	—	—
S243	**100 FR.** *D.1874.*			
	a. Issued note. Black w/deep red text, border and counterfoil. Back deep red.	—	—	—
	p. Black w/brown text, border and counterfoil. Proof.	—	—	—

1877 ND ISSUE

#S244-S246 w/o vignette, and smaller size.

		GOOD	FINE	XF
S244	**20 FR.** ND (1877). Green unpt.	—	—	—
S245	**50 FR.** ND (1877). Blue unpt.	—	—	—
S246	**100 FR.** ND (1877). Red unpt.	—	—	—

1883-93 CONCORDAT ISSUE

#S247-S249 like #S108-S110.

		GOOD	FINE	XF
S247	**50 FR.** 1883-93.	—	—	—
S248	**100 FR.** 1883-93.	—	—	—
S249	**500 FR.** 1883-93.	—	—	—

CAISSE HYPOTHÉCAIRE DU CANTON DE FRIBOURG

Founded in 1854; note-issuing privilege terminated in 1881.

1856 ISSUE

		GOOD	FINE	XF
S251	**10 FR.** 18xx (ca.1856). Black on yellow unpt. Arms at top ctr., uniface. Remainder w/counterfoil.	—	Unc	225.00

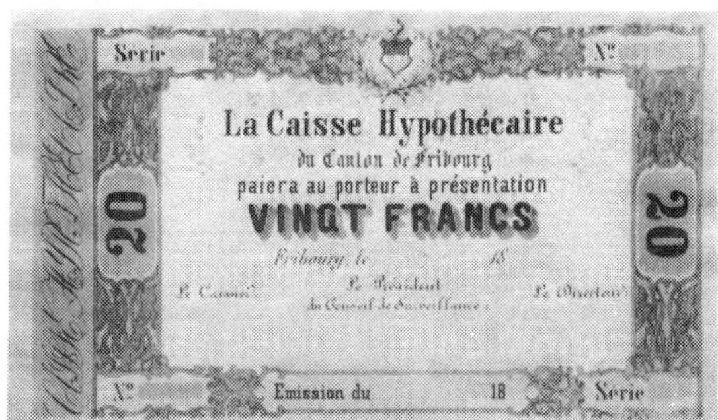

S252 20 Fr.
18xx (ca.1856). Black on lt. red unpt. Arms at top ctr., uniface. Remainder w/counterfoil. — Unc 200.00

		Good	Fine	XF
S253	**100 Fr.** 18xx (ca.1856). Green unpt. Arms at top ctr., uniface.			
	a. Issued note.	700.00	1250.	—
	r. Remainder w/counterfoil.	—	Unc	200.00

Crédit Agricole et Industriel de la Broye, Estavayer

Founded in 1866; note-issuing privilege terminated in 1910.

1866-77 Issue

#S261-S264 views of Estavayer and surroundings. Printer: J. J. Hofer, Zürich.

		Good	Fine	XF
S261	**10 Fr.** 1.12.1866. Gray paper. Remainder.	—	Unc	150.00
S262	**20 Fr.** 1.12.1866. Red paper. Remainder.	—	Unc	150.00

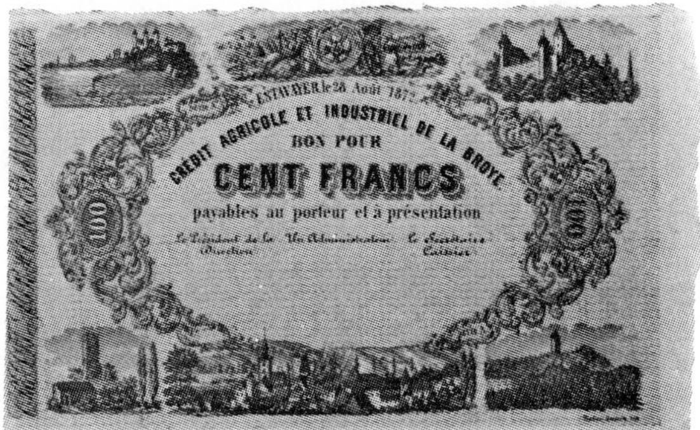

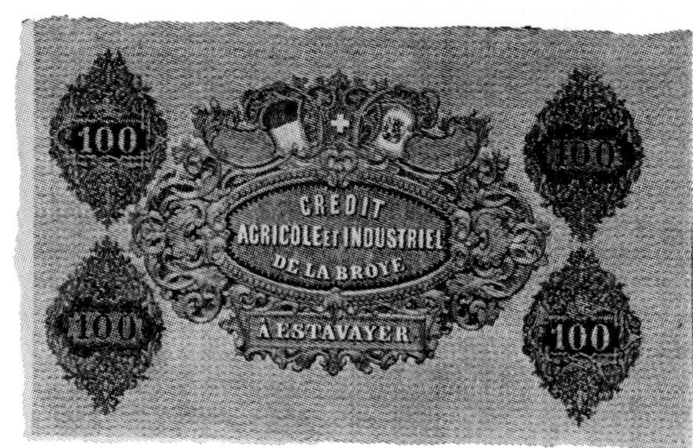

		Good	Fine	XF
S263	**100 Fr.** 28.8.1872. Blue on white paper. Remainder.	—	Unc	150.00
S264	**50 Fr.** 28.3.1877. Green on white paper. Green back. Remainder.	—	Unc	150.00

NOTE: A small hoard of unsigned remainders appeared on the market around 1970.

1883-1910 Concordat Issue

#S265 and S266 like #S108 and S109.

		Good	Fine	XF
S265	**50 Fr.** 1883-1910.	—	—	—
S266	**100 Fr.** 1883-1910.	—	—	—

Crédit Gruyérien, Bulle

Founded in 1871; note-issuing privilege terminated in 1890.

Emission du 1.1.1874

#S271 and S272 arms of *La Gruyère* (pelican) at top ctr., vignettes in border of Bulle and Estavayer, a cow herd, woman embroidering, and figures w/cornucopias and sheaves. Bank name within frame flanked by cherubs. Printer: J. J. Hofer, Zürich.

		Good	Fine	XF
S271	**20 Fr.** *D.1874.* Green w/black text and counterfoil. Back green; black text.	—	—	—
S272	**100 Fr.** *D.1874.* Brown w/black text and counterfoil. Back brown; black text.	—	—	—

1883-90 Concordat Issue

#S273 and S274 like #S108 and S109.

		Good	Fine	XF
S273	**50 Fr.** 1883-90.	—	—	—
S274	**100 Fr.** 1883-90.	—	—	—

Geneva

Banque de Genève

Founded in 1848; note-issuing privilege terminated in 1899.

1848-51 Issue

		Good	Fine	XF
S281	**100 Fr.** 1848. Blue paper.	—	—	—
S282	**500 Fr.** 1848. Green paper.	—	—	—
S283	**1000 Fr.** 1848.	—	—	—
S284	**20 Fr.** 1851. Red paper.	—	—	—

1873 Issue

		Good	Fine	XF
S285	**100 Fr.** 1873.	—	—	—

1883-99 Concordat Issue

#S286-S289 like #S108-S111.

		Good	Fine	XF
S286	**50 Fr.** 1883-99.	—	—	—
S287	**100 Fr.** 1883-99.	—	—	—
S288	**500 Fr.** 1883-99.	—	—	—
S289	**1000 Fr.** 1883-99.	—	—	—

Banque du Commerce de Genève

Founded in 1845; note-issuing privilege terminated in 1907.

#S291-S301 cantonal arms, freight in front of steam locomotive.

1846 Issue

		Good	Fine	XF
S291	**100 Fr.** 1846.	—	—	—
S292	**500 Fr.** 1846.	—	—	—
S293	**1000 Fr.** 1846.	—	—	—

1850 Issue

		Good	Fine	XF
S294	**100 Fr.** 1850.			
	a. Like #S291 but yellow guilloche.	—	—	—
	b. W/additional text: *En or ou en argent au cours legal français.*	—	—	—
S295	**500 Fr.** 1850.			
	a. Like #S292 but blue guilloche.	—	—	—
	b. W/additional text like #S294b.	—	—	—
S296	**1000 Fr.** 1850.			
	a. Like #S293 but w/pink unpt. added.	—	—	—
	b. W/additional text like #S294b.	—	—	—

1871 Issue

		Good	Fine	XF
S297	**50 Fr.** 1871.	—	—	—

1874 Issue

		Good	Fine	XF
S298	**50 Fr.** 1874.	—	—	—
S299	**100 Fr.** 1874.	—	—	—

1878 Issue

		Good	Fine	XF
S300	**50 Fr.** 1878.	—	—	—
S301	**100 Fr.** 1878.	—	—	—

1883-1907 Concordat Issue

#S302-S305 like #S108-S111.

		Good	Fine	XF
S302	**50 Fr.** 1883-1907.	—	—	—

		Good	Fine	XF
S303	**100 Fr.** 1883-1907.	—	—	—
S304	**500 Fr.** 1883-1907.	—	—	—
S305	**1000 Fr.** 1883-1907.	—	—	—

Banque Générale Suisse

Founded in 1853; liquidated in 1869. Printer: A. Bovet, Geneva.

1857 Issue

		Good	Fine	XF
S307	**20 Fr.** 1857.	—	—	—
S308	**50 Fr.** 1857.	—	—	—

B.F. Bonna, Genève

1840 Issue

		Good	Fine	XF
S309	**100 French Fr.** (ca.1840).	—	—	—

NOTE: With text: *1 day after sight* the French banker issuing #S309 wanted to circumvent the monopoly on note issue of the Banque de France.

Caisse d'Escompte de Genève

1856 Issue

		Good	Fine	XF
S311	**10 Fr.** 2.8.1856. Black on green unpt. Arms at upper ctr. Uniface. Printer: Pilet & Cougnard, Geneva.			
	a. Issued note.	—	—	—
	b. Cancelled, hand stamped: *ANNULÉ* and circular bank stamp.	250.00	600.00	—

Hentsch & Cie, Genève

1840 Issue

		Good	Fine	XF
S316	**100 French Fr.** (ca.1840).	—	—	—

NOTE: #S316 has the same text as #S309 in hopes of circumventing the Banque de France.

Lombard, Odier & Cie, Genève

Note-issuing privilege terminated in 1852.

1832 Issue

		Good	Fine	XF
S321	**100 Fr.** 1832. *Bon au Porteur.*	—	—	—

Glarus

Bank in Glarus

Founded in 1852; note-issuing privilege terminated in 1882.

1852 Issue

#S326-S327 Helvetia sitting at l., St. Fridolinus at ctr., head of Hermes in unpt. at r. Printer: OFZ.

		Good	Fine	XF
S326	**10 Fr.** 1852.	—	—	—
S327	**100 Fr.** 1852.	—	—	—

1864 ISSUE

#S328-S329 Helvetia sitting at l., St. Fridolinus at ctr., head of Hermes in unpt. at r.

		GOOD	FINE	XF
S328	**10 FR.** 1864.	—	—	—
S329	**100 FR.** 1864.	—	—	—

1876 ISSUE

#S330-S332 Helvetia sitting at l., St. Fridolinus at ctr., head of Hermes in unpt. at r. Printer: Dondorf & Naumann.

		GOOD	FINE	XF
S330	**50 FR.** 1876. Red.	—	—	—

		GOOD	FINE	XF
S331	**100 FR.** 14.6.1876. Green.			
	a. Issued note.	—	—	—
	b. Cancelled, hand stamped: *ANNULE*.	—	—	—
S332	**500 FR.** 1876. Blue.	—	—	—

LEIH-CASSA GLARUS

Founded in 1862; note-issuing privilege terminated in 1882.

1870 ISSUE

#S341-S343 factory at ctr., seated Helvetia at r.

		GOOD	FINE	XF
S341	**20 FR.** 1870. Blue.	—	—	—
S342	**50 FR.** 1870. Red.	—	—	—
S343	**100 FR.** 1870. Green.	—	—	—

GLARNER KANTONALBANK

Founded in 1884; note-issuing privilege terminated in 1910.

1884-1910 CONCORDAT ISSUE

#S346-S348 like #S108-S110.

		GOOD	FINE	XF
S346	**50 FR.** 1884-1910.	—	—	—
S347	**100 FR.** 1884-1910.	—	—	—
S348	**500 FR.** 1884-1910.	—	—	—

GRAUBÜNDEN

BANK FÜR GRAUBÜNDEN, CHUR

Founded in 1862; note-issuing privilege terminated in 1880.

1863 ND ISSUE

#S351-S353 interest-bearing state notes to the bearer and at sight. three allegorical figures at l. and r., arms above.

		GOOD	FINE	XF
S351	**50 FR.** ND (1863). Text on back.	—	—	—
S352	**100 FR.** ND (1863).	—	—	—
S353	**500 FR.** ND (1863).	—	—	—

1865-67 ISSUE

#S354-S357 Industry at l., farm couple symbolizing Agriculture at r.

		GOOD	FINE	XF
S354	**50 FR.** 1865. Brown paper.	—	—	—
S355	**100 FR.** 1865. Green paper.	—	—	—
S356	**500 FR.** 1865. Brown paper.	—	—	—
S357	**20 FR.** 1867. Black on blue and orange unpt.	—	—	—

GRAUBÜNDNER KANTONALBANK, CHUR

Founded in 1869; note-issuing privilege terminated in 1910.

1872-73 ISSUE

#S361-S365 Alps cottage and mountainscape w/bears.

		GOOD	FINE	XF
S361	**10 FR.** 1872. Yellow.	—	—	—
S362	**50 FR.** 1872. Green.	—	—	—
S363	**100 FR.** 1872. Blue.	—	—	—
S364	**500 FR.** 1872. Brown.	—	—	—
S365	**20 FR.** 1873. Red.	—	—	—

1883-1910 CONCORDAT ISSUE

#S366-S368 like #S108-S110.

		GOOD	FINE	XF
S366	**50 FR.** 1883-1910.	—	—	—

		GOOD	FINE	XF
S367	**100 FR.** 1883-1910.	—	—	—
S368	**500 FR.** 1883-1910.	—	—	—

LUCERNE

BANK IN LUZERN

Founded in 1857; note-issuing privilege terminated in 1907.

1857 ISSUE

#S371-S373 medallion w/steamer at l., view of Lucerne at ctr., train at r. Uniface. Series A.

		GOOD	FINE	XF
S371	**50 FR.** 1857. Yellow paper.	—	—	—
S372	**100 FR.** 1857. Blue paper.	—	—	—
S373	**500 FR.** 1857. White paper.	—	—	—

1866 ISSUE

#S374 and S375 Series B.

		GOOD	FINE	XF
S374	**100 FR.** 1866.	—	—	—
S375	**500 FR.** 1866.	—	—	—

1870-71 ISSUE

#S376 and S377 interest-bearing state notes. #S378 Series B.

		GOOD	FINE	XF
S376	**10 FR.** 1870.	—	—	—
S377	**100 FR.** 1870.	—	—	—
S378	**50 FR.** 1871.	—	—	—

1872 ISSUE

#S379-S381 Series C.

		GOOD	FINE	XF
S379	**50 FR.** 1872.	—	—	—
S380	**100 FR.** 1872.	—	—	—
S381	**500 FR.** 1872.	—	—	—

1873-75 ISSUE

#S382-S384 Series D.

		GOOD	FINE	XF
S382	**50 FR.** 1873.	—	—	—
S383	**100 FR.** 1873.	—	—	—
S384	**500 FR.** 1873.	—	—	—
S385	**100 FR.** 1875. Series E. Text added on back.	—	—	—

1877 ISSUE

#S386-S388 view of Lucerne, William Tell, girls and lion monument in Lucerne on face; woman's head on back. Printer: BWC.

		GOOD	FINE	XF
S386	**50 FR.** 1.1.1877.			
	a. Issued note.	—	—	—
	s. Specimen.	—	Unc	800.00

		Good	Fine	XF
S387	**100 Fr.** 1.1.1877.			
	a. Issued note.	—	—	—
	s. Specimen.	—	Unc	1000.

		Good	Fine	XF
S388	**500 Fr.** 1.1.1877.			
	a. Issued note.	—	—	—
	s. Specimen.	—	Unc	1200.

1883-1907 Concordat Issue

#S389-S391 like #S108-S110.

		Good	Fine	XF
S389	**50 Fr.** 1883-1907.	—	—	—
S390	**100 Fr.** 1883-1907.	—	—	—
S391	**500 Fr.** 1883-1907.	—	—	—

Luzerner Kantonalbank

Formerly the Kantonal-Spar-und Leihkasse Luzern. Note-issuing privilege terminated in 1910.

1892-1910 Concordat Issue

#S392-S395 like #S108-S111.

		Good	Fine	XF
S392	**50 Fr.** 1892-1910.	—	—	—

		Good	Fine	XF
S393	**100 Fr.** 1892-1910.	—	—	—
S394	**500 Fr.** 1892-1910.	—	—	—
S395	**1000 Fr.** 1892-1910.	—	—	—

Kantonal-Spar- und Leihkasse Luzern

Founded in 1850; name changed to Luzerner Kantonalbank in 1892.

1876-77 Issue

#S396-S398 like #S386-S388.

		Good	Fine	XF
S396	**50 Fr.** 31.10.1876.	—	—	—
S397	**100 Fr.** 1877.	—	—	—
S398	**500 Fr.** 1877.	—	—	—

Note: #S396-S398 from the Spar- und Leih-Cassa des Kantons Luzern. Same vignettes as #S386-S388.

1884-92 Concordat Issue

#S398A-S400 like #S108-S111.

		Good	Fine	XF
S398A	**50 Fr.** 1884-92.	—	—	—
S398B	**100 Fr.** 1884-92.	—	—	—
S399	**500 Fr.** 1884-92.	—	—	—
S400	**1000 Fr.** 1884-92.	—	—	—

Neuchatel

Banque Cantonale Neuchâteloise

Founded in 1854; liquidated in 1881. Reestablished in 1883; note-issuing privilege terminated in 1910.

1855-56 Issue

		Good	Fine	XF
S401	**100 Fr.** 1855. *Billet Provisoire.*	—	—	—

#S402-S405 view of Neuchatel, grape harvest and watchmaker's workshop.

		Good	Fine	XF
S402	**20 Fr.** 1856.	—	—	—
S403	**50 Fr.** 1856.	—	—	—
S404	**100 Fr.** 1856.	—	—	—
S405	**500 Fr.** 1856.	—	—	—

1859-74 Issue

		Good	Fine	XF
S406	**20 Fr.** 1859.	—	—	—
S407	**50 Fr.** 1859.	—	—	—
S408	**100 Fr.** 1872.	—	—	—
S409	**500 Fr.** 1874.	—	—	—

1883-1910 Concordat Issue

#S410-S412 like #S108-S110.

		Good	Fine	XF
S410	**50 Fr.** 1883-1910.	—	—	—
S411	**100 Fr.** 1883-1910.	—	—	—
S412	**500 Fr.** 1883-1910.	—	—	—

Banque Commerciale Neuchâteloise

Founded in 1883; note-issuing privilege terminated in 1907.

1883-1907 Concordat Issue

#S413-S415 like #S108-S110.

		Good	Fine	XF
S413	**50 Fr.** 1883-1907.	—	—	—
S414	**100 Fr.** 1883-1907.	—	—	—
S415	**500 Fr.** 1883-1907.	—	—	—

Banque de Fred: Perret & Co., Neuchâtel and Chaux deFonds

		Good	Fine	XF
S416	**100 Fr.** ND. Allegorical figure and beehive in ornate border.	—	—	—

Banque de Dépôt et d'Émission, Chaux de Fonds

Founded in 1848.

1848 Issue

		Good	Fine	XF
S417	**25 Fr.** 1848. Black and gray. Ornamental octagonal frame.	—	—	—
S418	**50 Fr.** 1848. Red paper. Similar to #S417.	—	—	—

Union Horlogère, Le Locle and La Chaux de Fonds

1858 Issue

		Good	Fine	XF
S419	**100 Fr.** (ca.1858). Interest-bearing note.	—	—	—

Nidwalden

Spar- und Leihkasse des Kantons Unterwalden nid dem Wald

Founded in 1879; name changed to Kantonale Spar-und Leihkasse von Nidwalden in 1891.

1879 ISSUE

#S421-S422 cantonal arms, Winkelried monument and woman's head.

		GOOD	FINE	XF
S421	**50 FR.** 1879.	—	—	—

		GOOD	FINE	XF
S422	**100 FR.** 1879. Lit. A.	—	—	—

1883-91 CONCORDAT ISSUE

#S423 and S424 like #S108 and S109.

		GOOD	FINE	XF
S423	**50 FR.** 1883-91.	—	—	—
S424	**100 FR.** 1883-91.	—	—	—

KANTONALE SPAR- UND LEIHKASSE VON NIDWALDEN, STANS

Formerly the Kantonale Spar- und Leihkasse von Nidwalden. Note-issuing privilege terminated in 1910.

1891-1904 CONCORDAT ISSUE

#S425 and S426 like #S108 and S109.

		GOOD	FINE	XF
S425	**50 FR.** 1891-1904.	—	—	—
S426	**100 FR.** 1891-1904.	—	—	—

OBWALDEN

OBWALDNER KANTONALBANK, SARNEN

Founded in 1887; note-issuing privilege terminated in 1910.

1887-1910 CONCORDAT ISSUE

#S427 and S428 like #S108 and S109.

		GOOD	FINE	XF
S427	**50 FR.** 1887-1910.	—	—	—

		GOOD	FINE	XF
S428	**100 FR.** 2.1.1887-1910. Dk. blue on tan unpt., black text. Blue-gray back.	—	—	—

ST. GALLEN

BANK IN ST. GALLEN

Founded in 1837; note-issuing privilege terminated in 1907.

1838 ISSUE

#S431-S433 uniface. Printer: Draper, Toppan, Longacre & Co., N.Y. & Phila.

		GOOD	FINE	XF
S431	**10 GULDEN** 18xx (ca. 1838). Black. Steamship at l., Hermes w/dog and key at upper ctr., steam passenger train at r. Remainder.	—	Unc	400.00
S432	**50 GULDEN** 18xx (ca.1838). Black. Newfoundland dog, beehive and rooster at l., steam trains at ctr., sheaf, plow and farm tools w/hills at r. Remainder.	—	Unc	800.00

		GOOD	FINE	XF
S433	**100 GULDEN** 18xx (ca.1838). Black. Seated allegorical figures at upper ctr., steam train at l. and r. Remainder.	—	Unc	500.00

1852 GULDEN ISSUE

#S434-S436 like previous three notes but w/stamping: *EFFECTIVE GULDEN ODER BRABANTERTHALER ZU FL. 2,42.* Litt. P-W (8 series).

		GOOD	FINE	XF
S434	**10 GULDEN** 18xx (ca.1852). Like #S431.	—	—	—
S435	**50 GULDEN** 18xx (ca.1852). Like #S432.	—	—	—
S436	**100 GULDEN** 18xx (ca.1852). Like #S433.	—	—	—

1852 FRANC ISSUE

#S437-S440 uniface. Printer: Toppan, Carpenter, Casilear & Co., New York and Phila.

		Good	Fine	XF
S437	**20 Fr.** 18xx (ca.1852). Black. Seated woman w/sheaf next to man w/anvil at l., shepherd w/sheep at upper ctr., beehive at bottom, woman w/grapes. at r. Remainder.	—	Unc	400.00

		Good	Fine	XF
S438	**50 Fr.** 18xx (ca.1852). Seated Justice at l., woman w/sheaf at r., train on bridge at upper ctr. Remainder.	—	Unc	500.00

		Good	Fine	XF
S439	**100 Fr.** 18xx (ca.1852). Woman harvesting at l., man w/3 horses at trough at top ctr., seated woman weaving at r. Remainder.	—	Unc	500.00

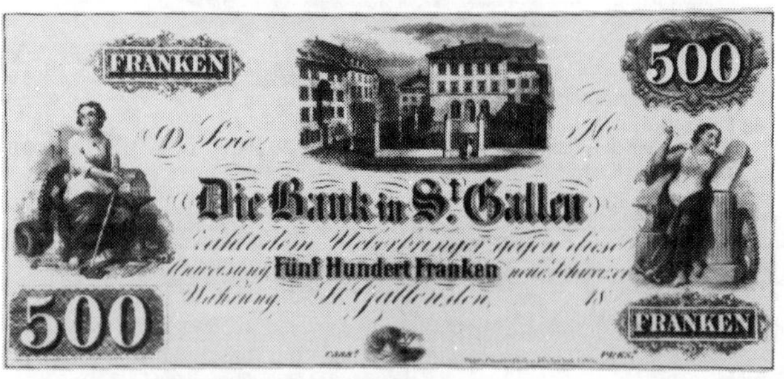

		Good	Fine	XF
S440	**500 Fr.** 18xx (ca. 1852). Seated woman w/hammer and anvil at l., bank at upper ctr., allegorical Art writing at r. Remainder.	—	Unc	600.00

1857 Issue

#S441-S444 like #S437-S440 but w/stamping: *RÜCKZAHLBAR IN SILBER ODER GOLD NAP. D'OR A FR. 20,-.*

		Good	Fine	XF
S441	**20 Fr.** 1857. Like #S437.	—	—	—
S442	**50 Fr.** 1857. Like #S438.	—	—	—
S443	**100 Fr.** 1857. Like #S439.	—	—	—
S444	**500 Fr.** 1857. Like #S440.	—	—	—

1873 Issue

		Good	Fine	XF
S445	**1000 Fr.** 1873. Swiss cross, woman's head, 2 boys holding shields. Printer: Dondorf & Naumann. Unissued remainder.	—	Unc	3000.

NOTE: #S445 was issued together with the Bank in Zürich, Bank in Basel and Kantonalbank von Bern.

1875 Issue

#S446-S449 similar to #S437-S440 but printed on different paper.

		Good	Fine	XF
S446	**20 Fr.** 1875. Similar to #S437.	—	—	—
S447	**50 Fr.** 1875. Similar to #S438.	—	—	—
S448	**100 Fr.** 1875. Similar to #S439.	—	—	—
S449	**500 Fr.** 1875. Similar to #S440.	—	—	—

1883-1907 Concordat Issue

#S450-S453 like #S108-S111.

		Good	Fine	XF
S450	**50 Fr.** 1883-1907.	—	—	—
S451	**100 Fr.** 1883-1907.	—	—	—
S452	**500 Fr.** 1883-1907.	—	—	—
S453	**1000 Fr.** 1883-1907.	—	—	—

Leih- und Sparkasse des Seebezirks, Uznach

Founded in 1848; note-issuing privilege terminated in 1852.

1848 Issue

		Good	Fine	XF
S454	**10 Gulden** 1848. Hermes and Fortune w/cornucopia.	—	—	—

St. Gallische Kantonalbank

Founded in 1868; note-issuing privilege terminated in 1910.

1868 Issue

#S455-S458 woman w/sickle near wheat field and apples at l., allegorical woman (Industry) near factory at r.

		Good	Fine	XF
S455	**20 Fr.** 1868-82. Green paper.	—	—	—
S456	**50 Fr.** 1868-82. Brown paper.	—	—	—

		Good	Fine	XF
S457	**100 Fr.** 1868-82. Green paper.	—	—	—
S458	**500 Fr.** 1868-82. Green paper.	—	—	—

1883-1910 Concordat Issue

#S459-S462 like #S108-S111.

		Good	Fine	XF
S459	**50 Fr.** 1883-1910.	—	—	—

		Good	Fine	XF
S460	**100 Fr.** 1883-1910.	—	—	—
S461	**500 Fr.** 1883-1910.	—	—	—
S462	**1000 Fr.** 1883-1910.	—	—	—

Toggenburger Bank, Lichtensteig

Founded in 1863; note-issuing privilege terminated in 1907.

1864 Issue

#S463-S465 view of Lichtensteig, woman at cotton machine, and Hermes. Uniface. Series A.

		Good	Fine	XF
S463	**10 Fr.** 1864.	—	—	—

		Good	Fine	XF
S464	50 Fr. 1864.	—	—	—
S465	100 Fr. 1864.	—	—	—

1865 Issue

#S466-S468 face like previous 3 notes. Back has value and arms of Lichtensteig.

		Good	Fine	XF
S466	10 Fr. 1865.	—	—	—
S467	50 Fr. 1865.	—	—	—
S468	100 Fr. 1865.	—	—	—

1883-1907 Concordat Issue

#S469-S471 like #S108-S110.

		Good	Fine	XF
S469	50 Fr. 1883-1907.	—	—	—
S470	100 Fr. 1883-1907.	—	—	—
S471	500 Fr. 1883-1907.	—	—	—

Schaffhausen

Bank in Schaffhausen

Founded in 1862; note-issuing privilege terminated in 1908.

1863 Issue

#S473-S475 arms of Schaffhausen surrounded by cornucopias w/money and flowers. Uniface. Printer: Theofil Beck, Schaffhausen.

		Good	Fine	XF
S473	50 Fr. 1863. Yellow paper.	—	—	—
S474	100 Fr. 1863. White paper.	—	—	—
S475	500 Fr. 1863. Blue paper.	—	—	—

1875 Issue

		Good	Fine	XF
S476	50 Fr. (ca.1875). Yellow paper. Allegorical Agriculture at l., arms of Schaffhausen at ctr., allegorical Industry at r.	—	—	—

1883-1908 Concordat Issue

#S477-S479 like #S108-S110.

		Good	Fine	XF
S477	50 Fr. 1883-1908.	—	—	—
S478	100 Fr. 1883-1908.	—	—	—
S479	500 Fr. 1883-1908.	—	—	—

Schaffhauser Kantonalbank

Founded in 1883; note-issuing privilege terminated in 1910.

1883-1910 Concordat Issue

#S480-S482 like #S108-S110.

		Good	Fine	XF
S480	50 Fr. 1883-1910.	—	—	—
S481	100 Fr. 1883-1910.	—	—	—
S482	500 Fr. 1883-1910.	—	—	—

Schwyz

Kantonalbank Schwyz

Founded in 1890; note-issuing privilege terminated in 1910.

1890-1910 Concordat Issue

#S483-S486 like #S108-S111.

		Good	Fine	XF
S483	50 Fr. 1890-1910.	—	—	—
S484	100 Fr. 1890-1910.	—	—	—
S485	500 Fr. 1890-1910.	—	—	—
S486	1000 Fr. 1890-1910.	—	—	—

Solothurn

Solothurner Kantonalbank

Formerly the Solothurnische Bank/Banque de Soleure; name change 1886. Note-issuing privilege terminated in 1910.

1886-1910 Concordat Issue

#S487-S490 like #S108-S111.

		Good	Fine	XF
S487	50 Fr. 1886-1910.	—	—	—
S488	100 Fr. 1886-1910.	—	—	—
S489	500 Fr. 1886-1910.	—	—	—
S490	1000 Fr. 1886-1910.	—	—	—

Solothurnische Bank
Bank de Soleure

Founded in 1857. Became the Solothurner Kantonalbank in 1886.

1858 Issue

#S491-S494 view of Solothurn.

		Good	Fine	XF
S491	20 Fr. 1858. Green paper.	—	—	—
S492	50 Fr. 1858. Yellow paper.	—	—	—
S493	100 Fr. 1858. Pink paper.	—	—	—
S494	500 Fr. 1858. Blue paper.	—	—	—

1872 Issue

#S495-S496 state notes.

		Good	Fine	XF
S495	500 Fr. 1872. Red.	—	—	—
S496	1000 Fr. 1872. Blue.	—	—	—

1873 Issue

#S497-S499 Hermes sitting, woman at spinning wheel near factory chimneys.

		Good	Fine	XF
S497	50 Fr. 1873.	—	—	—
S498	100 Fr. 1873.	—	—	—
S499	500 Fr. 1873.	—	—	—

1881 Issue

		Good	Fine	XF
S500	50 Fr. 1881. Gray.	—	—	—
S501	1000 Fr. 1881. Green.	—	—	—

1883-86 Concordat Issue

#S502-S505 like #S108-S111.

		Good	Fine	XF
S502	50 Fr. 1883-86.	—	—	—
S503	100 Fr. 1883-86.	—	—	—
S504	500 Fr. 1883-86.	—	—	—
S505	1000 Fr. 1883-86.	—	—	—

Thurgau

Thurgauische Hypothekenbank, Frauenfeld

Founded in 1851; note-issuing privilege terminated in 1908.

1852-54 Issue

		Good	Fine	XF
S506	10 Fr. 1852. White paper.	—	—	—
S507	50 Fr. 1852. Yellow paper.	—	—	—
S508	100 Fr. 1854. Yellow paper.	—	—	—

1858 Issue

#S509-S511 like previous three notes but ovpt: *IN SILBER UND GOLD*.

		Good	Fine	XF
S509	**10 Fr.** 1858. Like #S506.	—	—	—
S510	**50 Fr.** 1858. Like #S507.	—	—	—
S511	**100 Fr.** 1858. Like #S508.	—	—	—

1883-1908 Concordat Issue

#S512-S514 like #S108-S110.

		Good	Fine	XF
S512	**50 Fr.** 1883-1908.	—	—	—
S513	**100 Fr.** 1883-1908.	—	—	—
S514	**500 Fr.** 1883-1908.	—	—	—

Thurgauische Kantonalbank, Weinfelden

Founded in 1871; note-issuing privilege terminated in 1910.

1871 Issue

#S515-S518 Fortune w/crops, grapes and containers, allegorical Industry w/anvil, gear and locomotive at l., cantonal arms at r. Printer: OFZ.

		Good	Fine	XF
S515	**20 Fr.** 1871. Blue guilloche.	—	—	—
S516	**50 Fr.** 1871. Green guilloche.	—	—	—
S517	**100 Fr.** 1871. Orange guilloche.	—	—	—
S518	**500 Fr.** 1871. Red guilloche.	—	—	—

1883-1910 Concordat Issue

#S519-S521 like #S108-S110.

		Good	Fine	XF
S519	**50 Fr.** 1883-1910.	—	—	—
S520	**100 Fr.** 1883-1910.	—	—	—
S521	**500 Fr.** 1883-1910.	—	—	—

Ticino

Banca Cantonale Ticinese, Bellinzona

Founded in 1858; note-issuing privilege terminated in 1908.

1861 Issue

		Good	Fine	XF
S522	**5 Fr.** 1861. Ornamental design.	—	—	—
S523	**20 Fr.** 1861. Green paper. Ornamental design.	—	—	—
S524	**50 Fr.** 1861. Yellow paper. Head of Hermes and Fortune.	—	—	—
S525	**100 Fr.** 1861. Red paper. Girl from Ticino at l. and r.	—	—	—

1874-75 Issue

#S526-S528 printer: Carlo Trzaska, Milano.

		Good	Fine	XF
S526	**10 Fr.** 1874. Red guilloche. Arms at ctr.	—	—	—
S527	**20 Fr.** 1874. Green guilloche. Like #S526.	—	—	—
S528	**500 Fr.** 1875. White paper. Like #S526.	—	—	—

1884-1908 Concordat Issue

#S529-S532 like #S108-S111.

		Good	Fine	XF
S529	**50 Fr.** 1884-1908.	—	—	—
S530	**100 Fr.** 1884-1908.	—	—	—
S531	**500 Fr.** 1884-1908.	—	—	—
S532	**1000 Fr.** 1884-1908.	—	—	—

Banca della Svizzera Italiana, Lugano

Founded in 1873; note-issuing privilege terminated in 1907.

1874 Issue

#S533-S536 Buoni di Cassa.

		Good	Fine	XF
S533	**5 Fr.** 1874. Gray paper. Green guilloche. Back green.	—	—	—
S534	**10 Fr.** 1874. Gray paper. Green guilloche. Back brown.	—	—	—
S535	**20 Fr.** 1874. Gray paper. Brown guilloche. Back red.	—	—	—
S536	**50 Fr.** 1874. Green paper. Brown guilloche. Back red.	—	—	—

1877 Issue

#S537-S539 printer: ABNC.

		Good	Fine	XF
S537	**50 Fr.** 1877. Black on blue unpt. Boy at l., seated Abundance at ctr., arms at r. Back blue.			
	a. Issued note.	—	—	—
	p. Proof.	—	—	—

		Good	Fine	XF
S538	**100 Fr.** 1877. Black on green unpt. Arms at l., seated Helvetia at ctr., Industry at r. Back green.			
	a. Issued note.	—	—	—
	p. Proof.	—	—	—

		Good	Fine	XF
S539	**500 Fr.** 1877. Black on brown unpt. Arms at l., different portr. of seated Helvetia at ctr., allegorical woman at r. Back dk. brown.			
	a. Issued note.	—	—	—
	p. Proof.	—	—	—

1883-1907 Concordat Issue

#S540-S542 like #S108-S110.

		Good	Fine	XF
S540	**50 Fr.** 1883-1907.	—	—	—
S541	**100 Fr.** 1883-1907.	—	—	—
S542	**500 Fr.** 1883-1907.	—	—	—

NOTE: Facsimile reproductions, often offered as genuine notes, exist of 2 pieces: #S538 with serial #8859 and #S540 with serial #H2-0525. These copies were made to commemorate the centenary of the bank.

Banca Popolare di Lugano

Founded in 1888; note-issuing privilege terminated in 1910.

1888-1910 Concordat Issue

#S543-S545 like #S108-S110.

		Good	Fine	XF
S543	**50 Fr.** 1888-1910.	—	—	—
S544	**100 Fr.** 1888-1910.	—	—	—
S545	**500 Fr.** 1888-1910.	—	—	—

Credito Ticinese, Locarno

Founded in 1890; note-issuing privilege terminated in 1907.

1891-1907 Concordat Issue

#S546-S548 like #S108-S110.

		Good	Fine	XF
S546	**50 Fr.** 1891-1907.	—	—	—
S547	**100 Fr.** 1891-1907.	—	—	—
S548	**500 Fr.** 1891-1907.	—	—	—

Uri

Ersparniss-Cassa des Kantons Uri, Altdorf

Founded in 1837; note-issuing privilege terminated in 1910.

1878 Issue

#S549-S550 Tell's Chapel and Mt. Rütli at l. and r., cantonal arms at upper ctr.

		Good	Fine	XF
S549	**50 Fr.** 1.3.1878.	—	—	—
S550	**100 Fr.** 1.3.1878.	—	—	—

1883-1910 Concordat Issue

#S551 and S552 like #S108 and S109.

		Good	Fine	XF
S551	**50 Fr.** 1883-1910.	—	—	—
S552	**100 Fr.** 1883-1910.	—	—	—

Vaud

Banque Cantonale Vaudoise, Lausanne

Founded in 1845; note-issuing privilege terminated in 1910.

1846 Issue

#S553-S554 cantonal arms, Lake Geneva w/ship below, plow at beach, freight and anchor.

		Good	Fine	XF
S553	**10 Fünffrankentaler** 1846. White paper.	—	—	—
S554	**100 Fünffrankentaler** 1846. Pink paper.	—	—	—

NOTE: Facsimiles of #S554 were made for the centenary of the bank.

NOTE: The 20 Fünffrankentaler denomination was printed, but because of the poor quality of paper it was not released.

1847-53 Issue

		Good	Fine	XF
S555	**5 Fünffrankentaler** 1847.	—	—	—
S556	**20 Fünffrankentaler** 1853.	—	—	—

1856 Issue

		Good	Fine	XF
S557	**5 Fr.** 1856. Arms at ctr.	—	—	—
S558	**20 Fr.** 1856.	—	—	—
S559	**100 Fr.** 1856.	—	—	—
S560	**500 Fr.** 1856.	—	—	—

1864 Issue

		Good	Fine	XF
S561	**50 Fr.** 1864.	—	—	—
S562	**100 Fr.** 1864.	—	—	—
S563	**500 Fr.** 1864.	—	—	—
S564	**1000 Fr.** 1864.	—	—	—

1879 Issue

		Good	Fine	XF
S565	**1000 Fr.** 1879.	—	—	—

1883-1910 Concordat Issue

#S566-S569 like #S108-S111.

		Good	Fine	XF
S566	**50 Fr.** 1883-1910.	—	—	—
S567	**100 Fr.** 1883-1910.	—	—	—
S568	**500 Fr.** 1883-1910.	—	—	—
S569	**1000 Fr.** 1883-1910.	—	—	—

Banque Populaire de la Broye, Payerne

Founded in 1864; note-issuing privilege terminated in 1881.

1865-79 Issue

#S571-S572 church of Payerne and Qn. Berthe de Bourgogne riding, sheaf and agricultural tools.

		Good	Fine	XF
S571	**10 Fr.** 25.3.1865. Black on pink tint paper.			
	a. Stamping on back: *Mis en circulation le . . . 18 . . .* and handwritten date ca.1870.	150.00	300.00	—
	b. Handwritten on front: *Annule le 14 Juin 1871.*	150.00	300.00	—

		Good	Fine	XF
S572	**20 Fr.** 1865; 19.11.1879. Black type, green paper.			
	a. Stamping and date like #S571a.	—	—	—
	r. Unsigned remainder. 19.11.1879.	—	Unc	400.00

PHILIPPE GENTON, VEVEY

1840 ISSUE

		Good	Fine	XF
S574	**100 Fr.** (ca.1840).	—	—	—

NOTE: #S574 replaced letters of credit issued previously.

FELIX MARCEL, LAUSANNE

Note-issuing privilege terminated in 1845.

1843 ISSUE

		Good	Fine	XF
S576	**100 Fr.** 1843.	—	—	—

NOTE: The same text was used on #S576 as on #S309 and S316 to circumvent the Banque de France's authority.

WALLIS

BANQUE CANTONALE DU VALAIS, SITTEN

Founded in 1856; liquidated in 1870.

1858-63 ISSUE

#S581-S584 cantonal arms, uniface.

		Good	Fine	XF
S581	**20 Fr.** 1858. Cream paper.	—	—	—
S582	**50 Fr.** 1858. Red paper.	—	—	—
S583	**100 Fr.** 1858. Blue paper.	—	—	—
S584	**200 Fr.** 1858. White paper.	—	—	—
S585	**10 Fr.** 1863.	—	—	—

NOTE: 5 Fr. notes were authorized but none are known to exist.

CAISSE HYPOTHECAIRE & DE CRÉDIT DU VALAIS

1871 ISSUE

#S586-S586B Mercury seated w/anchor, canton shield at top ctr., Helvetia seated at l. Back canton shield flanked by value scroll. Wmk: Bank name. Printer: Spengler, Lith. Luzanne.

		Good	Fine	XF
S586	**50 Fr.** 1.8.1871. Black. Back blue. Remainder w/counterfoil.	—	Unc	400.00
S586A	**100 Fr.** 1.8.1871.	—	Unc	500.00
S586B	**500 Fr.** 1.8.1871. Red.	—	—	—

ZUG

ZUGER KANTONALBANK

Founded in 1892; note-issuing privilege terminated in 1910.

1893-1910 CONCORDAT ISSUE

#S587-S589 like #S108-S110.

		Good	Fine	XF
S587	**50 Fr.** 1893-1910.	—	—	—
S588	**100 Fr.** 1893-1910.	—	—	—
S589	**500 Fr.** 1893-1910.	—	—	—

ZÜRICH

BANK IN ZÜRICH

Founded in 1836; note-issuing privilege terminated in 1892.

1837 ISSUE

#S591-S592 angels' heads and two women w/Hermes' staff and cornucopia.

		Good	Fine	XF
S591	**10 Brabantertaler** 1837. Yellow.	—	—	—
S592	**100 Brabantertaler** 1837. White.	—	—	—

1840-52 ISSUE

#S593-S594 like previous two notes but ovpt: *ODER DEN WERTH IN WECHSELGELD.*

		Good	Fine	XF
S593	**10 Brabantertaler** 1840. Like #S591.	—	—	—
S594	**100 Brabantertaler** 1840. Like #S592.	—	—	—
S595	**10 Fünffrankentaler** 1847. (Not issued).	—	—	—
S596	**100 Fünffrankentaler** 1847. (Not issued).	—	—	—
S597	**50 Fr.** 1852. Stamping: *NACH WAHL DER BANK IN EFFEKTIVE FR. ODER DEUTSCHEM GELD ZU OFFIZIELLEM UMRECHNUNGSTARIF EINLÖSBAR.*	—	—	—
S598	**500 Fr.** 1852. Stamping like #S597.	—	—	—

1853 ISSUE

#S599-S600 like previous two notes but w/o stamping.

		Good	Fine	XF
S599	**50 Fr.** 1853. Like #S597.	—	—	—
S600	**500 Fr.** 1853. Like #S598.	—	—	—

1856-73 ISSUE

#S601 and S602 stamping: *EINLÖSUNG IN SILBER ODER NAP. D'OR.*

		Good	Fine	XF
S601	**50 Fr.** 1856.	—	—	—
S602	**500 Fr.** 1856.	—	—	—
S603	**1000 Fr.** 1873. Swiss cross, woman's head, 2 boys holding shields. Printer: Dondorf & Naumann. Remainder.	—	Unc	1500.

NOTE: #S603 was issued together with the Bank in St. Gallen, Bank in Basel and the Kantonalbank von Bern.

1874 ISSUE

		Good	Fine	XF
S604	**50 Fr.** 1874.	—	—	—
S605	**100 Fr.** 1874.	—	—	—
S606	**500 Fr.** 1874.	—	—	—

1883-92 CONCORDAT ISSUE

#S607-S610 like #S108-S111.

		Good	Fine	XF
S607	**50 Fr.** 1883-92.	—	—	—
S608	**100 Fr.** 1883-92.	—	—	—
S609	**500 Fr.** 1883-92.	—	—	—
S610	**1000 Fr.** 1883-92.	—	—	—

ZÜRCHER KANTONALBANK, ZÜRICH

Founded in 1869; note-issuing privilege terminated in 1910.

1870-72 ISSUE

#S611-S614 woman's head at l., lion holding shield at upper ctr., helmeted soldier's head at r.

		Good	Fine	XF
S611	**20 Fr.** 1870. Orange unpt.	—	—	—
S612	**50 Fr.** 1870. Green unpt.	—	—	—
S613	**100 Fr.** 1870. Blue unpt.	—	—	—
S614	**500 Fr.** 1870. Red unpt.	—	—	—

#S615-S620 interest-bearing Treasury notes.

		Good	Fine	XF
S615	**10 Fr.** 1870.	—	—	—
S616	**50 Fr.** 1870.	—	—	—
S617	**100 Fr.** 1870.	—	—	—
S618	**500 Fr.** 1870.	—	—	—
S619	**1000 Fr.** 1870.	—	—	—
S620	**5000 Fr.** 1870.	—	—	—
S621	**1000 Fr.** 1872. Dk. green unpt. Like #S611-S614.	—	—	—

1883-1910 CONCORDAT ISSUE

#S622-S625 like #S108-S111.

		Good	Fine	XF
S622	**50 Fr.** 1883-1910.	—	—	—
S623	**100 Fr.** 1883-1910.	—	—	—
S624	**500 Fr.** 1883-1910.	—	—	—
S625	**1000 Fr.** 1883-1910.	—	—	—

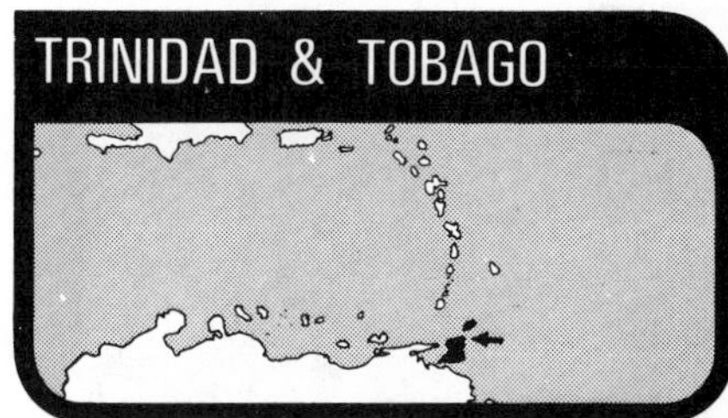

The Republic of Trinidad and Tobago, a member of the British Commonwealth situated 7 miles (11 km.) off the coast of Venezuela, has an area of 1,981 sq. mi. (5,130 sq. km.) and a population of 1.34 million. Capital: Port-of-Spain. The Island of Trinidad contains the world's largest natural asphalt bog. Birds of Paradise live on little Tobago, the only place outside of their native New Guinea where they can be found in a wild state. Petroleum and petroleum products are the mainstay of the economy. Petroleum products, crude oil and sugar are exported.

Trinidad and Tobago were discovered by Columbus in 1498. Trinidad remained under Spanish rule from the time of its settlement in 1592 until its capture by the British in 1797. It was ceded to the British in 1802. Tobago was occupied at various times by the French, Dutch and British before being ceded to Britain in 1814. Trinidad and Tobago were merged into a single colony in 1888. The colony was part of the Federation of the West Indies until Aug. 31, 1962, when it became an independent member of the Commonwealth of Nations. A new constitution establishing a republican form of government was adopted on Aug. 1, 1976. The president is Chief of State. The prime minister is Head of Government.

Notes of the British Caribbean Territories circulated between 1950-1964.

RULERS:

British to 1976

MONETARY SYSTEM:

1 Dollar = 100 Cents
5 Dollars = 1 Pound 10 Pence

TRINIDAD

Issued at Port of Spain.

BARCLAYS BANK (DOMINION, COLONIAL AND OVERSEAS)

Formerly the Colonial Bank.

1926 ISSUE

#S101-S104 crowned supported royal arms at ctr. Ovpt: Lg. *T* at upper r. Printer: BWC.

		GOOD	FINE	XF
S101	**5 DOLLARS** 1.9.1926. Black on pink and blue-green unpt. Back green.	300.00	850.00	—
S101A	**20 DOLLARS** 1.9.1926.	—	—	—

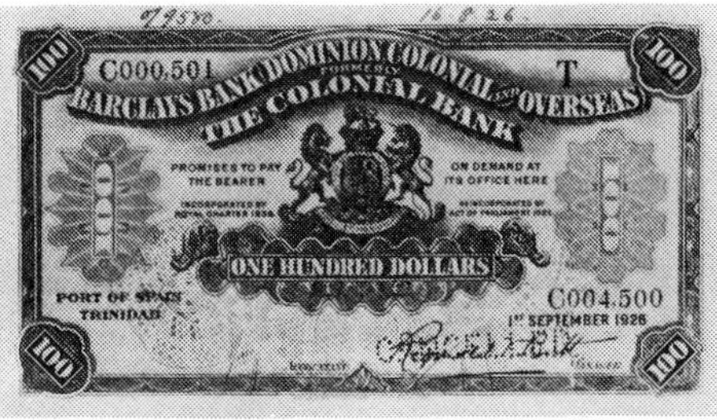

		GOOD	FINE	XF
S101B	**100 DOLLARS** 1.9.1926.	—	—	—

1937 ISSUE

#S102-S104 crowned supported royal arms at r. Ovpt: Lg. *T* at upper r.

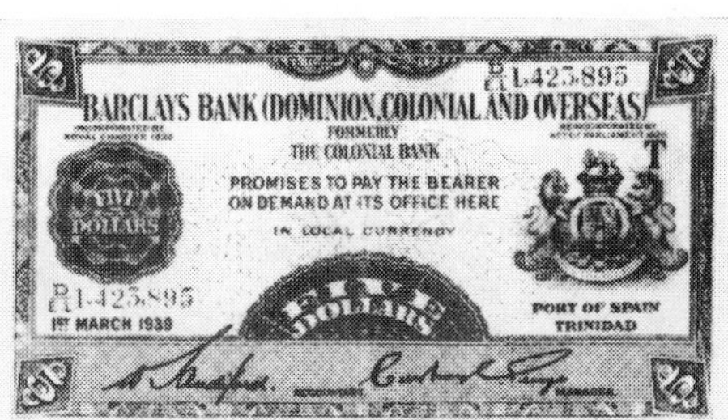

		GOOD	FINE	XF
S102	**5 DOLLARS** 1937-41. Purple on m/c unpt. back purple on blue unpt.			
	a. 1.5.1937; 1.2.1938; 1.3.1939.	200.00	400.00	700.00
	b. 1.3.1940; 1.2.1941.	150.00	300.00	600.00
	s. Specimen. 1.3.1939.	—	Unc	400.00
S103	**20 DOLLARS** 1937-40. Brown.			
	a. 1937; 1.3.1939; 1.3.1940.	500.00	1200.	—
	s. Specimen. 1.3.1939.	—	Unc	750.00

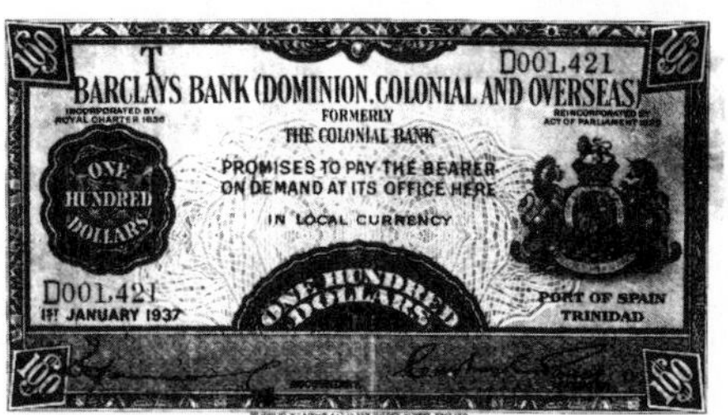

S104	**100 DOLLARS** 1937-40. Green.			
	a. Hand sign. at l. 1.1.1937.	550.00	1250.	—
	b. Printed sign. at l. 1.3.1939; 1.3.1940.	250.00	700.00	1500.
	s. Specimen. 1.3.1939.	—	Unc	750.00

CANADIAN BANK OF COMMERCE

Special designs issued in lg. size for British West Indies territories; not meant for circulation in Canada.

1921 ISSUE

#S111-S113 vertical ovpt: *TRINIDAD* at l. and r. on face. Printer: ABNC or CBNC.

		GOOD	FINE	XF
S111	**5 DOLLARS** 1.3.1921. Black on green and red-orange unpt. Seated woman w/lyre and water jug at ctr. Back green; Mercury at l. ctr., bank arms at ctr., allegorical woman w/sheaf at ctr. r.			
	a. Issued note.	375.00	600.00	1250.
	p. Proof. Printer: CBNC.	—	—	—
	s. Specimen.	—	—	—

		GOOD	FINE	XF
S112	**20 DOLLARS** 1.3.1921. Black on green and red unpt. Seated woman and globe at ctr. Back blue; like #S111.			
	a. Issued note.	950.00	2200.	—
	p1. Proof. Printer: CBNC.	—	—	—
	p2. Proof. Printer: ABNC.	—	—	—
	s. Specimen.	—	—	—

		GOOD	FINE	XF
S113	**100 DOLLARS** 1.3.1921. Black on olive and red unpt. Seated woman w/book and lamp at l. Back red; like #S111.			
	p1. Proof. Printer: CBNC.	—	—	—
	p2. Proof. Printer: ABNC.	—	—	—
	s. Specimen.	—	Unc	1650.

1939 ISSUE

#S116-S117 reduced size notes. Printer: CBNC.

		GOOD	FINE	XF
S116	**5 DOLLARS** 1.7.1939. Black on ochre and green unpt. Allegorical group at ctr. Back green; bank emblem at ctr.	200.00	500.00	850.00

NOTE: #S116 is similar to a regular Canadian issue made by this bank, although color and wording on the face distinguish it from its Canadian counterpart.

		GOOD	FINE	XF
S117	**20 DOLLARS** 1.7.1939. Black on red-orange unpt. Seated Neptune at l., 3 sirens at lower ctr. r., Mercury w/woman at r. Back blue. Like #S111.			
	a. Issued note.	400.00	1000.	—
	p. Proof.	—	—	—

COLONIAL BANK

Later became Barclays Bank.

1900'S ISSUE

		GOOD	FINE	XF
S119	**5 DOLLARS** 19xx. Curved *COLONIAL BANK* in ornate unpt. Specimen.	—	—	—

#S120-S132 printer: PBC.

		GOOD	FINE	XF
S120	**5 DOLLARS** 1.7.1901; 1.5.1903. Black on yellow unpt. Arms at upper ctr.	—	—	—

#S121 *Deleted*. See #S135.

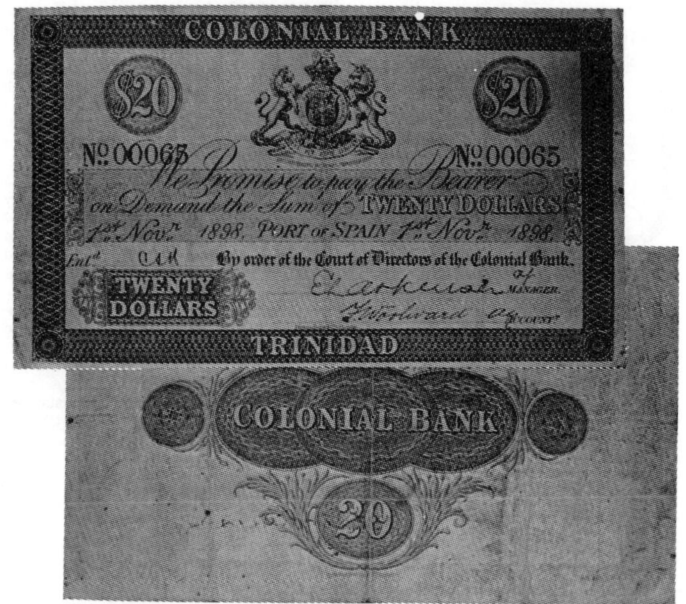

		GOOD	FINE	XF
S122	**20 DOLLARS** 1.11.1898. Black on tan unpt. Crowned supported royal arms at ctr. Back blue.	—	Rare	—

		GOOD	FINE	XF
S132	**20 DOLLARS** 19xx. Similar to #S122 but lg. curved *COLONIAL BANK* in ornate unpt. Specimen.	—	Rare	—

#S134 *Deleted*. See #S137.

1917-20 ISSUE

#S135-S137 crowned supported royal arms at upper ctr. Ovpt: lg. *T* at upper r.

		GOOD	FINE	XF
S135	**5 DOLLARS** 1917-20. Black on orange unpt. Back green.			
	a. Issued note. 1.1.1918; 1.3.1920.	400.00	1500.	—
	s. Specimen. 1.2.1917.	—	Unc	1000.

		Good	Fine	XF
S136	**20 Dollars** 1.11.1920. Specimen.	—	Unc	1500.

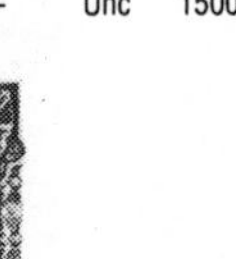

		Good	Fine	XF
S137	**100 Dollars** 1.11.1920. Specimen.	—	Unc	2000.

Royal Bank of Canada

1909 Provisional Issue

#S141-S143 vertical ovpt: *TRINIDAD* at l. and r., w/smaller vertical text: *PAYABLE AT PORT OF SPAIN, TRINIDAD* in red at l. ctr. Printer: ABNC.

		Good	Fine	XF
S141	**5 Dollars** 2.1.1909. Black on green and yellow unpt. Seated woman w/2 children at l. Back green and yellow.	700.00	1750.	—
S142	**20 Dollars** 2.1.1909. Black on blue and yellow unpt. Seated woman w/lion at ctr. Back blue and yellow.	—	Rare	—

		Good	Fine	XF
S143	**100 Dollars** 2.1.1909. Black on red-orange unpt. Seated allegory of Commerce at r. Back red-orange.			
	a. Issued note.	—	Rare	—
	s. Specimen.	—	—	—

1920 Issue

Notes designed specifically for circulation in the West Indies.

#S151-S153 lg. size notes. Printer: ABNC.

		Good	Fine	XF
S151	**5 Dollars = 1 Pound - 10 Pence** 2.1.1920. Black on green unpt. Steamship at ctr. Back green.			
	a. Sign. H. S. Holt at r.	350.00	750.00	1500.
	b. Sign. M. W. Wilson at r.	350.00	750.00	1500.

		Good	Fine	XF
S152	**20 Dollars = 4 Pounds - 3 Shillings - 4 Pence** 2.1.1920. Black on blue unpt. Sugar cane harvesting at ctr. Back blue.	—	Rare	—
S153	**100 Dollars = 20 Pounds - 16 Shillings - 8 Pence** 2.1.1920. Black on orange unpt. Seated woman w/island in background. Back orange. Specimen.	—	Rare	—

1938 Issue

#S161 and S162 sm. size notes. Printer: CBNC.

		Good	Fine	XF
S161	**5 Dollars = 1 Pound - 10 Pence** 3.1.1938. Similar to #S151.	175.00	350.00	900.00
S162	**20 Dollars = 4 Pounds - 3 Shillings - 4 Pence** 3.1.1938. Black on orange unpt. Back rose. Similar to #S152.	400.00	850.00	—

Union Bank of Halifax

Proposed issue of 1904. Notes never issued. Specimen only.

1904 Issue

#S171-S175 vertical ovpt: *TRINIDAD* at l. and r. and red ovpt: *PAYABLE AT PORT OF SPAIN TRINIDAD* horizontally across the face. Printer: BABNC.

		Good	Fine	XF
S171	**5 Dollars** 1.9.1904. Black on green unpt. Bank bldg. at ctr. Back green; fishermen on ship.	—	Unc	1350.

		GOOD	FINE	XF
S172	**10 DOLLARS** 1.9.1904. Black on ochre unpt. Crowned, supported royal arms at ctr. Back yellow-orange; like #S171.	—	Unc	1500.

		GOOD	FINE	XF
S173	**20 DOLLARS** 1.9.1904. Black on blue unpt. Woman w/flag sitting on bale at lower l., fishermen on boat at ctr., anchor and containers at lower r. Back blue; boy and dog on ship.	—	Unc	1650.

		GOOD	FINE	XF
S174	**50 DOLLARS** 1.9.1904. Black on red-brown unpt. Arms w/Indian and sailor. Back red-brown.	—	Unc	1750.

		GOOD	FINE	XF
S175	**100 DOLLARS** 1.9.1904. Black on red-brown unpt. Coast watcher at l., sailor at ctr. r. Back red.	—	Unc	2000.

WEST INDIA BANK

1841 ISSUE

		GOOD	FINE	XF
S181	**5 DOLLARS** 1.6.1841. Black. Crowned arms and palm trees upper ctr.	1500.	—	—

UNITED STATES

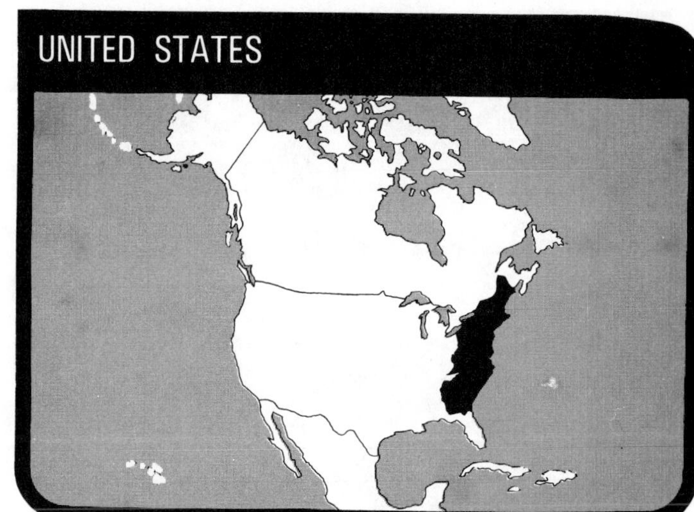

The area of the North American continent currently controlled by the United States of America was originally inhabited by numerous groups of Indian tribes. Some of these groups settled in particular areas, creating permanent settlements, while others were nomadic, traveling great distances and living off the land.

English explorers John and Sebastian Cabot reached Nova Scotia in what is today Canada in 1497; in 1534 the French gained a foothold with the explorations of Jacques Cartier. In 1541 the Spanish explorer Coronado traversed the south central portion of the country in what was to become the states of New Mexico, Texas, Nebraska and Oklahoma. In 1542 another Spaniard, Juan Cabrillo navigated north from Mexico along the Pacific coastline to California. The Spanish set up the first permanent settlement of Europeans in North America at St. Augustine, Florida in 1565. In 1607 the English settled in Jamestown, Virginia, and in 1620 at Plymouth, Massachusetts. This was followed closely by Dutch settlements in Albany and New York in 1624, and in 1638 the Swedes arrived in Delaware. From their foothold in Canada, French explorers pushed inland through the Great Lakes. Jean Nicolet explored what was to become Wisconsin in 1634, and in 1673 explorers Marquette and Joliet reached Iowa. In the 1650s the Dutch won the Swedish lands, and in 1664 the English gained control of the Dutch lands, thus giving the English control all along the Atlantic Coast. The resulting thirteen British colonies; New Hampshire, Vermont, Massachusetts, Rhode Island, Connecticut, New York, Pennsylvania, Delaware, Maryland, Virginia, North Carolina, South Carolina and Georgia formed the nucleus of what would become the United States of America.

From this point on tensions grew between the English, who could not expand westward from their settlements along the Atlantic Coast, and the French who had settled inland into the Ohio river valley. This dispute ended in 1763 after a war with the French loosing control of lands east of the Mississippi river. Manufacturing, textiles and other industry was developing at this time, and by 1775 about one-seventh of the world's production of raw iron came from the colonies. From 1771-1783 the war for American Independence was fought by the colonists against the English, and settled by the Peace of Paris in 1783. Americans gained control of lands south of the St. Lawrence and Great Lakes, and east of the Mississippi, with the exception of Florida which would remain under Spanish control until 1821. At the close of the war, the population was about 3 million, many of whom lived on self-sufficient family farms. Fishing, lumbering and the production of grains for export were becoming major economic endeavors. The newly independent states formed a loose confederation, but in 1787 approved the Constitution of the United States which is the framework for the goverment today. In 1789 it's first president, George Washington was elected, and the capitol was set up in New York City. In 1800 the capitol was moved to a planned city, Washington, D.C. where it remains.

Westward expansion was an inevitability as population grew. French territory west of the Mississippi, stretching to the northern Pacific was purchased in 1804 under the presidency of Thomas Jefferson, who then sent out Lewis and Clark on expedition of discovery. Spain granted independence to Mexico in 1821, which included lands which would become the states of California, New Mexico, Arizona and Texas. From 1836-1845 Texas was an independent republic, not joining the United States until 1845. Upon losing a war with the United States, Mexico ceded California (including most of Arizonia and New Mexico) to the United States in 1848. Gold was discovered in California that year, and western migration took off on overland wagon trains or around-the-horn sail and steam ships. Hawaii came under U.S. protection in 1851. As the country developed in the 19th century, the northern states increased in commerce and industry while the southern states developed a vast agricultural base through the use of slave labor. Northern political and social threats to slavery lead twelve southern states to secede from the Union in 1860 forming the Confederate States of America. The ensuing Civil War lasted until 1865, at which time slavery was abolished and the States reunited.

In 1867 Alaska was purchased from Russia. The transcontinental railroad was completed in 1869. The central region of the country west of the Mississippi River and east of the Rocky Mountains was the last to be developed, beginning after the Civil War, with the establishment of cattle ranches and farms. Between 1870 and 1891 the nomadic Native American population clashed with settlers and federal troops. By 1891 the Native Americans were confined to reservations.

At the close of the 19th century the United States embarked on a colonial mission of its own, with advances into Cuba, Puerto Rico, Panama, Nicaragua and the Philippines. This resulted in the Spanish-American War which was quickly decided, ending Spanish colonial dominance, and signaling the rise of the United States as a world power. Slow to enter both World Wars of the 20th century, it was a major contributor to the conclusion of both, making it one of the major nations of the 20th century. As the Spanish Milled Dollar achieved widespread acceptance throughout the American colonial period, it was a natural choice on which to base a national coinage system. The Spanish Milled Dollar had already been accorded legal tender status in several colonies, notably Massachusetts, Connecticut and Virginia and the others used it. Each colony had its own shilling exchange for a Spanish Milled Dollar ranging from 6 to 32 1/2 shillings. When the Continental Congress issued its first paper money to finance the revolution, the notes themselves promised to pay their face value in *Spanish milled dollars or the Value thereof in Gold or Silver*. The first quasi-official American coinage, the 1776 Continental *Dollar*, while not thus denominated, was struck in the size of the Spanish Milled Dollar.

While the denomination of *One Dollar* may have been a natural choice for a national monetary system, the problem of making change for that dollar was not. In 1782, Robert Morris, superintendent of Finance, proposed a coinage system based on a unit of 1/1440th part of a dollar which, he argued, would reconcile the different *official* values of the Spanish Milled Dollar in all the states. A year later, he submitted a series of copper and silver pattern coinage to Congress based on the basic unit of a quarter-grain of silver. The patterns are known to collectors today as the Nova Constellatio coinage. Other leading financiers saw the traditional division of the Spanish Milled Dollar into *eight reales*, or *bits* as they were familiarly known, as too unwieldy. Gouverneur Morris, assistant financier of the government then operating under the Articles of Confederation, proposed the simple solution of a decimal coinage ratio. With the support of Thomas Jefferson, who remarked, "The most easy ratio of multiplication and division is that of ten," and George Washington, who called it, "indispensably necessary," the decimal coinage proposal won out over more complicated plans. The dollar-decimal system was adopted on July 6, 1785, creating a silver dollar, with fractional coins, also in silver, in denominations of half (50¢), quarter (25¢), tenth (10¢) and twentieth (5¢) parts of a dollar, and copper pieces in denominations of 1/100th (1¢) and 1/200th (1/2¢) of a dollar.

Continental Currency: A total of 11 separate issues of paper currency were authorized by the Continental Congress to finance the war for American independence. The first issue was dated May 10, 1775, the date of the first session of the Continental Congress; the final issue was by Resolution of Jan. 14, 1779. In all, according to early American currency expert Eric P. Newman, a total of $241,552,780 worth of Continental Currency was issued.

Backed only by faith in the success of the Revolution, there was according to a Resolution of Congress a 40-to-1 devaluation by 1780, and in the end the bills were only redeemable at 1/100th of face value in interest-bearing bonds.

MONETARY SYSTEM:

Colonial & Confederation Period U.S. Constitutional Period
One Dollar was equal to:1 Dollar = 100 Cents
6 New England Shillings12 1/2 Cents U.S. = 1 Real (Spanish-American)
8 New York Shillings1 Dollar U.S. = 8 Reales (Spanish-American)
7 1/2 Middle States Shillings
6 Virginia Shillings
8 Carolina Shillings
32 1/2 Georgia Shillings

CONTINENTAL CURRENCY

MOTTOS

Various Latin mottos are found on Colonial, Continenal Currency, and early state issues as follows:
ACERVUS E PARVIS GRANDIS (Great accumulation from small things)
ANIMIS OPIBUSQUE PARATI (Prepared in spirit and in resources)
ARMIS CONCURRITE CAMPO (Run together on the field w/arms)
AUSPICIUM SALUTIS (An auspice of well-being)
AUT MORS AUT VICTORIA (Either death or victory)
AUT MORS AUT VICTORIA LAETA (Either death or victory is pleasing)
AUT MORS AUT VITA DECORA (Either death or an honorable life)
AUT NUMQUAM TENTES AUT PERFICE (Either finish or never begin)
CESSANTE VENTO CONQUIESCEMUS (When the wind dies down we rest)
CLARET AB ICTU (It shines from use)
COMMERCITO (Commerce) (Trade)
CONFEDERATION (Confederation)
CONSTANTIA DURISSIMA VINCIT (The firmest constancy will conquer)
CRESCIT SUB PONDERE VIRTUS (Virtue grows under pressure)
DEBELLARE BARBAROS RENOVA ANIMUM (Renew the spirit to fight the Barbarians)
DEPRESSA RESURGIT (Though crushed it comes back)
DEUS NOBISCUM (God be with us)
DEUS REGNAT EXULTET TERRA (God reigns, let the earth rejoice)
DIEU ET MON DROIT (God and my right)
DIVITIAE REIPUBLICAE DANT MIHI PRETIUM (The wealth of the republic gives me value)
DOMINUM GENEROSA RECUSAT (The well born refuses a master)
DULCE PRO PATRIA MORI (It is pleasing to die for one's country)
EN DAT VIRGINIA QUARTAM (Behold Virginia contributes one quarter of the arms)
ET DEUS OMNIPOTENS (And Almighty God)
ET IN SECULA SECULORUM FLORESCEBIT (An it will flourish for ages of ages)
ET SOLI ET MARTI (For the sun and for Mars)
EXITUS IN DUBIO EST (The outcome is in doubt)
FATA VIAM INVENIENT (The fates will find a way)
FIAT JUSTITIA RUAT COELUM (Let justice be done though the heavens fall)
FIDES PUBLICA (Public trust)
FORTIS A FORTE (Strength comes from strength)
FORTIS CADERE CEDERE NON POTEST (A brave man cannot fall)
FUGIO (I fly)
FUNDAMENTUM MIHI AERE PERENNIUS (A foundation for me more enduring than bronze)
GLORIAE FUNDAMENTUM FORTITUDO (Bravery is the foundation of glory)
HANC TUEMUR HAC NITIMUR (This we guard, for this we strive)
HINC OPES (Hence our wealth)
HIS ORNARI AUT MORI (To be decorated with these or to die)
HONI SOIT QUI MAL Y PENSE (Evil to him who evil thinks)
HONOR ET JUSTITIA (Honor and justice)
HORA PACIS & LIBERTATIS APPROPINQUAT (The time for peace and freedom is approaching)
IBI PATRIA UBI LIBERTAS (Our country is there, where is freedom)
ICH DIEN (I serve)
IMPAVIDE (Fearlessly)
INFELIX BRITANNIA (Unhappy England)
INFESTUS TANTUM INFESTIS (Hostile only to the hostile)
INFRACTO FOEDERE (By treaty unbroken)
IN RECTO DECUS (Honor in the right)
IN TE DOMINE SPERAMUS (In you, Lord, we have hope)
IN TE DOMINE SPERAVI (In you, Lord, I have hoped)
JUSTITIA (Justice)
JUSTITIA ADDIT FIDUCIAM (Justice adds trust)
LEX REGIT ARMA TUENTUR (Laws rule, arms guard)
LIBERTAS & NATALE SOLUM (Liberty and our native land)
MAGNIS INTERDUM PARVA NOCENT (Sometimes small things do harm to big ones)
MAJORA MINORIBUS CONSONANT (The large colonies in harmony with the small colonies)
MELIOR RESURGO (I return improved)
MELIOREM LAPSA LOCAVIT (Having fallen, it found a better place)
MINIME VIOLANDA FIDES (Trust by no means is to be violated)
MISERA SERVITUS OMNIS (All slavery is wretched)
MULTORUM SPEC (The hope of many)
MUTARE VEL TIMERE SPERNO (I refuse to change or to fear)
MUTUA DEFENSIO TUTISSIMA (Mutal defense is safest)
NEC ONUS NEC META GRAVABIT (Neither burden nor danger will force me down)
NE IMPROVISO (Not unexpectedly)
NEMO ME IMPUNE LACESSET (No one will provide me with impunity)
NIL DESPERANDUM (Nothing is to be despaired of)
NON DIU (Not for long)
NUSQUAM SUB MOLE FATISCIT (Nowhere does it weaken under weight)
PAR VIRIBUS VIRTUS (Virtue is equal to strength)
PAX REDDITA (Peace restored)
PER ARDUA SURGO (I rise through adversity)
PERENNIS (Everlasting)
PERSEVERANDO (By perseverance)
POSTERITATE (For posterity)
POST NUBILA PHOEBUS (After dark clouds comes the sun)
POST TENEBRAS LUX (After darkness, light)
PRAEMIUM INDUSTRIAE (The reward of industry)
PRO ARIS & FOCIS (For altars and the hearth)
PRO BONO PUBLICO (For the public good)
PRO LIBERTATE (For freedom)
PROVIDENTIA NOSTRIS PRAESIDEAT (Let foresight guide our people)
QUARENDA PECUNIA PRIMUM EST (Money has to be sought first)
QUID NON VIRTUTE EFFICIENDUM (What is not to be accomplished by virtue)
QUIS SEPARABIT (Who will separate)
RESTITUIT REM (He has restored the situation)
SALUTARIS SIBI PARENTIBUS QUE (Fortunate for itself and its parents)
SERENABIT (It will be calm)
SE SUSTULIT IPSA (It raises itself up)
SIC FLORET RESPUBLICA (Thus let the nation flourish)
SIC SEMPER TYRANNIS (Ever thus to tyrants)
SIC TRANSIT GLORIA MUNDI (Thus passes the glory of the world)
SI RECTE FACIES (IF you perform righteously)
SPERANDUM (One must hope)
SPES MENTIS SOLATIO (Hope is the consolation of the mind)
SUB CLYPEO (Under divine protection)
SUB VERTUTE SPERAMUS (With morality we have hope)
SUME EX SCELERATO SANGUINE POENAM (Exact punishment from guilty blood)
SUSTINE VEL ABSTINE (Either survive or refrain)
SUSTINET QUI TRANSTULIT (He who transplants sustains himself)
TERRA LIBERA NOTAM PRAETII IN ME POSUIT (A free land placed a mark of value on me)
THE ACTAEON. IRAM PRUDENTIA VINCIT (The Actaeon. Wisdom overcomes anger)
TRIBULATIO DITAT (Affliction enriches)
TURBAT SED EXTOLLIT (It disturbs but it elevates)
TUTA PEDAMINE VIRTUS (Honor safe in its support)
ULTIMA RATIO (The final reckoning)
UNO EODEMQUE IGNI (With one and the same flame)
UT QUOCUNQUE PARATUS (As prepared in every way)
UTRUM HORUM MAVIS ACCIPE (Accept whichever of these you prefer)
VI CONCITATE (Driven by force)
VIM PROCELLARUM QUADRENNIUM SUSTINUIT (For four years it has withstood the force of storm)
VIM VI REPELLAMUS (By force let us repel force)
VIS UNITATIS (The power of unity)
VOX POPULI (The voice of the people)

REFERENCES:

All government notes of the United States, since issue of the Demand Notes of 1861, are still valid as legal tender. The different types of currency are treated in a number of specialized catalogs such as the following:

Friedberg, Robert; *Paper Money of the United States.*
Hickman, John and Oakes, Dean; *Standard Catalog of National Bank Notes.*
Krause, Chester L. and Lemke, Robert F.; *Standard Catalog of United States Paper Money.*

Detailed information, as given in these catalogs, is not repeated here. The following listing is limited to the individual types and their principal varieties.

COLONIAL

CONTINENTAL CONGRESS

FIRST ISSUE, MAY 10, 1775

#S101-S110 black. Printer: Hall & Sellers, PA.

#S101-S108, S110 printed on thick rag paper w/blue fibers.

		VG	VF	UNC
S101	**1 DOLLAR** 10.5.1775. W/motto: *DEPRESSA RESURGIT* on emblem w/weighted bowl on acanthus plant. Ragweed and 2 willow leaves on back.	40.00	85.00	200.00
S102	**2 DOLLARS** 10.5.1775. W/motto: *TRIBULATIO DITAT* on emblem w/grain being threshed by a flail. Raspberry and 2 filbert leaves on back.	30.00	65.00	180.00
S103	**3 DOLLARS** 10.5.1775. W/motto: *EXITUS IN DUBIO EST* on emblem w/an eagle attacking a heron. Skeletonized elm and maple fruit leaves on back.	30.00	65.00	180.00
S104	**4 DOLLARS** 10.5.1775. W/motto: *AUT MORS AUT VITA DECORA* on emblem w/wild boar charging into spear. Skeletonized maple fruit leaf on back.	30.00	65.00	180.00

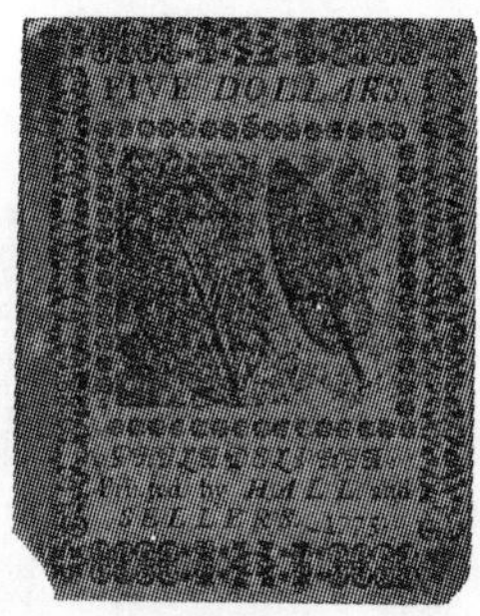

		VG	VF	UNC
S105	**5 DOLLARS** 10.5.1775. W/motto: *SUSTINE VEL ABSTINE* on emblem w/hand gathering food and bleeding because of pricks from thorns. Betony and sage leaves on back.	30.00	65.00	180.00

S106 6 DOLLARS — VG 30.00 | VF 65.00 | UNC 180.00
10.5.1775. W/motto: *PERSEVERANDO* on emblem w/beaver gnawing down tree. Buttercup leaf on back.

S107 7 DOLLARS — VG 30.00 | VF 65.00 | UNC 180.00
10.5.1775. W/motto: *SERENABIT* on emblem w/severe storm at sea. Buttercup leaf on back.

S108 8 DOLLARS — VG 30.00 | VF 65.00 | UNC 180.00
10.5.1775. W/motto: *MAJORA MINORIBUS CONSONANT* on emblem w/harp w/13 strings representing the 13 colonies. Henebit and 2 buttercups leaves on back.

S109 20 DOLLARS — VG 450.00 | VF 1000. | UNC 2500.
10.5.1775. Thin white paper. W/motto: *VI CONCITATE* on emblem w/strong wind blowing. W/motto: *CESSANTE VENTO CONQUIESCEMUS* on emblem w/sun shining on ships at sea on back.

S110 30 DOLLARS — VG 45.00 | VF 90.00 | UNC 250.00
10.5.1775. W/motto: *SI RECTE FACIES* on emblem w/wreath on a tomb. *VI CONCITATE* on l., emblem w/strong wind blowing, *CESSANTE VENTO CONQUIESCEMUS* on r. emblem w/sun shining on ships at sea on back.

NOTE: The 20 dollar notes were individually printed on thin white paper furnished by Benjamin Franklin. The 30 dollar notes were printed by inserting face and back forms into one position on the double sheet form and removing one of the smaller denominations.

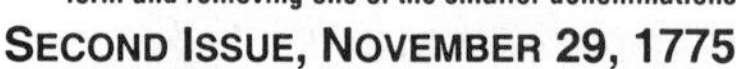

SECOND ISSUE, NOVEMBER 29, 1775

#S111-S118 black. Printer: Hall & Sellers, PA.

S111 1 DOLLAR — VG 45.00 | VF 90.00 | UNC 250.00
29.11.1775. Like #S101.

S112 2 DOLLARS — VG 20.00 | VF 50.00 | UNC 150.00
29.11.1775. Like #S102.

S113 3 DOLLARS — VG 20.00 | VF 50.00 | UNC 150.00
29.11.1775. Like #S103.

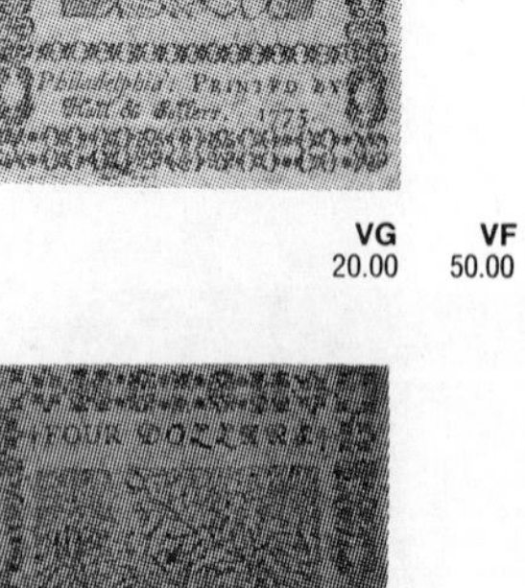

S114 4 DOLLARS — VG 20.00 | VF 50.00 | UNC 150.00
29.11.1775. Like #S104.

S115 5 DOLLARS — VG 20.00 | VF 50.00 | UNC 150.00
29.11.1775. Like #S105.

S116 6 DOLLARS — VG 20.00 | VF 50.00 | UNC 150.00
29.11.1775. Like #S106.

S117 7 DOLLARS — VG 20.00 | VF 50.00 | UNC 150.00
29.11.1775. Like #S107.

S118 8 DOLLARS — VG 20.00 | VF 50.00 | UNC 150.00
29.11.1775. Like #S108.

NOTE: Printings on blue paper are counterfeit detectors.

THIRD ISSUE, FEBRUARY 17, 1776

#S119-S130 printer: Hall & Sellers, PA.

#S119-S122 black. Sundial rebus at ctr. r. or l. Linked Colonies device on back.

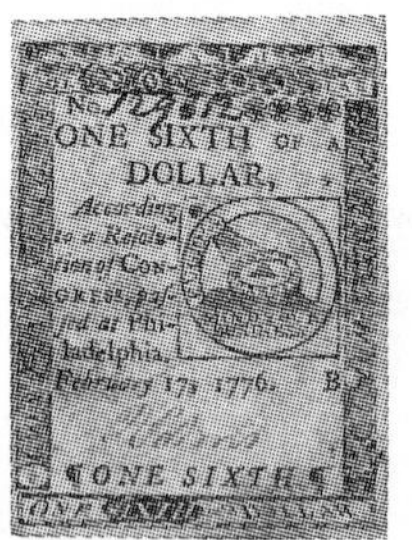

S119 1/6 DOLLAR — VG 35.00 | VF 75.00 | UNC 400.00
17.2.1776. *CURRENCEY* (error) at r.

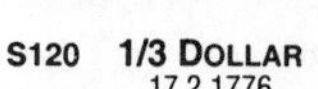

S120 1/3 DOLLAR — VG 35.00 | VF 75.00 | UNC 400.00
17.2.1776.

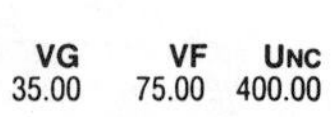

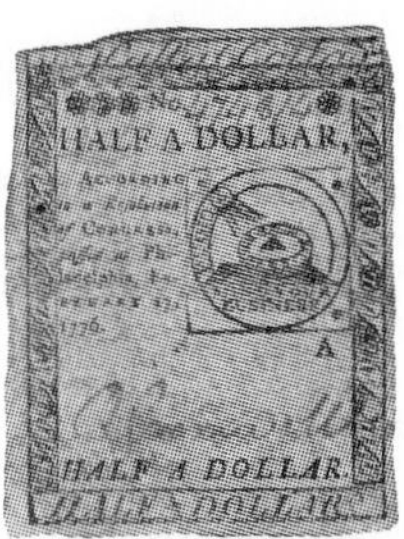

		VG	VF	UNC
S121	**1/2 DOLLAR** 17.2.1776.	35.00	75.00	400.00

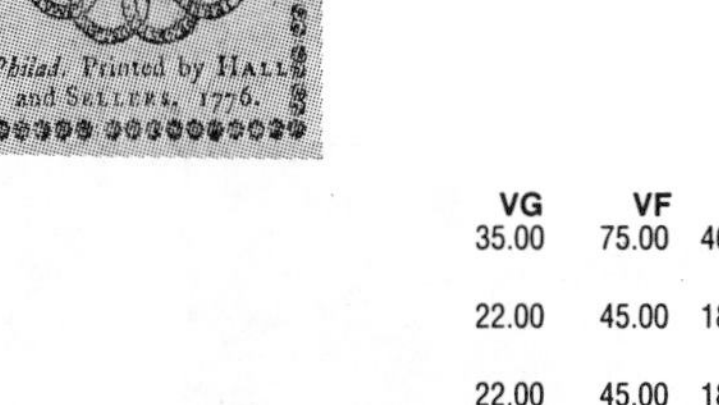

		VG	VF	UNC
S122	**2/3 DOLLAR** 17.2.1776.	35.00	75.00	400.00
S123	**1 DOLLAR** 17.2.1776. Like #S101.	22.00	45.00	180.00
S124	**2 DOLLARS** 17.2.1776. Like #S102.	22.00	45.00	180.00
S125	**3 DOLLARS** 17.2.1776. Like #S103.	22.00	45.00	180.00

		VG	VF	UNC
S126	**4 DOLLARS** 17.2.1776. Like #S104.	22.00	45.00	180.00
S127	**5 DOLLARS** 17.2.1776. Like #S105.	25.00	50.00	200.00
S128	**6 DOLLARS** 17.2.1776. Like #S106.	25.00	50.00	200.00
S129	**7 DOLLARS** 17.2.1776. Like #S107.	25.00	50.00	200.00
S130	**8 DOLLARS** 17.2.1776. Like #S108.	25.00	50.00	200.00

NOTE: Printings on blue paper are counterfeit detectors.

FOURTH ISSUE, MAY 9, 1776

#S131-S138 black. Printer: Hall & Sellers, PA.

		VG	VF	UNC
S131	**1 DOLLAR** 9.5.1776. Like #S101.	22.00	45.00	180.00

		VG	VF	UNC
S132	**2 DOLLARS** 9.5.1776. Like #S102.	22.00	45.00	180.00
S133	**3 DOLLARS** 9.5.1776. Like #S103.	22.00	45.00	180.00
S134	**4 DOLLARS** 9.5.1776. Like #S104.	22.00	45.00	180.00

		VG	VF	UNC
S135	**5 DOLLARS** 9.5.1776. Like #S105.	22.00	45.00	180.00
S136	**6 DOLLARS** 9.5.1776. Like #S106.	22.00	45.00	180.00
S137	**7 DOLLARS** 9.5.1776. Like #S107.	22.00	45.00	180.00
S138	**8 DOLLARS** 9.5.1776. Like #S108.	22.00	45.00	180.00

NOTE: Printings on blue paper are counterfeit detectors.

FIFTH ISSUE, JULY 22, 1776

#S139-S146 black. Printer: Hall & Sellers, PA.

		VG	VF	UNC
S139	**2 DOLLARS** 22.7.1776. Like #S102.	27.00	55.00	250.00

		VG	VF	UNC
S140	**3 DOLLARS** 22.7.1776. Like #S103.	27.00	55.00	250.00

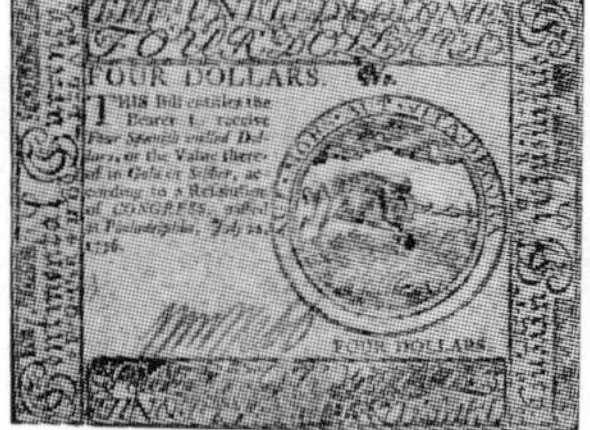

		VG	VF	UNC
S141	**4 DOLLARS** 22.7.1776. Like #S104.	27.00	55.00	250.00

		VG	VF	UNC
S142	**5 DOLLARS** 22.7.1776. Like #S105, except *B* in motto appears *H*.	27.00	55.00	250.00

		VG	VF	UNC
S143	**6 DOLLARS** 22.7.1776. Like #S106.	27.00	55.00	250.00
S144	**7 DOLLARS** 22.7.1776. Like #S107.	27.00	55.00	250.00

		VG	VF	UNC
S145	**8 DOLLARS** 22.7.1776. Like #S108.	27.00	55.00	250.00
S146	**30 DOLLARS** 22.7.1776. Like #S110.	27.00	55.00	250.00

NOTE: Printings on blue paper are counterfeit detectors.

SIXTH ISSUE, NOVEMBER 2, 1776

#S147-S154 black. Printer: Hall & Sellers, PA.

		VG	VF	UNC
S147	**2 DOLLARS** 2.11.1776. Like #S102.	25.00	55.00	200.00
S148	**3 DOLLARS** 2.11.1776. Like #S103.	25.00	55.00	200.00

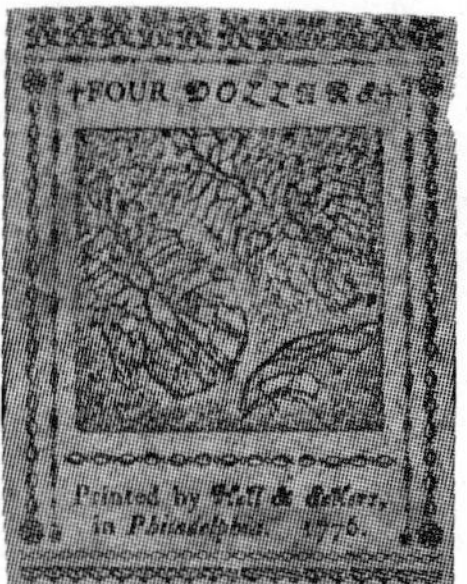

		VG	VF	UNC
S149	**4 DOLLARS** 2.11.1776. Like #S104.	25.00	55.00	200.00

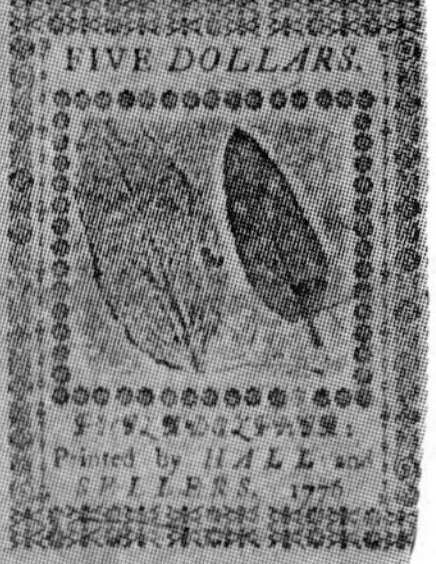

		VG	VF	UNC
S150	**5 DOLLARS** 2.11.1776. Like #S105, except *B* in motto appears as *H*.	25.00	55.00	200.00
S151	**6 DOLLARS** 2.11.1776. Like #S106.	25.00	55.00	200.00

		VG	VF	UNC
S152	**7 DOLLARS** 2.11.1776. Like #S107.	25.00	55.00	200.00
S153	**8 DOLLARS** 2.11.1776. Like #S108.	25.00	55.00	200.00

		VG	VF	UNC
S154	**30 DOLLARS** 2.11.1776. Like #S110.	25.00	55.00	200.00

NOTE: An additional issue of $500,000 in bills of 1/9, 1/6, 1/3, and 2/3 dollars was also authorized by the Nov. 2, 1776 Resolution, but these fractional denominations were never printed because the fractional denominations of the Feb. 17, 1776 issue were still being signed and were in adequate supply through the fall of 1777.

NOTE: Printings on blue paper are counterfeit detectors.

SEVENTH ISSUE, FEBRUARY 26, 1777

#S155-S162 black. Printer: Hall & Sellers, PA.

		VG	VF	UNC
S155	**2 DOLLARS** 26.2.1777. Like #S102.	28.00	60.00	225.00

		VG	VF	UNC
S156	**3 DOLLARS** 26.2.1777. Like #S103.	28.00	60.00	225.00

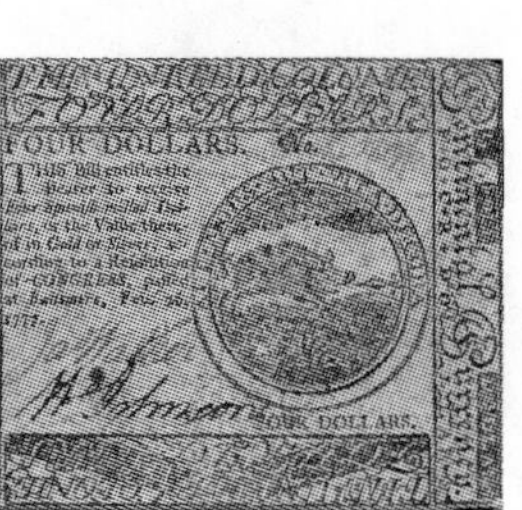
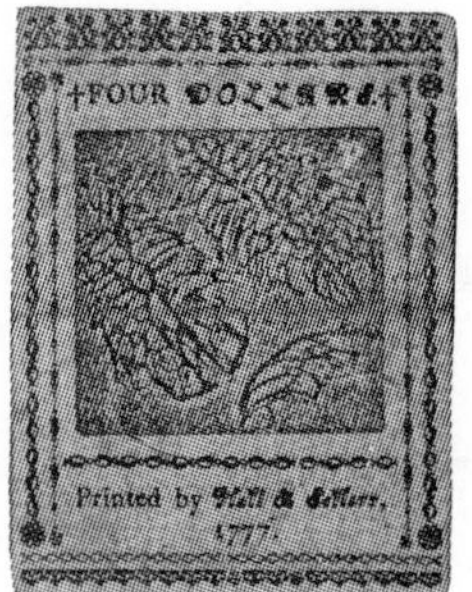

		VG	VF	UNC
S157	**4 DOLLARS** 26.2.1777. Like #S104.	28.00	60.00	225.00
S158	**5 DOLLARS** 26.2.1777. Like #S105, except *B* in motto appears as *H*.	28.00	60.00	225.00
S159	**6 DOLLARS** 26.2.1777. Like #S106.	28.00	60.00	225.00

		VG	VF	UNC
S160	**7 DOLLARS** 26.2.1777. Like #S107.	28.00	60.00	225.00

		VG	VF	UNC
S161	**8 DOLLARS** 26.2.1777. Like #S108.	28.00	60.00	225.00

		VG	VF	UNC
S162	**30 DOLLARS** 26.2.1777. Like #S110.	28.00	60.00	225.00

A word on pricing

When a note is marked RARE in the price columns, this note seldom appears on the market, or few are known in private hands. When dashes are in the price column, means that the note has not traded on the open market recently and a definitive value could not accurately be determined. Rare does not always mean expensive. A dashed price does not mean expensive or rare.

EIGHTH ISSUE, MAY 20, 1777

#S163-S170 black. Printer: Hall & Sellers, PA.

NOTE: #S163-S170 are the same style as the #S155-S162 except that the cuts for the top and bottom borders were modified to *United States* instead of *United Colonies*.

		VG	VF	UNC
S163	**2 DOLLARS** 20.5.1777. Like #S102.	45.00	135.00	425.00

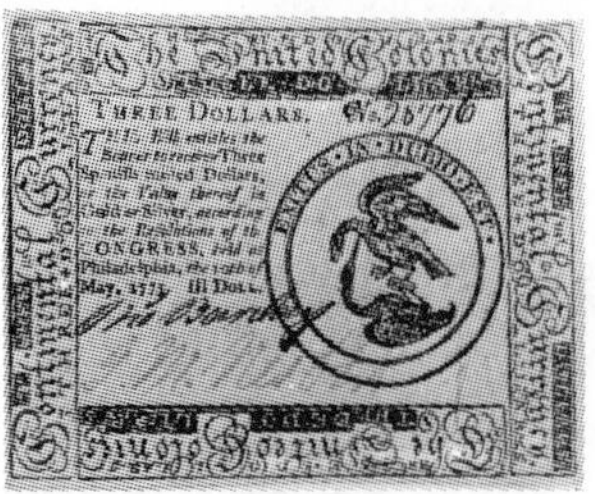

		VG	VF	UNC
S164	**3 DOLLARS** 20.5.1777. Like #S103.	45.00	135.00	425.00

		VG	VF	UNC
S165	**4 DOLLARS** 20.5.1777. Like #S104.	45.00	135.00	425.00
S166	**5 DOLLARS** 20.5.1777. Like #S105, except *H* in motto instead of *B*.	45.00	135.00	425.00
S167	**6 DOLLARS** 20.5.1777. Like #S106.	45.00	135.00	425.00
S168	**7 DOLLARS** 20.5.1777. Like #S107.	45.00	135.00	425.00
S169	**8 DOLLARS** 20.5.1777. Like #S108.	45.00	135.00	425.00
S170	**30 DOLLARS** 20.5.1777. Like #S110.	45.00	135.00	425.00

NOTE: Printings on blue paper are counterfeit detectors.

NINTH ISSUE, APRIL 11, 1778

#S171-S178 black. Printer: Hall & Sellers, PA.

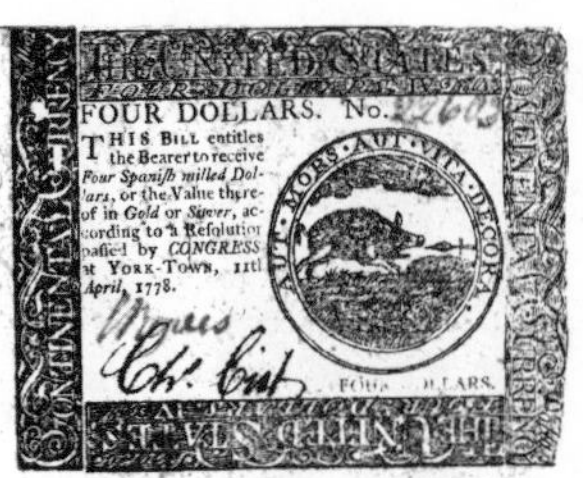

		VG	VF	UNC
S171	**4 DOLLARS** 11.4.1778. Face like #S104. Buttercup leaf on back.	225.00	500.00	1600.
S172	**5 DOLLARS** 11.4.1778. Face like #S105 w/undersigned *S* in motto. Willow leaf on back.	225.00	500.00	1600.
S173	**6 DOLLARS** 11.4.1778. Face like #S106. Sage leaf on back.	225.00	500.00	1600.
S174	**7 DOLLARS** 11.4.1778. Face like #S107. Grape and sage leaf on back.	225.00	500.00	1600.

		VG	VF	UNC
S175	**8 DOLLARS** 11.4.1778. Face like #S108. 3 sage leaves on back.	200.00	450.00	1600.
S176	**20 DOLLARS** 11.4.1778. Face like #S109. Buttercup leaf on back.	200.00	450.00	1600.

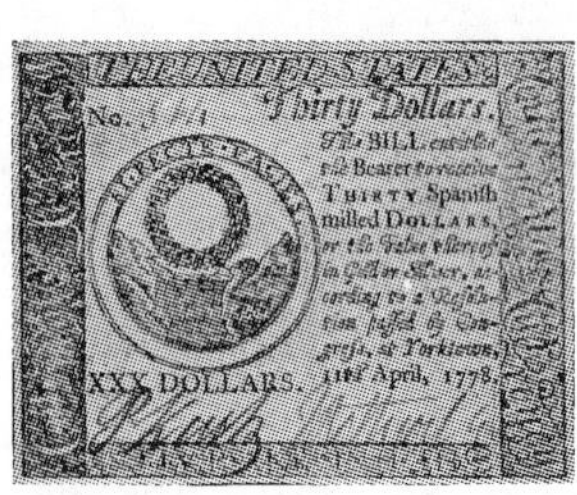

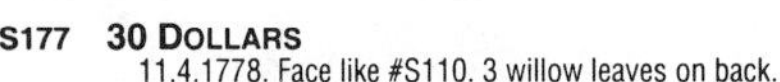

		VG	VF	UNC
S177	**30 DOLLARS** 11.4.1778. Face like #S110. 3 willow leaves on back.	200.00	450.00	1600.

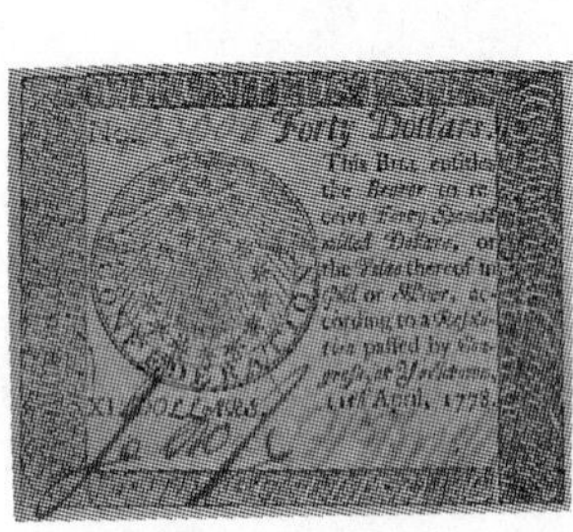

		VG	VF	UNC
S178	**40 DOLLARS** 11.4.1778. *CONFEDERATION* on emblem w/rays of an all-seeing eye shining on 13 stars surrounding a flame. Carrot leaf on back.	200.00	450.00	1600.

NOTE: Denominations below 4 dollars were eliminated, the 20 dollars reinstated, and a 40 dollar denomination added because of inflation.

NOTE: Printings on blue paper are counterfeit detectors.

TENTH ISSUE, SEPTEMBER 26, 1778

#S179-S186 black. Printer: Hall & Sellers, PA.

		VG	VF	UNC
S179	**5 DOLLARS** 26.9.1778. Face like #S105. Willow leaf on back.	25.00	55.00	160.00

		VG	VF	UNC
S180	**7 DOLLARS** 26.9.1778. Face like #S107. Grape and sage leaf on back.	25.00	55.00	160.00

		VG	VF	UNC
S181	**8 DOLLARS** 26.9.1778. Face like #S108. 3 sage leaves on back.	25.00	55.00	160.00
S182	**20 DOLLARS** 26.9.1778. Face like #S109. Buttercup leaf on back.	25.00	55.00	160.00

		VG	VF	UNC
S183	**30 DOLLARS** 26.9.1778. Face like #S110. 3 willow leaves on back.	20.00	50.00	150.00
S184	**40 DOLLARS** 26.9.1778. Like #S178.	20.00	50.00	150.00

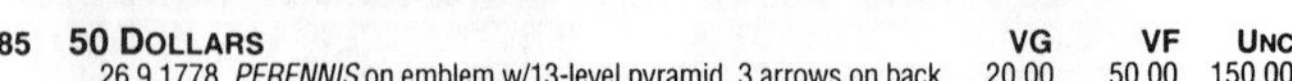

		VG	VF	UNC
S185	**50 DOLLARS** 26.9.1778. *PERENNIS* on emblem w/13-level pyramid. 3 arrows on back.	20.00	50.00	150.00

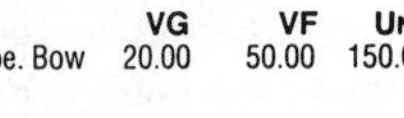

		VG	VF	UNC
S186	**60 DOLLARS** 26.9.1778. *DEUS REGNAT EXULTET TERRA* on emblem w/globe. Bow on back.	20.00	50.00	150.00

NOTE: Printings on blue paper are counterfeit detectors.

ELEVENTH ISSUE, JANUARY 14, 1779

UNCUT SHEET

HALF SHEET

#S187-S202 black and red. Printer: Hall & Sellers, PA.

		VG	VF	UNC
S187	**1 DOLLAR** 14.1.1779. Face like #S101. Back tansy leaf.	35.00	60.00	200.00
S188	**2 DOLLARS** 14.1.1779. Face like #S102. Back mulberry leaf.	35.00	60.00	200.00
S189	**3 DOLLARS** 14.1.1779. Face like #S103. Back rose leaf.	35.00	60.00	200.00

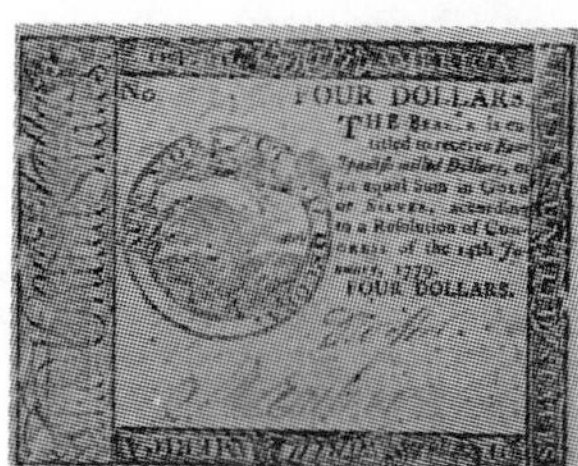

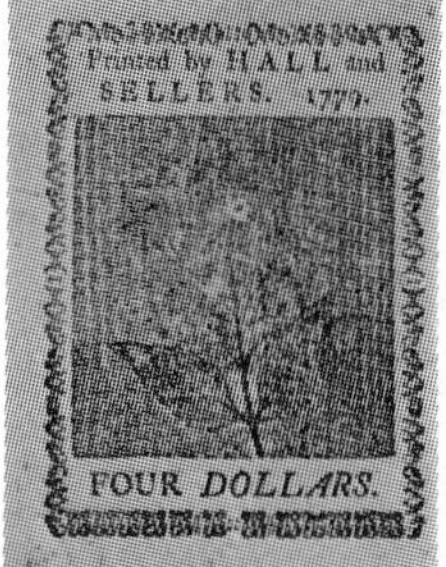

		VG	VF	UNC
S190	**4 DOLLARS** 14.1.1779. Face like #S104. Back mulberry leaf.	35.00	60.00	200.00

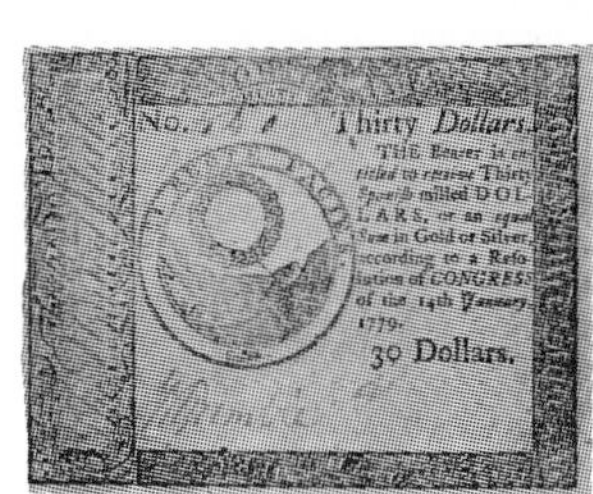

		VG	VF	UNC
S191	**5 DOLLARS** 14.1.1779. Face like #S105. Back fever few leaf.	35.00	60.00	200.00
S192	**20 DOLLARS** 14.1.1779. Face like #S109. Back grape leaf.	35.00	60.00	200.00

		VG	VF	UNC
S193	**30 DOLLARS** 14.1.1779. Face like #S110. Back climbing fumitory leaves.	30.00	50.00	180.00

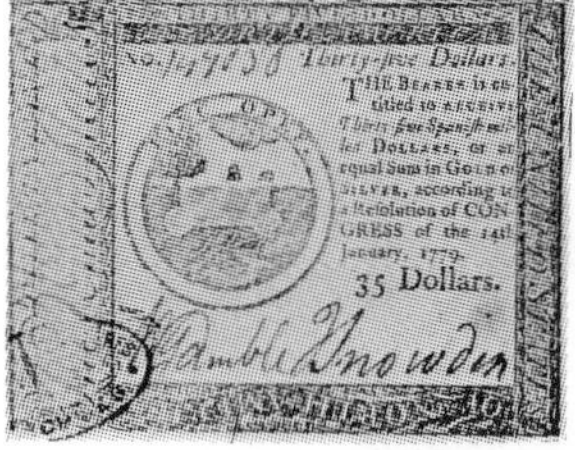

		VG	VF	UNC
S194	**35 DOLLARS** 14.1.1779. *HINC OPES* on emblem w/plow in a field. Back 2 willow leaves.	30.00	50.00	180.00

		VG	VF	UNC
S195	**40 DOLLARS** 14.1.1779. Face like #S178. Back poterium leaves.	30.00	50.00	180.00
S196	**45 DOLLARS** 14.1.1779. *SIC FLORET RESPUBLICA* on emblem w/beehives protected by a shed. Back ground ivy leaves.	30.00	50.00	180.00
S197	**50 DOLLARS** 14.1.1779. Face like #S185. Back parsley leaves.	30.00	50.00	180.00

		VG	VF	UNC
S198	**55 DOLLARS** 14.1.1779. *POST NUBILA PHOEBUS* on emblem w/sun coming out after storm. Back willow leaf and (?) leaf.	30.00	50.00	180.00
S199	**60 DOLLARS** 14.1.1779. Face like #S186. Back willow and poison hemlock leaf.	30.00	50.00	180.00

		VG	VF	UNC
S200	**65 DOLLARS** 14.1.1779. *FIAT JUSTITIA* on emblem w/hand holding balance scale. Back parsley leaves.	30.00	50.00	180.00
S201	**70 DOLLARS** 14.1.1779. *VIM PROCELLARIUM QUADRENNIUM SUSTINUIT* on emblem w/tree. Back maple leaf.	40.00	80.00	230.00
S202	**80 DOLLARS** 14.1.1779. *ET IN SECULA SECULORUM FLORESCEBIT* on emblem w/diamond superimposed on lg. tree. Back strawberry leaf.	50.00	100.00	280.00

NOTE: Printings on blue paper are counterfeit detectors.

1785-1787 INDENTS ISSUE

#S202A-S202F black. Sign. of J. Hardy or M. Hillegas.

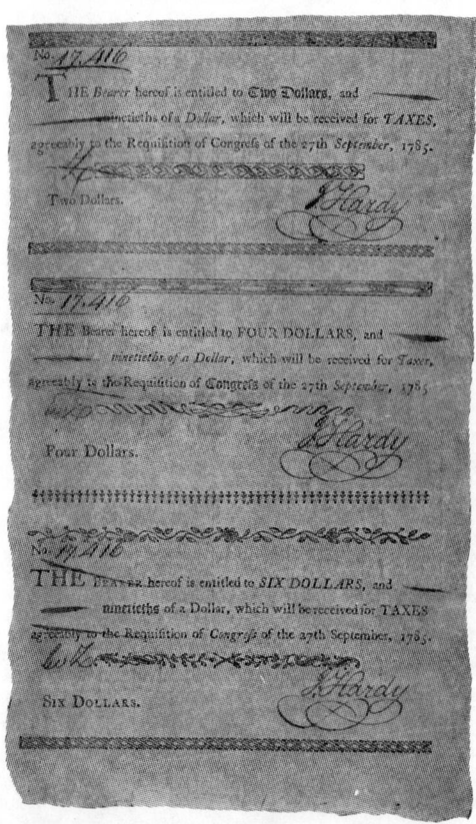

		VG	VF	UNC
S202A	**1 DOLLAR** 27.9.1785; 11.10.1787.	—	—	—
S202B	**2 DOLLARS** 27.9.1785; 11.10.1787.	—	—	—
S202C	**4 DOLLARS** 27.9.1785; 11.10.1787.	—	—	—
S202D	**6 DOLLARS** 27.9.1785; 11.10.1787.	—	—	—
S202E	**8 DOLLARS** 27.9.1785; 11.10.1787.	—	—	—
S202F	**25 DOLLARS** 27.9.1785; 11.10.1787.	—	—	—

BIBLIOGRAPHY

Newman, Eric P. *The Early Paper Money of America.* Fourth Edition, ©1997, Krause Publications, Inc., Iola, Wisconsin.

STATE ISSUES

ISSUES OF THE STATES

COLONIAL CURRENCY:

The colonial governments, continually plagued by the shortage of coins and currency began slowly to issue notes, and by 1730 most were. These early issues are rare. The notes from the revolutionary period are more frequently encountered, and some were signed by the same men who signed the Declaration of Independence. The newly independent states, as well as the Continental Congress, issued currency during the later war years and during the peace under the Articles of Confederation. These later notes are relatively common and popular.

STATE ISSUES:

Listings from the colonial area or era after 1776 and until the Civil War. They were sporadic at best. Some concentrate around the War of 1812.

CIVIL WAR ISSUES:

With their secession from the United States in 1861, the individual Confederate States began to issue currency notes to provide for their defense. Variously known as "notes," "warrants" or "bonds," these issues were promissory in nature, usually specifying redemption at some period after a peace was established between the U.S.A. and C.S.A. Redemption was sometimes promised in Confederate Treasury Notes, while other Southern States' notes did not specify with what the notes would be redeemed. As the Confederate States were occupied or surrendered, their wartime issues were invalidated, and the final defeat of the Confederacy in 1865 forced the repudiation of all such issues, the articles of peace making all debts engendered by the rebellion null and void.

POST CIVIL WAR ISSUES:

Sometimes known as "Carpetbagger" notes, these Southern State issues were necessitated by the ravaged economies of the area during the Reconstruction period. Some of the postwar notes were issued under strict control of the Federal military or civilian authority, while others were emitted by the states themselves under such guises as revenue bond scrip, emergency warrants, etc. Eventual economic recovery in the area led to a cessation of such notes.

TABLE OF CONTENTS

MISSOURI
State, 1821 .... #S1421-S1425
State Civil War, 1862-66 .... #S1431-S1456

NEW HAMPSHIRE
Colonial, 1709-76 .... #S1461-S1638
State, 1777-80 .... #S1639-S1647

NEW JERSEY
Colonial, 1709-76 .... #S1648-S1826
State, 1777-86 .... #S1827-S1861

NEW YORK
Colonial, 1709-76 .... #S1862-S2050
State, 1776-88 .... #S2051-S2090

NORTH CAROLINA
Colonial, 1722 .... #S2091-S2245
State, 1778-1824 .... #S2246-S2316
State Civil War, 1861-64 .... #S2321-S2375

PENNSYLVANIA
Colonial, 1723-76 .... #S2384-S2572
Commonwealth, 1777-85 .... #S2573-S2647

RHODE ISLAND
Colonial, 1710-76 .... #S2651-S2968
State, 1776 .... #S2969-S3043

SOUTH CAROLINA
Colonial, 1703-76 .... #S3101-S3263
State, 1776-86 .... #S3264-S3307
State Post Civil War, 1866-72 .... #S3311-S3327

TENNESSEE
State Post Civil War, 1875-83 .... #S3334-S3340

TEXAS
State Civil War, 1860-64 .... #S3395-S3438

VERMONT
State, 1781 .... #S3441-S3448

VIRGINIA
Colonial, 1755-75 .... #S3451-S3535
State, 1776-81 .... #S3536-S3674
State Civil War, 1861-62 .... #S3675-S3685

ALABAMA

STATE

ACT OF 19.12.1821 ISSUE

		GOOD	FINE	XF
S203	**6 1/4 CENTS** 1.6.1822.	—	—	—
S204	**12 1/2 CENTS** 1.6.1822. Stagecoach at top ctr.	200.00	350.00	550.00

		GOOD	FINE	XF
S205	**25 CENTS** 1.6.1822. Ox w/plow at top ctr.	350.00	500.00	800.00
S206	**37 1/2 CENTS** 1.6.1822.	—	—	—
S207	**50 CENTS** 1.6.1822.	—	—	—
S208	**75 CENTS** 1.6.1822.	—	—	—

ALABAMA

CIVIL WAR

1863 ISSUE

#S209-S213 engraved by J. T. Paterson & Co.

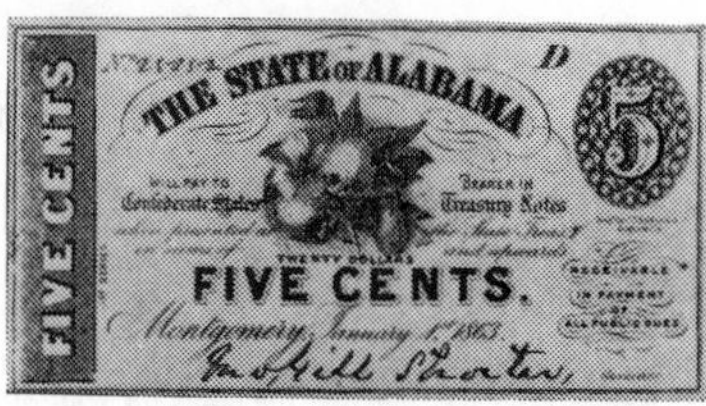

		VG	VF	UNC
S209	**5 CENTS** 1.1.1863. Black. Cotton balls at ctr.	12.50	20.00	30.00

		VG	VF	UNC
S210	**10 CENTS** 1.1.1863. Black. Tree w/map at ctr.	10.00	17.50	25.00

		VG	VF	UNC
S211	**25 CENTS** 1.1.1863. Black and red. Wagon load of cotton at ctr.			
	a. W/o SERIES.	9.00	14.00	25.00
	b. 2nd SERIES.	9.00	14.00	25.00
	c. 3rd SERIES.	9.00	14.00	25.00
S212	**50 CENTS** 1.1.1863. Black and blue. Tree w/map at ctr., woman at bottom r.			
	a. W/o SERIES.	9.00	14.00	25.00
	b. 2nd SERIES.	9.00	14.00	25.00

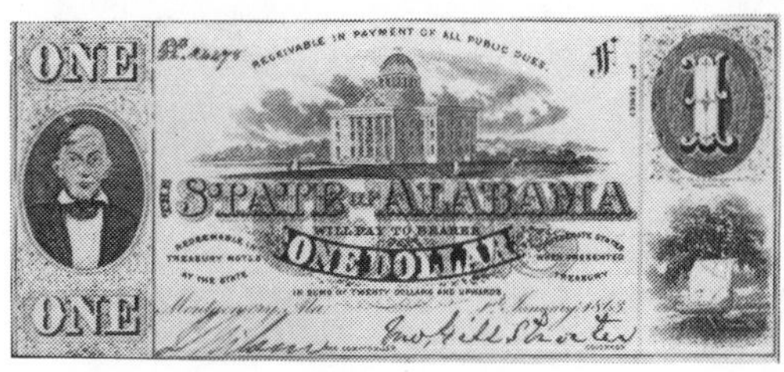

		GOOD	FINE	XF
S213	**1 DOLLAR** 1.1.1863. Black and green. Portr. Governor at l., State Capitol at ctr., tree w/map at r.			
	a. 1st SERIES.	8.00	12.50	20.00
	b. 2nd SERIES.	8.00	12.50	20.00

1864 ISSUE

#S214-S217 engraved by W. Keenan & Co.; Lith. & printed by J. T. Paterson & Co.

		GOOD	FINE	XF
S214	**5 DOLLARS** 1.1.1864. Black and green. Standing Liberty at l., overseer watching slaves at ctr., tree w/map at lower r.	15.00	35.00	85.00
S215	**10 DOLLARS** 1.1.1864. Black and green. Portr. Gov. Watts at ctr., tree w/map at bottom r.	15.00	35.00	85.00

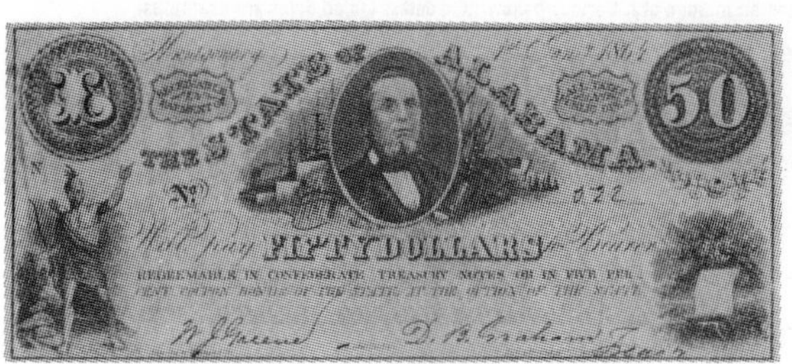

		GOOD	FINE	XF
S216	**50 DOLLARS** 1.1.1864. Black. Indian at lower l., portr. Gov. Watts at ctr., tree w/map at lower r. Back green.	35.00	75.00	175.00

S217 100 DOLLARS — GOOD 50.00 | FINE 100.00 | XF 200.00
1.1.1864. Black. Tree w/map at lower l., group of Indians at ctr., seated woman by water at lower r. Back green.

S218 50 DOLLARS — GOOD — | FINE Rare | XF —
17.2.1864. Similar to #S216 but back orange. Printer: J. T. Paterson & Co.

ARKANSAS

CIVIL WAR

ACT OF 1861 ISSUE

#S218A-S218C state coat-of-arms at top ctr. Blank certificates w/payee and value hand stamped. Handwritten dates. Printed in blue and red.

S218A 5 DOLLARS — GOOD 25.00 | FINE 50.00 | XF 100.00
16.9.1861. State coat-of-arms at top ctr.

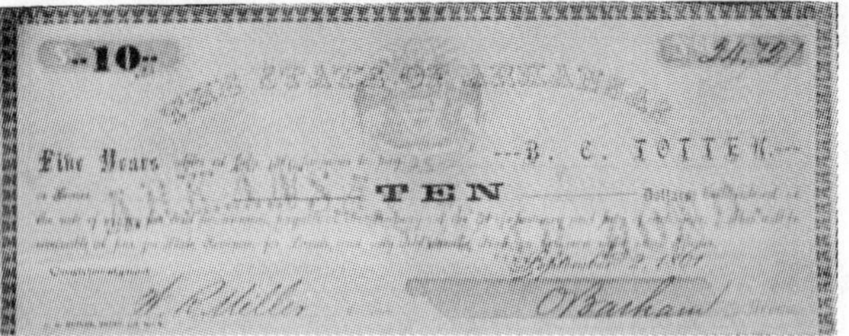

S218B 10 DOLLARS — GOOD 25.00 | FINE 50.00 | XF 100.00
16.9.1861.

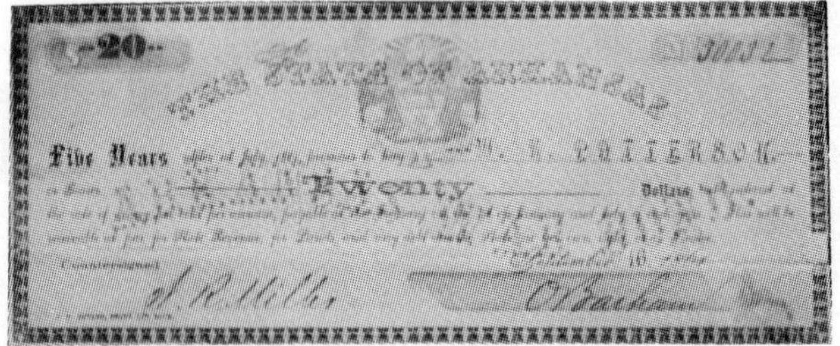

S218C 20 DOLLARS — GOOD 25.00 | FINE 50.00 | XF 100.00
16.9.1861.

1861 ON WAR BOND ISSUE

#S219-S222A Indian maiden at l. Various handwritten dates. Listed dates are examples.

	GOOD	FINE	XF
S219 1 DOLLAR			
30.12.1861. Black.			
a. White paper.	—	Rare	—
b. Blue paper.	200.00	350.00	500.00

	GOOD	FINE	XF
S220 2 DOLLARS 1861.	—	Rare	—
S221 3 DOLLARS 1861.	—	Rare	—
S222 10 DOLLARS 18.12.1861.	—	Rare	—
S222A VARIOUS HANDWRITTEN DENOMINATIONS (ca.1861).			
a. White paper.	150.00	275.00	475.00
b. Blue paper.	—	Rare	—

1861-62 FIRST ON AUDITOR'S WARRANT ISSUE

#S223 and S224 Indian maiden at l. Various handwritten dates. Listed dates are examples.

	GOOD	FINE	XF
S223 1 DOLLAR 9.1.1862. Blue paper.	—	Rare	—
S224 2 DOLLARS 1861-62. Blue paper.	—	Rare	—
S224A VARIOUS HANDWRITTEN DENOMINATIONS (ca.1861).			
a. White paper.	200.00	350.00	600.00
b. Blue paper.	—	Rare	—

1862 FIRST ON WAR BOND ISSUE

#S225-S227 Indian brave at l.

	GOOD	FINE	XF
S225 1 DOLLAR 3.1.1862. Black.			
a. White paper.	200.00	350.00	500.00
b. Blue paper.	200.00	350.00	500.00

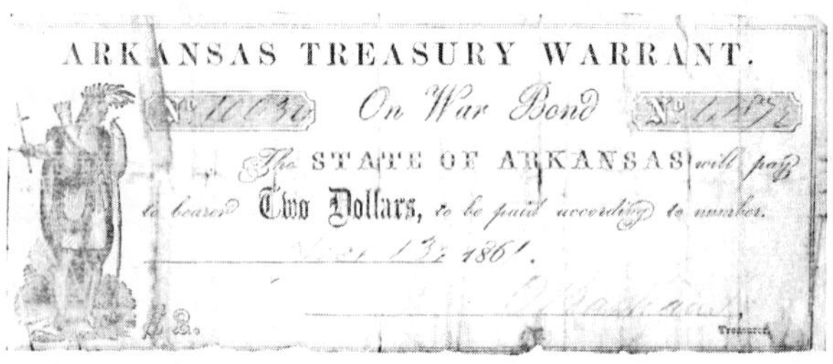

	GOOD	FINE	XF
S226 2 DOLLARS 1861-62.	200.00	350.00	500.00
S227 3 DOLLARS 1861-62.	—	Rare	—

1861-62 SECOND ON AUDITOR'S WARRANT ISSUE

#S228-S230 Indian brave at l.

	GOOD	FINE	XF
S228 1 DOLLAR 1861-62.	200.00	350.00	500.00
S229 2 DOLLARS 1861-62.	75.00	110.00	175.00
S229A 10 DOLLARS (ca.1861).	85.00	150.00	200.00
S229B VARIOUS HANDWRITTEN DENOMINATIONS (ca.1861).			
a. White paper.	—	Rare	—
b. Blue paper.	—	Rare	—

1862 SECOND ON WAR BOND ISSUE

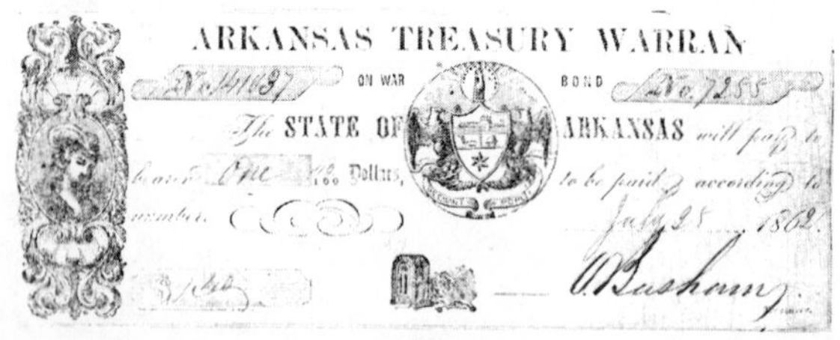

S230 1 DOLLAR — GOOD 100.00 | FINE 200.00 | XF 400.00
25.7.1862. Black and white. Bust of maiden at l., state arms at upper ctr.

1861-62 THIRD ON AUDITOR'S WARRANT ISSUE

	GOOD	FINE	XF
S230A 1 DOLLAR (ca.1861). White paper.	—	Rare	—
S230B VARIOUS HANDWRITTEN DENOMINATIONS (ca.1861). Bust of maiden in oval at l., Arkansas seal at ctr.			
a. White paper.	—	Rare	—
b. Blue paper.	—	Rare	—

#S231-S235 exist with *ARKANSAS TREASURY WARRANT* printed on back in green, red or blue on white or blue paper and sometimes inverted. Various handwritten dates 1862-63. The terms *ON WAR BOND* and *ON AUDITOR'S WARRANT* (by portr.) were removed from face plates in later issues. Certain notes were printed on the backs of bills of exchange. Printer: J. D. Butler.

		GOOD	FINE	XF
S231	1 DOLLAR 1862-63. Black. State arms at l., portr. Jefferson Davis at ctr.			
	a. W/*ON WAR BOND.*	20.00	50.00	80.00
	b. W/o *ON WAR BOND.*	30.00	50.00	85.00
	c. Printed on bills of exchange w/*ON WAR BOND.*	25.00	50.00	80.00
S232	2 DOLLARS 1862-63. Black. Similar to #S231. All serial letters B.			
	a. W/*ON WAR BOND.*	35.00	75.00	125.00
	b. W/o *ON WAR BOND.*	45.00	75.00	140.00
S233	3 DOLLARS 1862-63. Black. Similar to #S231.			
	a. W/*ON WAR BOND.*	50.00	85.00	150.00
	b. W/o *ON WAR BOND.*	75.00	125.00	185.00

		GOOD	FINE	XF
S234	5 DOLLARS 1862-63. Black. Black carrying cotton at l., portr. Governor H. M. Rector at top ctr., dog at bottom ctr.			
	a. W/*ON AUDITOR'S WARRANT.*	30.00	50.00	75.00
	b. W/o *ON AUDITOR'S WARRANT.*	30.00	50.00	75.00

		GOOD	FINE	XF
S235	10 DOLLARS 1862-63. Black. Black carrying cotton at l., portr. Samuel Adams at top ctr., dog at bottom ctr.			
	a. W/*ON AUDITOR'S WARRANT.*	30.00	50.00	75.00
	b. W/o *ON AUDITOR'S WARRANT.*	35.00	50.00	80.00

ARKANSAS

POST CIVIL WAR

ACT OF 16.3.1871 ISSUE

#S236-S240 various handwritten dates; listed dates are examples. Printer: NBNC.

		GOOD	FINE	XF
S236	1 DOLLAR 1873; 16.1.1874. Basket of corn at lower l., farmer seated w/sickle at ctr., foliage at lower r.	—	Rare	—
S237	2 DOLLARS 1872.	—	Rare	—
S238	5 DOLLARS 1872. Hunter at lower l., woman seated w/children at top ctr., woman walking w/girl at lower r.	—	Rare	—

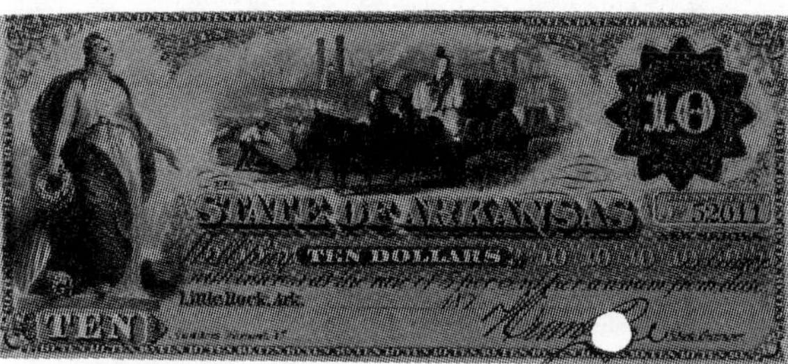

		GOOD	FINE	XF
S239	10 DOLLARS 187x. Brown and black. Standing Liberty at l., horse drawn load of cotton at top ctr. Back brown.			
	a. Issued note.	—	Rare	—
	b. Punched hole cancelled.	700.00	1250.	2000.
S240	10 DOLLARS 187x. Green and black. Back green.	—	Rare	—

ARKANSAS

TREASURER'S CERTIFICATES

ACT OF 20.1.1875 ISSUE

#S241 and S242 various handwritten dates; listed dates are examples.

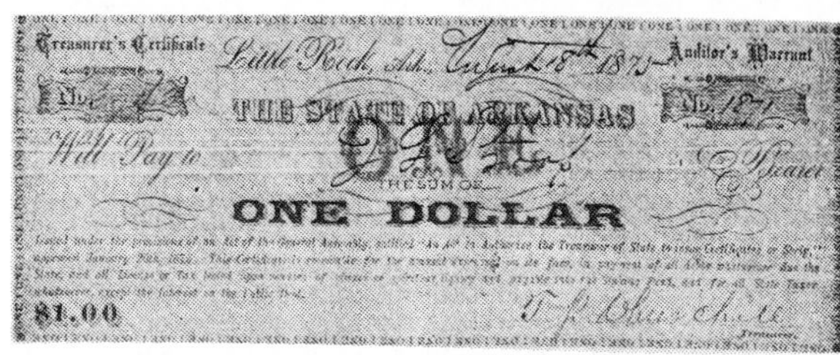

		GOOD	FINE	XF
S241	1 DOLLAR 13.3.1875; 18.8.1875. Black and red on green unpt.	—	Rare	—

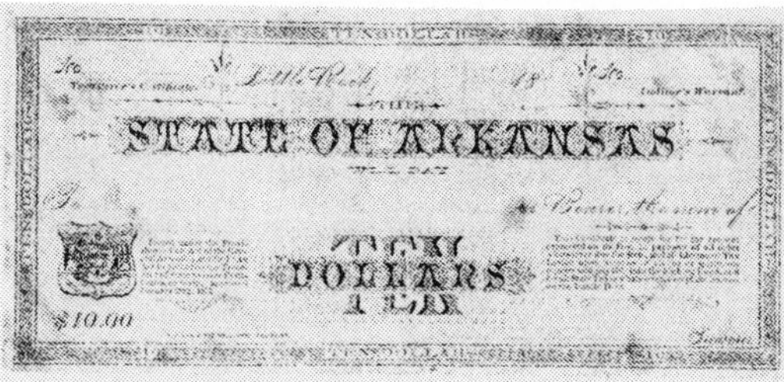

		GOOD	FINE	XF
S242	10 DOLLARS 18xx. Black on green unpt.	—	Rare	—

CALIFORNIA

IMPERIAL GOVERNMENT OF THE U.S.

In 1849 Joshua Norton came from the Cape of Good Hope in South Africa around Cape Horn to San Francisco. He was an astute investor and built a considerable fortune through real estate transactions. In 1855, he decided to try to corner the rice market and, as a consequence, lost his fortune. Three years of litigation and the loss of his fortune caused him to live in solitude. In 1859, Norton sent local newspapers a proclamation that he was becoming Norton I, Emperor of the United States. In the next 21 years, he was the toast of San Francisco. He was a perpetual "honored guest" and issued notes to his subjects for souvenirs and for payment of small debts.

MONETARY SYSTEM:

1 Dollar = 100 Cents

1872-79 ISSUE

#S242A-S244B various handwritten dates.

		GOOD	FNE	XF
S242A	25 CENTS ca.1872.	Reported Not Confirmed		

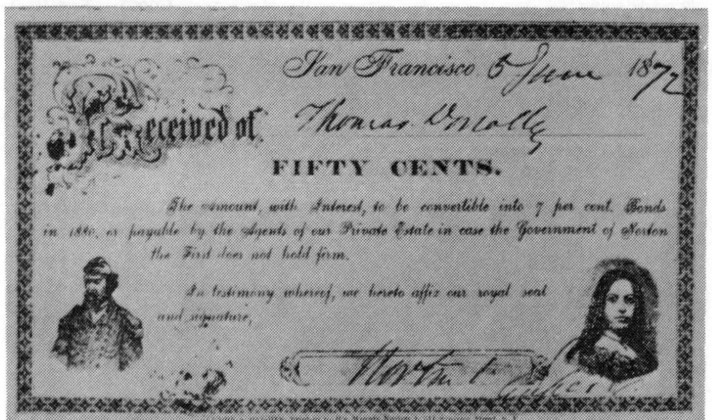

S243A 50 CENTS — GOOD — | FINE Rare | XF —
5.6.1872. Red printing. Norton at lower l., girl at lower r w/text: *CONVERTIBLE INTO 7% BONDS IN 1880.*

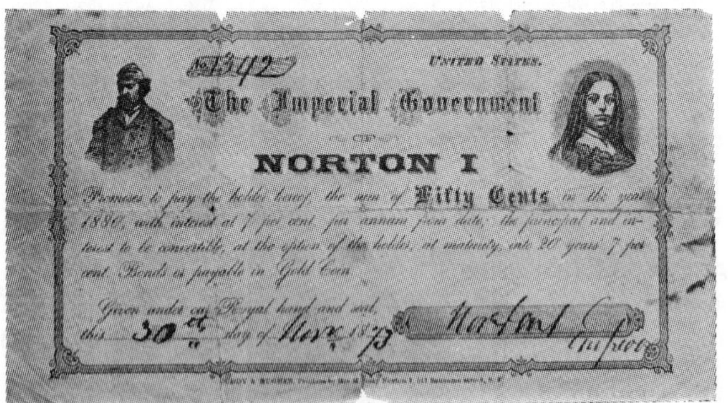

S243B 50 CENTS — GOOD — | FINE Rare | XF —
30.11.1873. Norton at upper l., girl at upper r.

S243C 50 CENTS — GOOD — | FINE Rare | XF —
11.3.1876. Standing Liberty w/shield and flag at l., Norton at upper r.

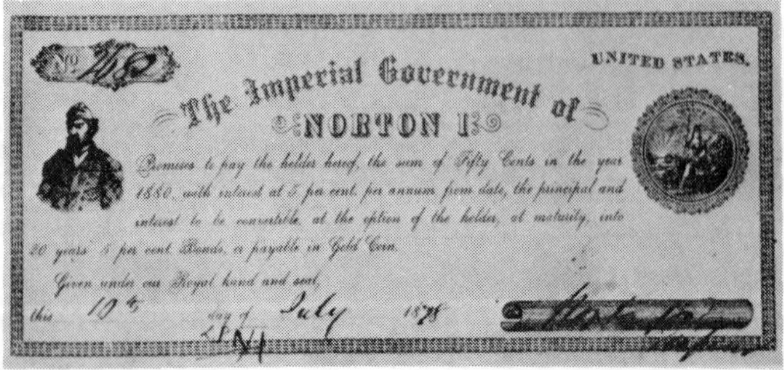

S243D 50 CENTS — GOOD — | FINE Rare | XF —
10.7.1878. Norton at l., California seal at r. w/text: *CONVERTIBLE INTO 5% BONDS IN 1880.*

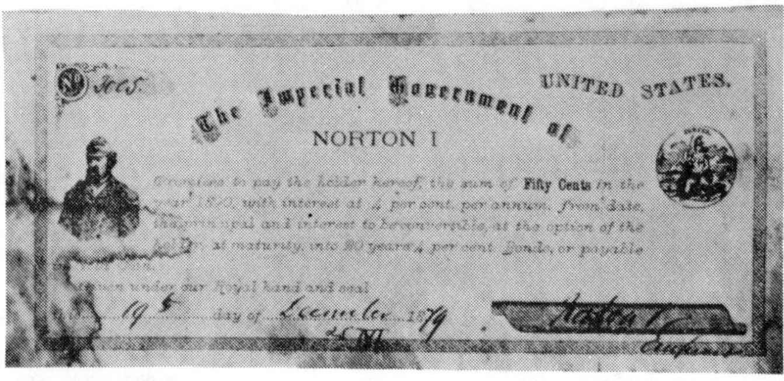

S243E 50 CENTS — GOOD — | FINE Rare | XF —
19.12.1879. Norton at l., California seal at r. w/text: *CONVERTIBLE INTO 4% BONDS IN 1890.*

S244A 75 CENTS
Written dates. ca.1873. — Reported Not Confirmed

S244B 1 DOLLAR
Written dates. ca.1873. — Reported Not Confirmed

CONNECTICUT

COLONIAL

1709 ISSUES

#S245-S252 black. W/motto: *SUSTINET QUI TRANSTULIT* on face.

		Good	Fine	XF
S245	**2 SHILLINGS** 12.7.1709.	—	—	—
S246	**2 SHILLING 6 PENCE** 12.7.1709.	—	—	—
S248	**5 SHILLINGS** 12.7.1709.	—	—	—
S249	**10 SHILLINGS** 12.7.1709.	—	—	—
S250	**20 SHILLINGS** 12.7.1709.	—	—	—
S251	**40 SHILLINGS** 12.7.1709.	—	—	—
S252	**5 POUNDS** 12.7.1709.	—	—	—

1709 MONOGRAMMED *AR* ISSUE

#S253-S260 black.

		Good	Fine	XF
S253	**2 SHILLINGS** 12.7.1709.	—	—	—
S254	**2 SHILLINGS 6 PENCE** 12.7.1709.	—	—	—
S255	**3 SHILLINGS** 12.7.1709.	—	—	—
S256	**5 SHILLINGS** 12.7.1709.	—	—	—
S257	**10 SHILLINGS** 12.7.1709.	—	—	—
S258	**20 SHILLINGS** 12.7.1709.	—	—	—
S259	**40 SHILLINGS** 12.7.1709.	—	—	—
S260	**5 POUNDS** 12.7.1709.	—	—	—

1713 FIRST REDATED ISSUE

#S261-S268 black. Scroll on back.

		Good	Fine	XF
S261	**2 SHILLINGS** May 1713 (- old date 12.7.1709).	—	—	—
S262	**2 SHILLINGS 6 PENCE** May 1713 (- old date 12.7.1709).	—	—	—
S263	**3 SHILLINGS** May 1713 (- old date 12.7.1709).	—	—	—
S264	**5 SHILLINGS** May 1713 (- old date 12.7.1709).	—	—	—
S265	**10 SHILLINGS** May 1713 (- old date 12.7.1709). Lamb.	—	—	—
S266	**20 SHILLINGS** May 1713 (- old date 12.7.1709). Deer.	—	—	—
S267	**40 SHILLINGS** May 1713. (- old date 12.7.1709). Horse.	—	—	—
S268	**5 POUNDS** May 1713 (- old date 12.7.1709). Lion.	—	—	—

1713 SECOND REDATED ISSUE

#S269-S276 black. Face plates were re-engraved in Boston in 1719. Flowers on back. Printer: Timothy Green.

		Good	Fine	XF
S269	**2 SHILLINGS** May 1713 (- old date 12.7.1709).	—	—	—
S270	**2 SHILLINGS 6 PENCE** May 1713; 12.7.1709.	—	—	—
S271	**3 SHILLINGS** May 1713 (- old date 12.7.1709).	—	—	—
S272	**5 SHILLINGS** May 1713 (- old date 12.7.1709).	—	—	—
S273	**10 SHILLINGS** May 1713 (- old date 12.7.1709).	—	—	—

		Good	Fine	XF
S274	**20 Shillings** May 1713 (- old date 12.7.1709).	—	—	—
S275	**40 Pounds** May 1713 (- old date 12.7.1709).	—	—	—
S276	**5 Pounds** May 1713 (- old date 12.7.1709).	—	—	—

1724 Issue

#S277-S280 black. Printer: Timothy Green.

		Good	Fine	XF
S277	**10 Shillings** 1.12.1724.	—	—	—
S278	**20 Shillings** 1.12.1724.	—	—	—
S279	**40 Shillings** 1.12.1724.	—	—	—
S280	**5 Pounds** 1.12.1724.	—	—	—

1727 Issue

#S281-S288 black. Printer: Timothy Green.

		Good	Fine	XF
S281	**2 Shillings** 7.11.1727.	—	—	—
S282	**2 Shilling 6 Pence** 7.11.1727.	—	—	—
S283	**3 Shillings** 7.11.1727.	—	—	—
S284	**5 Shillings** 7.11.1727.	—	—	—
S285	**10 Shillings** 7.11.1727.	—	—	—
S286	**20 Shillings** 7.11.1727.	—	—	—
S287	**40 Shillings** 7.11.1727.	—	—	—
S288	**5 Pounds** 7.11.1727.	—	—	—

1728 Issue

#S289-S292 black. Printer: Timothy Green.

		Good	Fine	XF
S289	**10 Shillings** Oct. 1728.	—	—	—
S290	**20 Shillings** Oct. 1728.	—	—	—
S291	**40 Shillings** Oct. 1728.	—	—	—
S292	**5 Pounds** Oct. 1728.	—	—	—

1729 Issue

#S293-S300 black. Printer: Timothy Green.

		Good	Fine	XF
S293	**2 Shillings** May 1729.	—	—	—
S294	**2 Shillings 6 Pence** May 1729.	—	—	—
S295	**3 Shillings** May 1729.	—	—	—
S296	**5 Shillings** May 1729.	—	—	—
S297	**10 Shillings** May 1729.	—	—	—
S298	**20 Shillings** May 1729.	—	—	—
S299	**40 Shillings** May 1729.	—	—	—
S300	**5 Pounds** May 1729.	—	—	—

1732 Issue

#S301-S308 black. *AMOR PATRIAE UICIT* on face. Printer: Timothy Green.

		Good	Fine	XF
S301	**2 Shillings** Aug. 1732.	—	—	—
S302	**2 Shillings 6 Pence** Aug. 1732.	—	—	—
S303	**3 Shillings** Aug. 1732.	—	—	—
S304	**5 Shillings** Aug. 1732.	—	—	—
S305	**10 Shillings** Aug. 1732.	—	—	—
S306	**20 Shillings** Aug. 1732.	—	—	—
S307	**40 Shillings** Aug. 1732.	—	—	—
S308	**5 Pounds** Aug. 1732.	—	—	—

1733 Issue

#S309-S316 black. Printer: Timothy Green.

		Good	Fine	XF
S309	**2 Shillings** 10.7.1733. Dove.	—	—	—
S310	**2 Shillings 6 Pence** 10.7.1733. Cock.	—	—	—
S311	**3 Shillings** 10.7.1733. Squirrel.	—	—	—
S312	**5 Shillings** 10.7.1733. Fox.	—	—	—
S313	**10 Shillings** 10.7.1733. Lamb.	—	—	—
S314	**20 Shillings** 10.7.1733. Deer.	—	—	—
S315	**40 Shillings** 10.7.1733. Horse.	—	—	—
S316	**5 Pounds** 10.7.1733. Lion.	—	—	—

1735 Redated Issue

#S317-S324 black. Printer: Timothy Green.

		Good	Fine	XF
S317	**2 Shillings** 1735. (- old date 10.7.1733). Dove.	—	—	—
S318	**2 Shillings 6 Pence** 1735. (- old date 10.7.1733). Cock.	—	—	—
S319	**3 Shillings** 1735 (- old date 10.7.1733). Squirrel.	—	—	—
S320	**5 Shillings** 1735 (- old date 10.7.1733). Fox.	—	—	—
S321	**10 Shillings** 1735 (- old date 10.7.1733). Lamb.	—	—	—
S322	**20 Shillings** 1735 (- old date 10.7.1733). Deer.	—	—	—
S323	**40 Shillings** 1735 (- old date 10.7.1733). Horse.	—	—	—
S324	**5 Pounds** 1735 (- old date 10.7.1733). Lion.	—	—	—

1740 First Redated Issue

#S325-S328 black. Printer: Timothy Green.

		Good	Fine	XF
S325	**10 Shillings** May 1740 (- old date 10.7.1733).	—	—	—
S326	**20 Shillings** May 1740 (- old date 10.7.1733).	—	—	—
S327	**40 Shillings** May 1740 (- old date 10.7.1733).	—	—	—
S328	**5 Pounds** May 1740. (- old date 10.7.1733).	—	—	—

1740 Issue

#S329-S336 black. Printer: Timothy Green.

		Good	Fine	XF
S329	**1 Shilling** 8.5.1740.	—	—	—
S330	**2 Shillings** 8.5.1740.	—	—	—
S331	**4 Shillings** 8.5.1740.	—	—	—
S332	**7 Shillings** 8.5.1740.	—	—	—
S333	**12 Shillings** 8.5.1740.	—	—	—
S334	**20 Shillings** 8.5.1740.	—	—	—
S335	**40 Shillings** 8.5.1740.	—	—	—
S336	**3 Pounds** 8.5.1740.	—	—	—

1740 Second Redated Issue

(Redated May 1740 on face; July 8, 1740 on back.)

		Good	Fine	XF
S337	**10 Shillings** May, 1740/8.7.1740 (- old date 10.7.1733). Lamb.	—	—	—
S338	**20 Shillings** May, 1740/8.7.1740 (- old date 10.7.1733). Deer.	—	—	—
S339	**40 Shillings** May, 1740/8.7.1740 (- old date 10.7.1733). Horse.	—	—	—
S340	**5 Pounds** May, 1740/8.7.1740 (- old date 10.7.1733). Lion.	—	—	—

1744 Redated Issues

#S341-S356 black. Printer: Timothy Green.

		Good	Fine	XF
S341	**1 Shilling** 10.5.1744 (- old date 8.5.1740).	—	—	—
S342	**2 Shillings** 10.5.1744 (- old date 8.5.1740).	—	—	—
S343	**4 Shillings** 10.5.1744 (- old date 8.5.1740).	—	—	—
S344	**7 Shillings** 10.5.1744 (- old date 8.5.1740).	—	—	—
S345	**12 Shillings** 10.5.1744 (- old date 8.5.1740).	—	—	—
S346	**20 Shillings** 10.5.1744 (- old date 8.5.1740).	—	—	—
S347	**40 Shillings** 10.5.1744 (- old date 8.5.1740).	—	—	—
S348	**3 Pounds** 10.5.1744 (- old date 8.5.1740).	—	—	—
S349	**1 Shilling** 11.10.1744 (- old date 8.5.1740).	—	—	—
S350	**2 Shillings** 11.10.1744 (- old date 8.5.1740).	—	—	—
S351	**4 Shillings** 11.10.1744 (- old date 8.5.1740).	—	—	—
S352	**7 Shillings** 11.10.1744 (- old date 8.5.1740).	—	—	—
S353	**12 Shillings** 11.10.1744 (- old date 8.5.1740).	—	—	—
S354	**20 Shillings** 11.10.1744 (- old date 8.5.1740).	—	—	—

		Good	Fine	XF
S355	**40 Shillings** 11.10.1744 (- old date 8.5.1740).	—	—	—
S356	**3 Pounds** 11.10.1744 (- old date 8.5.1740).	—	—	—

1744/45 Redated Issue

#S357-S364 black. Printer: Timothy Green.

		Good	Fine	XF
S357	**1 Shilling** 14.3.1744/45 (- old date 8.5.1740).	—	—	—
S358	**2 Shillings** 14.3.1744/45 (- old date 8.5.1740).	—	—	—
S359	**4 Shillings** 14.3.1744/45 (- old date 8.5.1740).	—	—	—
S360	**7 Shillings** 14.3.1744/45 (- old date 8.5.1740).	—	—	—
S361	**12 Shillings** 14.3.1744/45 (- old date 8.5.1740).	—	—	—
S362	**20 Shillings** 14.3.1744/45 (- old date 8.5.1740).	—	—	—
S363	**40 Shillings** 14.3.1744/45 (- old date 8.5.1740).	—	—	—
S364	**3 Pounds** 14.3.1744/45 (- old date 8.5.1740).	—	—	—

1746 Redated Issues

(Redated May 8, 1746.)

#S365-S376 black. Printer: Timothy Green.

		Good	Fine	XF
S365	**2 Shillings** 8.5.1746 (- old date 10.7.1733). Dove.	—	—	—

		Good	Fine	XF
S366	**2 Shilling 6 Pence** 8.5.1746 (- old date 10.7.1733). Cock.	—	—	—
S367	**3 Shillings** 8.5.1746 (- old date 10.7.1733). Squirrel.	—	—	—
S368	**5 Shillings** 8.5.1746 (- old date 10.7.1733). Fox.	—	—	—
S369	**1 Shilling** 8.5.1746 (- old date - 8.5.1740).	—	—	—
S370	**2 Shillings** 8.5.1746 (- old date 8.5.1740).	—	—	—
S371	**4 Shillings** 8.5.1746 (- old date 8.5.1740).	—	—	—
S372	**7 Shillings** 8.5.1746 (- old date 8.5.1740).	—	—	—
S373	**12 Shillings** 8.5.1746 (- old date 8.5.1740).	—	—	—
S374	**20 Shillings** 8.5.1746 (- old date 8.5.1740).	—	—	—
S375	**40 Shillings** 8.5.1746 (- old date 8.5.1740).	—	—	—
S376	**3 Pounds** 8.5.1746 (- old date 8.5.1740).	—	—	—

1755 Issues

#S377-S408 black. Printer: Timothy Green.

		Good	Fine	XF
S377	**9 Pence** 8.1.1755.	—	—	—
S378	**1 Shilling** 8.1.1755.	—	—	—
S379	**2 Shillings 6 Pence** 8.1.1755.	—	—	—
S380	**5 Shillings** 8.1.1755.	—	—	—
S381	**10 Shillings** 8.1.1755.	—	—	—
S382	**20 Shillings** 8.1.1755.	—	—	—
S383	**30 Shillings** 8.1.1755.	—	—	—
S384	**40 Shillings** 8.1.1755.	—	—	—
S385	**9 Pence** 13.3.1755.	—	—	—

		Good	Fine	XF
S386	**1 Shilling** 13.3.1755.	—	—	—
S387	**2 Shillings 6 Pence** 13.3.1755.	—	—	—
S388	**5 Shillings** 13.3.1755.	—	—	—
S389	**10 Shillings** 13.3.1755.	—	—	—
S390	**20 Shillings** 13.3.1755.	—	—	—
S391	**30 Shillings** 13.3.1755.	—	—	—
S392	**40 Shillings** 13.3.1755.	—	—	—
S393	**9 Pence** 27.8.1755.	—	—	—
S394	**1 Shilling** 27.8.1755.	—	—	—
S395	**2 Shillings 6 Pence** 27.8.1755.	—	—	—
S396	**5 Shillings** 27.8.1755.	—	—	—
S397	**10 Shillings** 27.8.1755.	—	—	—
S398	**20 Shillings** 27.8.1755.	—	—	—
S399	**30 Shillings** 27.8.1755.	—	—	—
S400	**40 Shillings** 27.8.1755.	—	—	—
S401	**9 Pence** 9.10.1755.	—	—	—
S402	**1 Shilling** 9.10.1755.	—	—	—
S403	**2 Shillings 6 Pence** 9.10.1755.	—	—	—
S404	**5 Shillings** 9.10.1755.	—	—	—
S405	**10 Shillings** 9.10.1755.	—	—	—
S406	**20 Shillings** 9.10.1755.	—	—	—
S407	**30 Shillings** 9.10.1755.	—	—	—
S408	**40 Shillings** 9.10.1755.	—	—	—

1758 Issue

#S409-S416 black. Printer: Timothy Green.

		Good	Fine	XF
S409	**9 Pence** 8.3.1758.	—	—	—
S410	**1 Shilling** 8.3.1758.	—	—	—
S411	**2 Shillings 6 Pence** 8.3.1758.	—	—	—
S412	**5 Shillings** 8.3.1758.	—	—	—
S413	**10 Shillings** 8.3.1758.	—	—	—
S414	**20 Shillings** 8.3.1758.	—	—	—
S415	**30 Shillings** 8.3.1758.	—	—	—
S416	**40 Shillings** 8.3.1758.	—	—	—

1759 First Issue

#S417-S424 black. Printer: Timothy Green.

		Good	Fine	XF
S417	**9 Pence** 7.2.1759.	—	—	—
S418	**1 Shilling** 7.2.1759.	—	—	—
S419	**2 Shillings 6 Pence** 7.2.1759.	—	—	—
S420	**5 Shillings** 7.2.1759.	—	—	—
S421	**10 Shillings** 7.2.1759.	—	—	—
S422	**20 Shillings** 7.2.1759.	—	—	—
S423	**30 Shillings** 7.2.1759.	—	—	—
S424	**40 Shillings** 7.2.1759.	—	—	—

1759 Second Issue

#S425-S432 black. Printer: Timothy Green.

		Good	Fine	XF
S425	**9 Pence** 8.3.1759.	1000.	—	—
S426	**1 Shilling** 8.3.1759.	1000.	—	—
S427	**2 Shillings 6 Pence** 8.3.1759.	1000.	—	—
S428	**5 Shillings** 8.3.1759.	1000.	—	—
S429	**10 Shillings** 8.3.1759.	1000.	—	—

		Good	Fine	XF
S430	20 Shillings 8.3.1759.	1000.	—	—
S431	30 Shillings 8.3.1759.	1000.	—	—
S432	40 Shillings 8.3.1759.	1000.	—	—

1759 Third Issue

#S433-S440 black. Printer: Timothy Green.

		Good	Fine	XF
S433	9 Pence 10.5.1759.	—	—	—
S434	1 Shilling 10.5.1759.	—	—	—
S435	2 Shillings 6 Pence 10.5.1759.	—	—	—
S436	5 Shillings 10.5.1759.	—	—	—
S437	10 Shillings 10.5.1759.	—	—	—
S438	20 Shillings 10.5.1759.	—	—	—
S439	30 Shillings 10.5.1759.	—	—	—
S440	40 Shillings 10.5.1759.	—	—	—

1760 Issue

#S441-S448 black. Printer: Timothy Green.

		Good	Fine	XF
S441	9 Pence 13.3.1760.	1000.	—	—
S442	1 Shilling 13.3.1760.	1000.	—	—
S443	2 Shillings 6 Pence 13.3.1760.	1000.	—	—
S444	5 Shillings 13.3.1760.	1000.	—	—
S445	10 Shillings 13.3.1760.	1000.	—	—
S446	20 Shillings 13.3.1760.	1000.	—	—
S447	30 Shillings 13.3.1760.	1000.	—	—
S448	40 Shillings 13.3.1760.	1000.	—	—

1761 Issue

#S449-S456 black. Printer: Timothy Green.

		Good	Fine	XF
S449	9 Pence 26.3.1761.	—	—	—
S450	1 Shilling 26.3.1761.	—	—	—
S451	2 Shillings 6 Pence 26.3.1761.	—	—	—
S452	5 Shillings 26.3.1761.	—	—	—
S453	10 Shillings 26.3.1761.	—	—	—
S454	20 Shillings 26.3.1761.	—	—	—
S455	30 Shillings 26.3.1761.	—	—	—
S456	40 Shillings 26.3.1761.	—	—	—

1762 Issue

#S457-S464 black. Printer: Timothy Green.

		Good	Fine	XF
S457	9 Pence 4.3.1762.	—	—	—
S458	1 Shilling 4.3.1762.	—	—	—
S459	2 Shillings 6 Pence 4.3.1762.	—	—	—
S460	5 Shillings 4.3.1762.	—	—	—
S461	10 Shillings 4.3.1762.	—	—	—
S462	20 Shillings 4.3.1762.	—	—	—
S463	30 Shillings 4.3.1762.	—	—	—
S464	40 Shillings 4.3.1762.	—	—	—

1763 Issue

#S465-S469 black. Printer: Timothy Green.

		Good	Fine	XF
S465	5 Shillings 12.5.1763.	1000.	—	—
S466	10 Shillings 12.5.1763.	1000.	—	—
S467	20 Shillings 12.5.1763.	1000.	—	—
S468	30 Shillings 12.5.1763.	1000.	—	—
S469	40 Shillings 12.5.1763.	1000.	—	—

1764 Issue

#S470-S478 black. Printer: Timothy Green.

		Good	Fine	XF
S470	9 Pence 8.3.1764.	—	Rare	—
S471	1 Shilling 8.3.1764.	—	Rare	—
S472	1 Shilling 6 Pence 8.3.1764.	—	Rare	—
S473	2 Shillings 8.3.1764.	—	Rare	—
S474	5 Shillings 8.3.1764.	—	Rare	—
S475	10 Shillings 8.3.1764.	650.00	—	—
S476	20 Shillings 8.3.1764.	650.00	—	—
S477	30 Shillings 8.3.1764.	650.00	—	—
S478	40 Shillings 8.3.1764.	650.00	—	—

1770 Issue

#S479-S483 black. Printer: Timothy Green.

		Good	Fine	XF
S479	2 Shillings 6 Pence 10.5.1770.	100.00	200.00	—
S480	5 Shillings 10.5.1770.	100.00	200.00	—
S481	10 Shillings 10.5.1770.	—	Rare	—
S482	20 Shillings 10.5.1770.	—	Rare	—
S483	40 Shillings 10.5.1770.	—	Rare	—

1771 Issue

#S484-S488 black. Printer: Timothy Green.

		VG	VF	Unc
S484	2 Shillings 6 Pence 10.10.1771.	80.00	165.00	—
S485	5 Shillings 10.10.1771.	80.00	165.00	—
S486	10 Shillings 10.10.1771.	80.00	165.00	—
S487	20 Shillings 10.10.1771.	80.00	165.00	—
S488	40 Shillings 10.10.1771.	80.00	165.00	—

1773 Issue

#S489-S493 black. Printer: Timothy Green.

		VG	VF	Unc
S489	2 Shillings 6 Pence 1.6.1773.	65.00	150.00	—
S490	5 Shillings 1.6.1773.	65.00	150.00	—
S491	10 Shillings 1.6.1773.	65.00	150.00	—
S492	20 Shillings 1.6.1773.	65.00	150.00	—
S493	40 Shillings 1.6.1773.	65.00	150.00	—

1775 First Issue

#S494-S498 black. Printer: Timothy Green.

		VG	VF	Unc
S494	2 Shillings 6 Pence 2.1.1775.	55.00	120.00	—
S495	5 Shillings 2.1.1775.	55.00	120.00	—
S496	10 Shillings 2.1.1775.	55.00	120.00	—
S497	20 Shillings 2.1.1775.	55.00	120.00	—
S498	40 Shillings 2.1.1775.	55.00	120.00	—

1775 Second Issue

#S499-S502 black. Printer: Timothy Green.

		VG	VF	Unc
S499	2 Shillings 6 Pence 10.5.1775.	90.00	265.00	—
S500	10 Shillings 10.5.1775.	75.00	220.00	—
S501	20 Shillings 10.5.1775.	70.00	200.00	—
S502	40 Shillings 10.5.1775.	27.00	80.00	—

1775 Third Issue

#S503-S507 black. Printer: Timothy Green.

		VG	VF	Unc
S503	2 Shillings 6 Pence 1.6.1775.	27.00	45.00	180.00
S504	6 Shillings 1.6.1775.	22.00	37.00	150.00
S505	10 Shillings 1.6.1775.	38.00	62.00	250.00
S506	20 Shillings 1.6.1775.	30.00	55.00	210.00

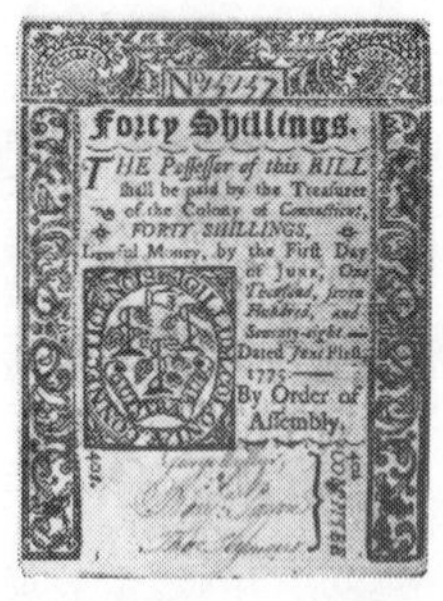

		VG	VF	UNC
S507	**40 SHILLINGS** 1.6.1775.	27.00	45.00	180.00

1775 FOURTH ISSUE

#S508-S513 black. Printer: Timothy Green.

		GOOD	FINE	XF
S508	**2 SHILLINGS** 1.7.1775.	20.00	75.00	—
S509	**2 SHILLINGS 6 PENCE** 1.7.1775.	20.00	75.00	—
S510	**6 SHILLINGS** 1.7.1775.	20.00	75.00	—
S511	**10 SHILLINGS** 1.7.1775.	20.00	75.00	—
S512	**20 SHILLINGS** 1.7.1775.	20.00	75.00	—
S513	**40 SHILLINGS** 1.7.1775.	20.00	75.00	—

CONNECTICUT

STATE

1776 FIRST ISSUE

#S514-S524 black. Printer: Timothy Green.

		VG	VF	UNC
S514	**1 SHILLING** 7.6.1776.	18.00	50.00	200.00
S515	**1 SHILLING 3 PENCE** 7.6.1776.	18.00	50.00	200.00
S516	**2 SHILLINGS** 7.6.1776.	18.00	50.00	200.00
S517	**2 SHILLINGS 6 PENCE** 7.6.1776.	15.00	40.00	165.00
S518	**3 SHILLINGS** 7.6.1776.	25.00	70.00	280.00

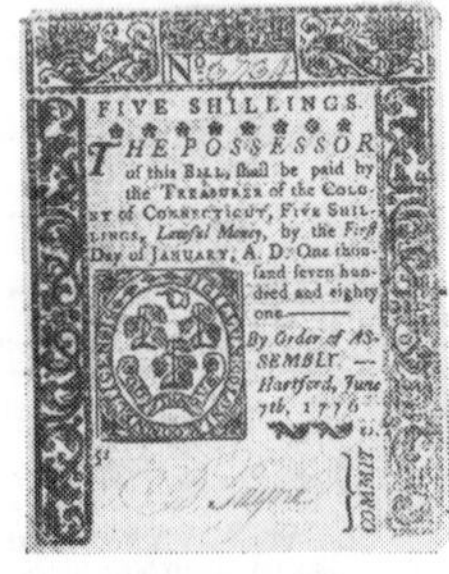

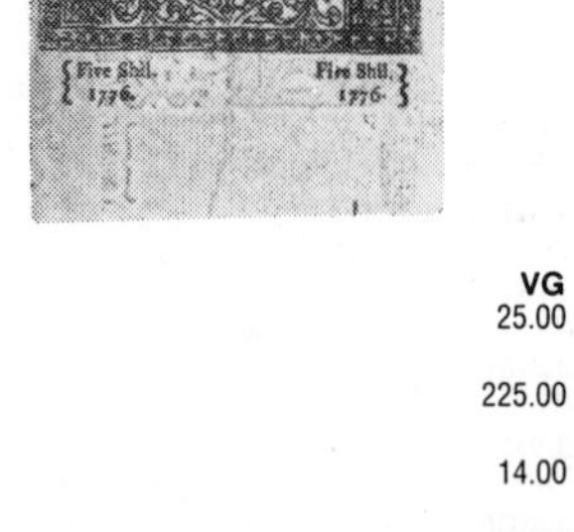

		VG	VF	UNC
S519	**5 SHILLINGS** 7.6.1776.	25.00	70.00	280.00
S520	**6 SHILLINGS** 7.6.1776.	225.00	—	—
S521	**10 SHILLINGS** 7.6.1776.	14.00	30.00	120.00
S522	**15 SHILLINGS** 7.6.1776.	18.00	50.00	200.00
S523	**1 POUND** 7.6.1776.	20.00	60.00	235.00
S524	**2 POUNDS** 7.6.1776.	100.00	—	—

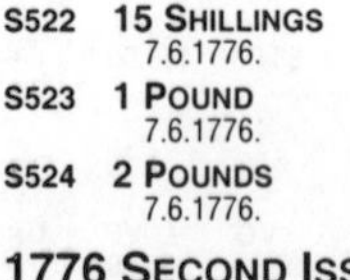

1776 SECOND ISSUE

#S525-S533 black. Printer: Timothy Green.

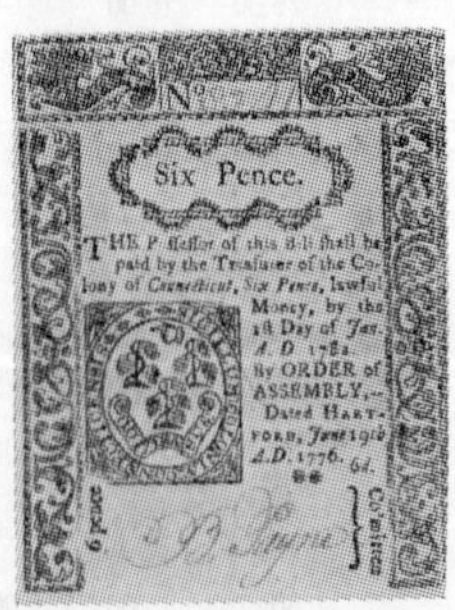

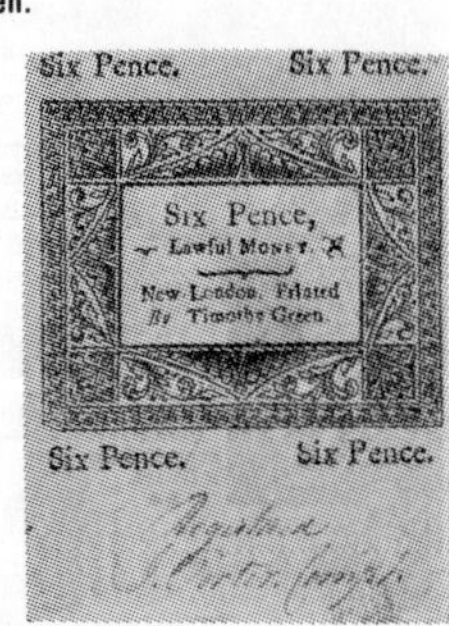

		VG	VF	UNC
S525	**6 PENCE** 19.6.1776.	12.50	25.00	90.00
S526	**9 PENCE** 19.6.1776.	15.00	35.00	125.00
S527	**1 SHILLING** 19.6.1776.	30.00	80.00	285.00

		VG	VF	UNC
S528	**1 SHILLING 3 PENCE** 19.6.1776.	25.00	55.00	200.00
S529	**1 SHILLING 6 PENCE** 19.6.1776.	22.50	45.00	165.00
S530	**2 SHILLINGS** 19.6.1776.	20.00	40.00	165.00
S531	**2 SHILLINGS 6 PENCE** 19.6.1776.	24.00	50.00	180.00
S532	**5 SHILLINGS** 19.6.1776.	20.00	40.00	145.00
S532A	**20 SHILLINGS** 19.6.1776.	28.00	75.00	270.00
S533	**40 SHILLINGS** 19.6.1776.	15.00	35.00	125.00

1777 ISSUE

#S534-S538 black. Uniface.

		VG	VF	UNC
S534	**2 PENCE** 11.10.1777.			
	a. White paper.	15.00	30.00	120.00
	b. Blue paper.	10.00	20.00	80.00

		VG	VF	UNC
S535	**3 PENCE** 11.10.1777.			
	a. White paper.	15.00	30.00	120.00
	b. Blue paper.	10.00	20.00	80.00
S536	**4 PENCE** 11.10.1777.			
	a. White paper.	15.00	30.00	120.00
	b. Blue paper.	10.00	20.00	80.00
S537	**5 PENCE** 11.10.1777.			
	a. White paper.	15.00	30.00	120.00
	b. Blue paper.	10.00	20.00	80.00
S538	**7 PENCE** 11.10.1777.			
	a. White paper.	15.00	30.00	120.00
	b. Blue paper.	10.00	20.00	80.00

1780 FIRST ISSUE

#S539-S545 black. Printer: Timothy Green.

		VG	VF	UNC
S539	**9 PENCE** 1.3.1780.	12.50	25.00	60.00
S540	**1 SHILLING 3 PENCE** 1.3.1780.	12.50	25.00	60.00
S541	**2 SHILLINGS 6 PENCE** 1.3.1780.	12.50	25.00	60.00
S542	**5 SHILLINGS** 1.3.1780.	12.50	25.00	60.00

		VG	VF	UNC
S543	**10 SHILLINGS** 1.3.1780.	12.50	25.00	60.00
S544	**20 SHILLINGS** 1.3.1780.	12.50	25.00	60.00
S545	**40 SHILLINGS** 1.3.1780.	12.50	25.00	60.00

1780 SECOND ISSUE

#S546-S552 black. Printer: Timothy Green.

		VG	VF	UNC
S546	**9 PENCE** 1.6.1780.	15.00	30.00	70.00

		VG	VF	UNC
S547	**1 SHILLING 3 PENCE** 1.6.1780.	15.00	30.00	70.00
S548	**2 SHILLINGS 6 PENCE** 1.6.1780.	15.00	30.00	70.00
S549	**5 SHILLINGS** 1.6.1780.	15.00	30.00	70.00
S550	**10 SHILLINGS** 1.6.1780.	15.00	30.00	70.00
S551	**20 SHILLINGS** 1.6.1780.	15.00	30.00	70.00
S552	**40 SHILLINGS** 1.6.1780.	15.00	30.00	70.00

1780 THIRD ISSUE

#S553-S560 black. Printer: Timothy Green.

		VG	VF	UNC
S553	**9 PENCE** 1.7.1780.	12.50	25.00	50.00
S554	**1 SHILLING** 1.7.1780.	12.50	25.00	50.00
S555	**1 SHILLING 3 PENCE** 1.7.1780.	12.50	25.00	50.00

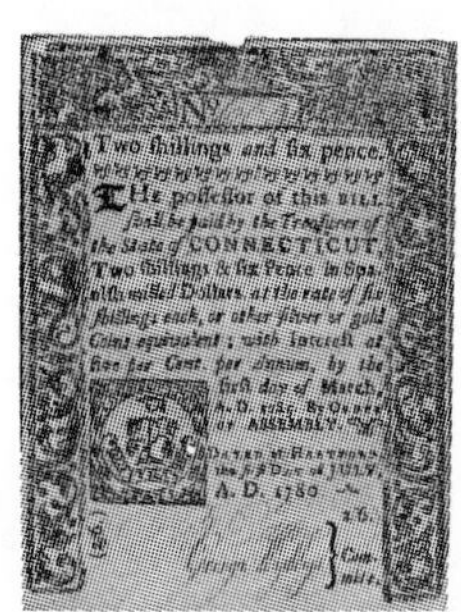

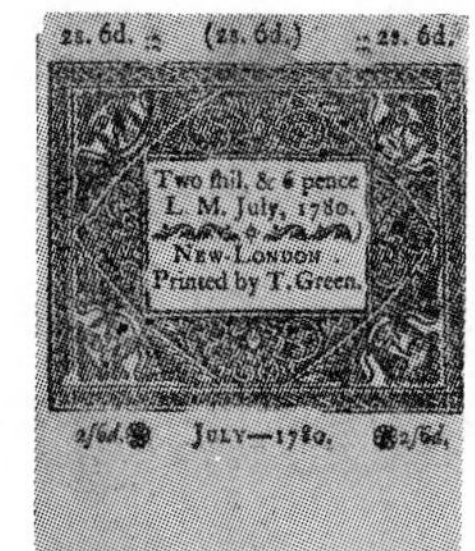

		VG	VF	UNC
S556	**2 SHILLINGS 6 PENCE** 1.7.1780.	12.50	25.00	50.00
S557	**5 SHILLINGS** 1.7.1780.	12.50	25.00	50.00
S558	**10 SHILLINGS** 1.7.1780.	12.50	25.00	50.00
S559	**20 SHILLINGS** 1.7.1780.	12.50	25.00	50.00
S560	**40 SHILLINGS** 1.7.1780.	12.50	25.00	50.00

DELAWARE

COLONIAL

1729 ISSUE

#S561-S568 black.

		GOOD	FINE	XF
S561	**1 SHILLING** 1729.	—	—	—
S562	**18 PENCE** 1729.	—	—	—
S563	**2 SHILLINGS** 1729.	—	—	—
S564	**2 SHILLINGS 6 PENCE** 1729.	—	—	—
S565	**5 SHILLINGS** 1729.	—	—	—
S566	**10 SHILLINGS** 1729.	—	—	—
S567	**15 SHILLINGS** 1729.	—	—	—
S568	**20 SHILLINGS** 1729.	—	—	—

1734 ISSUE

#S569-S576 black. Uniface. Printer: Benjamin Franklin.

		GOOD	FINE	XF
S569	**1 SHILLING** 1.3.1734.	—	—	—
S570	**18 PENCE** 1.3.1734.	—	—	—
S571	**2 SHILLINGS** 1.3.1734.	—	—	—
S572	**2 SHILLINGS 6 PENCE** 1.3.1734.	—	—	—
S573	**5 SHILLINGS** 1.3.1734.	—	—	—
S574	**10 SHILLINGS** 1.3.1734.	—	—	—
S575	**15 SHILLINGS** 1.3.1734.	—	—	—
S576	**20 SHILLINGS** 1.3.1734.	—	—	—

1739 ISSUE

#S577-S582 black. Uniface. Printer: Benjamin Franklin.

		GOOD	FINE	XF
S577	**1 SHILLING** 1.12.1739.	—	—	—
S578	**18 PENCE** 1.12.1739.	—	—	—
S579	**2 SHILLINGS** 1.12.1739.	—	—	—
S580	**2 SHILLINGS 6 PENCE** 1.12.1739.	—	—	—
S581	**5 SHILLINGS** 1.12.1739.	—	—	—
S582	**10 SHILLINGS** 1.12.1739.	—	—	—

1746 ISSUE

#S583-S590 black. Printer: Benjamin Franklin.

		GOOD	FINE	XF
S583	**1 SHILLING** 28.2.1746. Uniface.	—	—	—
S584	**18 PENCE** 28.2.1746. Uniface.	—	—	—
S585	**2 SHILLINGS** 28.2.1746. Uniface.	—	—	—
S586	**2 SHILLINGS 6 PENCE** 28.2.1746. Uniface.	—	—	—
S587	**5 SHILLINGS** 28.2.1746. Sea serpents on back.	—	—	—
S588	**10 SHILLINGS** 28.2.1746. Elephant and leaves on back.	—	—	—
S589	**15 SHILLINGS** 28.2.1746. Horse and sage leaf on back.	—	—	—
S590	**20 SHILLINGS** 28.2.1746. Lion and parsley on back.	—	—	—

1753 ISSUE

#S591-S596 black. Printer: Benjamin Franklin and David Hall.

		GOOD	FINE	XF
S591	**1 SHILLING** 1.1.1753. Uniface.	—	—	—
S592	**18 PENCE** 1.1.1753. Uniface.	—	—	—
S593	**2 SHILLINGS** 1.1.1753. Uniface.	—	—	—
S594	**2 SHILLINGS 6 PENCE** 1.1.1753. Uniface.	—	—	—
S595	**5 SHILLINGS** 1.1.1753. Sea serpents and blackberry leaf on back.	—	—	—
S596	**10 SHILLINGS** 1.1.1753. Elephant and leaves on back.	—	—	—

1756 ISSUE

#S597-S604 black. Printer: Benjamin Franklin and David Hall.

		GOOD	FINE	XF
S597	**1 SHILLING** 1.5.1756. Uniface.	—	—	—
S598	**18 PENCE** 1.5.1756. Uniface.	—	—	—

		GOOD	FINE	XF
S599	**2 SHILLINGS** 1.5.1756. Uniface.	—	—	—
		VG	VF	UNC
S600	**2 SHILLINGS 6 PENCE** 1.5.1756. Uniface.	—	—	—
S601	**5 SHILLINGS** 1.5.1756. Sea serpents and blackberry leaf on back.	150.00	—	—
S602	**10 SHILLINGS** 1.5.1756. Elephant and leaves on back.	150.00	—	—
S603	**15 SHILLINGS** 1.5.1756. Horse and sage leaf on back.	150.00	—	—
S604	**20 SHILLINGS** 1.5.1756. Lion and parsley on back.	150.00	—	—

1758 FIRST ISSUE

#S605-S612 black. Printer: Benjamin Franklin and David Hall.

		GOOD	FINE	XF
S605	**1 SHILLING** 1.3.1758.	—	—	—
S606	**18 PENCE** 1.3.1758.	—	—	—
S607	**2 SHILLINGS** 1.3.1758.	—	—	—
S608	**2 SHILLINGS 6 PENCE** 1.3.1758.	—	—	—
S609	**5 SHILLINGS** 1.3.1758. Back like #S586.	75.00	260.00	—
S610	**10 SHILLINGS** 1.3.1758. Elephant and maple leaf on back.	75.00	260.00	—
S611	**15 SHILLINGS** 1.3.1758. Back like #S588.	75.00	260.00	—
S612	**20 SHILLINGS** 1.3.1758. Lion and assorted leaves on back.	75.00	260.00	—

1758 SECOND ISSUE

#S613-S620 black. Printer: Benjamin Franklin and David Hall.

		GOOD	FINE	XF
S613	**1 SHILLING** 1.5.1758.	—	—	—
S614	**1 SHILLING 6 PENCE** 1.5.1758.	—	—	—
S615	**2 SHILLINGS** 1.5.1758.	—	—	—
S616	**2 SHILLINGS 6 PENCE** 1.5.1758.	—	—	—
S617	**5 SHILLINGS** 1.5.1758. Back like #S586.	100.00	350.00	—
S618	**10 SHILLINGS** 1.5.1758. Back like #S595.	100.00	350.00	—
S619	**15 SHILLINGS** 1.5.1758. Back like #S588.	100.00	350.00	—
S620	**20 SHILLINGS** 1.5.1758. Back like #S597.	100.00	350.00	—

1759 ISSUE

#S621-S629 black. Printer: Benjamin Franklin and David Hall.

		GOOD	FINE	XF
S621	**1 SHILLING** 1.6.1759. Uniface.	—	Rare	—
S622	**1 SHILLING 6 PENCE** 1.6.1759. Uniface.	—	Rare	—
S623	**2 SHILLINGS** 1.6.1759. Uniface.	—	Rare	—
S624	**2 SHILLINGS 6 PENCE** 1.6.1759. Uniface.	—	Rare	—
S625	**5 SHILLINGS** 1.6.1759. Sea serpents on back.	120.00	400.00	—

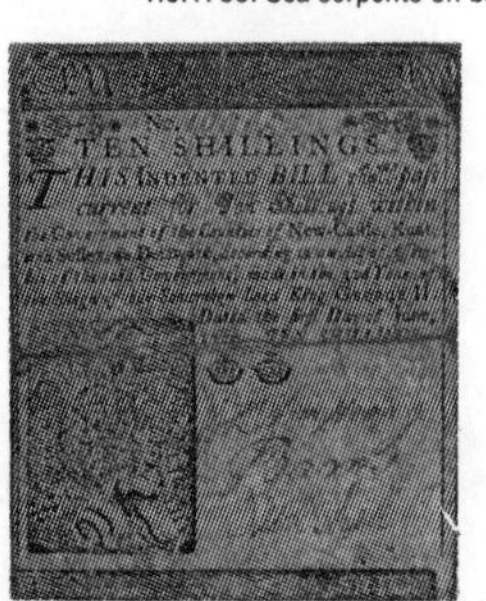

		GOOD	FINE	XF
S626	**10 SHILLINGS** 1.6.1759. Squirrel, elephant, and bird on back.	120.00	400.00	—
S627	**15 SHILLINGS** 1.6.1759. Horse on back.	120.00	350.00	—
S628	**20 SHILLINGS** 1.6.1759. Lion w/period over center of *Y* on back.	120.00	350.00	—
S629	**20 SHILLINGS** 1.6.1759. Lion w/period past right side of *Y* on back.	120.00	350.00	—

1760 ISSUE

#S630-S633 black and red. Printer: Benjamin Franklin and David Hall.

		GOOD	FINE	XF
S630	**20 SHILLINGS** 31.5.1760.	100.00	400.00	—
S631	**30 SHILLINGS** 31.5.1760. *I* omitted in ea. *THRTY.*	100.00	400.00	—
S632	**40 SHILLINGS** 31.5.1760. *D* reversed in borders.	100.00	400.00	—
S633	**50 SHILLINGS** 31.5.1760.	100.00	400.00	—

1776 ISSUE

#S634-S641 black. Thick paper containing blue fibres and mica flakes. Back w/cuts of a sheaf of wheat. Printer: James Adams.

		VG	VF	UNC
S634	**1 SHILLING** 1.1.1776.	18.00	50.00	150.00
S635	**18 PENCE** 1.1.1776.	18.00	50.00	150.00
S636	**2 SHILLINGS 6 PENCE** 1.1.1776.	18.00	50.00	150.00
S637	**4 SHILLINGS** 1.1.1776.	18.00	50.00	150.00
S638	**5 SHILLINGS** 1.1.1776.	18.00	50.00	150.00
S639	**6 SHILLINGS** 1.1.1776.	18.00	50.00	150.00

		VG	VF	UNC
S640	**10 SHILLINGS** 1.1.1776.	18.00	50.00	150.00
S641	**20 SHILLINGS** 1.1.1776.	18.00	50.00	150.00

DELAWARE

STATE

1777 ISSUE

#S642-S653 black. Thick paper containing blue fibres and mica flakes. Back w/cuts of a sheaf of wheat. Printer: James Adams.

		VG	VF	UNC
S642	**3 PENCE** 1.5.1777.	55.00	100.00	—
S643	**4 PENCE** 1.5.1777.	55.00	100.00	—
S644	**6 PENCE** 1.5.1777.	55.00	100.00	—
S645	**9 PENCE** 1.5.1777.	55.00	100.00	—
S646	**1 SHILLING** 1.5.1777.	55.00	100.00	—
S647	**1 SHILLING 6 PENCE** 1.5.1777.	55.00	100.00	—
S648	**2 SHILLINGS 6 PENCE** 1.5.1777.	55.00	100.00	—
S649	**4 SHILLINGS** 1.5.1777.	55.00	100.00	—
S650	**5 SHILLINGS** 1.5.1777.	55.00	100.00	—

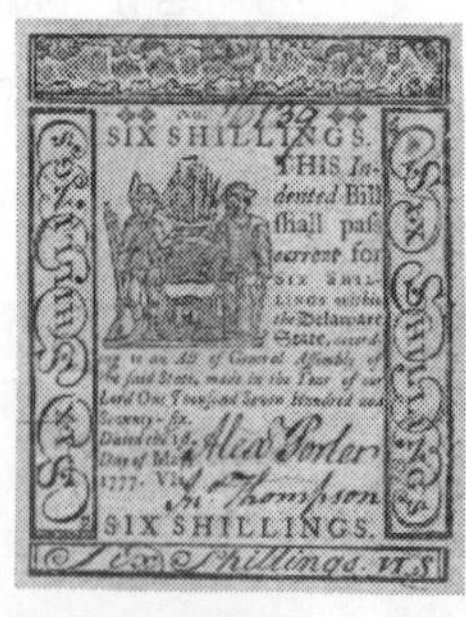

		VG	VF	UNC
S651	**6 SHILLINGS** 1.5.1777.	55.00	100.00	—
S652	**10 SHILLINGS** 1.5.1777.	55.00	100.00	—
S653	**20 SHILLINGS** 1.5.1777.	55.00	100.00	—

FLORIDA

AMELIA ISLAND

CUSTOM HOUSE ISSUE

		VG	VF	UNC
S655	**6 1/4 CENTS** 19.8.1817. Fernandina.	—	Rare	—

FLORIDA

TERRITORY

1829 TREASURY ISSUE

#S656-S660 various handwritten dates w/o vignettes.

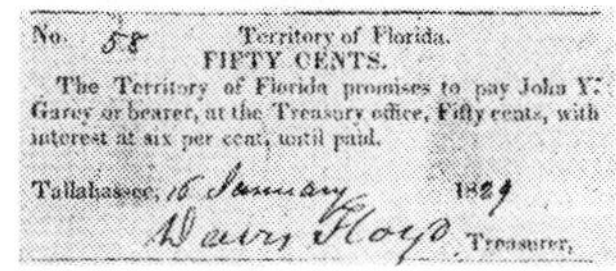
No. 58 Territory of Florida.
FIFTY CENTS.
The Territory of Florida promises to pay John Y. Garey or bearer, at the Treasury office, Fifty cents, with interest at six per cent, until paid.
Tallahassee, 16 January 1829
Davis Floyd Treasurer,

		VG	VF	UNC
S656	**50 CENTS** 16.1.1829.	—	Rare	—

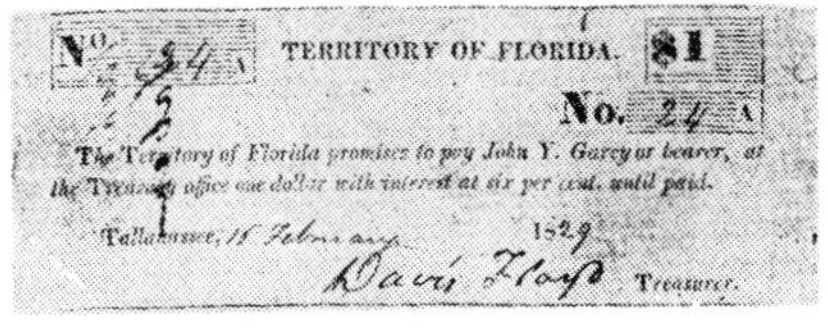
No. 34 TERRITORY OF FLORIDA. $1
No. 24
The Territory of Florida promises to pay John Y. Garey or bearer, at the Treasury office one dollar with interest at six per cent. until paid.
Tallahassee, 15 February 1829
Davis Floyd Treasurer.

		VG	VF	UNC
S657	**1 DOLLAR** 15.2.1829.	—	Rare	—
S658	**2 DOLLARS** 17.2.1829.	—	Rare	—
S659	**3 DOLLARS** 15.1.1829.	—	Rare	—
S660	**5 DOLLARS** 18.2.1829.	—	Rare	—

1829-30 ISSUE

#S661-S664 various handwritten dates. Uniface. Printer: N & S. S. Jocelyn, New Haven.

		GOOD	FINE	XF
S661	**1 DOLLAR** 1829; 24.5.1831. Black. Portr. G. Washington at l., Ceres w/eagle at top ctr.			
	a. Issued note.	450.00	950.00	—
	r. Remainder w/o sign.	400.00	850.00	—
S662	**2 DOLLARS** 12.6.1830. Black. Seated Ceres at l., Hope reclining at top ctr.			
	a. Issued note.	450.00	950.00	—
	r. Remainder w/o sign.	400.00	850.00	—
S663	**3 DOLLARS** 15.7.1830. Black. Justice at l., G. Washington at top ctr.			
	a. Issued note.	450.00	950.00	—
	r. Remainder w/o sign.	400.00	850.00	—

		GOOD	FINE	XF
S664	**5 DOLLARS** 15.7.1829; 1830. Black. Standing Liberty at l., Sir W. Raleigh at l. of Mercury at top ctr.			
	a. Issued note.	450.00	1000.	—
	r. Remainder w/o sign.	400.00	900.00	—

FLORIDA

CIVIL WAR

1861 ISSUES

#S665-S670 G. Washington at lower l., seated Tellus holding globe and spear at r. Various handwritten dates. Uniface. Printer: Hoyer & Ludwig.

		VG	VF	UNC
S665	**1 DOLLAR** 10.10.1861; 6.12.1861. Black *ONE* above seated Tellus at r.	60.00	110.00	200.00
S666	**1 DOLLAR** 1.12.1861; 6.12.1861. Similar to #S665 but w/o *ONE* above Tellus at r.	60.00	110.00	200.00
S667	**2 DOLLARS** 16.9.1861; 6.12.1861. *TWO* above Tellus at r.	60.00	110.00	200.00
S668	**2 DOLLARS** 10.10.1861. Similar to #S667 but w/o *TWO* above Tellus at r. and lg. 2's switched from l. to r.	70.00	125.00	210.00
S669	**3 DOLLARS** 9.10.1861. *THREE* above Tellus at r.	70.00	125.00	210.00
S670	**3 DOLLARS** 10.10.1861; 6.12.1861. Similar to #S669 but w/o *THREE* above Tellus at r.	70.00	125.00	210.00

#S671-S677 black. Seated Ceres at ctr. Engraved date.

		VG	VF	UNC
S671	**5 DOLLARS** 10.10.1861.	50.00	80.00	150.00
S672	**10 DOLLARS** 10.10.1861.	50.00	85.00	150.00
S673	**20 DOLLARS** 10.10.1861.	55.00	85.00	150.00
S674	**50 DOLLARS** 10.10.1861.	60.00	110.00	200.00
S675	**50 DOLLARS** 10.10.1861. Similar to #S674 but inverted *FIFTY* below *FLORIDA.*	60.00	110.00	200.00
S676	**50 DOLLARS** 10.10.1861. Similar to #S674 but *50* above *L* at l.	60.00	110.00	200.00

		VG	VF	UNC
S677	**100 DOLLARS** 10.10.1861.	45.00	95.00	185.00

1862 ISSUE

#S678-S682 black. Blacks picking cotton at l., seated Ceres, Commerce and Navigation at ctr. Printer: Hoyer and Ludwig.

		VG	VF	UNC
S678	**5 DOLLARS** 1.1.1862.	60.00	75.00	175.00
S679	**10 DOLLARS** 1.1.1862.	70.00	125.00	200.00
S680	**20 DOLLARS** 1.1.1862.	70.00	125.00	200.00
S681	**50 DOLLARS** 1.1.1862.	80.00	195.00	350.00

		VG	VF	UNC
S682	**100 DOLLARS** 1.1.1862.	160.00	300.00	400.00

1863 First Issue

#S683-S688 uniface or w/printing on back.

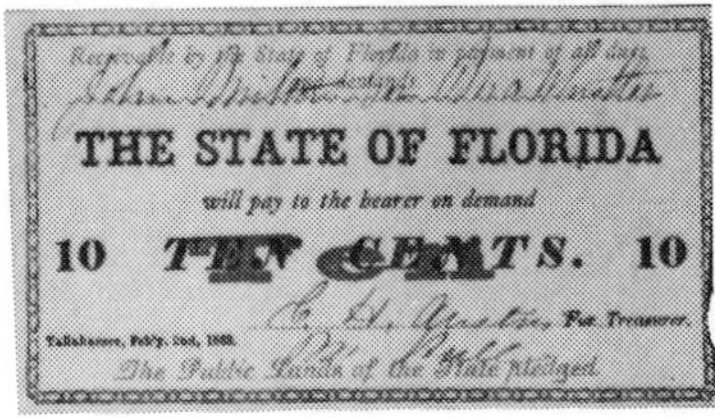

#S683

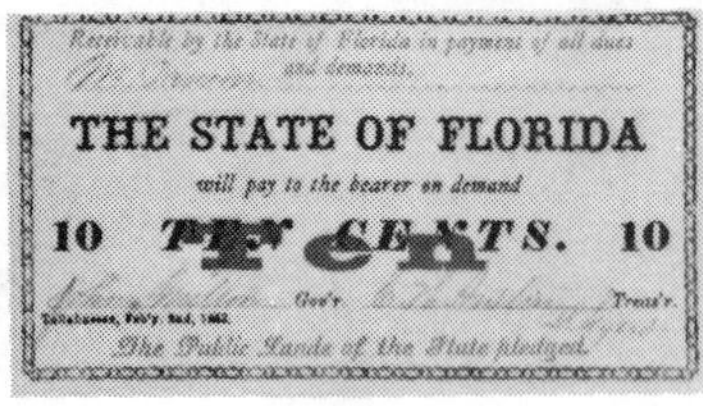

#S684

		VG	VF	Unc
S683	**10 Cents**			
	2.2.1863. Black, red, and blue. 1 sign. w/title: *For Treasurer.*			
	a. Uniface.	20.00	35.00	50.00
	b. Printed on Florida notes.	25.00	45.00	75.00
	c. Printed on Florida bonds.	25.00	45.00	75.00
S684	**10 Cents**			
	2.2.1863. Black, red and blue. Similar to #S683 but 2 sign. w/titles: *Gov'r.* and *Treas'r.*			
	a. Uniface.	13.00	20.00	40.00
	b. Printed on Florida notes.	—	Rare	—
	c. Printed on Florida bonds.	15.00	25.00	35.00

#S685

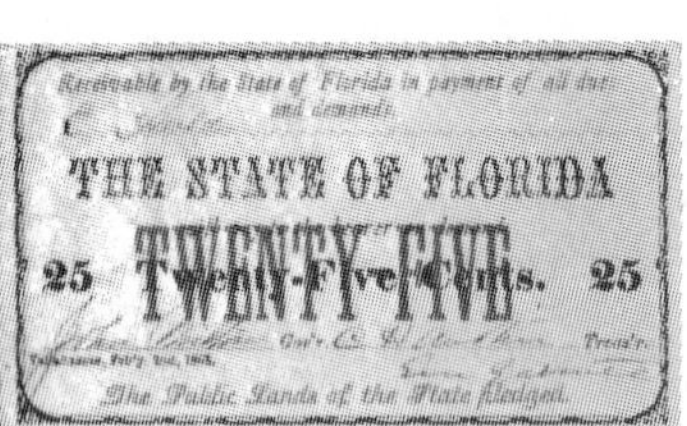

#S686

		VG	VF	Unc
S685	**25 Cents**			
	2.2.1863. Black, red, and blue. 1 sign. w/title: *For Treasurer.*			
	a. Uniface.	20.00	35.00	50.00
	b. Printed on Florida notes.	20.00	35.00	50.00
	c. Printed on Florida bonds.	20.00	35.00	50.00
S686	**25 Cents**			
	2.2.1863. Black, red, and blue. 2 sign. w/titles: *Gov'r* and *Treas'r.*			
	a. Uniface.	13.00	20.00	30.00
	b. Printed on Florida notes.	—	Rare	—
	c. Printed on Florida bonds.	25.00	45.00	75.00

#S687

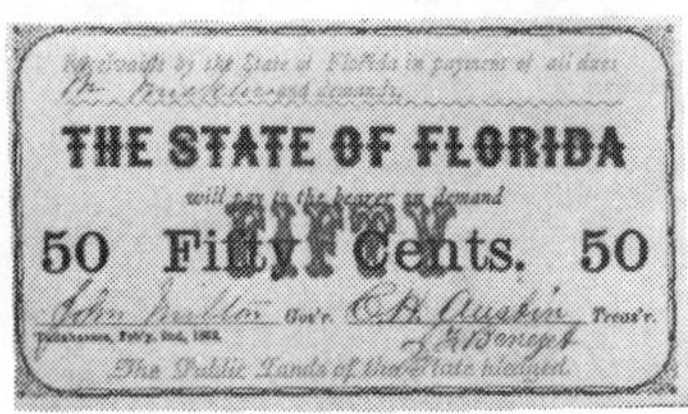

#S688

		VG	VF	Unc
S687	**50 Cents**			
	2.2.1863. Black, red, and blue. 1 sign. w/titles: *For Treasurer.*			
	a. Uniface.	25.00	35.00	50.00
	b. Printed on Florida notes.	30.00	50.00	100.00
	c. Printed on Florida bonds.	25.00	40.00	75.00
S688	**50 Cents**			
	2.2.1863. Uniface. Black, red, and blue. 2 sign. w/titles: *Gov'r.* and *Treas's.*			
	a. Uniface.	13.00	20.00	35.00
	b. Printed on Florida notes.	—	Rare	—
	c. Printed on Florida bonds.	—	Rare	—

1863 Second Issue

#S689-S693 2 allegorical figures in seal at upper l. except for #S692, seal is at r. Printer: Keatinge & Ball.

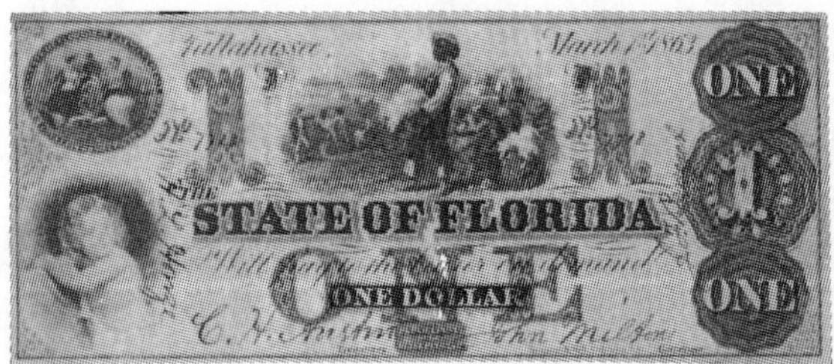

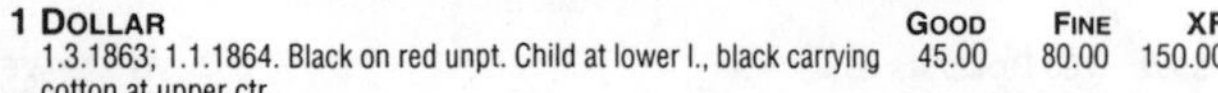

		Good	Fine	XF
S689	**1 Dollar** 1.3.1863; 1.1.1864. Black on red unpt. Child at lower l., black carrying cotton at upper ctr.	45.00	80.00	150.00

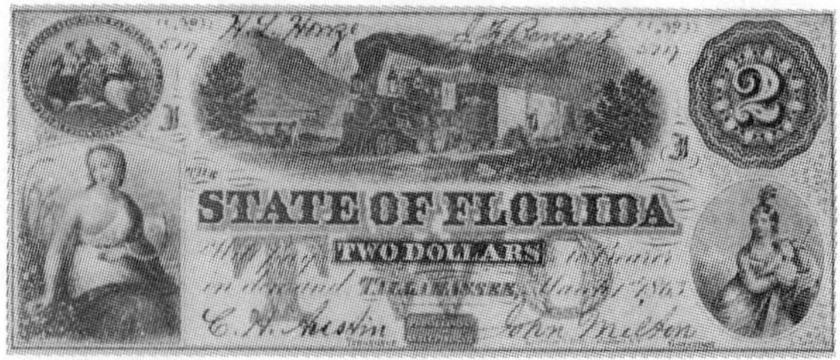

		Good	Fine	XF
S690	**2 Dollars** 1.3.1863; 1.1.1864. Black on red unpt. Ceres at lower l., steam passenger train at upper ctr., Indian maiden at lower r.	45.00	80.00	150.00

		Good	Fine	XF
S691	**3 Dollars** 1.3.1863; 1.1.1864. Black on red unpt. Buck at lower l., sailing ship at upper ctr., Hope at lower r.	50.00	90.00	165.00

		Good	Fine	XF
S692	**5 Dollars** 1.3.1863; 1.3.1864. Black on red unpt. Indian at l., seated Moneta at upper ctr.	45.00	90.00	150.00

		Good	Fine	XF
S693	**10 Dollars** 1.3.1863; 1.3.1864. Black on red unpt. Ship at lower l., seated Ceres at upper ctr., black w/cotton at lower r.	50.00	80.00	150.00

1865 Issue

		Good	Fine	XF
S694	**50 Dollars** 1.1.1865.	600.00	900.00	1500.

		Good	Fine	XF
S695	**100 Dollars** 1.1.1865.	700.00	1000.	2000.
S696	**500 Dollars** 1.1.1865.	—	Rare	—

Florida

Post Civil War

1860's Issue

		Good	Fine	XF
S697	**1 Dollar** 186x. Black and red. Washington at upper l.	—	Rare	—

		Good	Fine	XF
S698	**20 Dollars** 186x. Black on green unpt. Bust of A. Jackson on pedestal w/maiden seated holding shields at ctr., woman's head at upper r.	—	Rare	—

1870 Issue

		Good	Fine	XF
S699	**1 Dollar** 1.3.1870. Black and green. Farmer seated on fence holding scythe at upper l., seated Ceres on barrels at lower r. Printer: NBNC.	700.00	1250.	2000.

Georgia

Colonial

1755 Issue

#S710-S725 black.

		Good	Fine	XF
S710	**2 Pence** 1755.	—	—	—
S711	**3 Pence** 1755.	—	—	—
S712	**4 Pence** 1755.	—	—	—
S713	**6 Pence** 1755.	—	—	—
S714	**9 Pence** 1755.	—	—	—
S715	**1 Shilling** 1755.	—	—	—
S716	**1 Shilling 3 Pence** 1755.	—	—	—
S717	**1 Shilling 6 Pence** 1755.	—	—	—
S718	**2 Shillings** 1755.	—	—	—
S719	**2 Shillings 6 Pence** 1755.	—	—	—
S720	**3 Shillings** 1755.	—	—	—
S721	**3 Shillings 6 Pence** 1755.	—	—	—
S722	**4 Shillings** 1755.	—	—	—
S723	**5 Shillings** 1755. Bee.	—	—	—
S724	**10 Shillings** 1755. Bush and sickle.	—	—	—
S725	**20 Shillings** 1755. Woman operating thread winder.	—	—	—

1762 Issue

#S726-S744 black.

		Good	Fine	XF
S726	**2 Pence** 1762.	—	—	—
S727	**3 Pence** 1762.	—	—	—
S728	**4 Pence** 1762.	—	—	—
S729	**6 Pence** 1762.	—	—	—
S730	**9 Pence** 1762.	—	—	—
S731	**1 Shilling** 1762.	—	—	—
S732	**1 Shilling 3 Pence** 1762.	—	—	—
S733	**1 Shilling 6 Pence** 1762.	—	—	—
S734	**2 Shillings** 1762.	—	—	—
S735	**2 Shillings 6 Pence** 1762.	—	—	—
S736	**3 Shillings** 1762.	—	—	—
S737	**3 Shillings 6 Pence** 1762.	—	—	—
S738	**4 Shillings** 1762.	—	—	—
S739	**5 Shillings** 1762. Bee. Engraved.	—	—	—
S740	**5 Shillings** 1762. Indian. Typeset.	—	—	—
S741	**10 Shillings** 1762. Bush and sickle. Engraved.	—	—	—
S742	**10 Shillings** 1762. Ship. Typeset.	—	—	—
S743	**20 Shillings** 1762. Like #S725. Engraved.	—	—	—
S744	**20 Shillings** 1762. Red. Horse. Typeset.	—	—	—

1774 Issue

#S745-S749 black.

		Good	Fine	XF
S745	**1 Shilling** 1774.	—	—	—
S746	**2 Shillings** 1774.	—	—	—
S747	**2 Shillings 6 Pence** 1774.	—	—	—
S748	**5 Shillings** 1774.	—	—	—
S749	**10 Shillings** 1774.	—	—	—

1775 Issue

#S750 and S751 black.

		Good	Fine	XF
S750	**1 Shilling 6 Pence** 1775. Sheaf of wheat.	—	—	—
S751	**2 Shillings 6 Pence** 1775.	—	—	—

#S752-S756 black and red.

		Good	Fine	XF
S752	**5 Shillings** 1775. 1 crown.	—	—	—
S753	**10 Shillings** 1775. 2 crowns.	—	—	—
S754	**20 Shillings** 1775.	—	—	—
S755	**60 Shillings** 1775.	—	—	—
S756	**5 Pounds** 1775.	—	—	—

GEORGIA

STATE

1776 POUND STERLING ISSUE

#S757-S764 black.

No.	Denomination / Description	Good	Fine	XF
S757	**3 PENCE** 1776. 6 border varieties.	135.00	275.00	500.00
S758	**6 PENCE** 1776. 7 border varieties.	135.00	275.00	500.00
S759	**1 SHILLING** 1776. 3 border varieties.	135.00	275.00	500.00
S760	**1 SHILLING 6 PENCE** 1776. 5 border varieties.	135.00	275.00	500.00

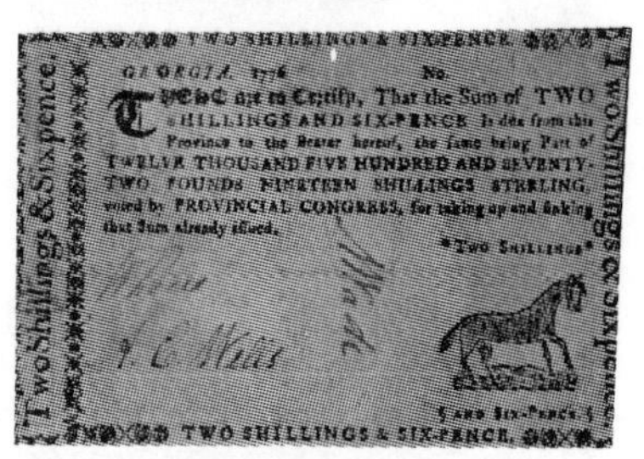

No.	Denomination / Description	Good	Fine	XF
S761	**2 SHILLINGS 6 PENCE** 1776. Horse. Denomination at l. and r.	150.00	300.00	550.00
S762	**2 SHILLINGS 6 PENCE** 1776. Horse. Ornaments at r.	150.00	300.00	550.00
S763	**5 SHILLINGS** 1776. Crown. 2 border varieties.	300.00	450.00	600.00
S764	**5 SHILLINGS** 1776. Crown. *SPERANDUM* on blue seal.	375.00	525.00	750.00

#S765 and S766 black and red.

No.	Denomination / Description	Good	Fine	XF
S765	**10 SHILLINGS** 1776. 3 border varieties.	325.00	475.00	700.00

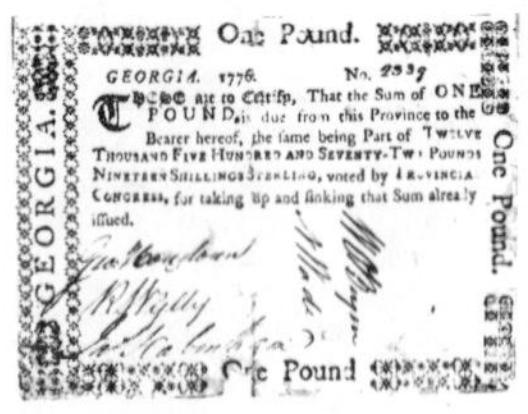

No.	Denomination / Description	Good	Fine	XF
S766	**1 POUND** 1776.	375.00	525.00	750.00

1776 DOLLAR ISSUE

#S767-S773 black and red; lt. blue circular seals.

No.	Denomination / Description	Good	Fine	XF
S767	**1 DOLLAR** 1776. Justice. *SUSTINE RECTUM* on seal. 2 border varieties.	110.00	225.00	375.00
S768	**2 DOLLARS** 1776. Floating jugs. *SI COLLIGIMUS FRANGIMUR* on seal. 2 border varieties.	110.00	225.00	375.00
S769	**2 DOLLARS** 1776. Liberty cap. *LIBERTAS CARIOR AURO* on seal.	130.00	270.00	425.00

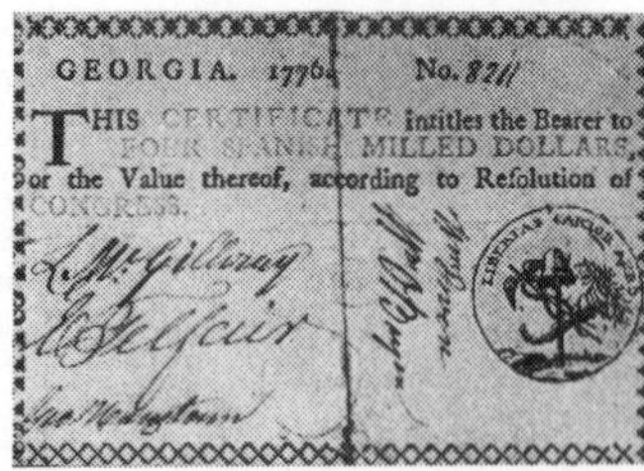

No.	Denomination / Description	Good	Fine	XF
S770	**4 DOLLARS** 1776. Liberty cap. *LIBERTAS CARIOR AURO* on seal. 4 border varieties.	110.00	225.00	375.00
S771	**4 DOLLARS** 1776. Floating jugs. *SI COLLIGIMUS FRANGIMUR* on seal.	130.00	270.00	425.00
S772	**10 DOLLARS** 1776. Millstone on palm tree. *OPPRESSA SURGIT* on seal. 2 border varieties.	135.00	300.00	450.00
S773	**20 DOLLARS** 1776. Rattlesnake. *NEMO ME IMPUNE LACESSET* on seal.	150.00	325.00	550.00

#S774-S777 black and red; maroon circular seals.

No.	Denomination / Description	Good	Fine	XF
S774	**2 DOLLARS** 1776. Floating jugs. *SI COLLIGIMUS FRANGIMUR* on seal.	160.00	250.00	410.00
S775	**4 DOLLARS** 1776. Liberty cap. *LIBERTAS CARIOR AURO* on seal.	160.00	250.00	410.00
S776	**10 DOLLARS** 1776. Millstone on palm tree. *OPPRESSA SURGIT* on seal.	165.00	275.00	435.00
S777	**20 DOLLARS** 1776. Rattlesnake. *NEMO ME IMPUNE LACESSET* on seal.	170.00	325.00	550.00

#S778-S785 black and red; orange or green circular seals.

No.	Denomination / Description	Good	Fine	XF
S778	**1 DOLLAR** 1776. Justice. *SUSTINE RECTUM* on orange seal. 9 border varieties.	100.00	190.00	425.00
S779	**1 DOLLAR** 1776. Like #S778 w/green seal.	175.00	325.00	625.00
S780	**2 DOLLARS** 1776. Floating jugs. *SI COLLIGIMUS FRANGIMUR* on orange seal. 4 or more border varieties.	140.00	230.00	475.00
S781	**2 DOLLARS** 1776. Like #S780 w/green seal. 5 or more border varieties.	145.00	275.00	625.00

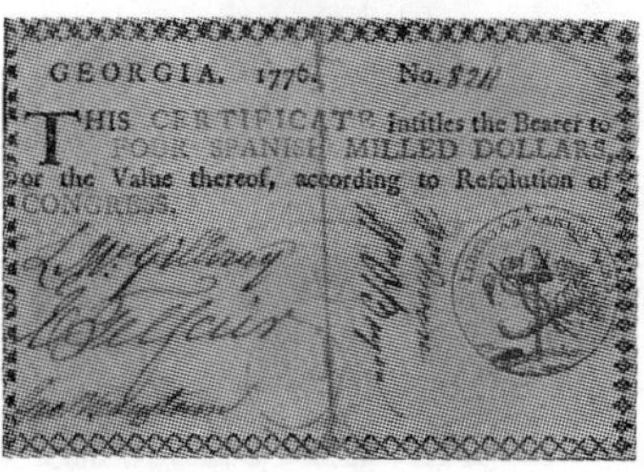

No.	Denomination / Description	Good	Fine	XF
S782	**4 DOLLARS** 1776. Liberty cap. *LIBERTAS CARIOR AURO* on orange seal. 3 border varieties.	140.00	235.00	475.00
S783	**4 DOLLARS** 1776. Like #S782 w/green seal.	240.00	520.00	1050.
S784	**10 DOLLARS** 1776. Millstone on palm tree. *OPPRESSA SURGIT* on orange seal. 3 border varieties.	170.00	320.00	625.00
S785	**20 DOLLARS** 1776. Rattlesnake. *NEMO ME IMPUNE LACESSET* on orange seal. 3 border varieties.	175.00	350.00	700.00

#S786 and S787 black.

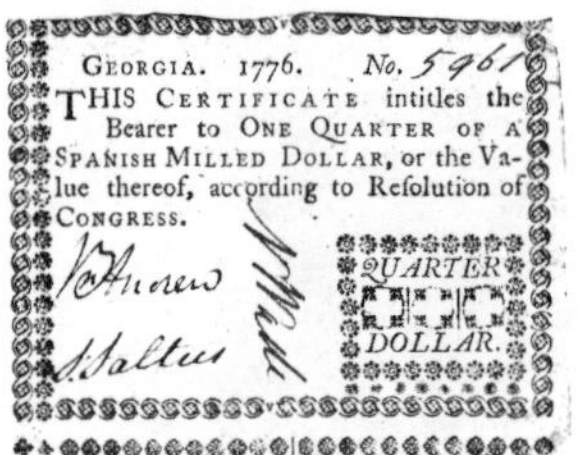

No.	Denomination / Description	Good	Fine	XF
S786	**1/4 DOLLAR** 1776. 8 border varieties.	140.00	240.00	400.00
S787	**1/2 DOLLAR** 1776. 4 border varieties.	150.00	275.00	425.00

#S788-S795 black and red.

No.	Denomination / Description	Good	Fine	XF
S788	**1 DOLLAR** 1776. Justice. *SUSTINE RECTUM* on blue-green seal. 8 border varieties.	150.00	250.00	600.00
S789	**4 DOLLARS** 1776. Liberty cap. *LIBERTAS CARIOR AURO* on blue-green seal. 2 border varieties.	1200.	1600.	2100.
S790	**2 DOLLARS** 1776. Flag, drum, gun and sword.	175.00	325.00	500.00

		VG	VF	Unc
S791	**3 DOLLARS** ND (1776). Crossed cannon.	375.00	600.00	—
S792	**4 DOLLARS** ND (1776). Frontiersman. 2 border varieties.	300.00	475.00	—
S793	**5 DOLLARS** ND (1776). Beehive. 2 border varieties.	325.00	500.00	—

		VG	VF	Unc
S794	**8 DOLLARS** ND (1776). Man holding a cane at r. 2 border varieties.	325.00	500.00	—
S795	**10 DOLLARS** ND (1776). Cannon.	400.00	600.00	—

1777 ISSUE

#S796-S805 black and red.

		VG	VF	Unc
S796	**2 DOLLARS** 1777. Floating jugs. *SI COLLIGIMUS FRANGIMUR* on blue-green seal. 4 border varieties.	325.00	650.00	—

No.	Description	VG	VF	Unc
S797	**3 Dollars** 1777. 9 border varieties w/typeset denomination design.	250.00	500.00	—
S798	**4 Dollars** 1777. Liberty cap. *LIBERTAS CARIOR AURO* on blue-green seal.	500.00	800.00	—
S799	**5 Dollars** 1777. Cannon. *ET DEUS OMNIPOTINCE* on blue-green seal. 9 border varieties.	200.00	400.00	—

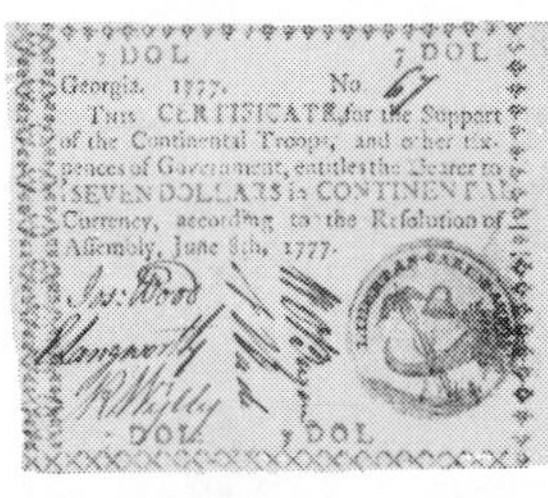

No.	Description	VG	VF	Unc
S800	**7 Dollars** 1777. Hand. *ULTIMA RADIO* on blue-green seal. 4 border varieties.	200.00	400.00	—
S801	**9 Dollars** 1777. Justice. *SUSTINE RECTUM* on blue-green seal. 4 border varieties.	200.00	400.00	—
S802	**11 Dollars** 1777. *SI COLLIGIMUS FRANGIMUR* on blue-green seal. 8 or more border varieties.	300.00	500.00	—
S803	**13 Dollars** 1777. Liberty cap. *LIBERTAS CARIOR AURO* on blue-green seal. 6 border varieties.	300.00	500.00	—
S804	**15 Dollars** 1777. Millstone on palm tree. *OPPRESSA SURGIT* on blue-green seal. 9 border varieties.	300.00	500.00	—

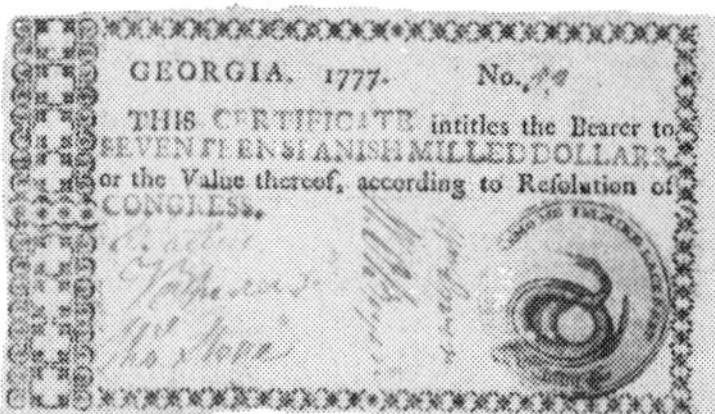

No.	Description	VG	VF	Unc
S805	**17 Dollars** 1777. Rattlesnake. *NEMO ME IMPUNE LACESSET* on blue-green seal. 6 border varieties.	350.00	500.00	—

Resolution of June 8, 1777

#S806-S814 black.

No.	Description	VG	VF	Unc
S806	**1/10 Dollar** 1777. Ship.	175.00	400.00	—
S807	**1/5 Dollar** 1777. Fenced house.	150.00	300.00	—
S808	**1/4 Dollar** 1777.	150.00	300.00	—
S809	**1/3 Dollar** 1777.	150.00	300.00	—
S810	**2/5 Dollar** 1777.	150.00	300.00	—
S811	**1/2 Dollar** 1777.	150.00	300.00	—
S812	**2/3 Dollar** 1777.	150.00	300.00	—
S813	**3/4 Dollar** 1777.	150.00	300.00	—
S814	**4/5 Dollar** 1777. 5 border varieties.	150.00	300.00	—

#S815-S830 black and red.

No.	Description	VG	VF	Unc
S815	**1 Dollar** 1777. Black in. Justice. *SUSTINE RECTUM* on red seal.	165.00	300.00	—
S816	**1 Dollar** 1777. Like #S815 but red *in.* 2 border varieties.	200.00	400.00	—
S817	**2 Dollars** 1777. Black *in.* Ship.	165.00	300.00	—
S818	**2 Dollars** 1777. Red *in.* Ship.	200.00	400.00	—
S819	**3 Dollars** 1777. Black *in.* Frontiersman.	165.00	300.00	—
S820	**3 Dollars** 1777. Red *in.* Frontiersman.	200.00	400.00	—
S821	**4 Dollars** 1777. Black *in.* Stag.	165.00	300.00	—
S822	**4 Dollars** 1777. Red *in.* Stag.	200.00	400.00	—
S823	**5 Dollars** 1777. Black *in.* Rattlesnake. *NEMO ME IMPUNE LACESSET* on dk. blue seal.	165.00	300.00	—
S824	**5 Dollars** 1777. Like #S823 but red *in.*	200.00	400.00	—
S825	**6 Dollars** 1777. Black *in.* Millstone on palm tree. *OPPRESSA SURGIT* on dk. blue seal.	165.00	300.00	—
S826	**6 Dollars** 1777. Like #S825 but red *in.*	200.00	400.00	—
S827	**7 Dollars** 1777. Black *in.* Liberty cap. *LIBERTAS CARIOR AURO* on dk. blue seal.	165.00	300.00	—
S828	**7 Dollars** 1777. Like #S827 but red *in.*	200.00	400.00	—
S829	**8 Dollars** 1777. Black *in.* Thirteen links. *C CONGRESS* on dk. blue seal.	165.00	300.00	—
S830	**8 Dollars** 1777. Like #S829 but red *in.*	200.00	400.00	—

Resolution of September 10, 1777

#S831-S833 black.

No.	Description	VG	VF	Unc
S831	**1/5 Dollar** 1777. 4 border varieties.	200.00	400.00	—
S832	**1/2 Dollar** 1777. 3 border varieties.	190.00	375.00	—
S833	**4/5 Dollar** 1777. 7 border varieties.	190.00	375.00	—

#S834-S841 black and red.

No.	Description	VG	VF	Unc
S834	**1 Dollar** 1777. Justice. *SUSTINE RECTUM* on red seal.	165.00	335.00	—
S835	**2 Dollars** 1777. Ship. Red seal.	165.00	335.00	—
S836	**3 Dollars** 1777. Frontiersman. Red seal.	165.00	335.00	—
S837	**4 Dollars** 1777. Stag. Red seal.	165.00	335.00	—
S838	**5 Dollars** 1777. Rattlesnake. *NEMO ME IMPUNE LACESSET* on dk. blue seal.	165.00	335.00	—
S839	**6 Dollars** 1777. Millstone on palm tree. *OPPRESSA SURGIT* on dk. blue seal.	165.00	335.00	—
S840	**7 Dollars** 1777. Liberty cap. *LIBERTAS CARIOR AURO* on dk. blue seal.	165.00	335.00	—
S841	**8 Dollars** 1777. Thirteen links. *C CONGRESS* on dk. blue seal.	165.00	335.00	—

1778 Issue

#S842-S844 black and red. Printer: W. Lancaster, Savannah.

		Good	Fine	XF
S842	**20 Dollars** 1778. Rattlesnake. *NEMO ME IMPUNE LACESSET* on greenish blue seal. 4 border varieties.	80.00	275.00	550.00
S843	**30 Dollars** 1778. Wild boar. *AUT MORS, AUT VICTORIA, LAETA* on greenish blue seal. 2 border varieties.	80.00	275.00	550.00

		Good	Fine	XF
S844	**40 Dollars** 1778. Dove and sword. *AUT PAX, AUT BELLUM, IN UTROQUE PARATUS* on greenish blue seal. 2 border varieties.	90.00	325.00	600.00

January 9, 1782 Resolve

		Good	Fine	XF
S845	**Various Amounts** 1782. Black.			
	a. First *C* in *confiscated* lower case.	—	—	—
	b. First *c* in *Confiscated* capitalized.	—	—	—

NOTE: No examples of #S845 are known officially signed.

NOTE: Denominations in pounds were inserted by hand.

1786 ISSUE

#S846-S851 black. Printed on Dutch paper. Wmk: *HONIG & ZOONEN*. Printer: John E. Smith, Augusta.

		GOOD	FINE	XF
S846	**6 PENCE** 16.10.1786.	500.00	750.00	—

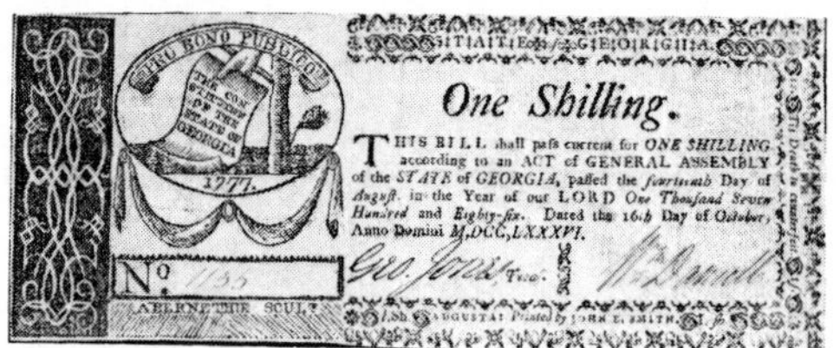

		GOOD	FINE	XF
S847	**1 SHILLING** 16.10.1786.	375.00	625.00	—
S848	**2 SHILLINGS 6 PENCE** 16.10.1786.	350.00	600.00	1100.
S849	**5 SHILLINGS** 16.10.1786.	250.00	500.00	1000.
S850	**10 SHILLINGS** 16.10.1786.	250.00	500.00	1000.

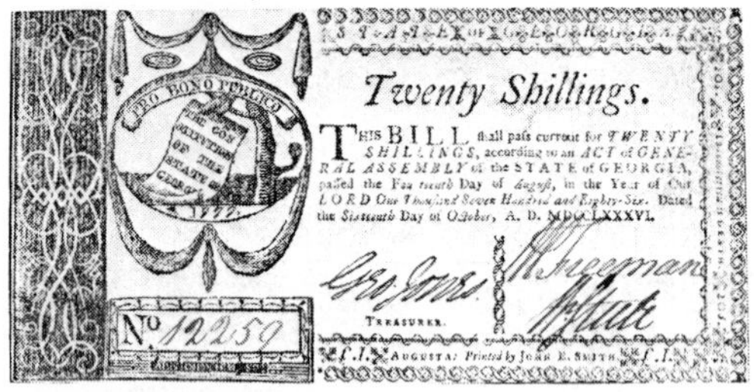

		GOOD	FINE	XF
S851	**20 SHILLINGS** 16.10.1786.	250.00	500.00	1000.

GEORGIA

CIVIL WAR

1862 ISSUE

#S852-S856 black and red. Engraved by Douglas.

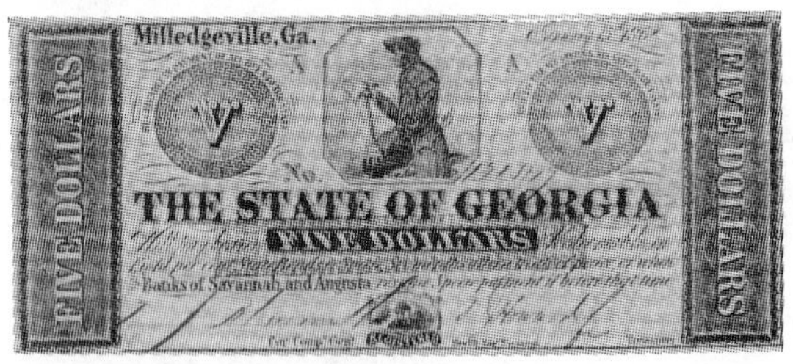

		VG	VF	UNC
S852	**5 DOLLARS** 15.1.1862. J. Oglethorpe in military dress at upper ctr. Back black. Treasury Seal. Printer: H. Engr.	12.50	20.00	35.00

		VG	VF	UNC
S853	**10 DOLLARS** 15.1.1862 Ceres holding grain at upper ctr., black Treasury Seal.	15.00	20.00	35.00
S854	**20 DOLLARS** 15.1.1862. Ceres holding grain at ctr., black Treasury Seal.	25.00	35.00	60.00

		VG	VF	UNC
S855	**50 DOLLARS** 15.1.1862. Justice at l. and r., Gov. Joseph E. Brown at l. and ctr. r., Ceres holding grain at ctr. 2 Treasury Seals.	25.00	40.00	60.00

		VG	VF	UNC
S856	**100 DOLLARS** 15.1.1862. Sailor at l. and r., Ceres holding grain at ctr. 2 Treasury Seals.	35.00	45.00	60.00

1863-64 ISSUES

#S857-S860 black. Engraved by R. H. Howell. Red or green Treasury Seal on back.

#S857

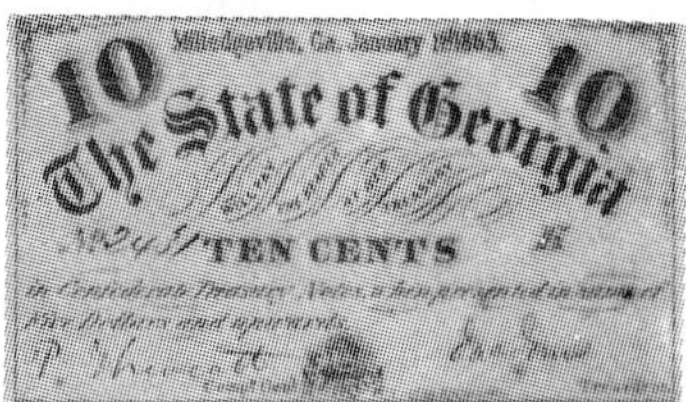

#S858

		VG	VF	UNC
S857	**5 CENTS** 1.1.1863.	9.00	12.50	20.00
S858	**10 CENTS** 1.1.1863.	9.00	12.50	20.00
S859	**15 CENTS** 1.1.1863.	20.00	35.00	50.00
S860	**20 CENTS** 1.1.1863.	60.00	130.00	180.00

#S861-S866 black. Engraver: Howell. Red or green Treasury Seal on back.

		VG	VF	UNC
S861	**25 CENTS** 1.1.1863.	9.00	12.50	20.00
S862	**50 CENTS** 1863-64. Red Treasury Seal. 3 workmen at upper ctr.			
	a. 1.1.1863.	9.00	15.00	20.00
	b. 1.1.1864	50.00	100.00	175.00

		VG	VF	UNC
S863	**1 DOLLAR** 1.1.1863; 1.1.1864. Green Treasury Seal. Steam passenger train at upper ctr.	20.00	30.00	85.00

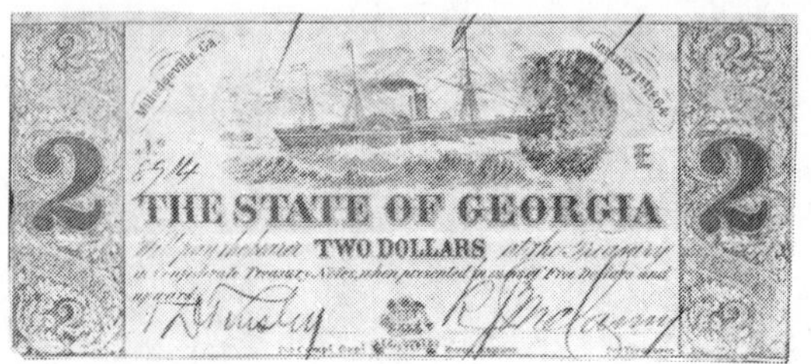

		VG	VF	UNC
S864	**2 DOLLARS** 1.1.1863; 1.1.1864. Green Treasury Seal. Steamship at upper ctr.	20.00	30.00	80.00

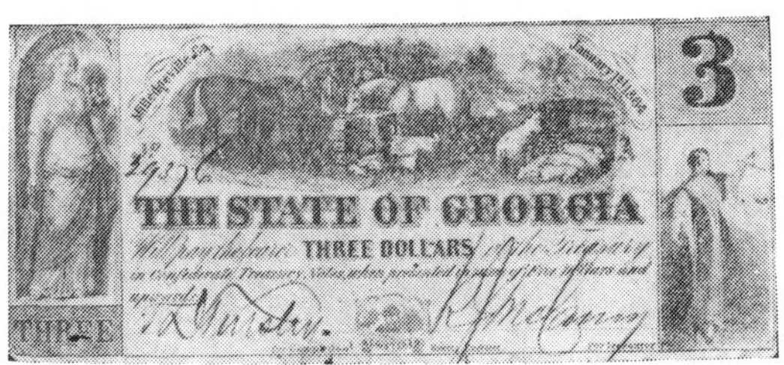

		VG	VF	UNC
S865	**3 DOLLARS** 1863-64. Standing Minerva at l., horses drinking at upper ctr., Justice holding scales at lower r.			
	a. 1.1.1863.	650.00	1000.	2500.
	b. 1.1.1864.	35.00	50.00	100.00
S866	**4 DOLLARS** 1863-64. Blacks picking cotton at lower l., Moneta reclining on chest at top ctr., black carrying sheaf at lower r.			
	a. 1.1.1863.	750.00	1200.	3500.
	b. 1.1.1864.	40.00	65.00	100.00

#S867-S869 engraved by Howell, Savannah. "Payable to State and Western & Atlantic Railroad."

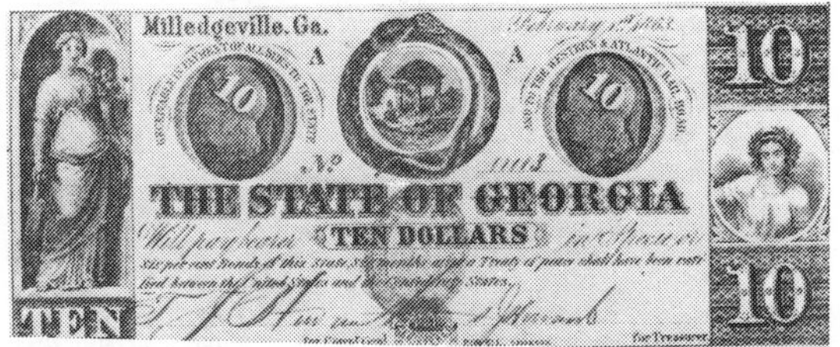

		VG	VF	UNC
S867	**10 DOLLARS** 1.2.1863. Black. Red Treasury Seal. Minerva at l., state arms within coil of rattlesnake at ctr., Ceres at r.	15.00	25.00	40.00

#S868-S869 black and red. Black Treasury Seal on back.

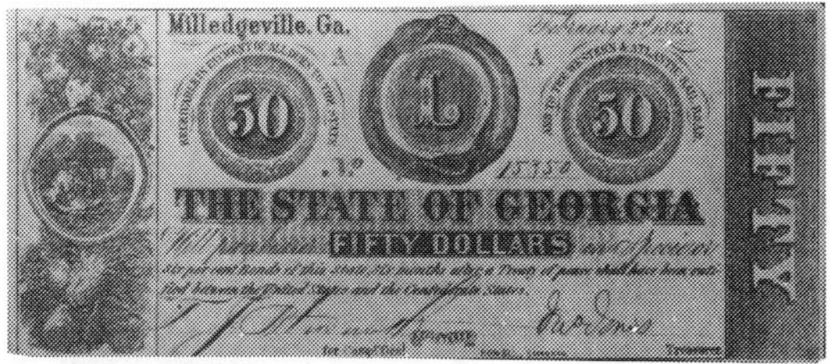

		VG	VF	UNC
S868	**50 DOLLARS** 2.2.1863. State arms at l., *L* at ctr. within coil of rattlesnake.	15.00	30.00	40.00

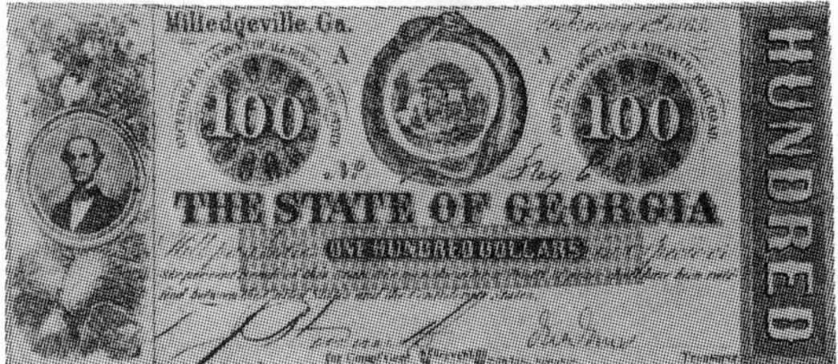

		VG	VF	UNC
S869	**100 DOLLARS** 2.1.1863. Portr. Gov. J. E. Brown at l., state arms within coil of rattlesnake at ctr.	20.00	35.00	50.00

ACT OF 25.12.1863; 1864 ISSUE

#S870-S875 redeemable on Dec. 25, 1864.

Moneta reclining on chest at top ctr. Engraved by Howell.

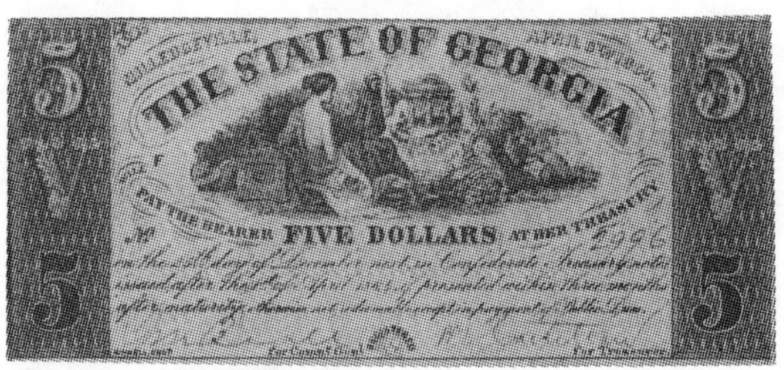

		VG	VF	UNC
S870	**5 DOLLARS** 6.4.1864. Black. Green Treasury Seal.	12.50	20.00	35.00
S871	**10 DOLLARS** 6.4.1864. Black. Green Treasury Seal.	15.00	25.00	45.00
S872	**20 DOLLARS** 6.4.1864. Black. Green Treasury Seal.	20.00	30.00	50.00
S873	**50 DOLLARS** 6.4.1864. Black and red.	25.00	40.00	75.00
S874	**100 DOLLARS** 6.4.1864. Black and red.	25.00	40.00	85.00

		VG	VF	UNC
S875	**500 DOLLARS** 6.4.1864. Black and red. Similar to #S870 but w/standing Minerva at l.	300.00	450.00	1000.

1865 ISSUE

#S876-S878 engraved by Howell. "Payable to State and Western & Atlantic Railroad."

		VG	VF	UNC
S876	**5 DOLLARS** 15.1.1865. Similar to #S852.	25.00	40.00	65.00

#S877 and S878 black Treasury Seal on back.

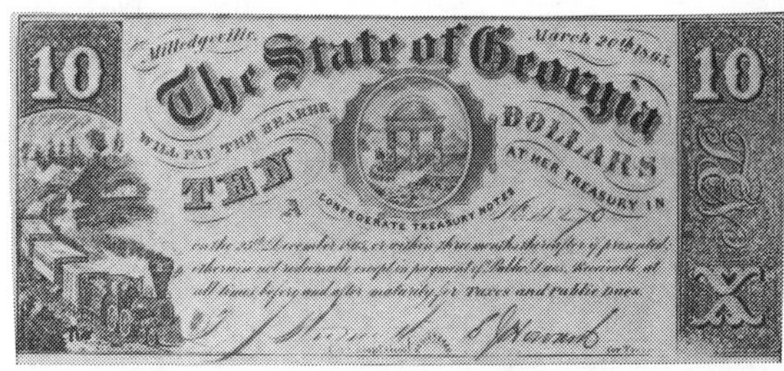

S877	**10 DOLLARS** 20.3.1865. Black. Steam train at lower l., state arms at ctr.	20.00	30.00	50.00

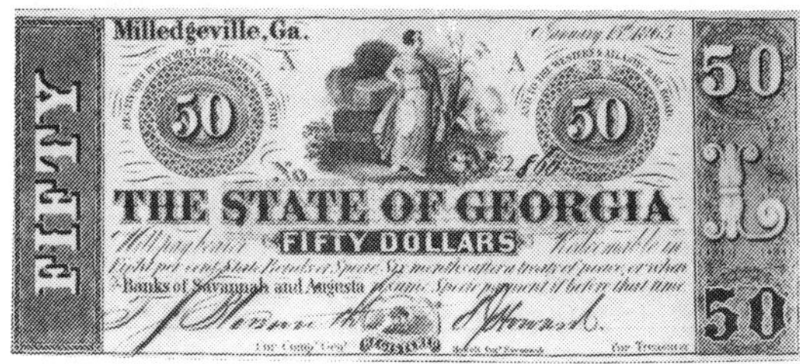

		VG	VF	UNC
S878	**50 DOLLARS** 15.1.1865. Black and red. Ceres holding grain at top ctr.	20.00	35.00	50.00

KANSAS

POST CIVIL WAR

Issued by the state to settle claims resulting from the Indian and Civil Wars.

1867 UNION MILITARY SCRIP ISSUE

#S881-S886 black. Uniface. Printer: CBNC.

		GOOD	FINE	XF
S881	**1 DOLLAR** 1.6.1867. Farmer plowing w/horses at upper l., allegorical Peace w/doves at ctr.	50.00	75.00	125.00

		Good	Fine	XF
S882	**5 Dollars** 1.6.1867. Union soldier w/horse talking w/blacksmiths at upper l.	50.00	75.00	125.00

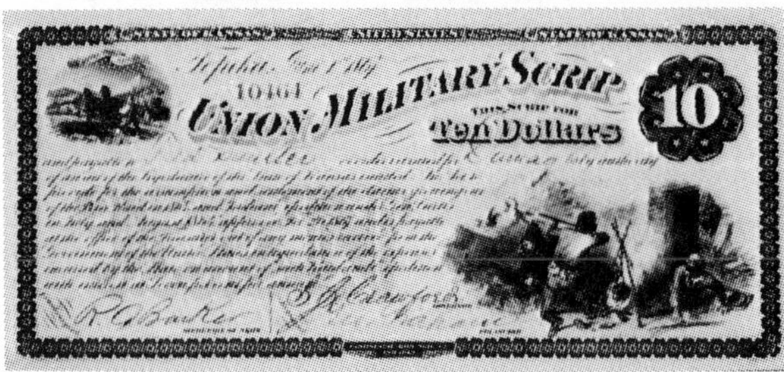

		Good	Fine	XF
S883	**10 Dollars** 1.6.1867. Farmer plowing w/horses at upper l., soldiers in action at lower r.	50.00	75.00	125.00

		Good	Fine	XF
S884	**20 Dollars** 1.6.1867. Farmer plowing w/horses at upper l., Liberty holding flag at ctr.	75.00	100.00	200.00

		Good	Fine	XF
S885	**50 Dollars** 1.6.1867. Farmer plowing w/horses at upper l., Indian on horseback hunting buffalo at lower l.	75.00	100.00	250.00

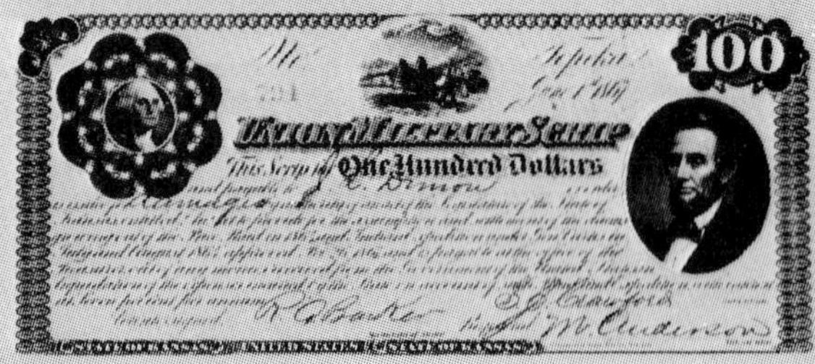

		Good	Fine	XF
S886	**100 Dollars** 1.6.1867. Portr. G. Washington at upper l., farmer plowing w/horses at top ctr., portr. A. Lincoln at r.	75.00	110.00	250.00

Louisiana

Spanish Administration

1790s Issue

		Good	Fine	XF
S886A	**25 Pesos** 24.6.1795. Black. Arms at upper ctr. Figures in 4 corners. Unsigned remainder.	—	Rare	—

Louisiana

Civil War

Act of January 23, 1862 Issue

#S887-S890 black. Seated Ceres at top ctr. Engraved by Douglas, New Orleans.

#S887, S889 printed on the backs of notes of The Commercial & Agricultural Bank of Texas.

		VG	VF	Unc
S887	**1 Dollar** 24.2.1862. Red protector: *ONE*. Printed on backs of various peso or dollar notes.	25.00	40.00	70.00
S888	**1 Dollar** 24.2.1862. Similar to #S887 but blue protector: *ONE*. Printed on backs of New Orleans notes.	25.00	35.00	65.00

#S889 and S890 printer: B. Duncan, Columbia, S.C.

		VG	VF	Unc
S889	**2 Dollars** 24.2.1862. Red protector: *TWO*. Printed on backs of various peso or dollar notes.	25.00	40.00	75.00
S890	**2 Dollars** 24.2.1862. Similar to #S889 but blue protector: *TWO*. Printed on backs of New Orleans notes.	20.00	35.00	60.00

Act of February 8, 1863 Issue

#S891-S893 w/o vignettes. Printed on the backs of The Exchange Office of Holly Springs, Mississippi Notes.

#S891 and S892 printer: B. Duncan, Columbia, S.C.

		VG	VF	Unc
S891	**1 Dollar** 24.2.1862. Black and green. Printed on backs of 5 dollar notes.	15.00	25.00	40.00

		VG	VF	UNC
S892	**2 DOLLARS** 24.2.1862. Black and green. Printed on backs of 10 or 20 dollar notes.	15.00	25.00	40.00
S893	**3 DOLLARS** 24.2.1862. Black and green. Printed on backs of 10 or 20 dollar notes.	15.00	25.00	50.00

		VG	VF	UNC
S894	**5 DOLLARS** 10.10.1862. Black. Vignette of the Confederacy striking down the Union above lazy *5* at ctr. Back green. Baton Rouge. Printer: B. Duncan, Columbia, S.C.	20.00	35.00	50.00

		VG	VF	UNC
S895	**5 DOLLARS** 10.3.1863. Black. Similar to #S894 but w/o lazy *5* at bottom ctr. Shreveport.	20.00	35.00	50.00

		VG	VF	UNC
S896	**20 DOLLARS** 10.3.1863. Red and black. Gen. P. G. T. Beauregard at ctr., wild man at r. Back blue.	30.00	50.00	125.00

		VG	VF	UNC
S897	**50 DOLLARS** 10.3.1863. Black. Gen. L. Polk at ctr., seated Liberty at lower r. Back green.	30.00	50.00	100.00

		VG	VF	UNC
S898	**100 DOLLARS** 10.3.1863. Black. Portr. Gov. T. Moore at upper l., State Capitol bldg. at top ctr., seated Liberty at lower r. Woman seated at ctr. on back.	35.00	65.00	125.00

1864 ISSUES

		VG	VF	UNC
S899	**25 CENTS** 1.3.1864. Black.			
	a. Uniface.	35.00	60.00	100.00
	b. Printed on backs of New Orleans notes.	35.00	60.00	100.00
	c. Printed on backs of bills of exchange.	35.00	65.00	110.00
S900	**50 CENTS** 1.3.1864. Black.			
	a. Uniface.	35.00	60.00	100.00
	b. Printed on backs of New Orleans notes.	15.00	20.00	40.00
	c. Printed on backs of bills of exchange.	15.00	20.00	40.00

#S901-S907 printer: South Western Print. Uniface. Also exist printed on backs of New Orleans notes.

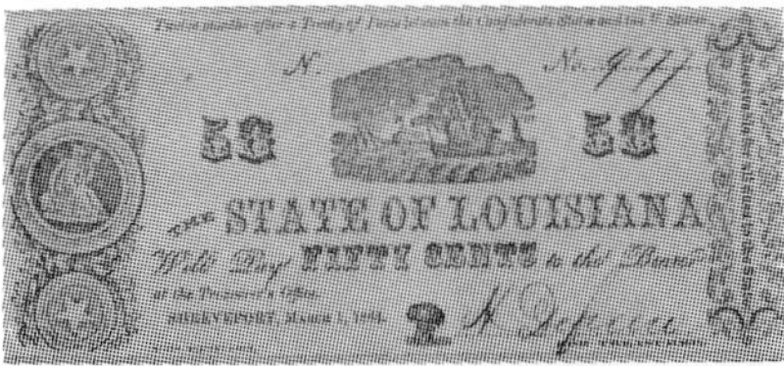

		VG	VF	UNC
S901	**50 CENTS** 1.3.1864. Seated Liberty at l., 3 ships at ctr.	10.00	15.00	25.00

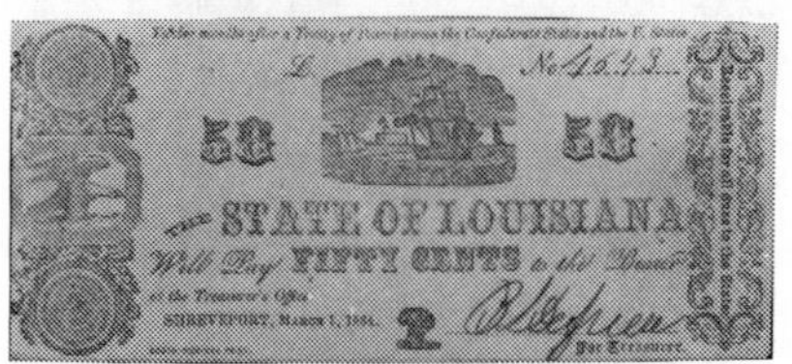

		VG	VF	UNC
S902	**50 CENTS** 1.3.1864. Black. Eagle at l., 3 ships at ctr.	10.00	15.00	30.00
S903	**1 DOLLAR** 1.3.1864. Black. Ship in oval at l.	10.00	15.00	30.00

		VG	VF	UNC
S904	**1 DOLLAR** 1.3.1864. Black. Standing Minerva at l., steamship at upper ctr.	10.00	15.00	30.00
S905	**1 DOLLAR** 1.3.1864. Black. Ship at l., Commerce leaning on bales of cotton at upper ctr.	10.00	15.00	30.00
S906	**1 DOLLAR** 1.3.1864. Black. Statue of Washington at l., Commerce leaning on bales of cotton at ctr.	10.00	15.00	30.00
S907	**1 DOLLAR** 1.3.1864. Black. Steam locomotive at l., sailing vessel at ctr.	8.00	12.00	25.00

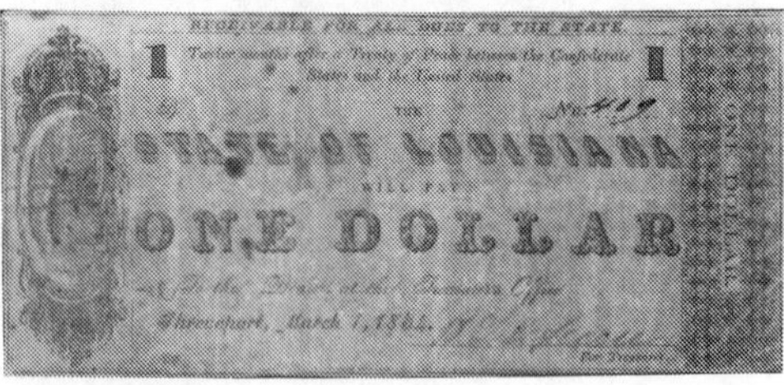

		VG	VF	UNC
S907A	**1 DOLLAR** 1.3.1864. Black. Passenger train in oval at l.	10.00	15.00	30.00

LOUISIANA

POST CIVIL WAR

1866 ISSUE

#S908-S910 black on green unpt. Various handwritten dates. Printer: ABNC.

		VG	VF	UNC
S908	**5 DOLLARS** 20.12.1866. Maiden's head at l. and r., Governor at r. Various handwritten dates 1866. Back green.	60.00	85.00	200.00
S909	**10 DOLLARS** 1.5.1866. G. Washington at l., dog on chest at top ctr., cotton ball at lower r.	150.00	200.00	325.00

		VG	VF	UNC
S910	**20 DOLLARS** 20.4.1866; 26.11.1866. Ships at dockside at upper l. ctr., portr. Thomas Jefferson at lower r. Various handwritten dates 1866. Back green.			
	a. Issued note.	125.00	175.00	250.00
	b. Punched hole cancelled.	100.00	150.00	200.00

MARYLAND

COLONIAL

Pound Sterling System

1733 ISSUE

#S911-S917 black. Printed on fine laid paper w/wmk: *MARYLAND*. Handwritten dates.

		VG	VF	UNC
S911	**1 SHILLING** 1733.	—	—	—

		VG	VF	UNC
S912	**1 SHILLING 6 PENCE** 1733.	—	—	—
S913	**2 SHILLINGS 6 PENCE** 1733.	—	—	—
S914	**5 SHILLINGS** 1733.	—	—	—
S915	**10 SHILLINGS** 1733.	—	—	—
S916	**15 SHILLINGS** 1733.	—	—	—
S917	**20 SHILLINGS** 1733.	—	—	—

NOTE: Signed notes of #S911-S917 are extremely rare.

1740 ISSUE

#S918-S924 black.

		VG	VF	UNC
S918	**1 SHILLING** 2.6.1740.	—	—	—
S919	**1 SHILLING 6 PENCE** 2.6.1740.	—	—	—
S920	**2 SHILLINGS 6 PENCE** 2.6.1740.	—	—	—
S921	**5 SHILLINGS** 2.6.1740.	—	—	—
S922	**10 SHILLINGS** 2.6.1740.	—	—	—
S923	**15 SHILLINGS** 2.6.1740.	—	—	—
S924	**20 SHILLINGS** 2.6.1740.	—	—	—

1748 ISSUE

#S925-S931 black. W/handwritten: *NEW BILL* on face.

		VG	VF	UNC
S925	**1 SHILLING** 1.10.1748.	—	—	—
S926	**1 SHILLING 6 PENCE** 1.10.1748.	—	—	—
S927	**2 SHILLINGS 6 PENCE** 1.10.1748.	—	—	—
S928	**5 SHILLINGS** 1.10.1748.	—	—	—
S929	**10 SHILLINGS** 1.10.1748.	—	—	—
S930	**15 SHILLINGS** 1.10.1748.	—	—	—
S931	**20 SHILLINGS** 1.10.1748.	—	—	—

1751 ISSUE

#S932-S938 black. Like #S925-S931 except the handwritten date is changed.

		VG	VF	UNC
S932	**1 SHILLING** 6.4.1751.	—	—	—
S933	**1 SHILLING 6 PENCE** 6.4.1751.	—	—	—
S934	**2 SHILLINGS 6 PENCE** 6.4.1751.	—	—	—
S935	**5 SHILLINGS** 6.4.1751.	—	—	—
S936	**10 SHILLINGS** 6.4.1751.	—	—	—
S937	**15 SHILLINGS** 6.4.1751.	—	—	—
S938	**20 SHILLINGS** 6.4.1751.	—	—	—

1756 ISSUE

#S939-S947 black. Printer: Jonas Green, Annapolis.

		VG	VF	UNC
S939	**6 PENCE** 14.7.1756.	—	—	—

		VG	VF	UNC
S940	**1 SHILLING** 14.7.1756.	—	—	—
S941	**1 SHILLING 6 PENCE** 14.7.1756.	—	—	—
S942	**2 SHILLINGS** 14.7.1756.	—	—	—
S943	**2 SHILLINGS 6 PENCE** 14.7.1756.	—	—	—
S945	**10 SHILLINGS** 14.7.1756.	—	—	—
S946	**15 SHILLINGS** 14.7.1756.	—	—	—
S947	**20 SHILLINGS** 14.7.1756.	—	—	—

1767 ISSUE

Dollar System

#S948-S958 black. Printed on thick paper. Printer: Jonas Green.

		VG	VF	UNC
S948	**1/9 DOLLAR** 1.1.1767.	45.00	110.00	—
S949	**1/6 DOLLAR** 1.1.1767.	45.00	110.00	—
S950	**2/9 DOLLAR** 1.1.1767.	45.00	110.00	—
S951	**1/3 DOLLAR** 1.1.1767.	45.00	110.00	—
S952	**1/2 DOLLAR** 1.1.1767.	45.00	110.00	—

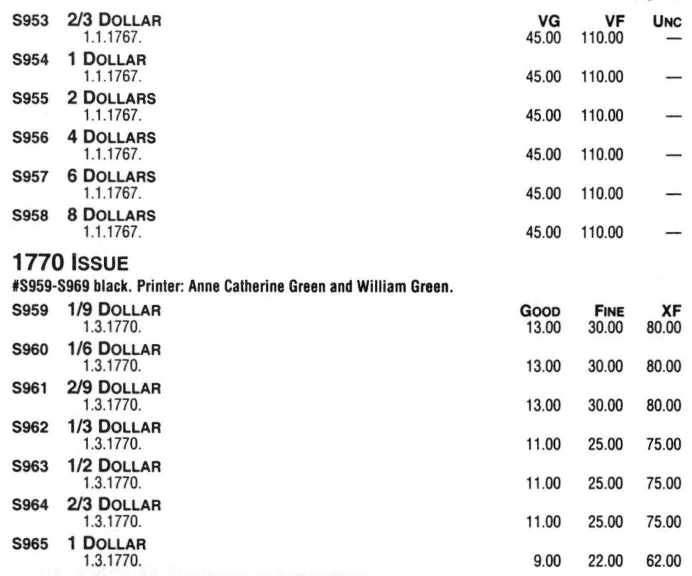

		VG	VF	UNC
S953	**2/3 DOLLAR** 1.1.1767.	45.00	110.00	—
S954	**1 DOLLAR** 1.1.1767.	45.00	110.00	—
S955	**2 DOLLARS** 1.1.1767.	45.00	110.00	—
S956	**4 DOLLARS** 1.1.1767.	45.00	110.00	—
S957	**6 DOLLARS** 1.1.1767.	45.00	110.00	—
S958	**8 DOLLARS** 1.1.1767.	45.00	110.00	—

1770 ISSUE

#S959-S969 black. Printer: Anne Catherine Green and William Green.

		GOOD	FINE	XF
S959	**1/9 DOLLAR** 1.3.1770.	13.00	30.00	80.00
S960	**1/6 DOLLAR** 1.3.1770.	13.00	30.00	80.00
S961	**2/9 DOLLAR** 1.3.1770.	13.00	30.00	80.00
S962	**1/3 DOLLAR** 1.3.1770.	11.00	25.00	75.00
S963	**1/2 DOLLAR** 1.3.1770.	11.00	25.00	75.00
S964	**2/3 DOLLAR** 1.3.1770.	11.00	25.00	75.00
S965	**1 DOLLAR** 1.3.1770.	9.00	22.00	62.00

		GOOD	FINE	XF
S966	**2 DOLLARS** 1.3.1770.	9.00	22.00	62.00
S967	**4 DOLLARS** 1.3.1770.	9.00	22.00	62.00
S968	**6 DOLLARS** 1.3.1770.	9.00	22.00	62.00
S969	**8 DOLLARS** 1.3.1770.	9.00	22.00	62.00

1774 ISSUE

#S970-S980 black. Similar to #S959-S969 but thinner paper containing mica flakes. Printer: Anne Catherine Green and Frederick Green.

		GOOD	FINE	XF
S970	**1/9 DOLLAR** 10.4.1774.	16.00	38.00	90.00
S971	**1/6 DOLLAR** 10.4.1774.	16.00	38.00	90.00
S972	**2/9 DOLLAR** 10.4.1774.	16.00	38.00	90.00

		GOOD	FINE	XF
S973	**1/3 DOLLAR** 10.4.1774.	14.00	35.00	85.00
S974	**1/2 DOLLAR** 10.4.1774.	14.00	35.00	85.00
S975	**2/3 DOLLAR** 10.4.1774.	14.00	35.00	85.00
S976	**1 DOLLAR** 10.4.1774.	13.00	30.00	78.00
S977	**2 DOLLARS** 10.4.1774.	13.00	30.00	75.00
S978	**4 DOLLARS** 10.4.1774.	13.00	30.00	78.00

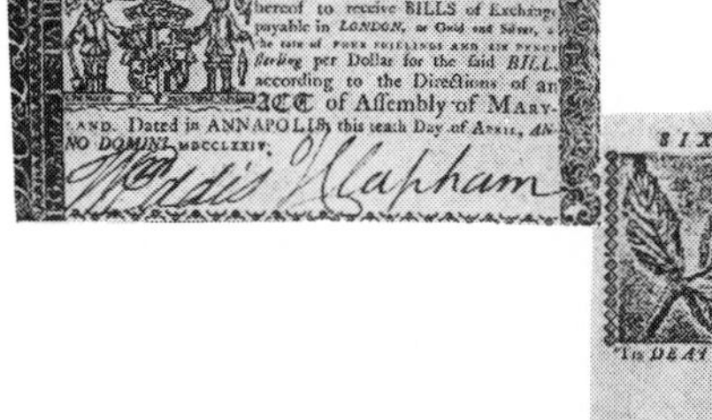

		GOOD	FINE	XF
S979	**6 DOLLARS** 10.4.1774.	13.00	30.00	78.00
S980	**8 DOLLARS** 10.4.1774.	13.00	30.00	78.00

1775 FIRST ISSUE

#S981-S988 black. Printer: Frederick Green.

		GOOD	FINE	XF
S981	**2/3 DOLLAR** 26.7.1775.	275.00	625.00	—
S982	**1 DOLLAR** 26.7.1775.	275.00	625.00	—

		GOOD	FINE	XF
S983	**1 1/3 DOLLARS** 26.7.1775.	275.00	625.00	—

		GOOD	FINE	XF
S984	**1 2/3 DOLLARS** 26.7.1775.	275.00	625.00	—
S985	**2 2/3 DOLLARS** 26.7.1775.	275.00	625.00	—
S986	**4 DOLLARS** 26.7.1775.	275.00	625.00	—

		GOOD	FINE	XF
S987	**8 DOLLARS** 26.7.1775.	275.00	625.00	—
S988	**16 DOLLARS** 26.7.1775.	275.00	625.00	—

1775 SECOND ISSUE

#S989-S1000 black. W/*SUB CLYPEO* on emblem w/shield at ctr. on back. Printer: Frederick Green.

		VG	VF	UNC
S989	**1/9 DOLLAR** 7.12.1775.	25.00	70.00	—
S990	**1/6 DOLLAR** 7.12.1775.	25.00	70.00	—
S991	**1/3 DOLLAR** 7.12.1775.	25.00	70.00	—
S992	**1/2 DOLLAR** 7.12.1775.	25.00	70.00	—
S993	**2/3 DOLLAR** 7.12.1775.	25.00	70.00	—
S994	**1 DOLLAR** 7.12.1775.	25.00	70.00	—
S995	**1 1/3 DOLLARS** 7.12.1775.	25.00	70.00	—
S996	**2 DOLLARS** 7.12.1775.	25.00	70.00	—
S997	**2 2/3 DOLLARS** 7.12.1775.	25.00	70.00	—
S998	**4 DOLLARS** 7.12.1775.	25.00	70.00	—
S999	**6 DOLLARS** 7.12.1775.	25.00	70.00	—

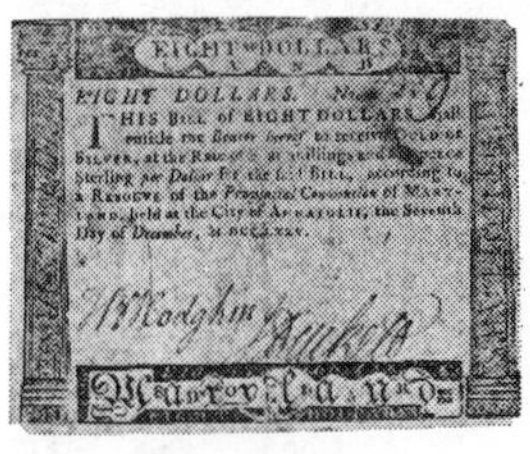

		VG	VF	UNC
S1000	**8 DOLLARS** 7.12.1775.	25.00	70.00	—

MARYLAND

STATE

1776 ISSUE

#S1001-S1012 black.

		VG	VF	UNC
S1001	**1/9 DOLLAR** 14.8.1776.	35.00	75.00	—
S1002	**1/6 DOLLAR** 14.8.1776.	35.00	75.00	—
S1003	**1/3 DOLLAR** 14.8.1776.	35.00	75.00	—
S1004	**1/2 DOLLAR** 14.8.1776.	35.00	75.00	—
S1005	**2/3 DOLLAR** 14.8.1776.	35.00	75.00	—
S1006	**1 DOLLAR** 14.8.1776.	35.00	75.00	—
S1007	**1 1/3 DOLLARS** 14.8.1776.	35.00	75.00	—

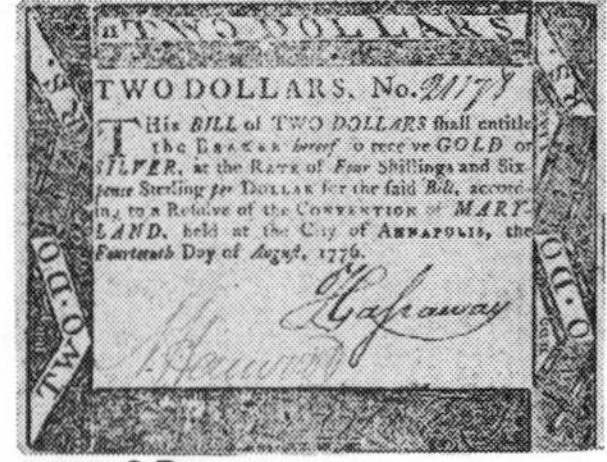

		VG	VF	UNC
S1008	**2 DOLLARS** 14.8.1776.	35.00	75.00	—
S1009	**2 2/3 DOLLARS** 14.8.1776.	35.00	75.00	—
S1010	**4 DOLLARS** 14.8.1776.	35.00	75.00	—
S1011	**6 DOLLARS** 14.8.1776.	35.00	75.00	—
S1012	**8 DOLLARS** 14.8.1776.	35.00	75.00	—

1780 FIRST ISSUE

#S1013-S1024 black. State arms on back. Printer: Frederick Green.

		VG	VF	UNC
S1013	**1/9 DOLLAR** 8.6.1780.	—	—	—
S1014	**1/6 DOLLAR** 8.6.1780.	—	—	—
S1015	**1/3 DOLLAR** 8.6.1780.	—	—	—
S1016	**1/2 DOLLAR** 8.6.1780.	—	—	—
S1017	**2/3 DOLLAR** 8.6.1780.	—	—	—
S1018	**1 DOLLAR** 8.6.1780.	—	—	—
S1019	**1 1/3 DOLLARS** 8.6.1780.	—	—	—
S1020	**2 DOLLARS** 8.6.1780.	—	—	—
S1021	**2 2/3 DOLLARS** 8.6.1780.	—	—	—
S1022	**4 DOLLARS** 8.6.1780.	—	—	—
S1023	**6 DOLLARS** 8.6.1780.	—	—	—
S1024	**8 DOLLARS** 8.6.1780.	—	—	—

1780 SECOND ISSUE

#S1025-S1032 black. Back black and red. Mica flaked paper. Wmk: *UNITED STATES*. Printer: Hall and Sellers, PA.

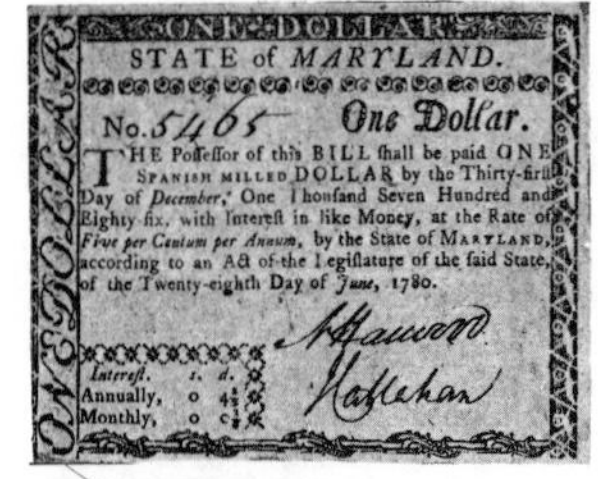

		VG	VF	UNC
S1025	**1 DOLLAR** 28.6.1780.	140.00	400.00	675.00
S1026	**2 DOLLARS** 28.6.1780.	140.00	400.00	675.00
S1027	**3 DOLLARS** 28.6.1780.	140.00	400.00	675.00
S1028	**4 DOLLARS** 28.6.1780.	140.00	400.00	675.00
S1029	**5 DOLLARS** 28.6.1780.	140.00	400.00	675.00
S1030	**7 DOLLARS** 28.6.1780.	140.00	400.00	675.00

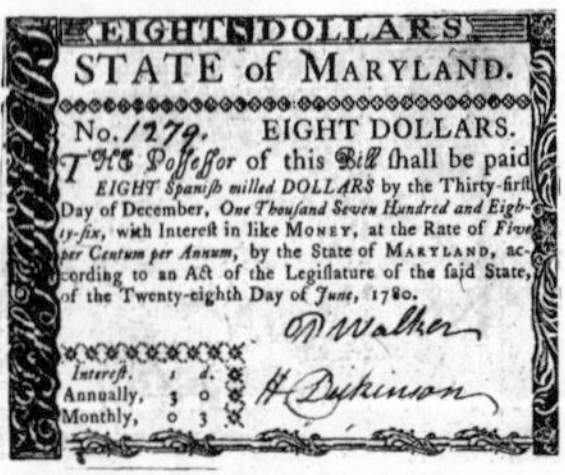

		VG	VF	UNC
S1031	**8 DOLLARS** 28.6.1780.	140.00	400.00	675.00
S1032	**20 DOLLARS** 28.6.1780.	140.00	400.00	675.00

1780 Third Issue

#S1033-S1036 black. Printer: Frederick Green.

		Good	Fine	XF
S1033	**1/15 Dollar** 17.10.1780.	—	—	—
S1034	**1/10 Dollar** 17.10.1780.	—	—	—
S1035	**1/6 Dollar** 17.10.1780.	—	—	—
S1036	**1/5 Dollar** 17.10.1780.	—	—	—

1781 First Issue

#S1037-S1044 black and red. Printer: Frederick Green.

		VG	VF	Unc
S1037	**1 Shilling** 10.5.1781.	400.00	800.00	—
S1038	**1 Shilling 6 Pence** 10.5.1781.	400.00	800.00	—
S1039	**2 Shillings 6 Pence** 10.5.1781.	400.00	800.00	—
S1040	**5 Shillings** 10.5.1781.	400.00	800.00	—
S1041	**7 Shillings 6 Pence** 10.5.1781.	400.00	800.00	—
S1042	**15 Shillings** 10.5.1781.	400.00	800.00	—
S1043	**30 Shillings** 10.5.1781.	400.00	800.00	—
S1044	**3 Pounds** 10.5.1781.	400.00	800.00	—

1781 Second Issue

#S1045-S1048 black.

		Good	Fine	XF
S1045	**3 Pence** 8.8.1781.	—	—	—
S1046	**4 Pence** 8.8.1781.	—	—	—
S1047	**6 Pence** 8.8.1781.	—	—	—
S1048	**9 Pence** 8.8.1781.	—	—	—

Massachusetts

Colonial

Pound Sterling System

1690 Issue

#S1051-S1054 black. Colony seal w/Indian.

		Good	Fine	XF
S1051	**5 Shillings** 10.12.1690.	—	—	—
S1052	**10 Shillings** 10.12.1690.	—	—	—
S1053	**20 Shillings** 10.12.1690.	—	—	—
S1054	**5 Pounds** 10.12.1690.	—	—	—
S1055	**2 Shillings** 3.2.1690.	—	—	—
S1056	**2 Shillings 6 Pence** 3.2.1690.	—	—	—
S1057	**3 Pounds** 3.2.1690.	—	—	—
S1058	**10 Pounds** 3.2.1690.	—	—	—

NOTE: 20 SHILLINGS notes are altered 2 SHILLINGS 6 PENCE notes.

1702 Issue

#S1059-S1066 black. Each denomination has differently shaped arms. Backs w/red scroll. Printer: John Allen.

		Good	Fine	XF
S1059	**2 Shillings** 21.11.1702. 2 varieties.	—	—	—
S1060	**2 Shillings 6 Pence** 21.11.1702. 2 varieties.	—	—	—
S1061	**5 Shillings** 21.11.1702.	—	—	—
S1062	**10 Shillings** 21.11.1702.	—	—	—
S1063	**20 Shillings** 21.11.1702. 3 varieties.	—	—	—
S1064	**40 Shillings** 21.11.1702.	—	—	—
S1065	**3 Pounds** 21.11.1702.	—	—	—
S1066	**5 Pounds** 21.11.1702.	—	—	—

1708 Issue

#S1067-S1076 black. Red ovpt: *AR* (Anna Regina). Backs w/red scroll.

		Good	Fine	XF
S1067	**2 Shillings** 21.11.1708.	—	—	—
S1068	**2 Shillings 6 Pence** 21.11.1708.	—	—	—
S1069	**3 Shillings** 21.11.1708.	—	—	—
S1070	**3 Shillings 6 Pence** 21.11.1708.	—	—	—
S1071	**5 Shillings** 21.11.1708.	—	—	—
S1072	**10 Shillings** 21.11.1708.	—	—	—
S1073	**20 Shillings** 21.11.1708.	—	—	—
S1074	**40 Shillings** 21.11.1708.	—	—	—

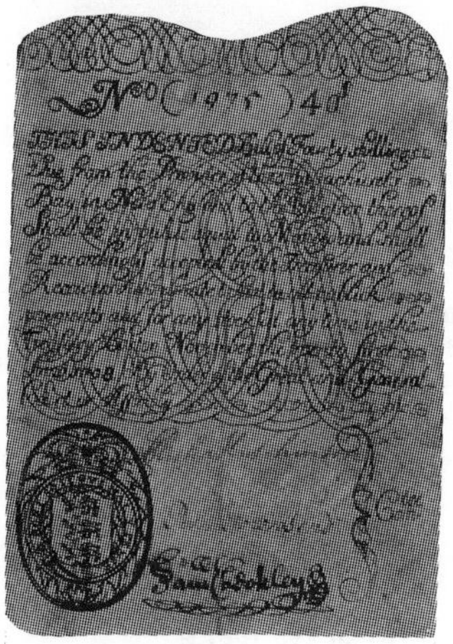

NOTE: Illustration of #S1074 is that of a counterfeit.

		Good	Fine	XF
S1075	**3 Pounds** 21.11.1708.	—	—	—
S1076	**5 Pounds** 21.11.1708.	—	—	—

1710 Issue

#S1077-S1088 black. Red ovpt: *AR* mirrored monogram.

		Good	Fine	XF
S1077	**2 Shillings** 31.5.1710.	—	—	—
S1078	**2 Shillings 6 Pence** 31.5.1710.	—	—	—
S1079	**3 Shillings** 31.5.1710.	—	—	—
S1080	**3 Shillings 6 Pence** 31.5.1710.	—	—	—

#S1081-S1088 red scroll on back.

		Good	Fine	XF
S1081	**4 Shillings** 31.5.1710.	—	—	—
S1082	**5 Shillings** 31.5.1710.	—	—	—
S1083	**10 Shillings** 31.5.1710.	—	—	—
S1084	**20 Shillings** 31.5.1710.	—	—	—
S1085	**40 Shillings** 31.5.1710.	—	—	—
S1086	**50 Shillings** 31.5.1710.	—	—	—
S1087	**3 Pounds** 31.5.1710.	—	—	—
S1088	**5 Pounds** 31.5.1710.	—	—	—

1711 Redated Issue

#S1089-S1096 black. Red ovpt: *AR* mirrored monogram. *1711* engraved r. of sign.

		Good	Fine	XF
S1089	**4 Shillings** 1711 (- old date 31.5.1710).	—	—	—
S1090	**5 Shillings** 1711 (- old date 31.5.1710).	—	—	—
S1091	**10 Shillings** 1711 (- old date 31.5.1710).	—	—	—
S1092	**20 Shillings** 1711 (- old date 31.5.1710).	—	—	—
S1093	**40 Shillings** 1711 (- old date 31.5.1710).	—	—	—
S1094	**50 Shillings** 1711 (- old date 31.5.1710).	—	—	—
S1095	**3 Pounds** 1711 (- old date 31.5.1710).	—	—	—
S1096	**5 Pounds** 1711 (- old date 31.5.1710).	—	—	—

1713 ISSUE

#S1097-S1104 black. Nature leaf print on back.

		Good	Fine	XF
S1097	1 SHILLING 14.10.1713.	—	—	—
S1098	1 SHILLING 6 PENCE 14.10.1713.	—	—	—
S1099	2 SHILLINGS 14.10.1713.	—	—	—
S1100	2 SHILLINGS 6 PENCE 14.10.1713.	—	—	—
S1101	3 SHILLINGS 14.10.1713.	—	—	—
S1102	5 SHILLINGS 14.10.1713.	—	—	—
S1103	10 SHILLINGS 14.10.1713.	—	—	—
S1104	20 SHILLINGS 14.10.1713.	—	—	—

1714 ISSUE

#S1105-S1108 black. Nature leaf print on back.

		Good	Fine	XF
S1105	30 SHILLINGS 26.5.1714.	—	—	—
S1106	40 SHILLINGS 26.5.1714.	—	—	—
S1107	60 SHILLINGS 26.5.1714.	—	—	—
S1108	100 SHILLINGS 26.5.1714.	—	—	—

1714-40 REDATED LOW DENOMINATION PLATE ISSUE

#S1109-S1112 black. Redated successively: 1714, 1718, 1719, 1721, 1722, 1723, 1725 ,1727, 1731, 1733, 1735, 1736, and 1740.

		Good	Fine	XF
S1109	12 PENCE 1714/40 (- old date 14.10.1713).	—	—	—
S1110	1 SHILLING 6 PENCE 1714/40 (- old date 14.10.1713).	—	—	—
S1111	24 PENCE 1714/40 (- old date 14.10.1713)	—	—	—
S1112	2 SHILLINGS 6 PENCE 1714/40 (- old date 14.10.1713).	—	—	—

1714-40 REDATED MIDDLE DENOMINATION PLATE ISSUE

#S1113-S116 black. Redated successively: 1714, 1716, 1716 w/star, 1718, 1719, 1721, 1722, 1723, 1724, 1725, 1725 w/cross, 1727, 1728, 1731, 1733, 1735, 1736, and 1740. The insignia following the 1716 and 1725 dates were added to identify the second issue of each of those years.

		Good	Fine	XF
S1113	3 SHILLINGS 1714/40 (- old date 14.10.1713).	—	—	—
S1114	5 SHILLINGS 1714/40 (- old date 14.10.1713).	—	—	—
S1115	10 SHILLINGS 1714/40 (- old date 14.10.1713).	—	—	—
S1116	20 SHILLINGS 1714/40 (- old date 14.10.1713).	—	—	—

1716-40 REDATED HIGH DENOMINATION PLATE ISSUE

#S1117-S1120 black. Redated successively: 1716, 1716 w/star, 1718, 1721, 1722, 1723, 1724, 1725, 1725 w/cross, 1727, 1733, 1735, 1736, and 1740.

		Good	Fine	XF
S1117	30 SHILLINGS 1716/40 (- old date 26.5.1714).	—	—	—
S1118	40 SHILLINGS 1716/40 (- old date 26.5.1714).	—	—	—
S1119	60 SHILLINGS 1716/40 (- old date 26.5.1714).	—	—	—
S1120	100 SHILLINGS 1716/40 (- old date 26.5.1714).	—	—	—

1722 ISSUE

#S1121-S1123 black.

		Good	Fine	XF
S1121	1 PENNY June 1722. Round shape.	—	—	—
S1122	2 PENCE June 1722. Rectangular shape.	—	—	—

		Good	Fine	XF
S1123	3 PENCE June 1722. Hexagonal shape.	—	—	—

1736 ISSUE

#S1124-S1131 black.

		Good	Fine	XF
S1124	10 PENCE 4.2.1736.	—	—	—
S1125	1 SHILLING 8 PENCE 4.2.1736.	—	—	—
S1126	3 SHILLINGS 4 PENCE 4.2.1736.	—	—	—
S1127	6 SHILLINGS 8 PENCE 4.2.1736.	—	—	—
S1128	10 SHILLINGS 4.2.1736.	—	—	—
S1129	20 SHILLINGS 4.2.1736.	—	—	—
S1130	30 SHILLINGS 4.2.1736.	—	—	—
S1131	40 SHILLINGS 4.2.1736.	—	—	—

1737 REDATED ISSUE

#S1132-S1139 black.

		Good	Fine	XF
S1132	10 PENCE 1737 (- old date 4.2.1736).	—	—	—
S1133	1 SHILLING 8 PENCE 1737 (- old date 4.2.1736).	—	—	—
S1134	3 SHILLINGS 4 PENCE 1737 (- old date 4.2.1736).	—	—	—
S1135	6 SHILLINGS 8 PENCE 1737 (- old date 4.2.1736).	—	—	—
S1136	10 SHILLINGS 1737 (- old date 4.2.1736).	—	—	—
S1137	20 SHILLINGS 1737 (- old date 4.2.1736).	—	—	—
S1138	30 SHILLINGS 1737 (- old date 4.2.1736).	—	—	—
S1139	40 SHILLINGS 1737 (- old date 4.2.1736).	—	—	—

#S1140-S1145 black. Printer: John Draper.

		Good	Fine	XF
S1140	1 PENCE 1737. Winged figures.	—	—	—
S1141	2 PENCE 1737. Angels w/fruit.	—	—	—
S1142	3 PENCE 1737. Lion.	—	—	—
S1143	4 PENCE 1737. Squirrel & turtle.	—	—	—
S1144	5 PENCE 1737. Circular frame.	—	—	—
S1145	6 PENCE 1737. Tree and Indian.	—	—	—

1741 ISSUE

#S1146-S1159 black. English and Massachusetts arms on face.

		Good	Fine	XF
S1146	2 PENCE 15.1.1741. Circle.	—	—	—
S1147	4 PENCE 15.1.1741. Square.	—	—	—
S1148	6 PENCE 15.1.1741. Hexagon.	—	—	—
S1149	8 PENCE 15.1.1741. Octagon.	—	—	—
S1150	1 SHILLING 15.1.1741. Oval.	—	—	—
S1151	2 SHILLINGS 15.1.1741. Square w/concave corners.	—	—	—
S1152	3 SHILLINGS 15.1.1741.	—	—	—
S1153	4 SHILLINGS 15.1.1741.	—	—	—
S1154	5 SHILLINGS 15.1.1741.	—	—	—
S1155	10 SHILLINGS 15.1.1741.	—	—	—
S1156	15 SHILLINGS 15.1.1741.	—	—	—
S1157	20 SHILLINGS 15.1.1741.	—	—	—
S1158	30 SHILLINGS 15.1.1741.	—	—	—
S1159	40 SHILLINGS 15.1.1741.	—	—	—

1742 REDATED ISSUE

#S1160-S1177 black. English and Massachusetts arms on face.

		Good	Fine	XF
S1160	2 PENCE 1742 (- old date 15.1.1741).	—	—	—
S1161	4 PENCE 1742 (- old date 15.1.1741).	—	—	—
S1162	6 PENCE 1742 (- old date 15.1.1741).	—	—	—
S1163	8 PENCE 1742 (- old date 15.1.1741).	—	—	—
S1164	1 SHILLING 1742 (- old date 15.1.1741).	—	—	—
S1165	2 SHILLINGS 1742 (- old date 15.1.1741).	—	—	—
S1166	3 SHILLINGS 1742 (- old date 15.1.1741).	—	—	—
S1167	4 SHILLINGS 1742 (- old date 15.1.1741).	—	—	—
S1168	5 SHILLINGS 1742 (- old date 15.1.1741).	—	—	—
S1169	10 SHILLINGS 1742 (- old date 15.1.1741).	—	—	—
S1170	15 SHILLINGS 1742 (- old date 15.1.1741).	—	—	—

		Good	Fine	XF
S1171	**20 Shillings** 1742 (- old date 15.1.1741).	—	—	—
S1172	**30 Shillings** 1742 (- old date 15.1.1741).	—	—	—
S1173	**40 Shillings** 1742 (- old date 15.1.1741).	—	—	—

#S1174-S1177 black. Denominations from changed plates.

		Good	Fine	XF
S1174	**3 Pence** 15.1.1741.	—	—	—
S1175	**9 Pence** 15.1.1741.	—	—	—
S1176	**15 Pence** 15.1.1741.	—	—	—
S1177	**2 Shillings 6 Pence** 15.1.1741.	—	—	—

1744 Issue

#S1178-S1191 black.

		Good	Fine	XF
S1178	**2 Pence** 20.6.1744. Circle.	—	—	—
S1179	**3 Pence** 20.6.1744. Octagon.	—	—	—
S1180	**4 Pence** 20.6.1744. Square.	—	—	—
S1181	**6 Pence** 20.6.1744. Hexagon.	—	—	—
S1182	**9 Pence** 20.6.1744. Square w/concave corners.	—	—	—
S1183	**1 Shilling** 20.6.1744. Oval. *44* in date reversed.	—	—	—
S1184	**15 Pence** 20.6.1744.	—	—	—
S1185	**2 Shillings 6 Pence** 20.6.1744.	—	—	—
S1186	**5 Shillings** 20.6.1744.	—	—	—
S1187	**10 Shillings** 20.6.1744.	—	—	—
S1188	**15 Shillings** 20.6.1744.	—	—	—
S1189	**20 Shillings** 20.6.1744.	—	—	—
S1190	**30 Shillings** 20.6.1744.	—	—	—
S1191	**40 Shillings** 20.6.1744.	—	—	—

1750 Issue

#S1192-S1197 black. Codfish at l., balancing scales at ctr., and pine tree at r. w/motto: *RESTITUIT REM.*

		Good	Fine	XF
S1192	**1/72 Dollar** 1750.	—	—	—
S1193	**1/24 Dollar** 1750.	—	—	—
S1194	**1/16 Dollar** 1750.	—	—	—
S1195	**1/12 Dollar** 1750.	—	—	—
S1196	**1/8 Dollar** 1750.	—	—	—
S1197	**1/4 Dollar** 1750.	—	—	—

1775 First Issue

#S1198-S1206 black. Printed on laid paper. Wmk: Crown over *GR* (Georgius Rex). Printer: Paul Revere.

		VG	VF	Unc
S1198	**6 Shillings** 25.5.1775.	1250.	3500.	—
S1199	**9 Shillings** 25.5.1775.	1250.	3500.	—
S1200	**10 Shillings** 25.5.1775.	1250.	3500.	—
S1201	**12 Shillings** 25.5.1775.	1250.	3500.	—

		VG	VF	Unc
S1202	**14 Shillings** 25.5.1775.	1250.	3500.	—
S1203	**15 Shillings** 25.5.1775.	1250.	3500.	—
S1204	**16 Shillings** 25.5.1775.	1250.	3500.	—
S1205	**18 Shillings** 25.5.1775.	1250.	3500.	—
S1206	**20 Shillings** 25.5.1775.	1250.	3500.	—

1775 Second Issue

#S1207-S1215 black. Printer: Paul Revere.

		Good	Fine	XF
S1207	**6 Shillings** 8.7.1775.	—	—	—
S1208	**9 Shillings** 8.7.1775.	—	—	—
S1209	**10 Shillings** 8.7.1775.	—	—	—
S1210	**12 Shillings** 8.7.1775.	—	—	—
S1211	**14 Shillings** 8.7.1775.	—	—	—
S1212	**15 Shillings** 8.7.1775.	—	—	—
S1213	**16 Shillings** 8.7.1775.	—	—	—
S1214	**18 Shillings** 8.7.1775.	—	—	—
S1215	**20 Shillings** 8.7.1775.	—	—	—

1775 Third Issue

#S1216-S1229 black. W/3 due dates. Man holding a sword in one hand and the Magna Charta in the other on back.

		Good	Fine	XF
S1216	**1 Shilling** 18.8.1775.	650.00	1850.	—

		Good	Fine	XF
S1217	**2 Shillings** 18.8.1775.	650.00	1850.	—
S1218	**2 Shillings 6 Pence** 18.8.1775.	650.00	1850.	—
S1219	**4 Shillings** 18.8.1775.	650.00	1850.	—
S1220	**5 Shillings** 18.8.1775.	650.00	1850.	—
S1221	**6 Shillings** 18.8.1775.	650.00	1850.	—
S1222	**7 Shillings 6 Pence** 18.8.1775.	650.00	1850.	—
S1223	**8 Shillings** 18.8.1775.	650.00	1850.	—
S1224	**10 Shillings** 18.8.1775.	650.00	1850.	—
S1225	**11 Shillings** 18.8.1775.	650.00	1850.	—
S1226	**12 Shillings** 18.8.1775.	650.00	1850.	—
S1227	**17 Shillings** 18.8.1775.	650.00	1850.	—
S1228	**20 Shillings** 18.8.1775.	650.00	1850.	—
S1229	**24 Shillings** 18.8.1775.	650.00	1850.	—
S1230	**30 Shillings** 18.8.1775.	650.00	1850.	—
S1231	**40 Shillings** 18.8.1775.	650.00	1850.	—

1775 Fourth Issue

#S1232-S1247 black. Similar to #S1216-S1230. Printer: Paul Revere.

		Good	Fine	XF
S1232	**8 Pence** 7.12.1775.	700.00	2100.	—
S1233	**1 Shilling 4 Pence** 7.12.1775.	700.00	2100.	—
S1234	**1 Shilling 6 Pence** 7.12.1775.	700.00	2100.	—
S1235	**2 Shillings 8 Pence** 7.12.1775.	700.00	2100.	—
S1236	**3 Shillings** 7.12.1775.	700.00	2100.	—
S1237	**3 Shillings 4 Pence** 7.12.1775.	700.00	2100.	—
S1238	**4 Shillings 6 Pence** 7.12.1775.	700.00	2100.	—

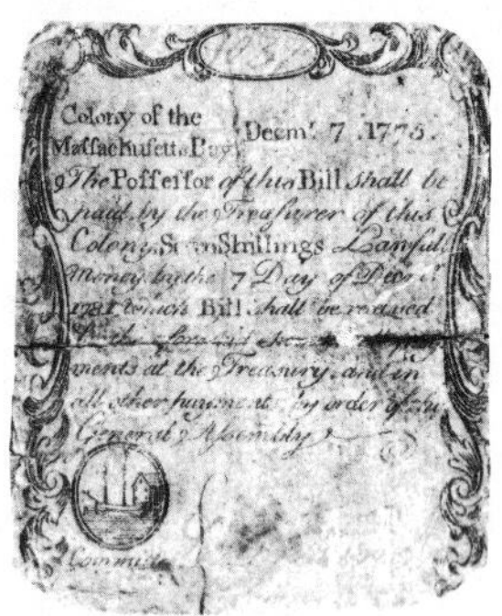

	Good	Fine	XF
S1239 7 Shillings 7.12.1775.	700.00	2100.	—
S1240 10 Shillings 7.12.1775.	700.00	2100.	—

	Good	Fine	XF
S1241 14 Shillings 7.12.1775.	700.00	2100.	—
S1242 16 Shillings 7.12.1775.	700.00	2100.	—
S1243 22 Shillings 7.12.1775.	700.00	2100.	—
S1244 28 Shillings 7.12.1775.	700.00	2100.	—
S1245 36 Shillings 7.12.1775.	700.00	2100.	—
S1246 42 Shillings 7.12.1775.	700.00	2100.	—
S1247 48 Shillings 7.12.1775.	700.00	2100.	—

Massachusetts

State

1776 First Issue

#S1248-S1271 black. Coarse paper w/2 due dates. Printer: Benjamin Edes.

	VG	VF	Unc
S1248 3 Pence 18.6.1776.	125.00	325.00	—
S1249 4 Pence 18.6.1776.	125.00	325.00	—
S1250 5 Pence 18.6.1776.	125.00	325.00	—
S1251 6 Pence 18.6.1776.	125.00	325.00	—
S1252 9 Pence 18.6.1776.	125.00	325.00	—
S1253 10 Pence 18.6.1776.	125.00	325.00	—
S1254 1 Shilling 18.6.1776.	125.00	325.00	—
S1255 1 Shilling 3 Pence 18.6.1776.	125.00	325.00	—
S1256 1 Shilling 8 Pence 18.6.1776.	125.00	325.00	—
S1257 2 Shillings 4 Pence 18.6.1776.	125.00	325.00	—

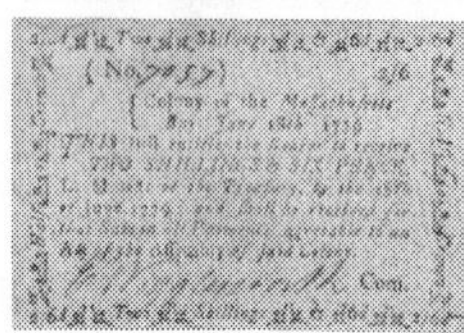

	VG	VF	Unc
S1258 2 Shillings 6 Pence 18.6.1776.	125.00	325.00	—
S1259 3 Shillings 6 Pence 18.6.1776.	125.00	325.00	—
S1260 4 Shillings 18.6.1776.	125.00	325.00	—

	VG	VF	Unc
S1261 4 Pence 18.6.1776.	125.00	325.00	—
S1262 5 Shillings 18.6.1776.	125.00	325.00	—
S1263 5 Shillings 4 Pence 18.6.1776.	125.00	325.00	—
S1264 6 Shillings 18.6.1776.	200.00	550.00	—
S1265 12 Shillings 18.6.1776.	200.00	550.00	—
S1266 18 Shillings 18.6.1776.	200.00	550.00	—
S1267 24 Shillings 18.6.1776.	200.00	550.00	—
S1268 30 Shillings 18.6.1776.	200.00	550.00	—
S1269 36 Shillings 18.6.1776.	200.00	550.00	—

	VG	VF	Unc
S1270 42 Shillings 18.6.1776.	200.00	550.00	—
S1271 48 Shillings 18.6.1776.	200.00	550.00	—

1776 Second Issue

#S1272-S1279 black. W/*COLONY* changed to *STATE* on face.

	Good	Fine	XF
S1272 10 Shillings 17.9.1776.	—	—	—
S1273 14 Shillings 17.9.1776.	—	—	—
S1274 16 Shillings 17.9.1776.	—	—	—
S1275 22 Shillings 17.9.1776.	—	—	—
S1276 28 Shillings 17.9.1776.	—	—	—
S1277 36 Shillings 17.9.1776.	—	—	—
S1278 42 Shillings 17.9.1776.	—	—	—
S1279 48 Shillings 17.9.1776.	—	—	—

1776 Third Issue

#S1280-S1303 black. Pine tree on back. Printers: Paul Revere and John Gill.

	VG	VF	Unc
S1280 2 Pence 18.10.1776.	150.00	300.00	1000.
S1281 3 Pence 18.10.1776.	150.00	300.00	1000.
S1282 4 Pence 18.10.1776.	150.00	300.00	1000.
S1283 6 Pence 18.10.1776.	150.00	300.00	1000.
S1284 8 Pence 18.10.1776.	150.00	300.00	1000.
S1285 9 Pence 18.10.1776.	150.00	300.00	1000.
S1286 1 Shilling 18.10.1776.	150.00	300.00	1000.
S1287 1 Shilling 6 Pence 18.10.1776.	150.00	300.00	1000.
S1288 2 Shillings 18.10.1776.	150.00	300.00	1000.
S1289 3 Shillings 18.10.1776.	150.00	300.00	1000.
S1290 4 Shillings 18.10.1776.	150.00	300.00	1000.
S1291 4 Shillings 6 Pence 18.10.1776.	150.00	300.00	1000.
S1292 6 Shillings 18.10.1776.	—	—	—
S1293 12 Shillings 18.10.1776.	—	—	—
S1294 18 Shillings 18.10.1776.	—	—	—
S1295 24 Shillings 18.10.1776.	—	—	—
S1296 30 Shillings 18.10.1776.	—	—	—

		VG	VF	UNC
S1297	36 SHILLINGS 18.10.1776.	—	—	—
S1298	42 SHILLINGS 18.10.1776.	—	—	—
S1299	48 SHILLINGS 18.10.1776.	—	—	—
S1300	54 SHILLINGS 18.10.1776.	—	—	—
S1301	60 SHILLINGS 18.10.1776.	—	—	—
S1302	66 SHILLINGS 18.10.1776.	—	—	—
S1303	72 SHILLINGS 18.10.1776.	—	—	—

1776 FOURTH ISSUE

#S1304-S1311 black. Like #S1272-S1279 but w/*MAGNA CHARTA* changed to *INDEPENDENCE* on back.

		VG	VF	UNC
S1304	10 SHILLINGS 17.11.1776.	—	—	—
S1305	14 SHILLINGS 17.11.1776.	—	—	—
S1306	16 SHILLINGS 17.11.1776.	—	—	—
S1307	22 SHILLINGS 17.11.1776.	—	—	—
S1308	28 SHILLINGS 17.11.1776.	—	—	—
S1309	36 SHILLINGS 17.11.1776.	—	—	—
S1310	42 SHILLINGS 17.11.1776.	—	—	—
S1311	48 SHILLINGS 17.11.1776.	—	—	—

1778 ISSUE

#S1312-S1323 black. Printers: Paul Revere and Thomas Fleet.

		GOOD	FINE	XF
S1312	2 PENCE 16.10.1778.	75.00	180.00	335.00
S1313	3 PENCE 16.10.1778.	75.00	180.00	335.00
S1314	4 PENCE 16.10.1778.	75.00	180.00	335.00

		GOOD	FINE	XF
S1315	6 PENCE 16.10.1778.	75.00	180.00	335.00
S1316	8 PENCE 16.10.1778.	75.00	180.00	335.00
S1317	9 PENCE 16.10.1778.	75.00	180.00	335.00
S1318	12 PENCE 16.10.1778.	75.00	180.00	335.00
S1319	1 SHILLING 6 PENCE 16.10.1778.	75.00	180.00	335.00
S1320	2 SHILLINGS 16.10.1778.	75.00	180.00	335.00

		GOOD	FINE	XF
S1321	3 SHILLINGS 16.10.1778.	75.00	180.00	335.00
S1322	4 SHILLINGS 16.10.1778.	75.00	180.00	335.00
S1323	4 SHILLINGS 6 PENCE 16.10.1778.	75.00	180.00	335.00

1779 ISSUE

#S1324-S1335 printers: Paul Revere and Thomas Fleet.

		VG	VF	UNC
S1324	1 SHILLING 1779.	150.00	300.00	—
S1325	1 SHILLING 6 PENCE 1779.	150.00	300.00	—
S1326	2 SHILLINGS 1779.	150.00	300.00	—
S1327	2 SHILLINGS 6 PENCE 1779.	150.00	300.00	—
S1328	3 SHILLINGS 1779.	150.00	300.00	—
S1329	3 SHILLINGS 6 PENCE 1779.	150.00	300.00	—

		VG	VF	UNC
S1330	4 SHILLINGS 1779.	150.00	300.00	—
S1331	4 SHILLINGS 6 PENCE 1779.	150.00	300.00	—
S1332	4 SHILLINGS 8 PENCE 1779.	150.00	300.00	—
S1333	5 SHILLINGS 1779.	150.00	300.00	—
S1334	5 SHILLINGS 4 PENCE 1779.	150.00	300.00	—
S1335	5 SHILLINGS 6 PENCE 1779.	150.00	300.00	—

1780 ISSUE

Dollar System

#S1336-S1343 black. Back red and black. Wmk: *UNITED STATES*. Printer: Hall and Sellers, PA.

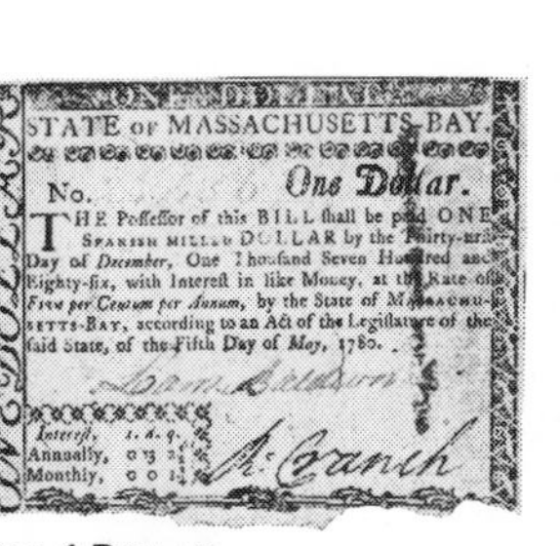

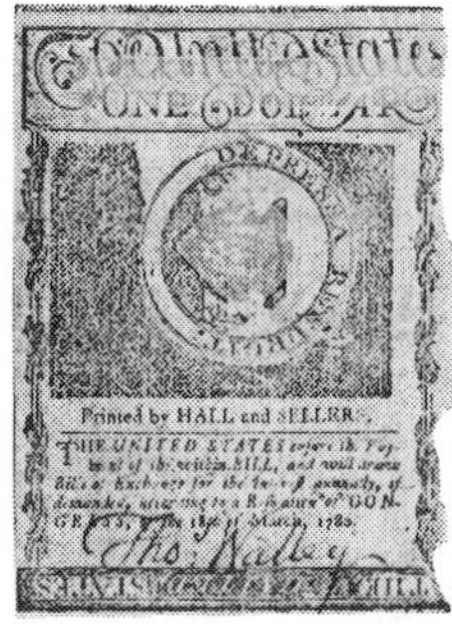

		VG	VF	UNC
S1336	1 DOLLAR 5.5.1780.	15.00	25.00	50.00
S1337	2 DOLLARS 5.5.1780.	15.00	25.00	50.00
S1338	3 DOLLARS 5.5.1780.	15.00	25.00	50.00
S1339	4 DOLLARS 5.5.1780.	15.00	25.00	50.00

		VG	VF	UNC
S1340	5 DOLLARS 5.5.1780.	15.00	25.00	50.00
S1341	7 DOLLARS 5.5.1780.	15.00	25.00	50.00

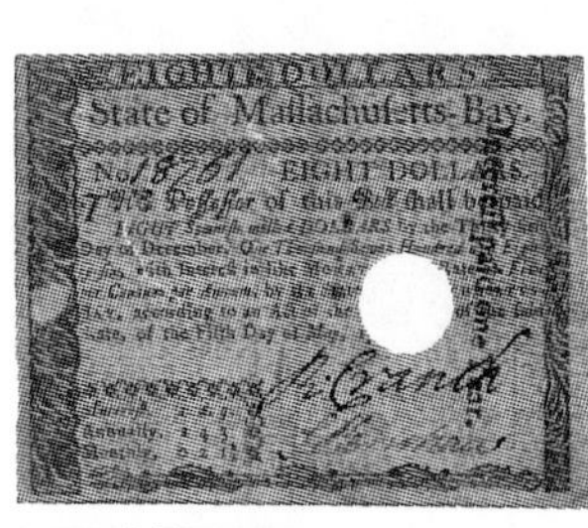

	VG	VF	UNC
S1342 8 DOLLARS 5.5.1780.	15.00	25.00	50.00
S1343 20 DOLLARS 5.5.1780.	15.00	25.00	50.00

MASSACHUSETTS

COMMONWEALTH

1781 TREASURY CERTIFICATES ISSUE

#S1344-S1347 black. Text in top border: *COMMONWEALTH OF MASSACHUSETTS*. Various handwritten dates.

	VG	VF	UNC
S1344 4 DOLLARS 1781.	—	—	—
S1345 6 DOLLARS 10.12.1781.	—	—	—
S1346 8 DOLLARS 1781.	—	—	—
S1347 16 DOLLARS 1781.	—	—	—

MICHIGAN

BRITISH OCCUPATION - WAR OF 1812

1815 FORT MICHILMACKINAC ISSUE

The fort on Michilmackinac Island, located in the Straits of Mackinac, was captured by the British and later restored to U.S.A. forces after the war ended.

	VG	VF	UNC
S1347A 4 DOLLARS 1.5.1815.	—	Rare	—

MINNESOTA

STATE

1855 AUDITOR'S OFFICE TREASURY ISSUE

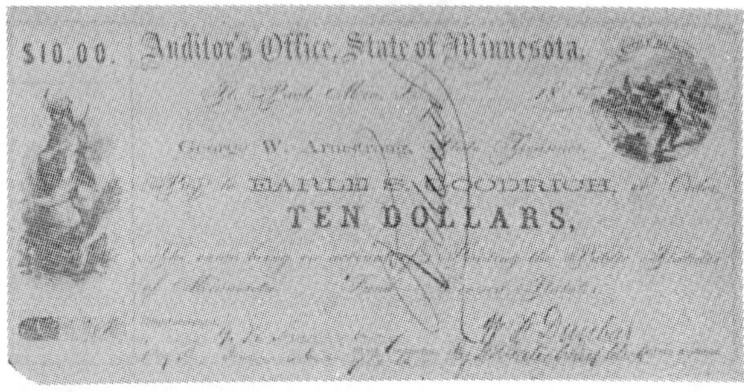

	GOOD	FINE	XF
S1348 10 DOLLARS 7.7.1855. Woman standing by another kneeling at l., farmer plowing by Indian on horseback at upper r.	85.00	175.00	—

JANUARY 29, 1858 AUTHORIZED ISSUE

#S1349-S1353 black. Various handwritten dates. Printer: Lith. by Louis Buechner, St. Paul, Minnesota.

	GOOD	FINE	XF
S1349 1 DOLLAR 1858.	42.50	85.00	—

	GOOD	FINE	XF
S1350 3 DOLLARS 20.3.1858.	65.00	175.00	—
S1351 5 DOLLARS 1858.	65.00	150.00	—

	GOOD	FINE	XF
S1352 10 DOLLARS 1858.	85.00	175.00	—

	GOOD	FINE	XF
S1353 20 DOLLARS 20.3.1858.	100.00	200.00	—

MISSISSIPPI

CIVIL WAR

1861 ISSUE

#S1360-S1362 various handwritten dates and "payable" dates of a year later. Printer: ABNC, New York and New Orleans.

	VG	VF	UNC
S1360 10 DOLLARS 1861-62; 19.1.1863. Black on red unpt. Portr. Gov. J. J. Pettus at lower l., black w/horses at top ctr., portr. woman at lower r.	100.00	175.00	300.00
S1361 20 DOLLARS 1861-62; 19.1.1863. Black on red unpt. Woman at lower r., mules pulling wagon load of cotton at top ctr., portr. Gov. J. J. Pettus at lower r.	100.00	175.00	300.00

	VG	VF	UNC
S1362 50 DOLLARS 1861-62; 19.1.1863. Black on red unpt. Portr. Gov. J. J. Pettus at upper l., mules pulling wagon at top ctr., black picking cotton at r. Uniface.	100.00	175.00	300.00

	VG	VF	UNC
S1363 100 DOLLARS 1861-62; 19.1.1863. Black on red-orange unpt. Proserpina at upper l., blacks gathering cotton at top ctr., portr. Gov. J. J. Pettus at lower r. Uniface.	90.00	200.00	350.00

1862 COTTON PLEDGED ISSUES

		VG	VF	UNC
S1364	**1 DOLLAR** 1862. Black on red unpt. Seated woman at upper l., steam passenger train at upper ctr., farmer holding sheaf at lower r. Green text: *COTTON PLEDGED.*			
	a. 1.4.1862.	25.00	50.00	75.00
	b. 1.5.1862.	25.00	50.00	75.00
S1365	**1 DOLLAR** 1.5.1862; 1.11.1862. Similar to #S1364 but blue text: *COTTON PLEDGED.*	25.00	50.00	75.00
S1366	**2 1/2 DOLLARS** 1.4.1862; 1.5.1862. Black on red unpt. Farmer standing w/sheaf at upper l., standing Indian w/tomahawk at lower r. Green text: *COTTON PLEDGED.*	25.00	50.00	75.00

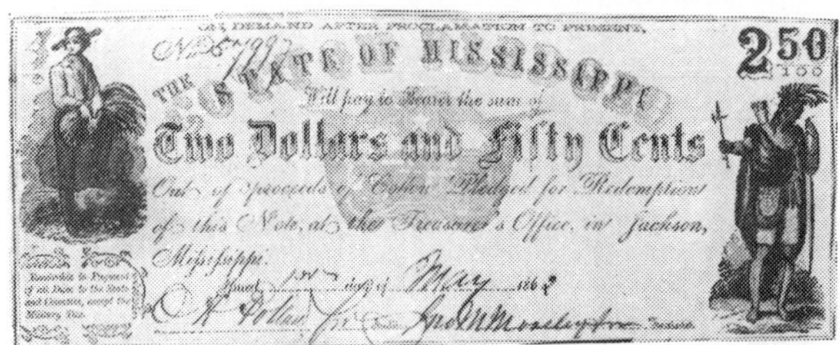

		VG	VF	UNC
S1367	**2 1/2 DOLLARS** 1.5.1862; 1.11.1862. Similar to #S1366 but w/blue text: *COTTON PLEDGED* in unpt.	35.00	50.00	90.00

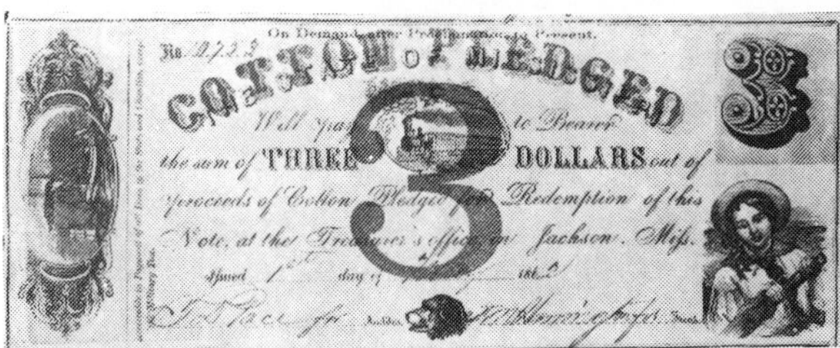

		VG	VF	UNC
S1368	**3 DOLLARS** 1.4.1862; 1.5.1862. Black on green unpt. Landscape in oval at l., steam passenger train at ctr., young boy at lower r. Green text: *COTTON PLEDGED.*	30.00	50.00	80.00
S1369	**3 DOLLARS** 1.5.1862; 1.11.1862. Similar to #S1368 but blue text: *COTTON PLEDGED.*	30.00	50.00	85.00

		VG	VF	UNC
S1370	**5 DOLLARS** 7.3.1862. Black on lt. green unpt. Woman at l., steam passenger train at ctr., sailing ship at lower r. Olive text: *COTTON PLEDGED.*	35.00	60.00	110.00
S1371	**5 DOLLARS** 7.3.1862. Black on pink unpt. Similar to #S1370.	35.00	60.00	110.00
S1372	**5 DOLLARS** 1862. Black w/o unpt. Similar to #S1370 but green text: *COTTON PLEDGED.*			
	a. 1.4.1862.	25.00	45.00	85.00
	b. Printed on backs of auditor's bills. 1.4.1862.	25.00	45.00	85.00
	c. 1.5.1862.	25.00	45.00	85.00
	d. Printed on backs of bills of exchange. 1.5.1862.	25.00	50.00	90.00
S1373	**10 DOLLARS** 7.3.1862. Black on lt. gray unpt. Woman w/balancing scales and sword at l., bldg. behind trees at r. Olive text: *COTTON PLEDGED.*	50.00	65.00	90.00
S1374	**10 DOLLARS** 7.3.1862. Black on pink unpt. Similar to #S1373.	50.00	65.00	90.00

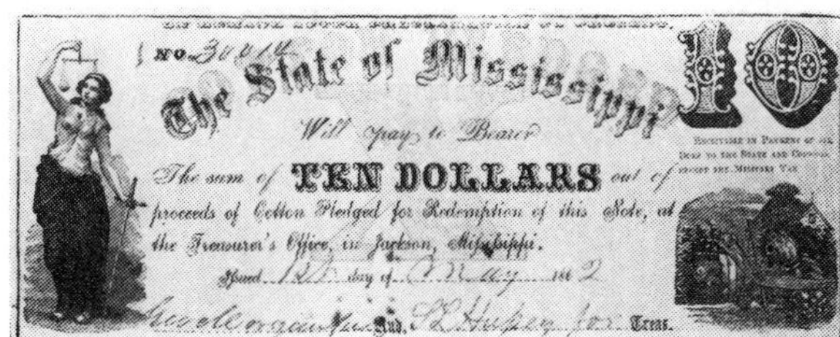

		VG	VF	UNC
S1375	**10 DOLLARS** 1862. Black w/o unpt. Similar to #S1373 but green text: *COTTON PLEDGED.*			
	a. 1.4.1862.	25.00	50.00	90.00
	b. Printed on backs of auditor's bills. 1.4.1862.	25.00	50.00	90.00
	c. 1.5.1862.	25.00	50.00	100.00
	d. Printed on backs of bills of exchange. 1.5.1862.	25.00	55.00	110.00

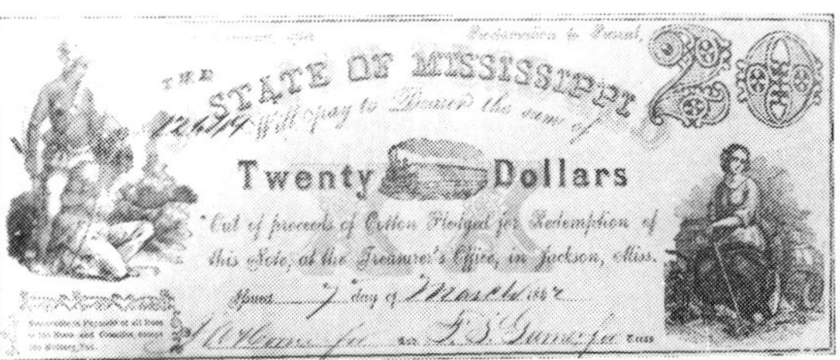

		VG	VF	UNC
S1376	**20 DOLLARS** 7.3.1862. Black on lt. gray unpt. 2 Indian braves at l., steam passenger train at ctr., seated woman at r. Olive text: *COTTON PLEDGED.*	35.00	60.00	125.00
S1377	**20 DOLLARS** 7.3.1862. Black on pink unpt. Similar to #S1376.	35.00	60.00	100.00

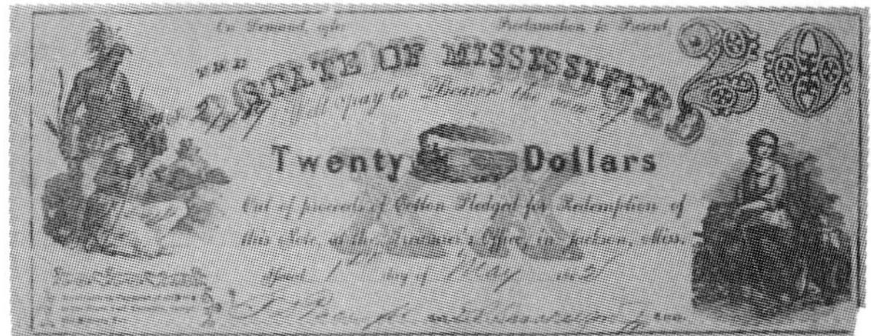

		VG	VF	UNC
S1378	**20 DOLLARS** 1862. Black w/o unpt. Similar to #S1376 but green text: *COTTON PLEDGED.*			
	a. 1.4.1862.	25.00	50.00	80.00
	b. Printed on backs of auditor's bills. 1.4.1862.	25.00	50.00	80.00
	c. 1.5.1862.	25.00	50.00	80.00
	d. Printed on backs of bills of exchange. 1.5.1862.	25.00	50.00	80.00
S1379	**50 DOLLARS** 7.3.1862. Black on lt. gray unpt. Indian brave at l., blacks picking cotton at r. Olive text: *COTTON PLEDGED.*	40.00	65.00	100.00
S1380	**50 DOLLARS** 7.3.1862. Black on pink unpt. Similar to #S1379.	35.00	60.00	100.00

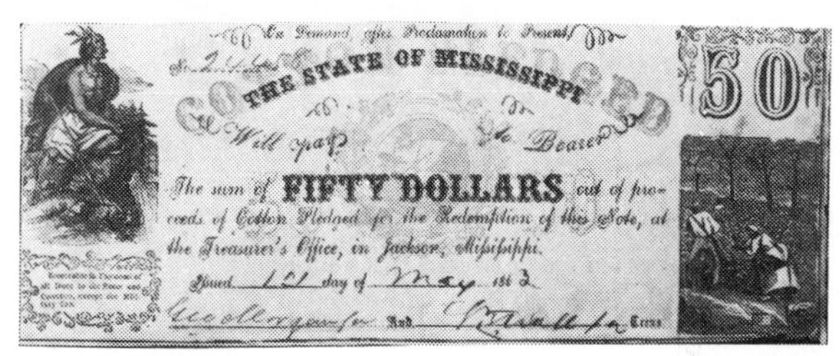

		VG	VF	UNC
S1381	**50 DOLLARS** 1862. Black w/o unpt. Similar to #S1379 but green text: *COTTON PLEDGED.*			
	a. 1.4.1862.	—	Rare	—
	b. Printed on backs of auditor's bills.	—	Rare	—
	c. 1.5.1862.	35.00	50.00	90.00
	d. Printed on backs of bills of exchange. 1.5.1862.	—	Rare	—
S1382	**100 DOLLARS** 7.3.1862. Black on lt. gray unpt. Woman standing at l. and r., steam train at ctr. Olive text: *COTTON PLEDGED.*	50.00	90.00	150.00
S1383	**100 DOLLARS** 7.3.1862. Black on pink unpt. Similar to #S1382.	—	Rare	—
S1384	**100 DOLLARS** 1862. Black w/o unpt. Similar to #S1382 but green text: *COTTON PLEDGED.*			
	a. 1.4.1862.	55.00	90.00	150.00
	b. 1.5.1862.	55.00	90.00	150.00
	c. Printed on backs of bills of exchange. 1.5.1862.	—	Rare	—

1862 FAITH OF THE STATE PLEDGED ISSUES

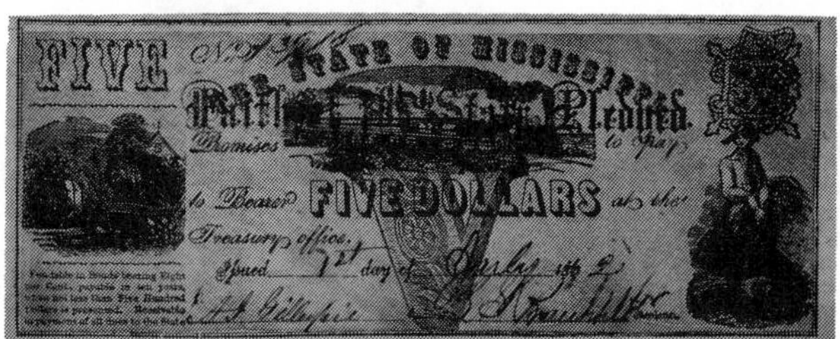

		VG	VF	UNC
S1385	**5 DOLLARS** 1862. Black. Plow at l., steam passenger train at top ctr., farmer holding sheaf of grain at lower r. Red text: *Faith of the State Pledged.*			
	a. 1.7.1862.	25.00	35.00	85.00
	b. Ovpt: *Re-Issue.* 1.7.1862.	30.00	45.00	90.00
	c. 1.11.1862.	25.00	35.00	85.00
	d. Ovpt: *Re-Issue.*. 1.11.1862.	25.00	45.00	90.00

	VG	VF	UNC
e. Printed on the backs of Mississippi Cotton Company notes. 1.11.1862.	50.00	60.00	135.00
f. Ovpt: *Re-Issue* on #S1385e.	35.00	50.00	100.00

S1386 5 DOLLARS
1.11.1862. Similar to #S1385 but blue text: *Faith of the State Pledged.*

	VG	VF	UNC
a. Issued note.	25.00	35.00	75.00
b. Ovpt: *Re-Issue.*	35.00	50.00	85.00

S1387 10 DOLLARS
1862. Black on red unpt. Seated woman at lower l., train at ctr., farmer at r. Red text: *Faith of the State Pledged.*

	VG	VF	UNC
a. 1.7.1862.	25.00	45.00	85.00
b. Ovpt: *Re-Issue.* 1.7.1862.	25.00	45.00	85.00
c. 1.11.1862.	25.00	45.00	85.00
d. Ovpt: *Re-Issue.* 1.11.1862.	25.00	45.00	85.00
e. Printed on backs of Mississippi Cotton Company notes. 1.11.1862.	25.00	45.00	85.00
f. Ovpt: *Re-Issue* on #S1387e.	25.00	45.00	85.00

S1388 10 DOLLARS
1.11.1862. Similar to #S1387 but blue text: *Faith of the State Pledged.*

	VG	VF	UNC
a. Issued note.	25.00	45.00	90.00
b. Ovpt: *Re-Issue.*	25.00	45.00	90.00
c. Printed on the backs of Mississippi Cotton Company notes.	25.00	45.00	90.00

S1389 20 DOLLARS
1862. Black on green unpt. Plow at upper l., steam passenger train at upper ctr., woman kneeling beside Indian maiden at lower r. Red text: *Faith of the State Pledged.*

	VG	VF	UNC
a. 1.7.1862.	25.00	45.00	85.00
b. Ovpt: *Re-Issue.* 1.7.1862.	30.00	50.00	90.00
c. 1.11.1862.	25.00	45.00	85.00
d. Ovpt: *Re-Issue.* 1.11.1862.	30.00	60.00	100.00
e. Printed on backs of Mississippi Cotton Company notes 1.11.1862.	40.00	65.00	100.00
f. Ovpt: *Re-Issue* on #S1389e.	45.00	80.00	150.00

S1390 20 DOLLARS
1.11.1862. Similar to #S1389 but blue text: *Faith of the State Pledged.*

	VG	VF	UNC
a. Issued note.	25.00	45.00	85.00
b. Ovpt: *Re-Issue.*	35.00	65.00	150.00

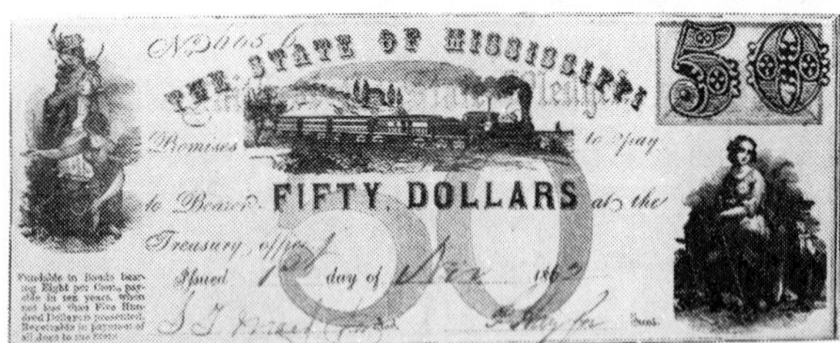

S1391 50 DOLLARS
1.11.1862. Black. Woman kneeling beside Indian maiden at upper l., steam passenger train at upper ctr, woman seated at lower r. Red text: *Faith of the State Pledged.*

	VG	VF	UNC
a. Issued note.	35.00	65.00	150.00
b. Ovpt: *Re-Issue.*	35.00	65.00	150.00

S1392 50 DOLLARS
1.11.1862. Similar to #S1391 but blue text: *Faith of the State Pledged.*

	VG	VF	UNC
a. Issued note.	45.00	75.00	150.00
b. Ovpt: *Re-Issue.*	45.00	80.00	150.00

S1393 100 DOLLARS
1.11.1862. Similar to #S1382 but red text: *Faith of the Sate Pledged.*

	VG	VF	UNC
a. Issued note.	—	Rare	—
b. Ovpt: *Re-Issue.*	—	Rare	—

S1394 100 DOLLARS
1.11.1862. Similar to #S1393 but blue text: *Faith of the State Pledged.*

	VG	VF	UNC
a. Issued note.	—	Rare	—
b. Ovpt: *Re-Issue.*	—	Rare	—

1864 ISSUE

#S1395-S1401 printer: J. T. Paterson & Co.

S1395 25 CENTS
1.5.1864. Black on red unpt. Cotton bolls at lower l.

VG	VF	UNC
12.50	20.00	35.00

S1396 50 CENTS
1.5.1864. Black on red unpt. Black hoeing field at lower l.

VG	VF	UNC
15.00	30.00	50.00

S1397 1 DOLLAR
1.5.1864. Black on red unpt. Ceres at lower l., steam passenger train at top ctr.

	VG	VF	UNC
a. W/imprint.	20.00	35.00	50.00
b. W/o imprint.	25.00	35.00	60.00

S1398 2 DOLLARS
1.5.1864. Black on red unpt. Sailor at lower l., sailing ship at top ctr.

	VG	VF	UNC
a. W/imprint.	25.00	35.00	50.00
b. W/o imprint.	25.00	30.00	50.00

S1399 3 DOLLARS
1.5.1864. Black on red unpt. Indian at lower l., Sentinel on duty at upper ctr.

VG	VF	UNC
30.00	45.00	65.00

S1400 20 DOLLARS
186x. Black on red and green unpt. Eagle w/shield at l., seated Indian at r. along bottom. Back green.

	VG	VF	UNC
a. W/green protector: *XX.*	—	Rare	—
b. W/o green protector: *XX* between eagle and seated Indian.	85.00	125.00	225.00

S1401 50 DOLLARS
186x. Black on red unpt. Similar to #S1400.

VG	VF	UNC
—	Rare	—

1865 ISSUE

		VG	VF	UNC
S1402	**50 DOLLARS** 1.4.1865. Black on green unpt. Indian at l., seated Commerce and Ceres at upper ctr. r. Back orange.	70.00	90.00	100.00

MISSISSIPPI

POST CIVIL WAR

1867 ISSUE

#S1403 various handwritten dates.

		VG	VF	UNC
S1403	**100 DOLLARS** 21.7.1867. Black and orange. Harbor scene at top ctr. Back green.	300.00	500.00	1000.

1870 ISSUE

#S1404-S1407 printer: CBNC.

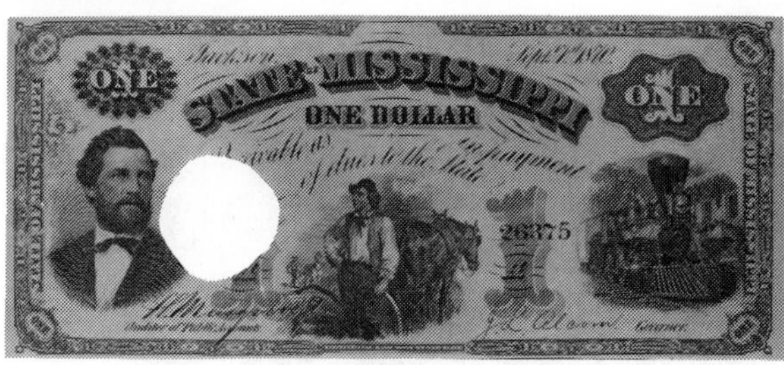

		VG	VF	UNC
S1404	**1 DOLLAR** 1.9.1870. Black and green. Gov. J. L. Alcorn at l., man w/horse and plow at lower ctr., steam locomotive at r. Back green.			
	a. Issued note.	75.00	150.00	275.00
	b. Punched hole cancelled.	15.00	30.00	50.00
S1405	**2 DOLLARS** 1.9.1870. Green and black. Gov. J. L. Alcorn at l., blacks loading cotton at lower ctr., steam train at lower r. Back green.			
	a. Issued note.	75.00	150.00	275.00
	b. Punched hole cancelled.	15.00	30.00	50.00

		VG	VF	UNC
S1406	**3 DOLLARS** 1.9.1870. Green and black. Gov. J. L. Alcorn at l., steamship in rough seas at ctr., eagle w/shield at r. Back green.			
	a. Issued note.	85.00	175.00	300.00
	b. Punched hole cancelled.	15.00	30.00	50.00

		VG	VF	UNC
S1407	**5 DOLLARS** 1.9.1870. Green and black. Woman at l., Gov. J. L. Alcorn at ctr., cotton boll at r. Back green.			
	a. Issued note.	75.00	150.00	275.00
	b. Punched hole cancelled.	15.00	30.00	50.00

ACT OF 10.2.1894 SPECIAL AUDITOR'S ISSUE

#S1411-S1413 black. Portr. man at l. Various handwritten dates, payable 1.1.1896. Printer: St. Louis Bank Note Co.

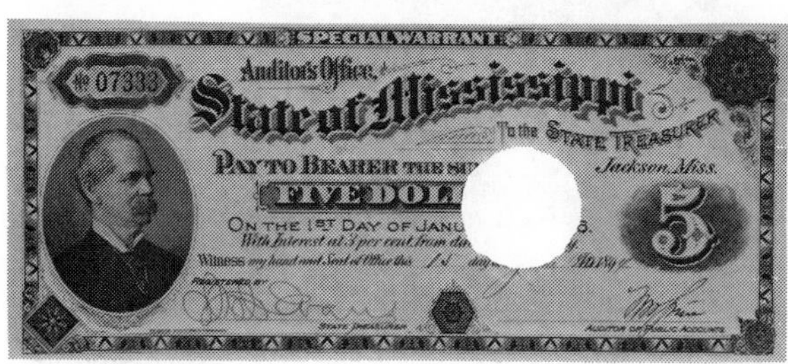

		VG	VF	UNC
S1411	**5 DOLLARS** 1894. Back green.			
	a. Issued note.	45.00	75.00	120.00
	b. Punched hole cancelled.	20.00	30.00	45.00
S1412	**10 DOLLARS** 1894. Back brown.			
	a. Issued note.	90.00	150.00	240.00
	b. Punched hole cancelled.	20.00	40.00	55.00
S1413	**20 DOLLARS** 1894.			
	a. Issued note.	85.00	145.00	225.00
	b. Punched hole cancelled.	27.50	45.00	75.00

ACT OF FEBRUARY 10, 1895 ISSUE

		VG	VF	UNC
S1415	**10 DOLLARS** 15.6.1895. Eagle at l. Back brown.			
	a. Issued note.	35.00	55.00	85.00
	b. Punched hole cancelled.	20.00	35.00	60.00

MISSOURI

STATE

1821 LOAN OFFICE CERTIFICATES ISSUE

		GOOD	FINE	XF
S1421	**50 CENTS** 1.10.1821. Black. Eagle at top ctr.	—	1600.	—
S1422	**1 DOLLAR** 1.10.1821. Black. Woman seated at top ctr.	—	Rare	—
S1423	**3 DOLLARS** 1.10.1821.	Reported Not Confirmed		
S1424	**5 DOLLARS** 1.10.1821. Black.	Reported Not Confirmed		
S1425	**10 DOLLARS** 1.10.1821. Black. Woman seated at top ctr.	—	Rare	—

MISSOURI

CIVIL WAR

1862 ISSUE

#S1431-S1433 engraver: A. Malus, New Orleans.

		VG	VF	UNC
S1431	**1 DOLLAR** 1.1.1862. Black on red unpt. Liberty at l., J. Davis at upper ctr., frontiersman at lower r.			
	a. White paper.	30.00	50.00	90.00
	b. Printed on backs of bills of exchange.	30.00	50.00	90.00
	c. Blue paper.	30.00	50.00	90.00
	d. Printed on backs of bills of exchange, blue paper.	30.00	50.00	90.00

S1432 2 DOLLARS
1.1.1862. Black on green unpt. Young girl at l., farmer w/horses and plow at top ctr., State arms at r.

	VG	VF	UNC
a. White paper.	35.00	50.00	100.00
b. Printed on backs of bills of exchange.	35.00	50.00	100.00
c. Blue paper.	—	Rare	—
d. Printed on backs of bills of exchange, blue paper.	—	Rare	—

S1433 3 DOLLARS
1.1.1862. Black on green unpt. Liberty at l., Gov. C. F. Jackson at top ctr., frontiersman at lower r.

	VG	VF	UNC
a. White paper.	—	Rare	—
b. Printed on backs of bills of exchange.	50.00	75.00	100.00
c. Blue paper.	25.00	45.00	75.00
d. Printed on backs of bills of exchange, blue paper.	25.00	45.00	75.00

#S1434 and S1435 engraver: D. Weil (w/o imprint).

S1434 5 DOLLARS
1.1.1862. Black. Seated Commerce on bale of cotton at top ctr.

	VG	VF	UNC
a. W/o imprint.	20.00	40.00	70.00
b. Blue paper w/imprint.	30.00	50.00	80.00
c. Blue paper w/o imprint.	30.00	40.00	70.00
d. W/text: *Prior to 1st, Nov'br 1861* rubberstamped or handwritten on back.	30.00	40.00	70.00

S1435 10 DOLLARS
1.1.1862. Black. Seated Ceres on horn of plenty w/sailing ship in l. background at top ctr.

	VG	VF	UNC
a. W/o imprint.	40.00	60.00	90.00
b. Blue paper w/imprint.	25.00	45.00	75.00
c. Blue paper w/o imprint.	25.00	50.00	80.00
d. W/text: *Prior to 1st, Nov'br 1861* rubberstamped or handwritten on back.	30.00	50.00	85.00

S1436 20 DOLLARS
1862-63. Black. Liberty at l., Ceres Volant at top ctr. Payable text: *Three Years after Date.* Engraver: A. Malus, New Orleans.

	VG	VF	UNC
a. 1.11.1862.	30.00	55.00	100.00
b. Blue paper. 1.11.1862.	45.00	75.00	125.00
c. 1.11.1863/62.	50.00	80.00	130.00
d. W/text: *Prior to 1st, Nov'br 1861* rubberstamped or handwritten on back.	30.00	55.00	100.00

S1437 20 DOLLARS
1862.63. Similar to #S1436 but payable text: *Five Years after Date.*

	VG	VF	UNC
a. 1.11.1862.	50.00	90.00	145.00
b. Blue paper. 1.11.1862.	45.00	80.00	135.00
c. 1.11.1863/62.	—	Rare	—
d. W/text: *Prior to 1st, Nov'br 1861* rubberstamped or handwritten on back.	45.00	85.00	140.00

MISSOURI

DEFENCE BOND

ACT OF 5.11.1861 ISSUE

#S1438-S1444 printer: Keatinge & Ball.

NOTE: Apparently no examples known w/genuine sign.

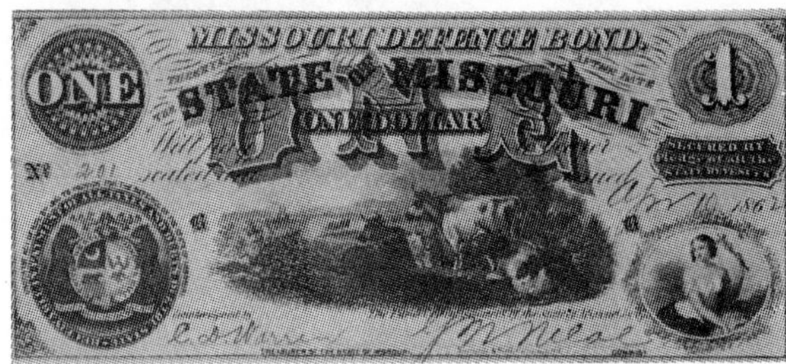

S1438 1 DOLLAR
186x. Black on red unpt. State arms at lower l., cattle in pasture at ctr., seated woman at lower r.

	VG	VF	UNC
a. Issued note.	—	—	—
r. Remainder w/o sign.	30.00	45.00	75.00

S1439 3 DOLLARS
186x. Black on red unpt. State arms at upper l., Ceres Volante at ctr. r., woman at lower r.

	VG	VF	UNC
a. Issued note.	—	—	—
r. Remainder w/o sign.	35.00	50.00	100.00

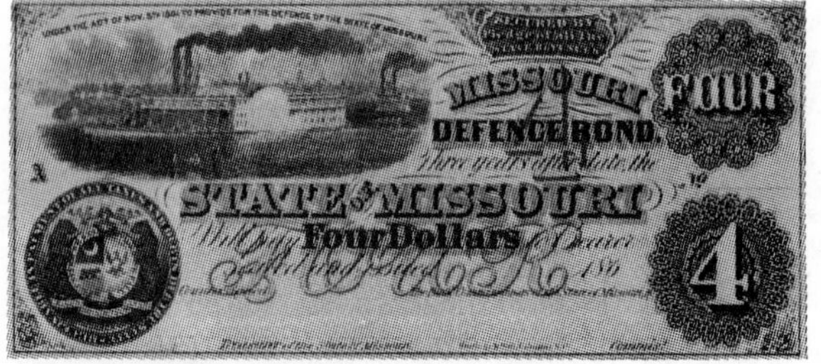

S1440 4 DOLLARS
186x. Black on red unpt. Mississippi riverboat at upper l. ctr. above state arms.

	VG	VF	UNC
a. Issued note.	—	—	—
r. W/o sign.	45.00	80.00	150.00

		VG	VF	UNC
S1441	**4 DOLLARS 50 CENTS** 186x. Black on red unpt. Ceres seated between Commerce and Navigation at l., state arms at lower r.			
	a. Issued note.	—	—	—
	r. Remainder w/o sign.	50.00	85.00	140.00

		VG	VF	UNC
S1442	**20 DOLLARS** 186x. Black on red unpt. Seated Liberty at upper l., riverboat at upper ctr., state arms at lower r. Back green.			
	a. Issued note.	—	—	—
	r. Remainder w/o sign.	40.00	70.00	125.00

		VG	VF	UNC
S1443	**50 DOLLARS** 186x. Black on red unpt. Ceres at lower l., blacks gathering cotton at upper r., state arms at lower r. Back green.			
	a. Issued note.	—	—	—
	r. Remainder w/o sign.	50.00	100.00	150.00

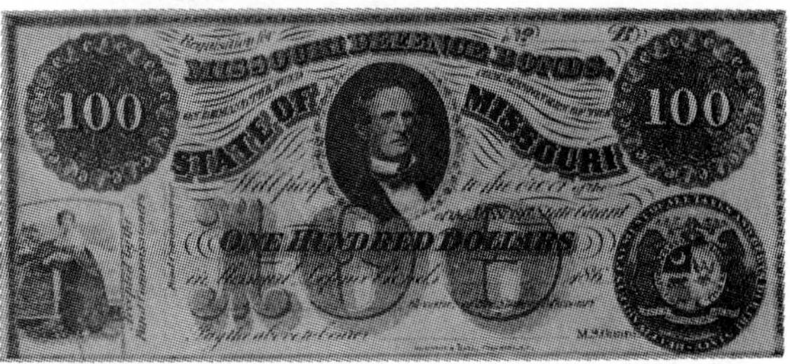

		VG	VF	UNC
S1444	**100 DOLLARS** 186x. Black on red unpt. Woman standing at lower l., portr. J. Davis at upper ctr., state arms at lower r. Back green.			
	a. Issued note.	—	—	—
	r. Remainder w/o sign.	50.00	100.00	150.00

MISSOURI

DEFENCE WARRANT

1862 ISSUE

#S1445 various handwritten dates.

		VG	VF	UNC
S1445	**10 DOLLARS** 23.2.1862. Black on green unpt.. State seal at upper l., girl at lower r. Plain green protector: *TEN*. Printer: A. McLean.	—	Rare	—

#S1446 printed or stamped dates.

		VG	VF	UNC
S1446	**10 DOLLARS** 28.2.1862. Similar to #S1445 but w/fancy green protector: *TEN*. Printer: A. McLean.	—	Rare	—

1864 ISSUE

#S1447-S1450 black. State arms at l. Printer: R. P. Studley & Co.

		VG	VF	UNC
S1447	**5 DOLLARS** 25.6.1864. Gen. F. Sigel at lower r.	—	Rare	—
S1448	**10 DOLLARS** 25.6.1864. Gen. I. Shepard at lower r.	—	Rare	—

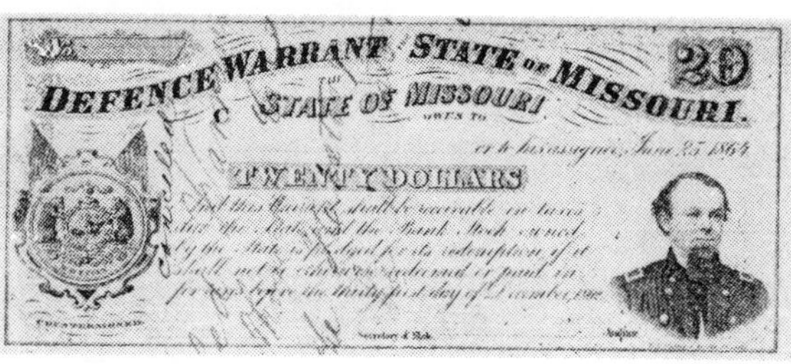

		VG	VF	UNC
S1449	**20 DOLLARS** 25.6.1864. Gen. J. Pope at lower r.	—	Rare	—

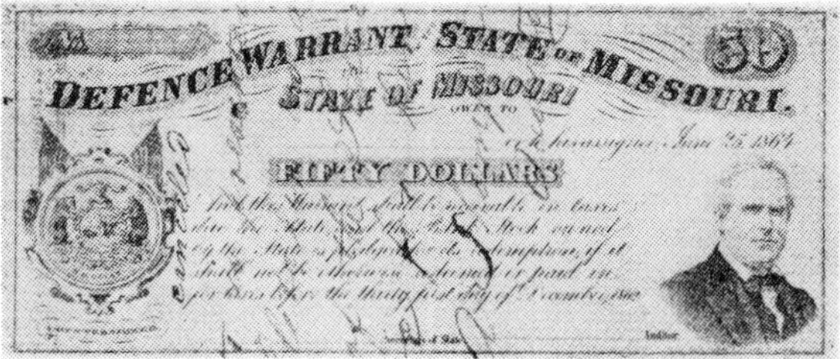

		VG	VF	UNC
S1450	**50 DOLLARS** 25.6.1864. Gov. W. P. Hall at lower r.	—	Rare	—

MISSOURI

UNION MILITARY BOND

ACT OF 9.3.1863 AND 20.2.1865 ISSUE

#S1451-S1456 various handwritten dates. Printer: ABNC.

		VG	VF	UNC
S1451	**1 DOLLAR** 1863-66. Black. Union officer at upper l., seated Liberty w/globe and eagle at r. Back green.	—	Rare	—
S1452	**3 DOLLARS** 1863-66. Black. Man at upper l., Liberty at ctr., state arms at lower r. Back green.	—	Rare	—
S1453	**5 DOLLARS** 1863.66. Black. Man w/horse at upper l., man at ctr. r. Back green.	—	Rare	—

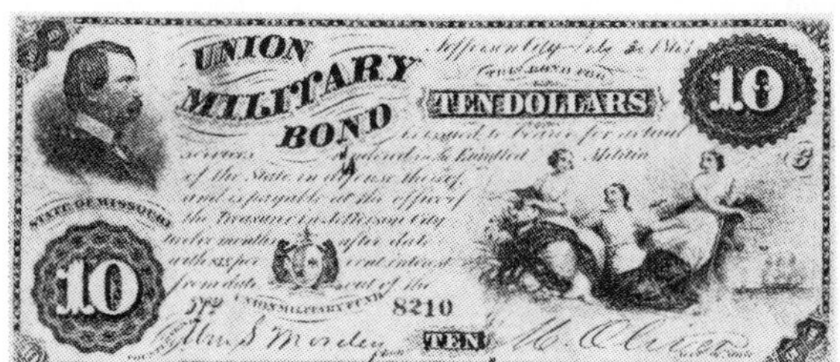

		VG	VF	UNC
S1454	**10 DOLLARS** 1863-66. Black. Gen. F. Blair at upper l., 3 reclining allegorical women at lower r. Back green.	—	Rare	—
S1455	**20 DOLLARS** 1863-66. Mountain at upper l., man at lower ctr. Proof.	—	Rare	—
S1456	**50 DOLLARS** 1863-66.	Reported Not Confirmed		

New Hampshire

Colonial

1709 Issue

Pound Sterling System

#S1461 and S1462 black and red. Uniface. Printer: Jeremiah Dummer.

	Good	Fine	XF
S1461 15 Shillings 1709.	—	—	—
S1462 50 Shillings 1709.	—	—	—

1717 Issue

#S1463-S1470 black. Printer: Jeremiah Dummer.

	Good	Fine	XF
S1463 1 Shilling 20.5.1717.	—	—	—
S1464 1 Shilling 6 Pence 20.5.1717.	—	—	—
S1465 4 Shillings 6 Pence 20.5.1717.	—	—	—
S1466 15 Shillings 20.5.1717.	—	—	—
S1467 25 Shillings 20.5.1717.	—	—	—
S1468 30 Shillings 20.5.1717.	—	—	—
S1469 3 Pounds 10 Shillings 20.5.1717.	—	—	—
S1470 4 Pounds 20.5.1717.	—	—	—

1714/17 Redated Issue

#S1471-S1474 black. Redated 1714.

	Good	Fine	XF
S1471 1 Shilling 1714 (- old date 20.5.1717).	—	—	—
S1472 1 Shilling 6 Pence 1714 (- old date 20.5.1717).	—	—	—
S1473 4 Shillings 6 Pence 1714 (- old date 20.5.1717).	—	—	—
S1474 25 Shillings 1714 (- old date 20.5.1717).	—	—	—

1717/17 Redated Issue

#S1475-S1478 black.

	Good	Fine	XF
S1475 1 Shilling 1717 (- old date 20.5.1717).	—	—	—
S1476 1 Shilling 6 Pence 1717 (- old date 20.5.1717).	—	—	—
S1477 4 Shillings 6 Pence 1717 (- old date 20.5.1717).	—	—	—
S1478 25 Shillings 1717 (- old date 20.5.1717).	—	—	—

1722 Redated Issue

#S1479-S1486 black. *CNH* (Colony of New Hampshire) monogram on back.

	Good	Fine	XF
S1479 1 Shilling 1722 (- old date 20.5.1717).	—	—	—
S1480 1 Shilling 6 Pence 1722 (- old date 20.5.1717).	—	—	—
S1481 4 Shillings 6 Pence 1722 (- old date 20.5.1717).	—	—	—
S1482 15 Shillings 1722 (- old date 20.5.1717).	—	—	—
S1483 25 Shillings 1722 (- old date 20.5.1717).	—	—	—
S1484 30 Shillings 1722 (- old date 20.5.1717).	—	—	—
S1485 3 Pounds 10 Shillings 1722 (- old date 20.5.1717).	—	—	—
S1486 4 Pounds 1722 (- old date 20.5.1717).	—	—	—

1726/27 Redated Issue

#S1487-S1494 black. Redated successively: 1724, 1725, 1726, and 1727.

	Good	Fine	XF
S1487 1 Shilling 1724/27 (- old date 20.5.1717). Boar.	—	—	—
S1488 1 Shilling 6 Pence 1724/27 (- old date 20.5.1717). Bear.	—	—	—
S1489 4 Shillings 6 Pence 1724/27 (- old date 20.5.1717). Camel.	—	—	—
S1490 15 Shillings 1724/17 (- old date 20.5.1717). Cod.	—	—	—
S1491 25 Shillings 1724/27 (- old date 20.5.1717). Double headed eagle.	—	—	—
S1492 30 Shillings 1724/27 (- old date 20.5.1717). Stag.	—	—	—
S1493 3 Pounds 10 Shillings 1724/27 (- old date 20.5.1717). Pine tree.	—	—	—
S1494 4 Pounds 1724/27 (- old date 20.5.1717). Indian.	—	—	—

1729 Redated Issue

#S1495-S1502 black.

	Good	Fine	XF
S1495 1 Shilling 1729. (- old date 20.5.1717). Boar.	—	—	—
S1496 1 Shilling 6 Pence 1729 (- old date 20.5.1717). Bear.	—	—	—
S1497 4 Shillings 6 Pence 1729. (- old date 20.5.1717). Camel.	—	—	—
S1498 15 Shillings 1729. (- old date 20.5.1717). Cod	—	—	—
S1499 25 Shillings 1729 (- old date 20.5.1717). Double headed eagle.	—	—	—
S1500 30 Shillings 1729 (- old date 20.5.1717). Stag.	—	—	—
S1501 3 Pounds 10 Shillings 1729 (- old date 20.5.1717). Pine tree.	—	—	—
S1502 4 Pounds 1729 (- old date 20.5.1717). Indian.	—	—	—

1737 Issue

#S1503-S1510 black.

	Good	Fine	XF
S1503 2 Shillings 1.4.1737.			
a. Issued note.	—	—	—
rp. Reprint.	—	—	—
S1504 3 Shillings 1.4.1737.			
a. Issued note.	—	—	—
rp. Reprint.	—	—	—
S1505 5 Shillings 1.4.1737. Crown.			
a. Issued note.	—	—	—
rp. Reprint.	—	—	—
S1506 10 Shillings 1.4.1737. Angel.			
a. Issued note.	—	—	—
rp. Reprint.	—	—	—
S1507 20 Shillings 1.4.1737. Black.	—	—	—
S1508 40 Shillings 1.4.1737.	—	—	—
S1509 60 Shillings 1.4.1737.	—	—	—
S1510 100 Shillings 1.4.1737.	—	—	—

1740 Redated Issue

#S1511-S1514 black. Redated Aug. 7, 1740.

	Good	Fine	XF
S1511 20 Shillings 7.8.1740 (- old date 1.4.1737).	—	—	—
S1512 40 Shillings 7.8.1740 (- old date 1.4.1737).	—	—	—
S1513 60 Shillings 7.8.1740 (- old date 1.4.1737).	—	—	—
S1514 100 Shillings 7.8.1740 (- old date 1.4.1737).	—	—	—

1742 Issue

#S1515-S1522 black. Motto: *DIEU ET MON DROIT* on state arms. Uniface.

	Good	Fine	XF
S1515 6 Pence 3.4.1742.	—	—	—
S1516 1 Shilling 3.4.1742.	—	—	—
S1517 2 Shillings 6 Pence 3.4.1742.	—	—	—
S1518 6 Shillings 3.4.1742.	—	—	—
S1519 7 Shillings 6 Pence 3.4.1742.			
a. Issued note.	—	—	—
rp. Reprint.	—	—	—
S1520 10 Shillings 3.4.1742.			
a. Issued note.	—	—	—
rp. Reprint.	—	—	—
S1521 20 Shillings 3.4.1742.			
a. Issued note.	—	—	—
rp. Reprint.	—	—	—
S1522 40 Shillings 3.4.1742.			
a. Issued note.	—	—	—
rp. Reprint.	—	—	—

1743 REDATED ISSUE

#S1523-S1530 black.

	Good	Fine	XF
S1523 6 PENCE 1743 (- old date 3.4.1742).	—	—	—
S1524 1 SHILLING 1743 (- old date 3.4.1742).	—	—	—
S1525 2 SHILLINGS 6 PENCE 1743 (- old date 3.4.1742).	—	—	—
S1526 6 SHILLINGS 1743 (- old date 3.4.1742).	—	—	—
S1527 7 SHILLINGS 6 PENCE 1743 (- old date 3.4.1742).	—	—	—
S1528 10 SHILLINGS 1743 (- old date 3.4.1742).	—	—	—

	Good	Fine	XF
S1529 20 SHILLINGS 1743 (- old date 3.4.1742).	—	—	—
S1530 40 SHILLINGS 1743 (- old date 3.4.1742).	—	—	—

1744 REDATED ISSUE

#S1531-S1538 black. Redated Feb. 1744(5).

	Good	Fine	XF
S1531 6 PENCE 1744 (- old date 3.4.1742).	—	—	—
S1532 1 SHILLING 1744 (- old date 3.4.1742).	—	—	—
S1533 2 SHILLINGS 6 PENCE 1744 (- old date 3.4.1742).	—	—	—
S1534 6 SHILLINGS 1744 (- old date 3.4.1742).	—	—	—
S1535 7 SHILLINGS 6 PENCE 1744 (- old date 3.4.1742).	—	—	—
S1536 10 SHILLINGS 1744 (- old date 3.4.1742).	—	—	—
S1537 20 SHILLINGS 1744 (- old date 3.4.1742).	—	—	—
S1538 40 SHILLINGS 1744 (- old date 3.4.1742).	—	—	—

1755 ISSUE

MONETARY SYSTEM

15 Shillings = 60 Shillings O.T. = 8 Spanish Reales

#S1539-S1548 black. Motto: *PRO ARIS & FOCIS* and expedition name of *Crown Point* on face.

	Good	Fine	XF
S1539 6 PENCE 3.4.1755. Squirrel in tree.	—	—	—
S1540 1 SHILLING 3.4.1755. Rabbit.	—	—	—
S1541 3 SHILLINGS 3.4.1755. Rooster.	—	—	—
S1542 3 SHILLINGS 9 PENCE 3.4.1755. Bird in flight.	—	—	—
S1543 5 SHILLINGS 3.4.1755. Bird in tree.	—	—	—
S1544 7 SHILLINGS 6 PENCE 3.4.1755. Bird on ground.	—	—	—
S1545 10 SHILLINGS 3.4.1755. Fox.	—	—	—
S1546 15 SHILLINGS 3.4.1755. Squirrel.	—	—	—
S1547 30 SHILLINGS 3.4.1755. Stag.	—	—	—
S1548 3 POUNDS 3.4.1755. Wings.	—	—	—

1756 FIRST REDATED ISSUE

#S1549-S1552 black. Redated Jan. 1, 1756.

	Good	Fine	XF
S1549 10 SHILLINGS 1.1.1756 (- old date 3.4.1755). Fox.	—	—	—
S1550 15 SHILLINGS 1.1.1756 (- old date 3.4.1755). Squirrel.	—	—	—
S1551 30 SHILLINGS 1.1.1756 (- old date 3.4.1755). Stag.	—	—	—
S1552 3 POUNDS 1.1.1756 (- old date 3.4.1755). Wings.	—	—	—

1756 SECOND REDATED ISSUE

#S1553-S1562 black. Redated Jan. 1, 1756.

	Good	Fine	XF
S1553 6 PENCE 1.6.1756 (- old date 3.4.1755).	—	—	—
S1554 1 SHILLING 1.6.1756 (- old date 3.4.1755).	—	—	—
S1555 3 SHILLINGS 1.6.1756 (- old date 3.4.1755).	—	—	—
S1556 3 SHILLINGS 9 PENCE 1.6.1756 (- old date 3.4.1755).	—	—	—
S1557 5 SHILLINGS 1.6.1756 (- old date 3.4.1755).	—	—	—
S1558 7 SHILLINGS 6 PENCE 1.6.1756 (- old date 3.4.1755).	—	—	—
S1559 10 SHILLINGS 1.6.1756 (- old date 3.4.1755).	—	—	—
S1560 15 SHILLINGS 1.6.1756 (- old date 3.4.1755).	—	—	—
S1561 30 SHILLINGS 1.6.1756 (- old date 3.4.1755).	—	—	—
S1562 3 POUNDS 1.6.1756 (- old date 3.4.1755).	—	—	—

1759 ISSUE

#S1563-S1566 black.

	Good	Fine	XF
S1563 6 PENCE 1759.	—	—	—
S1564 1 SHILLING 1759.	—	—	—
S1565 2 SHILLINGS 6 PENCE 1759.	—	—	—
S1566 10 SHILLINGS 1759.	—	—	—

1760 ISSUE

#S1567-S1570 black.

	Good	Fine	XF
S1567 6 PENCE 1.3.1760.	—	—	—
S1568 1 SHILLING 1.3.1760.	—	—	—
S1569 2 SHILLINGS 6 PENCE 1.3.1760. (Not issued).	—	—	—
S1570 10 SHILLINGS 1.3.1760.	—	—	—

1761 FIRST ISSUE

#S1571-S1574 black.

	Good	Fine	XF
S1571 6 PENCE 1.1.1761. (Not issued).	—	—	—
S1572 1 SHILLING 1.1.1761.	—	—	—
S1573 2 SHILLINGS 6 PENCE 1.1.1761.	—	—	—
S1574 10 SHILLINGS 1.1.1761.	—	—	—

1761 SECOND ISSUE

#S1575-S1578 black.

	Good	Fine	XF
S1575 6 PENCE 1.5.1761.	—	—	—
S1576 1 SHILLING 1.5.1761.	—	—	—
S1577 2 SHILLINGS 6 PENCE 1.5.1761.	—	—	—
S1578 10 SHILLINGS 1.5.1761.	—	—	—

1762 FIRST ISSUE

#S1579-S1582 black.

	Good	Fine	XF
S1579 6 PENCE 1.1.1762.	—	—	—
S1580 1 SHILLING 1.1.1762.	—	—	—
S1581 2 SHILLINGS 6 PENCE 1.1.1762.	—	—	—
S1582 10 SHILLINGS 1.1.1762.	—	—	—

1762 SECOND ISSUE

#S1583-S1586 black.

	Good	Fine	XF
S1583 6 PENCE (1.7.) 1762.	—	—	—
S1584 1 SHILLING (1.7.) 1762.	—	—	—
S1585 2 SHILLINGS 6 PENCE (1.7.) 1762.	—	—	—
S1586 10 SHILLINGS (1.7.) 1762.	—	—	—

1763 ISSUE

#S1587-S1590 black.

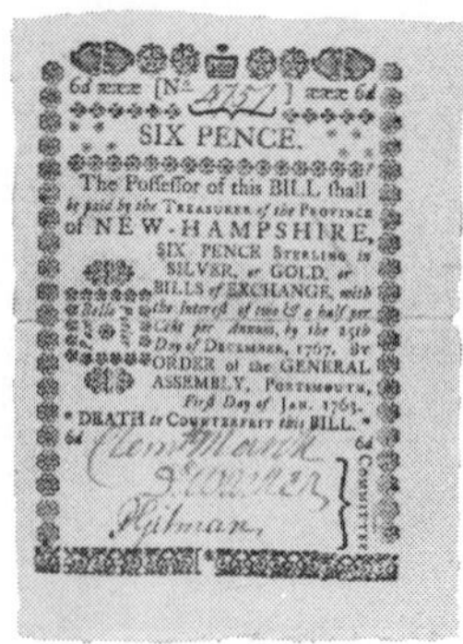

		GOOD	FINE	XF
S1587	**6 PENCE** 1.1.1763.	—	—	—
S1588	**1 SHILLING** 1.1.1763.	—	—	—
S1589	**2 SHILLINGS 6 PENCE** 1.1.1763.	—	—	—
S1590	**10 SHILLINGS** 1.1.1763.	—	—	—

1775 FIRST ISSUE

#S1591-S1594 black. 3 due date varieites. Printer: Paul Revere.

		GOOD	FINE	XF
S1591	**1 SHILLING** 20.6.1775. Lg. tree.	700.00	1800.	—
S1592	**6 SHILLINGS** 20.6.1775. Squirrel in tree.	700.00	1800.	—
S1593	**20 SHILLINGS** 20.6.1775. 2 leaves.	700.00	1800.	—
S1594	**40 SHILLINGS** 20.6.1775. Tree w/crossed trunks.	700.00	1800.	—

1775 SECOND ISSUE

#S1595-S1600 black.

		GOOD	FINE	XF
S1595	**6 PENCE** 25.7.1775.	225.00	500.00	—
S1596	**9 PENCE** 25.7.1775.	225.00	500.00	—
S1597	**1 SHILLING 6 PENCE** 25.7.1775.	225.00	500.00	—
S1598	**1 SHILLING 9 PENCE** 25.7.1775.	225.00	500.00	—
S1599	**2 SHILLINGS 6 PENCE** 25.7.1775.	225.00	500.00	—
S1600	**3 POUNDS** 25.7.1775.	225.00	500.00	—

1775 THIRD ISSUE

#S1601-S1605 black. 3 due date varieties.

		VG	VF	UNC
S1601	**5 SHILLINGS** 24.8.1775.	300.00	600.00	—
S1602	**10 SHILLINGS** 24.8.1775.	300.00	600.00	—
S1603	**15 SHILLINGS** 24.8.1775.	300.00	600.00	—
S1604	**30 SHILLINGS** 24.8.1775.	300.00	600.00	—
S1605	**3 POUNDS** 24.8.1775.	300.00	600.00	—

1775 FOURTH ISSUE

#S1606-S1616 black. 4 due date varieties.

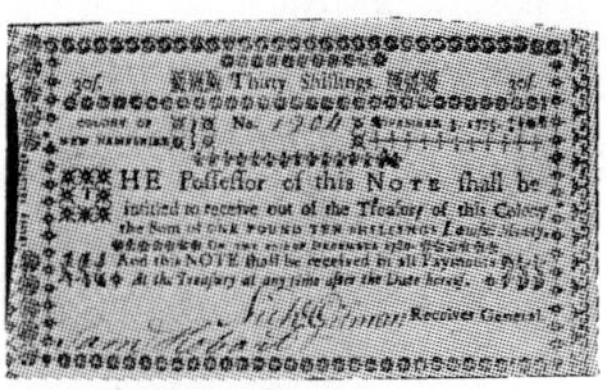

		VG	VF	UNC
S1606	**6 PENCE** 3.11.1775.	325.00	600.00	—
S1607	**9 PENCE** 3.11.1775.	325.00	600.00	—
S1608	**1 SHILLING 6 PENCE** 3.11.1775.	325.00	600.00	—
S1609	**1 SHILLING 9 PENCE** 3.11.1775.	325.00	600.00	—
S1610	**2 SHILLINGS 6 PENCE** 3.11.1775.	325.00	600.00	—
S1611	**3 SHILLINGS** 3.11.1775.	325.00	600.00	—
S1612	**5 SHILLINGS** 3.11.1775.	250.00	450.00	—
S1613	**10 SHILLINGS** 3.11.1775.	250.00	450.00	—
S1614	**15 SHILLINGS** 3.11.1775.	250.00	450.00	—
S1615	**30 SHILLINGS** 3.11.1775.	185.00	350.00	—
S1616	**40 SHILLINGS** 3.11.1775.	185.00	350.00	—

1776 FIRST ISSUE

#S1617-S1622 black. 4 due date varieties. Printer: Daniel Fowle, Portsmouth.

		VG	VF	UNC
S1617	**1 DOLLAR** 26.1.1776.	—	—	—
S1618	**2 DOLLARS** 26.1.1776.	—	—	—
S1619	**3 DOLLARS** 26.1.1776. Mottos: *SUB VERTUTE SPERAMUS* and *FOR LIBERTY* on face.	—	—	—
S1620	**4 DOLLARS** 26.1.1776. Mottos: *NIL DESPERANDUM* and *FOR LIBERTY* on face.	—	—	—
S1621	**5 DOLLARS** 26.1.1776. Mottos: *PRO BONO PUBLICO* and *LIBERTY & PROPERTY* on face.	—	—	—
S1622	**6 DOLLARS** 26.1.1776. Motto: *FOR DEFENCE OF AMERICAN LIBERTY* and name of committee members *MESHECH WEARE* and *LEVI DEARBORN* between ornaments on face.	—	—	—

1776 SECOND ISSUE

#S1623-S1632 black. 2 due date varieties. Uniface.

		GOOD	FINE	XF
S1623	**3 PENCE** 28.6.1776.	325.00	850.00	—
S1624	**4 PENCE** 28.6.1776.	325.00	850.00	—
S1625	**5 PENCE** 28.6.1776.	325.00	850.00	—
S1626	**7 PENCE** 28.6.1776.	325.00	850.00	—
S1627	**8 PENCE** 28.6.1776.	325.00	850.00	—
S1628	**10 PENCE** 28.6.1776.	325.00	850.00	—
S1629	**1 SHILLING** 28.6.1776.	325.00	850.00	—
S1630	**15 PENCE** 28.6.1776.	325.00	850.00	—
S1631	**2 SHILLINGS** 28.6.1776.	325.00	850.00	—
S1632	**4 SHILLINGS** 28.6.1776.	325.00	850.00	—

1776 THIRD ISSUE

Dollar System

#S1633-S1638 black. 4 due date varieties. Printer: Daniel Fowle, Portsmouth.

		GOOD	FINE	XF
S1633	**1 DOLLAR** 3.7.1776.	—	—	—
S1634	**2 DOLLARS** 3.7.1776.	—	—	—
S1635	**3 DOLLARS** 3.7.1776. Like #S1619.	—	—	—
S1636	**4 DOLLARS** 3.7.1776. Like #S1620.	—	—	—
S1637	**5 DOLLARS** 3.7.1776. Like #S1621.	—	—	—
S1638	**6 DOLLARS** 3.7.1776. Like #S1622.	—	—	—

NEW HAMPSHIRE

STATE

1777 ISSUE

Pound Sterling System

#S1639 and S1640 black. Various handwritten dates and denominations.

		GOOD	FINE	XF
S1639	**5 POUNDS** 1777. Black. *U-N-I-ON* in border.	—	—	—
S1640	**10 POUNDS** 1777. Black.	—	—	—

1780 ISSUE

Dollar System

#S1641-S1647 black. Back red and black. Wmk: *Confederation* in 2 lines. Printer: Hall & Sellers, PA.

		VG	VF	UNC
S1641	**1 DOLLAR** 29.4.1780.	125.00	300.00	600.00
S1642	**2 DOLLARS** 29.4.1780.	125.00	300.00	600.00

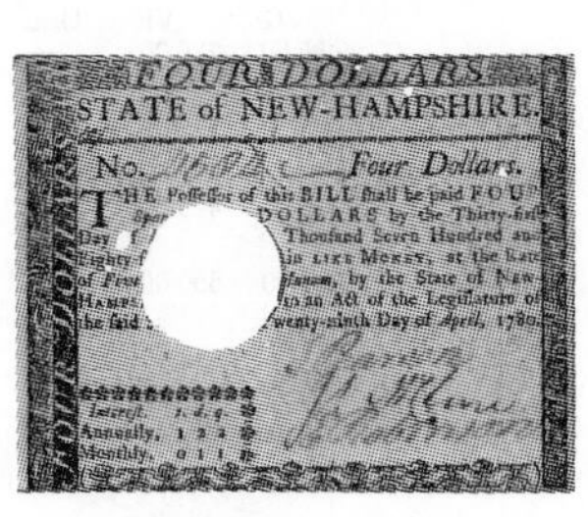

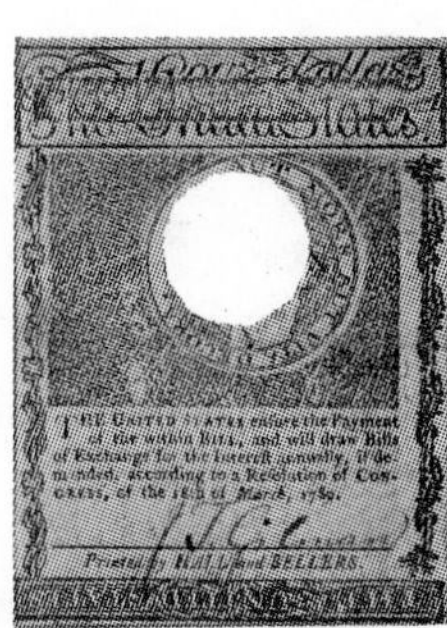

	VG	VF	UNC
S1643 4 DOLLARS 29.4.1780.	125.00	300.00	600.00
S1644 5 DOLLARS 29.4.1780.	125.00	300.00	600.00
S1645 7 DOLLARS 29.4.1780.	125.00	300.00	600.00
S1646 8 DOLLARS 29.4.1780.	125.00	300.00	600.00
S1647 20 DOLLARS 29.4.1780.	125.00	300.00	600.00

NEW JERSEY

COLONIAL

Pound Sterling System

1709 ISSUE

By mistake a design of the stub for identification was left out and English arms (3 lions) were used instead of British arms (shield).

#S1648-S1652 black.

	VG	VF	UNC
S1648 5 SHILLINGS 1.7.1709.	—	—	—
S1649 10 SHILLINGS 1.7.1709.	—	—	—
S1650 20 SHILLINGS 1.7.1709.	—	—	—
S1651 40 SHILLINGS 1.7.1709.	—	—	—
S1652 5 POUNDS 1.7.1709.	—	—	—

1711 ISSUE

#S1653-S1658 black.

	VG	VF	UNC
S1653 2 SHILLINGS 6 PENCE 14.7.1711.	—	—	—
S1654 5 SHILLINGS 14.7.1711.	—	—	—
S1655 10 SHILLINGS 14.7.1711.	—	—	—
S1656 20 SHILLINGS 14.7.1711.	—	—	—
S1657 40 SHILLINGS 14.7.1711.	—	—	—
S1658 5 POUNDS 14.7.1711.	—	—	—

1716 ISSUE

#S1659-S1667 black. Printer: William Bradford.

	VG	VF	UNC
S1659 2 SHILLINGS 24.1.1716 (7).	—	—	—
S1660 4 SHILLINGS 24.1.1716 (7).	—	—	—
S1661 5 SHILLINGS 24.1.1716 (7).	—	—	—
S1662 8 SHILLINGS 24.1.1716 (7).	—	—	—
S1663 10 SHILLINGS 24.1.1716 (7).	—	—	—
S1664 16 SHILLINGS 24.1.1716 (7).	—	—	—
S1665 20 SHILLINGS 24.1.1716 (7).	—	—	—
S1666 30 SHILLINGS 24.1.1716 (7).	—	—	—
S1667 40 SHILLINGS 24.1.1716 (7).	—	—	—

1724 ISSUE

#S1668-S1675 black. Printer: William Bradford.

	VG	VF	UNC
S1668 1 SHILLING 25.3.1724.	—	—	—
S1669 1 SHILLING 6 PENCE 25.3.1724.	—	—	—
S1670 3 SHILLINGS 25.3.1724.	—	—	—
S1671 6 SHILLINGS 25.3.1724.	—	—	—
S1672 12 SHILLINGS 25.3.1724.	—	—	—
S1673 15 SHILLINGS 25.3.1724.	—	—	—
S1674 30 SHILLINGS 25.3.1724.	—	—	—
S1675 3 POUNDS 25.3.1724.	—	—	—

1728 ISSUE

#S1676-S1684 black. Printer: Samuel Keimer.

	VG	VF	UNC
S1676 1 SHILLING 25.3.1728.	—	—	—
S1677 1 SHILLING 6 PENCE 25.3.1728.	—	—	—
S1678 3 SHILLINGS 25.3.1728.	—	—	—
S1679 6 SHILLINGS 25.3.1728.	—	—	—
S1680 12 SHILLINGS 25.3.1728.	—	—	—
S1681 15 SHILLINGS 25.3.1728.	—	—	—
S1682 30 SHILLINGS 25.3.1728.	—	—	—
S1683 3 POUNDS 25.3.1728.	—	—	—
S1684 6 POUNDS 25.3.1728.	—	—	—

1733 ISSUE

#S1685-S1693 black. Mottos: *DIEU ET MON DROIT* and *HONI SOIT QUI MAL Y PENSE* on face. Printer: Andrew Bradford.

	VG	VF	UNC
S1685 1 SHILLING 25.3.1733.	—	—	—
S1686 1 SHILLING 6 PENCE 25.3.1733.	—	—	—
S1687 3 SHILLINGS 25.3.1733.	—	—	—
S1688 6 SHILLINGS 25.3.1733.	—	—	—
S1689 12 SHILLINGS 25.3.1733.	—	—	—
S1690 15 SHILLINGS 25.3.1733.	—	—	—
S1691 30 SHILLINGS 25.3.1733.	—	—	—
S1692 3 POUNDS 25.3.1733.	—	—	—
S1693 6 POUNDS 25.3.1733.	—	—	—

1737 ISSUE

#S1694-S1702 black. Printer: Benjamin Franklin.

	VG	VF	UNC
S1694 1 SHILLING 25.3.1737.	—	—	—
S1695 1 SHILLING 6 PENCE 25.3.1737.	—	—	—
S1696 3 SHILLINGS 25.3.1737.	—	—	—
S1697 6 SHILLINGS 25.3.1737.	—	—	—
S1698 12 SHILLINGS 25.3.1737.	—	—	—
S1699 15 SHILLINGS 25.3.1737.	—	—	—
S1700 30 SHILLINGS 25.3.1737.	—	—	—
S1701 3 POUNDS 25.3.1737.	—	—	—
S1702 6 POUNDS 25.3.1737.	—	—	—

1746 ISSUE

#S1703-S1711 sage leaf on back. Printer: Benjamin Franklin.

	VG	VF	UNC
S1703 1 SHILLING 2.7.1746.	—	—	—
S1704 1 SHILLING 6 PENCE 2.7.1746.	—	—	—
S1705 3 SHILLINGS 2.7.1746.	—	—	—
S1706 6 SHILLINGS 2.7.1746.	—	—	—
S1707 12 SHILLINGS 2.7.1746.	—	—	—
S1708 15 SHILLINGS 2.7.1746.	—	—	—
S1709 30 SHILLINGS 2.7.1746.	—	—	—

#S1710 and S1711 black and red.

	VG	VF	UNC
S1710 3 POUNDS 2.7.1746.	—	—	—
S1711 6 POUNDS 2.7.1746.	—	—	—

1755 FIRST ISSUE

#S1712-S1720 black. Sage leaf on back. Printer: James Parker.

	VG	VF	UNC
S1712 1 SHILLING 15.5.1755.	—	—	—

No.	Denomination	Date / Description	VG	VF	UNC
S1713	1 SHILLING 6 PENCE	15.5.1755.	—	—	—
S1714	3 SHILLINGS	15.5.1755.	—	—	—
S1715	6 SHILLINGS	15.5.1755.	—	—	—
S1716	12 SHILLINGS	15.5.1755.	—	—	—
S1717	15 SHILLINGS	15.5.1755.	—	—	—
S1718	30 SHILLINGS	15.5.1755.	—	—	—
S1719	3 POUNDS	15.5.1755.	—	—	—
S1720	6 POUNDS	15.5.1755.	—	—	—

1755 SECOND ISSUE

#S1721-S1729 sage leaf on back. Printer: James Parker, Woodbridge.

No.	Denomination	Date / Description	VG	VF	UNC
S1721	1 SHILLING	8.9.1755.	—	—	—
S1722	1 SHILLING 6 PENCE	8.9.1755.	—	—	—
S1723	3 SHILLINGS	8.9.1755.	—	—	—
S1724	6 SHILLINGS	8.9.1755.	—	—	—
S1725	12 SHILLINGS	8.9.1755.	—	—	—
S1726	15 SHILLINGS	8.9.1755.	—	—	—
S1727	30 SHILLINGS	8.9.1755.	—	—	—

#S1728 and S1729 black and red.

No.	Denomination	Date / Description	VG	VF	UNC
S1728	3 POUNDS	8.9.1755.	—	—	—
S1729	6 POUNDS	8.9.1755.	—	—	—

1756 FIRST ISSUE

#S1730-S1738 sage leaf on back. Printer: James Parker.

No.	Denomination	Date / Description	VG	VF	UNC
S1730	1 SHILLING	26.1.1756. Black.	—	—	—
S1731	18 PENCE	26.1.1756. Black.	—	—	—
S1732	3 SHILLINGS	26.1.1756. Black.	—	—	—
S1733	6 SHILLINGS	26.1.1756. Black.	—	—	—
S1734	12 SHILLINGS	26.1.1756. Black.	—	—	—
S1735	15 SHILLINGS	26.1.1756. Black.	—	—	—
S1736	30 SHILLINGS	26.1.1756. Red.	—	—	—
S1737	3 POUNDS	26.1.1756. Red.	—	—	—
S1738	6 POUNDS	26.1.1756. Red and black.	—	—	—

1756 SECOND ISSUE

#S1739-S1747 sage leaf on back. Printer: James Parker.

No.	Denomination	Date / Description	VG	VF	UNC
S1739	1 SHILLING	22.6.1756. Black.	90.00	175.00	—
S1740	18 PENCE	22.6.1756. Black.	90.00	175.00	—
S1741	3 SHILLINGS	22.6.1756. Black.	90.00	175.00	—
S1742	6 SHILLINGS	22.6.1756. Black.	150.00	300.00	—
S1743	12 SHILLINGS	22.6.1756. Black.	150.00	300.00	—

No.	Denomination	Date / Description	VG	VF	UNC
S1744	15 SHILLINGS	22.6.1756. Black.	150.00	300.00	—
S1745	30 SHILLINGS	22.6.1756. Black and red.	400.00	950.00	—
S1746	3 POUNDS	22.6.1756. Black and red.	400.00	950.00	—
S1747	6 POUNDS	22.6.1756. Black and red. Back green.	400.00	950.00	—

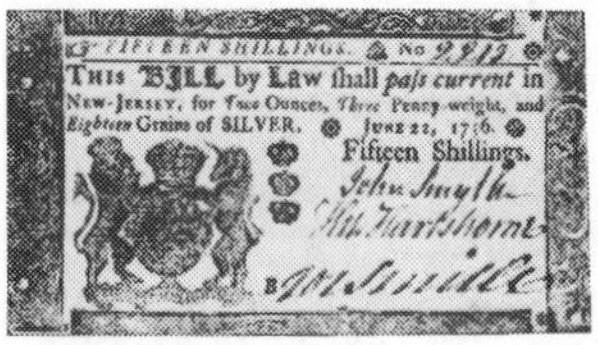

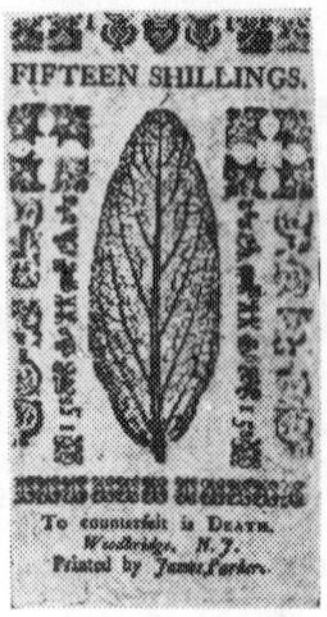

1757 FIRST ISSUE

#S1748-S1751 sage leaf on back. Printer: James Parker.

No.	Denomination	Date / Description	VG	VF	UNC
S1748	15 SHILLINGS	12.4.1757. Red. Back black.	85.00	225.00	—
S1749	30 SHILLINGS	12.4.1757. Red. Back black.	85.00	225.00	—
S1750	3 POUNDS	12.4.1757. Red. Back black.	175.00	425.00	—
S1751	6 POUNDS	12.4.1757. Red and black. Back green.	200.00	550.00	—

1757 SECOND ISSUE

#S1752-S1755 sage leaf on back. Printer: James Parker.

No.	Denomination	Date / Description	VG	VF	UNC
S1752	15 SHILLINGS	14.6.1757. Black.	120.00	—	—
S1753	30 SHILLINGS	14.6.1757. Black.	110.00	—	—
S1754	3 POUNDS	14.6.1757. Black.	150.00	—	—
S1755	6 POUNDS	14.6.1757. Red and black. Back black.	240.00	—	—

1757 THIRD ISSUE

			GOOD	FINE	XF
S1756	6 SHILLINGS	20.11.1757. Red and black. Back black.	35.00	150.00	—
S1757	15 SHILLINGS	20.11.1757. Red and black. Back black.	30.00	125.00	—
S1758	30 SHILLINGS	20.11.1757. Red and black. Back black.	24.00	90.00	—
S1759	3 POUNDS	20.11.1757. Red and black. Back black.	30.00	125.00	—
S1760	6 POUNDS	20.11.1757. Red and black. Back black.	90.00	375.00	—

1758 FIRST ISSUE

#S1761-S1765 sage leaf on back. Printer: James Parker.

			GOOD	FINE	XF
S1761	6 SHILLINGS	1.5.1758. Red and black. Back black.	25.00	85.00	—
S1762	15 SHILLINGS	1.5.1758. Red and black. Back black.	20.00	75.00	—
S1763	30 SHILLINGS	1.5.1758. Red and black. Back black.	18.00	62.00	—
S1764	3 POUNDS	1.5.1758. Red and black. Back black.	25.00	87.00	—
S1765	6 POUNDS	1.5.1758. Red and black. Back black.	42.00	275.00	—

1758 SECOND ISSUE

#S1766-S1774 sage leaf on back. Printer: James Parker.

			GOOD	FINE	XF
S1766	1 SHILLING	20.10.1758. Black.	35.00	165.00	—
S1767	18 PENCE	20.10.1758. Black.	50.00	210.00	—
S1768	3 SHILLINGS	20.10.1758. Black.	50.00	210.00	—
S1769	6 SHILLINGS	20.10.1758. Black.	60.00	250.00	—
S1770	12 SHILLINGS	20.10.1758. Black.	60.00	250.00	—
S1771	15 SHILLINGS	20.10.1758. Black.	72.00	300.00	—
S1772	30 SHILLINGS	20.10.1758. Red and black. Back black.	85.00	350.00	—
S1773	3 POUNDS	20.10.1758. Red and black. Back black.	135.00	—	—
S1774	6 POUNDS	20.10.1758. Red and brown. Back brown.	180.00	—	—

1759 ISSUES

#S1775-S1780 red and black. Sage leaf on back. Printer: James Parker.

			GOOD	FINE	XF
S1775	6 SHILLINGS	10.4.1759. Back black.	22.00	110.00	—
S1776	15 SHILLINGS	10.4.1759.	20.00	110.00	—
S1777	30 SHILLINGS	10.4.1759.	20.00	80.00	—
S1778	3 POUNDS	10.4.1759. Plate letter "A". O in Ounces is sometimes broken as to resemble C. Back black.	22.00	110.00	—
S1779	3 POUNDS	10.4.1759. Plate letter "B". Back black.	22.00	110.00	—
S1780	6 POUNDS	10.4.1759. Back black.	40.00	200.00	—

1760 ISSUE

#S1781-S1789 back black; sage leaf. Printer: James Parker.

			GOOD	FINE	XF
S1781	1 SHILLING	12.4.1760. Red and black.	20.00	100.00	—
S1782	18 PENCE	12.4.1760. Red and black.	22.00	110.00	—
S1783	3 SHILLINGS	12.4.1760. Red and black.	22.00	110.00	—
S1784	6 SHILLINGS	12.4.1760. Red and black.	25.00	125.00	—
S1785	12 SHILLINGS	12.4.1760. Red and black.	25.00	125.00	—

		Good	Fine	XF
S1786	**15 Shillings** 12.4.1760. Red and black.	25.00	125.00	—
S1787	**30 Shillings** 12.4.1760. Red and black.	25.00	125.00	—
S1788	**3 Pounds** 12.4.1760. Black.	35.00	175.00	—
S1789	**6 Pounds** 12.4.1760. Black.	50.00	250.00	—

1761 Issue

#S1790-S1794 red and black. Back black; sage leaf. Printer: James Parker.

No.	Denomination	VG	VF	Unc
S1790	**12 Shillings** 23.4.1761.	100.00	—	—
S1791	**15 Shillings** 23.4.1761.	60.00	—	—
S1792	**30 Shillings** 23.4.1761.	50.00	—	—
S1793	**3 Pounds** 23.4.1761.	70.00	—	—
S1794	**6 Pounds** 23.4.1761.	150.00	—	—

1762 Issue

#S1795-#S1799 red and black. Back black; sage leaf. Printer: James Parker.

No.	Denomination	VG	VF	Unc
S1795	**12 Shillings** 8.4.1762.	120.00	—	—
S1796	**15 Shillings** 8.4.1762.	80.00	—	—
S1797	**30 Shillings** 8.4.1762.	60.00	—	—
S1798	**3 Pounds** 8.4.1762.	80.00	—	—
S1799	**6 Pounds** 8.4.1762.	150.00	—	—

1763 Issue

#S1800-S1808 back black; sage leaf. Printer: James Parker.

No.	Denomination	VG	VF	Unc
S1800	**1 Shilling** 31.12.1763. Black.	15.00	50.00	100.00
S1801	**18 Pence** 31.12.1763.			
	a. Plate letters A; C.	17.00	60.00	120.00
	b. Plate letter B. *t* in *Penny-weight* is in italics instead of upright.	17.00	60.00	125.00
	c. Plate letter *D. PLATE* misspelled *PTATE.*	17.00	60.00	125.00
S1802	**3 Shillings** 31.12.1763. Black.	18.00	65.00	130.00
S1803	**6 Shillings** 31.12.1763. Black.	20.00	70.00	140.00

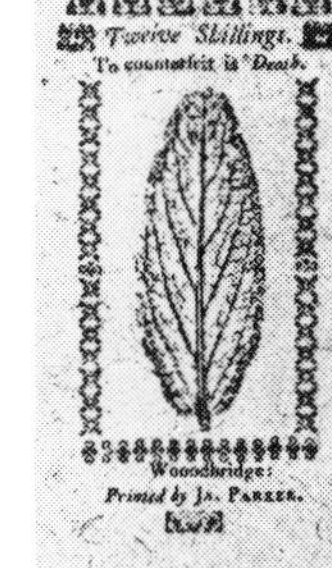

No.	Denomination	VG	VF	Unc
S1804	**12 Shillings** 31.12.1763. Black.	22.00	75.00	145.00
S1805	**15 Shillings** 31.12.1763. Black.	25.00	90.00	150.00
S1806	**30 Shillings** 31.12.1763. Red and black.	50.00	175.00	—
S1807	**3 Pounds** 31.12.1763. Red and black.	60.00	200.00	—
S1808	**6 Pounds** 31.12.1763. Red and blue.	120.00	400.00	1650.

1764 Issue

#S1809-S1813 red and black. Back black; sage leaf. Printer: James Parker.

No.	Denomination	VG	VF	Unc
S1809	**12 Shillings** 16.4.1764.	100.00	—	—
S1810	**15 Shillings** 16.4.1764.	55.00	—	—
S1811	**30 Shillings** 16.4.1764.	65.00	—	—
S1812	**3 Pounds** 16.4.1764.			
	a. Plate letters A; B; D.	70.00	—	—
	b. W/o plate letter. Solid sun.	70.00	—	—
	c. W/o plate letter. Split sun.	70.00	—	—
S1813	**6 Pounds** 16.4.1764.	200.00	—	—

1776 First Issue

#S1814-S1817 red and black. Back black; cut of leaf. Mica flaked paper. Wmk: *NEW JERSEY*. Printer: Isaac Collins, Burlington.

No.	Denomination	VG	VF	Unc
S1814	**6 Shillings** 20.2.1776.	45.00	110.00	—
S1815	**15 Shillings** 20.2.1776.	40.00	100.00	—

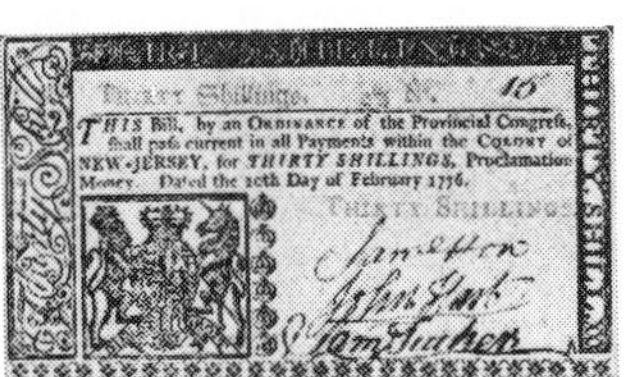

No.	Denomination	VG	VF	Unc
S1816	**30 Shillings** 20.2.1776.	32.00	80.00	—
S1817	**3 Pounds** 20.2.1776.	32.00	80.00	—

1776 Second Issue

#S1818-S1826 back black. Mica flaked paper. Wmk: *NEW JERSEY*. Printer: Isaac Collins.

#S1818-S1824 back black; leaf.

No.	Denomination	VG	VF	Unc
S1818	**1 Shilling** 25.3.1776. Red and black.	10.00	40.00	80.00
S1819	**18 Pence** 25.3.1776. Red and black.	11.00	45.00	90.00
S1820	**3 Shillings** 25.3.1776. Red and black.	13.00	52.00	105.00

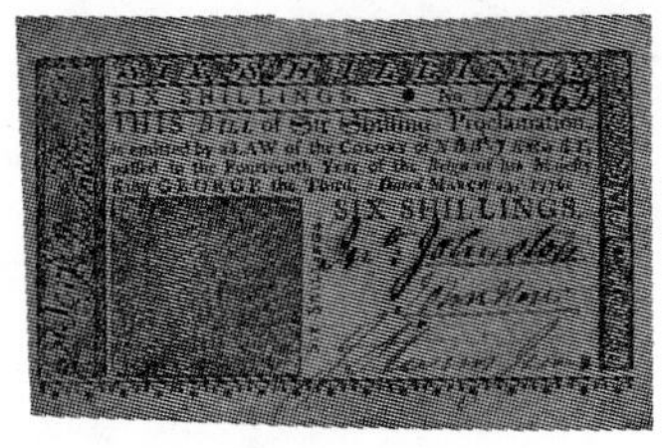

No.	Denomination	VG	VF	Unc
S1821	**6 Shillings** 25.3.1776. Red and black.			
	a. Plate letter A. Sm. coat-of-arms.	14.00	55.00	110.00
	b. Plate letter B. Lg. coat-of-arms.	15.00	60.00	120.00
S1822	**12 Shillings** 25.3.1776. Red and black.	15.00	60.00	120.00
S1823	**15 Shillings** 25.3.1776. Red and black.	18.50	75.00	150.00
S1824	**30 Shillings** 25.3.1776. Red and black.	25.00	100.00	200.00

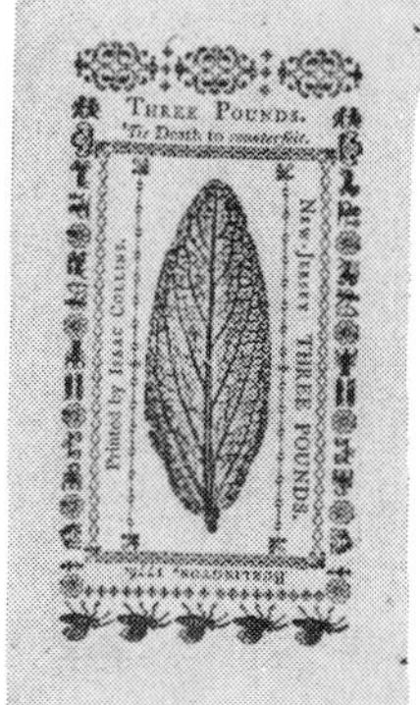

No.	Denomination	VG	VF	Unc
S1825	**3 Pounds** 25.3.1776. Red and blue. Back black; sage leaf and bees.	37.50	150.00	300.00
S1826	**6 Pounds** 25.3.1776. Red and blue. *RITTENHOUSE* in ctr. ornament at l. Back black; leaf.	57.50	225.00	450.00

New Jersey

State

1780 Issue

Dollar System

#S1827-S1834 black. Back red and black. Wmk: *UNITED STATES*. Printer: Hall & Sellers, PA.

		Good	Fine	XF
S1827	1 Dollar 9.6.1780.	40.00	90.00	190.00
S1828	2 Dollars 9.6.1780.	40.00	90.00	190.00
S1829	3 Dollars 9.6.1780.	40.00	90.00	190.00
S1830	4 Dollars 9.6.1780.	40.00	90.00	190.00
S1831	5 Dollars 9.6.1780.	40.00	90.00	190.00
S1832	7 Dollars 9.6.1780.	40.00	90.00	190.00
S1833	8 Dollars 9.6.1780.	40.00	90.00	190.00
S1834	20 Dollars 9.6.1780.	40.00	90.00	190.00

Act of 9.1.1781; 1781 Issue

Pound Sterling System

#S1835-S1844 black. N.J. state seal on face. Backs w/sage leaf stem printed opposite the side of the face of the Bill to differ from all previous issues. Printer: Isaac Collins, Trenton.

		VG	VF	Unc
S1835	6 Pence 1781.	75.00	200.00	350.00
S1836	9 Pence 1781.	75.00	200.00	350.00

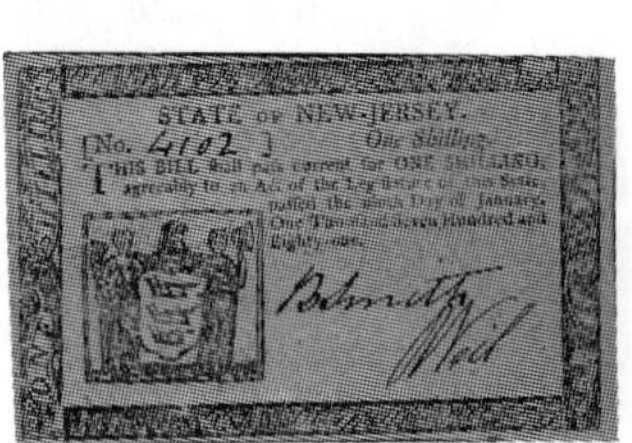

		VG	VF	Unc
S1837	1 Shilling 1781.	75.00	200.00	350.00
S1838	1 Shilling 6 Pence 1781.	75.00	200.00	350.00
S1839	2 Shillings 6 Pence 1781.	75.00	200.00	350.00
S1840	3 Shillings 6 Pence 1781.	75.00	200.00	350.00
S1841	3 Shillings 9 Pence 1781.	75.00	200.00	350.00
S1842	4 Shillings 1781.	75.00	200.00	350.00
S1843	5 Shillings 1781.	75.00	200.00	350.00

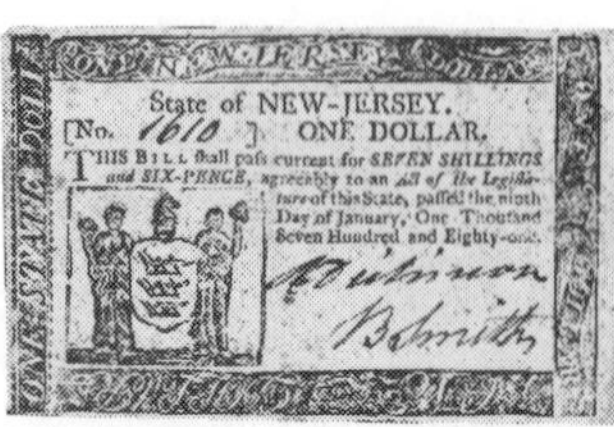

		VG	VF	Unc
S1844	7 Shillings 6 Pence or 1 Dollar 1781.	75.00	200.00	350.00

Act of Dec. 20, 1783; 1784 Issue

#S1845-S1853 black. Like #S1835-S1844. Wmk: *NEW JERSEY*. Printer: Isaac Collins.

		Good	Fine	XF
S1845	2 Shillings 6 Pence 1784.	—	—	—
S1846	3 Shillings 9 Pence 1784.	—	—	—
S1847	5 Shillings 1784.	—	—	—
S1848	7 Shillings 1784.	—	—	—
S1849	12 Shillings 1784.	—	—	—
S1850	15 Shillings 1784.	—	—	—
S1851	30 Shillings 1784.	—	—	—
S1852	3 Pounds 1784.	—	—	—
S1853	6 Pounds 1784.	—	—	—

1786 Issue

#S1854-S1861 red and black. Back black w/sage leaf stem printed opposite the r. side of the face w/SIC which apparently means Sculpist Isaac Collins. Wmk: *NEW JERSEY*. Printer: Isaac Collins.

		Good	Fine	XF
S1854	1 Shilling 1786. Plate letters A; B; C.	200.00	500.00	—
S1855	3 Shillings 1786. Plate letters A; B; C; D.	275.00	625.00	—

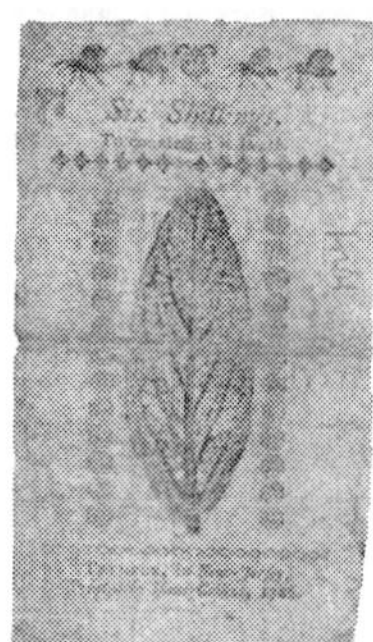

		Good	Fine	XF
S1856	6 Shillings 1786.			
	a. Plate letter A. Bees.	325.00	750.00	—
	b. W/o plate letter. Bees.	425.00	1000.	—
S1857	12 Shillings 1786.	425.00	1000.	—
S1858	15 Shillings 1786.	550.00	1200.	—
S1859	30 Shillings 1786.	850.00	1750.	—
S1860	3 Pounds 1786. Bees on back.	1200.	2400.	—
S1861	6 Pounds 1786.	1500.	3000.	—

New York

Colonial

1709 Issues

Pound Sterling System

#S1862, S1864, S1866-S1871 black. Uniface. Printer: William Bradford.

		Good	Fine	XF
S1862	5 Shillings 31.5.1709. *&* in fourth line of text.	—	—	—

		Good	Fine	XF
S1863	5 Shillings 31.5.1709. *d* in first, *and* is inverted.	—	—	—
S1864	10 Shillings 31.5.1709.			
	a. Text: w/*Lieut. Governor.*	—	—	—
	b. Text: w/*Lieut. Governour.*	—	—	—

#S1865 *Deleted*. See #S1846b.

		Good	Fine	XF
S1866	20 Shillings 31.5.1709.	—	—	—
S1867	40 Shillings 31.5.1709.	—	—	—
S1868	5 Pounds 31.5.1709.	—	—	—
S1869	25 Shillings 1.11.1709.	—	—	—
S1870	50 Shillings 1.11.1709.	—	—	—
S1871	5 Pounds 1.11.1709.	—	—	—

1709 Silver Plate Issue

Lion Daalder System

One Dutch silver *Lion Daalder* equalled 5 Shillings 6 Pence New York money of account or 13 pennyweights, 18 grains of silver plate.

		Good	Fine	XF
S1872	**4 Lyon Dollars** 1.11.1709.			
	a. Text: w/*Lieut. GOVERNOR.*	—	—	—
	b. Text: w/*Lieut. GOVERNOUR.*	—	—	—
S1874	**8 Lyon Dollars** 1.11.1709.	—	—	—
S1875	**16 Lyon Dollars** 1.11.1709.	—	—	—
S1876	**20 Lyon Dollars** 1.11.1709.	—	—	—

1711 Silver Plate Issue

Pound Sterling System

#S1877-S1885 black. *Fund* spelled *Fond*. Printer: William Bradford.

		Good	Fine	XF
S1877	**2 Shillings** 20.6.1711.	—	—	—
S1878	**4 Shillings** 20.6.1711.	—	—	—
S1879	**8 Shillings** 20.6.1711.	—	—	—
S1880	**16 Shillings** 20.6.1711.	—	—	—
S1881	**20 Shillings** 20.6.1711.	—	—	—
S1882	**40 Shillings** 20.6.1711.	—	—	—
S1883	**4 Pounds** 20.6.1711.	—	—	—
S1884	**8 Pounds** 20.6.1711. *C* is a different size in the 3rd *COLONY.*	—	—	—
S1885	**8 Pounds** 20.6.1711. First and last uses of *COLONY; C* is the same size.	—	—	—

1714 Silver Plate Issue

#S1886-S1897 black. Printer: William Bradford.

		Good	Fine	XF
S1886	**3 Shillings** 1.7.1714.	—	—	—
S1887	**6 Shillings** 1.7.1714.	—	—	—
S1888	**12 Shillings** 1.7.1714.	—	—	—
S1889	**15 Shillings** 1.7.1714.	—	—	—
S1890	**1 Pound 5 Shillings** 1.7.1714.	—	—	—
S1891	**1 Pound 10 Shillings** 1.7.1714.	—	—	—
S1892	**2 Pounds 10 Shillings** 1.7.1714.	—	—	—
S1893	**3 Pounds** 1.7.1714.	—	—	—
S1894	**5 Pounds** 1.7.1714.	—	—	—
S1895	**6 Pounds** 1.7.1714.	—	—	—
S1896	**7 Pounds 10 Shillings** 1.7.1714.	—	—	—
S1897	**10 Pounds** 1.7.1714.	—	—	—

1715 Silver Plate Issue

#S1898-S1904 black. Printer: William Bradford.

		Good	Fine	XF
S1898	**5 Shillings** 5.7.1715.	—	—	—
S1899	**10 Shillings** 5.7.1715.	—	—	—
S1900	**20 Shillings** 5.7.1715.	—	—	—
S1901	**40 Shillings** 5.7.1715.	—	—	—
S1902	**4 Pounds** 5.7.1715.	—	—	—
S1903	**5 Pounds** 5.7.1715.	—	—	—
S1904	**10 Pounds** 5.7.1715.	—	—	—

1717 Spanish Silver Issue

#S1905-S1915 black. Crowned arms of New York City. Printer: William Bradford.

		Good	Fine	XF
S1905	**2 Shillings** 28.11.1717.	—	—	—
S1906	**4 Shillings** 28.11.1717.	—	—	—
S1907	**6 Shillings** 28.11.1717.	—	—	—
S1908	**8 Shillings** 28.11.1717.	—	—	—
S1909	**10 Shillings** 28.11.1717.	—	—	—
S1910	**12 Shillings** 28.11.1717.	—	—	—
S1911	**16 Shillings** 28.11.1717.	—	—	—
S1912	**20 Shillings** 28.11.1717.	—	—	—
S1913	**40 Shillings** 28.11.1717.	—	—	—
S1914	**3 Pounds** 28.11.1717.	—	—	—
S1915	**4 Pounds** 28.11.1717.	—	—	—

1720 Silver Plate Issue

#S1916-S1920 black. Crowned arms of New York City. Printer: William Bradford.

		Good	Fine	XF
S1916	**1 Shilling** 10.11.1720.	—	—	—
S1917	**1 Shilling 6 Pence** 10.11.1720.	—	—	—
S1918	**2 Shillings 6 Pence** 10.11.1720.	—	—	—
S1919	**3 Shillings** 10.11.1720.	—	—	—
S1920	**3 Shillings 6 Pence** 10.11.1720.	—	—	—

1723 Silver Plate Issue

#S1921 and S1922 black. Printer: William Bradford.

		Good	Fine	XF
S1921	**3 Pounds 10 Shillings** 2.7.1723.	—	—	—
S1922	**4 Pounds 10 Shillings** 2.7.1723.	—	—	—

1724 First Issue

#S1923-S1929 black. Crowned arms of New York City. Printer: William Bradford.

		Good	Fine	XF
S1923	**1 Shilling 3 Pence** 10.7.1724.	—	—	—
S1924	**3 Shillings 9 Pence** 10.7.1724.	—	—	—
S1925	**7 Shillings 6 Pence** 10.7.1724.	—	—	—
S1926	**14 Shillings** 10.7.1724.	—	—	—
S1927	**1 Pound 12 Shillings** 10.7.1724.	—	—	—
S1928	**3 Pounds 4 Shillings** 10.7.1724.	—	—	—
S1929	**3 Pounds 12 Shillings** 10.7.1724.	—	—	—

1724 Second Issue

#S1930-S1939 black. Crowned arms of New York City. Printer: William Bradford.

		Good	Fine	XF
S1930	**1 Shilling** 22.7.1724.	—	—	—
S1931	**1 Shilling 6 Pence** 22.7.1724.	—	—	—
S1932	**2 Shillings** 22.7.1724.	—	—	—
S1933	**2 Shillings 6 Pence** 22.7.1724.	—	—	—
S1934	**3 Shillings** 22.7.1724.	—	—	—
S1935	**3 Shillings 6 Pence** 22.7.1724.	—	—	—
S1936	**4 Shillings** 22.7.1724.	—	—	—
S1937	**6 Shillings** 22.7.1724.	—	—	—
S1938	**8 Shillings** 22.7.1724.	—	—	—
S1939	**12 Shillings** 22.7.1724.	—	—	—

1726 Replacement Issue

#S1940-S1950 black. Crowned arms of New York City. The year of the note replaced is handwritten near top center.

		Good	Fine	XF
S1940	**1 Shilling** 16.11.1726.	—	—	—
S1941	**1 Shilling 3 Pence** 16.11.1726.	—	—	—
S1942	**1 Shilling 6 Pence** 16.11.1726.	—	—	—
S1943	**2 Shillings** 16.11.1726.	—	—	—
S1944	**2 Shillings 6 Pence** 16.11.1726.	—	—	—
S1945	**3 Shillings** 16.11.1726.	—	—	—
S1946	**3 Shillings 6 Pence** 16.11.1726.	—	—	—
S1947	**4 Shillings** 16.11.1726.	—	—	—
S1948	**6 Shillings** 16.11.1726.	—	—	—
S1949	**8 Shillings** 16.11.1726.	—	—	—
S1950	**12 Shillings** 16.11.1726.	—	—	—

1730 Replacement Issue

#S1951-S1954 black. Crowned arms of New York City. The year of the note replaced is handwritten near top center. Printer: William Bradford.

		Good	Fine	XF
S1951	**2 Shillings** 20.10.1730.	—	—	—
S1952	**5 Shillings** 20.10.1730.	—	—	—

		Good	Fine	XF
S1953	10 Shillings 20.10.1730.	—	—	—
S1954	20 Shillings 20.10.1730.	—	—	—

1734 Issue

#S1955-S1961 black. Crowned arms of New York City. Issued for fortifications. Printer: William Bradford.

		Good	Fine	XF
S1955	5 Shillings 15.11.1734.	—	—	—
S1956	10 Shillings 15.11.1734.	—	—	—
S1957	20 Shillings 15.11.1734.	—	—	—
S1958	2 Pounds 15.11.1734.	—	—	—
S1959	3 Pounds 15.11.1734.	—	—	—
S1960	5 Pounds 15.11.1734.	—	—	—
S1961	10 Pounds 15.11.1734.	—	—	—

1737 Issue

#S1962-S1968 black. Crowned arms of New York City. Uniface. Printer: John Peter Zenger.

		Good	Fine	XF
S1962	5 Shillings 10.12.1737.	—	—	—
S1963	10 Shillings 10.12.1737.	—	—	—
S1964	20 Shillings 10.12.1737.	—	—	—
S1965	2 Pounds 10.12.1737.	—	—	—
S1966	3 Pounds 10.12.1737.	—	—	—
S1967	5 Pounds 10.12.1737.	—	—	—

		Good	Fine	XF
S1968	10 Pounds 10.12.1737.	—	—	—

1739 Replacement Issue

#S1969-S1975 black. Crowned arms of New York City. Printer: William Bradford.

		Good	Fine	XF
S1969	5 Shillings 20.11.1739.	—	—	—
S1970	10 Shillings 20.11.1739.	—	—	—
S1971	20 Shillings 20.11.1739.	—	—	—
S1972	2 Pounds 20.11.1739.	—	—	—
S1973	3 Pounds 20.11.1739.	—	—	—
S1974	5 Pounds 20.11.1739.	—	—	—
S1975	10 Pounds 20.11.1739.	—	—	—

1746 Defence Issues

#S1976-S1985 black. Crowned arms of New York City at r. Printer: James Parker.

		Good	Fine	XF
S1976	2 Pounds 10.5.1746.	—	—	—
S1977	3 Pounds 10.5.1746.	—	—	—
S1978	5 Pounds 10.5.1746.	—	—	—
S1979	10 Pounds 10.5.1746.	—	—	—
S1980	10 Shillings 21.7.1746.	—	—	—
S1981	20 Shillings 21.7.1746.	—	—	—
S1982	2 Pounds 21.7.1746.	—	—	—
S1983	3 Pounds 21.7.1746.	—	—	—
S1984	5 Pounds 21.7.1746.	—	—	—
S1985	10 Pounds 21.7.1746.	—	—	—

1747 Defence Issue

#S1986-S1990 black. Crowned arms of New York City at l. Printer: James Parker.

		Good	Fine	XF
S1986	20 Shillings 25.11.1747.	—	—	—
S1987	2 Pounds 25.11.1747.	—	—	—
S1988	3 Pounds 25.11.1747.	—	—	—
S1989	5 Pounds 25.11.1747.	—	—	—
S1990	10 Pounds 25.11.1747.	—	—	—

1755 First Issue

#S1991-S1996 black. Crowned arms of New York City at r. White paper. Uniface w/dark coarse paper backs. Printer: James Parker.

		Good	Fine	XF
S1991	10 Shillings 25.3.1755.	—	—	—
S1992	20 Shillings 25.3.1755.	—	—	—
S1993	2 Pounds 25.3.1755.	—	—	—
S1994	3 Pounds 25.3.1755.	—	—	—
S1995	5 Pounds 25.3.1755.	—	—	—
S1996	10 Pounds 25.3.1755.	—	—	—

1755 Second Issue

#S1997-S2004 black. Crowned arms of New York City at l. White paper. Uniface w/dark coarse paper backs. Printer: James Parker.

		Good	Fine	XF
S1997	5 Shillings 12.5.1755.	—	—	—
S1998	10 Shillings 12.5.1755.	—	—	—
S1999	20 Shillings 12.5.1755.	—	—	—
S2000	2 Pounds 12.5.1755.	—	—	—
S2001	3 Pounds 12.5.1755.	—	—	—
S2002	4 Pounds 12.5.1755.	—	—	—
S2003	5 Pounds 12.5.1755.	—	—	—
S2004	10 Pounds 12.5.1755.	—	—	—

1755 Third Issue

#S2005-S2012 black. Crowned arms of New York City at l. White paper. Uniface w/dark coarse paper backs. Printer: James Parker.

		Good	Fine	XF
S2005	5 Shillings 15.9.1755.	—	—	—
S2006	10 Shillings 15.9.1755.	—	—	—
S2007	20 Shillings 15.9.1755.	—	—	—
S2008	2 Pounds 15.9.1755.	—	—	—
S2009	3 Pounds 15.9.1755.	—	—	—
S2010	4 Pounds 15.9.1755.	—	—	—
S2011	5 Pounds 15.9.1755.	—	—	—
S2012	10 Pounds 15.9.1755.	—	—	—

1756 First Issue

#S2013 black. Crowned arms of New York City at r. White paper. Uniface w/dark coarse paper back. Printer: James Parker.

		Good	Fine	XF
S2013	10 Pounds 16.2.1756.	—	—	—

1756 Second Issue

#S2014-S2018 black. Crowned arms of New York City at r. White paper. Uniface w/dark coarse paper backs. Printer: James Parker.

		VG	VF	Unc
S2014	20 Shillings 20.4.1756.	140.00	—	—
S2015	2 Pounds 20.4.1756.	200.00	—	—
S2016	3 Pounds 20.4.1756.	140.00	—	—
S2017	5 Pounds 20.4.1756.	100.00	—	—
S2018	10 Pounds 20.4.1756.	135.00	—	—

1758 Issue

#S2019 and S2020 black. Crowned arms of New York City at r. White paper. Uniface w/dark coarse paper backs. Printer: James Parker.

		VG	VF	Unc
S2019	5 Pounds 15.4.1758.	105.00	325.00	—

		VG	VF	Unc
S2020	10 Pounds 15.4.1758.	75.00	225.00	—

1759 Issue

#S2021-S2023 black. Crowned arms of New York City at r. Thin white paper. Printer: William Weyman.

		Good	Fine	XF
S2021	**2 Pounds** 2.4.1759.	40.00	125.00	—
S2022	**5 Pounds** 2.4.1759.	50.00	165.00	—
S2023	**10 Pounds** 2.4.1759.	45.00	145.00	—

1760 Issue

#S2024-S2026 black. Crowned arms of New York City at r. Printer: William Weyman.

		VG	VF	Unc
S2024	**2 Pounds** 21.4.1760.	85.00	150.00	—
S2025	**5 Pounds** 21.4.1760.	95.00	175.00	—
S2026	**10 Pounds** 21.4.1760.	95.00	175.00	—

1771 Issue

#S2027-S2033 black. Ornamental upper border, crowned arms of New York City. Thin laid paper. Printer: Hugh Gaine.

		VG	VF	Unc
S2027	**5 Shillings** 16.2.1771.	40.00	100.00	—
S2028	**10 Shillings** 16.2.1771.	40.00	100.00	—
S2029	**1 Pound** 16.2.1771.	45.00	115.00	—
S2030	**2 Pounds** 16.2.1771.			
	a. Comma after February. Stars on bottom border have 12 points.	45.00	115.00	—
	b. W/o comma after February. Stars on bottom border have 12 points.	45.00	115.00	—
	c. Stars on bottom border have 12 points except 7th from r.	45.00	115.00	—
	d. Stars on bottom border have 8 points.	45.00	115.00	—

		VG	VF	Unc
S2031	**3 Pounds** 16.2.1771.	45.00	115.00	—
S2032	**5 Pounds** 16.2.1771.	45.00	115.00	—
S2033	**10 Pounds** 16.2.1771.	45.00	115.00	—

1775 Spanish Silver Issue

Dollar System

#S2034-S2039 black. Crowned arms of New York City. Thick paper. Printer: John Holt.

		VG	VF	Unc
S2034	**1/2 Dollar** 2.9.1775. Planting of tree w/motto: *POSTERITATE* on back	40.00	120.00	—
S2035	**1 Dollar** 2.9.1775. Sheaf of wheat w/motto: *ACERVUS E PARVIS GRANDIS* on back.	40.00	120.00	—
S2036	**2 Dollars** 2.9.1775. 2 storks w/motto: *SALUTARIS SIBI PARENTIBUSQUE* on back.	40.00	120.00	—

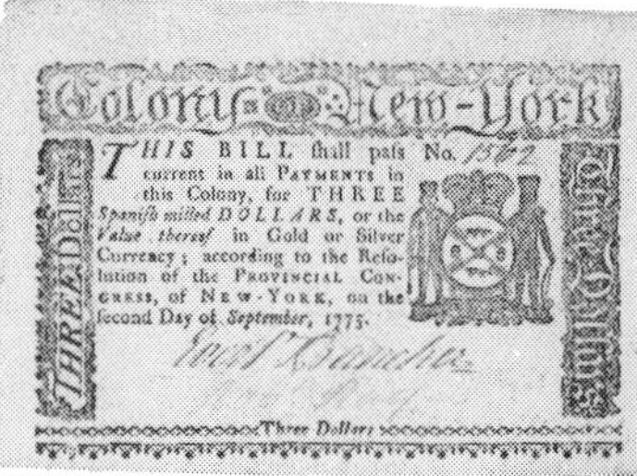

		VG	VF	Unc
S2037	**3 Dollars** 2.9.1775. Ten Commandments w/motto: *LEX REGIT ARMA TUENTUR* on back.	40.00	120.00	—
S2038	**5 Dollars** 2.9.1775. Candelabrum w/motto: *UNO EODEMQUE IGNI* on back.	40.00	120.00	—
S2039	**10 Dollars** 2.9.1775. Elephant w/motto: *PAR VIRIBUS VIRTUS* on back.	40.00	120.00	—

1776 Issue

#S2040-S2050 black. Thick paper. Printer: Samuel Loudon.

		VG	VF	Unc
S2040	**1/8 Dollar** 5.3.1776. Fire w/motto: *NON DIU* on back.	100.00	300.00	—

		VG	VF	Unc
S2041	**1/6 Dollar** 5.3.1776. Stork w/motto: *NE IMPROVISO* on back.	100.00	300.00	—
S2042	**1/4 Dollar** 5.3.1776. Book and candle w/motto: *CLARET AB ICTU* on back.	100.00	300.00	—
S2043	**1/3 Dollar** 5.3.1776. 3 wreaths w/motto: *HIS ORNARI AUT MORI* on back.	100.00	300.00	—
S2044	**1/2 Dollar** 5.3.1776. Planting of tree w/motto: *POSTERITATE* on back.	100.00	300.00	—
S2045	**2/3 Dollar** 5.3.1776. Eagle w/motto: *FORTIS A FORTE* on back.	100.00	300.00	—
S2046	**1 Dollar** 5.3.1776. Sheaf of wheat w/motto: *ACERVUS E PARVIS GRANDIS* on back.	100.00	300.00	—
S2047	**2 Dollars** 5.3.1776. 2 storks w/motto: *SALUTARIS SIBI PARENTIBUSQUE* on back.	150.00	500.00	—
S2048	**3 Dollars** 5.3.1776. Ten Commandments w/motto: *LEX REGIT ARMA TUENTUR* on back.	150.00	500.00	—
S2049	**5 Dollars** 5.3.1776. Candelabrum w/motto: *UNO EODEMQUE IGNI* on back.	150.00	500.00	—
S2050	**10 Dollars** 5.3.1776. Elephant w/motto: *PAR VIRIBUS VIRTUS* on back.	150.00	500.00	—

New York

State

1776 Issue

#S2051-S2053 black. Thick paper. Printer: Samuel Loudon.

		VG	VF	Unc
S2051	**1/16 Dollar** 13.8.1776.	35.00	70.00	200.00
S2052	**1/8 Dollar** 13.8.1776. Fire w/motto: *NON DIU* on back.	35.00	70.00	200.00
S2053	**1/4 Dollar** 13.8.1776. Book and candle w/motto: *CLARET AB ICTU* on back.	35.00	70.00	200.00
S2054	**1/2 Dollar** 13.8.1776. Planting of tree w/motto: *POSTERITATE* on back.	35.00	70.00	200.00
S2055	**2 Dollars** 13.8.1776. 2 storks w/motto: *SALUTARIS SIBI PARENTIBUSQUE* on back.	40.00	80.00	250.00
S2056	**3 Dollars** 13.8.1776. Ten Commandments w/motto: *LEX REGIT ARMA TUENTUR* on back.	40.00	80.00	250.00

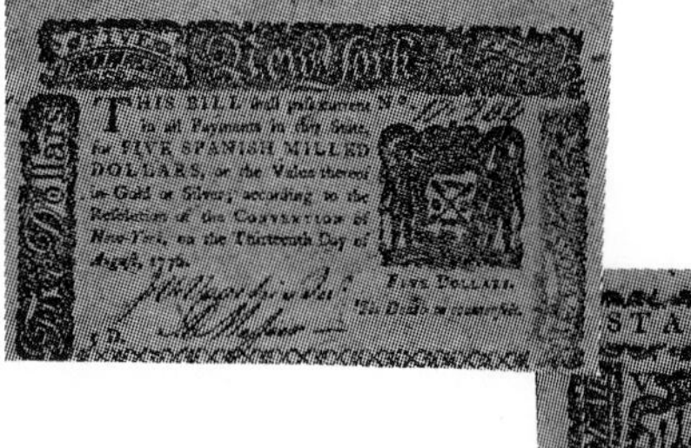

		VG	VF	Unc
S2057	**5 Dollars** 13.8.1776. Candelabrum w/motto: *UNO EODEMQUE IGNI* on back.	40.00	80.00	250.00
S2058	**10 Dollars** 13.8.1776. Elephant w/motto: *PAR VIRIBUS VIRTUS* on back.	40.00	80.00	250.00

1780 Issue

#S2059-S2066 black. Mica flaked paper. Wmk: *CONFEDERATION* in 2 lines. Back red and black. Printer: Hall & Sellers, PA.

		Good	Fine	XF
S2059	**1 Dollar** 15.6.1780.	200.00	425.00	—
S2060	**2 Dollars** 15.6.1780.	200.00	425.00	—
S2061	**3 Dollars** 15.6.1780.	200.00	425.00	—
S2062	**4 Dollars** 15.6.1780.	200.00	425.00	—
S2063	**5 Dollars** 15.6.1780.	200.00	425.00	—

No.	Denomination	Good	Fine	XF
S2064	**7 Dollars** 15.6.1780.	200.00	425.00	—
S2065	**8 Dollars** 15.6.1780.	200.00	425.00	—
S2066	**20 Dollars** 15.6.1780.	200.00	425.00	—

1781 Issue

#S2067-S2074 black. Some notes have a red printed endorsement ovpt: *Int. pd. one Year.* Printer: John Holt.

No.	Denomination	Good	Fine	XF
S2067	**1 Dollar** 27.3.1781. Liberty Cap.	—	—	—
S2068	**2 Dollars** 27.3.1781. Sword.	—	—	—
S2069	**3 Dollars** 27.3.1781.	—	—	—
S2070	**4 Dollars** 27.3.1781.	—	—	—
S2071	**5 Dollars** 27.3.1781.	—	—	—
S2072	**7 Dollars** 27.3.1781.	—	—	—
S2073	**8 Dollars** 27.3.1781. Justice.	—	—	—
S2074	**20 Dollars** 27.3.1781.	—	—	—

1786 Issue

#S2075-S2082 black. Arms of New York State. Printer: Samuel Loudon.

No.	Denomination	Good	Fine	XF
S2075	**5 Shillings** 18.4.1786.	—	—	—
		Good	Fine	XF
	a. *EXCELSIOR* in white.	—	—	—
	b. *EXCELSIOR* in black.	—	—	—
S2076	**10 Shillings** 18.4.1786.	—	—	—
S2077	**1 Pound** 18.4.1786.	—	—	—
S2078	**2 Pounds** 18.4.1786.	—	—	—
S2079	**3 Pounds** 18.4.1786.	—	—	—
S2080	**4 Pounds** 18.4.1786.	—	—	—
S2081	**5 Pounds** 18.4.1786.	—	—	—
S2082	**10 Pounds** 18.4.1786.	—	—	—

1788 Issue

#S2083-S2090 black and red. Thick paper. Back black. Printer: Hugh Gaine.

No.	Denomination	Good	Fine	XF
S2083	**5 Shillings** 8.2.1788.	—	—	—
S2084	**10 Shillings** 8.2.1788.	—	—	—
S2085	**1 Pound** 8.2.1788.	—	—	—
S2086	**2 Pounds** 8.2.1788.	—	—	—
S2087	**3 Pounds** 8.2.1788.	—	—	—
S2088	**4 Pounds** 8.2.1788.	—	—	—
S2089	**5 Pounds** 8.2.1788.	—	—	—
S2090	**10 Pounds** 8.2.1788.	—	—	—

North Carolina

Colonial

1722 Issue

Pound Sterling System

#S2091-S2100 black.

> **A word on pricing**
>
> When a note is marked RARE in the price columns, this note seldom appears on the market, or few are known in private hands. When dashes are in the price column, means that the note has not traded on the open market recently and a definitive value could not accurately be determined. Rare does not always mean expensive. A dashed price does not mean expensive or rare.

No.	Denomination	Good	Fine	XF
S2091	**12 Pence** 19.10.1722.	—	—	—
S2092	**2 Shillings** 19.10.1722.	—	—	—
S2093	**2 Shillings 6 Pence** 19.10.1722.	—	—	—
S2094	**5 Shillings** 19.10.1722.	—	—	—
S2095	**7 Shillings 6 Pence** 19.10.1722.	—	—	—
S2096	**10 Shillings** 19.10.1722.	—	—	—
S2097	**20 Shillings** 19.10.1722.	—	—	—
S2098	**40 Shillings** 19.10.1722.	—	—	—
S2099	**3 Pounds** 19.10.1722.	—	—	—
S2100	**5 Pounds** 19.10.1722.	—	—	—

1729 Issue

#S2101-S2111 black.

No.	Denomination	Good	Fine	XF
S2101	**12 Pence** 27.11.1729.	—	—	—
S2102	**2 Shillings** 27.11.1729.	—	—	—
S2103	**2 Shillings 6 Pence** 27.11.1729.	—	—	—
S2104	**5 Shillings** 27.11.1729.	—	—	—
S2105	**7 Shillings 6 Pence** 27.11.1729.	—	—	—
S2106	**10 Shillings** 27.11.1729.	—	—	—
S2107	**20 Shillings** 27.11.1729.	—	—	—
S2108	**40 Shillings** 27.11.1729.	—	—	—

No.	Denomination	Good	Fine	XF
S2109	**3 Pounds** 27.11.1729.	—	—	—
S2110	**5 Pounds** 27.11.1729. Denomination in red.	—	—	—
S2111	**10 Pounds** 27.11.1729.	—	—	—

NOTE: The illustration of #S2109 is that of a contemporary circulating counterfeit.

1734 Issue

#S2112-S2120 black.

No.	Denomination	Good	Fine	XF
S2112	**1 Shilling** 1734(5).	—	—	—
S2113	**2 Shillings 6 Pence** 1734(5).	—	—	—
S2114	**5 Shillings** 1734(5).	—	—	—
S2115	**10 Shillings** 1734(5).	—	—	—
S2116	**20 Shillings** 1734(5). Crowned lion.	—	—	—
S2117	**40 Shillings** 1734(5).	—	—	—
S2118	**3 Pounds** 1734(5).	—	—	—
S2119	**5 Pounds** 1734(5).	—	—	—
S2120	**10 Pounds** 1734(5). Winged stirrup.	—	—	—

1735 Issue

#S2121-S2129 black.

No.	Denomination	Good	Fine	XF
S2121	**1 Shilling** 1735.	—	—	—
S2122	**2 Shillings 6 Pence** 1735.	—	—	—

No.	Denomination / Description	GOOD	FINE	XF
S2123	**5 SHILLINGS** 1735.	—	—	—
S2124	**10 SHILLINGS** 1735.	—	—	—
S2125	**20 SHILLINGS** 1735. Crowned lion.	—	—	—
S2126	**40 SHILLINGS** 1735.	—	—	—
S2127	**3 POUNDS** 1735.	—	—	—
S2128	**5 POUNDS** 1735.	—	—	—
S2129	**10 POUNDS** 1735. Winged stirrup.	—	—	—

1748 ISSUE

#S2130-S2146 black.

		VG	VF	UNC
S2130	**4 PENCE** 4.4.1748. Denomination in circle.	175.00	—	—
S2131	**8 PENCE** 4.4.1748. Denomination in circle.	175.00	—	—
S2132	**1 SHILLING** 4.4.1748. Denomination in circle.	175.00	—	—
S2133	**1 SHILLING** 4.4.1748. Denomination in circle.	175.00	—	—
S2134	**2 SHILLINGS** 4.4.1748. Thistle.	175.00	—	—
S2135	**2 SHILLINGS 6 PENCE** 4.4.1748. Crowned rose.	175.00	—	—
S2136	**3 SHILLINGS** 4.4.1748. Plumes.	175.00	—	—
S2137	**5 SHILLINGS** 4.4.1748. Crown.	175.00	—	—
S2138	**6 SHILLINGS** 4.4.1748. Fleur-de-lys.	175.00	—	—
S2139	**7 SHILLINGS 6 PENCE** 4.4.1748. Harp.	175.00	—	—
S2140	**9 SHILLINGS** 4.4.1748. Crowned lion.	175.00	—	—
S2141	**10 SHILLINGS** 4.4.1748. Horse.	175.00	—	—
S2142	**15 SHILLINGS** 4.4.1748. Rampant lion.	175.00	—	—
S2143	**20 SHILLINGS** 4.4.1748. Unicorn.	175.00	—	—
S2144	**30 SHILLINGS** 4.4.1748. Winged stirrup.	175.00	—	—
S2145	**40 SHILLINGS** 4.4.1748. Drum, cannon and flags.	175.00	—	—

		VG	VF	UNC
S2146	**3 POUNDS** 4.4.1748. Fort Johnson and Union Jack.	175.00	—	—

1754 ISSUE

#S2147-S2158 black.

No.	Denomination / Description	GOOD	FINE	XF
S2147	**4 PENCE** 9.3.1754.			
	a. Key.	90.00	325.00	—
	b. Mountain lion.	90.00	325.00	—
	c. Monogram.	90.00	325.00	—
S2148	**8 PENCE** 9.3.1754.			
	a. Butterfly.	90.00	325.00	—
	b. Boar.	90.00	325.00	—
S2149	**1 SHILLING** 9.3.1754.			
	a. Swan.	90.00	325.00	—
	b. Bear.	90.00	325.00	—
	c. *NC* monogram.	90.00	325.00	—
S2150	**2 SHILLINGS 8 PENCE** 9.3.1754. Snail.	90.00	325.00	—
S2151	**4 SHILLINGS** 9.3.1754. Monogram.	90.00	325.00	—
S2152	**5 SHILLINGS** 9.3.1754. Squirrel.	90.00	325.00	—
S2153	**10 SHILLINGS** 9.3.1754. Bird.	90.00	325.00	—
S2154	**15 SHILLINGS** 9.3.1754. Armor.	75.00	250.00	—
S2155	**20 SHILLINGS** 9.3.1754. Crown.	75.00	250.00	—
S2156	**26 SHILLINGS 8 PENCE** 9.3.1754. Bible.	75.00	250.00	—
S2157	**30 SHILLINGS** 9.3.1754. House.	75.00	250.00	—
S2158	**40 SHILLINGS** 9.3.1754. Christ Church at Newbern.	75.00	250.00	—

Companion Volumes

Volume II – General Issues 1368-1960
Volume III – Modern Issues 1961-present

The Companion catalogs in the Standard Catalog of World Paper Money Series include two volumes on bank notes issued for national use. Those dated 1960 and before are in volume II, those dated 1961 and later are in volume III. Ordering information can be obtained from Krause Publications Book Division, 1-800-258-0929.

1756-57 ISSUE

#S2159-S2162 black.

No.	Denomination / Description	GOOD	FINE	XF
S2159	**5 POUNDS** 1756-57.	—	—	—
S2160	**10 POUNDS** 1756-57.	—	—	—
S2161	**20 POUNDS** 1756-57.	—	—	—
S2162	**50 POUNDS** 1756-57.	—	—	—

1757 ISSUE

#S2163-S2166 black.

No.	Denomination / Description	GOOD	FINE	XF
S2163	**10 SHILLINGS** 28.5.1757.			
	a. W/text: *per Cent.*	—	—	—
	b. W/text: *per Centum.*	—	—	—
S2164	**20 SHILLINGS** 28.5.1757.			
	a. W/text: *per Cent.*	—	—	—
	b. W/text: *per Centum.*	—	—	—
S2165	**40 SHILLINGS** 28.5.1757.			
	a. W/text: *per Cent.*	—	—	—
	b. W/text: *per Centum.*	—	—	—
S2166	**5 POUNDS** 28.5.1757.			
	a. W/text: *per Cent.*	—	—	—
	b. W/text: *per Centum.*	—	—	—

1757 SESSION ACT ISSUE

#S2167-S2170 black.

No.	Denomination / Description	GOOD	FINE	XF
S2167	**10 SHILLINGS** 21.11.1757.	—	—	—
S2168	**20 SHILLINGS** 21.11.1757.	—	—	—
S2169	**40 SHILLINGS** 21.11.1757.	—	—	—
S2170	**5 POUNDS** 21.11.1757.			
	a. W/text: *in Pay-ment of Taxes.*	—	—	—
	b. W/text: *in Payment of Taxes.*	—	—	—

1758 FIRST ISSUE

#S2171-S2173 black.

No.	Denomination / Description	GOOD	FINE	XF
S2171	**10 SHILLINGS** 4.5.1758.	—	—	—
S2172	**20 SHILLINGS** 4.5.1758.	—	—	—
S2173	**40 SHILLINGS** 4.5.1758.	—	—	—

1758 SECOND ISSUE

#S2174-S2176 black.

No.	Denomination / Description	GOOD	FINE	XF
S2174	**10 SHILLINGS** 22.12.1758.	—	—	—
S2175	**20 SHILLINGS** 22.12.1758.	—	—	—
S2176	**40 SHILLINGS** 22.12.1758.	—	—	—

1760 ISSUE

#S2177-S2188 black.

No.	Denomination / Description	GOOD	FINE	XF
S2177	**4 PENCE** 14.7.1760.	—	—	—
S2178	**6 PENCE** 14.7.1760.	—	—	—
S2179	**8 PENCE** 14.7.1760.	—	—	—
S2180	**1 SHILLING** 14.7.1760.	—	—	—
S2181	**2 SHILLINGS** 14.7.1760.	—	—	—
S2182	**2 SHILLINGS 8 PENCE** 14.7.1760.	—	—	—

		VG	VF	UNC
S2183	**5 SHILLINGS** 14.7.1760.	125.00	250.00	—
S2184	**10 SHILLINGS** 14.7.1760.	110.00	220.00	—
S2185	**20 SHILLINGS** 14.7.1760.	120.00	240.00	—
S2186	**30 SHILLINGS** 14.7.1760.	150.00	300.00	—

		VG	VF	UNC
S2187	**40 SHILLINGS** 14.7.1760.	150.00	300.00	—
S2188	**3 POUNDS** 14.7.1760.	150.00	300.00	—

1761 ISSUE

		VG	VF	UNC
S2189	**4 PENCE** 23.4.1761.	150.00	—	—
S2190	**6 PENCE** 23.4.1761.	150.00	—	—
S2191	**8 PENCE** 23.4.1761.	150.00	—	—
S2192	**1 SHILLING** 23.4.1761.	150.00	—	—
S2193	**2 SHILLINGS** 23.4.1761.	150.00	—	—
S2194	**2 SHILLINGS 6 PENCE** 23.4.1761.	150.00	—	—
S2195	**3 SHILLINGS** 23.4.1761.	180.00	350.00	—
S2196	**4 SHILLINGS** 23.4.1761.	180.00	350.00	—
S2197	**5 SHILLINGS** 23.4.1761.	180.00	350.00	—
S2198	**10 SHILLINGS** 23.4.1761.	180.00	350.00	—
S2199	**15 SHILLINGS** 23.4.1761.	180.00	350.00	—
S2200	**20 SHILLINGS** 23.4.1761.	180.00	350.00	—
S2201	**30 SHILLINGS** 23.4.1761.	300.00	500.00	—
S2202	**40 SHILLINGS** 23.4.1761.	300.00	500.00	—

		VG	VF	UNC
S2203	**3 POUNDS** 23.4.1761.	300.00	500.00	—

1768 ISSUE

#S2204-S2210 black.

		VG	VF	UNC
S2204	**2 SHILLINGS** Dec. 1768.			
	a. *1768* on 6th line.	75.00	200.00	—
	b. *1768* on 7th line.	75.00	200.00	—
S2205	**5 SHILLINGS** Dec. 1768.	80.00	250.00	—
S2206	**10 SHILLINGS** Dec. 1768.	80.00	250.00	—
S2207	**20 SHILLINGS** Dec. 1768.	80.00	250.00	—
S2208	**40 SHILLINGS** Dec. 1768.	80.00	250.00	—
S2209	**3 POUNDS** Dec. 1768.	100.00	350.00	—
S2210	**5 POUNDS** Dec. 1768.	100.00	350.00	—

1771 ISSUE

#S2211-S2219 black.

		VG	VF	UNC
S2211	**1 SHILLING** Dec. 1771.	65.00	120.00	350.00
S2212	**2 SHILLINGS 6 PENCE** Dec. 1771.			

		VG	VF	UNC
	a. Duck.	70.00	135.00	375.00

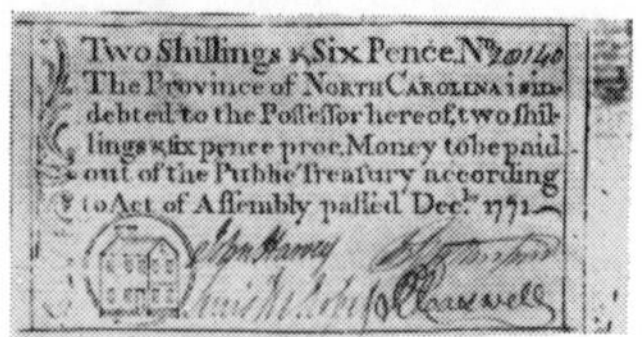

		VG	VF	UNC
	b. House.	70.00	135.00	375.00

NOTE: Shading on house strengthened in late printing.

		VG	VF	UNC
S2213	**5 SHILLINGS** Dec. 1771. Quill pens.	65.00	120.00	350.00

		VG	VF	UNC
S2214	**10 SHILLINGS** Dec. 1771. Ship. Shading on ship strengthened on late printing.	80.00	170.00	450.00
S2215	**1 POUND** Dec. 1771. Bear representing the constellation Ursa Minor.	80.00	170.00	500.00

NOTE: Shading on bear strengthened on late printing.

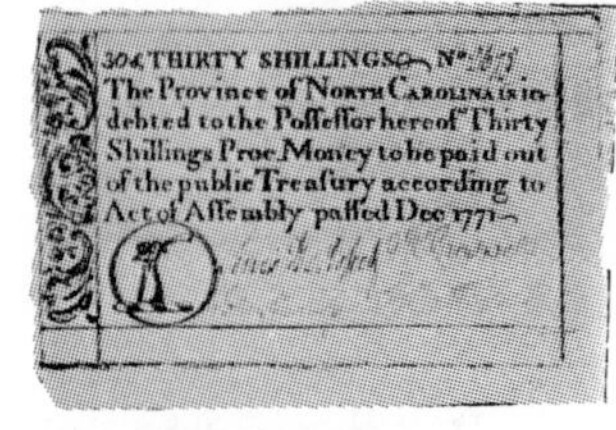

		VG	VF	UNC
S2216	**30 SHILLINGS** Dec. 1771. Hand holding dragger.	130.00	270.00	550.00
S2217	**2 POUNDS** Dec. 1771. Dove w/olive branch and motto: *PAX REDDITA MAY 1771.*	100.00	240.00	700.00
S2218	**3 POUNDS** Dec. 1771. *MAGNA CHARTA.*	90.00	200.00	600.00

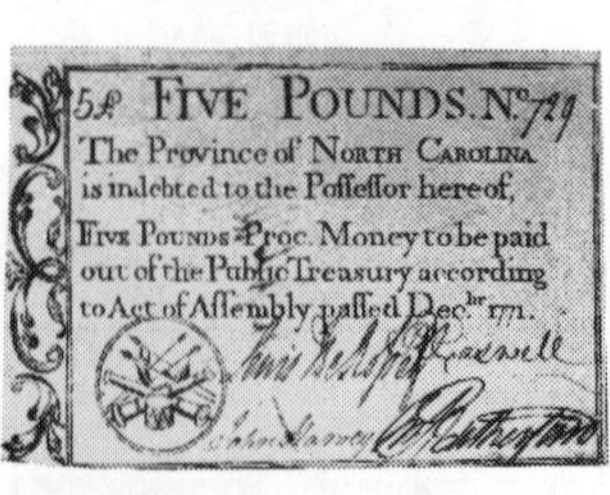

		VG	VF	UNC
S2219	**5 POUNDS** Dec. 1771. Drum, cannon, and flags.	135.00	300.00	725.00

1775 ISSUE

Dollar System

#S2220-S2228 black.

		VG	VF	UNC
S2220	**1/4 DOLLAR** 21.8.1775. Key.	150.00	325.00	800.00
S2221	**1/2 DOLLAR** 21.8.1775. Drum, cannon, and flags.	150.00	325.00	800.00

		VG	VF	UNC
S2222	**1 DOLLAR**			
	21.8.1775. Hermes w/motto: *12 UNITED COLONIES.*	150.00	325.00	800.00
S2223	**2 DOLLARS**			
	21.8.1775.	150.00	325.00	800.00
S2224	**3 DOLLARS**			
	21.8.1775. Masonic emblems.	150.00	325.00	800.00
S2225	**4 DOLLARS**			
	21.8.1775. Masonic emblems w/motto: *AERA OF MASONRY 1775.*	150.00	325.00	800.00
S2226	**5 DOLLARS**			
	21.8.1775. State House.	150.00	325.00	800.00
S2227	**8 DOLLARS**			
	21.8.1775. Britannia stabbing herself w/motto: *INFELIX BRITANNIA.*	150.00	325.00	800.00
S2228	**10 DOLLARS**			
	21.8.1775. 12 arms supporting Liberty cap w/motto: *HANC TUEMUR HAC NITIMUR.*	150.00	325.00	800.00

1776 ISSUE

#S2229-S2245 black. Thin laid paper. Some notes w/wmk: Partial crown.

		VG	VF	UNC
S2229	**1/16 DOLLAR**			
	2.4.1776.			
	a. Beetle.	160.00	240.00	475.00
	b. Butterfly.	160.00	240.00	475.00
	c. Cornucopia.	160.00	240.00	475.00
	d. Griffin.	160.00	240.00	475.00
	e. Nautilus.	160.00	240.00	475.00
	f. Vase of flowers.	160.00	240.00	475.00
S2230	**1/8 DOLLAR**			
	2.4.1776.			
	a. Dog.	160.00	240.00	475.00
	b. Heron.	160.00	240.00	475.00
	c. Lion.	160.00	240.00	475.00
	d. Monogram w/mirrored *H.*	160.00	240.00	475.00
	e. Monogram *JM.*	160.00	240.00	475.00
	f. Sculpin.	160.00	240.00	475.00
	g. Snake biting sword in scabbard.	160.00	240.00	475.00
	h. Steer.	160.00	240.00	475.00
S2231	**1/4 DOLLAR**			
	2.4.1776.			
	a. Bird flying.	160.00	240.00	475.00
	b. 3 fish.	160.00	240.00	475.00
	c. Hare.	160.00	240.00	475.00
	d. Monogram: *FB* in black script.	160.00	240.00	475.00
	e. Monogram: *NCSN* (State of North Carolina) in white script.	160.00	240.00	475.00
	f. Sea urchin.	160.00	240.00	475.00
	g. Shark.	160.00	240.00	475.00
	h. Tuna.	160.00	240.00	475.00

		VG	VF	UNC
S2232	**1/2 DOLLAR**			
	2.4.1776.			
	a. North American bear.	160.00	240.00	475.00
	b. Cock fight.	160.00	240.00	475.00
	c. Crown and pitcher.	160.00	240.00	475.00
	d. Hunter, dog and target. *HIT OR MISS.* W/o day in date.	160.00	240.00	475.00
	e. Monogram w/toothed border of triangles.	160.00	240.00	475.00
	f. Monogram w/toothed border of radial lines.	160.00	240.00	475.00
	g. Owl.	160.00	240.00	475.00
	h. Ship.	160.00	240.00	475.00
S2233	**1 DOLLAR**			
	2.4.1776.			
	a. Duck.	190.00	275.00	550.00
	b. Raccoon.	190.00	275.00	550.00
	c. Justice.	190.00	275.00	550.00
	d. Scroll w/denomination in black.	190.00	275.00	550.00
	e. Scroll w/denomination in white.	190.00	275.00	550.00
	f. Shaking encoiling bird.	190.00	275.00	550.00
S2234	**2 DOLLARS**			
	2.4.1776.			
	a. Deer.	190.00	275.00	550.00
	b. Fox.	190.00	275.00	550.00
S2235	**2 1/2 DOLLARS**			
	2.4.1776.			
	a. Hand holding 13 arrows. Motto: *VIS UNITATIS.*	190.00	275.00	550.00
	b. Liberty cap over altar. Motto: *LIBERTAS & NATALE SOLUM.*	190.00	275.00	550.00
S2236	**3 DOLLARS**			
	2.4.1776.			
	a. Alligator at top, beaver at l.	190.00	275.00	550.00
	b. Beehive.	190.00	275.00	550.00
S2237	**4 DOLLARS**			
	2.4.1776.			
	a. Bee.	190.00	275.00	550.00
	b. Sheaf of wheat.	190.00	275.00	550.00

		VG	VF	UNC
S2238	**5 DOLLARS**			
	2.4.1776.			
	a. Raven.	190.00	275.00	550.00
	x. Triton. Error *d2* instead of *2d.*	190.00	275.00	550.00
S2239	**6 DOLLARS**			
	2.4.1776.			
	a. Goat.	190.00	275.00	550.00
	b. Squirrel eating nut.	190.00	275.00	550.00

		VG	VF	UNC
S2240	**7 1/2 DOLLARS**			
	2.4.1776. U.S. flag w/3 stripes and Union Jack.	190.00	275.00	550.00
S2241	**8 DOLLARS**			
	2.4.1776.			
	a. Leopard.	190.00	275.00	550.00
	b. Rooster.	190.00	275.00	550.00
S2242	**10 DOLLARS**			
	2.4.1776.			
	a. Cupid.	190.00	275.00	550.00
	b. Peacock.	190.00	275.00	550.00
S2243	**12 1/2 DOLLARS**			
	2.4.1776. Bald eagle carrying broken arrows. Motto: *DEUS NOBISCUM.*	250.00	400.00	900.00
S2244	**15 DOLLARS**			
	2.4.1776. Boar.	220.00	325.00	800.00
S2245	**20 DOLLARS**			
	2.4.1776. Rattlesnake. Motto: *DON'T TREAD ON ME.*	220.00	325.00	800.00

NORTH CAROLINA

STATE

ACT OF AUGUST 8, 1778; 1778 ISSUE

#S2246-S2258 black. Both dark coarse mica flaked and thin unsized paper. Printer: James Davis.

		VG	VF	UNC
S2246	**1/8 DOLLAR**			
	1778. W/motto: *UNION HEARTS THE STRENGTH OF INTEREST.*	50.00	120.00	350.00
S2247	**1/4 DOLLAR**			
	1778. W/motto: *INDEPENDENCE.*	45.00	115.00	330.00
S2248	**1/2 DOLLAR**			
	1778. W/motto: *BEHOLD! A NEW WORLD.*	40.00	110.00	320.00
S2249	**1 DOLLAR**			
	1778.			
	a. W/motto: *LIBERTY AND PEACE, THE REWARD OF VIRTUOUS RESISTANCE.*	40.00	110.00	320.00
	b. W/motto: *VIRTUOUS COUNCILS THE CEMENT OF STATES.*	40.00	110.00	320.00
S2250	**2 DOLLARS**			
	1778. W/motto: *VIRTUOUS COUNCILS THE CEMENT OF STATES.*	40.00	110.00	320.00
S2251	**4 DOLLARS**			
	1778. W/motto: *A LESSON TO ARBITRARY KINGS, AND WICKED MINISTERS.*	40.00	110.00	320.00

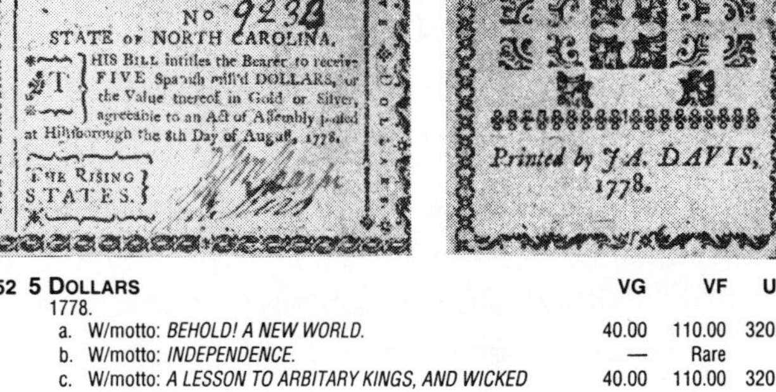

		VG	VF	UNC
S2252	**5 DOLLARS**			
	1778.			
	a. W/motto: *BEHOLD! A NEW WORLD.*	40.00	110.00	320.00
	b. W/motto: *INDEPENDENCE.*	—	Rare	—
	c. W/motto: *A LESSON TO ARBITARY KINGS, AND WICKED MINISTERS.*	40.00	110.00	320.00
	d. W/motto: *THE RISING STATES.*	40.00	110.00	320.00
S2253	**10 DOLLARS**			
	1778.			
	a. W/motto: *INDEPENDENCE.*	40.00	110.00	320.00
	b. W/motto: *PERSECUTION THE RUIN OF EMPIRES.*	40.00	110.00	320.00
	c. W/motto: *UNION OF HEARTS THE STRENGTH OF INTERESTS.*	40.00	110.00	320.00
S2254	**20 DOLLARS**			
	1778. W/motto: *AMERICAN VIRTUE TRIUMPHANT.*	50.00	120.00	350.00
S2255	**25 DOLLARS**			
	1778. W/motto: *SIC TRANSIT GLORIA MUNDI.*	60.00	130.00	375.00

No.	Description	VG	VF	UNC
S2256	**40 DOLLARS** 1778. W/motto: *FREEDOM OF SPEECH AND THE LIBERTY OF THE PRESS.*	85.00	150.00	450.00
S2257	**50 DOLLARS** 1778. W/motto: *THE RISING STATES.*	75.00	145.00	425.00
S2258	**100 DOLLARS** 1778. W/motto: *FREEDOM OR AN HONORABLE DEATH.*	100.00	175.00	475.00

1779 ISSUE

#S2259-S2265 black. Light coarse paper. Printer: Hugh Walker.

No.	Description	VG	VF	UNC
S2259	**5 DOLLARS** 15.5.1779.			
	a. Sm. *u* over *y* in *May.* W/motto: *BE FREEDOM AND INDEPENDENCE STEADILY PURSUED.*	50.00	100.00	—
	b. Umlaut over *e* in *Silver.* W/motto: *GOOD GOVERNMENT ALWAYS REVERE.*	50.00	100.00	—
S2260	**10 DOLLARS** 15.5.1779.			
	a. Sm. *u* over *y* in *May.* W/motto: *AMERICAN UNION FOR EVER.*	50.00	100.00	—
	b. Dash over *y* of *Assembly.* W/motto: *VIRTUE EXCELS RICHES.*	50.00	100.00	—
S2261	**20 DOLLARS** 15.5.1779. Umlaut over *e* of 2nd *the.* W/motto: *PEACE ON HONOURABLE TERMS.*	50.00	100.00	—
S2262	**25 DOLLARS** 15.5.1779.			
	a. *Q* instead of *O* in r. border. W/motto: *A FREE COMMERCE.*	65.00	125.00	—
	b. Top border lettering is mirrored image. Period after *No* is missing. W/motto: *AMERICAN FORTITUDE DISPLAYED.*	60.00	150.00	—
S2263	**50 DOLLARS** 15.5.1779. Circumflex over *e* in *Silver.* W/motto: *A RIGHTEOUS CAUSE THE PROTECTION OF PROVIDENCE.*	100.00	220.00	—
S2264	**100 DOLLARS** 15.5.1779. *Q* instead of *O* in r. border. W/motto: *A FREE COMMERCE.*	110.00	235.00	—
S2265	**250 DOLLARS** 15.5.1779. Circumflex over *e* in *Silver,* dash over first *i* in *Smithfield.* W/motto: *A RIGHTEOUS CAUSE THE PROTECTION OF PROVIDENCE.*	125.00	250.00	—

SESSION ACT OF APRIL 17, 1780; 1780 ISSUE

No.	Description	VG	VF	UNC
S2266	**50 DOLLARS** 1780.			
	a. W/motto: *INDEPENDENCE.*	—	—	—
	b. W/motto: *LIBERTY AND PEACE, THE REWARD OF VIRTUOUS RESISTANCE.*	—	—	—
	c. W/motto: *PERSECUTION THE RUIN OF EMPIRES.*	—	—	—

#S2267-S2275 black. Both thick and thin paper. Printer: James Davis.

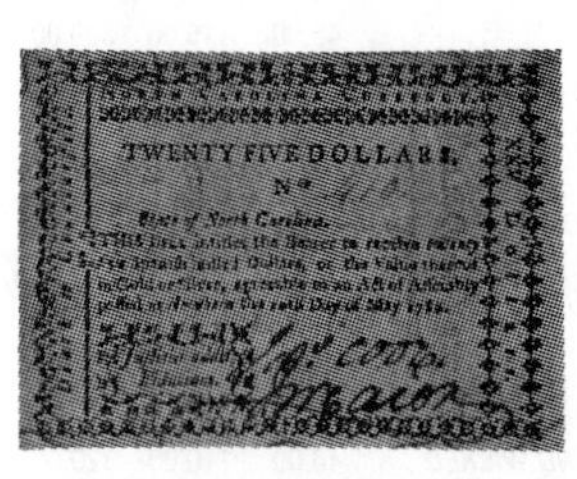

No.	Description	VG	VF	UNC
S2267	**25 DOLLARS** 10.5.1780.			
	a. W/motto: *DULCE PRO PATRIA MORI.*	50.00	120.00	—
	b. *S* is omitted from *DOLLARS* in text. W/motto: *HORA PACIS & LIBERTATIS APPROPINQUAT.*	50.00	120.00	—
	c. W/motto: *JUSTITIA ADDIT FIDUCIAM.*	50.00	120.00	—
	d. W/motto: *QUID NON VIRTUTE EFFICIENDUM.*	50.00	120.00	—
	e. Center bar of *F* in *FIVE* is missing. W/motto: *TERRA LIBERA NOTAM PRAEII IN ME POSUIT.*	50.00	120.00	—
	f. W/motto: *VIM VI REPELLAMUS.*	50.00	120.00	—
S2268	**50 DOLLARS** 10.5.1780. W/motto: *FUNDAMENTUM MIHI AERE PERENNIUS.*	60.00	150.00	—
S2269	**100 DOLLARS** 10.5.1780. W/motto: *FORTIS CADERE CEDERE NON POTEST.*	70.00	170.00	—
S2270	**200 DOLLARS** 10.5.1780. W/motto: *UT QUOCUNQUE PARATUS.*	100.00	250.00	—
S2271	**250 DOLLARS** 10.5.1780.			
	a. *T* in *This* in ornamented box. W/motto: *QUAERENDA PECUNIA PRIMUM EST.*	85.00	200.00	—
	b. *T* in *This* w/o box. Motto same as a.	85.00	200.00	—
S2272	**300 DOLLARS** 10.5.1780. W/motto: *AUT UMQUAM TENTES AUT PERFICE.*	100.00	250.00	—
S2273	**400 DOLLARS** 10.5.1780. W/motto: *MUTARE VEL TIMERE SPERNO.*	100.00	250.00	—
S2274	**500 DOLLARS** 10.5.1780.			
	a. *T* in *This* in ornamented box. W/motto: *DIVITIAE REIPUBLICAE DANT MIHI PRETIUM.*	90.00	225.00	—
	b. *T* in *This* w/o box. Motto same as a.	90.00	225.00	—
S2275	**600 DOLLARS** 10.5.1780. W/motto: *CRESIT SUB PONDERE VIRTUS.*	125.00	350.00	—

#S2276 *Deleted.*

1783 ISSUE

Pound Sterling System

#S2277-S2283 black. Printer: Thomas Davis, Halifax.

No.	Description	VG	VF	UNC
S2277	**6 PENCE** 17.5.1783. Bird.	250.00	—	—
S2278	**1 SHILLING** 17.5.1783.	250.00	—	—
S2279	**2 SHILLINGS** 17.5.1783. Corinthian column w/motto: *IN RECTO DECUS.*	250.00	—	—
S2280	**5 SHILLINGS** 17.5.1783.	250.00	—	—
S2281	**10 SHILLINGS** 17.5.1783. Ships w/motto: *COMMERCIO.*	250.00	—	—
S2282	**20 SHILLINGS** 17.5.1783			
	a. Justice w/motto: *DO AS YOU WOULD BE DONE BY.*	250.00	—	—
	b. Crown and book.	250.00	—	—
S2283	**40 SHILLINGS** 17.5.1783. Angel Gabriel and church.	250.00	—	—

1785 ISSUE

#S2284-S2291 black. Thick paper. Wmk: *NORTH CAROLINA.* Printer: Thomas Davis.

No.	Description	VG	VF	UNC
S2284	**6 PENCE** 29.12.1785. 13 stars.	250.00	—	—
S2285	**1 SHILLING** 29.12.1785. Wreath.	250.00	—	—
S2286	**2 SHILLINGS** 29.12.1785. Plough.	250.00	—	—
S2287	**2 SHILLINGS 6 PENCE** 29.12.1785. Phoenix. Motto: *MELIOR RESURGO.*	250.00	—	—
S2288	**5 SHILLINGS** 29.12.1785. Ship near fort.	250.00	—	—
S2289	**10 SHILLINGS** 29.12.1785. Crown and book.	250.00	—	—
S2290	**20 SHILLINGS** 29.12.1785. Angel Gabriel and church.	250.00	—	—
S2291	**40 SHILLINGS** 29.12.1785. Justice.	250.00	—	—

NOTE: Test specimens printed on blue paper.

ACT OF 1814; 1815 ISSUE

#S2292-S2298 printed date 1815, w/various handwritten day, month and 1816/1815. Listed dates are examples.

		GOOD	FINE	XF
S2292	**5 CENTS** 1815.	—	—	—
S2293	**10 CENTS** 1815.	—	—	—

		GOOD	FINE	XF
S2294	**20 CENTS** 4.1.1816/15.	—	—	—

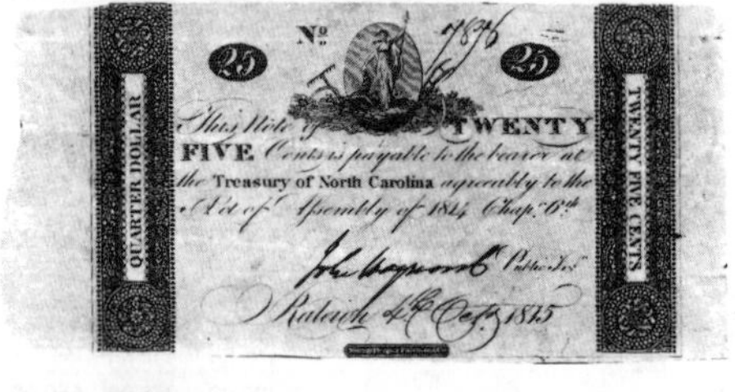

		GOOD	FINE	XF
S2295	**25 CENTS** 4.10.1815. Allegorical female w/spear at top ctr.	—	—	—
S2296	**30 CENTS** 1815.	—	—	—
S2297	**40 CENTS** 1815.	—	—	—

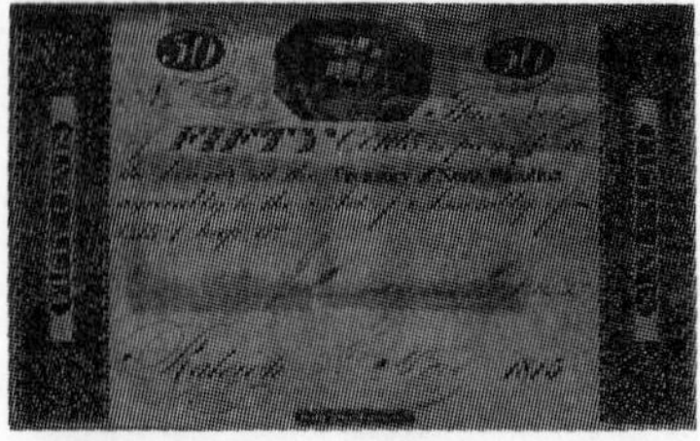

		GOOD	FINE	XF
S2298	**50 CENTS** 1815.	—	—	—

ACT OF 1816; 1817 ISSUE

#S2299-S2306 printed date 1817 w/various handwritten day and month.

		GOOD	FINE	XF
S2299	**5 CENTS** 1817.	—	—	—

		Good	Fine	XF
S2300	**6 1/4 Cents** 1817.	—	—	—
S2301	**10 Cents** 1817.	—	—	—
S2302	**12 1/2 Cents** 1817.	—	—	—
S2303	**20 Cents** 1817.	—	—	—
S2304	**25 Cents** 1817.	—	—	—

		Good	Fine	XF
S2305	**30 Cents** 1817.	—	—	—
S2306	**40 Cents** 1817.	—	—	—
S2307	**50 Cents** 1817.	—	—	—

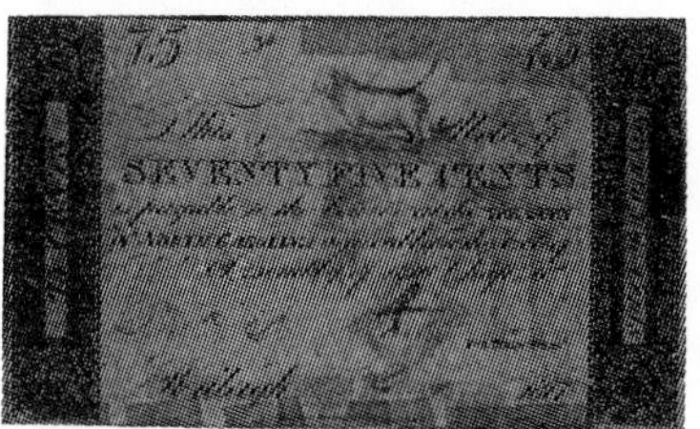

		Good	Fine	XF
S2308	**75 Cents** 1817.	—	—	—

Act of 1823; 1824 Issue

		Good	Fine	XF
S2309	**5 Cents** 1824.	—	—	—
S2310	**10 Cents** 1824.	—	—	—
S2311	**20 Cents** 1824.	—	—	—

		Good	Fine	XF
S2312	**25 Cents** 1824.	—	—	—

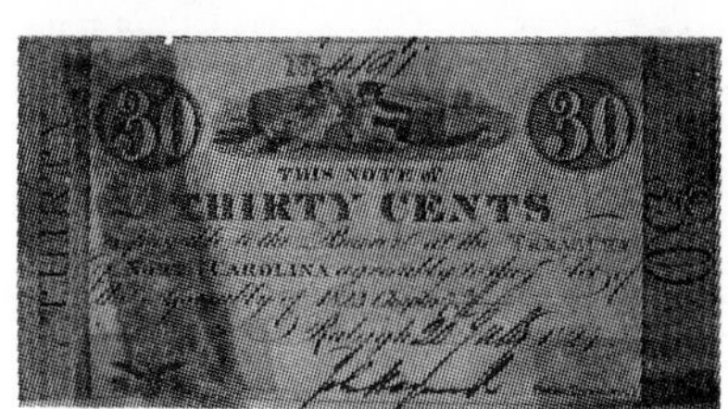

		Good	Fine	XF
S2313	**30 Cents** 1824. 2 cherubs at top ctr.	—	—	—
S2314	**40 Cents** 1824. Sir W. Raleigh at top ctr.	—	—	—
S2315	**50 Cents** 1824.	—	—	—
S2316	**75 Cents** 1824.	—	—	—

A word on date ranges

Often date ranges or specific dates are listed. These have been observed or reported by our contributors. If a note is outside the published range, it only means that it is a newly reported date, and not necessarily worthy of a premium value.

North Carolina

Civil War

Act of 28.6.1861; 1861 Issue

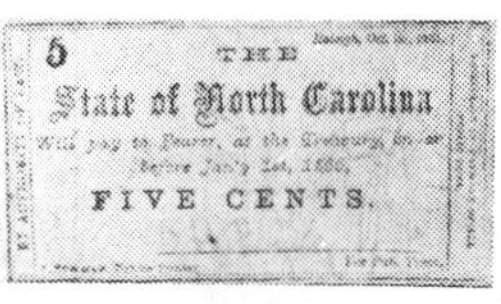

S2321

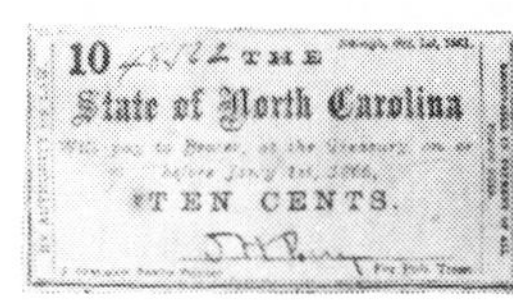

S2322

		VG	VF	Unc
S2321	**5 Cents** 1.10.1861. Black.			
	a. W/o wmk.	7.00	10.00	15.00
	b. Printed on backs of N. Carolina bonds.	10.00	26.00	50.00
	c. Wmk: *FIVE.*	9.00	15.00	40.00
	d. Wmk: *TEN.*	9.00	15.00	40.00
	e. Wmk: *T.C. & Co.*	—	Rare	—
S2322	**10 Cents** 1.10.1861.			
	a. W/o wmk.	7.00	10.00	25.00
	b. Wmk: *FIVE.*	10.00	35.00	60.00
	c. Wmk: *TEN.*	10.00	35.00	60.00
	d. Wmk: *T.C. & Co.*	—	Rare	—
S2323	**20 Cents** 1.10.1861. Black.			
	a. W/o wmk.	25.00	30.00	50.00
	b. Printed on backs of N. Carolina bonds.	20.00	35.00	60.00
	c. Wmk: *FIVE.*	20.00	35.00	60.00
	d. Wmk: *TEN.*	20.00	35.00	60.00
	e. Wmk: *T.C. & Co.*	—	Rare	—
S2324	**25 Cents** 1.10.1861. Black.			
	a. W/o wmk.	7.00	15.00	25.00
	b. Wmk: *FIVE.*	10.00	35.00	60.00
	c. Wmk: *TEN.*	10.00	35.00	60.00
	d. Wmk: *T.C. & Co.*	—	Rare	—

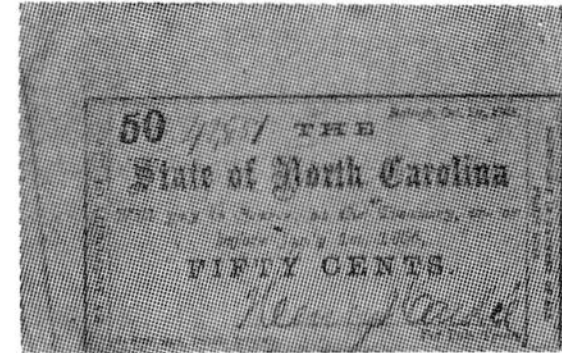

		VG	VF	Unc
S2325	**50 Cents** 1.10.1861. Black.			
	a. W/o wmk.	7.00	15.00	25.00
	b. Wmk: *FIVE.*	10.00	35.00	60.00
	c. Wmk: *TEN.*	10.00	35.00	60.00
	d. Wmk: *T.C. & Co.*	—	Rare	—

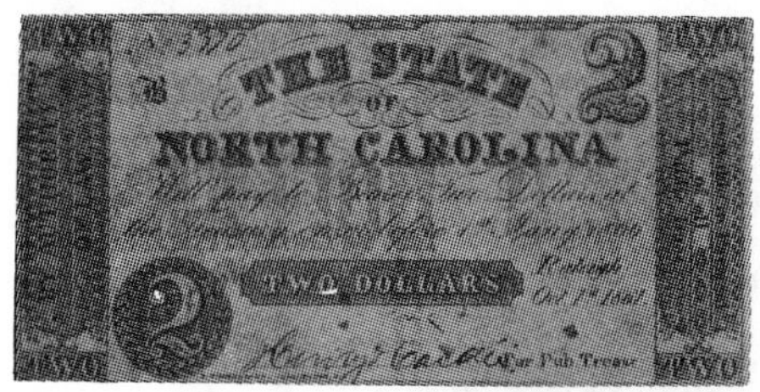

		VG	VF	Unc
S2326	**2 Dollars** 1, 2, 4 & 6.10.1861. Black. Printer: F. W. Bornemann.			
	a. W/o wmk.	7.00	15.00	35.00
	b. Red protector: *TWO DOLLARS* on back. 1.10.1861.	7.00	14.00	30.00
	c. Printed on backs of N. Carolina bank notes.	14.00	30.00	60.00
	d. Printed on backs of N. Carolina 1000 Dollar bonds.	30.00	60.00	150.00
	e. Wmk: *FIVE.* 4.10.1861.	25.00	40.00	65.00

#S2327 and S2328 standing Minerva at l., dog lying by strongbox at lower ctr. Printer: N. C. Inst. Deaf and Dumb Print.

S2327 1 Dollar

	VG	VF	Unc
1-5.10.1861. Black.			
a. Red protector: *ONE DOLLAR* on back.	15.00	20.00	50.00
b. Printed on backs of N. Carolina bank notes.	16.00	35.00	125.00
c. Printed on backs of N. Carolina bonds. 5.10.1861.	25.00	60.00	150.00

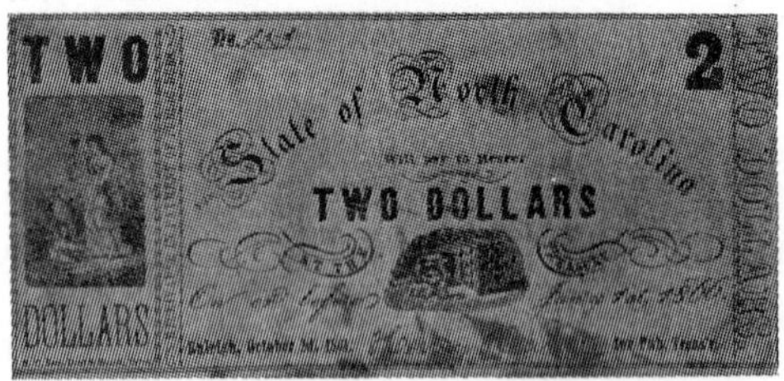

S2328 2 Dollars

	VG	VF	Unc
3.10.1861. Black. Red protector: *TWO DOLLARS* on back. Printed on backs of N. Carolina bank notes. 12-20 known.	1000.	1500.	—

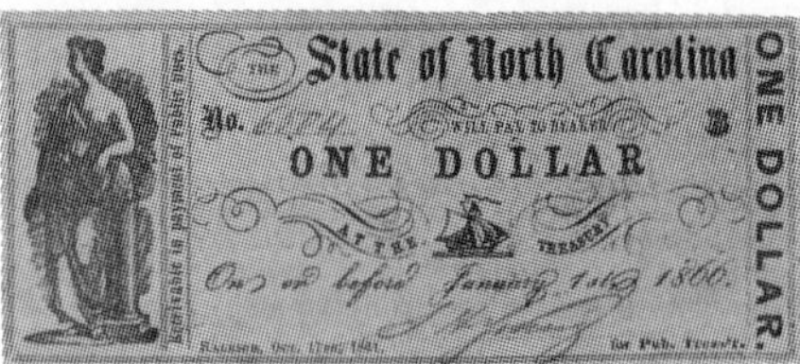

S2329 1 Dollar

	VG	VF	Unc
10-21.10.1861. Black. Standing Minerva at l., ship at ctr. Back lt. brownish pink. Series A; B. W/o imprint.			
a. W/o wmk.	6.00	9.00	25.00
b. Wmk: *FIVE.*	15.00	25.00	60.00
c. Wmk: *TEN.*	8.00	15.00	35.00
d. Wmk: *T.C. & Co.*	40.00	60.00	100.00

NOTE: #S2330 Interest bearing at six percent per annum, various handwritten dates. Printer: J. Manouvrier.

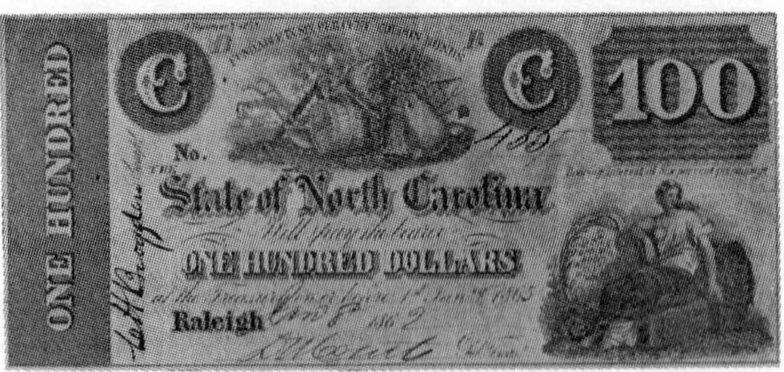

S2330 100 Dollars

	VG	VF	Unc
1.12.1861. Black. Agricultural tools at top ctr., seated Commerce at lower r.	500.00	800.00	1500.

1862 Issues

#S2331-S2337 various handwritten dates. Printer: J. Manouvrier.

S2331 20 Dollars

	VG	VF	Unc
1862. Black. Ceres Volant at top ctr.			
a. W/text: *FUNDABLE IN SIX PERCENT COUPON BONDS* in upper and lower borders.	20.00	45.00	125.00
b. Printed on backs of bills of exchange.	25.00	45.00	125.00
c. Printed on backs of N. Carolina bonds.	35.00	80.00	150.00

S2332 20 Dollars

	VG	VF	Unc
1862. Black. Like #S2331.			
a. Red ovpt: *FUNDABLE/ONLY/IN SIX PERCENT BONDS* on #S2331a.	20.00	45.00	125.00
b. Ovpt. on #S2331b.	15.00	38.00	95.00
c. Ovpt. on #S2331c.	35.00	80.00	125.00

S2333 50 Dollars

	VG	VF	Unc
1862. Black. Standing Liberty next to seated Ceres at top ctr. Red ovpt: *FIFTY DOLLARS* on back.	350.00	500.00	1200.

S2334 50 Dollars

	VG	VF	Unc
1862. Red ovpt: *FUNDABLE/ONLY/IN SIX PERCENT BONDS* on #S2333.	400.00	600.00	1250.

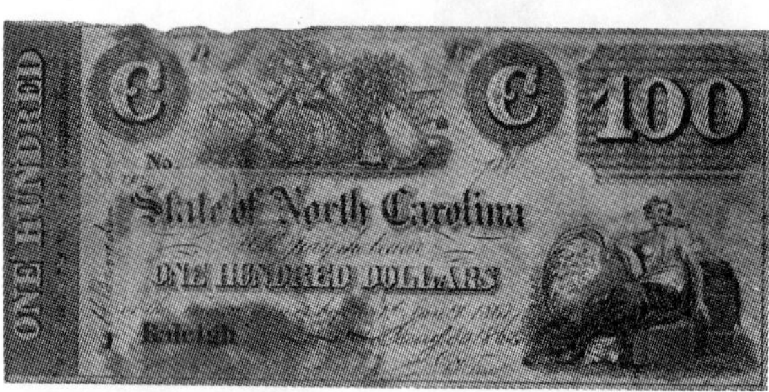

S2335 100 Dollars

	VG	VF	Unc
1862. Similar to #S2330 but w/o *Bearing Interest at Six percent . . .* at r.	—	Rare	—

S2336 20 Dollars

	VG	VF	Unc
1862. Similar to #S2331.			
a. W/text: *FUNDABLE IN EIGHT PERCENT COUPON BONDS* in top border and *RECEIVABLE IN PAYMENT OF ALL PUBLIC DEBTS* in lower border.	35.00	65.00	150.00
b. Printed on backs of bills of exchange.	30.00	60.00	150.00

S2337 20 Dollars

	VG	VF	Unc
1862. Black. Like #S2331.			
a. Red ovpt: *FUNDABLE/ONLY/IN SIX PERCENT BONDS* on #S2336a.	30.00	60.00	150.00
b. Ovpt. on #S2336b.	30.00	60.00	150.00

S2338 20 Dollars

	VG	VF	Unc
1862. Red vertical ovpt: *FUNDABLE* in 2 lines on #S2336a.	40.00	65.00	165.00

S2338A 20 Dollars

	VG	VF	Unc
1862. Similar to #S2331. Printed on backs of bills of exchange. w/text: *FUNDABLE . . .* in upper border but blocked out in lower border.	30.00	50.00	100.00

#S2339-S2349 various handwritten dates. Printer: J. Manouvrier.

S2339 10 Dollars

	VG	VF	Unc
1862. Black. Steam passenger train at ctr. Interest bearing at the rate of *SIX PERCENT* per annum in oval at r. Printed on backs of N. Carolina bonds.	30.00	65.00	125.00

S2340 5 Dollars

	VG	VF	Unc
1862. Black. Seated Ceres w/produce, sailing ship in background, steam train vertically at r.			
a. Issued note.	35.00	65.00	150.00
b. Printed on backs of bills of exchange.	35.00	65.00	150.00

S2341 5 Dollars

	VG	VF	Unc
1862.			
a. Red ovpt: *FUNDABLE/ONLY/IN SIX PERCENT BONDS* on #S2340a.	30.00	60.00	125.00
b. Red ovpt. on #S2340b.	30.00	65.00	125.00

		VG	VF	UNC
S2342	**10 DOLLARS**			
	1862. Similar to #S2339 but w/*FUNDABLE IN SIX PERCENT COUPON BONDS* in oval at r.			
	a. Issued note.	40.00	75.00	125.00
	b. Printed on backs of bills of exchange.	35.00	55.00	100.00
	c. Printed on backs of N. Carolina bonds.	35.00	55.00	100.00
S2343	**10 DOLLARS**			
	1862. Oval ovpt: *FUNDABLE. . .* at r. on #S2342.	45.00	75.00	140.00

		VG	VF	UNC
S2344	**5 DOLLARS**			
	1862. Black. Standing Liberty w/seated Ceres at top ctr., steam passenger train vertical at r.	35.00	65.00	125.00
S2345	**5 DOLLARS**			
	1862. Red ovpt: *FUNDABLE/ONLY/IN SIX PERCENT BONDS* on #S2344.	40.00	65.00	150.00
S2346	**10 DOLLARS**			
	1862. Similar to #S2342 but w/*FUNDABLE IN EIGHT PERCENT BONDS* at r.			
	a. W/o wmk.	40.00	55.00	125.00
	b. Wmk: *TEN*.	45.00	70.00	135.00

		VG	VF	UNC
S2347	**10 DOLLARS**			
	1862. Red ovpt: *FUNDABLE/ONLY/IN SIX PERCENT BONDS* on #S2346.	40.00	65.00	135.00
S2348	**20 DOLLARS**			
	1862. Black. Grain at l., steam passenger train at ctr. *FUNDABLE IN EIGHT PERCENT COUPON BONDS* in top border.	—	—	—
S2349	**20 DOLLARS**			
	1862. Red ovpt: *FUNDABLE/ONLY/IN SIX PERCENT BONDS* on #S2348.	50.00	65.00	150.00

NOTE: #S2348 and S2349 w/full upper and lower borders command a considerable premium.

		VG	VF	UNC
S2350	**3 DOLLARS**			
	1.5.1862. Black. W/o vignette or imprint.	—	Rare	—

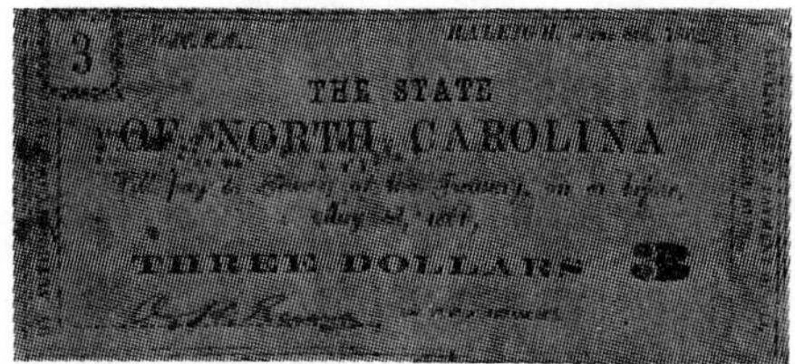

		VG	VF	UNC
S2351	**3 DOLLARS**			
	8.6.1862. Black. W/o vignette or imprint.	—	Rare	—

		VG	VF	UNC
S2352	**5 DOLLARS**			
	1.7.1862. Black. Standing Ceres at l., steamship at upper ctr.	—	—	—
S2353	**5 DOLLARS**			
	1862. Red ovpt: *FUNDABLE/ONLY/IN SIX PERCENT BONDS* on #S2352.	25.00	45.00	80.00
S2354	**4 DOLLARS**			
	1.8.1862. Black. W/o vignette.	—	Rare	—

NOTE: #S2352-S2354 full upper and lower borders command a considerable premium.

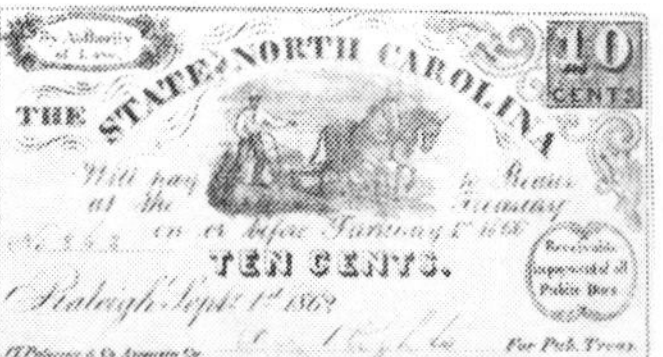

#S2355

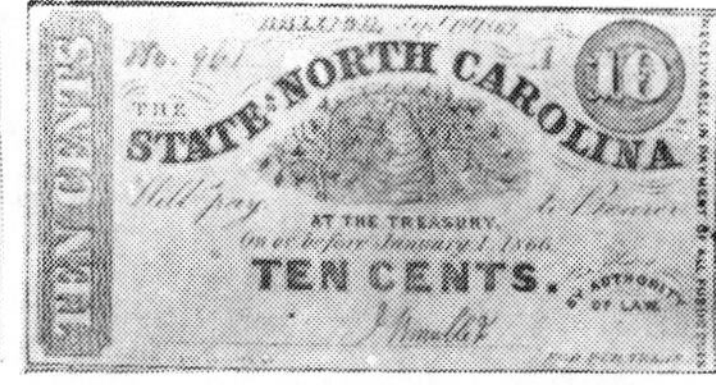

#S2356

		VG	VF	UNC
S2355	**10 CENTS**			
	1.9.1862. Black. Black plowing at ctr.	9.00	16.00	25.00
S2356	**10 CENTS**			
	1.9.1862. Black. Hornet's nest at ctr.	9.00	12.00	20.00

		VG	VF	UNC
S2357	**25 CENTS**			
	1.9.1862. Black. Ceres at lower l.			
	a. Issued note.	8.00	10.00	20.00
	b. Printed on backs of N. Carolina bonds.	12.00	20.00	30.00
	c. Printed on backs of N. Carolina banknotes.	12.00	20.00	30.00

		VG	VF	UNC
S2358	**50 CENTS**			
	1.9.1862. Black. Sailing ship at l. ctr.			
	a. Issued note.	8.00	10.00	20.00
	b. Printed on backs of N. Carolina bonds.	9.00	15.00	25.00

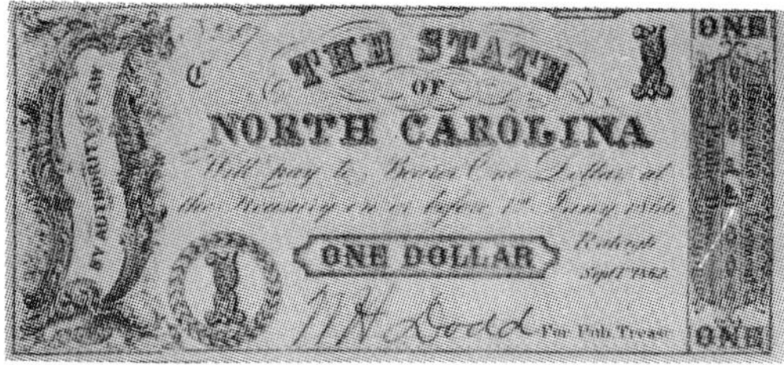

		VG	VF	UNC
S2359	**1 DOLLAR**			
	1.9.1862. Black.			
	a. W/o wmk.	7.00	10.00	20.00
	b. Wmk: *FIVE*.	25.00	50.00	100.00

1863 ISSUE

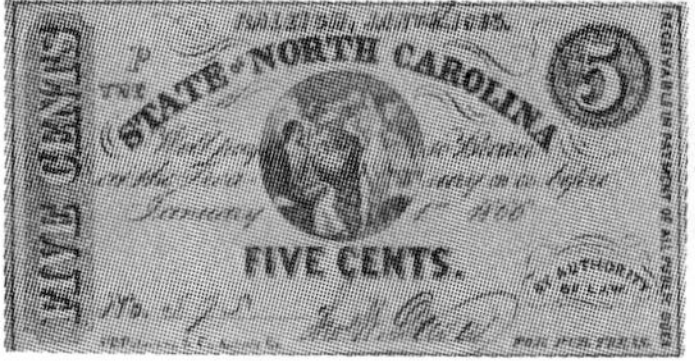

#S2360

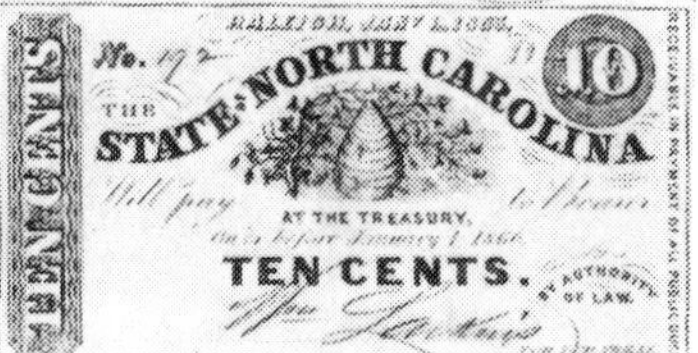

#S2361

		VG	VF	UNC
S2360	**5 CENTS**			
	1.1.1863. Black. Liberty and Peace at ctr.	5.00	9.00	14.00
S2361	**10 CENTS**			
	1.1.1863. Black. Hornet's nest at ctr.	5.00	9.00	15.00

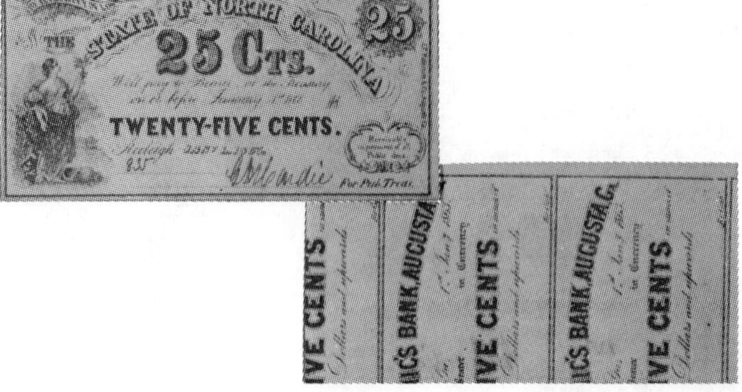

S2362 25 Cents

1.1.1863. Black. Ceres at l.

	VG	VF	Unc
a. W/o wmk.	10.00	12.00	20.00
b. Wmk: *WHATMAN.*	50.00	90.00	175.00
c. Printed on the backs of Georgia notes.	10.00	15.00	30.00
d. Printed on the backs of N. Carolina notes.	10.00	15.00	30.00

S2363 50 Cents

	VG	VF	Unc
1.1.1863. Black. Sailing ship at ctr.	10.00	12.00	15.00

S2364 75 Cents

	VG	VF	Unc
1.1.1863. Black. Standing Industry by beehive at ctr.	12.00	20.00	35.00

S2365 1 Dollar

	VG	VF	Unc
1.1.1863. Black. Commerce and Industry holding figure *1*.	7.00	11.00	25.00

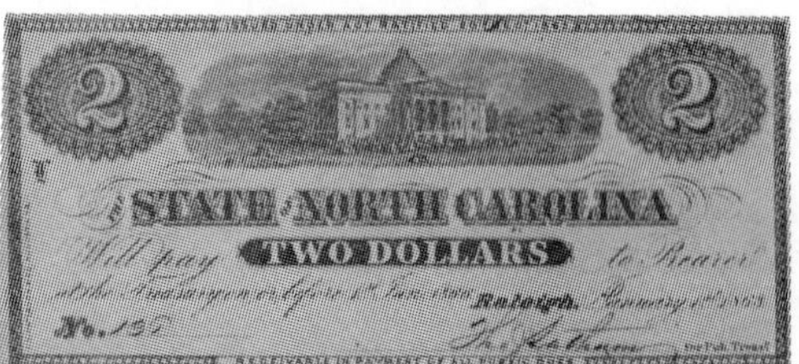

S2366 2 Dollars

	VG	VF	Unc
1.1.1863. Black. State Capitol in Raleigh at ctr.	7.00	10.00	20.00

S2367 3 Dollars

1.1.1863. Black. Standing Liberty by seated Ceres at top ctr.

	VG	VF	Unc
a. W/o wmk.	20.00	35.00	50.00
b. Wmk: *FIVE.*	20.00	45.00	75.00
c. Wmk: *TEN.*	20.00	45.00	75.00
d. Wmk: *T.C. & Co.*	40.00	70.00	125.00

S2368 5 Dollars

1.1.1863. Black. Ceres at l., sailing steamship at ctr.

	VG	VF	Unc
a. Issued note.	15.00	25.00	50.00
b. W/red handwritten text: *Fundable in six . . .*	35.00	70.00	125.00

S2369 5 Dollars

	VG	VF	Unc
1.1.1863. Black. N.C. standing Liberty at l., harbor and City of Wilmington at upper ctr., portr. D. W. Courts at lower r.	20.00	35.00	75.00

S2370 10 Dollars

	VG	VF	Unc
1.1.1863. Black on red unpt. State Capitol in Raleigh at ctr., portr. D. W. Courts at r.	15.00	30.00	75.00

S2371 20 Dollars

	VG	VF	Unc
1.1.1863. Like #S2348.	25.00	50.00	100.00

S2372 20 Dollars

1.1.1863. Black and red. Portr. Gov. Z. Vance at ctr.

	VG	VF	Unc
a. Plain paper.	25.00	45.00	90.00
b. Wmk: *J. Whatman. 1861* horizontal lines, arms or parts thereof.	25.00	45.00	90.00

S2373 50 Dollars

1.1.1863. Black and red. Portr. Gov. Z. Vance at ctr.

	VG	VF	Unc
a. Plain paper.	—	Rare	—
b. Wmk. Like #S2372b.	30.00	95.00	100.00

1864 Issue

#	Denomination	VG	VF	Unc
S2374	**25 Cents** 1.1.1864. Black. Standing Ceres at lower l. Blue protector: *25 Cts./Twenty-Five Cents.*	8.00	12.00	20.00
S2375	**50 Cents** 1.1.1864. Black. Sailing ship at ctr. Red protector: *50 Cts.*	9.00	15.00	30.00

Pennsylvania

Colonial

1723 First Issue

#S2384-S2391 black. Arms of the Penn family. Uniface.

#	Denomination	Good	Fine	XF
S2384	**1 Shilling** 17.1.1723.	—	—	—
S2385	**1 Shilling 6 Pence** 17.1.1723.	—	—	—
S2386	**2 Shillings** 17.1.1723.	—	—	—
S2387	**2 Shillings 6 Pence** 17.1.1723.	—	—	—
S2388	**5 Shillings** 17.1.1723.	—	—	—
S2389	**10 Shillings** 17.1.1723.	—	—	—
S2390	**15 Shillings** 17.1.1723.	—	—	—
S2391	**20 Shillings** 17.1.1723.	—	—	—

1723 Second Issue

#S2392-S2398 black. Arms of the Penn family. Uniface.

#	Denomination	Good	Fine	XF
S2392	**1 Shilling** 2.4.1723.	—	—	—
S2393	**2 Shillings** 2.4.1723.	—	—	—
S2394	**2 Shillings 6 Pence** 2.4.1723.	—	—	—
S2395	**5 Shillings** 2.4.1723.	—	—	—
S2396	**10 Shillings** 2.4.1723.	—	—	—
S2397	**15 Shillings** 2.4.1723.	—	—	—
S2398	**20 Shillings** 2.4.1723.	—	—	—

1726 Replacement Issue

#S2399-S2404 black.

#	Denomination	Good	Fine	XF
S2399	**1 Shilling** 25.3.1726.	—	—	—
S2400	**1 Shilling 6 Pence** 25.3.1726.	—	—	—
S2401	**2 Shillings** 25.3.1726.	—	—	—
S2402	**2 Shillings 6 Pence** 25.3.1726.	—	—	—
S2403	**5 Shillings** 25.3.1726.	—	—	—
S2404	**10 Shillings** 25.3.1726.	—	—	—

1729 Issue

#S2405-S2412 black. Arms of the Penn family. Uniface. Printer: Andrew Bradford.

#	Denomination	Good	Fine	XF
S2405	**1 Shilling** 15.9.1729.	—	—	—
S2406	**1 Shilling 6 Pence** 15.9.1729.	—	—	—
S2407	**2 Shillings** 15.9.1729.	—	—	—
S2408	**2 Shillings 6 Pence** 15.9.1729.	—	—	—
S2409	**5 Shillings** 15.9.1729.	—	—	—
S2410	**10 Shillings** 15.9.1729.	—	—	—
S2411	**15 Shillings** 15.9.1729.	—	—	—
S2412	**20 Shillings** 15.9.1729.	—	—	—

1731 Issue

#S2413-S2420 black. Printer: B. Franklin.

#	Denomination	Good	Fine	XF
S2413	**1 Shilling** 10.4.1731.	—	—	—
S2414	**1 Shilling 6 Pence** 10.4.1731.	—	—	—
S2415	**2 Shillings** 10.4.1731.	—	—	—
S2416	**2 Shillings 6 Pence** 10.4.1731.	—	—	—
S2417	**5 Shillings** 10.4.1731.	—	—	—
S2418	**10 Shillings** 10.4.1731.	—	—	—
S2419	**15 Shillings** 10.4.1731.	—	—	—
S2420	**20 Shillings** 10.4.1731.	—	—	—

1739 Issue

#S2421-S2428 black. Arms of the Penn family. Printer: B. Franklin.

#	Denomination	Good	Fine	XF
S2421	**1 Shilling** 10.8.1739. Uniface.	—	—	—
S2422	**18 Pence** 10.8.1739. Uniface.	—	—	—
S2423	**2 Shillings** 10.8.1739. Uniface.	—	—	—
S2424	**2 Shillings 6 Pence** 10.8.1739. W/text: *Pensilvania* (error). Uniface.	—	—	—
S2425	**5 Shillings** 10.8.1739. W/text: *Pensilvania* (error). Back leaves. Plate letter A; B.	—	—	—
S2426	**10 Shillings** 10.8.1739. W/text: *Pensilvania* (error). Back leaves. Plate letter A-D.	—	—	—
S2427	**15 Shillings** 10.8.1739. W/text: *Pensilvania* (error). Back leaves. Plate letter A; B.	—	—	—
S2428	**20 Shillings** 10.8.1739. W/text: *Pensilvania* (error). Back leaves. Plate letter A; B.	—	—	—

NOTE: The 4 highest denominations have *Pensilvania* deliberately misspelled to act as a secret check to detect alterations from the lower denominations.

1744 Issue

#S2429-S2433 black. Ams of the Penn family. Uniface. Printer: B. Franklin.

#	Denomination	Good	Fine	XF
S2429	**1 Shilling** 1.8.1744.	—	—	—
S2430	**18 Pence** 1.8.1744.	—	—	—
S2431	**2 Shillings** 1.8.1744.	—	—	—
S2432	**2 Shillings 6 Pence** 1.8.1744.	—	—	—
S2433	**5 Shillings** 1.8.1744.	—	—	—

1746 Issue

#S2434-S2437 black. Printer: B. Franklin.

#	Denomination	Good	Fine	XF
S2434	**4 Pence** 1.8.1746.	—	—	—
S2435	**6 Pence** 1.8.1746.	—	—	—
S2436	**9 Pence** 1.8.1746.	—	—	—
S2437	**20 Shillings** 1.8.1746. Arms of the Penn family. Back leaves. Plate letter A; B; C; D.	—	—	—

1749 Issue

#S2438-S2441 black. Arms of the Penn family. Uniface. Printer: B. Franklin and D. Hall.

#	Denomination	Good	Fine	XF
S2438	**3 Pence** 16.5.1749.	—	—	—
S2439	**4 Pence** 16.5.1749.	—	—	—
S2440	**6 Pence** 16.5.1749.	—	—	—
S2441	**9 Pence** 16.5.1749.	—	—	—

1755 Issue

#S2442-S2451 black. Arms of the Penn family. Printer: B. Franklin and D. Hall.

#S2442-S2449 uniface.

#	Denomination	VG	VF	Unc
S2442	**3 Pence** 1.10.1755.	—	—	—
S2443	**4 Pence** 1.10.1755.	—	—	—
S2444	**6 Pence** 1.10.1755.	—	—	—
S2445	**9 Pence** 1.10.1755.	—	—	—

		VG	VF	Unc
S2446	**1 Shilling** 1.10.1755.	—	—	—
S2447	**18 Pence** 1.10.1755.	—	—	—
S2448	**2 Shillings** 1.10.1755.	—	—	—
S2449	**2 Shillings 6 Pence** 1.10.1755.	—	—	—
S2450	**5 Shillings** 1.10.1755. Complex nature print of leaves on back.	400.00	—	—
S2451	**10 Shillings** 1.10.1755. Complex nature print of leaves on back.	350.00	—	—

1756 Issue

#S2452-S2459 black. Arms of the Penn family. Nature print of leaf on back. Plate letter: A; B. Printer: B. Franklin and D. Hall.

No.	Denomination	Good	Fine	XF
S2452	**1 Shilling** 1.1.1756. *Pennsilvania.*	115.00	300.00	—
S2453	**18 Pence** 1.1.1756. *Pensilvania.*	115.00	300.00	—
S2454	**2 Shillings** 1.1.1756. *Pensilvania.*	115.00	300.00	—
S2455	**2 Shillings 6 Pence** 1.1.1756. *Pennsylvania.*	115.00	300.00	—
S2456	**5 Shillings** 1.1.1756. *Pensilvania.*	115.00	300.00	—
S2457	**10 Shillings** 1.1.1756. *Pennsilvania.*	135.00	350.00	—
S2458	**15 Shillings** 1.1.1756. *Pennsylvania.*	135.00	350.00	—
S2459	**20 Shillings** 1.1.1756. *Pensylvania.*	135.00	350.00	—
S2460	**5 Shillings** 1.10.1756. *Pensilvania.*	100.00	275.00	—
S2461	**10 Shillings** 1.10.1756. *Pennsilvania.*	100.00	275.00	—
S2462	**15 Shillings** 1.10.1756. *Pennsylvania.*	100.00	275.00	—
S2463	**20 Shillings** 1.10.1756. *Pensylvania.*	100.00	275.00	—

1757 First Issue

#S2464-S2467 black. Arms of the Penn family. Nature print of leaf on back. Plate letter A; B. Printer: B. Franklin and D. Hall.

No.	Denomination	Good	Fine	XF
S2464	**5 Shillings** 10.3.1757. *Pensilvania.*	90.00	250.00	—
S2465	**10 Shillings** 10.3.1757. *Pennsilvania.*	90.00	250.00	—
S2466	**15 Shillings** 10.3.1757. *Pennsylvania.*	90.00	250.00	—
S2467	**20 Shillings** 10.3.1757. *Pensylvania.*	90.00	250.00	—

1757 Second Issue

#S2464-S2471 black. Arms of the Penn family. Nature print of leaf on back. Plate letter A; B. Printer: B. Franklin and D. Hall.

No.	Denomination	Good	Fine	XF
S2468	**5 Shillings** 1.7.1757. *Pensilvania.*	75.00	225.00	—
S2469	**10 Shillings** 1.7.1757. *Pensilvania.*	75.00	225.00	—
S2470	**15 Shillings** 1.7.1757. *Pennsylvania.*	75.00	225.00	—
S2471	**20 Shillings** 1.7.1757. *Pensylvania.*	75.00	225.00	—

1758 Issue

#S2472-S2479 black. Arms of the Penn family. Nature print of leaf on back. Printer: B. Franklin and D. Hall.

#S2472-S2475 uniface.

No.	Denomination	Good	Fine	XF
S2472	**1 Shilling** 20.5.1758.	—	—	—
S2473	**18 Pence** 20.5.1758.	—	—	—
S2474	**2 Shillings** 20.5.1758.	—	—	—
S2475	**2 Shillings 6 Pence** 20.5.1758.	—	—	—

#S2476-S2479 plate letter A; B.

No.	Denomination	Good	Fine	XF
S2476	**5 Shillings** 20.5.1757. *Pensilvania.*	85.00	240.00	—
S2477	**10 Shillings** 20.5.1758. *Pennsilvania.*	85.00	240.00	—
S2478	**15 Shillings** 20.5.1758. *Pennsylvania.*	85.00	240.00	—
S2479	**20 Shillings** 20.5.1758. *Pensylvania.*	85.00	240.00	—

1759 First Issue

#S2480-S2485 printer: B. Franklin and D. Hall.

		VG	VF	Unc
S2480	**5 Shillings** 25.4.1759. Black. *Pensilvania.*	135.00	325.00	—
S2481	**10 Shillings** 25.4.1759. Black. *Pennsilvania..*	135.00	325.00	—
S2482	**15 Shillings** 25.4.1759. Black. *Pennsylvania.*	110.00	250.00	—
S2483	**20 Shillings** 25.4.1759. Black. *Pensylvania.*	110.00	250.00	—

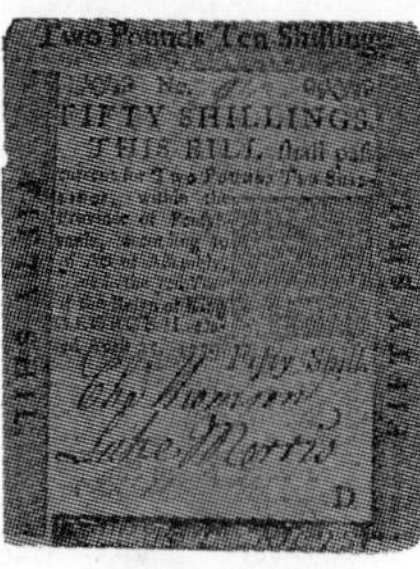

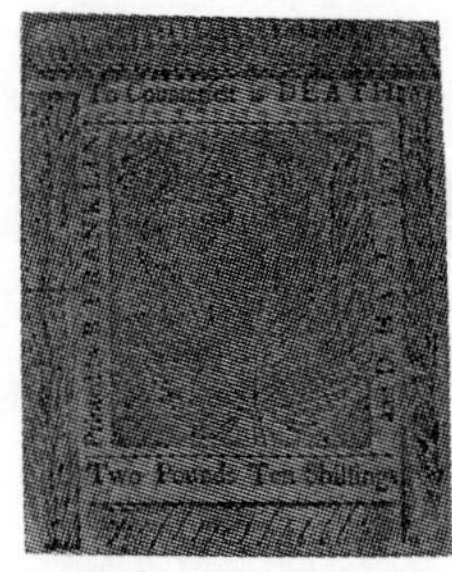

		VG	VF	Unc
S2484	**50 Shillings** 25.4.1759. Black and red. *Pensylvania.* Back black and red; nature print of leaves.	110.00	250.00	—

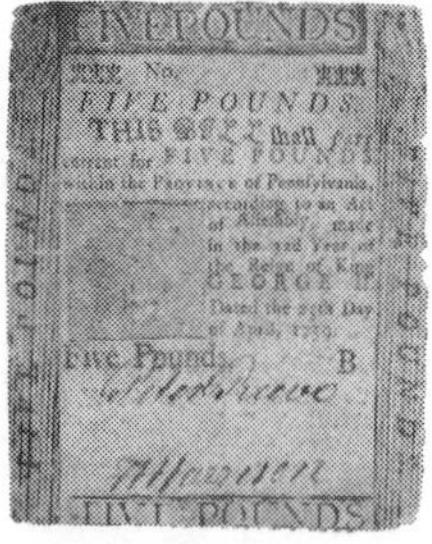

		VG	VF	Unc
S2485	**5 Pounds** 25.4.1759. Black and red. *Pennsylvania.* Back black and red; nature print of leaves.	110.00	250.00	—

1759 Second Issue

#S2486 and S2487 black and red. Nature print of leaves.

No.	Denomination	Good	Fine	XF
S2486	**50 Shillings** 21.6.1759. *Pensylvania.* Plate letter C; D.	—	—	—
S2487	**5 Pounds** 21.6.1759. *Pennsylvania.* Plate letter A; B.	—	—	—

1760 Issue

#S2488-S2496 arms of the Penn family. Printer: B. Franklin and D. Hall.

#S2488-S2495, S2497 plate letter A; B.

No.	Denomination	Good	Fine	XF
S2488	**3 Pence** 1.5.1760. Black.	—	—	—
S2489	**4 Pence** 1.5.1760. Black.	—	—	—
S2490	**6 Pence** 1.5.1760. Black.	—	—	—
S2491	**9 Pence** 1.5.1760. Black.	—	—	—

#S2492-S2494 nature prints of leaves on back.

		VG	VF	Unc
S2492	**5 Shillings** 1.5.1760. Black. *Pensilvania.*	150.00	325.00	—

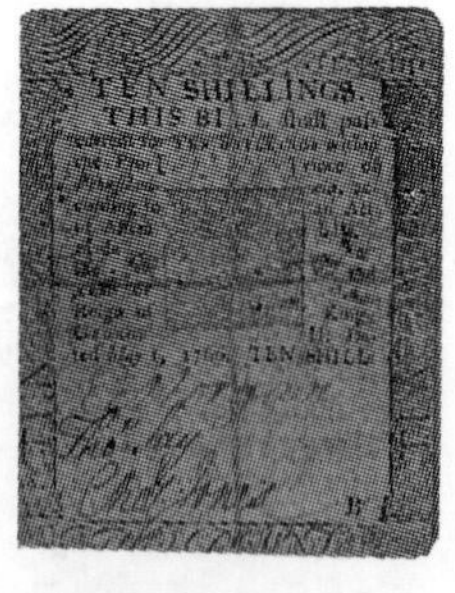

		VG	VF	Unc
S2493	**10 Shillings** 1.5.1760. Black. *Pennsilvania.*	150.00	325.00	—
S2494	**15 Shillings** 1.5.1760. Black. *Pennsylvania.*	135.00	275.00	—
S2495	**20 Shillings** 1.5.1760. Black. *Pennsylvania.*	110.00	240.00	—
S2496	**50 Shillings** 1.5.1760. Black and red. *Pensylvania.* Plate letter C; D. Back black and red; nature print of leaves.	110.00	240.00	—
S2497	**5 Pounds** 1.5.1760. Black and red. *Pennsylvania.*	110.00	240.00	—

NOTE: Notes printed on blue paper are counterfeit detectors.

1764 Issue

#S2498-S2508 black. Crowned supported British arms. Printer: B. Franklin and D. Hall.

#S2498-S2505, S2507 and S2508 plate letter A; B.

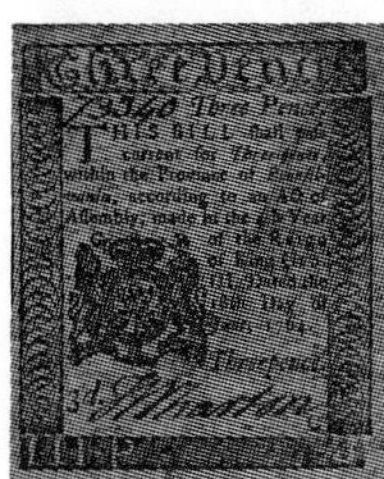

		VG	VF	UNC
S2498	**3 Pence** 18.6.1764. *Pennsilvania.*	120.00	225.00	—
S2499	**4 Pence** 18.6.1764. *Pensylvania.*	150.00	265.00	—
S2500	**6 Pence** 18.6.1764. *Pennsylvania.*	150.00	265.00	—
S2501	**9 Pence** 18.6.1764. *Pennsylvania.*	150.00	265.00	—

#S2502-S2508 backs w/nature print: leaf or leaves.

		VG	VF	UNC
S2502	**1 Shilling** 18.6.1764. *Pennsilvania.*	110.00	240.00	—
S2503	**1 Shilling 6 Pence** 18.6.1764.	110.00	240.00	—
S2504	**2 Shillings** 18.6.1764.	110.00	240.00	—
S2505	**2 Shillings 6 Pence** 18.6.1764. Black.	110.00	240.00	—
S2506	**5 Shillings** 18.6.1764. Black. *Pensylvania.* Plate letter A; B; C; D.	110.00	240.00	—
S2507	**10 Shillings** 18.6.1764. Black. *Pennsilvania.*	110.00	240.00	—
S2508	**20 Shillings** 18.6.1764. Black. *Pennsylvania.*	110.00	240.00	—

1767 Issue

#S2509-S2511 black. Arms of the Penn family. Nature print of leaves on back. Printer: David Hall and William Sellers.

		Good	Fine	XF
S2509	**40 Shillings** 15.6.1767. Plate letter A; B; C; D.	—	—	—
S2510	**4 Pounds** 15.6.1767. Plate letter A; B.	—	—	—
S2511	**6 Pounds** 15.6.1767. Plate letter A; B; C; D.	—	—	—

NOTE: Notes printed on blue paper are Test Notes.

1769 First Issue

#S2512-S2515 blacks. Arms of the Penn family. Nature print of leaves on back. Printer: David Hall and William Sellers.

		Good	Fine	XF
S2512	**8 Shillings** 1.3.1769. *Pensilvania.*	125.00	350.00	—
S2513	**12 Shillings** 1.3.1769. *Pensylvania.*	125.00	350.00	—
S2514	**1 Pound 10 Shillings** 1.3.1769. *Pennsylvania.* Plate letter A; B; C.	90.00	265.00	—
S2515	**3 Pounds** 1.3.1769. *Pennsilvania.* Plate letter A; B.	90.00	265.00	—

1769 Second Issue

#S2516-S2527 black. Arms of the Penn family. Printer: David Hall and William Sellers.

#S2516-S2523 uniface.

		VG	VF	UNC
S2516	**3 Pence** 10.3.1769. *Pensilvania.* Plate letter A; B; C.	120.00	450.00	—
S2517	**4 Pence** 10.3.1769. *Pennsilvania.* Plate letter A; B; C.	120.00	450.00	—
S2518	**6 Pence** 10.3.1769. *Pensylvania.* Plate letter A; B; C.	120.00	450.00	—
S2519	**9 Pence** 10.3.1769. *Pennsylvania.* Plate letter A; B; C.	120.00	450.00	—
S2520	**1 Shilling** 10.3.1769. *Pennsylvania.* Plate letter A; B; C; D.	75.00	300.00	—
S2521	**18 Pence** 10.3.1769. *Pennsylvania.* Plate letter A; B; C; D.	75.00	300.00	—

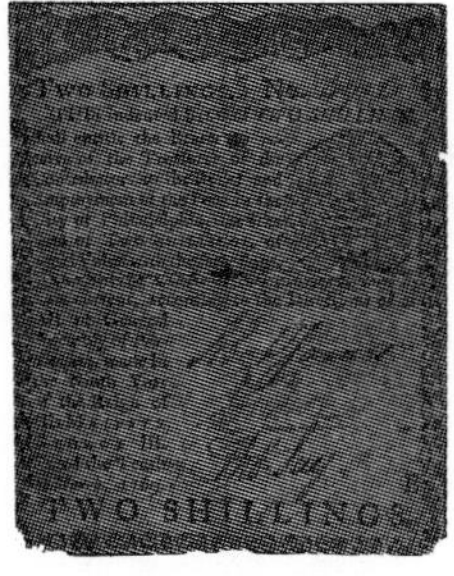

		VG	VF	UNC
S2522	**2 Shillings** 10.3.1769. *Pensilvania.* Plate letter A; B; C; D.	75.00	300.00	—
S2523	**2 Shillings 6 Pence** 10.3.1769. *Pensylvania.* Plate letter A; B.	75.00	300.00	—

#S2524-S2527 nature print of leaves on back.

		VG	VF	UNC
S2524	**5 Shillings** 10.3.1769. *Pennsylvania.* Plate letter A; B; C; D.	75.00	300.00	—
S2525	**10 Shillings** 10.3.1769. *Pensylvania.*			
	a. Asterisk follows date on face. 12 identical ornaments to r. of colon on lower border.	75.00	300.00	—
	b. W/o asterisk after date. 11 identical ornaments to r. of colon on lower border.	75.00	300.00	—
S2526	**15 Shillings** 10.3.1769. *Pennsylvania.*	75.00	300.00	—
S2527	**20 Shillings** 10.3.1769. *Pennsylvania.*	75.00	300.00	—

1771 Issue

#S2528-S2531 black and red. Arms of the Penn family. Nature prints of leaves on back. Paper w/mica flakes. Plate letter A; B. Printer: David Hall and William Sellers.

		VG	VF	UNC
S2528	**5 Shillings** 20.3.1771. *Pensilvania.*	35.00	100.00	300.00
S2529	**10 Shillings** 20.3.1771. *Pensylvania.*	35.00	100.00	300.00
S2530	**15 Shillings** 20.3.1771. *Pennsilvania.*	35.00	100.00	300.00

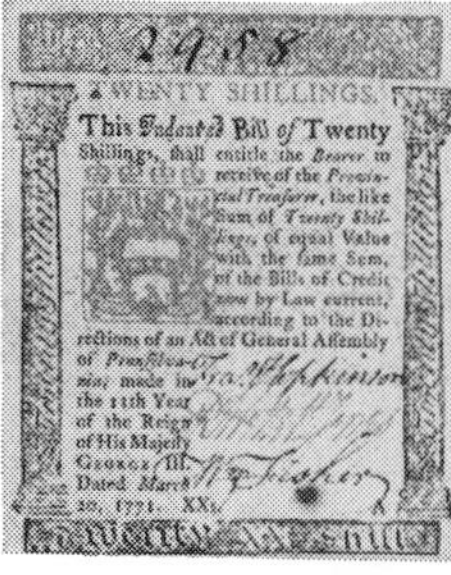

		VG	VF	UNC
S2531	**20 Shillings** 20.3.1771. *Pennsylvania.*	35.00	100.00	300.00

1772 Issue

#S2532-S2540 black. Arms of the Penn family. Printer: David Hall and William Sellers.

		VG	VF	UNC
S2532	**3 Pence** 3.4.1772. *Pennsylvania.* Plate letter A; B; C.	30.00	80.00	—
S2533	**4 Pence** 3.4.1772. *Pennsilvania.* Plate letter A; B; C.	30.00	80.00	—
S2534	**6 Pence** 3.4.1772. *Pensylvania.* Plate letter A; B; C.	30.00	80.00	—
S2535	**9 Pence** 3.4.1772. *Pensilvania.* Plate letter A; B; C.	30.00	80.00	—

#S2536-S2538 nature print of leaf.

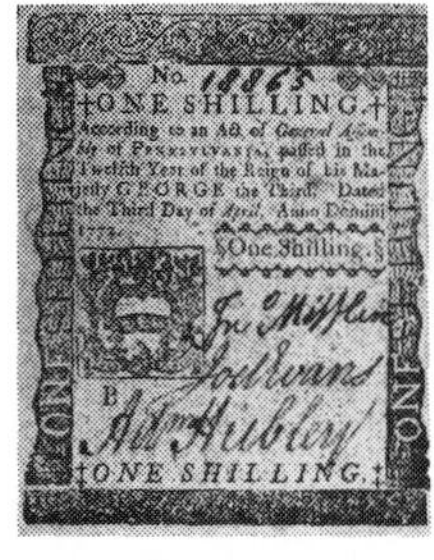

		VG	VF	UNC
S2536	**1 Shilling** 3.4.1772. Black. *Pennsylvania.* Plate letter A; B.	25.00	60.00	125.00
S2537	**18 Pence** 3.4.1772. Black. *Pennsilvania.* Plate letter A; B.	25.00	60.00	125.00
S2538	**2 Shillings** 3.4.1772. Black. *Pensylvania.* Plate letter A; B.	25.00	60.00	125.00
S2539	**2 Shillings 6 Pence** 3.4.1772. Black. *Pensilvania.* Plate letter A; B.	25.00	60.00	125.00
S2540	**40 Shillings** 3.4.1772. Black and red. *Pennsylvania.* Plate letter A; B; C; D.	50.00	150.00	—

1773 Issue

#S2540A-S2540H black and red. Arms of the Penn family. Paper w/mica flakes and blue fibres. Landscape on back.

		VG	VF	UNC
S2540A	**18 Pence** 1.10.1773. *Pennsilvania.*	18.00	40.00	100.00
S2540B	**2 Shillings** 1.10.1773. *Pennsylvania.*	18.00	40.00	100.00

		VG	VF	UNC
S2540C	**2 SHILLINGS 6 PENCE** 1.10.1773. *Pennsylvania.*	18.00	40.00	100.00

		VG	VF	UNC
S2540D	**5 SHILLINGS** 1.10.1773. *Pennsylvania.*	18.00	40.00	100.00

		VG	VF	UNC
S2540E	**10 SHILLINGS** 1.10.1773. *Pennsylvania.* Red *X.*	18.00	40.00	100.00
S2540F	**15 SHILLINGS** 1.10.1773. *Pensylvania.* Red *XV.*	18.00	40.00	100.00

		VG	VF	UNC
S2540G	**20 SHILLINGS** 1.10.1773. *Pennsylvania.* Red *1* (pound).	18.00	40.00	100.00
S2540H	**50 SHILLINGS** 1.10.1773. *Pennsilvania.* Red *L.*.	18.00	40.00	100.00

1773 LIGHTHOUSE CONSTRUCTION ISSUE

#S2540I-S2540M black. Arms of the Penn family. Lighthouse, sailing ship on back. Paper w/mica flakes. Printer: David Hall and William Sellers.

		VG	VF	UNC
S2540I	**4 SHILLINGS** 20.3.1773. Plate letter A; B.	25.00	55.00	200.00

		VG	VF	UNC
S2540J	**6 SHILLINGS** 20.3.1773. Arms upside down. Plate letter A.	25.00	55.00	200.00
S2540K	**6 SHILLINGS** 20.3.1773. Arms corrected. Plate letter B.	25.00	55.00	200.00
S2540L	**14 SHILLINGS** 20.3.1773. Plate letter A; B.	25.00	55.00	200.00
S2540M	**16 SHILLINGS** 20.3.1773. Plate letter A; B.	25.00	55.00	200.00

NOTE: Detector notes are printed on blue paper.

1775 LIGHTHOUSE CONSTRUCTION ISSUE

#S2540N-S2540Q black. Similar to #S2540I-S2540M. Plate letter A; B.

		VG	VF	UNC
S2540N	**4 SHILLINGS** 25.3.1775.	30.00	75.00	300.00

		VG	VF	UNC
S2540O	**6 SHILLINGS** 25.3.1775.	30.00	75.00	300.00
S2540P	**14 SHILLINGS** 25.3.1775.	30.00	75.00	300.00
S2540Q	**16 SHILLINGS** 25.3.1775.	30.00	75.00	300.00

1775 FIRST JAIL AND CORRECTIONAL INSTITUTION CONSTRUCTION ISSUE

#S2540R-S2540V red and black. Workhouse (Philadelphia City jail) on back. Paper w/mica flakes. Printer: David Hall and William Sellers.

		VG	VF	UNC
S2540R	**50 SHILLINGS** 10.4.1775. *Pennsilvania.* Plate letter C.	30.00	70.00	300.00
S2540S	**50 SHILLINGS** 10.4.1775. *Pennsylvania.* Plate letter D.	30.00	70.00	300.00
S2540T	**5 POUNDS** 10.4.1775. *Pensylvania.* Plate letter A.	30.00	70.00	300.00

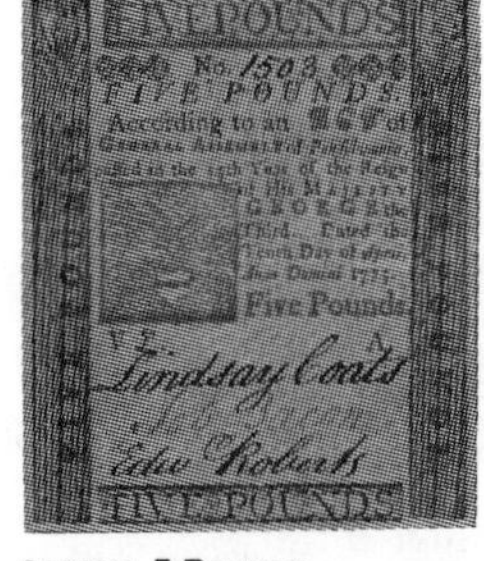

		VG	VF	UNC
S2540U	**5 POUNDS** 10.4.1775. *Pensilvania.* Plate letter B.	30.00	70.00	300.00

1775 SECOND JAIL AND CORRECTIONAL INSTITUTION CONSTRUCTION ISSUE

#S2541-S2544 black. Nature print of leaves on back. Paper w/mica flakes and blue fibres.

		VG	VF	UNC
S2541	**10 SHILLINGS** 20.7.1775.			
	a. Plate letter A. Reversed *S* on l. column. *Pennsilvania.*	25.00	55.00	150.00
	b. Plate letter B. Reversed *S* on r. column. *Pennsylvania.*	25.00	55.00	150.00
S2542	**20 SHILLINGS** 20.7.1775.			
	a. Plate letter A. Capital letters on r. column. *Pennsylvania.*	25.00	55.00	150.00
	b. Plate letter B. Capital letters on l. column. *Pennsilvania.*	25.00	55.00	150.00
S2543	**30 SHILLINGS** 20.7.1775.			
	a. Plate letter A. *Pensylvania.*	25.00	55.00	150.00

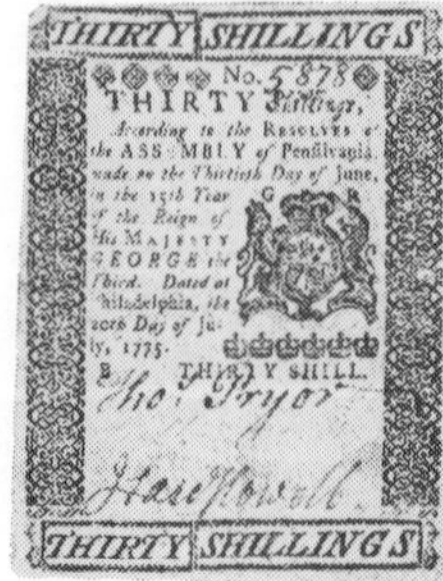

		VG	VF	UNC
	b. Plate letter B. *Pensilvania.*	25.00	55.00	150.00

		VG	VF	UNC
S2544	**40 SHILLINGS** 20.7.1775.			
	a. Plate letter A. *Pensilvania.*	25.00	55.00	150.00
	b. Plate letter B. *Pensylvania.*	25.00	55.00	150.00

1775 THIRD JAIL AND CORRECTIONAL INSTITUTION CONSTRUCTION ISSUE

#S2545-S2556 black. Arms of Penn family. Except for #S2552 nature print of leaf or leaves on back. Printer: David Hall and William Sellers.

		VG	VF	UNC
S2545	**3 PENCE** 25.10.1775. *Pennsylvania.*	15.00	30.00	100.00
S2546	**4 PENCE** 25.10.1775. *Pennsilvania.*	15.00	30.00	100.00

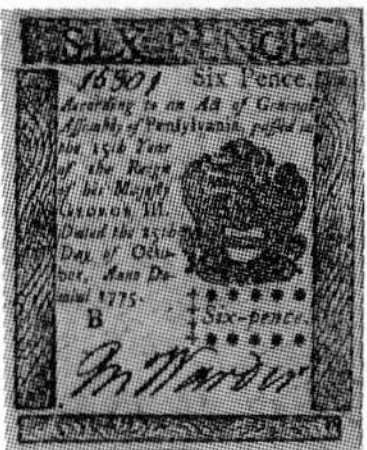

		VG	VF	UNC
S2547	**6 PENCE** 25.10.1775. *Pensylvania.*	15.00	30.00	100.00
S2548	**9 PENCE** 25.10.1775. *Pensilvania.*	15.00	30.00	100.00
S2549	**1 SHILLING** 25.10.1775. *S* for Smither in top border. *Pensylvania.*	15.00	30.00	100.00

		VG	VF	UNC
S2550	**18 PENCE** 25.10.1775. *Pennsilvania.*	15.00	30.00	100.00

		VG	VF	UNC
S2551	**2 SHILLINGS** 25.10.1775. *Pensylvania.*	15.00	30.00	100.00
S2552	**2 SHILLINGS 6 PENCE = 1/2 CROWN** 25.10.1775. *Pennsylvania.* Back chevron designs.	15.00	30.00	100.00
S2553	**5 SHILLINGS = 1 CROWN** 25.10.1775. *Pennsylvania.*	17.00	35.00	120.00
S2554	**10 SHILLINGS = 2 CROWNS** 25.10.1775. *Pennsylvania.*	17.00	35.00	120.00
S2555	**15 SHILLINGS = 3 CROWNS** 25.10.1775. *Pensilvania.*	17.00	35.00	120.00
S2556	**20 SHILLINGS = 4 CROWNS** 25.10.1775. *Pensylvania.*	17.00	35.00	120.00

1775 FOURTH JAIL AND CORRECTIONAL INSTITUTION

CONSTRUCTION ISSUE

#S2557-S2560 black. Crowned supported British arms. Nature print of leaf or leaves on back. Paper w/blue fibres. Printer: David Hall and William Sellers.

		VG	VF	UNC
S2557	**10 SHILLINGS** 8.12.1775.			
	a. Plate letter A. Reversed *S* on l. column.	15.00	30.00	90.00
	b. Plate letter B. Reversed *S* on r. column.	15.00	30.00	90.00
S2558	**20 SHILLINGS** 8.12.1775.			
	a. Plate letter A. Capital letters on r. column.	15.00	30.00	90.00
	b. Plate letter B. Capital letters on l. column.	15.00	30.00	90.00
S2559	**30 SHILLINGS** 8.12.1775. *Pensilvania.*	15.00	30.00	90.00

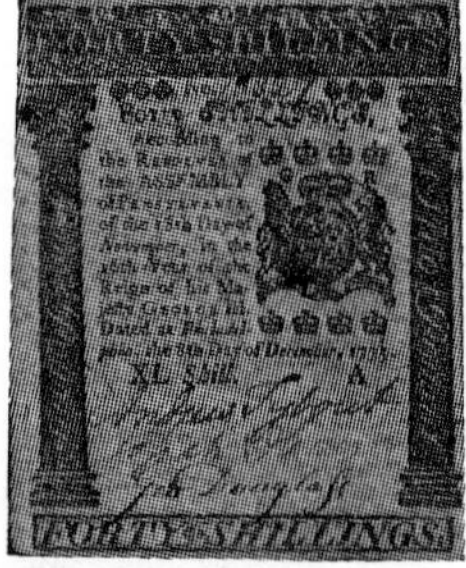

		VG	VF	UNC
S2560	**40 SHILLINGS** 8.12.1775. *Pensylvania.*	15.00	30.00	90.00

1776 JAIL AND CORRECTIONAL INSTITUTION CONSTRUCTION ISSUE

#S2561-S2572 black. Paper w/mica flakes and blue fibres. Printer: David Hall and William Sellers.

#S2561-S2564 arms of the Penn family.

		VG	VF	UNC
S2561	**3 PENCE** 25.4.1776. *Pennsylvania.*	12.00	28.00	70.00

		VG	VF	UNC
S2562	**4 PENCE** 25.4.1776. *Pensilvania.*	12.00	28.00	70.00
S2563	**6 PENCE** 25.4.1776. *Pensylvania.*	12.00	28.00	70.00
S2564	**9 PENCE** 25.4.1776. *Pensylvania.*	12.00	28.00	70.00

#S2565-S2572 crowned supported British arms. Nature print of leaf or leaves on back.

		VG	VF	UNC
S2565	**1 SHILLING** 25.4.1776. *Pennsylvania.*	15.00	30.00	80.00

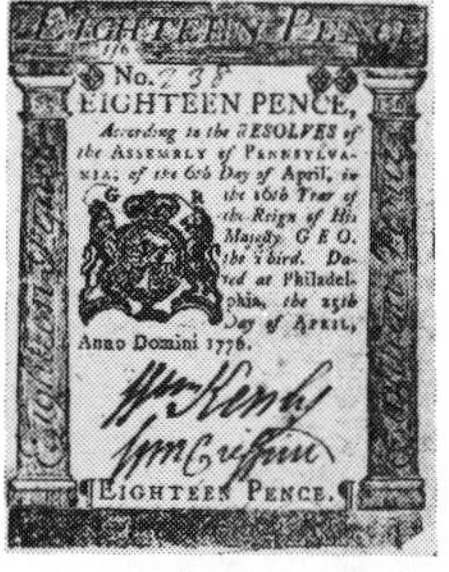

		VG	VF	UNC
S2566	**18 PENCE** 25.4.1776. *Pennsylvania.*	15.00	30.00	80.00
S2567	**2 SHILLINGS** 25.4.1776. *Pennsilvania.*	15.00	30.00	80.00
S2568	**2 SHILLINGS 6 PENCE** 25.4.1776. *Pennsylvania.*	15.00	30.00	80.00
S2569	**10 SHILLINGS** 25.4.1776.			
	a. Plate letter A. Reversed *S* on r. column. *Pennsylvania.*	18.00	45.00	100.00
	b. Plate letter B. Reversed *S* on l. column. *Pennsilvania.*	18.00	45.00	100.00
S2570	**20 SHILLINGS** 25.4.1776.			
	a. Plate letter A. Capital letters on r. column. *Pennsilvania.*	18.00	40.00	120.00
	b. Plate letter B. Capital letters on l. column. *Pennsylvania.*	18.00	40.00	120.00
S2571	**30 SHILLINGS** 25.4.1776.			
	a. Plate letter A. *Pensylvania.*	18.00	45.00	100.00
	b. Plate letter B. *Pensilvania.*	18.00	45.00	100.00
S2572	**40 SHILLINGS** 25.4.1776.			
	a. Plate letter A. *Pensylvania.*	18.00	45.00	100.00
	b. Plate letter B. *Pensilvania.*	18.00	45.00	100.00

PENNSYLVANIA

COMMONWEALTH

1777 FIRST ISSUE

#S2573-S2588 black. Arms of the Commonwealth of Pennsylvania. Wmk: *PENSYL/VANIA.* Red serial numbers. Plate letter A; B; C. Printer: John Dunlap.

		VG	VF	UNC
S2573	**3 PENCE** 10.4.1777.	12.00	30.00	100.00
S2574	**4 PENCE** 10.4.1777.	12.00	30.00	100.00

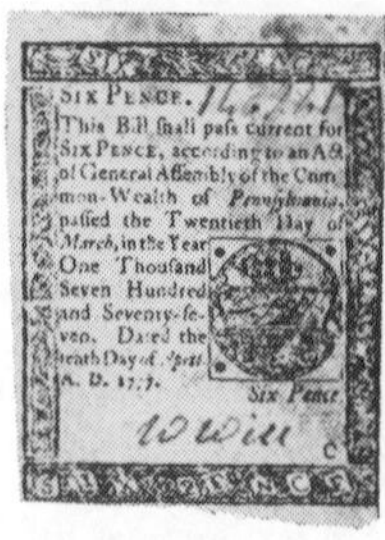

		VG	VF	UNC
S2575	**6 PENCE** 10.4.1777.	12.00	30.00	100.00
S2576	**9 PENCE** 10.4.1777.	12.00	30.00	100.00

#S2577-S2588 farm landscape on back.

		VG	VF	UNC
S2577	**1 SHILLING** 10.4.1777.	14.00	32.00	90.00
S2578	**1 SHILLING 6 PENCE** 10.4.1777.	14.00	32.00	90.00
S2579	**2 SHILLINGS** 10.4.1777.	14.00	32.00	90.00
S2580	**3 SHILLINGS** 10.4.1777.	14.00	32.00	90.00
S2581	**4 SHILLINGS** 10.4.1777.	14.00	32.00	90.00

		VG	VF	UNC
S2582	**6 SHILLINGS** 10.4.1777.	14.00	32.00	90.00
S2583	**8 SHILLINGS** 10.4.1777.	14.00	32.00	90.00
S2584	**12 SHILLINGS** 10.4.1777.	14.00	32.00	90.00
S2585	**16 SHILLINGS** 10.4.1777.	14.00	32.00	90.00

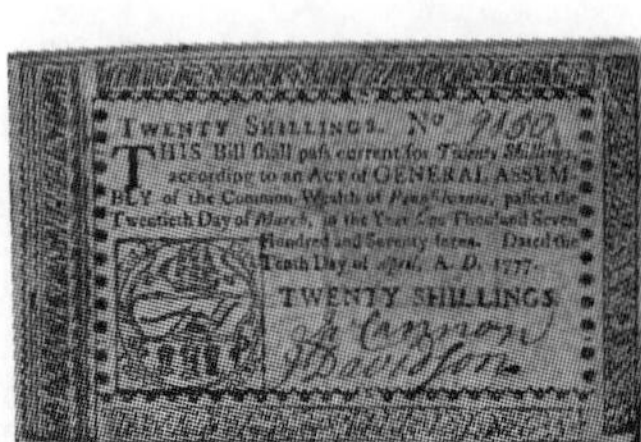

		VG	VF	UNC
S2586	**20 SHILLINGS** 10.4.1777.	14.00	32.00	90.00
S2587	**40 SHILLINGS** 10.4.1777.			
	a. Issued note.	18.00	50.00	110.00
	x. Back of 4 Pounds (error).	—	—	—
S2588	**4 POUNDS** 10.4.1777.			
	a. Issued note.	18.00	50.00	110.00
	b. Back of 40 Shillings (error).	—	—	—

1777 SECOND ISSUE

#S2589-S2600 red and black. Arms of the Commonwealth of Pennsylvania. Farm landscape on back.

		VG	VF	UNC
S2589	**1 SHILLING** 10.4.1777. Back red and black.	18.00	40.00	100.00
S2590	**1 SHILLING 6 PENCE** 10.4.1777. Back red and black.	18.00	40.00	100.00
S2591	**2 SHILLINGS** 10.4.1777. Back red and black.	18.00	40.00	100.00

		VG	VF	UNC
S2592	**3 SHILLINGS** 10.4.1777. Back red and black.	18.00	40.00	100.00
S2593	**4 SHILLINGS** 10.4.1777. Back red and black.	18.00	40.00	100.00
S2594	**6 SHILLINGS** 10.4.1777. Back red and black.	18.00	40.00	100.00
S2595	**8 SHILLINGS** 10.4.1777. Back red and black.	18.00	40.00	100.00
S2596	**12 SHILLINGS** 10.4.1777. Back red and black.	18.00	40.00	100.00
S2597	**16 SHILLINGS** 10.4.1777. Back red and black.	18.00	40.00	100.00
S2598	**20 SHILLINGS** 10.4.1777. Back red and black.	18.00	40.00	100.00
S2599	**40 SHILLINGS** 10.4.1777. Back black.	25.00	55.00	125.00
S2600	**4 POUNDS** 10.4.1777. Back black.	25.00	55.00	125.00

1780 FIRST ISSUE

#S2601-S2608 black. Wmk: *PENSYL/VANIA*. New set of nature prints of leaf or leaves on back. Printer: John Dunlap.

		GOOD	FINE	XF
S2601	**5 SHILLINGS** 29.4.1780.	—	—	—
S2602	**10 SHILLINGS** 29.4.1780.	—	—	—
S2603	**15 SHILLINGS** 29.4.1780.	—	—	—
S2604	**20 SHILLINGS** 29.4.1780.	—	—	—
S2605	**30 SHILLINGS** 29.4.1780.	—	—	—
S2606	**40 SHILLINGS** 29.4.1780.	—	—	—
S2607	**50 SHILLINGS** 29.4.1780.	—	—	—
S2608	**60 SHILLINGS** 29.4.1780.	—	—	—

1780 SECOND ISSUE

Dollar System

#S2609-S2616 black. Wmk: *CONFEDE/RATION*. Back red and black; similar to Continental Currency issue of 14.1.1779. Printer: David Hall and William Sellers.

		VG	VF	UNC
S2609	**1 DOLLAR** 1.6.1780.	250.00	600.00	—
S2610	**2 DOLLARS** 1.6.1780.	250.00	600.00	—
S2611	**3 DOLLARS** 1.6.1780.	250.00	600.00	—

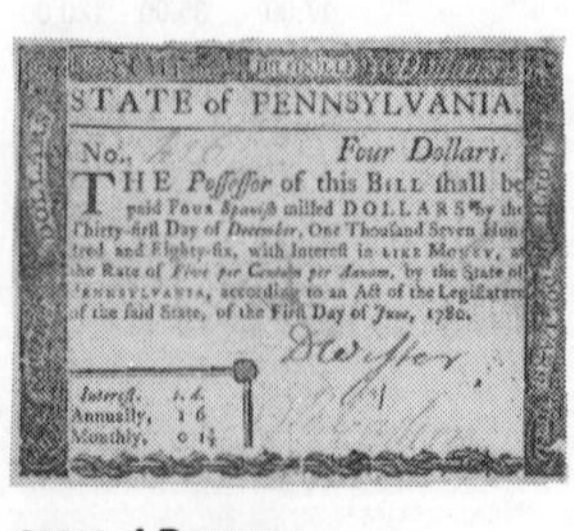

		VG	VF	UNC
S2612	**4 DOLLARS** 1.6.1780.	250.00	600.00	—
S2613	**5 DOLLARS** 1.6.1780.	250.00	600.00	—
S2614	**7 DOLLARS** 1.6.1780. *DOLLARS* misspelled *DOLLRAS* in upper r. border.	250.00	600.00	—
S2615	**8 DOLLARS** 1.6.1780.	250.00	600.00	—
S2616	**20 DOLLARS** 1.6.1780.	250.00	600.00	—

1781 Issue

#S2617-S2631 black. Wmk: *PENSYL/VANIA*. Printer: John Dunlap.

		VG	VF	Unc
S2617	**3 Pence** 20.4.1781.			
	a. Plate letter A. *Pence* misspelled *PENEE* at end of text.	75.00	225.00	450.00
	b. Plate letter B.	50.00	150.00	300.00
S2618	**6 Pence** 20.4.1781.			
	a. Plate letter A. Lower border words separated.	50.00	150.00	300.00
	b. Plate letter B. Lower border words too close.	50.00	150.00	300.00
S2619	**9 Pence** 20.4.1781.			
	a. Plate letter A. Lower border letters are black.	50.00	110.00	—
	b. Plate letter B. Lower border letters are white.	50.00	120.00	—
S2620	**1 Shilling 6 Pence** 20.4.1781.	85.00	235.00	400.00
S2621	**2 Shillings** 20.4.1781. Leaves on back.	85.00	235.00	400.00
S2622	**2 Shillings 6 Pence** 20.4.1781. Chevron designs on back.	85.00	235.00	400.00
S2623	**5 Shillings** 20.4.1781. Leaves on back.	85.00	235.00	400.00
S2624	**10 Shillings** 20.4.1781. Leaves on back.	95.00	260.00	450.00
S2625	**15 Shillings** 20.4.1781. Leaves on back.	95.00	260.00	450.00
S2626	**20 Shillings** 20.4.1781. Leaves on back.	95.00	260.00	450.00
S2627	**30 Shillings** 20.4.1781. Leaves, *Dunlap* misspelled *DNNLAP* on back.	95.00	260.00	450.00
S2628	**40 Shillings** 20.4.1781. Leaves on back.	95.00	260.00	450.00
S2629	**50 Shillings** 20.4.1781. Leaves on back.	95.00	260.00	450.00
S2630	**60 Shillings** 20.4.1781. Leaves on back.	150.00	350.00	600.00
S2631	**5 Pounds** 20.4.1781. Farm landscape on back.	200.00	450.00	750.00

1783 Treasury Issue

#S2632-S2639 black.

		Good	Fine	XF
S2632	**1/4 Dollar** 21.3.1783.	—	—	—
S2633	**1 Dollar** 21.3.1783.	—	—	—
S2634	**2 Dollars** 21.3.1783.	—	—	—
S2635	**3 Dollars** 21.3.1783.	—	—	—
S2636	**6 Dollars** 21.3.1783.	—	—	—
S2637	**12 Dollars** 21.3.1783.	—	—	—
S2638	**15 Dollars** 21.3.1783.	—	—	—
S2639	**20 Dollars** 21.3.1783.	—	—	—

1785 Issue

#S2640-S2647 black. Commonwealth Seal in various shapes. Wmk: *PENSYL/VANIA*. New type of nature and cloth designs on back. Printer: Francis Bailey.

		VG	VF	Unc
S2640	**3 Pence** 16.3.1785.	75.00	120.00	—
S2641	**9 Pence** 16.3.1785.	75.00	125.00	—
S2642	**1 Shilling 6 Pence** 16.3.1785.	75.00	125.00	—
S2643	**2 Shillings 6 Pence** 16.3.1785. *Bailey* misspelled *BAILLY* on back.	75.00	125.00	—
S2644	**5 Shillings** 16.3.1785.	85.00	150.00	—
S2645	**10 Shillings** 16.3.1785.	85.00	150.00	—

		VG	VF	Unc
S2646	**15 Shillings** 16.3.1785.	85.00	150.00	—
S2647	**20 Shillings** 16.3.1785.	85.00	150.00	—

Rhode Island

Colonial

1710 Issue

Pound Sterling System

#S2651-S2658 black. Arms of Rhode Island. Uniface.

		Good	Fine	XF
S2651	**2 Shillings** 16.8.1710.	—	—	—
S2652	**2 Shillings 6 Pence** 16.8.1710.	—	—	—
S2653	**5 Shillings** 16.8.1710.	—	—	—
S2654	**10 Shillings** 16.8.1710.	—	—	—
S2655	**20 Shillings** 16.8.1710.	—	—	—
S2656	**40 Shillings** 16.8.1710.	—	—	—
S2657	**3 Pounds** 16.8.1710.	—	—	—
S2658	**5 Pounds** 16.8.1710.	—	—	—

1715 Issue

#S2659-S2668 black. Arms w/motto: *IN TE DOMINE SPERAMUS*. Ornamental designs on back. Printer: Samuel Vernon.

		Good	Fine	XF
S2659	**12 Pence** 5.7.1715.	—	—	—
S2660	**2 Shillings 6 Pence** 5.7.1715.	—	—	—
S2661	**3 Shillings** 5.7.1715.	—	—	—
S2662	**4 Shillings 6 Pence** 5.7.1715.	—	—	—
S2663	**5 Shillings** 5.7.1715.	—	—	—
S2664	**10 Shillings** 5.7.1715.	—	—	—
S2665	**20 Shillings** 5.7.1715.	—	—	—
S2666	**40 Shillings** 5.7.1715.	—	—	—
S2667	**3 Pounds** 5.7.1715.	—	—	—
S2668	**5 Pounds** 5.7.1715.	—	—	—

1721 Redated Issue

#S2669-S2678 black.

		Good	Fine	XF
S2669	**12 Pence** 1721 (- old date 5.7.1715).	—	—	—
S2670	**2 Shillings 6 Pence** 1721 (- old date 5.7.1715).	—	—	—
S2671	**3 Shillings** 1721 (- old date 5.7.1715).	—	—	—
S2672	**4 Shillings 6 Pence** 1721 (- old date 5.7.1715).	—	—	—
S2673	**5 Shillings** 1721 (- old date 5.7.1715).	—	—	—
S2674	**10 Shillings** 1721 (- old date 5.7.1715).	—	—	—
S2675	**20 Shillings** 1721 (- old date 5.7.1715).	—	—	—
S2676	**40 Shillings** 1721 (- old date 5.7.1715).	—	—	—
S2677	**3 Pounds** 1721 (- old date 5.7.1715).	—	—	—
S2678	**5 Pounds** 1721 (- old date 5.7.1715).	—	—	—

1724 Redated Issue

#S2679-S2688 black.

		Good	Fine	XF
S2679	**12 Pence** 1724 (- old date 1721/5.7.1715).	—	—	—
S2680	**2 Shillings 6 Pence** 1724. (- old date 1721/5.7.1715).	—	—	—
S2681	**3 Shillings** 1724. (- old date 1721/5.7.1715).	—	—	—
S2682	**4 Shillings 6 Pence** 1724. (- old date 1721/5.7.1715).	—	—	—
S2683	**5 Shillings** 1724. (- old date 1721/5.7.1715).	—	—	—
S2684	**10 Shillings** 1724. (- old date 1721/5.7.1715).	—	—	—
S2685	**20 Shillings** 1724. (- old date 1721/5.7.1715).	—	—	—
S2686	**40 Shillings** 1724. (- old date 1721/5.7.1715).	—	—	—
S2687	**3 Pounds** 1724. (- old date 1721/5.7.1715).	—	—	—
S2688	**5 Pounds** 1724. (- old date 1721/5.7.1715).	—	—	—

1726 Redated Issue

#S2689-S2692 black.

No.	Denomination / Date	Good	Fine	XF
S2689	**12 Pence** 1726 (- old date 1724/21/5.7.1715).	—	—	—
S2690	**2 Shillings** 1726 (- old date 1724/21/5.7.1715).	—	—	—
S2691	**3 Shillings** 1726 (- old date 1724/21/5.7.1715).	—	—	—
S2692	**4 Shillings 6 Pence** 1726 (- old date 1724/21/5.7.1715).	—	—	—

1726 Issue

#S2693-S2698 black. Leaf and bird design on back.

No.	Denomination / Date	Good	Fine	XF
S2693	**5 Shillings** 14.6.1726.	—	—	—
S2694	**10 Shillings** 14.6.1726.	—	—	—
S2695	**20 Shillings** 14.6.1726.	—	—	—
S2696	**40 Shillings** 14.6.1726.	—	—	—
S2697	**3 Pounds** 14.6.1726.	—	—	—
S2698	**5 Pounds** 14.6.1726.	—	—	—

1728 Redated Issue

#S2699-S2708 black. Printer: Samuel Vernon.

No.	Denomination / Date	Good	Fine	XF
S2699	**12 Pence** 1728 (- old date 1726/24/21/5.7.1715).	—	—	—
S2700	**2 Shillings 6 Pence** 1728 (- old date 1726/24/21/5.7.1715).	—	—	—
S2701	**3 Shillings** 1728 (- old date 1726/24/21/5.7.1715).	—	—	—
S2702	**4 Shillings 6 Pence** 1728 (- old date 1726/24/21/5.7.1715).	—	—	—
S2703	**5 Shillings** 1728 (- old date 14.6.1726).	—	—	—
S2704	**10 Shillings** 1728 (- old date 14.6.1726).	—	—	—
S2705	**20 Shillings** 1728 (- old date 14.6.1726).	—	—	—
S2706	**40 Shillings** 1728 (- old date 14.6.1726).	—	—	—
S2707	**3 Pounds** 1728 (- old date 14.6.1726).	—	—	—
S2708	**5 Pounds** 1728 (- old date 14.6.1726).	—	—	—

1731 Redated Issue

#S2709-S2718 black. Printer: Samuel Vernon.

No.	Denomination / Date	Good	Fine	XF
S2709	**12 Pence** 1731 (- old date 1728/26/24/21/5.7.1715).	—	—	—
S2710	**2 Shillings 6 Pence** 1731 (- old date 1728/26/24/21/5.7.1715).	—	—	—
S2711	**3 Shillings** 1731 (- old date 1728/26/24/21/5.7.1715).	—	—	—
S2712	**4 Shillings 6 Pence** 1731 (- old date 1728/26/24/21/5.7.1715).	—	—	—
S2713	**5 Shillings** 1731 (- old date 1728/14.6.1726).	—	—	—
S2714	**10 Shillings** 1731 (- old date 1728/14.6.1726).	—	—	—
S2715	**20 Shillings** 1731 (- old date 1728/14.6.1726).	—	—	—
S2716	**40 Shillings** 1731 (- old date 1728/14.6.1726).	—	—	—
S2717	**3 Pounds** 1731 (- old date 1728/14.6.1726).	—	—	—
S2718	**5 Pounds** 1731 (- old date 1728/14.6.1726).	—	—	—

1733 Redated Issue

#S2719-S2728 black.

No.	Denomination / Date	Good	Fine	XF
S2719	**12 Pence** 1733 (- old date 1731/28/26/24/21/5.7.1715).	—	—	—
S2720	**2 Shillings 6 Pence** 1733 (- old date 1731/28/26/24/21/5.7.1715).	—	—	—
S2721	**3 Shillings** 1733 (- old date 1731/28/26/24/21/5.7.1715).	—	—	—
S2722	**4 Shillings 6 Pence** 1733 (- old date 1731/28/26/24/21/5.7.1715).	—	—	—
S2723	**5 Shillings** 1733 (- old date 1731/28/14.6.1726).	—	—	—
S2724	**10 Shillings** 1733 (- old date 1731/28/14.6.1726).	—	—	—
S2725	**20 Shillings** 1733 (- old date 1731/28/14.6.1726).	—	—	—
S2726	**40 Shillings** 1733 (- old date 1731/28/14.6.1726).	—	—	—
S2727	**3 Pounds** 1733 (- old date 1731/28/14.6.1726).	—	—	—
S2728	**5 Pounds** 1733 (- old date 1731/28/14.6.1726).	—	—	—

1737 Redated Issue

#S2729-S2732 black. Printer: Samuel Vernon.

No.	Denomination / Date	Good	Fine	XF
S2729	**12 Pence** 1737 (- old date 1733/11/5.7.1715).	—	—	—
S2730	**12 Shillings 6 Pence** 1737 (- old date 1733/11/5.7.1715).	—	—	—
S2731	**3 Shillings** 1737 (- old date 1733/11/5.7.1715).	—	—	—
S2732	**4 Shillings 6 Pence** 1737 (- old date 1733/11/5.7.1715).	—	—	—

1737 Issue

#S2733-S2736 black. Printer: Samuel Vernon, Jr.

No.	Denomination / Date	Good	Fine	XF
S2733	**1 Pound** 15.8.1737.	—	—	—
S2734	**2 Pounds** 15.8.1737.	—	—	—
S2735	**3 Pounds** 15.8.1737.	—	—	—
S2736	**50 Pounds** 15.8.1737.	—	—	—

1738 Redated Issue

#S2737-S2740 black. Printer: William Claggett.

No.	Denomination / Date	Good	Fine	XF
S2737	**1 Pound** 1738 (- old date 15.8.1737).	—	—	—
S2738	**2 Pounds** 1738 (- old date 15.8.1737).	—	—	—
S2739	**3 Pounds** 1738 (- old date 15.8.1737).	—	—	—
S2740	**5 Pounds** 1738 (- old date 15.8.1737).	—	—	—

1738 Issue

#S2741-S2746 black. Printer: William Claggett.

No.	Denomination / Date	Good	Fine	XF
S2741	**1 Shilling** 22.8.1738.	—	—	—
S2742	**2 Shillings 6 Pence** 22.8.1738.	—	—	—
S2743	**3 Shillings** 22.8.1738.	—	—	—
S2744	**5 Shillings 6 Pence** 22.8.1738.	—	—	—
S2745	**7 Shillings 6 Pence** (Seaven) 22.8.1738.	—	—	—
S2746	**10 Shillings** 22.8.1738.	—	—	—

1740 Issue

#S2747-S2754 black. Printer: John Coddington.

No.	Denomination / Date	Good	Fine	XF
S2747	**6 Pence** 2.12.1740.	—	—	—
S2748	**1 Shilling** 2.12.1740.	—	—	—
S2749	**1 Shilling 6 Pence** 2.12.1740.	—	—	—
S2750	**2 Shilling 6 Pence** 2.12.1740.	—	—	—
S2751	**5 Shillings** 2.12.1740.	—	—	—
S2752	**10 Shillings** 2.12.1740.	—	—	—
S2753	**20 Shillings** 2.12.1740.	—	—	—
S2754	**40 Shillings** 2.12.1740.	—	—	—

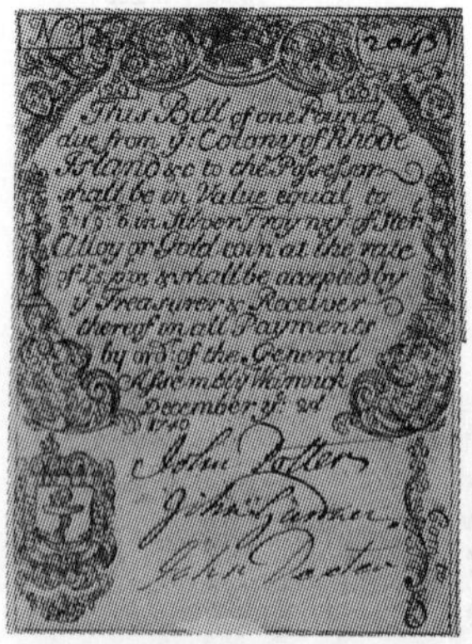

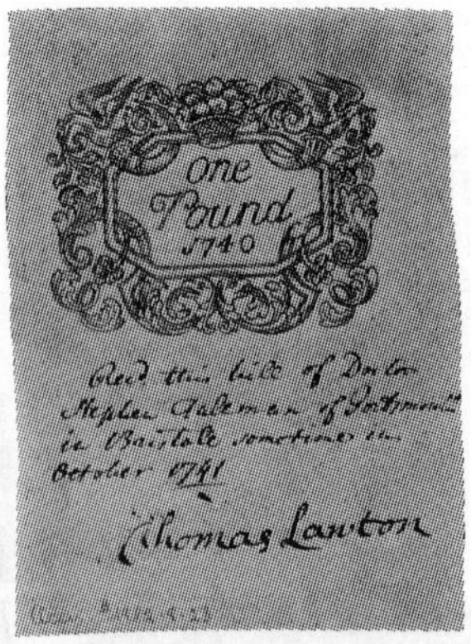

1741-42 Issue

#S2755-S2762 black. Arms w/motto: *IN TE DOMINE SPERAMUS*. Printer: William Claggett.

No.	Denomination / Date	Good	Fine	XF
S2755	**6 Pence** 2.2.1741/42.	—	—	—
S2756	**1 Shilling** 2.2.1741/42.	—	—	—
S2757	**1 Shilling 6 Pence** 2.2.1741/42.	—	—	—

		Good	Fine	XF
S2758	**2 Shillings 6 Pence** 2.2.1741/42.	—	—	—
S2759	**5 Shillings** 2.2.1741/42.	—	—	—
S2760	**10 Shillings** 2.2.1741/42.	—	—	—
S2761	**20 Shillings** 2.2.1741/42. Two angels.	—	—	—
S2762	**40 Shillings** 2.2.1741/42.	—	—	—

1743-44 Issue

#S2763-S2770 black.

		Good	Fine	XF
S2763	**4 Pence** 14.2.1743/44.	—	—	—
S2764	**6 Pence** 14.2.1743/44. *SPERAMUS* misspelled *SPEARMUS.*	—	—	—
S2765	**1 Shilling** 14.2.1743/44.	—	—	—

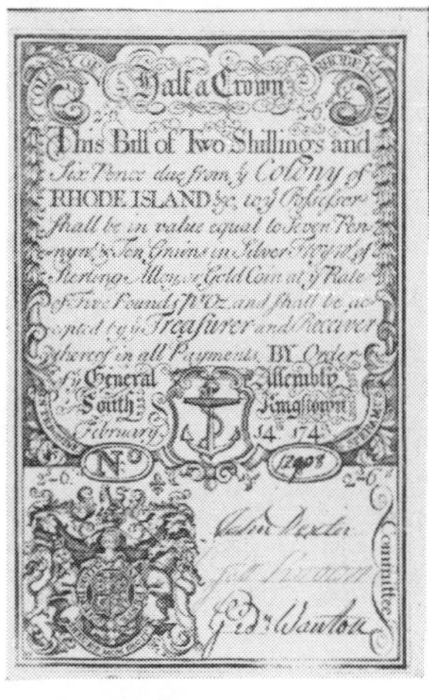

		Good	Fine	XF
S2766	**2 Shillings 6 Pence** 14.2.1743/44.	—	—	—
S2767	**5 Shillings** 14.2.1743/44.	—	—	—
S2768	**10 Shillings** 14.2.1743/44.	—	—	—
S2769	**20 Shillings** 14.2.1743/44.	—	—	—
S2770	**40 Shillings** 14.2.1743/44.	—	—	—

1743/44 Redated Issues

#S2771-S2802 black.

		Good	Fine	XF
S2771	**5 Shillings** 1744/45 (- old date 14./2.1743/44).	—	—	—
S2772	**10 Shillings** 1744/45 (- old date 14./2.1743/44).	—	—	—
S2773	**20 Shillings** 1744/45 (- old date 14./2.1743/44).	—	—	—
S2774	**40 Shillings** 1744/45 (- old date 14./2.1743/44).	—	—	—
S2775	**5 Shillings** 1745 (- old date 14./2.1743/44).	—	—	—
S2776	**10 Shillings** 1745 (- old date 14./2.1743/44).	—	—	—
S2777	**20 Shillings** 1745 (- old date 14./2.1743/44).	—	—	—
S2778	**40 Shillings** 1745 (- old date 14./2.1743/44).	—	—	—
S2779	**4 Pence** 1746 (- old date 14./2.1743/44).	—	—	—
S2780	**6 Pence** 1746 (- old date 14./2.1743/44).	—	—	—
S2781	**1 Shilling** 1746 (- old date 14./2.1743/44).	—	—	—
S2782	**2 Shillings 6 Pence** 1746 (- old date 14./2.1743/44).	—	—	—
S2783	**5 Shillings** 1746 (- old date 14./2.1743/44).	—	—	—
S2784	**10 Shillings** 1746 (- old date 14./2.1743/44).	—	—	—
S2785M	**20 Shillings** 1746 (- old date 14./2.1743/44).	—	—	—
S2786	**40 Shillings** 1746 (- old date 14./2.1743/44).	—	—	—
S2787	**4 Pence** 1746/47 (- old date 14./2.1743/44).	—	—	—
S2788	**6 Pence** 1746/47 (- old date 14./2.1743/44).	—	—	—
S2789	**1 Shilling** 1746/47 (- old date 14./2.1743/44).	—	—	—
S2790	**2 Shillings 6 Pence** 1746/47 (- old date 14./2.1743/44).	—	—	—
S2791	**5 Shillings** 1746/47 (- old date 14./2.1743/44).	—	—	—
S2792	**10 Shillings** 1746/47 (- old date 14./2.1743/44).	—	—	—
S2793	**20 Shillings** 1746/47 (- old date 14./2.1743/44).	—	—	—
S2794	**40 Shillings** 1746/47 (- old date 14./2.1743/44).	—	—	—
S2795	**4 Pence** 1747/48 (- old date 14./2.1743/44).	—	—	—
S2796	**6 Pence** 1747/48 (- old date 14./2.1743/14./2.1743/44). *SPEARAMUS* spelling corrected.	—	—	—
S2797	**1 Shilling** 1747/48 (- old date 14./2.1743/44).	—	—	—
S2798	**2 Shillings 6 Pence** 1747/48 (- old date 14./2.1743/44).	—	—	—
S2799	**5 Shillings** 1747/48 (- old date 14./2.1743/44).	—	—	—
S2800	**10 Shillings** 1747/48 (- old date 14./2.1743/44).	—	—	—
S2801	**20 Shillings** 1747/48 (- old date 14./2.1743/44).	—	—	—
S2802	**30 Shillings** 1747/48 (- old date 14./2.1743/44).	—	—	—

1750-51 Sterling Silver Coin Issue

#S2803-S2810 black. Issued in troy weights with value in "Old Tenor" on back.

		Good	Fine	XF
S2803	**2 Shillings O.T.** 18.3.1750/51.	—	—	—
S2804	**5 Shillings O.T.** 18.3.1750/51.	—	—	—
S2805	**8 Shillings O.T.** 18.3.1750/51.	—	—	—
S2806	**1 Pound O.T.** 18.3.1750/51.	—	—	—
S2807	**2 Pounds O.T.** 18.3.1750/51.	—	—	—
S2808	**4 Pounds O.T.** 18.3.1750/51.	—	—	—
S2809	**8 Pounds O.T.** 18.3.1750/51.	—	—	—
S2810	**16 Pounds O.T.** 18.3.1750/51.	—	—	—

1750/51 Redated Sterling Silver Coin Issue

#S2811-S2818 black. Issued in troy weights w/value in "Old Tenor" on back.

		Good	Fine	XF
S2811	**2 Shillings O.T.** 1755 (- old date 18.3.1750/51).	—	—	—

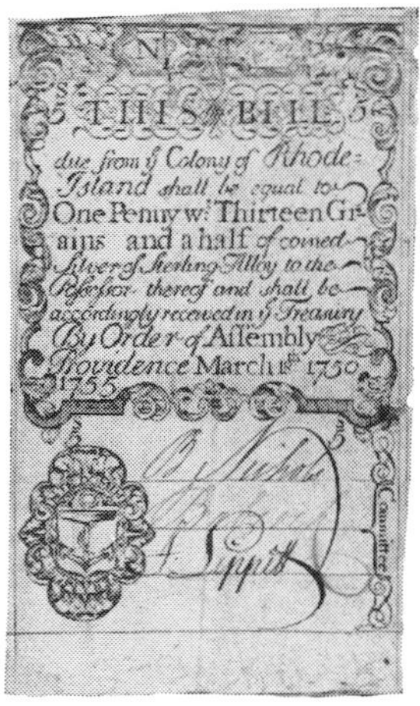

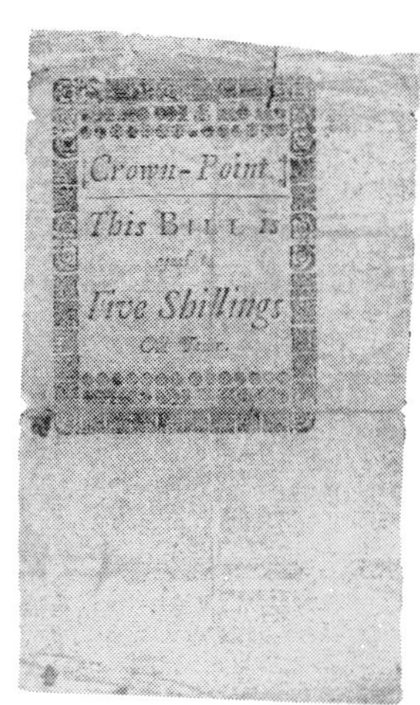

		Good	Fine	XF
S2812	**5 Shillings O.T.** 1755 (- old date 18.3.1750/51).	—	—	—
S2813	**8 Shillings O.T.** 1755 (- old date 18.3.1750/51).	—	—	—
S2814	**1 Pound O.T.** 1755 (- old date 18.3.1750/51).	—	—	—
S2815	**2 Pounds O.T.** 1755 (- old date 18.3.1750/51).	—	—	—
S2816	**4 Pounds O.T.** 1755 (- old date 18.3.1750/51). 1755 redating omitted.	—	—	—
S2817	**8 Pounds O.T.** 1755 (- old date 18.3.1750/51).	—	—	—
S2818	**16 Pounds O.T.** 1755 (- old date 18.3.1750/51).	—	—	—

1756 Issues

#S2819-S2836 black.

		Good	Fine	XF
S2819	**6 Pence** 27.2.1756.	—	—	—
S2820	**9 Pence** 27.2.1756.	—	—	—
S2821	**1 Shilling** 27.2.1756.	—	—	—

		Good	Fine	XF
S2822	2 Shillings 27.2.1756.	—	—	—
S2823	3 Shillings 27.2.1756.	—	—	—
S2824	5 Shillings 27.2.1756.	—	—	—
S2825	10 Shillings 27.2.1756.	—	—	—
S2826	20 Shillings 27.2.1756.	—	—	—
S2827	25 Shillings 27.2.1756.	—	—	—
S2828	6 Pence 8.1756.	—	—	—
S2829	9 Pence 8.1756.	—	—	—
S2830	1 Shilling 8.1756.	—	—	—
S2831	2 Shillings 8.1756.	—	—	—
S2832	3 Shillings 8.1756.	—	—	—
S2833	5 Shillings 8.1756.	—	—	—
S2834	10 Shillings 8.1756.	—	—	—
S2835	20 Shillings 8.1756.	—	—	—
S2836	25 Shillings 8.1756.	—	—	—

1758 First Issue

#S2837-S2843 black.

		Good	Fine	XF
S2837	6 Pence 8.5.1758.	—	—	—
S2838	1 Shilling 8.5.1758.	—	—	—
S2839	2 Shillings 8.5.1758.	—	—	—
S2840	5 Shillings 8.5.1758.	—	—	—
S2841	10 Shillings 8.5.1758.	—	—	—
S2842	20 Shillings 8.5.1758.	—	—	—
S2843	30 Shillings 8.5.1758.	—	—	—

1758 Second Issue

Probably same denominations as 8.5.1758. Dated 23.12.1758.

#S2844-S2850 *Reserved.*

1759 Issues

Probably same denominations as 8.5.1758. Dated 15.3.1759; 4.4.1759; 23.6.1759.

#S2851-S2858 *Reserved.*

1760 First Issue

#S2859-S2866 black.

		Good	Fine	XF
S2859	6 Pence 10.3.1760.	—	—	—
S2860	9 Pence 10.3.1760.	—	—	—
S2861	1 Shilling 10.3.1760.	—	—	—
S2862	2 Shillings 10.3.1760.	—	—	—
S2863	5 Shillings 10.3.1760.	—	—	—
S2864	10 Shillings 10.3.1760.	—	—	—
S2865	20 Shillings 10.3.1760.	—	—	—
S2866	30 Shillings 10.3.1760.	—	—	—

1760 Second Issue

#S2867-S2870 black.

		Good	Fine	XF
S2867	5 Shillings 12.5.1760.	—	—	—
S2868	10 Shillings 12.5.1760.	—	—	—
S2869	20 Shillings 12.5.1760.	—	—	—
S2870	30 Shillings 12.5.1760.	—	—	—

1762 First Issue

#S2871-S2879 black.

		Good	Fine	XF
S2871	3 Pence 20.3.1762.	—	—	—
S2872	6 Pence 20.3.1762.	—	—	—
S2873	9 Pence 20.3.1762.	—	—	—
S2874	1 Shilling 20.3.1762.	—	—	—
S2875	2 Shillings 20.3.1762.	—	—	—
S2876	5 Shillings 20.3.1762.	—	—	—
S2877	10 Shillings 20.3.1762.	—	—	—
S2878	20 Shillings 20.3.1762.	—	—	—
S2879	30 Shillings 20.3.1762.	—	—	—

1762 Second Issue

#S2880-S2883 black.

		Good	Fine	XF
S2880	5 Shillings 10.4.1762.	—	—	—
S2881	10 Shillings 10.4.1762.	—	—	—
S2882	20 Shillings 10.4.1762.	—	—	—
S2883	30 Shillings 10.4.1762.	—	—	—

1762 Third Issue

#S2884-S2887 black.

		Good	Fine	XF
S2884	5 Shillings 8.5.1762.	—	—	—
S2885	10 Shillings 8.5.1762.	—	—	—
S2886	20 Shillings 8.5.1762.	—	—	—
S2887	30 Shillings 8.5.1762.	—	—	—

1762 Fourth Issue

#S2888-S2897 black.

		Good	Fine	XF
S2888	3 Pence 1.11.1762.	—	—	—
S2889	6 Pence 1.11.1762.	—	—	—
S2890	9 Pence 1.11.1762.	—	—	—
S2891	1 Shilling 1.11.1762.	—	—	—
S2892	2 Shillings 1.11.1762.	—	—	—
S2893	3 Shillings 1.11.1762.	—	—	—
S2894	4 Shillings 1.11.1762.	—	—	—
S2895	5 Shillings 1.11.1762.	—	—	—
S2896	10 Shillings 1.11.1762.	—	—	—
S2897	20 Shillings 1.11.1762.	—	—	—

1766 Issue

#S2898-S2904 black.

		Good	Fine	XF
S2898	3 Pence 1.3.1766.	—	—	—
S2899	6 Pence 1.3.1766.	—	—	—
S2900	9 Pence 1.3.1766.	—	—	—
S2901	1 Shilling 1.3.1766.	—	—	—
S2902	2 Shillings 1.3.1766.	—	—	—
S2903	3 Shillings 1.3.1766.	—	—	—
S2904	5 Shillings 1.3.1766.	—	—	—

1767 Issue

#S2905-S2913 black.

		Good	Fine	XF
S2905	4 Pence 28.2.1767.	—	—	—
S2906	8 Pence 28.2.1767.	—	—	—
S2907	1 Shilling 28.2.1767.	—	—	—
S2908	2 Shillings 28.2.1767.	—	—	—
S2909	3 Shillings 28.2.1767.	—	—	—
S2910	4 Shillings 28.2.1767.	—	—	—
S2911	6 Shillings 28.2.1767.	—	—	—
S2912	10 Shillings 28.2.1767.	—	—	—
S2913	20 Shillings 28.2.1767.	—	—	—

1775 First Issue

#S2914-S2924 black. Printer: John Carter.

		VG	VF	Unc
S2914	6 Pence 3.5.1775.	150.00	—	—
S2915	9 Pence 3.5.1775.	150.00	—	—
S2916	1 Shilling 3.5.1775.	150.00	—	—
S2917	2 Shillings 3.5.1775.	150.00	—	—
S2918	3 Shillings 3.5.1775.	200.00	—	—
S2919	4 Shillings 3.5.1775.	200.00	—	—
S2920	5 Shillings 3.5.1775.	200.00	—	—
S2921	10 Shillings 3.5.1775.	200.00	—	—
S2922	20 Shillings 3.5.1775.	200.00	—	—
S2923	30 Shillings 3.5.1775.	200.00	—	—
S2924	40 Shillings 3.5.1775.	300.00	—	—

1775 Second Issue

#S2925-S2935 black.

		VG	VF	Unc
S2925	6 Pence 16.6.1775.	210.00	—	—
S2926	9 Pence 16.6.1775.	210.00	—	—
S2927	1 Shilling 16.6.1775.	210.00	—	—
S2928	2 Shillings 16.6.1775.	210.00	—	—
S2929	3 Shillings 16.6.1775.	300.00	—	—
S2930	4 Shillings 16.6.1775.	300.00	—	—
S2931	5 Shillings 16.6.1775.	300.00	—	—
S2932	10 Shillings 16.6.1775.	300.00	—	—
S2933	20 Shillings 16.6.1775.	300.00	—	—
S2934	30 Shillings 16.6.1775.	300.00	—	—
S2935	40 Shillings 16.6.1775.	425.00	—	—

1775 Third Issue

#S2936-S2946 black.

		VG	VF	Unc
S2936	6 Pence 29.6.1775.	210.00	—	—
S2937	9 Pence 29.6.1775.	210.00	—	—
S2938	1 Shilling 29.6.1775.	210.00	—	—
S2939	2 Shillings 29.6.1775.	210.00	—	—
S2940	3 Shillings 29.6.1775.	300.00	—	—
S2941	4 Shillings 29.6.1775.	300.00	—	—
S2942	5 Shillings 29.6.1775.	300.00	—	—
S2943	10 Shillings 29.6.1775.	300.00	—	—
S2944	20 Shillings 29.6.1775.	300.00	—	—
S2945	30 Shillings 29.6.1775.	300.00	—	—
S2946	40 Shillings 29.6.1775.	425.00	—	—

1775 Fourth Issue

#S2947-S2956 black.

		VG	VF	Unc
S2947	6 Pence 6.11.1775.	110.00	300.00	—
S2948	9 Pence 6.11.1775.	110.00	300.00	—
S2949	1 Shilling 6.11.1775.	110.00	300.00	—
S2950	2 Shillings 6.11.1775.	120.00	350.00	—
S2951	3 Shillings 6.11.1775.	140.00	400.00	—
S2952	5 Shillings 6.11.1775.	160.00	—	—
S2953	10 Shillings 6.11.1775.	180.00	—	—
S2954	20 Shillings 6.11.1775.	200.00	—	—
S2955	30 Shillings 6.11.1775.	225.00	—	—
S2956	40 Shillings 6.11.1775.	250.00	—	—

1776 Issue

#S2957-S2968 black. Printer: John Carter.

		VG	VF	Unc
S2957	6 Pence 15.1.1776.	135.00	300.00	—
S2958	9 Pence 15.1.1776.	135.00	300.00	—
S2959	1 Shilling 15.1.1776.	135.00	300.00	—
S2960	2 Shillings 15.1.1776.	140.00	325.00	—
S2961	3 Shillings 15.1.1776.	135.00	300.00	—
S2962	4 Shillings 15.1.1776.	135.00	300.00	—
S2963	5 Shillings 15.1.1776.	135.00	300.00	—
S2964	10 Shillings 15.1.1776.	135.00	300.00	—
S2965	20 Shillings 15.1.1776.	135.00	300.00	—
S2966	30 Shillings 15.1.1776.	135.00	—	—
S2967	40 Shillings 15.1.1776.	150.00	—	—
S2968	60 Shillings 15.1.1776.	185.00	—	—

Rhode Island

State

1776 First Issue

Pound Sterling System

#S2969-S2979 black. Printer: John Carter.

		VG	VF	Unc
S2969	9 Pence 18.3.1776.	200.00	360.00	—
S2970	1 Shilling 18.3.1776.	200.00	360.00	—
S2971	2 Shillings 18.3.1776.	200.00	360.00	—
S2972	3 Shillings 18.3.1776.	200.00	360.00	—
S2973	4 Shillings 18.3.1776.	200.00	360.00	—
S2974	5 Shillings 18.3.1776.	200.00	360.00	—
S2975	10 Shillings 18.3.1776.	200.00	360.00	—
S2976	20 Shillings 18.3.1776.	200.00	360.00	—
S2977	30 Shillings 18.3.1776.	200.00	360.00	—

#S2978 and S2979 uniface.

		VG	VF	Unc
S2978	40 Shillings 18.3.1776.	200.00	360.00	—
S2979	60 Shillings 18.3.1776.	200.00	360.00	—

1776 Second Issue

Dollar System

#S2980-S2994 black. Printer: John Carter.

#S2980 and S2981 uniface.

		VG	VF	Unc
S2980	1/16 Dollar 5.9.1776.	220.00	—	—
S2981	1/8 Dollar 5.9.1776.	220.00	—	—
S2982	1/4 Dollar 5.9.1776.	220.00	—	—
S2983	1/2 Dollar 5.9.1776.	220.00	—	—
S2984	1 Dollar 5.9.1776.	250.00	—	—
S2985	2 Dollars 5.9.1776.	—	—	—
S2986	3 Dollars 5.9.1776.	—	—	—
S2987	4 Dollars 5.9.1776.	—	—	—
S2988	5 Dollars 5.9.1776.	—	—	—
S2989	6 Dollars 5.9.1776.	—	—	—
S2990	7 Dollars 5.9.1776.	—	—	—
S2991	8 Dollars 5.9.1776.	—	—	—
S2992	10 Dollars 5.9.1776.	—	—	—
S2993	20 Dollars 5.9.1776.	—	—	—
S2994	30 Dollars 5.9.1776.	—	—	—

1777 FIRST ISSUE

#S2995-S3001 black. Denominations over $30 were handwritten, and issued in denominations requested by lender. Written dates.

		VG	VF	UNC
S2995	5 DOLLARS 1777.	—	—	—
S2996	6 DOLLARS 1777.	—	—	—
S2997	7 DOLLARS 1777.	—	—	—
S2998	8 DOLLARS 1777.	—	—	—
S2999	10 DOLLARS 1777.	—	—	—
S3000	20 DOLLARS 1777.	—	—	—
S3001	30 DOLLARS 1777.	—	—	—

1777 SECOND ISSUE

#S3002-S3010 black.

		GOOD	FINE	XF
S3002	1/36 DOLLAR 1777.	180.00	550.00	—
S3003	1/24 DOLLAR 1777.	180.00	550.00	—
S3004	1/18 DOLLAR 1777.	180.00	550.00	—
S3005	1/12 DOLLAR 1777.	180.00	550.00	—
S3006	1/9 DOLLAR 1777.	180.00	550.00	—
S3007	1/8 DOLLAR 1777.	180.00	550.00	—
S3008	1/6 DOLLAR 1777.	180.00	550.00	—
S3009	1/4 DOLLAR 1777.	215.00	650.00	—
S3010	1/3 DOLLAR 1777.	250.00	—	—

1778-79 ISSUE

Pound System

#S3011 black. Written dates.

		VG	VF	UNC
S3011	10 POUNDS	—	—	—

1780 FIRST ISSUE

#S3012-S3023 black. Printer: B. Wheeler.

		VG	VF	UNC
S3012	6 PENCE 6.1780.	—	—	—
S3013	9 PENCE 6.1780.	—	—	—
S3014	1 SHILLING 6.1780.	—	—	—
S3015	2 SHILLINGS 6.1780.	—	—	—
S3016	3 SHILLINGS 6.1780.	—	—	—
S3017	4 SHILLINGS 6.1780.	—	—	—
S3018	6 SHILLINGS 6.1780.	—	—	—
S3019	9 SHILLINGS 6.1780. Issued but not authorized.			
S3020	10 SHILLINGS 6.1780.	—	—	—
S3021	20 SHILLINGS 6.1780.	—	—	—
S3022	30 SHILLINGS 6.1780.	—	—	—
S3023	40 SHILLINGS 6.1780.	—	—	—

1780 SECOND ISSUE

#S3024-S3031 black. Back red and black. Printer: David Hall and William Sellers.

		VG	VF	UNC
S3024	1 DOLLAR 2.7.1780.	15.00	35.00	85.00
S3025	2 DOLLARS 2.7.1780.	15.00	35.00	85.00
S3026	3 DOLLARS 2.7.1780.	15.00	35.00	85.00

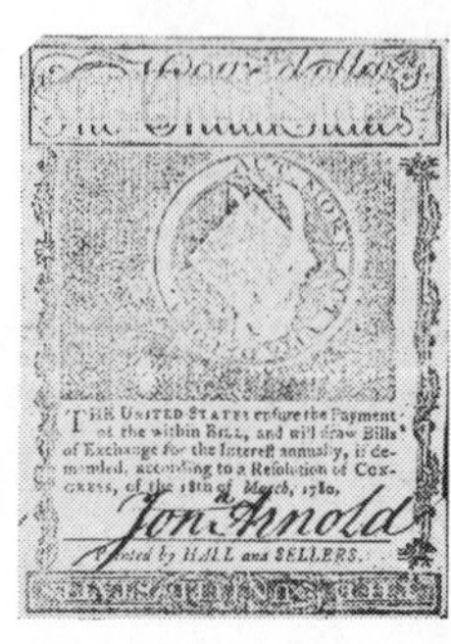

		VG	VF	UNC
S3027	4 DOLLARS 2.7.1780.	15.00	35.00	85.00
S3028	5 DOLLARS 2.7.1780.	15.00	35.00	85.00
S3029	7 DOLLARS 2.7.1780.	15.00	35.00	85.00
S3030	8 DOLLARS 2.7.1780.	15.00	35.00	85.00
S3031	20 DOLLARS 2.7.1780.	15.00	35.00	85.00

1786 ISSUE

#S3032-S3043 black. Printer: Southwick and Barber.

		VG	VF	UNC
S3032	6 PENCE 5.1786.	20.00	40.00	75.00
S3033	9 PENCE 5.1786.	20.00	40.00	75.00
S3034	1 SHILLING 5.1786.	20.00	40.00	75.00
S3035	2 SHILLINGS 6 PENCE 5.1786.	20.00	40.00	75.00
S3036	3 SHILLINGS 5.1786.	20.00	40.00	75.00
S3037	5 SHILLINGS 5.1786.	20.00	40.00	75.00

		VG	VF	UNC
S3038	6 SHILLINGS 5.1786.	20.00	40.00	75.00
S3039	10 SHILLINGS 5.1786.	20.00	40.00	75.00
S3040	20 SHILLINGS 5.1786.	20.00	40.00	75.00
S3041	30 SHILLINGS 5.1786.	20.00	40.00	75.00

		VG	VF	UNC
S3042	40 SHILLINGS 5.1786. Vertical format.	20.00	40.00	75.00

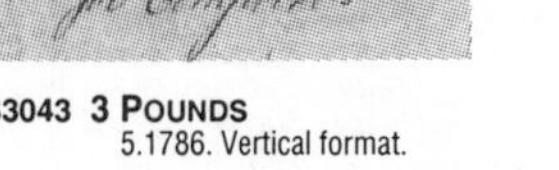

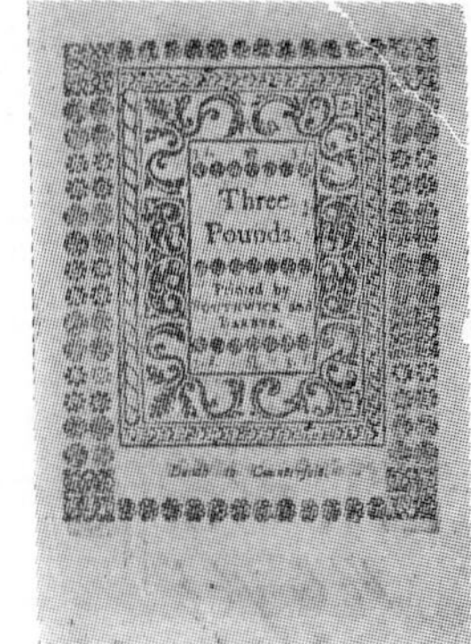

		VG	VF	UNC
S3043	3 POUNDS 5.1786. Vertical format.	30.00	65.00	100.00

SOUTH CAROLINA

COLONIAL

1703 ISSUE

Pound Sterling System

Known as "Country Bills."

#S3101 and S3110 black. Engraver: Joseph Massey.

		GOOD	FINE	XF
S3101	**50 SHILLINGS** 8.5.1703.	—	—	—
S3110	**20 POUNDS** 8.5.1703.	—	—	—

1707 ISSUE

#S3111-S3122 black.

		GOOD	FINE	XF
S3111	**20 SHILLINGS** 5.7.1707.	—	—	—
S3112	**40 SHILLINGS** 5.7.1707.	—	—	—
S3116	**4 POUNDS** 5.7.1707.	—	—	—
S3120	**10 POUNDS** 5.7.1707.	—	—	—
S3121	**20 POUNDS** 5.7.1707.	—	—	—
S3122	**20 SHILLINGS** 14.2.1707.	—	—	—

1708 ISSUE

#S3123 and S3124 black.

		GOOD	FINE	XF
S3123	**20 SHILLINGS** 24.4.1708.	—	—	—
S3124	**40 SHILLINGS** 24.4.1708.	—	—	—

1710 ISSUE

#S3125 and S3126 black.

		GOOD	FINE	XF
S3125	**5 SHILLINGS** 1.3.1710.	—	—	—
S3126	**10 SHILLINGS** 1.3.1710.	—	—	—

ACT OF 10.11.1711; 1712 ISSUE

Referred to as "Tusquerora Bills" because they were issued to aid North Carolina in defending itself against attacks of the Tusquerora Indians. The denominations are not known.

Known as "Bank Bills."

#S3131 and S3135 black.

		GOOD	FINE	XF
S3131	**5 SHILLINGS** 7.6.1712.	—	—	—
S3135	**20 POUNDS** 7.6.1712.	—	—	—

1715 ISSUE

		GOOD	FINE	XF
S3140	**4 POUNDS** 27.8.1715. Black.	—	—	—

ACT OF 24.3.1715(6); 1715(6) ISSUE

Authorized for military expenses and made legal tender by the June 30, 1716 Act. Denominations are not known.

1716 ISSUE

#S3145 and S3147 black.

		GOOD	FINE	XF
S3145	**5 POUNDS** 30.6.1716.	—	—	—
S3147	**20 POUNDS** 30.6.1716.	—	—	—

NOTE: Other denominations could exist.

ACT OF 4.8.1716

Denominations are not known.

ACT OF 20.2.1718; 1718(9) ISSUE

Known as "Rice Bills." Denominations are not known.

ACT OF 18.6.1720; 1720 ISSUE

Known as "Rice Bills." Denominations are not known.

1723 ISSUE

#S3161-S3172 black. Printer: Joseph Massey.

		GOOD	FINE	XF
S3161	**5 SHILLINGS** 1723. Crown above rose.	—	—	—
S3162	**6 SHILLINGS 6 PENCE** 1723. Crown above plume.	—	—	—
S3163	**7 SHILLINGS 6 PENCE** 1723.	—	—	—
S3164	**10 SHILLINGS** 1723. Plum w/motto: *ICH DIEN.*	—	—	—
S3165	**1 POUND** 1723.	—	—	—
S3166	**2 POUNDS** 1723.	—	—	—
S3167	**4 POUNDS** 1723.	—	—	—
S3168	**6 POUNDS** 1723.	—	—	—
S3169	**8 POUNDS** 1723.	—	—	—
S3170	**12 POUNDS** 1723.	—	—	—
S3171	**15 POUNDS** 1723.	—	—	—
S3172	**20 POUNDS** 1723.	—	—	—

1731 ISSUES

#S3173-S3189 black.

		GOOD	FINE	XF
S3173	**4 SHILLINGS 6 PENCE** 1731.	—	—	—
S3174	**5 SHILLINGS** 1731.	—	—	—
S3175	**7 SHILLINGS 6 PENCE** 1731. Thistle.	—	—	—
S3176	**20 SHILLINGS** 1731.	—	—	—
S3177	**2 POUNDS** 1731.	—	—	—
S3178	**3 POUNDS** 1731.	—	—	—
S3179	**4 POUNDS** 1731.	—	—	—
S3180	**6 POUNDS 5 SHILLINGS** 1731.	—	—	—
S3181	**10 POUNDS** 1731. Deer.	—	—	—
S3182	**12 POUNDS 10 SHILLINGS** 1731.	—	—	—
S3183	**15 POUNDS** 1731.	—	—	—
S3184	**20 POUNDS** 1731.	—	—	—
S3185	**5 POUNDS** 20.8.1731.	—	—	—
S3186	**6 POUNDS 5 SHILLINGS** 20.8.1731.	—	—	—
S3187	**12 POUNDS 10 SHILLINGS** 20.8.1731.	—	—	—
S3188	**25 POUNDS** 20.8.1731.	—	—	—
S3189	**50 POUNDS** 20.8.1731.	—	—	—

1736 ISSUE

#S3190 and S3191 black.

		GOOD	FINE	XF
S3190	**6 POUNDS** 5.3.1736.	—	—	—
S3191	**12 POUNDS** 5.3.1736.	—	—	—

1740 FIRST ISSUE

#S3192 and S3193 black.

		GOOD	FINE	XF
S3192	**4 POUNDS** 5.4.1740.	—	—	—
S3193	**8 POUNDS** 5.4.1740.	—	—	—

1740 SECOND ISSUE

#S3194 and S3195 black.

		GOOD	FINE	XF
S3194	**4 POUNDS** 19.9.1740.	—	—	—
S3195	**8 POUNDS** 19.9.1740.	—	—	—

1748 ISSUE

#S3196-S3205 black.

		GOOD	FINE	XF
S3196	**2 SHILLINGS 6 PENCE** 30.6.1748.	—	—	—
S3197	**5 SHILLINGS** 30.6.1748.	—	—	—
S3198	**6 SHILLINGS 3 PENCE** 30.6.1748.	—	—	—
S3199	**7 SHILLINGS 6 PENCE** 30.6.1748.	—	—	—
S3200	**10 SHILLINGS** 30.6.1748.	—	—	—
S3201	**1 POUND** 30.6.1748. Horse.	—	—	—
S3202	**2 POUNDS** 30.6.1748.	—	—	—
S3203	**5 POUNDS** 30.6.1748. Sheaf.	—	—	—
S3204	**10 POUNDS** 30.6.1748. Deer.	—	—	—
S3205	**20 POUNDS** 30.6.1748. Lion on crown.	—	—	—

NOTE: Illustration of #S3201 is that of a reprint.

1750-69 ISSUE

#S3206-S3210 black. Various handwritten dates. Backs elaborately engraved w/*JACOB MOTTE P. TREASURER.* Issued during his incumbency.

		GOOD	FINE	XF
S3206	**5 POUNDS** 1750-69.	—	—	—
S3207	**10 POUNDS** 1750-69.	—	—	—
S3208	**20 POUNDS** 1750-69.	—	—	—

		Good	Fine	XF
S3209	**30 Pounds** 1750-69.	—	—	—
S3210	**50 Pounds** 1750-69.	—	—	—

1752 Issue

#S3211-S3216 black.

		Good	Fine	XF
S3211	**5 Shillings** 16.5.1752.	—	—	—
S3212	**6 Shillings 3 Pence** 16.5.1752.	—	—	—
S3213	**1 Pound** 16.5.1752.	—	—	—
S3214	**2 Pounds** 16.5.1752.	—	—	—
S3215	**5 Pounds** 16.5.1752.	—	—	—
S3216	**10 Pounds** 16.5.1752.	—	—	—

1757 Issue

#S3217 and S3218 black.

		Good	Fine	XF
S3217	**10 Pounds** 6.7.1757.	—	—	—
S3218	**20 Pounds** 6.7.1757.	—	—	—

1760 Issue

#S3219 and S3220 issued primarily for expenses of Lyttleton's Expedition.

		Good	Fine	XF
S3219	**25 Pounds** 1760. Motto: *DEBELLARE BARBAROS RENOVA ANIMUM* around seal.	—	—	—
S3220	**50 Pounds** 1760.	—	—	—

#S3221 issued primarily for expenses of Middleton's Regiment.

		Good	Fine	XF
S3221	**20 Pounds** 1760. Black. Mottos: *SUME EX SCELERATO SANGUINE POENAM* around and *INFRACTO FOEDERE* within seal.	—	—	—

1761 Issue

#S3222-S3226 black.

		Good	Fine	XF
S3222	**2 Shillings 6 Pence** 25.7.1761.	—	—	—
S3223	**5 Shillings** 25.7.1761.	—	—	—
S3224	**7 Shillings 6 Pence** 25.7.1761.	—	—	—
S3225	**10 Shillings** 25.7.1761.	—	—	—
S3226	**1 Pound** 25.7.1761.	—	—	—

1762 Issue

		Good	Fine	XF
S3227	**2 Pounds** 29.5.1762. Black.	—	—	—

1770 Issue

#S3228-S3237 black.

		Good	Fine	XF
S3228	**2 Shillings 6 Pence** 1.1.1770.	—	—	—
S3229	**5 Shillings** 1.1.1770.	—	—	—
S3230	**6 Shillings 3 Pence** 1.1.1770.	—	—	—
S3231	**7 Shillings 6 Pence** 1.1.1770.	—	—	—
S3232	**10 Shillings** 1.1.1770.	—	—	—
S3233	**1 Pound** 1.1.1770.	—	—	—
S3234	**2 Pounds** 1.1.1770.	—	—	—
S3235	**5 Pounds** 1.1.1770.	—	—	—
S3236	**10 Pounds** 1.1.1770. Stag.	—	—	—
S3237	**20 Pounds** 1.1.1770. Lion on crown.	—	—	—

1775 Issue

#S3238-S3247 black. Printer: James Oliphant.

		VG	VF	Unc
S3238	**2 Shillings 6 Pence** 15.11.1775.	150.00	450.00	—
S3239	**5 Shillings** 15.11.1775.	150.00	450.00	—
S3240	**7 Shillings 6 Pence** 15.11.1775.	150.00	450.00	—
S3241	**10 Shillings** 15.11.1775.	150.00	450.00	—
S3242	**15 Shillings** 15.11.1775.	150.00	450.00	—
S3243	**20 Shillings** 15.11.1775.	150.00	450.00	—
S3244	**30 Shillings** 15.11.1775.	150.00	450.00	—
S3245	**2 Pounds** 15.11.1775. W/motto: *UTRUM HORUM MAVIS ACCIPE.*	150.00	450.00	—
S3246	**2 Pounds 10 Shillings** 15.11.1775. W/motto: *PRO LIBERTATE.*	150.00	450.00	—
S3247	**3 Pounds** 15.11.1775. W/motto: *ULTIMA RATIO.*	150.00	450.00	—

1776 Issue

#S3248-S3263 red and black. Printer: Peter Timothy.

		VG	VF	Unc
S3248	**1 Shilling 3 Pence** 6.3.1776.	250.00	600.00	—
S3249	**2 Shillings 6 Pence** 6.3.1776.	250.00	600.00	—
S3250	**3 Shillings 9 Pence** 6.3.1776.	250.00	600.00	—
S3251	**5 Shillings** 6.3.1776.	250.00	600.00	—
S3252	**6 Shillings 3 Pence** 6.3.1776.	250.00	600.00	—
S3253	**12 Shillings 6 Pence** 6.3.1776.	250.00	600.00	—
S3254	**17 Shillings 6 Pence** 6.3.1776.	250.00	600.00	—
S3255	**1 Pound** 6.3.1776.	250.00	600.00	—
S3256	**1 Pound 15 Shillings** 6.3.1776.	250.00	600.00	—
S3257	**2 Pounds** 6.3.1776.	250.00	600.00	—

		VG	VF	Unc
S3258	**2 Pounds 5 Shillings** 6.3.1776.	250.00	600.00	—
S3259	**3 Pounds** 6.3.1776.	250.00	600.00	—

#S3260-S3263 black. W/motto: *hite* and bluish paper.

		VG	VF	Unc
S3260	**15 Pounds** 6.3.1776. Rattlesnake attacking British lion. W/motto: *MAGNIS INTERDUM PARVA NOCENT.*	150.00	300.00	—
S3261	**25 Pounds** 6.3.1776. Flourishing tree and fallen tree. W/motto: *MELIOREM LAPSA LOCAVIT.*	150.00	300.00	—
S3262	**50 Pounds** 6.3.1776. Trophies. W/motto: *ANIMIS OPIBUSQUE PARATI.*	150.00	300.00	—
S3263	**100 Pounds** 6.3.1776. 13 hearts. W/motto: *QUIS SEPARABIT.*	150.00	300.00	—

South Carolina

State

1776 First Issue

Dollar/Pound Sterling System

#S3264-S3269 black. Thick brownish paper. Printer: Peter Timothy.

		VG	VF	Unc
S3264	**1 Dollar** 19.10.1776. Palm tree. W/motto: *NUSQUAM SUB MOLE FATISCIT.*	100.00	200.00	—
S3265	**2 Dollars** 19.10.1776. Tree. W/motto: *SE SUSTULIT IPSA.*	100.00	200.00	—
S3266	**4 Dollars** 19.10.1776. Elephant. W/moto: *INFESTUS TANTUM INFESTIS.*	100.00	200.00	—
S3267	**6 Dollars** 19.10.1776. Wind and waves. W/motto: *TURBAT SED EXTOLLIT.*	100.00	200.00	—
S3268	**8 Dollars** 19.10.1776. Wind on rock. W/motto: *IMPAVIDE.*	100.00	200.00	—
S3269	**10 Dollars** 19.10.1776. Drums and flags. W/motto: *TUTA PEDAMINE VIRTUS.*	100.00	200.00	—

1776 Second Issue

#S3270-S3277 black. Thick brownish paper. Printer: Peter Timothy.

		VG	VF	Unc
S3270	**1 Dollar** 23.12.1776. Tree. W/motto: *PER ARDUA SURGO.*	85.00	140.00	400.00

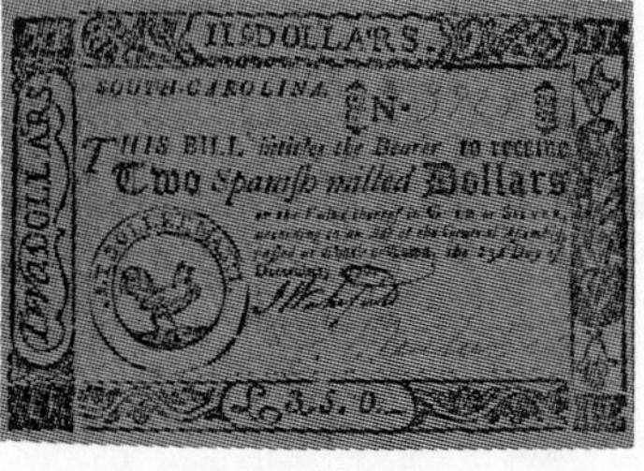

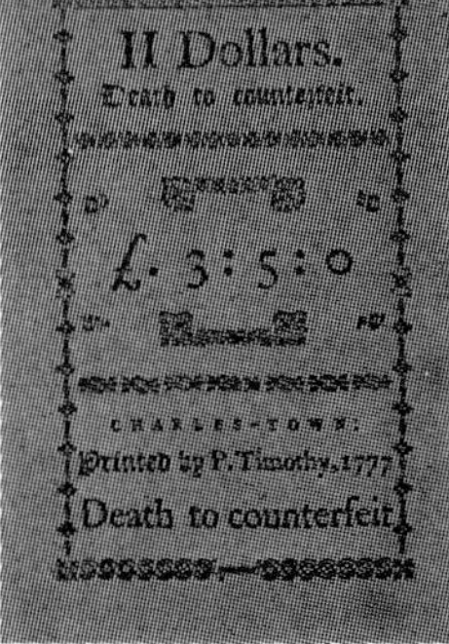

		VG	VF	UNC
S3271	**2 DOLLARS** 23.12.1776. Rooster. W/motto: *ET SOLIET MARTI.*			
	a. Regular date.	90.00	150.00	450.00
	b. Text on face is misdated December 23, 1777.	200.00	400.00	700.00
S3272	**3 DOLLARS** 23.12.1776. Oracle. W/motto: *FATA VIAM INVENIENT.*	90.00	150.00	400.00
S3273	**4 DOLLARS** 23.12.1776. Ship. W/motto: *THE ACTAEON. IRAM PRUDENTIA VINCIT.*			
	a. Regular date.	90.00	150.00	400.00
	b. Text on face is misdated December 23, 1777.	200.00	400.00	700.00
S3274	**5 DOLLARS** 23.12.1776. Horse. W/motto: *DOMINUM GENEROSA RECUSAT.*	120.00	180.00	450.00
S3275	**6 DOLLARS** 23.12.1776. Camel. W/motto: *NEC ONUS NEC META GRAVABIT.*	90.00	150.00	400.00

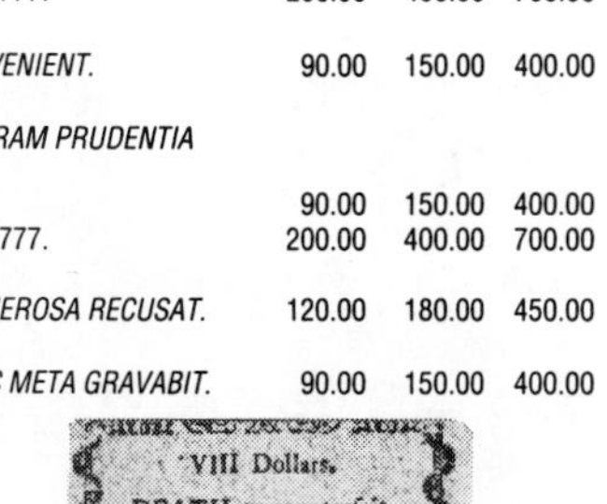

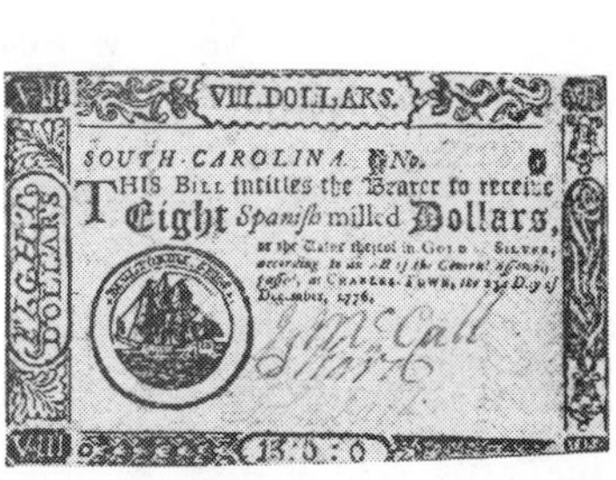

		VG	VF	UNC
S3276	**8 DOLLARS** 23.12.1776. Sailing ship . W/motto: *MULTORUM SPES.*	90.00	150.00	400.00
S3277	**20 DOLLARS** 23.12.1776. Bull. W/motto: *AUT MORS AUT VICTORIA.*	150.00	210.00	500.00

1777 ISSUE

#S3278 and S3279 black. Dk. brownish paper.

		VG	VF	UNC
S3278	**20 DOLLARS** 14.2.1777. Bird escaping from cage. W/motto: *IBI PATRIA UBI LIBERTAS.*	60.00	200.00	—
S3279	**30 DOLLARS** 14.2.1777. Man w/pack. W/motto: *MISERA SERVITUS OMNIS.*	60.00	200.00	—

1778 ISSUE

#S3280-S3287 black. Thin paper.

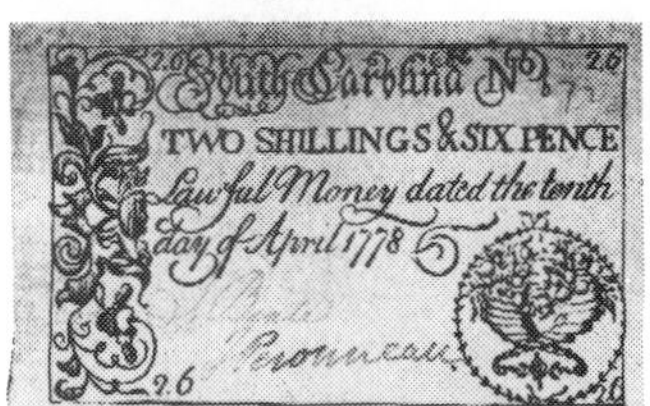

		VG	VF	UNC
S3280	**2 SHILLINGS 6 PENCE** 10.4.1778. Black. Cornucopiae.	40.00	135.00	300.00
S3281	**3 SHILLINGS 9 PENCE** 10.4.1778. Beaver.	40.00	135.00	300.00

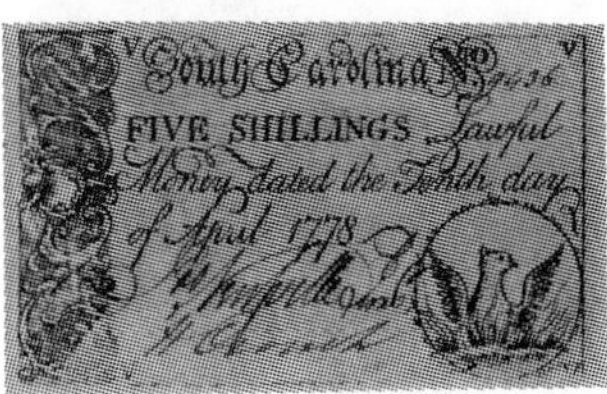

		VG	VF	UNC
S3282	**5 SHILLINGS** 10.4.1778. Phoenix.	40.00	135.00	300.00
S3283	**7 SHILLINGS 6 PENCE** 10.4.1778. Beehive.	50.00	150.00	350.00
S3284	**10 SHILLINGS** 10.4.1778. Palmetto.	40.00	135.00	300.00
S3285	**15 SHILLINGS** 10.4.1778. Sun.	50.00	150.00	350.00
S3286	**20 SHILLINGS** 10.4.1778. Horse.	50.00	150.00	350.00
S3287	**30 SHILLINGS** 10.4.1778. Hope and anchor.	50.00	150.00	350.00

1779 ISSUE

#S3288-S3294 black. White or blue paper.

		GOOD	FINE	XF
S3288	**40 DOLLARS** 8.2.1779. Ceres. W/motto: *MINIME VIOLANDA FIDES.* Angel blowing trumpet and holding book on back.	85.00	220.00	600.00
S3289	**50 DOLLARS** 8.2.1779. Providence and globe. W/motto: *PROVIDENTIA NOSTRIS PRAESIDEAT.* Atlas holding a boulder on back.	47.50	140.00	400.00

		GOOD	FINE	XF
S3290	**60 DOLLARS** 8.2.1779. Figure and cornucopia. W/motto: *MUTUA DEFENSIO TUTISSIMA.* Lyre, horns and flags on back.	85.00	220.00	600.00
S3291	**70 DOLLARS** 8.2.1779. Hope w/anchor. W/motto: *SPES MENTIS SOLATIO.* Prometheus bound and attacked by vulture on back.	47.50	140.00	400.00
S3292	**80 DOLLARS** 8.2.1779. Man w/sword. W/motto: *CONSTANTIA DURISSIMA VINCIT.* Shield and Liberty cap on back.	85.00	220.00	700.00
S3293	**90 DOLLARS** 8.2.1779. Warrior. W/motto: *ARMIS CONCURRITE CAMPO.* Hercules strangling a lion on back.	47.50	140.00	400.00
S3294	**100 DOLLARS** 8.2.1779. Athena. W/motto: *GLORIAE FUNDAMENTUM FORTITUDO.* Palmetto, drum and flags on back.	90.00	230.00	650.00

1786 FIRST ISSUE

Pound Sterling System

#S3295-S3303 black.

		GOOD	FINE	XF
S3295	**2 SHILLINGS 6 PENCE** 1786. W/motto: *FIDES PUBLICA.*	—	—	—
S3296	**5 SHILLINGS** 1786.	—	—	—
S3297	**10 SHILLINGS** 1786.	—	—	—
S3298	**1 POUND** 1786.	—	—	—
S3299	**1 POUND 10 SHILLINGS** 1786.	—	—	—
S3300	**3 POUNDS** 1786.	—	—	—
S3301	**5 POUNDS** 1786.	—	—	—
S3302	**10 POUNDS** 1786.	—	—	—
S3303	**20 POUNDS** 1786.	—	—	—

1786 SECOND ISSUE

#S3304-S3307 engraver: Abernethie of Charleston.

		GOOD	FINE	XF
S3304	**1 POUND** 1.5.1786. W/motto: *HONOR ET JUSTITIA.*	—	—	—
S3305	**2 POUNDS** 1.5.1786. W/motto: *PRAEMIUM INDUSTRIAE.*	—	—	—
S3306	**3 POUNDS** 1.5.1786. W/motto: *HINC OPES.*	—	—	—
S3307	**10 POUNDS** 1.5.1786. W/motto: *VOX POPULI.*	—	—	—

SOUTH CAROLINA

POST CIVIL WAR

1866 ISSUE

#S3311-S3314 printer: ABNC.

		GOOD	FINE	XF
S3311	**1 DOLLAR** 1.1.1866. Black and green. Similar to #S3321.	—	Rare	—
S3312	**2 DOLLARS** 1.1.1866. Black and green. Similar to #S3322.	—	Rare	—
S3313	**5 DOLLARS** 1.1.1866. Black and green. Similar to #S3323.	—	Rare	—
S3314	**10 DOLLARS** 1.1.1866. Black and green. Similar to #S3324.	—	Rare	—

ACT 2.3.1872 REVENUE BOND FIRST ISSUE

#S3318-S3319 steam train in vertical at l.

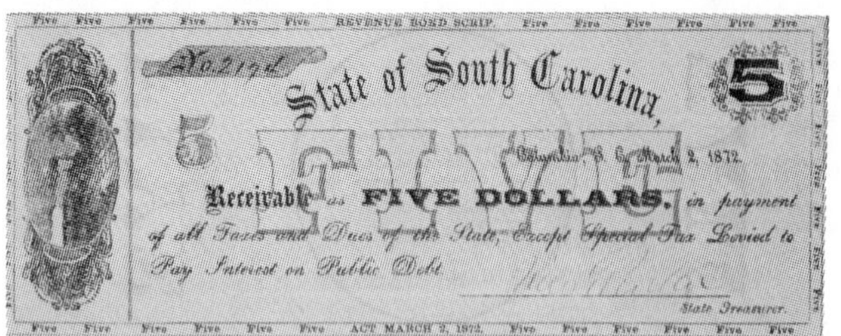

		VG	VF	UNC
S3318	**5 DOLLARS** 2.3.1872. Black on green unpt.	15.00	25.00	30.00
S3319	**10 DOLLARS** 2.3.1872. Black on green unpt.	10.00	12.00	30.00
S3319A	**100 DOLLARS** 2.3.1872. Palmetto tree at ctr., small dog and safe at lower r.	40.00	65.00	110.00

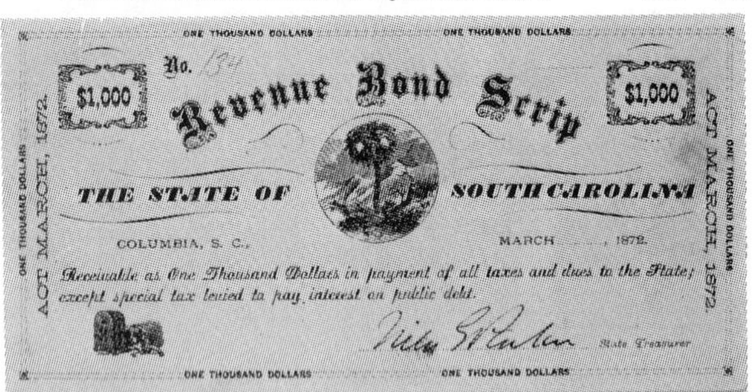

		VG	VF	UNC
S3320	**1000 DOLLARS** 1872. Black. Palmetto tree within circle at upper ctr., dog and safe at lower l. Handwritten dates.	—	Rare	—
S3320A	**5000 DOLLARS** 2.3.1872. Similar to #S3320.	—	Rare	—

ACT 2.3.1872 REVENUE BOND SECOND ISSUE

#S3321-S3326 printer: ABNC.

#S3321-S3334 similar to #S3311-S3314 but text: *REVENUE BOND SCRIP* on face.

		VG	VF	UNC
S3321	**1 DOLLAR** 2.3.1872. Green and black. Oxen pulling cart at upper l. ctr., 2 children in oval at upper ctr. r., maiden seated at lower r. Back green.	15.00	35.00	45.00

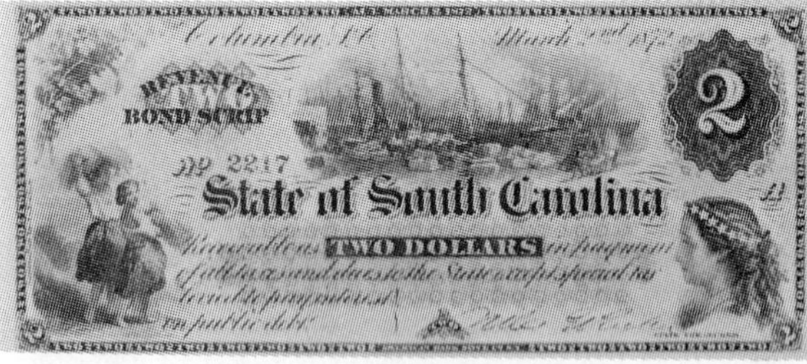

		VG	VF	UNC
S3322	**2 DOLLARS** 2.3.1872. Green and black. 2 young girls w/sheaves of grain at lower l., harbor scene at ctr. r., girl's head at lower r. Back green.	20.00	35.00	45.00

		VG	VF	UNC
S3323	**5 DOLLARS** 2.3.1872. Green and black. Gen. T. Sumter at lower l., Gen. F. Marion's *Sweet Potato Dinner* at top ctr., Gen. W. Moultrie at lower r. Back green.	20.00	35.00	45.00

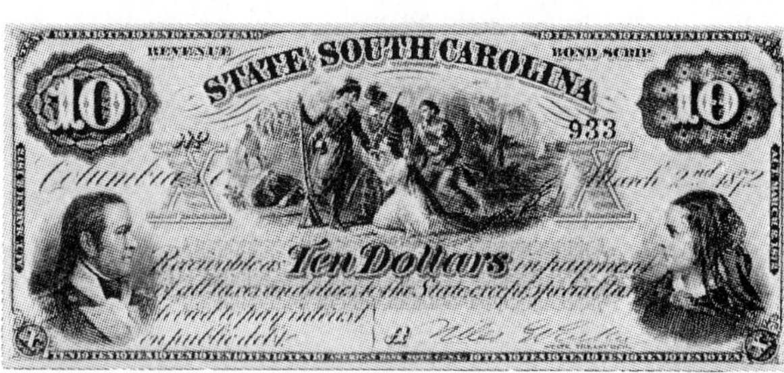

		VG	VF	UNC
S3324	**10 DOLLARS** 2.3.1872. Green and black. Revolutionary Gen. at lower l., Revolutionary scene of an Indian being captured at upper ctr., young girl at lower r. Back green.	20.00	35.00	45.00

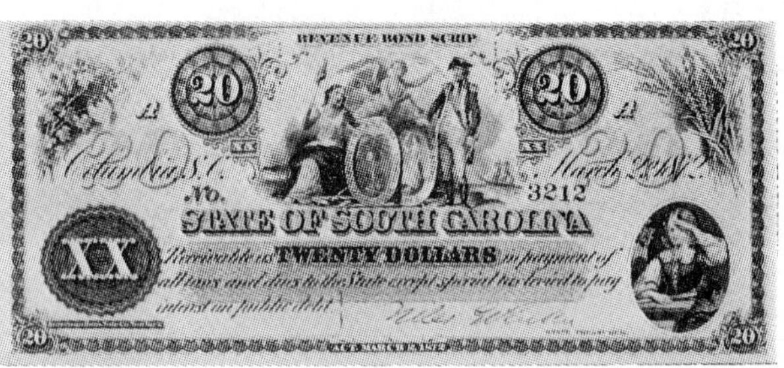

		VG	VF	UNC
S3325	**20 DOLLARS** 2.3.1872. Green and black. Liberty, soldier, and angel guarding state seals at upper ctr., young girl at lower r. Back green.	20.00	35.00	45.00

		VG	VF	UNC
S3326	**50 DOLLARS** 2.3.1872. Black. Horse drawn cart at l., portr. G. Washington at ctr., black carrying cotton at r.	20.00	40.00	55.00

#S3327 *Deleted.* See #S3320.

TENNESSEE

POST CIVIL WAR

1875 PAYABLE WARRANT ISSUE

#S3334-S3339 printer: ABNC.

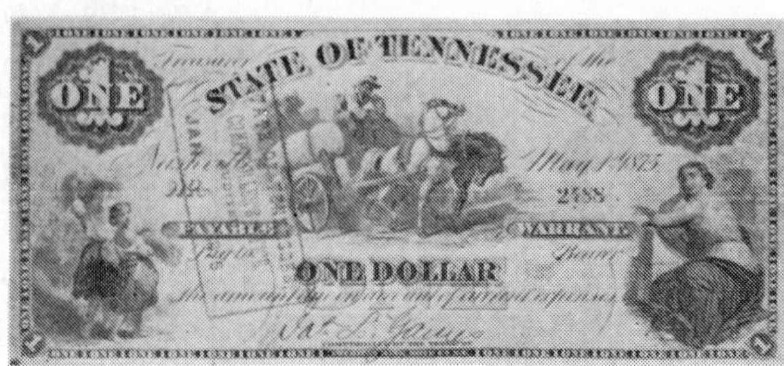

		VG	VF	UNC
S3334	**1 DOLLAR** 1.5.1875. Black on green unpt. 2 young girls w/sheaves of grain at lower l., horsedrawn cart at ctr., seated Ceres at lower r. Back green.			
	a. Issued note.	175.00	300.00	500.00
	b. Punched hole cancelled.	125.00	250.00	350.00

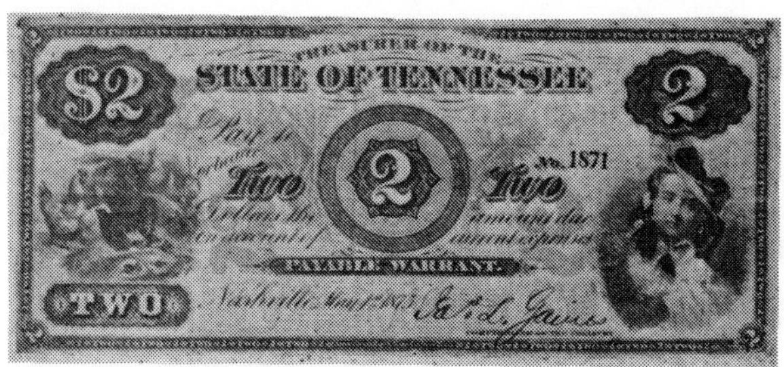

S3335 2 Dollars
1.5.1875. Black on green unpt. Chickens at l., young girl's head at lower r. Back green.

	VG	VF	Unc
a. Issued note.	175.00	300.00	450.00
b. Punched hole cancelled.	125.00	250.00	350.00

S3336 5 Dollars
1.5.1875. Black on green unpt. Black picking cotton at upper l., portr. man at lower r. Back green.

	VG	VF	Unc
a. Issued note.	200.00	325.00	550.00
b. Punched hole cancelled.	100.00	200.00	325.00

S3337 10 Dollars
1.5.1875. Black on green unpt. Boy gathering corn stalks at l., portr. A. Jackson at ctr. dog lying by safe at lower r. Back green.

	VG	VF	Unc
a. Issued note.	200.00	375.00	650.00
b. Punched hole cancelled.	175.00	165.00	200.00

S3338 20 Dollars
1.5.1875. Black on green unpt. Black picking cotton at upper l., young woman reclining at lower r. Back green.

	VG	VF	Unc
a. Issued note.	200.00	250.00	650.00
b. Punched hole cancelled.	95.00	125.00	160.00

S3339 50 Dollars
1.5.1875. Black on green unpt. Young girl w/puppy at l., man and horses w/plow at ctr., girl w/quill pen at lower r. Back green.

	VG	VF	Unc
a. Issued note.	250.00	450.00	750.00
b. Punched hole cancelled.	150.00	300.00	500.00

1883 Issue

S3340 1 Dollar
1.7.1883. Portr. of man at l. Bldg. at ctr. on back. Series D.

	VG	VF	Unc
a. Issued note.	125.00	175.00	300.00
b. Punched hole cancelled.	80.00	175.00	—

Texas

State

Civil War

1860-64 Treasury Warrant Civil Service Issues

#S3395-S3416 various handwritten dates.

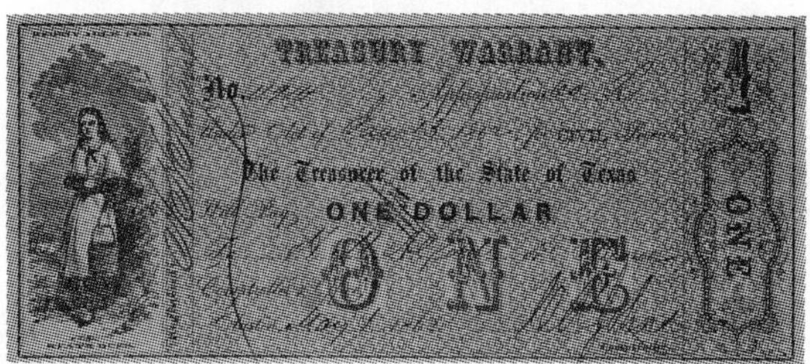

	VG	VF	Unc
S3395 1 Dollar 1860-64. Black on orange unpt. Milkmaid at l.	25.00	50.00	80.00

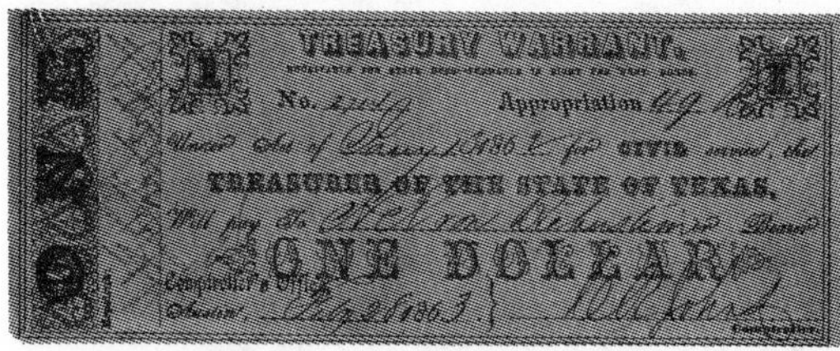

	VG	VF	Unc
S3396 1 Dollar 1860-64. Green and black. Ornate *ONE* vertically at l.	25.00	50.00	80.00

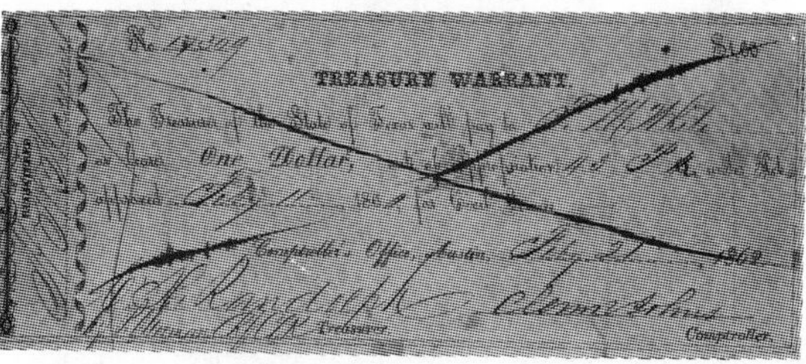

	VG	VF	Unc
S3397 1 Dollar 1860-64. Black. Sign. vertically at l.	25.00	45.00	75.00

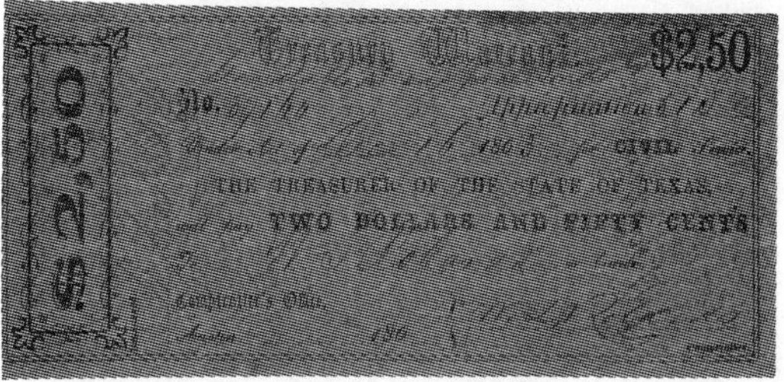

	VG	VF	Unc
S3398 2 1/2 Dollars 1860-64. Black. Lt. brown paper.	35.00	60.00	90.00

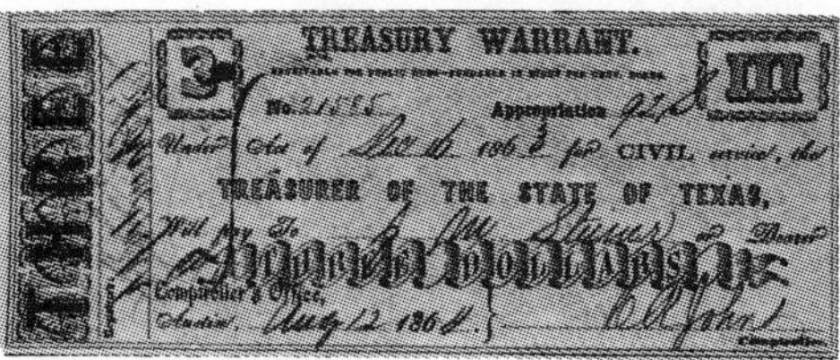

	VG	VF	Unc
S3399 3 Dollars 1860-64. Green and black.	30.00	45.00	80.00

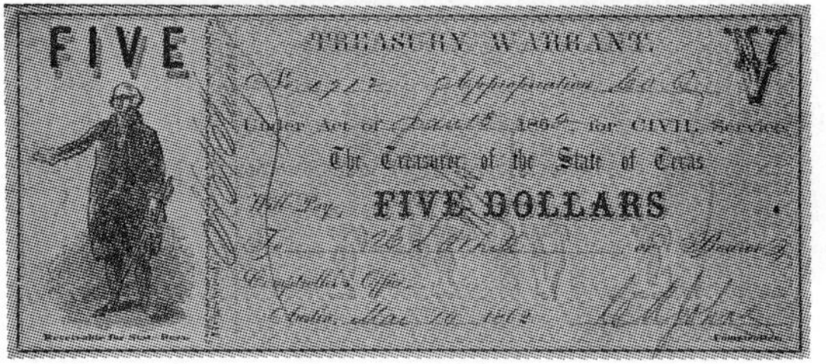

	VG	VF	UNC
S3400 5 DOLLARS 1860-64. Black on green unpt. Standing George Washington at l.	25.00	40.00	60.00
S3400A 5 DOLLARS 1860-64. Green and black. Similar to #S3399 w/ornate *FIVE* vertically at l.	25.00	40.00	60.00
S3401 5 DOLLARS 1860-64. Black. Similar to #S3397.	25.00	40.00	60.00

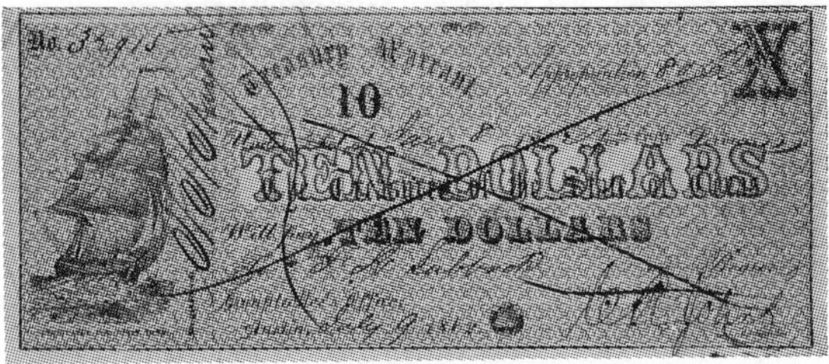

	VG	VF	UNC
S3402 10 DOLLARS 1860-64. Black on red unpt. Sailing ship at l.	25.00	40.00	60.00
S3403 10 DOLLARS 1860-64. Green and black. Similar to #S3399 w/ornate *TEN* vertically at l.	25.00	40.00	65.00
S3404 10 DOLLARS 1860-64. Black. Similar to #S3397.	25.00	40.00	60.00

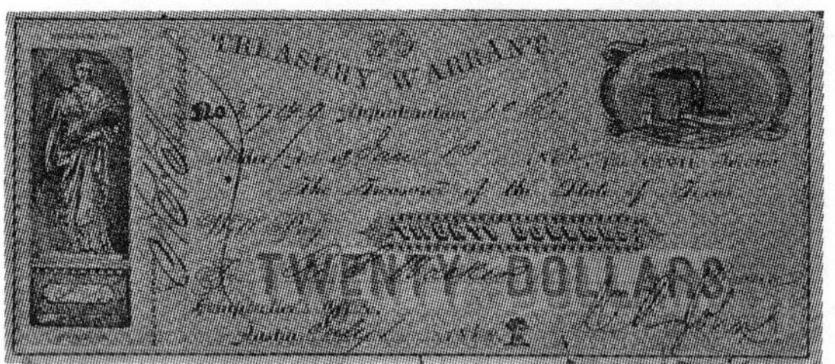

	VG	VF	UNC
S3405 20 DOLLARS 1860-64. Black on red unpt. Standing Ceres at l., steamboat at upper r.	30.00	55.00	90.00
S3406 20 DOLLARS 1860-64. Green and black. Similar to #S3399 w/ornate *TWENTY* vertically at l.	30.00	40.00	60.00
S3407 20 DOLLARS 1860-64. Black. Similar to #S3397.	25.00	35.00	60.00

	VG	VF	UNC
S3408 50 DOLLARS 1860-64. Black and green on yellow unpt. Steam passenger train vertically at l., ships at upper r.	25.00	50.00	75.00

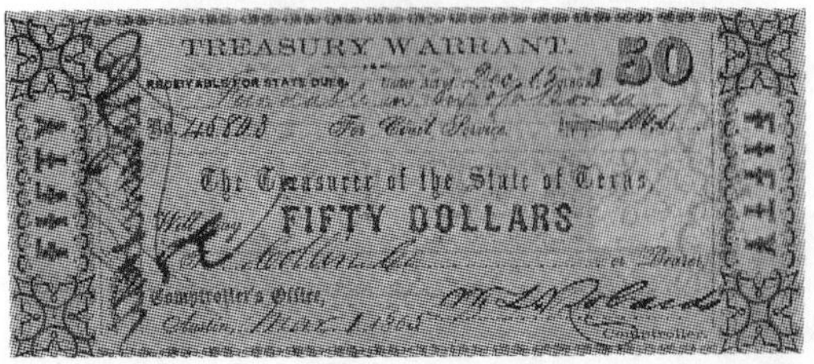

	VG	VF	UNC
S3409 50 DOLLARS 1860-64. Black. *FIFTY* vertically at l. and r. Back geen.	25.00	45.00	65.00
S3410 50 DOLLARS 1860-64. Black. Similar to #S3397.	25.00	45.00	65.00

	VG	VF	UNC
S3411 100 DOLLARS 1860-64. Black on red unpt. Sailing ship at upper ctr. r.	150.00	200.00	300.00
S3412 100 DOLLARS 1860-64. Black. Similar to #S3409 w/*ONE HUNDRED* vertically at l. and r. Back green.	40.00	75.00	150.00
S3413 100 DOLLARS 1860-64. Black.	150.00	200.00	300.00

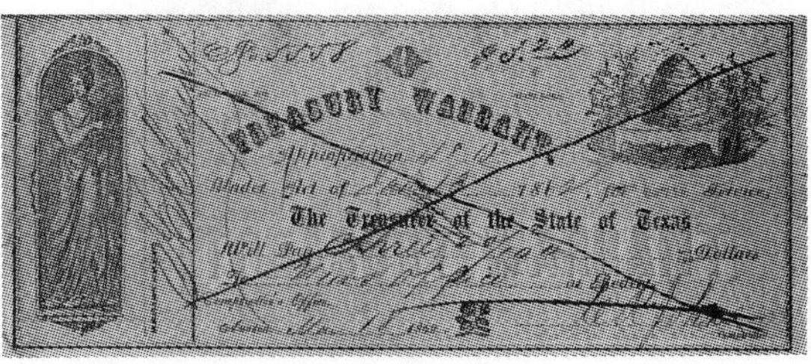

	VG	VF	UNC
S3414 WRITTEN DENOMINATIONS 1860-64. Black on blue unpt. Liberty at l., beehive at upper r.	25.00	45.00	70.00

	VG	VF	UNC
S3415 WRITTEN DENOMINATIONS 1860-64. Black on green unpt. Indian maiden at l., seated Ceres at ctr. r.	25.00	40.00	65.00
S3416 WRITTEN DENOMINATIONS 1860-64. Similar to #S3397.	25.00	40.00	65.00

1860-64 MILITARY SERVICE ISSUES

#S3417-S3448 similar to #S3395-S3416 except the word *Military* replaces *Civil*. Various handwritten dates.

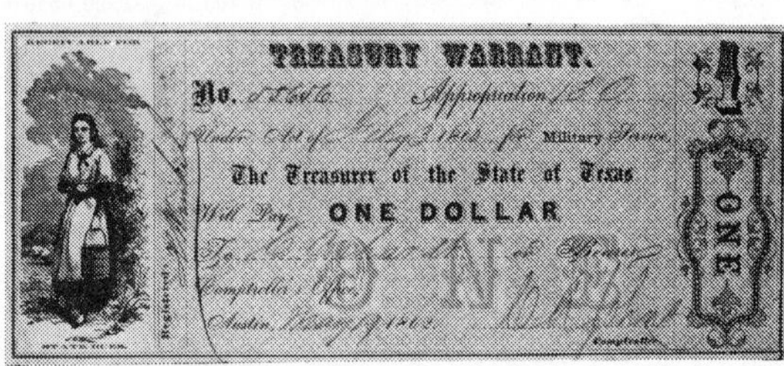

	VG	VF	UNC
S3417 1 DOLLAR 1860-64. Like #S3395.	25.00	35.00	65.00
S3418 1 DOLLAR 1860-64. Like #S3396.	25.00	35.00	65.00
S3419 1 DOLLAR 1860-64. Like #S3397.	25.00	35.00	65.00

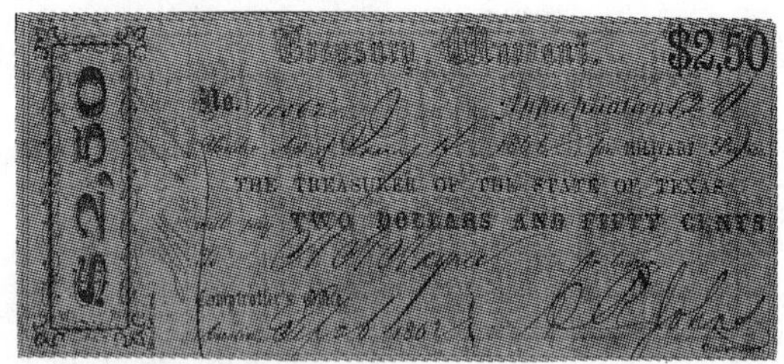

	VG	VF	UNC
S3420 2 1/2 DOLLARS 1860-64. Like #S3398.	25.00	45.00	70.00
S3421 3 DOLLARS 1860-64. Like #S3399.	25.00	50.00	75.00
S3422 5 DOLLARS 1860-64. Like #S3400.	25.00	40.00	70.00
S3423 5 DOLLARS 1860-64. Similar to #S3401.	25.00	40.00	70.00

	VG	VF	UNC
S3424 10 DOLLARS 1860-64. Like #S3402.	25.00	40.00	70.00

		VG	VF	UNC
S3425	**10 DOLLARS** 1860-64. Like #S3403.	25.00	40.00	70.00
S3426	**10 DOLLARS** 1860-64. Like #S3404.	25.00	40.00	70.00
S3427	**20 DOLLARS** 1860-64. Like #S3405.	25.00	40.00	70.00

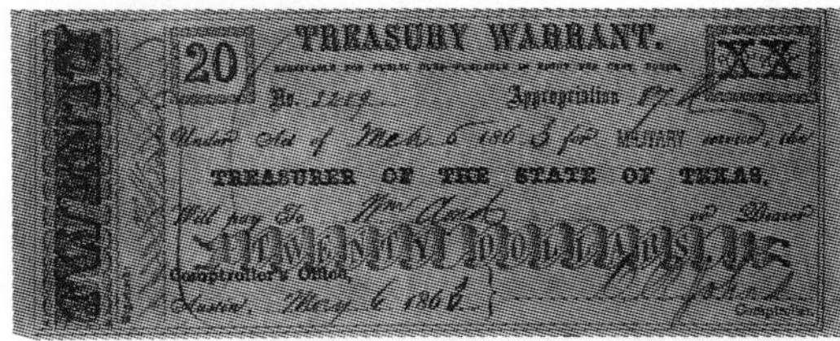

		VG	VF	UNC
S3428	**20 DOLLARS** 1860-64. Like #S3406.	25.00	40.00	65.00
S3429	**20 DOLLARS** 1860-64. Like #S3407.	18.00	25.00	50.00
S3430	**50 DOLLARS** 1860-64. Like #S3408.	20.00	35.00	60.00

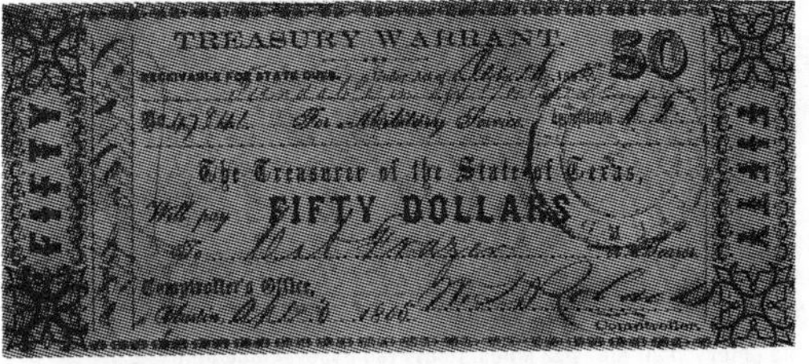

		VG	VF	UNC
S3431	**50 DOLLARS** 1860-64. Like #S3409.	30.00	45.00	75.00
S3432	**50 DOLLARS** 1860-64. Like #S3410.	30.00	45.00	75.00

		VG	VF	UNC
S3433	**100 DOLLARS** 1860-64. Like #S3411.	40.00	75.00	175.00
S3434	**100 DOLLARS** 1860-64. Like #S3412.	20.00	40.00	75.00
S3435	**100 DOLLARS** 1860-64. Like #S3413.	25.00	40.00	75.00
S3436	**VARIOUS HANDWRITTEN DENOMINATIONS** 1860-64. Like #S3415.	25.00	35.00	60.00

		VG	VF	UNC
S3437	**VARIOUS HANDWRITTEN DENOMINATIONS** 1860-64. Like #S3416.	25.00	35.00	55.00
S3438	**VARIOUS HANDWRITTEN DENOMINATIONS** 1860-64. Like #S3417.	25.00	35.00	55.00

PROVISIONAL ISSUES

Note: #S3395-S3416 are known w/*Military* handwritten over *Civil* while #S3417-S3438 are known w/*Civil* handwritten over *Military*.

VERMONT

STATE

1781 TREASURY ISSUE

#S3441-S3448 black. Seal that has 13 joined links and 1 loose link exemplifying Vermont's objection from being excluded from being one of the original colonies attaining statehood. W/motto: *VERMONT CALLS FOR JUSTICE.* Thin weak paper. Printer: Spooner and Green.

		FAIR	GOOD	VG
S3441	**1 SHILLING** February 1781.	1200.	2200.	3500.
S3442	**1 SHILLING 3 PENCE** February 1781.	1200.	2200.	3500.

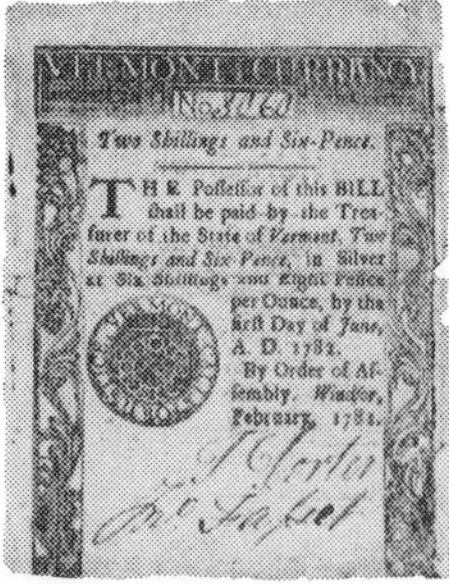

		FAIR	GOOD	VG
S3443	**2 SHILLINGS 6 PENCE** February 1781.	1200.	2200.	3500.
S3444	**5 SHILLINGS** February 1781.	1200.	2200.	3500.
S3445	**10 SHILLINGS** February 1781.	1200.	2200.	3500.
S3446	**20 SHILLINGS** February 1781.	1500.	2500.	3750.
S3447	**40 SHILLINGS** February 1781.	1750.	2750.	4000.
S3448	**3 POUNDS** February 1781.	2250.	3250.	4500.

VIRGINIA - COLONIAL

1755 FIRST ISSUE

Pound Sterling System
Denominations are not known.

1755 SECOND ISSUE

		GOOD	FINE	XF
S3451	**10 SHILLINGS** 11.12.1755.	—	—	—
S3454	**5 POUNDS** 11.12.1755.	—	—	—

NOTE: Several additional denominations apparently existed. #S3451 and S3454 are known only as counterfeits.

1757 ISSUE

#S3461-S3470 black. Virginia Colony seal on face w/motto: *EN DAT VIRGINIA QUARTAM.* Thin laid paper. Printer: William Hunter.

		GOOD	FINE	XF
S3461	**1 SHILLING** 8.6.1757.	—	—	—
S3462	**1 SHILLING 3 PENCE** 8.6.1757.	—	—	—
S3463	**2 SHILLINGS 6 PENCE** 8.6.1757.	—	—	—
S3464	**5 SHILLINGS** 8.6.1757.	—	—	—
S3465	**10 SHILLINGS** 8.6.1757.	—	—	—
S3466	**20 SHILLINGS** 8.6.1757.	—	—	—
S3467	**2 POUNDS** 8.6.1757.	—	—	—
S3468	**3 POUNDS** 8.6.1757.	—	—	—
S3469	**5 POUNDS** 8.6.1757.	—	—	—
S3470	**10 POUNDS** 8.6.1757.	—	—	—

1758 ISSUE

		GOOD	FINE	XF
S3470C	**10 POUNDS** 12.4.1758. Black. Virginia Colony seal at l.	—	Rare	—

#S3471-S3479 black. Larger Virginia Colony seal. Printer: William Hunter.

		GOOD	FINE	XF
S3471	**1 SHILLING** 12.10.1758.	—	—	—
S3472	**1 SHILLING 3 PENCE** 12.10.1758.	—	—	—
S3473	**2 SHILLINGS 6 PENCE** 12.10.1758.	—	—	—
S3474	**5 SHILLINGS** 12.10.1758.	—	—	—
S3475	**10 SHILLINGS** 12.10.1758.	—	—	—
S3476	**20 SHILLINGS** 12.10.1758.	—	—	—
S3477	**2 POUNDS** 12.10.1758.	—	—	—
S3478	**3 POUNDS** 12.10.1758.	—	—	—
S3479	**5 POUNDS** 12.10.1758.	—	—	—

1759 FIRST ISSUE

#S3480-S3488 black. Virginia Colony seal.

		GOOD	FINE	XF
S3480	**1 SHILLING** 5.4.1759.	—	—	—
S3481	**1 SHILLING 3 PENCE** 5.4.1759.	—	—	—

		Good	Fine	XF
S3482	2 SHILLINGS 6 PENCE 5.4.1759.	—	—	—
S3483	5 SHILLINGS 5.4.1759.	—	—	—

		Good	Fine	XF
S3484	10 SHILLINGS 5.4.1759.	—	—	—
S3485	20 SHILLINGS 5.4.1759.	—	—	—
S3486	2 POUNDS 5.4.1759.	—	—	—
S3487	3 POUNDS 5.4.1759.	—	—	—
S3488	5 POUNDS 5.4.1759.	—	—	—

1759 SECOND ISSUE

#S3490 and S3491 black. Virginia Colony seal.

		Good	Fine	XF
S3490	3 POUNDS 21.11.1759.	—	—	—
S3491	5 POUNDS 21.11.1759.	—	—	—

NOTE: Additional denominations may have been issued.

1760 FIRST ISSUE

#S3492-S3496 black. Virginia Colony seal.

		Good	Fine	XF
S3492	2 SHILLINGS 6 PENCE 11.3.1760.	—	—	—
S3493	5 SHILLINGS 11.3.1760.	—	—	—
S3494	2 POUNDS 11.3.1760.	—	—	—
S3495	3 POUNDS 11.3.1760.	—	—	—
S3496	5 POUNDS 11.3.1760.	—	—	—

1760 SECOND ISSUE

#S3497-S3505 black. Virginia Colony seal.

		Good	Fine	XF
S3497	1 SHILLING 24.5.1760.	—	—	—
S3498	1 SHILLING 3 PENCE 24.5.1760.	—	—	—
S3499	2 SHILLINGS 6 PENCE 24.5.1760.	—	—	—
S3500	5 SHILLINGS 24.5.1760.	—	—	—
S3501	10 SHILLINGS 24.5.1760.	—	—	—
S3502	20 SHILLINGS 24.5.1760.	—	—	—
S3503	2 POUNDS 24.5.1760.	—	—	—
S3504	3 POUNDS 24.5.1760.	—	—	—
S3505	5 POUNDS 24.5.1760.	—	—	—

1762 ISSUE

#S3506-S3512 black. Virginia Colony seal.

		Good	Fine	XF
S3506	2 SHILLINGS 6 PENCE 7.4.1762.	—	—	—
S3507	5 SHILLINGS 7.4.1762.	—	—	—
S3508	10 SHILLINGS 7.4.1762.	—	—	—
S3509	20 SHILLINGS 7.4.1762.	—	—	—
S3510	2 POUNDS 7.4.1762.	—	—	—
S3511	3 POUNDS 7.4.1762.	—	—	—
S3512	5 POUNDS 7.4.1762.	—	—	—

ACT OF NOV. 7, 1769; 1770 ISSUE

#S3513-S3515 black. Virginia Colony seal. Printer: William Rind.

		Good	Fine	XF
S3513	20 SHILLINGS 1770.	—	—	—
S3514	2 POUNDS 1770.	—	—	—
S3515	5 POUNDS 1770.	—	—	—

1771 TOBACCO ISSUE

#S3516-S3518 black. Virginia Colony seal. W/text: *TOBACCO* on face indicating these notes were to pay for tobacco lost by floods. Printer: William Rind.

		Good	Fine	XF
S3516	2 POUNDS 11.7.1771.	—	—	—
S3517	3 POUNDS 11.7.1771.	—	—	—
S3518	5 POUNDS 11.7.1771.	—	—	—

1773 ISSUE

#S3519-S3522 black. Virginia Colony seal.

		Good	Fine	XF
S3519	20 SHILLINGS 4.3.1773.	150.00	500.00	—
S3520	2 POUNDS 4.3.1773.	150.00	500.00	—

		Good	Fine	XF
S3521	3 POUNDS 4.3.1773.	150.00	500.00	—
S3522	5 POUNDS 4.3.1773.	150.00	500.00	—

1775 SMALL SIZE ISSUE

#S3523-S3531 black. Virginia Colony seal. Sm. size notes. Heavy rag paper w/blue fibres.

		VG	VF	Unc
S3523	1 SHILLING 3 PENCE 17.7.1775.			
	a. *And* in denomination in text.	50.00	120.00	—
	b. *&* in denomination in text.	50.00	120.00	—
	p. Proof of border cuts and arms only.	—	—	—
S3524	2 SHILLINGS 6 PENCE 17.7.1775.			
	a. *SIXPENCE* as one word.	50.00	120.00	—
	b. *Six Pence* as two words.	50.00	120.00	—
	p. Proof of border cuts and arms only.	—	—	—
S3525	5 SHILLINGS 17.7.1775.	50.00	120.00	—
S3526	7 SHILLINGS 6 PENCE 17.7.1775.	50.00	120.00	—
S3527	10 SHILLINGS 17.7.1775.	60.00	130.00	—
S3528	12 SHILLINGS 6 PENCE 17.7.1775.	60.00	130.00	—
S3529	20 SHILLINGS 17.7.1775. *FOUR CROWNS* misspelled *FOWR CROWNS* in r. border.	75.00	165.00	—
S3530	2 POUNDS 17.7.1775.	75.00	165.00	—

		VG	VF	Unc
S3531	3 POUNDS 17.7.1775.	75.00	165.00	—

1775 LARGE SIZE ISSUE

#S3532-S3535 black. Virginia Colony seal. Lg. size notes w/counterfoil at l.

		VG	VF	Unc
S3532	20 SHILLINGS = 1 POUND 17.7.1775.	150.00	300.00	—

		VG	VF	UNC
S3533	2 POUNDS 17.7.1775.	150.00	300.00	—
S3534	3 POUNDS 17.7.1775.	150.00	300.00	—

		VG	VF	UNC
S3535	5 POUNDS 17.7.1775.	150.00	300.00	—

VIRGINIA

STATE

1776 FIRST ISSUE

Dollar/Pound Sterling System

#S3536-S3549 black. Heavy rag paper w/blue fibers.

		GOOD	FINE	XF
S3536	1/6 DOLLAR = 1 SHILLING 6.5.1776. State arms.	20.00	80.00	—
S3537	1 SHILLING 3 PENCE 6.5.1776. Virginia Colony seal.			
	a. *And* in denomination in text.	30.00	110.00	—
	b. *&* in denomination in text.	30.00	110.00	—
S3538	1/3 DOLLAR = 2 SHILLINGS 6.5.1776. State arms.	20.00	80.00	—
S3539	2 SHILLINGS 6 PENCE 6.5.1776. Virginia Colony seal.			
	a. *SIXPENCE* as one word.	30.00	110.00	—
	b. *Six Pence* as two words.	30.00	110.00	—
S3540	5 SHILLINGS 6.5.1776. Virginia Colony seal.	35.00	130.00	—
S3541	7 SHILLINGS 6 PENCE 6.5.1776. Virginia Colony seal.	35.00	130.00	—
S3542	10 SHILLINGS 6.5.1776. Virginia Colony seal.	35.00	130.00	—
S3543	12 SHILLINGS 6 PENCE 6.5.1776. Virginia Colony seal.	35.00	130.00	—
S3544	20 SHILLINGS 6.5.1776. Virginia Colony seal. *FOUR CROWNS* misspelled *FOWR CROWNS*.	100.00	400.00	—
S3545	4 DOLLARS = 24 SHILLINGS 6.5.1776. State arms.	20.00	80.00	—
S3546	5 DOLLARS = 30 SHILLINGS 6.5.1776. State arms. Spanish 8 Reales.	20.00	80.00	—
S3547	2 POUNDS 6.5.1776. Virginia Colony seal.	100.00	400.00	—
S3548	3 POUNDS 6.5.1776. Virginia Colony seal.	100.00	450.00	—
S3549	4 POUNDS 6.5.1776. Virginia Colony seal.	100.00	400.00	—

1776 SECOND ISSUE

Dollar System

#S3550-S3559 black. State arms. Heavy rag paper w/blue fibers.

		VG	VF	UNC
S3550	1/6 DOLLAR 7.10.1776.	50.00	125.00	—
S3551	1/3 DOLLAR 7.10.1776.	50.00	125.00	—
S3552	2/3 DOLLAR 7.10.1776.	50.00	125.00	—
S3553	1 DOLLAR 7.10.1776. Spanish 8 Reales.	50.00	125.00	—

#S3554-S3559 w/motto: *SIC SEMPER TYRANNIS* misspelled *TYRANNUS*.

		VG	VF	UNC
S3554	4 DOLLARS 7.10.1776.	50.00	125.00	—
S3555	5 DOLLARS 7.10.1776.	50.00	125.00	—
S3556	6 DOLLARS 7.10.1776.	50.00	125.00	—
S3557	8 DOLLARS 7.10.1776.	50.00	125.00	—

		VG	VF	UNC
S3558	10 DOLLARS 7.10.1776.	50.00	125.00	—

		VG	VF	UNC
S3559	15 DOLLARS 7.10.1776.	50.00	125.00	—

1777 FIRST ISSUE

#S3560-S3569 black. Similar to #S3550-S3559 except printed date partly removed from cuts and replaced w/writing. Heavy rag paper w/blue fibers and mica flakes.

		VG	VF	UNC
S3560	1/6 DOLLAR 5.5.1777.	60.00	135.00	—
S3561	1/3 DOLLAR 5.5.1777.	60.00	135.00	—
S3562	2/3 DOLLAR 5.5.1777.	60.00	135.00	—
S3563	1 DOLLAR 5.5.1777. Spanish 8 Reales.	60.00	135.00	—
S3564	4 DOLLARS 5.5.1777.	60.00	135.00	—
S3565	5 DOLLARS 5.5.1777.	60.00	135.00	—
S3566	6 DOLLARS 5.5.1777.	60.00	135.00	—
S3567	8 DOLLARS 5.5.1777.	60.00	135.00	—
S3568	10 DOLLARS 5.5.1777.	60.00	135.00	—
S3569	15 DOLLARS 5.5.1777.	60.00	135.00	—

1777 SECOND ISSUE

#S3570-S3579 black. State arms. Same forms as #S3560-S3569. Heavy rag paper w/blue fibers.

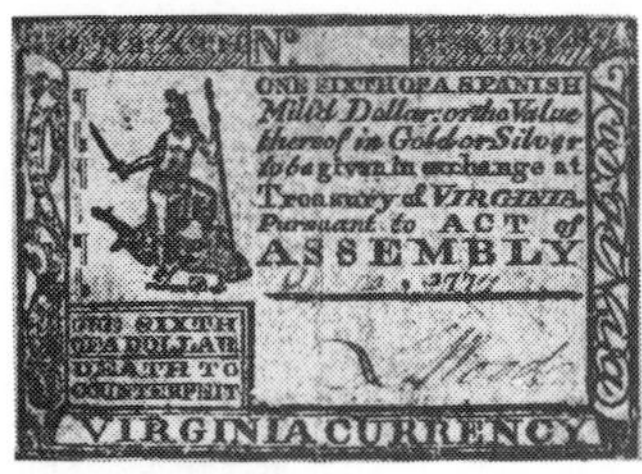

		VG	VF	UNC
S3570	1/6 DOLLAR 20.10.1777. Uniface.	40.00	110.00	350.00
S3571	1/3 DOLLAR 20.10.1777.	40.00	110.00	350.00
S3572	2/3 DOLLAR 20.10.1777.	40.00	110.00	350.00
S3573	1 DOLLAR 20.10.1777. Spanish 8 Reales.	40.00	110.00	350.00
S3574	4 DOLLARS 20.10.1777.	40.00	110.00	350.00
S3575	5 DOLLARS 20.10.1777.	40.00	110.00	350.00
S3576	6 DOLLARS 20.10.1777.	40.00	110.00	350.00
S3577	8 DOLLARS 20.10.1777.	40.00	110.00	350.00
S3578	10 DOLLARS 20.10.1777.	40.00	110.00	350.00
S3579	15 DOLLARS 20.10.1777.	40.00	110.00	350.00

1778 FIRST ISSUE

#S3580-S3587 black. State arms. Same forms as #S3560-S3569 and S3570-S3579. Various handwritten dates.

		GOOD	FINE	XF
S3580	1/6 DOLLAR 4.5.1778.	60.00	210.00	—
S3581	1/3 DOLLAR 4.5.1778.	60.00	210.00	—
S3582	2/3 DOLLAR 4.5.1778.	60.00	210.00	—

		Good	Fine	XF
S3583	**1 Dollar** 4.5.1778. Spanish 8 Reales.	60.00	210.00	—
S3584	**4 Dollars** 4.5.1778.	60.00	210.00	—
S3585	**5 Dollars** 4.5.1778.	60.00	210.00	—
S3586	**6 Dollars** 4.5.1778.	60.00	210.00	—
S3587	**8 Dollars** 4.5.1778.	60.00	210.00	—

1778 Second Issue

#S3588-S3599 black. Newly cut borders and state arms. *TYRANNIS* corrected on arms. Both thick rag paper w/blue fibres and thin laid paper.

		Good	Fine	XF
S3588	**1/6 Dollar** 4.5.1778.			
	a. Thick paper.	80.00	280.00	—
	b. Thin paper.	50.00	165.00	—
S3589	**1/4 Dollar** 4.5.1778.			
	a. Thick paper.	80.00	280.00	—
	b. Thin paper.	50.00	165.00	—
S3590	**1/3 Dollar** 4.5.1778.			
	a. Thick paper.	80.00	280.00	—
	b. Thin paper.	50.00	165.00	—
S3591	**2/3 Dollar** 4.5.1778.			
	a. Thick paper.	80.00	280.00	—
	b. Thin paper.	50.00	165.00	—
S3592	**1 Dollar** 4.5.1778.			
	a. Thick paper.	80.00	280.00	—
	b. Thin paper.	50.00	165.00	—
S3593	**3 Dollars** 4.5.1778.			
	a. Thick paper.	80.00	280.00	—
	b. Thin paper.	50.00	165.00	—
S3594	**4 Dollars** 4.5.1778.			
	a. Thick paper.	80.00	280.00	—
	b. Thin paper.	50.00	165.00	—
S3595	**5 Dollars** 4.5.1778.			
	a. Thick paper.	80.00	280.00	—
	b. Thin paper.	50.00	165.00	—
S3596	**6 Dollars** 4.5.1778.			
	a. Thick paper.	80.00	280.00	—
	b. Thin paper.	50.00	165.00	—
S3597	**7 Dollars** 4.5.1778.			
	a. Thick paper.	80.00	280.00	—
	b. Thin paper.	50.00	165.00	—
S3598	**10 Dollars** 4.5.1778.			
	a. Thick paper.	80.00	280.00	—
	b. Thin paper.	50.00	165.00	—
S3599	**15 Dollars** 4.5.1778.			
	a. Thick paper.	80.00	280.00	—
	b. Thin paper.	50.00	165.00	—

1778 Third Issue

#S3600-S3611 black. Thin laid paper.

#S3600-S3609 state arms.

		VG	VF	Unc
S3600	**1/6 Dollar** 5.10.1778.	55.00	150.00	—
S3601	**1/4 Dollar** 5.10.1778.	55.00	150.00	—
S3602	**1/3 Dollar** 5.10.1778.	55.00	150.00	—
S3603	**2/3 Dollar** 5.10.1778.	55.00	150.00	—
S3604	**1 Dollar** 5.10.1778.	55.00	150.00	—
S3605	**3 Dollars** 5.10.1778.	55.00	150.00	—
S3606	**5 Dollars** 5.10.1778.	55.00	150.00	—
S3607	**7 Dollars** 5.10.1778.	55.00	150.00	—
S3608	**10 Dollars** 5.10.1778.	55.00	150.00	—
S3609	**15 Dollars** 5.10.1778.	55.00	150.00	—
S3610	**50 Dollars = 15 Pounds** 5.10.1778.	105.00	300.00	—
S3611	**100 Dollars = 30 Pounds** 5.10.1778.	105.00	300.00	—

1779 Issue

#S3612-S3618 black. Thin laid paper.

#S3612-S3616 state arms.

		VG	VF	Unc
S3612	**3 Dollars** 3.5.1779.	75.00	200.00	—
S3613	**5 Dollars** 3.5.1779.	75.00	200.00	—
S3614	**7 Dollars** 3.5.1779.	75.00	200.00	—
S3615	**10 Dollars** 3.5.1779.	75.00	200.00	—
S3616	**15 Dollars** 3.5.1779.	75.00	200.00	—
S3617	**50 Dollars = 15 Pounds** 3.5.1779. Ship in l. border.	100.00	300.00	—
S3618	**100 Dollars = 30 Pounds** 3.5.1779. Ship in l. border.	100.00	300.00	—

1780 First Issue

#S3619-S3626 black. Backs red and black. Wmk: *CONFEDERATION* in 2 lines. Various handwritten dates. Printer: David Hall and William Sellers.

		VG	VF	Unc
S3619	**1 Dollar** 1.5.1780.	125.00	250.00	—
S3620	**2 Dollars** 1.5.1780.	125.00	250.00	—
S3621	**3 Dollars** 1.5.1780.	125.00	250.00	—
S3622	**4 Dollars** 1.5.1780.	125.00	250.00	—
S3623	**5 Dollars** 1.5.1780.	125.00	250.00	—
S3624	**7 Dollars** 1.5.1780.	125.00	250.00	—
S3625	**8 Dollars** 1.5.1780.	125.00	250.00	—
S3626	**20 Dollars** 1.5.1780.	125.00	250.00	—

1780 Second Issue

Dollar/Pound Sterling System

#S3627-S3638 black. Denominations on back. Very thin paper.

		VG	VF	Unc
S3627	**3 1/3 Dollars = 20 Shillings** 14.7.1780.	60.00	150.00	300.00
S3628	**6 2/3 Dollars = 2 Pounds** 14.7.1780.	60.00	150.00	300.00
S3629	**10 Dollars = 3 Pounds** 14.7.1780. *Bill* misspelled *Qill.*	60.00	150.00	300.00
S3630	**13 1/3 Dollars = 4 Pounds** 14.7.1780.	60.00	150.00	300.00
S3631	**15 Dollars = 4 Pounds** 14.7.1780.	60.00	150.00	300.00
S3632	**20 Dollars = 6 Pounds** 14.7.1780.	60.00	150.00	300.00
S3633	**35 Dollars = 10 Pounds 10 Shillings** 14.7.1780.	60.00	150.00	300.00
S3634	**45 Dollars = 13 Pounds 10 Shillings** 14.7.1780.	60.00	150.00	300.00
S3635	**55 Dollars = 15 Pounds 10 Shillings** 14.7.1780. *DOLLARS* misspelled *DOLLANS.*	60.00	150.00	300.00
S3636	**60 Dollars = 18 Pounds** 14.7.1780. *Bill* misspelled *DILL.*	60.00	150.00	300.00
S3637	**80 Dollars** 14.7.1780. Lower border text inverted.	60.00	150.00	300.00
S3638	**100 Dollars = 30 Pounds** 14.7.1780.	60.00	150.00	300.00

1780 Third Issue

#S3639-S3644 black. Denominations on back. Very thin paper.

		VG	VF	Unc
S3639	**50 Dollars = 15 Pounds** 16.10.1780.	50.00	125.00	300.00
S3640	**100 Dollars = 30 Pounds** 16.10.1780. *This* misspelled *Tnis.*	50.00	125.00	300.00
S3641	**200 Dollars = 60 Pounds** 16.10.1780.	50.00	125.00	300.00
S3642	**300 Dollars = 90 Pounds** 16.10.1780.	50.00	125.00	300.00
S3643	**400 Dollars = 120 Pounds** 16.10.1780. *HUNDRED* misspelled *HUNDNED.*	50.00	125.00	300.00
S3644	**500 Dollars = 150 Pounds** 16.10.1780. *Bill* misspelled *Qill.*	50.00	125.00	300.00

1780 Act for Clothing the Army Issue

#S3645-S3650 black. Uniface. Very thin laid paper. W/o control letters.

		VG	VF	Unc
S3645	**100 Dollars = 30 Pounds** 16.10.1780.	475.00	1000.	—
S3646	**200 Dollars = 60 Pounds** 16.10.1780.	475.00	1000.	—
S3647	**300 Dollars = 90 Pounds** 16.10.1780.	475.00	1000.	—
S3648	**400 Dollars = 120 Pounds** 16.10.1780. *HUNDRED* misspelled *HUNDNED.*	475.00	1000.	—
S3649	**500 Dollars = 150 Pounds** 16.10.1780. *Bill* misspelled *Qill.*	475.00	1000.	—
S3650	**1000 Dollars = 300 Pounds** 16.10.1780.	600.00	1350.	—

1781 First Issue

#S3651-S3658 black. Both very thin laid paper or thick laid paper.

		VG	VF	Unc
S3651	**20 Dollars = 6 Pounds** 1.3.1781.	60.00	135.00	425.00
S3652	**50 Dollars = 15 Pounds** 1.3.1781.	60.00	135.00	425.00
S3653	**80 Dollars = 24 Pounds** 1.3.1781.	60.00	135.00	425.00
S3654	**150 Dollars = 45 Pounds** 1.3.1781. *DOLLARS* misspelled *DOLLARAE.*	60.00	135.00	425.00
S3655	**250 Dollars = 75 Pounds** 1.3.1781. *DOLLARS* misspelled *DOLLAR8.*	60.00	135.00	425.00
S3656	**500 Dollars = 150 Pounds** 1.3.1781. *FIVE* misspelled *OIVE.*	60.00	135.00	425.00
S3657	**750 Dollars = 225 Pounds** 1.3.1781. POUN(D)S, *Bill* misspelled *Qill.*	70.00	150.00	465.00
S3658	**1000 Dollars = 300 Pounds** 1.3.1781.	80.00	170.00	500.00

1781 Second Issue

#S3659-S3674 black. Printer: John Dunlap, Philadelphia.

		VG	VF	Unc
S3659	**10 Dollars = 3 Pounds** 7.5.1781.	80.00	160.00	400.00
S3660	**15 Dollars = 4 Pounds 10 Shillings** 7.5.1781.	80.00	160.00	400.00
S3661	**25 Dollars = 7 Pounds 10 Shillings** 7.5.1781.	80.00	160.00	400.00
S3662	**30 Dollars = 9 Pounds** 7.5.1781.	80.00	160.00	400.00
S3663	**35 Dollars = 10 Pounds 10 Shillings** 7.5.1781.	80.00	160.00	400.00
S3664	**40 Dollars = 12 Pounds** 7.5.1781.	80.00	160.00	400.00
S3665	**50 Dollars = 15 Pounds** 7.5.1781.	80.00	160.00	400.00
S3666	**70 Dollars = 21 Pounds** 7.5.1781.	80.00	160.00	400.00
S3667	**75 Dollars = 22 Pounds 15 Shillings** 7.5.1781.	75.00	150.00	400.00
S3668	**100 Dollars = 30 Pounds** 7.5.1781.	75.00	150.00	400.00
S3669	**200 Dollars = 60 Pounds** 7.5.1781. *WF* in lower border.	75.00	150.00	400.00
S3670	**500 Dollars = 150 Pounds** 7.5.1781.	75.00	150.00	400.00
S3671	**1000 Dollars = 300 Pounds** 7.5.1781.	75.00	150.00	400.00
S3672	**1200 Dollars = 360 Pounds** 7.5.1781.	90.00	200.00	500.00
S3673	**1500 Dollars = 450 Pounds** 7.5.1781.	110.00	275.00	600.00
S3674	**2000 Dollars = 600 Pounds** 7.5.1781.	140.00	325.00	700.00

Virginia

Civil War

1861 Treasury Issue

#S3675-S3680 various handwritten dates. Engraver: Hoyer and Ludwig.

		VG	VF	Unc
S3675	**5 Dollars** 15.10.1861. Girl at lower l., seated Ceres in lg. *V* at r.	40.00	75.00	150.00

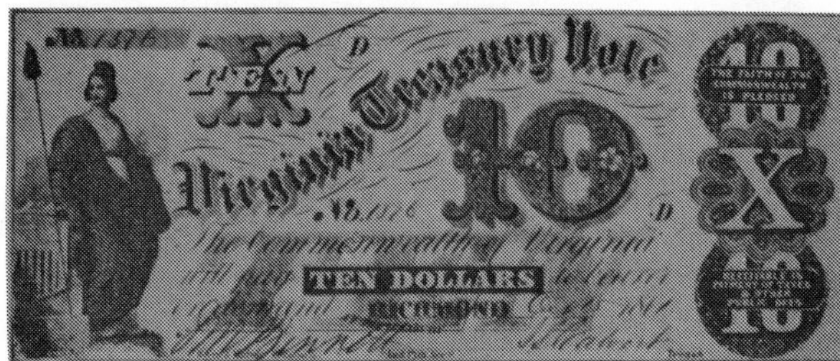

		VG	VF	Unc
S3676	**10 Dollars** 15.10.1861. Standing Liberty w/shield at l.	50.00	75.00	150.00

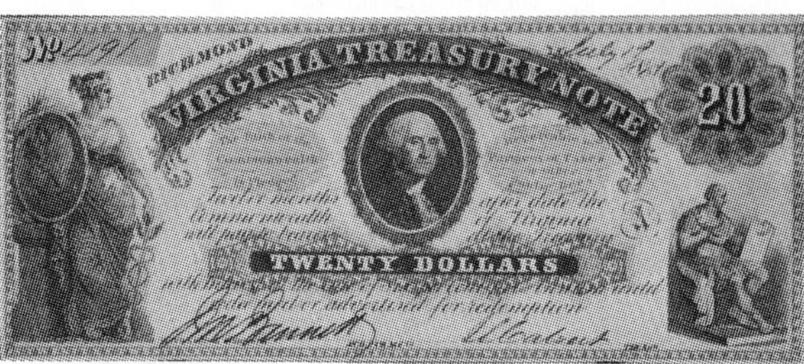

		VG	VF	Unc
S3677	**20 Dollars** 1.8.1861. Black on green unpt. Standing Minerva at l., portr. G. Washington at ctr., seated man reading script at r.	60.00	125.00	175.00

		VG	VF	Unc
S3678	**50 Dollars** 13.8.1861. Black on red unpt. Gladiator at l., Ceres and Commerce w/urn at top ctr., J. Tyler at r.	450.00	900.00	1850.

		VG	VF	Unc
S3679	**100 Dollars** 13.8.1861. Black on red unpt. Woman reclining at l., portr. G. Washington between seated woman and man in unpt. at ctr.	750.00	1500.	2500.
S3680	**500 Dollars** 25.9.1861. 3 women seated at l., portr. G. Washington at upper r.	—	Rare	—

1862 TREASURY ISSUE

#S3681-S3685 engraver: Keatinge & Ball.

	VG	VF	UNC
S3681 1 DOLLAR 1862. Black on red unpt. Portr. Gov. J. Letcher at l., seated Ceres at ctr.			
a. 15.5.1862.	8.00	13.00	35.00
b. 21.7.1862.	7.00	12.00	30.00
c. 21.10.1862.	8.00	15.00	30.00

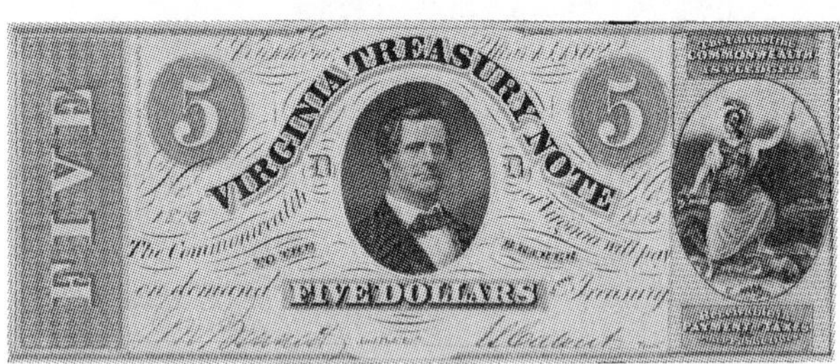

	VG	VF	UNC
S3682 5 DOLLARS 13.3.1862. Black on green unpt. Portr. Gov. J. M. Bennett at ctr., Gladiatorial figure at r. Plain paper.			
a. Wmk: *Hodgkinson & Co. Wookey Hole Mill.*	75.00	110.00	150.00
b. Wmk: *CSA.*	20.00	35.00	75.00
c. Wmk: *J. Whatman.*	50.00	75.00	125.00
S3683 10 DOLLARS 15.10.1862. Black on green unpt. Hercules in cartouche at l., seated Ceres at ctr., Gov. J. B. Floyd at r. Plain paper.			
b. Wmk: *FIVE.*	30.00	70.00	100.00
c. Wmk: *W.T.C.C. & Co.*	30.00	45.00	100.00
d. Wmk: *J. Green & Sons 1862.*	75.00	125.00	200.00

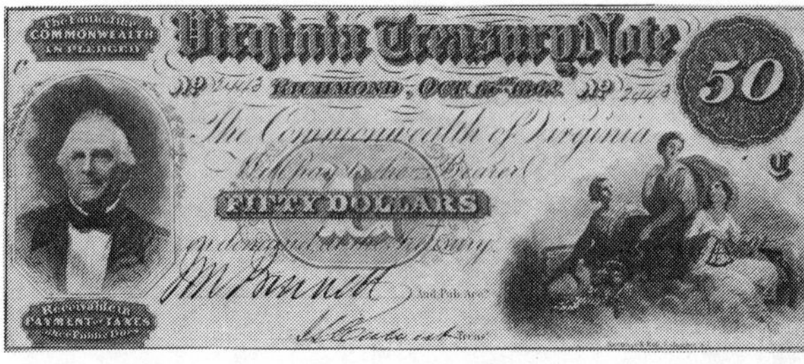

	VG	VF	UNC
S3684 50 DOLLARS 15.10.1862. Portr. Gov. J. M. Mason at l., seated Ceres between Commerce and Navigation at lower r.	40.00	75.00	125.00

	VG	VF	UNC
S3685 100 DOLLARS 15.10.1862. Black on orange unpt. Portr. G. Washington at l., portr. Gov. Letcher L. Washington at ctr., Indian girl at r.	50.00	85.00	175.00

The Oriental Republic of Uruguay (so called because of its location on the east bank of the Uruguay River) is situated on the Atlantic coast of South America between Argentina and Brazil. This most advanced of South American countries has an area of 68,536 sq. mi. (176,220 sq. km.) and a population of 3.27 million. Capital: Montevideo. Uruguay's chief economic asset is its rich, rolling grassy plains. Meat, wool, hides and skins are exported.

Uruguay was discovered in 1516 by Juan Diaz de Solis, a Spaniard, but settled by the Portuguese who founded Colonia in 1680. Spain contested Portuguese possession and, after a long struggle, gained control of the country in 1778. During the general South American struggle for independence, Uruguay's first attempt was led by gaucho soldier José Gervasio Artigas leading the Banda Oriental which was quelled by Spanish and Portuguese forces in 1811. The armistice was soon broken and Argentine forces from Buenos Aires cast off the Spanish bond in the Plata region in 1814, only to be reconquered by the Portuguese from Brazil in the struggle of 1816-20. Revolt flared anew in 1825 and independence was reasserted in 1828 with the help of Argentina. The Uruguayan Republic was established in 1830.

In 1919, a new constitution established a plural executive, but this was abolished in 1933. A presidential government existed from 1933 to 1951 at which time a collective form of leadership was formed through 1966. Strikes and riots in the 1960's brought the military to power until 1985 when Julio Maria Sanguinetti established a government of national unity.

MONETARY SYSTEM:

1 Patacón = 960 Reis
1 Peso = 8 Reales to 1860
1 Peso = 100 Centésimos
1 Doblon = 10 Pesos, 1860-1875

BANK ISSUES

STATE ISSUE

BANKS

BANCO COMERCIAL, MONTEVIDEO

1857 ISSUE

	GOOD	FINE	XF
S95 240 CENTÉSIMOS 21.9.1857. Black. Beehives at upper ctr.	—	—	—

1858 ISSUES

	GOOD	FINE	XF
S101 120 CENTÉSIMOS 1.10.1858. Brown. Printer: Lit. Mege.	400.00	—	—
S106 240 CENTÉSIMOS 1.10.1858. Black. Lion at upper ctr. Printer: Lit. Mege.	500.00	—	—

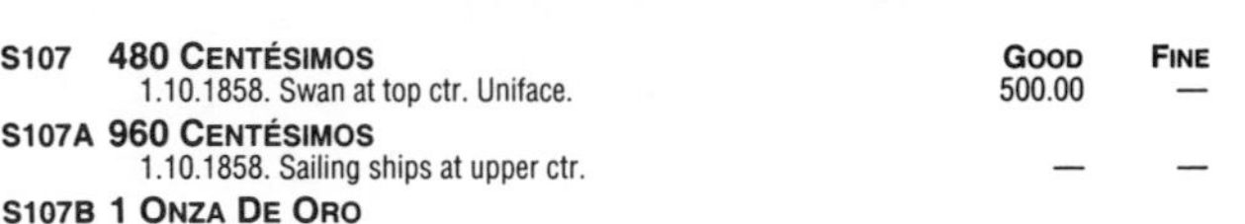

S107 480 CENTÉSIMOS	GOOD	FINE	XF
1.10.1858. Swan at top ctr. Uniface.	500.00	—	—

S107A 960 CENTÉSIMOS | | |
---|---|---|---
1.10.1858. Sailing ships at upper ctr. | — | — | —

S107B 1 ONZA DE ORO | | |
---|---|---|---
1.10.1858. Horse at upper ctr. | — | — | —

S108 1 ONZA DE ORO	GOOD	FINE	XF
1.10.1858. Wagon at ctr., city in background. Printer: H. Bradbury & Co.	1000.	—	—

1860 ISSUE

#S111-S113 printer: H. Bradbury & Co.

S111 240 CENTÉSIMOS	GOOD	FINE	XF
1.1.1860. Black. Orange paper.	400.00	—	—

S112 480 CENTÉSIMOS	GOOD	FINE	XF
1.1.1860. Black. Blue paper.	700.00	—	—

S113 960 CENTÉSIMOS	GOOD	FINE	XF
1.1.1860.	1000.	—	—

LAW OF 23.6.1862; 1863 ISSUE

S121 10 CENTÉSIMOS	GOOD	FINE	XF
3.1.1863. Medallic woman portr. at ctr. Printer: Lit. A. Hequet y Cohas Hnos.	300.00	—	—

#S122-S125A printer: BWC.

S122 20 CENTÉSIMOS	GOOD	FINE	XF
2.1.1863. Black. Yellow paper. Uniface.	150.00	—	—

S123 50 CENTÉSIMOS	GOOD	FINE	XF
2.1.1863. Black on brown unpt. Uniface.	300.00	—	—

		Good	Fine	XF
S124	**1 Peso** 2.1.1863. Black and lt. brown-orange. Green paper.	800.00	—	—

		Good	Fine	XF
S125	**1 Doblon** 2.1.1863. Woman at top ctr.			
	a. Issued note.	1000.	—	—
	p. Proof.	—	Unc	1200.
S125A	**2 Doblones** 2.1.1863. Similar to #S125.	—	—	—

Law of 23.6.1862; 1872 Issues

Law of 23.6.1862

		Good	Fine	XF
S126	**10 Pesos** 1.4.1872. Black, brown, green and salmon. Seated allegorical woman w/2 children at top center; woman's head at l. and r.	1000.	—	—
S128	**100 Pesos** 1.10.1872. Woman at l. and r. Payable text: *(en billetes de curso legal).*	—	—	—
S129	**100 Pesos** 1.10.1872. Two women at ctr.	—	—	—

1886 Issue

		Good	Fine	XF
S130	**10 Pesos = 1 Doblon** 1.10.1886. Standing allegorical figure at l., woman w/train and farm scene at ctr., woman at r. Printer: W&S.	—	—	—

Banco Comercial de Paysandú, Paysandú

1863 Issue

#S131-S136 printer: Lit. A. Hequet y Cohas Hnos, Montevideo. Uniface.

		Good	Fine	XF
S131	**5 Centésimos** 4.1.1863. Black. Dog running at ctr.			
	a. Issued note.	—	—	—
	b. Black oval handstamp: *BANCO COMERCIAL PAY-SANDU/AGENCIA DE MERCEDES* at r.	—	—	—
S133	**20 Centésimos** 4.1.1863. Black. Mountain w/sailboat at ctr. Blue paper.	—	—	—

		Good	Fine	XF
S133A	**25 Centésimos** 4.1.1863 printed date, 30.6.1865 hand dated. Black. Ostrich at ctr.	—	—	—
S134	**50 Centésimos** 4.1.1863.	—	—	—

		Good	Fine	XF
S135	**1 Peso** 4.1.1863; 28.2.1863. Black on blue unpt. Standing woman at l. and r., galloping stallion at ctr.			
	a. Issued note.	—	—	—
	b. Black oval handstamp: *BANCO COMERCIAL DE PAYSANDU/AGENCIA DE MERCEDES* at r. 4.1.1863.	—	—	—
S136	**2 Pesos** 4.1.1863. Green and black on pink paper. Bull at ctr.	—	—	—

1866 Issue

#S141-S149 printer: ABNC.

		Good	Fine	XF
S141	**20 Centésimos** 30.6.1866. Black on red unpt. Dog at lower l., plow and farm implements at upper ctr., allegorical women flanking shield at lower r. Uniface.	—	—	—
S142	**25 Centésimos** 30.6.1866. Black on blue unpt. Cherub at lower l. and r., girl's head at upper ctr.			
	a. Issued note.	—	—	—
	b. Blue oval handstamp: *AGENCIA DEL BANCO COMERCIAL DE PAYSANDU/MERCEDES* at r.	—	—	—
S143	**50 Centésimos** 30.6.1866. Black on blue-green unpt. Dog at upper l., young girl at lower r. Proof.	—	—	—
S144	**1 Peso** 30.6.1866. Black on brown unpt. 2 cherubs holding fruit at l., 3 farmers w/sheep at upper ctr., woman w/produce at r. Proof.	—	—	—

		Good	Fine	XF
S145	**2 Pesos** 30.6.1866. Black on green unpt. Portr. young woman at lower l., seated allegorical woman at upper ctr., young girl at lower r. Uniface.	—	—	—

		Good	Fine	XF
S148	**10 Pesos = 1 Doblon** 30.6.1866. Black on red-orange unpt. Seated woman at lower l., vaqueros w/cattle at upper ctr., woman at lower r. Back brown.	—	—	—
S149	**20 Pesos = 2 Doblones** 30.6.1866. Black on orange unpt. Woman at l., horse's head between Indian woman and allegorical woman at ctr., shield at r. Back green. Proof.	—	—	—

NOTE: Some issues of this bank have oval ovpt. at r. for *Agencia de Mercedes*.

Banco Comercial del Salto, Salto

1866 Issue

#S152-S159 printer: ABNC.

		Good	Fine	XF
S152	**20 Centésimos** 1.4.1866. Black on olive unpt. Beehive at lower l. and r., steamship at upper ctr. Proof.	—	—	—

		Good	Fine	XF
S153	**50 Centésimos** 1.4.1866. Black on green unpt. Dog on top of safe at upper ctr. Proof.	—	—	—
S154	**1 Peso** 1.4.1866. Black on orange unpt. Young girl at lower l., galloping stallion at upper ctr., bull's head at lower r.	—	—	—

		Good	Fine	XF
S157	**10 Pesos = 1 Doblon** 1.4.1866. Black on green unpt. Seated woman w/sheaf and sickle at lower l., vaquero chasing bull at upper ctr., young girl w/puppies at lower r.			
	a. Issued note.	—	—	—
	p. Proof.	—	—	—
S158	**20 Pesos = 2 Doblones** 1.4.1866. Black on orange unpt. Woman at lower l., seated allegorical woman holding sword w/child in wharf scene at upper ctr., eagle on cliff at lower r. Proof.	—	—	—

		Good	Fine	XF
S159	**50 Pesos = 5 Doblones** 1.4.1866. Black on green unpt. Man and dog at lower l., village scene at upper ctr., cow at lower r. Uniface.	—	—	—

Banco de Crédito Auxiliar, Montevideo

Law of 25.10.1887

#S161-S168 printer: CSABB, Buenos Aires.

		Good	Fine	XF
S161	**4 Centésimos** *L.1887.* Blue. Series A.			
	a. Signed and dated. 29.9.1888.	25.00	45.00	—
	r. Unsigned remainder.	—	Unc	5.00

		Good	Fine	XF
S162	**50 Centésimos** 1.10.1888. Black on rose or brown unpt. Series A.			
	a. Signed and dated.	—	—	—
	r. Unsigned remainder.	—	Unc	7.00

		Good	Fine	XF
S163	**10 Pesos** *L.1887.* Black on blue unpt. Shoreline at r. Back blue. Series A.			
	a. Signed and dated.	—	—	—
	r. Unsigned remainder.	—	—	—

		Good	Fine	XF
S164	**20 Pesos** *L.1887.* Black on green unpt. Harvest scene at ctr. Back green. Series B.			
	a. Signed and dated.	3.00	6.00	12.00
	r. Unsigned remainder.	—	Unc	8.00

		Good	Fine	XF
S165	**50 Pesos** *L.1887.* Black on tan unpt. 2 horses at l. Back orange. Series C.			
	a. Signed and dated. 1.1.1888-1.1.1889.	5.00	12.00	25.00
	r. Unsigned remainder.	—	Unc	9.00

NOTE: #S165a also has rectangular or round stamping on back for 8% interest paid, and a rectangular revenue adhesive stamp affixed to the back.

		Good	Fine	XF
S168	**1000 Pesos** *L.1887.* 2 allegorical figures standing at l. Cows at water on back. Series E.			
	a. Issued note.	—	—	—
	r. Unsigned remainder.	—	Unc	150.00

NOTE: Other denominations are reported, not confirmed.

Banco de España y Río de la Plata, Montevideo

1888 Issue

#S169 and S170 printer: ABNC.

		Good	Fine	XF
S169	**10 Pesos** 1.1.1888. Black on orange and green unpt. 2 allegorical women at l., sailors sighting land at ctr., cattle at r. Back orange; steam passenger train, allegorical woman w/shield and implements, and sailing ship at ctr.			
	a. Issued note.	—	—	—
	p. Proof.	—	—	—

		Good	Fine	XF
S170	**100 Pesos** 1.1.1888. Black on blue and brown unpt. C. Columbus, Indian woman and crowned shield at l., eagle at ctr., seated allegorical woman w/shield at r. Back dk. brown; girl at l., sailing ships at ctr. r. Proof.	—	—	—

Banco Franco-Platense, Montevideo

Some notes of this bank have branch office stampings on face.

Law of 1.5.1870; 1871 Issues

		Good	Fine	XF
S171	**10 Pesos = 1 Doblon** 1.5.1871. Black on orange and green unpt. Liberty w/caduceus and shields at l. Back brown. Printer: A. Hequet y Cohas Hos.			
	a. Signed.	20.00	50.00	—
	b. W/o sign.	5.00	10.00	25.00

#S172 and S173 printer: ABNC.

		Good	Fine	XF
S172	**10 Pesos = 1 Doblon** 1.8.1871. Black on orange unpt. 3 shields at l., reclining woman at dockside w/sailing ship at ctr., 2 young girls at r. Back orange.			
	a. Signed.	5.00	10.00	35.00
	b. W/o sign.	3.00	5.00	17.50

		Good	Fine	XF
S173	**20 Pesos = 2 Doblones** 1.8.1871. Black on orange unpt. 3 shields at l., ship on stormy sea at ctr., 2 young girls at r. Back orange.			
	a. Signed.	6.00	15.00	45.00
	b. W/o sign.	3.00	6.00	22.50

Banco Herrera, Eastman & Ca., Montevideo

1873 Issue

		Good	Fine	XF
S181	**10 Pesos** 1.1.1873. Black and blue. Portr. Mercury at upper l., portr. woman below, bldg. at r. Back lt. violet; head at l. and r. Printer: BWC.	—	Rare	—

Banco Inglés del Rio de la Plata, Montevideo

1885 Issue

#S191 and S194 printer: BWC.

		GOOD	FINE	XF
S191	**10 PESOS** 1.5.1885. Black on blue and yellow unpt. Allegorical woman at l. and r. Back black, blue, green and brown; cow, sheaf, ram and plant at ctr.			
	a. Issued note.	100.00	300.00	—
	b. Branch ovpt: *PAYSANDU.*	150.00	—	—
	c. Branch ovpt: *SALTO.*	150.00	—	—

		GOOD	FINE	XF
S194	**100 PESOS** 1.5.1885. Black on pink unpt. Standing Minerva w/shield and staff at l., animals around oval ctr. w/arms at top, woman at r. Back black on red and green unpt.; 2 horses pulling man in sm. cart at ctr.	600.00	—	—

BANCO ITALIANO, MONTEVIDEO

1867 ISSUE

#S201-S209 printer: ABNC.

		GOOD	FINE	XF
S201	**20 CENTÉSIMOS** 2.1.1867. Black on orange unpt. Boy w/cows at ctr. Back brown.			
	a. Issued note.	—	Rare	—
	b. 3-line black handstamp: *SUCURSAL DEL BANCO ITALIANO SAN CARLOS.*	—	—	—
	p. Proof. .	—	—	—

		GOOD	FINE	XF
S202	**50 CENTÉSIMOS** 2.1.1867. Black on green unpt. Gaucho on horse w/cattle and sheep at ctr. Back orange.			
	a. Issued note.	—	Rare	—
	p. Proof.	—	—	—

		GOOD	FINE	XF
S203	**1 PESO** 2.1.1867; 2.1.1869. Black on orange unpt. 4 cherubs w/numeral *1* at l., girl at top ctr. r. Back green.			
	a. Issued note.	—	Rare	—
	b. Square 3-line blue handstamp: *SUCURSAL DEL BANCO ITALIANO MERCEDES.*	—	—	—
	s. Specimen.	—	—	—
S204	**1 PESO** 2.1.1867. Black on green unpt. Like #S203. Blue ovpt: *SUCURSAL DEL BANCO ITALIANO MERCEDES* in square.	—	Rare	—

		GOOD	FINE	XF
S206	**10 PESOS = 1 DOBLON** 2.1.1867. Black on brown unpt. Justice at l., cherub at upper l. ctr. and ctr. r., allegorical woman w/barrels at r. Back orange; arms at ctr. Proof.	—	—	—

		Good	Fine	XF
S207	**20 Pesos = 2 Doblones** 2.1.1867. Black on dk. orange unpt. Young girl's head at lower l., winged allegorical woman blowing horn w/globe and condor at l. ctr., arms at lower r. Back blue. Proof.	—	—	—

		Good	Fine	XF
S208	**50 Pesos = 5 Doblones** 2.1.1867. Black on green unpt. C. Columbus sighting land at l., allegorical woman w/marine implements at upper ctr., cherub w/flowers at r. Back brownish purple. Proof.	—	—	—

		Good	Fine	XF
S209	**100 Pesos = 10 Doblones** 2.1.1867. Black on blue unpt. Allegorical woman leaning on anchor at l., sailor holding horn at upper ctr. r., cherub w/sheaf and sickle at lower r. Back dk. brown. Proof.	—	—	—

Banco Italiano del Uruguay, Montevideo

1887 Issues

#S212-S215 printer: ABNC.

		Good	Fine	XF
S212	**10 Pesos** 20.9.1887. Black on blue and brown-violet unpt. Portr. Cavour at lower l., 2 allegorical women standing w/2 flags and arms at ctr., portr. Garibaldi at lower r. Back blue on yellow unpt.; seated woman w/gear and bales at ctr.			
	a. Issued note.	—	Rare	—
	b. Branch ovpt: *MERCEDES.*	—	—	—
	r. Unsigned remainder.	—	Unc	17.50

		Good	Fine	XF
S214	**100 Pesos** 20.9.1887. Black on green and orange unpt. Portr. Kg. Vittorio Emanuele II at l., portr. C. Columbus at r. Back brown on yellow unpt.; cow at l., vaqueros w/cows at r.			
	a. Issued note w/sign. titles: PRESIDENTE/DIRECTOR GERENTE.	—	Rare	—
	b. Issued note w/o sign. titles.	—	—	—
	p. Proof.	—	—	—
	s. Specimen.	—	—	—

NOTE: Virtually all signed and issued notes of #S212 and S214 are cancelled. Remainders range generally from 30,000 to 50,000 for #S212 and above 7,000 for #S214.

		Good	Fine	XF
S215	**100 Pesos** 20.9.1887. Like #S214, but back green on yellow unpt. Remainder.	—	Unc	20.00

Banco Italo-Oriental, Montevideo

1889 Issue

#S222 and S225 printer: W&S.

		Good	Fine	XF
S222	**10 Pesos** 10.6.1889.	—	—	—

		Good	Fine	XF
S225	**100 Pesos** 10.6.1889. 3 allegorical women w/sheaves and other implements at ctr. Specimen.	—	Unc	300.00

Banco de Londres y Rio de la Plata, Montevideo

Law of 23.6.1862; 1865 Issue

#S231-S233 printer: BWC.

		Good	Fine	XF
S231	**20 Centésimos** 1.7.1865. Black and olive-gray. Galloping stallion at l., English arms at r.	—	—	—
S232	**50 Centésimos** 1.7.1865. Liberty standing at l., British shield at r.	—	—	—

		Good	Fine	XF
S233	**1 Peso** 1.7.1865. Black and blue-gray. Arms at l. and r.	—	—	—

1867 Issue

#S234 and S235 printer: BWC.

		Good	Fine	XF
S234	**20 Centésimos** 1.1.1867. Galloping stallion at l.	—	—	—
S235	**50 Centésimos** 1.1.1867. Bull at l.	—	—	—

1872 Issue

#S237 and S238 printer: BWC.

		Good	Fine	XF
S237	**20 Pesos = 2 Doblones** 1.1.1872. Black on lt. green and lt. brown unpt. Similar to #S238 but English arms at upper r.	—	—	—

		Good	Fine	XF
S238	**50 Pesos = 5 Doblones** 1.1.1872. Green and brown. Liberty standing w/sword, shield and flag at l., British shield at r.			
	a. Issued note.	—	—	—
	r. Unsigned remainder.	—	Unc	12.00

1870's Issue

#S239 and S240 printer: BWC.

		Good	Fine	XF
S239	**10 Pesos** 187-. Black on green and orange unpt. Like #S242. Back green. Unsigned remainder.	—	—	—
S240	**20 Pesos** 187-. Black on blue and orange unpt. Similar to #S239 but different figure at r. Back blue; head at l. and r. Unsigned remainder.	—	—	—

1883 Issue

#S242 and S245 printer: BWC.

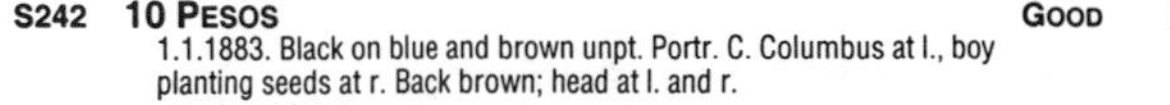

		Good	Fine	XF
S242	**10 Pesos** 1.1.1883. Black on blue and brown unpt. Portr. C. Columbus at l., boy planting seeds at r. Back brown; head at l. and r.			
	a. Issued note.	—	—	—
	r. Unsigned remainder.	—	Unc	8.00
S245	**100 Pesos** (date filled in). Black on yellow unpt. Portr. C. Columbus at l., boy running w/rope at r. Woman's head at ctr. on back.			
	a. Issued note.	—	—	—
	r. Unsigned remainder.	—	Unc	15.00

NOTE: Beware of notes falsely signed w/serial # over 415000 ($10.) (see #S245 illustration) or 60000 ($100.). Original issued notes must have a scalloped cutting line at l. margin.

Banco Mauá & Cia., Montevideo

1857 Issue

		Good	Fine	XF
S251	**240 Centésimos** 1.8.1857. Printer: BWC.	—	—	—

		Good	Fine	XF
S252	**480 Centésimos** 1.9.1857. Black on gray paper. Uniface.	200.00	550.00	—
S253	**960 Centésimos** 10.8.1857. Branch ovpt: *AGENCIA DEL BANCO MAUA PAYSANDU.* Printer: BWC.	—	—	—

1860-62 Issue

		Good	Fine	XF
S255	**240 Centésimos** 2.1.1861. Printer: Bradbury and Evans.	—	—	—
S256	**480 Centésimos** 2.1.1861.	—	—	—

#S257 and S258 printer: BWC.

		GOOD	FINE	XF
S257	**960 CENTÉSIMOS** 1.8.1861.	—	—	—

		GOOD	FINE	XF
S258	**1 ONZA DE ORO** 1860; 1862.	—	—	—

1863-65 ISSUE

#S261-S263 printer: BWC.

		GOOD	FINE	XF
S261	**20 CENTÉSIMOS** 2.1.1863. Black and green on rose paper.	40.00	125.00	—
S262	**50 CENTÉSIMOS** 2.1.1863. Orange and black on yellow paper.			
	a. Issued note.	40.00	125.00	—
	b. Branch ovpt: *AGENCIA DEL. . . PAYSANDU.*	—	—	—
	c. Blue branch ovpt: *AGENCIA DEL . . . SALTO.*	—	—	—

		GOOD	FINE	XF
S263	**1 PESO** 2.1.1863. Black on red unpt. Uniface.			
	a. Issued note.	50.00	200.00	—
	b. Branch ovpt: *AGENCIA DEL. . . SALTO.*	—	—	—
S265	**10 PESOS** 1865. Black and brownish-red. Oval branch stamping: *PAYSANDU.* Uniface.	—	—	—
S266	**20 PESOS** 2.1.1863. Blue and red, violet paper. Woman reclining at ctr.	—	—	—

Companion Volumes

Volume II – General Issues 1368-1960

Volume III – Modern Issues 1961-present

The Companion catalogs in the Standard Catalog of World Paper Money Series include two volumes on bank notes issued for national use. Those dated 1960 and before are in volume II, those dated 1961 and later are in volume III. Ordering information can be obtained from Krause Publications Book Division, 1-800-258-0929.

1865 ISSUE

#S271-S281 printer: BWC.

#S271-S273 portr. Irineo Evangelista de Souza, Vizconde de Mauá at l.

		GOOD	FINE	XF
S271	**20 CENTÉSIMOS** 1.7.1865. Black on green unpt. Child at top ctr.	50.00	200.00	—
S272	**50 CENTÉSIMOS** 1.7.1865. Black on red unpt. Pale rose paper. 2 children w/anvil at upper ctr.	50.00	200.00	—

		GOOD	FINE	XF
S273	**1 PESO** 1.7.1865. Black on green unpt., pale yellow paper. Child at top ctr.	50.00	200.00	—

#S276-S279 portr. V. Mauá at upper ctr.

		GOOD	FINE	XF
S276	**10 PESOS** 1.7.1865. Child at l.	—	—	—
S277	**20 PESOS** 1.7.1865. Black on green and red unpt. Boy at l. Back like face, but inverted w/o black print.	—	—	—

		GOOD	FINE	XF
S279	**100 PESOS** 1.7.1865. Blue and m/c. Cherub in boat at l., gaucho on galloping stallion at r. Uniface.	—	—	—

1869-70 ISSUE

		Good	Fine	XF
S281	**100 Pesos** 1.7.1869. Black, grayish blue and salmon. Portr. V. Mauá at ctr. Retrograde printing of frame but w/bust of Minerva at ctr. on back.	—	—	—

		Good	Fine	XF
S283	**10 Pesos = 1 Doblon** 1.9.1870. Liberty standing w/shield and anchor at l. Printer: Hequet y Cohas Hos.	—	—	—

		Good	Fine	XF
S284	**20 Pesos = 2 Doblones** 1.9.1870. Black on yellow and red unpt. Mercury and lion at l. Back green.	—	—	—

LAW OF 4.5.1870; 1871 ISSUE

#S291 and S292 printer: BWC.

		Good	Fine	XF
S291	**10 Pesos = 1 Doblon** 1.3.1871. Green. Portr. young girl at r.	40.00	150.00	—

		Good	Fine	XF
S292	**20 Pesos = 2 Doblones** 1.3.1871. Black on red and green, rose paper. Portr. woman at top ctr.	3.00	12.00	30.00

1875 ISSUE

#S301-S309 printer: BWC.

		Good	Fine	XF
S301	**20 Centésimos** 26.10.1875. Black on orange unpt. Portr. woman at l.	50.00	150.00	—

		Good	Fine	XF
S302	**50 Centésimos** 26.10.1875. Green, rose paper. Woman w/sickle and sheaf at l.	50.00	150.00	—

		Good	Fine	XF
S303	**1 Peso** 26.10.1875. Black on orange unpt. Yellow paper. Portr. Liberty at l., young bird at r. Back lt. brown.	75.00	250.00	—

		Good	Fine	XF
S304	**2 Pesos** 26.10.1875. Black on red unpt. Portr. Mauá at l., portr. woman at r. Back red.	50.00	200.00	—

		Good	Fine	XF
S305	**5 Pesos** 26.10.1875. Black on blue and red unpt. Pink paper. Barón Mauá at l., bull at upper ctr., Liberty at r. Back blue; 2 cameo heads.	—	—	—

		Good	Fine	XF
S309	**100 Pesos** 1.7.1869. Altered date. *75* written over *69*. Ovpt: *ORO SELLADO* on #S281.	—	Rare	—

1876 Issue

#S311-S315 like #S301-S305.

		Good	Fine	XF
S311	**20 Centésimos** 3.1.1876. Like #S301.	—	—	—
S312	**50 Centésimos** 3.1.1876. Like #S302.	—	—	—
S313	**1 Peso** 3.1.1876. Black and orange on yellow paper. Like #S303.	—	—	—
S314	**2 Pesos** 3.1.1876. Like #S304.	—	—	—
S315	**5 Pesos** 3.1.1876. Like #S305.	—	—	—

		Good	Fine	XF
S320	**50 Pesos** 1.1.1876. Farm implements at ctr., horse at r. Printer: NBNC.			
	p. Proof.	—	—	—
	r. Remainder w/o sign.	—	Unc	500.00

		Good	Fine	XF
S321	**100 Pesos** 1.1.1876. Black and blue. Harbor and city view of Montevideo at ctr. Back brown. Printer: NBNC.			
	a. Hand signed issued note. Scalloped cutting line at l.	—	—	—
	p. Proof.	—	—	—
	r. Remainder w/o sign., straight cutting line at l.	—	Unc	500.00

Banco Mercantil del Rio de la Plata, Montevideo

1873 Issue

#S333-S336 Minerva at ctr. Printer: BWC.

		Good	Fine	XF
S333	**10 Pesos** 1.9.1873. Black and green. Back green and red.	—	Rare	—
S334	**20 Pesos** 1.9.1873.	—	—	—
S335	**50 Pesos** 1.9.1873.	—	—	—
S336	**100 Pesos** 1.9.1873.	—	—	—

Banco Montevideano, Montevideo

1865 Issue

#S341 and S346 printer: Litog. Wiegeland, Montevideo.

		Good	Fine	XF
S341	**20 Centésimos** 1.8.1865. Black. Lg. denomination in unpt. at ctr.	—	—	—

		Good	Fine	XF
S346	**10 Pesos = 1 Doblon** 1.8.1865. Brown. Standing woman at l. in numeral *1*. Back blue.	—	—	—

1866 Issue

#S351-S359 printer: ABNC.

		Good	Fine	XF
S351	**20 Centésimos** 3.1.1866. Black on green unpt. Steamship at ctr. Back green.	—	—	—

		Good	Fine	XF
S352	**50 Centésimos** 3.1.1866. Black on green unpt. Cherub at lower l. and r., young girl's head at upper ctr.			
	a. Issued note.	—	—	—
	b. Branch ovpt: *SUCURSAL. . . DOLORES.*	—	—	—

		Good	Fine	XF
S353	**1 Peso** 3.1.1866. Black on green unpt. 2 children at lower l., galloping stallion at top ctr., bull's head at r. Uniface.	150.00	375.00	—

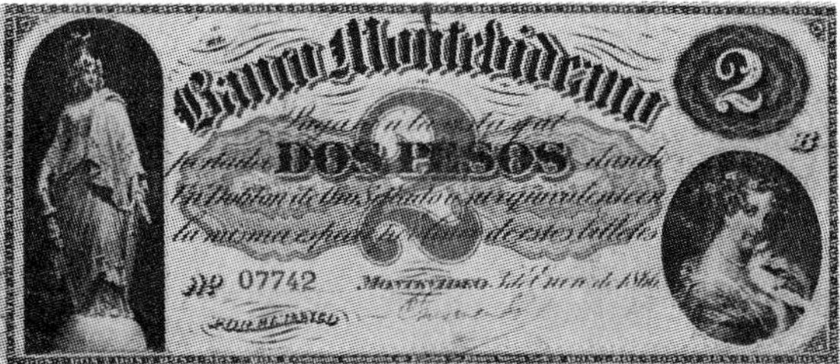

		Good	Fine	XF
S354	**2 Pesos** 3.1.1866. Black on green and red unpt. Statue of Freedom at l., woman w/bird at lower r. Lg. *2* in unpt. at ctr.	300.00	500.00	—
S356	**10 Pesos = 1 Doblon** 3.1.1866. Black on green unpt. Woman at lower l., woman reclining w/globe at top ctr., arms at r.	—	—	—

		Good	Fine	XF
S357	**20 Pesos = 2 Doblones** 3.1.1866. Black on green unpt. Sheep at upper l., man at lower r.	—	Rare	—
S358	**50 Pesos = 5 Doblones** 3.1.1866. Black on green unpt. Justice w/barrels and boxes at l., landing of Columbus at ctr., Columbus at r. Archive copy.	—	—	—
S359	**100 Pesos = 10 Doblones** 3.1.1866. Black on green unpt. Dog on top of safe at lower l., cattle watering in pond at upper ctr., horse at bottom ctr., man at lower r. Archive copy.	—	—	—

Banco Navia y Ca., Montevideo

Began operations in 1866, closed in 1874. The bank notes were nationalized under the Law of June 11, 1875 and were gradually retired from circulation.

1865 First Issue

#S361 and S362 printer: A. Hequet y Cohas Hos.

		Good	Fine	XF
S361	**1 Peso** 1.9.1865. Red.	—	Rare	—

		Good	Fine	XF
S362	**1 Doblon** 1.9.1865. Black and red on pink paper. Boy at top ctr. Back brown; ornate design.	—	Rare	—

1865 Second Issue

#S371-S379 printer: ABNC.

		Good	Fine	XF
S371	**20 Centésimos** 4.11.1865. Black on red-brown unpt. Sailor standing at top ctr. Back red-brown.	—	—	—

		Good	Fine	XF
S372	**50 Centésimos** 4.11.1865. Black on brown unpt. Galloping stallion at ctr.	—	—	—

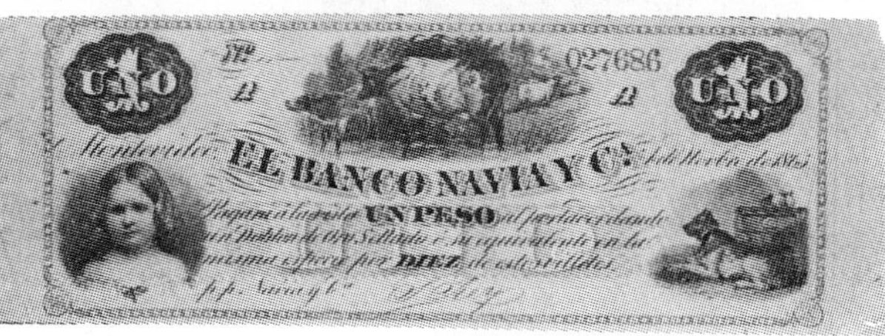

		Good	Fine	XF
S373	**1 Peso** 4.11.1865. Black on orange unpt. Girl's bust at lower l., cows at upper ctr., dog and safe at lower r.	—	—	—
S376	**10 Pesos = 1 Doblon** 4.11.1865. Black on green unpt. Girl and puppies at l., paddlewheel steamship *MONTEVIDEO* at upper ctr., anchor at r. Back green.	—	Rare	—

		Good	Fine	XF
S377	**20 Pesos = 2 Doblones** 4.11.1865. Black on green unpt. Seated Justice at lower l., 2 seated allegorical women w/shield at upper ctr., seated woman at lower r. Back lilac-brown.	—	Rare	—
S378	**50 Pesos = 5 Doblones** 4.11.1865. Black on green unpt. Cow at l., steamship, globe and train at ctr., Indian woman holding arrow at r. Back blue. Archive copy.	—	—	—

		Good	Fine	XF
S379	**100 Pesos = 10 Doblones** 4.11.1865. Black on green unpt. 2 sailors w/ship at lower l., seated woman w/sheaf at upper ctr., 2 children at lower r. Back brown.	—	Rare	—

Banco Oriental, Montevideo

1867-69 Issue

#S381-S387 printer: ABNC.

		Good	Fine	XF
S381	**20 Centésimos** 1.8.1867; 1.8.1869. Black on brown unpt. Gaucho pouring drink at l., gaucho smoking at r.	—	Rare	—

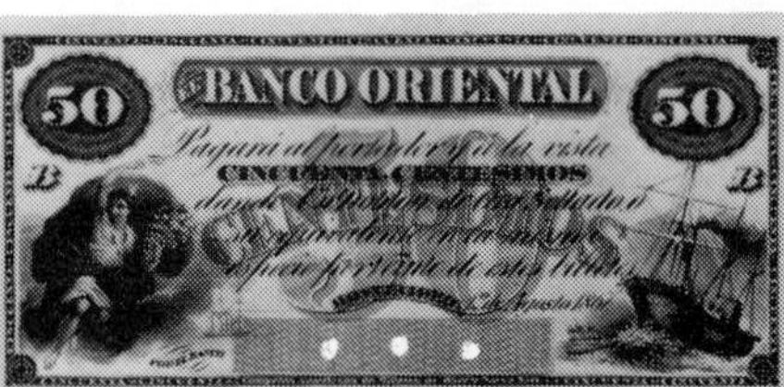

		Good	Fine	XF
S382	**50 Centésimos** 1.8.1867. Black on red-brown unpt. Allegorical figure w/cornucopia at l., steam/sailing ship at r. Uniface.			
	a. Issued note.	—	Rare	—
	p. Proof.	—	—	—

		Good	Fine	XF
S383	**1 Peso** 1.8.1867. Black on green unpt. Gaucho pouring drink at l., woman at r. Uniface.			
	a. Issued note.	80.00	200.00	—
	r. Remainder.	—	Unc	100.00
	s. Specimen.	—	—	—

		Good	Fine	XF
S384	**5 Pesos** 1.8.1867. Black on orange unpt. Allegorical woman holding sword seated by child on wharf at l., young boy at ctr. r. Back green.			
	a. Issued note.	—	Rare	—
	p. Proof.	—	—	—

		Good	Fine	XF
S385	**10 Pesos = 1 Doblon** 1.8.1867. Black on orange unpt. 2 standing allegorical women at l., arms at lower r. Back orange.			
	a. Issued note.	4.50	10.00	35.00
	p. Proof.	—	—	—

		Good	Fine	XF
S386	**20 Pesos = 2 Doblones** 1.8.1867. Black on dk. orange unpt. Allegorical woman leaning on sheaf at l., arms at r. Back blue.	4.50	10.00	40.00

		Good	Fine	XF
S387	**50 Pesos = 5 Doblones** 1.8.1867. Black on blue unpt. Seated woman beneath trees at l., arms at lower r. Back orange.	5.00	15.00	50.00

Banco de Paysandú

1862 Issue

#S388-S391 printer: Lit. de Mege y Willems, Montevideo. Uniface.

		Good	Fine	XF
S388	**120 Centésimos** 27.9.1862. Black. Sailing ship at upper ctr. Cream paper.	—	—	—

		GOOD	FINE	XF
S389	**240 CENTÉSIMOS** 27.9.1862. Black.	—	—	—

		GOOD	FINE	XF
S390	**480 CENTÉSIMOS** 27.9.1862. Black. 2 cows at upper ctr. Blue paper.	—	—	—

		GOOD	FINE	XF
S391	**960 CENTÉSIMOS = 1 PATACON** 27.9.1862. Black. 2 standing allegorical women at l. Blue-green paper.	—	Rare	—

BANCO POPULAR, MONTEVIDEO

LAW OF 23.6.1862; 1888 ISSUE

		GOOD	FINE	XF
S395	**10 PESOS** 5.11.1888. Black on lt. green unpt. Man in chariot w/bow and arrow at l. Back green; woman at ctr. Printer: A. Godel.			
	a. Issued note.	30.00	90.00	—
	r. Remainder.	5.00	10.00	25.00

BANCO DEL SALTO, SALTO

1858 ISSUE

		GOOD	FINE	XF
S401	**120 CENTÉSIMOS** 1.10.1858. Brown. Tree at upper ctr.			
	a. Issued note.	—	—	—
	r. Remainder.	—	Unc	100.00

		GOOD	FINE	XF
S403	**480 CENTÉSIMOS** 1.10.1858. Black. Sheep at ctr. Remainder.	—	—	—

		GOOD	FINE	XF
S404	**960 CENTÉSIMOS = 1 PATACON** 1.10.1858. Black on cream paper. Ostrich at ctr.	—	—	—

1863 ISSUE

#S411-S415 printer: BWC.

		GOOD	FINE	XF
S411	**5 CENTÉSIMOS** 2.1.1863. Black. Tree at upper ctr. Yellow paper. Uniface.	—	—	—
S412	**10 CENTÉSIMOS** 2.1.1863. Black. Tiger at ctr. Tan paper. Uniface.	—	—	—
S413	**20 CENTÉSIMOS** 2.1.1863. Black. Rooster at ctr. Yellow paper.	—	—	—
S414	**50 CENTÉSIMOS** 2.1.1863. Black. Deer at ctr. Blue paper.	—	—	—
S415	**1 PESO** 2.1.1863. Black. Sheep at upper ctr. Orange paper.	—	—	—

Banco Villaamil & Ca., Montevideo

Decreto 12.10.1876

		Good	Fine	XF
S417	**10 Pesos** *D.1876.* Black on tan and lt. blue unpt. Justice at l., allegorical woman w/beehive at r. Uniface. Printer: BWC.	—	—	—

Cambio de Monedas de Viñas y Ca., Montevideo

1873 Issue

		Good	Fine	XF
S418	**1 Peso** 1.8.1873. Black on orange unpt. Cherub w/numeral *1* at l. W/o sign. Printer: A. Hequet y Ca.	—	—	—

Comercio de Tacuarembo

1861 Issue

		Good	Fine	XF
S418D	**480 Centésimos** Feb. 1, 1861. Black. Sheep at upper ctr. r. Oval seal: *COMERCIO DE TACUAREMBO/480 CENTÉSIMOS* at l. Uniface.	—	—	—

Progreso Oriental, Montevideo

Though not legal tender, the notes of this issuer may have been more highly regarded than most other paper money issues. The guarantee on these notes specifically states that they are fully guaranteed by mortgages and that payment will be made in gold or silver regardless of the law.

1868 Issue

#S419-S423 printer: ABNC.

#S419-S420A authorization date of 14.2.1868 and guarantee text on back.

		Good	Fine	XF
S419	**1 Peso** 18xx (ca.1868). Black on orange unpt. Anchor at upper ctr. Back orange. Proof.	—	—	—

		Good	Fine	XF
S419A	**5 Pesos** 18xx (ca.1868). Black on blue unpt. Dog w/safe at upper ctr. Back blue. Proof.	—	—	—
S420	**10 Pesos** 18xx (ca.1868). Black on green unpt. Cherubs at l. and r., sailing ship at ctr. Back green. Proof.	—	—	—
S420A	**50 Pesos** 18xx (ca.1868). Black on brown unpt. Sailor at upper l., 3 allegorical women holding denomination numeral at r. Back brown. Proof.	—	—	—

#S421-S423 authorization date of 14.2.1868 and guarantee text on face.

		Good	Fine	XF
S421	**100 Pesos** 18xx (ca.1868). Black on red-orange unpt. Seated allegorical woman holding vase w/barrels, boxes and other implements, ships behind, at ctr. Back red-orange.	100.00	300.00	—

NOTE: All known examples of #S421 w/o sign. or date.

		Good	Fine	XF
S422	**100 Pesos** 18xx (ca.1868). Black on green unpt. Reclining allegorical woman w/coins, anchor and other marine implements at ctr. Back green. Proof.	—	—	—
S423	**1000 Pesos** 18xx (ca.1868). Black on brown unpt. Seated woman at l., sailor at r. Back brown.	—	—	—

Sociedád Auxiliar de Crédito y Alquileres, Montevideo

Law of 18.9.1889

		Good	Fine	XF
S426	**100 Pesos** *L.1889.* Lion at l. Printer: A. Godel, Montevideo. Remainder.	—	—	—

Sociedád de Cambios

1856 Issue

#S431-S437 w/o specific issuer, possibly prepared as samples or as uniform styles. Uniface.

		Good	Fine	XF
S431	**120 Reis** 5.1856. Red. Rooster at upper ctr.	—	—	—

		Good	Fine	XF
S432	**240 Reis** 5.1856. Blue. Ostrich at upper ctr.	—	—	—

		Good	Fine	XF
S433	**320 Reis** 5.1856. Brown. Buggy pulled by 4 horses at upper ctr.	—	—	—

		Good	Fine	XF
S434	**480 Reis** 5.1856. Orange. Ewe at upper ctr.	—	—	—

		Good	Fine	XF
S435	**640 Reis** 5.1856. Bridge at upper ctr.	—	—	—

		Good	Fine	XF
S436	**960 Reis = 1 Patacón** 5.1856. Trotting horse at upper ctr.	—	—	—

		Good	Fine	XF
S437	**2 Patacónes** 5.1856. Bull at upper ctr.	—	—	—

Sociedád de Cambios, Montevideo

1856 Issue

		Good	Fine	XF
S438	**120 Reis** 1.7.1856. Black. Sailing ships at upper ctr. Uniface.	—	—	—
S439	**240 Reis** 1.7.1856. Black.	—	—	—
S440	**480 Reis** 1.7.1856. Black.	—	—	—
S440A	**640 Reis** 1.7.1856. Black.	—	—	—
S440B	**960 Reis** 1.7.1856. Black.	—	—	—
S440C	**1920 Reis** 1.7.1856. Black.	—	—	—
S440D	**3840 Reis** 1.7.1856. Black.	—	—	—

Sociedád de Cambios Carmelo y Na (Nueva) Palmira

Most notes of this issue are similar to the previous listing.

1856 Issue

		Good	Fine	XF
S441	**120 Reis** 5.1856. Similar to #S431.	—	—	—

		Good	Fine	XF
S444	480 Reis 5.1856. Orange. Similar to #S434.	—	—	—

		Good	Fine	XF
S445	640 Reis 5.1856. Brown. Similar to #S435.	—	—	—
S447	2 Patacónes 5.1856. Black. Similar to #S437.	—	—	—

Sociedád de Cambios de Cerro Largo

ND Issue

		Good	Fine	XF
S451	480 Reis ND.	—	—	—

Sociedád de Cambios de Paysandú

1856 Issue

		Good	Fine	XF
S461	2 Patacónes 1856. Printer: Lit. Mege. Specimen.	—	—	—

1840's Issue

		Good	Fine	XF
S465	120 Reis 184x.	—	—	—

1864 Issue

#S466-S469 printer: Hequet y Cohas Hnos.

		Good	Fine	XF
S466	240 Reis 1864.	—	—	—
S467	480 Reis 1864.	—	—	—
S468	1 Patacón 1864.	—	—	—

1865 Issue

		Good	Fine	XF
S469	2 Patacónes = 1920 Reis 4.1.1865. Allegorical figures l. and r., bull at ctr.	—	—	—

Sociedád de Crédito Hipotecario

1868 Issue

#S471-S478 printer: A. Hequet y Cia.

		Good	Fine	XF
S471	2 Centésimos 30.9.1868. Black and green. Oval hand stamp on back.	30.00	80.00	—
S472	4 Centésimos 30.9.1868. Black and orange. Like #S471.	30.00	80.00	—
S472A	5 Centésimos 30.9.1868. Black on orange unpt. Like #S471.	—	—	—
S473	8 Centésimos 30.9.1868. Black and orange. Like #S471.	30.00	80.00	—

		Good	Fine	XF
S478	10 Pesos 1.11.1868. Black on gray unpt. Standing woman holding caduceus at l.	—	—	—

Sociedád Fomento Territorial, Montevideo

Interest-bearing notes: 1% per month payable to bearer.

1868 Issue

#S480-S482 uniface. Printer: Lit. A. Hequet y Cohas Hnos.

		Good	Fine	XF
S480	1 Peso 1.7.1868. Black on orange unpt. Boy w/torch and arms at l., value beneath.	40.00	—	—
S481	10 Pesos 1.6.1868. Black on green unpt. Boy w/torch, map of Uruguay and shield at l. Back gold.	7.00	15.00	35.00

		Good	Fine	XF
S482	20 Pesos 1.6.1868. Black on orange unpt. Like #S481. Back blue.	7.00	15.00	35.00

State

Departamento de Artigas

A most unusual issue was made in 1907 by the Departamento de Artigas as it took political contribution receipts and ovpt. them on the back as provisional bills of exchange. It is not known if these were ever issued.

1907 Provisional Billetes de Canje (Bills of Exchange) Issue

#S491 and S492 text on the back indicating type of note, issuer and date.

		Good	Fine	XF
S491	1 Peso 1907. Original receipt is Black and gray. Series 1.	—	—	—

		Good	Fine	XF
S492	5 Pesos 1907. Original receipt is blue and gray. Series 1.	—	—	—

NOTE: #S491 and S492 w/o text on back as shown are not believed to be items that could have circulated.

The Republic of Venezuela, located on the northern coast of South America between Colombia and Guyana, has an area of 352,145 sq. mi. (912,050 sq. km.) and a population of 24.17 million. Capital: Caracas. Petroleum and mining provide 90 percent of Venezuela's exports although they employ less than 2 percent of the work force. Coffee, grown on 60,000 plantations, is the chief crop.

Columbus discovered Venezuela on his third voyage in 1498. Initial exploration did not reveal Venezuela to be a land of great wealth. An active pearl trade operated on the off-shore islands and slavers raided the interior in search of Indians to be sold into slavery, but no significant mainland settlements were made before 1567 when Caracas was founded. Venezuela, the home of Bolívar, was among the first South American colonies to revolt against Spain in 1810. Independence was attained in 1821 but not recognized by Spain until 1845. Together with Ecuador, Panama and Colombia, Venezuela was part of "Gran Colombia" until 1830 when it became a sovereign and independent state.

MONETARY SYSTEM:

1 Bolívar = 100 Centimos, 1879-

BANKS

Banco de Carabobo, 188x. . . . . #S101-S104
Banco de Carácas, ca.1876-79. . . . . #S111-S124
Banco Carácas, 189x-1928. . . . . #S131-S157
Banco Colonial Britanico, 18xx . . . . #S161
Banco Comercial, 188x. . . . . #S166-S170
Banco Comercial de Maracaibo, ca.1916-33 . . . . #S171-S183
Banco de Londres y Venezuela, Limitado, 1865. . . . . #S185
Banco de Maracaibo, 188x-1935 . . . . #S190-S229
Banco Mercantil y Agrícola, 1934-35 . . . . #S231-S233
Banco Nacional de Venezuela, 1841 . . . . #S236
Banco Venezolano de Crédito, 1925-39 . . . . #S241-S248

Banco de Venezuela

First Bank Issue, 1862. . . . . #S251-S256
Second Bank Issue, 189x-1939 . . . . #S261-S315

GOVERNMENT

Compañía de Accionistas, 1856 . . . . #S321-S324
Compañía de Crédito, ca.1873 . . . . #S325-S329

STATE

Estado de Guayana, 1878-79 . . . . #S332-S354

LEPROSARIUM

Isla de Providencia, Leprosarios Nacionales, ca.1940 . . . . #S361-S370

BANKS

BANCO DE CARABOBO

Founded in December 1883 at Valencia, State of Carabobo. Absorbed by the Banco de Venezuela in 1890.

1880's ISSUE

#S101-S104 printer: ABNC.

		GOOD	FINE	XF
S101	**20 BOLÍVARES** 188x. Black on blue unpt. State arms at l., seated allegorical woman w/globe at ctr., national arms at r. Back blue. Proof.	—	—	—

		GOOD	FINE	XF
S102	**30 BOLÍVARES** 188x. Black on orange unpt. Allegorical woman w/beehive and sickle at l., state arms at ctr., national arms at r. Back orange. Proof.	—	—	—

		GOOD	FINE	XF
S103	**100 BOLÍVARES** 188x. Black on yellow unpt. State arms at l., allegorical woman w/plants at ctr., national arms at r. Back yellow. Proof.	—	—	—

		GOOD	FINE	XF
S104	**500 BOLÍVARES** 188x. Black on green unpt. State arms at l., allegorical woman w/implements, shield, train and sailing ship at ctr., national arms at r. Back green. Proof.	—	—	—

BANCO DE CARÁCAS

1876 ISSUE

Venezolano System.

#S111-S118 black on brown unpt. Printer: CABB.

#S111-S113 *CAPITAL 160,000 VENEZOLANOS.*

		GOOD	FINE	XF
S111	**5 VENEZOLANOS** 18xx (ca.1876). Allegorical woman w/boxes, globe and marine implements at ctr. Proof.	—	—	—

		GOOD	FINE	XF
S112	**20 VENEZOLANOS** 18xx (ca.1876). Columbus sighting land at ctr. Proof.	—	—	—
S113	**100 VENEZOLANOS** 20.11.1876. Explorer landing at ctr. Proof.	—	—	—

1877 ISSUE

#S116-S118 *CAPITAL V. 200,000.*

		GOOD	FINE	XF
S116	**5 VENEZOLANOS** 18xx (ca.1877). Proof.	—	—	—

		GOOD	FINE	XF
S117	**20 VENEZOLANOS** 18xx (ca.1877). Proof.	—	—	—

		GOOD	FINE	XF
S118	**100 VENEZOLANOS** 18xx (ca.1877). Proof.	—	—	—

1879 ISSUE

Bolívar System.

#S121-S124 *CAPITAL B. 1,300,000.* Printer: CABB.

		GOOD	FINE	XF
S121	**20 BOLÍVARES** 18xx (ca.1879). Black on brown unpt. Proof.	—	—	—

		GOOD	FINE	XF
S122	**100 BOLÍVARES** 18xx (ca.1879). Black on green unpt. Griffins at bottom ctr. Proof.	—	—	—

		GOOD	FINE	XF
S123	**500 BOLÍVARES** 18xx (ca.1879). Black on blue unpt. Horse at bottom ctr. Proof.	—	—	—
S124	**1000 BOLÍVARES** 18xx (ca.1879). Black on salmon unpt. Proof.	—	—	—

BANCO CARÁCAS

189X FIRST ISSUE

#S131-S142, S147-S155, S158-S159 allegorical woman w/sword and scale on back. Printer: HLBNC.

#S131-S134 ctr. sign. title: *PRESIDENTE DEL DIRECTORIO.*

		GOOD	FINE	XF
S131	**20 BOLÍVARES** 189x. Black on purple and lilac unpt. Liberty at l., cherub at lower r. Back red. Proof.	—	—	—
S132	**100 BOLÍVARES** 189x. Black on blue and tan unpt. Seated allegorical woman w/anchor and sailing ships at l., young girl at r. Back brown. Proof.	—	—	—
S134	**800 BOLÍVARES** 189x. Black on blue and orange orange unpt. 2 allegorical women w/cornucopias and other implements in harbor scene at l. Back blue. Proof.	—	—	—

189X SECOND ISSUE

#S136-S139 ctr. sign. title: *DIRECTOR.*

		GOOD	FINE	XF
S136	**20 BOLÍVARES** 189x. Like #S131.			
	p1. Back blue. Proof.	—	—	—
	p2. Back green. Proof.	—	—	—
	s1. Back blue. Specimen.	—	—	—
	s2. Back green. Specimen.	—	—	—

		GOOD	FINE	XF
S137	**100 BOLÍVARES** 189x; 22.3.1902/189x. Like #S132.	—	—	—

		GOOD	FINE	XF
S138	**400 BOLÍVARES** 189x; 1910. Black on blue and orange unpt. Seated allegorical woman w/globe at l.			
	a. Back orange. 189x; 29.8.1910/189x.	—	—	—
	p. Back green. Proof. 189x.	—	—	—

		Good	Fine	XF
S139	**800 Bolívares** 189x; 1.12.1910/189x. Like #S134. Series C. Proof.	—	—	—

1907 Issue

		Good	Fine	XF
S141	**20 Bolívares** 19xx (ca.1907). Black on green and yellow unpt. Like #S136. Series F.			
	p. Proof.	—	—	—
	s. Specimen.	—	—	—
S142	**100 Bolívares** 19xx (ca.1907). Black on green and lilac unpt. Like #S137. Series F.			
	p. Proof.	—	—	—
	s. Specimen.	—	—	—

19xx; 1914 Issue

#S146-S151 short text line: *A LA PRESENTACION DE ESTE BILLETE* beneath denomination words at ctr.

		Good	Fine	XF
S146	**10 Bolívares** 24.7.1914. Black on gold unpt. Ornate bldg. at ctr. Back red; arms at ctr. Series H. Printer: ABNC.	—	—	—
S147	**20 Bolívares** 19xx. Like #S141. Series G.			
	p. Proof.	—	—	—
	s. Specimen.	—	—	—
S149	**100 Bolívares** 19xx. Like #S142. Series G.			
	p. Proof.	—	—	—
	s. Specimen.	—	—	—
S150	**400 Bolívares** 19xx. Like #S138.	—	—	—
S151	**800 Bolívares** 19xx. Like #S139.	—	—	—

1925 Provisional Issue

#S153-S155 red ovpt: *PAGADERO EN LAS OFICINAS DEL BANCO* at l.

		Good	Fine	XF
S153	**20 Bolívares** 30.1.1925; 1.12.1928. Ovpt. around Liberty head on #S147.	—	—	—
S155	**100 Bolívares** ND (old date- 21.3.1911). Ovpt. on #S149.	—	—	—

1926-28 Regular Issue

#S157-S159 like #S146-S149, but longer text: *A LA PRESENTACION DE ESTE BILLETE EN LAS OFICINAS DEL BANCO* beneath denomination words at ctr.

		Good	Fine	XF
S157	**10 Bolívares** 26.3.1928. Like #S146. Series J.	—	—	—

		Good	Fine	XF
S158	**20 Bolívares** 19xx. Like #S147. Series J. Proof.	—	—	—
S159	**100 Bolívares** 9.4.1926. Like #S149. Series I.	—	—	—

NOTE: The following dates were listed in the fifth edition: 20 Bolívares, 30.3.1928; 100 Bolívares, 4.9.1922; 400 Bolívares, 30.3.1925; 800 Bolívares, 30.3.1925. Confirmation is needed to assign these dates to their proper variety listings.

Banco Colonial Britanico

This bank, a foreign branch of the Banco Colonial de Londres, was the first firm as such to be established in Venezuela. It began operations on July 29, 1839 and terminated its activities in 1849.

1839 Issue

		Good	Fine	XF
S161	**50 Pesos** 18xx. Black. English arms at upper ctr. Printer: PB&P. Specimen.	—	—	—

NOTE: Denominations of 5, 10, 20, and 100 Pesos are reported, not confirmed.

Banco Comercial

This bank began operations in Carácas on March 24, 1883, and became the Banco de Venezuela in 1890.

1880's Issue

#S166-S170 printer: ABNC.

		Good	Fine	XF
S166	**20 Bolívares** 188x. Black on red-orange unpt. Seated allegorical woman w/marine implements at l. Back red-orange. Proof.	—	—	—

		Good	Fine	XF
S167	**50 Bolívares** 188x. Black on gold unpt. Allegorical woman w/plants at l., ships at ctr. Back gold. Proof.	—	—	—

		Good	Fine	XF
S168	**100 Bolívares** 188x. Black on blue unpt. Allegorical woman seated w/produce and plants at l., Columbus and Indian woman at r. Back blue; arms at ctr. Proof.	—	—	—

		Good	Fine	XF
S169	**500 Bolivares** 188x. Black on salmon unpt. Columbus sighting land at l. Back salmon; 2 sailors at ctr. Proof.	—	—	—

		Good	Fine	XF
S170	**1000 Bolívares** 188x. Black on green unpt. National arms at l., horse at upper ctr., Columbus sighting land at r. Back green; steam passenger train at ctr. Proof.	—	—	—

BANCO COMERCIAL (DE MARACAIBO)

This bank was founded in 1916 with the name Banco Comercial. One note was issued bearing this form of the name. In 1920, the name was lengthened to include the city, and the second issue of notes appeared at that time.

1916 ISSUE

		GOOD	FINE	XF
S171	**10 BOLÍVARES** 19xx. Black on olive unpt. Portr. Gen. R. Urdaneta at ctr. Back olive; vaquero roping cattle at ctr. Printer: ABNC.			
	p. Proof.	—	—	—
	s. Series A. Specimen.	—	—	—

BANCO COMERCIAL DE MARACAIBO

1921 ISSUE

#S173 and S174 *CAPITAL Bs 400,000.* Printer: ABNC.

		GOOD	FINE	XF
S173	**10 BOLÍVARES** 1.5.1921; 1.2.1922. Similar to #S171.	—	—	—

		GOOD	FINE	XF
S174	**10 BOLÍVARES** 19xx. Black on m/c unpt. Similar to #S173. Proof.	—	—	—

1929 ISSUE

#S176-S179 *CAPITAL Bs 2,000,000.* Printer: ABNC.

		GOOD	FINE	XF
S176	**10 BOLÍVARES** 9.3.1929. Like #S174, but different capitalization amount.	—	—	—

		GOOD	FINE	XF
S177	**20 BOLÍVARES** 9.3.1929. Blue on m/c unpt. Oil field and steam passenger train at ctr. Back blue; dock scene w/ship, steam passenger train and truck at ctr.	—	—	—

		GOOD	FINE	XF
S179	**100 BOLÍVARES** 1.3.1929. Red on m/c unpt. Woman at l. Back red; market scene at ctr.	—	—	—

1933 ISSUE

#S181-S183 *CAPITAL Bs 2,000,000.* Printer: ABNC.

		GOOD	FINE	XF
S181	**10 BOLÍVARES** 19xx (ca.1933). Red on m/c unpt. Like #S176.	—	—	—
S182	**20 BOLÍVARES** 19xx (ca.1933). Green on m/c unpt. Like #S177.	—	—	—
S183	**100 BOLÍVARES** 19xx (ca.1933). Olive on m/c unpt. Like #S179.	—	—	—

NOTE: A 10 Bolívares dated 2.7.1925 was previously listed. Confirmation is needed to assign this date to the proper variety listing.

BANCO DE LONDRES Y VENEZUELA, LIMITADO

Founded 1862; closed 1865.

1865 ISSUE

		GOOD	FINE	XF
S185	**5 PESOS** 23.1.1865. Black on green unpt. Oval arms of City of London and of Venezuela at top ctr. *FIVE DOLLARS CURRENCY* on back.	—	Rare	—

BANCO DE MARACAIBO

Founded on July 20, 1882.

1882 ISSUE

#S190-S192 *CAPITAL B 160,000.* Sign. title: *PRESIDENTE DE LA ASEMBLEA DELAGATORIA.* Printer: ABNC.

		GOOD	FINE	XF
S190	**20 BOLÍVARES** 188x (ca.1882). Black on gold unpt. Sailing ships at l., seated allegorical woman w/bales at ctr., arms at r. Back gold. Proof.	—	—	—

		Good	Fine	XF
S191	**50 Bolívares** 188x (ca.1882). Black on green unpt. Sailor at l., woman pouring water at ctr., arms at r. Back green. Proof.	—	—	—

		Good	Fine	XF
S192	**100 Bolívares** 188x (ca.1882). Black on blue unpt. Arms and seated allegorical woman w/ship at l., seated allegorical woman w/bales, wheel and train at r. Back blue. Proof.	—	—	—

1885 Issue

#S195-S197 *CAPITAL B 320,000.* Sign. title: *PRESIDENTE DE LA ASEMBLEA DELAGATORIA.* Printer: ABNC.

		Good	Fine	XF
S195	**20 Bolívares** 188x (ca.1885). Like #S190. Proof.	—	—	—

		Good	Fine	XF
S196	**50 Bolívares** 188x (ca.1885). Like #S191. Proof.	—	—	—

		Good	Fine	XF
S197	**100 Bolívares** 188x (ca.1885). Like #S192. Proof.	—	—	—

1889 Issue

#S200-S203 sign. title: *PRESIDENTE DE LA ASEMBLEA DELAGATORIA.*

#S200-S202 *CAPITAL B 800,000.* Printer: ABNC.

		Good	Fine	XF
S200	**20 Bolívares** 188x (ca.1889). Like #S190. Proof.	—	—	—
S201	**50 Bolívares** 188x (ca.1889). Like #S191. Proof.	—	—	—
S202	**100 Bolívares** 188x (ca.1889). Like #S192. Proof.	—	—	—
S203	**200 Bolívares** 188x (ca.1889). Black on red-orange unpt. Helmeted Athena and allegorical woman at l., reclining woman at ctr., 2 allegorical women and arms at r. Back red-orange. Proof.	—	—	—

1897 Issue

#S205-209 sign. title: *PRESIDENTE DE LA ASEMBLEA DELAGATORIA.*

#S205, S207-S208 *CAPITAL B 1,250,000.* Printer: ABNC.

		Good	Fine	XF
S205	**20 Bolívares** 1.1.1897. Like #S200.			
	a. Issued note.	1200.00	2250.00	—
	p. Proof.	—	—	—
S206	**40 Bolívares** 189x (ca.1897). Black on green unpt. Similar to #S201, but minor plate differences. Back green. Proof.	—	—	—
S207	**100 Bolívares** 18xx (ca.1897). Like #S202. Proof.	—	—	—

		Good	Fine	XF
S208	**200 Bolívares** 18xx (ca.1897). Like #S203. Proof.	—	—	—

		Good	Fine	XF
S209	**400 Bolívares** 189x (ca.1897). Black on yellow unpt. Arms at lower l., standing allegorical woman w/book and plant at l., female portrait at ctr. r. Back yellow. Proof.	—	—	—

1908-09 Issue

#S211 and S212 partially engraved date: *19xx.* Sign. title: *PRESIDENTE DE LA ASEMBLEA DELAGATORIA.* Printer: ABNC.

		Good	Fine	XF
S211	**20 Bolívares** 19xx; 1908. Like #S190.			
	a. Ovpt: *RESELLADO* at l. 1.5.1908.	—	—	—
	s. Specimen. 19xx (ca.1907).	—	—	—

		Good	Fine	XF
S212	**40 Bolívares** 1.4.1909. Like #S206. Specimen.	—	—	—

1915-17 Issue

#S216-S222 r. sign. title: *SEGUNDO DIRECTOR PRINCIPAL.* Printer: ABNC.

S216 10 BOLÍVARES — Good / Fine / XF
1.1.1917/19xx. Black on purple unpt. Seated allegorical man w/scythe at l., arms at ctr., seated allegorical woman holding ship at r. Back purple. — — —

#S217 *Deleted.* See #S223.

S218 20 BOLÍVARES — Good / Fine / XF
1917/19xx. Like #S190.
- a. 1.1.1917/19xx. — — —
- p. Proof. 19xx (ca.1916). — — —

S219 40 BOLÍVARES — Good / Fine / XF
1917/19xx. Like #S206.
- a. 1.1.1917/19xx. — — —
- p. Proof. 19xx (ca.1916). — — —

S220 100 BOLÍVARES — Good / Fine / XF
1915/19xx. Like #S192.
- a. Ovpt. near bottom: *EN LAS OFICINAS DEL BANCO* and 2 sign. titles, black bar below. 15.1.1915/19xx. — — —
- p. Proof. 19xx (ca.1916). — — —

S221 200 BOLÍVARES
15.3.1915/19xx. Like #S203. Ovpt. at l.: *PAGADERO/EN LAS/OFICINAS DEL BANCO*, 2 sign. titles and black bar like #S220. — — —

S222 400 BOLÍVARES — Good / Fine / XF
1.1.1917/19xx. Like #S209. — — —

1924 ISSUE

S223 10 BOLÍVARES — Good / Fine / XF
19xx (ca.1924). Black on purple unpt. Similar to #S216. Capitalization at lower l., date area upper r. Series A. — — —

NOTE: #S223 is a transitional issue as it has close similarities to #S226.

1925-26 ISSUE

#S226-S229 reduced size: *CAPITAL B 2,500,000.* Printer: ABNC.

S226 10 BOLÍVARES — Good / Fine / XF
10.9.1925; 27.4.1933; 2.8.1934; 1.9.1935. Similar to #S223, but different capitalization. — 175.00 / 400.00 / —

NOTE: #S226 dated 1.7.1923 and 3.3.1925 were listed in the fifth edition. Confirmation is needed to ensure their proper inclusion in this listing.

S227 20 BOLÍVARES — Good / Fine / XF
19xx. Similar to #S190. Proof. — — —

S228 100 BOLÍVARES — Good / Fine / XF
20.5.1926. Similar to #S192. — — —

S229 500 BOLÍVARES — Good / Fine / XF
20.5.1926. Black on yellow and m/c unpt. Similar to #S222 but different allegorical woman at l. — — —

BANCO MERCANTIL Y AGRÍCOLA

1929-35 ISSUE

#S231-S233 bank arms at ctr., reclining allegorical figures supporting shield w/bank monogram at ctr. on back. Hand sign. Printer: ABNC.

		GOOD	FINE	XF
S231	**10 BOLÍVARES** 20.3.1934; 8.11.1935. Orange on m/c unpt. Cattle under trees at ctr.			
	a. Issued note w/date.	65.00	175.00	300.00
	r. Remainder, w/o date but w/2 hand sign.	—	—	65.00

		GOOD	FINE	XF
S232	**20 BOLÍVARES** 21.2.1927. Dk. green on m/c unpt. Ships and steam passenger train at loading area.			
	a. Issued note w/date.	75.00	200.00	—
	r1. Remainder, w/o date but w/2 hand sign.	—	—	65.00
	r2. Remainder, w/o date or sign.	—	—	50.00

		GOOD	FINE	XF
S233	**100 BOLÍVARES** 6.1.1929. Purple on m/c unpt. Reclining allegorical woman w/globe at ctr.			
	a. Issued note w/date.	80.00	225.00	—
	r1. Remainder, w/o date but w/2 hand sign.	—	—	90.00
	r2. Remainder, w/o date or sign.	—	—	90.00

BANCO NACIONAL DE VENEZUELA

Founded in June of 1841.

1841 ISSUE

		GOOD	FINE	XF
S236	**5 PESOS** 6.12.1841. Black. Sailing ship at l., arms at upper ctr., woman standing at r. Printer: NEBNC.	—	—	—

NOTE: A 20 Pesos denomination is reported, not confirmed.

BANCO VENEZOLANO DE CRÉDITO

1925-26 ISSUE

#S241-S243 printer: ABNC.

		GOOD	FINE	XF
S241	**10 BOLÍVARES** 27.7.1926; 28.12.1927; 28.6.1929. Red on yellow and m/c unpt. Woman w/basket on head at ctr. Back red; workers picking cotton at ctr.			
	a. Issued note.	200.00	—	—
	p. Proof.	—	—	—
	s. Specimen.	—	—	—

		GOOD	FINE	XF
S242	**20 BOLÍVARES** 2.11.1925; 24.5.1928; 4.12.1928. Green on m/c unpt. Vaqueros roping cattle at ctr. Back green; cows watering at ctr.			
	a. Issued note.	—	Rare	—
	p. Proof.	—	—	—
	s. Specimen.	—	—	—

		GOOD	FINE	XF
S243	**100 BOLÍVARES** 18.11.1925; 2.6.1926; 16.3.1928; 21.9.1928. Brown on m/c unpt. Reclining allegorical woman at l. Back brown; seated allegorical man on crate at ctr.			
	a. Issued note.	—	Rare	—
	p. Proof.	—	—	—
	s. Specimen.	—	—	—

1931 ISSUE

#S247 and S248 printer: W&S.

		GOOD	FINE	XF
S247	**20 BOLÍVARES** 31.8.1931; 31.10.1933; 11.4.1934; 28.8.1935; 14.1.1939. Green. Coffee pickers at ctr. Cattle at ctr. on back.			
	a. Issued note.	125.00	400.00	—
	s. Specimen.	—	—	—

		GOOD	FINE	XF
S248	**100 BOLÍVARES** 31.1.1931; 3.2.1933; 14.1.1939. Brown on m/c unpt. Allegorical woman w/tablet held by cherub at l. Mercury w/Cupid at ctr. on back.			
	a. Issued note.	—	—	—
	s. Specimen.	—	—	—

NOTE: Specimen notes (from salesman's sample books) have different colors than issued notes.

BANCO DE VENEZUELA (SINCE 1860'S)

There were two separate banks with this name, one in operation during the mid-19th century and the other much later. The second Banco de Venezuela exists today.

1862 ISSUE

		GOOD	FINE	XF
S251	**8 REALES = 1 PESO** 1.3.1862. Black. Uniface.	—	—	—
S256	**50 PESOS** 1.2.1862. Black. Red seal stamped at lower l. ctr. Uniface.	—	—	—

NOTE: A 5 Pesos of this issue is reported, not confirmed.

BANCO DE VENEZUELA (SINCE 1890)

This bank began operations on Aug. 18, 1890, a result of the transformation of the Banco Comercial and the absorption of the Banco de Carabobo. Business needs caused a number of varieties in the way of overprints and other modifications to appear on notes of this bank. Notes were issued until 1939.

NOTE: An 1899 provisional issue of #S271-S275 w/ovpt: *CAPITAL Bs 12,000,000* old capitalization is reported, not confirmed.

NOTE: A 1921 provisional issue of #S286-S289 w/dual ovpt: *CAPITAL Bs 24,000,000* and *PAGADERO EN LAS OFICINAS DEL BANCO* is reported, not confirmed.

1890'S ISSUE

#S261-S265 *CAPITAL B/8,000,000.* Printer: ABNC.

		GOOD	FINE	XF
S261	**20 BOLÍVARES** 189x (ca.1890). Black on yellow and brown unpt. Plowman and 2 horses at l. Portr. S. Bolívar at r. Back dk. brown; arms at ctr.			
	p. Proof.	—	—	—
	s. Specimen.	—	—	—

		GOOD	FINE	XF
S262	**40 BOLÍVARES** 18xx (ca.1890). Black on green and yellow unpt. Portr. S. Bolívar at l., cowboys roping cattle at ctr. r. Back green; arms at l.			
	p. Proof.	—	—	—
	s. Specimen.	—	—	—

		GOOD	FINE	XF
S263	**100 BOLÍVARES** 18xx (ca.1890). Black on yellow and red-orange unpt. Helmeted Minerva at upper l., cherub w/fish at ctr., Portr. S. Bolívar at r. Back red-orange; arms at ctr.			
	p. Proof.	—	—	—
	s. Specimen.	—	—	—
S264	**500 BOLÍVARES** 18xx (ca.1890). Black on blue and yellow unpt. Miners at l. ctr., Bolívar at r. Back blue; arms at l.			
	p. Proof.	—	—	—
	s. Specimen.	—	—	—

		GOOD	FINE	XF
S265	**1000 BOLÍVARES** 18xx (ca.1890). Black on orange and yellow unpt. Portr. S. Bolívar at l., allegorical woman w/industrial implements at ctr. r. Back orange; arms at ctr.			
	p. Proof.	—	—	—
	s. Specimen.	—	—	—

1897 ISSUE

#S271-S273 arms at ctr. on back; *CAPITAL B/15,000,000.* Printer: ABNC.

		GOOD	FINE	XF
S271	**20 BOLÍVARES** 189x (ca.1897). Black on green and yellow unpt. Vaquero and cattle at ctr. r. Back green. Proof.	—	—	—

		GOOD	FINE	XF
S272	**50 BOLÍVARES** 189x (ca.1897). Black on blue and yellow unpt. Seated allegorical woman w/pallette at r. Back blue.			
	p. Proof.	—	—	—
	s. Specimen.	—	—	—

S273 100 BOLÍVARES | GOOD | FINE | XF
19xx (ca.1900). Black on rose and yellow unpt. Allegorical woman kneeling at l., value at ctr., seated allegorical woman at r. Back red-orange.

	GOOD	FINE	XF
p. Proof.	—	—	—
s. Specimen.	—	—	—

S274 500 BOLÍVARES	GOOD	FINE	XF
19xx (ca.1900). Black on orange and rose unpt. Portr. S. Bolívar at l., reclining allegorical woman w/water vase and lyre at r. Back orange. Proof.	—	—	—

S275 1000 BOLÍVARES	GOOD	FINE	XF
189x (ca.1897). Black on green and blue unpt. Horses and handlers at l. and r., Portr. S. Bolívar at ctr. Back blue. Proof.	—	—	—

NOTE: Later notes (1900's) have minor plate and color differences from earlier (1890's) issues.

1910 PROVISIONAL ISSUE

S281 20 BOLÍVARES
19xx (ca.1910). Dual ovpt. on #S271, w/*CAPITAL Bs 12,000,000* under blacked out older capitalization at upper r. and w/text: *PAGADERO EN LAS/OFICINAS DEL BANCO* under vignette at lower r.

	GOOD	FINE	XF
a. Issued note.	—	—	—
p. Proof.	—	Unc	1000.
r. Remainder.	—	Unc	50.00

NOTE: Other denominations are reported, not confirmed. A group of #S281r surfaced in recent months.

1910 ISSUE

#S286-S289 w/text: *QUE SE PAGARÁN AL PORTADOR EN CARÁCAS A LA PRESENTACIÓN* (paid to the bearer in Carácas upon presentation); *CAPITAL Bs 12,000,000.* Arms at ctr. on back. Printer: ABNC.

S286 20 BOLÍVARES	GOOD	FINE	XF
19xx (ca.1910). Black on green and m/c unpt. Vaqueros herding cattle towards l. at ctr. Back green. Proof.	—	—	—

#S287 Held in reserve.

S288 100 BOLÍVARES	GOOD	FINE	XF
19xx (ca.1910). Black on brown and m/c unpt. Vaqueros and cattle towards r. at ctr. Back brown. Proof.	—	—	—

S289 500 BOLÍVARES	GOOD	FINE	XF
19xx (ca.1910). Black on blue and m/c unpt. Portr. S. Bolívar at l. Back blue.	—	—	—

1919 PROVISIONAL ISSUE

#S291 and S292 w/text: *PAGADERO EN LAS OFICINAS DEL BANCO* (payable in the offices of the bank) ovpt. near upper ctr. on face. Also wording: *EN CARÁCAS* blacked out in text line across ctr.

	GOOD	FINE	XF
S291 20 BOLÍVARES 29.1.1919. Black on green and m/c unpt. Like #S286 but w/alterations. Back green; arms at ctr.	250.00	550.00	—
S292 100 BOLÍVARES (ca.1919). Like #S288 but w/alterations.	—	Rare	—

NOTE: Other denominations are reported, not confirmed.

1916-21 ISSUE

#S293 and S294 w/text: *PAGADEROS AL PORTADOR EN LAS OFICINAS DEL BANCO* (payable to bearer in the offices of the bank). Three sign. titles and sign. Printer: ABNC.

	GOOD	FINE	XF
S293 100 BOLÍVARES 19xx (ca.1916-21). 15.6.1918. Similar to #S288, but different payable clause.	—	—	—
S294 500 BOLÍVARES 19xx (ca.1916-21). Similar to #S289, but different payable clause.	—	—	—

1921 ISSUE

#S297 and S298 *CAPITAL Bs 24,000,000.* Three sign. titles. Printer: ABNC.

S297 100 BOLÍVARES
19xx (ca.1921). Similar to #S288, but different capitalization amount. Proof.

	GOOD	FINE	XF
a. Issued note.	150.00	—	—
p. Proof.	—	—	—

		Good	Fine	XF
S298	**500 Bolívares** Aug. 1921. Similar to #S289, but different capitalization amount. Proof.	—	—	—

1924-26 Issue

#S301-S305 *CAPITAL Bs 24,000,000.* Two sign titles: *POR EL BANCO DE VENEZUELA* at l. and r. Printer: ABNC.

		Good	Fine	XF
S301	**20 Bolívares** 5.7.1925; 27.10.1926. Black on green and m/c unpt. Similar to #S286, but plate differences.	—	—	—

		Good	Fine	XF
S302	**50 Bolívares** 19xx (ca.1924). Black on orange and salmon unpt. Similar to #S272, but some plate differences. Back orange.	—	—	—

		Good	Fine	XF
S303	**100 Bolívares** 19xx (ca.1926). Black on brown and m/c unpt. Similar to #S288.	—	—	—

		Good	Fine	XF
S304	**500 Bolívares** 19xx (ca.1924). Black on blue and m/c unpt. Similar to #S289.	—	—	—

		Good	Fine	XF
S305	**1000 Bolívares** 19xx (ca.1926). Black on brown and yellow unpt. Similar to #S275, but some plate differences. Back gold.			
	p. Proof.	—	—	—
	s. Specimen.	—	—	—

1930-36 Issue

#S311-S315 guilloches changed from previous issues. *CAPITAL Bs 24,000,000.* Two sign. titles. Printer: ABNC.

		Good	Fine	XF
S311	**20 Bolívares** 1.6.1930; 29.2.1931; 30.10.1933; 29.4.1934; 29.11.1938. Black on m/c unpt. Similar to #S286.	175.00	400.00	—

		Good	Fine	XF
S312	**50 Bolívares** 27.9.1935-26.9.1939. Black on m/c unpt. Similar to #S272.	250.00	1500.	—

		Good	Fine	XF
S313	**100 Bolívares** 4.9.1931-9.11.1939. Black on m/c unpt. Similar to #S288.	—	—	—
S314	**500 Bolívares** 27.9.1935; 26.10.1935. Black on m/c unpt. Similar to #S289.	—	—	—

		Good	Fine	XF
S315	**1000 Bolívares** 31.1.1936. Similar to #S275.	—	—	—

Government

Compañía de Accionistas

This institution was organized in 1855. It issued notes and rendered services to the Treasury. It ceased operations in 1858.

1856 Issue

#S321-S322, S324 printer: Baldwin, Adams & Co., New York.

		Good	Fine	XF
S321	**5 Pesos** 18.2.1856. Black on red denomination in unpt. at ctr. Justice at l., reclining allegorical woman at upper ctr., seated woman at r. Uniface.	—	—	—
S322	**10 Pesos** (ca.1855).	—	—	—

#S323 Held in Reserve.

		Good	Fine	XF
S324	**100 Pesos** (ca.1855).	—	—	—

COMPAÑÍA DE CRÉDITO

This institution was organized on December 9, 1870 with part of its various functions acting on behalf of the government. It ceased operations on June 30, 1876.

1870 ISSUE

		GOOD	FINE	XF
S325	5 VENEZOLANOS 12.12.1870. Seated navigation at deckside at upper ctr.	—	—	—

1800'S ISSUE

#S326-S329 black, arms at ctr. Uniface. Printer: ABNC.

		GOOD	FINE	XF
S326	5 VENEZOLANOS 18xx (ca.1873). Proof.	—	—	—

		GOOD	FINE	XF
S327	10 VENEZOLANOS 18xx (ca.1873). Proof.	—	—	—
S328	50 VENEZOLANOS 18xx (ca.1873). Proof.	—	—	—

		GOOD	FINE	XF
S329	100 VENEZOLANOS 18xx (ca.1873). Proof.	—	—	—

STATE

ESTADO DE GUAYANA

#S331-S345 w/heading: *ESTADO DE GUAYANA*.

1878 FIRST ISSUE

#S331-S337 arms of Guayana at l., standing allegorical woman at r. Uniface. Printer: Lith. Sedille & Cie., Paris.

		GOOD	FINE	XF
S331	50 CENTÉSIMOS 31.8.1878. Purple.	—	Rare	—

		GOOD	FINE	XF
S332	1 VENEZOLANO 31.8.1878. Black. Similar to #S331.	—	Rare	—

		GOOD	FINE	XF
S333	2 VENEZOLANOS 31.8.1878. Black on lt. red unpt. Similar to #S331.	—	Rare	—
S334	4 VENEZOLANOS 1878. Blue. Similar to #S331.	—	Rare	—
S335	8 VENEZOLANOS 1878. Brown. Similar to #S331.	—	Rare	—
S337	20 VENEZOLANOS 1878. Black. Similar to #S331.	—	Rare	—

NOTE: Issued notes may have a circular state stamping on back.

1878 SECOND ISSUE

#S341-S345 similar to previous issue. Printer: The Hatch Lith. Co., N.Y.

		GOOD	FINE	XF
S341	50 CENTÉSIMOS ND (1878). Black. a. Green unpt. b. Pale purple unpt.	 — —	 Rare Rare	 — —
S342	1 VENEZOLANO 1878.	Reported Not Confirmed		

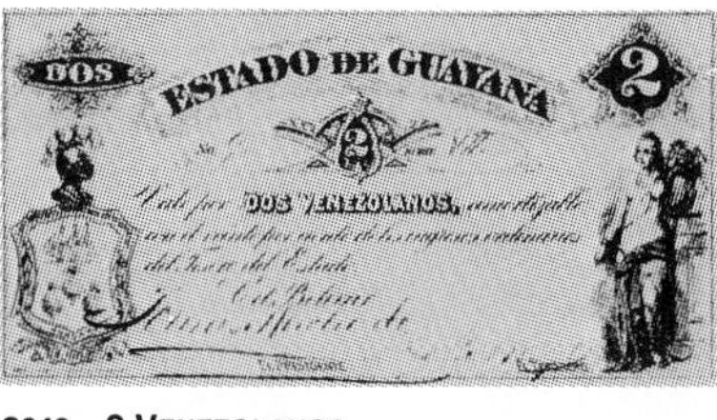

		GOOD	FINE	XF
S343	2 VENEZOLANOS 1878. Black on dk. red unpt.	—	Rare	—
S344	4 VENEZOLANOS 1878. Black and green.	—	Rare	—
S345	8 VENEZOLANOS 1878. Brown.	—	Rare	—

1879 ISSUE

#S351-S354 arms at l., Bolívar in unpt. at ctr. *ESTADO GUAYANA* heading. Dates filled in by hand. Printer: Hatch Lith. Co. (w/o imprint).

		GOOD	FINE	XF
S351	5 BOLÍVARES = 1 VENEZOLANO 31.12.1879. Green.	—	Rare	—

		Good	Fine	XF
S352	**10 Bolívares = 2 Venezolanos** 31.12.1879. Black on brown unpt. Back brown.	—	Rare	—

		Good	Fine	XF
S353	**20 Bolívares = 4 Venezolanos** 31.12.1879. Black on blue unpt. Back blue.	—	Rare	—
S354	**40 Bolívares = 8 Venezolanos** 31.12.1879. Black on yellow unpt.	—	Rare	—

Leprosarium

Isla de Providencia

Leproserias Nacionales - Ministerio de Sanidad y Asistencia Social

HAND STAMP VARIETIES:

TYPE I: *ESTADOS UNIDOS DE VENEZUELA ISLA DE PROVIDENCIA-ADMINISTRACION DEL LAZARETO.*

TYPE II: *E.E.U U. DE VENEZUELA Ministerio de Sanidad y Asistencia.*

1940 ND Series B Issue

#S361-S365 serial # on face, sailboat w/island in background at ctr. on face and back. Printer: Tip (ografía). Del Comercio-Carácas.

#S363-S365 w/hand stamp variety Type I.

		Good	Fine	XF
S361	**.25 Bolívar** ND(1940). Green.	Reported Not Confirmed		
S362	**.50 Bolívar** ND(1940). Orange.	Reported Not Confirmed		
S363	**1 Bolívar** ND(1940). Red-orange.	—	—	—
S364	**2 Bolívares** ND(1940). Purple.	35.00	60.00	90.00

		Good	Fine	XF
S365	**5 Bolívares** ND(1940). Grayish blue.	30.00	50.00	75.00

1940 ND Series C Issue

#S366-S370 serial # on face and back, sailboat w/island in background at ctr. on face and back. Printer: Edit (orial) Bellas Artes.

		Good	Fine	XF
S366	**.25 Bolívar** ND(1940). Green.	Reported Not Confirmed		
S367	**.50 Bolívar** ND(1940). Orange.	Reported Not Confirmed		

#S368-S370 w/hand stamp varieties Type I and II.

		Good	Fine	XF
S368	**1 Bolívar** ND(1940). Pale orange.	12.50	40.00	75.00
S369	**2 Bolívares** ND(1940). Purple.	20.00	60.00	90.00
S370	**5 Bolívares** ND(1940). Lt. blue.	45.00	75.00	125.00

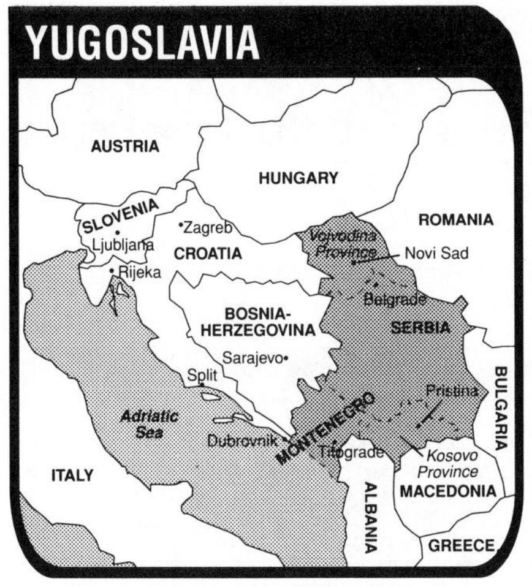

The Federal Republic of Yugoslavia is a Balkan country located on the east shore of the Adriatic Sea bordering Bosnia-Herzegovina and Croatia to the west, Hungary and Romania to the north, Bulgaria to the east, and Albania and Macedonia to the south. It has an area of 39,449 sq. mi. (102,173 sq. km.) and a population of 10.5 million. Capital: Belgrade. The chief industries are agriculture, mining, manufacturing and tourism. Machinery, nonferrous metals, meat and fabrics are exported.

The first South-Slavian State - Yugoslavia - was proclaimed on Dec. 1, 1918, after the union of the Kingdom of Serbia, Montenegro and the South Slav territories of Austria-Hungary; it then changed its official name from the Kingdom of the Serbs, Croats, and Slovenes to the Kingdom of Yugoslavia on Oct. 3, 1929. The Royal government of Yugoslavia attempted to remain neutral in World War II but, yielding to German pressure, aligned itself with the Axis powers in March of 1941; a few days later it was overthrown by a military-led coup and its neutrality reasserted. The Nazis occupied the country on April 17, and throughout the remaining years were resisted by a number of guerrilla armies, notably that of Marshal Josip Broz known as Tito. After the defeat of the Axis powers, a leftist coalition headed by Tito abolished the monarchy and, on Jan. 31, 1946, established a "People's Republic". Tito's rival General Draza Mihajlovic, who led the Chetniks against the Germans and Tito's forces, was arrested on March 13, 1946 and executed the following day after having been convicted by a partisan court.

The Federal Republic of Yugoslavia was composed of six autonomous republics: Serbia, Croatia, Slovenia, Bosnia-Herzegovina, Macedonia and Montenegro with two autonomous provinces within Serbia: Kosovo-Metohija and Vojvodina. The collapse of the Socialist Federal Republic of Yugoslavia during 1991-92 has resulted in the autonomous republics of Croatia, Slovenia, Bosnia-Herzegovina and Macedonia declaring their respective independence.

The Federal Republic of Yugoslavia was proclaimed in 1992; it consists of the former Republics of Serbia and Montenegro.

RULERS:

Peter I, 1918-1921
Alexander I, 1921-1934

REGIONAL - WWII

ФЕДЕРАЛНА ЦРНА ГОРА У ФЕДЕРАТИВНОЈ ДЕМОКРАТСКОЈ ЈУГОСЛАВИИИ ЦЕТИЊЕ

FEDERAL REGIME OF THE YUGOSLAV DEMOCRATIC FEDERATION CETINJE, MONTENEGRO

1945 ISSUE

#S101-S103 monthly depreciating redemption values on back.

		Good	Fine	XF
S101	**10 DINARA** 1.1.1945. Blue. People w/hands raised at l., burning house at r.	80.00	200.00	400.00
S102	**100 DINARA** 1.2.1945. Blue-green and yellow. Woman offering bearded man a drink.	150.00	375.00	750.00

		Good	Fine	XF
S103	**1000 DINARA** 1.2.1945. Lt. brown and brown. Horseman w/arm in sling.	130.00	325.00	650.00

REGIONAL MILITARY - WWII

GOSPODARSKO FINANCNI ODBOR OSVOBODILNE FRONTE

STATE FINANCE DEPARTMENT LIBERATION FRONT

1944 ND ISSUE

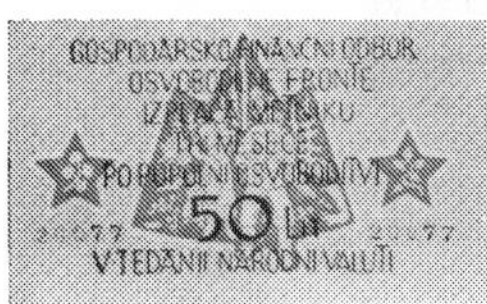

		Good	Fine	XF
S104	**50 LIT** ND. Orange w/dk. red text. Partisan family in woods at ctr. State seal at ctr. on back. Blue or black serial #.			
	a. Issued note.	1.00	4.00	12.50
	b. Hand stamp (cancelled).	.75	3.00	10.00

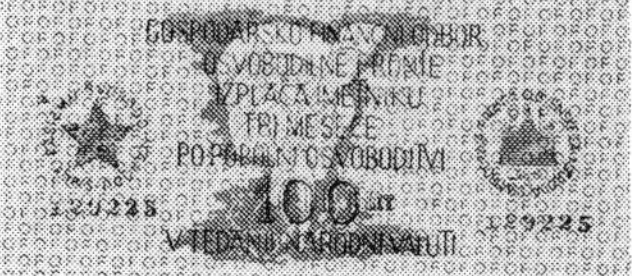

		Good	Fine	XF
S105	**100 LIT** ND. Lilac, brown and blue. Partisan carrying flag at ctr. on face and back.			
	a. Hand stamp, serial # and hand sign.	—	—	—
	b. W/o hand stamp or sign.	1.00	4.00	12.50
	c. W/o serial #.	.75	3.00	10.00
S106	**500 LIT** ND. Red-brown and gray-olive. (Not issued).	15.00	50.00	125.00
S107	**1000 LIT** ND. Red-brown and gray-olive. Soldiers at ctr.	20.00	62.50	150.00

		Good	Fine	XF
S108	**5000 LIT** ND. Red-brown and gray-olive.	40.00	120.00	250.00
S109	**10,000 LIT** ND. Red-brown and gray-olive. Partisans at ctr. Seal at ctr. on back.	50.00	150.00	300.00

DENARNI ZAVOD SLOVENIJE

MONETARY BANK OF SLOVENIA

1944 FIRST ISSUE

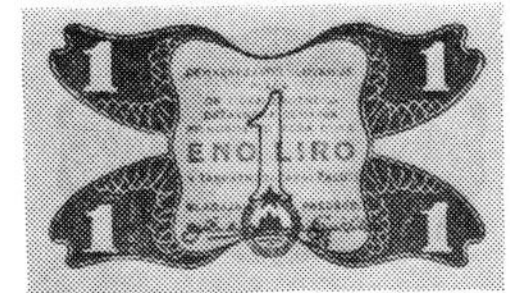

		VG	VF	Unc
S110	**1 LIRO** 20.2.1944-12.3.1944. Blue-green. "No." or letters w/serial #. Back brown.	2.00	6.00	15.00

		VG	VF	Unc
S111	**5 LIR** 20.2.1944-12.3.1944. Blue and lt. blue. 2 serial # varieties.	2.50	7.50	17.50

		VG	VF	UNC
S112	**10 LIR** 20.2.1944-12.3.1944. Red. 2 serial # varieties.	2.50	7.50	17.50

NOTE: German propaganda issue face like #S112, back w/*Ra denar je prau. . .* Value $60 in XF.

1944 SECOND ISSUE

#S113-S118 various date and sign. varieties. Wmk. paper.

		VG	VF	UNC
S113	**1 LIRO** 20.2.1944-12.3.1944. Blue on olive unpt. Red serial #.	2.00	6.00	15.00

		VG	VF	UNC
S114	**5 LIR** 20.2.1944-12.3.1944. Blue on gray-olive unpt. Red serial #.	2.50	7.50	17.50

		VG	VF	UNC
S115	**10 LIR** 20.2.1944-12.3.1944. Brown on gray-violet unpt. Black serial #.	2.50	7.50	17.50
S116	**50 LIR** 20.2.1944-12.3.1944. Green.	6.00	17.50	40.00

		VG	VF	UNC
S117	**100 LIR** 20.2.1944-12.3.1944. Brown on lt. brown unpt. Black serial #.	6.50	20.00	45.00

		GOOD	FINE	XF
S118	**VARIOUS DENOMINATIONS** Green.	16.50	50.00	120.00

NOTE: #S118 recorded in handwritten denominations of 1000, 1500, 3000 and 5000 Lir.

IZVRENI ODBOR OSVOBODILNE FRONTE SLOVENSKEGA NARODA

COMMITTEE OF THE SLOVENIAN GOVERNMENT LIBERTY FRONT

1943 RM ISSUE

#S119-S127 star behind woman w/loaf between farmer and blacksmith at r. 3% obligations.

		GOOD	FINE	XF
S119	**20 RM** 8.10.1943. Blue and red.	30.00	80.00	150.00
S120	**50 RM** 8.10.1943. Green and red.	30.00	80.00	150.00
S121	**100 RM** 8.10.1943. Green and red.	50.00	150.00	250.00
S122	**500 RM** 8.10.1943. Lilac and red.	60.00	180.00	300.00

1943 LIR ISSUE

		GOOD	FINE	XF
S123	**100 LIR** 8.10.1943. Blue and red.	60.00	180.00	300.00
S124	**500 LIR** 8.10.1943. Blue and red.	60.00	180.00	300.00

1943 ND LIT ISSUE

		GOOD	FINE	XF
S125	**100 LIT** ND (1943). Brown. Similar to #S127.	30.00	80.00	200.00
S126	**1000 LIT** ND (1943). Brown. Similar to #S127.	45.00	140.00	350.00

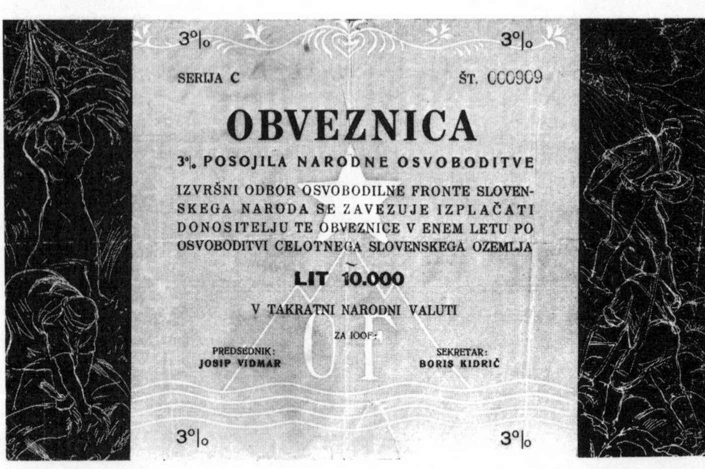

		GOOD	FINE	XF
S127	**10,000 LIT** ND (1943). Brown. Agricultural work at l. and r.	70.00	200.00	500.00

PARTISAN CERTIFICATES "POTRDILO" WWII

GLAVNO POVELJSTVO SLOVENSKIH PARTIZANSKIH CET LJUBLJANA

1942-45 ISSUE

#S128 various handwritten denominations and dates, crudely printed or duplicated.

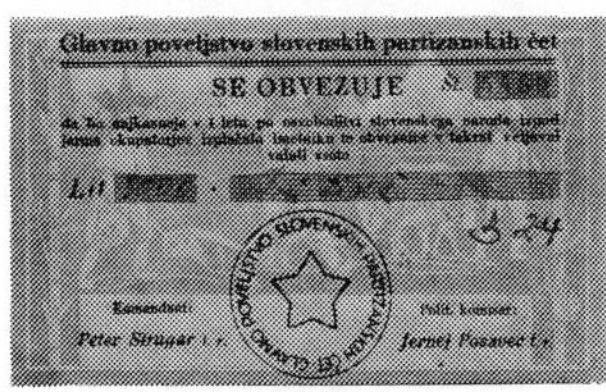

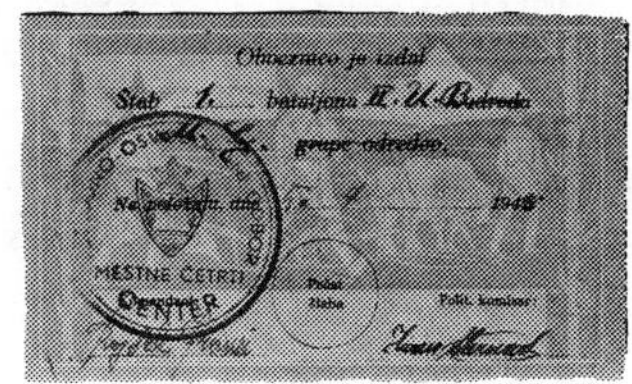

		GOOD	FINE	XF
S128	**VARIOUS DENOMINATIONS** 1942-45. Blue w/red text. Farmer and partisan plowing.	15.00	45.00	75.00

KANALSKI O.N. OO. (O.F.)

DISTRICT NATIONAL COMMITTEE OF THE LIBERATION FRONT FOR KANAL

1944-45 ISSUE

#S129 and S130 Tito at r. Various handwritten dates.

		GOOD	FINE	XF
S129	**100 LIR** 1944-45. Lilac.	50.00	150.00	400.00

		GOOD	FINE	XF
S130	**600 LIR** 1944-45. Lilac.	50.00	150.00	400.00

NARODNI OSVOBODILNI SVET ZA PRIMORSKO SLOVENIJO

NATIONAL LIBERATION COMMITTEE FOR THE SLOVENIAN COAST

1944-45 ISSUE

		GOOD	FINE	XF
S131	**100 LIR** 1944-45. Blue.	50.00	150.00	400.00
S132	**300 LIR** 1944-45. Blue.	50.00	150.00	400.00
S133	**400 LIR** 1944-45. Blue.	50.00	150.00	400.00

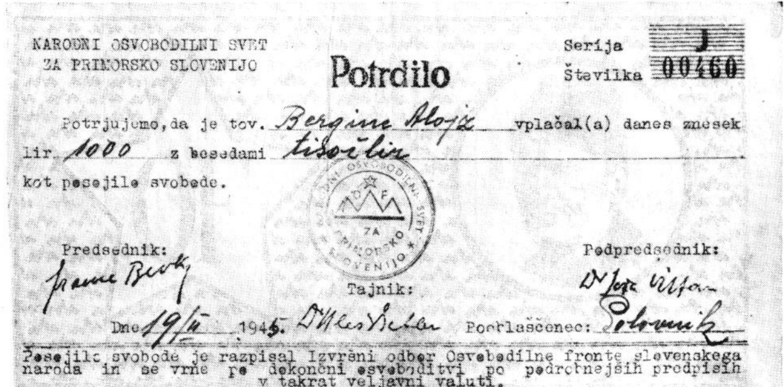

		GOOD	FINE	XF
S134	**1000 LIR** 1944-45. Purple. Tito at r.	50.00	150.00	400.00
S135	**2000 LIR** 1944-45. Blue.	50.00	150.00	400.00

		GOOD	FINE	XF
S136	**5000 LIR** 1944-45.	50.00	150.00	400.00
S137	**7000 LIR** 1944-45. Purple. Tito at r.	50.00	150.00	400.00
S138	**10,000 LIR** 1944-45. Green.	50.00	150.00	400.00

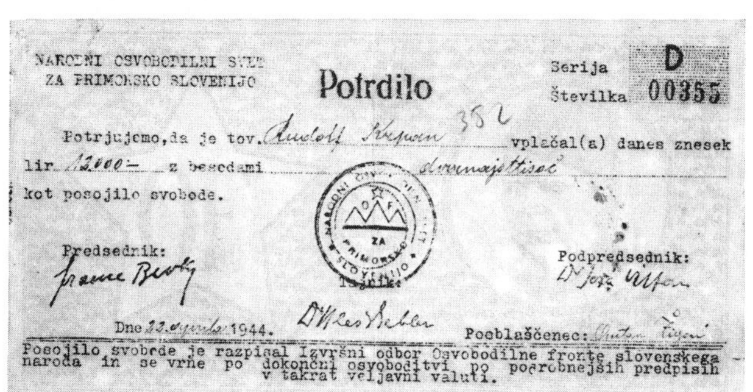

		GOOD	FINE	XF
S139	**12,000 LIR** 1944-45. Green. Tito at r.	50.00	150.00	400.00

OKROZNI ODBOR O.F. ZA PIVKO

DISTRICT COMMITTEE OF THE LIBERATION FRONT FOR PIVKO

1940'S ISSUE

		GOOD	FINE	XF
S140	**500 LIR** 194x. Red. W/o unpt.	50.00	150.00	400.00

OKROZNI ODBOR O.F. ZA JUZNO PRIMORSKO

DISTRICT COMMITTEE OF THE LIBERATION FRONT FOR PRIMORSKO DISTRICT

1940'S ISSUE

#S141 and S142 various dates.

		GOOD	FINE	XF
S141	**200 RM** 194x. W/o unpt.	50.00	150.00	400.00
S142	**250 RM** 194x. W/o unpt.	50.00	150.00	400.00

OKROZNI ODBOR O.F. ZA ZAPADNO PRIMORSKO

DISTRICT COMMITTEE OF LIBERATION FRONT FOR PRIMORSKO DISTRICT

1940'S ISSUE

#S143 and S144 various dates.

		GOOD	FINE	XF
S143	**128 LIR** 194x. Blue. Tito at r.	50.00	150.00	400.00
S144	**200 LIR** 194x. Similar to #S143.	50.00	150.00	400.00

Okrozni Odbor O.F. za Slov. Istro

District Committee of the Liberation Front for SlovenianIstria

1945 Issue

#S145-S148 various dates.

		Good	Fine	XF
S145	**100 Lir** 1945. Blue-gray.	50.00	150.00	400.00
S146	**400 Lir** 1945. Blue-gray.	50.00	150.00	400.00
S147	**500 Lir** 1945. Blue-gray.	50.00	150.00	400.00
S148	**1000 Lir** 1945. Blue-gray.	120.00	360.00	—

OOOF (Okrozni Odbor O.F.) za Brkine

District Committee of the Liberation Front for Brkine

1944 Issue

#S149 and S150 hand dated.

		Good	Fine	XF
S149	**600 Lit** 1944. Black. Outline of star and mountains at ctr.	50.00	150.00	400.00
S150	**1000 Lit** 1944. Similar to #S149.	50.00	150.00	400.00

Okrozni N.O.O. za Brkine

District National Committee of the Liberation Front for Brkine

1940's Issue

#S151 various dates.

		Good	Fine	XF
S151	**1000 Lir** 194x. Green. Tito at r.	50.00	150.00	400.00

Okrozni N.O.O. (Odbor O.F.) za Viparsko Okrozje

District National Committee of the Liberation Front Viparsko

1940's Issue

#S152 various dates.

		Good	Fine	XF
S152	**500 Lir** 194x. Black.	50.00	150.00	400.00

Okrozni Narodno Osvobodilni Odbor za Brda

District National Liberation Committee for Brda

1944 Issue

#S153-S157 various dates.

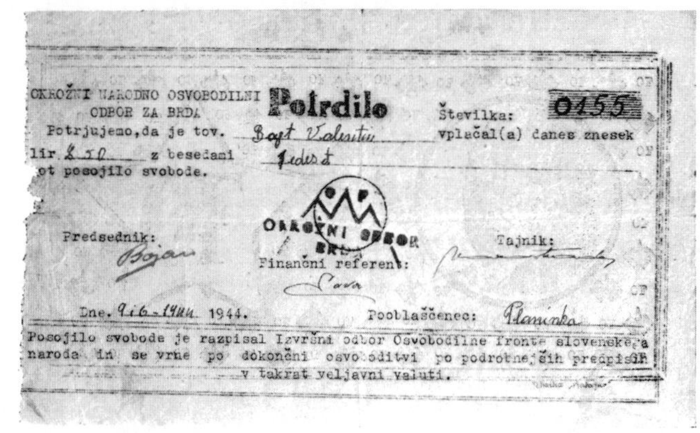

		Good	Fine	XF
S153	**50 Lir** 1944. Lilac. Tito at r.	50.00	150.00	400.00
S154	**300 Lir** 1944. Red-brown. Tito at r.	50.00	150.00	400.00
S155	**600 Lir** 1944. Brown.	50.00	150.00	400.00
S156	**2000 Lir** 1944. Gray. Similar to #S154.	50.00	150.00	400.00
S157	**10,000 Lir** 1944. Gray. Tito at r.	50.00	150.00	400.00

Okrozni N.O.O. za Kras

District National Liberation Committee for Kras

1944 Issue

#S158-S160 various dates.

		Good	Fine	XF
S158	**100 Lir** 1944.	50.00	150.00	400.00
S159	**200 Lir** 1944. Gray. Star at ctr.	50.00	150.00	400.00

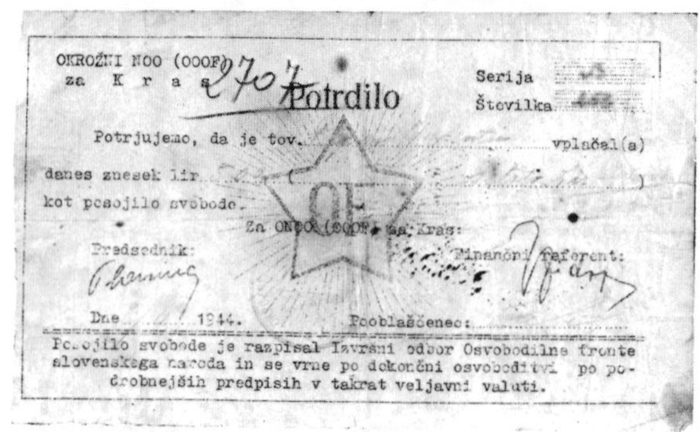

		Good	Fine	XF
S160	**500 Lir** 1944. Gray.	50.00	150.00	400.00

Okrozni N.O.O. za Gorisko

District National Liberation Committee for Gorisko

1940's Issue

#S161-S164 various dates.

		Good	Fine	XF
S161	**250 Lir** 194x. Green. Tito at r.	50.00	150.00	400.00
S162	**500 Lir** 194x. Brown. Tito at r.	50.00	150.00	400.00
S163	**1000 Lir** 194x. Green. Tito at r. w/ or w/o Italian text.	50.00	150.00	400.00
S164	**5000 Lir** 194x. Green.	50.00	150.00	400.00

Okrozni N.O.O. za Idrijsko

District National Liberation Committee for Idrijsko

1940's Issue

#S165-S167 various dates.

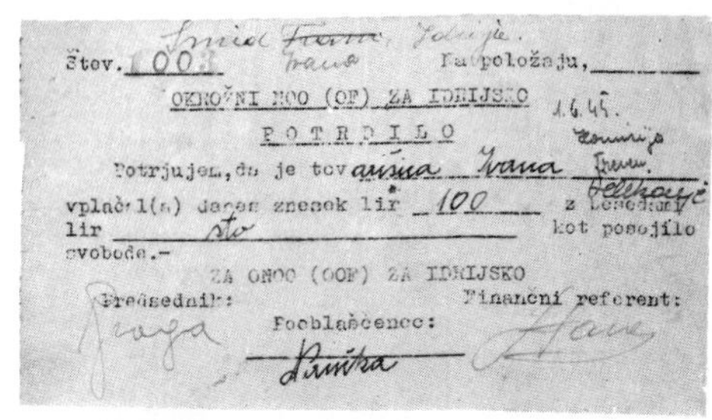

Štev. 1003 Na položaju,

OKROŽNI NOO (OF) ZA IDRIJSKO

POTRDILO

Potrjujem, da je tov

vplačal(a) danes znesek lir 100 z

lir sto kot posojilo

svobode.-

ZA ONOO (OOF) ZA IDRIJSKO

Predsednik: Finančni referent:

Pooblaščenec:

		GOOD	FINE	XF
S165	**100 LIR** 194x. Gray.	50.00	150.00	400.00
S166	**200 LIR** 194x. Black.	50.00	150.00	400.00
S167	**500 LIR** 194x. Black.	50.00	150.00	400.00

OKROZNI N.O.O. ZA BASKO

DISTRICT NATIONAL LIBERATION COMMITTEE FOR BASKO

1944-45 ISSUE

#S168-S175 hand dated.

		GOOD	FINE	XF
S168	**50 LIR** (ca.1944-45).	50.00	150.00	400.00
S169	**100 LIR** (ca.1944-45). Red star at r.	50.00	150.00	400.00
S170	**200 LIR** (ca.1944-45). Red star at r.	50.00	150.00	400.00
S171	**400 LIR** (ca.1944-45). Gray. Red star at r.	50.00	150.00	400.00

OF

Okrožni NOO (OOF) za Baško Štev. 654

POTRDILO.

Tov. je vplačal(a)

dne znesek Lir

(z besedami)

v posojilo svobode.

Za Baški ONOO (OOOF):

Predsednik: Finančni referent

Pooblaščenec:

		GOOD	FINE	XF
S172	**500 LIR** (ca.1944-45). Gray. Red star at r.	50.00	150.00	400.00
S173	**1000 LIR** (ca.1944-45).	50.00	150.00	400.00
S174	**2000 LIR** (ca.1944-45). Similar to #S172.	50.00	150.00	400.00
S175	**5000 LIR** (ca.1944-45).	50.00	150.00	400.00

OKROZNI N.O.O. ZA TOLMINSKO

DISTRICT NATIONAL LIBERATION COMMITTEE FOR TOLMINSKO

1940'S ISSUE

#S176 various dates.

		GOOD	FINE	XF
S176	**100 LIR** 194x. Blue. Tito at r.	50.00	150.00	400.00

OKROZNI N.O.O. ZA VIPAVSKO

DISTRICT NATIONAL LIBERATION COMMITTEE FOR VIPAVSKO

1940'S ISSUE

		GOOD	FINE	XF
S177	**10 LIR** ND. Gray.	50.00	150.00	400.00

POKRAJINSKI ODBOR O.F. ZA STAJERSKO

COMMITTEE OF THE LIBERATION FRONT FOR STAJERSKO

1940'S ISSUE

#S178 and S179 various dates.

		GOOD	FINE	XF
S178	**50 RM** 194x.	50.00	150.00	400.00
S179	**75 RM** 194x.	50.00	150.00	400.00

POKRAJINSKI ODBOR O.F. ZA GORENJSKO

COMMITTEE OF THE LIBERATION FRONT FOR GORENJSKO

1940'S ISSUE

		GOOD	FINE	XF
S180	**200 RM** 194x. Blue-gray. Tito at r.	50.00	150.00	400.00

HEJIRA DATE CONVERSION CHART

HEJIRA DATE CHART

HEJIRA (Hijra, Hegira), the name of the Muslim era (A.H. = Anno Hegirae) dates back to the Christian year 622 when Mohammed "fled" from Mecca, escaping to Medina to avoid persecution from the Koreish tribemen. Based on a lunar year the Muslim year is 11 days shorter.

*= Leap Year (Christian Calendar)

AH Hejira	AD Christian Date
1010	1601, July 2
1011	1602, June 21
1012	1603, June 11
1013	1604, May 30
1014	1605, May 19
1015	1606, May 19
1016	1607, May 9
1017	1608, April 28
1018	1609, April 6
1019	1610, March 26
1020	1611, March 16
1021	1612, March 4
1022	1613, February 21
1023	1614, February 11
1024	1615, January 31
1025	1616, January 20
1026	1617, January 9
1027	1617, December 29
1028	1618, December 19
1029	1619, December 8
1030	1620, November 26
1031	1621, November 16
1032	1622, November 5
1033	1623, October 25
1034	1624, October 14
1035	1625, October 3
1036	1626, September 22
1037	1627, September 12
1038	1628, August 31
1039	1629, August 21
1040	1630, July 10
1041	1631, July 30
1042	1632, July 19
1043	1633, July 8
1044	1634, June 27
1045	1635, June 17
1046	1636, June 5
1047	1637, May 26
1048	1638, May 15
1049	1639, May 4
1050	1640, April 23
1051	1641, April 12
1052	1642, April 1
1053	1643, March 22
1054	1644, March 10
1055	1645, February 27
1056	1646, February 17
1057	1647, February 6
1058	1648, January 27
1059	1649, January 15
1060	1650, January 4
1061	1650, December 25
1062	1651, December 14
1063	1652, December 2
1064	1653, November 22
1065	1654, November 11
1066	1655, October 31
1067	1656, October 20
1068	1657, October 9
1069	1658, September 29
1070	1659, September 18
1071	1660, September 6
1072	1661, August 27
1073	1662, August 16
1074	1663, August 5
1075	1664, July 25
1076	1665, July 14
1077	1666, July 4
1078	1667, June 23
1079	1668, June 11
1080	1669, June 1
1081	1670, May 21
1082	1671, May 10
1083	1672, April 29
1084	1673, April 18
1085	1674, April 7
1086	1675, March 28

AH Hejira	AD Christian Date
1087	1676, March 16*
1088	1677, March 6
1089	1678, February 23
1090	1679, February 12
1091	1680, February 2*
1092	1681, January 21
1093	1682, January 10
1094	1682, December 31
1095	1683, December 20
1096	1684, December 8*
1097	1685, November 28
1098	1686, November 17
1099	1687, November 7
1100	1688, October 26*
1101	1689, October 15
1102	1690, October 5
1103	1691, September 24
1104	1692, September 12*
1105	1693, September 2
1106	1694, August 22
1107	1695, August 12
1108	1696, July 31*
1109	1697, July 20
1110	1698, July 10
1111	1699, June 29
1112	1700, June 18
1113	1701, June 8
1114	1702, May 28
1115	1703, May 17
1116	1704, May 6*
1117	1705, April 25
1118	1706, April 15
1119	1707, April 4
1120	1708, March 23*
1121	1709, March 18
1122	1710, March 2
1123	1711, February 19
1124	1712, February 9*
1125	1713, January 28
1126	1714, January 17
1127	1715, January 7
1128	1715, December 27
1129	1716, December 16*
1130	1717, December 5
1131	1718, November 24
1132	1719, November 14
1133	1720, November 2*
1134	1721, October 22
1135	1722, October 12
1136	1723, October 1
1137	1724, September 29*
1138	1725, September 9
1139	1726, August 29
1140	1727, August 19
1141	1728, August 7*
1142	1729, July 27
1143	1730, July 17
1144	1731, July 6
1145	1732, June 24*
1146	1733, June 14
1147	1734, June 3
1148	1735, May 24
1149	1736, May 12*
1150	1737, May 1
1151	1738, April 21
1152	1739, April 10
1153	1740, March 29*
1154	1741, March 19
1155	1742, March 8
1156	1743, February 25
1157	1744, February 15*
1158	1745, February 3
1159	1746, January 24
1160	1747, January 13
1161	1748, January 2
1162	1748, December 22*
1163	1749, December 11
1164	1750, November 30
1165	1751, November 20
1166	1752, November 8*
1167	1753, October 29
1168	1754, October 18
1169	1755, October 7
1170	1756, September 26*
1171	1757, September 15
1172	1758, September 4
1173	1759, August 25
1174	1760, August 13*
1175	1761, August 2
1176	1762, July 28
1177	1763, July 12

AH Hejira	AD Christian Date
1178	1764, July 1*
1179	1765, June 20
1180	1766, June 9
1181	1767, May 30
1182	1768, May 18*
1183	1769, May 7
1184	1770, April 27
1185	1771, April 16
1186	1772, April 4*
1187	1773, March 25
1188	1774, March 14
1189	1775, March 4
1190	1776, February 21*
1191	1777, February 9
1192	1778, January 30
1193	1779, January 19
1194	1780, January 8*
1195	1780, December 28*
1196	1781, December 17
1197	1782, December 7
1198	1783, November 26
1199	1784, November 14*
1200	1785, November 4
1201	1786, October 24
1202	1787, October 13
1203	1788, October 2*
1204	1789, September 21
1205	1790, September 10
1206	1791, August 31
1207	1792, August 19*
1208	1793, August 9
1209	1794, July 29
1210	1795, July 18
1211	1796, July 7*
1212	1797, June 26
1213	1798, June 15
1214	1799, June 5
1215	1800, May 25
1216	1801, May 14
1217	1802, May 4
1218	1803, April 23
1219	1804, April 12*
1220	1805, April 1
1221	1806, March 21
1222	1807, March 11
1223	1808, February 28*
1224	1809, February 16
1225	1810, February 6
1226	1811, January 26
1227	1812, January 16*
1228	1813, January 4
1229	1813, December 24
1230	1814, December 14
1231	1815, December 3
1232	1816, November 21*
1233	1817, November 11
1234	1818, October 31
1235	1819, October 20
1236	1820, October 9*
1237	1821, September 28
1238	1822, September 18
1239	1823, September 7
1240	1824, August 26*
1241	1825, August 16
1242	1826, August 5
1243	1827, July 25
1244	1828, July 14*
1245	1829, July 3
1246	1830, June 22
1247	1831, June 12
1248	1832, May 31*
1249	1833, May 21
1250	1834, May 10
1251	1835, April 29
1252	1836, April 18*
1253	1837, April 7
1254	1838, March 27
1255	1839, March 17
1256	1840, March 5*
1257	1841, February 23
1258	1842, February 12
1259	1843, February 1
1260	1844, January 22*
1261	1845, January 10
1262	1845, December 30
1263	1846, December 20
1264	1847, December 9
1265	1848, November 27*
1266	1849, November 17
1267	1850, November 6
1268	1851, October 27

AH Hejira	AD Christian Date
1269	1852, October 15*
1270	1853, October 4
1271	1854, September 24
1272	1855, September 13
1273	1856, September 1*
1274	1857, August 22
1275	1858, August 11
1276	1859, July 31
1277	1860, July 20*
1278	1861, July 9
1279	1862, June 29
1280	1863, June 18
1281	1864, June 6*
1282	1865, May 27
1283	1866, May 16
1284	1867, May 5
1285	1868, April 24*
1286	1869, April 13
1287	1870, April 3
1288	1871, March 23
1289	1872, March 11*
1290	1873, March 1
1291	1874, February 18
1292	1875, February 7
1293	1876, January 28*
1294	1877, January 16
1295	1878, January 5
1296	1878, December 26
1297	1879, December 15
1298	1880, December 4*
1299	1881, November 23
1300	1882, November 12
1301	1883, November 2
1302	1884, October 21*
1303	1885, October 10
1304	1886, September 30
1305	1887, September 19
1306	1888, September 7*
1307	1889, August 28
1308	1890, August 17
1309	1891, August 7
1310	1892, July 26*
1311	1893, July 15
1312	1894, July 5
1313	1895, June 24
1314	1896, June 12*
1315	1897, June 2
1316	1898, May 22
1317	1899, May 12
1318	1900, May 1
1319	1901, April 20
1320	1902, April 10
1321	1903, March 30
1322	1904, March 18*
1323	1905, March 8
1324	1906, February 25
1325	1907, February 14
1326	1908, February 4*
1327	1909, January 23
1328	1910, January 13
1329	1911, January 2
1330	1911, December 22
1331	1912, December 11*
1332	1913, November 30
1333	1914, November 19
1334	1915, November 9
1335	1916, October 28*
1336	1917, October 17
1337	1918, October 7
1338	1919, September 26
1339	1920, September 15*
1340	1921, September 4
1341	1922, August 24
1342	1923, August 14
1343	1924, August 2*
1344	1925, July 22
1345	1926, July 12
1346	1927, July 1
1347	1928, June 20*
1348	1929, June 9
1349	1930, May 29
1350	1931, May 19
1351	1932, May 7*
1352	1933, April 26
1353	1934, April 16
1354	1935, April 5
1355	1936, March 24*
1356	1937, March 14
1357	1938, March 3
1358	1939, February 21
1359	1940, February 10*

AH Hejira	AD Christian Date
1360	1941, January 29
1361	1942, January 19
1362	1943, January 8
1363	1943, December 28
1364	1944, December 17*
1365	1945, December 6
1366	1946, November 25
1367	1947, November 15
1368	1948, November 3*
1369	1949, October 24
1370	1950, October 13
1371	1951, October 2
1372	1952, September 21*
1373	1953, September 10
1374	1954, August 30
1375	1955, August 20
1376	1956, August 8*
1377	1957, July 29
1378	1958, July 18
1379	1959, July 7
1380	1960, June 25*
1381	1961, June 14
1382	1962, June 4
1383	1963, May 25
1384	1964, May 13*
1385	1965, May 2
1386	1966, April 22
1387	1967, April 11
1388	1968, March 31*
1389	1969, March 20
1390	1970, March 9
1391	1971, February 27
1392	1972, February 16*
1393	1973, February 4
1394	1974, January 25
1395	1975, January 14
1396	1976, January 3*
1397	1976, December 23*
1398	1977, December 12
1399	1978, December 2
1400	1979, November 21
1401	1980, November 9*
1402	1981, October 30
1403	1982, October 19
1404	1983, October 8
1405	1984, September 27*
1406	1985, September 16
1407	1986, September 6
1408	1987, August 26
1409	1988, August 14*
1410	1989, August 3
1411	1990, July 24
1412	1991, July 13
1413	1992, July 2*
1414	1993, June 21
1415	1994, June 10
1416	1995, May 31
1417	1996, May 19*
1418	1997, May 9
1419	1998, April 28
1420	1999, April 17
1421	2000, April 6*
1422	2001, March 26
1423	2002, March 15
1424	2003, March 5
1425	2004, February 22*
1426	2005, February 10
1427	2006, January 31
1428	2007, January 20
1429	2008, January 10*
1430	2008, December 29
1431	2009, December 18
1432	2010, December 8
1433	2011, November 27*
1434	2012, November 15
1435	2013, November 5
1436	2014, October 25
1437	2015, October 15*
1438	2016, October 3
1439	2017, September 22
1440	2018, September 12
1441	2019, September 11*
1442	2020, August 20
1443	2021, August 10
1444	2022, July 30
1445	2023, July 19*
1446	2024, July 8
1447	2025, June 27
1448	2026, June 17
1449	2027, June 6*
1450	2028, May 25